India

Bryn Thomas
David Collins
Rob Flynn
Christine Niven
Sarina Singh
Dani Valent

D1586003

India

7th edition

Published by
Lonely Planet Publications
Head Office: PO Box 617, Hawthorn, Vic 3122, Australia
Branches: 155 Filbert St, Suite 251, Oakland, CA 94607, USA
               10a Spring Place, London NW5 3BH, UK
               71 bis rue du Cardinal Lemoine, 75005 Paris, France

Printed by
Colorcraft Ltd, Hong Kong

Photographs by

Sanjay Singh Badnor	Chris Beall	Paul Beinssen	Sara-Jane Cleland
David Collins	Michelle Coxall	Mark Daffey	Greg Elms
Hugh Finlay	Rob Flynn	Frances Linzee Gordon	Meera Govil
Sally Hone	Richard I'Anson	Margaret Jung	Leanne Logan
Adam McCrow	Bruce Mitchell	Christine Niven	Jane Rawson
Valerie Tellini	Bryn Thomas	Tony Wheeler	

Front cover: Open prayer book, Rajasthan (Lisl Dennis, Image Bank)

First Published
October 1981

This Edition
November 1997

National Library of Australia Cataloguing in Publication Data

India.

    7th ed.
    Includes index.
    ISBN 0 86442 491 4.

    1. India - Guidebooks. I. Thomas, Bryn, 1959-

915.40452

Bryn Thomas

Born in Zimbabwe, where he grew up on a farm, Bryn contracted an incurable case of wanderlust during camping holidays by the Indian Ocean in Mozambique.

An anthropology degree at Durham University in England earned him a job polishing the leaves of pot plants in London. He has also been a ski-lift operator, encyclopaedia seller and an English teacher in Cairo, Singapore and Tokyo. Travel on five continents has included a 2500km Andean cycling trip and 10 visits to India.

Bryn's first guide, the *Trans-Siberian Handbook*, was short-listed for the Thomas Cook Guidebook of the Year awards. He is co-author of LP's *Britain*.

David Collins

David was born in England but ran away as soon as he could. Desperate for an antidote to a quiet life in Bristol, he launched himself in a flurry of good intentions at Mother Teresa's mission in Calcutta. Rapidly realising that good intentions were not enough to save the world, the somewhat less starry-eyed 19-year-old tottered into a career in journalism, prostituting himself on some of the world's most obscure technical publications. Squandering the proceedings on a 'glamourous cities of the world' tour, David tried Santa Barbara, Sydney, and Ouagadougou on for size before settling into the cable-knit-sweater feel of Melbourne, where he now slaves on LP's web site.

Rob Flynn

Rob grew up as a surf grommit on Sydney's northern beaches. A certified dilettante, he ditched careers in medicine and anthropology to work as a garbo, car washer, house painter, gardener, rubber worker, truck driver, magazine editor, advertising copywriter and photographer between travels through India, Southeast Asia, Africa, Europe, Australia and the Pacific.

Rob joined Lonely Planet in 1993 and is currently the ringleader of LP's e-team, which is responsible for its award-winning web site among other electronic projects.

Christine Niven

Christine grew up in New Zealand, but after completing university left for the traditional overseas experience and has been travelling whenever the opportunity arises ever since.

Working for Lonely Planet has provided the perfect opportunity to mix business with pleasure. Christine has also co-authored the LP guide to *Sri Lanka*.

Sarina Singh

After finishing a business degree in Melbourne, a deep passion for travel lured Sarina to India. There she did a marketing executive traineeship with Sheraton Hotels, but later drifted into journalism. Writing mainly about India, assignments also took her to Pakistan, Kenya, Zanzibar, Nepal and the Middle East. After 3½ years in India, Sarina returned to Australia, did a post-graduate journalism course and wrote two television documentary scripts. Other Lonely Planet books she has worked on are *Rajasthan*, *Africa* and *Mauritius, Réunion & Seychelles*.

Dani Valent

Realising she was never going to be Noel Gallagher's guitar tech, Dani stashed her singlet and gaffer and was roadie no more. She moved on to pie-making in Port Melbourne, and then tea-trolley duty in LP's sales department. In between work on LP's *Australia*, *India* and the *Eastern Europe* shoestring, she is chief crumpet-toaster and anagram-monitor on LP's web site. She drives a shiny 1966 Holden sedan with a white roof and takes care not to park it under gum trees.

Prakash A Raj

Prakash was born in Nepal and studied for two years in Varanasi where he learnt to speak fluent Hindi. He spent five years at university in the USA and a year in the Netherlands. He travelled extensively in Europe and returned to Nepal where he worked on the Kathmandu English-language daily as a journalist and also for the Nepalese government's planning agency. Prakesh has also worked for the OECD in Paris, the UN secretariat in New York and is now working for the UNHCR in Asia. Prakash has written several books about Nepal and his life there in both English and Nepali.

From the Authors

Bryn Thomas I'd like to thank Jane for first inspiring me to go to India back in 1983, now ten visits ago. As Mark Tully says, 'It's very difficult to have halfway-house feelings about India. It either grabs you completely or turns you off.' This book has been a welcome excuse for frequent returns.

A project of this size requires the collaboration of many people for its success. Thanks, first, to the contributing authors, in particular to Christine Niven for completing her section under the worst circumstances imaginable. Thanks also to Doug Streatfeild-James, co-author of LP's new Goa guide, who largely updated the Goa section in this book.

At LP in Melbourne, thanks to Sue Galley, Sharan Kaur, Jane Rawson and all the other Martians involved in India 7. In Britain, thanks once again to Anna Jacomb-Hood for her help in sorting through the 1000s of letters we received from the last edition. In particular, thanks to Margaret Wilson, Bruce Cairns and Mike Rothbart.

In India, for help, advice, suggestions and/or companionship, I'm grateful to many people, including Lome Aseron in Delhi, Frederick Noronha in Goa, Michiel Aten in Mamallapuram, Bob Wright in Calcutta, intrepid French travellers Marie & Jean-Pierre Michaud in Tamil Nadu and Pondicherry, Larry Doffing, Velide Levithan, Justin Zaman, Bruno Lamonica, Yogev & Yuval Irit, Richard Fisk and James Smith. In Sikkim, thanks to Yeshi Dorjee, Pema Topgyal, Tshering Uden Bhutia, Satish Bardewa, and Dicey Tourists Charlie Colville and Juliet Bray. In the North-Eastern Region, I'd like to thank Jeeban Bora in Guwahati, Manik Chakraborti in Agartala, and Deepak in Shil-long. In the Andamans, I'm grateful to the Meshack family for all their hospitality, Sushila Tigga at the Government of India Tourist Office in Port Blair, and to Sam Hencher, Martin Kwast and Rowena Stone. And finally thanks to Naveen Singh in Delhi for the ceaseless flow of rubbish via the net.

David Collins Thanks to Anne Thornton for her patience, support and assistance with research. In India, special thanks to the helpful staff of the Government of India Tourist Office in Mumbai; Janaki Umesh Narayan, Department of Tourism, Mysore; U Srinath Mallya, KSTDC, Bangalore; Mysore rice merchant Ranganna for his careful driving and deft ability with punctured tyres; and Captain RK and the crew of Indian coast-guard vessel No 33 for rescuing me from a dull night in Karwar.

Thanks also to Aravind Narsipur in Bangalore and Kamlesh Amin of Transway International in Mumbai for mop-up research; Cathy Thornton for the magic camera; and Tony Miller in Bangalore for a brief glimpse into expat life and local dating rituals. At LP, thanks to Sharan for noticing my hand when it went up in the air, and to Sue and Rob Flynn for allowing me to stretch my legs.

Rob Flynn Thanks to the many people who shared their time, knowledge and tea & sandwiches, especially 'Rhino', DM Yadav at the Government of India Tourist Office in Aurangabad, Anant Songire, Shaikh Nasir, Jamsked Lord, Santosh Velkar, the Joseph family, B Jayachandran at the DTPC in Alappuzha, PA Antony, Michael O in Kovalam, the Tourist Desk in Ernakulam, Atui Asher, Prof Kabir Modi, Heinrich Hessler, Asif

Ahmed, R Saheer Kulkarni, the Tourist Information Centre in Kollam, Jx for the vodka and, of course, the flower girl of Cochin.

At home thanks to Anne, Sue, Sharan, Jane, Steve and Richard.

Sarina Singh Special thanks to Harendrapal Singh (Poshina) for looking after me so well in Gujarat, LK Jangid for his insights on Shekhawati, Anil Mulchandani (Ahmedabad), Madan Singh (tourist officer in Jaipur), and the much loved gang in Udaipur (they know who they are).

Thank you to fellow travellers – David Timms & Jessica Hardy (UK), John Sparks & Marcia Wiley (USA), Gabriela Foresti (Argentina), Christine Pockett (Peru), Miko Aubin (France) and Michelle Eilering (NZ) – for their feedback. Thanks also to travellers who wrote to LP about Rajasthan and Gujarat – I read each and every letter.

In Melbourne, I'm grateful to dad and Ajeet for their help and to mum – for giving the dog her regular flea rinse. At Lonely Planet, thanks to Sue and Sharan for their much appreciated guidance.

Personal thanks to Sanjay Singh Badnor for his vitality (and help in testing 'all-you-can-eat' Gujarati thalis!); Amit, Swati & Parth Jhaveri for keeping me amused in Mumbai and Jitendra Singh Rathore – for helping me sort out even the slightest problem.

Dani Valent Thanks to Michael Turner; Bubban, the best rickshaw-wallah in Jhansi; Ranjit K Guha Roy from Government of India Tourist Office in Calcutta; SK Pati from the Government of Orissa Tourist Office in New Delhi; the bus drivers who didn't quite kill me; the guy in Chowringhee with a suss hundred dollar bill; anyone who made me a half-decent breakfast. In the Netherlands: Dan, Lotte & Joey; Erik, Jackie (who doesn't even know it), Dennis, Han & Saskia. Oh yeah & Damo for Suck Face wardrobe. In Melbourne: Sue & Sharan for the job, my family, Col, Emma.

This Edition

For this seventh edition of *India*, Bryn Thomas coordinated the whole project. He also updated the introductory chapters, Delhi, West Bengal, Sikkim, North-Eastern Region, Goa, Chennai, Tamil Nadu and the Andaman & Nicobar Islands.

Christine Niven updated Punjab & Haryana, Himachal Pradesh, Jammu & Kashmir, Ladakh & Zanskar and parts of Uttar Pradesh.

Sarina Singh updated Rajasthan and Gujarat.

Rob Flynn updated Maharashtra, Andhra Pradesh and Kerala.

Dani Valent updated Bihar, Calcutta, Orissa and Madhya Pradesh.

David Collins updated parts of Uttar Pradesh, Mumbai and Karnataka.

Thanks to Garry Weare for updating the trekking sections.

This Book

When the first edition of this book emerged in 1981 it was the biggest, most complicated and most expensive project we'd tackled at Lonely Planet. It began with an exploratory trip to south India by Tony and Maureen to see what information would be needed. The following year Geoff Crowther, Prakash Raj, Tony and Maureen returned to India and spent a combined total of about a year of more-or-less nonstop travel. The second, third and fourth editions were researched by Tony, Prakash, Geoff and Hugh Finlay. The fifth edition was researched by Hugh, Tony, Geoff and Bryn Thomas. The sixth edition was researched by Hugh, Tony, Bryn, Prakash, Michelle Coxall, Leanne Logan and Geert Cole.

The first edition exceeded all our hopes and expectations: it instantly became our best-selling guide. In the UK it won the Thomas Cook Guidebook of the Year award and in India it became the most popular guide to the country – a book used even by Indians to explore their own country. It has continued to be one of Lonely Planet's most popular and successful guides.

From the Publisher

This book was coordinated by Jane Rawson. A cast of thousands helped out with the editing and proofing: Carolyn Papworth and Martin Hughes were thrown in at the deep end without floaties; Lindsay Brown tamed a vicious festivals table as well as picking up all Jane's lapses of concentration; Michelle Coxall took a break from child-rearing to cast an experienced eye over the manuscript; and Paul Harding, Janet Austin, Bethune Carmichael and Suzi Petkovski picked up the loose ends.

Coordinating the mapping of this book was a huge job, and it took a huge man to do it. Paul 'too big for his boots' Piaia not only coordinated mapping, but also did the layout, designed the colour sections and drew the climate charts.

Paul was ably assisted by a small army of mappers: Mark 'the marble' Germanchis, Adam 'I'm not doing that book anymore' McCrow and Geoff Stringer. Mark also contributed the gorgeous chapter ends and numerous illustrations. Other illustrators included Trudi Canavan, Tamsin Wilson, Margaret Jung and the multi-talented Adam, who also designed the cover and created the back cover map.

Valerie Tellini put her botanical arm to good use keeping Paul on the straight and narrow, while Sharan Kaur took on the awesome task of guiding Jane. Final artwork was checked by Sally Gerdan, Michelle Glynn, Valerie and Sharan. Sue Galley kept coming up with bright ideas.

Thanks
All those involved in producing this book greatly appreciate the contributions of those travellers who put so much effort into writing and telling us of their experiences. Your names appear on page 1163.

Warning & Request
Things change – prices go up, schedules change, good places go bad and bad places go bankrupt – nothing stays the same. So, if you find things better or worse, recently opened or long since closed, please tell us and help make the next edition even more accurate and useful.

We value all of the feedback we receive from travellers. Julie Young coordinates a team who read and acknowledge every letter, postcard and email, and ensure that every morsel of information finds its way to the appropriate authors, editors and publishers.

Everyone who writes to us will find their name in the next edition of the appropriate guide and will also receive a free subscription to our quarterly newsletter, *Planet Talk*. The very best contributions will be rewarded with a free Lonely Planet guide.

Excerpts from your correspondence may appear in new editions of this guide; in our newsletter, *Planet Talk*; or in updates on our Web site – so please let us know if you don't want your letter published or your name acknowledged.

Contents

Map Legend

BOUNDARIES

International Boundary
Regional Boundary
Disputed Boundary

ROUTES

Freeway
Highway
Major Road
Unsealed Road or Track
City Road
City Street
Railway & Station
Metro & Station
Walking Track
Walking Tour
Ferry Route
Cable Car or Chairlift

AREA FEATURES

Parks
Built-Up Area
Pedestrian Mall
Market
Christian Cemetery
Non-Christian Cemetery
Reef
Beach or Desert
Forest

HYDROGRAPHIC FEATURES

Coastline
River, Creek
Rapids, Waterfalls
Lake, Intermittent Lake
Canal
Swamp

SYMBOLS

○ CAPITAL — National Capital
◉ Capital — Regional Capital
CITY — Major City
● City — City
● Town — Town
● Village — Village

■ ▼ — Place to Stay, Place to Eat
⚏ ⚑ — Cafe, Pub or Bar
✉ ☎ — Post Office, Telephone
❶ $ — Tourist Information, Bank
◒ P — Transport, Parking
🏛 ⌂ — Museum, Youth Hostel
Å ↑ — Camping Ground, Golf Course
✚ ✚ — Church, Cathedral
☾ ✿ — Mosque, Synagogue
🔒 ⚉ — Temple, Sikh Temple
⊞ ⚏ — Buddhist Temple, Hindu Temple

○ 🅿 — Embassy, Petrol Station
✈ ✝ — Airport, Airfield
❖ ✿ — Shopping Centre, Gardens
⚐ 🐘 — Bird Sanctuary, Zoo
✚ ★ — Hospital, Police Station
← A25 — One Way Street, Route Number
🏛 ⚊ — Stately Home, Monument
✕ ▣ — Castle, Tomb
⌂ ⌂ — Cave, Hut or Chalet
▲ ☀ — Mountain or Hill, Lookout
⚓ ⚓ — Lighthouse, Shipwreck
)(◉ — Pass, Spring
✈ ⚏ — Beach, Swimming Pool
❦ ⚏ — Vineyard, Picnic Site
∴ — Archaeological Site or Ruins
Ancient or City Wall
Cliff or Escarpment, Tunnel

Note: not all symbols displayed above appear in this book

Map Index

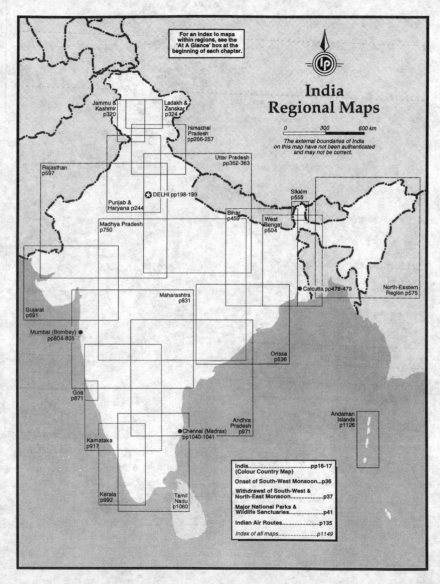

For an index to maps within regions, see the 'At A Glance' box at the beginning of each chapter.

India Regional Maps

0   300   600 km

The external boundaries of India on this map have not been authenticated and may not be correct.

Jammu & Kashmir p320

Ladakh & Zanskar p324

Himachal Pradesh pp266-257

Uttar Pradesh pp362-363

Rajasthan p597

DELHI pp198-199

Sikkim p558

Punjab & Haryana p244

Bihar p459

West Bengal p504

Madhya Pradesh p750

North-Eastern Region p575

Calcutta pp478-479

Maharashtra p831

Gujarat p691

Mumbai (Bombay) pp804-805

Orissa p536

Goa p871

Andhra Pradesh p971

Andaman Islands p1126

Karnataka p917

Chennai (Madras) pp1040-1041

Kerala p992

Tamil Nadu p1060

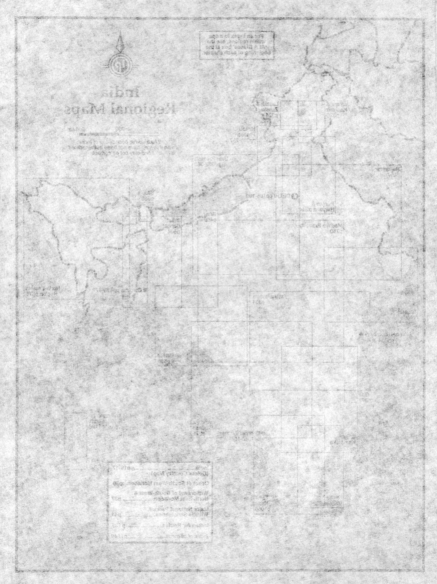

Introduction

India, it is often said, is not a country but a continent. From north to south and east to west, the people are different, the languages are different, the customs are different, the country is different.

There are few countries on earth with the enormous variety that India has to offer. It's a place that somehow gets into your blood. Love it or hate it you can never ignore India. It's not an easy country to handle, and more

than a few visitors are only too happy to finally get on to their flight and leave the place. Yet a year later they'll be hankering to get back.

It all comes back to that amazing variety – India is as vast as it is crowded, as luxurious as it is squalid. The plains are as flat and featureless as the Himalaya are high and spectacular, the food as terrible as it can be magnificent, the transport as exhilarating as

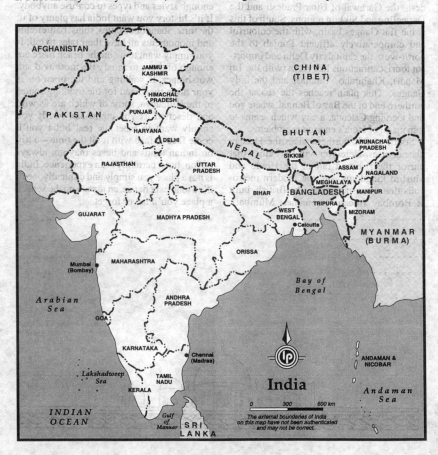

AFGHANISTAN

CHINA (TIBET)

JAMMU & KASHMIR

HIMACHAL PRADESH

PAKISTAN

PUNJAB

HARYANA

DELHI

BHUTAN

NEPAL

ARUNACHAL PRADESH

RAJASTHAN

UTTAR PRADESH

SIKKIM

ASSAM

NAGALAND

MEGHALAYA

MANIPUR

BANGLADESH

BIHAR

TRIPURA

MIZORAM

GUJARAT

MADHYA PRADESH

WEST BENGAL

Calcutta

MYANMAR (BURMA)

Mumbai (Bombay)

MAHARASHTRA

ORISSA

Bay of Bengal

Arabian Sea

ANDHRA PRADESH

GOA

KARNATAKA

Chennai (Madras)

ANDAMAN & NICOBAR

Lakshadweep Sea

TAMIL NADU

KERALA

India

0   300   600 km

Andaman Sea

INDIAN OCEAN

Gulf of Mannar

SRI LANKA

The external boundaries of India on this map have not been authenticated and may not be correct.

it can be boring and uncomfortable. Nothing is ever quite the way you expect it to be.

India is far from the easiest country in the world to travel around. It can be hard going, the poverty will get you down, Indian bureaucracy would try the patience of a saint, and the most experienced travellers find themselves at the end of their tempers at some point in India. Yet it's all worth it.

Very briefly, India is a triangle with the top formed by the mighty Himalayan mountain chain. Here you will find the intriguing Tibetan region of Ladakh and the astonishingly beautiful Himalayan areas of Himachal Pradesh, the Garhwal of Uttar Pradesh and the Darjeeling and Sikkim regions. South of this is the flat Ganges basin, with the colourful and comparatively affluent Punjab to the north-west, the capital city Delhi and important tourist attractions like Agra (with the Taj Mahal), Khajuraho, Varanasi and the holy Ganges. This plain reaches the sea at the northern end of the Bay of Bengal, where you find teeming Calcutta, a city which seems to sum up all of India's enormous problems.

South of this northern plain the Deccan plateau rises. Here you will find cities that mirror the rise and fall of the Hindu and Muslim kingdoms, and the modern metropolis that their successors, the British, built at Bombay (recently renamed Mumbai).

India's story is one of many different kingdoms competing with each other, and this is never more clear than in places like Bijapur, Mandu, Golconda and other centres in central India. Finally, there is the steamy south, where Muslim influence reached only fleetingly. Here Hinduism was least altered by outside influences and is at its most exuberant. The temple towns of the south are quite unlike those of the north and are superbly colourful.

Basically India is what you make of it and what you want it to be. If you want to see temples, there are temples in profusion with enough styles and types to confuse anybody. If it's history you want India has plenty of it; the forts, abandoned cities, ruins, battlefields and monuments all have their tales to tell. If you simply want to lie on the beach there are enough of those to satisfy the most avid sun worshipper. If walking and the open air is your thing then head for the trekking routes of the Himalaya, some of which are as wild and deserted as you could ask for. If you simply want to meet the real India you'll come face to face with it all the time – a trip on Indian trains and buses may not always be fun, but it certainly is an experience. India is not a place you simply and clinically 'see'; it's a total experience, an assault on the senses, a place you'll never forget.

SARA-JANE CLELAND

FRANCES LINZEE GORDON

SANJAY SINGH BADNOR

FRANCES LINZEE GORDON

PAUL BEINSSEN

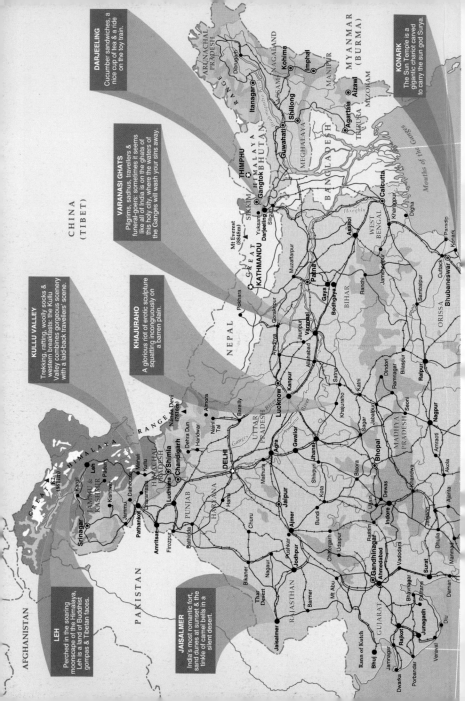

LEH
Perched on the soaring moonscape of the Himalaya, Leh is a land of Buddhist gompas & Tibetan faces.

KULLU VALLEY
Trekking, rafting, woolly socks & western breakfasts: the Kullu Valley combines gorgeous scenery with a laid-back travellers' scene.

JAISALMER
India's most romantic fort, sand dunes at sunset & the tinkle of camel bells in a silent desert.

KHAJURAHO
A glorious riot of erotic sculpture squatting incongruously on a barren plain.

VARANASI GHATS
Pilgrims, sadhus, travellers & funeral-goers: sometimes it seems like all of India is on the ghats of this holy city, where the waters of the Ganges will wash your sins away.

DARJEELING
Cucumber sandwiches, a nice cup of tea & a ride on the toy train.

KONARK
The Sun Temple is a gigantic stone chariot carved to carry the sun god Surya.

AFGHANISTAN

PAKISTAN

CHINA
(TIBET)

NEPAL

BHUTAN

BANGLADESH

MYANMAR
(BURMA)

JAMMU & KASHMIR
K2 (8611m)
Srinagar
Kargil
Leh
Padum
Kishtwar
Jammu

HIMACHAL PRADESH
Manali
Kullu
Dalhousie
Dharamsala
Shimla

PUNJAB
Pathankot
Amritsar
Ludhiana
Firozpur
Bathinda

CHANDIGARH

HARYANA
Hansi

DELHI

RAJASTHAN
Bikaner
Nagaur
Barmer
Jaisalmer
Thar Desert
Churu
Pushkar
Ajmer
Jodhpur
Bundi
Kota
Chittorgarh
Udaipur
Mt Abu
Chhotgarh

GUJARAT
Gandhinagar
Ahmedabad
Rann of Kutch
Bhuj
Jamnagar
Rajkot
Junagadh
Porbandar
Dwarka
Veraval
Diu
Bhavnagar
Palitana
Surat
Vadodara
Daman
Dhulia

UTTAR PRADESH
Nanda Devi (7816m)
Almora
Nainl Tal
Dehra Dun
Haridwar
Bareilly
Mathura
Agra
Gwalior
Jhansi
Kanpur
Lucknow
Ayodhya
Jaunpur
Allahabad
Varanasi
Gorakhpur

MADHYA PRADESH
Bhopal
Indore
Dewas
Ujjain
Ratlam
Shivpuri
Sagar
Satna
Katni
Khajuraho
Dhindori
Jabalpur
Seoni
Nagpur
Amraoti
Akola
Ajanta
Chhindwara
Bilaspur

BIHAR
Patna
Gaya
Bodhgaya
Muzaffarpur
Ranchi
Dhanbad

WEST BENGAL
Asansol
Calcutta
Hooghly
Kharagpur
Digha
Jamshedpur
Purulia

ORISSA
Bhubaneswar
Cuttack
Konark
Puri
Sambalpur
Raipur

SIKKIM
Gangtok
Yuksam
Darjeeling
Siliguri

ARUNACHAL PRADESH
Itanagar
Dibrugarh

NAGALAND
Kohima

ASSAM
Guwahati

MEGHALAYA
Shillong

MANIPUR
Imphal

MIZORAM
Aizawl

TRIPURA
Agartala

THIMPHU

KATHMANDU
Pokhara

Mt Everest (8848m)

GREAT HIMALAYA RANGE

Ganges River
Chambal River
Mahanadi River
Mouths of the Ganges

Ganganagar

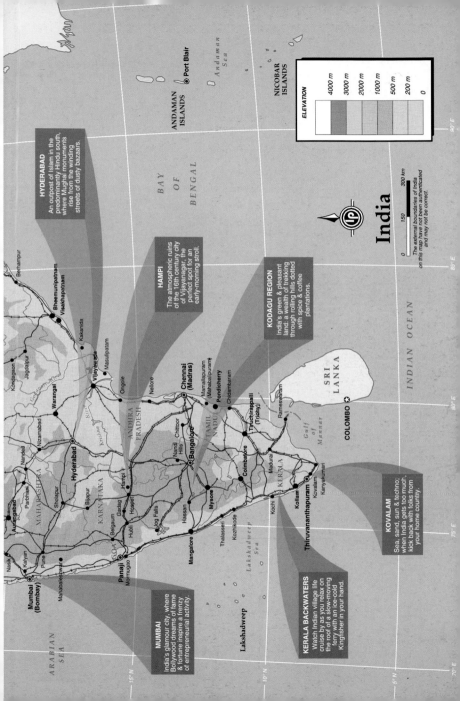

India

The external boundaries of India
on this map have not been authenticated
and may not be correct.

ELEVATION

	4000 m
	3000 m
	2000 m
	1000 m
	500 m
	200 m
	0

HYDERABAD
An outpost of Islam in the predominantly Hindu south, where Mughal monuments rise from the winding streets of dusty bazaars.

HAMPI
The atmospheric ruins of the 16th century city of Vijayanagar, the perfect spot for an early-morning stroll.

KODAGU REGION
India's green & pleasant land, a wealth of trekking through rolling hills dotted with spice & coffee plantations.

MUMBAI
India's glamour city, where Bollywood dreams of fame & fortune inspire a frenzy of entrepreneurial activity

KERALA BACKWATERS
Watch Indian village life cruise by as you relax on the roof of a slow-moving ferry with an ice-cold Kingfisher in your hand.

KOVALAM
Sea, sand, sun & techno; when India gets too much, kick back with folks from your home country.

ANDAMAN ISLANDS ● Port Blair

Andaman Sea

NICOBAR ISLANDS

BAY OF BENGAL

SRI LANKA

COLOMBO

Gulf of Mannar

INDIAN OCEAN

ARABIAN SEA

Lakshadweep Sea

Lakshadweep

0   150   300 km

Nasik
Kalyan
Mumbai (Bombay)
Pune
Mahabaleshwar

Aurangabad
Nanded
Parbhani
Sholapur
Bijapur
Belgaum

MAHARASHTRA

Kondagaon
Jagdalpur

Kakinada
Behrampur

Bheemunipatnam
Visakhapatnam

Nizamabad
Warangal
Hyderabad

ANDHRA PRADESH

Vijayawada
Masulipatam

Ongole

Nellore

Chennai (Madras)
Mamallapuram (Mahabalipuram)
Pondicherry
Chidambaram

Gadag
Hospet
Hampi
Hubli
Jog Falls

KARNATAKA

Chittoor
Nandi Hills
Bangalore

TAMIL NADU

Tiruchirappalli (Trichy)
Rameswaram

Hassan
Mysore
Coimbatore
Madurai

Thalasseri
Kozhikode
Mangalore

KERALA

Kochi
Kollam
Thiruvananthapuram
Kovalam
Kanyakumari

Panaji
Mormugao
GOA

Godavari River
Krishna River

Delhi & Mumbai

Top: Mumbai's dhobi ghats.
Left: Delhi's suburbs sprawl under a
    cloud of pollution.

Centre: The Taj Mahal Hotel, Mumbai's
    classiest place to stay.
Right: Jai Singh's observatory, Delhi.

Facts about the Country

For at least 4000 years, India's social and religious structures have withstood invasions, famines, religious persecutions, political upheavals and many other cataclysms. Few other countries could claim to have a national identity with such a long history behind it. To describe India as a land of contrasts is to state the obvious. Although there are many countries which would qualify for such a description in terms of their different ethnic groups, languages, religions, geography and traditions, few can match the vast scale and diversity to be found in India.

Change is inevitably taking place as modern technology reaches further and further into the fabric of society, yet essentially village India remains much the same as it has for thousands of years. So resilient are its social and religious institutions and, at the same time, so static, that it has either absorbed or thrown off all attempts to radically change or destroy them. Even in the fast-paced modern cities like Delhi, Mumbai (formerly known as Bombay) and Bangalore, what appears to be a complete change of attitude and lifestyle is only surface gloss. Underneath, the age-old verities, loyalties and obligations still rule people's lives.

There is possibly no other country where religion is so inextricably intertwined with every aspect of life. Coming to understand it can be a long process littered with pitfalls, particularly for those educated in the western liberal tradition with its basis in logic. For those people, 'Indian logic' can often seem bizarre, convoluted and even exasperating. Yet it encompasses a unique cosmology which is both holistic and coherent as well as being fascinating.

It's well to remember that India was the birthplace of two of the world's great religions (Hinduism and Buddhism) and one of its smallest (Jainism). It's also home to one of the world's few remaining communities of Parsis, adherents of the faith of Zoroastrianism.

The modern state itself is a relatively recent creation born out of a people's desire to throw off the yoke of colonialism. Even the mightiest of India's ancient civilisations did not encompass all of modern India, and today it is still as much a country of diversities as of unities. You may hear it said that there are many Indias. In terms of ethnic origin, language and geographical location, that is undoubtedly true, and it sometimes bedevils efforts at creating a national consciousness. Yet it's worth remembering that for the last 50 years, India has remained the world's largest democracy.

HISTORY
Indus Valley Civilisation
India's first major civilisation flourished for 1000 years from around 2500 BC along the Indus River valley in what is now Pakistan. Its great cities were Mohenjodaro and Harappa, where a civilisation of great complexity developed. The major city sites were discovered during this century and other, lesser cities have been subsequently unearthed at sites like Lothal, near Ahmedabad in India.

The origins of Hinduism can be traced all the way back to this early civilisation. The society was ruled by priests rather than by kings, and it was they who interceded with the gods, dictated social modes and determined such issues as land tenure. Clay figurines have been found at these sites suggesting worship of a Mother Goddess (later personified as Kali) and a male, three-faced god sitting in the attitude of a yogi attended by four animals (the prehistoric Siva). Black stone pillars (phallic worship associated with Siva) have also been discovered. Even at this time, certain animals were regarded as sacred, the most prominent being the humped bull (later, Siva's mount). The traditional Hindu fear of pollution and the need for ritual washing is also reflected in the intricate system of drains found at Harappa. There is even evidence of an organised system of garbage collection!

Comparatively little is known about the development and eventual demise of this civilisation. Their script has still not been deciphered, nor is it known why such an advanced civilisation collapsed so quickly following invasion by the Aryans.

Early Invasions & the Rise of Religions

The Aryan invaders swept south from central Asia between 1500 and 200 BC. They eventually controlled the whole of northern India as far as the Vindhya hills, and pushed the original inhabitants, the Dravidians, south. The invaders brought with them their nature gods, among whom the ones of fire and battle were predominant, as well as their cattle-raising and meat-eating traditions. Yet, even by the 8th century BC, the priestly caste had succeeded in reasserting its supremacy and the nature gods were displaced or absorbed into the concept of a universal soul (Brahman) to which the *aatman* (individual soul) was identical. These events are recorded in the literature of the time as the victory of Brahma over Indra (formerly the goddess of food and the law but later of thunder and battle). Indra supposedly led a bizarre double life, being a woman for one phase of the moon and then changing overnight into a man for the next phase. It was also during this period of transition (1500-1200 BC) that the Hindu sacred scriptures, the *Vedas*, were written.

The social order which reflected the assimilation of the Aryans and the supremacy of the priests became consolidated in the caste system, which survives to this day despite efforts by the central government to enhance the status of those at the bottom of the pile. Control over this social order was maintained by extremely strict rules designed to secure the position of the Brahmins (priests). Elaborate taboos were established concerning marriage, diet, travel, modes of eating and drinking and social intercourse. Within the system, each caste adopted its own unique set of rules with which to assert its superiority over those considered to be inferior. Anyone disregarding the rules would be cast out and driven away. Yet the priests could not have it all their own way. Despite the strictures concerning respect for the priests and for all animal life, the meat-eating traditions of the Aryans had to be accommodated. It's essentially from these times that the vague division between the meat-eating north and vegetarian south stems.

During the period when the Aryans were consolidating their hold on northern India, the heartland narrowly missed two other invasions from the west. The first was by the Persian king, Darius (521-486 BC), who annexed the Punjab and Sind but went no further. Alexander the Great reached India in his epic march from Greece in 326 BC, but his troops refused to march further than the Beas River, the easternmost extent of the Persian Empire he had conquered, and he turned back without extending his power into India itself. The most lasting reminder of his appearance in the East was the development of Gandharan art, that intriguing mixture of Grecian artistic ideals and the new religious beliefs of Buddhism.

Buddhism arose around 500 BC contemporaneously with Jainism and presented Brahmanical Hinduism with its greatest challenge. The appeal of both of these cosmologies was that they rejected the Vedas and condemned caste, though, unlike the Buddhists, the Jains never denied their Hindu heritage and their faith never extended beyond India.

Buddhism, however, drove a radical swathe through the spiritual and social body of Hinduism and enjoyed spectacular growth after Ashoka embraced the faith and declared it the state religion. Nevertheless, it gradually lost touch with the general population and faded as Hinduism underwent a revival between 200 and 800 AD, based on devotion to a personal god represented today by sects based on Rama and Krishna (*avatars*, or manifestations, of Vishnu). Yet such was the appeal of the greatest of India's spiritual teachers that the Buddha could not be sidelined and forgotten. He was therefore incorporated into the Hindu pantheon as yet another of the avatars of Vishnu. It was a prime example of the way in which Hinduism has absorbed spiritual competitors and heretical ideologies.

The Mauryas & Ashoka

Two centuries before Alexander made his long march east, an Indian kingdom had started to develop in the north of India. It expanded into the vacuum created by Alexander's departure when Chandragupta Maurya's empire came to power in 321 BC. From its capital at the site of present-day Patna, the Mauryan Empire eventually spread across northern India. The Mauryas set up a rigid and well-organised empire with a huge standing army paid for directly by the emperor. They also developed an efficient bureaucracy which kept tabs on everyone for the collection of taxes, tithes and agricultural produce. There were heavy penalties for those who evaded taxes and an extensive system of spies, but corruption was rife, and life for the ordinary peasant remained unrelentingly harsh.

The empire reached its peak under Emperor Ashoka, who converted to Buddhism in 262 BC. He left pillars and rock-carved edicts which delineate the enormous span of his empire. Ashokan edicts and pillars can be seen in Delhi, Gujarat, Orissa, Sarnath in Uttar Pradesh, and at Sanchi in Madhya Pradesh.

Ashoka also sent missions abroad, and in Sri Lanka his name is revered because he sent his son as a missionary to carry Buddhism to the island. The development of art and sculpture also flourished during his rule, and his standard, which topped many of his pillars, is now the seal of the modern state of India. Under Ashoka, the Mauryan Empire controlled more of India than probably any subsequent ruler prior to the Mughals or the British. Following his death, in 232 BC, the empire rapidly disintegrated and collapsed in 184 BC.

An Interlude, then the Guptas

A number of empires rose and fell following the collapse of the Mauryas. The successors to Alexander's kingdoms in the north-west expanded their power into the Punjab and this later developed into the Gandharan Kingdom. In the south-east and east, the Andhras or Telugus expanded inland from the coast, while the Mauryan Empire was replaced by the Sungas, who ruled from 184 to 70 BC. During this period, many Buddhist structures were completed and the great cave temples of central India were commenced. This was the period of the 'lesser vehicle' or *Hinayana* Buddhism, in which the Buddha could never be directly shown but was alluded to through symbols such as stupas, footprints, trees or elephants. Although this form of Buddhism probably continued until about 400 AD, it was already being supplanted by 100 AD by the 'greater vehicle' or *Mahayana* Buddhism.

In 319 AD, Chandragupta II founded the Gupta Empire, the first phase of which became known as the Imperial Guptas. His successors extended their power over northern India, first from Patna and later from other northern cities such as Ayodhya. The Imperial Guptas gave way to the Later Guptas in 455 AD and the Gupta period continued to 606 AD. The arts flourished during this period, with some of the finest work being done at Ajanta, Ellora, Sanchi and Sarnath. Poetry and literature also experienced a golden age. Towards the end of the Gupta period, however, Buddhism and Jainism both began to decline and Hinduism began to rise in popularity once more.

The invasions of the White Huns signalled the end of this era of history, although they were at first repelled by the Guptas. The Huns drove the Gandharas from the northwest region, close to Peshawar, into Kashmir. Subsequently, North India broke up into a number of separate Hindu kingdoms and was not really unified again until the coming of the Muslims.

Meanwhile in the South

In Indian history, events in one part of the country do not necessarily affect those in another. The kingdoms that rose and fell in the north of the country generally had no influence or connection with those in the south. While Buddhism and, to a lesser extent, Jainism were displacing Hinduism in the centre and north of India, Hinduism continued to flourish in the south.

The south's prosperity was based upon its long-established trading links with other civilisations. The Egyptians and, later, the Romans both traded by sea with the south of India. Strong links were also formed with parts of South-East Asia. For a time, Buddhism and, later, Hinduism flourished in the Indonesian islands, and the people of the region looked towards India as their cultural mentor. The *Ramayana*, that most famous of Hindu epics, is today told and retold in various forms in many South-East Asian countries. Bali is the only Hindu stronghold in South-East Asia today and, though it's clearly recognisable as such, its isolation from the heartland of Hinduism has resulted in considerable modification of the faith.

Other outside influences which came to the south of India in this period included St Thomas the Apostle, who is said to have arrived in Kerala in 52 AD. To this day, there is a strong Christian influence in the region.

Great empires that rose in the south included the Cholas, Pandyas, Cheras, Chalukyas and Pallavas. The Chalukyas ruled mainly over the Deccan region of central India, although at times their power extended further north. With a capital at Badami in Karnataka, they ruled from 550 to 753 AD before falling to the Rashtrakutas. They rose again in 972 and continued their rule through to 1190. Further south, the Pallavas pioneered Dravidian architecture with its exuberant, almost baroque, style. They also carried Indian culture to Java in Indonesia, Thailand and Cambodia.

In 850 AD, the Cholas rose to power and gradually superseded the Pallavas. They too were great builders, as their temple at Thanjavur indicates. They also carried their power overseas and, under the reign of Raja Raja (985-1014 AD), controlled almost the whole of southern India, the Deccan, Sri Lanka, and parts of the Malay peninsula and the Sumatran-based Srivijaya Kingdom.

First Muslim Invasions

While the Hindu kingdoms ruled in the south and Buddhism was fading in the north, Muslim power was creeping towards India from the Middle East.

Muslim power first made itself strongly felt on the subcontinent with the raids of Mahmud of Ghazni. Today, Ghazni is just a grubby little town between Kabul and Kandahar in Afghanistan, but from 1001 AD Mahmud conducted raids from here on an annual basis. In 1033, after his death, one of his successors actually took Varanasi. The raids stopped in 1038 when the expansionist Seljuk Turks took Ghazni.

These early visits, however, were little more than banditry, and it was not until 1192 that Muslim power arrived in India on a permanent basis. In that year, Mohammed of Ghori, who had been expanding his powers across the Punjab, moved his armies into India and took Ajmer. The following year, his general, Qutb-ud-din, took Varanasi and then Delhi. After Mohammed of Ghori was killed in 1206, Qutb-ud-din became the first of the Sultans of Delhi. Within 20 years, the Muslims had brought the whole of the Ganges basin under their control, but the Sultans of Delhi were never consistent in their powers. With each new ruler, the kingdom grew or shrank depending on personal abilities.

In 1297, Ala-ud-din Khilji pushed the borders south into Gujarat; his general subsequently moved further south, but could not maintain the extension. In 1338, Mohammed Tughlaq decided to move his capital south from Delhi to Daulatabad, near Aurangabad in Maharashtra. He marched most of Delhi's population south, but the site turned out to be unsuitable, and eventually he had to return north. Soon after, the Bahmani Kingdom arose and the Delhi Sultanate began to retreat north, only to be further weakened when Tamerlane (Timur) made a devastating raid from Samarkand into India in 1398. From then on, the power of this Muslim kingdom steadily contracted, until it was supplanted by another Muslim kingdom, that of the Mughals.

The Muslims were a somewhat different breed of invader. Unlike previous arrivals, they retained their own identity, and the contempt which they heaped on their infidel subjects prevented their absorption into the prevailing Hindu religious and social systems. Nevertheless, Hinduism survived and Islam found India relatively infertile ground for conversion. By the 20th century, after 800 years of Muslim domination, only 25% of the population had converted to Islam.

The Muslims could not rule without Hindu assistance, so many Hindus were inducted into the bureaucracy. This resulted in the development of a common language, Urdu, which is a combination of Persian vocabulary and Hindi grammar using Perso-Arabic script. It remains the language of large parts of northern India and of Pakistan.

Meanwhile in the South (again)

Once again, events in the south of India took a different path to those in the north. Just as the Aryan invasions never reached the south, so the early Muslim invasions failed to permanently affect events there. Between 1000 and 1300 AD, the Hoysala Empire, which had centres at Belur, Halebid and Somnathpur, was at its peak. It eventually fell to a predatory raid by Mohammed Tughlaq in 1328, and then to the combined opposition of other Hindu kingdoms.

Two other great kingdoms developed in the north of modern-day Karnataka – one Muslim and one Hindu. The Hindu kingdom of Vijayanagar was founded in 1336. Its capital was at Hampi, and it was probably the strongest Hindu kingdom in India during the period that the Muslim Sultans of Delhi were dominating the north.

At the same time, the Bahmani Muslim kingdom developed, but in 1489 it split into five separate kingdoms at Berar, Ahmednagar, Bijapur, Golconda and Ahmedabad. In 1520, Vijayanagar took Bijapur, but in 1565 the kingdom's Muslim opponents combined to destroy Vijayanagar in the epic Battle of Talikota. Later, the Bahmani kingdoms were to fall to the Mughals.

The Mughals (1527-1757)

These larger-than-life individuals ushered in a golden age of building, arts and literature, and spread their control over India to an extent rivalled only by Ashoka and the British. Their rise to power was rapid but their decline was equally quick. There were only six great Mughals; after Aurangzeb, the rest were emperors in name only.

The Mughals did more than simply rule, however – they had a passion for building which resulted in some of the greatest buildings in India – Shah Jahan's magnificent Taj Mahal ranks as one of the wonders of the world. Art and literature also flourished under the Mughals and the magnificence of their court stunned early European visitors.

The six great Mughals and their reigns were:

Babur	1527-1530
Humayun	1530-1556
Akbar	1556-1605
Jehangir	1605-1627
Shah Jahan	1627-1658
Aurangzeb	1658-1707

The Mughal emperor Akbar ruled from 1556 to 1605, and was probably the greatest of the Mughal rulers, who dominated northern India for three centuries.

Babur, a descendant of both Tamerlane and Genghis Khan, marched into the Punjab from his capital at Kabul in Afghanistan in 1525 to defeat the Sultan of Delhi at Panipat. This initial success did not totally destroy opposition to the Mughals, and in 1540 the Mughal Empire came to an abrupt but temporary end when Sher Shah defeated Humayun, the second great Mughal. For 15 years, Humayun lived in exile until he was able to return and regain his throne. By 1560, Akbar, his son and successor, who had come to the throne aged only 14, was able to claim effective and complete control of his empire.

Akbar was probably the greatest of the Mughals, for he not only had the military ability required of a ruler in that time, but he was also a man of culture and wisdom with a sense of fairness. He saw, as previous Muslim rulers had not, that the number of Hindus in India was too great to subjugate. Instead, he integrated them into his empire and made use of many Hindu advisers, generals and administrators. Akbar also had a deep interest in religious matters, and spent many hours in discussion with religious experts of

Shah Jahan, who ruled from 1627 to 1658, had a passion for building, and was responsible for one of the most stunning buildings in the world – the Taj Mahal.

all persuasions, including Christians and Parsis. He eventually formulated a religion which combined the best points of all those he had studied.

Jehangir followed Akbar and maintained his father's tolerance of other religions but took advantage of the stability of the empire to spend most of his time in his beloved Kashmir, eventually dying while en route there. His tomb is at Lahore in Pakistan. Shah Jahan, however, who secured his position as emperor by executing all male collateral relatives, stuck much more to Agra and Delhi. During his reign, some of the most vivid and permanent reminders of the Mughals' glory were constructed. Best known, of course, is the Taj Mahal, but that was only one of Shah Jahan's many magnificent buildings. Indeed, some say that it was his passion for building that led to his downfall, and that his son, Aurangzeb, deposed him in part to put a halt to his architectural extravagances. Shah Jahan also ditched Akbar's policy of religious tolerance in favour of a return to Islam. Yet it was during his reign that the British were granted their trading post at Madras in 1639.

The last of the great Mughals, Aurangzeb, devoted his resources to extending the empire's boundaries, but it was the punitive taxes which he levied on his subjects to pay for his military exploits and his religious zealotry that eventually secured his downfall. It was also during his reign that the empire began to rot from the inside, as luxury and easy living corroded the mettle and moral fibre of the nobles and military commanders. His austere and puritanical beliefs led him to destroy many Hindu temples and erect mosques on their sites, alienating the very people who were such an important part of his bureaucracy.

It didn't take long for revolts to break out on all sides and, with Aurangzeb's death in 1707, the Mughal Empire's fortunes rapidly declined. There were Mughal 'emperors' right up to the time of the Indian Mutiny, when the British exiled the last one and executed his sons, but they were emperors without an empire. In sharp contrast to the magnificent tombs of his Mughal predecessors,

Aurangzeb's tomb is a simple affair at Rauza, near Aurangabad.

The states which followed the Mughal Empire did, in some cases, manage to sustain themselves. In the south, the viceroyalty in Hyderabad became one of the British-tolerated princely states, one which lasted until Independence. The nawabs of Avadh in north India ruled eccentrically, flamboyantly and badly until 1856, when the British 'retired' the last nawab. In Bengal, the Mughals unwisely clashed with the British far earlier, and their rule was terminated by the Battle of Plassey in 1757.

The Rajputs & the Marathas

Mughal power was not replaced by another, greater power. It declined due to a number of factors and power passed to a number of other rulers.

Throughout the Muslim period in the north of India, there were still strong Hindu powers, most notably the Rajputs. Centred in Rajasthan, the Rajputs were a warrior caste with a strong and almost fanatical belief in the dictates of chivalry, both in battle and in the conduct of state affairs. Their place in Indian history is much like that of the knights of medieval Europe. The Rajputs opposed every foreign incursion into their territory, but were never united or sufficiently organised to be able to deal with superior forces on a long-term basis. Not only that, but when not battling foreign oppression they squandered their energies fighting each other. This eventually led to them becoming vassal states of the Mughal Empire, but their prowess in battle was well recognised, and some of the best military men in the emperors' armies were Rajputs.

The Marathas first rose to prominence with Shivaji who, between 1646 and 1680, performed feats of arms and heroism across most of central India. Tales of his larger-than-life exploits are still popular with wandering storytellers in small villages today. He is a particular hero in Maharashtra, where many of his wildest exploits took place, but he is also revered for two other things: as a lower-caste Sudra, he showed that great

leaders do not have to be Kshatriyas (soldiers or administrators), and he also demonstrated great abilities in confronting the Mughals. At one time, Shivaji was captured by the Mughals and taken back to Agra but, naturally, he managed to escape and continue his adventures.

Shivaji's son was captured, blinded and executed by Aurangzeb. His grandson was not made of the same sturdy stuff, but the Maratha Empire continued under the Peshwas, hereditary government ministers who became the real rulers. They gradually took over more and more of the weakening Mughal Empire's powers, first by supplying troops and then by actually taking control of Mughal land.

When Nadir Shah from Persia sacked Delhi in 1739, the declining Mughals were weakened further. But the expansion of Maratha power came to an abrupt halt in 1761 at Panipat. There, where Babur had won the battle that established the Mughal Empire over 200 years earlier, the Marathas were defeated by Ahmad Shah Durani from Afghanistan. Though their expansion to the west halted, the Marathas consolidated their control over central India and the region known as Malwa. Soon, however, they were to fall to India's final imperial power, the British.

Expansion of British Power

The British were not the first European power to arrive in India, nor were they the last to leave – both those honours go to the Portuguese. In 1498, Vasco da Gama arrived on the coast of modern-day Kerala, having sailed around the Cape of Good Hope. Pioneering this route gave the Portuguese a century of uninterrupted monopoly over Indian and Far Eastern trade with Europe. In 1510, they captured Goa, the Indian enclave they controlled right through to 1961. So rich was Goa during its heyday that it was known as the Lisbon of the East. In the long term, however, the Portuguese simply did not have the resources to hold onto a worldwide empire and they were quickly eclipsed when the British, French and Dutch arrived.

In 1612, the British made their first permanent inroad into India when they established a trading post at Surat in Gujarat. In 1600, Queen Elizabeth I had granted a charter to a London trading company giving it a monopoly on British trade with India. For 250 years, British power was exercised in India not by the government but by the East India Company, which developed from this initial charter. British trading posts were established on the eastern coast at Madras in 1640, at Bombay in 1668 and at Calcutta in 1690.

The British and Portuguese were not the only Europeans in India. The Danes and Dutch also had trading posts, and in 1672 the French established themselves at Pondicherry, an enclave that they, like the Portuguese in Goa, would hold even after the British had departed.

The stage was set for over a century of rivalry between the British and French for control of Indian trade. In 1746, the French took Madras, only to hand it back in 1749. In subsequent years, there was to be much intrigue between the imperial powers. If the British were involved in a struggle with one local ruler, they could be certain the French would be backing him with arms, men or expertise. In 1756, Siraj-ud-daula, the Nawab of Bengal, attacked Calcutta and outraged Britain with the 'black hole of Calcutta' incident. A year later, Robert Clive retook Calcutta and in the Battle of Plassey defeated Siraj-ud-daula and his French supporters, thus not only extending British power but also curtailing French influence. The victory ushered in a long period of unbridled profiteering by members of the East India Company until its powers were taken over by the British Government in the 19th century.

India at this time was in a state of flux – a power vacuum had been created by the disintegration of the Mughal Empire. The Marathas were the only real Indian power to step into this gap and they were more a collection of local kingdoms who sometimes cooperated, sometimes did not, than a power in their own right. In the south, where Mughal influence had never been great, the picture was confused by the strong British-French rivalry, as one ruler was played off against another.

This was never clearer than in the series of Mysore wars. In the 4th Mysore War (1789-99), that irritant to British power, Tipu Sultan, was killed at Srirangapatnam and British power took another step forward. The long-running British struggle with the Marathas was finally concluded in 1803, which left only the Punjab outside British control. Even that fell to the British in 1849 after the two Sikh wars.

It was during this time that the borders of Nepal were delineated, following a brief series of battles between the British and the Gurkhas in 1814. The Gurkhas were initially victorious but, two years later, were forced to sue for peace as the British marched on Kathmandu. As part of the price for peace, the Nepalese were forced to cede the provinces of Kumaon and Shimla, but mutual respect for each others' military prowess prevented Nepal's incorporation into the Indian Empire and led to the establishment of the Gurkha regiments of the British Army.

British India

By the early 19th century, India was effectively under British control. In part, this takeover had come about because of the vacuum left by the demise of the Mughals, but the British also followed the rules Akbar had laid down so successfully. To them, India was principally a place to make money, and the Indians' culture, beliefs and religions were left strictly alone. Indeed, it was said the British didn't give a damn what religious beliefs a person held so long as they made a good cup of tea. Furthermore, the British had a disciplined, efficient army and astute political advisers. They followed the policy of divide and rule with great success and negotiated distinctly one-sided treaties giving them the right to intervene in local states if they were inefficiently run; 'inefficient' could be, and was, defined as the British saw fit.

Even under the British, India remained a patchwork of states, many of them nominally independent but actually under strong British influence. This policy of maintaining 'princely states' governed by maharajas and nawabs (and a host of other titled rulers) continued right through to Independence, and caused a number of problems at that time. The British interest in trade and profit resulted in expansion of iron and coal mining, the development of tea, coffee and cotton growing, the construction of the basis of today's vast Indian rail network, and the commencement of irrigation projects which have today revolutionised agriculture.

In the sphere of government and law, Britain gave India a well-developed and smoothly functioning government and civil service structure. The fearsome love of bureaucracy which India inherited from Britain may be the downside to that, but the country reached Independence with a better organised, more efficient and less corrupt administrative system than most ex-colonial countries.

There was, however, a price to pay: colonies are not established for altruistic reasons. Cheap textiles from Britain's new manufacturing industry flooded into India, crippling local cottage industries. On one hand, the British outlawed *sati*, the Hindu custom of burning the wife on her husband's funeral pyre, but on the other hand they encouraged the system of *zamindars*. These absentee landlords eased the burden of administrative and tax collection for the British, but contributed to an impoverished and landless peasantry in parts of India – a problem which is still chronic in Bihar and West Bengal today.

The British also established English as the local language of administration. While this may have been useful in a country with so many different languages, and still fulfils a very important function in nationwide communication today, it did keep the new rulers at arm's length from the Indians.

The Indian Uprising

In 1857, less than half a century after Britain had taken firm control of India, the British had their first serious setback. To this day, the causes of the Indian Uprising, or Mutiny,

are hard to unravel. It's even hard to define if it really was the 'War of Independence' as it is referred to in India, or merely a mutiny. The causes were a run-down administration, the dismissal of local rulers, and a bullet lubricant. A rumour, quite possibly true, leaked out that a new type of bullet issued to the troops, many of whom were Muslim, was greased with pig fat. A similar rumour claimed that the bullets were actually greased with cow fat. Pigs, of course, are unclean to Muslims, and cows are holy to Hindus.

The British were slow to deny these rumours and even slower to prove either that they were incorrect or that changes had been made. The result was a loosely coordinated mutiny of the Indian battalions of the Bengal Army. Of the 74 battalions, seven (one of them Gurkhas) remained loyal, 20 were disarmed and the other 47 mutinied. The Uprising broke out at Meerut, close to Delhi, and soon spread across north India. There were massacres and acts of senseless cruelty on both sides, long sieges and protracted struggles, but in the end the struggle died out rather than came to a conclusive finish. It never spread beyond the north of India, and although there were brilliant self-made leaders on the Indian side, there was never any real coordination or common aim.

Post-Uprising

The British made two moves after the Uprising. First, they wisely decided not to look for scapegoats or to exact official revenge, although revenge and looting had certainly taken place on an unofficial level. Second, the East India Company was wound up and administration of the country was belatedly handed over to the British government. The remainder of the century was the peak period for the empire on which 'the sun never set', and India was one of its brightest stars.

Two parallel developments during the latter part of the 19th century gradually paved the way for the independent India of today. First, the British slowly began to hand over power and bring more people into the decision-making processes. Democratic systems began to be implemented, although the British government retained overall control. In the civil service, higher and higher posts were opened up for Indians instead of being reserved for colonial administrators.

At the same time, Hinduism began to go through another of its periodic phases of resurgence and adjustment. During the Mughal and early British periods, it had gradually lost much of its mass appeal, if only because of the demise of its once-great Hindu kingdoms. It was clearly time to drag the religion back into the present and re-establish its relevance for the common people. The main protagonists in this revival were reformers like Ram Mohan Roy, Ramakrishna and Swami Vivekananda, who pushed through sweeping changes in Hindu society and paved the way for the Hindu beliefs of today. Other reformers, such as Sri Aurobindo, attempted to meld Hindu philosophy with the rapidly emerging precepts of modern science.

It was largely as a result of their efforts that hybrid spiritual groups based on Hinduism and a variety of pre-Christian western mysticism also made their appearance in the early part of the 20th century. Societies like the Theosophical Society of Annie Besant and her guru, Krishnamurti, date from this period. Even modern occultist Aleister Crowley owed a debt to these popularisers of Hindu philosophy and mysticism.

Road to Independence
Opposition to British rule began to increase at the turn of the century. The 'Congress', which had been established to give India a degree of self-rule, now began to push for the real thing. Outside the Congress, hot-blooded individuals pressed for independence by more violent means. Eventually, the British mapped out a path towards independence similar to that pursued in Canada and Australia. However, WWI shelved these plans and events in Turkey – where Britain was at war with the Sultan (the spiritual leader of Muslims in India) – alienated many Indian Muslims. After the war, the struggle began

again in earnest, and its new leader was Mahatma Gandhi.

In 1915, Mohandas Gandhi returned from South Africa, where he had practised as a lawyer and devoted himself to fighting the racial discrimination faced by the country's many Indian settlers. In India, he soon turned his abilities to the question of independence, particularly after the infamous massacre at Amritsar in 1919 when a British army contingent opened fire on an unarmed crowd of protesters. Gandhi, who subsequently became known as the Mahatma, or great soul, adopted a policy of passive resistance, or *satyagraha*, to British rule.

The central pillar of his achievement was to broaden the scope of the independence struggle from the middle classes to the peasants and villagers. He led movements against the iniquitous salt tax and boycotts of British textiles, and for his efforts was jailed on a number of occasions. Not everyone involved in the struggle agreed with or followed

Mahatma Gandhi is often referred to as the 'Father of the Nation'. He spent many years campaigning against the British, using techniques of *satyagraha* (passive resistance).

Gandhi's policy of noncooperation and non-violence, yet the Congress Party and Mahatma Gandhi remained at the forefront of the push for independence.

By the time WWII was concluded, independence was inevitable. The war dealt a deathblow to colonialism and the myth of European superiority, and Britain no longer had the power or the desire to maintain a vast empire. Within India, however, a major problem had developed: the large Muslim minority had realised that an independent India would also be a Hindu-dominated India, and that despite Gandhi's fair-minded and even-handed approach, others in the Congress Party would not be so willing to share power.

Independence

The July 1945 Labour Party victory in the British elections brought a new breed of political leaders to power, and they realised that a solution to the Indian problem was imperative.

However, elections in India revealed an alarming growth of communalism. The country was divided along purely religious lines, with the Muslim League, led by Muhammad Ali Jinnah, speaking for the overwhelming majority of Muslims, and the Congress Party, led by Jawaharlal Nehru, representing the Hindu population. Mahatma Gandhi remained the father figure for Congress, but did not have an official role – and, as events were to prove, his political influence was slipping.

'I will have India divided, or India destroyed', were Jinnah's words. This uncompromising demand, Jinnah's egotistical bid for power over a separate nation, and Congress' desire for an independent greater-India proved to be the biggest stumbling blocks to the British granting independence. However, each passing day increased the prospects for intercommunal strife and bloodshed. In early 1946, a British mission failed to bring the two sides together and the country slid closer towards civil war. A 'Direct Action Day', called by the Muslim League in August 1946, led to the slaughter of Hindus in Calcutta,

followed by reprisals against Muslims. Attempts to make the two sides see reason had no effect. In February 1947, the British government made a momentous decision: the current viceroy, Lord Wavell, would be replaced by Lord Louis Mountbatten and independence would come by June 1948.

The Punjab region of northern India was already in a state of chaos, and the Bengal region in the east was close to it. The new viceroy made a last-ditch attempt to convince the rival factions that a united India was a more sensible proposition, but they – Jinnah in particular – remained intransigent. The reluctant decision was then made to divide the country. Only Gandhi stood firmly against the division, preferring the possibility of a civil war to the chaos he so rightly expected.

Neatly slicing the country in two proved to be an impossible task. Although some areas were clearly Hindu or Muslim, others had evenly mixed populations or were isolated 'islands' of Muslims surrounded by Hindu regions. The impossibility of attempting to divide all the Muslims from all the Hindus is illustrated by the fact that, after Partition, India was still the third-largest Muslim country in the world – only Indonesia and Pakistan had greater Muslim populations.

Unfortunately, the two overwhelmingly Muslim regions were on opposite sides of the country – Pakistan would inevitably have an eastern and western half divided by a hostile India. The instability of this arrangement was self-evident, but it took 25 years before the predestined split finally came and East Pakistan became Bangladesh. On top of this, the Sikhs would also find their 'homeland' split in half.

Other problems showed up only after independence was achieved. Pakistan was painfully short of the administrators and clerical workers with which India was so well endowed because these were not traditionally Muslim occupations. Many other occupations, such as moneylending and the menial tasks performed by the untouchables, had also been purely Hindu callings.

Mountbatten decided to follow a break-neck pace to independence and announced that it would come on 14 August 1947. Once the decision had been made to divide the country, there were countless administrative decisions to be made, the most important being the actual location of the dividing line. Since a locally adjudicated dividing line was certain to bring recriminations from either side, an independent British referee was given the odious task of drawing the line, knowing that its effects would be disastrous for countless people. The most difficult decisions had to be made in Bengal and the Punjab. In Bengal, Calcutta, with its Hindu majority, port facilities and jute mills, was divided from East Bengal, which had a Muslim majority, large-scale jute production, no mills and no port facilities.

The problem was far worse in the Punjab, where intercommunal antagonisms were already running at fever pitch. The Punjab was one of the most fertile and affluent regions of the country, and had large percentages of Muslims (55%), Hindus (30%) and a substantial number of India's Sikhs. It was clear that the Punjab contained all the ingredients for an epic disaster but, with the announcement of the dividing line only days after Independence, the resulting bloodshed was even worse than expected. Huge exchanges of population took place as Muslims moved to Pakistan and Hindus and Sikhs to India.

The dividing line cut neatly between the Punjab's two major cities – Lahore and Amritsar. Prior to Independence, Lahore's total population of 1.2 million included approximately 500,000 Hindus and 100,000 Sikhs. When the dust had finally settled, Lahore had a Hindu and Sikh population of only 1000.

For months, the greatest exodus in human history took place east and west across the Punjab. Trains full of Muslims, fleeing westward, were held up and slaughtered by Hindu and Sikh mobs. Hindus and Sikhs fleeing to the east suffered the same fate. The army sent to maintain order proved totally inadequate and, at times, all too ready to join the partisan carnage. By the time the Punjab chaos had run its course, over 10 million people had changed sides and even the most conservative estimates calculate that 250,000 people had been slaughtered. The true figure may well have been over half a million. An additional million people changed sides in Bengal, mainly Hindus heading west since few Muslims migrated from West Bengal to East Pakistan.

The division of the Punjab was not to be the only excuse for carnage. Throughout the British era, India had retained many 'princely states', and incorporating these into independent India and Pakistan proved to be a considerable headache. Guarantees of a substantial measure of independence convinced most of them to opt for inclusion into the new countries, but at the time of Independence there were still three hold-outs.

One was Kashmir, a predominantly Muslim state with a Hindu maharaja. In October 1948, the maharaja had still not opted for India or Pakistan when a rag-tag Pathan (Pakistani) army crossed the border, intent on racing to Srinagar and annexing Kashmir without provoking a real India-Pakistan conflict. Unfortunately for the Pakistanis, the Pathans had been inspired to mount their invasion by the promise of plunder, and they did so much plundering on the way that India had time to rush troops to Srinagar and prevent the town's capture. The indecisive maharaja finally opted for India, provoking the first, although brief, India-Pakistan war.

The UN was eventually persuaded to step in and keep the two sides apart, but the issue of Kashmir has remained a central cause for disagreement and conflict between the two countries ever since. With its overwhelming Muslim majority and its geographic links to Pakistan, many people were inclined to support Pakistan's claims to the region. To this day, India and Pakistan are divided in this region by a demarcation line (known as the Line of Actual Control), yet neither side agrees that this constitutes the official border.

The final stages of Independence had one last tragedy to be played out. On 30 January 1948, Gandhi, deeply disheartened by Partition and the subsequent bloodshed, was assassinated by a Hindu fanatic.

Independent India

Since Independence, India has made enormous strides and faced enormous problems. The mere fact that India has not, like so many developing countries, succumbed to dictatorships, military rule or wholesale foreign invasion is a testament to the basic strength of the country's government and institutions. Economically, it has made major steps forward in improving agricultural output, and its industries have expanded to the stage where India is one of the world's top 10 industrial powers.

Jawaharlal Nehru, India's first prime minister, tried to follow a strict policy of nonalignment. Yet, despite maintaining generally cordial relations with its former coloniser, and electing to join the Commonwealth, India moved towards the former USSR – partly because of conflicts with China and partly because of US support for arch-enemy Pakistan.

There were further clashes with Pakistan in 1965 and 1971, one over the intractable Kashmir dispute and the other one over

Jawaharlal Nehru, India's first prime minister, campaigned hard for Independence from Britain in the 1930s and 1940s.

Bangladesh. A border war was also fought with China in 1962 in the North-East Frontier Agency (NEFA; now referred to as the North-Eastern Region) and Ladakh, which resulted in the loss of Aksai Chin (Ladakh) and smaller areas in the NEFA. India continues to dispute sovereignty over these areas.

These outside events drew attention away from India's often serious internal problems, especially the failure to address rapid population growth.

Indira's India

Politically, India's major problem since Independence has been the personality cult that has developed with its leaders. There have only been three real prime ministers of stature – Nehru, his daughter Indira Gandhi (no relation to Mahatma Gandhi) and her son Rajiv Gandhi. Having won the 1966 election, Indira Gandhi faced serious opposition and unrest in 1975, which she countered by declaring a state of emergency – a situation which in many other countries might quickly have become a dictatorship.

During the emergency, a mixed bag of good and bad policies were followed. Freed of many parliamentary constraints, Gandhi was able to control inflation remarkably well, boost the economy and decisively increase efficiency. On the negative side, political opponents often found themselves behind bars, India's judicial system was turned into a puppet theatre, the press was fettered and there was more than a hint of personal aggrandisement, particularly in relation to her son, Sanjay Gandhi. His disastrous programme of forced sterilisations, in particular, caused much anger.

Despite murmurings of discontent, Gandhi decided that the people were behind her and in 1977 called a general election. Things did not go her way and her partially renamed Congress Party (Indira) was bundled out of power in favour of the Janata People's Party, a coalition formed with the sole purpose of defeating her. Once it had won, it quickly became obvious that Janata had no other cohesive policies. Its leader, Morarji Desai, seemed more interested in protecting cows, banning alcohol and getting his daily glass of urine than coming to grips with the country's problems. With inflation soaring, unrest rising and the economy faltering, nobody was surprised when Janata fell apart in late 1979. The 1980 election brought Indira Gandhi back to power with a larger majority than ever.

Indira Gandhi, the country's first woman prime minister, is still held in extremely high esteem. Her house in Delhi, where she was assassinated by one of her own bodyguards, is now a very popular museum.

India in the 1980s

Gandhi's political touch seemed to have faded as she grappled unsuccessfully with communal unrest in several areas, violent attacks on untouchables, numerous cases of police brutality and corruption, and the upheavals in the north-east and the Punjab. Then her son and political heir, the unpopular Sanjay, was killed in a light aircraft accident.

In 1984, Mrs Gandhi herself was assassinated by her Sikh bodyguards, clearly in reprisal for her earlier, and somewhat ill-considered, decision to send in the Indian Army to flush out armed Sikh radicals from the Golden Temple in Amritsar.

The radicals were demanding a separate Sikh state, to be named Khalistan. Regardless of the viability of such a land-locked state adjacent to a hostile Pakistan and what would have been a none-too-friendly India, her decision to desecrate the Sikhs' holiest temple was a disaster which led to large-scale riots, big problems in the army (in which Sikhs form a significant part of the officer corps), and a legacy of hate and distrust in the Punjab.

Meanwhile, Mrs Gandhi's son, Rajiv, an Indian Airlines pilot until his younger brother's death, quickly become the next heir to the throne, and was soon swept into power with an overwhelming majority and enormous popular support.

Despite his former lack of interest in politics, Rajiv Gandhi brought new and pragmatic policies to the country. Foreign investment and the use of modern technology were encouraged, import restrictions eased and many new industries were set up. They undoubtedly benefited the middle classes and provided many jobs for those who had been displaced from the land and migrated to the cities in search of work, but whether these policies were necessarily in the long-term best interests of India is open to question. They certainly projected India into the 1990s, woke the country from its partially self-induced isolationism, and broke its protectionist stance to world trade, but they didn't stimulate the rural sector.

Furthermore, his administration continually failed to quell unrest in the Punjab or Kashmir. It was also during his tenure in power that the Indian armed forces became bogged down in the turmoil in neighbouring Sri Lanka, caused by Tamil secessionists in that country demanding an independent state. Support for the Sri Lankan Tamils was clearly being supplied by their mainland brethren, and police activities in Tamil Nadu state aimed at rooting out sympathisers and curtailing the flow of arms and equipment made Rajiv a marked man.

There was also the Bofors scandal which dogged Rajiv's administration. Bribes were allegedly paid to members of the government to secure a contract to supply Swedish heavy artillery guns to the Indian army. It was even alleged that Rajiv, or at least his Italian-born wife, Sonia, were recipients of such bribes. The affair continues to be a thorn in the side of the Congress Party even 10 years on. During local elections in February 1997, other parties made much of the recent allegation that Italian businessman Otto Quattrocchi, a close friend of the Gandhis, received Rs 430 million for his part in the deal.

Following the November 1989 elections, Rajiv Gandhi's Congress(I) Party, although the largest single party in Parliament, was unable to form a government in its own right. As a result, a new National Front Government, made up of five parties, including the Hindu fundamentalist Bharatiya Janata Party (BJP), were to form the next government. Like the previous attempt to cobble together a government of national unity from minority parties with radically different viewpoints, it didn't last long and fresh elections had to be announced.

During the election campaign, disaster struck. While on a campaign tour of Tamil Nadu, Rajiv Gandhi, many of his aides and a number of bystanders were blown to bits by a bomb carried by a supporter of the Tamil Tigers. The assassination had clearly been planned in advance, and a massive police crackdown resulted in a shoot-out with Tamil mainland leaders and the arrest of several others.

Meanwhile, the septuagenarian Narasimha Rao assumed the leadership of the Congress(I) party and led it to victory at the polls. There were attempts, immediately after the assassination, to induce Rajiv's wife Sonia to assume the leadership, but she made it clear she had little interest in doing so. Nevertheless, she continues to be a powerful, behind-the-scenes influence.

India in the 1990s
Narasimha Rao shared Rajiv's determination to drag India (kicking and screaming, if necessary) into the economic realities of the 1990s, particularly after the collapse of the USSR, India's long-term ally and aid supplier. After years of languishing behind tariff barriers and a somewhat unrealistic currency exchange rate, the economy was given an enormous boost in 1992. The finance minister, Manmohan Singh, made the momentous step of partially floating the rupee against a basket of 'hard' currencies and legalising the import of gold by nonresident Indians.

Rao inherited a number of intractable problems which tested the mettle of his government. His biggest headache, though, was the simmering issue of communalism – that potentially explosive conflict between different religious groups, particularly between Hindus and Muslims, for which Ayodhya came to be a focus. This small town in central Uttar Pradesh is revered by Hindus as the birthplace of Rama. There are many Hindu temples here, but during Mughal times, the emperors razed several temples and constructed mosques on their sites. It was claimed that one of these mosques, the Babri Masjid, stood on the site of what was previously the Rama Temple. In December 1992 fundamentalist Hindus, egged on by the staunchly Hindu revivalist BJP (which controlled the UP state government), destroyed the mosque. Rioting followed in many cities across the north, extremists detonated bombs in Bombay and Delhi and several hundred people died.

Religious violence has also been unleashed by the practice of reserving government jobs and university places for members of so-called 'backward' classes, which generally means lower caste Hindus. This policy has been used by all parties to buy votes, but it has also caused outbreaks of violence across the country. This system also disaffects lower class Muslims because they don't qualify for places reserved for lower class Hindus. The reservation practice has gone a long way to undoing much of the work done by people such as Mahatma Gandhi, who worked tirelessly to improve the lot of the socially disadvantaged; once again, caste has been brought to the fore. The only bright spot in this whole issue is that as economic liberalisation takes hold, the private sector will expand at the expense of the public sector, so these policies will apply to a rapidly shrinking proportion of the economy.

The Kashmir issue again moved centre stage during the early 1990s, with demonstrations on both sides of the Line of Actual Control and an alarming increase in Jammu & Kashmir Liberation Front (JKLF) guerrilla activities in the Vale of Kashmir. Pakistan was almost certainly involved in encouraging, funding and supplying arms to the militants on the Indian side of the 'border' (which, of course, is denied), but reports suggest that the over-zealous activities of the Indian Army are also partially responsible for the upsurge in militancy. In 1995 the Charar-e-Sharif shrine and 1000 houses in the vicinity were burnt down, Kashmiris blaming the army. This led to riots in Srinagar. Incidents against tourists in Kashmir are on the increase. Six westerners were kidnapped in 1995; the body of one has been recovered and another escaped, but the fate of the others is unknown. In 1996 a family of Indian tourists were murdered on their Dal Lake houseboat.

Pakistan's support of the Kashmiri militants, both on its side of the 'border' (known as Azad Kashmir) and in the Vale itself, has rebounded. Kashmiri militants and their supporters on both sides have demanded nothing short of independence from both India and Pakistan. This demand is anathema to both India and Pakistan, but with the examples of the former USSR, Yugoslavia and Afghanistan, anything could happen.

Another problem has been the growth of secessionist movements in several parts of the country. This has often involved violent clashes between the people and police. In 1996, the prime minister gave his backing to the creation of a new state, Uttarakhand, in northern Uttar Pradesh. This will no doubt lead other secessionist movements (Jharkhand in Bihar/West Bengal, Gorkhaland in the Darjeeling region, and Bodoland in Assam) to intensify their fight for independence.

Developments in the Punjab have been encouraging. Elections were finally held under difficult circumstances in 1992, and Congress(I) secured power at state level, although only 24% of the electorate voted after the Akalis boycotted the polls. The elections in February 1997 saw a landslide victory for the Akali Dal-BJP alliance. The threat of terrorism in the area has waned considerably since.

As the Hindu fundamentalist parties such as the BJP and Shiv Sena have gained support in the last few years, the Congress Party has fallen out of favour with the people. In late 1994, they were dealt a severe blow with election routs in the states of Andhra Pradesh (Rao's home state) and Karnataka. It's hard to pinpoint the reasons for the voters' lack of confidence in the party, but there was definitely some backlash against corruption scandals and economic policies. The reduction of agricultural subsidies combined with high inflation (averaging 10%) made life even more difficult for millions of peasant farmers and labourers.

The 1996 general election was a disaster for Congress(I) , who were defeated by the BJP. The government formed by the BJP lasted less than two weeks, and was replaced by a coalition of 13 parties called the United Front, supported by Congress(I) and headed by HD Deve Gowda. In April 1997 he was replaced by Inder Kumar Gujral, the current prime minister. The current president, Kocheri Raman Narayanam, is the first Dalit to ever hold the post.

Despite all India's problems, it's worth remembering that half the people in the world who live in democratic societies live in India. Furthermore, despite its population problems, poverty, corruption and political opportunism, India manages (at least at the moment) to feed its own people without importing food, turns out hi-tech products, has a free and highly critical press, and hassles by security and customs officials are either nonexistent or minimal. This is a lot

India in the Record Books

In a country as large and diverse as India, where the weird and the wonderful are even more weird and wonderful than anywhere else, it comes as no surprise that the country holds many world records – although some of them are of dubious worth!

Obviously with its vast population, a number of records relate to crowds and people: the largest recorded assembly of people was an estimated 15 million at the Kumbh Mela festival at Allahabad in 1989 – a similar number attended the funeral of the Tamil Nadu chief minister in 1969; the largest single employer in the world is Indian Railways with 1,624,121 people on the payroll; the South Point High School in Calcutta has the largest enrolment with 11,683 regular students; and, in the world's largest democracy, the 1989 Lok Sabha elections produced quite a few records when 304,126,600 people voted for the 291 parties contesting the 543 seats at over 593,000 polling stations across the country!

India also has its fair share of biggest, longest and highest: Hero Cycles in Punjab is the world's largest manufacturer: in 1989 it built no less than 2,936,073 clunkers; the longest railway platform in the world (833m) is at Kharagpur in West Bengal; the State Bank of India has the most branches of any bank, with 12,203 across the country; the wettest place on earth is also in India, at Cherrapunji in Meghalaya, which in a one-year period copped a massive 26.46m; and pop star Lata Mangeshkar holds the record for the greatest number of recordings, with over 30,000 songs recorded in 20 Indian languages.

The bizarre and downright silly? Yes, India has them too. Indians hold the records for nonstop talking (360 hours), balancing on one foot (34 hours), clapping (58 hours, nine minutes), nonstop chanting (11,100 days and still rising), continuous typewriting (123 hours), standing still (over 17 years!), crawling (1,400 km), nonstop solo singing (262 hours), whistling (45 hours, 20 minutes), and walking with a full milk-bottle balanced on the head (65 km).

India also has the tree with the largest canopy – a banyan tree in the Calcutta Botanical Gardens covers 1.2 ha; the highest bridge in the world (5600m) is found on the Manali to Leh road; and, not surprisingly, the Howrah Bridge in Calcutta is the world's busiest – every day it carries almost 60,000 vehicles and innumerable pedestrians; while the Qutab Minar in Delhi, at 72.5m, is the tallest free-standing stone tower.

Indian disasters, both natural and otherwise, also feature in the record books. No-one could forget Bhopal, where 6000 people died and at least 200,000 others were injured, but in 1888, 246 people were killed in a hailstorm, while a dam which burst its banks in Gujarat killed at least 5000 in 1979.

Lastly, a record that's hardly likely to be challenged is that held by a Pune man who, in 1966, won a court case which had been filed by his ancestor 761 years earlier – the Indian bureaucracy in full swing! ■

more than you can say about many countries.

GEOGRAPHY & GEOLOGY

India has a total area of 3,287,263 sq km. This is divided into 25 states and seven directly administered union territories (including the capital, Delhi). The states are further subdivided into districts.

The Himalaya

The north of the country is decisively bordered by the long sweep of the Himalaya, the highest mountains on earth. They run from south-east to north-west, separating India from China. Bhutan in the east and Nepal in the centre actually lie along the Himalaya, as does Sikkim, Darjeeling, the northern part of

Uttar Pradesh, Himachal Pradesh and Jammu & Kashmir.

The Himalaya is one of the youngest mountain ranges in the world. Its evolution can be traced to the Jurassic era (80 million years ago) when the world's land masses were split into two: Laurasia in the northern hemisphere and Gondwanaland in the southern hemisphere. The land mass which is now India broke away from Gondwanaland and floated across the earth's surface, eventually colliding with Laurasia. The hard volcanic rocks of India were thrust against the soft sedimentary crust of Laurasia, forcing it upwards to create the Himalaya. This continental collision is still continuing with the mountains rising by up to 8mm each year.

The Himalaya are not a single mountain

range but a series of ranges with beautiful valleys wedged between them. The Kullu Valley in Himachal Pradesh and the Vale of Kashmir in Jammu & Kashmir are both Himalayan valleys, as is the Kathmandu Valley in Nepal. Kanchenjunga (8598m) is the highest mountain in India, although until Sikkim (and Kanchenjunga) were absorbed into India that honour went to Nanda Devi (7817m). Beyond the Himalaya stretches the high, dry and barren Tibetan plateau; in Ladakh, a small part of this plateau actually lies within India's boundaries.

The final southern range of the Himalaya, the Siwalik Hills, ends abruptly in the great northern plains of India.

The Northern Plain

In complete contrast to the soaring mountain peaks, the northern plain is oppressively flat and slopes so gradually that all the way from Delhi to the Bay of Bengal it drops only 200m. The mighty Ganges River, which has its source in the Himalaya, drains a large part of the northern plain and is the major river in India. The Brahmaputra, flowing from the north-east of the country, is the other major river of the north. In the north-west, the Indus River starts flowing through Ladakh in India but soon diverts into Pakistan to become that country's most important river.

The North-East

The north-eastern boundary of India is defined by the foothills of the Himalaya, which separate the country from Myanmar (Burma).

In this region, India bends almost entirely around Bangladesh and almost meets the sea on the eastern side.

Centre & South

South of the northern plains, the land rises up into the high plateau of the Deccan. The plateau is bordered on both sides by ranges of hills which parallel the coast to the east and west. The Western Ghats are higher and have a wider coastal strip than the Eastern. The two ranges meet in the extreme south in the Nilgiri Hills. The southern hill stations are in these hills: Matheran and Mahabaleshwar, near Mumbai in the Western Ghats; Ooty and Kodaikanal in the Nilgiri Hills. The major rivers of the south are the Godavari and the Krishna. Both rise on the eastern slope of the Western Ghats and flow across the Deccan into the sea on the eastern coast.

The West

On the western side, India is separated from Pakistan by three distinct regions. In the north, in the disputed area of Kashmir, the Himalaya forms the boundary between the two countries. The Himalaya drop down to the plains of the Punjab, which then merge into the Great Thar Desert in the western part of Rajasthan. This is an area of great natural beauty and extreme barrenness. It's hard to imagine that it was once covered by thick forests. Discoveries made by palaeontologists in 1996 suggest that the area was inhabited by dinosaurs and their ancestors as far back as 300 million years ago.

Redrawing State Boundaries

In 1996 it was announced by the prime minister that a new state would be created from the hill region of Uttar Pradesh, known as Uttarakhand. No date for the creation of the state was given, however.

When the states of modern India were created shortly after Independence, boundaries followed linguistic lines, creating some vast administrative units such as Madhya Pradesh. When the formerly large state of Assam was broken up in the 1960s, however, it was on political grounds – to control the Naga rebels. The government later favoured setting up Hill Councils to give greater autonomy to minority groups within larger states, as was done for the Gurkhas in the Darjeeling area.

Critics of the decision to create the new state of Uttarakhand claim that, as in Russia, it will encourage every minority group in the country to try for its own state. The Gurkhas may demand an independent Gorkhaland and the country could theoretically see the creation of five other new states: Bodoland, Jharkhan, Chhatisgarh, Vidharbha, and Telengana. ■

Finally, the Indian state of Gujarat is separated from the Sind in Pakistan by the unusual marshland known as the Rann of Kutch. In the dry season, this marshland dries out, leaving many isolated salt islands perched on an expansive plain. In the wet season, the marshland floods to become a vast inland sea.

CLIMATE

India is so vast that the climatic conditions in the far north have little relation to those of the extreme south. While the heat is building up to breaking point on the plains, the people of Ladakh, high in the Himalayas, will still be waiting for the snow to melt on the high passes.

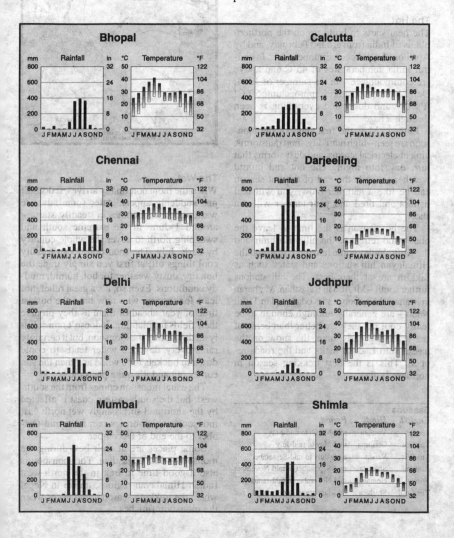

Basically, India has a three-season year – the hot, the wet and the cool. The best time to visit is during the winter (November through February), unless you are travelling to the northern Himalayan regions, where late spring and summer (April through August) is the best time. See the climate charts earlier in this section.

The Hot

The heat starts to build up on the northern plains of India from around February, and by April or May it becomes unbearable. In central India, temperatures of 45°C and above are commonplace – in the summer of 1994, Delhi had temperatures approaching 50°C! It's dry and dusty and everything is seen through a haze.

Later in May, the first signs of the monsoon are seen – high humidity, short rainstorms, violent electrical storms, and dust storms that turn day into night. The hot and humid weather towards the end of the hot season can be like a hammer blow; you will feel listless and tired and your temper will run short.

The hot season is the time to leave the plains and retreat to the hills. Kashmir and the Kullu Valley come into their own, and the Himalayan hill stations and states such as Sikkim are at their best. The hill stations further south – Mt Abu in Rajasthan, Matheran in Maharashtra, Ooty and Kodaikanal in Tamil Nadu – are generally not high enough to be really cool but they are better than being at sea level. By early June, the snow on the passes into Ladakh melts and the roads reopen. This is the best trekking season in northern India.

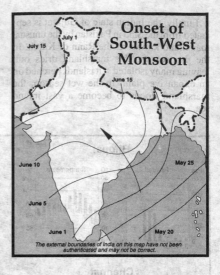

Onset of South-West Monsoon

The external boundaries of India on this map have not been authenticated and may not be correct.

Seasons

English	Hindi	Period
Spring	Vasanta	mid-March to mid-May
The Hot	Grishma	mid-May to mid-July
The Wet	Varsha	early-July to mid-September
Autumn	Sharada	mid-September to mid-November
Winter	Hemanta	mid-November to mid-January
The Cool	Shishira	mid-January to mid-March

The Wet

When the monsoon finally arrives, it doesn't just suddenly appear. After some advance warning, the rain comes in steadily, starting around 1 June in the extreme south and sweeping north to cover the whole country by early July. The monsoon doesn't really cool things off; at first you simply trade the hot, dry, dusty weather for hot, humid, muddy conditions. Even so, it's a great relief, not least for farmers who now have the busiest time of year ahead of them as they prepare their fields for planting. It doesn't rain solidly all day during the monsoon, but it certainly rains every day; the water tends to come down in buckets for a while and then the sun comes out and it's quite pleasant.

The usual monsoon comes from the south-west, but the south-eastern coast is affected by the short and surprisingly wet north-east monsoon, which brings rain from mid-October to the end of December.

Some places are at their best during the monsoon – like Rajasthan. The monsoon is also a good time to trek in the north-west Indian Himalayan regions, unlike in Nepal where the trekking season commences when the monsoon finishes.

Although the monsoon brings life to India, it also brings its share of death. Almost every year there are destructive floods and thousands of people are made homeless. Rivers rise and sweep away road and railway lines and many flight schedules are disrupted, making travel difficult during the monsoon.

The Cool

Finally, around October, the monsoon ends, and this is probably the best time of year in India. Everything is still green and lush but you don't get rained on daily. The temperatures are delightful, not too hot and not too cool. The air is clear in the Himalaya, and the mountains are clearly visible, at least early in the day. As the cool rolls on, Delhi and other northern cities become quite crisp at night in December and January. It becomes downright cold in the far north, but snow brings India's small skiing industry into action so a few places, such as the Kullu Valley, have a winter season too.

In the far south, where it never gets cool, the temperatures become comfortably warm rather than hot. Then, around February, the temperatures start to climb again, and before you know it you're back in the hot weather.

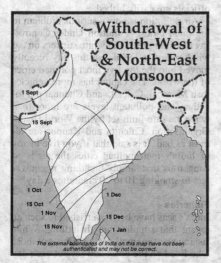

Withdrawal of South-West & North-East Monsoon

1 Sept
15 Sept
1 Oct
15 Oct
1 Nov
15 Nov
1 Dec
15 Dec
1 Jan

The external boundaries of India on this map have not been authenticated and may not be correct.

ECOLOGY & ENVIRONMENT

With a rapidly rising population making ever-increasing demands upon dwindling resources, India is living on borrowed time. Around the year 2000 the population will have passed one billion and it will become more and more difficult to feed them all. The rush to industrialise at any cost has left a trail of ecological disasters, the world's worst, Bhopal, amongst them.

Quite apart from the human pressures, many areas of the country are acutely susceptible to environmental degradation caused by the forces of nature. A major earthquake in Maharashtra killed over 10,000 people in 1994. The Himalayan region is a particularly fragile ecosystem, also prone to earthquakes. The monsoonal weather patterns mean that there are droughts in the dry season, destructive floods in the wet. Over 3000 people died in the torrential tropical storms that hit Andhra Pradesh in November 1996.

The basic environmental issues are outlined here. For more information, *This Fissured Land – An Ecological History of India*, by Madhav Gadgil & Ramchandra Guha, is recommended.

Deforestation

India's deforestation problems date from British times. Until the First Forest Act of 1865, all forests had been managed by the people who lived in and around them. With the government taking control of the forests to begin the large-scale timber extraction that has continued to this day, the people found themselves having to walk further and further each day to collect fuel and fodder. Forest cover in India has fallen to little more than 10%, an extremely serious situation for a country where so many depend on forests for their livelihood.

Probably the best known environmental organisation in the country is the Chipko Movement. In the 1970s, the women of the Himalayan regions of Uttar Pradesh embarked on a grassroots programme to save the forests in their area. Conforming to the Gandhian doctrine of *ahimsa* (nonviolence), these women were prepared to die for their cause, literally clinging to trees that were marked for felling – *chipko* means embrace. The model spread to many other parts of the country where forests were threatened by logging.

Land Degradation

Not only is the burgeoning population putting pressure on the land, but each year over 175 million ha of land are lost, mainly through water erosion. Valuable topsoil is swept away by the floods that come with the annual monsoons.

There's been a backlash against the so-called Green Revolution, when chemical fertilisers and high-yield grains were introduced on a large scale in the 1960s. Although production was more than tripled and India able to feed all its people, the land cannot stand such intensive use. To feed more than a billion mouths in the next century would require an increase in chemical farming.

Desertification is a serious problem in large areas of the country, particularly in Rajasthan.

Water

Increased demand upon supplies has caused India's water table to sink. Despite the high rainfall during the monsoon, 86% of rainwater runs into the sea. Monsoons cannot always be relied upon – in any five years two may be considered drought years. In desert regions it is not uncommon for one in three years to be stricken by drought. The quality of available water is low: up to 90% is said to be impure.

Projects to control and conserve water resources for irrigation and hydroelectric schemes are fraught with difficulties. The Narmada Valley Project is the most controversial project to date, a vast project of several large dams and hundreds of smaller ones providing water and power for Gujarat, Rajasthan, Madhya Pradesh and Maharashtra. The World Bank sanctioned a loan for the Sardar Sarovar in Gujarat and the Narmada Sagar in Madhya Pradesh. When completed, these two dams will submerge 350,000 ha of

forest and 200,000 ha of cultivated fields and displace nearly 400,000 people. A vigorous campaign is in progress to reduce the size of the dams. It has been calculated that if the height of the dam wall of the Sardar Sarovar were reduced by a mere 10m, 90% of the currently affected population would not have to be relocated.

Also highly controversial is the Tehri Dam project in the Uttarakhand region of Uttar Pradesh. Quite apart from the fact that 85,000 people will be displaced by its construction, this dam is being built in an area of considerable seismic activity. In 1991 a major earthquake in Uttarakhand killed 800 people. If the Tehri Dam were to burst, many towns, Rishikesh and Haridwar among them, would be destroyed.

Pollution

India holds the unenviable record of hosting the world's worst industrial disaster: Bhopal's gas leak, where more than 6000 people died and around 500,000 had their health destroyed as the result of toxic gas escaping from the Union Carbide factory. There are many other lesser examples of pollution by factories. Although the laws against pollution are some of the strictest in the world, officials are easily bribed.

Air pollution is now a serious problem in the main cities. 'Pollution Under Control' say the little green and white stickers on car windscreens in Delhi, but this city recently moved into the top five most polluted cities of the world. The capital has more vehicles than Mumbai, Calcutta and Chennai put together, and pollutant levels are more than twice the safe limit set by the World Health Organisation. Calcutta and Kanpur are almost as bad. It is said that if you live in any of India's metropolitan cities the air is so dangerous that simply breathing is equivalent to smoking 10 to 20 cigarettes a day!

Fisheries

India's seas have been overfished to such an extent that supplies are dwindling. While fishing was the small-scale preserve of those who lived on the coast and set out each day in their traditional log boats, stocks could keep pace. With the introduction of trawlers and factory fishing ships, some areas – the Kerala coast, for example – have been over-fished, leading to loss of livelihood for fishing families.

Inland, river habitats have become severely polluted and in many areas fish populations have simply died out.

Conservation

The concept of nature conservation is not new to India. Since time immemorial, wildlife here has enjoyed a privileged position of protection through religious ideals and sentiment. Early Indian literature, including the Hindu epics, the Buddhist Jatakas, the Panchatantra and the Jain strictures, teach nonviolence and respect for even lowly animal forms. Many of the gods are associated with certain animals: Brahma with the deer, Vishnu with the lion and cobra, Siva with the bull, and Ganesh with the elephant. The earliest known conservation laws were made in India in the 3rd century BC, when Emperor Ashoka wrote the Fifth Pillar Edict, forbidding the slaughter of certain wildlife and the burning of forests.

Unfortunately, during the recent turbulent history of India, much of this tradition has been lost. Extensive hunting by the British and Indian rajas, large-scale clearing of forests for agriculture, availability of guns, poaching, strong pesticides and the ever-increasing population have had disastrous effects on India's environment. Only around 10% of the country still has forest cover, and only 4% is protected within national parks and similar reserves. However, in the past few decades the government has taken serious steps towards environmental management and has established over 350 parks, sanctuaries and reserves.

FLORA & FAUNA

The following description of India's flora and fauna was originally written by Murray D Bruce and Constance S Leap Bruce.

The diversity of India's climate and topography is reflected in its rich flora and fauna. India is renowned for its tigers, elephants and rhinoceros, but these are just three of the more than 500 species of mammals living in the country. Conservation projects have been established to preserve some of them, but for some species, such as the Indian cheetah,

Heading for Extinction

While India has made a laudable effort to protect its endangered species by establishing wildlife sanctuaries, greed and corruption have undermined the success of these endeavours. The tiger is the symbol of the conservation effort, but with one killed almost every day in India, and less than 3000 remaining, it's unlikely that the tiger will survive far into the next century unless some very serious steps are taken. The Chinese folk medicine business places a high value on the animal, where the bones form the basis of 'tiger wine', believed to have healing properties. The penis is coveted for its alleged aphrodisiacal powers. The skin and claws can fetch up to US$6000 in Nepal.

National parks and sanctuaries are lucrative hunting grounds for poachers. Frequently, only main roads in parks are patrolled by often poorly paid guards, so poachers can trespass without fear of detection.

Industry poses another threat to India's wildlife. Vast tracts of wilderness designated as 'protected areas' have been denotified to make way for mining ventures. The Indian Aluminium Company has requested a portion of the Radhnagari Bison Sanctuary to mine bauxite. One-third of the Melghat Wildlife Sanctuary in Maharashtra was requisitioned for the construction of a dam. Other impediments include: the focussing of attention on Project Tiger, which has led to the neglect of other pressing problems; the lack of centre/state co-operation; inadequate staffing, funding and infrastructure; the use of some parks (such as Manas in Assam) as refuges by militants and other malcontents; and, most recently, the increased tourist traffic in ecologically fragile areas.

Without a concerted effort on the part of conservationists, and the requisite political will to effect meaningful conservationist policies, mausoleum-like museums will prove to be the final home of India's wildlife – stuffed tigers and lions will be all that remains of India's once rich wildlife heritage. ∎

protection has come too late – it was last seen in 1948.

Many deer and antelope species can be seen around the country, but these are now mostly confined to the protected areas because of competition with domestic animals and the effects of their diseases. They include graceful Indian gazelles (chinkaras); Indian antelopes (blackbucks); diminutive, four-horned antelopes (chowsinghas); large and ungainly looking blue bulls (nilgais); rare swamp deer (barasinghas); India's largest deer (sambars); beautiful spotted deer (chitals); the larger barking deer (muntjacs); and the tiny mouse deer (chevrotains).

Also seen are wild buffaloes, massive Indian bisons (gaurs), shaggy sloth bears, striped hyenas, wild pigs, jackals, Indian foxes, wolves, and Indian wild dogs (dhole), which resemble giant foxes but roam in packs in forests. Amongst the smaller mammals are mongoose, renowned as snake killers, and giant squirrels.

Cats include leopards or panthers, short-tailed jungle cats, and beautiful leopard cats. Monkeys include rhesus macaques, bonnet macaques and long-tailed common langurs.

India is blessed with over 2000 species and sub-species of birds. The diverse birdlife of the forests includes large hornbills, ser-pent eagles and fishing owls, as well as the elegant national bird, the peacock. Waterbirds, such as herons, ibises, storks, cranes, pelicans and others, are seen not only in parks but at numerous special waterbird sanctuaries. These sanctuaries contain large breeding colonies, and are of great importance for the countless migrating birds which visit India annually.

Among the other wildlife are over 500 species of reptiles and amphibians, including magnificent king cobras, pythons, crocodiles, large freshwater tortoises and monitor lizards. There are also 30,000 insect species, including some spectacularly large and colourful butterflies.

The vegetation, from dry desert scrub to alpine meadow, comprises some 15,000 species of plants.

Many of the wildlife sanctuaries, and some national parks, have been established in the former private hunting reserves of the British and Indian aristocracy. Often, the parks are renowned for one particular creature, such as Asian lions in Gir, Indian rhinoceros in Kaziranga, elephants in Periyar, and tigers in Kanha and Corbett; other areas have been established to preserve unique habitats such as lowland tropical rainforest or the mangrove forest of the Sunderbans.

National Parks & Sanctuaries

National parks and other protected areas in India are administered at the state level and are often promoted as part of each state's tourist attractions. To encourage more visitors, accommodation, road systems, transport and other facilities continue to be developed and upgraded.

Whenever possible, book in advance for transport and accommodation through the local tourist offices or state departments, and check if a permit is required, particularly in border areas. Various fees are charged for your visit (entrance, photography, etc) and

these are usually included in advance arrangements. Meals may also be arranged when you book, but in some cases you must take your own food supplies and have them prepared for you.

Some parks offer modern-style guest houses with electricity, while others only have dak-style bungalows. Facilities usually include van and jeep rides, and at some parks you can take a boat trip to approach wildlife more discreetly. Watchtowers and hides are also often available, and provide good opportunities to observe and photograph wildlife close up.

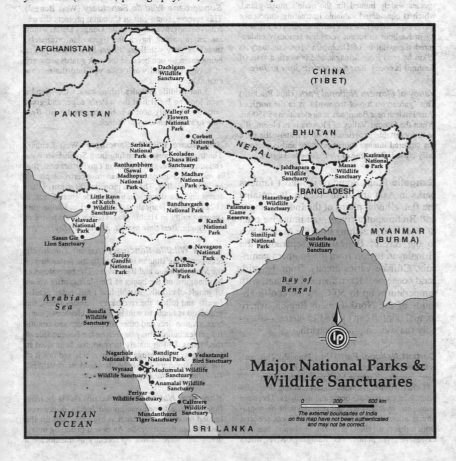

Major National Parks & Wildlife Sanctuaries

0   300   600 km

The external boundaries of India on this map have not been authenticated and may not be correct.

The main national parks, wildlife sanctuaries and reserves listed below are included in more detail in the relevant chapters.

Northern India This is a region of extremes, ranging from the snow-bound peaks and deep valleys of the Himalaya to flat plains and tropical lowlands.

Dachigam Wildlife Sanctuary (Kashmir) This sanctuary is in a very scenic valley with a large meandering river. The surrounding mountain slopes contain rare Kashmir stags (hangul), as well as black and brown bears. There are also musk deer, a small species widely hunted for the male's musk gland, which is considered valuable in treating impotence and is exported to Europe's perfumeries. The instability in Kashmir in recent years has seriously endangered the wildlife of Dachigam. The sanctuary is 22km by road from Srinagar, and is worth a visit (if Kashmir is open). *Best time to visit: June to July.*

Valley of Flowers National Park (Uttar Pradesh) This 'garden on top of the world' is in the north of Uttar Pradesh near Badrinath, at an elevation of 3500m. When the famous Valley of Flowers is in bloom, it's an unforgettable experience. Unfortunately, the park has suffered intense tourist pressure and is periodically closed. *Best time to visit: June to August.*

Gangetic Plain Some of the most famous parks in Asia are in this region. It contains the flat, alluvial plains of the Indus, Ganges and Brahmaputra rivers – an immense tract of level land stretching from the Arabian Sea to the Bay of Bengal and separating the Himalayan region from the southern peninsula. Climate varies greatly, from the arid, sandy deserts of Rajasthan and Gujarat, with temperatures up to 50°C, to the cool highlands of the North-Eastern Region, where annual rainfall can exceed 15 *metres* – allegedly the wettest place on earth.

Corbett National Park (Uttar Pradesh) This park is famous for its tigers, but it's not the best place to see these animals – Kanha in Madhya Pradesh is better.

Other wildlife includes chitals and hog deer, elephants, leopards, sloth bears and muntjacs. There are numerous watchtowers, but only daylight photography is allowed. The park has magnificent scenery, from sal forest (giant, teak-like hardwood trees) to extensive river plains. The Ramganga River offers

tranquil settings and good fishing. It's a bit touristy, but worth a visit. *Best time to visit: November to May.*

Hazaribagh Wildlife Sanctuary (Bihar) This is an area of rolling, forested hills with large herds of deer, as well as tigers and leopards. *Best time to visit: February to March.*

Palamau Game Reserve (Bihar) Palamau is smaller than Hazaribagh, but has good concentrations of wildlife, including tigers, leopards, elephants, gaurs, sambars, chitals, nilgais and muntjacs, as well as rhesus macaques, common langurs and (rarely) wolves. It is 150km south of Ranchi, with bungalows at Betla. *Best time to visit: February to March.*

Sunderbans Wildlife Sanctuary (West Bengal) This reserve, south-east of Calcutta, protects the extensive mangrove forests of the Ganges Delta, which are an important haven for tigers. Unfortunately, there's no way you'll see a tiger here unless you're being eaten by one because the park guards are wary of savage cats and won't take you into the narrow channels.

Other wildlife includes fishing cats, which can be seen looking for fish at the water's edge, and great birdlife. The only access is by chartered boat. *Best time to visit: February to March.*

Jaldhapara Wildlife Sanctuary (West Bengal) The tropical forests extending from South-East Asia end around here, and if you don't go further east, this is your best chance to see Indian rhinoceros, elephants and other wildlife. The area protects 100 sq km of lush forest and grasslands, cut by the wide Torsa River. It is 224km from Darjeeling, via Siliguri and Jalpaiguri (nearest railhead Hashimara). There's a rest house at Jaldhapara. *Best time to visit: March to May.*

Manas Wildlife Sanctuary (Assam) This lovely area bordering Bhutan is formed by the watershed of the Manas, Hakua and Beki rivers. The bungalows at Mothanguri, on the banks of the Manas, offer views of jungle-clad hills. Established trails enter nearby forests and follow the riverbanks. Besides tigers, the grassland is home to wild buffaloes, elephants, sambars, swamp deer and other wildlife; rare and beautiful golden langurs may be seen on the Bhutan side of the Manas. Unfortunately, the park has been used in recent times as a refuge by Bodo rebels and much of the infrastructure has been damaged or destroyed. *Best time to visit: January to March.*

Kaziranga National Park (Assam) This is the most famous place to see one-horned Indian rhinoceros, hunted almost to extinction as big game and for the Chinese apothecary trade. As an anti-poaching measure, plans were drawn up recently to translocate a number of animals to the Terai grasslands of Dudhwa National Park in Uttar Pradesh. However, this plan now seems to have been shelved, and the outlook for the rhino here is not good.

The park is dominated by tall (up to six metres) grasslands and *jheels* (swampy areas). The first sighting of a rhinoceros is always impressive; they can reach a height of over two metres and weigh more than two tonnes. Despite their appearance, rhinos are incredibly agile and fast. Spotting them in the tall grass may be difficult. Watch for egrets and other birds who use the rhino's armoured back as a perch, and listen for the 'churring' sound of a large animal moving through the grass. The best viewing areas are around the jheels, where they bathe. *Best time to visit: February to March.*

Sariska & Ranthambhore National Parks (Rajasthan)
Both of these areas provide good opportunities to see the wildlife of the Indian plains. Sariska is notable for night viewing and its nilgai herds. Unfortunately, it has recently become the haunt of hordes of loud and insensitive tourists who seem to have little regard for the very thing they have come to the park to see. Illegal mining also poses a threat to the park.

Ranthambhore (or Sawai Madhopur) is smaller, which can make seeing animals easier, and it is in a picturesque setting around a crocodile-filled lake. Its reputation as a place to spot the famous lake tigers is no more. Corrupt officials allowed illegal poaching to rapidly deplete the tiger population. The sanctuary is on the Delhi to Mumbai railway line, and is 160km south of Jaipur by road. *Best time to visit: February to June (Sariska); November to May (Ranthambhore).*

Keoladeo Ghana Bird Sanctuary (Rajasthan)
This is the best known and most touristy bird sanctuary (usually just called Bharatpur). It features large numbers of breeding waterbirds and thousands of migrating birds from Siberia and China, including herons, storks, cranes and geese. The network of crossroads and tracks through the sanctuary can increase opportunities to see the birds, deer and other wildlife. It is also on the Delhi to Mumbai railway line. *Best time to visit: September to February.*

Sasan Gir National Park (Gujarat)
This forested oasis in the desert is famous for the last surviving Asian lions (around 250 of them), but it also supports a variety of other wildlife, notably the chowsinghas and the crocodiles which live in Lake Kamaleshwar. The lake and other watering holes are good places to spot animals. The park is closed from mid-May to mid-October. *Best time to visit: December to April.*

Velavadar National Park (Gujarat)
This park, 65km north of Bhavnagar, protects the rich grasslands in the delta region on the west side of the Gulf of Khambhat (Cambay). The main attraction is a large concentration of beautiful blackbucks. There is a park lodge for visitors. *Best time to visit: October to June.*

Little Rann of Kutch Wildlife Sanctuary (Gujarat)
This sanctuary was designated for the protection of the desert region of north-west Gujarat. A variety of desert life can be found here, notably the surviving herds of the Indian wild ass *(khur)*. Also in residence are wolves and caracal (a large, pale cat with tufted ears). Access is difficult, but can be arranged at Bhuj. *Best time to visit: October to June.*

Madhav National Park (Madhya Pradesh)
This picturesque park close to Gwalior has open forests surrounding a lake. There are good opportunities for photographing various deer, including chinkaras, chowsinghas and nilgais. It is also home to tigers and leopards. *Best time to visit: February to May.*

Kanha National Park (Madhya Pradesh)
Kanha is one of India's most spectacular and exciting parks for both variety and numbers of wildlife. Originally proposed to protect a unique type of swamp deer (barasinghas), it is also an important area for tigers, chitals, blackbucks, gaurs, leopards and hyenas. The park is closed from 1 July to 31 October. *Best time to visit: March and April, although wildlife can be seen throughout the season, from November to May.*

Bandhavgarh National Park (Madhya Pradesh)
Bandhavgarh is smaller and less touristy than Kanha, has an impressive setting, and boasts an old fort on the cliffs above the plains. Although the park is not part of Project Tiger, tigers are occasionally seen. The park is closed from 1 July to 31 October. *Best time to visit: November to April.*

Navagaon National Park (Maharashtra)
This wildlife sanctuary, about 140km east of Nagpur, is home to small numbers of tiger, leopard and sloth bear. The terrain is hilly and the vegetation is largely deciduous forest interspersed with bamboo groves. The **Salim Ali Bird Sanctuary**, which is within the park, becomes a major nesting ground for many migratory bird species in winter. *Best time to visit: October to June.*

Similipal National Park (Orissa)
This reserve is a vast and beautiful area protecting India's largest region of sal forest. It has magnificent scenery and a variety of wildlife, including tigers (thought to number around 80), elephants, leopards, sambars, muntjacs and chevrotains. The park is closed from July to October. *Best time to visit: November to June.*

Southern India The Deccan peninsula is a triangular plateau ranging in altitude from 300 to 900m. It is intersected with rivers, and scattered with peaks and hills, including the Western and Eastern Ghats. The Ghats form a natural barrier to the monsoons and have created areas of great humidity and rainfall on the Malabar Coast, and drier regions on the mountains' leeward sides.

Sanjay Gandhi National Park (Maharashtra) This 104 sq km park, formerly known as Borivli, protects an important and scenic area close to Mumbai. Amongst the smaller types of wildlife to be seen are a variety of waterbirds. *Best time to visit: October to June.*

Taroba National Park (Maharashtra) This is a large park featuring mixed teak forests and a lake. Night viewing offers good opportunities to see tigers, leopards, gaurs, nilgais, sambars and chitals. The park is 45km from Chandrapur, south-west of Kanha National Park. You can arrange to stay in the park. *Best time to visit: March to May.*

Periyar Wildlife Sanctuary (Kerala) Periyar is a large and scenic park, comprising the watershed of a reservoir developed around a large, artificial lake. It is famous for its large elephant population, which can easily be seen by boat from the lake.

Other wildlife includes gaurs, Indian wild dogs and Nilgiri langurs, as well as otters, large tortoises and flights of hornbills. At the water's edge, you may see the flashing, brilliant hues of several kinds of kingfisher, perhaps even fishing owls. *Best time to visit: February to May.*

Jawahar National Park There was a recent proposal to merge Bandipur and Nagarhole national parks (Karnataka), Mudumulai Wildlife Sanctuary (Tamil Nadu), and Wynaad Wildlife Sanctuary (Kerala). Situated at the junction of the Western Ghats, the Nilgiri Hills and the Deccan plateau, the merging of these contiguous areas would protect the largest elephant population in India and one of the most extensive forested areas in the south. The mixed, diverse forests harbour leopards, gaurs, sambars, chitals, muntjacs, chevrotains, bonnet macaques and giant squirrels.

The very rich birdlife includes many spectacular species such as hornbills, barbets, trogons, parakeets, racquet-tailed drongos and streamer-tailed Asian paradise flycatchers. The two most popular areas are Bandipur and Mudumulai. This area should not be missed if you visit the south. *Best time to visit: January to June.*

Vedantangal Bird Sanctuary (Tamil Nadu) About 35km south of Chengalpattu, this is one of the most spectacular breeding grounds for water birds in India. Cormorants, egrets, herons, storks, ibises, spoonbills, grebes and pelicans come here to breed and nest for about six months from October/November to March, depending on the monsoons. At the height of the breeding season (December and January), you can see up to 30,000 birds at once. Many other species of migratory birds also visit the sanctuary. *Best time to visit: November to January.*

Calimere Wildlife Sanctuary (Tamil Nadu) Also known as Kodikkarai, this coastal sanctuary is 90km south-east of Thanjavur in a wetland area jutting into the Palk Strait, which separates India and Sri Lanka. It is noted for the vast flocks of migratory water fowl, especially flamingoes, which congregate here every winter. Blackbucks, spotted deer and wild pigs can also be seen. From April to June there's very little activity; the main rainy season is between October and December. *Best time to visit: November to January.*

Mundanthurai Tiger Sanctuary (Tamil Nadu) Mundanthurai is in the mountains near the border with Kerala. It's principally a tiger sanctuary, though it's also noted for chitals, sambars and rare lion-tailed macaques. The main rainy season is between October and December. Tiger sightings are apparently extremely infrequent. *Best time to visit: January to March, though it is open all year.*

Anamalai Wildlife Sanctuary (Tamil Nadu) This wildlife sanctuary is on the slopes of the Western Ghats along the border between Tamil Nadu and Kerala. Though recently renamed the Indira Gandhi Wildlife Sanctuary, most people still refer to it by its original name. It covers almost 1000 sq km and is home to elephants, gaurs, tigers, panthers, spotted deer, wild boars, bears, porcupines and civet cats.

In the heart of this beautiful forested region is the Parambikulam Dam, which has formed an immense plain of water that spreads into Kerala. *Best time to visit: February to June.*

GOVERNMENT & POLITICS

India has a parliamentary system of government with certain similarities to the US system. There are two houses – a lower house known as the Lok Sabha (House of the People) and an upper house known as the Rajya Sabha (Council of States).

The lower house has 544 members (excluding the speaker), all but two elected on a population basis (proportional representation).

Elections for the Lok Sabha are held every five years, unless the government calls an election earlier. All Indians over the age of 18 have the right to vote.

Of the 544 seats, 125 are reserved for the Scheduled Castes & Tribes (see the Society & Conduct section later in this chapter for details on these people). The upper house has 245 members. The lower house can be dissolved but the upper house cannot.

There are also state governments with legislative assemblies known as Vidhan Sabha. The two national houses and the various state houses elect the Indian president, who is a figurehead – the prime minister wields the real power.

There is a strict division between the activities handled by the states and by the national government. The police force, education, agriculture and industry are reserved for the state governments. Other areas are jointly administered by the two levels of government.

The central government has the controversial right to assume power in any state if the situation in that state is deemed to be unmanageable. Known as President's Rule, it has been enforced in recent years, either because the law and order situation has got out of hand – notably in Punjab from 1985 to 1992, Kashmir in 1990 and in Assam in 1991 – or because there is a political stalemate – such as occurred in Goa, Tamil Nadu, Pondicherry, Haryana and Meghalaya in 1991, and Nagaland in 1992.

The general election in 1996 was a disaster for the longstanding Congress Party, which won only 135 seats. The rise in popularity of the radical Hindu nationalist party, the BJP, culminated in their winning 177 seats – the largest number. Without a clear mandate, however, the government they formed lasted only 13 days.

The current government, headed by Inder Kumar Gujral, is a coalition of 13 parties collectively known as the United Front.

National Emblem, Flag & Anthem

The national flag is known as the tricolour. It features three horizontal bands of colour – from top to bottom saffron orange, white and dark green. The *chakhra* wheel in the centre of the flag is based on the design that appears on the famous Ashokan pillar at Sarnath.

The words of the national anthem are taken from a Hindi poem by Rabindranath Tagore. Tagore's English translation is as follows:

Thou art the ruler of the minds of all people,
Dispenser of India's destiny.
Thy name rouses the hearts of the Punjab,
Sind, Gujarat and Maratha.
Of the Dravid and Orissa and Bengal.
It echoes in the hills of the Vindhyas and Himalayas,
Mingles in the music of the Jamuna and the Ganges,
And is chanted by the waves of the Indian Sea.
They pray for the blessings and sing thy praise,
The saving of all people waits in thy hand,
Thou dispenser of India's destiny,
Victory, victory, victory to thee.

ECONOMY

Although India is a predominantly agricultural country, it has a large manufacturing base and is one of the world's major industrial powers. The economic reforms of the last few years are now enabling India to attract multinationals who want to tap into the huge Indian market.

Agriculture

The agriculture sector, for so long the mainstay of the Indian economy, now accounts for only about 20% of GDP, yet still employs over 50% of the population. For some years after Independence, India depended on foreign aid to meet its food needs, but in the last 40 years food production has risen steadily, mainly due to an increase in irrigated areas and the widespread use of high-yield seeds, fertilisers and pesticides. The country is a net exporter of food grains.

The main crops are rice (annual yield of 81 million tonnes) and wheat (55 million tonnes), but it's the cash crops such as tea and coffee which are the export earners. India is the world's largest producer of tea, with an annual production of around 740 million kg, of which around 210 million tonnes is exported. Virtually all Indian tea is grown in the states of Assam, West Bengal, Kerala and

Tamil Nadu. India also holds around 30% of the world spice market, with exports of 123,000 tonnes per year.

Other significant crops grown and used domestically are rubber, with an annual production of around 547,000 tonnes, and coconuts, with production running to about one billion nuts annually.

Industry

For many years India's industrial sector was strictly controlled by the central government, but the level of central intervention has decreased markedly over the past decade. Since Narasimha Rao initiated sweeping economic reforms in mid-1991, foreign investment has poured in.

One reason for the eagerness of foreign companies to establish operations in India is to gain access to the 300 million Indians who have an annual income of more than US$700 and the 100 million who earn more than US$1400. Both these groups have high enough disposable incomes to purchase consumer goods.

In purely economic terms, the results of the reforms have been impressive, with economic growth reaching 12.1% in 1996-97, with record levels of exports and foreign exchange reserves. Predictably, the 37% of the population who live on or below the poverty line have been little affected. The reforms led to an increase in inflation which has wavered between 7% and 15% over the last three years. Despite the existence of a large middle class, the national per capita income is still only Rs 12,000 per annum, or around Rs 33 per day.

Although things are improving, most industries are still hopelessly inefficient, use outdated technology and equipment, produce inferior goods unsuitable for export, are often dangerous places to work, and are polluting the environment at an incredible rate. However, virtually everything you come across in Indian shops is still made locally by Indian companies, which is quite an amazing achievement given that the country had very little industrial diversity at the time of Independence.

Tribals

For most people, it comes as a surprise to learn that more than 50 million Indians belong to tribal communities distinct from the great mass of Hindu caste society. These Aadivasi, as they are known in India, have origins which precede the Vedic Aryans and the Dravidians of the south. For thousands of years they have lived more or less undisturbed in the hills and densely wooded regions which were regarded as unattractive by the peasantry of more dynamic populations. Many still speak tribal languages not understood by the politically dominant Hindus, and they follow archaic customs foreign to both Hindus and Muslims alike.

Although there was obviously some contact between the tribals and the Hindu villagers on the plains, this rarely led to friction since there was little or no competition for resources and land. All this changed dramatically when improved communications opened up previously inaccessible tribal areas, and rapid growth of the Indian population led to pressure on resources. In the space of just over 40 years, the vast majority of tribal people have been dispossessed of their ancestral land and turned into impoverished labourers exploited by all and sundry. The only region where this has not taken place and where tribals continue to manage their own affairs is Arunachal Pradesh, in the extreme north-east of India. Only here can it be said that the tribes have benefited from contact with modern civilisation and are managing to hold their own.

Elsewhere in India, and especially in Madhya Pradesh, Andhra Pradesh, Bihar, and the Andaman & Nicobar Islands, a shocking tale of exploitation, dispossession and widespread hunger has unfolded with the connivance and even encouragement of officialdom. It's a record which the government would prefer to forget about and which it vehemently denies. Instead, it points to the millions of rupees which it says have been sunk into schemes to improve the condition of the aborigines. Although some of this aid has got through, corruption has claimed much of it.

It's unlikely that any genuine effort will be made to improve the lot of the tribals in peninsular India, given the pressure for land. What is far more likely is that the erosion of their cultures and traditions will continue until they eventually 'disappear' as distinct tribes. ■

Textiles account for around 25% of exports, but engineering goods, marine products, chemicals, and, increasingly, high-tech items such as computer software, are all important exports. The major import is oil and petroleum products, accounting for around 25% of imports.

POPULATION & PEOPLE

India has the second largest population in the world, exceeded only by that of China. It had 439 million people in 1961, 547 million in 1971, 687 million in 1981, and 843 million in 1991. Estimates for 1997 put the figure at 968 million. Despite extensive birth control programmes, it is still growing far too rapidly for comfort – around 2% per year.

Despite India's many large cities, the country is still overwhelmingly rural. It is estimated that about 290 million of the total population live in urban areas, but with increasing industrialisation the shift from village to city continues.

The Indian people are not a homogeneous group. It is quite easy to tell the difference between the shorter Bengalis of the east, the taller and lighter-skinned people of the centre and north, the Kashmiris with their distinctly Central Asian appearance, the Tibetan people of Ladakh, Sikkim and the north of Himachal Pradesh, and the dark-skinned Tamils of the south. Despite these regional variations, the government has managed to successfully establish an 'Indian' ethos and national consciousness.

Although India is overwhelmingly Hindu, there are large minorities of other religions. These include around 110 million Muslims, making India one of the largest Muslim countries in the world, much larger than any of the Arab Middle East nations. Christians number about 23 million, Sikhs 19 million, Buddhists 6.9 million and Jains 4.7 million. About 7% of the population is classified as 'tribal'. They are found scattered throughout the country, although there are concentrations of them in the north-eastern corner of the country, as well as in Bihar, Orissa, Madhya Pradesh and Andhra Pradesh.

EDUCATION

There are 820,000 schools in the country, 573,000 for primary education. Operation Blackboard, launched in 1987 to bring literacy to 100 million adults in the 15-35 age group by 1997, failed mainly because of lack of funds. The literacy rate is 54% nationally, up from 44% in 1981. Men are generally more literate than women – 64% to 39% respectively. The literacy rate varies hugely from state to state – Kerala boasts 91% literacy, while in Bihar and Rajasthan it's 38%. Amongst the Scheduled Castes & Tribes, the literacy rates are abysmally bad – 28% among men and 9% among women.

SOCIETY & CONDUCT
The Caste System

The caste system is one of India's more confusing mysteries – how it came about, how it has managed to survive for so long and how much harm it causes are all topics of discussion for visitors to India. Its origins are hazy, but it seems to have been developed by the Brahmins or priest class in order to maintain its superiority. Later, it was probably extended by the invading Aryans who felt themselves superior to the indigenous pre-Aryan Indians. Eventually, the caste system became formalised into four distinct classes, each with rules of conduct and behaviour.

At the top are the Brahmins, who are the priests and the arbiters of what is right and wrong in matters of religion and caste. Next come the Kshatriyas, who are soldiers and administrators. The Vaisyas are the artisan and commercial class and, finally, the Sudras are the farmers and the peasant class. These four castes are said to have come from Brahma's mouth (Brahmins), arms (Kshatriyas), thighs (Vaisyas) and feet (Sudras).

Beneath the four main castes is a fifth group, the untouchables. These people, members of the so-called Scheduled Castes, literally have no caste. They perform the most menial and degrading jobs. At one time, if a high-caste Hindu used the same temple as an untouchable, was touched by one, or even had an untouchable's shadow cast across them, they were considered polluted and had to go through a rigorous series of rituals to be cleansed.

Today, the caste system has been weakened but it still has considerable power, particularly among less educated people. Gandhi put great effort into bringing the untouchables into society, including renaming them the 'Harijans' or 'Children of God'. Recently, the word Harijan has lost favour, and the use of it in official business has been banned in Madhya Pradesh. The term the members of these groups prefer is Dalit, meaning Oppressed or Downtrodden.

It must be remembered that being born into a certain caste does not limit you strictly to one occupation or position in life, just as being black in the USA does not mean you are poverty stricken and live in Harlem. Many Brahmins are poor peasants, for example, and hundreds of years ago the great Maratha leader Shivaji was a Sudra. None of the later Marathas, who controlled much of India after the demise of the Mughals, were Brahmins. Nevertheless, you can generalise that the better-off Indians will be of higher caste and that the 'sweeper' you see cleaning the

---

Everyone in their Place

We were sampling breakfast in Le Meridien Hotel in New Delhi. Third world or not, this is a decidedly first-world hotel. The glass elevators soar up 20-plus floors in the huge atrium and the nightly room rate probably equates pretty close to the average Indian's annual income. But there, in the middle of this luxury, was somebody crawling across the floor towards us with a dirty wash-rag in his hand. Why?

'Why?' is a question you often find yourself asking in India. Why hasn't the mop handle been invented yet? Or why can't this fancy five-star hotel afford mop handles for its workers? In this case, the answer was probably that anybody crawling around on his hands and knees washing the floor is obviously pretty low caste and people higher up the caste ladder *like* to see the lower castes down there where they reckon they belong. Standing up to wash the floor, five-star or not, would be getting far too uppity! Better the lower castes stay down on their knees.

Tony Wheeler (Aus)

---

toilet in your hotel will be a Dalit. In fact, when Indian Airlines appointed its first Dalit flight attendant, it was front-page news in Indian newspapers.

How can you tell which caste a Hindu belongs to? Well, if you know that their job is a menial one, such as cleaning streets, or in some way defiling, such as working with leather, they are a Dalit. But for most Hindus, you can't really tell which caste they belong to. However, if you see a man with his shirt off and he has the sacred thread looped round one shoulder, he belongs to one of the higher castes, but then Parsis also wear a sacred thread. Sikhs, Muslims and Christians do not have caste.

In many ways, the caste system also functions as an enormous unofficial trade union, with strict rules to avoid demarcation disputes. Each caste has many subdivisions, so that the servant who polishes the brass cannot, due to their caste, also polish silver. Many of the old caste rules have been considerably relaxed, although less educated or more isolated Hindus may still avoid having a lower-caste person prepare their food for fear of becoming polluted. Better educated people are demonstrably none too worried about shaking hands with a caste-less westerner though! Nor does the thought of going overseas, and thus losing caste completely, carry much weight these days.

The caste system still produces enormous burdens for India, however. During the last few years, there have been frequent outbreaks of violence towards members of the Scheduled Castes and so-called backward classes ('tribals', and those who are poor or poorly educated for reasons other than caste). In an effort to improve the lot of these people, the government reserves huge numbers of public sector jobs, parliamentary seats and university places for them. With nearly 60% of the jobs reserved, many well-educated people are missing out on jobs which they would easily get on merit. In 1994, some state governments (such as Karnataka) raised the reservation level even higher in an effort to win mass support. In 1991, and again in 1994, there were serious protests against the raising of the quotas. At least 100 people died or were seriously injured in self-immolation incidents in the 1991 protests. The current president is a Dalit, the first ever, but it is yet to be seen whether this will have any effect on wider perceptions of the Dalit caste.

It's important to remember that the western medieval ideal of heaven was developed in part to keep the peasants in their place – behave yourself, work hard, put up with your lot and you'll go to heaven. Probably caste developed in a similar fashion – your life may be pretty miserable but that's your *karma*; knuckle under and you may be born into a better one next time around.

Women in Society

India is a country of great hardship, and the people who face the worst of it are generally the women. It is a cruel paradox that at a time when India's prime minister was arguably the world's most powerful woman, 75% of the country's women had little education, few rights, strenuous and poorly paid jobs, and little prospect of anything better.

Problems for Indian women begin at birth. Even now, boys are considered more desirable than girls because they offer parents security in old age – traditionally, the sons remain in their parents' house even after marriage. Girls are often seen as a burden on the family, not only because they leave the family when married, but also because an adequate dowry must be supplied. Consequently, girls may get less food, and their education is neglected.

Arranged marriages are still the norm rather than the exception. A village girl may well find herself married off while still in her early teens to a man she has never met. She then goes to live in his village, where she is expected not only to do manual labour (at perhaps half the wages that a man would receive for the same work), but also raise children and keep house. This might involve a daily trek of several km to fetch water, as much again to gather firewood, and a similar amount again to gather fodder for domestic animals. She would have no property rights

should her husband own land, and domestic violence is common; a man often feels it is his right to beat his wife. In many ways, her status is little better than that of a slave.

For the urban, middle-class woman, life is materially much more comfortable, but pressures still exist. She is much more likely to be given an education, but only because this will make her marriage prospects better. Once married, she is still expected to be mother and home maker above all else. Like her village counterpart, if she fails to live up to expectations – even if it is just not being able to give her in-laws a grandson – the consequences can be dire, as the practice of 'bride burning' is not uncommon. On a daily basis, there are newspaper reports of women burning to death in kitchen fires, usually from 'spilt' kerosene. The majority of these cases, however, are either suicides – desperate women who could no longer cope with the pressure from their parents-in-law – or outright murders by in-laws who want their son to remarry someone they consider to be a better prospect.

A married woman faces even greater pressure if she wants to divorce her husband. Although the constitution allows for divorcees (and widows) to remarry, few are in a position to do this simply because they are considered outcasts from society – even her own family will turn their back on a woman who seeks divorce, and there is no social security net to provide for her. A marriage in India is not so much a union based on love between two individuals, but a social contract joining two people and their families. It is then the responsibility of the couple to make the marriage work, whatever the obstacles; if the marriage fails, both husband and wife are tainted, but the fall-out for the woman is far worse. Divorce rates are, not surprisingly, low.

While this is the downside of being a woman in India, the picture is not all gloomy. In the past decade or so, the women's movement has had some successes in improving the status of women. Although the professions are still very much male dominated, women are making inroads – in 1993, the first women were inducted into the armed forces, and they account for around 10% of all parliamentarians.

For village women, it's much more difficult to get ahead, but groups such as SEWA (Self Employed Women's Association) in Ahmedabad have shown what's possible. Here, poor and low caste women, many of whom work only on the fringes of the economy, have been organised into unions, giving them at least some lobbying power against discriminatory and exploitative work practices. SEWA has also set up a bank, giving many poor women their first access to a savings or lending body, since conventional banks were unwilling to deal with people of such limited means. (See the boxed SEWA section in the Gujarat chapter for more information.)

Although attitudes towards women are slowly changing, it will be a long time before they gain even a measure of equality with men. For the moment, their power lies in their considerable influence over family affairs and so remains largely invisible.

Birth Control

India had a birth control blitz in the early 1970s. Slogans and posters appeared all over the country, and the infamous 'transistor radio in exchange for sterilisation' campaign began. More sinister still was the brief campaign during the emergency era, when squads of sterilisers terrorised the country and people were afraid to go out after dark. This wayward campaign harmed India's birth control programme severely.

It wasn't until the mid-1980s that population control was once again a government priority – Rajiv Gandhi mounted an ambitious project, with the target of 1.3 billion Indians by the year 2050. By then India will have overtaken China as the world's most populous country.

Getting Married

One place where the caste system is still well entrenched is the choosing of marriage partners. You only need to read a few of the 'matrimonial' advertisements which appear in many places, including the national Sunday newspapers (and even these days on the Internet) to realise that marriage across the 'caste bar', even among wealthy, well-educated or higher caste people, is basically not on. The majority of marriages are still arranged by the parents, although 'love marriages' are becoming more common, particularly in urban centres.

When a couple are choosing a partner for their son or daughter, a number of factors are taken into consideration: caste of course is pre-eminent, but other considerations are beauty and physical flaws – the matrimonial ads can seem brutally frank in this regard – and a horoscope for the would-be partner is often called for. Many potential matches are rejected simply because the astrological signs are not propitious. The financial status of the prospective partner's family is also taken into account.

Another facet of marriage is the pernicious dowry. A dowry was originally a gift to the bride from her parents, so she would have something of her own and would in turn be able to provide a dowry to her own daughters. These days, however, the dowry is a matter of status for the bride's family – the bigger the dowry and grander the ceremony, the greater the prestige to the family.

Although the practice is officially outlawed, a dowry is still expected in the majority of marriages. For poorer families, the marriage can become a huge financial burden. Many families have to borrow money, either for their daughter's dowry or to stage a lavish ceremony and feast (or both), usually at outrageous rates of interest. The end result is that for the rest of their lives they are indebted to the feared moneylenders, or become bonded labourers.

The amount of an expected dowry varies, but it is never small. The main determining factor is the level of education and social standing of the young man; a dowry of at least US$20,000 would be expected from the family of a young woman hoping to marry a graduate of a foreign university, a doctor or other highly paid professional. A 'Green Card' (American residence card) is also highly desirable, and the holder of one can command a high price.

The official age for marriage is 18 years, but this is widely ignored – 8% of girls aged between 10 and 14 are married, and nearly 50% of females aged between 15 and 19 are married, although the average age for marriage is 18.3 for women and 23.3 for men. Virginity is also of vital importance, and it is often listed among the woman's attributes in the matrimonial columns. ∎

Although there has been some success at slowing the growth rate, the picture isn't promising. Many experts feel that the solution to the population problem in India is to educate women, particularly in rural communities. Literate, educated women are much better equipped to understand the need for limiting the size of families and the population. Decreasing the mortality rate among small children is also seen as a significant factor in reducing the desire for large families. As long as children are seen as a source of security in old age, and while male heirs are so avidly desired, it is going to be difficult to successfully limit population growth.

Although educating women is an important part of the programme, the emphasis is once again on sterilisation, with women the main target. It seems men are unwilling to volunteer for a vasectomy. In regional areas, social workers are recruited to find 'volunteers' for the operation. As an incentive, they are paid a small fee for every person encouraged to go through with it. There is also a small financial incentive offered to people who undergo sterilisation.

Another part of the family planning drive involves widespread use of the media – particularly TV. The two-child family is portrayed as the ideal, and the use of contraceptives, especially condoms, is encouraged.

Female infanticide

Such is the desire to have male children rather than female that the government has had to pass legislation to prohibit the abortion of healthy foetuses, the modern equivalent of the age-old practice of infanticide. In 1994 'sex determination' clinics had been banned but abortions, following examinations in illegal ultrasound clinics, continued.

The problem is worst in Punjab & Haryana where the ratio of women to men has now fallen to 85:100; in Rajasthan it's 91:100. By comparison, in sub-Saharan Africa it's 102:100, and in industrialised countries there's an average of 106 women to every 100 men.

Some states are countering the problem by offering grants to parents who have girls – Rs 1500 in Rajasthan. ■

Indian Clothing

Many travellers start wearing Indian clothes while in India – after all, much of it is a lot more appropriate to India's climate than jeans and T-shirts. The best known Indian outfit is the *sari*. It is also the one piece of clothing which is very difficult for western women to wear properly. This supremely graceful attire is simply one length of material, a bit over a metre in width and five to nine metres long. It's worn without any pins, buttons or fastenings. The tightly fitted, short blouse worn under a sari is a *choli*. The final length of the sari, which is draped over the wearer's shoulder, is known as the *pallav* or *palloo*.

The sari is not the only women's costume in India. Kashmiri and Sikh women wear loose pyjama-like trousers. Over these trousers, known as *salwars*, they wear a long, loose tunic known as a *kameez*. This attire is comfortable and 'respectable'. A *churidhar* is similar to the salwar but tighter fitting. Over this goes a collarless or mandarin-collar *kurta* – an item of clothing worn by both men and women which is also popular in the west.

Although the overwhelming majority of Indian women wear traditional costume, many Indian men wear quite conventional western clothing. Indeed, a large proportion of India's consumer advertising appears to be devoted to 'suitings and shirtings' – the material made for tailor-made, western-style business suits and shirts. You can easily get a suit made to measure, although the styling is likely to be somewhat dated. The collarless jackets, known as 'Nehru jackets', are a popular buy among travellers. These khadi (homespun cloth) coats are best bought at the government khadi emporiums found in the major cities.

The traditional *lungi* originated in the south and today is worn by women as well as men. It's a short length of material worn rather like a sarong. The lungi can be rolled up but should be lowered when sitting down or when entering someone's home or a temple. A *dhoti* is like a longer lungi but with a length of material pulled up between the legs, effective but a long way from elegant!

A dhoti is a more formal piece of attire than a lungi, however. Pyjama-like trousers, worn by country folk, are known as *lenga*. Striped pyjamas are casual and very comfortable but

---

How to Wear a Sari

If you've ever wondered how Indian women manage to keep their saris in position without any fastenings, here's how it's done:

1. With your left hand hold the inside end of the sari material.
2. Tuck the top border of the inner end of the sari into your petticoat, keeping the hem of the sari just above the floor.
3. Keeping the sari at the same height off the floor wind the material round to the front.
4. Make sure the sari is still held firmly – tuck it in a little if necessary.
5. Fold most of the rest of the material into pleats, starting at the right.
6. Hold the pleats firmly making sure the bottom hem is at floor level.
7. Tuck in the pleats, letting them fall straight.
8. Wind the remaining material around you and over your left shoulder. ■

---

they're looked upon as a labourer's outfit; not something to wear to a fancy restaurant or to somebody's home.

There are many religious and regional variations in costume, such as the brightly mirrored Rajasthani skirts and their equally colourful tie-dye materials. In Ladakh, the women wear superbly picturesque Tibetan costumes with high 'top hats'. The men wear long dressing-gown-like coats. Muslim women, of course, wear much more staid and all-covering attire than their Hindu sisters. More traditional Muslim women wear the all-enveloping, tent-like *burkha*.

Dos & Don'ts

Religious Etiquette Particular care should be taken when attending a religious place (temple, shrine) or event. Dress and behave appropriately – don't wear shorts or singlet tops (this applies to men and women) and do not smoke or hold hands. Remove your shoes before entering a holy place, and never touch a carving or statue of a deity. In some places, such as mosques, you will be required to cover your head. For religious reasons, do not touch local people on the head and similarly never direct the soles of your feet at a person, religious shrine, or image of a deity, as this may cause offence. Never touch another person with your feet. When visiting Buddhist temples and religious sites always walk around them in a clockwise direction.

Photographic Etiquette You should be sensitive about taking photos of people, especially women, who may find it offensive – always ask first. Taking photos at a death ceremony, or a religious ceremony or of people bathing (in baths or rivers) may cause offence. Don't use flash photography in prayer rooms in gompas or to take pictures of murals of any kind.

Guest & Food Etiquette Don't touch food or cooking utensils that local people will use. You should use your right hand for all social interactions, whether passing money or food or any other item. Eat with your right hand only.

Puja

Puja is the Hindu term for ritual worship. It covers the rites undertaken either in the day-to-day worship of a god, or those used when asking for special favours. While puja is usually made to some physical representation of a god, it can also be made to trees, animals or even to the tools used by the devotee.

Puja takes many forms, but there are rules for every form laid down in the *Shastras* and *Agamas*, Hindu holy texts. While any Hindu can perform a puja, a priest will often be called in when a special puja is required.

Firstly the puja room, the home of the god, is purified and decorated. Temples and bigger homes will have a special puja room, but many people use a cupboard or a corner of the kitchen. Hymns and mantras are sung to the god, and he or she is often symbolically awakened with cymbals or bells. Gifts, including food, are given to the god, and acts which represent washing, dressing and decorating the god take place. Other forms of puja may include offering fire to the god, walking clockwise around it, or receiving gifts of sacred ash or water from the god. Particularly special pujas may include a procession, where the *darshana* – or presence – of the god can be felt. ■

If you are invited to dine with a family, take off your shoes if they do and wash your hands before taking your meal. The hearth is the sacred centre of the home, so never approach it unless you have been invited to do so.

Never enter the kitchen unless you have been invited to do so, and always take your shoes off before you go in. Similarly, never enter the area where drinking water is stored unless you have removed your shoes. Do not touch terracotta vessels in which water is kept – you should always ask your host to serve you.

Washing Nudity is completely unacceptable and a swimsuit must be worn even when bathing in a remote location.

LANGUAGE

There is no one 'Indian' language as such. This is part of the reason why English is still widely spoken 50 years after the British left India and why it's still the official language of the judiciary.

Eighteen languages are recognised by the constitution, and these fall into two major groups: Indic, or Indo-Aryan, and Dravidian. Additionally, there are over 1600 minor languages and dialects listed in the latest census. The scope for misunderstanding can be easily appreciated!

The Indic languages are a branch of the Indo-European group of languages (to which English belongs), and were the language of the Central Asian peoples who invaded what is now India. The Dravidian languages are native to south India, although they have been influenced by Sanskrit and Hindi over the years.

Most of the languages have their own script, and these are used along with English. In some states, such as Gujarat, you'll hardly see a word of English, whereas in Himachal Pradesh virtually everything is in English. For a sample of the different scripts, look at a Rs 5 or larger banknote where 14 languages are represented. As well as Hindi and English there's a list of 12 other languages; from the top, they are: Assamese, Bengali, Gujarati, Kannada, Kashmiri, Malayalam, ·Marathi, Oriya, Punjabi, Sanskrit, Tamil, Telugu and Urdu.

Major efforts have been made to promote Hindi as the national language of India and to gradually phase out English. A stumbling block to this plan is that while Hindi is the predominant language in the north, it bears little relation to the Dravidian languages of the south; subsequently very few people in the south speak Hindi. It is from here, particularly the state of Tamil Nadu, that the most vocal opposition to the adoption of Hindi comes, along with the strongest support for the retention of English.

For many educated Indians, English is virtually their first language, and for the

The 18 main languages in India are:

Hindi The most important Indian language, although it is only spoken as a mother tongue by about 20% of the population – mainly in the area known as the Hindi-belt, the cow-belt or Bimaru, which includes Bihar, Madhya Pradesh, Rajasthan and Uttar Pradesh. This Indic language is the official language of the Indian government, the states already mentioned, plus Haryana and Himachal Pradesh.

Assamese State language of Assam, and spoken by nearly 60% of that state's population. Dates back to the 13th century.

Bengali Spoken by nearly 200 million people (mostly in what is now Bangladesh), and the state language of West Bengal. Developed as a language in the 13th century.

Gujarati State language of Gujarat, it is an Indic language.

Kannada State language of Karnataka, spoken by about 65% of that state's population.

Kashmiri Kashmiri speakers account for about 55% of the population of Jammu & Kashmir. It is an Indic language written in the Perso-Arabic script.

Konkani Konkani is a Dravidian language spoken by people in the Goa region.

Malayalam A Dravidian language, and the state language of Kerala.

Manipuri An Indic language of the north-east region.

Marathi An Indic language dating back to around the 13th century, Marathi is the state language of Maharashtra.

Nepali Nepali is the predominant language of Sikkim, where around 75% of the people are ethnic Nepalis.

Oriya An Indic language, it is the state language of Orissa where it is spoken by 87% of the population.

Punjabi Another Indic language, this is the state language of the Punjab. Although based on the same script as Hindi (Devanagari), it is written in a 16th century script, known as Gurumukhi, which was created by the Sikh guru, Guru Angad.

Sanskrit One of the oldest languages in the world, and the language of classical India. All the *Vedas* and classical literature such as the *Mahabharata* and the *Ramayana* were written in this Indic language.

Sindhi A significant number of Sindhi speakers are found in what is now Pakistan, although the greater number are in India. In Pakistan, the language is written in a Perso-Arabic script, while in India it uses the Devanagari script.

Tamil An ancient Dravidian language at least 2000 years old, and the state language of Tamil Nadu. It is spoken by 65 million people.

Telugu The Dravidian language spoken by the largest number of people, it is the state language of Andhra Pradesh.

Urdu Urdu is the state language of Jammu & Kashmir. Along with Hindi, it evolved in early Delhi. While Hindi was largely adopted by the Hindu population, the Muslims embraced Urdu, and so the latter is written in the Perso-Arabic script and includes many Persian words. ■

large number of Indians who speak more than one language, English is often their second tongue. Thus it is very easy to get around India with English, but it's always good to know at least a little of the local language. There are Hindi language schools in all the larger cities, but one place which has been recommended is Landour Language School (☎ (0135) 631467), Mussoorie, Uttar Pradesh 248179.

Hindi

See Lonely Planet's *Hindi/Urdu Phrasebook* for a comprehensive list of Hindi words and phrases.

Hello/Goodbye.	*namaste*
Excuse me.	*maaf kijiyeh*
Please.	*meharbani seh*
Yes/No.	*haan/nahin*
big	*bherra*
small	*chhota*
today	*aaj*
day	*din*
night	*raat*
week	*haftah*
month	*mahina*
year	*saal*
medicine	*dava-ee*
egg	*aanda*

fruit	*phal*
vegetables	*sabzi*
sugar	*chini*
butter	*makkhan*
rice	*chaaval*
water	*paani*
tea	*chai*
coffee	*kaafi*
milk	*dudh*
Do you speak English?	*kya aap angrezi samajhte hain?*
I don't understand.	*meri samajh men nahin aaya*
Where's a hotel?	*hotal kahan hai?*
How far is ...?	*... kitni duur hai?*
How do I get to ...?	*... kojane ke liyeh kaiseh jaana parega?*
How much?	*kitneh paiseh?/ kitneh hai?*
This is expensive.	*yeh bahut mehnga hai*
Show me the menu.	*mujheh minu dikhaiyeh*
The bill please.	*bill de dijiyeh*
What is your name?	*aapka shubh naam kya hai?*
What's the time?	*kitneh bajeh hain?*
How are you?	*aap kaiseh hain?*
Very well, thank you.	*bahut acha, shukriya*

Beware of *acha*, that all-purpose word for 'OK'. It can also mean 'OK, I understand what you mean, but it isn't OK'.

Tamil

Although Hindi is promoted as the 'official' language of India, it won't get you very far in the south, where Tamil reigns supreme (although English is also widely spoken). Tamil is a much more difficult language to master and the pronunciation is not easy.

Hello.	*vanakkam*
Goodbye.	*sendru varugiren*
Excuse me.	*mannithu kollungal*
Please.	*dhayavu seidhu*
Yes/No.	*aamam/illai*

big	*periyadhu*
small	*siriyadhu*
today	*indru*
day	*pagal*
night	*iravu/rathiri*
week	*vaaram*
month	*maadham*
year	*aandu*
medicine	*marundhu*
ice	*panikkatti*
egg	*muttai*
fruit	*pazhlam*
vegetables	*kaaikari*
sugar	*sarkarai/seeni*
butter	*vennai*
rice	*saadham/soru*
water	*thanner*
tea	*thenneer*
coffee	*kapi*
milk	*paal*
Do you speak English?	*neengal aangilam pesuveergala?*
I don't understand.	*yenakku puriyavillai*
Where is a hotel?	*hotel yenge irrukindradhu?*
How far is ...?	*yevallavu dhooram ...?*
How do I get to ...?	*haan yeppadi selvadhu ...?*
How much?	*yevvallvu?*
This is expensive.	*idhu vilai adhigam*
Show me the menu.	*saapatu patiyalai kamiungal*
The bill please.	*vilai rasidhai kodungal*
What is your name?	*ungal peyar yenna?*
What is the time?	*ippoludhu mani yevallavu?*
How are you?	*neengal nalama?*
Very well, thank you.	*nandri, nandraga irukkindren*

Numbers

Whereas we count in tens, hundreds, thousands, millions and billions, the Indian numbering system goes tens, hundreds, thousands, hundred thousands, ten millions. A hundred thousand is a *lakh*, and 10 million is a *crore*.

These two words are almost always used in place of their English equivalent. Thus you will see 10 lakh rather than one million, and one crore rather than 10 million. The numbers are generally written that way too – three hundred thousand appears as 3,00,000 not 300,000, and ten million, five hundred thousand would appear as 1,05,00,000 (one crore, five lakh) not 10,500,000. If you say something costs five crore or is worth 10 lakh, it always means 'of rupees'.

When counting from 10 to 100 in Hindi, there is no standard formula for compiling numbers – they are all different. Here we've just given you enough to go on with!

	Hindi	Tamil
1	ek	onru
2	do	irandu
3	tin	moonru
4	char	naangu
5	panch	ainthu
6	chhe	aaru
7	saat	ezhu
8	aath	ettu
9	nau	onpathu
10	das	pathu
11	gyaranh	padhinondru
12	baranh	pannirendu
13	teranh	padhimundru
14	chodanh	padhinaangu
15	pandranh	padhinainthu
16	solanh	padhinaaru
17	staranh	padhinezhu
18	aatharanh	padhinettu
19	unnis	patthonpathu
20	bis	irubadhu
21	ikkis	irubadhiondru
22	bais	irubadhirandu
23	teis	irubadhimoonru
24	chobis	irubadhinaangu
25	pachis	irubadhiainthu
26	chhabis	irubadhiaaru
27	sattais	irubadhiezhu
28	athais	irubadhiettu
29	unnattis	irubadhionpathu
30	tis	muppathu
35	paintis	muppathiainthu
40	chalis	narpathu
45	paintalis	narpathiainthu
50	panchas	aimbathu
55	pachpan	aimbathiainthu
60	saath	arubathu
65	painsath	arubathiainthu
70	sattar	ezhbathu
75	pachhattar	ezhubathiainthu
80	assi	enbathu
85	pachasi	enabathiainthu
90	nabbe	thonooru
95	pachanabbe	thonootriainthu
100	so	nooru
200	do so	irunooru
1000	ek hazaar	aayiram
2000	do hazaar	irandaayiram
100,000	lakh	lacham
ten million	crore	kodi

Facts for the Visitor

PLANNING

When to Go

Most foreign visitors visit India in the cooler winter months from November to March. For the Himalaya, it's too cold in winter – April through September is the season here, although there are regional variations according to the onset and departure of the monsoon. For more information about when to go where, see the Climate section in the previous chapter.

Maps

Lonely Planet's *India Travel Atlas* breaks the country down into over 100 pages of maps, and so gives unequalled coverage. It is fully indexed and the book format means it is easy to refer to, especially on buses and trains.

The Lascelles 1:4,000,000 map of *India, Pakistan, Nepal, Bangladesh & Sri Lanka* is probably the most useful general map of India. Its biggest failing is that it does not always include places of great interest but small population – Khajuraho, for instance. The Bartholomews map is similar, and is widely available in India as well as overseas.

The Nelles Verlag series gives more detailed coverage, but you need to carry five maps to cover the whole country. They are excellent maps, but they're not widely available in India.

Locally, Nest & Wings produces a reasonable series of maps for Himalaya regions. The Survey of India has maps covering all of India. In Delhi their shambolic office is opposite the tourist office on Janpath. The maps are not all that useful since the government will not allow production of anything at a reasonable scale which shows India's sea or land borders, and many of them date back to the 1970s. It is illegal to take any Survey of India map of larger than 1:250,000 scale out of the country.

The Government of India tourist office has a number of excellent giveaway city maps and also a reasonable all-India map. State tourist offices do not have much in the way of maps, but the Himachal Pradesh office has three excellent trekking maps which cover the trekking routes in that state.

What to Bring

The usual travellers' rule applies – bring as little as possible. It's much better to have to

---

Indian Maps

Getting maps of India 'right' is a real headache. In early 1995 imported atlases and copies of Encyclopaedia Britannica were banned in India because the Indian government didn't like the way they portrayed the country's borders. We have had the same problem with this book. The main problem is Kashmir where Pakistan claims they own the lot, India claims it owns the lot and the reality is there's a 'line of control' through the middle with Indian troops on one side and Pakistani troops on the other. Showing the actual line of control is not good enough; the whole lot has to be shown as part of India and even then a disclaimer has to be added to the map, presumably in case the government decides their border extends even further.

We used to put 'Government of India Statement – the external boundaries of India are neither correct nor authenticated' on any potentially problematic maps with disputed borders, but midway through the life of one edition of this book the government decided that this wasn't good enough. By saying it was a government statement perhaps it could be interpreted that only the government believed it! So we had to reprint books for the Indian market with a new disclaimer. The absurdity of these rules is indicated by history books with disclaimers about the borders of India tagged on to maps of India under the Emperor Ashoka two millenniums ago! Turn on the BBC satellite TV news and you'll see maps the government can't put statements on; it's said the politicians just have to close their eyes or switch off the TV. ∎

---

get something you've left behind than find you have too much and need to get rid of it. Remember that clothes are easily and cheaply purchased in India.

In the south of India you can count on short-sleeves weather year-round, but in the north it gets cool enough to require a sweater or light jacket in the evenings during the winter. In the far north it will get down to freezing and you will need all the cold-weather gear you can muster.

Modesty rates highly in India, as in most Asian countries. Although men wearing shorts is accepted as a western eccentricity, they should at least be of a decent length. Wearing shorts or a T-shirt in a more formal situation is definitely impolite. A reasonable clothes list would include:

- underwear and swimming gear
- one pair of cotton trousers
- one pair of shorts (men only)
- one long (ankle-length) cotton skirt (women)
- a few T-shirts or short-sleeved cotton shirts
- sweater for cold nights
- one pair of sneakers or shoes plus socks
- sandals
- flipflops (thongs; handy to wear when showering)
- lightweight jacket or raincoat
- a set of 'dress up' clothes
- sun hat

Bedding A sleeping bag can be a hassle to carry, but can serve as something to sleep in (and avoid unsavoury looking hotel bedding), a cushion on hard train seats, a seat for long waits on railway platforms or a bed top-cover (since cheaper hotels rarely give you one).

If you're trekking in the north then a sleeping bag will be an absolute necessity. An increase in specialist trekking companies in the Himalaya means that it is now possible to hire trekking gear, including sleeping bags, near some popular trailheads, but the quality is not what you'll find in the west. A sheet sleeping bag, like those required by youth hostels in the west, can be very useful, particularly on overnight train trips or if you don't trust the hotel's sheets. Mosquito nets

are also rare, so your own sheet or sheet sleeping bag will also help to keep mosquitoes at bay (and thus reduce the risk of malaria).

Some travellers find that a plastic sheet is useful for a number of reasons, including to bedbug-proof unhealthy looking beds. Others have recommended an inflatable pillow as a useful accessory. These are widely available for Rs 40.

Toilet Paper Indian sewerage systems are generally overloaded enough without having to cope with toilet paper as well. However, if you can't adapt to the Indian method of a jug of water and your left hand, toilet paper is widely available throughout the country in all but the smallest towns. A receptacle is sometimes provided in toilets for used toilet paper – don't put paper or sanitary napkins in toilets.

Toiletries Soap, toothpaste and other toiletries are readily available. A sink plug is worth having since few cheaper hotels have plugs. A nailbrush can be very useful. For women, tampons are available in most major places; sanitary pads are more widely available, however.

Men can safely leave their shaving gear at home. One of the pleasures of Indian travel is a shave in a barber shop every few days. With AIDS becoming more widespread in India, however, choose a barber's shop that looks clean, avoid roadside barbers, and make sure that a fresh blade is used. For just a few rupees you'll get the full treatment – lathering, followed by a shave, then the process is repeated, and finally there's the hot, damp towel and sometimes talcum powder, or even a scalp massage.

Miscellaneous Items It's amazing how many things you wish you'd brought with you when you're in India. For budget travellers, a padlock is a virtual necessity. Most cheap hotels and quite a number of mid-range places have doors locked by a flimsy latch and padlock. You'll find having your own sturdy lock on the door does wonders for your peace of mind.

A knife (preferably Swiss Army) has a whole range of uses, and can be particularly good for peeling fruit. Some travellers rhapsodise about the usefulness of a miniature electric element to boil water in a cup. A sarong is a handy item – it can be used as a bed sheet, an item of clothing, an emergency towel, and a pillow on trains.

Bring insect repellent. You can pick up an electric mosquito zapper in Delhi or Jaipur. Power cuts are not uncommon ('load shedding' as it is euphemistically known) and there's little street lighting at night, so a torch (flashlight) and candles are essential. A mosquito net can be very useful.

If you wear glasses, bring along a spare set and your spectacle prescription. Earplugs are useful to shut out the din in some hotels. Eye shades can also be handy.

A sun hat and sunglasses are essential. A water bottle should always be by your side; if you're not drinking bottled water, have water purification tablets (which also reduces the amount of plastic bottles seen on dumps around India). High-factor sunscreen cream is becoming more widely available, but it's *expensive*! Lip balm is especially useful in the desert and mountain regions, where the sun can really pack a punch.

Some travellers bring a reasonably heavy-duty chain to secure their pack to the luggage racks of trains and buses. Some women carry a high-pitched whistle which may act as a deterrent to would-be assailants. See the Health section later in this chapter for details about medical supplies.

How to Carry It Where to put all this gear? Well, for budget travellers the backpack is still the best carrying container. Many packs these days are lockable, otherwise you can make it a bit more thief-proof by sewing on tabs so you can padlock it shut. It's worth paying the money for a strong, good quality pack as it's much more likely to withstand the rigours of Indian travel.

An alternative is a large, soft, zip bag with a wide shoulder strap. This is obviously not an option if you plan to do any trekking. Suitcases are only for jet-setters!

Lots of plastic bags will keep your gear in some sort of order and will also be invaluable for keeping things dry should your pack get rained on.

SUGGESTED ITINERARIES

With such a mind-boggling array of amazing things and places to see, it can be difficult deciding which ones to visit in the time you have available.

The following itineraries assume you have a month to spend in India. They take in the highlights of a region and hopefully will help you make the most of your time. They also assume that you don't want to spend the greater part of your time actually travelling between places – many first-time visitors to India make the mistake of trying to see too much in too short a period of time, and end up tired and frustrated.

><><><><><><><><><><><><><><><><
Warning
Lonely Planet strongly advises against travelling to the regions of Jammu and Kashmir. While the Indian Government has not placed restrictions on visiting Jammu and Kashmir, it is still foolhardy to visit these regions, particularly when it is possible that the Al-Faran or an associated organisation may attempt to take further hostages. The situation is exacerbated by the naïve advice offered by members of the J&K Tourist Office in Delhi who, even after western hostages were taken in July 1995, persist with the notion that the situation in Kashmir is under control. It is, therefore, essential to contact your embassy in Delhi for up-to-date information. ■
><><><><><><><><><><><><><><><><

Rajasthani Colour
Delhi – Agra – Bharatpur – Jaipur – Shekhawati – Bikaner – Jaisalmer – Jodhpur – Pushkar – Bundi – Chittorgarh – Udaipur – Aurangabad (Ajanta and Ellora caves) – Mumbai (Bombay).

This route gives you a taste of just about everything – Mughal architecture, including, of course, the Taj Mahal, wildlife, the desert, Hindu temples, hippie hangouts, Rajput exuberance, unusual Islamic architecture and the superb Buddhist paintings and sculptures of the Ajanta and Ellora caves. Mumbai and Delhi are both cities where you could happily spend a week, although a couple of days in each is usually all there's time for. Travel is by bus and train, except for the Udaipur to Aurangabad leg which can be flown.

Mughals, Jains & the Portuguese – India West

Delhi – Agra – Jaipur – Pushkar – Jodhpur – Ranakhpur – Udaipur – Bhuj – Rajkot – Junagadh – Sasan Gir – Diu – Palitana – Ahmedabad – Mumbai (Bombay).

Gujarat offers the chance to get off the well-beaten tourist circuit and is well worth any time spent there. The route takes in not only Rajasthan but also the best of what Gujarat has to offer – the tribal cultures of the Rann of Kutch in the far west of the state, the fortified town of Junagadh with some fine buildings and the magnificent Jain temples atop Girnar Hill, Sasan Gir – the last home of the Asian lion, Diu – the old Portuguese enclave with its beaches, Palitana – another town with hilltop Jain temples, and Ahmedabad – the busy city which has, among other things, the Gandhi Ashram. Travel is by bus and train.

Hindu & Mughal Heartlands

Delhi – Jaipur – Agra – Varanasi – Khajuraho – Jhansi – Sanchi – Mandu – Aurangabad – Mumbai (Bombay).

Madhya Pradesh is another state that is largely untouristed but has enough places of interest to make a visit worthwhile. The Hindu temples at Khajuraho are the big attraction, but Sanchi and Mandu between them have fine examples of Buddhist, Hindu and Afghan architecture.

Varanasi, one of the holiest places in the country, Agra, with the incomparable Taj Mahal, and the caves of Ajanta and Ellora are other attractions on this route.

Hill Stations & the Himalaya

Delhi – Dalhousie – Dharamsala – Shimla – Manali – Leh – Delhi.

Travel in this part of the country is generally by bus and, because of the terrain, is slow. This is a good route to follow if you're in India during the summer, when the heat on

---

Hill Stations

Although they may take the credit for having popularised the concept of the hill station, the British cannot claim to have invented it. Back in Mughal times the emperors retreated into the Himalaya to avoid the searing heat of mid-summer on the plains. Their favourite spot was Kashmir.

In the 19th century, British troops exploring the country discovered that the incidence of disease was much lower in the cooler hills. In 1819 a hospital was opened in Shimla and the first hill station was established. As the British presence in India grew, other hill stations were built and it became the custom to dispatch women and children to them for the summer months. They eventually developed into temporary capitals, with all the machinery of government decamping to the hills in the summer. Darjeeling was Calcutta's summer capital, and Shimla was Delhi's.

The cooler climate was certainly healthier but it seemed to infect most foreign residents with severe cases of nostalgia and they soon made their hill stations into little corners of England, building bungalows with names like 'Earl's Court', 'Windamere' and 'Windsor Cottage'. During the summer season they were great social centres with balls, theatrical performances and an endless round of dinner parties. The main thoroughfare was almost always known as The Mall and closed to all but pedestrians – as long as they were not Indian.

Today, most hill stations have become holiday resorts for middle class Indian tourists, often on their honeymoon. Although they are dilapidated shadows of the preserves of the elite which they once were, they're nonetheless great fun to visit. The journey there is usually interesting in itself – often by narrow-gauge railway (up to Shimla, Darjeeling or Matheran, for example). Some hill stations are built around a lake, as at Nainital and Kodaikanal, and most have superb views and good walks along the surrounding ridges. ∎

the plains becomes unbearable, and in fact the road from Manali to Leh is only open for a couple of months a year when the snow melts.

The hill stations of Shimla and Dalhousie hark back to an era that is rapidly being consigned to history; Dharamsala is a fascinating cultural centre, being the home of the exiled Tibetan leader His Holiness the Dalai Lama; Manali in the Kullu Valley is simply one of the most beautiful places in the country, while the two day bus trip from there to Leh, high on the Tibetan plateau, is incredibly rough but equally memorable – it's one of the highest motorable roads in the world. Leh is the capital of Ladakh and centre for another unique Himalayan culture. There are direct flights from Leh back to Delhi.

Trekkers and adventure seekers are well catered for at various places on this route. From Manali there are literally dozens of treks, ranging from a couple of days to a couple of weeks, into places such as the remote Zanskar Valley. Leh, too, is a centre for trekkers, and the Markha Valley is a popular trip. Trekking agencies in Manali and Leh can arrange everything, or you can strike out on your own.

Palaces, Temples & Holy Cities

Delhi – Jaipur – Agra – Jhansi – Khajuraho – Jabalpur – Kanha – Varanasi – Calcutta.

Starting from Delhi, this route gives you a taste of Rajasthan and includes the Taj Mahal. Jhansi is the station for the bus journey to the famous temples of Khajuraho, but it's worth stopping at Orchha, 18km from Jhansi, to see this well-preserved old city of palaces and temples. From Khajuraho, a three hour bus journey brings you to Satna for trains to Jabalpur. A boat trip through the Marble Rocks is the main attraction here. Next stop is Kanha National Park where the chances of seeing a tiger are good, and then it's back to Jabalpur to pick up a train to the holy city of Varanasi. There are direct trains from here to Calcutta, one of the most fascinating cities in the country.

Flight-Pass Route

Delhi – Agra – Khajuraho – Varanasi – Bhubaneswar – Calcutta – Andaman & Nicobar Islands – Darjeeling (Bagdogra) – Delhi.

For US$500/750 you can buy a flight pass on Indian Airlines for two/three weeks. Distance becomes no object and you can visit as many places as you like, within the time limit. This suggested itinerary links a number of the more exotic and distant places as well as 'musts' like the Taj. From Delhi fly to Agra, on to Khajuraho the next day and continue to Varanasi two days later. Next stop is the temple city of Bhubaneswar before taking the flight to Calcutta. An early-morning departure brings you to Port Blair, the capital of the Andaman & Nicobar Islands, for a few days at this rarely visited tropical paradise. With a three week pass you could also nip up to Darjeeling (3½ hours by bus from the airport at Bagdogra), changing planes in Calcutta, on your way back to Delhi.

Temples & Ancient Monuments – Central & South India

Chennai (Madras) – Kanchipuram – Mamallapuram (Mahabalipuram) – Pondicherry – Kumbakonam – Thanjavur – Tiruchirappalli – Madurai – Kodaikanal – Udhagamandalam (Ooty) – Mysore – Bangalore – Belur/Halebid/ Sravanabelagola – Hampi – Badami – Bijapur – Mumbai (Bombay).

This route takes in a small slice of modern India plus a popular travellers' beach resort, a glimpse of ex-French India along with the experimental international community settlement of Auroville, and several days in the mountains bordering Tamil Nadu and Kerala. Transport is by train and bus plus the use of a one day Indian Tourism Development Corporation (ITDC) bus ex-Mysore or ex-Bangalore to the temple towns of Belur, Halebid and Sravanabelagola.

Temples & Beaches – South India

Chennai (Madras) – Mamallapuram – Pondicherry – Thanjavur – Tiruchirappalli – Madurai – Kanyakumari – Thiruvananthapuram – Kovalam Beach – Kollam – Alappuzha – Kochi – Bangalore & Mysore – Hampi – Bijapur – Mumbai (Bombay).

This route, a variation of the above, gives you a much broader perspective of southern India and takes you through the tropical paradise of Kerala with its beaches, backwaters, Kathakali dance-dramas and historical Indo-European associations. It also includes some of the major temple complexes of Tamil Nadu, the palaces of Mysore, the Vijayanagar ruins of Hampi and the Muslim splendour of Bijapur. Transport is by train, bus and boat. If time is getting short by the time you reach Bangalore, flights are available from there to Mumbai.

HIGHLIGHTS

India can offer almost anything you want, whether it's beaches, forts, amazing travel experiences, fantastic spectacles or even a search for yourself. Listed here are just a few of those possibilities and where to start looking.

Beaches

People generally don't come all the way to India just to laze on a beach – but there are some superb beaches if you're in that mood. On the west coast, at the southern end of Kerala, there's Kovalam and Varkala; further north, Goa has a whole collection of beautiful beaches complete with soft white sand, gentle lapping waves and swaying palms. If you find it a little overcommercialised these days then head for the tiny ex-Portuguese island of Diu off the southern coast of Saurashtra (Gujarat), or to southern Karnataka, where the ex-Goa crowd are now throwing down their bedrolls.

Over on the east coast you could try the beach at Mamallapuram in Tamil Nadu. From the shore temple the beaches stretch north towards Chennai and there are some fine places to stay. In Orissa the beach at Gopalpur-on-Sea is clean and quiet.

While they're not easily accessible, some of the beaches in the Andamans are straight out of a holiday brochure for the Caribbean – white coral sand, gin-clear water and multi-coloured fish and coral.

Beach	State	Page
Kovalam	Kerala	999
Varkala	Kerala	1005
Various	Goa	869
Diu	Gujarat	716
Mamallapuram	Tamil Nadu	1061
Konark	Orissa	551
Gopalpur-on-Sea	Orissa	553
Various	Andaman Islands	1125

Faded Touches of the Raj

Although the British left India 50 years ago, there are many places where you'd hardly know it. Much of India's government system, bureaucracy, communications, sports (the Indians are crazy over cricket) and media are British to the core, but you'll also find the British touch in more unusual, enjoyable and amusing ways.

Relax in true British style with afternoon tea at Glenary's Tea Rooms in Darjeeling and later retire for a preprandial cocktail in front of the open fire in the lounge of the Windamere Hotel. There you can await the gong which summons you to dinner.

If you prefer your fading Edwardian splendour served southern-style, you can stay at the Hotel Metropole in Mysore. The twee Home Counties rural atmosphere of the Woodlands Hotel or Fernhill Palace Hotel in Udhagamandalam (Ooty) has a very Raj feel. The Tollygunge Club in Calcutta is run by a Brit and is also a great place to stay.

Sight	Place	State	Page
Victoria Memorial	Calcutta	WB	477
Tollygunge Club	Calcutta	WB	494
St Paul's Cathedral	Calcutta	WB	485
Glenary's Tea Rooms	Darjeeling	WB	525
Windamere Hotel	Darjeeling	WB	524
Gymkhana Club	Darjeeling	WB	524
Mysore Palace	Mysore	Ka	934
Hotel Metropole	Mysore	Ka	934
Lalitha Palace	Mysore	Ka	934
Fernhill Palace	Udhagamandalam	TN	1117
Woodlands Hotel	Udhagamandalam	TN	1117
Hotel Brijraj Bhawan	Kota	R	634
Victoria Terminus	Mumbai	Mah	810
Secretariat Buildings	Delhi		193
The Residency	Lucknow	UP	425
Naini Tal Boat Club	Nainital	UP	408

Abbreviations of States
Ka – Karnataka   Mah – Maharashtra
R – Rajasthan   TN – Tamil Nadu
UP – Uttar Pradesh   WB – West Bengal

Other particularly British institutions include Victoria Terminus railway station in Mumbai, and the Lutyens-designed secretariat buildings in Delhi. The Naini Tal Boat Club is an old British club with a lakeside ballroom which was once the preserve of only true-blue Brits (the famous British hunter, Jim Corbett, having been born in Nainital, was refused membership). The Gymkhana Club in Darjeeling still has its original snooker tables, Raj ghosts and cobwebs. Perhaps more nostalgic than all these is St Paul's Cathedral (Calcutta), which is stuffed with memorials to the Brits who didn't make it home, plus a Burne-Jones stained-glass window.

Freak Centres

India has been the ultimate goal of the on-the-road hippie dream for years, and somehow the 1960s still continues in India's kind climate. Goa has always been a great freak centre. The beaches are an attraction at any time of the year and every full moon is the occasion for a great gathering of the clans – but Christmas is Goa's peak period when half the freaks in India seem to flock to its beaches. There are occasional 'purges' of the Goan beaches which shouldn't worry most people, but the purist die-hards have decided this is too uncool and have moved to more remote locations.

Further south at Kovalam the fine beaches attract a steady clientele. The holy lake of Pushkar in Rajasthan has a smaller, semipermanent freak population drawn by the quiet, spiritual atmosphere of this holy town. The technicolour Tibetan outlook on life (they've got a way with hotels and restaurants too) works well in Kathmandu, so why not in India – you'll find Dharamsala and Manali, both in Himachal Pradesh, also have longer-term populations of visitors. Hampi, capital of the Vijayanagar kingdom, has only a small number of visitors but is definitely on the circuit. Finally, Puri (Orissa) and Mamallapuram (Tamil Nadu) both have temples and beaches, a sure-fire freak combination.

Centre	State	Page
Various	Goa	869
Pushkar	Rajasthan	627
Kovalam	Kerala	999
Dharamsala	Himachal Pradesh	272
Manali	Himachal Pradesh	301
Hampi	Karnataka	955
Puri	Orissa	543
Mamallapuram	Tamil Nadu	1061

Colourful Events

India is a country of festivals and there are a number of places and times that are not to be missed. They start with the Republic Day Festival in Delhi each January – elephants, a procession and military might with Indian princely splendour.

Also early in the year is the Desert Festival in Jaisalmer, Rajasthan.

In June/July the great Car Festival (Rath Yatra) in Puri is another superb spectacle as the gigantic temple car of Lord Jagannath makes its annual journey, pulled by thousands of eager devotees.

In Kerala, one of the big events of the year is the Nehru Cup Snake Boat Races on the backwaters at Alappuzha (Alleppey), which take place on the second Saturday of August.

September/October is the time to head for the hills to see the delightful Festival of the Gods in Kullu. This is part of the Dussehra Festival, which is at its most spectacular in Mysore. November is the time for the huge and colourful Camel Festival at Pushkar in Rajasthan. Finally, at Christmas where else is there to be in India than Goa?

Festival	Place	State	Page
Republic Day Festival	Delhi	D	193
Desert Festival	Jaisalmer	R	595
Car Festival	Puri	O	534
Snake Boat Races	Alappuzha	Ke	989
Dussehra	Mysore	Ka	915
Festival of the Gods	Kullu	HP	254
Camel Fair	Pushkar	R	595
Christmas	various	Go	869

Abbreviations of States

D – Delhi	Go – Goa	HP – Himachal Pradesh
Ka – Karnataka	Ke – Kerala	O – Orissa
R – Rajasthan		

Deserted Cities

There are a number of places in crowded India where great cities of the past have been deserted. Fatehpur Sikri, near Agra, is the most famous, as Akbar founded, built and left this impressive centre in less than 20 years. Hampi, the centre of the Vijayanagar Empire, is equally impressive. Not too far from there are the ancient centres of Aihole and Badami. Some of the great forts that follow are also deserted cities.

Site	State	Page
Fatehpur Sikri	Uttar Pradesh	374
Hampi	Karnataka	955
Aihole & Badami	Karnataka	962

Great Forts

India has more than its share of great forts – many of them now deserted – to tell of its tumultuous history. The Red Fort in Delhi is one of the most impressive, but Agra Fort is an equally massive reminder of Mughal power at its height. A short distance south is the huge, impregnable-looking Gwalior Fort. The Rajputs could build forts like nobody else and they've got them in all shapes and sizes and with every imaginable tale to tell. Chittorgarh Fort is tragic, Bundi and Kota forts are whimsical, Jodhpur Fort is huge and high, Amber Fort simply beautiful and Jaisalmer the essence of romance.

Way out west in Gujarat, there are the impressive forts of Junagadh and Bhuj built by the princely rulers of Saurashtra.

Further south there's Mandu, another fort impressive in its size and architecture but with a tragic tale to tell. Further south again at Daulatabad it's a tale of power, ambition and not all that much sense with another immense fort which was built and soon deserted. Important forts in the south include Bijapur and Golconda.

Naturally the European invaders had their forts too. You can see Portuguese forts in Goa, Bassein, Daman and Diu, the last being the most impressive. The British also built their share: Fort St George in Chennai is open to the public and has a fascinating museum. Those built by the French, Dutch and Danes are, regrettably, largely in ruins, although the ruins also have a certain appeal.

Fort	State	Page
Red Fort	Delhi	194
Agra	Uttar Pradesh	366
Chittorgarh	Rajasthan	641
Bundi	Rajasthan	638
Kota	Rajasthan	634
Jodhpur	Rajasthan	666
Amber	Rajasthan	612
Jaisalmer	Rajasthan	596
Junagadh	Gujarat	726
Bhuj	Gujarat	739
Daman	Gujarat	711
Diu	Gujarat	716
Mandu	Madhya Pradesh	787
Gwalior	Madhya Pradesh	751
Daulatabad	Maharashtra	861
Bassein	Maharashtra	829
Bijapur	Karnataka	964
Golconda, Hyderabad	Andhra Pradesh	970
Warangal	Andhra Pradesh	982
Chapora	Goa	899
Aguada	Goa	890
St George, Chennai	Tamil Nadu	1038

TOURIST OFFICES
Local Tourist Offices

Within India the tourist office story is somewhat blurred by the overlap between the national and state tourist offices. In addition to the national (Government of India) tourist office, each state also maintains its own tourist office, and this can lead to some confusion.

The state tourist offices vary widely in their efficiency and usefulness. Some of them are very good, and some of them are completely hopeless.

In many states the tourism ministry also runs a chain of tourist bungalows which generally offer good accommodation at very reasonable prices. You can usually find the state tourist office in the local tourist bungalow (where there is one).

The overlap between the national and state tourist offices often causes wasteful duplication. Both offices might produce a brochure on place A, while neither produces anything on place B.

To add to the confusion, in addition to the Government of India tourist office, in many places you will also find an office of the Indian Tourism Development Corporation (ITDC). The latter is more an actual 'doing'

Gurus & Ashrams

The search for gurus is becoming increasingly popular in Western culture, and thousands visit India each year to receive *darshan* (an audience with a guru, or literally 'a glimpse of God'). The word guru traditionally means either 'the dispeller of darkness' or 'heavy with wisdom'.

Most gurus live in an ashram, which means 'place of striving', a reflection of the Hindu belief that life is a continuous struggle through a series of reincarnations that eventually leads to *moksha* (spiritual salvation). An ashram is established when a guru stays in one place and disciples congregate around him, in time buying land, building facilities and making donations. Most ashrams in India are the legacies of dead gurus.

Ashrams are peppered throughout India – any place of striving can be called an ashram, be it a commercial complex or a person's home, where like-minded people gather to explore their spirituality. Visiting any ashram can be a learning experience and visiting a guru can change your life.

Some ashrams are more reputable than others and, if possible, attend one where a guru resides. The ashrams of living gurus reflect the disposition of the founder and their perception of the needs of their disciples. For example, if you visit Ma Amritanandamayi's ashram in Kerala you will be put to work and at another you might be expected to practice up to four hours meditation per day.

Many ashrams have codes of conduct which can include daily bathing, the avoidance of unnecessary chat or, in the case of Sai Baba's ashrams, when you do talk to do so softly and lovingly. Most ashrams are vegetarian and you may also be asked to abstain from eggs, tobacco, alcohol, and garlic and onions (considered aphrodisiacs). Most people in the ashrams wear white, the colour of purity, and you will feel more comfortable if you don't stand out. Suitable white clothing can be bought or made inexpensively near any ashram.

Most ashrams don't require notice of your arrival but, if you are unsure, check in advance. Talk to locals and other travellers to see which ashram or guru might best suit you. Also many of the gurus sometimes move around without much notice so investigate to avoid disappointment.

The atmosphere surrounding the ashram can have a profound and deeply moving effect on visitors. While this can be a rewarding experience it is urged to use common sense and discernment.

Movement	Place	State	Page
Various	Rishikesh	UP	397
Krishna Consciousness	Vrindaban	UP	379
Poonjaji	Lucknow	UP	423
Theosophical Society	Chennai	TN	1038
Krishnamurti Foundation	Chennai	TN	1038
Ramana Maharishi	Tiruvannamalai	TN	1073
Sri Aurobindo	Pondicherry	TN	1074
Ma Amritanandamayi	Amritapuri	Ke	990
Ramakrishna	Calcutta	WB	476
Sai Baba	Puttaparthi	AP	988
Raja Yoga	Mt Abu	R	658
Osho	Pune	Mah	844
Tibetan Buddhism	Dharamsala	HP	272
Buddhism	Bodhgaya	B	469

Abbreviations of States

AP – Andhra Pradesh	B – Bihar
HP – Himachal Pradesh	Ke – Kerala
Mah – Maharashtra	R – Rajasthan
TN – Tamil Nadu	UP – Uttar Pradesh
WB – West Bengal	

Poonjaji

organisation than a 'telling' one. For example, the ITDC will actually operate the tour bus on the tour for which the tourist office sells tickets.

The ITDC also runs a series of hotels and travellers' lodges around the country under the Ashok name. States may also have a tourist transport operation equivalent to the national ITDC, so in some cities you might find that there's a national and a state tourist operator as well as a national and a state tourist office! Of course, this still doesn't guarantee that you'll be able to find the information you're after.

Tourist Offices Abroad

The Government of India Department of Tourism maintains a string of tourist offices in other countries where you can get brochures, leaflets and some information about India. The tourist office leaflets and brochures are often very informative and worth getting hold of. On the other hand, some of the foreign offices are not always as useful for obtaining information as those within the country. There are also smaller 'promotion offices' in Osaka (Japan) and in Dallas, Miami, San Francisco and Washington DC (USA).

Australia
    Level 2, Picadilly, 210 Pitt St, Sydney NSW 2000
    (☎ (02) 9264 4855; fax 9264 4860)
Canada
    60 Bloor St West, Suite No 1003, Toronto, Ontario
    M4W 3B8 (☎ (416) 962 3787; fax 962 6279)
France
    8 Blvd de la Madeleine, 75009 Paris
    (☎ 01 42 65 83 86; fax 01 42 65 01 16)
Germany
    Kaiserstrasse 77-III, D-6000 Frankfurt-am-
    Main-1 (☎ (069) 235423; fax 234724)
Italy
    Via Albricci 9, 20122 Milan
    (☎ (02) 804952; fax 202 1681)
Malaysia
    Wisma HLA, Lot 203 Jalan Raja Chulan, 50200
    Kuala Lumpur (☎ (03) 242 5285; fax 242 5301)
Netherlands
    Rokin 9-15, 1012 KK Amsterdam
    (☎ (020) 620 8991; fax 638 3059)
Singapore
    United House, 20 Kramat Lane, Singapore 0922
    (☎ 235 3800; fax 235 8677)
Sweden
    Sveavagen 9-11, S-III 57, Stockholm 11157
    (☎ (08) 215081; fax 210186)
Switzerland
    1-3 Rue de Chantepoulet, 1201 Geneva
    (☎ (022) 732 1813; fax 731 5660)
Thailand
    Kentucky Fried Chicken Bldg, 3rd floor, 62/5
    Thaniya Rd, Bangkok 10500 (☎ (02) 235 2585)
UK
    7 Cork St, London W1X 2LN (☎ (0171) 437
    3677; 24 hour brochure line ☎ (01233) 211999;
    fax (0171) 494 1048)
USA
    30 Rockefeller Plaza, 15 North Mezzanine, New
    York NY 10112 (☎ (212) 586 4901; fax 582 3274)
    3550 Wilshire Blvd, Suite 204, Los Angeles CA
    90010 (☎ (213) 380 8855; fax 380 6111)

VISAS & DOCUMENTS

Passport

You must have a passport with you all the time; it's the most basic travel document. Ensure that your passport will be valid for the entire period you intend to remain overseas. If your passport is lost or stolen, immediately contact your country's embassy or consulate in Delhi; see the Information section in the Delhi chapter.

Visas

Virtually everybody needs a visa to visit India. The application is (in theory) straightforward and the visas are usually issued with a minimum of fuss.

Tourist visas come in a variety of flavours and are shown in the visa table below. Note that with a three month visa, your entry to India must be within 30 days from the date of issue of the visa. Also, the six month visa is valid from the date of issue of the visa, not the date you enter India. This means that if you enter India five months after the visa was issued, it will be valid only for one month, not the full six months. If you enter India the day after it was issued, you can stay for the full six months. We get many letters from travellers who get caught out, thinking a six month visa gives them a six month stay in India.

Very few embassies issue one year tourist visas, although travellers have recently reported that it is possible to obtain a one year Indian visa in the Netherlands, valid from date of issue.

Duration	Valid From	Entries	Extendible
15 days	entry to India	single	No
15 days	entry to India	double	No
3 months	entry to India	multiple	No
6 months	issue of visa	multiple	Yes

Currently, for a 15 day/three month/six month visa, Brits pay UK£3/13/26, and Aussies pay A$17/40/70. Most other nationalities are charged much the same.

Nepal According to a recent report from travellers, it is no longer possible to get a new Indian visa in Kathmandu if you already have a six month visa in your passport. Some travellers have managed to get a short visa extension, however, by having their current visas changed to three/six months from date of entry instead of from date of issue.

Pakistan The high commission in Islamabad is quite efficient, although if there is an Indian embassy in your home country they may have to fax there to check that you are not a thief, wanted by the police or in some other way undesirable. The process takes a few days, and of course you have to pay for the fax.

Sri Lanka In addition to the Indian Embassy in Colombo, travellers have reported that it is possible to obtain an Indian visa in Kandy. Visas take approximately one week to be issued. The office is located on the uphill road 100m after the Royal Palace Park, on the left, near the Castle Hill Guest House.

Thailand It now takes four working days for non-Thai nationals to obtain an Indian visa.

Visas for Neighbouring Countries

Bhutan Although Bhutan is an independent country, India has firm control over foreign policy and most other things. Applications to visit Bhutan must be made through the Director of Tourism, Ministry of Finance, Tachichho Dzong, Thimpu, Bhutan; or through the Bhutan Foreign Mission (☎ (011) 609217; fax 687 6710), Chandragupta Marg, Chanakyapuri, New Delhi 110021, India; or through the Bhutanese mission in New York. And don't hold your breath – unless you have high-up Indian connections or a personal friend in the Bhutanese aristocracy, you needn't expect to get a permit. Very few permits are issued for overland travel. The only way around these restrictions is to book an organised tour, and these don't come cheap.

Myanmar (Burma) The embassy in Delhi is fast and efficient and issues four week visas.

There is *no* Burmese consulate in Calcutta, although there is one in Kathmandu in Nepal and Dhaka in Bangladesh.

Nepal The Nepalese Embassy in Delhi is on Barakhamba Rd, New Delhi, quite close to Connaught Place, not out at Chanakyapuri like most other embassies. It is open Monday to Friday from 10 am to 1 pm. Single entry, 30 day visas take 24 hours and cost US$25 (payable in rupees). A 30 day visa is available on arrival in Nepal for US$25, and can be extended, but doing so involves rather a lot of form filling and queueing – it's better to have a visa in advance, if possible.

There is a consulate in Calcutta, and it issues visas on the spot. You'll need one passport photo and the rupee equivalent of US$25.

Sri Lanka Most western nationalities do not need a visa to visit Sri Lanka, but there are diplomatic offices in Delhi, Mumbai, and Chennai.

Thailand There are Thai embassies in Delhi and Calcutta. One month visas cost about US$10 and are issued in 24 hours. They can be extended in Thailand. If you are flying into and out of Thailand and don't intend to stay more than 15 days, a visa is not required, but you cannot extend your period of stay.

Visa Extensions Only six month tourist visas are extendible. If you want to stay in India beyond the 180 days from the date of issue of your visa, *regardless of your date of entry into India*, you're going to have to try to extend your visa. Extensions are not given as a matter of routine. If you have already been in the country for six months, it can be difficult to get an extension, and then you may only be given a month. If you've been in India less than six months the chances are much better. A one month extension costs anything from Rs 600 to Rs 800, and four photos are required.

Applications for visa extensions can be made at Foreigners' Registration offices (see below), and in all state and district capitals at the office of the Superintendent of Police.

If you stay beyond four months you are also supposed to get income tax clearance before you leave. See the upcoming Tax Clearance Certificates section for details.

Foreigners' Registration Offices Visa extensions are issued by Foreigners' Registration offices. The main offices include:

Calcutta
   237 Acharya JC Bose Rd (☎ (033) 247 3301)
Chennai
   Shashtri Bhavan Annex, 26 Haddows Rd
   (☎ (044) 827 8210)
Delhi
   1st Floor, Hans Bhavan, Tilak Bridge, New Delhi
   (☎ (011) 331 9489)
Mumbai
   Special Branch II, Annexe 2, Office of the Commissioner of Police (Greater Mumbai), Dadabhoy Naoroji Rd (☎ (022) 262 0446)

Tax Clearance Certificates
If you stay in India for more than 120 days you need a tax clearance certificate to leave the country. This supposedly proves that your time in India was financed with your own money, not by working in India or by selling things or playing the black market.

Basically all you have to do is find the Foreign Section of the Income Tax Department in Delhi, Calcutta, Chennai or Mumbai and turn up with your passport, visa extension form, any other similar paperwork and a handful of bank exchange receipts (to show you really have been changing foreign currency into rupees officially). You fill in a form and wait anything from 10 minutes to a couple of hours. You're then given your tax clearance certificate and away you go. We've never yet heard from anyone who has actually been asked for this document on departure.

Photocopies
It's a good idea to carry photocopies of your important travel documents, which obviously should be kept separate from the originals in the event that these are lost or stolen.

Take a photocopy of the first page of your passport (with your personal details and

photograph), as well as a copy of the page with your Indian visa. A photocopy of your travel insurance policy could be handy. Keep a record of the travellers cheques you have exchanged, where they were encashed, the amount and serial number. Encashment receipts should also be kept separate from your travellers cheques. Photocopy your airline ticket and your credit card. It's not a bad idea to leave photocopies of your important travel documents with a friend or relative at home.

Restricted Area Permits
Even with a visa you are not allowed everywhere in India. Certain places require special additional permits. These are covered in the appropriate sections in the main text, but briefly they are:

Andaman Islands For those flying in, permits for a stay of up to 30 days are issued on arrival at the airport in Port Blair. If you're arriving by ship, you need a permit in advance; the shipping company won't let you buy a ticket without one. Permits are obtainable from an embassy or consulate abroad, from the Ministry of Home Affairs in Delhi, or from the Foreigners' Registration offices in Chennai or Calcutta.

Getting the permit in Delhi could take several days; in Calcutta or Chennai it's generally a few hours. If you think there's a chance you might visit the Andamans on your Indian trip, get a permit when you get your Indian visa; it costs nothing and could save time later.

Lakshadweep A permit for these islands west and south-west of Kerala state is problematic. Only one island is currently open to foreigners. See the Lakshadweep section at the end of the Kerala chapter for full details.

North-Eastern Region This area is opening up. No permits are now needed for Assam, Meghalaya and Tripura.

A permit is still required for Manipur. The other three states in this area (Arunachal Pradesh, Mizoram and Nagaland) are much harder to get into. Theoretically, permits are granted to tourists in groups of four or more people on a tour arranged through a travel agent. Don't hold your breath when applying as they can take months to come through, if at all. It helps if you have a reference from an Indian who has political clout.

Permits allow for a maximum 10 day stay in each state. In practice things are, predictably, a lot different; you may get only three to five days for Manipur, and getting permission to visit Nagaland is currently extremely difficult.

Sikkim A 15 day permit is issued either while you wait or within two or three hours (depending on where you apply for it) – see the Sikkim chapter for full details.

Onward Tickets

Many Indian embassies and consulates will not issue a visa to enter India unless you are holding an onward ticket, which is taken as sufficient evidence that you intend to leave the country.

Travel Insurance

A travel insurance policy to cover theft, loss and medical problems is a wise idea. There is a wide variety of policies and your travel agent will have recommendations. The international student travel policies handled by STA Travel, Council Travel and other student travel organisations are usually good value. Some policies offer a range of medical-expense options. The more expensive options are chiefly for countries like the USA which have extremely high medical costs. Check the small print:

Some policies specifically exclude 'dangerous activities', which can include motorcycling and even trekking. If such activities are on your agenda you don't want that sort of policy. A locally acquired motorcycle licence may not be valid under your policy.

You may prefer a policy which pays doctors or hospitals direct rather than you having to pay on the spot and claim later. If you have to claim later make sure you keep all documentation. Some policies ask you to call back (reverse charges) to a centre in your home country where an immediate assessment of your problem is made. Keep a photocopy of your policy, with this number, separate from the original, for reference in the event that the latter is stolen.

Check if the policy covers ambulances, an emergency helicopter airlift out of a remote region, or an emergency flight home with a medical escort. If you have to stretch out you will need two seats and somebody has to pay for them!

Driving Licence & Permits

If you are planning to drive in India, get an International Driving Permit from your local national motoring organisation. In some centres, such as Delhi, it's possible to hire motorcycles. An International Permit can also be used for other identification purposes, such as plain old bicycle hire.

Other Documents

A health certificate, while not necessary in India, may well be required for onward travel. Student cards are virtually useless these days – many student concessions have either been eliminated or replaced by 'youth fares' or similar age concessions. Similarly, a Youth Hostel (Hostelling International – HI) card is not generally required for India's many hostels, but you do pay slightly less at official youth hostels if you have one.

It's worth having a batch of passport photos for visa applications and for obtaining permits to remote regions. If you run out, Indian photo studios will do excellent portraits at pleasantly low prices.

EMBASSIES
Indian Embassies Abroad

India's embassies, consulates and high commissions include:

Australia
    3-5 Moonah Place, Yarralumla, ACT 2600
    (☎ (02) 6273 3999; fax 273 3328)
    Level 27, 25 Bligh St, Sydney, NSW 2000
    (☎ (02) 9223 9500; fax 9223 9246)
    15 Munro St, Coburg, Melbourne, Vic 3058
    (☎ (03) 9384 0141; fax 9384 1609)
    The India Centre, 49 Bennett St, Perth, WA 6004
    (☎ (09) 221 1485; fax 221 1206)

Bangladesh
120 Road 2, Dhamondi, Dhaka
(☎ (02) 503606; fax 863662)
1253/1256 OR Nizam Rd, Mehdi Bagh,
Chittagong (☎ (031) 211007; fax 225178)

Belgium
217 Chaussee de Vleurgat, 1050 Brussels
(☎ (02) 640 9802; fax 648 9638)

Bhutan
India House Estate, Thimpu, Bhutan
(☎ (0975) 22162; fax 23195)

Canada
10 Springfield Rd, Ottawa K1M 1C9
(☎ (613) 744 3751; fax 744 0913)

China
1 Ri Tan Dong Lu, Beijing
(☎ (01) 532 1908; fax 532 4684)

Denmark
Vangehusvej 15, 2100 Copenhagen
(☎ (045) 3118 2888; fax 3927 0218)

France
15 rue Alfred Dehodencq, 75016 Paris
(☎ 01 40 50 70 70; fax 01 40 50 09 96)

Germany
Adenauerallee 262, 53113 Bonn 1
(☎ (0228) 54050; fax 540 5153)

Israel
4 Kaufman St, Sharbat House, Tel Aviv 68012
(☎ (03) 584585; fax 510 1431)

Italy
Via XX Settembre 5, 00187 Rome
(☎ (06) 488 4642; fax 481 9539)

Japan
2-2-11 Kudan Minami, Chiyoda-ku, Tokyo 102
(☎ (03) 3262 2391; fax 3234 4866)

Myanmar (Burma)
545-547 Merchant St, Yangon (Rangoon)
(☎ (01) 82550; fax 89562)

Nepal
Lainchaur, GPO Box 292, Kathmandu
(☎ (071) 411940; fax 413132)

The Netherlands
Buitenrustweg 2, 252 KD, The Hague
(☎ (070) 346 9771; fax 361 7072)

New Zealand
180 Molesworth St, Wellington
(☎ (04) 473 6390; fax 499 0665)

Pakistan
G5 Diplomatic Enclave, Islamabad
(☎ (051) 814371; fax 820742)
India House, 3 Fatima Jinnah Rd, Karachi
(☎ (021) 522275; fax 568 0929)

South Africa
Sanlam Centre, Johannesburg
(☎ (011) 333 1525; fax 333 0690)

Sri Lanka
36-38 Galle Rd, Colombo 3
(☎ (01) 421 605; fax 446 403)

Thailand
46 Soi 23 (Prasarnmitr), Sukhumvit Rd, Bangkok
(☎ (02) 258 0300; fax 258 4627)
113 Bumruangrat Rd, Chiang Mai 50000
(☎ (053) 24-3066; fax 24-7879)

UK
India House, Aldwych, London WC2B 4NA
(☎ (0171) 836 8484; fax 836 4331)
8219 Augusta St, Birmingham B18 6DS
(☎ (0121) 212 2782; fax 212 2786)

USA
2107 Massachusetts Ave NW, Washington DC
20008 (☎ (202) 939 7000; fax 939 7027)
3 East 64th St, Manhattan, New York, NY 10021-
7097 (☎ (212) 879 7800; fax 988 6423)
540 Arguello Blvd, San Francisco, CA 94118
(☎ (415) 668 0662; fax 668 2073)

Foreign Embassies & High Commissions in India

Most foreign diplomatic missions are in the nation's capital, Delhi, but there are also quite a few consulates in the other major cities of Mumbai, Calcutta and Chennai. Embassies and consulates in New Delhi include the following (the telephone area code for New Delhi is 011):

Australia
1/50-G Shantipath, Chanakyapuri
(☎ 688 8223; fax 687 4126)

Austria
EP-13 Chandragupta Marg, Chanakyapuri
(☎ 601238; fax 688 6929)

Bangladesh
56 Ring Rd, Lajpat Nagar-III
(☎ 683 4668; fax 683 9237)

Belgium
50-N Shantipath, Chanakyapuri
(☎ 608 295; fax 688 5821)

Bhutan
Chandragupta Marg, Chanakyapuri
(☎ 609217; fax 687 6710)

Canada
7/8 Shantipath, Chanakyapuri
(☎ 687 6500; fax 687 0031)

China
50-D Shantipath, Chanakyapuri
(☎ 600328; fax 688 5486)

Denmark
11 Aurangzeb Rd (☎ 301 0900; fax 301 0961)

Finland
E-3 Nyaya Marg, Chanakyapuri
(☎ 611 5258; fax 688 6713)

France
2/50-E Shantipath, Chanakyapuri
(☎ 611 8790; fax 687 2305)

Germany
6/50-G Shantipath, Chanakyapuri
(☎ 688 9144; fax 687 3117)
Ireland
13 Jor Bagh Rd (☎ 461 7435; fax 469 7053)
Israel
3 Aurangzeb Rd (☎ 301 3238; fax 301 4298)
Italy
50-E Chandragupta Marg, Chanakyapuri
(☎ 611 4355; fax 687 3889)
Japan
4-5/50-G Shantipath, Chanakyapuri
(☎ 687 6581)
Myanmar (Burma)
3/50-F Nyaya Marg, Chanakyapuri
(☎ 600251; fax 687 7942)
Nepal
Barakhamba Rd (☎ 332 8191; fax 332 6857)
The Netherlands
6/50-F Shantipath, Chanakyapuri
(☎ 688 4951; fax 688 4856)
New Zealand
50-N Nyaya Marg, Chanakyapuri
(☎ 688 3170; fax 687 2317)
Norway
50-C Shantipath, Chanakyapuri
(☎ 687 3532; fax 687 3814)
Pakistan
2/50-G Shantipath, Chanakyapuri
(☎ 600603; fax 637 2339)
South Africa
B-18 Vasant Marg, Vasant Vihar
(☎ 611 9411, 611 3505)
Spain
12 Prithviraj Rd (☎ 379 2085; fax 379 3375)
Sri Lanka
27 Kautilya Marg, Chanakyapuri
(☎ 301 0201; fax 301 5295)
Sweden
Nyaya Marg, Chanakyapuri
(☎ 687 5760; fax 688 5401)
Switzerland
Nyaya Marg, Chanakyapuri
(☎ 604225; fax 687 3093)
Thailand
56-N Nyaya Marg, Chanakyapuri
(☎ 605679; fax 687 2029)
UK
50 Shantipath, Chanakyapuri
(☎ 687 2161; fax 687 2882)
USA
Shantipath, Chanakyapuri (☎ 600651)

CUSTOMS

The usual duty-free regulations apply for India; that is, one bottle of whisky and 200 cigarettes.

You're allowed to bring in all sorts of western technological wonders, but big items, such as video cameras, are likely to be entered on a 'Tourist Baggage Re-Export' form to ensure you take them out with you when you go. This also used to be the case with laptop computers, but some travellers have reported that it is no longer necessary. It's not necessary to declare still cameras, even if you have more than one.

Note that if you are entering India from Nepal you are not entitled to import anything free of duty.

MONEY
Costs

From top to bottom: if you stay in luxury hotels, fly everywhere, and see a lot of India in a very short trip, you can spend a lot of money. India has plenty of hotels at US$50 or more a day and some where a room can cost US$200 plus. At the other extreme, if you scrimp and save, stay in dormitories or the cheapest hotels, always travel 2nd class on trains, and learn to exist on *dhal* and rice, you can see India on less than US$7 a day.

Banknotes
Indian currency notes circulate far longer than in the west and the decision has now been taken not to reprint Rs 1, Rs 2 and Rs 5 notes. The small notes in particular become very tatty – some should carry a government health warning! A note can have holes right through it (most do in fact, as they are bundled together with staples when new) and be quite acceptable, but if it's slightly torn at the top or bottom on the crease line then it's no good and you'll have trouble spending it. Even a missing corner makes a bill unacceptable. If you do receive a torn note, the answer is to simply accept it philosophically or think of clever uses for it. Use it for tips or for official purposes. I'd love to pay the Rs 300 departure tax with 300 totally disreputable Rs 1 notes – although someone who did just that wrote to say he had some trouble getting them to accept it! Some banks have special counters where torn notes will be exchanged for good ones, but who wants to visit banks more than necessary? ■

Most travellers will probably be looking for something between these extremes. If so, you'll stay in reasonable hotels with the sort of standard provided by the tourist bungalows in many states – a clean but straightforward room with fan cooling and bathroom. You'll eat in regular restaurants but occasionally splash out on a fancy meal when you're in a big town. If you mix your travel, you'll try 2nd class most of the time, and opt for 1st class only if you're travelling on a long overnight trip; you'll take auto-rickshaws rather than always looking for a bus. In that case India could cost you something like US$15 to US$25 a day on average. It totally depends on what you're looking for.

As everywhere in Asia, you get pretty much what you pay for, and many times it's worth paying a little more for the experience. That old-fashioned Raj-style luxury is part of India's charm and sometimes it's foolish not to lay out the money and enjoy it.

Carrying Money

A money belt worn around your waist beneath your clothes is probably one of the safest ways of carrying important documents such as your passport and travellers cheques on your person. Some travellers prefer a pouch attached to a string which is worn around the neck, with the pouch against the chest concealed beneath a shirt or jumper. It is now possible to purchase innocuous looking leather belts from travel goods suppliers which have a secret compartment in which you could hide your 'emergency stash'.

Travellers Cheques

Although it's usually not a problem to change travellers cheques, it's best to stick to the well known brands – American Express, Visa, Thomas Cook, Citibank and Barclays – as more obscure ones may cause problems. Occasionally a bank won't accept a certain type of cheque – Visa and Citibank in particular – and for this reason it's worth carrying more than one flavour.

A few simple measures should be taken to facilitate the replacement of travellers cheques, should they be stolen (see Stolen Travellers Cheques in the Dangers & Annoyances section later in this chapter).

Credit Cards

Credit cards are widely accepted at midrange and upmarket hotels, for buying rail and air tickets, and in many shops.

On a MasterCard, Visa card, or Japanese Credit Bureau card you can now get cash advances (in rupees) on the spot in main cities. With American Express you can get dollar or sterling travellers cheques in Delhi, but you must have a personal cheque to cover the amount, although counter cheques are available if you ask for them.

International Transfers

Don't run out of money in India unless you have a credit card against which you can draw travellers cheques or cash. Having money transferred through the banking system can be time consuming. It's usually straightforward if you use a foreign bank, Thomas Cook or American Express in Delhi; elsewhere it may take a fortnight and will be a hassle.

Currency

The rupee (Rs) is divided into 100 paise (p). There are coins of five, 10, 20, 25 and 50 paise, Rs one, two and five, and notes of Rs one, two, five, 10, 20, 50, 100 and 500, although in 1996, the Reserve Bank of India decided to stop printing notes of Rs one, two and five.

You are not allowed to bring Indian currency into the country or take it out of the country. You are allowed to bring in unlimited amounts of foreign currency or travellers cheques, but you are supposed to declare anything over US$10,000 on arrival.

One of the most annoying things about India is that no-one ever seems to have *any* change, and you'll find on numerous occasions you'll be left waiting for five minutes while a shopkeeper hawks your Rs 100 note around other shops to secure change.

Currency Exchange

In Delhi and other gateway cities you can change most foreign currencies or travellers cheques – Australian dollars, Deutschmarks, yen or whatever – but for the rest of the country it's best to stick to US dollars or pounds sterling. Thomas Cook and American Express are both popular travellers cheques, and can be exchanged readily in most major tourist centres.

At the time of going to press, the exchange rates were as follows:

A$1	=	Rs 27.20
C$1	=	Rs 26.00
DM1	=	Rs 20.80
FFr1	=	Rs 6.00
Jap ¥ 100	=	Rs 32.00
Nep Rs100	=	Rs 63.00
NZ$1	=	Rs 25.00
Sin$1	=	Rs 25.00
UK£1	=	Rs 58.50
US$1	=	Rs 35.70

Outside the main cities, the State Bank of India is usually the place to change money, although occasionally you'll be directed to another bank, such as the Bank of Baroda. In the more remote regions, few banks offer exchange facilities, so utilise the banks in the main tourist centres. Some banks charge an encashment fee, which may be levied for the entire transaction, or on each cheque. Find out how much the bank is going to charge to exchange your cheques before you sign them.

Black Market

The rupee is a fully convertible currency; that is, the rate is set by the market not the government. For this reason there's not much of a black market, although you can get a couple of rupees more for your dollars or pounds cash. In the major tourist centres you will have constant offers to change money. There's little risk involved although it is officially illegal.

Encashment Certificates

All money is supposed to be changed at official banks or moneychangers, and you are supposed to be given an encashment certificate for each transaction. In practice, some people surreptitiously bring rupees into the country with them – they can be bought at a discount price in places such as Singapore or Bangkok. Indian rupees can be brought in fairly openly from Nepal and again you can get a slightly better rate there.

Banks will usually give you an encashment certificate, but occasionally they don't bother. It is worth getting them, especially if you want to re-exchange excess rupees for hard currency when you depart India.

The other reason for saving encashment certificates is that if you stay in India longer than four months, you have to get an income tax clearance. See Tax Clearance Certificates earlier in this chapter for details.

Tipping

In tourist restaurants or hotels, where service is usually tacked on in any case, the normal 10% figure usually applies. In smaller places, where tipping is optional, you need only tip a few rupees, not a percentage of the bill. Hotel porters expect Rs 5 to Rs 10; other possible tipping levels are Rs 2 for bike-watching, Rs 10 or Rs 15 for train conductors or station porters performing miracles for you, and Rs 5 to Rs 15 for extra services from hotel staff.

POST & COMMUNICATIONS
Post

The Indian postal and poste restante services are generally excellent. Expected letters are almost always there and letters you send almost invariably reach their destination, although they take up to three weeks. American Express, in its major city locations, offers an alternative to the poste restante system.

Have letters addressed to you with your surname in capitals and underlined, followed by the poste restante, GPO, and the city or town in question. Many 'lost' letters are simply misfiled under given (Christian) names, so always check under both your names. Letters sent via poste restante are held for one month only, after which, if unclaimed, they are returned to the sender.

Baksheesh

In most Asian countries tipping is virtually unknown, but India is an exception to that rule – although tipping has a rather different role in India than in the west. The term *baksheesh* encompasses tipping and a lot more besides. You 'tip' not so much for good service, but to get things done.

Judicious baksheesh will open closed doors, find missing letters and perform other small miracles. Tipping is not necessary for taxis nor for cheaper restaurants, but if you're going to be using something repeatedly, an initial tip will ensure the standards are kept up – this may explain why the service is slower every time in your hotel restaurant for example. Keep things in perspective though. Demands for baksheesh can quickly become never-ending. Ask yourself if it's really necessary or desirable before shelling out.

Many westerners find this aspect of Indian travel the most trying – the constant demands for baksheesh and the expectations that because you're a foreigner, you'll tip. However, from an Indian perspective, baksheesh is an integral part of the system – it wasn't invented simply to extract money from tourists. Take some time to observe how Indians (even those who are obviously not excessively wealthy) deal with baksheesh situations; they always give something, and it's expected and accepted by both sides.

Although you may not consider yourself well off, think of how an Indian who earns Rs 500 a month sees you. Foreigners who spend their whole time trying to fight the system, instead of rolling with it philosophically, inevitably find themselves constantly involved in vitriolic and unpleasant arguments with people over what is, in the end, a pittance. No-one would be naive enough to suggest that all demands for baksheesh are justified, or that the amount demanded is always reasonable; however, if you can accept the fact that this is how things work here, and tip fairly, chances are you'll find that things are a whole lot easier.

Although most people think of baksheesh in terms of tipping, it also refers to giving alms to beggars. Wherever you turn in India you'll be confronted by beggars – many of them (often handicapped or hideously disfigured) genuinely in dire need, others, such as kids hassling for a rupee or a pen, obviously not.

All sorts of stories about beggars do the rounds of the travellers' hangouts, many of them with little basis in fact. Stories such as rupee millionaire beggars, people (usually kids) being deliberately mutilated by their parents so they can beg, and a beggars' Mafia are all common.

It's a matter of personal choice how you approach the issue of beggars and baksheesh. Some people feel it is best to give nothing to any beggar as it 'only encourages them' and to contribute by helping out at Mother Teresa's or similar; others give away loose change when they have it; unfortunately, others insulate themselves entirely and give nothing in any way. It's up to you.

Whether or not you decide to give to beggars on the street, the 'one pen, one pen' brigades should be firmly discouraged. ■

You can buy stamps at larger hotels, saving a lot of queueing in crowded post offices.

Postal Rates It costs Rs 6 to send a postcard or aerogramme anywhere in the world from India, and Rs 11 for a standard letter (up to 20g).

Posting Parcels Most people discover how to do this the hard way, in which case it'll take half a day. Go about it as described below, which can still take up to an hour:

- Take the parcel to a tailor and tell him you'd like it stitched up in cheap linen. Negotiate the price first.
- Go to the post office with your parcel and ask for the necessary customs declaration forms. Fill them in and glue one to the parcel. The other will be

stitched onto it. To avoid excise duty at the delivery end it's best to specify that the contents are a 'gift'. Be careful how much you declare the contents to be worth. If you specify over Rs 1000, your parcel will not be accepted without a bank clearance certificate. You can imagine the hassles involved in getting one of these, so always state the value as less than Rs 1000.

- Have the parcel weighed and franked at the parcel counter.

Note that small parcels up to two kg (considered 'packets' rather than 'parcels') can be sent at letter mail rates, which are much cheaper than parcel rates. For example, a compact 500g parcel sent airmail to Australia is only Rs 150 instead of about Rs 750.

If you are just sending books or printed

matter, these can go by bookpost, which is considerably cheaper than parcel post, but the package must be wrapped a certain way: make sure that the package can either be opened for inspection along the way, or that it is just wrapped in brown paper or cardboard and tied with string, with the two ends exposed so that the contents are visible. To protect the books, it might be worthwhile first wrapping them in clear plastic. No customs declaration form is necessary for such parcels.

The maximum weight for a bookpost parcel is two kg, which costs Rs 210 (seapost) to destinations around the world. Rates for airmail bookpost are: 200g, Rs 45; 250g, Rs 54; 500g, Rs 102; 760g, Rs 159; one kg, Rs 195; 1260g, Rs 252; 1500, Rs 288; two kg, Rs 363.

Be cautious with places which offer to mail things to your home address after you have bought them. Government emporiums are usually OK. In New Delhi, some places offer a comprehensive parcel packing service and will also offer to post the parcel for you. No matter how many travellers' testimonies you are shown guaranteeing that parcels arrived at their destinations, it pays to take the parcel to the post office yourself.

Sending parcels in the other direction (to you in India) is an extremely hit-and-miss affair. Don't count on anything bigger than a letter getting to you. And don't count on a letter getting to you if there's anything of market value inside it.

Telephone
The telephone system in India is generally very good. Most places are hooked up to the STD/ISD network, so making interstate and international calls is simplicity itself from even the smallest town.

Everywhere you'll come across private STD/ISD call booths with direct local, interstate and international dialling. These phones are usually found in shops or other businesses, but are well signposted with large 'STD/ISD' signs advertising the service. A digital meter lets you keep an eye on what the call is costing, and gives you a printout at the end. You then just pay the shop owner

– quick, painless and a far cry from the not so distant past when a night spent at a telegraph office waiting for a line was not unusual. Direct international calls from these phones cost around Rs 70 per minute, depending on the country you are calling. To make an international call, you will need to dial the following:

00 (international access code from India) + country code (of the country you are calling) + area code + local number

In some centres, STD/ISD booths may offer a 'call back' service – you ring your folks or friends, give them the phone number of the booth and wait for them to call you back. The booth operator will charge about Rs 2 to Rs 3 per minute for this service, in addition to the cost of the preliminary call. Advise your caller how long you intend to wait at the booth in the event that they have trouble getting back to you. The number your caller dials will be as follows:

(caller's country international access code) + 91 (international country code for India) + area code + local number (booth number)

The Central Telegraph offices/Telecom offices in major towns are usually reasonably efficient. Some are open 24 hours.

Home Country Direct Phone Numbers

Country	Number
Australia	0006117
Canada	000167
Germany	0004917
Italy	0003917
Japan	0008117
The Netherlands	0003117
New Zealand	0006417
Singapore	0006517
Spain	0003417
Taiwan	00088617
Thailand	0006617
UK	0004417
USA	000117

Also available is the Home Country Direct service, which gives you access to the international operator in your home country. You can then make reverse charge (collect) or credit card calls, although this is not always easy. If you are calling from a hotel beware of exorbitant connection charges on these sorts of calls. You may also have trouble convincing the owner of the telephone you are using that they are not going to get charged for the call. The countries and numbers to dial are listed in the Home Country Direct Phone numbers table on the previous page.

Fax

Fax rates at the telegraph offices (usually at or near the central post office) are Rs 60 per page for neighbouring countries, Rs 95 per page to other Asian destinations, Africa, Europe, Australia and New Zealand, and Rs 110 to the USA and Canada. Main telegraph offices are open 24 hours. Rates within India are Rs 30 per page for A4 size transmissions, and Rs 15 for A4/2 sheet transmissions. It's also possible to receive faxes at telegraph offices.

Many of the STD/ISD booths also have a fax machine for public use but they cost between 5% and 30% more than government telegraph offices.

Email

There are offices where you can send and receive email in only the largest cities (Delhi, Chennai etc) – see the Information sections in the relevant chapters. While this is the cheapest way to send text, offices often charge more for receiving email than for receiving a fax.

Telegram

It's also still possible to send telegrams. From telegraph offices the cost is around Rs 2.50 per word.

BOOKS

India is a great place for reading – there's plenty to read about, there's plenty of time to read on those never-ending bus or train trips, and when you get to the big cities you'll find plenty of bookshops where you can purchase the reading matter.

India is one of the world's largest publishers of books in English. After the USA and the UK, it's up there with Canada or Australia as a major English-language publisher. You'll find a great number of interesting books on India by Indian publishers, which are generally not available in the west.

Indian publishers also do cheap reprints of western bestsellers at prices far below western levels. A meaty Leon Uris or Arthur Hailey novel, ideal for an interminable train ride, will often cost less than US$5. The favourite western author is probably PG Wodehouse – 'Jeeves must be considered another incarnation of Vishnu', was one explanation.

Recently published British and American books also reach Indian bookshops remarkably fast and with very low mark-ups. If a bestseller in Europe or America has major appeal for India they'll often rush out a paperback in India to forestall possible pirates.

Lonely Planet

It's pleasing to be able to say that for more information on India and its neighbours, and for travel beyond India, most of the best guides come from Lonely Planet!

Lonely Planet's handy pocket-sized city guide *Delhi* has more information on the country's capital. The Himalaya is well covered, with both a trekking guide and a regular travel guide (*Indian Himalaya*). *Trekking in the Indian Himalaya* is by Garry Weare, who has spent years discovering the best trekking routes in the Himalaya, and his guide is full of practical descriptions and excellent maps. There are also Lonely Planet guides to Rajasthan and *Goa*, for travellers spending more time in these regions.

Lonely Planet guides to other countries in the South Asian region include: *Nepal, Trekking in the Nepal Himalaya, Tibet, Karakoram Highway, Pakistan, Bangladesh, Myanmar, Sri Lanka, Maldives*, and *South-East Asia*.

Guidebooks

First published in 1859, the 22nd edition of *A Handbook for Travellers in India, Pakistan, Nepal, Bangladesh & Sri Lanka* (John Murray, London, 1975) is that rarest of animals, a Victorian travel guide. If you've got a deep interest in Indian architecture and can afford the somewhat hefty price, then take along a copy of this immensely detailed guidebook. Along the way you'll find a lot of places where the British army made gallant stands, and more than a few statues of Queen Victoria – most of which have been replaced by statues of Mahatma Gandhi.

For relatively cheap but excellently produced photo-essays of the subcontinent, try Insight Guides' *Rajasthan* and *India* by APA Productions. The Nelles Guides' *Northern India* and *Southern India* (Nelles Verlag, 1990) are similar general guides with good photographs and text but skimpy hard information. In a similar vein is Odyssey Guides' *Delhi, Agra & Jaipur*.

If you're planning on doing a trek in Ladakh you'll find the detailed route descriptions and maps in *Leh & Trekking in Ladakh* (Trailblazer Publications, 1996) very useful.

There are a great number of regional and local guidebooks published in India. Many of them are excellent value and describe certain sites (the Ajanta and Ellora caves or Sanchi for example) in much greater detail than is possible in this book. The guides produced by the Archaeological Survey of India are particularly good. Another good guide, this time on the painted *havelis* (merchants' mansions) of a small region in Rajasthan, is *The Painted Towns of Shekhawati* (Mapin Publishing, 1994), by Ilay Cooper, which comes complete with street maps. It's available in the bookshops of Jaipur.

Books on wildlife are difficult to get, but bird-watchers may find the *Collins Handguide to the Birds of the Indian Subcontinent* useful. It doesn't cover all the birds by any means but it does have the best illustrations and text, and if you're not a very serious bird-watcher you will probably find it useful. Visitors to Kashmir and Sikkim can use *Birds*

of Nepal, which includes notes on these two regions. Insight Guides' *Indian Wildlife* (APA, 1988) is available from major bookshops in India and is valuable if you're keenly interested in visiting national parks.

Railway buffs should enjoy *India by Rail* (Bradt Publications, 1997) by Royston Ellis.

Travel Writing

John Keay's *Into India* (John Murray, London, 1973) is a fine general introduction to travelling in India even though it was written nearly 25 years ago.

In Rajasthan (Lonely Planet, 1996) by Royina Grewal gives a fascinating insider's view of the people and places encountered in the state; this book is one of the many exciting titles in Lonely Planet's travel literature series, Journeys. Robyn Davidson's *Desert Places* (Viking, UK, 1996) is an account of the author's journey by camel with the Rabari (Rajasthani nomads) on their annual migration through the Thar Desert. It gives a compelling insight into both the plight of the nomads and the solo woman traveller in Rajasthan.

Slowly Down the Ganges by Eric Newby is an entertaining boat-trip tale, bordering, at times, on sheer masochism!

Karma Kola by Gita Mehta is accurately subtitled 'the marketing of the mystic east'. It amusingly and cynically describes the unavoidable and hilarious collision between India looking to the west for technology and modern methods, and the west descending upon India in search of wisdom and enlightenment.

India File by Trevor Fishlock (Indian paperback by Rupa, Delhi, 1984) is a very readable collection of articles on India by the *Times* correspondent. The chapter on sex in India is often hilarious. An updated second edition is available.

Subtitled *A Year in Delhi*, William Dalrymple's wonderful *City of Djinns* (Flamingo, 1994) delves into this city's fascinating – and in many respects largely overlooked – history. Dalrymple turns up a few surprises in his wanderings around Delhi, and the book is written in a light style which makes it accessible to even hardened non-history readers.

Ved Mehta has written a number of interesting personal views of India. *Walking the Indian Streets* (Penguin paperback) is a slim and highly readable account of the culture shock he went through on returning to India after a long period abroad. *Portrait of India* is by the same author.

Ronald Segal's *The Crisis of India* (Penguin, London, 1965) is written by a South African Indian on the theme that spirituality is not always more important than a full stomach. *The Gunny Sack* by MG Vassanji explores a similar theme, this time from the point of view of a group of Gujarati families who migrated to East Africa in Raj times but retain their connections with India. It's a good read and has been dubbed 'Africa's answer to Midnight's Children' by certain literary critics.

Frank Smythe's *Valley of Flowers* (Hodder & Stoughton, 1938) is a classic travelogue, and fascinating reading for anyone interested in the western Himalaya's flora and fauna.

Third Class Ticket by Hilary Ward is an interesting account of the culture shock experienced by a group of Bengali villagers as they explore the country for the first time. *Unveiling India* (Penguin) by Anees Jung is a contemporary documentary on women in India. *An Indian Attachment* by Sarah Lloyd is an interesting and unsentimental account of an Englishwoman's life in small villages in Punjab and Uttar Pradesh.

For an assessment of the position of women in Indian society, it is well worth getting hold of *May You Be the Mother of One Hundred Sons* (Penguin, 1991) by Elisabeth Bumiller. The author spent 3½ years in India in the late 1980s and interviewed Indian women from all walks of life. Her book offers some excellent insights into the plight of women in general and rural women in particular, especially with regard to arranged marriages, dowry deaths, *sati* and female infanticide.

Chasing the Monsoon by Alexander Frater (Penguin India, 1990) is an Englishman's account of, as the title suggests, a journey

north from Kovalam in Kerala all the way to one of the wettest places on earth (Cherrapunji in Meghalaya), all the while following the onset of the monsoon as it moves north across the country. It's a fascinating insight into the significance of the monsoon, and its effect on people.

Goddess in the Stones by Norman Lewis is an interesting account of the author's travels through Bihar and the tribal villages of Orissa.

Finally, no survey of personal insights into India can ignore VS Naipaul's two controversial books *An Area of Darkness* and *India – A Wounded Civilisation*. Born in Trinidad, but of Indian descent, Naipaul tells in the first book of how India, unseen and unvisited, haunted him and of the impact upon him when he eventually made the pilgrimage to the motherland. In the second book he writes of India's unsuccessful search for a new purpose and meaning for its civilisation. His most recent book, *A Million Mutinies Now*, is also excellent.

Novels
Plenty of authors have taken the opportunity of setting their novels in a country as colourful as India. Rudyard Kipling, with books like *Kim* and *Plain Tales from the Hills*, is the Victorian English interpreter of India *par excellence*. In *A Passage to India*, EM Forster perfectly captures that collision of incomprehension between the English and the Indians. It is a very readable book.

Much more recent but again following that curious question of why the English and Indians, so dissimilar in many ways, were so similar in others, is Ruth Prawer Jhabwala's *Heat & Dust*. The contemporary narrator of the tale also describes the backpacker's India in a flawless fashion.

Probably the most widely acclaimed Indian novel in recent times was Salman Rushdie's *Midnight's Children*, which won the Booker Prize. It tells of the children who were born, like modern India itself, at the stroke of midnight on that August night in 1947 and how the life of one particular 'midnight's child' is inextricably intertwined with events in India itself. Rushdie's follow-up, *Shame*, was set in modern Pakistan. His sardonic treatment of the post-Independence rulers of India and Pakistan in these two novels upset quite a few over-inflated egos. His novel *The Satanic Verses* inflamed Muslim passions to the limit and resulted in Iran's now-deceased Ayatollah Khomeini pronouncing a death sentence on him. The book is banned in India. Rushdie's latest book, *The Moor's Last Sigh* revolves around Bal Thakeray's defamation case. Thakeray is the leader of Shiv Sena, currently in power in Maharashtra.

Vikram Seth's epic novel about post-Independence India, *A Suitable Boy*, is already a classic. It is set in the newly independent India of the 1950s, and centres around a Hindu mother's search for a suitable husband for her daughter. It ranges far and wide and touches on most aspects of Indian culture, as well as important historical issues of the time, such as the abolition of the *zamindar* system, the fall-out from Partition, Hindu-Muslim conflict and general elections. It is well worth the effort – although at 1300-odd pages it is a bit of a monster to carry!

Paul Scott's *The Raj Quartet* and *Staying On* are other important novels set in India. The big 'bestseller' Indian novel of recent years was the monster tome *Far Pavilions* by MM Kaye. Women's magazine romance in some ways, it has some interesting angles on India.

Nectar in a Sieve by Kamala Markandaya is an interesting account of a woman's life in rural India. See the Calcutta chapter for more on *City of Joy*, the 1986 bestseller in Europe and India which has been made into a popular film.

Kushwant Singh is one of India's most published contemporary authors and journalists, although he seems to have as many detractors as fans. One of his more recent offerings is simply titled *Delhi* (Penguin India, 1990). This novel spans a 600 year time frame and brings to life various periods in Delhi's history through the eyes of poets, princes and emperors. It is ingeniously spiced with short dividing chapters describing the author's peripatetic affair with a *hijda* (hermaphrodite) whore and his own age-induced and overindulgent activities which play havoc with his libido. As the author states: 'History provided me with the skeleton. I covered it with flesh and injected blood and a lot of seminal fluid into it'. It's a lively and essential read!

Kushwant Singh has also written the harrowing *Train to Pakistan* on the holocaust of Partition, the humorous *India – An Introduction*, and a collection of short stories, published in hardback, some of which are superb.

Also extremely well known and highly regarded are the books of RK Narayan. Many were set in the fictional town of Malgudi, and offer unique glimpses and insights into Indian village life. They're excellent reading. His most well known works include: *Swami & His Friends*, *The Financial Expert, The Guide, Waiting for the Mahatma* and *Malgudi Days*.

If you prefer pulp in the form of Dallas-type financial double-dealing, adultery and sex in the boardroom among the Mumbai stock market elite, try Shobha De's series of upmarket Mills & Boon-type novels. One of the most recent was *Sisters*.

History & Culture

If you want a thorough introduction to Indian history then look for the Pelican two volume *A History of India*. In volume one Romila Thapar follows Indian history from 1000 BC to the coming of the Mughals in the 16th century. Volume two by Percival Spear follows the rise and fall of the Mughals through to India since Independence. At times both volumes are a little dry, but if you want a reasonably detailed history in a handy paperback format they're worth having. More cumbersome, but offering more detail, is the 900 page paperback *Oxford History of India* by Vincent Smith.

The Wonder that was India by AL Basham gives detailed descriptions of the Indian civilisations, origins of the caste system and social customs, and detailed information on

Hinduism, Buddhism and other religions in India. It is also very informative about art and architecture. It has a wealth of background material on ancient India without being overly academic.

Christopher Hibbert's *The Great Mutiny – India 1857* (Penguin, London, 1980) is a single-volume description of the often lurid events of the Mutiny. This readable paperback is illustrated with contemporary photographs.

Plain Tales from the Raj, edited by Charles Allen (Futura paperback, London, 1976), is the delightful book derived from the equally delightful series of radio programmes of the same name. It consists of a series of interviews with people who took part in British India on both sides of the table. Extremely readable and full of fascinating little insights into life during the Raj era.

British historian Bamber Gascoigne's *The Mughals* is an excellent combination of informed and interesting historical text and glossy pictures. It's well worth the Rs 500 price tag.

The Nehrus & the Gandhis (Picador, 1988) by Tariq Ali is a very readable account of the history of these families and hence of India this century.

Freedom at Midnight is one of India's best-selling books. Authors Larry Collins and Dominique Lapierre have written other equally popular modern histories, but you could hardly ask for a more enthralling series of events than those that led to India's independence in 1947. In India you can find *Freedom at Midnight* in a cheap Bell Books paperback (Vikas Publishing, Delhi, 1976).

Highness – the Maharajas of India by Ann Morrow (Grafton Books, 1986) provides an illuminating, if at times sycophantic, insight into the rarefied and extravagant lives of these Indian rulers during the days of the Raj and since Independence.

For a good insight into the country since Independence there is *From Raj to Rajiv – 40 Years of Indian Independence* (BBC Books UK, Universal Book Stall, Delhi, 1988). It is written by old India hand and former BBC correspondent Mark Tully, and Zareer Masani.

Two current-affairs books which are well worth reading are *Bhopal – the Lessons of a Tragedy* by Sanjoy Hazarika and *Riot after Riot – Reports on Caste & Communal Violence in India* by MJ Akbar. Both are published by Penguin.

For those interested in the continuing and often shocking and sad story of India's treatment of its tribals, there is the scholarly *Tribes of India – the Struggle for Survival* by Christoph von Fürer-Haimendorf (Oxford University Press, 1982).

Autobiography of an Unknown Indian and *Thy Hand, Great Anarch!: India 1921-1952* are two autobiographical books by one of India's most prominent contemporary writers, Nirad Choudhuri. They are an excellent account of the history and culture of modern India.

The Royal Palaces of India, with text by George Michell and photographs by Antonio Martinelli (Thames & Hudson, London, 1994), is the most comprehensive book to the forts and palaces of India. The text is complemented with excellent photographs, and there are also some archaeological maps. It's incredibly detailed, giving information on the kitchen layout, bathrooms, women's quarters, and more.

Religion

If you want a better understanding of India's religions there are plenty of books available in India. The English series of Penguin paperbacks are amongst the best and are generally available in India. In particular, *Hinduism* by KM Sen (Penguin, London, 1961) is brief and to the point. If you want to read the Hindu holy books these are available in translations: *The Upanishads* (Penguin, London, 1965) and *The Bhagavad Gita* (Penguin, London, 1962). *Hindu Mythology*, edited by Wendy O'Flaherty (Penguin, London), is an interesting annotated collection of extracts from the Hindu holy books. It's convenient if you don't want the whole thing.

A Classical Dictionary of Hindu Mythology & Religion by John Dowson (Rupa, Delhi, 1987) is an Indian paperback reprint of an old English hardback. As the name suggests, it is in dictionary form and is one of the best sources for unravelling who's who in Hinduism. There's also *Indian Mythology* by Jan Knappert (Harper Collins, Delhi, 1992), a paperback encyclopedia.

Penguin also has a translation of the *Koran*. To gain some insight into Buddhism, Guy Claxton's *The Heart of Buddhism* (Aquarian Press, London, 1992) is a good place to begin. *A Handbook of Living Religions*, edited by John R Hinnewls (Pelican, London, 1985), provides a succinct and readable summary of all the various religions you will find in India.

An excellent, detailed and dispassionate introduction to 16 of India's best known gurus and religious teachers is *Guru – the Search for Enlightenment* by John Mitchiner (Viking, 1991, available in India).

Also Recommended

Readers have recommended numerous other books such as *Eating the Indian Air* by John Morris; *The Gorgeous East* by Rupert Croft-Cooke; *Delhi is Far Away* and *The Grand Trunk Road* by John Wiles; and books by Jan & Rumer Godden. *A Princess Remembers* (Rupa, 1995) by Gayatri Devi, wife of the last maharaja of Jaipur, makes interesting reading if you're travelling to Rajasthan. Irish wanderer Dervla Murphy heads south in her book *On a Shoestring to Coorg. An Indian Summer* by James Cameron (Penguin) is an autobiographical account of independence and south India.

There are some wonderful Indian comic books dealing with Hindu mythology and Indian history.

Phrasebooks

Lonely Planet has the subcontinent well covered, with phrasebooks for Hindi/Urdu, Bengali and Sinhalese.

ONLINE SERVICES

There are numerous online services relevant to India, but services come and go with some frequency. Check the Lonely Planet Web site on the Internet (http://www.lonelyplanet.com) for up-to-date information about online services.

CINEMA
Indian Films

The Indian film industry is the largest in the world in purely volume terms – in 1995, a massive 795 films were registered for classification with the censorship board! There are more than 12,000 cinemas across the country, and at least five times as many 'video halls'. The vast proportion of what is produced are your average Bollywood 'masala movies' – cheap melodramas based on three vital ingredients: romance, violence and music. Most are dreadful, but it's cheap escapism for the masses, a chance to dream.

However, for all the dross churned out, India has produced some wonderful films from brilliant directors, foremost among them being Satyajit Ray. Ray first came into the scene in the 1950s when his film *Pather Panchali* gained international recognition. For the next 40 years Ray turned out consistently excellent work, and in 1992, shortly before he died, he was awarded an Oscar, which was presented to him at his bedside in Calcutta where he was seriously ill. His best films include *Pather Panchali, Apur Sansar, Ashani Sanket* and *Jana Aranya*.

Shot on the streets of Mumbai is the excellent film *Salaam Bombay* by Mira Nair. It concentrates on the plight of the street children in Mumbai, and won the Golden Camera Prize at Cannes in 1989. Also directed by Mira Nair is *Kama Sutra*, released in 1997. Its theme of sensuality and sexuality in 16th century India has shocked the Bollywood establishment, which until very recently prohibited the depiction of even chaste kisses between romantic protagonists on celluloid. Another film which provoked controversy in India is *Bandit Queen*, directed by Shekhar Kapur, which is based on the life of the female *dacoit* (outlaw), Phoolan Devi.

Other notable Indian directors include

Mrinal Sen, Ritwik Ghatak, Shaji N Karuns, Adoor and Aravindan.

Foreign Films

A number of foreign films have been made about India over the years. Keep your eyes open for a showing of Louis Malle's two part film *Phantom India*. Running to about seven hours in all, this is a fascinating in-depth look at contemporary India. At times it's very self-indulgent and is now somewhat dated, but as an overall view it can't be beaten – it has been banned in India. The Australian ABC TV has produced two excellent documentary series on India, one titled *Journey into India*, the other *Journey into the Himalayas*. Both of them, but particularly the former, are worth seeing if you get a chance.

Of course the epic *Gandhi* was a major film, spawning a host of new and reprinted books on the Mahatma. *Heat & Dust* has also been made into an excellent film, as has *A Passage to India* and *Far Pavilions*. The film version of Lapierre's *City of Joy* was filmed in Calcutta in 1992 at a purpose-built slum. Directed by Roland Joffe (of *The Killing Fields*) with the principal character played by Patrick Swayze, it attracted a lot of flak from the West Bengal government which felt it was yet another condescending look at India's poor, but the critics, in general, felt otherwise.

NEWSPAPERS & MAGAZINES

English-language dailies include the *Times of India*, the *Hindustan Times*, the *Indian Express* and the *Statesman*; many feel the *Express* is the best of the bunch.

Weekly news magazines include *Frontline*, *India Today*, *The Week*, *Sunday* and the *Illustrated Weekly of India*. They're widely available at bookshops and railway and bus stations.

There's a very wide range of general interest magazines published in English in India – everything from *Computers Today* to *Auto Indian*, from *Cosmopolitan* to *Naughty Boy*! *Time* and *Newsweek* are only available in the main cities, and anyway, once you've become used to Indian prices they seem very

expensive. You can also find newspapers like the *Herald Tribune* and *Guardian* and magazines like *Der Spiegel* and its English, French and Italian clones in the major cities and at expensive hotels but, again, they're not cheap.

One thing you'll quickly find is that newspapers and magazines become public property on trains and buses. By your side you may have your virgin copy of *Time* magazine on which you have lashed out to help pass the time on a long train journey, and are just waiting for the right moment to start reading it. If a fellow passenger spots it, you'll be expected to hand it over, and it will then circulate until you go and collect it. If this annoys you, keep any reading matter out of sight until you are ready to use it.

TV

The revolution in the TV network has been the introduction of cable TV. It's amazing to see satellite dishes even in the remotest villages. The result is that viewers can tune in to the BBC and, broadcasting from Hong Kong, Murdoch's Star TV, Prime Sports and Channel V (an MTV-type music channel). Z TV is a local Hindi cable channel. The national broadcaster is Doordarshan.

PHOTOGRAPHY

Film

Colour print film processing facilities are readily available in larger cities. Film is relatively cheap and the quality is usually (but not always) good. Kodak 100 colour print film costs around Rs 140 for a roll of 36. Always check the use-by date on local film stock. Heat and humidity can play havoc with film, even if the use-by date hasn't been exceeded. Developing costs are around Rs 25, plus Rs 5 per photo for printing.

If you're taking slides bring the film with you. Colour slide film is only available in the major cities. Colour slides can be developed only in Delhi, and quality is not guaranteed – take your film home with you. Kodachrome and other 'includes developing' film will have to be sent overseas.

Equipment

A UV filter permanently fitted to your lens will not only cut down ultraviolet light, but will protect your lens. Spare batteries should be carried at all times. Serious photographers will consider bringing a tripod and fast film (400 ASA) for temple and fort interior shots.

Exposure

In general, photography is best done in the early morning and late afternoon. The stark midday sun eliminates shadows, rendering less depth to your photographs.

Restrictions & Photographing People

Be careful what you photograph. India is touchy about places of military importance – this can include railway stations, bridges, airports, military installations and sensitive border regions. Some temples prohibit photography in the *mandapa* (forechamber of a temple) and inner sanctum. If in doubt, ask. Some temples, and numerous forts and palaces, levy a fee to bring a still camera or video camera onto the premises. You have to pay up front – generally around Rs 25 for a still camera and Rs 50 for a video camera – and there's no refund if you decide not to take any pictures after all.

Some people are more than happy to be photographed, but care should be taken in pointing cameras at women. Again, if in doubt, ask. A zoom is a less intrusive means of taking portraits – even when you've obtained permission to take a portrait, shoving a lens in your subject's face can be disconcerting. A reasonable distance between you and your subject will help to reduce your subject's discomfort, and will result in more natural shots.

Protecting Your Camera & Film

Film manufacturers warn that, once exposed, film should be developed as quickly as possible; in practice the film seems to last, even in India's summer heat, without deterioration for months. Try to keep your film cool, and protect it in water and air-proof containers if you're travelling during the monsoon. Silica gel sachets distributed around your gear will help to absorb moisture.

It's worthwhile investing in a lead-lined (X-ray proof) bag, as repeated exposure to X-ray (even so-called 'film proof' X-ray) can damage film. *Never* put your film in baggage which will be placed in the cargo holds of aeroplanes. It will probably be subjected to large doses of X-ray which will spoil or completely ruin it.

TIME

India is 5½ hours ahead of GMT/UTC, 4½ hours behind Australian EST and 10½ hours ahead of American EST. It is officially known as IST – Indian Standard Time, although many Indians prefer to think it stands for Indian Stretchable Time!

ELECTRICITY

The electric current is 230-240V AC, 50 cycles. Electricity is widely available in the main towns and cities and tourist destinations. Sockets are of a three round-pin variety, similar (but not identical) to European sockets. European round-pin plugs will go into the sockets, but as the pins on Indian plugs are somewhat thicker, the fit is loose and connection is not always guaranteed.

You can buy small immersion elements, perfect for boiling water for tea or coffee, for Rs 50. For about Rs 70 you can buy electric mosquito zappers. These are the type that take chemical tablets which melt and give off deadly vapours (deadly for the mosquito, that is). There are many different brands and they are widely available – they come with quaint names such as Good Knight.

WEIGHTS & MEASURES

Although India is officially metricated, imperial weights and measures are still used in some areas of commerce. A conversion chart is included on the inside back cover of this book.

LAUNDRY

All of the top-end hotels, most of the mid-range hotels and some of the budget hotels and guest houses offer a laundry service, and costs are minimal.

HEALTH

Travel health depends on your predeparture preparations, your daily health care while travelling and how you handle any medical problem that does develop. While the potential dangers can seem quite frightening, in reality few travellers experience anything more than upset stomachs.

Predeparture Planning

Immunisations The further off the beaten track you go the more necessary it is to take precautions. Be aware that there is often a greater risk of disease with children and in pregnancy.

Plan ahead for getting your vaccinations: some of them require more than one injection, while some vaccinations should not be given together. It is recommended you seek medical advice at least six weeks before travel.

Record all vaccinations on an International Health Certificate, available from your doctor or government health department.

Discuss your requirements with your doctor, but vaccinations you should consider for this trip include:

Hepatitis A The most common travel-acquired illness after diarrhoea which can put you out of action for weeks. Havrix 1440 is a vaccination which provides long term immunity (possibly more than 10 years) after an initial injection and a booster at six to 12 months.

Gamma globulin is not a vaccination but is ready-made antibody collected from blood donations. It should be given close to departure because, depending on the dose, it only protects for two to six months.

Typhoid This is an important vaccination to have where hygiene is a problem. Available either as an injection or oral capsules.

Diphtheria & Tetanus Diphtheria can be a fatal throat infection and tetanus can be a fatal wound infection. Everyone should have these vaccinations. After an initial course of three injections, boosters are necessary every 10 years.

Meninogócoccal Meningitis Healthy people carry this disease; it is transmitted like a cold and you can die from it within a few hours. There are many carriers and vaccination is recommended for travellers to certain parts of India and Nepal. A single injection will give good protection for three years. The vaccine is not recommended for children under two years because they do not develop satisfactory immunity from it.

Hepatitis B This disease is spread by blood or by sexual activity. Travellers who should consider a hepatitis B vaccination include those visiting countries where there are known to be many carriers, where blood transfusions may not be adequately screened or where sexual contact is a possibility. It involves three injections, the quickest course being over three weeks with a booster at 12 months.

Polio Polio is a serious, easily transmitted disease, still prevalent in many developing countries. Everyone should keep up to date with this vaccination. A booster every 10 years maintains immunity.

Rabies Vaccination should be considered by those who will spend a month or longer in the country, especially if they are cycling, handling animals, caving, travelling to remote areas, or for children (who may not report a bite). Pretravel rabies vaccination involves having three injections over 21 to 28 days. If someone who has been vaccinated is bitten or scratched by an animal they will require two booster injections of vaccine; those not vaccinated require more.

Japanese B Encephalitis This mosquito-borne disease is not common in travellers. Consider the vaccination if spending a month or longer in a high risk area, making repeated trips to a risk area or visiting during an epidemic. It involves three injections over 30 days. The vaccine is expensive and has been associated with serious allergic reactions so the decision to have it should be balanced against the risk of contracting the illness – talk to your doctor.

Tuberculosis TB risk to travellers is usually very low. For those who will be living with or closely associated with local people in high risk areas, there may be some risk. As most healthy adults do not develop symptoms, a skin test before and after travel to determine whether exposure has occurred may be considered. A vaccination is recommended for children living in these areas for three months or more.

Malaria Medication Antimalarial drugs do not prevent you from being infected but do kill the malaria parasites during a stage in their development and significantly reduce the risk of becoming very ill or dying.

Expert advice on medication should be sought, as there are many factors to consider including the area to be visited, the risk of exposure to malaria-carrying mosquitoes, the side effects of medication, your medical history and whether you are a child or pregnant.

Travellers to isolated areas in high risk countries may like to carry a treatment dose of medication for use if symptoms occur.

Malaria is a risk throughout the year in all parts of India below 2000m. The only places where there is no risk are in parts of the states of Himachal Pradesh, Jammu & Kashmir and Sikkim.

Health Insurance Make sure that you have adequate health insurance. See Travel Insurance under documents in the Facts for the Visitor chapter for details.

Travel Health Guides If you are planning to be away or travelling in remote areas for a long period of time, you may like to consider taking a more detailed health guide.

Staying Healthy in Asia, Africa & Latin America, Dirk Schroeder, Moon Publications, 1994. Probably the best all-round guide to carry; it's compact, detailed and well organised.
Travellers' Health, Dr Richard Dawood, Oxford University Press, 1995. Comprehensive, easy to read, authoritative and highly recommended, although it's rather large to lug around.
Where There is No Doctor, David Werner, Macmillan, 1994. A very detailed guide intended for someone, such as a Peace Corps worker, going to work in an underdeveloped country.
Travel with Children, Maureen Wheeler, Lonely Planet Publications, 1995. Includes advice on travel health for younger children.

There are also a number of excellent travel health sites on the Internet. From the Lonely Planet home page there are links at (http://www.lonelyplanet.com/health/ health.htm/h-links.htm) to the World Health Organisation, the US Centers for Disease Control & Prevention and Stanford University Travel Medicine Service.

Other Preparations Make sure you're healthy before you start travelling. If you are going on a long trip make sure your teeth are OK. If you wear glasses take a spare pair and your prescription.

If you require a particular medication take an adequate supply, as it may not be available locally. Take part of the packaging showing the generic name, rather than the brand, which will make getting replacements easier. To avoid any problems, it's a good idea to have a legible prescription or letter from your doctor to show that you legally use the medication.

Basic Rules

Food There is an old colonial adage which says: 'If you can cook it, boil it or peel it you

---

Medical Kit Check List

Consider taking a basic medical kit including:

☐ **Aspirin** or paracetamol (acetaminophen in the US) – for pain or fever.

☐ **Antihistamine** (such as Benadryl) – useful as a decongestant for colds and allergies, to ease the itch from insect bites or stings, and to help prevent motion sickness. Antihistamines may cause sedation and interact with alcohol so care should be taken when using them; take one you know and have used before, if possible.

☐ **Antibiotics** – useful if you're travelling well off the beaten track, but they must be prescribed; carry the prescription with you.

☐ **Loperamide** (eg Imodium) or Lomotil for diarrhoea; prochlorperazine (eg Stemetil) or metaclopramide (eg Maxalon) for nausea and vomiting.

☐ **Rehydration** mixture – for treatment of severe diarrhoea; particularly important for travelling with children.

☐ **Antiseptic** such as povidone-iodine (eg Betadine) – for cuts and grazes.

☐ **Multivitamins** – especially for long trips when dietary vitamin intake may be inadequate.

☐ **Calamine lotion** or **aluminium sulphate spray** (eg Stingose) – to ease irritation from bites or stings.

☐ **Bandages** and Band-aids

☐ **Scissors, tweezers** and a **thermometer** (note that mercury thermometers are prohibited by airlines).

☐ **Cold and flu tablets** and throat lozenges. Pseudoephedrine hydrochloride (Sudafed) may be useful if flying with a cold to avoid ear damage.

☐ **Insect repellent, sunscreen, chap stick** and **water purification tablets**.

☐ **A couple of syringes**, in case you need injections in a country with medical hygiene problems. Ask your doctor for a note explaining why they have been prescribed.

can eat it...otherwise forget it'. Vegetables and fruit should be washed with purified water or peeled where possible. Beware of ice cream which is sold in the street or anywhere it might have been melted and refrozen; if there's any doubt (eg a power cut in the last day or two) steer well clear. Shellfish such as mussels, oysters and clams should be avoided as well as undercooked meat, particularly in the form of mince. Steaming does not make shellfish safe for eating.

If a place looks clean and well run and the vendor also looks clean and healthy, then the food is probably safe. In general, places that are packed with travellers or locals will be fine, while empty restaurants could be questionable. The food in busy restaurants is cooked and eaten quite quickly with little standing around and it is probably not reheated.

Water The number-one rule is *be careful of the water* and especially ice. If you don't know for certain that the water is safe assume the worst. Reputable brands of bottled water or soft drinks are generally fine, although in some places bottles may be refilled with tap water. Only use water from containers with a serrated seal – not tops or corks. Take care with fruit juice, particularly if water may have been added. Milk should be treated with suspicion as it is often unpasteurised, though boiled milk is fine if it is kept hygienically.

Tea or coffee should also be OK, since the water should have been boiled.

Water Purification The simplest way of purifying water is to boil it thoroughly. Vigorously boiling should be satisfactory; however, at high altitude water boils at a lower temperature, so germs are less likely to be killed. You will need to boil it for longer in these environments.

Consider purchasing a water filter for a long trip. There are two main kinds of filter. Total filters take out all parasites, bacteria and viruses, and make water safe to drink. They are often expensive, but they can be more cost effective than buying bottled water. Simple filters (which can even be a nylon mesh bag) take out dirt and larger foreign bodies from the water so that chemical solutions work much more effectively; if water is dirty, chemical solutions may not work at all. It's very important when buying a filter to read the specifications, so that you know exactly what it removes from the water and what it doesn't. Simple filtering will not remove all dangerous organisms, so if you cannot boil water it should be treated chemically. Chlorine tablets (Puritabs, Steritabs or other brand names) will kill many pathogens, but not some parasites such as giardia and amoebic cysts. Iodine is more effective in purifying water and is available in tablet form (such as Potable Aqua). Follow the

---

Nutrition

If your food is poor or limited in availability, if you're travelling hard and fast and therefore missing meals, or if you simply lose your appetite, you can soon start to lose weight and place your health at risk.

Make sure your diet is well balanced. Cooked eggs, tofu, beans, lentils (dhal in India) and nuts are all safe ways to get protein. Fruit you can peel (bananas, oranges or mandarins for example) is usually safe (melons can harbour bacteria in their flesh and are best avoided) and a good source of vitamins. Try to eat plenty of grains (including rice) and bread. Remember that although food is generally safer if it is cooked well, overcooked food loses much of its nutritional value. If your diet isn't well balanced or if your food intake is insufficient, it's a good idea to take vitamin and iron pills.

In hot climates make sure you drink enough – don't rely on feeling thirsty to indicate when you should drink. Not needing to urinate or small amounts of very dark yellow urine is a danger sign. Always carry a water bottle with you on long trips. Excessive sweating can lead to loss of salt and therefore muscle cramping. Salt tablets are not a good idea as a preventative, but in places where salt is not used much, adding salt to food can help. ■

directions carefully and remember that too much iodine can be harmful.

Medical Problems & Treatment

Self-diagnosis and treatment can be risky, so you should always seek medical help. Although we do give drug dosages in this section, they are for emergency use only. Correct diagnosis is vital.

An embassy, consulate or five-star hotel can usually recommend a good place to go for advice. In some places standards of medical attention are so low that for some ailments the best advice is to get on a plane and go somewhere else. Antibiotics should ideally be administered only under medical supervision. Take only the recommended dose at the prescribed intervals and use the whole course, even if the illness seems to be cured earlier. Stop immediately if there are any serious reactions and don't use the antibiotic at all if you are unsure that you have the correct one. Some people are allergic to commonly prescribed antibiotics such as penicillin or sulpha drugs; carry this information when travelling eg on a bracelet.

Environmental Hazards

Altitude Sickness Lack of oxygen at high altitudes (over 2500m) affects most people to some extent. The affect may be mild or severe and occurs because less oxygen reaches the muscles and the brain at high altitude, requiring the heart and lungs to compensate by working harder. Symptoms of Acute Mountain Sickness (AMS) usually develop during the first 24 hours at altitude but may be delayed up to three weeks. Mild symptoms include headache, lethargy, dizziness, difficulty sleeping and loss of appetite. AMS may become more severe without warning and can be fatal. Severe symptoms include breathlessness, a dry, irritative cough (which may progress to the production of pink, frothy sputum), severe headache, lack of coordination and balance, confusion, irrational behaviour, vomiting, drowsiness and unconsciousness. There is no hard-and-fast rule as to what is too high: AMS has been fatal at 3000m, but 3500 to 4500m is the usual range.

Everyday Health

Normal body temperature is up to 37°C or 98.6°F; more than 2°C (4°F) higher indicates a high fever. The normal adult pulse rate is 60 to 100 per minute (children 80 to 100, babies 100 to 140). As a general rule the pulse increases about 20 beats per minute for each 1°C (2°F) rise in fever.

Respiration (breathing) rate is also an indicator of illness. Count the number of breaths per minute: between 12 and 20 is normal for adults and older children (up to 30 for younger children, 40 for babies). People with a high fever or serious respiratory illness breathe more quickly than normal. More than 40 shallow breaths a minute may indicate pneumonia. ■

Treat mild symptoms by resting at the same altitude until recovery, usually a day or two. Paracetamol or aspirin can be taken for headaches. If symptoms persist or become worse, however, *immediate descent is necessary*; even 500m can help. Drug treatments should never be used to avoid descent or to enable further ascent.

The drugs acetazolamide (Diamox) and dexamethasone are recommended by some doctors for the prevention of AMS, however their use is controversial. They can reduce the symptoms, but they may also mask warning signs; severe and fatal AMS has occurred in people taking these drugs. In general we do not recommend them for travellers.

To prevent acute mountain sickness:

- Ascend slowly – have frequent rest days, spending two to three nights at each rise of 1000m. If you reach a high altitude by trekking, acclimatisation takes place gradually and you are less likely to be affected than if you fly directly to high altitude.
- It is always wise to sleep at a lower altitude than the greatest height reached during the day if possible. Also, once above 3000m, care should be taken not to increase the sleeping altitude by more than 300m per day.
- Drink extra fluids. The mountain air is dry and cold and moisture is lost as you breathe. Evaporation of sweat may occur unnoticed and result in dehydration.
- Eat light, high-carbohydrate meals for more energy.
- Avoid alcohol as it may increase the risk of dehydration.
- Avoid sedatives.

Fungal Infections Fungal infections occur more commonly in hot weather and are usually found on the scalp, between the toes or fingers, in the groin and on the body (ringworm). You get ringworm (which is a fungal infection, not a worm) from infected animals or other people. Moisture encourages these infections.

To prevent fungal infections wear loose, comfortable clothes, avoid artificial fibres, wash frequently and dry carefully. If you do get an infection, wash the infected area at least daily with a disinfectant or medicated soap, and rinse and dry well. Use an antifungal cream or powder like tolnifate (Tinaderm). Try to expose the infected area to air or sunlight as much as possible and wash all towels and underwear in hot water, change them often and let them dry in the sun.

Heat Exhaustion Dehydration and salt deficiency can cause heat exhaustion. Take time to acclimatise to high temperatures, drink sufficient liquids and do not do anything too physically demanding.

Salt deficiency is characterised by fatigue, lethargy, headaches, giddiness and muscle cramps; salt tablets may help, but adding extra salt to your food is better.

Anhydrotic heat exhaustion, caused by an inability to sweat, is quite rare. It is likely to strike people who have been in a hot climate for some time, rather than newcomers.

Heatstroke This serious, occasionally fatal, condition can occur if the body's heat-regulating mechanism breaks down and the body temperature rises to dangerous levels. Long, continuous periods of exposure to high temperatures and insufficient fluids can leave you vulnerable to heatstroke.

The symptoms are feeling unwell, not sweating very much (or at all) and a high body temperature (39°C to 41°C or 102°F to 106°F). Where sweating has ceased the skin becomes flushed and red. Severe, throbbing headaches and lack of coordination will also occur, and the sufferer may be confused or aggressive. Eventually the victim will become delirious or convulse. Hospitalisation is essential, but in the interim get victims out of the sun, remove their clothing, cover them with a wet sheet or towel and then fan continually. Give fluids if they are conscious.

Hypothermia Too much cold can be just as dangerous as too much heat. If you are trekking at high altitudes or simply taking a long bus trip over mountains, particularly at night, be prepared. In some parts of the country such as the Himalaya you should always be prepared for cold, wet or windy conditions even if you're just out walking or hitching.

Hypothermia occurs when the body loses heat faster than it can produce it and the core temperature of the body falls. It is surprisingly easy to progress from very cold to dangerously cold due to a combination of wind, wet clothing, fatigue and hunger, even if the air temperature is above freezing. It is best to dress in layers; silk, wool and some of the new artificial fibres are all good insulating materials. A hat is important, as a lot of heat is lost through the head. A strong, waterproof outer layer (and a 'space' blanket for emergencies) are essential. Carry basic supplies, including food containing simple sugars to generate heat quickly and fluid to drink.

Symptoms of hypothermia are exhaustion, numb skin (particularly toes and fingers), shivering, slurred speech, irrational or violent behaviour, lethargy, stumbling, dizzy spells, muscle cramps and violent bursts of energy. Irrationality may take the form of sufferers claiming they are warm and trying to take off their clothes.

To treat mild hypothermia, first get the person out of the wind and/or rain, remove their clothing if it's wet and replace it with dry, warm clothing. Give them hot liquids – not alcohol – and some high-kilojoule, easily digestible food. Do not rub victims, instead allow them to slowly warm themselves. This should be enough to treat the early stages of hypothermia. The early recognition and treatment of mild hypothermia is the only way to prevent severe hypothermia, which is a critical condition.

Jet Lag Jet lag is experienced when a person travels by air across more than three time zones (each time zone usually represents a one-hour time difference). It occurs because many of the functions of the human body (such as temperature, pulse rate and emptying of the bladder and bowels) are regulated by internal 24 hour cycles. When we travel long distances rapidly, our bodies take time to adjust to the 'new time' of our destination, and we may experience fatigue, disorientation, insomnia, anxiety, impaired concentration and loss of appetite. These effects will usually be gone within three days of arrival, but to minimise the impact of jet lag:

- Rest for a couple of days before departure.
- Try to select flight schedules that minimise sleep deprivation; arriving late in the day means you can go to sleep soon after you arrive. For very long flights, try to organise a stopover.
- Avoid excessive eating (which bloats the stomach) and alcohol (which causes dehydration) during the flight. Instead, drink plenty of non-carbonated, non-alcoholic drinks such as fruit juice or water.
- Avoid smoking.
- Make yourself comfortable by wearing loose-fitting clothes and perhaps bringing an eye mask and ear plugs to help you sleep.
- Try to sleep at the appropriate time for the time zone you are travelling to.

Motion Sickness Eating lightly before and during a trip will reduce the chances of motion sickness. If you are prone to motion sickness try to find a place that minimises movement – near the wing on aircraft, close to midships on boats, near the centre on buses. Fresh air usually helps; reading and cigarette smoke don't. Commercial motion-sickness preparations, which can cause drowsiness, have to be taken before the trip commences. Ginger (available in capsule form) and peppermint (including mint-flavoured sweets) are natural preventatives.

Prickly Heat Prickly heat is an itchy rash caused by excessive perspiration trapped under the skin. It usually strikes people who have just arrived in a hot climate. Keeping cool, bathing often, drying the skin and using a mild talcum or prickly heat powder or resorting to air-conditioning may help.

Sunburn In the tropics, the desert or at high altitude you can get sunburnt surprisingly quickly, even through cloud. Use a sunscreen, hat, and barrier cream for your nose and lips. Calamine lotion or Stingose are good for mild sunburn. Protect your eyes with good quality sunglasses, particularly if you will be near water, sand or snow.

Infectious Diseases

Diarrhoea Simple things like a change of water, food or climate can all cause a mild bout of diarrhoea, but a few rushed toilet trips with no other symptoms is not indicative of a major problem.

Dehydration is the main danger with any diarrhoea, particularly in children or the elderly as dehydration can occur quite quickly. Under all circumstances *fluid replacement* (at least equal to the volume being lost) is the most important thing to remember. Weak black tea with a little sugar, soda water, or soft drinks allowed to go flat and diluted 50% with clean water are all good. With severe diarrhoea a rehydrating solution is preferable to replace minerals and salts lost. Commercially available oral rehydration salts (ORS) are very useful; add them to boiled or bottled water. In an emergency you can make up a solution of six teaspoons of sugar and a half teaspoon of salt to a litre of boiled or bottled water. You need to drink at least the same volume of fluid that you are losing in bowel movements and vomiting. Urine is the best guide to the adequacy of replacement – if you have small amounts of concentrated urine, you need to drink more. Keep drinking small amounts often. Stick to a bland diet as you recover.

Lomotil or Imodium can be used to bring relief from the symptoms, although they do not actually cure the problem. Only use these drugs if you do not have access to toilets eg if you *must* travel. For children under 12 years Lomotil and Imodium are not recommended. Do not use these drugs if the person has a high fever or is severely dehydrated.

In certain situations antibiotics may be required: diarrhoea with blood or mucous (dysentery), any fever, watery diarrhoea with fever and lethargy, persistent diarrhoea not improving after 48 hours and severe diarrhoea. In these situations gut-paralysing drugs like Imodium or Lomotil should be avoided.

A stool test is necessary to diagnose which kind of dysentery you have, so you should seek medical help urgently. Where this is not possible the recommended drugs for dysentery are norfloxacin 400mg twice daily for three days or ciprofloxacin 500mg twice daily for five days. These are not recommended for children or pregnant women. The drug of choice for children would be co-trimoxazole (Bactrim, Septrin, Resprim) with dosage dependent on weight. A five-day course is given. Ampicillin or amoxycillin may be given in pregnancy, but medical care is necessary.

Amoebic dysentery is more gradual in the onset of symptoms, with abdominal pain and vomiting less likely; fever may not be present. It will persist until treated and can recur and cause other health problems.

Giardiasis is another type of diarrhoea. The parasite causing this intestinal disorder is present in contaminated water. The symptoms are stomach cramps, nausea, a bloated stomach, watery, foul-smelling diarrhoea and frequent gas. Giardiasis can appear several weeks after you have been exposed to the parasite. The symptoms may disappear for a few days and then return; this can go on for several weeks. Tinidazole, known as Fasigyn, or metronidazole (Flagyl) are the recommended drugs. Treatment is a 2gm single dose of Fasigyn or 250mg of Flagyl three times daily for five to 10 days.

Hepatitis Hepatitis is a general term for inflammation of the liver. It is a common disease worldwide. The symptoms are fever, chills, headache, fatigue, feelings of weakness and aches and pains, followed by loss of appetite, nausea, vomiting, abdominal pain, dark urine, light-coloured faeces, jaundiced (yellow) skin and the whites of the eyes may turn yellow. **Hepatitis A** is transmitted by contaminated food and drinking water. The disease poses a real threat to the western traveller. You should seek medical advice, but there is not much you can do apart from resting, drinking lots of fluids, eating lightly and avoiding fatty foods. People who have had hepatitis should avoid alcohol for some time after the illness, as the liver needs time to recover.

Hepatitis E is transmitted in the same way, it can be very serious in pregnant women.

There are almost 300 million chronic carriers of **Hepatitis B** in the world. It is spread through contact with infected blood, blood products or body fluids, for example through sexual contact, unsterilised needles and blood transfusions, or contact with blood via small breaks in the skin. Other risk situations include having a shave, tattoo, or having your body pierced with contaminated equipment. The symptoms of type B may be more severe and may lead to long term problems. **Hepatitis D** is spread in the same way, but the risk is mainly in shared needles.

Hepatitis C can lead to chronic liver disease. The virus is spread by contact with blood – usually via contaminated transfusions or shared needles. Avoiding these is the only means of prevention.

HIV & AIDS HIV, the Human Immunodeficiency Virus, develops into AIDS, Acquired Immune Deficiency Syndrome, which is a fatal disease. HIV is a major problem in many countries. Any exposure to blood, blood products or body fluids may put the individual at risk. The disease is often transmitted through sexual contact or dirty needles – vaccinations, acupuncture, tattooing and body piercing can be potentially as dangerous as intravenous drug use. HIV/AIDS can also be spread through infected blood transfusions; some developing countries cannot afford to screen blood used for transfusions.

If you do need an injection, ask to see the syringe unwrapped in front of you, or take a needle and syringe pack with you.

Fear of HIV infection should never preclude treatment for serious medical conditions.

Intestinal Worms These parasites are most common in rural, tropical areas. The different worms have different ways of infecting people. Some may be ingested on food including undercooked meat and some enter through your skin. Infestations may not show up for some time, and although they are generally not serious, if left untreated some can cause severe health problems later. Consider having a stool test when you return home to check for these and determine the appropriate treatment.

Meningococcal Meningitis This very serious disease attacks the brain and can be fatal. There are recurring epidemics in northern India and Nepal.

A fever, severe headache, sensitivity to light and neck stiffness which prevents forward bending of the head are the first symptoms. There may also be purple patches on the skin. Death can occur within a few hours, so urgent medical treatment is required.

Trekkers to rural areas of Nepal should be particularly careful, as the disease is spread by close contact with people who carry it in their throats and noses, spread it through coughs and sneezes and may not be aware that they are carriers. Lodges in the hills where travellers spend the night are prime spots for the spread of infection.

Treatment is large doses of intravenous penicillin, or chloramphenicol injections.

Sexually Transmitted Diseases Gonorrhoea, herpes and syphilis are among these diseases; sores, blisters or rashes around the genitals, discharges or pain when urinating are common symptoms. In some STDs, such as wart virus or chlamydia, symptoms may be less marked or not observed at all especially in women. Syphilis symptoms eventually disappear completely but the disease continues and can cause severe problems in later years. While abstinence from sexual contact is the only 100% effective prevention, using condoms is also effective. The treatment of gonorrhoea and syphilis is with antibiotics. The different sexually transmitted diseases each require specific antibiotics. There is no cure for herpes or AIDS.

Typhoid Typhoid fever is a dangerous gut infection caused by contaminated water and food. Medical help must be sought.

In its early stages sufferers may feel they have a bad cold or flu on the way, as early symptoms are a headache, body aches and a fever which rises a little each day until it is around 40°C (104°F) or more. The victim's pulse is often slow relative to the degree of fever present – unlike a normal fever where the pulse increases. There may also be vomiting, abdominal pain, diarrhoea or constipation.

In the second week the high fever and slow pulse continue and a few pink spots may appear on the body; trembling, delirium, weakness, weight loss and dehydration may occur. Complications such as pneumonia, perforated bowel or meningitis may occur.

The fever should be treated by keeping the victim cool and giving them fluids as dehydration should be watched for. Ciprofloxacin 750mg twice a day for 10 days is good for adults.

Chloramphenicol is recommended in many countries. The adult dosage is two 250mg capsules, four times a day. Children aged between eight and 12 years should have half the adult dose; and younger children one-third the adult dose.

Insect-Borne Diseases
Filariasis, leishmaniasis, lyme disease, typhus and yellow fever are all insect-borne diseases, but they do not pose a great risk to travellers. For more information on them see Less Common Diseases at the end of this section.

Malaria This serious and potentially fatal disease is spread by mosquito bites. If you are travelling in endemic areas it is extremely important to avoid mosquito bites and to take tablets to prevent this disease. Symptoms range from fever, chills and sweating, headache, diarrhoea and abdominal pains to a vague feeling of ill-health. Seek medical help immediately if malaria is suspected.

Without treatment malaria can rapidly become more serious and can be fatal.

If medical care is not available, malaria tablets can be used for treatment. You need to use a malaria tablet which is different to the one you were taking when you contracted malaria. The treatment dosages are mefloquine (two 250mg tablets and a further two six hours later), fansidar (single dose of three tablets). If you were previously taking mefloquine then other alternatives are halofantrine (three doses of two 250mg tablets every six hours) or quinine sulphate (600mg every six hours). There is a greater risk of side effects with these dosages than in normal use.

Travellers are advised to prevent mosquito bites at all times. The main messages are:

- wear light coloured clothing
- wear long pants and long sleeved shirts
- use mosquito repellents containing the compound DEET on exposed areas (prolonged overuse of DEET may be harmful, especially to children, but its use is considered preferable to being bitten by disease-transmitting mosquitoes)
- avoid highly scented perfumes or aftershave
- use a mosquito net impregnated with mosquito repellent (permethrin) – it may be worth taking your own
- impregnating clothes with permethrin effectively deters mosquitoes and other insects

Dengue Fever There is no preventative drug available for this mosquito-spread disease which can be fatal in children. A sudden onset of fever, headaches and severe joint and muscle pains are the first signs before a rash develops. Recovery may be prolonged.

Japanese B Encephalitis This viral infection of the brain is transmitted by mosquitoes. Most cases occur in rural areas as the virus exists in pigs and wading birds. Symptoms include fever, headache and alteration in consciousness. Hospitalisation is needed for correct diagnosis and treatment. There is a high mortality rate among those who have symptoms; of those that survive many are intellectually disabled.

Cuts, Bites & Stings
Rabies is passed through animal bites. See Less Common Diseases for details of this disease.

Bedbugs & Lice Bedbugs live in various places, but particularly in dirty mattresses and bedding, evidenced by spots of blood on bedclothes or on the wall. Bedbugs leave itchy bites in neat rows. Calamine lotion or Stingose spray may help.

All lice cause itching and discomfort. They make themselves at home in your hair (head lice), your clothing (body lice) or in your pubic hair (crabs). You catch lice through direct contact with infected people or by sharing combs, clothing and the like. Powder or shampoo treatment will kill the lice and infected clothing should then be washed in very hot, soapy water and left in the sun to dry.

Insect Bites & Stings Bee and wasp stings are usually painful rather than dangerous. However in people who are allergic to them severe breathing difficulties may occur and require urgent medical care. Calamine lotion or Stingose spray will give relief and ice packs will reduce the pain and swelling. There are some spiders with dangerous bites but antivenenes are usually available. Scorpion stings are notoriously painful and can actually be fatal. Scorpions often shelter in shoes or clothing.

There are various fish and other sea creatures which can sting or bite dangerously or which are dangerous to eat. Again, local advice is the best suggestion.

Cuts & Scratches Wash well and treat any cut with an antiseptic such as povidone-iodine. Where possible avoid bandages and Band-aids, which can keep wounds wet. Coral cuts are notoriously slow to heal and if they are not adequately cleaned small pieces of coral can become embedded in the wound. Avoid coral cuts by wearing shoes when walking on reefs, and clean any cut thoroughly with an antiseptic. Severe pain, throbbing, redness, fever or generally feeling unwell suggest infection and the need for antibiotics promptly as coral cuts may result in serious infections.

Jellyfish Local advice is the best way of avoiding contact with these sea creatures which have stinging tentacles. Dousing in vinegar will de-activate any stingers which have not 'fired'. Calamine lotion, antihistamines and analgesics may reduce the reaction and relieve the pain.

Leeches & Ticks Leeches may be present in damp rainforest conditions; they attach themselves to your skin to suck your blood. Trekkers often get them on their legs or in their boots. Salt or a lighted cigarette end will make them fall off. Do not pull them off, as the bite is then more likely to become infected. Clean and apply pressure if the point of attachment is bleeding. An insect repellent may keep them away.

You should always check all over your body if you have been walking through a potentially tick-infested area as ticks can cause skin infections and other more serious diseases. If a tick is found attached, press down around the tick's head with tweezers, grab the head and gently pull upwards. Avoid pulling the rear of the body as this may squeeze the tick's gut contents through the attached mouth parts into the skin, increasing the risk of infection and disease. Smearing chemicals on the tick will not make it let go and is not recommended.

Snakes To minimise your chances of being bitten always wear boots, socks and long trousers when walking through undergrowth where snakes may be present. Don't put your hands into holes and crevices, and be careful when collecting firewood.

Snake bites do not cause instantaneous death and antivenenes are usually available. Immediately wrap the bitten limb tightly, as you would for a sprained ankle, and then attach a splint to immobilise it. Keep the victim still and seek medical help, if possible with the dead snake for identification. Don't attempt to catch the snake if there is a possibility of being bitten again. Tourniquets and sucking out the poison are now comprehensively discredited.

Women's Health

Gynaecological Problems Sexually transmitted diseases are a major cause of vaginal problems. Symptoms include a smelly discharge, painful intercourse and sometimes a burning sensation when urinating. Male sexual partners must also be treated. Medical attention should be sought and remember in addition to these diseases HIV or hepatitis B may also be acquired during exposure. Besides abstinence, the best thing is to practise safe sex using condoms.

Antibiotic use, synthetic underwear, sweating and contraceptive pills can lead to fungal vaginal infections when travelling in hot climates. Good personal hygiene, and loose-fitting clothes and cotton underwear will help to prevent these infections.

Fungal infections, characterised by a rash, itch and discharge, can be treated with a vinegar or lemon-juice douche, or with yoghurt. Nystatin, miconazole or clotrimazole pessaries or vaginal cream are the usual treatment.

Pregnancy It is not advisable to travel to some places while pregnant as some vaccinations normally used to prevent serious diseases are not advisable in pregnancy eg yellow fever. In addition, some diseases are much more serious for the mother (and may increase the risk of a stillborn child) in pregnancy eg malaria.

Most miscarriages occur during the first three months of pregnancy. Miscarriage is not uncommon, and can occasionally lead to severe bleeding. The last three months should also be spent within reasonable distance of good medical care. A baby born as early as 24 weeks stands a chance of survival, but only in a good modern hospital. Pregnant women should avoid all unnecessary medication, vaccinations and malarial prophylactics should still be taken where needed. Additional care should be taken to prevent illness and particular attention should be paid to diet and nutrition. Alcohol and nicotine, for example, should be avoided.

Less Common Diseases

The following diseases pose a small risk to travellers, and so are only mentioned in passing. Seek medical advice if you think you may have any of these diseases.

Cholera This is the worst of the watery diarrhoeas and medical help should be sought. Outbreaks of cholera are generally widely reported, so you can avoid such problem areas. *Fluid replacement is the most vital treatment* – the risk of dehydration is severe as you may lose up to 20 litres a day. If there is a delay in getting to hospital then begin taking tetracycline. The adult dose is 250mg four times daily. It is not recommended for children under nine years nor for pregnant women. Tetracycline may help shorten the illness, but adequate fluids are required to save lives.

Filariasis This is a mosquito-transmitted parasitic infection found in India. Possible symptoms include fever, pain and swelling of the lymph glands; inflammation of lymph drainage areas; swelling of a limb or the scrotum; skin rashes and blindness. Treatment is available to eliminate the parasites from the body, but some of the damage already caused may not be reversible. Medical advice should be obtained promptly if the infection is suspected.

Leishmaniasis A group of parasitic diseases transmitted by sandfly bites, found in many parts of the India. Cutaneous leishmaniasis affects the skin tissue causing ulceration and disfigurement and visceral leishmaniasis affects the internal organs. Seek medical advice as laboratory testing is required for diagnosis and correct treatment. Avoiding sandfly bites is the best precaution. Bites are usually painless and itchy are yet another reason to cover up and apply repellent.

Lyme Disease Lyme disease is a tick-transmitted infection which may be acquired throughout Asia. The illness usually begins with a spreading rash at the site of the tick bite and is accompanied by fever, headache, extreme fatigue, aching joints and muscles and mild neck stiffness. If untreated, these symptoms usually resolve over several weeks but over subsequent weeks or months disorders of the nervous system, heart and joints may develop. Treatment works best early in the illness. Medical help should be sought.

Rabies Rabies is a fatal viral infection found in many countries. About 30,000 people a year die from rabies, a great many of them in India. Many animals can be infected (such as dogs, cats, bats and monkeys) and it is their saliva which is infectious. Any bite, scratch or even lick from a warm-blooded, furry animal should be cleaned immediately and thoroughly. Scrub with soap and running water, and then apply alcohol or iodine solution. Medical help should be sought promptly to receive a course of injections to prevent the onset of symptoms and death.

Tetanus Tetanus occurs when a wound becomes infected by a germ which lives in soil and in the faeces of horses and other animals. It enters the body via breaks in the skin. All wounds should be cleaned promptly and adequately and an antiseptic cream or solution applied. Use antibiotics if the wound becomes hot, throbs or pus is seen. The first symptom may be discomfort in swallowing, or stiffening of the jaw and neck; this is followed by painful convulsions of the jaw and whole body. The disease can be fatal.

Tuberculosis (TB) TB is a bacterial infection usually transmitted from person to person by coughing but may be transmitted through consumption of unpasteurised milk. Milk that has been boiled is safe to drink, and the souring of milk to make yoghurt or cheese also kills the bacilli. Travellers are usually not at great risk as close household contact with the infected person is usually required before the disease is passed on.

Typhus Typhus is spread by ticks, mites or lice. It begins with fever, chills, headache and muscle pains followed a few days later by a body rash. There is often a large painful sore at the site of the bite and nearby lymph nodes are swollen and painful. Typhus can be treated under medical supervision. Seek local advice on areas where ticks pose a danger and always check your skin (including hair) carefully for ticks after walking in a danger area such as a tropical forest. A strong insect repellent can help, and serious walkers in tick areas should consider having their boots and trousers impregnated with benzyl benzoate and dibutylphthalate.

Plague There was an outbreak of pneumonic plague in 1994 in Surat, Gujarat, although the risk to travellers was tiny.

Hospitals

Although India does have a few excellent hospitals such as the Christian Medical College Hospital in Vellore, Tamil Nadu, the Breach Candy Hospital in Mumbai and the All India Institute of Medical Sciences in Delhi, most Indian cities do not have the quality of medical care available in the west. Usually hospitals run by western missionaries have better facilities than government hospitals where long queues are common. Unless you have something very unusual, these Christian-run hospitals are the best places to head for in an emergency.

India also has many qualified doctors with their own private clinics which can be quite good and, in some cases, as good as anything available anywhere in the world. The usual fee for a clinic visit is about Rs 100; Rs 250 for a specialist. Home calls usually cost about Rs 150.

WOMEN TRAVELLERS

Foreign women in India have always been seen by Indian men as free and easy, based largely on what they believed to be true from watching cheap western soapies. Women have been hassled, stared at, spied on in hotel rooms, and often groped, although the situation was rarely threatening.

Recently, however, the situation has become more difficult for women travellers, mainly because the 'sexual revolution' which

swept the west 30 years ago has now hit India. Movies and magazines are much more explicit, and the widespread billboard advertisements for condoms often quote passages from the *Kama Sutra* and depict naked or semi-naked women and men. The message getting through to the middle-class Indian male is that sex before and outside of marriage is less of a taboo than in the past, and so foreign women are seen as even more free and easy than ever before.

Unwanted attention can entail staring, provocative comments, or even groping or inappropriate body contact when in crowded places. It is not only western women who are subjected to this form of treatment, which is known in India as Eve teasing.

Close attention to standards of dress will go a long way to minimising problems for female travellers. The light cotton drawstring skirts that many foreign women pick up in India are really sari petticoats and to wear them in the street is rather like going out half dressed. Ways of blending into the Indian background include avoiding sleeveless blouses, skirts that are too short and, of course, the bra-less look. Remember that *lungis* are only acceptable wear for women in the state of Kerala.

Getting stared at is something which you'll have to get used to. Don't return male stares, as this will be considered a come-on; just ignore them. Dark glasses can help. Other harassment likely to be encountered includes obscene comments, touching-up and jeering, particularly by groups of youths.

Getting involved in inane conversations with men is also considered a turn-on. Keep discussions down to a necessary minimum unless you're interested in getting hassled. If you get the feeling he's encroaching on your space, the chances are that he is. A firm request to keep away is usually enough. Firmly return any errant limbs, put some item of luggage in between you and if all else fails, find a new spot. You're also within your rights to tell him to shove off!

When travelling on buses and trains in the south (particularly in rural Tamil Nadu), women may find men reluctant to sit next to them. Even if you offer the neighbouring seat to a man standing in the crowded aisle, it's likely that he'll shake his head and mumble something about 'getting off at the next stop'. The fact that the next stop is two hours down the track is inconsequential. Likewise, Indian women from rural areas will often stand rather than sit next to a man.

It must be said that the further you get from the heavily touristed areas, the fewer problems you'll encounter. The south is also generally more relaxed than the north.

Being a woman also has some advantages. There is often a special ladies' queue for train tickets or even a ladies' quota and ladies' compartments. One woman wrote that these ladies' carriages were often nearly empty – another said that they were full of screaming children. Special ladies' facilities are also sometimes found in cinemas and other places.

GAY & LESBIAN TRAVELLERS

While overt displays of affection between members of the opposite sex, such as cuddling and hand-holding, are frowned upon in India, it is not unusual to see Indian men holding hands with each other or engaged in other close affectionate behaviour. This does not necessarily suggest that they are gay. The gay movement in India is confined almost exclusively to larger cities and Mumbai is really the only place where there's a gay 'scene'. Since marriage is seen as very important, to be gay is a particular stigma – most gays stay in the closet or risk being disowned by their families.

As with relations between heterosexual western couples travelling in India – both married and unmarried – gay and lesbian travellers should exercise discretion and refrain from displaying overt affection towards each other in public.

Legal Status

Homosexual relations for men are illegal in India. Section 377 of the national legislation forbids 'carnal intercourse against the order of nature' (that is, anal intercourse). The penalties for transgression can be up to life imprisonment. Because of this gay travellers

could be the subject of blackmail – take care. There is no law against lesbian relations.

Publications & Groups

Bombay Dost is a gay and lesbian publication available from 105 Veena Beena Shopping Centre, Bandra (W) Mumbai; The People Tree, 8 Parliament St, New Delhi; and Classic Books, 10 Middleton St, Calcutta. Support groups include Bombay Dost (address above); Pravartak, Post Bag 10237, Calcutta, West Bengal 700019; Sakhi (Lesbian Group), PO Box 3526, Lajpat Nagar, New Delhi 110024; and Sneha Sangama, PO Box 3250, RT Nagar, Bangalore 560032.

DISABLED TRAVELLERS

Travelling in India can entail some fairly rigorous challenges, even for the able-bodied traveller – long bus trips in crowded vehicles between remote villages and endless queues in the scorching heat at bus and train stations can test even the hardiest traveller. If you can't walk, these challenges are increased many-fold. Few buildings have wheelchair access; toilets have certainly not been designed to accommodate wheelchairs; footpaths, where they exist (only in larger towns), are generally riddled with holes, littered with obstacles and packed with throngs of people, severely restricting mobility.

Nevertheless, many disabled travellers are taking on the challenge of travel in India. Seeing the mobility impaired locals whizz through city traffic at breakneck speed in modified bicycles might even serve as inspiration! If your mobility is restricted you will require a strong, able-bodied companion to accompany you, and it would be well worth considering hiring a private vehicle and driver.

SENIOR TRAVELLERS

Unless your mobility (see above) or your vision is impaired or you're in any other way incapacitated, and if you're in reasonable health, there is no reason why the senior traveller should not consider India as a potential holiday destination. It may be helpful to discuss your proposed trip with your local GP.

Go for it!

I have visited India many times before but never in a wheelchair as a disabled person. As India is so rewarding, it is worth the effort to see it despite the lack of facilities we are used to in the west.

I am 55 and have MS. I can walk two or three steps with support which does help but I was carried up and down steps very willingly where necessary. I have enough money to use medium price hotels with ground floor rooms and to take taxis when necessary. Even a car and driver for a few days isn't too expensive and Indians are expert at getting things like wheelchairs into boots of cars. It would, however, be almost impossible to do without a willing companion, not only for the pushing and pulling (pavements are never smooth) but to see if a restaurant, shop, hotel or temple is feasible. That saves a lot of time.

There is always plenty of manpower available if people are shown what to do, and paying for it or tipping is obviously welcome. In the same way you can hire a nurse and the rate of exchange is such that it is very cheap to us. Bathrooms in the modest hotels are actually better than in the expensive ones. They are big, have western loos, marble or cement floors and shower taps come out of the wall about three feet from the ground with a tap at that level too. Loos out and about are the biggest problem. I solved it by taking a fold up stool with me and a 'slipper' potty which slots underneath so I could get into a loo (often it is the squat kind) and balance somewhat precariously.

Every disabled person is different and I find that thinking through every eventuality beforehand and taking whatever kit is essential is important. It would be difficult to buy things especially for the disabled but Indians are very good at making do and mending. You can then be prepared to be very surprised at how you can survive and how much you can enjoy a holiday in India.

Margaret Wilson (UK)

TRAVEL WITH CHILDREN

The numbers of intrepid souls travelling around India accompanied by one, or even two, young children, seems to be on the increase. Children can often enhance your encounters with local people, as they often possess little of the self-consciousness and sense of the cultural differences which can inhibit interaction between adults. Nevertheless, travelling with children can be hard work, and ideally the burden needs to be shared between two adults. For more information, see the Health section earlier in this chapter, and get hold of a copy of Lonely Planet's *Travel with Children* by Maureen Wheeler.

DANGERS & ANNOYANCES
Theft

Never leave those most important valuables (passport, tickets, health certificates, money, travellers cheques) in your room; they should be with you at all times. Either have a stout leather passport wallet on your belt, or a passport pouch under your shirt, or simply extra internal pockets in your clothing. On trains at night keep your gear near you; padlocking a bag to a luggage rack can be useful, and some of the newer trains have

loops under the seats which you can chain things to. Never walk around with valuables casually slung over your shoulder. Take extra care on crowded public transport.

Thieves are particularly prevalent on train routes where there are lots of tourists. The Delhi to Agra *Shatabdi Express* service is notorious; Delhi to Jaipur, Jaipur to Ajmer and Jodhpur to Jaisalmer, Varanasi to Calcutta, Delhi to Mumbai and Agra to Varanasi are other routes to take care on. Train departure time, when the confusion and crowds are at their worst, is the time to be most careful. Just as the train is about to leave, you are distracted by someone while his or her accomplice is stealing your bag from by your feet. Airports are another place to be careful, especially when international arrivals take place in the middle of the night, when you are unlikely to be at your most alert.

From time to time there are also drugging episodes. Travellers meet somebody on a train or bus or in a town, start talking and are then offered a cup of tea or something similar. Hours later they wake up with a headache and all their gear gone, the tea having been full of sleeping pills. Don't accept drinks or food from strangers no matter how friendly they seem, particularly if you're on your own. This has even happened to people travelling in 1st class compartments who have fallen for a well-dressed, well-spoken conperson.

Beware also of your fellow travellers. Unhappily there are more than a few backpackers who make their money go further by helping themselves to other people's.

Remember that backpacks are very easy to rifle through. Don't leave valuables in them, especially during flights. Remember also that something may be of little or no value to a thief, but to lose it would be a real heartbreak to you – like film. Finally, a good travel insurance policy helps.

If you do have something stolen, you're going to have to report it to the police. You'll also need a statement proving you have done so if you want to claim on insurance.

Insurance companies, despite their rosy promises of full protection and speedy settlement of claims, are just as disbelieving as the Indian police and will often attempt every devious trick in the book to avoid paying out on a baggage claim.

Note that some policies specify that you must report an item stolen to the police within a limited amount of time of your observing that it is missing.

Stolen Travellers Cheques If you're unlucky enough to have things stolen, some precautions can ease the pain. All travellers cheques are replaceable, although this does you little immediate good if you have to go home and apply to your bank. What you want

is instant replacement. Furthermore, what do you do if you lose your cheques and money and have a day or more to travel to the replacement office? The answer is to keep an emergency cash-stash in a totally separate place. In that same place you should keep a record of the cheque serial numbers, proof of purchase slips, encashment vouchers and your passport number.

American Express makes considerable noise about 'instant replacement' of their cheques but a lot of people find out, to their cost, that without a number of precautions 'instantly' can take longer than you think. If you don't have the receipt you were given when you bought the cheques, rapid replacement will be difficult. Obviously the receipt should be kept separate from the cheques, and a photocopy in yet another location doesn't hurt either. Chances are you'll be able to get a limited amount of funds on the spot, and the rest will be available when the bank has verified your initial purchase of the cheques. American Express has a 24 hour number in Delhi (☎ (011) 687 5050) which you must ring within 24 hours of the theft.

LEGAL MATTERS

If you find yourself in a sticky legal predicament, contact your embassy. You should carry your passport with you at all times.

In the Indian justice system it seems the burden of proof is on the accused, and proving one's innocence is virtually impossible. The police forces are often corrupt and will pay 'witnesses' to give evidence.

Carbon-Monoxide Poisoning

Lonely Planet recommends that travellers do not use fires as a means of heating in hotel rooms. The Indian police have confirmed that a number of deaths from carbon-monoxide poisoning occur each year. The tragic story below explains why you should especially avoid burning charcoal or other fuels which give off toxic fumes.

On 25 January 1996, we had the heartbreaking news our precious son John and his beautiful girlfriend Lisa had been found dead in their hotel room in Darjeeling. Apparently the weather was freezing, and on asking for some heating, they were brought a bucket of charcoal. Unfortunately, ventilation was almost nonexistent and they died from carbon-monoxide poisoning.

Diane Stevens

Drugs

For a long time India was a place where you could indulge in all sorts of illegal drugs (mostly grass and hashish) with relative ease – they were cheap, readily available and the risks were minimal. These days things have changed. Although dope is still widely available, penalties for possession, use and trafficking in illegal drugs are strictly enforced. If convicted on a drugs-related charge, sentences are long *(minimum* of 10 years), even for minor offences, and there is no remission or parole. In some cases it has taken three years just to get a court hearing.

In the past year 16 Brits have been arrested on drugs charges at Delhi airport. If you partake in drugs, be aware of the risks.

BUSINESS HOURS

Government offices are open from 10 am to 5 pm, Monday to Saturday, and are closed every second Saturday. Banks are open from 10 am to 2 pm Monday to Friday, and 10 am to noon on every second Saturday. Travellers cheque transactions usually cease 30 minutes before the official bank closing time. In some tourist centres there may be foreign exchange offices that stay open for longer hours. Shops and offices are usually closed on Sunday and public holidays.

HOLIDAYS & FESTIVALS

Owing to its religious and regional variations, India has a great number of holidays and festivals. Most of them follow the Indian lunar calendar and therefore change from year to year according to the Gregorian calendar. Muslim holidays and festivals, which follow the Islamic calendar, are listed at the end of this section.

January

Republic Day Republic Day on 26 January celebrates the anniversary of India's establishment as a republic in 1950; there are activities in all the state capitals but most spectacularly in Delhi, where there is an enormously colourful military parade. As part of the Republic Day celebrations, three days later a *Beating of the Retreat* ceremony takes place outside Rashtrapati Bhavan, the residence of the Indian president, in Delhi.

Pongal This Tamil festival marks the end of the harvest season. It is observed on the first day of the Tamil month of Thai, which is in the middle of January. The festivities last four days and include such activities as the boiling-over of a pot of *pongal* (a mixture of rice, sugar, dhal and milk), symbolic of prosperity and abundance. On the third day, cattle are washed, decorated and even painted, and then fed the pongal. In Andhra Pradesh the festival is known as *Makar Sankranti*.

Vasant Panchami To celebrate this spring festival, held on the 5th day of Magha, it is traditional to dress in yellow. In some places, especially in West Bengal, Saraswati, the goddess of learning, is honoured. Books, musical instruments and other objects related to the arts and scholarship are placed in front of the goddess to receive her blessing.

February-March

Holi This is one of the most exuberant Hindu festivals, with people marking the end of winter by throwing coloured water and powder *(gulal)* at one another. In tourist places it might be seen as an opportunity to take liberties with foreigners; don't wear good clothes on this day, and be ready to duck. On the night before Holi, bonfires are built to symbolise the destruction of the evil demon Holika. It's mainly a northern festival; in the south, where there is no real winter to end, it is not widespread. In Maharashtra, this festival is known as Rangapanchami and is celebrated with dancing and singing.

Sivaratri This day of fasting is dedicated to Lord Siva, who danced the *tandava* on this day. Temple processions are followed by the chanting of mantras and anointing of lingams.

Indian Lunar Months & Their Gregorian Equivalents	
Chaitra	March-April
Vaishaka	April-May
Jyaistha	May-June
Asadha	June-July
Sravana	July-August
Bhadra	August-September
Asvina	September-October
Kartika	October-November
Aghan	November-December
Pausa	December-January
Magha	January-February
Phalguna	February-March

March-April

Mahavir Jayanti This Jain festival marks the birth of Mahavira, the founder of Jainism.

Ramanavami In temples all over India the birth of Rama is celebrated on this day. In the week leading up to Ramanavami, the *Ramayana* is widely read and performed.

Good Friday This Christian holiday is also celebrated in India.

Gangaur This Rajasthani festival honours Siva and Parvati. The Rajasthani women are at their most colourful, and can be seen dancing, praying and singing near any Siva idol.

May-June

Buddha Jayanti This 'triple blessed festival' celebrates Buddha's birth, enlightenment and attainment of nirvana. Processions of monks carrying sacred scriptures pass through the streets of Gangtok (Sikkim) and other towns, The festival falls on the full moon of the fourth lunar month (late May or early June).

June-July

Rath Yatra (Car Festival) Lord Jagannath's great temple chariot makes its stately journey from his temple in Puri, Orissa, during this festival. Similar but far more grandiose festivals take place in other locations, particularly in the Dravidian south. Lord Jagannath is one of Krishna's names, and the main procession in Puri celebrates Krishna's journey to Mathura to visit his aunt for a week! The images of his brother (Balarama) and sister (Subhadra) are also carried in the parade.

Teej Another Rajasthani festival, Teej celebrates the onset of the monsoon. Idols of the goddess Parvati are paraded through the streets, amid much singing and dancing.

July-August

Naag Panchami This festival is dedicated to Ananta, the serpent upon whose coils Vishnu rested between universes. Offerings are made to snake images, and snake charmers do a roaring trade. Snakes are supposed to have power over the monsoon rainfall and keep evil from homes.

Raksha Bandhan (Narial Purnima) On the full-moon day of the Hindu month of Sravana, girls fix amulets known as *rakhis* to their brothers' wrists to protect them in the coming year. The brothers reciprocate with gifts. Some people also worship the Vedic sea-god deity Varuna on this day.

August

Independence Day This holiday on 15 August celebrates the anniversary of India's independence from the UK in 1947. The prime minister delivers an address from the ramparts of Delhi's Red Fort.

Drukpa Teshi This festival celebrates the first teaching given by the Buddha. It is held on the fourth day of the sixth month.

August-September

Janmashtami The anniversary of Krishna's birth is celebrated with happy abandon in tune with Krishna's own mischievous moods. Although it is a national holiday, Agra, Bombay and Mathura (his birthplace) are the main centres of celebration. Devotees fast all day until midnight.

Ganesh Chaturthi This festival, held on the fourth day of the Hindu month Bhadra, is dedicated to Ganesh. It is widely celebrated all over India, but with particular enthusiasm in Maharashtra. In every village, shrines are erected and a clay Ganesh idol is installed. Firecrackers explode at all hours, and each family buys a clay idol of Ganesh. On the day of the festival the idol is brought into the house, where it is kept and worshipped for a specified period before being ceremoniously immersed in a river, tank or the sea. As Ganesh is the god of wisdom and prosperity, Ganesh Chaturthi is considered to be the most auspicious day of the year. It is considered unlucky to look at the moon on this day.

Shravan Purnima After a day-long fast, high-caste Hindus replace the sacred thread which they always wear looped over their left shoulder.

September-October

Dussehra This is the most popular of all the Indian festivals and takes place over 10 days, beginning on the first day of the Hindu month of Asvina. It celebrates Durga's victory over the buffalo-headed demon Mahishasura. In many places it culminates with the burning of huge images of the demon king Ravana and his accomplices, symbolic of the triumph of good over evil. In Delhi it is known as Ram Lila (Life story of Rama), with fireworks and re-enactments of the *Ramayana*, while in Mysore and Ahmedabad there are great processions. In West Bengal the festival is known as Durga Puja and in Gujarat it's Navratri (Festival of Nine Nights). In Kullu, in the north, the festival takes place a little later than elsewhere.

Gandhi Jayanti This is a solemn celebration of Gandhi's birthday on 2 October with prayer meetings at the Raj Ghat in Delhi where he was cremated.

October-November

Diwali (or *Deepavali*) This is the happiest festival of the Hindu calendar, celebrated on the 15th day of Kartika. At night, countless oil lamps are lit to show Rama the way home from his period of exile. Today, the festival is also dedicated to Lakshmi (particularly in Bombay) and to Kali in Calcutta. In all, the festival lasts five days. On the first day, houses are thoroughly cleaned and doorsteps are decorated with intricate *rangolis* (chalk designs). Day two is dedicated to Krishna's victory over Narakasura, a legendary tyrant. In the south on this day, a pre-dawn oil bath is followed by the donning of new clothes. Day three is spent in worshipping Lakshmi, the goddess of fortune. Traditionally, this is the beginning of the new financial year for companies. Day four commemorates the visit of the friendly demon Bali whom Vishnu put in his place. On the fifth day men visit their sisters to have a tika put on their forehead.

Diwali has also become the Festival of Sweets. Giving sweets has become as much a part of the tradition as the lighting of oil lamps and firecrackers. Diwali is also celebrated by the Jains as their New Year's Day.

Govardhana Puja This is a Hindu festival dedicated to that holiest of animals, the cow.

November-December

Nanak Jayanti On this day, the birthday of Guru Nanak, the founder of the Sikh religion, is celebrated.

Christmas Day This is also a holiday in India.

Muslim Holidays

The dates of the Muslim festivals are not fixed, as they fall about 11 days earlier each year.

Id-ul-Fitr This festival celebrates the end of Ramadan, the Muslim month of fasting. Falls on about 29 January 1998 and 18 January 1999.

Id-ul-Zuhara This festival commemorates Abraham's attempt to sacrifice his son. Falls on 30 March 1998 and 20 March 1999.

Muharram This 10 day festival commemorates the martyrdom of Mohammed's grandson, Imam Hussain. Falls on 29 April 1998 and 18 April 1999.

Milad-un-Nabi This festival celebrates the birth of Mohammed. Falls on 7 July 1998 and 27 June 1999.

ACTIVITIES
Camel Safaris

It seems just about everyone in Rajasthan is offering camel safaris these days. An old favourite is in the environs of Jaisalmer, in western Rajasthan, where it's possible to take a safari lasting from one day up to a week or more. There are other operators in Pushkar, Shekhawati and Bikaner. See the Rajasthan chapter for more details.

Cycling & Motorcycling

There are few organised tours but it's not difficult or expensive to organise things for yourself. See the Bicycle and Motorcycle sections in the Getting Around chapter.

Diving

There are dive schools in Goa, the Lakshadweep Islands and the Andaman Islands. The dive school in South Andaman is a recommended place to do the internationally recognised PADI Open Water Diver Certificate course – see that chapter.

Horse Riding & Polo

Horses are available in many of the tourist areas, the hill stations and Himalaya regions in particular. There are a few specialist operators in Rajasthan who offer horse safaris. See that chapter for more details.

Kayaking & River Rafting

The Mountaineering Institute & Allied Sports in Manali can arrange two week kayaking trips on the Beas River in October and November for US$140. See under Manali in the Himachal Pradesh chapter for details.

River rafting expeditions are possible on the Beas River in Himachal Pradesh, on the Ganges and its tributaries in Uttarakhand (northern Uttar Pradesh), on the Indus and Zanskar rivers in Ladakh and Zanskar, and on the Teesta River in the West Bengal hills. Travel agencies in Gangtok (Sikkim) can also organise trips on the Teesta. See the relevant chapters for details.

Mountaineering

Mountaineering expeditions interested in climbing peaks over 6000m need to obtain clearance from the Indian Mountaineering Foundation (IMF; ☎ (011) 671211; fax 688 3412), Benito Juarez Rd, Anand Niketan, New Delhi, 110021.

For information on mountaineering expeditions to less lofty heights in Uttar Pradesh, contact the Trekking & Mountaineering Division (☎ (01364) 32648), Garhwal Mandal Vikas Nigam (GMVN), Laksmanjhula Rd, Muni-ki-Reti, Rishikesh. Trekking and mountaineering equipment can be hired here.

Skiing

India's premier ski resort is at Auli, near Josimath in northern Uttar Pradesh. UP Tourism offers very competitive ski packages, which include ski hire, tows, lessons and accommodation. The ski season at Auli extends from the beginning of January to the end of March. See the Uttar Pradesh chapter for details.

There are also less developed resorts in Himachal Pradesh, at Solang Nullah, north of Manali, and near Shimla, at Kufri and Narkanda.

Trekking

With some of the highest mountains in the world, it's hardly surprising that India has some spectacular trekking regions, although the trekking industry is not as developed as it is in Nepal. The main areas are Ladakh, Himachal Pradesh, northern Uttar Pradesh, the Darjeeling area (West Bengal) and Sikkim. See those chapters and Lonely Planet's *Trekking in the Indian Himalaya* for more details.

Wildlife Safaris

Elephant-back safaris are available at the larger wildlife sanctuaries and are highly recommended. They are usually very good value and the best way to get close to other animals.

Adventure Tour Operators

Local tour operators are listed under town headings. The following trek and tour outfits are all based in Delhi:

Amber Tours Pty Ltd
Flat 2, Dwarka Sadan, C-42 Connaught Place (☎ (011) 331 2773; fax 331 2984). It offers yoga and mystic tours, river rafting, trekking, fishing for the mahseer, and private jet or helicopter flights over the Himalaya.

Himalayan River Runners
188-A Jor Bagh, (☎ (011) 615736). It offers a range of rafting expeditions in the western Himalaya.

Mercury Himalayan Explorations
Jeevan Tara Bldg, Parliament St (☎ (011) 312008). Mercury specialises in organised treks in the western Himalaya.

Shikhar Travels
209 Competent House, 14 Middle Circle, Connaught Circus (☎ (011) 331 2444; fax 332 3660). Shikhar specialises in trekking and mountaineering tours and can also organise mountaineering expeditions for beginners.

World Expeditions
Ground Floor, MG Bhawan-1, 7 Local Shopping Centre, Madangir (☎ (011) 698 3358; fax 698 3357). It has operated world-class Himalayan tours and treks since 1975.

COURSES

Language

The Landour Language School, near Mussoorie in northern Uttar Pradesh, offers three month beginners' courses in Hindi, as well as more advanced courses. At McLeod Ganj it's possible to learn Tibetan either at the Library of Tibetan Works & Archives or from private teachers. In Darjeeling, beginners' courses in Tibetan are available at the Manjushree Centre of Tibetan Culture. For all these courses, see the relevant chapters for details.

Philosophy & Religion

Courses in aspects of Tibetan Buddhism and culture are offered in McLeod Ganj, Darjeeling, Choglamsar (near Leh) and Leh. Indian Hinayana Buddhism can also be studied in McLeod Ganj and Gaya. See the relevant chapters for details of these courses.

Rishikesh is the place to head if you're interested in staying at an ashram and learning about aspects of Hindu philosophy, including yoga and meditation.

See the Gurus & Religion boxed section in the Facts about the Country chapter for more information.

VOLUNTARY WORK

Numerous charities and international aid agencies have branches in India and, although they're mostly staffed by locals, there are some opportunities for foreigners. Though it may be possible to find temporary volunteer work when you are in India, you'll probably be of more use to the charity concerned if you write in advance and, if they need you, stay for long enough to be of help. A week on a hospital ward may go a little way towards salving your own conscience, but you may actually do not much more than get in the way of the people who work there long-term.

Some areas of voluntary work seem to be more attractive to volunteers than others. One traveller commented that there was no difficulty getting foreign volunteers to help with the babies in the orphanage where he was working but few came forward to work with the severely mentally handicapped adults.

Overseas Aid Agencies

For information on specific charities in India, contact the main branches in your own country. For long-term posts, the following organisations may be able to help or offer advice and further contacts:

Australian Volunteers Abroad: Overseas Service Bureau Programme
    PO Box 350, Fitzroy Vic 3065, Australia
    (☎ (03) 9279 1788; fax (03) 9416 1619)
Co-ordinating Committee for International Voluntary Service
    c/o UNESCO, 1 rue Miollis, F-75015 Paris, France (☎ (01) 45 68 27 31)
Council of International Programs (CIP)
    1101 Wilson Blvd Ste 1708, Arlington VA 22209, USA (☎ (703) 527 1160)
International Voluntary Service (IVS)
    St John's Church Centre, Edinburgh EH2 4BJ, UK (☎ (0131) 226 6722)
Peace Corps of the USA
    1990 K St NW, Washington DC 20526, USA (☎ (202) 606 3970; fax 606 3110)
Voluntary Service Overseas (VSO)
    317 Putney Bridge Rd, London SW15 2PN, UK (☎ (0181) 780 2266; fax 780 1326)

Aid Programmes in India

Following are some of the programmes operating in India which may have opportunities for volunteers:

Himachal Pradesh Long-term visitors at McLeod Ganj are always welcome to teach English to newly arrived Tibetan refugees. Check at the Library of Tibetan Works & Archives in Gangchen Kyishong, near McLeod Ganj.

Ladakh The Mahabodhi International Meditation Centre (PO Box 22, Leh, Ladakh, 194 101 Jammu & Kashmir state, India), which operates a residential school for poor children, requires volunteers to assist with teaching and secretarial work. Contact the centre at the above address, or through their head office at 14 Kalidas Rd, Gandhinagar, Bangalore, 560 009 (☎ (0812) 260684; fax 260292).

If you have a particular interest in Ladakh and have some educational or agricultural experience, there are two organisations in Leh which may be able to use your experience and enthusiasm: the Ladakh Ecological Development Group (LEDeG), Leh, Ladakh, 194101 (☎ (01982) 3746; fax 2484); and the Student's Educational & Cultural Movement of Ladakh (SECMOL), PO Box 4, Leh, Ladakh, 194101 (☎ 3676).

Rajasthan SOS Worldwide runs over 30 programmes across India. The society looks after orphaned, destitute and abandoned children, who are cared for by unmarried women, abandoned wives and widows. In Jaipur, SOS has a fine garden-surrounded property, and cares for over 144 children and young adults. Volunteers are welcome at the centre, to teach English, help the children with their homework and simply to join in their games. For more information contact SOS Children's Village, Opposite Pital Factory, Jhotwara Rd, Jaipur, 302016 (☎ (0141) 322393; fax 318140).

The Urmul Trust provides primary health care and education to the people of the remote villages in Rajasthan; raises awareness among the women of the desert of their rights and privileges in society; and promotes the handicrafts of rural artisans with profits going directly to artisans. There is volunteer work available in social welfare, teaching English, health care, and other projects. Even if you don't have skills in these areas, Urmul may have positions in implementation and overseeing of projects. Contact the secretary at the Urmul Trust (☎ (0151) 523093), inside Urmul Dairy, Ganganagar Rd, Bikaner (adjacent to the bus terminal).

Les Amis du Shekhawati (70 rue Bonaparte, 75006 Paris) is one of a number of charities whose aim is to safeguard and preserve India's crumbling architectural heritage – in this case the havelis and paintings of the Shekhawati region in Rajasthan. Ramesh Jangid is the president of the association. He welcomes volunteers keen to preserve the paintings of Shekhawati and can be contacted at the Ramesh Jangid Tourist Pension (☎ (01594) 22129), Nawalgarh.

Jaisalmer in Jeopardy is a UK charity which operates several architectural restoration programmes in this desert city. Jaislamer is suffering from the combined pressures of population growth and tourism; the primitive infrastructure cannot withstand these pressures. For more information contact Sue Carpenter, 20E Redcliffe Gardens, London SW10 9EX (☎ & fax (0171) 460 8592).

West Bengal Mother Teresa's Missionaries of Charity headquarters, the 'Mother House', is at 54A Lower Circular Rd in Calcutta. For information about volunteering, contact the London branch: International Committee of Co-Workers, Missionaries of Charity, 41 Villiers Rd, Southall, Middlesex, UK (☎ (0181) 574 1892).

In Darjeeling, the Nepali Girls' Social Service Centre may be able to offer voluntary work on an informal basis to travellers interested in teaching English, art or musical instruments. Also in Darjeeling, people interested in teaching English to Tibetan refugees should contact the Tibetan Refugee Self-Help Centre.

ACCOMMODATION

India has a very wide range of accommodation possibilities apart from straightforward hotels.

Youth Hostels

Indian youth hostels (HI – Hostelling International) are generally very cheap and sometimes in excellent condition with superb facilities. They are, however, often some distance from the town centres. You are not usually required to be a YHA (HI) member (as in other countries) to use the hostels, although your YHA/HI card will generally get you a lower rate. The charge is typically Rs 15 for members, Rs 30 for nonmembers. Nor do the usual rules about arrival and departure times, lights-out or not using the hostel during the day apply.

There are also some state government youth hostels in main cities but they tend to be very badly run.

Government Accommodation

Back in the days of the British Raj, a whole string of government-run accommodation units were set up with labels like Rest Houses, Dak Bungalows, Circuit Houses, PWD (Public Works Department) Bungalows, Forest Rest Houses and so on. Today most of these are reserved for government officials, although in some places they may still be available for tourists, if there is room. In an approximate pecking order the Dak Bungalows are the most basic; they often have no electricity and only essential equipment in out-of-the-way places. Rest Houses are next

up and at the top of the tree comes the Circuit Houses, which are strictly for travelling VIPs.

Tourist Bungalows

Usually run by the state government, tourist bungalows often serve as replacements for the older government-run accommodation units. Tourist bungalows are generally excellent value, although they vary enormously in facilities and level of service offered.

They often have dorm beds as well as rooms – typical prices are around Rs 40 for a dorm bed, and Rs 120 to Rs 350 for a double room. The rooms have a fan, two beds and bathroom; air-con rooms are often also available at around Rs 500. Generally there's a restaurant or 'dining hall' and often a bar. The local branch of the state government tourist office is often at the tourist bungalow.

Almost every state has some towns where the tourist bungalow is definitely the best place to stay. Their biggest drawback is that, in common with state-run companies virtually anywhere, the staff may be less than 100% motivated – in some cases they are downright lazy and rude – and maintenance is not what it might be.

In tourist bungalows, as in many other government-run institutions in India, such as the railways, you will find a curiously Indian institution: the 'complaints book'. In this you can write your complaints and periodically someone higher up the chain of command comes along, reads the terrible tales and the tourist bungalow manager gets his knuckles rapped. In disputes or other arguments, calling for the complaints book is the angry customer's best weapon; it's the one thing which minions seem to be genuinely afraid of. In many places the complaints book can provide interesting and amusing reading.

Railway Retiring Rooms

These are just like regular hotels or dormitories except they are at the railway stations. To stay here you are generally supposed to have a railway ticket or Indrail Pass. The rooms are, of course, extremely convenient if you have an early train departure, although they can be noisy if it is a busy station. They are often very cheap and in some places they are also excellent value. Some stations have retiring rooms of definite Raj pretensions, with huge rooms and enough furniture to do up a flat or apartment back home. They are usually excellent value, if a little institutional in feel, and are let on a 24 hour basis. The main problem is getting a bed, as they are very popular and often full.

Railway Waiting Rooms

For emergency accommodation when all else fails or when you just need a few hours rest before your train departs at 2 am, waiting rooms are a free place to rest your weary head. The trick is to rest it in the (usually empty) 1st class waiting room and not the crowded 2nd class one. Officially you need a 1st class ticket to be allowed to use the 1st class room and its superior facilities. In practice, luck, a 2nd class Indrail Pass or simply your foreign appearance may work. In some places your ticket will be checked.

Cheap Hotels

There are cheap hotels all over India, ranging from filthy, uninhabitable dives (but with prices at rock bottom) up to quite reasonable places in both standards and prices. Ceiling fans, mosquito nets on the beds, private toilets and bathrooms are all possibilities, even in rooms which cost Rs 120 or less per night for a double.

Throughout India hotels are defined as 'western' or 'Indian'. The differentiation is basically meaningless, although expensive hotels are always western, cheap ones Indian. 'Indian' hotels will be more simply and economically furnished but the acid test is the toilet. 'Western' hotels have a sit-up-style toilet; 'Indian' ones usually (but not always) have the traditional Asian squat style. You can find modern, well-equipped, clean places with Indian toilets and dirty, dismal dumps with western toilets. Some places even have the weird hybrid toilet, which is basically a western toilet with footpads on the edge of the bowl!

Although prices are generally quoted in this book for singles and doubles, most hotels will put an extra bed in a room to make a triple for about an extra 25%. In some smaller hotels it's often possible to bargain a little if you really want to. On the other hand these places will often put their prices up if there's a shortage of accommodation.

Many hotels, and not only the cheap ones, operate on a 24 hour system. This can be convenient if you check in at 8 pm, as it gives you until 8 pm the following day to check out. Conversely, if you arrive at 8 am one day it can be a nuisance to have to be on the streets again by 8 am the next day. There are, however, considerable regional variations. Some hotels maintain a noon checkout; hill stations often operate on a 9 am (or even 7 am!) checkout. Make sure you know the checkout time at your hotel. Some hotels will offer a half-day rate if you want to stay a few extra hours.

Expensive Hotels

You won't find 'international standard' hotels throughout India. The big, air-con, swimming-pool places are generally confined to the major tourist centres and the large cities. There are a number of big hotel chains in India. The Taj Group has some of India's flashiest hotels, including the luxurious Taj Mahal Intercontinental in Mumbai, the romantic Rambagh Palace in Jaipur and the Lake Palace in Udaipur. Other interesting hotels are the Taj Coromandel in Chennai, the Fort Aguada Beach Resort in Goa and the Malabar Hotel in Kochi (Cochin). The Oberoi chain is as well known outside India as within. Clarks is a small chain with popular hotels in Varanasi and Agra, among other places. Other hotel chains include Welcomgroup (affiliated with Sheraton), Ritz, Casino, and the Air India-associated Centaur hotels.

In addition, there is the government-operated ITDC group which usually append the name 'Ashok' to their hotels. There's an Ashok hotel in virtually every town in India, so that test isn't foolproof, but the ITDC places include a number of smaller (but higher-standard) units in places like Sanchi or Konark where accommodation possibilities are limited. The ITDC has been under attack in India for some time about its overall inefficient operation, financial losses and poor standards in its hotels. Privatisation was mooted at one stage as a way of raising capital and improving service, but this is still yet to happen and standards remain unchanged.

Most expensive hotels operate on a noon checkout basis.

You may be able to negotiate a discount on air-con rooms in December and January since air-con often isn't necessary then.

Home Stays
Staying with an Indian family can be a real education. It's a change from dealing strictly with tourist-oriented people, and the differences and curiosities of everyday Indian life can be very interesting.

Home-stay accommodation is organised on an official basis in Rajasthan. The cost is anything from Rs 150 upwards, depending on the level of facilities offered. The tourist offices in the main cities of Rajasthan (including Jaipur, Jodhpur and Bikaner) have comprehensive lists of the families offering this service. It's known as the Paying Guest Scheme and is administered by the Rajasthan Tourism Development Corporation. In Chennai and Mumbai it is known as Paying Guest Accommodation.

Other Possibilities
There are YMCAs and YWCAs in many of the big cities – some of these are modern, well equipped and cost about the same as a mid-range hotel (but are still good value). There are also a few Salvation Army Hostels – in particular in Mumbai, Calcutta and Chennai. There are a few camping places around India, but travellers with their own vehicles can almost always find hotels with gardens where they can park and camp.

Free accommodation is available at some Sikh gurdwaras (temples) where there is a tradition of hospitality to visitors. It can be interesting to try one, but please don't abuse this hospitality and spoil it for other travellers.

At many pilgrimage sites there are dharamsalas and choultries, places which offer accommodation to pilgrims, and travellers are often welcome to use these. This particularly applies at isolated sites such as Ranakhpur in Rajasthan. The drawback here (especially with Jain choultries) is that no leather articles are allowed inside.

Taxes & Service Charges
Most state governments impose a variety of taxes on hotel accommodation (and restaurants). At most rock-bottom hotels you won't have to pay any taxes. Once you get into the top end of budget places, and certainly for mid-range accommodation, you will have to pay something. As a general rule, you can assume that room rates over about Rs 250 will attract a 10% (sometimes just 5%) tax. Most mid-range and all luxury hotels attract a 10% to 15% loading.

Another common tax, which is additional to the above, is a service charge which is pegged at 10%. In some hotels, this is only levied on food, room service and use of telephones, not on the accommodation costs. At others, it's levied on the total bill. If you're trying to keep costs down, don't sign up meals or room service to your room bill and keep telephone use to a minimum if you know that a service charge is levied on the total bill.

Rates quoted in this book are the basic rate only unless otherwise indicated. Taxes and service charges are extra.

Seasonal Variations
In popular tourist places (hill stations, beaches and the Delhi-Agra-Rajasthan triangle), hoteliers crank up their prices in the high season by a factor of two to three times the low-season price.

The definition of the high and low seasons obviously varies depending on location. For the beaches and the Delhi-Agra-Rajasthan triangle it's basically a month before and two months after Christmas. In the hill stations and Kashmir, it's usually April to July when the lowlands are unbearably hot. In some locations and at some hotels, there are even higher rates for the brief Christmas/New Year period, or during major festivals such as Diwali and Dussehra.

Conversely, in the low season(s), prices at even normally expensive hotels can be surprisingly reasonable.

Touts

Hordes of accommodation touts operate in many towns in India – Agra, Jaipur and Varanasi in particular – and at any international airport terminal. Very often they are the *rickshaw-wallahs* who meet you at the bus or railway station. The technique is simple – they take you to hotel A and rake off a commission for taking you there rather than to hotel B. The problem with this procedure is that you may well end up not at the place you want to go to but at the place that pays the best commission. Some very good cheap hotels simply refuse to pay the touts and you'll then hear lots of stories about the hotel you want being 'full', 'closed for repairs', 'no good any more' or even 'flooded'. Nine chances out of 10 they will be just that – stories.

Touts do have a use though – if you arrive in a town when some big festival is on, or during peak season, finding a place to stay can be very difficult. Hop in a rickshaw, tell the driver in what price range you want a hotel, and off you go. The driver will know which places have rooms available and unless the search is a long one you shouldn't have to pay the driver too much. Remember that he will be getting a commission from the hotel too.

FOOD

Despite the very fine meals that can be prepared in India, you'll often find food a great disappointment. In many smaller centres there is not a wide choice and you'll get bored with rice, mushy vegetables and dhal. When you're in larger cities where the food can be excellent, take advantage of it.

Contrary to popular belief, not all Hindus are officially vegetarians. Strict vegetarianism is confined more to the south, which has

not had the meat-eating influence of the Aryan and later Muslim invasions, and also to the Gujarati community. For those who do eat meat, it is not always a pleasure to do so in India – the quality tends to be low (most chickens give the impression that they died from starvation) and the hygiene is not all that it might be. Beef, from the holy cow, is strictly taboo of course – and leads to interesting Indian dishes like the mutton-burger. Where steak is available, it's usually buffalo and found only in Muslim restaurants. Pork is equally taboo to the Muslims and is generally only available in areas where there are significant Christian communities (such as Goa), or among the Tibetans in Himachal Pradesh and Sikkim. If you're a non-vegetarian you will end up eating a lot more vegetarian food in India.

Although you could travel throughout India and not eat a single curry, Indian interpretations of western cuisine can be pretty horrific; in smaller places it's usually best to stick to Indian food.

Meals served on trains are usually palatable and reasonably cheap. At most stops you will be besieged by food and drink sellers. Even in the middle of the night that raucous cry of 'Chai! Chai!' or 'Ah, coffee coffee coffee!' will inevitably break into your sleep. The sheer bedlam of an Indian station when a train is in is a part of India you never forget.

If, after some time in India, you do find the food is getting you down physically or psychologically, there are a couple of escapes. It is very easy for budget travellers to lose weight in India and feel lethargic and drained of energy. The answer is to increase your protein intake – eat more eggs, which are readily available. It also helps to eat more fruit and nuts, so buy bananas, mandarin oranges or peanuts, all easily found at stations or in the markets. Many travellers carry multi-vitamins with them. Another answer, if you're travelling on a budget, is to occasionally splash out on a meal in a fancy hotel or restaurant – compared to what you have been paying it may seem amazingly expensive, but try translating the price into what it would cost at home.

There are considerable regional variations from north to south, partly because of climatic conditions and partly because of historical influences. In the north, as already mentioned, much more meat is eaten and the cooking is often 'Mughal style' (often spelt 'Mughlai') which bears a closer relationship to food of the Middle East and Central Asia. The emphasis is more on spices and less on chilli. In the north, grains and breads are eaten far more than rice.

In the south more rice is eaten, there is more vegetarian food, and the curries tend to be hotter – sometimes very hot. Another feature of southern vegetarian food is that you do not use eating utensils; food is always eaten with fingers (of the right hand only). Scooping up food that way takes a little practice but you soon become quite adept at it. It is said that eating this way allows you to get the 'feel' of the food, as important to south Indian cuisine as the aroma or arrangement are to other cooking styles. It also offers the added protection that you never need worry if the eating utensils have been properly washed.

In the most basic Indian restaurants and eating places, known as *dhabas* or *bhojanalyas*, the cooking is usually done right out the front so you can see exactly what is going on and how it is done. Vegetables will be on the simmer all day and tend to be overcooked and mushy to western tastes. In these basic places *dhal* (curried lentil gravy) is usually free but you pay for *chapatis, parathas, puris* or rice. Vegetable preparations, dhal and a few chapatis make a passable meal for around Rs 15. If you order half-plates of the various dishes brewing out the front you get half the quantity at half the price and get a little more variety. With chutneys and a small plate of onions, which come free, you can put together a reasonable vegetarian meal for Rs 30, or non-vegetarian for Rs 45. In railway station restaurants and other cheaper restaurants always check the prices and add up your bill. If it's incorrect, query it.

At the other end of the price scale, there are many restaurants in India's five star hotels that border on the luxurious and by western standards are absurdly cheap. Paying US$15 for a meal in India seems exorbitant after you've been there for a while, but check what a meal in your friendly local Hilton would cost you. Many of the international-standard hotels offer all-you-can-eat buffet deals. One place to which *every* traveller goes for a splurge is the Lake Palace in Udaipur where, for around US$13, you can treat yourself to a range of dishes in one of India's most luxurious settings – including a dance show and the boat fare. For budget travellers it makes a very pleasant change from dhal and rice.

Finally, a couple of hints on how to cope with curry. After a while in India you'll get used to even the fiercest curries and will find western food surprisingly bland. If, however, you do find your mouth is on fire, don't reach for water; in emergencies that hardly helps at all. Curd (*dahin*, yoghurt) or fruit do the job much more efficiently.

Curry & Spice

Believe it or not, there is no such thing as 'curry' in India. It's an English invention, an all-purpose term to cover the whole range of Indian food spicing. *Carhi*, incidentally, is a Gujarati dish, but never ask for it in Kumaon where it's a very rude word!

Although all Indian food is certainly not curry, this is the basis of Indian cuisine. Curry doesn't have to be hot enough to blow your head off, although it can if it's made that way. Curry most definitely is not something found in a packet of curry powder. Indian cooks have about 25 spices on their regular list and it is from these that they produce the curry flavour. Normally the spices are freshly ground in a mortar and pestle known as a *sil-vatta*. Spices are usually blended in certain combinations to produce *masalas* (mixes). *Garam masala* ('hot mix'), for example, is a combination of cloves, cinnamon, cardamom, coriander, cumin and peppercorns.

Popular spices include saffron, an expensive flavouring produced from the stamens of certain crocus flowers. This is used to give rice that yellow colouring and delicate fragrance. (It's an excellent buy in India, where a one gram packet costs around Rs 35 – you'll pay about 10 times more at home.) Turmeric also has a colouring property, acts as a preservative and has a distinctive smell and taste. Chillies are ground, dried or added whole to supply the heat. They come in red and green varieties but the green ones are the hottest. Ginger is supposed to be good for the digestion, while many masalas contain coriander because it is said to cool the body. Strongly aromatic cardamom is used in many desserts and in rich meat dishes. Other popular spices and flavourings include nutmeg, poppy seeds, caraway seeds, fenugreek, mace, garlic, cloves, bay leaves and curry leaves.

Breads & Grains

Rice is, of course, the basic Indian staple, but although it is eaten throughout the country, it's all-important only in the south. The best Indian rice, it is generally agreed, is found in the north where Basmati rice grows in the Dehra Dun Valley. It has long grains, is yellowish and has a slightly sweetish or *'bas'* smell. In the north (where wheat is the staple) rice is supplemented by a whole range of breads known as *rotis* or *chapatis*. In the Punjab a roti is called *phulka*. Western-style white sliced bread is widely available, and it's generally pretty good.

Indian breads are varied but always delicious. Simplest is the chapati/roti, which is simply a mixture of flour and water cooked on a hotplate known as a *tawa*. Direct heat blows them up but how well that works depends on the gluten content of the wheat. Note that Hindus use their tawa concavely, Muslims convexly! A *paratha* is also cooked on the hotplate but ghee is used and the bread is rolled in a different way. There are also parathas that have been stuffed with peas or potato. Deep-fried bread which puffs up is known as a *puri* in the north and a *luchi* in the east. Bake the bread in a clay (tandoori) oven and you have *naan*. However you make them, Indian breads taste great. Use your chapati or paratha to mop or scoop up your curry.

Found all over India, but originating from the south, are *dosas*. These are basically paper-thin pancakes made from lentil and rice flour. Curried vegetables wrapped inside a dosa makes it a *masala dosa* – a terrific snack meal. An *idli* is a kind of south Indian rice dumpling, often served with a spicy curd sauce *(dahin idli)* or with spiced lentils and chutney; it is a popular breakfast dish in the south. *Papadams* are crispy deep-fried lentil-flour wafers often served with *thalis* or other meals. An *uttapam* is like a dosa.

Outside the Delhi Jama Masjid, you may see 'big' chapatis known as *rumali roti* (handkerchief bread).

Basic Dishes

Curries can be vegetable, meat (usually chicken or lamb) or fish, and the all-important spices will be fried in ghee (clarified butter) or vegetable oil to release their flavours and aromas. North or south, curries will be accompanied by rice, but in the north you can also choose from the range of breads.

There are a number of dishes which aren't really curries but are close enough to them for western tastes. *Vindaloos* have a vinegar marinade and tend to be hotter than most curries. Pork vindaloo is a favourite dish in Goa. *Kormas*, on the other hand, are rich, substantial dishes prepared by braising. There are both meat and vegetable kormas. *Navratan korma* is a very tasty vegetable dish using nuts, while a *malai kofta* consists of cheese-and-vegetable balls in a rich, cream-based sauce. *Dopiaza* literally means 'two onions' and is a type of korma which uses onions at two stages in its preparation.

Probably the most basic of Indian dishes is dhal. Dhal is almost always there, whether as an accompaniment to a curry or as a very basic meal in itself with chapatis or rice. In the very small rural towns dhal and rice is just about all there is on the menu. The favourite dhal of Bengal and Gujarat is yellow *arhar*, whereas in Punjab it is *black urad*. The common green lentils are called *moong*; *rajmaa* (kidney beans) is the Heinz 57 varieties of dhal!

Other basic dishes include *mattar paneer* – peas and cheese in gravy; *saag gosht* – spinach and meat; *aalu dum* – potato curry; *palak paneer* – spinach and cheese; and *aalu chhole* – diced potatoes and spicy-sour chickpeas. Some other vegetables include *paat gobi* (cabbage), *phuul gobi* (cauliflower), *baingan* (eggplant or brinjal) and *mattar* (peas).

Tandoori & Biryani

Tandoori food is a northern speciality and refers to the clay oven in which the food is cooked after first being marinated in a mixture of herbs and yoghurt. Tandoori chicken is a favourite. This food is not as hot as curry dishes and usually tastes terrific.

Biryani (again chicken is a popular biryani dish) is another northern Mughal dish. The meat is mixed with a deliciously flavoured, orange-coloured rice which is sometimes spiced with nuts or dried fruit. A Kashmiri biryani is basically fruit salad with rice.

A *pulao* is flavoured rice often with pulses and with or without meat. You will also find it in other Asian countries further west. Those who have the idea that Indian food is always curry and always fiery hot will be surprised by tandoori and biryani dishes.

Regional Specialities

Rogan josh is straightforward lamb curry, always popular in the north and in Kashmir where it originated. *Gushtaba*, pounded and spiced meatballs cooked in a yoghurt sauce, is another Kashmiri speciality. Still in the north, *chicken makhanwala* is a rich dish cooked in a butter sauce.

Many coastal areas have excellent seafood, including Mumbai where the *pomfret*, a flounder-like fish, is popular; so is Bombay duck, which is not a duck at all but another fish dish. *Dhansaak* is a Parsi speciality found in Mumbai – lamb or chicken cooked with curried lentils and steamed rice. Further south, Goa has excellent fish and prawns; in Kerala, Kochi (Cochin) is famous for its prawns.

Another indication of the influence of Central Asian cooking styles on north Indian food is the popularity of kababs. You'll find them all across north India with a number of local variations and specialities. The two basic forms are *seekh* (skewered) or *shami* (wrapped). In Calcutta *kati kababs* are a local favourite. Another Bengali dish is *dahin maach* – curried fish in yoghurt sauce, flavoured with ginger and turmeric. Further south in Hyderabad you could try *haleen*, pounded wheat with a lightly spiced mutton gravy.

Lucknow is famous for its wide range of kebabs and for *dum pukht* – the 'art' of steam pressure cooking, in which meat and vegetables are cooked in a sealed clay pot.

Side Dishes

Indian food generally has a number of side dishes to go with the main meal. Probably the most popular is *dahin* – curd or yoghurt. It has the useful ability of instantly cooling a fiery curry – either blend it into the curry or, if it's too late, you can administer it straight to your mouth. Curd is often used in the cooking or as a dessert and appears in the popular drink *lassi*. *Raita* is another popular side dish consisting of curd mixed with cooked or raw vegetables, particularly cucumber (similar to Greek *tzatziki)* or tomato.

Sabzi is curried vegetables, and *baingan bharta* is a puréed eggplant dish. *Mulligatawny* is a soup-like dish which is really just a milder, more liquid curry. It's a dish adopted into the English menu by the Raj. Chutney is pickled fruit or vegetables and is the standard relish for a curry.

Thalis

A *thali* is the all-purpose Indian dish. Although it is basically a product of south India, you will find restaurants serving thalis or 'plate meals' (veg or non-veg) all over India. Often the sign will simply announce 'Meals'. In addition, there are regional variations like the particularly sumptuous and sweet Gujarati thalis.

The name is taken from the 'thali' dish in which the meal is served. This consists of a metal plate with a number of small metal bowls known as *katoris* on it. Sometimes the small bowls will be replaced by simple indentations in the plate; in more basic places the 'plate' will be a big, fresh banana leaf. A thali consists of a variety of curry vegetable dishes, relishes, a couple of papadams, puris or chapatis and a mountain of rice. A fancy thali may have a *pataa*, a rolled leaf stuffed with fruit and nuts. There'll probably be a bowl of curd and possibly even a small dessert or paan.

Thalis are consistently tasty and good food value, but they have two other unbeatable plus points for the budget traveller – they're cheap and they're usually 100% filling. Thalis can be as little as Rs 10 and will rarely cost much more than Rs 30 at the very most, though Gujarati thalis are the exception and you'll consistently be paying Rs 40 to Rs 50 for these at reasonable restaurants. Most are 100% filling because they're normally 'all you can eat'. When your plate starts to look empty they come round, add another mountain of rice and refill the katoris. Thalis are eaten with fingers, although you may get a spoon for the curd or dhal. Always wash your hands before you eat one

– a sink or other place to wash your hands is provided in a thali restaurant.

Snacks

Chaat is the general term for snacks, while *namkin* is the name for the various spiced nibbles that are sold prepackaged – although one waiter I encountered referred to them as 'bitings'. *Channa* is spiced chickpeas *(gram)* served with small puris. *Sambhar* is a soup-like lentil and vegetable dish with a sour flavour. See the Fast Food colour section for a further description of Indian snacks.

Western Food

Sometimes Indian food simply becomes too much and you want to escape to something familiar and reassuring. The Indian-food blues are particularly prone to hit at breakfast time – somehow idlis never really feel like a breakfast. Fortunately that's the meal where

---

Fancy a vegetarian snake?

One of the delights of Indian menus is their amazing English. Start the morning, for example, with corn flaks, also useful for shooting down enemy aircraft. Or perhaps corn flex – Indian corn flakes are often so soggy they'll do just that.

Even before your corn-whatever you should have some tea, and what a variety of types of tea India can offer. You can try bed tea, milk tea, light tea, ready tea, mixed tea, tray tea, plain tea, half set tea and even (of course) full set tea. Eggs also offer unlimited possibilities: half-fried eggs, pouch eggs (or egg pooch), bolid eggs, scimbled eggs, skamal and egg tost, sliced omelettes, skerem boil eggs (interesting combination there), bread omelt, or simply aggs. Finally, you could finish off breakfast with that popular Scottish dish – pordge, or maybe porch with hunney.

Soup before a meal? – how about French onion soap, or that old favourite, crap soup? Or you could start your meal with Scotch brath, mughutoni, or perhaps a parn coactale. Follow that up with some dal fly. There are some amazing interpretations of western dishes, like the restaurant that not only had Napoleon spaghetti but also Stalin spaghetti! Fried fish with fresh feces might not taste too good; perhaps a seezling plator or vegetable augrotten sounds more like it? Or simply a light meal – well, why not have a sandwitch or a vegetable pup? Feeling strong – then try a carate salad, or a vegetable cutlass.

Chickens come in for some pretty amazing treatment, too, with chicken buls, bum chicken, chicken cripes, chicken manure, chicken merrylens and possibly the all-time classic: chicken katan blueinside chess – no, I don't have any idea what it is either!

If you want a drink how about orange squish or that popular Indian soft drink Thumps Up?

Chinese dishes offer a whole new range of possibilities, including mashrooms and bamboo sooghts, spring rolos, American chopsy, vege chapsey, Chinies snakes, vegetable chop off, vegetable nuddles, plane fried rice and park fried rice.

Finally for dessert you could try apple pai, apple filter, sweet pannking with hanni or banana panecake, or treat yourself to leeches & cream, or even semenolina pudding!

Travellers have sent in lots more menu suggestions since the first edition of this book, like tired fruit juice (tinned, you know), plane tost (the stuff they serve on Indian Airlines?), profit roles (at an expensive Delhi hotel), omlet & began, two eggs any shape, loose curds, curds bath, tomatoe stuff, scram bled eggs, chicken poodle soup, screambled eggs, banana frilters, pain-apple cream and chocolet padding. Or something even Colonel Sanders hasn't thought of yet – fried children and child juice. ∎

you'll find an approximation to the west most easily obtained. All those wonderful Indian varieties of eggs can be had – half-fried, omelettes, you name it.

Toast and jam can almost always be found, and very often you can get cornflakes and hot milk, although Indian cornflakes would definitely be rejects from Mr Kellogg's production line. The Scots must have visited India too, because porridge is often on the breakfast menu and is usually good.

That peculiar Raj-era term for a midmorning snack still lives – tiffin. Today tiffin means any sort of light meal or snack. One western dish which Indians seem to have come to terms with is chips (French fries). Unfortunately ordering chips is very much a hit and miss affair – sometimes they're excellent, and at other times truly dreadful. Some Indian cooks call potato chips 'Chinese potatoes', and 'finger chips' is also quite common.

Other Cuisines
Other Asian foods, apart from Indian, are often available. There's still a small Chinese population in India, particularly in Calcutta and Mumbai. You can find Chinese food in the larger cities, and Mumbai and Bangalore in particular have excellent Chinese food.

Elsewhere, Chinese food (or Indian interpretations of it) features on most menus in mid-range or better restaurants. The results are highly unpredictable, but the food is usually rather bland and stodgy.

In the north, where many Tibetans settled following the Chinese invasion of Tibet, you'll find Tibetan restaurants in places such as Darjeeling, Dharamsala, Gangtok, Kalimpong and Manali.

In the big gateway cities, and other large cities such as Bangalore, restaurants featuring cuisines, such as French, Thai, Japanese or Italian, are becoming more common. They are usually confined to the luxury hotels, and are therefore priced accordingly.

McDonald's, Kentucky Fried Chicken and Domino's Pizza have arrived although they currently have only a handful of branches. Indian quality control standards seem to be slowing their advance. Politics has played a part, too. In 1996 Delhi's Hindu fundamentalist-controlled municipal council managed to get the first KFC branch closed down for low cleanliness standards. On this basis all restaurants throughout the capital would have to be closed down!

Desserts & Sweets
Indians have quite a sweet tooth and an amazing selection of desserts and sweets to satisfy it. The desserts are rice or milk-based, and often consist of various nuts, or they may be pastries dripping in sweet syrup.

Kulfi is a delicious pistachio-flavoured sweet similar to ice cream and is widely available. You can, of course, also get western-style ice cream all over India. The major brands, such as Vadelal, Go Cool, Kwality (now in partnership with UK's Walls) and Havmor, are safe and very good. *Ras gullas* are another very popular Indian dessert; they're sweet little balls of cream cheese flavoured with rose water.

Gulaab jamuns are a typical example of small 'things' in syrup – they're fried and made from thickened boiled-down milk (known as *khoya*) and flavoured with cardamom and rose water. *Jalebis*, the orange-coloured squiggles with syrup inside, are made of flour coloured/flavoured with saffron. *Ladu* are yellow coloured balls made from chickpea flour.

Barfi is also made from khoya and is available in flavours like coconut, pistachio, chocolate or almond. *Sandesh* is another milk sweet; it's a particular favourite in Calcutta. *Payasam* is a sweet southern drink made from coconut milk, mango pulp, cashews and spices. *Gajar ka halwa* is a translucent, vividly coloured sweet made from carrot, sweet spices and milk.

Many Indian sweets are covered in a thin layer of silver, as are some of the desserts. It's just that: silver beaten paper-thin. Don't peel it off, it's quite edible. There are countless sweet shops with their goodies all lined up in glass showcases. Prices are around Rs 50 for a kg but you can order 50g or 100g at a time or simply ask for a couple of pieces.

FAST FOOD

No matter where you are in the world today, you won't find it hard to find a 'curry' – and given a handful of different spices and a lentil or two anyone can enjoy an authentic Indian meal without having to set foot on the subcontinent. But one kind of Indian food is impossible to copy at home, and that's precisely because it's a unique experience as well: street food. From the mouthwatering masala dosa made on the railway platform in Mysore, to the fiery little vegetable curry served with a few puris in its own 'takeaway' container of a banana leaf and some twigs, the range of delicious foods that are whipped up out in the open and meant for immediate comsumption is really amazing.

Vendors squat beside their *karais* (wok-like vessels) full of bubbling oil, or *tawas* (hotplates), while the crowds jostle around and shout out their orders for their *bhajas* (deep-fried crispy veg cakes), *beguni* (eggplant slices dipped in a *besan* (chickpea flour) batter and deep fried) or *aloo bonda* (round balls of spiced mashed potatoes covered in the same batter and deep fried). Lucknow loves its *aloo tikki* (flat potato cake with a lentil stuffing, served with a sweet & sour tamarind sauce and yoghurt), and some say *bhel puri* is Mumbai's favourite snack: look out for the colourful wagons on Chowpatty Beach and join the queues for this irresistible nibble made from crunchy dal and chickpeas, spices, chutney, potatoes, onions, mint, coriander, tomatoes and yoghurt.

The further north you go, the more you find streetside set-ups grilling lamb kebabs over hot coals, and serving them wrapped up with yoghurt in warm bread. The flavour of *pakoras* (battered and deep fried veg), *samosas* (pastry triangles stuffed with spiced veg or meat) and bhajas, fresh from the boiling ghee of a vendor's karai, is so far beyond even the best that you've tried in restaurants back home, that you might find yourself pining for these taste sensations long after you've forgotten exactly how astonishing the Taj looked in the early morning light.

GREG ELMS

MARGARET JUNG

Top: Fresh turmeric.

Left : Indian sweets aren't just delicious, they also come in gorgeous hand-made carry boxes.

Bottom: A street vendor cooks samosas in a karai.

BRYN THOMAS

GREG ELMS

GREG ELMS

Indians are renowned for their sweet teeth, and the range of sweets that you'll see on display in the streets is breathtaking. Fairyland silver and gold, rich yellow, deep brown and pale milky white confections are made from the simplest of ingredients (ghee, milk, sugar) but make the most unbelievably rich, sweet, decadent concoctions. You'll find them everywhere, usually sold by big fat men who obviously take an active role in quality control.

Top and centre: Thalis, or 'plate meals', are a delicious all-you-can-eat lunch found throughout south India.

Bottom: A fraction of the huge range of sweets sold in India.

GREG ELMS

Use your common sense when you're out in the open. Join the longest queue (you wouldn't dine in an empty restaurant; don't buy from a smelly, lonely stallholder) and do your own cursory health inspection: you can't with impunity walk into a restaurant's kitchen to suss out the freshness of the ingredients and the state of the chef's fingernails and hair, but on the street it's all there on display for you. Enjoy!

GREG ELMS

GREG ELMS

Top: Delicious street snacks eaten in the open are a highlight of Indian travel.

Bottom: Masala dosa epitomises Indian snacking: cheap, filling and absolutely delicious.

Food Markets

Some of the most colourful scenes you'll see in India are the food markets that you'll come across in every city and town. Many of these are weekly events, with people coming in from the surrounding districts to buy and sell produce. Others may be a collection of fruit and vegetable sellers who set up at a particular spot each day. The larger cities usually have purpose-built markets.

With vegetarianism being so widespread, most markets are devoted purely to fruit, vegetables, herbs and spices. Markets selling meat, poultry or fish are kept apart and are often found in the Muslim part of town.

GREG ELMS

Top: Roadside vendors, like this one in Cochin, sell everything from coconuts to conditioner.

Bottom: Selling betel leaves for paan in the Devaraja Market, Mysore.

GREG ELMS

These shops often sell curd, as well as sweet curd which makes a very pleasant dessert. Sweets include all sorts of unidentifiable goodies; try them and see.

Fruit

If your sweet tooth simply isn't sweet enough to cope with too many Indian desserts, you'll be able to fall back on India's wide variety of fruit. It varies all the way from tropical delights in the south to apples, apricots and other temperate-region fruits in the north. Some local specialities include cherries and strawberries in Kashmir, and apricots in Ladakh and Himachal Pradesh. Apples are found all over this north-western region but particularly in the Kullu Valley of Himachal Pradesh.

Melons are widespread in India, particularly watermelons, which are a fine thirst quencher when you're unsure about the water and fed up with soft drinks. Try to get the first slice before the flies discover it. Green coconuts are even better and there are coconut stalls on many city street corners, especially in the south. When you've drunk the milk the stall-holder will split the coconut open and cut you a slice from the outer shell with which to scoop the flesh out.

Mangoes are delicious and are widespread in summer. Bananas are also found virtually all over India, particularly in the south; pineapples are found in West Bengal and Kerala as well as elsewhere. You don't see oranges all over the place (lots in Kerala and throughout the Ganges plain though), but tangerines are widespread in central India, particularly during the hot season. You can go through an awful lot of them in a day.

Paan

An Indian meal should properly be finished with *paan* – the name given to the collection of spices and condiments chewed with betel nut. Found throughout eastern Asia, betel is a mildly intoxicating and addictive nut, but by itself it is quite inedible. After a meal you chew paan as a mild digestive.

Paan sellers have a whole collection of little trays, boxes and containers in which they mix either *saadha* 'plain' or *mithaa* 'sweet' paans. The ingredients may include, apart from the betel nut itself, lime paste (the ash not the fruit), the powder known as *catachu*, various spices and even a dash of opium in a pricey paan. The whole concoction is folded up in a piece of edible leaf which you pop in your mouth and chew. When finished you spit the leftovers out and add another red blotch to the pavement. Over a long period of time, indulgence in paan will turn your teeth red-black and even addict you to the betel nut. Trying one occasionally won't do you any harm.

DRINKS
Non-Alcoholic Drinks

Tea & Coffee Indians make some of the most hideously over-sweetened, murkily-milky excuses for tea that you'll ever see. Still, many travellers like it and it is cheap. At railway stations it is often served in small clay pots, which you then smash on the ground when empty.

Better tea can be obtained if you ask for 'tray tea', which gives you the tea, the milk and the sugar separately and allows you to combine them as you see fit. Unless you specify otherwise, tea is 'mixed tea' or 'milk tea', which means it has been made by putting cold water, milk, sugar and tea into one pot and bringing the whole concoction to the boil, then letting it stew for a long time. The result can be imagined.

Tea is more popular in the north, while in the south coffee, which is generally good, is the number one drink. It's almost impossible to get a decent cup of coffee in the north. Even in an expensive restaurant instant coffee is almost always used. The branches of the Indian Coffee House are one of the few places with decent coffee.

Water In the big cities, the water is chlorinated and safe to drink, although if you've just arrived in India, the change from what you are used to drinking is in itself enough to bring on a mild dose of the shits.

Outside the cities you're on your own. Some travellers drink the water everywhere

Paan-Wallahs

In India, as the red-stained walls and floors bear witness, the chewing of paan is something of a national obsession. Even the smallest village will have a paan-wallah, sitting cross-legged in front of a pile of paan leaves and tins of ingredients in a shop which is often not much more than a niche in a wall.

Although most paans cost around Rs 1 there are rumours of paan-wallahs who have become millionaires. In spite of reduced sales after the introduction of factory-prepared packets of paan masala, with low overheads and high turnover, the owners of some paan shops are undoubtedly very wealthy.

At Prince Pan Centre, in Daryaganj in Delhi, the city's rich will pay over Rs 100 for the best preparation.

Apart from the usual ingredients of lime, betel nut and catachu, every paan-wallah has his or her secret recipe which may include tobacco, flower essences or even silver and gold leaf. Among the numerous varieties of paan is one subtly named *palang tor* ('bed breaker') that is sometimes given to the groom on his wedding night. Thought to contain rhino-horn and other traditional aphrodisiacs, its ingredients are more usually cocaine or opium, resulting in a performance that is likely to be an illusion to the groom and a disappointment to the bride. ■

and never get sick, others are more careful and still get a bug. Basically, you should not drink the water in small towns unless you know it has been boiled, and definitely avoid the street vendors' carts everywhere. Even in the better class of hotel and restaurant, the water is usually only filtered and not boiled. The local water filters remove solids, but don't remove bacteria. Water is generally safer in the dry season than in the monsoon when it really can be dangerous.

Water-purifying tablets are available from pharmacies and camping shops in the west, but not in India. See the Health section for more information.

Mineral Water Most travellers to India these days avoid tap water altogether and stick to mineral water. It is available virtually everywhere, and comes in one litre plastic bottles. The price ranges from Rs 12 to Rs 20 in the shops, Rs 18 to Rs 70 in restaurants. Brand names include Bisleri, India King, Officer's Choice, Honeydew and Aqua Safe.

Virtually all the so-called mineral water available is actually treated tap water. A re-

cent reliable survey found that 65% of the available mineral waters were less than totally pure, and in some cases were worse than what comes out of the tap! Generally, though, if you stick to bottled water, any gut problems you might have will be from other sources – food, dirty utensils, dirty hands, etc (see under Basic Rules in the Health section earlier).

The best (real) mineral water is from Pondicherry, available in the south.

Soft Drinks Soft drinks are a safe substitute for water although they tend to have a high sugar content. Coca-Cola got the boot from India a number of years back for not co-operating with the government, but both they and Pepsi Cola are back with a vengeance. There are many indigenous brands with names like Campa Cola, Thums Up, Limca, Gold Spot or Double Seven. They are reasonably priced at around Rs 9 for a 250ml bottle (more in restaurants). They're also sickly sweet.

Juices & Other Drinks One very pleasant escape from the sickly sweet soft drinks is

Beer

India's climate being what it is, there are few travellers who don't relish a wee drop of the amber nectar at the end of a hot, dusty day or as an accompaniment to the setting sun at a beach cafe. There are a plethora of different brands, some of which are only brewed locally and others on a national basis.

In terms of taste, consistent quality, popularity and availability nationwide, the top five bottled beers would be Kingfisher, UB Export Lager, Kalyani Black Label, Black Knight and London Pilsner, which average around 5%. There are others which are usually only available locally but which are just as good such as Goa Pilsner Dry, Hamburg Pils, Khajuraho and Haywards. Draught beer (usually Kingfisher or London Pilsner) is also becoming more common in the big cities. Occasionally you'll come across obscure local brands, and these vary from quite OK to totally undrinkable – 'like the dregs after a party, minus the cigarette butts' was one assessment.

Beers which purport to be strong or even super strong (around 8% v/v) with dangerous names like Bullet, Hit and Knock Out are definitely in the 'hangovers installed and serviced' category and should be imbibed in moderation.

Since most beers are lagers, they should always be drunk as cold as possible. This is often not a fact appreciated by bar owners, so feel the bottle first before allowing the waiter to pop the top. Some beers, especially the stronger varieties, are totally unpalatable served in any way other than ice-cold.

Beer and other alcoholic drinks have always been regarded in India as luxury items and are frowned on by the Hindu and Muslim elites alike. As a result, they're heavily taxed by most state governments (except Pondicherry, Sikkim and Goa) making the price of a bottle of beer three to four times the price of a thali meal.

Despite this disparity, brewing is a growth industry and bars proliferate, except in Gujarat and Andhra Pradesh states where prohibition is in force. Prohibition was a common feature in many states during the 1960s and its legacy survives (especially in Tamil Nadu) in the form of 'permit rooms' which are so dark you can't even see the drink in front of you. The overall impression is that you ought not to be involved in such a nefarious activity as drinking beer. Other states have a much more enlightened attitude, so bars are well lit, there's contemporary music playing and they're often the centre of social activity. They do, however, maintain licenced hours – commonly 11 am to 3 pm and 5 to 11 pm unless you're also eating.

Neither Pondicherry, Sikkim nor Goa have ever suffered from the approbation of rabid prohibitionists and it's there you'll find not only the cheapest beers (as low as Rs 23) but there are also no licenced hours – only the barperson's willingness to stay awake.

The majority of non-vegetarian restaurants these days also serve alcoholic drinks but you will never find them in vegetarian restaurants – they remain the preserve of those who eschew such impurities. ■

apple juice, sold for Rs 5 per glass from the Himachal fruit stands found at many railway stations. Also good are the small cardboard boxes of various fruit juices, especially mango. For Rs 7 these are excellent, if a little sweet.

Coconut milk, straight from the young green coconut, is a popular drink, especially in the south. Another alternative to soft drinks is soda water – Bisleri, Spencer's and other brands are widely available. Not only does it come in a larger bottle, but it is also cheaper – generally around Rs 4. With soda water you can get excellent, and safe, lemon squash sodas.

Falooda is a popular drink made with milk, nuts, cream and vermicelli strands. Finally there's lassi, that oh so cool, refreshing and delicious iced curd (yoghurt) drink.

Alcoholic Drinks

Alcohol is relatively expensive – a bottle of Indian beer can cost anything from Rs 23 up to Rs 160 in a flash hotel; Rs 40 to Rs 70 is the usual price range. In some states (such as Goa, Sikkim and Pondicherry) it is very cheap, and in some very expensive. Indian beers have delightful names like Golden Eagle, Rosy Pelican, Cannon Extra Strong, Bullet, Black Label, Knock Out, Turbo, Kingfisher, Guru or Punjab. They're not too bad if you can find them cold, but most tend to be insipid. Avoid overindulgence or you'll wake up late in the morning feeling thoroughly disoriented with a thumping headache to boot. Preservatives (sulphur dioxide in the main) are lavishly used to combat the effects of climate on 'quality'.

Beer and other Indian interpretations of

western alcoholic drinks are known as IMFL − Indian Made Foreign Liquor. They include imitations of Scotch and brandy under a plethora of different brand names. The taste varies from hospital disinfectant to passable imitation Scotch. Always buy the best brand.

With the continuing freeing up of the economy, it is likely that in the near future well-known foreign brands of beer and spirits will be available.

Local drinks are known as Country Liquor and include *toddy*, a mildly alcoholic extract from the coconut palm flower, and *feni*, a distilled liquor produced from fermented cashew nuts or from coconuts. The two varieties taste quite different.

Arak is what the peasants drink to get blotto. It's a clear, distilled rice liquor and it creeps up on you without warning. Treat it with caution and only ever drink it from a bottle produced in a government-controlled distillery. *Never, ever* drink it otherwise − hundreds of people die or are blinded every year in India as a result of drinking *arak* produced in illicit stills. You can assume it contains methyl alcohol (wood alcohol).

The only state in India which is 'dry' is Gujarat (excluding Daman and Diu). You cannot buy beer or any other liquor for love nor money, except at the most expensive hotels and even then you'll have to consume it in your room. Bars don't exist.

SPECTATOR SPORT

India's national sport (obsession almost) is cricket. There's something about a game with as many idiosyncrasies and peculiarities as cricket which simply has to appeal to the Indian temperament. During the cricket season, if an international side is touring India and there is a test match on, you'll see crowds outside the many shops which have a TV, and people walking down the street with a pocket radio pressed to their ear. Test matches with Pakistan have a particularly strong following as the rivalry is intense. One thing you can count on is that most Indians will know the names of the entire touring cricket team and, if you come from the same country but don't know their

names, then you may well be regarded as mentally retarded. On the other hand, if you do have an interest in cricket, it can be a great way to start up conversations.

India is also one of the world leaders in hockey, and has several Olympic gold medals to its credit − although none since 1980. In the 1996 Olympics the country's only medal was a tennis bronze, won by Leander Paes.

Soccer has a keen following, particularly in Calcutta.

THINGS TO BUY

India is packed with beautiful things to buy. The cardinal rule when purchasing handicrafts is to bargain and bargain hard. You can get a good idea of what is reasonable in quality and price by visiting the various state emporiums and the Central Cottage Industries Emporiums which can be found in Delhi, Calcutta, Mumbai, Chennai, Bangalore and Hyderabad. You can inspect items at these places from all over the country. Because prices are fixed, you will get an idea of how hard to bargain when you purchase similar items from regular dealers.

As with handicrafts in any country, don't buy until you have developed a little understanding and appreciation. Rushing in and buying the first thing you see will inevitably lead to later disappointment and a considerably reduced stash of travellers cheques.

Be careful when buying items which include delivery to your home country. You may be told that the price includes home delivery and all customs and handling charges. Inevitably this is not the case, and you may find yourself having to collect the item yourself from your country's main port or airport, pay customs charges (which could be as much as 20% of the item's value) and handling charges levied by the airline or shipping company (up to 10% of the value). If you can't collect the item promptly, or get someone to do it on your behalf, exorbitant storage charges may also be charged.

Carpets

It may not surprise you that India produces and exports more hand-crafted carpets than

Iran, but it probably is more of a surprise that some of them are of virtually equal quality.

In Kashmir, where India's best carpets are produced, the carpet-making techniques and styles were brought from Persia even before the Mughal era. The art flourished under the Mughals and today Kashmir is packed with small carpet producers. Persian motifs have been much embellished on Kashmiri carpets, which come in a variety of sizes – three by five feet, four by six feet and so on. They are either made of pure wool, wool with a small percentage of silk to give a sheen (known as silk touch) or pure silk. The latter are more for decoration than hard wear. Expect to pay from Rs 7000 for a good quality four-by-six

carpet and don't be surprised if the price is more than twice as high.

Other carpet-making areas include Badhoi and Mirzapur in Uttar Pradesh or Warangal and Eluru in Andhra Pradesh. In Kashmir and Rajasthan, the coarsely woven woollen *numdas* are made. These are more primitive and folksy, and consequently cheaper, than the fine carpets. Around the Himalaya and Uttar Pradesh *dhurries*, flat-weave cotton warp-and-weft rugs are woven. In Kashmir *gabbas* are appliqué-like rugs. The many Tibetan refugees in India have brought their craft of making superbly colourful Tibetan rugs with them. A three-by-five Tibetan rug will be less than Rs 1000. Two of the best

A Warning!

In touristy places, particularly Agra, Jaipur, Varanasi, Delhi and Calcutta, take extreme care with the commission merchants – these guys hang around waiting to pick you up and cart you off to their favourite dealers where whatever you pay will have a hefty margin built into it to pay their commission. Stories about 'my family's place', 'my brother's shop' and 'special deal at my friend's place' are just stories and nothing more.

Whatever you might be told, if you are taken by a rickshaw driver or tout to a place, be it a hotel, craft shop, market or even restaurant, the price you pay will be inflated. This can be by as much as 50%, so try to visit these places on your own. And don't underestimate the persistence of these guys. I heard of one desperately ill traveller who virtually collapsed into a cycle rickshaw in Agra and asked to be taken to a doctor – he ended up at a marble workshop, and the rickshaw driver insisted that, yes, indeed a doctor did work there! The high-pressure sales techniques of both the runners and the owners is the best in the world. Should you get up and leave without buying anything, the feigned anger is just that. Next time you turn up (alone), it will be all smiles – and the prices will have dropped dramatically.

Another trap which many foreigners fall into occurs when buying with a credit card. You may well be told that if you buy the goods, the merchant won't forward the credit slip for payment until you have received the goods, even if it is in three months time – this is total bullshit. No trader will be sending you as much as a postcard until he or she has received the money, in full, for the goods you are buying. What you'll find in fact is that within 48 hours of you signing the credit slip, the merchant has telexed the bank in Delhi and the money will have been credited to his or her account.

Also beware of any shop which takes your credit card out the back and comes back with the slip for you to sign. It has occurred that, while out of sight, the vendor will imprint a few more forms, forge your signature, and you'll be billed for items you haven't purchased. Get them to fill out the slip right in front of you.

If you believe any stories about buying anything in India to sell at a profit elsewhere, you'll simply be proving (once again) that old adage about separating fools from their money! Precious stones and carpets are favourites for this game. Merchants will tell you that you can sell the items in Australia, Europe or the USA for several times the purchase price, and will even give you the (often imaginary!) addresses of dealers who will buy them. You'll also be shown written statements, supposedly from other travellers, documenting the money they have supposedly made – it's all a scam. The stones or carpets you buy will be worth only a fraction of what you pay. Don't let greed cloud your judgement. It seems that with every edition of this book we make the warnings longer and more explicit, and yet we still get a steady trickle of letters from people with tales of woe, and they usually concern scams we specifically warn about!

While it is certainly a minority of traders who are actually involved in dishonest schemes, virtually all are involved in the commission racket, so you need to shop with care – take your time, be firm and bargain hard. Good luck! ■

Child Labour & the 'Smiling Carpet'

In India hundreds of thousands of children, mostly poor and virtually all uneducated, work in factories across the country. This is despite the Child Labour Prohibition & Regulation Act of 1986, which prohibits the employment of children below the age of 14 in hazardous industries.

The carpet-weaving industry employs an estimated 300,000 children, mostly in Uttar Pradesh state. The children are in demand because their small, nimble fingers are ideal for intricate weaving work, and, of course, being young, they get minimal wages. The conditions the children work under are generally atrocious – up to 16 hour working days, poor lighting and dangerous workplaces are all common.

In an effort to combat this exploitation of children, in 1992 the UN children's fund (UNICEF), the Indo-German Export Promotion Council (IGEP) and a group of nongovernment organisations came up with the 'Smiling Carpet' label – a label which was to be attached to any carpet produced without child labour. Also throwing its weight behind the project was the South Asian Coalition Against Child Servitude (SACACS). These bodies lobbied to ban the export of Indian child-made carpets.

Predictably, there has been opposition to the new label from the carpet manufacturers/exporters and the government, who say there are insufficient controls within the industry to allow for detailed inspection and therefore legitimate labels. Nevertheless, the movement has the support of German carpet importers, who are paying 1% more for their carpets and using this extra money to establish a fund to aid the child workers.

Despite the opposition, the scheme is gaining credibility and increasing numbers of manufacturers are getting involved. While it is obviously not going to put an end to child labour, the 'Smiling Carpet' label is a major achievement. ■

places to buy them are Darjeeling and Gangtok.

Unless you're an expert it is best to get expert advice or buy from a reputable dealer if you're spending large amounts of money on carpets. Check prices back home too; many western carpet dealers sell at prices you would have difficulty matching even at the source.

Papier Mâché

This is probably the most characteristic Kashmiri craft. The basic papier-mâché article is made in a mould, then painted and polished in successive layers until the final intricate design is produced. Prices depend upon the complexity and quality of the painted design and the amount of gold leaf used. Items include bowls, cups, containers, jewellery boxes, letter holders, tables, lamps, coasters, trays and so on. A cheap bowl might cost only Rs 25, a large, well-made item might approach Rs 1000.

Pottery

In Rajasthan interesting white-glazed pottery is made with hand-painted blue-flower designs – it's attractively simple. Terracotta images of the gods and children's toys are made in Bihar.

Metalwork

Copper and brass items are popular throughout India. Candle holders, trays, bowls, tankards and ashtrays are made in Mumbai and other centres. In Rajasthan and Uttar Pradesh the brass is inlaid with exquisite designs in red, green and blue enamel. *Bidri* is a craft of north-eastern Karnataka and Andhra Pradesh, where silver is inlaid into gunmetal (for more details see the Bidriware of Bidar boxed section at the end of the Karnataka chapter). Hookah pipes, lamp bases and jewellery boxes are made in this manner.

Jewellery

Many Indian women put most of their wealth into jewellery, so it is no wonder that so much of it is available. For western tastes the heavy folk-art jewellery of Rajasthan has particular appeal. You'll find it all over the country, but particularly in Rajasthan. In the north you'll also find Tibetan jewellery, even chunkier and more folk-like than the Rajasthani variety.

If, on the other hand, you're looking for fine jewellery as opposed to folk jewellery, you may well find that much of what is produced in India is way over the top.

Leatherwork

Of course Indian leatherwork is not made from cow-hide but from buffalo-hide, camel, goat or some other substitute. *Chappals*, those basic sandals found all over India, are the most popular purchase. In craft shops in Delhi you can find well-made leather bags, handbags and other items. Kashmiri leather shoes and boots, often of quite good quality, are widely found, along with coats and jackets of often abysmally low quality.

Kanpur in Uttar Pradesh is the country's major city for leatherwork.

Textiles

This is still India's major industry and 40% of the total production is at the village level where it is known as *khadi*. There are government khadi emporiums (known as Khadi Gramodyog) around the country, and these are good places to buy handmade items of homespun cloth, such as the popular 'Nehru jackets' and the *kurta pajama*. Bedspreads, tablecloths, cushion covers or material for clothes are other popular khadi purchases.

There is an amazing variety of cloth styles, types and techniques around the country. In Gujarat and Rajasthan material is embroidered with tiny mirrors and beads to produce the mirrorwork used for dresses, stuffed toys and wall hangings. Tie-dye work is also popular in Rajasthan and Kerala.

In Kashmir embroidered materials are made into shirts and dresses. Fine shawls and scarves of pashmina goats' wool are popular buys in the Kullu Valley. Phulkari bedspreads or wall hangings come from the Punjab. Another place which is famous for its embroidery is Barmer, near the Pakistani border and south-west of Jaisalmer in Rajasthan. Batik is a fairly recent introduction from Indonesia but already widespread; kalamkari cloth from Andhra Pradesh and Gujarat is an associated but far older craft.

Silks & Saris

Silk is cheap and the quality is often excellent. The 'silk capital' these days is Kanchipuram in Tamil Nadu, although Varanasi is also popular, especially for silk saris.

If you are buying a silk sari, it helps to know a bit about both the silk and the sari. Saris are 5½ metres long, unless they have an attached blouse *(choli)*, in which case they are six metres. Sari silk is graded and sold by weight – in grams per metre.

Bronze Figures

In the south, delightful small images of the gods are made by the age-old lost-wax process. A wax figure is made, a mould is formed around it and the wax is melted and poured out. The molten metal is poured in and when it's solidified the mould is broken open. Figures of Siva as dancing Nataraj are amongst the most popular.

Woodcarving

In the south, images of the gods are also carved out of sandalwood. Rosewood is used to carve animals – elephants in particular. Carved wooden furniture and other household items, either in natural finish or lacquered, are also made in various locations. In Kashmir intricately carved wooden screens, tables, jewellery boxes and trays are carved from Indian walnut. They have a similar pattern to the decorative trim of houseboats.

Paintings

Reproductions of the beautiful old miniatures are painted in many places, but beware of paintings claimed to be antique – it's highly unlikely that they are. Also note that quality can vary widely; low prices often mean low quality, and if you buy before you've had a chance to look at a lot of miniatures and develop some appreciation you'll inevitably find you bought unwisely. Udaipur (Rajasthan) has some good shops specialising in modern reproductions.

In Kerala, and, to a lesser extent, Tamil Nadu, you'll come across vibrant miniature paintings on leaf skeletons enclosed on a printed card depicting domestic and rural scenes as well as gods and goddesses.

Antiques

Articles over 100 years old are not allowed to be exported from India without an export clearance certificate. If you have doubts

Dhobi-Wallahs

When you travel in India there's hardly any need for more than one change of clothes. Every day there will be a knock on your door and the laundry boy will collect all those dusty, sweaty clothes you wore yesterday, and every evening those same clothes will reappear – washed and ironed with more loving care than any washing-powder-ad mum ever lavished upon anything. And all for a few rupees per item. But what happened to your clothes between their departure and their like-new return?

Well, they certainly did not get anywhere near a washing machine. First of all they're collected and taken to the *dhobi ghat*. A ghat is a series of steps near a lake or river, a *dhobi-wallah* is a washerperson, so the dhobi ghat is where the dhobi-wallahs ply their trade and wash clothes. In big cities, dhobi ghats will be huge places with hundreds of dhobi-wallahs doing their thing with thousands of articles of clothing.

Upon arrival at the ghat, the clothes are separated – all the white shirts are washed together, all the grey trousers, all the red skirts, all the blue jeans. By now, if this was the west, your clothes would either be hopelessly lost or you'd need a computer to keep track of them all. Your clothes are soaked in soapy water for a few hours, following which the dirt is literally beaten out of them. No multiprogrammed miracle of technology can wash as clean as a determined dhobi-wallah, although admittedly after a few visits to the Indian laundry your clothes do begin to look distinctly thinner. Buttons also tend to get shattered, so bring some spares. Zips sometimes fare likewise.

Once clean, the clothes are strung out on miles of clothesline to quickly dry in the Indian sun. They're then taken to the ironing sheds where hundreds of ironers wielding primitive irons press your jeans like they've never been pressed before. Not just your jeans – your socks, your T-shirts, even your underwear will come back with knife-edge creases. Then the Indian miracle takes place. Out of the thousands upon thousands of items washed that day, somehow your very own brown socks, blue jeans, yellow T-shirt and red underwear all find their way back together and head for your hotel room. A system of marking clothes, known only to the dhobis, is the real reason behind this feat. They say criminals have been tracked down simply by those telltale 'dhobi marks'. ∎

about any item and think it could be defined as an antique, you can check with branches of the Archaeological Survey of India.

Other Things to Buy

Marble inlay pieces from Agra are pleasant reminders of the beauty of the Taj. They come as either simple little pieces or larger items like jewellery boxes. Appliqué work is popular in many places, such as Orissa.

Indian musical instruments always have an attraction for travellers, although you don't see nearly as many backpackers lugging sitars or tablas around as you did 15 years ago. A more portable Indian music buy might be records or tapes. Certain Indian streets in major cities now resemble Taipei, Bangkok, Bali and Singapore

in having street stalls and shops offering the full range of 1960s through to contemporary western music, though they're often pirated and on inferior tapes. You're looking at around Rs 50 per tape.

THINGS TO SELL

With the opening of the Indian market many western technological items that were once good things to sell in India are now available here. Cameras, tape recorders and VCRs are as dead as a dodo in terms of making a profit. In any case, VCRs might well be entered into your passport to ensure they leave the country with you. But there's always a market, particularly in Calcutta, Delhi and Chennai, for your bottle of duty-free whisky.

Getting There & Away

AIR
Buying Tickets

Your plane ticket will probably be the single most expensive item in your budget. Some of the cheapest tickets have to be bought months in advance, and some popular flights sell out early. Talk to other recent travellers – they may be able to stop you making some of the same old mistakes. Look at the ads in newspapers and magazines, and watch for special offers. Then phone around travel agents for bargains. (Remember that airlines, except at times of inter-airline war, do not supply the cheapest tickets.) Find out the fare, the route, the duration of the journey and any restrictions on the ticket. (See Restrictions in the Air Travel Glossary in this chapter.) Then sit back and decide which is best for you.

You may discover that those impossibly cheap flights are 'fully booked, but we have another one that costs a bit more...' Or the flight is on an airline notorious for its poor safety standards and leaves you in the world's least favourite airport in mid-journey for 14 hours. Or they claim only to have the last two seats available for that country for the whole of July, which they will hold for you for a maximum of two hours. Don't panic – keep ringing around.

If you are travelling from the UK or the USA, you will probably find that the cheapest flights are being advertised by obscure bucket shops whose names haven't yet reached the telephone directory. Many such firms are honest and solvent, but there are a few rogues who will take your money and disappear, to reopen elsewhere a month or two later under a new name. If you feel suspicious about a firm, don't give them all the money at once – leave a deposit of 20% or so and pay the balance when you get the ticket. If they insist on cash in advance, go somewhere else. And once you have the ticket, ring the airline to confirm that you are actually booked on the flight.

You may decide to pay more than the rock-bottom fare by opting for the safety of a better-known travel agent. Firms such as STA Travel, who have offices worldwide, Council Travel in the USA or Travel CUTS in Canada are not going to disappear overnight, leaving you clutching a receipt for a nonexistent ticket, but they do offer good prices to most destinations.

Once you have your ticket, write its number down, together with the flight number and other details, and keep the information somewhere separate. If the ticket is lost or stolen, this will help you get a replacement.

It's sensible to buy travel insurance as early as possible. If you buy it the week before you fly, you may find, for example, that you're not covered for delays to your flight caused by industrial action.

Warning: Reconfirmation
It is essential to reconfirm your return flight home at least 72 hours prior to departure. Some travellers have reported that failure to do so resulted in cancelled seats and several anxious days trying to secure new seats for their return journey – not a pleasant way to spend your last days in India! ■

Travellers with Special Needs

If you have special needs of any sort – you've broken a leg, you're vegetarian, travelling in a wheelchair, taking the baby, terrified of flying – you should let the airline know as soon as possible so that they can make arrangements accordingly. You should remind them when you reconfirm your booking (at least 72 hours before departure) and again when you check in at the airport. It may also be worth ringing around the airlines before you make your booking to find out how each one of them can handle your particular needs.

Air Travel Glossary

Apex Tickets Apex stands for Advance Purchase Excursion fare. These tickets are usually between 30% and 40% cheaper than the full economy fare, but there are restrictions. You must purchase the ticket at least 21 days in advance (sometimes more) and must be away for a minimum period (normally 14 days) and return within a maximum period (90 or 180 days). Stopovers are not allowed, and if you have to change your dates of travel or destination, there will be extra charges to pay. These tickets are not fully refundable – if you have to cancel your trip, the refund is often considerably less than what you paid for the ticket. Take out travel insurance to cover yourself in case you have to cancel your trip, for instance due to illness.

Baggage Allowance This will be written on your ticket; you are usually allowed one 20kg item to go in the hold, plus one item of hand luggage. Some airlines which fly transpacific and transatlantic routes allow for two pieces of luggage (there are limits on their dimensions and weight).

Bucket Shops At certain times of the year and on certain routes, many airlines fly with empty seats. This isn't profitable and it's more cost-effective for them to fly full, even if that means having to sell a certain number of drastically discounted tickets. They do this by off-loading them onto bucket shops (UK) or consolidators (USA), travel agents who specialise in discounted fares. The agents, in turn, sell them to the public at reduced prices. These tickets are often the cheapest you'll find, but you can't purchase them directly from the airlines. Availability varies widely, so you'll not only have to be flexible in your travel plans, you'll have to be quick off the mark as soon as an advertisement appears in the press.

Bucket-shop agents advertise in newspapers and magazines and there's a lot of competition – especially in places like Amsterdam and London, which are crawling with them – so it's a good idea to telephone first to ascertain availability before rushing from shop to shop. Naturally, they'll advertise the cheapest available tickets, but by the time you get there, these may be sold out and you may be looking at something slightly more expensive.

Bumped Just because you have a confirmed seat doesn't mean you're going to get on the plane – see Overbooking.

Cancellation Penalties If you have to cancel or change an Apex or other discount ticket, there may be heavy penalties involved; insurance can sometimes be taken out against these penalties. Some airlines impose penalties on regular tickets as well, particularly against 'no show' passengers.

Check-In Airlines ask you to check in a certain time ahead of the flight departure (usually two hours on international flights). If you fail to check in on time and the flight is overbooked, the airline can cancel your booking and give your seat to somebody else.

Confirmation Having a ticket written out with the flight and date on it doesn't mean you have a seat until the agent has confirmed with the airline that your status is 'OK'. Prior to this confirmation, your status is 'on request'.

Courier Fares Businesses often need to send their urgent documents or freight securely and quickly. They do it through courier companies. These companies hire people to accompany the package through customs and, in return, offer a discount ticket which is sometimes a phenomenal bargain. In effect, what the courier companies do is ship their freight as your luggage on the regular commercial flights. This is a legitimate operation – all freight is completely legal. There are two shortcomings, however: the short turnaround time of the ticket, usually not longer than a month; and the limitation on your luggage allowance. You may be required to surrender all your baggage allowance for the use of the courier company, and be only allowed to take carry-on luggage.

Discounted Tickets There are two types of discounted fares – officially discounted (such as Apex – see Promotional Fares) and unofficially discounted (see Bucket Shops). The latter can save you more than money – you may be able to pay Apex prices without the associated Apex advance booking and other requirements. The lowest prices often impose drawbacks, such as flying with unpopular airlines, inconvenient schedules, or unpleasant routes and connections.

Economy-Class Tickets Economy-class tickets are usually not the cheapest way to go, though they do give you maximum flexibility and they are valid for 12 months. If you don't use them, most are fully refundable, as are unused sectors of a multiple ticket.

Full Fares Airlines traditionally offer first class (coded F), business class (coded J) and economy class (coded Y) tickets. These days there are so many promotional and discounted fares available that few passengers pay full fare.

Lost Tickets If you lose your airline ticket, an airline will usually treat it like a travellers' cheque and, after inquiries, issue you with a replacement. Legally, however, an airline is entitled to treat it like cash, so if you lose a ticket, it could be forever. Take good care of your tickets.

MCO A Miscellaneous Charges Order is a voucher for a given amount, which resembles an airline ticket and can be used to pay for a specific flight with any IATA (International Air Transport Association) airline. MCOs, which are more flexible than a regular ticket, may satisfy the onward ticket requirement, but some countries are now reluctant to accept them. MCOs are fully refundable if unused.

No Shows No shows are passengers who fail to show up for their flight for whatever reason. Full-fare no shows are sometimes entitled to travel on a later flight. The rest of us are penalised (see Cancellation Penalties).

Open Jaw Tickets These are return tickets which allow you to fly to one place but return from another, and travel between the two 'jaws' by any means of transport at your own expense. If available, this can save you backtracking to your arrival point.

Overbooking Airlines hate to fly with empty seats, and since every flight has some passengers who fail to show up (see No Shows), they often book more passengers than they have seats available. Usually the excess passengers balance those who fail to show up, but occasionally somebody gets bumped. If this happens, guess who it is most likely to be? The passengers who check in late.

Promotional Fares These are officially discounted fares, such as Apex fares, which are available from travel agents or direct from the airline.

Reconfirmation You must contact the airline at least 72 hours prior to departure to 'reconfirm' that you intend to be on the flight. If you don't do this, the airline can delete your name from the passenger list and you could lose your seat.

Restrictions Discounted tickets often have various restrictions on them, such as necessity of advance purchase, limitations on the minimum and maximum period you must be away and restrictions on breaking the journey or changing the booking or route.

Round-the-World Tickets These tickets have become very popular in the last few years; basically, there are two types – airline tickets and agent tickets. An airline RTW ticket is issued by two or more airlines that have joined together to market a ticket which takes you around the world on their combined routes. It permits you to fly pretty well anywhere you choose using their combined routes as long as you don't backtrack: that is, you must keep moving in roughly the same direction east or west. Other restrictions are that you (usually) must book the first sector in advance and cancellation penalties then apply. There may be restrictions on how many stopovers you are permitted. The RTW tickets are usually valid for from 90 days up to a year.

Quite a few of these combined-airline RTW tickets go through India, including ones in combination with Air India which will allow you to make several stopovers within India. RTW tickets typically cost around A$1950 to A$2400, UK£560 to UK£940 and US$1250 to US$2500.

The other type of RTW ticket, the agent ticket, is a combination of cheap fares strung together by an enterprising travel agent. These may be cheaper than airline RTW tickets, but the choice of routes will be limited.

Standby This is a discounted ticket where you only fly if there is a seat free at the last moment. Standby fares are usually only available directly at the airport, but sometimes may also be handled by an airline's city office. To give yourself the best possible chance of getting on the flight you want, get there early and have your name placed on the waiting list. It's first come, first served.

Student Discounts Some airlines offer student-card holders 15 to 25% discounts on their tickets. The same often applies to anyone under the age of 26. These discounts are generally only available on ordinary economy-class fares. You wouldn't get one, for instance, on an Apex or a RTW ticket, since these are already discounted.

Tickets Out An entry requirement for many countries is that you have an onward or return ticket, in other words, a ticket out of the country. If you're not sure what you intend to do next, the easiest solution is to buy the cheapest onward ticket to a neighbouring country or a ticket from a reliable airline which can later be refunded if you do not use it.

Transferred Tickets Airline tickets cannot be transferred from one person to another. Travellers sometimes try to sell the return half of their ticket, but officials can ask you to prove that you are the person named on the ticket. This may not be checked on domestic flights, but on international flights tickets are usually compared with passports.

Travel Periods Some officially discounted fares, Apex fares in particular, vary with the time of year. There is often a low (off-peak) season and a high (peak) season. Sometimes there's an intermediate or shoulder season as well. At peak times, when everyone wants to fly, both officially and unofficially discounted fares will be higher, or there may simply be no discounted tickets available. Usually the fare depends on your outward flight – if you depart in the high season and return in the low season, you pay the high-season fare. ■

Flying with Children Children under two travel for 10% of the standard fare (or free, on some airlines), as long as they don't occupy a seat. They don't get a baggage allowance either. Bassinets should be provided by the airline if requested in advance; these will take a child weighing up to about 10kg. Children between two and 12 can usually occupy a seat for half to two-thirds of the full fare, and do get a baggage allowance. Strollers can often be taken as hand luggage.

Round-the-World Fares
Round-the-World (RTW) fares are very competitive and are a popular way to travel to India. See the Air Travel Glossary box item in this chapter for more information.

Cheap Tickets in India
Although you can get cheap tickets in Mumbai (Bombay) and Calcutta, it is in Delhi that the real wheeling and dealing goes on. There are a number of bucket shops around Connaught Place, but enquire with other travellers about their current trustworthiness. And if you use a bucket shop, double check with the airline itself that the booking has been made.

One-way fares from Delhi to London are from around US$270 on Aeroflot, a bit less from Mumbai. It's well worth paying about US$50 more for something more reliable such as Emirates. Delhi–Hong Kong–San Francisco costs around US$750.

Although Delhi is the best place for cheap tickets, many flights between Europe and South-East Asia or Australia pass through Mumbai; it's also the place for flights to East Africa. Furthermore, if you're heading east from India to Bangladesh, Myanmar (Burma) or Thailand you'll probably find much better prices in Calcutta than in Delhi, even though there are fewer agents.

Africa
There are plenty of flights between East Africa and Mumbai due to the large Indian population in Kenya. Typical fares from Mumbai to Nairobi are around US$500 return with either Ethiopian Airlines, Kenya Airways, Air India or Pakistan International Airlines (PIA, via Karachi).

Aeroflot operates a service between Delhi and Cairo (via Moscow).

Australia & New Zealand
Advance-purchase return fares from the east coast of Australia to India range from A$1250 to A$1500 depending on the season and the destination in India. Fares are slightly cheaper to Chennai (Madras) and Calcutta than to Mumbai or Delhi. From Australia fares are cheaper from Darwin or Perth than from the east coast. The low travel period is from March to September; peak is from October to February.

Tickets from Australia to London or other European capitals with an Indian stopover range from A$1200 to A$1350 one way and A$2000 to A$2500 return, again, depending on the season.

Return advance-purchase fares from New Zealand to India range from NZ$1800 to NZ$1900 depending on the season.

STA Travel and Flight Centres International are major dealers in cheap airfares in both Australia and New Zealand. Check the travel agents' ads in the Yellow Pages and ring around.

Bangladesh
Bangladesh Biman and Indian Airlines fly from Calcutta to Dhaka (US$57) and Chittagong (US$73) in Bangladesh. Many people use Biman from Calcutta through to Bangkok – partly because they're cheap and partly because they fly through Yangon (Rangoon) in Myanmar. Biman should put you up overnight in Dhaka on this route but be careful – it appears they will only do so if your ticket is specifically endorsed that you are entitled to a room. If not, tough luck – you can either camp out overnight in the hot transit lounge or make your way into Dhaka on your own, pay for transport and accommodation, and get hit for departure tax the next day.

Continental Europe
Fares from continental Europe are mostly far more expensive than from London.

Amsterdam, however, can be a good place for a cheap ticket, but make sure the travel agent you use has an 'SGR' certificate or you may never see your money again. The cheapest return ticket is around DFL1000 (UK£375) to Delhi/Mumbai. Excursion fares can be much more – DFL2400 (UK£900).

From Paris to Mumbai/Delhi, return excursion fares range upwards from FFr7880 (UK£980; about one-third the standard return economy fare).

From Frankfurt to Mumbai/Delhi, return excursion fares are around DM1950 (UK£820).

Malaysia

Not many travellers fly between Malaysia and India because it is cheaper from Thailand, but there are flights between Penang or Kuala Lumpur and Chennai. You can generally pick up one-way tickets for the Malaysian Airline System (MAS) flight from Penang travel agents for around RM$780, which is rather cheaper than the regular fare. Other fares include Kuala Lumpur-Mumbai for RM$700 one way and RM$1275 return, and Kuala Lumpur-Delhi for RM$700 one way and RM$1070 return.

On Biman, a one-way ticket between Kuala Lumpur and Mumbai costs US$280 and includes a night in a five-star hotel in Dhaka.

The Maldives

Thiruvananthapuram (Trivandrum)-Malé costs US$70. This is cheaper than flying to the Maldives from Colombo in Sri Lanka.

Myanmar

There are no land crossing points between Myanmar and India (or between Myanmar and any other country), so if you want to visit Myanmar your only choice is to fly there. Myanma Airways flies Calcutta-Yangon; Bangladesh Biman flies Dhaka-Yangon.

If you are coming from Bangkok via Myanmar, the one-way Bangkok-Yangon-Calcutta fare is around US$240 with Thai, or US$225 on Myanma Airways.

Calcutta-Yangon costs US$160 on Indian Airlines.

Nepal

Royal Nepal Airlines Corporation (RNAC) and Indian Airlines share routes between India and Kathmandu. Both airlines give a 25% discount to those under 30 years of age on flights between Kathmandu and India; no student card is needed.

Delhi is the main departure point for flights between India and Kathmandu. The daily one-hour Delhi to Kathmandu flight costs US$142.

Other cities in India with direct air connections with Kathmandu are Mumbai (US$282), Calcutta (US$96) and Varanasi (US$71). The flight from Varanasi is the last leg of the popular Delhi-Agra-Khajuraho-Varanasi-Kathmandu tourist flight.

If you want to see the mountains as you fly into Kathmandu from Delhi or Varanasi, you must sit on the left side.

Pakistan

Pakistan International Airlines (PIA) and Air India operate flights from Karachi to Delhi for US$75 and Lahore to Delhi for about US$140. Flights are also available between Karachi and Mumbai.

Singapore

Singapore is a great cheap-ticket centre and you can pick up Singapore-Delhi tickets for about S$900 return.

Sri Lanka

Because the ferry service from India is out of operation, flying is now the only way to reach Sri Lanka.

There are flights to and from Colombo and Mumbai, Chennai, Tiruchirappalli or Thiruvananthapuram (Trivandrum). Flights are most frequent on the Chennai-Colombo route (US$71).

Thailand

Bangkok is the most popular departure point from South-East Asia into Asia proper because of the cheap flights from there to Calcutta, Yangon in Myanmar, Dhaka in Bangladesh or Kathmandu in Nepal. The popular Bangkok-Kathmandu flight is about

US$220 one way and US$400 return. You can make a stopover in Myanmar on this route and do a circuit of that fascinating country. Bangkok-Calcutta via Myanmar is about US$270 one way.

The UK

Various excursion fares are available from London to India, but you can get better prices through London's many cheap-ticket specialists. Check the travel page ads in the *Times, Business Traveller* and the weekly 'what's on' magazine *Time Out*; or check give-away papers like *TNT*. Two reliable London shops are Trailfinders, 194 High St Kensington, London W8 7RG (☎ (0171) 938 3939), or 46 Earls Court Rd, London W8 (☎ (0171) 938 3366); and STA Travel, 74 Old Brompton Rd, London SW7 (☎ (0171) 937 9962), or 117 Euston Rd, London NW1. Also worth trying are Quest Worldwide (☎ (0181) 547 3322) at 29 Castle St, Kingston, Surrey KT1 1ST, and Bridge the World (☎ (0171) 911 0900) at 1-3 Ferdinand St, Camden Town, London NW1. SD Enterprises (☎ (0181) 903 3411; fax 903 0392) at 103 Wembley Park Dr, Wembley, Middlesex, is particularly useful.

From London to Delhi, fares range from around UK£300/350 one way/return in the low season, or UK£350/450 one way/return in the high season – cheaper short-term fares are also available. The cheapest fares are usually with Middle Eastern or Eastern European airlines. You'll also find very competitive air fares to the subcontinent with Bangladesh Biman or Air Lanka. Thai International always seems to have competitive fares despite its high standards. Lufthansa has some of the best deals but, on these special offers, once you've bought the ticket no changes to dates of travel are allowed.

Some travel companies offer packages to Goa and Kerala at competitive rates which include accommodation, breakfast, and transfers – check with travel agents and travel page ads in newspapers and magazines. There are also a few packages including charter flights between London and Agra.

If you want to stop in India en route to Australia expect to pay around UK£500 to UK£600. You might find fares via Karachi (Pakistan) or Colombo (Sri Lanka) slightly cheaper than fares via India.

Most British travel agents are registered with the Association of British Travel Agents (ABTA). If you have paid an ABTA-registered agent for your flight and they go out of business, ABTA will guarantee a refund or an alternative. Unregistered bucket shops are riskier but are also sometimes cheaper.

The USA & Canada

The cheapest return air fares from the US west coast to India are around US$1350. Another way of getting there is to fly to Hong Kong and get a ticket from there. Tickets to Hong Kong cost about US$450 one way and around US$725 return from San Francisco or Los Angeles; in Hong Kong you can find one-way tickets to Mumbai for US$300 depending on the carrier. Alternatively, you can fly to Singapore for around US$600/US$850 one way/return, or to Bangkok for US$470/760 one way/return.

From the east coast you can find return tickets to Mumbai or Delhi for around US$950. The cheapest one-way tickets will be around US$650. An alternative way of getting to India from New York is to fly to London and buy a cheap fare from there.

Check the Sunday travel sections of papers like the *New York Times, San Francisco Chronicle/Examiner* or *Los Angeles Times* for cheap fares. Good budget travel agents include the student travel chains STA Travel or CIEE. The magazine *Travel Unlimited* (PO Box 1058, Allston, Mass 02134) publishes details of the cheapest air fares and courier possibilities for destinations all over the world from the USA.

Fares from Canada are similar to US fares. From Vancouver the route is like that from the US west coast, with the option of going via Hong Kong. From Toronto it is easier to travel via London.

The *Toronto Globe & Mail* and the *Vancouver Sun* carry travel agents' ads. The magazine *Great Expeditions* (PO Box 8000-411, Abbotsford BC V2S 6H1) is useful.

LAND

Drivers of cars and riders of motorbikes will need the vehicle's registration papers, liability insurance and an international drivers' permit in addition to their domestic licence. Beware: there are two kinds of international permit, one of which is needed mostly for former British colonies. You will also need a *carnet de passage en douane*, which is effectively a passport for the vehicle, and acts as a temporary waiver of import duty. The carnet may also need to have listed any more expensive spares that you're planning to carry with you, such as a gearbox. This is necessary when travelling in many countries in Asia, and is designed to prevent car import rackets. Contact your local automobile association for details about all documentation.

Liability insurance is not available in advance for many out-of-the-way countries, but has to be bought when crossing the border. The cost and quality of such local insurance varies wildly, and you will find in some countries that you are effectively travelling uninsured.

Anyone who is planning to take their own vehicle with them needs to check in advance what spares and petrol are likely to be available. In India, unleaded fuel is available only in Delhi, Mumbai, Calcutta and Chennai.

Cycling is a cheap, convenient, healthy, environmentally sound and above all fun way of travelling.

For more details on driving your own vehicle in India, or cycling in the country, see the Getting Around chapter.

Bangladesh

The main crossings are at Benapol/Haridaspur on the Calcutta route and Chilahati/Haldibari on the Darjeeling route. The Tamabil/Dauki border crossing, in the north-east corner on the Meghalaya route, opened in 1995. The border with Tripura is also open and you can cross between Akaur and Agartala.

No exit permit is required to leave Bangladesh. If border officials mention anything about a permit, remain steadfast. However, if you enter Bangladesh by air and exit via

land, you do need a road permit, which can be obtained from the Passport & Immigration office, 2nd floor, 17/1 Segunbagicha Rd in Dhaka, and if you are driving from Bangladesh in your own vehicle, two permits are required: one from the Indian High Commission (☎ 504897), House 120, Road 2, Dhanmondi in Dhaka, and one from the Bangladesh Ministry of Foreign Affairs (☎ 883260), Pioneer Rd (facing the Supreme Court), Segun Bagicha in the centre of Dhaka.

We have received in over recent years letters from travellers who have crossed at Bhurungamari (south-east of Haldibari)/Changrabandha (an alternative route from Darjeeling), Hili/Balurghat and Godagari/Lalgola, both north of Benapol/Haridaspur. These lesser crossings witness so few westerners that everyone assumes they're closed. Getting the truth from Indian and Bangladeshi officials is virtually impossible, so crossing the border on these lesser routes is never certain.

Dhaka to Calcutta The Dhaka to Calcutta route is the one used by the majority of land travellers between Bangladesh and India. Coming from Dhaka it's wise to book your seat on the bus at least a day in advance. The buses that operate overnight between Dhaka and the border are direct. Buses only depart from 8 to 11 pm; they reach Benapol (the Bangladeshi border town) at dawn. From Benapol to the border, it's about 10 minutes by cycle-rickshaw (Tk 5). There are no buses in the daytime between the border and Benapol. Crossing the border takes an hour or so with the usual filling in and stamping of forms. From the border at Haridaspur, on the Indian side, to Bangaon, it's about 10km (Rs 15, 20 minutes by cycle-rickshaw, or Rs 70 by auto-rickshaw). It's possible to change money at Bangaon, and the rate is better than at the border.

Alternatively, you can take a Coaster (minibus) from Jessore to Benapol (Tk 12), from where you can proceed to the border and India.

Chilahati to Darjeeling The Bangladesh border point is at Chilahati, and this can be reached by train, although it's much quicker to take the bus. From Chilahati to Haldibari (the Indian border checkpoint), it's a seven km walk along a disused railway line. The trip from Haldibari to New Jalpaiguri takes two hours and costs Rs 9 by train. From New Jalpaiguri to Darjeeling you can take the fast buses or the slower more picturesque toy train. Note that changing money in Chilahati is virtually impossible. There are money-changers at Haldibari.

Sylhet to Shillong In the early 1970s, the route between Shillong in Meghalaya and Sylhet in Bangladesh was closed on the Indian side to both regional and international traffic because of problems in Assam caused by the influx of illegal immigrants from Bangladesh. In 1995, the permit requirement was dropped; it may take a while before crossing here becomes problem free. If you're travelling by bus and border officials demand such a permit, you may have to educate them.

It takes 2½ hours to get to Tamabil from Sylhet by bus, and it's a 15 minute hike to the border. It is then a further 1.5km walk to Dauki in India, from where buses run to Shillong, a 3½ hour trip. From Shillong, at an elevation of 1496m, if it's not cloudy the views over Bangladesh are superb.

Europe
The classic way of getting to India has always been overland. Sadly, events in the Middle East and Afghanistan have turned the cross-Asian flow into a trickle. Afghanistan is still off-limits but the trip through Turkey, Iran and into Pakistan is straightforward.

The Asia overland trip is certainly not the breeze it once was, but it is definitely possible. Many travellers combine travel to the subcontinent with the Middle East by flying from India or Pakistan to Amman in Jordan or one of the Gulf states. A number of the London-based overland companies operate their bus or truck trips across Asia on a regular basis. Check with Exodus (☎ (0181)

675 5550), 9 Weir Rd, London SW12 0LT, UK; Encounter Overland (☎ (0171) 370 6951), 267 Old Brompton Rd, London SW5 9LA, UK; or Top Deck Travel (☎ (0171) 370 4555) for more information.

For more detail on the Asian overland route see the Lonely Planet guides to Pakistan, Iran and Turkey.

Nepal
There are direct buses from Delhi to Kathmandu, but these generally get bad reports from travellers. It's cheaper and more satisfactory to organise this trip yourself.

For more details of the land routes into Nepal see the Uttar Pradesh, Bihar and West Bengal chapters in this book. The most popular routes are from Raxaul (near Muzaffarpur), Sunauli (near Gorakhpur), and Kakarbhitta (near Siliguri). If you are heading straight to Nepal from Delhi or elsewhere in western India then the Gorakhpur to Sunauli route is the most convenient. From Calcutta, Patna or most of eastern India, Raxaul to Birganj is the best entry point. From Darjeeling it's easiest to go to Kakarbhitta.

To give an idea of costs, a 2nd-class rail ticket from Delhi to Gorakhpur costs US$6 and buses from Gorakhpur to the border and then on to Kathmandu cost another US$6.

There are other roads into Nepal from northern Bihar to the east of Birganj but they are rarely used by travellers, and a couple of them are closed. One such is the crossing between Jogbani (near Purnia) and Biratnagar. Additionally, the narrow-gauge railway from Jaynagar (near Darbhanga) which crosses the border to Janakpur (an attractive Nepalese city famous as the birthplace of Sita) is also closed.

It is also possible to cross the border at Nepalganj, Dhangadi and Mahendrenagar in the far west of Nepal. The entry at Mahendrenagar, just over the border from the northern Uttar Pradesh village of Banbassa, is the most interesting possibility. It may take a while for things to start operating smoothly, but when they do, this will present an interesting alternative route to/from Delhi. It takes 12 hours on the Delhi-Mahendrenagar route, nine hours for Mahendrenagar-Nepalganj, and 16 hours for Nepalganj-Kathmandu. See under Banbassa in the Uttar Pradesh chapter for more details on this route.

Pakistan

At present, due to the continuing unstable political situation between India and Pakistan, there's only one border crossing open. This may change.

Lahore to Amritsar The crossing at Attari is open daily to all traffic. It may be worth checking the situation in the Punjab with the Home Ministry in Delhi or the Indian High Commission in Islamabad, Pakistan, before you travel, as this could change if there are major problems either side of the border.

For the Lahore to Amritsar train you have to buy one ticket from Lahore to Attari, the Indian border town, and another from Attari to Amritsar. The train departs Lahore daily at 11.30 am and arrives in Amritsar at 3 pm after a couple of hours at the border passing through immigration and customs. Going the other way, you leave Amritsar at 9.30 am and arrive in Lahore at 1.35 pm. Pakistan immigration and customs are handled at Lahore station. Sometimes, border delays can make the trip much longer.

From Amritsar you cannot buy a ticket until the morning of departure and there are no seat reservations – arrive early and push. Moneychangers offer good rates for Pakistan rupees on the platform. Travellers have reported that whichever direction you're travelling, the exchange rate between Indian and Pakistan rupees is more advantageous to you on the Pakistan side of the border, but you can change Indian rupees to Pakistani rupees or vice versa at Wagah (the Pakistani border town) and in Amritsar – no matter what the Pakistanis may tell you!

Few travellers use the road link between India and Pakistan. It's mainly of interest to people with vehicles or those on overland buses. By public transport the trip from Lahore entails taking a bus to the border at Wagah between Lahore and Amritsar,

walking across the border and then taking another bus or taxi into Amritsar.

From Lahore, buses and minibuses depart from near the general bus station on Badami Bagh. The border opens at 9.15 am and closes at 3.30 pm. If you're stuck on the Pakistan side you can stay at the *PTDC Motel*, where there are dorm beds and double rooms.

South-East Asia

In contrast to the difficulties of travelling overland in central Asia, the South-East Asian overland trip is still wide open and as popular as ever. From Australia the first step is to Indonesia – Timor, Bali or Jakarta. Although most people fly from an east-coast city or from Perth to Bali, there are also flights from Darwin and from Port Hedland in the north of Western Australia. The shortest route is the flight between Darwin and Kupang on the Indonesian island of Timor.

From Bali you head north through Java to Jakarta, from where you either travel by ship or fly to Singapore or continue north through Sumatra and then cross to Penang in Malaysia. After travelling around Malaysia you can fly from Penang to Chennai in India or, more popularly, continue north to Thailand and eventually fly out from Bangkok to India, perhaps with a stopover in Myanmar. Unfortunately, crossing by land from Myanmar to India (or indeed to any other country) is forbidden by the Myanmar government.

An interesting alternative route is to travel from Australia to Papua New Guinea and from there cross to Irian Jaya; then to Sulawesi in Indonesia. There are all sorts of travel variations possible in South-East Asia; the region is a delight to travel through, it's good value for money, the food is generally excellent and healthy, and all in all it's an area of the world not to be missed. For full details see Lonely Planet's guide *South-East Asia*.

SEA

The ferry service from Rameswaram in southern India to Talaimannar in Sri Lanka has been suspended for some years due to the unrest in Sri Lanka. This was a favourite route for shipping arms and equipment to the Tamil guerrilla forces in the north of the country. The service between Penang and Chennai also ceased some years ago.

The shipping services between Africa and India only carry freight (including vehicles), not passengers.

DEPARTURE TAX

For flights to neighbouring countries (Pakistan, Sri Lanka, Bangladesh, Nepal) the departure tax is Rs 100, but to other countries it's Rs 750. The airport tax applies to everybody, even to babies who do not occupy a seat. The method of collecting the tax varies but generally you have to pay it before you check in, so look out for an airport tax counter as you enter the check-in area.

INSURANCE

Regardless of how you plan to travel to India, it's worth taking out travel insurance. For more information, see Visas & Documents in the Facts for the Visitor chapter.

ORGANISED TOURS

There are numerous foreign eco-travel and adventure travel companies which can provide unusual and interesting trips in addition to companies that provide more standard tours. There are too many to include them all here; check newspapers and travel magazines for advertisements, and journals such as *Earth Journal* (USA) for listings. Companies that organise tours to various parts of India include the following:

Australasia

Peregrine Adventures
258 Lonsdale St, Melbourne, 3000, Australia (☎ (03) 9663 8611). Also offices in Sydney, Brisbane, Adelaide, Perth and Hobart.

Venturetreks
164 Parnell Rd (PO Box 37610), Parnell, Auckland, New Zealand
(☎ (09) 379 9855; fax (09) 377 0320)

World Expeditions
3rd Floor, 441 Kent St, Sydney, 2000, Australia (☎ (02) 9264 3366; fax (02) 9261 1974)
1st Floor, 393 Little Bourke St, Melbourne, 3000, Australia
(☎ (03) 9670 8400; fax (03) 9670 7474)

UK

Encounter Overland
267 Old Brompton Rd, London SW5 9JA
(☎ (0171) 370 6845)

Exodus Expeditions
9 Weir Rd, London SW12 OLT
(☎ (0181) 673 0859)

Imaginative Traveller (international reservation office)
14 Barley Mow Passage, Chiswick, London W4 4PH, UK (☎ (081) 742 3113; fax (081) 742 3046)

USA

Adventure Center
1311 63rd St, Suite 200, Emeryville, CA 94608
(☎ (800) 227-8747)

All Adventure Travel, Inc.
PO Box 4307, Boulder, CO 80306
(☎ (303) 440-7924)

Asian Pacific Adventures
826 S. Sierra Bonita Ave, Los Angeles, CA 90036
(☎ (800) 825-1680)

Inner Asia Expeditions
2627 Lombard St, San Francisco, CA 94123
(☎ (415) 922-0448; fax (415) 346-5535)

Getting Around

AIR
Domestic Air Services

India's major domestic airline, the government-run Indian Airlines, flies extensively throughout the nation and into neighbouring countries. Some services are operated by its subsidiary, Alliance Air. The country's international carrier, Air India, also operates domestic services, principally on the Mumbai (Bombay)-Delhi, Mumbai-Calcutta, Delhi-Calcutta and Mumbai-Chennai (Madras) routes.

There are also several independent operators. The best of them (indeed the best airline in India) is Jet Airways, serving 27 cities across the country. NEPC Airlines (Fokker 49 seaters) and its subsidiary Skyline NEPC (Boeing 737s) cover 50 destinations between them. Sahara India links a dozen cities. Even smaller are the regional airlines – Gujarat Airways, UP Air, Archana Airways and Jagson Airlines. Two other operators, East-West and Modiluft, had both suspended operations in early 1997 but may resume services later in the year – your travel agent may be able to give you information on this.

Reservations

Indian Airlines has computerised booking at all but the smallest offices, so getting flight information and reservations is relatively simple – it's just getting to the head of the queue that takes the time. Nevertheless, all flights are heavily booked and you need to plan as far in advance as possible.

The private operators are all reasonably efficient, and most have computerised booking.

For most airlines, tickets must be paid for with foreign currency or by credit card, or rupees backed up by encashment certificates. Change, where appropriate, is given in rupees.

Infants up to two years old travel at 10% of the adult fare, but only one infant can travel at this fare per adult. Children two to 12 years old travel at 50% fare. Indian nationals aged 65 and over also qualify for a 50% discount. There is no student reduction for overseas visitors, but there is a youth fare for people 12 to 30 years old. This allows a 25% reduction.

Refunds on adult tickets attract a charge of Rs 100 and can be made at any office. There are no refund charges on infant tickets.

The Fight for the Skies

Until partial deregulation in the early 1990s, state-run Indian Airlines had a virtual monopoly on services. There was little incentive to pay much heed to that nuisance known as the customer. In-flight service was lousy, the food barely edible, delays and cancellations frequent, and reservations difficult to make. Air travel within India was rather a fraught affair.

In 1992-3 came a rush of new small airlines, known as Air Taxi Operators (ATOs). Not only has this given the air traveller a choice of airlines on many routes, it has also forced Indian Airlines to pull its finger out in a major way in an effort to compete. The result is that the overall standard of service has improved, despite many pilot defections to the ATOs, lured by lucrative salaries.

It's certainly not all clear skies, though. In turning down a proposal for a new joint venture airline between Tata and Singapore International Airlines, the government has shown that although a foreign company may now own a 40% stake in an Indian airline company the proposal will not automatically be given the go-ahead – particularly if it feels the venture might threaten Indian Airlines. The result is that many of the smaller operators are underfunded fly-by-night operations that come and go. Damania won the best airline award for two years running but has now been absorbed by NEPC. East-West has been grounded since 1996 by disputes over fees to government and debts. Modiluft is fighting a lawsuit with its partner Lufthansa and its planes are also currently grounded.

Few of the airlines are making money; some are losing spectacular amounts. Air India's losses were Rs 400 crore (about US$115 million) for 1996-7, Indian Airlines lost Rs 40 crore. 'The airline business is in the biggest mess it's ever been in' (*Business India*, 9 February 1997). ■

If a flight is delayed or cancelled, you cannot refund the ticket. If you fail to show up 30 minutes before the flight, this is regarded as a 'no-show' and you forfeit the full value of the ticket.

Indian Airlines accepts no responsibility if you lose your tickets. They absolutely will not refund lost tickets, but at their discretion may issue replacements.

Indian Airlines Office Addresses

(distance from the office to the airport in brackets)

Agartala (12 km)
  Khosh Mahal Bldg, Central Rd
  (☎ (0381) 225470)
Agra (7 km)
  Hotel Clarks Shiraz, 54 Taj Rd
  (☎ (0562) 360948)
Ahmedabad (10 km)
  Airlines House, Lal Darwaja
  (☎ 140, (079) 352211)
Allahabad (12 km)
  Tourist Bungalow, MG Rd (☎ (0532) 602832)
Amritsar (11 km)
  48 The Mall (☎ (0183) 225321)
Aurangabad (10 km)
  Dr Rajendra Prasad Marg (☎ (02432) 25496)
Bagdogra (14 km)
  Hotel Sinclairs, Mallaguri, Siliguri
  (☎ (03556) 26689)
Bangalore (13 km)
  Housing Board Bldg, Kempegowda Rd
  (☎ (080) 221 1914)
Bhavnagar (8 km)
  Diwanpara Rd (☎ (0278) 26503)
Bhopal (11 km)
  Bhadbhada Rd, TT Nagar (☎ (0755) 550480)
Bhubaneswar (4 km)
  Unit 1, Raj Path, Bapuji Nagar (☎ (0674) 402380)
Bhuj (6 km)
  Outside Waniawad Gate, Station Rd
  (☎ (0735) 21433)
Calcutta (16 km)
  Airlines House, 39 Chittaranjan Ave
  (☎ (033) 263135, 266869)
Chandigarh (11 km)
  SCO-186-187-188 Sector 17C
  (☎ (0172) 544034)
Chennai (18 km)
  19 Marshalls Rd, Egmore
  (☎ (044) 825 1677, 141, 827 7888)
Chittagong, Bangladesh (23 km)
  Hotel Agrabad (☎ 502814)
Coimbatore (12 km)
  Civil Aerodrome, Peelamedy (☎ (0422) 212208)

Colombo, Sri Lanka (32 km)
  95 Sir Baron Jayatilaka Mawatha (☎ 323136)
Darjeeling
  Bellevue Hotel, Chowrasta (☎ (0354) 54230)
Delhi (20 km)
  Malhotra Bldg, Connaught Place
  (☎ (011) 331 0517)
  PTI Building, Sansad Marg (☎ 371 9168)
  Domestic Terminal (24 hours) (☎ 141)
Dhaka, Bangladesh (17 km)
  Sharif Mansion, Motijheel (☎ 503693)
Dibrugarh (16 km)
  CIWTC Bungalow, Assam Medical College Rd
  (☎ (0373) 20114)
Dimapur (3 km)
  Dimapur-Imphal Rd (☎ (03862) 20875)
Gangtok
  Tibet Rd (☎ (03592) 23099)
Goa (30 km)
  Dempo Building, D Bandodkar Marg, Panaji
  (☎ (0832) 224067)
Guwahati (23 km)
  Paltan Bazar (☎ (0361) 564400)
Gwalior (12 km)
  Tansen Marg, Barrar (☎ (0751) 326872)
Hyderabad (16 km)
  Secretariat Rd (☎ (0842) 237698)
Imphal (8 km)
  Mahatma Gandhi Rd (☎ (03852) 220999)
Indore (9 km)
  Dr R S Bhandari Marg (☎ (0731) 431595)
Jaipur (13 km)
  Tonk Rd (☎ (0141) 514407)
Jammu (6 km)
  Tourist Reception Centre, Veer Marg
  (☎ (0191) 542735)
Jamnagar (10 km)
  Indra Mahal, Bhind Bhanjan Rd
  (☎ (0288) 78569)
Jodhpur (5 km)
  Airport Rd (☎ (0291) 36757)
Jorhat (7 km)
  Tarajan Rd, Garhali (☎ (0376) 320011)
Karachi, Pakistan (19 km)
  Hotel Inter-Continental (c/o PIA) (☎ 568 1577)
Kathmandu, Nepal (6 km)
  26 Durbar Marg (☎ 419649)
Khajuraho (5 km)
  Khajuraho Hotel (☎ (076861) 2035)
Kochi (Cochin) (6 km)
  Durbar Hall Rd, Ernakulam (☎ (0484) 370236)
Kozikhode (Calicut)
  Eroth Centre, Bank Rd (☎ (0495) 55343)
Leh (8 km)
  Ibex Guest House (☎ (01982) 2276)
Lucknow (14 km)
  Clarks Avadh, 5 Mahatma Gandhi Marg
  (☎ (0522) 246623)

Madurai (12 km)
    Pandyan House, 7A West Veli St
    (☎ (0452) 26795)
Malé, Maldives (5 km)
    Beach Hotel (☎ 323003)
Mangalore (20 km)
    Hathill Rd, Lalbagh (☎ (0824) 414300)
Mumbai (26 km)
    Army & Navy Bldg, MG Rd
    (☎ (022) 287 6161, 202 3031)
Mysore
    Hotel Mayura Hoysala, 2 Jhansi Lakshmi Bai Rd
    (☎ (0821) 516943)
Nagpur (11 km)
    242A Manohar Niwas, Rabindranath Tagore Rd,
    Civil Lines (☎ (0712) 533962)
Patna (8 km)
    South Gandhi Maidan (☎ (0612) 227310)
Port Blair (3 km)
    Tagore Marg (☎ (03192) 21108)
Pune (10 km)
    39 Dr Ambedkar Rd (☎ (0212) 659939, 140)
Raipur (16 km)
    LIC Bldg (☎ (0771) 526707)
Rajkot (4 km)
    Angel Chamber, Station Rd (☎ (0281) 33329)
Ranchi (13 km)
    Welfare Centre, Main Rd (☎ (0651) 203042)
Silchar (26 km)
    Red Cross Rd (☎ (03842) 20096)
Srinagar (14 km)
    Air Cargo Complex Bldg, Shervani Marg
    (☎ (0194) 77370)
Tezpur (16 km)
    Jankin Rd (☎ (03804) 20083)
Thiruvananthapuram (Trivandrum) (6 km)
    Mascot Hill Bldg, Museum Rd
    (☎ (0471) 438288)
Tiruchirappalli (8 km)
    Southern Railway Employees Co-op Credit
    Society Bldg, Dindigul Rd (☎ (0431) 462233)
Tirupathi (15 km)
    Hotel Vishnupriya, Ranigunta Rd (☎ 22349)
Udaipur (24 km)
    LIC Bldg, outside Delhi Gate (☎ (0294) 410999)
Vadodara (Baroda) (6 km)
    University Rd, Fateh Ganj (☎ (0265) 328596)
Varanasi (22 km)
    Mint House Motel, Vadunath Marg, Cantonment
    (☎ (0542) 45959)
Visakhapatnam (16 km)
    Jeevan Prakash, LIC Bldg Complex
    (☎ (0891) 546501)

Air Passes

The Indian Air Routes chart details the main Indian Airlines and private airlines domestic routes and fares. The private airlines usually charge the same as Indian Airlines on identical routes, although it can be lots more.

Indian Airlines also has a 'Discover India' pass which costs US$500/750 for 15/21 days. This allows unlimited travel on domestic routes and can be reasonable value if you have lots of long flights. There's also a 25% youth discount if you're under 30. The other pass is the 'India Wonder Fare'; it's US$300 for a week's unlimited travel between cities within a regional group: north, west, south and east. Unless changing planes you may visit each place within the group only once.

Skyline NEPC operates a scheme similar to the Discover India pass for US$250/275 for 7/10 days, and US$500/750/900 for 15/21/30 days, but their network is not as comprehensive as Indian Airlines.

Private Airline Domestic Operators
Ahmedabad
    East West ☎ 423311
    Jet Airways ☎ 656 1290, 786 8307
    Modiluft ☎ 466228
    NEPC Airlines ☎ 642 6295, 786 8681
    Sahara India ☎ 656 4049, 786 6071
Agartala
    Sahara India ☎ 23387
Aurangabad
    East West ☎ 24949, 84600
    Jet Airways ☎ 487091, 484269
    NEPC Airlines ☎ 484601
Bagdogra
    Jet Airways ☎ 435876, 450590
    NEPC Airlines ☎ 436263, 450925
    Sahara India ☎ 434929, 450074
Bangalore
    East West ☎ 558 6874, 526 8494
    Jet Airways ☎ 227 6620, 526 1926
    ModiLuft ☎ 558 2199
    NEPC Airlines ☎ 559 4850, 526 2842
    Sahara India ☎ 558 6976, 526 2531
Bhavnagar
    NEPC Airlines ☎ 411191
Bhubaneswar
    NEPC Airlines ☎ 413612
Bhuj
    Gujarat Airways ☎ 25198
Calcutta
    Archana Airways ☎ 292471
    East West ☎ 745179, 552 8782
    Jet Airways ☎ 240 8192, 511 8836
    ModiLuft ☎ 299864
    NEPC Airlines ☎ 475 9652, 552 8779
    Sahara India ☎ 242 9067, 551 9545

Chennai (Madras)
East West ☎ 827 7007, 234 0551
Jet Airways ☎ 855 5353, 234 6557
ModiLuft ☎ 826 0048
NEPC Airlines ☎ 434 5538, 234 8421
Sahara India ☎ 826 3661, 233 0056
Coimbatore
East West ☎ 210286
Jet Airways ☎ 212034, 575387
NEPC Airlines ☎ 216741, 576312
Delhi
Archana Airways ☎ 329 5768
East West ☎ 372 1510, 328 5126
Jagson Airlines ☎ 372 1593
Jet Airways ☎ 685 3700, 329 5404
Sahara India ☎ 332 0013, 548 1351
ModiLuft ☎ 647 7903
NEPC Airlines ☎ 332 2525, 329 5577
UP Air ☎ 464 6290, 329 5126
Dharamsala
Jagson Airlines ☎ 23361
Diu
Gujarat Airways ☎ 2180
Goa
East West ☎ 224108, 513071
Jet Airways ☎ 221472, 511005
ModiLuft ☎ 227577
NEPC Airlines ☎ 229233, 511933
Sahara India ☎ 226291, 510043
Guwahati
Jet Airways ☎ 520202, 84131
NEPC Airlines ☎ 560765, 84127
Sahara India ☎ 548676, 84128
Hyderabad
East West ☎ 526518, 815932
Jet Airways ☎ 231263, 840382
ModiLuft ☎ 243783
NEPC Airlines ☎ 241660, 842054
Sahara India ☎ 202836, 842054
Indore
Jet Airways ☎ 409437, 410452
NEPC Airlines ☎ 433922, 410219
Jaipur
East West ☎ 516809, 551901
Jet Airways ☎ 377051, 551733
NEPC Airlines ☎ 365118
Sahara India ☎ 553525, 550018
Jaisalmer
Jagson Airlines ☎ 52759
Jorhat
Jet Airways ☎ 325657
NEPC Airlines ☎ 325258
Jodhpur
East West ☎ 37343, 37516
Jagson Airlines ☎ 43813
Kochi (Cochin)
East West ☎ 363542, 369592
Jet Airways ☎ 369582, 666509

ModiLuft ☎ 367772
NEPC Airlines ☎ 367720, 668558
Kozhikode (Calicut)
East West ☎ 361632
Jet Airways ☎ 356518, 722375
NEPC Airlines ☎ 65147
Kullu
Archana Airways ☎ 65630
Jagson Airlines ☎ 65222
UP Air ☎ 65364
Madurai
East West ☎ 31767, 30995
NEPC Airlines ☎ 541382, 24530
Mangalore
East West ☎ 440541, 752650
Jet Airways ☎ 440694, 752709
NEPC Airlines ☎ 455032, 752931
Mumbai (Bombay)
Archana Airways ☎ 284 6535, 617 7442
East West ☎ 643 6678
Jet Airways ☎ 285 5086, 610 2772
ModiLuft ☎ 363 5380
NEPC Airlines ☎ 610 7068, 611 3545
Sahara India ☎ 283 2446, 615 0948
Patna
NEPC Airlines ☎ 221155
Sahara India ☎ 661109, 228307
Porbandar
Gujarat Airways 41889
Pune
East West ☎ 625862, 663881
Jet Airways ☎ 637181, 685591
NEPC Airlines ☎ 637441, 24008
Sahara India ☎ 500327
Rajkot
East West ☎ 40422
NEPC Airlines ☎ 57966, 57870
Srinigar
Modiluft ☎ 452524
Jet Airways ☎ 475511, 33041
Thiruvananthapuram (Trivandrum)
East West ☎ 463569, 541969
Jet Airways ☎ 327635, 451424
NEPC Airlines ☎ 441005
Udaipur
ModiLuft ☎ 526374, 655281
NEPC Airlines ☎ 521513
Vadodara (Baroda)
East West ☎ 452741
Jet Airways ☎ 337051, 555938
NEPC Airlines ☎ 333180, 426001
Varanasi
NEPC Airlines ☎ 46337
UP Air ☎ 43795
Visakhapatnam
East West ☎ 564119
NEPC Airlines ☎ 574151, 559492
(Where two numbers are given, the first is the main
office, the second the airport office)

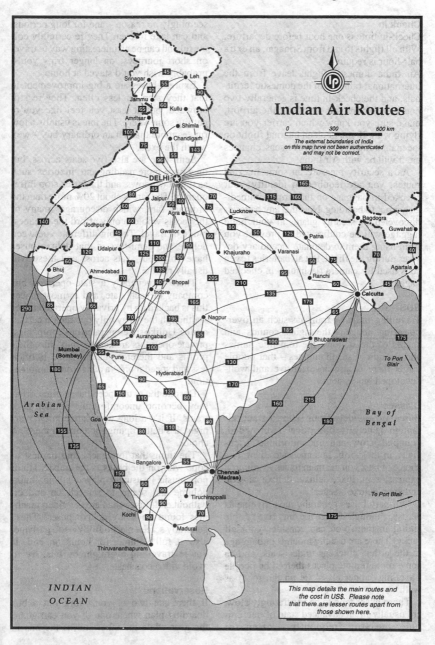

Indian Air Routes

0   300   600 km

The external boundaries of India
on this map have not been authenticated
and may not be correct.

Srinagar
Leh
45
40
55
90
Jammu
65
60
Kullu
Amritsar
100
90
Shimla
75
Chandigarh
143
96
55

DELHI
45
80
Jaipur
50
40
70
115
190
165
160
Lucknow
75
Bagdogra
60
75
Agra
Jodhpur
60
80
Gwalior
50
125
Patna
Guwahati
140
45
110
60
Khajuraho
Varanasi
40
Udaipur
120
125
200
90
50
75
70
Bhuj
60
Ahmedabad
90
135
60
95
Ranchi
60
Agartala
45
70
40
Indore
Bhopal
205
210
135
175
Calcutta
290
85
65
165
65
70
Nagpur
195
185
Aurangabad
55
100
Bhubaneswar
175
Mumbai
(Bombay)
55
55
Pune
100
130
To Port
Blair
180
Hyderabad
90
170
65
190
110
130
80
160
215
Goa
80
110
80
180
Bay of
Bengal
Arabian
Sea
155
135
Bangalore
55
Chennai
(Madras)
150
95
60
60
Tiruchirappalli
To Port Blair
90
Kochi
90
70
175
90
Madurai
Thiruvananthapuram

INDIAN
OCEAN

This map details the main routes and
the cost in US$. Please note
that there are lesser routes apart from
those shown here.

Check In

Check-in time is one hour before departure. With all flights to and from Srinagar, an extra half-hour is required.

Air India domestic flights leave from the international rather than the domestic terminals, and the check-in time is generally two hours, so before you set off for the airport, make sure you know which carrier you are flying with. If you book an internal flight on the main trunk routes from overseas, chances are it will be with Air India.

As a security measure on some internal routes, you are required to identify your checked-in baggage on the tarmac immediately prior to boarding. Note that any batteries discovered by security guards in your hand luggage will be confiscated to prevent you from using them to detonate incendiary devices during the flight. Put all batteries (even cells used for camera flashguns) in checked baggage.

BUS

Travelling India by train has such an overpowering image – the sights, sounds and smells of the stations, the romantic names and exotic old steam engines – that people forget there is also an extensive and well-developed bus system.

Classes

Buses vary widely from state to state, although generally bus travel is crowded, cramped, slow and uncomfortable, especially in the north. In some states there is a choice of buses on the main routes – ordinary, express, semi-luxe, deluxe, deluxe air-con and even deluxe sleeper!

Ordinary buses generally have five seats across, although if there are only five people sitting in them you can consider yourself lucky! There are usually mounds of baggage in the aisles, chickens under seats, and in some more remote places there'll be people travelling 'upper class' (ie on the roof) as well.

These buses tend to be frustratingly slow, are usually in an advanced state of decrepitude and stop frequently – often for

seemingly no reason – and for long periods, and can take forever. They're certainly colourful and can be an interesting way to travel on short journeys; on longer trips you'll probably wish you'd stayed at home.

Express buses are a big improvement in that they stop far less often. They're still crowded, but at least you feel like you're getting somewhere. The fare is usually a few rupees more than on an ordinary bus – well worth the extra.

Semi-luxe are also five seats across, but they have more padding and 'luxuries' such as tinted windows, and the buses stop infrequently. The fare is about 20% more than the ordinary fare, which discourages many of the locals who can only afford the cheapest mode of travel. The big difference between deluxe and semi-luxe is that deluxe buses have only four seats across and these will usually recline.

There is generally a state-operated bus company in each state, and in most places this is backed up by privately operated buses – although they may only operate on certain routes. Unlike state-operated bus companies, private operators are keen to maximise their profits and therefore maintenance is often less and speed more – a dangerous combination.

Despite the extra speed buses often offer, they become uncomfortable sooner than trains. If it's a long trip, particularly overnight, it's better opting for a train if there's a choice.

The thing that foreigners find hardest to cope with on the buses is the music. Hindi pop music is usually played at maximum volume and seems to screech on and on without end. Just as bad are the video machines found on many deluxe buses. These generally screen macho Bollywood garbage, also at full volume, for hours on end. If you're travelling overnight by bus, try to avoid video coaches.

Reservations

If there are two of you, work out a bus boarding plan where one of you can guard the gear while the other storms the bus in search of a seat. The other accepted method is to pass a newspaper or article of clothing through the open window and place it on an empty seat, or ask a passenger to do it for you. Having made your 'reservation' you can then board the bus after things have simmered down. This method rarely fails.

The big advantage of buses over trains is that they go more frequently and getting one involves comparatively little predeparture hassle. You can, however, often make advance reservations for a small additional fee, but this usually only applies to express, semi-luxe and deluxe services. Private buses should always be booked in advance.

At many bus stations there is a separate women's queue. You may not notice this because the relevant sign (where it exists at all) will not be in English and there may not be any women queuing. Usually the same ticket window will handle the male and the female queue, taking turns. What this means is that women can usually go straight to the front of the queue (beside the front of the male queue) and get almost immediate service.

Baggage

Baggage is generally carried for free on the roof, so it's an idea to take a few precautions. Make sure it's tied on properly and that nobody dumps a tin trunk on top of your gear. At times a tarpaulin will be tied across the baggage – make sure it covers your gear adequately.

Theft is sometimes a problem so keep an eye on your bags at chai stops. Having a large, heavy-duty bag into which your pack will fit can be a good idea, not only for bus travel but also for air travel.

If someone carries your bag onto the roof, expect to pay a few rupees for the service.

Toilet Stops

On long-distance bus trips, chai stops can be far too frequent or, conversely, agonisingly infrequent. Long-distance trips can be a real hassle for women travellers – toilet facilities are often hopelessly inadequate.

TRAIN

The Indian Railways system is the world's fourth-largest, with a route length of over 60,000km. Every single day more than 7000 passenger trains run, carrying over 10.5 million passengers and connecting 7100 stations. It's also the world's largest single employer with a shade over 1.6 million employees!

The first step in coming to grips with Indian Railways is to get a timetable. *Trains at a Glance* (Rs 15) is a handy, 100 page guide covering all the main routes and trains. It is usually available at major railway stations, and sometimes on newsstands in the larger cities.

If you can't find *Trains at a Glance*, a regional timetable provides much the same information, including the more local train services and a pink section with timetables for the major mail and express trains (the fast ones) throughout the country. Unfortunately, these are also often unavailable!

There is also the 300 page *Indian Bradshaw* (Rs 50) which covers every train service throughout the country. It's more detailed than most people need and it can be frustratingly difficult to find things, but for serious exploring it's invaluable. Published monthly, it's not widely available but you can usually find it on the bookstalls at major city railway stations. Thomas Cook's *Overseas Timetable* has good train timetables for India, although it's not available in India.

The timetables indicate the km distance between major stations. A table in front shows the fares for distances from one km to 5000km for the various train types. With this information it is very easy to calculate the fare between any two stations. Unless otherwise indicated, the fares quoted in this guide are based on the faster ('express' rather than 'passenger') trains.

A factor to consider with Indian trains is that getting there may not always be half the fun but it is certainly 90% of the experience. Indian rail travel is unlike any other sort of travel in any other place on earth. At times it can be uncomfortable or incredibly frustrating (since the trains are not exactly fast) but an experience it certainly is. Money aside, if you simply want to get from A to B, fly. If getting from A to B is as much a part of

India as what you see at both ends, then take the train.

During and shortly after the monsoon, rail services can be drastically affected by floods and high rivers, particularly in low-lying areas along the Ganges basin or where major rivers reach the sea, such as the coastal region of Andhra Pradesh.

Classes

There are generally two classes – 1st and 2nd – but there are a number of subtle variations on this basic distinction. For a start there is 1st class and 1st-class air-con. The air-con carriages only operate on the major trains and routes. The fare for 1st-class air-con is considerably more than double normal 1st class. A slightly cheaper air-con alternative is the air-con two-tier sleeper, which costs about 25% more than 1st class. These carriages are a lot more common than 1st-class air-con, but are still only found on the major routes.

Between 1st and 2nd class there are two more air-con options: the air-con three-tier sleeper and air-con chair car. The former has three levels of berths rather than two, while the latter, as the name suggests, consists of carriages with aircraft-type layback seats. Once again, these carriages are only found on the major routes, and the latter only on day trains. The cost of air-con three-tier is about 70% of the 1st-class fare; air-con chair is about 55% of the 1st-class fare.

Types

What you want is a mail or express train. What you do not want is a passenger train. No Indian train travels very fast, but at least the mail and express trains keep travelling more of the time. Passenger trains spend a lot of time at a lot of stations and are subject to interminable delays, which quickly becomes very boring unless you have a keen interest in small-town stations. According to figures

---

The Konkan Railway

The British may have scratched a spiderweb of railway lines across the map of India but they left one blank space: the Konkan coast from Mumbai down through Maharashtra to Goa and on through Karnataka to Mangalore, just north of the border with Kerala. Hills, ravines, rivers, floodplains and swamps made railway construction an intimidating prospect and as a result connections down the coast have always been slow going and hard work. The 760-km Konkan Railway, nearing completion, will change all that. The cost, both financial and environmental, has been enormous.

In order to fund the project, the government formed the Konkan Railway Company in 1990. The Ministry of Railways bought 51% of the Rs 6 billion-worth of shares, the rest were divided between the governments of Maharashtra, Goa, Karnataka and Kerala. (Although the line does not actually pass through Kerala the state will benefit from better communications with Mumbai.) The remaining Rs 15 billion was to be raised through market borrowings against the issue of tax-free bonds. However, it has proved rather harder to raise the finance and the project has also been the subject of several political scandals.

The biggest railway project in South Asia this century has been a formidable engineering undertaking with 140 rivers to cross, nearly 2000 bridges in all and over 10% of the total distance made up of either bridges or tunnels.

The line should now be open in both directions as far as the north and south borders of Goa. In Goa itself two tunnels (one near Old Goa, the other in the north) are proving as troublesome as Goa's environmental lobby has been. Those opposing the construction of the line rightly argued that it would cause soil erosion and deforestation, that it passed too close to archaeological monuments, and that it would affect water levels. Damage to the complex system of irrigation between fields has resulted in stagnant pools in which mosquitoes responsible for the spread of Japanese encephalitis now breed. The railway company argues that the line, being a far more direct route, will not only save time but will also slash Rs 2 billion per annum off the national fuel bill.

When the line opens completely, probably in early 1998, the journey time between Mumbai and Goa will be cut from 20 hours to 10 and from Mumbai to Mangalore from 44 hours to 18. It will be the fastest railway line in India, capable of handling trains travelling at speeds of up to 160km/h. ∎

published by Indian Railways, express/mail trains average 47.1km/h, passenger trains 27.2km/h – if you had any ideas about going places in a hurry, you might as well forget it! Passenger trains are usually 2nd class only; 2nd-class fares on passenger trains are less than on a mail or express train over the same route.

Air-con 'superfast' express services operate on certain main routes, and because of tighter scheduling and fewer stops they are much faster. India's top rail services are the *Rajdhani Express* trains, connecting most of the largest cities, and the *Shatabdi Express* trains, which tend to be even faster but don't usually operate overnight services. A separate fare structure applies to both these trains as meals are usually included. The *Rajdhani* and *Shatabdi* services are claimed to average around 130km/h.

Gauge

There are three gauge types in India: broad, metre and narrow, and what you want nearly as much as a mail or express train is broad gauge. In broad gauge the rails are 1.676m apart; metre gauge is, as it says, one metre wide; narrow gauge is either 0.762m (two feet six inches) or 0.610m (two feet).

Broad gauge has a major advantage – it is much faster. It also gives a smoother ride. The carriages are much the same between broad gauge and metre gauge, but on narrow gauge they are much, much narrower and the

accommodation very cramped. In areas where there are no broad-gauge lines it may be worth taking a bus, which will often be faster then the metre-gauge trains. A major engineering undertaking to convert metre-gauge to broad-gauge is now underway.

Life on Board

It's India for real on board the trains. In 2nd class, unreserved travel can be a nightmare since the trains are often hopelessly crowded, and not only with people – Indians seem to be unable to travel without the kitchen sink and everything that goes with it. Combined with the crowds, the noise and the confusion there's the discomfort. Fans and lights have a nasty habit of failing at prolonged stops, just when there's no air moving through the carriage, and toilets can get more than a little rough towards the end of a long journey.

Worst of all are the stops. Trains seem to stop often, interminably and for no apparent reason. Often it's because somebody has pulled the emergency stop cable because they are close to home – well, so it's said; some people deny this. Still, it's all part of life on the rails and part of the railway experience.

In 2nd-class reserved it's a great deal better since, in theory, only four people share each bench, but there's inevitably the fifth, and sometimes even the sixth, person who gets the others to bunch up so they can get at

Indian Rail Fares						
Distance (km)	*1st class (air-con)*	*1st class*	*Air-con chair*	*2nd-class express, sleepers*	*2nd-class express, seat*	*2nd-class passenger*
50	Rs 205	Rs 92	Rs 72	Rs 62	Rs 17	Rs 9
100	Rs 329	Rs 139	Rs 85	Rs 62	Rs 26	Rs 14
200	Rs 495	Rs 223	Rs 137	Rs 62	Rs 49	Rs 26
300	Rs 693	Rs 310	Rs 191	Rs 90	Rs 68	Rs 36
400	Rs 887	Rs 395	Rs 233	Rs 113	Rs 85	Rs 43
500	Rs 1048	Rs 464	Rs 275	Rs 135	Rs 102	Rs 50
1000	Rs 1713	Rs 756	Rs 420	Rs 219	Rs 166	Rs 72
1500	Rs 2316	Rs 1014	Rs 561	Rs 272	Rs 207	Rs 89
2000	Rs 2878	Rs 1259	Rs 681	Rs 309	Rs 235	Rs 106

least part of their bum on the seat. This normally doesn't happen at night or in 1st class, where there are either two or four people to a compartment and the compartment doors are lockable.

Costs

Fares operate on a distance basis. The timetables indicate the distance in km between the stations and from this it is simple to calculate the cost between any two stations. If you have a ticket for at least 400km you can break your journey at the rate of one day per 200km so long as you travel at least 300km on the first sector. This can save a lot of hassle buying tickets and also, of course, results in a small saving.

The Indian Rail Fares table in this section indicates fares for set distances.

Reservations

The cost of reservations is nominal – it's the time it takes which hurts, although even this is generally getting better as computerised reservation becomes more widespread.

In Delhi, Mumbai, Calcutta and Chennai there are special tourist booking facilities at the main booking offices. These are for any foreign tourists and they make life much easier. The people at these offices are generally very knowledgeable (although you will be surprised how often you find other railway booking clerks who really know their stuff). They will often give you excellent advice

---

Running out of Steam

If you imagined that rail travel in India meant riding the rails behind a puffing steam train you'll be disappointed. Until the late 1980s, however, there were as many as 3000 steam locos still running. In 1993 a decision was taken to speed up considerably the gradual modernisation programme that had been going on for years, with the result that there are now less than 200 steam locos left in service, and how many of these will still be running by the end of the year is anybody's guess. There is a massive broad-gauge electrification programme going on which along with the well publicised broad gauging of most of the metre gauge, has allowed the cascading of diesels to lesser routes.

As far as peninsular India is concerned, steam is extinct, with the exception of the Sunday service on the Ooty line, when that is running. The situation can change almost overnight, but the latest information I have gives the situation as three narrow gauge lines still steam operated, and three widely separated and unconnected pockets of metre gauge steam.

Broad Gauge

Broad gauge steam is dead, apart from a couple of preserved locos working an odd turn on 'The Palace on Wheels' tourist charter train. The last working broad-gauge locos were a few of the light axle load WL class based at Firozpur in the Punjab. Largely by chance I was fortunate enough to see them in operation in 1995 literally two days before the last one ran. They were in the most terrible condition, their life having been extended by almost one year due to the woeful unreliability of the replacement Diesel Multiple Units.

Metre Gauge

Assam Quite a bit of steam working remains east of Guwahati, though with conversion of the main line to broad gauge well under way it is unclear how far into 1997 this will continue.
Bihar The lines between the Ganges and Nepal have been some of the last major concentrations of steam working, even including a couple of expresses. However, massive conversion to broad gauge in the last year has decimated this and only the lines from Saharsa to Forbesganj and Mansi seem likely to still be steam worked by 1997.
Rajasthan, Gujarat & Madhya Pradesh The Western Railway is surprisingly providing the largest concentration of steam working in an area bounded by Chittorgarh, Rajkot, Ahmedabad and Mhow, with Ahmedabad being the last major city to see steam working, including the last steam hauled expresses – train Nos 9643/4 to and from Udaipur. It is reported that the railway unions here have so far resisted dieselisation in order to protect jobs, but despite the fact that major overhauls are still being carried out on locos, failure is common and timekeeping is appalling. It is therefore uncertain how long the authorities can let the current situation continue, and random diesel substitution for failed steam engines is already quite common. However, the scenic Chittorgarh-Udaipur-Ahmedabad line does

and suggest connections and routes which can save you a lot of time and effort.

At other major stations with computerised reservation offices, such as Ahmedabad and Jaipur, one ticket window will deal with foreign tourists and other minorities (such as 'Freedom Fighters'!). These windows are generally queue-free, so check to see if one exists.

Reservations can be made up to six months in advance and the further in advance you make them the better. Your reservation ticket will indicate which carriage and berth you have, and when the train arrives you will find a sheet of paper fixed to each carriage listing passenger names beside their appropriate berth number. Usually this information is also posted on notice boards on the platform. It is Indian rail efficiency at its best.

As at many bus stations, there are separate women's queues, usually with a sign saying 'Ladies' Queue'. Usually the same ticket window handles the male and female queue, taking one at a time. This means that women can go to the front of the queue, next to the first male at the window, and get almost immediate service.

Reservation costs are Rs 30 in air-con 1st class, Rs 20 in 1st class and air-con chair class, Rs 15 in a 2nd-class three-tier sleeper, and Rs 10 in 2nd-class sitting. There are very rarely any 2nd-class sitting compartments with reservations. There are also some superfast express trains that require a supplementary charge.

If the train you want is fully booked, it's often possible to get an RAC (Reservation

---

give the casual tourist the best chance of getting a ride behind steam, though make sure you are not on a tight schedule at the far end. The daytime passenger trains (Nos 85/6) run at a most relaxing pace through beautiful countryside and are recommended.

Narrow Gauge
Pulgaon to Arvi This 762 mm gauge, 35 km line off the main Mumbai to Nagpur line in central Madhya Pradesh is operated by little ZP Pacifics. It is operated by Central Railway but apparently may be owned by a UK company. It is not known whether there are any plans for dieselisation.
Bankura to Rainagar Again 762 mm, this time running for 97 km through rural West Bengal, north west of Calcutta. Bankura is the district capital not far from the temple city of Bishnupur (Vishnupur), but Rainagar is a station set in the middle of fields with not a house in sight and the nearest road 500m away. There is only one train a day leaving Bankura at 5.30 am (give or take an hour) and if you want to see what Indian rail travel used to be like give it a try.

I took the overnight passenger train from Calcutta arriving in Bankura at about 4 am. By the time we had found the narrow gauge platform the three coaches were already packed. It was still dark and with no lights on the train (and at that point no engine), we were wondering what to do next when I spotted the locked guard's compartment. He spoke a little English and although he considered us mad to want to travel on his train when there were air-conditioned expresses to our ultimate destination of Barddhaman (bus from Rainagar), we were given VIP treatment throughout the day, getting introduced to every railway official along the way, offered numerous cups of chai, and getting to drive the engine. All in all a wonderful day and in many ways the highlight of a three week trip. The engines are again miniature Pacifics, this time CC class built in Glasgow around 1906. Again the line is not owned by Indian Railways and although there may be longterm plans to broad gauge it, steam seems likely to continue for some time yet.
New Jalpaiguri to Darjeeling Only 610 mm gauge with tiny blue engines, this 90 km mountain railway is a must for any enthusiast, if it is running! The problem is that each monsoon part of the trackbed seems to get washed away, and as all freight and most of the passenger traffic now goes by road, the line has no strategic significance, so it takes months before repairs are completed. It is usually the bottom section that gets washed out, so if there is no sign of a train at New Jalpaiguri, take a taxi or bus to Kurseong and you'll probably find the train there to take you the rest of the way. Probably India's most famous railway, it is a fantastic though very slow journey as the line climbs, switches back on itself and criss-crosses the road on hairpin bends. Apparently it is to stay steam worked until at least the end of the century.

Malcolm Moscrop (UK)

Against Cancellation) ticket. This entitles you to board the train and have seating accommodation. Once the train is moving, the TTE (Travelling Ticket Examiner) will find a berth for you, but it may take an hour or more. This is different from a wait-listed ticket, which does not give you the right to actually board the train (should you be so cheeky you can be 'detrained and fined'). The hassle with RAC tickets is that you will probably get split up if there are two or more of you.

If you've been unable to get a reservation, it's worth getting on the train in any reserved carriage. Although there's the risk of a small fine for 'ticketless travel', most TTEs are sympathetic. If there is a spare berth/seat they'll allot you one, and charge the normal fare plus reservation fee. If all the berths/seats are already reserved you'll simply be banished to the crush and confusion in the unreserved carriages. This trick only works well for day travel. At night sleepers are generally booked out well in advance so if you can't get one (or an RAC ticket), then sitting up in 2nd class is your only choice.

If you plan your trip well ahead, you can avoid all the hassles by booking in advance from abroad. A good Indian travel agent will book and obtain tickets in advance and have them ready for you on arrival. As an alternative to buying tickets as you go along, it's possible to buy a ticket from A to Z with all the stops along the way prebooked. It might take a bit of time sitting down and working it out at the start, but if your time is limited and you can fix your schedule rigidly, this can be a good way to go.

Refunds

Booked tickets are refundable but cancellation fees apply. If you present the ticket more than one day in advance, a fee of Rs 10 to Rs 50 applies, depending on the class. Up to four hours before you lose 25% of the ticket value; within four hours before departure and up to three to 12 hours after departure (depending on the distance of the ticketed journey) you lose 50%. Any later than that and you can keep the ticket as a souvenir.

Tickets for unreserved travel can be refunded up to three hours after the departure of the train, and the only penalty is a Rs 10 per passenger fee.

When refunding your ticket, you are officially entitled to go straight to the head of the queue (if there isn't a dedicated window for refunds), the rationale being that the spot you are surrendering may be just the one required by the next person in the queue.

Sleepers

There are 2nd-class and 1st-class sleepers, although by western standards even 1st class is not luxurious. Bedding is available, but only on certain 1st class and air-con two-tier services, and then only if arranged when booking your ticket. First-class sleepers are generally private compartments with two or four berths in them, sometimes with a toilet as well. Usually the sleeping berths fold up to make a sitting compartment during the day. First-class air-con sleepers are more luxurious, and much more expensive, than regular 1st-class sleepers.

Second-class sleepers are known as three-tier. They are arranged in doorless sections each of six berths. During the day the middle berth is lowered to make seats for six or eight. At night they are folded into position, everybody has to bed down at the same time, and a TTE ensures that nobody without a reservation gets into the carriage. Broad-gauge, three-tier sleeping carriages also have a row of narrow two-tier (upper and lower) berths along one side. These are not only narrower than the 'inside' berths, but are about 20 cm shorter, so that for the average person stretching right out is not possible. When reserving 2nd-class berths, always write 'inside' on the 'Accommodation Preference' section of the booking form. Sleeping berths are only available between 9 pm and 6 am.

For any sleeper reservation you should try to book at least several days ahead. There is usually a board in each station indicating what is available or how long before the next free berth/seat comes up on the various routes. At the major city stations this is usually computerised and TV screens give a continuous read-out. Once you've selected a particular train and date, you must fill in a reservation form. Do this before you get to the front of the queue. The forms are usually found in boxes around the reservation hall. The demand for 1st-class sleepers is generally far less than for 2nd class.

At most major stations there's usually a separate section or counter(s) in the booking hall (often called 'Tourist Cell'!) which deals with the tourist quota. Only foreigners and nonresident Indians are allowed to use this facility. Here you can make your reservations in relative comfort away from the madding crowds *but* you must pay in foreign currency (cash or travellers cheques in US dollars or pounds sterling only) or with rupees backed up by exchange certificates, and any change will be given in rupees.

Lastly, when deciding which train to take along any route, you may come up against that major source of bewilderment – the Indian custom of naming a train without indicating where it goes. On the timetable or state-of-reservation board at a station you could, for example, see the *Brindavan Express* or the *Cholan Express* etc. But where do they go to? It might be the train you want, but it might not. This is where your *Trains at a Glance* or *Indian Bradshaw* comes in. If you don't have one, you'll have to ask – and that's going to soak up time. Tourist offices can usually help by suggesting the best trains but there isn't always a tourist office. It's something you'll just have to come to terms with.

Getting a Space Despite Everything

If you want a sleeper and there are none left then it's time to try and break into the quotas. Ask the stationmaster (often a helpful man who speaks English) if there is a tourist quota, station quota or a VIP quota. The latter is often a good last bet because VIPs rarely turn up to use their quotas.

If all that fails then you're going to be travelling unreserved and that can be no fun at all. To ease the pain get yourself some expert help. For, say, Rs 10 baksheesh you can get a porter who will absolutely ensure you get a seat if it's humanly possible. If it's

a train starting from your station, the key to success is to be on the train before it arrives at the departure platform. Your porter will do just that, so when it rolls up you simply stroll on board and take the seat he has warmed for you. If it's a through train then it can be a real free-for-all, and you can be certain he'll be better at it than you are – he'll also not be encumbered with baggage or backpacks.

Women can ask about the Ladies' Compartments which many trains have and which are often a refuge from the crowds in other compartments.

Left Luggage

Most stations have a left luggage facility (quaintly called a cloak room) where backpacks can be left for Rs 2 per day. This is a very useful facility if you're visiting (but not staying in) a town, or if you want to find a place to stay, unencumbered by gear. The regulations state that any luggage left in a cloak room must be locked, although this is not strictly enforced.

Special Trains

A special 'Palace on Wheels' makes a regular circuit around Rajasthan – you not only travel by train, you stay in the 'fit for a maharaja' carriages. See the Rajasthan chapter for more details.

The Royal Orient Express is a similar luxury service that operates between Delhi and Ahmedabad via Rajasthan.

The English organisation, Butterfield's Indian Railway Tours, operates regular train tours of India using a special carriage in which you travel, eat and sleep. The carriage is hooked on to regular trains and is left on the sidings of various towns you visit. The accommodation facilities are basic but you cover a lot of India, and using the railway in this way brings you into much closer contact with people than you'd get on a usual package tour staying in upmarket hotels. Tours from 16 to 29 days are available, and prices start from around UK£900. For more information contact Butterfield's Railway Tours (☎ (01262) 470230) Burton Fleming, Driffield, East Yorks YO25 0PQ, UK. Butterfield's can also be contacted through the Madras Hotel, Connaught Circus, Delhi.

Indrail Passes

Indrail passes permit unlimited travel on Indian trains for the period of their validity, but they are expensive and not good value. To get the full value out of any of the passes you need to travel around 300km per day; with the speed of Indian trains that's at least six hours travelling!

Although the pass covers the cost of reservations, it doesn't get you to the front of the queue, so is of little help there, and you join in the waitlist like everybody else if the train is fully booked. The only occasion when it's going to save you time is if you want to travel unreserved on a train, when you can simply hop on without queuing for a ticket. As these journeys are likely to be far fewer and shorter than those when you want to have a reserved berth, it's not much of a gain.

The average visitor to India might cover around 3000km in a month by rail. An air-con Indrail Pass for this would cost US$550; to buy the tickets as you go along would cost around US$100 to US$160, depending on the number and length of the journeys; even if you did 6000km, you still wouldn't come close to getting your money's worth. It's the same story with the other class passes: a 2nd class, one month pass costs US$125, the individual tickets for 3000km of travel would cost around US$12 to US$25. See the Indian Rail Fares table for the cost of Indrail passes.

Children aged five to 12 years pay half-fare. Indrail passes can be bought overseas through some travel agents or in India at certain major railway offices. Payment in India can be made only in either US dollars or pounds sterling, cash or travellers cheques, or in rupees backed up with exchange certificates. Second-class passes are not available outside India. Indrail passes cover all reservation and berth costs at night. They

---

Palace on Wheels

The RTDC *Palace on Wheels* is a special tourist train service which operates weekly tours of Rajasthan, departing from Delhi every Wednesday from September to April. The itinerary takes in Jaipur, Chittorgarh, Udaipur, Ranthambhore National Park, Jaisalmer, Jodhpur, Bharatpur and Agra. It's a hell of a lot of ground to cover in a week, but most of the travelling is done at night. In 1995 the carriages were converted to run on broad gauge, but since Udaipur is still metre gauge, the three hour journey between Chittorgarh and Udaipur is currently made by bus.

Originally, this train used carriages which once belonged to various maharajas, but these became so ancient that newer carriages were refurbished to look like the originals. They were also fitted with air-conditioning. The result is a very luxurious mobile hotel, and it can be a memorable way to travel if you have limited time and limitless resources.

The cost includes tours, entry fees, accommodation on the train plus all meals. Rates per person per day are US$240 for triple occupancy, US$300 for double occupancy and US$425 for single occupancy. Children between five and 12 years of age are charged half fare. It's a very popular service and bookings must be made in advance at the RTDC Tourist Reception Centre, Bikaner House, Pandara Rd, New Delhi (☎ (011) 338 1884; fax 338 2823), or at the Tourist Reception Centre, Office Annexe, RTDC Hotel Swagatam, Jaipur (☎ (0141) 319531; fax 316045). ■

SANJAY SINGH BADNOR

cannot be extended if you wish to keep on travelling. The main offices in India which handle Indrail passes are:

Calcutta
> Railway Tourist Guide, Eastern Railway, Fairlie Place
> Central Reservation Office, South-Eastern Railway, Esplanade Mansion

Chennai
> Central Reservation Office, Southern Railway, Chennai Central

Delhi
> Railway Tourist Guide, New Delhi Railway Station

Mumbai
> Railway Tourist Guide, Western Railway, Churchgate
> Railway Tourist Guide, Central Railway, Victoria Terminus

Indrail Pass Prices in US$

Days	Air-Con	1st Class	2nd Class
7	300	150	80
15	370	185	90
21	440	220	100
30	550	275	125
60	800	400	185
90	1060	530	235

CAR

Few people bring their own vehicles to India. If you do decide to bring a car or motorcycle to India it must be brought in under a carnet, a customs document guaranteeing its removal at the end of your stay. Failing to do so will be very expensive.

Renting

Self-drive car rental in India is not widespread, but it is possible. Both Budget and Hertz maintain offices in the major cities. Given India's crazy driving conditions it's far better, and much more straightforward, to hire a car and driver. By western standards the cost is quite low, certainly cheaper than a rent-a-car (without driver) in the west. Almost any local taxi will quite happily set off on a long-distance trip in India. Enquiring at a taxi rank is the easiest way to find a car

– you can also ask your hotel to book one for you, although this will cost slightly more.

Trips are either 'one-way', in which case they cost around Rs 8 per km, or a 'running trip', which costs around Rs 4 per km. This is because the one-way fare is set on the basis of returning empty to the starting point. A running trip means a minimum of 250km a day, so if you take a car for four days it's going to cost at least Rs 4000 (1000km at Rs 4 per km). If you're going to drive 250km from A to B on day one, spend two days in B, then drive 250km back to A on day four, it's exactly the same cost to take a taxi each way as to take one taxi and have the driver wait for you for two days. And they will wait – your driver will stretch himself out on the back seat and be ready to go when you turn up for the return trip. An air-con car will cost about twice as much as a non air-con vehicle.

Long-distance car hire with driver is becoming an increasingly popular way of getting around parts of India. Spread amongst say four people, it's not overly expensive and you have the flexibility to go where you want when you want.

Self-drive in a small car (Maruti-Suzuki) costs from around Rs 900 per 24 hours (150km minimum) plus Rs 4 per extra km. Fuel is extra, and a deposit of Rs 3000 will be refunded if there's no damage whatsoever to the car – a scratch constitutes 'damage'.

Buying

Buying a car is expensive and not worth the effort unless you intend to stay for months.

Road Conditions

Because of the extreme congestion in the cities and the narrow bumpy roads in the country, driving is often a slow, stop-start process – hard on you, the car and fuel economy. Service is so-so in India, parts and tyres not always easy to obtain, though there are plenty of puncture-repair places. All in all driving is no great pleasure except in rural areas where there's little traffic.

Fuel

Petrol is expensive relative to the west and

when compared to the cost of living in India – around Rs 20 per litre – but diesel is much cheaper at around Rs 9 per litre. Petrol is readily available in all larger towns and along main roads, so there is no need to carry spare fuel. You can now get unleaded petrol in Delhi, Mumbai, Calcutta and Chennai.

MOTORCYCLE

Travelling around India by motorcycle has become increasingly popular in recent years, and it certainly has its attractions – motoring along the backroads through small un-touristed villages, picnics in the wilds, the freedom to go when and where you like – making it the ideal way to get to grips with the vastness that is India.

You'll still get a sore bum, you'll have difficult and frustrating conversations and you'll get fed up with asking directions, receiving misleading answers, and getting lost,

but you'll also have adventures not available to the visitor who relies on public transport.

This section is based largely on information originally contributed by intrepid Britons Ken Twyford and Gerald Smewing, with updates from Jim & Lucy Amos and Bill Keightley.

What to Bring

An International Driving Licence is not mandatory, but is handy to have.

Helmets (required in the main cities) should definitely be brought with you. Although Indian helmets are cheap (Rs 500 to Rs 1000), it is often hard to find one that fits well, and the quality is rather suspect. You are not required by law to wear a helmet, but you'd be silly not to. If required, leathers, gloves, boots, waterproofs and other protective gear should also be brought from your home country.

Road Safety

In India there are 155 road deaths daily – 70,000 in the last year – which is an astonishing total in relation to the number of vehicles on the road. In the USA, for instance, there are 43,000 road fatalities per year, but it also has more than 20 times the number of vehicles.

The reasons for the high death rate in India are numerous and many of them fairly obvious – starting with the congestion on the roads and the equal congestion in vehicles. When a bus runs off the road there are plenty of people stuffed inside to get injured, and it's unlikely too many of them will be able to escape in a hurry. One newspaper article stated that 'most accidents are caused by brake failure or the steering wheel getting free'!

Many of those killed are pedestrians involved in hit-and-run accidents. The propensity to disappear after the incident is not wholly surprising – lynch mobs can assemble remarkably quickly, even when the driver is not at fault!

Most accidents are caused by trucks, for on Indian roads might is right and trucks are the biggest, heaviest and mightiest. You either get out of their way or get run down. As with so many Indian vehicles they're likely to be grossly overloaded and not in the best of condition. Trucks are actually licensed and taxed to carry a load 25% more than the maximum recommended by the manufacturer. It's staggering to see the number of truck wrecks by the sides of the national highways, and these aren't old accidents, but ones which have obviously happened in the last 24 hours or so – if they haven't been killed, quite often the driver and crew will be sitting around, wondering what to do next.

The karma theory of driving also helps to push up the statistics – it's not so much the vehicle which collides with you as the events of your previous life which caused the accident.

If you are driving yourself, you need to be extremely vigilant at all times. At night there are unilluminated cars and ox carts, and in the daytime there are fearless bicycle riders and hordes of pedestrians. Day and night there are the crazy truck drivers to contend with. Indeed, at night, it's best to avoid driving at all along any major trunk route unless you're prepared to get off the road completely every time a truck is coming in the opposite direction! The other thing you have to contend with at night is the eccentric way in which headlights are used – a combination of full beam and totally off (dipped beams are virtually unheard of). A loud horn definitely helps since the normal driving technique is to put your hand firmly on the horn, close your eyes and plough through regardless. Vehicles always have the right of way over pedestrians and bigger vehicles always have the right of way over smaller ones. ■

A few small bags will be a lot easier to carry than one large rucksack. A tent and sleeping bag are handy where accommodation is scarce.

Renting

Motorcycles can be rented from companies in several places in India (Delhi and Goa, for example) for a negotiable price, including insurance. Costs are around Rs 7000 per month or Rs 200 to Rs 300 per day. You'll have to leave a deposit (returnable) of about US$500.

Buying & Selling

India does not have used-vehicle dealers, motorcycle magazines or weekend newspapers with pages of motorcycle classified advertisements. To purchase a secondhand machine one simply needs to enquire. A good place to start is with mechanics. They are likely to know somebody who is selling a bike. In Delhi the area around Hari Singh Nalwa St in Karol Bagh is full of places buying, selling and renting motorcycles. One place that has been recommended by several

Indian Vehicles

In 1951 the number of motorised vehicles on India's roads totalled 300,000. The figure had climbed to 5.4 million by 1981 and shot to 26.5 million in.1996. India's metropolitan vehicle population has tripled since 1990 with dire results for the environment.

In the closed market following Independence the Indian motorist had to choose between a few license-built cast-offs from the west. When the Morris Oxford was replaced by a newer model in the UK in the mid 1950s, production shifted to Calcutta, where it has continued ever since as the Hindustan Ambassador. Variety was added in the early 1960s with an old version of the Fiat 1100D, renamed the Pal Padmini. Later the Fiat 124 was introduced. For a while the Triumph Herald was produced here, in a five-door version known as the Standard Gazel. Hindustan bought the rights to a 1970s Vauxhall which has now become the Hindustan Contessa. Sipani Autos had a brief fling with Reliant, producing a four-wheel version of the fibreglass three-wheel Robin. They had similarly unsuccessful joint ventures with the Rover 2000 and the Austin Montego estate.

The big story, however, is the Maruti, a locally assembled Japanese Suzuki minicar, minivan and 4WD, put together in the abortive Sanjay Gandhi 'people's car' factory near Delhi. They've swept the country and you now see them everywhere in surprisingly large numbers.

With this joint venture the floodgates opened and new arrivals on the Indian roads include the Ford Escort (complete with wood-effect dash and touted as a luxury vehicle), the Peugeot 309, Fiat Uno, Daewoo Cielo, Opel Astra, and the Mercedes 220 – all assembled in India. Soon to follow are Honda and Skoda.

Marutis start at around Rs 201,000 new. Ambassadors (now with safety belts!) start from around Rs 330,000. More expensive versions now have Isuzu engines and five-speed gearboxes. A Mercedes 220 will set you back Rs 2,250,436.

India's truck and bus industry is quite well developed, with companies like Tata and Ashok Leyland turning out sturdy trucks which you see all over India, and also in a number of other countries (Britain now imports Tata pickups). Here too there has been a Japanese onslaught; modern Japanese trucks have appeared. All Japanese vehicle builders in India must have at least 50% Indian ownership. The name thus becomes an Indo-Japanese hybrid, so you get Maruti-Suzuki, Hindustan-Isuzu, Allwyn-Nissan, Swaraj-Mazda and Honda-Kinetic.

The active motorcycle and motor scooter industry has also experienced rapid growth. The motorcycles include the splendid Enfield India – a replica of the old British single-cylinder 350cc Royal Enfield Bullet of the 1950s. Enthusiasts for the old British singles will be delighted to see these modern-day vintage bikes still being made. Purists will be horrified by the diesel version. Motor scooters include Indian versions of both the Italian Lambretta and the Vespa. When production ceased in Italy, India bought the manufacturing plant from them lock, stock and barrel.

There is a variety of mopeds but the assembly of small Honda, Suzuki and Yamaha motorcycles is widespread and they are becoming as familiar a sight on the roads of India as in South-East Asia. The arrival of Japanese manufacturing companies in India has provided some insightful culture clashes. A *Time* magazine article some years ago noted that Honda had found it impossible to instil the Japanese-style team spirit at the Hero-Honda plant near Delhi. Workers didn't mind rubbing shoulders with the management – but not with the Dalits (untouchables), please. And despite having quality inspectors, unknown in Japanese plants where everybody is a quality inspector, the rejection rate at the end of the assembly line was 30% against 3% in Japan. ■

travellers is Inder Motors (☎ (011) 572 5879), 1744/55 Hari Singh Nalwa St.

To buy a new bike, you'll have to have a local address and be a resident foreign national. However, unless the dealer you are buying from is totally devoid of imagination and contacts, this presents few problems. When buying secondhand, all you need to do is give an address.

New bikes are generally purchased through a showroom. When buying secondhand it is best to engage the services of an 'auto consultant'. These people act as go-betweens to bring buyers and sellers together. They will usually be able to show you a number of machines to suit your price bracket. These agents can be found by enquiring, or may sometimes advertise on their shop fronts.

For around Rs 500 (which usually covers a bribe to officials) they will help you get the papers through the bureaucracy. Without their help this could take a couple of weeks.

The overall appearance of the bike doesn't seem to affect the price greatly. Dents and scratches don't reduce the cost much, and added extras don't increase it by much.

When the time comes to sell the bike, don't appear too anxious to get rid of it and don't hang around in one town too long as word gets around the auto consultants and the offers will get smaller as the days go by. If you get a reasonable offer, grab it. Regardless of which bike it is, you'll be told it's the 'least popular in India' and other such tales.

Ownership Papers A needless hint perhaps, but do not part with your money until you have the ownership papers, receipt and affidavit signed by a magistrate authorising the owner (as recorded in the ownership papers) to sell the machine. Not to mention the keys to the bike and the bike itself!

Each state has a different set of ownership transfer formalities. Get assistance from the

---

Getting There is Half the Fun

A lot of travel in India can be indescribably dull, boring and uncomfortable. Trains take forever, buses fall apart and shake your fillings loose, even Indian Airlines sometimes manages to make your delay time far longer than your flying time.

Despite the hassles there are a fair number of trips where getting there is definitely half the fun. Trains, of course, are the key to Indian travel. The narrow-gauge line to Darjeeling, which winds back and forth on its long climb up to the hill station, is the last remaining steam-powered line and the trip up (or down) is half the fun of visiting Darjeeling. Other 'toy trains' include the run up to Matheran, just a couple of hours outside Mumbai; the 'rack train' which makes the climb to Ooty from Mettupalayam in Tamil Nadu; and the narrow-gauge line which connects the hill station of Shimla (Himachal Pradesh) with Kalka on the plains.

Then there is the delightful backwater trip through the waterways of Kerala between Kollam (Quilon) and Alappuzha (Alleppey) – not only is the trip fascinating, it's absurdly cheap.

Indian buses are generally a refined form of torture but the two-day trip between Manali in Himachal Pradesh and Leh in Ladakh is too good to miss. The bus route from Darjeeling or Kalimpong to Gangtok in Sikkim is pretty good too, as is the climb up to Kodaikanal from Madurai in Tamil Nadu. Finally, flying into Leh you cross the full width (and height!) of the Himalaya – there could hardly be a more spectacular flight in the world.

agent you're buying the machine through or from one of the many 'attorneys' hanging around under tin roofs by the Motor Vehicles Office. They will charge you a fee of up to Rs 300, which will consist largely of a bribe to expedite matters.

Alternatively you could go to one of the many typing clerk services and request them to type out the necessary forms, handling the matter cheaply yourself – but with no guarantee of a quick result.

Check that your name has been recorded in the ownership book and stamped and signed by the department head. If you intend to sell your motorcycle in another state then you will need a 'No Objections Certificate'. This confirms your ownership and is issued by the Motor Vehicles Department in the state of purchase, so get it immediately when transferring ownership papers to your name. The standard form can be typed up for a few rupees, or more speedily and expensively through one of the many attorneys.

Insurance & Tax As in most countries it is compulsory to have third-party insurance. The New India Assurance Company or the National Insurance Company are just two of a number of companies who can provide it. The cost for fully comprehensive insurance is around Rs 1000 for 12 months, and this also covers you in Nepal.

Road tax is paid when the bike is bought new. This is valid for the life of the machine and is transferred to the new owner when the bike changes hands.

Which Bike?
The big decision to make is whether to buy new or secondhand. Obviously cost is the main factor, but remember that with a new bike you are less likely to get ripped off as the price is fixed, the cost will include free servicing and you know it will be reliable. Old bikes are obviously cheaper and you don't have to be a registered resident foreign national, but you are far more open to getting ripped off, either by paying too much or by getting a dud bike.

Everyone is likely to have their own preferences, and so there is no one bike which suits everybody. However, here is a rundown of what's readily available.

Mopeds These come with or without gears. As they are only 50cc capacity, they are really only useful around towns or for short distances.

Scooters There are the older design Bajaj and Vespa scooters, or the more modern Japanese designs by Honda-Kinetic and others. The older ones are 150cc while the Honda is 100cc and has no gears.

Several readers have written in praise of this form of transport. Scooters are economical to buy and run, are easy to ride, have a good resale value, and most have built-in lockable storage. The 150cc Bajaj Cheetak costs Rs 28,400, and has plenty of power and acceleration for Indian road conditions. It's reliable as long as the plug is kept clean; newer models have electronic ignition so there's no need to adjust the points.

A big plus for the scooter is the spare tire. I've experienced a puncture nearly every 1500km and believe me, pushing a dead motorcycle through the hot Indian sun is a pain. Wheel removal on a scooter is a breeze – five nuts and that's it. No dirty chains to screw around with, no broken spokes to replace. Another inherent plus of this machine is the front end, which protects the rider from numerous surprise projections as well as mud and other flying excretions. Let someone else ride deafening Enfields with their greasy temperamental chains, no spare tire and gas tank between their legs. I'll take a 'bulletproof' scooter any day!

Bill Keightley (USA)

100cc Motorcycles This is the area with the greatest choice. The four main Japanese companies – Honda, Suzuki, Kawasaki and Yamaha – all have 100cc, two-stroke machines, while Honda and Kawasaki also have four-stroke models.

There's little to differentiate between these bikes; all are lightweight, easy to ride, very economical and reliable, with good resale value. They are suitable for intercity travel on reasonable roads, but they should not be laden down with too much gear. Spares and servicing are readily available. The cost of a new bike of this type is about Rs 35,000 to Rs 40,000.

If you're buying secondhand avoid the Rajdoot 175 XLT, based on a very old Polish model, and the Enfield Fury which has a poor gearbox, spares that are hard to come by and a low resale value.

Bigger Bikes The Enfield Bullet is the classic machine and is the one most favoured among foreigners. Attractions are the traditional design, thumping engine sound, and the price, which is not much more than the new 100cc Japanese bikes. It's a wonderfully durable bike, easy to maintain and economical to run, but mechanically they're a bit hit and miss, largely because of poorly engineered parts and inferior materials – valves and tappets are the main problem areas. Another drawback is the lack of an effective front brake – the small drum brake is a joke, totally inadequate for what is quite a heavy machine. The Bullet is also available in a 500cc single-cylinder version. It has a functional front brake and 12V electrics which are superior to the 350's 6V. If you opt for a 350cc, consider paying the Rs 5000 extra to have the 500cc front wheel fitted.

If you are buying a new Enfield with the intention of shipping it back home, it's definitely worth opting for the 500cc as it has features – such as folding rear foot-rest and longer exhaust pipe – which most other countries require. The emission control regulations in some places, such as California, are so strict that there is no way these bikes would be legal. You may be able to get around this by buying an older bike, as the regulations often only apply to new machines. Make sure you check all this out before you go lashing out on a new Enfield, only to find it unregisterable at home. The price is around Rs 58,000, or Rs 65,000 for the 500cc model. There's a hopelessly underpowered diesel version for Rs 66,000.

The Yezdi 250 Classic (or Monarch/Deluxe) is a cheap and basic bike. It's a rugged machine, and one which you often see in rural areas.

The Rajdoot 350 is an imported Yamaha 350cc. It's well engineered, fast and has good brakes. Disadvantages are that it's relatively uneconomical to run, and spares are hard to come by. These bikes are also showing their age badly as they haven't been made for some years now. They cost around Rs 12,000.

If you've Rs 530,000 to spare, the BMW F650 is now available in India.

Some Indian Rules of the Road

Drive on the Left Theoretically vehicles keep to the left in India – as in Japan, Britain or Australia. In practice most vehicles keep to the middle of the road on the basis that there are fewer potholes in the middle than on the sides. When any other vehicle is encountered the lesser vehicle should cower to the side. Misunderstandings as to status can have unfortunate consequences.

Overtaking In India it is not necessary to ascertain that there is space to complete the overtaking manoeuvre before pulling out. Overtaking can be attempted on blind corners, on the way up steep hills or in the face of oncoming traffic. Smaller vehicles unexpectedly encountered in mid-manoeuvre can be expected to swerve apologetically out of the way. If a larger vehicle is encountered it is to be hoped that the overtakee will slow, pull off or otherwise make room for the overtaker.

Use of Horn Although vehicles can be driven with bald tyres or nonexistent brakes, it is imperative that the horn be in superb working order. Surveys during the research for the last edition revealed that the average driver uses the horn 10 to 20 times per km, so a 100km trip can involve 2000 blasts of the horn. In any case the horn should be checked for its continued loud operation at least every 100m. Signs prohibiting use of horns are not to be taken seriously. ∎

On the Road

It must be said that, given the general road conditions, motorcycling is a reasonably hazardous endeavour, and one best undertaken by experienced riders only – you don't want to discover on the Grand Trunk Road with a lunatic in a Tata truck bearing down on you that you don't know how to take evasive action! Hazards range from families of pigs crossing the road to broken-down vehicles abandoned in the middle of the road.

Route-finding can be very tricky. It's certainly much easier to jump on a bus and leave the navigating to someone who knows the way. The directions people give you can be very interesting. It is invariably a 'straight road', although if pressed the person might also reveal that the said straight road actually involves taking two right turns, three left turns and the odd fork or two. Pronunciation can also cause problems, particularly in country areas.

On the whole people are very welcoming, and curious about how you are coping with the traffic conditions.

Generally you can park the bike and not have things stolen from it. The biggest annoyance is that people seem to treat parked motorcycles as public utilities – handy for sitting on, using the mirror to do the hair, fiddling with the switches – but they don't deliberately do any damage. You'll just have to turn all the switches off and readjust the mirrors when you get back on.

Run-ins with the law are not a major problem. The best policy is to give a smile and a friendly wave to any police officers, even if you are doing the opposite of what is signalled.

In the event of an accident, call the police straight away, and don't move anything until the police have seen exactly where and how everything ended up. One foreigner reported spending three days in jail on suspicion of being involved in an accident, when all he'd done was taken a child to hospital from the scene of an accident.

Don't try to cover too much territory in one day. As such a high level of concentration is needed to survive, long days are tiring

and dangerous. On the busy national highways expect to average 50km/h without stops; on smaller roads, where driving conditions are worse, 10km/h is not an unrealistic average. On the whole you can expect to cover between 100km and 150km in a day on good roads.

Night driving should be avoided at all costs. If you think driving in daylight is difficult, imagine what it's like at night when there's the added hazard of half the vehicles being inadequately lit (or not lit at all), not to mention the breakdowns in the middle of the road.

Putting the bike on a train for really long hauls can be a convenient option. You'll pay about as much as the 2nd-class passenger fare for the bike. It can be wrapped in straw for protection if you like, and this is done at the parcels office at the station, which is also where you pay for the bike. The petrol tank must be empty, and there should be a tag in an obvious place detailing name, destination, passport number and train details.

Repairs & Maintenance

Anyone who can handle a screwdriver and spanner in India can be called a mechanic, or *mistri*, so be careful. If you have any mechanical knowledge it may be better to buy your own tools and learn how to do your own repairs. This will save a lot of arguments over prices. If you are getting repairs done by someone, don't leave the premises while the work is being done or you may find that good parts have been ripped off your bike and replaced with bodgy old ones.

Original spare parts bought from an 'authorised dealer' can be rather expensive compared to the copies available from your spare-parts wallah. If you're going up to Ladakh, take basic spares with you (valves, piston rings and rocker rods) as they are not easily available there.

If you buy an older machine you would do well to check and tighten all nuts and bolts every few days. Indian roads and engine vibration tend to work things loose, and constant checking could save you rupees and trouble. Check the engine and gearbox oil level regularly. With the quality of oil it is advisable to change it and clean the oil filter every couple of thousand km.

Punctures Chances are you'll be requiring the services of a puncture-wallah at least once a week. They are found everywhere, often in the most surprising places, but it's advisable to at least have tools sufficient to remove your own wheel and take it to the puncture-wallah (*punkucha wallah* in Hindi).

Given the hassles of constant flat tyres, it's worth lashing out on new tyres if you buy a secondhand bike with worn tyres. A new rear tyre for an Enfield costs around Rs 600.

Fuel Should you run out, try flagging down a passing car (not a truck or bus since they use diesel) and beg for some. Most Indians are willing to let you have some if you have a hose or siphon and a container. Alternatively, hitch a truck ride to the nearest petrol station. One route on which you will have to carry spare fuel (10 litres) is the Leh-Manali road.

Organised Motorcycle Tours
Classic Bike Adventure (☎ (0832) 273351; fax 276124, 277343), Casa Tres Amigos, Socol Vado No 425, Assagao, Bardez, Goa, is a German company that organises bike tours on well-maintained Enfields with full insurance. Tours last two to three weeks and cover Rajasthan, the Himalaya between Kullu-Manali and Gangotri, and the south from Goa. Costs are from DM2450 to DM3680. See the Getting Around section in the Goa chapter for more information.

Ferris Wheels (☎ & fax 61 (02) 9904 7419), 61 Elizabeth St, Artarmon, NSW 2065, Australia, also organises tours through the Himalaya and Rajasthan on classic Enfields.

BICYCLE
The following information comes from Ann Sorrel, with updates from various travellers.

Every day millions of Indians pedal along the country's roads. If they can do it so can you. India offers an immense array of

challenges for a long-distance cyclist: there are high-altitude passes and rocky dirt tracks; smooth-surfaced, well-graded highways with roadside restaurants and lodges; coastal routes through coconut palms; and winding country roads through coffee plantations. There are city streets with all manner of animal and human-powered carts and vehicles and the spectacular bazaars. Hills, plains, plateaus, deserts – you name it, India's got it!

Nevertheless, long-distance cycling is not for the faint of heart or weak of knee. You'll need physical endurance to cope with the roads and the climate, plus you'll face cultural challenges – 'the people factor'.

Cycling in India is tough. Think how hard you want to travel before you go. But for all its chaos, dust and bumpy roads India is a beautiful country. The birds will thrill you, the animals and children will delight you and the warmth and generosity of the people will win you over. During one elevenses break a skinny old man appeared herding his cows. He immediately offered us his only bit of sugarcane. It made me feel very humble and it's typical of the Indians we met. It's a hard country to leave.

Ian & Allie Smith (UK)

Information
Before you set out, read some books on bicycle touring such as the Sierra Club's *The Bike Touring Manual* by Rob van de Plas (Bicycle Books, 1993). Cycling magazines provide useful information including listings for bicycle tour operators and the addresses of spare-parts suppliers. They're also good places to look for a riding companion.

For a real feel of the adventure of bike touring in strange places, read Dervla Murphy's classic *Full Tilt – From Dunkirk to Delhi on a Bicycle*, Lloyd Sumner's *The Long Ride* or Bettina Selby's *Riding the Mountains Down* (subtitled 'A Journey by Bicycle to Kathmandu').

Your local cycling club may be able to help with information and advice. In the UK, the Cyclists Touring Club (☎ (01483-417217; fax 01484-426994) 69 Meadrow, Godalming, Surrey GU7, has country touring sheets that are free to members. The International

Bicycle Fund (☎ (206) 628-9314), 4887 Columbia Drive South, Seattle, Washington 98108-1919, USA, has two useful publications: *Selecting and Preparing a Bike for Travel in Remote Areas* and *Flying With Your Bike*.

If you're a serious cyclist or amateur racer and want to contact counterparts while in India, there's the Cycle Federation of India; contact the Secretary, Yamun Velodrome, New Delhi.

Using Your Own Bike

If you are going to keep to sealed roads and already have a touring bike, by all means consider bringing it. Mountain bikes, however, are especially suited to countries such as India. Their smaller, sturdier construction makes them more manoeuvrable, less prone to damage, and allows you to tackle rocky, muddy roads unsuitable for lighter machines.

There is a disadvantage: your machine is likely to be a real curiosity and subject to much pushing, pulling and probing. If you can't tolerate people touching your bicycle, don't bring it to India.

Spare Parts If you bring a bicycle to India, prepare for the contingencies of part replacement or repair. Bring spare tyres, tubes, patch kits, chassis, cables, freewheels and spokes. Ensure you have a working knowledge of your machine. Bring all necessary tools with you as well as a compact bike manual with diagrams in case the worst happens and you need to fix a rear derailleur or some other strategic part. Indian mechanics can work wonders and illustrations help overcome the language barrier. Roads don't have paved shoulders and are very dusty, so keep your chain lubricated.

Most of all, be ready to make do and improvise.

Although India is officially metricated, tools and bike parts follow 'standard' or 'imperial' measurements. Don't expect to find tyres for 700cc rims, although 27 x 1¼ tyres are produced in India by Dunlop and Sawney. Some mountain bike tyres are available but the quality is dubious. Indian

bicycle pumps cater to a tube valve different from the Presta and Schraeder valves commonly used in the west. If you're travelling with Presta valves (most high-pressure 27 x 1¼ tubes) bring a Schraeder (car type) adaptor. In India you can buy a local pump adaptor, which means you'll have an adaptor on your adaptor. Bring your own pump as well; most Indian pumps require two or three people to get air down the leaky cable.

In major cities Japanese tyres and parts (derailleurs, freewheels, chains) are available, but pricey – although so is postage, and transit time can be considerable. If you receive bike parts from abroad beware of exorbitant customs charges. Say you want the goods as 'in transit' to avoid these charges. They may list the parts in your passport!

For foreign parts try Metre Cycle, Kalba Devi Rd, Mumbai, or its branch in Thiruvananthapuram (Trivandrum); the cycle bazaar in the old city around Esplanade Rd, Delhi; Popular Cycle Importing Company on Popham's Broadway, Chennai; and Nundy & Company, Bentinck St, Calcutta. Alternatively, take your bicycle to a cycle market and ask around – someone will know which shop is likely to have things for your 'special' cycle. Beware of Taiwanese imitations and do watch out for tyres which may have been sitting collecting dust for years.

Luggage Your cycle luggage should be as strong, durable and waterproof as possible. Don't get a set with lots of zippers, as this makes pilfering easier. As you'll be frequently detaching luggage when taking your bike to your room, a set designed for easy removal from the racks is a must: the fewer items, the better. *(Never* leave your bike in the lobby or outside your hotel – take it to bed with you!)

Bike luggage that can easily be reassembled into a backpack is also available, just the thing when you want to park your bike and go by train or foot.

Theft If you're using an imported bike, try to avoid losing your pump (and the water bottle from your frame) – their novelty makes them particularly attractive to thieves. Don't leave anything on your bike that can easily be removed when it's unattended.

Don't be paranoid about theft – outside the major cities it would be well-nigh impossible for a thief to resell your bike as it would stand out too much. And not many folk understand quick-release levers on wheels. Your bike is probably safer in India than in western cities.

Buying & Selling a Bike in India

Finding an Indian bike is no problem: every town will have at least a couple of cycle shops. Shop around for prices and remember to bargain. Try to get a few extras – bell, stand, spare tube – thrown in. There are many brands of Indian clunkers – Hero, Atlas, BSA, Raleigh, Bajaj, Avon – but they all follow the same basic, sturdy design. A few mountain-bike lookalikes have recently come on the market, but most have no gears. Raleigh is considered the finest quality, followed by BSA which has a big line of models including some sporty jobs. Hero and Atlas both claim to be the biggest seller. Look for the cheapest or the one with the snazziest plate label.

Once you've decided on a bike you have a choice of luggage carriers – mostly the rat-trap type varying only in size, price and strength. There's a wide range of saddles available but all are equally bum-breaking. A stand is certainly a useful addition and a bell or airhorn is a necessity. An advantage of buying a new bike is that the brakes actually work. Centre-pull and side-pull brakes are also available but at extra cost and may actually make the bike more difficult to sell. The average Indian will prefer the standard model.

Sportier 'mountain bike' styles with straight handlebars are popular in urban areas. In big cities and touristy areas it's also possible to find used touring bikes left by travellers. Also check with diplomatic community members for bikes.

Reselling is no problem. Count on getting about 70% of what you originally paid if it was a new bike. A local cycle-hire shop will probably be interested or you could ask the proprietor of your hotel if they know any prospective purchasers.

Spare Parts As there are so many repair 'shops' (some consist of a pump, a box of tools, a tube of rubber solution and a water pan under a tree), there is no need to carry spare parts, especially as you'll only own the bike for a few weeks or months. Just take a roll of tube-patch rubber, a tube of Dunlop patch glue, two tyre irons and the wonderful 'universal' Indian bike spanner, which fits all the nuts. There are plenty of puncture-wallahs in all towns and villages who will patch tubes for a couple of rupees, so chances are you won't have to fix a puncture yourself anyway. Besides, Indian tyres are pretty heavy duty, so with luck you won't get too many flats.

On the Road

The 'people factor' makes a bike ride in India both rewarding and frustrating. Those with Indian bikes are less likely to be mobbed by curious onlookers. A tea stop with an imported bike can attract a crowd of 50 men and boys eagerly commenting on the bike's operation – one points to the water-bottle saying 'petrol', another twists the shifter lever saying 'clutch', another squeezes a tyre saying 'tubeless' or 'airless', yet others nod knowingly as 'gear system', 'automatic' and 'racing bike' are mouthed. In some areas you'll even get 'disco bike'!

The worst scenario is stopping on a city street for a banana, looking up as you are pushing off to find rickshaws, cyclists and pedestrians all blocking your way! At times the crowd may be unruly – schoolboys especially. If the mob is too big, call over a lathi-wielding policeman. The boys will scatter pronto! Sometimes the hostile boys throw rocks. The best advice is to keep pedalling; don't turn around or stop, and don't leave your bike and chase them as this will only incite them further. Appeal to adults to discipline them. Children, especially boys seven to 13 years old, are unruly and dangerous in crowds. Avoid riding past a boys' school at recess.

Routes

You can go anywhere on a bike that you would on trains and buses, with the added pleasure of seeing all the places in between.

Try to avoid the major highways up north like the NH1 through Haryana, and the NH2 – the Grand Trunk Road between Delhi and Calcutta. They're plagued by speeding buses and trucks. Other national highways can be pleasant – often lonely country roads well marked with a stone every km. A basic knowledge of Hindi will help you to translate the signs, although at least one marker in five will be in English.

Another option is to follow canal and river paths. It's also possible in some areas to bike along railway tracks on maintenance roads. Do make enquiries before venturing off road.

If mountain bicycling is your goal give serious consideration to Himachal Pradesh as well as the hill stations of South India.

Crossing international borders with a bicycle is relatively uncomplicated. India has border crossings with Pakistan, Nepal and Bangladesh. Unlike a car or motorcycle, papers need not be presented. Do not be surprised, however, if the bike is thoroughly inspected for contraband!

Distances

If you've never cycled long distances, start with 20 to 40km a day and increase this as you gain stamina and confidence. Cycling long distances is 80% determination and 20% perspiration. Don't be ashamed to get off and push the bike up steep hills. For an eight hour pedal a serious cyclist and interested tourist will average 90 to 130km a day on undulating plains, or 70 to 100km in mountainous areas.

Accommodation

There's no need to bring a tent. Inexpensive lodges are widely available, and a tent pitched by the road would merely draw crowds. There's also no need to bring a stove and cooking kit (unless you cannot tolerate Indian food), as there are plenty of tea stalls and restaurants (called hotels). When you want to eat, ask for a hotel. When you want

a room ask for a lodge. On major highways you can stop at *dhabas*, the Indian version of a truck stop. The one with the most trucks parked in front generally has the best food (or serves alcohol). Dhabas have *charpoys* (string beds) to serve as tables and seats or as beds for weary cyclists. You should keep your cycle next to you throughout the night. There will be no bathroom or toilet facilities but plenty of road noise. Dhabas are not recommended for single women riders.

Eating at dhabas is probably for the adventurous. We tried a couple but that was enough. The food was unpleasant and the water unsafe. So for lunch we opted for banana sandwiches eaten on a grassy verge. Bananas are cheap (Rs 6 per kg) and white (milk) bread is widely available. Sugar cane too was a great reviver and very juicy. We still got people coming up for a chat or just to stare but it wasn't as intimidating as in the dhabas.

Ian & Allie Smith (UK)

Directions

Asking directions can be a real frustration. Approach people who look like they can speak English and aren't in a hurry. Always ask three or four different people just to be certain, using traffic police only as a last resort. Try to be patient; be careful about 'left' and 'right' and be prepared for instructions like 'go straight and turn here and there'.

Transporting your Bike

Sometimes you may want to quit pedalling. For sports bikes, air travel is easy. With luck airline staff may not be familiar with procedures, so use this to your advantage. Tell them the bike doesn't need to be dismantled and that you've never had to pay for it. Remove all luggage and accessories and let the tyres down a bit.

Bus travel with a bike varies from state to state. Generally it goes for free on the roof. If it's a sports bike stress that it's lightweight. Secure it well to the roof rack, check it's in a place where it won't get damaged and take all your luggage inside.

Train travel is more complex – pedal up to the railway station, buy a ticket and explain you want to book a cycle for the journey.

You'll be directed to the luggage offices (or officer) where a triplicate form is prepared. Note down your bike's serial number and provide a good description of it. Again leave only the bike, not luggage or accessories. Your bike gets decorated with one copy of the form, usually pasted on the seat, you get another, and God only knows what happens to the third. Produce your copy of the form to claim the bicycle from the luggage van at your destination. If you change trains en route, *personally* ensure the cycle changes too!

Final Words

Just how unusual is a cycle tourist in India? At a guess, currently 2000 foreign cyclists tour for a month or more each year somewhere on the subcontinent. That number appears to be growing rapidly. Perhaps 5000 Indians tour as well – mostly young men and college students. 'Kashmir to Kanyakumari' or a pilgrimage to holy places are their most common goals.

HITCHING

Hitching is not a realistic option. There are not that many private cars streaking across India so you are likely to be on board trucks. You are then stuck with the old quandaries of: 'Do they understand what I am doing?', 'Should I be paying for this?', 'Will the driver expect to be paid?', 'Will they be unhappy if I don't offer to pay?', 'Will they be unhappy if I offer or will they simply want too much?'. But it is possible.

However, it is a very bad idea for women to hitch. Remember India is a developing country with a patriarchal society far less sympathetic to rape victims than the west, and that's saying something. A woman in the cabin of a truck on a lonely road is perhaps tempting fate.

BOAT

Apart from ferries across rivers (of which there are many), the only real boating possibilities are the trips through the backwaters of Kerala – not to be missed (see the Kerala chapter for more details) and the jetfoil bet-

ween Mumbai and Goa (see the Mumbai chapter).

The only other ferries connecting coastal ports are those from Calcutta and Chennai to the Andaman Islands (see Getting There & Away in the Port Blair section of the Andaman & Nicobar Islands chapter).

LOCAL TRANSPORT

Although there are comprehensive local bus networks in most major towns, unless you have time to familiarise yourself with the routes you're better off sticking to taxis, auto-rickshaws, cycle-rickshaws and hiring bicycles. The buses are often so hopelessly overcrowded that you can only really use them if you get on at the starting point and get off at the terminus.

A basic ground rule applies to any form of transport where the fare is not ticketed or fixed (unlike a bus or train), or metered – agree on the fare beforehand. If you fail to do that you can expect enormous arguments and hassles when you get to your destination. And agree on the fare clearly – if there is more than one of you make sure it covers all of you. If you have baggage make sure there are no extra charges, or you may be asked for more at the end of the trip. If a driver refuses to use the meter, or insists on an extortionate rate, simply walk away – if he really wants the job the price will drop. If you can't agree on a reasonable fare, find another driver.

The Airport

There are official buses, operated by the government, Indian Airlines or some local co-operative, to most airports in India. Where there aren't any, there will be taxis or auto-rickshaws. There are some airports close enough to town to get to by cycle-rickshaw.

When arriving at an airport anywhere in India, find out if there's a prepaid taxi booth inside the arrival hall. If there is, pay for one there. If you don't do this and simply walk outside to negotiate your own price, you'll invariably pay more. Taxi drivers are notorious for refusing to use the meter outside airport terminals. Confusingly, in some airports (Delhi in particular) there may be several prepaid taxi booths. The one with the lowest prices is the official one.

Taxi

There are taxis in most towns in India, and most of them (certainly in the major cities) are metered. Getting a metered fare is rather a different situation. First of all the meter may be 'broken'. Threatening to get another taxi will usually fix it immediately, except during rush hours.

Secondly the meter will almost certainly be out of date. Fares are adjusted upwards so much faster and more frequently than meters are recalibrated that drivers almost always have 'fare adjustment cards' indicating what you should pay compared to what the meter indicates. This is, of course, wide open to abuse. You have no idea if you're being shown the right card or if the taxi's meter has actually been recalibrated and you're being shown the card anyway. In states where the numbers are written differently (such as Gujarat) it's not much use asking for the chart if you can't read it!

The only answer to all this is to try and get an idea of what the fare should be before departure (ask information desks at the airport or your hotel). You'll soon begin to develop a feel for what the meter says, what the cards say and what the two together should indicate.

Auto-Rickshaw

An auto-rickshaw is a noisy three-wheel device powered by a two-stroke motorcycle engine with a driver up front and seats for two (or sometimes more) passengers behind. They don't have doors (except in Goa) and have just a canvas top. They are also known as scooters or autos.

Although they are all made by Bajaj, it's amazing how the designs differ from town to town. Design seems to be unique to a particular town: in Chittorgarh in Rajasthan, for example, the auto-rickshaws are fitted with an extra seat facing backwards, and so they can carry four people (although they'll often carry eight or more!).

They're generally about half the price of a taxi, usually metered and follow the same ground rules as taxis.

Because of their size, auto-rickshaws are often faster than taxis for short trips and their drivers are decidedly nuttier – hair-raising near-misses are guaranteed and glancing-blow collisions are not infrequent; thrillseekers will love it!

In busy towns you'll find that, when stopped at traffic lights, the height you are sitting at is the same as most bus and truck exhaust pipes – copping dirty great lungfuls of diesel fumes is part of the fun of auto-rickshaw travel. Also their small wheel size and rock-hard suspension makes them supremely uncomfortable; even the slightest bump will have you instantly airborne. The speed humps and huge potholes found everywhere are the bane of the rickshaw traveller – pity the poor drivers.

Tempo

Somewhat like a large auto-rickshaw, these ungainly looking three-wheel devices operate rather like minibuses or share-taxis along fixed routes. Unless you are spending large amounts of time in one city, it is generally impractical to try to find out what the routes are. You'll find it much easier and more convenient to go by auto-rickshaw.

Cycle-Rickshaw

This is effectively a three-wheeler bicycle with a seat for two passengers behind the rider. Although they no longer operate in most of the big cities except in the old part of Delhi and parts of Calcutta, you will find them in all the smaller cities and towns, where they're the basic means of transport.

Fares must always be agreed on in advance. Avoid situations where the driver says something like: 'As you like'. He's hoping you are not well acquainted with correct fares and will overpay. Invariably no matter what you pay in situations like this, it will be deemed too little and an unpleasant situation often develops. This is especially the case in heavily touristed places, such as Agra and Jaipur. Always settle the price beforehand.

It's quite feasible to hire a rickshaw-wallah by time, not just for a trip. Hiring one for a day or several days can make good financial sense.

Hassling over the fares is the biggest difficulty of cycle-rickshaw travel. They'll often go all out for a fare higher than it would cost you by taxi or auto-rickshaw. Nor does actually agreeing on a fare always make a big difference – there is a greater possibility of a post-travel fare disagreement when you travel by cycle-rickshaw than when you go by taxi or auto-rickshaw – whether they are metered or not.

Other Transport

In some places, tongas (horse-drawn two-wheelers) and victorias (horse-drawn carriages) still run.

Calcutta has a large tram network and India's first underground. Mumbai, Delhi and Chennai have suburban trains.

Once upon a time there used to be people-drawn rickshaws, but today these only exist in parts of Calcutta, although from January 1997 they were officially banned by the West Bengal government.

Bicycle Rental

India is a country of bicycles – it's a great way to get around the sights in a city or make longer trips – see the section on touring India by bicycle earlier in this chapter. Even in the smallest towns there will be a shop which rents bikes. They charge from around Rs 3 to Rs 5 per hour or around Rs 15 per day. In tourist areas (such as hill stations) and places where foreigners are common (like Goa) you'll probably pay about double the normal rate.

If you should be so unfortunate as to get a puncture, don't worry: you'll soon spot men sitting under trees with puncture-repair outfits at the ready – it'll cost just a few rupees to fix it.

If you're travelling with small children and would like to ride a lot, consider getting a bike seat made. If you find a shop making cane furniture they'll make up a child's bicycle seat from a sketch. Get it made to fit on a standard-size rear carrier and it can be securely attached with a few lengths of cord.

ORGANISED TOURS

At almost any place of tourist interest in

Cycle-rickshaws are a common form of transport in Indian towns and cities. A lucky rickshaw-wallah may get the contract to take school children to and from school, and thereby have at least a certain amount of guaranteed daily income.

On Ancestors' Stomping Ground

Barely 22 years old, fresh out of university and with a burning passion to spread my wings, I began a journey that had a distinct beginning, but no conceivable end. Back then I had no inkling that what started out as a one year career opportunity, would end up being a 3½ year 'pilgrimage', paramount in navigating my life.

I was packing my bags, gulping down malaria tablets and setting off to explore my country of descent after a lifetime of hearing about it. My folks had raised me with a profound awareness and veneration of my ancestry, forever reiterating the importance of nurturing my heritage. But somehow, to a child, their portrayals of India seemed alien – even lacklustre through repetition – dampening the curiosity to venture beyond their interpretations.

On the plane bound for New Delhi, I really contemplated for the first time what lay ahead. India had always been like a cryptic jigsaw puzzle, teasing me with fluid pieces that refused to fit together. And then it struck me. All perceptions of *my* motherland had literally been sculpted by secondary sources – television, relatives, books, strangers on the net, even rumours...I had been a jaded observer of my own cultural fabric.

From the very beginning, India completely swathed my being. The first few months were spent attempting to compartmentalise everything around me – a deluded and futile quest. Despite initial trepidation, I took to the roads, determined to perfect the art of manoeuvring my little car through the tumultuous traffic of downtown Delhi. After a showdown with a cantankerous bus that had a vendetta against one-way streets, the golden rule of driving gelled firm: might is right. I later discovered that this 'rule' permeated much of life in India.

My lineage was often a passport to glowing opportunities, inviting me to experience India in a more esoteric dimension than most other travellers. Many Indians willingly shared their lives, allowing me privileged access to places, people, matters of the soul. From the money-saving angle, my Indian appearance occasionally acted as a vaccination against being ripped off by unscrupulous shopkeepers and rickshaw-wallahs. Alas, this immunity rapidly evaporated if I uttered any words – it ain't easy taming an Aussie accent!

One thing I never quite acclimatized to were the unrelenting stares. With an Indian appearance, I thought I'd melt into the crowd. For a while, the reason for such tenacious scrutiny eluded me and I became intensely introspective. Just as my identity was becoming jagged around the edges, the clouds cleared. Apparently I was a somewhat perplexing creature – an enigmatic fusion of east and west. Possessing certain Indian traits but evincing the demeanour of a 'typical' foreigner, I was an Indian – yet not an Indian, a foreigner – yet not a foreigner! I had two options: learn to live with the intrusive stares, or mitigate my western 'idiosyncrasies'. I opted for the former rather than repress the person that I was.

India had an uncanny way of making me grapple with jumbled emotions. Conflicting perspectives constantly aroused inner reflection. Attitudes towards me varied wildly. There were Indians who accepted me with open arms, proud of my link with India. And then there were those who impetuously condemned me as a misguided product of the western world. This was rarely conveyed in words, rather in one swift and stinging scowl. It ignited some riveting thought on the complex and prickly realm of migration, assimilation, expectations, limitations and misconceptions.

Going back to my ancestral land was an extraordinarily intimate and invigorating experience. There were times when I felt incredibly isolated and vulnerable, seeking solace by trying to straighten winding roads – trying to make sense of India's disorientating unpredictability, its tangle of contrasts and contradictions. Solace only came when I surrendered the security of structure, allowing India to play a cardinal role in shaping each moment. That's when I made the transition from being an onlooker to a participant. Everything changed.

Sarina Singh

Sarina Singh is an Australian writer of Indian descent. Her grandparents migrated to Fiji from northern India; her parents settled in Australia when she was just eight months old. A twist of fate landed her a marketing executive traineeship with Sheraton Hotels in India, but she later fell into journalism. After several years in India as a freelance journalist and foreign correspondent, Sarina returned to Melbourne where she continues to write. ■

India, and quite a few places where there's not much tourist interest, there will be tours operated either by the Government of India tourist office, the state tourist office or the local transport company – sometimes by all three. These tours are usually excellent value, particularly in cities or places where the tourist sights are widespread. You probably couldn't get around Delhi on public transport as cheaply as you could on a tour.

These tours are not strictly for western tourists; you will almost always find yourself outnumbered by local tourists. Despite this the tours are usually in English – possibly the only common language for the middle-class Indian tourists in any case. These tours are an excellent place to meet Indians.

The big drawback is that many of them try to cram far too much into too short a period of time. If a tour looks too hectic, you're better off doing it yourself at a more appropriate pace or taking the tour simply to find out to which places you want to devote more time.

You can never be too careful

Like most travellers I've had numerous close calls and near misses. This story is to remind you that no matter how experienced you are, not matter how many times you've eluded serious injury or even death, and no matter how confident you feel as a result, you are still vulnerable.

I have never had a serious accident or illness in my life; as a traveller I have never been in a situation that I couldn't get out of. I also thought I was well informed on health problems and risks and knew what to do if things went wrong. Well, I was in for a surprise during my trip to northern India in 1996.

I had hired a driver and jeep to take me into and out of Ladakh. When the time came to leave Leh, the weather towards Manali had deteriorated so much that we both decided it was too risky to return that way. We opted to go via Kashmir; my driver was from Srinagar and knew the roads and the situation there. After a day of looking around Srinagar and servicing the vehicle, we set off for Delhi, a two-day journey. We headed off down the Jammu road, which is flat, straight and sealed all the way through the Vale of Kashmir. I remember telling the driver about the dengue fever outbreak in Delhi, but that's the last thing I remember.

A little over an hour later our vehicle smashed into a Tata truck at 120km/h, head on. The truck driver was apparently overtaking a bus and was roaring down our side of the road. The impact smashed in our car to within a couple of feet of the front seats. The driver smashed face-first into the centre of the steering wheel. I must have seen the collision coming (I was in the front passenger seat) and crouched down with my arms around my head and my feet under the dashboard to brace myself against the impact. As it turned out, I came out of all this relatively lightly; numerous cuts and bruises and several fractures in my legs, but no head, internal or spinal injuries, thank heavens. The driver, on the other hand, died a few days later in Srinagar General Hospital.

OK, so I survived. What happened next put me in as much danger as the accident itself. While my memory of what then happened is poor, I am told that the army extricated me from the car and took me to the police station – where all luggage and personal belongings (including my money belt which was around my waist and under my clothes!) were confiscated. I was then put in a car and taken, without ID, money or belongings, to the hospital in Srinagar where the care was basic, to say the least.

I don't think I would have lived through this episode had it not been for a family friend of the driver, who, thank god, went and phoned my embassy in Delhi and told them to fly me out. I was beyond helping myself. The same person who rang the embassy also helped persuade the police to return my belongings, so I got my passport and travellers cheques back (although all my cash was gone). I was at this hospital for four days during which I survived mainly on teaspoonfuls of water administered by a 'helper' arranged through the person I've described above. When the medivac (an Indian doctor with a stretcher) arrived from Delhi I was asked whether I was insured. Yes, I was, but I only knew that I had bought the insurance through STA Travel; I couldn't remember the name of the insurance company. All that information was in my money belt. I hadn't actually heard the world 'medivac' at that stage; I had no idea how to arrange one or what my rights were under the insurance policy.

Throughout all of this I was in quite a lot of pain, very weak and probably in shock. I was appalled that someone had died. For the first few days in Delhi (of which I have only hazy memories) I didn't care what happened to me and unfortunately it was during this time that I underwent medical treatment that caused untold problems later; namely malaria and golden staph.

Three weeks after arriving in Delhi I was flown to Melbourne; just in time, really, because I don't think I would otherwise have survived the malaria. Recovery is proving to be a rather slow process because of complications resulting from those fateful few days in Delhi. There are some things which I now consider mandatory for travellers, and even though they may seem self-evident it's amazing how many people (including experienced travellers) choose to ignore them. You *must* have travel insurance, you should have a contact at home or at your embassy who can help you if things go wrong, and if things *do* go wrong you should get home as soon as humanly possible. For more information on how to stay safe in India, see the health and travel insurance sections in the Facts for the Visitor chapter.

Christine Niven

SACRED INDIA

PAUL BEINSSEN

India is a biryani of religions – contrasting flavours and colours jumbled together to make a tantalising blend. There is probably more diversity of religions and sects in India than anywhere else on earth. Apart from having nearly all the world's great religions represented, India was the birthplace of Hinduism and Buddhism, a vital supporter of Zoroastrianism (one of the world's oldest religions) and home to Jainism (an ancient religion unique to India).

India is also the guru centre of the world. Since the Beatles first took up with the Maharishi, westerners have flocked to the country to bask in the presence of holies such as Sai Baba and Osho.

Whether your interest is deeply spiritual or coolly academic, India's kaleidoscope of religions will confuse, infuriate and probably alienate you – but understanding it will bring you closer to the heart of India.

PAUL BEINSSEN

Title page: Dressed in Krishna's colour – blue – two girls worship before an image of the god at the Jagannath Temple in Delhi. (photograph by Sally Hone).

Facing page: A devotee of Hanuman, the monkey god, studies a sacred text.

Left: Dressed as the goddess Kali, this man travels the country spreading prayer and seeking boons.

TONY WHEELER

HINDUISM

India's major religion, Hinduism, is practised by approximately 80% of the population – over 670 million people. Only in Nepal, the Indonesian island of Bali, the Indian Ocean island of Mauritius and possibly Fiji, do Hindus also predominate, but in terms of numbers of adherents, it is the largest religion in Asia. It is one of the oldest extant religions, with firm roots extending back to beyond 1000 BC.

The Indus Valley civilisation developed a religion which bore a close relationship to Hinduism. Later, this religion was influenced by the combined religious practices of the southern Dravidians and the Aryan invaders who arrived in the north of India around 1500 BC. Around 1000 BC, the Vedic scriptures were introduced, providing the first loose framework for the religion.

Hinduism today has a number of holy books, the most important being the four *Vedas* (divine knowledge) which are the foundation of Hindu

GREG ELMS

Facing page: Despite the crowds of pilgrims and gawping tourists, it is still possible to find a peaceful, meditative ghat in the Hindu holy city of Varanasi.

Left: A Jaipur Hindu plays the part of Hanuman, monkey god and Rama's ally.

philosophy. The *Upanishads* are contained within the *Vedas* and delve into the metaphysical nature of the universe and soul. The *Mahabharata* (Great War of the Bharatas) is an epic poem containing over 220,000 lines. It describes the battles between the Kauravas and Pandavas, who were descendants of the Lunar race. It also includes the story of Rama, and the most famous Hindu epic, the *Ramayana*, was probably based on this. The *Ramayana* is highly revered by Hindus, perhaps because a verse in the introduction says 'He who reads and repeats this holy life-giving *Ramayana* is liberated from all his sins and exalted with all his posterity to the highest heaven'. The *Bhagavad Gita* is a famous episode of the *Mahabharata* where Krishna relates his philosophies to Arjuna.

Basically, the religion postulates that we will all go through a series of rebirths or reincarnations that eventually lead to *moksha*, the spiritual salvation which frees us all from the cycle of rebirths. With each rebirth we can move closer to or further from eventual moksha; the deciding

Women make their early morning devotions at a Hindu temple in Khajuraho.

PAUL BEINSSEN

factor is our karma, which is literally a law of cause and effect. Bad actions during our lives result in bad karma, which ends in a lower reincarnation. Conversely, if our deeds and actions have been good, we will reincarnate on a higher level and be a step closer to eventual freedom from rebirth.

Dharma, or the natural law, defines the total social, ethical and spiritual harmony of our lives. There are three categories of dharma, the first being the eternal harmony which involves the whole universe. The second category is the dharma that controls castes and the relations between castes. The third dharma is the moral code which an individual should follow.

The Hindu religion has three basic practices. They are *puja*, or worship (see the puja aside in the Facts About the Country chapter), the cremation of the dead, and the rules and regulations of the caste system (see the Society & Conduct section of the Facts About the Country chapter).

Hinduism is not a proselytising religion since you cannot be converted. You're either born a Hindu or you are not; you can never become one. Nevertheless, Hinduism has attracted many westerners, and India's 'export gurus' are many and successful.

A guru is not so much a teacher as a spiritual guide, somebody who by example or simply by their presence indicates what path you should follow. In a spiritual search one always needs a guru.

PAUL BEINSSEN

SARA-JANE CLELAND

Top: Devotees at Varanasi avail themselves of the Ganges' holy water.

Bottom: Women pray for their husbands' well-being during the Kawachot Festival in Varanasi.

HINDU GODS

Westerners have trouble understanding Hinduism principally because of its vast pantheon of gods – traditionally there are 330 million Hindu gods and demons. In fact you can look upon all these different gods simply as manifestations of *brahman* or godhead. This one omnipresent god has three main physical representations. Brahma is the creator, Vishnu is the preserver and Siva is the destroyer and reproducer. Each of these gods has a consort, or female aspect, and the gods and their consorts have many different manifestations. Each god also has a vehicle on which they ride, and a symbol.

Brahma, the creator, is the least approachable of the Hindu gods. He is considered to be impersonal and infinite, unable to be comprehended through the senses. Brahma is usually represented as having four bearded heads and four arms, which hold a sceptre, a drinking bowl, a bow and the Vedas, which emanated from his mouths. Brahma's vehicle is a white swan or goose. In his knowable form his consort is Sarasvati, sometimes said to also be Brahma's daughter. She is the goddess of science, speech and music and the inventor of Sanskrit, and she carries a stringed instrument called a *veena*.

Vishnu, the preserver or sustainer, is associated with 'right action'. He behaves as a lawful, devout Hindu, and protects and sustains all that is good in the world. In some ways Vishnu is similar to Christ – he is considered the redeemer of humanity, a knowable god. He sits on a couch made from the coils of a serpent and In his hands he holds two symbols, the conch shell and the discus. Vishnu's vehicle is the half-man half-eagle known as the Garuda. The Garuda is benevolent and has a deep dislike of snakes. Vishnu's consort is the beautiful Lakshmi (Laxmi), who came from the sea and is the goddess of wealth, prosperity, honour and love. She is often represented sitting on a lotus flower.

Vishnu has had nine incarnations, including Rama, Krishna and Gautama Buddha, and it is said that he will come again.

The *Ramayana* is the story of Rama's battle with the demon king Ravana. Rama's consort is Sita, and his brother Lakshmana and servant Hanuman, the monkey god, are also widely worshipped.

Krishna's story is told in the *Mahabharata*, the tale which incorporates the Bhagavad Gita, a guide to caste law in the form of a dialogue between Krishna and Arjuna. Krishna's mischievous nature, his peasant background

From left to right: Ganesh, elephant-headed son of Siva and Parvati; Vishnu, the preserver; Siva, the destroyer.

GREG ELMS   GREG ELMS   GREG ELMS

and his legendary exploits with the *gopis* have made him one of the most popular gods. His consorts are Radha (the head of the gopis), Rukmani and Satyabhama. Krishna is often blue and plays a flute.

Siva, the destroyer, is the agent of death and destruction, without which growth and rebirth could not take place. He is represented with either one or five faces, and four arms which may hold fire, a drum, a horn or a trident, or take the positions of protection or action. He is often surrounded by an arch of flame, and sometimes has a third eye. His matted hair is said to carry Ganga, the goddess of the river Ganges, in it. Siva's creative role is phallically symbolised by his representation as the frequently worshipped lingam. One of Siva's incarnations is Nataraj, the cosmic dancer ,whose dance shook the cosmos and created the world.

Siva's consort is Parvati, the beautiful. Parvati is the daughter of the Himalayas and is considered the perfect wife. She is a form of the mother goddess Devi, whose body is India and who also appears as Durga, the terrible (who holds weapons in her 10 hands, rides a tiger and slays the demons of ignorance) and Kali, the fiercest of the gods (who demands sacrifices and wears a garland of skulls).

Siva and Parvati have two children. Ganesh is the elephant-headed god of prosperity and wisdom, and is probably the most popular of all the gods. Ganesh obtained his elephant head due to his father's notorious temper. Coming back from a long trip, Siva discovered Parvati in her room with a young man. Not pausing to think that their son might have grown up a little during his absence, Siva lopped his head off! He was then forced by Parvati to bring his son back to life but could only do so by giving him the head of the first living thing he saw – which happened to be an elephant. Ganesh's vehicle is a rat.

Siva and Parvati's other son is Kartikkaya or Skanda, the god of war, whose vehicle is a peacock. In the south of India, Siva and Parvati's sons are known Ayappan and Murugan, although Ayappan is sometimes said to be the son of Siva and Vishnu in female form.

Of course, these descriptions only skim the surface of Hinduism. Hindu gods are part of the fabric of everyday life, interwoven with people's beliefs about food, family and financial success. It may well be impossible for non-Hindus to ever come to grips with this religion, as densely populated as the country it calls home.

CHRIS BEALL

Many-armed Skanda, god of war, rides his peacock across the Sri Meenakshi Temple in Madurai.

SARA-JANE CLELAND

SADHUS

A sadhu is an individual on a spiritual search. They're easily recognised – half-naked and smeared in dust with matted hair and beard, what few clothes they wear are usually saffron coloured. If they follow Siva they may carry a trident.

Sadhus have often decided that their business and family life have reached a natural conclusion and that it is time to throw everything temporal aside. They may perform feats of self-mortification and travel great distances around the country.

GREG ELMS

RICHARD I'ANSON

Facing page and this page: Although they may once have been the village postman or a succesful businessman, sadhus renounce their material lives and wander the country, homeless, on a personal spiritual quest.

HINDU WEDDINGS

Hindu weddings are usually colourful, lavish affairs. Vast sums are shelled out by the bride's father to put on a show worthy of both his own status and that of the bridegroom's family.

In a typical ceremony, the two extended families gather on an auspicious day to celebrate. The bride often remains out of sight in the house until the time of the ceremony. The groom *(barr)* arrives to much fanfare, having paraded through the streets, often on horseback, wearing a *sehra* (garland). The parade (*baraat*) is accompanied by a brass band (which usually pays small attention to minor details such as melody, harmony and rhythm), and the whole spectacle is lit by men carrying fluorescent tubes, all wired together in a vast and dangerous clump of spaghetti leading to a generator carried at the rear of the procession.

The wedding ceremony centres around the *havan*, or sacred fire, which the couple circle seven times after the priest has placed a *tika* (see the Tika section on page 175), on the forehead of each.

The bride, surrounded by female family and friends, is kept out of sight before a wedding in Rajasthan.

SANJAY SINGH BADNOR

GREG ELMS

GREG ELMS

Top: The bride and groom must wait until a priest has placed tikas on their foreheads before circling the sacred fire.

Bottom: Blessings all round at a wedding in Bangalore.

Holy Cows

India has nearly 200 million cattle, which are vitally important as farm machinery. Their religious protection probably first developed to safeguard them during droughts or famine when they might have been killed off. One of the most amazing sights in India, especially for the first-time visitor, is the number of cows roaming the streets and rummaging through the concrete bins where waste vegetable matter is tipped.

A cow in its best gear for the Pongal Festival, Mahabalipuram, Tamil Nadu.

GREG ELMS

TIKA

The tika is the forehead markings with which most adult Hindu (and sometimes Christian) women adorn themselves. On a man it is referred to as a tilak, although these days the word tika has become common for both sexes. The mark takes many forms, and can be applied either by the wearer or by a temple priest as a sign of blessing.

The markings are usually made from a red vermilion paste *(sindoor)*, white sandalwood paste or ash *(vibhuti)*, and can be used to denote sects. Although there's a multitude of marks, they can be roughly divided into two main groups: three horizontal bars indicate the person is a Shaivite (follower of Siva); vertical stripes indicate a Vaishnavite (follower of Vishnu). The central stroke on a Vaishnavite's forehead is usually red, representing the radiance of the goddess Lakshmi (the wife of Vishnu in his incarnation as Narayan).

The small circle which a married woman places on her forehead is known as a *bindi* ('zero'). These are usually bought ready-made from the market and have become almost a fashion accessory, with every imaginable shape and colour to match the occasion. You'll also come across a wide variety of used bindis stuck to the mirrors in hotel bathrooms!

GREG ELMS

Brightly coloured tika powders sculptured for sale at the Devarajan market in Mysore.

HOLY HINDU CITIES

Of India's many sacred cities, seven are considered particularly holy. Varanasi, Haridwar, Ayodhya, Mathura, Dwarka, Kanchipuram and Ujjain are known as *tirthas* – fords that enable pilgrims to cross from the world of earthly suffering to a divine plane. As such, they are pilgrimage centres and also auspicious places to die.

Varanasi and Haridwar are important sites on the river of life, the Ganges. Other cities are the birthplaces of gods – Rama was born in Ayodhya, Krishna in Mathura. Badrinath, Puri, Rameswaram and Dwarka are traditionally considered the corners (north, east, south and west) of mother India, and some pilgrims attempt to make a journey which visits all four.

SARA-JANE CLELAND

Facing page: The Ganges laps at a sunken temple in Varanasi as boats glide by.

Left: Pilgrims at the Sun Temple in Konark, Puri, one of India's traditional four corners.

RICHARD I'ANSON

BUDDHISM

Although there are only about 6.6 million Buddhists in India, the religion is of great importance because it had its birth here and there are many reminders of its historic role. Strictly speaking Buddhism is not a religion, since it is not centred on a god, but a system of philosophy and a code of morality.

Buddhism was founded in northern India in about 500 BC when Siddhartha Gautama, born a prince, achieved enlightenment. Gautama Buddha was not the first Buddha, but the fourth, and is not expected to be the last 'enlightened one'. Buddhists believe that the achievement of enlightenment is the goal of every being, so eventually we will all reach Buddhahood.

The Buddha never wrote down his dharma, or teachings, and a subsequent schism resulted in the development of two major Buddhist schools. The Theravada (Doctrine of the Elders), or Hinayana (Small Vehicle), holds that the path to nirvana, the eventual aim of all Buddhists, is an individual pursuit. In contrast, the Mahayana (Large Vehicle) school holds that the combined belief of its followers will eventually be great enough to encompass all of humanity and bear it to salvation. The less austere and ascetic Mahayana school is considered by some to be a soft

RICHARD I'ANSON

RICHARD I'ANSON

Facing page: A novice monk prays at the Tiske Gompa in Ladakh.

Top: Novices at the Dali monastery in Darjeeling study to become monks.

Bottom: Music is an integral part of morning devotions at the Tiske Gompa, Ladakh.

option. Today, it is chiefly practised in Vietnam, Japan and China, while the Hinayana school is followed in Sri Lanka, Myanmar (Burma), Cambodia and Thailand. There are other, sometimes more esoteric, divisions of Buddhism such as the Hindu-Tantric Buddhism of Tibet which you can see in Ladakh and other parts of north India.

The Buddha renounced his material life to search for enlightenment but, unlike other prophets, he found that starvation did not lead to discovery. Therefore, he developed his rule of the 'middle way': moderation in everything. The Buddha taught that all life is suffering but that suffering comes from our sensual desires and the illusion that they are important. By following the 'eight-fold path' these desires will be extinguished and a state of *nirvana*, where we are free from their delusions, will be reached. Following this process requires going through a series of rebirths until the goal is eventually reached and no more rebirths into the world of suffering are necessary. The path that takes you through this cycle of births is *karma*, but this is not simply fate. Karma is a law of cause and effect: your actions in one life determine the role you will play and what you will have to go through in your next life.

CHRIS BEALL

The Buddha summarised his teachings into the Four Noble Truths:

1 existence comprises conflict, dissatisfaction, sorrow and suffering
2 this state is caused by selfish desire
3 it is possible to escape from this and attain nirvana
4 the key to achieving this is to follow the eight-fold path

Eight-Fold Path

- right understanding (uninhibited by superstition or delusion)
- right thought (as befits human consciousness and intelligence)
- right speech (honest and compassionate)
- right action (peaceful and honest)
- right mode of living (without causing harm to other living creatures)
- right endeavour (self-discipline and control)
- right mindfulness (having an alert and contemplative mind)
- right concentration (deep contemplation of the realities of life)

Above: A pilgrim spins prayer wheels at Rumtek monastery in Sikkim.

The Buddha first enunciated the eight-fold path to five ascetics, former companions on his pilgrimage, at present-day Sarnath. This first sermon was known as the *Dhammacakkappavattana-sutta* (Setting in Motion the Wheel of Truth). He maintained that it is inappropriate to follow two extremes, that is, self-indulgence and self-mortification. By avoiding these two extremes the Buddha had discovered the 'Middle Path'.

The Buddha died in Kushinagar (near Gorakhpur) in about 480 BC, reputedly after eating poisonous mushrooms.

In India, Buddhism developed rapidly when it was embraced by the great Emperor Ashoka. As his empire extended over much of India, so Buddhism was carried forth. He also sent out missions to other lands to preach the Buddha's word, and his own son is said to have carried Buddhism to Sri Lanka. Later, however, Buddhism began to contract in India because it had never really taken a hold on the great mass of people. As Hinduism revived, Buddhism in India was gradually reabsorbed into the older religion. Today, Hindus regard the Buddha as another incarnation of Vishnu.

At its peak, magnificent structures were erected wherever the religion held sway. The earlier Theravada form of Buddhism, however, did not believe in the representation of the Buddha in human form. His presence was always alluded to in Buddhist art or architecture through symbols such as the bo tree (under which he was sitting when he attained enlightenment), the elephant (which his mother saw in a dream before he was born) or the wheel of life. Today, however, even Theravada Buddhists produce Buddha images.

BRYN THOMAS

Prayer flags along the Dzongri Trek, Sikkim. As the wind blows through these flags, the prayers written on them are carried up to heaven.

HUGH FINLAY

ISLAM

Muslims, followers of the Islamic religion, constitute India's largest religious minority. They number about 105 million in all, almost 10% of the country's population. This makes India one of the largest Islamic nations in the world. India has had two Muslim presidents and several cabinet and state chief ministers since Independence. Islam is the most recent and widespread of the Asian religions; it predominates from the Mediterranean across to India and is the major religion east of India in Bangladesh, Malaysia and Indonesia.

The religion's founder, the prophet Mohammed, was born in 570 AD at Mecca, now part of Saudi Arabia. His first revelation from Allah (God) occurred in 610, and this and later visions were compiled into the Muslim holy book, the Koran. As his purpose in life was revealed to him, Mohammed began to preach against the idolatry for which Mecca was then the centre. Muslims are strictly monotheistic and believe that to search for God through images is a sin. Muslim teachings correspond closely with the Old Testament of the Bible, and Moses and Jesus are both accepted as Muslim prophets, although Jesus is not believed to be the son of God.

Converts to Islam have only to announce that 'There is no god but Allah and Mohammed is his prophet' to become Muslim. Friday is the Muslim holy day and the main mosque in each town is known as the Jama Masjid or Friday Mosque. One of the aims of every Muslim is to make the pilgrimage (hajj) to Mecca and become a hajji.

In the 12th century all of north India fell into Muslim hands. Eventually, the Mughal Empire controlled most of the subcontinent, and from here it was spread by Indian traders into South-East Asia. For around 600 years Islam held sway, to a greater or lesser degree, over the north of the country. But despite its long period of control, Islam never managed to make great inroads into Hindu society and religion. Converts were principally from the lowest castes, with the result that at Partition Pakistan found itself with a shortage of the educated clerical workers and government officials

RICHARD I'ANSON

Facing page: A Muslim contemplates the Koran outside the Ahmed Shah Mosque in Ahmedabad.

Left: Unrolling prayer rugs for the morning devotions at the Jama Masjid in Delhi.

with which India is so liberally endowed. However, the effects of Muslim influence in India are particularly visible in its architecture, art and food.

For more information on the history of Islam in India, see the History section of the Facts about the Country chapter.

A Muslim pilgrim visiting Delhi's Jama Masjid, India's largest mosque.

RICHARD I'ANSON

SALLY HONE

MARGARET JUNG

Top: Morning prayers during the Baqr-id Festival in Nizamuddin village, Delhi.

Bottom: The tomb of Humayun – one of India's great Islamic Mughal rulers – in Delhi.

MICHELLE COXALL

SIKHISM

There are 18 million Sikhs in India, mostly in the Punjab. They are the most visible religious group because of the five symbols introduced by Guru Gobind Singh to help Sikh men easily recognise each other. They are known as the five *kakkars* and are: *kesh* – uncut hair (symbol of saintliness); *kangha* – the wooden or ivory comb (symbol of cleanliness); *kuccha* – shorts (symbol of alertness); *kara* – the steel bracelet (symbol of determination); and *kirpan* – the sword (for the defence of the weak). Because of their kesh, Sikh men wear their hair tied up in a bun and hidden by a turban. Wearing kuccha and carrying a kirpan came about because of the Sikhs' military tradition – they didn't want to be tripping over a long dhoti or be caught without a weapon. Normally the sword is simply represented by a tiny image set in the comb. With his beard, turban and upright, military bearing, the Sikh is hard to miss!

The Sikh religion was founded by Guru Nanak, who was born in 1469, to bring together the best of Hinduism and Islam. Its basic tenets are similar to those of Hinduism, but without caste distinctions and pilgrimages to rivers, although Sikhs still make pilgrimages to holy sites.

They worship at temples known as gurdwaras, baptise their children (when they are old enough to understand the religion) in a ceremony known as *pahul* and cremate their dead. The holy book of the Sikhs is the *Granth Sahib*, which contains the works of the 10 Sikh gurus together with Hindu and Muslim writings. The last guru died in 1708.

In the 16th century, Guru Gobind Singh introduced military overtones into the religion in an attempt to halt persecution of Sikhs. A brotherhood, known as the Khalsa, was formed. From that time most Sikhs have borne the surname Singh, which means Lion (although just because a person has the surname Singh doesn't mean they are necessarily a Sikh).

Sikhs believe in one god and are opposed to idol worship. They practise tolerance and love of others, and will offer shelter to anyone who comes to their gurdwaras. Because of their get-on-with-it attitude to life they are one of the more affluent groups in Indian society. They have a well-known reputation for mechanical aptitude.

GREG ELMS

Facing page: A Sikh displays the khanda set in his turban. The khanda, the symbol of Sikhdom, is made up of a double-edged sword which cleaves truth from lies, a circle which represents the perfection of god, and two kirpans, reminding Sikhs of their equal responsibility to spirituality and society.

Left: Amritsar, the Sikh holy city, is named after this pool surrounding the city's Golden Temple.

JAINISM

The Jain religion is contemporaneous with Buddhism and bears many similarities to both it and Hinduism. It was founded around 500 BC by Mahavira, the 24th and last of the Jain prophets, known as *tirthankars* or Finders of the Path. The Jains now number only about 4.5 million but are found all over India, predominantly in the west and south-west. They tend to be commercially successful and have an influence disproportionate to their actual numbers.

The religion originally evolved as a reformist movement against the dominance of priests and the complicated rituals of Brahminism, and it rejected the caste system. Jains believe that the universe is infinite and was not created by a deity. They also believe in reincarnation and eventual spiritual salvation, or *moksha*, through following the path of the tirthankars. One factor in the search for salvation is *ahimsa*, or reverence

LEANNE LOGAN

Facing page: Broken statues inside a Jain temple.

Left: The 17m high statue of fordmaker Gomateshvara at Sravanabelagola.

for all life and the avoidance of injury to all living things. Due to this belief, Jains are strict vegetarians and some monks actually cover their mouths with a piece of cloth in order to avoid the risk of accidentally swallowing an insect.

The Jains are divided into two sects, the white-robed Shvetambara and the Digambara. The Digambaras are the more austere sect; their name literally means Sky Clad since, as a sign of their contempt for material possessions, they do not even wear clothes. Not surprisingly, Digambaras are generally monks who are confined to a monastery! The famous Sravanabelagola shrine in Karnataka state, south India, is a Digambara temple.

The Jains constructed extraordinary temple complexes, notable for the large number of similar buildings clustered together in the one place. The temples also feature many columns, no two of which are ever identical. Their most spectacular 'temple city' is at Palitana in eastern Gujarat – a mountain-top fortress filled with hundreds of beautiful temples. Down south, Sravanabelagola in Karnataka, though only a village, is also a holy site – it is home to the 17m high sculpture of Gomateshvara, the world's tallest monolithic statue.

BRYN THOMAS

Top: A Jain temple complex in Khajuraho.

Bottom: A temple at Jaisalmer displays the decorative splendour for which Jains are renowned.

GREG ELMS

ZOROASTRIANISM

This is one of the oldest religions on earth and was founded in Persia by the prophet Zarathustra (Zoroaster) in the 6th or 7th century BC. He was born in Mazar-i-Sharif in what is now Afghanistan. At one time, Zoroastrianism stretched all the way from India to the Mediterranean, but today it is found only around Shiraz in Iran, Karachi in Pakistan and Mumbai in India. The followers of Zoroastrianism are known as Parsis because they originally fled to India to escape persecution in Persia.

Zoroastrianism was one of the first religions to postulate that there is an omnipotent and invisible god. Their scripture is the *Zend-Avesta*, which describes the conflict between the forces of good and evil. Their god is Ahura Mazda, who is symbolised by fire. Humanity ensures the victory of good over evil by following the principles of *humata* (good thoughts), *hukta* (good words) and *huvarshta* (good deeds).

Parsis worship in fire temples and wear a *sadra*, or sacred shirt, and a *kasti*, or sacred thread. Flames burn eternally in their fire temples and are worshipped as a symbol of their god. Because Parsis believe in the purity of elements, they will not cremate or bury their dead since this might pollute the fire, earth, air or water. Instead, they leave the bodies in 'Towers of Silence' where they are soon cleaned off by vultures.

Although there are only about 85,000 Parsis, they can be very influential in a wide range of spheres, and even acted as a channel of communication between India and Pakistan when the two countries were at loggerheads. Their numbers are gradually declining because of the strict requirements that a Parsi must only marry another Parsi. The offspring of mixed liaisons are not regarded as true Parsis.

CHRISTIANITY & JUDAISM

India has around 22 million Christians. There have been Christian communities in Kerala since the coming of Christianity to Europe (St Thomas the Apostle is supposed to have arrived here in 54 AD). The Portuguese, who unlike the English were as enthusiastic about spreading their brand of Christianity as making money from trade, left a large Christian community in Goa. Generally, however, Christianity has not been greatly successful in India, if success is counted in number of converts. The first round of Indian converts to Christianity were generally those from the ruling classes, and subsequently they were mainly from the lower castes. There are, however, two small states (Mizoram and Nagaland) where Christians form a majority of the population. A quarter of the population of Kerala and a third of Goa are also Christian. The Christian festivals of Good Friday and Christmas Day are both celebrated in India.

There are small Jewish communities in a number of cities, but the Jews of Kochi (Cochin) in Kerala are of special interest because a group claims to have arrived here in 587 BC.

Back page: An offering is dwarfed by the gigantic foot of Gomateshvara – one of Jainism's 'ford makers' – in Karnataka. (photograph by David Collins).

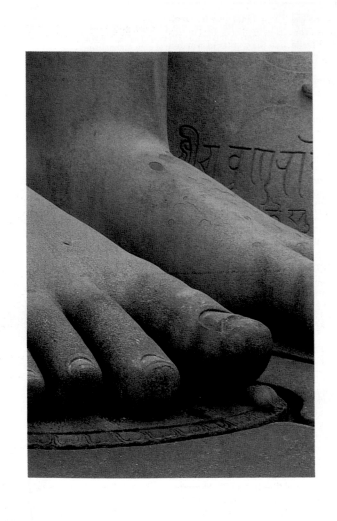

Delhi

Delhi is the capital of India and its third-largest city. The city actually consists of two parts. Old Delhi was the capital of Muslim India between the 17th and 19th centuries. In Old Delhi you will find many mosques, monuments and forts relating to India's Muslim history. The other Delhi is New Delhi, the imperial city created as the capital of India by the British. It is a spacious, open city and contains many embassies and government buildings.

In addition to its historic interest and role as the government centre, Delhi is a major travel gateway. It is one of India's busiest entrance points for overseas airlines, the hub of the north Indian travel network, and a stop on the overland route across Asia. The city of Delhi covers most of the Delhi Union Territory, which is a federal district similar to Washington DC.

Not many travellers have a lot of good things to say about Delhi, and air pollution has now become so bad here it's said to be the world's second dirtiest city (after Mexico City). It does, however, have a long and fascinating history and there are plenty of interesting things to see.

HISTORY

Delhi has not always been the capital of India, but it has played an important role in Indian history. The settlement of Indraprastha, which featured in the epic *Mahabharata* over 3000 years ago, was located approximately on the site of present-day Delhi. Over 2000 years ago, Pataliputra (near modern-day Patna) was the capital of Emperor Ashoka's kingdom. The Mughal emperors made Agra the capital through the 16th and 17th centuries. Under the British, Calcutta was the capital until the construction of New Delhi in 1911.

There have been at least eight cities around modern Delhi, and the old saying that whoever founds a new city at Delhi will lose it has come true every time – most recently

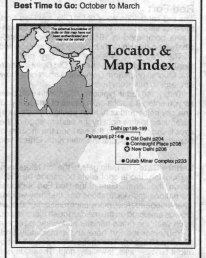

DELHI AT A GLANCE

Population: 11.3 million
Area: 1485 sq km
Main Languages: Hindi, Urdu, Punjabi & English
Telephone Area Code: 011
Best Time to Go: October to March

Locator & Map Index

Delhi pp198-199
Paharganj p214 ● Old Delhi p204
● Connaught Place p208
◎ New Delhi p206

● Qutab Minar Complex p233

Highlights

- Red Fort, Jama Masjid and a walk round Old Delhi
- Rajpath and Lutyens' parliament buildings
- Shopping in the many varied markets and emporia

Festivals

Republic Day Parade – Rajpath – 26 January
Independence Day – Red Fort – 15 August
Crafts Mela – late August

for the British who founded New Delhi in 1911. The first four cities were to the south around the area where the Qutab Minar stands. Indraprastha, the earliest known Delhi, was centred near present-day Purana Qila. At the beginning of the 12th century the last Hindu kingdom of Delhi was ruled by the Tomara and Chauthan dynasties and was also near the Qutab Minar and Suran Kund, now in Haryana.

This city was followed by Siri, constructed by Ala-ud-din near present-day Hauz Khas in the 12th century. The third Delhi was Tughlaqabad, now entirely in ruins, which stood 10km south-east of the Qutab Minar. The fourth Delhi dates from the 14th century and was also a creation of the Tughlaqs. Known as Jahanpanah, it also stood near the Qutab Minar.

The fifth Delhi, Ferozabad, was sited at

A REGIONAL HIGHLIGHT

Red Fort

The red sandstone walls of Lal Qila, the Red Fort, extend for two km and vary in height from 18m on the river side to 33m on the city side. Shah Jahan started construction of the massive fort in 1638 and it was completed in 1648. He never completely moved his capital from Agra to his new city of Shahjahanabad in Delhi because he was deposed and imprisoned in Agra Fort by his son Aurangzeb.

The Red Fort dates from the very peak of Mughal power. When the emperor rode out on elephant-back into the streets of Old Delhi it was a display of pomp and power at its most magnificent. The Mughal reign from Delhi was a short one, however: Aurangzeb was the first and last great Mughal emperor to rule from here.

Today, the fort is typically Indian, with would-be guides leaping forth to offer their services as soon as you enter. It's still a calm haven of peace if you've just left the frantic streets of Old Delhi, however. The city noise and confusion are light years away from the fort gardens and pavilions. The Yamuna River used to flow right by the eastern edge of the fort, and filled the 10m deep moat. These days the river is over one km to the east and the moat remains empty. Entry to the fort is Rs 2 (free on Friday) from the kiosk opposite the main gate. Check your change.

Lahore Gate The main gate to the fort takes its name from the fact that it faces towards Lahore, now in Pakistan. If one spot could be said to be the emotional and symbolic heart of the modern Indian nation, the Lahore Gate of the Red Fort is probably it. During the struggle for independence, one of the nationalists' declarations was that they would see the Indian flag flying over the Red Fort in Delhi. After independence, many important political speeches were given by Nehru and Indira Gandhi to the crowds amassed on the *maidan* (open place or square) outside, and on Independence Day (15 August) each year, the prime minister addresses a huge crowd from the gate.

You enter the fort here and immediately find yourself in a vaulted arcade, the **Chatta Chowk** (Covered Bazaar). The shops in this arcade used to sell the upmarket items that the royal household might fancy – silks, jewellery, gold. These days they cater to the tourist trade and the quality of the goods is certainly a little lower, although some still carry a royal price tag! This arcade of shops was also known as the Meena Bazaar, the shopping centre for ladies of the court. On Thursdays the gates of the fort were closed to men; only women were allowed inside the citadel.

The arcade leads to the **Naubat Khana**, or Drum House, where musicians used to play for the emperor, and the arrival of princes and royalty was heralded from here. There's a dusty **Indian War Memorial museum** (free) upstairs. The open courtyard beyond the Drum House formerly had galleries along either side, but these were removed by the British Army when the fort was used as their headquarters. Other reminders of the British presence are the monumentally ugly, three storey barrack blocks which lie to the north of this courtyard.

Diwan-i-Am The Hall of Public Audiences was where the emperor would sit to hear complaints or disputes from his subjects. His alcove in the wall was marble-panelled and set with precious stones, many of which were looted following the Mutiny/Uprising. This elegant hall was restored as a result of a directive by Lord Curzon, the viceroy of India between 1898 and 1905.

Diwan-i-Khas The Hall of Private Audiences, built of white marble, was the luxurious chamber where the emperor would hold private meetings. Centrepiece of the hall (until Nadir Shah carted it off to Iran in 1739) was the magnificent Peacock Throne. The solid gold throne had figures of peacocks standing behind it, their beautiful colours resulting from countless inlaid precious stones. Between them was the figure of a parrot carved out of a single emerald.

This masterpiece in precious metals, sapphires, rubies, emeralds and pearls was broken up, and

Feroz Shah Kotla in present-day New Delhi. Its ruins contain an Ashoka pillar, moved here from elsewhere, and traces of a mosque in which Tamerlane prayed during his attack on India.

Emperor Sher Shah created the sixth Delhi at Purana Qila, near India Gate in New Delhi today. Sher Shah was an Afghan ruler who defeated the Mughal Humayun and took control of Delhi. The Mughal emperor, Shah Jahan, constructed the seventh Delhi in the 17th century, thus shifting the Mughal capital

A REGIONAL HIGHLIGHT

the so-called Peacock Throne displayed in Tehran simply utilises various bits of the original. The marble pedestal on which the throne used to sit remains in place.

In 1760, the Marathas also removed the silver ceiling from the hall, so today it is a pale shadow of its former glory. Inscribed on the walls of the Diwan-i-Khas is that famous Persian couplet:

If there is a paradise on earth
it is this, it is this, it is this.

Royal Baths Next to the Diwan-i-Khas are the *hammams* or baths – three large rooms surmounted by domes, with a fountain in the centre – one of which was set up as a sauna! The floors used to be inlaid with *pietra dura* work, and the rooms were illuminated through panels of coloured glass in the roof. The baths are closed to the public.

Shahi Burj This modest, three storey octagonal tower at the north-eastern edge of the fort was once Shah Jahan's private working area. From here water used to flow south through the Royal Baths, the Diwan-i-Khas, the Khas Mahal and the Rang Mahal. Like the baths, the tower is closed to the public.

Moti Masjid Built in 1659 by Aurangzeb for his own personal use, the small and totally enclosed Pearl Mosque, made of marble, is next to the baths. One curious feature of the mosque is that its outer walls are oriented exactly to be in symmetry with the rest of the fort, while the inner walls are slightly askew, so that the mosque has the correct orientation with Mecca.

Other Features The **Khas Mahal**, south of the Diwan-i-Khas, was the emperor's private palace, divided into rooms for worship, sleeping and living.

The **Rang Mahal** or Palace of Colour, further south again, took its name from the painted interior, which is now gone. This was once the residence of the emperor's chief wife, and is where he ate. On the floor in the centre is a beautifully carved marble lotus, and the water flowing along the channel from the Shahi Burj used to end up here. Originally there was a fountain made of ivory in the centre.

There is a small Museum of Archaeology in the **Mumtaz Mahal**, still further south along the eastern wall. It's well worth a look, although most visitors seem to rush through the Red Fort, bypassing the museum.

Another museum that's worth seeing is the newly-opened **Svatantrata Sangrama Sangrahalaya** (Museum of the Independence Movement), to the left before the Naubat Khana, amongst the army buildings. The independence movement is charted with photos, letters, newspaper cuttings and several impressive dioramas. Did the Rani of Jhansi really ride into battle with a baby strapped to her back? There's no charge for entry.

Gardens Between all the exquisite buildings were highly formal *charbagh* gardens, complete with fountains, pools and small pavilions. While the general outline and some of the pavilions are still in place, the gardens are not what they once were.

Sound & Light Show Each evening an interesting sound & light show recreates events of India's history, particularly those connected with the Red Fort. There are shows in English and Hindi, and tickets (Rs 20) are available from the fort. The English sessions are at 7.30 pm from November through January, 8.30 pm from February to April and September-October, and at 9 pm from May to August. It's well worth making the effort to see this show, but make sure you are well equipped with mosquito repellent. ■

DELHI

Pollution Alert

The number of vehicles on Delhi's roads has tripled since 1990. Their uncontrolled emissions together with the foul smoke that belches from numerous factories around the city is poisoning the air. More than a third of the population is said to suffer from some kind of respiratory complaint. The level of carbon monoxide at traffic intersections can be as high as 5000mg per cubic metre, 50 times the WHO standard. On windless days it's especially bad and a dark veil hangs over the city.

Little is being done to save Delhi earning the title of world's most polluted city. Cars with black smoke pouring from their tail pipes carry stickers that read 'Pollution Under Control'. In 1997 the municipal council took the dramatic step of banning smoking in public places. Given that simply to breath Delhi's foul air is equivalent to smoking 20 cigarettes a day (40 a day if you're in the thick of the traffic), this is unlikely to achieve a reduction in the growing number of deaths from respiratory diseases.

If you're asthmatic don't stay too long in Delhi. ■

from Agra to Delhi; his Shahjahanabad roughly corresponds to Old Delhi today and is largely preserved. His Delhi included the Red Fort and the majestic Jama Masjid (a *masjid* is a mosque). Finally, the eighth Delhi, New Delhi, was constructed by the British – the move from Calcutta was announced in 1911 but construction was not completed, and the city officially inaugurated, until 1931.

Delhi has seen many invaders through the ages. Tamerlane plundered it in the 14th century; the Afghan Babur occupied it in the 16th century, and in 1739 the Persian emperor, Nadir Shah, sacked the city and carted the Kohinoor Diamond and the famous Peacock Throne off to Iran. The British captured Delhi in 1803, but during the Indian Uprising of 1857 it was a centre of resistance against the British. Prior to Partition, Delhi had a very large Muslim population and Urdu was the main language. Now Hindu Punjabis have replaced many of the Muslims, and Hindi predominates.

William Dalrymple's excellent *City of Djinns* is a wonderfully entertaining introduction to Delhi's past and present.

ORIENTATION

Delhi is a relatively easy city to find your way around although it is very spread out. The section of interest to visitors is on the west bank of the Yamuna River and is divided basically into two parts – the tightly packed streets of Old Delhi and the spacious, planned areas of New Delhi.

Old Delhi is the 17th century walled city of Shahjahanabad, with city gates, narrow alleys, the enormous Red Fort and Jama Masjid, temples, mosques, bazaars and the famous street known as Chandni Chowk. Here you will find the Delhi railway station and, a little further north, the main interstate bus station near Kashmir Gate. Near New Delhi railway station, and acting as a sort of 'buffer zone' between the old and new cities, is Paharganj. This has become the budget travellers' hangout, and there are many popular cheap hotels and restaurants in this area.

New Delhi is a planned city of wide, tree-lined streets, parks and fountains. It can be further subdivided into the business and residential areas around Connaught Place and the government areas around Rajpath to the south. At the east end of Rajpath is the India Gate memorial and at the west end is Rashtrapati Bhavan, the residence of the Indian president.

The hub of New Delhi is the great circle of Connaught Place and the streets that radiate from it. Here you will find most of the airline offices, banks, travel agents, the various state tourist offices and the national one, more budget accommodation and several of the big hotels. The Regal Cinema, at the south side of the circle, and the Plaza Cinema, at the north, are two important Connaught Place landmarks and are very useful for telling taxi or auto-rickshaw drivers where you want to go.

Janpath, running off Connaught Place to the south, is one of the most important streets, with the Government of India tourist office, the Student Travel Information Centre in the Imperial Hotel and a number of other useful addresses.

South of the New Delhi government areas are Delhi's more expensive residential areas, with names like Defence Colony, South Extension, Lodi Colony, Greater Kailash and Vasant Vihar. The Indira Gandhi International Airport is to the south-west of the city, and about halfway between the airport and Connaught Place is Chanakyapuri, the diplomatic enclave. Most of Delhi's embassies are concentrated in this modern area and there are several major hotels here.

The 200 page *A to Z Road Guide for Delhi* includes 60 area maps, and is a good reference if you are venturing further into the Delhi environs. It's available at most larger bookstores or at the Delhi Tourism Development Corporation.

INFORMATION
Tourist Offices

The Government of India tourist office (☎ 332 0005) at 88 Janpath is open Monday to Friday from 9 am to 6 pm and Saturday from 9 am to 2 pm. The office has a lot of information and brochures on destinations all over India, but none of it is on display – you have to know what you want and ask for it. They have a good giveaway map of the city, and can also help you find accommodation.

In the arrivals hall at the international airport terminal there is a tourist counter (☎ 329 1171) open around the clock. Here, too, they can help you find accommodation although, like many other Indian tourist offices, they may tell you the hotel you choose is 'full' and steer you somewhere else when actually your selected hotel is not full at all.

There is a Delhi Tourism Corporation office (☎ 331 3637) in N Block, Connaught Place. They also have counters at New Delhi, Old Delhi, and Nizamuddin railway stations, as well as at the Interstate bus station (☎ 251 2181) at Kashmir Gate.

Most of the state governments have information centres in Delhi, and the offices for Assam (☎ 334 5897), Bihar (☎ 372 3371), Gujarat (☎ 373 2107), Karnataka (☎ 336 3862), Maharashtra (☎ 336 0773), Manipur (☎ 336 4026), Orissa (☎ 336 4580), Tamil Nadu (☎ 336 4651) and West Bengal (☎ 373 2840) are all on Baba Kharak Singh Marg, which runs off Connaught Place.

The offices for Haryana (☎ 332 4910), Himachal Pradesh (☎ 332 5320) and Uttar Pradesh (☎ 332 2251) are in the Chandralok Building at 36 Janpath.

Rajasthan (☎ 332 2332) has its tourist office at Bikaner House, near India Gate.

Jammu & Kashmir (☎ 332 5373), Kerala (☎ 331 6541), Madhya Pradesh (☎ 332 1187) and Punjab (☎ 332 3055) have their offices in the Kanishka Shopping Centre between the Yatri Niwas and Kanishka hotels.

Others include: Andaman & Nicobar Islands (☎ 687 1442), A&N Bhavan, Chanakyapuri (behind Chanakya Cinema); Goa (☎ 462 9968), 18 Amrita Shergil Marg; Meghalaya (☎ 301 5503), 9 Aurangzeb Rd; Sikkim (☎ 301 3026), at Sikkim Bhavan, Chanakyapuri; and Tripura (☎ 301 4607), Tripura Bhavan, Chanakyapuri.

There are several listings guides available from newsstands – *Delhi City Guide*, *Genesis*, and *Delhi Diary* among them. *First City* (Rs 20) is a monthly society magazine which gives some useless gossip on what the city's social set are up to, but it's worth having a look at because it also has good listings of cultural events.

Warning Steer clear of the dozen or so 'tourist information centres' across the road from New Delhi railway station. None of them are tourist offices as such, despite bold claims to the contrary; they are simply travel agents, and many are simply out to fleece unsuspecting visitors – both foreign and Indian.

If you are going to make a booking at the foreign tourist booking office at the station you may well be approached by touts from these shops who will insist the office you want is closed and try to steer you to the shonky travel agents and rake off a commission. Don't be tempted by offers of cheap bus fares or hotels.

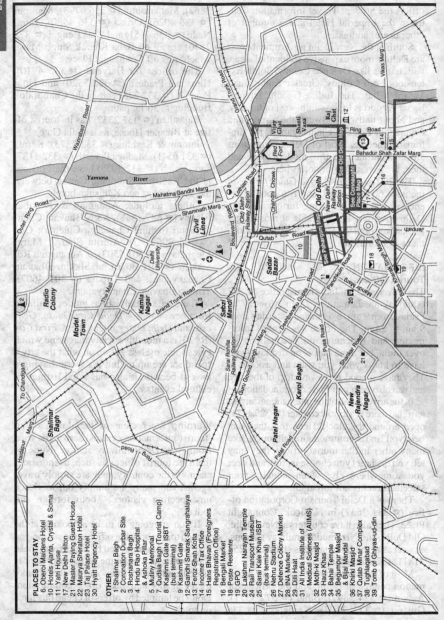

PLACES TO STAY

6 Oberoi Maidens Hotel
10 Hotels Ajanta, Crystal & Soma
11 Yatri House
17 New Delhi Hilton
21 Master Paying Guest House
22 Maurya Sheraton Hotel
23 Taj Palace Hotel
30 Hyatt Regency Hotel

OTHER

1 Shalimar Bagh
2 Coronation Durbar Site
3 Roshanara Bagh
4 Hindu Rao Hospital
5 Mutiny Memorial & Ashoka Pillar
7 Qudsia Bagh (Tourist Camp)
8 Kashmiri Gate ISBT (bus terminal)
9 Kashmiri Gate
12 Gandhi Smarak Sangrahalaya
13 Feroz Shah Kotla
14 Income Tax Office
15 Hans Bhavan (Foreigners' Registration Office)
16 Bengali Market
18 Poste Restante
19 GPO
20 Lakshmi Narayan Temple
24 Rail Transport Museum
25 Sarai Kale Khan ISBT (bus terminal)
26 Nehru Stadium
27 Defence Colony Market
29 Dilli Haat
31 All India Institute of Medical Sciences (AIIMS)
32 Moth-ki Masjid
33 Hauz Khas
34 Bahai Temple
35 Begumpur Masjid & Bijai Mandal
36 Khirki Masjid
37 Qutab Minar Complex
38 Tughlaqabad
39 Tomb of Ghyas-ud-din

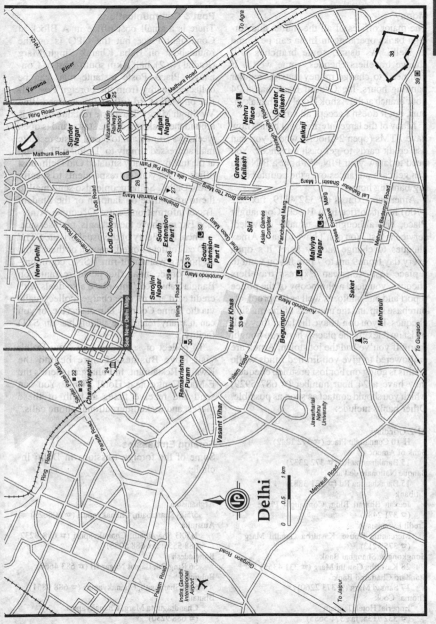

Delhi

0   0.5   1 km

DELHI

Money

The major offices of all the Indian and foreign banks operating in India can be found in Delhi. As usual, some branches will change travellers cheques, some won't. If you need to change money outside regular banking hours, the Central Bank has a 24 hour branch at the Ashok Hotel in Chanakyapuri, but it doesn't accept all currencies.

Many of the large international banks now have ATMs (open 24 hours) where you can use credit cards to get cash advances. You need to know your PIN. Without a PIN you can get cash advances over the counter during banking hours.

American Express (☎ 332 4119; fax 332 1706) has its office in A Block, Connaught Place, and although it's usually crowded, service is fast. You don't have to have Amex cheques to change money here. It's open every day from 9 am to 7 pm. If you want to replace lost American Express travellers cheques, you need a photocopy of the police report and one photo, as well as the proof-of-purchase slip and the numbers of the missing cheques. If you don't have the latter they will insist on telexing the place where you bought them. If you've had the lot stolen, Amex are empowered to give you limited funds while all this is going on. For lost or stolen cheques, they have a 24 hour number (☎ 687 5929) which you should contact as soon as possible. Other banks include:

ANZ Grindlays
    H-10 Connaught Place (☎ 372 1242)
Bank of America
    15 Barakhamba Rd (☎ 372 2332)
Banque Nationale de Paris
    15 Barakhamba Rd (☎ 331 3883)
Citibank
    Jeevan Bharati Bldg, Connaught Place
    (☎ 371 2484)
Credit Lyonnais
    Mercantile House, Kasturba Gandhi Marg
    (☎ 375 5213)
Hongkong & Shanghai Bank
    28 Kasturba Gandhi Marg (☎ 331 4355)
Standard Chartered Bank
    17 Sansad Marg (☎ 373 2260)
Thomas Cook
    Imperial Hotel, Janpath
    (☎ 332 7135; fax 371 5685)

Post & Communications

There is a small post office in A Block at Connaught Place but the GPO is on the roundabout on Baba Kharak Singh Marg (Radial No 2), half a km south-west of Connaught Place. Poste restante mail can be collected nearby from the Foreign Post Office on Market Rd (officially renamed Bhai Vir Singh Marg). The poste restante office is around the back and up the stairs, and is open weekdays from 9 am to 5 pm. Poste restante mail addressed simply to 'Delhi' will end up at the inconveniently situated Old Delhi post office, so ask your correspondents to specify 'New Delhi'. Some people also send mail to the tourist office on Janpath or the Student Travel Information Centre. Of course, American Express have their clients' mail service.

There are plenty of the usual private STD/ISD call offices dotted around, or there's the 24 hour, government-run VSNL communication office near the poste restante on Bangla Sahib Rd. This place also deals with credit card and reverse charge (collect) calls via the Home Country Direct service, or you can use any telephone which has an STD facility.

To collect or send email in New Delhi, visit Roye Business Centre behind the Kwality Restaurant. In Paharganj there's the E-Mail Centre near Hotel Vishal. You can send and receive faxes at both of these places, and make international phone calls.

Foreign Embassies

Some of the foreign missions in Delhi include:

Afghanistan
    5/50F Shantipath, Chanakyapuri (☎ 606625)
Australia
    1/50G Shantipath, Chanakyapuri (☎ 688 8232,
    688 5556; fax 688 5088)
Bangladesh
    56 Ring Rd, Lajpat Nagar III (☎ 683 4668)
Belgium
    50N Shantipath, Chanakyapuri (☎ 688 9851)
Bhutan
    Chandragupta Marg, Chanakyapuri
    (☎ 688 9230)

Canada
    7/8 Shantipath, Chanakyapuri
    (☎ 687 6500; fax 687 6579)
China
    50D Shantipath, Chanakyapuri (☎ 600328)
Denmark
    11 Aurangzeb Rd (☎ 301 0900)
Finland
    E3 Nyaya Marg, Chanakyapuri
    (☎ 611 5258; fax 688 6713)
France
    2/50E Shantipath, Chanakyapuri
    (☎ 611 8790; fax 687 2305)
Germany
    6/50G Shantipath, Chanakyapuri (☎ 604861)
Indonesia
    50A Niti Marg, Chanakyapuri (☎ 611 8646)
Iran
    5 Barakhamba Rd (☎ 332 9600)
Iraq
    169 Jor Bagh Rd (☎ 461 8011)
Ireland
    13 Jor Bagh Rd (☎ 462 6733; fax 469 7053)
Israel
    3 Aurangzeb Rd (☎ 301 3238)
Italy
    50E Chandragupta Marg, Chanakyapuri
    (☎ 611 4355)
Japan
    50G Shantipath, Chanakyapuri (☎ 687 6581)
Kenya
    66 Vasant Marg, Vasant Vihar (☎ 687 6540)
Malaysia
    50M Satya Marg, Chanakyapuri (☎ 601297)
Myanmar (Burma)
    3/50F Nyaya Marg, Chanakyapuri (☎ 600251)
Nepal
    Barakhamba Rd (☎ 332 8191)
Netherlands
    6/50F Shantipath, Chanakyapuri (☎ 688 4951)
New Zealand
    50N Nyaya Marg, Chanakyapuri (☎ 688 3170)
Norway
    50C Shantipath, Chanakyapuri
    (☎ 687 3532; fax 687 3814)
Pakistan
    2/50G Shantipath, Chanakyapuri (☎ 600601)
Palestine
    D1/27 Vasant Vihar (☎ 614 6605)
Russia
    Shantipath, Chanakyapuri (☎ 611 0641)
Singapore
    E6 Chandragupta Marg, Chanakyapuri
    (☎ 688 5659)
South Africa
    B-18 Vasant Marg, Vasant Vihar (☎ 611 9411)
Spain
    12 Prithviraj Rd (☎ 379 2085)

Sri Lanka
    27 Kautilya Marg, Chanakyapuri (☎ 301 0201)
Sweden
    Nyaya Marg, Chanakyapuri (☎ 687 5760)
Switzerland
    Nyaya Marg, Chanakyapuri
    (☎ 604 225; fax 687 3093)
Syria
    28 Vasant Marg, Vasant Vihar (☎ 614 0233)
Thailand
    56N Nyaya Marg, Chanakyapuri (☎ 611 8103)
UK
    50 Shantipath, Chanakyapuri
    (☎ 687 2161; fax 687 2882)
USA
    Shantipath, Chanakyapuri
    (☎ 688 7033, 611 3033)

See under Visas in the Facts for the Visitor chapter for more details on obtaining visas in Delhi for other countries.

Visa Extensions & Other Permits

Hans Bhavan, near the Tilak Bridge railway station, is where you'll find the Foreigners' Registration Office (☎ 331 9489). Come here to get permits for restricted areas such as Arunachal Pradesh. Four photos are required for permits. The office is open weekdays from 9.30 am to 1.30 pm and 2 to 4 pm.

The Foreigners' Registration Office can issue 15 day visa extensions if you just need a few extra days before you leave the country. To apply for a longer visa extension, first you have to collect a form from the Ministry of Home Affairs at Khan Market which is then taken to the Foreigners' Registration Office (about a Rs 20 rickshaw ride away). You can usually get 15 days free, but a one month extension costs Rs 725 (four photos required). When (and if) the extension is authorised, the authorisation has to be taken *back* to the Home Office, where the actual visa extension is issued.

Since it's extremely difficult to get an extension on a six month visa, you may be approached by people offering to forge your visa for a longer stay. Don't fall for this one, as the authorities will check your details carefully against their computer records when you leave India. There are heavy fines and you won't be allowed to visit India again.

If you need a tax clearance certificate before departure, the Foreign Section of the Income Tax Department (☎ 331 7826) is just around the corner from Hans Bhavan in the Central Revenue Building on Vikas Marg. Bring exchange certificates with you, though it's quite likely nobody will ask for your clearance certificate when you leave the country. The office is closed from 1 to 2 pm.

Export of any object over 100 years old requires a permit. If in doubt, contact the Director, Antiquities, Archaeological Survey of India, Janpath (☎ 301 7220).

Libraries & Cultural Centres

The American Center (☎ 331 6841) is at 24 Kasturba Gandhi Marg and is open from 9.30 am to 6 pm. It has an extensive range of books. The British Council Library (☎ 371 0111) is at 17 Kasturba Gandhi Marg and is open Tuesday to Saturday from 10 am to 6 pm. It's much better than the US equivalent, but officially you have to join to get in. Other cultural centres include: Alliance Francaise (☎ 644 0128), D-13 South Extension Part II; Italy (☎ 644 9193), Golf Links Rd; Japan (☎ 332 9803), 32 Ferozshah Rd; and Russia (☎ 332 9102), 24 Ferozshah Rd.

India International Centre (☎ 461 9431), beside the Lodi Tombs, has lectures each week on art, economics and other contemporary issues by Indian and foreign experts.

Sangeet Natak Akademi (☎ 338 7248), at 35 Ferozshah Rd, is the main performing arts centre and has substantial archive material.

World Wide Fund for Nature India (☎ 469 3744), 172-B Lodi Estate, has excellent computerised environmental records, a good library, and an eco-shop selling handicrafts and books. It's open Monday to Friday from 9.30 am to 5.30 pm.

Travel Agencies

In the Imperial Hotel, the Student Travel Information Centre (☎ 332 7582) is used by many travellers and is the place to renew or obtain student cards, although their tickets are not usually as cheap as elsewhere.

Some of the ticket discounters around Connaught Place are real fly-by-night operations, so take care. Those that have been recommended by readers include Aerotrek Travels (☎ 371 5966) in the Mercantile Building in E Block; Cozy Travels (☎ 331 2873), BMC House, 1-N Connaught Place; Tripsout Travel (☎ 332 2654), 72 Tolstoy Lane; Y Tours & Travel, at the YMCA; Tan's Travel (☎ 332 1490), 72 Janpath; Outbound Travel (☎ 603902) at B-2/50 Safdarjang Enclave. In Paharganj, Aa Bee Travels (☎ 752 0117) is based at Hare Rama Guest House but has several links to the more popular travellers' hotels in this area.

For more upmarket travel arrangements, both within India and for foreign travel, there are a number of places, mostly around Connaught Place. These include: Cox & Kings (☎ 332 0067), Sita World Travels (☎ 331 1133) and the Travel Corporation of India (☎ 331 2570).

Bookshops

There are a number of excellent bookshops around Connaught Place – a good place to look for interesting Indian books or to stock up with hefty paperbacks to while away those long train rides. Some of the better shops include: the New Book Depot at 18 B Block, Connaught Place; the English Book Depot; the Piccadilly Book Store, 64 Shankar Market, the Oxford Book Shop opposite N Block on the Outer Circle, Connaught Place; and Bookworm at 29B Radial Rd No 4, Connaught Place. Prabhu Book Service in Hauz Khas Village has an interesting selection of secondhand and rare books.

There are plenty of pavement stalls at various places around Connaught Place, with the major concentration on Sansad Marg, near the Kwality Restaurant. They have a good range of cheap paperbacks, and will often buy them back from you if they are returned in a reasonable condition. Almost next door to the Kwality Restaurant is People Tree, which sells books about the environment, and eco-friendly crafts.

The largest stockist of Lonely Planet guides is Bahri Sons, opposite the main gate at Khan Market.

Film & Photography
The Delhi Photo Company, at 78 Janpath close to the tourist office, processes both print and slide film quickly, cheaply and competently.

Medical Services
If you need medical attention in Delhi, the East West Medical Centre (☎ 462 3738, 469 9229), near the Delhi Golf Course at 38 Golf Links Rd, has been recommended by many travellers, diplomats and other expatriates. All the rickshaw-wallahs know where it is. It's well equipped and the staff know what they're doing. A consultation costs Rs 220, which is high by Indian standards, but if you want good treatment...

For 24 hour emergency service, try the All India Institute of Medical Sciences (☎ 661123, 686 4581) at Ansari Nagar. Other reliable places include the Dr Ram Manohar Lohia Hospital (☎ 331 1621), Baba Kharak Singh Marg; and the Ashlok Hospital (☎ 608407) at 25A Block AB, Safdarjang Enclave.

There's a 24 hour pharmacy at Super Bazaar in Connaught Place.

Ambulance services can be phoned on ☎ 102.

Motorcycle Shops
If you are in the market for a new Enfield motorcycle, try Essaar on Jhandi Walan Extension, Karol Bagh. For second-hand bikes and parts, try Inder Motors (☎ 572 8579) or Madaan Motors, also in Karol Bagh.

OLD DELHI
See the **Red Fort** regional highlight on p194.

The old walled city of Shahjahanabad stands to the west of the Red Fort and was at one time surrounded by a sturdy defensive wall, only fragments of which now exist. The **Kashmir Gate**, at the northern end of the walled city, was the scene of desperate fighting when the British retook Delhi during the Mutiny. West of here, near Sabzi Mandi, is the British-erected **Mutiny Memorial** to the soldiers who lost their lives during the uprising. Near the monument is an **Ashoka pillar**,

and like the one in Feroz Shah Kotla, it was brought here by Feroz Shah Tughlaq.

Chandni Chowk
The main street of Old Delhi is the colourful shopping bazaar known as Chandni Chowk. It's hopelessly congested day and night, a sharp contrast to the spacious streets of New Delhi. At the east (Red Fort) end of Chandni Chowk, there is a **Digambara Jain temple** with a small marble courtyard surrounded by a colonnade. There's an interesting **bird hospital** here, run by the Jains; entry is free but donations are gratefully accepted.

Next to the *kotwali* (old police station) is the **Sunehri Masjid**. In 1739, Nadir Shah, the Persian invader who carried off the Peacock Throne when he sacked Delhi, stood on the roof of this mosque and watched while his soldiers conducted a bloody massacre of Delhi's inhabitants.

At the west end of Chandni Chowk is the **Fatehpuri Mosque**, which was erected in 1650 by one of Shah Jahan's wives.

Jama Masjid
The great mosque of Old Delhi is both the largest in India and the final architectural extravagance of Shah Jahan. Begun in 1644, the mosque was not completed until 1658. It has three great gateways, four angle towers and two minarets standing 40m high and constructed of alternating vertical strips of red sandstone and white marble.

Broad flights of steps lead up to the imposing gateways. The eastern gateway was originally only opened for the emperor, and is now open on Fridays and Muslim festivals. The general public can enter by the north or south gate (Rs 10). Remove your shoes. Those people considered unsuitably dressed (bare legs for either men or women) can hire robes at the northern gate.

The courtyard of the mosque can hold 25,000 people. For Rs 6 (Rs 10 with a camera) it's possible to climb the southern minaret – if you're a man or you have one with you. The views in all directions are superb – Old Delhi, the Red Fort and the polluting factories beyond it across the river,

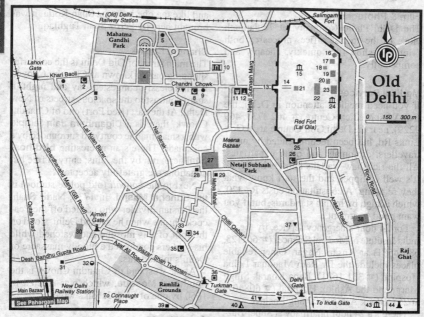

Old Delhi

0   150   300 m

PLACES TO STAY
3   Bharat Hotel & Star
    Guest House
28 Hotel New City Palace
29 Hotel Bombay Orient
    & Karim's Restaurant
31 Rail Yatri Niwas
39 Hotel Ranjit
40 Tourist Camp

PLACES TO EAT
7   Ghantewala Sweet
    Shop
37 Moti Mahal Restaurant
41 Chor Bizaare
42 Tandoor Restaurant

OTHER
1   Gadodia Market
2   Fatehpuri Masjid
4   Town Hall
5   Delhi Public Library

6   Jain Svetambara
    Temple
8   Sunehri Masjid
9   Sisganj Gurdwara
10 Begum Samru's
    Palace
11 Gauri Shankar Temple
12 Digambara Jain
    Temple & Bird
    Hospital
13 Red Fort's Lahore
    Gate & Ticket Kiosk
14 Chatta Chowk
15 Museum of
    Independence
    Movement
16 Shahi Burj
17 Hammams
18 Moti Masjid
19 Diwan-i-Khas
20 Khas Mahal
21 Naubat Khana

22 Diwan-i-Am
23 Rang Mahal
24 Mumtaz Mahal &
    Museum
25 Red Fort's Delhi Gate
26 Sunehri Masjid
27 Jama Masjid
30 Madrassa of
    Ghazi-ud-din
32 DTC Buses No 780
    (Airport) & No 505
    (Qutab Minar)
33 Bishan Swaroup Haveli
34 Sultan Raziya's Tomb
35 Kalan Masjid
36 Tomb of Hazrat Shah
    Turkman & Holy
    Trinity Church
38 Zinat-ul Masjid
43 Gandhi Memorial
    Museum
44 Gandhi Memorial

and New Delhi to the south. You can also see one of the features that the architect Lutyens incorporated into his design of New Delhi –

the Jama Masjid, Connaught Place and Sansad Bhavan (Parliament House) are in a direct line. There's also a fine view of the

Red Fort from the east side of the mosque. Women should take care on the dark staircase of the tower; several women have written to say they have been molested by Indian men here and had to fight to get away.

Coronation Durbar Site

This is a must for incurable Raj fans looking for their fix of nostalgia. It's north of Old Delhi and is best reached by auto-rickshaw. In a desolate field stands a lone obelisk – this is where, in 1877 and 1903, the durbars were enacted.

It was also here in 1911 that King George V was declared emperor of India. If you look closely you can still see the old boy – a statue of him rises ghost-like out of the bushes nearby, where it was unceremoniously dumped after being removed from the canopy midway along Rajpath, between India Gate and Rashtrapati Bhavan. Further inspection reveals other imperial dignitaries languishing in the scrub. These days this historic bit of spare ground is used for backyard cricket matches and is a place for young men to teach their girlfriends how to ride the family scooter.

FEROZ SHAH KOTLA

Erected by Feroz Shah Tughlaq in 1354, the ruins of Ferozabad, the fifth city of Delhi, can be found at Feroz Shah Kotla, just off Bahadur Shah Zafar Marg between the old and new Delhis. In the fortress-palace is a 13m high sandstone **Ashoka pillar** inscribed with Ashoka's edicts (and a later inscription). The remains of an old mosque and a fine well can also be seen in the area, but most of the ruins of Ferozabad were used for the construction of later cities.

RAJ GHAT

North-east of Feroz Shah Kotla, on the banks of the Yamuna, a simple square platform of black marble marks the spot where Mahatma Gandhi was cremated following his assassination in 1948. A commemorative ceremony takes place each Friday, the day he was killed.

Jawaharlal Nehru, the first Indian prime minister, was cremated just to the north at Shanti Vana (Forest of Peace) in 1964. His daughter, Indira Gandhi, who was killed in 1984, and grandsons Sanjay (1980) and Rajiv (1991) were also cremated in this vicinity.

The Raj Ghat area is now a beautiful park. The **Gandhi Memorial Museum** here is well worth a visit; a macabre relic is the pistol with which Gandhi was assassinated. Entry is free; it's open daily except Monday, from 9.30 am to 5.30 pm.

NEW DELHI
Connaught Place

Located at the northern end of New Delhi, Connaught Place is the business and tourist centre. It's a vast traffic circle with an architecturally uniform series of colonnaded buildings around the edge, mainly devoted to shops, banks, restaurants, and airline offices. It's spacious but busy, and you're continually approached by people willing to provide you with everything imaginable, from an airline ticket for Timbuktu to having your fortune read.

Shoeshine Sir?

Thought you should hear about a scam being operated by shoeshine boys in Delhi at the moment.

They will pester you to shine your shoes. You decline as you happen to be wearing trainers or, in my case, suede. You look down to point this out and find a dollop of shit has found its way onto your shoe. You then agree to have this wiped off and a second boy arrives. They do a good job of cleaning your shoes and demand Rs 350 payment! They then become quite aggressive as you remonstrate. I ended up paying Rs 30. I saw several others caught in the same manner and was pestered again later on and found to my amazement another dollop of shit on my shoe. I guess they must have some kind of shitgun to get the stuff there so accurately!

Graeme Jackson (UK)

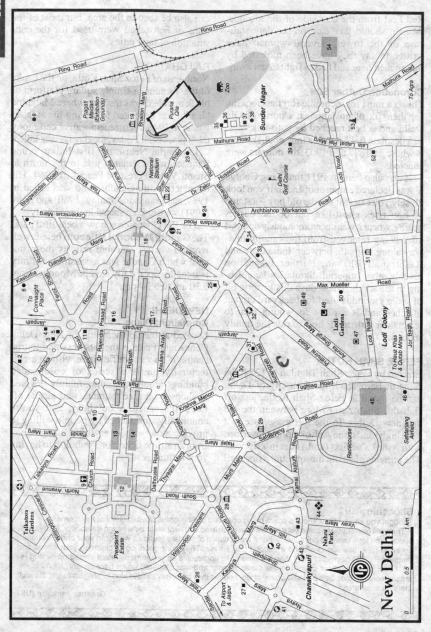

New Delhi

0   0.5   1 km

In 1995 the inner and outer circle were renamed Rajiv Chowk and Indira Chowk (the son within the mother); but everyone still calls it CP (Connaught Place) despite the signs.

Jantar Mantar

Only a short stroll down Sansad Marg (Parliament St) from Connaught Place, this strange collection of salmon-coloured structures is one of Maharaja Jai Singh II's observatories. The ruler from Jaipur constructed this observatory in 1725 and it is dominated by a huge sundial known as the Prince of Dials. Other instruments plot the course of heavenly bodies and predict eclipses.

Lakshmi Narayan Temple

Situated due west of Connaught Place, this garish modern temple was erected by the industrialist BD Birla in 1938. It's dedicated to Lakshmi, the goddess of prosperity and good fortune, and is commonly known as Birla Mandir.

Rajpath

The Kingsway is another focus of Lutyens' New Delhi. It is immensely broad and is flanked on either side by ornamental ponds. The Republic Day parade is held here every 26 January, and millions of people gather to enjoy the spectacle.

At the eastern end of Rajpath lies the India Gate, while at the western end lies Rashtrapati Bhavan, now the president's residence, but built originally for the viceroy. It is flanked by the two large Secretariat buildings, and these three buildings sit upon a small rise, known as Raisina Hill.

India Gate

This 42m high stone arch of triumph stands at the eastern end of the Rajpath. It bears the names of 85,000 Indian Army soldiers who died in the campaigns of WWI, the North-West Frontier operations of the same time and the 1919 Afghan fiasco.

Rashtrapati Bhavan

The official residence of the President of India stands at the opposite end of the Rajpath from

PLACES TO STAY

2	YWCA International Guest House	7	Rabindra Bhavan	24	Pandara Market
3	Ashok Yatri Niwas Hotel	8	Appu Ghar	28	Nehru Museum
4	Janpath Hotel	9	Church of the Redemption	29	Indira Gandhi Memorial Museum
5	Kanishka Hotel	10	Sansad Bhavan (Parliament House)	30	Gandhi Smriti
11	Le Meridien Hotel	12	Rashtrapati Bhavan	32	Israeli Embassy
25	Taj Mahal Hotel	13	Secretariat (North Block)	33	Khan Market
26	Diplomat Hotel	14	Secretariat (South Block)	38	Sunder Nagar Market
27	Vishwa Yuvak Kendra & Youth Hostel	15	Vijay Chowk	40	UK Embassy
31	Claridges Hotel	16	Indira Gandhi National Centre for the Arts	41	US Embassy
34	Ambassador Hotel	17	National Museum	42	Australian Embassy
35	Maharani Guest House	18	India Gate	44	Santushti Shopping Centre
36	Kailash Inn & La Sangrita Tourist Home	19	Crafts Museum	45	Safdarjang Tomb
37	Jukaso Inn	20	Children's Park	46	Indian Airlines (24 hours)
39	Oberoi Hotel	21	Bikaner House (Rajasthan Tourist Office & Deluxe buses to Jaipur)	47	Mohammed Shah's Tomb
43	Hotels Ashok & Samrat	22	National Gallery of Modern Art	48	Bara Gumbad Mosque
52	Lodhi Hotel	23	Sher Shah's Gate & Khairul Manzil Masjid	49	Sikander Lodi's Tomb
OTHER				50	India International Centre
1	Ram Manohar Lohia Hospital			51	Tibet House
6	Max Mueller Bhavan			53	Nizam-ud-din's Shrine
				54	Humayun's Tomb

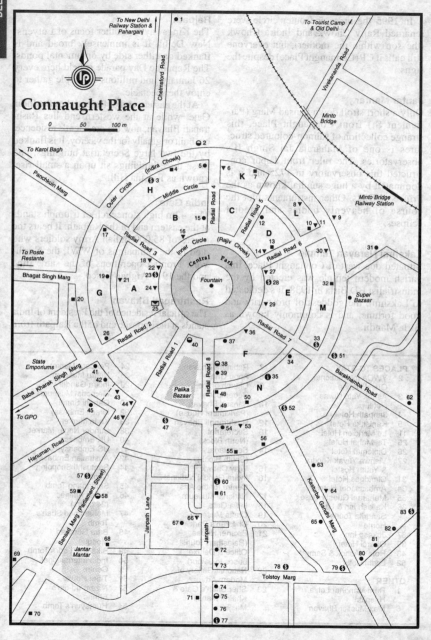

Connaught Place

To New Delhi Railway Station & Paharganj

To Tourist Camp & Old Delhi

Chelmsford Road

Vivekananda Road

Minto Bridge

Minto Bridge Railway Station

0   50   100 m

To Karol Bagh

Panchkuin Marg

Outer Circle

Middle Circle

Inner Circle

(Indira Chowk)

(Rajiv Chowk)

Central Park

Fountain

To Poste Restante

Bhagat Singh Marg

Radial Road 3

Radial Road 4

Radial Road 5

Radial Road 6

Radial Road 7

Radial Road 2

Radial Road 1

Radial Road 8

Barakhamba Road

State Emporiums

Baba Kharak Singh Marg

To GPO

Hanuman Road

Palika Bazaar

Kasturba Gandhi Marg

Sansad Marg (Parliament Street)

Janpath Lane

Janpath

Jantar Mantar

Tolstoy Marg

To New Delhi

H

B

A

G

C

D

E

F

K

L

M

N

India Gate. Completed in 1929, the palace-like building is an interesting blend of Mughal and western architectural styles, the most obvious Indian feature being the huge copper dome. To the west of the building is a Mughal garden which occupies 130 ha. If you want to visit it, this garden is only open to the public in February.

Prior to Independence this was the viceroy's residence. At the time of Mountbatten, India's last viceroy, the number of servants needed to maintain the 340 rooms and its extensive gardens was enormous. There were 418 gardeners alone, 50 of them boys whose sole job was to chase away birds!

Secretariat Buildings
The north and south Secretariat buildings lie either side of Rajpath on Raisina Hill. These imposing buildings, topped with *chhatris* (small domes), now house the ministries of Finance and External Affairs respectively.

Sansad Bhavan
Although another large and imposing building, Sansad Bhavan, the Indian parliament

	PLACES TO STAY				
4	Hotel 55	44	El Arab Restaurant	47	Citibank & Air India
7	York Hotel	46	Kwality Restaurant	51	Scotiabank
10	Nirula's Hotel	49	Wimpy	52	Hongkong & Shanghai
13	Hotel Palace Heights	53	Croissants Etc		Bank
17	Hotel Marina	64	Parikrama Restaurant	54	Oxford Bookshop
20	Alka Hotel	66	Bankura Cafe	57	Standard Chartered &
32	Hotel Bright, Hotel	73	Sona Rupa		Allahabad Banks
	Blue & Andhra Bank		Restaurant	58	Bus 433 to Bahai
48	Hotel Metro & Nirula's		& Royal Nepal		Temple & Bus 620
	(branch)		Airlines		to Youth Hostel &
50	Hotel Central Court				Chanakyapuri
55	Ringo Guest House		**OTHER**	60	Government of India
56	Sunny Guest House	1	Railway Booking Office		Tourist Office &
59	Park Hotel	2	Bus 620 to Youth		Delhi Photo
61	Janpath Guest House		Hostel &		Company
68	Mr SC Jain's Guest		Chanakyapuri	62	East-West Airlines,
	House	3	ANZ Grindlays Bank		Emirates Air &
69	YMCA Tourist Hotel	5	Plaza Cinema		Wheels Rent-a-Car
70	YWCA International	12	Odeon Cinema	63	American Center
	Guest House	15	Bookworm	65	British Council
71	Imperial Hotel,	19	NEPC Airlines/Skyline	67	Map Sales Office
	Thomas Cook &		NEPC	72	Lufthansa
	Student Travel	23	American Express	74	Central Cottage
	Information Centre	25	Post Office		Industries
		26	Malaysian & Royal		Emporium
	PLACES TO EAT		Jordanian	75	Bus 505 to Qutab
6	Gola Restaurant		Airlines, El Al		Minar
8	Delhi Durbar & Minar	28	ANZ Grindlays Bank	76	Japan Airlines
	Restaurants	31	Shankar Market	77	Haryana, Himachal
9	Yamu's Panchayat	33	Bank of Baroda		Pradesh, Uttar
11	Nirula's Restaurants	34	Aeroflot		Pradesh & West
14	Embassy Restaurant	35	Delhi Tourism		Bengal Tourist
16	Cafe 100, Zen & Volga	37	Cathay Pacific Airlines		Offices
	Restaurants	38	EATS Airport Bus	78	Deutsche Bank
18	Keventers	39	Indian Airlines	79	Credit Lyonnaise
21	Fa Yian Restaurant	40	Pre-paid Autorickshaw	80	United & Sahara
22	Wenger's		Kiosk & Motorcycle		Indian Airlines
24	El Rodeo Restaurant		Rickshaws to Old	81	KLM
27	Kovil		Delhi	82	ModiLuft
29	United Coffee House	41	Khadi Gramodyog	83	Bank of America,
30	Domino's Pizza		Bhavan		Banque
36	The Host	42	Regal Cinema		Nationale deParis
43	Gaylord	45	Roye Business Centre		& Saudia Airlines
			(Email)		

building, stands almost hidden and virtually unnoticed at the end of Sansad Marg, or Parliament St, just north of Rajpath. The building is a circular colonnaded structure 171m in diameter. Its relative physical insignificance in the grand scheme of New Delhi shows how the focus of power has shifted from the viceroy's residence, which was given pride of place during the time of the British Raj when New Delhi was conceived.

Permits to visit the parliament and sit in the public gallery are available from the reception office on Raisina Rd, but you'll need a letter of introduction from your embassy.

MUSEUMS & GALLERIES
National Museum

Located on Janpath just south of Rajpath, the National Museum has a good collection of Indian bronzes, terracotta and wood sculptures dating back to the Mauryan period (2nd to 3rd century BC), exhibits from the Vijayanagar period in south India, miniature and mural paintings, and costumes of the various tribal peoples. The museum is definitely worth visiting and is open Tuesday to

Miniature painting:
tranquil scenes from times past.

Sunday from 10 am to 5 pm. Admission is Rs 0.50. There are film shows each afternoon.

Right next door is the Archaeological Survey of India office. Publications available here cover all the main sites in India. Many of these are not available at the particular sites themselves.

National Gallery of Modern Art

This gallery stands near India Gate at the eastern end of Rajpath, and was formerly the Delhi residence of the Maharaja of Jaipur. It houses an excellent collection of works by both Indian and colonial artists.

It is open daily from 10 am to 5 pm; admission is free.

Nehru Museum & Planetarium

Located on Teen Murti Rd near Chanakyapuri, the residence of the first Indian prime minister, Teen Murti Bhavan, has been converted into a museum. Photographs and newspaper clippings on display give a very fascinating insight into the history of the independence movement. There's a planetarium in the grounds (shows at 11.30 am and 3 pm).

The museum is open Tuesday to Sunday from 10 am to 5 pm. Admission is free.

Rail Transport Museum

This museum at Chanakyapuri will be of great interest to anyone fascinated by India's exotic collection of railway engines. The exhibit includes an 1855 steam engine, still in working order, and a large number of oddities such as the skull of an elephant that charged a mail train in 1894, and lost. See the boxed section (Running out of Steam) in the Getting Around chapter for more details.

The museum is open Tuesday to Sunday from 9.30 am to 5 pm; entry is Rs 5 (plus Rs 10 for a camera).

Tibet House

This small museum has a fascinating collection of ceremonial items brought out of Tibet when the Dalai Lama fled following the Chinese occupation. Downstairs is a shop selling a wide range of Tibetan handicrafts. There are often lecture/discussion sessions.

The museum is in the Institutional Area, Lodi Rd, and open weekdays from 9.30 am to 1 pm and 2 to 5.30 pm. Admission is Rs 1.

Crafts Museum

Located in the Aditi Pavilion at the Pragati Maidan Exhibition Grounds, Mathura Rd, this museum contains a collection of traditional Indian crafts in textiles, metal, wood and ceramics. The museum is part of a 'village life' complex where you can visit rural India without leaving Delhi. Opening hours are daily from 9.30 am to 4.30 pm. Admission is free.

Indira Gandhi Memorial Museum

The former residence of Indira Gandhi at 1 Safdarjang Rd has also been converted into a museum. On show are some of her personal effects, including the sari (complete with blood stains) she was wearing at the time of her assassination. Striking a somewhat macabre note is the crystal plaque in the garden, flanked constantly by two soldiers, which protects a few brown spots of Mrs Gandhi's blood on the spot where she actually fell after being shot by two of her Sikh bodyguards in December 1984.

Other Museums

The **Museum of Natural History** is opposite the Nepalese Embassy on Barakhamba Rd. Fronted by a large model dinosaur, it has a collection of fossils, stuffed animals and birds, and a 'hands on' discovery room for children. It's open Tuesday to Sunday from 10 am to 5 pm.

There is a **National Philatelic Museum** hidden in the post office at Dak Bhavan, Sardar Patel Chowk on Sansad Marg (Parliament St). It's closed on Saturday and Sunday. At Indira Gandhi International Airport there is an **Air Force Museum**, open daily except Tuesday from 10 am to 1.30 pm.

PURANA QILA

Just south-east of India Gate and north of Humayun's Tomb and the Nizamuddin railway station is the old fort, Purana Qila. This is the supposed site of Indraprastha, the original city of Delhi. The Afghan ruler, Sher Shah, who briefly interrupted the Mughal Empire by defeating Humayun, completed the fort during his reign from 1538-45, before Humayun regained control of India. The fort has massive walls and three large gateways.

Entering from the south gate you'll see the small octagonal red sandstone tower, the Sher Mandal, later used by Humayun as a library. It was while descending the stairs of this tower one day in 1556 that he slipped, fell and received injuries from which he later died. Just beyond it is the Qila-i-Kuhran Mosque, or Mosque of Sher Shah, which, unlike the fort itself, is in a fairly reasonable condition.

There's a small archaeological museum just inside the main gate, and there are good views of New Delhi from atop the gate. A new sound & light show should now be underway. Timings and tickets (Rs 25) are available from the tourist office.

ZOO

The Delhi Zoo, on the south side of Purana Qila, is not terribly good. The cages are poorly labelled and in winter many of the animals are kept inside. There are white tigers though. The zoo is open daily except Friday; and it's popular at weekends with Delhiites who come here to tease the animals. Entry is Rs 0.50.

HUMAYUN'S TOMB

Built in the mid-16th century by Haji Begum, senior wife of Humayun, the second Mughal emperor, this is an early example of Mughal architecture. The elements in its design – a squat building, lighted by high arched entrances, topped by a bulbous dome and surrounded by formal gardens – were to be refined over the years to the magnificence of the Taj Mahal in Agra. This earlier tomb is thus of great interest for its relation to the later Taj. Humayun's wife is also buried in the red-and-white sandstone, black-and-yellow marble tomb.

Other tombs in the garden include that of Humayun's barber and the Tomb of Isa

Khan, a good example of Lodi architecture. Entry to Humayun's Tomb is Rs 0.50, except on Friday when it is free. An excellent view can be obtained over the surrounding country from the terraces of the tomb.

NIZAM-UD-DIN'S SHRINE

Across the road from Humayun's Tomb is the shrine of the Muslim Sufi saint, Nizam-ud-din Chishti, who died in 1325 aged 92. His shrine, with its large tank, is one of several interesting tombs here. The construction of Nizam-ud-din's tank caused a dispute between the saint and the constructor of Tughlaqabad, further to the south of Delhi (see Tughlaqabad in the upcoming Greater Delhi section for details).

Other tombs include the later grave of Jahanara, the daughter of Shah Jahan, who stayed with her father during his imprisonment by Aurangzeb in Agra's Red Fort. Amir Khusru, a renowned Urdu poet, also has his tomb here, as does Atgah Khan, a favourite of Humayun and his son Akbar. Atgah Khan was murdered by Adham Khan in Agra. In turn Akbar had Adham Khan terminated and his grave is near the Qutab Minar.

It's worth visiting the shrine at around sunset on Thursdays, as it is a popular time for worship, and *qawwali* singers start performing after the evening prayers.

LODI GARDENS

About three km to the west of Humayun's tomb and adjoining the India International Centre are the Lodi Gardens. In these well-kept gardens are the tombs of the Sayyid and Lodi rulers. Mohammed Shah's Tomb (1450) was a prototype for the later Mughal-style tomb of Humayun, a design which would eventually develop into the Taj Mahal. Other tombs include those of his predecessor Mubarak Shah (1433), Ibrahim Lodi (1526) and Sikander Lodi (1517). The Bara Gumbad Mosque is a fine example of its type of plaster decoration.

SAFDARJANG TOMB

Beside the small Safdarjang airport, this tomb was built in 1753-54 by the Nawab of Avadh for his father, Safdarjang, and is one of the last examples of Mughal architecture before the final remnants of the great empire collapsed. The tomb stands on a high terrace in an extensive garden. Entry is Rs 0.50; free on Friday.

HAUZ KHAS

Situated midway between Safdarjang and the Qutab Minar, this area was once the reservoir for the second city of Delhi – Siri – which lies slightly to the east. Interesting sights here include Feroz Shah's Tomb (1398) and the remains of an ancient college. It was around this area that Tamerlane defeated the forces of Mohammed Shah Tughlaq in 1398. Hauz Khaus is now one of the more chic suburbs in the city; there are some excellent restaurants and shops here.

Also part of the old city of Siri is the Moth ki Masjid, which lies some distance to the east of Hauz Khas. It is said to be the finest mosque in the Lodi style.

BAHAI TEMPLE

Lying to the east of Siri is this building shaped like a lotus flower. Completed in 1986, it is set amongst pools and gardens, and adherents of any faith are free to visit the temple and pray or meditate silently according to their own religion. It looks spectacular at dusk, particularly from the air, when it is floodlit, but is rather disappointing close up.

Bus No 433 from opposite the Park Hotel on Sansad Marg near Connaught Place stops not far from the temple.

SWIMMING POOLS

The New Delhi Municipal Corporation has its pool at Nehru Park, near the Ashok Hotel in Chanakyapuri.

Most of the deluxe hotels have pools, and several allow nonresidents' use – for a fee. It's Rs 350 to use the pool at the Kanishka, Rs 550 at the Imperial. Claridges no longer lets nonresidents use their pool.

In the winter months many hotel pools are closed, which is hardly surprising given the weather. The pool at the Sheraton is heated and open year-round, but to hotel guests only.

ORGANISED TOURS

Delhi is very spread out, so taking a city tour makes a lot of sense. Even by public transport, getting from, say, the Red Fort to the Qutab Minar is comparatively expensive.

Two major organisations arrange Delhi tours – beware of agents offering cut-price (and sometimes inferior) tours. The ITDC, operating under the name Ashok Travels & Tours (☎ 332 2336), has tours which include guides and a luxury coach. Their office is in L Block, Connaught Place, near Nirula's Hotel, but you can book at the tourist office on Janpath or at the major hotels. Delhi Tourism (☎ 331 4229), a branch of the city government, arranges similar tours and their office is in N Block, Middle Circle.

A five-hour morning tour of New Delhi costs Rs 100 with ITDC. Starting at 8 am, the tour includes the Qutab Minar, Humayun's Tomb, India Gate, the Jantar Mantar and the Lakshmi Narayan Temple. The afternoon Old Delhi tour for Rs 85 starts at 2.15 pm and covers the Red Fort, Jama Masjid, Raj Ghat, Shanti Vana and Feroz Shah Kotla. If you take both tours on the same day it costs Rs 175.

Tours further afield include ITDC day tours to Agra for Rs 500.

PLACES TO STAY

If Delhi is your first stop in India, you'd be well advised to phone or fax from abroad several days in advance to book your accommodation. The hotels that are reasonable value fill up quickly, leaving greenhorns easy prey to hotel touts. These guys will stop at nothing to earn their fat commissions by getting you into the rip-off joints.

Places to Stay – bottom end

Delhi is no bargain when it comes to cheap hotels. You can easily pay Rs 150 for the most basic single room – a price that elsewhere in India will generally get you a double with bath.

There are basically two areas for cheap accommodation. Most travellers head for Paharganj near New Delhi railway station –

this is about midway between Old Delhi and New Delhi.

The alternative area is around Janpath at the southern side of Connaught Place in New Delhi, but it's a little more expensive and there's less choice.

There are also a number of rock-bottom hotels in Old Delhi itself. They're colourful but generally noisy and too far away from New Delhi's agents, offices, airlines and other facilities for most travellers, especially given the difficult public transport situation.

Camping The *Tourist Camp* (☎ 327 2898) is one of the cheapest places to stay and is surprisingly popular. It's some distance from Connaught Place but is well served by buses. Most of the overland operators arrange accommodation here. Run by retired Indian Army officers, the camp is actually in Old Delhi, near Delhi Gate on Jawaharlal Nehru Marg, across from the JP Narayan Hospital (Irwin Hospital), only two km from Connaught Place. You can camp with your own tent (Rs 40), or there are basic rooms with shared bathrooms for Rs 110/160. They're nothing flash, but OK; this place generally gets good recommendations from travellers. There's a basic restaurant and a left-luggage room.

Qudsia Gardens Tourist Camp (☎ 252 3121) is the alternative, and it's right across the road from the Interstate bus station. Camping costs Rs 50 per person, or there are ordinary rooms for Rs 110/140, and deluxe doubles for Rs 180. It's convenient for an early morning bus departure, but little else.

Connaught Place & Janpath Area There are several cheap lodges or guest houses near the Government of India tourist office. They're often small and cramped, but you meet lots of fellow travellers; they're also conveniently central and there are often dormitories for shoestring travellers. Since many of these places are so popular, you may find that your first choice is full. If so, simply stay at one of the others until a room becomes available – it's unlikely you'll have to wait more than a day.

DELHI

Ringo Guest House (☎ 331 0605), 17 Scindia House (down a small side street near the tourist office) has been a travellers' institution for many years, and it has its fair share of detractors as well as fans. Nevertheless, it's still popular. Beds in crowded, 14-bed dorms are Rs 75; rooms with common bath are Rs 110/200 and doubles with private bath are Rs 260 to Rs 300. The rooms are very small but it's clean enough and the showers and toilets are well maintained. Meals are available in the rooftop courtyard. You can also store luggage for Rs 7 per item per day.

Sunny Guest House (☎ 331 2909), 152 Scindia House, is a very similar set up to Ringo Guest House, and a few doors further along the same side street. Dorm beds are Rs 75, singles/doubles with common bath are Rs 110/200, and it's Rs 280 to Rs 300 for a double with bath attached. Again, the rooms are small but the place has a sort of shabby charm, and this, along with the location, is

what attracts so many people. The left-luggage facility is also Rs 7 per item per day.

Mr SC Jain's Guest House (☎ 332 3484), 7 Pratap Singh, has been a minor legend among travellers since the early 1980s. There are tolerably grubby rooms for Rs 150/250, all with common bath. This place is hardly the Ritz and gets mixed reviews. Some say they find the owner an interesting guy to talk to, others say it's badly-run. Just off Janpath Lane, the guest house is very conveniently located. (If you're looking for the other minor legend in the area, Mrs Colaco, she's closed down her guest house and sold up).

Hotel Blue (☎ 332 9123), 126 M Block, Connaught Place, opposite Super Bazaar and above Hotel Bright, has singles/doubles for Rs 150/250 with common bath, and Rs 300/450 with bath attached. There's a pleasant sitting area on the balcony overlooking Connaught Place. It's reasonable value for this

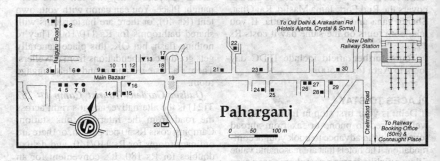

Paharganj

0   50   100 m

To Old Delhi & Arakashan Rd
(Hotels Ajanta, Crystal & Soma)

New Delhi
Railway Station

To Railway
Booking Office
(50m) &
Connaught Place

PLACES TO STAY			
1	Hotel Kelson	17	Hotel Navrang
3	Metropolis Tourist Home	18	Hotel Payal
		21	Camran Lodge
4	Hotel Star View	22	Hotel Namaskar
5	Hotels Sapna Deluxe & Satyam	23	Hotel Bright Guest House
9	Hotel Vishal & Hare Krishna Guest House	24	Hotel Star Palace
		25	Hotel Down Town
10	Anoop Hotel	26	Kiran Guest House
11	Ankush Guest House	27	Kailash Guest House
12	Hotel Vivek	28	Royal Guest House
14	Ajay Guest House	29	Traveller Guest House
15	Hare Rama Guest House	30	Hotel Kanistha

PLACES TO EAT	
7	Khosla Cafe
13	Pitta Factory & Felafel Restaurant
16	Diamond Cafe

OTHER	
2	Imperial Cinema
6	E-mail Centre
8	Book Exchange & Bicycle Hire
19	Vegetable Market
20	Paharganj Post Office

part of Delhi but nothing to write home about.

Hotel Palace Heights (☎ 332 1419) in D Block, Connaught Place, is a moderately priced place close to Nirula's. It's on the 3rd floor of an office building and has a huge balcony that's great for breakfast or afternoon tea. Rooms cost Rs 250/300 with air-cooler but common bath, or there are air-con doubles with bath for Rs 500.

Paharganj Area Directly opposite New Delhi railway station's front entrance is the start of Main Bazaar, a narrow road which stretches due west for about a km. Because of its proximity to the station it has become a major accommodation centre for Indians and foreigners alike, and these days also seems to be a magnet for Russians on shopping sprees. Virtually anything you'd care to name – from incense to washing machines – is sold in this bustling market. There are any number of cheap hotels along this road, offering varying degrees of comfort and quality.

Hotel Kanishta (☎ 525365) is not the quietest of places as it's very close to the station and Qutab Rd. The air-cooled rooms with bath, TV and balcony are best and cost Rs 200/250.

Traveller Guest House Inn (☎ 354 4849), 4360 Main Bazaar, is run by a very friendly manager and has clean rooms, though some are without windows. There are no singles; doubles with attached bath are Rs 180. A nice triple with TV and attached bath (hot water geyser) costs Rs 250.

Royal Guest House (☎ 753 5880), 4464 Main Bazaar (just off to the left), has a range of good rooms and a welcoming owner. Doubles cost Rs 150 with common bath, Rs 220 with bath attached.

Kailash Guest House (☎ 777 4993) is at No 4469. It's modern and clean enough, although many of the rooms face inwards and can be a bit stuffy; those with windows are fine. It's good value at Rs 100/150 with common bath, and Rs 150/220 for a double/triple with attached bath. Hot water is available free by the bucket. The list of regulations

at reception is intriguing: 'Possession of any thigh is objectionable under law'!

Kiran Guest House (☎ 526104) is virtually an identical twin to the Kailash next door, and prices are similar at Rs 100/150 with common bath.

Hotel Bright Guest House (☎ 752 5852), at No 1089-90, is one of the cheapest places in Paharganj, though not particularly friendly. Rooms around a small courtyard cost Rs 80/90 with common bath, Rs 150 for a double with bath.

Hotel Star Palace (☎ 752 8584) is down the side lane to the left just before Hotel Bright. With clean rooms from Rs 200/250 with attached bath and TV it's been recommended by several readers.

Hotel Down Town (☎ 355 5815) is down the same side lane as the Star Palace. They charge Rs 125/150 for good clean rooms with common bath, Rs 150/200 with bath attached.

Hotel Namaskar (☎ 752 1234), 917 Chandiwalan, is down a narrow alley to the right, not far beyond the Hotel Bright Guest House. This is a very friendly place run by two brothers, and they go out of their way to make sure you are comfortable. All rooms have windows and attached bath, and there's a geyser on each floor so there's plenty of hot water for your buckets. Luggage is stored free of charge for guests (although there's not always space). Rooms cost Rs 150/200, and there are also rooms with three (Rs 300) and four (Rs 400) beds. It's an excellent place, and they can also arrange cheap bus tickets.

Camran Lodge (☎ 526053), 1116 Main Bazaar, is a funky old place built into the side of the old mosque. It bills itself as a 'Trusted lodging house for distinguished people'. The rooms are small and shabby, but cheap at Rs 60/120 with common bath, Rs 150 for a double with bath attached. Hot water by the bucket is free.

Hotel Navrang (☎ 753 1922), 6 Tooti Chowk, is down a side street to the right off the vegetable market. It's a large place with relatively clean, basic rooms on five floors: Rs 60/80 for singles/doubles with common bath, Rs 800/100 with bath attached. This hotel seems to attract an interesting crowd of travellers – musicians, bikers, cyclists – and it's very popular.

Hotel Payal (☎ 520867), 1182 Main Bazaar, has a flash marble lobby and rooms from Rs 125/200 with common bath, Rs 150/250 with bath attached. It's often full.

Hotel Vivek (☎ 777 7062), 1534-50 Main Bazaar, often has quite a few foreigners staying, partly because of the restaurant on the ground floor. The rooms are pretty standard and smallish – Rs 150/180 with attached bath and hot water by the bucket, Rs 280/300 for rooms with hot showers, and air-con rooms for Rs 470/490.

Ajay Guest House (☎ 354 3125), 5084 Main Bazaar, is down a side lane to the left. It's always crowded with travellers and currently one of the most popular places to stay in Paharganj. The rooms are clean, the hot water system is reliable, there's a good restaurant and excellent pastries at the German Bakery in the foyer. All rooms have bathrooms attached and cost Rs 150/190/230 for single/double/triple. Checkout is 24 hours.

Hare Rama Guest House (☎ 529273) is right opposite the Ajay and just as popular, particularly with Israeli travellers. There are 65 rooms, some much nicer than others (not all have windows). They cost Rs 100/170 with common bath, Rs 180 to Rs 200 for doubles with bath attached. There's a travel agent, Aa Bee Travels, and a restaurant open 24 hours.

Ankush Guest House (☎ 751 9000), at No 1558, is another place popular with travellers. There are single rooms with common bath at Rs 80, or doubles/triples with attached bath for Rs 130/170.

Hotel Vishal (☎ 753 2079), a little further along, is similar, and has two good restaurants on the ground floor. Rooms cost Rs 150/180 with bath attached.

Hare Krishna Guest House (☎ 753 3017), 1572 Main Bazaar, is a good place run by friendly people. It has nice, clean rooms for Rs 160/200, and there are good views from the roof where there's a 24 hour restaurant shared with the Anoop Hotel next door.

Anoop Hotel (☎ 529366) is at No 1566. It's quite modern and clean, and is good

value for money. The rooms, which have attached bath and hot water, are a decent size and are marble-lined, which makes them cool, although a bit tomb-like. They're well worth the Rs 160/220 cost (Rs 160 for a double with common bath). The biggest attraction of this place, however, is the rooftop terrace and snack bar. Checkout is 24 hours.

Hotel Sapna Deluxe (☎ 524066) is very basic and a bit tatty around the edges, but habitable and cheap at Rs 70/90 with common bath, and Rs 120 for a double with attached bath.

Hotel Satyam (☎ 525200), next to the Sapna, is a step up the scale, with clean rooms for Rs 150/200 with attached bath. The front rooms can be noisy, but that's true of all the places along Main Bazaar.

Hotel Star View (☎ 355 6300), 5136 Main Bazaar, is a more upmarket place with a range of doubles from Rs 275 to Rs 975. All have windows, attached bathrooms and TV.

Metropolis Tourist Home (☎ 753 5766; fax 752 5600), at 1634 Main Bazaar, is the top hotel in the area. Clean, comfortable, air-con doubles with attached bath and fridge cost Rs 660 including taxes. There's a good restaurant here.

Hotel Kelson (☎ 752 7070) is one of several similar hotels on Rajguru Rd, just off Main Bazaar. It's a clean and modern place, but the rooms are definitely on the small side, and many lack windows. However, it's good value at Rs 150/200 with TV and attached bath, or Rs 450 for a double with air-con. Free tea and coffee seems to be the permanent special offer at most of the hotels on this street.

Major's Den (☎ 752 9599) at 2314 Lakshmi Naryan St, behind the Imperial Cinema, is clean, well run and a good place to stay. All rooms have bath attached and cost from Rs 200/275 to Rs 275/350. 'A small haven of peace' was how one traveller described the guest house.

Still in Paharganj, there's a whole group of places on Arakashan Rd, which is just to the north of New Delhi railway station, past the Desh Bandhu Gupta Rd flyover (see the

Old Delhi map). These are definitely at the top end of the budget category, and charge from around Rs 200, but they are mostly modern and pretty well equipped.

Hotel Soma (☎ 752 1002), at 33 Arakashan Rd, is one of the cheaper places in this area. The clean and modern rooms are a good size, and range from Rs 200/250 to Rs 500/600 (air-con).

Hotel Ajanta (☎ 752 0925), at 36 Arakashan Rd, gets mixed reviews – it's worth seeing more than one room as some are better than others. All rooms have attached bath with hot water, and the deluxe rooms have TV and phones. The charge is Rs 355/455 for deluxe, and Rs 785 for air-con.

Hotel Crystal (☎ 753 1639) is a few doors along from the Ajanta. The rooms are quite good, and it's Rs 325/425 for a room with TV, fridge and attached bath. They also have a few cheaper rooms.

Rail Yatri Niwas (☎ 331 3484), on the Ajmer Gate side of New Delhi railway station, has rooms at Rs 150/250 with attached bath and dorm beds for Rs 70. To stay there you have to arrive in Delhi by train and have the ticket to prove it.

Old Delhi There's a group of hotels around the south-western corner of the Jama Masjid, and many more along Matya Mahal, the road which runs due south of the same mosque. These places are fine if you like the hustle and bustle, and if you don't mind being away from the business and restaurant centre of Connaught Place.

Hotel New City Palace (☎ 327 9548) is right behind the mosque. The front rooms have windows but also get the early morning call from the mosque. The hotel boasts it's a 'home for palatial comfort', which is perhaps overstating things, but it is clean and modern, and the management is friendly. Double rooms with attached bath with hot water cost Rs 250; with air-con it's Rs 325.

Hotel Bombay Orient (☎ 328 6253) on Matya Mahal, not far from the southern gate of the Jama Masjid, is also good. It's clean and well kept, and singles/doubles with

common bath are Rs 100/200, doubles with attached bath Rs 150/250.

Bharat Hotel (☎ 235326) is at the west end of Chandni Chowk on the opposite side of the road from the eastern gate of Fatehpuri Masjid. It's an old rambling place with a few small courtyards and quite a bit of atmosphere. The rooms are a bit gloomy and the 25 watt bulbs used to illuminate them certainly don't help. Nevertheless, it's cheap and cheerful, with rooms for Rs 100/150.

Star Guest House (☎ 292 1127), 186 Katra Baryan, is near the Bharat. It's more modern than the Bharat and has tolerably grubby rooms for Rs 100/160 with common bath.

Other Areas The *Youth Hostel* (☎ 301 6285) is in Chanakyapuri, at 5 Nyaya Marg. Dorm beds cost Rs 30. With the inconvenient location, and the fact that this place takes members only, it's not really a great proposition.

Vishwa Yuvak Kendra – International Youth Centre (☎ 301 3631), also out at Chanakyapuri on Nyaya Marg, is not so hot either. Dorm beds are Rs 50, rooms Rs 650, but there is a good cheap canteen.

Retiring rooms are available at both New and (Old) Delhi railway stations, but they fill up quickly and are very noisy. The retiring rooms at the airport can be useful, however, and they're at both the domestic (Terminal I; ☎ 329 5126) and international (Terminal II; ☎ 545 2011) sections of the airport. You can use them if you have a confirmed departure within 24 hours of your arrival by plane, but you'll need to ring in advance as demand far outstrips supply. They cost Rs 200/350 for an air-con single/double. The tourist information officer at the desk at the airport may insist that the retiring rooms are 'full' and try to direct you to a hotel from which the officer gets commission.

Places to Stay – middle

Again, there are few bargains in this price range in Delhi. There's currently a luxury tax of 10% on rooms over Rs 500 (not included in prices below), and some places also levy an additional service charge of 5% to 10%.

The Ys There are three YMCA or YWCA places, all of which take either sex. They're all very popular so you'll need to book ahead.

The *YMCA Tourist Hotel* (☎ 336 1915; fax 374 6032) is on Jai Singh Rd, near the Jantar Mantar. Although it has a strong institutional feel and is no great bargain, it's still very popular with foreigners as it's well located, clean and has good facilities including a reliable travel agent. There are gardens, a swimming pool, lounge and a restaurant with western, Indian and Mughlai cuisine. Despite what the touts may tell you if you arrive in Delhi late at night, the hotel is open 24 hours, and credit cards are accepted. The rooms cost Rs 350/595 with common bath, and Rs 700/1170 with air-con and attached bath. There's also an additional 5% service charge, the 10% luxury tax on rooms over Rs 500 and a temporary membership charge of Rs 10, valid for one month. Breakfast is included.

YWCA International Guest House (☎ 336 1517; fax 334 1763), at 10 Sansad Marg (Parliament St), has singles/doubles for Rs 450/725 (plus 10% service charge, and the 10% luxury tax on rooms over Rs 500); all rooms have bath and air-con. It's conveniently located near Connaught Place and has a good restaurant, where a set breakfast is Rs 45.

YWCA Blue Triangle Family Hostel (☎ 336 0133; fax 336 0202) is on Ashoka Rd just off Sansad Marg (Parliament St). It's clean, well run and has a restaurant. Rates, including breakfast, are Rs 400/750 for an ordinary room, or Rs 550/850 with air-con; all rooms have bathroom attached. There's also a temporary membership fee of Rs 10 but currently no service charge. It's only about a 10 minute walk from the heart of Connaught Place.

Connaught Place & Janpath Area There are several mid-range hotels around Janpath and Connaught Place.

Janpath Guest House (☎ 332 1935) is a few doors down from the tourist office at 82-84 Janpath. It's reasonably well kept, and the staff are friendly; the rooms, though, are claustrophobically small and most don't have a proper window. Singles/doubles with air-cooling cost Rs 400/475, Rs 900/1100 with air-con.

ITDC Ashok Yatri Niwas (☎ 332 4511) is just a 10 minute walk from Connaught Place on Ashoka Rd at the intersection with Janpath. Rooms in this high-rise, government-run hotel cost Rs 450/600/700 for singles/doubles/four-beds (plus 10% luxury tax) with attached bath. The rooms are a reasonable size and some have been renovated recently, but none has a phone, TV or room service. There's a self service cafe (pick your dish from the pictures on the wall and pay in advance) and a good restaurant. This place gets very mixed reviews – 'a managerial disaster that's been setting the standard for lousy service for some years now', say some – others think it's reasonable value for Delhi. Very much depends on the room you get.

Hotel Bright (☎ 332 0444) is at 85 M Block Connaught Circus, opposite the Super Bazaar. There's definitely nothing bright about this place, but it's not too bad; rooms cost Rs 550/660 with attached bath. Avoid the ones facing the road, which can be noisy. They occasionally have a few cheaper rooms.

Hotel 55 (☎ 332 1244; fax 332 0769), at 55 H Block Connaught Circus, is well designed with air-con throughout. Rooms with balcony and bath are Rs 800/1100. Since this place has won the Best One Star Hotel Award two years running, rates have shot up and it's now overpriced.

Alka Hotel (☎ 344 4328; fax 373 2796) is also centrally located at 16 P Block Connaught Circus and has air-con singles/doubles for Rs 1150/1800. As is typical of many places in this area, most of the rooms don't have windows. There's a very good vegetarian restaurant and a 24 hour coffee shop.

Hotel Metro (☎ 331 3856), on N Block, is better than initial impressions might indicate. There are large rooms and the place is surprisingly quiet for such a central location. Singles/doubles cost Rs 650/800 with common bath, Rs 800/1000 with attached bath and air-con.

Hotel Central Court (☎ 331 5013), N Block, has rooms from Rs 950/1350 with air-con and attached bath. It's nothing special, but there's a pleasant terrace and an astro-palmist is on call.

York Hotel (☎ 332 3769) in K Block is clean but fairly characterless, and the rooms cost Rs 1195/2000. Those at the back are quieter.

Nirula's Hotel (☎ 332 2419; fax 335 3957) is on L Block, Connaught Place, right beside the Nirula restaurants and snack bars. Singles/doubles range from Rs 1195/2200 in this small but good standard hotel. Advance bookings are advisable.

Sunder Nagar In a peaceful residential neighbourhood near the zoo there are several small hotels set back from the main road. All rooms have attached bath, air-con and Star TV. Luxury tax (currently 10%) must be added to all prices below.

Maharani Guest House (☎ 469 3128), 3 Sunder Nagar, has a flashy foyer and comfortable rooms from Rs 1190/1700.

Kailash Inn (☎ 461 7401), at No 10, is much smaller than the Maharani and around the corner on the square. It's a friendly place with good clean rooms from Rs 1100/1400.

La Sangrita Tourist Home (☎ 469 4541), at No 14 Sunder Nagar, is probably the best value of all these places. Rooms with nice soft beds are Rs 1195/1395 and there's a small garden.

Jukaso Inn (☎ 469 0308), 50 Sunder Nagar, is not to be confused with the place of the same name on Connaught Circus. It's a glitzy hotel with rooms from Rs 1190/ 1740, very popular with business people.

Other Areas There are two excellent private guest houses to the west of Connaught Place. The small inconvenience of being further from the heart of things is compensated for by the friendly and relaxed atmosphere you find at these places. Advance bookings are advisable during the high season.

Master Paying Guest House (☎ 574 1089) is at R-500 New Rajendra Nagar, a Rs

30 auto-rickshaw ride from Connaught Place. This small and friendly place is in a quiet residential area and the helpful owner has worked hard to create a home-like atmosphere. It has large, airy and beautifully furnished doubles from Rs 350/500 to Rs 750, and there's a 25% discount during summer. Bathrooms (not attached) are probably the cleanest you'll see in India! Light meals are available, there's a pleasant rooftop terrace, and car hire for extended trips can also be arranged. 00-91-11

Yatri House (☎ 752 5563) is at 3/4 Rani Jhansi Rd, which is opposite the junction of Panchkuin Marg (Radial No 3) and Mandir Marg, about one km west of Connaught Place. It's calm, secure and there are trees, a lawn and a small courtyard at the back. The good-sized rooms cost from Rs 800, all with attached bath, and are kept spotlessly clean. For Rs 350 they'll meet you at the airport, there's car hire available for sightseeing trips, and air tickets can be arranged.

MR. PURI —

Places to Stay – top end

Prices at Delhi's top hotels have increased dramatically over the past three years. To the prices below you can expect to add taxes of at least 20%.

Four Star Unless otherwise stated, these four star places do not have a swimming pool:

Ambassador Hotel (☎ 463 2600; fax 463 2252) is a small hotel at Sujan Singh Park, a short distance south of India Gate. There are 81 rooms costing US$80/110. Until the rooms are renovated, which no doubt they will be since the hotel has just been taken over by the Taj Group, they are overpriced. The hotel has a noted vegetarian restaurant, coffee shop and bar.

Connaught Hotel (☎ 346 4225; fax 334 0757) is due west of Connaught Place, on Bhagat Singh Marg. It offers restaurants, 24 hour room service and car rental. Rooms cost from US$105/110 with breakfast.

Diplomat Hotel (☎ 301 0204; fax 301 8605), 9 Sardar Patel Marg, south-east of Rashtrapati Bhavan, is a smaller place with just 25 rooms from Rs 4000/4500, a restaurant and bar.

Hotel Hans Plaza (☎ 331 6861; fax 331 4830), Tolstoy Marg, is conveniently central with rooms from US$150/160.

Hotel Janpath (☎ 332 0070; fax 332 7083) is run by the ITDC with typically indifferent service. This large hotel has a good position on Janpath. Rooms start at Rs 1500/2350.

Hotel Kanishka (☎ 332 4422; fax 332 4242) is another ITDC hotel. Overpriced at US$100/130, it's one of the few places in this class to have a swimming pool.

Hotel Marina (☎ 332 4658; fax 332 8609), on the outer circle of Connaught Place in G Block, is quite smart. The rooms, mostly with windows, are Rs 1900/2400 including buffet breakfast.

Oberoi Maidens Hotel (☎ 252 5464; fax 291 5134), 7 Sham Nath Marg, is inconveniently located north of Old Delhi, but the building itself is a verandahed colonial relic and is very pleasant, as is the large garden. It also has a swimming pool. Rooms start at US$85/105.

Five Star If you're looking for a little more luxury, try one of the following hotels.

Claridges Hotel (☎ 301 0211; fax 301 0625) at 12 Aurangzeb Rd is south of Rajpath in New Delhi. It's a very comfortable, older place, with four good restaurants, a swimming pool and a health club. It's probably the best-value five star hotel, with singles/doubles from US$145.

Imperial Hotel (☎ 332 5332; fax 332 4542) is conveniently situated on Janpath near the centre of the city. It's a pleasantly old-fashioned hotel with a pool and a big garden – wonderful for breakfast – and it's surprisingly quiet given its central location. Rooms are from US$160.

Park Hotel (☎ 373 2477; fax 373 2025) on Sansad Marg (Parliament St) lacks character but is in a very central location only a block from Connaught Place. This hotel has a swimming pool, a superb Spanish restaurant and a business centre. Rooms are US$220.

Hotel Samrat (☎ 603030; fax 688 7047) is just behind the Ashok Hotel in Chanakyapuri, and also run by the ITDC. Delhiites regard this government-run place as a joke and wouldn't think of staying here. If you must, rooms are US$120/140. 'The worst hotel experience of my life', was one reader's comment.

Five Star Deluxe If you're looking for somewhere near the airport, the flashy new **Radisson Hotel Delhi** (☎ 613 7373) is nearing completion and is just three km from the international terminal.

Centaur Hotel (☎ 565 2223; fax 565 2256) has rooms at US$150/170. It's on Gurgaon Rd, two km from the international terminal and five from the domestic terminal. However, it's easy enough to get to and from the airport from all of the hotels in the south of the city.

Ashok Hotel (☎ 611 0101; fax 687 3216), 50B Chanakyapuri, is the 563 room flagship of the ITDC hotel fleet. Need we say more? Singles/doubles cost from US$225/265.

New Delhi Hilton (☎ 332 0101; fax 332 5335), formerly the Holiday Inn Crowne Plaza, is a modern 445 room hotel which is very centrally located just off Barakhamba Rd, east of Connaught Place. It boasts every conceivable mod con, including an open-air swimming pool on a 3rd floor terrace, and it also has a floor of nonsmoking rooms. Standard singles/doubles cost US$295/315, and there are more expensive suites available.

Hyatt Regency (☎ 618 1234; fax 618 6633), with 518 rooms, is in the south of New Delhi, between Hauz Khas and Chanakyapuri. Facilities include a fitness centre, in-house movies, restaurants, bar and coffee shop. For all this you pay US$275 for a double room.

Hotel Le Meridien (☎ 371 0101; fax 371 4545) is another very modern place with a stunning atrium. This 355 room hotel has a swimming pool, restaurants and 24 hour coffee shop. The rates are US$275/300 for standard singles/doubles.

Hotel Oberoi New Delhi (☎ 436 3030; fax 436 0484) is south of New Delhi near the

Purana Qila. Services include a 24 hour business centre, travel desk, swimming pool and secretarial services. Rooms cost from US$305/335.

Hotel Maurya Sheraton (☎ 611 2233; fax 615 5555) is west of Chanakyapuri on Sardar Patel Marg, the road to the airport. Apart from a high level of comfort, the hotel boasts two excellent restaurants, a solar-heated swimming pool (the only one in Delhi) and a disco. It has 500 rooms costing from US$350.

Taj Mahal Hotel (☎ 301 6162; fax 301 7299), at 1 Man Singh Rd, is a luxurious place that is fairly central but quiet. It has all the usual facilities including a swimming pool; singles/doubles start at US$275/305.

Taj Palace Hotel (☎ 301 0404; 301 1252), is near the Maurya Sheraton on Sardar Patel Marg, and fairly convenient for the airport. Rooms are US$275/300.

PLACES TO EAT

Delhi has an excellent array of places to eat – from a dhaba house with dishes for less than Rs 10 up to top-of-the-range restaurants where a meal for two can top Rs 4000!

The western fast food chains are moving in, but slowly. Most are currently located in the upmarket suburbs, far from the tourist areas. McDonald's is 10km south of Connaught Place in Vasant Vihar, KFC is equally far away in New Friends Colony, and Pizza Hut is out at Shanti Niketan.

Janpath & Connaught Place

There are many Indian-style fast-food places in this area. Their plus point is that they have good food at reasonable prices and are clean and healthy. A minus point for some of them is they have no place to sit – it's stand, eat and run. They serve Indian food (from samosas to dosas) and western food (burgers to sandwiches).

Cheap Probably the most popular and long running of these fast-food places is *Nirula's*, which does a wide variety of light snacks, both Indian and western. They've also got good cold drinks, milk shakes and ice cream, or they will pack you a lunch box – ideal to take on train trips. The ice-cream parlour is amazingly busy, and is open from 10 am to midnight. The main Nirula's is on L Block on the outer circle, and there are various other outlets dotted throughout suburban Delhi. Above the ice-cream parlour is a sit-down restaurant called *Pot Pourri*, which is always busy. The smorgasbord salad bar is quite good value at Rs 95, other dishes less so. Half tandoori chicken is Rs 75. It's a good place for breakfast, which is served from 7.30 am. Also upstairs at Nirula's is the *Chinese Room*, with Chinese dishes in the Rs 120 to Rs 180 range, and a very congenial bar (beer is Rs 80).

Cafe 100, on B Block, is a very popular semi self-service place that's giving Nirula's a run for their money. There are Indian snacks, burgers from Rs 28, a wide range of ice creams, and an excellent buffet upstairs for Rs 145 (noon to 3, and 7 to 11 pm).

Croissants Etc, 9 Scindia House, Connaught Place, has an excellent range of filled croissants, rolls and cakes. You can either take them away or eat in and watch Channel V.

Wimpy, the well-named but busy British hamburger chain, is on Janpath at N block. For hamburgers read lamb-burgers. The burgers are fair imitations but, again, if you're used to Indian prices, spending Rs 60 on a burger and Coke seems like reckless extravagance.

Domino's Pizza opened in Connaught Place in 1997. It's the real thing but not cheap. Small/medium/large pizzas range from 60/110/160 to Rs 105/190/275. For free delivery phone ☎ 373 6880.

Sona Rupa Restaurant on Janpath does good north and south Indian vegetarian food (excellent dosas) and has a bizarre self-service system. It's very good value.

Don't Pass Me By, in the same lane as the Ringo and Sunny guest houses, is a popular little place which caters to international tastes. It's great for breakfast. Other places close by include the *Anand, New Light, Kalpana, Swaram* and *Vikram* restaurants.

Keventers, the small milk bar on the corner of Connaught Place and Radial Rd No 3, round the corner from American

Express, has good fresh milk. Shakes are Rs 10 to Rs 25.

Wenger's on Connaught Place is a cake shop with an awesome range of little cakes which they'll put in a cardboard box and tie up with a bow so you can self-consciously carry them back to your hotel room for private consumption. Chocolate eclairs are Rs 14, a whole chocolate cake costs Rs 90.

More upmarket The *Embassy* restaurant on D Block has excellent veg and non-veg food. Chicken a la Kiev is Rs 99.75, chicken tandoori Rs 92.75. It's popular among office workers.

Kovil in E Block is one of the best places for south Indian vegetarian food.

Vega, at the Hotel Alka, specialises in vegetarian food cooked Delhi style (in pure ghee but without onion and garlic). A thali costs Rs 135.

United Coffee House, also on E Block, is quite plush with a very pleasantly relaxed atmosphere, good food and some of the best coffee in Delhi.

Kwality Restaurant on Sansad Marg is clean and very efficient and the food's good value. The menu is the almost standard non-vegetarian menu you'll find at restaurants all over India. Main courses are in the Rs 70 to Rs 100 range. This is also a good place for non-Indian food if you want a break.

El Arab Restaurant, right on the corner of Sansad Marg and the outer circle of Connaught Place, has an interesting Middle Eastern menu with most dishes under Rs 100. Downstairs here is the more expensive *Cellar*.

Fa Yian on A Block, Middle Circle, is owned and run by Chinese, and quite authentic. There's a set Chinese meal for Rs 100.

The Host, which serves excellent Indian and Chinese food, is in F Block. It's extremely popular with well-heeled Indians, but it ain't cheap.

Zen Restaurant is on B Block. Its focus is Chinese and Japanese food. Prices are reasonable: there's pork from Rs 75, lamb from Rs 85 and chicken from Rs 105.

El Rodeo, is a restaurant serving good Mexican food on A Block near American

Express; it's worth visiting just for the sight of waiters in cowboy suits! Main dishes are around Rs 150.

Gaylord is one of the priciest, plushest restaurants in Connaught Place, with big mirrors, chandeliers and excellent Indian food. Main dishes are Rs 150 to Rs 200, but the high quality of the ingredients makes this a worthwhile splurge.

Parikrama revolving restaurant on Kasturba Gandhi Marg is an interesting place to eat. Unlike many places of this ilk where the first-class views are supposed to distract you from decidedly second-class food, the fare here is excellent but pricey. Main dishes are around Rs 200, beer costs Rs 90. It's open daily for lunch and dinner, and for drinks from 3 to 7 pm.

Yamu's Panchayat is where the wealthy go to round off their meal with some of the most pricey paans in the city. They range from Rs 5 to Rs 50 and some contain edible silver leaf.

Paharganj Area
In keeping with its role as a travellers' centre, Main Bazaar in Paharganj has a handful of cheap restaurants which cater almost exclusively to foreign travellers. They are all up towards the western end of Main Bazaar.

Pitta Factory is a new stand-up fast food place down a side street by the Hotel Vivek. Pitta with schnitzel costs Rs 40, felafel is Rs 30. The *Felafel Restaurant* is nearby.

German Bakery, in the foyer of the Hotel Ajay, does excellent sandwiches and snacks. There are some interesting choices – a baguette filled with pepper cheese for Rs 35 or a farmer's loaf sandwich with tuna or yak's cheese for Rs 25. There's a wide range of cakes.

Lords Cafe in the Hotel Vishal has an extensive menu and cheap food. The pepper steaks (Rs 30) are pretty good.

Diamond Cafe, opposite the Hotel Vivek is very similar to Lords.

Appetite Restaurant is in the Hotel Vishal. This place has similar food to the others, but is a bit more upmarket. The pizzas here are popular, but what is even more popular is the fact that this place has Star TV; international sports broadcasts, especially cricket, draw big audiences.

Metropolis Restaurant, in the hotel of the same name just past Rajguru Rd, is the best place to eat. With most main dishes around Rs 125, it's much more expensive than the other Main Bazaar cheapies.

Old Delhi

In Old Delhi there are many places to eat at the west end of Chandni Chowk.

Inderpuri Restaurant has a good selection of vegetarian dishes, and *Giani* has good masala dosas.

Ghantewala, near the Siganj Gurdwara on Chandni Chowk, is reputed to have some of the best Indian sweets in Delhi. The stalls along the road in front of the Jama Masjid are very cheap.

ISBT Workers' Canteen, in the Interstate bus station, has good food at low prices.

Karim's, down a lane across from the south gate of the Jama Masjid, is very well known for its excellent non-veg food. There's everything from kebabs to the richest Muglai dishes in this large restaurant, and prices are reasonable.

Tandoor, at the Hotel President on Asaf Ali Rd near the tourist camp, is an excellent place with the usual two-waiters-per-diner service and a sitar playing in the background. The tandoori kitchen can be seen through a glass panel.

Chor Bizaare is close by in the same street in the Hotel Broadway. They've certainly put some effort into decorating this place with an eclectic mix of bits and pieces collected from various markets – a four-poster bed, an old sports car (now used as a salad bar) and an old cello. The food is good but pricey; expect to pay Rs 600 to Rs 800 for a meal for two.

Moti Mahal Restaurant, around the corner on Netaji Subhash Marg in Daryaganj, has been going for 50 years and is still noted for its tandoori dishes.

South Delhi

There are good eating options in the area south of Connaught Place, but you'll need a taxi or transport to get to most of them.

Basil & Thyme, in the swish Santushti shopping centre in Chanakyapuri, is still quite hip. The food's good and the service excellent. Main dishes are around Rs 150.

Defence Colony is one of the upmarket residential suburbs in south Delhi. The *market* here draws middle-class Delhi-wallahs and their families in numbers in the evenings, especially on weekends.

Colonel's Kababz is a very popular stand-up kebab, tandoori and seafood place, although most diners remain in their cars and are served by scurrying waiters!

The *Sagar* restaurant here offers what is reckoned to be the best south Indian food in Delhi.

Village Bistro is a restaurant complex in Hauz Khaus incorporating a number of eating places, including *Al Capone* (Italian and Continental), *Darbar*, *Mohalla*, *Great Wall of China*, *Golconda Terrace* (spicy Andhra Pradesh dishes and good views). Other Hauz Khas restaurants include *Sukhotthai* (Thai), *Osaka* and *Duke's Place*, which is a pleasant Italian place with live jazz some nights.

Karim's, in Nizamuddin, offers some of the best Mughlai cooking in the city. There's a second branch behind the Jama Masjid in Old Delhi.

International Hotels

Many Delhi residents reckon that the best food in the capital is at the large hotels.

Claridges – The restaurants at this hotel are very good value and they're interesting places to eat. The *Dhaba* offers 'rugged roadside' cuisine, and is set up like a typical roadside cafe; the *Jade Garden* serves Chinese food in a bamboo grove setting; *Pickwicks* offers western food, and the decor is 19th century England; while outdoor *Corbetts* gets its inspiration from Jim Corbett of man-eating tiger fame, and so has a hunting camp theme, complete with recorded jungle sounds. As might be expected, meat features prominently on the menu. All restaurants are moderately priced – most main dishes are under Rs 200.

Imperial Hotel – This is a great place for an alfresco breakfast in the pleasant garden.

At the *Tavern Restaurant* main dishes are Rs 180 to Rs 225. Heavenly chocolate mousse is Rs 100. Prices at the less formal *Garden Party* are 10% lower.

Ambassador Hotel – There are upmarket thalis for Rs 130 at the vegetarian restaurant *Dasaprakash*.

Park Hotel – If you're staying at one of the Ys, treat yourself to the all-you-can-eat buffet breakfast for Rs 234 including taxes. The dinner buffet costs Rs 411. There's also the new Spanish restaurant, *Las Meninas*; the chef's from Santander, the decor's very stylish. Tapas are from Rs 150, main dishes Rs 300 to Rs 400.

Le Meridien – Buffet lunch or dinner costs Rs 525 including taxes and includes a superb range of mouth-watering western and Indian cuisine. There's also an excellent Chinese restaurant, the *Golden Phoenix*, where main dishes are around Rs 300.

Oberoi – The *Baan Thai* is probably the best Thai restaurant in Delhi. Count on Rs 1000 for two.

Maurya Sheraton – The *Bukhara* is one of the best restaurants in the city. It has many Central Asian specialities, including tandoori cooking and dishes from the Peshawar region in north-west Pakistan. Another restaurant here is the *Dum Phukt*, named after the cuisine first invented by the *nawabs* of Avadh (Lucknow) around 300 years ago. The dishes are covered by a pastry cap when cooked, so the food is steamed as much as anything else. It's quite distinctive and absolutely superb.

Taj Mahal Hotel – The *House of Ming* is a popular Sichuan Chinese restaurant with main dishes around Rs 300. The best French restaurant in town is the *Longchamp*, at the top of this hotel. A three-course lunch is Rs 795, dinner is a snip at Rs 1750 – plus 17% taxes. The chef used to run a Michelin star restaurant in Britain.

ENTERTAINMENT

Indian dances are held each evening at 6.45 pm at the *Parsi Anjuman Hall* on Bahadur Zafar Marg, opposite Ambedkar Stadium (near Delhi Gate). They're well worth attending;

phone ☎ 623 4689 for details. The *India International Centre* (☎ 461 9431), at 40 Max Mueller Road, is another regular classical dance venue.

For films there are a number of cinemas around Connaught Place, but the fare is typically Hindi mass-appeal movies; seats range from Rs 25 to Rs 50. For something a little more cerebral, the *British Council* (☎ 371 0111) on Kasturba Gandhi Marg often screens good foreign films, and the other cultural centres are also worth trying.

Delhi's strict licensing laws certainly don't help its nightlife scene. Most bars and discos are at the five star hotels. The discos at these hotels are quite exclusive and entry is usually restricted to members and hotel guests; couples and women stand a better chance of being admitted than unaccompanied men.

El Rodeo, the bar-restaurant on Connaught Place (see Places to Eat), has a cover charge of Rs 150 after 7.30 pm if you only want to drink and not eat. Draught beer is Rs 60.

Jazz Bar at the Maurya Sheraton is very good, with live jazz each evening, but drinks are expensive – over Rs 200!

Someplace Else is a bar-disco at Park Hotel. Entry is Rs 300 per couple; beer is Rs 210.

CJ's is a night club at Le Meridien Hotel. Entry is Rs 500 per couple.

THINGS TO BUY

Good buys include silk products, precious stones, leather and woodwork, but the most important thing about Delhi is that you can find almost anything from anywhere in India. If this is your first stop in India, and you intend to buy something while you are here, then it's a chance to compare what is available from all over the country. If this is your last stop and there was something you missed elsewhere in your travels, Delhi provides a chance to find it.

Two good places to start are in New Delhi, near Connaught Place. The Central Cottage Industries Emporium is on Janpath. In this building you will find items from all over India, generally of good quality and reasonably priced. Whether it's woodcarvings, brasswork, paintings, clothes, textiles or furniture, you'll find it here. Along Baba Kharak Singh Marg, two streets round from Janpath, are the various state emporiums run by the state governments. Each of them display and sell handicrafts from their state.

There are many other shops around Connaught Place and Janpath. By the Imperial Hotel are a number of stalls and small shops run by Tibetan refugees and rapacious Kashmiris selling carpets, jewellery and many (often instant) antiques.

In Old Delhi, Chandni Chowk is the famous shopping street. Here you will find carpets and jewellery, but you have to search the convoluted back alleys. In the narrow street called Cariba Kalan, perfumes are made as well.

Main Bazaar in Paharganj has a good range. You can find an interesting variety of perfumes, oils, soaps and incense at two places (both signposted), one near the Hotel Vivek and another near the Camran Lodge. Take advantage of all the free testers. Monday is the official weekly holiday for the shops in Main Bazaar, and many are closed on that day, although a surprising number remain open seven days a week.

In recent years the Karol Bagh Market, two km west of Connaught Place along Panchkuin Marg (Radial Rd No 3), has become even more popular than Connaught Place or Main Bazaar.

Just south of the Purana Qila, beside Dr Zakir Hussain Rd and across from the Hotel Oberoi New Delhi, is the Sunder Nagar Market, a collection of shops selling antiques and brassware. The prices may be high but you'll find fascinating and high-quality artefacts. Shops in the major international hotels often have high-quality items, at equally high prices.

Opposite the Ashok Hotel in Chanakyapuri is the Santushti shopping arcade. There's a string of small upmarket boutiques here with a good range of crafts and high prices to match.

Hauz Khas Village in south Delhi has become a very interesting little shopping enclave.

GETTING THERE & AWAY

Delhi is a major international gateway to India; for details on arriving from overseas see the introductory Getting There & Away chapter. At certain times of the year international flights out of Delhi can be heavily booked so it's wise to make reservations as early as possible. This particularly applies to some of the heavily discounted airlines out of Europe – check and double-check your reservations and make sure you reconfirm your flight.

Delhi is also a major centre for domestic travel, with extensive bus, rail and air connections.

Air

The domestic terminals (Terminals IA & IB of the Indira Gandhi International Airport) are 15km from the centre, and the international terminal (Terminal II) is a further five km. There's a free IAAI bus between the two terminals, or you can use the EATS service (see the Getting Around section later).

If you're arriving at New Delhi Airport from overseas, there's 24 hour State Bank of India and Thomas Cook foreign-exchange counters in the arrivals hall, after you go through customs and immigration. Once you've left the arrivals hall you won't be allowed back in. The service is fast and efficient.

Many international flights arrive and depart at terrible hours of the morning. Take special care if this is your first foray into India and you arrive exhausted and jet-lagged. If you're leaving Delhi in the early hours of the morning, book a taxi the afternoon before. They'll be hard to find in the night. See Other Areas in the Places to Stay – bottom end section in this chapter for information about the retiring rooms at the airport.

Several airlines now require you to have the baggage you're checking in X-rayed and sealed, so do this at the machines just inside the departure hall before you queue to check in. For international flights the departure tax (Rs 300) must be paid at the State Bank counter in the departures hall, also before check-in.

DELHI

Facilities at the international terminal include a dreadful snack bar, bookshop and banks. Once inside the departure lounge there are a few duty-free shops with the usual inflated prices, and another terrible snack bar where you have the privilege of paying in US dollars. There's also the Ashok Restaurant, with possibly some of the worst food of any international airport.

Indian Airlines Indian Airlines has a number of offices. The Malhotra Building office (☎ 331 0517) in F Block, Connaught Place, is probably the most convenient. It is, however, fairly busy at most times. It's open daily except Saturday from 10 am to 5 pm.

There's another office in the PTI Building (☎ 371 9168) on Sansad Marg, open daily except Sunday from 10 am to 5 pm.

At the old Safdarjang airport there's a 24 hour office (☎ 141), and this can be a very quick place to make bookings.

Transport Scams in Delhi

While London cabbies catch the latest instalment of *EastEnders* and New York taxi drivers discuss the recent ball game, one imagines that Delhi taxi wallahs spend their spare time concocting ever more devious scams to separate the dumb tourists from their money.

We all know that when the taxi wallah or auto-rickshaw wallah says the hotel you ask to be taken to is 'full' or 'closed', that it's probably not true and he only wants to suggest one that will pay him a fat commission. Nevertheless, this straightforward bit of trickery still ensnares a few first-timers. There are, however, far more subtle scams than that about.

Delhi Riots Scam You arrive at the airport in the early hours of the morning, jet-lagged and exhausted, and hop in a taxi for the city centre. You give the name of a hotel and off you go. After a few km the driver suggests that it may not be such a great idea to go to that hotel because the 'road is closed'. You immediately recognise this as a scam along the lines of 'hotel full' and 'hotel burnt down' and insist to be taken there. After another few km the driver says there are 'riots' in Delhi. Playing along you say that's no problem, you want to be dropped at the hotel you asked for. Suddenly the taxi is flagged down by a man in uniform – a policeman as far as you are concerned. There's a heated exchange in Hindi. The driver turns to you and says he doesn't want to go on as the rioting is very bad and many people have been killed. With the policeman there the picture looks altogether different to you. You let the driver take you to the hotel of his choice. It turns out to be rather more expensive than you'd expected, but you're safe. At breakfast a travel agent appears and sells you a trip to Rajasthan – leaving immediately. Would never happen to you? It has to more than a few foreign travellers.

The auto-rickshaw wallahs have a similar scam set up where they meet a bogus policeman down a side street, he says there are Hindu-Muslim riots in Paharganj and you land up in a rip-off hotel, usually in Karol Bagh.

EATS Scam We're not suggesting that an organisation with such a venerable name as the Ex-Servicemen's Air Link Transport Service isn't operated by honourable people, but they don't seem to be dropping foreigners exactly where they should these days. As you near Connaught Place a group of predatory auto-rickshaws gathers in the wake of the bus. Finally the bus stops and everyone has to get off – into the hands of these rickshaw wallahs. A popular stop (for the drivers, that is) is Ajmer Gate, the 'wrong' side of New Delhi railway station for Paharganj. Here there's a phoney Government of India tourist office, complete with sign, that looks like the real thing. Some travel agents may get aboard the bus and tell you that you have to register at this office. Lies, all lies, of course. If they say they'll take you to, say, the YMCA, make sure they do rather than dropping you a couple of km away.

Hotel Reservations Scam Coming out of the railway station a cycle-rickshaw wallah meets you and says he'll take you to any hotel you want for Rs 5. Since it's usually any hotel *they* want for Rs 5, you agree. After a few minutes the rickshaw wallah stops outside a travel agent. 'Check your room reservation for free', he says. You say there's no need but since it's free... Inside they ask where you're staying, dial the number and pass the phone to you. The 'receptionist' answers, asks your name, and then says they're very sorry but they've had to cancel your reservation as they'd double booked. What you don't know is that the 'receptionist' was actually in the room next door, you weren't speaking to the hotel at all. Naturally the travel agent is quick to suggest alternative accommodation. ■

Business-class passengers can check in by telephone on ☎ 329 5166. For prerecorded flight departure information, ring ☎ 143.

Indian Airlines flights depart from Delhi to all the major Indian centres. Check-in at the airport is 75 minutes before departure. Note that if you have just arrived and have an onward connection to another city in India, it may be with Air India, the country's international carrier, rather than the domestic carrier, Indian Airlines. If that is the case, you must check in at the international terminal (Terminal II) rather than the domestic terminal.

Other Domestic Airlines As well as the offices listed below, all the private airlines have offices at the airport's domestic terminal. There are currently no East-West or Modiluft flights operating.

Archana Airways
    41A Friends Colony East, Mathura Rd
    (☎ 684 2001)
East-West Airlines
    DCM Bldg, Barakhamba Rd (☎ 375 5167)
Jagson Airlines
    12E Vandana Bldg, 11 Tolstoy Marg
    (☎ 372 1593)
Jet Airways
    3E Hanslaya Bldg, Barakhamba Rd
    (☎ 372 4727)
ModiLuft
    Vandana Bldg, Tolstoy Marg (☎ 371 2222)
NEPC Airlines/Skyline NEPC
    G39 4th Floor, Pawan House, Connaught Place
    (☎ 332 2525)
Sahara Indian Airlines
    Ambadeep Bldg, Kasturba Gandhi Marg
    (☎ 332 6851)
UP Air
    A-2, Defence Colony (☎ 464 6290)

International Airlines International airlines that fly to Delhi include the following:

Aeroflot
    Cozy Travels, BMC House, 1st Floor, 1-N Connaught Place (☎ 331 2873)
Air Canada
    Suite 1421, New Delhi Hilton (☎ 372 0014)
Air France
    7 Atma Ram Mansion, Connaught Circus
    (☎ 331 7054)

Air India
    Jeevan Bharati Bldg, Connaught Place
    (☎ 331 1225)
Air Lanka
    Student Travel Information Centre, Imperial Hotel, Janpath (☎ 332 6843)
British Airways
    DLF Bldg, Sansad Marg (Parliament St)
    (☎ 332 7428)
Cathay Pacific
    Tolstoy House, Tolstoy Marg (☎ 332 3919)
Delta Airlines
    Chandralok Bldg, 36 Janpath (☎ 332 5222)
Druk Air (Bhutan)
    Chandralok Bldg, 36 Janpath (☎ 331 0990)
El Al
    G-57 Connaught Place (☎ 332 3960)
Emirates
    18 Barakhamba Rd (☎ 332 4665)
Gulf Air
    Indrapakash Bldg, 320 Barakhamba Rd
    (☎ 332 3352)
Iran Air
    Ashok Hotel, Chanakyapuri (☎ 610 0101)
Iraqi Airways
    Ansal Bhawan, Kasturba Gandhi Marg
    (☎ 331 7415)
Japan Airlines
    Chandralok Bldg, 36 Janpath (☎ 332 4858)
Kazakhstan Airlines
    Hotel Janpath (☎ 332 4889)
KLM
    7 Tolstoy Marg (☎ 332 6822)
Kuwait
    DCM Bldg, 16 Barakhamba Rd,
    (☎ 231 4221)
Lufthansa
    56 Janpath (☎ 332 3310)
Malaysian Airlines
    G Block, Connaught Place (☎ 332 4308)
Pakistan International Airlines (PIA)
    Ranjit Hotel, Maharaja Ranjit Singh Rd
    (☎ 373 7791)
Royal Jordanian Airlines
    G-56 Connaught Place (☎ 332 0635)
Royal Nepal Airlines
    44 Janpath (☎ 332 0817)
SAS
    Ambadeep Bldg, Kasturba Gandhi Marg
    (☎ 335 2299)
Singapore Airlines
    Hindustan Times Bldg, Kasturba Gandhi Marg
    (☎ 332 6373)
South African Airways
    B Block, Connaught Place (☎ 332 7503)
Swissair
    DLF Centre, Sansad Marg (☎ 332 5511)
Syrian Arab Airlines
    66 Janpath (☎ 371 2266)

Domestic Flights from Delhi

Destination	Time (hours)	IC	JA	D2	9W	F5	4S	S2	M9	UZ	Fare (US$)
Agra	0.40	1d	-	-	-	-	-	-	-	-	40
Ahmedabad	1.25	2d	-	-	1d	-	-	-	4w	-	105
Amritsar	1.00	2w	-	-	1d	-	-	-	-	-	75
Aurangabad	3.30	4w	-	-	-	-	-	-	-	-	135
Bagdogra	1.55	3w	-	-	1d	-	-	-	-	-	165
Bangalore	2.40	2d	-	-	-	-	1d	6w	1d	-	205
Bhopal	2.00	6w	-	-	-	-	-	-	-	-	90
Bhubaneshwar	3.00	1d	-	-	-	-	-	-	-	-	175
Calcutta	2.05	3d	-	-	2d	-	-	6w	-	2d	160
Chandigarh	1.00	3w	-	-	-	1d	-	-	-	-	55
Chennai (Madras)	2.30	2d	-	1d	-	-	6w	-	6w	-	210
Dibrugarh	3.45	5w	-	-	-	-	-	-	-	-	219
Goa	2.00	1d	-	-	-	-	-	-	3w	-	190
Guwahati	2.25	5w	-	-	1d	-	-	5w	-	-	190
Gwalior	0.50	3w	-	-	-	-	-	-	-	-	50
Hyderabad	2.00	2d	-	-	-	-	-	1d	6w	-	165
Imphal	3.45	2w	-	-	-	-	-	-	-	-	215
Indore	2.15	6w	-	-	-	-	-	-	-	-	105
Jaipur	0.40	2d	-	-	-	1d	-	-	-	1d	45
Jammu	1.10	1d	-	-	1d	-	-	-	3w	-	90
Jodhpur	1.55	6w	2w	-	-	-	-	-	-	-	80
Khajuraho	2.00	1d	-	-	-	-	-	-	1d	-	75
Kochi (Cochin)	4.05	1d	-	-	-	-	-	-	-	-	270
Kulu	1.30	-	1d	-	10w	-	-	-	-	-	123
Leh	1.15	4w	-	-	-	-	-	-	-	-	90
Lucknow	0.50	1d	-	-	-	-	-	-	1d	1d	70
Mumbai (Bombay)	1.50	6d	-	2d	5d	-	1d	1d	2d	-	140
Nagpur	1.25	1d	-	-	-	-	-	-	-	-	120
Patna	1.25	1d	-	-	-	-	-	-	3w	-	115
Pune	2.00	1d	-	-	-	-	-	-	-	-	165
Raipur	1.40	1d	-	-	-	-	-	-	-	-	155
Rajkot	2.30	1d	-	-	-	-	-	-	-	1d	235
Ranchi	2.55	1d	-	-	-	-	-	-	-	-	150
Shimla	1.10	-	3w	-	-	-	4w	-	-	-	96
Srinagar	1.15	1d	-	-	1d	-	-	-	-	-	100
Thiruvananthapuram (Trivandrum)	5.10	6w	-	-	-	-	-	-	-	-	290
Udaipur	1.55	11w	-	-	-	-	4w	-	-	-	80
Vadodara	2.45	1d	-	-	-	-	-	-	-	-	120
Varanasi	1.15	2d	-	-	-	-	-	-	1d	3w	95

*Airline abbreviation codes:

IC – Indian Airlines	9W – Jet Airways	S2 – Sahara Indian Airlines
JA – Jagson Airlines	F5 – Archana Airways	M9 – ModiLuft**
D2 – Skyline NEPC	4S – East West**	UZ – UP Air

** Currently no operations

Tarom Romanian
    Antariksh Bhawan, Kasturba Gandhi Marg
    (☎ 335 4422)
Thai International Airways
    Park Royal Hotel, America Plaza, Nehru Place,
    Chanakyapuri (☎ 623 9988)
Turkmenistan Airlines
    BMC House, Connaught Place (☎ 332 8129)
United Airlines
    Amba Deep Bldg, Kasturba Gandhi Marg
    (☎ 335 3322)
Uzbekistan Airlines
    Hotel Janpath (☎ 332 0070)

International Flights The only international
route served by Indian Airlines from Delhi is
the daily flight to Kathmandu (US$142).

Bus
The main bus station is the Interstate bus
terminal (ISBT) at Kashmir Gate, north of
the (Old) Delhi railway station. It has 24 hour
left-luggage facilities, a State Bank of India
branch, post office, pharmacy, and restaurant. City buses depart from here to locations
all around Delhi (☎ 296 8836). State government bus companies operating from here are:

Delhi Transport Corporation (☎ 331 5085) – book-
    ings from 8 am to 8 pm.
Haryana Roadways (☎ 252 1262) – bookings from
    6.15 am to 12.30 pm and 2 to 9.30 pm. Reserva-
    tions can also be made at the Haryana Emporium
    from 10 am to 5 pm.
Himachal Pradesh Roadways (☎ 251 6725) – book-
    ings from 7 am to 7 pm.
Punjab Roadways (☎ 296 7842) – bookings from 8
    am to 8 pm.
Rajasthan Roadways (☎ 251 8705) – bookings from
    7 am to 9 pm. Bookings can also be made at
    Bikaner House (☎ 383469) just south of Rajpath
    from 6 am to 7 pm.
Uttar Pradesh Roadways (☎ 296 8709) – bookings
    from 6 am to 9 pm.

Rajasthan Buses popular with travellers include the frequent and fast service to Jaipur
(Rs 74, 5½ hours). Deluxe buses for Jaipur
leave from Bikaner House, take five hours
and cost Rs 136, or Rs 234 for the less
frequent air-con services.

North of Delhi For Himalayan destinations
buses are the only option, but it's more pleasant

to take a train for the first part of the journey.
Shimla is accessible by both train and bus;
direct day buses are Rs 115 (10 hours), overnight deluxe buses are around Rs 200.
Alternatively you could take the bus to
Chandigarh (Rs 70, five hours) and the narrow gauge train from there. There are also
direct buses to Dharamsala (13 hours), Manali (16 hours), Dehra Dun (seven hours),
Haridwar (eight hours), Naini Tal (nine
hours), and Jammu (14 hours).

You can buy tickets for the private buses
to these destinations at agents in Connaught
Place and Paharganj.

South of Delhi From the Sarai Kale Khan
ISBT, close to Nizamuddin railway station,
there are frequent departures for Agra (Rs 52
to Rs 75 depending on class, five hours),
Mathura and Gwalior. It's generally quicker
to go by train to all these places, though.
There's a city bus link between this station
and Kashmir Gate ISBT.

Kathmandu Around Paharganj and the other
travellers' hangouts you'll see posters advertising direct buses to Kathmandu – these take
around 36 hours. Most travellers seem to find
that it's cheaper, more comfortable and better
value to do the trip by train to Gorakhpur (Uttar
Pradesh), and then take buses from there.

A number of travellers have also entered
Nepal at the border crossing just east of the
northern Uttar Pradesh village of Banbassa.
There are daily buses to this village from
New Delhi. See the Uttar Pradesh chapter for
more details.

Train
Delhi is an important rail centre and an excellent place to make bookings. There is a
special foreign tourist booking office
upstairs in New Delhi railway station, open
Monday to Saturday from 7.30 am to 5 pm.
This is the place to go if you want a tourist-
quota allocation, are the holder of an Indrail
Pass or want to buy an Indrail Pass. It gets
very busy and crowded, and it can take up to
an hour to get served. If you make bookings
here tickets must be paid for in foreign

DELHI

Major Trains from Delhi

Destination	Train Name & Number	Departure Time *	Distance (km)	Duration (hours)	Fare (Rs) (2nd/1st)
Agra	2180 *Taj Exp*	7.15 am HN	199	4.35	49/223
	2002 *Shatabdi Exp***	6.15 am ND		1.55	275/530
Bangalore	2430 *Rajdhani Exp***	9.30 am HN Sat	2444	35.00	1210/3850
	2628 *Karnataka Exp*	9.15 pm ND		41.00	342/1482
Calcutta	2302 *Rajdhani Exp***	5.15 pm ND	1441	18.00	1015/2895
	2304 *Poorva Exp*	4.30 pm ND		24.00	270/995
Chennai (Madras)	2622 *Tamil Nadu Exp*	10.30 pm ND	2194	33.20	324/1359
Gorakhpur	2554 *Vaishali Exp*	7.45 pm ND	758	13.00	186/642
Jaipur	2901 *Pink City Exp*	5.45 am SR***	308	6.00	72/318
	Shatabdi Exp **	6.15 am ND		4.25	350/685
Jammu Tawi	4645 *Shalimar Exp*	4.10 pm ND	585	14.00	153/528
Lucknow	4230 *Lucknow Mail*	10.00 pm ND	487	9.15	134/464
	2004 *Shatabdi Exp* **	6.20 am ND		6.25	450/900
Mumbai (Bombay)	2952 *Rajdhani Exp***	4.00 pm ND	1384	17.00	825/2835
	1038 *Punjab Mail*	6.00 am ND		26.00	263/965
Shimla	4095 *Himalayan Queen*	6.00 am ND	364	11.00	82/368
Udaipur	9617 *Garib Nawas Exp*	5.45 am SR***	739	17.45	181/632
Varanasi	2382 *Poorva Exp*	4.30 pm ND	764	12.20	186/649

*Abbreviations for train stations: ND – New Delhi, OD – Old Delhi, HN – Hazrat Nizamuddin, SR – Sarai Rohilla
** Air-con only; fare includes meals and drinks.
*** May revert to Old Delhi – check when you buy ticket

currency (US dollars and pounds sterling only, and your change will be given in rupees), or with rupees backed up by bank exchange certificates.

The main ticket office is on Chelmsford Rd, between New Delhi railway station and Connaught Place. This place is well organised, but it's also incredibly busy. Take a numbered ticket from the counter as you enter the building, and then wait at the allotted window.

It's best to arrive first thing in the morning, or when it reopens after lunch. The office is open Monday to Saturday from 7.45 am to 1.50 pm and 2 to 9 pm. On Sunday it's open until 1.50 pm only.

Remember that there are two main stations in Delhi – Delhi railway station in Old Delhi, and New Delhi railway station at Paharganj. New Delhi is much closer to Con-

naught Place, and if you're departing from the Old Delhi railway station you should allow adequate time to wind your way through the traffic snarls of Old Delhi. Between the Old Delhi and New Delhi stations you can take the No 6 bus for Rs 1.

There's also the Nizamuddin railway station south of the New Delhi area where some trains start or finish. It's worth getting off here if you are staying in Chanakyapuri or anywhere else that's south of Connaught Place.

Some trains between Delhi and Jaipur, Jodhpur and Udaipur currently operate to and from Sarai Rohilla station rather than Old Delhi – it's about 3.5km northwest of Connaught Place on Guru Govind Singh Marg. The exception is the *Shatabdi Express* to Jaipur, which operates from New Delhi.

GETTING AROUND

Delhi is large, congested, and the buses get hopelessly crowded. The alternative is a taxi, auto-rickshaw or bicycle.

The Airport

Although there are a number of options, airport-to-city transport is not as straightforward as it should be, due to predatory taxi and auto-rickshaw drivers who prey on the unwary – usually first-time visitors. See the warning in the Delhi Transport Scams boxed item.

Bus The Ex-Servicemen's Air Link Transport Service (EATS; ☎ 331 6530) has a regular bus service between the airport (both terminals) and Connaught Place. The fare is Rs 25 and they will drop you off at most of the major hotels en route if you ask – although this doesn't include Paharganj. In Connaught Place the service leaves from the old Vayudoot office next door to Indian Airlines, between 4 am and 11.30 pm.

When leaving the international terminal, the counter for the EATS bus is just to the right as you exit the building. This is probably the best, although not the quickest, way into the city if you arrive late at night (see the warning about pre-paid taxis in the Taxi section that follows).

There is also a regular DTC bus service that runs from the airport to New Delhi railway station and the Interstate bus station; it also costs Rs 25. At New Delhi railway station it uses the Ajmer Gate (east) side. There is also a public bus to the airport (No 780) from the Super Bazaar at Connaught Place, but it can get very crowded.

Taxi What you want from the airport is not just a pre-paid taxi, but the right pre-paid taxi. In the arrival hall is a long line of 'Pre-paid taxi' booths ranging in price from Rs 350 to Rs 180. Look for the Delhi Traffic Police Pre-Paid Taxi Booth which is where you'll get the lowest price. You'll be given a voucher which you have to present at the booth just outside the airport building.

We've had reports of a number of travellers who have been given the run around by unofficial pre-paid taxis in the middle of the night; they get taken to a hotel, told it's full, then on to another hotel (often in Karol Bagh) and intimidated into staying there at vastly inflated prices (up to US$150). This seems to happen only once the driver has established that the person hasn't been to India before, and only in the middle of the night when it's difficult to get your bearings and there are few other vehicles about.

Bear in mind that if you do head into the centre late at night, most budget hotels are closed (and firmly locked) from around midnight until at least 6 am, so unless you have arranged a late arrival in advance, your options are limited. If you do take a taxi from the airport late at night, before getting into the vehicle make an obvious point of noting down the registration number. Read the boxed item on Delhi Transport Scams; if the driver is not prepared to go where *you* want to go, find another taxi. If this is your first trip to India it is probably best to wait in the terminal building until daylight when there is much less risk of getting led astray and your surroundings are far less intimidating.

At the domestic terminal, the taxi booking desk is just inside the terminal and charges Rs 110 to Connaught Place, plus Rs 2 per bag. The taxi-wallahs outside will try for more.

Bus

Avoid buses during the rush hours. Whenever possible try to board (and leave) at a starting or finishing point, such as the Regal and Plaza cinemas in Connaught Place, as there is more chance of a seat. There are some seats reserved for women on the left-hand side of the bus. The Delhi Transport Corporation runs some buses, others are privately owned, but they all operate along the same set routes.

Useful buses include bus No 505 to the Qutab Minar from the Super Bazaar, or from Janpath opposite the Imperial Hotel. Bus No 101 runs between the Kashmir Gate Interstate bus station and Connaught Place. Bus Nos 620 and 630 will take you between Connaught Place (from outside the Jantar

Mantar) and Chanakyapuri. Bus Nos 101, 104 and 139 run between the Regal Cinema bus stand and the Red Fort. A short bus ride (like Connaught Place to Red Fort) is only about Rs 2.

Taxi & Auto-Rickshaw

All taxis and auto-rickshaws are metered but the meters are invariably out of date, allegedly 'not working' or the drivers will simply refuse to use them.

If you're anywhere near Connaught Place and need an auto-rickshaw pick one up from the very useful pre-paid booth near Palika Bazaar. Otherwise, you'll need to negotiate a price before you set out and this will always be more than it should be. At places like New Delhi railway station or the airport, where there are always plenty of police hanging around, you can generally rely on the meter being used because it's too easy to report a driver.

At the end of a metered journey you will have to pay according to a scale of revised charges. Drivers are supposed to carry cards but if you demand to see one, strangely enough they won't be able to find it. Fare charts are, however, also printed in *Delhi City Guide* (Rs 15, available from newsagents). Currently, when the meter in an auto-rickshaw reads Rs 5/10 you must pay Rs 8.45/17; in a taxi if it reads Rs 10/20 you must pay Rs 16.55/33.75. If you have a chart, pay what you think is the right price and leave it at that. Rest assured that no-one is going to be out of pocket, except yourself, despite hurt or angry protestations to the contrary.

Connaught Place to the Red Fort should cost around Rs 60 by taxi or Rs 30 by auto-rickshaw, depending on the traffic. From 11 pm to 5 am there is a 20% surcharge for auto-rickshaws and 25% in taxis.

There are also unusual six-seater Harley Davidson motorcycle rickshaws running fixed routes at fixed prices. From Connaught Place their starting point is Palika Bazaar and drivers chop their way through the traffic as far as the fountain in Chandni Chowk via the Red Fort in Old Delhi. They cost Rs 3 per

person and are good value, especially during rush hours.

Car Rental

Given Delhi's hectic traffic, you're better off taking a taxi than trying to drive yourself. You'll also save money. If you must rent a car, try Wheels (☎ 372 2150), 18 Barakhamba Rd; or Hertz (☎ 619 7188), Ansal Chambers, Bhikaji Cama Place.

Bicycle & Cycle-Rickshaw

Although traffic and pollution are bad in Old Delhi and around Connaught Place, the bicycle is an excellent way of getting around the sights to the south. Even the Qutab Minar is accessible if you don't mind a bit of exercise, although attempting this in summer might be a bit ambitious. There are very few places to hire bikes, however. In Paharganj, there's a small cycle-hire shop near Rajguru Rd.

Cycle-rickshaws are banned from the Connaught Place area and New Delhi itself, but they can be handy for travelling between the northern edge of Connaught Place and Paharganj, and around Old Delhi.

Greater Delhi

KHIRKI MASJID & JAHANPANAH

This interesting mosque with its four open courts dates from 1380. The nearby village of Khirki also takes its name from the mosque.

Close to the mosque are remains of the fourth city of Delhi, Jahanpanah, including the high Bijai Mandal platform and the Begumpur Mosque with its multiplicity of domes.

TUGHLAQABAD

The massively strong walls of Tughlaqabad, the third city of Delhi, are east of the Qutab Minar. The walled city and fort with its 13 gateways was built by Ghiyas-ud-din Tughlaq. Its construction involved a legendary quarrel with the saint Nizam-ud-din – when the Tughlaq ruler took the workers whom Nizam-ud-din wanted for work on his shrine, the saint cursed the king, warning that his city would be inhabited only by shepherds. Today that is indeed the situation.

The dispute between king and saint did not end with curse and counter-curse. When the king prepared to take vengeance on the saint, Nizam-ud-din calmly told his followers (in a saying that is still current in India today): 'Delhi is a long way off'. Indeed it was, for the king was murdered on his way from Delhi in 1325.

The fort walls are constructed of massive blocks and outside the south wall of the city is an artificial lake with the king's tomb in its centre. A long causeway connects the tomb to the fort, both of which have walls that slope inward.

Getting There & Away
The easiest way to visit Tughlaqabad is to combine it with a visit to the Qutab Minar, and catch a bus from there.

QUTAB MINAR COMPLEX
The buildings in this complex, 15km south of Delhi, date from the onset of Muslim rule in India and are fine examples of early-Afghan architecture. The Qutab Minar itself is a soaring tower of victory which was started in 1193, immediately after the defeat of the last Hindu kingdom in Delhi. It is nearly 73m high and tapers from a 15m diameter base to just 2.5m at the top.

The tower has five distinct storeys, each marked by a projecting balcony. The first three storeys are made of red sandstone, the fourth and fifth of marble and sandstone. Although Qutab-ud-din began construction of the tower, he only got to the first storey. His successors completed it and, in 1368, Feroz Shah Tughlaq rebuilt the top storeys and added a cupola. An earthquake brought the cupola down in 1803 and an Englishman replaced it with another in 1829. However, that dome was deemed inappropriate and was removed some years later.

Today, this impressively ornate tower has a slight tilt, but otherwise has worn the centuries remarkably well. The tower is closed to visitors, and has been for some years after

a stampede during a school trip led to a number of deaths.

Quwwat-ul-Islam Masjid
At the foot of the Qutab Minar stands the first mosque to be built in India, the Might of Islam Mosque. Qutab-ud-din began construction of the mosque in 1193, but it has had a number of additions and extensions over the centuries. The original mosque was built on the foundations of a Hindu temple, and an inscription over the east gate states that it was built with materials obtained from demolishing '27 idolatrous temples'. Many of the elements in the mosque's construction indicate their Hindu or Jain origins.

Altamish, Qutab-ud-din's son-in-law, surrounded the original mosque with a cloistered court built between 1210 and 1220. Ala-ud-din added a court to the east and the magnificent Alai Darwaza gateway in 1300.

Iron Pillar This seven metre high pillar stands in the courtyard of the mosque and has been there since long before the mosque's construction. A six line Sanskrit inscription indicates that it was initially erected outside a Vishnu temple, possibly in Bihar, and was

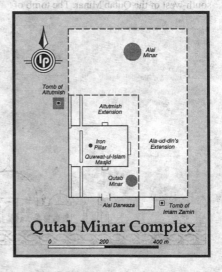

Qutab Minar Complex

0   200   400 m

DELHI

raised in memory of the Gupta King Chandragupta Vikramaditya, who ruled from 375 to 413.

What the inscription does not tell is how it was made, for the iron in the pillar is of quite exceptional purity. Scientists have never discovered how this iron, which is of such purity that it has not rusted after 2000 years, could be cast with the technology of the time. It is said that if you can encircle the pillar with your hands whilst standing with your back to it, your wish will be fulfilled.

Alai Minar
At the same time Ala-ud-din made his additions to the mosque, he also conceived a far more ambitious construction programme. He would build a second tower of victory, exactly like the Qutab Minar, except it would be twice as high! When he died the tower had reached 27m and no-one was willing to continue his overambitious project. The uncompleted tower stands to the north of the Qutab Minar and the mosque.

Other Features
Ala-ud-din's Alai Darwaza gateway is the main entrance to the whole complex. It was built of red sandstone in 1310 and stands just south-west of the Qutab Minar. The tomb of Imam Zamin stands beside the gateway, while the tomb of Altamish, who died in 1235, is by the north-west corner of the mosque.

A short distance west of the enclosure, in Mehrauli village, is the Tomb of Adham Khan who, according to legend, drove the beautiful Hindu singer Rupmati to suicide following the capture of Mandu (see Mandu in the Madhya Pradesh chapter). When Akbar became displeased with him he ended up being heaved off a terrace in the Agra Fort. Also in Mehrauli, a large new Shakti Pitha temple complex is under construction.

South of the enclosure is the Jain Ahimsa Sthal, and an impressive four metre statue in pink granite of Mahavir.

There are some summer palaces in the area and also the tombs of the last kings of Delhi, who succeeded the last Mughals. An empty space between two of the tombs was intended for the last king of Delhi, who died in exile in Rangoon, Burma (Myanmar), in 1862, following his implication in the 1857 Indian Uprising.

Getting There & Away
You can get out to the Qutab Minar on a No 505 bus from the Ajmer Gate side of New Delhi railway station, or from Janpath, opposite the Janpath Hotel.

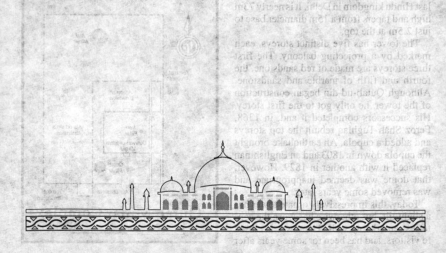

PLACES OF WORSHIP

HINDU TEMPLES

Hindu temples predominate in India, from the mysterious 13th century Sun Temple at Konark in Orissa, to the technicolour glory of Madurai's Sri Meenakshi in Tamil Nadu.

DESIGN & FUNCTION

For Hindus, the square is the perfect shape (a circle isn't perfect because it implies motion), so temples are always based on a square ground plan. Extremely complex rules govern the siting, design and building of each individual temple, based on numerology, astronomy, astrology and religious law. These are so complicated and so important that it's customary for each temple to harbour its own particular set of calculations as though they were religious texts.

Each temple is dedicated to a particular god. The temple is used exclusively for religious rites. However, because Hinduism has so many rites and festivals, there's always something happening and the temple is often a de facto community centre.

ETIQUETTE FOR VISITORS

Dress conservatively, remove your shoes before entering, and do not attempt to enter the sanctum.

EXAMPLES OF HINDU TEMPLES

Bhubaneswar, in Orissa, is known as temple town, and claims to contain over 500 temples. Orissa is also home to the Sun Temple at Konark. India's south is littered with Deccan Hindu temples, including the magnificent Hoysala temples of Belur and Halebid in Karnataka, Venkateshwara – one of India's richest temples – at Tirumala in Andhra Pradesh, and the 125 temples of the holy city of Kanchipuram in Tamil Nadu.

The Mukteshvara Temple in Bhubaneswar, Orissa, was built in the late 10th century. It is one of the most highly decorated of Bhubaneswar's 500 plus temples.

BUDDHIST TEMPLES

India's Buddhist temples are mostly found on the slopes of the Himalaya, in Himachal Pradesh, Ladakh & Zanskar and Sikkim, although one of Buddhism's holiest sites is Bodhgaya, in Bihar.

DESIGN & FUNCTION

The first Buddhist temples were *stupas*, hemispherical mounds which were built to house relics of the Buddha. Unlike the temples of other religions, these included no internal space where worshippers could pray – instead, Buddhists circumambulated the stupas to show their respect. Later, these stupas were incorporated into *chaityas*, a long hall with the stupa at one end. From these, *viharas* were developed – cells were built around a quadrangle with a stupa or Buddha figure at one end. Originally these were cut from rock, but later they were built of brick.

ETIQUETTE FOR VISITORS

When circumambulating a stupa or any other Buddhist site, it is important to always walk in a clockwise direction.

EXAMPLES OF BUDDHIST TEMPLES

Bodhgaya in Bihar – the site of the Buddha's enlightenment and home to the Mahabodhi temple – is an important Buddhist pilgrimage centre. Maharashtra's spectacular rock-cut temples – the caves of Ajanta and Ellora – are largely dedicated to Buddha. The gompas of Ladakh are spiritual centres for Tibetan Buddhism and there's and important temple at the monastery in Dharamsala, the town in Himachal Pradesh where the Dalai Lama now lives.

The Mahabodhi Temple in Bodhgaya, Bihar, stands on the site of a temple erected in the 3rd century BC. The temple is home to a descendant of the bodhi tree under which the Buddha gained enlightenment.

MOSQUES

Some of India's most spectacular mosques are relics of the Mughals, who ruled much of India on and off from 1525 until the early 18th century. Most mosques are found in the north of the country.

DESIGN & FUNCTION

Despite their sometimes astounding beauty and great variety of design, mosques are essentially simple buildings, providing a large space for communal prayer. Larger mosques may have a school attached.

Mosques are usually built around a rectangular courtyard with a tank at its centre. Three sides of the courtyard are cloistered while the fourth is the entrance to the prayer hall.

India's oldest mosques bear witness to Islamic architectural innovation: Muslim invaders introduced both the arch and mortar masonry to India

The Jama Masjid, or 'Friday Mosque', is where the community gathers for prayer on Friday, Islam's holy day. Smaller, local mosques are used for prayer on other days of the week.

ETIQUETTE FOR VISITORS

You must remove your shoes before entering a mosque. Find out if visitors are permitted at prayer times – often they are not. Many mosques admit women visitors, but some don't. Both men and women must cover their arms and legs. A few larger mosques have robes for visitors who are not appropriately dressed.

EXAMPLES OF MOSQUES

Delhi's Jama Masjid is one of India's most spectacular mosques and features traditional *ablaq* stonework. The Jama Masjid at the deserted city of Fatehpur Sikri in Uttar Pradesh is said to be modelled on that of Mecca, and incorporates some Hindu design elements. The ruined Adhai-din-ka-jhonpra in Ajmer, Rajasthan, was converted from a Jain temple in 1198 by Muhammad Ghori.

The Jama Masjid, or Friday Mosque, in Delhi is the country's largest mosque. It's said that 25,000 worshippers can cram into its courtyard.

SIKH TEMPLES

Sikhism doesn't recognise caste or class, so everyone becomes involved in ceremonies. Communal meals are a feature of temple activities. Often accommodation is offered free of charge.s

DESIGN & FUNCTION

Sikh temple is called a *gurdwara*. Outside there is a flagpole, called a *nishan sahib*, flying a triangular flag with the Sikh insignia. There is no special requirement for the design of the building. Sikhs worship only one god and are opposed to idol worship. You'll probably see pictures of the Gurus (the spiritual leaders who founded Sikhism), especially the first, fifth and 10th (last) Gurus. The wisdom of the Gurus is contained in the *Guru Granth Sahib*, a book written by Arjun, the fifth Guru, in the early 17th century. It has become an object of veneration in itself and is regarded as the 'living' Guru.

ETIQUETTE FOR VISITORS

Sikhism is an egalitarian religion and everyone is welcome to enter the temple. However, you must remove your shoes and you are supposed to cover your head.

EXAMPLES OF SIKH TEMPLES

The Golden Temple in Amritsar, Punjab, is the paragon of Sikh Temples. This holiest shrine of Sikhism, also known as the Hari Mandir, blends Hindu and Muslim styles of architecture.

Gurdwara Damdama Sahib, one of Delhi's eight Sikh temples, marks the place where Guru Gobind Singh met with emperor Bahadur Shah, Aurang-zeb's son

JAIN TEMPLES

Jains take their temple building very seriously: constructing temples is one of the ways to attain good karma, and consequently Jain temples are often found in huge concentrations. Shatrunjaya in Gujarat, for example, is a complex made up of 863 temples.

While Jainism was founded around 500 BC, it didn't become widely spread until the 1st century AD. Most Jain temples date from between 1000 and 1300, when the Solani dynasty of western India was patronising the religion. Many of these temples are still in use today.

DESIGN & FUNCTION

Jain temples are quite similar to Hindu temples, with the main difference being the number of cells built to hold images. Many Jain temples hide their spectacular interiors behind a non-descript wall. This reflects the Jain belief that everyone has the seed of perfection within them, despite our flawed exteriors – beauty is found within.

In many cases Jain temples follow the complex mathematical Hindu model. Most are aligned along an east-west axis, and as the sun rises it shines through the entrance. Temples may be either cut from rock or built free-standing.

EXAMPLES OF JAIN TEMPLES

The hilltop temple complex of Shatrunjaya, the Place of Victory, in Gujarat, is one of the most evocative Jain memorials in India. The Dilwara temples of Mt Abu, in Rajasthan, are renowned as the country's finest Jain architecture.

The Jain temple complex at Ranakpur in Rajasthan is one of the country's largest. One hundred metres square, it has 29 halls supported by 1444 pillars.

Punjab & Haryana

The Punjab was probably the part of India which suffered the most destruction and damage at the time of Partition, yet today it is far and away the most affluent state in India. No natural resource or advantage gave the Punjabis this enviable position; it was sheer hard work.

Prior to Partition the Punjab extended across both sides of what is now the India-Pakistan border, and what was its capital, Lahore, is now the capital of the Pakistani state of Punjab. The grim logic of Partition sliced the population of the Punjab into a Muslim region and a Sikh and Hindu region. As millions of Sikhs and Hindus fled eastward and equal numbers of Muslims fled west, there were innumerable atrocities and killings on both sides.

More recently, Sikh political demands have racked the state. In 1984, extremists occupied the Golden Temple in Amritsar and were only evicted after a bloody battle with the Indian army. The terrorist activities of five extremist groups continued into the early 1990s, putting the Punjab firmly off-limits to travellers. Support for these groups has dwindled, things are quiet now, and it's safe to visit.

The major city in the Punjab is Amritsar, the holy city of the Sikhs, but it is so close to the Pakistani border that it was thought wise to build a safer capital further within India. At first Shimla, the old imperial summer capital, was chosen, but Chandigarh, a new planned city, was conceived and built in the 1950s to serve as the capital of the new Punjab.

In 1966, however, the Punjab was to undergo another split. This time it was divided into the predominantly Sikh and Punjabi-speaking state of Punjab and the state of Haryana. At the same time some of the northern parts of the Punjab were hived off to Himachal Pradesh. Chandigarh, on the border of Punjab and Haryana, remained the capital of both states until 1986 when the

PUNJAB & HARYANA AT A GLANCE

PUNJAB
Population: 21.4 million
Area: 50,362 sq km
Capital: Chandigarh
Main Language: Punjabi
Literacy Rate: 57%
Best Time to Go: October to March

HARYANA
Population: 17.8 million
Area: 44,212 sq km
Capital: Chandigarh
Main Language: Hindi
Literacy Rate: 55%
Best Time to Go: October to March

The external boundaries of India on this map have not been authenticated and may not be correct.

Amritsar p249
Golden Temple p243

Chandigarh p245

Locator & Map Index

DELHI

Highlights
- The Golden Temple at Amritsar in the early morning light
- The chilling atmosphere of the Martyrs' Gallery, Jallianwalal Bagh, Amritsar

government announced that it would be handed over to Punjab in an attempt to placate the Sikhs. However, with the continued violence in Punjab this didn't take place,

A REGIONAL HIGHLIGHT

Golden Temple, Amritsar

The holiest shrine of the Sikh religion, also known as the Hari Mandir, is in the centre of the old part of Amritsar. The temple itself is surrounded by the pool which gave the town its name, and is reached by a causeway. Open to all, it's a beautiful place, especially early in the morning. However, at the weekends it can get quite crowded.

Restoration work to repair the damage done when the Indian army stormed the Golden Temple in 1984 has largely been completed.

Pilgrims and visitors to the Golden Temple must remove their shoes and cover their heads before entering the precincts. No smoking is allowed; photography is permitted from the Parikrama, the marble walkway that surrounds the sacred pool. An English-speaking guide is available at the information office near the clock tower which marks the temple's main entrance. The information office has a number of interesting publications including one eclectic booklet entitled *Human Hair – Factory of Vital Energy!*

GREG ELMS

Hari Mandir Standing in the middle of the sacred pool, the Golden Temple is a two storey marble structure reached by a causeway known as the Gurus' Bridge. The lower parts of the marble walls are decorated with inlaid flower and animal motifs in the *pietra dura* style of the Taj Mahal. Once inside the temple, pilgrims offer sweet doughy *prasaad* to the attendants, who take half to distribute to everyone as they leave the temple.

The architecture of the Golden Temple is a blend of Hindu and Muslim styles. The golden dome (said to be gilded with 100kg of pure gold) is supposed to represent an inverted lotus flower. It is inverted, turning back to the earth, to symbolise the Sikhs' concern with the problems of this world. The dome is currently being re-covered in gold donated by the Sikh community of Birmingham, Britain.

Granth Sahib Four priests at key positions around the temple keep up a continuous reading in Punjabi from the Sikhs' holy book. The reading is broadcast by loudspeaker. The original copy of the Granth Sahib is kept under a pink shroud in the Golden Temple during the day and at around 10 pm each evening is ceremoniously returned to the Akal Takhat (Sikh Parliament) building. The morning processional ceremony takes place at 4 am in summer, 5 am in winter.

Sikh Museum The Central Sikh Museum is upstairs in the clock tower and comprises a gallery of paintings telling the story of the Sikhs and their martyrs.

although eventually it will. In the meantime, Chandigarh remains the capital of the two states, yet is administered as a Union Territory from Delhi.

Although the Punjab is predominantly an agricultural state, it also has a number of thriving industries including Hero Bicycles at Ludhiana – India's (and the world's) biggest bicycle manufacturer.

From the traveller's point of view, the area has just one attraction – the beautiful Golden Temple in Amritsar. Apart from that, the states are mainly places of transit to and from Pakistan or the Indian Himalaya.

Haryana

If you're going from Delhi to almost any major attraction in the north of India – Jaipur, Agra, Amritsar – you will need to go through Haryana. The state itself is notable for having virtually no tourist attractions.

A REGIONAL HIGHLIGHT

Akal Takhat The Shiromani Gurdwara Parbandhak Committee, or Sikh Parliament, traditionally meets in this building, which is why it was a target for the Indian army in 1984. It has since been completely rebuilt.

Guru Ka Langar & Gurdwaras All Sikh temples have a community kitchen, and in this one volunteers prepare free meals for up to 30,000 people every day. The food is very basic – chapatis and lentils – and is prepared and dished out daily in an orderly fashion. Nearby are the gurdwaras, offering free accommodation to all. Pilgrims are well provided for and there's a good library, a post office, bank and railway booking agent.

Other Buildings To the south of the temple enclosure is a garden in which stands the **Baba Atal Tower**. The tall **Ramgarhia Minars**, scarred by tank fire, stand outside the temple enclosure. ■

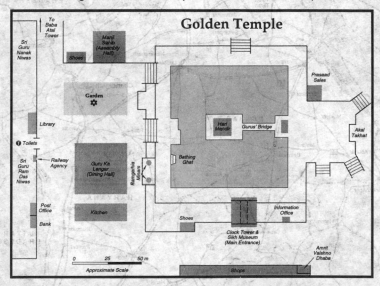

Golden Temple

To make up for this, the Haryanans have built a series of 'service centres' along the main roads – motel-restaurant-service station complexes named after birds found in the state – that can make travelling through the area a real pleasure. Typically the complexes may have a camping site, camper huts (usually for around Rs 200) and rooms (in the Rs 350 to Rs 400 range if they have air-con, and cheaper without). Some places also have dormitories. All have restaurants, and some of these serve fast food. For details on the location, facilities and costs of service centres, pick up a pamphlet from the Haryana Government Tourist Bureau in Delhi (Chanderlok Building, 36 Janpath) or from the tourist office in Chandigarh (Sector 17B).

The **Suraj Kund Crafts Mela**, one of Haryana's higlights, takes place in the first two weeks of February. You buy direct from the craftspeople, quality is very high and prices lower than in the state emporia. Suraj Kund is only 10km from Delhi.

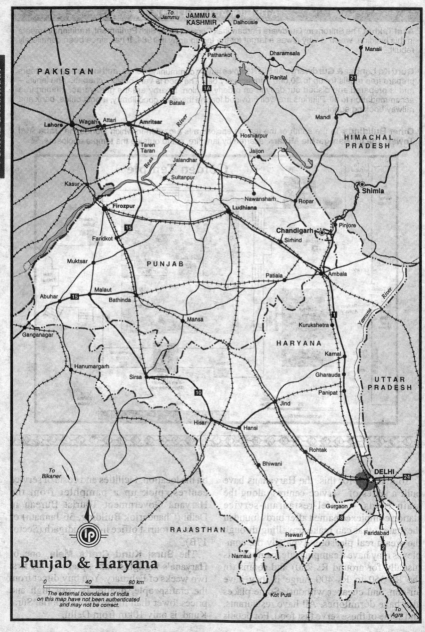

Punjab & Haryana

0   40   80 km

The external boundaries of India
on this map have not been authenticated
and may not be correct.

CHANDIGARH

Pop: 619,000   Tel Area Code: 0172

Construction of Chandigarh from a plan by the French architect Le Corbusier began in the 1950s. Although to many western visitors it appears to be a rather sterile and hopelessly sprawling city, Indians are very proud of it and Chandigarh's residents feel that it is a good place to live.

Orientation

Chandigarh is on the edge of the Siwalik Hills, the outermost edge of the Himalaya. It is divided into 47 numbered sectors, separated by broad avenues. The bus terminal, modern shopping centre, and many of the restaurants are in Sector 17. As the railway station is eight km out of Chandigarh, buses are much more convenient than trains.

Information

Tourist Offices The Chandigarh tourist office (☎ 704614), which is upstairs in the bus terminal, is open from 9 am to 5 pm Monday to Friday and 9 am to 1 pm Saturday. One floor up is Punjab Tourism (☎ 704570). Haryana Tourism (☎ 702955) is in Sector 17B.

Himachal Tourism and UP Tourism have offices beside the Hotel Jullundur.

Money The major banks (Bank of Baroda, State Bank of India) are in Sector 17 near Haryana Tourism. An efficient, fast alternative, also in Sector 17 near the banks, is Wall Street Finance, which accepts most travellers cheques and is open 9.30 am to 6 pm Monday to Saturday.

Post & Communications The GPO, in Sector 17, is open Monday to Friday from 9 am to 4 pm. STD and ISD booths that also offer fax services can be found in sectors 17 and 22.

Government Buildings

The Secretariat and the Vidhan Sabha (Legislative Assembly) buildings are in Sector 1. Between 10 am and noon you can go to the top of the Secretariat, from where there is an

```
Chandigarh
        0    0.5    1 km
```

PLACES TO STAY
1	Puffin Guesthouse
6	YMCA
7	Hotel Mount View
14	Chandigarh Yatri Niwas
16	Panchayat Bhavan
19	Hotel Shivalik View
20	Hotels Pankaj, Alankar & Amar
24	Hotels Sunbeam & Jullundur
25	Hotels Piccadily & Divyadeep
28	Aroma Hotel

PLACES TO EAT
11	Wimpy Restaurant
15	Mehfil Restaurant
21	Indian Coffee House & Keelam Cinema
22	Kwality Restaurant
26	Sai Sweets & Tasty Bite
27	Golden Dragon & Singh's Chicken

OTHER
2	Secretariat
3	Vidhan Sabha (Legislative Assembly)
4	High Court
5	Rock Garden
8	Museum & Art Gallery
9	Foreigners' Registration Office
10	Rose Garden
12	Haryana Tourism
13	GPO
17	Indian Airlines
18	Air India
23	Tourist Office & Bus Station

excellent view over Chandigarh. The huge open hand here is a symbol of unity, and is supposed to be the centrepiece of the government sector.

Rock Garden
This strange and whimsical fantasy has grown and grown over the years and is now very extensive. It's open from 9 am to 1 pm and 3 to 7 pm from 1 April to 30 September. The rest of the year it opens and closes an hour earlier in the afternoons. Entry is Rs 2.

Close by is the artificial **Sukhna Lake**, where you can rent rowing boats or just stroll round its two km perimeter.

Museum & Art Gallery
The art gallery in Sector 10 is open daily except Monday and contains a modest collection of Indian stone sculptures dating back to the Gandhara period, together with some miniature paintings and modern art. The adjacent museum has fossils and implements of prehistoric humans found in India. Opening hours are 10 am to 5 pm Wednesday to Sunday. Entry is Rs 1.

Rose Garden
The rose garden in Sector 16 is claimed to be the biggest in Asia and contains more than a thousand varieties of roses.

Places to Stay – bottom end
Chandigarh isn't over-endowed with rock-bottom budget accommodation.

Panchayat Bhavan is one of the least expensive options. However, it's an institutional block with a sports club atmosphere – all smelly socks and towel-flicking. Dorm beds cost Rs 12 or there are doubles for Rs 150.

Chandigarh Yatri Niwas (☎ 545904) is on the corner of sectors 15 and 24, rather anonymously hidden behind a block of flats. Singles/doubles cost Rs 150/200, or Rs 200/250 with air-cooling. There is a cafeteria.

Hotel Jullundur (☎ 706777), opposite the bus terminal, is more of a conventional hotel with double rooms with TV, attached bath and constant hot water for Rs 275.

City Hotel (☎ 708992), behind the Jullundur, has singles/doubles from Rs 150/200; some rooms have attached bath.

Places to Stay – middle
About 500m north-west of the bus terminal there are three bottom to middle-range hotels side by side in Sector 22, which all offer reasonable rooms. There are several other options nearby.

Amar (☎ 703608) charges Rs 300 for reasonable doubles (Rs 450 with air-con) and has a good restaurant.

Alankar (☎ 708801) has doubles from Rs 400.

Hotel Pankaj (☎ 709891) has singles/doubles from Rs 385/415.

Hotel Divyadeep (☎ 705191) on Himalaya Marg (on the southern edge of Sector 22) has rooms with fan for Rs 140/170, Rs 190/220 with air-cooling and Rs 250/300 with air-con.

Aroma Hotel (☎ 700045), just past the traffic lights, about 10 minutes walk from the bus terminal, is very comfortable. Rooms are from Rs 750/850. The place is clean and well kept and there's a restaurant and coffee shop.

Places to Stay – top end
Hotel Sunbeam (☎ 708100-7) is near the bus stand. Pleasant air-con rooms cost from Rs 795/995.

Hotel Piccadilly (☎ 707571) is nearby on Himalaya Marg. It charges Rs 1290/1790 for singles/doubles and is popular with business people.

Hotel Mount View (☎ 547882) is set in peaceful gardens in Sector 10. It has air-con rooms for Rs 1300/1600, a restaurant and coffee shop, swimming pool and health club.

Places to Eat
Chandigarh has many places to eat and there's plenty of variety, from western-style fast food to Chinese and Indian regional dishes. Haryana is a dry state so you won't be able to buy alcoholic drinks.

Royal, *Vince* and *Punjab* restaurants can be found in the row of shops on Udyog Path opposite the bus terminal. They serve inexpensive, standard Indian food.

Singh's Chicken, around the corner on Himalaya Marg, has a good range of chicken dishes.

Golden Dragon Chinese restaurant nearby is cheaper than it looks and the food is good.

Tasty Bite, a ritzy takeaway place with decent burgers and south Indian snacks is near the Golden Dragon.

Bhoj Restaurant at the Hotel Divyadeep serves slightly expensive vegetarian food in glossy surroundings.

Chopstix 2, a Chinese place, is handy if you're staying in the Panchayat Bhavan (it's across the road).

Wimpy, the British hamburger chain, is to the north of Chopstix in Sector 9.

There are lots of places to eat in the Sector 17 shopping centre.

Hot Millions (near Air India) serves fast food; nearby is the **Indian Coffee House**.

Mehfil, and in the same street, **Ghazal** are Chandigarh's top two restaurants. Their menus are the standard mix of Continental, Chinese and Indian.

Things to Buy
Woollen sweaters and shawls from the Punjab are good buys, especially in the Government Emporium. The Sector 17 shopping centre is probably the most extensive in India.

Getting There & Away
Air Indian Airlines (☎ 544539), in the Sector 17 shopping complex, is open from 9.30 am to 7 pm. It has three flights a week each to Delhi, Mumbai and Amritsar and once-a-week flights to Leh. Archana (☎ 546399) has a daily flight to Delhi.

Bus Chandigarh has a huge and noisy bus terminal. For the five hour trip to Delhi there are nearly 200 buses every day, departing round the clock. Ordinary buses cost Rs 70, deluxe buses are Rs 140. Some other destinations include Shimla (four hours, Rs 100 deluxe), Manali (10 hours, Rs 131 ordinary),

Dharamsala (10 hours, Rs 88 ordinary), Amritsar (six hours, Rs 77 express) and Jaipur (Rs 272 deluxe, 12 hours).

Train Buses are more convenient than trains to or from Chandigarh; if you prefer to travel by train, however, reservations can be made at the office (☎ 704382) upstairs in the bus terminal. It's open from 8 am to 8 pm.

It is 245km from Delhi to Chandigarh and the twice-daily *Shatabdi Express* does the journey in just three hours. The fare is Rs 300 in an air-con chair car, and Rs 595 in executive class.

Kalka is just 25km up the line, and from there it takes nearly six hours to reach Shimla on the narrow-gauge mountain railway.

Getting Around
The Airport The airport is 11km to the south of Sector 17 and it's Rs 250 by taxi or Rs 57 by auto-rickshaw.

Local Transport Chandigarh is much too spread out to get around on foot. The extensive bus network is the cheapest way of getting around. Bus No 1 runs by the Aroma Hotel as far as the government buildings in Sector 1, and bus No 37 runs to the railway station from the bus terminal.

If you're planning a longer trip across the city consider taking an auto-rickshaw, of which there aren't so many. There is a pre-paid auto-rickshaw stand behind the bus terminal. A sign lists all the set fares, but rickshaw-wallahs may offer lower rates when business is slack. From the railway station to the bus terminal should cost around Rs 34.

Bicycle is the best form of transport, but hire shops are hard to find; ask at your hotel.

AROUND CHANDIGARH
Pinjore
The **Yadavindra Gardens** at Pinjore were designed by Fidai Khan, Aurangzeb's foster brother, who also designed the Badshahi Mosque in Lahore, Pakistan. Situated 20km from Chandigarh, near Kalka, the gardens include the Rajasthani Mughal-style **Shish**

Mahal palace. Below it is the Rang Mahal and the cubical Jal Mahal. There is an otter house, and other animals can be seen in the mini-zoo near the gardens. The fountains only operate on weekends.

There are hourly buses from Chandigarh, which stop by the entrance to the gardens.

CHANDIGARH TO DELHI

There are many places of interest along the 260km route from Chandigarh to Delhi. The road, part of the Grand Trunk Road, is one of the busiest in India.

Karnal & Kurukshetra

Karnal is mentioned in the *Mahabharata*, and it was here that Nadir Shah, the Persian who took the Peacock Throne from Delhi, defeated the Mughal emperor, Mohammed Shah, in 1739. The **Kurukshetra tank** has attracted as many as a million pilgrims during eclipses, when the water is believed to be especially purifying.

Gharaunda

The gateways of an old Mughal serai (rest house) stand to the west of this village, 102km north of Delhi. Shah Jahan built *kos minars* (milestones) along the road from Delhi to Lahore and serais at longer intervals. Most of the kos minars still stand but there is little left of the various serais.

Panipat

Panipat, 92km north of Delhi, is reputed to be one of the most fly-infested places in India – due, it is said, to a Muslim saint buried here. He is supposed to have totally rid Panipat of flies, but when the people complained that he had done too good a job he gave them all the flies back, multiplied by a thousand.

Sultanpur

There are many birds, including flamingoes, at Sultanpur's bird sanctuary 46km southwest of Delhi. September to March is the best time to visit, and you can stay at the *Rosy Pelican* (☎ 85242) complex. To get there take a blue Haryana bus from Delhi to Gurgaon, and then take a Chandu bus to Sultanpur.

DELHI TO SIRSA

This route takes you north-west through Haryana towards the Punjab and Pakistan, south of the Delhi to Amritsar route. From Delhi the railway line runs through **Rohtak**, 70km north-west of Delhi, which was once a border town between the Sikhs' and Marathas' regions, and were the subject of frequent clashes.

Hansi, north-west of Rohtak, was where Colonel Skinner died. (Skinner's Horse, the private cavalry regiment he founded in the 1790s, was responsible for the conquest of large areas of northern India for the East India Company.) **Sirsa**, 90km further northwest, is an ancient city but little remains apart from the city walls.

Punjab

AMRITSAR

Pop: 784,000   Tel Area Code: 0183

Founded in 1577 by Ram Das, the fourth guru of the Sikhs, Amritsar is both the centre of the Sikh religion and the major city of Punjab state. The name means Pool of Nectar, referring to the sacred tank around which the Sikhs' Golden Temple is built. Although Amritsar itself is just another dusty Indian city, the Golden Temple is an exceptionally beautiful and peaceful place.

The original site for the city was granted by the Mughal emperor, Akbar, but in 1761 Ahmad Shah Durani sacked the town and destroyed the temple. It was rebuilt in 1764, and in 1802 was roofed over with copper-gilded plates by Ranjit Singh and became known as 'the Golden Temple'. During the turmoil of the Partition of India in 1948, Amritsar was a flash point for the terrible events that shook the Punjab.

During unrest in the Punjab in the early 1980s the Golden Temple was occupied by Sikh extremists who were finally evicted by the Indian army in 1984 with much bloodshed. This action was a contributing factor to Indira Gandhi's subsequent assassination.

The temple was again occupied by extremists in 1986. The damage wrought on the Golden Temple by the tanks of the Indian army has now been repaired, and things are quiet again.

The Sikhs are justifiably proud of their capital city and the Golden Temple, and travellers have commented on their friendliness and helpfulness.

Orientation

The old city is south-east of the main railway station and is surrounded by a circular road which used to contain the massive city walls.

There are 18 gates still in existence but only the north gate, facing the Ram Bagh gardens, is original. The Golden Temple and the narrow alleys of the bazaar area are in the old city.

The more modern part of Amritsar is north-east of the railway station, where you will also find the beautiful gardens known as Ram Bagh, Mall Rd and 'posh' Lawrence St. The bus terminal is two km east of the railway station on the road to Delhi.

Information

Tourist Offices The tourist office (☎ 231482) is in the former youth hostel, now occupied

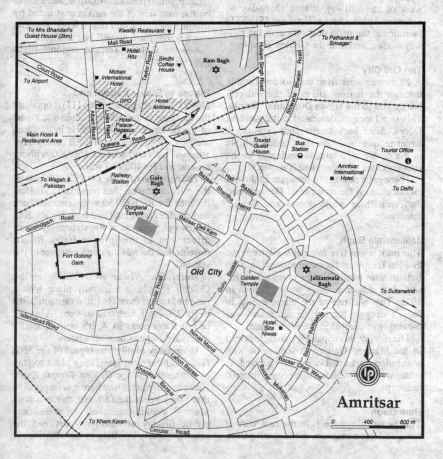

by the army, one km east of the bus terminal. It has very little information and is closed at weekends. The information office at the Golden Temple is very helpful.

Money There are numerous money changers in Links Rd, opposite the railway station. There is a Bank of Punjab branch office at the Golden Temple.

Post & Communications There is a post office at the Golden Temple that sells stamps (open Monday to Saturday 9 am to 6.30 pm). The main post office is on Court Rd north-west of the railway station (Monday to Saturday 9 am to 5 pm). There are ISD/STD facilities at the main post office, at the railway station, and near the Golden Temple.

The Old City
A 15 minute walk from the Golden Temple through the narrow alleys of the old city brings you to the Hindu **Durgiana Temple**. This small temple, dedicated to the goddess Durga, dates back to the 16th century. A larger temple, built like the Golden Temple in the centre of a lake, is dedicated to the Hindu deities, Lakshmi and Narayan.

There are a number of mosques in the old city, including the mosque of **Mohammed Jan** with three white domes and slender minarets.

Jallianwala Bagh
This park is just five minutes walk from the Golden Temple and commemorates the 2000 Indians who were killed or wounded at this site, shot indiscriminately by the British in 1919. This was one of the major events in India's struggle for independence and was movingly re-created in the film *Gandhi*.

The story of this appalling massacre is told in the Martyrs' Gallery. A section of wall with bullet marks still visible is preserved, as is the well into which some people jumped to escape.

Ram Bagh
This beautiful garden is in the new part of town and has a museum in the small palace built by the Sikh Maharaja Ranjit Singh. The museum has a weapons from Mughal times and some portraits of the ruling houses of the Punjab. It's closed on Wednesday.

Other Attractions
Fort Gobind Garh, in the south-west of the city, has been taken over by the Indian army and is now off limits. It was built in 1805-09 by Ranjit Singh, who was also responsible for constructing the city walls.

Taren Taran is an important Sikh tank about 25km south of Amritsar. There's a temple, which predates Amritsar, and a tower on the east side of the tank, constructed by Ranjit Singh. It's said that a leper who can swim across the tank will be cured.

See the **Golden Temple** regional highlight on p242.

Places to Stay – bottom end
Hotel Palace-Pegasus (☎ 65111) is opposite the entrance to the railway station and is one of the better choices; the hotels in this area are generally pretty scruffy. All rooms have attached bath and cost Rs 150/200 without air-con and Rs 400/600 with.

Tourist Guest House (☎ 553830), east of the railway station, has reasonable singles/doubles for Rs 100/150 with common bath and doubles with attached bath for Rs 200. Watch out for touts at the station who will direct you to the inferior *Hotel Tourist Bureau*, just outside the north entrance of the station.

Hotel Sita Niwas (☎ 54092) near the Golden Temple is a friendly place with a range of rooms from Rs 150 (common bath) to Rs 750 (with bath and air-con). A bucket of hot water costs Rs 4. It's built around a courtyard and can be a little noisy.

Hospitality to pilgrims is part of the Sikh faith, and the most interesting place to stay in Amritsar is at the *Golden Temple* itself. However, if you do stay here it is imperative that you respect the fact that this is a holy place – smoking, alcohol, drugs and any public display of familiarity between the sexes is grossly insulting to the Sikhs.

The gurdwaras *Sri Guru Ram Das Niwas* and *Sri Guru Nanak Niwas* are staffed by volunteers. Accommodation is free but you must pay a deposit of Rs 50 (returnable on departure) and you can stay for up to three days. There's a large dorm, bedding is provided and the toilets and shower block are in the centre of the courtyard. There's no pressure from any of the staff but a donation is expected – and you shouldn't forget to make one. Doubles with attached bath are sometimes available for foreigners in the Sri Guru Nanak Niwas.

The *Sri Guru Hargobind Niwas*, a new guest house nearby, costs Rs 50.

Places to Stay – middle

Hotel Airlines (☎ 64848), on Cooper Rd near the railway station has reasonable rooms, if a bit tatty. They range from Rs 275/330 (ordinary) to Rs 550/660-770 (air-con). All have attached bathroom and there's a pleasant sun terrace and restaurant.

Grand Hotel (☎ 62424), near the Hotel Palace-Pegasus opposite the railway station, is not such good value. Rooms are Rs 375, and with air-con Rs 600.

Hotel Blue Moon is on Mall Rd in the new area of the city and about one km from the railway station. The rooms are similarly priced and quite pleasant.

Amritsar International Hotel (☎ 555991), Punjab Tourism's centrally air-conditioned hotel, is a modern building near the bus terminal. Rooms with attached bath cost from Rs 475/550.

Mrs Bhandari's Guest House (☎ 222390), at 10 The Cantonment, is a delightful place to stay and consequently very popular. Rooms are Rs 650/740 with air-con and Rs 500/600 without. Mrs Bhandari herself has since retired but the place is efficiently run by her two daughters. The kitchen ('Commando Bridge') is spotless and the bedrooms stuck in a now very fashionable 1950s time warp. Meals are available – breakfast is Rs 100, lunch and dinner Rs 150/200 veg/non-veg. The guest house is set in a large peaceful garden with a swimming pool (Rs 50; open May to August). Camping charges (with own equipment) are Rs 80 per person.

Places to Stay – top end

Hotel Ritz (☎ 66027), at 45 Mall Rd, has a gym and swimming pool, and overpriced air-con rooms at Rs 950/1250.

Mohan International Hotel (☎ 227803), on Albert Rd, is Amritsar's top hotel, with rooms from Rs 950/1400 with bathtubs in the attached bathrooms. It has air-con, a swimming pool (Rs 75 for non-guests) and a good restaurant.

Places to Eat

It's interesting to join the pilgrims for a basic meal at the Guru ka Langar at the *Golden Temple*; there's no charge but you should make a donation when you eat here.

Opposite the clock-tower entrance to the temple are a number of cheap dhabas.

Amrit Vaishno Dhaba (at the end of the group, opposite the information office) does good chana bhatura (spiced chickpeas with fried Indian bread).

Kwality Restaurant is one of several mid-range restaurants near the Ram Bagh on Mall Rd. It has main dishes for around Rs 60.

South Land, where masala dosas cost Rs 15, and *Salads Plus* nearby have cheaper snacks.

Sindhi Coffee House opposite Ram Bagh offers full meals at prices similar to Kwality's, and snacks such as French toast with cheese.

Kasar de Dhawa near the Durgiana Temple and the telephone exchange in the old city, is one of Amritsar's cheaper places. Parathas and other vegetarian dishes are the speciality here, and you can eat well for around Rs 30.

Mrs Bhandari's Guest House serves British-style food; Rs 200 for a non-veg lunch or dinner. Non-guests should book in advance.

Things to Buy

Woollen blankets, shawls and sweaters are supposed to be cheaper in Amritsar than in other places in India, as they are locally manufactured. Katra Jaimal Singh, near the telephone exchange in the old city, is a good shopping area.

Getting There & Away

Air The Indian Airlines office (☎ 66433) is just north of Mall Rd at 367 Green Ave. Amritsar is linked by a four times weekly Indian Airlines flight to Delhi (US$75) and Srinagar (US$65).

Bus The bus journey to Delhi (10 hours, Rs 121) is less comfortable than going by train. There are also early-morning buses to Dehra Dun (10 hours, Rs 115), Shimla (10 hours, Rs 115), Dalhousie and Dharamsala.

There are frequent buses to Pathankot (three hours, Rs 28), Chandigarh (six hours, Rs 63) and Jammu (five hours, Rs 48) for Srinagar. There are privately operated buses to Jammu or Chandigarh (Rs 180) but these do not go from the bus terminal. Tickets must be bought in advance from the agents near the railway station.

Getting to Rajasthan from Amritsar can be a pain unless you go via Delhi. It's possible to get a direct bus as far as Ganganagar (just over the Rajasthan border); the journey takes around 10 hours.

Train There are direct rail links to Delhi (447km, Rs 47/388 in ordinary 2nd/1st class) in eight to 10 hours, but the daily *Shatabdi Express* does the journey in just over seven hours. Tickets are Rs 420/840 in chair car/executive class. The *Amritsar-Howrah Mail* links Amritsar with Lucknow (850km, 17 hours), Varanasi (1251km, 23 hours) and Calcutta (1829km, 38 hours).

To/From Pakistan The rail crossing point is at Attari, 26km from Amritsar, and the *4607 Indo-Pak Express* leaves Amritsar daily at 9.30 am, reaching Lahore in Pakistan at 1.35 pm. However, it can be delayed for hours at the border. In the other direction, the train doesn't always stop in Amritsar.

The road crossing at Wagah, 32km from Amritsar, is quicker. The border is open from 9 am to 4 pm daily and there are frequent

buses from Amritsar (one hour, Rs 12). Taxis cost Rs 300 to Rs 400.

Neem Chameli Tourist Complex, operated by Punjab Tourism, at Wagah, has dorm beds and cheap doubles.

See the introductory Getting There & Away chapter for further details.

Getting Around

The airport is 15km from the city centre. An auto-rickshaw should cost around Rs 70, a taxi Rs 150.

Auto-rickshaws charge Rs 25 from the station to the Golden Temple. The same trip on a cycle-rickshaw will cost Rs 15.

PATHANKOT

Pop: 165,000   Tel Area Code: 0186

The town of Pathankot in the extreme north of the Punjab, 107km from Amritsar, is important to travellers purely as a crossroad. It's the gateway to the Himachal Pradesh hill stations of Dalhousie and Dharamsala, and on the route to Jammu and Srinagar. Otherwise it's a dull little place, although there's the picturesque **Shahpur Kandi Fort** about 13km north of the town on the River Ravi.

Places to Stay & Eat

Hotel Tourist (☎ 20660) is outside the railway station (turn right). It's a basic place with rooms from Rs 60/125 with attached bath, and a reasonable restaurant. *Hotel Green* nearby is similar.

Hotel Airlines (☎ 20505), by the post office, is a clean but slightly gloomy hotel with rooms from Rs 100/150, all with TV and attached bath.

Getting There & Away

The dusty bus stand and the railway station are only 300m apart, on opposite sides of the road. There are buses to Dalhousie (four hours, Rs 35), Dharamsala (4½ hours, Rs 40), Chamba (5½ hours, Rs 53), and Jammu. You can also get taxis for these longer trips next to the bus stand; to either Dalhousie or Dharamsala it's two hours and Rs 720, try for a reduction if things are quiet.

PATIALA
Pop: 300,000
Located a little south of the road and railway lines from Delhi to Amritsar, Patiala was once the capital of an independent Sikh state. There is a museum in the Motibagh Palace of the Maharaja in the Baradari Gardens.

SIRHIND
Pop: 34,600
This was once a very important town and the capital of the Pathan Sur dynasty. In 1555, Humayun defeated Sikander Shah here and a year later his son, Akbar, completed the destruction of the Sur dynasty at Panipat. From then until 1709 Sirhind was a rich Mughal city, but clashes between the declining Mughal and rising Sikh powers led to the city's sacking in 1709 and complete destruction in 1763.

The Pathan-style **tomb of Mir Miran** and the later Mughal **tomb of Pirbandi** Nakshwala, both ornamented with blue tiles, are worth seeing. The **Salabat Beg Haveli** is probably the largest private home remaining from the Mughal period. South-east of the city is an important Mughal serai.

LUDHIANA
Pop: 1.14 million   Tel Area Code: 0161
The textile centre of India, Ludhiana was the site of a great battle in the First Sikh War. The world's largest bicycle manufacturer, Hero Bicycles, which produces nearly three million bikes annually, is based here.

There's little here to see; but if you're sick, the Christian Medical College Hospital (affiliated with the hospital of the same name in Vellore in Tamil Nadu) is a good place to

head for. Established in 1895, it was the first school of medicine in Asia.

Hotel City Heart (☎ 740240), five minutes walk from the railway station and just beyond the clock tower, is a comfortable, modern hotel with a good restaurant and bar. Air-con rooms cost Rs 1100/1400.

JALANDHAR
Pop: 578,000   Tel Area Code: 0181
Only 80km south-east of Amritsar, this was once the capital of an ancient Hindu kingdom. It survived a sacking by Mahmud of Ghazni nearly a thousand years ago and later became an important Mughal city. The town has a large serai built in 1857.

Kings Hotel (☎ 225031), a few minutes walk from the bus stand, has reasonable rooms for Rs 500/650.

Skylark Hotel (☎ 221002), a couple of intersections further east, has good rooms from Rs 310/395.

Kamal Palace (☎ 58462) a km from the bus station is more upmarket with rooms from Rs 1000.

SOUTH-WEST PUNJAB
The railway line from Sirsa (Haryana) to Firozpur passes through **Bathinda**, which was an important town of the Pathan Sur dynasty.

Faridkot, 350km north-west of Delhi and close to the Pakistan border, was once the capital of a Sikh state of the same name and has a 700 year old fort.

Firozpur, almost on the border, is 382km north-west of Delhi; prior to Partition, the railway line continued to Lahore, now in Pakistan.

Himachal Pradesh

Himachal Pradesh – the land of eternal snow peaks – takes in the transition zone from the plains to the high Himalaya and, in the trans-Himalayan region of Lahaul and Spiti, actually crosses that mighty barrier to the Tibetan plateau.

The Kullu Valley with its developed and tourist-oriented economy can be considered the backbone of the state. Off to the east is the Parbati Valley (popular with long-stay visitors). In the Chamba and Kangra regions can be found typical British hill stations. The residence of the Dalai Lama is in Upper Dharamsala, known as McLeod Ganj, which has become a centre for Buddhism, as well as the headquarters of the Tibetan Government in Exile. Shimla, the famous colonial hot-weather capital, remains Himachal's seat of government.

The bleak, high altitude regions of Lahaul, Spiti and Kinnaur were opened to foreigners in 1992. Permits (easily obtained) are necessary to visit some parts. The predominant influence here is Tibetan Buddhism.

See Lonely Planet's *Trekking in the Indian Himalaya* and *Indian Himalaya* for detail on trekking in this region.

History

The regions that today comprise Himachal were in ancient times crossed by trade routes to Tibet (over the Shipki La) and Central Asia (via the Baralacha La and Leh), and in addition commanded the Sach Pass that led to Kashmir. Rajas, Ranas and Thakurs ran their rival *rahuns* and *thakurais*, the regions over which they presided, making Himachal a patchwork quilt of tiny states. Only Kangra and Kullu (and later Chamba) had the power to break out of the petty feuding system.

Several Himachal states had kings from Bengal, the best known of these states being Mandi, which was founded in 1527. With the exception of the bigger states, most of the later hill states were founded by Rajput adven-

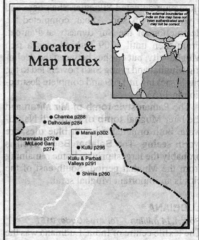

HIMACHAL PRADESH AT A GLANCE

Population: 5.6 million
Area: 55,673 sq km
Capital: Shimla
Main Languages: Hindi, Pahari
Literacy Rate: 63%
Best Time to Go: mid-May to mid-October (trekking); late December to March (winter sports)

Locator & Map Index

The external boundaries of India on this map have not been authenticated and may not be correct.

- Chamba p288
- Dalhousie p284
- Manali p302
- Dharamsala p272
- McLeod Ganj p274
- Kullu p296
- Kullu & Parbati Valleys p291
- Shimla p260

Highlights

- Kalpa, the legendary home of Siva, surrounded by peaks and forests and criss-crossed with ancient winding streets
- The crumbling colonial charm of Shimla, a sprawling town set among cool hills
- For a taste of Tibet, McLeod Ganj, home to the Dalai Lama and the Tibetan Government in Exile
- The temples, art gallery and haunted castle of Nagger

Festivals

Shivrati Festival – Mandi – February/March
Sui Mata Festival – Charnba – March/April
Ladarch Festival – Kibber – July
Minjar Festival – Chamba – late July/early August

turers from the plains in the early medieval period.

A REGIONAL HIGHLIGHT

The Temples of Chamba

Chamba, capital of the Pahari kings for 1000 years, boasts some of northern India's finest and best preserved temples.

Lakshmi Narayan Temple Complex The six temples in this complex, all featuring exquisite sculpture, are representative of the Shikhara style, although they have distinctive characteristics which are found only in the temple architecture of the Chamba Valley. Three of the temples are dedicated to Vishnu, and three to Siva. The largest (and oldest) temple in the group is that of Lakshmi Narayan (Vishnu), which is directly opposite the entrance to the complex. According to tradition it was built during the reign of the founder of Chamba, Raja Sahil Varman, in the 10th century AD. It was extensively renovated in the 16th century by Raja Partap Singh Varna. The image of Lakshmi Narayan enshrined in the temple dates from the temple's foundation. Some of the fine sculptures around the temple include those of Vishnu and Lakshmi, Narsingh (Vishnu in his lion form), and Krishna with the *gopis* (milkmaids). A small niche at the back harbours a beautiful sculpture of a goddess churning the ocean with Sheshnag, the snake of Vishnu, to bring the poison up from the bottom.

The fourth temple from the right, the Gourishankar Temple, is dedicated to Siva. Its stone carving of the Ganges and Yamuna rivers personified as goddesses on either side of the door frame is renowned.

The complex is open from 6 am to 12.30 pm and 2.30 to 8.30 pm.

Chamunda Devi Temple A terrace before this hilltop temple gives an excellent view of Chamba with its slate-roof houses (some of them up to 300 years old), the River Ravi and the surrounding countryside. It's a steep 30 minute climb along a path that begins above the bus stand, passing en route a small rock outcrop smeared with saffron, which is revered as an image of the goddess of the forest, Banasti. When you reach the road, you can either follow it to the left or go up the steep staircase.

The temple is dedicated to Durga in her wrathful aspect as Chamunda Devi. In front of the temple is her vehicle, a lion. Almost the entire wooden ceiling of the *mandapa* (forechamber) is richly carved, featuring animal and floral motifs, and depictions of various deities. From it are suspended numerous brass bells, offered to the goddess by devotees.

Just before ascending the steps to the temple is a small pillar bearing the footprints of the goddess. Behind the temple is a very old, small Shikhara-style temple dedicated to Lord Siva.

Hariral Temple This fine stone Shikhara-style temple, at the north-west side of the Chowgan, near the fire station, dates from the 11th century. It is dedicated to Vishnu, and enshrines a fine triple-headed image of Vaikuntha Vishnu reputedly made from eight different materials. In April 1971, the statue was stolen from the inner sanctum. It was discovered by Interpol on a ship destined for the USA seconds before the boat was to sail, and was returned to Chamba. At the rear of the temple is a fine sculpture of Lord Vishnu astride six horses.

Sui Mata Temple About 10 minutes walk from the Chamunda Devi Temple is a small modern temple dedicated to Sui Mata. Colourful paintings around the interior walls of the temple tell the story of Sui, a Chamba princess who gave her life for the inhabitants of Chamba. Women and children can be seen here laying wildflowers before the temple in devotion to Sui Mata.

Bajreshwari Devi Temple This ancient temple is about 10 minutes walk from Sui Mata (take the little path to the right just before passing the last few houses of Chamba). The temple conforms to the Shikhara style, and is topped by a wooden *amalaka* (fluted medallion-shaped flourish). The sanctum enshrines an image of Bajreshwari (a form of Durga), although it is difficult to make out beneath its garlands of flowers. The entire surface of the temple is elaborately carved, featuring two friezes of rosettes at the lower levels. It is fronted by two stone columns with richly carved capitals and bases. A form of ancient script called *takri* can be seen crudely incised on the right column, and on other spots around the temple. In the niche on the west side of the temple is an image of Undavi, the goddess of food, with a bowl and a ladle. At the rear of the temple, Durga can be seen slaying the giant Mahisasur and his buffalo vehicle. The giant is dwarfed by Durga, who is standing astride him with her foot on the buffalo. On either side of the door jambs, the rivers Yamuna and Ganges are personified as goddesses holding pitchers of water.

Other Temples The diminutive **Surara temples** are found down a series of alleyways in the area called Muhala, back down in Chamba, about 10 minutes walk from the Bajreshwari Temple.

Behind the City Police Office is the **Champavati Temple,** dedicated to the daughter of Raja Sahil Varman. The dimly lit *mandapa* features four solid wooden carved pillars featuring floral and bird motifs. ∎

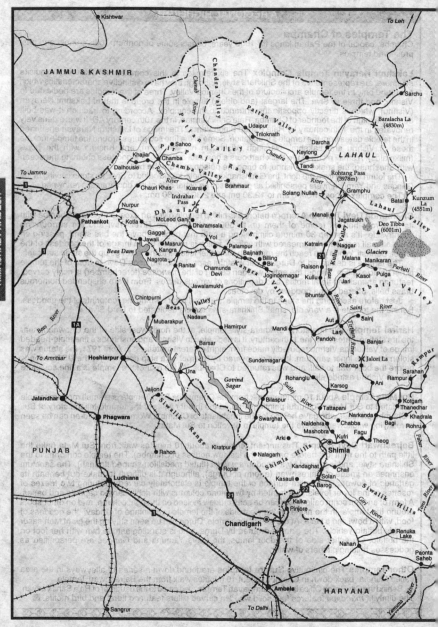

JAMMU &
KASHMIR

Spiti River

Lingti Valley

Shilla
(7026m)

Kibber

Spiti Valley

Kaza

SPITI

Dankar   Tabo   Sumdo

CHINA
TIBET

Pin Valley

Nako

Leo Pargial
(6791m)

Pin River

Manerang
(6593m)

KINNAUR

Puh

River

Kalpa   Rekong Peo   Morang

Valley

Nichar   Tapri

Wangtu

Sutlej

Kinnaur Kailash
(6050m)

Sangla

Sangla

Valley

UTTAR
PRADESH

LP

Himachal Pradesh

To
Dehra Dun

0   30   60 km

The external boundaries of India
on this map have not been authenticated
and may not be correct.

Rajaji Wildlife
Sanctuary

The first westerners to visit the region were Jesuit missionaries in search of Prester John's legendary land. The British discovered Himachal after their wars with the Sikhs and the Gurkhas. And upon the subsequent discovery that Himachal was ideal for growing apples, an American missionary, the Reverend NS Stokes, developed the Kotgarh orchards (his family still runs them). Little bits of England were created at Shimla, Dalhousie and Dharamsala during the late 19th century. In the early part of this century a railway was built to Shimla and another was laid through the Kangra Valley. In the interior, however, feudal conditions remained: men were forced to work without pay and women were regarded as chattels.

The new state of Himachal Pradesh comprising only six districts was formed in 1948. By 1966, the Pahari-speaking parts under Punjab administration, including Kangra, Kullu, Lahaul and Spiti, were added. Full statehood was achieved in 1971.

Geography

Himachal Pradesh is dominated by mountains, and associated rivers and valleys. The highest peaks are Shilla (7026m), Manerang (6597m) and Shipki (6608m).

There are several major rivers running through the state including the Beas River (pronounced 'bee-ahs') which flows through the Kullu Valley, the Chenab River in Lahaul and Spiti and the Spiti River, which joins the Sutlej River in Kinnaur.

A lot of Himachal Pradesh can be easily segregated according to the various valleys. Lahaul and Spiti is a series of valleys stretching from the Chandra Valley in the north-west to the Lingti Valley along the Spiti River. The Kullu Valley stretches from Mandi to Manali. The Parbati Valley follows the Parbati River, which branches off the Beas River. The Kangra Valley stretches from Mandi to Shahpur, near Pathankot. To the north of the Kangra Valley, on the other side of the Dhauladhar Range, is the Chamba Valley, which is separated from the remote Pattan Valley (upper Chenab River Valley) by the Pir Panjal Range.

Tourist Offices

The Himachal Pradesh Tourist Development Corporation (HPTDC) has a central reservation office at Daizy Bank Estate in Shimla, which can arrange bookings for HPTDC hotels.

In season, the HPTDC organises 'deluxe' buses for tourists between the major centres. HPTDC buses are more expensive than public buses, but are quicker and far more comfortable. The HPTDC also organises daily sightseeing tours out of Dharamsala, Shimla and Manali.

HPTDC offices elsewhere in India can also provide worthwhile information:

Calcutta
    25 Carmac St (☎ (033) 446 8477)
Chandigarh
    SCO: 1048-49, Sector 22B (☎ (0172) 43569)
Chennai (Madras)
    28 Commander-in-Chief Rd (☎ (044) 472966)
Delhi
    Chandralok Bldg, 36 Janpath
    (☎ (011) 332 4764)
Mumbai (Bombay)
    36 World Trade Centre, Cuffe Parade
    (☎ (022) 219191)

Permits

Inner Line Permits are usually required for some of Lahaul and Spiti, and Kinnaur. Regulations, and their implementation, have noticeably relaxed in recent times. Check the current regulations with the relevant authorities or other travellers.

Foreigners can travel between Leh and Manali without a permit. A permit is not usually required for travel between Leh, or Manali, and Kaza, the capital of the Spiti subdistrict (although some travellers have reported that they needed a permit). From Tabo to Rekong Peo, you need a permit, but from Rekong Peo to Shimla, no permit is required.

Permits can be obtained from the District and Sub-District Magistrates' offices in most regional centres. It is better to get them in Kaza or Rekong Peo so you don't waste any of your seven day permit just getting to these places.

Shimla

Pop: 123,000   Tel Area Code: 0177

Shimla was once part of the Nepalese kingdom, and called *Shyamala*, another name for the goddess Kali, but Shimla never gained any fame until it was first 'discovered' by the British in 1819. Three years later, the first 'British' house was erected, and by 1864 Shimla had become the summer capital of India. After the construction of the Kalka to Shimla railway line in 1903, Shimla really boomed. Following independence, Shimla was initially the capital of the Punjab, then it became the capital of Himachal Pradesh.

Today, Shimla is a lovely, sprawling town, set among spectacular, cool hills, with plenty of crumbling colonial charm. It has very good facilities, although accommodation, particularly in the high season, is expensive.

Orientation & Information

There are only two roads in the central part of Shimla. The Mall runs from the far west into the centre of town to the lower eastern side. In the centre it meets Scandal Corner – immortalised by Rudyard Kipling. The mall area known as The Ridge runs from Scandal Corner to the Christ Church. Cart Rd circles the southern part of Shimla, and is where the bus and taxi stands and railway station are located. The rest of Shimla is connected by masses of unnamed, steep lanes and steps. There is also a passenger lift connecting Cart Rd to The (eastern) Mall.

The HPTDC tourist office at Scandal Corner provides basic local information and maps, offers a taxi service, organises tourist buses and handles bookings for Archana Airways. It's open from 9 am to 9 pm every day in season; from 9.30 am to 5 pm in the off season. All banks are open from about 10 am to 2 pm, weekdays; and from 10 am to noon on Saturday. The State Bank of India, along The (western) Mall, charges Rs 20 per transaction, plus Rs 3 for every travellers cheque cashed. The two little, chaotic Punjab National Bank branches, either side of the

Indian Coffee House, change money, with no fee, and offer friendly, albeit slow, service. The main post office, not far from Scandal Corner, is open from 10 am to 6 pm, Monday to Saturday; 10 am to 4 pm on Sunday and public holidays. The Central Telegraph Office (CTO) (fax 204026), west of Scandal Corner is the best place to make telephone calls, and to send and receive faxes; it's open 24 hours.

Himachal State Museum & Library
About 2½km west of Scandal Corner, the State Museum has a good collection of statues, coins, photos and other items from around Himachal Pradesh. There is also a useful library, full of historical books, and the daily English-language newspapers. The museum is free, and is open daily from 10 am to 1.30 pm and from 2 to 5 pm; it's closed on Monday and public holidays.

Viceregal Lodge & Botanical Gardens
The Viceregal Lodge, also known as Rashtrapati Niwas, is based on Observatory Hill. It was formerly the residence of the British viceroy Lord Dufferin, and is where many decisions affecting the destiny of the subcontinent were made. Incredibly, every brick of the six storey building was carried here by mule (the train hadn't been built at that stage). The lodge was eventually finished in 1888.

Here there are magnificently kept lawns, botanical gardens, and a small cafe. The lodge now houses the Indian Institute of Advanced Study.

The lodge is a pleasant two km walk further west from the museum – about 4½km from Scandal Corner. It's open daily from 9 am to 8.30 pm in summer, and closes a little earlier during the rest of the year. It costs Rs 6 for a guided tour of the lodge (closed between 1 and 2 pm), or Rs 3 to look around the gardens only.

Himalayan Aviary
Right next to the entrance of the institute complex is the Himalayan Bird Park or Aviary. As expected, it has a collection of species found around Himachal Pradesh, such as the Himalayan monal (the state bird of Himachal Pradesh), various types of pheasants, and the national bird of India, the Indian peafowl. The aviary is open daily (closed on Monday) from 10 am to 5 pm. Entry is Rs 5, but a still camera costs an extra Rs 25, and a video camera, Rs 100.

Christ Church & St Michael's Cathedral
The second oldest church in northern India (the oldest is in Ambala), the Christ Church, overlooking The Ridge, was built between 1846 and 1857. The clocks were added three years later, but none of them now work. One of Shimla's major landmarks, the church is also renowned for its stained glass windows. You can discreetly have a look inside the church, or attend English-language services every Sunday during the tourist season. The other main church in Shimla is St Michael's Cathedral, just below the Central Telegraph Office.

Jakhu Temple
Dedicated to the monkey god, Hanuman, Jakhu Temple is at an altitude of 2455m near the highest point of the Shimla ridge, east of the town centre. It offers a fine view over the surrounding valleys, out to the snow-capped peaks, and over Shimla itself. Appropriately, there are many monkeys around the temple. It's a steep 45 minute walk from Scandal Corner. Take the footpath that goes past the Hotel Dreamland to the south. Sunrise is a good time to be here.

Bazaars
There are two main bazaar, or *mandi*, areas in Shimla. Just below the western end of The (eastern) Mall, the frantic Sabzi Mandi, also known as Lower Bazaar, is a maze of twisting, steep lanes full of stalls selling food and just about everything imaginable. Prices here for meals, and other things, are generally cheaper than places along The Mall. Beyond The Ridge, the small, busy Lakkar Bazaar is the place to buy souvenirs, although most shops seem to sell fairly tacky wooden stuff.

HIMACHAL PRADESH

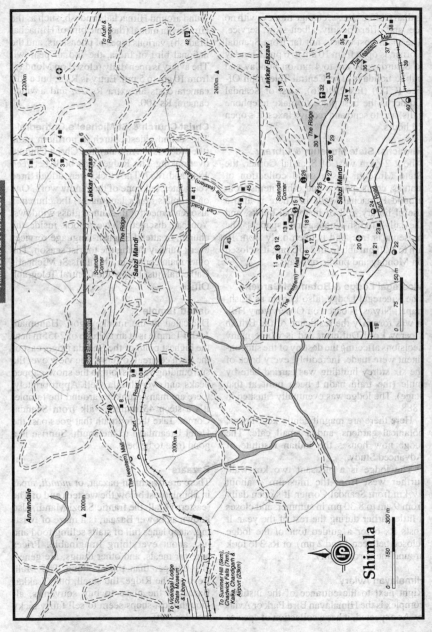

Shimla

PLACES TO STAY
1 Hotel Auckland
2 Hotels Chanakya & White
3 Hotels Ashoka & Shimla View
4 Hotels Diplomat & Snow View
6 Hotels Uphar & Dreamland
8 Hotels Gulmarg & Fontaine Bleau
9 Hotel Prakash
10 Hotels Dalziel & Classic
13 YWCA
21 Thakur Hotel
23 Hotel Basant & High Way Lodge
33 YMCA
35 Hotel Bridge View & Doegar Hotel
38 Hotel Samrat
41 Hotel Crystal Palace
43 HPTDC Hotel Holiday Home
44 Oberoi Clarke's Hotel
45 Hotels Shingar & Sangeet

PLACES TO EAT
16 Indian Coffee House
17 The Devicos Restaurant
18 Alfa Restaurant
25 Baljee's & Fascination Restaurants
29 Himani's
30 Ashiana, Goofa & Quick Bite Restaurants
31 Toran & Tripti's Restaurants
34 Park Cafe
36 Shere-e-Punjab
37 Embassy Restaurant

OTHER
5 Indira Gandhi Hospital
7 State Bank of India
11 Central Telegraph Office
12 UCO Bank
14 Main Post Office
15 ANZ Grindlays Bank
19 Railway Station & Reservation Office
20 Deen Dayal Upadhayay (Ripon) Hospital
22 Bus Station
24 Kalka-Shimla Taxi Union Stand
26 HPTDC Tourist Office
27 Galety Theatre
28 Maria Brothers
32 Christ Church
39 Passenger Lift
40 Vishal Himachal Taxi Operators' Union Stand
42 Jakhu Temple

Walks

Apart from a promenade along The Mall and the walk to the Jakhu Temple, there are a great number of interesting walks around Shimla. For more information on places further afield, refer to the Around Shimla section.

The Glen, about four km west of Scandal Corner, is one of the former playgrounds of rich British colonialists. The turnoff is on the way to the State Museum, and goes through the other lovely area of **Annandale**. This was the site of a famous racecourse, where cricket and polo are still played.

Summer Hill is five km away, on the Shimla-Kalka railway line, and has pleasant, shady walks. It's also famous because Mahatma Gandhi stayed at the Raj Kumari Amrit Kaur mansion on Summer Hill.

Chadwick Falls are 67m high, but are only really worth visiting during or just after the monsoons – from July to October. The falls are seven km from Shimla and can be reached via Summer Hill.

Prospect Hill is about five km west of Shimla, and a 15 minute climb from Boileauganj. The hill is a popular picnic spot with fine views over the surrounding country. The **Kamna Devi Temple** is nearby.

Sankat Mochan, seven km from Shimla, on the road to Chandigarh, has a Hanuman temple, and fine views of Shimla. It can also be reached by taxi.

Tara Devi Temple is 10km from Shimla. It is dedicated to Tara Devi, Goddess of the Stars. It is situated on top of a hill, and another, dedicated to Lord Siva, is nearby. It's about three km up a path from the Tara Devi station on the Shimla to Kalka railway, or you can take a taxi there.

Organised Tours

The HPTDC organises daily sightseeing tours in season (book at the office on The Mall). There are tours to Kufri, Fagu and Naldehra (Rs 125), and, for great views, to Narkanda via Fagu and Theog (Rs 145); to the lovely, historic Chail region (Rs 125); and to the hot springs at Tattapani, via Naldehra (Rs 125).

The YWCA (☎ 72375; fax 211016) organises treks in Himachal Pradesh for Rs 800 per person per day. They will also organise jeep safaris to Kinaur, Spiti and Lahaul for US$70 per day for two people. Advance notice of at least a week is required for these tours.

HIMACHAL PRADESH

Places to Stay

Accommodation in Shimla is expensive, particularly during the peak seasons. But in the off season, or when business is quiet, prices drop substantially, sometimes by as much as half.

Places to Stay – bottom end

If you're on a low budget, the cheapest areas are around the bus station, and along Cart Rd, heading east from the bus station.

The *YMCA* (☎ 72375; for men and women) has singles/doubles/triples for Rs 100/200/280 with common bath; there is one double with attached bath for Rs 280. There is also a Rs 40 temporary membership fee. Thali meals are available for Rs 40/55 veg/non-veg and there is a late-night coffee shop (entry Rs 25). In the off season the YMCA doesn't drop its prices, so no longer represents good value. It's not far behind the Christ Church, up a laneway from The Ridge.

The *YWCA* (☎ 203081; also for men and women), above the main post office, is better value. It's a convenient, friendly old place, with great views. Large rooms range from Rs 100 to Rs 150; there is a Rs 10 temporary-membership fee. Meals cost an extra Rs 15.

Hotel Himachal, a little south of the railway station (look for the hotel sign), has ordinary singles/doubles, often windowless, for Rs 125/150.

Vikrant Hotel (☎ 3602), off the laneway that goes to the Himachal, has rooms for Rs 150 (common bath) and Rs 250 (attached bath).

Thakur Hotel (☎ 77545) is big and a little better, with large rooms for Rs 100/180.

Along the busy Cart Rd, east from the bus station, are several cheap places:

Hotel Basant (☎ 78381) is a well run, friendly place. Singles with common bath cost Rs 85; singles/doubles with attached bath are from Rs 110/165. Hot water comes by the bucket, at Rs 5.

Hotel Kohinoor (☎ 20008) is more expensive and right in front of the bus station. Rooms with attached bath and running hot water cost about Rs 200.

Around the Lakkar Bazaar area, a steep climb past The Ridge, there are several places which are reasonably priced:

Hotel Snow View (☎ 3244) has pretty good singles/doubles from Rs 150/250.

Hotel Ridge View (☎ 4859) has rooms from Rs 160 to Rs 400, with TV and hot water, and offers 50% discounts in the off season – like many other places. To find it, just follow the signs from the Christ Church.

Hotel Uphar (☎ 77670) is clean and friendly. Rooms with attached bath and hot water cost Rs 150/200, and Rs 260 with a view.

Hotel Ashoka (☎ 78166) has rooms for Rs 175/275, and is of a similar standard to Uphar.

Hotel Shimla View (☎ 203244) has rooms with a common bath for Rs 125.

Actually on The Mall, a short distance from Scandal Corner, are one or two noisy but handy places:

Hotel Loveena (☎ 202035), above the Indian Coffee House on The (western) Mall, has rooms for Rs 400 with views and TV, which cost half that in the off season.

Hotel Minerva (☎ 72043), 90 The (eastern) Mall, has nice, but small, singles/doubles for Rs 125/195 with bath and TV.

Hotel Gulmarg (☎ 3168) across the road from the State Bank of India has a TV and hot water in each of its rooms. In the huge rambling hotel complex, there are charmless and windowless economy rooms from Rs 150, and 'Honey Moon' rooms up to Rs 850.

Hotel Fontaine Bleau (☎ 3549) next door to the Gulmarg is quaint, family-run and has a nice landlady who speaks English well. Rooms with a share bathroom cost from Rs 175 to Rs 300.

The *retiring rooms* at the Shimla railway station are standard Indian Railways issue if you're getting an early or late train. Comfortable but noisy rooms cost Rs 150 – with a 50% discount in the off season.

Places to Stay – middle

The majority of rooms in this range will usually include TV (often cable), and a bathroom with hot water. They are particularly good value in the off season, when a nice double room with cable TV and hot water costs about Rs 200.

F 202038
F 223098
FAX T:223919 223098
0091- (0) 177

Just off The (western) Mall, a short walk up from the railway station, there are three reasonable places:

Hotel Prakash (☎ 213321) has rooms from Rs 400 to Rs 600.

Hotel Classic (☎ 5463), friendly and comfortable, has rooms for Rs 250/400 with good views.

Hotel Dalziel (☎ 72691) has rooms starting at the very negotiable price of Rs 280.

North of The Ridge, and around the Lakkar Bazaar area, are several good places, but it is a little inconvenient, and a steep climb up here:

Hotel Chanakya (☎ 211232), is clean and comfortable, with double rooms from Rs 380.

Hotel Diplomat (☎ 72001) has rooms from Rs 400, or Rs 500 with a view.

Hotel White (☎ 5276) has rooms ranging from Rs 200 to Rs 850. Those upstairs are better.

Hotel Dreamland (☎ 5057) is good value, and is popular, with rooms at about the same price.

Hotel Auckland (☎ 72621) is a very pleasant place, with rooms from Rs 440.

Around the lower end of The (eastern) Mall, near the passenger lift, is a gaggle of newish places:

Hotel Bridge View (☎ 78537) has great views and rooms from Rs 330.

Doegar Hotel (☎ 211927) above Bridge View, and arguably better, has rooms from Rs 350.

Hotel Samrat (☎ 78572) has a range of rooms, many of them small, starting at Rs 470.

Hotel Crystal Palace (☎ 75588) at the bottom of the lift has rooms for Rs 500 for rooms at the back, more for a view.

There are two good places across from the Oberoi Clarke's Hotel, at the bottom end of The (eastern) Mall.

Hotel Shingar (☎ 72881) has rooms for Rs 600, to Rs 800 with a view. It's well run and good value.

Hotel Sangeet (☎ 202506) nearby is another good place. Standard rooms are Rs 500; better rooms with views cost Rs 700.

HPTDC's *Hotel Holiday Home* (☎ 212890) is on Cart Rd. It's friendly, well set up with a bar and coffee shop, but it's inconveniently located, and doesn't give off-season discounts. Rates start at Rs 400 for the cheapest rooms, and up to Rs 2000, including meals, for a deluxe room.

Places to Stay – top end

Woodville Palace Resort (☎ 72763), two km south past the Oberoi Clarke's Hotel on The (eastern) Mall is an ivy-covered building constructed in 1938 by Raja Rana Sir Bhagat Chandra, the ruler of the former princely state of Jubbal. It's a small place, set among very pleasant gardens. Double rooms (high season) are Rs 2900, and suites cost Rs 4650 – bookings are recommended.

Oberoi Clarke's Hotel (☎ 212991), down the far end of The (eastern) Mall, past the lift, is one of Shimla's earliest hotels. The luxurious rooms in this Tudor style building cost US$56/112 (no discounts, here, thank you) including the compulsory three meal 'American Plan'.

Places to Eat

There are several parlours selling (safe) ice cream, plenty of bakeries, and sweet and chocolate shops in Shimla. Just about every place serves hot, western breakfasts, but many don't open until about 9 am – Shimla is not a place for early starters.

Western Cuisine The *Embassy Restaurant*, not far from the top of the lift on The (eastern) Mall is self-serve and no-nonsense, and has great individual pizzas and hamburgers, as well as Indian and Chinese food.

The Devicos Restaurant, on The (western) Mall, near Scandal Corner, is a clean, trendy place that does good, but a little overpriced, fast food.

Park Cafe, just down The (eastern) Mall and up some stairs, also does great western treats, and Indian food. It's recommended for milkshakes, breakfasts, and laid-back late-evening music listening.

Oberoi Clarke's Hotel has a buffet for Rs 195 plus tax. A carafe of Australian red wine costs Rs 345.

The HPTDC has a building on The Ridge with three places to eat.

HIMACHAL PRADESH

HIMACHAL PRADESH

Ashiana is about the best (and most expensive) place around the area for decor and service.

Goofa, downstairs, is nowhere near as classy or good, but serves a reasonable (and early) breakfast.

Quick Bite in the same complex as the Ashiana has cheap pizzas, and Indian food – or, for a combination of both, try their 'keema pizza'.

Indian Shimla has a lot of places serving Indian food, primarily southern Indian.

Baljee's along The (eastern) Mall has a delicious range of Indian and western food, and the service is good. Prices can be a little high (but the seats are very comfortable).

Fascination, the associated restaurant upstairs, is similarly priced and just as popular.

Alfa Restaurant, near Scandal Corner, is about the same standard, price and popularity as Baljee's.

Himani's, at 49 The (eastern) Mall, does tasty southern Indian snacks and meals, and has a bar.

Rendezvous, right on Scandal Corner, has Indian and Thai food, moderate prices but slow service.

Bakeries There are many bakeries along The Mall. They sell an amazing selection of sweet pastries, with icing and cream.

Trishool's, next to the Gaiety Theatre, is recommended.

Baljee's has a bakery counter at the front, and is a great place for morning or afternoon teas.

Krishna Bakers, along The (eastern) Mall, does good burgers, cakes and pastries.

Drinks The *Indian Coffee House*, along The (western) Mall, is where traditionally dressed waiters serve great coffee (but no tea) and south Indian snacks.

Himani's has a bar, and so does the *Rendezvous*, on Scandal Corner, but it is dingy and unwelcoming. There are several small bars on the 1st floors of buildings along The Mall. The expensive hotels usually serve alcohol.

Entertainment

Probably the most popular, and best, entertainment is to stroll along The Mall and The Ridge (vehicle-free!). This is especially pleasant in the evenings when the views and lights are wonderful. An ice-skating rink is open in winter – follow the signs from Scandal Corner.

The lovely old *Gaiety Theatre* often has shows or recitals, particularly in the tourist season.

There are several *cinemas*, but they usually play the inevitable Hindi love epic or a dubbed Chinese kung-fu classic. The local daily newspaper *The Himachal Times* (Rs 1) has information on local things to do.

Getting There & Away

Air Jagson Airlines flies to/from Delhi (US$96) every Tuesday, Thursday and Saturday as part of a milk run, which also connects Shimla with Kullu (US$67). Archana Airways flies to Delhi on Monday, Wednesday, Friday and Sunday for the same price as Jagson.

Archana Airways bookings are possible at the HPTDC office at Scandal Corner. Jagson Airlines is represented by Span Tour & Travels (☎ 52220), 4 The (western) Mall. Airline bookings can be made at travel agencies along The Mall. The Jubbarhatti airport is 23km south of Shimla.

Bus The large Shimla public bus station on Cart Rd has no information booth, no timetables are displayed in English and most of the destinations listed on the buses are in Hindi.

However, there is a very handy private computer-booking booth at the station, where the employees speak English, and you can book a ticket up to one month ahead on any public bus.

There are public buses to Narkanda every 30 minutes (Rs 26); to Rampur every 30 minutes (Rs 56) – change buses in Rampur for Sarahan; and to Paonta Saheb/Nahan (Rs 72/55) – take the daily Dehra Dun bus. For other local places, such as Tattapani; Kasauli; places on the way to Kalka; and places on the way to Narkanda such as Kufri and

Theog, catch one of the regular local buses along Cart Rd.

Buses go every day to other more distant places in Himachal Pradesh: to Manali (11 hours), there are two ordinary (Rs 114) and two deluxe buses (Rs 152); three semideluxe buses go to Dharamsala (10 hours, Rs 1); 10 go to Bilaspur/Mandi (Rs 40/88); one overnight bus goes to Dalhousie (Rs 170); five or six a day go to Kullu (Rs 100) via Mandi; and three buses leave every day for Chamba.

There is one overnight, and one early-morning deluxe bus to Delhi (10 hours, Rs 250) and ordinary buses every hour; to Chandigarh (Rs 50), ordinary buses leave about every 30 minutes; one bus a day goes to Dehra Dun (nine hours, Rs 96).

Travel agencies along The Mall offer private 'deluxe' buses to Manali and Delhi. These are neither regular nor reliable, and run almost always in the peak season when there is high demand, and after the bus from Manali or Delhi arrives with passengers. Prices change according to demand and the season.

The HPTDC offers daily buses, in season, to Manali (Rs 225); to Dharamsala (overnight; Rs 170); and overnight/day buses to Delhi (Rs 225/350) via Chandigarh (Rs 80). It also promises deluxe buses for the two day trip to Kaza, the capital of Lahaul and Spiti, for Rs 400, but these buses only leave when there is enough demand (which is not often). All HPTDC buses should be booked at the tourist office at Scandal Corner.

Train The railway reservation office (☎ 3021) at the station can arrange bookings for the Shimla to Kalka railway, and for other trips in northern India. The booking office is open from 10 am to 5 pm, Monday to Saturday; 10 am to 2 pm on Sunday.

The train journey to Shimla involves a change from broad gauge to narrow gauge at Kalka, a little north of Chandigarh. The narrow-gauge trip to Shimla takes about five hours (less by rail car). If you're travelling from Shimla to Chandigarh, you can catch the train to Solan (three hours), then take a bus to Chandigarh from there. As you

approach Shimla, don't make the mistake of getting off at the Summer Hill railway station.

There are three classes: 2nd class (Rs 14), which uses old coaches with wooden seats, and can be crowded; chair car (Rs 97), which is modern and comfortable; and 1st class (Rs 134; Rs 159 by rail car), which is definitely the way to travel, if you can afford it. Normally, there are four daily trains each way between Shimla and Kalka, and usually three more in season. Trains from Kalka to Shimla or vice versa can be cancelled if there is not enough demand.

The best and most reliable way to travel from Delhi to Shimla by train in one trip is to catch the *Himalayan Queen* from New Delhi station at 6 am. It arrives in Kalka at about 11.40 am. When you get in, cross to another platform from where the 12.20 pm toy train leaves, arriving in Shimla at 5.05 pm. In the opposite direction, the only way to do the Shimla to Delhi trip in one day is to catch the 10.15 am train from Shimla, which connects with the *Himalayan Queen* at Kalka and pulls into New Delhi station at 9.40 pm.

Taxi There are three agencies with fixed-price taxis – which are almost impossible to bargain down, even in the off season. They are the Kalka-Shimla Taxi Union (☎ 78225) on Cart Rd, right opposite the Tourist Reception Centre; the Pre-Paid Taxi Service, which can be booked at the HPTDC office at Scandal Corner; and the Vishal Himachal Taxi Operators' Union (☎ 77136), at the bottom of the lift on Cart Rd. All are about the same price, although the HPTDC taxis often cost a little more.

Taxis are either 'gypsy jeeps' or 'multivans' which take three passengers, plus driver; or the Ambassador taxi, which can take four passengers, plus driver.

Examples of taxi fares from Shimla, which may include an extra charge for fuel, are: one day sightseeing tours to Naldehra, Fagu and other places, Rs 300 to Rs 500; one way to Chandigarh, Rs 800; to Kalka, Rs 600; to Rampur, Rs 700; to Manali, Rs 1800;

to Kullu, Rs 1600; to Dharamsala, Rs 1800; to Rekong Peo/Kalpa, Rs 1200; to Dehra Dun, Rs 1500; and to Delhi, Rs 2400.

Getting Around
The Airport A fixed-price taxi costs Rs 300 from the airport to Shimla, but if you are staying anywhere along or near The Mall, you may have to walk the last bit yourself anyway. In season, the HPTDC normally runs a bus service (Rs 50) to/from the airport to connect with flights to/from Delhi.

Passenger Lift Around 500m from Scandal Corner, along The (eastern) Mall, there is a lift which goes down to Cart Rd, finishing next to the Vishal Himachal taxi stand. In fact, it is two lifts, connected by a walkway – the Rs 3 ticket is good for a one-way trip on either lift.

Porters At the bus or railway stations you will be besieged by porters who will offer to carry your luggage for Rs 4 to Rs 20, depending on weight and distance. A porter is not a bad idea, especially when you arrive. From the railway station, for instance, it's a long, steep climb to The Mall, particularly to somewhere like the Hotel Dreamland. Porters double as hotel touts.

Around Shimla

There are a number of points of interest in the environs of Shimla that can be visited on day trips from the hill station, including Kasauli to the south-west, where it's possible to take some fine short walks; the village of Kufri, to the east, where you can hire horses for rides to surrounding areas; and Naldehra, en route to the hot springs at Tattapani (see under Sutlej River Valley), which has a fine golf course.

SHIMLA TO KALKA
The road from Shimla to Kalka is windy but good, and lined with cafes and restaurants offering gorgeous views. Buses ply the road regularly, but visitors usually take the famous Shimla to Kalka train. You can get off and on the train at most stations along the way. If the train doesn't actually stop, it certainly goes slow enough to allow passengers to get off or on easily. Refer to Getting There & Away in the Shimla section for more information.

Solan
Tel Area Code: 01792
Solan is known as the home of the Mohan Meakan brewery, built in 1835, and is the capital of the Solan district. It pretends to be another hill station but doesn't have the scenery, facilities or charm of nearby Shimla.

Barog
Barog is not a bad place for a day trip by train from Shimla. There are nice walks nearby, including that to the Churdhar mountain (3650m).

HPTDC's *Hotel Pinewood* (☎ 6125) has rooms (some with great views) from Rs 350 to Rs 1000 with hot water and TV. There are several other mid-range places from about Rs 200.

The railway *retiring rooms* cost from Rs 50 to Rs 100.

Kasauli
Tel Area Code: 01793
About 12km from the main road between Shimla and Kalka, Kasauli is a charming place. It's a good detour between Shimla and Kalka, a popular side trip from Shimla, or an alternative to staying in Shimla.

There are numerous lovely walks around Kasauli, including to **Sanawar**, another picturesque hill town, and the location of a famous colonial college. Only about four km away, **Monkey Point** has no monkeys (unlike Shimla) but it's a nice walk there, with great views. These days, the area is owned by the Indian Airforce, so you'll have to get their permission (at the gates) as you walk to Monkey Point.

Places to Stay & Eat The *Alasia Hotel* (☎ 72008) costs from Rs 300.

Maurice Hotel (☎ 72074) has good value singles/doubles from Rs 150/250.

Anchal Guest House (☎ 72052) is OK at Rs 200 a room.

Mahamaya Palace (☎ 8448) virtually opposite the bus stand is relatively new and has doubles for Rs 400 to Rs 600 including TV, hot water, telephone and views.

HPTDC's *Hotel Ros Common* (☎ 72005) has rooms with TV from Rs 400 to Rs 750, and is set in a nice location. The restaurant is OK.

Getting There & Away Regular local buses connect Shimla with Kasauli. By train, get off at the Dharampur station, and catch a local bus, or hitch a ride to cover the 12km to Kasauli. A one-way taxi from Shimla to Kasauli costs about Rs 250.

Kalka

Past the unexciting industrial town of Parwanoo, and just over the border into Haryana, Kalka is the start/finish for the toy train trip to/from Shimla. There is nothing to see or do, and nowhere to stay in Kalka, so get on the train to somewhere else. About five km southwest of Kalka, on the Chandigarh road, is the attractive Yadavindra (or Mughal) gardens at **Pinjore**. A one-way taxi from Shimla to Kalka costs Rs 600.

WILDFLOWER HALL

Wildflower Hall, at **Chharabra**, 13km from Shimla, is the former residence of the British commander-in-chief, Lord Kitchener. Before it was severely damaged by fire in 1994, the HPTDC ran the place as the *Wildflower Hall Hotel*. Check with the HPTDC office in Shimla for the latest on whether/ when it's opening.

Woodrina (☎ (4499) is an alternative place to stay where rooms cost Rs 800 to Rs 1000.

CHAIL

Tel Area Code: 01792

Chail was created as the summer capital of the princely state of Patiala by the maharaja after he was expelled from Shimla. The town is built on three hills – one is topped by the Chail Palace, one by the village itself, and the other by the SnowView mansion.

Three km from the village is the world's highest **cricket ground** (2444m), built in 1893. There is also a **wildlife sanctuary** three km from Chail with a limited number of deer and birds. This is also great hiking country.

Places to Stay & Eat

HPTDC's *Palace Hotel* (☎ 48343) has a range of suites, cottages, log huts, and rooms set among 70 acres of lawns. Modest luxury starts at Rs 650 for a double, and moves up to Rs 3500 for the 'Maharaja suite'. There is a top-class restaurant, cafe and bar.

HPTDC's *Hotel Himneel* is more modest with rooms for Rs 400.

Hotel Deodar has rooms from Rs 100.

Monal Tourist Lodge has reasonable rooms from Rs 250.

Getting There & Away

Chail can be reached from the Shimla to Kalka road via Kandaghat, or more commonly via the turnoff at Kufri. A return taxi from Shimla, via Kufri, costs Rs 550. There are irregular local buses (more in the high season) to Chail from Shimla and Chandigarh.

EAST OF SHIMLA

Kufri

Kufri is a nondescript little village, but there are a few things to do and see. The nearby countryside offers some great hiking, including to nearby Mahasu peak. Horses can be hired for Rs 30 to Rs 160 for trips around the valleys and hills.

The **Himalayan Nature Park** has a collection of animals and birds unique to Himachal Pradesh, but you won't see much unless you have your own vehicle or you're on a tour. There is a Rs 10 entrance fee, plus extra charges for cameras, and it's open from 10 am to 5 pm every day. Nearby, the **Indira Tourist Park** has great views, the HPTDC's

Cafe Lalit, horse riding and a chance to have your photo taken standing next to a yak.

Kufri is promoted for its skiing (from December to February) but the snow isn't reliable and the location isn't particularly good. Inquire at the Kufri Holiday Resorts or the HPTDC office in Shimla for details of current costs and package deals. In winter, tobogganing is a popular and cheaper alternative.

Places to Stay & Eat The *Hotel Snow Shelter*, on the main road in the village, has cosy rooms, great views, and hot water at a reasonable Rs 250 for a double.

Kufri Holiday Resorts (☎ 28341) has rooms that cost from Rs 2250.

Atri Food Center and *Deluxe Food Corner* serve reasonable food.

Getting There & Away Kufri is one of the stops for the regular buses that travel between Shimla and Narkanda and Rampur. A one-way taxi from Shimla to Kufri costs about Rs 200.

Fagu
Fagu is another unexciting village, but it serves as a good base for exploring the fantastic nearby countryside.

HPTDC's *Hotel Peach Blossom* (☎ 285522 – bookings recommended, and vital in season) is the only hotel. The six rooms are enormous, and have old fireplaces. They cost from Rs 275 to Rs 350 a double. Taxis and buses can drop you off at Fagu easily.

NARKANDA
Halfway between Shimla and Rampur, Narkanda is basically a truck stop town, but it is a popular place for hiking (Hattu Peak is only six km away) and for skiing, in season.

Skiing
The ski season here lasts from January to mid-April. Narkanda is not as well set up for skiing as the other major site in the region, Solang Nullah, north of Manali.

The HPTDC office in Shimla or the HPTDC's Tourist Bungalow in Narkanda can provide details of current skiing courses. All inclusive seven-day packages cost from about Rs 2000, which is a lot cheaper than at Solang Nullah. There are good opportunities for cross-country skiing around Narkanda if you have the equipment and experience.

Places to Stay & Eat
HPTDC's *Tourist Bungalow* is 250m up a lane from the main road (look for the sign).

Hotel Hatu (☎ 8430) has rooms with cable TV for Rs 750, plus a restaurant.

Hotel Mahamaya (☎ 8448) has lovely, large rooms with hot water, balcony and views for the upmarket price of Rs 550. It will possibly offer discounts in the off season.

Hotel Snow View dorms cost Rs 39, and a private room, with bathroom, costs Rs 220; amazing views and friendly staff are added attractions. Look for the sign from the village centre.

Cafe Vasant, near the Snow View and set in a large, old room, is the best place to eat.

Getting There & Away
Local buses travel in either direction along the main road at least every 30 minutes. A return taxi from Shimla will cost about Rs 600.

NORTH OF SHIMLA
Mashobra & Craignano
About 11km from Shimla is Mashobra, a small village where donkeys rule the streets. There are pleasant walks around the place, including to Sipi, where there is a fair every May and a wooden **temple** dedicated to Lord Siva. The resort of Craignano is about three km from Mashobra, along a lovely trail.

Places to Stay & Eat The *rest house* in Craignano can be booked through the Forest Department (☎ 72911) in Shimla.

Gables Resorts (☎ 28376) is the only place to stay in or near Mashobra. It offers rural luxury from Rs 850 upwards.

Mashobra has a couple of *dhabas*.

Naldehra
Fifteen km further north, Naldehra is a pleasant little village. It is mostly famous for

having one of the oldest and highest golf courses in India. There is even a temple – the **Mahunag Temple** – in the middle of the course. The charges are Rs 50 green fees for 18 holes (twice around the course); Rs 15 to hire golf clubs; and Rs 40 for a caddy; and a wad of rupees for replacing lost golf balls.

Places to Stay & Eat The *Hotel Golf Glade & Restaurant* (☎ 287739) has six luxurious log cabins from Rs 950 to Rs 3000, and rooms from Rs 450.

Paradise Restaurant on the main road is the only reasonably good place to eat outside of the hotel.

SUTLEJ RIVER VALLEY
Tattapani

Tattapani is famous only for its hot sulphurous springs. They are not as well developed or as nice as the ones in Vashisht, near Manali, or Manikaran, along the Parbati Valley. Tattapani is probably not worth visiting just for the springs, but the setting is great, and the village is small and relaxed. The hot water is piped from a section of the Sutlej River to the two guesthouses on the bank.

Places to Stay & Eat HPTDC's *Tourist Bungalow* (☎ 286649) has four clean, sparse rooms from Rs 100 to Rs 200. Dorms (20 beds in a room) cost Rs 30, but they are often booked out in the high season. At the back of the hotel, the hot water 'deluxe' individual baths cost Rs 20 with soap and towel, or Rs 10 in a common, dirty pool.

Spring View Paying Guest House is very basic, but friendly and relaxed, and rooms cost Rs 80. A soak in the pool costs Rs 10.

Tourist Inn offers old-world style, and great views, but nothing much else for an unbeatable Rs 15 – bring everything: sleeping bags, pillows etc. It's not easy to find: head up a lane about 100m to the left from the bridge before the other guesthouses, and turn sharp left again.

Hotel Springdale is a cheap option in the nearby village of Sunni, about five km away.

Getting There & Away Get off the bus just after the bridge which is about 10 minutes past Sunni. The guesthouses and springs are about 200m further up alongside the river. The village is up a laneway on the left before the guesthouses. A local bus leaves Shimla every hour or so from Cart Rd to Tattapani and then visits other villages further north before heading back on the main Bilaspur to Mandi road. A return taxi from Shimla to Tattapani costs Rs 575, which includes some waiting time while you soak your weary limbs.

Rampur

Rampur was once on ancient trade routes between India and Tibet, and is a former centre of the mighty Bushahr Empire which spread into Kinnaur. The Lavi Fair is held in Rampur every November. Rampur is not a particularly exciting place to stay overnight, but there are one or two things to see if you do stop.

The major attraction is the **Padam Palace** built in 1925, located on the side of the main road. You cannot go inside, but there are lovely gardens, flanked by a **Hindu temple**, which you can wander around. The older part of town, by the river and below the palace, is the most interesting place to explore, and to stay. It's a maze of tiny lanes, full of shops and Hindu and Buddhist temples, such as the (Buddhist) **Sri Sat Nahan Temple**, built in 1926.

Places to Stay & Eat Not far from the bus station, *Narindra* (☎ 33155), is not bad value for Rs 80 a double.

Hotel Bhagwati (☎ 33117) – look for the huge sign on its roof – remains popular. Doubles start at Rs 100.

Highway Home Guest House, on the main road as you come from Shimla, is the same price and standard.

Himgiri Hotel & Restaurant (☎ 33176), in the old part of Rampur, has ordinary singles/doubles for Rs 30/45.

Cafe Sutlej is worth the one km walk from the palace towards Shimla for views and good food.

The old town has plenty of *dhabas*, and several pretty good *bakeries*.

HIMACHAL PRADESH

Getting There & Away Rampur is a major transport hub, so is well connected by buses. There are buses every 30 minutes between 5.30 am and 4 pm from Rampur to Narkanda, and then on to Shimla. To Rekong Peo and Kalpa, there are three buses a day; one bus goes each day to Kaza, leaving at 1.30 am; and a 6.30 am bus leaves every day for Kullu. A return taxi from Shimla to Rampur will cost Rs 700.

Sarahan
Tel Area Code: 01702

Former summer capital of the Bushahr Empire, Sarahan (1920m) is a wonderful little village in a beautiful region of deodar forests. It is definitely worth a visit – there are spectacular views and trekking opportunities to nearby villages such as Ranwin, and Bashal peak.

The main attraction is the **Bhimakali Temple**, which dominates Sarahan village. In the Indo-Tibetan architectural style, Bhimakali has smaller temples inside dedicated to Lord Narsingh and Lord Raghunath, some silver decorations, other images from the Hindu and Buddhist religions, and a small **museum**. There are some entry rules. You must wear a cap (which can be borrowed from inside the temple); no cameras or leather goods (belts, wallets etc) are allowed (they can be left with the guards); and shoes must be removed.

Places to Stay & Eat Inside the temple complex are three clean, quiet *rooms* for Rs 100 to Rs 150 with bathroom and a dorm with beds for Rs 25 each. Opposite is a new wing with six large and spotless doubles with attached bath and hot water for Rs 200 to Rs 300.

Bushair Guest House next to the temple entrance has clean, large rooms, with bathroom, for Rs 100.

HPTDC's *Hotel Shrikhand* (☎ 7434), set over the edge of a cliff, dominates the view as you come up the hill. Large, quiet, comfortable rooms, with TV and hot water, are good value. They start at Rs 300, and cost Rs

650 in the modern wing. The dorms cost Rs 45. The restaurant here is good.

There are a few *dhabas* in the village.

Getting There & Away From Shimla, buses go every 30 minutes to Rampur, from where there are several daily buses to Sarahan. Alternatively, take any other bus going along the main road, get off at the dismal little junction of Jeori, where the road up to Sarahan starts, and wait for a local bus (every hour or two) up the steep 17km road. A taxi from Jeori to Sarahan will cost about Rs 100.

To get from Sarahan to Shimla in one day, take the 6.30 or 7.30 am daily bus. To Rekong Peo or Kalpa in one day, take the early bus to Shimla, get off at Jeori, and wait for one of the hopelessly crowded buses heading east from Rampur or Shimla. A taxi from Rampur to Sarahan costs about Rs 200 and will save a lot of time.

Kangra Valley

The beautiful Kangra Valley starts near Mandi, runs north, then bends west and extends to Shahpur near Pathankot. To the north the valley is flanked by the Dhauladhar Range, to the side of which Dharamsala/ McLeod Ganj clings. There are a number of places of interest along the valley, including McLeod Ganj, home of the Dalai Lama and headquarters of the Tibetan Government in Exile.

The main Pathankot to Mandi road runs through the valley, and there is a narrow-gauge railway line from Pathankot as far as Jogindernagar. The Kangra school of painting developed in this valley.

BAIJNATH
The small town of Baijnath, 46km to the south-east of Dharamsala, is an important pilgrimage place due to its ancient stone **Baidyanath Temple**, sacred to Siva as Lord of the Physicians. It is said to date from 804 AD, although according to tradition it was built by the Pandavas, the heroes of the

Mahabharata, when they were in exile following the slaying of their kin, the Kauravas.

Baijnath itself is a chaotic and ramshackle town, although the Dhauladhar provides a fine backdrop.

The *PWD Rest House* (owned by the Public Works Department), a 10 minute walk from the temple on the Palampur side of town, has doubles with good views for Rs 104 if you should find yourself stuck here.

Cafe Bharva, on the right is as you enter Baijnath from Palampur, has fine views out over the valley, and a range of Indian cuisine.

The narrow-gauge railway line passes through Baijnath. To Pathankot it's Rs 24 (six hours), and to the end of the line, at Jogindernagar, it's Rs 7 (three hours). The station is at Paprola, one km from the main bus stand.

TARAGARH & TASHIJONG GOMPA

Taragarh lies five km north-west of Baijnath on the Palampur road. There is no settlement here as such.

Palace Hotel (☎ (018946) 3034), in what was the extraordinary summer palace of Dr Karan Singh, the son of the last maharaja of Jammu & Kashmir. It is set in beautiful gardens complete with tennis court, aviary, swimming pool and brass statues of deer. Doubles range from Rs 600; the suites, which are beautifully furnished with old bureaus and dressers, cost up to Rs 1500. You can hire mountain bikes (Rs 25 per hour) from the hotel to tour the environs, including the **Tashijong Gompa**, visible in the distance, two km to the north of the hotel. The gompa is the focus of a small Tibetan community who hail from Kham province in Tibet.

PALAMPUR
Tel Area Code: 01894

A pleasant little town surrounded by tea plantations, Palampur is 30km south-east of Dharamsala and stands at 1260m. The main road runs right through Palampur and there are some fine walks around the town. A four day trek takes you from Palampur to **Holi** via the Waru La, or in a shorter walk you can visit

the **Bundla chasm**, from which a waterfall drops into the Bundla Stream.

Places to Stay & Eat

HPTDC's *Hotel T-Bud* (☎ 4031) is one km north of Main Bazaar. It has doubles with attached bath for Rs 400 and Rs 500, and a four bed suite for Rs 700.

Baghla Guest House, opposite the bus stand, has very basic rooms for Rs 40, and there's no hot water.

Hotel Sawhney (☎ 30888), in Main Bazaar, has basic doubles for Rs 150, or with TV, Rs 200.

Joy Restaurant in Main Bazaar has cheap fare, including a very good egg chicken dosa for Rs 30.

Aahaar Real Value Foods near the Joy Restaurant has a variety of ice cream.

Sapan Restaurant, opposite the post office in Main Bazaar, has Indian and Chinese cuisine.

Getting There & Away

The new bus stand is one km south of Main Bazaar; a taxi will charge Rs 15. Buses to Dharamsala take two hours and cost Rs 15. To Mandi, it's four hours and Rs 36, and to Pathankot, four hours and Rs 45. Palampur is on the narrow-gauge line between Pathankot and Jogindernagar. There are several trains daily between Palampur and either Nagrota to the west (for Dharamsala), or the end of the line at Jogindernagar, to the east.

CHAMUNDA DEVI TEMPLE

From Palampur the road leaves the wide green valley, passing through tea plantations and a pleasant wooded area, before descending to the settlement around the colourful Chamunda Devi temple complex on the bank of the Baner River, 10km to the west. Chamunda is a particularly wrathful form of Durga; the idol in the main temple is considered so sacred that it is completely concealed beneath a red cloth.

Shaksi Restaurant, to the right of the temple before the car park, is one of several places to stay here. Doubles with attached bath are Rs 220, and there's 24 hour hot water.

HIMACHAL PRADESH

Buses between Dharamsala and Palampur will drop you at the Chamunda Devi Temple on request.

DHARAMSALA

Pop: 19,200   Tel Area Code: 01892

While Dharamsala is synonymous with the Tibetan Government in Exile, the actual headquarters of the government is about four km above Dharamsala at Gangchen Kyishong, and most travellers head up to McLeod Ganj, strung along a high ridge 10km above Dharamsala.

Dharamsala itself is a busy bazaar town, and few travellers base themselves here, although Kotwali Bazaar, at the foot of the roads leading up to McLeod Ganj, is an interesting and colourful market, and you can visit the Kangra Art Museum, which has examples of the miniature paintings for which the Kangra Valley was once renowned.

Orientation & Information

Tourist Office & Money The HPTDC's tourist office (☎ 23107) is in Kotwali Bazaar. It's open Monday to Saturday from 10 am to 5 pm. Jagson Airlines (☎ 24928) is near the tourist office.

The main branch of the State Bank of India is near the tourist office in Kotwali Bazaar. Only American Express and Thomas Cook travellers cheques in US dollars and pounds sterling are accepted. Further down the main road is the Punjab National Bank, which also accepts other major travellers cheques in various currencies.

Kangra Art Museum

This museum is a few minutes walk down from the tourist office. In addition to the miniature paintings from the famous Kangra school of art, which flourished in the Kangra Valley in the 17th century, the museum has elaborately embroidered costumes of Kangra tribal people, woodcarvings and tribal jewellery. It's open Tuesday to Sunday from 10 am to 5 pm. Entry is free.

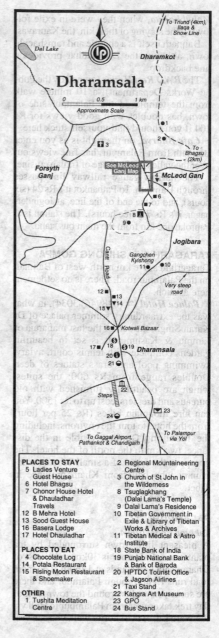

Dharamsala

0   0.5   1 km
Approximate Scale

To Triund (4km),
Ilaqa &
Snow Line

Dal Lake

Dharamkot

To Bhagsu (2km)

Forsyth Ganj

See McLeod Ganj Map

McLeod Ganj

Jogibara

Gangchen Kyishong

Very steep road

Kotwali Bazaar

Dharamsala

Steps

To Gaggal Airport,
Pathankot & Chandigarh

To Palampur via Yol

PLACES TO STAY
5 Ladies Venture Guest House
6 Hotel Bhagsu
7 Chonor House Hotel & Dhauladhar Travels
12 B Mehra Hotel
13 Sood Guest House
16 Basera Lodge
17 Hotel Dhauladhar

PLACES TO EAT
4 Chocolate Log
14 Potala Restaurant
15 Rising Moon Restaurant & Shoemaker

OTHER
1 Tushita Meditation Centre
2 Regional Mountaineering Centre
3 Church of St John in the Wilderness
8 Tsuglagkhang (Dalai Lama's Temple)
9 Dalai Lama's Residence
10 Tibetan Government in Exile & Library of Tibetan Works & Archives
11 Tibetan Medical & Astro Institute
18 State Bank of India
19 Punjab National Bank & Bank of Baroda
20 HPTDC Tourist Office & Jagson Airlines
21 Taxi Stand
22 Kangra Art Museum
23 GPO
24 Bus Stand

Places to Stay & Eat

Sood Guest House on Cantt Rd, Kotwali Bazaar, has doubles/triples for Rs 220 with attached bath (hot water available in buckets for Rs 5). A 50% discount is offered during the monsoon.

B Mehra Hotel, a few doors up on the opposite side of the road to Sood has grimy doubles (with brilliant views!) for Rs 100 with attached bath. Singles with common bath are Rs 75.

HPTDC's *Hotel Dhauladhar* (☎ 24926) has standard rooms for Rs 400/500, and deluxe rooms for Rs 562/750. There's a restaurant and bar, as well as a billiard room for guests.

Basera Lodge (☎ 22234), just before the Hotel Dhauladhar, has basic double rooms with attached bath and hot water for Rs 250.

Rising Moon Restaurant, opposite the Sood Guest House on Cantt Rd, has continental breakfasts, and Tibetan cuisine. It's run by a very friendly Tibetan man.

Potala Restaurant, up a narrow flight of stairs opposite, has good vegetarian and non-vegetarian Tibetan and Chinese cuisine.

Things to Buy

The shoemaker Chhotu Ram, in the store bearing the sign 'Specialist in Dingo Shoes', on Cantt Rd, close to the Rising Moon Restaurant, makes fine men's leather shoes to order from Rs 450.

Getting There & Away

Buses for the 30 minute trip (Rs 5) up to McLeod Ganj depart every 30 minutes throughout the day. There are buses every hour to Pathankot between 5.45 am and 5 pm (3½ hours, Rs 39); to Mandi at 4, 5 and 11 am and 6 pm (six hours, Rs 55), which continue to Kullu (10 hours, Rs 100) and Manali (12½ hours, Rs 115).

Beware of low-hanging power lines if you are riding on the roof of the bus between Manali and Dharamsala.

Buses to Shimla leave at 5.30, 6 and 8.30 am, and 5, 5.10, 7 and 7.45 pm. It takes 10½ hours, and costs Rs 109 on ordinary services, and Rs 170 for the deluxe service.

There are numerous services to Chandigarh between 5.30 am and 9.30 pm (nine hours, Rs 86). To Delhi, there are ordinary services at 2, 5 and 9.30 pm, and a deluxe service at 6 pm (13 hours, Rs 155 ordinary, Rs 300 deluxe). There's an 8.30 am service to Dalhousie (six hours, Rs 58) which continues to Chamba (eight hours, Rs 75). To Dehra Dun there's one service at 9 pm (14 hours, Rs 160).

To the right of the bus terminal building is a steep staircase which leads up to the vegetable market at Kotwali Bazaar. If you walk through the market and turn left at the main road, after about five minutes you'll come to the taxi stand on your left. Here you can hire a Maruti van up to McLeod Ganj for Rs 80.

AROUND DHARAMSALA
Norbulinka Institute

This complex is about 14km from McLeod Ganj and four km from Dharamsala, set amid Japanese-influenced gardens with shady paths, wooden bridges across small streams and tiny waterfalls. Norbulinka has been established to teach and preserve traditional Tibetan art, such as woodcarving, *thangka* painting, goldsmithing and embroidery.

Nearby is the **Dolmaling Nunnery**, where the Women's Higher Studies Institute is shortly to be opened, offering nuns courses at advanced levels in Buddhist philosophy.

There is a *guesthouse* at Norbulinka with doubles for Rs 550, and suites for Rs 850.

To get here, catch a Yol-bound bus and ask to be let off at Sidhpur, near the Sacred Heart School. At this crossroad is a signpost to Norbulinka, from where it is about a 20 minute walk. A taxi from McLeod will cost Rs 130.

McLEOD GANJ
Tel Area Code: 01892

Before Upper Dharamsala, or McLeod Ganj (named after the Lieutenant Governor of Punjab, David McLeod), was established in the mid-1850s as a British garrison, it was the home of the seminomadic Gaddi tribe. There is still a sizeable number of Gaddi families in the villages around McLeod Ganj. The British developed the settlement as an important administrative centre for the Kangra region, but following a major earthquake on 4 April 1905, moved the centre to Lower Dharamsala, 10km by road below McLeod Ganj.

Today McLeod Ganj is best known as the headquarters of the Tibetan Government in Exile, and is the home of the 14th Dalai Lama, Tenzin Gyatso.

Orientation & Information

The heart of McLeod Ganj is the bus stand. From here roads radiate to various points around the township, including that back

down to Dharamsala, which passes en route the church of St John in the Wilderness and the cantonment area of Forsyth Ganj. Other roads lead to the villages of Dharamkot and Bhagsu. To the south of the bus stand is the main bazaar area, along the sides of two parallel roads. Temple Rd proceeds to the

PLACES TO STAY
6	Paljor Gakyil Guest House
7	Kalsang Guest House
15	Tashi Khansar Guest House
16	Green Hotel & Tibetan Women's Association
19	Hotel Tibet & Take Out
22	Shangrila Guest House
24	Hotel Snow Palace
26	Kailash Hotel & Bhakto Restaurant
27	Om Guest House
28	Drepung Loseling Guest House
29	Tibetan Ashoka Guest House
41	International Guest House
42	Surya Resorts, Hotel Natraj & Hotel Him Queen

PLACES TO EAT
11	McLlo Restaurant
12	Friend's Corner & Bombay Studios
20	Cafe Shambhala & Malabar
30	Gakyi Restaurant
32	Aroma Restaurant
34	Ashoka Restaurant & Tibetan Handicrafts Society
38	Dreamland Restaurant

OTHER
1	Occidental Bookshop & Bedi Travels
2	Dharamsala Bookshop & Himachal Travel
3	Taxi Stand
4	Telecom Office
5	Yeti Trekking
8	Tara Herbal Gift Shop
9	Nowrogee Store
10	Bus Stand
13	Potala Tours & Travels
14	Tibetan Youth Congress
17	Green Shop
18	Branch Security & Tibetan Welfare Offices
21	Video Hall
23	Tibetan Bookshop & Information Centre
25	Chorten & Prayer Wheels
31	Video Hall
33	Office of Tibetan Handicrafts
35	Dr Yeshi Dhonden's Clinic
36	State Bank of India
37	Bookworm
39	Pema Youdon
40	Post Office
43	Eagle Height Trekkers & Travellers

McLeod Ganj

To Glenmore Cottages & Dharamsala (via Forsyth Ganj)

To TCV & Dal Lake

To Regional Mountaineering Centre, Tushita Retreat Centre & Dharamkot

To TIPA

To Bhagsu

To Dip Tse-Chok Ling Gompa

Bridle Path to Dharamsala

Temple Road

Jogibara Road

Mall Road

0   25   50 m
Approximate Scale

To Dalai Lama's Temple & Library of Tibetan Works & Archives

To Hotel Bhagsu

To Chocolate Log, Library of Tibetan Works & Archives & Dharamsala

Dalai Lama's temple, about 800m to the south, from where it's possible to take a shortcut down to the administrative area of Gangchen Kyishong, where you'll find the Library of Tibetan Works & Archives, a walk of some 20 minutes. The other road through the bazaar, Jogibara Rd, wends its way down to Gangchen Kyishong in about three km via the village of Jogibara.

Money The State Bank of India is near the post office. It's open weekdays from 10.30 am to 12.30 pm and Saturday from 10.30 to 11.30 am. It changes American Express and Thomas Cook travellers cheques in US dollars and pounds sterling only.

Post & Communications The post office is on Jogibara Rd, just past the State Bank of India. To post parcels you need to complete a customs form (in triplicate!), which you can get at the Office of Tibetan Handicrafts, opposite the State Bank of India for Rs 3. This form is not required for book postage. There are several places that offer a parcel-packing service, including a couple on Jogibara Rd. Pema Youdon, opposite the post office, also offers a parcel-packing service. Letters sent c/poste restante are held for one month.

The telecom office is up a flight of stairs behind the bus stand, and has a fax facility (Rs 116 per page). The fax number is 24528, and in theory you can receive faxes here. The office is open Monday to Saturday from 8 am to 8 pm; the fax is turned off on the weekends. Faxes can also be sent and received at Bombay Studios, behind the McLlo Restaurant. The fax number is 23002, and this place also has email facilities.

Down at Gangchen Kyishong in the library compound is the Computer Resource Centre, above the Department of Information & International Relations (the building with the circular glass windows). You can send a one page email message here for Rs 60, and receive messages for Rs 15. The address is tcrc@cta.unv.ernet.in. The centre also has computers for hire (Rs 50 per hour).

Travel Agencies A reliable outfit is Potala

Tours & Travels (☎ 22587; fax 24327), opposite the Hotel Tibet. Down near Tsuglagkhang (the Dalai Lama's temple) is Dhauladhar Travels (☎ 23158), which arranges domestic and international bookings. Some agencies, including Bedi Travels (☎ 22359), will reconfirm international flight tickets for a small fee.

Trekking Outfits Eagle Height Trekkers & Travellers (☎ 24330), on the Hotel Bhagsu road, can organise porters and guides, as well as arrange treks in the Kullu and Chamba valleys, Lahaul and Spiti and Ladakh, from US$40 per day including porter, guide, cook, meals, tents and sleeping bag. Transport is extra. Yeti Trekking (☎ 22887) also arranges tailor-made treks to these areas, with accommodation in huts and houses. They can be found in a fine old building reached through a gate off the Dharamkot road.

Regional Mountaineering Centre This centre (☎ 24897) is about 15 minutes walk north of McLeod on the Dharamkot road. Here you can get advice on treks and mountaineering in the Chamba and Kangra valleys, and it's also possible to hire gear including sleeping bags, foam mattresses, rucksacks and tents. It's not possible to hire specialised mountaineering equipment; for this, the closest place is the Mountaineering Institute & Allied Sports in Manali, and equipment is subject to availability.

You can also purchase Survey of India trekking maps (Rs 15); it's a good idea to advise the centre if you are planning a trek in the region.

Bookshops & Newsagencies There's an excellent selection of new books at the Bookworm, up the road to the right of the State Bank of India. The Occidental Bookshop, on the Dal Lake road, has a very good selection of secondhand books. The Tibetan Bookshop & Information Centre on Jogibara Rd has a comprehensive selection of books on the Tibetan struggle for independence and Tibetan Buddhism. National English-language dailies arrive after 12.30 pm at the Nowrogee Store, at the bus stand.

Tibetan Publications *Chö-Yang* is a glossy journal published by the Department of Religion & Culture. There are currently seven volumes, which include scholarly essays on Buddhism and Tibetan culture. Other journals published in McLeod include the *Tibetan Bulletin*, which is published in Tibetan, Hindi, French and English, and *Rangzen* (Freedom), published by the Tibetan Youth Congress.

Voluntary Work
If you're interested in teaching English to newly arrived refugees, check at the Library of Tibetan Works & Archives.

Organised Tours
Taxi operators have devised fixed-rate taxi tours to points of interest around McLeod Ganj and in the Kangra Valley. A local sightseeing tour taking in the Bhagsunag Temple, Tsuglagkhang (the Dalai Lama's temple) and Dal Lake is Rs 180. A tour to the colourful Hindu temple at Chamunda, the Hindu ashram at Tapovan, and to Palampur and Baijnath is Rs 650. To Kangra Fort and the Shakti Temple at Jawalamukhi, it's Rs 1000.

Activities
The Occidental Bookshop on Mall Rd, just beyond the bus stand, hires out horses for Rs 550 per day. A guide is an additional Rs 200 per day. You can also hire horses at the Dharamsala Bookshop, nearby.

Buddhist Philosophy Courses
About 20 minutes walk above McLeod, on a path off the road to Dharamkot (passing en route a colony of monkeys), is the Tushita retreat centre (☎ 22866; fax 21328). The path heads off to the right near a small white temple just beyond the Regional Mountaineering Centre. Tushita offers residential courses plus retreat accommodation (Rs 35 per day in a dorm; Rs 65 per day for a single with attached bath). There is a small library here (books cannot be borrowed), which is open to students and nonstudents, and there are books on Buddhism for sale. The office at Tushita is open Monday to Saturday from 9.30 to 11.30 am and 1 to 4.30 pm.

Behind Tushita is the new Dhamma Sikhara Vipassana Meditation Centre, which offers courses in Indian Hinayana Buddhism.

Down at the library, in Gangchen Kyishong, classes in aspects of Buddhist philosophy are led by Tibetan lamas and translated into English. They take place on weekdays, and

---

Cleaning Upper Dharamsala Project
This new project is an innovation of the Welfare Office and a young Dutch man who helped raise money for the project. It consists of four 'green workers' – generally new arrivals from Tibet – who collect about 40 to 50kg of recyclable goods from homes and businesses around McLeod each day, including paper, glass, metals and plastics, which are then sold. At Nechung and Namgyal gompas, the Dialectic School and Gaden Chuling Nunnery there are special baskets with separate receptacles for different materials. These are emptied once a week and the materials are then separated. So far the amount received from selling recyclables covers little more than the salary of one green worker, but profits are secondary to the goal of raising environmental awareness and promoting a cleaner township.

Another initiative under the Welfare Office is the Green Shop, on the Bhagsu road. This shop sells rechargeable batteries, hand-painted T-shirts, natural cosmetics and boiled and filtered water. In the off season, 25 to 30 bottles of water are sold each day. In the peak season, this increases to 100 to 120 bottles per day. Posters on environmental issues, in Hindi, have been posted in villages around McLeod, and the project officers plan to work in cooperation with the Indian community.

Tourists can support the project and help promote a cleaner McLeod by having their mineral-water bottles refilled at the Green Shop, and by encouraging hotel owners to separate garbage and give it to the green workers, rather than throwing it on dumps. ■

cost Rs 100 per month. If you're not sure you want to commit yourself to extended studies, it's possible to attend the first class free.

Other Courses

Pema Youdon is a friendly Tibetan woman who teaches Tibetan language from her home opposite the post office. It costs Rs 40 per hour, and there is a discount for two hour sessions. It's also possible to study the Tibetan language at the Library of Tibetan Works & Archives. Classes are held on weekdays for both beginners and advanced students, and it costs Rs 200 per month.

It's possible to receive private tuition in the Tibetan performing arts at the Tibetan Institute of Performing Arts (TIPA), about 15 minutes walk from McLeod along the TIPA road. The cost is Rs 50 per hour, with instructors providing tuition for one to two hours per day for up to 15 days.

Tibetan Offices & Institutions

As the headquarters of the Tibetan Government in Exile are in McLeod Ganj there are numerous offices and organisations concerned with Tibetan affairs and the welfare of the refugee community. These include the Tibetan Welfare Office, the Planning Council, Tibetan Youth Congress, Tibetan Children's

His Holiness the Dalai Lama, leader of the Tibetan people.

An Audience with His Holiness the Dalai Lama

The Dalai Lama is so much in demand that a private audience at his residence in Dharamsala is now very difficult to arrange. You can try, however, by contacting his private office in McLeod Ganj at least four months in advance. You're much more likely to be able to meet him face to face by attending a public audience. Contact his private office to find out when the next public audience is being held.

Meeting this 14th incarnation of Chenresig, Tibetan Buddhism's deity of Universal Compassion, is no ordinary event. Not so much because of his title, nor even because of the high degree of reverence in which he is held by the Tibetan people; but more because of how it feels to be in his company. As an American friend put it: 'When you look at him, he is the size of a normal human being; but when you look away; you realise that his presence is filling the whole room'.

After waiting, strangely nervous, in the anteroom, we were ushered into his reception room for our audience with His Holiness, which seemed to speed by in a flash. However, several strong impressions remain, including the way in which he gives his whole attention to questions. He really listens, and pauses before replying, to give consideration to the subject matter. He responds rather than reacts to the issue under discussion. There is a wisdom in his thinking which comes through clearly in his words, filled as they are with common sense and realism.

I remember his direct and friendly gaze, his firm handshake, and an almost palpable sense of compassion. He also has a superb sense of humour, often remarked upon by those who meet him. He laughs often and easily – and what a laugh! He throws back his head to release a deep, thorough chuckle which rises from his abdomen and expresses pure mirth. It is kind laughter, and highly infectious.

As our audience came to a close, he accompanied us to the door. With each of us in turn, he took one of our hands in both of his. Bowing slightly over the joined hands, he looked up into our faces and beamed. Following this farewell, we seemed to be walking inches above the streets of McLeod Ganj. And we just couldn't stop smiling.

Vyvyan Cayley

Village (TCV), Yongling Creche & Kindergarten and the Tibetan Women's Association. Interested visitors are welcome at many of these.

All offices and institutions are open from 9 am to 5 pm on weekdays (closed for lunch between 1 and 2 pm in summer, and noon to 1 pm in winter), other than on Tibetan holidays and three Indian national holidays (26 January, 15 August and 2 October).

Tibetan Institute of Performing Arts (TIPA)

This institute promotes the study and performance of the Tibetan performing arts to ensure the preservation of these rich manifestations of Tibetan culture.

In April each year TIPA convenes an opera festival, which also includes folk dancing and contemporary and historical plays. There is also a three day festival from 27 May, the anniversary of the foundation of TIPA. Details of these and other performances at TIPA are posted around McLeod Ganj.

Tsuglagkhang (Dalai Lama's Temple)

This is the most important Buddhist monument in McLeod Ganj. Although a relatively modest structure, it enshrines three magnificent images, including an enormous (three metre high) gilt statue of Shakyamuni (Buddha), and to the left (facing Tibet), statues of Avalokitesvara (Chenresig, the Tibetan deity of compassion, of whom the Dalai Lama is considered an incarnation), and Padmasambhava, or Guru Rinpoche, the Indian scholar who introduced Buddhism and Tantric teachings to Tibet in the 8th century.

Also housed in the temple are a collection of sacred texts known as the *Khagyur*, which are based on the teachings of the Buddha, and have been translated from the original Sanskrit, as well as the *Tangyur*, which are translations of commentaries based on the Buddha's teachings and recorded by Indian scholars. They include works on Buddhist philosophy, art, literature, astrology and medicine.

Dip Tse-Chok Ling Gompa

This beautiful little gompa lies at the bottom of a steep track which leads off the laneway past the Om Guest House. The main prayer hall houses an image of Shakyamuni, as well as two enormous drums covered in goat skin and painted around the rim, which were made by monks at the gompa. Also here are some superb butter sculptures, which are made during Losar (Tibetan New Year), and destroyed during Losar the following year. Fine and detailed sand mandalas are also made here.

Library of Tibetan Works & Archives

The library, down at Gangchen Kyishong, halfway between Kotwali Bazaar and McLeod (take the shortcut down past the Dalai Lama's temple), is the repository of Tibet's rich literary heritage, containing about 40% of Tibet's original manuscripts, as well as an excellent general reference library on the Himalayan regions and a photographic archive.

Tibetan Medical & Astrological Institute

This institute is at Gangchen Kyishong, about five minutes walk below the main entrance to the library area. There's a museum, library, research unit, and a college at which Tibetan medicine and astrology is taught. It's possible to have a life horoscope prepared for US$30.

The museum (opened on request) has a well displayed exhibition of materials used in Tibetan medicines.

St John in the Wilderness

Dharamsala was originally a British hill resort, and one of the most poignant memories of that era is the pretty church of St John in the Wilderness. It's only a short distance below McLeod on the main road towards Dharamsala.

Walks

There are many fine walks and even finer views around McLeod Ganj. The sheer rock wall of Dhauladhar rises behind the township. Interesting walks include the two km stroll to **Bhagsu**, a popular picnic spot, where there is an old temple sacred to Siva, a spring, slate quarries and a small waterfall. You can continue on beyond here on the ascent to the snow line. Dal Lake is now polluted, and it's not one of the most attractive spots in the region. About three km from McLeod Ganj brings you to the little village of **Dharamkot**, where you'll enjoy a fine view. From Dharamkot, you can continue to Bhagsu and walk back to McLeod along the main Bhagsu road.

An eight km trek from McLeod Ganj will bring you to **Triund** (2827m) at the foot of Dhauladhar. It's a steep but straightforward ascent, with the path veering off to the right across scree just beyond Dharamkot. The views of Dhauladhar from here are stunning. It's another five km to the snow line at **Ilaqa**. A *Forest Rest House* here provides overnight accommodation.

From Ilaqa, it's possible to continue over the Indrahar Pass to the Chamba Valley. See under Treks out of Dharamsala later in this chapter.

From the village of **Jogibara**, which lies between McLeod Ganj and Gangchen Kyishong, a village path leads down into the valley and up the opposite side, from where you can walk along a path to the end of the ridge, affording fine views down over Dharamsala. A shorter walk is around **Tsuglagkhang**. Take the road to the left past the entrance to the temple, and after a few minutes, where the road veers around to the left (towards Gangchen Kyishong), a small path leads off to the right, eventually looping all the way around the Dalai Lama's residence back to the entrance to the temple. The path is flanked by colourful mani stones and prayer flags, and at one section there is a series of small prayer wheels. As you are effectively circumambulating the sacred temple, this walk should be made in a clockwise direction only.

Places to Stay – bottom end
International Guest House (☎ 22476), two minutes walk down past the post office on Jogibara Rd, has singles/doubles with common bath for Rs 90/135, or with attached bath with geyser for Rs 200/250.

Ladies Venture (☎ 22559), further down Jogibara Rd past the *Chocolate Log* (see under Places to Eat), is a very quiet place with a pleasant garden. Rooms with attached bath are Rs 150/250; sharing a bathroom with one other room costs Rs 125/175. Hot water can be provided with 30 minutes advance notice.

Kailash Hotel (☎ 22344), very centrally located, opposite the *chorten*, has doubles/triples for Rs 70/80, all with common bath (with 24 hour hot water). Rooms at the back have great views, but are pretty rustic.

Om Guest House (☎ 24313), on a path leading down from the bus stand behind the Kailash, has singles/doubles with common bath for Rs 35/70, all with valley views. Hot water in buckets is Rs 8, and there's a good restaurant.

Shangrila, on the other side of the chorten, has doubles with common bath for Rs 70, and bucket hot water available for Rs 10.

Hotel Snow Palace (☎ 22291), behind the Shangrila, has budget singles/doubles with common bath for Rs 40/60-80, or singles/doubles with attached bath and hot shower for Rs 135/180. There are also deluxe rooms with valley views.

Tibetan Ashoka Guest House (☎ 22763), further down Jogibara Rd, and down an alley beside the Drepung Loseling Guest House, has a range of rooms. Doubles with common bath are Rs 66, ground floor rooms with attached bath are Rs 170, and top floor rooms, some with balconies, are around Rs 225. The cheaper rooms are quite small and dark, but not bad value.

Kalsang Guest House (☎ 21609) on the TIPA Rd has a range of rooms, including tiny singles with common bath for Rs 45, and doubles with common bath for Rs 80 and Rs 90. Doubles with hot showers but no external windows are Rs 190, or there are rooms with great views upstairs for Rs 210 and Rs 280. You can get a hot shower in the common bathroom for Rs 10, but 30 minutes advance notice is required. Taxes are extra.

HIMACHAL PRADESH

Paljor Gakyil Guest House (☎ 21571), above the Kalsang, has singles/doubles with common bath for Rs 50/90, doubles with attached bath (cold water) from Rs 90 to Rs 110, or with hot water, Rs 132 to Rs 265.

Green Hotel, a long-time favourite with travellers, is at the end of McLeod on the Bhagsu road. Small spartan rooms with common bath are Rs 50/70, and with attached bath, Rs 150, or Rs 250 for deluxe rooms. Some rooms have great valley views, and there's a good restaurant.

Tashi Khansar Guest House, opposite the Green, has single rooms with common bath (with hot water) for Rs 80, and singles/ doubles with attached bath for Rs 130/145, some with excellent views.

Dip Tse-Chok Ling Gompa, about 300m down a path which leads off the laneway beyond the Om Guest House, has several rooms. It's a beautiful, peaceful place, although the precipitous staircase down to the gompa would make it difficult to approach after dark. Rooms are Rs 80, and have fine views down over the valley.

Zilnon Kagyeling Nyingmapa Gompa is also a possible place to stay. It's about one km from McLeod on the Bhagsu road (below TIPA). Rooms are Rs 60, and a hot shower is Rs 10. There is a rooftop *cafe* here.

For genuine research scholars and students attending classes at the Library of Tibetan Works & Archives, there are a limited number of rooms, some with attached kitchens. Rents range from Rs 400 to Rs 1200 per month.

Places to Stay & Eat – middle & top end

Drepung Loseling Guest House (☎ 21087) is popular with long-term volunteers. It has doubles with attached bath and cold shower for Rs 150, or with a hot shower for Rs 190 and a view Rs 250. The more expensive rooms have their own balcony and great valley views. There's also a dorm with beds for Rs 30, and breakfast is served in the dining hall downstairs.

Hotel Tibet (☎ 21587), a few steps from the bus stand on the Bhagsu road, has standard doubles for Rs 440 through to deluxe

rooms for Rs 600. All rooms are carpeted and have cable TV and attached bath. There's a very good restaurant and bar here.

Hotel Natraj (☎ 22529), past the Bookworm, has doubles on the ground floor for Rs 400, and semideluxe rooms for Rs 600; neither of these have views. Deluxe rooms with good views are Rs 800. There's 24 hour hot water, a roof terrace and a restaurant and bar.

Hotel Him Queen (☎ 21861), further along from the Natraj, has ordinary doubles for Rs 750, superdeluxe and VIP rooms for Rs 1000 and Rs 1250 respectively, and a roof-terrace restaurant.

Surya Resorts (☎ 21868), near the Him Queen, has standard deluxe rooms for Rs 1440/1600, or deluxe rooms for Rs 2500. A 50% discount is offered in the off season. All rooms have good valley views.

HPTDC's *Hotel Bhagsu* (☎ 3191) has a range of doubles from Rs 500 to Rs 1000. There's a good restaurant here, and the hotel has its own roller-skating rink (see the Dharamsala map).

Chonor House Hotel (☎ 22006; fax 22010), close to the Dalai Lama's temple, behind Dhauladhar Travels, has rooms from Rs 500; they are decorated with traditional Tibetan artefacts (see the Dharamsala map).

Glenmore Cottages (☎ 25010), about two km above McLeod along a track which branches off the main Dharamsala road, has comfortable accommodation in five peacefully located cottages. Rates are Rs 700, Rs 990 and Rs 1500, and all rooms have heaters and geysers.

Places to Eat

Chocolate Log, a few minutes walk down past the post office on Jogibara Rd, is an old favourite, serving western dishes such as pizza (Rs 15 per slice), various types of cakes (chocolate, black forest, banana), and cheese macaroni.

Friend's Corner serves good food and prices are reasonable.

McLlo Restaurant, above the bus stand, has an extensive menu, good food and a bar.

Hotel Tibet's restaurant has a convivial

bar and an extensive menu featuring Tibetan and Indian cuisine.

Take Out is a new place beneath the Hotel Tibet where you can buy freshly baked bread, cakes and doughnuts.

Bhakto Restaurant, beneath the Kailash, has traditional mutton momos for Rs 14, and filling noodle soup for Rs 12. It's popular with local Tibetans, and is usually only open around lunch time.

Malabar, on the opposite side of the chorten, on Jogibara Rd, is a pleasant little place serving good Indian, Chinese and continental cuisine.

Cafe Shambhala near the Malabar is also popular.

Gakyi Restaurant on Jogibara Rd serves delicious muesli (Rs 30). In the morning you can also get freshly baked brown bread here for Rs 20.

Green Hotel's restaurant is very popular, and has a range of home-made cakes, as well as good Indian and Chinese cuisine.

Om Guest House is also popular. The quite good vegie burger here is served with salad, a banana and chips, and there's a good sound system.

Ashoka Restaurant on Jogibara Rd serves excellent chicken korma. Also good is the tandoori chicken (Rs 45 for a half serve), chicken Mughlai (Rs 60), or the malai kofta.

Aroma Restaurant near the Ashoka has Israeli cuisine.

Yak opposite the Aroma serves delicious momo soup (Rs 15).

Dreamland Restaurant is a good place to go for salads (chicken, gado gado).

Hotel Bhagsu's restaurant has very good food and cold beers. However, it's a dark, gloomy and cavernous place. On sunny days, tables are set up in the gardens, and you can eat out here, a much more pleasant proposition.

Things to Buy

Tibetan textiles such as bags, *chubas* (the dress worn by Tibetan women), hats and trousers can be found at the Office of Tibetan Handicrafts, opposite the State Bank of India. Here you can have a chuba made to order with your own fabric (Rs 70), or with fabric supplied by the centre (from Rs 350 to Rs 450). Opposite is the Tibetan Handicrafts Society. The society employs about 145 people, many of them newly arrived refugees, in the weaving of Tibetan carpets which incorporate traditional Tibetan designs. Fine New Zealand wool carpets, with some 90,000 to 95,000 knots per sq m, cost Rs 1681 per sq m, while those of Indian wool are Rs 1477 per sq m. The society can pack and post purchases home, and visitors are welcome to watch the carpet makers at work on traditional looms.

Tara Herbal Gift Shop, near the bus stand, has traditional Tibetan herbal incense and books on Tibetan medicine. At the Green Shop, on the Bhagsu road, you can buy handpainted T-shirts and handmade paper.

Entertainment

There are two video halls in the town centre on Jogibara Rd. They show new releases each evening, with the programme posted out the front. Tickets are Rs 5 to Rs 10. The Hotel Bhagsu, at the end of the Bookworm road, has it's own roller-skating rink, and hires out skates for Rs 20 per hour.

Getting There & Away

Air The closest airport to McLeod Ganj and Dharamsala is at Gaggal, 15km south of Dharamsala. At the time of writing, flights had been suspended, but it may pay to check with Potala Tours & Travels and Dhauladhar Travels or with Jagson's agent, East West Travel Services (☎ 25261), above the Bank of Baroda.

Bus The HRTC (Himachal Roadways Transport Corporation) booking office is at the bus stand. There's a daily bus to Manali at 6 pm (11 hours, Rs 125) and a direct bus to Dehra Dun at 7.30 pm (12 hours, Rs 164). There's also a direct service to Manali at 5.30 am (Rs 115). The deluxe service to Delhi leaves at 5 pm (12 hours, Rs 300), and there's a semi-deluxe service at 8.30 pm (Rs 225).

Potala Tours & Travels, opposite the Hotel Tibet, has a deluxe service to Delhi, which arrives at Connaught Place at 6 am (Rs 325). Numerous other agencies book deluxe bus trips. Quoted prices at Himachal Travels (☎ 22723), on Mall Rd, just above the bus stand, were: Shimla (leaving Dharamsala at 7 pm; 11 hours, Rs 195); Manali 12 hours, Rs 250; Leh (via Manali), departing McLeod at 9 pm, arriving Manali at 6 am; then departing Manali at 7 am, arriving Leh the following evening (with an overnight stop en route) at 5 pm. The cost is Rs 950.

Bedi Travels (☎ 22359), also on Mall Rd, can book ordinary bus tickets to Dalhousie and on to Chamba. Buses depart at 5 am, arriving Dalhousie (Rs 55) at 10.30 am, and Chamba (Rs 73) at 1.30 pm.

Train Many travel agencies will book train tickets for services out of Pathankot, down on the plains in the Punjab. Generally a Rs 25 booking fee is levied. There's a railway booking office at the bus stand in Dharamsala, but it has only a very tiny quota of tickets. It's only open between 10 and 11 am, and is closed on Sunday.

The closest railway station to McLeod is at the small village of Nagrota, 20km south of Dharamsala. Nagrota is on the small narrow-gauge line which serves the Kangra Valley, connecting Pathankot with the small settlement of Jogindernagar, 58km northwest of Mandi. It's a slow, five hour haul between Nagrota and Pathankot – the bus is much faster – but if you have the time, it's worthwhile taking the four hour trip between Nagrota and Jogindernagar, which wends through the Kangra Valley affording fine views of the Dhauladhar Range to the north. To Jogindernagar, trains from Nagrota leave at 7.02 am and 2.08 pm (Rs 9), passing through Palampur (one hour) and Baijnath (two hours).

Getting Around
An auto-rickshaw to Bhagsu is Rs 30. A taxi is Rs 35. To hire a taxi for the day, covering less than 80km, costs Rs 500.

There are buses for the 40 minute trip to Dharamsala from the bus stand every 30 minutes between 4.15 am and 8.30 pm.

AROUND McLEOD GANJ
Dusallan & Bhagsu
Many travellers planning to stay long-term rent rooms from villagers in the settlements around McLeod Ganj. Between McLeod and Bhagsu, below the Bhagsu road (take the path beside the Green Hotel) is the tiny village of **Dusallan**. The first place you come to on your right as you enter the village has several rooms for rent. Rates are around Rs 30 per day, including a bucket of hot water, and some have magnificent views down over the terraced fields. A few steps away is a large yellow house which has some very good rooms for rent, and there's a hot shower here. Inquire with the friendly fellow at the *Rajpal Cafe* on the Dharamkot road in McLeod.

Two km from McLeod is the village of **Bhagsu**, which has a small temple sacred to Lord Siva, which was built by the Raja of Kangra, Dharam Chand, in the 16th century.

Hotel Triund is a brand new place on the left as you enter Bhagsu. Deluxe rooms are Rs 700, superdeluxe rooms are Rs 800, and the VIP suites are Rs 1000. All rooms are carpeted and have TV and hot water.

Trimurti has good cheap vegetarian food.

Bhagsu Cafe down near the temple is the best place in town for a cappuccino, and you can also get cakes here from the German bakery. The bakery itself is above the primary school. Here you can get freshly baked bread and croissants.

Paradise Cafe has an extensive menu and good food.

Shiva Cafe is a good spot for chai, above the waterfall in Bhagsu.

From Bhagsu you can continue to the little village of **Dharamkot**.

Om Tara Bakery in Dharamkot is run by a German woman, and you can get fresh home-cooked goods here, and good German bread.

SOUTH & EAST OF DHARAMSALA
Kangra
Tel Area Code: 01892
There is little to see in this ancient town, once the seat of the Chand Dynasty, which ruled

over the princely state of Kangra. It lies 18km almost directly south of Dharamsala, but at one time it was a place of considerable importance. The famous **temple of Bajreshwari Devi** was of such legendary wealth that every invader worth their salt took time to sack it. Mahmud of Ghazni carted off a fabulous fortune in gold, silver and jewels in 1009. In 1360 it was plundered once again by Tughlaq but it was still able to recover and, in Jehangir's reign, was paved in plates of pure silver. The temple is in the bazaar, at the end of a labyrinthine series of alleyways flanked with stalls selling *prasaad*.

The British took possession of the ancient fort of Kangra, 2½km south of modern Kangra, according to the terms of the Jawalamukhi Treaty in 1846, and established a garrison. The disastrous earthquake that shook the valley in 1905 destroyed the fort and the temple, though the latter has since been rebuilt.

Nagar Kot, the ancient fort, is a beautiful place, perched high on a windswept ridge overlooking the confluence of the Manjhi and Baner rivers. It can be reached from Kangra by auto-rickshaw (Rs 25).

The State Bank of Patiala, next to the post office on Dharamsala Rd, has foreign exchange facilities.

Places to Stay There's a *PWD guesthouse* at Purana (old) Kangra, near the fort.

Hotel Maurya (☎ 65875), near the post office, is one of several places to stay in Kangra. It has singles for Rs 100 and Rs 125, and doubles for Rs 150, all with attached bath and hot water.

Hotel Jai (☎ 5568), further down Dharamsala Rd, has rooms at the same rate.

Getting There & Away Kangra's bus stand is on Dharamsala Rd. From here it is 1½km to the temple. There are buses to Dharamsala every 15 minutes throughout the day (45 minutes, Rs 7). Kangra has two railway stations: Kangra station is accessible by road, but Kangra Mandir station lies 500m from the nearest road, where auto-rickshaws lie in wait to ferry you around the city. A taxi from McLeod Ganj to Kangra will cost Rs 375.

Masrur

South-west of Dharamsala via Gaggal is the small settlement of Masrur, where there are 15 richly carved rock-cut temples in the Indo-Aryan style which were hewn from the sandstone cliffs in the 10th century AD. They are partly ruined but still show their relationship to the better known and much larger temples at Ellora in Maharashtra. This is a beautiful, peaceful place, fronted by a small artificial lake and a pleasant lawn compound. The sculptures are badly eroded, but three crude statues of Sita, Rama and Lakshmi can still be made out in the dimly lit sanctum of the central temple. Several more badly damaged sculptures can be seen leaning against the low wall by the lake in front of the temples.

Getting There & Away A taxi from McLeod Ganj will charge around Rs 550 to get to Masrur, and the road affords some magnificent views, particularly on the section between Gaggal and Masrur.

Jawalamukhi

Lying in the south of the Kangra Valley, 34km south of Kangra, is the temple of Jawalamukhi, the goddess of light. Pilgrims descend into a tiny square chamber where a priest, while intoning a blessing on their behalf, ignites natural gas emanating from a copper pipe, from which a blue flame, worshipped as the manifestation of the goddess, briefly flares. The temple is one of the most sacred sites in the Kangra Valley, and is topped by a golden spire, the legacy of a wealthy devotee.

Places to Stay The *Hotel Jawalaji* (☎ (01970) 2280) has doubles from Rs 300 to Rs 650, all with attached bath. Dorm beds here are Rs 45.

Getting There & Away Buses to Dharamsala (Rs 25) leave throughout the day from the stand below the road leading up to the temple.

Nurpur

Only 24km from Pathankot on the Dharamsala road, this town was named by Jehangir, after his wife, Nurjahan. Nurpur Fort is now in ruins, but still has some finely carved reliefs. A ruined temple dedicated to Krishna, also finely carved, stands within the fort, which looms over the main road.

A *PWD rest house* (☎ (01893) 2009) here, with large and very clean double rooms, costs Rs 105.

Chamba Valley

Separated from the Kangra Valley to the south by the high Dhauladhar Range and the remote Pattan Valley to the north by the Pir Panjal Range is the beautiful Chamba Valley,

through which flows the Ravi River. For over 1000 years this region formed the princely state of Chamba, the most ancient state in northern India. Few travellers find their way here, and of those that do, few continue down the valley beyond the hill station of Dalhousie. The valley is renowned for its fine *shikhara* temples, with excellent examples in the beautiful town of Chamba, 56km from Dalhousie, and at the ancient capital of Brahmaur, a further 65km down the valley to the south-east. Brahmaur is also the starting point for some fine treks, including that to the sacred lake of Manimahesh, and across the high Kugti Pass to the Chandra Valley and Lahaul.

DALHOUSIE

Pop: 10,100 Tel Area Code: 018982

Sprawling over and around five hills at around 2000m, Dalhousie was, in the British era, a sort of 'second string' hill station,

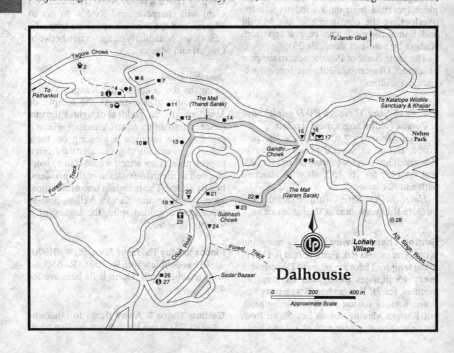

Dalhousie

mainly used by people who lived in Lahore. It was acquired from the raja of the princely state of Chamba by the British, and was a place frequented by those who could not aspire to Shimla. The settlement was named after Lord Dalhousie, then viceroy of India, by David McLeod (after whom McLeod Ganj was named). Today Dalhousie's population includes around 1100 Tibetan refugees.

Orientation

Dalhousie is very spread out; most of the shops are clustered around Gandhi Chowk, about a 15 minute walk up from the bus stand. Gandhi Chowk is connected to Subhash Chowk, also with a high concentration of hotels and restaurants, by The Mall – actually two roads, the highest of which is a pedestrian-only road locally known as Garam Sarak (Hot Road) as it receives more sunshine than the other road, known as Thandi Sarak (Cold Road). A road also connects the bus stand with Subhash Chowk, about a 15 minute walk uphill.

Be careful if you are walking along Garam Sarak between Gandhi and Subhash chowks at night. It's badly illuminated, and some sections are in pitch darkness. Bring a flashlight.

There are many registered porters around the bus stand. In the off season, they charge Rs 15 between the bus stand and Gandhi Chowk, and Rs 10 to Subhash Chowk. Expect to pay double in the season.

Information

Tourist Office The tourist office (☎ 2136) is on the top floor of the building by the bus stand. It's open Monday to Saturday from 10 am to 5 pm, and during the tourist season on Sunday until 1 pm. During the season it runs full-day tours to points of interest around Dalhousie including Khajiar and Chamba, for Rs 80.

Money The Punjab National Bank is about five minutes walk from Subhash Chowk, next to the Aroma-n-Claire Hotel. It's the only bank that exchanges travellers cheques, but there are no foreign transactions on Wednesday.

Post Office The post office is on Gandhi Chowk.

Travel Agencies Span Tours & Travels (☎ 5341; fax 2841) can book luxury coaches during the season to Delhi, Manali and Dharamsala, and can also make train and air reservations.

Newsagencies You can get English-language newspapers at Neelam Studio photographic store at the bus stand, and at Dayal News Agency on Gandhi Chowk.

Things to See & Do

With its dense forest, old British houses and colourful Tibetan community, Dalhousie can be a good place to spend a few days.

PLACES TO STAY		PLACES TO EAT			9	Bus & Taxi Stands
2	Youth Hostel	15	Kwality Restaurant		11	Cinema
4	Glory Hotel & Restaurant	16	Lovely Restaurant		13	Himachal Handloom Industry Emporium
6	Hotel Mount View	19	Moti Mahal Restaurant		17	Post Office
7	Hotel Grand View	20	Restaurant Preet Palace		18	Tibetan Handicrafts Showroom & Bengali Sweet Shop
10	Hotel Satpushp	24	Shere-e-Punjab & Amritsari Dhabas			
12	HPTDC Hotel Geetanjali					
14	Hotel Shangrila	**OTHER**			25	St Francis Catholic Church
21	Hotel Goher	1	English Cemetery		27	Punjab National Bank
22	Hotel Green's	3	Tourist Office		28	Satdhana Spring
23	Hotel Craigs	5	Dalhousie Club			
26	Aroma-n-Claire Hotel	8	Tibetan Market & Span Tours & Travels			

HIMACHAL PRADESH

About midway along Garam Sarak, between Gandhi and Subhash chowks, you'll pass brightly painted low-relief pictures of Tibetan deities, including Padmasambhava and Avalokitesvara (Chenresig), as well as script bearing the sacred mantra 'Om Mani Padmi Hum'. Close to Gandhi Chowk is a rock painting of Tara Devi, and a little shrine has been constructed here. There's a **Tibetan market** just above the bus stand.

Kalatope Wildlife Sanctuary is 8½km from the main post office. To take a vehicle into the sanctuary, you require a permit from the District Forest Officer in Chamba. There's a checkpoint at **Lakkar Mandi**, on the perimeter of the sanctuary, which has stupendous mountain views. It's possible to get a taxi here (Rs 150 return), and walk three km into the sanctuary. The sanctuary is home to a variety of species including the black bear and barking deer, as well as an abundant variety of bird life. There's a *Forest Rest House* here, but to reserve a room, you'll need to contact the District Forest Officer (DFO) in Chamba (☎ 2639; dial the area code 85 if you're ringing from Dalhousie, 018992 from elsewhere).

From April until November, Lakkar Mandi is home to an itinerant group of villagers who originally hail from Mandi, in the Kangra Valley. Their main source of income is derived from preparing charcoal which they sell to the hotels in Dalhousie.

On the way to Panch Pulla (Five Bridges) along Ajit Singh Rd, there's a small, and easily missed, freshwater spring known as **Satdhana**.

Places to Stay

Dalhousie has plenty of hotels, although a fair number of them have a run-down, left-by-the-Raj feel to them. Prices fluctuate with the seasons. It's fairly congested during the peak Indian holiday periods, and getting accommodation at this time can be extremely difficult.

The *youth hostel* (☎ 2189), rather grubby but friendly, is about a five minute walk from the bus stand. Rates remain constant all year and are Rs 20 in the dorm for members (Rs 40 for nonmembers), or there are doubles with attached bath for Rs 60 (Rs 80 for nonmembers). The hostel is closed between 10 am and 5 pm.

Glory Hotel & Restaurant (☎ 2533), right on the bus stand, has singles/doubles for Rs 75/150, both with attached bath and free hot water in buckets. Rooms are clean, if a little musty.

Hotel Satpushp (☎ 2346), south of the bus stand also offers cheap rooms. Doubles range from Rs 100 to Rs 400, with good discounts in the off season.

Hotel Goher (☎ 2253), in the Subhash Chowk area, has singles with common bath for Rs 75, and doubles with attached bath from Rs 110 (with cold water) to Rs 350 (with hot water and TV). Some rooms are being renovated, so prices may increase.

Aroma-n-Claire Hotel, on Court Rd, about five minutes walk to the south of Subhash Chowk was constructed in the 1920s with materials especially shipped from Belgium. Rates range from Rs 450 to Rs 1200. It's slightly ramshackle, but has wonderful eclectic decorations and rooms of all shapes and sizes.

HPTDC's *Hotel Geetanjali* (☎ 2155) is just off Thandi Sarak, on the hill just above the bus stand. It's a slightly run-down, old building. Rooms are enormous, and all have attached baths with hot water. The dining hall has magnificent views. Doubles cost from Rs 350 (30% reduction in the off season).

Hotel Shangrila (☎ 2134), near Geetanjali, has a range of doubles from Rs 200. All rooms have views of the Pir Panjal, and the more expensive ones have a separate sitting area.

Hotel Green's (☎ 2167), about five minutes walk from Gandhi Chowk on Garam Sarak, has doubles for Rs 400, Rs 500 and Rs 600, and a 30% discount is offered in the off season. All rooms have attached bath and colour TV.

Hotel Craigs (☎ 2124) further along Garam Sarak has one single for Rs 100, and doubles for Rs 250, Rs 350 and Rs 400. It's a somewhat dilapidated place, but it's in a quiet location with fine views out over the valley.

Hotel Grand View (☎ 2823), just above the bus stand, has doubles for Rs 800, and double suites for Rs 1000. This is a beautifully maintained place, and better value than other hotels in the same price category. A 30% discount is offered in the off season.

Hotel Mount View (☎ 2120), near the Grand View and with less character, has singles for Rs 275, and doubles for Rs 500, Rs 700 and Rs 900, including breakfast and one other meal.

Places to Eat

There are numerous places to eat, but many are high on price and low on quality. The dhabas are the best value, and Dalhousie's are a cut above the usual Indian dhaba.

Restaurant Preet Palace, right on Subhash Chowk, features Mughlai, Kashmiri and Chinese cuisine, and prices are reasonable.

Moti Mahal Restaurant near the Preet Palace also has a bar.

Royal Dhaba, on Court Rd, just off Subhash Chowk, is cheap, and portions are generous.

Amritsari and *Sher-e-Punjab* dhabas nearby are also worth checking out.

Lovely Restaurant, at Gandhi Chowk, is open all year, and there's a sun terrace with outdoor seating. The menu features South Indian and Chinese cuisine.

Kwality Restaurant, also at Gandhi Chowk, has an extensive menu, and this place is very popular.

A *Tibetan restaurant* in the Tibetan Market, above the bus stand, serves fried momos for Rs 10, and very cheap chow mein.

Things to Buy

Dalhousie is a good place to pick up a woollen shawl. Himachal Handloom Industry Emporium on Thandi Sarak has a good selection. At the Tibetan Handicraft Centre (☎ 2119), three km from Gandhi Chowk along the Khajiar road, you can have Tibetan carpets made to order. There are over 180 traditional designs to choose from. The Tibetan Handicraft Centre Showroom is on a road leading away from Gandhi Chowk that runs parallel to Garam Sarak. Here you can buy carpets, bags and purses. The shops nearby sell a range of goods, including Kashmiri shawls.

Getting There & Away

The booking office at the bus stand is open daily from 9 am to 5 pm (closed between 2 and 3 pm). There is one bus to Jammu at 10.10 am (seven hours), and one to Dharamsala at 8.30 am (six hours, Rs 60). There are several buses daily to Pathankot (three hours, Rs 42), and one daily service to Shimla (12 hours, Rs 130). Buses to Khajiar leave at 9.30 and 10.30 am, and 4 pm (one hour, Rs 12), and to Chamba at 6.45 and 4 pm (three hours, Rs 30).

Quoted rates at the taxi stand were: Pathankot, Rs 800; Chamba, Rs 650; Khajiar, Rs 420; Brahmaur, Rs 1800; and Kalatope, Rs 320.

Getting Around

From the bus stand to Gandhi Chowk, taxis charge Rs 30, and to Subhash Chowk, Rs 36.

KHAJIAR

Tel Area Code: 018992

This grassy *marg*, or meadow, is 22km from Dalhousie towards Chamba, and you can get here by bus or on foot, a day's walk. Over a km long and nearly a km wide, it is ringed by pine trees with a lake in the middle. There's a **golf course** here and the 12th century **Khajjinag Temple**, with fine woodcarving on the cornices, and some crude carvings of the five Pandavas, the heroes of the *Mahabharata*, which were installed in the temple by Raja Balbhadra Varman in the 16th century.

It's possible to do a circuit of the marg by horseback (Rs 40 for 15 minutes).

Places to Stay & Eat

HPTDC's *Hotel Devdar* (☎ 8233) has cottages right on the edge of the marg for Rs 500, and doubles for Rs 550. There's also a dorm with beds for Rs 50.

Parul Guest House (☎ 8244) behind the temple has pleasant rooms overlooking the marg for Rs 500, and a good off-season discount.

The **PWD Guest House** on the east side of the marg has very pleasant rooms with attached bath for Rs 106. Bookings should be made through the Executive Engineer in Dalhousie (☎ (018982) 2145).

Sharma Confectionary Store, near the temple, has a variety of meals, and is very busy during the season.

Getting There & Away

Buses from Dalhousie to Khajiar leave at 9.30 and 10.30 am and 4 pm (one hour, Rs 12). From Khajiar, they return at 8.30 am and 4 pm. To Chamba, they depart at 12.15 and 5.30 pm (one hour, Rs 12). If the 9.30 am bus from Dalhousie is running, you could spend the day at Khajiar, and proceed on to Chamba that evening at 5.30 pm. A taxi from Khajiar to Chamba is Rs 450.

CHAMBA

Pop: 19,000   Tel Area Code: 018992

It's a beautiful, if somewhat hair-raising 56km trip from Dalhousie to Chamba. The views down over the terraced fields are spectacular, with tiny villages clinging to the

HIMACHAL PRADESH

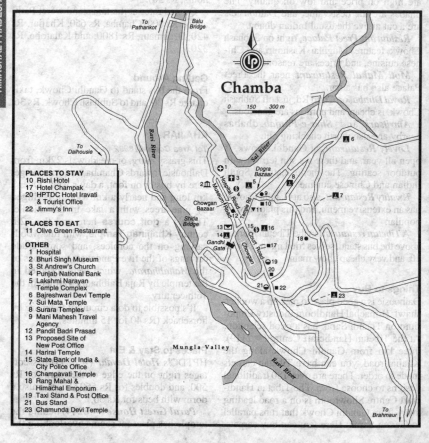

PLACES TO STAY
10 Rishi Hotel
17 Hotel Champak
20 HPTDC Hotel Iravati
     & Tourist Office
22 Jimmy's Inn

PLACES TO EAT
11 Olive Green Restaurant

OTHER
1   Hospital
2   Bhuri Singh Museum
3   St Andrew's Church
4   Punjab National Bank
5   Lakshmi Narayan
     Temple Complex
6   Bajreshwari Devi Temple
7   Sui Mata Temple
8   Surara Temples
9   Mani Mahesh Travel
     Agency
12 Pandit Badri Prasad
13 Proposed Site of
     New Post Office
14 Harirai Temple
15 State Bank of India &
     City Police Office
16 Champavati Temple
18 Rang Mahal &
     Himachal Emporium
19 Taxi Stand & Post Office
21 Bus Stand
23 Chamunda Devi Temple

sheer slopes of the valley. Chamba lies in a valley at an altitude of 926m – quite a bit lower than Dalhousie, so it's warmer in the summer. Perched on a ledge flanking the Ravi River, it has often been compared to a medieval Italian village and is famed for its ancient temples.

For 1000 years prior to Independence, Chamba was the headquarters of a district of the same name, and was ruled by a single dynasty of maharajas. The town was founded by Raja Sahil Varman, who shifted the capital here from Brahmaur.

Chamba has a grassy promenade known as the Chowgan. The town is a busy trading centre for villagers from the surrounding hills. The **Minjar Festival** is held each year in late July/early August.

The **Sui Mata Festival** is held in March/April. Sui Mata was a Chamba princess who gave her life for her people.

See the **Chamba Temples** regional highlight on p255.

Orientation & Information

The tourist office (☎ 2671) is in the Hotel Iravati on Court Rd, and there's a divisional tourism development office (☎ 4002) in the white building adjacent to the Iravati.

You can arrange porters and guides at the Mani Mahesh Travel Agency, close to the Lakshmi Narayan temple complex. Porters are Rs 150 per day, guides are Rs 200, and the friendly staff can also tailor treks in the environs of Chamba, as well as rock climbing and snow trekking. You can also hire a guide to provide a commentary on Chamba's beautiful temples (Rs 100).

You can get English-language newspapers at Pandit Badri Prasad, Museum Rd, Chowgan Bazaar.

Rang Mahal

The Rang Mahal, or Old Palace, now houses the **Himachal Emporium**. Here you can purchase *rumals* – small cloths featuring very fine silk embroidery, a traditional craft executed by the women of Chamba which dates back almost 1000 years. The stitching is very fine, and the reverse side of the cloth features a mirror image of the design – there is no evidence of knots or loose threads. Popular images include Krishna and Radha, and those of Gaddi shepherds. A finely stitched rumal can take up to a month to complete, and costs from Rs 200 to Rs 300.

You can also purchase from the showroom here repoussé brass plates and Chamba shawls, and above the showroom is a workshop where you can see the shawls being made. An elaborately decorated shawl can take up to 45 days to make on a traditional wooden loom.

The emporium is open Monday to Saturday from 10 am to 1 pm and 2 to 5 pm.

Bhuri Singh Museum

This museum has an interesting collection representing the art and culture of this region – particularly the miniature paintings of the Basohli and Kangra schools. Also here are some of the murals which were recovered from the Rang Mahal after it was damaged by fire. The museum is open Tuesday to Friday, Sunday and every second Saturday from 10 am to 5 pm. Entry is free.

Gandhi Gate

This bright orange gateway at the south-west side of the Chowgan was built in 1900 to welcome Viceroy Lord Curzon to the city. This was the main entrance into the city before the new road was built.

Places to Stay & Eat

HPTDC's *Hotel Iravati* (☎ 2671), only a few minutes walk from the bus stand on Court Rd, has doubles with attached bath for Rs 400, Rs 500 and Rs 600. There's 24 hour room service, rooms are spotless and there's a good restaurant (nonguests welcome).

Hotel Champak (☎ 2774), also run by the HPTDC, behind the post office, has large doubles with common bath for Rs 125, and with attached bath and hot water, they're Rs 175. There's also a dorm with beds for Rs 45.

Jimmy's Inn (☎ 4748), opposite the bus stand, has comfortable rooms from Rs 125, all with attached bath. Hot water is available in buckets for Rs 5.

Rishi Hotel (☎ 4343) is on Temple Rd, right opposite the Lakshmi Narayan temple complex. Doubles for Rs 125 have attached bath with cold water. The cheaper rooms are at the back, and are a little gloomy. There's also a three-bed dorm with beds for Rs 40, and a good dining hall where you can sample the local dish Chamba madhra – kidney beans with curd and ghee.

Orchard Hut is in a lovely tranquil spot 12km from Chamba. There are tents for Rs 50 per person, or very basic lodging for Rs 30. With all meals, it's Rs 175. Check at the Mani Mahesh Travel Agency.

Olive Green Restaurant is upstairs on Temple Rd, in Dogra Bazaar. It's a very quiet and clean place, with good, reasonably priced veg and non-veg dishes.

Chamba is known for its chukh – a chilli sauce consisting of red and green peppers, lemon juice, mustard oil and salt. You'll find it in most of the provision stores in Dogra Bazaar for around Rs 22 a jar.

Getting There & Away

There are several buses daily for the (somewhat nerve-shattering) trip to Brahmaur (three hours, Rs 28). To Dharamsala there are buses at 6 am, 1.30 and 9.45 pm (10 hours, Rs 80). To Khajiar, buses leave at 7 am and 1.30 and 5.10 pm (one hour, Rs 12). To Dalhousie, they depart at 6 am and 6 pm (three hours, Rs 35). There are several buses daily to Pathankot (five to six hours, Rs 55).

To Khajiar, a reserve taxi will cost Rs 300; to Brahmaur, it's Rs 400.

Getting Around

A taxi from the town up to Chamunda Temple costs about Rs 50 return.

BRAHMAUR
Tel Area Code: 01090

Sixty-four km south-east of Chamba is the ancient slate-roofed village of Brahmaur, at 2195m. It's a spectacular trip along a fairly precarious road up the Ravi River valley,

passing through the village of Holi, which is surrounded by apple orchards.

Before Raja Sahil Varman founded the new capital at Chamba in 920 AD, Brahmaur was the ancient capital of the princely state of Chamba for over 400 years, and the well preserved temples are a testament to its wealth.

Brahmaur is a centre for the seminomadic Gaddis, pastoralists who move their flocks up to the alpine pastures during the summer, and descend to Kangra, Mandi and Bilaspur in the winter.

There are some fine treks which commence from Brahmaur; see Lonely Planet's *Indian Himalaya* and *Trekking in the Indian Himalaya* for details. The Mountaineering & Allied Sports Sub-Centre (☎ 236) can arrange guides and porters.

Kullu & Parbati Valleys

The Kullu Valley and (to a lesser extent) the Parbati Valley, were always popular places which managed to retain a very peaceful and unhurried atmosphere. With the troubles in Kashmir, however, the valleys, including Manali, have largely replaced the Kashmir Valley, as they are safer places to enjoy outdoor activities, see the countryside, and hang out.

Originally known as Kulanthapitha, meaning the 'End of the Habitable World', the first recorded inhabitants of the Kullu Valley date back to the first century. The first capital was at Jagatsukh, then moved to Naggar, before the British moved it to Kullu town. The Kullu Valley, about 80km long and often less than two km wide, rises northward from Mandi at 760m to the Rohtang Pass at 3980m, the gateway to Lahaul and Spiti.

In the south, the valley is little more than a narrow, precipitous gorge, with the Beas River sometimes a sheer 300m below the narrow road. The Beas is fed by melting snow through its northern and eastern tributaries, and further south by the monsoons, which often result in floods. The Parbati Valley joins the Kullu Valley at Bhuntar, and

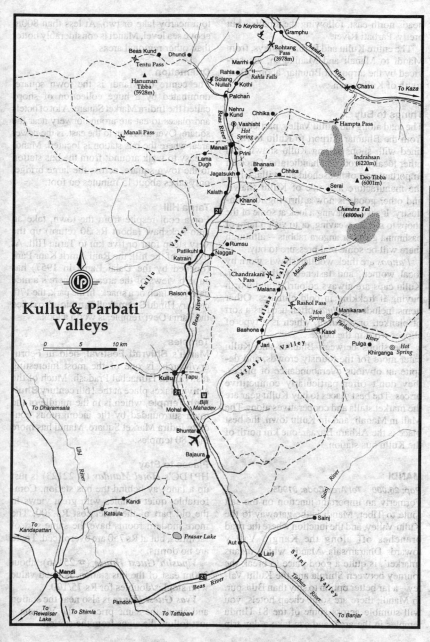

Kullu & Parbati Valleys

0   5   10 km

To Keylong

Gramphu

Chandra River

Rohtang Pass (3978m)

To Kaza

Chatru

Marrhi

Rahla
Solang Nullah
Kothi
Palchan

Rahla Falls

Nehru Kund

Beas Kund
Tentu Pass

Dhundi

Hampta Pass

Chhika

Vashisht Hot Spring
Vashisht Kund

Manali Pass

Hanuman Tibba (5928m)

Manali
Prini
Bhanara
Chhika
Serai

Indrahsan (6220m)
Deo Tibba (6001m)

Lama Dugh
Jagatsukh
Kalath
Khanol

Chandra Tal (4800m)

Beas River

Kullu Valley

Patlikuhl
Katrain

Rumsu
Naggar

Chandrakani Pass

Malana Valley

Malana River

Raison

Malana

Rashol Pass

Manikaran

Beas River

Baahona

Hot Spring

Parbati River

Kasol

Pulga

Hot Spring

Khirganga

Kullu
Tapu

Bijli Mahadev

Jari

Parbati Valley

Mohal

Bhuntar

To Dharamsala

Uhl River

Bajaura

Sainj River

Kandi
Kataula

Prasar Lake

Sainj

To Kandapattan

Aut

Larji

Sainj Valley

Mandi

Pandoh

Tirthan River

To Rewalsar Lake
To Shimla
To Tattapani

Beas River

To Banjar

HIMACHAL PRADESH

heads north-east, following the smaller, but pretty, Parbati River.

The entire Kullu and Parbati valleys, from Mandi to Manali and Manikaran, are serviced by the airport at Bhuntar, about 10km south of Kullu town.

Things to Buy
The road along the Kullu Valley, particularly from the Bhuntar Airport to Kullu town, is lined with shops selling Kullu shawls and other locally produced handicrafts. Once an important part of household and village life, the manufacture and sale of Kullu shawls and other goods is now a thriving local industry. It's worth having a look at some of the shops to see the weaving, or to visit a farm of pashmina goats or angora rabbits – although there will be some real pressure to buy.

Pattoos are thick woollen shawls worn by local women, and fastened with a *gachi*. Kullu caps are always colourful, and worth buying if trekking in cold climates. Other items include a *gudma*, often used as a sort of blanket, or a *pullan*, which is a type of slipper worn in the home.

The shops between Bhuntar and Kullu cater more for the touristy crowds, and despite an obvious overabundance of places, they don't offer particularly competitive prices. The best places to buy Kullu gear are the market stalls and cooperatives along The Mall in Manali; and, in Kullu town, the best place is the Akhara Bazaar, one km north of the Kullu bus station.

MANDI
Pop: 26,000   Tel Area Code: 01905

Formerly an important junction on the salt route to Tibet, Mandi is the gateway to the Kullu Valley, and the junction where the road branches off along the Kangra Valley towards Dharamsala. Mandi, which means 'market', is quite a good place to break the journey between Shimla and the Kullu Valley – a far better option to stay than Bilaspur. In Mandi, there are some cheap hotels, you will stumble across some of the 81 Hindu temples in the area, and can take a day trip to a nearby lake or two. At less than 800m above sea level, Mandi is considerably hotter than other regional areas.

Orientation
The centre of Mandi is the town square, dominated by a huge collection of shops called the Indira Market Square. A lot of hotels and places to eat are around or very near the square. Over the river, to the east, is the newer area, where the bus station is located. Mandi is easy to walk around; from the bus station to the town square, across the large bridge, only takes about 15 minutes on foot.

Tarna Hill
For a cool respite from the town, take an auto-rickshaw (about Rs 30 return) up the very steep four or five km to Tarna Hill. At the top of the hill, the Rani Amrit Kaur Park (opened by the Dalai Lama in 1957) has superb views of the area, and there's a nice cafe for lunch or a snack. In the park, the 17th century Hindu **Syamakali Temple**, also called the Tarna Devi Temple, is worth a look.

Temples
Mandi's **Shivrati Festival**, held in February/March, is one of the most interesting festivals in Himachal Pradesh. Much of the activity takes place at the 16th century **Bhutnath Temple**, which is in the middle of the town surrounded by the incongruous concrete Indira Market Square. Mandi has more than 80 temples.

Places to Stay
HPTDC's *Hotel Mandav* (☎ 22123) is just up a laneway behind the bus station. Comfortable, quiet doubles with great views in the old part of the hotel cost Rs 200. The more modern rooms have the same sort of facilities, but at Rs 750 are overpriced. There are no dorms.

Vipasha Guest House (☎ 25116), about 300m east of the bus station, is good value with singles/doubles for Rs 75/100.

Vyas Guest House is also near the station and about the same price as the Vipasha – just follow the signs from the station.

Along the road across the bridge from the bus station, there are a number of cheap, although noisy, places for about Rs 40/60. The better hotels are the *Hotel Anand* (☎ 22515), which is cramped but reasonably clean; the *Hotel Koyal* (☎ 22248); and the *Sangam Hotel* (☎ 22009), which offers some views.

Around the town square, there are places of all types and prices. They include: *Hotel Standard* (☎ 22948) which charges Rs 65 for a double with attached bath; *Hotel Shiva* (☎ 24211) with rooms from Rs 90 to Rs 225 – good value with TV and hot water, but a little noisy.

Just behind the square, in areas known as Gandhi Chowk and Moti Bazaar, there are several mid-range places like the *Hotel Parth* (☎ 22003) and the *Evening Palace* (☎ 3318), which charge about Rs 300 a room.

Raj Mahal (☎ 22401) is a rambling place at the back of a decrepit building at the town centre, next to the district library. Set around large gardens, comfortable rooms cost Rs 97/125, while the rooms for Rs 200/275 are considerably better.

Hotel Mayfair (☎ 22570), across the square, is a modern place. Doubles cost from Rs 330 to Rs 550, with TV, attached bath and constant hot water.

Places to Eat

Copacabana Bar & Restaurant at the Raj Mahal is a popular, open-air place where good food is served.

Hotel Mandav is worth the walk up for a good selection, breakfasts, and the bar in the next room.

The HPTDC *Cafe Shiraz*, just behind the square, serves so-so food, although their curried 'finger chips' (French fries) are not bad.

Hotel Mayfair on the Indira Market Square is a bit classier and has views.

Hotel Standard in the same area has good, cheap food.

Hotel Shiva nearby is also pretty good.

Plenty of dhabas and stalls selling just about everything are scattered around the market.

Getting There & Away

Bus As the junction for the Kangra and Kullu valleys, Mandi is well served by local public buses. The bus station – where you can make advanced bookings – is across the river in the eastern part of the town.

There are buses every hour or so to Shimla via Bilaspur; approximately every hour up the Kullu Valley road to Pandoh, Bhuntar (for the airport and Manikaran), Kullu and Manali; and along the Kangra Valley road, to Dharamsala and any place on the way, such as Jogindernagar, at least 10 times a day.

Taxi Taxis congregate outside the bus station, and at a stand on the eastern side of the Indira Market Square. A one-way trip by taxi from Mandi to Kullu costs Rs 550.

Getting Around

If you need a lift around town, or up to Tarna Hill, an auto-rickshaw is the best value.

AROUND MANDI

Rewalsar Lake

Tel Area Code: 01905

Rewalsar Lake is high up in the hills, 24km south-west of Mandi and set beside the village of Rewalsar. It's a lovely area, with some pretty scenery, and is worth a day trip out, or an overnight stay.

The small lake is revered by Buddhists because it is where Padmasambhava departed for Tibet. Every year, shortly after the Tibetan New Year (February or March), many Buddhists make a pilgrimage here, especially from Dharamsala.

Hindus also revere the lake because it was where Rishi Lomas did his penance as a dedication to Lord Siva, who, in return, gave Rishi the seven lakes in the vicinity, including Rewalsar.

As you enter the lake area, the **Drikung Kagyud Gompa**, immediately on the right, is full of friendly monks who will show you around. The **Tso-Pema Ogyen Heru-kai Nyingmapa Gompa & Institute** may be a bit of a mouthful, but it's worth a visit. Built in the 19th century, it has a little museum, some friendly monks and colourful murals.

Around the lake, there are three **Hindu temples** dedicated to Rishi Lomas, Lord Siva and Lord Krishna. Outside one of the Hindu temples, hundreds of feverish fish in the lake, and menacing monkeys beside the lake, eagerly wait to be fed.

The Sikhs have the huge **Guru Govind Singh Gurdwara**. It was built in 1930 by Raja Joginder Sen, and dedicated to Govind Singh, who stayed at the Rewalsar Lake for a month.

Places to Stay & Eat The HPTDC *Hotel Rewalsar* (☎ 80252) has dorm beds for Rs 45, and nice doubles from Rs 200 to Rs 400, all with a balcony (although most do not actually overlook the lake). The Drikung Kagyud Gompa offers cosy little rooms in its *Peace Memorial Inn* for Rs 30; more rooms will be finished soon.

Hotel Rewalsar, a few good Tibetan cafes around the Tso-Pema Gompa, and several Indian dhabas along the main road are the only places to eat.

Getting There & Away Rewalsar isn't actually on the way to anywhere, so you will have to travel to and from Mandi, whether you stay overnight in Rewalsar or not. Buses from Mandi go to Rewalsar village, adjacent to the lake, every 30 or 40 minutes, so it is an easy day trip along a pretty, but fairly rough, road. A return auto-rickshaw from Mandi costs about Rs 150; a taxi is quicker and more comfortable but more expensive at Rs 250 return.

MANDI TO KULLU
Pandoh
About two km north of Pandoh, the impressive **Pandoh Dam** diverts water from the Beas River along two 12km tunnels to Baggi. The water then joins the Sutlej River near Bilaspur, eventually feeding into the huge artificial Govind Sagar.

There is nowhere to stay at Pandoh or at the dam.

HPTDC's *Jai Tarang* cafe serves reasonable food – if it's open. A one-way/return taxi from Mandi costs Rs 150/200; a return taxi from Kullu costs Rs 450. On the main road, eight km past Pandoh towards Kullu, is the revered **Hongi Hindu Temple**, set among dramatic cliffs. Your bus or taxi driver will probably stop here to give a small prayer.

Sainj Valley
The Kullu Valley road passes the dismal little village of Aut, about 20km past Pandoh. Aut functions as a turnoff to the Sainj Valley, and as the true start of the Kullu Valley. Only a few km along the road through the Sainj Valley is the pretty village of Larji, from where there is a turnoff to the village of Sainj. Larji, set at the spectacular junction of the Sainj and Tirthan rivers, is a centre for trout fishing, but you will need a licence from Kullu. The road along the Sainj Valley continues as far as Banjar.

Bajaura
Back on the main road, 15km south of Kullu, is the village of Bajaura. It's the home of **Basheshar Mahadev**, the largest stone temple in the Kullu Valley. Built in the 8th century from carved stone blocks, the temple has fine carvings and sculptures.

Raj Guest House, about 500m north of the village, is good value at about Rs 50 a room.

Bhuntar
Bhuntar's claim to fame is its airport, which serves all of the Kullu and Parbati valleys, and the bridge across the Beas River leading to the Parbati Valley. Otherwise, Bhuntar is not a particularly pleasant place, and not worth a stop or stay. Several of the airlines have offices in or near Bhuntar. (Refer to Getting There & Away in the Kullu section for details.)

Places to Stay & Eat Bhuntar is only 10km from Kullu, but if you have an early or late departure or arrival, staying at Bhuntar may be handy. Just north of the airport gate, there are several very basic places.

The *Ratan Guest House*, the *Beas Valley Guest House* and the *Airlines Hotel* are all about Rs 70 a room.

Near the bridge to the Parbati Valley, about 500m towards Kullu, there are some places in the middle range with TV, hot water, and modern rooms.

The *Hotel Sunbeam* (☎ 5190) has singles/doubles for Rs 150/250. The *Hotel Trans Shiva* (☎ 65623) has rooms from Rs 300.

The *Hotel Amit* (☎ 65123) has rooms from Rs 200 to Rs 500.

Hotel Airport-End, one of the better places, is opposite the airport entrance. It has clean but noisy rooms for a negotiable Rs 250.

Around the airport entrance and in the streets, several dhabas serve basic food, and some have great fresh fruit juices. Otherwise, any of the reasonable hotels have fairly good restaurants.

Getting There & Away As the regional airport and the junction for the Parbati Valley, Bhuntar is well served by buses, which leave from outside the airport entrance. Most buses go to Kullu, where you may have to change for another bus for places further north. Some direct buses do go as far north as Manali, and as far south as Chandigarh. All buses between Manali and any place south of Kullu stop at, or very near, Bhuntar.

From the bus/taxi stand outside the airport entrance, taxis can take you to just about anywhere. To Kullu, it costs Rs 80; to Mandi, Rs 480; and to Manali, Rs 425.

KULLU
Pop: 16,000   Tel Area Code: 01902
At an altitude of 1200m, Kullu is the district headquarters of the valley but is not the main tourist centre – that honour goes to Manali. Kullu is reasonably set up with hotels and other facilities, and is not a bad place, especially around Dhalpur, but many visitors don't bother to stay long in Kullu as there are nicer places around the valleys.

Orientation
Kullu is small enough to walk around. The maidan (field) area at Dhalpur, where Kullu's festivals are held, is the nicest part of town. The 'centre' of town is probably the area around the taxi stand. From there a busy footpath heads towards the large bus station area (don't take the road if walking; it's longer) called Sarwari, full of shops and cheap guesthouses. The road from the bus station then heads towards Manali through Akhara Bazaar, which is a good place to buy Kullu shawls and other handicrafts.

Information
The helpful HPTDC tourist office (☎ 22349) is by the maidan at Dhalpur. It's open daily from 9 am to 7 pm in summer, and from 10 am to 5 pm in winter. HPTDC buses leave from outside the office.

The only place that changes money is the State Bank of India, which is on the maidan in Dhalpur. It's open from 10 am to 1.30 pm, weekdays; on Saturday, from 10 to 11.30 am. This branch won't accept Citicorp or Visa travellers cheques. The main post office, up from the taxi stand, is open from 10 am to 5 pm, Monday to Saturday, but is a bit slow.

If you want a permit for Lahaul and Spiti or Kinnaur, the District Magistrate's Office is located at the Dhalpur maidan, to the back of the small Dhalpur bus stand. However, it's better to get your permit in Keylong, Kaza or Rekong Peo. (Refer to the Lahaul and Spiti or Kinnaur sections for more information.)

Temples
In the north of the town, the **Raghunath Temple** is dedicated to the principal god in the valley. Although it's the most important temple in the area, it's not terribly interesting and is only open from 5 pm. Three km from Kullu, in the village of Bhekhli, is the **Jagannathi Devi Temple**. It's a stiff climb, but from the temple there are great views over Kullu. Take the path off the main road to Akhara Bazaar after crossing the bridge. Alternatively, take a return taxi for Rs 250, or an auto-rickshaw for far less. The temple area is now also used as a jumping off point for the occasional, irreverent hang-glider.

Places to Stay

Like Manali, and most places along the Kullu Valley, prices for hotels and guesthouses in town, vary according to the season, and, more commonly, the current tourist demand. Prices aren't too bad, as you can shop around and get a good discount. Below are prices for the high season – but they vary considerably from one week to another.

Accommodation can be divided into three areas: the nice, and more convenient, at Dhalpur maidan; the noisy but cheapest, at Akhara Bazaar, which is on the road from the bus station towards Manali; and around the busy bus station itself.

Places to Stay – bottom end & middle

Dhalpur The *Hotel Bijleshwar View* (☎ 22677), right behind the tourist office, remains incredibly popular, and good value. The cheaper rooms cost Rs 125; the larger, newer ones, with a balcony, are Rs 250. All rooms have hot water.

HPTDC's *Hotel Sarvari* (☎ 22471), a little south of the maidan and a short walk off the main road, has doubles from Rs 400 to Rs 500, and dorm beds at Rs 50.

Hotel Rohtang (☎ 22303) on the maidan is good value at Rs 200 a room, and Rs 450 for a room with four beds, but some rooms are dark.

Hotel Daulat (☎ 22358) nearby has rooms with a balcony for Rs 200 and more.

Hotel Aroma Classic also on the maidan has economy rooms for Rs 300, and full facilities for up to Rs 500.

Fancy Guest House (☎ 2681) is across the other (eastern) side of the maidan, towards the river.

Sa-Ba Tourist Home nearby is better and offers single rooms for Rs 75, and doubles for Rs 150.

Akhara Bazaar The *Beas View Hotel* is popular, so is often full.

Alankar Guest House (☎ 22785) is about the best choice. Rooms cost Rs 100/150, and dorms are Rs 35, in a nice and friendly atmosphere.

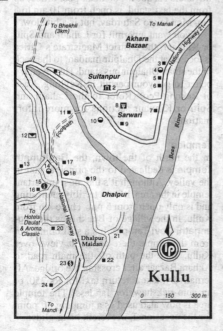

PLACES TO STAY	
1	Vimay & Sangam Guesthouses
3	Central Hotel
5	Alankar Guest House
6	Beas View Hotel
7	Luxmi Guest House
9	The Nest
11	Aadikya Guest House
13	Bhaga Sidh Guest House
16	Hotel Bijleshwar View
17	Hotel Shobla & Restaurant
20	Hotel Rohtang & Restaurant
21	Sa-Ba Tourist Home
22	Fancy Guest House
24	Hotel Sarvari & Restaurant

OTHER	
2	Palace
4	Naggar Bus Stop
8	Raghunath Temple
10	Main Bus Station
12	Main Post Office
14	Taxi Stand
15	Tourist Office & Mona Cafe
18	Dhalpur Bus Stand
19	District Magistrate's Office
23	State Bank of India

Hotel Naman (☎ 22667), with rooms for Rs 100/150, and a good restaurant, is opposite the bus stop to Naggar. Any further out than the Naman is not convenient to facilities in Kullu.

Central Hotel (☎ 22482) at Rs 50/100 is another possibility.

Bus Station Area The *Aadikya Guest House* is on the path that connects the central taxi stand area with the main bus station, and right by the bridge. Rooms for Rs 100/180 have TV, attached bath and hot water.

Vimay and *Sangam* guesthouses further back, along the main road, are OK.

The Nest near the bus station has enormous double rooms for Rs 250, or Rs 400 with two double beds in the one room.

Luxmi Guest House and the *Naravan Guest House* are just a couple of the convenient but unavoidably noisy places around the bus station for up to Rs 100 a double.

Places to Stay – top end
Hotel Shobla (☎ 22800) in the centre of town has some luxury rooms from Rs 550 to Rs 935, plus about Rs 345 for three meals. A few places south of Kullu, on the way to the airport, are in the top-end range, but inconvenient unless you have your own transport.

Hotel Vaishali is one of the best here, with doubles from Rs 650. It also handles Archana Airways bookings, and is more convenient and easier to find than the Archana Airways office near Bhuntar.

Places to Eat
HPTDC's *Monal Cafe* by the tourist office serves good meals (particularly recommended is the puri bhajee), and snacks.

Hotstuff just opposite is a great place for pizzas, soup and just about everything else. Plenty of other cheap places around the bus stand, or the central taxi stand, serve basic Tibetan and Indian food.

Hotel Rohtang has nice views of Dhalpur maidan, with a good selection and prices; it's very good for breakfast.

Hotel Aroma Classic near the maidan

looks expensive, but isn't – the setting, service and selection make it a good option.

Hotel Shobla has the best views, all the service you would expect, and good food at prices which aren't outrageous (individual pizzas are Rs 30; omelettes, Rs 15).

Getting There & Away
Air Jagson Airlines (☎ 65222) flies to/from Delhi every day for US$123; and also links Bhuntar with Shimla (US$67) every Tuesday, Thursday and Saturday.

Bus Kullu has a large, busy bus station, with timetables displayed in English, and an advance-booking system. The bus stop at the Dhalpur maidan is only good if you're going to nearby places to the south, such as Bhuntar, and, maybe, the Parbati Valley, but these buses may be full by the time they get to Dhalpur from the main Kullu bus station. For any bus out of Kullu, it is better to go to the large station, and get a seat or ticket as soon as you can.

Along the Kullu and Parbati valleys, there are several daily public buses to Mandi – or take any bus going to Shimla or Delhi; to Shimla, there are four buses each day; to Manikaran, a bus leaves every 30 minutes or so, or take a bus to Bhuntar and change there; and there is a bus every 15 or 20 minutes along the main road on the western side of the Beas River between Kullu and Manali. To Naggar, there is a bus stop in Akhara Bazaar, about two km north of the main bus station. Buses to Naggar leave there every few hours.

There are three public buses every day (one overnight) to Dharamsala; and to Bajaura, Aut and the Sainj Valley, as far as Banjar, buses leave every hour or so. Regular daily express public buses go to Delhi (14 hours; Rs 200). These go via Chandigarh. Direct daily buses to Chandigarh also leave several times a day.

The HPTDC runs daily buses in season from its office in Dhalpur to Dharamsala (Rs 200), Manali (Rs 75), Shimla (Rs 200), Delhi (Rs 375) and Chandigarh (Rs 250).

Bookings can be made in advance at the tourist office.

Travel agencies in Kullu sell tickets for deluxe private buses 'from Kullu', but these are just really part of the trips from Manali organised by bus companies in Manali.

Taxi Taxis from Kullu to Manali cost Rs 550 via the normal, quicker National Highway 21 (on the western side of the river), or more if you take the slower, but more scenic, route via Naggar. Long-distance taxis can be taken to Mandi for Rs 550; to Chandigarh, Rs 2200; to Delhi, Rs 4000; to Dharamsala and to Shimla, Rs 2000.

The Kullu Taxi Operators' Union (☎ 22332) is just north of the Dhalpur maidan. It also offers three hour local sightseeing tours (Rs 450) to nearby temples and the inevitable Kullu shawl factory. The minimum charge is Rs 35; the charge for waiting is Rs 40 per hour; and prices are fixed. To the airport, the set price is Rs 80.

Getting Around

An auto-rickshaw is handy to get around, particularly if you have some heavy gear, or want to visit the nearby temples. From Dhalpur to the bus station should cost about Rs 10, or to the airport at Bhuntar, Rs 40.

PARBATI VALLEY
Jari

Jari is halfway along the Parbati Valley – about 19km from Bhuntar. It has recently been developed to cater for the hippie crowd who have spilled over from Manikaran, or who prefer Jari's peace and cheap rooms.

There are several cheap, friendly, basic places to stay:

Om Shiun Guest House (☎ 73202) has doubles/triples, but some have no windows, for Rs 50/100.

Roman Guest House, at about the same price as the Om Shiun, is OK.

Krishna Guest House is a little cheaper.

Ratna and **Village** guesthouses, other converted family homes, are further back from the main road, far quieter, more relaxed and cost about Rs 50 per person.

Deepak Restaurant on the main road is the best and most popular place for food.

Rooftop Cafe on top of the Om Shiun Guest House has great views.

Parbati Valley buses will stop in Jari if required. A one-way taxi from Kullu to Jari is Rs 325.

Kasol

Kasol is another tiny village along the Parbati Valley road which has become a hangout. It's very pretty, in a lovely setting among pines and streams with some trout. The village is actually divided into 'Old Kasol', on the Bhuntar side of the bridge, and 'New Kasol', on the Manikaran side.

Rainbow Cafe & Guest House in New Kasol attracts the most foreigners. It has a few rooms for Rs 60 a double, and serves western food and eastern 'herbs' all day. Others stay in rooms at the back of village shops and homes.

Manikaran
Tel Area Code: 01902

Famous for its hot springs, which apparently cure anything from rheumatism to bronchitis, and are hot enough to boil rice, Manikaran is another place where many foreigners have forgotten to leave. Manikaran means 'jewel from the ear' in Sanskrit. According to the local legend, a giant snake took earrings from Parvati while she was bathing and then snorted them through its nose to create spaces where the hot springs spewed forth.

The town is split in two, over both sides of the very loud Parbati River. Almost all of the guesthouses, places to eat and temples are on the northern side, where no vehicles are allowed. The first bridge you see as you approach from Bhuntar is a footbridge which leads to the hot springs under the enormous Sikh temple, and then out into the village. The second bridge is at the end of the Parbati Valley road, where there is a taxi and bus stand. There is no place to change money in Manikaran; the nearest bank is in Kullu town.

Temples The town is revered by followers of the Hindu and Sikh religions. The Hindu temple **Shri Ramchander** dominates the centre of the town. It's a quiet place where you can discreetly have a look around. Indian sadhus and western freaks huddle around outside the temple trying to get some sunshine. As you enter Manikaran, you cannot escape the extraordinary sight of the **Shri Guru Nanak Dev Ji** Sikh gurdwara.

Baths There are three alternatives: the hot baths (separate for men and women) under the Sikh temple; for a 20 minute bath, the Hotel Parvati charges Rs 15 for one person or Rs 20 for two; or there are baths in most local guesthouses.

Places to Stay Like the rest of the region, prices vary according to demand.

HPTDC's *Hotel Parvati* (☎ 738235) has clean doubles at Rs 300, which is not good value around here.

Sharma Guest House has good value doubles for Rs 50. It is close to the first footbridge – follow the signs around the village.

Padha Guest House (☎ 748228) nearby is of a similar standard. It charges Rs 60 a double, and has a balcony overlooking the loud river.

Places to Eat Manikaran is now set up for short and long-term foreigners.

Hot Spring serves delicious pizzas. *O-Rest* does similar food, and is popular. *Holy Palace* has reasonable Italian and Israeli food. *SSMP* and *Shiva Restaurant* are nearer the gurdwara.

Getting There & Away Buses between Kullu and Manikaran leave every 30 minutes or so, or, alternatively, take a regular bus going to Bhuntar, and catch another on to Manikaran. Buses link Manikaran with Manali six times a day (Rs 35). Another option is a day trip from Manali on a tourist bus for Rs 140, which stops off at Kasol for a quick look, on the way.

A return taxi from Manali to Manikaran

will cost Rs 900. A fixed-price taxi from the taxi stand at the end of the road into Manikaran will cost Rs 350 to Bhuntar (one way), and Rs 400 to Kullu (one way).

Around the Parbati Valley

From Manikaran, a well defined trail leads to the village of **Pulga** (four to five hours). The next stage continues on up the Parbati Valley to the hot springs at **Khirganga**, where Siva sat and meditated for 2000 years. Here there are a number of tea houses to spend the night before returning directly to Manikaran in one long stage. Porters and guides can be hired in Manikaran.

On the other side of the river from Jari is the interesting Malana Valley. **Malana** (2652m) can be reached in a full day trek from Jari. There are about 500 people in Malana and they speak a peculiar dialect with strong Tibetan elements. It's an isolated village with its own system of government and a caste structure so rigid that it's forbidden for visitors to touch either the people or any of their possessions. It's very important to respect this custom; wait at the edge of the village for an invitation to enter.

KULLU TO MANALI

There are a number of interesting things to see along both sides of the 42km valley between Kullu and Manali. There are two Kullu to Manali roads: the main highway runs along the west bank of the Beas, while the rougher but more scenic road goes along the eastern bank, through Naggar.

Raison

Thirteen km from Kullu, Raison lies at a particularly wide and low part of the Kullu Valley.

The HPTDC *Camping Site* (☎ 83516) is right on the river. A hut with two bedrooms costs Rs 500, and a pretty camping spot is Rs 50.

Saga Guest House is above the river in the village.

Katrain

Katrain is on one of the widest points in the Kullu Valley.

The HPTDC's *Hotel Apple Blossom* (☎ 83136) has doubles from Rs 250, and a five bed dorm for Rs 45 per bed. The hotel has great views, but is looking a bit old and tired these days.

Nangdraj Guest House is cheap, family-run and the only other place in the village worth staying at.

Patlikuhl

Patlikuhl is the largest village between Kullu and Manali, and almost exactly halfway between the two towns.

Beas River Guest House near the bridge is one of the few places to stay. Doubles cost Rs 50.

Avtar Guest House (☎ 83271) has similar basic facilities for Rs 75 a room. Being so close to the lovely village of Naggar, just across the river, there seems little or no need to stay at Patlikuhl.

Travellers have reported that the State Bank of Potalia at Patlikuhl is a good place to change travellers cheques. In fact, if you have anything but Thomas Cook and American Express, this bank may be the only place in the Kullu Valley, including Manali, that will change your travellers cheques.

Naggar
Tel Area Code: 01902

Naggar is a lovely little village, set on a hill and surrounded by forests. Naggar can be visited in a day trip from Manali or Kullu, but if you have time Naggar is worth stopping over for a night or two.

Naggar Castle Naggar was capital of the Kullu Valley for nearly 1500 years. The castle, built about 500 years ago as the raja's headquarters, was converted to a hotel in 1978. The quaint old castle is built around a courtyard with verandahs right around the outside, providing stupendous views over the valley. Inside the courtyard is a small **temple** containing a slab of stone with an intriguing legend about how it was carried there by wild bees. There is also a small **museum**.

Temples The grey sandstone Siva **temple of Gauri Shankar** is at the foot of the small bazaar below the castle and dates from the 11th or 12th century. Almost opposite the front of the castle is the curious little **Chatar Bhuj Temple** dedicated to Vishnu. Higher up the hill is the pagoda-like **Tripura Sundri Devi Temple** and higher still, on the ridge above Naggar, the **Murlidhar Krishna Temple**.

Roerich Gallery One km past the castle is the Roerich Gallery, a fine old house displaying the artwork of both the eccentric Professor Nicholas Roerich, who died in Naggar in 1947, and his son, Svetoslav Roerich, who died in Bangalore in 1993. Its location is delightful and the views over the valley are great. It's open daily from 9 am to 1 pm, and from 2 to 5 pm.

Places to Stay

The HPTDC *Castle Hotel* (☎ 47816), reputedly haunted, has a good range of accommodation. The more basic rooms cost Rs 200, and others cost from Rs 350 to Rs 800. Dorm beds (10 in a room) for Rs 50 are often booked out. Try to book in advance – it is very popular.

Poonam Mountain Lodge & Restaurant (☎ 47812) is near the castle. The owner is helpful and rents trekking gear. Good singles/doubles with hot water, overlooking the temple, cost Rs 100/120.

Hotel Ragini is in the middle range. It costs Rs 300 a room, with balcony, hot water and nice wooden decor in the rooms.

Sheetal Guest House has older rooms with share bath for Rs 75/125, and up to Rs 400 for more luxury.

Places to Eat

Hotel Ragini and the *Castle Hotel* have good, clean restaurants.

Cinderella Restaurant at the Sheetal Guest House is also worth a try.

Poonam Restaurant is one of several places that caters to backpackers.

Getting There & Away Naggar Castle and the guesthouses are at the top of a steep two km path off the eastern Kullu to Manali road. To reach the castle, get off the bus at the village on the main road, and walk up, or take one of the auto-rickshaws that mill around. Buses go directly between the village of Naggar (on the main road) and Manali six times a day (Rs 9). Alternatively, just wait by the road for a reasonably regular Kullu to Manali bus.

A return taxi from Manali to Naggar Castle will cost Rs 350; a return taxi from Kullu is Rs 450. Another way is to get the bus to Patlikuhl (there are more buses along the western side of the river) from either Manali or Kullu. Then take a taxi from Patlikuhl to Naggar Castle – or even walk, but it's steep, and about five km. From Bhuntar airport, a taxi to Naggar Castle is Rs 400.

Manali

Pop: 4200   Tel Area Code: 01902
At the northern end of the Kullu Valley and the Beas River sits the ancient site, but the modern town, of Manali. It doesn't have the colonial history or charm of Shimla, nor the culture and spectacular setting common in Lahaul and Spiti and Kinnaur. But it is a pleasant, if overdeveloped, town with a lovely nearby countryside of forests and orchards for hiking, and there are good facilities for visitors.

In the 70s and 80s, Manali was very much a 'scene'. In the summer, the town would attract numerous western hippies and travellers drawn by the high quality marijuana that grows in the area. A lot of these people have moved to the nearby villages of Dhungri and Vashisht, or to Manikaran and Pulga, along the Parbati Valley. Now the character of Manali has changed considerably. With literally hundreds of hotels and guesthouses, it's one of the most popular places in the country for honeymooning Indian couples.

Legend has it that Manu stepped off a boat in Manali to recreate human life after floods had devastated the world – Manali means 'home of Manu'.

Orientation & Information
Manali is based on one street – The Mall. National Highway 21 on the left side of the Beas coming from the Kullu Valley becomes the busy, noisy Mall, which is not nearly as charming as its namesake in Shimla. For tourist information go to the HPTDC Tourist Reception Centre, which is the small, white hut, under the Hotel Kunzam. Open from 10 am to 5 pm in summer (fewer hours in winter), the Tourist Reception Centre should not be confused with the far larger HPTDC Tourism Marketing Office (☎ 52116) next door. This office sells bus tickets for HPTDC buses and makes reservations for HPTDC skiing courses, and hotels. The Marketing Office also has a useful noticeboard for the use of visitors.

Travel Agencies Of the many travel agencies in Manali, the following places, run by locals, are reliable, have been long established, and organise their own tours:

Antrek Tours
    Manu Market (☎ 52292), which specialises in rock climbing and skiing
Chandra Trekkers & Expeditions
    The Mall, near UCO Bank (☎ 85269), for trekking
Druk Expeditions
    Model Town, a little west of the Gozy Restaurant (☎ 53135), for trekking and mountaineering
Himalayan Adventurers
    The Mall, next to the UCO Bank (☎ 53050), for trekking and rafting
Himalayan Journeys
    The Mall, near the State Bank of India (☎ 52365), for just about anything
North Face Adventure Tours
    The Mall, near the Mount View Restaurant (☎ 52441), for paragliding and skiing
Snowbird Adventures
    Manu Market (☎ 52586), for trekking, mountain-bike trekking and skiing

Dhungri Temple
The Dhungri or Hadimba Temple is a four storey wooden building in the middle of a

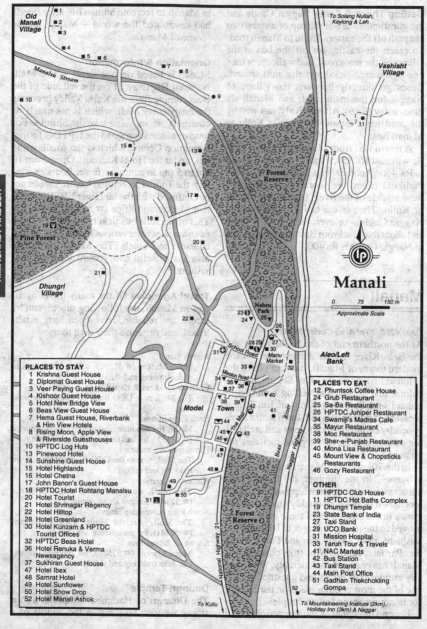

Manali

Approximate Scale
0   75   150 m

PLACES TO STAY
1 Krishna Guest House
2 Diplomat Guest House
3 Veer Paying Guest House
4 Kishoor Guest House
5 Hotel New Bridge View
6 Beas View Guest House
7 Hema Guest House, Riverbank & Him View Hotels
8 Rising Moon, Apple View & Riverside Guesthouses
10 HPTDC Log Huts
13 Pinewood Hotel
14 Sunshine Guest House
15 Hotel Highlands
16 Hotel Chetna
17 John Banon's Guest House
18 HPTDC Hotel Rohtang Manalsu
20 Hotel Tourist
21 Hotel Shrinagar Regency
22 Hotel Hilltop
28 Hotel Greenland
30 Hotel Kunzam & HPTDC Tourist Offices
32 HPTDC Beas Hotel
36 Hotel Renuka & Verma Newsagency
37 Sukhiran Guest House
47 Hotel Ibex
48 Samrat Hotel
49 Hotel Sunflower
50 Hotel Snow Drop
52 Hotel Manali Ashok

PLACES TO EAT
12 Phuntsok Coffee House
24 Grub Restaurant
25 Sa-Ba Restaurant
26 HPTDC Juniper Restaurant
34 Swamiji's Madras Cafe
35 Mayur Restaurant
38 Moc Restaurant
39 Sher-e-Punjab Restaurant
45 Mona Lisa Restaurant
45 Mount View & Chopsticks Restaurants
46 Gozy Restaurant

OTHER
9 HPTDC Club House
11 HPTDC Hot Baths Complex
19 Dhungri Temple
23 State Bank of India
24 Taxi Stand
29 UCO Bank
31 Mission Hospital
33 Tarun Tour & Travels
41 NAC Markets
42 Bus Station
43 Taxi Stand
44 Main Post Office
51 Gadhan Thekchoking Gompa

Old Manali Village

Manalsu Stream

Forest Reserve

Pine Forest

Dhungri Village

To Solang Nullah, Keylong & Leh

Vashisht Village

Aleo/Left Bank

Nehru Park

School Road

Mission Road

Manu Market

Model Town

The Mall

Beas River

Naggar Highway

Forest Reserve

National Highway 21

To Kullu

To Mountaineering Institute (2km), Holiday Inn (3km) & Naggar

HIMACHAL PRADESH

forested parkland, known as the Dhungri Van Vihar. Erected in 1553, the temple is dedicated to the goddess Hadimba. According to a local legend, Bhima killed the evil Hadimb, and married his sister Hadimba. She then became a goddess, who is worshipped at times of disaster. The temple has intricate carvings of dancers and characters from various Hindu stories, and horns of bulls and other animals decorate the walls. It is a very popular picnic spot for Indian tourists. Every May, there is a major festival at the temple.

On foot, follow the sign to the temple from the road out to the HPTDC Log Huts. Alternatively, walk past the Hotel Hilltop towards the Hotel Shrinagar Regency or the monstrous Hadimba Palace, through the apple orchards and past dozens of empty concrete guesthouses. It is an easy 20 minute walk; if you need directions, ask a local. A new road now goes all the way to the entrance of the park, near the temple, so a taxi or auto-rickshaw is another option.

Gadhan Thekchokling Gompa
Built by Tibetan refugees in the late 1960s, the gompa has some brightly coloured frescoes and a mid-size Buddhist statue. On the outside wall there is a list of Tibetan martyrs killed during the Chinese occupation from 1987 to 1989. The gompa, open from 6 am to 7 pm, dominates the 'Tibetan area' around the bottom of The Mall.

Old Manali
The original settlement of Manali is situated about three km north-west of the current 'new' Manali. Old Manali is a lovely area of old guesthouses and orchards, where livestock wander at will. Past most guesthouses, the small **Manu Maharishi Temple** is where Manu meditated after he arrived in the area. To get to Old Manali, follow the road to the left at the top of The Mall and follow the signs – the village is across the bridge, and up the left hand road.

Markets
The Tibetan market, spread around the back of the Hotel Ibex, is a bit lifeless, but has many stalls selling shawls and other woollen clothes, and souvenirs – and it offers more choice and better prices than in Leh. Around the bus station, there are a few more stalls, and the NAC Markets, at the back of the bus station, have souvenir stalls and some travel agencies. The older Manu Market, along the eastern side of The Mall, has plenty of travel agencies, hairdressers, dhabas, and a good vegetable market.

Activities
Rafting Some basic rafting is available along the Beas River. Trips generally start at Mohal, halfway between the Bhuntar airport and Kullu town, and go onto Bajaura, a few km south of Kullu town – a total distance of about 10km.

The rafting season on the Beas generally lasts from May to mid-June, and, depending on the monsoon, from mid-September to mid-October. Himalayan Adventurers offer one day trips for about Rs 1250 per person, and Snowbird Adventures charges Rs 700.

Paragliding In summer, paragliding can be organised on the slopes of Solang Nullah, north of Manali, by the Himalayan Eagle Paragliding School (run by North Face Adventure Tours), Himalayan Adventurers, and Snowbird Adventures. Snowbird runs a one day course for Rs 650 per person; a week-long beginners' course, which costs Rs 4200; and a two week course for US$420. These prices include accommodation (if applicable), food, equipment and a guide, but not transport.

Skiing Skiing for beginners is possible at Solang Nullah from January to March; the later the better, because January is very cold. Refer to the section on Solang Nullah, in Around Manali, for details of courses there. Courses and tours can be arranged there, or through Manali-based agencies listed earlier in this section. Skiing in summer, between April and June, is possible at Rohtang Pass, north of Manali. This has not been developed yet, and involves camping and skiing in generally rugged conditions. Ski gear can be rented from Snowbird Adventures, the Mountaineering Institute (see below), and North Face Adventure Tours. All the gear you'll need for a day's skiing will cost about Rs 250.

Helicopter skiing can be organised through Himalayan Journeys, if you have the money, experience and courage.

Mountaineering Institute & Allied Sports

The institute (☎ 52342) is located about three km south of The Mall, not far from the Hotel Manali Ashok.

The institute runs basic and advanced courses in mountaineering, rock climbing, skiing (refer to the Solang Nullah section for more details on its skiing courses), trekking and water sports. A prospectus is available from the institute for Rs 5.

Organised Tours

Tours are organised by the HPTDC Tourism Marketing Office, where you buy tickets, and by local private bus companies. They may be touristy, but are often the cheapest and easiest way to visit some local places, especially if you're on your own and you can't share the cost of a taxi.

Each bus agency offers four identical trips. One is to Rohtang Pass (3978m) to feel some snow, via Nehru Kund (lake), Kothi and Marrhi for views, for Rs 145 per person. The second is to the village of Naggar, to visit the castle and art gallery, stopping at the Jagatsukh temples, with a side trip to Solang Nullah, for Rs 130. The third is along Parbati Valley, as far as Manikaran, stopping at Vaishno Temple, and maybe even to an angora rabbit farm, for Rs 175. The fourth is a local trip to the Dhungri Temple, and Vashisht, and not much else – all of which you can walk to easily.

Places to Stay

Prices are listed in hotel receptions, and are fixed by the government. Nevertheless, many places offer 'off-season discounts' or drop their prices if things are slack. Some charge an arbitrary 10% luxury tax.

Places to Stay – bottom end

Budget accommodation can be easily found in the nearby villages of Old Manali, Vashisht (see Around Manali section) and Dhungri – there are few cheap places in Manali itself.

Manali The *Sukhiran Guest House* (☎ 52178) at the back of The Mall remains one of the best value places in Manali. They'll charge you Rs 150 a double, with some dorm beds (eight in a room) available for Rs 30. A bucket of hot water is available for a little more.

Hotel Greenland (☎ 52122) at the top of The Mall is popular, clean and convenient for about Rs 200 to Rs 250 a room.

Hotel Renuka (☎ 52309) further down in The Mall has good singles/doubles for Rs 200/300, with hot water and balcony.

Samrat Hotel (☎ 52356) past the Hotel Ibex has doubles from Rs 350.

Sunflower (☎ 52419) and *Snow Drop*, in the Tibetan area near the gompa, offer clean, airy rooms in the range of Rs 100 to Rs 150. There are numerous basic guesthouses in the vicinity.

Old Manali The road to Old Manali starts to the left of the fork at the top of The Mall. At the bridge, just follow the signs advertising places to stay.

Near the HPTDC Club House are: *Hotel Riverbank* at about Rs 300 a double; *Hotel Him View*, with good value rooms from Rs 75; and the *Hema Guest House* for up to Rs 350 a double.

At the village itself are: *Hotel New Bridge View* with rooms from Rs 100; the *Veer Paying Guest House*, charging Rs 150 for a double with attached bath; the *Kishoor Guest House* with a nice garden setting for about the same; the nearby *Diplomat Guest House*, which has good views; and the *Beas View Guest House*.

Krishna Guest House, further on, is pleasant and run by a nice family. Rooms cost a reasonable Rs 75/120.

Dhungri A newer, alternative hangout to Old Manali and Vashisht, Dhungri village is an easy two km from The Mall. Old village family homes have been converted to guesthouses with cheap rooms and share bathrooms.

Freedom Paying Guest House costs Rs 100 a double.

Deodar Retreat has very basic rooms for a bit less.

Scenic Cottage is probably the best value from the small selection for the same price. More places are being built. (Refer to the Dhungri Temple section for more details on how to get here.)

Places to Stay – middle
A lot of the mid-range places are new concrete hotels all lined up in the charmless, uninspiring 'suburb' called Model Town, about halfway along The Mall, and one block to the west. Each hotel offers almost identical facilities – usually including TV and hot water – for an almost identical price of Rs 350/450 for a single/double, in season. But this is a good area for off-season bargains; many places offer rooms at half the normal price. Of the dozens to choose from, some of the better hotels (close to the post office) are: the *Mona Lisa* (☎ 52447), the *Hotel Shishar* (☎ 52745), the *Lhasa Hotel* (☎ 52134) and the *Premier Hotel* (☎ 52473).

Most of the other places in this range are on the main road between Manali and Old Manali, catering mainly for the Indian family and honeymoon market. There are dozens of places, all of which offer TV, hot water and, often, some seclusion in lovely gardens. Some of the best include:

Hotel Tourist (☎ 52297), where rooms with balcony cost from Rs 400 to Rs 850.

John Banon's Guest House (☎ 52335), in an old Raj building, has clean, large rooms for Rs 500 plus – not to be confused with the super swish, very expensive Banon Resorts nearby.

Sunshine Guest House (☎ 52320), in another older building, has a nice lawn, and rooms from Rs 250 to Rs 400.

Hotel Highlands (☎ 52399) further up has rooms from Rs 250 to Rs 450.

Other good choices in the area include:

Pinewood Hotel (☎ 52118) has rooms form Rs 550 to Rs 800, and is also run by the Banon family.

Hotel Chetna (☎ 52245) has lovely views of the pine forest and rooms from Rs 500 to Rs 700.

The HPTDC runs several places – bookings can be made at the HPTDC Tourism Marketing Office on The Mall.

Beas Hotel, on the eastern side of The Mall, has great views of the river, and rooms from Rs 200 to Rs 500.

Hotel Rohtang Manalsu (☎ 52332), on the road to the Dhungri Temple, is a nice place, with good views across the valley. Doubles cost Rs 400 to Rs 600.

Places to Stay – top end
Many of these places provide little extra in the way of service and facilities than the better places in the middle range, so think twice before choosing one.

Holiday Inn (☎ 52262) has all the luxury you would expect, but is several km from town. Rooms, including meals, cost from Rs 2000.

Hotel Manali Ashok (☎ 52331), halfway between the Holiday Inn and the town, has luxurious rooms with views from Rs 1400.

Hotel Shrinagar Regency (☎ 52252) in the western part of town has doubles from Rs 1400.

HPTDC's *Log Huts* (☎ 52407), just off the road to Old Manali, cost from Rs 2500 to Rs 3500 for two bedrooms.

Hotel Ibex (☎ 52480) conveniently located on The Mall has rooms from Rs 700 to Rs 1000.

HPTDC's *Hotel Kunzam* (☎ 53197) at the top of The Mall is new and has good rooms ranging from Rs 750 to Rs 1500.

Places to Eat
There is no shortage of great places to eat in the area. While Manali caters for all visitors, Old Manali, Vashisht (see Around Manali section) and Dhungri cater primarily for the budget backpacker crowd.

HIMACHAL PRADESH

Manali The *Sa-Ba* in Nehru Park, at the top of The Mall, serves western food such as hamburgers, pizzas and milkshakes.

Grub, opposite Sa-Ba serves good pancakes.

HPTDC's *Juniper Restaurant*, right near the bridge, offers a vast selection, in a good setting, but with higher prices.

Sher-e-Punjab, on The Mall, has a sterile setting, but its Indian food (as well as pizza and pasta) is recommended.

Gozy Restaurant at the bottom of The Mall has a good selection of authentic Punjabi and Gujarati food.

Mayur Restaurant, down a little alley called Mission Rd, just off The Mall, is very popular, and has cosy decor.

Swamiji's Madras Cafe nearby serves large thalis for Rs 35.

Sangam, *Meehak* and *Neel Kamal*, in the hotels of the same name, are also worth a try.

Mount View Restaurant and, next door, *Chopsticks*, both halfway along The Mall, are cosy, friendly places where you can order genuine Chinese food – and not just chop suey – as well as momos or sukiyaki. They also have handy noticeboards for messages.

Moc Restaurant, near the Sukhiran Guest House, also serves similar, but slightly lower-priced, Asian food.

Mona Lisa, opposite the bus station, is popular for its Indian and western food at good prices.

Kamal and *Himalaya* are two good dhabas along The Mall. In the Manu Market, there are also a couple of even cheaper dhabas.

Phuntsok Coffee House, Tibetan-run and at the junction of the Naggar Highway and the road to Vashisht, has excellent apple, banana or walnut cakes/pies with custard.

Old Manali The best places are over the bridge, and up the road towards the village. They are easy to find. There are several outdoor places with great settings along the river, and it's worth a stroll out there even if you're staying elsewhere. They all cater for westerners, so you'll be lucky to find any real Indian cuisine.

Ish Cafe is deservedly popular. *Shiva Cafe* nearby has good Italian food, and serves Israeli cuisine. *German Bakery*, near the bridge, offers fresh goodies. *Beas View Guest House* serves great breakfasts, as well as freshly baked rolls and strudels. *Little Tibetan Cafe* nearby serves wholesome, cheap Tibetan food. *Moondance Garden* opposite is another laid-back, outdoor place.

Dhungri The *Our Freedom Cafe* near the guesthouses serves some basic meals, as well as cooked breakfasts.

Entertainment

The HPTDC *Club House*, near the bridge on the way to Old Manali, offers some activities. For a Rs 5 one-day temporary membership, you have access to the nice, but pricey, bar and restaurant, and a library where you can read (but not borrow) English-language books. Some indoor games, such as table tennis and snooker, can be played for a few extra rupees.

The HPTDC *Vashisht Hot Bath Complex* is worth visiting to bathe in the hot sulphur water. (See the Around Manali section for details.)

The only place to find a drink is a very dingy bar in the Manu Market, or the expensive HPTDC hotels, which seem to have a monopoly on serving alcohol. There is a movie house on The Mall (if you want to see the latest Hindi love epic).

Things to Buy

There are plenty of places to buy clothes and souvenirs in Manali, particularly along The Mall. Prices are generally negotiable. Some of the better places are the Tibet Emporium, near the post office, or any of the cooperatives run by local women, such as the Kullu/Kashmir Shawl Emporium, on The Mall. For a top quality pashmina shawl (pashmina is shorn from the underbelly of the Ladakh snow goat) expect to pay upward of Rs 10,000. Traditional pillbox-style hats (Afghan, Kullu and Kinnauri) are quite cheap.

Roadside stalls spring up in the evenings, especially around the Gozy Restaurant and the bus station. The Tibetan Market has a good range of thangkas, silver and turquoise jewellery, and music cassettes.

For an indulgence, try some locally made pickles, jams and juices. Natural oils for massages and shampoos are available from a shop on The Mall that sells nothing else.

Getting There & Away

Air The nearest airport is Bhuntar airport, south of Kullu town, an inconvenient 50km from Manali. There are no flights between Manali/Kullu (Bhuntar) and Leh. Refer to Getting There & Away in the Kullu town section for details on flights that serve the Kullu region.

Bus There are two booths – open from 9 am to noon, and from 2 to 5 pm – at the bus station which provide computerised booking services. You can book a ticket up to a month in advance.

The companies which do long-distance trips from Manali (and local sightseeing tours – refer to the earlier Organised Tours section) are listed below. Tickets for long-distance bus trips can be bought from the respective bus companies, or from any other travel agency in Manali.

Enn Bee Tours & Travels, The Mall (opposite the bus station) (☎ 2650)
Ibex Travels, Hotel Ibex, The Mall (☎ 52480)
Swagtam Tours, Mission Rd (☎ 52390)
Tarun Tour & Travels, just off The Mall (☎ 52688)

Leh Several daily deluxe and public buses connect Manali with Leh from about June to late September – a little later according to the weather and the demand. This is a long, but truly spectacular, ride over two days, with a stopover at a tent site.

Kullu & Parbati Valleys Public buses regularly go between Manali and Kullu town (two hours, Rs 17). They travel along both sides of the Beas River, but mostly via the quicker, western bank (if the road has been

repaired since the devastating flood of 1995). To Naggar (one hour, Rs 9), there are six daily buses from Manali, leaving every hour or so from 9.30 am.

Along the Parbati Valley, six public buses leave Manali from 6.30 am to 1.30 pm every day to Manikaran (Rs 35).

Other Places To Delhi (16 hours), every day in summer, there is one public 'deluxe' bus (Rs 435), two overnight HPTDC buses, and usually several private buses. Private companies and the HPTDC (both for the same price) also run daily buses, in season, to Shimla (10 hours, Rs 225), Dharamsala (10 hours, Rs 170), and Chandigarh (10 hours, Rs 250). With demand, there may be private buses to Jammu and Dalhousie.

There are three daily public buses to Dharamsala (Rs 115); two to Keylong (seven hours, Rs 60); five to Delhi (Rs 215); six to Chandigarh (Rs 151), leaving in the early morning; four to Shimla (Rs 122); and five to Mandi (five hours, Rs 53).

Taxi Long-distance taxis are available from the taxi union stands on The Mall. To Leh, a taxi costs a hefty Rs 10,000. A one-way taxi from Manali to Kullu is Rs 500.

Truck Trucks congregate along the two roads into Manali, usually just on the outskirts of town. To Leh, a lift should cost about Rs 300. Trucks are not a real option between Manali and Kullu or Manikaran because buses are so regular and cheap.

Motorcycle Refer to the Leh to Manali section in the Ladakh & Zanskar chapter for details on this mode of travel.

Getting Around

The Airport For buses between Bhuntar airport and Manali, take a regular Bhuntar-Kullu and a regular Kullu-Manali bus. A taxi between Manali and Bhuntar costs Rs 425.

The official office for Archana Airways is Ambassador Travels (☎ 52110), next to the State Bank of India. Jagson Airlines (☎ 52476) has an office at shop 24, NAC Markets.

Taxi There are two taxi stands, both on The Mall, run by the HPTDC. Aanchal Taxi Operators' Union may be contacted around the clock on ☎ 52120/52135. Prices are fixed.

Three-Wheelers Auto-rickshaws, known locally as three-wheelers, go to Dhungri, Old Manali and Vashisht for very negotiable prices.

Bicycles Himalayan Journeys rents mountain bikes for Rs 125 per day. Snowbird Adventures will organise mountain-bike treks.

AROUND MANALI
Vashisht

Vashisht is a lovely little village with hot springs, high up the mountainside, about four km from The Mall by road. There is a decaying temple in the village dedicated to Vashisht Muni and Lord Rama.

The footpath and road to Vashisht go straight past the HPTDC Vashisht Hot Baths Complex, open every day from 7 am to 7 pm. A 30 minute soak in a private pool costs Rs 40 a single, Rs 50 a double, and Rs 10 for every extra person. A towel costs an extra Rs 2. The common public baths (separate areas for men and women) in the Vashisht village are free, but do not look very hygienic. These baths are open from 5 am to 9 pm every day.

Places to Stay Vashisht is a popular place for long-term budget travellers, who are attracted by its cheap facilities, great setting, and the availability of locally grown 'horticultural products'.

Dharma, a bit of a walk behind the temple, and the *Amrit*, *Dolnath* and *Kalptaru* guesthouses all offer very similar, no-frills, older-style accommodation, usually with share bathroom, for about Rs 60 a room.

Prachi Hotel & Restaurant is newer and also serves fresh trout.

Sanam and *Janata*, down the road from the village, have basic rooms from Rs 60.

New Surabhi has nice rooms and a *real* bath with hot water for Rs 350.

Hotel Bhrigu and the *Hotel Valley View* next door, offer good rooms, and great views, for Rs 250 a room.

Places to Eat The *cafe* at the HPTDC Hot Baths Complex serves hot and cold drinks, and a selection of pretty good Chinese and Indian food.

Rose Garden Inn, next door, with great views, has pricey, but delicious, Italian and other 'continental' food.

Hari Om Cafe Bijurah in the village is popular for its snacks.

Super Bake, next to the temple, serves wonderful baked goodies. *Kathmandu Cafe*, also by the temple, provides cheap and authentic food.

Ranu or the *Zodiac Cafe*, next to the Sanam Guest House, are good places to hang out.

Freedom Cafe, just down the road from Super Bake, serves pretty good western food and cold drinks.

Hotel Bhrigu and the nearby *Hotel Valley View* offer something a bit more upmarket, with views. The Bhrigu serves a great vegetarian thali for Rs 35.

Getting There & Away Vashisht is connected by a good road, so a three-wheeler can take you there. On foot, it's quicker not to take the road. About 200m past the turnoff by road to Vashisht, take an unmarked trail up, which starts opposite a small dhaba. If in doubt, ask a local; it is a commonly used trail, which goes all the way to the Hotel Valley View, via the HPTDC Hot Baths.

Vashisht to Solang Nullah

The main northern road from Manali to Rohtang Pass is dotted with little villages, and some hotels.

Laxmi Guest House is one of a few places to stay at Bahang.

From Bahang you can explore and admire the nearby, dramatic **Jogni waterfalls**. Nehru Kund is famous as the place where former Prime Minister Nehru relaxed in 1958 and

1960 after sorting out India's problems, and tasted the delights of a nearby spring.

Hotel Ekant, a big hotel with rooms from Rs 500, is practically all that's here.

Solang Nullah

Some of Himachal Pradesh's best ski slopes are at Solang Nullah, about 14km north-west of Manali. There are 2½km of runs, with black, red and blue routes mainly for beginners, and one 300m ski lift. February and March are the best months to ski; January is bitterly cold, and Christmas time can be busy with Indian tourists. But don't disregard Solang if it isn't snowing; the area is very pretty in spring and summer. There are several options for skiing courses. (Refer to the Travel Agencies section under Manali for details of agencies there involved in skiing.)

The HPTDC organises seven day skiing packages. These include accommodation in Manali (inconvenient if the road between Manali and Solang is snowed under), food, lessons and some sightseeing for Rs 3200 per person, excluding transport to Solang.

The Raju Paying Guest House, through Antrek Tours in Manali, offers seven to 10-day packages, including accommodation, all meals, porters and instruction, for Rs 600 per day; Rs 200 extra per day for ski-gear hire. The Friendship Hotel in Solang offers similar week-long packages.

Manali-based agencies North Face Adventure Tours and the Hotel Ibex offer similar packages, with accommodation in Solang.

Snowbird Adventures (also Manali-based) has a five day basic or intermediate course costing Rs 5000, including transport, accommodation (Solang), food, gear and an instructor. Five day all-inclusive advanced courses are Rs 10,000. A one day all-inclusive trip with some skiing and horse riding costs Rs 1000. Cross-country skiing/trekking costs Rs 1200 per person per day, all inclusive.

The Mountaineering Institute & Allied Sports runs basic, intermediate and advanced all-inclusive 16 day courses for US$220, which includes rental of gear, food and dormitory accommodation near the slopes – but not transport.

Places to Stay & Eat The *Friendship Hotel* has large rooms for Rs 300, and Rs 150 for smaller rooms with a common bathroom.

Raju Paying Guest House has large doubles with nice wood panelling for Rs 300, or Rs 500 for a room with up to four beds.

North Face offers a more basic, but still comfortable place to stay and caters mainly to prearranged skiing packages.

Each hotel serves large plates of simple vegetarian food, accompanied by loads of tea. There are several other good restaurants around the village catering to tourists, but these are usually closed in the off season.

Getting There & Away A bus leaves Manali at noon and 1 pm every day to Solang Nullah (Rs 5). A nicer way is to take the bus to Palchan, the turnoff to Solang Nullah from the main road, and then walk for about an hour to Solang through gorgeous countryside. If you're fit you can head north along the western side of the Beas River along any trail starting from Old Manali. It's about a 12km hike.

Lahaul & Spiti

Lahaul and Spiti, the largest district in Himachal Pradesh, is a vast area of high mountains and narrow valleys bounded by Ladakh and Tibet to the north, Kinnaur to the east and the Kullu Valley to the south. Lahaul is often regarded as a midway point en route to Leh and the Indus Valley, but has more to offer travellers. Spiti has only recently been opened to foreign tourists attracted to the isolated Buddhist gompas and villages.

The Rohtang Pass linking the Kullu Valley and Lahaul was completed in the 1960s. More recently a motorable road was constructed from Lahaul to Spiti over the Kunzum La. Both roads are closed because of snow for several months of the year.

History

In the 10th century, upper Lahaul was united with Spiti and Zanskar as part of the vast Lahaul-West Tibet kingdom sometimes referred to as Guge. After Ladakh's defeat by the Mongol-Tibetan armies in the 18th century, Lahaul was split into two regions. Upper Lahaul came under the influence of the Kullu raja, while lower Lahaul, across to the district of Pangi, came under the influence of the courts of Chamba. The more geographically isolated Spiti remained part of Ladakh.

In 1847, Kullu and Lahaul came under the British administration as a division of the Kangra state. Spiti came under the Kangra administration two years later. The region's trails were upgraded, and bridges were constructed along the main trading highways that linked Kullu, Lahaul and Spiti.

While the Nonos, or rulers, of Spiti tended to confine their trading activities to the Tibetan borderlands, the Hakurs of Lahaul secured many valuable trade agreements with Kullu and the towns to the south. To maintain these agreements many of the Hakurs set up bases in the Kullu Valley – a situation that has continued to the present day.

People & Culture

In Spiti, most people are Buddhists, and colourful gompas dominate the villages and village life. In Lahaul, about half of the population is Buddhist, while the other half is Hindu. In some Lahauli temples and homes, it is not unusual to see idols from both religions side by side.

The people of Lahaul and Spiti congregate into communal groups *(kotchis)*, which are then divided into smaller groups *(puttees)*. Farms, which are usually inherited by the eldest son, rely on natural springs or complicated irrigation systems, to grow their crops.

The main crops are barley *(no)*, wheat *(do)*, potatoes *(aalu)*, feed for the goats, sheep and yaks, and hops (Lahaul and Spiti is the only area in India where hops are grown). *Kuth*, a herb reputedly endowed with medicinal powers, is exported to Europe.

The main indigenous language of the area is Bhoti, which is very similar to Tibetan; there are several distinct, but mutually comprehensible, dialects. The very handy word *jule*, which in Ladakh means hello, goodbye,

please and thank you, is also used in Lahaul and Spiti.

Permits

An Inner Line Permit is only necessary if you're travelling between Tabo and Rekong Peo, the capital of Kinnaur.

Seven day permits are available from the Senior District Magistrate (SDM) in Kaza, Keylong and Rekong Peo, from the Deputy Commissioner in Kullu or Shimla, and from the Ministry of Home Affairs in Delhi. They are best obtained in Kaza or Rekong Peo. In Kaza, you will need a group of four people to apply (as it is often difficult to get a group together this requirement isn't strictly enforced); three passport-sized photos (but this has also often been waived – there is nowhere in Kaza to have photos taken); an application form from the Magistrate's office; and a lot of patience – the whole process could take up to a day.

Despite what may be written on the permit, you can stay in any village and camp anywhere along the main road between Kaza and Rekong Peo; you can travel on any form of public or private transport; and you can travel alone or in a group of any size.

KAZA

Tel Area Code: 01906

Kaza is the major transport hub of vast eastern part of Himachal Pradesh, and is the administrative centre of the subdistrict of Spiti. It is an easy-going place to spend a few days – to rest from the arduous bus trips, or to wait for your permit if you're going on to Kinnaur.

Orientation & Information

Kaza can be easily divided into two areas. The 'old town', south of the current bus stand, is a maze of little shops, hotels and houses. The 'new town', a collection of government buildings, including the District Magistrate's office (look for the Indian flag), is over the creek. The State Bank of India doesn't change travellers cheques, but may be able to exchange small denomination US bills.

Places to Stay & Eat

Sakya's Abode (☎ 254) in the new town is run by a helpful family and set in a lovely garden. Good rooms cost Rs 200; a bucket of hot water, Rs 5.

Milarepa's Guest House next door is good value, but a bit scruffy – rooms cost Rs 100.

Hotel Sharma and the *Hotel City*, both near the current bus stand in the old town, and *Ladakhi Hotel* next to the large chorten, further down in the old town, cost from Rs 50 to Rs 80 a room.

Zambala Hotel & Restaurant (☎ 250) next to the State Bank is slightly upmarket with large rooms for Rs 150.

Sakya's Abode does good Spitian food, basic Indian meals, and breakfast.

Lyul Cafe and *Flax* in the old town serve thukpa and momos. Zambala's restaurant, however, is better.

Whispering Willows in the old town has a restaurant that's more inviting than the very small, rocky camping site of the same name next door.

Getting There & Away

The Taxi Operators' Union in Kaza has no stand or office; if you want to hire a taxi, your guesthouse will find a local with a car. Taxi fares are high because of the lack of competition and petrol transportation costs. The first hour of waiting is free, then it's Rs 50 per hour.

The bus stand is in the top end of the old town, near the creek, but a new bus station will be built soon. Get to the bus early to make sure that you get a seat, or a ticket. A bus to Rekong Peo (12 hours, Rs 77) leaves Kaza at 6 am. There is a bus between Kaza and Shimla on alternate days (two days, Rs 195) via Rekong Peo; and one or two daily buses to/from Manali (12 hours, Rs 115). There are also irregular buses between Kaza and Keylong (eight hours).

AROUND KAZA
Dankar Gompa

Built nearly 1000 years ago, Dankar Gompa has a spectacular rocky setting. Once the site of the capital of Spiti, and then a jail, the gompa has more than 150 monks, some outstanding thangkas (usually locked away), sculptures, frescoes and a statue of Dhyan Buddha (Thinking Buddha). Some of the gompa was destroyed during a particularly harsh winter in 1989. Herbs growing here are claimed to cure lung and heart complaints.

Getting There & Away From Kaza to Dankar, take one of the irregular local buses directly there, or any other bus going in that direction. Get off at the village of Scihiling, from where there is a steep eight km walk (including an altitude increase of about 600m); if you are lucky, there might be a daily bus between Scihiling and Dankar. A return taxi from Kaza to the Dankar Gompa costs Rs 700; or just to Scihiling, Rs 500 return.

Ki Gompa & Kibber

Ki, the oldest and largest gompa in Spiti, about 14km from Kaza, was built by Ringchen Zangpo and belongs to the Gelukpa order. The gompa was invaded three times in the 19th century by Ladakhis, Dogras and Sikhs. It was damaged by fire, and was partially destroyed by an earthquake in 1975. A modernised head lama (he often wears jeans) leads the hundred or so monks, who spend their days training, painting or playing music.

The gompa (under restoration; donations welcome) is famous for its priceless collection of ancient thangkas, including Tibetan silk thangkas up to 800 years old, and frescoes depicting the life of Padmasambhava. No photos are allowed. There are a few trinkets for sale.

About 11km from Ki village is the small village of Kibber, also known as Khyipur. It claims to be the highest village in the world, at 4205m, although Gete (4270m), another village about seven km east of Ki, has a better claim to this honour. Kibber was a part of the overland salt trade centuries ago, and is a pretty little place. The Ladarch Festival in Kibber each July attracts Buddhists from all over the region.

Places to Stay & Eat Kibber has three small guesthouses.

Sargaung Guest House, *Parang La Guest House* and *Sargong Hotel* offer no-frills rooms for about Rs 50, and are easy to find. They also offer some very basic food. It may be possible to stay at the Ki Gompa if you ask.

Getting There & Away Some travellers have attempted to walk to both Ki and Kibber from Kaza in one day, but it is a very long walk (about 22km from Kaza to Kibber). From Kaza, head along the northern road for about four km, cross the bridge (there are signs) and then the steep road starts. The Ki Gompa is actually about three km by road above the Ki village. There is an unmarked turnoff to the gompa, but you will see the gompa clearly from the road.

In summer, a bus leaves Kaza every day to Ki and Kibber at 8 am. This will allow you time to see Ki village or Ki Gompa while the bus goes to, and comes back from, Kibber, but you won't be able to see both Ki and Kibber in one day. A return taxi from Kaza to both the Ki Gompa and Kibber costs Rs 500; to only Ki and back, Rs 300; or to only Kibber and back, Rs 450.

Pin Valley

Pin Valley starts just south of Dankar, along the Pin River. The valley is reputedly famous for its wildlife – tourist agencies refer to it as the 'Land of Ibex and Snow Leopard' – but you are likely to see little else but marmots. Along the valley there are several gompas following different forms of Buddhism to that normally found in Lahaul and Spiti. The village of **Guling** has a gompa, which belongs to the Nyingmapa order, where you can stay. The most important gompa in the valley is the 600-year-old gompa at **Kungri**, a few km from the main road down the valley.

This is trekking and camping country. Public transport is scarce, and guesthouses nonexistent, although there is a government rest house at **Sangam**. Buses from Kaza go about 25km along the valley road as far as the village of Mud. Alternatively, get off the bus on the main Lahaul and Spiti road, walk

to Attargo, the gateway to the valley, and wait for a lift.

Tabo Gompa

Tabo Gompa is one of the most important in all of the Tibetan Buddhist world, and is planned as the place where the current Dalai Lama will retire. It was built in 996 AD by The Great Translator, Ringchen Zangpo, who brought artists from Kashmir to decorate the gompa. Designed in a western Tibetan style, the gompa houses impressive murals, and sculptures. There are eight temples in the complex, all at ground level and some dating from the 10th century. A new **painting school** founded by the Dalai Lama is also there.

On the other side of the road, opposite Tabo village, there are some **caves**, known locally as *duwang*, with some famous ancient murals. The caves have been damaged over the years, but are being gradually restored. You will have to ask for directions to find them. The 1000 year anniversary of the Tabo Gompa was held in June 1996.

A few rooms may be available at the gompa, for a donation, or at the Forest Department and PWD *rest houses* in the village.

Himgiri Restaurant, near the bus stop, serves very ordinary food, but you will have little or no other choice.

Tabo is two hours one way by bus from Kaza. It's a time-consuming day trip, but it may be the only option until some places to stay are built at Tabo village. From Kaza to Tabo, take the 6 am bus, which goes on to Rekong Peo, and catch any afternoon bus back.

Thang Yud Gompa

About 13km north of Kaza, and seven km from Gete, the 14th century Thang Yud Gompa, also known as Hikim, belongs to the rare Sakyapa order. There are no roads or public transport to this secluded gompa. It involves a steep trek, and you'll need reliable directions from local people.

KAZA TO KEYLONG

From Kaza, the main road through Lahaul and Spiti continues towards Udaipur and beyond, turns north at Tandi towards Leh via

Keylong, or goes south at Gramphu towards Manali. The first main village along the road is Losar, about 60km from Kaza. It is pleasant enough, but has little to recommend a stopover. A little further on is the **Kunzum La** (4551m). From the pass, a 12km trail goes to the lovely **Chandra Tal** ('moon lake'), at about 4250m, and continues to Baralacha La, on the road to Leh.

Batal is the starting point for treks to nearby **Bara Shigri** ('big glacier'). It's up to 10km long and one km wide, and one of the longest glaciers in the Himalaya. Get off at Gramphu (or Keylong) if you want to continue on to Manali. Khoksar is desolate and regarded as the coldest place in Himachal Pradesh. Sissu, which has a rest house where you may be able to stay, is the location of the revered **Lord Geypan Temple** – not currently open for tourists.

The road continues on to Gondla, the starting point for a visit to the **Guru Ghantal Gompa** at the village of Tupchiling, a steep four km away. Founded about 800 years ago, but repaired extensively about 30 years ago, the gompa is linked to the one at Stakna, near Leh in Ladakh, and belongs to the Drukpa order. Guru Ghantal is built from wood, and renowned for its carvings and idols of Padmasambhava.

KEYLONG
Tel Area Code: 019002
Located on a fertile plain, Keylong, the capital of Lahaul and Spiti, is a reasonable place to break up the journey from Leh to Manali (although you're almost at Manali anyway), or to base yourself for day trips to nearby gompas.

Places to Stay & Eat
The *Tourist Bungalow*, run by the HPTDC, has a few doubles at Rs 300, and some dorm beds (10 in a room) for Rs 45. During the summer (June to late September), tents are also set up, and cost Rs 150 for two people.

Lamayuru (some rooms can be dark and dirty), *Geypa Hotel* and *Hotel Gang Steng* are other reasonable places with singles/ doubles for about Rs 80/120.

Hotel Snowland, in the higher range, has good but overpriced rooms from Rs 300.

All hotels will serve something reasonable to eat, or try one of the tea houses around the town. The *Lamayuru*'s restaurant is one of the better places. It has good food and music and a pleasant atmosphere.

Getting There & Away
Two daily buses travel directly between Keylong and Manali (Rs 60). To Kaza, there are irregular buses in season. The main way in and out of Keylong is to catch one of the regular buses that travel between Leh and Manali in summer. The comfortable HPTDC bus costs Rs 100 from Keylong to Manali, or Rs 600 from Keylong to Leh (plus tent accommodation and food); private buses cost slightly less; and the public bus will cost about half the HPTDC price depending on which class you choose, or which is available.

Plenty of trucks ply the busy road and are a great alternative. (Refer to the Leh to Manali section in the Ladakh & Zanskar chapter for more details on travel to and from Keylong.)

AROUND KEYLONG
Khardong Gompa
The 900-year-old gompa at Khardong, formerly a capital of Lahaul, is only four km from Keylong. Of the Gelukpa order, this is the largest gompa in the area with about 30 lamas and *chomos* (nuns). There are good frescoes, some old prayer drums, a large Buddha statue and a famous library of ancient scriptures. The trail to the gompa starts on the other side of the Bhaga River.

Shashur Gompa
Three km from Keylong is the Shashur Gompa. Dedicated to a Zanskari lama, it was built in the 16th century and is of the Gelukpa order. The five metre thangka is famous in the region. An annual festival, held every June or July (depending on the Tibetan calendar), is renowned for the mask dances performed by the lamas.

Kinnaur

Tel Area Code: 017852

Kinnaur is a district of Himachal Pradesh situated between the Shimla district and the Tibetan border. The region was derestricted and opened up to tourism in 1991. Travel to and around Kinnaur is now possible with easy-to-obtain permits.

Kinnaur is bounded to the north by the formidable Zanskar Range that provides the border with Tibet. To the south, the main Himalaya Range forms the backdrop of the region including the impressive Kinnaur Kailash Range, with the peaks Kinnaur Kailash (6050m), Jorkanden (6473m) and Phawarang (6349m), that provides an effective barrier to the monsoon rains. South of the Kinnaur Kailash Range is the popular Sangla Valley, which has been described as one of the most scenic in the entire Himalaya.

The road up the Sutlej Valley – the Hindustan Highway – remains open for most of the year. The ideal time to visit the popular Sangla Valley is either in the springtime from April to the end of May or in the autumn in September and October.

People & Culture

Because of regular mentions in ancient Hindu texts, including the *Ramayana*, Kinnauris have always regarded themselves as a distinct people of the Aryan group. Nearer the Tibetan border, Tibetan and Mongol features are also obvious. Most Kinnauris follow a mixture of Hinduism, which they gained from the area's ancient links with the rest of India, and Tibetan Buddhism. Especially near the borders of Tibet, villagers often have a Hindu and Buddhist name, and lamas continue to influence village life. Attempts by missionaries to introduce Christianity to the Kinnaur region in the 19th century never succeeded.

Barley and wheat are the dominant crops, and peas and potatoes are often grown. Kinnauris like to eat meat; tradition forbids them to consume chicken; and there is a burgeoning fishing industry around the Baspa and Spiti rivers. They enjoy alcohol *(ghanti)*, such as *angoori* grape wine and *arak* made from fermented barley.

Kinnauri (often called Homskad) is the major indigenous language, which has about 12 different dialects. One of these is called Sangnaur, and is only spoken in the village of the same name, near Puh.

Permits

From the Shimla region, you can travel as far as Rekong Peo, Kalpa and the Sangla Valley without a permit. For travel to northern Kinnaur and as far as Tabo in Spiti, you currently need a permit. These can be obtained from the Senior District Magistrate's office in Shimla, Keylong, Kullu and Chamba, or the Sub-District Magistrate's office in Rampur and Nichar. However, they are easier to get in Rekong Peo, Keylong or Kaza. (Refer to the Lahaul and Spiti section for further details on permits from Kaza.)

The only place to obtain a permit in Kinnaur is the district capital, Rekong Peo. The permit is valid for seven days but can be easily extended in Rekong Peo or Kaza. The permit allows you to travel from Rekong Peo to Kaza and back; from Kaza onwards you do not usually need to get another permit (although some travellers have required one, so check for the current situation). In Rekong Peo, you must apply for the permit in a group of at least four. You can travel alone, however, or in a group of less than four, and by any available public or personal transport. To get a permit you must:

- provide three passport-size photos – there are photo booths in Rekong Peo
- get a 'letter of introduction' from a travel agency. The Mandala travel agency (next to the Mayur Guest House) in Rekong Peo charges a pricey Rs 100 per person, but is about the only place to get a letter
- complete an application form, available at the travel agent or the magistrate's office
- make a photocopy of the front pages of your passport (with your personal details and photo) – there are several places which will do this in Rekong Peo

• take all the above documentation to the magistrate's office, a three-storey building just below the bus stop. The whole process may take an entire day

You can ignore the rules on the old forms. For instance, they state that: a) you are not allowed 'any night halt' – you *are* allowed to stay anywhere along the main road, but there is little choice anyway, and you can camp; b) you 'shall not resort to photography' – there is no restriction, but be careful around any sensitive or military areas; and c) you cannot carry any 'maps' – you are allowed to do this, but the maps aren't very good anyway. But you should never venture too close to the Tibetan border or too far from the main roads. The checkpoints between Rekong Peo and Kaza are at Jangi, Chango and Sumdo.

REKONG PEO

Up a side road from the main thoroughfare through Kinnaur are the two main towns of Kalpa, the former capital, and Rekong Peo, the current capital of Kinnaur. Both places have the most stupendous settings in probably all of Himachal Pradesh – anywhere up the road will give you incredible views of the mighty Kinnaur Kailash mountain, among several others, at around 6000m. While it may lack the charm of nearby Kalpa, Rekong Peo is probably a better place to stay because it has better facilities and transport connections, and it is where you will have to apply and wait for your permit anyway, if going on further to Kinnaur or Lahaul and Spiti.

Orientation & Information

Rekong Peo is very small; everything is within a yak's spit of the bus stop in the centre of the village. The banks here do not change foreign currencies. There are plenty of little shops around the bus stop, and up a lane to the north of the bus stop. At these shops, you can take photocopies of permits and passports, and stock up on some necessities (mineral water is not sold around here) for the trip to Lahaul and Spiti, where village shops have very, very limited supplies.

A brightly coloured gompa, the **Kinnaur Kalachakra Celestial Palace**, is about a 20 minute steep walk above the village, just behind the radio station. There is a huge outdoor Buddha statue, in an area overrun by apple orchards, and facing the mighty Kinnaur Kailash mountain.

Places to Stay & Eat

Hotel Snow View is opposite the bus stand and, therefore, noisy. It has clean rooms and hot water for Rs 200 a double.

Hotel Fairyland is 200m from the bus stop. A room costs Rs 200, and there is hot water. The views from some of the rooms are great.

Mayur Guest House, next to the Fairyland, has dingy rooms for about Rs 80. Very ordinary dorm beds, which cater for the bus crowd stopping overnight, cost Rs 30.

There are a few tea shops along the main street, but the best bet for food is the *Snow View* or the *Fairyland*.

Getting There & Away

The chaotic little ticket booth, about 80m from where the buses actually stop, sells tickets for all buses, but most people just get on the bus and pay the conductor. There are occasional buses to Powari, at the turnoff to Rekong Peo on the main road, and to Kalpa – but it is certainly quicker to get a taxi to these places. A daily bus from Rekong Peo goes to Kaza (12 hours, Rs 77) at 7 am; several buses each day, starting from 4.30 am, go to Shimla (10 hours); and there's one bus a day to Rampur. Unfortunately, some of these buses do not originate in Rekong Peo or Kalpa, so they are often hopelessly full by the time they arrive.

A one-way/return taxi ride to Kalpa costs Rs 100/150; a one-way ride to Powari costs Rs 100.

KALPA

Known as Chini when it was the main town in Kinnaur, Kalpa is the legendary winter home of Siva; during the winter, the god is said to retire to his Himalayan home here and indulge his passion for hashish. In the month of Magha (January/February), the gods of Kinnaur supposedly meet here for an annual conference with Siva. Kalpa was also a favourite resting place for several high-level British colonialists.

Kalpa is a tiny collection of narrow lanes, seven km and 600m higher in altitude up a windy road from Rekong Peo. What it lacks in facilities, Kalpa makes up with atmosphere, charm and history. The road between Rekong Peo and Kalpa takes you through a pretty area of forests, overshadowed by peaks. The walk can be shorter, but still steep, if you go straight up the hill rather than follow the road.

Places to Stay & Eat
The *Timber Lane Trekking Camps* is 600m from the village centre. It's in a great location, and has some luxuries like hot water, but they only have glorified tents, for which they charge Rs 650 per person. The whole place packs up and goes back to Delhi from October to May.

Circuit Rest House, now renovated for tourists, is far better value. A huge double room, with bathroom and fireplace, with spine-tingling views of Kinnaur Kailash just outside, costs Rs 250. It is about a two km walk from Kalpa. It is best to take a one-way taxi there (Rs 100) from the bus stop at Rekong Peo.

Getting There & Away
There are irregular buses between Kalpa and Rekong Peo. Long-distance buses to/from Rekong Peo often do not go through Kalpa, so for bus transport out of Kalpa, you will probably have to get to Rekong Peo first. If you can find one, a taxi may take you from Kalpa to Rekong Peo for Rs 100; or Rs 150, return.

SANGLA VALLEY
The Sangla Valley is also called the Baspa Valley because it follows the 95km long Baspa River. The valley is a remote area, full of wildlife and dominated by spectacular mountains.

Sangla village has a **temple** dedicated to Nagesh. From the village, you can trek about

two km to Kamru which has a five storey wooden **fort**. Kamru is a former capital of the Bushahr Empire which once ruled Kinnaur. The valley road continues to Rakchham, which means 'rock bridge'. The 44km valley road finishes at Chitkul, where there are three **temples**, dedicated to the goddess Mathi, built about 500 years ago.

REKONG PEO TO SUMDO
From Rekong Peo to Kaza in Lahaul and Spiti, there is no official accommodation. If you make arrangements in Shimla, Kaza or Rekong Peo, you may be able to stay at the rest houses owned by the PWD at Puh, Jangi, Yangthang and Morang. Alternatively, there are plenty of suitable camping sites along the way.

Southern Himachal Pradesh

Tel Area Code: 01702

There are several areas of interest in the southern regions of the state, including the old settlement of Nahan, and the picturesque Renuka Lake. If you're heading for the hill station of Mussoorie in northern Uttar Pradesh, you'll find you'll need to travel via Paonta Saheb, on the border, which has an ancient Sikh gurdwara.

NAHAN
Nahan was founded in the early 17th century by Raja Karan Prakash. Now the headquarters of the Sirmour district, Nahan is set in a pretty area of southern Himachal Pradesh, on a good road linking Shimla with Dehra Dun. Nahan hosts a festival called Sawan Dwadshi at the end of the monsoon season, when over 50 idols of Hindu gods are placed in a pool of water at a nearby temple. Nahan is a good place to break a journey, to use as a base for a day trip to the nearby Renuka Lake, and to enjoy some hiking in the countryside.

Nahan is actually built on two levels above each other on a hillside and linked by the steep main road. One level is dominated by the football ground, next to the Lytton Memorial building – this is the best place to base yourself. The other level is around the bus stand.

Places to Stay & Eat

Hotel Renuka, opposite the football ground, has singles/doubles with attached bath for Rs 75/100, but the rooms downstairs are windowless and uninspiring.

Keshav Guest House (☎ 2459), at the back of the Lytton Memorial on Hindu Ahram Rd, has good, quiet doubles for Rs 100.

Hotel Renuka has a good, small restaurant. *New Mehek Restaurant* nearby is OK.

Getting There & Away

The daily Shimla to Dehra Dun bus goes through Nahan (Rs 55), and other regular local buses also go to Dehra Dun from Nahan. About every hour, crowded buses leave Nahan for Dadahu, near Renuka Lake, and others go to Paonta Saheb. You can get off or on the bus at the Nahan bus station or outside the Hotel Renuka. A one-way taxi from Shimla to Nahan (or to Renuka Lake) costs Rs 1200.

RENUKA LAKE

About an hour by bus from Nahan is Renuka Lake or Renukaji, which is fed by underground springs. A week-long festival is celebrated here in November.

To enjoy the lake, walk along the three km circular track, or walk seven km up a path to the **Jamu Peak** for great views. You can also hire a small rowboat from the Hotel Renuka for Rs 30 per half-hour; a tour in a motorboat, in season, costs Rs 100. The lake has plenty of large (protected) fish. Around the lake there are thousands of gorgeous butterflies, a small **aviary** with local birds, a **wildlife park** (open in the tourist season) with some deer, and several Hindu **temples**, including the Parashuruma.

Places to Stay & Eat

HPTDC's *Hotel Renuka* (☎ 8339) is the only place to stay around the lake area.

Comfortable rooms in secluded gardens, with a children's playground, range from Rs 300 to Rs 550, with TV and hot water. It is worth booking ahead before you make the trip to Renuka Lake.

The *Hotel Renuka* has a good restaurant. Near the entrance to the wildlife park, several stalls have hot and cold drinks and serve some basic meals.

Getting There & Away

About every hour, a bus from Nahan goes to Dadahu, from where you can walk (40 minutes) to the lake, but some buses do continue on to the lake. A one-way taxi from Shimla to the lake will cost Rs 1200.

PAONTA SAHEB

On the Uttar Pradesh Border is the uninteresting town of Paonta Saheb. Dedicated to the 10th Sikh guru, Govind Singh, who lived there between the ages of 16 and 20, the town's gurdwara is an impressive place, situated right on the river. During the Holi festival in March, the temple overflows with pilgrims.

Inside the temple, there's a small **museum** dedicated to Govind Singh. Below the gurdwara is the **Yamuna Temple**. Rules for entry are the same for all Sikh temples: bring a head covering (or borrow one from a counter on the right at the temple entrance); take off your shoes (and if you value them, leave them at a counter on the left at the temple entrance); and then wash your feet.

Places to Stay

HPTDC's *Hotel Yamuna* (☎ 2341) is about 100m from the entrance to the temple. It is the best option. Doubles cost Rs 200 to Rs 600. The very few budget options are awful.

Getting There & Away

The daily Shimla to Dehra Dun bus goes through Paonta Saheb (Rs 72). There are other regular local buses to Shimla, via Nahan, and to Dehra Dun. Two daily buses directly connect Paonta Saheb with Delhi. A taxi from Shimla to Paonta Saheb costs Rs 1500 one way.

Jammu & Kashmir

The regions of Jammu and Kashmir (J&K for short) form part of a vast state which includes Ladakh. Srinagar is J&K's summer capital, while the city of Jammu, further south on the plains, is the winter capital. Jammu and Kashmir (as distinct from Ladakh) have been subject to political unrest since the late 1980s. The following information is intended for background only; travellers are advised to contact their embassy in Delhi before travelling to these regions.

J&K is a state with wide cultural and geographical contrasts. The Kashmir Valley is a fertile, verdant region enclosed by the high snow-capped ridges of the Pir Panjal to the west and south, and the main Himalaya Range to the east. Its population is predominantly Muslim, with a rich Islamic history that can be traced back to the 14th century. South of the Kashmir Valley is the region of Jammu. It includes the city of Jammu, situated on the North Indian plains, a short distance from the rolling Siwalik hills. North of the Siwaliks, the rest of the Jammu region is drained by the Chenab River whose vast catchment area includes several narrow valleys that extend deep into the high Himalaya. The region of Jammu is predominantly Hindu, although there are small Muslim communities in the vicinity of Banihal and Kishtwar immediately south of the Kashmir Valley.

The political violence in the Kashmir Valley since the late 1980s has discouraged most

JAMMU & KASHMIR AT A GLANCE

Population: 8.8 million
Area: 222,236 sq km
Capital: Srinagar (summer), Jammu (winter)
Main Languages: Kashmiri, Dogri, Urdu, Ladakhi
Literacy Rate: 26.2%
Best Time to Go: May to September

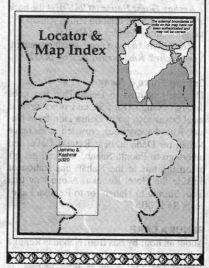

Locator & Map Index

Jammu & Kashmir p320

The external boundaries of India on this map have not been authenticated and may not be correct.

Warning
Lonely Planet strongly advises against travelling to the regions of Jammu and Kashmir. While the Indian government has not placed restrictions on visiting Jammu and Kashmir, it is still foolhardy to visit the regions particularly when there is still a danger of kidnapping. It is essential to contact your embassy in Delhi for up-to-date information. ■

travellers from visiting the region. Until 1989, a stay on the famous houseboats of Dal Lake close to the city centre of Srinagar was considered a must for anyone visiting northern India, while the treks out of Gulmarg, Sonamarg and Pahalgam were among some of the most popular in the Himalaya. Before the outbreak of violence, more than 600,000 Indian tourists and 60,000 foreign tourists visited Kashmir throughout the summer season, from early June until mid-October. Since 1990, this figure has been reduced to a handful of travellers and even these have now been 'warned off' the region following the tragic events of July 1995 when six foreign trekkers were taken hostage by a little-known guerrilla group called the Al-Faran. One American managed to escape, but a Norwegian man was murdered the following month. At the time of writing, the other four men remain captive.

In the region of Jammu, the situation is no better. There have been sporadic bomb blasts in the city of Jammu since 1992, as separatist groups have stepped up their campaigns. The town of Kishtwar has also been subject to separatist activity, and the Indian Army has actively discouraged foreigners from the area.

In spite of this, there are no special permits necessary to visit J&K. In July 1990, certain areas of the Kashmir Valley were declared 'disturbed areas'. That is to say, the Indian military and reserve police forces in Kashmir were given extraordinary powers of arrest, similar to the situation in the Punjab after 1984. However, there are no restrictions on movement in the state except the ones which were already in force, such as the ban on travel close to the India-Pakistan cease-fire line, or to areas under curfew.

HISTORY

J&K has always been a centre of conflict for independent India. When India and Pakistan became independent, there was much controversy over whether the region should be annexed to India or Pakistan. The population was predominantly Muslim but J&K was not a part of 'British India'. It was a 'princely state', ruled by a Hindu maharaja, in whose hands was left the decision of whether to merge with Muslim Pakistan or Hindu India. As told in *Freedom at Midnight*, by Larry Collins & Dominique Lapierre, the indecisive maharaja only made his decision when a Pathan group from North-West Pakistan was already crossing his borders, and the inevitable result was the first Indo-Pakistani conflict.

Since that first conflict, in October 1948, Kashmir has remained a flash point between the two countries. A substantial part of the region is now Indian and the rest (Azad Kashmir) is claimed by Pakistan; both countries claim all of it.

Since 1989, militant activity in Kashmir has increased substantially and it's estimated that as many as 20,000 Kashmiris have died in the fighting.

In 1990 the J&K state government was dissolved and the state was placed under direct rule from Delhi (President's Rule). In November 1995, the independent Election Commission rejected the Indian Government's request for elections in the province because J&K was too unstable. The Kashmiri opposition parties (and the Pakistan Government, which assists the Muslim secessionists) planned to boycott the elections. However, the elections went ahead in September 1996 and were won by the National Conference Party (a pro-India, regional party), under the leadership of Farooq Abdullah. By October Kashmir had its own elected government, ending the direct rule from Delhi, with Abdullah as chief minister.

JAMMU REGION

Jammu

Pop: 257,000   Tel Area Code: 0191

Jammu is J&K's second-largest city and its winter capital. In summer it is a sweltering, uncomfortable contrast to the cool heights of Kashmir. From October onwards it becomes much more pleasant. Jammu is actually two towns. The old town sits on a hilltop overlooking the river, and several km away across the river is the new town of Jammu Tawi.

Jammu to Srinagar

On the Jammu to Srinagar route are the hill resorts of Kud, Patnitop and Batote. The important Sudh Mahadev Shiva temple is situated eight km from Kud and Patnitop. Also on this route is Sanasar, a beautiful valley which is a centre for the Gujar shepherds each summer.

During the winter months, Srinagar was often completely cut off from the rest of India before the Jawarhar Tunnel was completed. The 2½km long tunnel is 200km from Jammu and 93km from Srinagar and has two separate passages; inside it's very

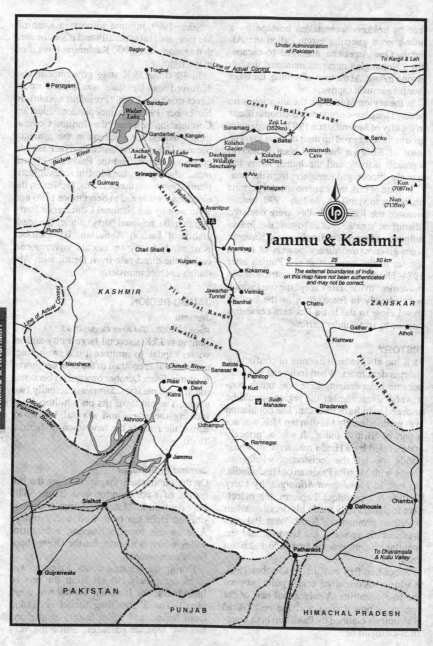

Jammu & Kashmir

The external boundaries of India
on this map have not been authenticated
and may not be correct.

0   25   50 km

Under Administration
of Pakistan

Line of Actual Control

To Kargil & Leh

Great Himalaya Range

Drass

Zoji La
(3529m)

Sonamarg

Baltal

Sanku

Kolahoi
Glacier

Amarnath
Cave

Kolahoi
(5425m)

Kun
(7087m)

Nun
(7135m)

Dachigam
Wildlife
Sanctuary

Aru

Pahalgam

Harwan

Dal Lake

Anchar
Lake

Kangan

Gandarbal

Wular
Lake

Bandipur

Tragbal

Bagtor

Panzgam

Jhelum River

Gulmarg

Srinagar

Jhelum River

Kashmir Valley

Avantipur

1A

Anantnag

Kokarnag

Verinag

Chatru

ZANSKAR

Galhar

Atholi

Kishtwar

Chari Sharif

Kulgam

Jawarhar
Tunnel

Banihal

Punch

KASHMIR

Pir Panjal Range

Siwalik Range

Chatru

Pir Panjal Range

Naoshera

Chenab River

Batote

Sanasar

Patnitop

Bhadarwah

Riasi

Katra

Vaishno
Devi

Kud

Sudh
Mahadev

Line of Actual Control

Official Indo-
Pakistan Border

Akhnoor

Udhampur

Ramnagar

Jammu

Sialkot

Chamba

Dalhousie

Gujranwala

Pathankot

To Dharamsala
& Kulu Valley

PAKISTAN

PUNJAB

HIMACHAL PRADESH

damp and full of vehicle-emission fumes. From Banihal, 17km south of the tunnel, the Kashmiri region begins and people speak Kashmiri as well as Dogri. At the northern end of the tunnel is the green, lush Vale of Kashmir.

KASHMIR VALLEY

This is one of the most beautiful regions of India but since 1989 it has been racked by political violence.

The Mughal rulers of India were always happy to retreat from the heat of the plains to the cool green heights of Kashmir, and indeed Jehangir's last words, when he died en route to the 'happy valley', were a simple request for 'only Kashmir'. The Mughals developed their formal garden-style art to its greatest heights in Kashmir.

One of Kashmir's greatest attractions was undoubtedly the Dal Lake houseboats. During the Raj period Kashmir's ruler would not permit the British (who were as fond of Kashmir's cool climate as the Mughals) to own land here. So they adopted the solution of building houseboats – each one a little bit of England, afloat on Dal Lake. A visit to Kashmir, it was often said, was not complete until you had stayed on a houseboat.

Srinagar
Pop: 725,000   Tel Area Code: 0194
Srinagar, the summer capital of Kashmir, stands on Dal Lake and the picturesque Jhelum River.

It is a city with a distinctly Central Asian flavour. Indeed the people look different from those in the rest of India; and when you head south from Srinagar it is always referred to as 'returning to India'.

The old city is situated in the vicinity of the Hari Parbat Hill and includes the labyrinth of alleyways, mosques and houses that constitute the commercial heart of the city. The more modern part of the city is situated

further up the Jhelum River (above its famous seven bridges), which sweeps through Srinagar.

East of the city is Dal Lake, much of it a maze of intricate waterways. Dal comprises a series of lakes, including Nagin Lake some 8km from the city centre. Most of the more modern houseboats are located on these lakes. The famous Mughal gardens, including the Shalimar Bagh and Nishat Bagh, are located on the far (east) side of Dal Lake.

Pahalgam
Pahalgam is about 95km east of Srinagar, at an altitude of 2130m. Situated at the junction of the East and West Lidder rivers, Pahalgam was a popular trekking base before the present troubles. The Shri Amarnath yatra endures, however, and each year in July-August thousands of Hindu pilgrims approach the Armanath Cave from this area.

Gulmarg
The large meadow of Gulmarg is 52km south-west of Srinagar at 2730m. The name means Meadow of Flowers and in spring it's just that. Also once a popular trekking base, Gulmarg used to be India's premier skiing resort.

Srinagar to Kargil
Sonamarg, at 2740m, is the last major town before Ladakh, and until the terrorist activity began, it was an excellent base for trekking. Its name means Meadow of Gold.

Baltal, an army camp, is right at the foot of the Zoji La (3529m). **Zoji La** is the watershed between Kashmir and Ladakh – on one side you have the green lush scenery of Kashmir while on the other side everything is barren and dry. Drass is the first main village after the pass. From here it's another 56km to Kargil.

JAMMU & KASHMIR

Ladakh & Zanskar

Ladakh – the land of high passes – marks the boundary between the peaks of the western Himalaya and the vast Tibetan Plateau. Opened up to tourism in 1974, Ladakh has been variously described as 'the Moonland', 'Little Tibet' and even 'the last Shangri La'. Whatever the description, it's one of the most remote regions of India.

The high culture of Ladakh is Buddhist, with its close cultural and trading connections with Tibet. This is particularly evident in the most populated region of Leh and the Indus Valley, with its many whitewashed *gompas* (monasteries) and forts perched on top of sugarloaf mountains. Padum, the capital of the more remote Zanskar Valley, shares this Buddhist heritage. Kargil and the Suru Valley, the third main region of Ladakh, is predominantly Muslim and shares a cultural affinity with Baltistan (in Pakistan since Indian Partition in 1947).

You do not need a permit to travel to Zanskar, Leh, or along the major routes to Srinagar and Manali. However, don't stray too close to sensitive border areas.

HISTORY

Ladakh's earliest inhabitants were the Khampas, nomads who grazed their yaks on the high, windswept pastures. The first settlements, along the upper Indus, were established by Mons, Buddhist pilgrims on their way from India to Mt Kailash in Tibet. The remnant tribe of Drukpas (or Dards, as they are known in some areas), who today live near Khalsi, claim descent from Alexander's Macedonian army.

In the 9th century Ladakh's influence extended beyond the Indus Valley and during this time many forts and palaces, including Shey, were constructed. In the late 14th century a Tibetan pilgrim, Tsong Khapa, introduced to Ladakh a Buddhist order headed by the first Dalai Lama. The new order, known as Gelukpa, flourished and led

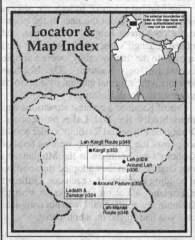
to the founding of gompas at Tikse, Likir and Spituk.

In the ensuing years, Balti-Kashmir armies launched various attacks against Ladakh which in the 16th century fell subject to the rule of Ali Mir of Baltistan. But its fortunes were revived under the rule of Singe Namgyal (1570-1642) who, in addition to territorial gains, established Leh as his capital and constructed a palace there. During the early 17th century, the Ladakhi royal family assisted Drukpa monks to establish gompas at Hemis and Stakna.

Soon Ladakhi forces were called on to face a combined Mongol-Tibetan army and help was sought from the Kashmir governor. This involved symbolic tribute to the Mughal empire and the mosque in Leh bazaar was the price Aurangzeb extracted.

After the conflict with Tibetan forces, trade relations resumed and Leh was able to

Festivals of Ladakh

Festivals are an integral part of Ladakhi religion and agriculture, usually coinciding with the commemoration of religious events, and the end of the harvest. These festivals often used to take place in winter, but many have now moved to the summer to coincide with another important part of the year: the tourist season. Major festivals are held each year at Spituk, Matho, Hemis, and most other gompas in the region. The annual dates for these gompa festivals, which are determined according to the Tibetan lunar calendar, are listed below.

Now that tourism is flourishing in the region, the annual Ladakh Festival has been extended and is now held in the first two weeks of September in a blatant attempt to prolong the tourist season. Nevertheless, the festival should not be missed. Regular large, colourful displays of dancing, sports, ceremonies and exhibitions are held throughout Ladakh, but mainly in Leh, which has the highest population and receives the most visitors.

The first day of the festival starts with a spectacular march through the main streets of Leh. People from all over Ladakh, monks in yellow and orange robes, polo and archery troupes and Tibetan refugees from Choglamsar, walk proudly in traditional costume, wearing the tall, bright *perak* hats and the curled *papu* shoes. The march culminates in a day long cultural display at the polo ground in Leh. (If you want the best view of the opening ceremonies, ignore the march and go early to the polo ground to get a good seat.)

Other activities during the two weeks include mask dances, which are serious and hypnotic when performed by monks, or cheeky and frivolous when performed by small children. There are also archery and polo competitions, concerts and other cultural programmes throughout Ladakh. From year to year, handicraft, food, wildlife and thangka exhibitions are held in Leh. The tourist offices in Leh hand out free programmes which list the locations and dates of the various activities.

Apart from Leh, other smaller, associated festivals are held in Changspa, Tangtse (near Pangong Tso), Shey, Basgo, Korzok (on the shore of Tso Moriri) and Biama (in the Dha-Hanu region). In the Nubra Valley, Diskit and Sumur hold the biggest festival outside Leh, with camel races, 'warfare demonstrations' (not quite as violent as they sound), ibex and peacock dances, traditional marriage ceremonies, some sword dancing from Baltistan, flower displays and archery competitions.

Following are the dates of festivals until 1999 celebrated at the gompas of Ladakh & Zanskar.

Gompa	1997	1998	1999
Chemrey	Nov 27-28	Nov 17-18	Nov 5-6
Diskit	Feb 5-6	Feb 24-25	Feb 14-15
Hemis	July 15-16	July 4-5	June 23-24
Karsha	July 21-22	July 11-12	
Leh	Feb 5-6	Feb 24-25	Feb 14-15
Likir	Feb 5-6	Feb 24-25	Feb 14-15
Matho	Feb 21-22	March 12-13	March 1-2
Phyang	Aug 5-6	July 25-26	July 14-15
Spituk	Jan 7-8	Jan 26-27	Jan 15-16
Stok	Feb 15-16	March 6-7	March 24-25
Taktok	Aug 13-14	Aug 3-4	July 23-24
Tikse	Nov 17-18	Nov 6-7	Oct 27-28
Losar	Dec 30	Dec 19	Dec 8

(The New Year Festival is celebrated at all gompas.)

The Hemis Festival features chaams danced by monks in elaborate masks.

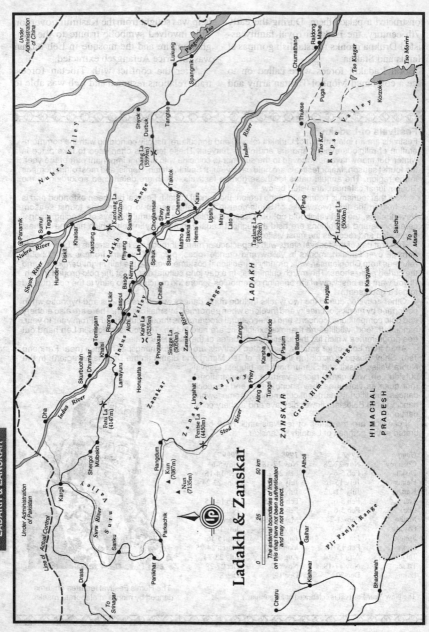

Ladakh & Zanskar

0   25   50 km

The external boundaries of India
on this map have not been authenticated
and may not be correct.

re-establish its influence over Zanskar and further south to Lahaul and Spiti. Ladakh's fortunes changed again in the 1830s when the Dogra army from Jammu invaded Ladakh and exiled its king to Stok. The Dogras were led by the famous general Zorawar Singh, who was appointed by the first maharaja of Kashmir, Gulab Singh.

Ladakh became an integral part of the maharaja's vast state in 1846 and remained under the control of Jammu & Kashmir after independence until some administrative autonomy was granted in 1995. Ladakh is still a sensitive area and its borders with both Pakistan and China have been disputed. India's war with China in 1962 exacerbated the problem and was one of the main reasons why Ladakh was closed to outsiders until 1974. While China and India are approaching accord on the border dispute, some heavy fighting continues between India and Pakistan (above 6000m in the eastern Karakoram region). This costly warfare – a million US dollars a day since 1988 – ensures a significant military presence in Ladakh. Travellers are forbidden to go near the border area.

GEOGRAPHY
Ladakh is bordered to the south by the main Himalaya Range, including the impressive snow-capped peaks of Nun (7135m) and Kun (7087m), the highest peaks in the Kashmir Himalaya. North and parallel to the Himalaya is the Zanskar Range, which is the main range between the Himalaya and the Indus Valley. The region is drained by the Zanskar River, which flows into the Indus River just below Leh, and the Suru River which flows into the Indus downstream of Kargil.

The Stok Range immediately south of Leh is an impressive outlier north of the Zanskar Range, while north of Leh is the snow-capped Ladakh Range. North of the Ladakh Range the Nubra and Shyok rivers drain the huge peaks of the eastern Karakoram including Rimo 1 (7385m) and Teram Kangri 1 (7464m), which define the northern border of Ladakh.

In the east of Ladakh are several scintillating lakes including the Pangong Tso (lake)

forming the border with Tibet and the Tso Moriri set in a high-altitude desert characteristic of the Tibetan Plateau.

TRAVEL TAX
As a result of the formation of the Ladakh Autonomous Hill Council, a tourist entry tax of US$10 per foreign tourist has been introduced. This will be collected at the various entry points into Ladakh (eg at Upshi – on the road from Manali). It will also be collected at the airport from tourists arriving by air. An additional US$20 will be levied on tourists visiting the newly opened areas of the Nubra Valley, Pangong Tso, Tso Moriri and the Dha-Hanu region.

Travellers have reported that if they use a non-Ladakhi vehicle (ie a car with a Delhi or Manali number plate) to visit one of the gompas on the tourist circuit from Leh, they've been fined Rs 500 for not having a 'gompa ticket' (Rs 20) supposedly available from the taxi union in Leh. No one seemed to know anything about a 'gompa ticket' in Leh so, no doubt, this is just another devious scam to watch out for.

LANGUAGE
Ladakhi is the main language used by most indigenous people. Once similar to Tibetan, Ladakhi has now changed considerably, and there are disparate dialects. If you only remember one word, it will be the all-purpose *jule* (pronounced 'JOO-lay'), which means hello, goodbye, please and thank you.

Useful Words

yes	*kasa*
no	*man*
how much/many	*tsam*
good	*demo*
rupee	*kirmo*
milk	*oma*
rice	*dras*
meat	*sha*
water	*chhu*
sugar	*khara*
I don't understand	*hamago*

Geographical & Climatic Terms

In Ladakh, life is completely dominated by the weather and geography. Here are a few words you may hear or see:

bridge	*zampa*
ice	*kang*
mountain	*ri*
river	*tsangspo*
stream	*tokpo*
wind	*lungspo*
cold	*tangmo*
lake	*tso*
mountain pass	*la*
snow	*ka*
summer	*yar*
winter	*rgun*

Numbers

1	*chig*
2	*nyis*
3	*sum*
4	*zhi*
5	*nga*
6	*truk*
7	*dun*
8	*gyet*
9	*gu*
10	*chu*

Leh

Pop: 25,500   Tel Area Code: 01982

Leh is located in a small valley just to the north of the Indus Valley. Until 1947 it had close trading relations with Central Asia, with yak trains setting off from the Leh bazaar to complete the stages over the Karakoram Pass to Yarkand and Kashgar. Today Leh is an important strategic centre for India. The large military presence is a reminder that the region of Ladakh is situated along India's sensitive borders with both Pakistan and China.

Leh's character changed when Ladakh was opened up to foreign tourists in 1974. Since then, well over 100 hotels have been established and many of the shops in the main bazaar have been converted to sell Ladakhi arts and crafts.

Leh is dominated by the dilapidated nine storey Leh Palace, home of the Ladakhi royal family before they were exiled to Stok in the 1830s. Above the palace at the top of the Namgyal Hill is the Victory Fort, built to commemorate Ladakh's victory over the Balti-Kashmir armies in the early 16th century.

The old town of Leh, situated at the base of Namgyal Hill, is a labyrinth of alleyways and houses stacked with dry wood and dung, which is collected for fuel to withstand the long winter months. To the south of the old town is the polo ground where weekly matches are contested between Leh and the outlying villages of the Indus Valley. The mosque at the head of the Leh bazaar was commissioned by the Mughal emperor Aurangzeb.

In Changspa, an outlying village of Leh, there are important Buddhist carvings dating back to the 8th and 9th centuries when Ladakh was converted to Buddhism. Close by is the village of Sankar, the site of a modern gompa which serves much of the Leh Valley. The gompa is attended by some 15 to 20 monks from the gompa at Spituk. It seems surprising that Leh does not have a more impressive gompa; even the King's Gompa at the palace is run down and administered by a monk seconded from Hemis.

Orientation

Leh is small enough to find your way around easily. The road from the airport goes past the new and old bus stands, then turns into the main street, Main Bazaar Rd, where there are plenty of shops and restaurants. South of the Leh Palace, around Fort Rd, is the most popular area for places to eat, sleep and spend money. About two km west of town and out of Leh is the village of Changspa, with its many guesthouses and long-term visitors.

Information

Tourist Offices The Tourist Reception Centre (☎ 52297) is three km south of the town centre, on the road to the airport. For general inquiries the small counter in the same building as the Foreign Exchange, next to the Tourist Bungalow on Fort Rd, is far handier. Both tourist offices are open from 9 am to 6 pm daily except Sunday (the Tourist Reception Centre, however, is open from 10 am to 4 pm on Saturday). There is a small tourist information counter at the airport, but this really just handles Foreigner's Registration Forms. The airport arrivals area has an informative video presentation about the region.

Permits Permits are not required for Leh. However, you must fill out a Foreigners' Registration Form at the airport, and again at your hotel. For permits to the newly opened regions of Ladakh, you have to go to a travel agency and then to the District Magistrate's Office (☎ 52210), open normal business hours, just above the polo ground. For more details on permits, refer to the Ladakh Regions section later in this chapter.

Money Changing money is really only possible at the Forex (Foreign Exchange) counter next to the Tourist Bungalow, although some travellers have had luck at the State Bank of India. The Forex is open Monday to Friday from 10.30 am to 1.30 pm and on Saturday from 10.30 am to noon. You must fill out two copies of a currency form and wait.

Post & Communications The main post office – open Monday to Saturday from 10 am to 1 pm and 2 to 5 pm – is hopelessly inconvenient, more than three km south of the centre of Leh. The smaller post office on the corner of Fort and Main Bazaar roads is open from 10 am to 4 pm, closed on Sunday. The poste restante at the main post office is not particularly reliable.

All around Leh are small telephone booths with long-distance facilities. Calls within India cost Rs 30 to Rs 40 per minute; to Australia/New Zealand and Europe, Rs 85; and to USA/Canada, Rs 98. Faxes are a far more expensive method of communication (Rs 3 per second for international faxes), but machines are available. Prices change

periodically; if in doubt, check the schedule of charges in the telephone directory.

Travel Agencies Many travel agencies operate in Leh in the summer. Almost all agencies work on a commission basis, selling tickets for other agencies' buses and tours.

Recommended travel agencies include: Druk Travels in the Hotel Ibex, opposite the taxi stand on Fort Rd (although the manager is often absent); Kailash Expeditions (near the Instyle German Bakery) on Fort Rd; Yak Tail Travels (☎ 52318), in the hotel of the same name; Yungdung Tours & Travels, opposite the taxi stand; Rimo Expeditions, near the Hotel Khang-la-Chhen; Yasmin Trek & Tour, which is near the Hotel Ibex; and Gypsy's World (☎ 52735) near Hotel Yak Tail on Fort Rd.

Equipment Hire Several travel agencies hire out sleeping bags, tents and so on, but the gear can be of low quality and poorly maintained. Check the gear carefully before you take it. Places which rent gear include: Snow Leopard, opposite the taxi stand; Royal Express, near the Hotel Ibex; and the Traveller Shop (☎ 52248) on Fort Rd, towards the Indian Airlines office. Approximate rental prices per day are: two-person tent, Rs 60; sleeping bag, Rs 50; and gas stove, Rs 10.

Rafting Agencies Several agencies in Leh run white-water rafting trips on the Indus and Zanskar rivers. Rafting is not especially popular, as the rivers aren't particularly good or reliable, and the season only lasts from about early July to mid-September. A three-hour, calm trip from Hemis to Choglamsar costs Rs 750 per person. Better rafting from Nimmu to Alchi or to Khalsi will cost Rs 1200 for the day. Longer, customised rafting trips for the adventurous cost about US$65 per day, including all transport, gear, food and a guide.

Two of the better travel agencies in Leh which handle rafting trips are Indus Himalayan Explorers (☎ 52735), opposite the taxi stand in Fort Rd; and Rimo Expeditions (see Travel Agencies above).

LADAKH & ZANSKAR

Bookshops & Libraries Both the Artou Bookshop and Lost Horizon Books have great selections on Ladakh and Tibet, as well as novels. The Tibetan Handicraft Emporium, on Main Bazaar Rd, is also good for Tibetan literature. Bookworm, near the Hotel Ga-Idan Continental on Old Fort Rd, has a selection of secondhand books (English, French, German, Japanese) and will buy back the books at half their selling price.

Next to the Hotel Bijou, the small Leh District Library is a good place to read (mainly old) books about Ladakh, and recent issues of English-language newspapers and

magazines. It is open Monday to Saturday from 10 am to 4 pm. The Ladakh Ecological Development Group (LEDeG) runs a very good library with books on local issues and ecological matters. For books on Buddhism and Tibet, try the Tibetan library in Choglamsar.

Newspapers & Magazines Daily English-language Indian newspapers can be obtained at Parkash Booksellers, next to the German Bakery. The bilingual (English and Ladakhi) quarterly magazine *Ladags Melong* (Rs 20) is a great source of information on Ladakhi

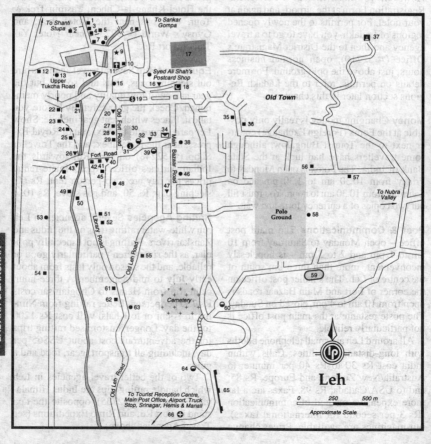

To Shanti Stupa
To Sankar Gompa
Upper Tukcha Road
Syed Ali Shah's Postcard Shop
Old Town
Old Fort Road
Fort Road
Main Bazaar Road
Library Road
Old Leh Road
Cemetery
Polo Ground
To Nubra Valley
To Tourist Reception Centre, Main Post Office, Airport, Truck Stop, Srinagar, Hemis & Manali

Leh

0   250   500 m
Approximate Scale

culture, education, history and so on. It is not easy to find in Leh, but try the library, SECMOL (see the following SECMOL section), or the major bookshops.

Film & Photography Several places along Fort and Main Bazaar roads sell print and slide film, but always check the expiry date. The Gemini Lab on Fort Rd, opposite the Hotel Yak Tail, does a pretty good job with developing print (not slide) film.

Courses Buddhist study centres have been set up in both Leh and nearby Choglamsar. The Mahabodi International Meditation Centre in Leh (look for the sign on the way to the Shanti Stupa) has summer meditation sessions at 5.30 pm daily except Sunday. The Centre also holds popular five to 10 day study camps near Temisgam and at Dewachan, near Choglamsar.

Laundry There are numerous laundries in Leh.

Snow White has a few outlets, including a convenient one opposite the State Bank of India. The Dzomsa (literally: meeting place) laundry at the Old Fort Road end of Upper Tuckha Road is run by a women's cooperative; clothes are washed several km away from town and the soapy water poured into a pit in the desert to avoid polluting the streams. Laundry charges for same-day service don't vary much from place to place. Expect to pay around Rs 8 for a T-shirt, Rs 15 for jeans and Rs 10 for a shirt.

Medical Services Leh is at an altitude of 3505m, so it is important to acclimatise to avoid Acute Mountain Sickness (AMS). If you suspect you are suffering from the symptoms of AMS, medical advice is available (☎ 52014 from 10 am to 4 pm or ☎ 52360 from 4 pm to 10 am). For more information on AMS, see the Health section in the Facts for the Visitor chapter. Leh has several clinics and pharmacies which can dispense advice

PLACES TO STAY
1 Two Star Guest House
2 Rainbow Guest House
3 Karzoo Guest House
4 Odzer Guest House
5 Maryul Guest House
6 Antelope Guest House
7 Tsemo La Hotel
10 Khan Manzil Guest House
12 Hotel Omasila, Eagle Guest House, Otsal, Asia, Larchang Guest Houses
21 Jigmet Guest House
22 Ti Sei Guest House
23 Dehlux Hotel
24 Indus Guest House
25 Bimla Guest House
27 Hotel Lingzi
29 Hotel Ga ldan Continental
35 Tak Guest House
36 Old Ladakh Guest House
41 Dreamland Hotel & Restaurant
42 Hotel Yak Tail & Restaurant
44 Hotel Rockland

45 Khangri Hotel
49 Padma Guest House
50 Hotel Choskar
51 Pangong Hotel
52 Kang La
54 Mandala Hotel
55 Chospa Guest House
56 Palace View Hotel
57 Sabila Guest House
61 Hotel Dragon
62 Hotel Hills View

PLACES TO EAT
14 Mentokling Restaurant
16 Bakery Stalls
20 German Bakery & Tibetan Restaurant
26 Instyle German Bakery
33 Tibetan Friends Corner Restaurant
40 Summer Harvest Restaurant
43 Tibetan Kitchen
47 Mughal Darbar Restaurant

OTHER
8 LEDeG Centre
9 Police Station
11 Morovian Church

13 Mahabodi International Meditation Centre
15 Artou Bookshop
17 Leh Palace
18 Mosque
19 State Bank of India
28 Bookworm
30 Vegetable Market
31 Tourist Office & Foreign Exchange
32 HPTDC Bus Office & Modiluft Office
34 Post Office
37 Namgyal Tsemo Gompa
38 Lost Horizon Books
39 Taxi Stand & Union Office
46 Tibetan Handicraft Emporium
48 Leh District Library
53 Indian Airlines
58 District Magistrate's Office
59 National Archery Stadium
60 Old Bus Stand
63 SECMOL Centre
64 New Bus Stand
65 Mani Wall
66 SNM Hospital

LADAKH & ZANSKAR

and medicines for low-level complaints, but for anything serious the Sonam Narbu Memorial (SNM) Hospital (☎ 52014) is nearly three km south of Leh.

Leh Palace

Looking for all the world like a miniature version of the Potala in Lhasa, Tibet, Leh Palace was built in the 17th century but is now deserted and dilapidated. Try to find a monk to unlock the preserved, but now unused, central prayer room. If you can't get in, don't despair; there is no shortage of more interesting, spectacular gompas near Leh.

Namgyal Tsemo Gompa

The Tsemo (Red) Gompa, built in 1430, contains a fine three-storey-high Buddha image and ancient manuscripts and frescoes. It's open from 7 to 9 am. Another gompa above the Tsemo Gompa is ruined, but the views of Leh from here are superb. The steep laneway starts from the road to the Leh Palace.

Sankar Gompa

It's an easy stroll to the Sankar Gompa, a couple of km north of the town centre. (A return taxi costs Rs 115.) This interesting little gompa, which belongs to the Gelukpa order, is only open from 7 to 10 am and from 5 to 7 pm. The gompa has electric lighting so an evening visit is worthwhile. Upstairs, as well as a library and great views from the roof, there is an impressive representation of Avalokitesvara (Chenresig, the Buddhist deity of Compassion) complete with 1000 arms and 1000 heads.

Shanti Stupa

Looming impressively, especially at night when it is well lit-up, this *stupa* (Buddhist religious monument) was built by a Japanese man whose intention was to spread Buddhism by building temples throughout the world. With some financial assistance from the Japanese government, it was opened by the Dalai Lama in 1985.

From the top, there are great views. The stupa is located at the end of the road which goes through Changspa, about three km from Fort Rd. If on foot, there is a very, very steep set of steps – not to be attempted if you have just arrived in Leh. By taxi (Rs 120 return) or with your own transport, a longish, winding (but less steep) road goes straight to the top.

There are five rooms at the stupa (which can be rented for Rs 100 per night) and an empty looking restaurant. Staying here will offer the greatest views of Leh, but it is a long way down to your favourite eatery!

Ladakh Ecological Development Group

The Ladakh Ecological Development Group (LEDeG), founded in 1983, initiates and promotes 'ecological and sustainable development which harmonises with and builds on the traditional culture'. This includes environmental and health education, strengthening the traditional system of organic farming, and publishing books in the local language.

The video *Ancient Futures – Learning from Ladakh* can be viewed any day except Sunday at 4.30 pm at the LEDeG Centre, next to the Tsemo-La Hotel, but a minimum audience of 10 people is required. It's well worth seeing for an insight into Ladakh, and the problems associated with tourism. There are also study groups at the centre every Wednesday at 10.30 am. The library is popular; and the handicraft shop has a good, if a little pricey (but it is non-profit), selection of locally made goods. For further information about the LEDeG, contact: Ladakh Project, 21 Victoria Sq, Clifton, Bristol, BS84ES, UK; or Ladakh Project, PO Box 9475, Berkeley, CA 94709, USA.

Students' Educational & Cultural Movement of Ladakh (SECMOL)

SECMOL (☎ 52421) was founded in the late 1980s to organise cultural shows and youth activities and to promote traditional art forms. People interested in conducting English conversation classes may join in the summer camps at Phey village near the Phyang Monastery (board and food will cost you about Rs 70 a day). The camps are aimed at preparing young people for the state exams, which are in English. Volunteers may also participate in a project at Phey constructing solar houses using traditional building materials. SECMOL produces a local magazine, *Ladags Melong*, and a Ladakhi phrasebook. The SECMOL centre (open 10 am to 4.30 pm daily except Sunday) is on Old Leh Rd.

Places to Stay

There is plenty of choice when it comes to hotels and guesthouses in Leh, although most are only open during the tourist season (July to mid-September). Technically, prices are set by the local tourist authorities, but what you pay depends more on demand – prices can soar in the peak season, especially after the arrival of a full flight. In low season, even a day or two after the peak season ends, prices can drop dramatically, sometimes by up to 50%. Prices quoted here are for the high season, but, remember, the cost of a hotel will change from day to day. Many places will also charge an arbitrary 'service tax' of about 10%.

Electricity can be spasmodic, so torches (flashlights) and candles may be needed. Before paying extra for hot water, inquire how regular it is; often it may only run for one or two hours a day. If you're staying for some time in Leh, it is worth checking into one place for the first night, then spending your first day, while acclimatising, finding a place that really suits.

Budget accommodation can be found in three main areas: the old town, which is a little noisy and smelly, but has character; the 'newer', greener areas along and not far from Fort Rd; and in the village of Changspa. Most other accommodation is in the newer parts of Leh.

Places to Stay – bottom end

Old Town Under the Leh Palace, along a quiet road to the Sankar Gompa, are several good places.

Antelope Guest House, popular for its friendliness and garden setting, has singles/ doubles for Rs 80/150.

Hotel Kailash, a little further up the road and surrounded by a walled garden and fields,

has doubles from Rs 150, all with common bathroom.

Old Ladakh Guest House, one of Leh's first budget places, has rooms with common bathroom for Rs 80/150, with attached bath for Rs 300.

There are several good places in the area between the Old Ladakh Guest House and the polo ground, with similarly priced rooms and facilities to those above.

Shalimar Guest House is a clean, friendly and popular place.

Tak Guest House, also popular, has rooms with common bath for Rs 150.

The larger *Palace View Hotel* has rooms for Rs 100 with common bath, Rs 150 with attached bath.

Sabila Guest House has rooms with common bath for Rs 100/150.

Khan Manzil Guest House, further afield near Syed Ali Shah's postcard shop (see the Things to Buy section later in this chapter), has reasonable rooms for Rs 80/100 for singles/doubles with common bath.

Firdous Hotel, beside the archery stadium, is a friendly little place with doubles for Rs 80, or Rs 120 with attached bath.

Changspa Changspa, about 15 minutes walk from the town centre, is a very popular place for budget travellers. Many of the older places are basic, with outside bathrooms, but are usually very friendly, and surrounded by colourful gardens. Following are recommended places among the dozens around or on the way to Changspa.

Eagle Guest House has singles/doubles for around Rs 80/120.

The *Tsavo Guest House* is a very basic, authentic Ladakhi home with doubles from Rs 80.

The *Otsal*, *Asia* and *Larchang* guesthouses have reasonable singles/doubles for around Rs 80/100.

Along the road to the Shanti Stupa, past Changspa, a bit of a walk from town, are dozens of other nice family-run guesthouses – just look for the signs on the road.

Rinchens Guest House has clean doubles with attached bath.

The *Oriental Guest House*, run by a very friendly family, has doubles from around Rs 100.

The *Karzoo Guest House* has plain singles/doubles with common bath for Rs 60/120 – bucket of hot water included – and there's a lovely garden.

The *Maryul Guest House* is a new place with hot water. A sizeable upstairs room with common bath and a nice view over the garden is Rs 150-200, Rs 250 with attached bath. Rooms downstairs are Rs 150 with common bath.

The *Two-Star Guest House* offers fairly basic rooms with common bath for Rs 80/150, with attached bath for Rs 130/200.

The *Mansoor Guest House* has a nice family atmosphere.

The friendly *Rainbow Guest House* has singles/doubles with common bath for Rs 100/150.

Other Areas Down Old Leh Rd are old favourites within the range of Rs 100 to Rs 200, usually with a shared bathroom. They include:

Spic-n-Span (☎ 52238), the *Singge Palace* (☎ 52422), and the *Chospa Guest House*, which has its own in-house astrologer.

Along the lane known as Library Rd (which the library isn't actually on) there are several good places.

Pangong Hotel is a little in the mid-range, but has airy, bright singles/doubles with hot water for Rs 200/300.

The popular *Kang La* next door has small, cosy rooms with bathroom for Rs 100.

The *Hotel Hills View* (☎ 2258) has rooms for Rs 100/150 with common bath, Rs 250 for a double with attached bath.

The *Nezer View Guest House*, near Spic-n-Span is recommended. It has rooms from Rs 150 with common bath.

Hotel Dragon nearby has rooms with attached bath and hot water for Rs 400-600/1800.

Up the lane beside the Instyle German Bakery are several guesthouses.

Ti-sei Guest House has a nice garden and a traditional Ladakhi kitchen.

The *Dehlux Hotel* has rooms with common bath for Rs 60/120 and one large glassed-in room (No 10) for Rs 150.

Jigmet Guest House, not far away on Upper Tukcha Rd, is tidy and has large rooms for Rs 200 with common bath and Rs 300 with attached bath.

The *Stream View Guest House*, next door at No 39 (there's no sign), has very pleasant rooms with common bath for Rs 80/150.

Camping The only camp site is at *Zen*, in Changspa. For Rs 30, you can place your tent on a small piece of turf. If you have a tent, you may be able to put it up at the back of a guesthouse for about the same price.

Places to Stay – middle

A few of the places which used to be in the 'bottom end' range are a little overpriced despite improvements. These include several along the lane beside the Instyle German Bakery.

Bimla Guest House has singles/doubles for about Rs 200/300 without a bathroom (expect to pay Rs 50-100 more for rooms with hot water and great views).

The *Indus Guest House* has doubles with hot water for Rs 300.

There are several options on or near Fort Rd.

Yasmin Guest House (opposite Hotel Rockland) has good doubles with attached bath and hot water for Rs 400.

Hotel Choskar has similarly priced doubles to the above.

Hotel Rockland is a little more expensive.

Places to Stay – top end

Prices for these places are high, and offer little value; a room may have some form of heating or air-conditioning, and hot water, but no other extras. Many places offer an 'American Plan', which includes three meals for an additional Rs 400 to Rs 500 per day. It may seem a reasonable deal, but there are plenty of good cheap places to eat in Leh, and why always eat at the same place?

Tsemo-La Hotel (☎ 52790; Rs 600/1200); the central *Khangri Hotel* (☎ 52311; Rs 900-

1100), the *K-Sar Palace* (☎ 52348; from Rs 900/1200) and the similarly priced *Mandala Hotel* are all top-end places. Centrally located around Fort Rd are the *Hotel Lingzi*, the *Hotel Yak Tail* (☎ 52118; from Rs 900/110), the *Hotel Omasila* (Rs 1500/1800) and the *Hotel Ga-Idan Continental* (☎ 52436; from Rs 1250/1500).

Places to Stay – winter

Almost every place to stay in Leh closes in winter, mainly because no one can get to the place. Prices at those places which remain open in the off season are still high because of a charge for room heating, which is certainly needed as the temperature in winter can plummet to about -35°C.

The only places which reliably open in winter are the first and original *Old Ladakh Guest House*, which has remained open every day since 1974; the *Hotel Ibex*, opposite the taxi stand on Fort Rd; and the *Khangri Hotel* (where you will be put up for free if your Indian Airlines flight is cancelled).

Places to Eat

There is no shortage of places to eat in Leh (although supplies are sometimes scarce), and it's a joy to sample various types of food from a multitude of good places. Almost all places serve a range of cuisines. If you want to eat at a popular place in the peak season, you'll need to get there before 7 pm to get a table.

Indian Cuisine On Main Bazaar Rd *Mughal Darbar* is recommended. Although the servings are small, a great meal will only set you back about Rs 70 per person.

Poora Barba, opposite the Hotel Yak Tail on Fort Rd, is the place for no-frills, cheap Indian food, such as filling plates of vegetable curries and rice.

Tibetan Cuisine Leh has a sizeable Tibetan refugee population, which naturally has influenced the cuisine and increased the number of Tibetan restaurants. Along Main Bazaar Rd, mostly on the 2nd or 3rd floors,

are several good, cheap (and well signed) places to try Tibetan specialities, including: *Kokonor Tibetan Restaurant*, the *Wok Tibetan Kitchen* and the two *Amdo* cafes, which also serve reasonable western and Chinese food.

The *Budshah Inn*, near the mosque, serves Kashmiri and Tibetan treats.

The *Tibetan Kitchen*, at the western end of Fort Rd, has pleasant decor and good service, and the varieties of Tibetan cuisine are explained on posters and menus for the uninitiated. It will do a famous *gyarhcee* (Tibetan hotpot) for at least four people with a day's notice.

The *Dreamland Restaurant*, centrally located in the hotel of the same name, is popular for its Tibetan specialities, among other types of food.

The unpretentious *Tibetan Restaurant Devi*, near the State Bank of India, has maintained its reputation for cheap, nourishing food.

La Montessori, on Main Bazaar Road, serves up big portions of very tasty Chinese, Tibetan and some western favourites, and is popular with local monks.

The *Tibetan Friends Corner Restaurant*, near the taxi stand, is another established local favourite.

Western Cuisine The *Yak Tail* is good, if a little pricey, and is one of the few places that serves beer.

The *Centerpoint* on Fort Rd, above the Tsomo Hotel, has nice decor and a good selection, including Ladakhi dishes at reasonable prices.

The *Summer Harvest* opposite is very popular, and deservedly so.

Bakeries As well as fresh cinnamon rolls and other tasty things, the bakeries in Leh serve good western food such as pasta, hamburgers and large, hot breakfasts.

Instyle German Bakery on Fort Rd is a great place for a cup of coffee, sandwiches and breakfast, including piping hot porridge.

The *German Bakery* at the top of Old Fort

LADAKH & ZANSKAR

Rd is very popular; specialities include lasagne and a big set-price breakfast (Rs 40).

The *Mona Lisa Bakery*, close to the State Bank of India, is small but good for tea and freshly baked goodies.

Hot, fresh Indian and Tibetan bread can be bought in the early morning from several unmarked *bakery stalls* in the street behind the mosque – follow the sign to the Antelope Guest House towards Sankar Gompa. Get there early to watch them make the bread. It is great with locally made jam.

Bars If you're desperate for a bottle of Turbo Extra Strong Lager, there are a couple of bars.

Penguin Bar is at the back of the Instyle German Bakery.

Namra Bar, dark and seedy, is opposite the Hotel Yak Tail.

The open-air *Mentokling Restaurant* and the *Mona Lisa*, near the LEDeG Centre, are relaxing places for a meal, a drink and western popular music.

Entertainment
The Cultural & Traditional Society (CATS) puts on a cultural show each summer evening opposite the Hotel Yak Tail at 6 pm (which is not particularly pleasant if you have a room nearby).

In competition with the CATS show, the Ladakh Artists' Society of Leh puts on a show of Ladakhi songs and dances every day in summer at 5.30 pm outside the Leh Palace. It's an entertaining show, at a great location. Bring a torch (flashlight) for the walk back. Each show costs Rs 50.

While they *are* set up for tourists, these shows are likely to be the closest you'll get to seeing traditional songs and dances, and to try (if you dare) some Ladakhi gur-gur. It's a good idea to avoid the front rows unless you want to become part of the spectacle at the end of the show.

Things to Buy
Prices in Leh are generally quite high; you may find exactly the same Tibetan-inspired item for less in Kashmir, Dharamsala or

Nepal. For Tibetan goods, try places around Choglamsar (several km south of Leh), the Tibetan Handicraft Shop near the entrance to the airport, or the Tibetan Handicrafts Emporium on Main Bazaar Rd.

If you are around Leh at the time of the Ladakh Festival (first two weeks of September), there are good exhibitions and stalls selling local handicrafts and clothes. Syed Ali Shah's postcard shop near the old town makes an interesting visit; the postcards are actually photos the proprietor himself has taken over the years.

Getting There & Away
Air From June to September Indian Airlines (IA) has return flights between Leh and Delhi (US$90) at least four times a week, and weekly flights to and from Chandigarh (US$60). There are also direct flights once a week from Leh to Srinagar (US$45), and two times a week to Jammu (US$55). They can be a useful, indirect, way of getting out of Leh if the Leh to Delhi flights are hopelessly overbooked.

From October to May IA generally flies into Leh four times a week from Delhi, but this depends greatly on weather conditions. When flights from Leh are delayed, IA will pay for passengers' overnight accommodation in Leh.

Modiluft (☎ 52386), whose office is opposite the No 1 taxi stand in Leh, also flies between Delhi and Leh.

Fares and timetables change fairly frequently and it always pays to get the latest information from the airline offices themselves.

At the time of writing, Archana Airways (AA), which normally concentrates on flying around Himachal Pradesh, planned to commence flights between Leh and Delhi, and between Leh and Kargil.

IA warns passengers it cannot depart Leh with more than 70 to 80 passengers because of the altitude, climatic conditions and short runway. So, at peak periods, flights can be heavily overbooked. To avoid this, book well ahead but be prepared for disappointment. If you can't get a booking in economy class, it's worth trying for 1st class (US$135 to Delhi). Another option is to get to the airport early on the day you want to go, because even if you are waitlisted up to number 100, there is still a good chance you will get on a flight, as a sudden improvement in conditions may result in a larger passenger load.

The Indian Airlines office (☎ 52255) in Leh is on the extension of Fort Rd, in a small, white building. The office is open from 10 am to 5 pm every day – 10 am to noon on Sunday – with a lunch break from 1 to 2 pm. It is worth getting to the office early to avoid the crowds of frantic people confirming their flights.

Bus There are only two overland routes to Leh: the road from Srinagar, and the road from Manali in Himachal Pradesh. A complication when trying to leave Leh for Srinagar or Manali is that you may not be able to buy tickets on the local buses (or private buses at the end of the season) until the evening before departure, because buses may not turn up from either of these places. Thus you can't be certain you will be leaving until the last moment. Try to book ahead if possible, especially in peak season, at the new bus stand in Leh, from where the public buses leave.

Srinagar The Leh to Srinagar road is usually open from the beginning of June to October, but in practice the opening date varies. The trip takes two days, about 12 hours travel on each day, with an overnight halt at Kargil. There are three classes of public buses, but you may not get the class you want on the day you want. J&KSRTC buses to Kargil/Srinagar cost Rs 130/258 (A Class) and Rs 97/194 (B Class). A Class has push-back seats. The buses leave Leh at 5.30 am every day, in season.

At the time of researching, the regular deluxe/tourist private buses, which used to connect Srinagar and Leh, were cancelled due to lack of demand.

Manali The Leh to Manali road is open for a shorter period, usually from July to mid-

September, sometimes up to mid-October; again, the opening and closing dates depend on climatic conditions. There is a good selection of private and public buses for this route, indicating its popularity. (For more information on the buses and the trip, refer to the Leh to Manali section later in this chapter.)

Jeep & Taxi Long-distance jeeps and taxis are an expensive but useful alternative to the buses.

'Indian jeeps' take five passengers, while 'Japanese jeeps' and Ambassador taxis take four passengers, plus driver. Fares are listed at taxi stands in Leh and Kargil. Extra charges are Rs 250 if staying overnight; waiting for the second and third hours (the first is free) is set at Rs 105 per hour.

The two day trip from Leh to Manali (including an overnight stop) will cost about Rs 10,770. A trip from Leh, via Lahaul and Spiti, on to Shimla and back to Leh, over five or six days would be fantastic, but very expensive at about Rs 25,000. If hiring a jeep or taxi for a long trip, try to get a driver who speaks English and knows the area. This is not always possible because the next driver on the Taxi Union list gets the fare, regardless of his talents. Taxi drivers in Leh and Kargil are unionised; they must wear uniforms and go through union checkpoints on all routes outside Leh.

While officially 'fixed', jeep and taxi fares for longer, more expensive trips are certainly negotiable.

Truck Trucks are a worthy and acceptable method of travelling to Manali, or to places on the way. Talk to the drivers at the truck stop on the way to the airport in Leh.

Getting Around
The Airport The bus service from Leh to the airport was not running at the time of writing. Rates for jeeps and taxis are set at Rs 70 to Leh, or Rs 100 to Changspa.

Bus All public buses leave from the new bus stand, where it's difficult to secure information on schedules. Both tourist offices have

an updated, but often incomplete, timetable for public buses. To get to the new bus stand, walk through the areas with the *chortens*, like everyone else; don't follow the long road.

Jeep & Taxi A taxi from the old and new bus stands to Fort Rd, for those tired from a long journey and/or with loads of gear, will cost about Rs 20. Costs for day trips to nearby gompas are: to Sankar, Shanti and Spituk, Rs 450; to Shey, Tikse and Stok, Rs 588; and to just about every nearby gompa mentioned in the following Around Leh section, Rs 1492.

Taxis in Leh congregate around three designated stands; they generally don't go around the streets looking for customers – you will have to approach them. Taxi drivers accept only the union rate; fares are listed at the taxi stands. The biggest stand, No 1 on Fort Rd, is open from 7 am to 7 pm, but there are taxis hanging around Fort Rd in the very early morning, waiting for fares to the airport or the new bus stand. Taxi stand No 2 is at the old bus stand, where a few old taxis loiter; and No 3 is at the new bus stand, but you may find it hard to get a taxi here.

Motorcycle Vespa scooters can be rented for about Rs 500 per day, plus petrol, from several places: Oasis Travels on the way to the Indian Airlines office; Yati Travels, opposite the small post office on Main Bazaar Rd; Nezer View Guest House on Old Leh Rd; and Yasmin Trek & Tour on Fort Rd. Motorcycle rental is likely to become more readily available and hopefully cheaper, but there will be restrictions on how far from Leh you can travel. Ensure that you have comprehensive insurance.

Bicycle Bicycle rental is just catching on. Mountain bikes – a great way to visit the more accessible villages (but you may have to walk up to the gompas, anyway) – can be hired from the Lost Horizon travel agency opposite the Hotel Yak Tail. Rental is Rs 200 per day, but this price may be reduced as more competition comes along.

AROUND LEH

There are many beautiful gompas and villages which make good day trips from Leh. The main places are described here; for a more comprehensive listing refer to Lonely Planet's *Indian Himalaya*.

Choglamsar

Choglamsar has become an important centre for Tibetan Buddhism and the study of Tibetan culture and history. Around the Tibetan refugee camp, just off the main road from Leh, there is a Tibetan library, medical centre, handicraft shops, study centre,

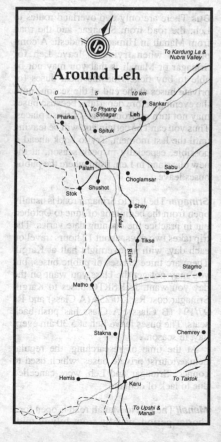

bookshops, plenty of restaurants, and the Central Institute of Buddhist Studies.

Any of the buses heading south from Leh will drop you off at Choglamsar, or a one-way taxi will cost Rs 130. There are a couple of crummy guesthouses along the very noisy main road.

Hemis Gompa

Also known as Chang-Chub-Sam-Ling (or the Lone Place of the Compassionate Person), Hemis Gompa, 45 km south of Leh, belongs to the Drukpa order and was founded in the early 17th century. Now it is one of the most accessible, famous and, therefore, most visited gompas.

The gompa has an excellent library, well preserved frescoes showing some Kashmiri influence, and good Buddha figures. The largest *thangka* in Ladakh, over 12m long, is at Hemis, but is only exhibited every 11 years. To commemorate the birth of the renowned Indian sage, Padmasambhava, the famous annual Hemis Festival is held on the 9th to 11th days of the 5th Tibetan month. (See the Ladakh Festivals aside earlier in the chapter for details.)

There are no guesthouses near the gompa, only one or two in the village, a long walk away. Several places near the gompa allow camping: you can set up your own tent next to the gompa for Rs 35, or rent a pre-set two person tent for Rs 50. Book at the nice outdoor restaurant, next to the gompa entrance, which serves unexciting but welcome Chinese food, tea and beer. Hemis is worth an overnight stay to explore the **Kotsang Hermitage Gompa**, a one-hour walk along a trail behind the gompa. There are also some **caves** nearby.

Daily buses leave Leh for Hemis at 9.30 am and 4 pm, returning to Leh at 6.30 am and 12.30 pm. The times are not great, but allow you an hour or so to look around if you are on a day trip from Leh. Return taxis from Leh cost Rs 783.

Matho Gompa

Built in the 16th century, Matho holds an annual festival during which the monks and novices go into trances and self-inflict wounds which appear to leave no marks. The five km road between Matho and Stakna Gompa is impassable for vehicles, but it's possible to walk. Take the bus to Hemis, get off at the sign to the Stakna Gompa, walk to Matho via Stakna and return the same way. Alternatively, take the bus from Leh to Matho (leaves Leh at 9 am and 5 pm; returns 10 am and 6 pm). A taxi to Stakna and Matho from Leh costs about Rs 800. There is no accommodation in Matho, but it's possible to camp.

Shey Gompa

Shey, 15km south of Leh, was the former summer palace of the kings of Ladakh. The gompa, still partially used, is being restored. There is a small library and a collection of thangkas, and some stupas and mani walls nearby. The 12m Shakyamuni Buddha statue, made of copper but gold plated, is the largest in the region, built by King Singge Namgyal's son. More crumbling **chortens** are scattered around the nearby fields.

Shey is easy to get to and can be easily combined with a visit to Tikse by any form of transport. Catch any bus from Leh going to Tikse or Hemis and disembark at Shey; by taxi, it will cost Rs 240 return. The only place to stay is the pleasant and large *Shil Kar Hotel & Restaurant*, near the road up to the gompa. Rooms with bathroom cost Rs 150.

Spituk Gompa

On a hilltop above the Indus River and only eight km from Leh, the Spituk Gompa was built in the 15th century under the Gelukpa order. It is next to the airport, and so has an ugly view at the front, but the back looks onto the pretty local village. The two prayer rooms have some nice Buddha statues, only unveiled once a year during the annual festival held usually in January.

Spituk has nowhere to stay or eat, as it is so close to Leh. From Leh to Spituk is a long, hot walk; a bike would be ideal. Alternatively, take one of the buses from Leh which go past Spituk every 15 minutes or so. Taxis from Leh cost Rs 195 return.

Stakna Gompa

The gompa at Stakna – which means Tiger's Nose – is another set spectacularly on the Hemis side of the Indus River. Built by King Singge Namgyal's stepbrother, as part of the Drukpa order, it is not difficult to get to, and can be combined with a trip to Matho on the same day (see the earlier Matho section).

To get there, take the Leh-Hemis bus, and get off at the sign by the road to the gompa. Cross the bridge and walk for 30 minutes across the shadeless fields and up the steep path. A return taxi from Leh costs Rs 580. There is no guesthouse in the village, but it should be possible to camp back near the Indus.

Stok Gompa & Museum

Over the bridge from Choglamsar, the Stok Gompa is where the last king of Ladakh died in 1974. Built in 1814, it is a popular place because it is so easy to get to. There are over 80 rooms, only a few of which are open to the public.

The museum has a unique display of rare ornaments from the royal family, thangkas, and traditional clothing and jewellery. Entry is Rs 20 and it's open in summer from 8 am to 8 pm. Photography is not permitted. The gompa, which has some fine masks and frescoes, is behind the museum. Don't wander near the Telecom plant.

The only nearby place to stay is the elegant *Hotel Highland*, just under the museum (there's no sign). There are other smaller places to stay towards the main road. Direct buses leave Leh at 7.30 am and 5 pm. Alternatively, try to get there by mountain bike or motorcycle. A return taxi from Leh will cost Rs 370.

Tikse Gompa

About 17km south of Leh, this gompa, part of the Gelukpa order, has an important collection of Tibetan books in its library, some excellent artwork and a new Maitreya temple. It's a busy place, with almost incessant chanting and music, and there is a good chance to witness a *puja* . Go to the roof for great views of the valleys and villages. There

is even a small (and welcome) cafe and shop. The gompa is open daily from 7.30 am to 6 pm. Permission is required to use video or movie cameras.

The only place to stay in Tikse is the *Skalzang Chamba Hotel*, right at the start of the trail leading to the gompa. It is a well run and pleasant place with a small garden. The cost is Rs 130 per room, including meals. Students (male only) of Buddhism, but not ordinary backpackers, may be able to stay at the gompa.

A bus from Leh to Tikse leaves about every hour. Alternatively, take the Hemis bus, which leaves Leh at 9.30 am and 4 pm. From the bus stop, it is a fair walk up to the gompa, as usual. A return taxi from Leh will cost Rs 365.

Ladakh Regions

This section deals with areas which have been recently opened up to travellers (with permits) by the Indian authorities.

PERMITS

Permits are required for all foreigners (including non-Ladakhi and non-Zanskari Indians) travelling to the four newly opened areas in Ladakh: the Nubra Valley, Pangong Tso, Tso Moriri and the Dha-Hanu region. Recently, these permits and their enforcement have become less strict. Check the current regulations.

At the time of researching, permits were only valid for seven days, and although four people must *apply* for a permit together, checkpoints do not require that you actually *travel* together. Take your permits with you at all times – there are several checkpoints along most roads. If you need a group, leave messages around noticeboards in Leh, or get a travel agency to organise things.

First, a 'letter of introduction' from a travel agency is necessary, even though you don't have to go on an organised tour. Travel agencies in Leh will charge about Rs 50 per person for the letter. Several travel agencies are willing to find some old photocopies of other passports to help 'fill up' the required numbers for your 'group'. Ask discreetly at agencies or check with other travellers.

Second, fill out the application form, which your travel agent will have. List every place you may go to, within the permitted regions. Then take a copy of the front page of your passport (ie with your personal details and photo), and Indian visa. Take it all to the District Magistrate's Office in Leh (open 10 am to 4 pm daily except Sunday and public holidays), just above the polo ground. And wait. It is worth considering paying your travel agent another Rs 80 to Rs 100 per person to organise the permit. This includes a special 'fee' for speedy service at the Magistrate's Office.

Take a photocopy of the permit for yourself. These permits must be shown at checkpoints. Hotels in the regions may also require details of your permit.

Consider others if you are thinking of breaking your permit regulations, by going to restricted areas or overstaying your allotted seven days. If you do break the rules, you will be in trouble, your travel agency will be severely penalised, and regulations are likely to become stricter, affecting future travellers.

CLIMATE

The average summer (June to September) and winter (October to May) temperatures for the four regions are:

Region	Max	Min
Nubra Valley	28/15°C	-3/-15°C
Pangong Tso	18/5°C	-12/-25°C
Tso Moriri	17/6°C	-10/-22°C
Dha-Hanu region	29/15°C	-3/-15°C

WHAT TO BRING

For the two lake regions, Pangong Tso and Tso Moriri, there are no guesthouses, or shops to buy supplies (although this is likely to change soon). You must take all your own food, as well as sleeping and cooking equipment – which can be hired in Leh. In the more populated Dha-Hanu and Nubra Valley areas, there are a few guesthouses for accommodation

and food, and small shops for basic supplies. To liven up a boring plate of *dhal* and rice or *thukpa* (Tibetan soup) or to please locals if you are willing to share, it's a good idea to bring some canned meat and fresh vegetables from Leh if visiting the remote villages in Dha-Hanu and Nubra.

Even at the height of summer, temperatures in some valleys can be extremely cold. A sleeping bag and warm clothes are vital in all areas. The days can be hot, causing dry skin and sunburn, so a good hat, sunscreen and so on are important. Other items worth considering are torches (flashlights) and candles, as electricity, if there is any, is unreliable in all regions. Consider bringing binoculars to admire the wildlife, which is guaranteed to disappear when you get too close.

ORGANISED TOURS

Tours, organised by reputable travel agencies in Leh, are the easiest, most comfortable, but, naturally, most expensive way to go. If you want to pay more for a guide and some comfort, make sure the tour is not just a local taxi-driver-cum-guide, because you can organise one of them yourself at the taxi stand in Leh for far less. Demand, as well as the quality of jeep, tent accommodation, food, destination and guide, affects the price of organised tours, but a rough idea of the costs per day per person for an upmarket trip are: US$40 to US$60 for a five day package to the Nubra Valley; US$50 to US$65 for three days at Pangong Tso; and US$55 to US$70 for four days to Tso Moriri.

NUBRA VALLEY

The Nubra Valley – *nubra* means green – used to be on the trading route which connected Tibet with Turkistan, and was the envy of Turkistan, which invaded it several times. Also known as the Valley of Flowers, Nubra has always been well cultivated and fertile, with the best climate in Ladakh, so grains and fruits, such as apples and apricots, have always been plentiful. The Nubra population is 90% Buddhist.

The valley is a wonderful area to visit, dominated by an incredible broad, empty valley between the Nubra and Shyok rivers. Camels are common near Hunder. There are pretty, small villages, dense forests and some wildlife, but, inevitably, the area is becoming slowly more affected by the increasing number of travellers who make the effort to visit. Remember that your permit only allows you to travel as far as Hunder along the southern valley, and to Panamik in the northern valley.

Festivals

The Nubra Valley isn't as crowded with gompas as the area around Leh, so festivals tend to be less religious and more sport-oriented. As part of the annual Ladakh Festival in the first two weeks of September, there are many activities in the Nubra Valley which should not be missed, including a camel safari between Diskit and Hunder. Activities are generally centred in the main villages of Diskit and Sumur.

Leh to Kardung

The road to the Nubra Valley goes through the highest motorable pass in the world at Kardung La (5602m). The pass is almost permanently covered in fog and snow, and is likely to be bitterly cold at the top regardless of the time of year. A free cup of hot *chai*, (tea) near the 'highest temple in the world' – Jai Kardungla Babe – is most welcome. In the summer, you may see the world's highest traffic jam of trucks and buses too.

The road between Leh and Khalsar is reasonable, except between the miserable road-building camps of South Pullu and North Pullu, just before and after Kardung La, where the road is atrocious. Near the pass, there are many places to stop for views, if you can, such as the intriguing-sounding Siachen Taggles' Gate.

The road then continues to Kardung village, which, most disappointingly, has no tea stall, one very basic shop, and an unused Government Rest House.

Khalsar

The Nubra Valley really starts at the village of Khalsar, where there *are* several tea houses and some hotels for about Rs 30 to Rs 50 per room. The better two are *L Tonyot*, which also serves good dhal and rice, and the *Wisnu Hotel*. The road then divides just before the village of Lughzhun, the left fork going to Hunder and beyond in the valley following the Shyok River, and the right heading north to Panamik and beyond, following the Nubra River.

Diskit

To Diskit, the road suddenly turns left, along an awesome, wide and dry riverbed for about three km. Truck and bus drivers know where to turn off (there are no signs), so if you have your own transport, ask and follow the other vehicles. Diskit is about 10km further up the hill.

The **Diskit Gompa**, with about 70 monks, is the oldest – over 350 years old – and the biggest of its kind in the Nubra Valley.

Between Diskit and Hunder is an area of **sand dunes**, not unlike the Saharan regions (if you can ignore the snow-capped Alps-like mountains in the background!).

Places to Stay & Eat About 50m from the gompa, *Olthang Guest House & Camping* has a nice garden and costs Rs 150 per room, with attached bathroom.

Shahen Hotel, on the main street in the village, is very basic for about Rs 50 a room – you may have to find someone to open the hotel and take your money.

Sand Dune Hotel in the village has been recommended.

Hunder

Hunder is a pretty village, set among lots of trees and mingling streams. It is nicer than Diskit, but Diskit, the bigger village of the two, has slightly better facilities. From Diskit, it is only about seven km to Hunder; some visitors enjoy the walk between the villages, either along the main road or across the sand dunes (but watch out for wild camels!).

The **gompa** at Hunder is about a two km walk above the village, including a short, steep, rocky climb. It is completely deserted and quite eerie. There is only a small Buddha statue and some damaged frescoes, but the climb is worth it for the views and atmosphere. Don't wander too far up the road – there's a heavy military presence.

Places to Stay & Eat The *Nerchung Pa*, owned by the local headmaster, is one of the better places. It is friendly, set in a nice garden, costs Rs 150 per person including three meals, and is impossible to find; ask locals for directions.

Camping sites are being developed, but their rumoured prices – over Rs 1000 per night for a pre-set two person tent with meals – are outrageous. Hopefully, prices will decrease with time and competition. Alternatively, find a spot near the village to camp for free. There is no electricity this far up the valley, so torches and candles are necessary, and should be brought from Leh.

Sumur

Sumur, a major village along the Nubra River side of the valley, is a pretty place worth exploring.

The **Samtanling Gompa** at Sumur, over 150 years old, is a large complex with seven temples. Inaugurated by the Dalai Lama in 1962, it is a busy, friendly place with about 45 children busy chanting or cultivating apples and apricots. The prayer rooms that are open to the public house an impressive collection of thangkas and excellently restored frescoes.

By road, it is a fair distance from Sumur village to the gompa: about three km south towards the village of Tegar, from where a three km road to the gompa starts. It's far quicker on foot, as you can go up the hill from the village and avoid the road, but you will have to ask directions. It can be confusing because the gompa near the start of the road to the Samtanling Gompa is actually the Tegar Gompa. The Samtanling Gompa is the more colourful one, and is situated closer to Sumur.

Places to Stay & Eat The *Hotel Sumur* is on the main road. It's rather dingy, but offers rock-bottom prices.

Tsering Angchok Hotel is another no-frills place but cheapish at Rs 70 per person – just follow the signs from the main road.

Stakrey Guest House, owned by the local headmaster, is further up (ask directions). For about Rs 200 per person including three meals, you get good, friendly service and mountain views.

Hotel Yarab Tso just opposite the road leading to the Samtanling Gompa, near the village of Tegar, is more upmarket. For an overpriced Rs 975, you get a large, clean room and immaculate bathroom with hot water. (This is the first of several, similarly priced places being built around the Nubra Valley.)

Samtanling Gompa is an accommodation option only if you are a serious (male) Buddhist student.

Some shops near the main road in Sumur stock limited supplies, and there are tea stalls serving basic food.

Panamik

Panamik is another small village, famous for centuries for its **hot springs**, and as the first or last stop along the ancient trade route between Ladakh and central Asia. While Panamik may be a long way to come for some hot springs, they are worth visiting if you're in the Nubra Valley.

The water, which is meant to cure rheumatism, among other ailments, is pumped in by pipe from the Nubra River, about two km from the village. It is usually easier for men to have a bath or shower; unfortunately, women will have to be a bit more modest and careful about their attire. There are also a couple of craft shops in the village, where you can buy some weaving and woodcarvings.

The 250 year old **Ensa Gompa** is a fair walk from the village – a couple of hours at least. It is further than it seems and not really worth the effort; relax and enjoy the hot springs instead. If you do want to get to the gompa, walk about five km to Hargam, then cross the bridge for some more walking. Some travellers have tried to cross the river by swimming or wading, and many have nearly come to a tragic end. Be sensible and take the bridge.

Places to Stay & Eat Currently, there is one guesthouse, which costs Rs 150 for a big double room; dhal, rice and tea will cost more. More guesthouses – and camping sites – are very likely to be built in the near future. There are one or two small shops for supplies, but they offer little. Panamik does not yet have electricity.

Getting There & Away
As with most of Ladakh, the road to the Nubra Valley (because of the very high Kardung La), and, therefore, the valley itself, is only open for three to four months of the year, from about June to September.

Air Indian Airlines (IA) reportedly wants to commence flights, probably from Delhi, direct to Hunder, where there is a military airfield which can be converted to accommodate civilian aircraft.

If flights to the Nubra Valley do start, there are serious implications for the infrastructure of the region which could not yet cope with a tourist influx, and it will presumably increase the availability of associated transport, such as taxis and local buses, in the region.

Bus Buses travel from Leh to both sides of the Nubra Valley every few days. The time-tables are irregular, so check with local bus and tourist agencies. The buses are slow and crowded, as expected in this region, but fun. Buses between Leh and Diskit travel on Monday and Friday (at least five hours, Rs 54); they leave Leh at 5.30 am. Buses from Diskit to Panamik and back go on Monday and Wednesday. The bus will drop you off in the main street of Diskit, a little way off the main road. A bus to Sumur and on to Panamik (Rs 66) leaves Leh at 5.30 am on Monday and Wednesday.

Truck Lifts on trucks, even military ones – in fact, anything travelling along the roads to, and around, the Nubra Valley – is quite acceptable for tourists and locals alike. As usual, negotiate a fare (around the cost of the bus fare, ie Rs 60), and prepare yourself for a rough old ride.

Taxi Hiring jeeps or taxis may be the only alternative; with a group it is often a good option. A one-way/return taxi to Diskit from Leh will cost Rs 3050/4025. A taxi from Leh to Panamik will cost about Rs 3200, or Rs 4270 return. A return trip from Leh visiting Diskit, Hunder, Sumur and Panamik for three days will cost about Rs 8000 per taxi. If there are taxis around Diskit, they will offer full-day tours of the area on the southern side of the valley for Rs 860; or Rs 1300 for both sides. From Diskit to Panamik, it will be Rs 1000/1290; from Diskit to Sumur, Rs 650/840.

PANGONG TSO
The salty Pangong Tso – Pangong means hollow – is the highest lake in Ladakh at about 4300m, and is flanked by massive peaks over 6500m high. The lake is 150km long but only four km at its widest. It extends almost in a straight line way into Tibet; in fact, only a quarter of the lake is in India.

Pangong Tso is a good side-trip from Leh: it involves less bone-crushing travel, transport is cheaper because it is closer to Leh, and less time is needed to see it than other regions. Permits allow travel from Leh to Pangong Tso via Karu, Chang La, Durbuk, Tangtse, Lukung and only as far as Spangmik, the first village on the north-western side of the lake.

The area around Tangtse, on the way to the lake, is of historical significance, as it was an important stop on ancient trade routes. There is a small **gompa** and some **inscriptions**, possibly 1000 years old, on the rocks around the area, but these are hard to locate.

Places to Stay & Eat
There are no guesthouses in the villages except a *Government Rest House* in Tangtse, which is not strictly for tourists, so you will have to bring your own tents and all your own supplies. Official camping sites are at Durbuk, Tangtse, Lukung and Spangmik;

otherwise, just take your pick of any unofficial spot in the countryside. Lukung is about the best area for camping. There are several little villages along the lake, and on the way to it, but they offer little, if anything, in the way of supplies.

Getting There & Away
From Leh, the road is reasonable to the military town of Karu, goes through the Chang La pass (5599m), and then becomes terrible down to Tangtse, another military site. The road then alternates between very bad and barely adequate until Lukung, and then to Spangmik, which is as far as your permit will allow; a 4WD vehicle is necessary for this section.

By Indian or Japanese jeep from Leh the cost of a one-way/return fare to Tangtse is Rs 2500/3300. A more leisurely two day return trip, which is about all you may need, will cost Rs 5000 per vehicle from Leh. You may be able to fit in a side trip to the gompas at Tikse and Chemrey along the way to Tangtse.

There are occasional buses from Leh to Tangtse, but taking a bus will severely limit your ability to explore the area, as there is no local public transport.

TSO MORIRI & TSO KAR
Known as 'mountain lake', Tso Moriri is located in the Rupsu Valley, only about 140km, but a rough and tumble six or so hours by jeep, from Leh. The lake is about 28km long, eight km at its widest and at an elevation of over 4000m. Surrounded by barren hills, which are backed by snow-covered mountains, Tso Moriri is not in a really spectacular setting, but it's a good place to relax, visit the nearby **gompas** and walk around the lake area. On the way from Leh to Tso Moriri is another brackish lake, the smaller Tso Kar, or 'white lake'.

This is an area of nomadic people, known as Khampas, who can often be seen taking advantage of the summer and moving herds of goats, cows and yaks from one grazing spot to another. Khampas live in large, movable, family tents or in solid winter-proof brick huts.

Another great aspect of this region is the amount of wildlife – the best (accessible) place in Ladakh for it. Commonly seen are wild asses (known as *kiangs*), foxes and cuddly marmots busy waking up from their last hibernation, or preparing for the next. On the lakes, you may see large flocks of black-necked geese.

Tso Moriri
The small collection of huts on the shore of Tso Moriri is also called Tso Moriri. Here you must register and show your permit. You can pitch your tent here, but there is nothing stopping you from camping anywhere else. Tso Moriri village does have a toilet.

Korzok
A path at the back of the huts for a km or so leads to the delightful village of Korzok, inhabited by friendly people. The **gompa** here is quite unusual because it is inhabited predominantly by about 30 women, who often spend their days making beautiful garments for themselves, but which are not for sale (or not yet). The gompa was built in about 1850, replacing one destroyed during a Dogra invasion.

Tso Kar
On Tso Kar, there is a small **gompa** at the village of Thukse, a collection of solid brick huts set up for the dramatic winters. You will have to find the monk to let you in. On a slight – and legal – detour off the track linking Tso Kar and Tso Moriri is the smaller lake of **Tso Kiagar**.

Places to Stay & Eat
In short, there is nowhere to stay in the region at all – though this may change as demand increases. You must bring your own tents and all equipment. There are pre-set tents at the astronomical price of Rs 800 per two-person tent at Tso Moriri village; these are set up for upmarket, organised tour groups. Some building was going on at Tso Moriri village at the time of writing, so small shops selling limited supplies may be set up soon.

There is no place to eat in the region, so, again, bring your own food and cooking equipment. This is a very fragile environment, so take out, and back to Leh, everything that you bring in – cans, bottles, papers, *everything*.

Getting There & Away

There are two ways by which your 4WD jeep is physically able, and permitted, to enter or leave the region. The first route is over the Mahe bridge (near Raldong, along the Indus Valley road), through Puga, and then to one or both lakes. The other route is the road south from Upshi, over the Taglang La (5328m), then a detour off the road – look out for the yellow sign. Once you get off any main road, there are no signs (or maps) at all.

No public transport goes remotely near the lakes. The area has no signposts and quality maps are nonexistent, so motorcycles or mountain bikes are not recommended unless you have a guide. There will be very few people around to give you directions.

Taxi A round trip from Leh to Tso Moriri over three days will cost about Rs 8100 via Tso Kar and Taglang La, or the shorter, more direct way is Rs 6500. From Leh, a two day round trip just to Tso Kar will be Rs 4200. Travel agencies in Leh can organise a three day 'jeep safari' from Rs 7000 to Rs 9500 per vehicle, including meals and tent accommodation, depending which way you go.

TREKS IN LADAKH

Treks out of Leh and the Indus Valley include the trek from Spituk just below Leh to the Markha Valley and Hemis Gompa and the trek from Lamayuru Gompa to Chiling village alongside the Zanskar river. These treks can be completed from the end of June until the middle of October, when the first of the winter snows settle on the high passes. Proper acclimatisation is essential on both these treks and a few days in Leh (3505m) are recommended before setting off.

There are many trekking agencies in Leh offering inclusive treks with a guide, pack horses, food and supplies for around US$50 per day. When making your own arrangements

pack horses can be hired from Spituk or Lamayuru for around Rs 200 per horse per day. It is recommended that all camping gear including sleeping bag and tent are brought with you even on *inclusive* treks, as the gear provided may not be adequate. Food supplies should also be carried with you from Leh as the village lodges and tea houses are not available on all stages of the treks.

Spituk to Markha Valley & Hemis via the Kongmaru La

From Spituk Gompa the trail follows the open desert plain south of the Indus river before entering the Jingchen Valley. An extra day should be reserved for acclimatisation in the vicinity of the village of Rumbak before continuing to the base of the Ganda La (4920m). From the pass there are views north to the Zanskar Range before descending to the Markha Valley and the village of Skiu. It's a further stage to Markha, a substantial village with a small gompa, before a long and gradual climb to the yak grazing pastures at Nimaling, set beneath the impressive peak of Kangyaze (6400m).

The Kongmaru La (5030m) is the highest pass on the trek and affords great views north across the Indus Valley to the snow capped peaks of the Ladakh Range. From the pass there is a steep descent through narrow gorges to the settlement of Chogdo. The final stage to Hemis Gompa can be completed in four to five hours with time to visit the gompa before catching the bus back to Leh.

Stage 1	Spituk to Rumbak (6 to 7 hours)
Stage 2	Rumbak to Yurutse & camp (4 to 5 hours)
Stage 3	Yurutse to Skiu via the Ganda La (6 to 7 hours)
Stage 4	Skiu to Markha (7 to 8 hours)
Stage 5	Markha to Nimaling (7 to 8 hours)
Stage 6	Nimaling to Chogdo via Kongmaru La (6 hours)
Stage 7	Chogdo to Hemis (4 to 5 hours)

Lamayuru to Chiling via the Konze La & Dung Dung La

From Lamayuru the trek crosses the Prinkiti La (3750m) to the village and ancient gompa at Wanlah. It's a further stage to the village of Hinju at the base of the Konze La. An extra day should be reserved here for acclimatisation before ascending the Konze La (4950m). From the pass there are impressive views of the East Karakoram Range before the trail down via the open meadows to the village of Sumdo Choon. From Sumdo Choon it is a further stage to the yak herders encampment at the base of the Dung Dung La. Views from the Dung Dung La (4820m) are rewarded with views of the Zanskar Range and a bird's eye view of the swirling Zanskar River before a long and tiring descent to the village of Chiling. .

From Chiling you can either return to Leh by jeep or bus or extend your trek by heading up the Markha Valley. The trek from Chiling to the village of Skiu in the Markha Valley can be completed in three hours. It then takes a further four stages to reach Hemis Gompa and the Indus Valley.

Stage 1	Lamayuru to Wanlah via Prinkiti La (3 to 4 hours)
Stage 2	Wanlah to Hinju (4 to 5 hours)
Stage 3	Hinju to Sumdo Chinmu via Konze La (6 hours)
Stage 4	Sumdo Choon to Dung Dung La base (3 hours)
Stage 5	Camp to Choon via Dung Dung La (6 hours)

Likir to Temisgam

This trek can be completed in a day if you are fit! From Likir Gompa the trail crosses a small pass to the village of Yantang a short distance from Rizdong Gompa. The next stage leads to the village of Hemis-Shukpachu. It is a further short stage over two minor passes to the roadhead at Temisgam. The trek can be completed throughout the year, horses can be hired from Likir, and supplies and a tent must be brought from Leh.

Road building will eventually render this trek obsolete. Until then there is a daily bus service to Likir, and a bus from Temisgam back to Leh each day around midday, making it possible to complete the third stage of the trek and be back in Leh that evening.

Stage 1	Likir to Yangtang (4 to 5 hours)
Stage 2	Yangtang to Hemis-Shukpachu (3 hours)
Stage 3	Hemis-Shukpachu to Temisgam (3 to 4 hours)

Leh to Manali

This road was opened to foreigners in 1989 and has become increasingly popular as an alternative to the once well-worn Srinagar-Leh route.

The road to Manali is the world's second-highest motorable road, reaching an elevation of 5328m at Taglang La. As only about half of the total distance of 485km between Leh and Manali is paved, it can be a rough journey. Whatever form of transport, it will take at least two days, with an overnight stop at a tent camp, probably in Sarchu or Darcha.

It is not uncommon for there to be sudden changes in weather, even in the mid-summer month of August, causing delays of several days. While it may be sunny in Leh, it is worth having some cold and wet weather gear with you in the bus because the weather, especially around the very high passes, can be very cold and/or wet. The road is usually open between early June and mid-October.

LEH TO UPSHI

Leaving Leh, from the main road you will get your last glimpse (or your first, if coming from Manali) of the magnificent gompas at Tikse, Shey and Stok. For an hour or so before Upshi, along a paved but dusty road, there are plenty of ugly military sites, such as at Karu, where there is the turnoff to the Pangong Tso area, and to the gompas at Taktok and Chemrey.

UPSHI

The first checkpoint of Upshi is the turnoff south to Manali. Although permits are not needed for this trip, foreigners have to register at the police hut. If travelling on a bus with plenty of other foreigners, there is enough time for tea, an 'omlate', or to stock up on supplies of chocolate and other goodies.

In Upshi, there are a couple of desperate-looking places to stay at the junction, at about Rs 50 per room, but there seems little point, as it is not far from Leh.

UPSHI TO TAGLANG LA

At Miru, the crumbling little **gompa** is worth a look. It's on the nearby hill, surrounded by chortens. There is nowhere to stay or eat, but plenty of camping sites. Lato has a huge **chorten** on the side of the road, but there is no village to speak of. Rumtse is another small village, with an empty Tourist Bungalow (which may be open at another time) and

To Srinagar
Leh
To Taktok &
Tikse
Pangong Tso
Indus River
Karu
35km
Chemrey
Upshi
49km
Miru
64km
Leh-Manali
Lato
70km
Route
Rumtse
79km
To Chumathang
Not to Scale
& Tso Moriri
Taglang La
(via Mahe)
Distances in km from Leh
(5328m)
109km
Pang
184km
To Tso Kar
& Tso Moriri
Lachlung La
(5060m)
209km
To Padum
Sarchu
263km
Patseo
326km
Darcha
340km
Baralacha La
(4883m)
To Udaipur &
299km
Triloknath
Bhaga River
Keylong
372km
Jispa
347km
HIMACHAL
PRADESH
Tandi
386km
Chandra
Gondla
Sissu
Khoksar
390km
398km
414km
Grampu
Kunzum La
Rohtang Pass
419km
(4551m)
(3978m)
To
434km
River
Kaza
Manali
Batal
485km
To Delhi

some tent hotels which also serve food. From here the road starts to climb for about three hours to Taglang La (5328m), where there's a little shrine and the world's highest 'Gents Urinal' and 'Ladies Urinal'. The bus stops for a rest and a look around, but if you're coming from Manali and haven't acclimatised to the altitude, take it easy.

TAGLANG LA TO LACHLUNG LA

Not long after Taglang La, the road surprisingly flattens out along a valley, and becomes paved. If going on to Tso Moriri or Tso Kar, you will have to look out for the sign (refer to the earlier Ladakh Regions section). The road to Pang is good, through a windswept valley, then becomes hopelessly potholed. Five km before Pang, the road descends through a dramatic series of **gorges** before reaching the tea-house settlement.

Pang, at the bottom of these gorges, has several restaurants in tents set up by the river, where most buses stop for lunch. A plate of rice, dhal and vegetables costs about Rs 20, and you may be able to stock up on mineral water and biscuits. Most tents have a mattress where you can unroll your sleeping bag for Rs 50 per night.

At 5060m, Lachlung La is the second-highest pass on the Leh to Manali road. Nearby is an incredible 20km of switchback roads, including a spine-tingling 21 'loops', or hairpin bends, on one side of one mountain.

SARCHU

Sarchu, just over the state line in Himachal Pradesh, is where most buses stop overnight. It is just a collection of tents, stretching over 15km or so, which all pack up for eight months of the year (ie October to May). Just opposite the striped Himachal Pradesh Tourist Development Corporation (HPTDC) tent camps, you must register, again, with the police. Your bus driver may collect passports and do it himself – either way it involves a lot of waiting.

HPTDC buses stop at HPTDC's own **tent camps**, which are the best of the lot: clean, two-person tents with camp beds and lots of blankets are Rs 115 per person. A tent kitchen

LADAKH & ZANSKAR

does passable dhal and rice for dinner, and omelettes for breakfast, for about Rs 40.

Public and other private bus drivers seem to have some sort of 'arrangement' with other tent site owners, so you may have little choice but to stay in a tent camp not even remotely as good as the HPTDC site, but for around the same price. Although the driver will try to dissuade you, you can sleep on the bus for free, where it will be warmer. There are plenty of places to put your own tent.

Just over the bridge from the HPTDC camp are several *tent restaurants* which serve dhal and rice, tea, omelettes, curried noodles and, for those long cold evenings, a shot (or bottle) of whisky or *chang* (Tibetan rice beer).

BARALACHA LA
It's only a short climb to this 4883m pass, which means 'crossroads pass' because it is a double pass linking both the upper Chandra and Bhaga valleys with the Lingti Valley and vast Lingti plains around Sarchu. About an hour further on is the **police checkpoint** at Patseo. Here the road begins to hug the Bhaga River to Tandi, where it meets the Chandra River.

DARCHA
Darcha is the other major tent site on this road. Faster buses from Leh, or slower ones from Manali, may stay here, depending on the time and the state of the road around Baralacha La, but Sarchu is more commonly used as a stopover. Like Sarchu, Darcha is just a temporary place, with some crummy tents for hire, and a few tent restaurants in the area. There is a police checkpoint. Shortly after Darcha, you pass through Jispa, where there is yet another large army camp.

Darcha is the start of a popular trekking option to Padum, and in winter it is the only way. From here, you can also trek into places such as Hemis (about 11 days). If you have your own transport, try to get to the little lake of **Deepak Tal** about 16km from Darcha. It is a great spot for camping and exploring.

KEYLONG TO MANALI
Keylong is the first town of any size on the journey from Leh to Manali, and the administrative centre of Lahaul and Spiti. From Keylong, it isn't far to the T-junction at Tandi. From here a road goes sharply to the north-west along the Chenab River to the little-visited parts of Himachal Pradesh towards Udaipur and the famous temple site of **Triloknath**.

The road to Manali heads south-east and climbs steadily past Gondla, Sissu and Khoksar. There are Public Works Department (PWD) rest houses, which you may be able to use, in all three places, but nothing much else. At **Sissu**, there is a nice **waterfall** nearby, set under spectacular peaks. Further on, at Gramphu, the road continues to climb along Lahaul and Spiti – get off at Gramphu or at Keylong if you want to continue to Kaza – or heads south to Manali.

Rohtang Pass (3978m) – not high, but treacherous all the same – starts the descent to Manali.

Refer to the Himachal Pradesh chapter for more details on the towns of Keylong and Manali.

GETTING THERE & AWAY
Bus
As the road goes up to 5328m at its highest point, most people suffer the effects of altitude (eg headaches, nausea) from the rapid ascent, unless they have spent time acclimatising in Leh.

If you plan to fly one way, then fly into Leh and take the bus out because the effects of the altitude gain on the Leh-Manali journey will not be so great as doing the journey in the other direction.

All buses leave Leh at about 6 am to get an early start for the long haul to the overnight stop. Make sure you know your bus number because at this early hour, in darkness, it can be quite confusing finding your bus among several others.

Three types of buses travel between Leh and Manali; all of which generally run daily during the season, more often if there is demand. Most bus services will not start until about early July and then cease in about mid-September, possibly later, if there is

LADAKH & ZANSKAR

demand and the weather holds. Late in the season, the availability of buses from Leh depends on the demand in the other direction, ie from Manali to Leh. From Manali, it is easy to get a connection on a deluxe bus almost straight away to Delhi (about Rs 400) or to many other places; less for the public bus.

HPTDC Bus The most comfortable bus is operated by the HPTDC. Bookings and departures are from the HPTDC office on Fort Rd in Leh, or the HPTDC Marketing Office (☎ 2116) on The Mall, Manali. Tickets cost Rs 700 (Rs 600 from Leh to Keylong), or Rs 1000 including a tent, dinner and breakfast in Sarchu. This extra Rs 300 is not worth it, as you can stay in the same tent and order the same meals yourself in Sarchu for about half the price. Try to book your bus ticket as far in advance as you can, especially if you intend travelling at the end of the season.

Private Bus Many other privately owned (by travel agencies in Manali) buses offer a slightly cheaper, and slightly less comfortable, alternative. All private buses cost around the same: about Rs 600, plus accommodation and food in Sarchu or Darcha – but the price can, and does, change according to the demand. In Leh, you must buy your tickets from one of the travel agencies, which means you probably won't know what bus you have a ticket for until you get on. In Manali, bookings can, and should be, made directly with the bus agencies themselves (any of the travel agencies in Manali can also sell you a ticket). Some of the bus companies in Manali servicing the Leh to Manali route on a regular basis are:

Enn Bee Tours & Travels, The Mall, opposite the bus station (☎ 2650)
Ibex Tours, Hotel Ibex, The Mall (☎ 2480)
Swagtam's Tours, Mission Rd (☎ 2390)
Tarun Tours & Travels, just off the Mall (☎ 2688)

Public Bus The third alternative is the far less comfortable and generally slower, but certainly cheaper, public bus. They leave, according to demand, every one or two days from Leh and Manali at about 4 am. 'Super Deluxe' (a bit of a misnomer) costs Rs 490; 'A Class' is Rs 475; and 'B Class' is Rs 350. Subtract about Rs 70 from the fare if you plan to get off at Keylong.

Truck
Trucks are often quicker than buses, and should be cheaper. They may not stop at Sarchu, but instead drive throughout the night, which is not a great idea; or they may stop overnight anywhere alongside the road – also not a great idea. Trucks can be more comfortable if there are only a couple of people in the cabin. Plenty of trucks travel this route, in season. It is just a matter of getting to the area where the trucks stop in Leh and Manali very, very early – or better, organise a lift the day before. The cost should be about half the tourist bus price, and a little less than the cheapest bus – about Rs 300.

Taxi
Another option – which is not outrageous if in a group – is a taxi between Leh and Manali for a 'fixed' (but in reality negotiable) Rs 10,770. This can be arranged at the Taxi Union on Fort Rd in Leh, or on The Mall, Manali.

Motorcycle
Motorcycles are an increasingly popular means of travelling between Leh and Manali, and places beyond. (Refer to the Getting Around chapter for details.) This, of course, gives you the option of taking several days to admire the spectacular scenery.

It is worth remembering that there are no villages between Leh and Keylong, so you will have to take all your spare parts, particularly spare chains and tubes – and enough spare parts to get out of Leh, because Leh doesn't have much to offer either. Some tent sites may sell limited petrol at twice the Leh or Manali price; there are petrol stations at Tandi and Keylong, but nowhere else. At all times, it is advisable to wear cold and wet-weather gear throughout the trip, including boots, because the road is always muddy, wet and dusty in places. It seems unnecessary to advise that you take it easy. And look out for trucks and buses at all times!

Leh to Kargil

This section refers to places on, or near, the main road from Leh to Kargil. The places below are listed in order of distance from Leh.

A number of buses ply the 231km to Kargil. Trucks are also a good option for a lift and for hitching between villages. Taxis may seem outrageous but with a group sharing the cost you can visit several gompas on the way to, say, Alchi or Lamayuru. A taxi from Leh to Alchi, stopping at Phyang, Basgo, Likir and Rizong, will cost about Rs 1200 – about US$10 each in a group of four.

PHYANG

Not far past Spituk (refer to the earlier Around Leh section for details on Spituk), a long, roughish track off the main road leads to the pretty village of Phyang. **Mani walls** lead to the little-visited gompa, which was built around the 15th century by King Tashi Nam-

gyal and now houses about 45 monks who belong to the Kagyupa order.

Direct buses from Leh leave daily at 8 am, 2 and 5 pm. Hitching is not really possible as very few vehicles make the detour to Phyang. Taxis from Leh cost Rs 350 or Rs 470 return. From Phyang, a trekking route almost parallel to the main road passes through some lovely villages such as Likir and Temisgam, before returning to the main road near Khalsi.

NIMMU

Nimmu is a pleasant place to stop for tea. About eight km east, towards Leh, is the junction of the differently coloured Indus and Zanskar rivers. If you can, get out and admire this really spectacular sight. To get to Nimmu, take any bus going from Leh beyond Nimmu, or a one-way/return taxi from Leh costs Rs 520/650.

BASGO

It's only six km further on to Basgo, which was the capital of lower Ladakh, before the Ladakh kingdom was united at Leh. The 400 year old gompa is up some winding, steep

tracks. It is often deserted, so ask around for one of the handful of monks in the village to open up. The prayer room in the Ser Zung Temple has great frescoes; another temple has an enormous gold and copper statue of the Maitreya Buddha (the coming Buddha), and some elaborate roof and wall frescoes. The views from the roof are wonderful.

The *Lagung Guest House*, next to the gompa, offers basic but reasonable accommodation. Daily buses from Leh go direct to Basgo at 1 and 4 pm (these times are changeable, so check at the tourist office in Leh for an update); or catch one of the daily buses to Alchi or beyond. A one-way/return taxi to Basgo from Leh costs Rs 575/650.

LIKIR

Located five km north of the main road, just before Saspul, is another magnificent gompa, overlooking the village of Likir. Known as the Klu-kkhyil (water spirits) Gompa, it was founded in the 14th century, and was the first gompa in Ladakh known to have been built under the direction of Tibetan monks. The present gompa was rebuilt in the 18th century, re-dedicated to the Gelukpa order, and is now inhabited by almost 150 friendly monks, who offer free tea to visitors and are happy to show you around.

To stay in Likir, return to the village, about 30 minutes walk across the fields. The *Lharjan Guest House* has a vicious dog and a landlady who speaks no English at all. Far more hospitable is the pleasant *Norboo Guest House*, with a large, authentic Ladakhi kitchen. Rooms here, including all meals, are good value at Rs 100 per person. A bus to Likir village, which continues to the gompa, leaves Leh every day at 3 pm. A one-way/return taxi from Leh costs Rs 760/ 850.

ALCHI

Alchi is a busy village with several good places to stay and eat, and masses of stalls selling handicrafts.

The Alchi Gompa is the only one in the Ladakhi region on flat ground, so no knee-breaking climb is involved. The gompa was founded in the 11th century by The Great

Translator, Ringchen Zangpo, on his return from India, which accounts for the Indian, and particularly Kashmiri, influences.

The three-storey **Dharma Wheel Gompa**, actually run by the gompa in Likir, is noted for its massive Buddha statues. Within the complex, there are other statues made of clay, lavish woodcarvings, the only examples of Kashmiri-style wall paintings in the area, and many chortens around the village. Unfortunately, some of the frescoes showing the life of Buddha have been rather badly restored. But thanks to some help from German experts, all may not be lost or irrecoverable.

Places to Stay & Eat

Choskpor, in the village a short distance from the gompa, offers good and simple doubles/triples for Rs 70/80, and basic meals in a nice garden. It's very popular.

Zimskhang Guest House, on the lane leading to the temple, is not as good value; rooms cost Rs 150 with common bath and Rs 400 with attached bath.

Royal Chhoksar, a new hotel opposite, was under construction at the time of writing.

Pota La Guest House, behind the chai shops where the buses stop, has airy rooms for Rs 150. It also has a restaurant and camping site (Rs 20 per tent).

The nearby *Samdup Ling Guest House* is of a similar price and standard.

Lotsava Guest House near the village has rooms for Rs 50/80. It is simple, with shared bathroom, but good value.

Getting There & Away

There is one direct bus to Alchi every day, leaving Leh at 3 pm. Otherwise, take any of the other daily buses to places beyond Alchi, get off at the blue sign to 'Alchi Chhoskor Gompa' near the bridge (tee it up with the bus conductor or driver), then walk for an hour along the path to Alchi, or take the short cut, scrambling over the hills near the first bend in the road. A one-way taxi from Leh, direct to Alchi, is Rs 850.

SASPUL

Saspul is a village on the main road, over the river from the turnoff to Alchi. Apparently there is a small **cave temple** nearby, but nobody seems to know much about it. While Saspul is nice enough, Alchi has far more to offer. The *Chakzoth Guest House*, on the main road in Saspul, has small rooms for Rs 30 to Rs 40.

RIZONG

About six km along a steep, rocky track north of the main road is the start of the area containing the nunnery of Julichen and the gompa of Rizong.

There is no village at Rizong, but you may be able to stay at the gompa (men only) or the nunnery (women only); bring your own supplies. Alternatively, near the turnoff to Rizong, about 200m towards Alchi on the main road, is the pleasant *Uletokpo Camping Ground*, which is set among apricot trees.

There is no direct bus to Rizong from Leh, so it is a matter of getting a bus bound for beyond Lamayuru. If coming from Alchi, it is not difficult to hitch a ride on a truck or bus for 20 minutes between the turnoffs for Alchi and Rizong. As an alternative, a one-way taxi from Leh to the bottom of the walk up to the gompa will set you back Rs 1035.

KHALSI

This is a major military area, where your passport will be checked regardless of where you are going, and your permit checked if you're going to the Dha-Hanu region.

LAMAYURU

After exploring villages in the area, it comes as a surprise to find that Lamayuru is a scruffy little place. But it is completely overshadowed by one of the most famous and spectacularly set gompas in Ladakh.

The gompa, part of the Kagyupa order, is not as interesting as others; it's the location that makes it special. The oldest known gompa in Ladakh, dating back beyond the 10th century, it has been destroyed and restored several times over the centuries. There are renowned collections of carpets, thangkas

and frescoes. Criminals were once granted asylum here (not any more, you'll be glad to know!) which explains one previous name for the gompa: Tharpa Ling or 'place of freedom'. Try to get there early to witness a mesmerising puja. Several km south of Lamayuru is the small **Wanlah Gompa**, set on the popular trekking route to Padum in Zanskar.

Places to Stay & Eat

Gompa Hotel is one of the better places to stay on the main road above the gompa, but only if you are not going to explore Lamayuru village or the gompa – there are marginally better, quieter places to stay in the village.

Shangrila Hotel, near the main road, has nice views and doubles with common bath for Rs 50, with attached bath for Rs 120.

Tasigar, above the post office, is very basic but costs just Rs 20 per person.

Dragan (just follow the ubiquitous signs) offers large rooms with share bathroom for Rs 100 per room.

Monastery Hotel at the gompa itself offers very basic accommodation: Rs 25 for a bed and a bucket of hot water (there are no bathrooms).

Getting There & Away

There are no buses from Leh or Kargil directly to Lamayuru, so take the Leh to Kargil/Srinagar bus and get off at the truck stop at the top of the village. A better option is a ride on one of the many trucks that stop there. Trucks leave Lamayuru early morning; ask around at the truck stop for expected departure/arrival times. A one-way taxi in one long day from Leh costs Rs 1775. You can easily walk from the main road to the gompa, and to the village along a road which may be finished soon.

MULBEKH

From Lamayuru the road passes Fatu La (4147m), the highest pass on the route, then Namika La (3760m) before suddenly turning into a lovely green valley. Mulbekh is the last sign of Buddhism before you shortly head into the Muslim-dominated regions near Kargil and beyond.

Mulbekh's main claim to fame is the impressive 8m **Chamba statue**, an image of a future Buddha, cut into the rock face and dating back to about 700 AD. Unfortunately, all buses stop for food and a rest at the village of Wakha, two km from Mulbekh, so this gives you no opportunity to inspect the statue on the way, but you can see it from the bus window.

There are also two gompas, **Serdung** and **Gandentse**, which offer great views of the valley. As in other smaller villages, it is wise to inquire if the gompa is open before making the ascent.

The only place worth staying in Mulbekh is the *Paradise Hotel and Restaurant* (Rs 50 a double with common bath), right opposite the Chamba statue. From Leh, take the Kargil/Srinagar bus. Mulbekh makes a decent day trip from Kargil. A couple of buses leave Kargil for Mulbekh every day. A return taxi from Kargil plus an hour or so in Mulbekh will cost Rs 750.

SHERGOL

About seven km further on towards Kargil, along a fertile valley, is the small village of Shergol. Meaning 'Lord of the Morning Star', Shergol is set on the opening of the Wakha River, and has a tiny **cave gompa** perched halfway up the steep, eastern slope of the mountain. It is almost deserted, and is really for those who can't get enough of gompas and stiff walks up mountains. The view, of course, is magnificent. Below the gompa is a **nunnery**.

Kargil & the Suru Valley

The valleys of Suru, Drass, Wakha and Bodkarbu lie midway between the alpine valleys of Kashmir and the fertile reaches of the Indus Valley and Ladakh. The region is politically part of India, ethnically part of Baltistan and geographically an integral part of Ladakh.

KARGIL
Tel Area Code: 01985

Until 1947 Kargil was an important trading centre linking Ladakh with Gilgit (Pakistan) and the lower Indus Valley. There were also important trading links between the villages of the Suru Valley and the Zanskar Valley, and even 20 years ago it was not uncommon to see yak trains making their way from Padum all the way into the Kargil bazaar.

Continuing political problems in Kashmir have seriously affected the number of visitors to Kargil and the hotels survive at present from the handful of visitors making their way from Leh to Padum and the Zanskar Valley.

The people of Kargil are mostly Shia Muslims: Arabic script is everywhere; women are rarely seen, and if so, are usually veiled; and mosques dominate the town.

Orientation & Information

Kargil, situated next to the roaring Suru River, is the second largest town in Ladakh but is really little more than one long main road called the Main Bazaar Rd, with lots of little lanes jutting off (watch out for wide trucks!). Along the Main Bazaar Rd are plenty of places with long-distance and international telephone facilities, as well as the post office and the State Bank of India, which changes money (Amex and Thomas Cook travellers cheques only) from 10 am to 2 pm weekdays.

There is no electricity during the day, but this should improve with the completion of a huge hydroelectric station nearby. If you have time, walk up Hospital Rd for some decent views of the area. There are also nice fields and villages across the Qatilgah Bridge, at the end of Balti Bazaar Rd.

The Tourist Reception Centre, not to be confused with any similarly named government office, is now next to the taxi stand, just off the main road. It's open from 10 am to 8 pm in summer and till 3.30 pm in winter. Trekking equipment can be hired here: a sleeping bag costs Rs 16 per day, boots (Dolomite) Rs 10 per day, tents (two person,

CHRISTINE NIVEN

BRYN THOMAS

RICHARD I'ANSON

RICHARD I'ANSON

Ladakh & Zanskar

Top: The colours of prayer flags represent earth, fire, clouds, sky and water.

Centre Left: Stupa overlooking Leh.

Centre Right: A shepherd pastures his flock at Sonamarg, the golden meadow.

Bottom: Buddhist prayer stones.

RICHARD I'ANSON

RICHARD I'ANSON

Ladakh & Zanskar
Top: Lamayuru Gompa towers above the village of Lamayuru.
Bottom: Hanging a prayer flag brings luck, prosperity and long life.

Rhundho) Rs 40 per day. No permits are needed for the area. There are no travel or trekking agencies in Kargil.

Places to Stay

Kargil used to be full of grotty places to stay overnight for those travelling between Srinagar and Leh, or onwards to Zanskar. There are still a couple of places on the Main Bazaar Rd, but they are really awful – it is not hard to get somewhere better. Near the bus stand area, but thankfully not affected too much by its noise, are the following places.

Crown Hotel has reasonable singles/doubles for Rs 80/100, with dirty common bathrooms.

The large, rambling *Hotel International* next door is slightly nicer with singles/doubles for Rs 100/150.

The *J&KTDC Tourist Bungalows* in Kargil are infrequently used.

Hotel Greenland (☎ 2324), further south near the taxi stand, has quiet rooms with a verandah, some with nice bathrooms (some with hot water) from Rs 100 per room.

Mid-range accommodation includes:

Hotel Siachen (☎ 2221), where singles/doubles cost Rs 300/450; it has a very nice garden, hot water and is good value.

Caravan Sarai (☎ 2278) in upper Kargil is a nice place, catering for the upmarket trekking crowd, with bed and breakfast, hot water and views for Rs 1000/1400.

D'Zojila (☎ 2360), a little out of Kargil, is also a reasonable place, with singles/doubles for Rs 500/600 including attached bath and hot water.

Places to Eat

There is not much to recommend the restaurants in Kargil – it really isn't set up for long-term visitors. Your hotel will probably do some bland Chinese dishes and some eggs and bread for breakfast. On and near the Main Bazaar Rd are some small restaurants – the *Naktul*, *Shashila* and *Popular Chacha*

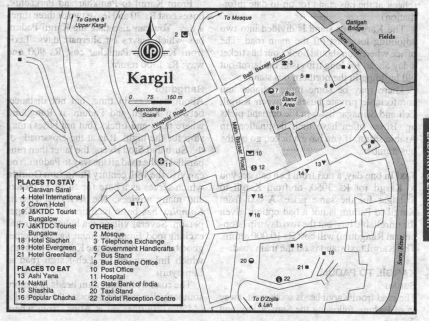

To Goma &
Upper Kargil

To Mosque

Qatilgah
Bridge

Fields

Kargil

0   75   150 m
Approximate
Scale

Suru River

Batti Bazaar Road

Hospital Road

Main Bazaar Road

Bus
Stand
Area

Suru River

To D'Zojila
& Leh

PLACES TO STAY
1 Caravan Sarai
4 Hotel International
5 Crown Hotel
9 J&KTDC Tourist Bungalow
17 J&KTDC Tourist Bungalow
18 Hotel Siachen
19 Hotel Evergreen
21 Hotel Greenland

PLACES TO EAT
13 Ashi Yana
14 Naktul
15 Shashila
16 Popular Chacha

OTHER
2 Mosque
3 Telephone Exchange
6 Government Handicrafts
7 Bus Stand
8 Bus Booking Office
10 Post Office
11 Hospital
12 State Bank of India
20 Taxi Stand
22 Tourist Reception Centre

LADAKH & ZANSKAR

– all of which proudly display advertisements claiming they serve 'Chine's' food. Also worth a try is the *Ashi Yana*. The restaurant at Hotel Siachen serves a good breakfast and, discreetly in the evenings, a bottle of beer, but watch for overcharging.

Getting There & Away
Air Indian Airlines and Archana Airways plan to launch regular flights to Kargil (which has India's second-highest airport) from Leh and Delhi, but at the time of researching, no details were available.

Bus There are early morning daily buses from Kargil to Leh and Kargil to Srinagar, both costing Rs 98 in 'B Class'and Rs 130 in 'A Class'. Towards Leh, there are also two daily buses to Mulbekh and one to Shergol; towards Srinagar, there are regular daily buses to nearby Drass.

There are at least two buses a day to nearby Panikhar and Parkachik. To Padum, in Zanskar, there is a 3 am bus on alternate days (check at the bus stand for up-to-date information).

The Kargil bus stand is divided into two adjoining lots, just off the main road. The office where you should book your bus ticket a day ahead for long trips is in the burnt-out old building in the northern bus stand.

There may be some more reliable and comfortable private buses between Kargil, Leh and Srinagar if/when the demand picks up. Buses often have their destinations in Arabic script. If you have a ticket, go by the bus number.

Taxi In one day, a taxi from Leh can get you to Kargil for Rs 3050, or from Kargil to Srinagar for the same price. A taxi from Kargil to Padum is not a bad option, given the unreliable bus, but the two day trip (stopping at Rangdum) will cost Rs 10,000 return. The Kargil taxi stand is on the main road.

KARGIL TO PADUM
Sanku
The road from Kargil heads south-west, away from Padum, following the Suru Valley and Suru River. It is still predominantly inhabited by Muslims, who converted to Islam in the 15th century; a **Muslim shrine**, dedicated to Sayed Mir Hashim, is located in Karpo-Khar near Sanku. Sanku can also be reached from Drass, west of Kargil on the main road to Srinagar, on a two to three day trek.

There is a bus from Kargil to Sanku every day at 3 pm (Rs 16). At Sanku, accommodation is limited to a *Government Rest House*, which may be rented, and a *J&KTDC Tourist Bungalow*.

Panikhar
Further down the Suru Valley, Panikhar and Parkachik are the places to get off and admire, or even get closer to, the twin mountains of Nun (7135m) and Kun (7087m). It is a lovely area in summer, often full of flowers. In Panikhar, the best accommodation option is a room at the comfortable *J&KTDC Tourist Bungalow*. At the time of researching, with the lack of tourists in the area, it was a bargain Rs 80 per double.

From Kargil to Panikhar and Parkachik, buses cost Rs 30 and leave two or three times a day. You can also take the Kargil-Padum bus which leaves on alternate days. Taxis from Kargil to Panikhar cost Rs 900 one way; Rs 1300 return.

Rangdum
About halfway in time, but not distance, between Kargil and Padum, is Rangdum, where taxis and trucks (but not buses) may stop for the night. It is at the crossroads of the Suru and Stod rivers; the latter then runs parallel to the road all the way to Padum. You can visit the 18th century **Rangdum Gompa** which serves as a base for about 35 monks and many novices. The *J&KTDC Tourist Complex* has basic facilities for Rs 80 per person. Several village tea houses offer unexciting food. From Rangdum, there is another good trek, east through the Kanji La (5255m) which links up with the Leh-Kargil road at Lamayuru.

The road from Rangdum heads in a more southerly direction and crosses the Pentse La (4450m). Further on is Ating, from where you can visit the **Zongkul Gompa**. As you approach Padum, the valley becomes more populous, with plenty of small villages such as Tungri, Phey and Sani.

Zanskar

The isolated region of Zanskar consists of a number of small mountain-locked valleys to the south of Ladakh.

In mid-1995, following political unrest in Zanskar, foreign trekkers were discouraged from visiting the region. However, a resolution of the issues seems to have been achieved and Zanskar leaders issued a statement in January 1996 saying that there will be no further impediment to foreign tourists who may 'come and go freely as before'.

PADUM

Padum, the administrative headquarters of the Zanskar region, was once an ancient capital. It's not a particularly attractive place, with incongruous government buildings that were constructed when the road from Kargil was completed in 1981. This has resulted in

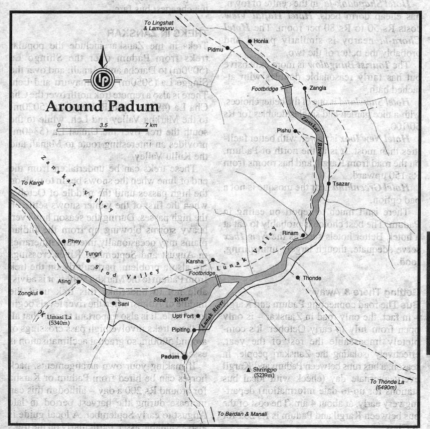

Around Padum

To Lingshat & Lamayuru

Pidmu

Honia

Footbridge

Zangla

Pishu

Zanskar River

To Kargil

Tsazar

Phey

Tungri

Karsha

Footbridge

Rinam

Lunak Valley

Ating

Stod Valley

Zongkul

Sani

Stod River

Upti Fort

Pipiting

Lunak River

Thonde

Umasi La (5340m)

Padum

Shringpo (5239m)

To Thonde La (5490m)

To Bardan & Manali

0   3.5   7 km

the town gaining a character similar to road-heads everywhere. Vehicles are repaired, diesel cans are discarded and much that is not used is disposed of here. The main *camp site* and the small *hotel area* is close to the newly constructed mosque (the only one in the Zanskar region) which serves the small Sunni Muslim community living here.

Padum is also the starting point for a number of difficult long-distance treks.

Places to Stay & Eat
There's a limited choice of just a few basic guesthouses.

Hotel Shapodok-la, in the centre of town, has cheap dorm beds. *Hotel Haftal View* costs Rs 50 to Rs 80 per room. The *Hotel Chora-la* nearby is similarly priced and probably the better of the two.

The *Tourist Bungalow* is more expensive but has fairly reasonable doubles with attached bath.

Hotel Snowland is one of the better choices, with a nice garden and singles/doubles for Rs 50/100.

Hotel New Ibex is newer, with better facilities than most. It is in the north of Padum, on the road from Kargil, and has rooms from Rs 150 upward.

Hotel Greenland near the mosque is not a bad option.

There isn't much to report on eating in Padum. The best choice is probably to eat at a hotel. Better hotels such as the *New Ibex* serve adequate, though largely uninspiring, food.

Getting There & Away
Bus The road connecting Padum and Kargil – in fact, the only road in Zanskar – is only open from July to early October. It's completely impassable the rest of the year, effectively isolating the Zanskari people. In season, a bus runs between Padum and Kargil every alternate day (check with local bus stations for up-to-date information) departing very early, at about 4 am. The cost of the bus between Kargil and Padum is Rs 202 for A Class.

Taxi By taxi, it costs Rs 10,000 return from Kargil to Padum (no-one with a vehicle in Padum will do the journey from Padum in reverse), but with a group to cut costs, this is a great way to really admire the amazing scenery. This trip would be done over two days, stopping about halfway at Rangdum.

Truck Trucks occasionally go along this route, but not nearly as often as the Srinagar-Leh road, because so few people live in and around Zanskar. Nevertheless, hitching rides on a truck, if you can find one, is normal practice, and most drivers will take you for a negotiable fee, maybe about the same as the cheapest bus fare.

TREKS IN ZANSKAR
Treks in the Zanskar include the popular treks from Padum over the Shingo La (5090m) to Darcha and Manali; and over the Singge La (5050m) to Lamayuru and Leh. There is also a remote trek north over the Cha Cha La (4950m) and Rubrang La (5020m) to the Markha Valley and Leh, while to the south the trek over the Umasi La (5340m) provides an interesting route to Manali and the Kullu Valley.

These treks can be undertaken from the end of June when the snows begin to melt on the high passes until the middle of October when the first of the winter snows settle on the high passes. During the season however, heavy storms blowing up from the Indian plains may occasionally interrupt itineraries in August and September. River crossings are also a problem, particularly on the trek from Padum to the Markha Valley; it is advisable not to undertake this trek until the middle of August when the river levels begin to subside. It is also important to note that all of these treks involve high pass crossings of around 5000m, so gradual acclimatisation is essential.

If making your own arrangements, pack horses can be hired from Padum or Karsha for around Rs 200 a day – although this can increase during the harvest period in late August to early September. A local guide is also a valuable asset, particularly on the treks from Padum to the Markha Valley. They are also necessary for the trek over the Umasi La to Manali, a trek that can only be completed with porters normally hired from the village of Zongkul close to Padum. Budget for around Rs 2000 to Rs 2500 per porter for the stages over the pass. Thereon pack horses are available for around Rs 200 per day.

Camping gear including a tent and sleeping bag must be brought with you as there are a number of stages on all of the treks in the Zanskar where there are no villages to stay for the night. Food supplies must also be brought from Leh or Kargil.

Padum to Darcha via Shingo La

This trek follows a well defined route up the Tsarap Valley for the first three stages before diverting to Phugtal Gompa, one of the oldest monasteries in the Zanskar. The trek continues through a number of villages to the highest settlement at Kargyak. From here it is a further stage to the base of the Shingo La (5090m) before crossing the Great Himalaya Range. A final stage brings you to the road-head at Darcha from where you can bus or truck it to Leh or Manali.

Stage 1	Padum to Mune (6 hours)
Stage 2	Mune to Purne (8 hours)
Stage 3	Purne to Phugtal Gompa & Testa (6 hours)
Stage 4	Testa to Kargyak (7 hours)
Stage 5	Kargyak to Lakong (6 to 7 hours)
Stage 6	Lakong to Rumjak via the Shingo La (6 to 7 hours)
Stage 7	Rumjak to Darcha (6 to 7 hours)

Padum to Lamayuru via Singge La

This trek commences from either Padum or from Karsha Gompa. The initial stages of the trek follow the true left bank of the Zanskar river before diverting towards the Hanuma La (4950m) and Lingshat Gompa. It is a further stage to the base of the Singge La (5050m) before crossing the Zanskar Range. From the pass there are dramatic views of the Zanskar gorges while to the south are the snow capped peaks of the Great Himalaya Range. The Singge La is not a particularly demanding pass crossing and the gradual

descent to the village of Photaksar can be completed in one stage.

From Photaksar the trail crosses the Sisir La (4850m) to the village of Honupatta. It is a further stage to the ancient monastery at Wanlah before crossing the Prinkiti La (3750m) to Lamayuru Gompa and onward transport by bus or truck to Leh.

Stage 1	Padum to Karsha (2 hours)
Stage 2	Karsha to Pishu (4 to 5 hours)
Stage 3	Pishu to Hanumil (4 to 5 hours)
Stage 4	Hanumil to Snertse (5 hours)
Stage 5	Snertse to Lingshat via the Hanuma La (5 to 6 hours)
Stage 6	Lingshat to Singge La base (5 to 6 hours)
Stage 7	Camp to Photaksar via Singge La (5 to 6 hours)
Stage 8	Photaksar to Honupatta via the Sisir La (6 hours)
Stage 9	Honupatta to Wanlah (5 hours)
Stage 10	Wanlah to Lamayuru via Prinkiti La (3 to 4 hours)

Padum to Manali via Umasi La

This challenging trek over the main Himalaya Range heads up the Zanskar Valley past Tungri village to Zongkul monastery. It is a further stage to the base of the Umasi La. The climb to the pass crosses a series of glaciers and includes a steep section just below the pass. From the Umasi La (5340m) there are panoramic views of the Great Himalaya before a short descent to a large rock overhang where the porters insist on sheltering overnight. There follows a long descent to the Buddhist settlement at Suncham. Allow two stages from here to the village of Atholi before heading up the Chandra Valley to the village of Kilar and the newly constructed road to the Kullu Valley and Manali.

Stage 1	Padum to Zongkul Gompa (6 to 7 hours)
Stage 2	Zongkul to Umasi La base (6 to 7 hours)
Stage 3	Camp to Rock overhang via Umasi La (7 hours)
Stage 4	Rock camp to Suncham (8 hours)
Stage 5	Suncham to Marchel (3 hours)
Stage 6	Marchel to Atholi (8 hours)
Stage 7	Atholi to Shoal (3 hours)
Stage 8	Shoal to Istahari (6 to 7 hours)
Stage 9	Istahari to Kilar (6 to 7 hours)

LADAKH & ZANSKAR

Padum to Leh via Cha Cha La, Rubrang La & the Markha Valley

This challenging trek is followed by only a handful of trekkers each season. From Padum the trail heads north to the village of Zangla before diverting from the Zanskar Valley to the Cha Cha La (4950m). From the pass there are uninterrupted views south towards the Great Himalaya Range. Heading north the trail enters a series of dramatic gorges that support rare wildlife including brown bear, bharal and snow leopard. It takes a minimum of two stages to reach the Rubrang La (5020m) and the crest of the Zanskar Range before a steady descent to the villages of the Markha Valley. From Markha village it takes a further three stages to cross the Kongmaru La (5030m) to Hemis monastery and the Indus Valley.

Stage 1	Padum to Zangla (7 hours)
Stage 2	Zangla to Cha Cha La base (3 hours)
Stage 3	Base camp to Gorge camp via Cha Cha La (6 hours)
Stage 4	Gorge camp to Tilat Sumdo (6 hours)
Stage 5	Tilat Sumdo to Rubrang La base (5 to 6 hours)
Stage 6	Base camp to Markha via Rubrang La (6 hours)
Stage 7	Markha to Nimaling (7 to 8 hours)
Stage 8	Nimaling to Chogdo via Kongmaru La (6 hours)
Stage 9	Chogdo to Hemis (4 to 5 hours)

Uttar Pradesh

Often referred to as the cow belt or Hindi belt, Uttar Pradesh has been the most dominant state in Indian politics and culture since Independence, producing seven of India's 10 prime ministers. This is partly because it's the nation's most populous state – it has as many inhabitants as Brazil – and partly because of the central role the region plays in the religious landscape of Hindus. The Ganges River, which forms the backbone of Uttar Pradesh, is the sacred river of Hinduism, and four of the religion's seven holy towns are in the state, including Varanasi, the holiest of them all. Uttar Pradesh is also a place of major importance to Buddhists, for it was at Sarnath, just outside Varanasi, that the Buddha first preached his message of the middle way.

Most of Uttar Pradesh consists of the vast Ganges plain, an area of awesome flatness which often floods dramatically during the monsoon. The people of this area are predominantly poorly educated farmers, whose unequal share in the wealth and resources enjoyed by the state's urbanites is a matter of social concern. In stark contrast to the plains, the scenic north-western corner has hill stations sprinkled along the foothills of the Himalaya, boasts excellent trekking and rises to form some of the highest mountains in India.

History

Over 2000 years ago the area that became Uttar Pradesh was part of Ashoka's great Buddhist empire. Muslim raids from the north-west began in the 11th century, and by the 16th century the region was part of the famed Mughal Empire whose capital was for some time at Agra and Fatehpur Sikri.

Following the decline of the Mughal Empire, the nawabs of Avadh rose to prominence in the central part of the region and were responsible for turning Lucknow into a flourishing centre for the arts. When the British East India Company deposed the last

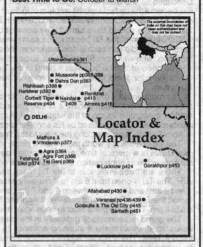

UTTAR PRADESH AT A GLANCE

Population: 166.63 million
Area: 294,411 sq km
Capital: Lucknow
Main Language: Hindi
Literacy Rate: 41.7%
Best Time to Go: October to March

Locator & Map Index

The external boundaries of India on this map have not been authenticated and may not be correct.

Uttarakhand p361
Mussoorie pp388-389
Dehra Dun p383
Rishikesh p386
Haridwar p392
Corbett Tiger • Nainital •
Reserve p404   p409
Ranikhet
p415
Almora p416

DELHI

Mathura &
Vrindavan p377
Agra p364
Fatehpur   Agra Fort p366
Sikri p374 Taj Ganj p369
Lucknow p424   Gorakhpur p453
Allahabad p430
Varanasi pp438-439
Godaulia & The Old City p445
Sarnath p451

Highlights

- The Taj Mahal at sunset and the deserted city of Fatehpur Sikri
- The ghats at Varanasi
- Studying yoga at Rishikesh
- Looking for tigers in Corbett Tiger Reserve
- Kicking back in the hill station of Nainital

Festivals

Magh Mela – Sangam – January/February
Taj Mhotsav – Agra – February
Buddha Purnima – Sarnath – May
Krishna's birthday – Gokul – July/August
Lucknow Festival – Lucknow – November/December
Shi'ite Muharram – Lucknow – dates vary

nawab, the Mutiny of 1857 began at Meerut, and its most tragic events took place in Lucknow and Kanpur. Agra was later merged with

Avadh and the state became known as United Province. It was renamed Uttar Pradesh (Northern State) after Independence.

In recent times Uttar Pradesh has become the main focus for the Hindu chauvinist party, the BJP. The dispute at Ayodhya over the construction of a Hindu temple on the site of a mosque brought the state to flash point in 1992. It also led to riots and killings in other parts of India. The dispute remains unresolved and is currently before the Allahabad High Court.

A REGIONAL HIGHLIGHT

Taj Mahal

Described as the most extravagant monument ever built for love, this poignant Mughal mausoleum has become the de facto tourist emblem of India. It was constructed by Emperor Shah Jahan in memory of his second wife, Mumtaz Mahal, whose death in childbirth in 1631 left the emperor so heartbroken that his hair is said to have turned grey overnight.

Construction of the Taj began in the same year and was not completed until 1653. In total, 20,000 people from India and central Asia worked on the building. The main architect is believed to have been Isa Khan, who was from Shiraz in Iran. Experts were also brought from Europe – Austin of Bordeaux and Veroneo of Venice both had a hand in the Taj's decoration – which allowed the British to delude themselves for some time that such an exquisite building must certainly have been designed by a European.

The most unusual (but almost certainly apocryphal) story about the Taj is that there might well have been two of them. Shah Jahan, it is said, intended to build a second Taj as his own tomb in black marble, a negative image of the white Taj of Mumtaz Mahal. Before he could embark on this second masterpiece he was deposed by his son, Aurangzeb. Shah Jahan spent the rest of his life imprisoned in Agra Fort, looking out along the river to the final resting place of his wife.

The Taj is definitely worth more than a single visit as its character changes with the light during the day. Dawn is a magical time, and it's virtually deserted. Friday tends to be impossibly crowded and not conducive to appreciating this most serene of monuments.

There are three entrances to the Taj (east, south and west); the main entrance is on the western side. The Taj is open from 6 am to 7 pm daily except Monday. Entry costs Rs 105 at sunrise (between 6 and 8 am) and sunset (between 4 and 7 pm), and Rs 15 between 8 am and 4 pm. There's no charge to visit the Taj on Friday, and between 1 April and 30 September the cheaper period extends from 7.30 am to 5 pm. There are plans afoot to once again open the Taj on full-moon nights, probably up until 10 pm.

The grand red sandstone **gateway** in the interior forecourt is inscribed with verses from the Koran in Arabic. It would make a stunning entrance to the Taj, but unfortunately these days you only exit through here. The entrance is now through a small door to the right of the gate, where everyone has to undergo a security check. Food, cigarettes, matches and a hundred other items (including, thankfully, *paan*) are not allowed to be taken inside. There's a cloakroom nearby for depositing things for safekeeping. Cameras are permitted, though there are signs on the walkway approaching the Taj forbidding photography within about 100m of the building. This rule is not enforced and everybody flagrantly ignores it. Taking photographs inside the mausoleum will, however, attract attention.

Paths leading from the gate to the Taj are divided by a long **watercourse** in which the Taj is reflected. The ornamental gardens through which the paths lead are set out along classical Mughal *charbagh* lines – a square quartered by watercourses. To the west is a small **museum** that's open daily except Monday and Friday between 10 am and 5 pm. It houses original architectural drawings of the Taj, information on the semiprecious stones used in its construction, and some nifty celadon plates, said to split into pieces or change colour if the food served on them contains poison. Entry to the museum is free.

The Taj Mahal itself stands on a raised marble platform on the northern edge of the ornamental gardens. Tall, purely decorative, white **minarets** grace each corner of the platform – as the Taj Mahal is not a mosque, nobody is called to prayer from them. Twin red sandstone buildings frame the building; the one on the western side is a mosque, the identical one on the eastern side is purely for symmetry. It cannot be used as a mosque because it faces in the wrong direction.

The central Taj structure has four small domes surrounding the bulbous central dome. The **tombs** of Mumtaz Mahal and Shah Jahan are in a basement room. Above them in the main chamber are false tombs, a common practice in mausoleums of this type. Light is admitted into the central chamber by finely cut marble screens. The echo in this high domed chamber is superb, and there is always somebody there to demonstrate it.

In late 1996 the state was placed under direct rule from Delhi when elections resulted in a hung assembly. After five months of political stalemate the BJP, who won the most seats, formed a coalition government with the BSP, an anti-caste secular party at the opposite end of the political spectrum. This uneasy coalition will be responsible for handling the Central government's proposal to create Uttarakhand, a new state carved out of the Kumaon and Garhwal regions of north-western Uttar Pradesh.

A REGIONAL HIGHLIGHT

Ironically, the perfect symmetry of the Taj is disrupted only by the tomb of the man who built it. When Shah Jahan died in 1666, Aurangzeb placed his casket next to that of Mumtaz Mahal. His presence, which was never intended, unbalances the mausoleum's interior.

Although the Taj is amazingly graceful from almost any angle, it's the close-up detail which is really astounding. Semiprecious stones are inlaid into the marble in beautiful patterns using a process known as *pietra dura*. The precision and care which went into the Taj Mahal's design and construction is just as impressive whether you view it from across the river or from arm's length.

Taj Apocryphal Story Number 376

There are more apocryphal stories surrounding the Taj Mahal than there are coke-based industries. According to one tale, after 22 years of waiting, Shah Jahan was finally informed that his masterpiece had been completed. Keen to see it, he asked how long it would take to dismantle the scaffolding draping the mausoleum. 'At least several months', replied an official. Shah Jahan, understandably impatient, decreed that anyone who helped untie the scaffolding could keep the pieces for themselves. It took only a single day for the Taj to be whisked clean of building materials, and ready for the emperor's inspection. ∎

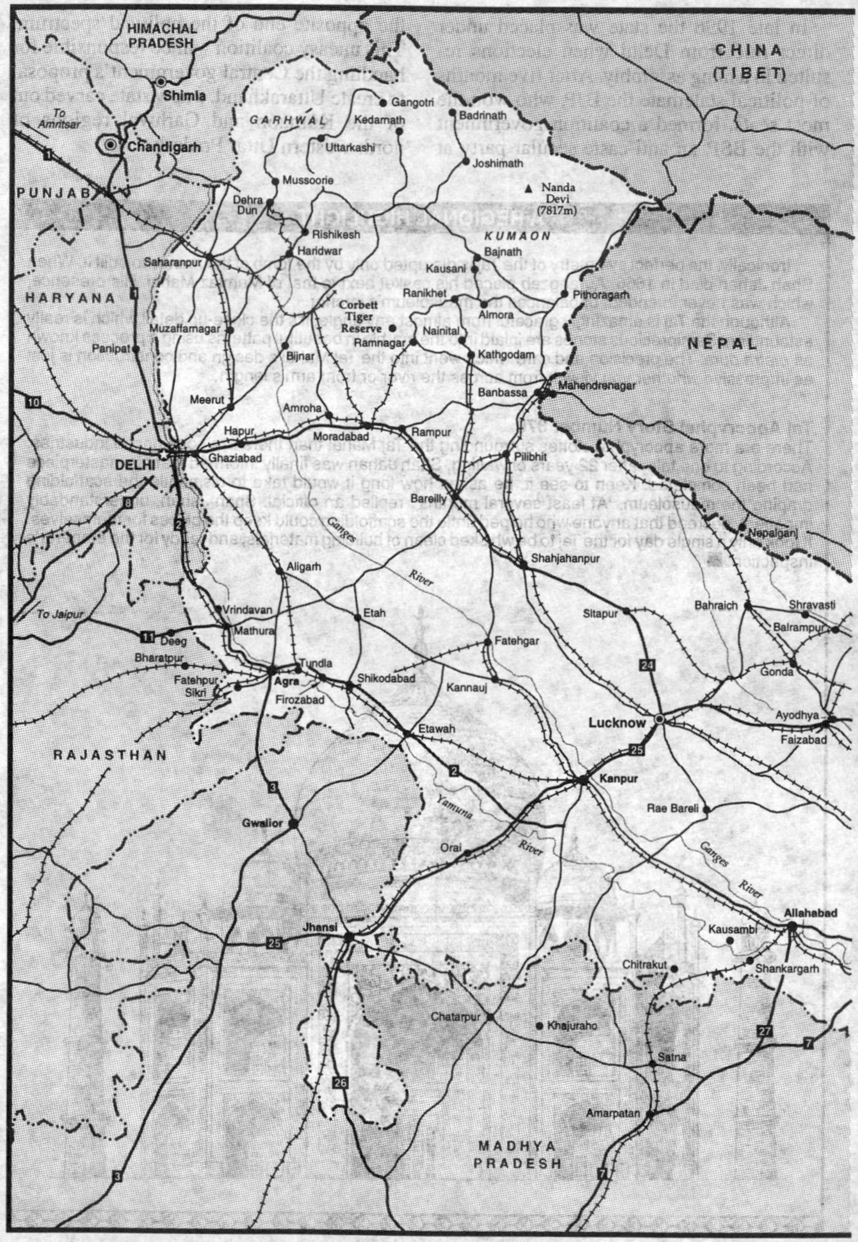

UTTAR PRADESH

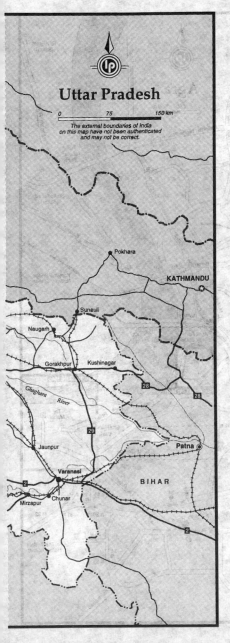

Information

Most major Indian cities have UP Tourism offices:

Ahmedabad
   303 Ashwamedh House, 5 Smriti Kunj, Navrangpura (☎ (0121) 400752)
Calcutta
   12A Netaji Subashi Rd (☎ (033) 220-7855)
Chandigarh
   SCO 1046-47, 1st Floor, Sector 22B (☎ (0172) 707649)
Chennai (Madras)
   28 Commander-in-Chief Rd (☎ (044) 828-3276)
Delhi
   Chandralok Bldg, 36 Janpath, Delhi (☎ (011) 332-2251; fax 371-1296)
Lucknow
   Chitrahar Bldg, 3 Naval Kishor Rd (☎ (0522) 223-3632)
Mumbai (Bombay)
   World Trade Centre, Cuffe Parade, Colaba (☎ (022) 218-5458)

Agra Region

AGRA

Pop: 1,118,800   Tel Area Code: 0562

In the 16th and 17th centuries, Agra was the capital of India under the Mughals, and its superb monuments date from this era. They include a magnificent fort and the building which many people come to India solely to see – the Taj Mahal. Away from its handful of imposing monuments, there's little to distinguish Agra from any other northern Indian city: it has the usual dense chowk, a large cantonment, lots of predatory rickshaw-wallahs and highly polluted air. The Yamuna River, which flows through the city and is the backdrop to the Taj and Agra Fort, has become an open sewer – scientists recently declared it incapable of supporting any life form.

It's possible to day trip to Agra from Delhi, and there's an excellent train service making this eminently practicable. However, Agra is worth more than a flying visit, particularly if you intend to see the nearby deserted city of Fatehpur Sikri. The Taj certainly deserves more than a single visit if you want to appreciate

PLACES TO STAY
5   Hotel Rose
7   Hotels Sheetal & Sakura
9   Lauries Hotel
10 Major Bakshi's Tourist
    Home
11 Tourist Rest House
12 Agra & Akbar Hotels
13 Hotel Prem Sagar
15 Agra Ashok Hotel
19 Hotel Jaiwal & Kwality
    Restaurant
23 Hotel Akbar Inn
25 Clarks Shiraz Hotel &
    Indian Airlines
29 Park Plaza
30 Hotel Amar & Mansingh
    Palace
31 Taj View Hotel & Mayur
    Tourist Complex
32 Mughal Sheraton
33 Upadhyay's Mumtaz
    Guest House
34 Highway Inn
35 Hotel Safari

PLACES TO EAT
17 Zorba the Buddha
20 Park Restaurant &
    Lakshmi Vilas
27 Only Restaurant

OTHER
1   Chini Ka Rauza
2   Itimad-ud-daulah
3   Jama Masjid
4   Agra Fort Bus Stand
6   Idgah Bus Stand
8   Foreigner's Registration
    Office
14 GPO
16 Government of India
    Tourist Office
18 Andhra Bank
21 Police Station
22 Telegraph Office
24 Archaeological Survey
    of India
26 UP Tourist Office
28 State Bank of India

Agra

0   250   500 m

To Aligarh
(83km)

Balkeshwar Road

Aligarh Road

Ram
Bagh

National Highway 2 Bypass

To
Shikodabad
(63km)

Kanpur Road

1

Karbala Road

Kalicharan Tiwari Road

Pandit

Yamuna River

Nehru Road

Chhil Int Rd

To Dayal Bagh
Temple (2km)

To Sikandra (4km)
Mathura (56km) &
Delhi (204km)

Raja
Mandi
Railway
Station

Marg

Ramratan

To Bharatpur

Panchkuiyan Road

Bhagat Singh
Marg

Capt   Naresh
Road

Khari Bazar

Hospital Road

Belan

Ganj

Yamuna Bridge
Railway Station

Ghalibpura Road

M G Road

Mantola Road

P Marg

Jama Masjid Road

Chhata Road

3

Agra Fort
Railway Station

Fort

See Agra Fort Map

See Taj Ganj Map

Salyed Ali Nabi Marg

Fatehpur   Sikri   Road

To Fatehpur
Sikri (40km)

4

Yamuna Kinara Road

Taj Mahal

Shahjahan
Park

Taj
Mahal

Golf Course

12

FM Cariappa Road

Chhip Tola Road

Kachahri Road

Namner Road

Mahatma Gandhi Road

5

8

6
7

9

10

11

14

15

16

17
18

19 20

Gwalior Road

Fatehad Road

23   24
The Mall

Taj Road

28   29

30

31   32

33

To The Trident
Hotel (1.5km)

34

35

Gough Road

25

27

26

Taj Road

Sadar
Bazaar

21

Station   Road

Fatehpur

Sikri Road

13

Agra Cantonment
Railway Station

To Airport (7km) &
New Bakshi House

Ajmer   Road

To Bharatpur

Prithvi Raj Road

Grand   Parade Road

To Gwalior
(118km)

22

To Aligarh

how its appearance changes under different light.

History

Badal Singh is credited with building a fort on the site of the present Agra Fort in 1475, but this didn't stop Sikandar Lodi making his capital on the opposite bank of the Yamuna in 1501. Babur defeated the last Lodi Sultan in 1526 at Panipat, 80km north of Delhi, and Agra then became the Mughal capital. The city reached the peak of its magnificence between the mid-16th and mid-17th centuries under the reigns of Akbar, Jehangir and Shah Jahan. It was during this period that the fort, Taj Mahal and Agra's major tombs were built. In 1638 Shah Jahan built a new city in Delhi, and Aurangzeb moved the capital there 10 years later.

In 1761 Agra fell to the Jats, who looted its monuments, including the Taj Mahal. It was taken by the Marathas in 1770, before the British wrested control in 1803. There was heavy fighting around the fort during the Mutiny of 1857, and after the British regained control, they shifted the administration of the North Western Provinces to Allahabad. Agra has since developed as an industrial centre.

Orientation

Agra is on the western bank of the Yamuna River, 204km south of Delhi. The old part of

the city and the main marketplace (Kinari Bazaar) are north-west of the fort. The spacious British-built cantonment is to the south, and the main road running through it is called The Mall. The commercial centre of the cantonment is Sadar Bazaar.

The labourers and craftsmen who toiled on the Taj set up home immediately south of the mausoleum. This area of congested alleyways is known as Taj Ganj and today it contains most of Agra's budget hotels. The 'tourist class' hotels are predominantly in the area south of here.

Agra's main railway station, Agra Cantonment, is west of Sadar Bazaar. The city's major bus stand, Idgah, is nearby. Agra's airport is seven km west of the city.

Information

The Government of India tourist office (☎ 363959) is at 191 The Mall, and is open from 9 am to 5.30 pm weekdays and 9 am to 1 pm Saturday. It has maps of Agra and an informative brochure on Fatehpur Sikri. There's a helpful UP tourist office (☎ 360517) at 64 Taj Rd and also a tourist information counter (☎ 368598) at Agra Cantonment railway station.

The State Bank of India branch south of Taj Ganj and the Andhra Bank in Sadar Bazaar are the best places to change money. You'll find the GPO, with its sloppy poste restante

---

Wear & Tear on the Face of Eternity

Although one of Akbar's court officials was moved to record that 'Agra is a great city having esteemed healthy air', this is no longer the case. The World Health Organization has classified Agra as a 'pollution intensive zone'. The city's coke-based industries and vehicle emissions are so befouling that visibility can be reduced to several hundred metres on a clear day. There is great concern that pollution is eroding the Taj, since sulphur dioxide, which settles on the mausoleum as sulphuric acid, is causing the marble to discolour and flake.

The political will to counter the effects of pollution was slow to develop, though new industries within a 10,000 sq km exclusion zone were banned. The Supreme Court has since ordered nearly 300 coke-based industries in this area to either move out or switch over to gas. Meanwhile, the government has prevented vehicles from entering the precincts of the Taj, restricted parking within a 500m radius of the building, and planted thousands of trees in the Taj Protected Forest immediately east of the mausoleum in a bid to soak up harmful pollutants. Critics argue that these measures do not go far enough, since the amount of suspended particles in the air is said to be five times the maximum level the Taj can handle without sustaining damage. The Taj is now closed on Monday for cleaning.

Travellers can help these initiatives to save the Taj by not taking auto-rickshaws or taxis to or from the mausoleum. ∎

facility, on The Mall, opposite the Government of India tourist office. If you're looking for reading material, the small bookshop in the Taj View Hotel carries stock in both English and French.

The Foreigners Registration Office (☎ 367563) is at 16 Idgah Colony, not far from the Idgah bus stand. If you need medical treatment, the Jaggi Nursing Home (☎ 360315), in the area south of Taj Ganj, comes highly recommended by travellers.

The Archaeological Survey of India (☎ 363506) is at 22 The Mall. You need to make a booking here if you want to stay at the Archaeological Survey Rest House when visiting Fatehpur Sikri.

Agra Fort

Construction of the massive red sandstone Agra Fort on the bank of the Yamuna River was begun by Emperor Akbar in 1565, though additions were made up until the rule of his grandson, Shah Jahan. In Akbar's time the fort was principally a military structure, but during Shah Jahan's reign it had partially become a palace.

The auricular fort's colossal double walls rise over 20m in height and measure 2½km in circumference. They are encircled by a fetid moat and contain a maze of buildings which form a small city within a city. Unfortunately not all buildings are open to visitors, including the white marble Pearl Mosque, regarded by some as the most beautiful mosque in India.

The Amar Singh Gate to the south is the sole entry point. It's open from 6 am to 5.30 pm daily; admission is Rs 15, except on Friday when there's no charge. There's a lot to see in the fort, so you may find a guide useful.

Diwan-i-Am The Hall of Public Audiences was built by Shah Jahan and replaced an earlier wooden structure. His predecessors had a hand in the hall's construction, but the throne room, with its typical inlaid marble work, indisputably bears Shah Jahan's influence. This is where the emperor met officials and listened to petitioners. Beside the Diwan-i-Am is the small **Nagina Masjid** or Gem Mosque. A door leads from here into the **Ladies' Bazaar**, where female merchants came to sell goods to the ladies of the Mughal court. No males were allowed to enter the bazaar except Akbar, though according to one apocryphal story he still enjoyed visiting in female disguise.

Diwan-i-Khas The Hall of Private Audiences was also built by Shah Jahan, between 1636 and 1637. It's where the emperor received important dignitaries or foreign ambassadors. The hall consists of two rooms connected by three arches. The famous Peacock Throne was kept here before being moved to Delhi by Aurangzeb. It was later carted off to Iran and its remains are now in Tehran.

Octagonal Tower The exquisite Musamman Burj or Octagonal Tower stands close to the Diwan-i-Khas and the small, private Mina Masjid. This is where Shah Jahan died after seven years' imprisonment in the fort. The tower looks out over the Yamuna and is traditionally considered to have one of the most poignant views of the Taj, but Agra's pollution is now so thick that it's difficult to

1 Moti Masjid (Pearl Mosque)
2 Ladies' Bazaar
3 Nagina Masjid
4 Diwan-i-Am
5 Diwan-i-Khas
6 Shish Mahal
7 Octagonal Tower
8 Bookshop
9 Mina Masjid
10 Anguri Bagh
11 Khas Mahal
12 Jehangir's Palace
13 Hauz-i-Jehangri
14 Ticket Office
15 Amar Singh Gate

Yamuna River

To Taj Mahal

Agra Fort

0   100   200 m

To Taj Mahal

see. The tower has been badly damaged over the years and at the time of writing it was closed for conservation work.

Jehangir's Palace Akbar is believed to have built this palace, the largest private residence in the fort, for his son. This was one of the first signs of the fort's changing emphasis from military to luxurious living quarters. The palace also displays an interesting blend of Hindu and central Asian architectural styles – a contrast to the Mughal style which had developed by the time of Shah Jahan.

Other Buildings Shah Jahan's **Khas Mahal** is a beautiful white marble structure used as a private palace. The rooms underneath it were intended as a cool retreat from the summer heat. The **Shish Mahal** or Mirror Palace is reputed to have been the harem dressing room and its walls are inlaid with tiny mirrors. The **Anguri Bagh** or Grape Garden probably never had any grapevines but was simply a small, formal Mughal garden. It stood in front of the Khas Mahal.

In front of Jehangir's Palace is the **Hauz-i-Jehangri**, a huge bowl carved from a block of stone. One story says Jehangir's wife, Nur Jahan, made attar of roses in the bowl; it's also fabled to have been used for preparing bhang. The **Amar Singh Gate** takes its name from a maharaja of Jodhpur who slew the imperial treasurer in the Diwan-i-Am in 1644 and, in a bid to escape, is said to have ridden his horse over the fort wall near here. Not surprisingly, the unlucky horse did not survive the fall – though it is now immortalised in stone; Amar Singh did not survive Shah Jahan's wrath. Justice tended to be summary in those days; there is a shaft leading down to the river where those who made themselves unpopular with the great Mughals were hurled without further ado.

See the **Taj Mahal** regional highlight on p360.

Jama Masjid

Across the railway tracks from the Delhi Gate of Agra Fort is the Jama Masjid, built by Shah Jahan in 1648. An inscription over the main gate indicates that it was built in the name of Jahanara, Shah Jahan's favourite daughter, who was eventually imprisoned with Shah Jahan by Aurangzeb. The mosque has no minarets but its sandstone domes have striking marble patterning.

Itimad-ud-daulah

On the opposite bank of the Yamuna, north of the fort, is the exquisite Itimad-ud-daulah – the tomb of Mirza Ghiyas Beg. This Persian gentleman was Jehangir's *wazir*, or chief minister, and his beautiful daughter Nur Jahan later married the emperor. Nur Jahan constructed the tomb between 1622 and 1628 in a style similar to the tomb she built for Jehangir near Lahore in Pakistan.

Interestingly, many of its design elements foreshadow the Taj, construction of which started only a few years later. The Itimad-ud-daulah was the first Mughal structure totally built from marble and the first to make extensive use of pietra dura, the marble inlay work which is so characteristic of the Taj. Though small and squat compared to its more famous cousin, its human scale is attractive. Extremely fine marble latticework passages admit light to the interior, and the beautifully patterned surface of the tomb is superb. It's well worth a visit.

The Itimad-ud-daulah is open from 6 am to 5 pm daily; admission is Rs 12 except on Friday when it's free.

Akbar's Mausoleum

The sandstone and marble tomb of Akbar, the greatest of the Mughal emperors, lies in the centre of a peaceful garden grazed by deer at Sikandra, four km north-west of Agra. Akbar started its construction himself, blending Islamic, Hindu, Buddhist, Jain and Christian motifs and styles, much like the syncretic religious philosophy he developed called Deen Ilahi. When Akbar died, the mausoleum was completed by his son, Jehangir, who significantly modified the original plans. This accounts for its somewhat cluttered architectural lines.

Like Humayun's Tomb in Delhi, it's an interesting place to study the gradual evolution in design that culminated in the Taj Mahal. Very tame langur monkeys hang out on the walkway waiting to be fed. The stunning southern gateway is the most impressive part of the complex. It has three-storey minarets at each corner and is built of red sandstone strikingly inlaid with white marble abstract patterns. The ticket office is located here, to the left of the arched entrance. The mausoleum is open from 6.30 am to 5.30 pm; entry is Rs 12, except on Friday when it is free. A video camera permit costs Rs 25.

Sikandra is named after Sikandar Lodi, the Delhi sultan who ruled from 1488 to 1517, immediately preceding the rise of Mughal power on the subcontinent. He built the **Baradi Palace**, in the mausoleum gardens. Across the road from the mausoleum is the **Delhi Gate**. Between Sikandra and Agra are several tombs and two *kos minars*, or milestones.

Local buses heading to Sikandra run along MG Rd from the Agra Fort bus stand. They cost Rs 3. Auto-rickshaws charge around Rs 60 for the return trip with an hour's waiting time at the tomb.

Other Attractions

The alleyways of **Kinari Bazaar**, or old marketplace, start near the Jama Masjid. There are several distinct areas whose names are relics of the Mughal period, although they don't always bear relation to what is sold there today. The **Loha Mandi** (Iron Market) and **Sabji Mandi** (Vegetable Market) are still operational, but the **Nai Ki Mandi** (Barber's Market) is now famous for textiles. Something entirely different is for sale in the **Malka Bazaar**, where women beckon to passing men from upstairs balconies. In the butcher's area next to the leather market, watch out for the festering bloody animal skins that are piled high in the streets.

The white marble **Dayal Bagh Temple** of the Radah Soami religion has been under construction since 1904 and is not expected to be completed until some time next century. If you're lucky, you may get to see pietra dura inlaid marblework in process. Although the building is architecturally

unremarkable, the level of artisanship has to be admired. Dayal Bagh is two km north of Agra and can be reached by bus or bicycle.

The squat and smelly **Chini Ka Rauza** (China Tomb), one km north of the Itimad-ud-daulah, is the mausoleum of Afzal Khan, a poet and high official in the court of Shah Jahan. Its exterior was once covered in brightly coloured enamelled tiles, but due to years of neglect, the remaining tile work only hints at the building's former glory.

Ram Bagh, the earliest of India's Mughal gardens, is also forlorn. You'll need to use a lot of imagination to picture how it must have looked in 1528 when it was constructed by Babur. It's on the riverbank 500m north of the Chini Ka Rauza and is open from 6 am to 5 pm daily; admission is Rs 2, free on Friday.

Swimming

The following hotels allow non-guests to use their pools for a fee: Lauries Hotel (Rs 100), Hotel Amar (Rs 100), Agra Ashok Hotel (Rs 150) and the Clarks Shiraz Hotel (Rs 300). The pool at the Ashok is best.

Organised Tours

Guided tours depart from the Government of India tourist office at 9.30 am and proceed to Agra Cantonment railway station to pick up passengers arriving from Delhi on the *Taj Express*, which pulls in at 9.45 am. The tours include the Taj Mahal, Agra Fort and a rather hasty visit to Fatehpur Sikri. They finish at 6 pm so day trippers can catch the *Taj Express* returning to Delhi at 6.45 pm. Buy tickets (Rs 125) from the tourist office, or from the tourist information counter at the railway station on arrival.

Places to Stay – bottom end

Agra's paying guest scheme enables you to stay with local families for between Rs 200 and Rs 400. Contact the tourist information counter at the railway station when you arrive.

Taj Ganj Area There are plenty of hotels in this compact area immediately south of the Taj. Many of them boast views of the famous building, but often it's just wishful thinking.

Shanti Lodge and Hotel Kamal have uninterrupted views from their rooftops, and the Taj Khema has a decent view from a hummock in its garden. However, the government is currently struggling to stop hotels in Taj Ganj from 'encroaching' on the monument and ruining the skyline around it, so you may want to think twice about encouraging their skyward growth.

Hotel Sidhartha (☎ 331238), not far from the Taj's western gate, is a clean, friendly, spacious place built motel-style around a central courtyard. Singles/doubles with attached bath and bucket hot water start from Rs 80/100, and with hot water on tap from Rs 150/225.

Hotel Sheela (☎ 331194), near the Taj's eastern gate, is surrounded by a large garden and has doubles with attached bath and hot water for between Rs 100 and Rs 250. The cheaper rooms are excellent value.

Hotel Raj (☎ 331314) is another good choice. Clean, modern rooms with common bath start from Rs 50/100 and rooms with

attached bath and hot water from Rs 75/150. Air-con doubles go for Rs 300 and dorm beds for Rs 40.

Hotel Kamal (☎ 330126) has OK singles with common bath for Rs 80, and doubles/triples with attached bath for Rs 120/200. It has a prime view of the Taj from the sitting area on the roof and gets positive reviews from travellers.

Shanti Lodge (☎ 330900) gets mixed reviews, but it has a decent view of the Taj from its rooftop eating area. Cramped and slightly shabby rooms with attached bath cost from Rs 80/100 or Rs 150 for doubles with 'views' of the Taj through a fly screen and a grubby window. Some rooms are definitely better than others.

Hotel Pink (☎ 330115), by the Taj's eastern gate, is a modest place set around a small courtyard draped in crimson bougainvillea. All rooms have attached bath and range from Rs 60/100 with bucket hot water to Rs 150 for a double with hot water on tap.

Hotel Taj Khema (☎ 330140) is a ramshackle, overpriced UP Tourism hotel east of the Taj. Rooms with common bath cost Rs 125/150, with attached bath Rs 250/300 and with air-con Rs 450/500. Between October and March, tents are attached to toilet blocks and euphemistically called 'Swiss Cottages'. It costs Rs 200/250 to experience this delight. The hotel's saving grace is the excellent view of the Taj from the artificial hill in the garden.

Hotel White House (☎ 330907) is an average place with rooms with attached bath and hot water for Rs 80/100. Room number six is the most fetching room.

Shahjahan Lodge (☎ 331159) in the heart of Taj Ganj has dorm beds for Rs 20, and good-value rooms with common bath from Rs 25/50 and with attached bath from Rs 40/80.

Indo Guest House (no phone), near the Taj's southern gate, is a clean, basic, family-run affair where singles with common bath cost Rs 40 and rooms with attached bath and hot water are Rs 60/80.

Hotel Sikander (☎ 330279) next door is a similar standard and charges Rs 60/100 for rooms with attached bath.

Taj Ganj

1 Museum	9 Police Station
2 Hotel Sheela	10 Joney's Place
3 Hotel Taj Khema	11 Shahjahan Lodge
4 Hotel Pink	12 Saeed Place
5 Indo Guest House,	13 Shankari Vegis
Hotel Sikander &	Restaurant
Hotel Noorjahan	14 Hotel Kamal
6 Hotel Raj	15 Shanti Lodge
7 Hotel Sidhartha	16 Hotel White House
8 Lucky Restaurant	17 Raja Bicycle Store

Yamuna River

Taj Mahal

0   75   150 m

To Agra Fort (2km)

Main Entrance

Shahjahan Park

To Shilpgram

Tonga Stand

To State Bank of India

Shahjahan Gardens Road

Fatehbad Rd

Taj Road

UTTAR PRADESH

Hotel Noorjahan (no phone) nearby has cheap air-cooled rooms from Rs 25/40 with common bath and Rs 50 for attached bath and hot water. It's basic but clean enough, and it has a small restaurant that's inordinately proud of its buffalo steaks.

South of Taj Ganj There are several options south of Taj Ganj.

Hotel Safari (☎ 360110) on Shamsabad Rd is popular, clean and very good value. Air-cooled singles/doubles with attached bath and hot water cost Rs 85/100. There are also air-con rooms for Rs 200/300. Some rooms have bathtubs and all are supplied with towel, soap and toilet roll.

Highway Inn (☎ 332758) nearby is popular with overlanders for its camping facilities which cost Rs 30 per person. Rooms are not such good value at Rs 110/160 with common bath and Rs 200/300 with attached bath.

Upadhyay's Mumtaz Guest House (☎ 332277) at 3/7 Vibhav Nagar, a quiet residential street, has good air-cooled rooms with attached bath and hot water for Rs 100/150. There's a small garden and several terraces on the roof.

Sadar Places to stay in the Sadar area include the following:

Tourist Rest House (☎ 363961) on Kachahari Rd is an excellent place to stay. It has spotless, comfortable rooms set around a central courtyard, and soap, a towel and toilet roll are provided. The place is managed by two benign brothers who also own the Hotel Safari south of Taj Ganj. Air-cooled singles/doubles with attached bath and hot water are an absolute bargain at Rs 65/85. Don't confuse this place with the Tourist Rest House near Agra Fort bus stand or Kapoor Tourist Rest House, a real dive near a busy intersection on Fatehpur Sikri Rd.

Hotel Akbar Inn (☎ 363212) is on The Mall, midway between Sadar and Taj Ganj. It has rooms with common bath from Rs 30/45 and with attached bath and hot water from Rs 80/100. You can also camp here for Rs 15 per person. Rooms in the main building are good value, while those in the separate wing

are not. Don't confuse this place with the Hotel Akbar mentioned later in this section.

Major Bakshi's Tourist Home (☎ 363829) has been popular for so many years that people still talk about when Julie Christie stayed here. Comfortable, well-furnished, spotless rooms with attached bath start from Rs 175/350 and a four-bed room costs Rs 600. It's a peaceful place and about as close as you'll get to staying with a family without partaking in the paying guest scheme.

Agra Hotel (☎ 363331) on Field Marshal Cariappa Rd is a large, crumbling, dowdy place caught in a time warp. It's very friendly and peaceful and has a good range of rooms starting from Rs 150/200, all with attached bath, hot water and some amazing antediluvian plumbing. Air-cooling is Rs 50 extra and air-con doubles cost Rs 450.

Hotel Akbar (☎ 363312) next door has plain but OK singles/doubles/triples with attached bath and hot water for Rs 60/120/140; air-cooling is Rs 25 extra. This place has big plans, which include a swimming pool. At the time of writing only the 'To the swimming pool' sign had been erected and this pointed at a large swampy sewer – still, you never know your luck.

Hotel Jaiwal (☎ 262442) is on the main drag of Sadar Bazaar close to shops and restaurants. Fine, bland air-cooled rooms with attached bath and hot water cost between Rs 200/300 and Rs 300/400. Air-con rooms are Rs 400/500. It's a bit pricey but not bad. Don't be confused by the more modern section at the back which is part of the same establishment even though it operates under the name Pawan Hotel.

Elsewhere There are several other budget options elsewhere in Agra.

Hotel Rose (☎ 369786) at 21 Old Idgah Colony is convenient for Idgah bus stand. Good singles/doubles with attached bath cost from Rs 95/105. Air-con rooms go for Rs 405/450 and dorm beds for Rs 40.

Hotel Sakura (☎ 369793) is even closer to Idgah bus stand, and private buses to Rajasthan depart from right outside. Rooms with attached bath range from Rs 100/150 to

Rs 150/250. The more expensive rooms are fine, but avoid the cheaper rooms.

Hotel Sheetal (☎ 369420) next door has a range of rooms from Rs 150/250.

Hotel Prem Sagar (☎ 267408) at 264 Station Rd is the best of a cluster of budget hotels just east of Agra Cantonment railway station. Doubles/triples with attached bath and bucket hot water cost Rs 175/225 and are fine for a night.

The *retiring rooms* at the station have dorm beds for Rs 25, doubles for Rs 100 and air-con doubles for Rs 200.

Places to Stay – middle
Mayur Tourist Complex (☎ 332302) has interesting cottage-style rooms arranged around a lawn with a swimming pool. Air-cooled singles/doubles will cost you Rs 600/750 and air-con rooms are Rs 700/900. The hotel is efficiently run and it has a pretty good restaurant.

Hotel Amar (☎ 331885) has gaudy air-con rooms from Rs 900/1100, plus a small swimming pool and a gym.

Lauries Hotel (☎ 364536) is an established hotel where Queen Elizabeth II is claimed to have stayed on a visit to India in 1963. You'd hardly believe it, since it's certainly not by royal appointment now. The rooms are large and clean but a bit pricey at Rs 550/675. You can also camp here for Rs 50. Its swimming pool is open during the hotter months.

New Bakshi House (☎ 368159) is an upmarket guest house at 5 Laxman Nagar, between the railway station and the airport. The owner is the son of the late Major Bakshi whose namesake guest house is in the Sadar area. Comfortable doubles in this well-equipped, clean place range from Rs 750 to Rs 1050. It's often full, so phone in advance.

Places to Stay – top end
All the top-end hotels are air-conditioned and have pools.

The Trident (☎ 331818; fax 331827) on Fatehbad Rd is a low-rise Mughal-style hotel where singles/doubles are excellent value at Rs 1195/2350.

Agra Ashok Hotel (☎ 361223; fax 361620) is a well-managed, pleasant place to stay despite being part of the Indian Tourism Development Corporation chain. Room rates are Rs 1195/2300.

Mansingh Palace (☎ 331771; fax 330202) has been recently renovated, and rooms in this three-star hotel cost from Rs 1195/2300.

Park Plaza (☎ 331870; fax 330408) is a new squeaky-clean hotel nearby offering rooms for Rs 1195/2195.

Clarks Shiraz Hotel (☎ 361421; fax 361428) may be a long-standing Agra landmark but the rooms are showing signs of age for a hotel that charges US$100/110.

Taj View (☎ 331841; fax 331860) is a five-star member of the Taj Group of hotels. Rooms with a distant view of the Taj Mahal cost US$110/130; rooms without views are US$100/120.

Mughal Sheraton (☎ 331701; fax 331730) is Agra's top hotel. It boasts all the usual luxuries and has standard rooms for US$175/190 and a whopping US$290/305 for rooms with a medium-range view of the Taj Mahal.

Places to Eat
Taj Ganj Area In the Taj Ganj area there are a huge number of makeshift eateries catering to budget travellers, many of them on rooftops or terraces. Their cooking facilities are minimal and hygiene is not always quite what it might be. Food tends to be mainly vegetarian – and a quick peek at the butcher shops near the main square may convince you that this is not such a bad thing. Beer can be 'arranged' in most places and 'special' lassis are widely available.

Joney's Place is one of the area's longest running establishments and one of the few places with excellent food. The decor is a tad unsettling but it serves great western breakfasts, good Indian and Israeli food, and is justly famous for its banana lassis.

Shankara Vegis Restaurant has rooftop and street-level dining. It tries its hand at Indian veg, Chinese, spaghetti and western breakfasts. Meals cost roughly Rs 30 to Rs 45. There are plenty of games available if you run out of conversation.

Saeed Place is one of Taj Ganj's original travellers' restaurants and it still turns out acceptable interpretations of Israeli food for between Rs 10 and Rs 30, even though it rarely has customers now that rooftop eating is the rage.

Lucky Restaurant has the usual have-a-go-at-everything menu but it's one of the more convivial places to hang out. Apart from the open-sided ground floor area, there are a few tables on the roof, which has views of the Taj.

Elsewhere Although Agra has a fine tradition of Mughlai food, you would never know it from the food dished up in its restaurants. For quality Mughlai cuisine, you'll need to dip into the luxury hotels – and also into your wallet.

Dasaprakash, in the Meher Cinema complex behind the Agra Ashok Hotel, serves tasty and highly regarded south Indian food.

Zorba the Buddha in Sadar Bazaar is a spotlessly clean, non-smoking, Osho-run vegetarian restaurant. Excellent main dishes cost around Rs 40 to Rs 50, and you can polish one off with a Nutty Coffee flavoured with cinnamon and cashew nuts. The restaurant is closed each year between mid-May and mid-July.

Kwality Restaurant is a comfortable aircon place with the usual cover-all-bases menu. Veg fare costs around Rs 30 and non-veg around Rs 55. There's an acceptable bar next door.

Lakshmi Vilas is a cheap south Indian veg restaurant nearby, recommended for its 22 varieties of dosa.

Park Restaurant is a pricey but popular open-air burger and pizza joint on the same stretch.

Only Restaurant, at the Taj Ganj end of The Mall, is highly rated by locals and you may be urged to eat here. However, standards need to double and prices halve before it becomes a viable option. You're much better off trying the restaurants in *Clarks Shiraz* and the *Mughal Sheraton* if you want to enjoy sumptuous food.

Don't forget to try the local speciality, ultra-sweet candied pumpkin peitha.

Things to Buy

Agra is well known for leather goods, jewellery, *dhurrie* weaving and marble items inlaid with coloured stones, similar to the pietra dura work on the Taj. Sadar Bazaar and the area south of Taj Ganj are full of emporiums of one kind or another, but prices here are more expensive than in the bazaars of the old part of the city. The best jewellery shops are around Pratapur, also in the old part of Agra, though you can still pick up precious stones cheaper in Jaipur.

About one km along the road running from the eastern gate of the Taj is Shilpgram, a crafts village and open-air emporium. During the Taj Mhotsav Festival in February it hosts live performances of music and dance; the rest of the time it has displays of crafts from all over the country. Prices are certainly on the high side, but the quality is good and the range hard to beat.

Read the warning in the Things to Buy section of the Facts for the Visitor chapter since quite a few tourists manage to get ripped off in Agra. The easiest way to avoid pitfalls is not to let rickshaw-wallahs persuade you to visit shops on the way to your destination – you'll pay inflated prices to cover the cost of commission. It's also best to avoid the cool young men on mopeds who claim to be students who want to learn about your country. An invitation to visit their home will inevitably lead you straight to a craft shop. Lastly, don't be tempted by the unconvincing scams which promise handsome profits in return for helping a shop export goods to your home country – somewhere along the line your credit card will take a beating.

Getting There & Away

Air The Indian Airlines office (☎ 360948) is at the Clarks Shiraz Hotel. It's open daily from 10 am to 1 pm and from 2 to 4.30 pm. Agra is on the popular daily tourist shuttle from Delhi to Agra, Khajuraho, Varanasi and back again. It's only a 40 minute flight from

Delhi to Agra. Fares from Agra are: Delhi US$40, Khajuraho US$60, and Varanasi US$80.

Bus Most buses leave from the Idgah bus stand. Buses to Delhi (five hours, Rs 69), Jaipur (six hours, Rs 76) and Mathura (1½ hours, Rs 17) depart every hour. Buses to Fatehpur Sikri (1½ hours, Rs 12) leave every 30 minutes. There's one bus to Khajuraho (10 hours, Rs 84) at 5 am. Slower buses to Mathura (two hours, Rs 17) also depart from the Agra Fort bus stand. Rajasthan government buses depart from a small booth outside Hotel Sheetal, close to the Idgah bus stand. Buses leave here every hour for Jaipur (six hours, Rs 91 deluxe), but you should book a day in advance.

Train There is no tourist quota allotment on trains from Agra, so booking a sleeper, especially to Varanasi, can be difficult. Try to plan as far in advance as possible. If you can't book a seat on the train that you want, you can always go to Delhi and make use of the tourist quota there.

Agra is on the main Delhi to Mumbai (Bombay) line. The fastest train to Delhi is the daily air-con *Shatabdi Express* (two hours, Rs 275 in air-con chair car class). It leaves Delhi at 6.15 am and departs from Agra for the return trip at 8.18 pm, making it ideal for day-tripping.

A much cheaper alternative is the daily *Taj Express* (2½ hours, Rs 49/233 in 2nd/1st class). It leaves Delhi at 7.15 am and departs from Agra for the return trip at 6.45 pm. This gives you less time in Agra but it conveniently connects with the organised tour (see Organised Tours, above). Plenty of other expresses operate between the two cities, most taking between three and 3½ hours. Take great care at New Delhi station; miscreants are aware that this is a popular tourist route and work overtime at parting unwary visitors from their valuables.

There are some direct trains to Mughalserai (12½ hours, Rs 153/528 in sleeper/1st class) near Varanasi, but most of the expresses running between Delhi and Calcutta do not

stop at Agra. So if you're heading to or from Varanasi (which is on this line), it may be more convenient to utilise Tundla or Firozabad stations, east of Agra, where most expresses stop. A bus between Firozabad and Agra takes 1½ hours and costs Rs 13; to Tundla it takes about an hour.

There are also direct trains to Mumbai (23 to 29 hours, Rs 261/940 in sleeper/1st class) Goa, Chennai (Madras) and Thiruvananthapuram (Trivandrum). If you're heading north towards the Himalaya there are trains through Agra which continue past Delhi – you don't have to stop and get another ticket.

Agra's rail connections to cities in Rajasthan have been disrupted by Rajasthan's conversion from metre gauge to broad gauge. Services have been reduced, though there's still a broad-gauge evening service to Jaipur from Agra Fort station at 7.50 pm. It takes six hours and is 2nd class only.

Getting Around
The Airport Agra's Kheria Airport is seven km from the centre of town and three km west of Idgah bus stand. From Taj Ganj, taxis charge around Rs 75 and auto-rickshaws Rs 30.

Taxi & Auto-Rickshaw Tempos operate on set routes: from the Agra Fort bus stand to Taj Ganj it's just Rs 2. Taxis and auto-rickshaws are unmetered so be prepared to haggle. An auto-rickshaw from Taj Ganj to Agra Cantonment railway station is less than Rs 20, and to the fort it's around Rs 10.

Prepaid transport is available from Agra Cantonment railway station to Taj Ganj (Rs 38/62 by rickshaw/taxi), Sadar Bazaar (Rs 17/35) and to the Taj Mahal and back with an hour's waiting time (Rs 42/62). Some travellers are now choosing not to take motorised transport to the Taj in an effort to reduce harmful pollutants in the mausoleum's vicinity (see the boxed story in this section). A prepaid rickshaw for local sightseeing costs Rs 222 for a full day or Rs 122 for half a day; taxis cost Rs 332 for a full day locally, or Rs 452 if you also want to go to

Fatehpur Sikri. These fares are higher than normal but save the hassle of bargaining.

Cycle-Rickshaw & Bicycle Agra is very spread out and not conducive to walking since hordes of cycle-rickshaw wallahs pursue would-be pedestrians with unbelievable persistence. Many visitors get frustrated by this but the rickshaw-wallahs often speak good English and have a finely-tuned sense of humour. They can also be useful sources of local information. Don't take any nonsense from rickshaw-wallahs who offer to take you from A to B via a few marble or jewellery shops.

From Taj Ganj to the heart of Sadar Bazaar is Rs 10, which is about the most you need to pay to get anywhere in Agra. Although cycle-rickshaws are the most environmentally friendly way to get around – certainly to the Taj – they are not particularly suited to Agra's diffuseness. If you're heading from the fort to the Taj, it's almost quicker to walk

than catch a cycle-rickshaw since this stretch consists of a long, slow incline.

The simple solution to Agra's transport problem is to hire a bicycle. The city is sufficiently traffic-free to make cycling an easy proposition and avoiding rickshaw-wallahs will increase your enjoyment of the city three-fold. Raja Bicycle Store, near the Taj Ganj tonga and rickshaw stand, hires bicycles for Rs 5 per hour, Rs 15 for half a day and Rs 30 for a full day. Insist on getting a decent bike.

FATEHPUR SIKRI
Pop: 29,280   Tel Area Code: 05619

This magnificent fortified ghost city was the capital of the Mughal Empire between 1571 and 1585, during the reign of Emperor Akbar. A few years earlier, it had been nothing more than a stone-cutters' village. Legend says that Akbar, despite his army of wives, was without a male heir when he made a pilgrimage to Sikri to see the Muslim saint

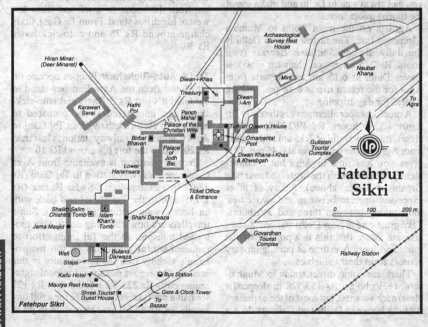

Fatehpur Sikri

Shaikh Salim Chishti. The saint foretold the birth of three sons, and when this came true Akbar was so impressed that he pledged to build a city at Sikri.

Just 14 years later, the city was abandoned as suddenly and dramatically as it had been built, possibly due to difficulties with the water supply. Akbar moved his capital to Lahore and within 20 years Fatehpur Sikri was deserted and has remained that way ever since. When Akbar returned to the area in 1598 he set up shop in Agra, which led some to conclude that the city had been nothing more than an emperor's whim. Today, thanks to the durable red sandstone and a lot of work by the Archaeological Survey of India, Fatehpur Sikri is a perfectly preserved example of a Mughal city at the height of the empire's splendour.

During his stay in Fatehpur Sikri, Akbar spent much time studying religions other than Islam. From discussions with Hindus, Jains, Parsis and recently arrived Portuguese Jesuits from Goa, he developed a new religion called Deen Ilahi, which attempted to combine elements from all major religions. Fatehpur Sikri itself can be seen as a similar synthesis: a place where Islamic architecture fuses with Hindu and Jain decorative art.

Most people visit Fatehpur Sikri as a day trip from Agra, but it can be an atmospheric place to stay. Spending the night here would allow you to watch the impressive sunset over the ruins. The best viewpoint is from the top of the city walls, a two km walk to the south.

Orientation & Information

The deserted city lies along the top of a ridge, 40km west of Agra. The village, with its bus stand and railway station, is at the bottom of the ridge's southern face.

The historic enclosure is open from 6 am to 5.30 pm; entry is Rs 5, free on Friday. A video camera permit is Rs 25. Note that the Jama Masjid and the tomb of Shaikh Salim Chishti are outside the city enclosure so there's no entry fee to visit them. The function and even the names of many buildings remain contentious so you may find it useful to hire a guide. Licensed guides cost around

Rs 40 and loiter near the ticket office; unlicensed guides solicit tourists at the Buland Darwaza.

Jama Masjid (Dargah Mosque)

Fatehpur Sikri's beautiful mosque contains elements of Persian and Hindu design and is said to be a copy of the mosque at Mecca. The main entrance is through the impressive 54m high **Buland Darwaza**, the Gate of Victory, constructed to commemorate Akbar's victory in Gujarat. A Koranic inscription inside its archway quotes Jesus saying: 'The world is a bridge, pass over it but build no house upon it. He who hopes for an hour may hope for eternity', which seems highly appropriate considering the fate of the city. Just outside the gateway is a deep well and, when sufficient numbers of tourists assemble, local daredevils leap from the top of the entrance into the water.

In the northern part of the courtyard is the superb white marble *dargah* or **tomb of Shaikh Salim Chishti**, built in 1570. Just as Akbar came to the saint four centuries ago looking for a son, childless women visit his tomb today. The carved marble lattice screens *(jalis)* are probably the finest examples of such work you'll see anywhere in the country. The saint's grandson, Islam Khan, also has his tomb within the courtyard. The eastern gate of the mosque, known as the **Shahi Darwaza** (King's Gate), was the one used by Akbar.

Palace of Jodh Bai

North-east of the mosque is the ticket office and entrance to the old city. The first building inside the gate is a palace, commonly but wrongly ascribed to Jodh Bai, Jehangir's Hindu mother and the daughter of the Maharaja of Amber.

The architecture is a blend of styles with Hindu columns and Muslim cupolas. The **Hawa Mahal** (Palace of the Winds) is a projecting room whose walls are made entirely of stone latticework. The ladies of the court may have sat inside to keep an unobtrusive eye on events below.

Birbal Bhavan

Thought to have been built either by or for Akbar's favourite courtier, Raja Birbal, this elegant building provoked Victor Hugo, the 19th century French author, to comment that it was either a very small palace or a very large jewellery box. Birbal, who was a Hindu and noted for his wit and wisdom, unfortunately proved to be a hopeless soldier and lost his life, and most of his army, near Peshawar in 1586. The palace fronts onto the **Lower Haramsara**, which was once believed to be an enormous stable, with nearly 200 enclosures for elephants, horses and camels. This is now thought to be where the palace maids lived. The stone rings still in evidence were more likely to have been used to secure curtains than to fetter pachyderms.

Karawan Serai & Hiran Minar

The Karawan Serai or Caravanserai was a large courtyard surrounded by the hostels used by visiting merchants. The Hiran Minar (Deer Minaret), which is actually outside the fort grounds, is said to have been erected over the grave of Akbar's favourite elephant. Stone elephant tusks protrude from the 21m tower from which Akbar is said to have shot at deer and other game which were driven in front of him. The flat expanse of land stretching away from the tower was once a lake and still occasionally floods today.

Palace of the Christian Wife

Close to the Jodh Bai Palace, this house was used by Akbar's Goan Christian wife, Maryam, and at one time was gilded throughout – giving it the name the Golden House.

Panch Mahal

This whimsical five storey palace was probably once used by the ladies of the court and originally had stone screens on the sides. These have now been removed, making the open colonnades inside visible. Like a house of cards, each of the five storeys is stepped back from the previous one until the top floor consists of only a tiny kiosk. The lower floor has 84 columns, no two of which are exactly alike.

Treasury

For a long time this building was known as Ankh Micholi, which translates roughly as 'hide and seek' – a game the emperor is supposed to have played here with ladies of the harem. However, current thinking suggests that the building was the imperial treasury – an idea supported by the curious struts carved with sea monsters who are believed to protect the treasures of the deep. Near one corner is a small canopied enclosure known as the Astrologer's Seat, where Akbar's Hindu guru may have sat while instructing him. A more mundane explanation is that the court treasurer parked himself here to watch the dosh being counted.

Diwan-i-Khas (Jewel House)

The exterior of the Hall of Private Audiences is plain, but its interior design is unique. A carved stone column in the centre of the building flares to support a flat-topped 'throne' some six metres high. Narrow stone bridges radiate from the corners of the room and meet at the throne. The function of the building is disputed: some think Akbar spent much time on the 'throne' (so to speak) discussing and debating with scholars of different religious persuasions; others believe it to be the perch from which he meted out justice. Another possibility is that this was where the emperor was weighed at the commencement of the Persian New Year.

Diwan-i-Am

Just inside the gates at the north-eastern end of the deserted city is the Hall of Public Audiences, which consists of a large open courtyard surrounded by cloisters. Beside the Diwan-i-Am is the **Pachisi Courtyard**, set out like a gigantic game board. It is said that Akbar played the game pachisi here, using slave girls as the pieces.

Other Monuments

Musicians would play from the **Naubat Khana**, at one time the main entrance to the city, as processions passed beneath. The entrance road then ran between the mint and the treasury before reaching the Diwan-i-Am. The

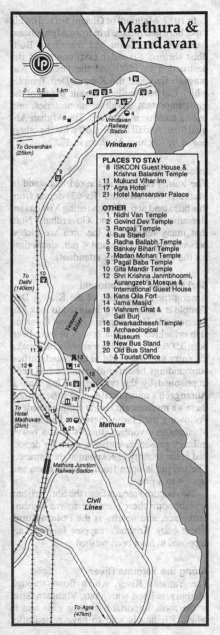

Mathura & Vrindavan

0   0.5   1 km

To Goverdhan
(25km)

Vrindavan
Railway
Station

Vrindavan

To Delhi
(140km)

Yamuna River

To Hotel
Madhuvan
(2km)

Mathura

Mathura Junction
Railway Station

Civil
Lines

To Agra
(47km)

PLACES TO STAY
8   ISKCON Guest House &
    Krishna Balaram Temple
11 Mukund Vihar Inn
17 Agra Hotel
21 Hotel Mansarovar Palace

OTHER
1   Nidhi Van Temple
2   Govind Dev Temple
3   Rangaji Temple
4   Bus Stand
5   Radha Ballabh Temple
6   Bankey Bihari Temple
7   Madan Mohan Temple
9   Pagal Baba Temple
10 Gita Mandir Temple
12 Shri Krishna Janmbhoomi,
    Aurangzeb's Mosque &
    International Guest House
13 Kans Qila Fort
14 Jama Masjid
15 Vishram Ghat &
    Sati Burj
16 Dwarkadheesh Temple
18 Archaeological
    Museum
19 New Bus Stand
20 Old Bus Stand
    & Tourist Office

Khwabgah, in front of the Daftar Khana, or record office, was Akbar's own sleeping quarters. Beside the Khwabgah is the tiny but elaborately carved **Rumi Sultana** or Turkish Queen's House. Near the Karawan Serai, badly defaced elephants still guard the **Hathi Pol**, or Elephant Gate.

Outside the Jama Masjid are the remains of the small stone-cutters' mosque. Shaikh Salim Chishti's cave was supposedly at this site and the mosque predates Akbar's imperial city. There's also a **Hakim's House** (Doctor's House), and a fine **hammam**, or Turkish bath, beside it.

Places to Stay & Eat

The *Archaeological Survey Rest House* is by far the cheapest place to stay. It costs only Rs 9 but advance bookings must be made at the Archaeological Survey of India (☎ (0562) 363506), 22 The Mall, Agra.

Maurya Rest House (☎ 2348) is the most pleasant of the budget hotels in the village. There are basic singles/doubles with common bath for Rs 70/100 and doubles with attached bath from Rs 150. It's well run by a friendly family, and food is available in the small, shady courtyard. Two of the brothers play the sitar and tabla and there are occasional impromptu concerts in the evening.

Shree Tourist Guest House (☎ 2276) has six clean rooftop rooms from Rs 70/100.

Govardhan Tourist Complex (☎ 2222) is a new hotel offering air-cooled doubles with attached bath and bucket hot water from Rs 200. Dorm beds go for Rs 100.

Gulistan Tourist Complex (☎ 2490) is a sympathetically designed upmarket UP Tourism operation with rooms from Rs 400/450 or from Rs 650/750 with air-con. Prices drop Rs 100 between March and September. It has a courtyard garden, a restaurant and a misconceived bar. It's a nice place to stay but not great value: if you eat western breakfasts, there's no alternative to the outrageously overpriced set breakfast costing Rs 75.

Kallu Hotel, a basic restaurant near the Buland Darwaza, serves thalis for Rs 25. There are plenty of snack and soft-drink vendors around all the entrances to the enclosures. Fatehpur Sikri's speciality is khataie, the biscuits you'll see piled high in the bazaar.

Getting There & Away
Tour buses only stop for an hour or so at Fatehpur Sikri, so if you want to spend longer (which is recommended) it's worth catching a bus from Agra's Idgah bus terminal (1½ hours, Rs 12). Buses depart every 30 minutes. There are also four trains a day to Fatehpur Sikri from Agra Fort (one hour, Rs 7).

You can spend a day in Fatehpur Sikri and continue on to the world-renowned bird sanctuary at Bharatpur in the evening. Buses depart from Fatehpur Sikri's bus stand every 30 minutes.

MATHURA
Pop: 272,500   Tel Area Code: 0565
This area, popularly known as Brij Bhoomi, is a major pilgrimage place for Hindus. Krishna, the popular incarnation of Vishnu, is believed to have been born in Mathura (Muttra) and the area is closely linked with many episodes in his early life. Nearby is Vrindavan (Vrindaban) where Krishna 'sported' with his *gopis* (milkmaids) and where the Hare Krishnas have their headquarters.

Although Mathura has been an important centre for the arts, the region's significance is largely incorporeal. Its material attractions certainly pale in comparison to the rich associations drawn from Hindu mythology.

History
Mathura is an ancient cultural and religious centre. The Buddhist monasteries that were built here received considerable patronage from Ashoka, and Mathura was mentioned by Ptolemy and by the Chinese visitors Fa Hian (who visited India in 401-410 AD) and Hiuen Tsang (634 AD). By Hiuen Tsang's visit, the population of Mathura's 20 monasteries had dropped from 3000 to 2000 as Buddhism in the region began to give way to Hinduism.

In 1017, Mahmud of Ghazni arrived on his rape, burn and pillage trip from Afghanistan, damaging the Hindu and remaining Buddhist shrines. Sikandar Lodi continued the destruction in 1500 and the fanatical Aurangzeb flattened the Kesava Deo Temple, which had been built on the site of one of the most important Buddhist monasteries, and built a mosque in its place. The Afghan Ahmad Shah Abdali finished off what the others began by torching Mathura in 1757.

Information
The tourist office is at the old bus stand in Mathura. Guided tours (Rs 42) depart from this bus stand at 6.30 am, visiting Vrindavan, Barsana, Nandgaon and Goverdhan. Note that many temples in the area are closed between about 11 am and 4 pm, siesta time for the deities and their attendants.

Shri Krishna Janmbhoomi
Among the foundations of the Kesava Deo Temple is a small room designed to look like a prison cell. Here pilgrims file past the stone slab on which Krishna is said to have been born 3500 years ago. He was obliged to make his entry into the world in these undignified surroundings because his parents had been imprisoned by the tyrannical King Kansa. Aurangzeb's mosque rises above the site and there's a more recent Hindu temple beside it. Following the clashes between Hindus and Muslims in Ayodhya, there's now a heavy military presence; cameras must be deposited at the security checkpoint at the entrance. The temple is open from 6 am to noon and from 4 to 8 pm.

Two hundred metres from the Shri Krishna Janmbhoomi there's an alternative Krishna birthplace, and nearby is the **Potara-Kund**, where baby Krishna's nappies (diapers) are supposed to have been washed.

Along the Yamuna River
The Yamuna River, which flows through Mathura, is lined with ghats. **Vishram Ghat** is the most important bathing ghat and is where Krishna is said to have rested after

killing King Kansa. You can hire a boat for a spell on the river for Rs 20 for half an hour; turtles are often seen in the water here.

The **Sati Burj**, beside Vishram Ghat, is a four storey tower built by the son of Behari Mal of Jaipur in 1570 to commemorate his mother's *sati*. Aurangzeb knocked down the upper storeys, but they have since been rebuilt.

The ruined fort, **Kans Qila**, on the riverbank, was built by Raja Man Singh of Amber; Jai Singh of Jaipur built one of his observatories here, but it has since disappeared.

Set back from the river are the **Jama Masjid**, which was built by Abo-in Nabir Khan in 1661, and the **Dwarkadheesh Temple**. Built in 1814 by Seth Gokuldass of Gwalior, Dwarkadheesh is Mathura's main temple and is dedicated (surprise, surprise) to Krishna.

Archaeological Museum
The Archaeological Museum is worth visiting to see its superb collection of the Mathura school of ancient Indian sculpture. This includes the famous and impressive 5th century standing Buddha found here. It's open daily except Monday from 10.30 am to 4.30 pm (7.30 am to 12.30 pm from 16 April to 30 June). Admission is free.

Places to Stay & Eat
International Guest House(☎ 405888), next to Shri Krishna Janmbhoomi, is excellent value with singles/doubles with common bath costing Rs 25/40 and doubles with attached bath from Rs 60. It has a garden and a cheap vegetarian restaurant.

Agra Hotel (☎ 403318), overlooking the river on Bengali Ghat, is highly recommended. Air-cooled rooms with attached bath, hot water and character cost from Rs 100/200 and air-con doubles are Rs 450.

Mukund Vihar Inn (☎ 404055) has plain, clean, air-cooled doubles with attached bath and hot water for Rs 300 or air-con rooms for Rs 500. It's set in a fun park so is highly recommended if you enjoy fooling around with paddleboats, toy trains and merry-go-rounds.

Hotel Mansarovar Palace (☎ 408686) is more upmarket but nothing special at Rs 400/500 for air-cooled rooms with attached bath and hot water or Rs 600/700 for air-con. It has a veg/non-veg restaurant which claims to be run on 'scientific and hygienic principles'.

Hotel Madhuvan (☎ 404064; fax 401884) is the top hotel in the area. It's a three-star establishment with rooms for Rs 500/650 or Rs 700/850 with air-con. There's a swimming pool that non-guests can use for Rs 100, and also a restaurant and bar. It's a Rs 10 cycle-rickshaw ride from the new bus stand.

Getting There & Away
Mathura is 47km north-west of Agra and 141km south of Delhi. From the new bus stand, there are buses to Delhi every half hour (3½ hours, Rs 42) and to Agra every 45 minutes (1½ hours, Rs 17). There are slower and less frequent buses to Agra from the old bus stand as well.

The fastest train to Delhi is the *Taj Express*, which departs Mathura at 7.35 am (1¾ hours, Rs 37/175 in 2nd/1st class). Mathura also has direct trains to Agra (one hour, Rs 18/95), Bharatpur, Sawai Madhopur (for Ranthambhore) and Kota.

AROUND MATHURA
Vrindavan
This is where Krishna indulged in adolescent pranks like flirting with gopis in the forests and stealing their clothes while they bathed in the river. Little now remains of the legendary forests and the river has meandered away from most of Vrindavan's bathing ghats, but this dusty town still attracts huge numbers of pilgrims.

The bulky red sandstone **Govind Dev Temple** is the most impressive building in Vrindavan. The name means Divine Cowherd – in other words Krishna. It's well worth picking your way through the bat droppings and hordes of monkeys to see its vaulted ceiling. Architecturally it's one of the most advanced Hindu temples in northern India and was built in 1590 by Raja Man Singh of Jaipur. It was originally seven storeys high but Aurangzeb lopped off the top four floors.

The **Rangaji Temple** dates from 1851 and is a bizarre mixture of architectural styles, including a Rajput entrance gate, a soaring south Indian *gopuram* and an Italianate colonnade. At the entrance are two amusing electronic puppet shows telling the stories of the *Ramayana* and the *Mahabharata*. Non-Hindus are not allowed in the middle enclosure of the temple where there's a 15m gold-plated pillar.

There are said to be 4000 other temples in Vrindavan, including the popular **Bankey Bihari**, **Radha Ballabh** (built in 1626), **Madan Mohan**, the 10 storey **Pagal Baba**, and the **Nidhi Van**.

The International Society of Krishna Consciousness (ISKCON) (☎ (0565) 442596) has its Indian base in Vrindavan. At its white marble **Krishna Balaram Temple** complex is a mausoleum dedicated to the sect's founder, Swami Prabhupada, who died in 1977. Every year several hundred westerners attend courses and seminars here. Phone the society for details.

Places to Stay & Eat The *ISKCON Guest House* (☎ (0565) 442478) at the ISKCON complex has clean rooms with attached bath, bucket hot water and very hard beds where you can stay for a 'donation' of Rs 200. It's also possible to stay in some of Vrindavan's *ashrams*. The restaurant at the ISKCON guest house is the best place to eat in this veg-only town. It serves thalis for Rs 40 and other meals for less than Rs 20.

Getting There & Away Tempos ply the 10km stretch between Mathura and Vrindavan. They depart from Mathura's new bus stand and Shri Krishna Janmbhoomi, and cost Rs 4. The trip takes about 15 minutes and can get very squashy. Auto-rickshaws are more comfortable but charge around Rs 50 one way. There are three steam trains each way a day on the metre-gauge line between Mathura and Vrindavan – one in the early morning, one mid-afternoon and the other in the evening.

Gokul & Mahaban
Krishna was secretly raised in Gokul, 16km south of Mathura. Hordes of pilgrims flock here during his birthday festival each July/August. It's best to get to Gokul by auto-rickshaw. It costs around Rs 100 return, including waiting time.

Mahaban, 18km south-east of Mathura, is where Krishna spent some of his youth.

Barsana & Goverdhan
Krishna's consort Radha was from Barsana, 50km north-west of Mathura. This is an interesting area to be during the festival of Holi when the women of Barsana attack the men of nearby Nandgaon with coloured water. Buses to Barsana depart from Mathura's new bus stand.

Krishna is said to have protected the inhabitants of Goverdhan from Indra's wrath (rain) by holding a hilltop, neatly balanced on top of his finger, over the town for seven days and nights. Goverdhan is 25km west of Mathura, on the road to Deeg.

Uttarakhand

Uttarakhand, the Land of the North, is the name given to the northern part of Uttar Pradesh. It's an area of hills, mountains and lakes; the western half is known as Garhwal and the eastern part is Kumaon.

Here are popular hill stations, including Nainital and Mussoorie, and many trekking routes – most of them little known and even less used. As Indo-Chinese relations improve, sensitive border areas previously closed to foreign trekkers and mountaineers are opening up. In the summer, pilgrims walk to the source of the holy Ganges near Gangotri, not far from the border with China. Gangotri is one of the four main Himalayan *yatra* (pilgrimage) destinations, the others being Badrinath, Kedarnath and Yamunotri

– collectively known as the Char Dham. More accessible pilgrimage centres include Haridwar and Rishikesh, where the Ganges leaves the Himalaya and joins the plains for its long trip to the sea.

You can enter Nepal from northern Uttar Pradesh. See under Banbassa at the end of this section for details.

Information

UP Tourism has offices in most major tourist centres (see under Information at the beginning of this chapter). The Garhwal and Kumaon regions also have tourist organisations:

Garhwal Mandal Vikas Nigam (GMVN), and Kumaon Mandal Vikas Nigam (KMVN), whose offices can be found in many larger towns. GMVN headquarters is in Dehra Dun, and a trekking and mountaineering division is in Rishikesh. There is a network of GMVN and KMVN tourist bungalows throughout Uttarakhand, with rates that vary according to the season.

Five day mountain cycling tours from Nainital and six day tours from Chaukori, (both in Kumaon) are organised by UP Tourism. Contact UP Tourism's Delhi office for details.

The organisation also operates package tours during the yatra season (April to November) to the Char Dham temples of Garhwal. Packages ex Delhi feature luxury bus and accommodation and a seven day tour to Badrinath and Kedarnath (Rs 2255); there's also a 13 day tour to the four temples (Rs 3680).

As well as its coach tours to the Char Dham during the yatra season, UP Tourism offers taxi packages. A seven day package departing from Delhi to Kedarnath and Badrinath is Rs 4005 per person for twin accommodation. Seven day taxi packages to Kedarnath and Badrinath from Delhi are Rs 5445 per person.

MEERUT
Pop: 980,000   Tel Area Code: 0121
Only 70km north-east of Delhi, this is where the 1857 Mutiny broke out, when Meerut was the largest garrison in northern India. There's little to remember that event by today – just the cemetery near St John's Church, which also has the grave of General Ochterlony, whose monument dominates the Maidan in Calcutta. The **Suraj Khund** is the most interesting Hindu temple in Meerut and there's a **Mughal mausoleum**, the Shahpir, near the old Shahpir Gate.

Meerut is a green revolution boom town and the new-found wealth, indicated by the many well-stocked stores, has led to inter-communal tensions.

Sardhana, 18km north of Meerut, is the palace of Begum Samru. She converted to Catholicism and built the basilica here in 1809, which has an altar of white Jaipur marble. The begum's tomb can be found in the basilica.

There are several hotels in Meerut; the best is the *Hotel Shaleen* and there's also the cheaper *Anand Hotel* – both in the Begum Bridge area.

SAHARANPUR
Pop: 431,000
Situated 178km north of Delhi, the industrial city of Saharanpur is a major railway junction.

The large **botanical gardens**, known as the Company Bagh, are over 175 years old.

DEHRA DUN
Pop: 424,500   Tel Area Code: 0135
Also spelt Dehra Doon, this pleasant town is situated in a valley in the Siwaliks, foothills of the Himalaya. The hill station Mussoorie can be seen, 34km away, on the high mountain range above Dehra Dun.

Dehra Dun is at the centre of a forest area and the impressive Forest Research Institute is here. The town is a major academic and research centre and a base for the Indian Military Academy and the Survey of India (which sells large-scale maps of many Indian cities). There are also several prestigious boarding schools including the Doon School, India's most exclusive private school, where Rajiv Gandhi was educated.

Orientation
The clock tower is the hub of the town and most of the budget hotels are near it or close to the railway station. The top-end hotels are all in the area known as Astley Hall, north of the clock tower. The main market is Paltan Bazaar; sold here is high quality basmati rice, for which the region is famous.

Information
Tourist Offices For information on Dehra Dun itself head for the Tourist Information Bureau (☎ 23400) at 9B Astley Hall, Rajpur Rd. It's open from 10 am to 5 pm daily except Sunday and has money exchange facilities.

UP Tourism (☎ 653217) and GMVN (☎ 654371) both have offices at the Hotel Drona, near the Delhi bus stand at 45 Gandhi Rd. They're both open Monday to Saturday from 10 am to 5 pm (closed for lunch between 1 and 2 pm).

Money The State Bank of India is close to the clock tower, at 11-A Rajpur Rd, in the Windlass Shopping Complex, beneath the Hotel Ambassador. Most travellers cheques are accepted, but *not* Visa. The Tourist Information Bureau at Astley Hall will exchange

Dehra Dun

OTHER
1 Tapkeshwar Temple
2 Forest Research Institute
3 Wadia Institute of Himalayan Geology
4 Doon School
5 Survey of India
12 GMVN Tourist Office
13 Central Bank
13 Dehra Dun Tourist Information Bureau
15 BJ Travels
19 Clock Tower
21 Delhi Bus Stand
22 UP Tourism, GMVN Tourist Office & Hotel Drona
26 Mussoorie Bus Stand

PLACES TO STAY
6 Hotel Madhuban
8 Hotel Meedo's Grand & Doon Guest House
9 The White House
11 Hotel Daichi
16 Hotel Ambassador & State Bank of India
20 Hotel Rang Mahal
23 Oriental Hotel & Sammaan Veg Restaurant
24 Victoria Hotel
27 Hotel Meedo

PLACES TO EAT
10 The Vegetarian & Daddy's
14 Kumar Restaurant & Motel Himshri
18 Motimahal & A-One Grill
25 Vishal & Kasturbi Restaurants

Rispana River
Rishpana River
To Mussoorie (34km)
To Tapovan (3km) & Sahastradhara (14km)
To Sahastradhara (14km)
Rajpur Road
Astley Hall Area
Eastern Canal Road
Subhash Road
Gandhi Park
Paltan Bazaar
New Road
Kaonli Road
Bindal (intermittent)
Railway Station
To Saharanpur (66km)
Chakrata Road
Kaulagarh Road
ONGC Chowk
Tons Nadi
General Mahadev Singh Road
Botanical Gardens
Pearson Road
To Shimla (221km)

0   0.5   1 km

all major travellers cheques, and give cash advances on Visa and American Express credit cards – it takes about three days for the money to come through. The Central Bank, Astley Hall area, on Rajpur Rd near the Hotel President, is one of the few banks that will exchange Visa travellers cheques.

Travel Agencies BJ Travels (☎ 657888), about 200m north of the main post office at 15-B Rajpur Rd, has a computerised reservation system and can provide instant confirmation on domestic and international flights. To arrange treks, contact Bajaj Tours & Trekking (☎ 624425), S Gurcharan Singh, 14A National Rd, Luxman Chowk, or Trek Himalaya Tours (☎ 653005). For inquiries in person, call into the Bengali Sweet Shop at the clock tower.

Bookshops Natraj Booksellers, at 17 Rajpur Rd, next to the Motel Himshri, has an extensive selection of books on environmental issues, with particular emphasis on the Indian Himalaya. There's also a hefty selection of Penguin titles. Around the corner at 15 Rajpur Rd, the English Book Depot also has an excellent range.

Film & Photography For photographic requirements, advice and excellent service, Harish Studio, in the Motel Himshri complex, is a good place to head.

Forest Research Institute
Established by the British earlier this century the FRI is now reputedly one of the finest institutes of forest sciences in the world and houses an excellent museum. It's set in large botanical gardens, with the Himalaya providing a spectacular backdrop.

The institute is open Monday to Friday from 10 am to 5 pm and entry is free. To get there take a Vikram (six-seater tempo) from the clock tower to the institute gates.

Other Things to See
The **Wadia Institute of Himalayan Geology** has a museum that's open Monday to Friday from 10 am to 5 pm.

Tapkeshwar Temple is dedicated to Siva. It's beside a stream, which (when flowing) is directed onto the lingam. A large fair is held here on Sivaratri day (usually in March).

Other places to visit include the **Lakshman Sidh Temple**; the village of **Sahastradhara** (14km east of Dehra Dun) with cold sulphur springs and a Tourist Rest House (Rs 150 for double; book through the GMVN in Dehra Dun); and the **Robbers' Cave**, a popular picnic spot just beyond Anarwala village, eight km from Dehra Dun. Take a local bus to Anarwala and walk the remaining 1½km. The **Survey of India** has its headquarters off Rajpur Rd, four km from the clock tower. You can buy maps from the map shop. It's open 10 am to 5 pm weekdays.

Places to Stay – bottom end
Oriental Hotel (☎ 627059) is pretty basic but cheap enough with singles/doubles for Rs 70/125. There's a restaurant.

Victoria Hotel has fairly grubby rooms built around a courtyard for Rs 70/120 with attached bath (bucket hot water costs Rs 3).

Hotel Meedo (☎ 627088) has rooms for Rs 150/230-245 with attached baths. Those at the back are quieter. There's a rather sleazy bar next door, but the Meedo itself is clean and friendly. (Don't confuse this place with the top-end Hotel Meedo's Grand.)

The White House (☎ 652765) is a good place (if a little run down) in a quiet garden setting. Singles/doubles start at Rs 125/175; air-coolers are available for Rs 50 a day. It's a popular place so it may pay to book ahead. A three-wheeler from the stations will cost about Rs 15; a Vikram Rs 2 (get off at Kanak Cinema).

Hotel Daichi (☎ 658107), on 6 Mahant Laxman Dass Rd, has good value rooms with attached bath plus hot water for Rs 165/275; more for air-cooling.

Doon Guest House (☎ 657171) has rooms for Rs 150/200 with bath and bucket hot water.

Railway retiring rooms at the station will cost you Rs 100 per double or Rs 30 for a dorm bed.

STREET VENDORS

One of the most interesting aspects of travel in India is the wide variety of goods and services offered by pavement vendors – everything from stocks and shares to a replacement tooth! The ones you'll see most often are the shoe-repair wallahs and pavement barbers, whose tools of the trade may be nothing more than a razor, scissors and the all-important mirror for customers to admire themselves in.

The pavement dentist often has an impressive display of dentures and teeth, and an array of implements straight out of the Middle Ages. Ear-cleaners also ply their trade on the streets, and are easily recognised by their small red turbans, into which they stick their various picks and prods.

Then there are the unemployed who sell various items on commission from shops. You might see a boy trying to sell half a dozen pairs of black socks, another with pens, padlocks or cheap and nasty plastic toys. It's hard to see how some of them make any money at all; the commission on a Rs 2 plastic comb can't be worth a lot, and how many can you sell in a day anyway?

In the hot season, men with large metal water carts do a good trade at 25 paise a glass, as do ice-cream sellers with their decorated white carts. It's probably best to avoid the water carts, and only buy well-known brands of ice cream, such as Kwality, Havmore and Milkfood.

HUGH FINLAY

GREG ELMS

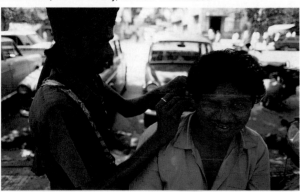

SARA-JANE CLELAND

Top: Glass bangles, worn by most Indian women, for sale at a roadside stall.

Left Top: A sight you're unlikely to see anywhere else in the world – a Mumbai man submits himself to the attentions of an ear cleaner.

Left Bottom: Shoe-repair wallahs fix everything from chappals to Nikes.

HENNA MARKINGS

Marking the hands and feet with henna, a plant extract, is a popular practice in many places, but especially in Rajasthan. When mixed with water, the green powder forms a reddish dye, which is then used to paint intricate patterns on the skin. This is usually done using thin plastic stencils bought cheaply in the bazaar, although there are still people who make a living from painting the designs freehand. Once applied, the dye can't be washed off, but gradually fades after about 10 days.

The Urdu word 'henna' comes from Arabic; Hindi speakers generally use the word *mehndi*, which is also used to describe the pre-marriage ceremony when henna patterns are drawn on the bride's hands and feet.

MEERA GOVIL

Top: Intricate henna patterns are traditionally worn by brides, but are also popular with travellers.

Right: A roadside vendor applying henna patterns.

MEERA GOVIL

Places to Stay – middle & top end

Most of Dehra Dun's middle to top-end accommodation can be found on Rajpur Rd.

Hotel Ambassador (☎ 655831), 11A Rajpur Rd, has air-cooled singles/doubles with colour TV from Rs 225/325.

Motel Himshri (☎ 653880) at 17 Rajpur Rd has ordinary rooms from Rs 250/350; larger deluxe rooms cost Rs 450/550.

Hotel President (☎ 658880), 6 Astley Hall, has air-cooled singles/doubles for Rs 600/800, and a restaurant, bar and coffee shop.

Hotel Meedo's Grand (☎ 657171) at 28 Rajpur Rd, three km from the railway station, has comfortable rooms for Rs 500/700. There's a restaurant and bar.

Hotel Madhuban (☎ 659990), north of Hotel Meedo's Grand at 97 Rajpur Rd, has a mini golf course and air-con singles/doubles for Rs 1150/1700.

Hotel Ajanta Continental (☎ 659596), north of Hotel Madhuban, has rooms from Rs 760/1000, and a restaurant, bar and swimming pool.

Hotel Drona (☎ 654371) at 45 Gandhi Rd, next to the Delhi bus station, is run by GMVN. Dorm beds (men only) cost Rs 100. Reasonably large, clean rooms with attached bath and hot water cost Rs 320/425; Rs 475/630 with air-con. There's a restaurant and bar (a beer costs Rs 50) and a 10% mid/ off-season discount.

Osho Resorts (☎ 659544), 111 Rajpur Rd, describes itself as a 'retreat with a waterfall'. It's part of the Bhagwan Rajneesh organisation. Rooms start at Rs 220/290; there are also wooden huts. Videos of the late guru are available for viewing and there's a meditation centre as well as a vegetarian restaurant.

Places to Eat

Kumar, on Rajpur Rd near Motel Himshri, serves up some of the best vegetarian food in town. Recommended are the gajar ka halwa (made from carrot, spices and milk) and the makki ki roti, saron ka saag (corn roti with mustard-leaf spinach) with lassi, which costs Rs 40.

A hundred metres south is another *Kumar* that serves non-veg and Chinese food.

Motimahal, one of the best in a string of eateries on the opposite side of Rajpur Rd, serves good veg and non-veg dishes.

The *A-One Grill* serves takeaway tandoori chicken and kebabs from 8 pm until late.

The *Punjab Restaurant* is inexpensive.

Vegetarian by the Hotel President dishes up inexpensive (Rs 30 and under) but tasty meals.

Daddy's offers Mughlai, South Indian and Chinese food.

Sammaan Veg Restaurant near the Oriental Hotel in Paltan Bazaar serves filling thalis for Rs 30.

Standard Confectioners near the Vegetarian restaurant is one of several good bakeries in Dehra Dun.

Grand Bakers in Paltan Bazaar is another one; there are several good *sweet shops* near the clock tower.

Getting There & Away

Air Jolly Grant Airport is 24km from the city. It's not currently served by any airline although at the time of writing UP Airways (Delhi ☎ (011) 463-8201) was planning flights from Delhi and Lucknow.

Bus The Mussoorie bus stand, by the railway station on Haridwar Rd, is for destinations in the hills. There are frequent departures to Mussoorie (1½ hours, Rs 15). Other buses go to Nainital (11 hours, Rs 121), Uttarkashi (seven hours, Rs 78) and Tehri (four hours, Rs 51).

The Delhi bus stand, beside the Hotel Drona, serves destinations on the plains. The seven hour trip to Delhi costs Rs 137 deluxe, Rs 94 semideluxe, Rs 76 ordinary. Deluxe buses leave hourly between 5.15 am and 10.30 pm; ordinary buses leave every 15 to 30 minutes.

Other destinations include: Haridwar (1½ hours, Rs 16); Rishikesh (1½ hours, Rs 12.50); Lucknow (1.30 and 6 pm, up to 16 hours, Rs 162 or Rs 179 express); Shimla via Paonta Saheb, Solan and Kumar Hatti (ie via the hills – departures at 5.30, 6.30, 8.30 10.30 and 11.30 am, seven hours, Rs 82) or via Saharanpur, Ambala and Chandigarh (ie via the plains – 7.25 and 9.15 am, nine hours, Rs 114); Dharamsala (12.30 pm, 15 hours, Rs 160); and Kullu (14 hours, Rs 180) and Manali (16 hours, Rs 195), departing at 3.15 pm.

Train Services to Dehra Dun, the terminus of the Northern Railway, include the speedy *Shatabdi Express*, leaving New Delhi at 6 am daily (except Tuesday) and reaching Haridwar at 10.45 am and Dehra Dun at 11.45 am. Chair car/1st class costs Rs 325/630 to Haridwar, and Rs 350/685 to Dehra Dun.

The *Mussoorie Express* is an overnight train service from Delhi to Dehra Dun. It leaves Old Delhi station at 10.25 pm, arriving at Haridwar at 6 am and Dehra Dun at 7.50 am. On the return journey, it leaves Dehra Dun at 9.30 pm, Haridwar at 11.20 pm, arriving at Old Delhi at 7 am.

The *Doon Express* operates between Lucknow and Dehra Dun. The 545km journey costs Rs 144/494 in 2nd/1st class. There are also services from Dehra Dun to Calcutta, Varanasi and Mumbai.

Taxi There's a share taxi stand in front of the Mussoorie bus stand on Haridwar Rd. Taxis leave for Mussoorie when full (five passengers required), and depart every hour or so between 6 am and 6 pm (1¼ hours, Rs 52). You'll have more luck if you hang around the taxi stand when trains disgorge their passengers from Delhi. A second share-taxi stand is by the Hotel Prince, on Rishikesh Rd. Taxis and jeeps (called 'trekkers' by locals) depart when full for Rishikesh (Rs 12), Haridwar (Rs 14), and Paonta Saheb, just over the border in eastern Himachal Pradesh (Rs 18). The trekker stops one km before the border, from where you can catch a rickshaw into Himachal Pradesh.

To reserve a whole taxi to Mussoorie will cost Rs 200; to other destinations expect to pay the following during the off season: Rishikesh (Rs 200), Haridwar (Rs 300), Uttarkashi (Rs 1000), Shimla (Rs 1600), and Nainital (Rs 1800). During the peak seasons, you'll be stung for at least Rs 100 more.

Getting Around
Tempo & Auto-Rickshaw Six-seater tempos (Vikrams) belch diesel fumes all over the city, but are a cheap way to get around. They run on fixed routes for about half the price of an auto-rickshaw ride. Route No 1 runs from the clock tower along Rajpur Rd.

Car Cars can be hired through GMVN at its Rajpur Rd and Hotel Drona offices. You may be able to negotiate better rates through Ventures Rent a Car (☎ 22724), at 87 Rajpur Rd.

MUSSOORIE
Pop: 33,600   Tel Area Code: 0135
At an altitude of 2000m and 34km beyond Dehra Dun, Mussoorie has been a popular hill station since it was 'discovered' in 1823 by a Captain Young. There are over 100 hotels jostling for the views across the Dun Valley to accommodate the hordes of tourists from Delhi in the hot season. It can be quite peaceful in the off season and there are good walks along the mountain ridges.

Orientation
The Mall connects Gandhi Chowk with Kulri Bazaar, two km away. Buses from Dehra Dun go to the Library bus stand (Gandhi Chowk) or Picture Palace (Kulri Bazaar), but not both; make sure you get the one you want, as The Mall is closed to traffic during the high season.

Information
Tourist Offices There's a very helpful UP tourist office (☎ 632863) towards the Kulri Bazaar end of The Mall, near the ropeway station, and a GMVN office (☎ 632984) at the Hotel Garhwal Terrace, about 500m further west along The Mall. There's a small GMVN booth (☎ 631281) at the Library bus stand at Gandhi Chowk which runs tours to Kempty Falls (three hours, Rs 25); Mussoorie Lake (Rs 15, high season only); and full-day tours (October and November only, Rs 100) which include the picnic site of Dhanolti, set amid deodar forests and with

excellent views of the Himalaya; and the Surkhanda Devi Temple, perched at 3050m and also affording magnificent views of a 300km long stretch of the Himalaya.

Money The State Bank of India at Kulri Bazaar will exchange American Express travellers cheques in US dollars only, and Thomas Cook and MasterCard cheques in US dollars and pounds sterling only. There's an encashment fee of Rs 25. The Bank of Baroda, Kulri Bazaar (beneath The Tavern restaurant), exchanges most travellers cheques, including Visa and Citicorp.

Travel Agencies Ambica Travels (☎ 632238) at the Hotel Hill Queen, Upper Mall Rd, The Mall (west) can book deluxe buses to Delhi (10.30 am and 10.30 pm, non air-con, and 11 am and 10 pm, air-con). They also book air and train tickets. Hire cars can be arranged through Kulwant Travels (☎ 632717), at the Masonic Lodge bus stand, or Harry Tours & Travels (☎ 632507), also at this bus stand.

Trekking Outfits & Tour Operators A respected trek operator is Trek Himalaya Tours (☎ 631366; fax 631302), at Powy's Cottage, Hakman's Compound (take the path down beside the UP tourist office). Neelamber Badoni here can arrange treks in the Garhwal area, and jeep safaris to Kinnaur, Spiti and Ladakh, as well as sorting out the paperwork and necessary permits for these areas. It is also possible to hire tents (Rs 50 to Rs 80 per day), sleeping bags (Rs 25 to Rs 30), mats (Rs 5) and rucksacks here. Harry Tours & Travels (see Travel Agencies above) can also organise treks.

Bookshops There's a good selection of books (including Penguins and regional guide books) and maps at Cambridge Booksellers and Chander Book Depot, both at Kulri Bazaar.

Medical Services You could try St Mary's Hospital (☎ 632845). James Chemist is a well-stocked dispensary near the Picture

Palace; so too is A Kumar & Co, beneath the library at the west end of The Mall.

Things to See & Do
A ropeway runs up to **Gun Hill** (Rs 25 return, 9 am to 7 pm daily and until 10 pm between 15 May and 15 July). For early-morning views of the Himalaya including Bandar Punch (6315m), you have to walk up. At the top, photo agencies will (if you like) dress you up in sequinned Garhwal national dress and take your photo for Rs 30.

The walks around Mussoorie offer great views. **Camel's Back Road** was built as a promenade and passes a rock formation that looks like a camel – hence the name. You can rent ponies or cycle rickshaws (Rs 60). Another good walk takes you down to Happy Valley and the **Tibetan Refugee Centre** where there's a temple and a small shop selling hand-knitted sweaters. An enjoyable longer walk (five km) takes you through Landour Bazaar to **Childers Lodge** (Lal Tibba), the highest point in Mussoorie, and Sisters' Bazaar.

GMVN runs tours in summer to **Kempty Falls** (Rs 30) and **Dhanolti** (Rs 100) where there are good views of the Himalaya.

Language Courses
The Landour Language School (☎ 631467) in the Sisters' Bazaar area has introductory courses in Hindi. Private lessons cost Rs 50 an hour and group lessons Rs 25 an hour. Contact the principal, Mr Chitranjan Datt, Landour Language School, Landour Cantt, Mussoorie, 248179.

Places to Stay
With so many hotels competing for your custom, prices vary enormously according to the season. Rates given here are for the off season (November to March) but you may be able to negotiate a further reduction at this time. Note that some hotels are closed in January and February. Prices rise by up to 300% in the summer and finding anywhere to stay during the Hindu festivals of Dussehra or Diwali can be very difficult. Porters from either bus stand to any hotel expect Rs 20.

Places to Stay – bottom end
Kulri Bazaar & The Mall (East End) Budget accommodation in this area includes the following.

Hotel Broadway (☎ 632243) was a small English guest house run by a Miss Lee until 1954 when it was bought by the current owner, Mr Malik. It's a friendly, well-kept place with some nice views, and is deservedly popular. Doubles cost from Rs 100; there are a few singles for Rs 50.

Hotel Valley View (☎ 632324) on The Mall has clean rooms for Rs 100/150. There is a non-veg dining hall.

Hotel Clarks (☎ 632393) has plenty of Raj-era character and boasts a billiard room with a full-size table. The rooms themselves are a little shabby; they range from Rs 150 to Rs 550.

Hotel Vikram (☎ 632932), near the Tilak Memorial Library, has doubles for Rs 75 to Rs 299, with bucket hot water supplied to guests in the cheaper rooms.

Library Area & The Mall (West End)
There are some good budget options at the west end of The Mall.

Hotel Laxmi Palace (☎ 632774) is a new place with clean, pleasant rooms. Singles/doubles cost Rs 100/250.

Whispering Windows (☎ 632020) (also known as Hotel Upstairs & Downstairs) is handy to the Library bus stand and right on The Mall. It has rooms for Rs 175 to Rs 275.

Hotel India (☎ 632359), just above The Mall, is run by a friendly Sikh family. It has doubles with attached bath for Rs 150 to Rs 350. The water is solar heated.

Hotel Prince (☎ 632674) nearby, is an interesting old building with great views, but the rooms seem rather neglected (upstairs rooms are better). A double with attached bath and hot water costs Rs 250.

Landour Bazaar
The *Hotel Nishima* (☎ 632227) is right in the busy market area. Basic rooms cost Rs 100/150.

Places to Stay – middle & top end
Kulri Bazaar & The Mall (East End) The *Hakman's Grand Hotel* (☎ 632959) is a place for Raj-era nostalgia buffs; there is even a cash register in the lobby calibrated in annas.

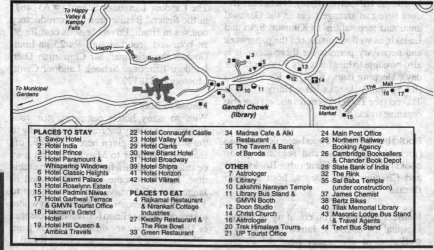

PLACES TO STAY		
1 Savoy Hotel	22 Hotel Connaught Castle	34 Madras Cafe & Alki
2 Hotel India	23 Hotel Valley View	Restaurant
3 Hotel Prince	29 Hotel Clarks	36 The Tavern & Bank
5 Hotel Paramount &	30 New Bharat Hotel	of Baroda
Whispering Windows	31 Hotel Broadway	
6 Hotel Classic Heights	39 Hotel Shipra	OTHER
9 Hotel Laxmi Palace	41 Hotel Horizon	7 Astrologer
13 Hotel Roselynn Estate	42 Hotel Vikram	8 Library
15 Hotel Padmini Niwas		10 Lakshmi Narayan Temple
17 Hotel Garhwal Terrace	PLACES TO EAT	11 Library Bus Stand &
& GMVN Tourist Office	4 Rajkamal Restaurant	GMVN Booth
18 Hakman's Grand	& Nirankari Cottage	12 Doon Studio
Hotel	Industries	14 Christ Church
19 Hotel Hill Queen &	27 Kwality Restaurant &	16 Astrologer
Ambica Travels	The Rice Bowl	20 Trek Himalaya Tourrs
	33 Green Restaurant	21 UP Tourist Office

24 Main Post Office
25 Northern Railway
Booking Agency
26 Cambridge Booksellers
& Chander Book Depot
28 State Bank of India
32 The Rink
35 Sai Baba Temple
(under construction)
37 James Chemist
38 Bertz Bikes
40 Tilak Memorial Library
43 Masonic Lodge Bus Stand
& Travel Agents
44 Tehri Bus Stand

Map labels: To Happy Valley & Kempty Falls; Happy Valley Road; To Municipal Gardens; Gandhi Chowk (library); Tibetan Market; The Mall

The rooms, which may not be to everyone's taste, cost Rs 300.

Hotel Shipra (☎ 632662), near the Masonic Lodge bus stand, has well-appointed rooms from Rs 1250 to Rs 1450, and a restaurant and bar.

Hotel Horizon (☎ 632899) is a new place opposite Hotel Shipra with thick pile carpets, Star TV and views across the valley. Doubles cost Rs 900; there's a 40% discount off season.

Hotel Connaught Castle (☎ 632210) is up a long driveway leading off the Upper Mall Rd. It's a modern place with marble corridors and luxurious rooms from Rs 1650.

Hotel Garwhal Terrace (☎ 632682) is a renovated GMVN place. Rooms, all with Star TV, cost Rs 495. Dorm beds cost Rs 60. There are two restaurants.

Library Area & The Mall (West End) Top-end accommodation in this area includes some fine old Raj relics.

Hotel Paramount (☎ 632352), right on The Mall, is run by a friendly Sikh man. Rooms, although a little small, are reasonably airy and cost Rs 200 to Rs 500.

Hotel Roselyn Estate (☎ 632201), 250m east along The Mall, has doubles (on the shabby side) from Rs 400. There's a non-veg restaurant.

Hotel Classic Heights (☎ 632514), a short distance south of the library, has a range of rooms from Rs 495/795 (40% less in the off season). The hotel's travel counter can arrange trekking, fishing and horse riding.

Hotel Padmini Nivas (☎ 632793), about 600m east of the library, once belonged to the Maharaja of Rajpipla. Doubles start from Rs 450; an apartment costs Rs 1300. The old world atmosphere is enhanced by a rose garden and wicker chairs on the patio. There's also a Gujarati vegetarian restaurant.

Savoy Hotel (☎ 632010) is a huge place covered with ivy and replete with faded touches of the Raj, including moth-eaten deer heads. It's also said to have a resident ghost, one Lady Gore Ormsby, whose death allegedly provided inspiration for Agatha Christie's first novel *The Mysterious Affair at Styles*. Rooms (with three meals) start at Rs 995/1795; 10% less in the off season.

Sisters' Bazaar The *Hotel Dev Dar Woods* (☎ 632644) is in a lofty wooded location by Sisters' Bazaar. Popular with foreigners at the nearby language school, it's an interesting

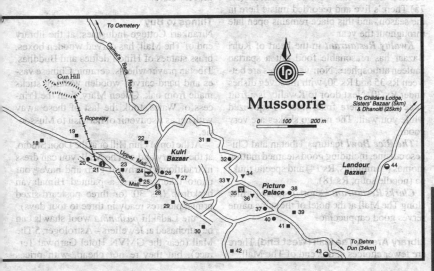

place to stay. Rooms cost Rs 250 including breakfast; three meals are included for the same price if you stay more than 15 days.

Places to Eat

Most of the better hotels have their own restaurants, and there are a lot of very good (and good value) restaurants in the Kulri Bazaar area. Due to a steep hike in licensing fees, many restaurants no longer have bars. Off-season, restaurants generally close around 10 to 10.30 pm.

Kulri Bazaar & The Mall (East End) The
Madras Cafe specialises in south Indian food, with the menu featuring 24 different types of dosa (Rs 10 to Rs 30). There are also idlis (steamed rice cakes) with dhal, and vadas (deep fried veg doughnuts).

Alki Restaurant is a few doors down, with south Indian and Chinese dishes. Here a sweet kulfi faluda (kulfi ice cream with faluda: long chickpea-flour noodles) costs Rs 15.

Green Restaurant has good vegetarian food; try the cheese korma (Rs 28).

The Tavern, near the Bank of Baroda, specialises in Mughlai and Chinese cuisine; The reshmi kabab (tender chicken kebab cooked in the tandoor) is excellent (Rs 75).There's live and recorded music here in the season, and this place remains open late throughout the year.

Kwality Restaurant in the heart of Kulri Bazaar has reasonable food but a spartan canteen atmosphere. Non-veg dishes are between Rs 35 and Rs 50, with most veg dishes under Rs 30. Next door to Kwality is a fruit juice stand, where fresh juice is squeezed while you wait. The mango shakes are very good.

The Rice Bowl features Tibetan and Chinese cuisine, including good steamed mutton momos (dumplings, Rs 14) and special thukpa (noodle soup, Rs 18).

Clarks Restaurant a short distance further along The Mall at the hotel of the same name serves good cappuccino.

Library Area & The Mall (West End) There
are fewer choices at this end of The Mall.

Whispering Windows is a popular spot for watching the holiday makers promenading along The Mall. During the season there's dancing to recorded music on the tiled floor.

The *Rajkamal Restaurant*, next door, has good cheap veg and non-veg food, and a dignified, ancient waiter resplendent in brass-buttoned livery.

Swiss Cafe next to the Hotel Paramount has Chinese and Indian food, as well as a selection of muffins and Danish pastries during the season.

Savoy Hotel meals are not cheap, with non-veg dishes around Rs 90, but you may be rewarded with a glimpse of the ghost of Lady Gore Ormsby (who probably expired at the sight of the bill). If you're feeling really magnanimous, you can shout your dining companions to a bottle of Moët et Chandon (Rs 1500), or a 25ml shot of Johnnie Walker Blue Label (Rs 395). Beers are Rs 80. Advance reservations are essential.

Sisters' Bazaar
Superb cheddar cheese (Rs 150 to Rs 175 per kg; not made during the monsoon) and home-made produce such as peanut butter, jams and chutneys can be found at *A Prakash & Co*, a long-established grocery store.

Things to Buy

Nirankari Cottage Industries, at the library end of The Mall, has carved wooden boxes, brass statues of Hindu deities and Buddhas, Tibetan prayer wheels, ceramic Chinese vases and hand-carved wooden walking sticks made from oak. Queen Mary, then the Princess of Wales, took the last of these away with her as a souvenir of her visit to Mussoorie.

At the top of Gun Hill or at the Doon Studio, at the library end of The Mall, you can dress in traditional Garhwali garb and have your photo taken against a painted Himalayan backdrop (Rs 30 for three postcard-sized prints; pictures ready in three to four days).

Pure Ladakhi *pashmina* wool shawls can be purchased at Jewellers – Astrologer, 5 The Mall (near the GMVN Hotel Garhwal Terrace), but they're not cheap, with prices starting at Rs 7000, up to Rs 60,000 for antique Jamawar shawls, produced on wooden looms, and employing a method now lost.

Getting There & Away

There are numerous buses from the Mussoorie bus stand (next to the railway station) in Dehra Dun to Mussoorie between 6.30 am and 8.30 pm (1½ hours, Rs 15). These go either to the Library bus stand (Gandhi Chowk) or Kulri Bazaar (Masonic Lodge bus stand). When travelling to Mussoorie from the west or north (ie Jammu) by train, it is best to get off at Saharanpur and catch a bus from there to Dehra Dun or Mussoorie, if there's no convenient train connection.

Buses to Dehra Dun leave half-hourly to hourly from the Library and Masonic Lodge stands (Rs 13). For Delhi, there's a deluxe overnight service from the Library bus stand (Rs 135), and an ordinary express overnight service (Rs 86.50) from the Masonic Lodge stand.

Buses to Hanuman Chatti (for Yamunotri) originate in Dehra Dun and collect passengers in Mussoorie at the Library bus stand (10 am, seven hours, Rs 80).

The Tehri bus stand is for buses to Tehri (five hours, Rs 30) and connections to Uttarkashi and Gangotri. The trip may be rough, but takes in some marvellous mountain scenery.

With at least 24 hours notice, train tickets can be arranged through the Northern Railway booking agency (☎ 632846), at the Kulri Bazaar end of The Mall. The office is open Monday to Saturday from 10 am to 4 pm, and Sunday from 8 am to 2 pm.

Reserve taxis from the Library bus stand and the Masonic Lodge bus stand go to many destinations, including Rishikesh (2½ hours, Rs 500 to Rs 600), Haridwar (three hours, Rs 600), Sister's Bazaar (30 minutes, Rs 120 one way, Rs 180 return with a half-hour wait), Delhi (seven hours, Rs 1500) and Uttarkashi (for Gangotri, 5½ hours, Rs 1400).

Getting Around

The Mall is closed to traffic for most of the year, so to traverse the two km between Kulri Bazaar and the library area, you can either walk, rent a pony (officially Rs 15 per km), or take a hand-drawn rickshaw (pulled by two rickshaw-wallahs and often pushed by a third). Expect to pay Rs 30 from the Picture Palace and Kulri Bazaar to the UP tourist office, and about Rs 15 to Rs 20 from the tourist office to the library (ie Rs 45 from Kulri Bazaar to the library).

At the time of writing, Bertz Bikes, from where it used to be possible to rent 100cc motorcycles from their shop on the road heading towards Landour Bazaar, was closed, but they may reopen in the near future.

HARIDWAR

Pop: 218,500   Tel Area Code: 0133

Haridwar's propitious location, at the point where the Ganges emerges from the Himalaya to begin its slow progress across the plains, makes it a particularly holy place. There are many ashrams here but you may find Rishikesh (24km to the north) more pleasant, especially if you wish to study Hinduism. Haridwar means Gateway to the Gods, but it seems like any another noisy town.

Every 12 years the Kumbh Mela attracts millions of pilgrims who bathe here. Kumbh Mela takes place every three years, consecutively at Allahabad, Nasik, Ujjain and Haridwar. It is next due to take place in Haridwar in 1998.

Orientation

Buses pull into the UP Roadways bus stand at the south-west end of town, on Railway Rd, the long road which runs parallel to the Upper Ganges Canal, connecting this end of town with Har ki Pairi (the main ghat), about 2½km north-east. The railway station is opposite the UP Roadways bus stand. The canal is traversed by the Laltarao Bridge, which you'll cross if you're coming from Rishikesh. The road over the bridge meets Railway Rd; the north-eastern section of Railway Rd (ie from Laltarao Bridge to Har ki Pairi) is known locally as Upper Rd. There are places to stay and eat scattered along the length of Railway Rd, with a lot of budget options in the area known as Shiv Murti, just to the north-east of the bus stand. Behind Har ki Pairi, running parallel to the canal, is the busy market area known as Bara Bazaar.

Information

Tourist Offices The GMVN tourist office (☎ 424240) is on Upper Rd, directly opposite the Laltarao Bridge. It's open Monday to Saturday from 10 am to 5 pm. You can book Char Dham packages here, but the best source of local information is Sanjeev Mehta at Mohan's Fast Food, Railway Rd (see the Places to Eat section). Sanjeev is a keen photographer, and spends most of his free time stalking through the jungle endeavouring to capture its inhabitants on film. UP Tourism's regional office (☎ 427370; open daily from 10 am to 5 pm) is based at the Rahi Motel, further west down Railway Rd, past the UP Roadways bus stand.

Money The Bank of Baroda, next door to the

Hotel Mansarovar International, exchanges American Express and Thomas Cook travellers cheques in US dollars and pounds sterling only. The State Bank of India on Sadhu Bela Marg also has foreign exchange facilities.

Post & Communications The main post office is on Upper Rd (Railway Rd) about 200m north-west of Laltarao Bridge. The Foreigners' Registration Office is next door.

Trekking Outfits & Tour Operators Ashvani Travels (☎ 424581), at 3 Upper Rd, can organise trekking (including equipment), white-water rafting (September to March) and ski packages to Auli (January and February). They can also provide guides and porters to take visitors around the salient spots of Haridwar.

Things to See

Haridwar is a very old town, mentioned by the Chinese scholar/traveller Hiuen Tsang in

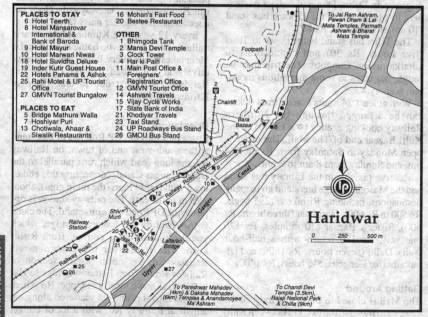

PLACES TO STAY
6 Hotel Teerth
8 Hotel Mansarovar International & Bank of Baroda
9 Hotel Mayur
10 Hotel Marwari Niwas
18 Hotel Suvidha Deluxe
19 Inder Kutir Guest House
22 Hotels Panama & Ashok
25 Rahi Motel & UP Tourist Office
27 GMVN Tourist Bungalow

PLACES TO EAT
5 Bridge Mathura Walla
7 Hoshiyar Puri
13 Chotiwala, Ahaar & Siwalik Restaurants

16 Mohan's Fast Food
20 Bestee Restaurant

OTHER
1 Bhimgoda Tank
2 Mansa Devi Temple
3 Clock Tower
4 Har ki Pairi
11 Main Post Office & Foreigners' Registration Office
12 GMVN Tourist Office
14 Ashvani Travels
15 Vijay Cycle Works
17 State Bank of India
21 Khodiyar Travels
23 Taxi Stand
24 UP Roadways Bus Stand
26 GMOU Bus Stand

To Jai Ram Ashram, Pawan Dham & Lal Mata Temples, Parmath Ashram & Bharat Mata Temple

Footpath

Chairlift

Bara Bazaar

Railway Road (Upper Road)

Canal

Ganga's

Shiv Murti

Railway Station

Railway Road

Laltarao Rd

Laltarao Bridge

Upper Rd

Haridwar

0   250   500 m

To Pareshwar Mahadev (4km) & Daksha Mahadev (6km) Temples & Anandamoyee Ma Ashram

To Chandi Devi Temple (3.5km), Rajaji National Park & Chilla (9km)

the 7th century AD, but its many temples were constructed comparatively recently, and are of little historical interest, although they do have many idols and illustrated scenes from the Hindi epics.

The main ghat, **Har ki Pairi** ('the footstep of God'), is supposed to be at the precise spot where the Ganges leaves the mountains and enters the plains. Consequently the river's power to wash away sins at this spot is superlative and endorsed by a footprint Vishnu left in a stone here. The ghat is on the west bank of a canal through which the Ganges is diverted just to the north. Each evening at sunset priests perform the Ganga Aarti, or river worship, ceremony here, when lights are set on the water to drift downstream while priests engage in elaborate rituals. Non-Hindus were once forbidden to step on the ghat, but in a new spirit of rapprochement, foreign visitors may now join the throngs of Hindu pilgrims. The glare from the sun's rays reflecting off the water and marble paved bridges is phenomenal – if you're here at noon, bring sunglasses.

In addition to the main ghat, a series of smaller ghats extends along the canal bank, with large orange and white life-guard towers at intervals to ensure that bathing pilgrims don't get swept away.

On the north side of the canal, between Har ki Pairi and the Upper Rd, is the colourful **Bara Bazaar**. Along with the usual religious paraphernalia (*prasaad* – food offered to the gods – images of the deities, religious pamphlets, etc) are scores of tiny stalls crammed along both sides of the bazaar selling an assortment of goods including tiffins, shawls, ayurvedic medicines, brassware, glass bangles, wooden whistles, bamboo canes and cane baskets.

It is worth taking the chairlift (Rs 20 return) to the **Mansa Devi Temple** on the hill above the city. The lift is not exactly state of the art, but it's well maintained. It operates between 8 am and noon, and 2 and 5 pm. If you're feeling energetic, you can walk up (1½km) and enjoy the view down over the city and the ghats at your leisure. Vendors sell colourfully packaged prasaad of coconuts,

marigolds and other offerings to take up to the goddess. Mansa is one of the forms of Shakti Durga. Photography is forbidden in the temple.

Four km to the south of Haridwar is the brand new **Pareshwar Mahadev Temple**. The temple, which was inaugurated by the late former president of India, Gyani Zail Singh, houses a sacred lingam reputedly made of mercury. The **Daksha Mahadev Temple** (also known as Shri Dakheswar) is two km further along this route, on the river bank at Khankhal. Daksha, the father of Sati (Siva's first wife), performed a sacrifice here but neglected to invite Siva. Sati was so angry at this unforgivable indiscretion that she managed to spontaneously self-immolate! Opposite this temple is the **Anandamoyee Ma Ashram**, which, since the death of this Bengali guru who counted among her devotees Indira Gandhi, has become an enormous mausoleum.

Other temples and buildings of note in the environs of Haridwar include the **Bhimgoda Tank**, about one km to the north of Har ki Pairi. The tank is said to have been formed by a blow from Bhima's knee – Bhima is the brother of Hanuman. About 150m further north, on the Rishikesh road, is the **Jai Ram Ashram**. Here the usual multicoloured deities characteristic of Hindu temples are strangely absent. Pristine white sculptures are in, and depict the gods and the demons battling for the waters of humanity. Also here are electronically animated scenes from the Hindu epics.

About 500m further along this road, a turn-off to the right at a (usually) dry river bed leads in a further 500m to the **Pawan Dham Temple**. This temple is famed for its fantastic glass and mirrorwork, and its elaborately garbed idols.

About one km further along this road, on the left, is the extraordinary **Lal Mata Temple**, which was completed in 1994. This is a replica of the Vaishno Devi Temple in Jammu & Kashmir, and it is completely faithful to the original – right down to the artificial hill on which the replica is sited. Adjacent is a perpetually frozen ice lingam, a replica of that in the Amarnath Cave in Jammu & Kashmir.

Further along this road, which eventually rejoins the main Rishikesh road, is the **Parmath Ashram**, which has fine images of the goddess Durga. The road proceeds past the **Bharat Mata Temple**, looking like an apartment block with a central dome. It's eight storeys high and there's a lift to the top for lazy pilgrims. On the top floor is an image of Lord Shankar (Siva). Just before this route rejoins the main Rishikesh road is the **Sapt Rishi Ashram**, about five km from Haridwar, named after the seven *rishis* (Hindu saints) who prayed here for the good of humanity. According to tradition, in order to please the seven rishis who were meditating in seven different locations, the Ganges split into seven streams here. Tempos (Vikrams) ply this route.

Chandi Devi, erected on Nhil Hill by a Kashmiri raja, Suchet Singh, in 1929, and a number of other temples in the hills are reached by an approximately four km walk to the south-east. Municipal approval has been granted for the construction of a ropeway cable car from Haridwar to Chandi Devi.

You may see large **river turtles** on the banks of the Nildhara River, near Haridwar, which is over two km broad during the monsoon.

Places to Stay
Hotel Mayur (☎ 427586), Upper Rd (near the chairlift), has very basic singles/doubles for Rs 110/165 in the off season, and Rs 165/265 in the peak season (May and June). Rooms have attached baths, air-coolers and geysers, and those at the front are larger.

Hotel Marwari Niwas (☎ 427759) is down the laneway beside the Mayur, in the area known as Subzi Mandi. Air-cooled doubles are Rs 220, and rooms with air-con are Rs 500. Rooms are set around a well, and all have running hot water and Star TV. Room service is available.

Hotel Mansarovar International (☎ 426501), on Upper Rd, towards Bara Bazaar, is relatively new. Comfortable but drab

singles/doubles with air-coolers cost Rs 450/800, and with air-con, Rs 650/735. A 15% to 20% discount applies off season, and there's a good restaurant (the Swagat). Credit cards are accepted.

Hotel Teerth (☎ 425311), in the heart of Bara Bazaar, is set right on the river, with great views over Har ki Pairi. Air-cooled doubles are Rs 650, air-con are Rs 850. All rooms have balconies facing the river, the staff are friendly and helpful and there's a restaurant.

There's a cluster of budget and mid-range hotels in the area called Shiv Murti, just to the north-east of the bus stands and railway station.

Hotel Kailash (☎ 427789), Railway Rd (the western end of Upper Rd), has air-cooled doubles for Rs 250 and air-con doubles for Rs 550. Some of the rooms have balconies, and there's a restaurant.

Hotel Panama (☎ 427506), just down the road from the Bestee Restaurant on Jasharam Rd, has cheap singles/doubles at Rs 45/90 with attached bath (bucket hot water available). Rooms are small and a little dark but clean; tea, toast and cold drinks are available through room service.

Hotel Ashok (☎ 427328), a few doors down, has basic singles with attached bath (cold water only) for Rs 75. Doubles with common bath are Rs 150, or with attached bath (running hot water), Rs 225. Air-cooled deluxe doubles are Rs 425, and air-con doubles are Rs 825. Rooms are spotless, and there's a travel desk and dining hall.

Hotel Suvidha Deluxe (☎ 427423) is about five minutes walk away, in a quiet location at Sharwan Nath Nagar. Pleasant singles/doubles, all with colour TV, are Rs 450/550 with air-cooler, Rs 700/800 with air-con, and there's a restaurant.

Rahi Motel (☎ 426430) is handy to the bus stands, but in a quiet location. It's also the home of UP Tourism's regional tourist office. Air-cooled singles/doubles are Rs 360/370; with air-con, they're Rs 560/650. Rates include breakfast, and there is also a six bed dorm (Rs 50). All rooms have colour TV, and there's a restaurant.

Inder Kutir Guest House (☎ 426336) is a friendly, family-run place close to the Upper Ganges Canal, at Sharwan Nath Nagar. Air-cooled singles/doubles are Rs 150/300, and there's a dining hall.

GMVN's *Tourist Bungalow* (☎ 426379) is in a peaceful location right on the river, outside the main part of town in Belwala. Singles/doubles are Rs 395/480. Dorm beds are Rs 50. There's no restaurant, but meals can be brought to your room.

Places to Eat
As a holy pilgrimage place, alcohol and meat are strictly prohibited; in fact, imbibing the one or consuming the other is a prosecutable offence. There is, however, a good selection of vegetarian restaurants.

Bestee Restaurant, in the Shiv Murti area, close to the Hotel Panama, has good shakes (in season, try the delicious cheiku shake – cheiku is a small brown fruit similar in appearance to a potato, but sweet). There are also snacks such as vegie rolls (Rs 14) and cutlets (Rs 13), and for breakfast you can wash down your porich (!) with a chocolate lassi (Rs 16).

Hoshiyar Puri has been serving thalis for over 50 years, and they're still good value. The special thali features cheese korma, mut-tar panir, dhal and kheer (rice pud).

Bridge Mathura Walla sweet shop in the heart of the Bara Bazaar has a range of sticky temptations including ras malai (Rs 5) – a milk and sugar based sweet served in a ban-ana leaf plate, floating in sugar syrup and sprinkled with pistachio nuts; rabri, a similar milky confection; and wedges of cashew-nut-studded halwa. Bhaturas (whopping big puris served with aalu and mattar) are also a cheap eat in the bazaar.

Mohan's Fast Food, close to Shiv Murti, in the Chitra Cinema Compound, Railway Rd, is deservedly popular. There are the usual offerings such as pizza and vegie burgers, with a few special Gujarati dishes thrown in for good measure, such as batata vada – four pakoras, green mint chutney and chilli (Rs 15), and pao bhaji – two buns with minced vegetables served in a thali with salad (Rs 15). There's also an astonishing range of ice creams and sundaes, and the friendly owner, Sanjeev Mehta, has a wealth of knowledge on sights around Haridwar, and on the Rajaji National Park.

Opposite the GMVN tourist office are three good upmarket dining places.

The *Ahaar Restaurant*, the pick of the bunch, specialises in Punjabi, South Indian and Chinese cuisine. It's downstairs next door to the Ahaar ice-cream parlour.

The long-running *Chotiwala*, a few doors down, has good Punjabi food.

The *Siwalik*, on the corner, is a multicuisine restaurant that specialises in Gujarati dishes.

Getting There & Away
Bus The UP Roadways bus stand (☎ 427037) is at the south-west end of Station Rd. Buses leave every 30 minutes for Rishikesh (one hour, Rs 7) and Dehra Dun (1½ to two hours, Rs 14). For Mussoorie, you'll need to change at Dehra Dun. There are ordinary bus services every 30 minutes up to 11.30 pm to Delhi (eight hours, Rs 53.50), and early morning and late afternoon and evening services to Agra (12 hours, Rs 100).

Buses for Shimla leave at 8 and 9.30 am (14 hours, Rs 95); to Nainital, at 5.30, 8.45, 9.15, 9.30 and 10.30 am (seven hours, Rs 80); to Almora at 5, 5.30 and 7 am (10 hours, Rs 107); to Ranikhet at 6.30 am and 4.30 pm (nine hours, Rs 89); and to Tehri (five hours, Rs 40) and Uttarkashi (10 hours, Rs 80) at 5.30, 6.30, 8.30 and 9.30 am.

For the Char Dham (Yamunotri, Gangotri, Badrinath and Kedarnath), you'll need to find your way to Rishikesh. As many of the buses to these pilgrimage sites leave in the wee hours, you'd do better to stay overnight in Rishikesh at one of the hotels opposite the Yatra bus stand.

To get to Chilla (for Rajaji National Park), catch a Kandi-bound bus from the Garhwal Motor Owners' Union (GMOU) stand near the Rahi Motel. Buses leave at 7 and 9 am, and return at noon and 4 pm (Rs 7).

Train See the Dehra Dun section for details of trains between Haridwar and Delhi. Other direct trains connect Haridwar with Calcutta (1472km, 35 hours), Mumbai (1649km, 40 hours), Varanasi (894km, 20 hours) and Lucknow (493km, 11 hours).

Taxi The Taxi Drivers & Owners Association (☎ 427338), open 24 hours, is directly opposite the bus stand. Posted rates are as follows: Rishikesh (Rs 200), Dehra Dun (Rs 300), Mussoorie (Rs 500), Tehri (Rs 700), Uttarkashi (Rs 1000); Hanuman Chatti (for Yamunotri – Rs 2800), Gangotri (Rs 2800), Delhi (Rs 900), Chilla (for Rajaji National Park – Rs 200 one way, Rs 300 return), Ranikhet (Rs 1700), Almora (Rs 1800), Nainital (Rs 1500) and Shimla (Rs 2500). A nine day tour to the Char Dham is Rs 8000 (transport only). You may get more competitive rates from the travel agents on Jasharam Rd in the Shiv Murti area such as Shakti Wahini Travels (☎ 427002) or Khodiyar Travels (☎ 423560).

During May and June, share taxis ply between the taxi stand and Rishikesh, Dehra Dun and Mussoorie, and possibly Chilla.

Getting Around
You can get from the railway station or UP Roadways bus stand to Har ki Pairi by cycle-rickshaw for Rs 7 or Vikram for Rs 3.

Low-tech rattle-you-senseless bicycles can be hired from Vijay Cycle Works, Railway Rd (near the Hotel Aarti), but for Rs 1.50 per hour, or Rs 10 per day, who's complaining?

RAJAJI NATIONAL PARK
This beautiful park, covering 820 sq km in the forested foothills east of Haridwar, is best known for its wild elephants, numbering around 150 in all. Unfortunately their future is in question since human competition for land has severed their traditional migration route, which once stretched from here to the area which is now part of Corbett Tiger Reserve, 170km to the east. Plans for a 'migration corridor' would involve moving several villages and have become bogged down in the usual bureaucracy. Nevertheless, increasing ecological awareness has brought about some advances, with large ducts having been constructed under the Chilla-Rishikesh road to enable the migrating animals to pass beneath.

As well as elephants, the park contains some rarely seen tigers and leopards, chital (spotted deer), which can be seen in herds of up to 250 at one time, sambar (India's largest species of deer), wild boars, sloth bears, barking deer, porcupines, jungle fowls, hornbills and pythons.

Open from mid-November to mid-June, the entry fee is Rs 100 for up to three days, and Rs 50 for each additional day. Entry into the park is not permitted between sunset and sunrise. Photography fees are Rs 50 for a still camera, Rs 500 for a video camera.

The (rather unattractive) village of **Chilla**, 13km east of Haridwar, is the only area which currently has an infrastructure in place for visitors. From Chilla it is possible to take elephant rides (Rs 50 per person, up to four people; Rs 200 for solitary would-be *mahouts*, or elephant masters) into the park. Official hire rates for jeeps (available from Chilla) are Rs 20 per km. The Forest Ranger's office is close to the tourist bungalow at Chilla; pay entry fees and book elephant rides here. Chilla has become the adoptive home of Raja, a baby elephant, who became an orphan when his mother, and several other elephants, were struck and killed by a train on the Rishikesh Rd.

One km beyond the entry gate is a *machaan* (hide), previously used by hunters, but now a vantage point from where visitors can unobtrusively view the park's inhabitants.

It may be possible to visit tribal villages in the park, where Gujars, who still live in their traditional clay huts and tend buffaloes, greet visitors with bowls of fresh, warm buffalo milk. Check at the Forest Ranger's bungalow in Chilla, or contact Sanjeev at Mohan's Fast Food, Railway Rd, Haridwar.

Places to Stay
The *Tourist Rest House* at Chilla is run by the GMVN. Here it's Rs 265 in a standard double, Rs 400 in an air-cooled double, and

there are dorm beds for Rs 65; you may also be able to camp in the grounds.

Nine *Forest Rest Houses* are dotted around the park. Double rates at Beribara, Ranipur, Kansrao, Kunnao, Phandowala, Satyanarain and Asarodi are all Rs 150; at Motichur and Chilla, rates are Rs 300. At these places, other than at Chilla, you'll need to bring your own food. For bookings contact the Chief Forest Officer, Tilak Rd, Dehra Dun, or write to the Director, Rajaji National Park office, 5/1 Ansari Marg, Dehra Dun (☎ 621669).

Getting There & Away

Buses to Chilla leave from the Garhwal Motor Owners' Union (GMOU), Haridwar, close to the Rahi Motel, en route to Kandi. They depart at 7 and 9 am, and return at noon and 4 pm (Rs 7). If there are enough passengers, share taxis leave from the taxi stand opposite the UP Roadways bus stand or from Chandi Ghat, opposite Har ki Pairi (Rs 10). The official rate for a reserve taxi to Chilla from Haridwar is Rs 200 one way, Rs 300 return (although ensure that the driver knows how much time you plan to spend at the park). You could also cycle to Chilla; bikes are available for hire in Haridwar (see under Haridwar's Getting Around section).

To walk to Chilla from Haridwar, cross the Laltarao Bridge and walk to the roundabout, then turn left onto the Rishikesh road. Just before the cable bridge over the Ganges canal, turn right. After 100m you'll reach a dam; cross the dam and turn left, where a short walk will bring you to a small artificial lake. Here you'll see migratory birds, including Siberian cranes, ducks and other water fowl; in the evening wild animals, including elephants, come here to drink (although you should beware of wild elephants at dusk). The road flanking the lake leads to Chilla, five km distant.

AROUND CHILLA

Fourteen km north-east of Chilla, two km off the Chilla-Rishikesh road, is the small village of **Bindevasani**. Local buses ply between the village and both Chilla and Haridwar, with the section between Chilla and the turn-off to

Bindevasani at a high elevation, affording good views out over the national park. There's a small temple sacred to Durga (Siva's consort in her fierce form) a steep 15 to 20 minute walk above the village. The temple itself is not of great interest, but it commands an excellent position, overlooking the *sangam* (confluence) of the Bindedhara and Nildhara rivers.

Fourteen km north of Bindevasani is Nilkantha, with its Mahadev Temple, dedicated to Siva. From Nilkantha, it is possible to continue to **Lakshman Jhula** (see the Rishikesh section), the suspension bridge which traverses the Ganges to the north-east of Rishikesh. The trail follows the original pilgrim trail, which affords magnificent forest scenery – beware of wild elephants, especially at dusk.

There are *dharamsalas* (pilgrims' rest houses) at Nilkantha, but you'll need to be prepared to camp out, and will require provisions, at Bindevasani.

RISHIKESH

Pop: 82,000   Tel Area Code: 01364

In spite of its claim to being the 'Yoga Capital of the World', Rishikesh is a quieter and more easy-going place than Haridwar. Surrounded by hills on three sides, it lies at 356m. The holy Ganges (almost clear here) flows through the town and, as in Haridwar, there are many ashrams along its sandy banks. This is an excellent place to stay and study yoga, meditation and other aspects of Hinduism.

Back in the 60s Rishikesh gained instant fame as the place where the Beatles came to be with their guru, the Maharishi Mahesh Yogi. Rishikesh is also the starting point for trips to Himalayan pilgrimage centres like Badrinath, Kedarnath and Gangotri.

Orientation

The main administrative and commercial sector is to the south of the (usually dry) Chandrabhaga River; the main and Yatra bus stands are here, as well as the main post office, banks and hotels. If you arrive by jeep

OTHER

1 Vanmali gita Yogashra
2 Lakshman Temple
3 Kailashanand Mission Ashram
4 Purnanand Yogashram
7 Post Office
8 Ramjharokha Ashram
9 Shivanand Ashram
11 Omkarananda Ashram
12 Yoga Niketan Ashram
14 Mahesh Yogi Ayurvedic Centre
15 Omkarananda Ganga Sadan
17 Clock Tower
18 Blue Hills Travels
19 Gita Bhavan
20 Swarg Ashram
23 Parnath Niketan Ashram
24 Vanprasth Ashram
25 Sri Ved Niketan Ashram
27 GMVN Tourist Office & Green Adventure Tours
28 Andhra Ashram
31 Mahesh Yogi Ashram
33 Yatra Bus Stand
34 Bank of Baroda
38 Ajay Travels & Hotel Neelkanth
39 Main Post Office
40 Bharat Mandir
41 Triveni Ghat
42 UP Tourist Office
44 Taxi Stand
45 Main Bus Stand
46 Yoga Study Centre

PLACES TO STAY

1 High Bank Peasants & Bhandari Swiss Cottages
4 Rama Guest House
22 Bombay Kshetra
23 Green Hotel
26 SMVN Tourist Rest House
29 Swiss Cottage
30 Nirajan Cottage
32 Hotels Suruchi & Adarsh
36 Inderlok Hotel, Jungle Vibes & State Bank of India
43 Hotel Gangotri
47 Hotel Ganga Kinare

PLACES TO EAT

5 Ganga Darshan Restaurant
10 Choliwala
16 Madras Cafe & Amrita House & Library
35 Neelam Restaurant
37 Anjali Restaurant & Triveni Travels

To Nilkantha Mahadev (12km)

Lakshman Jhula

Shivanand Jhula

To Deoprayag (63km)

Swarg Ashram

Chandrabhaga

Ganga River

Chandrabhaga Gate

Kailash Gate

Lakshman Jhula Road

Rishilok

Muni ki Reti

Chandrabhaga River

Dehra Dun Road

To Kunjapuri, Tehri & Gangotri

Ghat Road

Haridwar Road

Railway Station Road

Railway Station

Koyalgati

To Dehra Dun (43km)

To Haridwar (20km)

Rishikesh

0   250   500 m

you will probably be dropped on Haridwar Rd in this commercial area. The northern extension of Haridwar Rd is called Lakshman Jhula Rd. It goes past the GMVN tourist office to Shivanand Jhula; most of the temples and ashrams are to be found on either side of the river here. Lakshman Jhula (*jhula* means bridge) is two km north. Here there are more ashrams and temples.

Information

Tourist Offices The helpful UP tourist office (☎ 30209) is on Railway Station Rd. It's open Monday to Saturday from 10 am to 5 pm (lunch from 1.30 to 2 pm). The GMVN tourist office (☎ 30372) is in the area known as Muni ki Reti (open Monday to Saturday from 10 am to 5 pm; closed for lunch between 2 and 3 pm). It's set a little back from Lakshman Jhula Rd, near Kailash Gate.

Money The State Bank of India is next to the Inderlok Hotel on Railway Station Rd. It exchanges most major travellers cheques, but *not* Visa or MasterCard. If you're carrying either of these, try the Bank of Baroda, near the Yatra bus stand.

Travel Agencies Ajay Travels (☎ 32897), beneath the Hotel Neelkanth on Ghat Rd in the commercial district, can arrange taxis and bus travel to the Char Dham and elsewhere. Similar services are offered by Blue Hills Travels (☎ 31865), in the Swarg Ashram area.

Trekking Outfits & Tour Operators At the GMVN tourist office (☎ 30372) you can book Char Dham packages, and there's also a Trekking & Mountaineering division (☎ 32648) where you can hire tents, rucksacks, sleeping bags and mountaineering equipment, as well as book treks. Rates for treks start at Rs 1325 per day (minimum of three people required), including transport by deluxe coach or taxi, all meals, porters, guides and accommodation in tourist rest houses or tents. Treks include a nine day Har ki Dun trek, a 10 day trek to the lake of Rup Kund, an eight day trek to the Valley of Flowers, and a 14 day trek to the Khatling Glacier (all during the summer months only).

Triveni Travels (☎ 32989; fax 32881) on Railway Station Rd can arrange white-water rafting at Brahmpuri, 10km from Rishikesh, or the more exhilarating rapids at Shivpuri, 18km from Rishikesh. Cost is Rs 550 and includes transport, lunch, life jackets and helmets with two to three hours racing the rapids down the Ganges. A minimum of five people is required. They also have caving expeditions through the 200m long Vishitha *gufa* (cave), 16km from Rishikesh near Shivpuri (Rs 500), and half-day elephant safaris in the Rajaji National Park (Rs 800), as well as trekking and Char Dham packages.

Apex Adventure Tours (☎ 32804), at Muni ki Reti next door to the GMVN office, offers rafting and trekking packages at comparable rates, and also has rock-climbing expeditions (for beginners and more experienced climbers).

Himalayan River Runners (☎ 615736), 188A Jor Bagh, Delhi, offers white-water rafting expeditions ex Delhi on the Alaknanda and Ganges rivers between Rudraprayag and Rishikesh, or shorter expeditions on the Ganges between Deoprayag and Rishikesh.

From their camp at Kaudiyala near Rishikesh, UP Tourism offers rafting packages. Prices start at Rs 350 per day for rafting, Rs 150 for meals, and Rs 65 for share lodging (or Rs 100 for single occupancy).

From Rishikesh, UP Tourism offers coach and taxi tours to the Char Dham. A four day bus tour to Badrinath is Rs 1320, including share accommodation. To Yamunotri and Gangotri, a seven day tour departs each Friday during the yatra season (Rs 2050).

A 10 day taxi package to the Char Dham is Rs 5610 per person. The six day taxi package ex–Rishikesh to Kedarnath and Badrinath is Rs 3400 per person.

Things to See

The **Triveni Ghat** is an interesting place to be at dawn, when people make offerings of milk to the river and feed the surprisingly large fish. After sunset, priests set floating lamps on the water in the Ganga Aarti (river worship) ceremony. Nearby is the **Bharat Mandir**, the oldest temple here.

The suspension bridge **Lakshman Jhula** was built in 1929 to replace a rope bridge. This is where Rama's brother Lakshmana is said to have crossed the river on a jute rope, and the old **Lakshman Temple** is on the west bank. Across the river are some turreted oddities, including the 13 storey **Kailasha-nand Mission Ashram**. There's a good view from the top. It's a pleasant two km walk along this bank to the Shivanand Jhula.

Pilgrims take Ganga water to offer at **Nil-kantha Mahadev**, a four hour walk from Lakshman Jhula on the east bank. There are fine views on the way up to the temple at 1700m but take something to drink and start early as it can get very hot. It's now possible to make the journey by bus.

There are also great views from **Kunja-puri**, in the hills north of Rishikesh. It's a three km walk from Hindola Khal (45 minutes by bus from Rishikesh), which all buses to Tehri pass through.

Places to Stay
City Centre, Chandrabhaga & Rishilok While not as colourful as the Swarg Ashram and Lakshman Jhula areas, there are some good choices in these areas.

Hotel Gangotri (☎ 31139) is in a good location on Ghat Rd. Ordinary singles/doubles cost

---

Yoga & Meditation Courses

Studying aspects of Hinduism has, naturally, become somewhat commercialised at Rishikesh. However, once you've found a place to suit your needs, spending some time here can be a fulfilling experience. There are many ashrams to choose from; only a few are listed below. Most charge between Rs 50 and Rs 125 per day for a basic room; some also include three meals in this price. It's worth talking to other travellers first and going to a few classes at different ashrams to find a guru who gets through to you.

Many ashrams post up a 'code of conduct' advising you to bathe daily, avoid unnecessary chatting, and abstain from eggs, meat, fish, liquor, onions, garlic, tobacco and *paan*. Notices also state that women are not allowed into temples or the courtyard when having *masik dharma* (menstruating). Helpful hints for the practice of yoga include such tips as: 'Those who are suffering from pus in the ear or displacement of the retina should avoid topsy turvy poses'.

An **International Yoga Festival**, organised by UP Tourism, is held annually from 2 to 7 February. Seven-day packages including meals, accommodation and transport to venues from your hotel and air-con deluxe coach transfer from Delhi are US$470/500/940 for singles/doubles/triples. Advance bookings can be made through: the Director, UP Tourism, Chitrahar Building, 3 Naval Kishor Rd, Lucknow (☎(0522) 223 3632).

Yoga Niketan (☎ 30227) is located in a peaceful spot high above the main road in Muni-ki-Reti. It has been recommended by several travellers for the serious study of yoga but you must stay for a minimum of 15 days. The charge of Rs 125 per day covers all meals and the basic courses but many people opt for the additional courses which cost extra.

Sri Ved Niketan Ashram is a popular ashram with over 100 rooms arranged around a large courtyard. Rooms are Rs 40, or Rs 50 with attached bathroom; meals are Rs 15. It's a very relaxed place and you don't have to join the yoga class (6.30 am) or the evening lectures. Courses cost Rs 300 for a week.

Shivanand Ashram (The Divine Life Society), founded by Swami Shivanand, is a well-known ashram and the society has branches in many countries. You can stay for short-term study or for longer three-month courses, although to do this you need to contact them two months in advance (fax 431190), or simply drop by for the daily lectures at 10 am and 5 pm.

The **Yoga Study Centre** (☎ 431196) at Koyalgati runs three-week courses for beginners, intermediate and advanced students. Payment is by donation and accommodation can be arranged.

Omkarananda Ashram runs courses in a building near the Shivananda Arch, below Yoga Niketan. Hatha yoga classes are held daily except Sunday at 5.30 pm. There is also instruction in Indian classical dance.

Mahesh Yogi Ashram above Ved Niketan has courses on transcendental meditation. Six-month courses cost Rs 5000. To reserve a place write to: Mahesh Yogi Ashram, Shankaracharya Nagar, Rishikesh, 249201. ■

Rs 150/225, air-cooled rooms Rs 275/350, and air-con rooms Rs 450/550. All rooms have attached bath (cold water only; bucket hot water free). The air-con rooms at the front of the hotel have private balconies and a *joola* (bamboo chair) suspended from the ceiling! The restaurant here is open in the season only.

Inderlok Hotel (☎ 430555), diagonally opposite, has standard singles/doubles for Rs 350/450, or with air-con, Rs 550/650. Rooms are cool and comfortable, all with colour TV. The hotel also has a travel desk.

Hotel Suruchi (☎ 430356), right beside the Yatra bus stand, is built around a spacious atrium. Standard singles/doubles cost Rs 175/250; air-cooled rooms are Rs 250/350. Attached baths have cold water only, but bucket hot water is free. The restaurant here is very reasonably priced.

Hotel Adarsh (☎ 455101) nearby has fairly ordinary singles and doubles that cost Rs 100, some with attached baths; dorm beds are Rs 35. The hotel has a dining hall.

Hotel Ganga Kinare (☎ 430566) is a bit of a hike from the centre, about two km south of Railway Station Rd at 16 Virbhadra Rd. However, it's in a lovely peaceful spot on the west bank of the Ganges, and rooms are very well appointed, some (the more expensive ones!) having beautiful river views. All rooms are centrally air-conditioned, and singles/doubles cost Rs 990/1090, or Rs 1090/1190 with better views. Free meditation classes are held on the terrace, and guests can use the hotel's rowing boats. There's also a reference library on yoga, a travel desk which can arrange trekking, rafting, skiing, cycling and wildlife and cultural tours, and a reasonably priced restaurant. Evening prayers take place on the hotel's private ghat.

Swiss Cottage (no phone) on the north side of the Chandrabhaga River is run by Swami Brahmananda, a disciple of Swami Shivananda. Rooms are set around a shady courtyard. Singles, doubles and triples are all Rs 50; some with attached bath. No meals are provided, but self-catering is OK. If this place is booked up, ask here for directions to the nearby *Norwegian Cottage*. It's equally as friendly, if not quite as atmospheric.

Tourist Rest House (☎ 430373), run by the GMVN in the area known as Rishilok, is set in lovely grounds. It's a little pricey, with ordinary singles/doubles with common bath for Rs 120/140, or with attached bath, Rs 280/450. Bucket hot water is available for Rs 2, and there's a restaurant.

Swarg Ashram Area There are a couple of guest houses and a choice of two ashrams on this east side of the river, over the Shivanand Jhula.

Green Hotel (☎ 431242), down a quiet lane, has clean, if spartan, rooms at Rs 75/125 for singles/doubles. Larger doubles with air-coolers are Rs 250, hot water is free by the bucket and there's a good restaurant.

Rama Guest House (no phone), behind the Green Hotel, has clean doubles with common bath for Rs 60 (there's one *tiny* single for Rs 40). The guest house is run by a very friendly man who hails from Chennai, but there's no restaurant.

Vanprasth Ashram is right on the Ganges, at the south end of Swarg Ashram, about a 10 minute walk from the Shivanand Jhula. There are lovely flower gardens, and a resident yoga teacher, but you don't have to attend classes if you don't want to. Doubles (facing the Ganges) and triples are Rs 75 with attached bath (cold water only), and there's a room which can accommodate up to six people (Rs 300). There's a canteen, but you can use the ashram's kitchen facilities (free). Gas cylinders may be hired for Rs 15 per day. Foreign visitors can only stay between 1 November and 31 March.

Sri Ved Niketan Ashram next door to Vandprasth is an unmissable orange and turquoise edifice. There are daily yoga and meditation classes (see under Yoga & Meditation, above), but no pressure to attend. Large but spartan singles/doubles are Rs 70 with attached bath (cold water only; bucket hot water free). The upstairs rooms at the front have good views over the Ganges.

Lakshman Jhula Area The following places are furthest from the bus and train stations (at least four km), but it's a colourful and interesting area.

Bombay Kshettra (no phone) is on the east side of the river. It's an atmospheric old building with rooms ranging from Rs 40 to Rs 70, depending on the size, all with common bath, and set around a pleasant courtyard.

High Bank Peasants Cottage (☎ 431167) is set in beautiful flower gardens high above the Ganges. Take the road to the left, one km before Lakshman Jhula; the cottage is about 500m up this road. Rooms are about Rs 300 with attached bath (hot water free in buckets), and the balcony has wicker chairs were you can sit and contemplate the Ganges. Discounts are offered for stays of over a week. Each morning Lisa, the family dog, brings the newspaper up from the front gate. Good homely Indian meals (not too spicy!) using vegies from the garden are available, and you can arrange treks and river rafting here.

Bhandari Swiss Cottage (no phone) is just above High Bank Peasants. Rooms are plain but OK, and cost Rs 100 for singles or doubles with common bath. Meals are available, and there are great views from the balcony.

Places to Eat

Rishikesh is a holy pilgrimage town, and is therefore strictly vegetarian.

Indrani at the Inderlok Hotel has a good range of Chinese cuisine (Cantonese and Manchurian), as well as specials such as rajmah – seasoned kidney beans (Rs 25) and gajjar halwa in season (Rs 15).

Anjali Restaurant, further down Railway Station Rd towards Triveni Ghat, has very cheap dishes (most under Rs 10) in its mirrored dining hall-cum-*dhaba* .

Neelam Restaurant, run by the helpful Mr Singh, is a low-key place in a small lane just off Haridwar Rd. It's popular with westerners, who are tempted here by dishes such as macaroni (Rs 15), minestrone (Rs 12), and good rice pud, as well as the standard Indian fare.

Madras Cafe, on the west side of Shivanand Jhula, has a good range of dosa, and if you don't like it hot, you can ask the cook to

exercise restraint with the spices. There are also good lassis and cold coffee.

Amrita House & Library, closer to the bridge, is a groovy little eatery with books for perusing while you tuck into your banana, raisin and curd pancakes. Neem honey is for sale at Rs 125 for 500g, yellow cheese is Rs 40 for 100g, and there's soft and garlic cheeses too (both Rs 30 for 100g).

Chotiwala, across the Shivanand Jhula, in Swarg Ashram, is a long-time favourite for rooftop dining. The filling special thali is Rs 30, and there's a good range of Kwality ice cream. Next door (further away from the river) is another restaurant of the same name which isn't quite as popular.

Tripti Restaurant at the Hotel Suruchi has excellent fare, including dhal makhani – black lentils and red kidney beans with cream and butter – Rs 15, and the sublime Suruchi sundae with hot chocolate sauce and nuts (Rs 12).

Ganga Darshan Restaurant, opposite the Bombay Kshettra, is set right on the river, and has cheap, filling thalis for Rs 15, as well as south Indian food (dosa, idlis, etc).

Things to Buy

Rishikesh is a good place to pick up a *rudraksh mala*, the strings of beads used in *puja* (offerings) made from the nuts of the rudraksh tree. Prices start from around Rs 80, with beads of the smaller nuts commanding higher prices. Flanking the waterfront on the east side of the river, in the Swarg Ashram area, are dozens of stalls selling devotional accoutrements such as prasaad, scriptural booklets and cassettes, as well as shawls and ayurvedic medicines. There's also a good range of ayurvedic medicines made from herbs collected from the Himalaya at the Mahesh Yogi Ayurvedic Centre, on Lakshman Jhula Rd, opposite the pathway up to Yoga Niketan Ashram.

It may seem a strange sort of purchase in the spiritual heartland of Rishikesh, but Mukesh at Jungle Vibes (next to the Inderlok Hotel on Railway Station Rd) sells hand-made didgeridoos.

Getting There & Away

Bus From the main bus stand (☎ 30066) there are buses to Haridwar every 30 minutes from 4.30 am to 10.30 pm (one hour, Rs 7), and numerous buses to Dehra Dun between 6.30 am and 8 pm (1½ hours, Rs 10.50). Between 4.30 am and 10.30 pm there are hourly buses to Delhi. The trip takes around six hours and costs Rs 60 (ordinary), Rs 175 (semideluxe) or Rs 212 (super deluxe).

There's one bus at 8.15 am to Ramnagar (six hours, Rs 57.50) which continues to Nainital (8½ hours, Rs 88). To Shimla, you'll need to find your way to Dehra Dun, from where there are several services between 5.30 and 11.30 am (seven hours, Rs 82).

From the Yatra bus stand during the pilgrimage season, buses leave regularly for Badrinath between 3.30 am and 4 pm (14 hours, Rs 117); Kedarnath at 3.45, 4.15 and 5 am, and 12.30 and 1 pm (12 hours, Rs 85); and Uttarkashi at 3.45, 5.30, 8, 10 and 11.30 am and 12.30 pm (seven hours, Rs 60); the 5.30 am bus to Uttarkashi continues to Gangotri (12 hours, Rs 102). There's one bus to Hanuman Chatti, the roadhead for Yamunotri, at 7 am (10 hours, Rs 94).

Train Bookings can be made at the railway station (☎ 131) from 10 am to 4 pm (closed for lunch from 1.30 to 2 pm). The station has a small allocation of seats for Haridwar. There are trains to Haridwar at 6.40 and 9.15 am, 2.10, 3.15 and 6.40 pm (Rs 4). The 6.40 am service arrives at Delhi at 5.20 pm. The 6.40 pm train connects with the *Mussoorie Express* for Delhi and with overnight trains to Lucknow and Agra. The 2.10 pm train connects with the *Jammu Tawi* express to Pathankot and Jammu.

Taxi & Jeep Official (off-season) reserve taxi rates are: Delhi, Rs 1000; Dehra Dun, Rs 250; Mussoorie, Rs 500; Uttarkashi (for Gangotri), Rs 900; Tehri, Rs 550; Haridwar, Rs 180; and Ranikhet, Rs 1800. Expect to pay 20% to 50% more during summer. The main office for the Taxi Operators' Union (☎ 30413) is on Haridwar Rd, just over Ghat Rd. Official rates for the Char Dham are Rs 7500, or for Badrinath and Kedarnath only, Rs 4200.

You can flag down share jeeps (called trekkers) for Dehra Dun anywhere along the Dehra Dun Rd. Cost to Dehra Dun is Rs 12. You may be able to get a share taxi to Haridwar from the main bus stand (Rs 20). An alternative (and grubbier) proposition is to pick up a shared Vikram anywhere along the Haridwar Rd (Rs 10).

Getting Around

Vikrams run from Ghat Rd junction up to Shivanand Jhula (Rs 3) and Lakshman Jhula (Rs 5). Shivanand Jhula is a pedestrian-only bridge, so you'll have to lump your backpack across if you're planning to stay on the east side of the Ganges (ie in the Swarg Ashram area). On the east bank of the river, a seat in a jeep between Lakshman Jhula and Shivanand Jhula costs Rs 3.

For Rs 3 you can cross the river to Swarg Ashram between 8 am and 7 pm by boat (particularly auspicious).

UTTARKASHI DISTRICT

This northern district of Uttarakhand is best known for its two major pilgrimage centres: Gangotri, near the source of the Ganges, and Yamunotri, by the source of the Yamuna.

Uttarkashi

Uttarkashi, 155km from Rishikesh, is the administrative headquarters of the district. Several trekking companies operate from here and the town is also the base for the Nehru Institute of Mountaineering, where Bachhendri Pal, the first Indian woman to climb to the summit of Mt Everest, was trained. The town is pleasantly sited on the banks of the Bhagirathi River, drawing pilgrims to its Vishwanatha Temple, sacred to Siva. It's possible that you'll wind up here looking for a bed before proceeding further north to Gangotri. You can stock up on supplies here if you're planning a trek further north, although the town has more to offer. On the day of Makar Sakranti, which usually falls in January, the town hosts a colourful fair, when deities are borne aloft into the town on palanquins from outlying villages. Accommodation in Uttarkashi includes the GMVN *Traveller's Lodge* (☎ 2222), where spacious singles/doubles with common bath are Rs 90/120.

Yamunotri

Yamunotri is the source of the Yamuna River, the second-most sacred river in India after the Ganges. It emerges from a frozen lake of ice and glaciers on the Kalinda Parvat at an altitude of 4421m. The temple of the goddess Yamunotri is on the left bank of the river and, just below it, there are several hot springs. Buses go as far as Hanuman Chatti from Mussoorie or Rishikesh. From Hanuman Chatti, the trek to Yamunotri takes five to six hours, but there's a *Tourist Rest House* just past the halfway point, at Jankichatti. You can also stay at Yamunotri in the *dharamsalas*. Pilgrims cook their food in the boiling water of the hot springs.

CORBETT TIGER RESERVE
Tel Area Code: 05945

Established in 1936 as India's first national park, Corbett is famous for its wide variety of wildlife and its beautiful location in the foothills of the Himalaya by the Ramganga River. With the inclusion of the Sonanadi Wildlife Sanctuary to the west, Corbett has grown from 520 to 1318 sq km.

It may seem incongruous for a national park to be named after a famous British hunter – Jim Corbett is best known for his book *The Man-Eaters of Kumaon*, and was greatly revered by local people for shooting tigers that had developed a liking for human flesh. However, he was instrumental in setting up the reserve and eventually shot more wildlife with his camera than with his gun.

Seeing a tiger here is dependent on chance, since the animals are no longer baited or tracked (unlike at Kanha in Madhya Pradesh). However, your best chance to see one

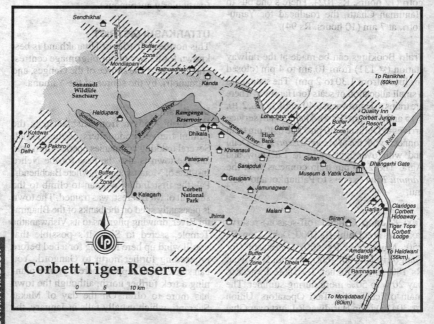

Corbett Tiger Reserve

is if you come late in the season (April to mid-June) and stay in the park for several days.

More commonly seen wildlife includes the wild elephant, langur monkey (black face, long tail), rhesus macaque, peacock, and several types of deer including chital (spotted deer), sambar, hog deer and barking deer. There are also crocodiles, the odd-looking gavial or gharial (a thin-snouted, fish-eating crocodile often spotted from High Bank), monitor lizards, wild boars and jackals. Leopards (referred to as panthers in India) are occasionally seen.

Corbett is also a bird-watcher's paradise, and since the creation of the Ramganga Reservoir on the Ramganga River, large numbers of waterfowl have been attracted here.

Orientation & Information

The Corbett Tiger Reserve encompasses both the original Corbett National Park, comprising the eastern side of the reserve, and the Sonanadi Wildlife Sanctuary, forming the

---

Saving the Tiger

More than 20 years after the launch of a major project aimed at saving India's tigers, conservationists are making another concerted bid to save the animals from extinction.

Project Tiger, as the first conservation effort came to be known, was launched in 1973, a year after a census (the first one conducted) that showed that the number of big cats in the wild was only about 1800. The demands of Chinese folk medicine, which regards the bones and flesh of the animal as having powerful medicinal qualities, placed a high price on the tiger. As well as the threat from poachers, tiger habitat was rapidly dwindling as India's population spiralled. Project Tiger was launched with the assistance of the World Wide Fund for Nature (WWF). Corbett was the first Project Tiger reserve. The number of reserves has grown from nine in the mid 1970s to 23 today.

The tiger population appeared to grow and by the late 1980s the project was being lauded; the population was estimated at around 4000 – a considerable success story. But in the 1990s the Chinese market in tiger bones continued to thrive, sightings of tiger in India's national parks were becoming rarer and experts began questioning the methods used for estimating tiger numbers. Officials in India claim that pug marks are like human fingerprints: no two are the same. Prints are, however, rarely clear enough to be told apart and this may be part of the reason for numbers having been exaggerated over the years. It's just as likely that the numbers have been deliberately inflated to hide the large-scale poaching that has been going on, often (as in the case of Ranthambhore in Rajasthan) involving government officials.

The poaching trade is extremely lucrative and has traditionally centred on barter, the bones being exchanged for *shatoosh*, the underwool of the endangered Tibetan antelope (the animal is slaughtered in order to obtain this wool). In 1996 the sale of shawls and other products made from shatoosh was banned throughout India. Much of the trade passed through Delhi and the Tibetan camps near the city, the bones being smuggled into China via the old trade routes through Tibet.

The most recent all-India tiger population census, conducted in 1993, showed that just 3750 tigers survived, down from 4334 in 1989. The fall in numbers prompted renewed efforts aimed at saving the tiger, culminating in the launch of a new project in 1995 with funding help from the WWF. It involves boosting public awareness of the tigers' plight; mobilising local support (eg, encouraging those who depend on the forest for a living to protect the tiger, the rationale being if the tiger remains, the forest and therefore human livelihood will similarly be protected from destruction); and fostering international cooperation in an attempt to stem the trade in tiger bones. ∎

western side of the reserve. There is an elaborate tourist infrastructure in place in the national park itself, and a busy reception centre at **Ramnagar**, outside the park on its south-eastern perimeter. There is a second reception centre at **Kotdwar**, on the south-western edge of the park.

The Tiger Reserve is open from mid-November to mid-June but you should avoid the crowded weekends. The gates are closed at sunset and no night driving is permitted. **Dhikala**, in the reserve, is the main accommodation centre. It's 51km north-west of Ramnagar, the nearest railhead, and is the headquarters of Project Tiger. Access to Dhikala is from the **Dhangarhi Gate**, about 20km to the north of Ramnagar. Outside Corbett there are some expensive resorts and a few hotels in Ramnagar.

At Dhikala there's a library where interesting wildlife films are shown (free) in the evenings. The elephant rides at sunrise and sunset are not to be missed and cost Rs 100 each for four people for about two hours. During the day you can sit in one of the observation posts to unobtrusively watch for animals. When the park is closed, elephant rides are available at Dhangarhi Gate.

At **Bijrani** there's an interpretation centre and restaurant. It's sometimes possible to get elephant rides from here, although as there are only four elephants, priority is given to those staying overnight. There's a State Bank of India in Ramnagar which exchanges travellers cheques.

Permits & Photographic Fees Two types of permits are available: day-visit permits and permits for overnight stays. The former can be obtained from access points around the perimeter of the reserve, clockwise from Ramnagar, and including Ramnagar itself, these are: Kalagarh, Pakhro, Kotdwar and Sendhikhal. Permits for an overnight stay must be obtained from the park reception centre at Ramnagar (☎ 85489; fax 85376) where some accommodation can be booked. The office is near the bus stand on the Ranikhet road, and is open daily, including holidays, from 8 am to 1 pm and 3 to 5 pm.

Forest rest houses in the Sonanadi Wildlife Sanctuary can be booked at the new reception centre at Kotdwar (☎ (01382) 8235), open Monday to Saturday from 10 am to 5 pm. You can also obtain overnight permits here. It's also possible to book some accommodation through UP Tourism in Delhi (☎ (011) 332-2251), while the three double rooms at Khinanauli (Rs 1500) must be booked through the Chief Wildlife Warden in Lucknow (☎ (0522) 283902).

Charges given in this section are for foreign nationals; Indians are charged about two-thirds less. At the reception centres you must pay an entry fee of Rs 350 for a stay of up to three days, then Rs 175 per day. There's no charge for a still camera but a video or movie camera cost a whacking Rs 5000. To take a car into the park is Rs 100, plus another Rs 100 (full day) or Rs 50 (half day) for a (compulsory) guide, available at Amdanda Gate, the closest gate to Ramnagar. At Dhangarhi Gate it's Rs 100 for the day, even if you will not be there for the duration.

Places to Stay & Eat

Most of the accommodation is at Dhikala, but there are forest rest houses in both the national park and the Sonanadi Wildlife Sanctuary. Elephant rides are available at Dhikala and Bijrani, but bear in mind that if you stay outside these areas, your chances of spotting wildlife are reduced to sightings from the rest houses themselves, as venturing into the reserve on foot is prohibited.

Dhikala There's a wide range of accommodation but the prices charged for foreigners mean that it's not good value.

The *Log Huts* has a very basic dormitory (like three-tier train sleepers!) for Rs 50.

The *Tourist Hutment* has better value triples (Rs 240). An extra charge (Rs 25) is made for mattresses and sheets in these places. Both places can be booked at the reception centre at Ramnagar.

Cabins are more comfortable – doubles are Rs 450 and must be booked through the Chief Wildlife Warden in Lucknow (see the Orientation & Information section).

The *Old Forest Rest House*, also bookable through Lucknow, has double rooms (Rs 600).

The *New Forest Rest House* is cheaper at Rs 450, and can also be booked through Lucknow.

There are two restaurants, one run by KMVN, and another run by a private operator.

Other Forest Rest Houses With your own transport and food, you can stay in the forest rest houses at **Sultan** and **Malani** (doubles for Rs 150), **Sarapduli** or **Gairal** (doubles for Rs 450), all in the Corbett National Park (ie the east end of the reserve). There is no electricity at any of these places, although the rest house at Sarapduli has its own generator. Bring a torch (flashlight). All these places can be accessed from the Dhangarhi Gate.

Bookings should be made with the Chief Wildlife Warden, Lucknow. Even if you have booked your accommodation in advance, you will still need to check in at the reception centre at Ramnagar to obtain overnight permits to enter the park.

There is also a forest rest house at **Bijrani**, in the south-eastern corner of the reserve. Singles/ doubles are Rs 250/450, and bookings must be made at the reception office in Ramnagar. Access to Bijrani is via the Amdanda Gate.

There are also forest rest houses in the reserve buffer areas of **Dhela**, **Jhirna** and **Kalagarh**, on the southern perimeter of the reserve, and at **Lohachaur**, in the buffer zone to the north of the national park. Doubles at all of these cost Rs 150. You should bring a flashlight and your own food. Bookings must be made at Ramnagar and the rest houses are not available between June and November.

There are a number of forest rest houses in the **Sonanadi Wildlife Sanctuary** at the western end of the reserve, including those at **Sendhikhal**, **Mondiapani**, **Rathuadhab**, **Haldupara** and **Kanda** (actually just over the boundary in the Corbett National Park). Again there is no electricity and you'll need to bring your own food. Double rates in all

of these are Rs 150, and they must be booked through the reception office at Kotdwar. Write in advance to the Sub-Divisional Officer, Kotdwar Reception Centre, Sonanadi, Kotdwar, UP.

Ramnagar Note that if you use Ramnagar as a base you'll have to rent a jeep and you won't be able to go out on elephant rides in the centre of the park, as day visits to Dhikala are not permitted.

The KMVN *Tourist Bungalow* (☎ 85225), next to the reception centre, has good doubles from Rs 300 to Rs 400. Dorm beds are Rs 30.

The *Hotel Everest* (☎ 85099) has clean and comfortable rooms for Rs 100 to Rs 200 between 15 November and 15 June, and Rs 70 to Rs 125 at other times. Hot water is available in buckets for Rs 4, and room service is available. The hotel is in a side street about two blocks up from the reception centre.

The *Hotel Govind* (☎ 85615), near the bus stand, has rooms with common bath. Doubles cost Rs 60, Rs 70 and Rs 80, and there's a good restaurant downstairs featuring Indian and Chinese cuisine.

Private Resorts There are several upmarket resorts strung along the Ramnagar to Ranikhet road, all outside the reserve precincts.

Tiger Tops Corbett Lodge (☎ 85279; Delhi (011) 644 4016), seven km from Ramnagar, is a very luxurious place with prices to match: Rs 3600 per person per night; a single supplement is 40% extra. Prices include all meals and two day-visits to the reserve during the season. There are elephant rides, jeep trips and a swimming pool, and a wildlife slide show in the evenings. Between 16 June and 14 November, a 40% discount is offered. Despite the name, it's not part of the company that operates the famous resort in Chitwan (Nepal).

Claridges Corbett Hideaway (☎ 85959; Delhi (011) 301 0211) has accommodation in attractive ochre cottages set in an orchard of mango trees. Air-con double rooms cost Rs 3300, and rates include all meals. Staff can arrange bird-watching and nature-trail excursions, and mountain bikes are available for hire for Rs 50 per hour. A 50% discount is offered when the reserve is closed.

Quality Inn Corbett Jungle Resort (☎ & fax 85230), in the Kumeria Forest Reserve, has attractive cottages high above the river for Rs 2600, including all meals. This place features its own in-house elephant (named Ramkali), so rides are assured. Jeep safaris are run in the morning and evening (Rs 350 per person), and include entrance fees, toll charges and guides. When the reserve is closed, double rates here are Rs 1800.

Getting There & Away
Buses for Delhi depart Ramnagar approximately every hour, with the first service leaving at 5.30 am and the last at 8 pm (seven hours, Rs 68). Tickets can be booked at the Delhi Transport Corporation, hidden in the back room of the Anand Mistham Bhandar sweet shop, in a side street two blocks up from the reception centre.

Services for other destinations in Kumaon are booked at the Kumaon Motor Owners' Union (KMOU) office, near the petrol pump on the Ranikhet road, on the opposite side to the reception centre. To Nainital, there are services at 6 am and 2.30 pm (3½ hours, Rs 25). The Ranikhet services depart at 4 and 9.30 am (4½ hours, Rs 39) and continue to Almora (6½ hours, Rs 60). Ramnagar is connected by train with the busy railway junction of Moradabad. A nightly service leaves Ramnagar at 8.40 pm, arriving into Delhi at 5 am. The railway station is 1½km south of the reception centre.

Getting Around
There is a local bus service from Ramnagar to Dhikala which leaves at 3 pm (2½ hours, Rs 10), and from Dhikala to Ramnagar at 9 am. None of the other places in the park are served by buses. Jeeps can usually only be rented at Ramnagar, and will cost about Rs 1000 per day. Book through the KMVN Tourist Bungalow. Safaris on foot are strictly prohibited. The only other mode of transport is the ubiquitous elephant.

NAINITAL
Pop: 35,700   Tel Area Code: 05942

At 1938m in the Kumaon Hills, this attractive hill station was once the summer capital of Uttar Pradesh. The hotels and villas of this popular resort are set around the peaceful Naini lake or *tal*, hence the name.

Nainital is very much a green and pleasant land that immediately appealed to the homesick Brits, who were reminded of the Cumbrian Lake District. It was 'discovered' by a Mr Barron and he had his yacht carried up here in 1840. The Nainital Boat Club, whose wooden clubhouse still graces the edge of the lake, became the fashionable focus of the community. Disaster struck on 16 September 1880 when a major landslip occurred, burying 151 people in the Assembly Halls area and creating the recreation ground now known as the Flats.

This is certainly one of the most pleasant hill stations to visit and there are many interesting walks through the forests to points with superb views of the Himalaya.

The high season (when Nainital is packed and hotel prices double or triple) corresponds to school holidays. Avoid Christmas and the New Year, mid-April to mid-July and mid-September to early November.

Orientation & Information
During the season, The Mall is closed to heavy vehicles for most of the day. Cyclerickshaws take passengers along the 1½km Mall between the bazaars at Tallital ('lake's foot'), at its south end, and Mallital ('lake's head'), to the north-west. The bus stand is in Tallital. Hotels and guest houses can be found here, as well as along the entire length of The Mall and in the Mallital area. Most of the top-end hotels are about 10 to 15 minutes walk to the west of Mallital in the area known as Sukhatal.

There is a post office near the bus stand in Tallital and the main post office is in Mallital.

There are several banks in Mallital which exchange travellers cheques, including the State Bank of India, the Bank of Baroda and the Allahabad Bank. The helpful UP tourist

Nainital

To Laria Kanta

Snow View
(2270m)

Ropeway

To Bhim Tal
(23km) &
Almora
(68km)

Tallital

To Hanumangarh (3km),
Observatory (4km) &
Kathgodam (35km)

Naini Lake
(Nainital)

The Mall

The Flats

Mallital

Sukhatal

To China
Peak

To Delhi
(289km)

To Deopatta

Dorothy's Seat
(2292m)

0   150   300 m

PLACES TO STAY
1 Shervani Hilltop Inn
2 Vikram Vintage Inn
3 Youth Hostel
4 Swiss Hotel
6 Holiday Inn Nainital
7 KMVN Naina Tourist
   Rest House
9 Kohli Cottage
12 Hotel Belvedere
17 Alps Hotel & Modern
20 Book & General Store
21 Claridges Naini Retreat
24 Standard Hotel
25 Hotel City Heart
31 Hotel Grand
36 Alka Hotel
39 Evelyn Hotel
40 Hotel Elphinstone
41 Hotel Gauri Niwas
42 Hotel Lake View
45 Hotel Prashant
47 KMVN Sarovar Tourist
   Rest House

OTHER
5 St John's Church
8 Allahabad Bank
10 Bank of Baroda
11 Main Post Office
14 Jama Masjid
15 State Bank of India
18 Pony Hire
19 Gurney House
21 Naina Devi Temple
22 Assembly Rooms
23 Nainital Boat Club
27 Nainital Mountaineering
30 Naini Billiards &
   Nairains (Bookshop)
32 UP Tourist Office
33 Gadhan Kunkyop Ling Gompa
34 Library
38 Church of St Francis
43 KMVN Tourist Office
   (Parvat Tours)
44 Post Office
45 Bus Stand
46 Railway Booking Agency

PLACES TO EAT
13 Sher-e-Punjab & Prem
16 Moti Mahal
26 Capri, Flattis &
   Rasoi
28 Embassy & Purohit's
29 Kwality
35 Pahun Restaurant

UTTAR PRADESH

office (☎ 35337) is towards the Mallital end of The Mall.

The Nainital Mountaineering Club (☎ 35051), CRST Inter College Building (take the road behind the Central Hotel), runs courses and can give advice on treks and expeditions in the area. Mr CL Sah at the club can help arrange guides and porters, or put you in touch with an English-speaking guide for nature walks in the environs of Nainital, and the club also hires out equipment. The District Forestry Officer can be contacted on ☎ 35145, or at his residence on ☎ 35230.

There's a good selection of English-language books (and a special section on the Kumaon region), at Narains, on The Mall near Naini Billiards. You can also get English-lanuage newspapers here. Books (and just about everything else!) can be found at the Modern Book and General Store; English-language newspapers arrive after 11 am, and there's an excellent selection of the *Adventures of Tintin*.

Naini Lake

This attractive lake is said to be one of the emerald green eyes of Siva's wife, Sati. She had jumped into a sacrificial bonfire and as her mourning husband dragged her charred remains across the country, various append-ages dropped off. India is now littered with places 'formed' by parts of her body. Her eye falling here makes this a holy spot and the popular **Naina Devi Temple** is by the north-ern end of the lake. Nearby is a small Tibetan market.

You can rent rowboats and pedal boats for around Rs 50 per hour from a number of places along The Mall. The **Nainital Boat Club** has a few yachts for Rs 60 per hour. It costs Rs 300 for a three-day temporary club membership, which gives you access to the club's facilities (including the bar, restau-rant, ballroom and library). The club is less exclusive than it once was. Once Jim Corbett was refused membership because he was born in India, and hence was not a *pukkah sahib*.

St John's Church

Built in 1847, this church contains a brass memorial to the victims of the famous land-slip. The few bodies that could be uncovered from the rubble were buried in the church's graveyard.

Snow View & Tibetan Gompa

A chairlift (ropeway), officially called the 'Aerial Express', takes you up to the popular Snow View at 2270m. The lift is open from 9.30 am to 1 pm and 2 to 5 pm and costs Rs 20 (one way). The Rs 30 return ticket gives you only one hour at the top and a set time for your return. Alternatively, it's a pleasant two km walk up past Gadhan Kunkyop Ling Gompa (Tibetan monastery; see below). At the Mallital end of The Mall, near The Flats, beautifully groomed horses and mountain ponies are available for hire, offering a pleas-ant alternative to the steep walk up to Snow View. The cost is about Rs 40 per hour.

At the top there are powerful binoculars (Rs 2) for a close-up view of Nanda Devi (7817m) which was, as the old brass plate here tells you, 'the highest mountain in the British Empire'. Nanda Devi was India's highest peak until Sikkim (and thus Kang-chenjunga) was absorbed into the country. For Rs 15 you can be dressed in Kumaoni traditional dress and have your photo taken with a spectacular Himalayan backdrop. There's a small marble temple dedicated to Dev Mundi housing images of Durga, Siva, Sita, Rama, Lakshman and Hanuman.

A walk up to Snow Peak can take in the tiny **Gadhan Kunkyop Ling Gompa** of the Gelupka order (of which the Dalai Lama is the spiritual leader). Take the road behind the Standard Hotel, from where a path branches off towards the gompa (the colourful prayer flags are visible from the road). The gompa serves Nainital's small (and mostly itinerant) Tibetan community. Most of the Tibetan families travel to Nainital in the summer season to sell sweaters and shawls, and in winter descend to the plains.

Other Walks

There are several other good walks in the area, with views of the snow-capped moun-tains to the north. **China Peak** (pronounced

'Cheena'), also known as Naini Peak, is the highest point in the area (2610m) and can be reached either from Snow View or from Mallital (five km). Climb up in the early morning when the views are clearer.

A four km walk to the west of the lake brings you to **Dorothy's Seat** (2292m), also known as Tiffin Top, where a Mr Kellet built a seat in memory of his wife, killed in a plane crash. From Dorothy's Seat it's a lovely walk to **Land's End** (2118m) through a forest of oak, deodar and pine. The walk will take about 45 minutes, and in the early morning you may see jungle fowl or goral (mountain goats). From Land's End there are fine views out over the lake of Khurpa Tal.

From the Jama Masjid, at the north-west corner of the lake, you can walk in 30 minutes to **Gurney House**, where Jim Corbett lived. This two storey wooden dwelling is now a private residence, but the caretaker may let you look inside.

Hanumangarh & Observatory
There are good views and spectacular sunsets over the plains from this Hanuman temple, three km south of Tallital. Just over one km further on is the state observatory, which should be open Monday to Saturday from 10 am to 5 pm, but check at the tourist office before you head out. There is a free slide show between 1.30 and 3 pm.

Other Activities
The reading room at the **library**, right on the lake shore about halfway along The Mall between Mallital and Tallital, is a good place to escape the frenetic activity on The Mall, particularly in the late afternoon, when reflections from the lake create a lovely rippling effect on the walls and ceiling. Bibliophiles will appreciate the old wooden card files and hundreds of old volumes, and there are current newspapers for visitors' perusal. It's open in summer from 7.30 to 10.30 am and 5.30 to 8.30 pm, and in winter, from 8.30 to 10.30 am and 4 to 7 pm.

At the Mallital end of The Mall is **Naini Billiards**. It's open daily, and costs Rs 35 per hour. Coaching is available for Rs 10 per hour. **Fishing** gear can be hired at **Bhim Tal**, an overrated excursion spot 23km to the east of Nainital. You will require a permit which is issued here by the Fisheries Officer.

Organised Tours
Package tours can be booked at either of the two KMVN rest houses. A two day tour to Kausani is Rs 200 by bus, or Rs 1200 by taxi. To Jageshwar, a two day tour costs Rs 100 by bus or Rs 1200 by taxi. A six day tour to Badrinath and Kedarnath is Rs 600 by bus or Rs 6000 by taxi. Prices include dormitory accommodation, transfers and evening meals.

Parvat Tours (☎ 35656), run by KMVN, is at the Tallital end of The Mall. The office is run by helpful and efficient staff keen to promote their new range of adventure and recreational activities which include mountain cycling, river rafting, canoeing, hang-gliding and paragliding. They arrange high and low-altitude trekking, including winter trekking, and run regular tours such as day trips to Corbett National Park (Rs 900 return by taxi, or Rs 150 by luxury bus). Luxury bus trips to Delhi can also be booked here (see the Getting There & Away section below).

Places to Stay
There are over 100 places to stay, from gloomy budget guest houses to five-star hotels. During the peak season, school holidays and during the festivals of Dussehra and Diwali, prices can triple, and finding anywhere to stay can be a major hassle.

Places to Stay – bottom end
Tallital & The Mall (South End) There are several good budget choices at the Tallital end of the lake on the road which runs above and parallel to The Mall at its south end.

Hotel Lake View (☎ 35532), Ramji Rd, run by the gracious Mr and Mrs Shah, has doubles in the season from Rs 150 to Rs 450 (Rs 100 to Rs 200 in the off season). All rooms have attached bath; bucket hot water is Rs 4. Views from the balcony extend from the plains, over Tallital, across the lake and to Mallital. The more expensive rooms are at the front of the building.

Hotel Gauri Niwas (no phone), also on Ramji Rd, has double rooms with geysers and lake views from Rs 200 to Rs 250; gloomy windowless rooms at the back (bucket hot water Rs 3) are Rs 100 and Rs 150. A 50% to 60% discount applies off season.

Hotel Prashant (☎ 35347) in the same area has doubles ranging from Rs 150 to Rs 400, with the more expensive rooms having better views; the cheaper rooms are a bit shabbier. All rooms have attached baths, and running hot water in the morning. The hotel has a dining hall. A 50% discount applies off season.

Mallital & Sukhatal In the heart of Mallital, *Kohli Cottage* (☎ 36368), is opposite the Allahabad Bank. In the season, doubles are Rs 200 and Rs 250, all with attached bath and hot water. In the off season, doubles are from Rs 100. Rooms are light and airy, and the manager is friendly and helpful. There are good views from the roof terrace.

Standard Hotel (☎ 35602), in a good location at the end of The Mall just before you reach Mallital, has fairly ordinary rooms, but some have great views out over the lake. Singles with common bath are Rs 450 and doubles with attached bath are Rs 650.

Alps Hotel (☎ 35317) is a rather creaky centurian, but has enormous double rooms for Rs 200 with attached bathroom. A 50% to 60% discount is offered in the off season, and there's a lovely old broad balcony for watching the promenaders on The Mall.

The *Youth Hostel* (☎ 36353) is set in a peaceful wooded location, about 20 minutes walk west of Mallital. Beds (with lockers) in the dorms cost Rs 12 for members, Rs 22 for nonmembers. There are also two double rooms with common bath for the same rates. Filling vegetarian thalis (Rs 13) are available in the dining hall, and you can inquire about the Pindari Glacier and other treks here.

Places to Stay – middle & top end
Tallital & The Mall (South End) Middle and top-end accommodation at this end of The Mall is limited.

Sarovar Tourist Rest House (☎ 35570), run by KMVN, is very handy to the bus stand. From 1 May to 15 July, doubles/four-bed rooms are Rs 500/600, and beds in the spotless dorm (with terrific lake views) are Rs 40. Between 15 September and 15 November, rates are Rs 350/425, and Rs 35 in the dorm, and during the rest of the year, rates are Rs 200/250, or Rs 30 in the dorm. Rooms are comfortable, and some have very good views over the lake.

Hotel Elphinstone (☎ 35534), right on The Mall, has doubles from Rs 250 to Rs 400. All rooms face the lake (other than those at Rs 250), and all have attached bathrooms. There's a pretty garden terrace, complete with a bust of Queen Victoria bearing a plaque with the inscription 'Victoria the Good'. A 40% discount is offered in the off season.

Evelyn Hotel (☎ 35457) is a large building further north along The Mall. Double rates range from Rs 400 to Rs 900, 50% less in the off season. To get to the cheapest rooms entails a strenuous climb up a seemingly endless series of stairs, but the views over the lake are excellent, and rooms are comfortable. There are several large and sunny roof terraces.

Alka Hotel (☎ 35220), also on The Mall, has economy doubles for Rs 600, and standard doubles for Rs 900 (Rs 400 and Rs 600 in the off season). All rooms have running hot and cold water and piped music.

Mallital & Sukhatal Sukhatal has the bulk of the top-end places.

Hotel Grand (☎ 35406) is at the Mallital end of The Mall. Singles/doubles are Rs 500/700, suites (with separate sitting area) are Rs 900. There's running hot water in the morning only. Hotel Grand is only open between 15 April and 15 November. Off season, a discount of Rs 100 is offered. There's a lovely wide shady balcony with potted geraniums, from where there are good lake views.

Hotel Belvedere (☎ 35082) was formerly the palace of the Raja of Awagarh. Take the road which leads up behind the Bank of Baroda. Doubles start from Rs 800, or with a separate sitting area, Rs 950. Enormous double suites are Rs 1200. Some of the rooms have very good lake views, or you can look out over the lake from the wicker chairs on the shady verandah. Mr and Mrs Singh are the gracious hosts, and they offer a discount of 40% in the off season.

Hotel City Heart (☎ 35228) is directly opposite the Nainital Mountaineering Club on the road behind the Standard Hotel. It's run by the effervescent Mr Pramod, a bass guitarist in an Indian heavy metal rock band. Doubles are very good value, with prices ranging from Rs 450 to Rs 1100. The cheaper rooms have no views, but are large, comfortable and spotless; the more expensive rooms have superlative views of the lake. There's a good roof terrace, and a cheery atmosphere enhanced by dozens of pretty potted plants. A discount of 50% to 60% is offered in the off season.

Naina Tourist Rest House (☎ 36374) is a KMVN place at Sukhatal, about one km from Mallital on the road towards Delhi. Dorm beds are available and doubles from 1 May to 15 July range from Rs 450 to Rs 550; from 15 September to 15 November, rates are Rs 250 to Rs 350, and in the off season, Rs 150 to Rs 225.

Swiss Hotel (☎ 36013) is a very good choice about 10 minutes walk west of Mallital, in a peaceful location, and set in pretty gardens. Run by the Nanda family, the Swiss has comfortable, airy rooms, some with views over the garden. Doubles are Rs 1200, suites are Rs 1500 and four-bed rooms are Rs 1800, all 25% less in the off season. Rates include breakfast and dinner. Mr Nanda's son is a keen naturalist, and can arrange bird and butterfly-spotting excursions around Nainital.

Shervani Hilltop Inn (☎ 36304), formerly the residence of a maharaja, is 15 minutes walk from Mallital. Rooms aren't that special, but are quite comfortable, and the flower garden is spectacular. In the off season this is a good mid-range choice, with room-only rates at Rs 600 to Rs 650. In the season, doubles are Rs 1465 to Rs 1665, including breakfast and dinner.

Vikram Vintage Inn (☎ 35877) is in a secluded location about 20 minutes walk west of Mallital, in Sukhatal. Doubles are Rs 1212, and checkout is a generous 11 am. There's billiards and table tennis, and the staff at the reception desk can arrange a private consultation with a palmist/numerologist (Rs 200 for 30 minutes).

Claridges Naini Retreat (☎ 35105), in a quiet spot above Mallital, has doubles for Rs 2150 including breakfast and one other meal. Guests can hire golf sets for Rs 75.

Holiday Inn Nainital (☎ 36031), Grasmere Estate, about 10 minutes walk northwest of Mallital, has luxuriously appointed rooms, most with lake views, from Rs 2600 to Rs 4000. There's a disco, two restaurants and Nainital's only bar. Rates are 30% to 40% less in the off season.

Places to Eat

There's a wide range of eating establishments along the length of The Mall, and all of the top-end hotels have their own restaurants (visitors welcome).

Sher-e-Punjab is in a small cul-de-sac in Mallital's main bazaar. As its name suggests, it features Punjabi cuisine.

Prem Restaurant is just around the corner, with Punjabi and south Indian cuisine.

Moti Mahal, opposite the north side of The Flats, specialises in Punjabi cuisine.

There is a *fresh fruit juice stall* that does shakes and lassis too, beneath the Standard Hotel, Mallital.

Capri Restaurant, near the Standard Hotel at The Mallital end of The Mall, has Indian, Chinese and Continental cuisine. It's popular, and often full at lunchtime. Non-veg dishes are around Rs 50.

The *Rasoi Vegetarian Restaurant*, next door, has good thalis and pizza.

Flattis Restaurant, with prices similar to Capri, is another popular eatery which features mutton and chicken sizzlers.

The *Embassy*, also in this area, is considered one of the best restaurants by locals. There is a conspicuous absence of ashtrays, and the menu features veg and non-veg cuisine, with main dishes between Rs 65 and Rs 90.

Purohit's, next door to the Embassy, serves vegetarian south Indian cuisine. There's alfresco dining with views across the lake, and filling thalis for Rs 32.

Kwality, also at the Mallital end of The Mall, is set right on the water's edge. It's a bit rowdy at lunchtime, but prices are reasonable, with most main dishes under Rs 50, and there is also an ice-cream parlour.

Pahun Restaurant (*pahun* means 'guest'), further down The Mall, about halfway between Tallital and Mallital, is excellent. This place features traditional Kumaoni cuisine such as aalu ke gutke (fried potato with masala), badeel (fried chickpea patties served with chutney or relish), and the sweet sooji ke pue (deep-fried semolina and curd balls). If you want to sample a variety of Kumaoni dishes, try the special Kumaoni thali (Rs 60). Advance notice is required, so advise the friendly staff in the morning if you plan to dine here in the evening. Prices are very reasonable, with most dishes under Rs 20. Pahun is closed Monday.

There are two restaurants at the Holiday Inn Nainital, Grasmere Estate: the multicuisine ***Kumaon***, and the ***Lotus Garden***, serving Chinese cuisine. This hotel also has Nainital's only bar, the ***Viceroy***. Main dishes in the restaurants cost between Rs 75 and Rs 120; sweets around Rs 40. If you're hanging out for a Continental breakfast, the buffet breakfast bar has croissants, Danish pastries, cereals, scrambled eggs, etc, for Rs 100. Cocktails in the bar are Rs 100, and a beer will set you back Rs 90.

Getting There & Away

Air The nearest airport is Pantnagar, 71km south, but it's not currently served by any scheduled flights.

Bus Buses leave from the bus stand at Tallital every 30 minutes for the railhead at Kathgodam (1½ hours, Rs 30). There's a deluxe service to Delhi at 8.30 am (nine hours, Rs 148) and an ordinary service at 8.45 am (Rs 90). Many private agencies book

deluxe coach tickets to Delhi, and KMVN have their own luxury services; air-con coaches are Rs 230.

Buses to Bhim Tal leave at 8 and 8.30 am, 1.45, 3.15, 4, 4.30 and 6 pm (one hour, Rs 9). To Ramnagar buses leave at 8.45 am and 2, 3 and 3.45 pm (3½ hours, Rs 25). To Almora there are services at 7 and 10 am and noon (three hours, Rs 28). Buses for Ranikhet leave at 6.30 am, 12.30 and 2.30 pm (3½ hours, Rs 25). To Kausani there's one service at 10 am (five hours, Rs 48), and there's also only one daily service to Pithoragarh at 7 am (9½ hours, Rs 75). To Bareilly, buses leave at 7.15 am, 1.30 and 2.30 pm (five hours, Rs 38). To Haridwar, buses depart at 5, 6 and 7 am, 4.30 and 8 pm (eight hours, Rs 96).

There's only one direct service to Rishikesh, at 5 am (nine hours, Rs 105). To Dehra Dun, ordinary buses leave at 6 and 7 am and 4.30 pm (10 hours, Rs 94), and there's a deluxe service at 8 pm (Rs 170). A daily bus to Song (for the Pindari Glacier trek) leaves Bhowali, 11km from Nainital at the junction of the main routes to Ranikhet and Almora, at 10 am (six hours).

Train Kathgodam (35km south) is the nearest railway station; the railway booking agency, near the bus stand, has a quota for trains to Delhi, Lucknow and Calcutta. The *Ranikhet Express* departs Old Delhi station at 11 pm, arriving into Kathgodam at 6.30 am. It departs Kathgodam at 8.45 pm, arriving into Old Delhi station at 4.50 am (Rs 97/403 in 2nd/2nd air-con class). The office is open from 9.30 am to 4 pm.

Taxi & Jeep When full, share jeeps leave from the bus stand for the bazaar at Bhowali (30 minutes, Rs 50). Share taxis depart when full for Kathgodam and Haldwani (Rs 30).

Getting Around
The official rate for a rickshaw from Tallital to Mallital is Rs 3; tickets can be purchased at the booths at either end of The Mall.

RANIKHET
Tel Area Code: 05966
North of Nainital and at an altitude of 1829m, this peaceful hill station offers excellent views of the snowcapped Himalaya including Nanda Devi (7817m). It's an important army town and the headquarters of the Kumaon Regiment. There are a couple of churches that have been converted into tweed and shawl mills with hand-operated looms.

Still in its infancy as a tourist destination, Ranikhet is a delightful place to spend time. There are several good walks – to **Jhula Devi Temple** (one km south of West View Hotel) and the orchards at **Chaubatia** (three km further on), and there's even a golf course with a 300km panoramic view of the Himalaya!

The tourist office (☎ 2227) is by the UP Roadways bus stand.

Places to Stay & Eat
There are several hotels in the bazaar area between the bus stands.

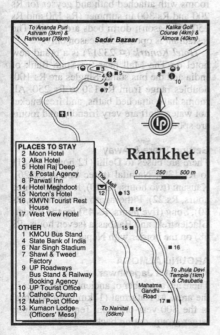

PLACES TO STAY
2 Moon Hotel
3 Alka Hotel
5 Hotel Raj Deep & Postal Agency
6 Parwati Inn
14 Hotel Meghdoot
15 Norton's Hotel
16 KMVN Tourist Rest House
17 West View Hotel

OTHER
1 KMOU Bus Stand
4 State Bank of India
7 Nar Singh Stadium
7 Shawl & Tweed Factory
9 UP Roadways Bus Stand & Railway Booking Agency
10 UP Tourist Office
11 Catholic Church
12 Main Post Office
13 Kumaon Lodge (Officers' Mess)

Hotel Raj Deep is the best of the cheap places, with doubles for Rs 45, or Rs 125 with bathroom, and a vegetarian restaurant.

Alka Hotel has doubles from Rs 150 and a pleasant balcony with mountain views.

Hotel Tribhuwan has a range of rooms in three buildings – doubles with balconies from Rs 100 and more expensive rooms in the house below.

Moon Hotel has overpriced rooms at Rs 150/250 but the restaurant is quite good (main dishes cost from Rs 35 to Rs 50).

Parwati Inn, once quite impressive, has rapidly deteriorated and, at Rs 175 for the cheapest rooms, is also overpriced.

The other places to stay are about four km from the bazaar in a peaceful wooded location.

The *Hotel Meghdoot* (☎ 2475) charges Rs 200 for a large clean double, and has a good restaurant.

Nearby, *Norton's Hotel* (☎ 2377) is a Raj leftover with doubles from Rs 150 to Rs 250. It's closed between December and March.

The *Tourist Rest House* (☎ 2297) is a good place with rooms at Rs 150 (with kitchens) and dorm beds at Rs 20.

The *West View Hotel* (☎ 2261) is another former Raj establishment. For Rs 325/525 there are large rooms with panelled ceilings and fireplaces; in the afternoon there's tea and croquet on the lawn.

Getting There & Away
As with the other hill stations in the Kumaon region, Kathgodam is the nearest railhead. There are buses to Kathgodam (four hours, Rs 32), Nainital (three hours, Rs 25), Almora (three hours, Rs 22), Kausani (3½ hours, Rs 26), Ramnagar (five hours, Rs 37), Delhi (12 hours, Rs 106 to Rs 132) as well as to Lucknow, Haridwar and Badrinath. Buses depart from the UP Roadways and the KMOU bus stands.

ALMORA
Pop: 53,507   Tel Area Code: 05962
This picturesque hill station, at an altitude of 1650m, is one of the few not created by the

British. Some 400 years ago it was the capital of the Chand rajas of Kumaon.

Almora is larger than Ranikhet and Kausani, and has an interesting bazaar, good views of the mountains and some great walks. The eight km walk up to the **Kasar Devi Temple** is recommended – this is where Swami Vivekananda came to meditate. The area has the reputation of being something of a 'power centre' and some travellers rent houses and stay for months. Attractions for tourists include the **Himalaya Woollen Mills** above the Holiday Home, and the town **museum**. The clock tower was built in 1842 and carries the motto 'Work as if thou hadst to live for aye, Worship as if thou wert to die today'. There's a Siva shrine in the room below it.

Beside the Savoy Hotel is the UP tourist office (☎ 22180). High Adventure (☎ 23445) and Discover Himalaya (☎ 23507) can organise treks in the area.

Places to Stay & Eat

There are several hotels in the bazaar.

The *Tourist Cottage*, by the Glory Restaurant, has very basic rooms from Rs 50.

Hotel Pawan, further up the street, is much cleaner with singles/doubles from Rs 83/131 with attached bathrooms, and billiards upstairs.

The large *Hotel Shikhar* (☎ 22395) is the best, with a wide range of good rooms from Rs 80 to Rs 500. The restaurant is also good, with main dishes from Rs 30 to Rs 40.

The *Glory Restaurant*, nearby, is recommended for vegetarian food.

Many people prefer the hotels outside the bazaar as they're more peaceful.

Kailash Hotel ('Junction of East and West Managed by House Wives') is interesting, and most travellers seem to enjoy the eccentricities of the guest house itself and its elderly proprietors, Mr and Mrs Shah. Mrs Shah's cooking is good and her herbal teas excellent. There are doubles from Rs 125 in summer, and dorm beds for Rs 40.

Savoy Hotel is in the same area, with rooms from Rs 200 with attached bath; 25% less off season.

Renuka Hotel (☎ 22860) is directly opposite the main post office and has fair value rooms with attached bath and geyser for Rs 200 and Rs 300 in summer (Rs 150 and Rs 250 off season); dorm beds are Rs 50. The restaurant is open in the season only.

Hotel Konark (☎ 23217) is a brand new hotel on The Mall near the State Bank of India and the bus stand. Singles are Rs 100, doubles range from Rs 150 to Rs 250. All rooms have attached baths, and free bucket hot water. Staff are very friendly, and rooms are spotless.

Getting There & Away

There are buses to Delhi (12 hours, Rs 111 to Rs 139), Nainital (three hours, Rs 26), Kausani (two hours, Rs 20), Ranikhet (three hours, Rs 22), Pithoragarh (seven hours, Rs 40), Song (five hours, Rs 45) for the Pindari Glacier trek, and Banbassa (seven hours, Rs 68) on the border with Nepal.

AROUND ALMORA
Katarmal & Jageshwar

There are a number of ancient temple sites in the area. At Katarmal (17km from Almora) is the 800-year-old Sun Temple. A much larger group, dating back to the 7th century

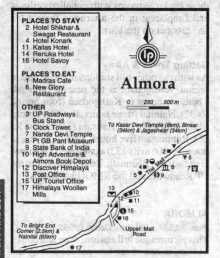

PLACES TO STAY
2 Hotel Shikhar &
   Swagat Restaurant
4 Hotel Konark
11 Kailas Hotel
14 Renuka Hotel
16 Hotel Savoy

PLACES TO EAT
1 Madras Cafe
6 New Glory
   Restaurant

OTHER
3 UP Roadways
   Bus Stand
5 Clock Tower
7 Nanda Devi Temple
8 Pt GB Pant Museum
9 State Bank of India
10 High Adventure &
   Almora Book Depot
12 Discover Himalaya
13 Post Office
15 UP Tourist Office
17 Himalaya Woollen
   Mills

Almora

0   250   500 m

To Kasar Devi Temple (8km), Binsar (34km) & Jageshwar (34km)

The Mall

Upper Mall Road

To Bright End Corner (2.5km) & Nainital (65km)

AD, is 34km away at Jageshwar in an attractive valley of deodars. There's a *Tourist Rest House* (Rs 100 for doubles) and a small museum at Jageshwar.

PITHORAGARH

Pop: 42,113   Tel Area Code: 05964

Situated at 1815m, Pithoragarh is the main town of a region that borders both Tibet and Nepal. It sits in a small valley that has been called 'Little Kashmir' and there are a number of picturesque walks in the area. You can climb up to **Chandak** (seven km) for a view of the Pithoragarh Valley.

There's a KMVN *Tourist Lodge* here, with doubles from Rs 200, and several other hotels. There are buses to Almora, Nainital, Haldwani, Delhi and Tanakpur (the railhead, 158km south).

KAUSANI

Tel Area Code: 059628

For an even closer view of the Himalaya, Kausani, 51km north of Almora, is the place to head for. At 1890m, it's a peaceful village that is perfect for quiet contemplation. Gandhi stayed at the Anasakti Ashram in 1929 and was inspired by the superb Himalayan panorama, and the Hindi poet laureate Sumitra Nandan Pant grew up here.

Among the numerous hikes in the area, the 14km walk to the 12th century temples at **Baijnath** is definitely worth it. Don't follow the road, as it's six km further, but ask for the path through the forest.

Places to Stay & Eat

Uttarakhand Tourist Lodge (☎ 84112), at the top of the stairs leading up from the bus stand, has basic doubles with attached bath on the ground floor for Rs 75 and on the 1st floor for Rs 200. Good discounts are offered in the off season, and all rooms face the snows. The lodge has a good restaurant serving Continental and Indian cuisine.

Hotel Prashant, on Ashram Rd, has a range of budget rooms, with singles from Rs 50, doubles from Rs 100 to Rs 300, and four-bed rooms from Rs 200 to Rs 400.

Cheaper rooms may be gloomy, but this is a popular place, and a 50% discount applies off season.

Anasakti Ashram (Gandhi Ashram) has accommodation by donation. It has a good library that is open to all, and an indicator on the terrace that's useful for mountain identification.

The upmarket *Krishna Mount View* (☎ 84108), nearby, has doubles with Star TV and running hot water for Rs 600 to Rs 1200, with a 40% off-season discount. All rooms face the snows.

The *Vaibhav Restaurant* at the Krishna Mount View features Mughlai and Gujarati cuisine. Main non-veg dishes are between Rs 55 and Rs 95, and there's a good range of sweets, including sooji halwa, a wheat and sugar-based dessert (Rs 20).

The KMVN *Tourist Rest House* (☎ 84106) is a couple of km beyond the village. It's very good value and has doubles from Rs 200 with great views, balconies and hot water. There are dorm beds for Rs 50, and good off-season discounts.

The *Amar Holiday Home* (☎ 84115) is an excellent choice, on Ashram Rd, about 10 minutes walk from the bus stand. Rooms are set in a beautiful garden and there are panoramic views of the snows. Singles/doubles with attached bath (bucket hot water) are Rs 150/450, 50% less in the off season.

Below the TV mast, the *Hill Queen Restaurant* is a popular place to eat.

The *Sunrise Restaurant*, nearby, has good basic food in a rustic setting, and it's run by friendly fellows.

Getting There & Away

Buses to Almora depart approximately every hour between 7 am and 3 pm (2½ hours, Rs 23), continuing to Nainital (six hours, Rs 45). There are a couple of services to Ranikhet between 7 am and 2 pm (four hours, Rs 23). To visit the beautiful stone temples at Baijnath, 20km to the north, take a Bhageshwar-bound bus. They leave approximately every hour between 6 am and 6 pm. The trip to Baijnath takes 30 minutes (Rs 10), and to Bhageshwar, it's 1½ hours (Rs 16).

For Karanprayag and destinations further north, there's one direct bus at 7 am (three hours, Rs 42).

The town's only taxi will charge Rs 200 to Rs 250 one way to Baijnath (Rs 350 to Rs 400 return).

BANBASSA

Banbassa is the closest Indian village to the Nepalese border post of Mahendrenagar, and it's possible to enter Nepal at this point. There are daily buses from Delhi (12 hours) and Banbassa is also connected by rail to Bareilly. From Almora there's a daily bus leaving at 7.30 am (seven hours, Rs 68).

From Banbassa, you can catch a rickshaw (20 minutes) to the border and across to Mahendrenagar. There are direct night buses from Mahendrenagar to Kathmandu, but they take a gruelling 25 hours. The countryside is beautiful and fascinating, so it's much better to travel during the day and to break the journey at Nepalganj. If you can't get a direct bus for the nine hour trip from Mahendrenagar to Nepalganj, take a bus to Ataria (at the junction for Dhangadhi) and from there to Nepalganj. There are plenty of buses from Nepalganj to Kathmandu (day and night journeys, 16 hours) and to Pokhara (night, 15 hours).

TREKS IN GARHWAL & KUMAON

Although only a handful of trekkers visit this region there are some superb trekking opportunities, including the treks in the vicinity of important pilgrimage sites such as Badrinath, Yamunotri, Kedarnath, Gangotri and Hem Kund close to the Valley of the Flowers. There is also a trek out of Gangotri to Gaumukh and the sacred source of the Ganges, a delightful trek to Dodi Tal from the pilgrim town of Uttarkashi, and a trek to Har ki Dun and Ruinsara Lake from the hill station of Mussoorie.

Nanda Devi (7817m), the highest mountain completely in India, is also an attraction for trekkers. Treks that follow the outer rim of the Nanda Devi Sanctuary are well worth considering, and include the Kuari Pass trek out of Joshimath; the trek to Rup Kund beneath Trisul (7120m); the trek to the Pindari Glacier to the south of the Nanda Devi Sanctuary; and the Milam Glacier trek to Nanda Devi East (7434m). It is important to note that trekking into the Nanda Devi Sanctuary has been closed since 1983 and there are no signs that the Indian government will lift this restriction.

The best time to trek in Garhwal and Kumaon is either in the pre monsoon period from mid-May until the end of June, or in the post monsoon season that extends from mid-September until mid-October. In July and August the region is subject to monsoonal rains, but it is the best time to appreciate the wildflowers in the high altitude *bugyals* (meadows) including the Valley of the Flowers.

UP Tourism's two regional subsidiaries, Garhwal Mandal Vikas Nigam (GMVN) and Kumaon Mandal Vikas Nigam (KMVN) can organise inclusive treks, while there are a number of agencies in Uttarkashi, Nainital and Mussoorie who can make similar arrangements. Budget for around US$40 to US$50 per day. If making your own arrangements then porters are normally available at the roadhead for around Rs 100 per day, and guides from Rs 250 per day upwards. The GMVN and the KMVN at Rishikesh, Uttarkashi and Joshimath have stocks of sleeping bags and tents for hire, although supplies may be limited.

Food supplies can be bought at Mussoorie, Nainital or Uttarkashi before continuing on to the roadhead. On some treks, including the trek to Har ki Dun, the trek to Gaumukh and the trek to the Pindari Glacier, there are many tea houses or PWD Rest Houses that provide both food and accommodation. On other treks, including the trek to Dodi Tal and Hanuman Chatti, the trek to Kuari Pass, Rup Kund and the Milam Glacier, it is essential to bring your own supplies.

Har ki Dun Valley & Ruinsara Lake

This trek follows a tributary of the Tons River to the beautiful meadow of Har ki Dun. The initial stages of the trek lead through well-established settlements to the highest village at Seema. It is a further stage to Har ki Dun where a day or two could be spent exploring the side valleys north of the Swargarohini peaks. It is also possible to extend the trek by returning to Seema and trekking to Ruinsara Lake where there are fine views of Swargarohini 1 (6525m).

Stage 1	Sankri to Taluka (3 hours)
Stage 2	Taluka to Seema (5 to 6 hours)
Stage 3	Seema to Har ki Dun (4 to 5 hours)
Stage 4	Har ki Dun to Dev Thach (3 hours)
Stage 5	Dev Thach to Ruinsara Lake & return (7 hours)
Stage 6	Dev Thach to Sankri (6 hours)

Uttarkashi to Hanuman Chatti via Dodi Tal

From Uttarkashi there is short bus ride to the roadhead at Sangam Chatti before trekking to the village of Agoda. It's a further stage to Dodi Tal, an idyllic lake set in a forest of oak, pine, deodar and rhododendron. From Dodi Tal there is a short ascent to the Darwa Pass (4150m) before trekking along the alpine ridges to gain magnificent views of Bandarpunch (6316m). An intermediary camp is necessary before descending to the Hanuman Ganga and the pilgrim town of Hanuman Chatti from where there are regular buses to Uttarkashi or Mussoorie.

Stage 1	Sangam Chatti to Agoda (2 to 3 hours)
Stage 2	Agoda to Dodi Tal (6 hours)
Stage 3	Dodi Tal to Seema camp via Darwa Pass (6 to 7 hours)
Stage 4	Seema to Hanuman Chatti (4 hours)

Gangotri to Gaumukh & Tabovan

The popular pilgrimage destination of Gangotri can be reached from Rishikesh by bus via Tehri and Uttarkashi, a 10 to 12 hour journey. The trek to the source of the holy Ganges starts from the village of Gangotri and follows a bridle trail along the true right of the Bhagirathi River. There are a number of established pilgrim rest stops with adequate shelter and food on the way to Gaumukh (3890m) (cow's mouth – *gau* means cow, and *mukh* is mouth), the true source of the Ganges.

Beyond Gaumukh the going gets harder with a demanding stage across moraine to the meadow at Tabovan. From the camp there are inspiring views of Shivling (6543m), while Bhagirathi peaks including Bhagirathi 1 (6856m) rise dramatically on the far side of the Gangotri Glacier.

Stage 1	Gangotri to Bhojbasa (6 to 7 hours)
Stage 2	Bhojbasa to Gaumukh (2 hours)
Stage 3	Gaumukh to Tabovan & return (5 to 6 hours)
Stage 4	Gaumukh to Gangotri (6 hours)

Valley of the Flowers & Hem Kund

The fabled Valley of the Flowers was 'discovered' by the British mountaineer Frank Smythe in the 1930s. Throughout the summer months from the middle of June to the middle of September the valley is an enchanting sight with an impressive array of wildflowers, and snow clad peaks including Nilgiri Parbat (6474m) standing in bold relief against the skyline. The valley is nearly 10km long and two km wide, and is divided by the Pushpawati stream, into which several tiny streams and waterfalls merge. Heavy traffic in the Valley has led authorities to create a national park with restrictions: no overnight camping is permitted.

Many local buses operate between Joshimath and Govind Ghat, the starting point for the trek. From Govind Ghat there is a gradual ascent along a well-maintained pilgrim trail to the camp at Ghangaria – the base from where day walks can be made into the Valley of the Flowers. From Ghangaria, you can follow the Laxma Ganga to the lake at Hem Kund – quite a steep climb. In the Sikh holy book, the *Granth Sahib*, Hem Kund is the fabled lake by which Guru Gobind Singh meditated in a previous life.

Stage 1	Govind Ghat to Ghangaria (7 hours)
Stage 2	Ghangaria to Valley of the Flowers & return (6 hours)
Stage 3	Ghangaria to Hem Kund & return (8 hours)
Stage 4	Ghangaria to Govind Ghat (5 hours)

Joshimath to Ghat via the Kuari Pass

Although the trek over the Kuari Pass is also known as the Curzon Trail (Lord Curzon was an enthusiastic Himalayan hiker), the Curzon party did not actually cross the pass but abandoned their attempt after being attacked by wild bees a few stages before the crossing.

From Joshimath there is a daily bus service to the village of Auli, where you commence the trek. Starting out, there are uninterrupted views up the Rishi Ganga to the Nanda Devi Sanctuary. The trail then winds through a series of pastures and shepherd camps affording panoramic views of Dunagiri (7066m) and the Chaukhamba massif including Chaukhamba 1 (7138m) on the far side of Joshimath. The best views of Nanda Devi (7816m) are gained from a day walk along the ridge above the pass.

From the Kauri Pass (3640m) there is a steep descent to the meadow at Dakwani before the hike to the shepherd camp at Sutoli. It's a further two stages across the forested ridges and past small villages high above the Birthi Ganga to the village of Ramni. The final stage continues down to the roadhead at Ghat where jeeps and buses complete the 30km to Nandaprayag on the Joshimath to Rishikesh road.

Stage 1	Auli to Chitraganta (6 to 7 hours)
Stage 2	Chitraganta to Dakwani via the Kuari Pass (4 to 5 hours)
Stage 3	Dakwani to Ghangri (7 hours)
Stage 5	Ghangri to Ramni (5 to 6 hours)
Stage 6	Ramni to Ghat (3 hours)

Ghat to Mundoli via Rup Kund

Set beneath the towering summit of Trisul (7120m), Rup Kund is sometimes called the Mystery Lake, due to the many human skeletons which have been found here. Every 12 years thousands of devout pilgrims make an arduous trek when following the Raj Jay Yatra from Nauti village, near Karnaprayag. The pilgrims are said to be led by a four-horned ram which takes them from here to Rup Kund. A golden idol of the goddess Nanda Devi is carried by the pilgrims on a silver palanquin.

The first stage of the trek ascends from Ghat to the village of Ramni before following a trail through mixed forest and traditional Hindu villages to the large village of Wan. The trail to Rup Kund then climbs through oak, pine and rhododendron forest to the alpine camp at Badni Bugyal. The views from this *bugyal* (high altitude meadow) are among the finest in the West Himalaya. To the east are the peaks beyond Joshimath, while to the south east, the Great Himalaya Range extends as far as the eye can see across western Garhwal. To the south the foothills descend to the Indian plains, and Trisul (7120m) provides an impressive northern backdrop.

It's a further stage to the camp at Bhogabasa. From here you can reach Rup Kund with time to return to Badni Bugyal the same day. From Badni Bugyal there are a number of short cuts across the bugyals and down to the trail between Wan and Mandoli. From Mandoli there are buses (Rs 15) and jeeps to Debal and onward connections to Gwalden and Nainital.

Stage 1	Ghat to Ramni (5 hours)
Stage 2	Ramni to Sutol (6 to 7 hours)
Stage 3	Sutol to Wan (5 hours)
Stage 4	Wan to Badni Bugyal (5 hours)
Stage 5	Badni Bugyal to Bhogabasa (4 to 5 hours)
Stage 6	Bhogabasa to Rup Kund & return to Badni Bugyal (6 to 7 hours)
Stage 7	Badni Bugyal to Mandoli (6 to 7 hours)

Song to the Pindari Glacier

The Pindari Glacier flowing from Nanda Kot (6861m) and Nanda Khat (6611m) is on the southern rim of the Nanda Devi Sanctuary.

From Almora there's an early morning bus to Song where you commence the trek. The first stage is all uphill following a well-marked trail through forests of quercus oak and horse chestnut and across open meadows to Dhakri Khal (2830m). Impressive views from the pass include Trisul (7120m) and Nanda Khat (6611m). The trail then winds down to the Pindari Valley and follows the course of the Pindari River through luxuriant forest to the meadow at Phurkiya.

It's an additional stage across meadows to get to the terminal moraine of the Pindari Glacier at Zero Point (3650m), beneath the impressive backdrop of Nanda Khat (6611m), Changuch (6322m) and Nanda Kot (6861m).

Stage 1	Song to Dhakri via Dhakri Khal (6 to 7 hours)
Stage 2	Dhakri to Dwali (6 to 7 hours)
Stage 3	Dwali to Phurkiya (3 hours)
Stage 4	Phurkiya to Pindari Glacier & return to Dwali (7 to 8 hours)
Stage 5	Dwali to Dhakri (6 to 7 hours)
Stage 6	Dhakri to Song (5 to 6 hours)

Munsyari to the Milam Glacier

The Milam Valley to the east of Nanda Devi has recently been opened to trekkers. Although no special permits are needed to complete this trek you will need to show your passport and register with the Indo-Tibet Border Police (ITBP) at Milam.

The trek includes magnificent views of Nanda Devi (7817m), and takes in villages in the upper sections of the Milam Valley which were the recruiting ground for the famous Pundits, the Indian explorers who mapped out much of Tibet for the Indian Ground Survey in the later decades of the 19th century.

There is an early morning bus from Almora to the town of Munsyari, where you commence the trek. The initial stages follow the course of the Gori Ganga past Hindu villages and mixed forests of chestnut and bamboo. The trail then enters impressive gorges, where the Gori Ganga forges its way through the crest of the Great Himalaya Range. It's a further stage to the village of Martoli, which is the turn-off point for the trek to the base of Nanda Devi East. From Martoli it's an easy walk to Milam with views en route of the remarkable East Face of Nanda Devi.

Until 1962 Milam and the nearby villages maintained close trading ties with Tibet. Nowadays this is as far as villagers and trekkers are allowed to go, although you are normally permitted to continue for three km to view the Milam Glacier and the peaks of Rishi Pahar (6992m), Hardeol (7151m) and Tirsuli (7074m).

Stage 1	Munsyari to Lilam (4 hours)
Stage 2	Lilam to Bodgwar (6 to 7 hours)
Stage 3	Bodgwar to Martoli (5 to 6 hours)
Stage 4	Martoli to Milam (4 hours)
Stage 5	Milam to Bodgwar (8 hours)
Stage 6	Bodgwar to Lilam (6 to 7 hours)
Stage 7	Lilam to Munsyari (4 hours)

AULI

This skiing resort, the best equipped in the country, boasts five km-long slopes which drop from an altitude of 3049m to 2519m. Prospective travellers in the cable car will be reassured to learn from the glossy Auli ski resort brochure that it incorporates 'remote controlled hydrauwlic and pneumetic braking system...electronic circuitry with telemetry and storm warning devices to minimise human error'. There's also a 500m-long ski lift.

Open from January to March, Auli is 15km from Joshimath. GMVN operates the resort and has *Tourist Rest Houses* at Joshimath (☎ (01389) 2118) and Auli (☎ (013712) 2226). Skis and boots can be hired here (Rs 100 per day) and seven or 14 day ski packages, including all meals, lodging, equipment, hire and lessons, are offered for Rs 1600/ 2800. To book, write in advance to the General Manager, GMVN, 74/1 Rajpur Rd, Dehra Dun, UP (☎ (0135) 656817; fax 24408).

Central Uttar Pradesh

ALIGARH

Pop: 562,330

Formerly known as Koil, this was the site of an important fort as far back as 1194. During the collapse of the Mughal Empire, the region was fought for by the Afghans, Jats, Marathas and Rohillas – first one coming out on top, then another. Renamed Aligarh (High Fort) in 1776, it fell to the British in 1803 despite French support for its ruler Scindia. The **fort** is three km north of the town, and in its present form dates from 1524.

Aligarh is best known today for the **Aligarh Muslim University** where the 'seeds of Pakistan were sown'. Muslim students from all over the Islamic world come here to study.

ETAWAH

This town rose to importance during the Mughal period, only to go through the usual series of rapid changes during the turmoil that followed the Mughals' decline. The **Jama Masjid** shows many similarities to the mosques of Jaunpur, and there are **bathing ghats** on the riverbank below the ruined fort.

KANNAUJ

Only a few dismal ruins indicate that this was the mighty Hindu capital of the region in the 7th century AD. It quickly fell into disrepair after Mahmud of Ghazni's raids. This was where Humayun was defeated by Sher Shah in 1540, and forced to temporarily flee India. There's not much to see now – just an archaeological museum, a mosque and the ruins of the fort.

KANPUR

Pop: 2,470,000   Tel Area Code: 0512
Although Lucknow is the capital of Uttar Pradesh, Kanpur is the state's largest city. It's a major industrial centre which attracts few tourists and has the unfortunate distinction of being one of the most polluted cities in the world.

Some of the most tragic events of the 1857 Mutiny took place here when the city was known as Cawnpore. General Sir Hugh Wheeler defended a part of the cantonment for almost a month but, with supplies virtually exhausted, he surrendered to Nana Sahib, only to be massacred with most of his party at Sati Chaura Ghat. Over 100 women and children were taken hostage and imprisoned in a small room. Just before relief arrived, they were murdered and their dismembered bodies thrown down a well.

General Neill, their avenger, behaved just as sadistically. Some of the mutineers he captured were made to drink the English blood that still lay in a deep pool in the murder chamber. Before being executed,

Hindus were force-fed beef and told they would be buried; Muslims got pork and the promise of cremation.

Things to See

There's not much to see in Kanpur, though you can visit the site of **General Wheeler's entrenchment**, just over a km from Kanpur Central railway station. Nearby is **All Souls' Memorial Church**, which has poignant reminders of the tragedy of the Mutiny. There's a large zoo at Allen Park, a few km northwest of The Mall.

The main shopping centre, **Navin Market**, is famous for its locally produced cotton goods. Kanpur is a good place to find cheap leather shoes and bags.

Places to Stay & Eat

Kanpur has a string of overpriced hotels along The Mall, which is where you'll probably have to stay since the city's budget hotels, located around the railway station, do not accept non-Indians. It is a Rs 5 cyclerickshaw ride from Kanpur Central railway station to The Mall. All the hotels below provide room service.

The *retiring rooms* at Kanpur Central railway station are excellent value in the circumstances and have certainly improved since Eric and Wanda Newby spent a sleepless night here on their way down the Ganges in 1963. Dorm beds cost Rs 50, doubles Rs 125 and air-con doubles Rs 325 for 24 hours. Rates are roughly half this if you stay less than 12 hours.

Meera Inn (☎ 319972) on The Mall has good air-cooled singles/doubles with attached bath and hot water for Rs 275/425.

The Attic (☎ 311691), just north of The Mall at 15/198 Vikramajit Singh Rd, is a Raj-era bungalow in a pleasant garden. Air-con rooms cost Rs 500/600 which, for Kanpur, is good value.

Hotel Meghdoot (☎ 311999; fax 310209) on The Mall is the city's top hotel. Air-con rooms cost Rs 1000/1400. It has two expensive restaurants, a bar, and a swimming pool on the roof.

Getting There & Away

Kanpur has plenty of connections to Delhi (around six hours, Rs 94/427 in 2nd/1st class) and Calcutta (16 to 25 hours, Rs 225/768 in sleeper/1st class). There are also trains to Mumbai (around 24 hours, Rs 261/940), Allahabad (around three hours), Varanasi (around six hours), Agra (six hours) and Lucknow (1½ hours); and plenty of buses to Lucknow (two hours, Rs 28).

JHANSI

Jhansi is a major transport hub for the north of Madhya Pradesh (MP) and is the most popular transit point for Khajuraho. Though it's actually in Uttar Pradesh, it's included in the MP chapter of this book. For details, see the Northern Madhya Pradesh section of that chapter.

LUCKNOW

Pop: 1,917,000   Tel Area Code: 0522

The capital of Uttar Pradesh rose to prominence as the centre of the nawabs of Avadh. These decadent Muslim rulers controlled a region of north-central India for about a century after the decline of the Mughal Empire. Most of the interesting monuments in Lucknow date from this period. The nawabs were:

Burhan-ul-mulk	1724-39
Safdar Jang	1739-53
Shuja-ud-Daula	1753-75
Asaf-ud-Daula	1775-97
Sa'adat Ali Khan	1798-1814
Ghazi-ud-din Haidar	1814-27
Nasir-ud-din Haidar	1827-37
Mohammad Ali Shah	1837-42
Amjad Ali Shah	1842-47
Wajid Ali Shah	1847-56

The capital of Avadh was moved from Faizabad to Lucknow during the reign of Asaf-ud-Daula. After Sa'adat Ali Khan, the rest of the Avadh nawabs were uniformly hopeless at running affairs of state. Wajid Ali Shah was so extravagant and indolent that to this day his name is regarded by many in India as synonymous with lavishness. However, the nawabs were great patrons of the arts, especially dance and music, and Lucknow's reputation as a city of culture and gracious living stems from this time.

In 1856 the British annexed Avadh, exiling the incompetent Wajid Ali Shah to a palace in Calcutta with an annual pension of UK£120,000. The annexation was one of the sparks that ignited the Indian Mutiny in 1857. Lucknow became the scene for some of the most dramatic events of the Mutiny. The British residents of the city held out in the Residency for 87 harrowing days, only to be besieged again for a further two months after being relieved.

Despite its rich cultural associations, Lucknow is not a particularly attractive city and it suffers from extremely high levels of pollution. However, the huge crumbling mausoleums of the nawabs and the pock-marked ruins of the Residency can make it an interesting place to visit. Lucknow has recently become popular with western followers of the octogenarian guru, Poonjaji, who spends some of the year here. If you're interested, the Carlton Hotel may be able to tell you if he's in town.

Orientation

Lucknow is very spread out. The historic monuments are mainly in the north-western part of the old city, near the Gomti River. The narrow alleys of Aminabad are the main shopping area. Hazratganj is the modern, fashionable district where you'll find most of the budget and mid-range hotels.

Information

Tourist information is available at the Hotel Gomti from UP Tours (☎ 211463). It's a branch of UP Tourism and runs half-day sightseeing tours of Lucknow (Rs 50) departing at 9.45 am. The main tourist office (☎ 226205) is hidden down an alley off Station Rd. It's open from 10 am to 5 pm daily except Sunday. There's also a useful information booth at Charbagh railway station which sells maps of the city for Rs 2.

The State Bank of India on Ashok Marg is the most convenient place to change money in Hazratganj. There's a British Council Library (☎ 242144) next to Hazratganj's

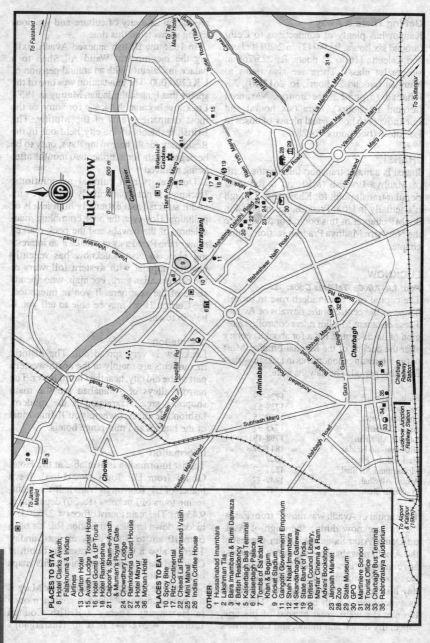

Lucknow

PLACES TO STAY
8   Hotel Clarks Avadh,
    Falaknuma & Indian
    Airlines
13 Carlton Hotel
15 Avadh Lodge Tourist Hotel
16 Hotel Gomti & UP Tours
18 Hotel Ramkrishna
21 Capoor's, Sham-e-Avadh
    & Muman's Royal Cafe
24 Chowdhury Lodge
27 Ramkrishna Guest House
34 Hotel Mayur
36 Mohan Hotel

PLACES TO EAT
10 Spicy Bite
17 Ritz Continental
22 Cheadi Lal Ramprasad Vaish
25 Mini Mahal
26 Indian Coffee House

OTHER
1   Hussainabad Imambara
2   Lakshman Tila
3   Bara Imambara & Rumi Darwaza
4   British Residency
5   Kaiserbagh Bus Terminal
6   Kaiserbagh Palace
7   Tombs of Sa'adat Ali
    Khan & Begum
9   Cricket Stadium
11 Gangotri Government Emporium
12 Shah Najaf Imambara
14 Sikandarbagh Gateway
19 State Bank of India
20 British Council Library,
    Mayfair Cinema & Ram
    Advani Bookshop
23 Janpath Market
28 Zoo
29 State Museum
30 GPO
31 Martiniere School
32 Tourist Office
33 Charbagh Bus Terminal
35 Rabindralaya Auditorium

UTTAR PRADESH

Mayfair Cinema. It's open from 10.30 am to 6.30 pm from Tuesday to Saturday. Ram Advani, on the other side of the cinema, is an excellent bookshop.

Bara Imambara
The Bara or Great Imambara (an *imambara* is the tomb of a Shi'ite Muslim holy man) was built in 1784 by Asaf-ud-Daula as a famine relief project. The central hall of the Imambara, at 50m long and 15m high, is one of the largest vaulted galleries in the world. An external stairway leads to an upper floor laid out as an amazing labyrinth known as the *bhulbhulaiya*; a guide may be useful since the dark passages stop abruptly at openings which drop straight to the courtyard below. Entry to the labyrinth is Rs 10.

There's a mosque with two tall minarets in the courtyard complex but non-Muslims are not allowed in. To the right of this is a 'bottomless' well. The Imambara complex is open from sunrise to 6 pm.

Beside the Bara Imambara, and also built by Asaf-ud-Daula, is the imposing **Rumi Darwaza**, a replica of an entrance gate built in Istanbul. 'Rumi' (relating to Rome) is the term Muslims applied to Istanbul when it was still Byzantium, the capital of the eastern Roman Empire.

Lakshman Tila, the high ground on the southern bank of the River Gomti nearby, was the original site of the town which became known as Lucknau in the 15th century. Aurangzeb's Mosque now stands on this site.

Hussainabad Imambara
Also known as the Chhota, or Small Imambara, this was built by Mohammad Ali Shah in 1837 to serve as his own mausoleum. Thousands of labourers worked on the project to gain famine relief. The large courtyard encloses a raised rectangular tank with small imitations of the Taj Mahal on each side. One of them is the tomb of Mohammad Ali Shah's daughter, the other that of her husband. The main building of the Imambara, topped by a golden dome, contains the tombs of Ali Shah and his mother. The nawab's silver-covered

throne, other paraphernalia of state and lots of tacky chandeliers are stored here. It's open from 6 am to 5 pm.

The decaying **watchtower** opposite the Hussainabad Imambara is known as Satkhanda, or the Seven-Storey Tower, but it actually has four storeys because construction was abandoned when Ali Shah died in 1840. A 67m-high defunct **clock tower**, reputedly the tallest in the country, overlooks the Hussainabad Tank nearby. A *baradari* or **summer house**, built by Ali Shah, fronts onto the tank. It houses portraits of the nawabs of Avadh.

West of the Hussainabad Imambara is the **Jama Masjid** which was started by Mohammad Ali Shah and completed after his death.

Residency
Built in 1800 for the British Resident, this group of buildings became the stage for the most dramatic events of the 1857 Mutiny – the Siege of Lucknow.

The British inhabitants of the city all took refuge with Sir Henry Lawrence in the Residency upon the outbreak of the Mutiny. In total there were 3000 people crammed into the Residency's grounds, including 800 British soldiers, 700 loyal native troops, 150 European volunteers, 550 women and children, and some 700 Indian servants. The Residency was technically indefensible, but those seeking shelter expected relief to arrive in a matter of days.

In fact it was 87 days before a small force under Sir Henry Havelock broke through the besiegers to the remaining half-starved defenders. But once Havelock and his troops were within the Residency, the siege immediately recommenced. It continued unabated from 25 September to 17 November, when final relief arrived with Sir Colin Campbell. Only 980 of the original inhabitants survived the ordeal. Many who did not die from bullet wounds succumbed to cholera, typhoid or smallpox.

The Residency has been maintained as it was at the time of the final relief, and the shattered walls are still scarred by cannon shot. Even since Independence little has changed. The only major work done on the place was the unveiling of an Indian Martyrs' Memorial directly opposite.

There's a **model room** in the main Residency building which is worth visiting to get your bearings from the rather tatty model. Downstairs you can see the cellars where many of the women and children lived throughout the siege. The **cemetery** at the nearby ruined church has the graves of 2000 men, women and children, including that of Sir Henry Lawrence, 'who tried to do his duty' according to the famous inscription on his weathered gravestone.

The Residency is open from sunrise to sunset, but the model room is open only from 9 am to 5.30 pm. Admission is Rs 2, except on Friday when it's free.

Other Attractions
The plain **Shah Najaf Imambara**, opposite the Carlton Hotel, is the tomb of Ghazi-ud-din Haidar who died in 1827. The interior is used to store garish chandeliers and *tazia*, elaborate creations of wood, bamboo and silver paper which are carried through the streets during the Muharram Festival. The Imambara is open from 6 am to 5 pm.

Sikandarbagh, the scene of pitched battles in 1857, is a partially fortified garden with a modest gateway bearing the nawabs' fish emblem. The **botanical gardens**, the home of the National Botanical Research Institute, are nearby.

The stately **tombs** of Sa'adat Ali Khan and his wife are close to the remnants of **Kaiserbagh Palace** on the south-eastern edge of the large roundabout near the cricket stadium. Cannons mounted on the tombs during the siege of Lucknow were effective in delaying Havelock from relieving the Residency.

The dusty Lucknow **zoo** in the Banarsi Bagh is open from 8 am to 5 pm daily except Monday. The **State Museum**, which contains an impressive collection of stone sculptures, is also here. It's open from 10.30 am to 4.30 pm daily except Monday.

The **Martiniere School** on the eastern edge of the city was designed by the Frenchman Major-General Claude Martin as a palatial home. His architectural abilities were, to say the least, a little confused – Gothic gargoyles were piled merrily atop Corinthian columns to produce a finished product which a British marquess sarcastically pronounced was inspired by a wedding cake. Martin died in 1800 before his home could be completed, but left the money and directions that it should become a school. 'Kim', the boy hero of Kipling's story of the same name, went to school here. The school can be visited but you need to get permission from the principal first.

Special Events
The spirit of the nawabs returns during the **Lucknow Festival** between 25 November and 5 December. There are processions, plays,

---

The Siege of Lucknow
The published accounts of the siege of Lucknow combine tales of derring-do with traces of domestic comedy wrung from the British contingent's struggle to maintain a stiff upper lip in the face of adversity.

Several accounts were written by women, some of whom at first seemed more troubled by the shortage of good domestic help than by being surrounded by tens of thousands of bloodthirsty mutineers. This changed during the drawn-out months of the siege, by the end of which they were said to be able to judge the weight of shot being fired into the compound better than the men.

In *The Siege of Lucknow*, Julia Inglis (whose husband took command on the death of Sir Henry Lawrence) flatly records the day-to-day horrors of life in the Residency:
July 1st – ...Poor Miss Palmer had her leg taken off by a round shot to-day, she, with some other ladies, having remained in the second storey of the Residency house, though warned it was not safe... July 4th – Poor Sir Henry (Lawrence) died to-day, after suffering fearful pain... July 8th – Mr Polehampton, one of our chaplains, was shot through the body to-day whilst shaving... October 1st – I was with Mrs Couper nearly all day, watching her baby dying... ∎

kathak dancing, *ghazal* and sitar recitals during the 10 day festival of nostalgia.

Lucknow is a good place to see the **Shi'ite Muharram** celebrations (dates vary from year to year) since it has been the principal Indian Shi'ite city since the nawabs arrived. The activity during Muharram, which centres on the Bara Imambara, can get intense as penitents scourge themselves with whips; keep a low profile.

Places to Stay – bottom end

There are plenty of hotels in Lucknow but good budget accommodation is in fairly short supply. Most travellers head for the Hazratganj area.

Chowdhury Lodge (☎ 221911), down an alley opposite the GPO, has singles/doubles with attached bath from Rs 100/130 and air-cooled rooms from Rs 160/240. Some rooms don't have windows but they're fine if you can handle being woken each morning at a godforsaken hour with offers of bed tea and a shave. The lodge has 24 hour checkout and charges extra for sheets, blankets and buckets of hot water.

Hotel Ramkrishna (☎ 280380) on Ashok Marg is a standard Indian hotel with clean air-cooled singles/doubles/triples with attached bath and hot water for Rs 150/195/270, and air-con rooms for Rs 495. It also has a small restaurant. Checkout is 24 hours.

Ramkrishna Guest House (☎ 272472) on Park Rd has fairly good air-cooled doubles from Rs 170 and air-con doubles for Rs 490.

Capoor's (☎ 223958) is a long-established hotel located on MG Rd in the heart of Hazratganj, but rooms with attached bath and bucket hot water are not great value at Rs 250. Air-cooled rooms are Rs 400 and air-con Rs 650. Checkout is 24 hours.

Avadh Lodge Tourist Hotel (☎ 282861) near Sikandarbagh is a tatty, atmospheric place which feels a bit like staying in a fusty old natural history museum. A previous owner was an unfortunately good shot and large quantities of the local fauna, including the now rare gharial (fish-eating crocodile), decorate the walls. Varied singles/doubles/triples with attached bath and hot water cost Rs 180/280/350; air-con is Rs 160 extra.

There are a few options in the noisy area near the railway stations.

The *retiring rooms* are the best value with dorm beds for Rs 25, doubles for Rs 115 and air-con rooms for Rs 160 for a 24 hour period. Rates drop by about 40% if you stay less than 12 hours.

Hotel Mayur (☎ 451824) has rooms with attached bath for Rs 200/250 and air-con doubles for Rs 450. It's not bad value for Lucknow.

Mohan Hotel (☎ 454216) has dorm beds for Rs 80, or Rs 100 in an air-con dorm. Fine but overpriced air-cooled rooms with attached bath start from Rs 250/350. Checkout is 24 hours.

Places to Stay – middle & top end

Carlton Hotel (☎ 224021; fax 229793) was once a palace and is still an impressive building with a musty air of decaying elegance. Large rooms with character and attached bath cost Rs 350/450 and Rs 550/900 with

---

Lucknow Cuisine

The refined palates of the nawabs have left Lucknow with a reputation for rich Mughlai cuisine. The city is famous for its wide range of kebabs and for *dum pukht* – the 'art' of steam pressure cooking, in which meat and vegetables are cooked in a sealed clay pot. Huge paper-thin chapatis *(rumali roti)* are served in many small Muslim restaurants in the old city. They arrive folded up and should be eaten with a goat or lamb curry like *bhuna ghosht* or *roghan josh. Kulfi falooda*, ice cream with cornflour noodles, is a popular dessert, and there are several places in Aminabad that serve it. The sweet orange-coloured rice dish known as *zarda* is also popular. In the hot months of May and June, Lucknow has some of the world's finest mangoes, particularly the wonderful *dashhari* variety grown in the village of Malihabad, west of the city. ■

air-con. The extensive gardens make it a relaxing place to stay.

Hotel Gomti (☎ 220624) is a UP Tourism operation with overpriced but good air-cooled rooms with attached bath and hot water for Rs 350/400 and air-con rooms for Rs 600/700. The hotel has a restaurant, coffee shop and a popular bar.

Hotel Clarks Avadh (☎ 216500; fax 216507) has rooms with good views from Rs 2200/2500 but you'll need to pay Rs 3300/3700 to stay on the 'Privilege Floor' to really get five-star facilities and service. There's a restaurant, coffee shop and bar, but no pool.

Taj Mahal Hotel (☎ 393939; fax 392282) is much better value but inconveniently located in Gomti Nagar, east of the city. Rooms cost from Rs 2000/3000. It has a restaurant specialising in Lucknow cuisine, a coffee shop, bar and pool.

Places to Eat

Hazratganj's MG Rd is lined with restaurants, snack bars and western-style fast-food joints.

Muman's Royal Cafe, next to Capoor's, is the best restaurant on MG Rd. It has good veg/non-veg Indian and Chinese food, prompt service and a civilised ambience. The excellent chaat stall outside does a roaring trade in tasty snacks costing only Rs 8.

Sham-e-Avadh, in Capoor's, serves decent veg/non-veg fare (Rs 25 to Rs 45), Chinese food and western breakfasts.

Cheadi Lal Ramprasad Vaish has great coffee, juices and ice cream, which are consumed by flocks of customers standing on the pavement outside. It's on MG Rd but poorly marked. It's the place next to the Lop Stop fast-food joint.

Mini Mahal nearby has a good selection of Indian sweets and pastries.

The *Indian Coffee House* is where the local intelligentsia used to meet over a coffee and snack. It's an unhurried place conducive to hanging out, unlike most of the other eateries around MG Rd. It serves a few snacks and, surprisingly, pretty bad coffee.

Ritz Continental is an upmarket vegetarian restaurant around the corner from the Hotel Ramkrishna. It serves good snacks, Indian and Chinese food, and pizzas (Rs 30 to Rs 50).

Spicy Bite, in the Tulsi Theatre Building, is rated highly by locals. Acceptable pizzas cost from Rs 42 and burgers Rs 28.

Falaknuma, in Hotel Clarks Avadh, is one of the best places to try Lucknow cuisine. Main courses are expensive but the food is good and the restaurant has great views across the city.

Entertainment

The *Rabindralaya auditorium* (☎ 455670), opposite Charbagh railway station, hosts classical music, dance and theatrical performances. The *Mayfair Cinema* in Hazratganj often shows English-language movies. If you want a drink, the *Hotel Gomti* has the best of Lucknow's few bars.

Things to Buy

The bazaars of Aminabad and Chowk are interesting to wander through, even if you're not buying. In the narrow lanes of Aminabad you can buy *attar* – pure essential oils extracted from flowers in the traditional manner. In Chowk, you'll find a bird-sellers district known as Nakkhas; pigeon-keeping and cockfighting have been popular in Lucknow since the time of the nawabs.

The Gangotri government emporium in Hazratganj sells local handicrafts, including the hand-woven embroidered cloth known as *chikan* for which Lucknow is famous.

Getting There & Away

Air The Indian Airlines office (☎ 220927) is at the Hotel Clarks Avadh. It operates daily flights to Delhi (US$70), four flights a week to Mumbai (US$200) and three a week to Patna (US$75) and Calcutta (US$125).

Sahara India Airlines (☎ 377675) has six flights a week to Varanasi (US$48), Delhi (US$67) and Mumbai.

Bus There are two bus terminals: Charbagh, near the railway stations, and Kaiserbagh. From Charbagh there are regular departures to Kanpur (two hours, Rs 28) and Allahabad (five hours, Rs 66), and early-morning and evening buses to Varanasi (8½ hours, Rs 90) and Agra (10 hours, Rs 130). From Kaiserbagh there are buses to Delhi (12 hours, Rs 168), Gorakhpur (seven hours, Rs 88) and Faizabad (three hours, Rs 41).

Train The two main stations, Charbagh and Lucknow Junction, are side by side; the former handles Northern Railway trains and the latter those of North Eastern Railway. Effectively this means Charbagh handles all trains between New Delhi and Calcutta, while Lucknow Junction handles many of the trains heading to cities in the south.

The *Shatabdi Express* runs between Lucknow and Delhi (6½ hours, Rs 450 in air-con chair class) via Kanpur (1½ hours, Rs 140). There are plenty of regular expresses to both Delhi (eight to nine hours, Rs 101/464 in 2nd/1st class) and Calcutta (around 23 hours, Rs 219/744 in sleeper/1st class). Other express trains go to Allahabad (four hours, Rs 34/160 in 2nd/1st class), Varanasi (five to six hours, Rs 72/318), Faizabad (three hours, Rs 27/139), Gorakhpur (five to six hours, Rs 66/297) and Mumbai (27 hours, Rs 265/973 in sleeper/1st class). Overnight trains to Agra take between six and seven hours.

Getting Around
The Airport Amausi Airport is 15km southwest of Lucknow. Taxis charge around Rs 150 for the trip so if you don't have much baggage it's worth catching a tempo from Charbagh railway station for Rs 4.

Local Transport Tempos are the best way to get around. They run along fixed routes connecting Charbagh railway station with the GPO (Hazratganj), Sikandarbagh, Kaiserbagh (for the bus terminal) and Chowk (for the imambaras). Most journeys cost around Rs 3. There are plenty of cycle-rickshaws but few auto-rickshaws. A cycle-rickshaw between the railway stations and Hazratganj costs locals Rs 5 but foreigners can expect to pay Rs 10. From Hazratganj to the imambaras, it costs Rs 10; for a day's sightseeing it's around Rs 50.

ALLAHABAD
Pop: 1,006,400   Tel Area Code: 0532
The city of Allahabad is 135km west of Varanasi at the confluence of two of India's most important rivers – the Ganges and the Yamuna (Jumna). The mythical Saraswati River, the River of Enlightenment, is also believed to join them here. The confluence, known as the *sangam*, is considered to have great soul-cleansing powers and all pious Hindus hope to bathe here at least once in their lifetime. Hundreds of thousands bathe here every January-February and once every 12 years the Kumbh Mela, the world's largest gathering of pilgrims, draws millions to the confluence for a holy dip.

Allahabad has a fort built by Akbar, which overlooks the confluence of the rivers, and also the Nehru family home, Anand Bhavan. Not many foreign travellers pause in this friendly city, but it's an interesting, relaxing and worthwhile stop, especially if you're partial to Indian-style espressos and sidewalk cafes.

History
Built on a very ancient site, Allahabad was known in Aryan times as Prayag, and Brahma himself is said to have performed a sacrifice here. The Chinese pilgrim Hiuen Tsang described visiting the city in 634 AD, and it acquired its present name in 1584, under Akbar. Later Allahabad was taken by the Marathas, sacked by the Pathans and finally ceded to the British in 1801 by the Nawab of Avadh.

It was in Allahabad that the East India Company officially handed over control of India to the British government in 1858, following the Mutiny. The city was a centre of the Indian National Congress and at the conference here in 1920, Mahatma Gandhi proposed his programme of nonviolent resistance to achieve independence.

Orientation & Information
Allahabad's Civil Lines is an area of broad avenues, Raj-era bungalows, modern shops and some outdoor eating stalls. The main

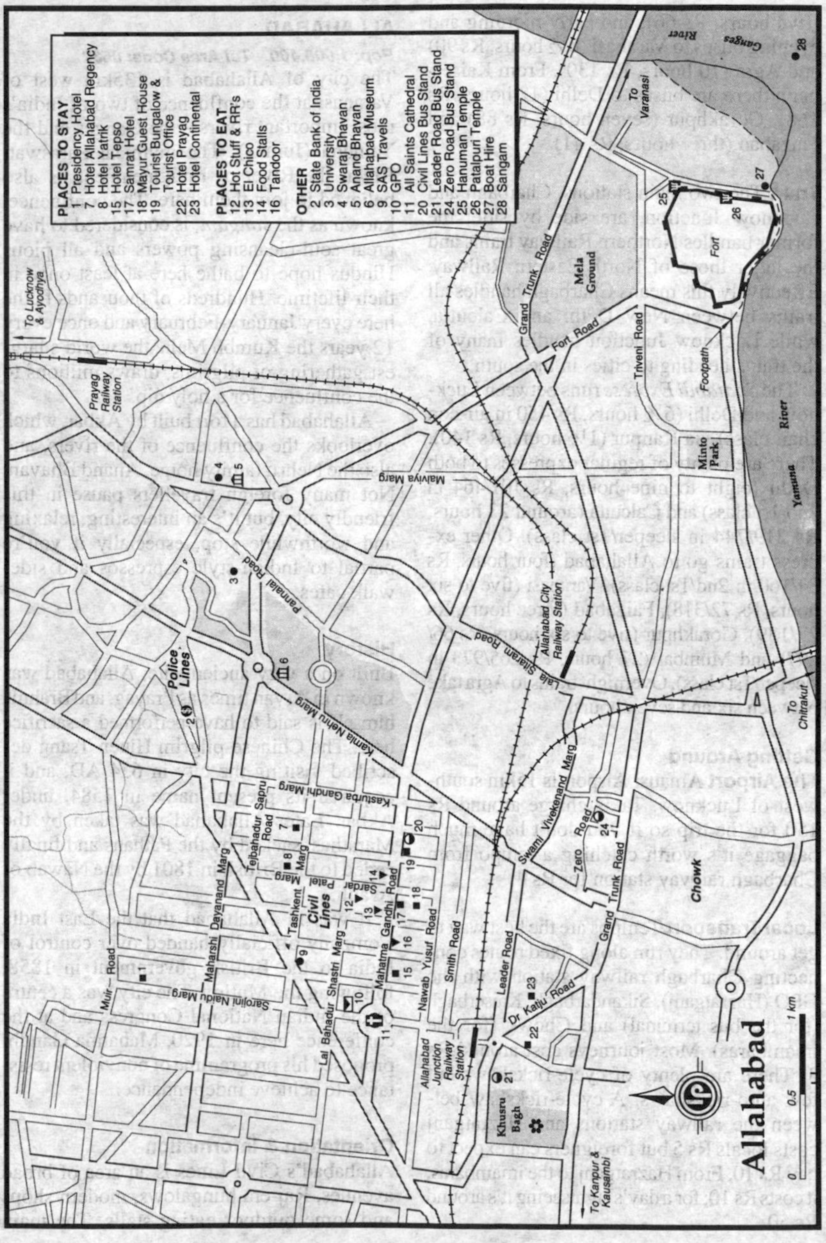

Allahabad
PLACES TO STAY
1 Presidency Hotel
7 Hotel Allahabad Regency
8 Hotel Yatrik
15 Hotel Tepso
17 Samrat Hotel
18 Mayur Guest House
19 Tourist Bungalow & Tourist Office
22 Hotel Prayag
23 Hotel Continental
PLACES TO EAT
12 Hot Stuff & RR's
13 El Chico
14 Food Stalls
16 Tandoor
OTHER
2 State Bank of India
3 University
4 Swaraj Bhavan
5 Anand Bhavan
6 Allahabad Museum
9 SAS Travels
10 GPO
11 All Saints Cathedral
20 Civil Lines Bus Stand
21 Leader Road Bus Stand
24 Zero Road Bus Stand
25 Hanuman Temple
26 Patalpuri Temple
27 Boat Hire
28 Sangam
To Lucknow & Ayodhya
Prayag Railway Station
To Varanasi
Ganges River
Yamuna River
Mela Ground
Fort
Grand Trunk Road
Fort Road
Triveni Road
Footpath
Minto Park
Malviya Marg
Pannalal Road
Police Lines
Kamla Nehru Marg
Allahabad City Railway Station
Lala Sitaram Road
To Chitrakut
Kasturba Gandhi Marg
Tejbahadur Sapru Road
Swami Vivekenand Marg
Zero Road
Chowk
Maharshi Dayanand Marg
Tashkent Marg
Patel Marg
Sardar Patel Marg
Civil Lines
Mahatma Gandhi Road
Lal Bahadur Shastri Marg
Nawab Yusuf Road
Smith Road
Leader Road
Dr Katju Road
Muir Road
Sarojini Naidu Marg
Allahabad Junction Railway Station
Khusru Bagh
To Kanpur & Kausambi
0 0.5 1 km

bus terminal is also here. It's divided from the dense, older part of town, known as Chowk, by Allahabad Junction railway station.

There's a Tourist Bungalow and office on MG Rd. The main branch of the State Bank of India in Police Lines is the place to change money. SAS Travels (☎ 623598) is an Indian Airlines agency but no flights operate from Allahabad's airport.

Sangam

At this point the shallow, muddy Ganges meets the clearer, deeper, green Yamuna. During the month of Magha (mid-January to mid-February) pilgrims come to bathe at this holy confluence for the festival known as the **Magh Mela**. Astrologers calculate the holiest time to enter the water and draw up a 'Holy Dip Schedule'. The most propitious time of all happens only every 12 years when the massive **Kumbh Mela** takes place. There's a half-mela (Ardh Mela) every six years.

An enormous temporary township springs up on the vacant land on the Allahabad side of the river and elaborate precautions have to be taken for the pilgrims' safety – in the early 1950s, 350 people were killed in a stampede to the water (an incident recreated in Vikram Seth's novel, *A Suitable Boy*).

Sunrise and sunset can be spectacular here. Boats out to the confluence are a bit of a tourist trap and what you pay very much depends on how many other people are around. Next to the fort you should be able to share a boat for about Rs 15 or hire a whole boat for Rs 40. It's more interesting sharing with Indians on a pilgrimage since you'll then appreciate the spot's religious significance.

Fort

Built by Akbar in 1583, the fort stands on the northern bank of the Yamuna, near the confluence with the Ganges. It has massive walls and three gateways flanked by high towers. It's most impressive when viewed from the river, so if you don't catch a boat out to the sangam it's worth walking along the riverbank footpath which skirts the fort's southern wall.

The fort is in the hands of the army so prior permission is required for a visit. Officially, passes can be obtained from the Defence Ministry Security Officer but the amount of patience required to get a permit is out of all proportion to the sights to be seen. Apart from one Mughal building, the only item of antiquity in the restricted area is an **Ashoka pillar** dating from 232 BC. Its inscription eulogises the victories of Samudragupta and contains the usual edicts.

Patalpuri Temple & Undying Tree A small door in the fort's eastern wall leads to the one portion of the fort you can visit without

Kumbh Mela

According to Hindu creation myths, the gods and demons once fought a great battle for a *kumbh* (pitcher) containing the nectar of immortality. Vishnu got his hands on the container and spirited it away, but during his flight four drops of nectar spilt on the earth – at Allahabad, Haridwar, Nasik and Ujjain. The fight lasted 12 days but the gods finally triumphed and got to quaff the nectar – a scene often portrayed in illustrations of Hindu mythology.

A huge *mela* (fair) is held at each of the four places the sacred nectar fell once every 12 years (since one day in the life of the gods equates to 12 years in the life of mortals). It is due to take place in Haridwar in 1998 and then in Allahabad in 2001. The Allahabad Kumbh Mela is the largest and holiest mela of them all – some say the largest religious gathering that takes place anywhere on earth. Unsubstantiated estimates of the numbers who came to bathe in the Ganges and Yamuna during Allahabad's last Kumbh Mela in 1989 ran as high as 20 million, though it was probably lower than this. The event is noted for the huge number of Hindu holy men it attracts, especially the naked sadhus or *nagas* of militant Hindu monastic orders.

Mark Tully's *No Full Stops in India* has a fascinating chapter on the politics, logistics and significance of Allahabad's last Kumbh Mela. ■

permission – the underground Patalpuri Temple which contains the 'Undying Banyan Tree'. Also known as Akshai Veta, this tree is mentioned by Hiuen Tsang, who tells of pilgrims sacrificing their lives by leaping to their deaths from it in order to seek salvation. This would be difficult now as there's not much of it left.

Hanuman Temple This popular temple, open to non-Hindus, is unusual because the Hanuman idol is reclining rather than upright. It is said that every year during the floods the Ganges rises so that it can touch the feet of the sleeping Hanuman before it starts receding.

Anand Bhavan
This shrine to the Nehru family must be the best kept museum in the country, which indicates the high regard in which this famous dynasty is held in India. The family home was donated to the Indian government by Indira Gandhi in 1970. The exhibits in the house show how this well-off family became involved in the struggle for Indian independence and produced four generations of astute politicians – Motilal Nehru, Jawaharlal Nehru, Indira Gandhi and Rajiv Gandhi.

Visitors walk around the verandahs of the two storey mansion looking through glass panels into the rooms. You can see Nehru's bedroom and study, the room where Mahatma Gandhi used to stay during his visits and Indira Gandhi's room, as well as many personal items connected with the Nehru family. A quick look at the bookshelves (full of Marx and Lenin) indicate where India's post-Independence faith in socialism sprang from. The house is open daily, except Monday, between 9.30 am and 5 pm. It's free to see the ground floor but costs Rs 2 to go upstairs.

In the manicured garden is an outbuilding housing a pictorial display of Jawaharlal Nehru's life. A **planetarium**, built in the grounds in 1979, has hourly shows between 11 am and 4 pm; tickets cost Rs 8.

Next door is **Swaraj Bhavan**, where Motilal Nehru lived until 1930 and where Indira Gandhi was born. A Hindi and English audio-visual presentation called *The Story of Independence* is shown daily except Monday between 11 am and 1.30 pm, and between 2 and 4.15 pm. It lasts a little under an hour and costs Rs 5.

Other Attractions
Close to the railway station is **Khusru Bagh**, a scrappy walled garden which contains the tomb of Prince Khusru, son of Jehangir, who was executed by his father. Nearby is the unoccupied tomb intended for his sister and the tomb of his Rajput mother, who was said to have poisoned herself in despair at Khusru's opposition to his father.

All Saints Cathedral was designed by Sir William Emerson, the architect of the Victoria Memorial in Calcutta. Its brass memorial plaques show that even for the sons and daughters of the Raj, life was not all high teas and pink gins. The inscriptions morbidly record the causes of death: 'died of blood poisoning', 'died in a polo accident' and, probably even more likely today, 'died in a motor accident on the road to Nainital'. It is open from 8 to 10 am and has services in English on Sunday.

Allahabad Museum has galleries devoted to local archaeological finds, including terracotta figurines from Kausambi. It also has natural history exhibits, an art gallery and artefacts donated by the Nehru family. The museum is open daily from 10.30 am to 4.30 pm except Monday. Admission is Rs 2. Not far away, opposite the university, is the house where Rudyard Kipling lived, but it isn't open to the public.

Minto Park, near the Yamuna, is where Lord Canning read out the declaration by which Britain took over control of India from the East India Company in 1858. The **Nag Basuki Temple** is mentioned in the Puranas and is on the bank of the Ganges, north of the railway bridge.

Places to Stay – bottom end
Budget hotels can be found in the peaceful Civil Lines area and immediately south of Allahabad Junction railway station.

The **Tourist Bungalow** (☎ 601440) at 35 MG Rd is a clean UP Tourism operation set back from the road in a well-tended garden, though noise still filters through from the adjacent bus stand. Good, spacious singles/doubles with attached bath cost from Rs 175/225 and air-con rooms Rs 450/500. Cheaper rooms do not have hot water, which can make washing decidedly nippy in the cool season. It's good value if you can put up with the staff, who consider guests a minor irritant to the smooth functioning of the hotel.

Mayur Guest House (☎ 420250), just off MG Rd, has acceptable, smallish rooms with attached bath, hot water and TV from Rs 120/150 and air-con rooms for Rs 375/475.

Hotel Tepso (☎ 623635) has rooms with common bath for Rs 60/85 and attached bath for Rs 165/225. It's seen better days and is not particularly good value.

Hotel Prayag (☎ 604430) is a typical good budget Indian hotel, south of Allahabad Junction railway station. It has a variety of rooms starting from Rs 60/80 with common bath and from Rs 105/135 for attached bath. Air-con doubles go for Rs 425.

Hotel Continental (☎ 652629) in the next street east is an airless place with basic but OK rooms with TV, attached bath and hot water in the mornings from Rs 120/160, and air-con doubles for Rs 400. It operates on the 24 hour checkout system.

There are numerous other places to stay in this price bracket along Dr Katju Rd.

The **retiring rooms** at Allahabad Junction railway station cost Rs 120 for a double with attached bath and Rs 40 in a dorm for 24 hours. The tariff is roughly half this if you stay less than 12 hours.

Places to Stay – middle & top end

All the mid-range and top-end hotels are in the Civil Lines area.

Hotel Allahabad Regency (☎ 601519) is a tranquil two-star establishment, set in a garden environment, with air-con rooms from Rs 600/700. It has a nice pool which is open only between April and September.

Hotel Yatrik (☎ 601713; fax 601434) is a smart, modern establishment of a similar

standard nearby on Sardar Patel Marg. Air-con rooms cost Rs 700/900. It has a lovely garden and a good pool open between April and September. Non-guests can use the pool at the management's discretion. Checkout is 24 hours.

Presidency Hotel (☎ 623308; fax 623897) is in a quiet residential area just north of Civil Lines. Modern, neat, air-con rooms cost from Rs 725/775. Its pool is open year-round.

Samrat Hotel (☎ 604888; fax 604987), in an alley just off MG Rd, has rooms with attached bath for Rs 450/650 and air-con rooms for Rs 550/750. It's clean, but over-priced considering the signs of wear and tear.

Places to Eat

Outdoor eating is all the rage in Allahabad. Many semipermanent stalls set up tables and chairs on the footpath of MG Rd in the evening, making it a popular, atmospheric and cheap area to eat. There's a good sidewalk **coffee stall** in front of Hotel Tepso, one of many in the area boasting an espresso machine. The **potato chaat stand** directly in front of El Chico serves fantastic snacks for Rs 3.

Shamiana is one of the few established food stalls on MG Rd open all day. It dishes up excellent noodles for just Rs 12 and OK masala dosa for Rs 10.

Chicken King and neighbouring **Spicy Bite**, a little further west, are stalls serving cheap and tasty veg/non-veg and Chinese food.

There's nothing much to distinguish between Allahabad's handful of proper restaurants, which try to cover every possible base by offering veg/non-veg Indian, Chinese and Continental fare. They feel rather bland after dining outdoors at the stalls, and none serve alcohol.

El Chico is arguably the best of the bunch, though meals are not cheap at Rs 40 to Rs 75. It also has a good pastry and sweet shop.

RR's and **Tandoor** focus more closely on Indian food. Main dishes are Rs 30 to Rs 60 in the former and Rs 45 to Rs 65 in the latter.

Hot Stuff is a western-style fast-food joint with pizzas for Rs 35, burgers and a good range of ice cream.

UTTAR PRADESH

There are many basic restaurants in the old town, plus several dhaba places close to the railway station along Dr Katju Rd. The bar in the Tourist Bungalow in Civil Lines is a cosy place to sink a beer.

Getting There & Away
Allahabad is a good place from which to travel to Khajuraho, since there are numerous express trains to Satna (four hours, Rs 47/204). The *Patna-Kurla Express* leaves at 7.40 am, leaving plenty of time to catch a bus from Satna to Khajuraho (four hours). Buses from Allahabad to Satna take several hours longer than express trains.

There are no flights to Allahabad; the nearest airport is at Varanasi.

Bus From the Civil Lines bus stand, beside the Tourist Bungalow, there are regular buses to Varanasi (three hours, Rs 37), Lucknow (five hours, Rs 66), Faizabad (five hours, Rs 53) and Gorakhpur (eight hours, Rs 89) via Jaunpur. There are three buses to Sunauli (12 hours, Rs 120) if you're heading to Nepal.

Train The main railway station is Allahabad Junction, in the centre of the city. There are connections to Varanasi (three hours, Rs 36/170 in 2nd/1st class) and Lucknow (four hours, Rs 34/160). There are also expresses to Delhi (10 hours, Rs 163/556 in sleeper/1st class), Calcutta (15 hours, Rs 195/669) and Mumbai (24 hours, Rs 261/951).

Getting Around
There are plenty of cycle and auto-rickshaws for hire. Use the back exit at Allahabad Junction railway station to reach Civil Lines. A cycle-rickshaw from the railway station to the Civil Lines bus stand costs only a couple of rupees. It's a Rs 12 cycle-rickshaw ride from the railway station to the fort and Rs 6 from MG Rd to Anand Bhavan.

AROUND ALLAHABAD
Bhita
Excavations at this site on the Yamuna River, 18km south of Allahabad, have revealed the remains of an ancient fortified city. Layers of occupation dating from the Gupta period (320-455 AD) back to the Mauryan period (321-184 BC) and perhaps even earlier have been uncovered. There's a museum with stone and metal seals, coins and terracotta statues. It's best to get here from Allahabad by taxi.

Garwha
The ruined temples in this walled enclosure are about 50km south-west of Allahabad, eight km from Shankargarh – the last three km have to be completed on foot.

The major temple has 16 beautifully carved stone pillars, and inscriptions reveal that the temples date back to the Gupta period at the very least. Some of the better sculptures from Garwha are now on display in the State Museum in Lucknow. Transport connections to Shankargarh are not good, so consider hiring a taxi in Allahabad.

Kausambi
This ancient Buddhist centre, once known as Kosam, is 63km south-west of Allahabad on the way to Chitrakut. It was the capital of King Udaya, a contemporary of the Buddha, and the Enlightened One is said to have preached several sermons here. There's a huge **fortress** near the village which contains the broken remains of an **Ashoka pillar**, minus any pre-Gupta period inscriptions. Buses depart irregularly from Allahabad's Leader Rd bus stand.

Chitrakut
It was here that Brahma, Vishnu and Siva are believed to have been 'born' and taken on their incarnations, which makes this town a popular Hindu pilgrimage place. **Bathing ghats** line the Mandakini River and there are over 30 temples in the town. UP Tourism has a *Tourist Bungalow* here, and there are a number of other cheap hotels and basic restaurants. The town is close to the border with Madhya Pradesh, 132km from Allahabad and 195km from Khajuraho. Buses depart from Allahabad's Zero Rd bus stand.

FAIZABAD

Pop: 207,600   Tel Area Code: 0527

Faizabad was once the capital of Avadh but rapidly declined after the death of Bahu Begum, the wife of Nawab Shuja-ud-Daula. Most of the Islamic buildings in Faizabad were built at her behest, and her mausoleum is said to be the finest of its type in Uttar Pradesh. Her husband also has an impressive mausoleum. There are three large mosques in the market (chowk) area and pleasant gardens in Guptar Park, where the temple from which Rama is supposed to have disappeared stands. The town makes a convenient base for visiting nearby Ayodhya.

Places to Stay & Eat

There are a couple of good hotels in the Civil Lines area, about 1½km west of the chowk, but both are on the main Lucknow to Gorakhpur road so avoid the front rooms. If your pack isn't too heavy you can walk to the hotels from the bus stand; the railway station is a Rs 5 cycle-rickshaw ride away.

Hotel Shan-e-Awadh (☎ 813586) is a clean, efficiently run place where singles/ doubles with attached bath and hot water cost from Rs 120/150 and air-con rooms are Rs 395/450. Its restaurant turns out decent veg/non-veg and Chinese fare and has coffee so frothy you could mistake it for a cappuccino if you've been in India long enough.

Hotel Tirupati (☎ 813231) next door is also good value with rooms with attached bath and hot water from Rs 120/150 and air-con rooms for Rs 350/450. It also has a restaurant.

Abha Hotel (☎ 812550) is the best of several places on a side street near the Majestic cinema in the chowk area. It has acceptable rooms with attached bath for Rs 100/135, a veg/non-veg restaurant and a large contingent of monkeys. It's a Rs 10 cycle-rickshaw ride from the railway station and Rs 5 from the bus stand.

Getting There & Away

Faizabad has fairly good train connections, including expresses to Lucknow (three hours, Rs 27/139 in 2nd/1st class) and Varanasi (four to six hours, Rs 49/223).

There are numerous buses from the quiet bus stand on the Lucknow-Gorakhpur Rd, 750m west of Hotel Shan-e-Awadh. Connections include Gorakhpur (three hours, Rs 35), Lucknow (three hours, Rs 41), Allahabad (five hours, Rs 53) and Sunauli (Rs 76). Tempos to Ayodhya (Rs 3.50) depart from the main road, about 50m from the clock tower in the chowk area.

AYODHYA

Pop: 48,000   Tel Area Code: 05276

Ayodhya, six km from Faizabad, is one of Hinduism's seven holy cities. It's a major pilgrimage centre since it is not only the birthplace of Rama, it's also connected with many events in the *Ramayana*. Unfortunately, its name has become synonymous with rising Hindu fanaticism since the fateful day on 6 December 1992 when a Hindu mob destroyed a mosque they believed had been built on the site of a temple marking Rama's birthplace. The event sent shock waves throughout India and threatened the nation's secular framework.

The Atharaveda described Ayodhya as 'a city built by gods and being as prosperous as paradise itself' although today it's just a small, dusty town with an amazing abundance of temples and monkeys. It sees few foreigners, and anyone intending to visit should keep an eye on the latest developments in the temple-mosque saga. Give the town a wide berth if there's rioting.

Babri Masjid – Ram Janam Bhumi

The **Babri Masjid** was constructed on the site of Rama's birth by the Mughals in the 15th century. The mosque was little used and was eventually closed to Muslims by the civil authorities and limited Hindu *puja* was permitted inside.

By 1990, Rama had been appropriated by Hindu fundamentalists to justify their calls for a Hindu India. Their plans to build a temple to Rama (the Ram Mandir) in place of the mosque led to outbreaks of violence

UTTAR PRADESH

between local Hindus and Muslims. A fragile court order called for the maintenance of the status quo and armed guards surrounded the mosque and attempted to keep the two communities apart.

In late 1992, a Hindu mob stormed the site and destroyed the Babri Masjid, erecting a small Hindu shrine known as **Ram Janam Bhumi** in its place. The destruction sparked riots across India and caused unrest in neighbouring Muslim countries.

The government, which owns the site, has promised to build a temple here if it is decided a temple was here before the mosque. In late 1994 the Indian High Court wisely refused to adjudicate on the issue. The matter currently rests with the Allahabad High Court.

There is a massive security presence at the temple/mosque site, since it's the country's most volatile flash point. You will probably be searched. Cameras are prohibited, and you cannot safely deposit them. Carry your passport. Once through the checks, you enter a narrow caged path lined by police.

The site is open between 7 and 10 am and from 2 to 5 pm. From Faizabad, take the small road that turns left off the main Faizabad-Ayodhya road next to the Hanuman temple. If you arrive by tempo, ask the driver to drop you at the Hanuman temple.

Other Attractions
The **Hanumangadhi** is dedicated to Hanuman, who is believed to have lived in a cave here while guarding the Janam Bhumi. It was built within the thick white walls of a fortress and there are good views from the ramparts. There are more than 100 other temples in Ayodhya, including the **Kanak Mandir** and several **Jain shrines.**

Places to Stay
Pathik Niwas Saket (☎ 52435), the UP Tourist Bungalow near the railway station, is the only acceptable place to stay in Ayodhya. Singles/doubles with attached bath cost from Rs 80/100, air-con rooms are Rs 250/300 and a bed in the dorm costs Rs 30. There's a lacklustre vegetarian restaurant and a tourist office.

Getting There & Away
There are regular tempos shuttling along the main road between Ayodhya and Faizabad for Rs 3.50.

SHRAVASTI
The extensive ruins of this ancient city and Jetavana Monastery are near the villages of Saheth-Maheth. Here the Buddha performed the miracle of sitting on a 1000-petalled lotus and multiplying himself a million times while fire and water came from his body. Ashoka was an early pilgrim and left a couple of pillars to commemorate his visit.

The site can be reached from Gonda, 50km north-west of Ayodhya. The nearest railway station is Gainjahwa, on the Gonda-Naugarh-Gorakhpur loop. The nearest large town is 20km away at Balrampur.

Varanasi Region

VARANASI
Pop: 1,279,000   Tel Area Code: 0542
The city of Siva on the bank of the sacred Ganges is one of the holiest places in India. Hindu pilgrims come to bathe in the waters of the Ganges, a ritual which washes away all sins. It is also an auspicious place to die, since expiring here ensures release from the cycle of rebirths and an instant passport to heaven. It's a magical city where the most intimate rituals of life and death take place in public on the city's famous ghats (steps which lead down to the river). It's this accessibility to the practices of an ancient religious tradition that captivates so many visitors.

In the past, the city has been known as Kashi and Benares, but its present name is a restoration of an ancient name meaning the city between two rivers – the Varuna and Asi.

It has been a centre of learning and civilisation for over 2000 years, and claims to be one of the oldest living cities in the world. Mark Twain obviously thought it looked the part when he dropped by on a lecture tour, since he told the world that 'Benares is older than history, older than tradition, older even than legend, and looks twice as old as all of them put together'. The old city does have an antique feel but few buildings are more than a couple of hundred years old thanks to marauding Muslim invaders and Aurangzeb's destructive tendencies.

Orientation

The old city of Varanasi is situated along the western bank of the Ganges and extends back from the riverbank ghats in a labyrinth of alleyways too narrow for traffic. Godaulia is just outside the old city, and Lahurabir is to the north-east, separated from the cantonment by the railway line.

One of the best ways to get your bearings in Varanasi is to remember the positions of the ghats, particularly important ones like Dasaswamedh Ghat. The alleyways of the old city can be disorienting, but the hotels here are well signposted. The big 'international hotels' and the Government of India tourist office are in the cantonment north of Varanasi Junction railway station. The TV tower is the most obvious landmark in this area.

Information

Tourist Offices The best place for information is the friendly Government of India tourist office (☎ 343744) at 15B The Mall in the cantonment. It's open weekdays from 9 am to 5.30 pm, and Saturday from 9 am to 1 pm. The UP tourist office (☎ 43413) in the Tourist Bungalow is a waste of space, but there's a useful tourist information booth at Varanasi Junction railway station.

Money If you're staying in the cantonment, the State Bank of India near the Hotel Surya is the most convenient place to change money, though it's fussy about accepting American Express travellers cheques in pounds sterling. There are also exchange facilities in several upmarket cantonment hotels. If you're staying near Dasaswamedh Ghat, the State Bank of India changes US dollar and pounds sterling Thomas Cook travellers cheques. The lobby of Shanti Guest House has a moneychanger with slightly lower rates who

accepts all major cheques and deals in 35 currencies. The Bank of Baroda and the Andhra Bank on Dasaswamedh Rd provide cash advances on major credit cards.

Post & Communications The Varanasi GPO is a short cycle-rickshaw ride north of the old city. The poste restante here is open from 10 am to 5 pm Monday to Saturday. In the cantonment, there's a post office at the Central Telegraph Office (CTO). You can make international and STD calls from the CTO 24 hours a day.

Visa Extensions The Foreigners' Registration Office is in Srinagar Colony, Siddgiri Bagh, Sigra. Head west along Luxa Rd away from the river and turn right just before the Theosophical Society on the left. Follow this road until it ends at a T-junction; the office is 50m to the right.

Books & Bookshops *Benares: City of Light* by Diana Eck (Princeton University Press) has information on each ghat and temple, and a good introduction to Hinduism. The *Pioneer* is an informative local English-language newspaper. The Universal Book Company in Godaulia is an excellent bookshop.

Medical Services & Police The Heritage Hospital (☎ 313977) is close to the main gate of Benares Hindu University. The closest police station (☎ 330653) to the old city is between the Town Hall and the GPO.

Ghats

Varanasi's principal attraction is the long string of ghats which line the western bank of the Ganges. Most are used for bathing but there are also several 'burning ghats' where bodies are cremated. The best time to visit the ghats is at dawn when the river is bathed in a magical light and pilgrims come to perform puja to the rising sun.

There are over 100 ghats in Varanasi, but Dasaswamedh Ghat is probably the most convenient starting point. A short boat trip from Dasaswamedh to Manikarnika Ghat can be an interesting introduction to the river.

To Mughalsarai (12km)

Kashi Railway Station

Kashi Station Road

To Sarnath

Varanasi City Railway Station

Rajghat Road

Grand Trunk Road

Varanasi River

Ganges River

Deranagar Road

Panch Koshi Road

Lahurabir

Kabir Chaura Marg

Chaitganj Marg

Premchand Marg

Maqbul Alam Road

Queen's College Rd

To Azamgarh, Gorakhpur, Sarnath & Gazipur

Raja Bazar Road

Kaudiya Kon Marg

Patal Nagar

Cantonment

Varanasi Junction Railway Station

Grand Trunk Road

To Allahabad

Vidyapeeth Road

Aurangabad Road

Cantonment Station Road

Station Road

To Airport & Jaunpur

See Godaulia & The Old City Map

OTHER

1 Private buses to Sarnath
2 Foreigner's Registration Office
4 Scindia Ghat
7 Civil Court
9 Indian Airlines
10 Govt of India Tourist Office & Rewarding Tours & Travel
11 TV Tower
12 Central Telegraph Office & Post Office
14 Auto-Rickshaws to Godaulia
15 Bus Stand
21 Sanskrit University
23 Auto-Rickshaws to Sarnath
25 Raj Ghat
26 Prahlad Ghat
27 Trilochan Ghat
28 Gai Ghat
30 Town Hall
31 Police Station
32 GPO
33 Alamgir Mosque
34 Panchganga Ghat
35 Ram Ghat
36 Bharat Mata Temple

40 Foreigner's Registration Office
41 Scindia Ghat
42 Manikarnika Ghat (Burning Ghat)
44 Mir Ghat
45 Dasaswamedh Ghat
46 Rana Ghat
48 Kedar Ghat
49 Harishchandra Ghat (Burning Ghat)
50 Hanuman Ghat
51 Shivala Ghat
53 Anandmayee Ghat
54 Bachraj Ghat
55 Tulsidas Ghat
56 Asi Ghat
57 Durga & Tulsi Manas Temples
58 Nagwa Ghat
59 Heritage Hospital
60 Auto-Rickshaws to Old City
61 Malaviya Bhavan
62 Bharat Kala Bhavan
63 New Vishwanath Temple
64 Ram Nagar Fort & Museum

PLACES TO STAY

3 Hotel Surya, Hotel Shalimar & State Bank of India
4 Hotel Ideal Tops
5 Hotel Clarks Varanasi
6 Hotel Varanasi Ashok
8 Hotel de Paris
13 Hotel Taj Ganges
14 Hotels India, Vaibhav & Temples Town & Palm Springs
16 Hotel Sandona & El Parador
17 Nar Indra
18 Tourist Bungalow, Hotel Relax & Most Welcome Restaurant
19 Hotel Avaneesh
20 Hotel Hindustan International
22 Pradeep Hotel & Poonam Restaurant
24 Hotels Ajaya & Buddha
29 Hotel Barahdari
37 Hotel Varuna
38 Hotel Garden View
39 Hotel Siddarth
52 Sandhya Guest House

PLACES TO EAT

47 Sindhi Restaurant

Varanasi

0   250   500 m

Ram Nagar Road

Pontoon Bridge (Nov-Jun)

Ferry

Ram Nagar Road

University Road

Benares Hindu University

Harishchandra Marg

Asi River

Asi Road

Lanka Road

Sonarpura Road

Durgakund Road

Mandapura Rd

Sheopurwa Marg

Luxa Road

Panch Koshi Road

Alternatively, if the water level is low, you can simply walk from one ghat to the next. This way you're among the throng of people who come to the edge of the Ganges not only for a ritual bath, but to do yoga, offer blessings, buy paan, sell flowers, get a massage, play cricket, have a swim, get a shave, and do their karma good by giving money to beggars.

The city extends from Raj Ghat, near the major road and rail bridge, to Asi Ghat, near the university. The **Asi Ghat** is one of the five special ghats which pilgrims are supposed to bathe at in sequence during the ritual route called Panchatirthi Yatra. The order is Asi, Dasaswamedh, Adi Keshava, Panchganga and finally Manikarnika. Much of the **Tulsidas Ghat** has fallen down towards the river. The **Bachraj Ghat** is Jain and there are three riverbank Jain temples. Many of the ghats are owned by maharajas or other princely rulers, such as the very fine **Shivala Ghat** owned by the Maharaja of Varanasi. The **Dandi Ghat** is the ghat of ascetics known as Dandi Panths, and nearby is the very popular **Hanuman Ghat**.

The **Harishchandra** or Smashan Ghat is a secondary burning ghat. It's one of the oldest ghats in the city. Above the crowded **Kedar Ghat** is a shrine popular with Bengalis and south Indians. **Mansarowar Ghat** was built by Man Singh of Amber and named after the Tibetan lake at the foot of Mt Kailash, Siva's Himalayan home. **Someswar** or Lord of the Moon Ghat is said to be able to heal diseases. The **Munshi Ghat** is very picturesque, while **Ahalya Bai's Ghat** is named after the Maratha woman ruler of Indore.

The **Dasaswamedh Ghat's** name indicates that Brahma sacrificed (*medh*) 10 (*das*) horses (*aswa*) here. It's one of the most important ghats and is conveniently central. Note its statues and the shrine of Sitala, goddess of smallpox.

Raja Man Singh's **Man Mandir Ghat** was built in 1600 but was poorly restored in the last century. The northern corner of the ghat has a fine stone balcony and Raja Jai Singh of Jaipur erected one of his unusual observatories on this ghat in 1710.

The **Mir Ghat** leads to the Nepalese Temple, which has erotic sculptures. The **Jalsain Ghat**, where cremations take place, virtually adjoins **Manikarnika Ghat**, one of the oldest and most sacred in Varanasi. Manikarnika is the main burning ghat and one of the most auspicious places that a Hindu can be cremated. Bodies are handled by outcasts known as *chandal*, and they are carried through the alleyways of the old city to the holy Ganges on a bamboo stretcher swathed in cloth. You'll see huge piles of firewood stacked along the top of the ghat, each log carefully weighed on giant scales so that the price of cremation can be calculated. There are no problems watching cremations, since at Manikarnika death is simply business as usual, but leave your camera at your hotel.

Above the steps here is a tank known as the Manikarnika Well; Parvati is said to have dropped her earring here and Siva dug the tank to recover it, filling the depression with his sweat. The **Charandpaduka**, a slab of stone between the well and the ghat, bears footprints made by Vishnu. Privileged VIPs are cremated at the Charandpaduka. There is also a temple dedicated to Ganesh on the ghat.

Dattatreya Ghat bears the footprint of the Brahmin saint of that name in a small temple nearby. **Scindia Ghat** was originally built in 1830 but was so huge and magnificent that it collapsed into the river and had to be rebuilt. The **Ram Ghat** was built by the Raja of Jaipur. The **Panchganga Ghat**, as its name indicates, is where five rivers are supposed to meet. Dominating the ghat is Aurangzeb's smaller mosque, also known as the Alamgir Mosque, which he built on the site of a large Vishnu temple erected by the Maratha chieftain Beni Madhav Rao Scindia. The **Gai Ghat** has a figure of a cow made of stone upon it. The **Trilochan Ghat** has two turrets emerging from the river, and the water between them is especially holy. **Raj Ghat** was the ferry pier until the road and rail bridge was completed here.

Golden Temple (Vishwanath Temple)

The most sacred temple in Varanasi is dedicated to Vishveswara – Siva as Lord of the

Universe. The current temple was built in 1776 by Ahalya Bai of Indore, and the 800kg of gold plating on the towers, which gives the temple its colloquial name, was provided by Maharaja Ranjit Singh of Lahore some 50 years later. Non-Hindus are not allowed into the temple but can view it from the upper floor of a house across the street.

There has been a succession of Siva temples in the vicinity for at least the past 1500 years, but they were routinely destroyed by Muslim invaders. Aurangzeb continued this tradition, knocking down the previous temple and building his **Great Mosque** over it. Armed guards protect the mosque since the BJP has declared that, after Ayodhya, the mosques at Varanasi and Mathura are its next targets. Be discreet if taking photographs in this area as the soldiers sometimes disapprove.

Next to the Vishwanath Temple is the **Gyan Kupor Well** (Well of Knowledge). The faithful believe drinking its water leads to a higher spiritual plane, though they are prevented from doing so by both tradition and a strong security screen. The well is said to contain the Siva lingam removed from the previous temple and hidden to protect it from Aurangzeb.

Durga Temple

The Durga Temple is commonly known as the Monkey Temple due to the many frisky monkeys that have made it their home. It was built in the 18th century by a Bengali maharani and is stained red with ochre. The small temple is built in north Indian Nagara style with a multi-tiered *sikhara*. Durga is the 'terrible' form of Siva's consort Parvati, so at festivals there are often sacrifices of goats. Non-Hindus can enter the courtyard but not the inner sanctum.

Tulsi Manas Temple

A short walk south of the Durga Temple is the modern marble sikhara-style Tulsi Manas Temple, built in 1964. Its walls are engraved with verses and scenes from the *Ram Charit Manas*, the Hindi version of the *Ramayana*.

Its author, poet Tulsi Das, lived here while writing it.

You can watch figures performing scenes from Hindu mythology on the 2nd floor for Rs 1. The temple is open from 5.30 am to noon and 3.30 to 9 pm.

Benares Hindu University

Varanasi has long been a centre of learning and that tradition is continued today at the Benares Hindu University, built in 1917. It was founded by the great nationalist Pandit Malaviya as a centre for education in Indian art, music, culture and philosophy, and for the study of Sanskrit. The five sq km campus houses the **Bharat Kala Bhavan** which has a fine collection of miniature paintings, sculptures from the 1st to 15th centuries and old photographs of Varanasi. It's open from 11 am to 4.30 pm (7.30 am to 12.30 pm in May and June) but is closed on Sunday. BHU is a 20 minute walk or a short rickshaw ride from the Durga Temple.

Varanasi is an important pilgrimage destination, and the streets are full of sadhus.

New Vishwanath Temple

It's about a 30 minute walk from the gates of the university to the new Sree Vishwanath Temple, which was planned by Pandit Malaviya and built by the wealthy Birla family of industrialists. Pandit Malaviya wished to see Hinduism revived without its caste distinctions and prejudices – accordingly, unlike many temples in Varanasi, this temple is open to all, irrespective of caste or religion. The interior has a Siva lingam and verses from Hindu scriptures inscribed on the walls. The temple is supposed to be a replica of the earlier Vishwanath Temple destroyed by Aurangzeb. It's open between 4 am and noon, and 1 and 9 pm. From Godaulia it costs around Rs 8 by cyclerickshaw or Rs 25 by auto-rickshaw to reach the temple.

Ram Nagar Fort & Museum

On the opposite bank of the river, this 17th century fort is the home of the former Maharaja of Benares. It looks most impressive from the river, though the decrepit planking of the pontoon bridge you cross to reach it is somewhat of a distraction. During the monsoon, access is by ferry. The interesting museum here contains old silver and brocade palanquins for the ladies of the court, gold-plated elephant howdahs, an astrological clock, macabre elephant traps and an armoury of swords and old guns. The fort is open from 9 am to noon and 2 to 5 pm; entry is Rs 4.

Bharat Mata Temple

Dedicated to 'Mother India', this unadorned temple has a marble relief map of India instead of the usual images of gods and goddesses. The temple was opened by Mahatma Gandhi and is worth a visit if you're staying nearby.

Activities

River Trips A boat ride on the Ganges has become one of the must-dos of a visit to Varanasi. It's customary to do the trip early in the morning when the light is particularly atmospheric. Even if you're not staying near the river, it's easy to organise a boat for sunrise as rickshaw-wallahs are keen to get a pre-dawn rendezvous arranged for the trip to the river. Get the rickshaw-wallah to take you to a large ghat such as Dasaswamedh, since there will be a number of boats to choose from. Travellers have reported being taken to smaller ghats where there was only one boat, placing them in a poor bargaining position.

The government rate for hiring a boat capable of holding up to four people is supposedly set at Rs 45 per hour; for a boat that can seat up to 10 people it's Rs 60 per hour. You'll undoubtedly have to remind boatmen of these rates since tourists frequently pay much more. Be sure to agree on a price before getting into a boat.

Swimming If the sight of pilgrims bathing in the Ganges makes you want to have a splash yourself, the following hotels permit non-guests to use their pools: Hotel Hindustan International (Rs 100), Hotel Varanasi Ashok (Rs 100), and Hotel Clarks Varanasi (Rs 150). Clarks has the best pool.

Yoga The Malaviya Bhavan at the university offers courses in yoga and Hindu philosophy. For the less committed, the Shanti Guest House runs morning and evening yoga classes which cost Rs 50.

Steam Baths & Massage The Hotel Surya offers steam baths for just Rs 35, and body massages to men for Rs 100 and to women (inexplicably) for Rs 150. You can get a vigorous head, neck and back massage at Dasaswamedh Ghat for Rs 10.

Organised Tours

Rewarding Tours & Travels (☎ 348546), next to the Government of India tourist office in the cantonment, operates a tour of Varanasi which includes hotel pick-up, a dawn boat ride on the Ganges, visits to several temples and the university, and an excursion to Sarnath. The tour begins at 5.30 am, finishes at 11.30 am and costs Rs 200.

Government guides can be hired at the Government of India tourist office if you want to be shown the city at your own pace.

They cost Rs 345 for a full day and Rs 230 for half a day.

Places to Stay

There are three main accommodation areas in Varanasi: the old city, Lahurabir and the cantonment. Wherever you intend to stay in Varanasi, be firm when giving instructions to your rickshaw-wallah when you first arrive. Since they get paid high commissions, they are keen to direct new arrivals to specific hotels. Don't listen to any nonsense about the hotel of your choice being 'closed', 'full up', 'burnt down' or 'flooded'. For places in the old city, it's better to just ask the rickshaw-wallah for Dasaswamedh Ghat and walk to the hotel from there, since rickshaws won't be able to negotiate the alleyways anyway.

Note that most hotels drop their rates by up to 50% in the low season between April and July.

There's a paying guest scheme in operation in Varanasi if you want to stay with a local family. Contact the Government of India tourist office for details.

Places to Stay – bottom end & middle

Old City & Ghats Area The old city is the place to look for budget hotels if you don't mind living in cramped conditions. The area is certainly the city's most atmospheric and there are several good lodges right on the river with superb views along the ghats. Nearly all the hotels have rooftop terraces to relax on. At the time of writing, several buildings with river views were being converted into three-star hotels so accommodation options may soon be wider.

Vishnu Rest House (no phone) is an excellent place right on the bank of the river. It's more spacious than most hotels in this area and has terraces offering great views of the river. Fine singles with attached bath cost Rs 60 and doubles between Rs 90 and Rs 150. Don't confuse it with the Real Vishnu Guest House or various other similarly named lodges which deliberately try to feed off its success.

Kumiko House Pension (☎ 324308) is another good place. It has only four small rooms and a dorm but is spotlessly clean and has excellent views. It's run by a friendly Japanese woman and her Indian husband and is extremely popular with Japanese travellers. A space in the dorm will set you back only Rs 20. Singles/doubles with common bath cost Rs 50/100 and a double with attached bath Rs 150. Check what time the door is locked if you're venturing out for the night.

Sita Guest House (no phone) also has fine river views from some rooms though it's not as well run as its neighbours. Rooms with common bath cost from Rs 60/150 and doubles with attached bath and hot water Rs 250.

Scindhia Guest House (☎ 320319), to the north of this area, has clean rooms with superb views over Scindia Ghat. It charges Rs 80/100 with common bath and Rs 100/125 for attached bath and hot water in the morning and evening. Doubles with attached bath, a balcony and air-cooling go for Rs 175. The management is not keen on drug use. Some travellers have found the hotel unwelcoming.

Alaknanda Guest House (☎ 327177), just north of Dasaswamedh Ghat, is a good place to try if the above establishments are full and you desperately want a room with a view. Fairly rudimentary rooms with attached bath costs Rs 60/90, or there are doubles with river views, air-coolers and hot water for Rs 150.

You don't need a river view to enjoy the old city and many travellers prefer the places in the alleys set back from the ghats.

Yogi Lodge (☎ 322588) has long been a favourite with budget travellers and it's efficiently run by a friendly family. Dorm beds cost from Rs 30, and small rooms with common bath cost from Rs 60/80. Like many other popular hotels in the old city, its success has spawned countless similarly named inferior places.

Golden Lodge nearby is a quiet place with basic rooms with common bath for Rs 50 and doubles with attached bath and hot water for Rs 75. Checkout is 10.30 am.

Sri Venkateswar Lodge (☎ 322357), behind the Siva temple on Dasaswamedh Ghat

Rd, is a quiet place with vibrantly painted blue rooms. It charges Rs 50/80 for a room with common bath and from Rs 120 for doubles with attached bath and hot water. The management is helpful and not overly keen on noxious substances.

Trimurti Guest House (☎ 323554) is very popular and good value with dorm beds for Rs 25, rooms with common bath for Rs 40/60 and doubles with attached bath and hot water for Rs 80.

Shanti Guest House (☎ 322568) is just off an alleyway leading to Manikarnika Ghat. It's very popular and has a 24 hour rooftop restaurant that has great views of the old city and the river. Spartan rooms with common bath start from Rs 30/50. Doubles with attached bath and lukewarm water go for between Rs 100 and Rs 150. Unfortunately the place has few outward facing windows and the slightest noise reverberates through the building – you'll certainly know about it when your neighbour decides to go for a dawn boat ride or suddenly gets the runs.

Sandhya Guest House (☎ 313292) is just a few minutes walk from Shivala Ghat, and in a quiet location by the Shivala post office. It's run by a friendly, helpful manager and has an eating area on the roof where you can chow down on home-made soups and brown bread. Clean rooms with common bath cost Rs 50/60 and with attached bath Rs 60/90. You can sleep on the roof on a bedroll for 'whatever you feel like paying'.

Godaulia The hotels on or near Dasaswamedh Ghat Rd are a bit more spacious but less interesting than those in the alleyways of the old city. Try to avoid rooms that front onto the main road as this area is noisy.

Seema Hotel (☎ 352686) has clean singles/doubles with attached bath and hot water for Rs 200/250 and air-con rooms for Rs 400/450.

Hotel Samman (☎ 322241) is better value. Basic but fine rooms with attached bath start from Rs 70/120. Checkout time is 24 hours.

Tripti Hotel (☎ 322346) is also good value, with a fine terrace and clean rooms with

common bath for just Rs 35/70 and doubles with attached bath for Rs 90.

Hotel Ganges (☎ 321097) is a large, characterless hotel, slightly overpriced at Rs 150/215 for rooms with attached bath and Rs 325/425 with air-con.

Lahurabir Area The Lahurabir area is not particularly interesting and is inconveniently located for anything other than the railway station and bus terminal. However it does have several good-value budget and mid-priced hotels, so may be to your liking if you want to keep out of the crush of the old city.

Hotel Buddha (☎ 343686) is the best low-budget hotel in the area. It's in a nice old building set back from the road and it has high ceilings and a verandah. Spartan but spacious singles/doubles with attached bath and hot water cost from Rs 100/150. There are also a few tiny rooms with common bath for Rs 80/100. The hotel food is pretty good and sensibly priced, and the staff are friendly and helpful.

Hotel Ajaya (☎ 343707), in front of the Hotel Buddha, has clean, pleasant rooms with attached bath for Rs 140/200 and air-cooled rooms for Rs 250/300. Checkout is based on the 24 hour system.

Hotel Avaneesh (☎ 350730) on Station Rd is a modern place with small but comfortable air-con rooms from Rs 300/375.

Pradeep Hotel (☎ 344963) is a three-star establishment offering some good rooms with attached bath, hot water and TV from Rs 300/350 and air-con rooms for Rs 500/600.

Hotel Barahdari (☎ 330040) is east of Lahurabir, not far from the GPO, and only a short walk from the alleyways of the old city. It's well run by a friendly Jain family and has a vegetarian restaurant and a peaceful garden. Comfortable, air-cooled rooms with attached bath, hot water and TV cost Rs 275/300, and air-con rooms Rs 450/500.

Hotel Varuna (☎ 358524) is in a quiet area south-west of Lahurabir. It's a friendly place that tries hard to please. Decent rooms with attached bath and hot water cost from Rs 150/200, or Rs 400/475 with air-con.

Hotel Siddharth (☎ 358161; fax 352301), on busy Vidyapeeth Rd, lacks atmosphere but has quality rooms with attached bath, hot water and TV for Rs 225/300, or Rs 375/450 with air-con.

Hotel Garden View (☎ 362716) nearby has neither a view nor a garden but it has a friendly manager and some travellers seem to like it. Rooms with attached bath and hot water start from Rs 175/200.

Railway Station Area There are lots of cheap hotels close to Varanasi Junction railway station if you need to be close to transport options. Most

supply bucket hot water during the cool season.

The *Tourist Bungalow* (☎ 43413) is quite popular since it has a pleasant garden. Dorm beds cost just Rs 30. Singles/doubles with attached bath go for Rs 150/175 and air-con rooms Rs 400/500.

Hotel Relax (☎ 343503) is cheaper, with rooms with attached bath costing from Rs 100/125 and air-cooled rooms Rs 125/175. It has 24 hour checkout and, like the other hotels lining this street, does good business when the Tourist Bungalow is full.

Hotel Sandona (☎ 46555), next to the El

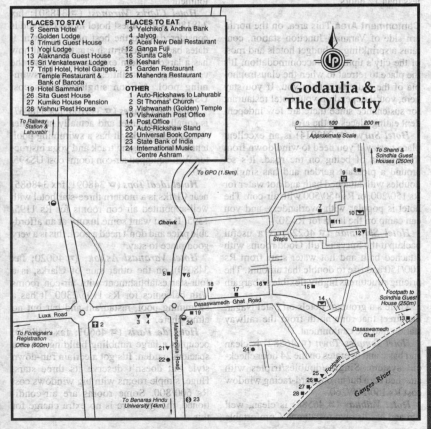

PLACES TO STAY
5 Seema Hotel
7 Golden Lodge
8 Trimurti Guest House
11 Yogi Lodge
13 Alaknanda Guest House
15 Sri Venkateswar Lodge
17 Tripti Hotel, Hotel Ganges, Temple Restaurant & Bank of Baroda
19 Hotel Samman
26 Sita Guest House
27 Kumiko House Pension
28 Vishnu Rest House

PLACES TO EAT
3 Yelchiko & Andhra Bank
4 Jalyog
6 Aces New Deal Restaurant
12 Ganga Fuji
16 Sunita Cafe
21 Keshari
21 Garden Restaurant
25 Mahendra Restaurant

OTHER
1 Auto-Rickshaws to Lahurabir
2 St Thomas' Church
9 Vishwanath (Golden) Temple
10 Vishwanath Post Office
14 Post Office
20 Auto-Rickshaw Stand
22 Universal Book Company
23 State Bank of India
24 International Music Centre Ashram

Godaulia & The Old City

0   100   200 m
Approximate Scale

To Railway Station & Lahurabir

To GPO (1.5km)

Chowk

Steps

Luxa Road

Dasaswamedh Ghat Road

Mandarpura Road

To Foreigner's Registration Office (600m)

To Benares Hindu University (4km)

To Shanti & Scindhia Guest Houses (250m)

Footpath to Scindhia Guest House (250m)

Dasaswamedh Ghat

Ganges River

UTTAR PRADESH

Parador restaurant, has clean, spartan singles/doubles/triples with attached bath for Rs 100/150/200 – about the cost of a main course next door.

Nar Indra (☎ 343586) is one of several hotels lining the noisy Grand Trunk Rd, right outside the railway station. Clean, simple rooms with TV cost Rs 100/125 with common bath, Rs 155/210 with attached bath and Rs 300/350 with air-con. It has 24 hour checkout and a veg/non-veg restaurant.

The *retiring rooms* at Varanasi Junction railway station have dorm beds for Rs 25, rooms for Rs 60/115 and air-con doubles for Rs 160. Rates drop by about 40% if you stay less than 12 hours.

Cantonment Area This area, on the northern side of Varanasi Junction station, contains a sprinkling of budget hotels and most of the city's upmarket accommodation. It's the place to retreat to when the claustrophobia of the old city gets to you. If you stay here, you'll depend on your hotel restaurant for sustenance since there are few independent eating places in the area.

Hotel Surya (☎ 343014) is an excellent place to stay if you need to wind down from the rigours of being on the road. It's set around a pleasant garden and has singles/doubles with attached bath and hot water for Rs 150/200, or Rs 450/500 with air-con. The hotel is popular with overlanders, and you can camp on the lawn for Rs 30.

Hotel Shalimar (☎ 46227) is a useful backup if the Surya is full. Good rooms with attached bath and hot water start from Rs 100/150 and rise to double that amount. The pricing structure is highly flexible so bargain hard.

There's a group of hotels on Patel Nagar, the street that runs north from the railway station into the cantonment.

Hotel Temples Town (☎ 46582) is clean and basic and operates on the 24 hour checkout system. Singles/doubles/triples with attached bath but no outward-facing window cost Rs 150/200/260.

Hotel Vaibhav (☎ 46588) is clean, well run and has its own restaurant. Comfortable rooms with attached bath, hot water and TV cost Rs 250/350 and air-con rooms Rs 375/450.

Hotel India (☎ 342912) is more upmarket, though some of the cheaper rooms lack windows. Rooms with attached bath and hot water start from Rs 300/400. Air-con rooms with bathtubs start from Rs 500/600 and rise to Rs 700/950 in the semi-luxurious modern wing. The hotel has an excellent restaurant, a cellar bar and a scrappy rooftop eating area.

Places to Stay – top end
Nearly all the top-end hotels are in the cantonment.

Hotel Clarks Varanasi (☎ 348501; fax 348186) is the oldest hotel in the city and is considered to be the best place in town. It dates back to the British era, though it now has a large modern extension. It boasts the usual range of facilities plus a good swimming pool. Air-con singles/doubles cost US$80/90.

Hotel Taj Ganges (☎ 345100; fax 348067) is equally upmarket and actually has better rooms than Clarks. It has a swimming pool, tennis court, jogging track and yoga instructor. Well-equipped air-con rooms cost US$95/110.

Hotel Ideal Tops (☎ 348091; fax 348685) near Clarks is a modern three-star hotel with well-appointed air-con rooms for Rs 1195/1395. If you want some luxury at an affordable price and don't need a pool, this is a very good place to stay.

Hotel Varanasi Ashok (☎ 46020; fax 348089), on the other side of Clarks, is a four-star establishment with air-con rooms with balconies for Rs 1195/2300. It has a swimming pool, restaurant and bar but no atmosphere.

Hotel de Paris (☎ 46601; fax 348520) occupies a large rambling building set in a spacious garden. It's got a certain run-down style but doesn't deserve its three stars. Huge, simple rooms with big windows cost Rs 600/800. Some rooms are air-conditioned, though there is no extra charge for this.

Hotel Hindustan International (☎ 351484; fax 350931) is the only luxury hotel outside the cantonment. It's a modern four-star concrete block in the centre of the city offering air-con rooms for US$38/70. Facilities include a swimming pool, a massage centre, a snug bar and a restaurant where your stomach will feel a lot more stable if you don't concentrate on the decor.

Places to Eat
Godaulia & the Old City The food in the old city is pretty uninspiring and standards of hygiene are not all that they might be. Cafes offer a standard travellers' menu consisting of western breakfasts and snacks that mostly involve giving their jaffle machine a serious work out. Indian food tends to be oily and there are plenty of restaurants where no matter what you order, every dish that comes out of the kitchen looks exactly the same. On the other hand, Varanasi is well known for its sweets and high quality paan. The alleyways of the old city are full of shops offering ample opportunity to indulge in either. If you arrive during mango season, try the locally grown variety known as Langda Aam.

Shanti Guest House, *Yogi Lodge*, *Trimurti Guest House* and *Vishnu Rest House* all have restaurants popular with travellers. Shanti and Vishnu both have excellent views.

Ganga Fuji, not far from the Golden Temple, is a snug place offering western breakfasts and Indian, Chinese and Japanese meals for between Rs 25 and Rs 30. There's live classical Indian music in the evenings.

Aces New Deal Restaurant has been popular with travellers for snacks and breakfast for years. The menu is extremely varied, as are the reports about the food. It has a ramshackle courtyard with a rustic view of a bullock yard.

Garden Restaurant is a relaxing little rooftop eatery with the usual travellers' menu. It also has veg/non-veg Indian food for between Rs 20 and Rs 35.

Mahendra Restaurant is the first cafe to score a river frontage at a ghat. It's a modest little operation with just a few outdoor tables and benches near the cluster of riverfront lodges upstream from Dasaswamedh Ghat. It opens at 6.30 am, which is handy for those out and about on the river at dawn.

There's a number of eateries along Dasaswamedh Ghat Rd offering Indian food.

Jalyog by the main roundabout in Godaulia has Indian-style breakfasts of puris and vegetables, known as kachauri. The place's sign is mainly in Hindi but as it was established nearly 100 years ago everyone knows where it is. Its samosas (Rs 2) may well be the best thing you eat while in Varanasi.

Keshari, down a small alley off Dasaswamedh Ghat Rd, is spotlessly clean and has an extensive menu offering veg/non-veg meals and snacks. Main dishes are around Rs 25.

Temple Restaurant in the Hotel Ganges has an interesting 1st floor view of Dasaswamedh Ghat Rd. It serves good veg/non-veg Indian fare, Chinese food and western breakfasts. Most main dishes are between Rs 20 and Rs 40.

Sunita Cafe is a modest vegetarian eatery in an alley off Dasaswamedh Ghat Rd serving good masala dosa, snacks and light meals. Nothing costs over Rs 14.

Yelchiko is a basement restaurant-cum-bar serving standard Indian-Chinese-Continental fare for between Rs 25 and Rs 45. Its popularity has less to do with the quality of the food and more to do with the fact that it's the only restaurant around the old city where you can get a beer (Rs 55).

Sindhi Restaurant in Bhelupura, near the Lalita Cinema, prepares good vegetarian food. Rickshaw-wallahs all know the cinema but not the restaurant.

Railway Station & Lahurabir Areas There are several places to choose from in these areas.

Most Welcome Restaurant, near the Tourist Bungalow, is a cute little eatery with cheap veg/non-veg fare and western breakfasts. Prices are between Rs 15 and Rs 25. It claims to be recommended by all the guide books of the world, which is pretty good for a place no bigger than the average western kitchen.

The *Tourist Bungalow* has a dull veg/non-veg restaurant with reasonable food and a bar.

The *Poonam Restaurant* in the Pradeep Hotel has decent Indian food, good service and charges between Rs 45 and Rs 85 for main dishes.

Hotel Buddha has a pleasant terrace and garden restaurant, serving reasonably priced veg/non-veg fare, western breakfasts and snacks. There are a few basic dhaba-type places in the street behind the hotel if you want cheap Indian food.

El Parador is the neighbourhood's gastronomy centre. It has an eclectic menu offering Greek, Mexican and Italian dishes. Its insistence on using only the finest available ingredients explains the pricey Rs 100 to Rs 130 for main courses.

Cantonment Area Hotel restaurants are the best bet in this area.

Canton Restaurant at the Hotel Surya serves good veg/non-veg fare, western standbys and, despite its name, just a few Chinese dishes. The restaurant overlooks the hotel garden and a lazy breakfast on the lawn makes a great start to the day. The staff are friendly and extremely efficient. Mains are between Rs 35 and Rs 50; beer is a tad pricey at Rs 70.

Palm Springs in the Hotel India has excellent Indian cuisine. A full meal costs under Rs 100 per head but it's worth every paise. If you can order the Huggy Buggy without laughing hysterically you should win a prize.

Hotel Clarks and the *Hotel Taj Ganges* are the places to go if you want to dine in style.

Entertainment

Varanasi is not renowned for its nightlife. About the only choice, other than the cinemas showing Bollywood fare, are the classical music recitals held at 8 pm on Wednesday and Saturday at the *International Music Centre Ashram* not far from Dasaswamedh Ghat. Major classical concerts are also occasionally held at *Nagari Natak Mandali*. Check the *Pioneer* for details.

If you are distressed about the lack of entertainment options, the Government Bhang Shop may alleviate your concern with hash cookies for Rs 30 and opium chocolate Rs 20. It's on the way to the Shanti Guest House from the chowk.

Things to Buy

Varanasi is famous throughout India for silk brocades and beautiful Benares saris. However, there are lots of rip-off merchants and commission people at work. Invitations to 'come to my home for tea' will inevitably mean to somebody's silk showroom, where you will be pressured into buying things.

There's a market west of the GPO called Golghar where the makers of silk brocades sell directly to local shops. You can get cheaper silk brocade in this area than in the big stores in the chowk area, but you must be careful about the quality. Mixtures of silk and cotton can look very like pure silk to the untrained eye. Pilikothi, a Muslim area north-east of the GPO, also has good silk.

Varanasi is also renowned for its ingenious toys, musical instruments and expensive Bhadohi carpets. There's a range of local products in the fixed-price Cottage Industries Exposition in the cantonment but since it's opposite the Hotel Taj Ganges the prices aren't fixed at the bottom end of the market.

Getting There & Away

Air Varanasi is on the popular daily tourist shuttle route linking Khajuraho (US$60), Agra (US$80) and Delhi (US$95). There are also four Indian Airlines flights a week to Lucknow (US$50) and Mumbai (US$190). The Indian Airlines office (☎ 345959) is in the cantonment near the Hotel de Paris. Office hours are 10 am to 1.15 pm, and 2 to 5 pm.

Sahara India Airlines (☎ 343094) has daily flights to Mumbai except Saturday and flights to Delhi and Lucknow daily except Sunday.

Bus Varanasi's bus stand is a few hundred metres north-east of Varanasi Junction railway station. It's a fairly sleepy depot and there's no timetable information in English. There are frequent express buses to Jaunpur

DAVID COLLINS

PAUL BEINSSEN

Varanasi
Top: Dawn breaks over the river and the ghats.
Bottom Left: Boating on the still waters of the holy Ganges.

RICHARD I'ANSON

BRUCE MITCHELL

MARK DAFFEY

Taj Mahal
Top Left: Detail of the Taj's delicate pietra dura work.
Top Right: The Taj draws pilgrims and tourists alike.
Bottom: The majestic symmetry of India's best-known monument.

(1½ hours, Rs 20), Allahabad (three hours, Rs 37), Lucknow (8½ hours, Rs 90), Faizabad (seven hours, Rs 66) and Gorakhpur (6½ hours, Rs 69).

No buses run direct to Khajuraho so take a train to Satna and a bus to Khajuraho (four hours) from there.

Train Varanasi Junction (also known as Varanasi Cantonment) is the main station. Foreign tourist quota tickets can be purchased at a ticket office near the UP Tourism information booth in the main station building. This office is open daily except Sunday between 10 am and 5 pm. If it's closed, go to the separate reservation centre building on the left as you approach the station. It's open Monday to Saturday from 8 am to 8 pm, and on Sunday from 8 am to 2 pm.

Not all trains between Delhi and Calcutta stop at Varanasi Junction but most halt at

Mughalserai, 12km south of Varanasi. This is a 45 minute ride by bus (Rs 3), tempo (Rs 10) or auto-rickshaw (Rs 50) along a congested stretch of the Grand Trunk Road. You can make reservations at Varanasi Junction railway station for trains leaving from Mughalserai.

Travellers should keep a close eye on their baggage while on trains heading to Varanasi. The tourist information booth at Varanasi Junction reckons hardly a day goes by without a traveller arriving on the platform without their backpack.

To/From Nepal There are regular ordinary buses from Varanasi's bus stand to Sunauli (eight hours, Rs 91) and deluxe buses (eight hours, Rs 130) at 10 am and 10 pm. Plenty of travel agents and lodges offer 'through' tickets to Kathmandu and Pokhara (Rs 300). This involves spending a night in spartan

Major Trains from Varanasi

Destination	Train Number & Name	Departure Time *	Distance (km)	Duration (hours)	Fare (Rs) (2nd/1st)
Calcutta	2382 Poorva Exp	5.00 am V	678	11.00	167/590
	3010 Doon Exp	4.15 pm V		15.00	
Chennai (Madras)	6040 Ganga Kaveri Exp	5.45 pm V	2144	41.00	321/1344
Delhi	2301 Rajdhani Exp**	12.38 am MS	764	9.00	710/2005
	2381 Poorva Exp	8.00 pm V	792	12.00	186/649
	4057 Kashi Vishwanath Exp	2.00 pm V		16.30	186/649
Gorakhpur	5104 Intercity Exp	5.50 am V	231	5.00	57/252
Lucknow	4227 Varuna Exp	5.25 am V	302	4.30	72/318
Mumbai (Bombay)	1066 Ratnagiri Exp	5.45 pm V	1509	28.00	276/1026
	1028 Dadar-Gorakhpur Exp	11.05 am V		33.00	
New Jalpaiguri	5652 Lohit Exp	6.35 pm MS	848	15.00	198/670
Patna	3484 Farrakka Exp	3.20 pm V	228	5.30	56/249
Puri	8476 Neelachal Exp	8.05 pm V	1061	23.00	229/796
Satna	5218 Kurla Exp	2.50 pm V	236	7.00	57/252

* Abbreviations for train stations: V – Varanasi Junction, MS – Mughalserai
** Air-con only; fare includes meals and drinks

All trains run daily except:
Ratnagiri 1066 only Tue/Thur/Fri
Ganga Kaveri 6040 only Mon/Wed
Poorva 2381 only Wed/Thur/Sun
Poorva 2382 only Mon/Tue/Fri
Rajdhani 2301 only Mon/Tue/Wed/Fri/Sat
Neelachal 8476 only Tue/Fri/Sun

accommodation in Sunauli and a change of buses at the border. Doing it yourself is not only cheaper but gives you a choice of accommodation and buses at the border.

It's not worth catching a train to the border since the line from Gorakhpur to Sunauli is metre gauge, though you could catch an express train to Gorakhpur and pick up a bus to Sunauli from there.

Indian Airlines has a daily flight to Kathmandu (US$71), but it can be difficult getting a seat. If you can't get on the plane and don't want to experience the long bus journey, Rewarding Tours & Travels (☎ 348546) can arrange a car to Kathmandu for up to four people for US$225. The trip takes 12 hours.

Getting Around
The Airport Babatpur Airport is 22km northwest of the city. A bus runs from the Vaibhav Hotel in the cantonment at 10.30 am and 2.30 pm via the Government of India tourist office and the Indian Airlines office. It also operates at irregular hours according to the Indian Airlines schedule. The fare is Rs 25 and it takes around 45 minutes. Telephone ☎ 46477 for reservations. If you bargain hard you should get an auto-rickshaw to the airport for around Rs 70. In the opposite direction, rickshaw-wallahs charge only Rs 25 since they assume they'll pick up a commission at the hotel where they drop you. Taxis charge around Rs 125 to the airport, but ask for at least twice as much.

Bus Local buses are very crowded unless you can get on at the starting point. Godaulia is the midtown bus stop, just an easy walk from the ghats. Lanka is the bus stop closest to Benares Hindu University. Between the railway station and Godaulia, a bus costs around Rs 1.

Auto-Rickshaw & Tempo These operate on a share basis with fixed prices (Rs 1 to Rs 3) along set routes. They can be the best way to get around the city cheaply, although not when you have hefty baggage. You can, of course, still hire an auto-rickshaw for a

'private' trip but you'll have to agree a price since they do not have meters.

From the stand outside the northern entrance of Varanasi Junction railway station it's Rs 2 (share) or Rs 7 (private) to the cantonment TV tower. There's a stand outside the southern entrance for destinations including Lahurabir and Godaulia (Rs 5 share, Rs 20 private).

The Varanasi Hotel Association is attempting to establish a prepaid taxi and auto-rickshaw stand at the railway station to curb hassles on arrival.

Cycle-Rickshaw & Bicycle It won't take long walking the streets before you start perceiving yourself as transport bait for cycle-rickshaw-wallahs. Figures quoted for trips usually start five times the price instead of just double, and some rickshaw-wallahs in the cantonment are cheeky enough to quote prices in US dollars. A trip between the railway station and Dasaswamedh Ghat should cost about Rs 10. From the cantonment hotels to Dasaswamedh Ghat is around Rs 15 and to Lahurabir around Rs 7.

SARNATH
The Buddha came to this hamlet, 10km north-east of Varanasi, to preach his message of the 'middle way' to nirvana after he achieved enlightenment at Bodhgaya. Later, the great Buddhist emperor Ashoka erected magnificent stupas and monasteries here.

Sarnath was at its peak when the indefatigable Chinese traveller Fa Xien visited the site early in the 5th century AD. When Hiuen Tsang, another Chinese traveller, dropped by in 640 AD, Sarnath had 1500 priests, a stupa nearly 100m high, Ashoka's mighty stone pillar and many other wonders. The city was known as the Deer Park, after the Buddha's famous first sermon, *The Sermon in the Deer Park*.

Soon after, Buddhism went into decline and when Muslim invaders destroyed and desecrated the city's buildings, Sarnath became little more than a shell. It was not until 1836 when British archaeologists started excavations that Sarnath regained some of its past glory. It's now a major Buddhist centre.

Most of Sarnath's monuments are set in landscaped gardens, making it a pleasant place to spend half a day. During the Buddha Purnima Festival in May, Sarnath celebrates the birth of the Buddha with a big fair and a procession. Although you may be able to arrange to stay in some of Sarnath's monasteries, you'd be better off going to Bodhgaya or Dharamsala if you're interested in studying Buddhism.

Dhamekh Stupa

This 34m stupa dominates the site and is believed to mark the spot where the Buddha preached his famous sermon. In its present form it dates from around 500 AD but was probably rebuilt a number of times. The geometrical and floral patterns on the stupa are typical of the Gupta period, but excavations have revealed brickwork from the Mauryan period – around 200 BC. Originally there was

1 Burmese Monastery	11 Mahabodhi Society
2 Monastery Ruins	12 Auto-Rickshaw &
3 Ashoka Pillar	Tempo Stands
4 Main Shrine	13 Anand
5 Sri Digamber Jain	14 Chinese Monastery
Temple	15 Post Office
6 Dhamekh Stupa	16 Tourist Bungalow
7 Mulgandha Kuti	17 Japanese Monastery
Vihar & Bo Tree	18 Tibetan Monastery
8 Museum Ticket Office	19 Chaukhandi Stupa
9 Thai Monastery	20 Rangoli Garden
10 Archaeological Museum	Restaurant

Sarnath

a second stupa, Dharmarajika Stupa, but this was reduced to rubble by 19th century treasure seekers.

The nearby **Jain temple**, built in 1824, is thought to mark the birthplace of the 11th Jain tirthankar, Shreyanshnath.

Main Shrine & Ashoka Pillar

Ashoka is said to have meditated in the building known as the 'main shrine'. The foundations are all that can now be seen, and to the north of it are the extensive ruins of the monasteries.

Standing in front of the main shrine are the remains of Ashoka's pillar. At one time this stood over 20m high, but the capital is now in the Sarnath Archaeological Museum, significantly shortening the column. An edict issued by Ashoka is engraved on the remaining portion of the column.

Archaeological Museum

The main attraction at this excellent archaeological museum is the superb capital from the Ashokan pillar. It has the Ashokan symbol of four back-to-back lions which has been adopted as the state emblem of modern India. Below this are representations of a lion, elephant, horse and bull. The lion is supposed to represent bravery, the elephant symbolises the dream Buddha's mother had before his birth, and the horse recalls that Buddha left his home on horseback in search of enlightenment.

Other finds from the site include figures and sculptures from Sarnath's Mauryan, Kushana and Gupta periods. Among them is the earliest Buddha image found at Sarnath and many images of Hindu gods dating from the 9th to 12th centuries. The museum is open from 10 am to 4.45 pm daily except Friday; entry is Rs 2.

Mulgandha Kuti Vihar

This modern Mahabodhi Society temple has a series of frescoes by the Japanese artist Kosetsu Nosi in the interior. A bo tree growing here was transplanted in 1931 from the tree in Anuradhapura, Sri Lanka, which in turn is said to be an offspring of the original tree under which the Buddha attained enlightenment. There's a group of statues here showing the Buddha giving his first sermon to his five disciples. The temple is closed between 11.30 am and 1.30 pm.

Other Temples & Deer Park

You can visit the modern temples in the Thai, Chinese, Tibetan, Burmese and Japanese monasteries.

North of the Mulgandha Kuti Vihar is the deer park, where unhappy-looking deer forage in the dust. There are also some Indian birds and waterfowl.

Places to Stay & Eat

The *Tourist Bungalow* has rooms with common bath for Rs 125 and attached bath for Rs 200. There's also a basic dorm costing Rs 35 per bed, and a restaurant serving the standard tourist bungalow fare.

Anand is a basic south Indian snack place. *Rangoli Garden Restaurant* is the place to go if you're looking for something more substantial.

Getting There & Away

Most visitors day trip from Varanasi. An autorickshaw for the 20 minute journey costs Rs 25. Local buses depart frequently from Varanasi's Civil Court (Rs 2) in the cantonment and from Varanasi Junction railway station (Rs 3). A few local trains stop at Sarnath, though currently the only convenient train returning from Sarnath to Varanasi is at 6.40 pm.

CHUNAR

Chunar Fort, overlooking the Ganges, has had a succession of owners representing most of India's rulers over the last 500 years. Sher Shah took it from Humayun in 1540, Akbar recaptured it for the Mughals in 1575 and in the mid-18th century it passed to the nawabs of Avadh. They were shortly followed by the British, whose gravestones here make interesting reading. Chunar's other claim to fame is that Ashoka's edicts were carved onto pillars made from the locally quarried sandstone. Chunar is 36km south-west of Varanasi and can be reached by bus.

JAUNPUR

Pop: 160,000   Tel Area Code: 05452

This bustling town 58km north-west of Varanasi sees few travellers but is of interest to architectural historians for its mosques, which are built in a unique style that is part Islamic and part Hindu and Jain.

Founded by Feroz Shah Tughlaq in 1360 on an ancient site, Jaunpur became the capital of the independent Muslim Sharqui kingdom. The most impressive mosques were constructed between 1394 and 1478. They were built on the ruins of Hindu, Buddhist and Jain temples and shrines, and are notable for their odd mixture of architectural styles, their two storey arcades and large gateways, and their unusual minarets. Jaunpur was sacked by Sikandar Lodi, who left only the mosques undamaged. The Mughals took over in 1530.

The bus stand is south of the Gomti River, a Rs 5 cycle-rickshaw ride from the 16th century stone **Akbari Bridge**, which crosses to the northern part of town where most of the mosques and Jaunpur Junction railway station are located. The sights are spread out over two or three sq km so a cycle-rickshaw can be useful, and the wallahs can also act as guides.

The modest but well-maintained **Jaunpur Fort**, built by Feroz Shah in 1360, overlooks the Gomti River. Continue 500m north of here and you come to the **Atala Masjid**, built in 1408 on the site of a Hindu temple dedicated to Atala Devi. Another 500m northwest is the largest and most impressive of the mosques, the **Jama Masjid**, built between 1438 and 1478.

Other places to see include the **Jhanjhri Masjid**, the **tombs of the Sharqui sultans**, the **Char Ungli Masjid** and the **Lal Darwaza Masjid**.

Places to Stay & Eat

Jaunpur is not set up for visitors, which is why the few travellers who come here tend to day trip from Varanasi.

Hotel Amber (☎ 63201), near the fort, has basic but acceptable singles/doubles with attached bath for Rs 55/70.

The small *dhabas* near Jaunpur Junction railway station and in the bazaars are as fancy as the eating opportunities get.

Getting There & Away

There are regular buses to and from Varanasi (1½ hours, Rs 20). A few express trains connect Jaunpur Junction with Varanasi (1½ hours, Rs 20), Faizabad (three hours, Rs 36) and Lucknow (six hours, Rs 57).

Eastern Uttar Pradesh

GORAKHPUR

Pop: 575,000   Tel Area Code: 0551

Most travellers happily pass straight through Gorakhpur on their way to or from Nepal. This is hardly surprising since the city is infamous for its annual plagues of flies and mosquitoes and even the local tourist office candidly tells visitors 'there are no sights in Gorakhpur'. The city is, however, the head-quarters of the North Eastern Railway and is a useful rail junction.

Gorakhpur is named after the sage Yogi Gorakhnath. The temple that bears his name is a couple of kilometres north-west of the city centre and is worth visiting if you have time to fill in between transport connections. The city is also home to well-known Hindu religious publishers Geeta Press. A visit to their office will result in a pile of invaluable English-language books being offered to you with titles like 'How to lead a household life'. These make excellent presents to friends back home with a sense of humour.

Information

There's a helpful tourist office at the railway station and a less useful one on Park Rd (☎ 335450). The State Bank of India on Bank Rd deals only with US dollar or pounds sterling American Express travellers cheques.

Places to Stay

The best places to stay in Gorakhpur are central and close to the few decent restaurants in the city. It costs Rs 5 to reach them by cycle-rickshaw from the railway station.

Hotel Yark-Inn (☎ 338233) is efficient and friendly and has singles/doubles with attached bath from Rs 80/140 or air-con rooms for Rs 350/400.

Hotel Marina (☎ 337630) has big, clean rooms from Rs 140/175 with attached bath and TV, and air-con doubles from Rs 325. Checkout is 24 hours.

Hotel President (☎ 337654), in front of Hotel Marina, is more expensive but not as good value at Rs 225/300 for rooms with attached bath and TV or Rs 450 for air-con. Checkout is 24 hours.

If you intend to catch the 5 am bus to Sunauli then the hotels opposite the railway station are the closest to the bus stand. Unfortunately they're nothing special and the area can be so noisy that you may not need to set your alarm.

Hotel Elora (☎ 330647) is the best of this bunch if you manage to score one of the

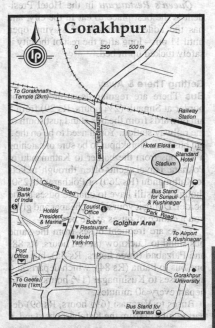

Gorakhpur

0   250   500 m

To Gorakhnath Temple (2km)

Railway Station

Maharana Road

Hotel Elora

Standard Hotel

Stadium

Cinema Road

State Bank of India

Bus Stand for Sunauli & Kushinagar

Park Road

Hotels President & Marina

Tourist Office

Bobi's Restaurant

Golghar Area

To Airport & Kushinagar

Hotel Yark-Inn

Post Office

To Geeta Press (1km)

Gorakhpur University

Bus Stand for Varanasi

rooms at the back. They have balconies overlooking a large playing field and are sheltered from the worst of the noise. They cost from Rs 80/125 with attached bath and TV and Rs 225/300 for air-con. Checkout is 24 hours.

Standard Hotel (☎ 336439) has pleasant rooms with attached bath for Rs 125/150/200. The hotel has the mosquito problem under a semblance of control thanks to netting on the windows, but this can make rooms hot from late March onwards.

The *retiring rooms* at the railway station cost Rs 65/100 with attached bath, and Rs 125/220 with air-con. Dorm beds go for Rs 30.

Places to Eat
There aren't many places in Gorakhpur catering to visitors so you could do worse than try the small outdoor eateries near the railway station.

Bobi's at the Ambar Hotel in the city centre has decent veg/non-veg fare and serves pastries and ice cream.

Queen's Restaurant in the Hotel President is the best place to eat in the city, and has the added advantage of staying open until 11 pm – long after the rest of the city is safely tucked up in bed.

Getting There & Away
Bus There are regular departures for the border at Sunauli (2¾ hours, Rs 29) from 5 am onwards from the bus stand just south of the railway station. You'll need to be on the 5 am bus from Gorakhpur to be sure of catching a day bus from the border to Kathmandu or Pokhara. Travel agents offer 'through' tickets to Kathmandu (Rs 260) or Pokhara (Rs 250) though you still have to change buses at the border. Doing it yourself is cheaper and gives you a choice of buses at the border.

There are frequent buses from the same bus stand to Lucknow (seven hours, Rs 88) and Faizabad (three hours, Rs 35), but only one bus to Patna (Rs 84), which departs at 6 am. Buses to Kushinagar (1½ hours, Rs 16) depart every 30 minutes.

Buses to Varanasi (6½ hours, Rs 69) depart regularly from the Katchari bus stand, a

Rs 4 cycle-rickshaw ride south-east of the city centre.

Train Gorakhpur has direct rail connections with Varanasi (five hours, Rs 57/252 in 2nd/1st class); Lucknow (five to six hours, Rs 65/291); Delhi (15 hours, Rs 188/656 in sleeper/1st class); Calcutta (18 to 22 hours, Rs 202/689); and Mumbai (1690km, 30 to 34 hours, Rs 267/1116).

There are also metre-gauge trains to Nautanwa, which is eight km short of the border at Sunauli. It's much faster and more convenient to get to Sunauli by bus.

KUSHINAGAR
Tel Area Code: 05563
The Buddha is reputed to have breathed his last words, 'Decay is inherent in all component things' and expired at Kushinagar. Pilgrims now come in large numbers to see the remains of his brick **cremation stupa**, the reclining Buddha figure in the **Mahaparinirvana Temple**, the modern **Indo-Japan-Sri Lanka Buddhist Centre** and the numerous Buddhist monasteries here. The tourist office opposite the Myanmar monastery is extremely helpful and makes up for its lack of printed material by being pretty nifty at hand-drawn cartography.

Places to Stay
For a donation you can stay in the Chinese, Myanmar and Tibetan monasteries. If you're on a budget this is your best bet, otherwise be prepared to day trip from Gorakhpur.

Pathik Nivas (☎ 7138), the UP Tourist Bungalow, is in a garden setting and has good but overpriced singles/doubles ranging from Rs 350/450 with attached bath and hot water to superdeluxe air-con rooms for Rs 850/950. Its pricey restaurant charges Rs 30 just for a bottle of water.

Lotus Nikko Hotel (☎ 7239) is a three-star establishment popular with Japanese visitors touring India's Buddhist sites. It charges US$60/110 for its cheapest rooms and boasts a Japanese restaurant and a Japanese bathhouse.

Getting There & Away

Kushinagar is 55km east of Gorakhpur and there are frequent buses (1½ hours, Rs 16) between the two towns. The Kushinagar bus stand is several km from the temples and monasteries, but it's possible to flag down buses heading to Gorakhpur anywhere along the main road.

SUNAULI

Tel Area Code: 05522

This sleepy village straddling the Nepalese border is little more than a bus stop, a couple of hotels, a few shops and a 24-hour border post. There's a much greater range of facilities on the Nepalese side, where the atmosphere is decidedly more upbeat. You're free to wander back and forth between the Indian and Nepalese parts of Sunauli without going through any formalities. Doing this carrying a backpack, however, is likely to attract attention.

The Nepalese border post is actually called Belhiya but everyone refers to it as Sunauli. Nepalese visas are available from the immigration office here between 6.30 am and 7 pm. Visas cost US$15 for 15 days or US$25 for 30 days, payable in US dollars or Nepalese rupees but not in travellers cheques. Make sure you have an encashment certificate if you intend to pay in Nepalese rupees.

The easy-to-miss Indian immigration checkpoint is on the right-hand side of the road heading towards Nepal, about 200m from the border post.

The State Bank of India in Sunauli does not change money, but there are numerous foreign exchange offices on the Nepalese side offering competitive rates. Note that you can pay for bus tickets and just about anything else in Indian rupees on the Nepalese side of the border.

At the time of writing, the exchange rate was Rs 1 = NRs 1.59.

Places to Stay & Eat

Hotel Niranjana (☎ 4901), one of UP Tourism's establishments, is a clean and friendly place 700m from the border. It has singles/doubles with attached bath, hot water and air cooling for Rs 200/225, some air-con rooms for Rs 315/350 and a dorm for Rs 35. The restaurant serves unexciting but acceptable fare.

Sanju Lodge (☎ 4919) is closer to the border post. It's fairly rudimentary but has pleasant common areas and a bed in a clean but crowded dorm costs only Rs 25. Rooms cost Rs 40/60 with common bath and Rs 120/150 with attached bath and hot water.

There are several good, cheap hotels, plenty of open-air restaurants and a sudden blitz of beer advertisements on the Nepalese side of the border, where most travellers prefer to stay.

Getting There & Away

Buses to Indian cities depart from the Sunauli bus stand on the edge of town, about one km from the border post. There are plenty of buses to and from Gorakhpur (2¾ hours, Rs 29) and direct buses to Varanasi (eight hours, Rs 90 to Rs 130) and Lucknow (12 hours, Rs 145).

If you're entering India at Sunauli, be wary of touts offering onward combined bus/rail tickets, since these are not 100% reliable. It's easy enough to arrange onward train travel yourself at the Gorakhpur or Varanasi railway stations.

To/From Nepal Private buses leave from the Nepalese side of the border for Kathmandu roughly every hour between 4.30 and 11.30 am (nine hours, NRs 105), and between 4.30 and 8 pm (11 hours, NRs 132). Buses to Pokhara leave equally regularly between 4.50 and 11 am (nine hours, NRs 105) and also in the evening at 6.45 and 8.30 pm (11 hours, NRs 125). Travelling during the day is preferable – at night it not only takes longer and costs more, you also miss the great views on the journey.

You should get a ticket in advance at the booking office at the bus stand, though you can only buy tickets on the day of your departure. The office opens at 4 am.

Government 'Sajha' buses leave for Kathmandu from Bhairawa, four km north of Sunauli, at 6.45 and 8 am (NRs 104), and at

6.30 and 7 pm (NRs 130). They're very popular and bookings should be made a day in advance. Tickets are sold from a kiosk near the Hotel Yeti in Bhairawa, on the main road from Sunauli. A cycle-rickshaw from the border to Bhairawa costs Rs 2.

There are no government buses to Pokhara. Numerous buses ply the 22km stretch between Bhairawa and Lumbini, the birthplace of the Buddha. They depart from the bus stand , which is about a km north of the Hotel Yeti.

Bihar

Passing along the Ganges in the area that is now Bihar, the Buddha prophesied that a great city would arise here, but that it would always be in danger from 'feud and fire and flood'. Over 250 years later, in the 3rd century BC, Ashoka ruled from Pataliputra, now Patna. It's difficult to imagine that this city, the capital of one of the most backward and depressed states in the country, was then the largest city in the world and capital of the greatest empire in India.

The name Bihar is derived from the word *vihara*, meaning monastery. Bihar was a great religious centre for Jains, Hindus and, most importantly, Buddhists. It was at Bodhgaya that the Buddha sat under the bo tree and attained enlightenment, and a descendant of that original tree still flourishes there today. Nearby Nalanda was a world-famous Buddhist university in the 5th century AD, while Rajgir was associated with both the Buddha and the Jain apostle Mahavira.

Today the Buddha's predictions continue to come true. The rivers periodically flood, causing disastrous problems for Bihar's dense population, which scratches a bare living from the soil. Per capita income is low, yet the Chotanagpur plateau in the south produces 40% of India's mineral wealth. Bihar's literacy rate is one of the lowest in the country, the state is considered to have the most widespread corruption and the state government is chronically short of money. Innovative projects, such as Cowherds' Schools, where boys can bring their cattle with them to classes, have typically failed due to widespread funds skimming. Civil servants and teachers get paid only every now and then – Bihar's teachers recently marched through Patna in their underwear to bring attention to their plight. 'Feud and fire' take the form of outbreaks of inter-caste warfare and violence – *dacoity* (banditry) is still widespread in Bihar.

Few travellers spend much time here, most just passing through Patna on their way

BIHAR AT A GLANCE

Population: 95.9 million
Area: 173,877 sq km
Capital: Patna
Main Language: Hindi
Literacy Rate: 38%
Best Time to Go: October to March

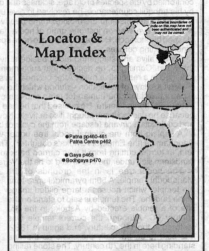

Locator & Map Index

Patna pp460-461
Patna Centre p462

Gaya p468
Bodhgaya p470

Highlights
* Soaking up the Buddhist vibe under Bodhgaya's bodhi tree
* The wild elephants in Palamau National Park

to Calcutta or Kathmandu. However, Bodhgaya is an excellent place to visit if you want to study Buddhism, and Rajgir, Nalanda and Sasaram are interesting places that are not on the tourist trail.

Warning The extreme poverty in Bihar means tourist buses are a favourite target of dacoits. In late 1996 two busloads of Taiwanese tourists on their way from Rajgir to Bodhgaya were robbed and assaulted by armed criminals

A REGIONAL HIGHLIGHT

Mahabodhi Temple, Bodhgaya

The Mahabodhi Temple marks the spot where the Buddha gained enlightenment and set out on his life of preaching. It is one of the four most important sites for Buddhist pilgrims.

Legend tells that the birth of the prince of the Sakya clan who was to become the Buddha was attended by great portents and prophesies. He was named Siddhartha (one whose aim is accomplished) because at his birth (in about 560 BC in Lumbini, now in Nepal) a soothsayer predicted that he would attain a position of immense power, either as a secular ruler or as a religious leader. Further predictions warned that if he ever laid eyes on the sufferings of the world he would have no choice but to follow the latter course and give up his family's kingdom.

His father, the king, anxious that this shouldn't happen, ensured that he was surrounded with youth, beauty and good health. He grew up happily, got married and had a son. As he grew older, however, the soothsayer's prediction came true. Outside the palace, among his father's subjects, he was confronted by the spectres of old age, sickness and death. Observing a wandering ascetic, and impressed by his tranquil countenance, he resolved to give up his privileged life in a search for absolute truth.

Subjecting himself to the most extreme deprivations, he spent nearly six years as an ascetic. He is said to have lived on just one grain of rice a day, fasting until he could feel his backbone when he clasped his stomach. He is also reputed to have spent long periods sitting on thorn bushes and sleeping among rotting corpses.

Barely alive and staggering along beside a river near Bodhgaya one day, he fainted and fell into the water. Coming to, he decided that such mortifications were counterproductive to his quest, and indulged in a restorative meal. After his meal he settled down beneath a bodhi tree to meditate.

After 49 days of meditation – during which he was tempted and terrified by Mara, the Lord of Death – he realised that the human lot is an endless cycle of birth and death to which people are bound because of human desire. He realised that he had been unable to achieve enlightenment as an ascetic because he desired it and sought it so actively. Now that he had ceased to desire he became enlightened and could attain nirvana (escape from the cycle of birth and death into a state of perfect bliss).

A sapling from the original bodhi tree under which the Buddha sat was carried to Sri Lanka by Sanghamitta (the Emperor Ashoka's daughter). That tree now flourishes at Anuradhapura in Sri Lanka and, in turn, a cutting from it was carried back to Bodhgaya when the original tree here died. A red sandstone slab under the tree is said to be the Vajrasan, or diamond throne, on which the Buddha sat.

The bodhi tree is in the grounds of the Mahabodhi Temple. A 50m pyramidal spire tops the temple, which houses a large gilded image of the Buddha. The temple is said to stand on the site of a temple erected by Ashoka in the 3rd century BC. Although the current temple was restored in the 11th century, and again in 1882, it is said to be basically the same as the one standing here in the 7th century. The stone railing around the temple, parts of which still stand, was originally thought to date from Ashoka's time but is now considered to be from the Sunga period around 184-172 BC. The carved and sculptured railing has been restored, although parts of it now stand in the museum in Calcutta and in the Victoria & Albert Museum in London. Stone stupas, erected by visiting pilgrims, dot the temple courtyard.

The temple is looking a little drab and dirty these days, planned cleaning and restoration work stalled somewhere between bureaucracy and the bottom line. Many stupas and icons have been removed or vandalised, and repair efforts have been haphazard; earthen slabs even stand in for granite in some cases. Nevertheless, this is an evocative site.

Entry to the temple grounds is free, but there is a Rs 5 charge for cameras.

For more information on Buddhism, see the Sacred India colour section earlier in the book. ∎

Buddha shown in the *bhumisparsa mudra*, as he would have meditated under the bodhi tree.

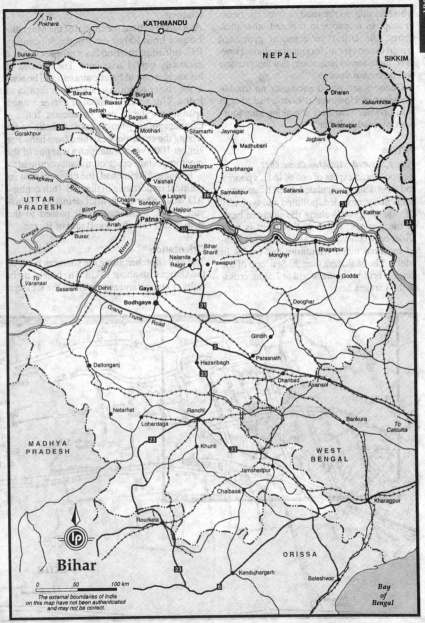

Bihar

0   50   100 km

The external boundaries of India
on this map have not been authenticated
and may not be correct.

who had dug up the road to force the buses to stop. In response to this and other incidents, the Bihar government promised armed escorts for all foreign travellers. However, there are no indications that this promise will be carried through.

Chances are you'll encounter no trouble whatsoever. However, it's not a bad idea to split up your valuables if making long journeys by road in Bihar.

PATNA

Pop: 1,285,470   Tel Area Code: 0612

As you would expect of one of India's poorest and most densely populated states, Bihar's capital is noisy, crowded, polluted and typically chaotic. It sprawls along the southern bank of the Ganges, which at this point is very wide; between Varanasi and Patna, it is joined by three major tributaries and triples in width. The Mahatma Gandhi Seti, one of the longest bridges in the world at 7.5km, crosses the Ganges here.

History

Ajatasatru shifted the capital of the Magadha Empire from Rajgir early in the 5th century BC, fulfilling the Buddha's prophecy that a great city would arise here. The remains of his ancient city of Pataliputra can still be seen at the site in Kumrahar, a southern district of Patna. This was the capital of a huge empire spanning a large part of ancient India – Chandragupta Maurya and Ashoka were among the emperors who ruled from here. For almost 1000 years Pataliputra was one of the most important cities on the subcontinent.

Renamed Azimabad, the city regained its political importance in the mid-16th century AD when Sher Shah, after defeating Humayun, made it his capital. It passed to the British in 1764 after the Battle of Buxar.

Orientation

The city stretches along the southern bank of the Ganges for about 15km. The hotels, main railway station and airport are in the western

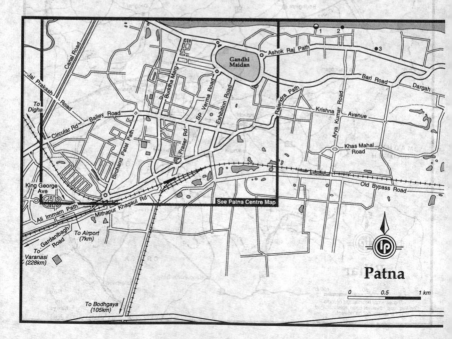

Patna

half of Patna, known as Bankipur, while the older and more traditional area is to the east, in Patna City. The 'hub' of the new Patna is at Gandhi Maidan. The main market area is Ashok Raj Path, which starts from Gandhi Maidan.

Two important roads near the railway station, Fraser and Exhibition Rds, have officially had their names changed to Muzharul Haque Path and Braj Kishore Path respectively, but everyone still uses the old names. On the other hand, Gardiner Rd is now referred to as Birchand Patel Path.

Information

The state tourist office (☎ 225411) is on Fraser Rd next to the petrol pump; enter through the Chef Restaurant entrance. There are also counters at the railway station and the airport, but don't expect much from them. There's a Government of India tourist office (☎ 345776), inconveniently located south of the railway line.

Trade Wings, behind the Maurya Patna Hotel, is a good place to change foreign currency and travellers cheques, or to get cash out against credit cards.

There are a couple of reasonable bookshops on Fraser Rd near the Satkar International Hotel, and a British Library (☎ 224198) on Bank Rd near the Biscomaun Bhavan by Gandhi Maidan.

Golghar

Overlooking the maidan, this huge building, shaped like a beehive, was constructed in 1786 as a granary to store surpluses against possible famines. It was built by Captain John Garstin at the instigation of the British administrator, Warren Hastings, and although the Bihar government is making use of it now, it has hardly ever been filled. Standing about 25m high with steps winding around the outside to the top, the Golghar provides a fine view over the town and the Ganges.

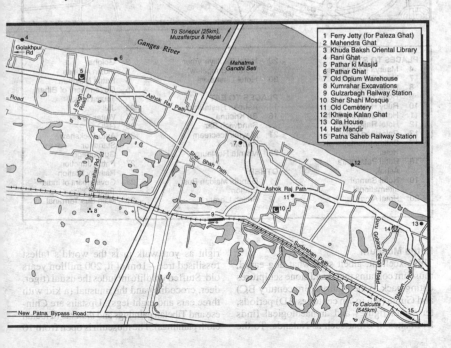

1 Ferry Jetty (for Paleza Ghat)
2 Mahendra Ghat
3 Khuda Baksh Oriental Library
4 Rani Ghat
5 Pathar ki Masjid
6 Pathar Ghat
7 Old Opium Warehouse
8 Kumrahar Excavations
9 Gulzarbagh Railway Station
10 Sher Shahi Mosque
11 Old Cemetery
12 Khwaje Kalan Ghat
13 Qila House
14 Har Mandir
15 Patna Saheb Railway Station

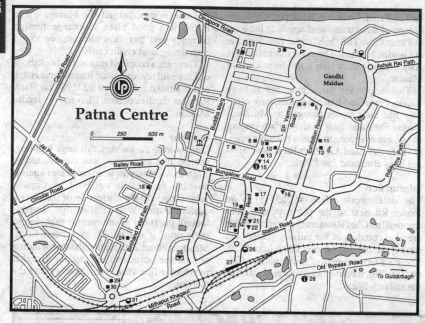

Patna Centre

0   250   500 m

PLACES TO STAY
4   Maurya Patna Hotel
7   Hotel President
8   Hotel Parker
9   Hotel Yash
10   Ruby Hotel
11   Hotel Swayam Sidhi
12   Hotel Rajkumar
13   Rajasthan Hotel
17   Satkar International
     Hotel
18   Hotel Pataliputra
     Ashok
19   Hotel Samrat
     International
20   Hotel Amar

29   Hotel Kautilya Vihar
     (Tourist Bungalow)
30   Hotel Chanakya

PLACES TO EAT
14   Ashoka Restaurant
16   Sri Krishna
     Sandwich Bar
21   Mayfair Icecream
     Parlour
22   Mamta Restaurant

OTHER
1   Gandhi Maidan Bus
     Station
2   British Library

3   Golghar
5   Indian Airlines
6   Patna Museum
15   Government of Bihar
     Tourist Office
23   Jail
24   Water Tower
25   GPO
26   Auto-Rickshaw
     Stand for
     Gulzarbagh
27   Patna Junction
     Railway Station
28   Government of India
     Tourist Office
31   Main Bus Terminal

Patna Museum

This excellent, albeit somewhat dog-eared, museum contains metal and stone sculptures dating back to the Maurya (3rd century BC) and Gupta (4th to 7th centuries AD) periods, terracotta figures and archaeological finds from sites in Bihar such as Nalanda. To the right as you walk in is the world's tallest fossilised tree – 16m of it, 200 million years old. Stuffed wildlife includes the usual (tiger, deer, crocodile) and the unusual (a kid with three ears and eight legs). Upstairs are Chinese and Tibetan paintings and *thankas* (Tibetan cloth paintings). The museum is open from 10 am to 4.30 pm; closed on Monday. Entry costs Rs 5.

Kumrahar Excavations

The remains of Pataliputra, the ancient capital of Ajatasatru (491-459 BC), Chandragupta (321-297 BC) and Ashoka (274-237 BC), have been uncovered in Kumrahar, south of Patna. The main points of interest are the assembly hall (a few large pillars are all that remain) dating back to the Mauryan period, and the foundations of the brick Buddhist monastery known as Anand Bihar. There's a small display of some of the clay figures and wooden beams discovered here.

The Kumrahar excavations are fairly esoteric, however, and are likely to attract only those with a keen interest in archaeology and India's ancient history. They are set in a pleasant park open daily (except Monday) from 9 am to 5 pm; entry costs Rs 5. Shared auto-rickshaws between Patna Junction railway station and Gulzarbagh pass right by here and cost Rs 3.

Har Mandir

At the eastern end of the city, in the Chowk area of old Patna, stands one of the holiest Sikh shrines. Built of white marble by Ranjit Singh, it marks the place where Gobind Singh, the 10th and last of the Sikh gurus, was born in 1660.

Not only must you go barefoot within the temple precincts, but your head must be covered. They lend cloths for this purpose at the entrance.

Qila House (Jalan Museum)

Built on the foundations of Sher Shah's fort, Qila House contains an impressive private collection of antiques, including a dinner service that once belonged to George III, Marie Antoinette's Sèvres porcelain, Napoleon's four-poster bed, Chinese jade and Mughal silver filigree. Phone ☎ 642354 for permission to visit.

Khuda Baksh Oriental Library

Founded in 1900, this library has a renowned collection of very rare Arabic and Persian manuscripts, Mughal and Rajput paintings, and oddities like the Koran inscribed in a book only 25mm wide. The library also contains the only books to survive the sacking of the Moorish University of Cordoba in Spain.

Other Attractions

Non-Hindus are welcome at the modern **Mahavir Mandir**, dedicated to the popular god, Hanuman. At night this place is lit up in garish pink and green neon – you can't possibly miss it as you leave the main railway station.

The heavy, domed **Sher Shahi**, built by the Afghan ruler Sher Shah in 1545, is the oldest mosque in Patna. Other mosques include the squat **Pathar ki Masjid** and the riverbank **Madrassa**.

Gulzarbagh, to the east of the city, was the site of the East India Company's **opium warehouse**. The building is currently occupied by a state government printing works.

Organised Tours

The state tourist office operates a day trip which includes Patna, Rajgir, Nalanda and Pawapuri. It runs on Saturday and Sunday, and the cost is Rs 125. For departure times, contact the tourist office or Hotel Kautilya Vihar (tourist bungalow).

Places to Stay – bottom end

Fraser Rd is Patna's hub, and a lot of the cheaper hotels are tucked away in lanes off the main street.

Hotel Amar (☎ 224157) has rooms with bathrooms for Rs 80/105. This is the most pleasant of the string of places off Fraser Rd, down the lane opposite the Hotel Samrat International.

Hotel Parker, up the other end of Fraser Rd, is OK but rather dark, with rooms from Rs 50/65.

Ruby Hotel, on the next block, is spartan and charges Rs 50/70 for rooms with attached bathrooms.

Hotel Rajkumar (☎ 655011), on Exhibition Rd, isn't bad. Rooms are Rs 75/120.

Hotel Swayam Sidhi (☎ 655312) is a

recommended new hotel. Clean, spacious rooms with attached bathrooms are Rs 190/250, but there are no air-coolers.

Hotel Yash (☎ 227210), with clean singles/doubles from Rs 150/200 and air-con doubles for Rs 450, is another good small place.

Retiring rooms at the station are Rs 30 for dorm beds, Rs 90 for doubles, or Rs 150 with air-con.

Places to Stay – middle

There are enough operators fighting for your rupee to ensure standards stay relatively high.

Hotel Kautilya Vihar (Tourist Bungalow) (☎ 225411) is in 'R-block' on Birchand Patel Path. Recent renovations have priced it out of budget tourist range: dorm beds are around Rs 100 but the rooms shoot up to Rs 400 a double (Rs 600 with air-con).

Hotel President (☎ 220600) is down a side street off Fraser Rd and has rooms from Rs 300/350 or Rs 550/650 with air-con. All rooms have attached bath and hot water.

Hotel Samrat International (☎ 220560; fax 226386) on Fraser Rd is a good mid-range hotel, with single/doubles from Rs 475/550, or with air-con at Rs 750/850; it boasts the first solar hot-water system in the state.

Satkar International Hotel (☎ 220551; fax 220556) is one of the few places with a noon checkout. Rooms cost Rs 600/725.

Rajasthan Hotel (☎ 225102) is also on Fraser Rd. It's Rs 310 for standard rooms, or Rs 555 with air-con (no single rates).

Places to Stay – top end

Luxury hotels do not condescend to join the Fraser Rd bustle.

Hotel Chanakya (☎ 223141; fax 220598), near the tourist bungalow, is a centrally air-conditioned three-star place that charges Rs 1050/1500 for singles/doubles.

Maurya Patna (☎ 222061; fax 222069) overlooks Gandhi Maidan and is Patna's top hotel. You can count on the usual mod cons, including a pool. Rooms cost from Rs 1195/2000.

Hotel Pataliputra Ashok (☎ 226270) is similar at Rs 1195/1800.

Places to Eat

Patna has plenty of places to eat, many of which are along Fraser Rd, not far from the railway station.

Mayfair Icecream Parlour is a clean and popular place with good masala dosas and other snacks, as well as 16-odd ice-cream flavours.

Mamta Restaurant has main dishes for Rs 30 and beer is Rs 45.

Ashoka Restaurant is further up Fraser Rd. It's rather dark but the non-vegetarian food (Chinese, tandoori) is good.

Rajasthan Hotel, not far from the Ashoka, has the best vegetarian restaurant in the city. It's not cheap but the food is excellent and they have a good range of ice creams.

Gaurav's Restaurant at Hotel Swayam Sidhi is another good vegetarian restaurant.

Sri Krishna Sandwich Bar, round the corner on Dak Bungalow Rd, has pizzas, sandwiches and sweets.

Getting There & Away

Air Indian Airlines (☎ 226433) has daily flights between Patna and Delhi (US$115), Calcutta (US$75) and Ranchi (US$50). Three flights a week connect Patna with Lucknow (US$75). Sahara Air has one flight a day to Varanasi.

Bus The main bus terminal is at Harding Park, just west of Patna Junction railway station. It's a large place with departure gates spread out along the road. Buses for Siliguri (12 hours, Rs 120), Gaya (four hours, Rs 35), Rajgir (three hours, Rs 26), Ranchi (nine hours, Rs 92) and Sasaram (six hours, Rs 35) go from Gate 7. Buses for Raxaul (seven hours, Rs 45) on the Nepalese border go from Gate 6, via Muzaffarpur.

The Gandhi Maidan bus stand is used by government buses to many places in Bihar. There are night buses to Ranchi and a deluxe bus to Siliguri (Rs 125, departing at 3 pm). There's also a deluxe night bus to Raxaul (seven hours, Rs 55, departing at 10 pm).

Train Patna Junction is the main railway station. The fastest trains on the Calcutta to Delhi line take 12 hours to Delhi (992km, Rs 166/768 in 2nd/1st) and 5½ hours to Calcutta (545km, Rs 109/494 in 2nd/1st). There are a number of direct trains daily to Varanasi (228km, five hours); Gaya (92km, two hours); Ranchi (591km, 10 hours); and Mumbai; and a weekly service to Chennai.

If you're heading to Darjeeling or the north-east region, the fast *North East Express* from Delhi leaves Patna at 10 pm, arriving in New Jalpaiguri (Siliguri) at 7 am. From Patna to New Jalpaiguri it's 636km and Rs 190/700 in 2nd/2nd class air-con.

To/From Nepal There are no direct trains from Patna to the border town of Raxaul (you have to change at Muzaffarpur) so the buses are faster. From the main bus terminal, there are hourly morning departures, less frequent afternoon services, and other departures from the government bus stand. Buses take seven hours and cost Rs 45.

Getting Around
The Airport The airport is seven km west of the city centre. Indian Airlines runs a bus service from their office by the Gandhi Maidan. Otherwise, you can get there by cycle-rickshaw for Rs 25. Taxis charge about Rs 100.

Auto-Rickshaw Shared auto-rickshaws shuttle back and forth between the main Patna Junction railway station and Gulzarbagh for Rs 5 per person. The other main route is from the Patna Junction railway station to Gandhi Maidan bus stand (Rs 3).

PATNA TO NEPAL
Sonepur
A month-long cattle fair is held in October/November at Sonepur, 25km north of Patna. It takes place around the full moon at Kartika Purnima, the most auspicious time to bathe at the confluence of the Ganges and the Gandak here. This is probably the largest animal fair in Asia, and not only cattle but all types of animals are traded here. At the Haathi Bazaar, elephants change hands for anything from Rs 10,000 to Rs 100,000, depending on age and condition. If you'd like to purchase an alternative form of transport, Mark Shand's *Travels on my Elephant* is essential reading for the modern mahout.

Vaishali
As long ago as the 6th century BC, Vaishali was the capital of a republic. It's the birthplace of Mahavira, one of the Jain *tirthankars*, and was where the Buddha preached his last sermon. There's very little to see – an **Ashoka pillar** (with its lion capital intact), a couple of dilapidated **stupas** (one contains an eighth of the Buddha's ashes) and a small **museum**. There are guided tours from Patna or buses from Lalganj and Muzaffarpur. There's a *tourist bungalow* at Vaishali where rooms are Rs 100/125.

Muzaffarpur
Pop: 282,120
Apart from being a bus-changing point on the way to the Nepal border, Muzaffarpur is of limited interest. This is a poverty-stricken, agriculturally backward area. There are a number of places to stay.

Hotel Deepak has reasonable food and very spartan rooms for Rs 60/80.

Hotel Elite, near the railway station on Saraiya Gunj, is more expensive at Rs 135 a double.

Motihari & Raxaul
North of Muzaffarpur, the area becomes even poorer. Motihari, where George Orwell was born, is a small provincial town which is also the district headquarters. Raxaul is right on the border and is virtually a twin town with Birganj, just across the border in Nepal. Both towns are crowded and dirty. Cycle-rickshaws take 20 minutes (Rs 10) to get from the border (open 4 am to midnight) to the bus stand in Birganj. Nepalese visas are available at the border for US$25. Be warned that US currency *only* is accepted as payment for visas at this border.

Places to Stay This is not a place to stick around.

Hotel Kaveri in Raxaul has rooms for Rs 45/65.

Hotel Ajanta is better. It's down a side road near the bus stand and charges Rs 50/80 for a room with common bath. Alternatively, you can cross the border and stay in equally unattractive Birganj.

Getting There & Away There are several buses a day from Raxaul to Patna (seven hours, Rs 45) and more to Muzaffarpur. Beware of touts selling combined bus/train tickets: it's much more reliable to organise things yourself.

From Birganj there are morning and evening buses to Kathmandu taking around 12 hours (Rs 60) or Pokhara (10 hours, Rs 55). To Kathmandu most buses take the much longer road via Narayanghat and Mugling, rather than the dramatically scenic Tribhuvan Highway via Naubise.

PATNA TO VARANASI
Sasaram

If you want to stop off between Varanasi and Gaya or Patna, you might consider having a look at the impressive **mausoleum of Sher Shah**, who died in 1545. Built of red sandstone and standing in the middle of a large artificial pond, it's particularly striking in the warm light of sunset. The 46m high dome has an impressive 22m span, which is four metres wider than the dome of the Taj Mahal.

Sasaram is a chaotic dustbowl on the Grand Trunk Road, the famous Indian highway that was built by Sher Shah in the mid-16th century. There's also the **tomb of Hassan Khan** (Sher Shah's father) and several other Muslim monuments.

There are more Muslim tombs at **Maner**. At **Dehri**, 17km from Sasaram, the railway and the Grand Trunk Road cross the River Son on a three km bridge. The hill fort of **Rohtas** is 38km from here.

The Grand Trunk Road

India's Grand Trunk Road (GTR) runs the breadth of the country, from the Pakistan border near Amritsar to Calcutta. It has been in existence for many centuries, and is by far the busiest road in the country. Rudyard Kipling described the Grand Trunk Road as a 'river of life', and many of the events in his novel *Kim* take place along it.

During the time of Ashoka's rule, pillars of edicts were placed along the road. In Mughal times it was *kos minars* (milestones) which were placed by the roadside, as the royal *kos* was the base unit for measuring long distances. Also of great importance were the *serais* (rest houses), established by many rulers over time but particularly during the Mughal era. These evolved from basically postal relay stations into establishments which became the focal point for commerce in many areas, and housed government officials; some were more grandiose constructions which even the emperor himself used when he passed through. The Nurmahal-ki-serai on the outskirts of Agra was one particularly grand serai, as was the New Delhi serai of Begum Sahib, eldest daughter of Shah Jahan.

One of the rulers with greatest influence over the appearance of the GTR was the emperor Jehangir, who planted avenues of trees (*khayabans*) along it to provide shade for travellers along the route. So pleasant was the road that it became known as 'the Long Walk' among European travellers in the 17th century. Unfortunately the decline of the Mughal Empire also saw a decline in the trees, as maintenance ceased.

The only significant realignment of the road was under the British, when the East India Company sought a more direct route between Calcutta and Varanasi on the mid-Ganges Plain; prior to that the road followed the sweeping bend of the Ganges through Bengal. After the realignment in 1781 the British renamed it the New Military Road, but this fell into disuse and the present route via Varanasi was completed in 1838.

The Grand Trunk Road today is still a vital part of the Indian road network. If you were to sit at a roadside *dhaba* (basic truckers' cafe) somewhere in rural India and observe the passing parade for a day or two, you would get a vivid picture of Indians on the move – oil tankers from Assam, Tata trucks from Punjab, barefoot sadhus on a Ganga pilgrimage, farmers steering overloaded ox-carts, wayward cows, schoolkids on bicycles and women on foot. You'd probably also suffer industrial deafness from the racket. ■

Places to Stay The *Tourist Lodge* is the best place to stay. Turn left onto the Grand Trunk Road outside the railway station and it's by the second petrol station, 15 minutes walk away. Doubles are Rs 50, or Rs 60 with attached bathrooms.

Getting There & Away There are frequent buses for Patna (five hours, Rs 40). For Varanasi and Gaya it's better to take a train as buses start at Dehri, 17km away, and few stop here. There are only two trains direct from Varanasi, but it's also possible to take a local bus from outside Varanasi railway station to Mughalserai (17km, Rs 5), from where there are frequent passenger trains to Sasaram (three hours, Rs 17).

PATNA TO GAYA
Nalanda

Founded in the 5th century BC, Nalanda was one of the world's great universities and an important Buddhist centre until it was sacked by the Afghans in the 12th century. When the Chinese scholar and traveller Xuan Zhang was here in the early 7th century AD, there were 10,000 monks and students in residence.

The brick-built remains are extensive and include the **Great Stupa**, with steps, terraces and a few intact votive stupas around it, and the monks' cells. There's an interesting **archaeological museum** (closed on Friday; Rs 1) housing the Nalanda University seal, sculptures and other remains found on the site. Pilgrims venerate the Buddha figures in spite of signs saying 'Do not offer anything to the objects in the museum'! Buy a guidebook at the booking office for Rs 3.

The newest building here is the **Hiuen Tsang Memorial Hall**, built as a Peace Pagoda by the Chinese. Xuan Zhang spent five years here as both student and teacher.

There's also an international centre for the study of Buddhism, established in 1951. There are Burmese, Japanese and Jain *dharamsalas* at Nalanda as well as a *PWD Rest House*.

Getting There & Away Shared Trekkers (jeeps) cost Rs 3 from Rajgir to Nalanda village, and from there it's Rs 5 for the 10

minute ride on a shared tonga to the university site. Take another jeep (Rs 3) from Nalanda village to Bihar Sharif for buses to Patna (3½ hours, Rs 20).

Rajgir
Tel Area Code: 06119

This was the capital of the Magadha Empire until Ajatasatru moved to Pataliputra (Patna) in the 5th century BC. Today, Rajgir is a minor Indian holiday centre. In winter, visitors are drawn by the hot springs and the healthy climate of this hilly region, 19km south of Nalanda.

Rajgir is an important Buddhist pilgrimage site since the Buddha spent 12 years here, and the first Buddhist council after the Buddha attained nirvana was held here. It's also an important place for Jains, as the Mahavir spent some time in Rajgir and the hills are topped with Digambara shrines. A mention in the *Mahabharata* also ensures a good supply of Hindu pilgrims.

Orientation & Information The main road passes about half a km west of the town. On it are the railway station and bus stand, and there are a number of hotels in this area.

There's a tourist office by the hot springs, which are about one km south of town along the main road.

Things to See Most people rent a tonga for half a day to see the sites, as they're spread out over several km. This costs about Rs 50, but, with the brutal way these horses are treated, you might prefer to take a taxi.

Main sites include parts of the ruined city, caves and places associated with Ajatasatru and his father Bhimbisara, whom he imprisoned and murdered. The pink building by the crowded hot springs is the **Lakshmi Narayan Temple**.

There's also a Burmese temple, an interesting **Jain exhibition** (Rs 5), a modern Japanese temple and on the top of Ratnagiri Hill, three km south of the hot springs, the **Japanese Shanti Stupa**, reached by a chairlift (10 am to 5 pm daily; Rs 10 return).

Places to Stay & Eat Accommodation prices vary widely depending on the season. High season is October to March.

Hotel Anand, near the bus stand, is one of the cheaper places. Gloomy rooms cost Rs 40/60. The hotel serves dosas for Rs 12.

Hotel Siddharth, south of town near the hot springs, is set within a pleasant walled courtyard. Rooms are Rs 75/120 with attached bathrooms.

Hotel Rajgir (☎ 5266) has a garden and the rooms are OK at Rs 65/125 with attached bathrooms.

Hotel Centaur Hokke (☎ 5245), three km west of the hot springs, is Rajgir's top hotel. It's a very pleasant, Japanese-designed place. Rooms, either Japanese or western-style, are US$78/112 (meals are an extra US$40 per person per day). The restaurant here is moderately expensive, and serves Indian and Japanese food. If you are staying elsewhere and want to eat here, you'll have to hire a cycle-rickshaw or tonga to take you and wait while you eat to take you back again.

Getting There & Away Rajgir is on a branch line, with daily trains to Patna, but the buses are faster (four hours, Rs 26). You may need to change at Bihar Sharif. There are also buses to Gaya (three hours, Rs 20) and Pawapuri. For Nalanda take a shared jeep for Rs 3.

Pawapuri

Mahavira, the final tirthankar and founder of Jainism, died and was cremated here in about 500 BC. It is said that the demand for his sacred ashes was so great that a large amount of soil was removed around the funeral pyre, creating the lotus-filled tank. A marble temple, the **Jalmandir**, was later built in the middle of the tank and is now a major pilgrimage spot for Jains. You can get here by bus from Rajgir or Bihar Sharif.

GAYA

Pop: 373,120 Tel Area Code: 0631

Gaya is about 100km south of Patna. Just as nearby Bodhgaya is a major centre for Buddhist pilgrims, Gaya is a centre for Hindu pilgrims. Vishnu is said to have given Gaya the power to absolve sinners. Pilgrims offer *pindas* (funeral cakes) at the ghats along the river here, and perform a lengthy circuit of the holy places around Gaya, to free their ancestors from bondage to the earth.

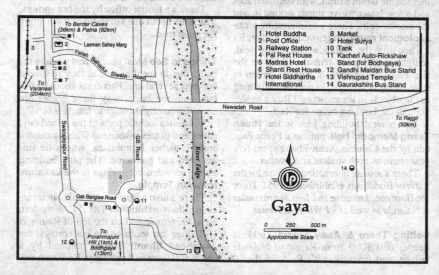

1 Hotel Buddha	8 Market
2 Post Office	9 Hotel Surya
3 Railway Station	10 Tank
4 Pal Rest House	11 Kacheri Auto-Rickshaw
5 Madras Hotel	Stand (for Bodhgaya)
6 Shanti Rest House	12 Gandhi Maidan Bus Stand
7 Hotel Siddhartha	13 Vishnupad Temple
International	14 Gaurakshini Bus Stand

Gaya

0   250   500 m

Approximate Scale

If you're on your way to Bodhgaya but only reach Gaya after dark, spend the night here – there have been a number of night-time muggings on the Gaya to Bodhgaya road.

There's a tourist office at the railway station. The nearest foreign exchange facility is in Bodhgaya.

Vishnupad Temple
In the crowded central part of the old town, this *sikhara*-style temple was constructed in 1787 by Queen Ahalya Bai of Indore on the banks of the River Falgu. Inside the temple the 40cm 'footprint' of Vishnu is imprinted in solid rock and surrounded by a silver-plated basin, although non-Hindus are not allowed to enter.

During the monsoon, the river carries a great deal of water but it dries up completely in winter. You can see cremations taking place on the riverbanks.

Other Attractions
A flight of 1000 stone steps leads to the top of the **Brahmajuni Hill**, one km south-west of the Vishnupad Temple. There's a good view over the town from the top. Gaya has a small **archaeological museum** (closed on Monday) near the tank.

A **temple of Surya**, the sun god, stands 20km to the north at Deo. The **Barabar Caves**, dating back to 200 BC, are 36km north of Gaya. These are the 'Marabar' caves of EM Forster's *A Passage to India*. Two of the caves contain Ashokan inscriptions. To get there take the train to Bela, a tonga from there for 10km and it's then a five km walk to the two groups of caves.

Places to Stay & Eat
There are many places to stay around the station, most of them spartan but OK for a short pause.

Hotel Buddha (☎ 23428) is down the lane opposite the railway station. Rooms are Rs 85/120 (plus Rs 20 if you want a TV).

Pal Rest House (☎ 433139), set back from the road, is quiet and cheap, with rooms with bathroom for Rs 75/105.

Shanti Rest House and *Madras Hotel* are similar places.

Hotel Surya (☎ 24004) is a Rs 5 cycle-rickshaw ride from the railway station, with doubles for Rs 140 with attached bathrooms, or Rs 190 with water heater and air-cooler.

Hotel Siddhartha International (☎ 21254) caters to upmarket pilgrims. Rooms cost US$22/29, or US$30/37 with air-con. There's a good non-vegetarian restaurant with main dishes around Rs 35 and a Continental breakfast at Rs 40.

All over Bihar you will see stalls selling the popular puff-pastry sweet known as khaja, which originated in a village between Gaya and Rajgir. Catch them as they come out of the oil – the flies are as partial to them as the Biharis are.

Getting There & Away
Buses to Patna (four hours, Rs 35) and Ranchi (seven hours, Rs 50) leave from the Gandhi Maidan bus stand. Buses to Rajgir (three hours, Rs 30) leave from the Gaurak-shini bus stand, which is across the river.

Gaya is on the main Delhi to Calcutta railway line and there are direct trains to Delhi, Calcutta, Varanasi, Puri and Patna.

Auto-rickshaws from the railway station should cost Rs 90 for the 13km trip to Bodh-gaya but they'll try for twice as much. From the Kacheri auto-rickshaw stand, which is a 25 minute walk from the station, it's Rs 4 for a seat, plus Rs 2 for a rucksack. Watch your head on the low roof in the back, though, or you'll attain a state of unconsciousness before you reach Bodhgaya!

Getting Around
It's Rs 5 by cycle-rickshaw to the Kacheri auto-rickshaw stand (for Bodhgaya) or to the Gaurakshini bus stand (for Rajgir) from the railway station.

BODHGAYA
Pop: 25,585   Tel Area Code: 0631
The four most holy places associated with the Buddha are Lumbini, in Nepal, where he was born; Sarnath, near Varanasi, where he

first preached his message; Kushinagar, near Gorakhpur, where he died; and Bodhgaya, where he attained enlightenment. For the traveller, Bodhgaya is probably the most interesting of these four places, being much more of a working Buddhist centre than an archaeological site. It's the most important Buddhist pilgrimage site in the world.

The focal point is the Mahabodhi Temple. The bo tree growing here is said to be a direct descendant of the original tree under which the Buddha sat, meditated and achieved enlightenment. World interest in Buddhism is increasing and there are a number of new monasteries and temples being built here.

Buddhists from all over the world flock to Bodhgaya, along with many westerners who come here to learn about Buddhism and meditation. Bodhgaya is small and quiet and, if you are not planning to stay long, a day is quite sufficient to see everything. The best time to visit Bodhgaya is when the Tibetan pilgrims come down from Dharamsala,

during the winter. The Dalai Lama often spends December here. When the Tibetans leave in mid-February they seem to take some of the atmosphere of the place with them.

Information

There's a tourist office opposite the Mahabodhi Temple. It is open daily from 10 am to 5 pm, but is less than helpful.

Monasteries

Most countries with a large Buddhist population have a temple or monastery here, usually built in a representative architectural style. Thus the Thai temple looks very much like the colourful *wats* you see in Thailand. The Tibetan temple and monastery was built in 1934 and contains a large prayer wheel. The Tibetans have two other places here, the Sakya Monastery and the Karma Temple.

The Burmese, who led the campaign to restore the Mahabodhi Temple in the 19th century, built their present monastery in

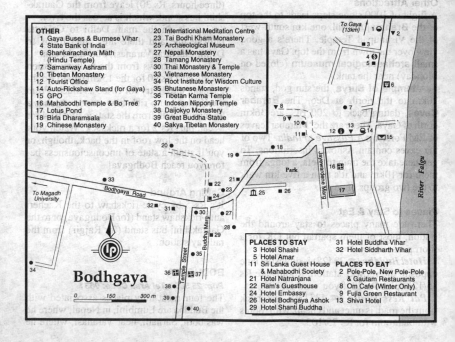

OTHER
1 Gaya Buses & Burmese Vihar
4 State Bank of India
6 Shankaracharya Math (Hindu Temple)
7 Samanway Ashram
10 Tibetan Monastery
12 Tourist Office
14 Auto-Rickshaw Stand (for Gaya)
15 GPO
16 Mahabodhi Temple & Bo Tree
17 Lotus Pond
18 Birla Dharamsala
19 Chinese Monastery
20 International Meditation Centre
23 Tai Bodhi Kham Monastery
25 Archaeological Museum
27 Nepali Monastery
28 Tamang Monastery
30 Thai Monastery & Temple
33 Vietnamese Monastery
34 Root Institute for Wisdom Culture
35 Bhutanese Monastery
36 Tibetan Karma Temple
37 Indosan Nipponji Temple
38 Daijokyo Monastery
39 Great Buddha Statue
40 Sakya Tibetan Monastery

PLACES TO STAY
3 Hotel Shashi
5 Hotel Amar
11 Sri Lanka Guest House & Mahabodhi Society
21 Hotel Natranjana
22 Ram's Guesthouse
24 Hotel Embassy
26 Hotel Bodhgaya Ashok
29 Hotel Shanti Buddha
31 Hotel Buddha Vihar
32 Hotel Siddharth Vihar

PLACES TO EAT
2 Pole-Pole, New Pole-Pole & Gautam Restaurants
8 Om Cafe (Winter Only)
9 Fujia Green Restaurant
13 Shiva Hotel

Bodhgaya

0   150   300 m

1936. The Japanese temple (Indosan Nipponji) has a beautiful image of the Buddha brought from Japan – across the road is the Daijokyo Temple. There are also Chinese, Sri Lankan, Bhutanese, Vietnamese and Nepali monasteries. The Tai Bodhi Kham Monastery is being built by Buddhist tribes from Assam and Arunachal Pradesh. Korea, Taiwan and Bangladesh are also working on monasteries.

Other Attractions

The **archaeological museum** (open 10 am to 5 pm daily except Friday) has a small collection of Buddha figures and pillars found in the area. The Hindu Shankaracharya Math has a **temple**, and there's a sculpture gallery in the grounds. Across the river are the Dungeshwari and Suraya **temples**.

The 25m **Great Buddha Statue** in the Japanese Kamakura style was unveiled by the Dalai Lama in 1989. There's a plan to build a Maitreya Buddha statue over 100m high in Bodhgaya as a symbol of world peace.

See the **Mahabodhi Temple** regional highlight on p458.

Meditation Courses

Courses and retreats take place in the winter, mainly from November to early February.

Some of the most accessible courses are run by the Root Institute for Wisdom Culture (☎ 400714), set in a peaceful location on the edge of Bodhgaya. They run basic five-day meditation courses and hold retreats. Travellers who have spent some time here all seem impressed, not only with the courses but by the way the Institute is working to put something back into the local community with health, agricultural and educational projects.

Courses are also run by the International Meditation Centre (☎ 400707) near Magadh University (five km from Bodhgaya), and at their centre closer to town. The annual insight meditation (Vipassana) and spiritual inquiry retreats take place from 7 to 17 January, 17 to 27 January, and 28 January to 4 February at the Thai Monastery. Led since 1975 by Christopher Titmuss, the retreats have spaces for 130 people, and the all-inclusive cost is US$50. Write in advance to Gaia

House (☎ (01803) 813188), West Ogwell, Near Newton Abbot, Devon TQ12 6EN, UK or (from mid-October) to Thomas Jost, Bodhgaya Post Office, Gaya District, Bihar 824 231, India. Meditation courses are also offered at the Burmese and Tibetan monasteries, and at the Dhammabodhi Vipassana Meditation Centre (☎ 400437), near Magadh University. Some courses are advertised on the noticeboard in the Om Cafe.

If you're interested in working on social development projects in the area, contact the Samanway Ashram.

Places to Stay

Prices given are for the high season (October to March), when room rates can be almost double the low-season rates.

Tourist Bungalows No 1 and *No 2* are next door to each other and have been given more imaginative names: the *Hotel Buddha Vihar* (☎ 400445) only has dormitory accommodation at Rs 100 a bed. *Hotel Siddharth Vihar* (☎ 400445) has doubles with attached bathrooms for Rs 500.

Ram's Guesthouse (☎ 400644) is a new family-run place. A dorm bed is Rs 75 and doubles are Rs 200, all with shared bathroom. There's a tent-restaurant here.

Sri Lanka Guest House, a Mahabodhi Society place, is popular and well run. They accept donations of around Rs 75 for rooms with attached bath.

Hotels Amar and *Shashi* are on the road to Gaya. They are basic little places with doubles for around Rs 100.

If you're planning a longer stay or don't mind roughing it a little, it's possible to stay at some of the monasteries.

The *Burmese Monastery*, which has a peaceful garden, is particularly popular with westerners for its study courses. The rooms are extremely basic and you're expected to make a donation of Rs 20 per night. Dignified conduct is expected, but unfortunately some travellers have abused the monastery's hospitality by breaking the rules.

The *Japanese Monastery* is another place where western visitors have made themselves unpopular and they may not be keen to let you in. It's clean and comfortable but packed out with Japanese tour groups during the season.

The *Bhutanese Monastery* is a good place where rooms without bath cost between Rs 30 and Rs 50.

The *Tibetan Monastery* is somewhat more spartan and a bit cheaper. Other places you could try include the *Sakya Tibetan Monastery*, and the *Thai* and *Nepalese monasteries*.

There's a spate of building going on in Bodhgaya, mostly of middle and top-price hotels.

Hotel Shanti Buddha (☎ 400534) is one of the more established mid-price options. Comfortable rooms cost Rs 300 per person.

Hotel Embassy (☎ 400711) passes the white-glove test. Rooms are Rs 500/700.

Hotel Natranjana (☎ 400475) is similar, with doubles from Rs 400.

ITDC Hotel Bodhgaya Ashok (☎ 22708) has singles/doubles at Rs 900/1400, or Rs 1195/2280 with air-con.

Places to Eat

The standard of food here is pretty low out of season and surprisingly high during winter, when the pilgrims arrive.

Mahabodi Canteen at the Sri Lanka Guest House is a reliable place serving quite reasonable Chinese food.

Shiva Hotel, near the tourist office, tries to cater to western tastes, with mixed results.

The best places are tent-restaurants opposite the Burmese Vihar.

Pole-Pole, *New Pole-Pole* and the *Gautam* restaurants all have varied menus, good tape collections and are popular. The Gautam also has a bakery in winter.

There are also several restaurants run by Tibetans behind the Tibetan Monastery. Most operate in tents and only open during the December to February season, but there are some perennial places.

Om Cafe is well established, and is a popular meeting place.

Fujia Green serves Tibetan and Chinese grub year-round.

Sculptural Symbolism

Buddha images throughout India are for the most part sculptured according to strict rules found in Buddhist art texts from the 3rd century AD. The way the monastic robes drape over the body, the direction in which the hair curls, the proportions for each body part are all to some degree canonised by these texts. The tradition does leave room for innovation, however, allowing the various 'schools' of Buddhist art to distinguish themselves.

Most Buddha figures wear a simple long robe which appears to be transparent – the body is usually clearly visible underneath. Often the Buddha will be wearing a halo, and in some earlier sculptures his hair is shown coiled.

Indian Buddha figures can be distinguished from those of other countries by their body type. A similar male body type appears in all Indian religious sculpture, whatever the faith – broad shoulders and chest, slim waist and a slightly pot belly.

One aspect of the Buddhist tradition that almost never varies is the posture (*asana*) and hand position (*mudra*) of Buddha images. There are four basic postures and positions: standing, sitting, walking and reclining. The first three are associated with the daily activities of the Buddha, such as teaching, meditating and offering refuge to his disciples.

Abhaya One or both hands extend forward, palms out, fingers pointing upward, to symbolise the Buddha's offer of protection or freedom from fear to his followers. This mudra is most commonly seen in conjunction with standing or walking Buddhas.

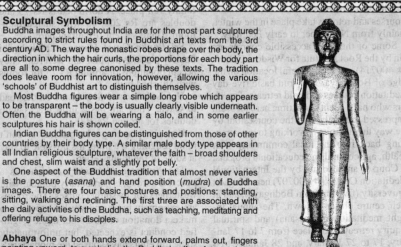

In the *abhaya* mudra, the extended palm bestows grace on the worshipper.

Getting There & Away

Bodhgaya is 13km from Gaya, and share auto-rickshaws shuttle back and forth. They're phenomenally overloaded: a total of up to 15 people (plus animals, goods and so on) travel on a vehicle intended for three! The fare is Rs 4 (or Rs 90 to rent the whole auto-rickshaw).

There are frequent buses to Gaya (Rs 4), and these are also very crowded. They leave regularly from outside the Burmese Vihar.

SOUTHERN BIHAR

Ranchi

Tel Area Code: 0651

At 652m, Ranchi doesn't really deserve its title of hill station, especially since it has now lost most of its tree cover. In British times it was Bihar's summer capital, with a reputation as a health resort. The Kanke hospital for the mentally handicapped is the best known in the country and was formerly a stop on the local tourist office's city tour.

Bhumisparsa In this classic mudra the right hand touches the ground while the left rests in the lap. This hand position symbolises the point in the Buddha's legendary life story when he sat in meditation beneath the bodhi tree and vowed not to budge from the spot until he gained enlightenment. Mara tried to interrupt the Buddha's meditation by invoking a series of distractions (including tempests, floods, feasts and nubile young maidens); the Buddha's response was to touch the earth, thus calling on nature to witness his resolve.

Vitarka or **Dhammachakka** When the thumb and forefinger of one hand (vitarka) or both hands (dhammachakka) form a circle with the other fingers curving outward the mudra evokes the first public discourse on Buddhist doctrine.

Dhyana Both hands rest palms up on the Buddha's lap, with the right hand on top, signifying meditation. ■

In the *bhumisparsa* mudra, Buddha is unmoved by worldly distractions.

The *dhammachakka* mudra symbolises Buddha's role as teacher.

In the *dhyana* mudra, the Buddha is shown as he would have appeared in meditation.

One of the most interesting things to see here is the **Jagannath Temple**, a small version of the great Jagannath Temple at Puri, which celebrates its own, smaller festival of the cars. It's six km south-west of Ranchi and visitors are welcome.

There are a number of hills on the edges of Ranchi for sunset views over the rocky landscape. There's also a Tribal Research Institute with a **museum** here.

Places to Stay & Eat There are numerous hotels around the bus stand.

Hotel Konark (☎ 307840) is the best small place. It's friendly, with clean singles/ doubles at Rs 100/125 with attached bathrooms and a good restaurant.

Hotel Paradise, at Rs 80/100, is another good place.

Hotel Yuvraj (☎ 300403), reputedly 'a house of respectable living', is 15 minutes from the station and has rooms from Rs 250/350.

Hotel Yuvraj Palace (☎ 300805), nearby, is centrally air-conditioned and has rooms from Rs 900/1100. This is Ranchi's best hotel.

Getting There & Away Ranchi has good air, bus and train connections. The railway station is 500m from the bus stand. There are buses to Gaya (seven hours, Rs 50), Hazaribagh (three hours, Rs 23) and Netarhat (four hours, Rs 28). A through bus to Puri takes 15 hours.

Hazaribagh

This pleasant leafy town lies 107km north of Ranchi, at an altitude of 615m. About the only reason for coming here would be to visit **Hazaribagh National Park**, 19km to the north.

Hotel Upkar (☎ (06546) 2246) is the best hotel in Hazaribagh, and good value with singles/doubles for Rs 90/120.

The *Tourist Lodge* or *Forest Rest House* are the places to stay in the park itself.

The railway station, Hazaribagh Rd, is 67km from the town. There are private mini-buses for Gaya (Rs 28, four hours) from outside the bus terminal.

Palamau National Park

This park, 140km west of Ranchi, is part of Project Tiger, but it's also one of the best

---

Project Elephant

Project Tiger is probably India's most visible attempt at wildlife conservation in recent years, and following on from that is Project Elephant – or *Gajatme* – first launched in 1992. It is structured roughly along the lines of Project Tiger, with a number of key areas set aside specifically for the elephant – 11 areas in the states of Bihar, Orissa, Assam, Meghalaya, Tamil Nadu, Kerala and Uttar Pradesh have been identified and gazetted as elephant reserves.

The prime function of these reserves is to guarantee the elephant's habitat, and, equally importantly, to protect the animals from poachers. Unlike the African elephant, tusks are found on only the male Indian elephant, and so it has been selectively targeted by poachers, resulting in a serious imbalance of the sexes. This imbalance is at its most extreme in Periyar National Park in Kerala, where out of a population of 1000 animals only five are adult males.

Other aims of the project include trying to limit damage to crops and people by elephants, establishing and managing corridors between reserves, and identifying 'problem' populations. ■

places in central India to see wild elephants. When the waterholes begin to dry up in March/April, Palamau's 100 elephants are easiest to spot. Jeep safaris can be organised in Betla, the park's access point, and you should expect to pay around Rs 6 per km for spins around the park's 250 sq km. There are also treetop and ground-level hideaways where you can spy on the animals without being seen yourself.

Accommodation is mostly in Betla, but you can also stay further afield in Daltonganj (24km from Betla).

The *Forest Rest House* or *Tourist Lodge*, both in Betla, are reasonable places to stay.

Betla is most easily accessible by road from Ranchi, but if you're coming from the north, there are buses to Betla from Gaya (240km) as well.

Parasnath

Just inside the Bihar state boundary from West Bengal, and only a bit north of the Grand Trunk Road, Parasnath is the major Jain pilgrimage centre in the east of India. Like so many other pilgrimage centres, it's perched on top of a steep hill and is reached by a stiff climb on foot. Rich Calcuttan Jain pilgrims are carried up in palanquins by porters.

The 24 temples, representing the Jain tirthankars, stand at an altitude of 1366m. Parasnath, the 23rd tirthankar, achieved nirvana at this spot 100 years after his birth in Varanasi.

Calcutta

Densely populated and polluted, Calcutta is often an ugly and desperate place that to many people sums up the worst of India. Yet it's also one of the country's more fascinating centres and has some scenes of rare beauty. Certainly the people are a friendly bunch and Bengali humour is renowned throughout India.

Don't let the squalor of first impressions put you off this city. There are a lot of jewels to be discovered and they're not far from the surface. However, Calcutta is not a good introduction to India and is best visited after you've had a chance to get used to some of the country's extremes.

Economically, Calcutta is suffering: the port has been silting up, making navigation from Calcutta down to the sea steadily more difficult and limiting the size of ships that can use the port. The Farakka Barrage (250km north of Calcutta), designed to improve the river flow through the city, has been the subject of considerable dispute between India and Bangladesh because it will also affect the flow of the Ganges through Bangladesh.

Furthermore, Calcutta has been plagued by chronic labour unrest resulting in a decline of its productive capacity. The situation is summed up in the city's hopeless power-generation system. Electrical power in Calcutta is so on-again off-again that virtually every hotel, restaurant, shop or small business has to have some sort of standby power generator or battery lighting system. The workers are blamed, the technicians are blamed, the power plants are blamed, the coal miners are blamed, even Indian railways are blamed for not delivering the coal on time, but it's widely pointed out that Mumbai, for example, certainly doesn't suffer the frequency and extent of power cuts that are a way of life in Calcutta.

The Marxist government of West Bengal has come in for much criticism over the chaos currently existing in Calcutta but, as it

---

CALCUTTA AT A GLANCE

Population: 12 million
Main Language: Bengali
Telephone Area Code: 033
Best Time to Go: November to March

Locator & Map Index

The external boundaries of India on this map have not been authenticated and may not be correct.

Calcutta pp478-479
BBD Bagh (Dalhousie Square) p487
Chowringhee p492

---

is also pointed out, their apparent neglect and mismanagement of the city is combined with a considerable improvement in the rural environment. Threats of flood or famine in the countryside no longer send hordes of refugees streaming into the city as in the past.

Despite all these problems Calcutta is a city with a soul, and one which many residents are inordinately fond of. The Bengalis, so ready to raise arms against the British in the struggle for independence, are also the poets and artists of India. The contrast between the Mumbai and Calcutta movie industries more or less sums it up. While Mumbai, the Hollywood of India, churns out movies of amazing tinsel banality, the smaller number of movie makers in Calcutta make non-commercial gems that stand up to anything produced for sophisticated western audiences. Calcuttans are so proud to be Bengali, that when hometown bowler Saurav Ganguly was omitted from India's squad, cricket-mad fans boycotted the game at Calcutta's Ranji Stadium.

Amongst the squalor and confusion Calcutta has places of sheer magic: flower sellers beside the misty, ethereal Hooghly River; the majestic sweep of the Maidan; the arrogant bulk of the Victoria Memorial; the superb collection of archaeological treasures exhibited in the Indian Museum. They're all part of this amazing city, as are massive Marxist and trade union rallies which can block traffic in the city centre for hours at a time. There's never a dull moment!

History

Calcutta isn't an ancient city like Delhi, with its impressive relics of the past. In fact, it's largely a British creation which dates back only some 300 years and was the capital of British India until the beginning of this century.

In 1686, the British abandoned Hooghly, their trading post 38km up the Hooghly River from present-day Calcutta, and moved downriver to three small villages – Sutanati, Govindpur and Kalikata. Calcutta takes its name from the last of those three tiny settlements. Job Charnock, an English merchant who later married a Brahmin's widow whom he dissuaded from becoming a *sati*, was the leader of the British merchants who made this move. At first the post was not a great success and was abandoned on a number of occasions, but in 1696 a fort was laid out near present-day BBD Bagh (Dalhousie Square) and in 1698, Aurangzeb's grandson gave the British official permission to occupy the villages.

Calcutta then grew steadily until 1756, when Siraj-ud-daula, the Nawab of Murshidabad, attacked the town. Most of the British inhabitants escaped, but those captured were packed into an underground cellar where, during the night, most of them suffocated in what became known as 'the black hole of Calcutta'.

Early in 1757, the British, under Clive of

A REGIONAL HIGHLIGHT

Victoria Memorial

At the southern end of the Maidan stands the Victoria Memorial, the most solid reminder of British Calcutta – in fact probably the most solid reminder of the Raj to be found in India. The Victoria Memorial is a huge white-marble museum, a strange combination of classical European architecture with Mughal influences or, as some have put it, an unhappy British attempt to build a better Taj Mahal.

The memorial was conceived by Lord Curzon, and the money for its construction was raised from 'voluntary contributions by the princes and peoples of India'. The Prince of Wales (later King George V) laid the foundation stone in 1906 and it was opened by another Prince of Wales (later the Duke of Windsor) in 1921.

Whether you're interested in the British Raj period or not, the memorial is an attraction not to be missed. It tells the story of the British Empire in India at its peak, just when it was about to begin its downhill slide. The imposing statue of Queen Victoria, at her bulky and least amused best, fronts the memorial and sets the mood for all the displays inside.

Inside you'll find portraits, statues and busts of almost all the main participants in British-Indian history. Scenes from military conflicts and events of the Mutiny/Uprising are illustrated. There are some superb watercolours of Indian landscapes and buildings made by travelling Victorian artists. A Calcutta exhibit includes many early pictures of the city and a model of Fort William. Queen Victoria appears again, much younger and slimmer than her statue outside. There's also a piano she played as a young girl and other memorabilia. A huge painting depicts King Edward VII entering Jaipur in a regal procession in 1876. French guns captured at the Battle of Plassey are on exhibit along with the black stone throne of the nawab whom Clive defeated. To top it all off, there is a good view over the Maidan from the balcony above the entrance.

The booklet *A Brief Guide to the Victoria Memorial* is available in the building. The memorial is open daily except Monday from 10 am to 3.30 pm, and until 4.30 pm in summer. Entry costs Rs 2. The informative sound & light show runs daily except Monday, from November to May. The English-language programme starts at 8.15 pm. Tickets are Rs 10 (Rs 5 for children). ∎

CALCUTTA

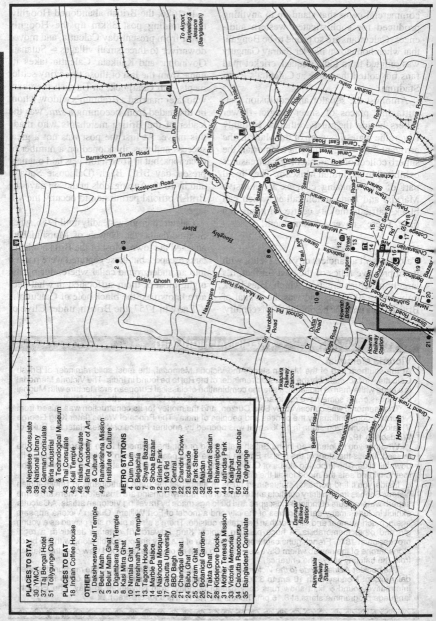

PLACES TO STAY
30 YMCA
37 Taj Bengal Hotel
51 Tollygunge Club

PLACES TO EAT
18 Indian Coffee House

OTHER
1 Dakshineswar Kali Temple
2 Belur Math
3 Belur Math Ghat
4 Digambara Jain Temple
5 Kasi Mitra Ghat
8 Nimtala Ghat
11 Pareshnath Jain Temple
13 Tagore House
14 Marble Palace
16 Nakhoda Mosque
17 Calcutta University
20 BBD Bagh
21 Chandpal Ghat
24 Babu Ghat
25 Outram Ghat
26 Botanical Gardens
28 Kidderpore Docks
31 Mother Teresa's Mission
33 Victoria Memorial
34 Calcutta Racecourse
35 Bangladeshi Consulate

38 Nepalese Consulate
39 National Library
40 German Consulate
42 Birla Industrial
   & Technological Museum
43 Thai Consulate
45 Kali Temple
46 Italian Consulate
48 Birla Academy of Art
   & Culture
49 Ramakrishna Mission
   Institute of Culture

METRO STATIONS
4 Dum Dum
6 Belgachia
7 Shyam Bazaar
9 Shoba Bazaar
12 Girish Park
15 MG Rd
19 Central
22 Chandni Chowk
23 Esplanade
29 Park Street
32 Maidan
36 Rabindra Sadan
41 Bhawanipore
44 Jatindas Park
47 Kalighat
50 Rabindra Sarobar
52 Tollygunge

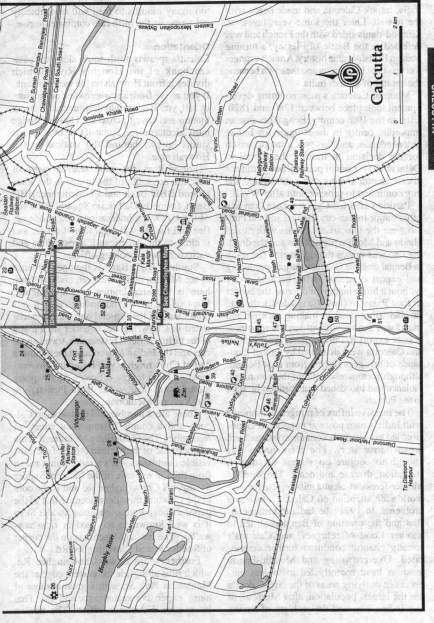

CALCUTTA

India, retook Calcutta and made peace with the nawab. Later the same year, however, Siraj-ud-daula sided with the French and was defeated at the Battle of Plassey, a turning point in British-Indian history. A much stronger fort was built in Calcutta and the town became the capital of British India.

Much of Calcutta's most enduring development took place between 1780 and 1820. Later in the 19th century, Bengal became an important centre in the struggle for Indian independence, and this was a major reason for the decision to transfer the capital to Delhi in 1911. Loss of political power did not alter Calcutta's economic control, and the city continued to prosper until after WWII.

Partition affected Calcutta more than any other major Indian city. Bengal and the Punjab were the two areas of India with mixed Hindu and Muslim populations and the dividing line was drawn through them. The result in Bengal was that Calcutta, the jute-producing and export centre of India, became a city without a hinterland, while across the border in East Pakistan (now Bangladesh), the jute (a plant fibre used in making sacking and mats) was grown without anywhere to process or export it. Furthermore, West Bengal and Calcutta were disrupted by tens of thousands of refugees fleeing from East Bengal, although fortunately without the communal violence and bloodshed that Partition brought to the Punjab.

The massive influx of refugees, combined with India's own postwar population explosion, led to Calcutta becoming an international urban horror story. The mere name was enough to conjure up visions of squalor, starvation, disease and death. The work of Mother Teresa's Calcutta mission also focused worldwide attention on Calcutta's festering problems. In 1971, the India-Pakistan conflict and the creation of Bangladesh led to another flood of refugees, and Calcutta's already chaotic condition further deteriorated. Overcrowding and Muslim-Hindu tensions have recently led to violent outbreaks in outlying areas of the city. Calcutta has the largest population, after Mumbai, of any Indian city, and the problem of having too many mouths to feed will undoubtedly get worse as the birth rate continues to rise.

Orientation

Calcutta sprawls north-south along the eastern bank of the Hooghly River, which divides it from Howrah on the western bank. If you arrive from anywhere west of Calcutta by rail, you'll come into the immense Howrah Station and have to cross the Howrah Bridge into Calcutta proper. Some of Calcutta's worst slums sprawl behind the station on the Howrah side.

For visitors, the more relevant parts of Calcutta are south of the bridge in the areas around BBD Bagh and Chowringhee. BBD Bagh, formerly Dalhousie Square, is the site of the GPO, the international telephone office and the West Bengal tourist office, and is close to the American Express office and various railway booking offices.

South of BBD Bagh is the open expanse of the Maidan along the river, and east from here is the area known as Chowringhee. Most of the cheap and middle-range hotels (and many of the top-end ones) are concentrated in Chowringhee, together with many of the airline offices, restaurants, travel agencies and the Indian Museum. At the southern end of Chowringhee you'll find the Government of India tourist office on Shakespeare Sarani, and, nearby, the Birla Planetarium and Victoria Memorial.

There are a number of landmarks in Calcutta and a couple of important streets to remember. The Ochterlony Monument at the northern end of the Maidan is one of the most visible landmarks – it's a tall column rising from the flat expanse of the Maidan. Sudder St runs off Chowringhee Rd and is the core of the Calcutta travellers' scene. Most of the popular cheap hotels are along Sudder St so it is well known to any taxi or rickshaw-wallah. The Indian Museum is on the corner of Sudder St and Chowringhee Rd.

Further south down Chowringhee Rd, which runs alongside the eastern edge of the Maidan, is Park St, with a great number of more expensive restaurants and the Thai International Airlines office. The newest

BRYN THOMAS

RICHARD I'ANSON

BRYN THOMAS

Calcutta

Top: Rows of Ambassadors under the Howrah Bridge.
Bottom Left: Selling vegetables in the New Market.
Bottom Right: One of Calcutta's fast-disappearing human-pulled rickshaws.

RICHARD I'ANSON

Away from the crowds, Calcutta.

landmark is the cable bridge (Vidyasagar Setu) over the Hooghly, finished in 1994. Although it was supposed to relieve the crush on the old Howrah Bridge, the new bridge is now almost as chaotic itself.

Street Names Getting around Calcutta is slightly confused by the habit of renaming city streets, particularly those with Raj-era connotations. However, many street signs still display the old names, while some maps show old names and others show new ones; taxi-wallahs inevitably only know the old names. It's going to be a long time before Chowringhee Rd becomes Jawaharlal Nehru Rd. There's a certain irony that the street the US Consulate is on was renamed Ho Chi Minh Sarani!

Information

Tourist Offices The Government of India tourist office (☎ 242 1402; fax 242 3521) is at 4 Shakespeare Sarani and is very helpful. They can give you (somewhat dated) computerised printouts of any destination in India.

The West Bengal tourist office (☎ 248

8271) is at 3/2 BBD Bagh – the opposite side to the post office. It is open Monday to Friday from 10.30 am to 5.30 pm. Both the state and national tourist offices (☎ 511 8299) have counters at the airport, and West Bengal has an office at Howrah Station (☎ 660 2518) open daily from 7 am to 1 pm.

Some other states have tourist offices here including the more obscure North-Eastern Region states, Sikkim and the Andaman & Nicobar Islands. They are as follows:

Andaman & Nicobar Islands
3A Auckland Place (☎ 247 5084)
Arunachal Pradesh
4B Chowringhee Place (☎ 248 6500)
Assam
8 Russell St (☎ 298331)
Bihar
26B Camac St (☎ 247 0821)
Madhya Pradesh
Chitrakoot Bldg, 6th floor, 230A AJC Bose Rd (☎ 247 8543)
Manipur
26 Roland Rd (☎ 747075)
Meghalaya
9 Russell St (☎ 290797)
Mizoram
24 Old Ballygunge Rd (☎ 748279)
Nagaland
11 Shakespeare Sarani (☎ 242 5269)
Orissa
55 Lenin Sarani (☎ 244 3653)
Sikkim
5/2 Russell St (☎ 297516)
Tripura
1 Pretoria St (☎ 242 3836)

To find out exactly what's happening on the cultural front, get hold of a free copy of the leaflet *Calcutta This Fortnight* from any tourist office.

Money American Express (☎ 248 0623; fax 248 8096) is at 21 Old Court House St. The Thomas Cook office (☎ 247 4560; fax 247 5854) is in the Chitrakoot Building, 230 AJC Bose Rd.

On Chowringhee Rd there are branches of the State Bank of India and ANZ Grindlays (near Park St metro station). ANZ Grindlays has another branch on Shakespeare Sarani. The Banque National de Paris has a branch

Calcutta's Renamed Roads	
Old Name	*New Name*
Ballygunge Store Rd	Gurusday Rd
Bowbazar St	Bepin Behary Ganguly
Buckland Rd	Bankim Ch Rd
Chowringhee Rd	Jawaharlal Nehru Rd
Harrington St	Ho Chi Minh Sarani
Harrison Rd	Mahatma Gandhi Rd
Kyd St	Dr M Ishaque Rd
Lansdowne Rd	Sarat Bose Rd
Lindsay St	Neille Sengupta Sarani
Lower Chitpur Rd	Rabindra Sarani
Lower Circular Rd	Acharya Jagadish Chandra Bose Rd
Machuabazar St	Madan Mohan St & Keshab Sen St
Mirzapore St	Suryya Sen St
Theatre Rd	Shakespeare Sarani
Wellesley St	Rafi Ahmed Kidwai Rd
Wellington St	Nirmal Chunder St

at BBD Bagh, next to the West Bengal tourist office. Next door again, in the crumbling Stephen Building, is RN Dutt, a licensed private moneychanger who deals with just about any currency you can think of. On Sudder St there are a few licensed money-changers. Travellers' Express Club, at 20 Mirza Ghalib St, is one of the few places you can change money on a Sunday.

The State Bank of India has a 24 hour counter in the new terminal building at the airport.

Post & Communications The large Calcutta GPO is on BBD Bagh and has an efficient poste restante and a philatelic bureau for stamp collectors. The New Market post office is far more conveniently located if you're staying in the Sudder St area. The Park St post office is useful if you're staying in that area and more reliable for posting parcels than the GPO. There are people here who will handle the whole process for you (prices negotiable) and even the officials are friendly and helpful.

The Telephone Bhavan is on BBD Bagh, while the Central Telegraph Office is at 8 Red Cross Place. There are lots of places to make international calls and faxes from, most with 'computerised' meters. American citizens only can make collect calls to the USA from the US Consulate.

International telephone calls are no problem but it takes several attempts to get through on a local call. When you eventually succeed, you invariably find that the number has been changed, although now that most numbers have seven digits, this problem should ease.

Foreign Consulates Some of the useful addresses in Calcutta include:

Bangladesh
    9 Circus Ave (☎ 247 5208)
Bhutan
    48 Tivoli Court, Pramothesh Barua Sarani (☎ 241301)
Denmark
    3 Netaji Subhas Rd (☎ 248 7476)

France
    26 Park St (☎ 290978), inside the courtyard on the right-hand side of Alliance Française
Germany
    1 Hastings Park Rd (☎ 479 1141)
Italy
    3 Raja Santosh Rd (☎ 479 2426)
Japan
    12 Pretoria St (☎ 242 2241)
Nepal
    1 National Library Ave (☎ 479 1173)
Russia
    7 Alipore Ave (☎ 479 7006)
Thailand
    18B Mandeville Gardens (☎ 440 7836)
UK
    1 Ho Chi Minh Sarani (☎ 242 5171)
USA
    5/1 Ho Chi Minh Sarani (☎ 242 3611)

The Nepalese Embassy is open from 10 am to 1 pm and 2 to 4 pm, and visas are issued while you wait.

The nearest Myanmar (Burmese) consulates are in Dhaka, Kathmandu and Delhi. For visas to Bangladesh, travellers have to go to Delhi even though there's an embassy here.

The Thai Consulate is hard to find. It's probably best to take a taxi, though the No 102 bus will get you close to it. It's near South Point School (not South Point High School) and closes at 11.45 am.

Visa Extensions & Permits The Foreigners' Registration Office (☎ 247 3301) is at 237 AJC Bose Rd. Visa extensions are granted here (but you'll need a very good story). Permits for the Andaman Islands are issued here too, but it's easier to buy your permit on arrival in Port Blair. Tax clearance certificates are available from Room 11, 4th floor, Income Tax Building, Bentinck St.

Travel Agencies Travellers' Express Club at 20 Mirza Ghalib St (Free School St) offers competitive prices on airline tickets and keen service.

Books & Bookshops Geoffrey Moorhouse's classic 1971 study *Calcutta* is available as a Penguin paperback. More recently, VS Naipaul has some interesting chapters on Calcutta in his *India – A Million Mutinies*

CALCUTTA

Now. Dominique Lapierre's *City of Joy* is *de rigeur* reading among travellers to Calcutta and is available in paperback (pirated or otherwise) at almost every bookshop. It's dangerous to criticise this book given the guru-like status that many readers accord him, but many parts of the book seem a little fanciful though otherwise interesting. What it certainly has done is to put the Anand Nagar slums in Howrah onto the tourist circuit, but we have a nagging feeling that this is pure voyeurism. When the book was filmed in 1991 a brand new slum was specially built as the set.

The main bookshop area is along College St, opposite the university. In the same building as the Indian Coffee House here, Rupa has a good range including its own publications. Newman's, the publishers of the Bradshaw railway timetable, runs one of Calcutta's oldest bookshops, in the same block as the Great Eastern Hotel.

The Cambridge Book & Stationery Company at 20D Park St is a good small bookshop. Further down Park St towards Chowringhee Rd, the Oxford Book Shop is larger and also has some specialised stock. Classic Books, at 10 Middleton Row, has a wide variety of both Indian and western books, and the owner, Bharat, is a mine of information. Booklands is a small bookstall at the eastern end of Sudder St, and there are more small swap 'n sell places as you turn left into Mirza Ghalib St. The Village Bookshop is probably the best for fiction.

At the end of January a large book fair is held on the Maidan.

Camera Repairs & Musical Instruments

Behind the YMCA at 24 Chowringhee Rd, Latif's is recommended for camera repairs. Camera Craft at 24 Park St, on the 1st floor, is also good. The best place for strings, tunings, repairs and negotiable prices on musical instruments is Braganza & Co at 2A Marquis St. The character who runs it really knows his instruments. Another good place is J Reynold & Co, 15 Mirza Ghalib St, where there's a great selection of instruments.

Medical Services

Dr Paes at Vital Medical Services (☎ 242 5664), 6 Ho Chi Minh Sarani, is open between 8 and 10 am. The Wockhardt Medical Centre (☎ 475 4046) is at 2/7 Sarat Bose (Lansdowne) Rd, and hours are 10 am to noon. Alternatively, medical queries should be directed to any of the large hospitals.

Indian Museum

Conveniently situated on the corner of Sudder St and Chowringhee Rd, the Indian Museum was built in 1875. It's certainly the largest and probably the best museum in India, and one of the best in Asia. Unfortunately, it appears to have been starved of funds in recent years and many of the exhibits are literally falling apart. Some of the display cases are so dusty you can hardly see into them. Its widely varied collection includes oddities such as a whole roomful of meteorites. Other exhibits include the usual fossils, stuffed animals, skeletons, deformed foetuses and so on. There are a number of unique fossil skeletons of prehistoric animals, among them giant crocodiles and an amazingly big tortoise.

The art collection has many fine pieces from Orissan and other temples, and superb examples of Buddhist Gandharan art – an interesting meeting point between Greek artistry and Buddhist ideals that produced Buddha images and other sculptures of great beauty.

The museum is open daily except Monday from 10 am to 5 pm. Between December and February it closes half an hour earlier. Entry is Rs 3.

Maidan & Fort William

After the events of 1756, the British decided there would be no repetition of the attack on the city and set out to replace the original Fort William, in the Maidan, with a massive and impregnable new fort. First they cleared out the inhabitants of the village of Govindpur and in 1758 laid the foundations of a fort. By the time it was completed in 1781, the fort had cost them the awesome total, for those days, of £2 million. Around the fort a huge expanse of jungle was cut down to give the cannons a clear line of fire but, as usually happens, the fort has never fired a shot in anger.

The fort is still in use today and visitors are only allowed inside with special permission (rarely granted). Even the trenches and deep fortifications surrounding the fort's massive walls seem to be out of bounds.

The area cleared around Fort William became the Maidan, the 'lungs' of modern Calcutta. This huge green expanse stretches three km north to south and is over a km wide. It is bound by Strand Rd along the river to the west and by Chowringhee Rd, lined with shops, offices, hotels and eating places, to the east. The stream known as Tolly's Nullah forms its southern boundary, and here you will find a racecourse and the Victoria Memorial. In the north-west corner of the Maidan is Eden Gardens, while Raj Bhavan overlooks it from the north.

Within the gardens are cricket and football fields, tennis courts, ponds, trees and even musical fountains. Cows graze, political discussions are held, people stroll across the grounds or come for early morning yoga sessions. And of course the place is used, like any area of open land in India, as a public toilet.

Ochterlony Monument Now officially renamed the Shahid (Martyr's) Minar, this 48m column towers over the northern end of the Maidan. It was erected in 1828 and named after Sir David Ochterlony, who is credited with winning the Nepal War (1814-6). The column is an intriguing combination of Turkish, Egyptian and Syrian architectural elements.

There's a fine view from the top of the column, but permission to ascend (not granted for the first and last week of each month) must be obtained from police headquarters, which is on Lal Bazaar St. It's only open Monday to Friday and you should simply ask for a 'monument pass' at the Assistant Commissioner's office on the 2nd floor.

Eden Gardens In the north-west corner of the Maidan are the small and pleasantly laid-out Eden Gardens. A tiny Burmese pagoda was brought here from Prome, Myanmar (Burma) in 1856; it's set in a small lake and is extraordinarily picturesque. The gardens were named after the sister of Lord Auckland, the former governor general. The Calcutta Cricket Ground (Ranji Stadium), where international Test and one-day matches are held, is also within the gardens.

Near the gardens you can take a pleasant walk along the banks of the Hooghly River. Ferries run across the river from several ghats and there are plenty of boat operators

---

Calcutta Mounted Police

Every day at around 5 am, 25 officers of the Calcutta Mounted Police force mount up at the stables in Chowringhee and head off around Calcutta's 25 sq km Maidan for the first of the day's half dozen or so sorties. This practice has been going on for the last 150 years.

The force was first formed in the 1840s, and its role then was to carry communications between the city's administrators and the port's harbourmaster. At that time the force consisted of just one senior officer and two juniors. As the city grew, however, the force was enlarged, and its duties increased to include the patrolling of the city's Maidan, which was notorious as the hangout of undesirables – thieves, muggers and prostitutes all frequented it. The force was gradually expanded to its present number of 98 horses, 105 men and as many grooms.

In the early days all officers of the Mounted Police were British; only after Independence was the first non-British officer appointed (an Anglo-Indian). The ranks were recruited from Uttar Pradesh, Kashmir and Rajasthan.

These days the main role of the force is to keep the city's sports fans in order. A big football or cricket match may draw a crowd of 90,000 excited fans to the Maidan, and outbreaks of violence are not uncommon. Other duties include forming the guard of honour for visiting dignitaries.

The horses themselves are all bred in India specifically for the force, and cost around Rs 30,000 each. In the past, when cash was less of a worry, they were imported direct from Australia. ∎

around offering to take you out on the water for a short cruise.

See the **Victoria Memorial** regional highlight on p477.

St Paul's Cathedral

Built between 1839 and 1847, St Paul's Cathedral is one of India's most important churches. It's east of the Victoria Memorial at the south end of the Maidan. The steeple fell during an earthquake in 1897 and was redesigned and rebuilt. Inside, there's some interesting memorials and stained glass, including the west window by Sir Edward Burne-Jones. It's open to visitors from 9 am to noon, and from 3 to 6 pm. Sunday services are at 7.30 and 8.30 am, and 6 pm.

Birla Planetarium

This planetarium, near the Government of India tourist office, is one of the largest in the world. For Rs 8 you'll get a much better view of the stars in here than in the polluted atmosphere outside. There are shows in English every day, but as times vary, check in advance (☎ 248 1515). Beware of pickpockets, especially in the queue outside.

Nehru Children's Museum

This small museum, conveniently situated at 94/1 Chowringhee Rd, is worth visiting for its models depicting the Hindu epics, the *Ramayana* and the *Mahabharata*. It's open daily except Monday from 11.30 am to 8.30 pm; admission is Rs 2.

Kali Temple

Rebuilt in 1809 on the site of a much older temple, Kalighat (as it is also known) is the actual temple from which Kalikata (anglicised to Calcutta) takes its name. According to legend, when Siva's wife's corpse was cut up, one of her fingers fell here. Since then it has been an important pilgrimage site.

Kali represents the destructive side of Siva's consort and demands daily sacrifices. In the morning goats have their throats slit here to satisfy the goddess' bloodlust. During the day many poor people come here for a free feed. This is an extremely busy (and grubby) temple, and you'll be latched on to by temple 'priests' who will whisk you around and ask for a donation of Rs 100 for a 'small bag of rice'!

Mother Teresa's **Hospital for the Dying**

Mother Teresa

Mother Teresa, the 'Saint of the Gutters', has come to epitomise selflessness in her dedication to the destitute, the suffering and the dying. Born Agnes Gonxha Bojaxhiu in Serbia in 1910 to Albanian parents, she joined the Irish Order of Loreto nuns in 1929 and was sent to Darjeeling as a teacher. Moving to a school in Calcutta in 1937 she was horrified at the numbers of poor people left to die on the streets of the city because there was nowhere else for them to go. She began to feel that behind the secure walls of the nunnery she was too far removed from the people she wanted to help.

The Missionaries of Charity was Mother Teresa's new order, formed in 1950. Among their vows is the promise 'to give wholehearted and free service to the poorest of the poor'. This vow was put into action with the setting up of several homes including Nirmal Hriday (the home for the dying), Shanti Nagar (for lepers) and Nirmala Shishu Bhavan (the children's home). There are now homes in many other places, staffed not only by nuns but also by volunteers or co-workers.

For all her saintliness, Mother Teresa is not without her critics. Germaine Greer, for example, has accused her of being a religious imperialist, although anyone who has spent some time with the nuns and seen them at work could hardly call them Bible-bashing evangelists. Mother Teresa herself has said that hers is contemplative work. Her inspiration is spiritual and Christian but it is put into practice mainly by ministering to physical needs. In 1979 her work achieved world recognition when she was awarded the Nobel Peace Prize.

Old age has finally slowed Mother Teresa down, and with three major operations in the last five years, worldwide attention keeps track of her heartbeat almost as keenly as her pacemaker does. In early 1997, Mother Teresa resigned her position at the Missionaries due to bad health, and was replaced by Sister Nirmala.

If you are considering undertaking voluntary work in India, see the relevant section in the Facts for the Visitor chapter. ∎

Destitute is right next door to the temple and you are welcome to visit.

The temple is about two km directly south of St Paul's Cathedral and is easily accessible by metro (Kalighat station).

Zoo & Horticultural Gardens

South of the Maidan, Calcutta's 16 hectare zoo was opened in 1875. Some of the animals are displayed in near natural environments, others in the pitiful conditions characteristic of Third World zoos. It's open from sunrise to sunset; admission is Rs 2.

Just south of the zoo on Alipore Rd are the pleasant and quiet horticultural gardens. They're open from 8 am to 5 pm; admission is Rs 1.

Howrah Bridge

Until 1943, the Hooghly River was crossed by a pontoon bridge which had to be opened to let river traffic through. There was considerable opposition to construction of a bridge due to fears that it would affect the river currents and cause silting problems. This problem was eventually avoided by building a bridge that crosses the river in a single 450m span – there are no pylons at all within the river.

The cantilevered bridge, also known as Rabindra Setu, is similar in size to the Sydney Harbour Bridge but carries a flow of traffic which Sydney could never dream of –

with a daily stream of nearly 60,000 vehicles, and pedestrians too numerous to count, it is the busiest bridge in the world. It's intriguing to stand at one end of the bridge at morning rush hour and watch the procession of double-decker buses come across. They heel over like yachts in a heavy wind due to the weight of passengers hanging onto the sides. In between are lumbering bullock carts, hordes of bicycles and even the odd car. During the morning and evening rush hours it can take 45 minutes to get across. The ferries running from below Howrah Station are a more convenient way to cross the river and give you a good view of the bridge.

The second bridge, Vidyasagar Setu, two km downriver, was an on-off project for 22 years but was finally completed in 1994. The problem now is that the approach roads to it are too narrow to handle the amount of traffic that uses the bridge, and there are no funds left for further development.

BBD Bagh (Dalhousie Square)

When Calcutta was the administrative centre for British India, BBD Bagh was the centre of power. On the north side of the square stands the huge Writers' Building, which dates from 1880 (when clerical workers were known as writers). The East India Company's writers have now been replaced by modern-day ones employed by the West Bengal state government, and this is where

---

India's Bakda-Wallahs

In India it's possible to buy just about anything from pavement hawkers. On the streets around Calcutta's Stock Exchange behind the Writers' Building, and indeed around the 20 other stock exchanges throughout the country, you'll find the wooden tables of the *bakda-wallahs*, the hawkers who distribute application forms for new share issues.

Apart from a wooden table, the only prerequisite for setting up as a bakda-wallah is about Rs 600 to register with a broker to handle the forms. What is more important, however, is good contacts and a nose for a bargain stock. A good bakda-wallah will not only help the investor fill in the forms, but should be able to give dependable tips about which stocks are hot. He may also go as far as to lodge the forms on behalf of the investors, often after the official closing dates if his bank contacts come through.

While it is a competitive business, a bakda-wallah can expect a very tidy monthly income of around Rs 3000, and those with an established clientele and impeccable contacts can earn 10 times that in a good month. His fee is between 1.25% and 1.8% of the value of the shares sold through him.

With the economic liberalisation of the past few years, the trading in stocks has increased dramatically, and the small investor would be lost without the bakda-wallah. ■

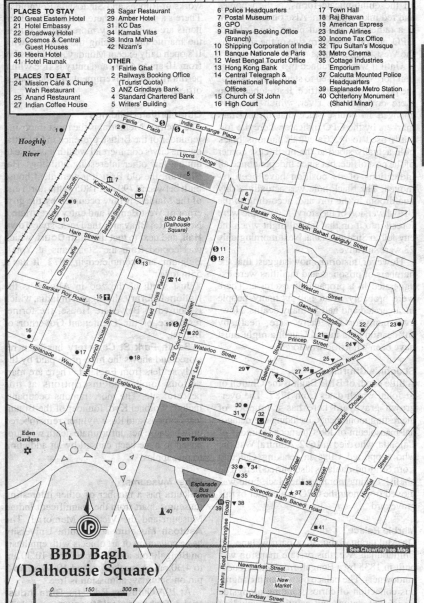

PLACES TO STAY
20 Great Eastern Hotel
21 Hotel Embassy
22 Broadway Hotel
26 Cosmos & Central Guest Houses
36 Heera Hotel
41 Hotel Raunak

PLACES TO EAT
24 Mission Cafe & Chung Wah Restaurant
25 Anand Restaurant
27 Indian Coffee House

28 Sagar Restaurant
29 Amber Hotel
31 KC Das
34 Kamala Vilas
38 Indra Mahal
42 Nizam's

OTHER
1 Fairlie Ghat
2 Railways Booking Office (Tourist Quota)
3 ANZ Grindlays Bank
4 Standard Chartered Bank
5 Writers' Building

6 Police Headquarters
7 Postal Museum
8 GPO
9 Railways Booking Office (Branch)
10 Shipping Corporation of India
11 Banque Nationale de Paris
12 West Bengal Tourist Office
13 Hong Kong Bank
14 Central Telegraph & International Telephone Offices
15 Church of St John
16 High Court

17 Town Hall
18 Raj Bhavan
19 American Express
23 Indian Airlines
30 Income Tax Office
32 Tipu Sultan's Mosque
33 Metro Cinema
35 Cottage Industries Emporium
37 Calcutta Mounted Police Headquarters
39 Esplanade Metro Station
40 Ochterlony Monument (Shahid Minar)

BBD Bagh (Dalhousie Square)

all the quintuplicate forms, carbon copies and red ink come from. Also on BBD Bagh is a rather more useful place, the Calcutta GPO, and on the eastern side of the square is the West Bengal tourist office.

Until it was abandoned in 1757, the original Fort William used to stand on the site of the present-day post office. It stretched from there down to the river, which has also changed its course since that time. Brass markers by the GPO indicate where the fort walls used to be. Calcutta's famous black hole actually stood at the north-east corner of the post office, but since Independence all indications of its position have been removed. The black hole was actually a tiny guardroom in the fort and, according to the British version of the story, 146 people were forced into it on that fateful night when the city fell to Siraj-ud-daula. Next morning only 23 were still alive.

However, historians now suggest that the numbers of prisoners and fatalities were exaggerated in a propaganda exercise. There were probably about half as many people incarcerated and half as many deaths. However many or few there were, death by suffocation on a humid Calcutta night must have been a horrific way to go.

St John's Church

A little south of BBD Bagh is the Church of St John, which dates from 1787. The overgrown graveyard here has a number of interesting monuments, including the octagonal mausoleum of Job Charnock, founder of Calcutta, who died in 1692. Admiral Watson, who supported Clive in retaking Calcutta from Siraj-ud-daula, is also buried here. The obelisk commemorating the black hole was moved from near the GPO to a corner of this graveyard.

Marble Palace

On Muktaram Babu St, a narrow lane off Chittaranjan Ave, this private mansion was built in 1835 by a Bengali *zamindar* (feudal landowner). The palace houses an incongruous collection of curios standing alongside significant statues and paintings (including

works of Rubens and Sir Joshua Reynolds). There's a private zoo here too, but the inhabitants are only slightly more animated than the marble lions gracing the palace lawns. It's open daily except Monday and Thursday from 10 am to 4 pm, and entry is free with a permit from the Government of India tourist office.

Other British Buildings

The Victoria Memorial is the most imposing reminder of the British presence in Calcutta, but the city's commercial wealth gave rise to quite a few other interesting buildings. **Raj Bhavan**, the old British government house built between 1799 and 1805 at the north end of the Maidan, is now occupied by the governor of West Bengal and entry is restricted. Next to Raj Bhavan is the Doric-style **Town Hall**, and next to that the **High Court**, which was copied from the Staadhaus at Ypres, Belgium, and completed in 1872. It has a 55m tower.

Just south of the zoo in Alipore is the **National Library**, the biggest in India, which is housed in Belvedere House, the former residence of the Lieutenant-Governor of Bengal.

South Park St Cemetery has been restored and shows the high price paid by the early settlers from England. There are marvellous tombs and inscriptions at this peaceful site. The more famous occupants include Colonel Kyd, founder of the Botanical Gardens, and Rose Aylmer, remembered only because her unfortunate death was supposed to have been caused by an addiction to pineapples!

Other Museums

Calcutta has a number of other interesting museums apart from the magnificent Indian Museum and the Victoria Memorial. The **Asutosh Museum** at Calcutta University has a collection of art objects with emphasis on Bengali folk art. It is open from 10.30 am to 4.30 pm on weekdays, and 10.30 am to 3 pm on Saturday; admission is free.

At 19A Gurusday Rd is the **Birla Industrial & Technological Museum**, open daily except Monday from 10 am to 5 pm; admission is Rs 1. Those philanthropic (and very wealthy) Birlas have also provided the **Birla Academy of Art & Culture** at 109 Southern Ave, open daily except Monday from 4 to 8 pm; admission is Rs 1. It has a good collection of sculpture and modern art. The huge Birla-built **Rada Krishna Temple** is just around the corner from the Industrial & Technological Museum.

The **Academy of Fine Arts**, on Cathedral Rd beside the cathedral in Chowringhee, has a permanent exhibition and runs an artists' studio. There are cultural shows in the evening. The academy is open daily except Monday from 3 to 8 pm; entry is Rs 1.

The rambling old **Tagore House** is a centre for Indian dance, drama, music and other arts. This is the birthplace of Rabindranath Tagore, India's greatest modern poet, and his final resting place. It's just off Rabindra Sarani, north of BBD Bagh, and is open from 10 am to 5 pm weekdays, to 2 pm on Saturday and is closed on Sunday.

Next door to the GPO there's a small **postal museum**.

Pareshnath Jain Temple

This temple, in the north-east of the city, was built in 1867 and dedicated to Sheetalnathji, the 10th of the 24 Jain *tirthankars*. The temple is an ornate mass of mirrors, coloured stones and glass mosaics. It overlooks a garden, and is open daily from 6 to 11.30 am and 3 to 7 pm.

Nakhoda Mosque

North of BBD Bagh, this is Calcutta's principal Muslim place of worship. Built in 1926, the huge Nakhoda Mosque is said to accommodate 10,000 people and was modelled on Akbar's tomb at Sikandra near Agra. The red sandstone mosque has two 46m minarets and a brightly painted onion-shaped dome. Outside the mosque, every day except Sunday, you can buy attar, which is perfume made from essential oils and flower fragrances.

Belur Math

North of the city, on the west bank of the Hooghly River, is the headquarters of the Ramakrishna Mission, Belur Math. Ramakrishna, an Indian philosopher, preached the unity of all religions. He died in 1886, and his follower Swami Vivekananda founded the Ramakrishna Mission in 1897. There are now branches all over India. Belur Math, the movement's international headquarters, was founded in 1899. It is supposed to represent a church, a mosque and a temple, depending on how you look at it. Belur Math is open daily from 6.30 to 11 am and from 3.30 to 7 pm, and admission is free.

The Mission's **Institute of Culture**, which has a library, reading rooms and lecture halls, is in the south of the city near Dhakuria railway station.

Dakshineswar Kali Temple

Across the river and north of Belur Math is this Kali temple where Ramakrishna was a priest, and where he reached his spiritual vision of the unity of all religions. The temple was built in 1847 and is surrounded by 12 other temples, dedicated to Siva.

Botanical Gardens

The extensive Botanical Gardens are on the west bank of the Hooghly River. They stretch for over a km along the riverfront and occupy 109 hectares. The gardens were originally founded in 1786 and initially administered by Colonel Kyd. It was from these gardens that the tea now grown in Assam and Darjeeling was first developed.

The gardens' prime attraction is the 200-year-old banyan tree, claimed to have the second largest canopy in the world (the largest is in Andhra Pradesh). It covers an area of ground nearly 400m in circumference and continues to flourish despite having its central trunk removed in 1925 because of fungus damage. The palm house in the centre of the gardens is also well worth a visit.

The gardens are over the Howrah Bridge, 19km from Chowringhee on a bus heading for Sibpur. However, it's much more pleasant to go by ferry, and there are frequent departures from Chandpal and Babu Ghats (Rs 3). The gardens are open from sunrise to sunset, and although they tend to be very crowded on Sunday, on other days they are peaceful and make a pleasant escape from the hassles and crowds of Calcutta.

Organised Tours

The Government of India tourist office (☎ 242 1402) at 4 Shakespeare Sarani has a full-day tour for Rs 75, departing daily (except Monday) at 8 am from their office. It covers Belur Math, Dakshineswar Temple, the Jain temple, the Victoria Memorial, the Indian Museum, the Nehru Children's Museum and the zoo.

The West Bengal tourist office (☎ 248 8271) at 3/2 BBD Bagh has a similar tour for Rs 70 or a second tour which crams in even more for Rs 100. One of the problems with sightseeing in Calcutta is that an awful lot of time is spent just sitting in traffic jams.

Bus tours are also conducted for the various festivals and pujas around the state – consult *Calcutta This Fortnight* or a tourist office for details. West Bengal Tourism operates weekly trips to the Sunderbans Wildlife Sanctuary from October to March. See the Sunderbans section in the West Bengal chapter for more information.

Places to Stay – bottom end

Calcutta suffers from a shortage of good cheap places to stay. Budget travellers' accommodation is centred on Sudder St, running off Chowringhee Rd beside the Indian Museum. Aim to arrive in Calcutta before noon or you may have great difficulty in finding a cheap bed.

The *Salvation Army Red Shield Guest House* (☎ 245 0599) at 2 Sudder St is popular with volunteers working for Mother Teresa. It has dorm beds from Rs 40 and private double rooms from Rs 80 to Rs 200. The more expensive rooms have a bath. The guest house is clean and well kept, and great value if you can get in.

Hotel Maria (☎ 245 0860), further down Sudder St, is equally popular, with dorm beds for Rs 50. There are also singles/doubles for Rs 100/150 with common bathroom, and Rs 150/200 with bath. They have a strict no drugs, no alcohol policy.

Hotel Paragon (☎ 244 2445), at 2 Stuart Lane, and *Modern Lodge* (☎ 243-4690), opposite at No 1, are two of Calcutta's most popular budget establishments. The Paragon has dorm beds at Rs 45 (downstairs) and Rs 50 (upstairs), tiny singles/doubles with common bath for Rs 90/110 and doubles with bath from Rs 120. The ground floor rooms are rather gloomy but there's a pleasant courtyard upstairs. Modern Lodge is similar. The rooftop area is a popular meeting place in the evening, and tea and soft drinks are available.

Hotel Hilson (☎ 249 0864), at 4 Sudder St, has clean singles with common bath for Rs 125, doubles with bath from Rs 350 and some triples at Rs 400.

Shilton Hotel (☎ 245 1512) has singles/doubles with attached bathrooms for Rs 175/250.

Mansukh Guest House (☎ 249 8231), 25 Marquis St, promises 'an experience that remains'. Our experience was 16 hours without electricity, but management assures us this was a one-off! Double rooms start at Rs 250, and hike to Rs 400 for dog-boxes with air-con.

Hotel Oriental (☎ 294295), where all rooms are Rs 300 and there's no air-con, is the big place opposite.

Times Guest House (☎ 245 1796) is a friendly Sikh-run place near the Blue Sky Cafe. Doubles with common bath are Rs 100, and Rs 150 with private bath.

Tourist Inn (☎ 244 9818), nearby, is fairly clean with rooms with common bath for Rs 75/150.

Centrepoint Guest House (☎ 244 8184) is around the corner from Sudder St, at 20 Mirza Ghalib St. It's a bustling, popular place. Double rooms are Rs 175 or Rs 350 with air-con, and there's a lounge with TV. There's no single room rate, but there are plans for a dormitory on the top floor.

Hotel Palace (☎ 244-6214), down Chowringhee Lane, has rooms for Rs 125/200 with attached bath, or Rs 400 with TV and air-con.

Timestar Hotel (☎ 245 0028) is in Tottee Lane, next to 4 Sudder St. It's Rs 140/200 for rooms with bath.

East End Hotel (☎ 298921) is south of

Sudder St, on Dr M Ishaque Rd. This is an old, well-maintained place run by friendly people. It has singles/doubles with attached bath for Rs 200/350.

Neelam Hotel (☎ 299198), right opposite, is better value with singles/doubles for Rs 150/250 and air-con for Rs 400.

Classic Hotel (☎ 290256) is nearby, down an alley off Mirza Ghalib St. Singles with common bath are Rs 115. Doubles with bath are Rs 205, or Rs 450 with air-con. Hot water is available free by the bucket.

Calcutta has a collection of Ys but they're often full.

The *YMCA* (☎ 249 2192) at 25 Chowringhee Rd is a big, gloomy building which is popular with Indian businesspeople. All accommodation includes early-morning tea, breakfast and dinner; the rooms have attached baths. There are dorm beds for Rs 220, singles/doubles for Rs 325/460 or Rs 560/730 with air-con.

Another *YMCA* (☎ 244 3814), at 42 Surendra Nath Banerji Rd, has simple rooms starting at Rs 100.

The *YWCA* (☎ 297033), 1 Middleton Row, is a grand old place – it's airy and spotless and has a beautiful tennis court. It's good value at Rs 255/410 with common bath and all meals, or Rs 500/610 with attached bath and all meals.

Lean-budget options in other parts of Calcutta are limited, although there are a number of cheapish guest houses in BBD Bagh and a group of cheaper hotels near New Market. Railway station accommodation is also a possibility.

Hotel Raunak (☎ 244 2285), along Corporation Place near New Market, has large rooms with bathroom for Rs 150/200.

Cosmos Guest House (☎ 261383), on Chittaranjan Ave in BBD Bagh, has spic and span rooms starting at Rs 175/215.

Retiring rooms at Howrah railway station are Rs 130 for doubles with attached bathrooms.

Railway Yatri Nivas (☎ 660 1742), in the new building next door, has dorm beds for Rs 75 and doubles with attached bathrooms for Rs 250, or Rs 390 with air-con. You can

only stay here with a train ticket for 200km or more, and then only for three nights. There are also *retiring rooms* at Sealdah and, for transit passengers, at Calcutta Airport. Check at the reservations desk at the terminal.

Places to Stay – middle

There's a bunch of mid-range places within easy walking distance of BBD Bagh.

Central Guest House (☎ 274876) is a recommended hotel that's good value with clean singles/doubles for Rs 190/250. All rooms have attached bathrooms. The hotel fronts onto Chittaranjan Ave but the entrance is round the back at 18 Prafulla Sarkar St.

Hotel Embassy (☎ 279040) is the old place on nearby Princep St. Singles/doubles with attached bath, TV and phone are Rs 300/350. Air-con doubles cost Rs 500.

Broadway Hotel (☎ 263930; fax 264151) is one block east. There's a range of rooms from Rs 160 for a single with common bathroom to doubles/triples/quads for Rs 320/410/500 with attached bath, TV and phone. It's popular and often full.

You'll find some moderately priced hotels in among Chowringhee's scungy and pocket-plungy establishments.

Hotel Lindsay (☎ 244 1039; fax 245 0310), 8A Lindsay St, is a clean new hotel with singles/doubles for Rs 400/500 or Rs 650/750 with air-con.

Gujral Lodge (☎ 244 0392) has spacious rooms at Rs 170/520 with attached bath. It's behind Hotel Lindsay, on the 2nd floor.

CKT Inn (☎ 244 0047), 12A Lindsay St, is a small friendly place with rooms for Rs 555/721, which includes all taxes and service charges. The rooms are air-con and have TVs and attached bathrooms. It's often full.

Hotel Plaza (☎ 244 6411) at 10 Sudder St has boxy windowless rooms for Rs 375 with attached bath, or Rs 475 with air-con.

Astoria Hotel (☎ 244 9679; fax 244 8589), 6/2 Sudder St, is all air-con. Spacious rooms with bath, colour TV and telephone are Rs 550/660.

Heera Hotel (☎ 228 0663) at 28 Grant St, just north of New Market, is a modern place

CALCUTTA

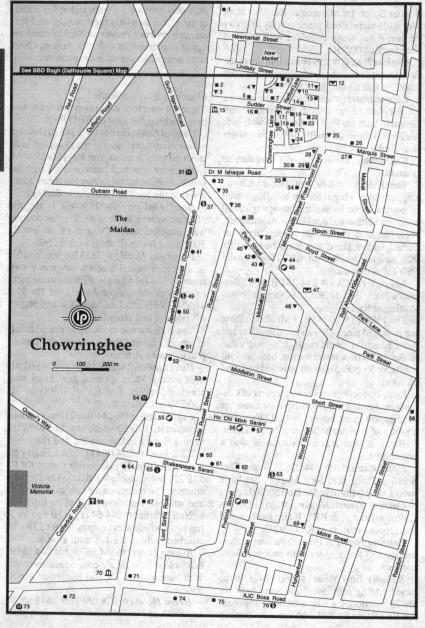

See BBD Bagh (Dalhousie Square) Map

Newmarket Street

New Market

Lindsay Street

Red Road

Dufferin Road

Guru Nanak Road

Outram Road

The Maidan

Chowringhee

0   100   200 m

Queen's Way

Victoria Memorial

Cathedral Road

Jawaharlal Nehru Road (Chowringhee Road)

Dr M Ishaque Road

Russel Street

Park Street

Middleton Row

Middleton Street

Little Russel Street

Ho Chi Minh Sarani

Shakespeare Sarani

Lord Sinha Road

Pretoria Street

Camac Street

Mirza Ghalib Street (Free School Street)

Ripon Street

Royd Street

Rafi Ahmed Kidwai Road

Park Lane

Park Street

Short Street

Wood Street

Loudon Street

Moira Street

Hungerford Street

Rawdon Street

AJC Bose Road

Sudder Street

Hafford Lane

Marquis Street

Market Street

Middleton Row

with carpeted rooms and attached bath for Rs 300/375, or Rs 550/700 with air-con.

Places to Stay – top end

If you happen upon Calcutta cashed up and ready to splurge, there are plenty of places happy to accommodate.

The *Tollygunge Club* (☎ 473 2316; fax 473 1903) is set on 44 hectares on the southern edge of Calcutta. It's not only a wonderfully relaxing place to stay, but is also just the place to get an idea of how the other half lived and played in the days of the Raj. It's run by an Englishman, Bob Wright, along exclusive lines set down almost 100 years ago. The elegant clubhouse was once the mansion at the centre of a large indigo plantation, now a championship golf course. Sitting by the swimming

pool here, with a cold beer or an excellent club sandwich, it's hard to believe you're still in Calcutta. Tolly (as it's affectionately called) is now the playground of the city's elite. As well as an indoor and an outdoor pool, there are grass and clay tennis courts, two squash courts, a croquet lawn, billiards, badminton and table tennis, and a stable full of ponies. As a foreign visitor, so long as you telephone, fax, or write in advance (120 DP Sasmal Rd, Calcutta 700 033), you may stay here and have temporary membership allowing you to use the facilities. Guests are expected to be reasonably tidy but jackets and ties are not necessary. The cheapest rooms are in 'Hastings' and these cost Rs 950/1000, with air-con and attached baths. The 'Grandstand' cottages cost Rs 1700/1800

CALCUTTA

PLACES TO STAY		PLACES TO EAT		43	Thai International,
1	Oberoi Grand Hotel	3	Zaranj Restaurant		Flury's, Peter Cat &
2	YMCA	4	Khalsa Restaurant		Silver Grill
5	Lytton Hotel	6	Oasis Restaurant	45	French Consulate
7	Fairlawn Hotel	10	Fiesta Restaurant	47	Park St Post Office
8	Gujral Lodge & City	11	Kathleen's Bakery	49	State Bank of India
	Express	17	Blue Sky Cafe	50	American Center
	Supermarket	24	Abdul Khalique Hotel	51	British Airways, RNAC,
9	Hotel Lindsay & CKT	25	Shamiana Bar & Gypsy		Air France, Citibank
	Inn		Fast Food		& ANZ Grindlays
13	Centrepoint Guest	28	Hong Kong Restaurant		Bank
	House & Travellers'	35	Peiping Restaurant	52	Cathay Pacific & KLM
	Express Club	36	Trinca's Gulnar	55	British High
14	Hotels Plaza & Astoria		Restaurant		Commission
16	Salvation Army Guest	40	Junior Brothers	56	US Consulate
	House	44	Golden Dragon	57	Vital Medical Services
18	Hotel Maria		Restaurant	59	Swissair
19	Hotel Paragon	48	Waldorf Restaurant	61	British Council
20	Hotel Palace	69	Hare Krishna Bakery &	63	ANZ Grindlays Bank
21	Timestar Hotel		ISKCON	64	Birla Planetarium
22	Shilton Hotel			65	Government of India
23	Modern Lodge &	**OTHER**			Tourist Office
	JoJo's Restaurant	12	New Market Post	66	St Paul's Cathedral
26	Mansukh Guest House		Office	67	Air India
27	Hotel Oriental	15	Indian Museum	68	Japanese Consulate
30	Neelam Hotel	29	Off cum On Rambo	70	Nehru Children's
33	East End Hotel		Bar		Museum
34	Classic Hotel	32	Bangladesh Biman	71	Aeroflot
38	Park Hotel & Kwality		Airlines & Lufthansa	72	Rabindra Sadan
	Restaurant	37	Standard Chartered	74	Foreigners'
46	YWCA		Bank & ANZ		Registration Office
53	Old Kenilworth Hotel		Grindlays Bank	76	Thomas Cook
58	Hotel Rutt Deen	39	Oasis, Moulin Rouge,		
60	New Kenilworth Hotel		Olypub, Bar BQ &	**METRO STATIONS**	
62	Astor Hotel		Blue Fox	31	Park St
75	Hotel Hindustan	41	Japan Airlines	54	Maidan
	International	42	Singapore Airlines	73	Rabindra Sadan

and have small sitting areas overlooking the golf course. Most rooms in Tolly Towers or Tolly Terrace are similarly priced. There's a 10% surcharge on the prices above. The club is a 10 minute walk from Tollygunge metro station.

'Old' Kenilworth Hotel (☎ 242 5325), 7 Little Russell St in Chowringhee, is an ageing place full of character. It's run by long-time Calcutta resident, Mrs Joyce Purdy, and is an old colonial-style house in its own grounds. Some people enjoy the character of the place and its somewhat eccentric proprietor, others complain that it's dilapidated and the service lacking. Large doubles with sitting areas are Rs 750, or Rs 1000 with air-con. All the rooms have a bath.

Great Eastern Hotel (☎ 248 2311; fax 248 0289), 1-3 Old Court House St (south of BBD Bagh), is a rambling Raj-style hotel. Although it's distinctly tatty round the edges, its 200 rooms are often full by late morning. Air-con doubles are Rs 1050/1450. There are a number of restaurants and a coffee shop with the peculiar name, 'Dragon in Sherry's'.

Fairlawn Hotel (☎ 245 1510; fax 244 1835), 13A Sudder St, is a piece of Calcutta where the Raj still lives, albeit in a decidedly eccentric manner which you may find quaintly amusing or downright irritating. Edmund Smith and his Armenian wife, Violet, the couple who still run the hotel more than 45 years after Independence, look like they've been time-warped from Brighton in the 1950s.

Most of the rooms are air-conditioned and have TV and phone, but the bathrooms are a bit on the primitive side and the hot water is sporadic. The doubles at US$50 are much better value than the singles at US$45, as the latter seem to be an afterthought. This tariff includes three meals (variable western food), plus afternoon tea in the garden. Service can be abrupt to the point of rudeness, which many people find off-putting. A 20% discount is offered from April to September. The hotel has its own well and water filtration equipment.

Lytton Hotel (☎ 249 1872; fax 249 1747), 14 Sudder St, is a good choice as far as modern

places go. Centrally air-con singles/doubles are Rs 1100/1600 with attached bathroom and TV. It's a popular place, so get there early in the day if possible.

Hotel Rutt Deen (☎ 247 5240; fax 247 5210), 21B Loudon St, is a good three-star place with singles/doubles from Rs 800/900 with air-con.

Astor Hotel (☎ 242 9957; fax 242 5136), 15 Shakespeare Sarani, is in a good location and has air-con singles/doubles from Rs 944/1322 (including tax). The hotel has a very pleasant garden and there are daily barbecues.

New Kenilworth Hotel (☎ 242 8394; fax 242 5136), 1-2 Little Russell St, has old and new wings but all rooms are air-con, have a fridge, TV and attached bath. Basic rates are US$60/70.

ITDC Airport Ashok (☎ 552 9111; fax 552 9137), at the airport, is modern, and convenient for passengers in transit. Singles/doubles with air-con cost Rs 3800/4200. It has all the facilities you would expect of a five-star hotel.

Hotel Hindustan International (☎ 247 2394; fax 247 2824), at 235/1 AJC Bose Rd, has 212 rooms at US$130/150.

Park Hotel (☎ 249 3121; fax 249 7343), at 17 Park St, is more expensive. It costs US$200/220 for air-con singles/doubles. There's a restaurant, bar and pool.

Oberoi Grand Hotel (☎ 249 2323; fax 249 1217), 15 Chowringhee Rd, is pretty plain externally but very grand inside. Rooms start at US$205/235. There are three restaurants, and beneath the palm trees in the central courtyard there's a swimming pool. The Oberoi Grand has long been acknowledged as Calcutta's best hotel and the jewel in the Oberoi crown.

Taj Bengal (☎ 248 3939; fax 248 1766), at the southern end of the Maidan, is a plush competitor for gold-carded clientele. It has all the mod cons you'd expect, and an opulent atrium with a waterfall. Singles/doubles are US$220/240, with more expensive suites.

Places to Eat

Cheap Finding good food at reasonable prices is no problem in the Chowringhee/

Sudder St area and everyone seems to have their own favourite place.

Blue Sky Cafe, halfway down Sudder St, is always packed with travellers and does excellent breakfasts and snacks. They have good curd with fruit, milk shakes, fresh juice, great porridge and a range of burgers and snacks. You'll probably find it hard to start the day anywhere else.

Places less geared to the western traveller are cheaper.

Abdul Khalique Hotel is just south of Sudder St. You can get a delicious egg-roll (wrapped in newspaper) for Rs 5 and a cup of tea for Rs 1.

Khalsa Restaurant, along the street opposite the Salvation Army Guest House, has been popular with both locals and travellers for many years.

Oasis Restaurant is in the same street. The menu choices are wider, but the bill hits harder.

Taj Continental, opposite the entrance to Stuart Lane, is cheaper and the food is good.

Shamiana Bar & Restaurant is one of several places on Mirza Ghalib St. It's clean and offers Indian and Chinese food.

Gypsy Fast Food is close by and similar.

Cafe 48 has good veg thalis.

Fiesta Restaurant serves basic Mughal food in Hartford Lane, which runs between Sudder and Lindsay Sts.

JoJo's Restaurant is also off Sudder St, but on the other side. It's open for breakfast, lunch and dinner and all dishes are under Rs 25.

Kamala Vilas, in a small side street off Chowringhee Rd near the Metro Cinema, is good for no-frills south Indian vegetarian food.

Hare Krishna Bakery, on the corner of Middleton and Russell Sts, is the place for good bread and takeaway snacks. Go early for the excellent brown bread.

Kathleen's Bakery is nearer Sudder St and has greater variety. This is where the Calcuttans who can afford to eat cake indulge themselves.

Princess Restaurant, adjoining Kathleen's Bakery, is a good place for a full meal.

They do good tandoori food, and most main courses will cost you around Rs 50. A beer is also Rs 50 and there's a wide range of ice creams.

Nizam's is also within reach of the Sudder St area, around the corner from the Elite Cinema. It's very popular among Calcuttans for mutton and chicken rolls, kebabs and Muslim food. Kebab rolls start at Rs 8.

Junior Brothers is a comfortable, cheap Indian restaurant tucked in among the ritzy options on Park St. Main dishes are under Rs 30.

There are good places closer to BBD Bagh, in the neighbourhood around Chittaranjan Ave.

Mission Cafe is a good choice for a stand-up snack, with masala dosas for Rs 14 and espresso coffee for Rs 7.

Chung Wah Chinese Restaurant, with its private wooden booths, looks like something out of Shanghai in the 1930s. Beer is Rs 50 and main dishes are around Rs 40; they have good value set lunches in their branch around the corner.

Anand Restaurant is probably the best vegetarian restaurant in the city. It's a smart place but main dishes are good value at Rs 20.

Chinese food on a menu doesn't always translate into Chinese food on a plate. Calcuttans say the place to go for really good cheap Chinese food is the Tangra area, but it's in the west of the city and you'll need a taxi to get there. Luckily, there are a few places closer to home which hit the mark more often than not.

Children in Calcutta: a city with soul.

How Hua, on Mirza Ghalib St, has northern Chinese dishes such as jiaozi, which is a bit like Tibetan momo.

Hong Kong Restaurant is reasonable, as is the *Golden Dragon*.

Silver Grill, *Bar BQ* and *Peiping* are all good Chinese restaurants on Park St.

Waldorf Restaurant, back on Mirza Ghalib St, turns a hand to Thai food.

Whether the topic is last week's Diwali fashions or next week's Marxist revolution, Calcutta's cacophonous cafes and sugar-soaked sweet shops are good places to work that jaw.

The *Indian Coffee House*, near Calcutta University, is an institution. For years it was the meeting place of the city's intellectuals. Nowadays it's mostly younger undergraduates who congregate beneath the faded portrait of Rabindranath Tagore in this large cafe. Nevertheless it's a good place to meet people and is convenient for a coffee and snack if you've been looking round the many bookshops in this area. There's a much more central branch on Chittaranjan Ave, and a sign warns that the management 'reserves the right to maintain the dignity of the coffee shop'.

Indra Mahal is a great place to try Bengali sweets. It's on Chowringhee Rd just up from the Oberoi Hotel. Bengali specialities are Mughal paratha and misthi dhoi (curd sweetened with jaggery).

KC Das, on Lenin Sarani near the corner of Bentinck St, is another famous sweet shop.

Flury's, on Park St in Chowringhee, is the place for a more sedate tea and cake session.

Curiously, it's hard to find real Bengali food in Calcutta unless you dine at a Bengali's home.

Suruchi, on Elliot Rd, by the Mallik Bazaar bus stop, is just about the only restaurant specialising in this cuisine.

More Expensive Most of the upmarket restaurants are on Park St and there are a whole stack to choose from.

Kwality Restaurant is at 17 Park St, beside the Park Hotel. The menu is small, with main dishes around Rs 50, but it's a good place to eat. Nearby is the similar *Tandoor*.

Trinca's Gulnar Restaurant next to the Park Hotel is better. The food is excellent but quite expensive and you'll have to pay a surcharge if, as is usual, there's a band playing.

Oasis Restaurant does excellent fish & chips with vegetables for Rs 66.

Blue Fox and *Moulin Rouge* have menus as un-Calcutta-sounding as their names!

Peter Cat, round the corner on Middleton Row, near the YWCA, is a good place to come for a meal or just a few drinks. The menu includes excellent kebabs, and a saucy section headed 'aphrodisiacs for the harem'.

Belt-loosening dining experiences are possible all over central Calcutta.

Amber Hotel (☎ 248 6520) is right in the centre of town at 11 Waterloo St (the narrow street that runs by the Great Eastern Hotel). The food is excellent and it is often voted by residents of Calcutta as the best place to eat in the city. Prices are very reasonable, with most dishes around Rs 40, and the tandoori items are very good. Ring to reserve a table.

Sagar Restaurant, nearby, is owned by the same people.

Astor Hotel, on Shakespeare Sarani, has a pleasant garden that's good for a relaxing drink (beers are Rs 60) or a barbecue (daily between 6 and 11 pm). On Saturday evenings there's live music here.

Fairlawn Hotel, on Sudder St, does it English-style, for residents and non-guests alike. The set lunches and dinners can be fun and are certainly different, announced by a gong and served in impatient style by uniformed waiters. You sit where you're told, but at least you can help yourself. Check the day's menu (posted at reception) before you decide to eat here. The food varies but is generally OK and, at Rs 110 for lunch and Rs 130 for dinner, very good value. The garden in front of the hotel is an excellent place for afternoon tea or a beer in the evening, although the mosquitoes are very friendly and the drinks dry up at 8 pm *sharp*.

Zaranj Restaurant, also on Sudder St, has a waterfall flowing through its middle. It's as expensive as its decor with most dishes around Rs 125, but is packed with rich Calcuttans who say it's worth it. If money is no object you could also try the restaurants at the Oberoi Grand and the Taj Bengal.

Entertainment

Calcutta is famous for its culture – film, poetry, music, art and dance all have their devotees here. Programmes are listed in the daily newspapers or in the leaflet *Calcutta This Fortnight*, available free from the tourist offices.

A dance-drama performance, Bengali poetry reading or a similar event takes place on most nights at the *Rabindra Sadan* (☎ 247 2413) on Cathedral Rd. Foreign films and retrospectives are shown at the *Nandan* complex nearby, and many of the cinemas in Chowringhee show recent release US movies. There are often drama performances in English at the Kala Mandir (☎ 247 9086), 48 Shakespeare Sarani, and musical programmes at the *Sisir Mancha* (☎ 248 1451), 1/1 AJC Bose Rd.

Every Saturday and Sunday at 5.30 pm the *Hotel Hindustan International* has a 'dances of India' show. Entry is free.

Bars & Discos In the Sudder St area, the *Sun Set Bar* at the Lytton Hotel is a good place for a drink. This bar is popular with travellers, young expatriate workers and local young people involved on the fringes of the tourist trade. It's a friendly place and they have a good music system. Similar is the open-air bar in the forecourt of the *Fairlawn Hotel* where there's always an interesting crowd.

There are plenty of other, much more basic, bars, some with bizarre names like *Off cum On Rambo Bar* (!) on Mirza Ghalib St, and *Olypub*, a pretty seedy restaurant and bar on Park St near the Moulin Rouge.

Quite a few of the larger hotels have discos which go on until early morning. The best of them is probably the *Pink Elephant*, at the Oberoi Grand Hotel, where you can get down Wednesday, Friday and Saturday night

and Sunday afternoon. It's Rs 150 for solo cruisers, or Rs 250 for a couple.

Thursday is a 'dry' day in Calcutta and the only places where you can get alcoholic drinks are in the four and five-star hotels, although some places seem to disregard this ruling. Several of the licensed restaurants are closed on Thursday.

Things to Buy

There are numerous interesting shops along Chowringhee Rd selling everything from carpets to handicrafts. The Central Cottage Industries Emporium at 7 Chowringhee Rd is quite good. The shops along the entrance arcade to the Oberoi Grand Hotel are interesting but not as entertaining as Chowringhee's amazing variety of pavement vendors who sell everything from water pistols to underwear to dancing dolls. Calcutta's administration is trying to move the street hawkers to (as yet unbuilt) underground markets in an attempt to clear the footpaths, but the unionised street merchants have so far resisted attempts to budge them.

Amid this mêlée are runners from other shops, particularly the New Market, looking for customers. Naturally, 'their' shop is only 'just round the corner', but this is rarely true. If you follow them, it's going to take up quite a bit of your time and the prices of the goods which you're invited to examine will be relatively high. After all, it's a long way back and a lot of wasted time for them to find another punter.

New Market, formerly Hogg Market, is Calcutta's premier place for bargain shopping. Here you can find a little of almost everything, and it is always worth an hour or so of wandering around. A particularly good bargain, if you're flying straight home from Calcutta, is caneware. This is ridiculously cheap compared to prices in the west and is, of course, very light if rather bulky.

Between Sudder St and New Market is an expensive air-con market. In the basement is City Express Supermarket offering fully computerised checkouts and at least one supermarket helper per customer, some even involved in product promotion!

There's another good street market (mainly clothes) along Lenin Sarani in the evenings.

Down Sudder St or in the lanes running off both sides, those in search of highs derived from the plant kingdom are attended to by touts offering a range of services. Discretion is the key word.

Getting There & Away

Air Most airline offices are around Chowringhee. Indian Airlines is on Chittaranjan Ave, and it also has an office in the Great Eastern Hotel. Other airline offices are:

Aeroflot
    58 Chowringhee Rd (☎ 242 9831)
Air France
    41 Chowringhee Rd (☎ 297161)
Air India
    50 Chowringhee Rd (☎ 242 2356)
Bangladesh Biman
    30C Chowringhee Rd (☎ 245 7309)
British Airways
    41 Chowringhee Rd (☎ 293430)
Cathay Pacific
    1 Middleton St (☎ 240 3312)
Damania Airways
    (☎ 475 5660)
East West Airlines
    2A Sarat Bose Rd (☎ 745179)
Indian Airlines
    39 Chittaranjan Ave (☎ 262548, 264433)
Japan Airlines
    35A Chowringhee Rd (☎ 298370)
KLM
    1 Middleton St (☎ 247 4593)
Lufthansa
    30A/B Chowringhee Rd (☎ 299365)
Modiluft
    2 Russell St (☎ 298437)
Royal Nepal Airlines (RNAC)
    41 Chowringhee Rd (☎ 298534)
Sahara India Airlines
    2A Shakespeare Sarani (☎ 242 9067)
SAS
    2/7 Sarat Bose Rd (☎ 747622)
Singapore Airlines
    18G Park St (☎ 292237)
Swissair
    46C Chowringhee Rd (☎ 242 4643)
Tarum Romanian
    228A AJC Bose Rd (☎ 240 5196)
Thai International
    18G Park St (☎ 299846)
Vayudoot
    29B Shakespeare Sarani (☎ 247 7062)

Calcutta is a good place for competitive air fares to other parts of Asia. You can expect to pick up tickets to Bangkok for around Rs 4400 and to Kathmandu for around US$72. Flights to Europe start around US$360, and to the east coast of the US for around US$610. Flights are usually with Air India, Indian Airlines, Thai International, Royal Nepal Airlines or Tarum Romanian.

Calcutta's Indian Airlines office (☎ 262546) is open 24 hours seven days a week. There's a tourist counter which rarely has anyone waiting in front of it so it's very quick. Even refunds or a change of flight date are no hassle.

As well as its domestic routes (see the Flights from Calcutta table), Indian Airlines also flies four international routes: to Dhaka (five times weekly, Rs 1420), Chittagong (weekly, Rs 1820), Bangkok (four times weekly, Rs 8400) and Kathmandu (six times weekly, US$96). Youth concessions are available.

Bus It's generally better to travel from Calcutta by train, although there are several useful bus routes to other towns in West Bengal.

The only buses which travellers use with any regularity are those from Calcutta to Siliguri and New Jalpaiguri (for Darjeeling). The 'Rocket Service' (!) costs Rs 145 and leaves Calcutta at 8 pm, arriving the next morning. It's much rougher than going by train.

Buses generally depart from the Esplanade bus stand area at the northern end of the Maidan, near Chowringhee Rd, but there are a number of private companies which have their own stands. Buses to and from the south generally use the bus stand near Fort William at Babu Ghat.

Train Calcutta has two major railway stations, both of them frenetic. Howrah, on the west bank of the Hooghly River, handles most trains into the city, but if you're going north to Darjeeling or the north-east region then the trains leave from Sealdah station on the east side of the Hooghly. Beware of pickpockets at both stations. At Howrah

Flights from Calcutta

Destination	Time (hours)	Frequency & Airline* Fare (d-daily, w-weekly) (US$)			
		IC	D2	9W	
Agartala	0.5	1d	-	-	45
Bagdogra	0.5	3w	-	-	70
Bangalore	2.2	1d	-	-	215
Bhubaneswar	0.5	5w	-	-	65
Chennai	2.0	2d	-	-	180
Delhi	2.0	3d	-	-	160
Dibrugarh	1.3	6w	-	-	85
Dimapur	2.1	2w	-	-	80
Guwahati	1.1	1d	-	-	60
Hyderabad	2.0	6w	-	-	170
Imphal	2.1	2w	-	-	70
Lucknow	2.2	3w	-	-	125
Mumbai	2.3	2d	2d	2d	185
Patna	0.5	3w	-	-	75
Port Blair	2.0	3w	-	-	175
Ranchi	0.5	2w	-	-	60

* Airline abbreviation codes:
IC – Indian Airlines   D2 – Damania Airways
9W – Jet Airways

station, platforms 1 to 16 are in the old main building, platforms 17 to 22 are in the new annex next door.

The tourist railway booking office is on the 1st floor at 6 Fairlie Place near BBD Bagh. It's fully computerised and has a tourist quota but can be very crowded with foreigners. It's open Monday to Saturday from 9 am to 1 pm and 1.30 to 4 pm, and on Sunday between 9 am and 2 pm. There's another booking office nearby, at 14 Strand Rd, from which you can buy advance tickets on routes into and out of Delhi, Chennai and Mumbai (get a form and join the correct queue; the tourist quota isn't accessible from this office). Bookings can be made up to 60 days before departure for all trains apart from the *Shatabdi Express*, for which bookings are only open within 15 days of departure.

Both these places attract long queues and the staff at Fairlie Place office demand to see exchange certificates if you pay in rupees.

There are other computerised booking offices which may be better for advance tickets out of Calcutta. The office at Tollygunge metro station is easy to get to and never seems to be very busy.

If you've just flown into Calcutta, it might be worth checking the rail reservation desk at the airport as they have an air-travellers' quota for same-day or next-day travel on the main expresses.

Boat See the Andaman & Nicobar Islands chapter for details on the shipping services from Calcutta.

Getting Around

The Airport The airport is 17km north-east of the city centre. A public minibus (No S10) runs from BBD Bagh to the airport for Rs 5. At the northern end of the Maidan, bus No L33 goes from the Esplanade bus stand to the airport, also for Rs 5. There's also an airport minibus from Babu Ghat. Check with Indian Airlines to see if their airport bus is up and running again.

If you want to take a taxi from the airport, it's cheaper to go to the prepaid kiosk where you'll be assigned one. It costs Rs 100 to Sudder St or the Oberoi Grand. In the opposite direction expect to pay at least an extra 25% or more. All the same, shared between four people, everyone gets out of it pretty lightly.

Incidentally, Calcutta's airport takes its name, Dum Dum airport, from the fact that this was the site of the Dum Dum Barracks, where the explosive dumdum bullet, banned after the Boer War, was once made.

Bus Calcutta's bus system is hopelessly crowded. It's an edifying sight to watch the double-decker buses come across Howrah Bridge during the rush hour. Fares are from Rs 1.20. Take a No S7 or S27 bus between Howrah station and Sudder St; ask for the Indian Museum. There is a secondary private minibus service, which is rather faster and slightly more expensive, with fares starting at Rs 1.60. You get good practice for your contortionist act in these little trundlers!

Major Trains from Calcutta

Destination	Train Number & Name	Departure Time *	Distance (km)	Duration (hours)	Fare (Rs) (2nd/1st)
Chennai	2841 *Coromandel Exp*	2.50 pm H	1636	27.30	218/995
Delhi	2305 *Rajdhani Exp***	1.45 pm H	1441	18.00	920/2630
	2381 *Poorva Exp*	9.15 am H		24.00	205/904
Mumbai VT	2860 *Gitanjali Exp*	12.30 pm H	1960	33.00	246/1218
New Jalpaiguri	3143 *Darjeeling Mail*	7.15 pm S	573	11.45	114/473
Patna	2381 *Poorva Exp*	9.15 am H	545	8.00	98/422
	3005 *Amritsar Mail*	7.20 pm H		9.40	109/449
Puri	8007 *Puri Exp*	10.15 pm H	500	10.00	108/444
Varanasi	2381 *Poorva Exp*	9.15 am H	670	10.30	128/542

* Abbreviations for train stations: H – Howrah, S – Sealdah
** Air-con only; fare includes meals and drinks

Beware of pickpockets on any of Calcutta's public transport.

Tram Calcutta has a public tram service, but the amazingly dilapidated trams are like sardine tins. They may be pollution-free but since they're a major cause of traffic jams, there's pressure to abolish them. Tram enthusiasts, including a sister society in Melbourne, Australia, have been campaigning to retain the trams and it looks like they've succeeded – for now. Local politicians are under pressure (especially in the wallet area) from bus companies to pull up the tracks and start pumping more diesel into Calcutta's 'air'. Fares start at Rs 1.20.

Metro India's first underground railway system is being built at minimum cost and in maximum time almost totally by hand. The soggy soil makes digging holes by hand no fun at all, and after each monsoon it takes half the time to the next monsoon simply to drain out what has already been dug. Nevertheless, the northern and southern sectors are open, and work is soon to proceed on an extension further to the south. It's the current southern sector, from Chandni Chowk to Tollygunge station, that is of most use to visitors, and there's a station near Sudder St. After using surface transport, you're in a different world down here. It's clean and efficient, although still chokingly crowded during peak hours. Movies are shown on platform TVs and the stations are all air-conditioned and well decorated (Rabindra Sadan has Tagore's poems on the walls). Trains run from 8.15 am to 9.15 pm, Monday to Saturday and from 3 to 9.15 pm on Sunday. Tickets cost from Rs 2.

Taxi Officially, taxi fares start at Rs 5 and go up by Rs 0.50 increments, but that can be more theory than practice. We found about a third of drivers willing to use the meter, another third who could be talked into it and a belligerent third who were as likely to use the meter as they were to offer a free ride and a picnic in the Maidan. There are plenty of taxis, so you can shop around, either for a metered ride or a reasonable negotiated price. The final cost is the meter reading plus 60%, as the meters are, predictably, out of date.

At Howrah station there's a prepaid taxi rank outside, and from here it will cost you Rs 25 to Sudder St, although it can take 15 minutes or more to get to the front of the queue. If you want to avoid the queue, other sharks will offer to take you for Rs 40.

Rickshaw Calcutta is the last bastion of the human-powered rickshaw, apart from at resorts like Mussoorie where they're just for the tourists. Calcutta's rickshaw-wallahs would not accept the new-fangled cycle-rickshaws when they were introduced elsewhere in India. After all, who could afford a bicycle? Most can't even afford their rickshaw and have to rent it from someone who takes the lion's share of the fares.

You may find it morally unacceptable to have a man pulling you around in a carriage – and these men are usually very thin, unhealthy and die early – but Calcutta's citizens are quite happy to use them. The only compensation is that they wouldn't have a job if people didn't use them and, as a tourist, you naturally pay more than local people. Calcutta's administration wants to ban the rickshaws, as part of a shortsighted traffic-management plan which equates slow-moving transport with slow-moving traffic. As it is, Calcutta's narrow lanes and poor drainage mean that jumping in a rickshaw is often the only way to get somewhere, bar walking.

These sort of rickshaws only exist in small parts of central Calcutta and they are restricted to the small roads. Across the river in Howrah or in other Calcutta suburbs, there are auto and cycle-rickshaws.

Ferry The ferries can be a quicker and a more pleasant way to get across the river than the congested Howrah Bridge. From Howrah to Chandpal Ghat or Fairlie Ghat there are several crossings an hour between 8 am and 8 pm. Ferries to the Botanical Gardens go from Chandpal Ghat or Babu Ghat. The fares are minimal.

West Bengal

At the time of Partition, Bengal was split into East and West Bengal. East Bengal became the eastern wing of Pakistan and later, with the disintegration of that country, Bangladesh. West Bengal became a state of India with Calcutta as its capital. The state is long and narrow, running from the delta of the Ganges River system at the Bay of Bengal in the south to the heights of the Himalaya at Darjeeling in the north.

There is not a great deal of interest in the state apart from these two extremes – Calcutta, with its bewildering maelstrom of noise, culture, confusion and squalor at one end; and Darjeeling, serene and peaceful, at the other.

Outside these two centres the intrepid traveller will find a number of places to consider visiting, either south of Calcutta on the Bay of Bengal or north along the route to Darjeeling. Few foreign tourists visit the ruined mosques of Malda, the palaces of Murshidabad, the temples of Vishnupur or the Sunderbans Wildlife Sanctuary. If you do, the friendly Bengalis will make you feel all the more welcome for being an exception to the rule.

History

Referred to as Vanga in the *Mahabharata*, this area has a long history that predates the Aryan invasions of India. It was part of the Mauryan Empire in the 3rd century before being overrun by the Guptas. For three centuries from around 800 AD, the Pala dynasty controlled a large area based on Bengal and including parts of Orissa, Bihar and modern Bangladesh.

Bengal was brought under Muslim control by Qutb-ud-din, first of the sultans of Delhi, at the end of the 12th century. Following the death of Aurangzeb in 1707, Bengal became an independent Muslim state.

Britain had established a trading post in Calcutta in 1698 which quickly prospered. Sensing rich pickings, Siraj-ud-daula, the

WEST BENGAL AT A GLANCE

Population: 74.5 million
Area: 87,853 sq km
Capital: Calcutta
Main Language: Bengali
Literacy Rate: 58%
Best Time to Go: October to March

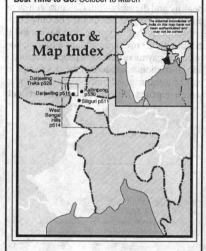

Highlights

- The quaint Britishness of Darjeeling, the archetypal hill station
- Toy train ride from New Jalpaiguri/Siliguri to Darjeeling
- Sandakphu/Phalut trek from Darjeeling

Festivals

Bathing Festival – Sagar Island – January
Mahesh Yatra (Car Festival) – Mahesh – June/July
Jhapan Festival – Vishnupur – August
Flower Festival – Kalimpong – October

Nawab of Bengal, came down from his capital at Murshidabad and easily took Calcutta in 1756. Clive defeated him the following year at the Battle of Plassey, helped by the treachery of Siraj-ud-daula's uncle, Mir

Jafar, who commanded the greater part of the nawab's army. He was rewarded by succeeding his nephew as nawab but after the Battle of Buxar in 1764, the British took full control of Bengal. For entertaining background reading on this period as seen through the eyes of a modern-day traveller, Peter Holt's book, *In Clive's Footsteps*, is recommended. The author is the five times removed great grandson of Clive.

Permits

Permission is necessary if you wish to visit the Sunderbans Wildlife Sanctuary. For

---

A REGIONAL HIGHLIGHT

Tea Plantations, Darjeeling

Tea is, of course, Darjeeling's most famous export. From its 78 gardens, employing over 40,000 people, it produces the bulk of West Bengal's crop, which is almost a quarter of India's total.

The tea from some of these estates is of very high quality. The world record for the highest price paid for tea is held by some fine leaves from the Castleton Estate in Darjeeling, for which a Japanese bidder paid US$220 per kg!

Although the area has just the right climatic conditions for producing fine tea bushes, the final result is dependent on a complex drying process. After picking, the fresh green leaves are placed 15 to 25 cm deep in a 'withering trough' where the moisture content is reduced from 70% to 80% down to 30% to 40% using high-velocity fans. When this is completed, the withered leaves are rolled and pressed to break the cell walls and express their juices onto the surface of the leaves. Normally two rollings at different pressures are undertaken, and in between rolls the leaves are sifted to separate the coarse from the fine. The leaves, coated with their juices, are then allowed to ferment on racks in a high-humidity room, a process which develops their characteristic aroma and flavour. This fermentation must be controlled carefully since either over or under-fermentation will ruin the tea.

This process is stopped by passing the leaves through a dry air chamber at 115˚C to 120˚C on a conveyer belt to further reduce the moisture content to around 2% to 3%.

The last process is the sorting of the tea into grades. In their order of value they are: Golden Flowery Orange Pekoe (unbroken leaves), Golden Broken Orange Pekoe, Orange Fannings and Dust (the latter three consisting of broken leaves).

In the last few years modern agricultural practices have been brought to the tea estates to maintain and improve their viability. The tea plantations were one of the first agricultural enterprises to use clonal plants in their replanting schemes, though most of the tea trees are at least 100 years old and nearing the end of their useful or even natural lives. The ageing plants and deteriorating soil causes grave concern, since tea not only earns the country valuable export revenue, but also provides much employment in the area. With the collapse of the USSR the Darjeeling tea planters lost their best customers and have had to look for new markets. Some have simply switched to growing cardamom, which is more profitable. There's not a big home market for Darjeeling; most Indians prefer the stronger Assam variety.

The most convenient plantation to visit is the Happy Valley Tea Estate, only two km from the centre of Darjeeling, where tea is still produced by the 'orthodox' method as opposed to the 'Curling, Tearing and Crushing' (CTC) method adopted on the plains. However, it's only worth going when plucking is in progress (April to November) because it's only then that the processing takes place. It's open daily from 8 am to noon and 1 to 4.30 pm, except on Monday and Sunday afternoon. An employee might latch on to you, whisk you around the factory and then demand some outrageous sum for his trouble; Rs 10 per person is not inappropriate. ∎

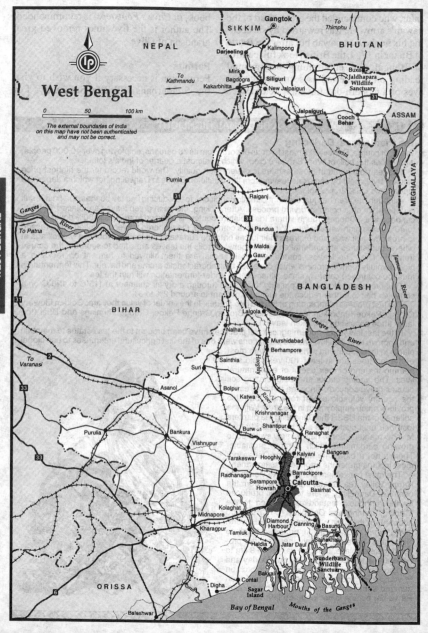

West Bengal

0   50   100 km

The external boundaries of India
on this map have not been authenticated
and may not be correct.

Sajnekhali and the Project Tiger areas, permits are available free of charge, while you wait (and wait …) at the Forest Department (G Block, 6th floor) in the Writers' Building, Calcutta. You must bring your passport. For other areas in the Sunderbans go to the Divisional Forest Officer (☎ 245 1037), 24 Parganas, 35 Gopalnagar Rd, Calcutta.

SOUTH OF CALCUTTA
Down the Hooghly
The Hooghly River is a very difficult river to navigate due to the constantly shifting shoals and sandbanks. Hooghly River pilots have to continuously stay in touch with the river to keep track of the frequent changes in its course. When the Howrah Bridge was constructed it was feared that it would cause severe alterations to the river's flow patterns. The tide rises and falls 3.5m at Calcutta and there is a bore, which reaches two metres in height, at the time of the rising tide. Because of these navigational difficulties and the silting up of the Hooghly, Calcutta is losing its importance as a port.

Falta, 43km downriver, was the site of a Dutch factory. The British retreated here in 1756 when Calcutta was captured by Siraj-ud-daula. It was also from here that Clive recaptured Calcutta. Just below Falta the Damodar River joins the Hooghly. The Rupnarain River also joins the Hooghly nearby and a little up this river is **Tamluk**, which was an important Buddhist centre over 1000 years ago. The James & Mary Shoal, the most dangerous on the Hooghly, is just above the point where the Rupnarain River enters. It takes its name from a ship which was wrecked here in 1694.

Diamond Harbour
A resort 51km south of Calcutta by road, Diamond Harbour is at the point where the Hooghly turns south and flows into the open sea. It can be reached by bus or train from Calcutta. Launches run from here to Sagar Island.

The *Sagarika Tourist Lodge* can be booked through West Bengal Tourism in Calcutta.

Haldia
The new port of Haldia is 96km south of Calcutta, on the west bank of the Hooghly. The port was constructed to try to regain the shipping lost from Calcutta's silting problems. There are regular buses between Calcutta and Haldia.

Sagar Island (Sagardwip)
At the mouth of the Hooghly, this island is considered to be the point where the Ganges joins the sea, and a great three day bathing festival takes place here in mid-January. A lighthouse marks the south-west tip of the island but navigation is still difficult for a further 65km south.

Digha
Close to the border with Orissa, 185km south-west of Calcutta on the Bay of Bengal, Digha is another self-styled 'Brighton of the East'. The beach is seven km long and very wide but if a beach holiday is what you want, carry on south to Puri or Gopalpur-on-Sea.

There are daily buses between Calcutta and Digha (Rs 32, six hours) departing Calcutta from 6.15 am. The Chandaneshwar Siva Temple is just across the border in Orissa, eight km from Digha.

Places to Stay The *Tourist Lodge* is run by West Bengal Tourism and has doubles from Rs 175 and meals at reasonable prices.

Digha has a wide range of other accommodation, including a *youth hostel*.

Bakkali
Also known as Fraserganj, this beach resort is not as busy as Digha, and a bit less polluted. It's 132km from Calcutta, on the east side of the Hooghly. West Bengal Tourism's *Tourist Lodge* has doubles for Rs 175 and dorm beds for Rs 50. From here you can get boats to the small island of Jambu Dwip to the south-west.

Sunderbans Wildlife Sanctuary
The innumerable mouths of the Ganges form the world's largest delta, and part of this vast mangrove swamp is a 2585 sq km wildlife

reserve that extends into Bangladesh. It's designated a World Heritage Site and as part of Project Tiger has one of the largest tiger populations of any of the Indian parks. Tourist agencies capitalise on this fact but few visitors get even a glimpse of one of the 250 well-hidden tigers.

You wouldn't want to get too close to these animals. Partial to human flesh, they kill about 20 people each year, lying in wait beside the narrow channels that crisscross the estuarine forest. Fishermen and honey collectors have now taken to wearing masks, painted with human faces, on the back of their heads since a tiger is less likely to attack you if it thinks you're watching it.

An entry in the visitors' book at Sajnekhali seems to sum up the feelings of many visitors to the Sunderbans: 'Who came here but here is not see tiger, his visited is not success'. However, the area has other attractions and you may see some wildlife, mainly spotted deer, wild pigs and monkeys. The journey here, by local boats and cycle-rickshaws through small traditional Bengali villages, can be fun. The whole area is wonderfully peaceful after frenetic Calcutta, and is teeming with birdlife.

There's a heron sanctuary (best between July and September) near Sajnekhali. At the Sajnekhali visitors' centre there's a crocodile enclosure, shark pond, turtle hatchery and an interesting Mangrove Interpretation Centre. From here boats are available for excursions through the mangroves; it's around Rs 500 for the whole day, or Rs 350 for a four hour trip, and you need a guide and boat permits. There are watchtowers here and at several other points around the park. In the south of the Sunderbans are two other sanctuaries at **Lothian** and **Halliday** islands, reached from Namkhana (three hours by bus from Calcutta).

Permission is required to visit the Sunderbans; see the permits section at the beginning of this chapter. There's a small entry fee to visit the reserve, payable at Sajnekhali.

Places to Stay The *Sajnekhali Tourist Lodge* at Sajnekhali charges Rs 275 for a double with attached bathroom, and there's

a basic restaurant here (western food is rarely available). The signs say 'Movement prohibited after evening' and they mean it. In 1991 a couple of tigers jumped over the fence and spent the night sniffing at the doors of the rooms where the tourists were sleeping!

Getting There & Away From October to March, West Bengal Tourism organises weekly boat tours, including food and accommodation (on board or in the Tourist Lodge). A two/three day trip costs Rs 800/1600. If you're expecting 'adventure at every corner', as the brochure suggests, forget it. 'More like a totally uneventful three-day picnic on the water', said one reader.

Travelling independently is rather more complex but could be more fun. From Calcutta it's quickest to get a bus to Sonakhali/Basunti (Rs 19, three hours) from Babu Ghat. Alternatively you can take the train to Canning (Rs 13, 1¼ hours), then cross the river to Dok Kart opposite (Rs 1) by *bod-booti* (small, overcrowded ferry) and go overland to Sonakhali by shared auto-rickshaw (Rs 6) or bus (Rs 3, 50 minutes). If you go via Canning you may be able to get a ride directly to Sajnekhali with one of the tour boats.

Continuing from Sonakhali/Basunti the next step is a boat to Gosava (Rs 6, 1¼ hours). From there get a cycle-rickshaw (no seats, just a wooden platform!) for the 40 minute ride to Pakhirala (Rs 15) for a boat across the river to Sajnekhali. There's also a direct boat (Rs 6) leaving Gosava at 1 pm to reach Sajnekhali at 3.30 pm. In the morning it departs from Sajnekhali at 8.30 am for Gosava.

A private boat to Sajnekhali costs Rs 600 from Canning or Rs 350 from Sonakhali/Basunti.

NORTH OF CALCUTTA
Serampore & Barrackpore
Twenty-five km from Calcutta on the Hooghly River, Serampore was a Danish centre until their holdings in India were transferred to the East India Company in 1845. The old **Danish church** and **cemetery** still stand. The

missionaries Ward, Marshman and Carey operated from here in the early 1800s.

Across the river is Barrackpore. A few dilapidated buildings are all that are left of the East India Company's cantonment here. There are also some gardens and a memorial to Gandhi by the river.

Mahesh, three km from Serampore, has a large and very old Jagannath temple. In June/July of each year the Mahesh Yatra (Car Festival) takes place here. It is second in size only to the great Car Festival of Jagannath at Puri, Orissa.

Chandernagore

Also known as Chandarnagar, this was one of the French enclaves in India which were handed over at the same time as Pondicherry in 1951. Situated on the banks of the Hooghly, 39km north of Calcutta, are several crumbling buildings dating from the French era. The first French settlers arrived here in 1673 and the place later became an important trading post, although it was taken by the British during conflicts with the French.

Hooghly & Satgaon

The historic town of Hooghly is 41km north of Calcutta and very close to two other interesting sites – Chinsura and Bandel. Hooghly was an important trading port long before Calcutta rose to prominence. In 1537 the Portuguese set up a factory here; before that time Satgaon, 10km further north, had been the main port of Bengal but was abandoned because of the river silting up. There are still a few traces of Satgaon's former grandeur, including a ruined **mosque**.

The Portuguese were kicked out of Hooghly in 1632 by Shah Jahan, after a lengthy siege, but were allowed to return a year later. The British East India Company also established a factory here in 1651. The **imambara**, built in 1836, with its gateway flanked by lofty minarets, is the main sight. Across the road is an older imambara, dating from 1776-7.

Chinsura

Only a kilometre or so south of Hooghly, Chinsura was exchanged by the Dutch for the British-held Indonesian island of Sumatra in 1825. There is a fort and the Dutch **cemetery**, with many old tombs, a km to the west.

Bandel

A couple of km north of Hooghly, and 43km from Calcutta, Bandel is the site of a Portuguese **church** and monastery which were built here in 1599. Destroyed by Shah Jahan in 1640, they were later rebuilt.

To get there, take the train to Naihati and then the hourly shuttle across the river.

Bansberia

Four km north of Bandel, Bansberia has the **Vasudev Temple**, with interesting terracotta wall carvings, and the **Hanseswari Temple**.

Vishnupur

Also spelt Bishnupur, this interesting town of terracotta temples is a famous cultural centre. It flourished as the capital of the Malla kings from the 16th to the early 19th centuries. The Mallas were great patrons of the arts.

Since there is no stone in the area, the traditional building material for important buildings was brick. The facades of the dozen or so **temples** here are covered with ornate terracotta tiles depicting lively scenes from the Hindu epics. The main temples to see are the highly decorated Jor Bangla, the large Madan Mohan, the pyramidal Ras Mancha and the Shyam Rai, built in 1643.

Vishnupur is in Bankura district, famous for its **pottery** (particularly the stylised Bankura horse) and **silk**. In the markets here you can also find metalwork, tussar silk and Baluchari saris, *ganjifa* (circular playing cards for a game long forgotten) and conch shell jewellery. In August, the Jhapan Festival draws snake charmers to honour the goddess Manasa who is central to the cult of snake worship.

Places to Stay Accommodation is very limited.

The *Tourist Lodge* (☎ (03244) 52013) is good, with dorm beds for Rs 50 and doubles for Rs 175 with attached bathroom, or Rs 300 also with air-con. It's about three km from the railway station. There are several cheaper hotels around the market.

Getting There & Away There are buses from Calcutta (Rs 29, 4½ hours). The *Purulia Express*, from Howrah, is the fastest train, taking 3½ hours.

Jairambati & Kamarpukur
Ramakrishna was born in Kamarpukur, 143km north-west of Calcutta, and there is a Ramakrishna Mission ashram here. Ramakrishna was a 19th century Hindu saint who did much to rejuvenate Hinduism when it was going through a period of decline during the British rule. Jairambati, five km away, is another important point for Ramakrishna devotees.

Shantiniketan
The Visvabharati University is at Shantiniketan, three km from Bolpur. The brilliant and prolific poet, writer and nationalist Rabindranath Tagore (1861-1941) founded a school here in 1901. It later developed into a university with emphasis on humanity's relationship with nature – many classes are conducted in the open air. Tagore went on to win the Nobel Prize in 1913 and is credited with introducing India's historical and cultural greatness to the modern world. In 1915 Tagore was awarded a knighthood by the British but he surrendered it in 1919 as a protest against the Amritsar massacre.

There are colleges of science, teacher training, Hindi, Sino-Indian studies, arts and crafts, and music and dance. Tagore called the place 'the cargo of my life's best treasure', but in the late 1990s he'd probably be saddened by the way the university has become much like any other in India. Lecturers are accused of nepotism, exam papers are leaked and graduates go for jobs with multinationals rather than with rural regeneration programmes as Tagore intended. Rich Bengalis are now building holiday homes in the area. Although it's still a very peaceful place,

there's little point in visiting unless you have a specific interest in Tagore.

There's a **museum** and **art gallery** within the Uttarayan complex where Tagore lived. They are open from 10.30 am to 1 pm and 2 to 4.30 pm Thursday to Monday, mornings only on Tuesday. The university is open to visitors in the afternoons (mornings only on Tuesday and during vacations) but closed on Wednesday, the day the university was founded.

Four km away is **Sriniketan**, started as a project to revitalise traditional crafts, such as *kantha* embroidery, weaving, batik and pottery.

Places to Stay The *International Guest House*, run by the university, has cheap accommodation and meals. There are also *university guest houses* if you're planning a long stay.

The *retiring rooms* at Bolpur railway station are good value.

Shantiniketan Tourist Lodge is run by West Bengal Tourism and is a good place with rooms for Rs 150/225 or Rs 325 to Rs 500 for an air-con double.

Chhuti Holiday Resort (☎ 52692), 241 Charupalli, is the top place. All rooms have bath attached and air-cooled singles/doubles are Rs 550/600, Rs 750/800 for air-con.

Getting There & Away The *3015 Shantiniketan Express* leaves Howrah daily at 9.55 am, reaching Bolpur at 12.25 pm. It departs from Bolpur at 1 pm for Howrah. For Darjeeling, there is the nightly *Darjeeling Mail* at 10.30 pm, which connects with the toy train at New Jalpaiguri. Many other trains stop here.

Nabadwip
Also known as Nadia, the last Hindu king of Bengal, Lakshman Sen moved his capital here from Gaur. It's an ancient centre of Sanskrit culture, 114km north of Calcutta. There are many temples at this important pilgrimage centre.

Mayapur

Across the river from Nabadwip, this is a centre for the ISKCON (Hare Krishna) movement. There's a large, white temple and gardens, and cheap accommodation is available in the *ISKCON Guest House*. A bus tour is run from Calcutta on Sunday (daily during the winter). Details are available from ISKCON (☎ 247 6075) at 3C Albert Rd, Calcutta.

Plassey (Palashi)

In 1757 Clive defeated Siraj-ud-daula and his French supporters here, a turning point in British influence in India. Plassey, or Palashi as it's now known, is 172km north of Calcutta. There's nothing to see here apart from the 15m memorial a couple of kilometres west of the village.

Berhampore

Eleven km south of Murshidabad is this large town, a notable centre for silk production. The Government Silk Research Centre is interesting to visit. In the old bazaar area of Khagra, in the northern part of Berhampore, the dilapidated mansions of European traders are quietly subsiding into the river.

Places to Stay & Eat The *Tourist Lodge* is good value and the best place to eat. Doubles are Rs 150 with attached bathroom, four-bed rooms are Rs 50 per bed and there are also air-con rooms for Rs 300. It's about 15 minutes from Berhampore Court railway station by cycle-rickshaw and close to the bus stand.

The *retiring rooms* at the railway station have a four-bed dorm.

Getting There & Away On this branch line between Sealdah and Lalgola, there are several trains a day from Calcutta (186km, four to six hours). There's a bus from Calcutta (Rs 35, five hours) leaving at 6.30 am, and other buses to Malda (Rs 22, 3½ hours), Bolpur (Rs 20, four hours) and Siliguri (Rs 75, seven hours).

Across the river is Khagraghat Rd station which is on the Howrah to Azimganj line.

Murshidabad

Pop: 34,100

When Siraj-ud-daula was Nawab of Bengal, this was his capital, and it was here that he was assassinated after the defeat at Plassey. Murshidabad was also the major trading town between inland India and the port of Calcutta, 221km south. Today it's an insignificant town on the banks of the Bhagirathi River; a chance to see typical rural Bengali life.

Cycle-rickshaw wallahs offer you guided tours of all the sites for around Rs 45 for a half day. This is a good idea as everything's fairly spread out. The main attraction is the **Hazarduari**, the classical-style Palace of a Thousand Doors built for the nawabs in 1837. In the recently renovated throne room a vast chandelier, a gift from Queen Victoria, is suspended above the nawab's silver throne. There are portraits of British dignitaries, an ivory sofa, ivory palanquins and silver sedan chairs. In the armoury downstairs is a cannon used at Plassey. It's open from 10 am to 4.30 pm daily except Friday.

Across the grass from the palace is the rapidly deteriorating **Great Imambara**. Murshid Quli Khan, who moved the capital here in 1705, is buried beside the impressive ruins of the **Katra Mosque**. Siraj-ud-daula was assassinated at the **Nimak Haram Deohri** (Traitor's Gate). The Jain **Parswanath Temple** is at Kathgola, and south of the railway station there's the **Moti Jhil**, or Pearl Lake, a fine place to view the sunset. It's worth taking a boat across the river to visit Siraj's **tomb** at Khusbagh, the Garden of Happiness. There are a number of other interesting buildings and ruins.

Places to Stay Accommodation here is very basic and rather overpriced; it's best to stay at Berhampore, although it's 11km away.

The *retiring rooms* at the railway station are the only bargain. They're Rs 40 for a double with attached bathroom.

Hotel Historical charges Rs 90 for a double; they may let you sleep on the roof.

Hotel Omrao is not bad, with singles for

Rs 80 and doubles with attached bathroom for Rs 150. There's a reasonable restaurant.

Hotel Manjusha, near the palace, has singles/doubles for Rs 100/175. It's a friendly place.

Getting There & Away Murshidabad is also on the Sealdah to Lalgola line and there are several trains daily from Calcutta (197km, four to six hours). For long-distance buses you must go to Berhampore.

Malda & English Bazaar

On the route to Darjeeling, 349km north of Calcutta, Malda is the base for visiting the ruined cities of Gaur and Pandua, although it's probably more famous now for its large Fajli mangoes. One reader wrote: 'You could probably kill yourself through overeating mangoes in this place! Gaur is delightful, one of the nicest places we visited in India, incredibly peaceful and beautiful'. Malda's not very interesting, but it has a small museum.

English Bazaar, also transliterated as Ingraj Bazar, is now a suburb of Malda. An English factory was established here in 1771. **Old Malda** is nearby, at the junction of the Kalindi and Mahananda rivers. It was once an important port for the former Muslim capital of Pandua.

Places to Stay & Eat There are *retiring rooms* and a good refreshment room at the railway station.

Malda Tourist Lodge is a reasonable place with an attractive garden. It's Rs 100 for a double with common bath, Rs 200 for a double with attached bath, and Rs 375 for an air-con double. The tourist office is here. A rickshaw from the railway station costs Rs 5.

Hotel Samrat, opposite, and *Hotel Natraj*, on the road to the bus stand, are similarly priced.

Hotel Purbanchal, with rooms from Rs 120/150 to Rs 400/500 with air-con, is the top place in town. It's 20 minutes from the station by rickshaw.

Getting There & Away Malda is directly connected by the main railway line to Calcutta

(344km, seven hours) and New Jalpaiguri (233km, five hours). There are buses to Siliguri (Rs 49, six hours) for Darjeeling, Berhampore (Rs 23, three hours) Murshidabad and Calcutta (Rs 55, eight hours).

Gaur

Twelve km south of Malda and right on the border with Bangladesh, Gaur was first the capital of the Buddhist Pala dynasty, then it became the seat of the Hindu Sena dynasty, and finally the capital of the Muslim nawabs. The ruins of the extensive fortifications and several large mosques are all that remain. (There are also some ruins on the other side of the ill-defined border.) Most impressive are the **Bara Sona Mosque** and the nearby brick **Dakhil Darwajah** built in 1425. **Qadam Rasul Mosque** enshrines a footprint of the Mohammed but it looks as if he was wearing thongs when he made it! Fath Khan's tomb is nearby and a sign informs you that he 'vomited blood and died on this spot'. There are still some colourful enamelled tiles on the **Gumti Gate** and **Lattan Mosque** but few left on the **Firoz Minar**, which you can climb for a good view.

Getting There & Away The monuments are very spread out and not all easy to find. Determined cycle-rickshaw wallahs offer half-day trips from Malda for anything up to Rs 120. Taxis cost Rs 300 and include Pandua.

Pandua

Gaur once alternated with Pandua as the seat of power. The main place of interest is the vast **Adina Mosque**, built by Sikandar Shah in the 14th century. Built over a Hindu temple, traces of which are still evident, it was one of the largest mosques in India but is now in ruins. Nearby is the **Eklakhi mausoleum**, so called because it cost Rs 1 lakh to build. There are also several smaller mosques. The dusty deer park, 2.5km across the highway in the 'forest', is not worth going to.

Getting There & Away Pandua is on the main highway (NH34), 18km north of Malda, and there are many buses that can drop you here. The main sites are at Adina, two km north of the village of Pandua, and right by the highway.

SILIGURI & NEW JALPAIGURI
Pop: 257,500   Tel Area Code: 0353

This crowded, sprawling, noisy place is the departure point for visits to Darjeeling, Kalimpong, Sikkim and the North-East states. Siliguri is the major trade centre for the north-east and eastern Nepal; a real boom town, it's packed with trucks and buses and not a pleasant place to stay for a moment more than necessary. New Jalpaiguri (known as NJP), the main railway junction, is eight km south of Siliguri, though there's effectively no break in the urban sprawl between the two places.

Orientation & Information

The towns of Siliguri and New Jalpaiguri comprise essentially just one north-south main road – Tenzing Norgay Rd. It's about four km from New Jalpaiguri railway station to Siliguri Town railway station, and a further four km from there on to Siliguri Junction railway station, behind the Tenzing Norgay Central bus terminal. You can catch the toy train (if it's running) from any of these railway stations. Bagdogra, 12km west of Siliguri is the airport serving this northern region.

The West Bengal Tourist Office (☎ 431974) is up a flight of stairs on Tenzing Norgay Rd, on the south side of the river. Here, it's possible to book accommodation in the Jaldhapara Wildlife Sanctuary (see later). There are tourist counters at the airport and railway stations.

The State Bank of India exchanges American Express travellers cheques in US dollars and pounds sterling only.

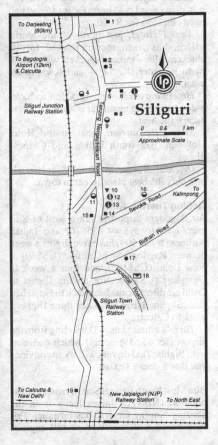

Siliguri

Approximate Scale 0   0.5   1 km

PLACES TO STAY
1   Hotel Sinclairs
2   Mainak Tourist Lodge & Indian Airlines
6   Tourist Services Agency Guest House
8   Siliguri Lodge
14 Hotel Chancellor
15 Hotel Vinayak & Jet Airways
19 Hotels Holydon, Baydanath & Miami Restaurant

PLACES TO EAT
5   Shere Punjab Hotel Restaurant
10 Anand Hotel Restaurant

OTHER
3   Mallagur Garage
4   Tenzing Norgay Central Bus Terminal & Share Jeeps
7   Assam Tourist Office
9   Sikkim Nationalised Transport (SNT) & Sikkim Tourism
11 Taxi Stand
12 State Bank of India
13 West Bengal Tourist Office
16 Share Jeep Stand
17 Railway Booking Office
18 GPO

WEST BENGAL

Permits for Sikkim These are available from Sikkim Tourism (☎ 432646) at the Sikkim Nationalised Transport (SNT) office diagonally opposite the bus terminal. Sikkim Tourism is open Monday to Saturday from 10 am to 4 pm.

Places to Stay
There's no reason to linger but if you arrive too late to catch a bus or train out there are dozens of hotels, many opposite the Tenzing Norgay Central bus terminal.

Tourist Services Agency Guest House is down the lane opposite the bus terminal. It's a friendly place but fills up fast. Singles/doubles are Rs 160/220, and hot water is available in buckets (Rs 5).

Siliguri Lodge is in a quiet spot next door to Sikkim Nationalised Transport. There's a pleasant garden, and rooms are very clean and airy. There are dorm beds for Rs 50 and doubles from Rs 130 with common bath or Rs 165 with bath attached.

Mainak Tourist Lodge (☎ 430986) is run by West Bengal Tourism. Non air-con rooms are Rs 400/500, and air-con doubles range from Rs 600 to Rs 1200. Rooms are clean and the staff friendly.

Hotel Chancellor (☎ 432360), on the corner of Sevoke and Tenzing Norgay roads, is a good place run by Tibetans. Small but comfortable singles are Rs 90, and doubles are Rs 165 without balcony or Rs 180 with balcony. Three/four bed rooms are Rs 210/260. The front rooms are a little noisy. Hot water in buckets, towels and mosquito zappers are provided.

Hotel Vinayak (☎ 431130), diagonally opposite the tourist office, is a good mid-range choice. Spotless and well appointed singles/doubles, all with attached bath, are Rs 250/350 without air-con, or Rs 650/725 with air-con. There's a good restaurant.

Hotel Holydon (☎ 423558) is convenient for NJP railway station. It has singles with common bath for Rs 99 and doubles with attached bath (hot water) for Rs 175 and Rs 240. The more expensive rooms are at the front, and are bright and airy. There's a small restaurant.

Hotel Baydanath is next door to Hotel Holydon. Very good singles/doubles with attached bath and running hot and cold water are Rs 175/240.

Hotel Sinclairs (☎ 522674) is two km north of the bus terminal. Non air-con rooms are Rs 600/725, air-con rooms are Rs 850/1100. There are money changing facilities, a swimming pool, good restaurant and bar.

Places to Eat
There are numerous places to eat along Hill Cart Rd.

Shere Punjab Hotel, opposite the bus terminal, has good cold beers for Rs 45 and half roast chickens for Rs 50.

Anand Hotel, just north of the tourist office, has been recommended for its chicken rolls – minced chicken with cardamom in batter (Rs 14) – and Kwality ice cream.

Hotel Vinayak has the usual Indian have-a-go-at-anything menu but is a good place to escape the heat.

Miami Restaurant, next to the Hotel Holydon, has south Indian and Chinese dishes.

Oriental Room, at Hotel Sinclairs, is probably the best place to eat in town.

Getting There & Away
Air Bagdogra airport is 12km west of Siliguri. Jet Airways (☎ 435876) and Indian Airlines (☎ 431509) have five flights a week between Bagdogra and Calcutta (US$69) or New Delhi (US$163), and four a week to Guwahati (US$41). Not all the flights to Delhi are direct, some backtrack to Guwahati first. Skyline NEPC also has three flights a week to Calcutta.

There's a direct bus to Darjeeling from the airport (Rs 65, 3½ hours) which connects with flights. Taxi drivers will try to convince you that it doesn't exist.

Bus Most North Bengal State Transport Corporation (NBSTC) buses leave from the Tenzing Norgay Central bus terminal. Private buses with services to hill regions

(Darjeeling, Gangtok etc) also have counters at the terminal. Note that if you are travelling to Jorethang in West Sikkim, you will require a trekking permit. See the Permits section in the Sikkim chapter for details.

For Darjeeling (Rs 28, three hours), NBSTC buses depart between 6.30 and 11.30 am. There's a bus at 7 am for Kalimpong (Rs 30, three hours), and services at 7.30 am and 2.30 pm for Mirik (Rs 23, 2½ hours).

The 'Rocket' services to Calcutta leave at 6, 7 and 8 pm (Rs 145, 12 hours). Other destinations include Malda (Rs 49, six hours), Berhampore (Rs 75, eight hours) and Patna (Rs 125, 12 hours). The bus to Patna leaves from Mallaguri Garage, a 10 minute walk north up Tenzing Norgay Rd.

For Guwahati, there's a NBSTC Rocket service from Tenzing Norgay terminal at 5 pm (Rs 160, 12 hours), and an ordinary service from Mallaguri Garage at 7.30 am (Rs 130).

Sikkim Nationalised Transport (SNT) buses leave every hour between 7 am and 4 pm from the SNT terminal for Gangtok (Rs 47, five hours). There's also a deluxe bus (Rs 80) at 7 am and 1 pm.

For Nepal, local buses leave from in front of the Tenzing Norgay Central bus terminal to Paniktanki (Rs 7, one hour), opposite the Nepal border town of Kakarbhitta. See the Darjeeling section for more details.

Train The *Darjeeling Mail* leaves Sealdah (Calcutta) at 7 pm (566km, 12 hours). Tickets are Rs 147/516 in 2nd/1st class. The return trip leaves New Jalpaiguri railway station at 6.45 pm, reaching Sealdah at 8.30 am. The *North East Express* is the fastest train to Delhi (1628km, 33 hours). It departs at 5.25 pm, travelling via Patna (636km, 16 hours). In the other direction this train continues to Guwahati (423km, 10 hours).

If the toy train from Siliguri/New Jalpaiguri to Darjeeling is running, tickets can be purchased from New Jalpaiguri, Siliguri Town or Siliguri Junction railway stations. As there are no advance reservations, it may be easier to pick up tickets at New Jalpaiguri, where the train originates, during the busy

peak season (May to mid-July). When operating, there is a daily service at 9 am, and during the peak season, another service at 7.15 am. The journey takes an interminable nine hours to cover the 88km up to the hill station, or four hours to Kurseong, 30km short of Darjeeling. Tickets cost Rs 14/116 in 2nd/1st class.

To reach Bangladesh you can take a train from New Jalpaiguri to Haldibari (the Indian border checkpoint). This takes two hours and costs Rs 13. From here it's a seven km walk along the disused railway line to the Bangladesh border point at Chiliharti, where there's a railway station.

There's a railway booking office on Bidhan Rd, just off Tenzing Norgay Rd. It's open Monday to Saturday from 8 am to 8 pm, and Sunday and holidays from 8 am to 2 pm.

Taxi & Jeep The fastest and most comfortable way of getting around the hills is by share jeep. There are a number of taxi stands where you can get share jeeps to destinations in the WB hills, and to Sikkim, including one on Sevoke Rd, and one outside Tenzing Norgay terminal. Share rates are: Darjeeling (2½ hours, Rs 45); Kalimpong (2½ hours, Rs 40); Mirik (two hours, Rs 35); and Gangtok (4½ hours, Rs 90). Back seats are Rs 5 to Rs 10 cheaper than those in the front.

From Bagdogra airport to Darjeeling, a taxi will cost Rs 650 or Rs 130 per seat.

Getting Around

From Tenzing Norgay Central bus terminal to New Jalpaiguri railway station, taxis will charge Rs 100, and auto-rickshaws about Rs 40. A cycle-rickshaw will cost about Rs 15 for the 40 minute trip from New Jalpaiguri railway station to Siliguri Junction, or Rs 20 to Tenzing Norgay Central bus terminal. There are infrequent bus services along this route (Rs 2).

If you are flying out of Bagdogra airport, you may be able to get a lift from Siliguri to the airport with airline staff. Check at the Jet Airways or Indian Airlines offices in Siliguri. A taxi between the airport and Siliguri costs Rs 120. A less expensive option is to take a taxi to Bagdogra bazaar (three km, Rs 30), and get a local bus from there into Siliguri (nine km, Rs 2).

JALDHAPARA WILDLIFE SANCTUARY

Although most visitors are keen to head for the hills after the chaotic strip of mayhem that is Siliguri, if you have time it's worth making the 135km trip east to this rarely visited sanctuary. It's a refuge for the Indian rhino, whose numbers are seriously threatened by poachers.

The best season to visit is from October to May, particularly in March and April when the wild animals are attracted by the growth of new grasses. Apart from about 35 rhinos, other animals found in the park environs are tigers (rarely seen), wild elephants, and various types of deer. You can take elephant safaris from Hollong, inside the park.

Places to Stay & Eat

Hollong Forest Lodge, within the park itself, has double rooms for Rs 400.

Jaldhapara Tourist Lodge is outside the park precincts at Madarihat. Doubles are Rs 570 and dorm beds are Rs 190, including all meals. Both of these places must be booked

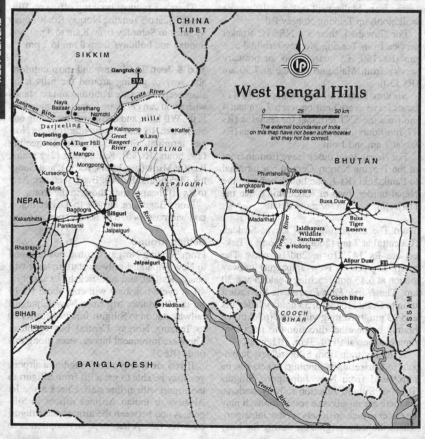

West Bengal Hills

0   25   50 km

The external boundaries of India on this map have not been authenticated and may not be correct.

CHINA
TIBET

SIKKIM

Gangtok

31A

Teesta River

Naya Bazaar Jorethang Namchi

Rangman River

Hills

Kaffer

Darjeeling
Darjeeling
Ghoom Kalimpong
Tiger Hill Great Lava
Mangpu Rangeet DARJEELING
River

Kurseong Mongpong

Mirik

Phuntsholing

BHUTAN

Langkapara Hat Totopara

Buxa Duar

NEPAL

Bagdogra Siliguri New Jalpaiguri

Kakarbhitta Paniktanki

31

JALPAIGURI

Teesta River

Madarihat Torsa River

Buxa Tiger Reserve

Jaldhapara Wildlife Sanctuary
Hollong

Bhadrapur

Jalpaiguri

Alipur Duar 31

BIHAR

Haldibari

Cooch Bihar

Islampur

COOCH BIHAR

ASSAM

BANGLADESH

Teesta River

WEST BENGAL

in advance through the Siliguri tourist office (☎ (0353) 431974), or the Government of West Bengal Tourist Development Corporation (☎ (033) 248 8271). WBTDC has packages including accommodation, all meals, and a one-hour elephant safari.

Getting There & Away
From Tenzing Norgay Central bus terminal in Siliguri, buses ply to Madarihat, nine km from Jaldhapara. The trip takes three hours and costs Rs 24. From here, a taxi to Hollong, inside the park, is Rs 100. To hire a taxi from Siliguri to Jaldhapara will cost about Rs 800. In theory, there is a daily train which leaves Siliguri at 11.30 am, arriving into Madarihat at 4 pm, but the service is erratic.

MIRIK
Being promoted as a 'new' hill station, Mirik is about 50km from both Siliguri and Darjeeling at an altitude of 1767m. The lake is the main attraction here and there's a 3.5km path around it. Since it's also the town's sewer it might not be wise to swim here. Mirik is surrounded by tea estates, orange orchards and cardamom plantations.

There are several places to stay. The rustic *Wooden Lodge*, on the main Darjeeling road, has doubles with common bath for Rs 80 and a good cheap restaurant.

Lodge Panchashil is down a small lane opposite the bank. There are rooms with attached bath from Rs 110/130. The manager is friendly and there's a pleasant rooftop terrace.

The flashy *Hotel Jagdeet*, on the main road has doubles from Rs 400.

There are four buses a day to Darjeeling (Rs 20, 2½ hours), and two to Siliguri (2½ hours).

KURSEONG
Kurseong is about halfway between Siliguri on the plains and Darjeeling. If you want to stay overnight there's the *Tourist Lodge*, with doubles from Rs 450, or the much cheaper *Jeet Hotel*.

DARJEELING
Pop: 83,000   Tel Area Code: 0354
Straddling a ridge at 2134m and surrounded by tea plantations, Darjeeling has been a popular hill station since the British established it as an R&R centre for their troops in the mid-1800s. People come here now, as they did then, to escape the heat, humidity and hassle of the north Indian plain. You get an indication of how popular Darjeeling is from the 70 or so hotels recognised by the tourist office and the scores of others which don't come up to its requirements. Here you will find yourself surrounded by mountain people from all over the eastern Himalaya who have come to work, to trade or – in the case of the Tibetans – as refugees.

Outside of the monsoon season (June to September), the views over the mountains to the snowy peaks of Kanchenjunga and down to the swollen rivers in the valleys are magnificent. Darjeeling is a fascinating place where you can see Buddhist monasteries, visit a tea plantation and see how the tea is processed, go for a ride on the chairlift (if it's reopened), spend days hunting for bargains in colourful markets and handicraft shops, or go trekking to high-altitude spots for closer views of Kanchenjunga.

Like many places in the Himalaya, half the fun is in getting there and Darjeeling has the unique attraction of its famous toy train. This miniature train loops and switchbacks its way up the steep mountainsides from New Jalpaiguri to Darjeeling.

History
Until the beginning of the 18th century the whole of the area between the present borders of Sikkim and the plains of Bengal, including Darjeeling and Kalimpong, belonged to the rajas of Sikkim. In 1706 they lost Kalimpong to the Bhutanese, and control of the remainder was wrested from them by the Gurkhas who invaded Sikkim in 1780, following consolidation of the latter's rule in Nepal.

These annexations by the Gurkhas, however, brought them into conflict with the

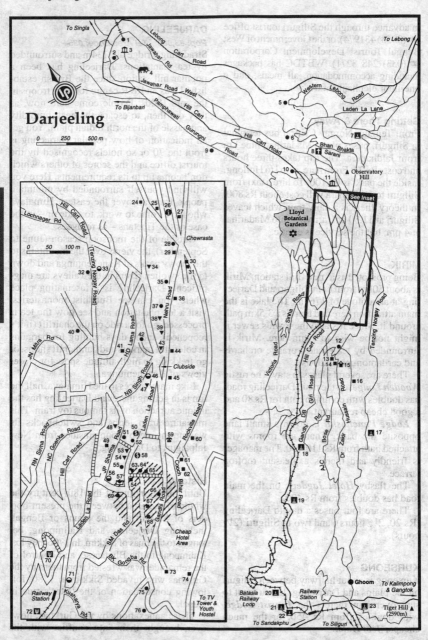

Darjeeling

British East India Company. A series of wars were fought between the two parties, eventually leading to the defeat of the Gurkhas and the ceding of all the land they had taken from the Sikkimese to the East India Company. Part of this territory was restored to the rajas of Sikkim and the country's sovereignty guaranteed by the British in return for British control over any disputes which arose with neighbouring states.

One such dispute in 1828 led to the dispatch of two British officers to this area, and it was during their fact-finding tour that they

spent some time at Darjeeling (then called Dorje Ling – Place of the Thunderbolt – after the lama who founded the monastery which once stood on Observatory Hill). The officers were quick to appreciate Darjeeling's value as a site for a sanatorium and hill station, and as the key to a pass into Nepal and Tibet. The officers' observations were reported to the authorities in Calcutta and a pretext was eventually found to pressure the raja into granting the site to the British in return for an annual stipend of Rs 3000 (raised to Rs 6000 in 1846).

WEST BENGAL

PLACES TO STAY		
13 Ratna Restaurant	43 Kev's (Keventer's Snack Bar)	26 Darjeeling Gorkha Hill Council Tourism Office
14 Triveni Guest House & Restaurant, Aliment Restaurant & Hotel	47 Dafey Munal Restaurant	28 Oxford Book & Stationery Co
15 Youth Hostel	48 New Dish Restaurant	32 Super Market & Trek & Tour Operators
16 Hotel Tower View	53 Park Restaurant & Hayden Hall	33 Buses, Jeeps & Taxis to Kalimpong, Siliguri & Sikkim
24 New Elgin Hotel	54 Golden Dragon Restaurant & Bar	
25 Hotel Alice Villa	63 Tibetan Restaurants	35 Curio Shops
27 Windamere Hotel		37 Das Studio
29 Pineridge Hotel & Trek-Mate	**OTHER**	40 Market
30 Bellevue Hotel, Tourist Office & Indian Airlines	1 Ropeway Station	42 Manjushree Centre of Tibetan Culture
	2 Snow Leopard Enclosure	46 Clubside Taxi Stand, Juniper Tours & Travels
31 Main Bellevue Hotel	3 Himalayan Mountaineering Institute & Museums	
36 Hotel Shangrila		50 ANZ Grindlays Bank
41 Hotel Seven Seventeen, Tibetan Medical & Astro Institute	4 Zoo	51 Clubside Tours & Travels
	5 Tibetan Refugee Self Help Centre	52 Foreigners' Registration Office
44 Darjeeling Club	6 Raj Bhavan	
45 Hotels Dekeling & Lunar, Dekevas Restaurant	7 Bhutia Busty Gompa	55 Nathmull's Tea Merchants
	8 Gymkhana Club & St Andrew's Church	56 Buses to Sikkim (Darjeeling Motor Service Co)
49 Hotel Tshering Denzongpa	9 Happy Valley Tea Estate	
60 Hotels Valentino, Continental & Daffodil	10 Deputy Commissioner's Office	57 Main Post Office
		58 State Bank of India
61 Rockville Hotel	11 Bengal Natural History Museum	59 Telegraph Office
62 Hotels Purnima & Broadway	12 TV Tower	64 Greenland Tours & Travels
65 Hotel Prestige	17 Aloobari Gompa	66 Himalayan Tours & Travels
67 Hotel Pagoda	18 Sonada Gompa	
68 Hotel Shamrock	19 Thupten Sangachoeling Gompa	69 Economic Pharmacy
73 Hotel Sinclairs		70 Maa Singha Temple
74 Palace Mahakal	20 Samdenchoeling Gompa	71 Taxis to Ghoom
	21 Ghoom (Yogachoeling) Gompa	72 Dhirdham Temple
PLACES TO EAT		75 Tibetan Refugee Self-Help Centre (Head Office)
34 Great Punjab Restaurant	22 Sakyachoeling Gompa	
38 Glenary's	23 Phin Sotholing Gompa	76 Nepali Girls' Social Service Centre
39 Hasty Tasty		

This transfer, however, rankled with the Tibetans who regarded Sikkim as a vassal state. Darjeeling's rapid development as a trading centre and tea-growing area in a key position along the trade route leading from Sikkim to the plains of India began to make a considerable impact on the fortunes of the lamas and leading merchants of Sikkim. Tensions arose, and in 1849 two British travellers, Sir Joseph Hooker and Dr Campbell, who were visiting Sikkim with the permission of the raja and the British government, were arrested. Various demands were made as a condition of their release, but the Sikkimese eventually released both prisoners unconditionally about a month later.

In reprisal for the arrests, however, the British annexed the whole of the land between the present borders of Sikkim and the Bengal plains, and withdrew the raja's annual Rs 6000 stipend. The stipend was later restored to his son.

These annexations brought about a significant change in Darjeeling's status. Previously it had been an enclave within Sikkimese territory, and to reach it the British had to pass through a country ruled by an independent raja. After the takeover, Darjeeling became contiguous with British territory further south and Sikkim was cut off from access to the plains except through British territory. This eventually led to the invasion of Sikkim by the Tibetans and the British military expedition to Lhasa.

When the British first arrived in Darjeeling it was almost completely forested and virtually uninhabited, though it had once been a sizeable village before the wars with Bhutan and Nepal. Development was rapid and by 1840 a road had been constructed, numerous houses and a sanatorium built and a hotel opened. By 1857 Darjeeling had a population of some 10,000.

The population increase was due mainly to the recruitment of Nepalese labourers to work the tea plantations established in the early 1840s by the British. Even today, the vast majority of people speak Nepali as a first language and the name Darjeeling continues to be synonymous with tea.

The immigration of Nepali-speaking peoples, mainly Gurkhas, into the mountainous areas of West Bengal, eventually led to political problems in the mid-1980s. Resentment had been growing among the Gurkhas over what they felt was discrimination against

The Toy Train

The 88km journey to Darjeeling from New Jalpaiguri or Siliguri on the famous miniature railway is certainly not the quickest way to get here but is nevertheless an experience that shouldn't be missed.

Until the late 1800s, all supplies for Darjeeling and all the tea exported had to be transported by bullock cart along aptly-named Hill Cart Rd. This was slow and expensive: rice that sold for Rs 98 a ton fetched Rs 240 a ton by the time it reached the hill station. Construction of the railway line commenced in 1879, and the little steam train made its maiden trip in 1880, carrying the viceroy 20km up to Tindharia. In 1881 the line was completed through to Darjeeling.

The whole line is an ingenious feat of engineering and includes five switchbacks and four complete loops. The last of these, known as the Batasia Loop, is five km short of Darjeeling and a popular spot for photographers.

Over the years there have been calls to pension off the elderly, unreliable, steam locomotives, the oldest of which (No 779) dates from 1892. In the last two years many of the country's steam engines have been shunted into the scrapyards. However, now that there are relatively few working steam lines, increased interest from rail enthusiasts and tourists should ensure the survival of Darjeeling's Toy Train. ∎

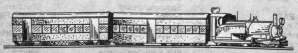

them by the government of West Bengal. Their language was not recognised by the Indian constitution and government jobs were thus only open to those who could speak Bengali.

The tensions finally came to a head in widespread riots throughout the hill country which continued for two years, and in which hundreds of people lost their lives and thousands were made homeless. Tourism came to a grinding halt and the Indian army was sent in to maintain some semblance of order. The riots were orchestrated by the Gurkha National Liberation Front (GNLF), led by Subash Ghising, which demanded a separate state to be known as Gorkhaland. The Communist Party of India (Marxist) was also responsible for a good deal of the violence since it was afraid of losing the support it had once enjoyed among the hill peoples.

A compromise was eventually hammered out in late 1988 whereby the Darjeeling Gorkha Hill Council (DGHC) was given a large measure of autonomy from the state government and fresh elections to the council were held. Darjeeling remains part of West Bengal but now has greater control over its own affairs.

Recently the authority of the GNLF has been challenged by the breakaway Akhil Bharatiya Gorkha League (ABGL) which is gaining support from the people. Following the prime minister's declaration in 1996 that the hill region of UP will become a separate state (Uttarakhand), there have been renewed demands for a separate Gorkhaland in the Darjeeling region.

Climate
For mountain views, the best time to visit Darjeeling is from mid-September to mid-December, although it gets pretty cold by December. The season resumes around mid-March and continues to mid-June but as the haze builds up the views become less clear. During the monsoon months (June to September), clouds obscure the mountains and the rain is often so heavy that whole sections of the road from the plains are washed away, though the town is rarely cut off for more than a few days at a time.

Average temperatures range from 8.5°C to 15°C in summer and from 1.5°C to 6°C in winter. It can get very cold indeed in winter, a real surprise if you've just come from Calcutta. If you go there during the monsoon, an umbrella – available cheaply in the market – is essential.

Tourist Tax
In October 1996 a tourist tax of Rs 3 was instigated, but following the burning down of the municipal building in Darjeeling (the result of an electrical fault, not arson by tourists!) this has yet to be collected. It may simply be added to hotel bills.

Orientation
Darjeeling sprawls over a west-facing ridge, spilling down the hillside in a complicated series of interconnecting roads and flights of steps. Hill Cart Rd has been renamed Tenzing Norgay Rd (even though Darjeeling already has another road by the same name) but the old name seems to stick. It's the main road through the lower part of the town, and the railway station and the bus and taxi stand are all on it. The most important route connecting this road with Chowrasta (the town square) at the top of the ridge is Laden La and Nehru Rds. The youth hostel is further back up the ridge, virtually at the high point.

Along these two roads are a fair number of budget hotels and cheap restaurants, the GPO, the bus terminals for Sikkim and Kathmandu, the Foreigners' Registration Office, the State Bank of India, curio shops and photographic supply shops. At the Chowrasta end of Nehru Rd and on Gandhi Rd above Laden La Rd are many of the mid-range hotels and restaurants. The bulk of the top-range hotels are clustered around Observatory Hill beyond Chowrasta. There are others along Dr Zakir Hussain Rd and AJC Bose Rd.

Information
Tourist Office The tourist office (☎ 54050) is below the Bellevue Hotel, Chowrasta. Staff are helpful and have reasonably up-to-date pamphlets and a map of Darjeeling for Rs 2. Buy

tickets (Rs 70) in advance here for the bus to Bagdogra airport. The office is open Monday to Friday from 10 am to 4.30 pm, but when it's closed you can get tickets for the airport bus at the Gorkha Hill Council Tourism office (☎ 54214) in the Silver Fir building opposite Hotel Alice Villa.

Money The State Bank of India and ANZ Grindlays are on Laden La Rd; most major travellers cheques are accepted.

Post & Communications The GPO is on Laden La Rd. You can send and receive faxes from the telegraph office (fax 54330), up the steps from Laden La Rd.

Permits for Sikkim The Foreigners' Registration Office is on Laden La Rd. To get a 15 day permit for Sikkim you must first visit the Deputy Commissioner's Office, otherwise known as the DM (District Magistrate). Then get an endorsement from the Foreigners' Registration Office and return to the DM to collect your permit. The DM's office is open for permit applications on weekdays from 11 am to 1 pm and 2 to 4 pm. The whole process takes about an hour. If you want to enter western Sikkim direct from Darjeeling (rather than first going to Gangtok), make sure that Naya Bazaar is one of the places listed on the permit.

Bookshops The Oxford Book & Stationery Company on Chowrasta is the best bookshop here. Several of the budget guest houses run book exchanges.

Medical Services If you need a doctor inquire at Puri & Co, a well-stocked chemist on Nehru Rd. The Tibetan Medical & Astro Institute (open weekdays, 9 am to noon and 2 to 4 pm) is at Hotel Seven Seventeen.

Trekking Outfits & Tour Operators There are several operators, some of whom also rent out equipment to individuals not taking their tours.

Trek-Mate (☎ 54074), at the Pineridge Hotel on Nehru Rd, is run by the enthusiastic Indra

Gongba. Indra can tailor treks in the Sikkim and Darjeeling areas, and special interest tours to temples and gompas. Clubside Tours & Travels (☎ 54646), JP Sharma Rd (off Laden La Rd), arranges treks and wildlife tours in North Bengal, Sikkim and Assam. Himalayan Tours & Travels (☎ 54544) organises treks and also leads mountaineering expeditions.

There are several good trekking agents in the Super Market complex, near the Bazaar bus stand on Hill Cart Rd. Himali Treks & Tours (☎ 52154) books treks and also hires equipment. It also does a half-day mountainbike tour (Rs 160); and rafting on the Teesta River. Other operators include Diamond Tours & Travels (☎ 53180) and Kasturi Tours & Travels.

Trekking gear can be hired from the youth hostel, but you must leave a deposit to cover the value of the articles you borrow (deposits returnable, less hire charges). Typical charges per day are: sleeping bag Rs 25, rucksack Rs 15, and jacket Rs 25. The hostel keeps a book in which trekkers write comments about the routes. Trek-Mate hires out equipment at comparable rates. Himali Treks & Tours lends dome tents for Rs 80.

Tiger Hill
The highest spot in the area at 2590m, Tiger Hill is near Ghoom, about 11km from Darjeeling. The hill is famous for its magnificent dawn views over Kanchenjunga and other eastern Himalayan peaks. On a clear day even Mt Everest is visible.

Every day a large convoy of battered Land Rovers leaves Darjeeling at 4.30 am, which means that in the smaller lodges you get woken up at this time every day, whether you like it or not. It can be very cold and very crowded at the top but coffee is available. There's a view tower and entry costs Rs 2 for the top or Rs 7 for the warmer VIP lounge. Halfway down the hill a temple priest causes a massive traffic jam by anointing the steering wheel of each vehicle for the return trip! Many take the jeep one way and then walk back – a very pleasant two hour trip.

The tourist office offers a tour for Rs 50

but most people go with the independent operators who charge a little less – around Rs 35/45 for a one-way/return trip. Some will even send a runner to your hotel at 4.30 am to make sure you don't wimp out!

Senchal Lake
Close to Tiger Hill is Senchal Lake, which supplies Darjeeling with its domestic water. It's a particularly scenic area and popular as a picnic spot with Indian holiday-makers.

Kanchenjunga Views
At 8598m this is the world's third-highest mountain. From Darjeeling, the best uninterrupted views are to be had from Bhan Bhakta Sarani. From Chowrasta, take the road to the right-hand side of the Windamere Hotel and continue about 300m.

Bhutia Busty Gompa
Not far from Chowrasta is this colourful monastery, with Kanchenjunga providing a spectacular backdrop. Originally a branch of the Nyingmapa sect's Phodang Monastery in Sikkim, it was transferred to Darjeeling in 1879. The shrine here originally stood on Observatory Hill. There's a library of Buddhist texts upstairs which houses the original copy of the *Tibetan Book of the Dead*.

Ghoom Gompa
More correctly known as Yogachoeling Gompa, this is probably the most famous monastery in Darjeeling and is about eight km south of town, just below Hill Cart Rd and the railway station near Ghoom. It enshrines an image of the Maitreya Buddha (the coming Buddha). Foreigners are allowed to enter the shrine and take photographs. A small donation is customary and the monks are very friendly.

Other Gompas
There are three other gompas in Ghoom: the very large but relatively uninteresting **Samdenchoeling**, the nearby and smaller **Sakyachoeling**, and the **Phin Sotholing**.

Nearer Darjeeling, on Tenzing Norgay Rd, **Aloobari Monastery** welcomes visitors. The

monks often sell Tibetan and Sikkimese handicrafts and religious objects (usually hand bells). If the monastery is closed ask at the cottage next door and they'll let you in.

Halfway between Ghoom and Darjeeling is the **Thupten Sangachoeling Gompa** at Dali. Westerners interested in Tibetan Buddhism often study here. A little closer to Darjeeling on the same road is the opulent **Sonada Gompa**.

Observatory Hill
Situated above the Windamere Hotel, this viewpoint is sacred to both Hindus and Buddhists. There's a Kali shrine here and the multicoloured prayer flags double as trapezes for the monkeys. Watch out for them as they can be aggressive.

Dhirdham Temple
The most conspicuous Hindu temple in Darjeeling, this is just below the railway station and is modelled on the famous Pashupatinath Temple in Kathmandu.

Bengal Natural History Museum
Established in 1903, a comprehensive but dusty collection of Himalayan and Bengali fauna is packed into this interesting museum. Among the 4300 specimens is the estuarine crocodile, the animal responsible for the greatest loss of human life in Asia. The museum is open daily except Thursday, from 10 am to 4 pm. Entry is Rs 1.

Zoological Park
Conditions for some of the animals here are barely tolerable, made worse by the fact that they have no escape from the Indian male tourists who show off by teasing them mercilessly. The zoo houses India's only collection of Siberian tigers, and some rare species such as the red panda. It's open daily from 8 am to 4 pm; entry is Rs 3.

Himalayan Mountaineering Institute (HMI) & Museums
Entered through the zoo, on Jawahar Rd West about two km from the town, the HMI runs courses to train mountaineers, and maintains

WEST BENGAL

a couple of interesting museums. The **Mountaineering Museum** contains a collection of historic mountaineering equipment, specimens of Himalayan flora and fauna and a relief model of the Himalaya. The **Everest Museum** next door traces the history of attempts on the great peak.

Sherpa Tenzing Norgay, who conquered Everest with Edmund Hillary in 1953, lived in Darjeeling and was the director of the institute for many years. He died in 1986 and his statue now stands beside his cremation spot just above the institute.

There are film shows at the institute and for Rs 1 you can view Kanchenjunga close up through a Zeiss telescope given to a Nepalese maharaja by Adolf Hitler.

The institute is open from 9 am to 1 pm and 2 to 4.30 pm, and entry costs Rs 3. There's a reasonable vegetarian restaurant by Sherpa Tenzing's statue.

Snow Leopard Breeding Programme
In contrast to the animals in the rest of the zoo the snow leopards are kept in a large separate enclosure on the way to the ropeway. These rare animals are reputedly less keen to breed in captivity than the panda (whose disinterest in sex is legendary) but they've had some success here. Much credit must be given to the devoted attentions of Kiran Moktan, who runs the programme and spends his days with the leopards. He welcomes interested visitors between 9 and 11 am and 2 to 3.30 pm, daily except Thursday, but you should not make too much noise. Ask to see his drawings as he's an accomplished artist.

Passenger Ropeway
At North Point, about three km from town, this was the first passenger ropeway (cablecar) to be constructed in India. It is five km long and connects Darjeeling with Singla Bazaar on the Little Ranjit River at the bottom of the valley. It's currently under renovation; phone ☎ 52731, or contact the tourist office to see if it's running again.

Botanical Gardens
Below the bus and taxi stand near the market, these gardens contain a representative collection of Himalayan plants, flowers and orchids. The hothouses are well worth a visit. The gardens are open between 6 am and 5 pm; entry is free.

Tibetan Refugee Self-Help Centre
A 20 to 30 minute walk from Chowrasta brings you down to this Tibetan centre. It was established in October 1959 to help rehabilitate Tibetan refugees who fled from Tibet with the Dalai Lama following the Chinese invasion. The centre produces superb carpets, woollens, woodcarvings and leatherwork, and has various Tibetan curios for sale (coins, banknotes, jewellery etc).

You can wander at leisure through the workshops and watch the work in progress. The weaving and dyeing shops and the woodcarving shop are particularly interesting, and the workers are very friendly.

Gymkhana Club
Membership of the Darjeeling Gymkhana Club costs Rs 30 per day. The word gymkhana is actually derived from the Hindi *geindkhana* (ball house). Ball games include tennis (mornings only, Rs 25 racquet and court hire), squash, badminton, table tennis and billiards. Roller-skating is also available.

The club must have been magnificent when it was the playground of the Raj; these days it's semi-derelict.

Other Activities
Beware of the pony-wallahs who congregate in Chowrasta. They'll come along with you as a guide and at the end you'll find you're paying for a second pony and for their guiding time! The usual charge is around Rs 35 an hour, but make sure of the price first.

See the **Tea Plantations** regional highlight on p503.

Courses
Three-month courses in Tibetan language are offered by the Manjushree Centre of Tibetan Culture (☎ 54159) at 8 Burdwan Rd.

If you'd like to volunteer to teach English try the Nepali Girls' Social Service Centre (☎ 52985).

Carbon-Monoxide Poisoning

Fires, charcoal burners in particular, are not recommended as a means of heating in hotel rooms. The Indian police have confirmed that a number of deaths from carbon-monoxide poisoning occur each year. Among them recently were two young travellers staying in Darjeeling. They had asked for some heating for their room and had been brought a bucket of burning charcoal. Unfortunately, ventilation in the room was almost nonexistent and they died in their sleep from carbon-monoxide poisoning.

If you're cold, take a tip from trekkers who fill their drinking bottles with boiling water at night to use as a hot water bottle (covered with a sock to prevent burning). In the morning the water can be drunk since having been boiled it will have been purified. More upmarket hotels usually provide their guests with proper hot water bottles. ∎

Places to Stay

There are a great number of places to stay: only a limited selection follows. Prices vary widely with the season; those listed are for the high season (15 March to 15 July and 15 September to 15 November). In the low season prices drop by 50% to 75%, less for bottom end places; discounts are negotiable.

Darjeeling suffers from chronic power and water shortages. Not all hotels have backup generators.

Places to Stay – bottom end

Many travellers head for the area around the youth hostel and TV tower, on or near Dr Zakir Hussain Rd. It's about a 20 minute (uphill!) walk from the railway station. If you're coming from Chowrasta, Dr Zakir Hussain Rd divides at the TV tower.

The **Youth Hostel**, at the top of the ridge on Dr Zakir Hussain Rd, has seen better days, and the wind whistles through the shabby dorms. For a bed it's Rs 20 for members, Rs 40 for nonmembers. There's a good travellers'

comment book, and the staff are informative about treks in the area.

Triveni Guest House & Restaurant (☎ 53114) is opposite the hostel. Beds in the dorm are Rs 25, there are singles/doubles with common toilet for Rs 40/80, or with attached toilet and bath, Rs 50/80. A double is around Rs 60 in the off season.

Aliment Restaurant & Hotel is near the Triveni. It has singles/doubles for Rs 50/80, and dorm beds for Rs 30. There's a good borrowing library, a useful travellers' comments book and a popular restaurant. One woman traveller wrote to say that a stay on their family farm in Mirik (invitation only) is probably a better experience for men than women.

Ratna Restaurant, also near the Triveni, has four charming and cosy double rooms for Rs 70, and a comfortable sitting room. This is a great place and very good value, too.

Hotel Tower View (☎ 54452) is a very popular place run by a friendly family. There's a range of rooms, from Rs 50 for a single with attached bath, Rs 70 for a double with great views and common bath, up to Rs 140 with views and attached bath. There's a convivial lounge area where tasty meals are dished up.

Hotel Tshering Denzongpa (☎ 53412), at 6 JP Sharma Rd, is an excellent, Sherpa-run place. Doubles range from Rs 200 to Rs 600. The more expensive rooms have better views. Hot water is available free in buckets. A 40% discount is offered in the off season.

Hotel Shamrock, Upper Beechwood Lane, run by an enthusiastic Sherpa family, is a popular place with travellers. To reach it from Laden La Rd, just beyond the post office, take the stone steps uphill that lead eventually to Gandhi Rd. Halfway up, Upper Beechwood Rd is the lane that branches to the right. Singles/doubles/triples cost Rs 75/160/175, some with attached bath. Hot water is available free in buckets. There are good views from the upstairs rooms which, with their wood panelling and sloping roofs, have a Swiss chalet ambience.

Hotel Pagoda is next door to the Shamrock. It has basic but pleasant doubles for Rs 160 with attached bath. There are cheaper

WEST BENGAL

doubles, but they're a bit gloomy. This is a good location, and the staff are friendly. There's a cosy TV room with a fireplace.

Hotel Prestige (☎ 52699) is on the stairway leading up from Laden La. All rooms have attached bath with geyser, and cost from Rs 200/400/600, with a 50% discount in the off season. The upstairs rooms are best. The hotel has a borrowing library.

Places to Stay – middle

There's a collection of mid-range (and almost identical) hotels along Cooch Bihar and Rockville roads, including the *Hotel Purnima* (☎ 53110), *Hotel Broadway* (☎ 53248) and *Rockville Hotel* (☎ 52513), all with doubles from Rs 250; the *Hotel Daffodil* (☎ 52605) and *Continental* (☎ 53196), with doubles from Rs 350, and the *Hotel Dil* (☎ 52773), at 12A Rockville Rd, which has cosy and very clean doubles/ triples for Rs 450/650. All these places offer good discounts in the off season.

Bellevue Hotel (☎ 54075), a charming old hotel right on Chowrasta, is a favourite in this price range. Fine old wood-panelled doubles range from Rs 700 to Rs 880, and all rooms have attached baths with hot water in the mornings. Room 49 (Rs 880) has the best views, as well as a separate sitting room. There's a cafe for guests only, which is a shame, as the views out over Chowrasta are excellent. Very good discounts are offered in the off season.

Main Bellevue Hotel (☎ 54178) is up the track beside the other Bellevue. This is a delightfully shabby Raj-era building with doubles/triples for Rs 500/550, and a special double with Kanchenjunga views for Rs 700. The hotel has a gracious and attentive manager and is set in a lovely established garden. In the off season the generous discounts make it very affordable.

Pineridge Hotel (☎ 54074) is on Nehru Rd, opposite the Bellevue Hotel. Doubles are Rs 500 to Rs 800; in the off season you should be able to get a room with attached bath for Rs 250/350 or less for single/double occupancy. The rooms are nice (some have bay windows and good views) but the hotel,

the Drum Druid in the Raj era, has definitely seen better days. It's a big place and partial renovation is still in progress.

Hotel Shangrila (☎ 54149) is above the restaurant of the same name. Enormous, light, airy rooms with fireplaces and polished wooden floors are Rs 800 (Rs 400 in the off season).

Hotel Dekeling (☎ 54159), 51 Gandhi Rd, on the top floor above the Dekevas Restaurant and owned by the same Tibetan family, is a popular place with travellers. Doubles are Rs 400 and Rs 665, all with attached bath. A 40% discount is offered in the off season. Many students studying at the Manjushree Centre of Tibetan Culture stay here longterm in the pleasant wood-panelled attic rooms (Rs 150 for singles with common bath).

Hotel Lunar (☎ 54194) is one floor below Hotel Dekeling. It's a small place with cosy rooms for Rs 750/900, bathrooms attached. There's a good vegetarian restaurant.

Hotel Valentino (☎ 52228), 6 Rockville Rd, has doubles from Rs 770 to Rs 1050, and some of the best views in Darjeeling. Rates include breakfast, and heaters are provided free in winter. Run by a Chinese family from Calcutta, the hotel has oriental *objets d'art* and a fountain which falls into a pool full of fat goldfish. This place is a pleasant discovery among some less salubrious prospects. There's an excellent Chinese restaurant.

Hotel Seven Seventeen (☎ 54717) is one of several hotels on HD Lama Rd. It's not a great location but this place is Tibetan-run and welcoming. There are rooms from Rs 600/700 with a 30% discount in the off season. The Tibetan Medical & Astro Institute is here.

Darjeeling Club (☎ 54349; fax 54348), above Nehru Rd, was the Tea Planters' Club in the days of the Raj. The downstairs doubles for Rs 600 are shabby, gloomy and chilly. Large, comfortable doubles upstairs are Rs 1800, or there are identical rooms, which are cheaper simply on account of having been allowed to get shabbier, for Rs 1000. There's a billiard room, a musty library, plenty of memorabilia and lots of nice sitting areas. There's a temporary membership charge of

Rs 50 per day, and rates are discounted by up to 40% in the off season.

Palace Mahakal (☎ 52026), behind Hotel Sinclairs, is an intimate, comfortable hotel. Singles/doubles/triples are Rs 700/1000/1400, plush super-deluxe rooms with great views are Rs 1000/1400/1700.

Places to Stay – top end

Windamere Hotel (☎ 54041; fax 54043) is undoubtedly the best place to stay in Darjeeling. This is one of the oldest hotels here and a gem of a leftover from the Raj. It's set in beautifully maintained gardens and consists of a main block with detached cottages and dining room. Guests are entertained by a pianist or string quartet at dinner; at tea there are cucumber sandwiches served by waitresses in starched aprons. The hotel has been owned since the 1920s by Mrs Tenduf-la, a Tibetan lady now in her 90s. She's still very much running the place and continues to play a mean game of pontoon.

Rooms are by no means luxurious, but are cosy and comfortable, and TVs are deliberately absent. Comfort is assured with little touches like heaters and hot-water bottles in the bedrooms, and a torch (flashlight) in case of power failure. Single rates are from US$70 to US$80, and doubles are US$110, including all meals. There's a 25% surcharge over Christmas.

New Elgin (☎ 54114; fax 54267), off Robertson Rd, is a delightful old place with resident labrador and pictures of the Queen on the walls. Rooms cost US$57/68 including meals. The staff are friendly and attentive, rooms are elegantly furnished, and hot water bottles are provided at night. There's a good restaurant, a bar and gardens.

Places to Eat

Around the TV Tower Most of the guest houses in this area have small restaurants, which saves you the trek down into town. They all have the usual travellers' menus that include pancakes and jaffles. The *Tower View* is popular, *Triveni Guest House* is very clean and the *Ratna* is very good value.

Laden La & Nehru Rds There are numerous cheap restaurants along Laden La Rd all clustered together between the State Bank of India and the post office. Several of them are Tibetan-run while the remainder offer Indian cuisine of various sorts. Most of them are pretty basic and could use a good scrub down. They include the *Golden Dragon, Vineet, Utsang, Potala, Lotus, Penang, Soatlee* and *Washington*.

Lhasa Restaurant is a very cheap and very basic Tibetan restaurant serving good momos and thukpa.

Park Restaurant has probably the best Indian cuisine in town. Tandoori items are mouthwatering – chicken sheek kebabs are Rs 45, chicken tikka masala costs Rs 55. Decor is Graeco-Roman greenhouse finished off with shower-room curtains, but the food is excellent.

Dekevas Restaurant is on Nehru Rd; it's very popular with travellers. Spicy Hong Kong chicken is Rs 40, special pizza with the works costs Rs 41 and is filling. There are also Tibetan specialities.

Dafey Munal Restaurant, by the Clubside taxi stand, offers chicken with chips for Rs 50 and ever popular 'chocolate pudding with fire' (!) for Rs 25.

Great Punjab Restaurant is down Robertson Rd, which leads off the Laden La/Nehru Rd intersection. It has delicious Punjabi vegetarian dishes, such as rajma (kidney beans masala) for Rs 20.

Kev's (Keventer's Snack Bar), on Nehru Rd, is a popular place for breakfast and there are wonderful views from the open terrace. They've got ham, bacon, sausages and cheese, but service can be tediously slow.

Hasty Tasty, further north up Nehru Rd, is a busy fast food and ice cream parlour with excellent south Indian dishes and good views over the valley.

Glenary's, is an excellent place with a definite ghost-of-the-Raj air to it. Downstairs is the bakery; if you arrive early enough you can get very good brown bread. They also have croissants (Rs 6), doughnuts (Rs 7), garlic bread (Rs 10) and a wonderful range of cakes (cherry, Madeira, Dundee) for Rs 30, and (in season) Christmas cake for Rs 150. Tea time here is still a special occasion upstairs in the restaurant where you can also have full meals. Fried sausages are Rs 60, roast chicken costs Rs 70 and you could round this off with tipsy pudding (trifle with rum and cream, Rs 25) and Irish coffee (Rs 40). Credit cards are accepted.

Hotel Restaurants Many of the hotels have restaurants that are also open to nonresidents.

New Embassy Chinese Restaurant, in the Hotel Valentino, is the best Chinese place in Darjeeling. Most main dishes are under Rs 60, but they close around 8 pm so you probably won't be let in after 7.30 pm.

Silver Restaurant at the New Elgin Hotel has an interesting set dinner menu for Rs 225. Book in advance.

Windamere Hotel is the place to go for a splurge. If you're not staying here, you must book in advance. It's a set menu which costs US$10.20. Here you are served a full western meal, such as roast chicken, followed by a full-on Indian meal of curry, rice and chapatis! But it's not just food you get for your money – you are entertained by a pianist or string quartet during dinner and afterwards you can retire to the drawing room for a brandy by the fire. You can also come here for tea (US$3) which includes the best Darjeeling tea, cucumber sandwiches and cakes, and the pianist tickling the ivories next door.

Things to Buy
Curios & Carpets Most curio shops are on Chowrasta and along Nehru Rd. All things Himalayan are sold here – thangkas, brass statues, religious objects, jewellery, woodcarvings, woven fabrics, carpets etc – but if you're looking for bargains you have to shop judiciously and be prepared to spend plenty of time looking. Thangkas in particular may look impressive at first sight, but on closer inspection of the cheaper offerings you will find that little care has been taken over the finer detail.

If you're looking for bronze statues, the real goodies are kept under the counter and cost in multiples of US$100! Woodcarvings tend to be excellent value for money. Most of the shops accept international credit cards.

West Bengal's Manjusha Emporium, on Nehru Rd, is a fixed-price shop selling Himalayan handicrafts, silk and handloomed products. There is also a market off Hill Cart Rd next to the bus and taxi stands. Here you can find excellent and relatively cheap patterned woollen sweaters. If you need an umbrella these can be bought here cheaply. Made out of bamboo, they are collectors' items themselves!

For Tibetan carpets, the cheapest place in the area is at Hayden Hall, opposite the State Bank of India on Laden La Rd. It's a women's co-operative – excellent value and well worth checking out.

Darjeeling Tea A packet of tea is a popular souvenir. First Flush Super Fine Tippy Golden Flowery Orange Pekoe I is the top quality. The price varies enormously; you'll pay anything from Rs 160 to Rs 3000 per kg! The way to test tea is to take a small handful in your closed fist, breathe firmly on it through your fingers and then open your hand and smell the aromas released. At least it'll look as if you know what you're doing even if you don't have a clue! Avoid the tea in fancy boxes as this is usually blended and comes from Calcutta. A good place is Nathmull's Tea Merchants, near the post office on Laden La Rd. Mr Vijay Sarda here will hold you in thrall as he waxes lyrical over the virtues of various teas.

Getting There & Away
Air The nearest airport is 90km away at Bagdogra, down on the plains near Siliguri. See under Getting There & Away in the Siliguri section earlier in this chapter for details.

Indian Airlines (☎ 54230) is below the Bellevue Hotel and is open daily from 10 am to 1 pm and 2 to 4 pm. The Jet Airways agent is Clubside Tours (☎ 54646), JP Sharma Rd (off Laden La). Juniper Travels (☎ 52625) is the agent for the three Nepali airlines that fly from Bhadrapur, just over the border, to Kathmandu (US$99).

Tickets for the airport bus (Rs 70) can be purchased at the tourist office.

Bus Most of the buses from Darjeeling leave from the Bazaar bus stand (Hill Cart Rd). To Gangtok, buses leave at 7.30 and 8 am, 1.15 and 1.30 pm (Rs 65, five hours). Buses for Siliguri leave every 20 minutes between 6.20 am and 5.30 pm (Rs 28, three hours). Every 40 minutes between 8.30 am and 3.15 pm, buses depart for Mirik (2½ hours, Rs 20). To Kalimpong, there's one bus at 8 am (3½ hours, Rs 36).

The agent for Sikkim Nationalised Transport (SNT) is the Darjeeling Motor Service Co (☎ 52101), 32 Laden La Rd. The office is open daily from 10 am to 1 pm only. There is one bus daily which leaves from opposite the office to Gangtok at 1 pm (Rs 65, five hours). There are no bus services to Jorethang, in West Sikkim.

There are numerous private operators who sell seats through agents. Rates don't vary much between them. At Greenland Tours & Travels (☎ 53190), 21 Beechwood Rd (on the steps near the Hotel Prestige, above the main post office) rates are as follows: Calcutta (Rs 200, 19 hours), Patna (Rs 190, 18 hours), Guwahati (Rs 220, 20 hours, change at Siliguri), New Jalpaiguri (Rs 60, four hours), Gangtok (Rs 70, five hours), Kalimpong (Rs 55, 2½ hours).

Kathmandu There are a number of companies which offer daily buses between Darjeeling and Kathmandu (Rs 275, 26 hours), but none of them actually has a direct service; you have to change buses at Siliguri. The usual arrangement is that the agents will sell you a ticket as far as Siliguri, but guarantee you a seat on the connecting bus with the same agency. You arrive at the border around 3 pm (Kakarbhitta is the name of the town on the Nepalese side), leave again round 4 pm and arrive in Kathmandu around 9 or 10 am the next day.

Most travellers prefer to do the whole trip

independently, although it involves four changes – bus from Darjeeling to Siliguri (Rs 28), bus (Rs 6) or jeep (Rs 25) from Siliguri to Paniktanki on the border, rickshaw across the border to Kakarbhitta (Rs 5), and bus from Kakarbhitta to Kathmandu (17 hours, Nepalese Rs 280). This is cheaper than the package deal, and you get a choice of buses from the border, plus you have the option of travelling during the day and staying over at places along the way. There are day buses from Kakarbhitta that stop at a number of other towns on the terai (Nepalese plains), including Janakpur, and night buses direct to Pokhara.

The nearest Nepalese consulate is in Calcutta, but visas are available at Paniktanki on the Indian side of the border for US$25 (which must be paid in cash). If you need to extend your visa, you can do so in Kathmandu.

Taxi & Jeep Prices for share/full jeeps are as follows: Siliguri Rs 45/550, Kalimpong Rs 55/700, Gangtok Rs 105/1200. Rates are Rs 5 lower for the less comfortable seats in the back. You can also get jeeps to various destinations in West Sikkim, including Jorethang (Rs 60/900, 2½ hours), Pemayangtse (Rs 2500, 4½ hours) and Yuksom (Rs 2600, five hours). The section between Darjeeling and Naya Bazaar (21km) is very steep, and during the monsoon it is subject to landslides. If the road is closed, you'll need to take a detour is via Teesta Bridge, which costs an additional Rs 500 (shared between the passengers).

The share jeep stand for destinations in Sikkim is to the right of the bus ticket office at the bus stand on Hill Cart Rd. The share jeep office for Kalimpong is at the south end of the taxi rank, beneath the staircase to the first level of the Super Market.

Train New Jalpaiguri/Siliguri is the railhead for all trains other than the narrow-gauge toy train. Reservations for major trains out of New Jalpaiguri can be made at the Darjeeling railway station (the toy train terminus) between

10 am and 4 pm daily (closed for lunch between 1 and 2 pm).

The toy train runs daily, although services during the monsoon are often disrupted due to the track being washed away. It leaves Siliguri at 9 am, arriving into Darjeeling at 5.30 pm. An additional service leaves Siliguri at 7.15 am during the peak season. The cost is Rs 14/116 in 2nd/1st class, with the return journey from Darjeeling leaving at 7 and 10 am.

It's a slow but interesting trip, although the black soot belched out by the little steam engine soon gets annoying, and the tiny carriages are extremely cramped, especially when filled with at least a dozen hefty foreigners and their backpacks. The best bet is to disembark at Kurseong (Rs 9/33, four hours) and from there take a bus (Rs 15) or a seat in a jeep (Rs 30) for the 1½ hour run to Darjeeling. This also gets you into Darjeeling before dark. For an even shorter trip, it's a pleasant ride from Darjeeling to Ghoom (Rs 3, 45 minutes).

Darjeeling-Sandakphu/Phalut Trek

The best months to trek in this region are April, May, October and November. There may be occasional showers during April and May but, in a way, this is the best time to go as many shrubs are in flower, particularly the rhododendrons. There may be occasional rains during the first half of October if the monsoon is prolonged. November is generally dry, and visibility is excellent during the first half of December, though it's usually cold by then. After the middle of December there are occasional snowfalls.

You don't need to bring much with you on this trek as there's accommodation along the way. Most places have quilts but in the high season it might be worth bringing your own sleeping bag (you can rent them in Darjeeling) in case there's not enough bedding to go round. Also, since you will be passing through valley bottoms as low as 300m and over mountain ridges as high as 4000m, you'll need clothing for a wide range of temperatures. Take rain gear whatever time of year you go, as the weather can be unpredictable. Acute Mountain Sickness (AMS) can occur at high altitudes. See the Health section in the Facts for the Visitor chapter for more details.

Although you can get basic meals along the way, everyone recommends bringing along some snacks like nuts, biscuits, raisins and chocolate. You'll need a water bottle – even a plastic mineral water bottle will do – as there are some stretches where there's no water or places to eat.

Guides and porters are not necessary but can be arranged through the youth hostel or the trekking agencies. A porter would cost around Rs 120 per day, a guide Rs 200 per day. If you don't take a guide, you should ask directions at every opportunity as the path is not always clear.

Before leaving Darjeeling you're advised to browse through the Darjeeling Youth Hostel's book in which trekkers write their comments about the routes.

This trek to the Himalayan viewpoint at Phalut (3600m) is the most popular trek in the area. It involves a short bus trip from Darjeeling to Manaybhanjang, from where you walk steadily towards the mountains via Sandakphu. Here you can turn back or continue to Phalut and walk down to Rimbik for a bus to Darjeeling. The trek can be done in the opposite direction but you'll spend more time walking with your back to the mountains.

There's a rough jeep track from Manaybhanjang through Sandakphu but it's not used much. If you prefer, Rs 3000 will get you a return trip from Darjeeling to Sandakphu by Land Rover.

Day 1: Darjeeling to Jaubari (8 to 9 hours)
Day 2: Jaubari to Sandakphu (5 to 6 hours)
Day 3: Sandakphu to Molley (4 to 5 hours)
Day 4: Molley to Gorkhey (5 to 6 hours)
Day 5: Gorkhey to Rimbik (6 to 7 hours)
Day 6: Rimbik to Darjeeling

Short Cut If you don't have time for a six day trek, you can go just as far as Sandakphu where there are also good views. Sandakphu is actually slightly higher than Phalut, although further back from the mountains. From here you can backtrack to Bikhay Bhanjang and cut straight across to Rimbik in five to six hours for a bus to Darjeeling. Bear in mind that there's no water or food on this stretch. ■

WEST BENGAL

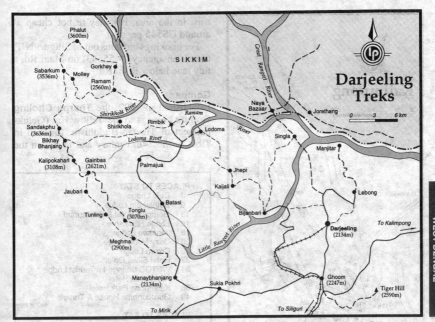

Darjeeling Treks

KALIMPONG

Pop: 46,500   Tel Area Code: 03552

Kalimpong is a bustling and rapidly expanding, though still relatively small, bazaar town set among the rolling foothills and deep valleys of the Himalaya at an altitude of 1250m. It was once part of the lands belonging to the rajas of Sikkim, until the beginning of the 18th century when it was taken from them by the Bhutanese. In the 19th century it passed into the hands of the British and thus became part of West Bengal. It became a centre for Scottish missionary activity in the late 19th century, and Dr Graham's orphanage and school is still running today.

Kalimpong's attractions include three monasteries, a couple of solidly built churches, an excellent private library for the study of Tibetan and Himalayan language and culture, a sericulture centre, orchid nurseries and fine views over the surrounding countryside. Although not many travellers bother to visit Kalimpong, there's enough

here to keep you occupied for a couple of days, and for the energetic there's some good trekking.

The most interesting part of a trip to Kalimpong is the journey there from Darjeeling via the Teesta River bridge. If you have no permit for Sikkim then the town is worth visiting just for the journey.

Orientation & Information

Though it's a much smaller town than Darjeeling, Kalimpong follows a similar kind of layout, straddling a ridge and made up of a series of interconnected streets and steps.

Life centres around the sports ground and east through the market. The bus stand and Chowrasta is also a busy area, and it's here that you find most of the cheap cafes and hotels. The Central Bank of India is at the north end of Main Rd; most major travellers cheques are accepted.

Gurudongma Travels (☎ 55204), Hill Top Rd, runs interesting cycling and trekking

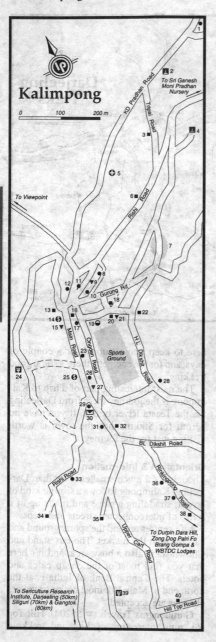

Kalimpong

0   100   200 m

To Sri Ganesh
Moni Pradhan
Nursery

To Viewpoint

Sports
Ground

To Sericulture Research
Institute, Darjeeling (50km)
Siliguri (70km) & Gangtok
(80km)

To Durpin Dara Hill,
Zong Dog Palri Fo
Brang Gompa &
WBTDC Lodges

trips in the area, but they're not cheap at around US$45 per day.

For bookings on trains out of Siliguri/NJP, there's an agency (☎ 55643) on Mani Rd, a tiny lane below Rishi Rd.

Gompas

Established in 1922, the **Tharpa Choling Gompa** belongs to the Yellow Hat (Gelukpa) sect of Tibetan Buddhism, founded in Tibet in the 14th century and to which the

PLACES TO STAY
3	Deki Lodge
6	Bethlehem Lodge
13	Gompu's Hotel & Restaurant
16	Lodge Himalshree
18	Janakee Lodge
20	Cozy Nook Lodge
22	Crown Lodge
32	Hotel Silver Oaks
34	WBTDC Shangri La Tourist Lodge
35	Himalayan Hotel
38	Kalimpong Park Hotel
40	Gurudongma House & Travels

PLACES TO EAT
9	Lark's Provisions
15	Ritu's Fast Food
21	Kalsang Restaurant
27	Ferrazzini's Bakery

OTHER
1	Dr Graham's Home
2	Tharpa Choeling Gompa
4	Thongsa Gompa & Mangal Dham Temple
5	Hospital
7	Market
8	Railway Booking Office
10	Kashi Nath Booksellers
11	Bhutia Shop
12	Arts & Crafts Co-op
14	Central Bank of India
17	SNT (Sikkim) Bus Office
19	Bus & Jeep Stand
23	Mintri Transport
24	Thakurbari Temple
25	State Bank of India
26	Speedways Travel Agency
28	Hill Crafts Institute
29	Foreigners' Registration Office
30	Sub Post Office
31	Town Hall
33	Cinema
36	Forest Development Corporation & Nature Interpretation Centre
37	Rishi Bankim Park
39	Kali Mandir

Dalai Lama belongs. It's a 40 minute walk (uphill) from town; take the path to the right off KD Pradhan Rd, just before the Milk Collection and Extension Wing Building.

Lower down the hill, the **Thongsa Gompa**, or Bhutanese Monastery, is the oldest monastery in the area and was founded in 1692. The present building isn't so old – the original was destroyed by the Gurkhas in their rampage across Sikkim before the arrival of the British.

Zong Dog Palri Fo-Brang Gompa, five km south of the town centre at the end of the ridge, was built in the mid-1970s at Durpin Dara Hill and was consecrated by the Dalai Lama. There are impressive wall paintings in the prayer room, and a rare three dimensional mandala upstairs. Mountain views are good from Durpin Dara Hill. This area is a big military camp, but you are free to walk or drive through it.

Flower Nurseries
Kalimpong produces 80% of India's gladiolis and is an important orchid-growing area; flowers are exported from here to many cities in northern India. The Sri Ganesh Moni Pradhan Nursery and the Udai Mani Pradhan Nursery are among the most important in the area. The Standard and the Universal Nurseries also specialise in cacti. There's a flower festival in Kalimpong in October.

Sericulture Research Institute
Silkworms are bred and silk is produced here. It is on the road to Darjeeling and can be visited between 9.30 am and 4 pm.

Dr Graham's Home
It takes less than an hour to walk from the town centre up through stands of bamboo to Dr Graham's Home, which was founded in 1900 on the lower slopes of Deolo Hill. The school was established to educate the children of tea-workers. There are now 1300 students and the grounds cover 193 hectares. Enrolment is open to all, but there is a reserve quota for children from economically deprived backgrounds. Visitors are welcome to the turn-of-the-century school buildings, and many people picnic in the attractive grounds.

From the school itself, it is a 40 minute walk to the summit of Deolo Hill, where there are fine views over Kalimpong.

Nature Interpretation Centre
On Rinkingpong Rd, and run by the Soil Conservation Division of the Ministry of Environment & Forests, the centre consists of a number of nicely put together dioramas which depict the effects of human activity on the environment. The centre is open daily, except Thursday, from 10 am to 4 pm; admission is free.

Places to Stay – bottom end
Kalimpong suffers from acute water shortages and many of the smaller places only have water by the bucket.

Lodge Himalshree (☎ 55070) is a small family place on the 3rd floor of a building on Ongden Rd. Despite the grubby communal staircase the rooms are very clean, and the owner is charming and helpful. Doubles/four-beds are Rs 120/200 with common bath, and there's one double with bath attached for Rs 250.

Cozy Nook Lodge (☎ 55541) has singles/doubles for Rs 120/200. The rooms are fine, but water comes in buckets and privacy is not what it might be.

Janakee Lodge (☎ 55479) is a good place with rooms from Rs 130/200 with common bath, Rs 180/260 with attached bathroom. Hot water is available in the morning.

Bethlehem Lodge (☎ 55182), Rishi Rd, is fairly new, well run and a good choice. Spotless rooms with attached bathrooms are good value at Rs 100/200.

Deki Lodge (☎ 55095), about a 10 minute walk north of the bus stand, is probably the most popular hotel with travellers. It's run by a very friendly and helpful family, and they can offer good suggestions about things to do in the Kalimpong area. Rooms cost Rs 80/150 with common bath, Rs 100/250 with attached bath (Rs 300 with geyser). There are hot showers in the common bathroom. Rustic

WEST BENGAL

doubles in the timber annexe behind the guesthouse are Rs 150 with attached bath.

Gompu's Hotel (☎ 55818) on Chowrasta is run by a friendly Tibetan family. Good singles/doubles are Rs 125/200 with attached bath. There's a good restaurant downstairs.

Crown Lodge (☎ 55846) is down a side street off HL Dikshit Rd. It's quiet, spacious and clean, and has rooms from Rs 250/350 with attached bathroom (hot showers in the mornings), TV in the double rooms, and free bed tea. There are good off-season discounts.

Places to Stay – middle
The few mid-range places are all out of the town centre to the south, along Rinkingpong Rd. Off-season discounts are available at most of these places.

Kalimpong Park Hotel (☎ 55304), about one km from the bus stand, is the pick of the bunch. The hotel is a very pleasant colonial bungalow, the former summer residence of the Maharaja of Dinajpur. The rooms are good value at Rs 550/600 with attached bath, hot water and TV, and those at the front have great views. There are rooms for the same price in the modern block at the rear, and although comfortable, they are far less attractive. The hotel has its own bar and restaurant.

WBTDC Tourist Lodges are run by the West Bengal Tourist Development Corporation (WBTDC). There are four lodges in Kalimpong, most quite far out and a hassle to get to without your own transport:

Shangri-La (☎ 55230), an old wooden building on the road down to the Teesta Bridge, is the closest. Doubles are from Rs 475 and dorm beds Rs 190 although this does include all meals.

The ***Hill Top*** (☎ 55654) has similar prices and is signposted off Rinkingpong Rd.

Morgan House (☎ 55384), is WBTDC's nicest lodge, a beautiful old ivy-covered Victorian building about three km from the town centre. There are rooms from Rs 600/1000 with attached bath (hot showers) and all meals included.

The adjacent ***Tashiding*** (☎ 55929), down a cobblestone path, is similarly priced. Rooms have a lovely outlook but are fairly basic.

Gurudongma House (☎ 55204), on Hill Top Rd, is another good place, set in a peaceful garden. It's about three km out, but General Jimmy Singh will pick up guests from the town centre. Singles/doubles are Rs 600/800, or three to four person tents are Rs 100. Meals are available.

Places to Stay – top end
Himalayan Hotel (☎ 55248; fax 55122), on Upper Cart Rd, is the best place to stay in Kalimpong. It is the beautiful former home of David MacDonald, who wrote *Twenty Years in Tibet* and *Land of the Lamas*. The hotel is still in the MacDonald family, now run by Tim (David's grandson) and Neelam MacDonald. They are most welcoming hosts, and can arrange walks in the neighbourhood, picnics and bird-watching trips. Singles/doubles are Rs 950/1300, or Rs 1400/2200 with all meals, plus 10% tax. The food is excellent and the chocolate cake served at tea time is surely the best on the subcontinent. The hotel is surrounded by superb gardens looking across to the peaks of Kanchenjunga.

Hotel Silver Oaks (☎ 55296), is a characterless modern hotel with pleasant views and comfortable rooms for US$57/68 including meals. It's close to the centre, 100m from the post office.

Places to Eat
Kalimpong cheese is a local speciality introduced by the Jesuits who established the Swiss dairy here. The dairy has now closed but cheese is still produced in the area. Similar to a slightly tart cheddar, it's very moreish and available at several shops including ***Lark's Provisions***, Rishi Rd. It costs Rs 120 per kg. Kalimpong lollipops are another speciality introduced by the sweet-toothed Jesuits, and shops still sell them.

Most restaurants close early; you'll have trouble getting a bite to eat after 9 pm, particularly in the off season. It might be worth finding out if the once popular Mandarin Restaurant (burnt down in 1996) has re-opened in a new location.

Kalsang Restaurant, Link Rd (behind Cosy Nook Lodge), is a lovely, rustic little place run by friendly Tibetans. Butter tea is Rs 3, and pork ghaytuk is Rs 15.

Ritu's Fast Food, Dambar Chowk, is a flashy snack bar with excellent chana bhatura (Rs 15) and good lassis (Rs 10).

Gompu's Restaurant, Dambar Chowk, is good for Tibetan and Chinese dishes. Chicken wonton soup (Rs 30) is good, and a beer costs Rs 42.

Ferrazzini's Bakery has snacks including delicious cheese crispies for Rs 1.50.

Himalayan Hotel requires advance bookings from nonresident diners. Breakfast is Rs 90, and lunch and dinner are Rs 180.

Things to Buy

Open Wednesday and Saturday, the market is definitely worth visiting, especially if you want to meet the locals.

The Bhutia Shop, Dambar Chowk, stocks traditional Bhutia crafts such as woodcarvings, as well as pastel paintings, embroidered bags and other items.

Kalimpong tapestry bags and purses, copperware, scrolls and paintings from Dr Graham's Home are sold at the Kalimpong Arts & Crafts Co-operative. Shops selling Tibetan jewellery and artefacts can be found in the streets to the east of Dambar Chowk.

Getting There & Away

Bus & Jeep There are frequent jeeps (Rs 45 for a back seat, Rs 55 for the front) for the three hour trip to Darjeeling. The buses are so much less frequent, slower and more uncomfortable that it's hardly worth the small cost saving. All transport, other than taxis, leaves from the Bazaar bus stand.

Buses for Siliguri cost Rs 30 for the three hour trip and should be booked in advance from one of the offices around the bus stand. The road to Siliguri follows the Teesta River after the bridge, so it's much cheaper and quicker than going via Darjeeling. The views are magnificent.

To Gangtok (Rs 36, 4½ hours), Sikkim Nationalised Transport (SNT) has two buses daily, at 8 am and 3 pm, and these should be booked in advance at the SNT office at the bus stand. There are also private buses and jeeps on this route.

Mintri Transport operates one bus daily to Siliguri and Bagdogra airport at 7 am from their office (which is also the Indian Airlines office; ☎ 55241) on Main Rd. The trip takes about three hours and costs Rs 90. Mintri Transport can also book flights, including those with Royal Nepal Airlines.

Bhutan From Kalimpong it is possible to visit Phuntsholing, just over the Bhutanese border, without a visa. There's a daily bus to Jaigaon, on the Indian side of the border, which leaves at 8.30 am (six hours, Rs 45). There are hotels and guesthouses at Phuntsholing, but not Jaigaon.

AROUND KALIMPONG

Teesta Bazaar, 16km from Kalimpong and where the road divides for Darjeeling and Siliguri, is becoming a centre for white water rafting activities. Johnny Gurkha (☎ 55374) is one operator based here. There are short trips from Rs 300 per person, and two-day trips including camping for Rs 1600 (plus, according to the brochure, 'evening full of fun 'n frolick')!

Lava, about 30km to the east of Kalimpong, is a small village with a small gompa. Tuesday is market day, and a good time to visit. There's a *Forest Rest House* (book ahead at the Forest Department office in Kalimpong), and buses and jeeps run regularly from Kalimpong. **Kaffer** is another small village east of Kalimpong, and it also has a *Forest Rest House*. Both of these places can be visited on treks from Kalimpong (ask at the Deki Lodge for details).

Thrill seekers should head for the **Samco Ropeway**, a chairlift installed by the Swedish as part of an aid programme to help villagers cross the Teesta River. If the idea of dangling from a piece of wire 30m above the water doesn't entice, give this a miss – it's definitely not for vertigo sufferers or heart patients! The ropeway is on the main Siliguri to Gangtok road, at a place known locally as 27th Mile. Catch any Siliguri bus from Kalimpong (Rs 20, 1½ hours).

Orissa

The tropical state of Orissa lies along the eastern seaboard of India, south of Bengal. Its main attractions are the temples of the capital Bhubaneswar, the long sandy beach at Puri and the great Sun Temple at Konark. These sites make a convenient and compact triangle, and Bhubaneswar is on the main Calcutta to Chennai (Madras) railway route.

Orissa is predominantly rural, with fertile green coastal plains rising to the hills of the Eastern Ghats. The majority of the population live on or below the poverty line, with annual per capita income one of the lowest in the country. Largely based on agriculture, Orissa's economy is often destabilised by natural disasters, including flood, drought, cyclone or tornado. However, flooding in the Mahanadi delta, which used to occur regularly, has been much reduced by the building of the Hirakud Dam. The state is mineral rich and is a big exporter of iron ore, with a large factory at Rourkela.

Few visitors venture outside the Bhubaneswar-Puri-Konark triangle, but although travel off the beaten track in Orissa is often rough, with few tourist facilities, it can be an interesting and rewarding experience. The Oriyas, 25% of whom are indigenous tribal peoples, are very friendly and hospitable.

History

Orissa's hazy past focuses with the reign of Kalinga. In 260 BC he was defeated by Ashoka, the great Indian emperor, near modern Bhubaneswar. The bloody battle left Ashoka with such a bitter taste in his mouth that he converted to Buddhism and spread that gentle religion far and wide. Buddhism soon declined in Orissa, however, and Jainism held sway until Buddhism reasserted itself in the 2nd century AD.

By the 7th century AD, Hinduism had, in turn, supplanted Buddhism. This was when Orissa's golden age began. Under the Kesari and Ganga kings the Orissan culture flourished – countless temples from that classical

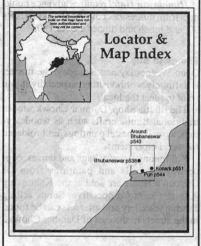

Highlights
* Puri, especially during the Rath Yatra
* Konark's mystery-shrouded Sun Temple
* Tigers, elephants and waterfalls in the beautiful forests of Similipal National Park

Festivals
Tribal Festival – Bhubaneswar – January
Chariot Festival – Lingaraj Mandir, Bhubaneswar – April
Rath Yatra – Puri – June/July
Dance Festival – Konark – December

period still stand today. The Oriyas managed to defy the Muslim rulers in Delhi until the region finally fell to the Mughals during the 16th century. Many of Bhubaneswar's temples were destroyed at that time.

A REGIONAL HIGHLIGHT

Sun Temple, Konark

The great temple of Konark (also known as Konarak) is three km from the coast, 36 km from Puri and 64 km from Bhubaneswar. Konark was constructed in the mid-13th century, but remarkably little is known about its early history. It's thought to have been built by the Orissan king Narashimhadev I, to celebrate his military victory over the Muslims. It is believed to have fallen into disuse in the early 17th century after being desecrated by one of Jehangir's envoys.

Originally nearer the coast (the sea has receded), Konark was visible from far out at sea and was known as the Black Pagoda by sailors, in contrast to the whitewashed temples of Puri. It was said to contain a great mass of magnetic iron which would draw unwary ships to the shore.

Until the early 1900s, Konark was simply an interesting ruin of impressive size. Then in 1904 debris and sand were cleared from around the temple base, and the sheer magnitude of its architect's imagination was revealed. The entire temple was conceived as a chariot for the sun god, Surya. Around the base of the temple are 24 gigantic carved stone wheels. Seven mighty stone horses haul at the temple and the immense structure is covered with carvings, sculptures, figures and bas-reliefs. It is not known if the temple was ever completed. If the tower was finished it would have soared to 70m, and archaeologists wonder if the sandy foundations could have supported such a structure. Part of the tower was still standing in 1837, but by 1869 had collapsed. Today the temple's interior has been filled in to support the ruins.

The main entrance, from the Tourist Bungalow side, is guarded by two stone lions crushing elephants. Steps rise to the main entrance, flanked by straining horses. The *jagamohan*, or assembly hall, still stands, but the *deul* behind it, in which the temple deity is kept, has collapsed (see the aside on Orissan temple architecture later in this chapter). The three impressive chlorite images of Surya have been restored to their positions, aligned to catch the sun at dawn, noon and sunset. Between the main steps up to the jagamohan and the entrance enclosure is an intricately carved dancing hall. To the north is a group of elephants and to the south a group of horses rearing and trampling men.

At the western end of the temple, the rubble from the collapsed deul has been cleared, allowing visitors to climb right down into the sanctuary. The image of the deity that was here is thought to have been moved to the Jagannath Temple in Puri in the 17th century.

Around the base of the temple and up the walls and roof is a continuous procession of carvings. Many are in the erotic style for which Konark, like Khajuraho in Madhya Pradesh, is famous. These erotic images of entwined couples, or solitary exhibitionists, can be minute images on the spoke of a temple wheel or life-size figures higher up the walls.

It's worth hiring a guide for an hour (about Rs 40) as they can show you interesting features and sculptures – such as the dancer with high-heeled shoes, giraffes and even a man treating himself for venereal disease! – which you would otherwise probably overlook. Just be sure that your guide is registered and wears his badge; unlicensed guides abound but are unreliable.

The temple looks particularly impressive in the evening as it's illuminated between 6 and 9 pm. ∎

ORISSA

Things to Buy

Orissa has a very wide and distinctive selection of handicrafts. Best known is probably the gorgeous appliqué work of Pipli. Brightly coloured patches of fabric, cut into animal and flower shapes, are sewn onto bed covers, cushions and beach umbrellas. The village of Raghurajpur is famous for its *patachitra*, or paintings on specially prepared cloth. Cuttack is known for its exquisitely delicate silver filigree jewellery.

More than 300,000 Orissans work as handloom weavers, producing numerous types of uniquely Orissan fabrics in silk and cotton.

Sambalpur is the centre of the area specialising in tie-dye and *ikat* fabrics. The complex ikat process involves tie-dying the thread before it is woven. This produces cloth with a slightly 'blurred' pattern which is particularly attractive.

At Puri you can buy strange little carved wooden replicas of Lord Jagannath and his brother and sister. Horoscopes and religious texts are traditionally inscribed on palm leaves in Orissa; you can find them at bazaars everywhere throughout the state. At Balasore, lacquered children's toys and wooden masks are manufactured.

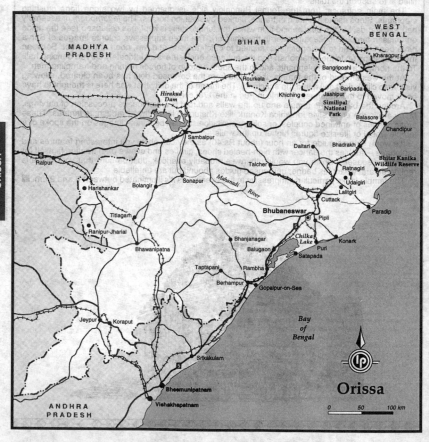

Orissa

BHUBANESWAR

Pop: 528,390   Tel Area Code: 0674

Although it was only in 1950 that the state capital was moved from overcrowded Cuttack to Bhubaneswar, the town's history goes back over 2000 years, as excavations at Sisuphal Garh, the remains of a ruined city, have shown.

Beside the site of the capital of ancient Kalinga, Bhubaneswar is known as Temple Town and Cathedral City on account of its many temples in the extravagant Orissan style. They date from the 8th to the 13th century AD, and it is said that at one time the Bindu Sagar tank had over 7000 temples around it. Today, the tour guides tell you that there are only 500, but even this seems like a bit of an exaggeration. Only about a dozen are of real interest, including the great Lingaraj Temple. It's one of the most important temples in India, but unfortunately is closed to non-Hindus.

During the last week of January the Tribal Festival is held here with dances, handicrafts and folk art on display.

Orientation & Information

A sprawling, rapidly expanding town, Bhubaneswar is divided by the railway line, which runs roughly north-south through the middle of it. The bus terminal is five km away on the western edge of town – further out from the centre than the airport. The temples are mainly in the south-east and the closest hotel to them,

the Panthanivas Tourist Bungalow, is within walking distance.

Orissa Tourism (☎ 431299) is down the lane by the Panthanivas Tourist Bungalow and has branches at the airport and the railway station (☎ 404715; open 24 hours). There is also a Government of India tourist office (☎ 432202) not far from the museum.

The Modern Book Depot has a good selection of maps and some pulpy English fiction.

Lingaraj Mandir

Surrounded by a high wall, the great temple of Bhubaneswar is off limits to all non-Hindus. Although the British Raj respected this ruling, it did not deter them from building a viewing platform beside the northern wall. It was put up for the visit of Lord Curzon and is still used by tourists today. You'll be asked for a donation at the platform and shown a book to 'prove' that some people give over Rs 1000. How much you give is up to you, but a few rupees is more than enough. In fact, you're now approached at many temples in Bhubaneswar with such persistence, you wonder whether these people really are the 'temple priests' they say they are. There is an official Rs 2 entry fee (waived on Friday) to some of the temple compounds, but there's often no-one there to collect your money.

The temple is dedicated to Tribhuvaneswar, or Lord of the Three Worlds, also known as Bhubaneswar. In its present form it dates from 1090 to 1104, although parts of it are

ORISSA

Orissan Temple Architecture

Orissan temples – whether the mighty Lingaraj in Bhubaneswar, the Jagannath in Puri, the Sun Temple at Konark or the many smaller temples – all follow a similar pattern. Basically there are two structures – the *jagamohan*, or assembly hall, and the *deul*, where the image of the temple deity is kept and above which the temple tower rises. The design is complicated in larger temples by the addition of other entrance halls in front of the jagamohan. These are the *bhoga-mandapa*, or hall of offering, and the *natamandir*, or dancing hall.

The whole structure may be enclosed by an outer wall, and within the enclosure there may be smaller, subsidiary temples and shrines. The most notable aspects of the temple design are the soaring tower and the intricate carvings that cover every surface. These may be figures of gods, men and women, plants and trees, flowers, animals and every other aspect of everyday life, but to many visitors it is the erotic carvings which create the greatest interest. They reach their artistic and explicit peak at Konark, where the close-up detail is every bit as interesting as the temple's sheer size. ■

over 1400 years old. The granite block, representing Tribhuvaneswar, is said to be bathed daily with water, milk and bhang. The temple compound is about 150m square and is dominated by the 40m high temple tower. More than 50 smaller temples and shrines crowd the enclosure. In the north-east corner, a small temple to Parvati is particularly interesting.

There is an annual chariot festival in the temple in April.

Bindu Sagar
The Ocean Drop Tank (Bindu Sagar), just north of the great temple, is said to contain water from every holy stream, pool and tank in India. When it comes to washing away sin, this tank washes the cleanest. There are a number of temples and shrines scattered around the tank, several with towers in imitation of the ones at the Lingaraj Temple. In the centre of the tank is a water pavilion where, once a year, the Lingaraj Temple's deity is brought to be ritually bathed.

Vaital Mandir
Close to the Bindu Sagar, this temple has a double-storeyed 'wagon roof', an influence from Buddhist cave architecture. It dates from

Bhubaneswar

0   1.5   3 km

To Nandankanan Zoo (25km) & Calcutta (437km)
To Cuttack (35km)
National Highway No 5
Sachivalaya Marg
Orissa Truck Rd
Maharishi College Road
Vidyok Marg
Azad Marg
Janpath
Bhubaneswar Road
Mahatma Gandhi Marg
Rail Path
Ekamra Marg
Railway Station
Forest Park
Puri Cuttack Road
Daya Canal
Gangua Nala
To Berhampur (160km) & Madras
Airport
To Madras (1232km)
Bindu Sagar
Mahatab Road
To Puri (60km) & Konark (64km)

the 8th century and was a centre of Tantric worship, the presiding deity being Chamunda (Kali). She can be seen in the dingy interior, although her necklace of skulls and the corpse she's sitting on are usually hidden beneath her temple robes.

Parsurameswar Mandir

Close to the main Bhubaneswar to Puri road, on the same side as the Lingaraj Temple, the Grove of the Perfect Beings is a cluster of about 20 smaller temples, including some of the most important in Bhubaneswar. The best preserved of the early temples is the Parsurameswar, a Siva temple built about 650 AD. It has interesting and lively bas-reliefs of elephant and horse processions, lattice windows and Siva images.

Mukteswar, Siddheswar & Kedargauri Temples

Not far from the Parsurameswar is the small 10th century Mukteswar Mandir, one of the most ornate temples in Bhubaneswar. The finely detailed carvings show a mixture of Buddhist, Jain and Hindu styles, but unfortunately some of the figures have been defaced. The carvings of dwarfs are particularly striking.

In front of the temple is a beautiful arched *torana* (architrave) clearly showing a Buddhist influence. The large green temple tank makes a perfect swimming pool for local children.

The later Siddheswar Mandir is in the same compound. Although plainer than the Mukteswar, it has a fine standing Ganesh figure.

Also by the road, across the path from the Mukteswar, the Kedargauri Mandir is one of the older temples at Bhubaneswar, although it has been substantially rebuilt.

Outside the Mukteswar compound there are chai shops and curio sellers.

Raj Rani Mandir

This interesting temple is surrounded by well-maintained gardens. It's one of the latest of the Bhubaneswar temples and is famous for its ornate *deul* (sanctuary), decorated with some of the most impressive Orissan temple sculptures. Around the compass points are statues of the eight *dikpalas* (temple guardians), who protect the temple, two for each side. Between them, nymphs, embracing couples, elephants and lions fill the niches and decorate the pillars. As it's no longer used for worship you are free to wander at will.

Brahmeswar Mandir

About a km east of the main road, the Brahmeswar Temple stands in a courtyard flanked by four smaller structures. It's notable for its very finely detailed sculptures with erotic

ORISSA

PLACES TO STAY		30	Panthanivas Tourist Bungalow	15	Capital (Old) Bus Stand
1	Oberoi Hotel			16	Market
3	Imperial Guest House			17	Indian Airlines
7	Hotel Prachi		PLACES TO EAT	18	State Bank of India
9	Hotel Swosti	10	Hare Krishna	28	Orissa State Museum
11	Yatri Nivas		Restaurant	29	ITDC Tourist Office
14	Bhubaneswar Hotel	13	Shanti Restaurant	31	Orissa Tourism
19	Central Lodge	22	South Indian Hotel	32	Vaital Mandir
20	Tourist Guest House			33	Parsurameswar
21	Hotels Bhagat Nivas, Padma & Pushpak		OTHER		Mandir
23	Kenilworth Hotel	2	Planetarium	34	Siddheswar & Mukteswar
24	Hotel Kalinga Ashok	4	Tribal Research Centre	35	Raj Rani Mandir
25	Hotel Odissi High	5	New Bus Station	36	Kedargauri
26	Park View Guest House	6	Khandagiri & Udayagiri Caves	37	Lingaraj Mandir
27	Venus & Swagat Inns	8	Post Office	38	Brahmeswar Mandir
		12	Modern Book Depot	39	Sisuphal Garh

and sometimes amusing elements. The temple dates from the 9th century.

State Museum

The museum is opposite the Hotel Kalinga Ashok and has an interesting collection focusing on Orissan history, culture and architecture and the various Orissan tribes. The museum is open from 10 am to 5 pm daily, except Monday; entry is Rs 2.

Tribal Research Centre (Museum of Man)

Although this is primarily an anthropological research centre, visitors are welcome. There's an interesting outdoor display of reconstructed houses of Orissan tribal people, including the Santal, Juang, Gadaba, Saora and Kondh. It's open daily from 10 am to 5 pm except Sunday and admission is free. Buses between the new bus terminal and the centre of town pass right by the museum.

Udayagiri & Khandagiri Caves

A couple of km south of the new bus terminal in Bhubaneswar, these two hills facing each other across the road are riddled with caves, some of them ornately carved. Most are thought to have been chiselled out for Jain ascetics in the first century BC.

On the right of the road, **Udayagiri**, or Sunrise Hill, has the more interesting caves, which are scattered at various levels up the hill; all are numbered. At the base of the hill, around to the right, is the two-storeyed Rani ka Naur or Queen's Palace Cave (cave 1). Both levels have eight entrances and the cave is extensively carved.

Return to the road via the Chota Hathi Gumpha (cave 3), with its carvings of elephants coming out from behind a tree. The Jaya Vijaya Cave (5) is double-storeyed and a bo tree is carved in the central compartment. Back at the entrance, ascend the hill to cave 9, the Swargapuri, and cave 14, the Hathi Gumpha or Elephant Cave. The latter is plain but an inscription relates in 117 lines

the exploits of its builder, King Kharaveli of Kalinga, who ruled from 168 to 153 BC.

Circle around the hill to the right, to the single-storeyed Ganesh Gumpha (10), which is almost directly above the Rani ka Naur. The carvings here tell the same tale as in the lower level cave but are better made. Retrace your steps to Cave 14, then on to the Pavana Gumpha or Cave of Purification and the small Sarpa Gumpha or Serpent Cave, where the tiny door is surmounted by a three-headed cobra.

Only 15m or so from this is the Bagh Gumpha (12) or Tiger Cave, entered through the mouth of the beast. The hill is topped by the foundations of some long-gone building. The oldest of these various caves date back to the 2nd century BC.

Across the road, **Khandagiri** offers a fine view back over Bhubaneswar from its summit. You can see the airport, the tower of the Lingaraj Temple rising behind it and, further away, the Dhauli Stupa. The steep path divides about a third of the way up the hill. The right path goes to the Ananta Cave (3), with carved figures of athletes, women, elephants and geese carrying flowers. The right path also leads to a series of Jain temples, and at the top of the hill is an 18th century Jain temple.

The caves are open from 8 am to 6 pm. There's a government restaurant here and lots of chai shops.

Getting There & Away No buses go specifically to the caves, but there are plenty which pass the nearby junction on the main Calcutta to Chennai highway. It's about Rs 3 from town, or you can get there by auto-rickshaw for about Rs 60.

Other Things to See

The partly excavated ruins at **Sisuphal Garh** are thought to be the remains of an Ashokan city. In the north of the city, the botanical gardens and regional plant reserve have a large collection of plants, including many cacti and the largest rose garden in India. The city's planetarium has shows hourly from 2 to 5 pm (4 pm in English) daily except Monday; tickets cost Rs 5.

Organised Tours

During the high season, tours operate daily except Monday from the Panthanivas Tourist Bungalow (☎ 431515). If you're pressed for time, you can take a long day tour through Pipli to Puri and Konark for Rs 100 (Rs 120 by air-con bus). By taxi this tour would cost upwards of Rs 650. Other day tours stay in and around Bhubaneswar, taking in the Nandankanan zoological park, the Udayagiri and Khandagiri caves and Dhauli (Rs 95, or Rs 120 air-con). However, these tours tend to linger at the zoo, and whiz through the caves and temples, so you might prefer to organise private transport.

Places to Stay – bottom end

There's a wide choice of budget accommodation in Bhubaneswar.

Yatri Nivas is a friendly place, very much like a youth hostel, although the location is inconvenient. Dorm beds start from Rs 20. There's a cheap restaurant here.

Hotel Bhagat Nivas (☎ 411545) is a recommended place that's good value, with singles/doubles with TV and attached bathroom from Rs 60/140. Air-con doubles start at Rs 360. It's clean and friendly.

Hotel Pushpak (☎ 415545) is close by and also cheap at Rs 100 for a double, or Rs 300 with air-con.

Hotel Padma (☎ 416626) is similar.

Venus Inn (☎ 401738) has singles/doubles from Rs 100/140 and a good south Indian restaurant downstairs.

Swagat Inn (☎ 408486) nearby has rooms for Rs 140/250, air-con doubles for Rs 400, and a fast-food restaurant.

Bhubaneswar Hotel (☎ 416977) is a popular place which has singles/doubles with attached bathrooms for Rs 100/150, or rooms with air-con for Rs 500.

Central Lodge (☎ 413803) is in a row of el cheapo lodges west of the railway tracks on Raj Path. Rooms are Rs 35/70 with attached bath. A sign in the reception area warns that 'deceased persons are not allowed in the lodge'.

Places to Stay – middle

If you can pay a little extra, there are some lovely places to stay.

Tourist Guest House (☎ 400857) is an extremely pleasant little place which well deserves its popularity. It's clean and comfortable with rooms for Rs 200/350 with attached bathrooms. Meals are available. If it's full, the same owner has two other guest houses which are just as welcoming but not so well located.

Park View Guest House (☎ 400664) is north of the airport on Ekamra Marg, in Forest Park, and has rooms from Rs 350/400, all with TV.

Imperial Guesthouse (☎ 415010) is closer to town. Rooms start at Rs 300/400.

Hotel Oddisi High (☎ 417084) is a spotless new hotel with rooms from Rs 300/400.

Panthanivas Tourist Bungalow (☎ 432515) isn't great value, and it has a nightmare checkout time (8 am), but it's close to the temples and has comfortable rooms. Doubles are Rs 250, or Rs 450 with air-con.

Places to Stay – top end

Bhubaneswar also caters for those who crave comfort, carpet and coddling.

Hotel Kalinga Ashok (☎ 431055) is almost opposite the museum. Singles/doubles cost from Rs 750/1000.

Kenilworth Hotel (☎ 433600; fax 433351) has a good reproduction of a Konark chariot wheel outside and is recommended for its position and facilities. Air-con rooms are Rs 1320/1550. There's a swimming pool here that non-guests can use for Rs 100 (closed between 10 am and 4 pm), a pastry shop, bookshop and resident masseur.

Hotel Prachi (☎ 402328; fax 403287) is a good air-conditioned place with rooms at Rs 1050/1250. Facilities include the 'Wim Bul Don' (a tennis court!) and a pool that non-guests can use for Rs 75.

Hotel Swosti (☎ 418253; fax 407524), on Janpath not far from the railway station, is a

ORISSA

good four-star hotel with rooms from Rs 1555/1995 including breakfast.

Oberoi Hotel (☎ 440890; fax 440898), on the outskirts of town, is at the top of the pile. Mimicking Orissan temple layout and design, it charges US$65/80 for rooms and has all mod cons, including swimming pool, health club, floodlit tennis courts and jogging track.

Places to Eat

There are many good, cheap south Indian places around the junction of Raj Path and Janpath.

South Indian Hotel is an excellent little place.

Hare Krishna Restaurant, run by the organisation itself, is the best vegetarian eatery in Bhubaneswar. It's a smart place with powerful air-con and excellent, though pricey, food (mains are around Rs 40).

Shanti Restaurant has a varied menu and the food is good and reasonably priced.

Panthanivas Tourist Bungalow has two restaurants, but they both serve up the same baffling attempts at Chinese and Continental dishes.

Sangam Restaurant at the Kenilworth Hotel is a recommended place for an evening out. During the dry season there are barbecues on the roof terrace.

Executive Restaurant at Hotel Swosti will make Odissi food with eight hours notice.

There are many vegetarian places in the temple area if you are down that way at lunchtime.

Aahar Restaurant near the Parsurameswar Temple serves a wide range of Bengali and Odissi dishes.

Things to Buy

Orissan handicrafts, including appliqué and ikat work, can be bought at the market off Raj Path. There are a number of shops, including the Orissa State Handloom Cooperative or Utkalika.

There's also the Orissa State Handicrafts Emporium, not far from the temples.

Getting There & Away

Air Indian Airlines (☎ 400533) has five flights a week between Bhubaneswar and Calcutta (US$65), and daily flights to Delhi (US$175). There are two flights a week to Chennai (US$160), and three to Nagpur (US$100) and Hyderabad (US$130). There are also four flights a week from Varanasi to Bhubaneswar (US$95), but nothing in the opposite direction.

Bus The impressive bus terminal (which looks more like an airport terminal) is on the main highway to Calcutta, five km northwest of the town centre. Buses to Cuttack, Puri and Konark still stop at the old Capital bus stand, which is much more conveniently located in the centre of town. The trip to Puri takes a little over an hour and costs Rs 12. Direct buses to Konark are Rs 15. Otherwise, take a Puri bus and change at Pipli, where the Konark road branches off.

From the new bus terminal there are three afternoon departures to Calcutta (Rs 100, overnight). Regular buses head for Cuttack (Rs 6, one hour) and Berhampur (Rs 40, five hours). There is one morning and one evening service for Sambalpur (Rs 85, nine hours). Private video coaches run to Baripada (Rs 73, seven hours).

Train Bhubaneswar is on the main Calcutta to Chennai railway line, so there are plenty of trains to these places. Many services from the north terminate at Puri. The crack *Rajdhani Express* departs from Calcutta at 10.45 am every Saturday and arrives in Bhubaneswar just over seven hours later. The fare for the 437km journey is Rs 560 in an air-con three-tier car. This train leaves Bhubaneswar every Sunday at 8.50 am for the return journey to Calcutta and goes on to Delhi (2077km, 24 hours).

There are also direct rail connections to Berhampur (166km, 2½ hours), Chennai (1226km, 24 hours), Varanasi (998km, 20 hours) and Agra (1874km, 39 hours).

Getting Around

The airport is very close to the town. There's no bus service and a taxi costs Rs 65 to the Tourist Bungalow or Rs 100 to the Oberoi.

A cycle-rickshaw costs only Rs 20, but you have to walk the last km between the entrance of the airport and the terminal.

Between the new bus terminal and the town centre you're up for Rs 30 by auto-rickshaw, or there are city buses to the old bus stand for Rs 3.

Cycle-rickshaws offer 'five temple' tours for around Rs 20, which cover the main temples; shorter journeys are around Rs 5.

Taxis have set rates which are available from the tourist office. They may be unwilling to drive you for those rates, but it's worth a try.

AROUND BHUBANESWAR
Dhauli

Around 260 BC, King Ashoka had his famous edicts carved onto a large rock halfway up a hill here at Dhauli, eight km south of Bhubaneswar just off the Puri road. After murdering large numbers of his family to gain power, then hundreds of thousands on the battlefield as he enlarged his empire, after his bloody victory at nearby Kalinga Ashoka finally 'saw the light' and converted to Buddhism.

Given his past record, Ashoka was wise to choose a pen name for these edicts, referring to himself as King Piyadasi (meaning He Who Looks on Everything with Kindness). In the edicts he tells his subjects, 'Meritorious is abstention from killing living creatures, meritorious is abstention from reviling the unorthodox..'

At the top of the hill is a dazzling white Peace Pagoda built by the Japanese in the 1970s, with older Buddha figures set into the modern structure.

You can get to the place where you turn off the main road on any Puri or Konark bus for Rs 4, and from there it's a three-km walk to Dhauli. Doing the trip by auto-rickshaw will cost about Rs 70.

Nandankanan Zoo

Famous for its white tigers, this zoo is 25km north of Bhubaneswar. There are also lion and tiger safaris in 'armoured buses', elephant rides and boating on the lake.

It's open daily from 7 am to 6 pm except Monday in summer, and from 7.30 am to 5 pm in winter. The nearest railway station is Barang, a couple of km from the zoo, or there are state transport buses from the Capital (old) bus stand in Bhubaneswar (Rs 5, two hours).

PURI
Pop: 142,665   Tel Area Code: 06752

The seaside resort of Puri, 60km from Bhubaneswar, is one of the four *dhams* (holiest Hindu pilgrimage places in India). Religious life in the city revolves around the great Jagannath Temple and its famous Rath Yatra, or Car Festival. It is thought that Puri was the hiding place for the Buddha tooth of Kandy before it was spirited away to Sri Lanka. There are similarities between the Rath Yatra and the annual Kandy procession.

Puri's other great attraction is its long sandy beach, which draws large numbers of

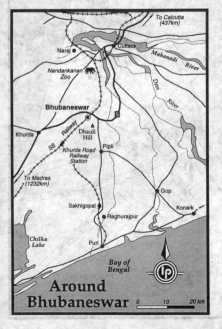

Around Bhubaneswar

0   10   20 km

Puri

Bay of Bengal

ORISSA

western travellers and Indians, especially during the October to January high season. Parts of the beach front are getting quite built up, but it can still be a relaxing place to spend a few days. Many Indian companies and government departments have vacation homes here, but the town is mostly visited by Bengali holiday-makers.

Early in November there's a lively festival of dance, music and drama in Puri.

Orientation

Grand Rd, a wide highway built to accommodate the hundreds of thousands of pilgrims who come to Puri for the Rath Yatra festival, runs from the Jagannath Temple to the Gundicha Mandir. The bus stand is at the eastern end of this road. Most hotels are along the seafront but there are two distinct beach areas – Indians to the west, foreign travellers to the east.

Information

The tourist office (☎ 22664) is on Station Rd and there's a counter at the railway station (☎ 23536).

The Loknath Bookshop on CT Rd is a good place to rent or buy second-hand books.

Money The State Bank of India offers the usual slow service for foreign exchange. The Andhra Bank near the post office handles credit-card cash advances.

Hotel Ghandara changes cash and travellers cheques and will advance cash on credit cards, but they charge 3% for the service. They're open seven days from 8 am to 8 pm. South-Eastern Railway Hotel also changes travellers cheques and foreign currency.

Warning A number of swimmers have come to grief in Puri's treacherous surf – see under Beach later in this section.

Jagannath Temple

The temple of Jagannath, Lord of the Universe and an incarnation of Vishnu, is unfortunately closed to non-Hindus. As at the Lingaraj Temple in Bhubaneswar, non-believers have to be content with looking over the wall, this time from the roof of the library opposite, but you won't see much inside the temple. An additional platform on the roof was built for the viceroy's visit in 1939. The library is open from 9 am to noon and from 4 to 8 pm; a donation is required.

ORISSA

PLACES TO STAY		39	Hotel Tanuja & Tanuja	22	Mickey Mouse
12	Hotel Sealand		Tribe Tours		Restaurant
13	South-Eastern	40	Holiday House	30	Raju's Restaurant
	Railway Hotel	41	Hotel Shankar		
15	Bay View Hotel		International	**OTHER**	
16	Hotel Dreamland	42	Hotel Holiday Resort	1	Gundicha Mandir
17	Hotel Love & Life	43	Youth Hostel	2	Bus Station
18	Hotel Ghandara	44	Hotel Samudra	3	Bhubaneswar Bus
19	Hotel Sea 'n Sand	45	Hotel Vijoya		Stand
23	Hotel Sri Balajee		International	4	Government Bhang
24	Lodge Happy	46	Mayfair Beach		Shop
	Haunt		Resort	5	Government Bhang
26	Hotel Akash	47	Hotel Repose		Shop
	International	48	Panthanivas Tourist	6	Jagannath Temple
27	Sagar Saikate		Bungalow	7	Library
	(New)	49	Hotel Nilachal Ashok	8	Andhra Bank
28	Krishna Lodge	51	Puri Hotel	9	GPO
29	Sagar Saikate (Old)	52	Victoria Club	11	Tourist Office
32	Pink House	53	Panthabhavan	14	Post Office
33	Leo Castle	54	Sea View Hotel	21	Temple
34	Hotel Nilambu			25	Government Bhang
35	Hotel Derby	**PLACES TO EAT**			Shop
36	Z Hotel	10	Lee Garden	31	Loknath Bookshop
37	Travellers' Inn &		Restaurant	38	Temple
	Tribe Tours	20	Harry's Cafe	50	State Bank of India

Watch out for the monkeys. There's a good collection of ancient palm-leaf manuscripts in the library and another 'donation' is required if you wish to take a look.

The temple makes Puri one of the four *dhams*, cardinal centres of pilgrimage (the others being Dwarka in the west, Badrinath in the north and Rameswaram in the south). Its considerable popularity amongst Hindus is also partly due to the lack of caste distinctions – all are welcome. Well, almost all – Indira Gandhi was barred from entering as she had married a non-Hindu.

The temple was built in its present form in 1198 and is protected by two surrounding walls. The outer enclosure is nearly square, measuring almost 200m on each side. The walls of the enclosure are six metres high. Inside, a second wall encloses the actual temple. The conical tower of the temple is 58m high and is topped by the flag and wheel of Vishnu, visible from far out to sea.

In front of the main entrance is a beautiful pillar, topped by an image of the Garuda, which originally stood in front of the temple at Konark. The main entrance is known as the Lion Gate due to the two stone lions guarding the entrance, and it is also the gate used in the chariot procession. The southern,

eastern and northern gates are guarded by statues of men on horseback, tigers and elephants respectively.

In the central *jagamohan* (see the aside on Orissan temple architecture earlier in this chapter), pilgrims can see the images of Lord Jagannath, his brother Balbhadra and sister Subhadra. Non-Hindus are not, of course, able to see them but the many shop stalls along the road outside the temple sell small wooden replicas. The curious images are carved from tree trunks, in a childlike caricature of a human face. The brothers have arms but the smaller Subhadra does not. All three are garlanded and dressed for ceremonies and the various seasons.

The temple employs 6000 men to perform the temple functions and the complicated rituals involved in caring for the gods. It has been estimated that in all, 20,000 people are dependent on Jagannath, and the god's immediate attendants are divided into 36 orders and 97 classes!

Gundicha Mandir

The Garden House, in which the images of the gods reside for the seven days of Rath Yatra, is off limits to non-Hindus. The walls enclose a garden where the temple is built.

Rath Yatra (Car Festival)

One of India's greatest annual events takes place in Puri each June or July, when the fantastic festival of the cars sets forth from the Jagannath Temple. It commemorates the journey of Krishna from Gokul to Mathura. The images of Jagannath, his brother and his sister are brought out from the temple and dragged in huge 'cars', known as *raths*, down the wide Grand Rd to the Gundicha Mandir (Garden House), over one km away.

The main car of Jagannath stands 14m high, over 10m sq, and rides on 16 wheels, each over two metres in diameter. It is from these colossal cars that our word 'juggernaut' is derived and, in centuries past, devotees were known to have thrown themselves beneath the wheels of the juggernaut in order to die in the god's sight. To haul the cars takes over 4000 professional car pullers, all employees of the temple. Hundreds of thousands of pilgrims (and tourists) flock from all over India to witness this stupendous scene. The huge and unwieldy cars take an enormous effort to pull, are virtually impossible to turn and, once moving, are nearly unstoppable.

Once they reach the other end of the road the gods take a week-long summer break, then they are reloaded onto the cars and trucked back to the Jagannath Temple, in a virtual repeat of the previous week's procession. Following the festival the cars are broken up and used for firewood in the communal kitchens inside the temple, or for funeral-pyre fuel. New cars are constructed each year. At intervals of eight, 11 or 19 years (or combinations of those numbers depending on various astrological occurrences), the gods themselves are also disposed of and new images made. In the past 150 years there have been new images in 1863, 1893, 1931, 1950, 1969, 1977 and 1996. The old ones are buried at a site near the northern gate. ∎

It's also known as the Aunt's House. Puri has a number of other temples, but most of these are off limits to non-Hindus.

Beach

Puri has a stretch of dirty sand where Indian pilgrims bathe in their customary fully attired manner. Don't come here expecting a tropical paradise. The beach is very wide and exposed and there's not a scrap of shade to be found.

Orissan fishermen, wearing conical straw hats, guide bathers out through the surf. They're unlikely to be much help should trouble arise, as one traveller reported, witnessing a rescue attempt: 'To our amazement the lifeguards turned back having done only 10 yards and the swimmer (or non-swimmer) disappeared for good. By then it was too late for anyone else to go. The victim was a young man of 19'. Another traveller reported two drownings in three days. The currents can be treacherous, so don't go out of your depth unless you're a very strong swimmer.

Past the travellers' beach to the east is the local fishing village.

As with all Indian beaches, this one doubles as a public lavatory, automatically flushed twice daily by the sea. Around the fishing village is the worst part, and it really can stink here in the afternoon when the catch is being gutted on the beach. The cleanest area is just a 15 minute walk to the east, past the fishing village, where the empty beach extends for miles.

Fishing

Many of the fishing families at Puri come from Andhra Pradesh. It's worth getting up before sunrise to watch them head out to sea. For a little baksheesh they'll take you with them – one traveller said, 'It was the highlight of my trip witnessing the dawn over the sea and fishing boats'. The crude construction of the boats is unusual – they're made of solid tree trunks and are enormously heavy. Buoyancy is achieved purely from the bulk of the wood. They're made in two or three pieces, split longways and bound together. When not in use they're untied and the pieces are laid out on the beach to dry. ■

Organised Tours

Tours operate out of Puri daily, except Monday, to Konark, Pipli, Dhauli, Bhubaneswar, Nandankanan and the Udayagiri and Khandagiri caves. They depart at 6.30 am from the Panthabhavan, and return at 6.30 pm. The cost is Rs 100. There's also a daily tour to Chilka Lake for Rs 85. Tribe Tours (☎ 24246; fax 24907) can organise a car and interpreter for visits to tribal areas in the south of Orissa.

Places to Stay

Puri's rickshaw-wallahs are notorious for telling tales about hotels – 'it's closed down', 'it's changed name', 'it's very expensive' – so they can take you to the place that pays them the best commission. Insist on going to the destination of your choice, and check it out for yourself.

Prices below are for the high season (October to February). You should be able to negotiate healthy discounts outside this period, especially at the mid-price places. Because most people arrive in Puri on overnight trains, checkout times can be as early as 7 am!

Places to Stay – bottom end

Most of the budget hotels popular with travellers are at the eastern end of the beach towards the fishing village, along or off Chakra Tirtha Rd (CT Rd to the rickshaw-wallahs).

The *youth hostel* (☎ 22424) has dormitory accommodation at Rs 40 per bed. The restaurant is recommended for its excellent Orissan-style thalis, but the hostel itself is a characterless place and the 10 pm curfew is a drag.

Bay View Hotel, in a scruffy English villa, is quiet and pleasant. Rooms start from Rs 40 (most with attached bathroom) and there's a nice verandah for sitting out on.

Hotel Dreamland (☎ 24122) is a small, recommended place with singles/doubles for Rs 50/80 and a friendly manager. It's set back from the road in a secluded garden.

Hotel Ghandara (☎ 24623; fax 22154) is more modern. Dorm beds are Rs 30 and rooms start from Rs 80 or Rs 100 with bath.

Hotel Love & Life (☎ 24433) is friendly, with dorm beds for Rs 25, rooms from Rs 50/100 and cottages for Rs 150/200.

Hotel Shankar International (☎ 23637), a good beach-front hotel on spacious grounds, has a wide range of rooms. Ground floor rooms with shared bathroom are Rs 60/80, upstairs rooms start at Rs 100/150, and huge sea-facing four-bed rooms with a balcony are Rs 400. There are six well-designed cottages in front of the main building, with TV, hot water and fridge, for Rs 350.

Hotel Tanuja (☎ 24823), by the Holiday House, has rooms with attached bathroom for Rs 60/120, and a pleasant garden.

Hotel Sea 'n Sand (☎ 23107), nearby, is a clean place with doubles for Rs 150, or Rs 250 with attached bathroom.

Z Hotel (that's Zed not Zee!) (☎ 22554) is an excellent place and popular with travellers. Formerly the palace of a very minor maharaja, it's an old, rambling building with large, airy rooms, many of them facing the sea. The management is easy-going, the hotel peaceful and the restaurant serves good seafood. There's a female-only dorm with beds for Rs 40. Singles/doubles with common bath cost Rs 100/200, while huge rooms with attached bath and balcony are Rs 300. There's a roof terrace for sunbathing.

Travellers' Inn (☎ 23592) is a basic lodge beside the Z. Singles/doubles are Rs 50/80 with common bathroom, or Rs 100 with attached facilities. There are several other similar places towards the beach here, including *Hotel Derby*, *Hotel Nilambu* and *Leo Castle*.

Pink House (☎ 22253) is a popular choice right on the beach. Basic rooms are Rs 60/120.

Hotel Sri Balajee (☎ 23388) is a good family-run place back on CT Rd. It's Rs 60/150 for standard rooms with attached bath, and Rs 250 for a double with a TV, air-cooler and phone. Each room has its own little verandah with table and chairs, not unlike an Indonesian *losmen*.

Lodge Happy Haunt (☎ 22355), next door, has some good balcony rooms (Rs 200).

Hotel Akash International (☎ 24204) is the ugly place opposite. Small rooms with attached bath are Rs 50/80.

Krishna Lodge (☎ 24357) is closer to the beach. Bright clean rooms with bathroom are Rs 60 a double.

Hotel Heera, also worth a look, is a new hotel behind the Akash.

Sagar Saikate (☎ 23253) has expanded into two buildings. The old part is right on the beach and looks like a small yellow castle (it was a fortified English villa). It has a great roof area, perfect for undisturbed sunbathing, and big, high-ceilinged rooms. Rooms here start at Rs 40/60 with common bath. The new part, with an entrance on CT Rd, is a little more expensive.

Santana Lodge (☎ 23491) is set back from the sea, deep into the fishing village. It's a recommended place run by a very friendly and helpful manager. Singles/doubles are Rs 30/60 with common bath. They have some rooms with attached bathroom for Rs 40/80. Meals can be included for an extra Rs 20. It's a Rs 10 cycle-rickshaw ride from the railway station. The area is known as Pentakota; the rickshaw-wallah may not know the hotel.

At the western end of the beach, along Marine Parade, there are many other hotels patronised almost exclusively by Indian pilgrims.

Sea View Hotel (☎ 23417) is rather run-down, with doubles from Rs 80.

Victoria Club (☎ 22005) is better and has doubles from Rs 150.

Puri Hotel (☎ 22114; fax 22744) claims to be Orissa's biggest and is very popular with middle-class Indians. Singles/doubles start from Rs 120/150. This is one of the few places with 24 hour checkout.

Places to Stay – middle & top end

Orissa Tourism's hotels are both reasonable and handy places if you want to organise tours.

Panthanivas Tourist Bungalow (☎ 22562) has doubles with attached bathroom for Rs 230 or Rs 475 with a sea view.

Panthabhavan (☎ 23526), on Marine Parade, is a gloomy converted palace. Doubles with attached bath are Rs 400.

There are several hotels along the beach from the Tourist Bungalow catering mainly to holidaying Calcutta-wallahs and their families.

Hotel Repose (☎ 23376) charges Rs 350 for sea-facing doubles, Rs 550 with air-con.

Hotel Vijoya International (☎ 22702) is a modern block with double rooms at Rs 400, or Rs 700 with air-con.

Hotel Samudra (☎ 22705) is the best of this group. It's right on the beach; most rooms have a balcony facing the sea and cost from Rs 250. Beware of the 7 am checkout time!

Hotel Sealand (☎ 23705) is a group of rather cramped cottages back on CT Rd costing Rs 350 or Rs 400 with air-con.

Holiday House (☎ 23782) is back to the east. It's relatively new and immaculately clean; good doubles with attached bathrooms are Rs 400 (extra for a sea view).

South-Eastern Railway Hotel (☎ 22063) is an old-world hotel that you may consider decidedly run down or charming and full of character. Rooms are Rs 400/500, or Rs 450/600 for more modern air-con rooms. Meals can be included for Rs 100 extra per person. The hotel has a pleasant lounge, bar, dining room, billiards room and an immaculate stretch of lawn. It also offers 24 hour checkout.

Hotel Holiday Resort (☎ 22440; fax 24370) is a big ugly lug of a place. Double rooms with balconies overlooking the sea are Rs 430; air-con cottages are Rs 830.

Mayfair Beach Resort (☎ 24041; fax 24242) is well located, and a lot of thought has gone into the design and layout. Comfortable air-con rooms with their own terrace cost from Rs 1300. This place has the only swimming pool in Puri, but it's only open to guests.

Hotel Nilachal Ashok (☎ 23639) is a pleasant place, but things get done slowly round here. Air-con rooms are Rs 1400.

Hotel Toshali Sands (☎ 22888) is a very secluded 'ethnic village resort', seven km from Puri on the road to Konark. A night in the cottages costs US$33/43. It's a three-km walk through the Balukhand Forest and Turtle Reserve to the private beach, but the hotel also has a swimming pool, which non-guests

can use for Rs 100. The food here is very good, although it's not cheap.

Places to Eat

The best food in Puri is the magnificent *prasad* cooked and blessed in the Jagannath Temple. Although non-Hindus aren't allowed in the temple, there's no prohibition against partaking of prasad, if you can find someone to buy it for you.

As far as the restaurants go, you can get some excellent seafood here – good tuna steaks and occasionally even lobster. Some of the restaurants along the travellers' end of the beach manage passable cakes and pies – and do an interesting line in apple pies with a special extra ingredient! Quite a few places close during the off-season.

Harry's, *Mickey Mouse* and *Xanadu* cater almost exclusively to travellers. They're all in a group near the Zed Hotel, and each has its admirers and detractors. They serve much the same food – poor imitations of western dishes, including banana, apple and cheese burgers – and service is typically very slow.

Raju's Restaurant is a cheap gathering place on the edge of the fishing village (look out for 'our crispy teat').

Pink House is best recommended for its view.

Z Hotel is the best of the restaurants in the budget hotels, but with most main dishes around Rs 35, a meal can be relatively pricey.

Om Restaurant, in Hotel Shankar, does quite good food.

There are a number of cafes at the western end of the beach and in the old town there are countless vegetarian places.

New Raj Restaurant is on Grand Rd, five minutes from the Jagannath Temple.

Lee Garden is a Chinese restaurant on Armstrong Rd.

South-Eastern Railway Hotel set dinners can be good for an evening out. The food is authentically Raj (often including puddings like trifle) and served in style by attentive uniformed waiters. It costs Rs 150 for five courses plus coffee, and you need to make a reservation.

ORISSA

Mayfair Beach Resort's restaurant is good but expensive. The dining room at the *Toshali Sands* is very good, but is really only convenient if you are staying there.

Things to Buy

Being a holy place, Puri is one of those delightfully eccentric Indian towns where the use of ganja is not only legal, but the government very thoughtfully provides for smokers' requirements at special bhang shops. Ganja is available here at Rs 40 a *tola* but it's not blowout stuff. You can also score opium at the same shops, where it'll cost you Rs 140 for 10 grams).

You'll come across quite a few craft and salespeople offering fabric, bead and bamboo work, especially along the western end of the beach. There are also plenty of people trying to sell snake and animal skins in such numbers that one dreads to think what is happening to the wildlife in the Orissan forests.

On Temple Rd and Swargadwar Rd there are numerous places selling Orissan handwoven ikat cloth. Some of this material is very attractive; you can buy it in lengths, or there are ready-made garments.

Getting There & Away

Bus Puri's bus stand is beside the Gundicha Mandir, though some of the private buses depart from around the nearby junction of Grand and Hospital Rds. Take one of the minibuses for the trip to Bhubaneswar (Rs 10, one hour) as they're much quicker than the big buses.

Between 6 am and 4.30 pm there are frequent departures for Konark (Rs 8, one hour), early morning services for Berhampur (Rs 50, 5½ hours) and Taptapani (Rs 75, eight hours), late afternoon departures for Sambalpur (Rs 90, nine hours) and one morning and one afternoon bus to Calcutta, but you'll probably find the trains are more comfortable for this route.

Train There are two overnight trains each way between Puri and Calcutta (500km, Rs 152/489 in 2nd/1st class) and three daily departures to Delhi (2140km, 30 to 36 hours). There are several trains between Puri and Bhubaneswar (Rs 15, two hours) but the buses are quicker.

If you're travelling to or from Chennai (1207km) and railway stations in the south it's not necessary to go via Bhubaneswar. Khurda Road, 44km from Puri, is a convenient junction that all trains pass through. The *Coromandel Express* passes through at 10 pm, arriving in Chennai at 5.30 pm the following day.

The railway booking office is computerised and is open Monday to Saturday from 8 am to noon and 12.30 to 3 pm. On Sunday, it's open only in the morning, It's advisable to book ahead during the pilgrim season when trains to Chennai and Calcutta are often booked out five to 10 days ahead. Reservations can also be made at the South-Eastern Railway Hotel; they have their own quotas so are worth trying when tickets are otherwise unavailable.

Getting Around

A cycle-rickshaw from the bus stand to the hotels along the beach is around Rs 10, less if they're pedalling to a commission. Buses shuttle between the Jagannath Temple and the bus stand and between the railway station and the bus stand for Rs 3.

The best way to get around is by bicycle, and there are several places at the travellers' end of the beach where you can rent one for Rs 15 per day. You can even roar off on an Enfield India (Rs 250 per day), or a less impressive Vespa scooter (Rs 200).

AROUND PURI
Raghurajpur

Famous for its *patachitra* painting, this artists' village, 10km from Puri, makes an interesting excursion. The paintings are done on cotton cloth that's coated with a mixture of gum and chalk and then polished before natural colours are applied.

The best way to get to the village is by taxi or bicycle, as it's 1.5km off the main road. From Puri, take the Bhubaneswar road for nine km, almost to Chandapur. Turn right before the bridge, cross the railway line, then follow the right fork through the coconut plantation for one km until you come to Raghurajpur.

Pipli

Twenty-three km from Puri, at the junction where the Konark road branches from the Bhubaneswar to Puri road, this small village is notable for its appliqué craft. The colourful materials are used to make temple umbrellas and wall hangings.

KONARK

Pop: 12,681   Tel Area Code: 06758

Konark consists of little more than the sun temple (see the beginning of this chapter) and a handful of shops, stalls and places to stay. Although most people make a day trip from Puri or Bhubaneswar, it's a wonderfully peaceful place to spend a few days, and the temple has even more atmosphere once the day-trippers have all gone home. However, there isn't a lot of accommodation here – yet. Several of the major hotel chains want to turn Konark into a new beach resort, but planning permission for their hotels has so far been withheld on environmental grounds.

Konark is protected as a UNESCO World Heritage Site.

If you come to Konark for the day you can take an early morning bus from Puri and a late bus back (or on to Bhubaneswar) in the afternoon, which will give you plenty of time to have a look at the temple.

An open-air theatre has been built near the temple and the Konark Dance Festival is staged here in early December. There's a smaller festival in February.

There's a tourist office in the Yatri Nivas.

Nine Planets' Shrine

The six-metre chlorite slab, once the architrave above the main entrance of the jagamohan, is now the centrepiece of a small shrine just outside the temple walls. The carved seated figures represent Surya (the sun), Chandra (the moon), Mars, Mercury, Jupiter, Venus, Saturn, Rahu and Ketu.

Archaeological Museum

Outside the temple enclosure is a museum (open from 10 am to 5 pm, closed Friday) containing many sculptures and carvings found during the temple excavation. Some of the small pieces (the statue of Agni, the

ORISSA

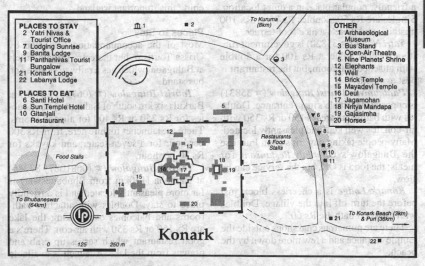

PLACES TO STAY
2 Yatri Nivas & Tourist Office
7 Lodging Sunrise
9 Banita Lodge
11 Panthanivas Tourist Bungalow
21 Konark Lodge
22 Labanya Lodge

PLACES TO EAT
6 Santi Hotel
8 Sun Temple Hotel
10 Gitanjali Restaurant

OTHER
1 Archaeological Museum
3 Bus Stand
4 Open-Air Theatre
5 Nine Planets' Shrine
12 Elephants
13 Well
14 Brick Temple
15 Mayadevi Temple
16 Deul
17 Jagamohan
18 Nritya Mandapa
19 Gajasimha
20 Horses

To Kuruma (8km)

Food Stalls

Restaurants & Food Stalls

To Bhubaneswar (64km)

To Konark Beach (3km) & Puri (36km)

Konark

0   125   250 m

fire god, for example) are particularly good. For more information, the Archaeological Survey of India's *Sun Temple – Konark* is on sale here but not at the temple itself.

Konark Beach

The sea is three km from the temple; you can walk there or hire a bicycle (Rs 20 per day from Yatri Nivas) or take a cycle-rickshaw. This part of the beach is much cleaner than at Puri, but beware of the strong current. It's also much quieter than Puri, but if there are any children about you're likely to attract their attention, since not many foreigners swim here. With miles of open sand, you can of course always move along the beach a bit. A number of chai shops sell drinks and snacks here.

See the **Sun Temple** regional highlight on p535.

Places to Stay & Eat

The cheapest accommodation is just south of the bus stand and is fairly basic.

Lodging Sunrise has doubles for Rs 40 with common bathroom.

Banita Lodge has rooms with attached bath for Rs 50.

Labanya Lodge (☎ 35824; fax 35860) is a friendly, popular place in a quiet location. Singles are Rs 50, doubles Rs 75 or Rs 100 upstairs, and there's a nice roof terrace.

Yatri Nivas (☎ 35820) is government run. It's excellent value at Rs 100 for a double with attached bathroom, but the restaurant is best avoided.

Panthanivas Tourist Bungalow (☎ 35831) is opposite the temple's main entrance. Doubles with bathroom are Rs 150 or Rs 350 with air-con. It's well kept and pleasantly located. Many people taking day trips from Puri use the Bungalow's *Gitanjali Restaurant* for meals; the food is OK, but the service can be slow.

Konark Lodge is a cheerless block just before the turn-off into the village. Doubles with attached bath are Rs 60.

There are numerous chai shops outside the temple entrance and a few more down by the beach.

Santi Hotel has meals for Rs 10.

Sun Temple Hotel is also a recommended place to eat.

Getting There & Away

Dilapidated buses and overcrowded mini-buses run along the coastal road between Puri and Konark (Rs 8, one hour). Some people even cycle the 36km from Puri and stay the night at Konark. Although it's a good flat road, make sure the bicycle you hire is in reasonable condition because there are few repair shops along the way.

CHILKA LAKE

South-west of Puri, Chilka Lake is dotted with islands and is noted for the many migratory birds which flock to the nesting sanctuary here in winter (December to January). The shallow lake is about 70km long and averages 15km wide, and is supposedly one of the largest brackish-water lakes in the country. It's separated from the sea only by a narrow sand bar. The railway line and the main road run along the inland edge of the lake. It's a peaceful enough place but probably of greatest interest to ornithologists. Environmental problems – such as siltation and commercial prawn fishing – are threatening this important wetland.

Places to Stay

Most of the accommodation is owned by Orissa Tourism, but there are private hotels at Balugaon, which has a railway station and bus stand.

Tourist Bungalow (☎ (06756) 20488) at Barkul (six km south of Balugaon) has doubles for Rs 250 or Rs 400 for air-con rooms. There are launches for hire here, from Rs 300 per hour for a seven-seater, and kayaks for Rs 30 per hour.

Tourist Bungalow (☎ (0681087) 87346) at Rambha (130km from Bhubaneswar) is far more pleasantly located and is a friendly place to stay. Doubles with attached bathrooms and balconies overlooking the lake are Rs 150 or Rs 350 with air-con. There's a good restaurant which serves up crab and prawns from the lake. A launch is available

ORISSA

for hire here or the fishermen will take you out for Rs 50 per hour.

Panthanivas is a new place on the lake at Satapada (50km south of Puri). Rooms with attached bath start at Rs 150.

GOPALPUR-ON-SEA
Tel Area Code: 0680

Gopalpur is a decaying little seaside resort, 18km south-east of Berhampur. The beach is attractive until you get close enough to smell it, but there are probably less nasty floaties in the sea here than at Puri.

Places to Stay & Eat
Prices vary according to season and demand, and you should be able to get a 50% discount on the high-season (November to January) prices given below if there aren't many people about.

The *youth hostel* is down the street beside Rohini's Restaurant. It's run-down but has beds for Rs 20.

Holiday Inn Lodge has singles/doubles for Rs 40/60 with attached bathroom. It's possible to cook your own food here. Follow the signs from the youth hostel.

Hotel Kalinga (☎ 82067) is right by the sea, with good singles/doubles for Rs 150/250 or Rs 250 for a four-bed room, all with attached bathrooms. It's well run and there's a restaurant here.

Hotel Holiday Home (☎ 82049), on the corner of the Beach Rd, has doubles from Rs 250.

Hotel Rosalin (☎ 82071) is opposite the fast-food stand by the beach. Rooms with attached bath are Rs 100/150.

Hotel Sea Side Breeze (☎ 82075) has ocean-facing doubles for Rs 250 as well as some cheaper rooms, and it's beside the beach.

Motel Mermaid (☎ 82050), also on Beach Rd, is flashier, with rooms from Rs 300/350, or you can pay an increased tariff and get veg or non-veg meals included. Non-guests can eat here with advance notice.

Hotel Song of the Sea (☎ 82347), near the lighthouse, is a new place with good views.

Doubles with sparkling bathrooms are Rs 500.

Oberoi Palm Beach Hotel (☎ 82021; fax 82300) is a luxurious low-key retreat in a coconut grove right by the sea. Rooms are from US$100/150, including all meals.

Hotel Rohini, on the main road, is a good value tandoor restaurant.

Getting There & Away
The only buses from Gopalpur are to Berhampur (Rs 4, 45 minutes) which is on the main Calcutta to Chennai railway line. A cycle-rickshaw for the three km between the railway station and the Berhampur bus stand costs Rs 10. From the bus stand there are regular departures to Bhubaneswar (Rs 38, five hours), overnight buses to Jeypur in the south for Rs 80 and regular buses to Taptapani (Rs 12, two hours).

TAPTAPANI
Apart from the small hot springs in this peaceful place in the hills west of Gopalpur, there's not much else to see, and it's really not worth a day trip. However, it would make a great winter splurge if you booked one of the two rooms at the *Panthanivas Tourist Bungalow* (☎ Podamari 2531), which have hot spring water channelled directly to the vast tubs (accommodating several people) in their Roman-style bathrooms. Double rooms cost Rs 500 and there are also ordinary rooms for Rs 225, with ordinary bathrooms.

Near **Chandragiri**, 36km away, there's a Tibetan refugee community and a temple. The Tibetans support themselves by breeding Tibetan long-haired dogs and weaving carpets, which you can buy here.

CUTTACK
Pop: 500,915   Tel Area Code: 0671

Only 35km north of Bhubaneswar, on the banks of the Mahanadi and Kathajuri rivers, Cuttack was the capital of Orissa until 1950. Today it's a chaotic and largely uninteresting place.

Only a gateway and the moat remain of the 14th century **Barabati Fort**. The stone

ORISSA

retaining wall on the Kathajuri River, which protects the city from seasonal floods, dates from the 11th century. The **Kadam Rasul** is a Muslim shrine which contains the Prophet's footprint.

Paradip, 90km east of Cuttack, is a major port and minor beach resort.

Places to Stay & Eat

Most visitors to Cuttack make a day trip from Bhubaneswar, but there are a number of comfortable hotels here.

Panthanivas Tourist Bungalow (☎ 621867) in Buxi Bazaar has doubles for Rs 200 or Rs 325 with air-con.

Hotel Neeladri (☎ 614221) has singles/doubles from Rs 150/250.

Hotel Ashoka's (☎ 613508) rooms are Rs 120/160 or Rs 350/400 with air-con.

Hotel Akbari Continental (☎ 622342) has air-con rooms for Rs 900/1100, and there is also a restaurant.

LALITGIRI, UDAIGIRI & RATNAGIRI

Buddhist relics and ruins can be found at these three hilltop complexes, north-east of Cuttack and about 100km from Bhubaneswar.

A gold casket, thought to contain **relics of the Buddha**, was discovered at Lalitgiri. Excavations are continuing. Eight km away is Udaigiri, with another **monastery complex** and a brick stupa.

The Ratnagiri site, five km beyond Udaigiri, has the most interesting and extensive **ruins** and is well worth a visit. The two large monasteries here flourished from the 6th to the 12th centuries AD. There are beautifully carved doorways, a large stupa and enormous Buddha figures.

From Cuttack there are buses to Lalitgiri only. Direct travel to Ratnagiri and Udaigiri entails an expensive taxi ride from Cuttack, or you can pick up a rickshaw near the Lalitgiri turn off.

The *Inspection Bungalow*, below the Lalitgiri hill in Patharajpur village, is the nearest accommodation.

BHITAR KANIKA WILDLIFE RESERVE

This sanctuary on the coast between Paradip and Chandipur was proclaimed largely to protect the nesting habitat of the 300,000-odd olive ridley marine turtles which come to the mouth of the Brahmani River here each winter to nest.

As yet there is little in the way of facilities. There is accommodation at the *Forest Rest House* in Dangmal, and in Chandbali, which you can get to from the main highway at Bhadrakh. The *Ray Lodge* (☎ (06797) 2201) has rooms for Rs 150.

BALASORE & CHANDIPUR

Balasore is the first major town in north Orissa on the railway line from Calcutta. It was once an important trading centre with Dutch, Danish, English and French factories. In 1634 it had the first British East India Company factory in Bengal. **Remina**, eight km away, has the Gopinath Temple, an important pilgrimage centre.

Chandipur, 16km away on the coast, is a beach resort where the beach extends five km at low tide and the sea can be very shallow. There are several buses a day from Balasore.

Places to Stay

Most of the accommodation is operated by Orissa Tourism.

Deepak Lodging, in Balasore, is pleasant and reasonably priced. Walk from the railway station to the main road, turn left and it's on the right-hand side, two blocks from the corner and across the street from the cinema.

Panthanivas Tourist Bungalow (☎ (06782) 72251), in Chandipur, has dorm beds for Rs 60, doubles for Rs 250 or Rs 425 with air-con. Cheaper private accommodation is available.

SIMILIPAL NATIONAL PARK

In the north-east of the state, 250km from Calcutta and 320km from Bhubaneswar, this park covers 2750 sq km and is part of Project Tiger. There are tigers (thought to number around 80), elephants and several types of deer among the many species here. The scenery is beautiful and varied, with hills, waterfalls and undisturbed forest in which the

ORISSA

wildlife manages to remain well hidden. The park is closed from July to October.

Tourist facilities are not well developed and you must bring money and food and arrange your own transport. The entrances to the park are on the western side at Jashipur, or more conveniently at Baripada. Your first stop has to be the Similipal park office (☎ (06792) 52593) at Baripada, to book your accommodation.

Forest Rest Houses (six) are dotted round the park. Doubles cost Rs 100. The one at Barheipani is recommended as it's near a 450m waterfall.

Aranya Niwas Tourist Lodge is at Lulung, about 10km inside the park (35km from Baripada). Double rooms cost Rs 300, or there's cheaper dorm accommodation.

Jashipur is accessible by bus (or train and bus via Bangriposhi) from Baripada. The *Tourist Lodge* in Jashipur is run by Mr Roy, who charges Rs 50 for a double. You can arrange to hire a jeep here (Rs 3.50 per km).

SAMBALPUR

Pop: 219,810   Tel Area Code: 0663

In the west, near the border with Madhya Pradesh, is the large town of Sambalpur. It's the heart of an **ikat weaving** district, and you can buy fabric in the main bazaar and in government co-operative shops. This area is right off the beaten tourist path, and you'll be something of a local attraction.

The town is promoted as a holiday destination by the Orissa Tourism Development Corporation largely, it seems, on account of the 24-km-long **Hirakud Dam**, built to control monsoon floods in the Mahanadi delta around Bhubaneswar.

Sonapur, 80km south, is another textile centre, and there are Tantric temples here.

The OTDC maintains tourist offices at the railway station and the Panthanivas Tourist Bungalow.

Places to Stay & Eat

Chances are you won't be in Sambalpur for long, but there are a few places which are fine for a short stay.

Indhrapuri Guest House (☎ 21712), right by the bus stand, has small rooms for Rs 30/40.

Rani Lodge, about five minutes walk away on the main street, is similar.

Hotel Uphar (☎ 21308) is a good place. Rooms with attached bath are Rs 175/225, although a 20% discount seems to be standard. There are also rooms at Rs 400/450 for air-con and colour TV. The restaurant here is not great.

Panthanivas Tourist Bungalow (☎ 21482) is on top of a small hill at the end of the main street. It's not brilliantly run or maintained, but there are good views from some rooms. A double with attached bath costs Rs 170, and Rs 325 with air-con.

Central Hotel, opposite the Indhrapuri Guest House, is a good place for cheap meals.

Hotel Uphar Palace's restaurant, on the main street, is a little more salubrious.

Getting There & Away

Bus The bus stand is in the centre of town. There are three buses daily for Puri (Rs 85, nine hours), but these leave in the afternoon and so arrive quite late. It's better to catch a morning bus for Cuttack (Rs 70, seven hours) and another from there to Puri.

On the main street outside the bus stand there are plenty of private companies with deluxe video coaches (night only) for Puri (Rs 100), Bhubaneswar (Rs 90) and Raipur (Rs 75). The state bus company also has a deluxe night bus to Bhubaneswar (Rs 80). Book in advance at the bus stand.

Train The railway station is about three km from the town centre, a rip-off Rs 30 by auto-rickshaw. There are direct trains to Bilaspur, Jhansi, Calcutta, Bhubaneswar (17 hours, via Vizianagram in Andhra Pradesh), Delhi and Chennai. Most of these trains also stop at Sambalpur *Road* railway station, which is a little closer to the centre.

OTHER ATTRACTIONS

In the north of Orissa, 50km south-west of Jashipur, **Khiching** was once an ancient capital and has a number of interesting temples (some in ruins) and a small museum. Further inland is the important industrial city of **Rourkela**, which has a major steel plant. A little north-west of Cuttack is the Siva temple of **Kapilas**.

Bronze-casting is done in the **Bolangir** area in the west of the state. **Harishankar**, west of Bolangir, has a number of temples and a waterfall. The twin villages of **Ranipur-Jharial** are 30km from Titlagarh and are noted

for the extensive collection of temples on a rock outcrop. They include a circular 64-*yogini* temple which, like the one at Khajuraho, once had 64 cells for figures of yoginis who attended to the goddess Kali.

Gupteswar Cave is 85km west of Koraput. This is in Orissa's large southern district, which is inhabited by several tribal peoples, including the Bonda.

Orissan Tribal People

No less than 62 distinct tribal groups of aboriginal people inhabited this region prior to the Aryan invasion of India. Officially known as 'tribals' – but also called *adivasis* – they constitute more than a quarter of the state's population and live mainly in the hilly areas outside the small coastal plain. Many have adopted the ways of the invader and, as far as the foreign visitor is concerned, may not seem to look or dress very differently to the average Aryan Orissan – though an anthropologist or a caste-conscious Indian would hardly agree. Others, such as the Bonda, who wear very little, are more obviously different.

Kondhs The most numerous of the tribals are the 950,000 Kondhs. They still practise colourful ceremonies, although animal sacrifices have been substituted for the human ones which the British took so much trouble to stop, particularly around Russelkonda (Bhanjanagar).

Juang The Juang number only around 30,000 and live in thatched huts decorated with white wall paintings. Their small villages are mainly in the central districts of Dhenkanal and Keonjhar to the north.

Santal There are about 500,000 Santal, living in the northern Mayurbhanj and Balasore districts, particularly around Baripada and Khiching. Their marriage system is interesting in that it involves several different methods for a woman to get her man, including *nir balak bapla* or 'marriage by intrusion'. Unable to hook him by any other method, she can just move in and if he and his parents can't get her out after a week or so, he must marry her!

Saoras This tribe, numbering over 300,000, is spread over a wide area in the central and southern districts. Saora children are revered within the tribe, but are also expected to pull their weight from an early age. There's no lower age limit on attending ceremonies, and smoking and drinking are permitted as soon as the child can do so without choking or vomiting.

Bonda The Bonda, known as the 'naked people', are renowned for their dormitories where young men and women are encouraged to meet for night-time fun and frolics. Only about 5000 Bonda remain in the hills of Koraput district. Women wear only a strip of cloth around their middle, long rows of beads and heavy metal neckbands.

Other major tribes are the Parajas, the colourful Godabas and the Koyas. Permission from the Orissa Home Ministry is needed to visit tribal villages, except for those along the main highways.

Tribal Tours

The concept of tribal tours is well-developed in Orissa, with most travel agents offering some sort of programme. Most of the tours are small-scale jeep trips, taking about seven days and costing US$200 per person, including meals, a driver and a guide, and the government permits required to enter tribal areas.

However, it's worth thinking about the cultural sensitivity of such tours and whether the insight they give into the threatened lives of the adivasis is a morally sound one. Events such as Bhubaneswar's Tribal Festival are undoubtedly a manufactured opening into the tribal world, but perhaps it is better that tribal people have the opportunity to present their culture when and where they wish, so that their villages may stay villages, and not become clusters of display homes. ∎

Sikkim

For many years, Sikkim was regarded as one of the last Himalayan 'Shangri-las' because of its remoteness, spectacular mountain terrain, varied flora and fauna and ancient Buddhist monasteries. It was never easy to visit and, even now, you need a special permit to enter, though this is easy to obtain (see the Permits section later in this chapter). All the same, access to the eastern part of Sikkim along the Tibetan border remains restricted, and trekking to the base of Kanchenjunga has to be organised through a recognised travel agency. Compared with other parts of the country, tourism in Sikkim is in its infancy.

Until 1975, Sikkim, or New House, was an independent kingdom, albeit under a treaty which allowed the Indian government to control Sikkim's foreign affairs and defence. However, following a period of political crises and riots in the capital, Gangtok, India annexed the country and Sikkim became the 22nd Indian state.

The move sparked widespread criticism, but tensions have now cooled. The central government has been spending relatively large sums of money to subsidise Sikkim's road building, electrification, water supply and agricultural and industrial development. Much of this activity was no doubt motivated by India's fear of Chinese military designs on the Himalayan region. Sikkim certainly now seems a more affluent place than its neighbour West Bengal, and being a tax-free zone no doubt helps further.

If you've been to Nepal you'll feel on familiar turf here: 75% of the population is Nepali and that's now Sikkim's main language.

History

The country was originally home to the Lepchas, a tribal people thought to have migrated from the hills of Assam, or possibly even from South-East Asia, around the 13th century. The Lepchas were peaceful forest foragers and small-crop cultivators who worshipped

---

SIKKIM AT A GLANCE

Population: 500,000
Area: 7214 sq km
Capital: Gangtok
Main Language: Nepali
Literacy Rate: 34%
Best Time to Go: March to August

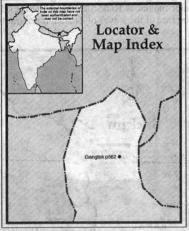

Locator & Map Index

Gangtok p562 ●

Highlights

- Buddhist monasteries
- Trekking to Kanchenjunga, at 8598m the third highest mountain in the world
- Magnificent rhododendrons and orchids

Festivals

Bhumchu – Tashiding Monastery – March
Saga Dawa – Gangtok – late May or early June
Drukpa Teshi – August
Pang Lhabsol – late August or early September
Dasain – October
Kagyat Dance – Gangtok, Pemayangste and Phodang – February
Loosong – last week of February
Losar – Pemayangste and Rumtek – early March

nature spirits. They still constitute some 18% of the total population of Sikkim.

SIKKIM

The Tibetans started to immigrate into Sikkim during the 15th century to escape religious strife between various Buddhist orders. In Tibet itself, the Gelukpa order (of which the Dalai Lama is the head) gradually gained the upper hand. In Sikkim, the Nyingma-pa order was introduced by three Tibetan lamas, Lhatsun Chempo, Kathok Rikzin Chempo and Ngadak Sempa Chempo. It was these lamas who consecrated the first *chogyal* or king, Phuntsog Namgyal, at Yuksom, which became the capital of the kingdom (it was later moved to Rabdentse, near Pelling). In the face of the waves of Tibetan immigrants,

the Lepchas retreated to the more remote regions. A blood brotherhood was eventually forged between their leader, Thekong Tek, and the Bhutia leader, Khye-Bumsa, and spiritual and temporal authority was imposed on the anarchistic Lepchas.

When the kingdom of Sikkim was founded, the country included the area encompassed by the present state as well as part of Eastern Nepal, the Chumbi Valley (Tibet), Ha Valley (Bhutan) and the Terai foothills down to the plains of India, including Darjeeling and Kalimpong.

Between 1717 and 1734, during the reign

The external boundaries of India on this map have not been authenticated and may not be correct.

of Sikkim's fourth chogyal, a series of wars fought with the Bhutanese resulted in the loss of much territory in the southern foothills, including Kalimpong, then a very important bazaar town on the trade route between Tibet and India. More territory was lost after 1780 following the Gurkha invasion from Nepal, though the invaders were eventually checked by a Chinese army with Bhutanese and Lepcha assistance. Unable to advance into Tibet, the Gurkhas turned south, where they came into conflict with the British East India Company. The wars between the two parties ended in the treaty of 1817, which delineated the borders of Nepal. The Gurkhas also ceded to the British all the Sikkimese territory they had taken; a substantial part was returned to the chogyal of Sikkim in return for British control of all disputes between Sikkim and its neighbours. The country thus became a buffer state between Nepal, Tibet and Bhutan.

In 1835, the British, seeking a hill station as a rest and recreation centre for their troops and officials, persuaded the chogyal to cede the Darjeeling area in return for an annual stipend. The Tibetans objected to this transfer of territory. They continued to regard Sikkim as a vassal state, and Darjeeling's rapid growth as a trade centre had begun to make a considerable impact on the fortunes of Sikkim's leading lamas and merchants.

Tensions rose and, in 1849, a high-ranking British official and a botanist, who were exploring the Lachen regions with the permission of both the Sikkim chogyal and the British government, were arrested. Although the two prisoners were unconditionally released a month later following threats of intervention, the British annexed the entire area between the present Sikkimese border and the Indian plains and withdrew the chogyal's stipend.

Further British interference in the affairs of this area lead to the declaration of a protectorate over Sikkim in 1861 and the delineation of its borders. The Tibetans, however, continued to regard these actions as illegal and, in 1886, invaded Sikkim to reassert their authority. The attack was repulsed

by the British, who sent a punitive military expedition to Lhasa in 1888 in retaliation. The powers of the Sikkimese chogyal were further reduced.

Keen to develop Sikkim, the British encouraged emigration from Nepal as they had done in Darjeeling, and a considerable amount of land was brought under rice and cardamom cultivation. This influx of labour continued right up until the 1960s, when the chogyal was constrained to prohibit further immigration.

The British treaties with Sikkim passed to India at independence. Demands within Sikkim for a democratic form of government as opposed to rule by the chogyal were growing. The Indian government supported these moves – it didn't want to be seen to be propping up an autocratic regime while doing its best to sweep away the last traces of princely rule in India itself.

The last chogyal, Palden Thondup Namgyal, came to the throne in 1963 and was not popular. He was married to an American, Hope Cook, who is chiefly remembered for having introduced crème de menthe to Gangtok society. The chogyal resisted demands for a change in the method of government until demonstrations threatened to get out of control. He was eventually forced to ask India to take over the country's administration.

In the 1975 referendum, 97% of the electorate voted for union with India. China, of course, refuses to accept Sikkim as part of India.

The current chief minister is Pawan Kumar Chamling of the Sikkim Democratic Front. His long-serving predecessor, Bahadar Bhandari, in common with most outgoing Indian politicians, is currently facing charges of 'acquiring assets disproportionate to his known sources of income'.

Tourist & Trekking Permits

You can stay in Sikkim for 15 days, with a further 15 day extension available in Gangtok from the Home Office (Tashiling Secretariat). Re-entry into Sikkim within three months is not possible, even if you leave Sikkim before your 15 day permit expires.

With a standard tourist permit you may visit Gangtok, Rumtek, Phodang and Pemayangtse. However, you must stick to the National Highway. A special endorsement (available from the permit office in Gangtok or the Gangtok Home Office) allows you to visit areas around Pemayangtse, including Khecheopari Lake and Tashiling Gompa.

While permits can be obtained through the Indian embassy in your home country when you apply for your Indian visa, they are easily obtained in India itself, either while you wait or within a few hours. You will need your passport and one photo, plus a photocopy of the front page of your passport (with expiry details and so on), and the page where your Indian visa is stamped; there's no charge. When applying for your permit, you must specify your date of entry into Sikkim.

Permits for Tsongo Lake (valid for a day visit only) and Yumthang (in North Sikkim; a nonextendible five day/four night permit) can only be obtained from the permit office in Gangtok, but as you must join a tour (minimum of four) to visit these two places, it's best to let the travel agency sort out the paper work for you.

The only area currently open in Sikkim for trekking is in the Dzongri area of West Sikkim. Trekking permits are in addition to the normal tourist permit and are issued at the permit office in Gangtok, or from the Government of Sikkim Tourist Information Centre in New Delhi (see below).

Two peaks in the Dzongri area of West Sikkim, Thingchen Khang and Jopunob (both just under 6000m), have been declared 'trekking peaks', which means that they are free of the usual royalty payment required for mountaineering peaks. Ascents may be combined with a trek in this area and are subject to the trekking regulations described above.

Permits are checked and your passport stamped when entering or leaving Sikkim, and at Legship and Yuksom.

Permits can be obtained from any of the following places:

Foreigners' Registration Offices
   Delhi, Mumbai (Bombay), Calcutta, Darjeeling
Resident Commissioner
   Government of Sikkim, 14 Panchsheel Marg, Chanakyapuri, New Delhi (☎ (011) 301 5346)
Sikkim Tourism Information Centre
   4C Poonam, 5/2 Russel St, Calcutta
   (☎ (033) 297516)
   SNT Bus Compound, Tenzing Norgay Rd, Siliguri (☎ (0353) 432646)

For more information, see the Trekking section at the end of this chapter.

Kanchenjunga National Park

Access to the heart of Kanchenjunga National Park, including the vast Zemu Glacier, is generally only permitted to mountaineering expeditions or experienced trekking parties using the services of a recognised travel agency. Gangtok travel agencies are best acquainted with the system and usually have the most useful contacts.

Mountaineering expeditions interested in climbing peaks over 6000m need to obtain clearance from the Indian Mountaineering Foundation (IMF; ☎ (011) 671211; fax 688 3412), Benito Juarez Rd, Anand Niketan, New Delhi 110021.

East Sikkim

Owing to its proximity to the Tibetan border, entry to most of East Sikkim by foreigners is prohibited. However, this region does encompass the capital, Gangtok, which is included on the standard tourist permit. Within the city and its immediate environs are some fascinating places to visit, including Rumtek Gompa, 24km to the west, the head of the Kagyu-pa order of Tibetan Buddhism.

GANGTOK
Pop: 85,000   Tel Area Code: 03592
The capital of Sikkim, Gangtok (which means 'hilltop'), occupies the west side of a long ridge flanking the Ranipul River. The scenery is spectacular and there are excellent

views of the entire Kanchenjunga Range from many points in the environs of the city.

Many people expect Gangtok to be a smaller version of Kathmandu. It's not, but it is an interesting and pleasant place to stay. Gangtok only became the capital in the mid-1800s (previous capitals were at Yuksom and Rabdentse) and the town has undergone rapid modernisation in recent years.

Gangtok has also become something of a hill station resort for holidaying Bengalis. The influx peaks during the 10 day Durga Puja holiday period at the end of September or early October, when Bengalis converge on the town en masse from the plains. It's a good time to give Gangtok a miss, as prices rise – especially for accommodation and local transport – and finding a room at *any* price can be a major headache.

Orientation

To the north is Enchey Gompa and the telecommunications tower. The palace of the former chogyal and the impressive Royal Chapel (the Tsuk-La-Khang) are lower down along the ridge. Nearby is the huge Tashiling, or Secretariat complex, and, below it, the relatively recently built Legislative Assembly, both executed in a traditional architectural style.

On a continuation of this ridge but much lower is the Namgyal Institute of Tibetology, an Orchid Sanctuary and, not far beyond the institute, a large *chorten* (Tibetan stupa) and adjoining gompa.

All the main facilities – hotels, cafes, bazaars, bus stand, post office, tourist office and the Foreigners' Registration Office – are either on, or very near, the main Darjeeling road (National Highway 31A).

Information

Tourist Office The helpful tourist office (☎ 23425) is at the top (north) end of MG Marg. In the season it's open daily, including holidays, from 9 am to 7 pm. Between June and August it's open Monday to Saturday from 10 am to 4 pm.

Money There's currently nowhere to cash Visa travellers cheques, but most other brands

can be exchanged at the State Bank of India near the tourist office.

Post & Communications The main post office is open Monday to Saturday. Faxes and telephone calls can be made at the telegraph office next door (open daily).

Permits Trekking permits for West Sikkim (ie north of Yuksom) can be obtained from the permit office in the same building as the tourist office. It's open Monday to Saturday from 10 am to 4 pm. To visit Tsongo Lake or North Sikkim, you need to be in a group of four and book a package through a travel agency; agencies will arrange requisite permits. Extensions can be applied for at the Home Office, Government of Sikkim, Tashiling Secretariat.

For more information on permits for Sikkim, see the permits section at the beginning of this chapter.

Tours Local tours operate on a point system, points referring to sites of interest around Gangtok. A seven point sightseeing trip taking in Enchey and Rumtek gompas, and the Namgyal Institute of Tibetology, among other places, takes four to five hours and costs Rs 100. Half-day tours also cover Rumtek but don't give you much time, and you'd be better off doing this yourself. The official rate to hire a taxi for a day to visit these sights is Rs 500.

Emergency Useful emergency contacts include the police (☎ 100/22033) and the hospital (☎ 22059).

Namgyal Institute of Tibetology

Established in 1958 and built in traditional style, this unique institute promotes research into Mahayana Buddhism and the language and traditions of Tibet. It has one of the world's largest collections of books and rare manuscripts on Mahayana Buddhism, many religious works of art and a collection of astonishingly beautiful and incredibly finely executed silk-embroidered thangkas. There are also relics of monks from the time of

SIKKIM

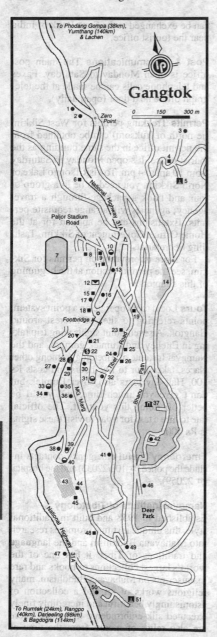

Gangtok

To Phodang Gompa (38km),
Yumthang (140km)
& Lachen

Zero
Point

0   150   300 m

To Rumtek (24km), Rangpo
(40km), Darjeeling (98km)
& Bagdogra (114km)

National Highway 31A

Paljor Stadium
Road

Footbridge

Tibet Road

MG Marg

Bhanu Path

Deer
Park

SIKKIM

PLACES TO STAY
4	Siniolchu Lodge
6	Hotel Superview Himalchuli & Yak & Yeti Travels
8	Nor-Khill Hotel
9	Hotel Mount View
11	Hotel Lhakhar
15	Hotel Tibet
18	Blue Heaven Lodge
19	Netuk House
21	Gangtok Lodge & New Kho-Chi Restaurant
23	Hotel Sonam Delek
25	Modern Central Lodge
26	Hotel Lhakpa
29	Green Hotel
34	Sunny Guest House
39	Denzong Inn
44	Hotel Tashi Delek
45	Hotel Laden La
48	Pine Ridge Hotel

PLACES TO EAT
20	Metro Fast Food

OTHER
1	Cottage Industries Emporium
2	Sikkim World Expeditions
3	Telecommunications Tower
5	Enchey Gompa
7	Stadium
10	SNT Bus Stand
12	Main Post Office & Telegraph Office
13	Yuksam Tours & Travels
14	Ridge Park, Flower Exhibition Centre & White Hall
16	Siniolchu, Mayur & Potala Tours & Travels
17	Tibetan Curio Store
22	State Bank of India
24	Blue Sky Tours & Travels
27	Sikkim Tours & Travels
28	Tourist Office
30	Chiranjilal Lalchand Dispensary
31	Children's Park Taxi Stand
32	Indian Airlines
33	Private Bus & Taxi Stands
35	Tashila Tours & Travels
36	Rural Artisans' Marketing Centre
37	Palace
38	Super Market Complex, Sikkim Trekking & Travel Services, Mahayana Tours & Travels
40	Lall Market Taxi Stand
41	Foreigners' Registration Office
42	Tsuk-La-Khang (Royal Chapel)
43	Lall Market
46	Tashiling Secretariat Complex
47	Forest Secretariat
49	Legislative Assembly
50	Namgyal Institute of Tibetology & Orchid Sanctuary
51	Chorten & Gompa

Ashoka, examples of Lepcha script, masks, and ceremonial and sacred objects, such as the *kapali*, a bowl made from a human skull, and the *varku*, a flute made from a thigh bone.

The institute has a number of religious art and craft works and books on Tibetan Buddhism for sale. The person who runs the publications shop is very interesting to talk to.

It's open Monday to Friday and every second Saturday from 10 am to 4 pm; entry is Rs 2. This is a sacred place, and footwear should be removed before entering.

Orchid Sanctuaries

Surrounding the institute, and itself enclosed by a peaceful forest, is the **Orchid Sanctuary**, where you can see many of the 454 species of orchid found in Sikkim. The best times to visit the sanctuary are April to May and the end of September to the beginning of December.

There is another, much larger, orchid sanctuary, called the **Orchidarium**, off the main road to Rangpo alongside the Rani Khola, a tributary of the Teesta. It is accessible by public bus and is also usually included on tours to Rumtek Gompa.

Up on top of the ridge, near White Hall, is a **Flower Exhibition Centre**, featuring orchids and seasonal flowers as well as bonsai. It's open from April to June and September until the end of November, from 10 am to 6 pm daily; entry is Rs 2. **White Hall** is the residence of the chief minister, and there are pleasant walks here through fine gardens. It's also a good walk from here to the deer park (see below).

Chorten & Gompa

The gold apex of this huge white chorten, surrounded by prayer flags, is visible from many points in Gangtok. Next to the chorten, about 500m beyond the Namgyal Institute, is a gompa for young lamas with a shrine containing huge images of Padmasambhava and his manifestation, Guru Snang-Sid Zilzon. As at other Buddhist gompas, the chorten is surrounded by prayer wheels.

Tsuk-La-Khang (Royal Chapel)

The Royal Chapel is the Buddhists' principal place of worship and assembly, and the repository of a large collection of scriptures. It's a beautiful and impressive building, and its interior is covered with murals. Lavishly decorated altars hold images of the Buddha, bodhisattvas and Tantric deities, and there are also a great many fine woodcarvings. The only time it's open to visitors is during Losar (the Tibetan New Year in late February/early March), when the famous dance portraying the triumph of good over evil is performed.

Deer Park

This popular viewpoint is on the edge of the ridge next to the Secretariat building. A good time to visit is around 8 am, when the deer are fed.

Enchey Gompa

Located above Siniolchu Lodge, about three km from the centre of town, Enchey Monastery is well worth a visit, particularly if you're in Gangtok when religious dances are performed in January (18th and 19th days of 12th lunar month).

Built in 1909, it's a relatively small place and is not as impressive as the other larger monasteries in Sikkim, but it does sit on a spectacular ridge overlooking Gangtok, and there are views across to Kanchenjunga.

Trekking Outfits & Tour Operators

You'll need the services of a recognised tour operator and at least four people in your trekking party if you want to travel to North Sikkim or do the Dzongri trek (Kanchenjunga). Operators in Gangtok charge between US$35 and US$60 per person per day, and also offer gompa tours, bird-watching tours, and white-water rafting. Equipment hire (sleeping bags etc) is available from some operators.

Sikkim Trekking & Travel Services
    Room No 1, Super Market Complex (☎ 23638; fax 22707 attn 'Sikkim Trekking'); not the cheapest, but it's very professional and was the

first outfit established in Sikkim; can also organise visits to Bhutan and the North-East Region.

Yak & Yeti Travels
Hotel Superview Himalchuli, NH 31A, Zero Point (☎ 22714; fax 24643); good value and run by the enthusiastic Satish Bardewa, who also has mountaineering experience.

Sikkim Tours & Travels
Church Rd, near the private bus stand (☎ 22188; fax 22707 attn 'Sikkim Tours'); Lukendra (Luke) here is a keen photographer, and can also organise tailor-made photography and bird-watching tours.

Siniolchu Tours & Travels
Paljor Stadium Rd (☎ 24457; fax 22707 attn 'Siniolchu'); also offers a wide range of tours, including a four day cultural tour of the gompas of Sikkim – US$120 per person with accommodation in tents.

Blue Sky Tours & Travels
opposite the Hotel Lhakpa on Tibet Rd (☎ /fax 23330); as well as treks to West Sikkim, this company also has tours to North Sikkim.

Sikkim World Expeditions
Zero Point, National Highway 31A (☎ 23494; fax 24195); also operates tours to North Sikkim.

Mahayana Tours & Travels
Room 23, Super Market Complex (☎ 23885; fax 22707 attn 'Mahayana'); offers a range of treks, including gompa treks and an eight day rhododendron trek from Yuksom to Bakhim, Dzongri, Phidong and Tsoska.

Yoksam Tours & Travels
National Highway 31A (☎ 23473; fax 22707 attn 'Yoksam'); organises treks to West Sikkim and tours to North Sikkim.

Potala Tours & Travels
Paljor Stadium Rd (☎ 22041); offers the usual range of treks at attractive prices.

Mayur Travels
Paljor Stadium Rd (☎ 24462); near Potala Tours, also organises local sightseeing trips.

Tashila Tours & Travels
National Highway 31A, opposite the private bus stand (☎ 22979; fax 22155); managed by Alok Raj Pradhan, who can also arrange special-interest tours such as high-altitude rhododendron and primula tours (the primulas are at their best in May and June).

Places to Stay

In the winter it's important to enquire about the availability of hot water and heating. A bucket of hot water for showering is available at most places (sometimes for a small extra charge), but heating is a rarity. Where an electric heater is available it will defi-

nitely cost you more. Very few places have single rooms, and there's often no discount for single occupancy of a double room.

Always enquire about low-season discounts wherever you stay. They vary between 15% and 30%, usually from around January to March, and in July and August.

Places to Stay – bottom end

Hotel Lhakpa (☎ 23002), Tibet Rd (above MG Marg), has very basic rooms with common bath for Rs 50/90, doubles with attached bath for Rs 150, and with geyser, Rs 200. There's a little bar downstairs with a good sound system, and the manager is a friendly, helpful fellow.

Modern Central Lodge (☎ 24670), Tibet Rd, is very popular with travellers. It's run by two friendly Sikkimese brothers, Sonam and Karma. Most rooms have attached baths, some with geysers. The brothers are compiling a very useful travellers' comment book, and have free maps with handy transport information. Dorm beds are Rs 30, singles are Rs 60, doubles with attached toilet are Rs 80 (these rooms are a little dark) or Rs 100 with good views. With attached bath, rooms cost from Rs 100/120 to Rs 180/200, the most expensive rooms having the best views and geysers in the bathrooms. There's a TV room, snooker room, restaurant, and roof terrace.

Green Hotel (☎ 23354) is on MG Marg, by the tourist office. There's a range of rooms, from Rs 120/150 with attached bath and hot water in buckets to Rs 200/250 for rooms with bath and geyser. The cheaper rooms are in the old block, and some are a little dark. There's a popular bar and restaurant.

Siniolchu Lodge (☎ 22074) is very cheap, and run by a friendly manager, but it's a long way from the centre and a strenuous hike uphill, just below the entrance to Enchey Gompa. Rooms with attached bath (hot water in buckets) are Rs 60/110, deluxe rooms with geyser are Rs 90/170. A taxi will charge Rs 20 to take you up here from the centre.

Hotel Laden La (☎ 23058) is a tiny place at the back of the Lall Market. Rustic rooms with common bath are Rs 85/160. Those at the front have great views down over the busy market. There's a bar downstairs.

Hotel Lhakhar (☎ 22198) is right opposite the SNT bus stand. Rooms with common bath cost Rs 80/150 and doubles/triples with attached bath are Rs 250/300. This is a pleasant place, run by a friendly Tibetan couple, with basic, but spotless rooms.

Blue Heaven Lodge (☎ 23827), Paljor Stadium Rd, is clean and friendly. All rooms have attached bathroom and constant hot water. Some rooms even have 'honeymoon' beds (just standard double beds but something of a rarity here). Rooms are from Rs 150/200 to Rs 275/350 – the more expensive ones come with a view.

Sunny Guest House (☎ 22179) is at the private bus stand. Doubles with common bath are Rs 160; doubles with attached bath are Rs 280 and Rs 320, the latter with a balcony and good views. This is a friendly place, and not bad value.

Places to Stay – middle

Most mid-range places add an additional 10% service charge to the bill.

Gangtok Lodge, diagonally opposite the tourist office on MG Marg, is friendly and central. Doubles are Rs 300 with attached bath (cold water, but there's a geyser in the common bathroom), or with a view, Rs 320. Good discounts are offered in the off season.

Pine Ridge Hotel (☎ 24958), near the Legislative Assembly, is run by the owners of Modern Central Lodge. All rooms have attached bath and range from Rs 325/400 to Rs 375/475. It's a good place but the cheaper rooms are quite small.

Hotel Sonam Delek (☎ 22566), on Tibet Rd, is pleasant. Doubles with common bath are Rs 175, or with attached bath Rs 450 (no view) and Rs 600 (with possibly the best views you'll get in Gangtok). A 40% discount is offered in the off season, and there's a good restaurant here.

Hotel Tibet (☎ 22523; fax 22707) is a popular choice. You'll be welcomed by a doorman in full traditional Tibetan dress. Rooms range from Rs 520/695 to Rs 1310/1750. There's 24 hour room service, foreign exchange facilities, a travel desk and a small bookshop with books on Tibetan issues. Most of the cheaper rooms are on the road side, and are a little small, as are the mid-range rooms on the valley side. The more expensive rooms are very plush, with traditional Tibetan decor. Its Snow Lion Restaurant has the best food in Gangtok.

Hotel Superview Himalchuli (☎ 22714) is a pleasant hotel with excellent views and very helpful staff. It's set just out of the main part of town towards Zero Point. Doubles/triples with attached bath are Rs 475/575, and there's also dormitory accommodation for Rs 50. There are good off season discounts, a bar, a garden restaurant, and a telescope for mountain viewing. Yak & Yeti Travels have their office here.

Hotel Mount View (☎ 23647) is on Paljor Stadium Rd. All rooms are doubles, but single occupancy is available. Singles/doubles range from Rs 270/385 to Rs 675/900. All are well appointed, and have attached baths with 24 hour hot water, and colour TVs.

Denzong Inn (☎ 22692) is in the Denzong Cinema complex, just outside Lall Market. Rooms with attached bath and geyser are Rs 300/400, and there's an enormous suite for Rs 1500 which could comfortably accommodate four people. Kitchen facilities cost an extra Rs 200 per day, and the hotel can provide utensils and gas. The cheaper rooms are nothing special, but some open onto a roof terrace with great Kanchenjunga views.

Places to Stay – top end

Hotel Tashi Delek (☎ 22991; fax 22362) is centrally located on MG Marg. The tiny ornate doorway opens onto an opulent lobby with traditional Tibetan woodcarving and Tibetan *objets d'art*. Singles/doubles are Rs 2200/2700, double suites are Rs 3500, and prices include all meals. In the low season they may offer rooms without meals for Rs 1800/1900. The double deluxe suites have great mountain views; the less-expensive rooms are comfortable, but not flash. There's a pleasant rooftop garden with great views of Kanchenjunga.

Netuk House (☎ 22374) is the home of an old Sikkimese family, the Denzongpas, and part of the 'Heritage Houses of the Himalayas' association which includes the Windamere in Darjeeling (they also take bookings for Netuk House). Rates are Rs 1400/2200 with all meals. There are just eight rooms, all with attached bath and constant hot water.

Nor-Khill Hotel (☎ 23186; fax 23187), above the stadium, was once the royal guesthouse. It's now a comfortable hotel with singles/doubles for Rs 2400/2800 including all meals, Rs 1800/2000 without. There's a travel desk, gift shop and foreign exchange, and the hotel is set in attractive gardens.

Places to Eat

Most of the hotels in Gangtok have their own restaurants and some of them are very good.

Modern Central Lodge, ***Hotel Lhakpa***, ***Hotel Lakhar***, *and* ***Green Hotel*** have restaurants which are popular with travellers. All offer cheap, tasty and filling meals in a variety of cuisines – usually Tibetan, Chinese and Indian – with some western alternatives such as pancakes. Chicken fried rice will set you back about Rs 25 at these places, tsampa is around Rs 15.

Oyster Restaurant, at the Hotel Sonam Delek, is a bit more upmarket. There are continental favourites such as French toast and banana pancakes, as well as Chinese, Indian and Tibetan cuisine. It's not too expensive: the chicken Kashmiri is Rs 40.

New Kho-Chi Restaurant & Bar is in a handy location beneath the Gangtok Lodge on MG Marg. There's an extensive Chinese and Indian menu, with most main dishes under Rs 50.

Metro Fast Food is a cheap South Indian snack bar opposite Gangtok Lodge. Masala dosas are Rs 15, and it's Rs 10 for a lassi.

Kikis Garden Restaurant is on the top floor of the Super Market complex. During the season there's a buffet here featuring Sikkimese cuisine, for Rs 70 per person. The restaurant is nothing flash, but there are great views of Kanchenjunga.

Blue Poppy Restaurant is at the Hotel Tashi Delek. They do good Sikkimese cuisine

but it must be ordered 12 hours in advance. Veg dishes range from Rs 30 to Rs 65, and non-veg dishes are Rs 70 to Rs 100.

Snow Lion Restaurant, at the Hotel Tibet, is without doubt the best place to eat in Gangtok. There's Tibetan cuisine, some Japanese and seafood dishes and good Indian food from their tandoor. It's not too expensive: most veg dishes are Rs 40, and nonveg dishes are Rs 50 to Rs 70. The delicious and filling chicken korma is Rs 55. The house special is Mandarin fish (Rs 375), but 24 hours advance notice is required.

There are also numerous little seedy bars with prices that are refreshingly cheap after West Bengal. A beer will set you back about Rs 26, and a peg of whisky, Rs 8. Note that full-moon and new-moon days are 'dry' days throughout Sikkim. Try *tumba* from a chang shop in the market – a large bamboo mug full of fermenting millet.

Things to Buy

The Cottage Industries Emporium specialises in hand-woven carpets, blankets, shawls, Lepcha weaves, patterned decorative paper and Choktse tables, exquisitely carved in relief. It's open daily during the season, and in the off season, daily except Sunday and every second Saturday, from 9 am to 3.30 pm. There are numerous other shops selling Tibetan handicrafts.

Getting There & Away

Air Bagdogra is the nearest airport. Indian Airlines (☎ 23099) has an agency on Tibet Rd.

Buses Sikkim Nationalised Transport (SNT) is the main bus operator to Gangtok, and they have plenty of services from their well-organised bus stand on Paljor Stadium Rd. Book as far in advance as possible, particularly during the Durga Puja holiday period. The booking office is open from 9 am to noon and 1 to 2 pm.

There are daily buses to Siliguri (Rs 47, five hours), Kalimpong (Rs 36, three hours), Darjeeling (Rs 65, seven hours) and Bagdogra (Rs 55, 4½ hours).

In addition to the SNT buses, there are

private buses which run from the private bus stand (adjacent to Sunny Guest House) to Siliguri, Darjeeling and Kalimpong. To Siliguri there are at least 10 buses daily (mostly in the afternoon), and to Darjeeling and Kalimpong at least two daily. They cost much the same as the SNT buses, and should be booked in advance at the private bus stand.

SNT buses for destinations within Sikkim are Gezing (for Pemayangtse) at 7 am (Rs 46, 4½ hours) – buses travel via Singtam, Rablonga, Kewzing and Legship (for connections to Tashiling and Yuksom); Rumtek at 4 pm (Rs 12, 1½ hours); Phodang at 7 and 8 am and 1.30 and 4 pm (Rs 16, 2½ hours); and Jorethang at 7 am and 2 pm (Rs 33, four hours).

Train There's a railway reservation counter at the SNT bus stand on Paljor Stadium Rd.

Taxi & Jeep Share jeeps are a faster and generally more comfortable alternative to buses.

At the private bus stand you can get share jeeps to Siliguri (Rs 85, 3½ hours), Darjeeling (Rs 105, four hours) and Kalimpong (Rs 50, 2½ hours).

From Children's Park, jeeps leave for destinations in West Sikkim such as Jorethang (Rs 55, three hours), Gezing (Rs 75, 5½ hours) and on to Pelling (Rs 95, six hours from Gangtok); and in North Sikkim to Phodang (Rs 35, two hours), as well as for Tsongo Lake (Rs 150, two hours, season only).

From Lall Market, you can get share jeeps to Rumtek and Tsongo Lake. During the season, share jeeps for Rumtek leave when full between 2 and 4 pm (Rs 30, one hour), and return between 6 am and 4 pm. In the off season, they leave between 11 am and 3 pm, and return between 6 and 8 am. Share jeeps for Tsongo Lake leave in the season only at 9 am and 2 pm (Rs 150, two hours), and return between noon and 2 pm.

Getting Around
The new city bus service, bitterly opposed by the taxi wallahs, should now be running along National Highway 31A.

All the taxis are new or near-new Maruti vans. Rs 20 will get you just about anywhere around town. To Rumtek you're looking at about Rs 280 return, including about an hour at the gompa.

AROUND GANGTOK
Rumtek Gompa
Rumtek, on the other side of the Ranipul Valley, is visible from Gangtok though it's 24km away by road. The monastery is the seat of the Gyalwa Karmapa, the head of the Kagyu-pa order of Tibetan Buddhism. The order was founded in the 11th century by Lama Marpa, the disciple of the Indian guru Naropa, and later split into several subsects, the most important of which are Druk-pa, Kagyu-pa and Karma-pa.

The main monastery is a recent structure, built by the Gyalwa Karmapa in strict accordance with the traditional designs of his monastery in Tibet. Visitors are welcome and there's no objection to your sitting in on the

Buddhist image in Rumtek monastery.

prayer and chanting sessions. They'll even bring you a cup of salted butter tea when it's served to the monks. Mural work here is exquisite and a visit is a must if you're interested in the Tibetan style of religious painting.

The main *chaam*, or religious dance, known as Tse Chu, is performed on the 10th day of the fifth lunar month (July), and depicts events in Guru Rimpoche's life. Another chaam, presenting the battle between good and evil, takes place two days before Tibetan New Year.

Most activity takes place in the late afternoon, but the gompa is open for visitors from 8 am to 5 pm in summer, and 10 am to 5 pm in winter. If you find the main door locked, ask around for someone to open it up for you, which they are quite happy to do.

If you follow the tarmac road for two or three km beyond Rumtek, through a gate off to the left you'll find another interesting, but smaller, monastery which was restored in 1983. Opposite is an old and run-down monastery with leather prayer wheels.

Places to Stay & Eat The *Sangay Hotel*, 100m down the motor road from the monastery, is a friendly little place. It's basic but clean, and blankets are provided. Rooms cost Rs 50/80 with common bath and hot water by the bucket. Cheap and basic meals are available.

Hotel Kunga Delek, where rooms are Rs 80/160, is opposite the main entrance.

Martam Resort (☎ (03592) 23314) is five km from Rumtek, in the village of Martam. Rooms cost Rs 1350/1800 with all meals. It's in a beautiful location in the middle of a paddy field, and staff here can arrange horse riding and treks in the surrounding area.

Getting There & Away There are buses and share jeeps to Rumtek from Gangtok. See Getting There & Away in the Gangtok section for details. If you feel like a bit of exercise, it's a very pleasant 12km walk (downhill) to the National Highway, from where it's easy to get a ride for the 12km (uphill!) trip to Gangtok.

Tsongo Lake
Lying 35km north-east of Gangtok, foreigners have recently been permitted to visit this lake; technically you should be in a group of four, and need to join a tour (US$12). Permits are valid for a day visit only. Numerous agencies in Gangtok offer tours to the lake, and can arrange the requisite permit.

North Sikkim

Previously foreigners were only permitted to travel as far north as Phodang, 38km by road to the north of Gangtok, which is accessible on the standard tourist permit. However, it is now possible to visit Yumthang, 102km further north via the villages of Mangan and Chungthang. At the time of writing it was necessary to make arrangements through a travel agency in Gangtok and join a tour with a minimum of four people.

PHODANG
Phodang Gompa, north of Gangtok along a winding but largely tarmac road, belongs to the same order (Kagyu-pa) as Rumtek, but is much smaller and less ornate than that gompa. After the 16th Karmapa fled from Tibet and before he installed himself in Rumtek in 1959, Phodang was the most important of Sikkim's three Kagyu-pa gompas (the third is Ralang Gompa). Here you can feel the timelessness of a part of Sikkim which tourists rarely visit. The gompa sits high up above the main road to Mangan and there are tremendous views down into the valley below.

Phodang is a fairly recent structure, although the original gompa here was founded, like Rumtek, in 1740. The gompa has a community of about 60 monks, many of them born in India after the Chinese occupation of Tibet. They're very friendly and are happy to show you around.

Opposite the gompa is a small community of nuns who belong to the same order. **Labrang Gompa**, two km further uphill beyond Phodang Gompa, was established in 1844, and belongs to the Nyingma-pa order. Beware of leeches when walking up here.

Places to Stay & Eat
The village of Phodang straddles the main Gangtok to Mangan road, and is about one km north of the turn-off to the gompas towards Mangan. There are a couple of basic places to stay here.

Yak & Yeti Lodge has clean rooms with common bath for Rs 50/80, and doubles with attached bath for Rs 120.

Northway Lodge has doubles with common bath for Rs 80, some with good views, and you can also get basic meals here.

Getting There & Away
See the Gangtok section for details of local buses and taxis to Phodang.

YUMTHANG VALLEY
The Yumthang Valley lies 140km north of Gangtok, at an elevation of 3564m. This region has recently been opened to foreigners, but trekking is still prohibited. The best time to visit is in April and May, when the rhododendrons are in full bloom. There are hot springs, covered by a wooden shelter. To get here, you'll need to join a tour, and local travel agencies can arrange the requisite permits. The road from Gangtok follows the Teesta River, crossing a spectacular gorge over the Rang Rang suspension bridge.

Western Sikkim

This area of Sikkim is attracting more and more visitors. Its main attractions, other than trekking up to Dzongri at the base of Kanchenjunga, are the two old monasteries of Pemayangtse and Tashiling, and hikes in the Pemayangtse area.

JORETHANG & NAYA BAZAAR
An important transport hub and administrative centre, Jorethang lies on the east side of the Rangeet River, only 30km north of

Darjeeling, and flanked by its twin city, Naya Bazaar.

Hotel Rangeet Valley, opposite the bus stand, has rooms with attached bath, nets and fans for Rs 100/200; the restaurant is very popular.

Hotel Namgyal, just past the bus stand towards the bridge, is the best place to stay. Singles/doubles/triples with attached bath are Rs 150/300/400, and are spotless.

From Jorethang, there are direct buses to Yuksom at 8 and 9.30 am (Rs 28, three hours), and to Legship at 11.30 am and 4.30 pm (Rs 12, one hour), continuing through to Gezing (2½ hours). There are share jeeps to Darjeeling (three hours), Gangtok (three hours), Siliguri (3½ hours), Gezing (2½ hours) and Legship (one hour).

LEGSHIP
Legship lies 100km west of Gangtok, and 27km north of Jorethang, on the banks of the Rangeet River. It's a chaotic and cluttered little village surrounded by wooded hills,

A Sikkimese woman displaying some of the region's distinctive jewellery.

and has a certain ramshackle appeal, with the colourful produce of fruit and vegie sellers piled in pyramids in wooden shacks flanking the main road. There's a police checkpost here.

GEZING

The road from Legship leaves the river and ascends high up above the village for 15km to Gezing (Gyalshing), an important transport junction. On Friday, villagers from outlying regions bring their produce into town and a colourful and busy market dominates the main square. Travellers cheques can be exchanged at the Central Bank of India, down a lane behind the town square.

Places to Stay

There are half a dozen hotels around the town square; most are pretty basic.

Hotel Kanchanzonga, above the square on the right, has doubles for Rs 80 with common bath.

Hotel Mayalu has rustic doubles/triples for Rs 50/75.

Hotel Attri (☎ (03593) 50602) is a new place above the square. Rooms are from Rs 350/450 with attached bath and constant hot water, and there are good views from the roof terrace.

Getting There & Away

There are SNT buses to Gangtok at 9 am and 1 pm (Rs 42, 4½ hours); and to Pelling (Rs 4, 30 minutes) at 8.30 am, 1 and 2 pm (many more buses on Friday). To Yuksom, buses leave at 1 and 2 pm (Rs 22, four hours); there are also buses to Tashiling, Jorethang and Siliguri. To get to Kalimpong, change buses at either Meli Bazaar or Teesta Bazaar; for Darjeeling change at Jorethang.

There are numerous share jeeps to Pelling (Rs 15), and also to Gangtok via Jorethang or Rablonga (both Rs 80, 4½ hours). There is one share jeep daily for Tashiling and Yuksom (Rs 50).

A taxi from the town square will charge Rs 200 to Pelling and Rs 600 to Jorethang.

PELLING & PEMAYANGTSE GOMPA

Tel Area Code: 03593

Pelling is a pleasant little town perched high on a ridge, 2.5km from Pemayangtse Gompa. There are great views north to Kanchenjunga and also to the south when the weather is clear.

Most travellers to western Sikkim use Pelling as their base. It offers the best budget accommodation and you can store gear while you trek.

The town has a post office, but no foreign exchange facilities. In Lower Pelling, the Cottage Industries Training Centre sells jumpers, hats and scarves.

Pemayangtse Gompa

Standing at a height of 2085m and framed on two sides by snowcapped mountains, Pemayangtse (Perfect Sublime Lotus) is one of the state's oldest and most important monasteries. It was founded in 1705, but was badly damaged in the earthquakes of 1913 and 1960. It has been reconstructed several times and belongs to the Nyingma-pa sect, which was established by Padmasambhava in the 8th century. All the sect's monasteries are characterised by a prominent image of this teacher, together with two female consorts, and this monastery is the head of all others in Sikkim. You can recognise followers of the sect by their red caps.

The monastery is a three storey structure filled with wall paintings and sculptures. On the third floor you'll find *Zandog-palri*, a seven-tiered painted wooden model of the abode of Guru Rimpoche, complete with rainbows, angels and the whole panoply of Buddhas and bodhisattvas on the third floor. The model was built single-handedly by the late Dungzin Rinpoche in five years.

In February each year the chaam, or religious dance, is performed by the monks. The exact dates are the 28th and 29th days of the 12th lunar month.

You can walk here from Pelling in about 40 minutes. SNT buses between Gezing and Pelling pass by the turnoff for Pemayangtse, from where it's a 10 minute walk.

Other Things to See

It's excellent walking territory around here – despite the leeches!

A 45 minute walk west from Pelling along a well-defined track through the forest brings you to **Sangachoeling Gompa**. The monastery predates Pemayangtse by some 10 years and is the second-oldest in Sikkim. As at Pemayangtse, the interior walls are highly decorated with paintings.

Further afield are the **Sangay Waterfalls**, 10km from Pelling along the road to Dentam.

Places to Stay & Eat

There's a bit of building going on in Pelling, and several new hotels should open soon.

Hotel Garuda (☎ 50614) is in the centre where the buses stop. It's a friendly place, popular with travellers, and there's excellent trekking information available. You can also store excess gear here while you trek. Dorm beds cost Rs 30, or there are rooms for Rs 70/80 with common bath (hot water by the bucket), doubles with bath attached for Rs 150, and a deluxe double with constant hot water for Rs 350. There's good cheap food (Rs 16 for fried cheese momos).

Hotel Kabur, in Upper Pelling, lacks the atmosphere of the Garuda, but is still OK. Doubles are Rs 200 with attached bath (no single tariff). There's also a restaurant here.

Sikkim Tourist Centre (☎ 50855) is between these two places. The rooms (all doubles) have attached bath with hot water and cost Rs 650 (Rs 700 with a view), including two meals.

Hotel Mt Pandim (☎ 50756) is two km outside Pelling, at the foot of the road leading up to Pemayangtse. Run by Sikkim Tourism, it's known to the locals as the 'Tourist Lodge'. Rooms with attached bath cost Rs 300/400 or Rs 400/550 for deluxe rooms with a view of Kanchenjunga, all plus 10% service charge. There's a restaurant. It's a nice peaceful place and the views from the garden are superb, but some rooms are a bit tatty and the service could be better.

Getting There & Away

Although a number of buses pass through Pelling, the choice is far greater from Gezing. It's a 50 minute steep downhill walk to Gezing, via the obvious shortcuts from opposite the Hotel Garuda.

From Pelling there are buses to Dentam (Rs 15), Gezing (Rs 4), Rimbi, Jorethang, Yuksom and Khecheopari Lake.

There's one jeep which does a daily run to Gangtok at 6 am (Rs 90). Tickets should be booked the day before at the paan stall between the Sikkim Tourist Centre and the Hotel Garuda.

There are numerous share jeeps down to Gezing on market day (Friday) in the morning.

KHECHEOPARI LAKE

Pronounced 'catch a perry', and sometimes spelt Khechepari, Khecheopalri or Khechupherei, this place is a popular objective for trekkers. The sacred lake lies in a depression surrounded by prayer flags and forested hills. Resist the temptation to swim, as it's a holy place. If you feel like a dip, you can swim in the river downhill from Pelling en route to the lake. Take care!

By the lakeshore is the small Lepcha village of **Tsojo**, and about 1.5km above the lake is the Khecheopari Gompa.

There is a *trekkers' hut* and a *pilgrims' hut* at the lake. The trekkers' hut is grimy and dark – not very salubrious. A bed at the pilgrims' hut will cost around Rs 40. A better bet would be to accept the hospitality offered by villagers. There are several chai shops at the lake. It gets very cold here at night, so bring warm gear with you.

By road the lake is about 27km from Pelling; the walking trail is shorter, but much steeper, and will take about 4½ hours.

From Khecheopari it is possible to continue on foot to Yuksom. The short cut is confusing, so ask for advice whenever you meet anyone en route. It should take three hours to cover the distance between the lake and Yuksom.

There's one bus daily between Pelling and Khecheopari, leaving Pelling at 3 pm (two hours), and returning at 7 am.

SIKKIM

TASHILING

The friendly little town of Tashiling is becoming popular with trekkers. Technically you should have your permit endorsed in Gangtok to come here but there's currently no checkpoint.

Tashiling Gompa

Founded around 1716, Tashiling Monastery is perched atop an almost conical hill between the Rangeet and Ratong rivers, a 45 minute slog on foot from Tashiling village. In Sikkim, only Pemayangtse Monastery is more sacred. The Bumchu festival is held here on the 15th day of the first month (during March).

Places to Stay & Eat

Blue Bird Hotel is a welcoming little place with rooms for Rs 40 and good dal bhat in the restaurant.

Hotel Laxmi also has a restaurant and rooms for Rs 30/60.

Siniolchu Guest House charges Rs 50 for a good room. Meals are served with the family.

Getting There & Away

There is one bus daily to Yuksom (3 pm), and in the morning it passes through at 8 am on the return journey to Legship and Gezing. Share jeeps that pass through Tashiling are usually full.

YUKSOM

Yuksom (also spelt Yoksum and Yuksam), 35km by road from Pemayangtse, is the furthest north you can get by road in Western Sikkim, and the trailhead for those intending to trek to Dzongri.

The **Dubdu Monastery**, an hour's walk uphill from Yuksom, was the first capital of Sikkim, and was where the first monarch of Sikkim was crowned in 1641. It's worth a visit, but there are no monks here and it's only opened during special Buddhist festivals.

Construction of the channel for the Rathong Hydel Project is now in full swing (despite strong objections from environmental groups),

with the headquarters of the colony just above the Yuksom.

Places to Stay & Eat

A large new hotel is under construction at the far end of the village. Most of the other places are in the centre near the police post.

Arpun Restaurant serves basic meals and has singles/doubles for Rs 50/100.

Hotel Wild Orchid has clean rooms for Rs 75/100.

Hotel Dzongrila has basic rooms for Rs 50/100, as well as good food, beer and tumba. It's run by a friendly, English-speaking family.

Hotel Demazong, across the road, has doubles with common bath for Rs 150.

Tourist Bungalow No 1 is behind the Hotel Demazong.

Tourist Bungalow No 2 is 500m north of Yuksom on the Dzongri Trail. Beds at both tourist bungalows are Rs 40 and you need to make reservations for them in Gangtok. There's no hot water at either of these places.

Getting There & Away

There is one bus daily (in the morning) to Gezing (Rs 22) via Tashiling and Legship; and also a share jeep to Gezing for Rs 50.

TREKS IN SIKKIM

Pelling-Khecheopari Trek

Linking some interesting villages together in West Sikkim it's possible to do a four day trek. You don't need a trekking permit for this but you should get your Sikkim permit endorsed in Gangtok to allow you to visit the area around Pemayangtse, including Khecheopari Lake and Tashiling Gompa.

The first stage takes you to the lake. For the second stage, if you go via a short cut to Yuksom it takes only three hours, heading downhill for the first hour, and then for the last two hours, ascending gradually to Yuksom. From Yuksom to Tashiling you can follow the road, taking some of the obvious short cuts. Then it's an easy one-hour walk along the road to Legship. Bring snacks as there's not much on offer along the way, and check with locals and other travellers for the best short cuts.

Stage 1   Pelling to Khecheopari (4 hours)
Stage 2   Khecheopari to Yuksom (3 hours)
Stage 3   Yuksom to Tashiling (6 hours)
Stage 4   Tashiling to Legship (1 hour)

Yuksom-Dzongri-Goecha La Trek

The most popular trek in Sikkim is from Yuksom to Dzongri and Goecha La for superb views of Kanchenjunga. To undertake this trek you must get together a group of at least four people and make arrangements through a recognised travel agency in Gangtok; they'll arrange your trekking permit. They usually charge from US$35 to US$60 per person per day, including food, yaks and porters. Make sure everyone is clear about exactly what will be provided – particularly the food. At overnight stops there are trekkers' huts which are the best bet if it's cold. At the height of the season there's not enough space in the huts and your trekking company will need to provide tents. Whatever the option it is imperative not to trek too high too quickly.

From Yuksom (1630m) the trail follows the Rathong Valley through unspoilt forests to Baktim (2740m) where there's a *forest rest house*. From Baktim there is a steep ascent to the village of Tsokha (3050m), where a couple of *lodges* provide overnight accommodation. Above Tsokha the trail enters magnificent rhododendron forests to an intermediary camp at Pethang (3760m). It's a wise idea to either bring tents and spend a night here or spend two nights at Tsokha to acclimatise. A further stage brings you to Dzongri (4025m) where there are *trekkers' huts*. From Dablakang, 200m above Dzongri there are excellent mountain views. You should spend two nights at Dzongri to acclimatise; walk up to Dzongri La (four hours return, 4415m) for great views of Kabru and Dome.

From Dzongri the trail drops steeply down to the river where there's a new *trekkers' hut*; you follow the river to Thangshing (3840m) where there's another *trekkers' hut*. The final stop is at the *trekkers' hut* at Samiti Lake (4200m) from which an early morning assault is made up to the head-spinning Goecha La (4940m) for the best views of Kanchenjunga. Then it's down to Thangshing for the night and back to Yuksom two days later.

Stage 1   Yuksom to Tsokha (7 hours)
Stage 2   Tsokha to Pethang (3 hours)
Stage 3   Acclimatisation day
Stage 4   Pethang to Dzongri (2 to 3 hours)
Stage 5   Acclimatisation day
Stage 6   Dzongri to Samiti Lake (7 hours)
Stage 7   Samiti Lake to Goencha La and down to Thangshing (9 to 10 hours)
Stage 8   Thanshing to Tsokha (6 to 7 hours)
Stage 9   Tsokha to Yuksom (5 to 6 hours)

SIKKIM

North-Eastern Region

The north-eastern region is the most varied and at the same time the least visited part of India. Before Independence the whole region was known as Assam Province, but it was finally split into seven separate states.

In many ways the north-east is unlike the rest of India. It is the country's chief tribal area, with a great number of tribes and many different languages and dialects – in Arunachal Pradesh alone over 50 distinct languages are spoken! These tribal people have many similarities to the hill tribes, who live across an arc that stretches from the eastern end of the Himalaya through Myanmar (Burma) and Thailand into Laos.

Also, the north-east has a high percentage of Christians, particularly in the more isolated and remote areas where the population is predominantly hill tribespeople.

For a number of reasons India has always been touchy about the north-east, although it recently lifted the permit requirement for foreign tourists visiting Assam, Meghalaya and Tripura. The north-east is a sensitive border zone where India meets Bhutan, China, Myanmar and Bangladesh. Equally important, the region is remote – only the narrow Siliguri corridor connects it to the rest of India, and before Independence the usual route to Assam would have been through Bangladesh. Today, it involves making a long loop north and then east. Roads have been improved dramatically but there are still very few of them compared to the rest of India.

As well as the perceived threat from across the borders, the north-east states have been wracked by internal problems. In the mid-1980s a whole series of strikes and riots in quick succession led to widespread violence and terrorism. There were a number of reasons for this unrest, including a feeling of central government neglect (poor transport links and lack of infrastructure development were the main complaints). Very little of the oil wealth from Assam, for example, found its way back for the state's industrial development.

N-E REGION AT A GLANCE

ASSAM
Population: 25 million
Area: 78,000 sq km
Capital: Guwahati

MANIPUR
Population: 2 million
Area: 22,300 sq km
Capital: Imphal

MEGHALAYA
Population: 2 million
Area: 22,400 sq km
Capital: Shillong

NAGALAND
Population: 1.4 million
Area: 17,000 sq km
Capital: Kohima

TRIPURA
Population: 3 million
Area: 10,400 sq km
Capital: Agartala

ARUNACHAL PRADESH
Population: 1 million
Area: 84,000 sq km
Capital: Itanagar

MIZORAM
Population: 820,000
Area: 21,000 sq km
Capital: Aizawl

Locator & Map Index

Highlights

- The Vaishanavaite monasteries of Majuli, the world's biggest river island
- Spotting a rhino from elephant-back in Kaziranga National Park
- Tawang Gompa, the most important gompa in the North East
- The pseudo Scottishness of Shillong hill station

Festivals

Ambuchi Festival – Guwahati – July

The whole region remained overwhelmingly agricultural.

But economic neglect and exploitation was only a minor issue. The main issue was about the inflow of 'foreigners' into the region. Military repression and economic stagnation, combined with high birth rates in Bangladesh, pushed thousands of Bangladeshis over the lightly policed borders into the north-eastern region. The influx was so great that, in some cases, it threatened to outnumber the indigenous population, and the demands for the Bangladeshis' repatriation became more and more strident. Such wholesale repatriation would have presented the central government with an extremely difficult problem since few of the 'foreigners' carried identification papers making it almost impossible to decide which of them had arrived recently and which had lived in the region for generations – legally or otherwise.

Lack of action in addressing the indigenous population's grievances, however, proved catastrophic. In 1983, wholesale massacres of 'foreigners' began to take place and photographs of their bodies floating down various tributaries of the Ganges and Brahmaputra rivers appeared in the world's press. The

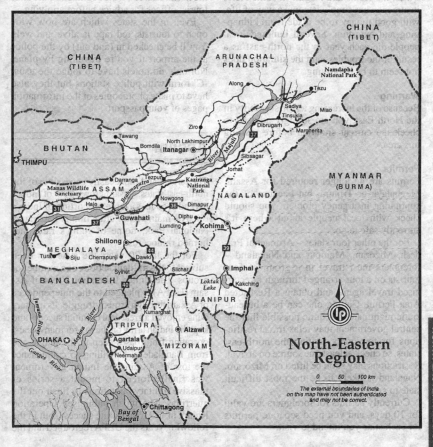

North-Eastern Region

The external boundaries of India on this map have not been authenticated and may not be correct.

0   50   100 km

killings eventually subsided but, in 1991, the states bordering Myanmar (Burma) were hit with more refugees following the Myanmar army's massive drive against the Muslim inhabitants in the country's north-west. As a result, tens of thousands of refugees fled over the border into Mizoram, Manipur and Nagaland.

Matters have been complicated by the demands of various ethnic minorities within the states themselves. In Assam, for example, the Bodos are demanding a homeland separate from the rest of the state. In Manipur, there is continued fighting between rival tribes, the Kukis and Nagas. In some states insurgency has simply become a way of life, with good money to be made from kidnapping and extortion. Several hundred local people die each year in the north-east as a result of the troubles; and the situation does not seem to be improving.

Warning
Because of the increasing terrorist activity in the North East, you are strongly advised to check the current situation before visiting this area.

Permits
Permits are no longer required for Assam, Meghalaya or Tripura, but because of the continuing insurgency problem you should check with local people about where it's currently safe to go.

For the other four states – Arunachal Pradesh, Mizoram, Manipur and Nagaland – foreigners must travel in a group of four tourists on a tour arranged through a recognised travel agent, and obtain a Restricted Area Permit. Getting one can be a bureaucratic nightmare. It's quite possible that the central government may relax travel restrictions for foreigners visiting the north-east states, so check at least one source on arrival. Restrictions may soon be lifted on Mizoram. Nagaland is likely to be the most difficult state to get a permit for.

Currently permits for foreigners are valid for 10 days, and you need separate permits for each state you intend to visit.

If your patience knows no bounds and you want to try your luck at getting into these states without going through a travel agent and being part of a group of four, you'll either need a very good excuse for visiting (a relative buried in the war graves in Kohima, for example) or friends in high places. Permits can be applied for at any overseas Indian consular office, or in India at the Ministry of Home Affairs, Foreigners' Division, Lok Nayak Bhavan, Khan Market, New Delhi 110003; and at Foreigners' Registration Offices in Delhi, Mumbai and Calcutta. Apply at least a month before you wish to visit the north-east. It's worth contacting the state tourist offices for advice before applying.

Even in the states which are now wide open to tourists, red tape is alive and well. You'll be checked in (and out) by the police at the airport if you're travelling by plane. Not only do hotels have to lodge the usual 'C' form with police stations but they also have to make photocopies of the information pages of your passport.

Assam

The largest and most easily accessible of the north-east states, Assam grows 60% of India's tea and produces a large proportion of India's oil. The main visitor attraction is Kaziranga National Park, home of India's rare one-horned rhinoceros.

For the last 20 years the state has been subject to the militant actions of a number of groups. The United Liberation Front of Assam (ULFA) is pledged to the independence of Assam through armed struggle. Its military wing enjoyed a great deal of initial success and kept the Indian army on the run for many years, operating from bases deep in the jungle and from Bangladesh. Unwilling to countenance the loss of Assam, the Indian government was finally forced to mount a series of massive military operations to flush out the guerrillas. The much publicised Operation Rhino, in 1991, had some success, but in the following years the ULFA regrouped and the bombings, kidnappings and killings have continued.

While the ULFA demand an independent Assam, the Bodo ethnic minority has been campaigning for the state to be split 50:50 with autonomy for their proposed Bodoland. There are now several Bodo groups, the most militant being the Bodo Liberation Tiger Force (BLTF). In December 1996 they bombed an express train just outside Guwahati, killing 33 people and injuring many others. In the same month the BLTF destroyed a bridge on the NH31 as a bus was crossing it.

The government's Unified Command counter insurgency operation is now in operation, and the army has a high profile. You are strongly advised to check on the current situation before visiting Assam.

GUWAHATI (Gauhati/Gawahati)
Pop: 660,000   Tel Area Code: 0361
Situated beside the impressively wide and muddy Brahmaputra River, Guwahati is Assam's sleepy capital. Once known as Pragjyotishpura (the Eastern City of Light) and mentioned in the Mahabharata, it has long been the most important town in the region. It's now the service centre for the oil industry and tea plantations; the world's largest tea auctions are held here.

Guwahati is a pleasant, relaxed place. There are numerous ancient Hindu temples in and around the town, but its main importance is as the gateway to the whole of the north-eastern region.

Orientation
Guwahati is split into two towns on either side of the river, but most places of interest and the offices are in the southern section. This is simply known as Guwahati (the northern section is North Guwahati).

The bus and railway stations are side by side. The busiest shopping areas are Fancy Bazaar and Paan Bazaar, both about one km west of the railway station.

Information
Assam Tourism's office (☎ 544475) is at the Tourist Lodge on Station Rd. It's open Monday to Friday from 10 am to 5 pm, and on Saturday until 1 pm. There's also a Government of India tourist office (☎ 547407) on BK Kakoti Rd. Neither office has much in the way of leaflets but they're keen to help. Meghalaya Tourism has a little office at the bus station.

Assam Tourism runs a city tour on Wednesday and Sunday from 9 am to 3 pm; tickets cost Rs 70. They also run two-day tours to Kaziranga for Rs 530.

ANZ Grindlays on GN Bordoloi Rd is a good place to change money. It's open Monday to Friday from 10 am to 3 pm, and until 12.30 pm on Saturday.

Network Travels (☎ 512700), GS Rd, is the Indian Airlines agent and can book other airlines. Jungle Travels (☎ 547862), GN Bordoloi Rd, is the American Express agent; they have package trips to Kaziranga.

Modern Book Depot, HB Rd, has a good range of books on the north-eastern region.

Guwahati Medical College Hospital (☎ 562159) is five km south of the centre off GS Rd.

Umananda Temple
The most interesting thing about this Siva temple is its location, on Peacock Island in the middle of the river. Ferries make regular crossings from 7 am to 5 pm, charging Rs 6 for a return trip.

Navagrah Temple
Situated on Chitrachal Hill to the east of the town, the Temple of the Nine Planets has long been known as a centre of astrology and astronomy. The nine planets are represented by nine linga inside the main temple.

Kamakhya Temple
Guwahati's best known temple is the Kamakhya Temple on Nilachal Hill, eight km west of the city. The temple is the centre for Shakti worship and Tantric Hinduism because when Siva sorrowfully carried away the corpse of his first wife, Shakti, her *yoni* fell here.

The temple was rebuilt in 1665 after being destroyed by Muslim invaders, but its origins are much older than that. It was probably an ancient Khasi sacrificial site, and sacrifices are still very much part of worshipping here. Groups of devotees arrive each morning with goats to offer to Shakti.

It attracts pilgrims from all over India, especially during the Ambuchi Festival which usually falls around July. This is a celebration of the end of the earth's menstrual cycle.

Leave your shoes with one of the *prasad* sellers near the entrance. Temple policy on admitting non-Hindus to the inner sanctum seems to vary from day to day – join the queue and try your luck. Inside it's dark and

a little eerie; and the floor's sticky with the blood of sacrificed goats.

You can get here on bus No 16 from the town centre.

Assam State Museum

This archaeological, ethnographic and natural history museum has recently been enlarged and is well worth a visit. Particularly interesting are the dioramas of Assamese tribal villages – in one you walk right through the reconstructed huts. There are also good displays of weavings, musical instruments and a large sculpture gallery.

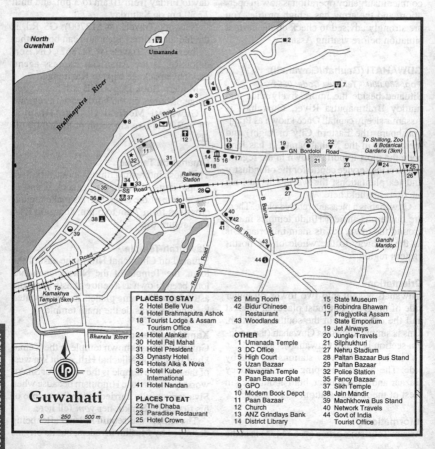

PLACES TO STAY
2 Hotel Belle Vue
4 Hotel Brahmaputra Ashok
18 Tourist Lodge & Assam Tourism Office
24 Hotel Alankar
30 Hotel Raj Mahal
31 Hotel President
33 Dynasty Hotel
34 Hotels Alka & Nova
36 Hotel Kuber International
41 Hotel Nandan

PLACES TO EAT
22 The Dhaba
23 Paradise Restaurant
25 Hotel Crown
26 Ming Room
42 Bidur Chinese Restaurant
43 Woodlands

OTHER
1 Umananda Temple
3 DC Office
5 High Court
6 Uzan Bazaar
7 Navagrah Temple
8 Paan Bazaar Ghat
9 GPO
10 Modem Book Depot
11 Paan Bazaar
12 Church
13 ANZ Grindlays Bank
14 District Library
15 State Museum
16 Robindra Bhawan
17 Pragjyotika Assam State Emporium
19 Jet Airways
20 Jungle Travels
21 Silphukhuri
27 Nehru Stadium
28 Paltan Bazaar Bus Stand
29 Paltan Bazaar
32 Police Station
35 Fancy Bazaar
37 Sikh Temple
38 Jain Mandir
39 Machkhowa Bus Stand
40 Network Travels
44 Govt of India Tourist Office

Guwahati

0   250   500 m

Bharalu River

To Kamakhya Temple (5km)

North Guwahati

Brahmaputra River

MG Road

Railway Station

SS Road

AT Road

Rehabari Road

B Barua Road

GS Road

GN Bordoloi Road

To Shillong, Zoo & Botanical Gardens (3km)

Gandhi Mandop

The museum is open daily except Monday, from 10 am to 4.15 pm (5 pm in summer). It's also closed on Sunday afternoon and on the second and fourth Saturday of each month. Entry is Rs 2.

Assam State Zoo & Botanical Gardens
The zoo & botanical gardens are about five km east of the railway station. The zoo is reasonably well managed and has tigers, leopards, and, of course, Assam's famous rhinos – plus the African two-horned variety for comparison. They're open daily except Friday; entry is Rs 3.

Places to Stay – bottom end
Prices of hotels listed here do not include tax, which is currently 10% on hotels costing Rs 100 to Rs 199, 15% on Rs 200 to Rs 299, and 20% on Rs 300 and above. To this some hotels also add a 10% service charge.

Hotel Alankar is about three km from the station, on GN Bordoloi Rd. It's good value and run by friendly people. There are dorm beds for Rs 25, singles with common bath for Rs 50, and rooms with bath attached for Rs 75/121. The rooms in the annexe at the back are quietest.

Hotel Alka is on MS Rd in Fancy Bazaar, right in the heart of the town. There are rooms with common bath for Rs 65/98, and three rooms with attached bath for Rs 145/200.

Tourist Lodge (☎ 544475), on Station Rd, is run by Assam Tourism which has an office here. Very close to the station, the lodge is rather shabby but not too bad. There are dorm beds for Rs 30 and doubles from Rs 170 which they'll occasionally rent as singles for Rs 100. All rooms have attached bath, and hot water is available in buckets. There's a basic restaurant.

Railway retiring rooms offer a range of accommodation from Rs 35 in the dorm to Rs 150 for an air-con double.

Hotel Nova (☎ 523464), SS Rd, is in busy Fancy Bazaar, about 1.5km west of the bus and railway stations. It's a good place although describing itself as a 'classic hotel for classy people' may be overstating it! There are rooms with attached bath from Rs 160/250 to Rs 280/45 (air-con) and they even take credit cards.

Places to Stay – middle
Hotel Kuber International (☎ 520807), HB Rd, is a well-known hotel, also in Fancy Bazaar. It's a little run-down but fine, and all rooms have bath attached. They cost Rs 200/300, or Rs 325/425 for air-con. The restaurant is quite good.

Hotel President (☎ 544979), GN Bordoloi Rd, is a reasonable place with rooms from Rs 275/400 with attached bath, and Rs 500/600 with air-con. It's also quite centrally located.

Hotel Belle Vue (☎ 540847), 'where the chirping of birds provides the wake-up call', is quite a long way from the centre but in a very peaceful, elevated location with views over the river. The rooms are large and all have attached bath and TV. Ordinary rooms cost Rs 625/750, deluxe rooms are Rs 825/950.

Hotel Nandan (☎ 540855) is a comfortable three-star place conveniently located on GS Rd, near the railway station. There are rooms without air-con from Rs 350/575, and with air-con from Rs 595/775. There's an excellent restaurant, a bar and all rooms have attached bathrooms and Star TV.

Places to Stay – top end
Hotel Raj Mahal (☎ 522476), AT Rd, is an imposing modern hotel south of the railway station. Centrally air-conditioned rooms cost from Rs 650/850 to Rs 850/1450.

Hotel Brahmaputra Ashok (☎ 541064; fax 540870), is in an excellent location right by the river on MG Rd. Rooms are large and airy and some have wonderful river views, so you can watch the dramatic sunset from the comfort of your bed. Singles/doubles are Rs 1195/1400. There's a restaurant and bar.

Dynasty Hotel (☎ 510496; fax 522112), on SS Rd and right in the centre of town, is a favourite with business people. The comfortable rooms all have air-con, attached bath and Star TV; prices range from Rs 950/1350 to Rs 3500 (for the suite).

Places to Eat

Fish is a big feature of Guwahati menus and can be very good. The most common fish are known locally as rahu, elish, puthi and chital; in cheap restaurants they range from Rs 7 to Rs 20 per plate.

All but the cheapest restaurants add 8% sales tax to the bill, and some also add a 10% service charge. No alcohol is available anywhere on the first day of each month, it being pay day.

Paradise Restaurant on GN Bordoloi Rd is the place to go to try local cuisine. Assamese thalis cost Rs 35/40 for veg/non-veg and the waiters will explain what everything is. It's open daily from 10 am to 3.30 pm and from 6 to 9.30 pm. Beer costs Rs 50 in the bar upstairs which closes at 7.30 pm.

The Dhaba, not far from Paradise Restaurant on the same road, is an open-air North Indian place. It's clean and good value – chicken Mughlai is Rs 33, mattar paneer is Rs 18.

Hotel Crown, GN Bordoloi Rd, near the flyover, is a very basic place serving fish curry rice for Rs 20.

Ming Room is hidden away under the flyover off GN Bordoloi Rd. As the name suggests it's a Chinese restaurant, currently the best in Guwahati. Freshwater prawns cost Rs 110; most non-veg dishes are around Rs 70.

Bidur Chinese Restaurant on GS Rd is cheap and does some Tibetan dishes. Momos are five for Rs 20. In the evening it closes at 7.30 pm.

Woodlands on GS Rd is a well-known south Indian vegetarian restaurant. A mini thali costs Rs 28, a large version is Rs 38. The food's good and the restaurant is air-con but you have to cross a stinking open sewer to reach it.

Utsav, at the Hotel Nandan, is an excellent upmarket north Indian restaurant that does very good tandoori items and naan. Chicken tikka is Rs 80.

Dynasty Hotel has Chinese and Indian restaurants, but they also do some western dishes including roast pork & apple sauce for Rs 75.

Things to Buy

The best places to buy silk and local crafts are the shops on GN Bordoloi Rd, including Pragjyotika Assam State Emporium.

Getting There & Away

Air The airport is 20km west of Guwahati. Indian Airlines (☎ 512700) has flights to/from Calcutta (US$60, daily), Delhi (US$190, five per week), Agartala (US$40, three per week) and Imphal (US$45, two per week). Jet Airways (☎ 522403) has a daily flight to Bagdogra (US$43) and five flights a week to Calcutta. Sahara India Airlines (☎ 547808) has five flights a week to Delhi and Dibrugarh (US$47).

NEPC Airlines (☎ 560765) has daily flights to Calcutta, Dimapur and Imphal and also flies to Jorhat, Lilabari and Silchar.

Bus The Paltan Bazaar bus stand is by the southern exit of the railway station. It's well organised and all the state transport companies are based here. The offices for private bus companies are also in this area and along GS Rd; the most reliable companies seem to be Blue Hill and Green Valley. There's also a second bus station known as Machkhowa bus stand with departures to many destinations including Hajo.

There are buses to Shillong (Rs 29, 3½ hours) every 30 minutes between 6 am and 5 pm; overnight buses to Siliguri (Rs 174, 13 hours), Agartala (Rs 237, 25 hours), and Imphal (Rs 265, 21 hours), among many others.

Within Assam, there are frequent departures for Tezpur (Rs 60, four hours), Kaziranga (Rs 90, 5½ hours), Jorhat (Rs 100, seven hours), and Sibsagar (Rs 120, eight hours). Green Valley has an air-con bus to Kaziranga for Rs 170.

Train The most convenient points from which to get to Guwahati are Calcutta and New Jalpaiguri.

From Calcutta (Howrah), it's 993km and about 24 hours to Guwahati on the *Kamrup Express* or 22 hours on the *Kanchenjunga Express* (to/from Sealdah) at a cost of Rs 219/756 in 2nd/1st class. These trains pass through New Jalpaiguri station at 7 am and 6.10 pm, respectively. There is also the *North East Express* which comes from New Delhi and passes through New Jalpaiguri at 9.40 am. The 422km journey from here to Guwahati takes about eight hours and costs Rs 120/421 in 2nd/1st class.

Faster and more expensive is the *Rajdhani Express* which leaves Delhi on Monday, Wednesday and Saturday at 5 pm, passing through New Jalpaiguri at 1.50 pm on Tuesday, Thursday and Sunday, reaching Guwahati at 8.30 pm. From Delhi it costs Rs 1250 in a three-tier air-con sleeper; Rs 515 from New Jalpaiguri.

The *Kamrup Express* continues east to Dibrugarh, and is metre gauge after Lumding. This line passes briefly through Nagaland with a stop at Dimapur, where you're not allowed to disembark without a permit for Nagaland.

Getting Around
There's an irregular airport bus (Rs 25) but most passengers share taxis into town (Rs 50).

There's no shortage of taxis, auto-rickshaws and cycle-rickshaws but the bus service is a cheap and easy way to get around; local people are very helpful in advising which bus to take.

If you want to get out on the river there are frequent ferry crossings from Paan Bazaar Ghat to North Guwahati (Rs 0.50).

AROUND GUWAHATI
Hajo
Located on the north bank of the Brahmaputra, 28km from Guwahati, Hajo is an important pilgrimage centre for Hindus, Buddhists and Muslims. Some Buddhists believe that Buddha attained nirvana here, Hindus worship at the Hayagriba Madhab Temple. For Muslims, the Pao Mecca Mosque is considered to have one-quarter (*pao*) the sanctity of the great mosque at Mecca. Numerous buses link Guwahati's Machkhowa bus stand with Hajo in a little over an hour.

Sualkuchi
Also across the river from Guwahati, 32km away, Sualkuchi is a famous silk-weaving centre best known for its muga silk which is naturally golden-coloured, not dyed. Endi and pat silks are also woven here, and prices are lower than in Guwahati. There is a regular ferry across the river and a bus several times daily.

Other Attractions
A popular picnic spot with small temples and a waterfall, **Basistha** is where the *rishi* or sage, Basistha, once lived. It's 12km from Guwahati and reached by one of the numerous city buses from GN Bordoloi Rd.

The beautiful natural lagoon at **Chandubi** is 64km from Guwahati. **Darranga**, 80km away on the Bhutan border, is a great winter trading area for the Bhutia mountain folk. **Barpeta**, with a monastery and the shrine of a Vaishnavite reformer, is 145km north-west of Guwahati.

TEZPUR
On the north bank of the Brahmaputra, 181km from Guwahati, Tezpur is a centre for the **tea** industry. The town still has a colonial feel to it and there's an old church by the maidan.

There are several ancient temples including the **Mahabhairava Temple**, and ancient Gupta sculptures at the ruins of **Da-Parbatia Temple**, five km to the west of Tezpur. In **Cole Park**, across from the Tourist Lodge, there are 9th century sculptures and excavated sections of the palace of a former king. At sunset you should climb **Agnigarh Hill** for a superb view of the river.

Places to Stay & Eat
Tourist Lodge, opposite Cole Park, is quite good and has a very friendly and helpful manager. Rooms are Rs 100/170 with attached bath and mosquito nets; dorm beds are Rs 30.

Hotel Meghdoot is on KK Rd, 500m from the bus stand. Rooms are Rs 65/90 and it's not bad.

Hotel Luit, near the bus stand, is the top hotel in town. There are rooms from around Rs 250/380, some with air-con. There's a good restaurant here.

Getting There & Away

Indian Airlines claims to have flights to Calcutta (US$70) via Imphal (US$45) on Tuesday and Saturday, but don't rely on them because they don't always operate.

Since Tezpur is on a branch line, buses are more useful than trains. There are frequent departures for Guwahati (Rs 60, four hours) and Kaziranga (Rs 24, 1½ hours). Arunachal Pradesh State Transport Corporation has services to Itanagar.

WILDLIFE PARKS

Swaying through the dew-covered grass at dawn on the back of an elephant and suddenly coming upon a lumbering rhino is a wonderful experience, and one of the main reasons people come to Assam. Kaziranga is the largest and most accessible of the parks, and it contains virtually the entire world population of Indian rhinos. Manas is the other main park but it's been closed off and on for many years because of insurgency problems; poaching has been a particular problem here. There are two smaller parks at **Orang** and **Sonai**.

If you're a non-Indian travelling on a tight budget it might be worth checking if the policy on two-scale pricing has been changed before venturing up here. In early 1997 the cost of an elephant ride was Rs 150 for Indians and Rs 750 for non-Indians.

Kaziranga National Park

North-east of Guwahati, on the banks of the Brahmaputra River, is the Kaziranga National Park, famous as the last major home of *Rhinoceros unicornis*. The 430 sq km park is thought to have a rhino population approaching 1300, although in 1904 they were on the verge of extinction. The park became a game sanctuary in 1926, and by 1966 the numbers had risen to about 400. They are now seriously threatened again, by poachers.

The park also has gaur, deer, elephants, tigers, bears and many water bird species, including pelicans, which breed here. The best way to observe the wildlife is from elephant-back, and the rhinos are said to have become accustomed to elephants carrying camera-toting tourists.

Information The park is open from November to April. The main gate is at Kohora. There's a tourist information centre (☎ 423) at Bonani Tourist Lodge, where you're required

Rhinoceros Unicornis

Assam is famous for its rare one-horned Great Indian Rhinoceros – when Marco Polo first saw one he thought he'd found the legendary unicorn. Once widely distributed across the northern floodplains of the subcontinent, the rhino has been hunted and displaced by humans and is now restricted to only a handful of wildlife reserves. In India, the greatest numbers are found in Kaziranga National Park.

Although its cause is less well publicised than that of the tiger, its numbers are even fewer – barely 1500 – and the majority of these are in just one area. Large and formidable, the rhino has few natural predators, but a naturally slow population growth makes them especially vulnerable to hunting. The

rhino's preferred habitat often coincides with human habitation and is increasingly sought for agriculture. As in Africa, political turmoil has provided a cover for poachers, and there is an ever-present market for rhino products. Powdered rhino horn is highly valued as a medicine in the east and can fetch up to almost US$40,000 a kilo. In India and Nepal there is little of a rhino's anatomy that is not prized for its aphrodisiac, medicinal or spiritual attributes. ■

to sign in. At the park headquarters here you can reserve accommodation, and book jeeps and elephant rides. A controversial two-level pricing policy is currently in place; prices for non-Indians/Indians are Rs 175/10 to enter the park, Rs 150/50 to bring a vehicle into the park, Rs 175/16 for a camera (plus Rs 35 if you have a telephoto lens), Rs 525/500 for a video, and Rs 750/ 150 for an elephant ride. To rent a jeep for up to nine people costs Rs 700 for 1½ hours.

Avoid organised tours to Kaziranga from Guwahati since they're too short (two days) and you'll spend most of that time on the bus (some nine hours in all) and have only one game drive. It's best to have at least three nights and four days in Kaziranga if you want to see anything.

Places to Stay & Eat There is a variety of accommodation around the park.

Forest Lodges must be reserved at the tourist office or park headquarters. Beds cost Rs 85 at *Bonashree* and *Kunjaban* and there are some doubles and four-bed rooms, all with bath attached; singles/doubles are Rs 350/450 at *Bonani*, which also has a restaurant; and at *Aranya*, the best of the Forest Lodges, there are air-con rooms for Rs 450/550 with attached bath and balcony, Rs 350/450 without. There's a good restaurant here.

Wild Grass Resort (☎ (037762) 681437) is a comfortable private resort about five km from Kohora. Accommodation is either luxury tents or a lodge. Doubles are Rs 750 (no singles). Their Jungle Plan for Rs 2100 per person per day includes accommodation, meals and trips into the park on elephant. For bookings contact the Guwahati office (☎ (0361) 596827), 107 MC Rd, Uzan Bazaar.

Getting There & Away The nearest airport is at Jorhat, 84km from the park. Furketing is the most convenient railway station, but it's still 72km away; from here buses and jeeps run to Kaziranga. Buses bound for Jorhat, Sibsagar and Dibrugarh from Guwahati (Rs 90, 5½ hours), 233km away, all pass the main gate. There's also an air-con bus (Rs 170) run by Green Valley, and Assam Tourism

runs a daily bus from the Tourist Lodge in Guwahati.

Manas Wildlife Sanctuary

In the foothills of the Himalaya, north-west of Guwahati, Manas Wildlife Sanctuary is on the Bhutan border, and a breathtakingly beautiful place. Three rivers run through the sanctuary, which has abundant bird and animal life. The rare pygmy hog and the golden langur (monkey) are among the notable animals here, although there are also some rhinos. Manas is part of Project Tiger, but many the tigers have been killed by poachers.

The park has been closed off and on for some years due to the Bodo rebels, who frequently shelter here to evade the authorities. It re-opened in 1996 but the tourist office were not advising people to visit. Check the current situation in Guwahati.

Information Manas is best from January to March, although there is excellent fishing from November to December. Mothangiri is the main town in the park but the tourist information centre (☎ 49) is on Barpeta Rd. Entry and camera charges are the same as for Kaziranga. Boats can be hired for excursions or fishing trips on the Manas River.

Places to Stay The *Manas Tourist Lodge* has rooms for Rs 100/170, or Rs 30 for a dorm bed; you can camp if you have a tent. The *forest bungalow* is cheaper, and includes bedding and mosquito nets. There is a *rest house* at the Barpeta Rd tourist centre.

Getting There & Away Guwahati, 176km away, has the nearest airport. Barpeta Rd, 40km from Mothangiri, is the nearest railway station. Transport from Barpeta Rd to Mothangiri must be arranged in advance. Some private bus companies run tours from Guwahati.

NORTH-EAST ASSAM
Jorhat

Eighty-four km beyond Kaziranga, Jorhat is the gateway to the north-east of Assam. You may need to spend the night here on the way to or from Majuli. It's not really feasible to do a day trip to Majuli from Jorhat.

Assam Tourism is at the Tourist Lodge. There's a State Bank of India branch on AT Rd, where travellers cheques can be cashed.

There's a reasonable choice of accommodation near the bus station. The *tourist lodge* has good rooms with attached bath for Rs 100/170; *Dipti Hotel* has clean rooms for Rs 120/190; and *Hotel Paradise* is the best choice with rooms for Rs 190/270.

There are four flights a week between Jorhat and Calcutta (US$80) on Indian Airlines and NEPC, both of which fly via Dimapur. Jet Airways has two flights a week to Calcutta; NEPC also flies to Bagdogra. There are numerous buses to Guwahati (Rs 100, seven hours), Sibsagar (Rs 13, 1½ hours), and Kaziranga (Rs 23, 2½ hours), as well as many other destinations in the north-east. Trains are less convenient as Jorhat is on a branch line.

Majuli

Majuli is famous as the world's biggest river island, but it's really most interesting for its *satras*, Hindu Vaishnava monasteries that are also centres for the arts. At the satras on Majuli, Vishnu is worshipped through dance dramas re-enacting the stories of the *Mahabharata*, and with music and poetry. Assamese Vaishnavites see Vishnu as the pre-eminent deity, without form rather like the god of western religions.

The main satras are at Kamalabari, Natun Kamalabari, Garmur, Samoguri, Aunati, Dakhinpat and Bengenaati. They're all about five km apart; taxis and auto-rickshaws are available. It's possible to stay at some satras but you should make a donation. The other alternatives are the *Circuit House* in Garmur, or lodgings with villagers.

There are ferries in the morning and afternoon from Neamati Ghat, 13km north of Jorhat. From the landing stage on Majuli there's usually a bus for the eight km journey to the island's capital, Garmur.

Sibsagar

Sibsagar, 55km from Jorhat, was the old

capital of the Ahom kings, who ruled Assam for the 600 years before the arrival of the British. It's now an important centre for the tea and oil industries.

The huge artificial lake, created by Queen Madambika in 1734, lies at the centre of the town. Beside the tank stands the Shivadol temple, at 33m the tallest Shiva temple in the country. Six km from the centre are the ruins of the 18th century palaces of Kareng Ghar and Talatal Ghar; 13km to the east is Gargaon Palace. Twelve km along the road to Jorhat is the Gaurisagar tank and three more temples.

There's an excellent *tourist lodge* by the tank, with rooms with bath attached for Rs 100/170. Assam Tourism's office is here. *Kareng Hotel* on Temple Rd is good value at Rs 70/120 and has a reasonable restaurant.

Simaluguri, the mainline railway station, is 20km from Sibsagar, but there are lots of buses – Guwahati (Rs 120, 8½ hours), Jorhat (Rs 13, 1½ hours).

SOUTH ASSAM

Assam's southern finger extends down as far as Tripura and Mizoram, and also has borders with Bangladesh and Manipur. Insurgency problems mean that you should take local advice before travelling here.

Haflong

This is Assam's only hill station, 85km north of Silchar. It's best known for Jatinga, nine km from Haflong, where flocks of birds are said to come to commit suicide on misty September nights. 'From the elevated watchtower one can see them yielding to their death wish and their little plummage dropping down', says the local tourist brochure. What actually happens is that migrating birds passing this way are attracted to lights set up by the villagers; the birds land and end up in the villagers' cooking pots.

There's a *tourist lodge* in Haflong with rooms for Rs 100/170, and several other budget choices. There are two very slow buses a day to/from Silchar (four hours).

Silchar

Silchar, in the far south of the state, is only of interest as a transport hub. There are flights to and from Calcutta, Guwahati and Imphal on Indian Airlines and NEPC Airlines, up to four times a week. There are also buses west to Shillong and Guwahati, south to Agartala and Aizawl, and east to Imphal and Kohima.

If you need to spend the night here there's the *tourist lodge* on Park Rd, with rooms for Rs 100/170.

Meghalaya

Created in 1972, this state is the home of the Khasi, Jaintia and Garo tribespeople. Their social organisation is notable for being matrilineal – property and wealth are passed through the female rather than the male line.

The hill station of Shillong is the state capital, while Cherrapunji, 58km away, was until recently said to be the wettest place on earth, with an average annual rainfall of 1150cm, nearly 40 feet! In one year 26.46m of rain fell. (Nearby Mawsynram recently took the title from Cherrapunji.) It's no wonder Meghalaya means Abode of Clouds!

With more than 150 caves in the limestone hills across the state, some of them several km long, Meghalaya is starting to attract the attention of international cavers.

SHILLONG

Pop: 255,000   Tel Area Code: 0364

From 1874 until 1905 Shillong was the capital of Assam and known as the Scotland of the East. Surrounded by pine trees and veiled in clouds, you can quite understand why it reminded the Brits so strongly of home. Standing at an altitude of 1496m it provided a welcome relief from the heat of the plains. They built a championship golf course (the world's wettest), and a polo ground, and soon the surrounding hills were dotted with neat Victorian bungalows and little churches.

Most of these still stand but in the centre of Shillong they've been joined by a multi-tude of ugly concrete buildings and the narrow roads are choked with traffic. Nevertheless, there are good walks in the area and interesting markets that attract tribespeople from outlying villages. It's a pleasant place to spend some time.

Orientation

Shillong is spread over several rolling hills. Ward's Lake, the botanical garden and the polo ground (all to the north) were formerly the European area; this is still a peaceful part of Shillong, and where some of the upmarket hotels are located. Police Bazaar is right at the centre of the town and the government bus stand, restaurants, more upmarket shops and many of the bottom end and middle hotels are here. About 1.5 km to the west is crowded Bara Bazaar and the private bus stand.

Information

The Meghalaya Tourism office (☎ 226220) is on Jail Rd in Police Bazaar. It's open Monday to Saturday from 7.30 am to 5 pm, and until noon on Sunday. If there's enough interest they run local tours (8.30 am to 2 pm; Rs 55) and trips to Cherrapunji (8 am to 4.30 pm; Rs 75 – bring a torch/flashlight for the caves). There's a Government of India tourist office (☎ 225632) nearby on GS Rd.

Travellers cheques can be cashed at the State Bank of India opposite the Shillong Club. Phone calls can be made at the telegraph office on Temple Rd or from any of the numerous STD places. You can send and receive faxes from the office next to the town's best bookshop, Modern Book Depot, on GS Rd.

For handicrafts there's Porbashree, the emporium by the Meghalaya Tourism office; also in the centre of Police Bazaar, on the corner of Kacheri Rd, there are shops selling finely woven baskets in a wide range of sizes. The most interesting market takes place in Bara Bazaar on Iewduh, which is the first day of the eight-day Khasi week. Khasi and Jaintia villagers come from all over eastern Meghalaya to buy and sell produce at the market.

Parks & Waterfalls

East of Police Bazaar, **Ward's Lake** was the focus of the European settlement. It's said that its construction was initiated by a bored Khasi prisoner who'd requested any kind of work to get him out of his cell. He was set to digging holes and filling them in again. When he hit a spring in this spot the civic engineer decided that a lake and gardens should be created; it was named after Sir William Ward, the Chief Commissioner. It's still quite an attractive place and there's boating on the lake.

About 1.5km south of Police Bazaar is **Lady Hydari Park**, which is at its best in April and October when the flowers are in bloom. There's also a mini zoo here; entry is Rs 2.

There are more gardens nearby at the **Crinolene Falls**, where there's also a swimming pool. As you might expect in a place so wet, there are numerous other waterfalls and beauty spots around Shillong.

Museums

The **State Museum** gives dusty coverage to the flora, fauna, culture and anthropology of the state. It's closed on Sunday and the 2nd and 4th Saturday of each month. More interesting is the **Butterfly Museum**, on Jaiaw Rd, 1.5km north of Police Bazaar, run by Wankhar & Co who breed butterflies and supply conservation organisations around the world. It's open Monday to Friday from 10 am to 4 pm, and on Saturday morning.

Other Things to See

In the **Anglican graveyard** the gravestones show that even for the privileged Brits, life could be short and death not always peaceful. There are a few gory inscriptions such as 'killed in the great earthquake' or 'murdered by headhunters'. If the graveyard's locked, get the key from the adjoining gatekeeper's house.

The town takes its name from the 1960m **Shillong Peak**, from which there are fine

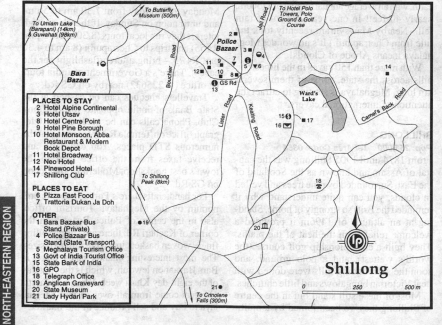

PLACES TO STAY
2 Hotel Alpine Continental
3 Hotel Utsav
8 Hotel Centre Point
9 Hotel Pine Borough
10 Hotel Monsoon, Abba Restaurant & Modern Book Depot
11 Hotel Broadway
12 Neo Hotel
14 Pinewood Hotel
17 Shillong Club

PLACES TO EAT
6 Pizza Fast Food
7 Trattoria Dukan Ja Doh

OTHER
1 Bara Bazaar Bus Stand (Private)
4 Police Bazaar Bus Stand (State Transport)
5 Meghalaya Tourism Office
13 Govt of India Tourist Office
15 State Bank of India
16 GPO
18 Telegraph Office
19 Anglican Graveyard
20 State Museum
21 Lady Hydari Park

Shillong

views. It's 10km from the centre, and a path winds up to the summit.

Sixteen km from Shillong, by the road to Guwahati is **Umiam Lake** (Barapani), a popular place for fishing and boating.

Places to Stay – bottom end

There are numerous cheap hotels (all fairly similar) in Police Bazaar, many on or around GS Rd.

Neo Hotel (☎ 224363), conveniently situated on GS Rd, has large admonitory notices such as 'A gentleman always keeps his walls and surroundings clean'. These seem to work– the place is clean and friendly. There are basic singles/doubles for Rs 60/125 with common bath, Rs 125/250 with bath attached. Fish curry rice is Rs 20 in the cheap restaurant.

Hotel Utsav (☎ 226715), Jail Rd, is opposite the bus stand. It's a reasonable place. Ordinary rooms with common bath are Rs 110/200; rooms with attached bath are Rs 150/250.

Hotel Broadway (☎ 226996), GS Rd, is good but a bit pricey. There are clean rooms for Rs 100/200 with common bath, Rs 290/400 with bath attached. There's a busy restaurant downstairs.

Hotel Monsoon (☎ 223316), GS Rd, is by Abba Restaurant. With attached bath rooms are Rs 125/225.

Hotel Pine Borough (☎ 220698) is down the lane beside Hotel Centre Point. It's quite popular with businesspeople on a tight budget and has rooms from Rs 140/230 to Rs 350 (for the executive suite). All have TV and bath attached; and there's a restaurant and travel agent.

Places to Stay – middle & top end

Government tax will currently add 10% to these prices, and some hotels also add a 5% to 10% service charge.

Hotel Centre Point (☎ 225210, fax; 227222), a landmark in the centre of Police Bazaar, has good singles/doubles from Rs 360/420 to Rs 700/750. All rooms have Star TV and attached baths, some even have double beds.

Shillong Club (☎ 226938) allows temporary members to use its residential wing. The club is not terribly grand, but rooms aren't expensive – Rs 240/425 with bathroom attached. Prices include membership and there's no tax.

Hotel Alpine Continental (☎ 220991), Thana Rd & Quinton Rd, is a good place with a wide range of rooms (all with baths attached) from Rs 250/550 to Rs 650/750.

Hotel Polo Towers (☎ 222340; fax 220090) is a modern hotel 1.5km north of Police Bazaar. It has all the usual mod-cons of a three-star hotel, with standard rooms for Rs 495/650 and deluxe rooms for Rs 695/850.

Pinewood Hotel (☎ 223116; fax 224176) is the most atmospheric place to stay, a wonderful Raj-era hotel that was built in the early 1900s. It's about two km from the centre and set in attractive grounds. The rooms have high ceilings and large comfortable beds, there are fires in the grates and tubs in the bathrooms. Rooms are good value at Rs 520/780. For Rs 840/1090, the suites are enormous and include a dressing room and sitting room.

There's a good restaurant still serving the kinds of dishes that must have been set before crusty Scots tea planters 70 years ago. Mushrooms on toast are Rs 33, fried fish with parsley butter is Rs 55. Orders are taken by the 'butler'.

The hotel is now in the hands of Meghalaya Tourism, who seem to be doing a reasonable job running it – for the moment at least.

Places to Eat

Some of the best restaurants are in the hotels. Try *La Galerie* at the Hotel Centre Point for Indian and Chinese dishes, and the *Pinewood Hotel* for Raj cuisine. There's a good range of restaurants in the Police Bazaar area.

Trattoria Dukan Ja Doh, down the small side road beside Hotel Centre Point, is a simple cafe where you can try Khasi fare. There's no menu but the delicacies include pig's brains with ginger for Rs 4 and Khasi fried rice for Rs 5.

Abba, GS Rd, is an excellent Chinese/Tibetan place. Chicken chow mein costs Rs 22, half a dozen momos are Rs 15; there are only a few tables.

Palace Restaurant is an Indian fast food cafe in Centre Point. Samosas are Rs 3, dosas Rs 15 and chana bhatura is Rs 15.

Eee Cee is a busy restaurant with good value Chinese and Indian dishes. It's a few doors up from the tourist office on Jail Rd.

Pizza Fast Food does what the name says, and quite well, from Rs 25 to Rs 70. It's just across the road from the tourist office.

Getting There & Away

Umroi airport is 32km from Shillong but out of action while the runway is upgraded. Currently, the nearest airport (and railway station) are at Guwahati in Assam. A good road runs through pineapple plantations for the 100km between Shillong and Guwahati; share taxis charge Rs 120. Share taxis and buses are sometimes available direct to Shillong from Guwahati airport.

From Shillong there are state transport buses from the Police Bazaar stand every half hour to Guwahati (Rs 29/39 for ordinary/deluxe, 3½ hours) and overnight buses to Silchar (Rs 93, 8½ hours) and Tura (Rs 125, 12 hours). Private companies such as Green Valley Travels have offices in Police Bazaar but their buses operate from the Bara Bazaar bus stand. A deluxe private bus to Agartala costs Rs 250 for the 18 hour journey. Local buses depart from Bara Bazaar.

There's a railway out agency at the Police Bazaar bus stand with quotas for three trains out of Guwahati.

AROUND SHILLONG

There are daily buses to **Cherrapunji**, 58km south of Shillong; if it's not raining the views from here over Bangladesh are superb. You can buy delicious honey in the market. Krem Mawmluh is a 4.5km-long cave near Cherrapunji. Meghalaya Tourism runs tours from Shillong.

The border post with Bangladesh is 1.5km from **Dawki**, 70km from Shillong and linked by a bus service. There's no Bangladesh embassy in Shillong; the nearest is in Agartala.

Mawsynram, which recently took the title of wettest place on earth from Cherrapunji, is 55km from Shillong. Mawjymbuin Cave is the other attraction near here. There are hot springs at **Jakrem**, 66km from Shillong.

In the Jaintia Hills, near Jowai, is Krem Um Lawan, which at 6.5km is India's longest cave.

GARO HILLS

There are numerous deep caves in the Garo Hills, in the west of the state around Siju, 150km from the district capital of Tura. Buses to Tura (Rs 125, 12 hours) from Shillong go via Guwahati.

Tripura

The tiny state of Tripura is the second smallest in the country with a population of only around three million, and is almost totally surrounded by Bangladesh. Tripura was once part of a large Hindu kingdom that was conquered by the Moghuls in 1733. It was taken over by the British in 1808, became a union territory of India in 1956 and a full state in 1972.

Over half the state is under forest, and it is said there are large reserves of natural gas. The largest single industry is handloom weaving. Although there are 19 scheduled tribes in Tripura the majority of the population is Bengali, with many immigrants from Bangladesh.

Perhaps the strongest reason for visiting Tripura is the fact that so few foreign visitors do – 14 in 1991, 0 in 1992, 2 in 1993, 50 in 1994 and 72 in 1995 (according to the latest available figures). Wherever you go people will be genuinely interested in talking to you. Locals stop you in the street, not, as is usually the case in the more touristed parts of India, to get you to buy something, but just to say hello. It's the perfect antidote to Jaipur!

Prospective visitors should, however, take local advice as to where it's currently safe to go. For the past few years Tripura's communist CPI (M) government has been trying to bring the several insurgent groups that terrorise the more inaccessible corners of the state under their control.

AGARTALA
Pop: 175,500   Tel Area Code: 0381

Tripura's sleepy capital was moved to its present site in 1850 by Maharaja Radha Krishna Kishore Manikya Bahadur. The town is dominated by the Ujjayanta Palace, built in Indo-Saracenic style in 1901. It's a pleasant enough place and the locals are very welcoming but there's not a lot to see.

Agartala is just two km from the border with Bangladesh. Visas are easily available at the embassy here.

Orientation & Information
The town is arranged on a modern grid plan so orientation is easy. The airport is 12km to the north, and Airport Rd brings you into the town by the Ujjayanta Palace. The main shopping street is HGB Rd, where the State Bank of India, museum and post office are all located.

Tripura Tourism (☎ 225930), located in the eastern wing of the palace, can be very helpful. For a minimum of 10 people they offer a tour around Agartala (Rs 52), Neermahal (Rs 48) and package tours from one to seven nights taking in most of the sights around the state for Rs 160 to Rs 1240. There's a Bangladesh tourist office at the embassy.

At the State Bank of India on HGB Rd there are sandbags in the doorway, no doubt in case of attack by militants.

Bangladesh Embassy The embassy (☎ 224807) is 1.5km north of Agartala just off Airport Rd. Ask for the Circuit House and it's down the lane beside Green Travels (opposite Assam Rifles). Open for visa applications Monday to Friday from 10 am to noon, you need to bring two photos and fill out an application form, then go to the State Bank of India on HGB Rd to deposit the visa fee in the embassy's account. Current fees are as follows: Australia (US$21), Canada (US$37), France (US$41), UK (UK£40), USA (US$21). Visas are ready for collection the following day between 3 and 4.30 pm; for an extra fee same-day visas are possible.

Things to See
Standing before a small lake, **Ujjayanta Palace** covers an area of almost one sq km. Since the building now houses the state legislative assembly it's not usually open to the public. However, if you go to the front gate between 3 and 4 pm (Monday to Saturday) they may give you an entry pass. In the grounds and open to all are the **Ummaneshwar Temple** and the **Jagannath Temple**, both painted a striking ochre colour. At the **Buddha Vihar** on Airport Rd, there are Burmese statues of the Buddha. There's a **mosque** near the motor stand.

The **State Museum** is by the roundabout on HGB Rd. It's worth a visit, the results of excavations within the state are on display, and there are old coins and ethnographic displays. It's open daily except Sunday from 10 am to 5 pm; entry is free.

Old Agartala, the former capital, is five km to the east. The Temple of Fourteen Deities here draws thousands of devotees in July for the Karchi Puja.

Places to Stay & Eat
Hotels in Tripura are all fairly basic but some have air-con rooms. Hotel tax is currently 10%; some places also add an additional 10% service charge.

Agartala Rest House, Motor Stand Rd, has some of the cheapest rooms in town – Rs 30 for an extremely basic single with common bath.

Hotel Minakshi (☎ 223430), Hawkers' Corner Rd (the side lane off HGB Rd), has basic rooms with attached bath for Rs 55/95, and deluxe rooms with constant hot water and TV for Rs 90/150. It's good value.

Hotel Ambar, just off HGB Rd, is also good. Rooms with attached bath, mosquito nets and TV cost Rs 88/165.

Hotel Moonlight & Restaurant, LNB Rd, is better known as a place to eat but also has some basic rooms for Rs 50/80.

Deep Hotel (☎ 227482), LNB Rd, is clean and popular. Rooms with attached bath cost Rs 120/200.

Royal Guest House (☎ 225652), Royal Compound, has good rooms from Rs 150/300 with attached bath, and Rs 300/400 plus air-con. Although there's really nothing royal about it, apart from the location, it's a friendly place. There's a good restaurant – a half tandoori chicken costs Rs 65.

Hotel Rajdhani (☎ 223387), BK Rd, says it is the first hotel in Tripura to have a lift installed. Ordinary rooms cost Rs 170/250 with attached bath. There are also air-con

rooms for Rs 290/450. Rooms are clean and come with mosquito nets. Room service is available.

Hotel Gujrat is a good place to eat, and there are veg and non-veg dishes. A thali costs Rs 20.

Hotel Indu, HGB Rd, is the place to go for a cheap meal. Rice is just Rs 2, dhal Rs 1, or you could splash out on fish curry for Rs 12. After prices like that, rooms aren't such brilliant value at Rs 50/80 with common bath.

Abhishek Restaurant, LNB Rd, has tables under umbrellas in the garden and small veg

and non-veg rooms inside. It's moderately priced – chicken korma is Rs 38, Thai chicken costs Rs 60.

Getting There & Away

Air Indian Airlines has daily flights to/from Calcutta (US$45) and three flights a week to/from Guwahati (US$40). It's likely that private airlines may also start services on these routes soon. From the airport, taxis/auto-rickshaws cost Rs 120/60.

Bus & Share Jeep There are three bus stands. From the TRTC state bus stand on Hospital Rd, there's a bus to Guwahati (Rs 237, 25 hours) via Shillong at 4 pm, daily except Sunday, and also buses for Silchar, Udaipur, Melaghar and Unakoti. Between Tellamura and Kumarghat all buses have an army escort in case of attack from insurgents.

Private buses leave from the chaotic Batala bus stand and the Motor Stand and some can be booked at the travel agencies on LNB Rd. Green Valley Travels has departures at 6 am and 2.30 pm for Guwahati (Rs 275) via Shillong (Rs 250). Sagar Travels has buses to Silchar for Rs 135 at the same times; they can also book air tickets.

From the Batala bus stand you can get share jeeps to Udaipur and Melaghar (for Neermahal). To both places seats cost Rs 15 in the front, Rs 11 at the back.

Train There is a computerised railway booking office at the TRTC bus stand, open Monday to Saturday from 8 am to 2 pm and on Sunday morning until noon. Although there's a railway line just seven km from Agartala in Bangladesh, the nearest within India is 140km north at Kumarghat.

Bangladesh Follow Akaura Rd 1.5km west to the border post, Rs 5 in a cycle-rickshaw. The border's open daily from 8 am to 5 pm. From the Bangladeshi side it's another five km to the railway station where there are trains to Dhaka (three hours) at 10.30 am and 6 pm.

SOUTH TRIPURA
Sepahijala Forest Sanctuary

The road south from Agartala runs through little villages of mud brick houses, past paddy fields and plantations of rubber and tea, 33km to Sepahijala Forest Sanctuary. Within the 18 sq km, some of it fenced, there are various species of deer and monkey and also a mini-zoo. Entry is Rs 3 and there are elephant rides for Rs 15. You can stay at the *Forest Dak Bungalow*.

Neermahal

South of Sepahijala one road continues 22km to Melaghar, one km from Rudrasagar Lake. On an island in the lake is Tripura's top attraction, the Moghul-style water palace of Neermahal. Now deserted and starting to fall into ruin, it dates from the beginning of the century. It's a beautifully peaceful place that attracts migrating birds in winter, however the lake itself is at its fullest and most impressive in the summer after the rains. On the lake shore, overlooking the palace, Tripura Tourism's *Sagarmahal Tourist Lodge* has doubles for Rs 80 with bath attached, and dorm beds for Rs 30. Make a reservation at the tourist office in Agartala. Outside the holidays you might get the whole place to yourself.

There are share jeeps from Agartala (Rs 15, 1½ hours) to Melaghar. Rickshaws charge Rs 4 down to the lake where there's a selection of boats for rent from Rs 6 per person or Rs 50 to Rs 80 for the whole boat. By the booking office (Rs 2 for entry to Neermahal), the *Co-operative Restaurant* serves fish from the lake for Rs 12. Most tourists come just for the day which is a very good reason to stay for a night at least.

Udaipur

Fifty-five km south of Agartala and 25km from Neermahal, Udaipur was the ancient Hindu capital. At the centre of Udaipur is the Jagannath Digthi tank, and on its banks the ruined Jagannath Temple which once held the famous Jagannath statue brought here from Puri in the 16th century. There are also several temples to Vishnu and the ruins of the old royal palace.

The **Tripura Sundari Temple**, four km from Udaipur, is the most famous temple in the south, built in the classic Bengali-hut style. It's also known as Matambari.

Share jeeps make frequent runs to Udaipur (Rs 15, 1½ hours). There are dorm beds for Rs 30 (three per room) at the *Matabari Pantha Niwas*, near the Tripura Sundari Temple.

NORTH TRIPURA

An ancient pilgrimage centre, **Unakoti**, 180km north of Agartala, is believed to date back to the 8th century. Several impressively large rock-cut images are set into the hills, and there are attractive waterfalls and pools. It's 10km from Kailasahar where the Forest Department has a *rest house*. Contact the Chief Conservator of Forests in advance (Airport Rd, Agartala). There are two buses a day to Kailasahar from Agartala (Rs 42, eight hours).

The railhead is at **Kumarghat**, linked by road to Agartala (Rs 35, 7½ hours) with at least two buses a day. There's accommodation here at *Uttarayan Pantha Nivas*, near the railway station, for Rs 30 per person.

Other States in the North-East

The only way into these states is on a group tour of at least four people, organised through a recognised travel agent; or with an personal invitation from a friend.

MIZORAM

Pop: 750,000

This finger-like extension in the extreme south-east of the region pokes between Myanmar and Bangladesh. The name means Hill People's Land – from Mizo, Man of the Hill, and Ram, Land. It's a picturesque place where the population is both predominantly tribal and overwhelmingly Christian. Under the British, the area was known as the Lushai

Hills, a name that persisted until 1972 when it became a Union Territory. For 20 years the Mizo National Front agitated for independence from Delhi, but in 1986 the Mizoram Peace Accord was signed and the region gained a measure of self government as a state in its own right.

If you can get a permit for Mizoram it's an interesting place to visit, more for the people than for any particular sight. The Mizos have the second highest literacy rate in India and many speak English.

Aizawl

Pop: 160,000   Tel Area Code: 0389

Mizoram's capital clings to the sides of a central ridge at an altitude of 1130m. The staff at Mizoram Tourism (☎ 21226), Chandmary, are friendly and helpful.

The **Bara Bazaar**, in the centre of town, is an interesting market. Good places for weavings and bags are the **Weaving Centre** and **Solomon's Cave**. Bamboo items are a good buy. The **Mizoram State Museum**, at Babu Tlang, has a good collection of traditional Mizo dress and implements. There's also a mini-zoo.

Luangmual is a small ridge-top village seven km from Aizawl. Apart from the pleasant views and budget accommodation at the *Yatri Niwas*, there's a good handicrafts centre.

Hotels in Aizawl include *Embassy* (☎ 22570), near the tourist office, with rooms for around Rs 150/200 and a good restaurant; and the similarly-priced *tourist lodge* at Chatlang, further from the centre. In Bara Bazaar, the *Hotel Ritz* is a little cheaper and has been recommended.

There are currently no flights into Mizoram and no railway lines. Road transport comes via Silchar, 175km north of Aizawl. There are day and night buses for the six hour journey. Capital Travels has a daily bus to Guwahati (Rs 275, 22 hours).

MANIPUR

Pop: 2 million

South of Nagaland, Manipur (which means jewelled land) borders with Myanmar. The state is inhabited by over two dozen different tribes, many of them Christians. Manipuri dancing is one of the great classical dance forms, which involves acrobatics on the part of the male dancers and slow graceful movements from the female dancers. The main sport is polo, and along with several other places in Asia, Manipur claims to have invented the game. Agriculture and weaving form the basis of the economy.

In the course of Manipur's long history there have been several invasions from Myanmar and numerous clashes with the Nagas. It became part of British India in 1926. During WWII it was occupied by the Japanese. For the last 10 years there have been violent disturbances not only by separatist groups, but also from ethnic conflict between Naga and Kuki tribes. Hundreds have been killed, thousands left homeless.

Travellers should check the current situation before attempting to visit Manipur.

Imphal
Pop: 210,000   Tel Area Code: 0385
The capital stands at an elevation of 790m, surrounded by wooded hills and lakes. The Vaishnavite **Shri Govindaji Temple** has two gold domes; ceremonial dances are often held here. Next to the temple are the ruins of the **Old Palace**. The **Khwairamband Bazaar**, or Ima Market, is probably the most interesting thing to see here and a great place to buy Manipuri wickerwork, basketry and weavings, as well as provisions, fruit and vegetables. It's run by women and is one of the biggest women's markets in India. There are also **war cemeteries** and an interesting **state museum**.

There's a range of accommodation, including air-con rooms, at the government-run *Hotel Imphal* (☎ 220459). Manipur Tourism is based here.

Imphal is linked by daily flights to Calcutta (US$70) on Indian Airlines and NEPC Airlines. There are also flights to Guwahati and Silchar. Kohima is 125km north of Imphal, Silchar 160km west; there are buses to both these places and also to Guwahati (Rs 265, 20 hours). There are no railway lines within Manipur.

Loktak Lake
Loktak Lake is the largest freshwater lake in the north-east, and much of it falls within the Keibul Lamjao National Park. Large areas of the lake are covered with thick matted weeds, and on this unique floating habitat live the local fishing people and some rare species that include the *sangai*, or Manipur dancing deer. There's a *tourist lodge* here.

NAGALAND
Pop: 1.55 million
South of Arunachal Pradesh and north of Manipur, the remote and hilly state of Nagaland is bordered by Myanmar. Getting a permit to visit is difficult owing to the political instability in the state.

The Nagas
The Nagas were once famous as head hunters. Animists until the arrival of the missionaries, they believed that the soul was lodged in the head, and that decapitation was the only way to release it from the body. Collecting these macabre trophies was thought to add to their good fortune as the souls released would look kindly on them for freeing them. The missionaries convinced them otherwise – over 90% are now Christians.

The Nagas' fighting spirit remains, however, and their demands for independence from India, which have been ongoing since the British left, have not always been peaceful. There are 16 Naga tribes, the Angamis, Rengmas, Aos, Konyaks, Wanchus, Semas and Lothas among them.

Kohima
Pop: 54,000   Tel Area Code: 0370
The capital of Nagaland, Kohima was where the Japanese advance into India was halted in April 1944. The well-maintained **war cemetery** is the main tourist sight; there's also an interesting **state museum**. On the hill above Kohima, **Bara Basti** (Kohima Village) was the original Naga settlement here. You can still find a few old traditional houses with crossed horns on their gables. The 20th century has caught up with Kohima, and you

need to get out into the hill villages to see traditional Naga ways of life.

Nagaland Tourism has rooms at the *tourist lodge* for Rs 85/100 and the *Yatri Nivas* for Rs 60/80. The top hotel is the *Hotel Japfu* (☎ 22721) with rooms for Rs 500/750.

The nearest airport and railhead are at Dimapur, four hours by road to the north. There are state buses from Guwahati (Rs 190, 16 hours).

Dimapur

Nagaland's gateway is also its commercial centre. Near the border with Assam, in the 13th century it was the Kacharis capital. Their huge decorative phallic symbols can still be seen. There's a range of accommodation including a *Tourist Lodge* with rooms from Rs 80/100, and the *Hotel City Tower*, Circular Rd, with rooms from Rs 250/350, some air-con, and a good restaurant.

Dimapur is an important air, bus, and train transportation hub. Indian Airlines and NEPC Airlines fly to Calcutta and Guwahati.

ARUNACHAL PRADESH
Pop: 1.01 million

The furthest north-east of the region, Arunachal Pradesh has borders with Bhutan, China and Myanmar (Burma) and is a mountainous, remote and predominantly tribal area. Eighty percent of the state is under forest.

Itanagar
Pop: 17,700   Tel Area Code: 0360

The capital, Itanagar, is near the Assam border. The nearest airport is 57km away at Lilabari in Assam. NEPC Airlines flies three times a week to Calcutta and Guwahati. The railhead, also over the border, is at Harmutti. **Ziro** is a hill station 160km north of Itanagar and 100km from Lilabari.

In Ganga Market the *Himalaya* has basic rooms at around Rs 80/120. *Hotel Arun Subansiri* (☎ 33258), Zero Point, has some very comfortable rooms for Rs 450/550. *Hotel Donyi Polo Ashok* (☎ 22626) is the top hotel with air-con rooms for Rs 850/1200.

Green Valley is a reliable operator with buses to Guwahati (Rs 130, nine hours).

West Arunachal Pradesh

In the far north-west, **Tawang Gompa** is in a superb location at 3400m, near the border with Bhutan. Dating from the mid 17th century, this is the most important monastery in the north-east. The sixth Dalai Lama was born here. It has an interesting collection of thangkas and a large gilded statue of the Buddha in the prayer hall. Getting here is certainly no picnic – it's 350km from the nearest airport at Tezpur in Assam and you have to cross the 4249m Se La. About halfway between Tezpur and Tawang is the attractive town of **Bomdila**.

East Arunachal Pradesh

In the east of the state **Tezu** is the nearest town to Parasuram Kund, a lake which attracts pilgrims for the festival in January.

Namdapha National Park borders Myanmar; tiger and leopard are among the many species here. Accommodation is available at Miao, the park headquarters.

Rajasthan

Rajasthan, the Land of the Kings, is India at its exotic and colourful best. This diverse state is the home of the Rajputs, a group of warrior clans who have controlled this part of India for 1000 years according to a code of chivalry and honour akin to that of the medieval European knights. While temporary alliances and marriages of convenience were the order of the day, pride and independence were always paramount. The Rajputs were therefore never able to present a united front against a common aggressor. Indeed, much of their energy was spent squabbling among themselves and the resultant weakness eventually led to their becoming vassal states of the Mughal Empire. Nevertheless, the Rajputs' bravery and sense of honour were unparalleled.

Rajput warriors would fight against all odds and, when no hope was left, chivalry demanded that *jauhar* be declared. In this grim ritual, the women and children committed suicide by immolating themselves on a huge funeral pyre, while the men donned saffron robes and rode out to confront the enemy and certain death. In some of the larger battles, tens of thousands of Rajput warriors lost their lives in this way. Three times in Chittorgarh's long history, the women consigned themselves to the flames while the men rode out to their martyrdom. The same tragic fate befell many other forts around the state. It's hardly surprising that Akbar persuaded Rajputs to lead his army, nor that subsequent Mughal emperors had such difficulty controlling this part of their empire.

With the decline of the Mughal Empire, the Rajputs gradually clawed back their independence through a series of spectacular victories, but then a new force appeared on the scene in the form of the British. As the Raj inexorably expanded, most Rajput states signed articles of alliance with the British which allowed them to continue as independent states, each with its own maharaja (or similarly titled leader), subject to certain

RAJASTHAN AT A GLANCE

Population: 49.7 million
Area: 342,239 sq km
Capital: Jaipur
Main Languages: Rajasthani & Hindi
Literacy Rate: 38.8%
Best Time to Go: mid-October to mid-March

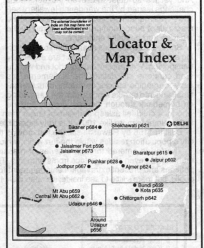

Highlights

- Grand palaces and mighty forts dotted throughout the state
- The placid and sacred town of Pushkar, and its spectacular Camel Fair
- The birds of Keoladeo Ghana National Park and the tigers and other wildlife of Ranthambhore and Sariska
- Camel safaris in the vast, bewitching desert around Jaisalmer
- The painted havelis of Shekhawati

Festivals

See the Festivals Calendar later in this chapter.

political and economic constraints. The British, after all, were not there for humanitarian reasons, but to establish an empire and gain a controlling interest in the economy of

Jaisalmer Fort

Jaisalmer Fort is the most alive of any museum, fort or palace that you're likely to visit in India. Shops – such as the 'Amba Beauty Parlour', where you can have your eyes decorated with kohl – lie mysteriously and seductively behind curtains and painted doors in alleys so narrow you have to breathe in to let others through. There are homes and hotels in the honeycombs – all sandstone and soft, surreal light; and shops and stalls swaddled in the kaleidoscopic mirrors and embroideries of brilliant Rajasthani cloth. And yet it's so quiet that even the ubiquitous challenge issued by the wandering jewellery sellers – 'yes madam, sir, you buy' – can't dispel the magic air of peace and protection offered by the massive and beautiful enclosure.

Sunsets and sunrises spent sitting or wandering around the ramparts of the fort are especially transporting. With ancient balls of shot and weathered cannons still dotting the battlements, it's easy to imagine specks on the far horizon materialising into terrible armies from the past, riding on horseback through the vast desert. Anyone who as a child fell asleep to dream of larger than life Aladdins and Ali Babas will think that one night in Jaisalmer is more like 1001. It is truly incredible.

Built in 1156 by Rawal Jaisal, the fort crowns the 80m high Trikuta Hill. About a quarter of the old city's population resides within the fort walls, which have 99 bastions around their circumference.

The fort is entered through a series of massive gates leading to a large courtyard. The former maharaja's seven storey palace fronts onto this. The square was formerly used to review troops, hear petitions and present extravagant entertainment for important visitors. Part of the palace is open to the public, but there's little to see inside; it's open daily from 8 am to 1 pm and 3 to 5 pm; entry is Rs 5. ∎

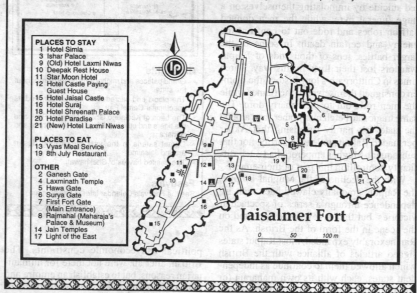

PLACES TO STAY
1 Hotel Simla
3 Ishar Palace
9 (Old) Hotel Laxmi Niwas
10 Deepak Rest House
11 Star Moon Hotel
12 Hotel Castle Paying
   Guest House
15 Hotel Jaisal Castle
16 Hotel Suraj
18 Hotel Shreenath Palace
20 Hotel Paradise
21 (New) Hotel Laxmi Niwas

PLACES TO EAT
13 Vyas Meal Service
19 8th July Restaurant

OTHER
2 Ganesh Gate
4 Laxminath Temple
5 Hawa Gate
6 Surya Gate
7 First Fort Gate
   (Main Entrance)
8 Rajmahal (Maharaja's
   Palace & Museum)
14 Jain Temples
17 Light of the East

Jaisalmer Fort

0   50   100 m

the subcontinent in the same way as the Mughals had done.

These alliances proved to be the beginning of the end for the Rajput rulers. Indulgence and extravagance soon replaced chivalry and honour so that, by the early 1900s, many of the maharajas spent much of their time travelling the world with an army of concubines and retainers, playing polo, racing horses, gambling and occupying whole floors of the most expensive hotels in Europe and America. While it suited the British to indulge them in this respect, their profligate waste of the resources of Rajputana (the land of the Rajputs) was socially and educationally detrimental. When India gained its independence, Rajasthan had one of the subcontinent's lowest life expectancy and literacy rates.

At Independence, India's ruling Congress Party was forced to make a deal with the nominally independent Rajput states in order to secure their agreement to join the new India. The rulers were allowed to keep their titles, their property holdings were secured and they were paid an annual stipend commensurate with their status. It couldn't last forever, given India's socialist persuasion, and the crunch came in the early 1970s when

Indira Gandhi abolished both the titles and the stipends and severely sequestered their property rights.

While some of the rulers have survived this by converting their forts into museums and their palaces into luxury hotels, many have fallen by the wayside, unable to cope with the financial and managerial demands of the late 20th century.

Although the fortunes of its former rulers may be in tatters, the culture of Rajasthan, with its battle-scarred forts, its palaces of breathtaking grandeur and whimsical charm, its riotous colours and even its romantic sense of pride and honour, is still very much alive. This visibility extends from the vibrant turbans and soup-strainer moustaches sported by the men and the flamboyant mirrored skirts and chunky silver jewellery of the women, to the amiable manner in which these people deal with you.

The state is diagonally divided into the hilly and rugged south-eastern region and the barren north-western Thar Desert, which extends across the border into Pakistan. Like many deserts, the Thar offers oases of magic and romance. There are plenty of historic cities, incredible fortresses awash with legends, and rare gems of impressionistic beauty, such as Udaipur. There are also a number of centres which attract travellers from far and wide, such as mellow Pushkar with its holy lake, and the bewitching desert city of Jaisalmer which resembles a fantasy from *The Thousand & One Nights*.

Rajasthan is one of India's prime tourist destinations, offering the traveller a potpourri of visual, culinary, spiritual and cultural experiences. Nobody leaves here without taking home priceless memories, a bundle of souvenirs, and an address book full of friends.

Festivals

Rajasthan has all the usual Hindu and Muslim festivals, some celebrated with special local fervour, as well as a number of festivals of its own.

Without a doubt, Rajasthan is best known for the immense and colourful Pushkar Camel Fair, held annually in November. This massive congregation of camels, cattle, livestock traders, pilgrims, tourists and filmmakers, is one of the planet's most incredible events. Other festivals include the Bikaner Camel Festival, Nagaur Fair and the Jaisalmer Desert Festival.

The dates of the fairs and festivals are determined by the lunar calendar. See the Festival Calendar below for details.

Art & Architecture

Rajasthan has various schools of miniature painting, the style largely deriving from the Mughal style but with some clear differences

Festival Calendar

Festival	Location	1998	1999	2000
Camel Festival	Bikaner	11-12 Jan	1-2 Jan	20-21 Jan
Nagaur Fair	Nagaur	3-6 Feb	24-27 Jan	12-15 Feb
Baneshwar Fair	Dungarpur	9-11 Feb	29-31 Jan	17-19 Feb
Desert Festival	Jaisalmer	9-11 Feb	29-31 Jan	17-19 Feb
Elephant Festival	Jaipur	12 Mar	1 Mar	19 Mar
Gangaur Fair	Jaipur	30-31 Mar	20-21 Mar	7-8 Apr
Mewar Festival	Udaipur	30-31 Mar	20-21 Mar	7-8 Apr
Summer Festival	Mt Abu	1-3 Jun	1-3 Jun	1-3 Jun
Teej Fair	Jaipur	26-27 Jul	14-15 Aug	2-3 Aug
Dussehra Mela	Kota	29 Sept to 1 Oct	17-19 Oct	5-7 Oct
Marwar Festival	Jodhpur	4-5 Oct	23-24 Oct	12-13 Oct
Camel Fair	Pushkar	1-4 Nov	20-23 Nov	9-11 Nov
Chandrabhaga Fair	Jhalawar	2-4 Nov	22-24 Nov	10-12 Nov

– in particular, the palace and hunting scenes are complemented by religious themes, relating especially to the Krishna legends. This art carried through to the elegant palaces built by the Rajputs when they were freed from confrontation with the Mughals. Many, such as Bundi, are liberally covered with colourful frescoes.

Most of Rajasthan's early architecture was damaged or destroyed by the first waves of Muslim invaders. Fragments remaining from that period include the Adhai-din-ka-Jhonpra in Ajmer, a mosque which is basically a converted Hindu temple, and the ruined temples at Osiyan, near Jodhpur. There are many buildings dating from the 10th to 15th centuries, including the superb Jain temples at Ranakpur and Mt Abu. Most of the great forts date, in their present form, from the Mughal period.

Accommodation
Palaces, Forts & Castles Rajasthan is famous for its superb palace hotels. The bulk of Rajasthan's maharajas have had to turn their palaces into hotels to make ends meet. The most renowned are Udaipur's super-luxurious Lake Palace Hotel and Shiv Niwas Palace Hotel, Jaipur's Rambagh Palace, and the Umaid Bhawan Palace in Jodhpur.

You don't have to spend a fortune to stay in a palace – there are plenty of other royal options which are more moderately priced. Many of these are known as Heritage Hotels, and they include *havelis* (traditional mansions built around a courtyard), forts and hunting lodges. Most tourist offices have a brochure listing Heritage Hotels.

Hotel Tariffs Most hotels in Rajasthan increase their room rates annually around the 1st October. The increase can be anything from 5% to as much as 50%.

Quite a few places also slap an additional tax (usually about 10%) on top of their advertised room rates. This extra charge goes by various names including: luxury tax, service tax, sales tax, extra tax or just plain old 'tax'.

Tourist Bungalows The RTDC (Rajasthan Tourism Development Corporation) operates a network of hotels in almost every large town. A few years ago they were often the best value in town, but their prices are no longer the bargain they once were. In addition, the fabric and services of most have severely deteriorated. However, for shoestringers, they frequently offer pretty cheap dormitory accommodation. The local tourist office (often called the Tourist Reception Centre), is usually in the RTDC hotel.

Homestay/Paying Guest House Accommodation Staying with an Indian family can be a real education, and the curiosities of everyday Indian life can be fascinating.

Rajasthan's Homestay or Paying Guest House Scheme currently operates in Jaipur, Jodhpur, Udaipur, Jaisalmer, Bikaner, Ajmer, Pushkar, Bundi and Mt Abu. The cost is anything from Rs 70 to Rs 800 per day, depending on the level of facilities offered. The scheme is administered by the RTDC and tourist offices have comprehensive lists of the participating families.

Getting Around
Bus Rajasthan has an extensive and reasonably good state bus system. On most sectors there is a choice of ordinary and express buses. You're advised to stick to expresses since the ordinary buses stop frequently, make a lot of frustrating detours, take a long time to get anywhere and are generally decrepit vehicles.

If you're taking a bus from a major bus stand, it's worth buying a ticket from the ticket office rather than on board the bus. It guarantees (or at least comes closer to guaranteeing) a seat, and you're also more likely to get on the right bus since the ticket clerk usually writes the bus registration number on your ticket. This can be an important consideration because timetables at bus stations are invariably in Hindi.

For long journeys make sure you go to the toilet beforehand, as stops can be infrequent and in less than desirable places (especially for women).

A number of private bus companies run luxury buses between the major towns, and many travellers prefer these to the state buses. Fares are higher than those on the state system but the buses are faster, more comfortable and don't take standing passengers. Their only drawback is that some are equipped with that curse known as the video cassette recorder, which is usually pumped up at full volume.

Train Travelling by train in Rajasthan was always a slow process because much of the track was metre gauge, narrower than the broad gauge as used in the rest of the country. As part of the national 'uni-gauge' drive, some of the lines have now been converted and most of the rest should be upgraded by 1999. This means that you're likely to find some parts of the rail system in Rajasthan out of action during your visit.

There are now fast broad-gauge connections between Delhi and Jaipur, Jaipur and Jodhpur, Jodhpur and Jaisalmer, and Jaipur/Jodhpur and Udaipur and Bikaner. Udaipur should be converted to broad gauge in 1998.

Train fares and schedules seem to constantly change in Rajasthan, so it's a good idea to double check details. Some trains can also book out quite quickly, so it's not a bad idea to make reservations well in advance.

The Palace on Wheels, one of India's most famous railway experiences, runs through Jaipur, Chittorgarh, Udaipur, Ranthambhore National Park, Jaisalmer, Jodhpur, Bharatpur and Agra. This train, a mobile hotel, is fitted out to look like a traditional maharaja's state carriage, and is an expensive but luxurious way to see the state. For more information, see the boxed aside in the Getting Around chapter.

Eastern Rajasthan

JAIPUR
Pop: 1.8 million   Tel Area Code: 0141
Jaipur, the vibrant capital of Rajasthan, is popularly known as the 'pink city' because of the pink-coloured buildings in its old city.

It sits on a dry lake bed in a somewhat arid landscape, surrounded by barren hills surmounted by forts and crenellated walls. This buzzing metropolis is certainly a place of wild contrasts and a veritable feast for the eyes. Vegetable-laden camel carts thread their way through streets jam-packed with cars, rickshaws, bicycles, tempos, motorbikes, and pedestrians frantically dodging the chaotic traffic. Traditionally dressed Rajput men sporting bright turbans and swashbuckling moustaches discuss village politics outside restaurants serving spaghetti Bolognese and American ice-cream sodas. Ramshackle roadside stalls selling *jootis* (traditional Rajasthani shoes) stand beside kitsch shops selling a mishmash of modern trinkets.

Jaipur has long outstripped the confines of its city wall and is today among the most tumultuous and polluted places in Rajasthan. Despite this, it seldom disappoints the first-time visitor.

History
The city owes its name, its foundation and its careful planning to the great warrior-astronomer Maharaja Jai Singh II (1693-1743). His predecessors had enjoyed good relations with the Mughals and Jai Singh was careful to preserve this alliance.

In 1727, with Mughal power on the wane, Jai Singh decided the time was ripe to move down from his somewhat cramped hillside fort at nearby Amber to a new site on the plains. He laid out the city, with its surrounding walls and six rectangular blocks, according to principles of town planning set down in the *Shilpa-Shastra*, an ancient Hindu treatise on architecture. In 1728, he built the remarkable observatory (Jantar Mantar) which is still one of Jaipur's main attractions.

Orientation
The walled 'pink city' is in the north-east of Jaipur, while the new parts have spread to the south and west. The city's main tourist attractions are in the old part of town. The principal shopping centre in the old city is Johari Bazaar, the jewellers' market. Unlike most other shopping centres in narrow alleys

of the budget and mid-range hotels and restaurants, the railway station, the bus terminal, the GPO, many of the banks and the modern shopping centre.

Information

Tourist Offices The Tourist Reception Centre (☎ 370180) is in the RTDC Tourist Hotel compound and is open daily except Sunday from 8 am to 7 pm. It has a range of literature and the staff are quite efficient and helpful. There's another tourist office (☎ 315714) on

platform No 1 at the railway station. It's open daily from 6 am to 8 pm.

The Government of India tourist office (☎ 372200) is in the Hotel Khasa Kothi and, although it has lots of glossy leaflets, there's little other information, so it's of limited use. It's open Monday to Friday from 9 am to 6 pm, and Saturday from 9 am to 1 pm.

Money You can change money at Thomas Cook (☎ 360940) on the 1st floor of Jaipur Towers on MI Rd. It's open daily except

PLACES TO STAY		PLACES TO EAT		42	Main Bus Terminal
3	Samode Haveli	20	Royal's	46	Polo Victory Cinema
16	Hotel Kailash	21	LMB Hotel &	49	Cathay Pacific
22	Hotel Sweet Dream		Restaurant	51	Alitalia, British
25	Hotel Bissau Palace	24	Bismiliah Restaurant		Airways & Air India
26	Hotel Meghniwas	53	Rainbow Restaurant	52	Jaipur Towers
27	Tirupati Guest House	57	Copper Chimney		(Thomas Cook &
28	Shapura House	58	Handi Restaurant &		Airline Agents)
29	Madhuban		State Bank of	55	GPO
30	Umaid Bhawan Guest		Bikaner & Jaipur	60	DHL Worldwide
	House	62	Chanakya Restaurant		Express
31	Marudhara Hotel	63	Lassiwala	61	Andhra Bank
32	Pipalda House	67	Golden Dragon	64	Skyline NEPC
33	Jaipur Inn		Restaurant & Bake	65	Book Corner
34	Hotel Jaipur Ashok		Hut	66	Raj Mandir Cinema
35	RTD Hotel Teej	68	Niro's & Natraj	69	Books & News Mart
37	RTD Hotel Swagatam		Restaurants	70	Singhpol
38	Rajputana Palace	71	Indian Coffee House	72	Rajasthali Emporium
	Sheraton				& Rajasthan
40	Hotel Khasa Kothi &	**OTHER**			Handloom House
	Government of India	1	Samrat Gate	73	UP Airways
	Tourist Office	2	Zorawar Gate	74	Ajmeri Gate
41	RTDC Hotel Gangaur	4	Gangapol	75	New Gate
43	Jai Mangal Palace	5	Char Gate	76	Lufthansa
44	Hotel Mangal	6	Govind Devji Temple	77	Sanganeri Gate
45	Hotel Arya Niwas	7	Jantar Mantar	78	Ghat Gate
47	Mansingh Hotel &		(Observatory)	79	Ram Niwas
	Central Bank of India	8	City Palace		Gardens
48	Hotel Neelam & Karni		Museum	80	Ravindra Rangmanch
	Niwas	9	Choti Chaupar		Art Gallery
50	Atithi & Aangan Guest	10	Iswari Minar Swarga	81	Zoo
	Houses		Sal	82	Central Museum
54	Jai Mahal Palace Hotel	11	Janta Manta		(Albert Hall)
56	RTD Tourist Hotel &		(Observatory)	83	Maharaja College
	Tourist Reception	12	Tripolia Gate	86	Registhan Tours
	Centre	13	Hawa Mahal	87	Anokhi
59	Evergreen Guest	14	Gopalj ka Rasta	90	Sawai Mansingh
	House & Hotel Pink	15	Jama Masjid		Hospital
	Sun	17	Haldio ka Rasta	92	Doll Museum
84	Hotel Diggi Palace	18	Ramganj Chaupar	93	Museum of Indology
85	Rajmahal Palace	19	Surajpol	94	Vidyadharji ka Bagh
88	Youth Hostel	23	Chandpol	95	Sisodia Rani Palace
89	Rambagh Palace	36	Sita World Travels		& Gardens
91	Narain Niwas Palace	39	Aravali Safari &		
	Hotel		Tours		

Sunday from 9.30 am to 6 pm. The State Bank of Bikaner & Jaipur, opposite the GPO, will change most travellers cheques. It's open daily except Sunday from 2 to 4 pm.

The Andhra Bank (☎ 369606), MI Rd, does cash advances on MasterCard and Visa. The Central Bank of India (☎ 317419), Anand Bldg, Sansar Chandra Marg, near the Mansingh Hotel, issues cash advances on MasterCard.

Post & Communications The GPO on MI Rd is quite efficient and there's a man at the entrance who sews up parcels, sealing them with wax. He is there everyday from 10 am to 4.30 pm and his prices are reasonable.

The DHL Worldwide Express office (☎ 362826) is in a lane off MI Rd at C-scheme, G-7A Vinoba Marg. It operates air freight around the world.

There are lots of round-the-clock local/long-distance telephone booths around Jaipur, and their charges are generally much cheaper than the hotels.

Bookshops There's a very good range of English-language hardbacks and paperbacks as well as magazines, guidebooks and maps at Book Corner, MI Rd, near Niro's restaurant. There's also an excellent collection in the bookshop at the Rambagh Palace.

Old City (Pink City)

The old city is partially encircled by a crenellated wall with a number of gates – the major gates are Chandpol, Ajmeri and Sanganeri. Broad avenues, over 30m wide, divide the pink city into neat rectangles.

It's an extremely colourful city and, in the evening light, the pink and orange buildings have a magical glow which is complemented by the brightly clothed Rajasthanis.

The major landmark in this part of town is the **Iswari Minar Swarga Sal** (Heaven Piercing Minaret), near the Tripolia Gate, which was built to overlook the city.

The main **bazaars** in the old city are Johari Bazaar (for jewellery and saris), Tripolia Bazaar (for brassware, carvings and lacquerware), Bapu Bazaar (for perfumes and textiles) and Chandpol Bazaar (for modern trinkets and bangles).

Hawa Mahal

Constructed in 1799, the Hawa Mahal, or Palace of the Winds, is one of Jaipur's major landmarks, although it is actually little more than a facade. This five storey building, which looks out over the main street of the old city, is a stunning example of Rajput artistry with its pink, semi-octagonal and delicately honeycombed sandstone windows. It was originally built to enable ladies of the royal household to look out on the city and thereby observe everyday life and processions. You can climb to the top of the Hawa Mahal for an excellent view over the city. The palace was built by Maharaja Sawaj Pratap Singh and is part of the City Palace complex. There's a small archaeological museum on the same site.

Entrance to the Hawa Mahal is from the rear of the building. To get there, go back to the intersection on your left as you face the Hawa Mahal, turn right and then take the first right again through an archway. It's open daily from 9 am to 4.30 pm. There's a small entry fee, plus a Rs 50 camera charge.

City Palace

In the heart of the old city, the City Palace occupies a large area divided into a series of courtyards, gardens and buildings. The outer wall was built by Jai Singh, but other additions are much more recent, some dating to the start of this century. Today, the palace is a blend of Rajasthani and Mughal architecture. The son of the last maharaja and his family still reside in part of the palace.

The seven storey Chandra Mahal is the centre of the palace and commands fine views over the gardens and the city. The ground and 1st floors of the Chandra Mahal form the **Maharaja Sawai Man Singh II Museum**. The apartments are well maintained and the museum has an extensive collection of paintings, weapons and royal costumes. The newer **Mubarak Mahal** forms part of this museum and was built by Maharaja Sawai Madho Singh II in the late 19th century.

Other points of interest in the palace include the **diwan-i-am**, or the hall of public audience, with its intricate decorations and manuscripts in Persian and Sanskrit, and the **diwan-i-khas**, or hall of private audience, with a marble-paved gallery.

Outside the buildings, you can see enormous silver vessels in which a former maharaja used to take holy Ganges water to England. Being a devout Hindu, he preferred not to risk the English water!

The palace and museum are open daily between 9.30 am and 4.30 pm. Entry is Rs 35, plus Rs 50 for camera, Rs 100 for a video. There are guides for hire inside the palace complex for Rs 100.

Jantar Mantar

Adjacent to the entrance to the City Palace is the Jantar Mantar, or observatory, begun by Jai Singh in 1728. Jai Singh's passion for astronomy was even more notable than his prowess as a warrior and, before commencing construction, he sent scholars abroad to study foreign observatories. The Jaipur observatory is the largest and the best preserved

Royalty at play: ivory door panel (18th century).

of the five he built, and was restored in 1901. Others are in Delhi (the oldest, dating from 1724), Varanasi and Ujjain. The fifth, the Muttra observatory, is gone.

At first glance, Jantar Mantar appears to be just a curious collection of sculptures but, in fact, each construction has a specific purpose, such as measuring the positions of stars, altitudes and azimuths, or calculating eclipses. The most striking instrument is the sundial with its 27m high gnomon. The shadow this casts moves up to four metres an hour.

The observatory is open daily from 9.30 am to 4.30 pm and admission is Rs 4 (free on Monday). Photography is discouraged by the usual Rs 50 fee for a camera, Rs 100 for a video.

Those interested in the theory behind the construction of these monumental instruments should buy a copy of *A Guide to the Jaipur Astronomical Observatory* by BL Dhama, which can be purchased on site.

Central Museum

This dusty collection is housed in the architecturally impressive Albert Hall in the Ram Niwas Gardens, south of the old city. Exhibits include portraits of the Jaipur maharajas, tribal costumes, miniature paintings, musical instruments and decorative arts. Entry to the museum is Rs 5 (free on Monday). It is open daily except Friday from 10 am to 4.30 pm. Photography is prohibited.

Other Attractions

The Ram Niwas Gardens also has a **zoo** with unhappy looking animals and a small crocodile breeding farm. Jaipur has a modern **art gallery** in the 'theatre' near the zoo. **Kripal Kumbh**, B18/A Shiva Marg, where Jaipur's famous blue pottery is made, can also be visited.

The **Museum of Indology** is an odd private collection of folk art objects and other bits and pieces of interest – there's everything from a map of India painted on a rice grain, to manuscripts (one written by Aurangzeb), jewellery, fossils, coins, old currency notes, clocks, watches and much more. The museum is in fact in a private house (although the living quarters seem to have been swallowed up by the collection), and is signposted off J Nehru Marg, south of the Central Museum. It's open daily from 8 am to 6 pm. Entry is Rs 35.

Finally, if you go to only one Hindi movie while you're in India, see it at the **Raj Mandir**, just off MI Rd. This opulent cinema is a Jaipur tourist attraction in its own right and is usually full, despite its immense size.

Organised Tours
Jaipur City The RTDC offers half day and full day tours of Jaipur and its environs. They visit the Hawa Mahal, Amber Fort, Jantar Mantar, City Palace and Central Museum (closed Friday), and include the inevitable stop at a craftshop.

A full day tour costs Rs 90 and lasts from 9 am to 6 pm, including a lunch break at Nahargarh Fort. Half day tours are a little rushed but otherwise OK. They cost Rs 60; timings are 8 am to 1 pm, 11.30 am to 4.30 pm and 1.30 to 6.30 pm. Tours depart daily from the railway station (according to demand), but you can also arrange to be collected from any of the RTDC hotels. Contact the Tourist Reception Centre or tourist office at the railway station for details.

Those who want to explore Jaipur at more leisure should hire an auto-rickshaw, cycle-rickshaw or bicycle.

Other Tours From 6 to 10 pm on Saturday and Sunday, there are RTDC tours (including veg dinner) to Nahargarh Fort (Rs 100) and Chokhi Dhani (Rs 130). These only operate if there are a minimum of 10 people, so check in advance to make sure it's on.

If you want a taste of rural Rajasthan, the Hotel Bissau Palace organises tours to their erstwhile hunting pavilion, *The Retreat*, about 27km from Jaipur. From here you are whisked away by camel cart to several nearby villages. It costs Rs 500 per person (for a minimum of six people) or Rs 750 per person (below six people). This includes transport, the village tour, and lunch. Bookings must be made in advance at the Hotel Bissau Palace (☎ 304371; fax 304628).

Festivals
Jaipur has a number of interesting festivals, including the Elephant Festival in March and the Teej Fair in July/August. For the exact dates, see the festival calendar at the start of this chapter.

Places to Stay
Getting to the hotel of your choice in Jaipur can be a huge problem. Auto-rickshaw drivers besiege most travellers who arrive by train (less so if you come by bus). Their persistence can be irritating to say the least, but just keep your cool and don't allow them to get the better of you. If you don't want to go to a hotel of their choice, they'll either refuse to take you at all or they'll demand at least double the normal fare. If you do go to the hotel of their choice, you'll pay through the nose for accommodation because the manager will be paying them a commission of at least 30% of what you are charged for a bed (and the charge won't go down for subsequent nights).

Unfortunately, many hotel owners cooperate with this 'mafia' but others refuse. It's invariably cheaper and generally more satisfactory in the long run to pay double the normal fare to be taken to the hotel of your choice.

Note that many hotels whack a 10% service charge on their advertised room rates. On the plus side, many places offer discounts of 25% to 40% in the low season (April to September).

If you wish to stay with an Indian family, contact the Tourist Reception Centre which has details of Jaipur's Paying Guest House Scheme.

Places to Stay – bottom end
Jaipur Inn (☎ 316821) in Bani Park, about a km west of Chandpol, is an old favourite with travellers. It's a well kept and friendly place run by retired Wing Commander RN Bhargava and his son. Rooms range from Rs 100/150 with common bath to Rs 400/500

with attached bath and private balcony. There's also a clean dormitory (Rs 60), and you can even camp on the lawn (Rs 35 per person) if you have your own tent. Meals are available and the rooftop terrace commands sensational views over Jaipur.

Evergreen Guest House (☎ 363446; fax 371934), off MI Rd, is another popular option, although it could do with a facelift. It's a large hotel, complete with restaurant, small swimming pool and buildings of various vintages arranged around a garden courtyard. Because of its size the personal touch has been lost. Dorm beds cost Rs 50. Singles/ doubles with attached bath and bucket hot water cost Rs 100/150 or Rs 200/250 with constant hot water and air-cooling, and air-con rooms are Rs 350/450.

Hotel Pink Sun (☎ 376753) is nearby if you find the Evergreen too much of a scene. Cheap but pretty uninspiring doubles cost Rs 150 with attached bath; and there are also a few singles with common bath for Rs 75.

Hotel Diggi Palace (☎ 373091; fax 370359), just off Sawai Ram Singh Marg, less than a km south of Ajmeri Gate, is a popular choice. Formerly the palace of the *thakur* (similar to a lord or baron) of Diggi, it has a pleasant garden and tranquil ambience. Basic singles/ doubles with common bath cost Rs 100/125 and doubles with private bath start from Rs 200. It's worth looking at a few rooms first, as some are better than others. Good meals are available in the restaurant.

Youth Hostel (☎ 375455) is inconveniently located out of town, and few foreigners stay here. There are tightly packed dorm beds (Rs 20 for members) as well as two double rooms for Rs 50.

Retiring Rooms at the railway station are handy if you're catching an early morning train. Dorm beds cost Rs 35 (men only), rooms with common bath are Rs 60/100 or Rs 80/150 with bath.

Marudhara Hotel (☎ 321912), D-240 Bani Park, has basic, somewhat tatty, singles/ doubles with attached bath for Rs 100/125.

Pipalda House (☎ 321925), nearby, is a touch better and offers doubles with common bath for Rs 150, or Rs 250 with bath attached.

Hotel Kailash (☎ 565372), opposite the Jama Masjid in the old city, has rooms ranging from Rs 100/110 with common bath to Rs 140/165 with attached bath.

Hotel Sweet Dream (☎ 314409), to the south in Nehru Bazaar, has reasonably good rooms from Rs 190/250 with bath – ask to see a few first as some are better than others. There's a veg restaurant on the rooftop.

Karni Niwas (☎ 365433), at C-5 Motilal Atal Marg, behind the Hotel Neelam, is a down-to-earth place run by a friendly family. Rooms are from Rs 225/275 with attached bath and constant hot water. Better rooms with air-con go for Rs 625/650 (some with private balcony).

Atithi Guest House (☎ 378679) is at 1 Park House Scheme, opposite All India Radio, between MI Rd and Station Rd. It's a well kept place, run by the amiable Shukla family. Clean rooms with air-cooling and attached bath cost Rs 300/350, deluxe rooms cost Rs 500/550. Meals are available.

Aangan Guest House (☎ 373449), next door, is another good family run place that's great value for money. Comfortable singles/ doubles with air-cooling and private bath go for Rs 150/200, Rs 175/250 for a larger room with TV, or Rs 450/500 with air-con. Meals are available.

Hotel Arya Niwas (☎ 372456; fax 364376) just off Sansar Chandra Marg, has rooms with attached bath from Rs 250/350 to Rs 450/550. Although this place is certainly well maintained, like many hotels that expand over the years, it has lost the personal touch and homely atmosphere that it once had. There's a pleasant front lawn and a large self-service restaurant (which may bring back memories of boarding school); they do great macaroni cheese (Rs 17).

Madhuban (☎ 200033; fax 202344), at D-237 Behari Marg, Bani Park, is perfect if you crave a homely ambience and peaceful setting. This small and friendly family run place has a nice garden and range of comfortable rooms. Air-cooled singles/doubles with attached bath cost Rs 300/350 or Rs 450/500 for a better room. Deluxe air-con rooms cost Rs 650/700. Meals are also available and there is a puppet show most evenings.

Shapura House (☎ 312293) is in the same area, at D-257 Devi Marg. Singles/doubles with air-cooling and attached bath cost Rs 350/400, while air-con rooms are Rs 450/500. They operate camel safaris and also have a horse-drawn carriage for sightseeing around Jaipur (Rs 1000 for two!).

RTDC Places The *Hotel Swagatam* (☎ 310595) near the Jaipur railway station is pretty good as far as RTDC places go, although it has something of an institutional feel to it. Dorm beds are Rs 50, singles/ doubles with attached bath are Rs 200/275, and deluxe rooms cost Rs 325/450. There's a relaxing lawn area, restaurant and bar.

Tourist Hotel (☎ 360238) is housed in the rambling former Secretariat building off MI Rd. It's desperately in need of renovation, but reasonably cheap. Dorm beds are Rs 50, singles/doubles are Rs 150/200, deluxe rooms with air-cooling are Rs 225/300; all rooms have attached bath and hot water.

Hotel Teej (☎ 322538) is a mid-range place but also has dorm beds for Rs 50. See the mid-range accommodation section for full details.

Places to Stay – middle
Hotel Meghniwas (☎ 322661; fax 321420), C-9 Sawai Jai Singh Highway, in Bani Park, has the homely atmosphere of a large guest house and is an excellent place to stay. Pleasant air-cooled rooms cost Rs 785/800, Rs 950/1000 with air-con, or Rs 1145/1195 for a suite. There's a quiet garden and a swimming pool. Breakfast costs Rs 95, lunch/dinner is Rs 195.

Umaid Bhawan Guest House (☎ 316184), D1-2A Bani Park, has air-cooled singles/doubles with attached bath from Rs 350/450, and air-con rooms from Rs 750/850. This place is not as impressive as the Hotel Meghniwas, but is still well run and clean.

LMB Hotel (☎ 565844; fax 562176) is right in the heart of the old city in Johari Bazaar. Although it's better known for its restaurant, the hotel does have fairly good rooms, and the location is hard to beat. Singles/doubles with bath start at Rs 775/975.

Hotel Neelam (☎ 372215; fax 367808), at A-3 Motilal Atal Marg, has good, if somewhat dark, rooms from Rs 400/450. There's also a veg restaurant.

Hotel Bissau Palace (☎ 304371; fax 304628), north of Chandpol, was built by the *rawal* (nobleman) of Bissau in the 1920s. Unlike most other royal abodes, you won't have to pay a fortune to stay here. Comfortable air-cooled rooms cost Rs 495/660 and air-con rooms are Rs 900/990. Like most palaces, some rooms have more character than others, so try to see a few before deciding. There's a fine restaurant, swimming pool, tennis court, shops and an interesting library. They can also arrange good village tours at their country estate, *The Retreat*, where Prince Charles and Princess Diana once visited (in happier days!) – see under Organised Tours, earlier in this section.

Hotel Khasa Kothi (☎ 375151), not far from the railway station, is quite a good choice, although in need of a revamp. Large rooms, all with air-cooling and attached bath, range from Rs 700/750 up to Rs 2500. Facilities include a swimming pool, bar and restaurant.

Narain Niwas Palace Hotel (☎ 561291; fax 563448), in the south of the city, is a delightful place to stay. It's oozing with old-world charm and has a swimming pool and relaxing garden. Well appointed suites filled with old furniture and fittings cost Rs 1195/1800. There's also a new annexe, decorated in traditional style, with rooms from Rs 1000/1350. The set breakfast/lunch/dinner costs Rs 100/225/225. The owners also operate the *Royal Castle Kanota*, 14km southeast of Jaipur.

RTDC Places The *Hotel Teej* (☎ 374373) in Bani Park is a rather characterless place. It has musty air-cooled rooms with bath for Rs 350/475, air-con rooms for Rs 550/600, and dorm beds for Rs 50. There's a bar and restaurant here.

Hotel Gangaur (☎ 371641) is just off MI Rd, and seems to be better maintained than

PAUL BEINSSEN

RICHARD I'ANSON

PAUL BEINSSEN

Rajasthan
Top: A camel driver with his charges.
Bottom Left: Palace of the Winds, Jaipur.
Bottom Right: Dawn at the Pushkar Camel Fair.

MARK DAFFEY

MICHELLE COXALL

Jaisalmer

Top : Looking across Jaisalmer to the ramparts of the Fort.
Bottom: Carpet sellers in the Fort take a break.

the average RTDC place. Air-cooled singles/ doubles cost Rs 400/500 and air-con rooms are Rs 550/650, all with bath and hot water. It's a bit noisy but there's a sunny courtyard, a restaurant and coffee shop.

Places to Stay – top end
Samode Haveli (☎ 47068; fax 602370) is in the north-east corner of the old city. This superb 200 year old building was once the town house of the rawal of Samode, who was also prime minister of Jaipur. There's a charming open terrace area, an impressive dining room, and a couple of breathtaking suites – one totally covered with original mirrorwork. Rooms cost Rs 1195/1600 or Rs 2395 for a suite. It's the ideal film set, and was, in fact, a location for the movie *Far Pavilions*.

Rambagh Palace (☎ 381919; fax 381098), south of the city, is the place to stay if you really want to pamper yourself. This grandiose and romantic palace, once the maharaja of Jaipur's residence, is now an upmarket hotel operated by the Taj Group. The cheapest singles/doubles are US$175/195. The better rooms cost US$315, and are far more sumptuous – if you're going to splurge, take one of these. Prices go right up to US$675 for the luxurious royal suites. If you can't afford to stay, at least treat yourself to an evening drink at the terrace bar.

Jai Mahal Palace Hotel (☎ 371616; fax 365237) is on the corner of Jacob and Ajmer Rds, south of the railway station. Also run by the Taj Group, this very pleasant place has rooms ranging from US$145/165 all the way up to US$500 for suites. Facilities include a swimming pool, bar and restaurant.

Rajmahal Palace (☎ 381757; fax 381887), on Sardar Patel Marg in the south of the city, is the smallest of the Taj Group's hotels. It is yet another formerly important building, this time the erstwhile British Residency. It is by no means as luxurious or as polished in service as the previous two hotels, but it still offers top of the range facilities, such as a pool and good restaurant. Rooms cost US$60/ 80 (US$37/60 from May to September), or US$325 for the suites. The huge forecourt is often used for wedding receptions.

Rajputana Palace Sheraton (☎ 360011; fax 367848) is between Station and Palace Rds, within walking distance of the railway station. Run by Welcomgroup, it's not a palace as the name suggests, but rather a modern five star hotel, tastefully designed and built around a swimming pool. Rooms range from US$135/150 right up to US$700. There's a coffee shop, bar, two swish restaurants, shopping arcade and health club (good for those who have indulged in one too many sticky Indian sweets!).

Hotel Clarks Amer (☎ 550616; fax 550013), J Nehru Marg, is less expensive at US$80/90, but it's inconveniently located about 10km south of the city centre. Facilities include a pool, coffee shop and restaurant.

Holiday Inn (☎ 609000; fax 609090) is just north of the old city on Amber Rd. It's set in rather bleak surroundings but the rooms are suitably comfortable, and cost from Rs 2200/2400.

Mansingh Hotel (☎ 378771; fax 377582), off Sansar Chandra Marg in the centre of town, has rooms from Rs 2500/3000, a swimming pool and two restaurants. This place is a little lacking in character though.

Hotel Jaipur Ashok (☎ 320091; fax 322999), Jai Singh Circle, Bani Park, is one of those hotels which was fine when it first opened but has been on the decline ever since. Run by ITDC, rooms cost Rs 1195/ 2200, and there's a pool that non-guests can use for Rs 100.

Places to Eat
Jaipur has a range of eating places to suit most tastes and budgets. Local licensing laws mean that only hotels can serve alcohol. This piece of legislation has been skilfully circumvented by some restaurants and beer may be served in glasses shrouded in paper napkins – or even served in a teapot and drunk out of cups. 'Special Tea', they call it!

Niro's on MI Rd, is a favourite with Indians and westerners alike. It's so popular, in fact, that you may have to wait for a table; the wait isn't usually too long. They offer veg and non-veg Indian, Chinese and Continental food. Baked fish Florentine costs Rs 110, while an American ice-cream soda will set you back a cool Rs 50.

LMB (Laxmi Mishthan Bhandar) in Johari Bazaar, near the centre of the old city, has food which 'promotes longevity, intelligence, vigour, health and cheerfulness'. This is one of Jaipur's most popular vegetarian restaurants; it also has amazingly pristine 1950s 'hip' decor. Main dishes range from Rs 35 to Rs 70. A dessert speciality is LMB kulfi, including dry fruits, saffron and cottage cheese (Rs 42). Out the front, a counter serves snacks, ice cream and an assortment of colourful Indian sweets.

Natraj Restaurant, near Niro's, is a vegetarian place that's also popular for its sweets and spicy nibbles. Their north Indian food is good; a Kashmiri curry costs Rs 52.

Chanakya Restaurant, further up MI Rd, is a little more expensive but still good. A veg steak sizzler (totally veg) is Rs 120, but most other main dishes are around Rs 55.

Handi Restaurant, in the same area, opposite the GPO, is tucked away at the back of the Maya Mansions building. It's nothing fancy as far as decor goes, but it offers great barbecue chicken (Rs 53 for half a chicken) and kebabs. Don't confuse this place with the Handi Bamboo Hut Restaurant (in the grounds of the RTDC Tourist Hotel).

Copper Chimney, not far from the Handi Restaurant, is a worthwhile treat. It offers excellent veg and non-veg Indian, Continental and Chinese cuisine; their Indian food is best. A main veg dish costs from Rs 40 to Rs 75. The ambience is pleasant, the service is attentive and the food is delicious.

Jaipur Inn boasts one of the city's only rooftop restaurants. It has superb views over Jaipur and is especially delightful at sunset. The Indian veg buffet dinner costs Rs 70. Non-residents should book in advance.

Indian Coffee House on MI Rd, off the street, next to Arrow men's wear, is good if you are suffering withdrawal symptoms from lack of a decent cup of coffee. Cheap south Indian food is also available. It's rather seedy inside and looks like the kind of place where shady deals are consummated – over a strong black coffee, of course.

Golden Dragon Restaurant, down the side street next to Niro's, has tasty Chinese cuisine, including Singapore noodles (Rs 50) and chicken Manchurian (Rs 65).

Bake Hut is nearby and offers a selection of mouth-watering pastries including donuts and Black Forest cake. Go on, lash out and worry about the calories later.

Rambagh Palace is the place to go for a really serious splurge. You couldn't find more opulent surroundings than at the dining room here, although the food gets mixed reports. The menu is heavy and so are the prices – a main dish will lighten your money belt by at least Rs 150.

Things to Buy

Jaipur is *the* place to shop until you drop! It has heaps of handicrafts ranging from grimacing papier-mâché puppets to exquisitely carved furniture. You'll have to bargain hard though – this city is accustomed to tourists with lots of money and little time to spend it.

Jaipur is especially well known for precious stones, which seem cheaper here than

Embroidery: a popular souvenir.

elsewhere in India, and is even better known for semi-precious gems. For precious stones, find a narrow alley called Haldion ka Rasta off Johari Bazaar (near the Hawa Mahal). Semi-precious stones are sold in another alley, called the Gopalji ka Rasta, on the opposite side of the street. There are many shops here which offer bargain prices, but you do need to know your gems. Marble statues, costume jewellery and textile prints are other Jaipur specialities.

Shops around the tourist traps, such as the City Palace and Hawa Mahal, are likely to be more expensive although they do have some interesting items including miniatures, handicrafts and relatively cheap clothes. The Rajasthali Emporium on MI Rd sells an interesting range of handicrafts from around the state. Rajasthan Handloom House is next door, with a range of excellent textiles. Another highly recommended place for textiles is Anokhi, at 2 Tilak Marg, not far from the Secretariat. It has a superb range of high quality textiles such as block-printed fabrics, tablecloths, bed covers, cosmetic bags and scarves.

Jaipur's salespeople can be incredibly persuasive and tenacious. Their hounding can sometimes drive you nuts, but just keep your sanity and ignore them. Most rickshaw-wallahs are right into the commission business and it's almost guaranteed that they'll be getting a hefty cut from any shop they take you to. Many unwary visitors get talked into buying things for resale at inflated prices. Beware of these 'buy now to sell at a profit later' scams – see the warning under Things to Buy in the Facts for the Visitor chapter for more details.

For fixed-price *khadi* (homespun cloth) and cotton, go to a Khadi Gramodyog shop. These government-run shops have a wide range and everything is handmade. There's one just inside Sanganeri Gate in Bapu Bazaar.

Getting There & Away

Air Numerous international airlines are based in Jaipur Towers on MI Rd, including Singapore Airlines, Thai Airlines, Air Canada, United Airlines and Air France.

For all domestic flights, it's easiest to book through any travel agent such as Satyam Travels & Tours (☎ 374490; fax 370843), located on the ground floor of the Jaipur Towers building. The office is open daily except Sunday from 10 am to 6 pm. The Indian Airlines office (☎ 514407) is a little out of town on Tonk Rd. Indian Airlines flies Delhi-Jaipur (US$45) daily, and most flights continue to Mumbai (Bombay), via any one or all of Jodhpur (US$60), Udaipur (US$60) and Aurangabad (US$110). There's also a direct flight to and from Mumbai (US$125) three times weekly.

Sahara Airlines (☎ 365741), UP Airways (☎ 378206), Skyline NEPC (☎ 365118), and ModiLuft (☎ 369693) also operate flights to various domestic destinations. These airlines tend to have erratic timetables, so check if, and when, they are operating. It's wise to make bookings well in advance with all airlines, especially during the busy tourist season.

Bus Buses to all of Rajasthan's main centres and to Delhi and Agra are operated by the Rajasthan State Transport Corporation (RSTC) from the main bus terminal (☎ 363277) on Station Rd. Some services are deluxe (essentially non-stop). The deluxe buses all leave from platform No 3, which is tucked away in the right-hand corner of the bus terminal. These buses should be booked in advance at the booking office, open from 8 am to 10 pm, also on platform No 3.

State transport deluxe buses depart every 15 minutes for Delhi (Rs 136, 5½ hours). There are also ordinary buses for Rs 74 and air-con coaches for Rs 234. Buses frequently depart to Agra (Rs 78, five hours) and to Ajmer (Rs 43, 2½ hours). Six deluxe buses per day take seven hours to reach Jodhpur and cost Rs 102. To Udaipur, there are four deluxe buses daily; they take about 10 hours and cost Rs 120. There are six buses daily to Kota (Rs 77, five hours). For Jaisalmer there is an ordinary bus (Rs 165, 15 hours), and a faster night bus (Rs 187, 13 hours).

A number of private companies cover the same routes, and also offer services to Ahmedabad, other cities in Gujarat and Mumbai.

RAJASTHAN

The buses are not as frequent as those operated by the RSTC and often travel at night. Avoid video buses unless you want a thumping headache the next morning!

Train Many of the lines into Jaipur have been converted to broad gauge. As other parts of the state's railway are converted expect disruptions to services.

The computerised railway reservation office (☎ 131133), at the station entrance, is open Monday to Saturday from 8 am to 8 pm, and Sunday from 8 am to 2 pm. Join the queue for 'Freedom Fighters & Foreign Tourists'.

See the table below for train services. Apart from the trains mentioned in this table, there are also services to Ajmer, Sawai Madhopur, Abu Road, Ahmedabad, Kota, Mumbai and Sikar.

Getting Around
The Airport The airport is 15km out of the city centre; a taxi costs at least Rs 160. To cut the cost, try to share with others.

Local Transport Jaipur has taxis, auto-rickshaws, cycle-rickshaws, tempos and a city bus service, which also operates to Amber. For taxis and rickshaws, make sure you negotiate a price before setting off and keep in mind that Jaipur is notorious for over-inflated local transport costs. A cycle-rickshaw from the station to the Jaipur Inn or Hotel Arya Niwas should cost about Rs 8,

and Rs 14 from the station to Johari Bazaar. However, if you're going to a hotel that doesn't pay commission to the driver, you'll be extremely lucky to get a ride for these prices. In such cases, expect to pay two to three times the usual price.

Bicycles can be hired from most bike shops around town as well as from some budget hotels. Most places charge about Rs 25 per day (you may be able to bargain this down to Rs 20).

AROUND JAIPUR
There are some interesting attractions around Jaipur and you can get to most of these places by bus. Alternatively there are organised tours (see under Organised Tours earlier in this section).

Amber
About 11km out of Jaipur, on the Delhi to Jaipur road, is Amber, the ancient capital of Jaipur state. Construction of the fort-palace was begun in 1592 by Raja Man Singh, the Rajput commander of Akbar's army. It was later extended and completed by the Jai Singhs before the move to Jaipur on the plains below. The fort is a superb example of Rajput architecture, stunningly situated on a hillside and overlooking a lake which reflects its terraces and ramparts.

You can climb up to the fort from the road in about 10 minutes, and cold drinks are available within the palace if the climb is a hot one. A seat in a jeep up to the fort costs

Major Trains from Jaipur					
Destination	Train Number & Name	Departure Time	Distance (km)	Duration (hours)	Fare (Rs) (2nd/1st)
Agra	2308 Howrah Exp	11.00 pm	237	6.55	79/359
	Marudhar Exp	3.00 pm	237	7.00	79/359
Bikaner	4737 Bikaner Exp	9.05 pm	519	10.05	119/497
New Delhi	2015 Shatabdi Exp	5.50 pm	259	4.50	215/412
	Intercity Exp	5.30 am	259	5.20	92/215
Jodhpur	2465 Intercity Exp	5.30 am	318	4.35	89/214
Udaipur	9615 Chetak Exp	10.00 pm	431	11.30	112/430
	2915 Pink City Exp	12.20 pm	431	11.10	104/408

Rs 15. Riding up on elephants is popular, though daylight robbery at Rs 250 per elephant one way (each carries up to four people).

An imposing stairway leads to the **diwan-i-am**, or hall of public audience, with a double row of columns and latticed galleries above. Steps to the right lead to the small **Kali Temple**. There's also the white marble **Shila Devi Temple**.

The maharaja's apartments are on the higher terrace – you enter through a gateway decorated with mosaics and sculptures. The **Jai Mandir**, or hall of victory, is noted for its inlaid panels and glittering mirror ceiling. Regrettably, much of this was allowed to deteriorate during the 1970s and 1980s but restoration work proceeds. Opposite the Jai Mandir is the **Sukh Niwas**, or hall of pleasure, with an ivory-inlaid sandalwood door, and a channel running right through the room which once carried cooling water. From the Jai Mandir you can soak in the fine views from the palace ramparts over the lake below.

Amber Palace is open daily from 9 am to 4.30 pm and entry costs Rs 4. Photographers are hit with the usual steep Rs 50 charge, Rs 100 for a video.

Getting There & Away There are frequent buses to Amber from near the Hawa Mahal and from the railway station in Jaipur (Rs 3, 20 minutes).

Royal Gaitor
The **cenotaphs** of the royal family are at Gaitor, on the road from Jaipur to Amber. The white marble cenotaph of Maharaja Jai Singh II is impressive and is decorated with carved peacocks.

Opposite the cenotaphs is the **Jal Mahal** (Water Palace) in the middle of a lake and reached by a causeway. Or at least it was in the middle of a lake; the water is now all but squeezed out by that insidious weed, the water hyacinth.

Nahargarh Fort
Nahargarh Fort, also known as the Tiger Fort, overlooks the city from a sheer ridge to the north, and is floodlit at night. The fort

was built in 1734 and extended in 1868. An eight km road runs up through the hills from Jaipur, and the fort can be reached along a zigzagging two km path. The views fully justify the effort; the entry fee is Rs 4.

There's a small restaurant on the top, and this is a great place to come at sunset. You can even stay up here at the fort, although there's only one double room (Rs 300) which should be booked at the Tourist Reception Centre in Jaipur.

Jaigarh Fort
The imposing Jaigarh Fort, built in 1726 by Jai Singh, was only opened to the public in mid-1983. It's within walking distance of Amber and offers a great view over the plains from the Diwa Burj watchtower. The fort, with its water reservoirs, residential areas, puppet theatre and the cannon, Jaya Vana, is open from 9 am to 4.30 pm. Entry is Rs 10, plus an additional charge of Rs 50 per car, Rs 20 for a camera and Rs 100 for a video.

Samode
The small village of Samode is nestled among rugged hills about 50km north of Jaipur, via Chomu. The only reason to visit it is if you can afford to stay in the beautiful **Samode Palace** (although strictly speaking it's not actually a palace, as it wasn't owned by a ruler but by one of his noblemen). Like the Samode Haveli in Jaipur, this attractive building was owned by the rawal of Samode. The highlight of the building is the absolutely exquisite diwan-i-khas, which is covered with completely original painting and mirror-work, and is probably the finest example of its kind in the country.

Samode Palace (☎ (01423) 4114; fax 4123, or book through the Samode Haveli in Jaipur (☎ (0141) 47068; fax 602370) has rooms for Rs 1195/2395. Breakfast/lunch/dinner costs Rs 200/350/350. Non-guests can visit the palace by paying a Rs 100 entry fee. Similarly priced luxurious tent accommodation is available three km away at *Samode Bagh*.

Getting There & Away To get here, you'll have to take a bus to Chomu (Rs 7, one hour) then catch another bus to Samode (Rs 4, 30 minutes).

Galta
The temple of the sun god at Galta is 100m above Jaipur to the east, a 2.5km climb from Surajpol. A deep, temple-filled gorge stands behind the temple and there are good views over the surrounding plain.

Sisodia Rani Palace & Gardens
Six km from the city on Agra Rd and surrounded by terraced gardens, this palace was built for Maharaja Jai Singh's second wife, the Sisodia princess. The outer walls are decorated with murals depicting hunting scenes and the Krishna legend.

Vidyadharji ka Bagh
Nestled in a narrow valley, this beautiful garden was built in honour of Jai Singh's chief architect and town planner, Vidyadhar.

Balaji
The Hindu exorcism temple of Balaji is about 1.5km off the Jaipur to Agra road, about 1½ hours by bus from Bharatpur. The exorcisms are sometimes very violent and those being exorcised don't hesitate to discuss their experiences.

Sanganer
The small town of Sanganer is 16km south of Jaipur and is entered through the ruins of two *tripolias*, or triple gateways. In addition to its ruined palace, Sanganer has a group of Jain temples with fine carvings to which entry is restricted. The town is noted for handmade paper and block printing.

BHARATPUR
Pop: 1,646,500   Tel Area Code: 05644
A must for those with an interest in ornithology, Bharatpur is renowned for its World Heritage-listed bird sanctuary, the Keoladeo Ghana National Park. The best time to visit the sanctuary is from October to February when many migratory birds can be seen, though their numbers vary from year to year.

In the 17th and 18th centuries, the town was an important Jat stronghold. Before the arrival of the Rajputs, the Jats inhabited this area and were able to retain a high degree of autonomy, both because of their prowess in battle and because of their chiefs' marriage alliances with Rajput nobility. They successfully opposed the Mughals on more than one occasion and their fort at Bharatpur, constructed in the 18th century, withstood an attack by the British in 1805 and a long siege in 1825. This siege eventually led to the signing of the first treaty of friendship between the Indian states of north-west India and the East India Company.

The town itself, which was once surrounded by an 11km wall (now demolished), is of little interest. It's probably a good idea to bring mosquito repellent with you, as the mozzies can be a hassle.

Information
The Tourist Reception Centre (☎ 22542) is at the RTDC Hotel Saras. It's open daily except Sunday from 10 am to 1.30 pm and 2 to 5 pm. A guidebook including a map is available at the park entrance. It contains a short history of the park and a seemingly endless list of bird species, but is otherwise of little help to anyone without an understanding of ornithology. Books on birdlife are also available at a bookshop inside the park, about 1.5km from the main gate.

You can change money at the State Bank of Bikaner & Jaipur, near the Binarayan Gate.

Keoladeo Ghana National Park
No less than 415 kinds of birds have been recorded at the Keoladeo sanctuary, 117 of which migrate from as far away as Siberia and China. The sanctuary was formerly a vast semi-arid region, filling with water during the monsoon season only to rapidly dry up afterwards. To prevent this, the maharaja of Bharatpur diverted water from a nearby irrigation canal and, within a few years, birds began to settle in vast numbers. It seems his primary concern was not the environment but, rather, his desire to take guests on shooting sprees. A 'bag' of over 4000 birds per day

was not unusual. The carnage continued until shooting was banned in 1964 and, today, some 80 types of ducks are among the species which nest in the sanctuary.

The food requirements of the bird population can be enormous and it's hard to believe that these shallow lakes would be capable of meeting it – yet they do. For example, as many as 3000 painted storks nesting in a sq km need about three tonnes of fish every day, which amounts to over 90 tonnes of fish over their 40 day nesting period – and that's just one species.

Entry to the park costs Rs 25, plus Rs 10

for a camera and Rs 100 for a video camera. There's also an entry fee for cycles (Rs 3), scooters (Rs 10) and cycle-rickshaws (Rs 5). Motorised vehicles are prohibited in the park, so the only way of getting around is by walking, bicycle or cycle-rickshaw. Only those cycle-rickshaws authorised by the government (recognisable by the yellow plate bolted onto the front) are allowed inside the park – beware of anyone who tells you otherwise! Although you don't pay entry fees for the drivers of these cycle-rickshaws, you'll be up for about Rs 25 per hour if you take one and they'll expect a tip on top of that. Some

PLACES TO STAY & EAT
5 Hotel Park Palace
12 Tourist Lodge
29 Falcon Guest House, Jungle Lodge & Spoonbill Hotel & Restaurant
30 RTDC Hotel Saras & Tourist Reception Centre
31 Hotels Eagle's Nest & Sangam
32 Hotels Sunbird & Pelican
33 Wilderness Camp
34 Bharatpur Forest Lodge

OTHER
1 Goverdhan Gate
2 GPO
3 Deviji Temple
4 Chandpol
6 Khumer Gate
7 Museum
8 Austdhatu Gate
9 Ketan Gate
10 Jaghina Gate
11 Surajpol
12 Mathura Gate
13 Hospital
15 Lohiya Gate
16 Ganga Temple
17 City Post Office
18 Jama Masjid
19 Library
20 Old Laxman Temple
21 Laxman Temple
22 Anah Gate
23 Main Bus Stand
24 Neemda Gate
25 Atalbund Gate
26 State Bank of Bikaner & Jaipur
27 Binarayan Gate
28 Old Bus Stand

Bharatpur

RAJASTHAN

of the drivers actually know a lot about the birds you'll see and can be very helpful, so a tip is a reasonable request. If you wish to hire an experienced ornithologist, this will cost around Rs 40 per hour. Guides can be hired at the park entrance or at the Tourist Reception Centre.

A good way to see the park is to hire a bicycle (there are bikes for hire outside the sanctuary for Rs 20 per day). This allows you to easily avoid the bottlenecks which inevitably occur at the nesting sites of the larger birds. It's just about the only way you'll be able to watch the numerous kingfishers at close quarters – noise or human activity frightens them away. A bicycle also enables you to avoid clocking up a large bill with a rickshaw driver. Some of the hotels rent bicycles and usually charge from Rs 20 to Rs 30 per day. If you plan to visit the sanctuary at dawn (one of the best times to see the birds), you should hire your bicycle the day before. The southern reaches of the park are virtually devoid of *Humanus touristicus* and so are much better than the northern part for serious birdwatching.

Boats can be hired from the ticket checkpoint for Rs 60 per hour. They are a very good way of getting close to the wildlife.

There's a small snack bar and drinks kiosk about halfway through the park, next to the Keoladeo Temple.

This is one bird sanctuary which even non-ornithologists should visit and in fact, many travellers rate it as a highlight of their visit to India. It is open daily from 6 am to 6 pm and is situated about five km south of the city centre.

Lohagarh Fort

The Lohagarh Fort, or Iron Fort, was built in the early 18th century and took its name from its supposedly impregnable defences. Maharaja Suraj Mahl, the fort's constructor and founder of Bharatpur, built two towers within the ramparts, the Jawahar Burj and Fateh Burj, to commemorate his victories over the Mughals and the British.

The fort occupies the entire small artificial island in the centre of the town, and the three palaces within its precincts are in an advanced state of decay. One of the palaces houses a small and largely unexciting museum. Exhibits include sculptures, paintings, weapons and animal trophies. The museum is open daily except Friday from 10 am to 4 pm; entry is Rs 2.

Places to Stay & Eat

There's a good range of accommodation in Bharatpur, although it can get very busy during holidays, particularly around Christmas and the New Year. Since the railway station is about five km from the park, it's best to stay somewhere between Mathura Gate and the park entrance.

Tourist Lodge (☎ 23742), near Mathura Gate, is a popular and cheap little budget place. There are small singles/doubles with common bath for Rs 40/60, or from Rs 50/70 with bath attached. Hot water is by the bucket (free), and meals are available. Bikes and binoculars can be rented for Rs 30 (each) per day.

RTDC Hotel Saras (☎ 23700) is one of a group of places between the main road and park entrance. It's right by the road and so cops a fair amount of traffic noise and is rather unkempt – not a great choice. Dorm beds are Rs 50, singles/doubles range from Rs 275/325 to Rs 525/650 with air-con. There is also a restaurant.

Hotel Eagle's Nest (☎ 25144; fax 23170) is directly opposite the RTDC hotel and has comfortable rooms from Rs 200/350 with bath. Meals are available.

Hotel Sunbird (☎ 25701; fax 25147) is further along the road, and the rooms in this popular place fill up quickly. Clean singles/doubles with attached bath and constant hot water cost Rs 200/300.

Hotel Pelican (☎ 24221) nearby, is equally good and is run by the same people as the Tourist Lodge. There are basic rooms with common bath for Rs 50/80, or doubles for Rs 150 with attached bath and hot water. Dorm beds go for Rs 50. The restaurant serves Indian, Continental and even a small selection of Israeli food. You can rent bikes here for Rs 30 per day.

Wilderness Camp (no phone), located in the eucalyptus grove near the Hotel Pelican, is a tented camp with overpriced singles/doubles for Rs 350/450. The mosquitoes here can be tenacious, so don't forget to bring plenty of repellent. This campsite is only open from 15 October to 15 February.

Spoonbill Hotel & Restaurant (☎ 23571), just behind the RTDC Hotel Saras, is a good choice, with singles/doubles with private bath for Rs 100/150. Meals are available and you can rent bikes for Rs 25 per day and binoculars for Rs 30 per day.

Jungle Lodge (☎ 25622), nearby, has decent rooms from Rs 125/150 with attached bath or Rs 150/200 for a better room.

Hotel Sangam (☎ 25616) and *Falcon Guest House* (☎ 23815) are other cheapies in this area. Expect to pay around Rs 170/220 for rooms with bath.

Hotel Park Palace (☎ 23783) is the closest hotel to the bus stand, not far from Khumer Gate. Clean rooms with bath start from Rs 170/220 and there's a restaurant. This place is well maintained and managed, making it a fine choice.

Bharatpur Forest Lodge (☎ 22760; fax 22864) is about one km beyond the entrance gate and is run by the ITDC. To enjoy the privilege of staying in the national park itself, you'll have to pay Rs 1195/2300. The rooms are very pleasant and, if you can afford it, this is one of the best places to stay. Meals are available (buffet lunch/dinner costs Rs 297), and there are money-exchange facilities for guests.

Getting There & Away

Bus There are buses to a number of destinations including Agra (Rs 19, 1½ hours), Fatehpur Sikri (Rs 8, one hour), Jaipur (Rs 47, 4½ hours), and Deeg (Rs 12, one hour).

Train Bharatpur is on the Delhi to Mumbai broad-gauge line. Be certain that the train you choose is going to stop at Bharatpur – not all do.

The metre-gauge line between Jaipur and Agra is currently being converted to broad gauge so you may find that it's closed.

The *Firozpur Janta Express* travels between Delhi and Bharatpur and covers the 175km trip in about 4½ hours. It costs Rs 50/190 in 2nd/1st class.

Getting Around

You can use auto-rickshaws, cycle-rickshaws and tongas to get around town. A cheaper option is to hire a bicycle for Rs 20 to Rs 30 a day (the more expensive ones are usually in better condition).

DEEG
Pop: 40,000

Very few travellers ever make it to Deeg, about 36km north of Bharatpur. This is a pity because this small town with its massive fortifications, stunning palace and busy market is much more interesting than Bharatpur itself. It's an easy day trip from Bharatpur, Agra or Mathura.

Built by Suraj Mahl in the mid-18th century, Deeg was formerly the second capital of Bharatpur state and the site of a famous battle in which the maharaja's forces successfully withstood a combined Mughal and Maratha army of some 80,000 men. Eight years later, the maharaja even had the temerity to attack the Red Fort in Delhi! The booty he carried off included an entire marble building which can still be seen.

Suraj Mahl's Palace (Gopal Bhavan)

Suraj Mahl's Palace has to be one of India's most beautiful and delicately proportioned buildings. It's also in an excellent state of repair and, as it was used by the maharajas until the early 1970s, most of the rooms still contain their original furnishings.

Built in a combination of Rajput and Mughal architectural styles, the 18th century palace fronts onto a tank, the Gopal Sagar, and is flanked by two exquisite pavilions which were designed to resemble pleasure barges. The tank and palace are surrounded by well maintained gardens which also contain the Keshav Bhavan, or Summer Pavilion, with its hundreds of fountains, many of which are still functional but usually only turned on for local festivals.

The palace is open daily from 9 am to noon and 1 to 6 pm; admission is Rs 2. Deeg's massive walls (up to 28m high) and 12 bastions, some with their cannons still in place, are also worth exploring.

Places to Stay

As Deeg is essentially an agricultural town and few visitors ever come here with the intention of stopping overnight, accommodation is very limited.

Dak Bungalow is, frankly, quite undesirable and you should only come here if you're really desperate for somewhere to stay. It's run down, and rooms are around Rs 100.

RTDC Motel Deeg (no phone), on the same road, is a much better choice with clean singles/doubles with private bath for Rs 250/ 300.

Getting There & Away

There are frequent buses between Deeg and Alwar (Rs 20, 2½ hours). Buses travel at least once every hour between Deeg and Bharatpur (Rs 12, one hour).

SARISKA NATIONAL PARK
Tel Area Code: 0144

Located 107km from Jaipur and 200km from Delhi, the sanctuary is in a wooded valley surrounded by barren mountains. It covers 800 sq km (including a core area of 498 sq km) and has bluebulls, sambar, spotted deer, wild boar and, above all, tigers. Project Tiger (see the boxed section in the Uttar Pradesh chapter for more information) has been in charge of the sanctuary since 1979.

As at Ranthambhore National Park, also in Rajasthan, this park contains ruined temples as well as a fort, pavilions and a palace (now a hotel) built by the maharajas of Alwar. The sanctuary can be visited year round, except during July/August when the animals move to higher ground. Best time for spotting wildlife is between November and June.

You'll see most wildlife in the evening, though tiger sightings are becoming more common during the day.

The best way to visit the park is by jeep and these can be arranged at the Forest Reception Office (☎ 41333) on Jaipur Rd. It costs Rs 75 per jeep and there's an admission fee of Rs 25 per person, plus Rs 10 for a camera and Rs 100 for a video.

Places to Stay

RTDC Hotel Tiger Den (☎ 41342) is quite a popular choice with travellers. It costs Rs 450/550 for air-cooled singles/doubles, or Rs 625/750 for air-con rooms. A cheaper option is the dormitory for Rs 50. The hotel has a bar and restaurant.

Hotel Sariska Palace (☎ 41322), near the park entrance, is the imposing former hunting lodge of the maharajas of Alwar. It's a very pleasant place to stay with comfortable rooms for Rs 1190/2000. There's also a swimming pool, quiet gardens, bar, restaurant and jeeps for hire.

Getting There & Away

Sariska is 35km from Alwar, which is a convenient town from which to approach the sanctuary. There are direct buses to Alwar from Delhi (Rs 60, 170km) and Jaipur (Rs 40, 146km). Frequent buses travel between Sariska and Alwar (Rs 10). Though some people attempt to visit Sariska on a day trip from Jaipur, this option is expensive and largely a waste of time.

ALWAR
Pop: 250,000   Tel Area Code: 0144

Alwar was once an important Rajput state. It emerged in the 18th century under Pratap Singh, who pushed back the rulers of Jaipur to the south and the Jats of Bharatpur to the east, and who successfully resisted the Marathas. It was one of the first Rajput states to ally itself with the fledgling British Empire, though British interference in Alwar's internal affairs meant that this partnership was not always amicable.

There is a tourist office (☎ 21868) opposite Company Garden, Nehru Bal Vihar. It's open daily except Sunday from 10 am to 1.30 pm and 2 to 5 pm. You can change travellers cheques at the State Bank of Bikaner & Jaipur, near the bus stand.

Bala Quila

This imposing fort, with its five km of ramparts, stands 300m above the city. Predating the time of Pratap Singh, it's one of very few forts in Rajasthan constructed before the rise of the Mughals. Unfortunately, because the fort now houses a radio transmitter station, it can only be visited with special permission.

Palace Complex

Below the fort sprawls the huge city palace complex, its massive gates and tank lined by a beautifully symmetrical chain of *ghats* and pavilions. Today, most of the complex is occupied by government offices, but there's an interesting government museum housed in the former City Palace. It's open daily except Friday from 10 am to 4.30 pm and entry is Rs 2. Some of the museum's exhibits include miniature writing, ivory slippers, and old musical instruments.

Places to Stay & Eat

RTDC Hotel Lake Palace (☎ 22991) at Siliserh is a good place to relax, though it is some 20km from Alwar. It's a fairly modest palace built by Vinay Singh, Alwar's third ruler, and it overlooks a picturesque lake. Rooms cost Rs 400/500, or Rs 700/800 with air-con. There's a bar and restaurant; a veg thali costs Rs 55.

Ashoka Hotel (☎ 21780), not far from the bus stand in Alwar, has cheap rooms for Rs 50/100. Nearby are three hotels which are similar in price and standard to the Ashoka. They are the *Ankur Hotel* (☎ 333025), *Hotel Atlantic* (☎ 21581) and *New Alanka Hotel* (☎ 20027).

Hotel Aravali (☎ 332883), near the railway station, is run by the eager-to-please Kakkar family and is a fine choice. It has a good range of accommodation to suit most budgets. Dorm beds cost Rs 50, singles/doubles with private bath start from Rs 200/250. There's a good restaurant, bar and pool.

RTDC Hotel Meenal (☎ 22852) is a mid-range place, charging from Rs 300/400 for air-cooled singles/doubles to Rs 450/550 for air-con rooms. There's a restaurant and bar here.

Neemrana Fort Palace (☎ (01494) 6005; fax (011) 4621112), about 75km north of Alwar, is an impressive fortified palace. Dating from the 15th century, the Rajput king Prithviraj Chauhan III reigned from here. Rooms are suitably luxurious and start from Rs 1200/1500. There's a good restaurant and pleasant walks around the fort.

Getting There & Away

From Alwar, there are frequent buses to Sariska (Rs 10), Bharatpur (Rs 30), Deeg (Rs 20), Jaipur (Rs 40), and Delhi (Rs 52).

There are also rail links with Jaipur and Delhi. The *Pooja Express* travels between Alwar and Delhi (Rs 48); the 9759 *Intercity* travels from Alwar to Jaipur (Rs 42).

SHEKHAWATI

The semi-desert Shekhawati region lies in the triangular area between Delhi, Jaipur and Bikaner. Starting around the 14th century, a number of Muslim clans moved into the area and the towns which developed in the region became important trading posts on the caravan routes emanating from the ports of Gujarat.

Although the towns have long since lost any importance they may once have had, what they have not lost is the incredible painted havelis constructed by the merchants of the region. Most of the buildings date from the 18th century to early this century, and such is their splendour that the area has been dubbed by some as the 'open air gallery of Rajasthan'. There are also forts, a couple of minor castles, stepwells, cenotaphs, and a handful of mosques.

The major towns of interest in the region are Fatehpur, Nawalgarh, Mandawa, Ramgarh and Jhunjhunu, although virtually every town has at least a few surviving havelis.

The tourist boom has still not caught up with Shekhawati, but with so much to see, and some interesting places to stay, it's an area well worth exploring. The best plan is to wander at random through these small towns. There's no chance of getting lost, and there are surprises around every corner.

RAJASTHAN

Guidebooks

For a full rundown of the history, people, towns and buildings of the area, it's worth investing in a copy of *The Painted Towns of Shekhawati* (Ilay Cooper). Unfortunately, the cheap edition is difficult to find and the new full-colour edition is expensive at Rs 600. The book gives details of the buildings of interest in each town, along with fine sketch maps of the larger towns in the area.

Most tourist offices have a free colour brochure with details of the main Shekhawati towns.

Getting There & Away

Access to the region is easiest from Jaipur or Bikaner. The towns of Sikar and Fatehpur are on the main Jaipur to Bikaner road and are served by many buses. From Jaipur the bus takes four hours to Fatehpur at a cost of Rs 43 and five hours to Jhunjhunu for Rs 55.

Churu is on the main Delhi to Bikaner railway line, while Sikar, Nawalgarh and Jhunjhunu have several daily passenger train links with Jaipur and Delhi.

Getting Around

The Shekhawati region is criss-crossed by narrow bitumen roads, and all towns are well served by buses, either RSTC or private ones. The local services to the smaller towns can get very crowded and riding 'upper class' (on the roof!) is quite acceptable – and often necessary.

If you have a group of four or five people, it's worth hiring a taxi for the day to take you around the area. It's usually easy to arrange in the towns which have accommodation, although finding a driver who speaks English can be a problem. The rate for a diesel Ambassador is Rs 3 per km usually with a minimum of 250 to 300km a day. Alternatively, you could opt for a camel or horse safari.

Havelis

With large amounts of money coming from trade, the merchants of Shekhawati were keen to build mansions on a grand scale. The popular design was a building which, from the outside, was relatively unremarkable, the focus being the one or more internal courtyards. This served the purposes of security and privacy for the women, as well as offering some relief from the fierce heat which grips the area in summer.

The main entrance is usually a large wooden gate leading into a small courtyard, which in turn leads into another larger courtyard. The largest mansions had as many as four courtyards and were up to six storeys high.

Having built a house of grand proportions, the families then had them decorated with murals, and it is these murals which are the major attraction today. The major themes found are Hindu mythology, history (both old and contemporary), folk tales, eroticism (many now defaced or destroyed), and – one of the most interesting – foreigners and their modern inventions such as trains, planes, telephones, record players and bicycles. Animals and landscapes are also popular.

It is thought that the complex and sophisticated murals on the interiors of the buildings were executed by specialist painters from outside the area, while the more crude exterior ones were done by the local masons, after they had finished building the haveli. Originally the colours used in the murals were all ochre-based, but in the 1860s artificial pigments were introduced from Germany. The predominant colours are blue and maroon, but other colours such as yellow, green and indigo are also featured.

Many of the havelis these days are not inhabited by the owners, who find that the small rural towns in outback Rajasthan have little appeal. Many are occupied just by a single *chowkidar* (caretaker), while others may be home to a local family. Not many are open as museums or for display, and consequently quite a few are either totally or partially locked. While the locals seem fairly tolerant of strangers wandering into their front courtyard, be aware that these are private places, so tact and discretion should be used – don't just blunder in as though you own the place. Local custom dictates that shoes should be removed when entering the inner courtyard of the haveli.

One unfortunate aspect of the tourist trade is also beginning to manifest itself here – the desire for antiques. A couple of towns have antique shops chock a block full of items ripped from the havelis – particularly doors and window frames, but anything that can be carted away is fair game. ∎

Shekhawati

0   15   30 km

Fatehpur

Fatehpur, just off the main Bikaner to Jaipur road, was established in 1451 as a capital for Muslim nawabs, but it was taken by the Shekhawat Rajputs in the 18th century.

One of the main points of interest is the **Mahavir Prasad Goenka Haveli**, which has some noteworthy paintings. Built in 1860, it has just a single courtyard, and the main feature is the painted room upstairs, which features mirrorwork and some fine murals. If you want to visit it, a small tip is usually expected by the man living here.

There's the remains of a large 17th century **baori** (stepwell) near the bus stand. Sadly it is half-full with rubbish, and is in a pitiful state of decay.

Places to Stay The *RTDC Hotel Haveli* (☎ (01571) 20293) is on the southern edge of town, less than a km from the bus stand. It's currently a pleasant place to stay – hopefully it won't deteriorate as it gets older, like most RTDC places. Dorm beds are Rs 50, single/double rooms range from Rs 150/200 to Rs 400/500 with air-con. Reasonably priced veg/non-veg meals are available and transport to other villages can be arranged.

Mandawa

The compact and busy little market town of Mandawa was settled in the 18th century, and was fortified by the dominant merchant families. Today it has some of the finest painted havelis in the region.

Of the havelis, the **Binsidhar Newatia Haveli** has some curious paintings on its outer eastern wall – a boy using a telephone, and other 20th century inventions such as an aeroplane and a car. The haveli is in the compound of the State Bank of Bikaner & Jaipur. The **Gulab Rai Ladia Haveli** has a number of interesting murals, as well as some defaced erotic images.

Places to Stay Cheap accommodation is a problem in Mandawa, so it's not a good idea to base yourself here if you're strapped for cash.

Hotel Castle Mandawa (☎ (01592) 23124; fax 23171) has a somewhat medieval atmosphere and is a wonderful place to stay if you can afford it. Tastefully designed rooms with private bath cost Rs 1150/1325, while deluxe rooms are Rs 1185/1650. Some rooms have more charm than others, so try to look at a few first. Breakfast/lunch/dinner costs Rs 140/250/275 and camel rides are available for Rs 300 per hour.

Desert Resort (☎ (01592) 23151) is a little inconveniently located out of the town centre, on the road to Mukundgarh. It's actually part of the Hotel Castle Mandawa operation and is also a very pleasant place to stay. Singles/doubles cost Rs 1150/1325.

Lakshminarayan Ladia Haveli is the only budget option in Mandawa with basic rooms from Rs 50 to Rs 100. It can be tough to find this place – for directions, contact Shyam Singh at the Gayetri Art Gallery near the Hotel Castle Mandawa.

Dundlod

Dundlod is a tiny village right in the heart of the Shekhawati region. The **fort** here dates back to 1750, though much of it is more recent. The diwan-i-khas, private audience hall, is still in very good condition and has stained glass windows.

Other attractions in Dundlod include the **Tuganram Goenka Haveli**, the **Jagathia Haveli**, and the **Satyanarayan Temple**.

The *Dera Dundlod Kila* (☎ (015945) 2519; Jaipur (0141) 366276), at the fort, offers comfortable accommodation for Rs 800/900 with attached bath and hot water. There are also suites for Rs 1000/1500. Breakfast/lunch/dinner costs Rs 80/180/200. Horse, camel and jeep safaris can be arranged – these are a terrific way of exploring the Shekhawati region.

Nawalgarh

The main building in this town is the **fort**, founded in 1737 but today largely disfigured by modern accretions. It houses two banks and some government offices. One of the main havelis is the **Anandi Lal Poddar Haveli**, built in the 1920s. Today it houses a school, but has many fine paintings; also worth a look is the **Hem Raj Kulwal Haveli**, the **Bhagton ki Haveli** and the **Khedwal Bhavan**.

Places to Stay & Eat The *Hotel Natraj* (☎ (01594) 22404) is in the bustling Sabzi Mandi (vegetable market), right outside the entrance to the fort. If you're on a shoestring budget, you can't beat this place. It's a very primitive Indian hotel with just a couple of spartan rooms for Rs 50/80 with common bath. Simple meals are also available.

Roop Niwas Palace (☎ (01594) 22008; fax 23388), about one km from the fort, is far more salubrious. It was formerly the country house of the thakur of Nawalgarh. Rooms with private bath and air-cooling cost Rs 700/900; try to look at a few rooms first as some are much nicer than others. Breakfast/lunch/dinner costs Rs 90/170/190. Horse rides are available for Rs 250 per hour, while a camel ride costs Rs 200 per hour.

Apani Dhani, or Eco Farm, is on the west side of the main Jaipur road. Rooms are decorated in traditional style, and alternative energy is used wherever possible. Pure veg meals, made with fresh vegies from the garden, are available. Rooms cost around Rs 500/600 with attached bath.

Jhunjhunu

Jhunjhunu is one of the largest towns of Shekhawati and is the current district headquarters. It has some of the region's most beautiful buildings and shouldn't be missed.

The town was founded by the Kaimkhani nawabs in the mid-15th century, and remained under their control until it was taken by the Rajput ruler Sardul Singh in 1730.

It was in Jhunjhunu that the British based their Shekhawati Brigade, a troop raised locally in the 1830s to try to halt the activities of the *dacoits* (bandits), who were largely local petty rulers who had decided it was easier to become wealthy by pinching other peoples' money than by earning their own.

The main item of interest here is the **Khetri Mahal**, a minor palace dating back to around 1770. It has very elegant lines and is architecturally the most sophisticated building in the region, although it's not in the greatest condition. From the top, there are sensational views of the whole town. The **Bihariji Temple** is from a similar period and contains some fine murals, although these too have suffered over the years. The **Modi Haveli** and the **Kaniram Narsinghdas Tibrewala Haveli**, both in the main bazaar, are covered with murals, and the latter is particularly interesting. The town also has a number of cenotaphs and wells.

Jhunjhunu is on the bus and railway routes, so it has good connections with other parts of the state. The **tourist office** (☎ 32909) is in the Hotel Shiv Shekhawati compound. It's open Monday to Saturday from 10 am to 1.30 and 2 to 5 pm.

Places to Stay Jhunjhunu has the widest range of accommodation of any of the Shekhawati towns, making it an excellent place to base yourself. The bus stand is one km south of the centre, and close to it are a number of hotels.

Hotel Sangam (☎ (01592) 32544) near the bus stand, has fairly good singles/doubles with attached bath (no hot water) for Rs 100/125, air-cooled rooms with hot water for Rs 150/250, and a few singles with common bath for Rs 50.

Hotel Khilhari (☎ (01592) 34525), opposite the Hotel Sangam, is also cheap, but definitely not as good. Rooms with attached bath go for Rs 60/150.

Hotel Shiv Shekhawati (☎ (01592) 32651; fax 32603) is in a quieter area on the eastern edge of town. This is the most popular hotel with travellers and deservedly so – it's great value for money. Squeaky clean rooms cost Rs 100/150 with common bath, Rs 350/400 with attached bath and air-cooling, and Rs 600/800 with air-con. Lunch/dinner costs Rs 150 (veg) or Rs 200 (non-veg). The friendly owner, Mr Laxmi Kant Jangid, is very knowledgeable about the Shekhawati area.

Hotel Jamuna Resort (☎ (01592) 32871; fax 32603), about a km away, is also owned by Mr Jangid. It only has a few rooms and there's also a swimming pool (which non-guests can use for Rs 50). Pleasant singles/doubles cost Rs 700/800, and each room is traditionally decorated with mirrorwork. There's a relaxing outdoor dining area that's also open to non-residents.

Ramgarh

The town of Ramgarh was founded by the powerful Poddar merchant family in 1791, after they had left the village of Churu following a disagreement with the thakur. It had its heyday in the mid-19th century and was one of the richest towns of the region.

The **Ram Gopal Poddar Chhatri** near the bus stand, and the **Poddar Havelis** near the Churu Gate are worth checking out. Down the side street near the well near the northern gate is one of the antique shops which seems to make its living from pieces ripped out of the buildings in the area.

Lakshmangarh

Dominating this town is the 19th century **fort**, built by Lakshman Singh, the Raja of Sikar. It has fine views down to the town which was laid out, like Jaipur, along a grid pattern. Some of the most interesting havelis here include the **Char Chowk Haveli**, the **Rathi Family Haveli** and the **Shyonarayan Kyal Haveli**.

AJMER

Pop: 477,000 Tel Area Code: 0145

South-west of Jaipur is Ajmer, a burgeoning town on the shore of the Ana Sagar, flanked by barren hills. Historically, Ajmer had considerable strategic importance and was sacked by Mohammed of Ghori on one of his periodic forays from Afghanistan. Later, it became a favourite residence of the mighty Mughals. One of the first contacts between the Mughals and the British occurred in Ajmer, when Sir Thomas Roe met with Jehangir here in 1616.

The city was subsequently taken by the Scindias and, in 1818, it was handed over to the British, becoming one of the few places in Rajasthan controlled directly by the British rather than being part of a princely state. The British chose Ajmer as the site for Mayo College, a prestigious school opened in 1875 exclusively for the Indian princes, but today open to all those who can afford the fees. Ajmer is a major centre for Muslim pilgrims during the fast of Ramadan, and has some impressive Muslim architecture. However for most travellers, Ajmer is essentially just a stepping stone to nearby Pushkar. It can make an ideal base if you can't get accommodation in Pushkar during the Camel Fair.

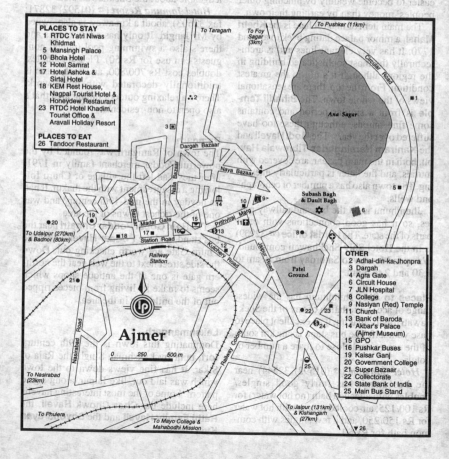

PLACES TO STAY
1 RTDC Yatri Niwas & Khidmat
5 Mansingh Palace
10 Bhola Hotel
12 Hotel Samrat
17 Hotel Ashoka & Sirtaj Hotel
18 KEM Rest House, Nagpal Tourist Hotel & Honeydew Restaurant
23 RTDC Hotel Khadim, Tourist Office & Aravali Holiday Resort

PLACES TO EAT
26 Tandoor Restaurant

OTHER
2 Adhai-din-ka-Jhonpra
3 Dargah
4 Agra Gate
6 Circuit House
7 JLN Hospital
8 College
9 Nasiyan (Red) Temple
11 Church
13 Bank of Baroda
14 Akbar's Palace (Ajmer Museum)
15 GPO
16 Pushkar Buses
19 Kaisar Ganj
20 Government College
21 Super Bazaar
22 Collectorate
24 State Bank of India
25 Main Bus Stand

Ajmer

Orientation & Information

The main bus stand is close to the RTDC Hotel Khadim on the east side of town. The railway station and most of the hotels are on the west side of town.

The tourist office (☎ 52426) is in the RTDC Hotel Khadim compound and has a good stock of literature. It's open daily, except Sunday, from 8 am to noon and 3 to 6 pm. There's also a small tourist information counter at the railway station. The State Bank of India, opposite the Collectorate, changes money. You can change money and get cash advances on credit cards at the Bank of Baroda on Prithviraj Marg opposite the GPO.

Ana Sagar

This artificial lake was created in the 12th century by damming the River Luni. On its bank is a pleasant park, the **Dault Bagh**, containing a series of marble pavilions erected in 1637 by Shah Jahan. It's popular for an evening stroll.

The lake tends to dry up if the monsoon is poor, so the city's water supply is taken from **Foy Sagar**, three km further up the valley. There are fine views from the hill beside the Dault Bagh.

Dargah

Situated at the foot of a desolate hill in the old part of town, this is one of India's most important places for Muslim pilgrims. The Dargah is the tomb of a Sufi saint, Khwaja Muin-ud-din Chishti, who came to Ajmer from Persia in 1192. Construction of the shrine was completed by Humayun and the gate was added by the Nizam of Hyderabad. Akbar used to make the pilgrimage to the Dargah from Agra once a year.

You have to cover your head in certain areas so don't forget to take a scarf or cap – you can buy one at the bazaar leading to the shrine.

As you enter the courtyard, removing your shoes at the gateway, a mosque constructed by Akbar is on the right. The large iron cauldrons are for offerings which are customarily shared by families involved in the shrine's upkeep. In an inner court, there is another mosque built by Shah Jahan. Constructed of white marble, it has 11 arches and a Persian inscription running the full length of the building.

The saint's tomb is in the centre of the second court. It has a marble dome and the actual tomb inside is surrounded by a silver platform. The horseshoes nailed to the shrine doors are offerings from successful horse dealers! Beware of 'guides' pestering for donations around the Dargah using the standard fake donation books or 'visitors registers' – you'll have to pay a generous donation if you sign up.

The tomb attracts hundreds of thousands of pilgrims every year on the anniversary of the saint's death, the Urs, in the seventh month of the lunar calendar (May/June). It's an interesting festival that's worth attending if you're in the area. As well as the pilgrims, sufis from all over India converge on Ajmer. You may even get to see a howling or whirling dervish.

Adhai-din-ka-Jhonpra & Taragarh

Beyond the Dargah, on the very outskirts of town, are the ruins of the Adhai-din-ka-Jhonpra mosque. According to legend, its construction, in 1153, took 2½ days, as its name indicates. Others say it was named after a festival lasting 2½ days. It was originally built as a Sanskrit college, but in 1198 Mohammed of Ghori seized Ajmer and converted the building into a mosque by adding a seven-arched wall in front of the pillared hall.

Although the mosque is now in need of restoration, it is a particularly fine piece of architecture – the pillars are all different and the arched 'screen', with its damaged minarets, is noteworthy.

Three km and a steep 1½-hour climb beyond the mosque, the Taragarh, or Star Fort, commands a superb view over the city. For those weary travellers who shudder at the thought of climbing up to the fort, you can now get there by car. This ancient fort was built by Ajaipal Chauhan, the town's founder. It was the site of much military activity during Mughal times and was later used as a sanatorium by the British.

RAJASTHAN

Akbar's Palace

Back in the city, not far from the GPO, this imposing building was constructed by Akbar in 1570 and today houses the Ajmer Museum, which is really not worth the bother. It's open daily except Friday from 10 am to 4.30 pm and there's a small entry fee.

Nasiyan (Red) Temple

The Red Temple on Prithviraj Marg is a Jain temple built last century and is definitely worth checking out. Its double-storey hall contains a fascinating series of large, gilt wooden figures from Jain mythology which depict the Jain concept of the ancient world. A sign in the temple warns that 'Smoking and chewing of beatles is prohibited'. The temple is open daily from 8.30 am to 4.30 pm and admission is Rs 2.

Places to Stay

Ajmer's budget hotels are generally dreary and rather indifferent towards travellers. They are OK for a night, but nearby Pushkar has far better (and friendlier) hotels. When leaving the railway station you'll probably be accosted by cycle and auto-rickshaw drivers all keen to take you 'anywhere' for Rs 5 or less – unfortunately 'anywhere' always means to a hotel where they receive commission. As in most parts of Rajasthan, this rickshaw 'mafia' has become a big problem in Ajmer.

The Paying Guest House Scheme operates in Ajmer, giving you the chance to live with an Indian family (it costs from Rs 70 to Rs 500). Contact the Tourist Reception Centre for details.

King Edward Memorial Rest House (☎ 20936), Station Rd, known locally as KEM, is to the left as you exit the railway station. This poorly maintained flophouse is a rambling old place with rooms ranging from Rs 50 for a '2nd class' single to Rs 75/125 for '1st class' singles/doubles and Rs 100/175 for deluxe rooms. Don't expect service with a smile here.

Nagpal Tourist Hotel (☎ 21603), near the KEM, is definitely a better choice. It offers a range of comfortable rooms with attached bath starting from Rs 125/300.

Hotel Ashoka (☎ 24729), also in this area, has basic rooms off a balcony for Rs 60/100. All rooms share a common bath.

Sirtaj Hotel (☎ 20096), nearby, is a fairly good place with rooms for Rs 80/150 with bathroom attached. This Sikh-run hotel has a restaurant serving Punjabi food; a main veg dish costs about Rs 25.

Bhola Hotel (☎ 23844), opposite the church and near Agra Gate, has singles/doubles for Rs 100/150 with bath. Hot water comes from the geyser outside the room, but there's no shortage. It's a reasonable place although it can get a bit noisy here at times. It has a good vegetarian restaurant.

RTDC Hotel Khadim (☎ 52490) is near the main bus stand, and like most RTDC places, customer service seems to be last on their list of priorities. Rooms with attached bath cost Rs 200/275 or Rs 300/425 with air-con. Dorm beds are available for Rs 50.

Aravali Holiday Resort (☎ 52089), next door, is cheaper and more homely. Singles/doubles with private bath and bucket hot water cost Rs 80/100, or Rs 150/175 for a better room with constant hot water.

RTDC Yatri Niwas Khidmat (☎ 52705), east of the lake on Circular Rd, is a bit remote, but better value and friendlier than the Hotel Khadim. It has rooms with attached bath for Rs 200/250.

Hotel Samrat (☎ 31805) is on Kutchery Rd, not far from the railway station. Though the rooms are on the small side and can be noisy, it's convenient for early morning departures with the private bus companies, as many have their offices nearby. Rooms with attached bath cost Rs 150/300. Be warned that some rooms cop a lot of traffic noise.

Mansingh Palace (☎ 425702; fax 425858) on Circular Rd, overlooking Ana Sagar, is Ajmer's only top-end hotel. Although it's comfortable enough, there is lack of attention to detail, and it's not great value at Rs 1195/2395. There's a bar and restaurant here.

Places to Eat

Bhola Hotel has a popular vegetarian restaurant; tasty thalis cost Rs 32, and there's also a good variety of other dishes.

Honeydew Restaurant near the KEM Rest House, has a selection of veg and non-veg food. Main dishes are around Rs 35; there's seating indoors and outdoors. They do pretty good pizzas (around Rs 40) and espresso coffee (Rs 12). You can also get a refreshing milkshake or ice cream here.

Tandoor Restaurant, south of the main bus stand, specialises in tandoori cuisine and offers an assortment of veg and non-veg fare; a tandoori chicken costs Rs 80.

Sheesh Mahal, at the Mansingh Palace, is Ajmer's best restaurant. There's a variety of veg and non-veg food; main dishes range from Rs 65 to Rs 160.

Getting There & Away
Bus There are buses from Jaipur to Ajmer every 15 minutes, some non-stop. The 131km trip costs Rs 45 and takes 2½ hours.

State transport buses also go to Jodhpur (Rs 70, 210km), Udaipur (Rs 95, 303km via Chittorgarh), Chittorgarh (Rs 53, 190km), Kota (Rs 68, 200km), Bundi (Rs 58, 165km), Ranakpur (Rs 59, 237km), Bharatpur (Rs 88, 305km) and Bikaner (Rs 79, 277km). In addition, buses frequently leave for Agra (Rs 104, 385km) and for Jaisalmer (Rs 137, 490km).

Also available are private buses to Ahmedabad, Udaipur, Jodhpur, Jaipur, Mt Abu, Jaisalmer, Bikaner, Delhi and Mumbai. Most of the companies have offices on Kutchery Rd. If you book your ticket to one of these destinations through an agency in Pushkar, they should provide a free jeep transfer to Ajmer to commence your journey. There are frequent buses from Ajmer to Pushkar (Rs 4) which leave from the bus stand near the GPO.

Train Ajmer is on the Delhi-Jaipur-Marwar-Ahmedabad line and most trains stop at Ajmer. To Jaipur, the *Pink City Express* travels daily, except Sunday, between Ajmer and Delhi (Rs 104/215 in 2nd/1st class) and Jaipur (Rs 38/188 in 2nd/1st class). The very comfortable *Shatabdi Express* travels daily, except Sunday, between Ajmer and Delhi (Rs 435/847 in ordinary/executive class) via Jaipur (Rs 215/412 in ordinary/executive class).

Refreshments are served, and are included in the ticket price. The train leaves Delhi at 6.15 am and arrives in Ajmer at 1.30 pm. Going in the other direction, the train leaves Ajmer at 3.10 pm and arrives in Delhi at 10.15 pm.

Getting Around
It's reasonably easy to get around Ajmer on foot, but there are plenty of auto and cycle-rickshaws, as well as some tongas. To travel anywhere in town by auto-rickshaw should cost you around Rs 15.

AROUND AJMER
Kishangarh
Located 27km from Ajmer, the small town of Kishangarh was founded by Kishan Singh in the early 17th century. Kishangarh is famous for its unique style of miniature painting, first produced in the 18th century.

Roopangarh Fort (☎ (01463) 3678 or Delhi (011) 665021), about 25km out of town, is a 17th century fort which has been converted into an interesting hotel by the maharaja and maharani of Kishangarh. Pleasant rooms cost Rs 1150/1475 with attached bath and there's a good restaurant. Village tours and horse-camel/jeep safaris can be arranged with advance notice.

Phool Mahal Palace, in Kishangarh, is in the process of being turned into an upmarket hotel by the maharaja and maharani. It's worth checking whether it's open yet.

PUSHKAR
Pop: 13,000   Tel Area Code: 0145
Pushkar is a mellow, serene and bewitching little town which attracts those in search of some respite from the tumult of India. In fact, many travellers who come here linger on for days, weeks, even years longer than they anticipated. Pushkar is right on the edge of the desert and is only 11km from Ajmer but separated from it by Nag Pahar, the Snake Mountain.

This traveller-friendly town clings to the side of the small Pushkar Lake with its many bathing ghats and temples. For Hindus, Pushkar is a very important pilgrimage centre and

RAJASTHAN

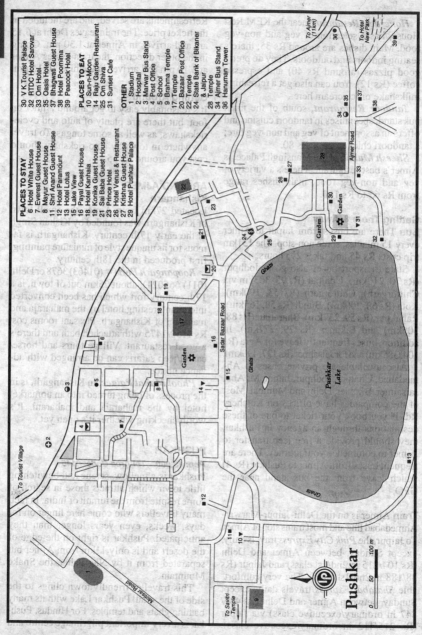

PLACES TO STAY
6   Hotel White House
7   Everest Guest House
8   Mayur Guest House
11 Shri Anand Guest House
12 Hotel Paramount
13 Hotel Lotus
15 Lake View
16 Payal Guest House
18 Hotel Kanhaia
19 Konika Guest House
21 Sai Baba Guest House
23 Prince Hotel
26 Hotel Venus & Restaurant
27 Krishna Guest House
29 Hotel Pushkar Palace
30 V K Tourist Palace
32 RTDC Hotel Sarovar
33 Om Hotel
35 Oasis Hotel
37 Bhagwati Guest House
38 Hotel Poornima
39 Peacock Hotel

PLACES TO EAT
10 Sun-n-Moon
14 Raju Garden Restaurant
25 Om Shiva
31 Sunset Cafe

OTHER
1   Stadium
2   Hospital
3   Marwar Bus Stand
4   Post Office
5   School
9   Brahma Temple
17 Temple
20 Bazaar Post Office
22 Temple
24 State Bank of Bikaner
    & Jaipur
28 Temple
34 Ajmer Bus Stand
36 Hanuman Tower

Pushkar

you'll see plenty of *sadhus* (individuals on a spiritual search). Unfortunately, after a poor monsoon the lake can be almost empty. This is a shame, as it's a big factor in the town's appeal.

Pushkar is perhaps best known for it's incredible Camel Fair which takes place here each November. At this time, the town is overflowing with tribal people from all over Rajasthan, pilgrims from all over India and film-makers and tourists from all over the world. And of course, there are hordes of camels and cattle. If you're anywhere within striking distance at the time, it's an event not to be missed.

There is no tourist office in Pushkar, but there are lots of travel agents and it's pretty easy to find your way around. You can change money at the State Bank of Bikaner & Jaipur. Camel rides and longer safaris are available year-round from a number of operators. Get your hotel, a travel agent, or other travellers to recommend a good safari operator.

Being a holy place, alcohol, meat and even eggs are banned.

Temples

Pushkar boasts temples, though few are as ancient as you might expect at such an important pilgrimage site, since many were desecrated by Aurangzeb and subsequently rebuilt. The most famous is the **Brahma Temple**, said to be one of the few temples in the world dedicated to this deity. It's marked by a red spire, and over the entrance gateway is the *hans*, or goose symbol, of Brahma,

who is said to have personally chosen Pushkar as its site.

The one hour trek up to the hilltop **Savitri Temple** overlooking the lake is best made early in the morning; the view is magical.

Ghats

Numerous ghats run down to the lake, and pilgrims are constantly bathing in the lake's holy waters. If you wish to join them, do it with respect – remove your shoes, don't smoke, refrain from kidding around and do not take photographs. This is not Varanasi and the pilgrims here can be very touchy about insensitive intrusions by non-Hindus.

Places to Stay

It can sometimes be difficult to find accommodation in Pushkar, especially if you arrive late in the day. Most hotels are nothing fancy, but they're generally clean and freshly white-washed. You should ask to see a few rooms before deciding, as many have a cell-like atmosphere owing to the tiny or non-existent windows. The mozzies can be a real nuisance here, so come armed with insect repellent. Be warned that most hotel tariffs skyrocket during the Camel Fair, when demand for rooms is exceptionally high.

Hotel Pushkar Palace (☎ 72001; fax 72226), near the lake, is the most popular place to stay and highly recommended. Once belonging to the maharaja of Kishangarh, today it's an upmarket hotel that also has some small but cheap budget rooms at Rs 150/200 with common bath. Well appointed rooms with

---

Camel Fair

The exact date on which the Camel Fair is held depends on the lunar calendar but, in Hindu chronology, it falls on the full moon of Kartik Purnima. Each year, up to 200,000 people flock to Pushkar for the Camel Fair, bringing with them some 50,000 camels and cattle for several days of pilgrimage, horse dealing, camel racing and spirited festivities. This is one of India's largest and most flamboyant festivals – don't forget to bring your camera and plenty of film.

Livestock traders take this fair very seriously. Many travel from hundreds of miles away with the sole intent of trading – a good camel can fetch a handsome sum.

In 1997 the fair is 11 to 14 November, in 1998 it's 1 to 4 November, in 1999 it's 20 to 23 November, and in 2000 it's 9 to 11 November. However, many travellers suggest that it's better to get here several days prior to these commencement dates to see the camel and cattle trading at its peak. ■

Pushkar Passports

You can tell a traveller who's been to the ghats in Pushkar by the red ribbon (the 'Pushkar Passport') tied around their wrist. Getting one can be an expensive procedure if you allow yourself to be talked into a more generous donation than you might otherwise have wanted to give. Priests, some genuine, some not, will approach you near the ghats and offer to do a puja. At some point during the prayers they'll ask you to tell Brahma how much you're going to give him, Rs 100 to Rs 400 being the suggested figure (although some travellers have been asked for much more!). Don't fall for this emotional blackmail – if you want to give just a few rupees, that's fine, although the 'priest' will probably tell you it's not enough and doesn't even cover the cost of his 'materials'. ■

attached bath range from Rs 350/450 for an air-cooled single/double to Rs 950/1050 with air-con and terrific lake views. There's a relaxing lawn area with chairs and tables and an excellent, though slightly pricey, restaurant.

RTDC Hotel Sarovar (☎ 72040) is next to the Hotel Pushkar Palace but approached from a different entrance. Set in its own spacious grounds at the far end of the lake and with a restaurant, it has more character than most other RTDC places. Singles/doubles with common bath cost Rs 100/150, Rs 200/250 with attached bath. Air-cooled rooms go for Rs 225/300 and lake view rooms cost Rs 300/400. There are also dorm beds for Rs 50.

VK Tourist Palace (☎ 72174), also in this area, is a popular cheapie with rooms from Rs 50/100 with common bath, Rs 125/150 with private bath. There's also a rooftop restaurant.

Hotel Venus (☎ 72323), nearby, offers a few double rooms with private bath for Rs 100, as well as a good rooftop restaurant. This hotel is run by Himmat Singh, a friendly guy who will enthusiastically answer any questions you may have about Pushkar.

Krishna Guest House (☎ 72091) and *Om Hotel* (no phone) are other cheap options in this area.

Hotel Poornima (☎ 72254), near the Ajmer bus stand, is built around a little courtyard and has rooms with attached bath for Rs 80/100.

Bhagwati Guest House (☎ 72423), nearby, has rooms from just Rs 40/60 with common bath. A double with attached bath costs Rs 100.

Oasis Hotel (☎ 72100), across the road, is a big place with rooms from Rs 100/150 with private bath.

Peacock Hotel (☎ 72093; fax 422974), on the outskirts of town, is a pretty good choice despite being rather far from the lake. There's a large, shady courtyard and a swimming pool. Singles/doubles range from Rs 150/200 with private bath to Rs 850/1000 for air-con rooms.

Hotel New Park (☎ 72464), also in this area, has well kept singles/doubles starting from Rs 300/450 with private bath. This is a peaceful place to stay and there's also a restaurant and pool.

Prince Hotel (no phone), closer to the lake, is basic but undeniably cheap. It has a small courtyard and rooms for Rs 40/70 with common bath, Rs 100 for a double with attached bath.

Sai Baba Guest House (no phone) nearby, is ideal for those on a tight budget. Basic rooms cost from Rs 30 with common bath. People often stay for a long time at this mellow little place, and the restaurant serves 'anything you like'!

Konika Guest House (no phone), not far from here, has clean doubles with attached bath for Rs 80.

Hotel White House (☎ 72147), north of the lake, is a pleasant place with fine views from the rooftop restaurant. Rooms cost Rs 60/100 with common bath and Rs 125/150 with private bath. Their mango tea (Rs 8) is refreshing.

Everest Guest House (☎ 72080), in the same area, is popular and a good choice if you're strapped for cash. It's a warren of a place, but its quiet and there are good views from the rooftop. Dorm beds are a mere Rs 20, while small singles/doubles cost Rs 30/60 with common bath and Rs 60/80 with bath attached. Meals can be arranged.

Mayur Guest House (☎ 72302), nearby, is a small place run by a friendly family. There are big rooms from Rs 80/100 with attached bath, Rs 30/50 without.

Payal Guest House (☎ 72163), right in the middle of the main bazaar, is another travellers' favourite. It's a relaxed and homely place with rooms from Rs 50/75 with common bath, and Rs 60/100 with private bath. The garden is home to two frolicking pet rabbits.

Lake View (☎ 72106) is across the road and does have very good views of the lake. Rooms in this popular hotel cost Rs 40/80 with common bath, while doubles with attached bath are Rs 120.

Shri Anand Guest House (no phone), northwest of the lake, is a very down-to-earth place run by a mother and daughter. Rooms are Rs 40/60, or Rs 80/100 with private bath.

Hotel Paramount (☎ 72428), nearby, has good views over the lake. Rooms with common bath go for Rs 70/100, Rs 100/200 with attached bath. The best room is No 111, with a small balcony and an attached bath (Rs 350).

Hotel Lotus (no phone), on the south side of the lake, is in a quiet location but has rather shabby rooms with common bath for Rs 40.

Hotel Kanhaia (☎ 72146), in Choti Basti, has doubles ranging from Rs 60 to Rs 150 and dorm beds for Rs 30.

JP's Tourist Village Resort (☎ 72067) is a little inconveniently located about two km out of town, but is a peaceful place to stay. Set in a pleasant garden, singles/doubles with attached bath start at Rs 100/140. There's also a swimming pool and restaurant.

Tourist Village During the Camel Fair, the RTDC sets up a tented 'Tourist Village' (☎ 72074) on the *mela* ground right next to the Camel Fair, with accommodation for up to 2000 people. It's a self-contained village with a dining hall, coffee shop, toilets, bathrooms

(bucket hot water), foreign exchange facilities, post office, medical centre, safe deposit, shopping arcade and tourist information counter.

There are several tented accommodation options (see below). To avoid disappointment, we strongly recommend you book well in advance (even as far as a year ahead), as tented accommodation is highly sought after during the fair.

RTDC Tourist Village has dormitory tents, each with 60 beds, at Rs 200 per person, and standard tents with singles/doubles with common bath for Rs 2000/2500, including all meals. There are also more upmarket 'Swiss cottage' tents with attached bath for Rs 3000/3500 and deluxe huts are Rs 3500/4000. These huts are open all year round, and are available for a significantly cheaper Rs 200/250 when the fair is not on.

Demand is high, so if you want to be sure of a bed, contact the General Manager, Central Reservations (☎ (0141) 310586 or 319353; fax 316045), RTDC Hotel Swagatam compound, Jaipur, well in advance. Full payment must be received 45 days in advance if you want to be sure of accommodation.

Royal Tents, owned by the maharaja of Jodhpur, are suitably luxurious and cost Rs 2000/4500 for a single/double. Reservations should be made through the Umaid Bhawan Palace in Jodhpur (☎ (0291) 33316; fax 35373).

Royal Desert Camp is another very good choice. The cheapest tents go for US$85/100, including all meals, while better tents cost US$100/115. Book through the Hotel Pushkar Palace in Pushkar (☎ 72001; fax 72226).

Places to Eat
Pushkar has plenty of good, reasonably priced eating places. Strict vegetarianism that forbids even eggs rather limits the range of ingredients, but the cooks make up for this with imagination. You can even get an eggless omelette in some places!

Although it's rarely printed in a menu, Pushkar is known for its 'special lassi' – a yoghurt and iced-water drink laced with *bhang* (a form of marijuana). If you do choose to indulge in this often potent concoction, just be aware that it doesn't agree with everyone. Some travellers have been stuck in bed for several miserable days after drinking it.

Buffet meals seem to have taken off in Pushkar in a big way, with many places offering all-you-can-eat meals for Rs 25 to Rs 40 – breakfast, lunch or dinner. It's safest to eat buffet meals at the busiest places where the food is more likely to be freshly cooked for each meal, rather than reheated.

Hotel Pushkar Palace has the best buffet in town, and you can dine in the restaurant or out in the garden. The set lunch/dinner costs Rs 90/110. There's also a small bakery here; a chocolate croissant costs Rs 15.

Sunset Cafe, nearby, has long been a popular hangout with travellers – a good place to swap stories about Goa, Nepal and beyond. This simple cafe offers a selection of snacks and pastries, as well as more substantial meals. The location by the lake shore is pleasant, especially at sunset, however the service and food get mixed reports.

Om Shiva (with the 'Om' written in Hindi), near the State Bank of Bikaner & Jaipur, is a good buffet place and reasonably priced.

Venus Restaurant, at the nearby Hotel Venus, has a nice rooftop restaurant that serves Indian, Continental, Chinese and Italian food. A special Indian thali is Rs 25, vegetarian pizza is Rs 25, and they also do refreshing fruit juices.

Raju Garden Restaurant, near the main bazaar area, has an assortment of western food such as oven-baked pizza (Rs 45) and baked potato. And if you're a Marmite addict, this place is usually stocked with some jars.

Sun-n-Moon, not far from the Brahma Temple, has tables around a bo tree, and offers a range of western fare such as pizzas and apple pie.

Things to Buy
Pushkar's main bazaar is a tangle of narrow lanes which are lined with an assortment of interesting little shops. It's especially good for embroidered fabrics such as wall hangings, bed covers, cushion covers and groovy shoulder bags. A lot of what is stocked here

actually comes from the Barmer district south of Jaisalmer and other tribal areas of Rajasthan. You'll have to haggle over prices, as Pushkar has long been exposed to tourists with money to burn and not much time to burn it. There's the usual nonsense about 'last price' quotes which aren't negotiable – take your time and visit a few shops. In between these shops are the inevitable clothing shops catering to styles which were in vogue in Goa and Kathmandu at the end of the 1960s. You may find occasional timeless items, but most of it is pretty clichéd.

The music shops (selling tapes and records), on the other hand, are well worth a visit if you're keen on picking up some examples of traditional or contemporary classical Indian music. The shops here don't seem to stock the usual banal current filmscore rages.

There are a number of bookshops in the main bazaar selling secondhand novels in various languages, and they'll usually buy them back for around 50% of what you pay.

Getting There & Away
To Pushkar, buses depart Ajmer frequently for Rs 4 (although it's only Rs 3 when going *from* Pushkar *to* Ajmer – because of the road toll; for cars the toll is Rs 10). It's a spectacular climb up and over the hills and you never know quite what to expect around each turn.

You could continue straight on from Pushkar to Jodhpur without having to backtrack to Ajmer, but the buses go there via Merta and can take a tiring eight hours. It's much faster to go to Ajmer and take the 4½ hour express bus.

There are some travel agencies in Pushkar offering tickets for private buses to various destinations – shop around for the best price. These buses all leave from Ajmer, but the agents should provide you with free transport to Ajmer in time for the departures. See the Ajmer section for destinations. For a small charge, some agents will book rail tickets for services ex-Ajmer.

Getting Around
There are no auto-rickshaws in the town centre, but it's a breeze to get around by foot.

Another good option is to hire a bicycle (Rs 4 per hour or Rs 25 per day).

RANTHAMBHORE NATIONAL PARK
Tel Area Code: 07462
Located near the town of Sawai Madhopur, midway between Bharatpur and Kota, Ranthambhore National Park is one of the prime examples of Project Tiger's conservation efforts in Rajasthan. Sadly, it also demonstrates the programme's overall failure; for it was in this park that government officials were implicated in the poaching of tigers for the Chinese folk medicine trade. According to the 1995 census, the park has a total of 27 tigers. There's still a reasonable chance of seeing one, but you should plan on two or three safaris. Other wildlife, especially the larger and smaller herbivores, are more numerous, and there's also a considerable bird population here. Even if you don't see a tiger, it's worth the effort for the scenery alone: in India it's not often you get the chance to visit such a large area of virgin bush.

The park itself covers some 400 sq km and its scenery is very beautiful. A system of lakes and rivers is hemmed in by steep high crags and on top of one of these is the extensive and well-preserved Ranthambhore Fort, built in the 10th century. The lower-lying ground alternates between open bushland and fairly dense forest and is peppered with ruined pavilions, chhatris and 'hides' – the area was formerly a hunting preserve of the maharajas.

A good network of four gravel tracks crisscrosses the park, and safaris are undertaken in open-sided jeeps driven by a ranger. If you've ever been on safari in Africa, you might think this is an unduly risky venture, but the tigers appear unconcerned by jeep loads of garrulous tourists touting cameras only metres away from where they're lying. No-one has been mauled or devoured – yet!

The best time to visit the park is between October and April, and the park is closed during the monsoon from 1 June to 1 October. Early morning and late afternoon are generally the best times for spotting wildlife.

Orientation & Information
There's a tourist office (☎ 20208) on Ranthambhore Rd, not far from the railway station. It's open daily except Sunday from 10 am to 1.30 pm and 2 to 5 pm.

The number of vehicles allowed into the park is strictly controlled. There are four trails within the park, and on each safari two or three jeeps take each trail. There are also large trucks (open-topped), called canters, seating 20 people, but they're limited to only two of the trails.

It's 10km from Sawai Madhopur to the first park gate, where you pay the entry fees, and a further three km to the main gate and the Jogi Mahal. The accommodation is strung out all the way along the road from the town to the park.

If you are taking photos, it's worthwhile bringing some 400 or 1000 ASA film, as the undergrowth is dense and surprisingly dark.

There's a Rs 25 entry fee to the park, plus Rs 10 for a camera. You'll also have to pay the entry fee of Rs 75 per jeep (the entry for canters is included in the ticket price). Excursions into the park must be booked at the booking office at the Project Tiger office (☎ 20223), and jeeps/canters can be booked with them. The office is open daily, except Sunday from 10 am to 1 pm and 2 to 5 pm. A seat in the canter costs Rs 75, and you can arrange to be picked up if your hotel is on the road between the town and the park. Jeeps cost Rs 575 per trip, and this can be shared by up to five people.

From October to February (winter), safari times are 7 am and 2.30 pm. From March to June (summer), they leave at 6.30 am and 3.30 pm. A guide should cost you about Rs 60.

Places to Stay
There's some basic accommodation in the town itself, while the better places are along the park road. When stepping off the train you may find yourself besieged by touts trying to drum up business. Don't be intimidated into staying somewhere you don't want to. It's worth noting that many of the hotels quote high prices, but they can usually be bargained down if things are quiet.

Unfortunately, owing to the activities of poachers, the wonderful Jogi Mahal, a former hunting lodge in an idyllic location by the lake, and the only place to stay within the park, is closed. It might be worth finding out if it has been reopened.

Retiring Rooms at the railway station have doubles with attached bath for Rs 100, and there's a dorm for Rs 35.

Hotel Swagat (☎ 20601) is about half a km from the railway station, right in the town. Although it's not the most savoury place, it's cheap. Doubles with common bath cost Rs 50, Rs 60/80 for singles/doubles with attached bath (bucket hot water), Rs 125 with running hot water.

Vishal Hotel (☎ 20504), in the same street, is better, with clean rooms from Rs 60/70 with attached bath (bucket hot water).

Sawai Madhopur Lodge (☎ 20541; fax 20718), about three km from the railway station, once belonged to the maharaja of Jaipur. Run by the Taj Group, it's ideal for those seeking comfort. There's a bar, restaurant, pool and lovely garden. Rooms are US$95/130 and there's also upmarket tented accommodation (with private bath) for US$75/110. Lunch/dinner costs Rs 240/280 plus tax.

Ankur Resort (☎ 20792), not far from the Sawai Madhopur Lodge, is a well kept and modern place with comfortable rooms, all with bath attached. The charge is Rs 400/550, but if it's not full you should be able to bargain this down. Meals are available and the staff are friendly.

Hotel Anurag Resort (☎ 20451) nearby, also has good rooms for Rs 300/400 or Rs 400/500 for a better room.

RTDC Vinayak Tourist Complex (☎ 21333), further along the road, has decent rooms with attached bath for Rs 400/500, and there's a good restaurant.

RTDC Castle Jhoomar Baori (☎ 20495) is stunningly located on a hillside, about seven km from the railway station. Formerly a royal hunting lodge, it's now a pleasant hotel with comfortable rooms. There's an attractive lounge as well as open rooftop areas, a bar and restaurant. Singles/doubles with private bath cost Rs 500/600. A 'panther

suite' costs Rs 650/800, while a 'tiger suite' is Rs 800/1000.

Hotel Tiger Moon (☎ Mumbai (022) 6433622; fax 6406399; Sawai Madhopur ☎ 6842; fax 21212) is a relaxing, upmarket resort at the end of the road. It has delightful bungalows for US$56/74 and there's also a swimming pool.

Hammir Wildlife Resort (☎ 20562) has reasonably good, if somewhat tatty, singles/doubles with bath from Rs 500/600.

Getting There & Away
Sawai Madhopur is on the main Delhi to Mumbai broad-gauge railway line and, as most trains stop here, there's a wide range to choose from. The *Frontier Mail* does the trip to Kota in about 2½ hours (Rs 56/149 in 2nd/1st class). To Agra the *Agra-Kota Passenger* takes about eight hours and costs Rs 105/249. The *Kota-Jodhpur Passenger* travels to Jaipur in about 2½ hours (Rs 30).

There are buses to Jaipur (Rs 40, four hours), Bundi (Rs 30, two hours), and Kota (Rs 36, four hours).

Getting Around
You can hire bikes for about Rs 20 per day at the shops just outside the main entrance to the railway station and at the east end of the main bazaar.

DHOLPUR
Although the town of Dholpur is in Rajasthan, this place can be more easily reached from Madhya Pradesh. Hence, details are given in that chapter.

Southern Rajasthan

KOTA
Pop: 640,000 Tel Area Code: 0744
Following the Rajput conquest of this area of Rajasthan in the 12th century, Bundi was chosen as the capital, with Kota as the land grant of the ruler's eldest son. This situation continued until 1624 when Kota became a

separate state, remaining so until it was integrated into Rajasthan following independence.

Building of the city began in 1264 following the defeat of the Bhil chieftains, but Kota didn't reach its present size until well into the 17th century, when Rao Madho Singh, a son of the ruler of Bundi, was made ruler of Kota by the Mughal emperor, Jehangir. Subsequent rulers have all added to the fort and palaces which stand here now.

Today, Kota serves as an army headquarters. It's also Rajasthan's industrial centre (mainly chemicals), powered by the hydroelectric plants on the Chambal River – the only permanent river in the state – and the nearby atomic plant. The latter made headlines in 1992 when it was revealed that levels of radioactivity in the area were way above 'safe' levels. Steady industrial growth has unfortunately contributed to Kota's proliferating level of pollution. Very few travellers make it here, which is a pity, because the Rao

Madho Singh Museum is particularly impressive.

Orientation & Information

Kota is strung out along the east bank of the Chambal River. The railway station is well to the north; the RTDC Hotel Chambal, a number of other hotels and the bus stand are in the middle; and Chambal Gardens, the Fort and the Kota Barrage are to the south.

The Tourist Reception Centre (☎ 27695) is at the RTDC Hotel Chambal. The staff here are helpful and a range of leaflets is available. It's open Monday to Saturday from 8 am to 6 pm.

City Palace & Fort

Standing beside the Kota Barrage, overlooking the Chambal River, the City Palace and Fort is one of the largest such complexes in Rajasthan. Some of its buildings are now occupied by schools, but most of the complex is open to the public. Entry is from the

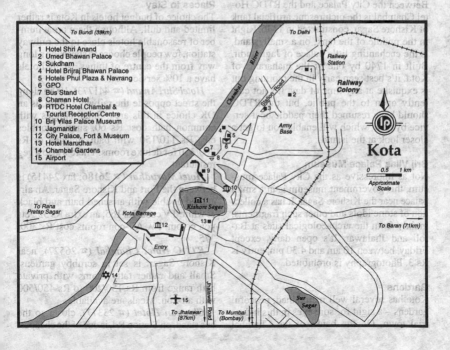

1	Hotel Shri Anand
2	Umed Bhawan Palace
3	Sukdham
4	Hotel Brijraj Bhawan Palace
5	Hotels Phul Plaza & Navrang
6	GPO
7	Bus Stand
8	Chaman Hotel
9	RTDC Hotel Chambal & Tourist Reception Centre
10	Brij Vilas Palace Museum
11	Jagmandir
12	City Palace, Fort & Museum
13	Hotel Marudhar
14	Chambal Gardens
15	Airport

To Bundi (39km)

To Delhi

Railway Station

Railway Colony

Chambal River

Station Road

Army Base

Kota

0   0.5   1 km
Approximate Scale

To Rana Pratap Sagar

Kota Barrage

Kishore Sagar

Entry

To Baran (71km)

To Jhalawar (87km)

Jhalawar Road

To Mumbai (Bombay)

Sur Sagar

south side through the **Naya Darwaza**, or New Gate.

The **Rao Madho Singh Museum**, in the City Palace, is excellent. It's on the right-hand side of the complex's huge central courtyard and is entered through a gateway topped by rampant elephants like those at the Bundi Fort. Inside, you'll find well displayed weapons, old costumes, stuffed beasts, and some of the best preserved murals in the state. The museum is open daily except Friday from 11 am to 5 pm. Entry is Rs 40, plus Rs 35 for a camera, Rs 75 for a video.

After visiting the museum, it's worth wandering around the rest of the complex just to appreciate how magnificent this place must have been in its heyday. Sadly, a lot of it is falling into disrepair, but there are some fine views over the old city, the river and the monstrous industrial complex with its enormous twin chimneys across the river.

Jagmandir

Between the City Palace and the RTDC Hotel Chambal is the picturesque artificial tank of Kishore Sagar, constructed in 1346. Right in the middle of the tank, on a small island, is the enchanting little palace of Jagmandir. Built in 1740 by one of the maharanis of Kota, it's best seen early in the morning but is exquisite at any time of day. It's not currently open to the public, but the RTDC should have resumed their paddle boat service by now, which will enable you to get a closer look at the island.

Brij Vilas Palace Museum

Not as impressive as the City Palace museum, this government museum is in a small palace near the Kishore Sagar. It has a collection of stone idols and other such fragments, mainly from the archaeological sites at Baroli and Jhalawar. It's open daily, except Friday, between 10 am and 4.30 pm; entry is Rs 3. Photography is prohibited.

Gardens

Kota has several well maintained, peaceful gardens – a sight for sore eyes in this industrial town. On the banks of the Chambal River, south of the Fort, are the **Chambal Gardens**. This is a popular spot for picnics and there's a small cafe here. The centrepiece is a murky pond well stocked with crocodiles. Once common all along the river, by the middle of this century crocodiles had been virtually exterminated through hunting. There are also some rare gharial – thin-snouted fish-eating crocodiles.

Just beside the RTDC Hotel Chambal are the **Chhattar Bilas Gardens**, a curious collection of somewhat neglected but impressive royal cenotaphs.

Organised Tours

There's a daily three hour city tour at 9 am for Rs 70. Enquire at the Tourist Reception Centre.

Regular half-hour boat cruises up the Chambal River depart daily from the Chambal Gardens. Tickets cost Rs 5 and are available from where the boat departs.

Places to Stay

The choice of budget hotels in Kota is rather limited and dull. Although there are a number of reasonable hotels close to the railway station, few people choose to stay such a long way from the centre of things. Many hotels have a 10% service tax.

Hotel Shri Anand (☎ 441773), 100m along the street opposite the railway station, is an OK choice in this area. Small singles with common bath cost Rs 60, singles/doubles cost Rs 110/150 with bath attached or Rs 200/350 for deluxe rooms. There's also a veg restaurant.

Hotel Marudhar (☎ 26186; fax 24415) is between the Fort and Kishore Sagar. An air-cooled double with attached bath and black & white TV costs Rs 165; an extra Rs 35 gets you colour TV. Air-con rooms cost Rs 300/375.

RTDC Hotel Chambal (☎ 26527), near Kishore Sagar, is set in scrubby gardens. Small and rather tatty rooms with private bath range from Rs 150/200 to Rs 450/500 with air-con. Meals are available.

Chaman Hotel (☎ 23377), closer to the bus stand, on Station Rd, is one of the cheapest (and grubbiest) places in Kota. Dingy rooms cost Rs 50/60 with common bath (bucket water). This seedy place is popular with truckes; single female travellers may feel uncomfortable staying here.

Hotel Phul Plaza (☎ 22356; fax 22614), near the GPO, offers a range of good rooms, all with attached bath and constant hot water. Air-cooled rooms cost Rs 220/320, air-con rooms are Rs 380/480 and deluxe rooms go for Rs 600/700. Meals are available.

Hotel Navrang (☎ 451253), next door, is a good place to stay, with comfortable air-cooled rooms with attached bath for Rs 300/400, or Rs 500/800 with air-con. Make sure you look at a few rooms first, as some definitely have loads more character than others. Decent meals are available here.

Hotel Brijraj Bhawan Palace (☎ 450529; fax 450057), located on an elevated site overlooking the Chambal River, is an excellent choice. Once a palace of the maharaos of Kota and also the former British Residency, this tranquil place is surrounded by well manicured gardens. Pleasant rooms cost Rs 800/1050, or Rs 1300 for a capacious suite. There are lots of airy verandas, a tennis court, cosy dining room and an attractive lounge. Unlike most palaces, this one is more homely than grand, and is one of Kota's most interesting places to stay.

Umed Bhawan Palace (☎ 25262; fax 451110) in the north of the town, is a more grandiose palace. Run by Welcomgroup, this is Kota's most upmarket hotel and is suitably luxurious. Set in beautiful gardens, it's got a restaurant, billiard room and even a badminton court. Singles/doubles cost from US$43/85.

Sukdham (☎ 20081; fax 441961), near the Umed Bhawan Palace, is considerably cheaper and a delightful place to stay. Singles/doubles with attached bath start at Rs 500/600, Rs 725/900 with air-con. Breakfast/lunch/dinner costs Rs 80/130/160.

Places to Eat
Most of the cheap restaurants are up by the railway station; there are very few around the RTDC Hotel Chambal or the bus stand. On the footpath outside the GPO, omelette and snack stalls set up in the early evening, and this can be a cheap way to eat.

Hotel Phul Plaza has a pretty good vegetarian restaurant; main dishes cost around Rs 35.

Hotel Navrang offers reasonably priced veg and non-veg food. Main dishes (non-veg) cost around Rs 45, a half butter chicken is Rs 60.

Umed Bhawan Palace is open to non-residents and has a set lunch/dinner for Rs 280 plus tax. Although the restaurant itself may not be that spectacular to look at, the food is good.

Hotel Brijraj Bhawan Palace has an intimate dining room that offers tasty Indian and Continental food; the set lunch/dinner costs Rs 125 plus tax. This delightful dining experience is only available to residents.

Getting There & Away
Bus There are bus connections to Ajmer (Rs 58), Chittorgarh (Rs 60), Jaipur (Rs 77), Udaipur (Rs 90) and other centres in Rajasthan. If you're heading into Madhya Pradesh, several buses a day go to such places as Gwalior, Ujjain and Indore. As with many places in Rajasthan, none of the timetables at the bus stand are in English.

Buses leave for Bundi every 30 minutes and the fare for the 50 minute journey is Rs 12. Tickets should be bought from window No 1 at the bus stand.

Train Kota is on the main broad-gauge Mumbai to Delhi line via Sawai Madhopur, so there are plenty of trains to choose from. For Sawai Madhopur, the 108km journey takes a bit over two hours at a cost of Rs 50/200 in 2nd/1st class. To Agra it's 343km at a cost of Rs 90, and to Jaipur the fare is Rs 50/200 in 2nd/1st class.

Getting Around
Minibuses link the railway station and bus stand (Rs 2). An auto-rickshaw should cost Rs 15 for this journey, although you'll probably be asked for more. Cycle-rickshaws are a cheaper option.

AROUND KOTA

One of Rajasthan's oldest temple complexes is at **Baroli**, 56km south-west of Kota on the way to Rana Pratap Sagar. Many of the temples were vandalised by Muslim armies but much remains and it warrants a visit. A lot of the sculptures from these **9th century temples** are displayed in the government museum in Kota.

There are hourly buses to Baroli from Kota (Rs 14).

JHALAWAR

Located 87km south of Kota, at the centre of an opium producing region, Jhalawar was the capital of a small princely state created in 1838. This little archaeological town is well off the beaten track and sees very few travellers. In the centre of town is the run-down **Jhalawar Fort** which today houses government offices. Also in town is a small **Government Museum** with a collection of sculptures, coins, weapons and paintings. It's open daily except Friday from 10 am to 4.30 pm (free entry).

In October/November the **Chandrabhaga Fair** is held on the banks of the Chandra-bhaga River, just outside Jhalrapatan (see below). On the last day of this fair, thousands of devotees take a holy dip.

The *RTDC Hotel Chandrawati* (☎ (07432) 30015) has singles/doubles with attached bath for Rs 150/175 or Rs 250/300 for better rooms. The **tourist office** is located here and is open daily except Sunday from 10 am to 5 pm.

There are hourly buses to Jhalawar from Kota (Rs 30, 2½ hours).

AROUND JHALAWAR

At **Jhalrapatan** ('city of temple bells'), seven km south of Jhalawar, are the ruins of a huge 10th century Surya Temple containing impressive sculptures as well as one of the best preserved idols of Surya (the sun god) in the whole of India. The well maintained 12th century Shantinath Jain Temple is also worth visiting.

If you're in this area, you should take a look at the imposing **Gagron Fort**, 10km

from Jhalawar. Very few tourists even suspect its existence, and if you like to explore in peace and quiet this place is perfect. Though perhaps not as famous as others like Chittorgarh, Jodhpur and Jaisalmer, the huge fort occupies a prominent place in the annals of Rajput chivalry and has been fought over for centuries.

The fort is open daily from sunrise to sunset and entry is free. There are local buses from Jhalawar every hour.

About 90km from Jhalawar near Kolvi town, there are ancient **Buddhist caves and stupas** atop a desolate hill. These extraordinary caves are believed to date back to the 5th century. It's a short climb to the top of the hill, where you'll find a number of large stupas, bat-filled meditation chambers and weathered statues of Buddha. This remarkable place is neglected and disintegrating, which is heartbreaking.

BUNDI

Pop: 77,000   Tel Area Code: 0747

Bundi is only 39km north-west of Kota and has a good deal more panache and rustic charm. It was the capital of a major princely state during the heyday of the Rajputs. Although its importance dwindled with the rise of Kota during Mughal times, it maintained its independence until its incorporation into the state of Rajasthan in 1947. Kota itself was part of Bundi until its separation in 1624 at the instigation of the Mughal emperor, Jehangir.

Today, Bundi is a picturesque little town with a somewhat medieval atmosphere. The town's Rajput legacy is well preserved in the shape of the massive Taragarh Fort, which broods over the town in the narrow valley below, and the imposing palace which stands beneath it. In this palace are found the famous Bundi murals – similar to those in the Rao Madho Singh Museum in Kota.

Many people visit Bundi on a day trip from Kota, but it's worth spending the night here. It's a good idea to bring enough rupees with you, as it's virtually impossible to change money here. There's a small, helpful tourist

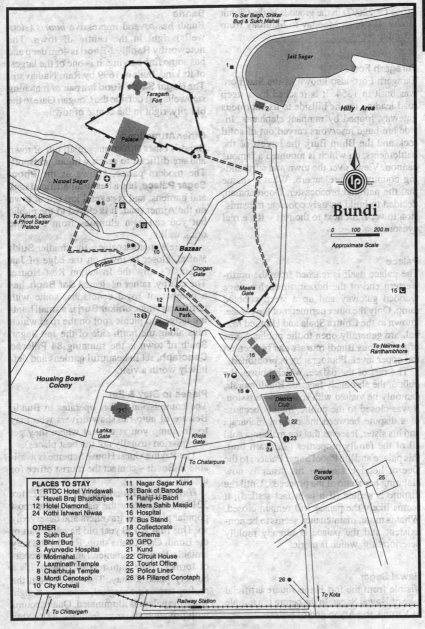

Bundi

0   100   200 m

Approximate Scale

To Sar Bagh, Shikar
Burj & Sukh Mahal

Jait Sagar

Hilly Area

Taragarh
Fort

Palace

Nawal Sagar

To Ajmer, Deoli
& Phool Sagar
Palace

Bazaar

Bypass

Chogan
Gate

Meera
Gate

Azad
Park

Housing Board
Colony

Lanka
Gate

Khoja
Gate

To Chatarpura

District
Club

To Nainwa &
Ranthambhore

Parade
Ground

To Kota

To Chittorgarh

Railway Station

PLACES TO STAY
1 RTDC Hotel Vrindawati
4 Haveli Braj Bhushanjee
12 Hotel Diamond
24 Kothi Ishwari Niwas

OTHER
2 Sukh Burj
3 Bhim Burj
5 Ayurvedic Hospital
6 Motimahal
7 Laxminath Temple
8 Charbhuja Temple
9 Mordi Cenotaph
10 City Kotwali

11 Nagar Sagar Kund
13 Bank of Baroda
14 Ranji-ki-Baori
15 Mera Sahib Masjid
16 Hospital
17 Bus Stand
18 Collectorate
19 Cinema
20 GPO
21 Kund
22 Circuit House
23 Tourist Office
25 Police Lines
26 84 Pillared Cenotaph

office (☎ 22697) in the grounds of the Circuit House. It's open Monday to Saturday from 10 am to 5 pm.

Taragarh Fort

Taragarh Fort, also known as the Star Fort, was built in 1354. It is reached by a steep road leading up the hillside to its enormous gateway, topped by rampant elephants. Inside are huge reservoirs carved out of solid rock and the Bhim Burj, the largest of the battlements, on which is mounted a famous cannon. Views over the town and surrounding countryside are superb. What a shame that the national broadcaster, Doordarshan, decided to build an ugly concrete transmission tower right next to the fort – it's a real eyesore.

Palace

The palace itself is reached from the north-western end of the bazaar, through a huge wooden gateway and up a steep cobbled ramp. Only the outer perimeter of the palace, known as the Chittra Shala and Ummed Mahal, are generally open to the public. Some of the famous Bundi **murals** can be seen on the upper level. Photography is prohibited.

The rest of the palace, which houses the bulk of the absolutely fantastic Bundi murals, can only be visited with special permission. It was closed to the public, mainly because of a dispute between the current maharaja and his sister. It seems that the maharaja sold all of the family properties (Taragarh Fort, this palace and the Phool Sagar Palace) to the Oberoi hotel chain, but his sister is now claiming her share of the proceeds. Until the dispute is settled (if it is in fact settled), it seems likely the palace will remain closed. What is more, maintenance seems to be non-existent and the palace is already rapidly deteriorating, which is tragic.

Nawal Sagar

Visible from the fort is the square artificial lake of Nawal Sagar. In the centre is a temple to Varuna, the Aryan god of water.

Baoris

Bundi has several impressive *baoris* (step-wells) right in the centre of town. The noteworthy **Raniji-ki-Baori** is 46m deep and has some fine carving. It is one of the largest of its kind, built in 1699 by Rani Nathavatji. The **Nagar Sagar Kund** is a pair of matching stepwells just outside the Chogan Gate to the old city, right in the centre of town.

Other Attractions

Bundi's other attractions are all out of town and are difficult to reach without transport. The modern palace, known as the **Phool Sagar Palace**, has a beautiful artificial tank and gardens, and is several km out of town on the Ajmer road. It is closed to the public but you can gain glimpses from over the brick wall.

There's another palace, the smaller **Sukh Mahal**, closer to town on the edge of Jait Sagar. It's now the Irrigation Rest House. The nearby, rather neglected **Sar Bagh**, has a number of royal cenotaphs, some with terrific carvings. **Shikar Burj** is a small hunting lodge and picnic spot on the road which runs along the north side of the Jait Sagar. South of town is the stunning **84 Pillared Cenotaph**, set in beautiful gardens and definitely worth a visit.

Places to Stay & Eat

The commission racket operates in Bundi. Beware of auto-rickshaw drivers who may try to dump you at a hotel where they get commission (usually not the best places).

The Paying Guest House Scheme is available in Bundi – contact the tourist office for details.

Haveli Braj Bhushanjee (☎ 32322; fax 32142), just below the palace, is the most popular place with travellers and deservedly so. This funky, 150 year old haveli is part of the Bundi Cafe Crafts shop. Run by the very amiable Braj Bhushanjee family (ancestors of former prime ministers of Bundi), it's a homely place to stay. The views from the rooftop terrace are magical, especially at night when the palace is illuminated. Quaint rooms with private bath range from Rs 200/300 to

VALERIE TELLINI

RICHARD I'ANSON

RICHARD I'ANSON

HUGH FINLAY

Rajasthan
Top: Jain sculptures at the Dilwara Temple, Mt Abu.
Middle: Details from the City Palace doors, Jaipur.
Bottom: Watching the day go by, Jaisalmer.

FRANCES LINZEE GORDON

MICHELLE COXALL

MICHELLE COXALL

Rajasthan

Top Left: A sugar cane seller at the Pushkar Camel Fair.

Top Right: Camel in the streets of Alwar.
Bottom: A painted Shekhawati haveli in the town of Lakshmangarh.

Rs 950 for the very best room. In the cheaper rooms hot water comes by the bucket. Tasty (though expensive) veg meals are available. If you arrive after hours, when the shop is closed, just ring the doorbell.

Kothi Ishwari Niwas (☎ 32414), opposite the tourist office, is not a bad choice, although it's not as atmospheric as the Haveli Braj Bhushanjee. Rooms with attached bath start at Rs 250/400 – the newer rooms are best. Good meals (veg and non-veg) are available. The owners are friendly and keen to help.

Hotel Diamond (☎ 22656), in the noisy and bustling bazaar area, has somewhat grimy singles/doubles with attached bath for Rs 50/100, Rs 150 for a deluxe room. The restaurant is OK; main dishes are around Rs 30 (veg only). This is not the most welcoming place for single female travellers.

RTDC Hotel Vrindawati (☎ 32473) out by Jait Sagar tank, has just two rooms for Rs 225/300. The rooms are nothing exciting, but the location is peaceful.

Things to Buy

There's an interesting collection of local souvenirs at the Bundi Cafe Crafts shop (at the Haveli Braj Bhushanjee), including miniatures and costume jewellery. And just so you can see what you're missing, ask to see their photos of the Bundi murals which were taken inside the closed part of the palace.

Although there isn't anything remarkable to buy in Bundi itself, you should take a stroll through the little markets just to soak in the medieval ambience of this town.

Getting There & Away

It takes about five hours by bus from Ajmer to Bundi (Rs 60). From Kota, it's only 50 minutes to Bundi (Rs 12). Buses also go to Sawai Madhopur (Rs 30) and Udaipur (Rs 90). For train service information ask at the tourist office.

Getting Around

The bus stand is at the Kota (south-east) end of town. It's relatively easy to find your way to the palace on foot through the bazaar –

once you pass through the city gate, there are only two main roads through town and the palace is visible from many points. Autorickshaws can also be hired from outside the bus stand. Bike riding is a pleasant and environmentally friendly way to explore the town. Bikes can be rented near the City Kotwali for Rs 3 per hour or Rs 20 per day.

CHITTORGARH (Chittor)
Pop: 84,500   Tel Area Code: 01472

The sprawling hilltop fort of Chittorgarh epitomises the whole romantic, doomed ideal of Rajput chivalry. Three times in its long history, Chittor was sacked by a stronger enemy and, on each occasion, the end came in textbook Rajput fashion as jauhar was declared in the face of impossible odds. The men donned the saffron robes of martyrdom and rode out from the fort to certain death, while the women and children immolated themselves on a huge funeral pyre. Honour was always more important than death.

Despite the fort's impressive location and colourful history, Chittor is off the main tourist circuit and sees surprisingly few visitors. It's well worth the detour – if you're pressed for time you could squeeze in a day trip to Chittor from Udaipur.

History

Chittor's first defeat occurred in 1303 when Ala-ud-din Khilji, the Pathan King of Delhi, besieged the fort in order to capture the beautiful Padmini, wife of the Rana's uncle, Bhim Singh. When defeat was inevitable, the Rajput noblewomen, including Padmini, committed jauhar and Bhim Singh led the orange-clad noblemen out to their deaths.

In 1535 it was Bahadur Shah, the sultan of Gujarat, who besieged the fort and, once again, the medieval dictates of chivalry determined the outcome. This time, the carnage was immense. It is said that 13,000 Rajput women and 32,000 Rajput warriors died following the declaration of jauhar.

The final sack of Chittor came just 33 years later, in 1568, when the Mughal emperor, Akbar, took the town. Once again, the fort was defended heroically but, once again, the odds were overwhelming and the women performed jauhar, the fort gates were flung open and 8000 orange-robed warriors rode out to their deaths. On this occasion, Maharana Udai Singh II fled to Udaipur where he re-established his capital. In 1616, Jehangir returned Chittor to the Rajputs but there was no attempt at resettlement.

Orientation & Information

The fort stands on a 280 ha site on top of a 180m high hill, which rises abruptly from the surrounding plain. Until 1568, the town of Chittor was also on the hilltop within the fort walls but today's modern town, known as Lower Town, sprawls to the west of the hill. A river separates it from the bus stand, railway line and the rest of the town.

The Tourist Reception Centre (☎ 41089) is near the railway station and has a wide range of literature. It's open Monday to Saturday from 10 am to 5 pm.

Fort

According to legend, Bhim, one of the Pandava heroes of the *Mahabharata*, is credited with the fort's original construction. All of Chittor's attractions are within the fort. A zigzag ascent of over one km leads through seven gateways to the main gate on the western side, the Rampol.

On the climb, you pass two chhatris, memorials marking spots where Jaimal and Kalla, heroes of the 1568 siege, fell during the struggle against Akbar. The main gate on the eastern side of the fort is know as the Surajpol. Within the fort, a circular road runs around the ruins and there's a deer park at the southern end. From the western end of the fort, there are fine views over the town and across the surrounding countryside, as well as a charming view of an enormous cement factory. There's even a little village in this part of the fort.

Today, the fort of Chittor is a virtually deserted ruin, but impressive reminders of its grandeur still stand. The main sites can all be seen in half a day (assuming you're not walking) but, if you like the atmosphere of ancient sites, then it's worth spending longer as this is a very mellow place and there are no hassles whatsoever. Entry to the fort is

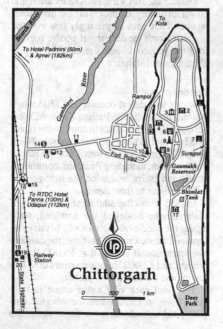

Chittorgarh

To Kota

To Hotel Padmini (50m) & Ajmer (182km)

Branch River

Gambheri River

Rampol

Fort Road

To Hotel Padmini

To RTDC Hotel Panna (100m) & Udaipur (112km)

Surajpol

Gaumukh Reservoir

Bhimlat Tank

Railway Station

State Highway

Deer Park

0   500   1 km

PLACES TO STAY	
11	Bhagwati Hotel
13	Natraj Tourist Hotel
15	Hotel Pratap Palace
19	Shalimar Hotel
20	Hotel Chetak

OTHER	
1	Tower of Fame & Mahavir Temple
2	Fateh Prakash Palace
3	Archaeological Museum & Office
4	Rana Kumbha Palace
5	Chhatris of Jaimal & Kalla
6	Kumbha Shyam & Meera Temples
7	Temple of Neelkanth Mahadev
8	Tower of Victory
9	Mahasati & Sammidheshwar Temple
10	Rawat Bagh Singh Memorial
12	Bus Stand
14	State Bank of India
16	GPO
17	Padmini's Palace
18	Tourist Reception Centre

free. Guides are available in the fort, usually at the Rana Kumbha Palace (see below) and charge around Rs 200.

Rana Kumbha Palace Entering the fort and turning right, you come almost immediately to the ruins of this palace. It contains elephant and horse stables and a Shiva temple. One of the jauhars is said to have taken place in a vaulted cellar. Across from the palace is the archaeological office and museum, and the treasury building or Nau Lakha Bhandar. The **Singa Chowri Temple** is nearby.

Fateh Prakash Palace Just beyond the Rana Kumbha Palace, this palace is much more modern (Maharana Fateh Singh died in 1930). It houses a small and poorly lit **museum**, and the rest of the building is closed. The museum is open daily, except Friday, from 10 am to 4 pm. Entry is Rs 2.

Tower of Victory Continuing anticlockwise around the fort, you come to the Jaya Stambh, or Tower of Victory. Erected by Rana Kumbha to commemorate his victory over Mahmud Khilji of Malwa in 1440, the tower was constructed between 1458 and 1468. It rises 37m in nine storeys and you can climb the narrow stairs to the eighth storey. Watch your head on the lintels! Entry is Rs 0.50, free on Friday.

Hindu sculptures adorn the outside of the tower, but the dome was damaged by lightning and repaired during the last century. Close to the tower is the Mahasati, an area where the ranas were cremated during Chittorgarh's period as the Mewar capital. There are many sati stones here. The **Sammidheshwar Temple** stands in the same area.

Gaumukh Reservoir Walk down beyond the temple and, at the very edge of the cliff, you'll see this deep tank. A spring feeds the tank from a carved cow's mouth in the cliffside – from which the tank got its name. The opening here leads to the cave in which Padmini and her compatriots are said to have committed jauhar.

Padmini's Palace Continuing south, you come to Padmini's Palace, built beside a large pool with a pavilion in its centre. Legend relates that, as Padmini sat in this pavilion, Ala-ud-din was permitted to see her reflection in a mirror in the palace. This glimpse was the spark that convinced him to destroy Chittor in order to possess her.

The bronze gates in this pavilion were carried off by Akbar and can now be seen in the fort at Agra. Continuing around the circular road, you pass the deer park, the Bhimlat Tank, the Surajpol and the Temple of Neelkanth Mahadev, before reaching the Tower of Fame.

Tower of Fame Chittor's other famous tower, the Kirti Stambha, or Tower of Fame, is older (probably built around the 12th century) and smaller (22m high) than the Tower of Victory. Built by a Jain merchant, it is dedicated to Adinath, the first Jain tirthankar, and is decorated with naked figures of the various tirthankars, thus indicating that it is a Digambara, or 'sky clad', monument. A narrow stairway leads through the seven storeys to the top.

Other Buildings Close to the Fateh Prakash Palace is the **Meera Temple**, built during the reign of Rana Kumbha in the ornate Indo-Aryan style and associated with the mystic-poetess Meerabai. The larger temple in this same compound is the **Kumbha Shyam Temple**, or Temple of Varah.

Across from Padmini's Palace is the **Kalika Mata Temple**, an 8th century Surya temple. It was later converted to a temple to the goddess Kali. At the northern tip of the fort is another gate, the **Lokhota Bari**, while at the southern end is a small opening from which criminals and traitors were hurled into the abyss.

Places to Stay & Eat
The *retiring rooms* at the railway station are a cheap, but rather mundane, option. Ordinary doubles cost Rs 65, or Rs 190 with air-con.

Shalimar Hotel (☎ 40842), near the railway station, has rooms for Rs 80/100 with common bath, or Rs 100/125 with bath attached.

Hotel Chetak (☎ 41588), also in this area, is a better choice. Rooms start at Rs 150/225 and hot water is available only in the mornings. There's also a good restaurant.

Natraj Tourist Hotel (☎ 41009), by the bus stand, is very basic but dirt cheap. Rooms cost Rs 30/45 with common bath, Rs 60/90 with bath; but you'll probably have to get them to change the sheets.

Bhagwati Hotel (☎ 42275), just over the river, is better, and has rooms starting at Rs 60/100 (bucket hot water).

RTDC Hotel Panna (☎ 41238) is closer to the town centre and is quite a good choice. It's a fairly modern place with dorm beds for Rs 50, singles/doubles with attached bathrooms for Rs 125/175, better rooms for Rs 225/300. There's a bar, and satisfying meals are available at the restaurant.

Hotel Pratap Palace (☎ 40099; fax 41042), between the bus stand and the RTDC Hotel Panna, is a favourite with travellers and a friendly place to stay. Air-cooled rooms cost Rs 375/425 with attached bath, or Rs 500/580 with air-con. There's a small bar and very good restaurant – a half tandoori chicken costs Rs 90; the set lunch/dinner is Rs 150/180. Village safaris can be arranged, as well as visits to their castle in Bijaipur (see below).

Hotel Padmini (☎ 41718), a little out of town by the Bearch River, has rooms for Rs 250/350, Rs 400/500 with air-con. The staff seem somewhat preoccupied here, but the vegetarian restaurant is good value; main dishes are around Rs 25.

Getting There & Away
Chittor is on the main bus and rail routes. By road, it's 182km from Ajmer, 158km from Bundi and 112km from Udaipur. There are frequent connections to these places. All the Kota buses go via Bundi (a slow 4½ hour trip).

It's possible to take an early bus from Udaipur to Chittorgarh (Rs 35, three hours), spend about three hours visiting the fort (by auto-rickshaw or bicycle), and then take a

late afternoon bus to Ajmer, but this is definitely pushing it.

Chittorgarh also has rail links with Ahmedabad, Udaipur, Ajmer, Jaipur and Delhi. The broad gauge line to Kota and Bundi would be convenient, except that the only passenger train on this route leaves Chittor at 2.50 pm, reaching Bundi at 6 pm and Kota at 7.15 pm.

Getting Around
It's six km from the railway station to the fort, less from the bus stand, and seven km around the fort itself, not including the long southern loop out to the deer park. To tour the fort, auto-rickshaws charge around Rs 90 from either the bus or railway station – make sure this includes waiting time at the various sites. Bicycles can also be rented near the railway station (Rs 3 per hour or Rs 20 per day), allowing you to explore the fort at leisure. As Indian bicycles rarely have gears, you may have to push the machine to the top – still, they're great once you get to the top, and for the journey back down.

AROUND CHITTORGARH
Bijaipur
Castle Bijaipur is a tranquil 16th century palace in this village, 40km south of Chittor. It's now an atmospheric hotel with pleasant rooms for Rs 800/850. Good meals are available; the set breakfast/lunch/dinner costs Rs 90/150/225. The amiable owners can organise interesting horse and jeep safaris to nearby villages – a half day village safari by jeep costs Rs 400 per person. To stay at the castle, book through the Hotel Pratap Palace in Chittor (☎ (01472) 40099; fax 41042).

There are daily RSTC buses from Chittor to Bijaipur for Rs 15.

Menal & Bijolia
Lying on the Bundi to Chittorgarh road, 48km from Bundi, Menal is a complex of Shiva temples built during the Gupta period. After a good monsoon, there's an impressive waterfall in this area.

Bijolia, 16km from Menal, was once a group of 100 temples. Today, only three are left standing, one of which has a huge figure of Ganesh.

Mandalgarh

A detour between Menal and Bijolia takes you to Mandalgarh. It is the third fort of Mewar built by Rana Kumbha – the others are the great fort of Chittorgarh and the fort at Kumbhalgarh.

Nagri

One of the oldest towns in Rajasthan, Nagri is 17km north of Chittor. Hindu and Buddhist remains from the Mauryan to the Gupta period have been found here.

Jagat

At this small town, 20km south of the road between Udaipur and Chittorgarh, is a small 10th century **Durga Temple**. There are some fine sculptures, including a couple of small erotic carvings, which have inspired some people to call the town the Khajuraho of Rajasthan (total nonsense!)

UDAIPUR

Pop: 366,000   Tel Area Code: 0294

Possibly no city in Rajasthan is quite as romantic as Udaipur, even though the state is replete with breathtaking hilltop fortresses, exotic fairytale palaces and gripping legends of medieval chivalry and heroism. The French Impressionist painters, let alone the Brothers Grimm, would have loved this place, and it's not without justification that Udaipur has been called the 'Venice of the East'.

Founded in 1568 by Maharana Udai Singh II – following the final sacking of Chittorgarh by the Mughal emperor, Akbar – Udaipur rivals any of the world-famous creations of the Mughals with its Rajput love of the whimsical and its superbly crafted elegance. The Lake Palace is certainly the best late example of this unique cultural explosion, but Udaipur is full of palaces, temples and havelis ranging from the modest to the extravagant. It's also proud of its heritage as a centre for the performing arts, painting and crafts. And, since water is relatively plentiful in this part of the state (in between the periodic droughts), there are plenty of green parks and gardens. Udaipur is very traveller friendly and is a fascinating place to simply wander around at leisure.

Until recent times, the higher uninhabited parts of the city were covered in forests but, as elsewhere in India, most of these have inevitably been turned into firewood. There is, however, a movement afoot to reverse this process.

The city was once surrounded by a wall and, although the gates and much of the wall over the higher crags remain, a great deal of it has disappeared.

In common with most Indian cities, Udaipur's urban and industrial sprawl goes beyond the city's original boundaries and pollution of various kinds can be discouraging. This will be your first impression of Udaipur if you arrive at the railway or bus stations. Ignore it and head for the old city where a different world is waiting for you.

Orientation & Information

The old city, bounded by the remains of a city wall, is on the east side of Lake Pichola. The railway station and bus stand are both just outside the city wall to the south east.

The Tourist Reception Centre (☎ 411535) is in the Fateh Memorial Building near Surajpol, less than a kilometre from the bus stand. The office is open Monday to Saturday from 10 am to 1.30 pm and 2 to 5 pm. There are also smaller tourist information counters at the railway station, airport and at the southern end of the City Palace complex.

The GPO is directly north of the old city, at Chetak Circle, but poste restante is at the post office at the junction of Hospital Rd and the road north from Delhi Gate, close to the RTDC Hotel Kajri.

Lake Pichola

The placid Lake Pichola was enlarged by Maharana Udai Singh II after he founded the city. He built a masonry dam, known as the Badipol, and the lake is now four km in length and three km wide. Nevertheless, it

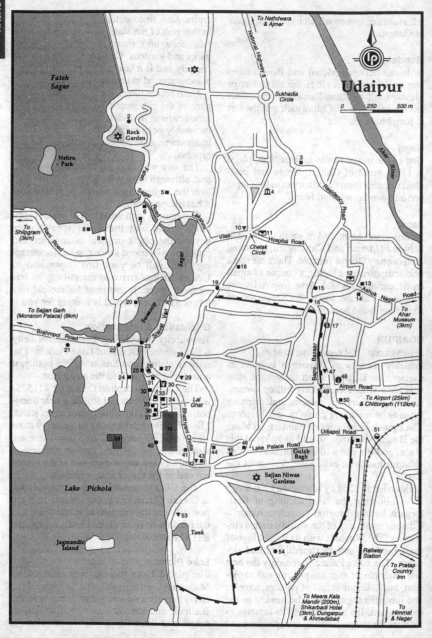

Udaipur

To Nathdwara & Ajmer

National Highway 8

Sukhadia Circle

0   250   500 m

Ahar River

Fateh Sagar

Nehru Park

Rock Garden

Fateh Sagar Road

Rani Road

To Shilpgram (3km)

To Sajjan Garh (Monsoon Palace) (8km)

Brahmpol Road

Lake Pichola

Jagmandir Island

Swaroop Vati Ror

Sikkat Viri Ror

Lakshmi Vilas

Chetak Circle

Hospital Road

Residency Road

Ashok Nagar Road

To Ahar Museum (3km)

Bapu Bazaar

Airport Road

To Airport (25km) & Chittorgarh (112km)

Udaipol Road

Lal Ghat

Bhattiyani Chotta

Lake Palace Road

Gulab Bagh

Sajjan Niwas Gardens

Tank

Udaipur Road

Railway Station

To Pratap Country Inn

National Highway 8

To Meera Kala Mandir (200m), Shikarbadi Hotel (3km), Dungarpur & Ahmedabad

To Himmat & Nagar

remains fairly shallow and can actually dry up in severe droughts. At these times, you can walk to the island palaces from the shore. Fortunately, this doesn't happen often. The City Palace extends a considerable distance along the east bank of the lake. South of the palace, a pleasant garden runs down to the lake. North of the palace, you can wander along the lake shore, where there are some interesting bathing and *dhobi* (laundry) ghats.

Out in the lake are two islands – Jagniwas and Jagmandir. **Boat rides**, which leave regularly from the City Palace jetty (known as Bansi Ghat), are worthwhile. These cost Rs 60 for half an hour, Rs 125 for one hour (the latter includes a visit to Jagmandir Island).

Jagniwas Island (Lake Palace Hotel) Jagniwas, the Lake Palace island, is about 1.5 ha in size. The palace was built by Maharana Jagat Singh II in 1754 and covers the whole island. Formerly the royal summer palace, today it is the ultimate in luxury hotels, with shady courtyards, fountains, lotus ponds and

even a small mango-tree-shaded swimming pool. Indeed, this is the perfect place to fall in love! It's truly magical but casual visitors are discouraged. It used to be possible to visit the palace for afternoon tea but now non-guests can only come over for lunch or dinner – and then only if the hotel is not full, which it often is. Hotel launches cross to the island from the City Palace jetty. The Lake Palace, along with the Shiv Niwas Palace and Monsoon Palace in Udaipur, were used as sets in the James Bond movie, *Octopussy*.

Behind Jagniwas is a much smaller island called **Arsi Vilas**, which has been used in recent times as a helipad.

Jagmandir Island The other island palace, Jagmandir, was commenced by Maharana Karan Singh, but takes its name from Maharana Jagat Singh (1628-52) who made a number of additions to it. It is said that the Mughal emperor, Shah Jahan, derived some of his inspiration for the Taj Mahal from this palace after staying here in 1623-24 while leading

PLACES TO STAY			Lake Ghat & Ratan	OTHER	
3	Mewar Inn	33	Palace Guest Houses	1	Saheliyon ki Bari
5	Laxmi Vilas Palace	34	Centre View Guest House	2	Pratap Smarak
	Hotel & Hotel Anand	35	Jagat Niwas Palace		(Moti Magri)
	Bhawan		Hotel & Kankarwa	4	Bhartiya Lok Kala
6	Gulab Niwas		Haveli		Museum
7	Hotel Hilltop Palace	36	Hotel Sai-Niwas	11	GPO
8	Hotel Lakend	37	Lake Corner Soni Paying	12	Poste Restante
9	Hotel Ram Pratap		Guest House	15	Indian Airlines
	Palace	39	Jagniwas Islan (Lake	16	Delhi Gate
13	RTDC Hotel Kajri		Palace Hotel)	17	Bank of Baroda
14	Prince, Alka & Ashok	41	Hotel Raj Palace	19	Hathipol
	Hotels	43	Rang Niwas Palace Hotel	21	Brahmpol
18	Ajanta Hotel	44	Ranjit Niwas Hotel	22	Ambapol
20	Hotel Natural	45	Hotels Mahendra	23	Chandpol
24	Wonder View Palace,		Prakash & Shambhu	28	Clock Tower
	Lake Pichola & Lake		Vilas	30	Jagdish Temple
	Shore Hotels	46	Haveli Hotel	38	City Palace, Museums,
25	Jheel Guest House	50	Hotel Apsara		Shiv Niwas Palace &
26	Hotel Gangaur Palace	52	Hotel Welcome		Fateh Prakash Palace
27	Hotel Badi Haveli &				Hotels
	Anjani Hotel		PLACES TO EAT	40	Bansi Ghat (City
31	Jag Niwas Guest	10	Berry's Restaurant		Palace Jetty)
	House	29	Mayur Cafe	48	Tourist Reception
32	Hotel Caravanserai,	42	Roof Garden Cafe		Centre
	Lalghat & Evergreen	47	Park View	51	Bus Stand
	Guest Houses &	49	16 Chef Restaurant &	54	Kishanpol
	Restaurant Natural		Surajpol		
	View	53	Cafe Hill Park		

a revolt against his father, Jehangir. Flanked by a row of enormous stone elephants, the island has an impressive chhatri carved from grey-blue stone. The view across the lake, to the city and its glorious golden palace, is a scene of rare beauty.

City Palace & Museums

The imposing City Palace, towering over the lake, is the largest palace complex in Rajasthan. Actually a conglomeration of buildings added by various maharanas, the palace manages to retain a surprising uniformity of design. Building was started by Maharana Udai Singh II, the city's founder. The palace is surmounted by balconies, towers and cupolas and there are fine views over the lake and the city from the upper terraces.

The palace is entered from the northern end through the Baripol of 1600 and the Tripolia Gate of 1725, with its eight carved marble arches. It was once a custom for maharanas to be weighed under the gate and their weight in gold or silver distributed to the populace.

The main part of the palace is now preserved as a museum with a large and varied collection. The museum includes the Mor Chowk with its beautiful mosaics of peacocks, the favourite Rajasthani bird. The Manak (or Ruby) Mahal has glass and porcelain figures, while Krishna Vilas has a remarkable collection of miniatures. In the Bari Mahal, there is a pleasant central garden. More paintings can be seen in the Zanana Mahal. The Moti Mahal has beautiful mirrorwork and the Chini Mahal is covered in ornamental tiles.

Enter the **City Palace Museum** through the Ganesh Deori, which leads to the Rai Angam, or Royal Courtyard. The museum is open from 9.30 am to 4.30 pm and admission is Rs 15. It costs Rs 30 for a camera, and a whopping Rs 200 for a video. A guide (Rs 90) is worthwhile. There's also a **Government Museum** (Rs 2) within the palace complex. Exhibits include a stuffed kangaroo (for homesick Aussies), a freaky monkey holding a small lamp and Siamese-twin deer. There's also more serious stuff like sculptures and paintings. In the large courtyard outside the City Palace Museum there are a number of pricey handicraft shops, a kiosk, and places to pick up film for your camera.

The other part of the palace is up against the lake shore and has been partly converted into two luxury hotels known as Shiv Niwas Palace and the Fateh Prakash Palace Hotels.

There's a stunning **Crystal Gallery** at the Fateh Prakash Palace Hotel in the City Palace complex. This rare collection of Osler's crystal was ordered from England by Maharana Sajjan Singh in 1877. Items include crystal chairs, tables and even beds! It's open daily from 10 am to 1 pm and 3 to 8 pm. The Crystal Gallery overlooks the grandiose **Durbar Hall**, formerly the royal hall of audience. Tastefully decorated, it features large portraits of former maharanas of Mewar (a most distinguished looking lot). And just wait until you feast your eyes upon the massive chandeliers – incredible!

Jagdish Temple

Located only 150m north of the entrance to the City Palace, this fine Indo-Aryan temple was built by Maharana Jagat Singh in 1651 and enshrines a black stone image of Vishnu as Jagannath, Lord of the Universe. A brass image of the Garuda is in a shrine in front of the temple and the steps up to the temple are flanked by elephants.

Fateh Sagar

North of Lake Pichola, this lake is overlooked by a number of hills and parks. It was originally built in 1678 by Maharana Jai Singh but, after heavy rains destroyed the dam, it was reconstructed by Maharana Fateh Singh. A pleasant lakeside drive winds along the east bank of the lake. In the middle of the lake is Nehru Park, a popular garden island with a boat-shaped cafe. You can get there by boat from near the bottom of Moti Magri for Rs 6 return. Pedal boats (Rs 40 for 30 minutes) are also available.

Pratap Smarak (Moti Magri)

Atop the Moti Magri, or Pearl Hill, overlooking Fateh Sagar, is a **statue** of the Rajput hero Maharana Pratap, who frequently defied the Mughals. The path to the top traverses elegant **gardens**, including a Japanese rock garden. The park is open daily from 9 am to 6 pm and admission is Rs 5.

Bhartiya Lok Kala Museum
The interesting collection exhibited by this small museum and foundation for the preservation and promotion of local folk arts includes dresses, dolls, masks, musical instruments, paintings and – the high point of the exhibits – puppets. It's certainly worth a visit. The museum is open daily from 9 am to 6 pm and entry costs Rs 7, plus Rs 10 for a camera and Rs 50 for a video. Regular free 15 minute puppet shows are staged daily. Longer puppet and cultural shows are held daily from 6 to 7 pm (Rs 20). Call ☎ 529296 for details.

Saheliyon ki Bari
The Saheliyon ki Bari, or Garden of the Maids of Honour, is in the north of the city. This small ornamental garden, with its fountains, kiosks, marble elephants and delightful lotus pool, is open from 9 am to 6 pm. Entry is Rs 2. They sometimes ask for Rs 2 to turn the fountains on.

Shilpgram
Shilpgram, a crafts village three km west of Fateh Sagar, was inaugurated by Rajiv Gandhi in 1989. It has traditional houses from four states – Rajasthan, Gujarat, Goa and Maharashtra – and there are daily demonstrations by musicians, dancers, or artisans from the various states. Although it's much more animated during festival times (usually in early December, but check with the Tourist Reception Centre), there's usually something happening.

The site covers 80 ha but most buildings are in a fairly compact area. It's open daily from 9 am to 6 pm, and there's a small entry fee.

Next to the site, *Shilpi Restaurant* serves good Indian and Chinese food. It also has a swimming pool (Rs 100), open from 11 am to 4 pm. There is no public transport to Shilpgram, so you'll have to come here by bicycle, auto-rickshaw or taxi.

Ahar Museum
Three km east of Udaipur are the remains of an ancient city. Here, you'll find a museum and nearby are the cenotaphs of the maharanas of Mewar. Although the museum is nothing to write home about, it has some very old earthen pottery, sculptures and other historic artefacts. It's open daily except Friday from 9.30 am to 4.30 pm and entry is Rs 2.

Other Attractions
Sajjan Niwas Gardens has pleasant lawns and a zoo – one traveller warns of the unfriendly dogs here. Beside Sajjan Niwas Gardens is the Rose Garden, or **Gulab Bagh**. Don't confuse the **Nehru Park** opposite Bapu Bazaar with the island park of the same name in Fateh Sagar. The city park has some strange topiary work, a giant cement teapot and children's slides incorporating an elephant and a camel.

On a distant mountain range is the **Monsoon Palace**, also known as Sajjan Garh. Constructed by Maharana Sajjan Singh in the late 19th century, this deserted and neglected palace is now owned by the government. Although the actual palace is closed to the public, the mountain on which it is situated is worth visiting purely for the sensational views. The round trip takes about 1½ hours. The palace is illuminated at night and from a distance looks like something out of a fairy tale.

Organised Tours
There's a daily five hour city tour that starts at 8 am from the RTDC Hotel Kajri and costs Rs 50. Depending on demand, an afternoon tour (2 to 7 pm) goes out to Eklingji, Haldighati and Nathdwara and costs Rs 80. Contact the Tourist Reception Centre for details. For information on boat tours, see under Lake Pichola earlier in this section.

Places to Stay – homestays
Udaipur pioneered the Paying Guest House Scheme in Rajasthan, and there are now over

200 families participating. Expect to pay Rs 100 to Rs 650, depending on the level of comfort and facilities you want. Contact the Tourist Reception Centre for details.

Places to Stay – bottom end

There are four main clusters of budget hotels in Udaipur, but those around the Jagdish Temple are definitely preferable to the others. Next best are those between the City Palace and the bus stand, along Lake Palace Rd and Bhattiyani Chotta. The third cluster is along the main road between the bus stand and the Delhi Gate. This is a noisy and polluted road and you have to be desperate or totally lacking in imagination to stay here. The last cluster is around the RTDC Hotel Kajri and, although it's better than staying on the main road, it's somewhat inconvenient.

Udaipur has countless small hotels and guest houses to suit all budgets, many with relaxing rooftop terraces which have superb lake views. Be warned that the commission system is notorious here and many travellers are bullied by auto-rickshaw drivers into staying at a hotel where the rickshaw 'mafia' gets commission (see under the Local Transport section).

Watch out for checkout times which vary greatly in Udaipur, and note that many places slap a 10% service charge on their advertised room rates.

Jagdish Temple Area You'll pay a little more for a hotel in this area, but there is hardly any traffic noise, most places have terrific views over the lake, and the central location is ideal. As it's the most popular area to stay, you get a lot of the 'yes have a look change money buy something' from the touts and shop owners, but this is not Agra.

Hotel Badi Haveli (☎ 412588), just north of the Jagdish Temple, is a popular place with fine views over the lake and old city. The 10 small rooms (two with private bath) are all different and range from Rs 80 with common bath to Rs 180 for the best rooms at the top.

Lalghat Guest House (☎ 525301), right by the lake, has a rooftop with great views over the water. It's another travellers' favourite,

with dorm beds for Rs 50, small rooms with common bath for Rs 75/100 and rooms with attached bath from Rs 200 to Rs 300. There are facilities for self-caterers, and a shop.

Evergreen Guest House (☎ 27823) is next door, with tidy rooms around a small courtyard. Basic singles/doubles cost Rs 60/80 with common bath, or Rs 100/150 with attached bath (free bucket hot water). There's also a good rooftop restaurant and the staff are friendly.

Jag Niwas Guest House (☎ 26267), nearby, offers squeaky clean rooms with bath from Rs 175 to 350. The management proudly advocates that: 'Honesty is our motto'.

Lake Ghat Guest House (☎ 521636), across the road from the Lalghat Guest House, is a friendly place with a wide range of accommodation, although not many of the rooms here have a view. Singles/doubles with bath start from Rs 125/200. There's also a good restaurant and terrace area.

Centre View Guest House (☎ 520039), nearby, has just a few rooms, all with common bath for Rs 40/60. There are no views but the family who run it are affable.

Lake Corner Soni Paying Guest House (no phone), closer to the lake, is owned by an adorable elderly couple. It has basic rooms for Rs 60/80 with common bath, Rs 100 for a double with bath attached. Vegetarian meals are available and there are great views from the rooftop.

Anjani Hotel (☎ 527670), near the Hotel Badi Haveli, is a modern place with a range of rooms from Rs 80/100 to Rs 150/250, all with attached bath and hot water. Try to get a room with a lake view.

Jheel Guest House (☎ 28321) is right at the bottom of the hill, by the ghat. Housed in an old haveli, doubles with common bath cost Rs 100, or Rs 225 for a larger room with bath and a view. The newer annexe across the road has better, but more expensive rooms. There's a relaxing rooftop restaurant overlooking the lake.

Lake Shore Hotel (no phone), south of Chandpol, away from the town, is a mellow place and has a terrace with fine views over the water. Rooms range from Rs 100 with common bath to Rs 300 with private bath; most have a lake view.

Hotel Natural (☎ 527879) is even further away, far removed from the hustle and bustle of town. It's a homely place in a secluded setting with friendly owners. Basic rooms cost Rs 60/100 with common bath, Rs 80/120 with bath attached. There's a rooftop restaurant serving hearty home-made food, cooked with tender loving care by Ritu.

Lake Palace Rd Area There are some popular budget hotels on and around Lake Palace Rd.

Haveli Hotel (☎ 28294) on Lake Palace Rd, has pretty good rooms with private bath ranging from Rs 125 to Rs 400.

Hotel Mahendra Prakash (☎ 522993), further along Lake Palace Rd, has doubles with attached bath ranging from Rs 100 to Rs 600. There's also a swimming pool here and the rooftop affords fine views of the City Palace.

Hotel Shambhu Vilas (☎ 29381), on the same road, has singles/doubles for Rs 150/250 with attached bath. They offer a discount if you stay for at least three nights. There's a good rooftop restaurant where the set lunch/dinner costs Rs 150/190.

Ranjit Niwas Hotel (☎ 525774), nearby, is a family run guest house and a homely place to stay. Dorm beds cost Rs 40, while single/double rooms with private bath cost Rs 100/175. There's a discount if you stay for three days or more. Meals are available.

Ashok Nagar Rd Area The location and standard of budget hotels in this area is not the best – few travellers choose to stay here.

RTDC Hotel Kajri (☎ 410501), at the traffic circle on Ashok Nagar Rd, has seen better days. With so many more interesting and better located hotels in Udaipur, there's little reason to stay here. There are dorm beds for Rs 50, and rooms with bath from Rs 200/275 to Rs 550/750.

Prince Hotel (☎ 414355), across the road from the RTDC, offers singles/doubles for Rs 60/100 and rooms with TV, attached bath and constant hot water for Rs 120/170.

Alka Hotel (☎ 414611), nearby, is a large,

somewhat drab place with singles/doubles from Rs 90/175 to Rs 125/250. The more expensive rooms are air-cooled and have constant hot water.

Ashok Hotel (☎ 411925), also in this area, is cheaper but unremarkable.

Bus Stand Area For those who don't mind the chaos and pollution of the main road, there are a number of choices.

Hotel Apsara (☎ 420400), north of the bus stand, is a huge place set back from the road. The rooms front onto an internal courtyard making them relatively quiet. Singles/doubles with attached bath cost Rs 75/125 to Rs 150/250.

Hotel Welcome (☎ 485375), opposite the bus stand, is one of the best places in this area. Rooms with private bath start from Rs 125/150.

Elsewhere If you don't mind staying well out of town, there are two decent budget options.

Mewar Inn (☎ 522090), well away from the centre of town on Residency Rd, is ideal if you're strapped for cash. It's an exceptionally cheap and down-to-earth place, but the rickshaw drivers hate it (because they receive no commission). Dorm beds are ridiculously cheap at Rs 12. Basic rooms go for just Rs 28/37, bigger rooms cost Rs 59 to Rs 79, and a discount is given to YHA members. A veg restaurant is on the rooftop and there are bicycles for hire (Rs 10).

Pratap Country Inn (☎ 583138; fax 583058), is an interesting retreat at Titadha village, about eight km outside Udaipur. Comfortable doubles with attached bath range from Rs 200 to Rs 800. Set in quiet surroundings, it's a secluded place with a very laid back atmosphere. Horse riding is available and they also organise longer safaris – from US$100 per person per day. An auto-rickshaw from Udaipur costs around Rs 40. Alternatively, if you want to get some exercise you could ride out here on a bike.

Places to Stay – middle
Rang Niwas Palace Hotel (☎ 523891), Lake Palace Rd, is one of the best mid-range options

and is deservedly popular. Set in well kept gardens, with a swimming pool, it's a very relaxed hotel with friendly owners. There's accommodation in the old building, formerly a royal guest house, and also comfortable rooms in the new building. Rooms with private bath range from Rs 300/350 to Rs 950/1100 for a suite. There's also a good restaurant.

Hotel Sai-Niwas (☎ 524909), just down the hill towards the ghat from the City Palace entrance, is also recommended. The rooms are imaginatively decorated (even the toilet!) and the more expensive ones have balconies with a lake view. Rooms (doubles only) with private bath cost Rs 500 to Rs 850, and there's a restaurant.

Ratan Palace Guest House (☎ 561153), not far from the Hotel Sai-Niwas, is good value for money. Neat double rooms with bath cost from Rs 250 to Rs 450. The terrace has lake views and tasty meals are available.

Hotel Caravanserai (☎ 521252), near the Evergreen Guest House, is a flash place that offers spotless rooms with private bath for Rs 750/800. There's also a pleasant rooftop restaurant.

Hotel Raj Palace (☎ 410364), at Bhattiyani Chotta, is a friendly place with rooms (doubles only) from Rs 150 to Rs 800, all with attached bath. Dorm beds are Rs 50. There's also a restaurant.

Jagat Niwas Palace Hotel (☎ 420133; fax 520023), right on the lake shore, has long been popular with travellers. This converted haveli has a relaxing restaurant with tremendous lake views. Rooms with common bath cost Rs 300; with attached bath they start from Rs 450.

Kankarwa Haveli (☎ 411457), next door, is also a very good choice. It has fine lake views and is well maintained. Squeaky clean rooms with attached bath start from Rs 350.

Wonder View Palace (☎ 522996; fax 412368), a little out of town south of Chandpol, has comfortable singles/doubles with private bath for Rs 300/400 or Rs 500/600 for deluxe rooms. There's also a rooftop restaurant.

Fateh Sagar Area If you want to get out of the centre of town, there are several good

options near Udaipur's other major lake, Fateh Sagar.

Hotel Ram Pratap Palace (☎ 528700; fax 520168) is an attractive modern haveli near the lake. It's a peaceful place and an excellent choice in this area. Pleasant singles/doubles with private bath start at Rs 550/650; most rooms have a balcony and lake view. The restaurant serves delicious meals and the rooftop terrace affords good views.

Hotel Lakend (☎ 23841; fax 523898), nearby, is a huge hotel with comfortable singles/doubles starting from Rs 500/600. There's a swimming pool, bar, restaurant and a nice garden running down to Fateh Sagar. They can also arrange visits to their resort at Jaisamand Lake (see the Around Udaipur section).

Hotel Anand Bhawan (☎ 523256; fax 523247), north-east of the Hotel Lakend, has good rooms for Rs 600/750. The restaurant serves veg and non-veg food.

Gulab Niwas (☎ 523644), nearby, is a small guest house in a delightful old lodge. Well kept air-cooled rooms with attached bath start at Rs 575/675. Set in a well manicured garden, this is a relaxing place to stay.

Places to Stay – top end
Lake Pichola Hotel (☎ 420197; fax 410575), south of Chandpol, is certainly the best of the lower priced top-range hotels. It's in an absolutely superb location with incomparable views of the ghats, Jagdish Temple and City Palace. Go up to the rooftop terrace to really soak in these magical views. Comfortable singles/doubles cost Rs 975/1000; many rooms have a balcony and lake view. The staff here are helpful and the restaurant serves tasty food.

Laxmi Vilas Palace Hotel (☎ 529711; fax 525536) is between Swaroop Sagar and Fateh Sagar lakes, up on the hill. It's a pleasant four star ITDC place where air-con rooms cost US$100/120. There's a bar, restaurant and swimming pool (Rs 165 for non-residents).

Hotel Hilltop Palace (☎ 561765), in the same area, is a modern hotel atop another hill. Rooms start at Rs 1195/1850 and although well kept, this place is somehow lacking in character. However, the rooftop boasts a sensational 360 degree view of Udaipur.

Shikarbadi Hotel (☎ 583201; fax 584841), located about three km out of town on the Ahmedabad road, is the perfect place to go for serenity and fresh air. Once a royal hunting lodge, it's now a relaxing hotel set in beautiful grounds with a swimming pool, small lake and deer park. Smart singles/doubles cost Rs 1050/2100. There's a quiet bar for a drink, as well as three restaurants. A stud farm on the premises offers horse rides as well as longer safaris.

Lake Palace Hotel (☎ 527961; fax 527974) which appears to be floating in the middle of Lake Pichola, is one of the world's most spectacular hotels. It's the very image of what a maharaja's palace should be like and most people with sufficient money would not pass up an opportunity to stay here. This swanky white palace has a bar, restaurant, little shopping arcade, open air courtyards, lotus ponds, and a small swimming pool. The cheapest rooms are US$180/200, while lavish suites cost US$310 to US$660. Needless to say, you will need to book well in advance to get a room.

Shiv Niwas Palace Hotel (☎ 528016; fax 528006) forms part of the City Palace complex, and is another atmospheric and swish palace-hotel. Rooms start at US$70 while magnificent suites range from US$200 to US$425. If you have an appetite for pure luxury, a suite is recommended. There's a restaurant, bar, holistic health centre, relaxing open air courtyard, and marble pool. A small bagpipe band strikes up a merry tune each evening near the hotel lobby. It's wise to also book well ahead here, as demand for rooms is high.

Fateh Prakash Palace Hotel (☎ 528016; fax 528006), also in the City Palace complex, is another excellent choice. This place is dripping with style and is ideal for those seeking some serious pampering. It has just nine rooms ranging from US$125 to US$225, which are plushly furnished with original palace pieces, including some exquisite Mewar paintings. There are two fine restaurants

(one on the rooftop), with brilliant views across the lake.

Places to Eat
There's a good range of restaurants in Udaipur, from sun-kissed rooftop cafes catering to budget travellers to lavish restaurants at the top-end hotels. Many of the budget restaurants try to lure customers by putting on a nightly screening of the James Bond movie *Octopussy*, which was partly filmed in Udaipur.

Mayur Cafe, near the Jagdish Temple, has long been a popular little place, serving good south Indian dishes such as masala dosa (Rs 15), as well as western alternatives such as Rajasthani pizza (Rs 30).

Restaurant Natural View, on the rooftop of the Evergreen Guest House, serves pizzas for around Rs 30, baked potatoes for Rs 20 and has an assortment of Chinese and Indian dishes.

Roof Garden Cafe, just around the corner from the Rang Niwas Palace Hotel, facing the City Palace, looks like the Hanging Gardens of Babylon. The food here is slightly expensive but there's a good menu and live Rajasthani folk music most nights. Fried fish and chips costs Rs 60.

Hotel Natural has a rooftop veg restaurant with scrumptious Indian, Chinese, Continental, Mexican and even Tibetan cuisine. A slice of cake, just like grandma used to bake, costs Rs 20.

Cafe Hill Park, south-west of the Sajjan Niwas gardens on a hill overlooking Lake Pichola, is worth a visit just for the views. This small cafe offers moderately priced Indian, Continental and Chinese fare.

Park View is opposite the park in the main part of town but there's absolutely no view. It serves tasty north Indian cuisine and is often packed with middle-class Indian families. Prices are reasonable – a half tandoori chicken costs Rs 43.

16 Chef Restaurant, nearby, is a well kept place that offers very reasonably priced vegetarian Indian, Continental and Chinese food. Sicilian spaghetti costs Rs 32; Indian dishes are around Rs 25.

Berry's Restaurant, on Chetak Circle, is more expensive but recommended for its Indian food.

Jagat Niwas Palace Hotel is good for a minor splurge and the restaurant boasts splendid views over the water. There's Indian and Continental cuisine; a main Indian veg dish costs around Rs 35.

Shiv Niwas Palace Hotel is more expensive but is a marvellous place for an unforgettable dining experience. There's seating indoors or in the pleasant open air courtyard by the pool. Their Indian food is best, and they do positively divine mango and strawberry ice cream. Indian classical music is performed each evening by the poolside, creating a magical ambience. Non-residents are welcome, but it's a good idea to book ahead.

Gallery Restaurant, at the Fateh Prakash Palace Hotel, is also highly recommended. Specialising in Continental cuisine, this intimate little restaurant has beguiling views across Lake Pichola. For a really romantic evening, come here at sunset for a drink, then enjoy the live Indian classical music while you dine. Or you could come here for afternoon tea, which is served from 3 to 5 pm. A 'full cream tea' costs Rs 100.

Lake Palace Hotel is, of course, the ultimate dining experience. While the food gets mixed reports, and the dining room is not the most impressive room in the palace, it's nevertheless well worth it just to see this unique hotel. Live sitar music accompanies the buffet dinner which is served from 7.30 to 10.30 pm and costs Rs 550. The buffet lunch is from 12.30 to 2.30 pm and costs Rs 450. Charges include the boat crossing. There's no guarantee that you'll be able to get in, though, since it's only possible to eat here when the hotel is not full. Reservations are essential, and reasonably tidy dress is expected.

Entertainment

From August to April there are one hour Rajasthani folk dance and music performances daily (except Sunday) at 7 pm at the **Meera Kala Mandir** (☎ 583176), Sector 11, Hiran Magari, near the Pars Theatre. It costs Rs 60

per person. There are a range of tribal dances, and also some more spectacular acts such as balancing numerous pots on top of the head while dancing on broken glass or unsheathed sabres. An auto-rickshaw to the auditorium from the City Palace area costs around Rs 25.

Many hotels (including some budget places) provide their own entertainment for guests – usually puppet shows or Rajasthani music and dancing.

Things to Buy

Udaipur has oodles of little shops selling a jumble of things, from funky western clothing to traditional antique jewellery. The town is popular for its local crafts, particularly miniature paintings in the Rajput-Mughal style. There's a good cluster of shops selling these on Lake Palace Rd, next to the Rang Niwas Palace Hotel, and others around the Jagdish Temple. Be prepared to bargain hard, as most places have ridiculously inflated prices for tourists.

Getting There & Away

Air Indian Airlines has at least one flight a day to Delhi (US$80), Jaipur (US$60), and Mumbai (US$95), and flights five times a week to Jodhpur (US$45) and Aurangabad (US$90). The direct flight between Udaipur and Aurangabad can save a great deal of bus or train time. The Indian Airlines office (☎ 410999) at Delhi Gate is open every day from 10 am to 1 pm and 2 to 5 pm.

UP Air (☎ 528666) has daily flights to Delhi (US$94), Mumbai (US$110) and Jaipur (US$68).

It's advisable to make flight reservations well in advance as they can get heavily booked, especially in the tourist season.

Bus Frequent RSTC buses run from Udaipur to other regional centres, as well as to Delhi and Ahmedabad. If you use these buses, make sure you take an express bus since the ordinary buses take forever, make innumerable detours to various towns off the main route and can be very uncomfortable.

Destinations served by express buses include Jaipur (Rs 120, nine hours, nine daily),

Ajmer (Rs 90, six hours, 11 daily), Kota/Bundi (Rs 90, six hours, six daily), Jodhpur (Rs 90, seven hours, five daily), and Chittorgarh (Rs 35, three hours, five daily). Express buses should be booked in advance.

There are quite a few private bus companies which operate to such places as Ahmedabad (Rs 100, six hours), Vadodara (Rs 140, eight hours), Mumbai (Rs 290, 16 hours), Delhi (Rs 180, 14 hours), Indore (Rs 125, 10 hours), Bikaner (Rs 160, 13 hours) and Mt Abu (Rs 80, five hours). Most have their offices along the main road from the bus stand. Book at least one day in advance.

Train Lines into Udaipur are currently metre gauge only, but scheduled to be converted to broad gauge sometime in 1998.

The best train between Delhi and Udaipur is the *Pink City/Garib Nawaz Express* which covers the 739km in 15½ hours, and goes via Jaipur, Ajmer and Chittorgarh. It leaves Delhi's Sarai Rohilla station daily except Sunday (daily except Saturday in the other direction), but you may need to change trains at Rewari (83km from Delhi) since the Delhi end of this metre-gauge route is being converted to broad gauge. Fares for the trip are Rs 179/625 in 2nd/1st class. This train operates during the day, so reaches its destination in the late evening. If you'd rather do the journey overnight and arrive at a more civilised hour, the *Chetak Express* does the trip, but it takes about 20 hours.

There's still a metre-gauge link between Udaipur and Jodhpur (221km). The trip costs Rs 95/318 in 1st/2nd class.

Taxi There are plenty of taxis willing to take you to places around Udaipur. Many drivers will show you a list of 'official' rates to places like Mt Abu, Chittor and Jodhpur. Shop around, as you can often get a better price from travel companies. And don't be afraid to engage in some friendly haggling – you're likely to get a better deal, especially if you require a taxi for several days. For travel out of town, remember that taxis generally charge return trip fares even if you're only going one way.

Getting Around

The Airport The airport is 25km from the city. Unfortunately there's no airport bus or auto-rickshaws. A taxi will set you back at least Rs 150 – try to split the cost by sharing with other people.

Local Transport Udaipur has a fairly decent city bus service. Auto-rickshaws and taxis are unmetered so you should agree on a fare before setting off. The standard fare for tourists anywhere within the city appears to be around Rs 20, and you'll be lucky to get it for less since there are too many tourists around who pay the first price asked.

The commission system is in place with a vengeance, so most rickshaw drivers will desperately try to drag you to a place of their choice rather than yours, especially if you want to go to the Lal Ghat area. If that's the case, just ask for the Jagdish Temple, as all the guest houses in that area are within easy walking distance of the temple. Some sneaky drivers will insist that the hotel of your choice has burnt down, suddenly closed, or the owner died in a freak accident! Don't be fooled by these far-fetched stories.

Udaipur is small enough and vehicle traffic slow enough to make getting around on a bicycle quite enjoyable. You can hire bicycles all over town for around Rs 3 an hour or Rs 20 per day. Rates tend to be higher at the places right by the tourist hotels.

AROUND UDAIPUR
Eklingji & Nagda

The little village of Eklingji, with a number of ancient temples, is only 22km north of Udaipur. The **Shiva temple** in the village itself was originally built in 734, although its present form dates from the rule of Maharana Raimal between 1473 and 1509. The walled complex includes an elaborately pillared hall under a large pyramidal roof and features a four faced Shiva image of black marble. The temple is open at rather odd hours: 5 to 6 am, 10 am to 1 pm and 5.30 to 8 pm (it's worth double checking timings, as they often change). Photography is not allowed. Avoid the temple on Monday (an auspicious day for devotees), as it can get very crowded.

At Nagda, about a km off the road and a km before Eklingji, are three old temples. The Jain temple of **Adbudji** is essentially ruined, but its architecture is quite interesting. The nearby **Sas Bahu**, or Mother and Daughter-in-Law, group has intricate architecture and carvings, including some erotic figures. You can reach these temples most conveniently by hiring a bicycle in Eklingji itself.

There are hourly RSTC buses from Udaipur to Eklingji for Rs 7.

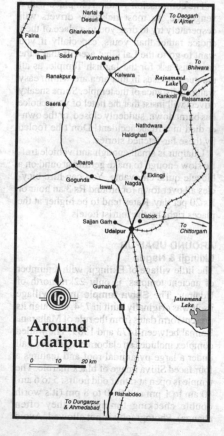

Around Udaipur

Haldighati

This site, 40km north of Udaipur, is where Maharana Pratap valiantly defied the superior Mughal forces of Akbar in 1576. This historically significant site is a battlefield and the only thing to really see is the chhatri to the warrior's horse, Chetak, a few km away.

Nathdwara

The important 18th century Vishnu temple of **Sri Nathji** stands here, 48km north of Udaipur, and it's an important shrine for Vaishnavite devotees. The black stone Vishnu image was brought here from Mathura in 1669 to protect it from Aurangzeb's destructive impulses. According to legend, when an attempt was later made to move the image, the getaway vehicle, a wagon, sank into the ground up to the axles, indicating that the image preferred to stay where it was!

Attendants treat the image like a delicate child, getting it up in the morning, washing it, putting its clothes on, offering it specially prepared meals and putting it down to sleep. It's a very popular pilgrimage site, and the temple opens and closes around the image's daily routine. It gets very crowded around 4.30 to 5 pm when Vishnu gets up after a siesta.

Nathdwara is also known for its *pichwai* paintings, which were first produced after the image of Vishnu was brought to the town.

The *RTDC Hotel Gokul* (☎ (02953) 30917) offers singles/doubles for Rs 250/300, and dorm beds for Rs 50.

RSTC buses leave from Udaipur to Nathdwara every hour (Rs 16).

Kankroli & Rajsamand Lake

Further north, at Kankroli, Dwarkadhish (an incarnation of Vishnu) has a **temple** similar to the temple at Nathdwara and opening hours here are similarly erratic.

Nearby is a lake created by the dam constructed in 1660 by Maharana Raj Singh. There are many ornamental arches and chhatris along the huge *bund* (embankment).

There are hourly RSTC buses from Udaipur for Rs 24.

Kumbhalgarh Fort

Eighty four km north of Udaipur, this is the most important fort in the Mewar region after Chittorgarh. It's a secluded place, built by Maharana Kumbha in the 15th century and, owing to its inaccessibility on top of the Aravalli range at 1100m, it was taken only once in its history. Even then, it took the combined armies of the Mughal emperor, Akbar, and those of Amber and Marwar to breach its defences. It was here that the rulers of Mewar retreated in times of danger. The walls of the fort stretch some 36km and enclose many temples, palaces, gardens and water storage facilities. The fort was renovated in the last century. It's open daily from sunrise to sunset and entry is free.

There's also a big **sanctuary** here, known for its wolves. The scarcity of waterholes between March and June makes this the best time to see animals. Other wildlife includes chowsingha (four horned antelope), leopard and sloth bear.

The *Aodhi Hotel* (☎ (02954) 4222; or bookings through the Shiv Niwas Palace Hotel (☎ (0294) 528016; fax 528006) in Udaipur) is by far the best place to stay. Rooms in this blissfully tranquil hotel cost Rs 1050/2100. There's a cosy bar, restaurant and swimming pool, and horse/jeep safaris can be arranged. This is a wonderful place to rejuvenate yourself.

Hotel Ratandeep (☎ (02954) 4217) is a much cheaper hotel, although it's a little far from the fort. Good rooms (all doubles) cost Rs 350 and dorm beds are Rs 100.

There are two RSTC buses a day from Udaipur (Rs 20, three hours) and private buses are also available. From where the bus drops you, it's a two to three km walk to the fort. If you want to hire a jeep, it's a good idea to come here as part of a small group and split the cost.

Ranakpur

The exceptionally beautiful Ranakpur complex is one of the largest and most important Jain temples in India. Sixty km north of Udaipur, it lies in a remote valley of the Aravalli range and is certainly worth seeing.

The main temple is the **Chaumukha Temple**, or Four Faced Temple, dedicated to Adinath. Built in 1439, this huge, superbly crafted and well kept marble temple has 29 halls supported by 1444 pillars, no two alike. Within the complex are two other Jain temples to **Neminath** and **Parasnath** and, a little distance away, a **Sun Temple**. One km from the main complex is the **Amba Mata Temple**.

The temple complex is open to non-Jains from noon to 5 pm. Shoes and all leather articles must be left at the entrance. Admission is free but there's a Rs 20 camera charge or Rs 100 for a video.

Places to Stay & Eat An overnight stay at Ranakpur breaks up the long trip between Udaipur and Jodhpur.

Maharani Bagh Orchard Retreat (☎ (02934) 3705; or bookings through Umaid Bhawan Palace (☎ (0291) 33316; fax 35373) in Jodhpur) is four km from Ranakpur and is the best place to stay. Set in a shady mango orchard, it offers comfortable accommodation in cottages for Rs 775/1075. Hearty meals are available; lunch or dinner costs Rs 200.

RTDC Hotel Shilpi (☎ (02934) 3674) is rather poorly run and has indifferent service. Singles/doubles go for Rs 175/200, deluxe rooms cost Rs 250/300, and dorm beds are Rs 50. Meals are available in the dining room.

The Castle (☎ (02934) 3733) is a much better option but more expensive, with rooms for around Rs 600/700.

Dharamsala (no phone) pilgrims' lodgings within the temple complex, has very basic accommodation for a donation. If you arrive at a meal time, you can get a thali in the dining hall, again for a small donation.

Getting There & Away Ranakpur is 39km from Falna Junction on the Ajmer to Mt Abu rail and road routes. There are frequent RSTC buses from Udaipur (Rs 24, 3½ to 4½ hours). Although it's possible to travel through from Ranakpur to Jodhpur or Mt Abu on the same day, it's hardly worth it since you'll arrive well after dark. Your best bet is to stay the night at Ranakpur and continue on the next day.

Narlai

Not too far from Ranakpur and Kumbhalgarh, Narlai can make an ideal base for exploration of the various attractions around Udaipur. It's also a good place to catch up on some serious relaxation.

Rawla Narlai (bookings through Ajit Bhawan (☎ (0291) 37410; fax 37774) in Jodhpur) has terrific rooms with attached bath and constant hot water for Rs 1190/1595. Good meals are available and tribal shows can be arranged with advance notice. Not far from the hotel are some old temples and a fine stepwell.

Ghanerao

About seven km from Narlai is the little town of Ghanerao.

Ghanerao Royal Castle (☎ (02934) 7335) has good, if somewhat run-down, rooms for Rs 800/1000 with private bath and bucket hot water. There's a restaurant here and jeep/walking treks can be organised.

Jaisamand Lake

Located 48km south-east of Udaipur, this stunningly located artificial lake, created by damming the Gomti River, was built by Maharana Jai Singh in the 17th century. It's one of the largest artificial lakes in Asia, and there are beautiful marble chhatris around the embankment, each with an elephant in front. The summer palaces of the Udaipur queens are also here and a wildlife sanctuary is nearby.

Jaisamand Island Resort (☎ (02906) 2222; or bookings through Hotel Lakend (☎ (0294) 23841; fax 523898) in Udaipur) is a modern hotel in a secluded position 20 minutes by boat across the lake. Comfortable rooms start at Rs 1150/2500, all with lake views.

Tourist Bungalow is a cheaper option on the shores of the lake.

There are frequent RSTC buses from Udaipur (Rs 15).

Dungarpur

Well off the beaten track, about 110km south of Udaipur, is the little town of Dungarpur. There's an interesting palace here that has been converted into a hotel.

Udai Bilas Palace (☎ (02964) 30808; fax 31008) is ideally located on the banks of a lake which attracts a variety of birdlife. Pleasant rooms cost Rs 1195/1650 and capacious suites go for Rs 2395. Bookings should be made in advance. Constructed of blue-grey stone, everything at this palace seems to have been left just as it was in those unhurried days before socialist India swept aside the princely states. A feature here is the intricately carved Ek Thambia Mahal (one pillared palace). Meals are available with advance notice.

The hotel can arrange a visit to the deserted old palace called **Juna Mahal**, built in the 13th century and filled with old frescoes, paintings and colourful glass inlay work.

Frequent RSTC buses travel to Dungarpur from Udaipur for Rs 30.

Each January/February the **Baneshwar Festival** is held at the Baneshwar Temple, situated about 70km from Dungarpur. This colourful event attracts thousands of Bhil tribals from around India.

MT ABU

Pop: 18,000   Tel Area Code: 02974

Mt Abu is Rajasthan's only hill station sprawling along a 1200m high plateau in the south of the state, close to the Gujarat border. It's a pleasant hot season retreat from the plains of both Rajasthan and Gujarat, but you won't find many western travellers here – apart from those who come to study at the Brahma Kumaris Spiritual University. Predominantly Indian visitors include many honeymooners and Gujarati families. Mt Abu's pace is easy going, although it can get terribly crowded with people and traffic during the summer months.

Mt Abu has more to attract visitors than just its cooler climate – it has a number of important temples, particularly the breathtaking Dilwara group of Jain temples, five km away. This is an important pilgrimage centre for Jains and boasts some of the finest marble carvings in all of Rajasthan, if not India. Also, like some other hill stations in India, Mt Abu has its own lake and heaps of small shops and eating places.

Orientation & Information

Mt Abu is on a hilly plateau about 22km long by six km wide, 27km from the nearest railway station, at Abu Road. The main part of the town extends along the road in from Abu Road, down to Nakki Lake.

The Tourist Reception Centre (☎ 3151) is opposite the bus stand and is open Monday to Saturday from 10 am to 1.30 pm and 2 to 5 pm. The GPO is on Raj Bhavan Rd, opposite the art gallery and museum. Several banks, including the Bank of Baroda, will change money.

Nakki Lake

Nakki Lake is virtually in the heart of Mt Abu and is a big attraction with tourists. The small lake takes its name from the legend that it was scooped out by a god, using only his nails, or *nakh*. It's a pleasant stroll around the lake – look for the strange **rock formations**.

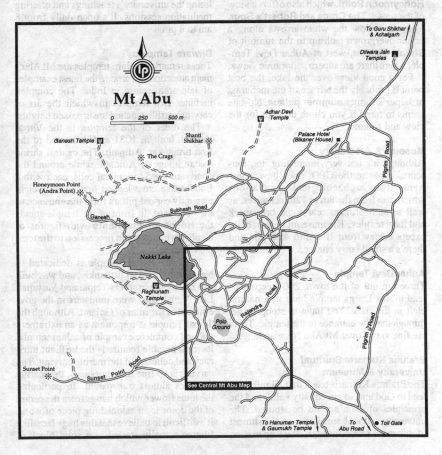
Mt Abu

The best known, Toad Rock, looks just like a toad about to hop into the lake. Others, like Nun Rock, Nandi Rock or Camel Rock, require more imagination. The 14th century **Raghunath Temple** stands beside the lake.

You can hire your own boat (Rs 25 for 30 minutes), or be rowed (Rs 4 per person).

Viewpoints
Of the various viewpoints around town, **Sunset Point** is the most popular. Hordes stroll out here every evening to catch the setting sun, the food stalls and all the usual entertainments. Other popular spots include **Honeymoon Point**, which also offers a view of the sunset, **The Crags** and **Robert's Spur**. You can follow the white arrows along a rather overgrown path up to the summit of **Shanti Shikhar**, west of Adhar Devi Temple, where there are superb panoramic views.

For a good view over the lake, the best point is probably the terrace of the maharaja of Jaipur's former **summer palace**. No-one seems to mind if you climb up here for the view and a photo.

Museum & Art Gallery
Although it's not very interesting, the museum, opposite the GPO, does have some items from archaeological excavations which date from the 8th to 12th centuries, as well as Jain bronzes, carvings, brasswork and local textiles. The museum is open daily except Friday from 10 am to 4.30 pm, and there's a small entry charge.

Adhar Devi Temple
Three km out of the town, 200 steep steps lead to this Durga temple built in a natural cleft in the rock. You have to stoop to get through the low entrance to the temple. There are fine views over Mt Abu from up here.

Brahma Kumaris Spiritual University & Museum
The Brahma Kumaris teach that all religions lead to God and so are equally valid, and the principles of each should be studied. The university's stated aim is the establishment of universal peace through 'the impartation of spiritual knowledge and training of easy raja yoga meditation'. There are over 4000 branches in 60 countries around the world and followers come to Mt Abu to attend courses at the spiritual university. To attend one of these residential courses you need to contact your local branch and arrange things in advance. You can, however, arrange for someone here to give you an introductory course (seven lessons) while you're in Mt Abu; this would take a minimum of three days. There's no charge – the organisation is entirely supported by donations.

There's a museum (free) in the town outlining the university's teachings and offering meditation sessions. It's open daily from 8 am to 8 pm.

Dilwara Temples
These remarkable Jain temples are Mt Abu's main attraction and among the finest examples of Jain architecture in India. The complex includes two temples in which the art of carving marble reached unsurpassed heights.

The older of the temples is the **Vimal Vasahi**, built in 1031 and dedicated to the first tirthankar, Adinath. The central shrine has an image of Adinath, while around the courtyard are 52 identical cells, each with a Buddha-like cross-legged image. Forty-eight elegantly carved pillars form the entrance to the courtyard. In front of the temple stands the **House of Elephants** with figures of elephants marching in procession to the temple entrance.

The later **Tejpal Temple** is dedicated to Neminath, the 22nd tirthankar, and was built in 1230 by the brothers Tejpal and Vastupal. Like Vimal, they were ministers in the government of the ruler of Gujarat. Although the Tejpal Temple is important as an extremely old and complete example of a Jain temple, its most notable feature is the brilliant intricacy and delicacy of the marble carving. The carving is so fine that, in places, the marble becomes almost transparent. In particular, the lotus flower which hangs from the centre of the dome is an astonishing piece of work. It's difficult to believe that this huge lace-like filigree actually started as a solid block of marble. The temple employs several full-time stone carvers to maintain and restore the work. There are three other temples in the enclosure, but they all pale beside the Tejpal and Vimal Vasahi.

The complex is open from noon to 6 pm. Photography is not allowed, and bags are thoroughly searched to prevent cameras being taken in. As at other Jain temples, all articles of leather (belts as well as shoes) have to be left at the entrance. You must also observe a number of other regulations which include 'bags, shoes, umbrellas, firearms not allowed' and 'moving hand-in-hand, hand on shoulders or waist is strictly prohibited'. And there's a dire warning for women: 'Entry of ladies in monthly course is strictly prohibited. Any lady in monthly course if enters any of the temples she may suffer'.

You can stroll out to Dilwara from the town in less than an hour, or take a share taxi for Rs 3 from opposite the Madras Cafe in the centre of town.

Organised Tours

The RTDC has five hour tours of all the main sites, leaving from the Tourist Reception Centre at 8.30 am and 1.30 pm (later in summer). The tours cost Rs 40 plus all entry and camera fees. The afternoon tour finishes at Sunset Point, and a notice warns that sunset is only included in the afternoon tour!

Places to Stay

There are a plethora of hotels in Mt Abu, with new ones continually springing up. Most are along or just off the main road through to Nakki Lake. The high season lasts from mid-March to mid-November. As most hotel owners raise prices to whatever the market will bear at those times, Mt Abu can be an expensive place to stay. The real peak time is from late April to mid-June, and a room of any kind for less than Rs 200 is hard to find. During the five days of Diwali (November), rooms are virtually unobtainable without advance booking. Avoid the place at this time.

In low season (with the exception of Christmas and New Year), discounts of up to 50% are available and mid-range accommodation can be an absolute bargain. Most places are definitely open to a bit of bargaining, and the rates generally get cheaper the longer you stay. The hotels usually have an ungenerous 9 am checkout time and many also levy a 10% tax.

At all times of the year there are plenty of touts working the bus and taxi stands. In the low season you can safely ignore them; at peak times they can save you a lot of legwork as they'll know exactly where the last available room is.

Paying Guest House accommodation is available in Mt Abu and ranges from about Rs 100 to Rs 500. Contact the Tourist Reception Centre for details.

Places to Stay – bottom end

Hotel Lake View (☎ 38659) overlooks picturesque Nakki Lake but, although the views are certainly good, it's really only an average hotel. In winter, there are singles with common bath from Rs 100, doubles with bath attached from Rs 100 to Rs 350. The minimum summer rate is Rs 250. Hot water is available between 6 and 11 am, and there's a pleasant terrace.

Hotel Panghat (☎ 3386), nearby, is better value. There are rooms with a lake view, attached bathroom and TV from Rs 125. Hot water is available from 7 to 9 am.

Hotel Nakki Vihar (☎ 3481), also in this lakeside area, has rooms from Rs 80 (some have a lake view).

Shree Ganesh Hotel (☎ 3591), up the hill towards the maharaja of Jaipur's old summer palace, is a popular place with travellers. It's in a quiet location and the owner is a friendly guy. Clean rooms with bath start from Rs 100 in the low season, Rs 350 in the high season. There are good views from the rooftop terrace. As this place is a little further from the centre of things, the high season rates tend to be a little more sensible than elsewhere, and bargaining is possible.

Hotel Rajdeep (☎ 3525), opposite the bus stand, is in an old building and some of the rooms are good value. A large double with attached bath is Rs 100 in winter. There's a small restaurant at the front of this hotel.

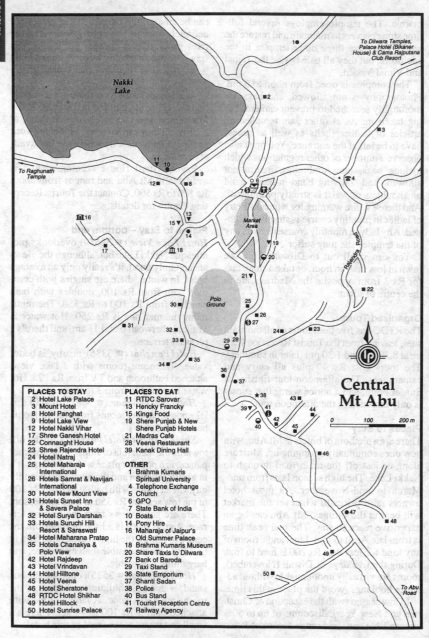

To Dilwara Temples,
Palace Hotel (Bikaner
House) & Cama Rajputana
Club Resort

*Nakki
Lake*

To Raghunath
Temple

Market
Area

Rajendra Road

Polo
Ground

Central
Mt Abu

0   100   200 m

To Abu
Road

PLACES TO STAY
2   Hotel Lake Palace
3   Mount Hotel
8   Hotel Panghat
9   Hotel Lake View
12 Hotel Nakki Vihar
17 Shree Ganesh Hotel
22 Connaught House
23 Shree Rajendra Hotel
24 Hotel Natraj
25 Hotel Maharaja
    International
26 Hotels Samrat & Navijan
    International
30 Hotel New Mount View
31 Hotels Sunset Inn
    & Savera Palace
32 Hotel Surya Darshan
33 Hotels Suruchi Hill
    Resort & Saraswati
34 Hotel Maharana Pratap
35 Hotels Chanakya &
    Polo View
42 Hotel Rajdeep
43 Hotel Vrindavan
44 Hotel Hilltock
45 Hotel Veena
46 Hotel Sheratone
48 RTDC Hotel Shikhar
49 Hotel Hillock
50 Hotel Sunrise Palace

PLACES TO EAT
11 RTDC Sarovar
13 Hencky Francky
15 Kings Food
19 Shere Punjab & New
    Shere Punjab Hotels
21 Madras Cafe
28 Veena Restaurant
39 Kanak Dining Hall

OTHER
1   Brahma Kumaris
    Spiritual University
4   Telephone Exchange
5   Church
6   GPO
7   State Bank of India
10 Boats
14 Pony Hire
16 Maharaja of Jaipur's
    Old Summer Palace
18 Brahma Kumaris Museum
20 Share Taxis to Dilwara
27 Bank of Baroda
29 Taxi Stand
36 State Emporium
37 Shanti Sadan
38 Police
40 Bus Stand
41 Tourist Reception Centre
47 Railway Agency

Hotel Veena (no phone) is nearby and similarly priced. There's not really a view of anything much from here, and while the main road is generally quiet by Indian standards, the noise can be annoying.

If you take the right-hand fork going up the hill opposite the taxi stand and polo ground, you'll find several other budget hotels.

Hotel Natraj (☎ 3532), near the Bank of Baroda, has reasonable rooms with private bath from Rs 150.

Shree Rajendra Hotel (☎ 3174), across the road, is one of the cheapest places here, with rooms from Rs 80 to Rs 250, all with attached bath. Bucket hot water costs Rs 4.

RTDC Hotel Shikhar (☎ 3129), back from the main road and up a steepish path, is a huge place with about 80 rooms. Although fairly popular, it's certainly not the best nor friendliest place in town. All rooms have attached bath; singles/doubles cost Rs 175/250 (with bucket hot water), deluxe rooms are Rs 325/400, and cottages are Rs 800. These are the year-round prices. There's also a restaurant.

On the far side of the polo ground there's a string of hotels, which are definitely mid-range in the high season but offer quite good rates in the low season.

Hotel Chanakya (☎ 3438) charges Rs 250 in the low season for a comfortable double with attached bath and constant hot water. In the high season it's Rs 550.

Hotel Saraswati (☎ 3237), nearby, is very good value. There are well kept doubles with bucket hot water for Rs 80, and a range of other rooms from Rs 100 to Rs 250. It's well run and a recommended place to stay, but the lilac and pink paint job is a bit radical. The vegetarian restaurant serves tasty Gujarati thalis (Rs 40).

Hotel Polo View (☎ 3487), *Hotel Surya Darshan* (☎ 3165), and *Hotel New Mount View* (☎ 38279), also in this area, all charge around Rs 250 for a room with attached bath.

Places to Stay – middle
Mount Hotel (☎ 3150) is in a peaceful location along the road to the Dilwara temples. It once belonged to a British army officer and has changed little since those days, except for a lick of paint. There are only a few rooms in this very homely place, and these cost Rs 250/300. Wholesome vegetarian meals (Rs 60) are available with advance notice. The owner is friendly and so is his dog, Spots.

Hotel Lake Palace (☎ 3254), just across from the lake, has doubles/triples with attached bath for Rs 600/800 in the high season; bargain hard in the low season and you should be able to slash at least 30% off these prices.

Hotel Sunset Inn (☎ 3194), on the western edge of Mt Abu, is a modern hotel that's well run. There are doubles from Rs 600, triples from Rs 700 and a 30% low-season discount. The restaurant serves satisfying meals.

Hotel Savera Palace (☎ 3354), nearby, is similarly priced but not as good.

Hotel Suruchi Hill Resort (☎ 3577), at the bottom end of the polo ground, has doubles for Rs 690 in the high season, and there's a 50% low-season discount.

Hotel Maharana Pratap (☎ 38667; fax 3576), at the end of this road, is a smart place with rooms from Rs 720, and a 50% discount in the low season.

Hotel Vrindavan (☎ 3147), not far from the bus stand, is a pleasant place with rooms from Rs 350 with TV and attached bath.

Hotel Sheratone (☎ 3544), in the same area, has airy doubles for around Rs 750.

Hotel Samrat (☎ 3153) and *Hotel Navijan International* (☎ 3173), on the main street, are basically the same hotel although they appear to be separate. Off-season rates in the Samrat are from Rs 550 for a double with bath and hot water; the Navijan is a little cheaper. Prices double in the high season.

Hotel Maharaja International (☎ 3161), directly opposite, is a little more upmarket.

Places to Stay – top end
Palace Hotel (Bikaner House) (☎ 38673; fax 38674), not far from the Dilwara Temples, is the most atmospheric hotel in Mt Abu. It has lovely gardens, a private lake, tennis courts, a billiard room and an excellent restaurant. Once the summer residence

of the maharaja of Bikaner, it is now managed by the maharaja's friendly and helpful son-in-law. Singles/doubles cost Rs 950/1175 all year round.

Cama Rajputana Club Resort (☎ 3163), nearby, is a large place that has comfortable rooms from Rs 1190/1690. There's a good restaurant serving Continental, Punjabi and Chinese cuisine.

Connaught House (☎ 3439; or bookings through the Umaid Bhawan Palace (☎ (0291) 33316; fax 35373) in Jodhpur), just east of the town, has undertones of an English cottage and is a homely place to stay. Owned by the maharaja of Jodhpur, it's set in its own pleasant gardens – the perfect place to sit back with a good book. As well as rooms in the delightful old building there's also a new wing. Singles/doubles with attached bath and constant hot water are Rs 950/1250. Meals are available and should be ordered in advance; the set lunch/dinner costs Rs 160.

Hotel Sunrise Palace (☎ 3573; fax 38775), at the southern end of Mt Abu, is yet another former summer residence of a Rajput maharaja (this time the maharaja of Bharatpur). It's a quiet and comfortable hotel with rooms ranging from Rs 650 to Rs 1450, and there's also a restaurant.

Hotel Hillock (☎ 3277), in the same area, is a flash place – large, spotlessly clean and well decorated, (although the outside of the building is quite ugly). Its year-round tariff is Rs 1190/1400. There's a restaurant, bar and pool.

Hotel Hilltone (☎ 38391; fax 38395) is closer to town and has a swimming pool, restaurant, bar, sauna and bookshop. It's a modern place with singles/doubles for Rs 950/1200; there's a 20% to 30% discount in the low season.

Places to Eat
Kanak Dining Hall, near the bus stand, is a popular place to eat. It's clean and offers excellent south Indian veg dishes and tasty lunchtime thalis for Rs 35; there's seating indoor and outdoors.

Veena Restaurant is further uphill, next to the junction at the bottom end of the polo ground. Its refillable Gujarati thalis (Rs 30) are among the best in town.

Shere Punjab Hotel, in the bazaar area, is in heavy duty competition with the nearby *New Shere Punjab Hotel*. The former has an excellent reputation; the latter is a bit cheaper. Both serve veg and non-veg food; each pours scorn on the other's catering abilities.

Madras Cafe, also in this area, is a pure veg place with an assortment of Indian and western fare. Pizzas cost Rs 20, vegie burgers are Rs 20 and masala dosas go for just Rs 12.

Kings Food, on the road leading down to the lake, has the usual have-a-go-at-anything menu and a good fresh juice stand.

Hencky Francky, nearby, was a fast food joint in a former life, but now this amazingly named place specialises in ice cream.

RTDC Sarovar is on the lake itself. It's a teashop in the form of a large dilapidated 'boat' that's closed in the low season.

Palace Hotel (Bikaner House) is the best place to go for a special meal. The delicious set lunch/dinner costs Rs 195 (veg), Rs 250 (non-veg). It's a good idea to make an advance reservation.

Things to Buy
Around Nakki Lake, there are numerous shops and stalls selling all sorts of cheap souvenirs. In the evening, the town really comes to life and this is an enjoyable time to do some leisurely browsing. Mt Abu is quite a good place to pick up knick-knacks for friends back home.

Getting There & Away
As you enter Mt Abu, there's a toll gate where bus and car passengers are charged Rs 5, plus Rs 5 for a car. If you're travelling by bus, this is an irksome hold up, as you have to wait until the collector painstakingly gathers the toll from each and every passenger (keep small change handy).

Bus From 6 am onwards, regular buses make the 27km climb from Abu Road up to Mt Abu (Rs 10, one hour). Some RSTC buses go all the way to Mt Abu, while others terminate at

Abu Road, so make sure you get the one you want.

The bus schedule from Mt Abu is extensive, and for many destinations you will find a direct bus faster and more convenient than going down to Abu Road and waiting for a train. To Udaipur, RSTC buses take seven hours at a cost of Rs 50. To Ajmer (Rs 118, eight hours) and Jaipur (Rs 159, 11 hours) there's one departure daily. For Ahmedabad there are many departures and the journey takes around seven hours (Rs 50).

Private buses are more expensive but are faster and more comfortable than state transport buses, and there's plenty of choice.

Train Abu Road, the railhead for Mt Abu, is on the (soon to be broad-gauge) line between Delhi and Ahmedabad via Jaipur and Ajmer.

In Mt Abu there's a railway agency at the HP service station, not far from the RTDC Hotel Shikar, which has quotas on most of the express trains out of Abu Road. It's open daily from 9 am to 1 pm and 2 to 4 pm (only until noon on Sunday).

From Abu Road, direct trains run to various destinations including Ajmer, Jodhpur, Jaipur, Ahmedabad and Agra. For Bhuj and the rest of the Kathiawar peninsula in Gujarat, change trains at Palanpur, 53km south of Abu Road.

Taxi A taxi, which you can share with up to five people, costs Rs 140 from Abu Road. To hire a jeep for local sightseeing costs around Rs 600 per day (but you may be able to bargain this down).

Getting Around

Buses from the bus stand go to the various sites in Mt Abu, but it takes a little planning to get out and back without too much hanging around. Some buses just go to Dilwara, while others will take you out to Achalgarh, so you'll need to decide which place to visit first, depending on the schedule. For Dilwara it's easier to take a share taxi, and these leave when full from opposite the Madras Cafe in the centre of town; the fare is Rs 3. There are

plenty of taxis with posted fares to anywhere you care to mention.

There are no auto-rickshaws in Mt Abu, but it's relatively easy to get around on foot. Porters with trolleys can be hired for a small charge to transport your luggage – weary travellers can even be transported in the trolley!

AROUND MT ABU
Achalgarh

The Shiva temple of **Achaleshwar Mahandeva**, 11km north of Mt Abu, has a number of interesting features, including a toe of Shiva, a brass Nandi and, where the Shiva lingam would normally be, a deep hole said to extend all the way to the underworld.

Outside, by the car park, three stone buffaloes stand around a tank while the figure of a king shoots at them with a bow and arrows. A legend states that the tank was once filled with ghee, but demons in the form of buffaloes came down and drank each night – until the king shot them. A path leads up the hillside to a group of colourful **Jain temples** with fine views out over the plains.

Guru Shikhar

At the end of the plateau, 15km from Mt Abu, is Guru Shikhar, the highest point in Rajasthan at 1721m. A road goes almost all the way to the summit. At the top is the **Atri Rishi Temple**, complete with a priest and good views all around.

Gaumukh Temple

Down on the Abu Road side of Mt Abu, a small stream flows from the mouth of a marble cow, giving the shrine its name. There is also a marble figure of the bull Nandi, Shiva's vehicle. The tank here, Agni Kund, is said to be the site of the sacrificial fire, made by the sage Vasishta, from which four of the great Rajput clans were born. An image of Vasishta is flanked by figures of Rama and Krishna.

ABU ROAD

This station down on the plains is the rail junction for Mt Abu. The railway station and bus stand are right next to each other on the edge of town. Although there are RSTC buses from Abu Road to other cities such as Jodhpur, Ajmer, Jaipur, Udaipur and Ahmedabad, there's little point in catching them here as they're all available from Mt Abu itself. Buses operated by private companies also run from Mt Abu.

There are a handful of basic hotels in the main market area which are OK for a night, but the hotels in Mt Abu are far preferable.

Retiring rooms at the railway station are convenient if you're catching an early morning train.

Western Rajasthan

JODHPUR

Pop: 770,000   Tel Area Code: 0291

Jodhpur stands at the edge of the Thar Desert and is the largest city in Rajasthan after Jaipur. The city is totally dominated by a massive fort, topping a sheer rocky hill which rises right in the middle of the town. Jodhpur was founded in 1459 by Rao Jodha, a chief of the Rajput clan known as the Rathores. His descendants ruled not only Jodhpur, but also other Rajput princely states. The Rathore kingdom was once known as Marwar, the Land of Death.

The old city of Jodhpur is surrounded by a 10km long wall, built about a century after the city was founded. From the fort, you can clearly see where the old city ends and the new begins. It's fascinating to wander around the jumble of winding streets in the old city, out of which eight gates lead. While Jaipur is known as the 'Pink City', Jodhpur is often referred to as the 'Blue City' because of its many blue-coloured houses which are best seen from the fort ramparts. Part of the film *Rudyard Kipling's Jungle Book*, starring Sam Neill and John Cleese, was shot in Jodhpur and yes, it was from here that those baggytight horse-riding trousers, jodhpurs, took their name.

As one of the closest major Indian cities to the border with Pakistan, Jodhpur has a large defence contingency. Don't dive for cover when you hear booming jet fighter planes above – Jodhpur is not under siege, the air force is simply undergoing its routine training exercise.

Orientation

The Tourist Reception Centre, railway stations and bus terminal are all outside the old city. High Court Rd runs from the Raika Bagh railway station, past the Umaid Gardens, the RTDC Hotel Ghoomar, and around beside the city wall towards the main station and the GPO. Most trains from the east stop at the Raika Bagh station before the main station – handy if you want to stay at the hotels on the eastern side of town.

Information

The Tourist Reception Centre (☎ 45083) is in the RTDC Hotel Ghoomar compound and is open daily except Sunday from 10 am to 6 pm. The Bank of Baroda, near the Hotel Arun, changes travellers cheques.

Meherangarh Fort

Still run by the maharaja of Jodhpur, the Majestic Fort is just that. Sprawled across a 125m high hill, this is the most formidable fort in fort-studded Rajasthan. A winding road leads up to the entrance from the city below. The first gate is still scarred by cannon ball hits, indicating that this was a fort which earned its keep. The gates include the **Jayapol**, built by Maharaja Man Singh in 1806 following his victory over the armies of Jaipur and Bikaner, and the **Fatehpol**, or Victory Gate, erected by Maharaja Ajit Singh to commemorate his defeat of the Mughals.

The final gate is the **Lahapol**, or Iron Gate, beside which there are 15 hand prints, the sati marks of Maharaja Man Singh's widows who threw themselves upon his funeral pyre in 1843. They still attract devotional attention and are usually covered in red powder.

Inside the fort, there is a series of courtyards and palaces. The **palace apartments** have evocative names like the Sukh Mahal, or Pleasure Palace, and the Phool Mahal, or

Flower Palace. They house a splendid collection of the trappings of Indian royalty, including an amazing collection of elephant *howdahs* (used when the maharajas rode their elephants in glittering procession through their capitals), miniature paintings from a variety of schools, superb folk musical instruments and the inevitable Rajput armoury, palanquins, furniture and costumes. In one room, there's even an exhibit of rocking cradles. Finally, there's an enormous and stunning tent, originally made for the Mughal emperors but carried off as booty by the Rajputs following one of their many battles.

The palace apartments are beautifully decorated and have delicately carved latticework windows of red sandstone.

At the southern end of the fort, old cannons look out from the ramparts over the sheer drop to the old town beneath. There's no guard rail and you can clearly hear voices and city sounds swept up by the air currents from the houses far below. The views from these ramparts are nothing less than magical. From here, you can also see the many houses painted blue to distinguish them as those of Brahmins. The **Chamunda Devi Temple**, dedicated to Durga, stands at this end of the fort.

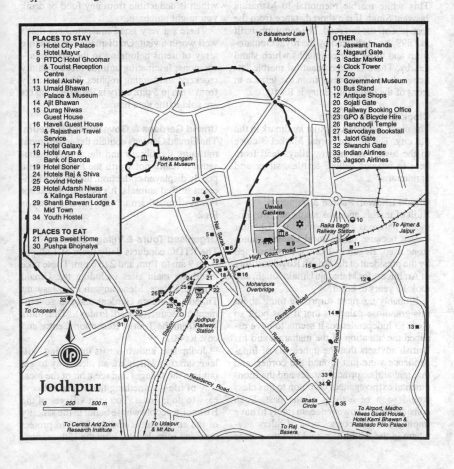

The fort is open daily from 9 am to 1 pm and 2 to 5 pm. Entry costs Rs 50 and there's a Rs 50 camera charge, Rs 100 for a video. Guides are available for around Rs 100, but they generally expect a small tip at the end. For weary travellers, an elevator will take you up to (but not down from) the top of the fort for Rs 10. A group of musicians usually sits outside the cafe near the museum entrance and strike up a merry Rajasthani number to herald your arrival – it helps set the mood and they, too, appreciate a tip.

Jaswant Thanda

This white marble memorial to Maharaja Jaswant Singh II is a short distance from the fort, just off the fort road. The cenotaph, built in 1899, was followed by the royal crematorium and three later cenotaphs which stand nearby. There is some beautiful marble latticework and fine views from the terrace in front of the cenotaph. Entry is Rs 10.

Clock Tower & Markets

The clock tower is a popular landmark in the old city. The vibrant Sardar Market is close to the tower, and narrow alleys lead from here to bazaars selling textiles, silver and handicrafts.

Umaid Bhawan Palace & Museum

Built of marble and pink sandstone, this immense palace is also known as the Chhittar Palace because of the local Chhittar sandstone used. Begun in 1929, it was designed by the president of the British Royal Institute of Architects for Maharaja Umaid Singh, and took 15 years to build.

Probably the most surprising thing about this grandiose palace is that it was built so close to Independence. It seems to have escaped the attention of the maharaja and his British advisers that the upheavals of Independence were just around the corner, and that maharajas, princely states and the monumental extravagances common to this class would soon be a thing of the past. Such considerations, however, seem rarely to have impinged on the consciences of rulers anywhere in the world. It is said that the palace was built as a royal job-creation programme to provide employment for thousands of local people during a time of severe drought.

Maharaja Umaid Singh died in 1947; his successor still lives in part of the building. The rest has been turned into a hotel – and what a hotel! While it lacks the charm of Udaipur's palace hotels, it certainly makes up for it in spacious grandeur. Few who could afford it would miss the chance of staying here, and the hotel corridors echo with languages from around the world. Unfortunately, the palace is not open to non-guests, unless you want to pay the fee of Rs 330, which is deductible from any food or drink you might purchase.

There's a very good museum here that's well worth a visit. On display is an amazing array of items belonging to the maharaja – weapons, fascinating antique clocks, dainty crockery, and hunting trophies. It's open daily from 9 am to 5 pm; entry is Rs 50 and tickets are sold in the gate house.

Umaid Gardens & Government Museum

The Umaid Gardens contain the government museum, the library and the zoo. The museum is really not worth the bother, with a poorly displayed collection, including moth-eaten stuffed animals. It's open daily except Friday from 10 am to 4.30 pm and entry is Rs 2.

Organised Tours & Village Safaris

The RTDC conducts daily tours of Jodhpur from 9 am to 1 pm and 2 to 6 pm. These take in all the main sites including the Umaid Bhawan Palace, Meherangarh Fort, Jaswant Thanda, Mandore Gardens and the government museum (closed Friday). The tours start from the Tourist Reception Centre and cost Rs 60.

Jodhpur is known for its interesting 'village safaris', which are an ideal way to get out into the villages and see a bit of the local way of life – something that it's not always easy to do in India. You visit villages of the Bishnoi, a people whose belief in the sanctity of the environment and the need to protect trees and animals dates from the 15th century.

A safari (by jeep) usually costs from Rs 350 to Rs 400 for a half day tour, including lunch (a minimum of three to six people is generally required).

The owner of the Madho Niwas Guest House (☎ 34486) conducts informative safaris for residents and non-residents. These cost Rs 350 per person for a half day safari (including a meal) and visit a variety of villages. Bookings must be made in advance. Several other hotels can also arrange safaris, including the Ajit Bhawan (☎ 37410) and Durag Niwas Guest House (☎ 39092). Alternatively, you can organise a safari through the Tourist Reception Centre (☎ 45083).

A private tour guide, the knowledgeable 65 year old Mr NL Tak (☎ 30637), has also been recommended for village safaris. He charges Rs 350 per person (including a meal).

Some travellers caution that if you book a safari through a travel agent it's important to choose carefully, as some are overpriced and poorly run.

Places to Stay – bottom end

Jodhpur operates the Paying Guest House Scheme with prices ranging from Rs 100 to Rs 700. Contact the Tourist Reception Centre for details.

Govind Hotel (☎ 22758), opposite the GPO, is a popular choice and is one of the best budget hotels in town. There are dorm beds for Rs 50, singles with common bath for Rs 60 and singles/doubles with bath attached for Rs 125/175. This is a very traveller friendly place so you won't have any hassles whatsoever. The rooftop restaurant commands magnificent views of the fort.

Shanti Bhawan Lodge (☎ 21689), just up the road opposite the Jodhpur railway station, has singles/doubles with common bath for Rs 70/150, rooms with attached bath and air-cooling are Rs 125/200, or Rs 500/700 for a bigger room with air-con. Some of the cheaper rooms are quite small and gloomy.

Hotel Soner (☎ 25732), *Hotel Galaxy* (☎ 25098), and the *Hotel Arun* (☎ 20238), are similarly priced hotels in this area. Expect to pay at least Rs 200 for a double with attached bath at any of these places.

Retiring rooms at the railway station are another cheap (but not very exciting) choice. Doubles with bath start from Rs 90.

Hotel Akshey (☎ 37327), opposite the Raika Bagh railway station, is quite a good choice, with dorm beds for Rs 40 while rooms with private bath start at Rs 150/200. There's also a restaurant and small garden.

There are some other budget options away from the railway station, including two family run guest houses which offer a very homely atmosphere.

Madho Niwas Guest House (☎ 34486), on Airport Rd, is definitely one of the most homely places to stay. Run by the very down-to-earth Dalvir Singh and his family, rooms are set around a quiet lawn area. Clean singles/doubles with private bath start at Rs 200/250. Meals are available; the Marwari style barbecue chicken is delicious. Good village safaris are available here (see earlier under Organised Tours & Village Safaris), and they can also arrange a sojourn at their relaxing country retreat *Ravla Bhenswara*, 130km from Jodhpur.

Durag Niwas Guest House (☎ 39092), closer to town, is another excellent choice and is run by a lovely family. Good double rooms with private bath range from Rs 200 to Rs 400 for a bigger room. Meals are also available. Don't confuse this guest house with the similarly named place next door.

RTDC Hotel Ghoomar (☎ 44010), on High Court Rd, offers singles/doubles with bath from Rs 200/300. There are dorm beds for Rs 50. There's a bar and restaurant here, as well as the Tourist Reception Centre.

The *Youth Hostel* (☎ 20150), near the Indian Airlines office, has dorm beds for Rs 20 for members, Rs 40 for non-members. Doubles with common bath cost Rs 100, doubles with attached bath cost Rs 120.

Places to Stay – middle

Hotel Karni Bhawan (☎ 32220; fax 33495), near the Madho Niwas Guest House, is a modern place with traditional touches. Set in well manicured gardens, comfortable singles/doubles with private bath start from Rs 1000/1100. Some rooms are imaginatively designed to depict a particular Indian festival. There's also a pool and fine restaurant.

Ajit Bhawan (☎ 37410; fax 37774), on Airport Rd, has long been popular with travellers. It has a series of modern stone cottages arranged around a relaxing garden. Cottages with private bath cost Rs 1300/1550, or Rs 2300/2500 for deluxe rooms. There's a restaurant, great swimming pool and village safaris are available. Although the setting of this hotel is indeed delightful, travellers have mixed reports about the service. Like many hotels that expand over the years, unfortunately the personal touch seems to be fading here, too.

Raj Basera (☎ 31973), towards the airport on Residency Rd, has pleasant cottages built around a central building for Rs 950/1050. There's also a restaurant; lunch/dinner costs Rs 195/225.

Hotel Adarsh Niwas (☎ 26936) is very convenient if you want to be close to the Jodhpur railway station. Plain but well kept air-cooled rooms with bath and TV cost Rs 500/650, Rs 700/950 with air-con. There's also a restaurant.

Places to Stay – top end

Umaid Bhawan Palace (☎ 33316; fax 35373) is undoubtedly Jodhpur's finest hotel and is *the* place to stay if you have a passion for pure luxury. This very elegant palace is owned by the maharaja of Jodhpur (who still occupies one wing) and the hotel is operated by Welcomgroup. There's an indoor swimming pool, tennis court, billiard room, shops, lush lawns and a vast dining hall. Rooms cost US$155/170, and suites range from US$300 to US$930. If you can possibly afford it, opt for a suite, as the cheaper rooms are suitably comfortable, but hardly palatial.

Ratanada Polo Palace (☎ 31910; fax 33118), on Residency Rd, has comfortable accommodation but is a rather characterless place. Singles/doubles cost Rs 3000/3500 and there's also a restaurant and swimming pool.

Places to Eat

While you're in Jodhpur, try a glass of makhania lassi, a delicious saffron-flavoured variety of that most refreshing of drinks.

Agra Sweet Home, opposite Sojati Gate, is so popular that in summer they claim to sell over 1500 lassis a day (at around Rs 9 per glass). Other popular dessert specialities in Jodhpur include mawa ladoo and the baklava-like mawa kachori. Dhood fini is a cereal dish consisting of fine threads of wheat in a bowl with milk and sugar.

Mid Town, in the Shanti Bhawan Lodge near the Jodhpur railway station, is popular – especially if you're waiting for a train. Items include vegie burgers for Rs 25 and thalis starting from Rs 40.

Kalinga Restaurant in the Hotel Adarsh Niwas has tasty non-veg Indian and Continental food. It charges Rs 30 to Rs 50 for veg dishes and Rs 55 to Rs 145 for non-veg dishes.

Govind Hotel has a popular rooftop veg restaurant which boasts stunning views of the fort. A veg pizza is Rs 35, and their masala milk (Rs 20) is refreshing.

The *refreshment room* on the 1st floor of the main railway station is not bad for a cheap and hearty feed. There's veg and non-veg food to munch on while waiting for your train.

Ajit Bhawan offers a buffet lunch/dinner for Rs 195/225, plus tax. Rajasthani folk music and dancing is put on most evenings. It's probably a good idea to book ahead.

Umaid Bhawan Palace is perfect for a dose of pampering. Its meals are served in the largest of the palace's halls and are accompanied by live Indian classical music. The tasty buffet lunch/dinner costs US$13/15 plus tax.

Things to Buy

The usual Rajasthani handicrafts are available here, but Jodhpur specialises in antiques. The greatest concentration of antique shops is along the road connecting the Ajit Bhawan with the Umaid Bhawan Palace. These shops are well known to western antique dealers who come here with wallets stuffed with plastic cards. As a result, you'll be hard pressed to find any bargains. Many places also sell cheaper replicas based on original antique designs.

Certain restrictions apply to the export of Indian items over 100 years old – see the section under Things to Buy in the Facts for the Visitor chapter for more details.

Getting There & Away

Air The Indian Airlines office (☎ 36757) is south of the centre on Airport Rd and is open daily from 10 am to 1 pm and 2 to 4.30 pm. It has flights four times a week to Delhi (US$80), Jaipur (US$60), Udaipur (US$45) and Mumbai (US$120).

Jagson Airlines (☎ 433813) and ModiLuft (☎ 48333) did not have fixed flight schedules at the time of writing, but it may be worth checking them out if they're still in business.

Bus RSTC buses and private luxury buses connect Jodhpur with a bunch of places around Rajasthan.

There are private buses to Udaipur (Rs 86, eight hours), Bikaner (Rs 71, six hours), Jaipur (Rs 105, seven hours), Ajmer (Rs 65, 4½ hours), Mt Abu (Rs 70, six hours), and Jaisalmer (Rs 70, six hours).

Train The booking office is on Station Rd, between the railway station and Sojati Gate. Demand for tickets can be heavy, so try to come here soon after you arrive in Jodhpur. There's a tourist quota and the office is open Monday to Saturday from 8 am to 8 pm, and only until 1.45 pm on Sunday.

At the main railway station is an International Tourists Bureau (☎ 39052), which has been set up to provide accommodation and assistance for foreign railway passengers. A sitting room and bathroom facilities are also available here.

There are superfast expresses between Delhi and Jodhpur (10 hours) and Ahmedabad and Jodhpur (eight hours). Fares for the 626km trip from Delhi are Rs 190/780 in 2nd/1st class. There's also a train to Agra, but the 439km journey takes around 20 hours and can get horrendously crowded.

To Udaipur there are trains which take

10½ hours to travel the 221km journey (Rs 60/262 in 2nd/1st class). Trains that link Jodhpur with Barmer, in the west of the state, take 5½ hours to cover the 113km trip (Rs 53/208 in 2nd/1st class). There's a day train, the *IJPJ Passenger*, in either direction between Jodhpur and Jaisalmer. The 295km trip takes around eight hours and costs Rs 90/301 in 2nd/1st class. There are plans to start a night service.

Getting Around

The Airport The airport is only five km from the centre of town. It costs about Rs 40 in an auto-rickshaw and Rs 100 in a taxi from the airport to the city, less when going from the city to the airport.

Taxi & Auto-Rickshaw There's a taxi stand near the main railway station – agree on a fare before setting off. Auto-rickshaw drivers can be rapacious, but most journeys in the town should cost no more than Rs 20. Beware of bossy drivers who insist on taking you to the hotel of their choice (usually not the best places) where they get commission.

Bicycle Jodhpur is a good place to explore by bicycle. You can hire a bike from several places near the GPO. The usual charge is about Rs 20 per day.

AROUND JODHPUR
Maha Mandir & Balsamand Lake

Two km north-east of the city is the Maha Mandir (Great Temple). It's built around a 100 pillared Shiva temple but is nothing to write home about. Five km further north is Balsamand Lake, a popular excursion spot.

Balsamand Palace offers comfortable accommodation in a serene setting. Singles/doubles go for Rs 1000/1800, and capacious suites are Rs 2400/3500. Bookings should be made through the Umaid Bhawan Palace in Jodhpur (☎ (0291) 33316; fax 35373).

Mandore

Situated nine km to the north of Jodhpur, Mandore was the capital of Marwar prior to the foundation of Jodhpur. Today, its extensive gardens with high rock terraces make it a popular local attraction. The gardens also contain the cenotaphs of Jodhpur rulers, including Maharaja Jaswant Singh and, largest and finest of all, the soaring memorial to Maharaja Ajit Singh.

The **Hall of Heroes** contains 15 figures carved out of a rock wall. The brightly painted figures represent Hindu deities or local heroes on horseback. The Shrine of 33 Crore (330 million) Gods is painted with figures of deities and spirits.

Rohet

Rohet Garh (☎ (02932) 66231) is a peaceful heritage hotel in this small village, 40km south of Jodhpur. Comfortable rooms cost Rs 1050/1200 and meals are available. Jeep/horse/camel safaris can be organised. This place seems to attract travel writers; Bruce Chatwin wrote *The Songlines* here and William Dalrymple began *City of Djinns*.

Luni

Fort Chanwa (☎ Jodhpur (0291) 84216) offers delightful accommodation in a pleasant setting. Tastefully decorated rooms cost Rs 1150/1300 and good meals are available; the set lunch/dinner costs Rs 195/250. There are some interesting walks in the area, and village safaris can be arranged with prior notice. This place is perfect if you want some respite from the tumult of travelling in India.

Osiyan

The ancient Thar Desert town of Osiyan, 65km north of Jodhpur, was a great trading centre between the 8th and 12th centuries when it was dominated by the Jains. The wealth of Osiyan's medieval inhabitants allowed them to build lavish and exquisitely sculptured temples, most of which have withstood the ravages of time. The largest of the Jain and Brahmanical temples is dedicated to Mahavira, the last of the Jain tirthankars. The sculptural detail on the Osiyan temples rivals that of the Hoysàla temples of Karnataka and the Sun Temple of Konark in Orissa. If you have the time, it's worthwhile visiting this place.

Camel Camp in Osiyan offers a range of tented accommodation in a magical location – atop a secluded sand dune overlooking the town. For budget travellers, there are tents with common bath for Rs 300 per person per night, while tents with attached bath go for Rs 999. Deluxe tents, inclusive of all meals and a half-day camel safari, cost Rs 3500. Longer camel safaris are also available. There's a relaxing bar and good restaurant. You must book in advance. Contact 'The Safari Club' (☎ (0291) 37023), High Court Colony, Jodhpur.

There are regular buses from Jodhpur to Osiyan (Rs 25, 1½ hours).

Nagaur

Nagaur, 135km north-east of Jodhpur, has a historic fort and palace and also sports a smaller version of Pushkar's Camel Fair. The **Nagaur Fair** takes place in January/February and attracts thousands of rural people from far and wide. As at Pushkar, the fair includes camel races and various cultural entertainment programmes.

Royal Tents are available for Rs 2000/4500. These luxurious tents must be booked in advance through the Umaid Bhawan Palace in Jodhpur (☎ (0291) 33316; fax 35373).

Sardar Samand Lake

The route to this wildlife centre, about 65km south-east of Jodhpur, passes through a number of colourful little villages.

Sardar Samand Lake Resort, formerly the maharaja of Jodhpur's summer palace, has now been converted into a pleasant hotel. Rooms cost Rs 1190/2390; lunch/dinner is available for Rs 350. There's also a stylish lakeside swimming pool that looks like something out of Vogue magazine. This place is a world away from the clamour of Jodhpur and can make a rejuvenating sojourn. Book at the Umaid Bhawan Palace in Jodhpur (☎ (0291) 33316; fax 35373).

JAISALMER

Pop: 46,500 Tel Area Code: 02992

Nothing else in India is remotely similar to Jaisalmer. Jodhpur certainly has one of the

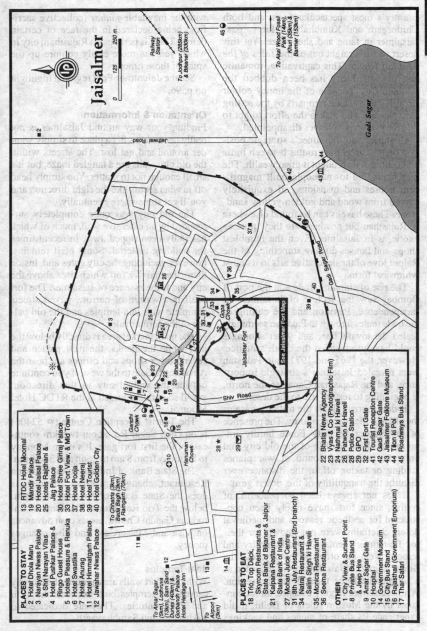

Jaisalmer

To Akal Wood Fossil
Park (14km) &
Khuri (35km) &
Barmer (153km)

To Jodhpur (285km)
& Bikaner (330km)

Railway
Station

Jethwai Road

Gadi Sagar

See Jaisalmer Fort Map

Jaisalmer Fort

Gopa
Chowk

Bhatia
Market

Gandhi
Chowk

Shiv Road

Hanuman
Chowk

Gadi Sagar Road

To Chhatris (3km),
Bada Bagh (3km)
& Ramgarh (70km)

To Amar Sagar
(5km), Lodhurva
(13km), Sam Sand
Dunes (42km),
Gorbandh Palace &
Hotel Heritage Inn

To
Airport
(3km)

0   125   250 m

PLACES TO STAY
2   Hotel Dhola Maru
3   Narayan Niwas Vilas
    & Shri Narayan Vilas
4   Hotel Pushkar Palace &
    Ringo Guest House
5   Hotels Pleasure & Renuka
6   Hotel Swastika
7   Hotel Anurag
11 Hotel Himmatgarh Palace
12 Jawahar Niwas Palace

13 RTDC Hotel Moomal
19 Mandir Palace
20 Hotel Jaisal Palace
25 Hotels Rajdhani &
    Jag Palace
30 Hotel Shree Giriraj Palace
33 Hotel Fort View, & Mid Town
37 Hotel Pooja
38 Hotel Neeraj
39 Hotel Tourist
40 Hotel Golden City

PLACES TO EAT
18 Trio, Top Deck,
    Skyroom Restaurants &
    State Bank of Bikaner & Jaipur
24 Kalpana Restaurant &
    State Bank of India
27 Mohan Juice Centre
31 8th July Restaurant (2nd branch)
34 Natraj Restaurant &
    Salim Singh ki Haveli
35 Monica Restaurant
36 Seema Restaurant

OTHER
1   City View & Sunset Point
8   Private Bus Stand
    & Jeep Hire
9   Amar Sagar Gate
10 Hospital
14 Government Museum
15 City Bus Stand
16 Rajasthali (Government Emporium)
17 Thar Safari

22 Bhatia News Agency
23 Vyas & Co (Photographic Film)
26 Nathmal ki Haveli
28 Patwon ki Haveli
29 Police Station
32 GPO
41 First Fort Gate
42 Tourist Reception Centre
43 Gadi Sagar Gate
44 Jaisalmer Folklore Museum
44 Tilon ki Pol
45 Roadways Bus Stand

country's most spectacular forts, and both Chittorgarh and Kumbhalgarh far surpass Jaisalmer in fame and sheer size. Yet this desert fort is straight out of the *Tales of the Arabian Nights*. This captivating, romantic and unspoiled city has been dubbed the 'Golden City' because of the honey colour imparted to its stone ramparts by the setting sun. No-one who makes the effort to get to this remote outpost leaves disappointed.

Centuries ago, Jaisalmer's strategic position on the camel train routes between India and central Asia brought it great wealth. The merchants and townspeople built magnificent houses and mansions, all exquisitely carved from wood and golden-yellow sandstone. These havelis can be found elsewhere in Rajasthan but nowhere are they quite as exotic as in Jaisalmer. Even the humblest shops and houses display something of the Rajput love of the decorative arts in its most whimsical form.

The rise of shipping trade and the port of Bombay saw the decline of Jaisalmer. At Independence, Partition and the cutting of the trade routes through to Pakistan seemingly sealed the town's fate, and water shortages could have pronounced the death sentence. However, the 1965 and 1971 Indo-Pakistan wars revealed Jaisalmer's strategic importance, and the Rajasthan Canal, to the north, is beginning to restore life to the desert.

Today, tourism rivals the military base as the pillar of the city's economy. The presence of the Border Security Force hardly impinges at all on the life of the old city and only the occasional sound of war planes landing or taking off in the distance ever disturbs the tranquillity of this desert gem.

It has not always been so peaceful, of course, since forts have rarely been constructed for aesthetic reasons and medieval desert chieftains were not known for their pacific temperaments. Chivalric rivalry and ferocity were the order of the day, and the Bhatti Rajputs of Jaisalmer were regarded as a formidable force throughout the region. While Jaisalmer largely escaped direct conquest by the Muslim rulers of Delhi, it did experience its share of sieges and sackings with the inevitable *jauhar* (collective sacrifice) being declared in the face of certain defeat. There is perhaps no Rajasthani city in which you can more easily conjure up the spirit of those times.

See the **Jaisalmer Fort** regional highlight on p596.

Orientation & Information

Finding your way around Jaisalmer is not really necessary – it's a place to simply wander around and get lost. The streets within the old city walls are a tangled maze, but it's small enough not to matter. You simply head off in what seems like the right direction and you'll get somewhere eventually.

The old city was once completely surrounded by an extensive wall, much of which has sadly been ripped away in recent times for building material. Some of it remains, however, including the city gates and, inside them, the massive fort which rises above the city and is the essence of Jaisalmer. The fort itself is a warren of narrow, paved streets complete with Jain temples and the old palace of the former ruler.

The main market area is directly below the hill, while the banks, the new palace and several other shops and offices are near the Amar Sagar Gate to the west. If you continue outside the walled city in this direction, you'll soon find yourself at the RTDC Hotel Moomal.

The Tourist Reception Centre (☎ 52406) is on Gadi Sagar Rd, about two km southeast of the first fort gate. It's open Monday to Saturday from 8 am to noon and 3 to 6 pm.

The State Bank of India, near the Kalpana Restaurant, changes travellers cheques, as does the State Bank of Bikaner & Jaipur, below the Trio Restaurant. The Bank of Baroda, at Gandhi Chowk, issues cash advances on Visa and MasterCard and also changes money.

Jain Temples

Within the fort walls are a group of beautifully carved Jain temples built between the 12th and 15th centuries. They are dedicated to Rikhabdev and Sambhavanth.

The Gyan Bhandar, a library containing some ancient manuscripts, is also in the temple complex. The temples are open daily from 8 am to noon and the library only opens between 10 and 11 am. Entry is free but it costs Rs 25 for a camera, Rs 50 for a video.

Havelis

The impressive mansions built by the wealthy merchants of Jaisalmer are known as havelis, and several of these fine sandstone buildings are still in beautiful condition.

There are no entry fees to most of the havelis, but some people are keen to get you to buy stone carvings and the like – there's some fine material to choose from.

Patwon ki Haveli This most elaborate and magnificent of all the Jaisalmer havelis stands in a narrow lane. It's divided into six apartments, two owned by the Archaeological Survey of India, two by families who operate craftshops here, and two private homes. There are murals on some of the inside walls as well as some mirrorwork.

Salim Singh ki Haveli This haveli was built about 300 years ago and part of it is still occupied. Salim Singh was the prime minister when Jaisalmer was the capital of a princely state, and his mansion has a beautifully arched roof with superb carved brackets in the form of peacocks. The mansion is just below the hill and, it is said, once had two additional wooden storeys in an attempt to make it as high as the maharaja's palace. The maharaja had the upper storeys of the prime minister's haveli torn down! There's a Rs 15 entry charge at this haveli and it's open from 8 am to 6 pm.

Nathmal ki Haveli This late 19th century haveli was also a prime minister's house. The left and right wings of the building were carved by brothers and are very similar, but not identical. Yellow sandstone elephants guard the building, and even the front door is a work of art.

Gadi Sagar Tank & Museum

This tank, south of the city walls, was once the water supply of the city and there are many small temples and shrines around it. A wide variety of water birds flock here in winter.

The attractive gateway which arches across the road down to the tank is said to have been built by a famous prostitute. When she offered to pay to have this gateway constructed, the maharaja refused permission on the grounds that he would have to pass under it on going down to the tank, and he felt that this would be way below his dignity. While he was away, she built the gate anyway, adding a Krishna temple on top so the king could not tear it down.

The small **museum** here has displays of folk art and entry costs Rs 5. Open daily from 9.30 am to 5.30 pm, exhibits include coins, textiles and Rajasthani musical instruments.

Organised Tours

Few travellers visit Jaisalmer without taking a camel safari into the desert. For details, see the information in the boxed section on Camel Safaris later in this chapter.

The Tourist Reception Centre offers a city sightseeing tour (Rs 50 per person) from 9 am to noon, and a sunset tour to the Sam sand dunes (Rs 90 per person).

Festivals

The annual Jaisalmer Desert Festival has camel races, dances, folk music, desert ballads and puppeteers. The RTDC sets up a special 'Tourist Village' at this time, similar to the one in Pushkar. The festival takes place over three days in January/February; see the boxed Festivals Calendar in this chapter for the exact dates.

Places to Stay

Jaisalmer is a very popular place, and many hotels, both cheap and not so cheap, have sprung up to meet the demand. More than anywhere else, the thing you'll notice first is the number of relentless touts who swarm around the bus and railway stations, frantically trying to grab the new arrivals. Unfortunately, some of them are less than honest about the service they provide – don't believe *anyone* who offers to take you 'anywhere you like' for Rs 3, and take with a grain of salt claims that the hotel you want to stay in is 'full', 'closed', 'no good any more' or has suffered some other inglorious fate. They'll only lead you to a succession of hotels, where of course they get commission if you stay.

Another word of advice – just check that you have in fact been taken to the hotel you asked for, as some cunning rickshaw drivers will hurry you into a different hotel where they get commission, get paid and disappear in a flash. If, after being carted from one hotel to another, you still insist on staying where *you* want and not where *they* want, you'll be dropped unceremoniously outside the main fort gate, from where you'll have to walk to the hotel of your choice. If you have made no decision about where to stay and just want a lift into the centre, then these people may be of use, but just be prepared for the roundabout tour and pressure to stay in a particular place.

Many of the popular budget hotels send their own vehicles to meet the bus or train. They display their own sign and offer free transport; otherwise you can take an auto-rickshaw.

Unfortunately, quite a few of the cheap places are really into the high-pressure selling of camel safaris. Some places can get quite ugly if you book a safari through someone else. Not only will they refuse to hold your baggage, but in many cases they'll actually evict you from the hotel!

As is so often the case in Rajasthani towns, if there's a festival on, prices skyrocket and accommodation of any kind can be hard to get. Many places offer off-season discounts between April and August – but you'd be crazy to come here during this time, as Jaisalmer becomes hellishly hot.

Places to Stay – bottom end
Town Area There's a wide choice of budget hotels along the two streets that run parallel to each other north of the Trio Restaurant.

Hotel Anurag (☎ 52596) has rooms starting

from Rs 60/80, less if you sign up for their safari.

Hotel Pushkar Palace (☎ 40817) offers doubles with attached bath for Rs 70, and rooms with common bath for Rs 30/40.

Ringo Guest House (☎ 53027), also in this area, gets mixed reports from travellers. Doubles with bath cost Rs 70 and there are cheaper rooms with common bath.

Hotel Swastika (☎ 52483) is a favourite with travellers and deservedly so. It's friendly and there are great views from the rooftop. Singles/doubles with common bath cost Rs 80/150 and rooms with bath are Rs 120/150. You even get a free cup of tea in the morning.

Hotel Pleasure (☎ 52323) is further up the street, and has rooms with common bath for Rs 40/60, Rs 65/80 with bath.

Hotel Renuka (☎ 52757), nearby, is a homely place with wonderful rooftop views. Singles/doubles with common bath cost Rs 40/50, and Rs 60/80 to Rs 80/100 with bath attached. Meals are available.

Across the other side of the old town is another group of budget hotels, close to the entrance to the fort.

Hotel Fort View (☎ 52214) is popular, mainly because of the fine views afforded from the roof and some of the rooms. Rooms start at Rs 44/55. There's also a couple of double/triple rooms with a fort view for Rs 150/250. The restaurant overlooks the small square below and the fort.

Hotel Shree Giriraj Palace (☎ 52268), also in this area, is a friendly place with a range of rooms from Rs 40/60 with common bath to Rs 60/80 with attached bath, or Rs 150 for a larger double. Dorm beds are Rs 20, and there's a rooftop restaurant.

Hotel Pooja (☎ 52608) is a small place to the east of the fort. It's in an old haveli, and rooms are Rs 40/60 with common bath, or there are more expensive rooms with attached bath. The rooms are pretty spartan, but cheap.

Hotel Tourist (☎ 52484) in the south of the town, rather out on a limb, has basic rooms for Rs 50/100 with attached bath.

Hotel Rajdhani (☎ 52746), not far from the Patwon ki Haveli, has clean rooms with attached bath and hot water from Rs 100/150. There's a rooftop vegetarian restaurant with fine views across to the fort.

Hotel Jag Palace (☎ 40438), directly opposite, has tidy rooms for Rs 150/300 with attached bath. Vegetarian meals are available.

Fort Area The *Deepak Rest House* (☎ 52665) has long been a hit with travellers. It's actually part of the fort wall and offers stunning views from its rooftop. Room No 9 (Rs 250) is the best one since it has its own balcony. Next best is room No 8 (Rs 150). Other doubles are upwards of Rs 50; Rs 80/100 for a single/double with attached bath. There's also a dorm for Rs 20, or you can sleep on the roof for just Rs 10. Some of the cheaper rooms are somewhat cell-like and have no views.

Star Moon Hotel (☎ 52910), next door, is even cheaper. There are small, somewhat stuffy rooms with common bath for Rs 40/70; the best room is No 11, which has an attached bathroom and desert views for Rs 200.

Hotel Laxmi Niwas (☎ 53065) has tiny rooms for Rs 50/100 with common bath, or rooms with bath for Rs 300/500. It also has a new annexe on the other side of the fort.

Hotel Paradise (☎ 52674) is on the far side of the main square from the palace as you come through the last gate into the fort. This popular place is a kind of haveli, with 23 rooms arranged around a leafy courtyard and sensational views from the roof. It has only a few cheap rooms from Rs 60/100 with common bath; good rooms with attached bath range from Rs 250 to Rs 550, depending on size and views. You can sleep on the roof for Rs 30.

Hotel Castle Paying Guest House (☎ 52988) has just a few double rooms ranging from Rs 100 to Rs 300. It's fairly basic but the family who run it are nice.

Places to Stay – middle
Town Area The *Hotel Jaisal Palace* (☎ 52717), not far from the Amar Sagar Gate, is a well maintained and efficiently run place. All rooms have attached bath with hot water and most cost Rs 390/440. The rooftop restaurant serves tasty veg food, and boasts magical views of the fort and town.

RTDC Hotel Moomal (☎ 52392) is pretty good value and quite pleasant, although it's out of the walled city. In the grounds there are thatched huts for Rs 325/400 with attached bathrooms. In the main building, dorm beds cost Rs 50, while single/double rooms with bath are Rs 325/400, air-cooled rooms are Rs 450/600 and rooms with air-con go for Rs 675/775. There's a restaurant, bar, and a beer shop.

Hotel Neeraj (☎ 52442), even further away from the centre than the RTDC hotel, offers overpriced singles/doubles with bath for Rs 550/750. It's clean and well run, but lacking in character.

Fort Area The *Hotel Suraj* (☎ 53023), near the Jain temples, is an interesting old haveli with rooms ranging from Rs 450 to Rs 650; all with private bath. Veg meals are available; lunch/dinner costs Rs 50/75.

Hotel Shreenath Palace (☎ 52907), nearby, is another haveli which oozes with atmosphere. Don't expect too many modern facilities here though, as this place is pretty authentic. Rooms cost Rs 250/300 (bucket hot water).

Places to Stay – top end
Hotel Jaisal Castle (☎ 52362; fax 52101) is a restored haveli in the south-west corner of the fort. Its biggest attraction is its position high on the ramparts looking out over the desert. Rooms with attached bathroom cost Rs 500/650. Some rooms are better than others, so look at a few first.

Jawahar Niwas Palace (☎ 52208), about one km west of the fort, is a beautiful sandstone palace, standing in its own sandy grounds. It's around 100 years old, and the exterior is more impressive than the interior. The rather plain rooms cost Rs 800/850 with attached bath. Meals are available.

Mandir Palace (☎ 52788) is another royal palace, just inside the town walls. It's also a beautiful building but a little run-down. The best room is number 11, which is decorated with coloured tiles and costs Rs 1500. Cheaper rooms cost Rs 550/750 with attached bath. The smaller doubles downstairs for Rs 400 are rather dark, stuffy and not recommended. Like the Jawahar Niwas Palace this place is very high on atmosphere but low on luxury.

Narayan Niwas Palace (☎ 52408; fax 52101), north of the fort, is a much slicker operation than the above three places. It's a modern hotel, not a palace, but it's been designed to simulate the atmosphere of a Rajput ruler's desert camp. The comfortable rooms surround a grassy courtyard and the place is festooned with local crafts and *objets d'art*. Rooms cost Rs 1295/1940, or Rs 1315/2240 with air-con. Meals are available and local musicians play in the courtyard while dinner (Rs 240) is served. There's also an indoor swimming pool and great views of the fort from the rooftop.

Shri Narayan Vilas (☎ 52283), next door, is an older and smaller hotel that has tried to capture the same atmosphere with mixed success. It is, however, a pleasant place to stay and significantly cheaper at Rs 525/650 for a room with attached bath, and Rs 725/850 with air-con. The rooms vary widely – try to see at least a couple before deciding.

Gorbandh Palace (☎ 53111; fax 52749), about 2.5km west of the fort, is a luxurious modern hotel with traditional designs. Constructed of local sandstone, the friezes around the hotel were sculpted by local artisans. Immaculate rooms start at Rs 1000/1250 and there's also a coffee shop, bar, restaurant, travel desk, and superb pool. Jeep/camel safaris can be arranged.

Hotel Heritage Inn (☎ 52769; fax 53038), next door to the Gorbandh Palace, is similarly priced.

Places to Eat

Like all travellers centres, Jaisalmer sports a clutch of budget restaurants/juice bars which seem to attract their own cliques of long time stayers. Hygiene is variable, though, and prices steadily rise in line with tourist numbers.

Monica Restaurant is a good rooftop place not far from the first fort gate. The thalis are excellent, and it's very popular in the early morning and evening.

Natraj Restaurant is just down the hill from the Monica. The open-air top floor has a fine view of the Salim Singh ki Haveli next door. The food is good and the prices are fairly reasonable; a chicken curry costs Rs 45.

Seema Restaurant, nearby, is slightly cheaper and offers a variety of veg and non-veg fare.

Mid Town, also near the fort gate, has pretty average food, but good rooftop views. A Rajasthani special thali costs Rs 40.

Trio, down near the Amar Sagar Gate, is one of Jaisalmer's longest running restaurants; although slightly more pricey than its neighbours, the food is tasty and well presented. A half chicken tandoori is Rs 85, spaghetti Bolognese is Rs 50. In the evening, musicians play as you dine.

Skyroom Restaurant, close by, is only a few rupees cheaper and on the top floor of an old haveli above the State Bank of India.

Kalpana Restaurant, in the same area, offers a variety of reasonably priced Indian, western and Chinese dishes.

Top Deck nearby, is popular and offers Indian, Continental and Chinese cuisine. Southern fried chicken costs Rs 55, veg dishes range from Rs 20 to Rs 35.

Gorbandh Palace has a pleasant restaurant which is open to non-residents and is the ideal place to go for a splurge. A satiating buffet breakfast/lunch/dinner costs Rs 175/325/400. A la carte dining is also available. It is about 2.5km west of the fort.

8th July Restaurant, located inside the fort above the square, is the perfect place to sit and watch the world go by. However, travellers have mixed reports about the food and service. The menu is purely vegetarian and largely caters to western tastes. Items include a 'foot long' with cheese and tomato (Rs 32) and pizza (Rs 40). There's another branch outside the fort but it's not as atmospheric.

Things to Buy

Jaisalmer is renowned for embroidery, Rajasthani mirrorwork, rugs, blankets, old stonework and antiques. Tie-dye and other fabrics are made at the Khadi Bhandar, north of the city. One traveller warns that you should watch out for silver items bought in Jaisalmer as the metal may be adulterated with bronze. Some rickshaw drivers may try to drag you only to shops (often expensive) where they receive commission.

Getting There & Away

Air At the time of writing, there were no flights operating to/from Jaisalmer, although it may be worth checking if this has changed.

Bus The main Roadways bus stand is some distance from the centre of town, near the railway station. Fortunately, all buses start from Gandhi Chowk, near Amar Sagar Gate, and then call at the main bus stand. Reservations are only really needed on the night buses, and these should be made at the main bus stand.

There are several daily RSTC buses to Jodhpur for Rs 65, or Rs 89 for a deluxe bus. To Bikaner a deluxe bus costs Rs 90 and takes about seven hours.

Every day there are frequent RSTC buses each way between Jaisalmer and Barmer (Rs 35, 3½ hours). There are also deluxe buses to Udaipur (Rs 160, 14 hours), Mt Abu (Rs 120, twelve hours), and Ahmedabad (Rs 130, twelve hours).

Train The reservations office at the railway station is open from Monday to Saturday from 10 am to 1 pm, 2 to 4 pm and on Sunday from 10 am to 1 pm.

There's a day train, the *IJPJ Passenger*, in either direction between Jodhpur and Jaisalmer. The 295km trip takes around eight hours and costs Rs 90/301 in 2nd/1st class. There are plans to also start a night service.

Getting Around

Unmetered taxis, auto-rickshaws and jeeps are available in Jaisalmer. From the railway station, expect to pay Rs 15 to the old town by auto-rickshaw.

Quite a few of the hotels provide their own transport from the station, which is free if you're going to stay there. Those hotels which own jeeps generally also hire them out for visits to the surrounding area. A visit to the sand dunes at Sam, for instance, costs around Rs 90 per person.

A good way to zip around Jaisalmer itself is to hire a bicycle. There are a number of hire places, including one in Gandhi Chowk just inside Amar Sagar Gate, and another just outside the main gate of the fort. Most places charge around Rs 3 per hour, Rs 20 per day.

AROUND JAISALMER

There are some fascinating places to see in the area around Jaisalmer, although it soon fades out into a barren sand dune desert which stretches across the lonely border into Pakistan.

Due to the lingering troubles in Punjab and alleged arms smuggling across the border from Pakistan, most of Rajasthan west of National Highway No 15 is a restricted area. Special permission is required from the Collector's office (☎ 52201) in Jaisalmer if you want to go there, and this is only issued in exceptional circumstances. The only places exempted are Amar Sagar, Bada Bagh, Lodhruva, Kuldhara, Akal, Sam, Ramkunda, Khuri and Mool Sagar.

Bada Bagh & Cenotaphs

About five km north of Jaisalmer, Bada Bagh is a fertile oasis with a huge old dam. Some of the city's fruit and vegetables are grown here and carried into the town each day by colourfully dressed women.

Above the gardens are royal cenotaphs with finely carved ceilings and equestrian statues of former rulers. In the early evening, this is a popular place to watch the setting sun turn Jaisalmer a delightful golden brown.

Amar Sagar

Seven km north-west of Jaisalmer, this once pleasant formal garden has now fallen into ruins. The lake here dries up several months into the dry season.

A beautifully carved **Jain temple** is being painstakingly restored by craftspeople brought in from Agra. Begun in the late 1970s, this monumental task is still continuing. Entry to the temple is free, but there's a Rs 25 camera charge, Rs 50 for a video.

Lodhruva

Further out beyond Amar Sagar, 15km from Jaisalmer, are the deserted ruins of this town which was the ancient capital before the move to Jaisalmer. The **Jain temples**, rebuilt in the late 1970s, are the only reminders of the city's former magnificence. The temple has an image of Parasnath, the 23rd tirthankar. In the temple is a hole from which a cobra is said to emerge every evening – only the 'lucky' can see it. Entry to the temple is free, but there's a Rs 25 camera charge, Rs 50 for a video.

Mool Sagar

Situated nine km directly west of Jaisalmer, this is another pleasant small garden and tank. It belongs to the royal family of Jaisalmer.

Camel Safaris

The most interesting means of exploring the desert around Jaisalmer is on a camel safari and virtually everyone who comes here goes on one of them. October to February is the best time.

Competition between safari organisers is cut-throat and standards vary considerably. This has resulted in many complaints when promises have been made and not kept. Touts will begin to hassle you even before you get off the bus or train; and, at the budget end of the market, hotel rooms can be as little as Rs 15 – providing you take the hotel's safari. Try to talk to someone at the Tourist Reception Centre in Jaisalmer, or to other travellers for feedback on who is currently offering good, reliable and honest service. Don't be pressured by agents who tell you that if you don't go on the trip leaving tomorrow there won't be another until next week. Naturally, they all offer *the best* safari and spare no invective in pouring scorn on their rivals.

The truth is more mundane. None of the hotels have their own camels – these are all independently owned – so the hoteliers and the travel agents are just go-betweens, though the hotels often organise the food and drink supplies. You need to consider a few things before jumping at what appears to be a bargain. Hotel owners typically pay the camel drivers around Rs 80 per camel per day to hire them, so, if you're offered a safari at Rs 120 per day, this leaves only a small margin for food and the agent's profit. It's obvious that you can't possibly expect three reasonable meals a day on these margins, but this is frequently what is promised. As a result, a lot of travellers feel they've been ripped-off when the food isn't what was offered. It's a moot point which of the parties ought to shoulder the responsibility for this – is it the agents who make impossible promises or the travellers who have unrealistic expectations?

The realistic minimum price for a basic safari is Rs 200 to Rs 300 per person per day. For this you can expect a breakfast of porridge, tea and toast, and lunch and dinner of rice, dhal and chapatis – pretty unexciting stuff. Blankets are also supplied, but you must bring your own mineral water. Of course the more you pay, the greater the level of comfort – tents, stretcher beds, better food, beer etc.

Two camel safari agents that are not linked to any hotels have been recommended. Sahara Travels (☎ 52609), by the fort gate, is run by Mr Bissa, alias Mr Desert. If you think you've seen his face before it's because he's India's Marlboro Man – the rugged model in the Jaisalmer cigarette ads. He is an amicable guy who seems keen to please. His basic tours cost Rs 300 a day for two to four days, or Rs 400 with a greater range of meals. Tented safaris start at Rs 500. Thar Safari (☎ 52722; fax 53214), at Gandhi Chowk by the Trio Restaurant, organises deluxe safaris for Rs 750 per day including tents, a guide and a choice of veg or non-veg food. For Rs 550 you get veg food only and sleep out under the stars.

However much you decide to spend, make sure you know exactly what is being provided and make sure it's there before you leave Jaisalmer. You should also make sure you know where they're going to take you. Attempting to get a refund on your return for services not provided is a waste of time.

Most safaris last three to four days and, if you want to get to the most interesting places, this is a bare minimum. Bring something very comfortable to sit on – many travellers neglect to do this and come back with terribly sore legs and/or backsides! A wide-brimmed hat (or Rajput-style turban), sun cream and a personal water bottle are also essential. It gets very cold at night so if you have a sleeping bag bring it along even if you're told that lots of blankets will be supplied.

If you're on your own it's worth getting a group of at least four people together before looking for a safari. Organisers will make up groups but four days is a long time to spend with people you might not get on with.

Sam Sand Dunes

A desert national park has been established in the Thar Desert near Sam village. One of the most popular excursions is to the sand dunes on the edge of the park, 42km from Jaisalmer. This is Jaisalmer's nearest real Sahara-like desert. It's best to be here at sunrise or sunset, and many camel safaris spend a night at the dunes. Just before sunset jeep loads of trippers arrive from Jaisalmer to be chased across the sands by tenacious camel owners offering short rides and young boys selling soft drinks. Yes, this place has become a massive tourist attraction, so don't set your heart on a solitary desert sunset experience. Despite the tourist frenzy however, this is still a bewitching place.

There are only two buses a day between Jaisalmer and Sam, so if you're only coming for the sunset you'll need to hire a taxi or take a tour (see under Organised Tours in the Jaisalmer section).

The usual circuit takes in such places as Amar Sagar, Lodhruva, Mool Sagar, Bada Bagh and Sam, as well as various abandoned villages along the way. Usually it's one person per camel, but check this when booking. The reins are fastened to the camel's nose peg, so the animals are easily steered. At resting points, the camels are completely unsaddled and hobbled. They limp away to browse on nearby shrubs while the cameleers brew sweet chai or prepare food. The whole crew rests in the shade of thorn trees by a tank or well.

It's a wonderful way to see the desert, which is surprisingly well populated and sprinkled with ruins. You constantly come across tiny fields of millet, girls picking berries or boys herding flocks of sheep or goats. The latter are almost always fitted with tinkling neck bells and, in the desert silence, it's music to the ears. Camping out at night in the Sam sand dunes, huddling around a tiny fire beneath the stars and listening to the camel drivers' yarns can be quite romantic. The camel drivers will expect a tip or gift at the end of the trip. If you've been happy with their services, don't neglect to do this. How much to give depends entirely on you.

Take care of your possessions, particularly on the return journey. A recent scam involves the drivers suggesting that you walk to some nearby ruins while they stay with the camels and keep an eye on your bags. The police station in Jaisalmer receives numerous reports of items missing from luggage but seems unwilling to help.

If you don't have the time, money or inclination to do an extended safari, there are any number of shorter options available. You could take a 2½ day trip which involves transport out to Sam by jeep, the return journey being made by camel. The cost of a trip like this is around Rs 750 per person – but you could try to bargain this down. For those with even less time, a one day, half-jeep/half-camel safari costs around Rs 300 per person. ■

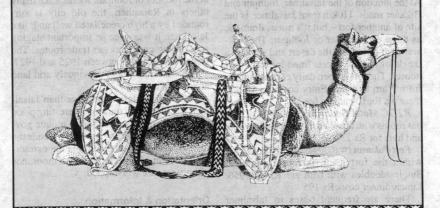

RAJASTHAN

RTDC Hotel Sam Dhani (☎ (02992) 52392) is the only place to stay here. Rooms go for Rs 125/175. Bookings can be made from the RTDC Hotel Moomal in Jaisalmer.

Khuri

Khuri is a village 40km south-west of Jaisalmer, out in the desert, in the touchy area near the Pakistan border. It's a peaceful place with houses of mud and straw decorated like the patterns on Persian carpets. Accommodation here is limited and quite expensive.

Mama's Guest House (☎ (02992) 8423) offers pricey accommodation in huts. The cheapest with shared bath and including meals will set you back Rs 350.

Khuri Guest House (☎ (02992) 8444), near the bus stand, is a more affordable option with rooms with common bath from Rs 125/250, including meals.

There are three daily buses between Jaisalmer and Khuri (Rs 12, two hours).

Akal Wood Fossil Park

Three km off the road to Barmer, 16km from Jaisalmer, are the fossilised remains of a 180 million year old forest. To the untrained eye it's not particularly interesting.

POKARAN

At the junction of the Jaisalmer, Jodhpur and Bikaner roads, 110km from Jaisalmer, is the site of another fort – but it's not as dramatic as those of Jaisalmer or Jodhpur. The Pokaran Fort rises from the desert and shelters a tangle of narrow streets lined by balconied houses. The fort is open daily except Sunday from 7 am to 6 pm. Entry costs Rs 15 and there's a Rs 10 camera fee.

RTDC Motel Godavan (☎ (02994) 2275) has rooms with attached bath for Rs 200/300, and huts for Rs 250/350.

Fort Pokaran (☎ (02994) 22274; fax 22279), within the fort itself, is more upmarket. Singles/doubles with bath are Rs 850/950. Lunch/dinner costs Rs 195.

There are frequent buses to Jaisalmer which take about 2½ hours and cost Rs 63.

BARMER

Barmer is a centre for woodcarving, carpets, embroidery, block printing and other handicrafts, and its products are famous throughout Rajasthan. Otherwise, this desert town, 153km south of Jaisalmer, isn't very exciting. There's no fortress here and the most interesting part is probably the journey to Barmer through small villages, their mud-walled houses decorated with the characteristic geometrical designs. There are two annual fairs in Barmer: the **Barmer Thar Festival** in early March and the **Barmer Cattle Fair** (held at nearby Tilwara) in March/April. For details, contact the Tourist Reception Centre in Jaisalmer.

Krishna Hotel (☎ (02982) 20785), on Station Rd, has clean air-cooled rooms for Rs 250/300 and air-con rooms for Rs 450/500.

Kailash Sarovar Hotel (☎ (02982) 20730), also on Station Rd, is slightly cheaper.

There are five daily buses between Barmer and Jaisalmer (Rs 40, 3½ hours). There are also frequent daily buses to Jodhpur (Rs 78, five hours).

Daily trains travel from Barmer to Jodhpur for Rs 60/220 in 2nd/1st class.

BIKANER
Pop: 493,000   Tel Area Code: 0151

This desert town in the north of the state was founded in 1488 by Rao Bika, a descendant of the founder of Jodhpur, Jodha. Like many others in Rajasthan, the old city is surrounded by a high crenellated wall and, like Jaisalmer, it was once an important staging post on the great caravan trade routes. The Ganga Canal, built between 1925 and 1927, irrigates a large area of previously arid land around Bikaner.

Although it's less impressive than Jaisalmer, Bikaner is still quite an interesting place to visit. There's a superb fort, a unique government camel breeding farm just outside the town, and 30km to the south is the extraordinary Karni Mata Temple where thousands of holy rats are worshipped.

Orientation & Information

The old city is encircled by a seven km long

city wall with five entrance gates, constructed in the 18th century. The fort and palace, built of the same reddish-pink sandstone as Jaipur's famous buildings, are outside the city walls.

The helpful Tourist Reception Centre (☎ 27445) is in the grounds of RTDC Hotel Dhola Maru. It's open daily except Sunday from 10 am to 5 pm.

You can change money at the State Bank of Bikaner & Jaipur, near the Thar Hotel.

Junagarh Fort

Constructed between 1588 and 1593 by Raja Rai Singh – a general in the army of the Mughal emperor, Akbar – the fort has a 986m long wall with 37 bastions, a moat and two entrances. The Surajpol, or Sun Gate, is the main entrance to the fort. The palaces within the fort are on the southern side and make a picturesque ensemble of courtyards, balconies, kiosks, towers and windows. A major feature of this fort and its palaces is the magnificent stone carving.

Among the places of interest are the **Chandra Mahal**, or Moon Palace, and the **Phool Mahal**, or Flower Palace, both decorated with paintings, mirrors, glass and carved marble panels.

Other palaces include the Hawa Mahal, Badal Mahal and Anup Mahal. The contents include the usual Rajput weapon collection, not to mention an old WWI biplane presented to Ganga Singh by the British. The Durga Niwas is a beautifully painted courtyard while the Ganga Niwas, another large courtyard, has a finely carved red sandstone front.

The fort is open daily from 10 am to 4.30 pm. Entry is Rs 50 and there's a Rs 25 camera charge, Rs 100 for a video. A guide is included in this price.

Lalgarh Palace

Three km north of the city centre, this red sandstone palace was built by Maharaja Ganga Singh (1881-1942) in memory of his father Maharaja Lal Singh. Although it's a grand building with overhanging balconies and delicate latticework, it's not the most beautiful of Rajasthani royal residences.

The **Shri Sadul Museum** covers the entire first floor of the palace. It has an assortment of exhibits, including personal possessions of former Bikaner rulers, old photos depicting royal hunts, and an extraordinary collection of the former maharaja's personal possessions – golf tees, camera, clothes, books, earplugs and even his electric toothbrush! There's also the usual depressing exhibition of Indian beasts, shot and stuffed. The museum is open daily except Wednesday from 10 am to 5 pm; entry is Rs 5. Photography is not allowed.

Other Attractions

The narrow smelly streets of the old city conceal a number of old havelis and a couple of notable **Jain temples**. The Bhandasar and Sandeshwar temples date from around the 15th century. The temples have colourful wall paintings and some intricate carving.

The **Ganga Golden Jubilee Museum** houses an interesting collection of sculpture, terracotta ware, coins, paintings, musical instruments and weapons. It's open daily except Friday from 10 am to 4.30 pm and there's a small entry fee.

There's a **Camel Festival** held in Bikaner each January (see the boxed Festival Calendar in this chapter for the exact dates), which is worth attending if you're in this area at the time.

Organised Tours

The Tourist Reception Centre can arrange tours to Deshnok (to see the Karni Mata Temple) and to the Gajner Wildlife Sanctuary. Each costs Rs 360 per person. You can also enquire about camel safaris here.

Places to Stay – bottom end

There are numerous budget options near the railway station. Station Rd is an amazingly busy thoroughfare so the noise level in any room fronting it can be diabolical – choose carefully. Bikaner has a shortage of good budget accommodation – most places are quite slovenly, but reasonably cheap.

The Tourist Reception Centre has a list of Paying Guest Houses. Expect to pay from Rs 85 to Rs 750.

Evergreen Hotel (☎ 23396), on Station Rd, is a fairly good choice, although some of the rooms can be a bit noisy. Singles/doubles with common bath go for Rs 60/90, and rooms with attached bath cost Rs 90/125. Hot water is by the bucket.

Hotel Deluxe (☎ 528127), next door, is similar in price and standards.

Hotel Akashdeep (☎ 26024), behind the Hotel Deluxe, is not as good. Rooms with private bath (bucket hot water) cost Rs 70/100.

Hotel Amit (☎ 28064), nearby, is a rather shabby place. Small, musty rooms with attached bath (and Indian-style toilets) cost Rs 125/150.

Hotel Shri Shanti Niwas (☎ 25025) is up the street opposite the railway station. The rooms are quite tatty but cheap at Rs 50/90 with common bath, Rs 65/110 with private bath.

Indre Lodge, a little further along the same street, is slightly better value. Singles/doubles cost Rs 60/100 with attached bath, but some of the rooms are a little gloomy.

Retiring rooms at the railway station charge Rs 50/95 with private bath (bucket hot water) and there are also more expensive air-con rooms. The dorm costs Rs 30.

Places to Stay – middle

Hotel Joshi (☎ 527700; fax 521213), on Station Rd near the railway station, is one of the best mid-range options. It's well run, comfortable and a convenient place to stay. Air-cooled singles/doubles with bath are Rs 225/290; for Rs 425/525 you get air-con. There's also a veg restaurant.

RTDC Hotel Dhola Maru (☎ 28621) is on Pooran Singh Circle, about one km from the centre of the city. Dorm beds are Rs 50, somewhat run-down singles/doubles with bath start from Rs 150/200. There's also a beer shop and restaurant.

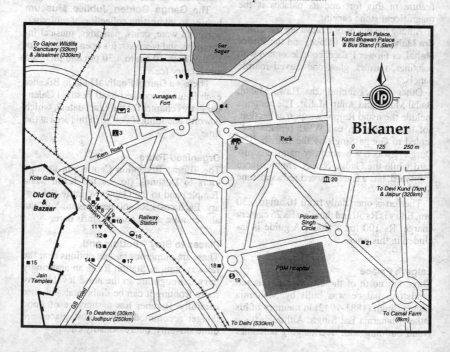

To Gajner Wildlife Sanctuary (32km) & Jaisalmer (330km)

To Lalgarh Palace, Kami Bhawan Palace & Bus Stand (1.5km)

Sur Sagar

Junagarh Fort

Kem Road

Kote Gate

Old City & Bazaar

Station Road

Railway Station

Jain Temples

GS Road

To Deshnok (30km) & Jodhpur (250km)

To Delhi (530km)

Park

Bikaner

0   125   250 m

Pooran Singh Circle

PBM Hospital

To Devi Kund (7km) & Jaipur (320km)

To Camel Farm (8km)

Thar Hotel (☎ 27180), on Hospital Rd, has rooms with bath from Rs 350/470. There's a non-veg restaurant here.

Hotel Meghsar Castle (☎ 527315; fax 522041), at 9 Gajner Rd, is an unchecked option that has recently been recommended by several travellers. Rooms with attached bath range from Rs 300 to Rs 800. If you do end up staying here, let us know how it was!

Places to Stay – top end
Lalgarh Palace Hotel (☎ 523963; fax 522253), north of the city centre, is part of the maharaja's modern palace and has well appointed singles/doubles for US$85/135. Rooms are tastefully decorated and there's a good bar and restaurant. Most evenings there's sitar and tabla music performed in the inner courtyard.

Karni Bhawan Palace (☎ 24887; fax 522408), not far from the Lalgarh Palace Hotel, is a more affordable option. Set in its own peaceful grounds, this recently renovated hotel has comfortable rooms for Rs 1150/2250. Good meals are available in the restaurant.

```
PLACES TO STAY
6   Hotel Deluxe
7   Hotel Akashdeep & Hotel Amit
8   Evergreen Hotel
10  Hotel Joshi
13  Hotel Shri Shanti Niwas
14  Indre Lodge
15  Hotel Bhanwar Niwas
18  Thar Hotel
21  RTD Hotel Dhola Maru & Tourist
    Reception Centre

PLACES TO EAT
9   Chhotu Motu Joshi Sweet Shop
11  Amber Restaurant

OTHER
1   Urmul Trust Shop
2   GPO
3   Ratan Behari Temple & Garden
4   Courts
5   Zoo
12  Bike Hire
16  Taxi Stand & Clock Tower
17  Victor Travels & Tours
19  State Bank of Bikaner & Jaipur
20  Ganga Golden Jubilee Museum
```

Hotel Bhanwar Niwas (☎ 61880) in the old city, is a popular choice and has delightful rooms for Rs 1175/2350. The building is made of attractive pink sandstone and the rooms are set around a courtyard. There's also a fine restaurant.

Places to Eat
Most of the restaurants in Bikaner are vegetarian, and some don't even serve eggs. Bikaner is noted for the spicy snacks known as namkin, sold in the shops along Station Rd, among other places.

Amber Restaurant is opposite the Hotel Joshi and serves good veg food. A tandoori cheese naan is Rs 26, an espresso coffee Rs 10 and most main dishes are around Rs 35.

Thar Hotel has satisfying veg and non-veg food; main dishes range from Rs 30 to Rs 55.

RTDC Hotel Dhola Maru offers veg and non-veg fare; a thali costs Rs 50 (veg), Rs 70 (non-veg).

Lalgarh Palace Hotel is open to non-residents and is the most upmarket place to eat; lunch/dinner costs US$10/11. It's a good idea to book ahead.

Chhotu Motu Joshi Sweet Shop, on Station Rd, has an assortment of tantalising gooey Indian sweets and is a favourite with the locals.

Things to Buy
On the right-hand side as you enter the fort is a very interesting craft shop, run by the Urmul Trust. Items sold here are of high quality and made by people from surrounding villages. Proceeds go directly to improve health and education projects in these villages. You can browse here without the usual constant hassles to buy.

Getting There & Away
Bus The bus stand is north of the city centre, almost opposite the road leading to the Lalgarh Palace Hotel. There are several RSTC buses daily between Bikaner and Jaisalmer (Rs 98, 7½ hours). Private companies also operate on this route.

The seven hour trip to Jaipur costs Rs 98 and there are at least six buses daily. A number of the Jaipur buses go via the Shek-hawati town of Fatehpur (Rs 48, 4½ hours).

Other places served by bus from Bikaner include Udaipur (Rs 158, 12 hours), Ajmer (Rs 79, eight hours), and Delhi (Rs 126, 11 hours).

Train The computerised booking office, open daily from 8 am to 8 pm (8 am to 2 pm on Sunday), is in the building to the right as you approach the station.

There are several trains to Jaipur (Rs 45/ 480 in 2nd/1st class), as well as to Jodhpur (Rs 40/250 in 2nd/1st class) and Delhi (Rs 105/412 in 2nd/1st class).

Getting Around
An auto-rickshaw should charge around Rs 15 for the trip between the bus and railway stations. There are bicycle hire places along Station Rd; most charge Rs 3 per hour.

AROUND BIKANER
Devi Kund
Eight km east of Bikaner, this is the site of the royal chhatris of many of the Bika dynasty rulers. The white marble chhatri of Maharaja Surat Singh is very imposing.

Camel Breeding Farm
This government-managed camel breeding station, eight km from Bikaner, is probably unique in Asia. There are hundreds of camels here and it's a great sight in the late afternoon as the camels come back from grazing. The British army had a camel corps drawn from Bikaner during WWI.

The farm is open Monday to Friday and every second Saturday from 3 to 5 pm. Entry is free and although photography is not al-lowed, some travellers say they have not been stopped from taking photos. Camel rides cost Rs 30 for 30 minutes.

Half the auto-rickshaw and taxi drivers in Bikaner appear to be on the lookout for tourists to take to the camel farm, but you need to bargain hard with them. For the round trip including a half hour wait at the farm, you'll pay around Rs 60 for an auto-rickshaw, Rs 110 for a taxi.

Gajner Wildlife Sanctuary
The lake and forested hills of this reserve, 32km from Bikaner on the Jaisalmer road, are inhabited by wildfowl and a number of deer and antelope. Imperial sand grouse mi-grate here in winter.

Gajner Palace Hotel (☎ (01534) 5001; or bookings through the Karni Bhawan Palace (☎ (0151) 24887; fax 522408) in Bikaner) is the erstwhile royal summer palace and is ideally situated on the banks of a lake. It's an impressive building made of red sandstone and is set in serene surroundings. Rooms start at Rs 1150/2250, and facilities include a restaurant, swimming pool and billiard room. Horse/jeep safaris can also be arranged.

Deshnok
Following the highly publicised 1994 out-break of plague in India, state governments have been attempting to reduce rat popula-tions with heavy use of pesticides. Of course, this being India, not all rats are on the death list. The thousands that inhabit the **Karni Mata Temple** in Deshnok are future incarna-tions of mystics and sadhus, so pest control here would be sacrilege.

A visit to this fascinating temple, dedi-cated to Karni Mata, an incarnation of Durga, is not for the squeamish. Once you've ad-mired the silver doors and marble carvings donated by Maharaja Ganga Singh, you plunge into the rats domain, hoping that some will scamper over your feet – most auspicious. Little boys sometimes pick them up by their tails and let them perch on your shoulders. Devotees buy prasad to offer to the rats, finishing off anything they may leave. Keep your eyes peeled for a white rat – it's consid-ered good fortune if you spot one. Eating prasad that has been salivated over by these holy rats also brings great fortune, but is not recommended for wimpish western constitu-tions.

The temple is open from 4 am to 10 pm and there's a Rs 10 camera charge, Rs 25 for a video. And remember, this is a place of worship, so don't conveniently forget to re-move your shoes!

Getting There & Away Deshnok is 30km from Bikaner along the Jodhpur road. There are buses every 15 minutes from Bikaner (Rs 12, 30 minutes). Taxi drivers don't seem keen to make this journey. You'll have to bargain hard for the round trip – expect to pay around Rs 230 for a taxi; make sure this includes at least 30 minutes at the temple. Some auto-rickshaws will also do the return trip for around Rs 165.

Music

The two main forms of Indian music are the southern Carnatic (folk) and the northern Hindustani Vedic (religious) traditions.

Of all Indian traditional folk music, Rajasthani music is perhaps the best known. In Rajasthan, music is an integral aspect of life: a party is not a party without folk musicians, and markets, weddings and theatrical performances always provide a stage for Rajasthani bands. Special songs are written for Diwali and Holi, as well as for the Opium festival, which is only celebrated by Rajput families.

The chants of the Langas and the Manganiars, professional singers, have their roots in ancient Rajasthani gypsy traditions, while many Rajasthani instruments were developed hundreds of years ago. The *kamycha* and *sarangi* are both ancient instruments which are still popular today. The sarangi is similar to the violin, but is made of goatskin, and played with a horsehair bow.

Many Rajasthani musicians are Muslims – Langas and Manganiars are exclusively Muslim – although they perform for mixed audiences. In the past, musicians played under the patronage of a landlord, usually a Hindu, but since the redistribution of large estates, most landlords lack the funds to keep on their musicians.

Indian music, has two basic elements, the *tala* and the *raga*. Tala is the rhythm and is characterised by the number of beats. *Teental* is a tala of 16 beats. The audience follows the tala by clapping at the appropriate beat, which in teental is at one, five and 13. There is no clap at the beat of nine since that is the *khali* or 'empty section', indicated by a wave of the hand.

The raga provides the melody; just as there are a number of basic talas so there are many set ragas. The classical Indian music group consists of three musicians who provide the drone, the melody and the rhythm. The musicians are basically soloists: they each select their own tala and raga, then zoom off in their separate musical directions and, to the audience's delight, meet every once in a while before again diverging.

Yehudi Menuhin, who has devoted much time and energy to understanding Indian music, suggests that it is much like Indian society: a group of individuals not working together but every once in a while meeting at some common point. Western music is analogous to western democratic societies: a group of individuals (the orchestra) who each surrender part of their freedom to the harmony of the whole.

Although Indian religious music has one of the longest continuous histories of any musical form, the music had never, until quite recently, been recorded in any written notation. Furthermore, notation is made virtually impossible because the musicians improvise, providing free-form variations on the basic tala-raga framework.

Best known of the Indian instruments are the sitar and the tabla. The sitar is the large stringed instrument popularised by Ravi Shankar in the west – and which more than a few westerners have discovered is notoriously difficult to tune. This is the instrument with which the soloist plays the raga. The tabla, a twin drum rather like a Western bongo, provides the tala. The drone, which runs on two basic notes, is provided by the oboe-like *shehnai* or the *tambura*.

It's Hindi film music, rather than *ghazals* (classical Urdu love songs), that you'll first come across on a visit to India. Most Hindi movies are really little more than vehicles for a series of hit songs that you'll hear played incessantly. Some of these tunes are adapted from the traditional folk music and songs of different regions. With the increasing interest in world music in the west, popularised versions of Indian folk music are becoming known outside the country. *Bhangra*, from the Punjab, is the most recent example.

Sitar The sitar is perhaps the best-known Indian instrument and probably evolved sometime in the 13th century. It is a long-necked lute with 20 curved metal frets and is plucked by the left-hand index finger fitted with a wire plectrum. The bridge of the sitar, which is rectangular, gives the instrument its characteristic sound.

Sitar

Tabla The tabla is the principal drum of north Indian music. It is actually a pair of drums played with fingers and wrists of both hands. The right-hand, smaller high-pitched drum is called tabla, and the left-hand one the bayan or dagga.

Sarangi The sarangi, developed to accompany vocal music, first became popular in the mid-17th century. It has the distinction of being the closest instrument to the human voice in its richness and melody and has long been associated with bards and mendicants. The sarangi was once described by Yehudi Menuhin as the instrument that 'most poignantly expresses the soul of Indian feeling and thought', but is ironically faced with oblivion since it has been largely surplanted by the harmonium.

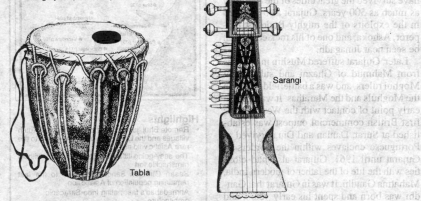

Sarangi

Tabla

Tambura An essential part of every Indian classical concert is the droning sound produced by the tambura. Popular all over the subcontinent, the instrument is called 'tanpura' in the north and 'tambura' in the south, and its construction also varies slightly depending on the place it's made.

Tambura

Gujarat

The west coast state of Gujarat is not one of India's busiest tourist destinations and although it is quite easy to slot Gujarat in between Mumbai (Bombay) and the cities of Rajasthan, few people pause to explore this interesting state.

If you want to go beyond history into the realm of legend, then Gujarat's Temple of Somnath was actually there to witness the creation of the universe! Along the south coast are the sites where many of the great events in Krishna's life took place.

On firmer historic footing, Lothal was the site of a Harappan or Indus Valley civilisation more than 4000 years ago. The main sites of this very ancient culture are now in Pakistan, but it is thought that Lothal may have survived the great cities of the Sindh by as much as 500 years. Gujarat also featured in the exploits of the mighty Buddhist emperor, Ashoka, and one of his rock edicts can be seen near Junagadh.

Later, Gujarat suffered Muslim incursions from Mahmud of Ghazni and subsequent Moghul rulers, and was a battlefield between the Moghuls and the Marathas. It was also an early point of contact with the West and the first British commercial outpost was established at Surat. Daman and Diu survived as Portuguese enclaves within the borders of Gujarat until 1961. Gujarat also had close ties with the life of the father of modern India, Mahatma Gandhi. It was in Gujarat that Gandhi was born and spent his early years, and it was to Ahmedabad, the main city of Gujarat, that he returned to wage his long struggle with the British for independence.

Gujarat has always been a centre for the Jains, and some of its most interesting sights are Jain temple centres like those at Palitana, and at Girnar Hill, near Junagadh. The Jains are an influential and energetic group and, as a result, Gujarat is one of India's wealthier states, with a number of important industries (particularly textiles and electronics) and the

GUJARAT AT A GLANCE

Population: 44.2 million
Area: 196,024 sq km
Capital: Gandhinagar
Main Language: Gujarati
Literacy Rate: 61.29%
Best Time to Go: October to March

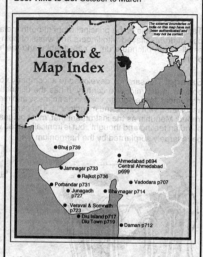

Highlights

* Remote Bhuj, jumping off point to the tribal Kutch villages and the Little Rann of Kutch – home to the rare Asiatic wild ass
* The easy-going little seaside town of Diu, with its ramshackle fort
* Sasan Gir Lion Sanctuary, home to the last remaining population of Asiatic lion
* Ahmedabad's fascinating Indo-Saracenic architecture

Festivals

See the Festivals boxed section later in this chapter.

dubious distinction of having the largest petrochemical complex in the country.

Apart from its Jain temples, Gujarat's major attractions include the last Asian lions

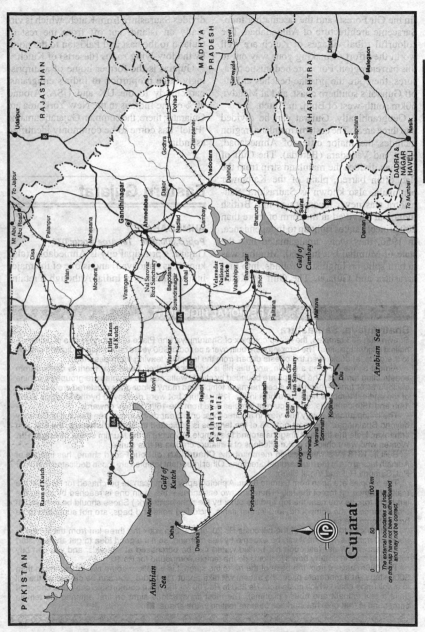

GUJARAT

Gujarat

The external boundaries of India
on this map have not been authenticated
and may not be correct.

0   50   100 km

(in the Gir Forest) and the fascinating Indo-Saracenic architecture of Ahmedabad. The colourful tribal villages of Kutch are well worth the effort of making your way out to this barren region. For more hedonistic pleasures, there are the pristine beaches at Diu, off Gujarat's southern coast, and at Mandvi, 60km south-west of Bhuj, in Kutch.

Geographically, Gujarat can be divided into three areas. The eastern (mainland) region includes the major cities of Ahmedabad, Surat and Vadodara (Baroda). The Gulf of Cambay divides the mainland strip from the flat, often barren, plain of the Kathiawar peninsula, also known as Saurashtra. Saurashtra was never incorporated into British India, but survived in the form of more than 200 princely states right up to Independence. In 1956, they were amalgamated into the state of Mumbai but in 1960, Mumbai was in turn split, on linguistic grounds, into Maharashtra and Gujarat. The Gulf of Kutch divides Saurashtra from Kutch, which is virtually an island, cut off from the rest of Gujarat to the east and Pakistan to the north by the low-lying *ranns* (deserts) of Kutch.

Gujarat is the former home of a surprisingly large proportion of India's emigrants, particularly to the UK and USA. Around 40% of the Indians in the New York area are Gujaratis; there, the common Gujarati surname 'Patel' has come to be commonly identified as Indian.

Eastern Gujarat

AHMEDABAD

Pop: 3,600,000   Tel Area Code: 079

Gujarat's principal city is Ahmedabad (also known as Amdavad) and is one of the major industrial cities in India. Although it retains

---

A REGIONAL HIGHLIGHT

Shatrunjaya, Saurashtra

Strewn with 863 temples, the hilltop complex of Shatrunjaya (the Place of Victory) is one of Jainism's holiest pilgrimage sites. The temples were built over a period of 900 years on a hilltop dedicated entirely to the gods; at dusk, even the priests depart from the temples, leaving them deserted.

Almost all the temples are Jain, and this hill is evidence of their belief that merit is derived from constructing temples. The hilltops are bounded by sturdy walls and the temples are grouped into nine enclosures or *tunks* – each with a central major temple and many minor ones clustered around. Some of the earliest temples here were built in the 11th century but were destroyed by the Muslims in the 14th and 15th centuries, so the current temples date from the 16th century onwards.

The hilltop affords a very fine view in all directions; on a clear day you can see the Gulf of Cambay beyond Bhavnagar. The most notable of the temples is dedicated to **Shri Adishwara**, the first Jain tirthankar. Note the frieze of dragons around this temple. Adjacent is the Muslim shrine of **Angar Pir**. Women who want children make offerings of miniature cradles at this shrine.

Built in 1618 by a wealthy Jain merchant, the **Chaumukh**, or Four-Faced shrine, has images of Adinath facing out in the four cardinal directions. Other important temples are those dedicated to Kumar Pal, Sampriti Raj and Vimal Shah.

The temples are open from 6 am to 6 pm. A photography permit can be purchased for Rs 20 at the main entrance on top of the hill. (There are two entrances – the main one is reached by taking the left-hand fork as you near the top and the other by the right-hand fork.) Shoes should be removed at the entrance to the compound, and leather items, including belts and bags, are not supposed to be brought onto the site.

A horse cart to the base of the hill costs Rs 20, or you can walk the three km from the village in about 30 minutes. The heat can be extreme by late morning, so it's a good idea to get an early start for the ascent. Water (although not bottled water) can be purchased at intervals, and you can buy refreshing curd in pottery bowls just outside the temple compound for Rs 10.

The 600m ascent from the base of the hill to the summit is a walk of some two km, up more than 3000 steps. At a moderate pace, the ascent will take about 1½ hours. You can be carried up the hill in a *doli* (rope chair) which costs from Rs 250 to Rs 700 for the most comfortable chair (the choice of quite a few affluent and obese pilgrims). The most conspicuous sight on first entering the temple compound is that of exhausted doli bearers resting in the shade. ■

little evidence of the Raj, it has been called the 'Manchester of the East' due to its many textile industries and its smokestacks. Ahmedabad is also very noisy and incredibly polluted; Relief Rd (Tilak Rd) gets the author's votes as one of the most polluted, congested and thoroughly chaotic strips of barely controlled mayhem in the country. It's a real rat race and only on Sunday mornings is there any respite.

Visitors in the hot season should bear in mind the derisive title given to Ahmedabad by the Moghul emperor, Jehangir: Gardabad, the City of Dust. Nevertheless, this comparatively little-visited city has a number of attractions for travellers, and is one of the best places to study the blend of Hindu and Islamic architectural styles known as the Indo-Saracenic.

The new capital of Gujarat, Gandhinagar, is 32km from Ahmedabad.

Things to Buy

With its busy modern textile works, it's not surprising that Gujarat offers a number of interesting buys in this line. Extremely fine, and often extremely expensive, patola silk saris are still made by a handful of master craftspeople in Patan. From Surat comes the *zari*, or gold-thread embroidery work. Surat is also a centre for silk saris. Less opulent, but still beautiful, are the block prints of Ahmedabad.

Jamnagar is famous for its tie-dye work, which you'll see throughout Saurashtra. Brightly coloured embroideries and beadwork are also found in Saurashtra, along with woollen shawls, blankets and rugs. Brass-covered wooden chests are manufactured in Bhavnagar, and Kutch is the centre for exquisite, fine embroidery. Most Gujarati handicrafts are on display at Gurjari or Handloom House, both on Ashram Rd, Ahmedabad. ∎

History

Over the centuries Ahmedabad has had a number of periods of grandeur, each followed by decline. It was founded in 1411 by Ahmed Shah (from whom the city takes its name) and in the 17th century was thought to be one of the finest cities in India. In 1615,

the noted English ambassador, Sir Thomas Roe, judged it to be 'a goodly city, as large as London' but in the 18th century, it went through a period of decline. Its industrial strength once again raised the city up, and from 1915, it became famous as the site of Gandhi's ashram and the place where he launched his celebrated march against the Salt Law.

Orientation

The city straddles the Sabarmati River. On the eastern bank, two main roads run east from the river to the railway station, about three km away. They are Relief Rd and Gandhi Rd. The busy road flanking the western bank of the Sabarmati is Sri R C Rd. This is the main road to the Gandhi Ashram and is called Ashram Rd at its northern end, although most locals refer to the entire road as Ashram Rd. The airport is off to the northeast of the city. Virtually all the old city walls are now demolished, but some of the gates remain.

Information

Gujarat Tourism publishes a range of brochures and maps. It has current information on forthcoming events and performances in Ahmedabad. The Ahmedabad edition of the *Times of India* has up-to-the-minute flight and rail information on page 2.

Tourist Office The helpful state tourist office Gujarat Tourism (☎ 449683) is just off Ashram Rd, across the river from the town centre. Opening hours are 10.30 am to 1.30 pm and 2 to 5.30 pm (closed Sunday). The office has good maps of Ahmedabad (Rs 4) and Gujarat state (Rs 20), and can also arrange tours and car hire. Ask rickshaw drivers for HK House on Ashram Rd – the tourist office is in this building, down the laneway near the South Indian Bank, or the BATA showroom (a more commonly known landmark).

Money The large State Bank of India branch at Lal Darwaja (the local bus stand) and the Bank of Baroda, at the west end of Relief Rd,

GUJARAT

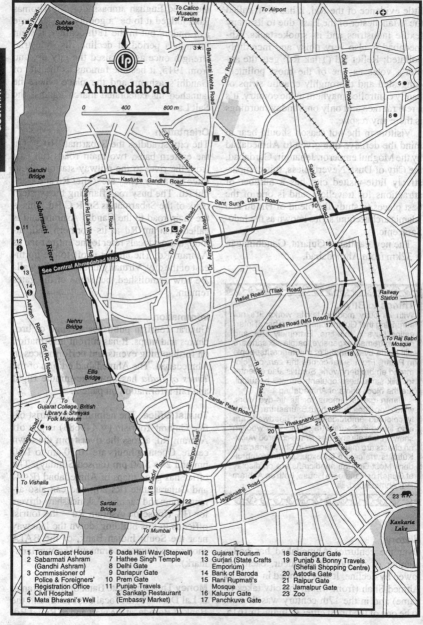

Ahmedabad

0   400   800 m

1 Toran Guest House	6 Dada Hari Wav (Stepwell)	12 Gujarat Tourism	18 Sarangpur Gate
2 Sabarmati Ashram	7 Hathee Singh Temple	13 Gurjari (State Crafts	19 Punjab & Bonny Travels
(Gandhi Ashram)	8 Delhi Gate	Emporium)	(Shefali Shopping Centre)
3 Commissioner of	9 Dariapur Gate	14 Bank of Baroda	20 Astodia Gate
Police & Foreigners'	10 Prem Gate	15 Rani Rupmati's	21 Raipur Gate
Registration Office	11 Punjab Travels	Mosque	22 Jamalpur Gate
4 Civil Hospital	& Sankalp Restaurant	16 Kalupur Gate	23 Zoo
5 Mata Bhavani's Well	(Embassy Market)	17 Panchkuva Gate	

both have money-changing facilities. The Bank of Baroda can give cash advances on Visa cards, and has a second branch on Ashram Rd.

Visa Extensions The Foreigners' Registration Office (☎ 333999) is in the office of the Commissioner of Police in Shahibaug, north of the city centre on Balvantrai Mehta Rd.

Post & Telecommunications The GPO is centrally located just off Relief Rd. The central telegraph office is just south of Sidi Saiyad's Mosque.

Libraries & Cultural Centres The British Library (☎ 656 0693) is at Bhaikaka Hall, near the Law Gardens, on the west side of the Sabarmati River. Informative lectures on topical issues are sometimes held here; when they are, announcements are published in the *Times of India*.

The Alliance Française (☎ 441551) is also on the west side of the river, at the rear of Gujarat College (between the college and the Law Gardens). The centre has information on French films which are sometimes screened in the city.

The Darpana Academy (☎ 445189), about one km north of Gujarat Tourism on Ashram Rd, has regular cultural programmes.

Bookshops There are a number of good bookshops at the Nehru Bridge end of Relief Rd. Sastu Kitab Ghar, near the Relief Cinema (on the opposite side of the road), has a good selection. Crossword also has an interesting range of books. It's at the Shree Krishna complex at Mithakali Six Roads, about one km from Gujarat Tourism.

Bhadra Fort & Teen Darwaja
Bhadra Fort was built by the city's founder, Ahmed Shah, in 1411 and later named after the goddess Bhadra, an incarnation of Kali. It now houses government offices and is of no particular interest. There is a post office in the former Palace of Azam Khan, within the fort. To the east of the fort stands the triple gateway, or Teen Darwaja, from which sultans used to watch processions from the palace to the Jama Masjid.

Jama Masjid
The Jama Masjid, built in 1423 by Ahmed Shah, is beside Mahatma Gandhi Rd, just to the east of the Teen Darwaja. Although 260 columns support the roof and its 15 cupolas, the two 'shaking' minarets lost half their height in the great earthquake of 1819, and another tremor in 1957 completed the demolition.

Much of this early Ahmedabad mosque was built using items salvaged from the

---

Festivals & Fairs
Gujarat has many fairs in its temple towns and small villages. They offer a chance to see religious festivals and celebrations and, in the villages, also provide an opportunity to see the finest examples of local handicrafts. The village of Ambaji, 177 km north of Ahmedabad, celebrates four major festivals each year. The Bhavnath Fair, held at the foot of Girnar Hill near Junagadh in the month of Magha (January/February), is a fine opportunity to hear local folk music and see folk dances.

In the week preceding Holi (February/March), the tribal Adivasi people have a major festival in the forested region called The Dangs, east of Surat near the Maharashtra border – it's known as the Dang Durbar. Krishna's birthday falls in August and his temple at Dwarka is the place to be for the celebration of the Janmashtami Festival held in his honour on this day. Along the coast at Madhavpur near Porbandar, the Madhavrai Fair is held in the month of Chaitra (March/April) to celebrate Krishna's elopement with Rukmini. In the same month, a major festival takes place at the foot of Pavagadh Hill at Champaner, near Vadodara, honouring the goddess Mahakali.

Somnath has a large fair at the full moon of Kartika Purnima in November/December. An important festival is held in honour of Shiva, the three-eyed one, or Trinetreshwar, in the month of Bhadra (August/September) in Tarnetar village – you'll see colourful local tribal costumes here.

Bhuj in Kutch hosts the annual Rann Festival in February/March. There are craft demonstrations, cultural programmes and tours to places of interest in the region. ■

demolished Hindu and Jain temples. It is said that a large black slab by the main arch is actually the base of a Jain idol, buried upside down for the Muslim faithful to tread on.

Tombs of Ahmed Shah & his Queens

The tomb of Ahmed Shah, with its perforated stone windows, stands just outside the east gate of the Jama Masjid. His son and grandson, who did not long survive him, also have their cenotaphs in this tomb. Women are not allowed into the central chamber. Across the street on a raised platform is the tomb of his queens – it's now really a market and in very poor shape compared to Ahmed Shah's tomb.

Sidi Saiyad's Mosque

This small mosque, which once formed part of the city wall, is close to the river end of Relief Rd. It was constructed by Sidi Saiyad, a slave of Ahmed Shah, and has beautiful carved stone windows depicting the intricate intertwining of the branches of a tree.

Ahmed Shah's Mosque

Dating from 1414, this was one of the earliest mosques in the city and was probably built on the site of a Hindu temple, using parts of that temple in its construction. It is to the south-west of the Bhadra Fort. The front of the mosque is now a garden.

Rani Rupmati's Mosque

A little north of the city centre, Rani Rupmati's Mosque was built between 1430 and 1440 and named after the sultan's Hindu wife. The minarets were partially brought down by the disastrous earthquake of 1819. Note the way the dome is elevated to allow light in around its base. As with so many of Ahmedabad's early mosques, this one displays elements of both Hindu and Islamic design.

'Marble trees' weave delicate patterns at Sidi Saiyad's Mosque.

Rani Sipri's Mosque

This small mosque is also known as the Masjid-e-Nagira, or Jewel of a Mosque, because of its extremely graceful and well-executed design. Its slender minarets again blend Hindu and Islamic styles. The mosque is said to have been commissioned in 1514 by a wife of Sultan Mahmud Begada after he executed their son for some minor misdemeanour, and she is in fact buried here. It's to the south-east of the city centre.

Sidi Bashir's Mosque & Shaking Minarets

Just south of the railway station, outside the Sarangpur Gate, the Sidi Bashir Mosque is famed for its shaking minarets, or jhulta minars. When one minaret is shaken, the other rocks in sympathy. This is said to be a protection against earthquake damage. It's a fairly fanciful proposition, and one which you'll be unable to verify, unless of course you happen to be on the spot during an earthquake.

Raj Babri Mosque

The Raj Babri Mosque, south-east of the railway station in the suburb of Gomtipur, also had shaking minarets, one of which was partially dismantled by an inquisitive Englishman in an unsuccessful attempt to find out how it worked.

A little to the north of the railway station, minarets are all that remain of a mosque which was destroyed in a battle between the Moghuls and Marathas in 1753.

Hathee Singh Temple

Just outside the Delhi Gate, to the north of the old city, this temple, as with so many Jain temples, is made of white marble. Built in 1848, it is dedicated to Dharamanath, the 15th Jain *tirthankar* (teacher).

Stepwells

Dada Hari Wav Stepwells (*wavs* or *baolis*) are strange constructions, unique to northern India, and Dada Hari Wav is one of the best. Built in 1501 by a woman of Sultan Begara's harem, it has a series of steps leading down

to lower and lower platforms terminating at a small, octagonal well. The depths of the well are cool, even on the hottest day, and it must once have been quite beautiful. Today, it is completely neglected and often bone dry, but it's a fascinatingly eerie place with galleries above the well and a small portico at ground level.

The best time to visit and photograph the well is between 10 and 11 am; at other times the sun doesn't penetrate to the various levels. Entry is free. Behind the well is the equally neglected mosque and *rauza* (tomb) of Dada Hari. The mosque has a tree motif like the one on the windows of Sidi Saiyad's Mosque.

Mata Bhavani's Well This well is a couple of hundred metres north of Dada Hari's. Ask children to show you the way. Thought to be several hundred years older, it is much less ornate and is now used as a crude Hindu temple.

Kankaria Lake

South-east of the city, this artificial lake, complete with an island summer palace, was constructed in 1451 and has 34 sides, each 60m long. Once frequented by Emperor Jehangir and Empress Nur Jahan, it is now a local picnic spot. There's a huge **zoo** and children's park by the lake, and the Ghattamendal pavilion in the centre houses an **aquarium**. To get there, take bus Nos 32, 42, 60, 152 or 153 from the Lal Darwaja bus stand (Rs 2.50).

Other Mosques & Temples

There's no shortage of mosques in Ahmedabad. If your enthusiasm for them is limited, don't go further than Sidi Saiyad's Mosque and the Jama Masjid. If you have real endurance, you could continue to **Dastur Khan's Mosque** near the Rani Sipri Mosque; also, the mosques of Haibat Khan, Saiyad Alam, Shuja'at Khan, Shaikh Hasan Muhammed Chisti and Muhafiz Khan.

For a complete change, you could plunge into the narrow streets of the old part of town and seek out the brightly painted **Swami**

Narayan Temple. Enclosed in a large court-yard, it dates from 1850. To the south of this Hindu temple are the nine tombs known as the Nau Gaz Pir, or Nine Yard Saints.

Other Attractions

In many streets, there are Jain bird-feeding places known as *parabdis*. Children catch and release pigeons for the fun of it. The older parts of the city are divided into totally separate areas known as *pols*. It's easy to get lost. The pleasant **Victoria Gardens** are at the east end of the Ellis Bridge.

On the sandy banks of the Sabarmati River, traditional block-printed fabrics are still stretched out to dry, despite the city's 70-plus large textile mills. The river dries to a mere trickle in the hot season.

Other places of interest in and around town include the ruined **Tomb of Darya Khan**, north-west of the Hathee Singh Temple. Built in 1453, the tomb has a particularly large dome. Nearby is the **Chhota Shahi Bagh**, across the railway line. Ladies of the harem used to live in the *chhota* (small) garden. In Saraspur, east of the railway line, the **Temple of Chintaman** is a Jain temple originally constructed in 1638 and converted into a mosque by Aurangzeb.

Museums

The excellent **Calico Museum of Textiles** (☎ 786 8172) exhibits antique and modern textiles including rare tapestries, wall hangings and costumes. Also on display are old weaving machines. The museum is in Sarabhai House, a former *haveli* (mansion), in the Shahi Bagh Gardens. You can only enter on a free guided tour. Tours depart at 10.15 am and 2.45 pm, and the museum is closed on Wednesday. To get there, take bus Nos 101, 102, 103 or 105 (Rs 3) out through the Delhi Gate.

The **Institute of Indology** beyond Gujarat College, near the Gujarat University campus, has an important collection of illustrated manuscripts and miniatures and one of the finest collections relating to Jainism in India. It's open daily from 11.30 am to 5.30 pm except Sunday.

The **NC Mehta Museum of Miniatures** at the Institute of Indology, has excellent examples of the various schools of Indian miniature painting. It's open Tuesday to Saturday from 9 to 11 am and 4 to 7 pm. The building was designed by Le Corbusier, who also had a hand in the new capital of Gandhinagar.

The **Shreyas Folk Museum**, about 2.5km west of the Sabarmati in the suburb of Ambavadi, displays the folk arts & crafts of Gujarat. It's open daily from 9 am to noon, and 3 to 5 pm except Wednesday. To get there, take bus No 34 or 200 (Rs 3). There is also the **National Institute of Design**, the **Tribal Research & Training Institute Museum**, and the **Philatelic Museum**.

There's a curious collection of cooking utensils at the **Utensils Museum** in the compound of the Vishalla restaurant. Items include nutcrackers, knives, cooking vessels and various other utensils. The museum is open daily from 10.30 am to 10.30 pm and entry costs Rs 3; photography is not allowed.

Sabarmati Ashram

Seven km from the centre of town, on the west bank of the Sabarmati River, this was Gandhi's headquarters during the long struggle for Indian independence. His ashram was founded in 1915 and still makes handicrafts, handmade paper and spinning wheels. Gandhi's spartan living quarters are preserved as a small museum and there is a pictorial record of the major events in his life. There's also a bookshop selling books by and about the Mahatma.

The ashram is open from 8.30 am to 6.30 pm (till 7 pm between April and September). Admission is free. At 8.30 pm on Sunday, Tuesday, Thursday and Friday evenings there is a sound & light show in English for a small charge. Bus Nos 81, 83/1 or 84/1 (Rs 3) will take you there. An auto-rickshaw will cost about Rs 25 with serious bargaining.

Organised Tours

The municipal corporation (☎ 535 2911) runs city tours from the local bus stand (Lal Darwaja) which depart daily at 8 am and 2 pm.

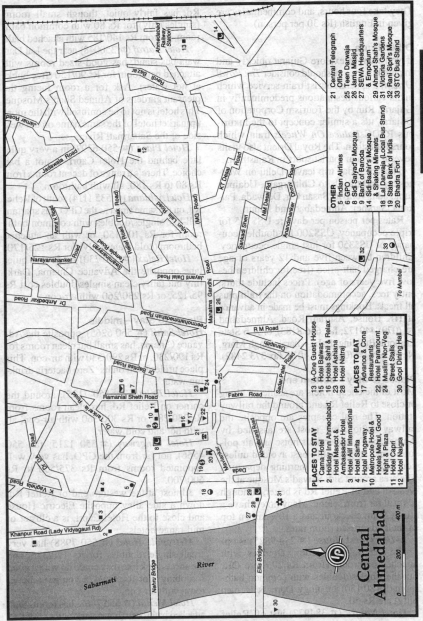

GUJARAT

Central Ahmedabad

Sabarmati

River

Nehru Bridge

Ellis Bridge

Khanpur Road (Lady Vidyagauri Rd)

0   200   400 m

PLACES TO STAY
1 Cama Hotel
2 Holiday Inn Ahmedabad;
   Hotel Mascot &
   Ambassador Hotel
3 Hotel Alif International
4 Hotel Sarita
7 Hotel Kingsway
10 Metropole Hotel &
   Hotels Mehul, Good
   Night & Plaza
11 Hotel Capri
12 Hotel Naigra

PLACES TO EAT
13 A-One Guest House
15 Hotel Balwas
16 Hotels Sahil & Relax
23 Hotel Ashiana
28 Hotel Natraj
17 Advance & Cona
   Restaurants
22 Hotel Paramount
24 Muslim Non-Veg
   Street Stalls
30 Gopi Dining Hall

OTHER
5 Indian Airlines
6 GPO
8 Sidi Sayyad's Mosque
9 Bank of Baroda
14 Sidi Bashir's Mosque
   & Shaking Minarets
18 Lal Darwaja (Local Bus Stand)
19 State Bank of India
20 Bhadra Fort
21 Central Telegraph
   Office
25 Teen Darwaja
26 Jama Masjid
27 SEWA Headquarters
   & Emporium
29 Ahmed Shah's Mosque
31 Victoria Gardens
32 Rani Sipri's Mosque
33 STC Bus Stand

To Mumbai

They take four hours, and commentaries are given in English (Rs 30 per person).

Other Tours

If you want to explore Gujarat quickly and in pure luxury, you should consider *The Royal Orient*, a special tourist train service which visits various destinations predominantly in Gujarat. Run by the Tourism Corporation of Gujarat, it's a similar concept to the luxurious RTDC *Palace On Wheels* train which tours Rajasthan. The Royal Orient also visits several popular tourist spots in Rajasthan.

The seven-day trip leaves Delhi on Wednesday and travels to Chittorgarh, Udaipur, Junagadh, Veraval, Sasan Gir, Delwada, Palitana, Sarkhej, Ahmedabad and Jaipur.

Rates per person per day are US$175 for triple occupancy, US$200 for double occupancy or US$350 for just single occupancy. Children between five and 12 years of age are charged half price (free for children below five years of age). Prices include tours, entry fees, accommodation on the train plus all meals. Bookings must be made in advance at HK House, Ashram Road, Ahmedabad (☎ (079) 449172; fax 656 8183), or A-6 State Emporia Building, Baba Kharak Singh Marg, New Delhi (☎ (011) 373 4015; fax 373 2482).

Places to Stay – bottom end

Most of the cheap hotels are scattered along or close to Relief Rd and around the railway station. The real cheapies are opposite the railway station, but most are assailed by Ahmedabad's horrendous noise and air pollution and are probably best avoided unless you have a very early morning departure. The area around Sidi Saiyad's Mosque at the western end of Relief Rd is better, although it's still far from serene. Many hotels have a stingy 9 am checkout and a 10% tax on top of their advertised room rates.

A-One Guest House (☎ 214 9823) is opposite the railway station. Doubles with attached bathroom (from Rs 200) are OK, but the singles/doubles with common bathroom (Rs 80/130) are dingy. Dorm beds (men only) are Rs 50.

Hotel Naigra (☎ 384977) just off Relief Rd, has fairly quiet, though small rooms (singles only) for Rs 80 with common bathroom, or from Rs 140/185 with attached bath.

Hotel Natraj (☎ 350048) near the Lal Darwaja bus stand, has good-sized rooms with attached bathroom for Rs 90/150 (free bucket hot water). Ask for a room facing the pleasant gardens of Ahmed Shah's Mosque. This hotel is not to be confused with the more upmarket hotel of the same name on the west side of the Sabarmati River.

Hotel Plaza (☎ 550 6397) in a very quiet lane behind the Hotel Capri, is not a bad choice. There's a range of decent rooms from Rs 80 to Rs 180, all with bathroom.

Hotel Ashiana (☎ 535 1114) south of Relief Rd, on the same street as the GPO, has spartan, cell-like singles/doubles with common bathroom for Rs 100/150, or with an attached bathroom (cold water only) for Rs 125/170.

Hotel Relax (☎ 550 7301) is down a quiet lane opposite the Advance Cinema. Dark, tiny but fairly clean singles/doubles cost Rs 95/125, or Rs 230/260 with air-con.

Places to Stay – middle

Hotel Sahil (☎ 550 6265), opposite the Advance Cinema, has small but clean rooms for Rs 190/230, or Rs 290/330 with air-con. This place prides itself on its 'Zero bacteria drinking water'.

Hotel Balwas (☎ 550 7135), around the corner on Relief Rd, has clean rooms from Rs 230/280, or Rs 300/360 with air-con, all with hot and cold water.

Hotel Kingsway (☎ 550 1215; fax 550 4566), not far from the GPO, has very well appointed rooms from Rs 375/500 to Rs 600/700.

Almost at the western end of Relief Rd, down a side alley opposite Electric House and close to the Hotel Capri, is a cluster of mid-range hotels.

Metropole Hotel (☎ 550 7988) has very small singles/doubles for Rs 170/325, and the sheets look like they could do with a good scrubbing. For Rs 375/425 you get a better room with air-con.

Hotel Mehul (☎ 550 7862) has rooms with attached bathroom (hot water) for Rs 150/200.

Rooms are large although a little shabby, and the service is rather unenthusiastic.

Hotel Good Night (☎ 550 7181) has rooms from Rs 225/300, or Rs 325/400 with air-con.

Hotel Capri (☎ 550 7143; fax 550 6646), also in this area, has pretty good rooms for Rs 325/375, or Rs 375/475 with air-con.

Hotel Sarita (☎ 550 1569) is in a quiet area close to the Indian Airlines office. Clean, modern rooms cost Rs 300/350, or Rs 400/450 with air-con.

Ambassador Hotel (☎ 550 2490; fax 550 2327) which runs parallel to the eastern bank of the Sabarmati River, has a range of rooms from Rs 250/300 to Rs 425/500 for a deluxe air-con room. However, this hotel is looking a little neglected compared to some of the new mid to top-range hotels which have sprung up along this road.

Hotel Alif International (☎ 550 0540) has singles/doubles starting at Rs 295/340, or Rs 350/475 with air-con.

Toran Guest House (☎ 748 3742) is a government-run place close to the river, right across the road from the Gandhi Ashram. Doubles cost Rs 350, or Rs 550 with air-con.

Places to Stay – top end
Holiday Inn Ahmedabad (☎ 550 5505; fax 550 5501), on Khanpur Rd, is unbeatable in terms of luxury. Sumptuous rooms range from Rs 3500/3700 to a whopping Rs 7000 for a suite, and the tariff includes a buffet breakfast. Decadent touches include an indoor swimming pool, jacuzzi, sauna, 24 hour coffee shop and two restaurants.

Hotel Mascot (☎ 550 3848; fax 550 3221), nearby, has rooms from Rs 1000/1300 and a courtesy airport service. It's less ostentatious than some of its grand neighbours, but is well appointed and has a good restaurant.

Cama Hotel (☎ 550 5281; fax 550 5285), further north along Khanpur Rd, has comfortable rooms for Rs 1900/2300. Facilities include a restaurant, coffee shop, pool and bookshop.

Places to Eat
Ahmedabad is a good place to sample a Gujarati thali. Many places offer all-you-can-eat thalis which make a cheap and very satisfying meal.

At the bottom end of the scale there's excellent Muslim (non-veg) street food available near Teen Darwaza on Bhathiyar Gali, a small street which runs parallel to Gandhi Rd, around the corner from the Hotel Ashiana. Each evening stalls are set up, and for around Rs 25 you can get a good feed. There are meat and fish dishes to choose from as well as vegetarian items. To get to this area, you'll have to walk through the live poultry market, where prospective chicken dishes are blissfully unaware of the fate which lies just a few metres away.

Gujarati Food
The strict vegetarianism of the Jains has contributed to Gujarat's distinctive regional cuisine. Throughout the state, you'll find the Gujarati version of the thali – it's the traditional all-you-can-eat vegetarian meal with an even greater variety of dishes than usual. It can, however, be overpoweringly sweet.

Popular dishes include *kadhi*, a savoury curry of yoghurt, fried puffs and finely chopped vegetables. *Undhyoo* is a winter speciality of potatoes, sweet potatoes, broad beans and aubergines roasted in an earthenware pot which is buried upside down (undhyoo) and a fire built on top. In Surat, the local variation of this dish has more spice and hot chilli. *Sev ganthia*, a crunchy fried chickpea-flour snack, is available from *farsan* stalls.

In winter, try Surat's *paunk*, a curious combination of roasted cereals; or *jowar*, garlic chutney and sugar. Then there's *kaman dhokla*, a salty, steamed chickpea flour cake, and *doodhpak*, a thick, sweetened, milk-based dessert with nuts. *Srikhand* is a yoghurt dessert spiced with saffron, cardamom, nuts and candied fruit. *Gharis* are rich sweets made of milk, clarified butter and dried fruits – another Surat speciality. In summer, *aam rasis* is a popular mango drink.

The Gujaratis make superb ice cream, available throughout western India under the brand name of Vadilal. It comes in about 20 flavours, some of which are seasonal. ■

Gopi Dining Hall, just off the west end of Ellis Bridge, near VS Hospital, is one of the most popular places for a thali. An all-you-can-eat Gujarati thali is Rs 40 (lunch) or Rs 55 (dinner).

Advance Restaurant, opposite the cinema of the same name, and the *Cona Restaurant*, a few doors down, open early and are good places for breakfast.

Hotel Paramount, close to Teen Darwaja, has Continental, Chinese and Indian cuisine, and you can dine in private curtained booths, with a massive crystal chandelier swinging overhead!

Cactus Restaurant at the Hotel Mascot, is perfect for a splurge. It serves Indian, Continental and Chinese dishes and there's live music on Monday and Thursday nights.

Sankalp Restaurant, off Ashram Rd near Dinesh Hall in the Embassy Market area, is worth a visit. This air-con restaurant boasts one of the longest dosas in India – four feet long! (Rs 201). The Rs 30 south Indian thalis also make a pleasant change from the sweet Gujarati cuisine.

Vishalla (☎ 403357) is an interesting rural complex on the southern edge of town in Vasana which evokes the atmosphere of a Gujarat village. Here, you'll dine in Indian fashion, seated on the floor, while watching puppet shows. It's not cheap, but the food is great. Lunch runs from 11 am to 2 pm and costs Rs 125, while dinner is from 7 to 11 pm and costs Rs 180. Dessert will cost you extra! The interesting Utensils Museum is located here (see under Museums earlier in this section).

Things to Buy

On Ashram Rd, just to the south of the tourist office, is the Gujarat state crafts emporium, called Gurjari. For hand-printed fabrics and other textiles, the Self-Employed Women's Association or SEWA (see the boxed section on SEWA) has two retail outlets: shop 21/22, Goyal Towers, near Jahnvi Restaurant, University Rd, on the western side of the Sabarmati, and at the eastern end of Ellis Bridge, opposite the Victoria Gardens. The headquarters is adjacent to the latter, and visitors are welcome.

Getting There & Away

Air The Indian Airlines office (☎ 550 3061) is on Relief Rd, close to the Nehru Bridge, on the right-hand side coming from the railway station.

Air India (☎ 642 5644) is in Premchand House, near the High Court building on Ashram Rd, west of the river. Ahmedabad has an

---

SEWA

The Self-Employed Women's Association, more commonly known by its acronym, SEWA, comprises more than 54,000 members, and is Gujarat's single largest union. Established in 1972, SEWA identifies three types of self-employed workers: hawkers and vendors, who sell their wares from carts, baskets or small shops; home-based workers such as weavers, potters and bidi rollers; and manual labourers and service providers such as agricultural labourers, contract labourers, construction workers, and laundry and domestic workers. More than 93% of all workers in India fall into one of these categories, and women constitute over half of these workers. However, SEWA recognises that frequently this 'work' is not considered to be 'employment', and the actual number of women workers is not known.

Adhering to a Gandhian philosophy of change through non-violent means, SEWA embodies three movements: the labour movement; the co-operative movement; and the women's movement. The aim of the organisation is to enable women to actively participate in the mainstream economy and to attain empowerment through financial autonomy. Self-employment is the keystone of the organisation and SEWA aims to assist its members by raising the profile of women in the social and political arenas. SEWA assists self-employed workers to organise into unions and cooperatives, so that ultimately they can control the fruits of their own labours. Policies and programmes are implemented in an endeavour to reflect the experience, needs and realities of the self-employed.

The two main goals of the movement are full employment and self-reliance, and the fulfilment of these goals is based on policies which focus on areas such as health and child care, literacy, appropriate housing and self-sufficiency. ■

international airport and there are direct flights with Air India to the UK and the USA.

Indian Airlines flies from Mumbai to Ahmedabad at least once a day (US$65), and there are twice-daily direct flights to Delhi (US$105). Other destinations are Vadodara (US$25, daily), Bangalore (US$180, four times weekly) and Chennai (Madras) (US$195, four times weekly). Twice weekly, flights to Mumbai have connections through to Goa (US$65).

Jet Airways (☎ 467886) has flights twice daily to Mumbai (US$65) and one daily flight to Delhi (US$105). ModiLuft's agent, Zen Travels (☎ 466228), can tell you if the airline's three weekly flights to Delhi are still running.

Bus Buses to Gandhinagar (Rs 5) depart every five minutes from Lal Darwaja or from one of the numerous stops on Ashram Rd.

Plenty of buses operate around Gujarat and to neighbouring states. The Gujarat State Transport Corporation (STC) buses are almost all standard-issue, battered meat wagons, but they're usually not too crowded and run to schedule.

If you're travelling long-distance, private minibuses are a more expensive but much quicker alternative. Punjab Travels (☎ 656 9200) Embassy Market, near Dinesh Hall just off Ashram Rd and only five minutes walk from Gujarat Tourism, has a number of intercity services, including: Ajmer and Jaipur at 5.30 pm (11 hours, Rs 120 and 15 hours, Rs 150); Bhavnagar at 7 and 11.30 am and 6 pm (four hours, Rs 50); Mumbai at 8.15 pm (15 hours, Rs 150); Bhuj at 9 pm (seven hours, Rs 100); Indore at 8.30 pm (10 hours, Rs 150); Junagadh at 9.30 pm (seven hours, Rs 70); Mt Abu at 10 pm (seven hours, Rs 100); Rajkot at 7 am (four hours, Rs 50); Udaipur at 9.30 pm (seven hours, Rs 80) and Veraval and Somnath at 9.30 pm (six hours, Rs 90).

Punjab Travels has another office in the Shefali Shopping Centre, 2.5km to the south on Pritamnagar Rd, the southern extension of Ashram Rd.

Another private bus company with numerous intercity services is Bonny Travels (☎ 657 6568), also at the Shefali Shopping Centre.

Train There is a computerised booking office to the left as you exit the main terminal. It's open Monday to Saturday from 8 am to 8 pm, and on Sunday from 8 am to 2 pm. Window No 6 handles the foreign tourist quota, which makes things much quicker. Train schedules and fares tend to change quite often so it's a good idea to double-check timetables.

Getting Around
The Airport An auto-rickshaw to the airport will cost at least Rs 85. A much cheaper option is a local bus from Lal Darwaja (Rs 4, bus Nos 103 or 105).

Local Transport Ahmedabad is well on the way to displacing Lagos as the world's craziest city as far as traffic is concerned. Venturing out in an auto-rickshaw is certainly a nerve-shattering experience. Most drivers are willing

Major Trains from Ahmedabad

Destination	Train Number & Name	Departure Time	Distance +20 (km)	Duration (hours)	Fare (Rs) (2nd/1st)
Baroda	2010 *Shatabdi Exp*	2.45 pm	100	1.30	150/300
Bhavnagar	9846 *Girnar Exp*	9.10 pm	268	8.05	97/303
Bhuj	65 *Bhuj Fast Pass*	8.25 pm	492	17.15	441
Dwarka	*Saurashtra Mail*	6.15 am	471	10.15	147/474
Delhi	2473 *Sarvodaya Exp*	12.00 pm	1098	16.15	255/1110
Mumbai	9102 *Gujarat Mail*	10.00 pm	491	8.55	150/364
Udaipur	9644 *Udaipur Exp*	11.15 pm	298	9.50	105/330

to use the meter, but at the end of the journey may ask for something utterly ridiculous. Ask to see the fare adjustment card; however, this is entirely in Gujarati, so you'll need to learn the Gujarati numbers to make any sense of it.

The local bus stand is known as Lal Darwaja, and is on the east side of the river, between Nehru and Ellis bridges. The routes, destinations and fares are all posted in Gujarati.

AROUND AHMEDABAD
Sarkhej

The suburb of Sarkhej, eight km south-west of Ahmedabad, is noted for its elegant group of buildings, including the **Mausoleum of Azam & Mu'assam**, built in 1457 by the brothers who were responsible for Sarkhej's architecture. The architecture here is interesting because the style is almost purely Hindu, with little of the Saracenic influence so evident in Ahmedabad.

As you enter Sarkhej, you pass the **Mausoleum of Mahmud Begara** and, beside the tank and connected to his tomb, that of his queen, Rajabai (1461). Also by the tank is the **Tomb of Ahmad Khattu Ganj Buksh**, a renowned Muslim saint and spiritual adviser to Ahmed Shah. The saint is said to have died in 1445 at the age of 111. Next to this is a fine mosque. Like the other buildings, it is notable for the complete absence of arches, a usual feature of Muslim architecture. The palace, with pavilions and a harem, is also around the tank.

The Dutch established a factory in Sarkhej in 1620 to process the indigo grown here.

Batwa

Ten km south-east of Ahmedabad, the suburb of Batwa has tombs of a noted Muslim saint (himself the son of another saint) and the saint's son. Batwa also has an important mosque.

Adalaj Wav

Nineteen km north of Ahmedabad, Adalaj Wav is one of the finest of the Gujarati stepwells, or baolis, with carvings depicting intricate motifs of flowers and birds. It was built by Queen Rudabai in 1499 and provided a cool and secluded retreat during the hot summer months.

Cambay

The old seaport of Ahmedabad is 92km to the south, at the northern end of the Gulf of Cambay. At the height of Muslim power in Gujarat, the entire region was known as Cambay and, when the first ambassadors arrived from England in 1583, they bore letters from Queen Elizabeth addressed to Akbar, the 'King of Cambay'. Dutch and Portuguese factories were established in the port before the British arrived, but the rise of Surat eclipsed Cambay and, when its port silted up, the city's decline was inevitable.

From Ahmedabad, it's a three hour bus trip from the STC bus stand to Cambay (Rs 24).

Nal Sarovar Bird Sanctuary

Between November and February, this 116 sq km lake, 60km south-west of Ahmedabad, is home to vast flocks of indigenous and migratory birds. Ducks, geese, pelicans and flamingos are best seen early in the morning and in the evening and the sanctuary is best visited as a day excursion by taxi, as buses are infrequent and there is no convenient accommodation. Desert Coursers (☎ (079) 448699), a family-run Ahmedabad tour outfit, takes personalised day tours to the sanctuary. Prices are Rs 1300 per person, including lunch.

You can hire a boat on Nal Sarovar with someone to punt you to the areas where the flamingos and pelicans are; but please avoid going too close and try to restrain the boatman from scaring the birds, as this causes them to fly away. One of the main reasons for the decline in population of some birds is excessive human disturbance. If possible, avoid weekends and holidays when it gets quite crowded.

Krys Kazmierczak, UK

Lothal

About 85km south-west of Ahmedabad, towards Bhavnagar, this important archaeological site was discovered in 1954. The city which stood here 4500 years ago is clearly related to the Indus Valley cities of Mohenjodaro and Harappa, both in Pakistan. It has the same neatly laid-out street pattern, the same carefully assembled brickwork and the same scientific drainage system.

The name Lothal actually means Mound of the Dead in Gujarati, as does Mohenjodaro in Sindhi. Excavations have revealed a dockyard – at its peak, this was probably one of the most important ports on the subcontinent. Seals discovered at the site suggest that trade may have been conducted with the civilisations of Mesopotamia, Egypt and Persia.

There is an **archaeological museum** at the site.

Utelia Palace is seven km from the archaeological site, by the Bhugavo River. Rooms at this grand palace cost Rs 1500 per person including meals. Trips to local villages, Nal Sarovar and Velavadar National Park can all be arranged.

Getting There & Away Lothal is a day trip from Ahmedabad. You can reach it by rail, disembarking at Bhurkhi on the Ahmedabad to Bhavnagar railway line, from where you can take a bus.

Modhera
The beautiful and partially ruined **Sun Temple of Modhera** was built by King Bhimdev I (1026-27) and bears some resemblance to the later, and far better known, Sun Temple of Konark in the state of Orissa, which it predates by some 200 years. Like that temple, it was designed so that the dawn sun shone on the image of Surya, the sun god, at the time of the equinoxes. The main hall and shrine are reached through a pillared porch and the temple exterior is intricately and delicately carved. As with the Temple of Somnath, this fine temple was ruined by Mahmud of Ghazni. The temple is open daily from 8 am to 6 pm.

Accommodation can pose a real problem here.

PWD Rest House is a possibility but foreigners often find it difficult to get a bed here.

Jilla Panchayat Rest House near the Sun

Temple has doubles for around Rs 80 to Rs 150, but it can also be a problem getting a room here.

Getting There & Away Modhera is 102km north-west of Ahmedabad. There are direct buses (3½ hours, Rs 30), or you can take the train to Mahesana and then catch a bus for the 26km trip to Modhera.

Unjha & Sidhpur
A little north of Mahesana and a base for those visiting the Modhera Temple, the town of Unjha is interesting for the marriage customs of the Kadwakanbis who live in this region. Marriages occur only once every 11 years and, on that day, every unmarried girl over 40 days old must be wed. If no husband can be found, a proxy wedding takes place and the bride immediately becomes a 'widow'. She later remarries when a suitable husband shows up.

There are a number of private guest houses at Unjha.

About 10km north of Unjha is Sidhpur where you'll find the very fragmented ruins of an ancient temple. This region was an important centre for growing opium poppies.

Patan
About 130km north-west of Ahmedabad, this was an ancient Hindu capital before being sacked by Mahmud of Ghazni in 1024. Now a pale shadow of its former self, it still has more than 100 **Jain temples** and is famous for its beautifully designed patola **silk saris**. There's also the renovated **Rani-ki-Vav**, a stepwell which boasts some of Gujarat's finest carvings. It's very impressive and certainly warrants a visit if you're in this area.

Hotel Neerav, about 500m from the bus stand, next to Kohinoor Cinema, has rooms ranging from Rs 50/100 to Rs 300/350.

Getting There & Away Patan is 25km north-west of the Mahesana railway station, which also serves as a departure point for Modhera. Buses from Ahmedabad take 3½ hours and cost Rs 40.

GUJARAT

Little Rann of Kutch

The Little Rann of Kutch, the barren expanse of 'desert' (actually salt plains) which divides Gujarat's western region of Kutch from the rest of Gujarat, is the home of the last remaining population of *khur* (Asiatic wild ass) in India. There's also a large bird population.

The Rann can be treacherously difficult to explore as the desert consists of salt deposited at a time when the area formed part of the delta of the River Indus. This means that rain can quickly turn parts of the desert into a sea of mud, and what to the untrained eye looks like solid ground may in fact be a thin crust of dry silt with soft mud underneath. Hence it is essential to have someone along who is familiar with local conditions.
Krys Kazmierczak, UK

The small town of **Zainabad**, 105km northwest of Ahmedabad, is very close to the Little Rann of Kutch. Desert Coursers (☎ (079) 448699) is a family-run tour company which organises interesting safari and cultural tours on the Rann.

Camp Zainabad (☎ (02757) 33322) offers *kooba* accommodation, traditional thatch-roofed huts (with attached bathrooms) in a very peaceful setting. It costs Rs 650 per person per night, including breakfast and dinner. The self-contained huts are pretty basic but comfortable and have been hand-painted by local Bajania people. The camp is run by the friendly Malik family, who operate Desert Coursers. It's advisable to make bookings in advance.

Getting There & Away From Ahmedabad, take a bus to Dasada, 12km north-east of Zainabad (two hours, Rs 23). From here there are local buses to Zainabad. There are also direct buses from Rajkot. Alternatively, taxis which take up to four people can be arranged through Desert Coursers for around Rs 4.50 per km.

GANDHINAGAR

Pop: 132,000 Tel Area Code: 02712 outside of Ahmedabad (dial 082 from Ahmedabad)

Although Ahmedabad became the capital of Gujarat state when the old state of Mumbai was split into Maharashtra and Gujarat in

1960, a new capital was planned 32km north-east on the west bank of the Sabarmati River. Named Gandhinagar after Mahatma Gandhi, who was born in Gujarat, it is India's second planned city after Chandigarh and, like that city, is laid out in numbered sectors, and is equally dull. Construction of the city commenced in 1965 and the secretariat was moved there in 1970.

Places to Stay & Eat

Youth Hostel (☎ 22364) in sector 16, charges Rs 40 for a bed and offers cheap meals.

Hotel Haveli (☎ 23905; fax 24057) in sector 11 is a more upmarket option. Rooms (doubles only) are from Rs 800 to Rs 1200, and there's a good restaurant here. Checkout is noon.

Getting There & Away

Buses from Ahmedabad cost Rs 5. They leave from Lal Darwaja, or from one of the numerous stops along Ashram Rd.

VADODARA (Baroda)

Pop: 1,200,000 Tel Area Code: 0265

Baroda was the capital of the princely Gaekwad state prior to Independence. Today Vadodara is a pleasant, medium-sized city with some interesting museums and art galleries and a fine park. The city's Fine Arts College attracts students from around the country and abroad.

Orientation & Information

The railway station, bus stand and a cluster of cheaper hotels are all on the west side of the Vishwarmurti River, which bisects the city. The state tourist office, Gujarat Tourism (☎ 427489) is on the ground floor of Narmada Bhavan, not far from the Kirti Mandir. It's open daily from 10.30 am to 6 pm except Sunday. There's also a Municipal Tourist Office (☎ 329656) opposite the railway station. Tilak Rd runs straight out from the station, across the river by Sayaji Bagh park and into the main part of town. The State Bank of India, near the Kirti Mandir, is open from 11 am to 3 pm Monday to Friday, and 11 am to 1 pm Saturday.

Sayaji Bagh & Vadodara Museum

This extensive park, encircled by a mini-railway, is a popular spot for an evening stroll. Within the park is the Vadodara Museum & Art Gallery, open daily except Thursday from 9.30 am to 4.45 pm. Entry costs Rs 2. The museum has various exhibits, while the gallery has Moghul miniatures and a collection of European masters. Also within the park grounds is a **planetarium**, where demonstrations are given each evening at 5 pm (in English); and a small **zoo**, which is open daily from 8 am to 11.30 am and 2 to 5.15 pm except Thursday; entry is Rs 1.

Maharaja Fateh Singh Museum

South of the centre, this royal art collection includes European works by Raphael, Titian and Murillo and examples of Greco-Roman, Chinese and Japanese art, as well as Indian exhibits. The museum is in the palace grounds and is open daily from 10.30 am to 5.30 pm except Monday. Entry costs Rs 10.

Other Attractions

The **Laxmi Vilas Palace** has a large collection of armour and sculptures and although not normally open to the public, foreigners can usually visit by making an advance booking (☎ 431819) and paying the whopping Rs 100 entry fee. The **Naulakhi Well**, a fine baoli, is 50m north of the palace.

Organised Tours

The Municipal Tourist Office conducts city tours every Tuesday, Wednesday and Friday from 2 to 6 pm (Rs 15 per person). On Saturday, Sunday and Monday, there's a longer tour from 2 to 9 pm, which also visits some places out of town (Rs 30 per person). Bookings should be made in advance.

Places to Stay – bottom end

Vadodara has limited budget accommodation and many hotels slap an additional tax on their advertised tariff.

Jagdish Hindu Lodge (☎ 330495) is not

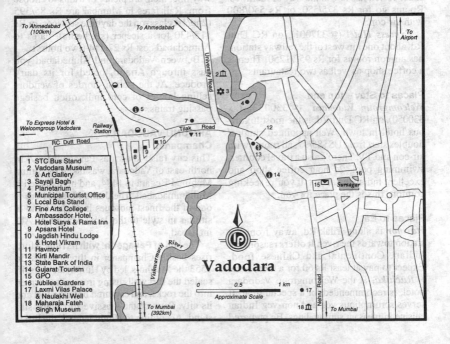

1 STC Bus Stand
2 Vadodara Museum & Art Gallery
3 Sayaji Bagh
4 Planetarium
5 Municipal Tourist Office
6 Local Bus Stand
7 Fine Arts College
8 Ambassador Hotel, Hotel Surya & Rama Inn
9 Apsara Hotel
10 Jagdish Hindu Lodge & Hotel Vikram
11 Havmor
12 Kirti Mandir
13 State Bank of India
14 Gujarat Tourism
15 GPO
16 Jubilee Gardens
17 Laxmi Vilas Palace & Naulakhi Well
18 Maharaja Fateh Singh Museum

To Ahmedabad (100km)
To Ahmedabad
To Airport
University Road
Tilak Road
Railway Station
To Express Hotel & Welcomgroup Vadodara
RC Dutt Road
Vishvamitri River
Sursagar
Nehru Road
To Mumbai
To Mumbai (392km)

Vadodara

0   0.5   1 km
Approximate Scale

too far from the railway station and has pretty gloomy rooms arranged around a courtyard. Singles/doubles with attached bathroom cost Rs 60/75.

Hotel Vikram (☎ 327737) is in the same street but a notch upmarket. It offers rooms with private bath for Rs 100/200, or Rs 200/300 with air-con.

Apsara Hotel (☎ 328251) is in the next street back towards the station. It's a well maintained place with rooms for Rs 150/180 with bathroom.

Places to Stay – middle

Ambassador Hotel (☎ 327653) is across the road from the Apsara. There are large, quiet rooms from Rs 200/330, or Rs 455/555 with air-con.

Rama Inn (☎ 330131), right next to the Ambassador, has rooms for Rs 375/525, or Rs 575/800 with air-con. There's also a swimming pool and restaurant.

Hotel Surya (☎ 336500), near the Ambassador Hotel, has less in the way of facilities. Rooms go for Rs 375/550, or Rs 550/800 with air-con.

Express Hotel (☎ 337001), on RC Dutt Rd, about one km west of the railway station, has air-con rooms for Rs 950/1250. There's a coffee shop as well as two restaurants.

Places to Stay – top end

Welcomgroup Vadodara (☎ 330033; fax 330050), on RC Dutt Rd, is the most luxurious hotel in town. Well appointed singles/doubles start from US$85/97, all rooms with air-con and TV. There's also a travel counter, swimming pool, 24 hour coffee shop and excellent Indian restaurant. If you're seeking comfort, this is the place for you.

Places to Eat

Havmor is along Tilak Rd, away from the station towards the river. It offers reasonable Indian, Continental and Chinese food. Expect to pay at least Rs 60 for a meal here.

Ruchika, at the Welcomgroup Vadodara hotel, is recommended for a special treat. It serves scrumptious veg and non-veg Indian cuisine in pleasant surroundings. Be prepared

to fork out a couple of hundred rupees to dine here. Otherwise try their coffee shop where the fare is cheaper.

Getting There & Away

Air Indian Airlines (☎ 328596) has flights from Vadodara to Mumbai (US$60), Delhi (US$120) and Ahmedabad (US$25). NEPC Airlines (☎ 337899) has daily flights to both Mumbai and Ahmedabad.

Bus The long-distance bus stand is 500m north of the railway station, and there are STC buses to many destinations in Gujarat, western Madhya Pradesh and northern Maharashtra. Buses to Ahmedabad leave at least every 30 minutes (Rs 27, 2½ hours).

The private companies all have their offices nearby.

Train Vadodara is 100km south of Ahmedabad by rail and 392km north of Mumbai. As it's on the main Mumbai to Ahmedabad railway line, there are plenty of trains to choose from. Rail fares to Mumbai are Rs 85/395 (2nd/1st class) on the daytime services, or Rs 115/430 for a sleeper (six hours). Fares to Ahmedabad cost Rs 27/114 (two hours).

Between Vadodara and Ahmedabad you pass through **Anand**, noted for its dairy produce. At the station, hordes of vendors selling bottles of cold milk often besiege passing trains.

AROUND VADODARA
Champaner

This city (also known as Pavagadh), 47km north-east of Vadodara, was taken by Sultan Mahmud Begara in 1484, and he renamed it Muhammadabad. The **Jama Masjid** here is one of the finest mosques in Gujarat and is similar in style to the Jama Masjid of Ahmedabad.

The **Hill of Pavagadh**, with its ruined fort, rises beside Champaner in three stages. In 1553 the Moghuls, led by Humayun himself, scaled the fort walls using iron spikes driven into the rocks, and captured both the fort and its city. Parts of the massive fort walls still stand. According to Hindu legend, the hill is actually a chunk of the Himalayan mountainside which the monkey god Hanuman carted off to Lanka in an episode of the *Ramayana*, hence the name Pavagadh, which means Quarter of a Hill.

Hotel Champaner (☎ 45641) is run by the state tourist organisation. Dorm beds cost Rs 30 per person and doubles are Rs 250.

Buses from Vadodara take one hour and cost Rs 10.

Dabhoi Fort
The 13th century fort of Dabhoi is 29km south-east of Vadodara. A fine example of Hindu military architecture, it is notable for the design of its four gateways – particularly the Hira, or Diamond Gate.

Dakor
Equidistant from Vadodara and Ahmedabad, the Temple of Ranchodrai in Dakor is sacred to Krishna and is a major centre for the Sharad Purnima festival in October or November.

Buses from Ahmedabad take 2½ hours and cost Rs 23.

BHARUCH (Broach)
Pop: 153,025
This very old town was mentioned in historical records nearly 2000 years ago. The **fort** overlooks the wide Narmada River from a hilltop and at its base is the **Jama Masjid**. On the riverbank, east of the city, is the **Temple of Bhrigu Rishi**, from which the city took its name, Bhrigukachba, later shortened to Bharuch.

SURAT
Pop: 1,674,000   Tel Area Code: 0261
Surat stands on the banks of the River Tapti and was once one of western India's major ports and trading towns. Parsis first settled in Surat in the 12th century; they had earlier been centred 100km south in Sanjan, where they had fled from Persia five centuries before. In 1573 Surat fell to Akbar after a prolonged siege. It then became an important Moghul trading port and also the point of departure for Mecca-bound Muslim pilgrims.

Surat soon became a wealthy city. In 1612, the British established a trading factory, followed by the Dutch in 1616 and the French in 1664.

Surat is no longer of any importance as a port, but it is a major industrial centre, especially for the manufacture of textiles and chemicals, and the processing and finishing of diamonds. The city is probably best known these days, however, as the site of an outbreak of pneumonic plague in 1994.

Despite its industrial importance Surat is of little interest to travellers, except those with a fascination for urban decay, mayhem, noise and pollution. If Ahmedabad is bad in this respect, Surat is horrific.

Orientation & Information
Surat is bordered on one side by the Tapti River and on the other by a brick wall. This wall was once an eight km long mud wall, but after the city was sacked in 1664 by the Mararha leader Shivaji, it was reconstructed in brick. The railway station, surrounded by

---

Sardar Sarovar Dam Project
The Narmada River has featured in the news both locally and internationally due to a large dam, the Sardar Sarovar, being constructed upstream of Bharuch near the village of Manibeli. This is part of a hugely extravagant US$6 billion project in the Narmada Valley to provide massive amounts of irrigation and electricity. The Sardar Sarovar dam is only a part of the entire project, which, if ever completed, will include 30 mega-dams, 135 medium dams and 3000 small dams.

The aim is laudable, but it's hard to see how the immediate disruption it causes will be effectively managed – the conservation lobby estimates that more than 100,000 people will need to be relocated as a result of the project, a further 200,000 will be affected by associated canal and dam works, and the homes of at least one million people will be submerged. Leading lobbyists have undertaken hunger strikes in protest at the dislocation of the inhabitants in the region, and to draw attention to the environmental problems it is envisaged the construction of this huge dam will cause. ■

many cheap hotels, is connected to the old fort beside the river by one of Surat's few wide roads.

Castle

Built in 1546, the castle is on the riverbank, beside the Tapti Bridge. Since most of it has been given over to offices it is no longer of great interest, but there is a good view over the city and river from its bastions. To get there, ask for the Tapti Bridge.

Cemeteries

The now very run-down, overgrown and neglected **English cemetery** is just beyond the Kataragama Gate, to the right of the main road. About 500m after the Kataragama Gate, you'll find the **Dutch cemetery**. There's a massive mausoleum of Baron Adriaan van Reede, who died in 1691. Adjoining the Dutch cemetery is the **Armenian cemetery**.

Other Attractions

Without a guide, you would have difficulty finding the remains of the **factories** and, in any case, there is little to indicate their former importance. They are near the IP Mission High School. The English factory is about midway between the castle and the Kataragama Gate, out of the old city.

Surat has a number of mosques and Jain, Hindu and Parsi temples. Nearby **Rander**, five km across the Hope Bridge, was built on the site of a very ancient Hindu city which had been taken by the Muslims in 1225. **Swally** (Suvali) was the old port for Surat, 19km to the west. It was off Swally, in 1615, that Portuguese colonial aspirations in India were ended by the British navy.

Places to Stay – bottom end

There are lots of hotels near the railway station but none stand out.

Rupali Guest House (☎ 423874) is in the rock-bottom bracket and is very basic. It has dorm beds for Rs 35, doubles with bathroom for Rs 130 and singles with common bathroom for Rs 70.

Simla Guest House (☎ 442339), on the street facing the station, is better but still

unremarkable. It has doubles with bath for Rs 200 and singles with common bath for Rs 90.

Sarvajanik Hotel (☎ 426159) is at the top end of this category, with singles/doubles with bath for Rs 170/270.

Places to Stay – middle

Hotel Central Excellency (☎ 425325; fax 441271) is a large hotel close to the railway station. It has rooms with private bath for Rs 400/550, with air-con for Rs 600/800. There's also a restaurant.

Hotel Yuvraj (☎ 413001), nearby, is another mid-range place with two vegetarian restaurants. All rooms have air-con and start at Rs 600/725. See a few rooms first, as some are better than others.

Embassy Hotel (☎ 443170; fax 443173), next door, has good rooms with bath from Rs 750/850.

Places to Stay – top end

Hotel Rama Regency (☎ 666565; fax 667294), near Bharti Park in Athwa Lines, five km from the central city area, is Surat's finest hotel. Air-con rooms with plenty of buttons and switches are Rs 2400/3400. Facilities include a swimming pool, health club, coffee shop and restaurant.

Places to Eat

Gaurav Restaurant, next to the Hotel Central Excellency, offers good south Indian dishes.

Hotel Rama Regency has a fine restaurant serving delicious (though pricey) Indian food. For something cheaper there's also a coffee shop in this hotel that serves a buffet dinner for Rs 180 plus tax.

Getting There & Away

Surat is on the main Mumbai to Ahmedabad railway line. The 263km trip to Mumbai takes between 4½ and 6½ hours and costs Rs 75/310, or Rs 95/310 for a sleeping berth. To Ahmedabad, the 229km trip takes from 3½ to 4½ hours and costs Rs 75/250.

AROUND SURAT

There are a number of beaches near Surat. Only 16km away, **Dumas** is a popular resort with locals. **Hajira** is 28km from the city and **Ubhrat** is 42km out, while **Tithal** is 108km away and only five km from Valsad on the Mumbai to Vadodara train line.

Twenty-nine km south of Surat, **Navsari** has been a headquarters for the Parsi community since the earliest days of their settlement in India. **Udvada**, only 10km north of Vapi, the station for Daman, has the oldest Parsi sacred fire in India. It is said that the fire was brought from Persia to Diu, on the opposite coast of the Gulf of Cambay, in 700 AD. **Sanjan**, in the extreme south of the state, is the small port where the Parsis first landed. A pillar marks the spot.

Places to Stay
Holiday Homes abound in this area. There's one at Hajira, with cottages for Rs 300 and double rooms for Rs 200. There's another place at Tithal (☎ (02632) 42731), where bungalows cost Rs 500 and single/double rooms are Rs 150/200.

DAMAN
Pop: 63,775 (Daman Town: 27,625)
Tel Area Code: 02636

Right in the south of Gujarat, the 56 sq km enclave of Daman was, along with Diu, taken from the Portuguese at the same time as Goa. For a time, Daman and Diu were governed from Goa but both now constitute the Union Territory of Daman & Diu, which is governed from Delhi. Daman is a laid back little town with a somewhat tropical flavour, although its beaches are rather drab and dirty.

Daman's main role now seems to be as a place to buy alcohol, since the surrounding state of Gujarat is completely 'dry'. The streets of Daman are lined with bars selling beer, 'Finest Scotch Whisky – Made in India' and various other spirits such as *feni* (distilled from fermented cashew nuts or coconuts). You are forbidden to take alcohol out of Daman into the dry state of Gujarat unless you obtain a permit. There are police checks as you leave Daman and alcohol without a permit will be confiscated.

The Portuguese seized Daman in 1531 and were officially ceded the region by Bahadur Shah, the last major Gujarati sultan, in 1559. There is still a lingering Portuguese flavour to the town, with its fine old forts and a number of churches, but it's definitely not a smaller version of Goa. The town is divided by the Daman Ganga River. The northern section is known as Nani Daman, or Little Daman, and contains the hotels, restaurants, bars and so on. In the southern part, known as Moti Daman, or Big Daman, government buildings and churches are enclosed within an imposing wall.

Information
The main post office is south of the river in Moti Daman, but there's a more convenient branch near the Hotel Sun n Sea in Nani Daman.

Churches
The **Se Cathedral** in the Moti Daman fort dates from the 17th century and is totally Iberian. It has recently been renovated and looks quite impressive. The **Church of Our Lady of the Rosary** has ancient Portuguese tombstones set into its cool, damp floor. The altar is a masterpiece of intricately carved, gold-painted wood. Light filters through the dusty windows, illuminating wooden panels painted with scenes of Christ and the apostles. The church is not always open; check with the vicar of the Se Cathedral for the key.

Other Attractions
You can walk around the ramparts of the **Nani Daman Fort** (Fort of St Jerome). They're a good place from which to watch the fish market and the activity of the small fishing fleet which anchors alongside.

Near the river on the Nani Daman side is an interesting **Jain temple**. If you inquire in the temple office, a caretaker should be able to show you around. The walls inside are completely covered with glassed-over 18th century murals depicting the life of Mahavira, who lived around 500 BC.

It's quite pleasant to wander around the wide streets of the old **Moti Daman**. The

GUJARAT

place has a very sleepy atmosphere, and the views across the river to Nani Daman from the ramparts near the lighthouse are not bad.

Places to Stay

Town Area Most of the cheaper hotels are on Seaface Rd. They are generally pretty basic and uninspiring.

Hotel Marina (☎ 34420), just off Seaface Rd, is one of the few surviving Portuguese-style houses. Rooms with bathroom cost Rs 150/175, or Rs 175/200 for deluxe rooms. There's a bar and restaurant downstairs.

Hotel Diamond (☎ 35135), near the taxi

stand, is a bit better. Decent rooms with bath cost Rs 200/250, and air-con rooms go for Rs 350. There's also a bar and restaurant.

Hotel Sovereign (☎ 35023; fax 34433), not far from the bus stand, is a friendly place which has rooms with private bath for Rs 175/225, or Rs 325/400 with air-con.

Hotel Gurukripa (☎ 35046), nearby, has OK, if somewhat musty, air-con rooms for Rs 375/425. There's a good restaurant here.

Devka Beach The best places to stay are at Devka Beach, a resort area about three km out of town (around Rs 20 for an auto-rickshaw).

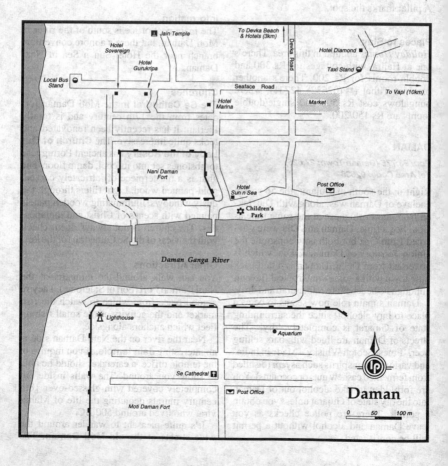

Daman

0   50   100 m

The beach is nothing great, but the ambience is serene and easy-going. Most of the hotels are all along one road.

Sandy Resort (☎ 34644) is one of the best options here. It's a friendly place which boasts a pool, restaurant and disco. Comfortable rooms start from Rs 550, all with air-con.

Hotel Miramar (☎ 34471; fax 34934) nearby is right on the beach but the staff seem a little indifferent. The rooms (all with air-con) start from Rs 650/750, while a sea-facing cottage costs Rs 1500. There's also a restaurant and disco.

Dariya Darshan Hotel (☎ 34476; fax 34286) is nearby and similarly priced.

Hotel Ashoka Palace (☎ 34239) is a cheaper option. It offers doubles with bath for Rs 350, Rs 500 with air-con.

Hotel Shilton (☎ 34558) next door is similarly priced. You should be able to bargain these last two hotels down by around 20% if they're not full.

Places to Eat

The best eating places are in the hotels.

Hotel Gurukripa has a popular air-con restaurant which offers veg and non-veg fare. The food is tasty, and most dishes cost around Rs 45.

A Kingfisher will set you back Rs 25 at any of Daman's numerous bars, but most hotels charge more (around Rs 32). If you fancy a drop of port wine, most bars charge about Rs 100 for a bottle.

In February, Daman is noted for *papri*, boiled and salted sweet peas served wrapped in newspaper. Crab and lobster are in season in October. *Tari* palm wine is a popular drink sold in earthenware pots.

Getting There & Away

Vapi station, on the main railway line, is the access point for Daman. Vapi is about 170km from Mumbai and 90km from Surat. The road from Daman to Surat would have to be one of the most congested in India so expect delays. It's the major route for trucks travelling between Mumbai and Ahmedabad.

It's about 10km from Vapi to Daman. Plenty of share taxis (Rs 10 per person) wait outside the railway station and leave frequently for Daman. The trip takes about 20 minutes. Also available are some ramshackle buses (Rs 2).

SAPUTARA

This cool hill resort in the south-east corner of the state is at an altitude of 1000m. It's a popular base for excursions to **Mahal Bardipara Forest Wildlife Sanctuary**, 60km away or the **Gira Waterfalls** (52km). Saputara means Abode of Serpents and there is a sacred snake image on the banks of the River Sarpagana.

Toran Hill Resort (☎ (02631) 37226) offers dorm beds for Rs 30, ordinary rooms for Rs 250, valley-view rooms for Rs 300, and mountain-view rooms for Rs 1500.

Saurashtra

The often bleak plains of Saurashtra on the Kathiawar peninsula are inhabited by friendly but reserved people. Those in the country are distinctively dressed – the men wear white turbans, pleated jackets (short-waisted and long-sleeved) and jodhpurs (baggy seat and drainpipe legs) and often sport golden stud earrings. The women are nearly as colourful as the women of Rajasthan and wear embroidered backless cholis, which are known by various names but most commonly as *kanjeri*.

The peninsula took its name from the Kathi tribespeople who used to roam the area at night stealing whatever was not locked into the many village forts, or *kots*. Around Kathiawar, you may notice long lines of memorial stones known as *palias* – men are usually depicted riding on large horses while women ride on wheels, showing that they were in carriages.

Although somewhat off the main tourist routes, Saurashtra is a pleasant area to travel around with very interesting – sometimes spectacular – temple sites and cities to explore, not to mention some beautiful beaches and the Sasan Gir Lion Sanctuary.

BHAVNAGAR
Pop: 448,800   Tel Area Code: 0278

Founded as a port in 1743, Bhavnagar is still an important trading post for the cotton goods manufactured in Gujarat. The Bhavnagar lock gate keeps ships afloat in the city's port at low tide. On the surface, Bhavnagar isn't the most exciting place to visit and few travellers get here. It does, however, have an interesting old bazaar area with overhanging wooden balconies, countless little shops, lots of local colour and not a tourist in sight.

Orientation & Information

Bhavnagar is a sprawling city with distinctly separate old and new sections. The bus stand is in the new part of town and the railway station is at the far end of the old town around 2.5km away. To complicate matters, private bus companies usually have their own depots; sometimes a long way from the bus stand.

There are no cheap hotels around the bus stand so if you're on a budget, take an auto-rickshaw into the old town. Even there, the choice is very limited.

Takhteshwar Temple

This temple sits on the highest hillock in Bhavnagar. The views over the city and out into the Gulf of Cambay are excellent but the temple itself is of minor interest.

Places to Stay – bottom end

The only cheap hotels in Bhavnagar are in the old bazaar area and there's very little choice. Note that many places add a 10% service tax on their room rates.

Shital Guest House (☎ 28360), Amba Chowk, Mali Tekra, right in the middle of the bazaar area, is not a bad choice. Simple singles/doubles with common bathroom cost Rs 40/80, doubles with bathroom cost Rs 100. Ask for a room with a balcony; the other rooms are gloomy.

Vrindavan Hotel (☎ 27391), not far from the Shital, is well signposted but the entrance

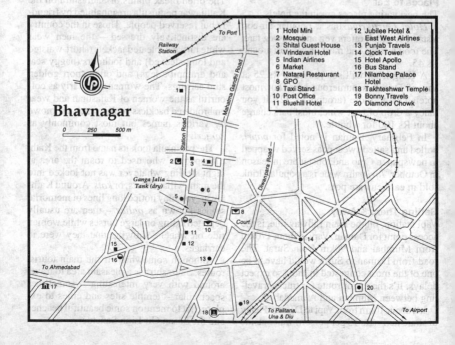

Bhavnagar

0   250   500 m

Ganga Jalia Tank (dry)

1 Hotel Mini	12 Jubilee Hotel &
2 Mosque	East West Airlines
3 Shital Guest House	13 Punjab Travels
4 Vrindavan Hotel	14 Clock Tower
5 Indian Airlines	15 Hotel Apollo
6 Market	16 Bus Stand
7 Nataraj Restaurant	17 Nilambag Palace
8 GPO	Hotel
9 Taxi Stand	18 Takhteshwar Temple
10 Post Office	19 Bonny Travels
11 Bluehill Hotel	20 Diamond Chowk

Railway Station

To Port

To Ahmedabad

Mahatma Gandhi Road

Station Road

Dwanpara Road

Court

To Palitana, Una & Diu

To Airport

can still be quite difficult to find. Entry is through an archway and across a courtyard; the steps leading to the reception area are directly opposite the archway. This large, old place has basic but clean singles/doubles with bathroom for Rs 100/150, or there are cheap dorm beds (Rs 35).

Hotel Mini (☎ 24415) on Station Rd, near the railway station, is one of the best budget hotels. It's clean and quiet and has singles/doubles from Rs 100/150 with attached bath. The staff are friendly and there's a dining hall.

Places to Stay – middle

Hotel Apollo (☎ 25249), directly opposite the bus stand, has fairly good rooms for Rs 320/430, or with air-con for Rs 450/600. There are money-changing facilities and the hotel has a non-veg restaurant.

Bluehill Hotel (☎ 26951), a little down the road from the taxi stand, is very well appointed, and has rooms with air-con from Rs 610/850. There are two veg restaurants.

Jubilee Hotel (☎ 20045) next door offers similar facilities, and rooms start at Rs 450/650, all with air-con.

Nilambag Palace Hotel (☎ 424241; fax 428072), west of the bus stand on the Ahmedabad road, is the most interesting place to stay – if you can afford it. This is a rambling former maharaja's palace and although it's not as swish as some other palace-hotels, it's still pleasant enough. Rooms cost Rs 1190/2390. There's also a swimming pool and restaurant.

Places to Eat

The best places to eat are in the hotels.

Hotel Apollo, Bluehill and *Jubilee Hotels* are all pretty reasonably priced and the food is satisfying.

Nilambag Palace Hotel is a more up-market choice, although the interior and service at the restaurant are pretty average. It's open to non-guests, and is reasonably priced considering it's a palace. Their Indian food is best; chicken Mughlai costs Rs 71.

Getting There & Away

Air The Indian Airlines office (☎ 26503) is north of the taxi stand, near the Ganga Jalia Tank. There are four flights a week to Mumbai (US$55). NEPC Airlines (☎ 411191) flies three times a week to Mumbai (US$60).

Bus State transport buses connect Bhavnagar with Ahmedabad and other centres in the region. For Una (and Diu) there are departures almost every hour from 5.30 am. The trip takes five hours and costs Rs 50. To Palitana there are departures every hour from 5 am for the 1½ hour journey (Rs 12). The timetable at the state bus stand in Bhavnagar is entirely in Gujarati.

The main private bus company is Punjab Travels (☎ 24582), opposite the Galaxy Cinema near the municipal office. It has buses to Ahmedabad every 30 minutes (Rs 55). Bonny Travels (☎ 29178) has departures for Ahmedabad (Rs 55). They also have a bus to Diu (six hours, Rs 55). The office is in the Madhav Darshan Complex, a huge aqua-coloured architectural nightmare near the Takhteshwar Temple. Bonny's sign is in Hindi.

Train Bhavnagar is 299km by rail from Ahmedabad. The trip takes about 5½ hours and costs Rs 70/260 in 2nd/1st class. There's one direct train daily, departing Bhavnagar at 5.30 am. To Palitana there are several daily trains which cover the 51km in about two hours (Rs 9).

Getting Around

An auto-rickshaw to the airport costs around Rs 60.

AROUND BHAVNAGAR
Valabhipur

About 42km north-west of Bhavnagar, this ancient city was once the capital of this part of India. Extensive ruins have been located and archaeological finds are exhibited in a museum, but there's little to see apart from scattered stones.

GUJARAT

Velavadar National Park

This park, located 65km north of Bhavnagar, is well known for its blackbucks. Blackbucks sport impressive horns which can be as long as 60cm in mature males. The best time to visit this park is from October to June.

PALITANA

Pop: 46,830   Tel Area Code: 02848

Situated 51km south-west of Bhavnagar, the town of Palitana is little more than a gateway to **Shatrunjaya**, the Place of Victory (see the regional highlight on p692).

Places to Stay

Palitana has scores of dharamsalas (pilgrims' rest houses) but unless you're a Jain, you're unlikely to be allowed to stay at any of them.

Hotel Sumeru (☎ 2327) on Station Rd is the best choice. It's a Gujarat Tourism enterprise which has rooms for Rs 280/335, or Rs 425/455 with air-con. Dorm beds are Rs 30, and there's a vegetarian restaurant.

Hotel Shravak (☎ 2428) opposite the bus stand, has basic singles/doubles/triples with bathroom for Rs 100/200/300 (free bucket hot water). There's also a dorm (men only) for Rs 25.

Places to Eat

Hotel Sumeru has a reasonably good restaurant with Gujarati thalis (Rs 38) as well as Punjabi and Continental dishes.

Jaruti Restaurant, beside the Shravak, is a wildly busy 24 hour snack place offering puris, sabzi, curd, roasted peppers and ganthia (varieties of fried dough).

Havmor is a popular ice cream parlour on the right as you approach the base of Shatrunjaya.

Getting There & Away

Bus If you're coming from the north, plenty of STC buses make the 1½ hour trip from Bhavnagar. The fare is Rs 10, or Rs 14 for the 'express' service. There are regular departures for Ahmedabad (five hours, Rs 55).

There is a direct bus to Una for Diu at 1 pm (five hours, Rs 40), or via Mahuva at 7 am (five hours, Rs 30). Whether you travel direct or via Mahuva, this is a trip from hell, along bumpy village roads in dilapidated old rattletraps.

Train Express trains make the trip from Ahmedabad in nine to 11 hours with a change at Sihor shortly before Palitana. There's a passenger service from Palitana (Rs 40) or an overnight express service (Rs 80/260 in 2nd/1st class). Local trains between Bhavnagar and Palitana take about 1½ hours (Rs 9).

DIU

Pop: 39,500 (Diu Town: 22,900)
Tel Area Code: 028758

This laid-back beach town was the first landing point for the Parsis when they fled from Persia, although they stayed only three years. Like Daman and Goa, Diu was a Portuguese colony until it was taken over by India in 1961. Along with Daman, it is still governed from Delhi as a Union Territory rather than as part of Gujarat. The former colony includes the island of Diu itself, about 13km long by three km wide, separated from the coast by a narrow channel. There are also two tiny mainland enclaves. One of these, on which the village of Ghoghla stands, is the entry point to Diu if you arrive through the town of Una.

Diu's crowning glory is the huge fort, a sight which justifies the long trip here. The northern side of the island, facing Gujarat, is tidal marsh and saltpans while the southern coast alternates between limestone cliffs, rocky coves and sandy beaches.

The somewhat windswept and arid island is riddled with quarries from which the Portuguese removed vast quantities of limestone to construct their fort, city walls, monuments and buildings.

The rocky and sandy interior reaches a maximum height of just 29m, so agriculture is limited although there are extensive stands of coconut and other palms. Branching palms (*Hyphaene* species) are very much a feature of the island and were originally introduced from Africa by the Portuguese.

Diu is a popular hangout with travellers and you'll probably see more foreigners here than anywhere else in Gujarat. Although the beaches are nothing compared to those of Goa, this is still a great place to let your hair down, sit back with a cold beer and watch the world drift by.

History
These days, it's hard to understand why the Portuguese should have been interested in holding such an apparently unimportant and isolated outpost, but between the 14th and 16th centuries, Diu was an important trading post and naval base from which the Ottoman Turks controlled the shipping routes in the northern part of the Arabian Sea.

Following an unsuccessful attempt to capture the island in 1531, during which Bahadur Shah, the Sultan of Gujarat, was assisted by the Turkish navy, the Portuguese finally secured control in 1535 by taking advantage of a quarrel between the sultan and the Moghul emperor, Humayun. Humayun had defeated Bahadur Shah the previous year and had forced him into exile in Malwa, but while he was distracted by clashes with the Afghan Sher Khan, Bahadur was able to return.

With pressure still being exerted by both the Portuguese and the Moghuls, Bahadur concluded a peace treaty with the Portuguese, effectively giving them control over the port at Diu. The treaty was soon cast to

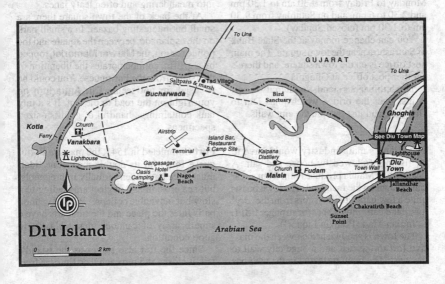

To Una

GUJARAT

To Una

Saltpans & marsh • Tad Village

Bucharwada

Bird Sanctuary

Ghoghla

Kotla

Ferry

Church

Vanakbara

Lighthouse

Airstrip

Terminal

Island Bar, Restaurant & Camp Site

Kalpana Distillery

Church

Malala

Fudam

See Diu Town Map

Lighthouse

Diu Town

Town Wall

Gangasagar

Oasis Camping Site

Hotel

Nagoa Beach

Jallandhar Beach

Chakratirth Beach

Sunset Point

Diu Island

Arabian Sea

0   1   2 km

the wind and, although both Bahadur Shah and his successor, Sultan Mahmud III, attempted to contest the issue, the peace treaty which was eventually signed in 1539 ceded the island of Diu and the mainland enclave of Ghoghla to the Portuguese. Soon after the signing of this treaty, the Portuguese began constructing their fort.

The Indian government appears to have an official policy of playing down the Portuguese era. Seven Rajput soldiers (six of them Singhs) and a few civilians were killed in Operation Vijay, which ended Portuguese rule. After the Indian Air Force unnecessarily bombed the airstrip and terminal, near Nagoa, it remained derelict until the late 1980s. The old church in Diu Fort was also bombed and is now a roofless ruin. It's said that the Portuguese blew up Government House to stop it falling into 'enemy' hands.

Information

The tourist office (☎ 2653) is on Bunder Rd, the main road which runs through Diu Town parallel to the waterfront. It's in the building on the waterfront, directly opposite the customs office. You can pick up a map of Diu Town here for Rs 10. The office is open from Monday to Friday from 9.30 am to 1.30 pm and 2.30 to 6 pm, and on Saturday from 9.30 am to 1.30 pm (closed Sunday).

You can change money at the State Bank of Saurashtra near the town square. The main post office is on the town square, and there's another post office at Ghoghla.

The Jethibai bus stand, for intercity buses, is just over the bridge which joins Diu to Ghoghla, and just outside the city walls.

Diu Town

The island's main industry would have to be fishing, followed by booze and salt. A distillery at Malala produces rum from sugar cane grown on the mainland. The town boasts quite a few bars where visitors from the 'dry' mainland can enjoy a beer (or stronger IMFL – 'Indian Made Foreign Liquor').

The town is sandwiched between the massive fort to the east and a huge city wall to the west. The main **gateway** in the wall has

carvings of lions, angels and a priest, while just inside the gate is a miniature chapel with an icon, dating from 1702.

Diu Town has three churches, although only one is fulfilling its original function. (It's said that there are now only about 15 Christian families left on the whole island.)

Access to **St Paul's** is through the adjacent school ground. This wonderful old church is suffering serious neglect, with beautiful old paintings slowly disintegrating, but it is still a peaceful place.

Nearby is St Thomas' Church, which houses the **Diu Museum**. There's an interesting collection of Catholic statues, including a somewhat disturbing statue of Christ prostrate on a bier, flanked by two angels. If you thought the Hindu pantheon was confusing, take a look at the bewildering collection of Christian saints. The third church is **St Francis of Assisi**, which has been converted into a hospital.

Unlike Daman, the buildings in Diu show a significant Portuguese influence. The town is a maze of narrow, winding streets and many of the houses are well ornamented and brightly painted. Further away from this tightly packed residential quarter, the streets turn into meandering and often leafy lanes.

At the back of the town square there's a small but interesting bazaar. In a small park on the esplanade, between the square and the police station, the **Marwar Memorial**, topped by a griffin, commemorates the liberation of the island from the Portuguese. You could be excused for not seeing **Diu Aquarium** on your right on the road to the fort. It's a tiny tank containing a handful of goldfish-sized specimens.

Fort Completed in 1541, the massive Portuguese fort with its double moat (one tidal) must once have been virtually impregnable, but sea erosion and neglect are leading to a slow but inevitable collapse. Piles of cannon balls litter the place and the ramparts have a superb array of cannons, many old yet in good condition.

Since the fort also serves as the island's jail, it closes at 5 pm each day. Entry is free.

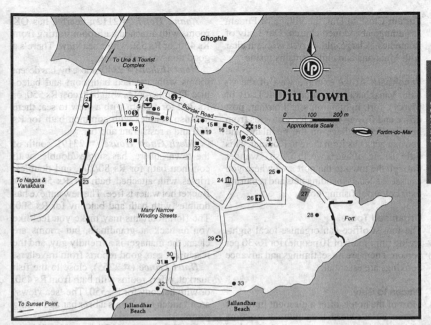

Diu Town

PLACES TO STAY
11 Hotel Prince
13 Nilesh Guest House
15 Hotel Alishan & Apana Hotel
16 Hotel Sanman
19 Hotel Mozambique
22 Hotel Samrat
31 Tourist Cottages

PLACES TO EAT
30 Jay Shankar Restaurant & Guest House

OTHER
1 Petrol Pump
2 Jethibai Bus Stand
3 Local Bus Stand
4 Oceanic Travels
5 Post Office
6 Town Square
7 Tourist Office
8 Chandani Bike Hire
9 Bazaar
10 State Bank of Saurashtra
12 Fish Market
14 Vegetable Market
17 Manisha Electronics (Moped Hire)
18 Public Gardens
20 Collectorate
21 Police
23 Jampa Gate
24 Diu Museum (St Thomas' Church)
25 Diu Aquarium
26 St Paul's Church
27 School
28 Deer Park
29 St Francis of Assisi
32 Summer House
33 Circuit House

Signs prohibit photography but no-one seems to observe this rule.

Around the Island
Beaches Temple and fort-satiated travellers used to head to **Nagoa** to catch up on some serious relaxation, and it's still a pleasant palm-fringed beach, largely deserted and safe for swimming. However, since the construction of a new road which stretches from the south of Diu Town's wall, joining up with the old Fudam Rd after about two km, access has now been provided to Diu's previously un-visited beaches in the south-east of the island. These include, from east to west, **Jallandhar**, **Chakratirth** and stunning **Sunset Point**.

GUJARAT

Fudam Close to Diu, the village of Fudam has a huge abandoned church, Our Lady of Remedies. A large, old, carved wooden altar with Madonna and child remains inside.

Vanakbara At the extreme west of the island, Vanakbara has a church (Our Lady of Mercy), fort, lighthouse, small bazaar, post office and fishing fleet. A ferry crosses from here to Kotla village on the mainland and you can get a bus from there to Kodinar. This little fishing village is worth a visit – wander through the town to the port area where you can see the locals mending nets and repairing their colourful fishing boats.

Organised Tours
The tourist office can organise local sightseeing (minimum of 10 people) for Rs 30 per person. There are no set timings and advance bookings are essential.

Places to Stay
Most of the hotels offer a discount in the off season, but it's worth bargaining at any time of the year, as many places will slash prices if they are not full. Prices below are for the peak season, which runs roughly from October to June.

Diu Town An old Portuguese-style house, *Hotel Mozambique* (☎ 2223) faces the vegetable market and is popular with budget travellers. Doubles/triples with common bathroom cost Rs 120/150, or Rs 150/200 with bath. All rooms have access to balconies with great views out over the channel between Diu Town and Ghoghla, and free bucket hot water is available.

Hotel Sanman (☎ 2342; fax 22844), an old Portuguese villa on Bunder Rd, halfway between the town square and the fort, is a popular little place and is often booked out. In previous incarnations it has been known as the Baron's Inn, the totally misleading Fun Club, and Pensão BeiraMar! Large, basic rooms (cold water only) with bathroom and good sea views cost Rs 75/200. The staff are friendly, and there's an atmospheric rooftop restaurant and bar.

Apana Hotel (☎ 2112), nearby, has OK rooms with attached bathroom starting from Rs 450, or Rs 550 with a sea view. There's a good non-veg restaurant.

Hotel Alishan (☎ 2340), close by, has decent rooms with attached bathroom and balconies. Double rooms with bath cost Rs 550, or Rs 700 for a room with a view to sea; there are also doubles with common bath for Rs 350 and a restaurant and bar.

Nilesh Guest House (☎ 2319), south of the town square, has singles/doubles with common bath for Rs 80/200, and doubles/triples with attached bath for Rs 500/600. Bucket hot water is free. The new annexe has doubles with bath and balcony for Rs 500. The floral curtains may make you feel like you're back at grandma's, but rooms are clean, the manager is a friendly guy, and the restaurant gets good reports from travellers.

Hotel Prince (☎ 2265), close to the fish market, offers rooms with bath from Rs 450, or with balcony for Rs 550. The 'sea views' aren't much but there's a beer bar and dining room.

Hotel Samrat (☎ 2354), a couple of blocks back from the town square, has rooms from Rs 250 (Rs 550 with air-con), and there are four-bed rooms for Rs 300. Rooms are well appointed, all with balconies, and room service is available. There's a good restaurant and bar and if the kitchen is not busy, the chef will cook fish bought by guests at the fish market for about Rs 50.

Jallandhar Beach Just out of Diu Town, *Tourist Cottages* (☎ 2654), are in a good location opposite Jallandhar Beach and about one km from the fort. Cottages with double or twin beds cost Rs 450. There are also four-person rooms (the second double bed is in a loft) for Rs 550. Many rooms have sea views, and there's a good restaurant and bar (non-guests welcome). If you don't mind being a little out of town, this is a very laid-back place, and is the closest accommodation to Sunset Point.

Jay Shankar Guest House (☎ 2424), nearby, has double rooms with attached bath for Rs 200. This small and homely guest house is at the same location as the Jay Shankar restaurant (see Places to Eat).

Nagoa Beach As it is forbidden to rent local cottages or freelance camp, accommodation is limited and the following are currently the only available options:

Oasis Camping Site, next to the Ganga Sagar Guest House, has tents for Rs 250 with light and fan. The site is only established between October and late June. Inquire at the tourist office (☎ 2653) in Diu Town.

Island Bar & Restaurant (no phone), on the Diu Town to Nagoa Beach road, has tents with light and fan for Rs 250 per tent from October to December, but the restaurant is open all year.

Ganga Sagar Guest House (☎ 2249) is the only hotel at Nagoa Beach, but some travellers say it's not a very friendly place to stay. Small rooms cost Rs 150/300 with bath. Meals are at set times, and if you are hungry outside these times, bad luck!

Ghoghla The *Tourist Complex* (☎ 2212) is in the village of Ghoghla on the mainland part of Diu. This is the first building in Diu after you come through the barrier which marks the border with Gujarat. Although relatively new, this place is already looking a little shabby. Air-con doubles cost Rs 450. There's a pleasant restaurant and bar, looking out over the sea.

Places to Eat

Beer and drinks are blissfully cheap in Diu – Rs 20 for a Kingfisher, although hotels usually charge a little more.

Hotel Sanman has a relaxing rooftop restaurant that's a popular hangout with travellers, especially in the evening. It has great sea views and is a wonderful place to sit back and chat over a drink. There's reasonably priced Indian and Chinese food; prawns masala costs Rs 40. The food is nothing to write home about, but the atmosphere is terrific.

Jay Shankar Restaurant, a little cafe on Jallandhar Beach, is run by the very friendly Motichand family. They manage to prepare

scrumptious (and cheap) dishes in their tiny kitchen. No alcohol is available.

Hotel Samrat and *Nilesh Guest House* also have good restaurants.

Hotel Mozambique has a bar with private drinking booths where shady deals can be sealed over a bottle of IMFL.

Food at Nagoa Beach is a problem; basically you need to bring it with you – there are no cafes at the beach.

Ganga Sagar Guest House might rustle up an omelette or toast at their bar if you're lucky.

Manali is a snack bar at Sunset Point which offers drinks and snacks only during the tourist season.

A restaurant on tiny Fortim-do-Mar, the little fortified island just to the north of the main town fort, was planned at the time of writing.

Getting There & Away

Air Gujarat Airways has a daily flight to Mumbai (US$80). The Gujarat Airways agent is Oceanic Travels (☎ 2180), located on the town square near the post office.

Bus Una is the access point for Diu, and there are direct buses to there from Bhavnagar, Palitana, Veraval and Talaja. Once in Una, you have to get yourself the 10 or so km to Ghoghla and Diu. Buses depart every 30 minutes from Una bus stand between 6.30 am and 8.15 pm (Rs 6). From Una, if you don't want to wait for a bus, walk the one km from the bus stand to Tower Chowk (ask directions), from where crowded share rickshaws take you to Ghoghla (Rs 5), and another share rickshaw on to Diu (Rs 3). An auto-rickshaw from Una costs about Rs 50.

There are a number of Gujarat STC buses which run all the way to Diu from places such as Veraval and Bhavnagar.

A quicker and more comfortable option to the STC buses are the private minibuses. At 7 pm, a bus leaves for Ahmedabad (10½ hours, Rs 90). There are regular departures between 6 am and 8 pm to Veraval (2½ hours, Rs 25), Junagadh (four hours, Rs 40), Rajkot (seven hours, Rs 60), and Porbandar (five hours Rs 55). There's a bus to Mumbai at 10 am (22 hours, Rs 200). Bookings for all buses should be made preferably 24 hours in advance.

Train Delwada, between Una and Ghoghla and only about eight km from Diu, is the nearest railhead. A share auto-rickshaw from there to Ghoghla costs about Rs 5. There's a direct train at 6 am from Delwada to Veraval (96km, Rs 27/114). There is also a daily service to Junagadh (164km, Rs 43/159) via Sasan Gir.

Getting Around
Auto-rickshaw drivers will demand Rs 50 to Una, but you may be able to bargain this down. To travel anywhere within the town of Diu itself should cost Rs 7. To Nagoa Beach, expect to pay Rs 35, and to Sunset Point, Rs 25. Share rickshaws to Ghoghla cost Rs 3 per person.

Cycling is a good way to get around Diu Town, although it can be a long, hot haul out to Nagoa or further afield to Vanakbara. Chandani Bike Hire at the back of the town square has bikes for Rs 20 per day. For more mobility with less effort, Manisha Electronics, next to the Hotel Sanman, rents out mopeds for Rs 120 per day plus fuel, or Rs 630 per week (discounted in the off season). Some of these old rattletraps have been known to break down, stranding riders in far-flung corners of the island – check the bike over carefully before heading off. You can also rent bicycles here.

Local buses from Diu Town to Nagoa Beach and Vanakbara leave from the bus stand opposite the petrol pump on Bunder Rd at 7 and 11 am, and 4 pm. From Nagoa, they depart for Diu Town from near the police post at 1, 5.30 and 7 pm (Rs 3).

VERAVAL
Pop: 107,835   Tel Area Code: 02876
On the south coast of Saurashtra is Veraval, which was the major seaport for Mecca pilgrims before the rise of Surat. It still has some importance as one of India's major

fishing ports (more than 1000 boats work from here), and as the base for a visit to Somnath Temple, five km south of the town.

Wooden dhows of all sizes, from fishing dinghies right up to ocean-going vessels, are still built totally by hand. The largest dhows still make the journey from here to Dubai and other Middle Eastern destinations, and you may see some of them loading or discharging cargo.

It's well worth a wander around the **port**, although photography is supposedly prohibited. If you're on a bicycle heading for Somnath, you can take a shortcut right through the port area. Apart from the port, there's not a lot to see in Veraval, despite its size.

Information
At the time of writing, no bank here would change travellers cheques. The State Bank of India near the railway station does change cash, however.

Places to Stay
Hotel Satkar (☎ 20120), close to the bus stand, is one of the best places to stay. Rooms are from Rs 100/150, or Rs 300/400 with air-con. All rooms have attached bathroom with hot water (mornings only), and the staff are quite obliging. Checkout is noon.

Hotel Kasturi (☎ 20248), nearby, has spacious rooms with private bath from Rs 80/150. There's hot and cold water in the attached bathrooms, and checkout is 10 am.

Toran Tourist Bungalow (☎ 20488), not far from the lighthouse, is a huge old place in a rather inconvenient location. It looks derelict, and has an atmosphere similar to the Addams Family home. Dusty rooms cost Rs 150/200 with ceiling fan. This place is somewhat redeemed by the views from some rooms of the nearby old nawab's palace (now a college).

Retiring Rooms at the railway station offer dorm beds for Rs 30; singles/doubles for Rs 60/70.

Chandrani Guest House (☎ 20356), near the railway station, has very basic doubles with bathroom for Rs 60.

GUJARAT

Places to Eat

Sagar Restaurant, which is about five minutes' walk from the bus stand towards the clock tower, is a pleasant air-con vegetarian restaurant.

Foodland Fast Food Restaurant, diagonally opposite, serves excellent bottomless Gujarati thalis for Rs 30. The service is super fast and the food is great.

Getting There & Away

Bus Daily buses run from the bus stand to Diu, Kodinar, Porbandar, Junagadh, Rajkot and Bhavnagar. There are regular departures for Sasan Gir (1½ hours, Rs 12). Neelam Travels (☎ 21602), opposite the bus stand, is the agent for the private bus companies.

There are half-hourly departures from the bus stand for Junagadh from 6.30 am daily (two hours, Rs 20); to Porbandar every half hour from 7 am (three hours Rs 35); to Diu every half hour from 8.30 am (2½ hours, Rs 25) and regular departures for Rajkot (five hours, Rs 43).

Train It's 431km from Ahmedabad to Veraval. Fares for the 11½-hour trip are Rs 118/352 in 2nd/1st class. There are also trains for

Sasan Gir at 8.45 am and 2 pm (two hours, Rs 9), and a daily passenger service to Delwada (for Diu) at 8.45 am with a change at Talala, arriving at 12.45 pm, or a direct train at 3.30 pm, arriving at 7.35 pm (Rs 33/114 in 2nd/1st class).

There is a daily train at 11.20 am to Rajkot, arriving at 4.30 pm (186km, Rs 48/178 in 2nd/1st class).

Getting Around

Bicycles can be hired opposite the bus stand, near Neelam Travels, for Rs 3 per hour, or Rs 20 per day.

An auto-rickshaw to Somnath, five km away, costs about Rs 25. There are local buses to Somnath for Rs 3.50. The local bus stand is near the long-distance STC stand.

SOMNATH
Temple of Somnath

This temple, at Somnath near Veraval and about 80km from Junagadh, has an extremely chequered past. Its earliest history fades into legend – it is said to have originally been built out of gold by Somraj, the moon god, only to be rebuilt by Rawana in silver, then by Krishna in wood and Bhimdev in stone.

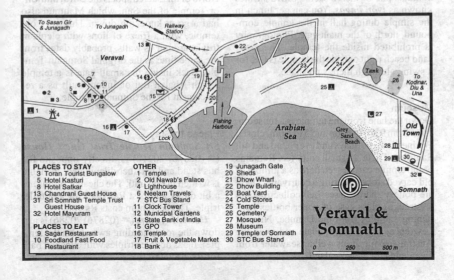

PLACES TO STAY
3 Toran Tourist Bungalow
5 Hotel Kasturi
8 Hotel Satkar
13 Chandrani Guest House
31 Sri Somnath Temple Trust Guest House
32 Hotel Mayuram

PLACES TO EAT
9 Sagar Restaurant
10 Foodland Fast Food Restaurant

OTHER
1 Temple
2 Old Nawab's Palace
4 Lighthouse
6 Neelam Travels
7 STC Bus Stand
11 Clock Tower
12 Municipal Gardens
14 State Bank of India
15 GPO
16 Temple
17 Fruit & Vegetable Market
18 Bank
19 Junagadh Gate
20 Sheds
21 Dhow Wharf
22 Dhow Building
23 Boat Yard
24 Cold Stores
25 Temple
26 Cemetery
27 Mosque
28 Museum
29 Temple of Somnath
30 STC Bus Stand

Veraval & Somnath

0   250   500 m

A description of the temple by Al Biruni, an Arab traveller, was so glowing that it prompted a visit in 1024 by a most unwelcome tourist – Mahmud of Ghazni. At that time, the temple was so wealthy that it had 300 musicians, 500 dancing girls and even 300 barbers just to shave the heads of visiting pilgrims.

Mahmud of Ghazni, whose raids on the riches of India are legendary, descended on Somnath from his Afghan kingdom and, after a two-day battle, took the town and the temple. Having looted its fabulous wealth, he destroyed it for good measure. So began a pattern of Muslim destruction and Hindu rebuilding which continued for centuries. The temple was again razed in 1297, 1394 and finally in 1706 by Aurangzeb, the notorious Moghul fundamentalist.

After the 1706 demolition, the temple was not rebuilt until 1950. Outside, opposite the entrance, is quite a large statue of SV Patel (1875-1950), who was responsible for the reconstruction. Inside there are fine views from the 2nd floor, as well as a photo collection (with English commentary) on the excavation and restoration of the seven temples.

The current temple was built to traditional patterns on the original site by the sea. It contains one of the 12 sacred Shiva shrines known as *jyoti lingas*. You can get lunch in the simple dining hall in the temple compound, north of the main gate. Photography is prohibited inside the temple. The greysand beach right outside the temple is OK for a swim, although there's no shade.

Museum

Down the lane from the temple is a museum, open from 9 am to noon and 3 to 6 pm, closed Wednesdays, holidays and every 2nd and 4th Saturday. There's a small entry fee. Remains of the temple can be seen here as a jumble of old carved stones littering a courtyard. There are pottery shards, a seashell collection and a (strange) glass case of water bottles containing samples from the Danube, Nile, St Lawrence, Tigris, River Plate and even the Australian Murray, as well as seawater from Tasmania and New Zealand.

Other Sites

The town of Somnath is entered from Veraval by the **Junagadh Gate**. This very ancient triple gate was the one which Mahmud finally broke through to take the town. Close to the second gate is an old **mosque** dating from Mahmud's time. The **Jama Masjid**, reached through the town's busy **bazaar**, was constructed using parts of a Hindu temple and has interesting bo tree carvings at all four corners. It is now a museum with a collection from many of these temples.

About a km before the Junagadh Gate, coming from Veraval, the finely carved **Mai Puri** was once a Temple of the Sun. This Hindu temple was converted into a mosque during Mahmud's time and is surrounded by thousands of tombs and palias (memorial stones). Two old tombs are close by and, on the shore, the **Bhidiyo Pagoda** probably dates from the 14th century.

To the east of the town is the **Bhalka Tirth** where Krishna was mistaken for a deer and wounded by an arrow while sleeping in a deerskin. The legendary spot is at the confluence of three rivers. You get to it through the small *sangam* (confluence gate), which is simply known as the Nana, or Small Gate. North of this sacred spot is the **Suraj Mandir**, or Temple of the Sun, which Mahmud also had a go at knocking down. This very old temple, with a frieze of lions with elephant trunks around its walls, probably dates from the same time as the original Somnath Temple. Back inside the small gate is a temple which Ahalya Bai of Indore built as a replacement for the Somnath Temple.

Places to Stay

Sri Somnath Temple Trust Guest House (☎ (02876) 20212) is directly opposite the bus stand and is rather dilapidated; its name is written in Gujarati. The cheaper rooms are a bit dingy and cost Rs 60/90 for a double/triple. The best room costs Rs 300.

Hotel Mayuram (☎ (02876) 20286) is just down the road (heading away from the temple). It has doubles/triples with attached bath for Rs 200/300.

GUJARAT

CHORWAD

Palace Beach Resort (☎ (02876) 88557), the summer palace of the Junagadh nawabs, is situated at the popular beach resort of Chorwad, 20km from Veraval (70km from Junagadh). It has been converted by the Gujarat State Tourism Department into a hotel surrounded by well-tended gardens, overlooking the sea. Doubles in the detached cottages cost Rs 375, and there are also other rooms from Rs 200 to Rs 500. Meals need to be ordered in advance.

SASAN GIR LION SANCTUARY

The last home of the Asiatic lion *(Panthera leo lersica)* is 59km from Junagadh via Visavadar. The sanctuary, which covers 1400 sq km, was set up to protect the lion and its habitat, and in this respect has been a success: since 1980 numbers have increased from less than 200 to an estimated 250. However, while the lions have been the winners, the local herders (the *maaldharis)* have lost valuable grazing land for their cattle.

Although the lions seem remarkably tame, in recent years they have reportedly been wandering further afield, well outside the limits of the sanctuary, in search of easy game – namely calves – which in earlier times was found within the park itself. The problem is compounded by the declining areas of forest outside the sanctuary, forcing villagers to forage for fuel within the sanctuary precincts, reducing the habitat of the lions.

The best time to visit the sanctuary is from December to April, and it is closed from 16 June to 15 October, even later if there has been a heavy monsoon.

Apart from the lions there are more than 30 species of other animals, including panthers, hyenas, foxes, wild boars and a number of species of deer and antelope. The deer include the largest Indian antelope (the nilgai), the graceful chinkara gazelle, the chowsingha and the barking deer. You may also see parrots, peacocks and monkeys.

The lions themselves are elusive but you'd be unlucky not to see at least one on a safari, although it would be safer to allow for a couple of trips if you're determined to see

one. Morning safaris are generally a better bet than those in the afternoons. Unfortunately the local guides are poorly trained and speak little English.

Whatever else you do, take a jeep and not a minibus. While the latter stick to the main tracks, the jeeps can take the small trails where you're much more likely to come across lions.

Before you can go on safari, you must get a permit. These are issued on the spot at the Sinh Sadan Forest Lodge office and cost Rs 15 per person for the first day (every additional day costs Rs 7.50), plus Rs 7.50 for a camera, Rs 15 for a video. Jeeps cost Rs 6 per km and can take up to six people. There are three main tracks in the park, so you will cover 25 to 35km, depending on the track your jeep is assigned to.

The guide's fee is set at Rs 20 (total, not per person), and if your guide's been keen and searched hard then a tip is certainly justified, otherwise it's up to you. Jeeps are available from the lodge office every day between 7 and 11 am and 3 and 6.30 pm during winter (October to February) and from 6.30 am during summer (March to June).

Twelve km from Sasan is the **Gir Interpretation Zone**, at Devalia, within the sanctuary precincts. The 4.12 sq km zone has a cross-section of the wildlife in Gir. No private vehicles are permitted in the zone; jeep hire (which includes waiting time while visitors are taking their tour) costs about Rs 150 from Sasan village. The cost to enter the zone, including a minibus mini-safari, permit and guide, is Rs 75 per person.

There are 25 species of reptiles in the sanctuary. A **crocodile-rearing centre** has been established next to Sinh Sadan Forest Lodge, where hatchlings are reared and then released into their natural habitat.

Places to Stay & Eat

There are only a few places to stay at Sasan Gir village. It's not a bad idea to make an advance booking, as rooms can suddenly fill up.

Sinh Sadan Forest Lodge (☎ 5540) is about a 10 minute walk from the railway station. It's a pleasant place to stay, although the staff are sometimes a little indifferent. A very aged film about the park is screened here most evenings at 7 pm. Comfortable doubles with private bath cost Rs 150, or Rs 450 with air-con. There's a restaurant (guests only) which serves thalis (Rs 25).

Gir Lodge (☎ 5521; fax 5528) down by the river, about 200m from the Sinh Sadan Forest Lodge, is an upmarket hotel surrounded by well maintained gardens and operated by the Taj Group. Well appointed singles/doubles cost Rs 1840/3795, or Rs 3865 for air-con suites. Checkout is noon. Their restaurant is open to non-guests.

Getting There & Away
STC and express buses travel between Junagadh and Veraval via Sasan Gir numerous times throughout the day. The 45km trip to Veraval takes 1½ hours (Rs 12). To Junagadh, the 59km trip takes around two hours (Rs 13). Trains run to Veraval (two hours, Rs 9) twice daily, to Delwada (for Diu) once daily at 8.30 am, and to Junagadh once a day (2½ hours, Rs 13).

JUNAGADH
Pop: 185,890   Tel Area Code: 0285
Junagadh is situated right at the base of the temple-studded Girnar Hill, and is the departure point for visits to the Gir Forest. This interesting and unspoilt town has some exotic old buildings, most in a state of disrepair, and is a fascinating place to explore, but very few tourists come here.

The city takes its name from the fort which enclosed the old city. Dating from 250 BC, the Ashokan edicts near the town testify to the great antiquity of this site. At the time of Partition, the Nawab of Junagadh opted to take his tiny state into Pakistan. However, the inhabitants were predominantly Hindu and the nawab soon found himself in exile, which perhaps explains the sorry state of his former palace and fort.

Information
The best source of information is Mr Sorathia,

the manager of the Hotel Relief – the town's unofficial tourist centre. The Bank of India, near Diwan Chowk, has money-changing facilities.

Junagadh's GPO is inconveniently located south of the city centre at Gandhigram. There's a branch in a small street just off MG Rd near the local bus stand. The telegraph office is on Jhalorapa Rd, near Ajanta Talkies.

Uparkot
This very old fort, from which the city derives its name (*jirna* means old), stands on the eastern side of Junagadh and has been rebuilt and extended many times over the centuries. In places, the walls are 20m high and an ornate triple gateway forms the entrance to the fort. It's said that the fort was once besieged for a full 12 years. In all, it was besieged 16 times. It is also said that the fort was abandoned from the 7th to 10th centuries and, when rediscovered, it was completely overgrown by jungle. The plateau-like area formed by the top of the old fort is covered in lantana scrub. Entry is Rs 1.

The **Jama Masjid**, the mosque inside the fort, was built from a demolished Hindu temple. Other points of interest include the **Tomb of Nuri Shah** and two fine baolis (stepwells) known as the **Adi Chadi** and the **Naughan**. The Adi Chadi is named after two of the slave girls who fetched water from it. The Naughan is reached by a magnificent circular staircase.

Cut into the hillside close to the mosque are some ancient **Buddhist caves** which are thought to be at least 1500 years old. These eerie double-storey caves have six pillars with very fine carvings. The soft rock on which Junagadh is built encouraged the construction of caves and wells, and there are other caves in Junagadh, including some thought to date back to the time of Ashoka.

Mahabat Maqbara
This stunning mausoleum of one of the nawabs of Junagadh is resplendent with silver doors and intricate architecture, including minarets encircled by spiralling stairways.

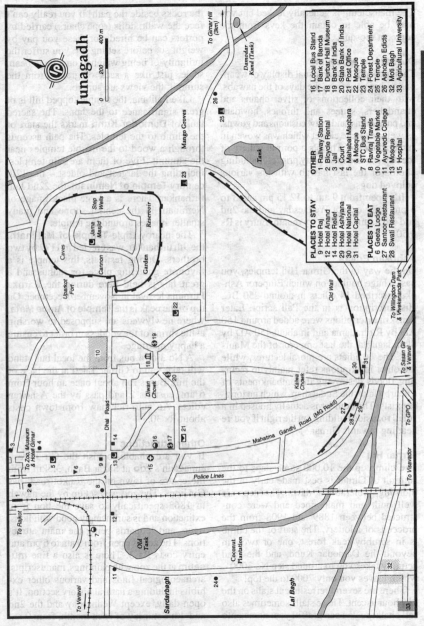

Junagadh

0   200   400 m

To Girnar Hill (3km)

Damodar Kund (Tank)

Mango Groves

Tank

Step Wells

Jama Masjid

Reservoir

Caves

Uparkot Fort

Cannon

Garden

Old Wall

To Willingdon Dam & Vivekananda Park

To Sasan Gir & Veraval

Old Wall

Kalwa Chowk

To GPO

Diwan Chowk

Dhal Road

Mahatma Gandhi Road (MG Road)

To Zoo, Museum & Hotel Girnar

Police Lines

To Rajkot

To Veraval

Old Tank

To Visavador

Coconut Plantation

Lal Bagh

Sardarbagh

To Sasan Gir & Veraval

OTHER
16 Local Bus Stand
17 Bank of Baroda
18 Durbar Hall Museum
19 Bank of India
20 State Bank of India
21 Post Office
22 Mosque
23 Temple
24 Forest Department
25 Temple
26 Ashokan Edicts
32 Moti Bagh
33 Agricultural University

1 Railway Station
2 Bicycle Rental
3 Jail
4 Court
5 Mahabat Maqbara & Mosque
7 STC Bus Stand
8 Ravraj Travels
10 Vegetable Market
11 Ayurvedic College
13 Mosque
15 Hospital

PLACES TO STAY
9 Hotel Raj
12 Hotel Anand
14 Hotel Relief
29 Hotel Ashiyana
30 Hotel National
31 Hotel Capital

PLACES TO EAT
6 Geeta Lodge
27 Santoor Restaurant
28 Swati Restaurant

The mausoleum is generally locked but you may be able to obtain the keys from the adjacent mosque.

Durbar Hall Museum

This museum has the usual display of weapons and armour from the days of the nawabs, with their collections of silver chains and chandeliers, settees and thrones, howdahs and palanquins, and a few cushions and gowns, as well as a huge carpet which was woven in Junagadh's jail. There's a portrait gallery of the nawabs and local petty princes, including photos of the last nawab with his various beloved dogs.

It's open from 9 am to 12.15 pm and 3 to 6 pm daily except Wednesday and the 2nd and 4th Saturday of every month. Entry is Rs 0.50.

Ashokan Edicts

On the way to the Girnar Hill temples, you pass a huge boulder on which Emperor Ashoka inscribed 14 edicts in around 250 BC. His inscription is in the Pali script. Later Sanskrit inscriptions were added around 150 AD by Rudradama and in about 450 AD by Skandagupta, the last emperor of the Mauryas. The 14 edicts are moral lectures, while the other inscriptions refer mainly to recurring floods destroying the embankments of a nearby lake, the Sudershan, which no longer exists. The boulder is actually housed in a small roadside building, on the right if you're heading towards Girnar.

Girnar Hill

The climb up the 10,000 stone steps to the summit of Girnar is best made early in the morning, preferably at dawn. The steps are well built and maintained and were constructed between 1889 and 1908 from the proceeds of a lottery. The start of the climb is in scrubby teak forest, one or two km beyond the Damodar Kund, and the road actually takes you to around step No 3000 – which leaves you only 7000 to the top!

There are several refreshment stalls on the 2½ hour ascent. These stalls sometimes also sell chalk, so you can graffiti your name onto

the rocks beside the path! If you really can't face the walk, dolis (rope chairs) carried by porters can be hired; for these you pay by weight so, before setting off, you suffer the indignity of being weighed on a huge beam scale, just like a sack of grain. From the summit, the views are superb.

Like Palitana, the temple-topped hill is of great significance to the Jains. The sacred tank of **Damodar Kund** marks the start of the climb to the temples. The path ascends through a wood to the marble temples near the summit. Five of them are Jain temples, including the largest and oldest – the 12th century **Temple of Neminath**, the 22nd Jain tirthankar. There is a large black image of Neminath in the central shrine and many smaller images around the temple.

The nearby triple **Temple of Mallinath**, the 9th tirthankar, was erected in 1177 by two brothers. During festivals, this temple is a favourite gathering place for sadhus and a great fair is held here during the Kartika Purnima festival in November/December. On top of the peak is the **Temple of Amba Mata**, where newlyweds are supposed to worship at the shrine of the goddess in order to ensure a happy marriage.

A No 3 or 4 bus from the local bus stand will take you to Girnar Taleti at the base of the hill. Buses run about once an hour from 6 am, cost Rs 2 and pass by the Ashokan edicts. An auto-rickshaw from town costs about Rs 30.

Other Attractions

If you are unable to visit the Gir Forest, Junagadh's **zoo** at Sakar Bagh, 3.5km from the centre of town on the Rajkot road, has Gir lions. The zoo was set up by the nawab in 1863 specifically to save the lion from extinction and is surprisingly good with lions, tigers and leopards being the main attractions. The zoo is open from 9 am to 6 pm and entry costs Rs 3. There is also a fine **museum** at the zoo with paintings, manuscripts, archaeological finds and various other exhibits including a natural history section. It's open daily, except Wednesday and the 2nd and 4th Saturday of each month, from 9 am to noon and 3 to 6 pm. Take a No 6 bus (Rs 2), or walk there by the old Majevadi Gate on your right.

The **Ayurvedic College** at Sadarbag on the western edge of town is housed in one of the former nawab's palaces, and has a small museum devoted to ayurvedic medicine. The staff are knowledgeable and it's a good place to obtain information on this ancient form of traditional medicine.

Other old constructions include the gate opposite the railway station on Dhal Rd, the clock tower near the central post office and the building opposite the Durbar Hall.

Places to Stay

Hotel Relief (☎ 20280) on Dhal Rd (the road leading to the fort), is a popular hangout for travellers. Singles/doubles with bathroom cost Rs 100/200, or Rs 440 for air-con rooms. Meals are also available. The friendly and helpful manager, Mr Sorathia, is a great source of information about local points of interest.

Hotel Raj (☎ 23961) nearby has small, clean rooms with attached bathroom for Rs 60/80. Dorm beds go for a mere Rs 20.

Hotel Anand (☎ 22657), on the same road but across the railway line, has rooms for Rs 125/200 (bucket hot water), or with air-con for Rs 220/500. Breakfast is available.

Hotel Girnar (☎ 21201) is a Gujarat Tourism hotel a little way out of town. It offers singles/doubles with bathroom for Rs 277/330 or Rs 425/440 with air-con. Most of the rooms are spacious and have a balcony (try to get one of these). The restaurant serves Gujarati veg thalis for Rs 35.

Retiring Rooms at the railway station are Rs 40/70; dorm beds are Rs 25.

There are a number of hotels around Kalwa Chowk, one of the two main squares in Junagadh, and although most of the good restaurants are down here, it's an inconvenient distance from the centre of town.

Hotel Capital (☎ 21442) may be grim, but it's hard to complain when singles/doubles with common bath cost just Rs 25/50.

Hotel National (☎ 27891), directly opposite, is much more savoury, with decent rooms from Rs 150/250, or air-con rooms for Rs

440/550. Checkout is 10 am, and there's a restaurant downstairs.

Hotel Ashiyana (☎ 20706), also in this area, has respectable rooms from Rs 75/125.

Places to Eat

Geeta Lodge, not far from the railway station, has all-you-can-eat thalis for Rs 23.

Santoor Restaurant, in a small lane just off MG Rd, has quick service and good veg food. This air-con restaurant is a pleasant surprise at the top of a fairly seedy-looking staircase. The sign out the front is in Gujarati.

Swati Restaurant, just down the road from the Hotel Ashiyana, is of a similar standard, and is popular with the locals. Main dishes (veg only) are around Rs 35.

Junagadh is famous for its fruit, especially kesar mangoes and *chiku* (sapodilla) which are popular in milkshakes in November/December.

Getting There & Away

Bus The timetable at the STC stand is entirely in Gujarati. Buses leave for Rajkot every 30 minutes (two hours, Rs 24), for Sasan Gir every hour (two hours, Rs 13 to Rs 19), and there are regular departures to other centres in the state.

Raviraj Travels (☎ 26988), beneath the Hotel Vaibhav, has deluxe minibuses to Rajkot every 10 minutes (two hours, Rs 25), and numerous departures to Ahmedabad (seven hours, Rs 70), Veraval (two hours, Rs 20), Una (four hours, Rs 40), Porbandar (two hours Rs 25), and to Bhuj (via Rajkot) (six hours, Rs 80,) as well as to other cities.

Train The *Somnath Mail* and *Girnar Express* run between Ahmedabad and Veraval via Junagadh. The *Somnath Mail* departs Junagadh at 7.05 pm, arriving in Ahmedabad at 4.20 am. The *Girnar Express* departs at 9.10 pm, arriving in Ahmedabad at 6.10 am. The 377km trip costs Rs 104/310 in 2nd/1st class.

To Veraval, there are additional services at 6.30 and 9.05 am, and 2.30 and 6 pm. The two-hour trip costs Rs 25/105 in 2nd/1st class. At 6 am there is a train to Sasan Gir (2½ hours, Rs 13), which continues on to

Delwada (for Una and Diu), arriving in Delwada at 12.30 pm (Rs 43/101 in 2nd/1st class). The *Veraval-Rajkot Mail* runs between Rajkot and Veraval via Junagadh, departing Junagadh for Rajkot at 1.15 pm. The 131km, four hour trip costs Rs 35/138 in 2nd/1st class.

Getting Around
Buses to Girnar Hill leave from outside the post office every hour from 6 am (Rs 2). An auto-rickshaw costs about Rs 30.

Junagadh's taxis seem to be mostly 1940s vintage Ford Plymouths, and there're dozens of them; probably the greatest concentration of working examples anywhere in the world!

Most auto-rickshaw trips around town should cost no more than Rs 6.

PORBANDAR
Pop: 178,700   Tel Area Code: 0286
On the south-east coast, about midway between Veraval and Dwarka, modern-day Porbandar is chiefly noted as the birthplace of Mahatma Gandhi. In ancient times, the city was called Sudamapuri after Sudama, a compatriot of Krishna, and there was once a flourishing trade from here to Africa and the Persian Gulf. The Africa connection is apparent in the number of Indianised Blacks, called Siddis, who form a virtually separate caste of Dalits.

Porbandar has several large cement and chemical factories and a textile mill. Dhows are still built here and fish-drying is an important activity, lending a certain aroma to the town!

Swimming at Chowpatty Beach is not recommended. This beach is used as a local latrine and there is a factory drain outlet by the Hazur Palace. Swimming is said to be OK a few km down the coast towards Veraval.

Information
The Bank of Baroda, beneath the Hotel Flamingo, and the State Bank of India, opposite, both have money-changing facilities.

Kirti Mandir
The Kirti Mandir, Gandhi's birthplace, houses one of India's many collections of Gandhi memorabilia. There is also an exhibit of photographs, some with English captions, and a small bookshop.

Nehru Planetarium & Bharat Mandir
Across the muddy creek, which is spanned by the Jynbeeli (once Jubilee) Bridge, are the Nehru Planetarium and the Bharat Mandir. Flocks of flamingos are an unexpected sight along the creek. Men and women enter the planetarium from the veranda by separate doors whose panels celebrate Indian nonalignment, showing Shastri with Kosygin on one side and Nehru with JFK on the other! The planetarium has afternoon sessions in Gujarati.

The large Bharat Mandir hall is in a charming garden opposite the planetarium. On the floor inside is a huge relief map of India and the building's pillars are brilliantly painted with bas-reliefs of more than 100 religious figures and legendary persons from Hindu epics.

Places to Stay
Nilam Guest House (☎ 20503), near the Municipal Gardens, has dusty rooms from Rs 100 with bucket hot water. Most of the windows face into the hall so rooms are quite dark.

Rajkamal Guest House (☎ 20374) on MG Rd is incredibly cheap at Rs 35/70 with attached bathroom (cold water), and is no worse than any of the other bottom-end places.

Hotel Flamingo (☎ 23123), also on MG Rd, is a friendly place with a very pleasant restaurant. Doubles cost Rs 200, or with air-con, from Rs 385. Some of the rooms have no external windows so although they're quite big, you may find them a little claustrophobic.

Hotel Sheetal (☎ 41821), opposite the GPO, is of a similar standard. All rooms have hot and cold water, and are reasonably well appointed. Prices start at Rs 150 for a double (no single rates).

Vaibhav Guest House (☎ 24000), near the Hotel Flamingo, has small rooms for Rs 100/160, or from Rs 300/350 with air-con. The sign out the front is in Gujarati.

Shree Kandhlikrupa Guest House (☎ 22655), near the railway station, offers good rooms with bath for Rs 100/200, and air-con rooms for Rs 400.

New Oceanic Hotel (☎ 20217) is a small villa on Chowpatty Beach. Its air-con rooms cost Rs 500/625 for doubles/triples, but although the sea is only a stone's throw away, only one room has a sea view! There's also a restaurant here.

Places to Eat

Aardash Restaurant on MG Rd has good, basic vegetarian food at reasonable prices.

Swagat Restaurant on the eastern end of MG Rd is a popular place and not expensive.

Hotel Flamingo has a delightful air-con restaurant which offers a wide range of Punjabi, Chinese and south Indian food; a main dish costs about Rs 40. Non-guests are welcome.

Marine Restaurant along the sea wall is a basic snack bar offering cheap eats in the evening. There are also other cheap snack places in this area.

GUJARAT

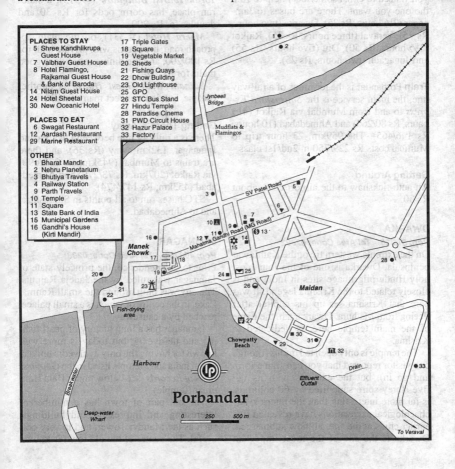

PLACES TO STAY
5 Shree Kandhlikrupa Guest House
7 Vaibhav Guest House
8 Hotel Flamingo, Rajkamal Guest House & Bank of Baroda
14 Nilam Guest House
24 Hotel Sheetal
30 New Oceanic Hotel

PLACES TO EAT
6 Swagat Restaurant
12 Aardash Restaurant
29 Marine Restaurant

OTHER
1 Bharat Mandir
2 Nehru Planetarium
3 Bhutiya Travels
4 Railway Station
9 Parth Travels
10 Temple
11 Square
13 State Bank of India
15 Municipal Gardens
16 Gandhi's House (Kirti Mandir)
17 Triple Gates
18 Square
19 Vegetable Market
20 Sheds
21 Fishing Quays
22 Dhow Building
23 Old Lighthouse
25 GPO
26 STC Bus Stand
27 Hindu Temple
28 Paradise Cinema
31 PWD Circuit House
32 Hazur Palace
33 Factory

Jynbeeli Bridge

Mudflats & Flamingos

SV Patel Road

Mahatma Gandhi Road (MG Road)

Manek Chowk

Fish-drying area

Harbour

Breakwater

Deep-water Wharf

Maidan

Chowpatty Beach

Effluent Outfall

Drain

Porbandar

0   250   500 m

To Veraval

Getting There & Away

Air Gujarat Airways has daily flights to Mumbai; NEPC Airlines has two flights weekly. Flights with both airlines cost US$85. Bookings can be made with Bhutiya Travels (☎ 41889).

Bus The STC bus stand is a 15 minute walk from MG Rd. There are regular services to Dwarka, Jamnagar, Veraval and Rajkot. The private bus companies have their offices on MG Rd, in the vicinity of the Hotel Flamingo. They only have signs in Gujarati so you'll need to enlist some local help to find the one you want. There are buses to Jamnagar (2½ hours, Rs 35), Dwarka (two hours, Rs 25), Veraval (three hours, Rs 35), Rajkot (3½ hours, Rs 50), Diu (five hours, Rs 55) and Junagadh (two hours, Rs 25).

Train Porbandar is the terminus of a railway line; the main service is the *Saurashtra Express* to and from Mumbai via Rajkot (4½ hours, Rs 80/260) and Ahmedabad (10 hours, Rs 146/465). The 959km, 23 hour trip to Mumbai costs Rs 229/750 in 2nd/1st class.

Getting Around

An auto-rickshaw to the airport costs about Rs 30.

DWARKA

Pop: 31,325   Tel Area Code: 02892

On the extreme western tip of the Kathiawar peninsula, Dwarka is one of the four most holy Hindu pilgrimage sites in India and is closely related to the Krishna legend. It was here that Krishna set up his capital after fleeing from Mathura. Dwarkanath, the name of the main temple here, is dedicated to Krishna.

The temple is only open to Hindus (though one visitor reported that you can sign a form and go in), but the exterior, with its tall five-storey spire supported by 60 columns, is far more interesting than the interior. Archaeological excavations have revealed five earlier cities at the site, all now submerged. Dwarka is the site of the most important

Janmashtami Festival which falls in August/September.

Dwarka's **lighthouse** is open to the public between 4.30 and 6 pm, and affords an excellent panoramic view from the top (Rs 1).

A little north of Dwarka, a ferry crosses from Okha to the **Island of Bet**, where Vishnu is said to have slain a demon. There are modern Krishna temples on the island.

A traveller advises to beware of the unfriendly dogs on this island.

Places to Stay & Eat

Toran Tourist Bungalow (☎ 313), a state-run place, has dorm beds for Rs 30 and doubles for Rs 200.

Meera Hotel (☎ 331), on the main approach road, has rooms with private bath for Rs 100/200, and the dining room does good thalis for Rs 20.

Satnam Wadi Guest House is another cheapie, but don't expect many facilities.

Getting There & Away

There is a railway line between Dwarka and Jamnagar, 132km away (Rs 36), and there are trains to Mumbai (945km, Rs 230/690) via Rajkot (207km, Rs 73/279) and Ahmedabad (453km, Rs 147/474).

STC buses run to all points in Saurashtra, and to Ahmedabad.

JAMNAGAR

Pop: 406,690   Tel Area Code: 0288

Prior to independence, the princely state of Jamnagar was ruled by the Jadeja Rajputs. The city was built around the small Ranmal Lake, in the centre of which is a small palace, reached by a causeway.

Jamnagar has a long history of pearl fishing and tie-dyeing, but today is more well known for having the only ayurvedic university in India and a temple listed in the *Guinness Book of Records* (see below under Bala Hanuman Temple).

The old part of town has a number of interesting and impressive old buildings, such as the Mandvi Tower, and is very colourful. The centre of the old town is known

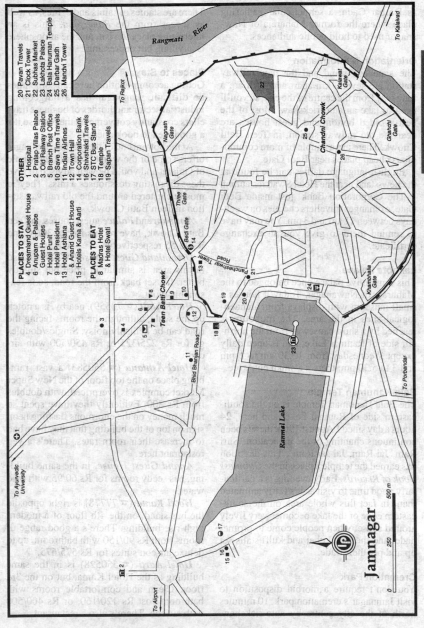

PLACES TO STAY
4 Dreamland Guest House
6 Anupam & Palace
   Guest Houses
7 Hotel Punit
9 Hotel President
13 Hotel Ashiana
   & Anand Guest House
15 Hotels Kama & Aarti

PLACES TO EAT
8 Madras Hotel
   & Hotel Swati

OTHER
1 Hospital
2 Pratap Villas Palace
3 Old Railway Station
5 Branch Post Office
10 Save Time Travels
11 Indian Airlines
12 Town Hall
14 Corporation Bank
16 Shivshakti Travels
17 STC Bus Stand
18 Temple
19 Sapan Travels
20 Pavan Travels
21 Clock Tower
22 Subhas Market
23 Lakhota Palace
24 Bala Hanuman Temple
25 Darbar Gadh
26 Manchi Tower

Rangmati River

To Kalavad

To Rajkot

Kalawat Gate

Chandni Chowk

Grhati Gate

Nagnath Gate

Three Gate

Bedi Gate

Pancheshwar Tower

Panchweshwar Road

Khambhalia Gate

To Ayurvedic University

To Porbandar

Teen Batti Chowk

Bhid Bhanjan Road

Ranmal Lake

To Airport

Jamnagar

0   250   500 m

as Darbar Gadh, a semicircular gathering place where the former Maharaja of Nawanagar used to hold public audiences.

Orientation & Information

The state bus stand and the new railway station are several km apart and both are a long way from the centre of the city, so you'll need to take an auto-rickshaw. Most of the best-avoided bottom-end guest houses are near the old railway station, in Teen Batti Chowk. There are a couple of more commodious cheap places near Bedi Gate.

English-language dailies can be found at the newsstand near the Hotel Swati restaurant.

The Corporation Bank, just inside Bedi Gate, exchanges travellers cheques on weekdays between 11 am and 3 pm. You may have to remind them to give you an exchange certificate.

Lakhota Palace

This diminutive palace once belonged to the Maharaja of Nawanagar. Today it houses a small museum with displays from archaeological sites in the area. The **museum** is reached by a short causeway from the northern side of Ranmal Lake, and is open daily except Wednesday from 10.30 am to 1 pm and 3 to 5.30 pm; there's a small entry fee.

Bala Hanuman Temple

The Bala Hanuman Temple is on the southeastern side of Ranmal Lake, and here, 24 hours a day since 1 August 1964, there's been continuous chanting of the invocation 'Shri Ram, Jai Ram, Jai Jai Ram'. This devotion has earned the temple a place in the *Guinness Book of Records*. Early evening is a particularly good time to visit as it's fairly animated then. In fact this whole area on the southeastern edge of the lake becomes very lively around sunset when people come to promenade, and the usual chai and kulfi stalls set up and ply their trade.

Cremation Park

You don't require a morbid disposition to visit Jamnagar's cremation park, 10 minutes north of the city centre by auto-rickshaw.

There are statues of saints and deities, as well as scenes from the *Ramayana*. This is an interesting place to visit, and the atmosphere is anything but depressing.

Places to Stay

Getting accommodation here can sometimes be difficult. Jamnagar has a burgeoning industrial sector and hordes of business travellers constantly converge on the town so it's a good idea to book ahead.

At the bottom end of the market, Jamnagar offers some of the worst hotels in the whole of Gujarat and you'd be well advised to give these disgusting dosshouses a miss. They're mostly clustered around the old railway station in Teen Batti Chowk.

Anupam and *Palace* guest houses, in Teen Batti Chowk, have rooms for Rs 30/70 and Rs 45/55 respectively.

Dreamland Guest House (☎ 70436), also in this area, is similar in price but slightly better. It's set back from the road, so is reasonably quiet.

Hotel Punit (☎ 70559), nearby, is a notch up the scale, although the rooms facing the road can be hellishly noisy. Singles/doubles go for Rs 225/325 or Rs 450/500 with aircon.

Hotel Ashiana (☎ 550583) a vast, rambling place on the top floor of the New Super Market complex is overpriced, with doubles from Rs 300. Evidently they have spent so much money on the enormous flashing neon sign on top of the building that they have had to increase their room rates. There's a veg restaurant here.

Anand Guest House, in the same building, has seedy rooms for Rs 60/95 with cold water.

Hotel Kama (☎ 77778) is right opposite the bus stand, on the 4th floor of a modern high-rise building. There's a good range of rooms from Rs 90/150 with bathroom, up to deluxe air-con suites for Rs 575/675.

Hotel Aarti (☎ 550528) is in the same building as the Hotel Kama, but on the 3rd floor. Clean and comfortable rooms with bathroom cost Rs 120/160, or Rs 400/500 with air-con. There's also a restaurant.

Hotel President (☎ 70516; fax 78634), Teen Batti Chowk, right in the centre of town, is Jamnagar's best hotel. Singles/doubles with private bath and constant hot water cost Rs 350/450, or Rs 500/600 with air-con. There's a restaurant and money-changing facilities.

Places to Eat
For cheap snack food in the evening try the various stalls that set up near the Bala Hanuman Temple. In the centre of town, in the Teen Batti Chowk area, there are plenty of small eating places.

Around Mandvi Tower in the heart of the old town there's an extraordinary array of 'sweetmeat' shops selling a wide variety of sweet and sticky creations.

Hotel Swati is a vegetarian place with an extensive range of reasonably priced south Indian, Jain and Punjabi dishes.

Madras Hotel, nearby, specialises in south Indian and Punjabi cuisine.

7 Seas Restaurant at the Hotel President offers veg and non-veg food; non-veg dishes are around Rs 35.

Getting There & Away
Air The Indian Airlines office (☎ 550211) on Bhid Bhanjan Rd is open from 10.30 am to 5 pm. Indian Airlines has four flights a week to Mumbai (US$80). Bookings can also be made with Save Time Travels (☎ 71739), between Bedi Gate and the town hall.

Bus There are STC buses to Rajkot every 30 minutes (Rs 20), and other departures to Dwarka, Porbandar, Bhuj, Junagadh and Ahmedabad.

Rather than compete with each other, the private bus companies have complicated bus bookings for travellers by each operating services to different destinations. Sapan Travels (☎ 71646) just off Pancheshwar Tower Rd, books buses to Rajkot (two hours, Rs 25) and to Ahmedabad (six hours, Rs 80). Pavan Travels (☎ 552002) on the same road, also has departures to Ahmedabad, as well as to Mumbai (20 hours, Rs 200). Shivshakti Travels (☎ 70091) in the basement of the building opposite the bus stand, has depar-

tures almost every 15 minutes to Rajkot, as well as services to Junagadh (three hours, Rs 30), Porbandar (2½ hours, Rs 35), and twice-daily departures to Bhuj (six hours, Rs 70).

Train There are direct trains from Mumbai and Ahmedabad via Rajkot. The fare for the 321km trip to Ahmedabad is Rs 115/275 for a 2nd/1st-class sleeper, or Rs 76/360 on the daytime service. The 813km trip to Mumbai costs Rs 212/700.

To Dwarka, the 132km journey takes three hours by express train, or a tedious 5½ hours on the daily 'fast passenger' service (Rs 36).

Getting Around
There is no minibus service to the airport, which is a long way out. Auto-rickshaw drivers demand at least Rs 30. A rickshaw from the bus stand to the Bedi Gate area costs about Rs 8. To the new railway station, about four km north of the city centre, expect to pay about Rs 15.

RAJKOT
Pop: 726,089   Tel Area Code: 0281
This bustling town was once the capital of the princely state of Saurashtra and is also a former British government headquarters. Mahatma Gandhi spent the early years of his life here. The Gandhi family home, the Kaba Gandhi no Delo, now houses a permanent exhibition of Gandhi items.

The prestigious Rajkumar College dates back to the second half of last century and is regarded as one of the best private schools in the country. It was one of five schools set up by the British for the education of the sons of nobility (*rajkumar* means prince).

Information
Rajkot has a helpful tourist office (☎ 234507), but it's hidden away behind the old State Bank of Saurashtra building on Jawahar Rd, almost opposite the Galaxy Hotel. It's open weekdays and the 1st and 3rd Saturday of the month, from 10.30 am to 6 pm (closed for lunch from 1.30 to 2 pm).

GUJARAT

The State Bank of India, to the north of the Jubilee Gardens, has money-changing facilities. Entry is from the rear of the building.

Watson Museum

The Watson Museum & Library in the Jubilee Gardens commemorates Colonel John Watson, Political Agent from 1886-89.

The entrance is flanked by two imperial lions and among the exhibits are copies of artefacts from Mohenjodaro, 13th century carvings, silverware, natural history exhibits and textiles as well as dioramas of local tribal costumes and housing styles.

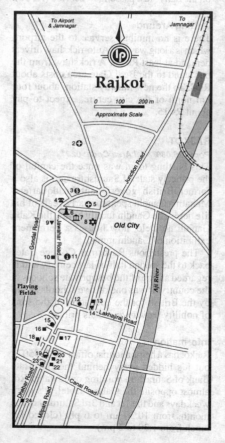

Perhaps the most startling piece is a huge marble statue of Queen Victoria seated on a throne, decidedly not amused. The museum is open daily except Wednesday from 9 am to 12.30 pm and 1.30 to 5.30 pm; there's a small entry fee.

Places to Stay – bottom end

Rajkot has a good range of accommodation. Note that many places add a 12% tax on their room rates. Lakhajiraj Rd, leading into the heart of the bazaar area, has a number of hotels.

Himalaya Guest House (☎ 222880), just off Lakhajiraj Rd, is a huge place with basic rooms with bathroom for Rs 75/150 (no hot water in the single rooms). Doubles are spacious, but singles are a little dark and pokey. The entrance is right inside the shopping complex over which it stands.

Hotel Jeel Guest House (☎ 231244), at the back of the centrally located bus stand, has cheap but grimy rooms with private bath for Rs 60/100 (bucket hot water).

Milan Guest House (☎ 235049), nearby, is a little better, with small singles from Rs

---

PLACES TO STAY
10 Galaxy Hotel
13 Himalaya Guest House
16 Vijay Guest House
17 Jyoti Guest House
18 Evergreen Guest House
21 Hotel Jeel Guest House
22 Milan Guest House
23 Hotel Samrat International
24 Hotel Tulsi

PLACES TO EAT
9 Havmor
14 Rainbow Restaurant

OTHER
1 Railway Station
2 Government Hospital
3 State Bank of India
4 Telegraph Office
5 Hospital
6 Gandhi School & Statue
7 Watson Museum & Library
8 Jubilee Gardens
11 Tourist Office
12 Library
15 Indian Airlines
19 STC Bus Stand
20 Private Bus Companies

60, and doubles with attached bath for Rs 100.

Jyoti Guest House (☎ 225271) is a little further from the bus stand, so is a fraction quieter. Rooms with bathroom cost Rs 100.

Evergreen Guest House (☎ 227052), only a few minutes walk from the bus stand, just off Dhebar Rd, is a good budget choice. Very small but tidy rooms with bath cost Rs 160 (doubles only).

Vijay Guest House nearby, is similarly priced and fairly reasonable value.

Places to Stay – middle
Galaxy Hotel (☎ 222904; fax 227053) is located on the 3rd floor of the Galaxy Commercial Centre on Jawahar Rd. It's one of the best mid-range places with rooms for Rs 280/420, or Rs 460/690 with air-con. The hotel has money-changing facilities for guests, but there's no restaurant.

Hotel Samrat International (☎ 222269), at the back of the bus stand, has well appointed rooms for Rs 260/400, or from Rs 450/650 with air-con; there's no restaurant here either.

Hotel Tulsi (☎ 231731; fax 231735), close by, is a very good choice, with comfortable and clean rooms for Rs 250/350, or Rs 375/550 with air-con. Meals are available with advance notice.

Places to Eat
Rainbow Restaurant, near the Himalaya Guest House, has tasty and cheap south Indian cuisine. There's an air-con section upstairs. This place has an impressive selection of ice cream: see if you can resist 'Nuts in Love'!

Havmor, up near the Jubilee Gardens, serves Indian, Chinese and western food.

Getting There & Away
Air The Indian Airlines office (☎ 227916) is on Dhebar Rd. Indian Airlines has four direct flights a week between Rajkot and Mumbai (US$65). NEPC (☎ 227330) and UP Air (☎ 225369) also have daily flights to Mumbai.

Bus STC buses connect Rajkot with Jamnagar, Junagadh, Porbandar, Veraval and Ahmedabad. The trip from Rajkot to Veraval via Junagadh takes about five hours and costs Rs 43. Rajkot to Jamnagar is a two hour journey and costs Rs 25.

There are also a number of private buses which operate to such places as Ahmedabad, Bhuj, Bhavnagar, Una (for Diu), Mt Abu, Udaipur and Mumbai. The offices of these companies are on the road behind the bus stand.

Train A number of broad-gauge express trains connect Rajkot with Ahmedabad, 246km away. Fares are Rs 57/266 in 2nd/1st class, and the trip takes about 5½ hours. There are other trains to and from Jamnagar (75km, Rs 25/128 in 1st/2nd class), Porbandar (221km, Rs 53/229 in 1st/2nd class), and Mumbai (738km, Rs 136/625 in 1st/2nd class). There's a metre-gauge service to Veraval (186km, Rs 47/213 in 1st/2nd class).

Getting Around
A rickshaw to the airport from the city centre costs about Rs 50; to the railway station, expect to pay Rs 15.

AROUND RAJKOT
Wankaner
There's a very interesting palace in the tiny town of Wankaner, about 38km from Rajkot. This striking palace (☎ (02828) 20000) looks like something straight out of a fairytale: it was built in 1907 and is a curious Greco-Roman Gothic Indo Scottish baronial extravagance.

As the royal family still live in the palace, guests are accommodated a couple of km away.

Oasis House is an original Art Deco building complete with indoor swimming pool. While hardly palatial, the rooms are comfortable, and meals are taken at the palace with the family. The charge is Rs 1200 per person, including meals.

There are regular buses to Rajkot every half hour, and Wankaner Junction is on the main railway line to Ahmedabad (Rs 84/249 in 2nd/1st class, 205km).

Morvi

North of Rajkot is Morvi, a friendly little town that's well off the main tourist track. There's an amazing 'swinging bridge' here that's definitely worth checking out if you're in the area. The suspended 19th century wooden bridge connects the old palace with the new palace, and yes, it actually shakes, creaks and rocks as you make your way across. The bridge overlooks a murky river (no crocodiles!) and has good views of the palace (closed to the public) and town. The swinging bridge is open daily from 7 am to 7 pm and there's a small entry fee.

Thakar Lodge (☎ (02822) 22378) about one km from the bus stand and near the vegetable market, is the best place to stay. Singles/doubles with attached bath cost Rs 100/300, Rs 250/500 for air-con rooms. There are cheaper rooms at their guest house next door. The restaurant serves an excellent all-you-can-eat Gujarati thali (Rs 50).

Buses travel frequently between Morvi and Rajkot (Rs 15), and there are also regular buses to Ahmedabad (Rs 50).

Surendranagar (Wadhwan)

This town on the route from Ahmedabad to Rajkot features the very old **Temple of Ranik Devi**, who became involved in a dispute between local rulers Sidh Raja (who planned to marry her) and Rao Khengar (who carried her off and did marry her). When Sidh Raja defeated Rao Khengar, Ranik Devi chose *sati* over dishonour and Sidh Raja built the temple as her memorial.

Tarnetar

Every year in the month of Bhadra (around September), the Trineteshwar Temple at Tarnetar, 65km north-east of Rajkot, hosts the three day **Tarnetar Fair**. The fair is most well known for the different *chhatris* (umbrellas) made specifically for the occasion, and as an opportunity to procure a spouse – one of the main functions of the fair is to enable villagers from the Bharwad community to form matrimonial alliances. Prospective candidates are appropriately bedecked in their finery,

making this fair an extraordinarily colourful spectacle.

According to legend, Arjuna once danced at this site, and the River Ganges flows into the tank here once a year.

Gondal

On the Rajkot to Junagadh road, south of Rajkot on the River Gondali, is the town of Gondal. Once the centre of a former prosperous princely state, it still has some impressive buildings. The Naulakaha Darbargadh palace (named after the nine lakhs it cost to build) is well worth a look.

Riverside Palace is an interesting place to stay in Gondal. It costs Rs 2000 per person including all meals and local sightseeing. The present royal family still has the Maharaja's collection of 30 or so vintage cars, and in the palace railway yard are two dilapidated royal rail carriages.

Kutch

The westernmost part of Gujarat is virtually an island; during the monsoon period from May onwards, it really is an island. The Gulf of Kutch divides Kutch (also known as Kachchh) from the Kathiawar peninsula. To the north, it is separated from the Sind region of Pakistan by the Great Rann of Kutch.

The salt in the soil makes this low-lying marsh area almost completely barren. Only on scattered 'islands' which rise above the salt level is there vegetation. During the dry season, the Rann is a vast expanse of hard, dried mud. Then, with the start of the monsoon in May, it is flooded first by sea water, then by the fresh water from rivers as they fill. Kutch is also separated from the rest of Gujarat to the east by the Little Rann of Kutch.

During the winter, the Gulf of Kutch is a breeding ground for flamingos and pelicans. The Asiatic wild ass lives in the Little Rann of Kutch and part of the area has been declared a sanctuary for this rare animal. Few tourists make it to this remote part of India.

BHUJ

Pop: 122,220   Tel Area Code: 02832

Bhuj, the major town of Kutch, is an old walled city – in the past the city gates were locked each night from dusk to dawn. You can lose yourself for hours in the intricate maze-like streets and alleyways of this fascinating town. There are walls within walls, attractive crenellated gateways, old palaces with intricately carved wooden pavilions, and striking, brightly decorated Hindu temples.

Bhuj resembles much of India before the tourist invasion, and you're much more likely to come across that disarming hospitality which was once the hallmark of rural India.

Unfortunately if there has been no monsoon, the picturesque lake remains dry.

Information

The tourist office (☎ 20004), housed in the Aina Mahal, is staffed by the very helpful Mr PJ Jethi, who is a mine of information on anything to do with Bhuj and Kutch. It's possible to arrange a guide (Rs 300 per day) through the tourist office. Ask Mr Jethi for details. The office is open daily from 9 am to 11.45, and 3 to 5.45 pm except Saturday. It

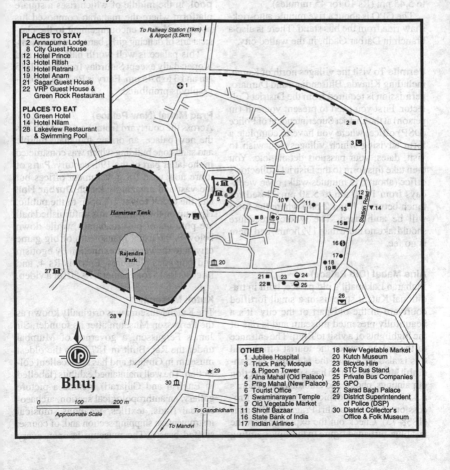

PLACES TO STAY
2 Annapurna Lodge
8 City Guest House
12 Hotel Prince
13 Hotel Ritish
15 Hotel Ratrani
19 Hotel Anam
21 Sagar Guest House
22 VRP Guest House & Green Rock Restaurant

PLACES TO EAT
10 Green Hotel
14 Hotel Nilam
28 Lakeview Restaurant & Swimming Pool

OTHER
1 Jubilee Hospital
3 Truck Park, Mosque & Pigeon Tower
4 Prag Mahal (New Palace)
5 Aina Mahal (Old Palace)
6 Tourist Office
7 Swaminarayan Temple
9 Old Vegetable Market
11 Shroff Bazaar
16 State Bank of India
17 Indian Airlines
18 New Vegetable Market
20 Kutch Museum
23 Bicycle Hire
24 STC Bus Stand
25 Private Bus Companies
26 GPO
27 Sarad Bagh Palace
29 District Superintendent of Police (DSP)
30 District Collector's Office & Folk Museum

Bhuj

To Railway Station (1km) & Airport (3.5km)
Hamirsar Tank
Rajendra Park
Station Road
To Gandhidham
To Mandvi

Approximate Scale 0 100 200 m

GUJARAT

sells a small booklet about Kutch for Rs 5, or there's a more informative one for Rs 25. Excellent postcards are also sold here for around Rs 5 each.

Changing money in Bhuj is a big problem. The State Bank of India on Station Rd offers money-changing facilities; however, it seems to favour Thomas Cook travellers cheques (weekdays, from noon to 3 pm). The Hotel Prince will change money for their guests.

If you feel like taking a refreshing dip, there's a swimming pool at the Lakeview Restaurant, at the south end of the lake. It's open to the public from 7 to 10 am, and 2.45 to 5.45 pm (Rs 10 for 45 minutes).

The GPO is about a five minute auto-rickshaw ride from the bus stand. There is also a branch in Darbar Gadh, in the walled city.

Permits To visit the villages north of Kutch, including Khavda, Bhirandiara and Dumaro, permission is required from the District Collector. First you need to present yourself (in person) at the District Superintendent of Police (DSP) office, where you have to complete a form advising which villages you wish to visit, dates, your passport details, etc. You then take this form to the District Collector's office (about five minutes walk; open weekdays from 10.30 am to 5.30 pm; closed for lunch between 1 and 2 pm) where the form will be authorised. The whole procedure should take no more than 1½ hours, and there is no fee.

Aina Mahal (Old Palace)

Maharao Lakhpatji's old palace, built in traditional Kutchi style, is in a small fortified courtyard in the old part of the city. It's a beautifully presented museum and is one of the highlights of a visit to Bhuj. The entrance to the palace houses the tourist office, and this is also the site of the **Maharao Madansinhji Museum**, which has a varied collection of paintings, photos and embroideries. There's a 15m long scroll depicting the Royal Procession of Maharao Shri Pragmalji Bahadur (1838-75). Check out the expression on the last blue-turbaned figure in this epic painting

– he looks quite peeved at having to ignobly bring up the rear of the procession!

The real attraction here, though, is the **Hall of Mirrors**, created by the master artisan, Ram Singh Malam, under the patronage of his poet-ruler, Maharao Shri Lakhpatji around the middle of the 18th century. A blend of Indian and European artistry (Ram Singh acquired his skills in Europe), the walls of the great hall are of white marble covered by mirrors separated by gilded ornaments, lighting being provided by elaborate candelabra, with shades of Venetian glass. Another remarkable feature is the **pleasure pool**, in the middle of which rises a square platform where the maharao composed his poems and gave encouragement to the classical arts of dancing girls, bards and musicians.

This palace is well worth half a day, and is open daily except Saturday from 9 to 11.45 am and 3 to 5.45 pm. Entry is Rs 3 and photography is prohibited.

Prag Mahal (New Palace)

Across the courtyard from the Aina Mahal is the new palace, an ornate Italianate marble and sandstone building which was constructed in the latter part of the 19th century. Parts of it are now used for government offices but the vast and amazingly kitsch **Durbar Hall** and the **clock tower** are open to the public. High up on the walls of this unfurnished hall are portraits of past maharaos, while down below is the usual mausoleum of big game driven to the verge of extinction by egotism and pompous pleasures. Entry is Rs 4, and its costs Rs 15 for a camera, Rs 50 for a video.

Kutch Museum

The Kutch Museum was originally known as the Fergusson Museum after its founder, Sir James Fergusson, a governor of Mumbai under the Raj. Built in 1877, it's the oldest museum in Gujarat and has an excellent collection. The well maintained exhibits (labelled in English and Gujarati) include a picture gallery, an anthropological section, archaeological finds, textiles, weapons, musical instruments, a shipping section and, of course, stuffed beasts. The museum is open every day except Wednesday and the 2nd and 4th Saturday of each month, from 9 to 11.30 am and 3 to 5.30 pm. Entry is Rs 0.50.

Sarad Bagh Palace

The last maharao died in the UK in 1991 and his palace to the east of the lake has been turned into a small museum. Set in spacious and beautifully tended gardens, the palace itself, built in 1867, is of very modest proportions, with just a drawing room downstairs and bedroom upstairs (closed). The dining room is in a separate building and on display here are a number of the maharao's personal possessions, including his video player. Also on display is his coffin, in which his body was brought back from the UK for cremation.

The palace is open from 9 am to noon and 3 to 6 pm daily except Friday; entry is Rs 1. There's also a Rs 15 camera charge, Rs 50 for a video.

Other Attractions

A huge old wall stretches around the hills overlooking the city. Unfortunately, you cannot explore around here as this is all a restricted military area.

The very colourful and richly decorated **Swaminarayan Temple** is near the Aina Mahal. It's open to the public from 7 to 11 am and 4 to 7 pm.

The **Bhartiya Sanscruti Darshan Kutch** (Folk Museum) houses an interesting private collection of beautiful textiles and artefacts, and also has reconstructions of typical village habitats. The museum is close to the Collector's Office, and you can visit by phoning the curator, Mr Rathod (☎ 21518).

Places to Stay – bottom end

There's a reasonably good range of accommodation in Bhuj, however many places whack a 'luxury tax' on top of their advertised room rates.

City Guest House (☎ 21067) is quite close to the old vegetable market and the palace. This traveller-friendly hotel is right in the middle of the walled city and has a courtyard area and a rooftop with good views over

Shroff bazaar. Small but clean doubles with private bath go for Rs 110. There are cheaper rooms with common bath for Rs 50/100. Free bucket hot water is available.

Hotel Ratrani (☎ 22388) is outside the bazaar, just off Station Rd. Singles/doubles with bathroom cost Rs 45/70 (bucket hot water), or Rs 90 for a double with constant hot water. The restaurant serves Gujarati thalis for Rs 20.

Hotel Ritish (☎ 24117) is a short walk north of the Hotel Ratrani and has clean, large rooms with attached bath (hot water in the mornings only) for Rs 75/150. There are also rooms with common bath for Rs 35/70 and dorm beds for Rs 25.

Sagar Guest House (☎ 21479), opposite the bus stand, has singles with common bath for Rs 40, and singles/doubles/triples with attached bath for Rs 60/90/125. Dorm beds are a mere Rs 20. The rooms are right above the street, so can get a bit noisy.

VRP Guest House (☎ 21388), around the corner, has clean and quiet rooms with common bath for Rs 40/60, and with attached bath for Rs 55/100. The sign is in Gujarati.

Annapurna Lodge (☎ 20831) is up near the truck park and has rooms with common bathroom for Rs 70 or with attached bathroom for Rs 60/100. Not exactly the quietest place in town, but it's cheap and friendly.

Places to Stay – middle

Hotel Anam (☎ 21390), on Station Rd, is definitely the best value in this price range. It has a range of squeaky clean rooms, all with bathroom and constant hot water, for Rs 160/300, or Rs 450/600 with air-con. There's a veg restaurant here that serves delicious Gujarati thalis.

Hotel Prince (☎ 20370; fax 50373), also on Station Rd, is equally good but pricey. Singles/doubles cost Rs 300/450, or Rs 950/1200 with air-con. There's a good non-veg restaurant and money-changing facility.

Places to Eat

Omlet Center, in the line of shops outside the bus stand, is good for a cheap breakfast.

Hotel Anam is the place to go for a really

serious feed. The restaurant offers tasty all-you-can-eat Gujarati thalis. An afternoon nap is recommended for those who over-indulge!

Green Rock restaurant in the same building as the VRP Lodge also serves excellent refillable thalis.

Hotel Prince has both veg and non-veg dishes, and is quite reasonably priced.

Hotel Nilam, opposite the Hotel Prince, is a popular vegetarian restaurant specialising in Punjabi and Chinese cuisine.

Green Hotel, down a small alley opposite the old vegetable market, offers cheap veg meals and snacks.

Things to Buy

If you are genuinely interested in the embroidery from villages in the Kutch region, get in touch with Mr AA Wazir (☎ 24187). He has a priceless collection of more than 3000 pieces, many of them very old, which he has gathered over the last 20 years or so. Some pieces are for sale (with prices starting at around Rs 200 and peaking at Rs 20,000). Remember, this is not a museum or shop, so don't expect the owner to show you each and every piece.

In the bustling Shroff Bazaar there are a range of reasonably priced shops, including some good embroidery and fabric places. Most places are open to bargaining.

Getting There & Away

Air The Indian Airlines office (☎ 21433) is open daily from 10 am to 12.30 pm and 1.30 to 4.30 pm. There are four flights weekly to Mumbai (US$85). Gujarat Airways (☎ 25198) also has four flights weekly to Mumbai (US$90). As the Indian Air Force has a base at the airport, there is tight security there.

Bus The private bus companies have their offices in the bus stand area, and have services to Rajkot (six hours, Rs 60), Mumbai (18 hours, Rs 450), Ahmedabad (seven hours, Rs 90 for a seat, or Rs 140 for a berth – yes, sleeper coaches!), and other areas in Gujarat. Patel Tours, Sahjanand Tours and MK Tours can all book sleeper coaches.

STC buses run to Jaisalmer in Rajasthan via Rathapur and Tarada (15 hours, Rs 163). For other places in Rajasthan, such as Abu Rd, Ajmer and Jaipur, you'll need to get a bus to Palanpur, and a second bus from there.

There are regular departures to the villages of Kutch; see Around Bhuj for details.

Train New Bhuj railway station is one km north of town down a little back road from the north gate (Sarpat Gate) of the old town. It's possible to travel to Ahmedabad via Palanpur (491km, 16 hours, Rs 128/382), but it's quicker to get a train or bus to Gandhidham to connect with the overnight *Gandhidham-Kutch Express* (300km, seven hours). The total rail fare ex-Bhuj is Rs 115/410 in 2nd/1st class.

To book a ticket, you don't have to face the hassle of going out to the railway station. For Rs 20, some travel agents will make the reservation for you. One place that offers this service is Hemal Travels (☎ 22491), near the bus stand.

Share Taxi A share taxi to Mandvi is Rs 20. They leave from the STC stand.

Getting Around

An auto-rickshaw to the railway station costs Rs 20, and to the airport, at least Rs 30. From Darbar Gadh to the bus stand shouldn't cost more than Rs 8.

There are places renting bicycles along the road outside the bus stand (Rs 3 per hour, Rs 20 per day). Scooters such as Vespas and Honda Heroes can be hired from the scooter hire shop close to the bus stand. However, they're not cheap, at Rs 200 to Rs 250 per day, though you may be able to negotiate a discount for a longer rental.

AROUND BHUJ
Gandhidham
Pop: 116,050   Tel Area Code: 02836
The new town of Gandhidham, near Kandla, was established to take refugees from the Sind following Partition. The town has nothing of interest, but if you are stuck here for a

night, there are two good hotels, each with a vegetarian restaurant.

Hotel Natraj (☎ 21955), opposite the bus stand, is a comfortable place with rooms from Rs 165/280 with attached bath.

Hotel Gokul (☎ 20068), nearby, is equally good with rooms from Rs 280/330.

The bus stand is about 200m diagonally to your right when leaving the railway station. Buses to Bhuj leave every 30 minutes (1½ hours, Rs 15).

Kutch Villages

The villages of the Kutch region each specialise in a different form of handicraft, and it would be easy to spend a week visiting some of them using Bhuj as a base. Due to their proximity to the Pakistan border, to visit the villages north of Bhuj you will require a permit signed by the Bhuj District Collector (see under Bhuj for details).

Some of the more important villages, (and the crafts they specialise in) include Bhujjodi (wool and cotton weaving), Padhar and Dhaneti (Ahir embroidery), Dhamanka (block printing), Lilpur (embroidery) and Anjar (nutcrackers, block printing and tie-dyeing). Several travellers warn of the children in Padhar and Dhaneti, who sometimes throw stones

Dholavira is a little village on a small 'island' north-east of Bhuj. Here, archaeologists have unearthed a city belonging to the Harappan (Indus Valley) civilisation.

For more information on the area, contact Mr Jethi at the tourist office in the Aina Mahal.

Places to Stay Accommodation in the villages is predictably limited.

Gandhi Ashram at Lilpur is a possibility with rooms for around Rs 70 per night including meals. Anjar village also has a couple of very basic guesthouses.

Getting There & Away There are buses to Anjar every 30 minutes from the bus stand in Bhuj. To Lilpur, there is one direct bus at 6.30 am (Rs 20), or take one of the many buses to Rapar and get another bus from there. Alternatively, ask the driver on the bus to Rapar to drop you off at the turn-off to Lilpur, and walk the three km to the village.

Than Monastery

About 60km from Bhuj, at the base of Dhinodar Hill, the Than Monastery is a good place to trek to. Permission is required from the District Collector in Bhuj to visit this area.

Dharamsala has extremely basic accommodation (by donation). It's considerate to try and limit your stay here to just a night or

Vernu

In Vernu, a tiny village with only 600 inhabitants on the southern edge of the Great Rann of Kutch, a self-imposed state of perpetual mourning has become a way of life. The villagers have been in mourning for over 250 years – ever since Venu Parmar, a Rajput chieftain, died fighting to protect the village from cattle thieves. In this village, cattle are not decorated, and festivals are conducted without the usual elaborate decorative touches such as garlands which make these events so colourful in other villages in this region. Even marriages are celebrated in distant villages, so as not to instil this sombre village with a spirit of gaiety or revelry. To do so would be to show disrespect to the soul of the brave Venu.

Venu was the younger brother of the Thakur of Muli, ruler of a princely state in Saurashtra. Learning of the plight of a group of villagers 70km distant who had been the victims of repeated acts of cattle theft by local dacoits (bandits or robbers), Venu valiantly went to their aid, and the battle which ensued, and in which Venu lost his life, is today the site of the village which bears his name ('Vernu' is a corruption of the warrior's name). According to legend, the indefatigable Venu lost his head at the site on which the temple dedicated to him stands today, but his body continued fighting until it dropped, four km distant!

A temple in the village dedicated to the chieftain is believed to bring death to those who sleep in it. The untimely demise of Captain James McMurdo, the first British resident of Kutch, who failed to heed local advice – only to be found dead in the temple the next morning – confirms the villagers' belief in its fatal powers. ■

two, because this place is really for pilgrims, not tourists.

There's a direct bus to Than at noon (Rs 16). Alternatively, you could take a bus to Nakatrana (Rs 12), west of Bhuj, and then another bus to Than (Rs 10). You will have to walk the last three km to the monastery, which is at the end of the road.

MANDVI
Pop: 40,670   Tel Area Code: 02834
Sixty km south-west of Bhuj, Mandvi is being promoted as a beach resort, and locals reckon its beaches are comparable with the best of those at Diu. It was once a walled port town famous for shipbuilding. This is a pleasant and unspoilt seaside town, but not many travellers venture out here.

Places to Stay & Eat
Vinayak Guest House (☎ 20366) has somewhat primitive rooms with common bath for Rs 20/40 (bucket hot water costs Rs 1).

Shital Guest House (☎ 21160) also has very basic rooms with common bath for Rs 40/60 and dorm beds for a mere Rs 15.

Vijay Villas Guest House (☎ 20043) is located in the Vijay Villas Palace compound, about eight km from Mandvi and 10 minutes

from a good beach. This secluded place has just a few double rooms with attached bath ranging from Rs 550 to Rs 650. There's a private beach for guests, but non-residents can use it for Rs 60. A thali is served at dinner for Rs 50 (order in advance). If there's nobody at the guest house when you get here, go to the nearby palace – you should find someone there to help you.

Zorba the Buddha, in the heart of the city, is a good place for cheap thalis (Rs 25).

Getting There & Away
Buses leave for Mandvi from the bus stand in Bhuj every 30 minutes (Rs 10). A share taxi from the Bhuj to Mandvi costs Rs 20.

A hovercraft service has been proposed between Mandvi and Mumbai. If this service does run, it will reduce the 19 hour trip by road to a speedy nine hour crossing.

LITTLE RANN OF KUTCH
Access to the Little Rann of Kutch, home of the last remaining population of khur (Asiatic wild ass) in India, is possible from either Bhuj or Ahmedabad. As a number of tours depart from Ahmedabad to this region, information has been included in the Around Ahmedabad section of this chapter.

Dharamanath
Indian saints and sadhus are renowned for the lengths to which they will go in their quests to attain spiritual salvation. From standing on nails to sealing themselves in caves for decades, acts of self-mortification seem limited only by the practitioner's imagination.

One of these spiritual warriors was Dharamanath, who journeyed to Kutch to find a tranquil spot in which to practise penance. He settled himself under a tree near Raipur and, whilst focusing on matters spiritual, depended on the people of Raipur to attend to his material needs. However, the Raipurians were not exactly forthcoming so, in a fit of rage, Dharamanath invoked a curse upon them. The city became desolate and its inhabitants hastily removed themselves to Mandvi. Dharamanath, overcome by remorse, resolved to climb the highest hill he could find, there to engage in a penance commensurate with his vengeful act. After being rejected by two hills, which refused to carry the burden of his guilt, he climbed *backwards* up a third hill – Dhinodar – and there proceeded to stand on his head – for 12 years. The gods, concerned at this excess, pleaded with Dharamanath to cease his penance. Dharamanath acceded – on condition that wherever his gaze fell, that region should become barren. Casting his gaze before him, the seas receded, leaving a barren, desolate wasteland – the Great Rann of Kutch.

On the highest peak of Dhinodar, a shrine dedicated to Dharamanath contains a red besmeared stone, which allegedly bore the head of the inverted ascetic during his extraordinary act of penance. ■

Madhya Pradesh

Madhya Pradesh is India's largest state and the geographical heartland of the country. Most of the state is a high plateau and in summer it can be very dry and hot. Virtually all phases of Indian history have left their mark on Madhya Pradesh, historically known as Malwa. There are still many pre-Aryan Gond and Bhil tribal people in the state, but Madhya Pradesh is overwhelmingly Indo-Aryan with the majority of the people speaking Hindi and following Hinduism.

Some of Madhya Pradesh's attractions are remote and isolated: Khajuraho, in the north of the state, is a long way from anywhere and most easily visited when travelling between Agra and Varanasi; Jabalpur, with its marble rocks, is in the centre of the state; Kanha National Park, famous for its tigers, is 160km south-east of Jabalpur.

Most of the state's other attractions are on or near the main Delhi to Mumbai railway line. From Agra, just outside the state to the north, you can head south through Gwalior (with its magnificent fort), Sanchi, Bhopal, Ujjain, Indore and Mandu. From there you can head west to Gujarat or south to the Ajanta and Ellora caves in Maharashtra.

Madhya Pradesh constitutes part of what is known as the Hindi belt, a region of northern India inhabited predominantly by Hindus. Politically it is dominated, not surprisingly, by the Hindu fundamentalist BJP. Since the demolition of the disputed mosque at Ayodyha and the subsequent political instability, the Congress Party has managed to gain some electoral ground; the BJP, however, still holds power.

History

The history of Madhya Pradesh goes back to the time of Ashoka, the great Buddhist emperor whose Mauryan Empire was powerful in Malwa. At Sanchi you can see the Buddhist centre founded by Ashoka, the most important reminder of him in India today. The Mauryans were followed by the Sungas and then by the Guptas, before the Huns swept across the state. Around 1000 years ago the Parmaras ruled in south-west Madhya Pradesh – they're chiefly remembered for Raja Bhoj, who gave his name to the city of Bhopal and also ruled over Indore and Mandu.

MADHYA PRADESH AT A GLANCE

Population: 72.3 million
Area: 443,446 sq km
Capital: Bhopal
Main Language: Hindi
Literacy Rate: 43%
Best Time to Go: September to February

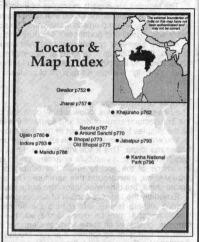

Locator & Map Index

The external boundaries of India on this map have not been authenticated and may not be correct.

Gwalior p752 ●
Jhansi p757 ●
● Khajuraho p762
Sanchi p767
● Around Sanchi p770
Ujjain p780 ● ● Bhopal p773
Indore p783 ● Old Bhopal p775
● Mandu p788
● Jabalpur p793
● Kanha National Park p796

Highlights

* Hanging out in Orchha's Jehangir Mahal
* Bicycle tours around Sanchi
* The 12,000-year-old cave paintings at Bhimbetka
* Sunset from Rupmati's Pavilion in Mandu
* The pink cliffs and wild water of the Marble Rocks

Festivals

Dance festival – Khajuraho – March
Navratri – Ujjain – September/October

MADHYA PRADESH

Khajuraho Temples

These temples were built during the Chandela period, a dynasty which survived for five centuries before falling to the Mughal onslaught. Khajuraho's temples almost all date from one century-long burst of creative genius from 950 to 1050 AD. Almost as intriguing as the sheer beauty and size of the temples is the question of why and how they were built here. Khajuraho is a long way from anywhere and was probably just as far off the beaten track 1000 years ago as it is today. There is nothing of great interest or beauty to recommend it as a building site, there is no great population centre here and during the hot season Khajuraho is very hot, dry, dusty and uncomfortable.

Having chosen such a strange site, how did the Chandelas manage to recruit the labour to turn their awesome dreams into stone? To build so many temples of such monumental size in just 100 years must have required a huge amount of human labour. Whatever their reasons, we can be thankful they built Khajuraho where they did, because its very remoteness helped preserve it from the desecration Muslim invaders were only too ready to inflict on 'idolatrous' temples elsewhere in India.

The temples are superb examples of Indo-Aryan architecture, but it's the decorations with which they are so liberally embellished that have made Khajuraho famous. Around the temples are bands of exceedingly fine and artistic stonework. The sculptors have shown many aspects of Indian life 1000 years ago – gods and goddesses, warriors and musicians, real and mythological animals.

But two elements appear over and over again and in greater detail than anything else – women and sex. Stone figures of *apsaras* or 'celestial maidens' appear on every temple. They pout and pose for all the world like pin-up models posing for the camera. In between are the *mithuna*, erotic figures, running through a whole *Kamasutra* of positions and possibilities.

Temple Terminology

The Khajuraho temples follow a fairly consistent design pattern unique to Khajuraho. Understanding the architectural conventions and some of the terms will help you enjoy the temples more. Basically all the temples follow a five-part or three-part layout.

You enter the temples through an entrance porch, known as the *ardhamandapa*. Behind this is the hall or *mandapa*. This leads into the main hall, or *mahamandapa*, supported with pillars and with a corridor around it. A vestibule or *antarala* then leads into the *garbhagriha*, the inner sanctum, where the image of the god to which the temple is dedicated is displayed. An enclosed corridor, the *pradakshina*, runs around this sanctum. The simpler three-part temples don't have a mandapa or pradakshina, but otherwise follow the same plan as the five-part temples.

Externally the temples consist of successive waves of higher and higher towers culminating in the soaring *sikhara* (spire), which tops the sanctum. While the lower towers, over the mandapa or mahamandapa, may be pyramid-shaped, the sikhara is taller and curvilinear. The ornate, even baroque, design of all these vertical elements is balanced by an equally ornate horizontal element from the bands of sculptures that run around the temples. Although the sculptures are superbly developed in their own right, they are also a carefully integrated part of the overall design – not some tacked-on afterthought.

The interiors of the temples are as ornate as the exteriors. The whole temple sits upon a high terrace, known as the *adisthana*. Unlike temples in most other parts of India, these had no enclosing wall but often had four smaller shrines at the corners of the terrace; many of them have now disappeared. The finely carved entrance gate to the temple is a torana, and the lesser towers around the main sikhara are known as *urusringas*.

The temples are almost all aligned east to west, with the entrance facing east. Some of the earliest temples were made of granite, or granite and sandstone, but all the ones from the classic period of Khajuraho's history are made completely of sandstone. At that time there was no mortar, so the blocks were fitted together.

The sculptures and statues play such an important part in the total design that many have their own terminology:

apsara – heavenly nymph, beautiful dancing woman.
mithuna – Khajuraho's most famous image, the sensuously carved, erotic figures which have been shocking people from Victorian archaeologists to busloads of blue-rinse tourists.
nayika – it's really impossible to tell a nayika from a surasundari, since the only difference is that the surasundari is supposed to be a heavenly creature while a nayika is human.
salabhanjika – female figure with tree, which together act as supporting brackets in the inner chambers of the temple. Apsaras also perform this bracket function.
sardula – a mythical beast, part lion, part some other animal or even human. Sardulas usually carry

A REGIONAL HIGHLIGHT

armed men on their backs, and can be seen on many of the temples. They all look like lions but the faces are often different. They may be demons or *asuras*.

surasundari – when a surasundari is dancing she is an apsara. Otherwise she attends the gods and goddesses by carrying flowers, water, ornaments, mirrors or other offerings. She also engages in everyday activities like washing her hair, applying make-up, taking a thorn out of her foot, fondling herself, playing with pets and babies, writing letters, playing musical instruments or posing seductively.

Western Group of Temples

The main temples are in the western group, conveniently close to the tourist part of Khajuraho. Most are contained within a fenced enclosure which is very well maintained as a park. The enclosure is open from sunrise to sunset and entry is Rs 5. This includes entry to the archaeological museum across the road, so don't lose your ticket. Admission is free on Friday. Ask at the ticket office about the excellent Archaeological Survey of India guidebook to Khajuraho. It's often out of stock, but is worth buying if available (Rs 12).

The temples are described here in a clockwise direction.

Lakshmi & Varaha Facing the large Lakshmana Temple are these two small shrines. The Varaha Temple, dedicated to Vishnu's boar incarnation or Varaha *avatar*, actually faces the Matangesvara Temple. Inside this small, open shrine is a huge, solid and intricately carved figure of the boar incarnation, dating from around 900 AD.

Lakshmana The large Lakshmana Temple is dedicated to Vishnu, although in design it is similar to the Kandariya Mahadev and Vishvanath temples. It is one of the earliest of the western enclosure temples, dating from around 930 to 950 AD, and is also one of the best preserved, with a full five-part floor plan and four subsidiary shrines. Around the temple are two bands of sculpture instead of the usual three; the lower one has fine figures of apsaras and some erotic scenes. Inside are excellent examples of apsaras acting as supporting brackets.

On the subsidiary shrine at the south-west corner you can make out an architect working with his students – it is thought this may be the temple's designer including himself in the grand plan. Around the base of the temple Is a continuous frieze with scenes of battles, hunting and processions. The first metre or two of the frieze consists of a highly energetic orgy, including one gentleman proving that a horse can be a person's best friend, while a stunned group of women look away in shock.

The temple platform gives you a good view of the Matangesvara Temple (see later in this section). It's outside the western enclosure and the only temple in this area that is still in use today.

Kandariya Mahadev The first of the temples on the common platform at the back of the western enclosure is not only the largest of the temples, it is also artistically and architecturally the most perfect. Built between 1025 and 1050, it represents Chandela art at its finest. Although the four subsidiary shrines which once stood around the main temple have long disappeared, the central shrine is in superb condition and shows the typical five-part design of Khajuraho temples.

The main spire is 31m high, and the temple is dedicated to Vishnu. The English archaeologist Cunningham counted 226 statues inside the temple and a further 646 outside – 872 in total with most of them nearly a metre in height. The statues are carved around the temple in three bands and include gods, goddesses, beautiful women, musicians and, of course, some of the famed erotic groups. The mithuna on the Kandariya Mahadev include some of the most energetic eroticism to be seen at Khajuraho.

Mahadeva This small and mainly ruined temple stands on the same base as the Kandariya Mahadev and the Devi Jagadamba. Although small and insignificant compared to its mighty neighbours, it houses one of Khajuraho's best sculptures – a fine sardula figure caressing a lion.

Devi Jagadamba The third temple on the common platform is slightly older than the Kandariya Mahadev and of a simpler, three-part design. It was probably originally dedicated to Vishnu, but later changed to Parvati and then Kali. Some students believe it may still be a Parvati temple and that the Kali image (or Jagadamba) is actually an image of Parvati, painted black. The sculptures around the temple are again in three bands. Many of the two lower band images are of Vishnu with sardulas in the inner recesses. But on the third and uppermost band the mithuna again come out to play, making this perhaps Khajuraho's most erotic temple.

A REGIONAL HIGHLIGHT

Chitragupta The fourth temple at the back of the western enclosure does not share the common platform with the other three. Similar in design to the Devi Jagadamba, this temple is probably slightly newer and is unique at Khajuraho in being dedicated to Surya, the sun god.

Attempts have obviously been made at restoration, but it is not in as good condition as other temples. Nevertheless it has some very fine sculptures that include processions, dancing girls, elephant fights and hunting scenes. In the inner sanctum, Surya can be seen driving his chariot and seven horses, while on the central niche in the south facade you can see an 11-headed statue of Vishnu. The central head is that of Vishnu himself; the 10 others are of his incarnations.

Parvati Continuing around the enclosure, you come to the Parvati Temple on your right. The name is probably incorrect since this small and not so interesting temple was originally dedicated to Vishnu and now has an image of Ganga riding on the back of a crocodile.

Vishvanath Temple & Nandi Believed to have been built in 1002, this temple has the complete five-part design of the larger Kandariya Mahadev Temple, but two of its four subsidiary shrines still stand. That it is a Siva shrine is made very clear by the large image of his vehicle, the bull Nandi, which faces the temple from the other end of the common platform. Steps lead up to this high terrace, flanked by lions on the northern side and elephants on the southern side.

The sculptures around the temple include the usual Khajuraho scenes, but the sculptures of women are particularly notable here. They write letters, fondle a baby, play music and, perhaps more so than at any other temple, languish in provocative poses.

Matangesvara Temple Standing next to the Lakshmana Temple, this temple is not within the fenced enclosure because it is still in everyday use, unlike all the other old Khajuraho temples. It may be the plainest temple here (suggesting that it was one of the first built) but inside it sports a polished lingam, 2.5m high.

Early in the morning, flower-sellers do a brisk trade in garlands for the statue of Ganesh outside. People drape them round the elephant-headed statue, say a prayer and as they walk away the flower-sellers whip them off to resell!

Chausath Yogini Standing beyond the tank, some distance from the other western group temples, this ruined temple is probably the oldest at Khajuraho, dating from 900 AD or earlier. It is also the only temple constructed entirely of granite and the only one not aligned east to west. Chausath means 64 – the temple once had 64 cells for figures of the 64 yoginis who attended the goddess Kali. A 65th cell sheltered Kali herself.

A further half km west is the **Lalguan Mahadev Temple**, a small, ruined shrine dedicated to Siva and constructed of granite and sandstone.

Eastern Group of Temples

The eastern group of temples can be subdivided into two groups. The first is made up of interesting Jain temples in the walled enclosure. The other four temples are scattered through the old village of Khajuraho (as distinct from the modern village near the western temples).

Jain Museum Outside the Jain enclosure is this modern circular gallery, filled with statues of the 24 tirthankars. It's open from 8 am to 5 pm (closed on Sunday) and entry is Rs 1.

Parsvanath The largest of the Jain temples in the walled enclosure is also one of the finest at Khajuraho. Although it does not approach the western enclosure temples in size, and does not attempt to compete in the sexual activity stakes, it is notable for the exceptional skill and precision of its construction, and for the beauty of its sculptures. Some of the best known figures at Khajuraho can be seen here, including the classic figure of a woman removing a thorn from her foot and another of a woman applying eye make-up. Although it was originally dedicated to Adinath, an image of Parsvanath was substituted about a century ago and the temple takes its name from this newer image.

Adinath Adjacent to the Parsvanath Temple, the smaller Adinath has been partially restored over the centuries. It has fine carvings on its three bands of sculptures and, like the Parsvanath, is very similar to the Hindu temples of Khajuraho. Only the striking black image in the inner sanctum indicates that it is Jain rather than Hindu.

A REGIONAL HIGHLIGHT

Shanti Nath This temple is a relatively modern one built about a century ago, but it contains many components from older temples around Khajuraho. The 4½m high statue of Adinath is said to have been sculptured in 1028. A triple-padlocked metal chest beside it is labelled 'secret donation box'. Groups of Digambara Jain pilgrims occasionally stay at the dharamsala here, their nakedness causing raised eyebrows amongst package tourists.

Ghantai Walking from the eastern Jain temple group towards Khajuraho village, you come to this small, ruined Jain temple. Only its pillared shell remains, but it is interesting for the delicate columns with their bell-and-chain decoration and for the figure of a Jain goddess astride a Garuda which marks the entrance.

Javari Walk through the village, a typical small Indian settlement, to this temple. Dating from around 1075 to 1100 AD, it is dedicated to Vishnu and is a particularly fine example of Khajuraho architecture on a small scale. The exterior has more of Khajuraho's maidens.

Vamana About 200m north of the Javari Temple, this temple is dedicated to Vamana, the dwarf incarnation of Vishnu. Slightly older than the Javari Temple, the Vamana Temple stands out in a field all by itself. It's notable for the relatively simple design of its sikhara. The bands of sculpture around the temples are, as usual, very fine with numerous celestial maidens adopting interesting poses.

Brahma & Hanuman Turning back (west) towards the modern village, you pass this granite and sandstone temple, one of the oldest at Khajuraho. It was actually dedicated to Vishnu and the definition of it as a Brahma temple is incorrect.

Taking the road directly from the modern village to the Jain enclosure, you pass a Hanuman Temple containing a large image of the monkey god. This 2½m statue has on it the oldest inscription here – 922 AD.

Southern Group of Temples
There are only two temples in the southern group, one of which is several km south of the river.

Duladeo A dirt track runs to this isolated temple, about a km south of the Jain enclosure. This is a later temple, and experts say that at this time the skill of Khajuraho's temple builders had passed its peak and the sculptures are more 'wooden' and 'stereotyped' than on earlier temples. Nevertheless, it's a fine and graceful temple with figures of women in a variety of pin-up poses and a number of mithuna couples.

Chaturbhuja South of the river, about three km from the village and a healthy hike down a dirt road, this ruined temple has a fine three metre high image of Vishnu.

Khajuraho's Erotica
The most frequently asked question by visitors to Khajuraho is why all the sex? One theory has it that the erotic posturing was a kind of *Kamasutra* in stone, a how-to-do-it manual for adolescent Brahmin boys growing up segregated from the world in special temple schools. Another claims that the figures were thought to prevent the temples being struck by lightning, by appeasing the rain god Indra. This old lecher is supposedly a keen voyeur who wouldn't want the source of his pleasure damaged.

Rather more convincing is the explanation that these are Tantric images. According to this cult, gratification of the baser instincts is one way to blot out the evils of the world and achieve final deliverance. *Bhoga* (physical enjoyment) and *yoga* (spiritual exercise) are seen as equally valid in this quest for nirvana.

Probably the most accurate theory is that the Khajuraho sculptors were simply representing life as it was viewed by their society, unhampered by Old Testament morality. In spite of the fact that modern visitors are drawn as much for reasons of prurience as for cultural appreciation, this is not pornography. Although there are certainly large numbers of erotic images here, many other day-to-day scenes are also shown. The carvings should be seen as a joyous celebration of all aspects of life.

For a map of the Khajuraho temples, see the Khajuraho town section later in this chapter. ■

MADHYA PRADESH

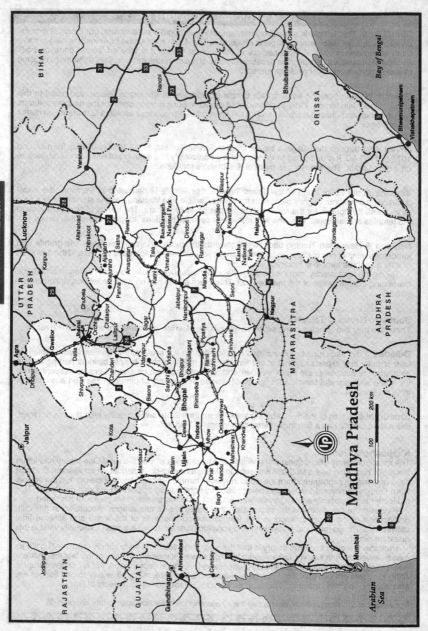

From 950 to 1050 AD the Chandelas constructed the fantastic series of temples at Khajuraho in the north of the state. Today Khajuraho is one of India's main attractions, drawing visitors from both India and overseas.

Between the 12th and 16th centuries, the region saw continuing struggles between Hindu and Muslim rulers or invaders. The fortified city of Mandu in the south-west was frequently the scene for these battles, but finally the Mughals overcame Hindu resistance and controlled the region. The Mughals, however, met their fate at the hands of the Marathas who, in turn, fell to the British.

Northern Madhya Pradesh

GWALIOR

Pop: 830,720   Tel Area Code: 0751

Just a few hours from Agra by train or road, Gwalior is famous for its old and very large fort. Within the fort walls are several interesting temples and ruined palaces. The dramatic and colourful history of the great fort goes back over 1000 years.

History

Gwalior's legendary beginning stems from a meeting between Suraj Sen and the hermit Gwalipa, who lived on the hilltop where the fort stands. The hermit cured Suraj Sen of leprosy with a drink of water from the Suraj Kund, which still remains in the fort. He then gave him a new name, Suhan Pal, and said his descendants would remain in power so long as they kept the name Pal. His next 83 descendants did just that, but number 84 changed his name to Tej Karan and – you guessed it – goodbye kingdom.

What is more certain is that in 1398 the Tomar dynasty came to power in Gwalior and, over the next several centuries, Gwalior Fort was the scene of continual intrigue and clashes with neighbouring powers. Man Singh, who came to power in 1486, was the greatest of these Tomar rulers. In 1505 he repelled an assault on the fort by Sikandar Lodi of Delhi, but in 1516 the fort was besieged by Ibrahim Lodi. Man Singh died early in the siege, but his son held out for a year before capitulating. Later the Mughals, under Babur, took the fort and held it until 1754 when the Marathas captured it.

For the next 50 years the fort changed hands on several occasions, including twice to the British. It finally passed into the hands of the Scindias, although the British retained control behind the scenes. At the time of the Indian Uprising in 1857, the maharaja remained loyal to the British but his troops didn't, and in mid-1858 the fort was the scene for some of the final, and most dramatic, events of the Uprising. It was near here that the British finally defeated Tantia Topi and it was in the final assault on the fort that the Rani of Jhansi was killed. See the Jhansi section in this chapter for more details on this heroine of the Uprising. There is a memorial to her in Gwalior.

The area around Gwalior, particularly between Agra and Gwalior, was until recent years well known for the dacoits (armed robbers) who terrorised travellers and villagers. In the Chambal River valley region you still see men walking along the roads carrying rifles.

Orientation & Information

Gwalior is dominated by its fort which tops the long hill to the north of Lashkar, the new town. The old town clings to the hill, north-east of the fort. The main market area, the Jayaji Chowk, is Lashkar's hub. Gwalior is a big place and everything is very spread out.

The tourist office (☎ 340370) is in the Hotel Tansen, about half a km south-east of the railway station.

You can change money at the State Bank of India in Lashkar, and at the Usha Kiran Palace.

Fort

Rising 100m above the town, the fort hill is about three km in length. Its width varies from nearly a km to less than 200m. The walls, which encircle almost the entire hilltop, are 10m high and imposingly solid. Beneath them, the hill face is a sheer drop away to the plains. On a clear day the view from the fort walls is superb: you can see over old Gwalior at the north-eastern end and far across the plains.

You can approach the fort from the south or the north-east. The north-eastern path starts from the archaeological museum and follows a wide, winding slope to the doors of the Man Singh Palace (Man Mandir). The southern entrance (Urbai Gate) is a long, gradual ascent by road, passing cliff-face Jain sculptures.

The climb can be sweaty work in the hot season. A taxi or auto-rickshaw up the southern road is probably the easiest way in. You can then walk down from the palace to the museum when you've looked around the fort. If you're walking both ways then it's better to go the other way: in at the north-east and out at the south. Drinks vendors are cannily situated at the top of both approaches, but there's no food available in the fort.

Check at the gates to see if the sound & light show is operating, as it's worth a look. Indian megastar Amitabh Bachchan is the narrator.

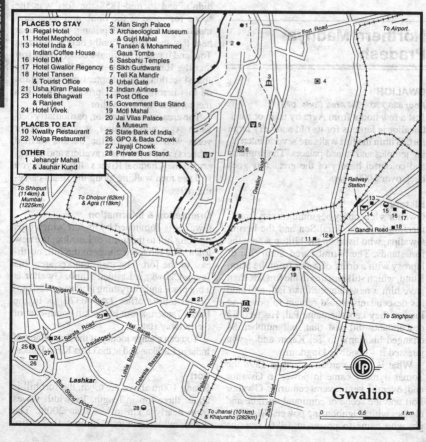

PLACES TO STAY
9 Regal Hotel
11 Hotel Meghdoot
13 Hotel India & Indian Coffee House
16 Hotel DM
17 Hotel Gwalior Regency
18 Hotel Tansen & Tourist Office
21 Usha Kiran Palace
23 Hotels Bhagwati & Ranjeet
24 Hotel Vivek

PLACES TO EAT
10 Kwality Restaurant
22 Volga Restaurant

OTHER
1 Jehangir Mahal & Jauhar Kund
2 Man Singh Palace
3 Archaeological Museum & Gujri Mahal
4 Tansen & Mohammed Gaus Tombs
5 Sasbahu Temples
6 Sikh Gurdwara
7 Teli Ka Mandir
8 Urbai Gate
12 Indian Airlines
14 Post Office
15 Government Bus Stand
19 Moti Mahal
20 Jai Vilas Palace & Museum
25 State Bank of India
26 GPO & Bada Chowk
27 Jayaji Chowk
28 Private Bus Stand

To Airport
Fort Road

To Shivpuri (114km) & Mumbai (1225km)
To Dholpur (62km) & Agra (118km)

Gwalior Road

Railway Station

Gandhi Road

To Singhpur

Laxmiganj New Road
Sarafa Road
Daulatganj
Nai Sarak
Lohia Bazaar
Dalwala Bazaar
Bus Stand Road
Palace Road
Jhansi Road

Lashkar

To Jhansi (101km) & Khajuraho (282km)

Gwalior

0   0.5   1 km

MADHYA PRADESH

There are several things to see in and around the fort, although most of the enclosed area is simply open space and fields. The admission charge is Rs 0.20.

Jain Sculptures The long ascent on the southern side climbs up through a ravine to the fort gate. Along the rock faces flanking this road are many Jain sculptures, some impressively big. Originally cut into the cliff faces in the mid-1400s, they were defaced by the forces of Babur in 1527 but were later repaired.

The images are in five main groups and are numbered. In the Arwahi group, image 20 is a 17m high standing sculpture of Adinath, while image 22 is a 10m high seated figure of Nemnath, the 22nd Jain tirthankar. The south-eastern group is the most important and covers nearly a km of the cliff face with more than 20 images.

Teli Ka Mandir This temple probably dates from the 9th century but has been recently restored. Its peculiar design incorporates a Dravidian roof with Indo-Aryan decorations (the whole temple is covered with sculptures). A Garuda tops the 10m high doorway. This is the highest structure in the fort.

Between the Teli Ka Mandir and the Sasbahu temples is a modern **Sikh gurdwara**, or temple.

Sasbahu Temples The 'mother-in-law' and 'daughter-in-law' temples stand close to the eastern wall about midway along that side of the fort. The two temples are similar in style, and date from the 9th to 11th centuries. The larger temple has an ornately carved base and figures of Vishnu over the entrances, and four huge pillars carry the heavy roof.

Man Singh Palace The palace, a delightfully whimsical building, is also known as the Chit Mandir or Painted Palace because of the tiled and painted decorations of ducks, elephants and peacocks. Painted blue, with hints of green and gold, it still looks very good today.

The palace was built by Man Singh between 1486 and 1516, and was repaired in 1881. It has four storeys, two of them underground and all of them now deserted. The subterranean ones are cool, even in the summer heat, and were used as prison cells during the Mughal period. The Emperor Aurangzeb had his brother Murad imprisoned and executed here. The east face of the palace, with its six towers topped by domed cupolas, stands over the fort entrance path.

Other Palaces There are other palaces clustered within the fort walls at the northern end. None is as interesting or as well preserved as the Man Singh Palace. The **Karan Palace**, or Kirti Mandir, is a long, narrow two-storey palace on the western side of the fort. At the northern end are the **Jehangir Palace** and **Shah Jahan Palace** with a very large and deep tank, the **Jauhar Kund**. It was here that the Rajput women of the harem committed mass *sati* after the raja was defeated in battle in 1232.

North-East Entrance There is a whole series of gates as you descend the worn steps of the path to the archaeological museum. The sixth gate, the **Hawa Gate**, originally stood within the palace but has been removed. The fifth gate, the **Hathiya Paur**, or Elephant Gate, forms the entrance to the palace.

Descending, you pass a Vishnu shrine dating from 876 AD known as **Chatarbhuj Mandir**, Shrine of the Four-Armed. A tomb nearby is that of a nobleman killed in an assault on this gate in 1518. From here a series of steps lead to rock-cut Jain and Hindu **sculptures** at the north-east of the fort. They are not as impressive as the sculptures on the southern side.

The interesting fourth gate was built in the 1400s and named after the elephant-headed god, Ganesh. There is a small pigeon house or **Kabutar Khana** here, as well as a small four-pillared **Hindu temple** to the hermit Gwalipa, after whom the fort and town were named.

The third gate dates from the same period as the Gujri Mahal and is known as the **Badalgarh**, after Badal Singh, Man Singh's uncle. It is also called the Hindola Gate, from the *hindol*, or swing, which used to stand here. The second gate, the Bansur, or Archer's Gate, has disappeared. The first gate is the **Alamgiri Gate**, dating from 1660. It was named after Aurangzeb, who took the title of Governor of Alamgiri in this region.

Archaeological Museum The museum is within the Gujri Mahal palace. Built in the 15th century by Man Singh for his favourite queen, Mrignayni, the palace is now rather deteriorated. There's a large collection of Hindu and Jain sculptures and copies of the Bagh Caves' frescoes. It's open daily except Monday from 10 am to 5 pm; admission is Rs 2 plus Rs 2 for a camera.

There's a small **museum** next to the Man Singh palace housing sculpture and carvings from around the fort. It's open daily except Friday from 10 am to 5 pm and admission is free.

Jai Vilas Palace & Museum

Located in the new town, which actually dates from 1809, this was the palace of the Scindia family. Although the current maharaja still lives in the palace, 35 rooms are now a museum. It's full of the bizarre items Hollywood maharajas are supposed to collect, such as Belgian cut-glass furniture (including a rocking chair), and what looks like half the tiger population of India, all shot, stuffed and moth-eaten. Modes of transport range from a Rolls Royce on rails to a German bubble car. Then there's a little room full of erotica, including a life-sized marble statue of Leda having her way with a swan. But the *pièce de résistance* is a model railway that carried brandy and cigars around the dining table after dinner.

The main durbar hall is quite impressive. The gold paint used around the room is said to weigh 58 kg, and the two giant chandeliers are incredible; they each hold 248 candles, are 12.5m high and weigh 3.5 tonnes apiece, so heavy that elephants were suspended from the ceiling to check that it could take the weight.

If you go there by auto-rickshaw, get dropped off at the museum, not at the palace entrance, as the two are far apart. The museum is open daily, except Monday, from 9.30 am to 5 pm; entry is Rs 50 (gulp) and photography is prohibited.

Old Town

The old town of Gwalior lies to the north and north-east of the fort hill. The 1661 **Jama Masjid** is a fine old building, constructed of sandstone quarried from the fort hill. On the eastern side of town is the fine **tomb of Mohammed Gaus**, a Muslim saint who played a key role in Babur's acquisition of the fort. It has hexagonal towers at its four corners, and a dome which was once covered with glazed blue tiles. It's a very good example of early Mughal architecture.

Close to the large tomb is the smaller **tomb of Tansen**, a singer much admired by Akbar. Chewing the leaves of the tamarind tree near his grave is supposed to do wonders for your voice (after munching here, I warbled my way tunefully around India)! It is a place of pilgrimage for musicians during December/January, when the tree tends to look unseasonally autumnal, stripped by visiting enthusiasts. To find it, follow the Fort Rd from the north-eastern gate for about 15 minutes and turn right onto a small road.

The **Moti Mahal** is an imposing edifice. It was formerly a palace, but these days it's government offices.

Places to Stay

The cheapest good places are near Bada Chowk in Lashkar, several km from the station.

Hotel Bhagwati (☎ 327428), on Nai Sarak, is excellent value. Rooms with attached bathroom are Rs 40/80, and there are good views of the fort from the terrace.

Ranjeet Hotel next door is much grottier and has rooms with common bathroom for Rs 45/85.

Hotel Vivek (☎ 427017), near Jayaji Chowk, is a better bet. It's friendly, if gloomy, and air-cooled rooms with attached bath cost Rs 100/150, or with air-con Rs 300/350.

Regal Hotel (☎ 331469) has great fort views from its roof terrace. There's a range of rooms from Rs 75/100, with common bathroom, to Rs 100/175 with bathroom and air-cooler. There are some air-con rooms. The restaurant is OK and serves beer.

Most of the mid-range places are near the railway station, but there are a few cheapies in the vicinity too.

Hotel India (☎ 341983) has dorm beds at Rs 60 and singles/doubles with attached bath from Rs 110/140. Air-coolers are available for Rs 40, or there are air-con rooms for Rs 340/400. The rooms aren't even approaching spotless and its proximity to the station means you get lots of atmosphere (read: noise and dust). It's run by the Indian Coffee Workers' Co-operative whose coffee houses you see in many Indian towns. There's one here too, staffed as usual by waiters in starched fan-shaped headgear.

Hotel DM (☎ 342083) is a peaceful place away from the hustle and bustle. Air-cooled rooms with decent attached bathrooms and flickering TVs are good value from Rs 155/185. The restaurant is a classic example of cheery Indian inefficiency.

Hotel Meghdoot (☎ 326148) is beside the Indian Airlines office. This is a gloomy place with scruffy air-cooled rooms from Rs 200/250 and some air-con rooms at Rs 300/350, all with attached bath and TV.

Hotel Tansen (☎ 340370), an MP Tourism place, is pleasantly situated in a shady area about one km from the station. It's not great value at Rs 300/350 for air-cooled singles/doubles, or Rs 525/599 with air-con.

Hotel Gwalior Regency (☎ 340670) has centrally air-conditioned rooms for Rs 550/675. Non-guests can use the health club for Rs 100 and the swimming pool for Rs 75.

Usha Kiran Palace (☎ 323213) is Gwalior's top hotel. Set in a garden near the Jai Vilas Palace, it was (as the name suggests) once a palace. It's not cheap at Rs 1050/1800, but it's cool and quiet.

Places to Eat

There's a good range of eating places in Gwalior and most hotels have restaurants.

The *Indian Coffee House* at the Hotel India is a good cheap place, with masala dosa for Rs 11 and other vegetarian snacks.

The *refreshment room* at the railway station is OK for a cheap vegetarian thali (Rs 13), and you may well be asked to sign the visitors' book!

Kwality Restaurant is an air-conditioned haven just a short stagger from the southern fort gate. Food here is good and fresh, and it's not much above street stall prices.

Volga Restaurant is near the Usha Kiran Palace. There's nothing Russian about it, but very good Indian food is served. Main dishes are around Rs 45.

The *Usha Kiran Palace's* restaurant is expensive (main dishes approach Rs 100), but the Indian dishes are good.

Getting There & Away

Air Indian Airlines (☎ 326872) has a thrice-weekly 'hopping' flight from Delhi (US$50) through Gwalior to Bhopal (US$60), Indore (US$80) and Mumbai (US$130), which also returns from Mumbai through the same cities.

Bus From the government bus stand there are regular services to Agra (three hours, Rs 33), Jhansi (three hours, Rs 31), Shivpuri (three hours, Rs 29) and Ujjain, Indore, Bhopal and Jabalpur. There are two buses each morning to Khajuraho (nine hours, Rs 72 or Rs 96 deluxe). There are also departures from the private bus stand in Lashkar.

Train Gwalior is on the main Delhi to Mumbai railway line. The superfast *Shatabdi Express* links Gwalior with Delhi (3¼ hours, Rs 324/466 in 2nd/1st class), Agra (1¼ hours, Rs 180/330), Jhansi (one hour, Rs 150/300) and Bhopal (4½ hours, Rs 380/530). If you've got the money but not the time you could use this reliable service for a day trip to Gwalior from Agra.

On other express trains it's five hours to Delhi (317km, Rs 94/317 in 2nd/1st), two hours to Agra (118km, Rs 35/146), 12 hours to Indore (652km, Rs 180/513) and 24 hours to Mumbai (1225km, Rs 255/794).

Getting Around

The Airport To or from the airport, auto-rickshaws charge around Rs 50. A taxi, if you find one, will sting you for around Rs 150.

Auto-Rickshaw & Tempo Auto-rickshaw drivers can rarely be persuaded to use their meters, so if you don't feel like bargaining, a tempo is a good option. The tempos run fixed routes around the city; the fare is Rs 4 from the railway station to Bada Chowk, the main square in Lashkar.

AROUND GWALIOR

The old summer capital of the Scindias was at Shivpuri, 114km south-west of Gwalior and 94km west of Jhansi. Set in formal gardens, the **chhatris** (tombs) are the main attraction here. With Mughal pavilions and *sikhara* spires, these beautiful memorials to the Scindia rulers are inlaid in *pietra dura* style, like the Taj Mahal. The chhatri of Madho Rao Scindia faces his mother's chhatri across the tank.

Nearby is **Madhav National Park**, essentially a deer park. On the edge of the park is the Sakhya Sagar lake. Swimming from the old boat club pier here might not be wise as there are crocodiles in the lake.

Places to Stay Most of the accommodation is in MP Tourism lodges, but there are a couple of private options, too.

Chinkara Motel (☎ (07492) 2297) is MP Tourism's place in Shivpuri. Singles/doubles are Rs 190/250.

Harish Lodge is on the main road right in the middle of town. Rooms here are cheaper and there is a restaurant.

Tourist Village (☎ (07492) 2600) is near Bhadaiya Kund and has comfortable rooms in attractive cottages for Rs 350/400, more with air-con.

Towards Agra

Between Gwalior and Agra, actually in a part of Rajasthan that separates Madhya Pradesh and Uttar Pradesh, is **Dholpur**. It was near here that Aurangzeb's sons fought a pitched battle to determine who would succeed him

as emperor of the rapidly declining Mughal Empire. The Shergarh Fort in Dholpur is very old and is now in ruins.

Near Bari is the **Khanpur Mahal**, a pavilioned palace built for Shah Jahan but never occupied.

Towards Jhansi

To the west of the railway line, 61km south of Gwalior towards Jhansi, a large group of white **Jain temples** is scattered along a hill. It's one of those strange, dream-like apparitions that so often seem simply to materialise in India. Sonagir is the nearest railway station.

Only 26km north of Jhansi is **Datia**, with the deserted seven-storey palace of Raj Bir Singh Deo. It's an impressive building, and some of the rooms still contain murals. It's worth the short bus trip from Jhansi. The town is surrounded by a stone wall and the palace is to the west.

CHANDERI

At the time of Mandu's greatest power, Chanderi was an important place, as indicated by the many ruined palaces, serais, mosques and tombs – all in a Pathan style similar to that of Mandu. The **Koshak Mahal** is a ruined Muslim palace which is still being maintained.

Today the town is chiefly known for its gold brocades and saris. Chanderi is 33km west of Lalitpur, which is 90km south of Jhansi on the main railway line. Accommodation in the town includes a *Circuit House* and the *Rest House* near the bus stand.

JHANSI

Pop: 456,895   Tel Area Code: 0517

Jhansi, situated 101km south of Gwalior, is actually just across the border in Uttar Pradesh, but for convenience we've included it here. Although Jhansi has played a colourful role in Indian history, most visitors to the town today go there simply because it's a convenient transit point for Khajuraho. This is the closest the Delhi to Mumbai railway line runs to Khajuraho, and there are good connections with Delhi and Agra; it's a punishing 5½ hour bus trip from Jhansi to Khajuraho.

History
In the 18th century, Jhansi became an important centre, eclipsing Orchha 18km to the south, but in 1803 the British East India Company got a foot in the door and gradually assumed control over the state. The last of a string of rajas died in 1853 and the British, who had recently passed a law letting them take over any princely state under their patronage if the ruler died without a male heir, pensioned the rani off and took full control.

Orientation & Information
The old city is behind the fort, which is three km from the railway station. The town is quite spread out so you'll need to use autorickshaws to get around.

The Uttar Pradesh and Madhya Pradesh state governments have tourist booths at the railway station, although neither of them is particularly good. There's also a UP tourist office at the Hotel Veerangana.

The State Bank of India is the only bank which deals with foreign currency, and even then only American Express travellers cheques. Hotel Sita and the Jhansi Hotel both have cash exchange services.

Jhansi Fort & Museum
Once used by the Indian army, the fort was built in 1613 by Maharaja Bir Singh Deo of Orchha. The British ceded the fort to the Maharaja of Scindia in 1858, but later exchanged it for Gwalior in 1866. There's nothing much to see, apart from the excellent views from the ramparts. Watch out for the band of aggressive monkeys by the temples here. It's open from sunrise to sunset daily, and entry is Rs 0.25 (waived on Friday, so you can buy an extra kernel of popcorn).

Just below the walls as you approach the fort is a bizarre blood-and-guts diorama (a

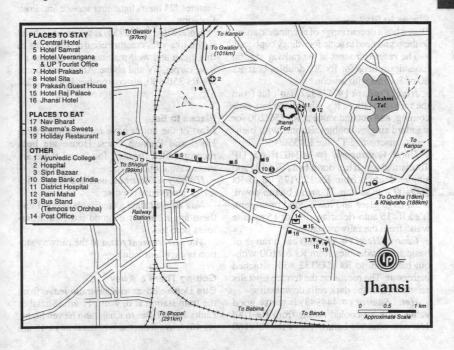

PLACES TO STAY
4 Central Hotel
5 Hotel Samrat
6 Hotel Veerangana
  & UP Tourist Office
7 Hotel Prakash
8 Hotel Sita
9 Prakash Guest House
15 Hotel Raj Palace
16 Jhansi Hotel

PLACES TO EAT
17 Nav Bharat
18 Sharma's Sweets
19 Holiday Restaurant

OTHER
1 Ayurvedic College
2 Hospital
3 Sipri Bazaar
10 State Bank of India
11 District Hospital
12 Rani Mahal
13 Bus Stand
   (Tempos to Orchha)
14 Post Office

To Gwalior (97km)
To Kanpur
To Gwalior (101km)
Lakshmi Tal
Jhansi Fort
To Kanpur
To Shivpuri (99km)
Railway Station
To Orchha (18km) & Khajuraho (188km)
To Bhopal (291km)
To Babina
To Banda

Jhansi

0   0.5   1 km
Approximate Scale

MADHYA PRADESH

Rani of Jhansi

The Rani of Jhansi was unhappy about being forcibly retired by the British in 1853, so when the Indian Mutiny burst into flame four years later, she was in the forefront of the rebellion at Jhansi. The British contingent in Jhansi were all massacred, but the following year the rebel forces were still quarrelling among themselves and the British retook Jhansi. The rani fled to Gwalior and, in a valiant last stand, she rode out against the British, disguised as a man, and was killed. She has since become a heroine of the Indian independence movement, a sort of central Indian Joan of Arc. ■

'life-like picturisation', according to the sign) depicting the battle where the Rani of Jhansi died.

Also below the fort is the government museum, which houses a small collection of 9th to 12th-century sculpture. It's open daily except Monday from 10.30 am to 4.30 pm.

Places to Stay

Jhansi has a decent range of accommodation, so there's no need to settle for a dingy cupboard.

The *retiring rooms* at the railway station have dorm beds for Rs 20; doubles cost Rs 80 or Rs 160 with air-con.

Hotel Prakash (☎ 448822) isn't far from the railway station. It's dilapidated but welcoming, and not bad value at Rs 150/200 for standard singles/doubles. Rooms with bathroom, air-con and TV are Rs 350/450.

Hotel Veerangana (☎ 442402) is a UP Tourism place. It has dorm beds (Rs 30) and singles/doubles from Rs 125/175 up to Rs 350/400 with air-con. Though a bit run-down, it's a large place and has a good restaurant. It's a Rs 15 auto-rickshaw ride, or 15 minute walk, from the railway station.

Central Hotel (☎ 440509) has a range of basic singles/doubles from Rs 65/100 without bathroom to Rs 100/132 with attached bathroom. The rooms on the terrace upstairs are nicer than the dark cells downstairs.

Hotel Samrat (☎ 444943) is pretty good value, with air-cooled rooms from Rs 100/150 with attached bathrooms or Rs 120/160

with TV as well. There's 24 hour checkout here.

Prakash Guest House (☎ 443133) is bright and airy, but it takes a couple of long-legged steps up the price scale. Air-cooled doubles with attached bath, colour TV and phone start at Rs 300. There's a pool here for guests' use and the restaurant is good.

Jhansi Hotel (☎ 470360) is one of the best in town. It was a hotel in British times and touches of the Raj are still evident. The horns of animals shot in the area line the verandah walls and in the hot season the old method of cooling is still used: *tatties* (large grass mats) are hung over the front of the hotel and kept damp to lower the air temperature as the water evaporates in the sun. Air-cooled doubles are Rs 475 and air-con rooms are Rs 475/575. The restaurant here is very good, and the bar is open all day.

Hotel Raj Palace (☎ 470554) is a modern place with air-cooled rooms from Rs 170/200, or with air-con Rs 275/325. The hotel features '24 hours lightning service and Posh Location'.

Hotel Sita (☎ 442956) is the place to head if you like your creature comforts. Rooms in this clean and well-maintained three-star all have carpet, TV and phone. Air-cooled rooms are Rs 350/400, air-con pushes it to Rs 525/575.

Places to Eat

Most of the hotels have restaurants (Jhansi Hotel and Prakash Guest House are both recommended for their food) and there are more casual options too.

Holiday Restaurant, near the Jhansi Hotel, is deservedly popular.

Nav Bharat runs a creditable second and there are a number of good ice-cream parlours here too.

The *refreshment room* at the railway station is excellent value.

Getting There & Away

Bus Deluxe buses to Khajuraho leave from the train station at 6, 7 and 11 am (Shatabdi Link). Local buses to Khajuraho (seven hours, Rs 46) leave from the bus stand at 11.45 am

MADHYA PRADESH

and 1.15 pm. Head to the bus stand for services to many other places including Gwalior (three hours, Rs 28; or Rs 40 for a luxury service which takes two hours), Shivpuri (three hours, Rs 26) and Datia (one hour, Rs 9). There's a daily bus to Indore leaving at 12 noon (12 hours, Rs 133). For Orchha, the tempos from here are better. They cost only Rs 6 for the 40 minute journey and leave when full.

Train Jhansi is on the main Delhi-Agra-Bhopal-Mumbai railway line and therefore has good rail connections. Tickets on the crack *Shatabdi Express* cost Rs 395/790 in 2nd/1st class for Delhi, Rs 220/460 for Agra, Rs 150/300 for Gwalior and Rs 340/655 for Bhopal. It departs at 10.47 am for Bhopal and 5.47 pm for Delhi.

Other expresses connect Jhansi with Delhi (414km, Rs 95/410), Agra (215km, three hours, Rs 54/241), Gwalior (97km, 1½ hours, Rs 27/139), Bhopal (291km, 4½ hours, Rs 88/400), Indore (555km, 10 hours, Rs 120/538) and Mumbai (1158km, 22 hours, Rs 179/828). There are also direct trains from Jhansi to Bangalore, Lucknow, Chennai, Pune and Varanasi.

Getting Around

The forecourt outside the railway station is filled with predatory auto-rickshaw drivers. They charge around Rs 20 for the trip to the bus stand; there are also tempos which will drop you there for Rs 3.

ORCHHA

Once the capital city of the Bundelas, Orchha is now just a village, set among a complex of well-preserved palaces and temples. It's definitely worth a visit. Tour groups do it in a couple of hours but it's a wonderfully relaxing place to stay, and you can even get a room in part of the palace here.

Orchha was founded in 1531 and remained the capital of a powerful Rajput kingdom until 1783, when nearby Tikamgadh became the new capital. Bir Singh Deo ruled from Orchha between 1605 and 1627 and built the Jhansi Fort. A favourite of the Mughal Prince

Salim, he feuded with Akbar and in 1602 narrowly escaped the emperor's displeasure; his kingdom was all but ruined by Akbar's forces. Then in 1605 Prince Salim became Emperor Jehangir, and for the next 22 years Bir Singh was a powerful figure. In 1627, Shah Jahan became emperor and Bir Singh once again found himself out of favour; his attempt at revolt was put down by the 13-year-old Aurangzeb.

Orchha's golden age was during the first half of the 17th century. When Jehangir visited the city in 1606, a special palace, the Jehangir Mahal, was built for him. Later, both Shah Jahan and Aurangzeb raided the city.

If you're wondering what all the numbers and arrows painted on the palace floors are, they're for the 1½ hour headset tour! Go-ahead MP Tourism has headsets that can be rented for Rs 25 (with Rs 500 deposit) from the Hotel Sheesh Mahal. In spite of – or perhaps because of – the breathless enthusiasm of the narrator, the recording really brings the empty palaces to life.

Palaces

The **Jehangir Mahal** is of impressive size and there are good views of the countryside from the upper levels. There's a small archaeological museum on the ground floor. Cameras attract a Rs 2 charge, and video cameras are not allowed. The **Raj Mahal** nearby has superb murals, but you may need to find the attendant to unlock some of the rooms. Below the Jehangir Mahal is the smaller **Raj Praveen Mahal**, a palace built near a garden. The *hammam* (baths) and camel stables are nearby.

Dinman Hardaul's Palace is also interesting, as is his story. The son of Bir Singh Deo, he committed suicide to 'prove his innocence' over an affair with his brother's wife, and has achieved the status of a local god through his martyrdom.

Temples

Orchha's impressive temples date back to the 17th century. They're still in use today and are visited regularly by thousands of devotees.

In the centre of the modern village is the **Ram Raja Temple** with its soaring spires. Originally a palace, it was turned into a temple when an image of Rama, temporarily installed, proved impossible to move. It now seems to have somehow made its way into the nearby **Chaturbhuj Temple**, where it is hidden behind silver doors. The **Lakshmi Narayan Temple** is linked to Ram Raja by a one km long path; it's worth the walk to see the well-preserved murals at the other end.

Other Attractions

The walled **Phool Bagh** gardens, a cool summer retreat, are also worth visiting. Other places to see include the dilapidated **Sundar Mahal** and the **chhatris** (memorials) to Orchha's rulers by the Betwa River.

Places to Stay & Eat

Orchha has limited budget accommodation, but it's not far back to Jhansi.

Hotel Mansarover, right in the centre of the village and run by the Special Area Development Authority (SADA), has clean rooms for Rs 50/75 with common bathroom (with a big marble tub but only cold water). There are two or three reasonable restaurants serving simple Indian food along the main street between the hotel and the bridge.

MP Tourism runs two places in Orchha, both of them relatively expensive. Orchha has no long-distance telephone lines, so if you want to book ahead do so through any MPTDC office. The nearest one is at Jhansi railway station (☎ (0517) 442622).

Betwa Cottages are half a km from the village, pleasantly set by the Betwa River. The cottages are in a spacious, well-tended although shadeless garden, and there are good views to the palace and the river. The cost is Rs 290/390 with air-cooling and Rs 590/690 with air-con.

Hotel Sheesh Mahal, in a converted wing of the Jehangir Mahal, must be the most romantic place to stay in Madhya Pradesh. There's one single for Rs 150, six singles/doubles for Rs 250/350 and an air-con suite for Rs 990. The best rooms are No 1 (the air-con suite) and No 2 below it. Both have

great views, even from the toilet! There's a restaurant here and it's a friendly place.

Getting There & Away

There are regular buses and tempos (Rs 6) from the Jhansi bus stand for the 18km journey to Orchha.

KHAJURAHO

Pop: 7665   Tel Area Code: 07686

Close behind the Taj and up there with Varanasi, Jaipur and Delhi, the temples of Khajuraho are one of India's major attractions. Once a great Chandela capital, Khajuraho is now a quiet village of just over 7000 people. In spite of all the tourist attention it's still a very mellow place to spend a few days.

Large numbers of visitors come to Khajuraho in March for the dance festival. This lasts 10 days and draws some of the best classical dancers in the country who perform by the western enclosure, with the floodlit temples providing a spectacular backdrop.

See the **Khajuraho Temples** regional highlight on p746.

Orientation

The modern village of Khajuraho is a cluster of modern buildings near the western group of temples. A km or so east of the bus stand is the old village of Khajuraho. Around it are the temples of the eastern group and to the south are two further groups of temples.

Information

Tourist Offices Khajuraho has a few tourist offices, but convincing a staff member to talk to you can be difficult.

The Government of India tourist office (☎ 2047) is in the modern village of Khajuraho. There is also an office at the airport. MP Tourism has a small stall at the bus stand, but the main office is hidden away at the Tourist Bungalow (☎ 2190) where the 'workers' are almost guaranteed of not being troubled by bothersome tourists.

Money As well as the usual opening hours, the State Bank of India is open for foreign currency transactions Monday to Friday between 4 and 6 pm and on Saturday from 3.30 to 4.30 pm. (The chhatri behind the bank is a memorial to Maharaja Pratap Singh Ju Deo.)

The Canara Bank down behind the bus stand is less busy than the State Bank of India. Money can be changed at Hotel Khajuraho Ashok, too.

Archaeological Museum

Close to the western enclosure, this museum has a fine collection of statues and sculptures rescued from around Khajuraho. It's small and worth a visit, but the attendants tend to hassle you for baksheesh. There's a wonderful dancing Ganesh figure in the entrance gallery. Admission is included in the western enclosure entrance fee and the museum is open from 10 am to 5 pm but is closed on Friday.

Opposite the museum, in the Archaeological Survey of India's compound beside the Matangesvara Temple, there are many more rescued sculptures – but this area is off limits.

Organised Tours

Government of India approved guides can be organised through the tourist offices or at Raja's Cafe. The cost is Rs 200/300 a half/full day for up to four people. Multilingual guides cost an extra Rs 100.

Places to Stay – bottom end

MP Tourism has quite a few hotels here and they're good value at the height of the season but overpriced at other times when private hotels reduce their prices. If there aren't many people here it's worth trying to get a reduction wherever you decide to stay. On arrival at the bus stand you'll be besieged by plenty of the usual rickshaw-wallahs offering Rs 5 rides – these are commission agents and you'll find hotel bargaining difficult if they take you to a hotel. Get them to drop you near the hotel of your choice.

The cheapest places are in the centre of the new village, close to the western group of temples.

New Bharat Lodge is very basic and not too clean. Doubles are Rs 50 with shared bathroom and from Rs 80 with attached bath.

Laxmi Guest House next door is clean and welcoming, if a little poky. Doubles with attached bathroom start at Rs 40. Nearby are two more cheap lodges in the same price range, *Yadav Lodge* (☎ 42223) and *Sita Lodge* (recently renovated). Yadav Lodge has some air-cooled rooms.

Yogi Lodge (☎ 2158) is the best of the cheapies; singles/doubles with attached bathroom start around Rs 50/70. Ask here about *Yogi Sharma's Ashram Lodge*, a large house with a garden about two km north.

Hotel Jain (☎ 2052) is an old favourite with travellers. There's a range of rooms from Rs 40/100 upwards, including air-cooled rooms. There's a good vegetarian restaurant on the terrace.

Hotel Surya (☎ 2145) next door is a step up the scale with a small garden and good rooms with attached bathroom for Rs 130/150, or Rs 500 with air-con. The upstairs rooms at the back (Rs 300) have a balcony and views over the fields.

Hotel Harmony (☎ 2135) is right beside the Surya. Comfortable rooms with attached bath are Rs 100/150 and there's a vegetarian restaurant. The small walled garden is immaculate.

Hotel Lakeside (☎ 2120) has very clean rooms set around a courtyard, right in the middle of the new village. Singles/doubles with attached bathroom and cooler cost from Rs 100/150.

Hotel Sunset View (☎ 2077) is being renovated, so prices will probably rise above the current rock bottom benchmark (Rs 50/60). Clean and with a nice garden, it should remain a reasonable place to stay. It's on the main road from the airport.

To the north of the modern village of Khajuraho are a number of hotels run by MP Tourism. Two of them scrape into a 'bottom end' listing.

Tourist Village (☎ 2128) has a peaceful and shady setting. It's a somewhat shabby collection of cottages (watch your head on the low doorways), decorated with local carpets and furnishings. A cottage with attached bathroom cost Rs 190 (Rs 50 extra if you want to use the air-cooler) and there's an open-air restaurant.

Hotel Rahil (☎ 2062) is a large concrete block nearby with an institutional feel to it. The dorms are small and clean with beds for Rs 50 and there are rooms with attached bathrooms and hot water for Rs 190/210.

Places to Stay – middle

MP Tourism hotels have the mid-price market just about sewn up.

Tourist Bungalow (☎ 2221) is a popular, convenient place, though it's showing signs of

age. Spacious air-cooled singles/doubles with attached bathroom cost Rs 250/ 300 and there's a restaurant.

Hotel Payal (☎ 2076) is a modern place with a garden and spacious singles/doubles for Rs 300/350 or Rs 540/590 with air-con. It's clean, well kept and there's an information booth. The restaurant is quite good but don't arrive too hungry because the service is slow.

Hotel Jhankar (☎ 2063) is MP Tourism's flagship here. Rooms are well decorated and also cost Rs 300/350 or Rs 540/590 for air-con, all with attached bathrooms and hot-

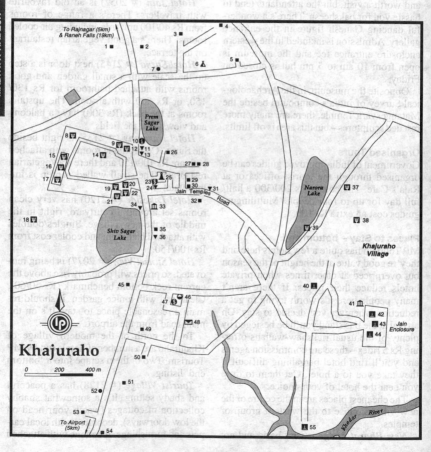

water heaters. The restaurant is not that great, but the beer is cold.

Hotel Marble Palace (☎ 2353) is a recommended new private hotel. The spacious rooms all have bathrooms with bathtubs and are pretty reasonably priced at Rs 150/250 for air-cooled rooms, and Rs 400/500 with air-con.

Places to Stay – top end

Most of the deluxe hotels are south of the modern village, where they attempt to outshine one another.

Hotel Chandela (☎ 2101; fax 2095) has air-con rooms for US$35/65, with comfortable beds, and bathtubs in the attached bathrooms. Diversions for when guests are 'templed out' include tennis, yoga, archery, croquet and badminton. Non-guests can use the swimming pool for Rs 100 or have a massage at the health club for Rs 125. There's a good bookshop, two excellent restaurants and a coffee shop.

Hotel Jass Oberoi (☎ 2085; fax 2088) has comparable tariffs and facilities. The hotel's pool is open to non-guests for Rs 150. The Oberoi has entertainment most evenings, open to all. From August to April there are folk dances (Rs 150). All year round there is a nightly puppet show, and a sitar and tabla recital (both free).

Hotel Clarks Bundela (☎ 2366), south of the Hotel Chandela, is good value at Rs 1195/2250 and also has a swimming pool. Discounts of up to 50% are available in the off-season.

Holiday Inn (☎ 2178), also south of the Hotel Chandela, is very tastefully furnished and the staff are helpful. Rooms are US$38/75. In keeping with the other places in this category, it has a pool, bar and two restaurants. The pool is open to non-guests for Rs 100.

Hotel Khajuraho Ashok (☎ 2024), a short walk north of the modern village, is an Indian Tourism Development Corporation (ITDC) gesture towards a classy hotel. It's Rs 1195/1400 single/double. Service is slow in the overpriced restaurant. You can use the swimming pool for Rs 100 as a non-guest.

Places to Eat

As the tourist industry hots up in Khajuraho, so does the range of eating places.

Raja's Cafe has been here almost 20 years and so has the Swiss woman who runs it. The large shady tree makes the restaurant's courtyard a popular gathering spot and there are good views over the temples from the terrace above. There's a wide range of food: the Swiss rostis (Rs 40) are a perennial favourite, the cheese and tomato parathas are excellent, and the waffles are a great way to fill the last corner of the belly. Tourist information and guides are also available here.

Jati Shankar Temple View, just next door, does an excellent vegetarian thali for Rs 15.

Lovely Restaurant, opposite the Archaeological Museum, is a good place for breakfast or a simple dinner.

Madras Coffee House, round the corner, isn't such good value. South Indian thalis are overpriced at Rs 50, but they have an extensive menu and plenty of other cheap dishes. If you're game you can try 'Porch with Hunney'.

Mediterraneo Restaurant is on Jain Temples Rd, opposite the Hotel Surya. The food is quite good and reasonably priced. The pasta dishes are better than the pizzas.

Shiva Janti Restaurant has a terrace overlooking the small Shiv Sagar. It's a good place to be in the early evening as the sun sets over the lake.

The top-end hotels all have good restaurants, but don't expect to get out of it cheaply – count on at least Rs 150 per person, plus drinks.

Getting There & Away

Getting to Khajuraho can be a major pain. It's really on the way from nowhere to nowhere, and is not near any railway station. Although many travellers slot it in between Varanasi and Agra, it involves quite a lot of slow bus travel over small country roads to cover not particularly great distances. Flying is a good alternative.

Air Indian Airlines (☎ 2035) have a daily Delhi-Agra-Khajuraho-Varanasi flight that returns by the same route to Delhi. It's probably the most popular tourist flight in India and can often be booked solid for days by tour groups. Unreliable ModiLuft flights ease the squeeze when they can afford fuel for their planes.

If you've got one of those middle-of-the-night international flights out of Delhi don't rely on flying in from Khajuraho the day before.

Indian Airlines' prices from Khajuraho are Agra US$60, Delhi US$75 and Varanasi US$60.

The Indian Airlines and ModiLuft offices are both next door to the Clarks Bundela Hotel.

Bus & Train From the west there are bus services from Agra (12 hours, Rs 160), Gwalior (nine hours, Rs 76; Rs 112 for a deluxe service) and Jhansi (5½ hours, Rs 72 deluxe). Jhansi is the nearest approach to Khajuraho on the main Delhi to Mumbai railway line, and there are half a dozen buses a day on this popular route. You can also go by train from Jhansi to Mahoba, 60km north of Khajuraho (2½ hours, Rs 20), and then catch a bus on to Khajuraho. The problem here is that there aren't many trains along this line, which connects Jhansi with Varanasi.

There is no direct route to Varanasi from Khajuraho. Satna (four hours from Khajuraho, Rs 29) is the nearest reliable railhead for travellers from Varanasi and the east. It's on the Mumbai to Allahabad line so there are plenty of connections. There are five buses daily from Satna to Khajuraho. However, it may not be possible to get from Varanasi to Khajuraho in one day as the last bus from Satna leaves at 3.30 pm. A good option is to take the overnight *Varanasi Kurla Express* from Varanasi at 11.30 pm, which gets you in to Satna at 6.30 am.

You can also get to Khajuraho from Varanasi via Mahoba, as described above from Jhansi.

There's a 7.30 am daily bus to Jabalpur (11 hours, Rs 75) but it is more comfortable to take a train from Satna.

Getting Around

The Airport There's an Indian Airlines airport bus; taxis charge Rs 80 for this short journey. If there aren't too many tourists about, you should be able to get a cycle-rickshaw to the airport for about Rs 30.

Khajuraho is famous for its erotic architecture.

Local Transport The best way to get around Khajuraho is by bicycle, since it's all flat and pleasantly traffic-free. Bicycles cost Rs 20 per day from several places in the new village. Cycle-rickshaws are a rip-off – hardly surprising given that rich tourists are willing to pay Rs 30 for the trip from the Hotel Chandela to the western temples!

It's a long walk to the eastern group of temples. If you're planning to take a cycle-rickshaw it's best to arrange a number of stops, including the southern temples and waiting time. You should be able to negotiate a half-day trip for around Rs 100.

AROUND KHAJURAHO
Dhubela
In the old fort in this town, 64km from Khajuraho along the road to Jhansi, there's a small **museum**. Exhibits include Shakti cult sculptures, weapons, clothes and other personal belongings of the Bundela kings.

Panna National Park
The road to Satna passes through this park lying along the River Ken, 32km from Khajuraho. It contains large areas of unspoilt forest and a variety of wildlife. There are tigers here but you'd be very lucky to see one. The numerous waterfalls in this area are popular picnic spots. Easy day trips from Khajuraho often also take in a visit to the **diamond mines** at Majhgawan, the **Rajgarh Palace** (soon to be converted into a hotel) and the **temples** of Panna town, 48km from Khajuraho.

The best time to visit is in the cooler months; in summer the park can be hotter than a furnace. The park is closed from June to October.

Access to the park is from the village of Madla, 22km from Khajuraho. Accommodation is available in the *Forest Rest House* outside the village. Another possibility is laying down with the leaves in *Giles' Tree House*. Ask at Raja's Cafe in Khajuraho.

Ajaigarh & Kalinjar Forts
At Ajaigarh, 80km from Khajuraho, is the large isolated hilltop fort, designed to protect the local population during attacks and sieges. It was built by the Chandelas when their influence in the area was on the decline. Kalinjar Fort, 25km north (just inside Uttar Pradesh) is much older, built during the Gupta period and mentioned by Ptolemy in the 2nd century AD.

SATNA
Tel Area Code: 07672
You may find it convenient or necessary to stay overnight here on your way to or from Khajuraho. The tourist office is at the railway station, but don't count on anyone being there.

Places to Stay & Eat
The choice is basically between proximity to the bus stand or the railway station.

Hotel India is a good place near the bus stand. Singles/doubles are Rs 90/120 with attached bathroom, and downstairs there's an excellent cheap restaurant. It's part of the Indian Coffee House chain.

Hotel Sahil nearby has very basic rooms for Rs 45/65.

MADHYA PRADESH

Hotel Glory has singles for Rs 50 but they're also very basic.

Hotel Park (☎ 23017) is in a slightly quieter location, with clean singles/doubles for Rs 80/120, air-cooled doubles for Rs 175, and air-con rooms for Rs 400. It's 1.5km from the railway station and has a vegetarian restaurant.

Hotel Chanakya (☎ 29732) isn't far from the railway station. Air-cooled rooms are Rs 190/230 and air-con rooms go for Rs 325/350.

Hotel Khajuraho (☎ 23330), behind the road leading from the station, is a decent place with air-cooled rooms at Rs 170/200 and the cheapest air-con in town (Rs 300).

Hotel Savera on the main street has a highly recommended restaurant, but it's expensive.

Getting There & Away

There are four buses to Khajuraho (four hours, Rs 29) between 6.30 am and 3.30 pm, and a morning bus through Rewa to Tala for Bandhavgarh National Park.

The railway station and the bus stand are about two km apart and cycle-rickshaws charge Rs 5, auto-rickshaws Rs 10. There are direct trains from Satna to Varanasi (316km, eight hours, Rs 97/506 in 2nd/2nd air-con class). Other direct expresses connect with Allahabad (180km, four hours), Calcutta, Mumbai and Chennai.

Central Madhya Pradesh

SANCHI

Tel Area Code: 07592

Beside the main railway line, 46km north of Bhopal, a hill rises from the plain. It's topped by some of the oldest and most interesting Buddhist structures in India. Although this site had no direct connection with the life of Buddha, it was the great Emperor Ashoka, Buddhism's most famous convert, who built the first stupas here in the 3rd century BC, and a great number of stupas and other religious structures were added over the succeeding centuries.

As Buddhism was gradually absorbed back into Hinduism in its land of origin, the site decayed and was eventually completely forgotten. In 1818 a British officer rediscovered the site, but in the following years amateur archaeologists and greedy treasure hunters did immense damage to Sanchi before a proper restoration was commenced in 1881. Finally, between 1912 and 1919, the structures were carefully repaired and restored to their present condition by Sir John Marshall.

Despite the damage which was wrought after its rediscovery, Sanchi is a very special place and is not to be missed if you're anywhere within striking distance. The site is one of the most evocative in India, and a good base for a number of interesting bicycle excursions.

Orientation & Information

Sanchi is little more than a small village at the foot of the hill on which the site is located. The site is open daily from dawn to dusk and tickets are available from the kiosk outside the museum. Entry costs Rs 5 (free on Friday) which covers both the site and the museum. It's worth buying a copy of the *Sanchi* guidebook (Rs 12), published by the Archaeological Survey of India. There's also a museum guidebook on sale here.

At the crossroads, the Mrignayni Emporium (closed Monday) sells local handicrafts including batik bed covers (from Rs 150), pillow cases (Rs 45), bell-metal figures, and wall hangings.

It's sometimes possible to visit the silkworm farm (Sericulture Centre). Ask at the MP Travellers' Lodge next door.

The quickest way up to the site is via the stone steps off to the right of the tarmac road. There's a drink stall by the modern *vihara* (monastery) on Sanchi hill, and Buddhist publications are for sale in the vihara. Following is a brief description of the buildings at the site; the *Sanchi* guidebook describes all these buildings, and many others, in much greater detail.

Archaeological Museum

This museum has a small collection of sculpture from the site. The most interesting pieces are the lion capital from the Ashoka pillar, a *yakshi* (maiden) hanging from a mango tree and a beautiful Buddha figure in red sandstone. It's open from 10 am to 5 pm daily except Friday.

Great Stupa

Stupa 1, as it is listed on the site, is the main structure on the hill. Originally constructed by Ashoka in the 3rd century BC, it was later enlarged and the original brick stupa enclosed

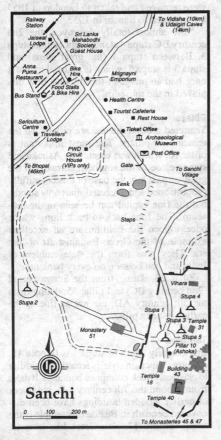

Sanchi

0   100   200 m

within a stone one. In its present form it stands 16m high and is 37m in diameter. A railing encircles the stupa and there are four entrances through magnificently carved gateways, or *toranas*. These toranas are the finest works of art at Sanchi and amongst the finest examples of Buddhist art in India.

Toranas The four gateways were erected around 35 BC and had all fallen down at the time of the stupa's restoration. The scenes carved onto the pillars and their triple architraves are mainly tales from the Jatakas, the episodes of the Buddha's various lives. At this stage in Buddhist art the Buddha was never represented directly – his presence was always alluded to through symbols. The lotus stands for his birth, the bo tree represents his enlightenment, the wheel his teachings and the footprint and throne symbolise his presence. Even a stupa itself is a symbol of the Buddha.

Walk around the stupa clockwise, as one should around all Buddhist monuments.

Northern Gateway The northern gateway, topped by a broken wheel of law, is the best preserved of the gateways. It shows many scenes from the Buddha's life, both in his last incarnation and in earlier lives. Scenes include a monkey offering a bowl of honey to the Buddha, whose presence is indicated by a bo tree. In another panel he ascends a road into the air (again represented by a bo tree) in the 'miracle of Sravasti'. This is just one of several miraculous feats he performs on the northern gateway – all of which leave his spectators stunned. Elephants, facing in four directions, support the architraves above the columns, while horses with riders and more elephants fill the gaps between the architraves.

Eastern Gateway One pillar on this gateway includes scenes of the Buddha's entry to nirvana. Across the front of the middle architrave is the 'great departure', where the Buddha (symbolised by a riderless horse) renounces the sensual life and sets out to find enlightenment. Maya's dream of an elephant standing on the moon, which she had when she conceived the Buddha, is also shown on one of the columns. The figure of a yakshi, hanging out from one of the architraves, is one of the best known images of Sanchi.

Southern Gateway The oldest of the gateways, this includes scenes of the Buddha's birth and also events from Ashoka's life as a Buddhist. At the rear of the top architrave there is another representation of the great departure. As on the western gateway, the tale of the Chhaddanta Jataka features on this gateway.

Western Gateway The western gateway, with the architraves supported by dwarfs, has some of the most interesting scenes at the site. The rear face of one of the pillars shows the Buddha undergoing the temptation of Mara, while demons flee and angels cheer his resistance. Mara also tempts on the back of the lowest architrave. The top front architrave shows the Buddha in seven different incarnations, but since he could not, at the time, be represented directly, he appears three times as a stupa and four times as a tree. His six incarnations prior to the seventh, Gautama Buddha, are known as the Manushi Buddhas.

The colourful events of the Chhaddanta Jataka are related on the front face of the bottom architrave. In this tale the Buddha, in a lower incarnation, took the form of a six-tusked elephant, but one of his two wives became jealous; she managed to reincarnate as a queen and then arranged to have the six-tusked elephant hunted and killed. The sight of his tusks, sawn off by the hunter, was sufficient for the queen to die of remorse! Pot-bellied dwarfs support the architraves on this gateway.

Other Stupas
There are many other stupas on the hill, some of them tiny votive ones less than one metre high. They date from the 3rd century AD. Eight were built by Ashoka but only three remain, including the great stupa. **Stupa 2**, one of the most interesting of the lesser stupas, is halfway down the hill to the west. If

you come up from the town by the main route you can walk back down via stupa 2. There are no gateways to this stupa, but the 'medallions' which decorate the surrounding wall are of great interest. Their design is almost childlike, but full of energy and imagination. Flowers, animals and people – some mythological – are found all around the stupa.

Stupa 3 stands north-east of the main stupa and is similar in design, though smaller in size, to the great stupa. It has only one gateway and is thought to have been constructed soon after the completion of the great stupa. Stupa 3 once contained relics of two important disciples of the Buddha. They were removed and taken to London in 1853 but returned to Sanchi in 1953.

Now almost totally destroyed, the 2nd century BC stupa 4 stands right behind stupa 3. Between stupa 1 (the great stupa) and stupa 3 is stupa 5, which is unusual in that it once had an image of the Buddha, now displayed in the museum.

Pillars
Scattered around the site are pillars and the remains of pillars. The most important is pillar 10, which was erected by Ashoka and stands close to the southern entrance to the great stupa. Only the base of this beautifully proportioned and executed shaft now stands, but the fine capital can be seen in the museum. The four back-to-back lions which once topped the column are an excellent example of the Greco-Buddhist art of that era. They now form the state emblem of India and can be seen on every bank note.

Pillar 25, dating from the Sunga period (2nd century BC) and pillar 35, dating from the 5th century AD, are not as fine as the earlier Ashoka pillar.

Temples
Immediately south of stupa 1 is **temple 18**, a *chaitya* which, in style, is remarkably similar to classical Greek-columned buildings. It dates from around the 7th century AD, but traces of earlier wooden buildings have been discovered beneath it. Beside this temple is the small **temple 17**, also Greek-like in style.

The large **temple 40**, slightly south-east of these two temples, in part dates back to the Ashokan period.

Temple 31, built originally during the 6th or 7th centuries but reconstructed during either the 10th or 11th centuries, is adjacent to stupa 5. This flat-roofed rectangular temple contains a well-executed image of the Buddha. This appears to have been moved here from another temple during the reconstruction of Temple 31, as it does not exactly fit the pedestal on which it is mounted.

Monasteries
The earliest monasteries on the site were made of wood and have long since disappeared. The usual plan is of a central courtyard surrounded by monastic cells. **Monasteries 45 and 47** stand on the higher, eastern edge of the hilltop. They date from the later period of building at Sanchi, a time of transition from Buddhism to Hinduism, and show strong Hindu elements in their design. There is a good view of the village of Sanchi below and Vidisha in the distance from this side of the hill.

Monastery 51 is partway down the hill on the western side toward stupa 2. Close to it is the **'great bowl'** in which food and offerings were placed for distribution to the monks. It was carved out of a huge boulder. The modern **vihara** on the hill was constructed to house the returned relics from stupa 3. The design is a poor shadow of the former artistry of Sanchi.

Places to Stay
It's possible to take in all that Sanchi has to offer in just two or three hours – less if you're pushed for time – so few people stay overnight. However, this is such a peaceful place that it's really worth spending the night here. Electricity cuts are frequent, so if you are planning to stay overnight, bring a torch (flashlight).

The *Sri Lanka Mahabodhi Society Guest House* (☎ 81239) is the best budget option in Sanchi. It's clean, if somewhat spartan. Rooms are in a tranquil garden setting and cost Rs 35/40 without/with attached bath

(cold water only). Ask around for the very friendly caretaker if it looks closed.

Jaiswal Lodge, over the road, has two rooms available, also for Rs 40, if the Guest House is full.

The *retiring rooms* at the railway station are clean and spacious, and cost Rs 60 per bed for the first 24 hours, Rs 90 thereafter.

Rest House, creaky, Gothic-looking and in a state of disrepair, has only two rooms, and is still not exactly cheap. A bed costs Rs 100 per person, but this includes breakfast and dinner. Visiting officials have priority on rooms (and we reckon they're welcome to them). If there's no-one around, ask at the house across the courtyard.

MP Tourism runs two places in Sanchi. *Tourist Cafeteria* (☎ 81243) has clean rooms for Rs 250/300. Rooms have ceiling fans, and there's a (hefty) Rs 50 surcharge to use the air-cooler. As the name suggests, snacks are available here and non-guests are welcome.

Travellers' Lodge (☎ 81223) is on the main road to Bhopal about 250m from the crossroads. All rooms have attached bathrooms and cost Rs 200/250, but you get hit with the same air-cooler surcharge. There's a restaurant here too.

Places to Eat
Dining in Sanchi is limited, but there's enough to keep you ticking.

Tourist Cafeteria is spotlessly clean and the dishes are good value at Rs 20 to Rs 25.

Travellers' Lodge is also good, but slightly more expensive.

Anna Purna Restaurant has the tastiest fare of the cluster of food stalls at the bus stand.

Getting There & Away
Bus Local buses connect Bhopal with Sanchi (and other towns and villages in the area) about every hour from dawn to dusk, but there are two possible routes. The longer route goes via Raisen (see the Around Sanchi section later in this chapter), takes three hours for the 68km trip and costs Rs 14. The shorter

route follows the railway line to Bhopal, takes 1¼ hours and costs Rs 12.

To Vidisha, buses depart from the Sanchi bus stand about every 30 minutes, and cost Rs 5. A rickshaw to Vidisha can be bargained down to about Rs 20.

Train Sanchi is on the main Delhi to Mumbai railway line, 46km north of Bhopal. Slow passenger trains (Rs 16) can take over two hours to get to Bhopal, but there are two express trains each day (Rs 20). The expresses depart Bhopal at 8 am and 2.40 pm, and depart Sanchi at 4 and 6 pm, so it's comfortably possible to visit Sanchi in a daytrip.

Getting Around
In Sanchi itself everything's within easy walking distance. For excursions to places nearby, like Vidisha (10km) and the Udaigiri caves (14km), you can rent bikes in Sanchi for Rs 2 per hour.

AROUND SANCHI
In the immediate vicinity of Sanchi there are more Buddhist sites, although none are of the scale or as well preserved as those at Sanchi. Most are within cycling distance. **Sonari**, 10km south-west of Sanchi, has eight stupas, two of them important. At **Satdhara**, west of Sanchi on the bank of the Beas River, there are two stupas, one 30m in diameter. Another eight km south-east is **Andher**, where there are three small but well-preserved stupas. These stupas were all discovered in 1851, after the discovery of Sanchi.

Vidisha
Pop: 109,695
Vidisha was important in Ashoka's time and it was from here that his wife came. Then it was known as Besnagar and was the largest town in the area. The ruins of the 2nd century BC Brahmanical shrine here show traces of lime mortar – the earliest use of cement in India. Finds from the site are displayed in the museum near the railway station.

From the 6th century AD the city was deserted for three centuries. It was renamed Bhilsa by the Muslims who built the now-ruined Bija Mandal, a mosque constructed from the remains of Hindu temples. From Sanchi you can reach Vidisha by bike (see Udaigiri below for directions), bus (Rs 5, every 30 minutes), train (Rs 10), or rickshaw (Rs 20).

Heliodorus Pillar
Between Vidisha and Udaigiri, one km north of the Udaigiri caves turnoff, is this inscribed pillar, known locally as the Khamb Baba pillar. It was erected in about 140 BC by Heliodorus, a Greek ambassador to the city from Taxila (now in Pakistan). The pillar celebrates his conversion to Hinduism. It's dedicated to Vishnu and worshipped by local fishers.

Udaigiri Caves
Cut into the sandstone hill, five km from Vidisha, are about 20 Gupta cave shrines dating from 320 to 606 AD; two are Jain, the other 18 Hindu. In cave 5 there is a superb image of Vishnu in his boar incarnation. Cave 7 was cut out for the personal use of King Chandragupta II. Cave 20 is particularly

interesting, with detailed Jain carvings. On the top of the hill are the ruins of a 6th century Gupta temple.

Getting There & Away From Bhopal take a Sanchi bus or train to Vidisha, and from there take a tonga or auto-rickshaw to the caves (Rs 50 including waiting time, with serious bargaining). To reach the caves by bike from Sanchi, cycle towards Vidisha until you cross the river (six km). One km further on turn left (or carry straight on if you want to visit Vidisha first). After three km you'll reach a junction in the colourful bazaar – turn left again. One km further is another left turn. Take this road for the caves (3.5km) or continue for one km for the Heliodorus Pillar.

Raisen
On the road to Bhopal, 23km south of Sanchi, the huge and colourful hilltop fort of Raisen has temples, cannons, three palaces, 40 wells and a large tank. This Malwa fort was built around 1200 AD, and although initially the centre of an independent kingdom, it later came under the control of Mandu. There are also ancient paintings in the caves in this area.

Gyaraspur
There are tanks, temples and a fort dating from the 9th and 10th centuries AD at this town, 51km north-east of Sanchi. The town's name is derived from the big fair which used to be held here in the 11th month, sometimes known as Gyaras.

Udayapur
Udayapur is 90km north of Sanchi. The large **Neelkantheswara Temple** here is thought to have been built in 1059 AD. It's profusely and very finely carved with four prominent decorated bands around the sikhara. The temple is aligned so that the first rays of the morning sun shine on the Siva lingam in the sanctum. It's a particularly fine example of Indo-Aryan architecture and is reached via the railway station at Bareth, which is seven km away.

BHOPAL
Pop: 1,278,030   Tel Area Code: 0755
The capital of Madhya Pradesh, Bhopal was built on the site of the 11th century city of Bhojapal. It was founded by the legendary Raja Bhoj who is credited with having constructed the lakes around which the city is built. The present city was laid out by the Afghan chief Dost Mohammed Khan, who was in charge of Bhopal during Aurangzeb's reign, but took advantage of the confusion following Aurangzeb's death in 1707 to carve out his own small kingdom.

Today, Bhopal has a multifaceted profile. There's the old city with its crowded marketplaces, huge old mosques, and the palaces of the former begums who ruled over the city from 1819 to 1926. To the north sprawl the huge industrial suburbs and the slums which these developments inevitably give rise to. The new city with its broad avenues, sleek high-rise offices and leafy residential areas lies to the west. In the centre of Bhopal are two lakes which, while providing recreational facilities, are also the source of its plagues of mosquitoes.

The city is also famous as the site of the world's worst industrial disaster. See the boxed section below on the Bhopal tragedy for more information.

Orientation
Both the railway station and bus stand are within easy walking distance of the main hotel area along Hamidia Rd. When arriving by train, you need to leave the station by platform No 4 or 5 to reach Hamidia Rd.

The new part of the city, which encompasses TT Nagar, site of most of the major banks, the tourist office and Indian Airlines, is a long way from either of the transport terminals so you'll have to take an auto-rickshaw or taxi. Old and New Bhopal are effectively separated by the Upper and Lower lakes.

Information
There are helpful and efficient tourist information counters at both the railway station

and airport. The headquarters of MP Tourism (☎ 554340) is in the Gangotri Complex, 4th floor, TT Nagar, in the new town. MP Tourism can book MP hotels and guest houses throughout the state. Five days advance booking is required. They can also arrange car hire (including driver) for Rs 5 per km (☎ 274289).

There's a 24 hour left-luggage facility at the railway station.

Shops in New Bhopal close on Monday, and in Old Bhopal, on Sunday. Businesses such as airlines and banks close at noon on Saturday and are also closed all day on Sunday.

Money You have to head over to TT Nagar if you want to change travellers cheques or cash. The State Bank of India (near the Rangmahal Talkies cinema, close to the tourist office), the State Bank of Indore (beneath the Hotel Panchanan) or the Allahabad Bank, Bhadbhada Rd, will do the requisite.

Post & Telecommunications The GPO and telegraph office are on Sultania Rd, Old Bhopal, near the Taj-ul-Masjid. Poste restante letters should be marked 'Bhopal GPO', or they will be directed to the central post office in TT Nagar. They appear to be held for

The Bhopal Disaster – Curing an Outrage with Neglect

On the night of 3 December 1984, 40 tonnes of deadly methyl icocyanate, a toxic gas used in the manufacture of pesticides by Union Carbide, a US-based multinational company, leaked out over the city of Bhopal. Carried by the wind, this deadly gas soon enveloped the sleeping city.

Unable to understand the sense of suffocation that overwhelmed them, the barely awake residents of Bhopal ran into the streets, falling by the roadside as they succumbed to the toxic gas. The majority of the 6000 immediate victims were Union Carbide workers and their families living in slums clustered on the perimeters of the factory. Children, elderly people and the disabled, who couldn't outdistance the spreading fumes, were particularly susceptible.

Panic and chaos ensued; officials intent on saving the lives of themselves and their families headed, literally, for the hills, leaving the bulk of the population to fend for themselves. Exact figures of those who perished in the disaster may never be known; local residents claim that the figures quoted by government officials are grossly unrepresentative. To date, the death toll stands at an estimated 16,000 people, and over half a million people have had their health permanently destroyed. Union Carbide's legacy is ongoing: toxic chemicals dumped and buried during the life of the factory have poisoned water supplies, further threatening the health of Bhopal's residents.

A report prepared by a team of international medical experts which was released on the 10th anniversary of the disaster has found that 'a substantial proportion of Bhopal's population' is suffering from 'genuine long-term morbidity', with victims exhibiting symptoms disturbingly similar to those suffered by AIDS victims – a breakdown of the immune system resulting in susceptibility to tuberculosis and respiratory problems. Unfortunately, medical services are inadequate, underfunded and corrupt, exacerbating the suffering of many patients. Since long-term monitoring of health problems was abandoned in late 1994, treatment is only symptomatic, and the drugs used are often harmful. Doctors employed in public hospitals commonly open private clinics, forcing the sick to pay for services they are entitled to free of charge.

Soon after the disaster, the Indian government demanded US$3 billion in compensation, but was persuaded to accept US$470 million or have the case drawn out for at least a decade. All criminal charges were dropped, Union Carbide renounced any liability for the accident, and the money was paid to the government. It was not until seven years after the disaster and after another 2000 people had died that a tiny portion of this money began to trickle down. So far US$90 million has been paid out to about one tenth of the almost 700,000 claimants. The remainder of compensation funds continue to filter their way through various pockets on the slow flow down to the victims.

Today Bhopal is a pleasant, cosmopolitan city, and residents are understandably reluctant to talk about the horror which suddenly enveloped their lives over a dozen years ago. Outside the now-closed factory, which lies just north of Hamidia Rd, a memorial statue to the dead is the only testimony to the tragedy of Bhopal.

Union Carbide (also operating as Everyday Industries) is a profitable business once more, and batteries produced by this company are available throughout the country. Read the small print when buying batteries in India. ■

collection until they have completely disintegrated.

Cultural Centres The Alliance Française (☎ 566595) is in Arera Colony. Officially services are for members only (Rs 100), but French visitors who are not members may be able to have a look at their French newspapers and journals.

Bookshops Bhadbhada Rd, between the State Bank of India and MP Tourism in TT Nagar, has a couple of bookshops with a small English-language range. Variety Book

House probably has the best selection, but their books are all pretty pulpy.

Taj-ul-Masjid
Commenced by Shah Jahan Begum, but never really completed, the Taj-ul-Masjid is one of the largest mosques in India. It's a huge pink mosque with two massive white-domed minarets and three white domes over the main building. The entrance to the mosque is not on Sultania Rd, despite the huge staircase here; you'll need to go around the corner and enter from busy Royal Market Rd.

MADHYA PRADESH

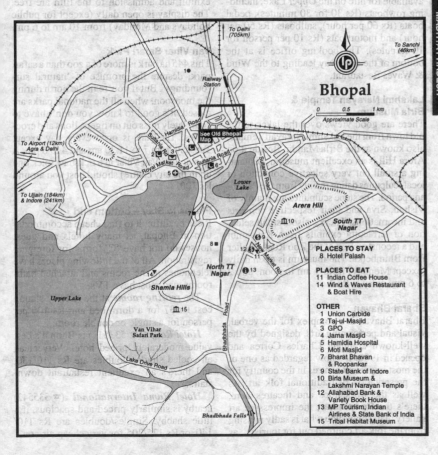

Bhopal

PLACES TO STAY
8 Hotel Palash

PLACES TO EAT
11 Indian Coffee House
14 Wind & Waves Restaurant & Boat Hire

OTHER
1 Union Carbide
2 Taj-ul-Masjid
3 GPO
4 Jama Masjid
5 Hamidia Hospital
6 Moti Masjid
7 Bharat Bhavan & Roopankar
9 State Bank of Indore
10 Birla Museum & Lakshmi Narayan Temple
12 Allahabad Bank & Variety Book House
13 MP Tourism, Indian Airlines & State Bank of India
15 Tribal Habitat Museum

Other Mosques

The **Jama Masjid**, built in 1837 by Qudsia Begum, is surrounded by the bazaar and has very squat minarets. The **Moti Masjid** was built by Qudsia Begum's daughter, Sikander Jahan Begum, in 1860. Similar in style to the Jama Masjid in Delhi, it is a smaller mosque with two dark-red minarets crowned by golden spikes.

Lakes

The larger Upper Lake covers six sq km and a bridge separates it from the Lower Lake. MP Tourism has a veritable flotilla of boats available for hire on the Upper Lake, including rowboats (Rs 30 for 30 minutes), pedal boats (Rs 60 per hour), sailboats (Rs 50 per hour) and motorboats (Rs 10 per person for 10 minutes). The booking office is at the bottom of the driveway leading to the Wind & Waves Restaurant.

Lakshmi Narayan Temple & Birla Museum

There are good views over the lakes to the old town from the Lakshmi Narayan Temple, also known as the Birla Mandir. Beside it on Arera Hill is an excellent museum, containing a small but very selective collection of local sculptures dating mainly from the Paramana period. The stone sculptures are mainly of Vishnu, Siva and their respective consorts and incarnations. There's also a small selection of terracotta exhibits from Kausambi and a reconstruction of the Zoo Rock Shelter from Bhimbetka. The museum is open daily (except Monday) from 9 am to noon, and 2 to 6 pm; entry is Rs 2.

Bharat Bhavan

Bharat Bhavan is a complex for the verbal, visual and performing arts, designed by the well-known architect Charles Correa and opened in 1982. It's now regarded as one of the most important centres in the country for the preservation of traditional folk art. As well as the workshops and theatres here, there's the **Roopankar**, the impressive art gallery that 'shows you what is sadly missing from the folk art churned out for tourists', as

one reader put it. Bharat Bhavan is in the Shamla Hills and is open daily except Monday from 2 to 8 pm; admission is Rs 1.

Tribal Habitat Museum (Museum of Man)

This interesting open-air exhibition of tribal buildings from all over India is at Rashtriya Manav Sangrahalaya in the Shamla Hills, on a 40 ha site overlooking the Upper Lake. Ancient rock-art shelters are encompassed within the exhibit area. There are craft and pottery demonstrations, and film shows on Saturday at 4 pm (one hour). Entry to the exhibit and admission to the film are free. The display is open daily (except for public holidays and Monday) from 10 am to 6 pm.

Van Vihar Safari Park

This 445 ha park is more of a zoo than a safari park, despite the promise of 'natural surroundings'. But if you're in the north during the monsoon, when all the national parks are closed, it's good to know you don't have to completely miss out on tigers, lions and crocodiles. The park is open every day except Tuesday from 7 to 11.30 am and 4 to 6 pm. A spin around Van Vihar in a rickshaw (pick one up in the city centre) should cost you around Rs 100.

Places to Stay – bottom end

It can be difficult to find cheap accommodation in Bhopal, as many hotels and guest houses do not have 'C' forms for foreigner registration. All of the following places have telephones in the rooms and attached bathrooms, and most have TVs.

The *retiring rooms* at the railway station cost Rs 37 for a dorm bed and Rs 100 per person for a single or double room.

Hotel Ranjit (☎ 533511) is Bhopal's best value moderately priced hotel. Very clean air-cooled singles/doubles are Rs 110/130, and there's an excellent restaurant downstairs.

Hotel Rama International (☎ 535542) nearby is similarly priced and spacious, if a little shabby. Singles/doubles are Rs 110/140, or Rs 175/205 for very cheap air-con.

Hotel Meghdoot (☎ 511375) has rooms from Rs 110/140. The rooms open onto the stairwell, so they could be noisy.

Hotel Sangam (☎ 542382) has basic but clean rooms from Rs 90/120 (no TV) to Rs 150/180. This place isn't well-maintained but it's set back from the main drag, so guests are spared the cacophony of Hamidia Rd.

Hotel Manjeet (☎ 536168) has singles/doubles without air-con from Rs 165/250, and with air-con from Rs 300/400.

Hotel Red Sea Plaza (☎ 535518) looms over the main Hamidia Rd junction. Singles/doubles are Rs 100/150, or Rs 250/300 with air-con. A deposit of Rs 500 is demanded on check-in!

Hotel Jalishan (☎ 535778) is centrally located on Hamidia Rd and has basic singles/doubles from Rs 120/200, or for Rs 350 with air-con. Checkout is 24 hours.

Places to Stay – middle

There's a good choice of mid-range hotels available in the city. Most have a very wide range of rooms from basic doubles to air-cooled and air-con rooms.

Hotel Taj (☎ 533162) has well-appointed rooms from Rs 100/250, or Rs 400/500 with air-con. There's an a la carte restaurant, but no bar.

Hotel Shivalik Gold (☎ 536000; fax 536101), behind the Taj, has comfortable and spotless rooms at Rs 175/225 or Rs 350/425 with air-con.

Hotel Shrimaya (☎ 535454) is also in this cluster of mid-range hotels on the north side of Hamidia Rd. Rooms here are Rs 155/225, or Rs 325/375 with air-con.

Hotel Ramsons International (☎ 535298) is at the back of this alley. It's gloomy and cavernous compared to its modern neighbours, and although the rooms are large and quiet, they aren't great value at Rs 150/225, or Rs 350/440 with air-con. Checkout is 24 hours.

Hotel Surya (☎ 536925) is a few doors down from Hotel Red Sea Plaza. Standard singles/doubles are Rs 175/225, and deluxe rooms with air-con are Rs 350/400.

Hotel Pathik (☎ 537251) is in a quiet area and has clean, straightforward rooms for Rs 170/210, or Rs 395/475 with air-con.

Hotel Blue Star (☎ 535526; fax 533045) is nearby. No-fuss rooms are good value at Rs 140/175, or Rs 350/400 with air-con.

Hotel Palash (☎ 553006) is an MP Tourism

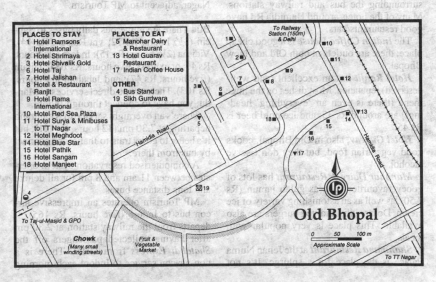

hotel. It's convenient if you have business in the TT Nagar area. Rooms are not cheap, however, at Rs 390/490 to Rs 590/690.

Places to Stay – top end
Those who can afford it head for the hills.

Residency Hotel (☎ 556002) is in Zone 1, MP Nagar. This three-star hotel is the only one in Bhopal with a swimming pool. Standard rooms are Rs 975/1140 and deluxe rooms are Rs 1120/1310.

Amer Palace Hotel (☎ 557127), close by, has standard rooms for Rs 950/1300 and deluxe rooms for Rs 1075/1425.

Hotel Lake View Ashok (☎ 541600; fax 541606) is a well-appointed hotel in the Shamla Hills with an excellent restaurant. All rooms have private balconies, and there are good views over the lake. Comfortable singles/doubles are Rs 1195/1600.

Jehan Numa Palace (☎ 540100; fax 540720), only a stone's throw away, was formerly a palace, built in the late 19th century. Rooms are from Rs 1450/1750; there's a restaurant and bar.

Places to Eat
The cheapest places to eat are the street stalls surrounding the bus and railway stations. Many of the hotels around Hamidia Rd have good restaurants/bars.

The *Indian Coffee House* is a good cheap place; there are outlets in both Old and New Bhopal.

Hotel Ranjit has an excellent (and well-deserved) reputation. Most dishes on the huge menu (there is even an 'everything' heading!) are around Rs 35, and ice-cold beer is Rs 45.

Hotel Guarav, also in Old Bhopal, cooks good vegetarian food, but they don't serve alcohol.

Manohar Dairy & Restaurant has lots of gooey favourites such as gulab jamun (Rs 7.50), as well as an astonishing variety of ice cream. Dosas, idlis and veg burgers are also available. This place is very popular with locals.

Shahnama Restaurant at the Jehan Numa Palace is the place for a splurge. It's not cheap, with main dishes from Rs 90, but the food is excellent.

Wind & Waves Restaurant is a (fairly ordinary) snack-stop at the boat-hire office on the Upper Lake.

Things to Buy
Bhopal's two main shopping areas are the New Market area, in New Bhopal, and the old market area, or Chowk, in Old Bhopal. Whilst similar items can be found in both markets, prices are much more reasonable in the Chowk, and the labyrinthine streets and alleys here make this a fascinating area to wander around – but count on getting totally lost! Here you'll find fine gold and silver jewellery, beautifully woven saris and hand-embroidered appliqué skirts at reasonable prices.

'Mrignayni' is the registered trade name for MP state handicraft merchandise – many retail shops carry Mrignayni products.

Getting There & Away
Air Indian Airlines (☎ 550480) has six flights weekly to Mumbai (US$100), Indore (US$40) and Delhi (US$90), and three flights weekly to Gwalior (US$60). The office is in TT Nagar, adjacent to MP Tourism.

Bus There are numerous daily buses to Sanchi (1½ hours, Rs 12; via Raisen, Rs 14); Vidisha (2½ hours, Rs 15); Indore (six hours, Rs 46; or express, five hours, Rs 100); Ujjain (five hours, Rs 47); and Jabalpur (11 hours, Rs 103). There are no direct services to Mandu; you have to connect through Indore.

There's an overnight service to Khajuraho departing at 7.30 pm (12 hours, Rs 111), but it's better to go by train to Jhansi and connect by bus from there.

A computerised reservation system operates between 11 am and 8 pm for all deluxe and long distance buses.

MP Tourism operates an impressive aircon bus to Indore (five hours, Rs 165). It departs from the railway station at 2.30 pm after having collected passengers off the *Shatabdi Express* from Delhi. There is a non-air-con service to Indore each morning at 8 am (Rs 100), and a daily minibus to Pachmarhi (five hours, Rs 100).

Train There's an efficient air-con reservation hall on the left as you exit the main terminal, and a separate counter for the *Shatabdi Express* within the terminal building itself.

Bhopal is on one of the two main Delhi to Mumbai railway lines. It's the terminus for the daily *Shatabdi Express*, which leaves New Delhi station at 6.15 am, reaching Bhopal at 2 pm and returning to New Delhi after a stop here of 40 minutes. Cheapest fares from Bhopal are Rs 340 for Jhansi (three hours), Rs 380 for Gwalior (4¼ hours), Rs 450 for Agra (5½ hours) and Rs 590 for New Delhi (7¾ hours).

Other express trains connect Bhopal with Delhi (705km, 10 to 12 hours, Rs 177/604 in 2nd/1st class), Mumbai (837km, 12 to 15 hours, Rs 198/670), Agra (506km, 8½ hours, Rs 137/469), Gwalior (388km, 6½ hours, Rs 111/388), Jhansi (291km, 4½ hours, Rs 89/310) and Ujjain (188km, three hours, Rs 62/230). Express trains leave for Sanchi (46km, one hour, Rs 20) at 8 am and 2.40 pm; there are numerous slower passenger trains to Sanchi and Vidisha.

For Khajuraho, travel to Jhansi and take a bus from there.

Getting Around
The Airport The airport is 12km from Old Bhopal. Fixed rates operate for both taxis (Rs 150) and rickshaws (Rs 80).

Local Transport Auto-rickshaw drivers almost always use their meters, except at night when you'll have to negotiate the fare. Minibuses for TT Nagar depart about every two minutes from in front of the Hotel Surya. The fare is Rs 2. A rickshaw costs about Rs 25.

AROUND BHOPAL
Bhojpur
The legendary Raja Bhoj (1010-53) not only built the lakes at Bhopal but also built another one, estimated at 400 sq km, in Bhojpur, 28km south-east of the state capital. History records that the lake was held back by massive earthen dams faced on both sides with huge blocks of sandstone set without mortar. Unfortunately, the lake no longer exists, having been destroyed by Hoshang Shah, the ruler of Mandu, in a fit of destructive passion in the early 15th century. It's said that the lake took three years to empty and that the climate of the area was radically affected by the loss of this enormous body of water.

What does survive here is the huge, partially completed **Bhojeshwar Temple**, which originally overlooked the lake. Dedicated to Siva, it has some very unusual design features and sports a lingam 2.3m high by 5.3m in circumference. The earthen rampart used to raise stones for the construction of the dome still remains. Nearby is another incomplete monolithic temple, this time a **Jain shrine** containing a colossal statue of Mahavira over six metres tall.

Bhimbetka
Like the Aboriginal rock paintings in the outback of Australia, the cave paintings of the Bushmen in the Kalahari Desert in Africa or the Palaeolithic Lascaux caves of France, the Bhimbetka caves are a must. Among forests of teak and sal in the craggy cliffs of an almost African setting 45km south of Bhopal, some 1000 rock shelters have been discovered. Almost half contain ancient paintings depicting the life and times of the different people who lived here.

Because of the natural red and white pigments which the painters used, the colours have been remarkably well preserved and it's obvious in certain caves that the same surface has been used by different people at different times. There's everything from figures of wild buffalo (gaur), rhinoceros, bears and tigers, to hunting scenes, initiation ceremonies, childbirth, communal dancing and drinking scenes, religious rites and burials.

The extent and archaeological importance of the site was only recently realised and dating is still not complete. The oldest paintings are believed to be up to 12,000 years old, whereas some of the crude, geometric figures probably date from as recently as the medieval period.

The caves are not difficult to find; a path connects the 15 that the local guide will show you. The **Zoo Rock Shelter** is one of the first you come to, famous for its variety of animal paintings. There's nothing here other than the caves so bring something to drink.

Getting There & Away From Bhopal, 45km away, take any bus to Hoshangabad or Itarsi (Rs 13) via Obaidullaganj, 50 minutes south of Bhopal. Get off 6.5 km after Obaidullaganj by the sign pointing right with '3.2' and some Hindi on it. Follow this sign, crossing the railway track for the 3.2 km walk to the hills in front of you. To get back you can flag down a truck on the main road. If you don't fancy the walk, pick up a rickshaw in Obaidullaganj. A taxi for the trip from Bhopal costs about Rs 600 return.

Other Places

Neori, only six km from Bhopal, has an 11th century Siva temple and is a popular picnic spot. **Islamnagar**, 11km from Bhopal on the Berasia Rd, is a hilltop palace built by Dost Mohammed Khan in the 18th century. In the palace's formal gardens, a highly decorated pavilion combines elements of the Afghan rulers' Islamic art and the local Hindus' decorative style. Any Berasia bus will drop you off here. At **Ashapuri**, six km north of Bhopal, there are ruined temples and Jain palaces with statues scattered on the ground. **Hathaikheda**, 10km out of Bhopal on the Raisen Rd, is a peaceful fishing spot. Also on the Raisen Rd, **Samardha**, 26km from Bhopal, has forest clearings just begging for a picnic blanket. **Chiklod**, 45km out, has a palace in a peaceful sylvan setting.

PACHMARHI

Pop: 14,700   Tel Area Code: 07578

Madhya Pradesh's peaceful hill station stands at an altitude of 1067m, and is 210km southeast of Bhopal. It was 'discovered' by a Captain Forsyth who realised the potential of the saucer-shaped valley as a health resort in 1857, when he first saw it from the viewpoint that now bears his name.

Although it's nothing like a Himalayan hill station, Pachmarhi is a very attractive place rarely visited by foreign tourists. The area draws quite a few artists, and gurus occasionally hold retreats up here. Every February/March up to 100,000 sadhus and tribals attend the **Sivaratri** celebrations at Mahadeo Temple, 10km south of Pachmarhi.

There are fine views out over the surrounding red sandstone hills, pools and waterfalls to bathe in, ancient **cave paintings** and some interesting walks through the sal forests. A recommended long day walk is to the hilltop shrine of **Chauragarh**, four km from Mahadeo. You can see the cave paintings at Mahadeo on the way. There's a golf course, a couple of churches and, if you don't feel like walking, bicycles for hire from the shop near New Hotel or in the bazaar.

Places to Stay & Eat

Most accommodation in Pachmarhi is run by MP Tourism or SADA, but there are a few private places springing up. High season is April to July and December/January; you should definitely negotiate discounts outside of these periods.

New Hotel (☎ 2017) is a large place operated by SADA. There's a wide range of rooms from Rs 100 for 'normal' to Rs 200 for 'super'. You can even get a 'bad' room for Rs 90. The restaurant here is reasonable with main dishes at around Rs 35.

Hotel Natraj (☎ 2151), opposite the bus stand, has double rooms from Rs 150.

Holiday Homes (☎ 2099) are a friendly budget choice, although they're two km out of town. Double rooms are Rs 225 plus Rs 75 for each extra person. Rooms have verandahs with cane chairs, and attached bathrooms with running hot water.

Nilamber Cottages (☎ 2039) are excellent. They're right beside the TV relay centre on the top of a hill so the views are great. Doubles with TV, air-cooler and attached bathroom with water heater are Rs 330.

Panchvati Huts & Cottages (☎ 2096) below the hill are not such good value with doubles from Rs 450, but the good *China Bowl* restaurant is here.

Nandanvan Cottages (☎ 2018) are better value at Rs 220 a double (Rs 250 deluxe).

Satpura Retreat (☎ 2097) is a former English bungalow with a large verandah, comfortable rooms and vast bathrooms. It's in a very quiet location along the Mahadeo road. Rooms are from Rs 325/375, or Rs 690/790 with air-con.

Amaltas (☎ 2098) was also a Raj bungalow and has rooms for Rs 375/425 with attached bathrooms but no air-con.

Rock End Manor (☎ 2079), halfway up the hill to the Nilamber Cottages, is the swankiest address in Pachmarhi. It used to be the local maharaja's golf retreat, but has recently been converted into an elegant heritage hotel. Rooms with panoramic views and all mod cons are Rs 1090/1190 single/double. *The Club* restaurant here serves Indian and Continental food and is quite reasonably priced.

Mahfil Restaurant, near the bus stand, has cheap dosas (Rs 12) and good veg burgers (Rs 12).

Getting There & Away
From the bus stand near the bazaar in Pachmarhi there's one early-morning bus to Bhopal (seven hours, Rs 55) and one MP Tourism minibus at 2.30 pm (five hours, Rs 100). There are departures every couple of hours to Pipariya (1½ hours, Rs 15). Jeeps also ply this route for Rs 40 per person or Rs 250 for the whole jeep. Signs by the winding road warn drivers that 'On the right is valley side – wobbling may mean suicide'!

PIPARIYA
Tel Area Code: 07576
Pipariya is the nearest road/rail junction to Pachmarhi, 47km away. It's on the railway line that runs from Mumbai to Jabalpur. Opposite the railway station, there's an excellent little MP Tourism *Tourist Motel* (☎ 22299) with doubles at Rs 130 (share bathroom) and a restaurant.

A local bus from Bhopal costs Rs 40 and takes six hours.

Western Madhya Pradesh

UJJAIN
Pop: 433,465   Tel Area Code: 0734
Only 56km from Indore, ancient Ujjain is one of India's holiest cities for Hindus. It gets its sanctity from a mythological tale about the churning of the oceans by the gods and demons in search of the nectar of immortality. When the coveted vessel of nectar was finally found, there followed a mad scramble across the skies with the demons pursuing the gods in an attempt to take the nectar from them. Four drops were spilt and they fell at Haridwar, Nasik, Ujjain and Prayag (Allahabad). As a result, Ujjain is one of the sites of the Kumbh Mela, which takes place here every 12 years. The 1992 Kumbh Mela drew millions to bathe here in the River Shipra.

Despite its relative obscurity today, Ujjain ranks equal as a great religious centre with such places as Varanasi, Gaya and Kanchipuram. Ujjain really comes alive during festival time, but the devotional vibe makes it a pleasant town year-round.

History
On an ancient trade route, Ujjain has a distinguished history whose origins are lost in the mists of time. It was an important city under Ashoka's father, when it was known as Avantika. Later it was so attractive to Chandragupta II (380-414 AD) that he ruled from here rather than from his actual capital, Pataliputra. It was at his court that Kalidasa, one of Hinduism's most revered poets, wrote the *Meghdoot*, with its famous lyrical description of the city and its people.

With the passing of the Guptas and the rise of the Parmaras, Ujjain became the centre of much turmoil in the struggle for control of the Malwa region. The last of the Parmaras, Siladitya, was captured by the Muslim sultans of Mandu, and Ujjain thus passed into the hands of Mughal vassals.

Muslim rule was sometimes violent, sometimes benign. An invasion by Altamish in 1234 resulted in the wholesale desecration of many temples, but that was halted during the reign of Baz Bahadur of Mandu. Bahadur himself was eventually overthrown by the Mughal emperor, Akbar. Later on, under Aurangzeb, grants were provided to fund temple reconstruction.

Following the demise of the Mughals, Maharaja Jai Singh (of Jaipur fame) became the governor of Malwa, and during his rule the observatory and several new temples were constructed at Ujjain. With his passing, Ujjain experienced another period of turmoil at the hands of the Marathas until it was finally taken by the Scindias in 1750. When the Scindia capital was moved to Gwalior in 1810, Ujjain's commercial importance declined rapidly.

Orientation & Information

The railway line divides the city: the old section, including the bazaar and most of the temples and ghats, are to the north-west of the city, and the new section is on the south-east side. The majority of hotels are in front of the railway station. Tourist information is available at the Hotel Shipra.

Temples

Mahakaleshwar Temple

The most important temple in Ujjain, the Mahakaleshwar Temple is dedicated to Siva. The temple enshrines one of India's 12 *jyoti lingam* – lingam believed to derive currents of power (*shakti*) from within themselves as opposed to lingam ritually invested with *mantra-shakti* by the priests.

The myth of the jyoti lingam (the lingam of light) stems from a long dispute for primacy between Brahma and Vishnu. During this dispute, according to legend, the earth split apart to reveal an incandescent column of light. To find the source of this column, Vishnu became a boar and burrowed underground while Brahma took to the skies in the form of an eagle. After 1000 years of fruitless

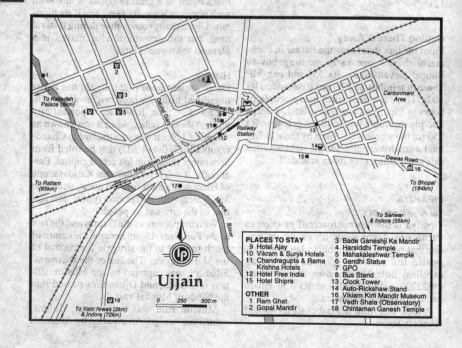

Ujjain

0   250   500 m

PLACES TO STAY
9 Hotel Ajay
10 Vikram & Surya Hotels
11 Chandragupta & Rama Krishna Hotels
12 Hotel Free India
15 Hotel Shipra

OTHER
1 Ram Ghat
2 Gopal Mandir

3 Bade Ganeshji Ka Mandir
4 Harsiddhi Temple
5 Mahakaleshwar Temple
6 Gandhi Statue
7 GPO
8 Bus Stand
13 Clock Tower
14 Auto-Rickshaw Stand
16 Vikram Kirti Mandir Museum
17 Vedh Shala (Observatory)
18 Chintaman Ganesh Temple

To Kaliadeh Palace (8km)

Mahakaleshwar Rd

Dewas Road

Cantonment Area

To Ratlam (85km)

Malgodown Road

Shipra River

To Bhopal (184km)

To Sanwar & Indore (55km)

To Yatri Niwas (2km) & Indore (72km)

Railway Station

MADHYA PRADESH

searching, Siva emerged from the lingam of light and both Brahma and Vishnu acknowledged that it was he who was the greatest of the gods.

The temple was destroyed by Altamish of Delhi in 1235 but restored by the Scindias in the 19th century. Non-Hindus are welcome to make the busy, jostling round of the many mini-temples in this evocative complex.

Bade Ganeshji Ka Mandir Above the tank near the Mahakaleshwar Temple, the large ornate statue of Ganesh here makes this temple a popular pilgrimage spot.

Harsiddhi Temple Built during the Maratha period, this temple enshrines a famous image of the goddess Annapurna. The two large pillars adorned with lamps were a special feature of Maratha art and are spectacular when lit at Navratri (Dussehra) in September/October.

Gopal Mandir The marble-spired Gopal Mandir was constructed by the queen of Maharaja Daulat Rao Scindia in the 19th century and is an excellent example of Maratha architecture.

The silver-plated doors of the sanctum have quite a history. They were originally taken from the temple at Somnath in Gujarat to Ghazni in Afghanistan and then to Lahore by Mahmud Shah Abdati. From there they were rescued by Mahadji Scindia and shortly afterwards installed in the temple. This is a very large temple but is easy to miss as it's buried in the bazaar.

Chintaman Ganesh Temple On the opposite bank of the River Shipra, this temple is believed to be of considerable antiquity. The artistically carved pillars of the assembly hall date back to the Parmara period.

Ghats
Since most of the temples are of relatively recent construction you may find more of interest on the ghats, especially at dawn and dusk when the locals frame their days with prayer. The largest ghat is Ram Ghat, fairly

close to the Harsiddhi Temple. The others are some considerable distance north of the centre.

Vedh Shala (Observatory)
Since the 4th century BC, Ujjain has been India's Greenwich (as far as Indian geographers were concerned), with the first meridian of longitude passing through it. Maharaja Jai Singh built one of his quirky observatories here between 1725 and 1730 AD. This one is smaller than those in Jaipur or Delhi but it's still in use and quite interesting. The very enthusiastic curator will demonstrate the function of the exhibits, but his English is a little hard to follow. Astrologers can purchase the complete year's astronomical ephemeris in both English and Hindi at the observatory for Rs 15.

Kaliadeh Palace
On an island in the Shipra River, eight km north of town, is the water palace of the Mandu sultans, constructed in 1458. River water is diverted over stone screens in the palace, and the bridge to the island uses carvings from the sun temple which once stood here. The central dome of the palace is a good example of Persian architecture.

With the downfall of Mandu, the palace gradually fell into ruin but was restored, along with the nearby sun temple, by Madhav Rao Scindia in 1920.

Places to Stay
There's quite a range of accommodation right opposite the railway station. Even the cheapest rooms seem to have attached bathrooms.

Hotel Vikram (☎ 25780) has small singles/doubles for Rs 50/60 and spacious rooms with TV for Rs 80/100. Avoid the grotty cells with shared bathrooms (Rs 30/40).

Hotel Surya (☎ 560747), next door, has rooms for Rs 65/75, or Rs 90/110 with TV. All rooms have running hot water.

Hotel Rama Krishna (☎ 25912) boasts 'well finished suits and self-contained too'. Rooms are Rs 125/150 or Rs 250/350 with air-con.

Hotel Chandragupta (☎ 25500), nearby, is not a bad choice, despite its manic, Fawlty

Towers atmosphere. Rooms range from Rs 55/80 to Rs 80/100, and bucket hot water is free. The cheaper rooms are a little dingy, but OK. Checkout is 24 hours.

Hotel Ajay (☎ 551354) is one of the best budget choices. It's around the corner from the railway station road where the bulk of the other cheapies are located, and is good value from Rs 70/90 (for a standard room) to Rs 140/180 (with TV and air-cooler). Hot water is available free by the bucket.

Hotel Free India (☎ 555457) is the large building opposite the Rama Krishna. Comfortable, large rooms with hot and cold water are Rs 150/165, and there's a vegetarian restaurant.

Retiring rooms at the railway station are Rs 70. Air-con are Rs 155; dorm beds Rs 30. There are two MP Tourism hotels.

The *Yatri Niwas* (☎ 551498) is inconveniently located two km from the city centre, and has only two rooms. Dorm beds cost Rs 50 and singles/doubles are Rs 190/250.

Hotel Shipra (☎ 551495), down a quiet road in a very pleasant setting, is Ujjain's top hotel. There's an impressive marble foyer, and the rooms are well appointed. Rooms range from Rs 300/350, to Rs 550/650 with air-con. The restaurant here is quite good, and there's a bar. To get to the Shipra from the railway station, exit at platform 7.

Places to Eat

There are a number of places to eat opposite the station.

Chanakya Restaurant, next to the Hotel Chandragupta, serves excellent vegetarian food and beer for Rs 35. Don't mistake the 'uroinal' here for the 'toilat'!

Sudama Restaurant next door has good vegetarian dishes for under Rs 30 but the breakfasts are spooky.

Nauratna Restaurant in the Hotel Shipra is not bad, although the size of the servings is a little modest, and beer is dear at Rs 70.

Getting There & Away

Bus There are frequent daily buses to Indore (56km, two hours, Rs 14) which are generally faster than the train, and to Bhopal (four

hours, Rs 57). There are currently no direct services to Mandu; you have to go via Indore. An early morning bus connects Ujjain with Kota in Rajasthan (Rs 75, 256km).

Train The overnight *Malwa Express* is the fastest link with Delhi. It takes 17½ hours to New Delhi (885km, Rs 140/689 in 2nd/1st), via Bhopal (184km, four hours, Rs 47/213), Jhansi (475km, nine hours, Rs 93/454), Gwalior (572km, 10½ hours, Rs 95/521) and Agra (690km, 13 hours, Rs 112/590).

The *Narmada Express* connects Ujjain with Indore (2¼ hours, Rs 24/118) and, heading east, Bhopal (184km, five hours, Rs 47/213), Jabalpur (540km, 12½ hours, Rs 88/489) and Bilaspur (929km, 25 hours, Rs 105/712).

The *Awantika Express* is the only direct service to Mumbai, leaving at 5.20 pm. The fare for the 639km journey is Rs 139/632. Alternatively, you can catch a passenger train to Nagda (1½ hours, Rs 14), to connect with the *Frontier Mail* which departs at 6 pm, arriving in Mumbai at 7 am (Rs 148/664).

The *Bhopal-Rajkot Express* to Ahmedabad departs at 8.30 pm and arrives at 10.15 am (Rs 95/436).

There is an efficient reservation hall to the left as you leave the station.

Getting Around

Many of Ujjain's sights are a long way from the centre of town so you'll probably find yourself using quite a few auto-rickshaws. Concerned at the reputation that Ujjain's rapacious rickshaw drivers had earned, the municipal authorities instituted a registration system at both the bus and railway stations. Drivers have to register the journey and fare with the police to ensure that tourists aren't ripped off!

INDORE

Pop: 1,278,690   Tel Area Code: 0731

Indore is not of great interest, but it's a good base for visiting Mandu. The city is a major textile-producing centre and at Pithampur, 35km away, Hindustan Motors, Kinetic Honda, Bajaj Tempo and Eischer all have factories. Indians call Pithampur the Detroit of India, and Indore is its gateway.

The Khan and Sarasvati rivers run through Indore. Although it is on an ancient pilgrimage route to Ujjain, nothing much happened here until the 18th century. From 1733, it was ruled by the Holkar dynasty who were firm supporters of the British, even during the Uprising.

Orientation

The older part of town is on the western side of the railway line, the newer part on the east. If arriving by train, leave the station by platform No 1 for the east side of town and by platform No 4 for the west side.

Information

The tourist office (☎ 430653) is by the Tourist Bungalow at the back of the RN Tagore Natya Griha Hall, RN Tagore Rd. You can make enquiries about tours to Mandu here. The office is open from 10 am to 5 pm.

There are sometimes exhibitions held at the magnificent Gandhi Hall (town hall). It's open to visitors daily from 10 am to 5 pm.

Travellers cheques can be changed at the State Bank of India near the GPO. The more centrally located State Bank of Indore on Yeshwant Niwas Rd has a foreign exchange licence but may be reluctant to extend its services in your direction.

Rupayana, beneath the Central Hotel, is a very good bookshop, and there's also quite a good selection at Badshah Book Shop, in the City Centre shopping complex further down MG Rd.

Rajwada

In the old part of town, the multi-storey gateway of the Rajwada or Old Palace looks out onto the palm-lined main square in the crowded streets of the Kajuri Bazaar. A mixture of French, Mughal and Maratha styles, the palace has been up in flames three times in its 200 year history. After a very serious

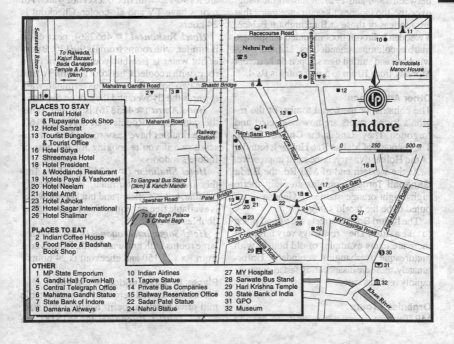

PLACES TO STAY
3 Central Hotel
   & Rupayana Book Shop
12 Hotel Samrat
13 Tourist Bungalow
   & Tourist Office
16 Hotel Surya
17 Shreemaya Hotel
18 Hotel President
   & Woodlands Restaurant
19 Hotels Payal & Yashoneel
20 Hotel Neelam
21 Hotel Amrit
23 Hotel Ashoka
25 Hotel Sagar International
26 Hotel Shalimar

PLACES TO EAT
2 Indian Coffee House
9 Food Place & Badshah
   Book Shop

OTHER
1 MP State Emporium
4 Gandhi Hall (Town Hall)
5 Central Telegraph Office
6 Mahatma Gandhi Statue
7 State Bank of Indore
8 Damania Airways
10 Indian Airlines
11 Tagore Statue
14 Private Bus Companies
15 Railway Reservation Office
22 Sadar Patel Statue
24 Nehru Statue
27 MY Hospital
28 Sarwate Bus Stand
29 Hari Krishna Temple
30 State Bank of India
31 GPO
32 Museum

To Rajwada,
Kajuri Bazaar,
Bada Ganapati
Temple & Airport
(9km)

To Indotels
Manor House

Indore

0   250   500 m

To Gangwal Bus Stand
(3km) & Kanch Mandir

To Lal Bagh Palace
& Chhatri Bagh

Racecourse Road

Nehru Park

Mahatma Gandhi Road

Shastri Bridge

Maharani Road

Railway
Station

Rani Sarai Road

Jawahar Road

Patel Bridge

Kiba Compound Road

Nasia Road

MY Hospital Road

Tuko Ganj

Yeshwant Niwas Road

RN Tagore Road

Agra-Mumbai Road

Khan River

Sarasvati River

conflagration in 1984, it's now not much more than a façade.

Kanch Mandir

On Jawahar Rd, not far from the Rajwada, is the Kanch Mandir or Seth Hukanchand Temple. This Jain temple is very plain externally, but inside is completely mirrored with pictures of sinners being tortured in the afterlife.

Museum

The museum, near the GPO, has one of the best collections of medieval and pre-medieval Hindu sculpture in Madhya Pradesh. Most are from Hinglajgarh in the Mandasaur district of western Madhya Pradesh and range from early Gupta to Paramana times.

The museum is open daily except Sunday from 10 am to 5 pm; entry is free.

Lal Bagh Palace

In the south-west of the city, surrounded by gardens, lies the grand Lal Bagh Palace, built between 1886 and 1921. It has all the usual over-the-top touches like entrance gates that are replicas of those at Buckingham Palace, a wooden ballroom floor mounted on springs, marble columns, chandeliers, stained-glass windows and stuffed tigers. Open daily except Monday from 10 am to 5 pm; entry is Rs 4.

Other Attractions

The chhatris, or memorial tombs, of the region's former rulers are now neglected and forgotten. They stand in the **Chhatri Bagh**. The cenotaph of Malhar Rao Holkar I, founder of the Holkar dynasty, is the most impressive.

At the western end of MG Rd, the **Bada Ganapati Temple** contains an eight metre high bright-orange statue of Ganesh – reputed to be the world's largest.

The **Kajuri Bazaar** streets are a good place to take a stroll. They're always very busy and there are many examples of old houses with picturesque overhanging verandahs. Unfortunately, these are disappearing fast as concrete rapidly replaces wood.

Organised Tours

MP Tourism operates day tours to Mandu

(Rs 140), Maheshwar (Rs 125), Omkareshwar (Rs 100) and Ujjain (Rs 100). Prices include lunch and afternoon tea. Ten passengers are needed for a tour to run, but you can generally count on Saturday and Sunday trips.

Places to Stay – bottom end

The railway station and the Sarwate bus terminal are only a few minutes walk apart, and it's in this area that you'll find the budget hotels. The area is lively, polluted and noisy.

Hotel Neelam (☎ 466001) is quite good value, with singles/doubles from Rs 85/120 to Rs 195/245 (with air-con), all with TV and VCR. Rooms are a little dingy, but clean, and all have hot and cold water.

Hotel Ashoka (☎ 477239), run by the same people as the Neelam, is also good value but the service is off-hand. Rooms are from Rs 90/140 to Rs 225/250 with air-con and TV, and checkout is 24 hours.

Hotel Payal (☎ 463202) is a friendly place very near the bus terminal. Spotless rooms are Rs 90/125 with free bucket hot water. All rooms have TV and air-cooler. Checkout is 24 hours.

Hotel Yashoneel (☎ 465286), next door, is similar, with rooms from Rs 90/130. Bucket hot water is free but you pay extra for a room with a cooler. Checkout is 9 am. To find these two hotels from the bus terminal, walk towards the flyover, and they're on the right.

Hotel Amrit (☎ 465876) is further along the same street. Rooms start at Rs 120/160. Some doubles have sexy round beds: try to score one if you're looking for the best of Indore's indoors.

Hotel Shalimar (☎ 462481), a little further from the bus terminal, is not exactly pristine, but it's cheap, and bucket hot water is available free on request. Very tiny singles/doubles are Rs 45/75.

Hotel Sagar International (☎ 462630) has large rooms with hot-water bath. Rooms cost from Rs 125/150 and checkout is 24 hours.

Places to Stay – middle & top end

Indore has a good selection of comfortable mid-price hotels, as befits a city of this size. The *Tourist Bungalow* (☎ 541818), on

RN Tagore Rd, is at the back of the Tagore Natya Griha Hall. Rooms are Rs 225/275, or Rs 350/400 with air-con.

Hotel Samrat (☎ 433889) is a large modern place. Comfortable rooms with TV are Rs 325/425, or Rs 425/525 with air-con. There's a very good restaurant and bar, and checkout is 24 hours.

Hotel Surya (☎ 431155) is another good choice. Standard rooms are Rs 425/600 and air-con rooms are Rs 500/675. Its restaurant is also very popular. All rooms have TV and VCR; most rooms have a balcony.

Central Hotel (☎ 435621) is a popular choice. Huge rooms with sitting areas are Rs 150/200, or Rs 400/500 with air-con.

Shreemaya Hotel (☎ 431941), opposite the more conspicuous Hotel President, has comfortable rooms from Rs 400/550.

Hotel President (☎ 433156; fax 532230) boasts a health club and sauna for guests. Well-appointed rooms are Rs 675/875, all with air-con. Checkout is 9 am.

Indotels Manor House (☎ 537301; fax 434864) is a four-star place with all the usual mod cons. Rooms cost from Rs 850/1050, and there's a good restaurant.

Places to Eat

There are several good places offering standard Indian fare close to the bus stand.

The *Indian Coffee House* is always a good, cheap choice. There's a branch on MG Rd, near the Central Hotel.

Food Place is a cafeteria serving tasty south Indian food. It's in the City Centre shopping complex on MG Rd.

Most of the hotels have restaurants and bars.

Woodlands Restaurant at the Hotel President is an excellent choice, and meals are very reasonably priced. The chef's special biryani (Rs 36) is a technicolour architectural extravaganza which has to be seen to be believed. The trick is getting it to your table before the elaborate edifice collapses.

Hotel Surya's restaurant is a great place for a splurge. Main (non-veg) dishes are from Rs 45 and beer costs Rs 55. In the Surya

Bar you can enjoy 'silent lights, sound of sips, soft & sweet heart music'.

Indore is famous for its variety of *namkin* – 'Prakash' brand is the best. If you're here during one of the festivals watch out for the *bhang gota* – samosas with added spice!

Things to Buy

The Kajuri Bazaar is only one of a number of colourful and lively bazaars in the vicinity of the Rajwada, specialising in gold and silverwork, cloth, leather work and traditional garments.

Getting There & Away

Air Indore Airport is nine km from the city. Indian Airlines (☎ 431595) has six flights a week to Mumbai (US$70). There are also six flights to Delhi (US$105), via Bhopal (US$40) and Gwalior (US$80).

Damania Airways (☎ 433922) has daily flights to Mumbai (Rs 1950).

Bus There are frequent departures from the Sarwate bus terminal to Ujjain (1½ hours, Rs 14). For Mandu, take a bus to Dhar (Rs 17) and another to Mandu from there (Rs 7). From Sarwate station there are buses to Dhar at 5, 6, 7, 8 and 9 am. From Gangwal bus stand, about three km west along Jawahar Rd, there are departures to Dhar every 30 minutes.

From the Sarwate bus stand there are two services to Aurangabad (for the Ajanta and Ellora caves): a morning service via Ajanta which departs at 5 am and an evening service direct to Aurangabad which leaves at 8.30 pm. Indore to Ajanta is Rs 95 (12 hours) and to Aurangabad, Rs 139 (15 hours). There's no direct bus to Ellora (change at Aurangabad).

Buses to Bhopal depart every 30 minutes (five hours, Rs 57). To Udaipur there are two early morning and three evening buses (12 hours, Rs 108).

There are a number of private bus companies between the bus and railway stations and RN Tagore Rd. Destinations include Mumbai (Rs 220), Pune (Rs 220), Nagpur (Rs 200), Jaipur (Rs 150), Gwalior (Rs 120),

Aurangabad (Rs 170) and Ahmedabad (Rs 120).

MP Tourism has a luxury service to Bhopal. It departs from the tourist office at 8 am, takes four to five hours, and costs a hefty Rs 165!

Train Indore is connected to the main broad-gauge lines between Delhi and Mumbai by tracks from Nagda via Ujjain in the west and Bhopal in the east. The daily *Malwa Express* leaves Indore at 6.30 pm for New Delhi (969km, 19 hours, Rs 231/734 in 2nd/1st), via Ujjain (1½ hours, Rs 24/118), Bhopal (264km, 5½ hours, Rs 62/283), Jhansi (555km, 10½ hours, Rs 111/503), Gwalior (652km, 12½ hours, Rs 166/769) and Agra (770km, 14 hours, Rs 177/823).

For Mumbai, the *Awantika Express* leaves Indore at 3.45 pm and arrives in Mumbai at 7 am (Rs 182/920 in 2nd/2nd air-con).

The other broad-gauge line runs from Indore to Bilaspur via Ujjain, Bhopal and Jabalpur. The *Narmada Express* departs Indore at 3 pm, reaching Jabalpur (600km, 15 hours, Rs 119/563) at dawn.

There is also a metre-gauge line through Indore. Services on this line run from Jaipur in Rajasthan (610km, 16 hours, Rs 175/556 in 2nd/1st class) via Indore south-east to Khandwa, Nizamabad and Secunderabad (787km, 24 hours, Rs 210/668).

The reservation office is in an ugly mauve and yellow building 30m along the small street opposite the railway station. It's open 8 am to 8 pm, Sunday 8 am to 2 pm, and you can also reserve places on trains departing from Delhi and Chennai.

Getting Around
The Airport The airport is nine km from the city. There's no airport bus; auto-rickshaws charge Rs 50 and taxis Rs 125.

Local Transport There are plenty of taxis, auto-rickshaws and tempos in Indore. The auto-rickshaws are cheap (most journeys are around Rs 5) and drivers will generally use their meters. Tempos operate along set routes and cost Rs 2 from point to point. The main

stands are in front of the railway station and at Gandhi Hall.

AROUND INDORE
Omkareshwar
This island at the confluence of the Narmada and Kaveri rivers has drawn Hindu pilgrims for centuries on account of its jyoti lingam, one of the 12 throughout India, at the Siva **Temple of Shri Omkar Mandhata**. (For an explanation of the myth of the jyoti lingam refer to the Mahakaleshwar Temple section under Ujjain earlier in this chapter.)

The temple is constructed from local soft stone which has enabled its artisans to achieve a rare degree of detailed work, particularly in the friezes on the upper parts of the structure.

There are other temples on this island including the **Siddhnath**, a good example of early medieval Brahminic architecture, and a cluster of other Hindu and Jain temples. Though damaged by Muslim invaders in the time of Mahmud of Ghazni (11th century), these temples and those on the nearby riverbanks remain essentially intact. The island temples present a very picturesque sight and are well worth visiting.

Places to Stay Many *dharamsalas* offer basic accommodation at Omkareshwar, but they're mainly for Hindu pilgrims.

Yatrika Guest House at Omkareshwar Mandir has singles/doubles around Rs 60/80.

Getting There & Away Omkareshwar Road, on the Ratlam-Indore-Khandwa line, is the nearest railway station. Omkareshwar itself is 12km from here by road. Local buses to Omkareshwar leave Indore (68km, Rs 20) at frequent intervals every morning until 10.30 am. There's one early morning bus from Ujjain (124km, Rs 33), and regular departures from Khandwa (68km, Rs 20).

Maheshwar
Maheshwar was an important cultural and political centre at the dawn of Hindu civilisation and was mentioned in the *Ramayana* and *Mahabharata* under its former name of

Mahishmati. It languished in obscurity for many centuries after that until revived by the Holkar queen, Rani Ahilyabai of Indore, in the late 18th century. It's from these times that most of the temples and the fort complex of this riverside town date.

The principal sights are the **fort**, which is now a museum displaying heirlooms and relics of the Holkar dynasty (open to the public), the three **ghats** lining the banks of the Narmada River, and the many-tiered **temples**, distinguished by their overhanging balconies and intricately worked doorways.

Maheshwar saris are famous throughout the country for their unique weave and beautifully complex patterns.

Places to Stay There is a *Government Rest House* and the *Ahilya Trust Guest House*.

Getting There & Away Maheshwar is best reached by road as the nearest railhead is 39km away. There is a direct bus from Indore at 2 pm (91km, Rs 25). Otherwise, local buses run to Maheshwar on a regular basis from Barwaha (57km, Rs 20) and Dhar (61km, Rs 20) both of which, in turn, can be reached by local bus from Indore (73km, Rs 21; and 56km, Rs 17 respectively).

Maheshwar is often included on bus tours from Indore to Mandu.

Dhar
Founded by Raja Bhoj, the legendary founder of Bhopal and Mandu, this was the capital of Malwa until Mandu rose to power. There are good views from the ramparts of Dhar's well-preserved **fort**. Dhar also has the large stone **Bhojashala Mosque** with ancient Sanskrit inscriptions, and the adjoining **tomb** of the Muslim saint Kamal Maula.

Dhar is best visited en route to or from Mandu, 33km away.

MANDU
Tel Area Code: 07292
The extensive and now mainly deserted hilltop fort of Mandu is one of the most interesting sights in central India. It's on an isolated outcrop separated from the tableland to the north by a deep and wide valley, over which a natural causeway runs to the main city gate. To the south of Mandu the land drops steeply away to the plain far below and the view is superb. Deep ravines cut into the sides of the 20 sq km plateau occupied by the fort.

Although it's possible to make a day trip from Indore, it's really worth spending the night here, although accommodation is limited. If you're visiting at the height of the season it might be a good idea to phone and book a room in advance. In the winter, Mandu is quite popular with foreign visitors (mainly French and Italian tour groups) but the local tourist season is during the monsoon, when the place turns green and the buildings are mirrored in the lakes.

Entry to Mandu costs Rs 1 per person (Rs 5 per car), although if you arrive by bus this is included in the fare. There are soft drink and fruit stalls at most of the major sites.

History
Mandu, known as the city of joy, has had a chequered and varied history. Founded as a fortress and retreat in the 10th century by Raja Bhoj (see the Bhopal section earlier in this chapter), it was conquered by the Muslim rulers of Delhi in 1304. When the Mughals invaded and took Delhi in 1401, the Afghan Dilawar Khan, Governor of Malwa, set up his own little kingdom and Mandu embarked on its golden age. Even after it was added to the Mughal Empire by Akbar, it retained a considerable degree of independence, until the declining Mughals lost control of it to the Marathas. The capital of Malwa was then shifted back to Dhar, and Mandu became a ghost town. For a ghost town, however, it's remarkably grandiose and impressive, and has one of the best collections of Afghan architecture in India.

Although Dilawar Khan first established Mandu as an independent kingdom, it was his son, Hoshang Shah, who shifted the capital from Dhar to Mandu and raised it to its greatest splendour.

Hoshang's son ruled for only a year before being poisoned by Mahmud Shah, who became king himself and ruled for 33 years. During his reign Mandu was in frequent and often bitter dispute with neighbouring powers.

In 1469, Mahmud Shah's son, Ghiyas-ud-din, ascended the throne and spent the next 31 years devoting himself to women and song, before being poisoned at the age of 80 by his son, Nasir-ud-din. The son lived only another 10 years before dying, some say of guilt. In turn his son, Mahmud, had an unhappy reign during which his underlings, like Gada Shah and Darya Khan, often had more influence than he did. Finally, in 1526, Bahadur Shah of Gujarat conquered Mandu.

In 1534 Humayun, the Mughal, defeated Bahadur Shah, but as soon as Humayun turned his back an officer of the former dynasty took over. Several more changes of fortune eventually led to Baz Bahadur taking power in 1554. In 1561 he fled from Mandu rather than face Akbar's advancing troops, and Mandu's period of independence ended. Although the Mughals maintained the fort for a time and even added some new minor buildings, its period of grandeur was over.

Orientation & Information

The buildings of Mandu can be divided into

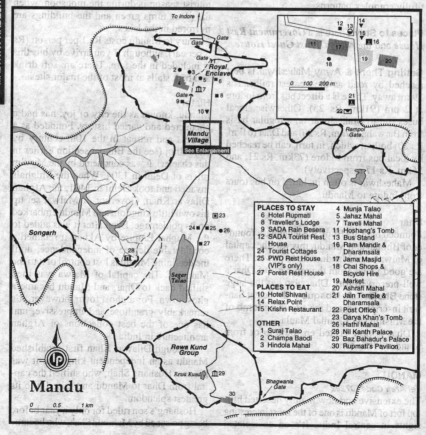

PLACES TO STAY
6 Hotel Rupmati
8 Traveller's Lodge
9 SADA Rain Besera
12 SADA Tourist Rest.
   House
24 Tourist Cottages
25 PWD Rest House
   (VIP's only)
27 Forest Rest House

PLACES TO EAT
10 Hotel Shivani
11 Relax Point
15 Krishn Restaurant

OTHER
1 Suraj Talao
2 Champa Baodi
3 Hindola Mahal

4 Munja Talao
5 Jahaz Mahal
7 Taveli Mahal
11 Hoshang's Tomb
13 Bus Stand
16 Ram Mandir &
   Dharamsala
17 Jama Masjid
18 Chai Shops &
   Bicycle Hire
19 Market
20 Ashrafi Mahal
21 Jain Temple &
   Dharamsala
22 Post Office
23 Darya Khan's Tomb
26 Hathi Mahal
28 Nil Kanth Palace
29 Baz Bahadur's Palace
30 Rupmati's Pavilion

three groups. When you enter the fort through the northern gates, your first stop is the ticket office. The road then swings south, past the Traveller's Lodge on your left and the Royal Enclave on your right. The Royal Enclave, Mandu's most impressive group of temples, stands on the northern shoulder of the fort, but is only accessible through Mandu village and entering from the south.

This small settlement is the only inhabited part of Mandu today and the buildings are known as the village group. Continuing on, you'll eventually reach the Rewa Kund group at the extreme south of the fort.

You can get a copy of the Archaeological Survey of India's excellent guidebook *Mandu* for Rs 11 from the Taveli Mahal in the Royal Enclave. There are many other buildings to see in Mandu.

The nearest bank for cashing travellers cheques is in Indore.

Royal Enclave Buildings

These are the only temples at Mandu for which you must pay admission. The enclosure is open from sunrise to sunset; entry is Rs 2.

Jahaz Mahal The Ship Palace is probably the most famous building in Mandu. It really is shiplike, being far longer (120m) than it is wide (15m), and the illusion is completed by the two lakes that flank it to the east and west.

It was built by Ghiyas-ud-din, son of Mahmud Shah for his harem, reputed to number more than 15,000 maidens. The Jahaz Mahal with its lookouts, arches, cool rooms and beautiful pool was their playground, but the only sighs you'll hear today are those of the wind whistling through the empty ruins.

Taveli Mahal Just south of the Jahaz Mahal this palace is now the Archaeological Survey of India's Antiquity Gallery. This small museum is open daily from 9.30 am to 5.30 pm except Friday (entry free). Exhibits include fragments of utensils and vessels found at the site, and some stone images.

Hindola Mahal Just north of Ghiyas' stately pleasure dome, this churchlike hall is known

as the Swing Palace because the inward slope of the walls is supposed to create the impression that the walls are swaying. The wide, sloping ramp at the northern end of the building is said to have been built to enable the ruler to be conveyed upstairs by elephant.

Champa Baodi To the west of the first two Royal Enclave structures is this interesting stepwell on the north shore of the lake. Its subterranean levels featured cool wells and bathrooms and it was obviously a popular hot-weather retreat.

Other Enclave Buildings Other buildings in the enclave include the 'house and shop' of Gada Shah and the 1405 **Mosque of Dilawar Khan**, one of the earliest Muslim buildings in Mandu.

Village Group Buildings

Jama Masjid This huge mosque built in 1454 dominates the village of Mandu. It is supposed to be the finest and largest example of Afghan architecture in India. Construction was commenced by Hoshang Shah, who patterned it on the great Omayyed Mosque in Damascus, Syria. The mosque features an 80m sq courtyard. It's open daily from 8.30 am to 5.30 pm.

Hoshang's Tomb Immediately behind the mosque is the imposing tomb of Hoshang, who died in 1435. Reputed to be India's oldest marble building, the tomb is entered through a domed porch. Light enters the interior through stone *jali* (carved marble lattice screens), typical of the Hindu influence on the tomb's fine design. It has a double arch and a squat, central dome surrounded by four smaller domes. It is said that Shah Jahan sent his architects to Mandu to study this tomb before they embarked upon the design of the Taj Mahal.

To one side of the tomb enclosure is a long, low colonnade with its width divided into three by rows of pillars. Behind is a long, narrow hall with a typically Muslim barrel-vaulted ceiling. This was intended as a shelter for pilgrims visiting Hoshang's tomb.

Ashrafi Mahal The ruin of this building stands directly across the road from the Jama Masjid. Originally built as a *madrasah* (religious college), it was later extended by its builder, Mahmud Shah, to become his tomb. The design was simply too ambitious for its builders' abilities and it later collapsed. The seven-storey circular tower of victory, which Mahmud Shah erected, has also fallen. A great stairway still leads up to the entrance to the empty shell of the building.

Jain Temple There are numerous buildings in this modern and ever-developing temple complex. The temples are richly decorated and feature tirthankars in marble, silver and gold, some with glinting jade eyes. Towards the back of the compound is a theme-park style Jain museum which includes a walk-on replica of Palitana, and a mural of colourful kitschy Jain homilies. One particularly explicit panel shows the terrible consequences of drinking and meat-eating: a drunk carnivore lies on the street with dogs pissing on him.

Rewa Kund Buildings
About three km south of the village group, past the large Sagar Talao tank, is the Rewa Kund group.

Baz Bahadur's Palace Baz Bahadur was the last independent ruler of Mandu. His palace, constructed around 1509, is beside the Rewa Kund and there was a water lift at the northern end of the tank to supply water to the palace. A curious mix of Rajasthani and Mughal styles, it was actually built well before Baz Bahadur came to power.

Rupmati's Pavilion At the very edge of the fort, perched on the hillside overlooking the plains below, is the pavilion of Rupmati. The Malwa legends relate that she was a beautiful Hindu singer, and that Baz Bahadur persuaded her to leave her home on the plains by building her this pavilion. From its terrace and domed pavilions Rupmati could gaze down on the Narmada River, which is now

dammed but which once wound across the plains far below.

It's a romantic building, the perfect setting for a fairytale romance – but one with an unhappy ending. Akbar, it is said, was prompted to conquer Mandu partly due to Rupmati's beauty. And when Akbar marched on the fort Baz Bahadur fled, leaving Rupmati to poison herself.

For maximum effect come here in the late afternoon to watch the sunset, or at night when the moon is full. Bring a bottle or a loved one – preferably both.

Darya Khan's Tomb & Hathi Mahal
To the east of the road, between the Rewa Kund and the village, are these two buildings. The Hathi Mahal, or Elephant Palace, is so named because the pillars supporting the dome are of massive proportions – like elephant legs. Nearby is the tomb of Darya Khan, which was once decorated with intricate patterns of mosaic tiles.

Nil Kanth Palace
This palace, at the end of one of the ravines which cuts into the fort, is actually below the level of the hilltop and is reached by a flight of steps down the hillside. At one time it was a Siva shrine, as the name – God with the Blue Throat – suggests. Under the Mughals it became a pleasant water palace with a cascade running down the middle. Though once one of Emperor Jehangir's favourite retreats, it has once again become a Siva temple and a playground for monkeys.

At the top of the steps, villagers sell the seeds of the baobab tree; Mandu is one of the few places in India where the baobab is found. It's difficult to miss – it's the tubby grey tree that looks as if it has been planted upside down with its roots in the air.

Organised Tours
Tours to Mandu are run from Indore. See Organised Tours under Indore earlier in this chapter for details. Local guides loiter around the bus stand offering their services. See Getting Around in this section.

Places to Stay & Eat

MP Tourism's two places should be booked at the tourist office in Indore (☎ (0731) 541818) if you want to be sure of a bed.

Traveller's Lodge (☎ 632221) has rooms at Rs 290/375 with bathroom and hot water, but there's a Rs 50 charge to use the air-cooler. Non-guests are welcome at the restaurant, which has an extensive menu.

Tourist Cottages (☎ 63235) are in a very pleasant location overlooking a lake. Rooms with attached bathroom cost Rs 290/375, or Rs 590/690 with air-con. Breakfast and dinner are served in the outdoor restaurant and non-guests are welcome.

Tourist Rest House is a SADA place. It's right opposite the Jama Masjid, and the rooms are basic but adequate, with attached bathrooms (hot water in buckets). The cost is only Rs 50 a double but they insist you deposit Rs 100 in case of 'dammig'.

Rain Besera is another SADA place – there's not always a caretaker in residence. Whilst rooms are large and clean, this place is not great value (Rs 200 a double with cold water bath), and it's hard to find. To get here, head towards the Royal Enclave from the village, past Hoshang's tomb, and take the turnoff to the left opposite the pink, rectangular building on your right, just past the SADA office. It's about five minutes walk up a dirt track.

Jain Dharamsala, at the Jain Temple, is recommended. Double rooms are Rs 100, or Rs 240 with private (cold water) bath.

Ram Dharamsala at Ram Mandir is much more basic. Cells with a mattress on the floor are Rs 40 or Rs 60 with a fan. Hot water is Rs 5 a bucket.

Hotel Rupmati (☎ 63270) has ten spacious rooms with patios backing onto a ravine. Clean rooms with modern bathrooms cost Rs 300/375 single/double. Air-con doubles are Rs 550, or you can pay a Rs 50 surcharge to use an air-cooler. There's a pleasant terrace restaurant with vegetarian dishes from Rs 20, and more expensive non-veg and Chinese dishes.

Forest Rest House accommodation is only possible if you reserve at the Forest Department in Dhar (☎ 22232).

Cheap vegetarian food is available at a couple of places at the main village intersection.

Relax Point has a limited selection but the samosas are delicious.

Krishn Restaurant, while still keeping it simple, has more choices.

Hotel Shivani, further north, back towards the Traveller's Lodge, serves up good, reasonably priced veg food.

Getting There & Away

There are numerous buses from Mandu to Dhar (1½ hours, Rs 7) from 5.30 am to 6 pm and lots of buses from there on to Indore (three hours, Rs 17).

For Bhopal, take the 5.30 am bus to Indore where you can connect with a bus to Bhopal (but not MP Tourism's deluxe coach to Bhopal). There are no direct buses from Mandu to Ujjain – you must change in Indore. The buses stop near the Jama Masjid.

The alternative to the erratic tours is to get a group together and hire a car. Taxis charge Rs 625 for the return journey from Indore. An overnight stay will incur another full day's charge. Organise through your hotel in Indore, or scout about outside the railway station or tourist office.

Getting Around

You can hire bikes from the shop on the south side of the Jama Masjid for Rs 20 a day or Rs 2 an hour. This is a great way to get around as the sights are quite far apart, and the terrain is relatively flat. On the other hand, this is a fine area for walking and it's pleasantly unpopulated.

There is one auto-rickshaw and three tempos here, and they hang around the bus stand. They'll try to sting you for Rs 150 for a three to four hour tour of Mandu's sights. It costs Rs 17 return from the village to Rupmati's Pavilion.

BAGH CAVES

The Bagh Caves are seven km from the village of Bagh and three km off the main road. Bagh is about 50km west of Mandu, on the road between Indore and Vadodara in

Gujarat. The Buddhist caves date from 400 to 700 AD and all were in extremely bad shape before restoration work began recently. The enthusiastic director of the restoration is also the curator at Mandu's Taveli Mahal Antiquity Gallery, so it's worth checking on the caves' progress here before you head out to Bagh. There's a **PWD Dak Bungalow** in Bagh village and an **Archaeological Survey Rest House** closer to the caves.

RATLAM & MANDSAUR
The railway line passes through Ratlam, capital of a former princely state whose ruler died in one of those tragically heroic Rajput battles against the might of the Mughals.

At Mandsaur, north of Ratlam, a number of interesting archaeological finds were made in a field three km from the town. Some of them are displayed in the museum at Indore. Two 14m high sandstone **pillars** are on the site, and an inscription commemorates the victory of a Malwa king over the Huns in 528 AD. In the **fort** are some fine pieces from the Gupta period.

Eastern Madhya Pradesh

JABALPUR
Pop: 1,065,025   Tel Area Code: 0761
Almost due south of Khajuraho and east of Bhopal, the large city of Jabalpur is principally famous today for the gorge on the Narmada River known as the Marble Rocks. It's also the departure point for a visit to the national parks of Kanha (160km away) and Bandhavgarh (197km).

Today Jabalpur is a major administrative and educational centre and the army headquarters for the states of Orissa and Madhya Pradesh. Jabalpur's active Christian community maintains an unusual number of Christian schools, colleges and churches scattered throughout the cantonment area. There are also about 500 students from East Africa studying at the university here.

History
The original settlement in this area was ancient Tripuri and the rulers of this city, the Hayahaya, are mentioned in the *Maha-bharata*. It passed successively into Mauryan and then Gupta control until, in 875 AD, it was taken by the Kalchuri rulers. In the 13th century it was overrun by the Gonds and by the early 16th century it had become the powerful state of Gondwana.

Though besieged by Mughal armies from time to time, Gondwana survived until 1789 when it was conquered by the Marathas. Their rule was unpopular, due largely to the increased activities of the thuggees who were ritual murderers and bandits. The Maratha were defeated in 1817 and the thuggees subdued by the British who developed the town in the mid-19th century.

Information
The tourist office (☎ 322111) is at the railway station, and is open daily from 6 am to 10 pm. They have the usual range of leaflets and can book MP Tourism accommodation for you at Kanha National Park, preferably a minimum of three days in advance, but they require a 100% deposit.

Money can be changed at the main branch of the State Bank of India and at Jackson's Hotel, where there's also a post office.

Things to See
The old **bazaar** of Jabalpur is huge and full of Indian smells, sights, sounds and goods for sale. The **Rani Durgavati Museum**, south of the bazaar, is open daily except Sunday from 10 am to 5 pm. **Madan Mahal**, a Gond fortress built in 1116 AD, is perched on top of a huge boulder on the route to the Marble Rocks. The Gonds, who worshipped snakes, lived in this region even before the Aryans arrived, and maintained their independence right up until Mughal times.

Places to Stay – bottom end
The cheap places to stay are almost all down by the bus stand, about three km from the railway station. Most are very cheap and very basic.

Hotel Sharda (☎ 315375), north of the bus stand, is reasonably clean with rooms from Rs 40/60 or Rs 60/80 with attached bathroom.

Hotel Natraj (☎ 310931), also in the heart of the bazaar area, is similar.

Hotel Mayur (☎ 310035) was renovating when we visited, but prices shouldn't creep much above Rs 50/75 for singles/doubles with a bathroom.

Hotel Rahul (☎ 325525) is a bit run-down but it's OK with rooms at Rs 80/110 with bathroom and hot water. Air-con rooms are Rs 250/300.

Swayam Hotel (☎ 325377) next door is cheaper at Rs 50/70, but this is a noisy street.

Places to Stay – middle & top end
There are three mid-range modern hotels close to each other.

Hotel Maruti (☎ 324677) is grubby but has a wide range of rooms from Rs 130/170 to Rs 300/375 with air-con.

Hotel Bluemoon (☎ 325146) next door is

cleaner, with air-cooled rooms for Rs 145/170, or for Rs 450/550 with air-con.

Hotel Roopali (☎ 325566) is the best of the lot but you pay for their cleaning rags. Air-cooled rooms are Rs 300/355 or Rs 450/550 for air-con and all rooms have attached bath and TV.

Jackson's Hotel (☎ 323412; fax 322066) in Civil Lines must have been the best hotel in town at one time; these days it's a bit shabby but still popular with travellers who don't mind spending a little extra. There's a range of rooms from Rs 175/250 for large singles/doubles, up to Rs 450/500 for air-con with TV and all with bathroom and hot water, and some with balconies overlooking the gardens. You can change travellers cheques, and excess baggage can be left here safely while you visit Kanha National Park.

Hotel Krishna (☎ 28984; fax 315153) is near the museum, with rooms from Rs 350/500 or Rs 600/700 with air-con. All rooms have attached bathrooms and TVs showing

MADHYA PRADESH

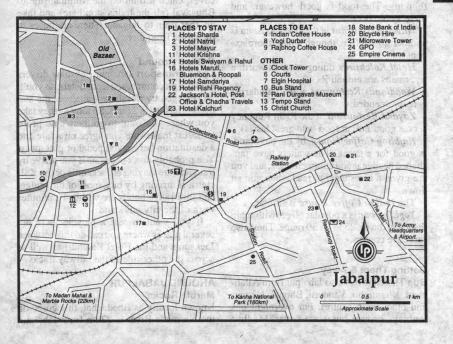

PLACES TO STAY
1 Hotel Sharda
2 Hotel Natraj
3 Hotel Mayur
11 Hotel Krishna
14 Hotels Swayam & Rahul
16 Hotels Maruti, Bluemoon & Roopali
17 Hotel Samdariya
19 Hotel Rishi Regency
22 Jackson's Hotel, Post Office & Chadha Travels
23 Hotel Kalchuri

PLACES TO EAT
4 Indian Coffee House
8 Yogi Durbar
9 Rajbhog Coffee House

OTHER
5 Clock Tower
6 Courts
7 Elgin Hospital
10 Bus Stand
12 Rani Durgavati Museum
13 Tempo Stand
15 Christ Church

18 State Bank of India
20 Bicycle Hire
21 Microwave Tower
24 GPO
25 Empire Cinema

Old Bazaar

Collectorate Road

Railway Station

To Army Headquarters & Airport

To Madan Mahal & Marble Rocks (22km)

To Kanha National Park (160km)

The Mall

Residency Road

Station Road

Jabalpur

0   0.5   1 km
Approximate Scale

in-house movies. There's a swimming pool and a good restaurant.

Hotel Kalchuri (☎ 321491) is a well-maintained MP Tourism operation close to the railway station. Singles/doubles cost Rs 290/390 with attached bathroom and hot water. Air-con rooms are Rs 575/650. There's a bar and restaurant, but the service is off-hand.

Hotel Rishi Regency (☎ 323261) is a three-star place near the State Bank of India. It's Rs 325/450, or Rs 550/675 with air-con.

Hotel Samdariya (☎ 316800; fax 316354) is a very modern place in a quiet location and has an excellent vegetarian restaurant. Rooms range from Rs 350/475 to Rs 600/750 with air-con.

Places to Eat
Most of the hotels have attached restaurants.

Grub Room at Jackson's Hotel has a rather wider choice than the usual Indian have-a-go-at-everything restaurant, but unfortunately much of it seems to be wishful thinking. The food is good, however, and there's cold beer.

Haveli Restaurant in the Hotel Krishna is another good place, though a little more expensive.

Hotel Kalchuri's dining room is worth a try; mains are around Rs 40.

Woodlands Restaurant at the Samdariya is recommended.

Zayaka Restaurant at the Rishi Regency serves good Indian food (and great lassis).

Rajbhog Coffee House, by the bus stand, is good for a snack. The waiters have fan-shaped headgear and cummerbunds, and you are given a newspaper to read when you sit down.

The *Indian Coffee House* is similar.

Yogi Durbar is a popular place, with main dishes in the Rs 25 to Rs 30 range. They also serve ice creams.

Getting There & Away
Bus There are buses to Jabalpur from Allahabad, Khajuraho, Varanasi, Bhopal, Nagpur and other main centres. For overnight bus journeys private buses are better. Madhya

Pradesh state transport buses are mostly in an advanced state of decay.

For Kanha National Park there are state transport buses to Kisli (6½ hours, Rs 40) at 7 and 11 am, or the optimistically named superfast bus (3½ hours, Rs 45) which runs according to demand and, presumably, the wish of the gods. The Kisli buses only run when the park is open (November to June). Take the 9 am Malakhand bus for Mukki (six hours, Rs 60).

There's one bus a day to Khajuraho (12 hours, Rs 100) leaving at 9 am but it's more comfortable to take the train to Satna from where there are regular bone-shattering buses to Khajuraho (four hours, Rs 29).

Train There are direct connections between Jabalpur and Satna (189km, three hours, Rs 42/213 in 2nd/1st class), Varanasi (505km, 13 hours, Rs 104/469) and Bhopal (336km, 7½ hours, Rs 100/354).

If you're heading for the Ajanta and Ellora caves, catch a train on the Mumbai line to Bhusaval (all the trains stop here) and take another train to Jalgaon. There are buses to the caves from there.

Getting Around
Local Transport Jabalpur rickshaw drivers all work on commission from hotels, so you'll be besieged by rickshaw-wallahs at the stations offering Rs 2 fares. So long as they take you where *you* want to go there's no problem. Just make sure you agree on a fare and a destination before you pedal or putt away. You probably don't need one if you arrive by train and are staying at Jackson's or the Kalchuri. If arriving by bus, most of the budget and mid-range hotels are within 10 minutes walk of the city bus stand.

If you want to rent a bicycle there are several places where you can do this between Jackson's and the Hotel Kalchuri as well as across the other side of the railway tracks.

AROUND JABALPUR
Marble Rocks
Known locally as Bhedaghat, this gorge on the Narmada River is 22km from Jabalpur.

The gleaming white and pink cliffs rise sheer from the clear water and are a very impressive sight, especially by moonlight. However it's been heavily promoted by MP Tourism and travellers' opinions on this tourist spot vary from 'truly spectacular' to 'a total bust'. It really all depends on when you come. Steer clear of the place at weekends and on full moon nights as it's usually packed with local tourists.

The best way to see the one km-long gorge is by shared rowboat – Rs 10 per person on a 20 seat boat. These go all day every day from October to June from the jetty at the bottom of the gorge.

The cliffs at the foot of the gorge are floodlit at night. At the head of the gorge is the **Dhuandhar** or Smoke Cascade. All around the falls are hundreds of stalls selling marble carvings, much of it fairly clichéd, but you can find some nice pieces if you shop around and bargain hard. Above the lower end of the gorge, a flight of over 100 stone steps leads to the **Chausath Yogini** or Madanpur Temple. The circular temple has damaged images of the 64 yoginis, or attendants of the goddess Kali.

Places to Stay & Eat Marble Rocks is a very mellow place to stay.

Motel Marble Rocks (☎ (0761) 83424) is run by MP Tourism and is the best place to stay. It overlooks the foot of the gorge and has an excellent restaurant. The motel is a comfortable ex-colonial bungalow and has only four rooms, for Rs 200/290 a single/double with bathroom, so it's best to book in advance. There are plenty of cheap cafes in the village.

In the village itself there are a couple of basic lodgings.

Getting There & Away Tempos run to the Marble Rocks from the city tempo stand near the museum in Jabalpur for Rs 4. Ask for the Tourist Motel, otherwise you'll end up at the head of the gorge, which is about a km further on.

An alternative way to get there is to hire a bicycle for the 22km trip. The road is busy but mostly flat with plenty of stalls to stop at along the way. Follow the road for Nagpur out of Jabalpur, then take the right fork below the Jain temples high on the hill. After about 15km turn left at the crossroads following the 'Bhedaghat 5 km' sign.

Narsinghpur
Narsinghpur (84km west of Jabalpur) is just a sleepy provincial town but worth visiting if you're interested in following the Sleeman trail (see the Thugs boxed section below). There's a fascinating account of Sleeman's anti-thug detective work in Sir Francis Tuker's *The Yellow Scarf*, and the novel *The Deceivers* by John Masters was based on Sleeman and the thugs.

You can visit **Narsingh Mandir**, an old temple with a honeycomb of underground tunnels beneath it. The caretaker will take you down to show the room where Sleeman cornered some of the thuggee leaders.

Thugs
It was from Narsinghpur in the early 19th century that Colonel Sleeman waged his war against the bizarre Hindu *thuggee* cult that claimed as many as a million lives over about 500 years. From as early as the 14th century, followers had roamed the main highways of India engaging in the ritual murder of travellers, strangling their victims with a yellow silk scarf in order to please the bloodthirsty goddess Kali.

Bizarre thuggee rites included sugar sacrifices and axe-worshipping ceremonies and they resisted infiltration by using secret signs and developing their own jargon.

It was largely due to Sleeman's efforts that the thuggee (from which the word 'thug' is derived) were wiped out. His campaign during the 1830s was sanctioned by the British governor-general Lord Bentinck and saw more than 400 thugs hanged and about 3000 imprisoned or banished, ensuring the virtual eradication of these scarf-wielding nasties. ∎

Places to Stay There are a few places where you can lay your head for thuggee dreams.

Lunawat Inn has doubles at Rs 100 and is near the station.

Nira Farm Guest House (☎ (07792) 30238) comprises just one basic double (Rs 100) and this must be arranged in advance. You can write to Mrs Prem Nagu at Nira Farm, By-pass Rd, Narsinghpur, Madhya Pradesh, or telephone. Mrs Nagu is an excellent cook and her husband, a retired colonel, is particularly knowledgeable about Sleeman as well as about places in the nearby Satpura Hills.

KANHA NATIONAL PARK

Kanha, 160km south-east of Jabalpur, is one of India's largest national parks, covering 1945 sq km including a 'core zone' of 940 sq km. The setting for Kipling's *Jungle Book*, it's a beautiful area of forest and lightly wooded grassland with many rivers and streams, and it supports an excellent variety of wildlife. It is also part of Project Tiger, one of India's most important conservation efforts. A scandal within this project, though, means tiger numbers may be decreasing. (See the boxed section on Project Tiger in the Uttar Pradesh chapter.)

Wildlife was first given limited protection here as early as 1933 but it wasn't until 1955 that the area was declared a national park. Additions to the park were made in 1962 and 1970. Kanha is a good example of what can be achieved under a determined policy of wildlife management: between 1973 and 1988 the tiger population increased from 43 to over 100, leopards from 30 to 62, chital (spotted deer) from 9000 to over 17,000, sambar from 1058 to 1853 and barasinga from 118 to 547. In spite of a serious outbreak of rinderpest in 1976, the numbers of gaur (Indian bison) rose from 559 to 671.

The park is very well organised and a popular place to visit. There's a good chance of sighting tiger, gaur and many herbivores.

Excursions into the park are made in the early morning and evening; no night driving is allowed. Between 1 July and 31 October, Kanha is completely closed owing to the monsoons. Although wildlife can be seen throughout the season, sightings increase as the weather gets hotter in March and April and the animals move out of the tree cover in search of water. The hottest months are May and June, when the temperature can reach 42°C in the afternoons. December and

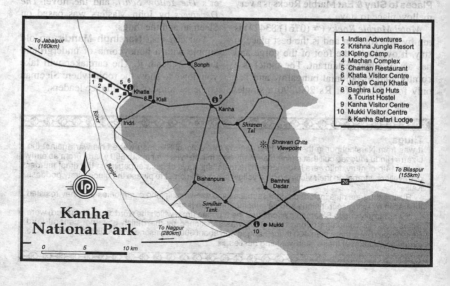

1 Indian Adventures
2 Krishna Jungle Resort
3 Kipling Camp
4 Machan Complex
5 Chaman Restaurant
6 Khatia Visitor Centre
7 Jungle Camp Khatia
8 Baghira Log Huts
  & Tourist Hostel
9 Kanha Visitor Centre
10 Mukki Visitor Centre
   & Kanha Safari Lodge

Kanha
National Park

To Jabalpur (160km)

Sonph

Khatia
Kisli
Indri

Kanha

Shravan Tal

Shravan Chita Viewpoint

To Bilaspur (155km)

Bishanpura

Bamhni Dadar

26

Sondhar Tank

To Nagpur (280km)

Mukki

0   5   10 km

January are the coldest months and, although it's warm enough to do without a sweater during the day, as soon as the sun sets the temperature quickly plunges to zero and below. Excursions into the park can be very cold so bring plenty of warm clothes.

There are no facilities for changing travellers cheques here. The nearest place to do this is Jabalpur. Petrol is available in Mandla. There's a telephone and small shop at Kisli but no petrol. Make sure you bring enough film. It needs to be fast film (400 ASA or higher) because of the low light of the early morning and evening excursions.

The local market at **Sarekha** on Friday draws the colourful Baiga tribal people and is worth going to.

There's a Rs 20 fee for entry to the park, plus a small charge for cameras.

Visitor Centres

In a joint project with the US National Park Service and the Indian Centre for Environment Education, three visitor centres have been set up. The interpretive displays in these centres at Khatia and Mukki gates and at Kanha itself are of a very high standard and well worth looking round. The Kanha display is the most impressive, with five galleries and a research hall. As well as displays of the animals and the environment, there's a novel sound & light show 'Encounters in the Dark'. Select the English or Hindi soundtrack and spend an enjoyable 20 minutes in a small dark room with five other people; 'there is no danger, all exhibits are artificial'!

A number of publications are on sale, including informative brochures, posters and postcards, and a small guide to the roadside markers installed as part of the project. There's also a full-colour handbook to the park for Rs 120. The visitor centres are open from 7 to 10.30 am and from 4 to 6 pm daily, and there are free film shows each evening at the Khatia Visitor Centre.

Places to Stay & Eat

Accommodation is strung out over a distance of about 6.5km along the road from Jabalpur,

so it's important that you get off the bus at the right place otherwise you're in for a lot of walking – there's hardly any other traffic along this road for most of the day.

Around the main gate at Kisli there are two places run by MP Tourism.

Tourist Hostel has three eight-bed dorms at Rs 190 a bed including all meals (vegetarian only) and hot showers. This is a pretty good deal.

Baghira Log Huts are nearby, but more expensive. Air-cooled rooms are Rs 490/540. There's a restaurant here with main dishes around Rs 25, and cold beer.

It's advisable to book these places in advance, though not essential if you're happy with a dorm bed. Bookings more than five days in advance have to be made at one of the following MP State Tourism offices and 100% payment is required:

Bhopal
    4th Floor, Gangotri, TT Nagar
    (☎ (0755) 553006)
Calcutta
    6th Floor, Chitrakoot Bldg, 230A, AJC Bose Rd,
    Calcutta 20 (☎ (033) 247 8543)
Delhi
    2nd Floor, Kanishka Shopping Plaza, 19 Ashok
    Rd (☎ (011) 332 1187).
Mumbai
    74 World Trade Centre, Cuffe Parade, Colaba
    (☎ (022) 218 7603)

Bookings between three and five days in advance have to be made through the tourist office (☎ (0761) 322111) at the railway station in Jabalpur. If you can't book more than three days in advance then this same tourist office can tell you what accommodation will be available.

There are a few private lodges at Khatia.

Jungle Camp Khatia is three km back towards Jabalpur at the Khatia Gate. There are 18 rooms with attached bathroom at Rs 100/200 including vegetarian thali meals. There's a nice thatched sitting area. This is probably a better place to be than at Kisli, since there are more jeeps here and in the evenings you can go to the film shows at the Khatia Visitor Centre.

MADHYA PRADESH

Machan Complex is a basic place charging Rs 30 for a dorm bed or Rs 100 for a double with attached bathroom. There are cheap meals here.

Chaman Restaurant, in a rustic blue and white building, has set vegetarian meals for Rs 20. It has a few singles/doubles/triples for Rs 50/80/120.

Motel Chandan has better doubles for Rs 150 with attached bathroom. There's a good restaurant here.

There's also privately run accommodation in the Kisli area.

Indian Adventures, the furthest from Kisli, is next to the ford across the river on the way in from Jabalpur. It has double chalets with bathrooms and an attractive open dining area with a fireplace. The staff are friendly and keen, and it's a good place to stay if there are other people there, but if you find yourself on your own, it can be quite lonely and isolated. It's also expensive at US$92 per person per day (US$72 twin share) including all meals and transport into and around the park (two game drives per day), except for the elephant rides which are extra. Their Maruti jeep is quiet and comfortable and they don't skimp on time.

Bookings should be made through Indian Adventures (☎ (022) 642 8244), 257 SV Road, Bandra, Mumbai 400050, at least 10 days in advance. Bookings less than 10 days in advance can be made through Chadha Travels (☎ (0761) 322178), Jackson's Hotel, Civil Lines, Jabalpur.

Krishna Jungle Resort nearby has 13 cottages and a swimming pool. Accommodation is Rs 400/450 or Rs 800/1200 including all meals. Bookings should be made through the Hotel Krishna in Jabalpur (☎ (0761) 28984; fax 315153).

Kipling Camp is the best place to stay at Kanha. Staffed by enthusiastic Brits and operated on the lines of an English house party, it's run by Bob Wright, who can be contacted through the Tollygunge Club (☎ (033) 473 4539; fax 473 1903), 120 DP Sasmal Rd, Calcutta 700 033. It's far from cheap at Rs 2600 per day (less if you stay for three nights or more), but prices also include all meals,

excursions into the park in open Land Rovers, guides, etc. It's also the home of Tara, the central character in Mark Shand's book *Travels on My Elephant*. She takes guests for rides in the surrounding forest and you can even join her for her daily bath in the river. Kipling Camp is open from 1 November to early May and all bookings must be made in advance. Arrangements can be made to meet you in Jabalpur (3½ hours by car), Bilaspur (6½ hours) or Nagpur (6½ hours). If you come via Nagpur you could break your journey at Kawardha Palace (see the Kawardha section later).

MP Tourism runs a hotel and visitor centre at Mukki, on the other side of the park from Kisli.

Kanha Safari Lodge is in a pleasant location and is hardly ever full so this is a good place to try if you can't get accommodation at Kisli. Singles/doubles cost Rs 350/425 or Rs 550/625 with air-con and there's a bar and restaurant. However, Mukki isn't easy to get to without your own transport.

Getting There & Away

There are direct state transport buses from the city bus stand in Jabalpur to Kisli Gate, twice daily at 7 am (six hours) and 11 am (seven hours) which cost Rs 50. Tickets go on sale about 15 minutes before departure. In the opposite direction, the buses depart from Kisli at around 8 am and 2.30 pm but the early bus can be late starting in winter. These are ramshackle old buses and crowded as far as Mandla though there are generally spare seats after that. Don't bring too much baggage as there's hardly anywhere to put it. On the Kisli to Jabalpur run you may have to change buses at Mandla.

The nearest railway station to Kisli is 1½ hours by bus at Chiraidongri. It's reached on a slow journey by narrow-gauge trains that will appeal to rail enthusiasts, via Nainpur from either Jabalpur or Gondia (between Nagpur and Raipur).

There's one bus a day from Jabalpur to Malakhand which passes through Mukki (six hours, Rs 60).

Getting Around

Jeeps are for hire at both Khatia and Kisli Gates and the cost is calculated on a per km basis. Expect to pay around Rs 600 (which can be shared by up to six people), plus Rs 100 per day for a compulsory guide. Park entry fees are extra. Park gates are open from sunrise to noon and 3 pm to sunset from 1 November to 15 February; sunrise to noon and 4 pm to sunset from 16 February to 30 April, and sunrise to 11 am and 5 pm to sunset from 1 May to 30 June. An average distance covered on a morning excursion would be 60km; less in the afternoon. At the height of the season there may not be enough jeeps to go round so book as soon as you arrive. As in other Indian national parks, drivers tend to drive too fast and not wait around long enough for game to appear. If you think they're being impatient, tell them to slow down.

Elephant Elephants are available for hire for Rs 50 per person per hour, either for an aimless trundle or for game-viewing safaris, when tigers may be sighted.

BANDHAVGARH NATIONAL PARK

This national park is 197km north-east of Jabalpur in the Vindhyan mountain range. It's not part of Project Tiger but tigers are occasionally seen here, more frequently late in the season. There are 25 tigers in the 'core' area of 105 sq km, but a buffer zone of 343 sq km has recently been added, along with another 25 tigers.

Bandhavgarh's setting is impressive. It's named after the ancient fort built on some 800m high cliffs. There's a temple at the fort which can be visited by jeep and below it are numerous rock-cut cave shrines.

The core area of the park is fairly small with a fragile ecology, but it supports such animals as nilgai, wild boar, jackal, gaur, sambar and porcupine as well as many species of birds. The ramparts of the fort provide a home for vultures, blue rock thrushes and crag martins.

Like Kanha, the park is closed for the middle part of the day, and completely from 1 July to 31 October. There's a small entry fee, and jeeps and guides can be hired.

Places to Stay & Eat

There's a small range of accommodation just outside the park gate in the village of Tala, and several cheap places to eat.

Tiger Lodge may be ornate-looking but it has the cheapest accommodation around: Rs 80 a double with fan.

Nature Resort charges Rs 60 for a bed in a tent. There are rooms at Rs 280 for a double.

White Tiger Forest Lodge (☎ (07653) 65308) is a good MP Tourism place, overlooking the river where the elephants bathe. Singles/doubles with attached bathroom cost Rs 390/450 or Rs 590/690 with air-con. The food is good and the waiters and manager all very friendly. Advance booking is advisable.

Bandhavgarh Jungle Camp is the former palace of the Maharaja of Rewa, and it's sometimes possible to stay there. It's an expensive place at more than Rs 1000 but this includes all food and visits to the park. The address for enquiries is 1/1 Rani Jhansi Rd, Delhi 110 055.

MADHYA PRADESH

White Tigers

The famous white tiger of Rewa was discovered as a cub near Bandhavgarh in 1951. He was named Mohun and as his mother had been shot he was reared by hand. Mated with one of his daughters in 1958, a litter of white cubs was produced and Mohun's numerous descendants can now be seen in several zoos around the world. The interesting thing about these white tigers is that although they have a white coat, they are not albinos. Their eyes are blue rather than pink, and with their dark stripes they are the result of a recessive gene. Inbreeding has led to their decline and the world population of white tigers has dropped from over 100 to about 20. The original white tiger can still be seen today – Mohun's stuffed body is in the Maharaja of Rewa's palace, now a hotel in Tala. ■

Getting There & Away

Umaria, 32km away on the Katni to Bilaspur railway line, is the nearest railhead. Local buses are available from there to Tala (three hours, Rs 12). From Satna connect through Rewa for the bus to Tala.

MANDLA & RAMNAGAR

Mandla is about 100km south-east of Jabalpur on the road to Kanha. Here there is a **fort** on a loop of the Narmada River built so that the river protects it on three sides while a ditch protects it on the fourth. Built in the late 1600s, the fort is now subsiding into the jungle although some of the towers still stand.

About 15km away is Ramnagar, with its ruined three-storey **palace** overlooking the Narmada. This palace, and the fort at Mandla, were both built by Gond kings, retreating south before the advance of Mughal power. Also near Mandla is a stretch of the Narmada where many temples dot the riverbank.

BHORAMDEO & KAWARDHA

At Bhoramdeo, 125km east of Kisli (Kanha), is a small and interesting 11th century **Siva temple** built in the style of the temples of Khajuraho. Carvings cover virtually every external surface, with deities indulging in the usual range of activities including the familiar sexual acrobatics. Unlike many Khajuraho temples, this one's still very much in use today. A cobra lives in the temple and is fed by the priests. A few km away there are two other temples, the **Mandwa Mahal** and the **Madanmanjari Mahal**, which date from the same time.

Places to Stay & Eat

Twenty km south of Bhoramdeo, well off the tourist trail, the Maharaja of Kawardha has opened part of his palace to guests.

Palace Kawardha (☎ 07741) 32408) is a delightfully peaceful place and you're made to feel very welcome here. As far as palaces go it's neither enormous nor particularly old (it was built in 1939), but it does have the touches you'd expect in a maharaja's palace – Italian marble floors, stuffed tigers and ancient English bathroom fittings. If you can

afford to stay here it's an experience not to be missed. It costs US$85 per person (with reductions for stays of more than one night). The price includes all meals (taken with the charming ex-maharaja and his family) and outings in the jeep – to the temples or into the hills. Open from 1 October to 30 April, reservations must be made in advance. Write to Margaret Watts-Carter, Palace Kawardha, Kawardha, District Rajnandgaon, Madhya Pradesh 491 995. Telephone connections to Kawardha are sporadic at best; you can also contact Ms Watts-Carter through her nominees in New Delhi (☎ (011) 684 0037; fax 682 2856; email delhi.hrh@axcess.net.in).

BILASPUR

Pop: 282,230   Tel Area Code: 07752

Bilaspur is a bustling city in the far east of Madhya Pradesh. It's the headquarters of the South-Eastern Railways, and while it has no 'attractions' to speak of, you may find it convenient to stop here if heading from Kanha National Park to Puri in Orissa.

The town of **Ratanpur**, 25km north, has a ruined fort and a number of small, artificial lakes, all made by the region's former Rajput rulers. There are plenty of local buses from Bilaspur (one hour, Rs 10).

Places to Stay & Eat

Natraj Hotel near the bus stand is well located on the main street, and has rooms from Rs 160.

Hotel Chandrika (☎ 5088), also on the main street, has singles/doubles for Rs 80/ 120 with attached bath, Rs 225/275 with TV and air-cooler, and Rs 350/400 with air-con. It also has a good bar and restaurant.

Getting There & Away

The bus stand is in the centre of town, and there are departures for Kawardha, Nagpur, Raipur and Mukki (for Kanha National Park).

The railway station is three km from the town centre. Bilaspur has rail connections with Jabalpur, Raipur, Bhopal, Sambalpur, Puri, Calcutta and Delhi.

Mumbai (Bombay)

Mumbai is the capital of Maharashtra and the economic powerhouse of India. It's an exhilarating city, fuelled by entrepreneurial energy, determination and dreams. Compared to the torpor of the rest of India, it can seem like a foreign country.

Mumbai is the finance capital of the nation, the industrial hub of everything from textiles to petrochemicals, and it's responsible for half the country's foreign trade. But while it has aspirations to become another Singapore, it's also a magnet to the rural poor. It's these new migrants who are continually re-shaping the city in their own image, making sure Mumbai keeps one foot in its hinterland and the other in the global marketplace.

Most travellers tend to stick around long enough only to reconfirm their plane tickets or organise transport to Goa, scared off by the city's reputation for squalor and the relatively high cost of accommodation. But Mumbai is a safe and charismatic city that fully rewards exploration. It has few 'sights', in the traditional sense of the word: instead it has a vital street life, decent nightlife, more bazaars than you could ever explore and personality by the bucketload.

To many visitors, Mumbai is the glamour of Bollywood cinema, cricket on the maidans on weekends, bhelpuri on the beach at Chowpatty and red double-decker buses. It is also the infamous Cages of the red-light district of Kamathipura, Asia's largest slums, communalist politics and powerful mafia dons. This tug-of-war for the city's soul is played out against a Victorian townscape more reminiscent of a prosperous 19th century English industrial city than anything you'd expect to find on the edge of the Arabian Sea. It's just one of the city's long list of contradictions that you'll have to come to terms with.

History

The seven islands that now form Mumbai were first home to the Koli fisherfolk, whose

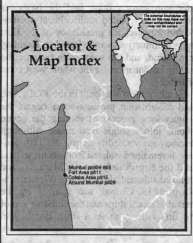

MUMBAI AT A GLANCE

Population: 15 million
Main Language: Hindi & Marathi
Telephone Area Code: 022
Best Time to Go: September to April

Locator & Map Index

Mumbai pp804-805
Fort Area p811
Colaba Area p815
Around Mumbai p828

Highlights

- Taking in the carnival atmosphere of Chowpatty Beach at night
- Catching a ferry to Elephanta Island to see the triple-headed carving of Siva
- Getting lost in the claustrophobic bazaars of Kalbadevi

shanties still occupy parts of the city shoreline today. The islands were ruled by a succession of Hindu dynasties, invaded by Muslims in the 14th century and then ceded to Portugal by the Sultan of Gujarat in 1534. The Portuguese did little to develop them before the major island of the group was included in Catherine of Braganza's dowry when she married England's Charles II in 1661. The British Government took possession of all seven islands in 1665 but leased them three years later to the East India Company for a meagre annual rent of UK£10.

Bombay soon developed as a trading port, thanks to its fine harbour and because merchants were attracted from other parts of India by the British promise of religious freedom and land grants. Migrants included sizeable communities of Parsis and Gujaratis, and south Indian Hindus fleeing Portuguese persecution in Goa. Their arrival, and that of later immigrant groups, laid the basis for Bombay's celebrated multicultural society. Within 20 years the presidency of the East India Company was transferred to Bombay from Surat, and the town soon became the trading headquarters for the whole west coast of India.

Bombay's fort was built in the 1720s, and land reclamation projects soon began the century-long process of joining the seven islands into a single land mass. Although Bombay grew steadily during the 18th century, it remained isolated from its hinterland until the British defeated the Marathas and annexed substantial portions of Western India in 1818. Growth was spurred by the arrival of steam ships and the construction of the first railway in Asia from Bombay to Thana in 1853. Cotton mills were built in the city the following year, and the American Civil War – which temporarily dried up Britain's supply of cotton – sparked Bombay's cotton boom. The fort walls were dismantled in 1864 and the city embarked on a major building spree as it sought to construct a civic townscape commensurate with its new found wealth. The opening of the Suez Canal in 1869 and the massive expansion of Bombay's docks cemented the city's future as India's primary port.

Bombay played a formative role in the struggle for Independence, hosting the first Indian National Congress in 1885 and the launch of the 'Quit India' campaign in 1942. After Independence the city became capital of the Bombay Presidency, but this was divided on linguistic grounds into Maharashtra and Gujarat in 1960. Since then, the huge number of rural (especially Maharashtran) migrants attracted by Bombay's commercial success has strained the city's infrastructure and altered its demographics. It has given rise to a pro-Marathi right-wing regionalist movement, spearheaded by the current Shiv Sena municipal government, which has shaken the city's multicultural foundations

A REGIONAL HIGHLIGHT

Chowpatty Beach

Nobody in their right mind would consider Chowpatty Beach an enticing place to frolic in the sun. By day it's nothing more than an unappealing stretch of baked sand rimmed by the filth washed up by the waters of Back Bay. The real action at Chowpatty starts at night, when the ugly surroundings disappear in the darkness and the skyscrapers of Malabar Hill light up like Christmas trees.

The locals come to Chowpatty to stretch their legs and indulge their kids as soon as the sun drops into the Arabian Sea. They're met by an eclectic mix of *bhelpuri* salesmen, masseurs, monkey trainers, con artists, paan-wallahs, mystics, card sharks, fairground operators and just about every other stock character you need for a typical Indian beach scene or Fellini movie. In the company of such a motley crew, it seems just about anything might happen.

The locals come seeking space, cool breezes and simple pleasures – and there's no reason why you can't too. You can taste some of the best bhelpuri and kulfi in Mumbai, get a vigorous head massage, be lectured on the finer points of Hindu philosophy, see human-powered ferris wheels, buy delicious groundnuts, take a few pot shots on the rifle range, play with archaic toys, eavesdrop on political rallies, and try to figure out who are the plants and who are the genuine gamblers at the card tables (you'll probably find they're all plants).

At Chowpatty, you'll be offered everything from balloon sculptures to ganga (often by the same person) and you'll meet everyone from snake charmers to smooth operators. It's the kind of place where you'll want to try a little bit of everything on offer except, perhaps, a romantic paddle along the seashore. When it's time to leave the magic world of roundabouts and pony rides, head back to the reality of Chowpatty Seaface – a noisy strip dominated by giant neon billboards enticing Mumbaikars with the more elusive pleasures of the First World. ∎

by discriminating against non-Maharashtrans and Muslims. This has increased communalist tensions, which erupted in murderous post-Ayodhya riots in 1992, followed by 13 bomb blasts which ripped through the city on a single day in March 1993. Shiv Sainaks were implicated in the former while the city's mafia got blamed for the latter – though the dividing line between the political establishment and organised crime has become harder to define of late.

In 1996 the Shiv Sena officially renamed the city Mumbai. Despite the fact that half the city's inhabitants live without water or electricity, Mumbai approaches the end of the millennium destined to become the second biggest city in the world. Nothing demonstrates its deteriorating environment better than a recent report which claims just breathing the air in Mumbai is equivalent to smoking 20 cigarettes a day. It is hoped that the satellite city of New Bombay, which is taking shape on the mainland, will relieve some of the pressures on the urban environment.

Orientation

Mumbai is an island connected by bridges to the mainland. The principal part of the city is concentrated at the southern claw-shaped end of the island. The southernmost peninsula is known as Colaba and this is where most travellers gravitate since it has a decent range of hotels and restaurants and two of the city's best known landmarks, the Gateway of India and the Taj Mahal Hotel.

Directly north of Colaba is the area known as the Fort, since this is where the old British fort once stood. Here you'll find most of the city's impressive colonial buildings, together with the GPO, Victoria Terminus (VT), offices and banks. The other major railway station is at Churchgate (planned to be renamed Chintaman Deshmukh Terminus), to the west, separated from the Fort by the interconnected grass areas known as maidans.

Further west is Marine Drive, which sweeps around Back Bay, connecting the high-rise modern business centre of Nariman Point with Chowpatty Beach and the classy residential area of Malabar Hill.

This whole area is known locally as South Mumbai and it ends roughly around Crawford Market. North of here, and in complete contrast, are the congested central bazaars of Kalbadevi, whose narrow alleys and traffic-clogged roads are on a much more human scale. The Goa ferry departs from Mumbai's dock, which occupies the eastern seaboard of the island.

To the north, across Mahim Creek, on what was once the separate island of Salsette, are the suburbs of Greater Mumbai. Here you'll find the two airports, Sahar International and the domestic Santa Cruz.

MUMBAI

What's in a name?

The city of Bombay officially became Mumbai in January 1996. Many locals are clearly in favour of the name change since it has been part of the democratically-elected Shiv Sena party's agenda for decades. They believe the new name reclaims the city's heritage and signifies its emergence from a colonial past. Others see the change as an assertion of Marathi identity (Mumbai is the Marathi name for the city) that is inappropriate for a multicultural city that was built by immigrants from all over India.

Supporters of 'Mumbai' believe that the city's name came from the goddess Mumba, worshipped by the original Koli inhabitants at the Mumbadevi temple which stood on the present site of Victoria Terminus. When the Portuguese arrived they called the harbour Bombaim. Depending on which side of the political divide you stand, this either stemmed from 'buan bahia', meaning 'good bay' in Portuguese, or is a corruption of the original Koli name. When the islands were donated to the British, they anglicised Bombaim into Bombay.

Although the political implications of the name change are highly charged, locals are pretty relaxed about it all and you'll hear one name as much as the other. The media and officialdom tend to refer to the city as Mumbai, but there are some fine attempts to straddle the fence: the local edition of the *Times of India*, for example, refers to 'Mumbai' in reports but retains a pull-out section titled the *Bombay Times*, the original name of the newspaper. ∎

MUMBAI

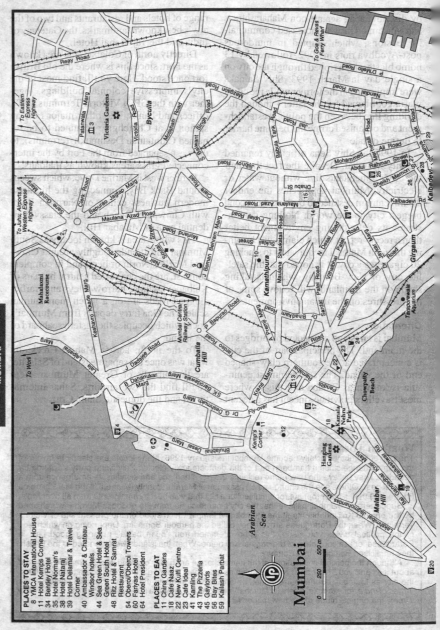

Mumbai

0   250   500 m

Arabian Sea

PLACES TO STAY
8   YMCA International House
11 Hotel Kemps Corner
34 Bentley Hotel
35 Hotel Norman's
38 Hotel Nataraj
39 Hotel Delamar & Travel
     Corner
40 Ambassador & Chateau
     Windsor hotels
44 Sea Green Hotel & Sea
     Green South Hotel
48 Ritz Hotel & Samrat
     Restaurant
54 Oberoi/Oberoi Towers
60 Fariyas Hotel
64 Hotel President

PLACES TO EAT
11 China Gardens
18 Cafe Naaz
22 New Kulfi Centre
23 Cafe Ideal
41 Kamling
43 The Pizzeria
45 Gaylords
56 Bay Bites
59 Kailash Parbat

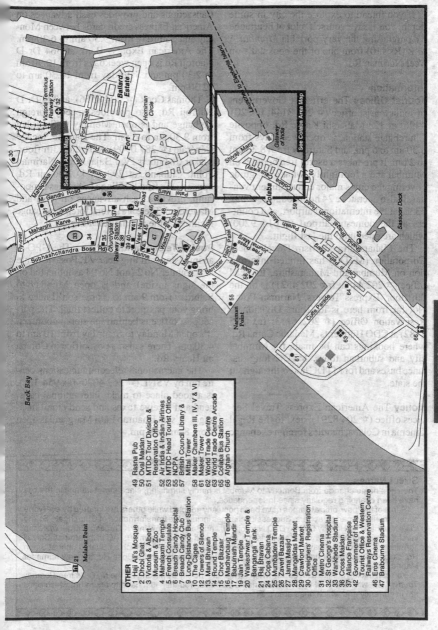

OTHER
1 Haji Ali's Mosque
2 Dhobi Ghat
3 Victoria & Albert Museum & Zoo
4 Mahalaxmi Temple
5 French Consulate
6 Breach Candy Hospital
7 Breach Candy Club
8 Long-Distance Bus Station
9 The Cages
10 Mani Bhavan
12 Towers of Silence
13 Mani Bhavan
14 Round Temple
15 Chor Bazaar
16 Madhavbaug Temple
17 Babulnath Mandir
19 Jain Temple
20 Walkeshwar Temple & Banganga Tank
21 Raj Bhavan
24 Copa Cabana
25 Mumbadevi Temple
26 Zaveri Bazaar
27 Jama Masjid
28 Mangaldas Market
29 Crawford Market
30 Foreigners' Registration Office
31 Metro Cinema
32 St George's Hospital
33 Wankhede Stadium
36 Cross Maidan
37 Alliance Française
42 Government of India Tourist Office & Western Railways Reservation Centre
46 Eros Cinema
47 Brabourne Stadium
49 Rasna Pub
50 Oval Maidan
51 MTDC Tour Division & Reservation Office
52 Air India & Indian Airlines
53 MTDC Head Tourist Office
55 British Council Library & Mittal Tower
58 Maker Chambers III, IV, V & VI
61 Maker Tower
62 World Trade Centre
63 World Trade Centre Arcade
65 Colaba Bus Station
66 Afghan Church

If you intend to explore the city in some depth, you'll save yourself a lot of heartache by purchasing the very portable *Mumbai A to Z* (Rs 110) from one of the bookstalls on Veer Nariman Rd.

Information

Tourist Offices The efficient Government of India tourist office (☎ 203 3144; fax 201 4496) at 123 Maharshi Karve Rd, opposite Churchgate station, is open weekdays from 8.30 am to 6 pm, and Saturday from 8.30 am to 2 pm. It produces a useful free booklet on Mumbai and a fortnightly 'what's on' guide covering the city's major entertainment venues. It also operates a 24 hour counter (☎ 832 5331) at the international airport, and counters at the domestic airport (☎ 614 9200) which are open until the last flight.

The Maharashtra Tourism Development Corporation (MTDC) has limited information on Mumbai and Maharashtra. Its head office (☎ 202 4482; fax 202 4521) is on the 9th floor, Express Towers, Nariman Point. Not far from here is its Tours Division & Reservation Office (☎ 202 6713; fax 285 2182) at CDO Hutments, Madame Cama Rd, where bookings can be made for Mumbai city and suburban tours, MTDC long-distance buses and for MTDC hotels throughout the state.

Money The American Express Travel Services office (☎ 204 8291), next to the Regal Cinema in Colaba, handles foreign exchange transactions and provides cash advances on American Express credit cards between Monday and Saturday from 9.30 am to 6.30 pm. The American Express Bank at 364 Dr D Naoroji Rd is open weekdays from 10.30 am to 2.30 pm and Saturday from 10.30 am to 12.30 pm.

Thomas Cook (☎ 204 8556), at 324 Dr D Naoroji Rd, also provides speedy foreign exchange and is open Monday to Saturday from 9.30 am to 6 pm. The Banque Société Générale (☎ 287 0909) is on the 13th floor, Maker Chambers IV, J Bajaj Marg, Nariman Point. Citibank, at 293 Dr D Naoroji Rd, opposite the Khadi Village Industries Emporium, provides cash advances on Visa and MasterCard. There are several foreign exchange facilities at the international airport.

Post & Telecommunications The GPO is an imposing building near VT. Poste restante is at counter No 2 (not No 93 as indicated on the signs inside) and is open Monday to Saturday from 9 am to 6 pm. You'll need to bring your passport to collect mail. The parcel post office is behind the stamp counters. It's open Monday to Saturday from 10 am to 4.30 pm. There's also a post office in Colaba on Henry Rd.

The international telecommunications centre run by VSNL (☎ 262 4020; fax 954 321), is a good place to make international calls, send and receive faxes and send email messages. It's on Bhaurao Patil Marg and is open from 8 am to 8 pm.

Street Names

The city's name change from Bombay to Mumbai is hardly surprising, since street names in the city have been changing regularly since Independence.

Some of the 'new' official names have been popularly adopted while others are ignored by everyone except municipal cartographers. Successful changes include the transformation of Churchgate St into Veer Nariman Rd, Hornby Rd into Dr D Naoroji Rd, and Rampart Row into K Dubash Marg – while the verdict is still out on Flora Fountain/Hutatma Chowk and Victoria Terminus (VT)/Chhatrapati Shivaji Terminus (CST). Others have failed to capture the popular imagination, such as Shahid Bhagat Singh Rd, Colaba Causeway's new official name, and Netaji Subhashchandra Bose Rd, the new name for Marine Drive.

You can make your life a lot easier when navigating the city by picking up the MTDC's free *Bombay Tourist Map*, which lists all the important name changes. You then just have to figure out which ones are in currency and which ones aren't. ■

Foreign Consulates Many countries maintain diplomatic representation in Mumbai. They include:

Australia
16th floor, Maker Towers, E Block, Cuffe Parade (☎ 218 1071)

Belgium
Morena, 11 ML Dahanukar Marg, Cumballa Hill (☎ 493 9261)

Canada
4th floor, Maker Chambers VI, J Bajaj Marg, Nariman Point (☎ 287 6028)

Denmark
L & T House, N Morarji Marg, Ballard Estate (☎ 261 8181)

France
2nd floor, Datta Prasad Bldg, 10 NG Cross Rd, off Dr G Deshmukh Marg, Cumballa Hill (☎ 495 0918)

Germany
10th floor, Hoechst House, Vinayak K Shah Rd, Nariman Point (☎ 283 2422)

Ireland
2nd floor, Royal Bombay Yacht Club, Shivaji Marg, Colaba (☎ 202 4607)

Italy
Kanchanjunga, 72 G Deshmukh Marg, Cumballa Hill (☎ 387 2341)

Japan
1 ML Dahanukar Marg, Cumballa Hill (☎ 493 3857)

Netherlands
International Building, Marine Lines Cross Rd 1, Churchgate (☎ 201 6750)

Singapore
9th floor, 94 Sakhar Bhavan, Nariman Point (☎ 204 3209)

Spain
Ador House, 6 K Dubash Marg, Fort (☎ 283 5232)

Sri Lanka
Ground floor, Sri Lanka House, 34 Homi Modi St, Fort (☎ 204 5861)

Sweden
1st floor, Bhupesh Gupta Bhavan, 85 Sayani Rd, Prabhadevi (☎ 436 0493)

Switzerland
10th floor, Maker Chambers IV, J Bajaj Marg, Nariman Point (☎ 288 4563)

Thailand
2nd floor, Krishna Bagh, 43 Bhulabhai Desai Marg, Cumballa Hill (☎ 363 1404)

UK
2nd floor, Maker Chambers IV, J Bajaj Marg, Nariman Point (☎ 283 0517)

USA
Lincoln House, 78 Bhulabhai Desai Marg, Cumballa Hill (☎ 363 3611)

Visa Extensions The Foreigners' Registration Office (☎ 262 0111 ext 266) is near the Police Commissioner's Office, just off Dr D Naoroji Rd. If you're walking north from the city, turn left into the laneway near the footbridge to VT.

Libraries & Cultural Centres The British Council Library (☎ 282 3530), on the 1st floor of Mittal Tower A Wing, Barrister Rajni Patel Marg, Nariman Point, is open Tuesday to Friday from 10 am to 5.45 pm and Saturday from 9 am to 4.45 pm. Membership costs Rs 400, but it's possible to read the British newspapers for free. You can read the French papers at Alliance Française (☎ 203 6187), 40 Sir V Thakersey Marg, on weekdays from 9.30 am to 5.30 pm and on Saturday until 1 pm.

Travel Agencies For personal service and discounted tickets you won't get much better than tiny Transway International (☎ 262 6066; fax 266 4465, email TRANSKAM.ETN @SMT.sprintrpg.ems.vsnl.net.in) on the 2nd floor of Pantaky House, 8 Maruti Cross Lane, off Maruti St, Fort. It can be a challenge to find but the service is worth the hunt – ask locals for the old Handloom House (now burnt down); Maruti St is behind it.

Space Travels (☎ 266 3258) at Nanabhay Mansion, Sir P Mehta Rd in the Fort, and Travel Corner Ltd (☎ 204 8565), down an alley next to Hotel Delamar on Veer Nariman Rd, are both reliable agencies. Thomas Cook and American Express also have helpful travel offices (see the Money section for details).

Bookshops & Publications The Nalanda Bookshop in the Taj Mahal Hotel is excellent, though a little more expensive than the well-stocked Strand Bookstall, just off Sir P Mehta Rd in the Fort. There's a motley selection of bookstalls under the arcades along Dr D Naoroji Rd and on Veer Nariman Rd just west of Flora Fountain, and a bookstand outside Cafe Mondegar on Colaba Causeway which has an assortment of paperbacks, maps and guides.

MUMBAI

City of Gold: the Biography of Bombay by Gillian Tindall is the standard historical work on the city. The city is an inspirational source for much of Salman Rushdie's fiction and it features strongly in *The Moor's Last Sigh* – a book which was almost banned locally due to its unflattering portrait of Shiv Sena supremo B⌐ Thackeray. It's also worth checking out the works of Booker bridesmaid Rohinton Mistry and the lightweight socialite dramas of Shobha Dé.

The *Times of India* and the *Indian Express* both have Mumbai editions; there's also a monthly Mumbai lifestyle magazine called *Island*.

Medical Services In an emergency, phone ☎ 102 for an ambulance. Breach Candy Hospital (☎ 363 2657) is at 60 Bhulabhai Desai Rd, Cumballa Hill.

Gateway of India & Taj Mahal Hotel

The Gateway of India is an exaggerated colonial marker conceived following the visit of King George V in 1911. The yellow basalt arch of triumph, derived from the Muslim styles of 16th century Gujarat, is located at the tip of Apollo Bunder. Officially opened in 1924, it was redundant just 24 years later when the last British regiment ceremoniously departed India through its archway. It became even more of an anachronism as passenger liner services to Bombay dried up. The gateway is now more like a disused back door, but it has become a popular emblem of the city and is a favourite meeting spot for locals in the evening. Touts, balloon sellers, postcard vendors and snake charmers have given it the hubbub of a bazaar.

The majestic Taj Mahal Hotel overlooks Apollo Bunder and has great views of the gateway from its top floor Apollo Bar. This Mumbai institution was built in 1903 by JN Tata, one of the city's great Parsi benefactors, supposedly after he was refused entry to one of the city's European hotels on account of being 'a native'. Nearby are statues of Swami Vivekananda and of the Maratha leader Shivaji astride his horse.

Colaba

The streets behind the Taj Mahal Hotel are the travellers' centre of Mumbai. **Colaba Causeway** (Shahid Bhagat Singh Marg) is the main thoroughfare running the length of much of the promontory. It passes close to **Sassoon Dock**, a scene of intense and pungent activity at dawn when colourfully-clad Koli fisherwomen sort the catch unloaded from fishing boats at the quay. The fish drying in the sun are *bombil*, which are deep fried to make Bombay Duck. Photography at the dock is forbidden unless you have permission from the Mumbai Port Trust.

Near the southern end of Colaba Causeway is the steepled Church of St John the Evangelist, also known as the **Afghan Church**. It was built in 1847 and is dedicated to the soldiers who died in the Sind campaign of 1838 and the First Afghan War of 1843. There are plenty of memorial plaques to those who 'courageously fell' or were 'noble defeated', some fine stained-glass windows and pews carved in such a way that soldiers could prop up their rifles while praying.

Prince of Wales Museum

The Prince of Wales Museum, between Colaba and Fort, was built to commemorate King George V's first visit to India in 1905 while he was still Prince of Wales, though it did not open until 1923. Designed by George Wittet in grand Indo-Saracenic style, it is set in an ornamental garden and boasts an impressive galleried central hall topped by a huge dome, said to have been inspired by the Golgumbaz in Bijapur. Its collection includes artefacts from Elephanta Island and Jogeshwari Caves, terracotta figurines from the Indus Valley, ivory carvings, statues, a huge range of miniatures and a gloomy portrait of Abraham Lincoln.

The museum is open from Tuesday to Saturday from 10.15 am to 6 pm; entry is Rs 5. Bags must be left at the entrance gate cloakroom.

National Gallery of Modern Art & Jehangir Art Gallery

The new National Gallery of Modern Art in

the revamped Sir Cowasji Jehangir Public Hall is a dramatic exhibition space showcasing Indian modern art. Its debut exhibition was of extremely high quality. The gallery is open daily except Monday between 10 am and 5 pm; entry is free.

The nearby Jehangir Art Gallery used to be the city's principal gallery. It hosts exhibitions of modern Indian art of varying quality and occasional touring exhibits. Signs in the gallery strangely request that visitors 'do not stick anything on the wall'. The gallery is open from 11 am to 7 pm daily and has a good cafe.

The Jehangir's rooftop has good views of a number of significant Victorian buildings opposite. These include the former **Watson's Hotel**, where the city's love affair with cinema began with the screening of the Lumiere Brothers' *Cinematographe* in 1896.

Bombay University & High Court

The two most impressive Victorian edifices lining Oval Maidan were built during the boom building years of the 1860s and 70s, following the dismantling of the fort walls. **Bombay University** was designed by Gilbert Scott of St Pancras Station fame and looks like a 15th century Florentine masterpiece dropped into the middle of an Indian metropolis. It consists of the exquisite **University Library** and the **Convocation Hall**. The site is dominated by the 80m high **Rajabai Tower**, whose clock used to play *God Save the Queen* and *Home Sweet Home* to mark the hour. Bombay University, the British Council and the Heritage Society are spearheading a campaign to restore these buildings to their former glory.

Statues of Justice and Mercy top the monolithic **High Court** building next door. It was built in Early English style by Colonel JA Fuller and was obviously designed to dispel any doubts about the weightiness and authority of the justice dispensed inside. Local stone carvers, who often worked independently, presumably saw things differently: they carved a blind ape holding the scales of justice on one of its pillars.

Flora Fountain

This cherished but undistinguished fountain stands at the established business centre of Mumbai. Though named after the Roman goddess of abundance, it was erected in 1869 in honour of Sir Bartle Frere, the Governor of Bombay who was responsible for dismantling the fort and shaping much of modern Mumbai. The whitewashed goddess shares the area with an ugly monument honouring those who died fighting to carve the state of Maharashtra out of the Bombay Presidency: hence the area's new name, Hutatma Chowk or Martyr's Square.

Dr D Naoroji Rd, named after the first Indian to become a British MP, heads northeast from the fountain towards VT. It's lined with the grand 19th century edifices of British commercial firms, though the street's elegant arcades are now clogged by hawkers stalls – a favourite local metaphor for the Indianisation of British Bombay.

Horniman Circle

This stately circle of buildings, laid out in the 1860s around the sole surviving section of Bombay's original Cotton Green, was the result of one of those periodic British attempts to stamp some discipline on the disorder of the Fort area.

The circle is overlooked from the east by the neoclassical **Town Hall**, which contains the Asiatic Library and Mumbai's municipal State Central Library. Behind the Town Hall, in the inaccessible dockland, are the **Mint** and the remains of the original **Bombay Castle**.

The peaceful park in the centre still contains the banyan tree which stockbrokers gathered under to trade shares in the early days of the Bombay Stock Exchange; the modern stock exchange, India's largest, has a more suitable home in the high-rise building to the south.

St Thomas' Cathedral nearby was begun as early as 1672 but remained unfinished until 1718. Its whitewashed interior contains poignant colonial memorials, including one to Henry Robertson Bower, Lieutenant of the Royal Indian Marine, 'who lost his life returning from the South Pole with Scott' – spare the man a thought when it's a sweltering 38 degrees outside.

Victoria Terminus (VT)

The city's most exuberant Gothic building looks more like a lavishly decorated cathedral or palace than anything as mundane as a transportation depot. It was designed by William Stevens as the headquarters of the Great Indian Peninsular Railway Company and was completed in 1887, 34 years after the first train in India left this site on its way to nearby Thana. Carvings of peacocks, gargoyles, monkeys, elephants and British lions are mixed up among the buttresses, domes, turrets, spires and stained-glass windows. Topping it all is a four metre high image of 'Progress' – though the rest of the building looks more like a celebration of Pandemonium. Don't wait until you have to catch a train to see it.

Marine Drive

Built on land reclaimed from Back Bay in 1920, Marine Drive (Netaji Subhashchandra Bose Rd) runs along the shoreline of the Arabian Sea from Nariman Point past Chowpatty Beach to the foot of Malabar Hill. It's one of Mumbai's most popular promenades and a favourite sunset-watching spot. You certainly won't be loitering on the sea wall long before you're engaged in conversation, even if it's with someone offering to show you how well their monkey can breakdance. Tourist brochures are fond of dubbing it the Queen's Necklace, because of the dramatic curve of its streetlights at night. It's altogether less spectacular during the day, though there are plans afoot to beautify the area.

Chowpatty Beach

Mumbai's famous beach is no place for a sunbathe or a dip. In fact, there's not much going on at Chowpatty at all during the day, but in the evening it develops a magical fairground atmosphere as locals come to stroll among the contortionists, masseurs, transvestites, balloon sellers, gamblers, fortune tellers, magicians, drug dealers, nut vendors,

ferris wheels and shooting galleries. In the middle of all this mayhem is a small Koli fishing community, where the original inhabitants of the island mend their nets and dry their fish oblivious to the shenanigans going on around them. Eating at the collection of stalls on the edge of the beach is a part of the Mumbai experience (see Places to Eat). The uninspiring **Taraporewala Aquarium** is on Marine Drive nearby.

Malabar Hill

On the northern promontory of Back Bay is the expensive residential area of Malabar Hill, favoured for its cool breezes and fine views over Back Bay. The colonial bungalows that peppered the hillside in the 18th century have now been replaced by the jerry-built apartment blocks of Mumbai's nouveau riche.

On the main road climbing Malabar Hill is a gaudy **Jain temple**, built in 1904, dedicated to the first Jain *tirthankar*, Adinath.

The formal **Hanging Gardens** (or Pherozeshah Mehta Gardens) on top of the hill are interesting only to study the courting rituals of coy Indian couples nestled among the bestial topiary, but there are superb views of the city from neighbouring **Kamala Nehru Park**.

Beside the Hanging Gardens, but carefully shielded from view, are the Parsi **Towers of Silence**. Parsis hold fire, earth and water as sacred so do not cremate or bury their dead. Instead the bodies are laid out within the towers to be picked clean by vultures (or crows). Elaborate precautions are taken to keep out ghoulish sightseers.

Towards the southern end of the promontory is the temple of **Walkeshwar**, the Sand Lord. According to the *Ramayana*, Rama rested here on his way to rescue Sita in Lanka and constructed a lingam of sand at the site. The original temple was built about 1000 years ago, though the current structure is much more recent. Just below the temple is the **Banganga Tank** which was built on the spot where water spouted when Rama shot a *bana* (arrow) into the ground. Bathing pilgrims and scores of curious kids make this neighbourhood an oasis from the world of luxury apartment blocks towering above.

At the end of the promontory is the inaccessible **Raj Bhavan**, the old British government headquarters and now the residence of Maharashtra's Chief Minister. At the foot of Malabar Hill's eastern slope, not far from Chowpatty Beach, is **Babulnath Mandir**, one of Mumbai's most popular Hindu temples.

Mani Bhavan
The building where Mahatma Gandhi stayed during his visits to Bombay between 1917-

34 has been turned into a small museum. Gandhi's room has remained untouched and there's a pictorial exhibit of incidents in Gandhi's life and a library of books by or about the Mahatma. Mani Bhavan is at 19 Laburnum Rd, near August Kranti Maidan where the campaign to persuade the British to 'Quit India' was launched in 1942. It's open daily from 9.30 am to 6 pm.

Haji Ali's Mosque
Situated at the end of a long causeway poking into the Arabian Sea is a whitewashed fairytale mosque containing the tomb of the

Fort Area

0   100   200 m

Azad Maidan

Ballard Estate

Horniman Circle

To Marine Drive

To Colaba

To Colaba

PLACES TO STAY
3 Hotel Manama
4 Railway Hotel
7 Hotel City Palace
12 Hotel Residency
13 Benazeer Hotel
18 Grand Hotel
19 Femandez Guest House
40 Hotel Lawrence

PLACES TO EAT
9 Suvidha
15 Star of Asia
23 Mocambo Cafe & Bar
29 Fountain Inn
31 Apoorva
37 Trishna
39 Wayside Inn

OTHER
1 Bus Stand
2 Central Railways Reservation Centre
5 GPO
6 Nagar Chowk
8 Studio

10 Fashion Street
11 Transway International
14 Khadi Village Industries Emporium
16 Strand Bookstall & Uttar Pradesh Emporium
17 Space Travels
20 The Mint
21 Kashmir Emporium
22 The Bombay Store
24 Thomas Cook
25 VSNL
26 Bookstalls
27 Flora Fountain
28 American Express Bank
30 Perfect Cargo Movers
32 Town Hall & Asiatic Library
33 St Thomas' Cathedral
34 High Court
35 University & Rajabai Clock Tower
36 Old Watson's Hotel & Indian Airlines
38 Rhythm House
41 Jehangir Art Gallery & Cafe Samovar
42 Prince of Wales Museum

Mahalaxmi Temple

An ancient temple dedicated to Mahalaxmi is known to have stood on a headland of Malabar Hill but it was destroyed by Muslim invaders who, according to local legend, threw an icon of the goddess into sea. When the British were constructing a sea wall joining Malabar Hill and Worli Island at the end of the 18th century, the local Hindu contractor claimed the goddess appeared to him in a dream and told him that, though several previous attempts to build a dyke had failed, his construction would be successful if he rebuilt the temple. Amazingly, a statue of the goddess was unearthed during construction of the wall and, upon the wall's completion, the contractor was granted land nearby where he built the temple to Mahalaxmi which stands today. Since Mahalaxmi is the goddess of wealth, the temple is one of the most popular in Mumbai. ■

Muslim saint Haji Ali. The saint is believed to have been a wealthy local businessman who renounced the material world and meditated on a nearby headland following a pilgrimage to Mecca. The mosque and tomb were built by devotees in the early 19th century. Alternative versions say Haji Ali died while on a pilgrimage to Mecca and his casket amazingly floated back to Bombay and landed at this spot.

The mosque can only be reached at low tide, when the causeway is lined with beggars suffering every imaginable affliction and deformity. There is nothing sombre about the building's cool courtyard, which is full of chattering families and refreshment stalls. The rocks exposed at low tide behind the mosque are a favourite spot to catch sea breezes.

Crawford Market

The colourful indoor Crawford Market or Phule Market, north of VT, is the last outpost of British Bombay before the tumult of the central bazaars begins. It used to be the city's wholesale produce market before this was strategically moved to New Bombay. Today it's where central Mumbai goes shopping for its fruit, vegetables and meat.

Bas reliefs by Rudyard Kipling's father, Lockwood Kipling, adorn the Norman-Gothic exterior, and an ornate fountain he designed stands buried beneath old fruit boxes at the market's centre. The animal market at the rear sells everything from sausage dogs to cockatoos, most kept in cruelly small cages. The meat market is for the brave only, though

it's one of the few places you can expect to be accosted and asked if you want to buy a bloody goat's head. Just south of the market, on the opposite side of Dr D Naoroji Rd, is the JJ School of Art, where Rudyard Kipling was born in 1865.

Kalbadevi

No visit to Mumbai is complete without a foray into the bazaars of Kalbadevi, north of Crawford Market. The narrow lanes of this predominantly Muslim area are hemmed in by laundry-draped *chawls*, and a seething mass of people bring Mumbai's traffic to a standstill. It's in complete contrast to the relative space, orderliness and modernity of South Mumbai. Apart from all the shopping opportunities (see the Things to Buy section later in this chapter), this is where you'll find the **Jama Masjid** and also the **Mumbadevi Temple** dedicated to the patron goddess of the island's original Koli inhabitants.

If you've taken a shine to some of the cute-looking cows in India, the precincts of the **Madhavbaug Temple** contain a cow shelter where you can drop in to feed, pat and scratch the holy beasts to your heart's content.

It's best to venture into this area without a clear destination in mind and just wander aimlessly around the bazaars; when you've had enough and need to get your bearings, head east until you hit the main thoroughfare of Mohammed Ali Rd.

Victoria Gardens

These gardens, north of the city centre, contain Mumbai's **zoo** and the **Victoria & Albert**

Museum, which houses interesting exhibits relating to the city's past. Just outside the museum is the large stone elephant removed from Elephanta Island, which gave the island its name. Nearby is a row of decaying statues of colonial officials removed from their high-profile pedestals in the city and parked here after Independence. The gardens, which have officially been renamed Veermata Jijabai Bhonsle Udyan, are open daily except Wednesday between 9 am and 6 pm. Entry to the museum is free; the zoo costs Rs 4.

Juhu

Luxury hotels and apartments line the southern end of Juhu Beach, a favourite haunt of Mumbai's movers and shakers. It's no place for a swim or a sunbathe, but on weekends and weekday afternoons there are horse and donkey rides, dancing monkeys, acrobats, cricket matches, toy sellers and every other type of Indian beach entertainment. North of Juhu is **Versova Beach**, home to Mumbai's largest Koli fishing community. Juhu is 18 km north of the city centre, not far from Mumbai's airports. Catch bus No 231 from Santa Cruz railway station.

Organised Tours

The Maharashtra Tourist Development Corporation (MTDC) has daily rushed tours of Mumbai departing at 9 am and 2 pm. They last four hours and cost Rs 60. They also run a suburban tour which covers similar turf but includes visits to Juhu, Kanheri Caves and fascinating places such as the Bandra Flyover and the domestic airport. This operates daily except Monday, departing at 9.15 am

and returning at 6.30 pm; it costs Rs 120. Tours depart from the MTDC Tours Division and Reservation Office on Madame Cama Rd and pick up passengers near the Gateway of India in Colaba.

Of more interest to travellers are the daily four hour MTDC guided tours of Elephanta Island. They depart hourly from the Gateway of India between 9 am and 2.15 pm and cost Rs 60. For details phone ☎ 202 6364. The MTDC plans to introduce guided horse-drawn carriage tours of Mumbai's illuminated architectural landmarks during evenings between November and May. These are expected to cost Rs 550. Call the MTDC (☎ 202 6713) for details.

The Government of India tourist office can arrange multilingual personal guides if you want to explore Mumbai at your own pace.

Activities

Swimming Mumbai is hot and sticky year-round but if you fancy a swim and are not staying at a luxury hotel, your choice is limited to a small pool at the Fariyas Hotel in Colaba (Rs 200 plus tax) or the exclusive Breach Candy Club on the shoreline at Bhulabhai Desai Rd. The latter has a huge pool built in the shape of India, a semi-indoor pool, a volleyball court, and an excellent cafe and bar – all set amid beautiful landscaped lawns. A day ticket costs Rs 200 on weekdays and Rs 300 on weekends.

Cricket Maidan cricket is a Mumbai institution, and you'll be welcome to join any informal games in progress. International

MUMBAI

Dhaba-Wallahs

If you're near VT or Churchgate railway stations around midday, look out for the crowds of dhaba-wallahs dressed in white and wearing Nehru caps who are waiting for the suburban trains to deliver lunches prepared by the wives or mothers of office workers. These home-cooked meals are packed into metal tiffin boxes, collected from suburban street corners all over the city, sorted according to destination and delivered to the desks of over 100,000 downtown office workers. This massive distribution system works without hiccup thanks to mysterious colour-coded notations on the lids that enable the often illiterate dhaba-wallahs to sort the lunches far quicker and more efficiently than Indian postal workers ever sorted the mail. ■

Festivals & Events

Elephanta Festival
This classical dance and music event on Elephanta Island is run under the auspices of the MTDC and will be held on 6-7 February in 1998 and 26-27 February in 1999.

Banganga Festival
Another of the MTDC's music festivals, this one will be held at the Banganga Tank on Malabar Hill on 10-11 January in 1998 and on 9-10 January in 1999.

(Ganesh) Chaturthi
This 10-day Hindu festival in August/September reaches a climax when large images of the elephant-headed god are immersed in the sea, notably off Chowpatty Beach. Its current form as a mass procession began only in 1893, when nationalists sought to harness the appeal of a Hindu festival. In recent years, the Shiv Sena has been accused of using the festival to promote its particular brand of Hindu chauvinism.

Diwali
Celebrated in Mumbai with particular gusto, Diwali's most significant days are marked by a barrage of firecrackers that turn Marine Drive into a war zone; traditional Diwali lamps are floated on the waters of Banganga Tank

Kala Ghoda
A celebration of arts and crafts held every Sunday from November through January on K Dubash Marg. It includes performing arts, and food and handicraft stalls. ■

Ganesh

cricket matches are played at Wankhede and Brabourne stadiums, just off Marine Drive.

Horse Racing Mumbai's horse-racing season runs from November to April. Races are held on Sunday at Mahalaxmi Race Course, optimistically named after the Hindu goddess of wealth. The big races are major social occasions.

Places to Stay
Mumbai is India's most expensive city to stay in, and pressure for accommodation – even at the bottom end of the market – is intense. There's no guarantee that you'll be able to find a room in your preferred price range on your first night, especially if you arrive late in the day. The standard of accommodation at the bottom end of the market is nothing to write home about.

Most travellers gravitate towards Colaba, which has plenty of budget and mid-range hotels. Although it's not a travellers ghetto, it does have a few of the disadvantages of other places where travellers congregate in large numbers: namely an environment artificially slanted towards foreign as much as Indian interests, and plenty of touts, vendors and taxi drivers of dubious morality. If you really want to pick up on the buzz of Mumbai, it's much better to stay in the Fort, where everyone is far too busy going about their business to take any notice of foreigners.

Wherever you decide to stay in Mumbai, taxi drivers may tell you that the hotel of your choice is 'full' in a bid to divert you to an establishment which pays commission: insist on going to the hotel that you requested.

If you want to stay with a local family, the Government of India tourist office has a list of private homes participating in Mumbai's paying guest scheme. Room rates range from Rs 150 to Rs 3000. The Pradhan family are centrally located and highly recommended.

Note that Mumbai's hotel rates generally rise every October.

Places to Stay – bottom end
Colaba The *Salvation Army Red Shield Hostel* (☎ 284 1824) at 30 Mereweather Rd is the cheapest place to stay in Colaba. A bed in a separate-sex dorm costs Rs 100 including breakfast or Rs 140 full board, which is great value if you're on a tight budget. A double with attached bath costs Rs 400 full board. The downside is that it's a little institutional, and the facilities are not always as clean as they should be. You'll need to make a reservation to secure a room, though dorms beds

are leased on a first-come first-served basis. The maximum stay is one week and check-out time is 9 am.

Hotel Volga II (☎ 282 4755), round the corner from Leopold Cafe & Bar on Nawroji Fardunji Rd, has doubles with common bath for Rs 350, with attached bath for Rs 375 and with air-con for Rs 400. The rooms consist of little more than a bed, but they're clean and you won't find air-con cheaper in Colaba.

Apollo Guest House (☎ 204 5540), on the 1st floor of the Mathuradas Estate Building on Colaba Causeway, has clean but cramped singles/doubles with common bath for Rs 240/340.

Carlton Hotel (☎ 202 0642), at 12 Mereweather Rd, is basic but rooms with common bath and TV cost just Rs 200/350; air-con doubles with attached bath are not such great value at Rs 650. It has a pleasant balcony, though the view of the brothel may not be what you bargained for.

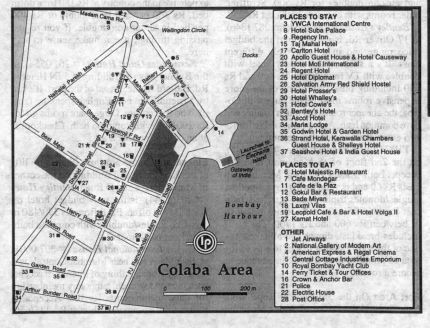

Hotel Prosser's (☎ 284 1715) at 2-4 Henry Rd is an acceptable budget hotel with a selection of rooms with common bath. They range from grubby little cells to spacious, airy doubles, but they all cost Rs 350/500.

Hotel Moti International (☎ 202 1654) at 10 Best Marg is a small establishment with a few good-value air-con doubles with attached bath for Rs 550.

Seashore Hotel (☎ 287 4237), on the 4th floor of Kamal Mansion on Arthur Bunder Rd, has windowless spartan rooms with common bath for Rs 250/350 or Rs 450 for doubles with water views. The entrance is just off Arthur Bunder Rd.

India Guest House (☎ 283 3769), on the 3rd floor of the same building, has rudimentary rooms with hardboard partitions that don't reach the ceiling for Rs 200/300 with common bath, and doubles with water views for Rs 320.

Maria Lodge (☎ 285 4081), in the Grants Building, Arthur Bunder Rd, has small but neat doubles with attached bath for Rs 300 and air-con doubles for Rs 500. Scruffier, older rooms with common bath cost Rs 250.

Bentley's Hotel (☎ 284 1474; fax 287 1846), at 17 Oliver Rd, is at the top of the budget price range and in a completely different class. It's a successful, friendly hotel with doubles with TV for between Rs 460 and Rs 790 including breakfast. Some of the more expensive rooms must be the largest in Colaba; the cheaper rooms are much smaller and have common bath. Air-con is available for Rs 175 extra. Reservations are recommended.

YWCA International Centre (☎ 202 0445), on the 2nd floor of 18 Madame Cama Rd, accepts both women and men. Membership costs Rs 60 and is valid for 90 days. Spotless singles/doubles/triples with attached bath cost Rs 496/975/1438 and require a deposit of between Rs 600 and Rs 1700. The tariff includes breakfast, dinner and all taxes. It's one of the most popular places to stay in the area so phone at least a week in advance to secure a room.

Fort Area On the 3rd floor at Rope Walk Lane, behind the Prince of Wales Museum,

Hotel Lawrence (☎ 284 3618), is one of the best budget hotels in Mumbai. Freshly painted singles/doubles/triples with common bath cost Rs 200/300/400 including taxes. Book at least 15 days in advance.

Benazeer Hotel (☎ 261 1725), in the heart of the Fort, at 16 Rustom Sidhwa Marg, has good air-con rooms with attached bath and TV for Rs 600. It's clean, friendly and well run.

Hotel City Palace (☎ 261 5515), opposite VT, has a huge range of clean singles/doubles/triples with attached bath and TV for Rs 575/725/875 or Rs 675/800/950 with air-con. Air-con broom closets with common bath go for Rs 325/475.

Hotel Manama (☎ 261 3412), at 221-226 P D'Mello Rd, has doubles (only) for Rs 350 with common bath, Rs 450 with attached bath and Rs 550 with air-con. It's an average place, whose main advantage is its proximity to VT, though some rooms have less than scenic views of the railway container depot.

The *retiring rooms* at VT must be the most expensive in the country at Rs 180 for a dorm bed, Rs 300 per bed in a double or Rs 400 per bed in an air-con double. If you're just passing through it can make sense to stay here.

Fernandez Guest House (☎ 261 0554), in the Balmer Lawrie Building at 5 JN Heredia Rd, Ballard Estate, is east of the Fort. It's run by a friendly but non-English speaking family who live on site. Large, bare rooms go for Rs 200/400 with common bath. Checkout is at an uncomfortable 8 am.

Elsewhere On the 3rd floor (there's no lift) of the Krishna Mahal Building on the corner of Marine Drive and D Road, *Bentley Hotel* (☎ 203 1244), is the only budget hotel on Back Bay. It offers B&B from Rs 390/480 in box-like singles/doubles with common bath. Checkout is 24 hours.

YMCA International House (☎ 307 0601) at 18 YMCA Rd, near Mumbai Central, is a long way from anything of interest. It accepts both men and women; temporary membership for three months costs Rs 100. Acceptable rooms with common bath cost Rs 435/660, with attached bath Rs 565/810 and with air-con Rs 665/920. The tariff includes breakfast and dinner, but a hefty room deposit is required.

Places to Stay – middle

Colaba At 30 PJ Ramchandani Marg, *Shelleys Hotel* (☎ 284 0229) overlooks the waters of Mumbai Harbour. It's an excellent place with a slight hint of the Raj about it. Huge air-con doubles (only) with attached bath, TV and fridge start from Rs 1080 and rise to Rs 2150 with water views. The more expensive rooms have oppressive decor.

Strand Hotel (☎ 288 2222; fax 284 1624), next door at No 25, is a little gloomier. Air-con singles/doubles with attached bath and TV start from Rs 1000/1300 and rise to Rs 1190/1500. The standard rooms are, once again, more pleasant than their deluxe counterparts.

Kerawalla Chambers Guest House (☎ 282 1089), above the Strand Hotel, has a range of clean, decent-sized rooms with attached bath, TV and fridge, starting at Rs 500 for a single and Rs 700 for an air-con double. Six rooms have water views and are good value at Rs 950 for a double.

Regent Hotel (☎ 287 1854; fax 202 0363), at 8 Best Marg, has well-appointed modern air-con rooms with TV and fridge. Singles/doubles/triples cost around Rs 1100/1700/1800 including taxes.

Hotel Causeway (☎ 282 7777), on the 3rd floor of the Mathuradas Estate Building on Colaba Causeway, has decent motel-style air-con doubles (only) with attached bath, TV and fridge from Rs 800.

Ascot Hotel (☎ 284 0020; fax 204 6449), *Godwin Hotel* (☎ 287 2050; fax 287 1592) and *Garden Hotel* (☎ 284 1476; fax 204 4290), all established hotels on Garden Rd, have air-con rooms with attached bath, TV and fridge from around Rs 1200/1600.

Hotel Cowie's (☎ 284 0232; fax 283 4203), at 15 Walton Rd, has average air-con rooms with attached bath, TV and fridge for Rs 1040/1300 including breakfast. The rooms are better than the unkempt common areas would suggest.

Hotel Whalley's (☎ 282 1802), at 41 Mereweather Rd, is one of the cheapest in this range but it's nothing special. Rooms cost Rs 450/550 with common bath, Rs 500/750 with attached bath, and Rs 650/900 with air-con. Breakfast is included in the price.

Hotel Diplomat (☎ 202 1661; fax 283 0000), at 24-26 Mereweather Rd, is popular with businesspeople. Air-con singles/doubles/triples with TV and fridge start from Rs 1240/1470/1635 including taxes. Reservations are recommended.

Regency Inn (☎ 202 0292; fax 287 3371), at 18 Lansdowne House, Mahakavi Bhushan Marg, has spacious air-con rooms with attached bath, TV and fridge for Rs 1200/1480 including taxes.

Hotel Suba Palace (☎ 202 0636; fax 202 0812) on Battery St is a comfortable, characterless three-star establishment with air-con singles/doubles/triples with TV and fridge for Rs 1360/1710/2050 including taxes.

Fort Area On the corner of Dr D Naoroji Rd and Rustom Sidhwa Marg, *Hotel Residency* (☎ 262 5525; fax 261 9164), is one of the few comfortable options in the heart of the Fort. It's a quiet, friendly and sensibly priced air-con hotel with immaculate singles/doubles with attached bath and TV from Rs 880/980.

Grand Hotel (☎ 261 8211; fax 262 6581) at 17 Shri Shivsagar Ramgulam Marg, Ballard Estate, fails to live up to its name, but it's a friendly enough three-star place that's popular with visiting businesspeople. Air-con doubles with attached bath, TV and dreary period furniture cost Rs 1800.

Railway Hotel (☎ 262 0775) at 249 P D'Mello Rd charges from Rs 600/750 for smallish rooms with attached bath, TV and fridge or from Rs 900/1050 with air-con. It's on a busy, unappealing street and a little overpriced, though the cheapest rooms are the best.

Marine Drive The *Sea Green Hotel* (☎ 282 2294), at 145 Marine Drive, and its adjacent twin *Sea Green South Hotel* (☎ 282 1613) are good value hotels charging Rs 1000/1150 for decent-sized air-con singles/doubles with

MUMBAI

attached bath, TV and fridge. All rooms are the same price, though some have sea views while others look, rather less appealingly, onto the struts of neighbouring Brabourne Stadium.

Hotel Delamar (☎ 204 2848), on the 2nd floor of 141 Marine Drive, is a similar but older establishment entered by a swirling Art Deco stairway. Rooms with common bath go for Rs 700/1050 and with attached bath for Rs 950/1160. Most rooms have air-con, but only three have sea views.

Hotel Norman's (☎ 203 4234), at 127 Marine Drive, has simple air-con rooms with common bath for Rs 750/900 or attached bath for Rs 1150. The back rooms are small and windowless but the front rooms are good value.

Chateau Windsor Hotel (☎ 204 3376; fax 202 6459) at 86 Veer Nariman Rd has spotless rooms with common bath for Rs 750/970 and singles/doubles/triples with attached bath for Rs 970/1190/1690. Air-con rooms go for Rs 1190/1690/1910.

Kemp's Corner At 131 August Kranti Marg, *Hotel Kemp's Corner* (☎ 363 4646) has air-con singles/doubles with attached bath and TV for Rs 900/1000, which is excellent value for a two-star hotel in such an upmarket area.

Airport There are a number of hotels in Vile Parle (pronounced 'Veelay Parlay'), a suburb close to the domestic terminal.

Hotel Aircraft International (☎ 612 1419), at 179 Dayaldas Rd, is one of the cheapest, with singles/doubles from Rs 650/700.

Hotel Avion (☎ 612 1467), on Nehru Rd, has rooms for Rs 1525/1825.

Hotel Transit (☎ 610 5812), off Nehru Rd, has rooms for Rs 1800/2700.

Juhu At 39/2 Juhu Beach, *Sea Side Hotel* (☎ 620 0293; fax 620 2306), has air-con singles/doubles with attached bath for Rs 1150/1500.

Kings Hotel (☎ 618 4381; fax 611 0059) at 5 Juhu Tara Rd has air-con rooms for Rs 1800.

Places to Stay – top end
Hotels in this category invariably have both state and central government taxes imposed on room tariffs and sometimes add their own service charge. These extras can amount to as much as 35% of your bill, though 20% is more common.

Colaba Near the Gateway of India, *Taj Mahal Hotel* (☎ 202 3366; fax 287 2711), is one of the best hotels in India. Rooms in the old part of the hotel cost from US$290/320, rising to US$325/355 with a sea view. Rooms in the modern wing are slightly cheaper at US$260/290. The Taj is a second home to Mumbai's elite and has every conceivable facility, including three restaurants, three bars, a coffee shop, disco and swimming pool.

Hotel President (☎ 215 0808; fax 215 1201), in the high-rise enclave that ruined once elegant Cuffe Parade, has rooms from Rs 5950/6450. The five-star hotel is part of the Taj Group and has a swimming pool and several good restaurants.

Fariyas Hotel (☎ 204 2911; fax 283 4992), two streets south of Arthur Bunder Rd on Justice Devshanker V Vijas Marg, is a comfortable, modern four-star establishment offering rooms from Rs 2800/3200. It has a small swimming pool, a restaurant and a popular bar.

Nariman Point & Marine Drive Overlooking Marine Drive and the Arabian Sea, *The Oberoi* (☎ 202 5757; fax 204 1505) competes strongly with the Taj Mahal Hotel in a bid to be Mumbai's most opulent hostelry. Singles/doubles cost from US$305/330 and the prestigious Kohinoor suite, where Michael Jackson stayed in 1996, goes for a cool US$1800.

The Oberoi Towers (☎ 202 4343; fax 204 3282) adjoins its younger sister hotel and has rooms from US$260/285. The two hotels have a plethora of facilities including a shopping complex, two swimming pools and five restaurants.

Ritz Hotel (☎ 285 0500; fax 285 0494) at 5 J Tata Rd, Churchgate, is a four-star hotel which lacks a pool but has plenty of character. Rooms start from Rs 3400/4200.

Ambassador Hotel (☎ 204 1131; fax 204 0004), on Veer Nariman Rd, is a four-star modern establishment close to Marine Drive. Its most remarkable feature is the freakish revolving restaurant sprouting from its roof which has superb views of Back Bay. Rooms cost from US$105/120 but the hotel has no pool.

Hotel Nataraj (☎ 204 4161; fax 204 3864), 135 Marine Drive, has decent rooms for Rs 3450/4400, some with sea views. It's a four-star hotel but has a limited range of facilities, targeted mainly at the conference brigade.

Airport One km from the international terminal, *Leela Kempinski* (☎ 836 3636; fax 836 0606), is an award-winning five-star establishment charging US$305/325 for singles/doubles.

Centaur Hotel (☎ 611 6660; fax 611 3535), right outside the domestic terminal, has all the usual five-star amenities. Rooms cost Rs 5500.

Juhu On the beach front at Balraj Sahani Marg, *Holiday Inn* (☎ 620 4444; fax 630 4452), has a relaxing ambience and decent rooms from US$200.

Ramada Hotel Palm Grove (☎ 611 2323; fax 611 3682), also on the beach front, is almost as good and slightly cheaper with singles/doubles for US$150/180.

Centaur Hotel Juhu Beach (☎ 611 3040; fax 611 6343), Juhu Tara Rd, has rooms from Rs 5500. There's an Air India reservation counter here.

Places to Eat

Mumbai has the best selection of restaurants of any Indian city. You could probably trace the history of the metropolis by trawling through the amazing variety of food available: Parsi dhansak, Gujarati thalis, Muslim kebabs, Mangalorean seafood and, of course, Mumbai's famous speciality bhelpuri – a tasty snack of crisp noodles, puffed rice, spiced vegetables, crushed puri, chutney and chillies. The city's delicious seafood is safe

to eat – even during the monsoon months. If you've just been to Chowpatty or Juhu and looked closely at the water, it's best to pretend that the fish came from the kitchen rather than the ocean. During mango season, be sure to try the delicious local Alphonso variety.

Colaba On Colaba Causeway *Leopold Cafe & Bar* is a Mumbai institution. Travellers arriving in Mumbai from less salubrious parts of India traditionally make it their first port of call. It has an extensive Continental, Chinese and veg/non-veg menu, and the quality of food is pretty good. Unfortunately its popularity has pushed prices up to nearly twice those of most other cafes and the staff are overdressed, offhand and not shy about letting you know that they expect to be tipped.

Cafe Mondegar may be cramped, but it's highly popular among budget travellers, mainly due to its convivial atmosphere and CD jukebox. Food ranges from Western breakfasts to Continental and Indian mains. Prices are similar to Leopold, though the food is not as good. Beer is consumed in large quantities in the evening, which only seems to make the surly waiters even more temperamental.

Piccadilly Restaurant on Colaba Causeway, a few blocks south of Leopold, is the place to go for cheap western breakfasts (around Rs 15) if you don't like the prices at Leopold and Mondegar.

Bade Miyan, a permanent evening street stall on Tulloch Rd, is a fun place to eat. It serves excellent grilled kebabs to customers milling on the street or seated at a motley assortment of benches on the side of the road. It has an enviable city-wide reputation, hence the Rs 30 cost of a kebab.

Kailash Parbat, at 1st Pasta Lane, is another Mumbai legend thanks to its inexpensive Sindhi-influenced pure veg snacks, such as *sev puri* and *dahi puri*, and the mouthwatering selection of sweets sold from its shop across the road.

Kamat Hotel is one of the better Indian restaurants on Colaba Causeway. It serves delicious and sensibly priced vegetarian food,

MUMBAI

such as masala dosas for Rs 18 and thalis for Rs 25.

Cafe de la Plaz, on the 2nd floor of the Metro Plaza complex on Colaba Causeway, is a tiny outdoor terrace cafe serving juices, burgers and sandwiches. It's a nice place to perch yourself to escape from the hubbub of the street, and to watch traffic accidents happening below.

Hotel Majestic, on the north side of Colaba Causeway, or *Laxmi Vilas*, on Nawroji Fardunji Rd, are the places to go for a big healthy cheap feed. They're both traditional plate-meal specialists, charging under Rs 20 for tasty thalis.

Tanjore, at the Taj Mahal Hotel, is a sumptuous restaurant with a select menu of tandoori dishes and thalis for between Rs 225 and Rs 545. It has Indian music and dance on Tuesday, Thursday and Saturday night. Formal dress is expected.

Fort In the Jehangir Art Gallery, located midway between Colaba and the Fort, *Cafe Samovar* serves moderately priced light meals on a pleasant jungly verandah. It's open daily between 11 am and 7 pm.

Wayside Inn, on K Dubash Marg, is one of the most comfortable places to hang out in central Mumbai. Dr Ambedkar must have felt that way, since he wrote the initial draft of the Indian Constitution at a table here. It looks like an Italian trattoria but actually serves nostalgic Raj fare, such as leek soup, roast chicken and even orange soufflé. Light meals cost around Rs 35, substantial dishes are around Rs 65. It's open daily until 7 pm.

Mocambo Cafe & Bar is a fine spot in the heart of the Fort serving a mixture of Indian and Continental fare. The beer is cold, the sandwiches are good, and the open street frontage lets you absorb the Fort's atmosphere.

Star of Asia is a friendly old Irani cafe dating back to 1938. It serves traditional veg/non-veg fare for around Rs 30, but has also branched out into salads, burgers and pizzas.

Suvidha, in the National Insurance Building at 204 Dr D Naoroji Rd, has excellent

South Indian vegetarian and Punjabi food for under Rs 20. Expect a long queue at lunchtime.

Fountain Inn, in Nanabhai Lane, is one of several galley-style moderately priced restaurant-bars in the Fort. It's a welcoming place with a vast menu ranging from tandoori crab to simple potato chaat.

Apoorva is an excellent Mangalorean seafood specialist whose mouthwatering crabs and prawn gassis are known throughout South Mumbai. Most seafood dishes cost around Rs 70.

Trishna (☎ 265 9644), at 7 Rope Walk Lane, is currently the rage among the city's foodies. The emphasis is on succulent seafood dishes, with most in the Rs 50 to Rs 250 price range. Non-seafood dishes are between Rs 50 and Rs 80. The king crab and surmai tikka are superb. Bookings are advisable.

Churchgate & Nariman Point There are hundreds of food vendors in the streets of Nariman Point catering to the area's office workers. They dish up tasty cheap fare and standards of hygiene are relatively high.

Bay Bites, at the end of J Bajaj Marg, is a snack shack set in a private garden looking over the water to Cuffe Parade. It's a good place for a cheap lunch and is a comfortable vantage point from which to watch Koli fishing boats heading out to sea.

The Pizzeria, on the corner of Marine Drive and Veer Nariman Rd, has the best pizzas in the city and beautiful views of the lights of Back Bay and Malabar Hill at night. Pizzas with the usual Western toppings, plus local variations, like 'Bombay Masala', start from Rs 65.

Kamling, on Veer Nariman Rd, is a modest but established Chinese restaurant serving inexpensive Cantonese fare.

Gaylords, on Veer Nariman Rd, is an expensive restaurant with a popular sidewalk cafe (often optimistically described as 'Parisian'). It's a pleasant spot for a snack, and the adjoining pastry shop serves delicious sweets and eclairs.

Samrat Restaurant, on J Tata Rd, Churchgate, is a smart, air-con, pure veg restaurant dishing up superb all-you-can-eat Gujarati thalis for Rs 75. It's immensely popular and one of the few thali restaurants in the city that lets you wash down your food with a beer.

Chowpatty Beach & Malabar Hill The stalls lining Chowpatty Beach in the evening are atmospheric spots to snack on bhelpuri, drink fresh juices and indulge in your favourite kulfi.

Cafe Ideal is an amiable Irani-style cafe on Chowpatty Seaface with a CD jukebox and the usual Continental-Chinese-Indian hybrid menu. Most dishes cost around Rs 30; beer is Rs 48.

New Kulfi Centre, opposite, has some of the most delicious kulfi in Mumbai. It's weighed in 100g slabs, cut into cubes, and served to customers clustered on the pavement outside. Prices range from Rs 12 to Rs 25.

Cafe Naaz, on the edge of Malabar Hill's Kamala Nehru Park, is a multi-tiered terrace cafe with superb views of Back Bay and Chowpatty Beach. It's a great place to loiter around sunset as the lights of Marine Drive come on.

China Garden (☎ 363 0841), in Om Chambers, Kemps Corner, is an elegant Chinese restaurant and cocktail bar. Locals unanimously agree that it has the best Chinese food in the city. Most main dishes are between Rs 120 and Rs 200; bookings are essential.

Entertainment

The Government of India tourist office publishes a free, fortnightly 'what's on' guide, but it doesn't extend much beyond the Taj Mahal Hotel and the National Centre for Performing Arts (NCPA). The entertainment

---

Bollywood & Masala Movies

Mumbai is the centre of India's huge Hindi film industry, producing around 200 full-length feature films a year. Forget the carefully crafted, thought-provoking Indian films that are occasionally released in the west – Mumbai films are overripe, technicolour escapist extravaganzas. They're known as 'masala movies' because they mix just about every possible ingredient – action, violence, music, dancing, romance and pat moralising – into one outrageous blend.

In many ways, Bollywood is reminiscent of the early decades of Hollywood studios: audiences are enthralled by the lives of stars and titillated by countless drooling fanzines; films are made on chaotic production schedules, according to coy censorship standards, and are heavily financed with black money.

To many westerners, masala movies are unadulterated rubbish. The usual criticism is that plots show no originality, characterisation is one-dimensional, fight scenes are woefully unconvincing, romances are sickly sweet, no-one ever has sex and the action is interrupted arbitrarily every five minutes for a compulsory song and dance routine. This perception isn't helped by the fact that Bollywood actors traditionally look like escapees from weight-watchers, since there's no glamour in being thin in India, and there are always far too many operatic gestures, heaving bosoms and fake moustaches.

The only problem with dismissing Bollywood's apparent artlessness is its phenomenal success. Stars are treated like gods and social commentators consider masala movies to be the collective dream of India in the same way Hollywood films are for America and much of the west.

Two things have happened since the introduction of satellite TV in India: movie theatres now have serious competition from TV, and masala filmmakers are beginning to be influenced by what they see beamed in from abroad – especially MTV. Actors are getting thinner, dress sense is getting cooler, and dance routines look more like funky Michael Jackson numbers than semaphore training. Much to the disgust of the powers that be, the patronising morality of traditional masala movies is getting ambiguous and the laughable wet-sari eroticism has begun to turn raunchy.

It's still a long way from serious social commentary, but the argument has always been that most Indians would prefer to escape from their circumstances for a few hours rather than have it portrayed larger-than-life on screen.

Unfortunately, there are no organised tours of Mumbai's film studios, but permission to visit sets may be possible if you contact the public relations officers of Film City (☎ 840 1533) in Goregaon, Natraj (☎ 834 2371) in Andheri, and RK Studio (☎ 556 3252) in Chembur. Otherwise you'll have to do what locals do: flick through the pages of *Cineblitz* and pay a visit to a downtown cinema. ∎

pages of the *Times of India* and the *Indian Express* have advertisements for most mainstream events.

Cinema The *Regal* cinema at the start of Colaba Causeway shows first-run English-language movies (Rs 25), but if you want to dip into the spirit of Mumbai check out a Bollywood blockbuster. The best places to do this are *Eros*, an Art Deco gem facing Churchgate railway station, or *Metro* on MG Rd.

Performing Arts The *NCPA* (☎ 283 3737), at the tip of Nariman Point, is the hub of Mumbai's music, dance and drama scene. In any given week, it might host Bengali theatre, dance troupes from Bihar and high-quality Indian classical music. It contains the Tata Experimental Theatre (which occasionally has English-language plays), the Centre for Photography as an Art Form and the Jehangir Nicolson Gallery. The box office is open between 9 am and 1.30 pm and from 4.30 to 6.30 pm.

Bars & Nightclubs Compared to most Indian cities, Mumbai has a relaxed attitude to alcohol. If you just want a drink in casual surroundings, *Cafe Mondegar* and *Leopold Cafe & Bar* (not the tacky pub upstairs) are where most travellers congregate in Colaba.

Fariyas Hotel has an English-style aircon tavern that's popular with Indians of both genders thanks to its giant video screen, loud music and good service.

Gokul Bar & Restaurant on Tulloch Rd is a serious drinking den. It can get pretty lively, though the fast-food seating arrangement doesn't allow much interaction between tables.

Crown & Anchor Bar, behind the Taj Mahal Hotel, is a tame version of Bangkok's Patpong Rd girlie bars, though the dress code is pure silk saris rather than mini-bikinis. It's a dark, unharassing pick-up joint where decorum is very much the name of the game. Drinks are fairly expensive, but it's worth a visit for the social anthropology lesson.

Studio, on Marzaban Rd, is the best pub-club in the Fort. It has semi-industrial decor,

discreet music and a clientele more interested in interacting with each other than the MTV video screen. There's a cover charge and queues at the door.

Rasna, in Churchgate, attracts a younger, brasher crowd who like neon lights, loud music and having to yell to hold a conversation. It's basically a nightclub without a dancefloor, and is couples-only.

Copa Cabana on Chowpatty Seaface is a small, civilised bar with decent background music, extended opening hours and an unconvincing Latin theme.

Most of Mumbai's discos are located in five-star hotels and entry is generally reserved for guests and members who have paid extortionate fees. *1900s* at the Taj Mahal Hotel is considered the best; *The Cellar* disco in Oberoi Towers is due to be replaced by a *Hard Rock Cafe*.

Things to Buy

Mumbai is India's great marketplace, and many people consider it to have the best shopping in the country. It's the textile and fashion centre of India, so you can pick up very cheap clothes, some of which you won't be embarrassed to wear.

You can save a small fortune by purchasing your backpacking wardrobe at 'Fashion Street', the stretch of stalls lining MG Rd between Cross and Azad maidans. If you want to buy Indian clothing, you could do worse than head to the Khadi Village Industries Emporium on Dr D Naoroji Rd, where time seems to have stopped somewhere in the 1940s. If you're looking for something hip, you're better off checking out the small cluster of boutiques on August Kranti Marg at Kemp's Corner.

The stalls lining Colaba Causeway and beneath the Victorian arcades of Dr D Naoroji Rd sell all the accessories you need, from leather belts and bags to toiletries and toys.

You can buy just about anything in the dense bazaars north of the Fort, it's only finding what you want that's the problem. Entire streets are often devoted to a single product since caste traditions remain stronger than capitalist marketing theories; this can make browsing a strange experience as you suddenly encounter shop after shop selling bathroom fittings or copper pipes. Some visitors consider the bazaars a spectacle rather than a place to shop, but it's a lot more fun doing both.

The main areas are Crawford Market (fruit and veg), Zaveri Bazaar (jewellery), Mangaldas Market (cloth), Dhabu St (leather goods) and Chor Bazaar (Mumbai's 'thieves' market'). You can pick up anything at Chor Bazaar, from car parts to Victorian porcelain – the traditional joke is that it was probably stolen from you in the first place. Mutton St in Chor Bazaar specialises in antiques, ingenious reproductions of the same, and miscellaneous junk. Don't place too much faith in authenticity or the lifespan of objects with mechanical parts.

You can pick up souvenirs from all over the country from the various state government emporiums. There's a swag of them in the World Trade Centre Arcade near Cuffe Parade and along Sir P Mehta Rd in the Fort. Central Cottage Industries Emporium in Colaba has the biggest selection of massproduced trinkets and handicrafts. Although most of the artefacts are fairly naff, its a convenient place to bulk purchase compulsory gifts. If you're looking for something that won't look incredibly tacky the moment you take it home, the Bombay Store on Sir P Mehta Rd is an elegant department store with rugs, cloth, home furnishings, books and designer bric-a-brac.

Rhythm House, near the Jehangir Art Gallery, has a huge selection of Indian classical and film music plus a range of western rock, pop and jazz. CDs will cost you around Rs 500 and cassettes Rs 60. See the Bookshops & Publications section earlier in this chapter to find out where to purchase reading material.

For shipping things out of India, contact Perfect Cargo Movers (☎ 283 1457) on the 4th floor of 56 Abdullabhia Currimjee Building, Jamabhoomi Marg, Fort. It's extremely reliable and can advise on customs regulations if you're thinking of purchasing something that you may have trouble exporting.

Getting There & Away

Air Mumbai is the main international gateway to India, with far more flights than Delhi, Calcutta or Chennai (Madras). It also has the busiest network of domestic flights. The international terminal (Sahar) is about four km away from the domestic terminal (Santa Cruz). They are 30km and 26km respectively north of Nariman Point in downtown Mumbai.

Most flights arrive in the middle of the night. So if you arrive without a hotel reservation and are wary of tramping around an unfamiliar city in the early hours of the morning, you may want to wait until dawn before heading into the city.

Facilities at Sahar include Government of India and MTDC tourist counters, a duty-free shop (US dollars only) and a prepaid taxi booth. If you're leaving India, you're advised to check in three hours before your flight departure. You can exchange any leftover rupees for a number of hard currencies at Sahar's 24 hour State Bank of India, opposite the check-in desks. This is also where you pay the Rs 300 departure tax charged on all international flights; do this *before* you check in.

Most international airline offices in Mumbai are in or close to Nariman Point. If you're leaving India from Mumbai, reconfirm your ticket several days before your departure.

Domestic Airlines Addresses of domestic carriers that service Mumbai include:

Indian Airlines
    Air India Building, Nariman Point (☎ 202 3031)
Jet Airways
    Amarchand Mansion, Madame Cama Rd
    (☎ 838 6111)
Sahara Indian Airlines
    Ground floor, Maker Chambers V, J Bajaj Marg,
    Nariman Point (☎ 283 2369)
Skyline NEPC
    Santa Cruz Airport, Vile Parle East (☎ 610 2546)

Domestic Flights from Mumbai There are regular flights to more than 35 Indian cities, including daily flights to Bangalore (US$110), Calcutta (US$185), Delhi (US$140), Goa

MUMBAI

(US$65), Jaipur (US$125), Kochi (US$135), Chennai (US$130) and Varanasi (US$190).

International Airlines Addresses of international airlines with offices in Mumbai include:

Aeroflot
    241/242 Nirmal Building, Barrister Rajni Patel Marg, Nariman Point (☎ 287 1942)
Air Canada
    Amarchand Mansion, Madame Cama Rd (☎ 202 1111)
Air France
    1st floor, Maker Chambers VI, J Bajaj Marg, Nariman Point (☎ 202 4818)
Air India
    Air India Bldg, Nariman Point (☎ 202 4142)
Air Lanka
    C Wing, Mittal Towers, Free Press Journal Marg, Nariman Point (☎ 284 4156)
Alitalia
    Industrial Assurance Bldg, Veer Nariman Rd, Churchgate (☎ 204 5023)
Biman Bangladesh Airlines
    199 J Tata Rd, Churchgate (☎ 282 4659)
British Airways
    Valcan Insurance Bldg, 202B Veer Nariman Rd, Churchgate (☎ 282 0888)
Cathay Pacific Airways
    Taj Mahal Hotel, Apollo Bunder, Colaba (☎ 202 9561)
Delta
    Taj Mahal Hotel, Apollo Bunder, Colaba (☎ 288 5652)
Emirates
    Ground floor, Mittal Chambers, 228 Nariman Point (☎ 287 1649)
Gulf Air
    Ground floor, Maker Chambers V, J Bajaj Marg, Nariman Point (☎ 202 1626)
Japan Air Lines
    Ground floor, Raheja Centre, Free Press Journal Marg, Nariman Point (☎ 287 4939)
Kenya Airways
    199 J Tata Rd, Churchgate (☎ 282 0064)
KLM
    Khaitan Bhavan, 198 J Tata Rd, Churchgate (☎ 283 3338)
Kuwait Airways
    Chateau Windsor, 86 Veer Nariman Rd, Churchgate (☎ 204 5351)
Lufthansa
    Ground floor, Express Towers, Nariman Point (☎ 202 3430)
Malaysian Airlines
    GSA Stic Travels & Tours, 6 Maker Arcade, Cuffe Parade (☎ 218 1431)

Pakistan International Airlines
    4th floor, B Wing, Mittal Towers, Free Press Journal Marg, Nariman Point (☎ 202 1598)
Qantas
    4th floor, Sakhar Bhavan, Nariman Point (☎ 202 9297)
SAS
    Podar House, 10 Marine Drive (☎ 202 7083)
Singapore Airlines
    Taj Mahal Hotel, Apollo Bunder (☎ 202 2747)
Swissair
    Ground floor, Maker Chambers VI, J Bajaj Marg, Nariman Point (☎ 287 2210)
Thai Airways International
    15 World Trade Centre Arcade, Cuffe Parade (☎ 218 7468)
TWA
    Amarchand Mansion, Madame Cama Rd (☎ 282 3080)

Bus Long-distance buses depart from the state road transport terminal close to Mumbai Central railway station. It's fairly chaotic and there is no information available in English. The state bus companies of Maharashtra, Goa, Gujarat, Karnataka and Madhya Pradesh all have offices here and bookings can be made (☎ 307 6622) between 8 am and 8 pm. There's only one government bus to Goa each day. It departs Mumbai at 5 pm and arrives in Panaji at 9 am the following day; tickets cost Rs 172.

Private long-distance buses depart from J Boman Behram Marg, near the entrance to the state road transport terminal, and there are numerous agents selling tickets from booths lining this street. If you're heading to Goa, it's much better to catch one of the more comfortable private buses than to take a government bus. Agents sell tickets to Goa for between Rs 200 and Rs 300 for deluxe buses and between Rs 400 and Rs 450 for air-con buses. Buses depart daily around 2.30 and 5.30 pm, and pick up passengers just south of the Metro Cinema on MG Rd. The journey takes 17 hours.

The MTDC operates daily deluxe buses to Mahabaleshwar (Rs 150, seven hours), Nasik (Rs 90), and Ganapatipule (Rs 160). All buses depart from the MTDC Tours Division and Reservation Office on Madame Cama Rd, where tickets should be purchased in advance. The MTDC also handles bookings for Ghadge Patil Transport's daily bus to Aurangabad (Rs 180, 12 hours), which departs from the same location at 7.45 pm.

Train Two railway systems operate out of Mumbai. Central Railways handles services to the east and south, plus a few trains to the north. It operates from Victoria Terminus (VT), which is also known as Chhatrapati Shivaji Terminus (CST). The reservation centre behind VT is open Monday to Saturday between 9 am and 1 pm, and 1.30 and 4 pm. Tourist-quota tickets and Indrail passes can be bought at counter No 8.

A few Central Railways trains depart from Dadar, several stops north of Mumbai Central. They include the *Chennai Express* and the *Dadar Express*, the two fastest trains to Chennai (Madras). You can still book tickets for these trains at VT. Trains operating on the functional stretches of the new Konkan Railway

(see the box section in the Getting Around chapter at the start of the book) also operate from here. Just to confuse the issue even more, a handful of useful expresses to Bangalore, Calcutta, Varanasi and Gorakhpur depart from Kurla, which is inconveniently located 16km to the north of VT.

The other railway system is Western Railways, which has services to the north from Churchgate and Mumbai Central stations. Bookings for trains departing from either station can be made at the reservation centre opposite Churchgate. It's open Monday to Saturday between 8 am and 8 pm, and until 2 pm on Sunday. Tourist-quota tickets and Indrail passes are issued on weekdays between 9.30 am and 1.30 pm and between 2 and 4.30 pm, and on Saturday from 9.30 am to 2.30 pm. There's also a reservation centre adjacent to Mumbai Central, but you cannot purchase tourist-quota tickets here.

Major Trains from Mumbai

Destination	Train Number & Name	Departure Time	Distance (km)	Duration (hours)	Fare (Rs) (2nd/1st)
Agra	1037 *Punjab Mail*	7.10 pm VT*	1344	21.30	261/940
Ahmedabad	2009 *Shatabdi***	6.25 am BC	492	7.00	430/865
	9101 *Gujarat Mail*	9.25 pm BC		9.00	135/464
Aurangabad	1003 *Devagiri Exp*	9.20 pm VT	375	7.15	110/376
	7617 *Tapovan Exp*	6.10 am VT		7.15	
Bangalore	6529 *Udyan Exp*	7.55 am VT	1210	24.30	247/876
Calcutta	2859 *Gitanjali Exp*	6.00 am VT	1960	33.30	309/1243
	8001 *Howrah Mail*	8.15 pm VT		36.00	
Chennai	1063 *Chennai Exp*	7.50 pm D	1279	24.00	251/917
Delhi	2951 *Rajdhani Exp***	4.55 pm BC	1384	17.00	000/2835
	2925 *Paschim Exp*	11.35 am BC		23.00	263/965
Kochi	1081 *Netravati Exp*	3.35 pm VT	1840	39.00	299/1190
Pune	2123 *Deccan Queen*	5.10 pm VT	191	3.30	48/217
	1007 *Deccan Exp*	6.40 am VT		4.30	
Varanasi	1065 *Ratnagiri Exp*	5.20 am K	1509	22.30	276/1026

* Abbreviations for train station: VT = Victoria Terminus; BC = Mumbai Central; D = Dadar; K = Kurla
** Air-con only; fare includes meals and drinks

Shatabdi 2009 runs/operates daily except Friday
Rajdhani 2951 runs/operates daily except Monday
Ratnagiri Express 1065 runs/operates Monday, Wednesday, Thursday only

If you're heading to Goa, keep your fingers crossed that the Konkan Railway is fully operational, otherwise you face an arduous 20 hour train journey via Miraj. When the Konkan Railway is open, travel time to Goa from Mumbai is expected to almost halve. Currently, it's much quicker and less hassle to catch a bus or the ferry.

See the train table for a selection of trains from Mumbai.

Boat The Mumbai to Goa ferry service is operated by Frank Damania. The modern, 400-seat, air-con jetfoil leaves Mumbai Friday to Sunday at 9.30 pm, and on Tuesday and Thursday at 10 am. The journey takes about eight hours. On the return leg it leaves Panaji daily, except Tuesday and Thursday, at 10 am. The fare is Rs1050/1250 in economy/business class, and includes meals. Children under two pay Rs100/125; children above two and under 12 pay 50% of the adult fare. For bookings contact the Frank Damania ferry terminal in Panaji (☎ (0832) 228711) or Mumbai (☎ (022) 374 3737; fax 374 3740).

Getting Around

The Airport An airport bus service operates between the Air India Building at Nariman Point and Santa Cruz (domestic) and Sahar (international) airports. The journey to Santa Cruz takes about one hour and costs Rs 40; to Sahar it takes about 1¼ hours and costs Rs 50. In peak hour, the trip through Mumbai's congested streets can take well over two hours, so don't cut things too fine. Baggage costs Rs 5 per piece.

From Nariman Point, departures are at 12.30, 4.15, 8.15, 10.15 and 11.30 am, and 1.15, 2.15, 3.45, 5.30, 7.15, 9.15 and 11.15 pm. From Sahar, departures are at 2.30, 6.30, 8, 9.30 and 11 am, at noon, and at 1.40, 2.30, 5, 7.30, 9.30 and 10.30 pm; the buses leave from Santa Cruz half an hour later. Tickets for the buses can be bought either at the booth outside the Air India building or on the buses themselves. There are also regular shuttle buses between the domestic and international terminals.

A taxi to the airports costs around Rs 200

from Colaba on the meter. During rush hours or at night you won't find a driver prepared to use the meter, so expect to pay more.

There's a prepaid taxi booth at the international airport, with set fares to various city destinations. It's Rs 225 to Colaba during the day and Rs 282 at night; slightly less to the Fort. Prepaid fares are higher than the meter rate but it saves haggling with taxi drivers.

Don't try to catch an auto-rickshaw from the airport to the city: they're prohibited from entering central Mumbai and will drop you only a few km down the road at Mahim Creek. Taxis loitering there will take maximum advantage of your predicament.

Bus Despite popular mythology, Mumbai's red double-decker buses are one of the best ways to travel short distances in the city, as long as you don't attempt this during rush hours. Fares generally cost only a couple of rupees and are paid to the conductor once you're aboard.

The problem with bus travel is figuring out where the buses go, since the route maps sold at newsstands are indecipherable. Useful buses from Colaba include: VT (Nos 1, 3, 11 and 124), Mumbai Central (No 124), Churchgate (No 123), Chowpatty (Nos 108 and 123), Dadar (Nos 4, 7 and 8) and Malabar Hill (No 108). If a bus number is followed by 'limited', this means it doesn't stop as frequently as regular buses; this is a good thing.

Unfortunately route numbers and destinations on the front of buses are written in Marathi; English signs have been relegated to the side. This means you have no idea where a bus is going until it's going past you. It's best to make as many friends as possible at the bus queue; somebody will always let you know when the right bus is coming.

Train Mumbai has efficient but overcrowded suburban electric trains, and it's virtually the only place in India where it's worth taking trains for intracity travel. Avoid rush hours when trains are so crowded that more people seem to be hanging onto the outside than are squashed inside. First class is only marginally less crowded; women should take advantage of the ladies-only carriages.

The main suburban route of interest to travellers is Churchgate to Mumbai Central (Rs 2/22 in 2nd/1st class) and onward to Dadar. There's a train every few minutes in either direction between 4.30 am and 1.30 am.

Taxi & Auto-Rickshaw Mumbai has a huge fleet of metered black-and-yellow taxis, but auto-rickshaws are confined to the outer northern suburbs. Taxis are the most convenient way to zip around the city but they're not cheap. You may have to approach a few vehicles before you find one willing to go where you want.

Taxi meters are out of date, so the fare is calculated using a conversion chart which all drivers carry – ask to see it at the end of the journey. The rough conversion rate is around 10 times the meter reading. The minimum fare is Rs 10.50 for the first 1.6 km and Rs 6.50 per km after this. Drivers use meters from dawn until late evening, but after midnight you'll probably have to negotiate a price.

If you're staying near the airport or in Juhu, you can catch auto-rickshaws to get around, though they are not allowed any closer to the city centre than Mahim Creek. Auto-rickshaws are metered but also use a conversion chart.

Car The ITDC's recommended rates for hiring a car with a driver are from Rs 750 per day or Rs 575 for half a day with limited km. Taxi drivers in Colaba quote around Rs 600 per day.

Boat There are plenty of ferries shuttling tourists between Apollo Bunder and Elephanta Island (see the Around Mumbai section later in this chapter), but little else of interest apart from a few ferries leaving Apollo Bunder for Mandwa and Alibag on the mainland south of Mumbai, and leaving Baucha Dhakka Wharf for Revas, also south of Mumbai.

AROUND MUMBAI
Elephanta Island

The rock-cut temples on Elephanta Island, nine km north-east of Apollo Bunder, are Mumbai's major tourist attraction. They are thought to have been created between 450 and 750, when the island was known as Gharapuri, the Fortress City. The Portuguese renamed it Elephanta because of a large stone elephant near the shore. This statue collapsed in 1814, and the British removed the remaining pieces to the Victoria Gardens where it was reassembled and still stands today.

Unfortunately the Portuguese took their traditional disdain for other religions to its usual lengths at Elephanta and did considerable damage to the sculptures, though their size, beauty and power remain impressive.

The caves are reached by a steep stairway, lined with handicraft and soft drink stalls, that begins near the ferry landing. Palanquins are available for those who need to be carried up. It costs Rs 5 to enter the cave area at the top of the hill.

There is one main cave with a number of large sculpted panels, all relating to Siva, and a separate lingam shrine. The most famous of the panels is the impassive Trimurti, or triple-headed Siva, where the god also takes the role of Brahma the creator and Vishnu the preserver. The central bust of Siva, its eyes closed in eternal contemplation, may be the most serene sight you witness in India.

There are also figures of Siva dancing the Tandava, the marriage of Siva and Parvati, Ravana shaking Kailasa, a scary carving of Siva killing the demon Andhaka, and one in which Siva appears as Ardhanari, uniting both sexes in one body.

The best time to visit Elephanta is during the week, since on weekends it has a carnival atmosphere that is not conducive to calm contemplation of the temples. On weekends a large queue forms before the triple-headed Siva as people wait their turn to use the sculpted figure as a photo prop.

When you've had your fill of the cave temples, the tree-top terrace of the MTDC's *Chalukya Restaurant & Beer Bar* at the head of the stairway is a fine spot to sit back

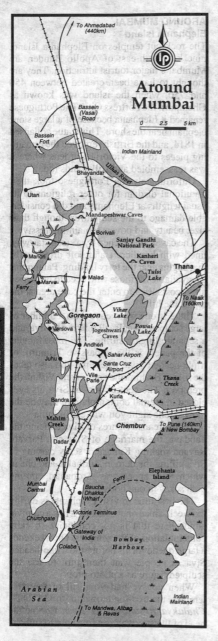

Around Mumbai

0   2.5   5 km

To Ahmedabad (440km)

Bassein (Vasai) Road

Bassein Fort

Indian Mainland

Bhayandar

Utan

Mandapeshwar Caves

Borivali

Manori

Sanjay Gandhi National Park

Kanheri Caves

Thana

Tulsi Lake

Marve

Malad

To Nasik (160km)

Ferry

Vihar Lake

Goregaon

Powai Lake

Versova

Jogeshwari Caves

Andheri

Sahar Airport

Juhu

Santa Cruz Airport

Vile Parle

Thana Creek

Bandra

Kurla

Mahim Creek

Chembur

To Pune (140km) & New Bombay

Dadar

Worli

Elephanta Island

Mumbai Central

Baucha Dhakka Wharf

Ferry

Churchgate

Victoria Terminus

Gateway of India

Bombay Harbour

Colaba

Arabian Sea

Indian Mainland

To Mandwa, Alibag & Revas

and take in the expansive views of Mumbai Harbour. Look out for the elderly gent patrolling the terrace with a slingshot to keep pesky monkeys at bay.

The government has been heavily criticised for its failure to maintain both the monument and the island's environment. Travellers can help MTDC initiatives by carrying any rubbish they generate back on the boat to Mumbai.

Getting There & Away Launches depart from Apollo Bunder by the Gateway of India. Ordinary boats cost Rs 40 return and luxury launches, which are met at Elephanta by a free tour guide, cost Rs 60. A good guide will increase your understanding and enjoyment. Tickets are sold by touts on the steps of the Gateway, and from booths nearby.

Both types of launch leave every half-hour from around 9 am to 2.30 pm. The voyage takes an hour and, though not particularly picturesque, does give an indication of the size of Mumbai's port. If you have a luxury ticket, you can return on any boat; if you have an ordinary ticket, you can return on any ordinary boat. The last boat leaves from Elephanta at 5.30 pm. During the monsoon, ordinary boats are suspended. For enquiries phone ☎ 202 6364.

An alternative to the launches is the catamaran which leaves daily from Apollo Bunder at 10 am and returns at 2 pm. The voyage takes 45 minutes and the fare is Rs 125. For catamaran enquiries phone ☎ 287 5473.

Ignore the hawkers at Apollo Bunder who try to persuade tourists that there's nothing to eat or drink on the island.

Sanjay Gandhi National Park
This 104 sq km protected area of forested hills on Mumbai's northern outskirts was formerly called the Borivali National Park. It's best known for the 109 **Kanheri Caves**, which line the side of a rocky ravine in the centre of the park. They were used by Buddhist monks between the 2nd and 9th centuries as *viharas* (monasteries) and *chaityas* (temples). The most impressive is cave 3, the Great Chaitya Cave, which has a long colonnade

of pillars and a five metre high *dagoba* at the back of the cave. Several other caves have interesting sculptures, though the majority are little more than shelters carved into the rock. Entry to the national park costs Rs 2; entry to the caves, a further five km from the park entrance, is another Rs 2.

There's a **Lion Safari Park** 500m inside the national park entrance. 'Safari trips' run daily except Monday between 9 am and 5 pm; entry is Rs 10. The park's natural wildlife, which includes a small population of tigers and panthers, is under serious threat from urban encroachment.

Getting There & Away Take the train from Churchgate to Borivali station (40 minutes) and then an auto-rickshaw for the six km to Kanheri caves. Be wary of rickshaw-wallahs who try to persuade you to keep the meter running while you explore the caves; if you fall for this trick, you'll return to the rickshaw to find the meter has been tampered with. On Sundays and public holidays there is a city bus service from Borivali station to the caves. Kanheri can also be visited (quickly) on the MTDC's suburban tour.

Mandapeshwar & Jogeshwari Caves

The Mandapeshwar Caves, north of Borivali, are of minor interest, though one of these Hindu caves was converted into a Portuguese church. The Jogeshwari Caves are much closer to the city, east of Jogeshwari railway station.

Manori Beach

This sleepy beach near the Portuguese-flavoured fishing village of Manori is a weekend retreat for wealthy Mumbai families and the scene of occasional beach parties. It's in a surprisingly rural environment, about 40km from the city centre.

Places to Stay The *Manoribel Hotel* (☎ 269 1301) has a selection of cottages set in a shady beachside grove strung with hammocks. They cost between Rs 600 and Rs 1300 on weekdays, and between Rs 750 and Rs 1750 on weekends. Double rooms are Rs 400 to Rs 500 weekdays; Rs 100 more on weekends. Full board is available for an extra Rs 310. Be sure to book in advance.

DoMonica Beach Resort (☎ 444 9735), 100m further north, charges Rs 150 per head. Full board is available for an extra Rs 220. Advance bookings are essential on weekends.

To get to Manori, take the suburban electric train from Churchgate to Malad, then bus No 272 to Marve. A ferry (Rs 2.50) shuttles across Manori Creek, and it's a pleasant two km walk or tonga ride from the Manori slipway to the beach and the hotels.

Bassein

The remains of the Portuguese fortified city of Bassein are on the northern side of the river which separates Greater Mumbai from the Indian mainland. After securing the area in 1534, the Portuguese built a city of such pomp and splendour – with a cathedral, five convents and 13 churches – that it came to be known as the Court of the North. In 1739 the Marathas besieged the city and the Portuguese surrendered after appalling losses. The weathered city walls are still standing and you can see the eerie ruins of some of the churches and the Cathedral of St Joseph. Bassein is 11km from the Bassein Road (Vasai Road in Marathi) railway station.

Maharashtra

Maharashtra is one of India's largest, most populous and economically important states. Its booming capital, Mumbai (Bombay), is also a major gateway for overseas visitors. From Mumbai most travellers head south to the beaches of Goa, south-east to Pune and its famous ashram, or north-east to the world-heritage cave temples of Ajanta and Ellora.

The jagged Western Ghats run parallel to the coast for the full length of the state and are dotted with inviting hill stations such as Matheran and Mahabaleshwar. Most of the state stands on the high Deccan plateau which stretches east some 800km from the ghats.

The Deccan was the epicentre of the 17th century Maratha Empire, which, under the rule of Shivaji, defied the Mughals and made a large part of central India its domain.

Maharashtra also has strong connections with Gandhi and the political actions that brought on India's independence. Gandhi was interned by the British at the Aga Khan's palace in Pune for two years after the Free India declaration, and his exemplary ashram is located at Sevagram in the far east of the state.

Today Maharashtran politics are dominated by the right-wing Shiv Sena (the army of Shiva) named after Shivaji. Headed by its charismatic founder, Bal Thackeray, the Sena was formed in the late 1960s to fight for 'Maharashtra for Maharashtrians', targeting non-Hindus and itinerant workers from the southern states in sometimes violent campaigns. It now panders to the broader Hindu communalism throughout the country, and in 1996 partnered the Hindu-fundamentalist BJP in an uneasy state- government coalition dubbed the 'saffron alliance'.

MAHARASHTRA AT A GLANCE

Population: 91 million
Area: 307,690
Capital: Mumbai
Main Language: Marathi
Literacy Rate: 63%
Best Time to Go: September to April (coast); September to mid-June (hill stations)

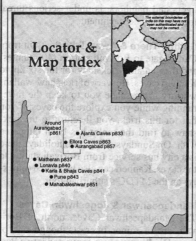

Locator & Map Index

The external boundaries of India on this map have not been authenticated and may not be correct.

Around Aurangabad p861
Ajanta Caves p833
Ellora Caves p863
Aurangabad p857
Matheran p837
Lonavla p840
Karla & Bhaja Caves p841
Pune p843
Mahabaleshwar p851

Highlights
- The toy-train ride to the hill station of Matheran
- The hand carved extravagance of Ellora's Kailasa Temple
- Meditating under Gandhi's pipal tree at the Sevagram ashram
- Delicious Alphonso mangoes

Festivals
Dance & Music Festival – Ellora – March
Ganesh Chaturthi & Pune Festival – Pune – Aug/Sept

Southern Maharashtra

THE KONKAN COAST
Maharashtra's Konkan Coast – the narrow strip between the Western Ghats and the Arabian Sea – is a region of deserted beaches, abandoned forts and isolated fishing communities, and is probably best known for its fresh produce, especially pomfret (a fish), avocados, and delicious Alphonso mangoes.

MAHARASHTRA

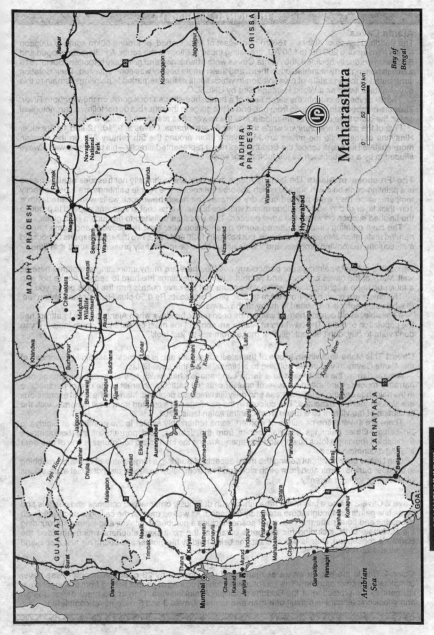

Maharashtra

Bay of Bengal

ORISSA

MADHYA PRADESH

ANDHRA PRADESH

KARNATAKA

GUJARAT

GOA

Arabian Sea

MAHARASHTRA

0   50   100 km

Raipur

Jagdalpur

Kondagaon

Chanda

Ramtek

Navagaon National Park

Nagpur

Sevagram

Wardha

Amaoti

Chikhaldara

Melghat Wildlife Sanctuary

Akola

Nanded

Warangal

Secunderabad
Hyderabad

Nizamabad

Gulbarga

Latur

Parbhani

Lonar

Buldhana

Khandwa

Burhanpur

Bhusawal

Fardapur

Ajanta

Jalna

Godavari River

Krishna River

Bijapur

Sholapur

Barsi

Pandharpur

Belgaum

Amalner

Dhulia

Jalgaon

Manmad

Ellora

Aurangabad

Paithan

Ahmednagar

Mumbai

Nasik

Trimbak

Kalyan

Thane

Matheran

Lonavla

Pune

Mund

Indapur

Satara

Mahabaleshwar

Chiplun

Ratnagiri

Ganpatipule

Kolhapur

Panhala

Miraj

Vita

Pratapgam

Daman

Surat

Malegaon

Tapti River

Chaul

Kashid

Janjira

A REGIONAL HIGHLIGHT

Ajanta Caves

The Buddhist caves of Ajanta – 166km north-east of Aurangabad, or around 60km south of Jalgaon – date from around 200 BC to 650 AD, predating those at Ellora to the south. As Ellora developed and Buddhism gradually declined, the Ajanta Caves were abandoned and gradually forgotten. But in 1819 a British hunting party stumbled upon them, and their remote beauty was soon unveiled. Their isolation contributed to the fine state of preservation in which some of their remarkable paintings remain to this day. Ajanta is listed as a World Heritage Site by UNESCO.

The 29 caves are cut into the steep face of a horseshoe-shaped rock gorge on the Waghore River. They are numbered in sequence from one end of the gorge to the other but do not follow a chronological order; the oldest are mainly in the middle and the newer ones are close to each end.

Five of the caves are *chaityas* while the other 24 are *viharas*. Caves 8, 9, 10, 12 and 13 are older Hinayana caves, while the others are Mahayana (from around the 5th century AD). In the simpler, more austere Hinayana school the Buddha was never represented directly – his presence was always alluded to by a symbol such as the footprint or wheel of law.

The 'Frescoes' of Ajanta The famous Ajanta 'frescoes' are technically not frescoes at all. A fresco is a painting done on a wet surface which absorbs the colour. The Ajanta paintings are more correctly tempera, since they were painted on a dry surface. The rough-hewn rock walls were coated with a 1cm thick layer of clay and cow dung mixed with rice husks. A final coat of lime was applied to produce the finished surface on which the artist painted. This was then polished to produce a high gloss.

The cave paintings initially suffered some deterioration after their rediscovery, and some heavy-handed restoration also caused damage, but between 1920 and 1922, two Italian art experts conducted a meticulous restoration process, and the paintings have been carefully preserved since that time.

Although the Ajanta paintings are particularly notable, there are many interesting sculptures here as well. Many of the caves are dark, and without a light the paintings are hard to see – if you're not with a tour, purchase a lighting ticket, which will ensure that the cave guards turn the lights on for you.

The caves are open daily from 9 am to 5.30 pm. Entry costs Rs 0.50 plus Rs 5 for the lighting fee. Flash photography is prohibited in many of the caves.

If possible, avoid coming here at weekends or on public holidays when Ajanta seems to attract half the population of India. The hawkers at Ajanta are some of the most persistent in south India – if you don't want to buy, don't accept 'gifts' or make promises to 'just look'.

Cave 1 This Mahayana vihara is one of the latest excavated and is the most beautifully decorated of the Ajanta Caves. If you prefer building to a climax, leave this cave till last.

A verandah at the front leads to a large congregation hall which has elaborate sculptures and narrative murals, surrounded by several smaller cells. Of particular interest is the use of perspective in the paintings and the details of dress and daily life which are depicted. Many of the facial expressions are also wonderfully executed. The colours in the paintings were created from local minerals, with the exception of the vibrant blue made from Central Asian lapis lazuli.

There are several fine paintings of women, some remarkably similar to the paintings at Sigiriya in Sri Lanka. Other paintings include scenes from the Jatakas, and portraits of the bodhisattvas Padmapani (holding a lotus flower) and Vajrapani. Among the interesting sculptures is one of four deer sharing a common head.

Don't leave cave 1 without seeing the three aspects of Buddha: a large statue of Buddha preaching in the deer park is illuminated from each side and then from below to reveal distinct facial expressions of solemnity, joy and serenity.

Cave 2 Cave 2 is also a late Mahayana vihara with deliriously ornamented columns and capitals and some fine paintings, though some are badly damaged. As well as murals, the ceiling is decorated with geometric and floral patterns. The mural scenes include a number of Jatakas and events surrounding the Buddha's birth, including his mother's dream of the six-tusked elephant which heralded the Buddha's conception. Details depict Gautama being held by his mother and taking his first steps, and the miracle of 1000 Buddhas.

Cave 4 This is the largest vihara at Ajanta and is supported by 28 pillars. Although it was never completed, the cave has some fine sculptures, including scenes of people fleeing from the 'eight great dangers' to the protection of the Buddha's disciple Avalokitesvara. One of the great dangers is an angry-looking elephant in pursuit of a man and woman. Caves 3 and 5 were never completed.

A REGIONAL HIGHLIGHT

Cave 6 This is the only two storey vihara at Ajanta, but parts of the lower storey have collapsed. Inside is a seated Buddha figure with an intricately carved door to the shrine. Upstairs the hall is surrounded by cells with fine paintings on the doorways.

Cave 7 Cave 7 is of unusual design in that the verandah does not lead into a hall with cells down the sides and a shrine room at the rear. Here there are porches before the verandah, which leads directly to the four cells and the elaborately sculptured shrine.

Cave 9 This is a chaitya and one of the earliest at Ajanta. Although it dates from the Hinayana period, two Buddha figures flanking the entrance door were probably later Mahayana additions. Similarly, the paintings inside, which are not in excellent condition, show signs of having been refurbished. Columns run down both sides of the cave and around the three metre high dagoba at the far end. At the front there is a horseshoe-shaped window above the entrance, and the vaulted roof has traces of wooden ribs.

Cave 10 This is thought to be the oldest cave (200 BC) and was the one first spotted by the British soldiers who rediscovered Ajanta. It is the largest chaitya and is similar in design to cave 9. The facade has collapsed and the paintings inside have been damaged, in some cases by graffiti dating from soon after the caves' rediscovery. The indentations in the floor near the left-hand wall were used for mixing paint pigments.

Cave 16 Some of Ajanta's finest paintings can be seen in this, one of the later vihara caves. It is thought that cave 16 may have been the original entrance to the entire complex, and there is a fine view of the river from the front of the cave. Two welcoming elephants guard the entrance. Best known of the paintings here is the 'dying princess': Sundari, wife of the Buddha's half-brother Nanda, is said to have fainted at the news that her husband was renouncing the material life (and her) in order to become a monk. This is one of the finest paintings at Ajanta. Nanda features in several other paintings, including one of his conversion by the Buddha.

Carved figures appear to support the ceiling in imitation of wooden architectural details, and there's a statue of Buddha seated on a lion throne teaching the eight fold path.

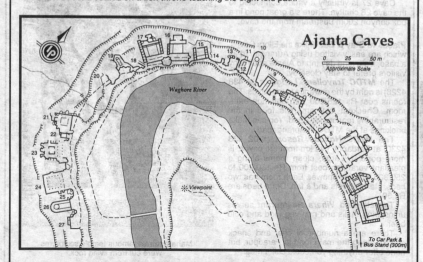

A REGIONAL HIGHLIGHT

Cave 17 This cave has the finest paintings at Ajanta. Not only are they in the best condition, they are also the most numerous and varied. They include beautiful women flying overhead on the roof while carved dwarfs support the pillars. One of Ajanta's best known images shows a princess, surrounded by attendants, applying make-up. In one there is a royal procession, while in another an amorous prince plies his lover with wine. In yet another panel the Buddha returns from his enlightenment to his own home to beg from his wife and astonished son.

A detailed panel tells the story of Prince Simhala's expedition to Sri Lanka. With his 500 companions he is shipwrecked on an island where ogresses appear as beautiful women, only to seize and devour their victims. Simhala escapes on a flying horse and returns to conquer the island.

Cave 19 The facade of this magnificent chaitya is remarkably detailed and includes an impressive horseshoe-shaped window as its dominant feature. Two very fine standing Buddha figures flank the entrance. Inside is a three tiered dagoba with a figure of the Buddha on the front.

There are also some fine sculptures and paintings, but one of the most striking is outside the cave to the west, where there is an image of the Naga king with seven cobra hoods arrayed around his head. His wife, hooded by a single cobra, is seated beside him.

Cave 24 Cave 24 would have been the largest vihara at Ajanta if it had been finished, and shows how the caves were constructed – long galleries were cut into the rock, and then the rock between them was broken through.

Caves 26 & 27 The fourth chaitya's facade has fallen and almost every trace of its paintings has disappeared. Nevertheless, there are some fine sculptures remaining. On the left wall is a huge figure of the 'reclining Buddha', lying back as he prepares to enter nirvana. Other scenes include a lengthy depiction of the Buddha's temptation by Mara.

In one scene Mara attacks the Buddha with demons, and then his beautiful daughters tempt him with more sensual delights. However, the Buddha's resistance is too strong, and the final scene shows a glum and dejected-looking Mara having failed to deflect the Buddha from the straight and narrow.

Cave 27 is virtually a vihara connected to the cave 26 chaitya. There's a great pond in a box canyon 200m upstream from the cave.

Places to Stay & Eat Unlike the Ellora Caves, which are easily visited using Aurangabad as a base, it's a long day trip to Ajanta and many visitors prefer to stay close by.

The **MTDC Travellers' Lodge** (☎ 02 438 4226) is right by the entrance to the caves. The rooms cost Rs 125/200 with common bathroom. Checkout is 9 am. The food in the restaurant is reasonably good. You can make bookings at the MTDC in Aurangabad.

The **MTDC Holiday Resort** (☎ 02 438 4230) at Fardapur, five km from the caves, is more popular. Large, clean rooms along a pleasant verandah cost from Rs 150/200 to 250/300 with hot shower. Each room has two beds, clean sheets and a fan. Dorm beds are Rs 50.

The attached **Vihara Restaurant** serves uninspiring thalis and non-veg food and cold beer.

There are a number of chai and snack shacks along the main road in Faradpur, but none offer anything you could call a meal.

Maharashtra's famous temple sculptures were cut from living rock.

A REGIONAL HIGHLIGHT

Getting There & Away For information on buses from Aurangabad or Jalgaon, see those sections.
The caves are four km off the main Aurangabad to Jalgaon road, and Fardapur is one km further down the main road towards Jalgaon. There are regular buses between Fardapur and Ajanta which cost Rs 4. Not all buses travelling along the main road call at Ajanta – so ensure you get on the right one to avoid a walk to the caves.
Shared taxis operate between the caves, Fardapur and Jalgaon. Prices are negotiable, but expect to pay around Rs 15 from Ajanta to Fardapur and Rs 50 to Jalgaon.
There's a 'cloakroom' at the Ajanta Caves where you can leave gear (Rs 2), so it is possible to arrive on a morning bus from Jalgaon, look around the caves, and continue to Aurangabad in the evening, or vice versa. If you want to visit Ajanta and Ellora in chronological order, visit Ajanta first. ■

Although the region is relatively undeveloped, a few travellers are already finding their way to the excellent beaches which fringe the coast. And the number of tourists is certain to increase rapidly in the foreseeable future following the opening in 1997 of the Konkan Railway, which connects Mumbai with Goa and Mangalore along the Konkan corridor. See the boxed section in the Getting Around chapter for further details on the progress of this railway.

Chaul

This old Portuguese settlement, located 40km south of Mumbai, was secondary in importance to Bassein. The Portuguese settled here in 1522 but relinquished it to the Marathas in the same year Bassein fell. There are a few remnants of Portuguese fortifications and a couple of ruined churches. The hilltop Muslim Korlai Fort stands on the opposite bank of the river, looking across to the Portuguese fort.

Ferries run to Revas from Mumbai's Baucha Dhakka ferry wharf and to Alibag from Apollo Bunder: it's a short bus ride from either of these to Chaul.

Kashid

Just 140km south of Mumbai, Kashid is Maharashtra's up-and-coming beach resort, boasting a 3km sweep of clean, undeveloped beach with good swimming. Facilities are still limited except for the burgeoning *Kashid Beach Resort* (☎ (02144) 85010; Mumbai ☎ 262 5406), which has split-level sea-view

doubles starting at Rs 600 (cheaper during the week), as well as a restaurant and pool.

Kashid is on the bus route from Mumbai to Murud (see below for getting there & away details).

Murud-Janjira

Just off the coast 160km south of Mumbai is the majestic island fortress of Janjira, the 16th century capital of the Siddis of Janjira, descendants of sailor-traders from the Horn of Africa. It is one of Maharashtra's most commanding coastal forts, stretched along an island a short distance off the tranquil fishing town of Murud and only accessible by local boat (20 mins, Rs 50).

The fort's 12m high walls made it impregnable to everyone, even the Marathas – Shivaji tried to conquer it by sea and his son, Sambhaji, even attempted to tunnel to it!

The *MTDC Holiday Resort* (☎ (021447) 4078; Mumbai ☎ 6174517) offers basic accommodation on the beach at Murud, 5km north of the fort. There's a variety of rooms available from Rs 400 to Rs 800 a double. Cottages sleeping four are Rs 1200, or Rs 1500 with air-con.

Getting There & Away Buses from Mumbai Central take around four hours to Kashid and a further hour to Murud. There are also two express Asiad buses a day (5.45 am and 12 noon; Rs 50), which take 3½ hours to Murud. The nearest railhead on the Konkan railway is Indapur.

MAHARASHTRA

Ganpatipule

Ganpatipule, on the coast 375km south of Mumbai, has another of Maharashtra's pristine and undeveloped beaches, but is better known for its *swayambhu Ganpati* or 'naturally formed' monolithic Ganesh, which attracts thousands of pilgrims from all over India.

Another 15km south is **Ratnagiri**, the largest town on Maharashtra's south coast. It was the birthplace of freedom fighter Lokmanya Tilak and the place where the British interned the last Burmese king, Thibaw, from 1886 until his death in 1916.

The *MTDC Holiday Resort* (☎ (02352) 35248) on the beach at Ganpatipule has a range of accommodation including tents (2 bed, Rs 125; 4 bed, Rs 225), non air-con/air-con doubles (Rs 350/500) and air-con 'Sea View Cottages' (Rs 1000).

The nearest railhead on the Konkan railway is Ratnagiri.

MATHERAN

Pop: 5500   Tel Area Code: 02148

Matheran ('jungle topped') is the nearest hill station to Mumbai and a refreshing break from the heat and noise of the capital. It's an undulating hilltop cloaked in shady trees and ringed by walking tracks which lead to lookouts that drop sheer to the plains. On a clear day the views are fantastic and it's possible to see (and supposedly even hear) Mumbai from Hart Point.

Hugh Malet, climbing the path known as Shivaji's Ladder, is credited with the 'discovery' of Matheran in 1850. It soon became a popular hill station during the days of the Raj, as the abundant shade and altitude (800m) made it slightly cooler than the plains below.

Matheran owes its tranquillity to a complete ban on motor vehicles (and bicycles), but on weekends, the town is overrun by day-trippers from Mumbai and the pleasant trails are wall to wall with people.

High season in Matheran runs from November to January and from mid-April to mid-June. In April and May and during Diwali in November you will need to book accommodation well in advance. During the monsoon (mid-June to early-October) Matheran virtually closes up. Few hotels and restaurants remain open, and the dirt walking trails and roads become very muddy. On the other hand, there are few people around, and the hotels that remain open reduce their tariffs significantly.

Getting to Matheran is half the fun; from Neral Junction you take a narrow-gauge toy train up the 21km route to the heart of the hill station. It's a two hour ascent (or 90 minute descent) as the train winds its way around the steep slopes and, at one point, passes through 'one kiss tunnel'. Alternatively, you can take a taxi or minibus from Neral to the Dasturi car park (the furthest point cars are permitted), from where you will have to walk (2km, 40 minutes) or hire a horse or hand-pulled rickshaw to Matheran.

Information

Entry to Matheran costs Rs 7 (Rs 2 for children). Arriving by train, you pay this leaving the Neral station. By road, you pay at the Dasturi car park.

The tourist information kiosk, opposite the station, is open daily during the high season and has a map of Matheran but not much else.

Few of the paths around town are lit at night – a torch may come in handy.

Walks & Views

Louisa Point, Panorama Point and Little Chouk Point have the finest views. Louisa Point is a great place to watch the sunset, especially during the week when you might have the bluff entirely to yourself. You can reach the valley below One Tree Hill down the path known as **Shivaji's Ladder**, so called because the Maratha leader is said to have used it.

Pleasant diversions include little **Charlotte Lake** (no swimming – it's the town water supply) and the Parsi and Hindu **cemeteries** near Rambaug Point.

Places to Stay

Matheran is very spread out and much of the accommodation is a 10 to 20 minute walk from the railway station. Many of the 'resort' hotels offer only full-board rates. As with most hill stations, the checkout time can be as early as 7 am. Off-season discounts typically range from 30% to 50%.

Places to Stay – bottom end

Budget accommodation in Matheran is limited. Most of it is along MG Marg and Kasturba Rd, which runs parallel to it.

Hotel Rangoli (☎ 30273), right opposite the station on MG Marg, has basic doubles for Rs 250 during the high season.

Khan's Cosmopolitan Hotel (☎ 30240),

also on MG Marg, is a rather primitive but well run place with a range of rooms. Doubles (no singles) with common bath are Rs 250/425 in the low/high season, including simple meals.

Hotel Meghdoot (☎ 30266) on Kasturba Rd offers grungy doubles for Rs 200/300 in the low/high season. No meals are available.

Hope Hall Hotel (☎ 30253) is a welcoming Christian-run lodge with simple but clean doubles for Rs 175/250 in the low/high season.

The *MTDC Tourist Camp* (☎ 30277) is next to the Dasturi car park, 2.5km north-east

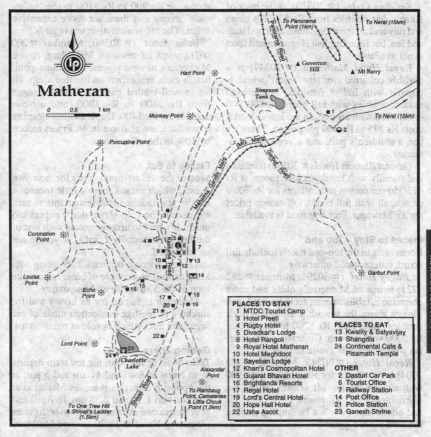

Matheran

To Panorama Point (1km)

To Neral (15km)

Panorama Road

Governor Hill

Mt Barry

Hart Point

Simpson Tank

Monkey Point

To Neral (15km)

Porcupine Point

MG Marg

Garbut Road

Mahatma Gandhi Marg

Coronation Point

Kasturba Road

Garbut Point

Louisa Point

Echo Point

Lord Point

Charlotte Lake

Alexander Point

To One Tree Hill & Shivaji's Ladder (1.5km)

Shivaji Road

To Rambaug Point, Cemeteries & Little Chouk Point (1.5km)

0   0.5   1 km

PLACES TO STAY	
1	MTDC Tourist Camp
3	Hotel Preeti
4	Rugby Hotel
5	Divadkar's Lodge
8	Hotel Rangoli
9	Royal Hotel Matheran
10	Hotel Meghdoot
11	Sayeban Lodge
12	Khan's Cosmopolitan Hotel
15	Gujarat Bhavan Hotel
16	Brightlands Resorts
17	Regal Hotel
19	Lord's Central Hotel
20	Hope Hall Hotel
22	Usha Ascot

PLACES TO EAT	
13	Kwality & Satyavijay
18	Shangrila
24	Continental Cafe & Pisamath Temple

OTHER	
2	Dasturi Car Park
6	Tourist Office
7	Railway Station
14	Post Office
21	Police Station
23	Ganesh Shrine

MAHARASHTRA

of the centre of town. Dorm beds are Rs 60, doubles range from Rs 200 to Rs 600 and there are larger cottages. There's a restaurant, and beer is available.

Places to Stay – middle

Divadkar's Lodge, in a pleasant location opposite the station, has musty but habitable doubles with attached bath for Rs 440. There's also a restaurant, but meals aren't included in the tariff.

Hotel Preeti (☎ 30202) is a friendly and quiet family oriented place with 'specious deluxe' doubles for Rs 440 and four-person rooms for Rs 1200, all with full board.

Sayeban Lodge (☎ 30519), at the back of Khan's, has doubles from Rs 550. It's clean and tidy and all the rooms have attached bath and fan, but little English is spoken and food is not available.

Royal Hotel Matheran (☎ 30247) is a garishly coloured two star 'resort' which is popular with Indian families. In the high season, doubles with full board cost Rs 900 or Rs 1300 with air-con. In the low season it costs Rs 275 to Rs 300 per person. There's a bar, a children's park and a vegetarian restaurant.

Gujarat Bhavan Hotel (☎ 30278) is relaxed and friendly with regular/deluxe rooms at Rs 475/550 per person and cottages for Rs 700 a person, all with full board. Off-season prices are 35% cheaper. Pure veg food is available.

Places to Stay – top end

Room rates in the top-end hotels include full board, unless stated otherwise.

Rugby Hotel (☎ 30291; Mumbai ☎ 282 1721) is one of Matheran's older and more charming establishments, set in tranquil rock gardens above the township. Bungalow-style doubles range from Rs 1200 to Rs 1700 or Rs 2000 with air-con. Gujarati and vegetarian western food is available.

Regal Hotel (☎ 30243; Mumbai ☎ 203 1004) has cottages for Rs 1200 or Rs 1900 with air-con. In the off season, prices are discounted 30%. All rooms have cable TV and phone and there's a swimming pool in the well-tended grounds.

Brightlands Resorts (☎ 30244; Mumbai ☎ 642 3856) is a lively place with a token swimming pool and disco nights. Rooms start at Rs 998 per person or Rs 1498 with air-con. In the off season, rooms are discounted 30% on a lodging-only basis (ie, no meals).

Lord's Central Hotel (☎ 30228; Mumbai ☎ 201 8008), presided over by the genial Mr Lord, has fading touches of the Raj and is the *only* hotel with views over the precipice. It's clean and quiet and there's a bar and a dining room renowned for its generously served, delicious homecooked meals. Doubles are Rs 650 to Rs 750 per person in the regular rooms, or Rs 900 to Rs 1100 in the 'valley view' rooms and there are more expensive suites. The off-season discount is 20%.

Usha Ascot (☎ 30360; Mumbai ☎ 200 0671), south of town on MG Marg, is one Matheran's newest places, boasting a pool, health club, restaurant and coffee shop, all set in well-tended gardens. Doubles range from Rs 2400 to Rs 3000, and air-con doubles are Rs 3400. Duplex villas, sleeping four adults, are also available. Prices reduce by 30% in the off season.

Places to Eat

Most of the 'resort' hotels cater for their own guests, which means there's little incentive for the few independent restaurants to turn out decent food. In short: don't expect too much. It's best to arrange meals with one of the hotels (especially *Lord's*) if you're not on full board.

There's a string of snack bars along MG Marg as well as a couple of basic restaurants such as the *Shangrila* and *Satyavijay*.

Matheran is famed for its honey and for chikki, a toffee-like confection made of gur sugar and nuts which is sold at many shops.

Getting There & Away

Train Most of the year, the toy train departs from Neral at 8.40 and 11 am and 5 pm; in the opposite direction it leaves Matheran at 5.45 am and 1.10 and 2.35 pm. In April and May there's one extra service from both points (departing Neral at 10.20 am and Matheran at 4.20 pm). During the monsoon there is only one train per day – it departs Neral at 8.40 am and Matheran at 1.10 pm. The fares are Rs 21/127 in 2nd/1st class. In Neral, the toy train terminus is at the east end of platform No 1.

From Mumbai, only a few of the Pune expresses stop at Neral Junction, including the *Deccan Express* (6.40 am from Mumbai VT, connecting with the 8.40 am toy train) and the *Miraj Express* (8.45 am from Mumbai VT, connecting with the 11 am toy train). Most (but not all) expresses from Mumbai stop at Karjat further down the line from Neral, from where you can backtrack to Neral on one of the frequent local trains. Alternatively, take a local Karjat-bound train from Mumbai VT and get off at Neral. The fare from Mumbai to Neral is Rs 25/126 in 2nd/1st class.

From Pune it's a similar story – either take one of the few Mumbai-bound expresses that stop at Neral (such as the *Sahyadri Express*) or one of the expresses that stop at Karjat and then take a local train to Neral. The fare from Pune to Neral is Rs 27/139 in 2nd/1st class.

If you're heading to Pune or Mumbai from Matheran, it's best to take any local train from Neral to Karjat to pick up one of the frequent trains from there.

There are no local trains between Karjat and Lonavla (for the Karla Caves), only the Mumbai to Pune expresses stop there.

It's a good idea to prebook the toy train back from Matheran to Neral in the high season as demand is heavy.

Taxi Taxis from Neral to Matheran cost around Rs 200 and take 20 to 30 minutes. If you want to share you may have to wait an hour or two for the taxi to fill up, depending on the season.

Getting Around
Horses and hand-pulled rickshaws are the only transport options in Matheran. Taxis and minibuses stop at the Dasturi car park, 2.5km (40 minutes walk) from the centre. From here, you can either walk (quickest along the railway line), hire a horse (Rs 50)

or a rickshaw (Rs 120) into the centre. It's a little quicker to walk into the centre than it is to hire a rickshaw, but if it's hot and your pack is heavy, consider the wheeled or hoofed option.

Horses can be hired for around Rs 100 per hour.

LONAVLA
Tel Area Code: 02114
Situated 106km south-east of Mumbai in the hills on the main railway line to Pune, Lonavla and nearby Khandala are twin hill resorts catering for weekenders and conference groups from Mumbai. The area has changed dramatically in recent years from a sleepy backwater into a major development area.

There is little of interest in the towns themselves, though Khandala does overlook a picturesque ravine with a fine wet-season waterfall. For most travellers Lonavla is simply the most convenient base from which to visit the Karla and Bhaja caves.

If you're game for something more energetic, the MTDC at Bhaja (☎ 82230) organises rock climbing at the Duke's Nose and other locations in the Karla hills.

Places to Stay – bottom end
There's no shortage of places to stay in Lonavla, most of them concentrated on the north side of the railway line.

Pitale Lodging & Boarding (☎ 72657) is delightfully ramshackle with wide verandahs and an old-world atmosphere. The staff are genial and there's a bar, garden restaurant and shady trees. It wouldn't suit everyone, but it's cheap at Rs 150 a double with common bath.

Adarsh Hotel (☎ 72353) is a little more comfortable, though it backs onto the bus stand, so avoid the rooms on that side. During the week doubles are Rs 200 or Rs 350 to 500 with TV; air-con suites are Rs 800. Rates increase 20% on weekends.

Hotel Chandralok (☎ 72921), across the road, is a clean, friendly place. Doubles start from Rs 350 including tax (Rs 100 per extra

MAHARASHTRA

person); air-con doubles are Rs 600. All rooms have attached bath with hot water. Superb Gujarati thalis are Rs 45 (Rs 60 with dessert).

Places to Stay – middle & top-end

Hotel Star Regency (☎ 73331; Mumbai ☎ 618 3708), Justice Telang Rd, is tucked down a quiet, leafy lane and has doubles from Rs 720 to Rs 1260 and suites for Rs 1800. They offer a package rate of Rs 3150 a double for two nights including breakfast, dinner and taxes.

Hotel Rama Krishna (☎ 73600; Mumbai ☎ 617 8111) is up on the main road and has doubles for Rs 600 or Rs 750 with air-con.

Biji's Kumar Resort (☎ 73091; Mumbai ☎ 604 5669), nearby, is newer and has a range of large comfortable rooms from Rs 1400 to Rs 2800, plus a wave pool and a bar. Both the Rama Krishna and the Kumar Resort have excellent open-air *restaurants*.

Fariyas Holiday Resort (☎ 73852; Mumbai ☎ 265 5317) offers five star luxury on a quiet hill on the western outskirts of town. It has an indoor swimming pool, health club, two restaurants and extensive gardens. Rooms are Rs 1195/2395 (extra person Rs 400).

Duke's Retreat (☎ 73817; Mumbai ☎ 261 0983), at Khandala, is perched on a precipice with stunning valley views. A 'standard' room will set you back a mere Rs 2900, while a deluxe room/cottage is Rs 3750, including breakfast, dinner and taxes.

Places to Eat

The best places to eat are at the hotels with restaurants mentioned above. Otherwise, try the *Lonavla Restaurant* on the main road which offers Sindhi-Punjabi veg and non-veg food as well as tandoori dishes. Close by is the *Mehfil Bar & Restaurant*, attached to the side of the noisy Hotel Gurukripa. There's an excellent *fruit market* in the bazaar, south of the railway station.

As in Matheran, the local speciality is chikki, a kind of nutty toffee.

Getting There & Away

Lonavla is on the main Mumbai to Pune road and railway line so there are plenty of trains and buses to/from both cities.

Bus Most of the state transport corporation (MSRTC) buses are pretty rough and, as they take up to four hours to get to Mumbai, you're better off using the trains.

Train All express trains between Mumbai and Pune stop at Lonavla. The trip to Mumbai (128km, three hours) costs Rs 34/160 in 2nd/1st class. To Pune (64km) there are express trains (one hour) and hourly shuttle trains (two hours) and the fare is Rs 21/99 in 2nd/1st class.

Getting Around

See the following section for details on getting to/from the caves.

KARLA & BHAJA CAVES

Dating from around the 2nd century BC, the superb rock-cut caves in the hills near Lonavla are among the oldest and finest examples of Hinayana Buddhist rock temple art in India.

1 Hotel Star Regency	7 Biji's Kumar Resort
2 Mehfil Bar & Restaurant	8 Adarsh Hotel
3 Pitale Lodging & Boarding	9 Hotel Chandralok
4 Lonavla Restaurant	& Restaurant
5 Bus Stand	10 Bank of Baroda
6 Hotel Rama Krishna	11 Post Office
& Restaurant	12 Fruit Market

To Karla & Bhaja Caves (11km) & Pune (64km)

To Fariyas Holiday Resort (2km), Khandala (5km) & Mumbai (106km)

Main Road

Justice Telang Road

Silver Road

Railway Station

To Mumbai

To Pune

Lonavla

0   50   100 m

MAHARASHTRA

At weekends and on holidays Karla is invaded by picnic mobs from Mumbai and Pune and devotees visiting the ugly modern Hindu temple at the entrance to the cave.

It's possible to visit the caves in a day trip from either Mumbai or Pune if you hire an auto-rickshaw from Lonavla for the day.

Karla Cave

It's a steep 20 minute climb from the carpark to the Karla Cave, the largest Hinayana Buddhist *chaitya* in India. Completed in 80 BC, the chaitya is around 40m long and 15m high, carved by monks and artisans from the living rock in imitation of more familiar wooden architecture.

A semi-circular 'sun window' filters light in towards the cave's representation of Buddha – a *dagoba*, protected by a carved wooden umbrella. The 37 pillars which form the circumambulatory aisles are each topped by kneeling elephants carrying seated figures. The roof of the cave is ribbed with teak beams said to be original. On the sides of the vestibule are carved elephant heads which once had ivory tusks.

A *stambha* (pillar) topped by four back-to-back lions, an image usually associated with

Ashoka, stands outside the cave and may be older than the cave itself. The Buddha images near the entrance were added during the later Mahayana Buddhist period.

There are some small, unadorned *viharas* further round the hillside, some of which have been converted into Hindu shrines.

Bhaja Caves & Forts

It's a rough 3km ride from the main road to the Bhaja Caves, but well worth the effort as the setting is lusher, greener, and more peaceful than nearby Karla. Thought to date from around 200 BC, ten of the 18 caves here are viharas, while cave 12 is an open chaitya, earlier than Karla, containing a simple dagoba but no sculpture.

Beyond this is a strange huddle of 14 stupas, five inside and nine outside a cave. The last cave on the south side has some fine sculptures; the caretaker will show you inside for a small 'donation'.

A few minutes walk past the last cave is a **waterfall** which may have enough water for a refreshing dip. In the hills above the caves are a couple of derelict, but atmospheric old forts – **Lohagad Fort**, which was twice taken by Shivaji, and **Visapur Fort**.

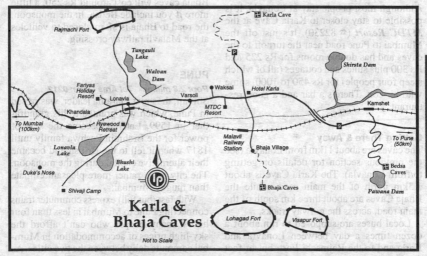

Karla & Bhaja Caves

Maharashtran Cave Architecture

Maharashtra's famous rock-cut caves have several distinct design elements. The Buddhist caves, which are generally the older ones, are either *chaityas* (temples) or *viharas* (monasteries). Chaityas are usually deep and narrow with a stupa at the end of the cave. There may be a row of columns down both sides of the cave and around the stupa.

The viharas are usually not as deep and narrow as the chaityas. Viharas were normally intended to be living quarters for the monks and usually have rows of cells along both sides. In the back there is often a small shrine containing an image of the Buddha. At Ajanta, the cliff face into which the caves are cut is very steep and there is often a small verandah or entrance porch in front of the main cave. At Ellora the rock face is more sloping and the verandah or porch element generally becomes a separate courtyard.

Cave architecture reached the peak of its complexity and design in the Hindu temples at Ellora, and particularly in the magnificent Kailasa Temple. These can hardly be called 'caves', for each temple is open to the sky. In design they are much like other temples of that era – except that instead of being built up from the bottom they were cut from the living rock from the top down. ■

Bedsa Caves

About 15km past the Karla/Bhaja turnoffs, and six km south-east of Kamshet station, are the **Bedsa Caves**. These caves see very few visitors, partly because of the 3km walk from Bedsa village to reach them and partly because the main cave – a chaitya thought to be later than Karla – is much poorer in design and execution. Still, it's worth a visit if you have an interest in early Buddhist architecture.

Places to Stay & Eat

Although most people stay at Lonavla, it is possible to stay closer to Karla Cave at the *MTDC Resort* (☎ 82230). It's just off the Mumbai to Pune road near the turnoff to the caves and has double rooms for Rs 225 and Rs 300 plus suites and cottages (all of which sleep four people) for Rs 450 to 1000, some with air-con. There's a bar and a good restaurant.

Getting There & Away

The caves are about 11km from Lonavla (see the previous section for details on getting to/from Lonavla). The Karla Cave is about 1.5km north of the main road, while the Bhaja Caves are about three km south of the main road, across the railway tracks.

Local buses are supposed to run about a dozen times a day between Lonavla and Karla and to the Rajmachi Fort, but in fact they run far less frequently and are chock-full when they arrive.

If you don't mind walking, you can get around comfortably in a day for about Rs 20. First, catch the 9 am bus from Lonavla to Karla Cave, then walk to Bhaja (five km, 1½ hours), walk back to Malavli railway station (three km, one hour) and catch a local train back to Lonavla.

Auto-rickshaws are plentiful and the price usually includes waiting time at the sites. A return trip from Lonavla to the Karla and Bhaja caves will cost around Rs 250, a little more if you include Bedsa. In the monsoon, the road to Bhaja is often closed to vehicles at the Malavli railway crossing.

PUNE

Pop: 2.8 million   Tel Area Code: 0212

Shivaji, the great Maratha leader, was raised in Pune, which was granted to his grandfather in 1599. Later it became the seat of power for the Brahmin Peshwa family until 1817 when it fell to the British and became their alternative capital during the monsoon. The city has a rather more pleasant climate than muggy Mumbai.

With fast (but full) express commuter trains connecting Pune to Mumbai in less than four hours, many people who can't afford the sky-high prices of accommodation in Mumbai commute daily between the two cities. As

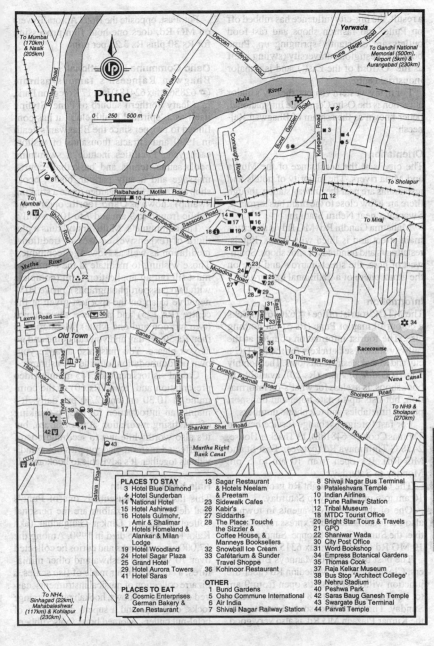

Pune

To Mumbai
(170km)
& Nasik
(205km)

0   250   500 m

Yerwada

To Gandhi National
Memorial (500m),
Airport (5km) &
Aurangabad (230km)

Mula   River

To Sholapur

To Mumbai

To Miraj

Old Town

Racecourse

Nava Canal

To NH9 &
Sholapur
(270km)

Murtha Right
Bank Canal

To NH4,
Sinhagad (22km),
Mahabaleshwar
(117km) & Kohlapur
(230km)

MAHARASHTRA

PLACES TO STAY	13 Sagar Restaurant	8 Shivaji Nagar Bus Terminal
3 Hotel Blue Diamond	& Hotels Neelam	9 Pataleshvara Temple
4 Hotel Sunderban	& Preetam	10 Indian Airlines
14 National Hotel	23 Sidewalk Cafes	11 Pune Railway Station
15 Hotel Ashirwad	26 Kabir's	12 Tribal Museum
16 Hotels Gulmohr,	27 Siddarths	18 MTDC Tourist Office
Amir & Shalimar	28 The Place: Touché	20 Bright Star Tours & Travels
17 Hotels Homeland &	the Sizzler &	21 GPO
Alankar & Milan	Coffee House, &	22 Shaniwar Wada
Lodge	Manneys Booksellers	30 City Post Office
19 Hotel Woodland	32 Snowball Ice Cream	31 Word Bookshop
24 Hotel Sagar Plaza	33 Cafétarium & Sunder	34 Empress Botanical Gardens
25 Grand Hotel	Travel Shoppe	35 Thomas Cook
29 Hotel Aurora Towers	36 Kohinoor Restaurant	37 Raja Kelkar Museum
41 Hotel Saras		38 Bus Stop 'Architect College'
	OTHER	39 Nehru Stadium
PLACES TO EAT	1 Bund Gardens	40 Peshwa Park
2 Cosmic Enterprises	5 Osho Commune International	42 Saras Baug Ganesh Temple
German Bakery &	6 Air India	43 Swargate Bus Terminal
Zen Restaurant	7 Shivaji Nagar Railway Station	44 Parvati Temple

a result, the big-city influence has rubbed off on Pune, and fashion shops and fast-food outlets are constantly springing up. Pune boasts a prestigious university (styling itself as the 'Oxford of the East'), and is a major industrial centre.

For many western visitors, the city's major attraction is the Osho Commune International, better known as the ashram of Bhagwan Rajneesh.

Orientation

The city is at the confluence of the Mutha and Mula rivers. The majority of hotels and restaurants are near the railway station, though there are a few close to the main bus terminal, Swargate, near Nehru Stadium.

Mahatma Gandhi Rd (MG Rd) is the city's main street and is lined with banks, hotels, restaurants and hundreds of shoe shops. South-west of here, the streets narrow and take on the atmosphere of a traditional bazaar-town.

Information

The MTDC tourist office (☎ 626867) stocks a colourful map of Pune (Rs 5) but nothing else. The tourist information counter at the railway station sells tickets for the MTDC's city and Mahabaleshwar bus tours. The monthly *Tourist Guide of Pune* (Rs 20), available in bookshops, is useless for what's-on information, but lists up-to-date hotel and transport prices, timetables and telephone numbers.

For fast foreign exchange service head to Thomas Cook (☎ 648188), 13 Thacker House, 2418 G Thimmaya Rd (between East St and MG Rd). It's open from 10 am to 5 pm Monday to Saturday.

The GPO on Connaught Rd is open from 10 am to 6 pm Monday to Saturday.

One of the best travel agents in town is also the local American Express representative: the Sunder Travel Shoppe, Sunder Plaza, 19 MG Rd (☎ 631848; fax 631534).

The best bookshop is Manneys Booksellers, Clover Centre, 7 Moledina Rd (near the junction with MG Rd); it's open from 9 am to 1 pm and from 4 to 8 pm daily except Sunday. The Word Bookshop, downstairs at the Kumar Plaza in MG Rd, is also very good.

FotoFast, opposite the Hotel Aurora Towers on MG Rd, does one-hour film processing for Rs 30 plus Rs 3.25 per print.

Osho Commune International

Bhagwan Rajneesh's famous ashram (☎ 628562; fax 624181) is at 17 Koregaon Park, in a leafy northern suburb of Pune. Styling itself as a 'spiritual health club', it has continued to prosper since the Bhagwan's death in 1990 and attracts thousands of visitors each year. Facilities include a swimming pool, sauna, tennis and basketball courts, massage and beauty parlour, bistro, bookshop and a five ha Zen garden (once a stinking swamp) known as **Osho Teerth**, open to the public from 6 to 9 am and 7 to 10 pm daily.

The commune's 'Multiversity' runs a plethora of (expensive) courses in traditional meditation as well as New Age techniques. Those wishing to meditate at the commune must fill out an application form (complete with two passport photographs), prove HIV-negative on an on-the-spot test given at the centre (Rs 125) and purchase three tunics (two maroon and one white). Meditation is then Rs 50 per day and you can come and go as you please. You must also arrange your own accommodation, outside the ashram.

Casual visitors can take a 45 minute video presentation and 'tour' (Rs 60) of the commune at 10.30 am and 2.30 pm daily. It's mainly an introduction for people thinking of practising meditation at the ashram, but it's also worthwhile just to see hundreds of disaffected maroon-clad yuppies being individuals together. It's advisable to book ahead.

Raja Kelkar Museum

This fascinating museum is one of Pune's real delights. The exhibits are the personal collection of Shri Dinkar Gangadhar (aka Kaka Kelkar) who died in 1990. Among the 17,000 or so artworks and curios he collected over 70 years are Peshwa and other miniatures, a coat of armour made of fish scales, a bizarre collection of musical instruments, carved doors and windows, hookah pipes, strange locks, oil lamps and a superb collection of betel-nut cutters, adorned brass footscrubbers,

Osho, the Bhagwan

Bhagwan Shree Rajneesh (1931-90), or Osho as he preferred to be called, was one of India's most popular and flamboyant 'export gurus' and without doubt the most controversial. He followed no particular religion, tradition or philosophy and his often acerbic criticism and dismissal of various religious and political leaders made him many enemies the world over. What particularly outraged his Indian critics was his advocacy of sex as a path to enlightenment, an approach which earned him the epithet 'sex guru' from the Indian press.

Rajneesh used a curious blend of Californian pop psychology and Indian mysticism to motivate his followers. His last technique, tagged The Mystic Rose, involved following a regime of laughing for three hours a day for one week, crying for three hours a day the next week, followed by becoming a 'watcher on the hill' (ie sitting) for three hours a day for another week. The Bhagwan felt that it was 'the most important breakthrough in meditation since Buddha's *vipassana*, created 25 centuries ago'. Indeed, he began to lean heavily towards Zen Buddhism in the years before his death and at one point, even declared himself to be the Buddha.

In 1981, Rajneesh went to the USA and set up the agricultural commune and ashram of Rajneeshpuram in Oregon. It was here that he drew the attention of the international media, and the ashram's notoriety (along with its highly publicised fleet of Rolls Royces) grew and grew. Eventually, with rumours and local paranoia about the ashram's activities running wild, and police turned up on the doorstep. The Bhagwan was charged with immigration fraud, fined US$400,000, and deported to India in November 1985.

In January 1987, Rajneesh took up residence again at the Pune ashram, and soon thousands of foreigners (mostly from Germany, Italy and Japan) were flocking to attend his nightly discourses and meditation courses. From early 1989 until his death, Rajneesh reverted to silence as he had done so once in America.

Before his death, the orange clothes and the *mala* (the string of beads and photograph of the Bhagwan worn around the neck), which used to be the distinctive mark of Bhagwan followers, had been discarded. This was done so that his followers could (according to the ashram press office) 'avoid harassment and molestation by the authorities'. Times have changed and these days there seems to be no such discrimination against the followers (who now get around in maroon). ∎

carved wooden noodle makers and hairdrying combs.

The museum is open from 8.30 am to 5.30 pm daily; entry is Rs 5 for Indians and Rs 30 for foreigners. To get the most from your visit, ask one of the knowledgeable attendants to show you around. The MTDC's city tour visits the museum briefly.

Shaniwar Wada

The ruins of this imposing, fortress-like palace stand in the old part of the city where the narrow and winding streets form a veritable maze. Built in 1736, the palace of the Peshwa rulers burnt down in 1828, but the massive walls still remain. Today there is a unkempt two hectare garden inside and signs proclaiming which rooms used to stand where. The palace is entered through sturdy doors studded with spikes designed to dissuade enemy elephants from leaning too heavily against the entrance. In a nearby street the Peshwa rulers used to execute offenders by having elephants trample them to death. Open daily from 8 am to 6.30 pm; entry is Rs 2.

Pataleshvara Temple

Just across the river on Jangali Maharaj Rd is the wonderful rock-cut Pataleshvara Temple (aka Panchalesvara Cave), a small 8th century temple similar in style to the much grander rock temple at Elephanta but never completed. More importantly, it's an active temple. In front of the excavation is a circular Nandi *mandapam*. Adjacent is the Jangali Maharaj ('Lord of the Jungle') temple, dedicated to a Hindu ascetic who died here in 1818.

Tribal Museum

Just south of the railway line and east of the railway station, this excellent museum (☎ 669471) documents the cultures of Maharashtran tribal communities, particularly those from the Sahyadri and Gondwana regions. It is open weekdays from 10 am to 5 pm. City bus tours do not call here.

MAHARASHTRA

Gardens

The **Empress Botanical Gardens** have fine tropical trees and a small zoo nearby. The moated **Saras Baug Ganesh Temple** is in Peshwa Park and has dozens of food stalls at night. The **Bund Gardens**, on the banks of the river, are a popular place for an evening stroll. The bridge here crosses the river to Yerwada and the Gandhi National Memorial.

Parvarti Hill & Temple

The **Parvati Temple** is on the southern outskirts of the town on a hilltop. There's a good view from the top, where the last Peshwa ruler is said to have stood and watched whilst his troops suffered defeat at the hands of the British at Kirkee.

Gandhi National Memorial

Across the river in Yerwada is this fine memorial set in 6.5 ha of gardens. Built by Imamsultan Muhammad Sha Agakhan III in 1892, it was the **Aga Khan's palace** until 1956 after which it became a school. In 1969 it was donated to India by the Aga Khan IV.

After Mahatma Gandhi delivered his momentous Quit India resolution in Bombay in 1942, the British interned him and other leaders of India's independence movement here for nearly two years. Both Kasturba Gandhi, the Mahatma's wife, and Mahadoebhai Desai, his secretary for 35 years, died here during this period of imprisonment. Their ashes are kept in **memorial tombs** *(samadhis)* in the gardens.

A photographic exhibition details some of the highlights of Gandhi's long career, but it is the simple personal effects (including a pair of sandals and a thermos) and the personal tragedies of the Mahatma during this period that leave the deepest impression. Film buffs will recognise the building from the movie *Gandhi*.

The memorial is open from 9 am to 5.45 pm daily; entry is Rs 2. The city tour stops here for around 30 minutes.

Organised Tours

Bus tours of Pune leave from the railway station at 8 am and 3 pm daily, take four hours and cost Rs 60. They cover all the main sights in a breathless rush. Book at the MTDC kiosk in the railway station's main hall.

Festivals

While **Ganesh Chaturthi** is celebrated all over India, the festival is most extravagant at Mumbai and, in more recent years, at Pune. Traditionally a household affair, it was converted into a public celebration a century ago when the freedom fighter, Lokmanya Tilak, used it to unite the masses for the freedom struggle. Ganesh (or Ganpati as he's often affectionately called) is, after all, the remover of obstacles.

At the end of the 11 day festival, plaster and clay images of Ganesh, some of them six metres high, are taken from homes and street *mandals* (shrines) and carried in huge processions to be immersed in water. In Mumbai this is done at Chowpatty Beach, in Pune it's done down by the river.

Kasturba & Mohandas Gandhi

MAHARASHTRA

The procession of Ganesh is the climax of the very popular **Pune Festival** – classical dance and music concerts, folk dance, a village festival including bullock cart races and wrestling. The opening ceremony features some of the country's best musicians and dancers, and is usually held around late Aug/early Sept, at which time Pune becomes very crowded.

Places to Stay – bottom end

Most of the cheapies close to the railway station are fleapits, but there are some in the area known as Wilson Gardens, directly opposite the station and behind the National Hotel, which are OK. There are good *retiring rooms* at the railway station.

Hotel Homeland (☎ 627158), Wilson Gardens, is a clean and efficient place in a big old house. Some rooms have TV and air-con. Rooms range from Rs 195/260 to Rs 375/445, all with attached bath. There's hot water in the morning and a small restaurant.

Hotel Alankar (☎ 620484), also in Wilson Gardens, has uninspiring doubles for Rs 250 with attached bath.

Milan Lodge (☎ 622024), nearby, has rooms for Rs 100/135 or Rs 205/275 with attached bath.

The *National Hotel* (☎ 625054), 14 Sassoon Rd, opposite the railway station, is the best choice in this range. Baha'i-run, it is a beautiful old mansion with verandahs and high ceilings (though some of the rooms have no windows). There are singles with common bath for Rs 100 and single/double/triple/quad rooms with attached bath or cottages

for Rs 200/270/320/370. Breakfast is available if ordered in advance; there's hot water in the morning only.

Hotel Shalimar (☎ 629191), around the corner in Connaught Rd, has endless numbers of singles/doubles with attached bath for Rs 180/210. Extras can bunk down on a mattress in the room for Rs 50.

Grand Hotel (☎ 668728), at the quieter end of MG Rd, is a crumbling old place on private grounds. Singles (beds separated by partition walls) cost Rs 70 with common bath. The double rooms with attached bath are better and go for Rs 220. The hotel has its own beer bar, patio and restaurant.

The *MTDC Hotel Saras* (☎ 430499) is handy if you want to be near Swargate bus terminal for an early morning getaway. It has decent singles/doubles starting at Rs 200/250.

Places to Stay – middle

Hotel Gulmohr (☎ 622773), 15A/1 Connaught Rd, at the bottom of this range, is within easy walking distance of the railway station. Rooms start at Rs 230/350 or at Rs 450/650 with air-con, some with a small balcony. There's hot water 24 hours a day, and a bar.

Hotel Ashirwad (☎ 628585), 16 Connaught Rd, is also close to the station and offers spacious rooms with balcony from Rs 495/600 or Rs 700/850 with air-con. Rooms have direct-dial phones and Star TV. There's a restaurant with good vegetarian food but no bar.

Hotel Amir (☎ 621841), next door at No 15, is seemingly modelled on a prison cell

---

Ganesh Mandals

'You must see them *all!*' our excited young guide Sheetal said as she led us through the dark, narrow backstreets of Pune, to an area where the biggest and most opulent mandals had been erected.

The source of her excitement was the mandals – elaborately decorated statues of the elephant-headed god, Ganesh, which had been set up to celebrate the Ganesh Chaturthi Festival. More than 1000 mandals dotted the city, and many of them were immense. In some cases, purpose-built platforms occupied entire street corners (sometimes blocking the whole street), and were illuminated with the best that Indian electrics can muster. Each mandal had a theme – either traditional or contemporary. Thus, one minute you could be looking at a majestic Ganesh seated in a regal parlour with peacocks and his devoted mother Parvati by his side; the next minute, 'Ganesh in Jurassic Park'! ■

block and some rooms are shabby and dark. Facilities include a bar, restaurants (veg and non-veg), coffee shop and a dreary shopping arcade. Rooms cost from Rs 795/1045, all with air-con.

Hotel Woodland (☎ 626161) is five minutes walk from the station, off Sadhu Vaswani Circle, and has a range of well-maintained rooms from Rs 750/850. There's an attached 'multi-cuisine vegetarian restaurant' and the hotel also offers complimentary airport transfers.

Hotel Sunderban (☎ 624949; fax 623535), 19 Koregaon Park, next door to the ashram, is beautifully kept and the best place to stay if you're visiting Osho or just wanting to soak up the New Age vibes. If a compulsory HIV test and maroon garb don't appeal, you could always meditate in the hotel's well-tended gardens. There's a wide variety of rooms available from US$13.

Places to Stay – top end

Hotel Sagar Plaza (☎ 622622; fax 622633), 1 Bund Garden Rd, off Moledina Rd, has air-con rooms from Rs 1600/1900-2100/2600. Facilities include a bar, coffee shop, speciality restaurant, small swimming pool and bookshop.

Hotel Aurora Towers (☎ 631818; fax 631826), 9 Moledina Rd at the junction of MG Rd, is also fully air-conditioned and has standard rooms for Rs 1550/1850 and deluxe doubles for Rs 2450; suites start at Rs 3295. Facilities include a shopping arcade, rooftop swimming pool with views over the city, bar, two restaurants and a 24 hour coffee shop.

Hotel Blue Diamond (☎ 625555; fax 627755), 11 Koregaon Rd, is a five star hotel just 10 minutes walk from the Osho ashram. Rooms start from Rs 2200/2500.

Hotel Executive Asoka (☎ 59618; fax 57391) at 5 University Rd, Sivajinagar, is similarly priced, and handy to the university and colleges west of the city.

Places to Eat

Sagar Restaurant, on the corner of Sassoon and Connaught Rds, is a big, clean place serving vegetarian meals from Rs 25. You can get toast and tea here for breakfast.

Hotel Neelam and *Hotel Preetam*, next door, are more intimate and offer reasonably priced veg and non-veg Indian and part-western dishes. The Preetam also serves cold beer.

The *sidewalk cafes* just south of the GPO are a good place to go in the evening for a cheap meal. They offer a variety of food and cold drinks.

Siddarths vegetarian restaurant, on the south side of Moledina Rd towards MG Rd, serves a variety of Punjabi and Chinese dishes and fresh juices on its open terrace.

The Place: Touché the Sizzler, just down the street, is a two tier air-con restaurant which specialises in sizzlers but also offers Indian, tandoori and continental dishes (Rs 70 to 100). The homemade orange marmalade ice cream (Rs 45) is delicious!

The part open-air *Kabir's*, opposite, offers cheaper Indian, Mughlai and tandoori dishes, as well as vegetarian pizzas and burgers. Both The Place and Kabir's serve cold beer.

The *Coffee House*, also on Moledina Rd, is a trendy hangout and definitely the place to be seen.

Cafétarium, in the atrium of the Sunder Plaza on MG Rd, is another spot for coffee and even a plate of pasta or a burger. It's open from 11 am to 11 pm.

Snowball, nearby, does a brisk trade in ice cream, milkshakes and juices.

Kohinoor Restaurant, a little further south on MG Rd, is always busy at lunchtime, serving thalis for Rs 18 and a range of other delicious veg meals.

Cosmic Enterprises German Bakery (a place you'll end up sooner or later if you're visiting Osho) is good for a fruit lassi (try the papaya), a half-decent cappuccino, and delicious pastries (oh yes, and lots of hugs!).

Zen Restaurant is right behind – just the ticket after a long day of *zazen*. There's always an interesting international crowd of Osho *sanyasins* at these places.

Getting There & Away

Air The Indian Airlines office (☎ 140 or 141)

PAINTING, SCULPTURE & ARCHITECTURE

Indian art and sculpture is basically religious in its themes and developments, and its appreciation requires at least some knowledge of the country's Buddhist and Hindu background.

Buddhist Influence

The earliest Indian artefacts (mainly small items of sculpture) were from the Indus Valley cities in modern-day Pakistan. It was not until the Mauryan era (4th to 2nd centuries BC) that India's first major artistic period flowered. This classical school of Buddhist art reached its peak during the reign of Ashoka (died 238 BC), and its superb sculpture can be seen at its best at Sanchi.

Close to Peshawar, now in Pakistan, Gandharan art combined Buddhism with a Greek influence brought by the descendants of Alexander the Great's invading army. During this period, the Buddha began to be represented directly in human form rather than by symbols such as the footprint or stupa.

Meanwhile, another school was developing at Mathura, between Agra and Delhi. Here, the Brahmin revival was having its effect on Buddhist art. It was in this school that the tradition of sculpturing *yakshis*, those well-endowed heavenly damsels, began.

During the Gupta period (320-600), Indian art experienced a golden age, and the Buddha images developed their present-day form – even today in Buddhist countries the representations of the Buddha's attitudes, clothing and hand positions have scarcely altered. However, this period saw the end of Buddhist art in India, as Hinduism began to reassert itself and a strongly Hindu tradition was developing in the south. Both schools of art produced metal-cast sculptures using the lost wax method, as well as larger sculptures in stone.

HUGH FINLAY

MARK DAFFEY

Top: A lovely 'apsara' plucks a thorn from her foot – one of the thousands of lively sculptures covering the Khajuraho temples.

Left : The colourful architecture of Sikkim's Rumtek Monastery is heavily influenced by Tibetan Buddhist tradition.

Hindu Influence

The following 1000 years saw a slow but steady development through to the exuberant medieval period of Indian Hindu art. This development can be studied at the caves of Ajanta and Ellora, where there are some of the oldest wall paintings in India, and the sculpture can be traced from the older, stiff and unmoving Buddhist sculptures through to the dynamic and dramatic Hindu figures.

These figures reached their culmination in the period when sculpture became an integral part of architecture – it is impossible to tell where building ends and sculpture begins. Some of the finest examples from this era can be seen in the Hoysala temples of Karnataka, the elaborate Sun Temple at Konark and the Chandelas' temples at Khajuraho. The architecture competes valiantly with the artwork, which manages to combine high quality with quite awesome quantity.

An interesting common element is the highly detailed erotic scenes. The heavenly maidens of an earlier period have blossomed into positions and possibilities that leave little to the imagination. Art of this period was not purely a representation of gods and goddesses. Every aspect of human life appeared in the sculptures, and it's pretty obvious that sex was considered a fairly important aspect of daily life!

Right: The Vittala Temple at Hampi is the pinnacle of Vijayanager sculpture and architecture.

Architecture and sculpture blend seamlessly in the Chandela temples of Khajuraho.

Mughal Influence

At first, the arrival of the Muslims and their intolerance of other religions and 'idols' caused enormous damage to India's artistic relics. The early invaders' art was chiefly confined to painting, but the Mughal era saw Indian art experience yet another golden age. The best known of the art forms they encouraged was the painting of miniatures. These delightfully detailed and brightly coloured paintings showed the events and activities of the Mughals in their magnificent palaces. Other paintings included portraits and studies of wildlife and plants.

At the same time, there was a massive revival of folk art; some of these developments embraced the Mughal miniature concepts but combined them with Indian religious arts. The popular Rajasthan or Mewar schools often included scenes from Krishna's life and escapades – Krishna is usually painted blue. Interestingly, this school followed the Persian-influenced Mughal school in its miniaturised and highly detailed approach, but made no use of the Persian-developed sense of perspective. As a result, the works are generally almost two-dimensional.

Right: The painted havelis of Rajasthan are an outdoor art gallery, combining Mughal, Rajput and western influences.

MICHELLE COXALL

is at 39 Dr B Ambedkar Rd, the main road to Mumbai. Air India (☎ 628190) is at 4 Hermeskunj Mangaldas Rd. NEPC Airlines' contact number is ☎ 625932.

Indian Airlines flies daily to Delhi (US$165), and four times weekly to Bangalore (US$115) and Chennai (US$140). NEPC flies to Bangalore (US$123) and Chennai (US$163) three times a week, and has two to three flights daily to Mumbai (US$70).

Bus Pune has three bus terminals: the Pune railway station terminal for points south including Goa, Belgaum, Kolhapur, Mahabaleshwar and Panchgani; the Shivaji Nagar terminal for points north and north-east – Ahmednagar, Aurangabad, Lonavla and Nasik; and the Swargate terminal for Sinhagad, Bangalore, Mangalore and Mumbai.

The MSRTC buses tend to be pretty rough and most travellers prefer to use the railway system. There are also plenty of private deluxe buses to most nearby centres but beware of going through agents as you may find yourself dumped on a regular MSRTC bus. Try Bright Star Tours & Travels (☎ 629666), Sadhu Waswani Square (the office is not signposted – it's inside the petrol station).

Train Pune is one of the Deccan's most important railway stations and all express and mail trains stop here. The computerised booking hall is to the left of the station as you face the entrance. For enquiries call ☎ 626575.

The *Deccan Queen* and *Pragati Express* are fast commuter trains to Mumbai and are

heavily subscribed. Other express and mail trains to Mumbai take four to five hours.

If you're heading for Matheran, the only express train which stops at Neral is the *Sahyadri Express* which leaves at 7.35 am. See the Matheran section for further details.

Taxi Long-distance share taxis (☎ 629657) (four passengers) connect Pune with Dadar in Mumbai around the clock. They leave from the taxi stand in front of Pune railway station and cost Rs 185 per person for the four hour trip. A similar service operates from Shivaji Nagar railway station to Nasik (Rs 180) and Aurangabad (Rs 220); call ☎ 323060 for bookings.

Getting Around
The Airport The airport is eight km northeast of the city. Indian Airlines operates an airport bus which departs from Hotel Amir and costs Rs 20 one way. An auto-rickshaw will cost Rs 35; a taxi, Rs 50.

Bus Local buses are relatively uncrowded. The bus you are most likely to use is the No 4, which runs from the bus terminal at Pune railway station to Swargate via the Shivaji Nagar terminal. The Marathi number '4' looks like an '8' with a gap at the top.

Auto-Rickshaws Auto-rickshaws are plentiful and the best option for most trips around town. Official rates are around Rs 4 per km (or around 4 times the rate shown on the out-of-date meters), but in most cases you'll

Train Services from Pune

Destination	Train number & name	Departure time	Distance (km)	Duration (hours)	Fare (Rs) (2nd/1st)
Bangalore	6529 *Udyan Exp*	12.20 pm	1019	33.00	230/809
Chennai	6011 *Mumbai-Madras Exp*	6.40 pm	1088	20.00	230/809
	1063 *Chennai Exp*	11.55 pm		20.05	
Delhi	1077 *Jhelum Exp*	5.35 pm	1595	27.45	278/1062
Hyderabad	7031 *Hyderabad Exp*	5.15 pm	600	13.15	155/528
Mumbai CST	2124 *Deccan Queen*	7.15 am	191	3.25	62/217
	2028 *Shatabdi Exp*	7.45 am		3.20	

need to negotiate a fare before you set off on your trip.

Bicycle Many of Pune's students get around by bicycle, but be warned – Pune has some of the most maniacal drivers in India. Bikes can be rented from most of the bicycle shops around town or from the stall near the entrance to the National Hotel.

AROUND PUNE
Sinhagad

Sinhagad, the Lion Fort, is 24km south-west of Pune and makes an excellent day trip. The nearly ruined fort stands on top of a steep hill, where there are also a number of old bungalows; including one where Gandhi met with the freedom fighter Tilak in 1915.

In 1670 Shivaji's general, Tanaji Malusre, led a force who scaled the steep hillside in the dark and defeated the unprepared forces of Bijapur. Legends about this dramatic attack relate that the Maratha forces used trained lizards to carry ropes up the hillside! There are monuments at the spot where Tanaji died, and also at the place where he lost his left hand before his death.

A motorable road winds up to the fort, but if you come by local bus it's a sweaty 1½ to two hour climb to the top, where you'll find a tea stall and cool drinks. It's a good idea to bring water and food with you.

Getting There & Away The Pune city bus No 50 runs frequently to Sinhagad village (from where you must walk) from 5.25 am until evening. It leaves from the bus stop 'Architect College' opposite Nehru Stadium and the trip (Rs 10) takes 45 minutes.

MAHABALESHWAR
Pop: 12,000   Tel Area Code: 02168

The terraced hills and fertile valleys of Maharashtra's most popular hill station (1372m) are a welcome escape from the noise and fumes of Mumbai and Pune. Mahabaleshwar has pleasant walks and panoramic lookouts (the sea is visible on a clear day), and the area has strong historical connections with Shivaji.

The station was founded in 1828 by Sir John 'Boy' Malcolm, and it was the summer capital of the Bombay presidency during the days of the Raj.

Like most hill stations, Mahabaleshwar closes up for the monsoon season (mid-June to mid-September). Local buildings are clad with *kulum* grass to prevent damage from the torrential rain – an unbelievable six *metres* of rain falls during the monsoon. Local tourists, especially students from Pune and Mumbai, now come to Mahabaleshwar simply to 'get wet'.

Information

You must pay a Road Passenger Tax of Rs 5 on arrival. Private vehicles must also pay a Rs 2 per day parking fee.

You can get a reasonable map of the hill station, including the walks, from most hotels.

Things to See & Do

Some faded traces of the Raj still persist in Mahabaleshwar in the many preserved and dilapidated buildings dotted around the town. The most evocative is **Mount Malcolm**, built as Government House and residence of 'Boy' Malcolm in 1829. Once a magnificent country residence with park-like gardens, a gazebo for alfresco dining and commanding views over the town and surrounding valleys, it's now derelict and overgrown.

On the hill behind the town stands **Christchurch**, also slowly falling apart, but with its beautiful stained glass window still intact; the squatters now occupying the church will happily allow you in for a peek.

Faring better after independence are the **Sir BD Petit Library** near the bus station and **The Club**, now a symbol of local prestige with its well-tended roses and 'members only' jogging track nearby – protected by barbed wire and walls topped with broken glass! Also worth a detour is **Morarji Castle**, where Mahatma Gandhi lived during 1945. Keep an eye out for the small tank and natural spring on the right-hand side as you walk up the driveway.

Most visitors come to Mahabaleshwar for the **walks and views**, which are impressive.

Elphinstone, Babington, Bombay and Kate's points offer fine views from the wooded plateau to the plains below. Arthur's Seat, 12km from Mahabaleshwar, looks out over a sheer drop of 600m to the Konkan coastal strip. There are pleasant **waterfalls** around Mahabaleshwar, such as Chinaman's, Dhobi's and Lingmala falls.

The small **Venna Lake**, about four km from Mahabaleshwar, has boating and fishing facilities.

In the village of **Old Mahabaleshwar** there are two ancient temples worth visiting. The Krishnabai, or Panchganga (Five Streams)

Mandir is said to contain the springs of five rivers, including the sacred Krishna river which issues from the mouth of a sculpted cow suckling a calf. The Mahabaleshwar Mandir is of interest for its naturally occurring lingam.

Organised Tours

In the high season, the MTDC (Maharashtra Tourism Development Corporation) organises tours of Mahabaleshwar, Pratapgarh Fort and Panchgani. Each tour costs Rs 40 per person and can be booked at the MTDC Holiday Resort.

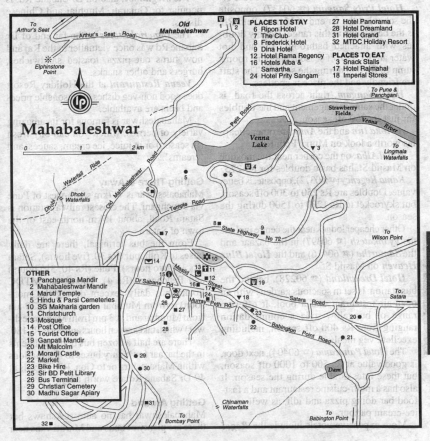

PLACES TO STAY
6 Ripon Hotel
7 The Club
8 Frederick Hotel
9 Dina Hotel
12 Hotel Rama Regency
16 Hotels Alba & Samartha
24 Hotel Prity Sangam
27 Hotel Panorama
28 Hotel Dreamland
31 Hotel Grand
32 MTDC Holiday Resort

PLACES TO EAT
3 Snack Stalls
17 Hotel Rajmahal
18 Imperial Stores

OTHER
1 Panchganga Mandir
2 Mahabaleshwar Mandir
3 Maruti Temple
5 Hindu & Parsi Cemeteries
10 SG Makharia garden
11 Christchurch
13 Mosque
14 Post Office
17 Tourist Office
19 Ganpati Mandir
20 Mt Malcolm
21 Morarji Castle
22 Market
23 Bike Hire
25 Sir BD Petit Library
26 Bus Terminal
27 Christian Cemetery
30 Madhu Sagar Apiary

Mahabaleshwar

Places to Stay

Mahabaleshwar has plenty of hotels but many are closed during the monsoon. The cheaper lodges are in the bazaar area, but don't expect rock-bottom prices. Prices rise dramatically during the high season (generally from November to January and mid-April to mid-June).

The *MTDC Holiday Resort* (☎ 60318), about two km from central Mahabaleshwar, has a variety of accommodation including dorm beds for Rs 50 per person, good doubles at Rs 200 to 300, and cottages and suites (three to four people) for Rs 400 to 700. A taxi from the bus stand costs Rs 30.

Hotel Prity Sangam (☎ 60437), opposite the school at the far end of Murray Peth Rd, is the best value in this range. Roomy doubles with attached bathroom, TV and hot water are Rs 350 off season; the same rooms jump to Rs 880 during the season. The staff are friendly and the place is spotless.

Hotel Sangam, right across the road, is under the same management and has doubles for just Rs 250 off season.

Ashoka Inn and the *Amir* are other cheapies worth a look on Murry Peth Rd.

Hotel Alba, on the corner near the mosque on Masjid St, has basic doubles for Rs 275.

Rama Regency (☎ 60372), opposite, is better value. Doubles are Rs 250 to 300 off season, but skyrocket to Rs 1200 to 1500 during the season.

Other cheaper lodges near the centre include the *Vyankatesh* (☎ 60397) in the bazaar and the *Samartha* (☎ 60416) and the *Hotel Blue Heaven* on Masjid St.

Hotel Dreamland (☎ 60228), behind the bus station, is set in spacious gardens with an open-air restaurant and a pool. It offers a range of bungalow-style accommodation ranging from Rs 400 off season, including excellent veg meals.

The *Hotel Panorama* (☎ 60404), next door, is good value at Rs 500 to 1000 off season, but these rates double during the season. It also has a multi-cuisine restaurant and a fast-food bar doing pizza and idli, as well as an ice-cream parlour.

More expensive hotels include the *Regal Hotel* (☎ 60001), *Dina Hotel* (☎ 60246) and *Fredrick Hotel* (☎ 60240). These places generally quote all-inclusive prices in the range of Rs 1000 to Rs 1800 per person per day during the season and around Rs 750, off season.

Places to Eat

The *Poonam* at the Shere Punjab Hotel on Dr Sabane Rd has good non-veg food, and the *Nukkad* next door is also popular.

Hotel Rajmahal, further up the road, serves thalis on an open-air terrace overlooking the bazaar.

The *Meghdoot*, also on Dr Sabane Rd, is popular for Gujarati, Mughlai and Chinese dishes.

The *Imperial Stores* at the far end of Dr Sabane Rd was once victualler to the Raj and now turns out pizza, toasted sandwiches, burgers and other snacks.

Veena Restaurant at the Holiday Resort does good non-veg dishes at reasonable prices and beers are available.

Mahabaleshwar is famous for its amazing variety of berries, which you can buy fresh (in season) or in juice, ice cream, sauces, and 'creams'.

Getting There & Away

Mahabaleshwar is 117km south-west of Pune via Panchgani. The closest railway station is Satara Road, about 15km north-east of the town of Satara.

From the bus terminal, there are daily buses to Kolhapur (Rs 30, five hours), Satara (Rs 18, two hours), Pune (Rs 40, 3½ hours) and Panchgani (Rs 4). There's an MTDC luxury bus daily (except during the monsoon) to/from Mumbai (it leaves at 6.30 am from Mumbai and at 3 pm from Mahabaleshwar) which takes seven hours and costs Rs 180.

There are half a dozen bus booking agents in the bazaar for luxury buses to destinations within Maharashtra or to Goa. RB Travels at 49 Dr Sabane Rd are worth a try.

Getting Around

Mahabaleshwar has no auto-rickshaws but there are plenty of taxis and Maruti vans near the bus station to take you around the main viewpoints or to Panchgani.

If you're here for a day or two, bicycling is the best option as there's little traffic to contend with, and the roads are relatively level. You can rent an old clunker for around Rs 5 an hour from the bicycle shop at the far end of the bazaar.

AROUND MAHABALESHWAR
Panchgani
Panchgani (Five Hills) is 19km east of Mahabaleshwar and just 38m lower. It's also a popular hill station, splendidly located, but overshadowed by its better known neighbour. It's famous today for its berry farms and orchards.

As in Mahabaleshwar, there's a variety of hotels. Cheaper places include the *Prospect Hotel* (☎ 40263), *Hotel Western* (☎ 40288) and the *Malas Guest House* (☎ 40321). The most expensive is the *Aman Hotel* (☎ 40211) with rooms from Rs 750/1000 in the low/high season. The *Hotel Five Hills* (☎ 40301) has rooms for Rs 500/700 and its *Silver Oaks Restaurant* is reasonably priced and serves excellent food.

Pratapgarh & Raigad Forts
Further afield are two impressive hill forts associated with Shivaji.

Built in 1656, Pratapgarh Fort dominates a high ridge 24km west of Mahabaleshwar and has spectacular views. It is connected with one of the more notable feats in Shivaji's dramatic life (see the Pratapgarh Protagonists boxed section for more details). Regular buses from Mahabaleshwar take about an hour

to the Fort, which is reached by a 500 step climb.

Seldom visited by travellers, Raigad (or Raigarh) Fort, 80km north-west of Mahabaleshwar, also has wonderful views from its isolated hilltop location, reached by a long, steep ascent. It was here that Shivaji was crowned in 1648 and where he died in 1680.

The MTDC operates some basic *accommodation* here including two large crash-on-the-floor dorms (Rs 20), and six four-bed rooms (Rs 200); book through the MTDC in Mumbai or Pune.

Satara
Satara houses a number of relics of the Maratha leader Shivaji. A building near the new palace contains his sword, the coat he wore when he met Afzal Khan and the *waghnakh* with which he killed him. The **Shivaji Maharaj Museum** is opposite the bus terminal.

Wasota fort in the south of the town has a colourful and bloody history, including being captured from the Marathas in 1699 by the forces of Aurangzeb, only to be recaptured in 1705 by means of a Brahmin who befriended the fort's defenders, then let in a band of Marathas.

Satara is 42km south of Mahabaleshwar on the main road from Pune to Belgaum and Goa. The nearest railhead is Satara Road, 15km away.

KOLHAPUR
Pop: 480,200   Tel Area Code: 0231
Kolhapur was once the capital of an important Maratha state. It's an interesting little town and worth exploring for a day or two if

---

Pratapgarh Protagonists
Outnumbered by the forces of Bijapur, Shivaji arranged to meet with the opposing General Afzal Khan. Neither was supposed to carry any weapon or wear armour. Neither, it turned out, could be trusted.

When they met, Afzal Khan pulled out a dagger and stabbed Shivaji, but the Maratha leader had worn a shirt of mail under his white robe, and concealed in his left hand was a *waghnakh*, a deadly set of 'tiger's claws'. This nasty weapon consisted of a series of rings to which long, sharpened metal claws were attached. Shivaji drove these claws into Khan and disembowelled him. Today a tomb marks where their encounter took place, and a tower was erected over the Khan's head. There is a statue of Shivaji in the ruined Pratapgarh Fort. ■

MAHARASHTRA

you're passing through. One of Kolhapur's maharajas died in Florence, Italy, and was cremated on the banks of the Arno where his *chhatri* (cenotaph) now stands. The last maharaja, Major General His Highness Shahaji Chhatrapati II, died in 1983.

The MTDC tourist office (☎ 659435), five minutes walk from the station in Station Rd, is open weekdays from 10 am to 6 pm and weekends from 8.30 am to noon and 4 to 6 pm.

Maharaja's Palace

The maharaja's 'new' palace, completed in 1881, houses the **Shahaji Chhatrapati Museum**, one of the most bizarre collections of memorabilia in India. The building was designed by 'Mad' Charles Mant, the British architect who fashioned the Indo-Saracenic style of colonial architecture (he practiced the style on several colonial buildings in Kolhapur) and is a cross between a Victorian railway station (clock tower included) and the Addams Family mansion.

The palace contains a weird and wonderful array of the old maharaja's possessions including his clothes, old hunt photos, silver peacock-shaped elephant saddles and the memorial silver spade he used to 'turn the first sod of the Kolhapur State Railway' in 1888.

But dominating every room in the palace are reminders of the maharaja's macabre passion: killing wild animals to decorate his palace. Skins cover floors and furniture, trophy heads stare blankly from the walls, ashtrays and coffee tables are made from tiger and elephant feet, lamp stands from ostrich legs and zebra hoofs. The variety of stuffed animals includes black bear, rhino, pangolin, panther and an entire pride of lions in a forest diorama! There's even a painting of the Maharani entitled 'The World's Greatest Woman Pig Sticker'.

The gun and sword collection could easily outfit a small army: dozens of swords, daggers, axes, pistols, punt guns and instruments of torture fill the armaments room. The most unusual piece (and befitting a maharaja) is a gold-plated, double-barrelled shotgun.

The palace is a few km north of the centre.

Rent a bicycle, or take an auto-rickshaw (Rs 10). Entry is Rs 5.

Other Things to See

The **Mahalakshmi Temple**, dedicated to the goddess Amba Bai, dominates the old town. Of particular interest is the carved ceiling of the columned mandapam. Nearby, the **Old Palace** still accommodates members of the maharaja's family, but in its cool atrium (open 10 am to 6 pm daily) you're more likely to find students poring over books under the benign gaze of a larger-than-life painted carving of the maharaja and a retinue of stuffed animals. An alley leads from the front of the palace to Kolhapur's famous **wrestling ground**, which resembles an enormous sandpit. Kolhapur has produced several Indian national wrestling champions, and you can see them training most days at 5 pm.

The Town Hall, built by Mant in 1872-76, is now a small but satisfying **museum**, housing pottery and bronze artefacts found during archaeological excavations on nearby **Brahmapuri Hill**, including a small bronze of the Greek god Poseidon holding his Siva-like trident.

For a respite from the city's bustle, head down to the sacred **ghats** on the Panchganga River or to **Lake Rankala**, five km from the railway station.

Places to Stay

The main hotel and restaurant area is around the square opposite the bus stand, 10 to 15 minutes walk from the centre of town and the railway station, where there are *retiring rooms*.

Hotel Chalukya (☎ 652996) has habitable doubles for Rs 150, slightly more with TV. There's hot water in the morning and extra beds cost Rs 40 per person.

Hotel Sahyadri (☎ 650929) is of a similar standard but can be noisy. Rooms are Rs 170/200.

Hotel Maharaja (☎ 652140) is marginally better at Rs 130/210 or Rs 300 for a four bed room with TV.

Hotel Girish (☎ 651236), just around the corner, is friendly and clean. It has rooms for

Rs 150/200, all with TV and phone. There's also a restaurant and a bar.

Ten minutes walk east of the bus station are three mid-range places. All face busy Station Rd, so rooms near the front can be noisy. *Hotel International* (☎ 652442) has rooms for Rs 225/275 to Rs 275/325 or Rs 400 with air-con, all with TV and phone. A veg restaurant is attached. *Hotel Ashoka Prestige* (☎ 654232) is a little more pricey with doubles costing Rs 480 without air-con. *Hotel Panchsil* (☎ 650517) is more comfortable than either, with rooms ranging from Rs 400/450 to Rs 450/500 or Rs 600/650 with air-con; suites are Rs 725 and there's a multi-cuisine restaurant.

Hotel Shalini Palace (☎ 620401) is the maharaja's old summer palace by Lake Rankala, five km from the bus stand or railway station. It dates back only to the 1930s but has plenty of regal grandeur. Rooms are Rs 300/450 or Rs 700/995 with air-con. Royal suites range from Rs 1500 to Rs 1800.

Places to Eat

The restaurants are also clustered around the bus-station square. The *Subraya Restaurant*, opposite Hotel Sahyadri, has north Indian veg and non-veg dishes, and regulation thalis. You could also head up the road to the restaurants at the *Hotel International* and *Hotel Panchsil*, where you'll pay around Rs 100 for a three course meal.

In the evening dozens of *snack stalls* set up opposite the bus stand, whipping up great omelettes and other goodies.

Getting There & Away

Bus There are daily departures for Satara, Bijapur, Mahabaleshwar, Pune, Ratnagiri and Belgaum. There are plenty of private bus companies around the square offering luxury coach services to Goa and other destinations.

Train The railway station is 10 minutes walk west of the bus station, towards the centre of town. The broad-gauge line connects Kolhapur via Miraj with Pune (eight hours) and Mumbai (13 hours) – take the daily *Koyna Express* or the overnight *Mahalaxmi Express*.

The *Maharashtra Express* zigzags 1220km through the state to Nagpur.

AROUND KOLHAPUR

Panhala

Panhala is a little-visited hill station (altitude 975m) 18km north-west of Kolhapur, and makes an interesting excursion from Kolhapur. The hilltop fort has a long and convoluted history: it was originally the stronghold of Raja Bhoj II in 1192, was captured by both the Mughals and the Marathas and was finally taken by the British in 1844. The **Pawala Caves** are nearby, as well as a couple of Buddhist cave temples.

Northern Maharashtra

NASIK

Pop: 834,000   Tel Area Code: 0253

This interesting town with its 200 temples and picturesque bathing ghats stands on the Godavari River, one of the holiest rivers of the Deccan. Nasik is one of four sites for the triennial Kumbh Mela, a huge Hindu gathering which takes place here every 12 years.

The town is about eight km north-west of the Nasik Road railway station, which is 187km from Mumbai.

Temples & Caves

Nasik's riverbanks are lined with ghats above which stand temples and shrines. Although there are no particularly notable temples, the **Sundar Narayan Temple**, to the west of the city, is worth a visit.

Other points of interest include the **Sita Gupta Cave** from which, according to the *Ramayana*, Sita, the deity of agriculture and wife of Rama, was supposed to have been carried off to the island of Lanka by the evil king Ravana. Near the cave, in a grove of large banyan trees, is the fine house of the Panchavati family. Also nearby is the Temple of **Kala Rama**, or Black Rama, in a 96 arched enclosure. The **Kapaleswar Temple** upstream is said to be the oldest in the town.

Kumbh Mela

The Kumbh Mela, purportedly the largest celebration of any kind on earth, alternates between Nasik, Allahabad, Ujjain and Haridwar every three years. *Kumbh* means 'pot' or 'cup', and in Hindu mythology, four drops of the nectar of immortality fell to earth, one in each of these places. For more details about this extraordinary pilgrimage, see the section under Allahabad in the Uttar Pradesh chapter.

Places to Stay & Eat

Hotel Siddharth (☎ 564288), on the Pune Rd about two km from the roundabout, is a large, well-kept place where singles/doubles are Rs 150/200 or Rs 250/300 with air-con.

Hotel Padma (☎ 576837), on Sharampur Rd opposite the central bus stand, has simple, clean rooms with attached bathroom for Rs 200/250.

Hotel Samrat (☎ 577211), near the central bus stand on Old Agra Rd, offers rooms without/with air-con for Rs 400/550. Its restaurant serves good Gujarati thalis and there's a bar.

Hotel Panchavati (☎ 571273), 430 Vakilwadi, is large and centrally located, offering clean, good-value rooms for Rs 350/550 or Rs 520/725 with air-con; there are cheaper rooms in its annexe. There's a couple of good restaurants and a bar here as well.

Wasan's Inn (☎ 570202) on Old Agra Rd is similarly priced and has its own restaurant.

Woodlands Restaurant, across the road from the Hotel Siddharth, serves excellent south Indian meals, but no alcohol.

Getting There & Away

Local buses and auto-rickshaws ply between the Nasik Road railway station and the town centre. The fastest train to Mumbai is the *Panchvati Express* which does the trip in 4½ hours, leaving at 7.09 am.

There are frequent buses to Mumbai but they're slower than the train as they get caught up in Mumbai's traffic chaos. Frequent buses also go to Aurangabad (200km, five hours) and Pune (209km, five hours).

AROUND NASIK
Pandu Lena

About eight km south of Nasik, close to the Mumbai road, is a group of 24 Hinayana Buddhist caves dating from around the 1st century BC to the 2nd AD. Cave 3 is a large vihara with some interesting sculptures. Cave 10 is also a vihara and almost identical in design to cave 3, although it is much older and finer in its detail. It is thought to be nearly as old as the Karla Cave near Lonavla. Cave 18 is a chaitya believed to date from the same time as the Karla Cave; it is well sculptured and its elaborate facade is particularly noteworthy.

Trimbak

From a spring high on a steep hill above Trimbak, 33km west of Nasik, the source of the Godavari River dribbles into the **Gangasagar bathing tank** whose waters are reputed to wash away sins. From this tiny start the Godavari eventually flows down to the Bay of Bengal, clear across India.

Also in Trimbak is the **Trimbakeshwar temple**, one of India's most sacred, containing one of 12 *jyotilingas* (naturally occurring lingams) of Siva. Although the temple is open to Hindus only, it is possible (and permitted) to see into the temple courtyard to the shrine from a convenient vantage point.

AURANGABAD

Pop: 682,000   Tel Area Code: 0240

Aurangabad has a number of attractions and could easily stand on its own were it not overshadowed by the famous Ellora and Ajanta caves nearby. The city is named after Aurangzeb, but earlier in its history it was known as Khadke.

Aurangabad is northern Maharashtra's largest city though it is remarkably uncrowded and quiet except for the occasional political rally.

Orientation

The railway station, tourist office and a variety of cheaper hotels and restaurants are clustered in the south of the town. The bus stand is 1.5km to the north. North-east of here is the crowded old town with its narrow streets and distinct Muslim quarter. The mid-range hotels are between the bus stand and railway station while the top-end places are dotted around town.

Information

The very helpful Government of India tourist office (☎ 331217) on Station Rd (West) has a decent range of brochures and will try to answer almost any query. It's open from 8.30 am to 6 pm on weekdays and until 1.30 pm on Saturday. The state tourist office (☎ 331513)

in the MTDC Holiday Resort, Station Rd (East), is open from 7 am to 7 pm but is not as useful. There are also information counters at the airport and railway station which open to meet arriving passengers.

Poste restante can be collected from the GPO at Juna Bazaar from 10 am to 5 pm Monday to Saturday.

Bibi-ka-Maqbara

The so-called 'poor-man's Taj Mahal' was built in 1679 as a mausoleum for Aurangzeb's wife, Rabia-ud-Daurani. It's a cheap imitation of the Taj in both design and execution

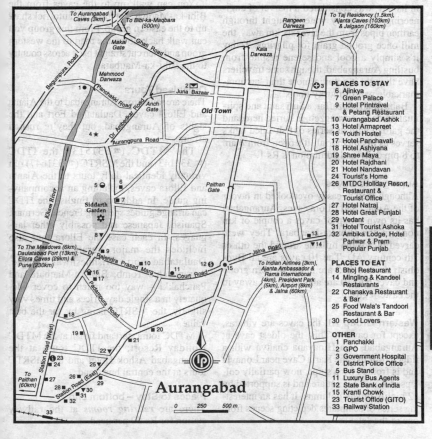

PLACES TO STAY
6 Ajinkya
7 Green Palace
9 Hotel Printravel & Petang Restaurant
10 Aurangabad Ashok
13 Hotel Armapreet
16 Youth Hostel
17 Hotel Panchavati
18 Hotel Ashiyana
19 Shree Maya
20 Hotel Rajdhani
21 Hotel Nandavan
24 Tourist's Home
26 MTDC Holiday Resort, Restaurant & Tourist Office
27 Hotel Natraj
28 Hotel Great Punjabi
29 Vedant
31 Hotel Tourist Ashoka
32 Ambika Lodge, Hotel Pariwar & Prem Popular Punjab

PLACES TO EAT
8 Bhoj Restaurant
14 Mingling & Kandeel Restaurants
22 Chanakya Restaurant & Bar
25 Food Wala's Tandoori Restaurant & Bar
30 Food Lovers

OTHER
1 Panchakki
2 GPO
3 Government Hospital
4 District Police Office
5 Bus Stand
11 Luxury Bus Agents
12 State Bank of India
15 Kranti Chowk
23 Tourist Office (GITO)
33 Railway Station

Aurangabad

0   250   500 m

MAHARASHTRA

– it simply looks awkward compared with the elegance and symmetry of the Taj; and where the Taj has gleaming marble, this tomb has flaking plaster. On the main gate an inscription reveals that it cost precisely Rs 665,283 and 7 annas to build. Still, it attracts hordes of visitors and would no doubt be considered a high point of Mughal architecture if the Taj did not exist. It's much more atmospheric at night, when it's floodlit.

It's open from sunrise to 10 pm and admission is Rs 2.

Panchakki

Panchakki takes its name from the mill that, in its day, was considered a marvel of engineering. Driven by water brought through earthen pipes from the river six km away, the mill once ground grain for pilgrims. Today it's simply a cool and serene respite from bustling Aurangabad, though some travellers have thought it nothing more than 'an unremarkable pair of murky pools'.

Baba Shah Muzaffar, a Sufi saint and spiritual guide to Aurangzeb, is buried here, and the garden with its series of fish-filled tanks serves as his memorial. It's open from 8 am to 8 pm daily and admission is Rs 1.

Aurangabad Caves

Although they're easily overlooked in favour of the Ajanta and Ellora caves, Aurangabad has its own group of caves a couple of km north of the Bibi-ka-Maqbara. They were carved out of the hillside around the 6th or 7th century AD. The 10 caves are all Buddhist; caves 1 to 5 are in the western group and caves 6 to 10 are about one km away in the eastern group.

Western Group All the caves are viharas, except for cave 4. This, the oldest cave at Aurangabad, is a Hinayana chaitya with a ridged roof like the Karla Cave near Lonavla and is fronted by a stupa, now partially collapsed. Cave 3 is square and is supported by 12 highly ornate columns. It has an interesting series of sculptures depicting scenes from one of the Jatakas.

Eastern Group Cave 6 is fairly intact and the sculptures of women are notable for their exotic hairstyles and ornamentation. There is a large Buddha figure here and Ganesh also makes an appearance. Cave 7 is the most interesting of the Aurangabad caves, particularly for its sculptures – the figures of women, scantily clad and ornately bejewelled, are indicative of the rise of Tantric Buddhism during this period.

To the left of Cave 7 a huge Bodhisattva prays for deliverance from the eight dangers: fire, the sword of the enemy, chains, shipwreck, lions, snakes, mad elephants and a demon (representing death).

You can walk up to the caves from the Bibi-ka-Maqbara or take an auto-rickshaw up to the eastern group. From this group you can walk back down the road to the western group and then cut straight back across country to the Bibi-ka-Maqbara.

Organised Tours

There are tours from Aurangabad to the Ajanta and Ellora caves, Daulatabad Fort and the sights of Aurangabad, but they're rushed affairs.

The MTDC (☎ 331513), the ITDC (☎ 331143) and the MSRTC (☎ 331647) run virtually identical daily tours to the Ajanta and Ellora caves, including an accompanying guide. In addition to English the ITDC can arrange guides speaking French, German, Spanish, Japanese and possibly other languages. In each case the Ellora tour also includes the major Aurangabad sites – Daulatabad Fort, Grishneshwar Temple, Aurangzeb's Tomb, Bibi-ka-Maqbara and Panchakki – way too much to cover adequately in a single day. Prices and times vary slightly, the MSRTC being by far the best value.

MTDC tours start and finish at the MTDC Holiday Resort; the ITDC tours at the Aurangabad Ashok Hotel and the MSRTC tours at the central bus stand.

Places to Stay – bottom end

There are *retiring rooms* at the railway station for Rs 50 per head.

Tours to Ajanta and Ellora from Aurangabad

Tours to Ellora

	Departs	Returns	Cost
MTDC	10.00 am	6.00 pm	Rs 110
ITDC	9.30 am	6.00 pm	Rs 100
MSRTC	8.00 am	4.30 pm	Rs 55

Tours to Ajanta

	Departs	Returns	Cost
MTDC	8.00 am	6.00 pm	Rs 140
ITDC	8.00 am	6.00 pm	Rs 135
MSRTC	8.00 am	5.30 pm	Rs 107

There's a string of cheap and basic places near the station with double rooms from Rs 50 to 70, including *Ambika Lodge* and *Hotel Pariwar*.

Hotel Tourist Ashoka (☎ 320020) is a little better and has rooms for Rs 100/250.

Green Palace and *Ajinkya* are the pick of the cheapies opposite the bus stand – basic rooms are around Rs 90/125.

The *youth hostel* (☎ 334892) on Station Rd (West), is a little tattered, but it's the cheapest place in town. Separate male and female dorms cost Rs 42 a head (Rs 22 for YHA members) and double rooms are Rs 90. There's a 10 pm curfew, hot water in the morning and meals are available.

Hotel Panchavati (☎ 25204), next to the youth hostel, has rooms for Rs 75/115 with attached bath, and hot water in the mornings. It's basic but the staff are amicable and there's a good restaurant and bar.

Shree Maya (☎ 333093), just around the corner, is well kept and friendly with rooms for Rs 100/150 and air-con doubles for Rs 350. Each room has TV and cold shower (but hot/cold bathtaps).

The two hotels on Station Rd (West) are good value and popular with backpackers. *Hotel Natraj* (☎ 24260) is a typical family run boarding house with rooms for Rs 90/100 with bathroom. The *Tourist's Home* (☎ 337212) next door has basic but very clean

rooms at Rs 60/100 to 70/125, all with bathroom.

Hotel Printravel (☎ 29707), on Station Rd (West) 600m south of the bus stand, has rooms for Rs 125/200, each with attached bath.

Hotel Ashiyana (☎ 29322) is a newish place just off Station Rd (West), offering clean rooms from Rs 100/150 with attached bath and TV.

Places to Stay – middle

Heading north along Station Rd (East) there are several mid-range hotels.

The *MTDC Holiday Resort* (☎ 34259) is set in its own shady grounds and has four-bed rooms with communal bathroom for Rs 200; doubles with bathroom are Rs 225 or Rs 400 with air-con. Mosquito nets are provided and there's a restaurant, a bar and a pleasant garden.

Hotel Nandavan (☎ 336314) about one km from the railway station is good value at Rs 140/190 with attached bathroom, 24 hour hot water and TV, or Rs 300/350 with air-con. There are two small restaurants and a bar.

Hotel Rajdhani (☎ 336503), is not terrific value at Rs 350/425 for standard rooms (Rs 425/495 with air-con), but planned renovations and an open-air coffee shop will certainly help.

Hotel Amarpreet (☎ 332521), out on Pt Nehru Marg (Jalna Rd) three km from the station towards the airport, is a little more expensive with rooms for Rs 425/525 or Rs 499/675 with air-con. It's comfortable, if a little rough around the edges, and has a restaurant, bar, coffee shop and travel desk.

Places to Stay – top end

Aurangabad Ashok (☎ 20520; fax 313328), Dr Rajendra Prasad Marg, is the cheapest in this range, with air-con rooms for Rs 1000/1500. This hotel has all the usual Ashok amenities but has seen better days.

Vedant (☎ 333844) is also central on Station Rd (East). This modern, multi-storey Quality Inn hotel has two restaurants, a bar, central air-con and swimming pool.

Rooms cost Rs 1330/2430 including breakfast, direct dial STD/ISD and TV.

Ajanta Ambassador (☎ 485211; fax 484367), out near the airport at Chikal Thana, is a five star hotel that has it all – swimming pool, bar, restaurants and shopping arcades. Prices start at around Rs 1200/2300 a single/double.

Welcomgroup Rama International (☎ 48541; fax 484768), nearby, offers similar luxury at similar rates.

President Park (☎ 486201; fax 532230), a very classy three star, is a little further out towards the airport and is excellent value at Rs 1100/1600, with deluxe suites for Rs 2350. The best feature of this hotel is its semi-circular swimming pool set in gardens with a poolside bar. It also has a travel desk, gym, multi-cuisine restaurant and coffee shop.

Taj Residency (☎ 332221) is a gleaming oasis on the northern fringes of town. The hotel sweeps around an immaculate garden and swimming pool. Well-appointed rooms start at Rs 1195/2375.

The Meadows (☎ 677412; fax 677416) is a cluster of small, modern bungalows set in their own spacious and irrigated gardens in a rural location about six km from Aurangabad on the road to Ellora. Rates are Rs 1400/2000, and facilities include satellite TV, pool, gym & sauna, children's playground, multi-cuisine restaurant and coffee shop.

Places to Eat

There's a clutch of rock-bottom restaurants along Station Rd (East), including the *Tirupati* and *Bharthi*, which both specialise in cheap south Indian meals.

Food Lovers garden restaurant is close by, and has the best ambience in town – earth floor, thatched walls and an ingenious cooling system on hot days. The Punjabi and Chinese food is delicious and if you spend Rs 100, you get a discount voucher for your next visit. It's open until midnight.

Foodwalas Tandoori Restaurant & Bar is further up Station Rd (East) and offers just what its name implies.

Chanakya Restaurant & Bar, a little further up the road, is another fine tandoori place.

Bhoj, on Dr Ambedkar Rd, is a popular 2nd floor restaurant serving expensive but excellent south Indian vegetarian food. It opens for breakfast from 7 am.

Petang Restaurant, nearby at Hotel Printravel, does a superb Rs 35 thali. You can wash it down with a mild beer (nothing 'strong' is available); this place stays open until quite late.

Mingling out on Jalna Rd has a reputation for tasty and even imaginative Chinese and Indian food. Prices range from Rs 40 to Rs 100 for mains.

The *Kandeel* next door is another popular dinner spot.

The *Vedant* has a buffet breakfast in the coffee shop for Rs 60 and a daily buffet lunch for Rs 99.

Getting There & Away

Aurangabad is off the main line but there are still direct trains from Mumbai and Hyderabad. Ajanta and Ellora are completely off the railway lines and are usually approached from either Aurangabad (Ellora 30km, Ajanta 106km) or from Jalgaon (Ajanta 60km). Jalgaon is on the main broad-gauge line from Mumbai to Allahabad.

Air The airport is about 10km east of town on the Jalna road. En route you'll find the Indian Airlines office (☎ 24864). The NEPC Airways office is in the President Park hotel, two km closer to the airport.

Indian Airlines has two flights daily to Mumbai (US$55) and NEPC also flies daily to Mumbai (US$70). On Monday, Tuesday, Thursday and Saturday there's an Indian Airlines flight to Udaipur (US$90), which continues to Jaipur (US$110) and Delhi (US$135).

Bus There are MSRTC buses from Aurangabad to Pune (six hours), Nasik (five hours), Indore and Mumbai (388km via Manmad, 400km via Pune). The MSRTC and MTDC also offer luxury overnight buses to Mumbai (12 hours, Rs 200). The luxury bus agents congregate around the corner where Dr Rajendra Prasad Marg becomes Court Rd.

To Ellora & Ajanta Caves Unless you're planning to take an organised tour from Aurangabad to Ajanta, you may find it more convenient to stay at Ajanta than to rely on local transport there and back.

There are local buses to Ellora (every half hour, Rs 10), Ajanta (four per day, 2½ hours, Rs 40), and to Jalgaon (hourly, 4½ hours, Rs 56).

Not all the Aurangabad to Jalgaon buses go right to Ajanta, so if it's the caves you specifically want and not Fardapur (the nearest village, four km away on the main road), make sure you get on the right bus.

Train Aurangabad is not on one of the main lines and has only sporadic services. There are two direct trains daily to/from Mumbai (375km) but are often heavily booked. The *Tapovan Express* departs at 2.55 pm and costs Rs 110/376 in 2nd/1st class but it gets you into Mumbai VT at 11.20 pm. The overnight *Devgiri Express* departs from Aurangabad at 9.40 pm and arrives at Mumbai at 5.45 am. Coming from Mumbai, the same train leaves at 9.20 pm and arrives at Aurangabad at 4.35 am.

Alternatively, you can get a bus or a local train to the nearest mainline station, Manmad, 113km north-west of Aurangabad, from where there are more frequent express trains to Mumbai.

If you are heading directly to the Ajanta Caves from Mumbai, it's best to get an express to Jalgaon and then a local bus to the caves, though this is still quite a gruelling day's travel (for details see the Jalgaon section).

To Hyderabad (Secunderabad), the daily *Devgiri Express* departs from Aurangabad at 4.45 am and the journey takes 14 hours. Alternatively, the *Aurangabad-Kacheguda Express* departs at 7.30 pm and arrives at Secunderabad at 9 am.

Getting Around

There are plenty of auto-rickshaw wallahs in Aurangabad who can double as excellent tour guides. Try those at the Aurangabad Ashok or MTDC Holiday Resort.

You can hire a bicycle from stalls near the bus stand and, as the town is not too hilly or the roads too busy, it's a good way to get around.

AROUND AURANGABAD

Daulatabad

Halfway (13km) between Aurangabad and the Ellora Caves is the magnificent hilltop fortress of Daulatabad. The **fort** is surrounded by five km of sturdy walls, while the central bastion tops a 200m high hill, which was originally known as Devagiri, the Hill of the Gods.

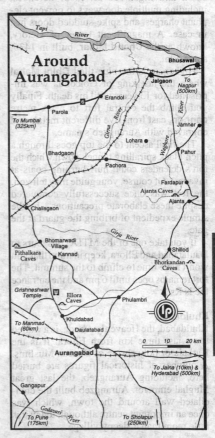

Around Aurangabad

In the 14th century it was renamed Daulatabad, the City of Fortune, by Mohammed Tughlaq. This somewhat unbalanced Sultan of Delhi conceived the crazy plan of not only building himself a new capital here, but marching the entire population of Delhi 1100km south to populate it. His unhappy subjects proceeded to drop dead like flies on this forced march, and 17 years later he turned round and marched them all back to Delhi. The fort remained.

It's worth making the climb to the top for the superb views over the surrounding country. Along the way you'll pass through a complicated and ingenious series of defences, including multiple doorways to prevent elephant charges, and spike-studded doors just in case. A magnificent tower of victory, known as the **Chand Minar**, built in 1435, soars 60m.

Higher up is the blue-tiled **Chini Mahal** where the last king of Golconda was imprisoned for 13 years until his death. Finally you climb the central fort to a six metre **cannon**, cast from five different metals and engraved with Aurangzeb's name.

The final ascent to the top goes through a pitch black spiralling tunnel, down which the fort's defenders could hurl burning coals at invaders. Of course, your guide may tell you, the fort was once successfully conquered despite these elaborate precautions – by the simple expedient of bribing the guard at the gate.

If you take one of the MTDC bus tours to Daulatabad and Ellora, keep in mind that you won't have time to climb to the summit. The fort remains open until 6 pm and the entrance fee is Rs 2.

Khuldabad

Khuldabad, the Heavenly Abode, is a walled town just three km from Ellora. It is the Karbala or holy shrine of Deccan Muslims. A number of historical figures are buried here, including Aurangzeb, the last great Mughal emperor. Aurangzeb built the crenellated wall around the town, which was once an important centre although today it is little more than a sleepy village.

The emperor's final resting place is a simple affair of bare earth in a courtyard of the **Alamgir Dargah** at the centre of the town. Aurangzeb's pious austerity extended even to his own tomb, for he stipulated that his mausoleum should be paid for with money he earned himself by manually copying out the Koran.

Within the building there is supposed to be a robe worn by the prophet Mohammed; it is only shown to the faithful once each year. Another shrine across the road from the Alamgir Dargah is said to contain hairs of the prophet's beard and lumps of silver from a tree of solid silver which miraculously grew at this site after a saint's death.

Grishneshwar

Close to the Ellora Caves in the village of Verul, the 18th century Grishneshwar temple has one of the 12 *jyotirlinga*s (naturally occurring lingams) in India, and is an important place of pilgrimage for Hindus.

ELLORA

The world-heritage listed cave temples of Ellora, about 30km from Aurangabad, are the culmination of Deccan rock-cut architecture.

Over five centuries, generations of Buddhist, Hindu and Jain monks carved monasteries, chapels and temples from a two km long escarpment and decorated them with a profusion of sculptures of remarkable imagination and detail. Because of the escarpment's gentle slope, in contrast to the sheer drop at Ajanta, many of the caves have elaborate courtyards in front of the main shrines. The caves run north-south and take on a golden radiance in the late-afternoon sun.

In all there are 34 caves at Ellora: 12 Buddhist (600-800 AD), 17 Hindu (600-900 AD) and five Jain (800-1000 AD). Whereas the caves at Ajanta chart the division of Buddhism into Hinayana and Mahayana schools, Ellora represents the renaissance of Hinduism under the Chalukya and Rashtrakuta dynasties, the subsequent decline of Indian Buddhism, and a brief resurgence of

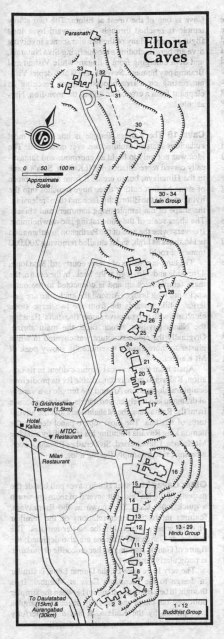

Ellora Caves

Parasnath

30 - 34
Jain Group

0   50   100 m
Approximate Scale

13 - 29
Hindu Group

To Grishneshwar
Temple (1.5km)

Hotel
Kailas

MTDC
Restaurant

Milan
Restaurant

To Daulatabad
(15km) &
Aurangabad
(30km)

1 - 12
Buddhist Group

Jainism under official patronage. The sculptural work at Ellora shows the growing influence of Tantric elements in India's three great religions, and their coexistence at one site indicates a prolonged period of religious tolerance.

The masterpiece of Ellora is the astonishing Kailasa Temple (cave 16). Dedicated to Siva, it is the world's largest monolithic sculpture, hewn from the living rock by 7000 labourers over a 150 year period. For three days in March the Kailasa Temple is the venue of the annual Ellora Dance & Music Festival.

Entry to Ellora is free except to the Kailasa Temple which costs Rs 0.50 plus another Rs 25 for a movie camera. Allow at least a half-day to visit Ellora and at least an hour for the Kailasa Temple; many visitors prefer to begin with the earlier Buddhist and Hindu caves (caves 1-15) as a prelude to Kailasa. The strong smell in some of the caves is bat guano.

Buddhist Caves

The southernmost 12 caves are all Buddhist viharas, except cave 10 which is a chaitya. While the earliest caves are quite simple, caves 11 and 12 are much more ambitious, probably in an attempt to compete with the more impressive Hindu temples which were built nearby.

Caves 1 to 4 Cave 1 is the simplest vihara and may have been a granary. Cave 2 is notable for its ornate pillars and its imposing seated Buddha facing the setting sun, his huge feet planted solidly on the earth. Caves 3 and 4 are earlier, simpler and less well preserved.

Cave 5 This is the largest vihara in this group, 18m wide and 36m long; the rows of stone benches indicate that it may have been an assembly or dining hall.

Caves 6 & 9 As well as the large seated Buddha in the shrine room, this ornate vihara also has a wonderful image of Tara (on the left), consort of the bodhisattva Avalokitesvara, and the Buddhist goddess of learning, Mahamayuri, looking remarkably similar to her Hindu equivalent, Saraswati. Cave 9 is notable for its wonderfully carved facade.

Cave 10 The Viswakarma or Carpenter's Cave is the only chaitya in the Buddhist group, and one of the finest in India. It takes its name from the ribs carved into the roof, in imitation of wooden beams; steps from the left of the courtyard lead to the balcony and upper gallery for a closer view of the ceiling and a frieze depicting amorous couples. A small, decorative window gently illuminates an enormous teaching Buddha; try sitting at his feet and intoning a few gentle *oms*, and imagine two hundred chanting monks doing the same.

Cave 11 The Do Thal (Two Storey) Cave is entered through its third, basement level, not discovered until 1876. Like cave 12 it probably owes its size to competition with the more impressive Hindu caves of the same period. The upper level is the most interesting and is reached by stairs on the left.

Cave 12 The enormous Tin Thal (Three Storey) Cave is entered through a courtyard. The (sometimes locked) shrine on the top floor contains a large seated Buddha flanked by his seven previous incarnations. The walls are carved with relief pictures, as in the Hindu caves.

Hindu Caves

Where calm and contemplation infuses the Buddhist caves, drama and dynamic energy characterise those of the Hindu group (Nos 13-29) in the middle of the escarpment. In scale, creative vision and skill of execution these are in a totally different league to the neighbouring Buddhist and Jain caves.

All these temples were cut from the top down, so that it was never necessary to use scaffolding – the builders began with the roof and moved down to the floor. It's worth contemplating the planning and coordination that was required over several generations – there was no way of adding a panel or a pillar if things didn't work out as expected.

Cave 14 The Ravana Ki Khai cave is a Buddhist vihara converted to a temple dedicated to Siva some time in the 7th century. Familiar scenes include Siva dancing the Tandava, a victory dance over the demon Mahisa; Siva playing chess with his wife Parvati; and Durga defeating the buffalo demon. Vishnu makes several appearances, including as Varaha the boar. Other panels depict the seven 'mother goddesses'; Kala and Kali, the skeletal goddesses of death; and Ravana attempting to shake Kailasa.

Cave 15 The Das Avatara (Ten Incarnations of Vishnu)

Cave is one of the finest at Ellora. The two storey temple is reached through its courtyard by a long flight of steps. Many of the familiar scenes involving Siva are here, including a mesmerising Siva Nataraja, and Siva emerging from a lingam while Vishnu and Brahma pay homage. Several panels also depict Vishnu: resting on a five hooded serpent; rescuing an elephant from a crocodile; and as the man-lion, Narasimha.

Cave 16 The Kailasa Temple is one of the most audacious feats of architecture ever conceived. The idea was not only to build an enormous and fantastically carved representation of Mt Kailasa, Siva's home in the Himalaya, but to create it from a single piece of stone by first cutting three huge trenches into the living rock of the Ellora cliff face and then 'releasing' the shape of the temple using hammers and chisels. The sheer scale of the undertaking is overwhelming. It covers twice the area of the Parthenon in Athens and is 1½ times as high, and it entailed removing 200,000 tonnes of rock!

The temple consists of a huge courtyard, 81m long, 47m wide and 33m high at the back. In the centre, the main temple rises up and is connected to the outer enclosure by a bridge. Around the enclosure are galleries, while towards the front are two large stone elephants with two massive stone 'flagstaffs' flanking the Nandi pavilion, which faces the main shrine. Originally the entire structure was covered in white plaster to more closely resemble the snowy peak of Mt Kailasa.

Apart from the technical genius evident in its creation, Kailasa Temple is remarkable for its prodigious sculptural decoration. Around the temple is a variety of dramatic and finely carved panels, depicting scenes from the Ramayana, the Mahabharata and the adventures of Krishna. The most superb panel depicts the demon king Ravana flaunting his strength by shaking Mt Kailasa. Unimpressed, Siva crushes Ravana's overweening pride by simply flexing a toe.

Other Caves The other Hindu caves pall beside the majesty of the Kailasa, but several of them are worth a quick look. Cave 21, known as the Ramesvara, features interesting interpretations of the familiar Shaivite scenes depicted in the earlier temples. The goddesses Ganga and Yamuna are also depicted; the figure of Ganga, standing on her crocodile or *makara*, is particularly notable.

The very large cave 29, the Dumar Lena, is similar in design to the Elephanta Cave at Mumbai. It is thought to be a transitional model between the simpler hollowed-out caves and the fully developed temples exemplified by the Kailasa. It has a wonderfully peaceful outlook over the nearby waterfall.

Jain Caves

The Jain caves mark the final phase of Ellora. They do not have the drama and high-voltage energy of the best Hindu temples nor are they as ambitious in size, but they balance this with their exceptionally detailed work. There are only five Jain temples, and they're 1km north of the last Hindu temple (cave 29) at the end of the bitumen road.

Cave 30 The Chota Kailasa or Little Kailasa is a poor imitation of the great Kailasa Temple and was never completed. It stands by itself some distance from the other Jain temples, which are clustered closely together.

Cave 32 The Indra Sabha (Assembly Hall of Indra) is the finest of the Jain temples. The ground-floor plan is similar to that of the Kailasa, but the upstairs area, reached by a stairway, is as ornate and richly decorated as downstairs is plain. There are images of the Jain tirthankars Parasnath and Gomateshvara, the latter surrounded by vegetation and wildlife. Inside the shrine is a seated figure of Mahavira, the 24th and last tirthankar, and founder of the Jain religion. Traces of paintings can still be seen on the roof of the temple.

Other Caves Cave 31 is really an extension of 32. Cave 33, the Jagannath Sabha, is similar in plan to 32 and has some particularly well-preserved sculptures. The final temple, the small cave 34, also has interesting sculptures. On the hilltop over the Jain temples a 5m high image of Parasnath looks down on Ellora.

Places to Stay & Eat

Hotel Kailas (☎ (02437) 41043) is the only place to stay at Ellora. It's close to the caves, and has a variety of accommodation. Attractive rooms with attached bath in individual cottages range from Rs 400 to Rs 700 or Rs 900 with air-con. The more expensive rooms have a view of the caves.

The *restaurant* at the hotel has both Indian and Chinese fare (thalis Rs 50), and is cheaper than the nearby *MTDC restaurant* which is intended for tour groups.

The *Milan Restaurant* across the road is better value than either and is adding a bar at the back.

Getting There & Away

See the Aurangabad section for details.

JALGAON
Tel Area Code: 0257

Jalgaon is on the main railway line from Mumbai to the country's north-east. It can make a convenient overnight stop en route to the Ajanta caves, 60km to the south.

Places to Stay

The three railway *retiring rooms* are good value at Rs 50/150 per person without/with air-con.

Hotel Plaza (☎ 227354), about 150m up from the railway station on the left-hand side, is one of several cheap hotels in Station Rd and is the best budget choice. It has spotless rooms with white tiled floors, attached bath and TV for Rs 125/180; extra beds are Rs 60. The manager is friendly and helpful.

Hotel Tourist Resort (☎ 225192) is on Nehru Chowk, up Station Rd and to the right, in all about 300m from the railway station. Rooms range from Rs 175/200 to Rs 265/300 or Rs 415/450 with air-con, all with attached bathroom.

Padmalaya Rest House, just behind the Hotel Tourist Resort, has simple rooms for Rs 100 per person but it's often full.

Hotel Galaxy (☎ 23578), next to the bus station, about one km from the railway station, has rooms with TV for Rs 150/250 and air-con doubles for Rs 450.

Getting There & Away

Several trains between Mumbai and Delhi or Calcutta stop briefly in Jalgaon. The trip to Mumbai (eight hours, 420km) costs Rs 119/410 in 2nd/1st class.

From Jalgaon there are frequent buses to Fardapur (Rs 20, 1½ hours); some of which continue to Ajanta and then on to Aurangabad. The railway and bus stations are about one km apart, a Rs 6 auto-rickshaw ride.

There are plenty of luxury bus offices in Station Rd, leading out of the railway station.

LONAR METEORITE CRATER

At the small village of Lonar, three hours by bus north-east of Jalna or 4½ hours south-

MAHARASHTRA

east of Ajanta, is a huge meteorite crater. Believed to be about 40,000 years old, the crater is two km in diameter and several hundred metres deep, with a shallow lake at the bottom. A plaque found at the rim near the town states that it is 'the only natural hypervelocity impact crater in basaltic rock in the world'.

There are several **Hindu temples** on the crater floor, and langur monkeys, peacocks and gazelles inhabit the bushes by the lake. The crater is only about five minutes walk from the bus stand – ask for directions to Lonar Tank.

It's possible to visit Lonar in a day en route between Fardapur and Aurangabad, but this would be rushing things.

The *MTDC Hotel* at the rim of the crater, about one km from the village, has two basic rooms for Rs 50 or you can spend the night in their 30 person tent for Rs 10 (no bedding provided).

From Lonar there are buses to Buldhana from where it's easy to catch a bus for the bumpy 1½ hour journey to Fardapur. Heading south from Lonar there are direct buses to Jalna, from where there are trains and buses to Aurangabad, a total journey of about five hours.

NAGPUR

Pop: 1.8 million   Tel Area Code: 0712

Situated on the River Nag, Nagpur is the orange-growing capital of India. It was once the capital of the central province, but was later incorporated into Maharashtra. Long ago it was a centre for the aboriginal Gond tribes who remained in power until the early 18th century, and many Gonds still live in the region.

In recent years there has been some desultory agitation for a separate Indian state of Vidarbha, which would have Nagpur as its capital.

On 18 October each year the town is host to thousands of Buddhists who come to celebrate the anniversary of Dr Ambedkar's conversion to Buddhism in 1956. Dr Ambedkar, a low-caste Hindu, was an important figure during the fight for independence, and was Law Minister and leader of the Scheduled Castes. An estimated three million low-caste Hindus followed him in converting to Buddhism.

There is little of interest to attract travellers, except those heading for Gandhi's ashram at Sevagram or taking a break on the long journey across the subcontinent.

Information

There's an MTDC office (☎ 533325) at Sanskritik Bachat Bhava, Sitabuldi, which has no information on Nagpur, but arranges bus and car tours to Wardha, Sevagram, Ramtek and Chikhaldara. There's a foreign exchange desk in the State Bank of India on Kingsway, 250m north of the railway station, open from 10.30 am to 2.30 pm Monday to Friday and until 12.30 pm on Saturday.

Places to Stay

If you arrive by train there's a number of budget and mid-range places to stay within walking distance. Make a right turn as you leave the station concourse, then right again across the bridge over the railway tracks, into Central Ave. A 10 minute walk brings you to a string of hotels.

Hotel Blue Diamond (☎ 727461), at 113 Dosar Chowk near Central Ave, has rooms for Rs 55/90 with common bath, Rs 100/155 with attached bath, or Rs 250/350 with air-con. It has a restaurant and bar.

Blue Moon (☎ 727460) at 129 Central Ave and the adjacent *Midland* (☎ 726131) are similar value.

Hotel Rajdhani (☎ 728773), nearby, has comfortable rooms ranging from Rs 200/325-325/400 or Rs 425/525 with air-con, all with TV and phone.

Pal Palace (☎ 724724) at 25 Central Ave is clean and quiet and is similarly priced.

Rawell Continental (☎ 523845), 7 Dhantoli, Wardha Rd, is centrally air-conditioned and more expensive, with rooms for Rs 750/900 and suites for Rs 1500.

The *Hotel Centre Point* (☎ 520910; fax 523093), 24 Central Bazaar Rd, Ramdaspeth, is about three km from the railway station. It has standard rooms for Rs 700/900 or Rs 850/1050 with air-con and suites for Rs 1800/2200. There's a swimming pool, restaurant and bar.

Jagsons Regency (☎ 228111; fax 224524), opposite the airport, is the city's top hotel and is slightly more expensive.

Getting There & Away

Indian Airlines (☎ 533962) has flights daily to Delhi (US$120) and Mumbai (US$100) and three times a week to Hyderabad (US$80), Calcutta (US$135) and Bhubaneshwar (US$100).

Nagpur Junction railway station and the main MSRTC bus terminal are roughly two km apart. Buses for Madhya Pradesh operate from a stand less than one km due south of the railway station. There are trains to Bangalore, Mumbai, Calcutta, Delhi and Hyderabad, among other places.

RAMTEK

About 40km north-east of Nagpur, Ramtek has a number of picturesque 600 year old **temples** surmounting the Hill of Rama. The old British cantonment of Kemtee is nearby, and a **memorial** to the Sanskrit dramatist Kalidasa is just along the road from the MTDC holiday resort which has a spectacular view of the town.

The *MTDC Holiday Resort* (☎ (07265) 55213) has dormitory beds and a few basic rooms; bookings can also be made through the MTDC office in Nagpur.

Regular buses make the one hour trip between Ramtek and the MSRTC bus stand in Nagpur.

SEVAGRAM

If you are at all interested in the life and philosophy of Mahatma Gandhi, it's well worth making the long trek to the heart of India to visit Sevagram, the Village of Service, where Gandhi established his ashram in 1933. For the 15 years from then until India achieved independence, Gandhi's headquarters was in some ways the alternative capital of India – the British considered it important

enough to install a phonebox here with a hotline to Delhi.

The ashram encompasses 100 acres of farmland, as well as residences and research centres. The original adobe huts of the ashram are still preserved, as are the Mahatma's personal effects, including his famous spinning wheel and spectacles.

The Centre of Science for Villages (Magan Sangrahalaya) is a museum intended to explain and develop Gandhi's ideals of village-level economics. There's a photo exhibit of events in the Mahatma's life at Mahadev Bhavan, which is beside the Kasturba Gandhi Hospital.

Ashramites can provide excellent guided tours of the ashram, as well as giving an explanation of Gandhi's life and his ideas. A non-denominational prayer service is held daily at 4.45 am and 6 pm under the pipal tree planted by Gandhi. Hand-spun *khadi* is for sale at the ashram, as are volumes of Gandhi's writings.

At **Paunar**, just three km from Sevagram, is the ashram of Vinoba Bhave, Gandhi's disciple. This persistent soul walked throughout India trying to persuade rich landlords to hand over tracts of land for redistribution to the landless and poor. The ashram, which is run almost entirely by women, is dedicated to the spirit of *swarajya*, or rural self-sufficiency.

On the banks of the nearby Paunar River is a **memorial** marking the place where some of Gandhi's ashes were scattered; hundreds of thousands of pilgrims visit the spot every February 12 to mark the anniversary of the Mahatma's death.

Places to Stay & Eat

The basic, clean *Yatri Nivas* at the Sevagram ashram offers accommodation and vegetarian meals for a nominal sum; donations are also welcome. Similar accommodation (though women are preferred) is available at Paunar.

The *MTDC* (☎ (07125) 3172) also offers basic accommodation in Wardha. Rooms are Rs 50/100.

Getting There & Away

The ashram can be reached from either Wardha or Sevagram railway stations, both of which are on the Central Railway. Express trains from Nagpur to Sevagram (76km) take a little over an hour; express MSRTC buses

also run between Nagpur and Wardha (2½ hours).

From Sevagram station an auto-rickshaw will cost around Rs 50. There are regular local buses to the ashram from Wardha (eight km; 20 minutes).

Goa

The former Portuguese enclave of Goa, one of India's gems, has enjoyed a prominent place in the travellers' lexicon for many years. The main reason for this is its magnificent palm-fringed beaches and renowned 'travellers' scene'. Yet it offers much more than just the hedonism of sun, sand and sea. Goa has a character quite distinct from the rest of India. Despite more than three decades of 'liberation' from Portuguese colonial rule, Roman Catholicism remains a major religion in Goa, skirts far outnumber saris, and the people display an easy-going tropical indulgence, humour and civility which you'll find hard to beat, even in Kerala.

Gleaming, whitewashed churches with Portuguese-style facades pepper the hillsides. There are paddy fields, dense coconut palm groves, and crumbling forts guarding rocky capes and estuaries. Markets are lively, colourful affairs, and siesta is widely observed during the hot afternoon hours. Carnival explodes onto the streets for four riotous days and nights prior to Lent.

There seems to be a total lack of the excessive shyness which Hindu women display towards men, and there are very good reasons for that. One of them relates to the Goan property laws which ensure that a married woman is entitled to 50% of the couple's estate – a far cry from what applies in the rest of India.

Goa has one of the highest literacy rates and boasts the third-highest GNP in the country. Farming, fishing, tourism and iron-ore mining form the basis of the economy, although the latter two sources of income are sometimes incompatible with the former. Mining has caused damage to paddy fields, and the five-star tourist resorts, with their swimming pools, have placed a heavy strain on water supplies needed by farmers.

Goans are better informed about their environment and what threatens it than many other Indians, and are more prepared to fight

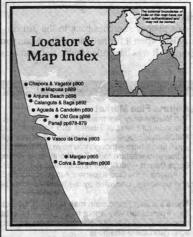

GOA AT A GLANCE

Population: 1.3 million
Area: 3659 sq km
Capital: Panaji
Main Languages: Konaki & Marathi, with a smattering of English & Portuguese
Literacy Rate: 77%
Best Time to Go: October to May – though April and May are very hot

Locator & Map Index

- Chapora & Vagator p900
- Mapusa p889
- Anjuna Beach p896
- Calangute & Baga p892
- Aguada & Candolim p890
- Old Goa p886
- Panaji pp878-879
- Vasco da Gama p903
- Margao p905
- Colva & Benaulim p908

The external boundaries of India on this map have not been authenticated and may not be correct.

Highlights

- Beaches to suit all tastes with a wide range of accommodation from five-star resorts to basic rooms
- The magnificent Portuguese cathedrals of Old Goa
- Nightlife – from laid-back beach bars to full moon raves under the coconut palms
- Some of the best seafood in India

Festivals

See Festivals boxed section later in this chapter.

for its protection. The Konkan Railway Corporation, currently completing the new railway line along the west coast to link Mumbai (Bombay) with Mangalore, had more trouble getting planning permission for the route through the tiny state of Goa than anywhere else on the 760km line. For an excellent overview of the state of the Goan environment, get a copy of *Fish Curry & Rice*, which is available from most bookshops.

Goa was part of the Union Territory of Goa, Daman & Diu until 1987 when it became the 25th state of the Indian Union. Daman & Diu remain a Union Territory, despite having the governor of Goa as lieutenant governor, and are covered in the Gujarat chapter of this book.

History

Goa's history stretches back to the 3rd century BC when it formed part of the Mauryan Empire. It was later ruled by the Satavahanas of Kolhapur at the beginning of the Christian era and eventually passed to the Chalukyans of Badami, who controlled it from 580 to 750 AD. Over the next few centuries it was ruled successively by the Shilharas, the Kadambas and the Chalukyans of Kalyani.

Goa fell to the Muslims for the first time in 1312, but the invaders were forced to evacuate it in 1370 by Harihara I of the Vijayanagar Empire, whose capital was at Hampi in present-day Karnataka state. The Vijayanagar rulers held on to Goa for nearly 100 years, and its harbours became important landing places for ships carrying Arabian horses to Hampi to strengthen the Vijayanagar cavalry.

In 1469, Goa was conquered by the Bahmani Sultans of Gulbarga. When this dynasty

---

A REGIONAL HIGHLIGHT

Anjuna Flea Market

The Wednesday flea market at Anjuna is a major attraction for people from all the Goan beaches. It's a wonderful blend of Tibetan and Kashmiri traders, colourful Gujarati tribal women and blissed-out 1960s-style hippies. It's quite a scene. Whatever you need, from a used paperback to a new swimsuit, you'll find it here – though you have to bargain hard to get a reasonable deal. There's also lots of good Indian and western food. Traditional-style fishing boats are available for transport to the market from Baga Beach – you'll see notices advertising this in Baga's restaurants.

Anjuna is the Goa experience in concentrated form, a syrup of hippies, ravers, handicrafts, hard-sell and sunshine, undiluted by the harsh realities of rural India. One traveller described it like this:

There's a San Franciscan man down on the hot baked sand. He has a brown beard and talks in that San Franciscan way about how he was here back in '71 – 'we were just saying, weren't we Karen, how it still has that *feel* about it ... there was an earthquake then, while I was away, now here I am again and there she goes'.

Karen laughs. She was talking to someone else in that animated boisterous San Franciscan way about delegating and networking, but now she joins in. 'His friends won't let him out anymore. They say he's the thread holding the plates together.' A whole circle of 40-somethings throw their hair back and laugh while a Brahmin bull noses around the circle's outside.

Close by on the sand, an Indian boy with Downs syndrome shadow boxes a dozen invisible Bruce Lees and holds a few enemies above his head before pitching them onto the sand metres away. A small crowd of kids has gathered to watch. They're workers resting. They're still swaddled head to toe in embroidered hats, waistcoats, lungis, tablecloths and shoulder bags, and rapt in the impromptu martial arts performance. The boy next to me sparkles with mirrors and giggles, and when I look at him he forgets to say, 'yes madam you looking now cheap price'.

A little Indian girl struggles up the beach carrying what looks like an old suitcase. She plops down on the sand in front of us and grins. Her suitcase is a squeezebox, and she works it with her small brown hand and sings out loud a plaintive song.

Up at the market the wind is blowing the silks around a bit, but the embroidered blankets suck in the heat and there's nowhere to hide from the desperate haggling – 'look sister, look madam, you *look*'.

One of the hippy stallholders starts to lose it in the too-bright sunlight. 'He hit me with the fucking bamboo!' he screams. 'Argh!' he screams again. His stall is right next to the one that has trip-inspired mushroom T-shirts and other surrealistic designs. The man selling these is so calm and at peace with the world that he can sit in full sun for hours, without having to move, nor sell a T-shirt. ∎

Goa

0   5   10 km

To Mumbai

MAHARASHTRA

KARNATAKA

Tarakhol
Querim
Pernem
Arambol
Chopdem
Slolim
Chapora
Vagator
Anjuna
Baga
Calangute
Candolim
Sinquerim Beach
Fort Aguada
Reis Magos
Gaspar Dias
Dona Paula

Pernem Railway Station
Aldona Fort
Mapusa Road Railway Station
Corjuem
Bicholim
Mapusa
Aldona
Shri Koteshwar Temple
Mayem Lake
Sanquelim
Valpoi

To Savantvadi (32km)

Panaji
Old Goa
Pilar

Mandovi River

Shri Magesh Temple
Shri Mahalsa Temple
Safa Shahouri Masjid
Ponda
Shri Shantadurga Temple
Shri Ramnath Temple

Bondla Wildlife Sanctuary
Tiskai

To Londa (111km), Dharwar (146km) & Belgaum (155km)

Mormugao
Vasco da Gama
Dabolim
Bogmalo

Agassaim
Cortalim
Verna

Cansaulim Railway Station

Molen

To Londa Junction & Castle Rock

Kulem
Dudhsagar Falls

Zuari River

Rachol
River

Molen Wildlife Sanctuary

Majorda
Colva
Benaulim

Margao

Sanvordem

Arabian Sea

Varca
Cavelossim
Mobor
Betul

Chinchinim
Cuncolim
Balli Railway Station

Sanguem
Quepem

Cabo da Rama

Agonda
Palolem
Canacona Island

Konkan Railway

Shri Mallikarjuna Temple
Chaudi
Cotigao Wildlife Sanctuary

Canacona Railway Station
Talpona

Polem

KARNATAKA

To Karwar (13km) & Jog Falls (489km)

Festivals

The *Christian* festivals in Goa take place on the following dates:

Date	Event
6 January	Feast of Three Kings at Reis Magos, Cansaulim and Chandor
2 February	Feast of Our Lady of Candelaria at Pomburpa
February/March	Carnival
Monday after 5th Sunday in Lent	Procession of the Franciscan Order at Old Goa
1st Sunday after Easter	Feast of Jesus of Nazareth at Siridao
16 days after Easter	Feast of Our Lady of Miracles at Mapusa
24 August	Festival of Novidades
1st fortnight of October	Fama de Menino Jesus at Colva
3rd Wednesday of November	Feast of Our Lady of the Rosary
3 December	Feast of St Francis Xavier at Old Goa
8 December	Feast of Our Lady of Immaculate Conception at Panaji and Margao
25 December	Christmas

Hindu festivals are harder to date because they depend on the Indian lunar calendar, but they include:

Date	Event
January	Festival of *Shantadurga Prasann* at the small village of Fatorpa, south of Margao in Quepem province. There is a night-time procession of chariots bearing the goddess, and as many as 100,000 people flock to the festival. The Shri Bodgeshwar *zatra*, or temple festival, takes place just south of Mapusa.
February	The three day zatra of Shri Mangesh takes place in the lavish temple of that name in the Ponda district. In the old Fontainhas district of Panaji, the Maruti zatra draws huge and colourful crowds. Maruti is another name for Hanuman.
March	In Goa, the festival of *Holi* is called *Shigmo*. There's a parade in Panaji and numerous temple festivals around Goa.

During the colourful and dramatic Procession of Umbrellas at Cuncolim, south of Margao, a solid silver image of Shantadurga is carried in procession over the hills to the original temple site wrecked by the Portuguese in 1580.

broke up, the area passed to the Adil Shahis of Bijapur, who made Goa Velha their second capital. The present Secretariat building in Panaji is the former palace of Adil Shah, and it was later taken over by the Portuguese viceroys as their official residence.

The Portuguese arrived in Goa in 1510 under the command of Alfonso de Albuquerque. They had tried to establish a base further south, but were opposed by the Zamorin of Calicut and faced stiff competition from the Turks, who controlled the trade routes across the Indian Ocean at the time.

Blessed as it is by natural harbours and wide rivers, Goa was the ideal base for the seafaring Portuguese, who wanted to control the spice route from the east. They were also possessed with the strong desire to spread Christianity. Jesuit missionaries led by St Francis Xavier arrived in 1542. For a while, Portuguese control was limited to a small area around Old Goa, but by the middle of the 16th century it had expanded to include the provinces of Bardez and Salcete.

The eventual ousting of the Turks and the fortunes made from the spice trade led to

Goa's golden age. The colony became the viceregal seat of the Portuguese Empire of the east, which included various East African port cities, East Timor and Macau. Decline set in, however, due to competition from the British, French and Dutch in the 17th century, combined with Portugal's inability to adequately service its far-flung empire.

Goa reached its present size in the 18th century after a series of annexations. In 1763, the provinces of Ponda, Sanguem, Quepem and Canacona were added, followed by Pednem, Bicholim and Satari in 1788.

The Marathas nearly vanquished the Portuguese in the late 18th century and there was a brief occupation by the British during the Napoleonic Wars in Europe. But it was not until 1961, when they were ejected by India, that the Portuguese finally disappeared from the subcontinent. The enclaves of Daman and Diu were also taken over at the same time.

Beaches

Goa is justifiably famous for its beaches, and westerners have been flocking to them since the early 1960s. They sometimes suffer from bad press in both the western and Indian media because of the real or imagined nefarious activities of a small minority of visitors.

While the beaches are still awash with budget travellers of all ages and degrees of affluence (or penury, depending on your point of view), there's also a large contingent of western package tourists who arrive by direct charter flight and stay in the resorts which have sprung up in the main centres. Indians from outside Goa also now come here in ever-increasing numbers.

The only problem is deciding which beach to head for. Much depends on how long you intend to stay. Renting a room at a hotel is an expensive way of staying long term and most budget travellers prefer either to rent a simple room at one of the beach cafes or to rent a private house on a monthly basis (shared, if desired, with a group of friends). Rooms and houses can be found at all the main centres, but there's heavy demand for the latter in the winter (high) season, so it might take you several days to track one down.

There's a wide range of accommodation at Colva, Benaulim, Calangute and Baga. Places to stay are generally more basic at Anjuna, Vagator and Chapora, which is where travellers tend to congregate. It's at these latter beaches that the full-moon parties are held. If you fancy somewhere that's less of a scene, Benaulim is an excellent choice. There's

---

Security

Goa's booming tourist industry has brought with it inevitable problems, crime being one of them. The temptation to get hold of tourist dollars has proved too strong in some cases, and recently there has been a spate of robberies (some of them violent). Much more disturbing has been a number of attacks on women travellers – many organisers of beach parties now strongly advise women not to wander off on their own.

The Goans are understandably concerned by the recent developments, and blame the incidents on criminals from neighbouring states. Some measures have been taken to discourage further attacks, although realistically their effectiveness is doubtful. Limited street lighting has been installed, and there are now security patrols on some beaches.

To put all this into context, Goa is still fairly safe compared to many places one could think of, and most visitors will have no problems whatsoever. It pays, however, to be wary. Don't walk alone along the beach at night, or go unaccompanied along dark, unlit village lanes if you can help it. The road from L'Amour Beach Resort back towards the village at Benaulim has been the scene of several muggings, in some of which chilli powder has been thrown into the eyes of the victims before their bags were snatched. If you are staying in a reasonable hotel or family house where there is a safe or similar facility, it is worth leaving your passport etc there rather than carrying it with you all the time. Women travellers should not walk alone in deserted areas at night.

Finally, if you're here in the low season avoid staying in isolated accommodation near the beach. During high season beach huts are fine because there are other travellers around, but there have been several cases of thieves targeting foreigners staying on their own. ■

good accommodation and the beach is relatively peaceful.

All these beaches are touristed, so if you want something quieter, you'll have to look further afield. Near the northern tip of Goa, Arambol (or Harmal as it's spelt on some maps) is still pretty much undeveloped, and there are empty stretches of sand both to the north and south of it. Betul, south of Colva, and Palolem, further south, are also good places to head for.

The Aguada, Bogmalo, Varca and Cavelossim beaches are essentially for affluent tourists staying at beach resorts.

Nudism & Local Sensibilities

Don't make the mistake of thinking that because Goa is so welcoming, friendly and liberal, that you're at liberty to disregard local sensibilities and prance around in your birthday suit whenever the mood takes you. Too many people did that in the late 1960s and 70s, and Goa became (in)famous for it. Signs on the main beaches now warn that nudism is illegal, and although that technically also includes going topless some women still do.

Ganja

In an effort to sanitise Goa for the package tourism market, there has recently been a spate of police crackdowns on drug users. Most of the 160 inmates in Aguada jail, 12 of them foreigners, are there on drug-related offences. One traveller wrote from the police lock-up in Mapusa to say that in Goa you can no longer expect to get off by paying a little baksheesh if you're caught. He was being held for possession of 15g of charas (hashish).

The standard sentence for possession of even a small amount of any drug is 10 years (plus a fine of Rs 100,000), and the police are increasingly targeting likely beaches and events. Think very carefully before succumbing to the weed which is, of course, still available. Read the warning in the Facts for the Visitor chapter.

Medical Services

If you're unlucky enough to be injured in a motorcycle accident – relatively common in Goa – the best bone specialist in Goa is Dr Bhale (☎ (0832) 217053), who runs a 24 hour X-ray clinic at Porvorim, four km north of Panaji on the NH17 road to Mapusa. The only brain scanner in the state is in Vasco da Gama, 30km from Panaji, at the Salgonkar Medical Research Centre (☎ (0834) 512524). There's currently nowhere to treat spinal injuries in Goa.

Accommodation

Accommodation prices in Goa are based on high, middle and low seasons. The high season covers the period from mid-December to late January, the middle (shoulder) period from October to mid-December and February to June, and the low season from July to September. Unless otherwise stated, prices quoted in this chapter are high season rates. If you're in Goa during the rest of the

---

Water Conservation

Take great care to use water as sparingly as possible because Goa's supplies are severely limited. Tourism in general has placed a heavy strain on the state's water resources, but the upmarket hotels carry most of the blame. In some areas, guests languish beside Olympic-sized swimming pools while just outside the gates the water supply to the locals is limited to a few hours a day. Some of the bigger hotels have drilled deep tube wells to syphon off their own supplies, but the effect has been to lower the water table in the area. Wells have dried up in some villages and been polluted with salt water in others.

Don't leave taps running. Even if your hotel has a bathtub in the bathroom, use the shower instead, or, best of all, use a bucket of water. If you're selecting a package tour or choosing an upmarket hotel to stay at, consider whether you want to condone the use of a swimming pool in such circumstances. Who needs a pool anyway when the Arabian Sea is just a short walk away? ■

year, then count on discounts of about 25% in the middle season and up to 60% in the low season.

At all times of year, there's a 5% luxury tax on rooms over Rs 100, 10% on rooms over Rs 500, and 15% for those over Rs 800. For most of the low budget places, the prices quoted here include this tax, but in mid and high budget hotels you can expect tax to be added to the bill.

Another thing to bear in mind is checkout times, which vary considerably and have no relation to the type of hotel you are staying in. Checkout times in some places can be as early as 8 am or as late as noon; while in other establishments, you get to rent the room on a 24 hour basis.

Getting There & Away

Air Goa's international airport, Dabolim, is 29km from Panaji, on the coast near Vasco da Gama. Most of India's domestic airlines operate services here, as well as several charter companies which fly into Goa direct from the UK and Germany.

There are numerous flights between Goa and Mumbai. Indian Airlines has a daily service (and an additional flight on Monday, Tuesday and Wednesday) for US$65. Also with daily services is Jet Airways (US$80), NEPC Skyline (US$76) and, if they're back in the air, Modiluft.

Indian Airlines has daily direct flights to and from Delhi (US$190), and flights to Bangalore five times a week (US$80), daily flights to Cochin (US$95) and five flights a week to Chennai (Madras) for US$110. Spanair has four flights a week to and from Pune (US$90).

Bus See the Getting There & Away section under Panaji for details of long-distance bus travel.

Train Goa's rail links with the rest of the country have been disrupted over the last few years by two major engineering projects. The first, the conversion of the lines from metre to broad gauge, is now complete.

The second project, the new 760km Konkan Railway from Mangalore, along the coast through Goa to Mumbai, is nearing completion. This is not easy terrain for railway construction: more than 10% of the line runs through tunnels, and 145 bridges have had to be built. The line is currently open from the north and from the south as far as the borders with Goa, the final hurdle being two tunnels in Goa. When these are completed, which should be by the time you read this, it should be possible to take a train from Mumbai and reach Goa 10 hours later. If tunnelling is seriously disrupted by the monsoon, however, the line may not be fully open until 1998.

Now that the conversion to broad gauge is complete, long-haul journeys are faster. Goa's two main stations are at Vasco da Gama and

---

Goan Food & Drink

Although food in Goa is much like food anywhere else in India, there are several local specialities, including the popular pork vindaloo. Other pork specialities include the Goan sausage, or *chourisso*, and the pig's liver dish known as *sarpotel*. *Xacuti* is a chicken or meat dish; *bangra* is Goan mackerel; *sanna* are rice 'cupcakes' soaked in palm toddy before cooking; *dodol* and *bebinca* are special Christmas sweets; and *Moira kela* are cooking plantains (banana-like fruit) from Moira village in Bardez. The plaintains were probably introduced from Africa and can be found in the vegetable market in Panaji close to the Indian Airlines office.

Although the ready availability (and low price) of commercially produced alcohol contrasts markedly with most other parts of India, the Goans also brew their own local varieties. Most common of these is *feni*, a spirit made from coconut or cashews. A bottle bought from a liquor shop costs only slightly more than a bottle of beer bought at a restaurant. Reasonably palatable wines are also being turned out. The dry white is not bad; the red is basically a port. As always, the quality depends on the price you pay. ∎

Margao. Seats and sleepers can be booked at either of these, or at the railway out-agency at counter No 5 in the Panaji bus terminal.

Trains to Bangalore take about 15 hours. Fares for the 689km trip are Rs 185/610 in sleeper class/1st class, or Rs 805 for air-con two-tier sleeper. The 720km trip to Mumbai (Rs 140/614 for 2nd/1st class) will take just 10 hours along the new Konkan Railway. The most useful stations in Goa are Mapusa Road for Mapusa, Old Goa for Panaji, and Margao.

Getting to Delhi from Goa takes about 44 hours and the fare for the 2200km trip is Rs 348/1410 in sleeper class/1st class, and Rs 1675 for air-con.

Taxi It takes 14 hours to drive the 600km from Mumbai to Goa, but this can be done over two days. You'll have to pay for the taxi's return trip, so the cost will be around Rs 6000. Shop around for the taxi that offers you the lowest rate per km.

Boat A flashy new catamaran service came into operation in November 1994 on the route between Mumbai and Panaji. Recently taken over by Frank Shipping (although most of the offices and timetables are still labelled in the name of the previous company, Damania), it does the return journey five times a week from October to May. From Goa to Mumbai it sails every Monday, Wednesday, Friday, Saturday and Sunday, departing at 10 am and arriving in Mumbai at 5.30 pm. Going the other way, on Tuesday and Thursday it departs Mumbai at 10 am, arriving in Panaji at 5.30 pm; on Friday, Saturday and Sunday, it leaves Mumbai at 10.30 pm, arriving at 6.30 am. Bookings can be made through travel agents or at the company's offices in Mumbai (☎ (022) 374 3737) and Panaji (☎ (0832) 228711).

It's an impressive service, but since the boat is only a few years old (Norwegian-designed and Singapore-built), tickets aren't cheap: Rs 1050/1250 for economy/business class. It's certainly more comfortable than going by plane but, apart from the half-hour cruise up the Mandovi River, the trip is really about as interesting as flying. Once out at sea, the catamaran is obliged to stay at least 15km from the coast to avoid fishing fleets, so there's nothing to see.

Getting Around

Bus The state-run Kadamba bus company is the main operator, although there are also many private companies. Buses are cheap and run to just about everywhere. Services are frequent and destinations at the bus stands are in English, so there are no worries about finding the bus you want. They are, however, fairly slow because they make frequent stops.

Car Rental Self-drive car rental is available in Goa, although it's expensive. Several companies have counters at the airport. Hertz (☎ (0832) 223998) charges from Rs 5950 for a week for a small Maruti-Suzuki. Wheels (☎ (0832) 224304) offer a three day rental with unlimited mileage for Rs 2700. It's often cheaper, however, to rent a taxi for a specific trip.

Motorcycle Rental Hiring a motorcycle in Goa is easy, and popular among many long-term travellers. The machines available are old Enfields (which often need loving care on the spark plugs), more modern Yamaha 100s and gearless Kinetic Honda scooters. Obviously what you pay for – with certain exceptions – is what you get, and prices also vary according to season. In peak season, on a daily basis, you're looking at up to Rs 300 for a scooter, Rs 400 for the smaller bikes and Rs 500 for an Enfield. Some places need your passport and a sizeable deposit before they'll let you go; others just want to know where you're staying.

While most bikes will have some sort of insurance, if you're involved in an accident you'll probably be required to pay for the damage to the rental bike, at the very least. Classic Bike Adventure (fax 262076), Casa Tres Amigos, Assagao, deals mainly with organised two to three week tours on well-maintained Enfields, but will sometimes also rent bikes. See the Getting Around chapter for details of their bike tours.

You should be aware that India has the worst record for road accidents in the world. Although Goan lanes are probably a little safer than the Grand Trunk Road, inexperienced, helmetless, foreigners on motorcycles are extremely vulnerable. Each season, more than a few tourists travel home in a box via the state mortuary in Panaji. Never forget that the Highway Code in India can be reduced to one essential truth – 'might is right'. On a motorcycle, you're pretty low on the hierarchy. Also make sure that the machine that you rent is in a reasonable state of repair, and watch out for pedestrians and animals on the roads. Goan pigs have an annoying habit of suddenly dashing out of the bushes and across the road when you're least expecting them.

Make sure that you carry the necessary paperwork (licence, registration and insurance) at all times because licence checks on foreigners are a lucrative source of baksheesh for the police. They may try for anything up to Rs 1000, but can usually be bargained down. Places to avoid are the towns (particularly Panaji, Margao and Mapusa) and Anjuna on market day (Wednesday).

If you're in the market for a new or used motorcycle, try Auto Guides on Dr Dada Vaidya Rd, near the Hotel Samrat, in Panaji. A new Enfield will set you back between Rs 47,000 and Rs 53,000, but they can arrange to ship it home for you.

Motorcycle Taxi Goa is the one place in India where motorcycles are a licensed form of taxi. If you don't mind travelling this way, they are much cheaper than other transport if you are travelling alone, and backpacks are no problem. Licensed motorcycles have a yellow front mudguard and are found in large numbers throughout the state.

Bicycle There are plenty of places to hire bicycles in all the major towns and beaches in Goa. Charges are around Rs 40 for a full day.

Boat One of the joys of travelling around Goa are the combined passenger/vehicle ferries which cross the many rivers in this small state. There are, however, bridges being built over several rivers which will eventually put the ferries out of business. The main ferries are:

Siolim to Chopdem – you may need this ferry for Arambol and places to the north. Services run at least every half hour from about 6.30 am until 10 pm; the crossing takes 10 minutes. Tickets cost Rs 0.75 for passengers; Rs 1.50 for motorcycles.

Querim to Terekhol – this ferry accesses Terekhol Fort, in the far north of the state. Services run approximately every half hour.

Dona Paula to Mormugao – this ferry runs between September and May only. There are frequent crossings but they are erratic and, at certain times of the day, you could find yourself waiting about two hours. The crossing takes 30 to 45 minutes; buses wait on either side for the arrival of boats. This is a passenger ferry only, but it's a pleasant way of getting from Panaji to Vasco da Gama. It stops running around 5 pm.

Old Goa to Diwar – ferries go every half hour.

Other Ferries – approximately 20 other ferry services operate throughout the state. These include: Panaji to Betim; Aldona to Corjuem; Pomburpa to Chorao; and Ribandar to Chorao.

North Goa

Goa neatly splits itself into two districts: North and South Goa. North Goa has the state capital, Panaji; the former capital of Old Goa, with its interesting churches and cathedrals; and a string of beaches that runs right up the coast to Maharashtra. These range from the developed places like Calangute, Baga and Candolim, to beaches such as Anjuna, Chapora and Vagator, which attract a colourful crowd of long-term residents and travellers. It's in these last three places that those famed midnight raves take place on full-moon nights. Arambol, in the far north, is rather quieter.

PANAJI (Panjim)
Pop: 93,000   Tel Area Code: 0832
Panaji is one of India's smallest and most pleasant state capitals. Built on the south

bank of the wide Mandovi River, it officially became the capital of Goa in 1843, though the Portuguese viceroys shifted their Residence from the outskirts of Old Goa to the former palace of Adil Shah in Panaji as early as 1759.

While most people pass through Panaji on their way to the beaches or to Old Goa (nine km to the east), the town is well worth a visit for its own sake. The atmosphere is easygoing and the people are very friendly. In the oldest part of the town, the Portuguese heritage has survived remarkably well: there are narrow winding streets, old houses with

overhanging balconies and red-tiled roofs, whitewashed churches and numerous small bars and cafes. Portuguese signs are still visible over many premises.

Information

Tourist Offices The tourist office (☎ 225715) is in the government-run Patto Tourist Home between the bus terminal and Ourem River (it's signposted). The staff here are keen and their information is reliable, but it is closed at weekends. Excellent maps of Goa and Panaji are available for Rs 12. There's also a useful tourist counter and railway out-agency

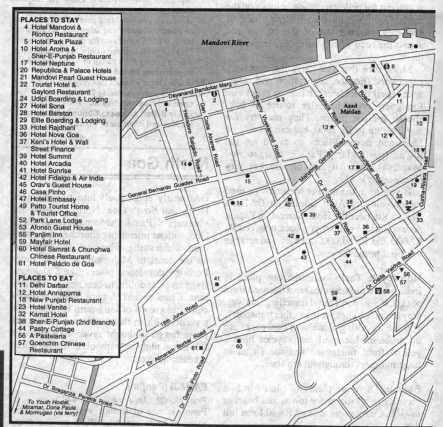

PLACES TO STAY
4 Hotel Mandovi &
  Riorico Restaurant
5 Hotel Park Plaza
10 Hotel Aroma &
  Sher-E-Punjab Restaurant
17 Hotel Neptune
20 Republica & Palace Hotels
21 Mandovi Pearl Guest House
22 Tourist Hotel &
  Gaylord Restaurant
24 Udipi Boarding & Lodging
27 Hotel Sona
28 Hotel Bareton
29 Elite Boarding & Lodging
33 Hotel Rajdhani
36 Hotel Nova Goa
37 Keni's Hotel & Wall
  Street Finance
39 Hotel Summit
40 Hotel Arcadia
41 Hotel Sunrise
42 Hotel Fidalgo & Air India
45 Orav's Guest House
46 Casa Pinho
47 Hotel Embassy
49 Patto Tourist Home
  & Tourist Office
52 Park Lane Lodge
53 Afonso Guest House
59 Panjim Inn
59 Mayfair Hotel
60 Hotel Samrat & Chunghwa
  Chinese Restaurant
61 Hotel Palácio de Goa

PLACES TO EAT
11 Delhi Darbar
12 Hotel Annapurna
18 New Punjab Restaurant
23 Hotel Venite
32 Kamat Hotel
38 Sher-E-Punjab (2nd Branch)
44 Pastry Cottage
56 A Pastelaria
57 Goenchin Chinese
  Restaurant

Mandovi River

Dayanand Bandokar Marg

Heliodoro Salgado Road

Gen Costa Alvares Road

General Bernardo Guedes Road

Ormuz Road

Malaca Road

Azad Maidan

Swami Vivekanand Road

Mahatma Gandhi Road

Dr P Shirgaonkar Road

Dr Pissurlekar Road

Cunha-Rivara Road

Dr Dada Vaidya Road

18th June Road

Dr Atmaram Borkar Road

Dr Gama Pinto Road

Dr Braganza Pereira Road

To Youth Hostel,
Miramar, Dona Paula
& Mormugao (via ferry)

GOA

at the bus terminal. It's open Monday to Saturday from 9 to 11.30 am and from 1.30 to 5 pm, and on Sunday from 9.30 am to 2 pm. A third counter, at the airport, is open for incoming flights.

There's a Government of India tourist office (☎ 223412) in the Communidade Building, Church Square. Also on this square is the Karnataka state tourist office (☎ 224110).

Money The State Bank of India is open from 10 am to 2 pm (until noon on Saturday). Thomas Cook opens from 9.30 am to 6 pm Monday to Saturday, and on Sunday (October to March only) from 10 am to 5 pm. Wall Street Finance is open 9.30 am to 6 pm Monday to Saturday.

Post & Communications The poste restante at the GPO is efficient. It's open from 9 am to 5 pm, Monday to Saturday.

International telephone calls are handled at the 24 hour central telegraph office, but it is quicker and only marginally more expensive to use one of the many private STD/ISD booths around town.

At Comtech Services (☎ 230431) you can send and receive faxes and email (Rs 45 per

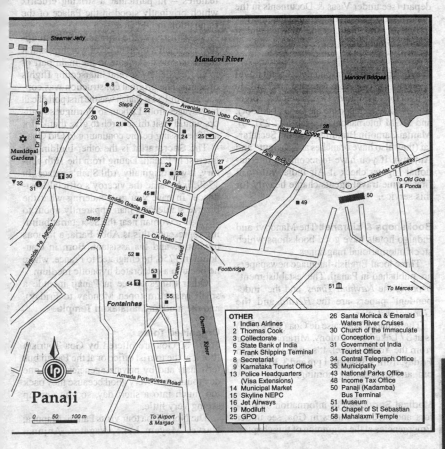

OTHER
1 Indian Airlines
2 Thomas Cook
3 Collectorate
6 State Bank of India
7 Frank Shipping Terminal
8 Secretariat
9 Karnataka Tourist Office
13 Police Headquarters
    (Visa Extensions)
14 Municipal Market
15 Skyline NEPC
16 Jet Airways
19 Modiluft
25 GPO
26 Santa Monica & Emerald
    Waters River Cruises
30 Church of the Immaculate
    Conception
31 Government of India
    Tourist Office
34 Central Telegraph Office
35 Municipality
43 National Parks Office
48 Income Tax Office
50 Panaji (Kadamba)
    Bus Terminal
51 Museum
54 Chapel of St Sebastian
58 Mahalaxmi Temple

Panaji

0   50   100 m

To Airport & Margao

page). It's 50m west of Hotel Arcadia on MG Rd.

Visa Extensions & Tax Clearance Visa extensions are not granted as a matter of course in Panaji. The more respectable you look, the more your application is likely to be viewed favourably. If you're unsuccessful here, Mumbai and Bangalore are the nearest alternatives. The Foreigners' Registration Office is in the centre of Panaji and is open from 9.30 am to 1 pm, Monday to Friday.

If you've stayed in India so long that you need a tax clearance certificate before you depart (see under Visas & Documents in the Facts for the Visitor chapter), the Income Tax Office is in the Shanta Building at the end of Emidio Gracia Rd.

Travel Agencies Reasonably efficient travel agencies include Aero Mundial (☎ 224831) at the Hotel Mandovi; Georgeson & Georgeson (☎ 223742) opposite the GPO (1st floor); and MGM International Travels (☎ 225150), Mamai Camotin Building, near the Secretariat (they also have branches at Calangute and Anjuna). If you have to reconfirm international flights, check if Air India will do it first. Some travel agents charge heavily for this service.

Bookshops & Libraries The Mandovi and Fidalgo hotels have good bookshops which stock international magazines.

Three local English-language newspapers are published in Panaji. The 'establishment' paper is the *Navhind Times*, and the 'independent' papers are the *Herald* and the *Gomantak Times*.

The Alliance Française de Goa (☎ 223274) is at 37 Lake View Colony, Miramar, not far from the Youth Hostel. It's open Monday to Friday, from 9.30 am to 1 pm and 3.30 to 6.30 pm, and on Saturday morning.

Medical Services For information on doctors and medical clinics in Goa, see under Emergencies at the beginning of this chapter.

Things to See
The old district, **Fontainhas**, is to the west of the Ourem River. It's an interesting area to walk around, with narrow streets, tiled buildings with overhanging balconies and an atmosphere more reminiscent of the Mediterranean than of India. There are numerous little bars rarely visited by foreigners. Even if you don't stay there, the **Panjim Inn** is a beautiful old building that's worth a visit.

At the centre of Fontainhas, the **Chapel of St Sebastian** stands at the end of a picturesque street. Although it dates only from the 1880s, it contains a number of interesting features – in particular a striking crucifix which originally stood in the Palace of the Inquisition in Old Goa.

The **Church of the Immaculate Conception** is Panaji's main place of worship, and it stands above the square in the main part of town, reached by several intersecting flights of stairs. The original construction was consecrated in 1541. Panaji was the first port of call for voyages from Lisbon, so Portuguese sailors would visit this church to give thanks for a safe crossing before continuing to Old Goa.

The **Secretariat** is the other building of interest in Panaji. Dating from the 16th century, it was originally Adil Shah's palace. In 1759, it became the viceroy's official Residence. In case you're wondering what the bizarre statue of a man apparently about to strangle a woman near the Secretariat building represents, this is Abbé Faria, a famous hypnotist, and his assistant. Born in Candolim in 1756, he emigrated to France, where he became a celebrated hypnotic medium.

Other things to see in Panaji include a small **museum** (open Monday to Friday), and the modern **Mahalaxmi Temple**.

Organised Tours
Tours of Goa are offered by Goa Tourism (book at the tourist office or at the Panaji bus terminal) and by private agencies. The one day tours aren't very good because they pack too much into a short day, so you end up seeing very little.

The North Goa tour visits Panaji, Mapusa, Narve, Mayem Lake, Vagator, Anjuna,

Calangute and Fort Aguada. The South Goa tours take in Miramar, Dona Paula, Pilar Seminary, Mormugao, Colva, Margao, Shantadurga Temple, Mangesh Temple and Old Goa. The tours cost Rs 70 (or Rs 100 for air-con buses) and depart daily at 9.30 am, returning to Panaji at 6 pm. Other tours are also available, including a two day tour to Dudhsagar Falls and the Bondla Wildlife Sanctuary (Rs 350).

There are also daily hour-long river cruises along the Mandovi River at 6 pm (Sunset Cruise) and 7.15 pm (Sundown Cruise) which cost Rs 55. They're good value and include a cultural programme of Goan folk songs and dances. Drinks and snacks are available. On full-moon nights, there are two-hour cruises from 8.30 pm for Rs 100; dinner is available. The government-operated *Santa Monica* leaves from the jetty next to the huge Mandovi Bridge. Other boats, operated by a private company, Emerald Waters, also leave from here. Similar, though slightly more expensive, cruises are offered, with some interesting variations, too. For Rs 500 you can take an all-day trip upriver to Old Goa. You arrive, as visitors did in the city's heyday, on the dock below the Viceroy's Arch, and two hours are allowed to see Old Goa itself.

Places to Stay
Note that throughout this chapter, unless otherwise stated, prices given are for the high season (mid-December to late January). For the shoulder season, prices drop by around 25% in the middle and top-end price ranges.

Whenever there is a religious festival in Goa – especially the festival of St Francis Xavier (several days on either side of 3 December) – it can be difficult to find accommodation in Panaji, especially at the small, inexpensive lodges. There is no accommodation at Old Goa.

Places to Stay – bottom end
Patto Tourist Home (☎ 227972), in a complex which includes the tourist office, is by the river, between the bus terminal and the town centre. It used to be a good bet, but beds in the single dormitory are no longer so easy

to get hold of, as the management won't let Indians and foreigners share the same room. Dormitory beds are Rs 50 in the high season and Rs 40 in the low season; double rooms are Rs 300. It has a restaurant and bar.

The *Youth Hostel* (☎ 225433) is at Miramar, three km west of Panaji, in a shady she-oak garden by the water. The drawbacks are the institutional air and the distance from the centre of Panaji. Dorm beds cost Rs 20 (Rs 40 for non-members) and there's a solitary double room with bathroom for Rs 70.

Udipi Boarding & Lodging is one of several good, cheap places to stay in the old part of town, in the narrow streets running parallel to the Ourem River. It has fairly basic double rooms for Rs 100, while the nearby *Elite Boarding & Lodging* has doubles for Rs 150, and a triple for Rs 200, all with private bathroom. There are also two double rooms (with a common bathroom) at the *Hotel Venite* restaurant for Rs 150.

Hotel Embassy (☎ 225172) is on Emidio Gracia Road. It costs Rs 325 for a good, clean double with attached bathroom.

The *Republica Hotel* (☎ 224630), on José Falcão Rd, at the back of the Secretariat, is an old place with fine views of the Mandovi River. All rooms have attached bathrooms. They charge Rs 150 for doubles, although this rises to Rs 250 in peak season.

Palace Hotel, next door to the Embassy, is for emergencies only. There are grubby cells for Rs 30/80, or equally dirty double rooms with attached bathroom for Rs 150. The atmosphere is gloomy and the very active Pentecostal church in one wing of the hotel will be an attraction to few.

Mandovi Pearl Guest House (☎ 223928) is just up the road from the Republica, at the back of the Tourist Hotel. It's very popular but as it has only four rooms it's often full. Large triples with attached bathroom go for Rs 350 (Rs 175 outside peak season).

Park Lane Lodge (☎ 220238) is one of the best of a number of other places in Fontainhas. Family-run, it's an old Portuguese house that has a variety of good clean rooms and a very pleasant relaxed atmosphere. A double with attached bathroom ranges from

Rs 210 in the shoulder season to Rs 300 during high season. They also have two slightly cheaper rooms with common bathroom, which they may let as singles. Also recommended is the nearby *Afonso Guest House* (☎ 222359), in the same street as the Chapel of St Sebastian. Spotlessly clean doubles with attached bathroom cost up to Rs 500 in peak season, but rapidly come down to more like half this by the end of February.

Orav's Guest House (☎ 226128), 31 January Rd, lacks the character of these last two places, but is also good. It's clean and well run, but checkout is 9 am. Doubles with attached bathroom are Rs 250, and the front rooms have little balconies.

Hotel Neptune (☎ 227747), Malaca Rd, offers doubles at Rs 300, or Rs 375 with air-con. All the rooms have bathrooms, and there's a restaurant and bar.

Places to Stay – middle

The *Tourist Hotel* (☎ 227103) is quite popular with travellers. It charges Rs 280/450 for doubles/triples, and Rs 450 for an air-con room. Prices drop by only about Rs 50 in the low season. Front rooms overlook the river but tend to be noisy, so try to get a back room. There's a terrace restaurant, bar, bookshop and a handicraft shop on the ground floor.

The *Hotel Samrat* (☎ 223318), Dr Dada Vaidya Rd, is a reasonable choice. Doubles/triples are Rs 500/550 (dropping by Rs 100 outside the peak season). Rooms are clean and all have attached bathrooms. There's a bar and a good Chinese restaurant in the building. Travellers cheques can be changed here, and credit cards are accepted.

Hotel Aroma (☎ 43519), Cunha-Rivara Rd, is a modern place which fronts onto the Municipal Gardens. The clean, airy double rooms with attached bathroom are relatively good value at Rs 350. The tandoori restaurant on the 1st floor is one of the best in Panaji.

Hotel Bareton (☎ 46405) is overpriced in the peak season, but shoulder season charges are much more reasonable: Rs 225/300 with

bathrooms attached and there is 24 hour hot water. Checkout time is 8.30 am.

Mayfair Hotel (☎ 223317), Dr Dada Vaidya Rd, is very pleasant. A double with attached bathroom is Rs 460. In the shoulder season, these rooms are good value at Rs 300; they also let them as singles for Rs 230.

Hotel Arcadia (☎ 220140) on MG Road is in the same league as the Mayfair. Clean, pleasant rooms are Rs 200/300 (more for a room with balcony or air-con).

The *Hotel Summit* (☎ 226736), Menezes Braganza Rd, is similar but more expensive at Rs 450 for a double with bathroom, and Rs 550 with air-con. Also worth considering is the similarly priced *Hotel Sun Rise* (☎ 220221), 18th June Rd, although it's often booked out by Indian business-wallahs.

Keni's Hotel (☎ 224581), 18th June Rd, is also fairly good value. Singles/doubles cost Rs 400/550; air-con doubles cost Rs 650 with bathroom, hot water and colour TV. The hotel includes a bar, restaurant and shopping arcade.

The *Panjim Inn* (☎ 226523) is by far the nicest, albeit the most expensive, place to stay in this price range. It's a beautiful 300-year-old mansion with a large 1st floor verandah and leafy garden. Run by a Tibetan family, it's a popular place and the staff are helpful and friendly. Singles/doubles cost Rs 450/585 with bathroom, plus 15% tax and an additional 12% between 21 December and 10 January. Try to see a few rooms because some are definitely better than others. There's a TV lounge, and good meals are available for guests.

Hotel Rajdhani (☎ 225362) is a good clean place, right in the centre on Dr Atmaram Borkar Rd. It charges Rs 415 for a double (plus Rs 80 for air-con) and there's a popular vegetarian restaurant downstairs. Checkout time is 10 am.

The *Hotel Palácio de Goa* (☎ 224289), Dr Gama Pinto Rd, is a glitzy place with doubles from Rs 545 (Rs 100 more for air-con). Some of the rooms have balconies, and there's a restaurant. Checkout time is 8 am.

Hotel Park Plaza (☎ 222601) is centrally located on Azad Maidan. The cheapest rooms in peak season are Rs 795/900, so it's not great value.

Places to Stay – top end

Hotel Mandovi (☎ 224405), Dayamond Bandokar, is the best of the top-end places. Rooms in this colonial hotel start at Rs 1375/1800. There's an excellent restaurant on the 1st floor and a pleasant bar on the balcony.

Hotel Nova Goa (☎ 226231), Dr Atmaram Borkar Rd, is the best of the modern hotels. Rooms cost Rs 1100/1800 for a single/double in peak season. There are also more expensive suites, and a shaded pool.

The *Hotel Fidalgo* (☎ 226291), 18th June Rd, also has a swimming pool, but is rather run down. Doubles start at Rs 1100.

Places to Eat

The *Hotel Venite*, 31 January Rd, has long been popular with travellers, although prices have risen considerably over the last few years. This attractive old place has polished wooden floors, flower-decked balconies overlooking the street and bags of atmosphere. The Goan and seafood cuisine is very good, the servings are generous and all the food is fresh. Goan sausages are Rs 75, as is another local dish, chicken cafrial. Fish balchão is Rs 75. Lobster and tiger prawns are also a speciality, but need to be ordered in advance. It's also a great spot for a cold beer or two during siesta. The Venite is open for breakfast, lunch and dinner daily except Sunday.

Udipi Boarding & Lodging, one street east of the Venite, also has a 1st floor restaurant with a balcony overlooking the street. Although it doesn't attract many foreigners, it's always crowded with Goans, and serves cheap, basic but tasty food.

Hotel Annapurna is a clean vegetarian restaurant around the back of the Hotel Aroma. Barefoot waiters serve excellent thalis for Rs 17, and there are dosas from Rs 10.

Gaylord Restaurant, upstairs at the Tourist Hotel, has a pleasant verandah overlooking the Mandovi River. It's a good place for breakfast, the food is reasonable and it's used by many travellers, though the lunch and dinner servings (especially of seafood) are very small.

Kamat Hotel, on the south side of the Municipal Gardens is part of the excellent chain of vegetarian restaurants. *New Punjab Restaurant*, diagonally opposite the Kamat Hotel, offers good, cheap Punjabi food and more expensive tandoori specials. It's closed on Thursday.

Sher-E-Punjab, at the Hotel Aroma, has the best tandoori in town. It serves excellent northern Indian food for around Rs 75 (per main dish). There's a second branch on 18th June Rd. Although it has a more extensive menu, it's not quite as good.

Delhi Darbar on MG Rd is another recommended tandoori place, though it's a little more expensive than the Sher-E-Punjab. It's one of the most popular restaurants in town and often fully booked in the later part of the evening.

The *Goenchin* (☎ 227614), just off Dr Dada Vaidya Rd, is an excellent Chinese restaurant but it's definitely a splurge option. It's open from 12.30 to 2.45 pm and 7.30 to 10.45 pm daily. Main dishes are around Rs 75, and specials range from Rs 100 to Rs 150.

Chunghwa, in the Hotel Samrat, is another good Chinese place. Prawns in garlic sauce cost Rs 75, and other main dishes are slightly cheaper. It's run by a Chinese family.

Riorico, at the Hotel Mandovi, is the best restaurant for Goan cuisine. Here you can try caldo verde (potato soup with spinach, Rs 40), fish/prawn balchão (cooked in a rich, spicy tomato sauce, Rs 110/125), peixe caldeirada (fish and potato stew with wine, Rs 160), and round the meal off with bebinca (the rich Goan sweet made from egg yolk and coconut, Rs 40).

For fruit juices, *Juicy Corner*, opposite the Secretariat, is a popular place with travellers. There are several pastry shops in Panaji: the best is probably the *Pastry Cottage*, near the Hotel Nova Goa. Also good is *A Pastelaria*, near the Goenchin Chinese restaurant.

Getting There & Away

Air Indian Airlines (☎ 223831) is at Dempo Building, D Bandodkar Marg, on the riverfront. It's open from 10 am to 1 pm and 2 to 5 pm. Air India (☎ 231101) is next to the Hotel Fidalgo on 18th June Rd. Other airlines with offices in Panaji include Moduluft (☎ 227577), Municipal Building, Near Church Square; Jet Airways (☎ 221472), Rizvi Chambers, Caetano Albuquerque Rd; and Skyline NEPC Ltd (☎ 220192), Liv In Apartments, General Bernardo Guedes Rd.

See the Getting There & Away section at the beginning of this chapter for flights to Goa's Dabolim airport, 29km from Panaji.

Bus Many private companies offer luxury/deluxe, superdeluxe and superdeluxe video buses to Mumbai, Bangalore, Pune and Mangalore from Panaji and Margao daily. The buses generally depart at night but if you have any designs on sleeping, avoid the video buses. Most of the companies have offices in Panaji, Mapusa and Margao.

The state-operated Kadamba buses are pretty good, and the booking office at the bus terminal is open daily from 9 am to 1 pm and 2 to 5.30 pm. Reservations (Rs 5) can be made up to 30 days in advance.

The trip to Mumbai is supposed to take 14 hours but can take up to 18. The cheapest fare for a luxury coach is Rs 224; air-con luxury is Rs 275. Most buses leave between 3 and 6 pm. Private operators have offices outside the entrance to the bus terminal, and their air-suspension coaches are the most comfortable (and expensive) way to do this trip. Paulo Holiday Makers (☎ 223736) has a daily overnight coach to Mumbai for Rs 350.

From the bus terminal, there are also services to Londa (where you can get a direct railway connection to Mysore every day), Hubli (a railway junction on the main Mumbai to Bangalore line, where you can also get trains to Gadag for both Bijapur and Badami, and Hospet and Hampi) and Belgaum. The bus to Hubli (Rs 53, seven hours) leaves at 7 am. From Hubli to Hospet is another 4½ hours.

There are daily buses to Mysore, which take 16 hours. Mangalore is an 11 hour trip for Rs 147 in a Kadamba luxury bus. Other buses include those to Pune (Rs 181) and

Bangalore (Rs 223). There are several buses daily to Karwar, the first major town across the southern border with Karnataka.

For journeys within Goa, some of the more popular routes from Panaji include:

Vasco da Gama & Mormugao – there are two ways of getting there. You can either go via the ferry from Dona Paula to Mormugao, or by road via Agassaim and Cortalim. Unless you know there will be a ferry waiting for you on arrival at Dona Paula, the route via Agassaim and Cortalim is the quicker of the two. Either way, it costs Rs 7 and takes about one hour.

Margao – you can get to Margao either via Agassaim and Cortalim or via Ponda. The former is the more direct route and takes about one hour at a cost of Rs 8. Via Ponda, it takes about an hour longer and costs Rs 11.

Old Goa – take one of the frequent buses going straight to Old Goa or any bus going to Ponda. The journey costs Rs 2.50 and takes 25 minutes.

Calangute – there are frequent services throughout the day and evening. The journey takes about 35 minutes and costs Rs 2.50.

Mapusa – buses cost Rs 3 and take about 25 minutes. Mapusa is pronounced 'Mapsa', and this is what the conductors shout. Change at Mapusa for Chapora.

Train If the Konkan Railway is now fully operational, the train to and from Mumbai should be a better bet than the buses. The nearest railway station to Panaji is 11km to the east, near Old Goa. See the Getting There & Away section at the start of this chapter.

Boat See the Getting There & Away and Getting Around sections at the start of this chapter for details of the daily catamaran service to and from Mumbai, and ferry crossings within Goa, respectively.

Getting Around
The Airport There is one bus a day (Rs 30) at 11.45 am from the Indian Airlines office in Panaji to Dabolim airport. A taxi costs about Rs 300 and takes about 40 minutes (Rs 312 from the pre-paid taxi stand at the airport to Panaji).

The Hotel Mandovi operates a bus to the airport which non-guests are sometimes allowed to use, if there's space. Check with the hotel the night before.

The cheapest way from the airport into Vasco is to wait at the small junction just outside the airport entrance. Infrequent buses from Dona Paula stop here en route to Vasco, from where there are frequent buses to Panaji.

Taxi & Auto-Rickshaw Taxis and auto-rickshaws are metered, but getting the drivers to use the meters is extremely difficult. Negotiate the fare before heading off. Typical taxi fares from Panaji include Rs 150 to Calangute and Rs 300 to Colva.

Other Transport See the Getting Around section at the start of this chapter for information on bike and motorcycle hire.

AROUND PANAJI

Three km west of Panaji is **Miramar**, Panaji's nearest beach, but it's neither particularly attractive nor a good place to swim. There's plenty of accommodation, including the Youth Hostel (see Places to Stay in Panaji), should you decide to stay.

Four km further along this road is **Dona Paula**, a small town with several resort complexes, that has grown up around a fishing village. The *Dona Paula Beach Resort* (☎ 227955), across the narrow peninsula from the harbour, is not bad and has a small private beach. Doubles with attached bathroom are Rs 730. Next door, the *Prainha* (☎ 224162) has peaceful gardens and a swimming pool, but it's more expensive: Rs 1150 for a non air-con double room. One km down the coast, the upmarket *Cidade de Goa* (☎ 221133), by Vaniguinim Beach, has all the five-star trimmings and double rooms for a hefty US$160 per night.

Frequent buses to Miramar and Dona Paula leave from Panaji's Kadamba bus terminal.

OLD GOA

Nine km east of Panaji, half a dozen imposing churches and cathedrals (among the largest in Asia) are all that remain of the Portuguese capital that was once said to rival Lisbon in

magnificence. Some of the old buildings have become museums maintained by the Archaeological Survey of India – a maintenance that is very necessary because if the lime plaster which protects the laterite structures is not renewed frequently, the monsoons will reduce the buildings to ruin.

History

Even before the arrival of the Portuguese, Old Goa was a thriving and prosperous city, and the second capital of the Adil Shahi dynasty of Bijapur. At that time, it was a fortress surrounded by walls, towers and a moat, and contained temples, mosques and the large palace of Adil Shah. Today, none of these structures remain except for a fragment of the gateway to the palace.

Under the Portuguese, the city grew rapidly in size and splendour, despite an epidemic in 1543 which wiped out a large percentage of the population. Many huge churches, monasteries and convents were erected by the various religious orders which came to Goa under royal mandates. The Franciscans were the first to arrive.

Old Goa's splendour was short-lived, however, because by the end of the 16th century, Portuguese supremacy on the seas had been replaced by that of the British, Dutch and French. The city's decline was accelerated by the activities of the Inquisition and another devastating epidemic which struck in 1635. Indeed, if it had not been for the treaty between the British and the Portuguese, it is probable that Goa would either have passed to the Dutch or been absorbed into British India.

The city muddled on into the early 19th century as the administrative capital of Portugal's eastern empire. In 1843, the capital was shifted to Panaji.

Information

The Archaeological Survey of India publishes the excellent booklet *Old Goa* by S Rajagopalan. It's available from the archaeological museum in Old Goa.

Se Cathedral

The largest of the churches in Old Goa, Se Cathedral was begun in 1562 during the reign of King Dom Sebastião (1557-8). It was substantially completed by 1619, though the altars were not finished until 1652. The cathedral was built for the Dominicans and paid for by the royal treasury out of the proceeds of the sale of crown property.

The building's style is Portuguese-Gothic with a Tuscan exterior and Corinthian interior. There were once two towers, one either side of the facade, but one collapsed in 1776. The remaining tower houses a famous bell, one of the largest in Goa, often called the Golden Bell because of its rich sound. The main altar is dedicated to St Catherine of Alexandria, and paintings on either side of it depict scenes from her life and martyrdom.

Convent & Church of St Francis of Assisi

This is one of the most interesting buildings in Old Goa. It contains gilded and carved woodwork, old murals depicting scenes from the life of St Francis, and a floor substantially made of carved gravestones – complete with family coats of arms dating back to the early 16th century. The church was built by eight Franciscan friars who arrived here in 1517 and constructed a small chapel consisting of three altars and a choir. This was later pulled down and the present building was built on the same spot in 1661.

The convent at the back of this church is now the **archaeological museum** (open Saturday to Thursday, 10 am to 5 pm; free entry). It is home to many portraits of the Portuguese viceroys, most of them inexpertly touched up or restored; fragments of sculpture from Hindu temple sites in Goa which show Chalukyan and Hoysala influences; stone Vetal images from the animist cult which flourished in this part of India centuries ago; and a model of a Portuguese caravel, minus the rigging.

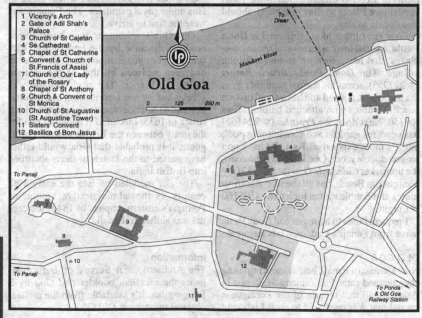

1 Viceroy's Arch
2 Gate of Adil Shah's Palace
3 Church of St Cajetan
4 Se Cathedral
5 Chapel of St Catherine
6 Convent & Church of St Francis of Assisi
7 Church of Our Lady of the Rosary
8 Chapel of St Anthony
9 Church & Convent of St Monica
10 Church of St Augustine (St Augustine Tower)
11 Sisters' Convent
12 Basilica of Bom Jesus

Old Goa

Mandovi River

To Diwar

To Panaji

To Panaji

To Ponda & Old Goa Railway Station

Se Cathedral, Old Goa's largest church.

Basilica of Bom Jesus

The Basilica of Bom Jesus is famous throughout the Roman Catholic world. It contains the tomb and mortal remains of St Francis Xavier who, in 1541, was given the task of spreading Christianity among the subjects of the Portuguese colonies in the east. A former pupil of St Ignatius Loyola, the founder of the Jesuit Order, St Francis Xavier's missionary voyages became legendary and, considering the state of transport at the time, were nothing short of miraculous.

Apart from the richly gilded altars, the interior of the church is remarkable for its simplicity. This is the only church which is not plastered on the outside (although it was originally). Construction began in 1594 and the church was completed in 1605. The centre of interest inside the church is, of course, the Tomb of St Francis. The construction of the tomb was underwritten by the Duke of Tuscany and executed by the Florentine sculptor Giovanni Batista Foggini. It took 10 years to build and was completed in 1698. The remains of the body are housed in a silver casket, which at one time was covered in jewels. On the walls surrounding it are murals depicting scenes from the saint's journeys, and one of his death on Sancian Island.

The **Professed House**, next door to the basilica, is a two storey laterite building covered with lime plaster. It was completed in 1585, despite much opposition to the Jesuits. Part of the building burned down in 1633 and was partially rebuilt in 1783. There's a modern **art gallery** attached to the basilica.

Church of St Cajetan

Modelled on the original design of St Peter's in Rome, this church was built by Italian friars of the Order of Theatines, who were sent by Pope Urban III to preach Christianity in the kingdom of Golconda (near Hyderabad). The friars were not permitted to work in Golconda, so settled at Old Goa in 1640. The construction of the church began in 1655. Historically, it's of much less interest than the other churches.

Church of St Augustine Ruins

All that is really left of this church is the enormous 46m tower which served as a belfry and formed part of the facade of the church. The few other remnants are choked with creepers and weeds, and access is difficult. The church was constructed in 1602 by Augustinian friars who arrived at Old Goa in 1587.

It was abandoned in 1835 due to the repressive policies of the Portuguese government, which resulted in the eviction of many religious orders from Goa. The church fell into neglect and the vault collapsed in 1842. In 1931, the facade and half the tower fell down, followed by more sections in 1938.

Church & Convent of St Monica

This huge three storey laterite building was completed in 1627, only to burn down nine years later. Reconstruction started the following year, and it's from this time that the buildings date. Once known as the Royal Monastery, due to the royal patronage which it enjoyed, the building is now used by the Mater Dei Institute as a nunnery and was inaugurated in 1964. Visitors are allowed inside if they are reasonably dressed. There are fading murals on the inside of the western walls.

The Incorrupt Body of St Francis Xavier

Goa's patron saint, Francis Xavier, had spent 10 years as a tireless missionary in South-East Asia when he died on 2 December 1552, but it was through his death that his greatest power in the region was released.

He died on the island of Sancian, off the coast of China. His servant is said to have emptied four sacks of quicklime into his coffin to consume his flesh in case the order came to return the remains to Goa. Two months later, the body was transferred to Malacca, where it was observed to be still in perfect condition – refusing to rot despite the quicklime. The following year, it was returned to Goa, where the people were declaring the preservation a miracle.

The Church was slower to acknowledge it, requiring a medical examination to establish that the body had not been embalmed. This was performed, in 1556, by the viceroy's physician, who declared that all internal organs were still intact and that no preservative agents had been used. He noticed a small wound in the chest and asked two Jesuits to put their fingers into it. He noted, 'When they withdrew them, they were covered with blood which I smelt and found to be absolutely untainted'.

In comparison to 16th and 17th century church bureaucracy, modern Indian bureaucracy seems positively streamlined, for it was not until 1622 that canonisation took place. By then, holy relic hunters had started work on the 'incorrupt body'. In 1614, the right arm was removed and divided between Jesuits in Japan and Rome, and by 1636, parts of one shoulder blade and all the internal organs had been scattered through South-East Asia. By the end of the 17th century, the body was in an advanced state of desiccation, and the miracle appeared to be over. The Jesuits decided to enclose the corpse in a glass coffin out of view, and it was not until the mid-19th century that the current cycle of 10 yearly expositions began. During the 54 days of the 1994-5 exposition, over one million pilgrims filed past the ghoulish remains.

The next exposition is not until November 2004, but if you're anywhere in the area on 3 December the annual celebration of the saint's day is well worth attending. ■

Other Buildings

Other monuments of minor interest in Old Goa are the Viceroy's Arch, Gate of Adil Shah's Palace, Chapel of St Anthony, Chapel of St Catherine, and the Church of Our Lady of the Rosary.

Getting There & Away

If you're a lover of old buildings and exotic ruins, you'll need the best part of a day to wander around Old Goa; otherwise, a morning or an afternoon will be sufficient.

There are frequent buses to Old Goa from the bus stand at Panaji (Rs 2.50, 25 minutes); buses from Panaji to Ponda also pass through Old Goa. Emerald Waters does a boat tour from Panaji (ask at the kiosks near the steamer jetty).

MAPUSA

Pop: 34,800   Tel Area Code: 0832

Mapusa (pronounced locally as 'Mapsa') is the main centre of population in the northern provinces of Goa and the main town for supplies if you are staying at either Anjuna

or Chapora. If you're staying at Calangute, Baga or Candolim, you have a choice of Panaji or Mapusa as a service centre.

There's not much to see in Mapusa, though the Friday market is worth a visit.

Places to Stay & Eat

Accommodation at the nearby beaches of Anjuna, Vagator and Chapora is far preferable to what's on offer in Mapusa.

Sirsat Lodge (☎ 262419) offers fairly basic rooms; doubles with common bathroom are Rs 80, and with attached bathroom are Rs 150.

Hotel Trishul (☎ 262700) is cheaper still; doubles with attached bathroom go for Rs 100, except over Christmas and Diwali, when all rooms are converted to take four people and cost Rs 240.

Hotel Vilena (☎ 263115) is a good, clean place with doubles at Rs 200, or Rs 300 with attached bathroom (and water heater).

The popular *Tourist Hotel* (☎ 262794), on the roundabout at the entrance to Mapusa, has a good range of rooms from Rs 180/220. There are also rooms with four/six beds for Rs 280/330. Hot water is available by the bucket, except in the air-con doubles (Rs 330), which have water heaters. There's an unremarkable restaurant on the 1st floor.

The *Satyaheera Hotel* (☎ 262849), near the Maruti Temple, is about the best Mapusa has to offer. Doubles range from Rs 300 to Rs 450 with air-con, all with bathroom attached. The *Ruchira*, reputed to be one of the best restaurants in Mapusa, is on the top floor. Main dishes are Rs 30 to Rs 45.

Getting There & Away
If the Konkan Railway is now fully operational, Mapusa Road (six km north-east of town) is the nearest station.

From the bus stand, there are buses to Mumbai (Rs 195 for a 'luxury' bus). Private operators have kiosks by the taxi and motorcycle stand. The most prestigious coach is the Aerowheels overnight air-con service to Mumbai, leaving at 3.30 pm. There are individual headsets, an on-board toilet, free snacks and soft drinks. Tickets cost Rs 450. Other operators offer cheaper services for Rs 250 to Rs 350.

There are frequent bus departures for Panaji (25 minutes, Rs 3), and buses at least hourly to Calangute (Rs 3) and Anjuna (Rs

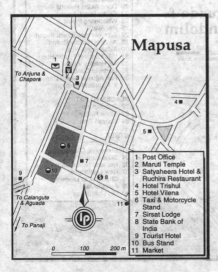

Mapusa

To Anjuna & Chapora

To Calangute & Aguada

To Panaji

0   100   200 m

1 Post Office
2 Maruti Temple
3 Satyaheera Hotel & Ruchira Restaurant
4 Hotel Trishul
5 Hotel Vilena
6 Taxi & Motorcycle Stand
7 Sirsat Lodge
8 State Bank of India
9 Tourist Hotel
10 Bus Stand
11 Market

4). Other buses go to Margao (Rs 17 by private express service), Chapora and Candolim. A motorcycle to Anjuna or Calangute costs Rs 40 and takes about 15 minutes. Rickshaws charge around Rs 60 and taxis about Rs 100.

FORT AGUADA & CANDOLIM
Tel Area Code: 0832
The beaches of North Goa extend from Fort Aguada in an almost uninterrupted 30km sandy stretch to the border with Maharashtra. Sinquerim, the beach below the fort, and Candolim are popular with package tourists, but independent travellers can also find accommodation here. These beaches tend to be quieter than Calangute, particularly at weekends. There are some pleasant places to stay, although there's nowhere for those on a very tight budget.

Guarding the mouth of the Mandovi River, **Fort Aguada** was built by the Portuguese in 1612. It's worth visiting the moated ruins on the hilltop for the views, which are particularly good from the old lighthouse. You can also visit the dungeons. There's no entry charge but the caretaker expects a hefty tip. Nearby, the new **lighthouse** can be visited from 4 to 5.30 pm (Rs 1); no photography is allowed from it.

To the east is **Aguada Jail**; most inmates (12 of them westerners) are in on drug charges. They're only allowed one visit a month, so although they usually appreciate visits from other foreigners, you need to make sure you won't be denying them the visit of someone they're expecting. You'll also need to contact your embassy for a list of names.

Places to Stay
Moving south from Calangute, the hotels become progressively more expensive. Prices listed below are for doubles with attached bathrooms in the high season. Some of these hotels are taken over entirely by package groups during this period.

There's a clutch of places ranging from Rs 300 to Rs 600 in an excellent position very close to the beach. These include the *Dona*

Florina Beach Resort, D'Mello's (rooms with balconies upstairs) and *Shanu Holiday Home*. There are even sea views from some of these places.

Next is a group of guest houses used by the cheaper end of the package market, with doubles during the peak season averaging around Rs 500 to Rs 600. Within a small area are the *Coqueiral Holiday Home* (☎ 276070), *Holiday Beach Resort* (☎ 276088), *Alexandra Tourist Centre* (☎ 276097) and *Monte Villa*. In the same bracket, on the other side of the road, is the *Sand Pebble* (☎ 279178). The nearby *Silver Sands Holiday Village*

(☎ 276744) is much more expensive over the peak period, charging Rs 1000 to Rs 1500.

Cheaper places in this area, with doubles around Rs 250, include *Manuel Guest House* and the friendly *Lobo's Guest House*. The *Pretty Petal Guest House* is a nice place, and worth the Rs 500 to Rs 600 room charges, but it's almost entirely turned over to tour operators nowadays. *Ave Maria* (☎ 277336) is also good value at Rs 500 for a double, and keeps some rooms free for independent travellers. The cheapest place in the area is *Ti Bhat* at Rs 250.

Slightly more upmarket is the *Tropicano*

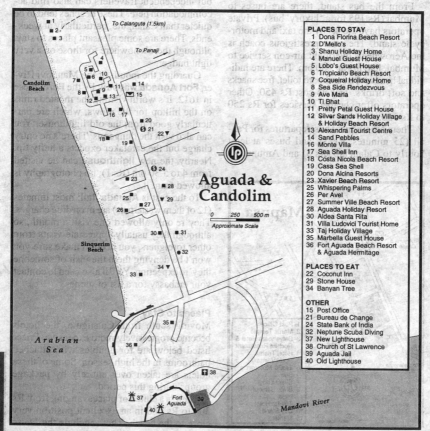

PLACES TO STAY
1 Dona Florina Beach Resort
2 D'Mello's
3 Shanu Holiday Home
4 Manuel Guest House
5 Lobo's Guest House
6 Tropicano Beach Resort
7 Coqueiral Holiday Home
8 Sea Side Rendezvous
9 Ave Maria
10 Ti Bhat
11 Pretty Petal Guest House
12 Silver Sands Holiday Village
    & Holiday Beach Resort
13 Alexandra Tourist Centre
14 Sand Pebbles
16 Monte Villa
17 Sea Shell Inn
18 Costa Nicola Beach Resort
19 Casa Sea Shell
20 Dona Alcina Resorts
23 Xavier Beach Resort
25 Whispering Palms
26 Per Avel
27 Summer Ville Beach Resort
28 Aguada Holiday Resort
30 Aldea Santa Rita
31 Villa Ludovici Tourist Home
33 Taj Holiday Village
35 Marbella Guest House
36 Fort Aguada Beach Resort
    & Aguada Hermitage

PLACES TO EAT
22 Coconut Inn
29 Stone House
34 Banyan Tree

OTHER
15 Post Office
21 Bureau de Change
24 State Bank of India
32 Neptune Scuba Diving
37 New Lighthouse
38 Church of St Lawrence
39 Aguada Jail
40 Old Lighthouse

Aguada & Candolim

To Calangute (1.5km)
To Panaji
Candolim Beach
Arabian Sea
Sinquerim Beach
0   250   500 m
Approximate Scale
Fort Aguada
Mandovi River

Beach Resort (☎ 277732), which charges Rs 600 for very pleasant little rooms with doors incorporating traditional Goan glazing – seashells! The *Sea Side Rendezvous* (☎ 276323) has a good restaurant, a small pool, and is also the base for Venture Sports, an outfit specialising in watersports.

Moving southwards, but remaining in the same sort of price range (Rs 500 to Rs 700), there's the *Sea Shell Inn* (☎ 276131), the *Casa Sea Shell* (☎ 277879), the homely *Per Avel* (☎ 277074), and the spotlessly clean *Summer Ville Beach Resort* (☎ 277075). The *Costa Nicola Beach Resort* (☎ 276343) is slightly more expensive at Rs 750 over Christmas, and is usually booked solid by package companies anyway.

Hotels (with pools) in the Rs 1000 to Rs 1500 range include the Portuguese-style villas of the *Aldea Santa Rita* (☎ 276868), and the *Aguada Holiday Resort* (☎ 276071). The *Dona Alcina Resorts* (☎ 277453) is more expensive still at Rs 2000 over peak season, although prices are below Rs 1000 before mid-December and after mid-January. The *Whispering Palms* (☎ 276141) is a package hotel, and charges independent travellers over Rs 3000 in peak season.

Villa Ludovici Tourist Home is one of only two places that have managed to preserve something of their colonial heritage. The owner is holding out against the developers, and this is a very pleasant place to stay. She charges Rs 350 with breakfast for two, Rs 250 in the shoulder season.

Marbella Guest House (fax 276308) is much more upmarket, a beautifully restored Portuguese villa hidden away down a quiet lane behind the Fort Aguada Beach Resort. Partly foreign-owned, there are six airy rooms, each superbly decorated in a different style. All rooms have a bathroom attached (one has a sunken marble tub) and the whole place is spotlessly clean. Rooms range from Rs 800 to Rs 1600 (Rs 650 to Rs 1300 in the shoulder season). It's highly recommended, but in the high season you'll need to book in advance.

The Taj Group (☎ 276201; fax 276044) operates a complex of three five-star deluxe hotels beside Sinquerim Beach, to the south of Candolim. The beachside *Taj Holiday Village* charges US$210 and has a watersports centre. Within the outer walls of the old fort, the *Fort Aguada Beach Resort* has rooms for US$225. Above it are the luxurious villas of the *Aguada Hermitage*, which have northern views and are priced at US$465 to US$575.

Places to Eat

Most of the hotels have restaurants attached, and down on the beach there are dozens more places to try – all of which serve excellent seafood, snacks and cold drinks.

Coconut Inn is one of the more established places in the area and is a pleasant, open-air, upmarket place to eat, though definitely not the restaurant to make for if you're after excitement. The food is good, but the choice of music (Unforgettable Oldies) just about sums it up. On Monday, there's a seafood barbecue and live music for Rs 295 per person – every guest gets a free jasmine garland!

The *Stone House* is a mellower place, with tables laid out in a raised garden, non-stop Marley and Dylan on the sound system, and suitably relaxed service.

The *Banyan Tree*, in the grounds of the Taj Holiday Village, is one of the best restaurants in the area. It's an open-sided affair serving excellent Thai and Chinese cuisine. Main dishes are from Rs 150.

Getting There & Away

Buses run from Panaji to Sinquerim (14km) and continue north to Calangute. A pre-paid taxi from the airport costs Rs 439.

CALANGUTE & BAGA
Tel Area Code: 0832

Seemingly not all that long ago, Calangute was the beach all self-respecting hippies headed for, especially around Christmas when psychedelic hell broke loose and the beach was littered with more budding rock stars than most people have hot dinners. If you enjoyed taking part in those mass pujas, with their endless half-baked discussions about

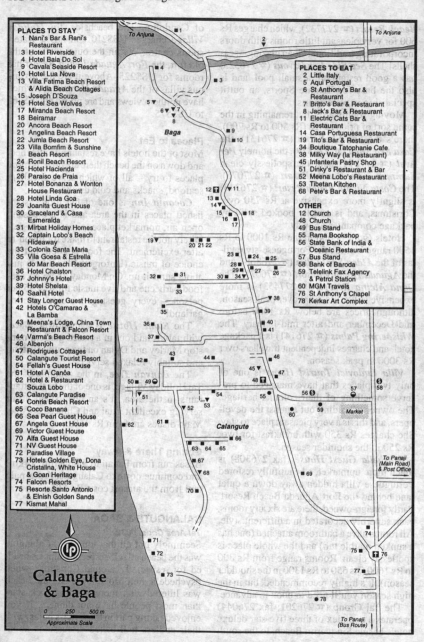

PLACES TO STAY
1 Nani's Bar & Rani's Restaurant
3 Hotel Riverside
4 Hotel Baia Do Sol
9 Cavala Seaside Resort
10 Hotel Lua Nova
13 Villa Fatima Beach Resort & Alidia Beach Cottages
15 Joseph D'Souza
16 Hotel Sea Wolves
17 Miranda Beach Resort
18 Beiramar
20 Ancora Beach Resort
21 Angelina Beach Resort
22 Jumla Beach Resort
23 Villa Bomfim & Sunshine Beach Resort
24 Ronil Beach Resort
25 Hotel Hacienda
26 Paraiso de Praia
27 Hotel Bonanza & Wonton House Restaurant
28 Hotel Linda Goa
29 Joanita Guest House
30 Graceland & Casa Esmeralda
31 Mirbat Holiday Homes
32 Captain Lobo's Beach Hideaway
33 Colonia Santa Maria
35 Vila Goesa & Estrella do Mar Beach Resort
36 Hotel Chalston
37 Johnny's Hotel
39 Hotel Shelsta
40 Saahil Hotel
41 Stay Longer Guest House
42 Hotels O'Camarao & La Bamba
43 Meena's Lodge, China Town Restaurant & Falcon Resort
44 Varma's Beach Resort
46 Albenjoh
47 Rodrigues Cottages
50 Calangute Tourist Resort
54 Fellah's Guest House
61 Hotel A Canôa
62 Hotel & Restaurant Souza Lobo
63 Calangute Paradise
64 Conria Beach Resort
65 Coco Banana
66 Sea Pearl Guest House
67 Angela Guest House
69 Victor Guest House
70 Alfa Guest House
71 NV Guest House
72 Paradise Village
73 Hotels Golden Eye, Dona Cristalina, White House & Goan Heritage
74 Falcon Resorts
75 Resorte Santo Antonio & Elnish Golden Sands
77 Kismat Mahal

PLACES TO EAT
2 Little Italy
5 Aqui Portugal
6 St Anthony's Bar & Restaurant
7 Britto's Bar & Restaurant
8 Jack's Bar & Restaurant
11 Electric Cats Bar & Restaurant
14 Casa Portuguesa Restaurant
19 Tito's Bar & Restaurant
34 Boutique Tatophanie Cafe
38 Milky Way (la Restaurant)
45 Infanteria Pastry Shop
51 Dinky's Restaurant & Bar
52 Meena Lobo's Restaurant
53 Tibetan Kitchen
68 Pete's Bar & Restaurant

OTHER
12 Church
48 Church
49 Bus Stand
55 Rama Bookshop
56 State Bank of India & Oceanic Restaurant
57 Bus Stand
58 Bank of Baroda
59 Telelink Fax Agency & Petrol Station
76 MGM Travels
76 St Anthony's Chapel
78 Kerkar Art Complex

To Anjuna

Baga

Calangute

Calangute & Baga

0 250 500 m
Approximate Scale

To Anjuna

To Panaji (Main Road) & Post Office

To Panaji (Bus Route)

GOA

'when the revolution comes' and 'the vibes, maaan', then this was just the ticket. You could frolic around with not a stitch on, be ever so cool and liberated, and completely disregard the feelings of the local inhabitants. You could get totally out of your head every minute of the night and day on every conceivable variety of ganja from Timor to Tenochtitlan, exhibit the most bizarre behaviour, babble an endless stream of drivel and bore everybody shitless. Naturally, John Lennon or The Who were always about to turn up and give a free concert. Ah, Woodstock! Where did you go?

Calangute's heyday as the Mecca of all expatriate hippies has passed. The local people, who used to rent out rooms in their houses for a pittance, have moved on to more profitable things, and Calangute has undergone a metamorphosis to become the centre of Goa's rapidly expanding package tourist market. The hotels and guest houses now stretch almost without a break from Calangute to Baga.

Calangute isn't one of the best Goan beaches: there are hardly any palms gracing the shoreline, some of the sand is contaminated with red soil and the beach drops pretty rapidly into the sea. There is, however, plenty going on, and people who find Colva too quiet may find Calangute more to their liking. However, the beach at Baga is better and the landscape is more interesting.

Information

Rama Bookshop offers a great range of books in many languages. You can buy, sell or exchange here.

The Kerkar Art Complex in South Calangute is well worth a visit. There's a gallery with paintings on sale by local artists and concerts of Indian classical music and dance on Tuesday and Saturday at 6.45 pm. Tickets are Rs 200.

Faxes can be sent and received at Telelink (fax 276124), near the petrol station. MGM Travels is nearby and there are several exchange offices that will change cash or travellers cheques. The Bank of Baroda, near

the market, will advance cash on a MasterCard or Visa card.

Places to Stay

Prices quoted here are for a double room with attached bathroom during the high season. Note that single rooms are rare in this area.

Central Calangute In the centre of Calangute are a number of popular budget options.

Angela Guest House (☎ 277269) offers doubles for Rs 300 to Rs 400 over Christmas. It's a popular place to stay, the rooms have fans and the staff are very friendly. If it's full, there are several other places nearby. The *Conria Beach Resort* and the *Calangute Paradise* have rooms during peak period at Rs 300 and Rs 250 respectively.

Hotel Souza Lobo has a great location right on the beach and has four clean, basic rooms for Rs 300. Hot water is available between 3 and 6 pm when the restaurant is closed.

Fellah's Guest House is a very basic place hidden away behind the souvenir shops. They charge Rs 200 to Rs 300 for a double with attached bathroom.

Hotel A Canôa (☎ 276082) has some nice rooms with sea views, and charges between Rs 150 to Rs 250; unfortunately it's often full.

Alfa Guest House (☎ 277358) is set back from the beach, with rooms from Rs 200 to Rs 250.

Victor Guest House (☎ 276966), also away from the beach, is very pleasant and has doubles with attached bathroom and hot water for Rs 300.

Coco Banana, near Angela Guest House, is very popular. Rooms in this mid-range establishment surround a quiet courtyard and are very clean. The beds are comfortable, fans are provided and the staff are friendly and helpful. Prices jump to Rs 800 in mid-December, but are more reasonable once the rush is over.

Sea Pearl Guest House, next door to Coco Banana, is run by the same people as the *A Canôa* and is slightly cheaper.

The government-owned *Calangute Tourist Resort* (☎ 276024) dominates the beach. The cottages constructed as an extension are rather more attractively designed. From October to June, rooms cost between Rs 220 and Rs 280 for a double, and Rs 390 a triple, all with bathroom and fan. Between 16 June and 30 September they cost Rs 150 to Rs 200, and Rs 300 respectively. There's also a dormitory for Rs 50 (Rs 40 in the low season).

Meena's Lodge, nearby, has doubles with common bathroom from Rs 150, next to the restaurant. There are also triples with attached bathroom for Rs 250 in a separate building.

Falcon Resort (☎ 277033), near Meena's Lodge, offers clean double rooms for around the Rs 300 mark.

Hotel O'Camarao is just north of the Tourist Resort and very close to the beach. Rooms are from Rs 250. Nearby *La Bamba* is similarly priced.

Varma's Beach Resort (☎ 276077), in the same area, is peaceful, friendly and rather exclusive, with the rooms set around a leafy courtyard. At Christmas, doubles cost Rs 1400 (Rs 1600 with air-con), although prices are more than halved by the start of March.

Albenjoh (☎ 276422) is a very good choice, with rooms from Rs 300 to Rs 400, all with attached bathroom. The more expensive rooms have adjoining balconies and the place is spotlessly clean. It's at the start of the Calangute to Baga road.

Rodrigues Cottages, nearby, has a few rooms at Rs 100 with attached bathroom.

South Calangute There are a few cheap places left in this area, but they're in the minority.

NV Guest House, in an excellent location, is the best of the lot. Run by a friendly family, they charge Rs 250 for a double. The restaurant, only a few metres from the beach, serves fresh seafood. For other budget options it's best to search around the back lanes that lead towards the beach.

Kismat Mahal (☎ 276067), near St Anthony's Chapel, is a friendly family-run place with doubles for Rs 300 (downstairs) and Rs 400 (upstairs) over the high season.

In the Rs 500 to Rs 1000 range, there's a group of small hotels notable only for their

position near the beach. The *Hotel Golden Eye* (☎ 277308) has a good restaurant. Next door is the *Hotel Dona Cristalina*, and beside it is the *White House* (☎ 276398). The *Hotel Goan Heritage* (☎ 276253), in the same area, has a swimming pool. Room prices shoot up to Rs 1500 at Christmas, dropping by around Rs 500 by mid-January.

Back from the beach there are a number of expensive resorts near St Anthony's Chapel, including *Elnish Golden Sands*, the *Resorte Santo Antonio* and *Falcon Resorts*. *Paradise Village* (☎ 276351) is a large complex that extends down to the beach. At the height of the season, it charges Rs 2200.

Calangute to Baga Many of the hotels in this area have been tarted up to pull in the package tourists, so it's no surprise that prices are relatively high.

Johnny's Hotel (☎ 277458) is a modern brick building close to the beach. Rooms here go for Rs 500 during the peak period and meals are available.

Hotel Chalston (☎ 276080), near Johnny's Hotel, is a monument to insensitive design and thoughtless planning. At Rs 600 (Rs 1200 for air-con rooms), the price is a joke.

The *Stay Longer Guest House* (☎ 277460) is the best of the smaller places to be found back on the main road heading north. It's run by a very friendly family; rooms are around Rs 400. The nearby *Saahil Hotel* has much the same prices. At Rs 600 the *Hotel Shelsta* (☎ 276069) is a bit more upmarket, with a pleasant garden.

Vila Goesa (☎ 277535), down the lane opposite the Shelsta, is an upmarket hotel in an attractive garden setting at the end of this lane, near the beach. Rooms are from Rs 1375.

Estrela do Mar Beach Resort (☎ 276014), near the Vila Goesa, is slightly cheaper and rather less well looked after. There's a garden and open-air restaurant here, too.

Graceland has a few small apartments for self-caterers, with attached kitchens, for around Rs 500. *Casa Esmeralda*, next door to Graceland, is a good bet and also charges around

Rs 500. *Joanita Guest House* (☎ 277166), near Casa Esmeralda, has good rooms with attached bathroom for Rs 250 to Rs 400. The rooms face a pleasant, shady garden.

Captain Lobo's Beach Hideaway (☎ 276103) is part of a group of three hotels in a small compound close to the beach. They're used almost exclusively by package tour companies. If rooms are available for individuals they charge anything from Rs 1000 to Rs 2000. Captain Lobo's has comfortable two-room units, each with a fridge. The *Colonia Santa Maria* (☎ 276011) and the *Mirbat Holiday Homes* are similar.

Hotel Linda Goa (☎ 276066) is one of a number of package tour hotels on the main road. Though it's looking a bit battered, it's probably the best value of the group, with rooms from Rs 500 to Rs 800. In the same area, with pools and rooms for around Rs 950, there's the *Sunshine Beach Resort* (☎ 276003), *Paraiso de Praia* (☎ 276768), *Villa Bomfim* (☎ 276105), *Ronil Beach Resort* (☎ 276183) and the *Beiramar* (☎ 276246). This last place doubles its prices over Christmas.

The *Ancora Beach Resort* (☎ 276096), down the next side lane (lined with persistent Kashmiri traders), is a reasonable place with attached restaurant and bar. Rooms are around Rs 400. Also down this lane are the over-priced *Jumla Beach Resort* (☎ 276102), and the *Angelina Beach Resort* (☎ 279268) – both around Rs 800.

Hotel Hacienda (☎ 277348) has some good rooms with bath and hot water for Rs 500; it's back on the main road. *Hotel Bonanza* (☎ 276010) across the road is more expensive at Rs 660, or Rs 860 with air-con.

Miranda Beach Resort, in the same area, has doubles for Rs 250 to Rs 300. The characterless *Hotel Sea Wolves* next door also charges Rs 250 for doubles with attached bathroom.

Baga If you're looking for a room or a house to rent ask at Jack's, Britto's or St Anthony's – the cluster of restaurants on the main road in the centre of Baga. There are also a number of houses and cottages for rent across the river, but they're often occupied by long-term visitors.

Joseph D'Souza (☎ 276831) offers basic rooms at around Rs 200 to Rs 250, in the old villa by Casa Portuguesa Restaurant.

Villa Fatima Beach Resort (☎ 277418), set back from the road amid the coconut palm groves, is a good hotel. It's a somewhat grandiose name for what is essentially a three storey building attached to a private house, but it's a very popular place to stay, especially long term, and the family who run it are pleasant. Double rooms with attached bathroom cost from Rs 200 for a courtyard room to Rs 400 for a room facing the sea. There's a restaurant and TV area, and you can rent a safety deposit box for Rs 50. It's often full in the high season.

Alidia Beach Cottages (☎ 276835) is slightly more upmarket, but is also a good place to stay. Over the Christmas fortnight, the very pleasant rooms here go for around Rs 800.

Hotel Riverside (☎ 276062) has pleasant rooms for Rs 700 in a quiet area.

Hotel Lua Nova (☎ 276288) has rooms looking out over rice fields and charges around Rs 950 in peak season. All rooms have a mini bar, and there's a small swimming pool in the shape of a guitar (or a cashew nut – depending how you look at it).

Hotel Baia Do Sol (☎ 722470), set in an attractive flower garden, charges around Rs 1000 but is closer to the beach. The *Cavala Seaside Resort* (☎ 276090) is cool and airy, and also has doubles with verandah and bathroom for around Rs 1000.

Nani's Bar & Rani's Restaurant (☎ 276313), across the river, has a few basic doubles with common bathroom for Rs 100, or Rs 350 with attached bathroom. This pleasant place is popular and getting a room can be difficult at times. To reach it, you cross over an extraordinary bridge which has to be seen to be believed. Somebody was evidently given an unlimited amount of concrete and told to construct the ugliest and most extravagant bridge they could imagine. There are several other houses with rooms to let on the peaceful northern bank of the river, and heading inland from here there are two large resort hotels about half a mile down the road.

Places to Eat

There are literally hundreds of small restaurants crammed into every available bit of space in Calangute, Baga and along the beach between the two. As you might expect, seafood features prominently on the menus.

Infanteria Pastry Shop is an excellent place for a croissant and coffee. There's also a good range of bread and cakes, and a few full meals.

Hotel Souza Lobo is an established favourite. It's a perfect place to watch the sunset or relax in the early afternoon (though it closes between 3 and 6 pm for the benefit of hotel residents). Service is off-hand but the food is very good. Pepper steak is Rs 50, whole grilled kingfish Rs 125, and tiger prawns Rs 350. It's also popular with the local feline population.

Pete's Bar & Restaurant, beside the Angela Guest House, is another good place to eat or sit around with a few cold beers. It's much more of a travellers' place than the Souza Lobo.

The **Tibetan Kitchen** offers momos and other Tibetan food in a relaxed setting, with magazines and board games available to encourage long stays. It's a good place to meet other travellers. The **Wonton House**, which is attached to the Hotel Bonanza, is good for Chinese dishes. Main courses cost between Rs 80 and Rs 100, but the food is good and the atmosphere is relaxed. **China Town**, by Meena's Lodge, is cheaper but hardly inspiring.

Mr Cater's, on the terrace in front of the Calangute Beach Resort, serves a range of north Indian and tandoori dishes, and is very reasonably priced.

The **Oceanic Restaurant**, near the State Bank of India, does excellent seafood. Tandoori shark is Rs 100, most other main dishes are between Rs 60 and Rs 100.

The **Boutique Tatophanie Cafe** is a slick place selling designer clothes and serving treats such as apple pie, chocolate cake and filter coffee.

The **Milky Way** serves ice creams, milkshakes and a range of snacks. In the evenings this turns into the upmarket **Le Restaurant**, where main dishes are around Rs 150.

Vila Goesa has an open-air restaurant with good food, and more reasonable prices – main courses cost about Rs 80 to Rs 100, and there's a good vegetarian selection.

Tito's Bar & Restaurant is the only nightspot to speak of, and it boasts a high-powered sound system and a large terrace which is usually packed by about 11 pm. Prices are more than you'd pay in other restaurants in Calangute and Baga. It's Rs 100 to get into the small disco (open till 3 am).

Casa Portuguesa Restaurant, set within the walled grounds of an old villa, has a unique old world charm. Among the specialities here are roast wild boar (Rs 105), galinha of chicken, and the mandatory tiger prawns. It's a good place for a splurge.

Jack's, **Britto's** and **St Anthony's** are probably the longest running of the beach bars, but there are many others.

Aqui Portugal, run by the same management as the Casa Portuguesa, is the smartest of the beach bars. This is beach cuisine with a difference: the floor is paved, the atmosphere is complemented by tasteful ferns and soft lighting, and the chefs sport full chefs' uniforms. It's a genuinely nice place to eat, and the prices are slightly lower than in the Casa.

Nani's Bar & Rani's Restaurant is a mellow place across the river. The food is good and the atmosphere relaxed.

Entertainment

See **Tito's Bar & Restaurant**, under Places to Eat, above.

Things to Buy

Calangute and Baga have been swamped by Kashmiri traders eager to cash in on the tourist boom. Their incessant hassling and pressure-selling can become tedious. There is, however, a good range of things to buy – Kashmiri carpets, embroideries, and papier-mâché boxes, as well as genuine and reproduction Tibetan and Rajasthani crafts.

Most things are well made but nothing is cheap. If you're going to buy, bargain very hard and don't be afraid to offer a price far below the first price suggested.

Getting There & Away

There are frequent buses to Panaji (Rs 2.50, 35 minutes) and Mapusa from Calangute. A taxi from Calangute or Baga to Panaji costs Rs 100 and takes about 20 minutes.

On Wednesday, boats leave regularly from Baga Beach for the Anjuna flea market.

Getting Around

Most of the buses between Panaji and this area terminate at Calangute; few continue on to Baga. Bicycles and motorcycles can be hired at many places in Calangute and Baga (see the Getting Around section at the start of this chapter) and touts cruise up and down looking for customers for their motorcycles.

ANJUNA

Tel Area Code: 0832

Famous throughout Goa for its Wednesday **flea market** (see the regional highlight on p870), this is the beach that everyone went to when Calangute had been filmed, recorded and reported into the sand. There's a weird and wonderful collection of over-landers, monks, defiant ex-hippies, gentle lunatics, artists, artisans, seers, searchers and peripatetic expats who normally wouldn't be seen outside the organic confines of their health-food shops in San Fran or London.

There's no point in trying to define what Anjuna is or what it's like – the only way to find out is to stay here for a while and make some friends. Full moon, which is often an excuse in itself for a party, is a particularly good time to be here.

Unlike Calangute, the place has retained its charm, although package tourism is beginning to make its presence felt. Nude bathing, on the other hand, is on the decline, as are drugs. Local outrage and official concern about the excesses of a certain minority has led to periodic clampdowns and an exodus to more remote beaches like Arambol to the north and Gokarn, over the border in Karnataka, to the south.

Information

You can have mail sent to Anjuna post office. Halfway between Nelson's Bar and the beach is a branch of MGM Travels, where you can make bookings and get flights confirmed.

The retail needs of the expatriate community are served by the Oxford Stores and the Orchard Stores which stand opposite each other. Here you can get everything from a loaf of bread to a Christmas turkey, and the shelves are piled high with 'exotic' goodies – Vegemite, Heinz baked beans etc. You can change money here and at several other places around the village.

Take great care of your possessions in Anjuna, particularly on party nights, as theft is a big problem. The bank has safety deposit boxes which you can use. You should take care not to waste water because there's an acute shortage, especially late in the season.

Places to Stay

There are guest houses around the village, and even a couple of hotels, but finding a place to stay during the high season can still be a problem. For those who plan to stay long term it can be even more difficult. Most of the available houses are rented for six months or a year by people who come back again and again, so you may have to make do with a very primitive shack to start with. Quite a few places have 'Rooms to Let' signs displayed, so head for these initially.

Accommodation prices given here are for the mid-December to late January high season. In November and February, they drop by about 30 to 50%.

Poonam Guest House (☎ 273247) is an attractive place built around a garden. The rooms here, all of which have attached bathrooms, are much in demand in peak season, and are priced accordingly: Rs 600 for a double with a sea view, Rs 500 for a room without the view, and Rs 800/1000 for the two newly built suites.

Mary's Holiday Home is slightly cheaper than the nearby Poonam; doubles with attached bathroom go for Rs 300 to Rs 400.

Sonic Guest House (☎ 273285) charges Rs 300 for double rooms with a common bathroom.

The new *Palmasol Cliff Resort* (☎ 273236) has double rooms with attached bathroom and hot water for Rs 410. *White Negro* (☎ 273326) is near Palmasol. The older rooms here, with common bathroom, are Rs 250. Basic rooms with attached bathroom are Rs 350, and there are 10 newly built doubles with bathrooms and hot water for Rs 500.

Red Cab Inn (☎ 274427) is a bit flash for any self-respecting backpacker, but great if you can afford your creature comforts. Doubles are Rs 450 (or Rs 350 with common bathroom). *Cabin Disco* (☎ 273254), back on the Mapusa road, charges Rs 150/200 for a single/double with common bathroom.

Starco Bar & Restaurant, nearby, is better value; the five double rooms, all with attached bathroom, go for Rs 200.

Coutino's Nest (☎ 274386) is recommended. It's a clean place with rooms for Rs 150 with common bathroom (hot shower). It's run by a friendly family and there's a pleasant sun terrace. *Motel Rose Garden* (☎ 273362) has eight reasonable rooms at the back, all with attached bathrooms, which range from

Rs 450 to Rs 750 in peak season. You couldn't get much closer to the beach, although the proximity to the Shore Bar means that it's not for party poopers.

Palacete Rodrigues (☎ 273358), on the outskirts of Anjuna, is an old colonial house built around a courtyard. Singles/doubles are Rs 400/500 and suites Rs 600. It's quite a pleasant place.

The Bougainvillea (☎ 273271; fax 262031) is an upmarket place, partly foreign-owned, and also on the outskirts of Anjuna. There's a swimming pool, a large garden, a bar and barbecue, and a pool room. In peak season, well-appointed rooms are Rs 1500 for a double and Rs 2000 for a suite.

Don João Resorts (☎ 274325), back in Anjuna, is a package hotel. If they have a room free in peak season (unlikely) they charge around Rs 1500.

Places to Eat

Anjuna has the usual beachside cafes, but

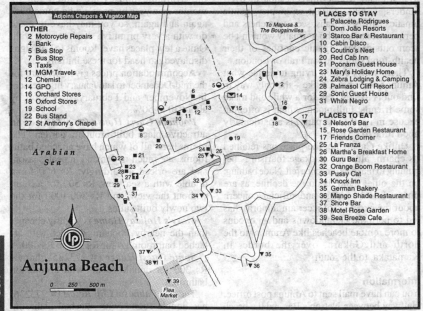

OTHER
2 Motorcycle Repairs
4 Bank
5 Bus Stop
7 Bus Stop
8 Taxis
11 MGM Travels
12 Chemist
14 GPO
16 Orchard Stores
18 Oxford Stores
19 School
22 Bus Stand
27 St Anthony's Chapel

Adjoins Chapora & Vagator Map

To Mapusa &
The Bougainvillea

*Arabian
Sea*

Anjuna Beach

0   250   500 m

Flea
Market

PLACES TO STAY
1 Palacete Rodrigues
6 Dom João Resorts
9 Starco Bar & Restaurant
10 Cabin Disco
13 Coutino's Nest
20 Red Cab Inn
21 Poonam Guest House
23 Mary's Holiday Home
24 Zebra Lodging & Camping
28 Palmasol Cliff Resort
29 Sonic Guest House
31 White Negro

PLACES TO EAT
3 Nelson's Bar
15 Rose Garden Restaurant
17 Friends Corner
25 La Franza
26 Martha's Breakfast Home
30 Guru Bar
32 Orange Boom Restaurant
33 Pussy Cat
34 Knock Inn
35 German Bakery
36 Mango Shade Restaurant
37 Shore Bar
38 Motel Rose Garden
39 Sea Breeze Cafe

GOA

there's some refreshingly different food available, partly because several places are run by foreigners staying here.

The **German Bakery** serves herbal teas and espresso coffee and all manner of other goodies. It's a great place to relax and read a book or meet up with friends. Main dishes are around Rs 50 and they do an excellent spinach and mushroom burger with hummus for Rs 40.

Motel Rose Garden is by the beach and has excellent seafood and cold beer.

The **Sea Breeze Cafe** has reasonable food with main dishes in the Rs 30 to Rs 40 range. **Knock Inn** is recommended for tandoori food. **La Franza** is also popular and serves huge portions.

White Negro is a popular bar and restaurant where the food is good and well presented. Main dishes are around Rs 50 to Rs 60.

Martha's Breakfast Home is, as the name suggests, a good place to start the day. There's good coffee and pancakes. The **Pussy Cat**, nearby, is another good place for lassi, ice cream, fruit juice and milk shakes.

Friends Corner, south of Oxford Stores, has a good range of food in pleasant surroundings.

Entertainment

For most people, the evening begins with several beers on the steps of the **Shore Bar**, watching the sun go down. It can get very crowded, particularly after the flea market, and the powerful sound system keeps people here until long after dark. The **Guru Bar** is another popular drinking spot.

The famous parties are usually held on full-moon nights, particularly over Christmas and the New Year, but there's also often something going on after the flea market. If not, the **Primrose Cafe** in Vagator stays open late and is a popular place to move on to. If there's a party in the area, they'll probably know about it. The motorcycle taxi-wallahs are also good sources of information.

Getting There & Away

There are buses every hour or so to Anjuna and Chapora from Mapusa. They can be very crowded, so it's usually a lot easier to take a motorcycle (about 15 minutes, Rs 50 to Rs 60) or to get a group together and hire a taxi.

Licence and insurance checks on foreigners who rent motorcycles are becoming more common, particularly on market day. See the warning under the Getting Around section at the beginning of this chapter for more details.

CHAPORA & VAGATOR
Tel Area Code: 0832

This is one of the most beautiful and interesting parts of Goa's coastline, and a good deal more attractive than Anjuna for either a short or a long stay. Much of the inhabited area nestles under a canopy of dense coconut palms, and Chapora village is dominated by a rocky hill on top of which sits an old Portuguese fort. The fort is fairly well preserved and worth a visit; the views from its ramparts are excellent.

Secluded, sandy coves are found all the way around the northern side of this rocky outcrop, though Vagator's main beaches face west towards the Arabian Sea. Little Vagator, the beach to the south, is very popular with travellers, and lots of people staying in Calangute and Baga come up here for the day.

Many westerners stay here on a long-term basis, but it's not a tourist ghetto. The local people remain friendly and, since the houses available for rent are widely scattered and there are several beaches and coves to choose from, it's really only on Little Vagator that you see large groups of travellers together in one place. However, although there's still no package tourism, the place is starting to change. The Sterling Vagator Beach Resort has been tarted up, and the large scale development which has just started to reach Anjuna looks set to continue up here eventually. Vagator is a major stop on the bus tours of north Goa, so for a few hours each day the nearest parts of the beach to the bus stop are flooded with day-trippers.

Places to Stay

Most people who come here stay for a long time. Initially, you'll have to take whatever is available and ask around, or stay at Ca-langute or Baga and 'commute' until you've found something. It helps if you get here before the real height of the season – try September and October when there are only a few people about and places have 'Rooms to Let' signs out. Accommodation in vil-lagers' houses costs from around Rs 60, with reductions for long-term letting.

Wherever you decide to live, make sure you have a torch (flashlight) handy. There are no street lights, and finding your way along the paths through coconut palms late at night when there's no full moon is a devil of a job. Houses for rent cost from around Rs 2000 a month upwards depending on their size, location and the length of the rental period. If you're only going to be here for the month over Christmas, you may have to pay two or three times the usual rate – presuming you can find a place to stay, that is.

Chapora The popular *Shertor Villa* has about 20 rooms and charges Rs 150 for a double with common bathroom (reductions for long stays). *Baba Restaurant* has eight doubles for Rs 150.

Sea View Guest House has some extremely basic rooms (little more than a mattress on the floor) from Rs 70 to Rs 100.

Helinda Restaurant (☎ 274345) has proba-bly the best rooms in Chapora. The place is clean and has a friendly, easy-going atmo-sphere, but is often booked solid; doubles with attached bathroom are Rs 250.

Vagator As well as trying the following guest houses, you can also ask for rooms at any of the local restaurants.

Dolrina Guest House (☎ 273382) has a good range of rooms and is run by a very friendly family. Doubles with common bath-room are Rs 230, Rs 260 with bath attached. The *Anita Lodge*, nearby, is cheaper, but basic.

Jolly Jolly Lester has good doubles with attached bathroom at Rs 350.

Reshma Guest House has singles/doubles with common bathroom for Rs 150/200, or Rs 300 with attached bathroom.

The *Royal Resort* (☎ 274365) is so expen-sive and so poorly run that it may be the only place with rooms available in peak season. At Rs 900/1200, this place is ridiculous but you should be able to get a good discount during the shoulder or low season. There's a pool non-guests can use for a nominal fee.

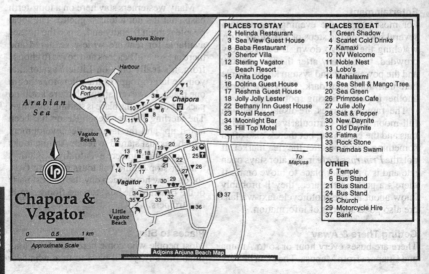

PLACES TO STAY
2 Helinda Restaurant
3 Sea View Guest House
8 Baba Restaurant
9 Shertor Villa
12 Sterling Vagator
   Beach Resort
15 Anita Lodge
16 Dolrina Guest House
17 Reshma Guest House
18 Jolly Jolly Lester
22 Bethany Inn Guest House
23 Royal Resort
34 Moonlight Bar
36 Hill Top Motel

PLACES TO EAT
1 Green Shadow
4 Scarlet Cold Drinks
7 Kamaxi
10 NV Welcome
11 Noble Nest
13 Lobo's
14 Mahalaxmi
19 Sea Shell & Mango Tree
20 Sea Green
26 Primrose Cafe
27 Julie Jolly
28 Salt & Pepper
30 New Daynite
31 Old Daynite
32 Fatima
33 Rock Stone
35 Ramdas Swami

OTHER
5 Temple
6 Bus Stand
21 Bus Stand
24 Bus Stand
25 Church
29 Motorcycle Hire
37 Bank

Chapora River
Harbour
Chapora Fort
Arabian Sea
Vagator Beach
Chapora
To Mapusa
Vagator
Little Vagator Beach

Chapora & Vagator

0   0.5   1 km
Approximate Scale

Adjoins Anjuna Beach Map

GOA

Bethany Inn Guest House is newly built. Only three rooms have been completed so far; there are two spacious doubles (Rs 450) and a larger family room, all with attached bathroom, hot water, and fridge.

Sterling Vagator Beach Resort ☎ 273276), on Vagator Beach, is the most upmarket place in this area. The resort, in palm-shaded grounds, comprises a main block containing the restaurant, bar and reception area, and two types of cottages. It's a friendly place and, as beach resorts go in Goa, quite good. Over peak season rooms cost Rs 1150/2350.

Hill Top Motel is set back a fair distance from Little Vagator Beach and has singles/doubles for Rs 90/160. Nearer the beach, several of the houses around the New Daynite restaurant have rooms to let.

The *Moonlight Bar* has five double rooms available for Rs 150 (common bathroom).

Places to Eat

There are numerous restaurants along the main street of Chapora village.

Scarlet Cold Drinks has excellent ice cream and fruit salad. *Green Shadow* has a range of Chinese, seafood and tandoori dishes all at reasonable prices.

Helinda is the cleanest and most pleasant of the Chapora restaurants, and the prices are good too. The other restaurants in the area are all pretty similar – *Baba Restaurant* is popular, as is *Noble Nest*.

Lobo's and *Mahalaxmi* are among several busy restaurants just above Vagator Beach. *Jolly Jolly Lester* is a friendly place with a good range of travellers' fare.

Sea Green serves up tasty Chinese food on a shady patio area, covered by an old parachute. Chilli prawns are Rs 45. *Mango Tree* also has a fair selection on offer.

Salt & Pepper offers fried mussels with chips and salad for Rs 70.

The *Old Daynite* and *New Daynite* are pleasantly shady places to while away a lazy afternoon.

Primrose Cafe is the place to go at night. It stays open late and has a great sound system.

Getting There & Away

There are fairly frequent buses to Chapora from Mapusa throughout the day. A bus to Vagator is almost as convenient. There are also occasional direct buses from Panaji which follow the coast instead of going via Mapusa. The bus stand is near the road junction in Chapora village. It's often easier and much quicker to rent a motorcycle from Mapusa or to get a group together and hire a taxi.

ARAMBOL (Harmal)

Some years ago, when the screws were tightened at Anjuna in an attempt to control what local people regarded as the more outrageous activities (nudism and drug use) of a certain section of the travelling community, the die-hards cast around for a more 'sympathetic' beach. Arambol, north of Chapora, was one of those which they chose.

Initially, only those willing to put up with very primitive conditions and a total lack of facilities came here. That has changed but development has so far been minimal, although there is talk of a golf course and resort being built here.

The seashore is beautiful and the village quiet and friendly, with just a few hundred locals, mostly fishing people, and a couple of hundred western residents in the November to February high season.

Buses from Mapusa stop at the modern part of Arambol, on the main road, where there's a church, a few shops, but no bank. From here, a side road leads one km down to the village, and the beach is about 500m further on. This main beach is a good place to swim but to the north are several much more attractive bays – follow the path over the headland. There are some chalets on the hillside of the first bay. Behind the second bay is a small freshwater pool that's very pleasant to lie about in. You can give yourself a mudbath with the mud that lines the bottom of this pool, said to be very good for the skin; there's a hot spring nearby.

Places to Stay & Eat

Long-term residents rent rooms from the villagers. The most basic places are often no more than four walls and a roof. You can rent mattresses, cookers and all the rest from the shops at the village.

The most pleasant accommodation is in the little *chalets* on the next bay north. They're basic – outside toilets and water from a spring – but the sea views are superb. At the height of the season these places are much in demand, and rooms are Rs 250.

Villa Oceanic, in the village, is a private house with several immaculately clean rooms, and a friendly atmosphere. All rooms are doubles with common bathroom, and cost Rs 150. The house is just back from the southern end of the beach, and is accessible from the road by a path that's difficult to follow – ask directions.

Laxmi Niwas, 500m back from the beach and above Ganesh Stores, has several double rooms at Rs 250 with attached bathroom.

Pitruchaya Hotel has very basic and rather depressing rooms with common bathroom for Rs 80 to Rs 100.

Mrs Naik Home is much more pleasant, and is consequently usually fully booked. It's on the road to the beach, and has doubles with attached bathroom for Rs 250 to Rs 300.

There are about 10 bars lining the main beach, in which all the usual fare is available. Set back from the beach, the *Garden of Meals* is open every evening and usually has a set special, which is different each night.

Getting There & Away

There are buses from Mapusa to Arambol every couple of hours which take three hours. Alternatively, get a group together and hire a taxi, but you'll have to pay the fare both ways since the driver is unlikely to be able to pick up passengers for the return journey.

There are boats every Wednesday to the Anjuna flea market: Rs 75 one way, or Rs 150 return.

TEREKHOL FORT

At Terekhol, on the north bank of the river of the same name, there's a small Portuguese fort with a little church (usually locked) within its walls. It's now a hotel, the *Hotel Tirakhol Fort Heritage* (☎ (0834) 782240;

fax 782326), and is an interesting, if slightly isolated, place to stay. There's little else here – even the beach is reached via the ferry – but the setting is spectacular, and the rooms in the old fort are unique. Doubles are Rs 850, and the deluxe suites (complete with a huge circular tub) cost Rs 1750.

The fort makes a good outing on a motorcycle, and you could stop for a swim on deserted Querim Beach, but there's very little to see at the fort itself apart from the views.

There are occasional buses from Mapusa or Pernem to Querim, on the south bank of the river, opposite Terekhol, and also between Arambol and Querim. The ferry between Querim and Terekhol runs every half hour between 6 am and 9.30 pm. A taxi from the airport to Terekhol is around Rs 600.

South Goa

Although the beaches of the southern district of Goa include travellers' centres like Colva and Benaulim, and a sprinkling of upmarket resort complexes, there's generally less tourist development here than in the north.

Margao is both the capital of the region and the transport hub. Goa's Dabolim Airport is near Vasco da Gama.

VASCO DA GAMA
Tel Area Code: 0834

Close to Mormugao Harbour and three km from Dabolim airport, Vasco da Gama is the terminus of the railway line into Goa. As the Konkan Railway becomes fully operational, however, even fewer travellers will need to venture up to this unexciting town. If you arrive in Goa by train, you can get off at Margao to reach Colva Beach; if you fly in, it's possible you may arrive too late to get much further than Vasco unless you're prepared to take a taxi.

Places to Stay

Twiga Lodge (☎ 512682), near the bus stand, is the most pleasant budget option. It's an old

Portuguese house run by Tony and Iva Pereira, who worked in Nairobi for a while (twiga is Swahili for giraffe). There is just one single and four doubles for Rs 80/100, and they tend to fill up quickly.

Hotel Westend (☎ 511575) has doubles at Rs 200. The rooms are clean and the management friendly.

The *Tourist Hotel* (☎ 513119), run by the Goa Tourist Development Corporation, is a good place that's centrally located. Doubles are Rs 220, dropping to Rs 180 in the low season; there are also some four-bedded rooms.

Hotel Gladstone (☎ 513966), on the eastern side of the old bus stand, is OK. Doubles are Rs 250, or Rs 350 with air-con. *Hotel Urvashi* (☎ 510273) is also very reasonable, with rooms for Rs 125/180, with bath attached.

Hotel Maharajah (☎ 514075) is probably the best of the mid-range bunch. Doubles range from Rs 275 to Rs 800. *The Citadel* (☎ 512097), near the Tourist Hotel, is more upmarket, but is quite good value – Rs 400, or Rs 500 for air-con rooms.

Hotel La Paz Gardens (☎ 512121; fax 513302) is the top hotel, with singles/doubles for Rs 900/1100.

Hotel Bismarck (☎ 512277; fax 518524) is pleasantly peaceful, and is used as a staging post by tour groups flying in and out of Dabolim. Rooms are Rs 550/700, or Rs 660/800 with air-con. It has a swimming pool (more of a paddling pool really).

Places to Eat

Nanking Chinese Restaurant, near Hotel La Paz Gardens, is a friendly place with good food. Szechuan chicken is Rs 40.

Goodyland is a fast-food joint near the Nanking, serving excellent pizzas (Rs 40), sausage rolls and ice cream.

Sweet N Sour, in the Hotel La Paz Gardens, is a more expensive Chinese place with an excellent reputation.

The vegetarian restaurant at the *Hotel Annapurna* is a good, cheap option, with thalis for Rs 18.

Getting There & Away

You can catch deluxe buses from the new bus stand to Mumbai (15 hours, Rs 205) and Bangalore (12 hours, Rs 222), and there are frequent buses to Margao (one hour, Rs 7) and Panaji (one hour, Rs 7). Change at Panaji for Mapusa and the beaches of north Goa.

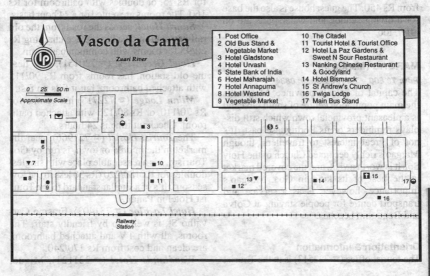

Vasco da Gama

Zuari River

0   25   50 m
Approximate Scale

1 Post Office
2 Old Bus Stand & Vegetable Market
3 Hotel Gladstone
4 Hotel Urvashi
5 State Bank of India
6 Hotel Maharajah
7 Hotel Annapurna
8 Hotel Westend
9 Vegetable Market
10 The Citadel
11 Tourist Hotel & Tourist Office
12 Hotel La Paz Gardens & Sweet N Sour Restaurant
13 Nanking Chinese Restaurant & Goodyland
14 Hotel Bismarck
15 St Andrew's Church
16 Twiga Lodge
17 Main Bus Stand

Railway Station

GOA

Long-distance private buses can be booked at the kiosks outside the railway station.

See Getting There & Away at the start of this chapter for information about trains from Vasco.

A taxi to the airport costs Rs 50.

BOGMALO

Eight km from Vasco, and only four km from the airport, is Bogmalo Beach. It's a small, sandy cove dominated by the five-star Park Plaza Resort, which evaded the restriction requiring all hotels to be built at least 500m from the beach. There's little here apart from the resort hotel and a few smaller places to stay (one with a diving centre attached), the reasonably pleasant beach, several expensive beach cafes, and the small village of Bogmalo.

Rooms at the *Park Plaza Resort* (☎ 513291; fax 512510) cost from US$170 plus taxes. There's a pool and all the usual trimmings you'd expect in a hotel of this calibre. In the village, not far from the beach, the *Petite Guest House* (☎ 555035) has doubles for around Rs 1000. Cheaper, and right on the beach, is *Joets Guest House* (☎ 555036), which has doubles with attached bathroom from Rs 450. The guest house is also the base for a diving school, and watersports are on offer, too.

MARGAO (Madgaon)

Pop: 79,800   Tel Area Code: 0834

The capital of Salcete province, Margao is the main population centre of south Goa and is a pleasant provincial town which still displays reminders of its Portuguese past. It's not of great interest to travellers, though Margao's richly decorated Church of the Holy Spirit is worth a visit, and the covered market is the best of its kind in Goa. Margao's importance, however, is as a service and transport centre for people staying at Colva and Benaulim beaches.

Orientation & Information

The tourist office (☎ 722513) is in the Tourist

Hostel, in the centre of town. The staff are friendly and helpful.

The main bus stand (Kadamba bus stand) is about 1.5km from the centre of town, on the road to Panaji.

The State Bank of India is opposite the Municipal Gardens. You can get advances on a Visa card at Canara Bank (across the road from the tourist office).

Paramount Travels (☎ 731150), next door to Longhuinos, can arrange tickets for the Frank Shipping (formerly Damania) catamaran to Mumbai. Menezes (☎ 720401), behind the Secretariat, is an Indian Airlines agent, but you'll get things done faster if you go direct to the office in Panaji.

The GPO is on the north side of the Municipal Gardens, but the poste restante (open only from 8.30 to 10.30 am and 3 to 4.30 pm) has its own office, 300m south-west of the GPO. Fax and email services are available from Business Inn, Kalika Chambers (on the same street as Food Affair).

Places to Stay

Rukrish Hotel (☎ 721709) is probably the best of the cheapies. It has good, clean singles with small balconies overlooking the street for Rs 75, or doubles with bathroom for Rs 160. The rooms are rented on a 24 hour basis.

Sanrit Hotel, across the road from the old railway station, is a basic place charging Rs 60/95 for rooms with common bathroom.

Hotel Greenview (☎ 720151), also near the old station, has rooms from Rs 90/115 with attached bathroom, but it fills up fast.

Milan Lodge (☎ 722715) has rooms for Rs 70/110, or Rs 80/125 with attached bathroom. Checkout time is 24 hours.

The *Tourist Hostel* (☎ 721966), near the market in the middle of town, is run by Goa Tourism. It's a reasonable place with singles/doubles for Rs 180/220 (Rs 30 less in the low season). It's of a similar standard to the Tourist Hotel in Panaji.

Hotel La Flor (☎ 731402), Erasmo Carvalho St, is well run by friendly staff. The rooms, all with TV and attached bathroom, are clean and cost from Rs 170/240.

Woodlands Hotel (☎ 221121), Miguel

Loyola Furtado Rd, is probably the best hotel in Margao. There's a wide range of rooms from basic singles/doubles with attached bathroom and TV for Rs 150/170 to air-con suites at Rs 500. There's also a bar and restaurant.

Places to Eat

The **Bombay Cafe** is a popular vegetarian place. You can't complain about the prices here: the most expensive item on the menu is the masala dosa – at Rs 6!

The **Kamat Hotel**, beside the Municipal Gardens, also offers no-frills south Indian

vegetarian dishes (nothing over Rs 10). There's a second branch by the Milan Lodge.

Tato, east of the Municipal Gardens, is the best vegetarian restaurant in Margao. A thali costs Rs 20, and the place is spotlessly clean.

Longuinhos, opposite the tourist office, is recommended for Goan cuisine. Goan sausages are Rs 25. They also do pastries, sweets and good tandoori dishes, and there's a busy bar: draught beer is Rs 12.

Woodlands Hotel has a restaurant that's good value – fish curry rice is Rs 21, fried chicken is Rs 31 (plus 10% service charge).

Food Affair is a subterranean restaurant

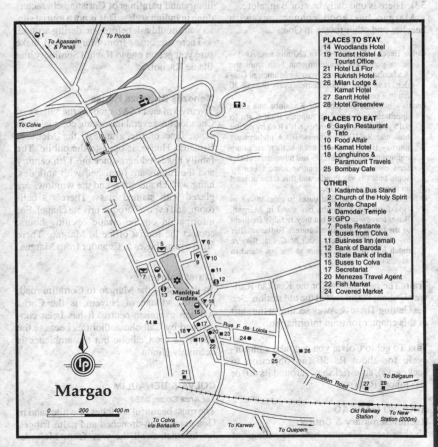

PLACES TO STAY
14 Woodlands Hotel
19 Tourist Hostel & Tourist Office
21 Hotel La Flor
23 Rukrish Hotel
26 Milan Lodge & Kamat Hotel
27 Sanrit Hotel
28 Hotel Greenview

PLACES TO EAT
6 Gaylin Restaurant
9 Tato
10 Food Affair
16 Kamat Hotel
18 Longhuinos & Paramount Travels
25 Bombay Cafe

OTHER
1 Kadamba Bus Stand
2 Church of the Holy Spirit
3 Monte Chapel
4 Damodar Temple
5 GPO
7 Poste Restante
8 Buses from Colva
11 Business Inn (email)
12 Bank of Baroda
13 State Bank of India
15 Buses to Colva
17 Secretariat
20 Menezes Travel Agent
22 Fish Market
24 Covered Market

Margao

0   200   400 m

near Tato that has tasty north Indian food and attentive service. Main dishes are Rs 50 to Rs 75. For nourishment of a spiritual nature the Divine Service Centre is conveniently located just across the road.

Gaylin is an excellent Chinese restaurant. It's very popular; main dishes are around Rs 60.

Getting There & Away

Bus From the Kadamba bus stand, buses leave at 2.30 and 5.30 pm for Mumbai (16 hours, Rs 232 for a luxury bus). There are five daily buses to Hubli (six hours, Rs 43), and seven buses for Belgaum (five hours, Rs 33). There is one daily bus for Bangalore.

Margao has good connections with beaches and other towns in Goa:

Colva Beach – buses to Colva (20 minutes, Rs 3 – some going via Benaulim) run both from the Kadamba bus stand and from the Municipal Gardens (east side), approximately every hour (7.30 am to 7 pm).

Panaji – buses depart from the Kadamba bus stand approximately every 15 minutes from 6 am to 9.15 pm, taking about an hour. It's Rs 8 by public bus, and Rs 10 by express. It's a picturesque journey, if you get a seat, because there are many old, whitewashed churches and monasteries to be seen en route. The alternative route taken by some buses is via Ponda, and this takes at least an hour longer (Rs 11).

Other Buses – you can find buses to most towns in Goa from the Kadamba bus stand in Margao. Buses leave when full, but they're fairly frequent to the major population centres. To the smaller towns, such as Betul, south of Colva, they're much less frequent: inquire at the bus stand in advance.

Train The new station for the Konkan Railway is about 800m east of the old station. See the Getting There & Away section at the start of this chapter for train information.

Taxi To get to Colva, you can take a motorcycle for about Rs 30 (no objection to backpacks), auto-rickshaw (around Rs 40) or taxi (about Rs 60).

AROUND MARGAO
Rachol Seminary & Church

Six km from Margao, near the village of Raia, is the Rachol Seminary and Church. The **Museum of Christian Art** here, which was partly funded by the Gulbenkian Foundation, has some interesting displays. These include textiles, some of the silver once used in the churches of Old Goa, a magnificent 17th century silver monstrance in the shape of a swan, and a mobile mass kit (complete with candlesticks) – standard issue for missionaries out in the jungle. The museum is open daily from 9.30 am to 12.30 pm and 2.30 to 5 pm, closed Monday.

The church dates from 1610 and the seminary has interesting architecture, a decaying library and paintings of Christian characters done in Indian styles. This is not a tourist site, so you should ask before wandering around.

There are buses from Margao, but make sure you get on one to Rachol Seminary, not Illa de Rachol.

Menezes Briganza House

Twenty km east of Margao, in the village of Chandor, are several interesting colonial mansions. One of the grandest, the Menezes Briganza House, is open to the public. The family has lived here since the 17th century and the rooms are furnished with antiques, hung with chandeliers, and the windows are glazed with stained glass. There's a ballroom, and even a baroque private chapel. For information on the erratic opening hours, contact the tourist office in Margao. There are frequent buses to Chandor from Margao.

Christ Ashram

To the east of the Margao to Cortalim road, near the village of Nuvem, is the Christ Ashram exorcism centre. It has been condemned by Catholic authorities because the trappings are Catholic but the ambience is definitely Hindu.

COLVA & BENAULIM
Tel Area Code: 0834

The most beautiful stretches of white sand in Goa extend sun-drenched and palm-fringed for kilometres all the way from Majorda, through Colva, Benaulim, Varca and Cavelossim, down to the point at Mobor.

Twenty years ago, precious little disturbed Colva, except the local fishing people who pulled their catch in by hand each morning, and a few of the more intrepid hippies who had forsaken the obligatory sex, drugs and rock & roll of Calangute for the soothing tranquillity of this paradise. Since there were only two cottages for rent and one restaurant (Vincy's), most people stayed either on the beach itself or in palm-leaf shelters, which they constructed themselves.

Those days are gone forever. The property speculators moved in swiftly, and you can see the results of their efforts – air-con resort complexes, close-packed ranks of tourist cottages, discos, trinket stalls and cold-drink stands. Between the bus park and beach, the small stream now runs black with pollution. You'll be lucky if you see a fisherman around the main area; most now have motorised trawlers which stand anchored in a line offshore. Likewise, you won't come across anyone sleeping on the beach these days or throwing up a palm-leaf shelter.

It's only fair to point out that this development is contained within relatively small areas. The dozen or so resort complexes which have sprung up along this 30km coastline are, for the most part, widely spaced and self contained. Colva itself has suffered, but much of the development here is in the small area around the end of the road from Margao – it's simplicity itself to get away from it. Walk two km in either direction, and you'll get close to what it used to be like before the cement mixers began chugging away. The area has a long way to go before it gets as developed as Calangute, or a lot of other beaches I could think of around the world.

Information

The nearest post office is in Colva village, where letters can be sent poste restante; you'll need to take your passport or similar proof of identity to collect mail. There's a small Bank of Baroda next to the church, and the Silver Sands Hotel will change travellers cheques. Thomas Cook has a mobile exchange van which parks outside Goa Tourism's Tourist Complex daily (in season) between 3 and 5 pm, and gives the best rates of all. You can send and receive faxes from the booth outside the Tourist Complex.

Places to Stay

Prices below are for the peak season: mid-December to late January. In November and February they drop by about 30 to 50%.

It's possible to rent houses long term in Colva and Benaulim – just ask around in the restaurants and shops. Most houses are a 20 minute walk from the beach. Prices vary enormously, depending on location, the size of the house and the season, but in high season you can expect to pay anything from around Rs 2000 a month up to Rs 10,000. Between November and March, competition for houses is stiff, so get there before then if possible.

Colva There's a wide choice of short-term accommodation in Colva. At the cheaper end of the market are the places strung out along the roads behind the beach, north of the main area.

Rodrickson Cottages is set back from the beach, but is reasonable value at Rs 70/120 for basic rooms with a shower and toilet behind a partition inside the rooms.

Hotel Tourist Nest (☎ 723944) is a rambling old Portuguese house that's similarly good value. Doubles are Rs 100 with common bathroom, or Rs 150 with attached bathroom. The *Garden Cottages* close by is similar.

Fishermen's Cottages is one of the closest places to the beach. Prices during peak season range from Rs 150 to Rs 200 for a double with bathroom, though it's not the cleanest place in Colva.

Lucky Star Restaurant (☎ 730069) has sea-facing doubles with attached bathroom for Rs 200, plus some cheaper rooms.

Vailankanni Cottages (☎ 737747) is one of several places right in the thick of things on the main street. Popular with travellers for the friendly atmosphere, rooms cost from Rs 150 to Rs 200 for a double with attached

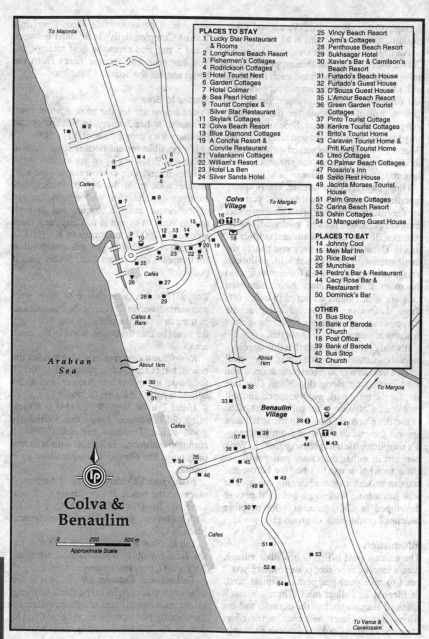

PLACES TO STAY
1 Lucky Star Restaurant & Rooms
2 Longhuinos Beach Resort
3 Fishermen's Cottages
4 Rodrickson Cottages
5 Hotel Tourist Nest
6 Garden Cottages
7 Hotel Colmar
8 Sea Pearl Hotel
9 Tourist Complex & Silver Star Restaurant
11 Skylark Cottages
12 Colva Beach Resort
13 Blue Diamond Cottages
19 A Concha Resort & Convite Restaurant
21 Vailankanni Cottages
22 William's Resort
23 Hotel La Ben
24 Silver Sands Hotel
25 Vincy Beach Resort
27 Jymi's Cottages
28 Penthouse Beach Resort
29 Sukhsagar Hotel
30 Xavier's Bar & Camilson's Beach Resort
31 Furtado's Beach House
32 Furtado's Guest House
33 D'Souza Guest House
35 L'Amour Beach Resort
36 Green Garden Tourist Cottages
37 Pinto Tourist Cottage
38 Kenkre Tourist Cottages
41 Brito's Tourist Home
43 Caravan Tourist Home & Priti Kunj Tourist Home
45 Liteo Cottages
46 O Palmar Beach Cottages
47 Rosario's Inn
48 Savio Rest House
49 Jacinta Moraes Tourist House
51 Palm Grove Cottages
52 Carina Beach Resort
53 Oshin Cottages
54 O Mangueiro Guest House

PLACES TO EAT
14 Johnny Cool
15 Men Mar Inn
20 Rice Bowl
26 Munchies
34 Pedro's Bar & Restaurant
44 Cacy Rose Bar & Restaurant
50 Dominick's Bar

OTHER
10 Bus Stop
16 Bank of Baroda
17 Church
18 Post Office
39 Bank of Baroda
40 Bus Stop
42 Church

To Majorda

Arabian Sea

Cafes

Colva Village

To Margao

Cafes

Cafes & Bars

About 1km

About 1km

To Margoa

Benaulim Village

Cafes

Cafes

Colva & Benaulim

0   250   500 m
Approximate Scale

To Varca & Cavelossim

GOA

bathroom. There are good meals and snacks available.

Blue Diamond Cottages (☎ 737909) is closer to the beach. This is an older place which offers good, clean rooms for Rs 250 with attached bathroom.

Jymi's Cottages (☎ 737752) is run by a friendly family and is very close to the beach just south of the main drag. The double rooms (with attached bathroom) are clean but basic and cost Rs 250.

Goa Tourism's **Tourist Complex** or **Tourist Cottages** (☎ 722287) is a two storey terrace of rooms facing the sea (each with its own balcony), a separate block of cottages, a restaurant, bar, reception area and garden. The rooms cost Rs 280 for a double with fan and bathroom, or Rs 450 with air-con. There's also a dormitory for Rs 50 per bed. The staff are friendly and the hotel is quite pleasant.

Hotel Colmar (☎ 721253) is popular, although it's fairly expensive over Christmas. There are doubles for Rs 450 with bath attached and also rooms for Rs 800, and cottages for Rs 1500. The hotel has its own restaurant, bar and money exchange facilities, and is used by overland tour groups.

Sea Pearl Hotel (☎ 730070) offers spotlessly clean doubles with attached bathroom for Rs 315. The staff are very friendly and helpful, and the restaurant is popular for its excellent seafood.

Sukhsagar Beach Resort (☎ 721888) is a reasonable place with doubles for Rs 320, or Rs 480 with air-con. All rooms have bathrooms with individual water heaters.

Hotel La Ben (☎ 722009) is a fairly characterless building on the main road. The rooms are clean and comfortable, however, and there's hot water, but the Rs 450 price tag for a double is probably a bit steep. There's a rooftop restaurant and bar.

Skylark Cottages (☎ 739261) charge Rs 315 for a double with bathroom, with a hot water shower. The rooms are clean and it's reasonable value.

Vincy Beach Resort (☎ 722276), once the only bar/restaurant in the area, has been through many changes. The original Indo-Portuguese structure has sadly long since disappeared and Vincy's has joined the 20th century with a vengeance. It now offers plain double rooms with attached bathroom (and individual water heaters) for Rs 350. There's a restaurant on the ground floor.

Colva Beach Resort (☎ 721975) is further away from the beach. There are doubles for Rs 600 and air-con doubles for Rs 800 during the peak season, although the prices drop significantly in the shoulder season.

William's Resort (☎ 721077) is a superior place charging Rs 770 for a double, or Rs 990 with air-con (tax not included). Non-guests can use the pool for Rs 25 per hour.

A Concha Resort (☎ 723593) is a long way back from the beach, near the church, but has good, clean rooms for Rs 690, and an excellent Chinese restaurant.

Silver Sands Hotel (☎ 721645) is in the centre of Colva. Doubles cost from Rs 950 (Rs 1200 over Christmas), not including tax. There's a swimming pool, health club, watersports and indoor games, an excellent bar and restaurant, live bands in the high season, and a travel counter.

Penthouse Beach Resort (☎ 731030) consists of a complex of Portuguese-style cottages built around a pool. Facilities and prices are similar to the Silver Sands.

Longhuinos Beach Resort (☎ 731645) is in an excellent location near the beach. The rooms are simply furnished but most have balconies and face the sea. Rates are from Rs 1200 for a double with attached bathroom and hot water. There's a small garden with direct access to the beach.

Majorda There are several resort complexes north of Colva, along Majorda Beach. They include: the Majorda Beach Resort (☎ 730241), which has 120 rooms costing Rs 4000 each over the peak season, but drops by about 50% by late February; and **The Regency Resort** (☎ 754180), which has well-appointed rooms for Rs 3500 (Rs 7000 over Christmas).

Benaulim If you hanker after the more tranquil parts of this coastline, then Benaulim

Beach, less than two km south of Colva, is the place to head for.

Furtado's Beach House is right on the beach; rooms with attached bathroom cost Rs 300.

Xavier's Bar, nearby, has slightly cheaper rooms at Rs 200. *Camilson's Beach Resort* (☎ 722917) has a few doubles at Rs 250, but most rooms cost between Rs 600 and Rs 900.

L'Amour Beach Resort (☎ 733720) has reasonable rooms with attached bathroom. They charge between Rs 275 and Rs 550. Most of the rooms are cottages, and are aligned so that they catch the sea breezes. *O Palmar Beach Cottages* (☎ 722901), opposite, is similar. Doubles are Rs 360 with fan and bathroom. Neither of these places has much in the way of shade, but they're both very close to the beach and are often full in the high season.

Most of the other places are scattered around the village of Benaulim, about one km back from the beach, where accommodation is cheaper.

Rosario's Inn (☎ 734167) is run by a charming family. It's very popular and has rooms with verandah and attached bathroom for Rs 150. There are also cheaper rooms with common bathroom.

Savio Rest House charges just Rs 50 for a room with common bathroom, or Rs 70 with attached bathroom. *Jacinta Moraes Tourist House* (☎ 722706), nearby, has good doubles at Rs 100 with bath.

Green Garden Tourist Cottages has two basic doubles for Rs 80. *Kenkre Tourist Cottages*, nearby, is excellent value at Rs 80 for a double with attached bathroom.

Liteo Cottages offers reasonable doubles with attached bathroom for Rs 250. *D'Souza Guest House* (☎ 734364), a short distance north along the road to Colva, is a small, excellent, upmarket guest house in a Goan bungalow with an extensive garden. Spotlessly clean rooms at this friendly, family-run place cost up to Rs 350 in peak season, but prices drop to half this at other times. They even accept credit cards! Also on this road is the *Pinto Tourist Cottage*, which has a few doubles for Rs 100.

Palm Grove Cottages (☎ 722533), further south, is an excellent place to stay. Set in a very peaceful garden, back from the beach, it has small rooms with attached bathroom for between Rs 175 and Rs 280, and larger rooms from Rs 500 to Rs 600. Comfortable rooms in the new building cost Rs 600 to Rs 650 with bathroom and hot water, or Rs 750 with air-con. The staff are most helpful and good meals are available in the shady, garden restaurant.

O Mangueiro Guest House has five doubles and a single that people often rent long term; the doubles go for Rs 80. There's a kitchen and common bathroom.

Oshin Cottages (☎ 722707) are in a very peaceful area, set back from the road. There are 12 doubles, all with attached bathrooms, for Rs 250.

Carina Beach Resort (☎ 734166) is currently the top hotel in Benaulim. It's a low-key affair with a garden and swimming pool. Rooms are Rs 880 to Rs 1200, but they have a few cheaper rooms without attached bathroom. A short way along the road, a new complex, the *Royal Goan Beach Club*, looks set to take over the top slot as soon as it is finished.

The old *Caravan Tourist Home* (☎ 737953) is in Maria Hall (the area around the second crossroads back from the beach). It has a beautifully furnished sitting room, although the bedrooms are more basic. Still, it's a pleasant place to stay, and has doubles from Rs 140 to Rs 200. *Priti Kunj Tourist Home*, next door, has large double rooms for Rs 150.

Brito's Tourist Home, nearby on the Margao road, is a fairly featureless place but is friendly and good value if you're on a tight budget – rooms are around Rs 120. You'll find the owner in the small general store attached.

Places to Eat

Colva The most popular places to eat (and drink) around Colva are the string of open-air, wooden restaurants which line the beach either side of where the road ends. They're all individually owned and, because of the competition, the standard of food is pretty high. Seafood is, of course, *de rigueur*, and the restaurants are well tuned in to what travellers like for breakfast. Cold beer and spirits are available, and virtually all of these places have a sound system.

It would be unfair to single out individual restaurants for special mention since every traveller has their favourite place and this often depends on the particular crowd which congregates there. This naturally changes constantly, but if a restaurant is full, this tends to be a fairly good indication that the food is good.

Further back from the beach are a number of popular places.

Men Mar Inn is a laid-back place with a book exchange and cheap food.

The *Convite* restaurant in the A Concha Resort has excellent Chinese food, although the prices are rather higher than many of the other places – main dishes cost Rs 60 to Rs 80, and small beers are Rs 25.

Johnny Cool, rapidly disappearing behind two new hotels under construction, has possibly the best selection of local beers in Colva.

The *Rice Bowl* serves good Chinese food for very reasonable prices.

The *Sea Pearl Hotel* is an excellent place for seafood; the kitchen must be one of the cleanest in India, and the selection is impressive. Specialities include doma fish, white and black pomfret, and baby shark, and you can follow it all up with a Goan speciality: bebinca – coconut pudding.

The *Hotel Colmar* has a restaurant with a pleasant ambience, although the food is sometimes rather disappointing.

The *Silver Star Restaurant*, at the Tourist Complex, has barbecues on the lawn, and they have good Mughlai dishes and seafood.

Munchies is one of several cheap open-air restaurants among the group of shops and souvenir stalls near the roundabout. It is hidden away on the beach side of the other places, and serves a selection of Indian and western food. It even has cappuccino coffee.

This whole area stays lively late into the night, and a short distance along the beach can be found what passes for Colva's nightlife.

Splash has a dance floor by the beach, as does the neighbouring bar, *Ziggy's*. Don't expect to find a huge party automatically, however. Much depends on the people who happen to turn up that night.

For a splurge, choose between *Longuinhos Beach Resort*, *Silver Sands Hotel* and *Penthouse Beach Resort*. The cuisine and service at these places is what you would expect from upmarket hotels and they all offer Goan, Indian and continental dishes. Both the Silver Sands and the Penthouse have live bands during the high season and dinner is often an 'all you can eat' smorgasbord for a set price.

Benaulim Almost all the beach shacks serve excellent seafood and cold beer.

L'Amour Beach Resort produces excellent tandoori food.

Pedro's Bar & Restaurant is a perennial favourite due to its convenient location.

Dominick's Bar, back in the village, is a meeting place for the older locals, but the restaurant just next to it is popular with foreigners, as is the restaurant in the *Palm Grove Cottages*.

Cacy Rose Bar & Restaurant in Benaulim village is a friendly family-run venture, and a good place to ask around for accommodation.

Getting There & Away

Buses run from Colva to Margao about every half hour (Rs 3, 20 minutes) between 7.30 am and about 7 pm. Buses from Margao to Benaulim are also frequent; some of them continue south to Varca and Cavelossim.

A taxi from Colva to Margao costs around Rs 60. Colva to Dabolim airport costs Rs 225, and to Panaji, it's Rs 300. All fares are negotiable. Motorcycle taxis charge Rs 30 between Margao and Colva. Backpacks are no problem.

Dominick's (the branch on Colva Beach) organises boat trips down the coast to Palolem for Rs 325, meals included. They also run a bus to Anjuna market every Wednesday.

Getting Around

There are plenty of places that rent bicycles (Rs 40 per day), mopeds (Rs 300), 100cc motorcycles (Rs 400) and Enfields (Rs 500). These are high season prices – they drop by 50% or more out of season. Negotiate for a lower price.

At low tide, you can cycle 15km along the beach to Mobor, at the southern end. It's possible to get a boat across the estuary to Betul and then cycle back via Margao.

If you're not planning on staying at any of the northern beaches, it's worth making the day trip to the Wednesday flea market at Anjuna. Trips are advertised at the beach bars and cost about Rs 85 to Rs 100. They take the best part of a day, but are worth it, because tackling this trip by public transport involves umpteen bus changes. It's also possible to hire one of the wooden ex-fishing boats to take you there, but get a group together because they're relatively expensive.

VARCA & CAVELOSSIM

Tel Area Code: 0834

The 10km strip of pristine beach south of Benaulim has become Goa's upmarket resort beach, with at least half a dozen hotels of varying degrees of luxury. As far as resorts go, some of them are quite good, and they are certainly isolated from anything which might disturb the peace. Access to the resorts is along the main road south from Benaulim. Prices given below are for the high season, which for these resort hotels tends to be from October to April. Over the Christmas peak period (21 December to 10 January), prices rise by about 40%; during the rest of the year they drop by about 40%.

Places to Stay

Varca Varca is five km south of Benaulim, and there are a couple of resorts here.

Resorte de Goa (☎ 745066; fax 745310) is a reasonably small place with rooms and villas set around a swimming pool. The beach is a short walk away and very quiet. The cheapest rooms are Rs 1850 but the villas at Rs 2150 are better.

Goa Renaissance Resort (☎ 745208; fax 745225), 500m beyond Resorte de Goa, is a true five-star establishment. All rooms have a balcony facing the sea, there's a pool, beach-side bar, and even a six-hole golf course. There's a couple of restaurants, and watersports are available. Rooms cost from US$207.

Cavelossim Cavelossim, seven km further south, is more developed. Several hotels are currently being built, and there's even a time-share resort under construction.

Gaffino's Beach Resort (☎ 746385) is a guest house with rooms for Rs 350/400 (Rs 300/350 outside the peak period). It's a good, clean place and perfect if all you want to do is get away from India and rub shoulders with the package tourists. The restaurant is very popular with people staying at the more expensive hotels nearby; main dishes are Rs 70 to Rs 100.

Dona Sylvia (☎ 746321; fax 746320), nearby, has a pool and is popular with package groups. Rooms cost Rs 3400 to Rs 5100 (Rs 4800 to Rs 7200 over Christmas). The *Old Anchor Resort* is 500m beyond. It's an older place with a reception area in an odd building that's supposed to resemble a Portuguese ship. There's a pool here too. Rooms are Rs 1190/2390 for a single/double; some could do with a lick of paint and a squirt of air freshener.

The *Holiday Inn Resort* (☎ 746303; fax 746333) has rooms arranged around a pool, just back from the beach. Doubles and singles alike go for Rs 4500.

The *Leela Beach Resort* (☎ 746363; fax 746352) is at the end of the road at Mobor, near the mouth of a small estuary. This well designed five-star deluxe complex is built around an artificial lagoon. The main building is very airy and catches the sea breezes. Rooms cost from US$235, although this goes up to US$330 over Christmas. The leisure facilities include tennis and squash courts, gym, pool and health spa, plus a full range of watersports. The beach is particularly good here, with palm trees providing welcome shade.

OTHER BEACHES

Opposite the narrow peninsula occupied by the Leela Beach Resort is the fishing village of **Betul**, reached either by boat or by bus from Margao (45 minutes, Rs 4) via Chinchinim or Cuncolim. North of the village, near the harbour, is the peaceful *Oceanic Tourist Hotel* (☎ (0834) 760301). It's a small place with double rooms with attached bathrooms from Rs 175. It takes about an hour to walk to Betul Beach from the hotel, so it's better to take a boat across the estuary to Mobor.

The road from Betul to Agonda winds over hills, past the old Portuguese fort of **Cabo de Rama**. There are now a couple of places to stay in **Agonda**, a little village by an empty two km stretch of sand. Both are about one km past the village, along the beach road. The *Dunhill Bar and Restaurant* (☎ (0834) 647328) has simple double rooms with common bathroom for Rs 100, and a shady bar and restaurant. Two hundred metres further down the track is *Carferns* (☎ 647235), which is slightly more basic, but charges the same price.

In the far south of Goa, at **Palolem**, is an impossibly beautiful palm-fringed cove of white sand that is becoming a popular spot for day-trippers from Colva and Cavelossim. There's accommodation at the *Palolem Beach Resort* (☎ (0834) 643054), a low-key affair with basic doubles at Rs 250 to Rs 300, and tents (better, since they catch the breeze) for Rs 150. Security seems to be pretty good, and there's a good restaurant. If this place is full, about 50m down the road from the beach is *Tonricks Royal Cottages* (☎ (0834) 643239), where doubles with attached bathroom go for Rs 350. Similarly priced is *Cocohuts*, which has some thatched beach huts built on stilts among the palm trees. There are also plenty of rooms available in villagers' houses.

There are only two buses a day from Margao to Palolem, but frequent services from Margao to Chaudi (Rs 8) – get off at the Palolem junction, 1.5km before Chaudi. It's then a two km ride in an auto-rickshaw (Rs 25); motorcycles charge Rs 15.

A couple of kilometres south of Palolem is **Rajbag**, an exposed but isolated stretch of sand. There's only one hotel, the *Molyma Hotel* (☎ (0834) 643028), Kindlebaga, Canacona. It's in a plantation of cashew trees, a long way back from the beach. The hotel is reasonable value at Rs 175/250 for a room with attached bathroom, but you really need your own transport to stay here.

PONDA

Although the central, inland town of Ponda is of no great interest, it does boast an old mosque and, in the surrounding area, numerous unique Hindu temples. There are regular buses from Panaji and Margao, but to get to the temples it's best to have your own transport.

When the Portuguese arrived in Goa, they destroyed every temple and mosque they could lay their hands on. As a result, temples in Goa are generally set back from the coast and comparatively new, although some date back about 400 years. The temples near Ponda have been rebuilt from originals destroyed by the Portuguese, and their lamp towers are a distinctive Goan feature.

Five of Goa's most important Hindu temples are close to Ponda, on the inland route between Panaji and Margao. The Siva temple of **Shri Mangesh** is at Priol-Ponda Taluka, about 22km from Panaji. This tiny 18th century hilltop temple, with its white tower, is a local landmark. Less than two km further down the road is **Shri Mahalsa**, a Vishnu temple.

About five km from Ponda are **Shri Ramnath** and **Shri Nagesh**, and nearby is the **Shri Shantadurga Temple**. Dedicated to Shantadurga, the goddess of peace, this temple sports an unusual, almost pagoda-like, structure with a roof made from long slabs of stone. Further south are the temples of **Shri Chandreshwar**, west of Quepem; **Shantadurga**, east of Betul; and **Shri Mallikarjuna**, east of Chauri.

The oldest mosque remaining in Goa is the

Safa Shahouri Masjid at Ponda, built by Ali Adilshah in 1560. It once matched the mosques at Bijapur in size and splendour, but was allowed to decay during the Portuguese period. Little remained of its former grandeur by the time the Portuguese left, but the Archaeological Survey of India has now undertaken its restoration using local artisans.

BONDLA WILDLIFE SANCTUARY
Up in the lush foothills of the Western Ghats, Bondla is a good place to see sambar and wild boar. It's the smallest of the Goan wildlife sanctuaries (eight sq km) but the easiest one to reach. It's 52km from Panaji and 38km from Margao.

There is a botanical garden, fenced deer park and a zoo which is better than most, with reasonably spacious enclosures. The zoo was originally established to house orphaned animals, but it's now also a breeding colony for the larger species of deer.

Bookings for accommodation should be made in advance at the office of the Department of Forestry, directly opposite the Air India office, and beside the Hotel Fidalgo, in Panaji. The accommodation is in chalets, which are very good value at under Rs 50, but they often get booked out. It may be easier to get a room on Thursdays, when the park is closed. This may not sound such a smart idea, but it's a very pleasant place to stay, and you're right at the sanctuary gates when they open at 9 am on Friday.

To get to Bondla, take a bus to Ponda, and then hire a taxi to the park (Rs 200). Alternatively, take the Molen bus as far as Tiskar, and catch a motorcycle taxi to the park (Rs 50). There is a minibus to get around the park, but it's easier (and quieter) to walk. The minibus is essentially for the deer park, which opens for an hour or so at 4 pm.

DUDHSAGAR FALLS
On the eastern border with Karnataka are Goa's most impressive waterfalls. They're particularly impressive if you're coming in by train soon after the monsoon, because the line crosses a bridge by the falls and the train often stops to let passengers get a good view. Dudhsagar is a two hour trip from Margao or 50 minutes from Kulem station. You can catch a morning train up and spend several hours at the falls – there are pools to swim in – before taking an afternoon train back. Timetables may change while the line is being upgraded.

MOLEN & COTIGAO WILDLIFE SANCTUARIES
These wildlife sanctuaries are larger than Bondla but you will need your own transport to get to them. There's a treetop watchtower in Cotigao but the animals manage to remain well hidden, so you won't see a lot.

Accommodation is available at Molen in the *Tourist Resort* (☎ (834) 600238). Doubles cost Rs 150, and meals are available for those who book in advance. There's no accommodation in the Cotigao sanctuary, although you can stay in the *Forest Rest House*, nearby, if you get permission from the Department of Forestry, opposite the Air India office in Panaji.

Karnataka

The Kannada-speaking state of Karnataka, formerly known as Mysore, has a finely balanced mix of natural attractions and superb historic architecture. It appeals equally to temple lovers, wildlife enthusiasts, trekkers and beach bums, yet much of the state sees few travellers compared to neighbouring Goa, Kerala and Tamil Nadu.

The state consists of a narrow coastal strip backed by the monsoon-drenched Western Ghats and a drier, cooler interior plateau that turns arid in the far north. It's a major producer of coffee, spices and betel nut, and supplies 60% of the country's silk. The capital, Bangalore, is the centre of India's science and technology industry and is one of the fastest growing cities in Asia.

Karnataka has a rich history, thanks to the rollcall of competing dynasties which rose and fell in this part of the country. To see the architectural legacy of these kingdoms, you need to explore the central plateau; to witness the beauty of the state's teak and rosewood forests, you need to explore the Western Ghats; and to enjoy the serenity of Karnataka's coastline, you need to come before developers take advantage of the new Konkan Railway and start meddling with this forgotten stretch of India's coast.

History

A multitude of religions, cultures and kingdoms have unrolled across the terrain of Karnataka, beginning in the 3rd century BC when Chandragupta Maurya, India's first great emperor, retreated to Sravanabelagola after he had renounced worldly ways and embraced Jainism. Many centuries later, the 17m high statue of Gomateshvara, which celebrated its 1000th anniversary in 1981, was erected at Sravanabelagola. In the 6th century, the Chalukyans built some of the earliest Hindu temples in India near Badami. All later south Indian temple architecture stemmed from their designs, and from those

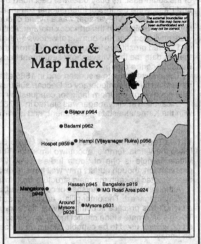

KARNATAKA AT A GLANCE

Population: 48.6 million
Area: 191,773 sq km
Capital: Bangalore
Main Language: Kannada
Literacy Rate: 56%
Best Time to Go: September to February

Locator & Map Index

- Bijapur p964
- Badami p962
- Hospet p958 • Hampi (Vijayanagar Ruins) p956
- Mangalore p949
- Hassan p945 Bangalore p919 • MG Road Area p924
- Around Mysore p938 • Mysore p931

Highlights

- Hiring a rickety old bike and cycling among the atmospheric ruins of Vijayanagar in the early morning
- Resting up from the travails of the road on Gokarna's laid-back beaches
- Clambering among the ruins and beautiful cave temples in the sandstone canyon at Badami

Festivals

Vairamudi – Melkote – March/April
Dussehra – Mysore – October
Muharram – Hospet – dates vary

by the Pallavas at Kanchipuram and Mahabalipuram in Tamil Nadu.

Other important Indian dynasties, such as the Cholas and the Gangas, have also played their part in Karnataka's history, but it was

A REGIONAL HIGHLIGHT

The Ruins of Vijayanagar

Vijayanagar, or Hampi as it is often called these days, was once the capital of one of the largest Hindu empires in Indian history. Founded by the Telugu princes Harihara and Bukka in 1336, it reached the height of its power under Krishnadevaraya (1509-29), when it controlled the whole of the peninsula south of the Krishna and Tungabhadra rivers, except for a string of commercial principalities along the Malabar coast.

Comparable to Delhi in the 14th century, the city, which covered an area of 33 sq km, was surrounded by seven concentric lines of fortification and was reputed to have had a population of about half a million. It maintained a mercenary army of over one million according to the Persian ambassador, Abdul Razak, and ironically included Muslim mounted archers to defend it from the Muslim states to the north.

Vijayanagar's wealth was based on control of the spice trade to the south and the cotton industry of the south-east. Its busy bazaars, described by European travellers such as the Portuguese Nunez and Paes, were centres of international commerce.

The religion of Vijayanagar was a hybrid of current Hinduism, with the gods Vishnu and Siva being lavishly worshipped in the orthodox manner. At the same time, Jainism was also prominent. Brahmins were privileged; sati (the burning of widows on the funeral pyres of their husbands) was widely practised and sacred prostitutes frequently worked from the city's temples. Brahmin inscriptions discovered on the site date the first Vijayanagar settlement back to the 1st century AD and suggest that there was a Buddhist centre nearby.

The empire came to a sudden end in 1565 after the disastrous battle of Talikota when the city was ransacked by the confederacy of Deccan sultans (Bidar, Bijapur, Golconda, Ahmednagar and Berar), thus opening up southern India for conquest by the Muslims.

Excavation at Vijayanagar was started in 1976 by the Archaeological Survey of India in collaboration with the Karnataka state government, and is still continuing.

Vittala Temple From the eastern end of Hampi Bazaar an obvious track, navigable only on foot, leads left to the Vittala Temple, about two km away. The undisputed highlight of the ruins, the 16th century Vittala Temple is one of south India's three World Heritage Monuments. It's in a good state of preservation, though purists may well have reservations about the cement-block columns which have been erected to keep the main structure from falling down.

Although it was never finished or consecrated, the temple's incredible sculptural work is the pinnacle of Vijayanagar art. The outer pillars are known as the musical pillars as they reverberate when tapped, although this practice is being actively discouraged as the pillars are somewhat the worse for wear. There's an ornate stone chariot in the temple courtyard containing an image of Garuda. The chariot's stone wheels used to be capable of turning. It costs Rs 5 to enter the temple complex, though it's free on Friday.

Sule Bazaar & Achyutaraya Temple Halfway along the path from Hampi Bazaar to the Vittala Temple, a track to the right leads to deserted Sule Bazaar, which gives you some idea of what Hampi Bazaar might have looked like if it hadn't been repopulated. At the southern end of this area is the Achyutaraya Temple, whose isolated location at the foot of Matunga Hill makes it even more atmospheric than the Vittala Temple.

Royal Enclosure Area This area of Hampi is quite different from the northern section, since most of the rounded boulders which once littered the site have been used to create a mind-boggling proliferation of beautiful stone walls. It's a two km walk from the Achyutaraya Temple on a poorly signposted track, so most people get to it from the Hampi Bazaar-Kamalapuram road. This area is easily navigable by bicycle since a decent dirt road runs through the heart of it.

Within various stone-walled enclosures here are the rest of Hampi's major attractions, including the **Lotus Mahal** and the **Elephant Stables**. The former is a delicately designed pavilion in a walled compound known as the Zenana Enclosure. It's an amazing synthesis of Hindu and Islamic style and it gets its name from the lotus bud carved in the centre of the domed and vaulted ceiling.

The Elephant Stables is a grand building with domed chambers, which once housed the state elephants. It costs Rs 5 to enter the Zenana Enclosure, except on Friday when it's free.

Further south are the Royal Enclosure, with its various temples and elaborate waterworks, plus the **Underground Temple** and the impressive **Queen's Bath**. ■

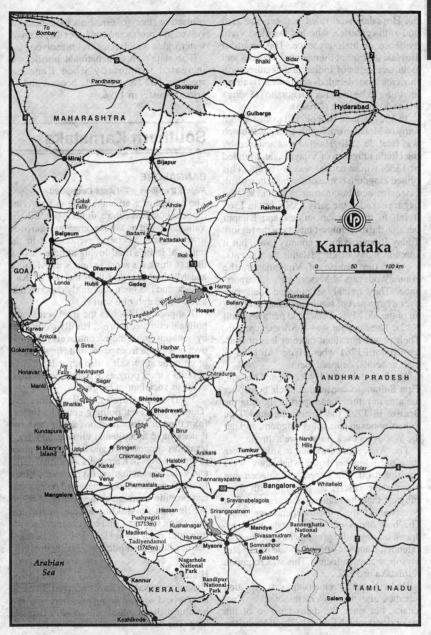

Karnataka

0   50   100 km

the Hoysalas, who ruled between the 11th and 14th centuries, who left the most vivid evidence of their presence. The beautiful Hoysala temples at Somnathpur, Halebid and Belur are gems of Indian architecture, with intricate and detailed sculptures rivalling anything to be found at Khajuraho (Madhya Pradesh) or Konark (Orissa).

In 1327, Hindu Halebid fell to the Muslim army of Mohammed Tughlaq, but his triumph was brief. In 1346, Halebid was annexed by the Hindu kingdom of Vijayanagar, founded in 1336, whose capital was at Hampi. This ruined kingdom is one of the most beautiful, extensive and fascinating in India. Vijayanagar peaked in the early 1550s, but in 1565 it fell to the Deccan sultans and Bijapur became the most important city of the region. Today Bijapur is just a country town, but it contains many striking Islamic monuments.

After the demise of Vijayanagar, the Hindu Wodeyars of Mysore grew in importance. They quickly established their rule over a large part of southern India, including all of the old Mysore state and parts of Tamil Nadu. Their capital was at Srirangapatnam. Their power remained more or less unchallenged until 1761 when Hyder Ali (one of their generals) deposed them.

The French helped Hyder Ali and his son, Tipu Sultan, to consolidate their hold over the area in return for support in fighting the British. In 1799 the British defeated Tipu Sultan, annexed part of his kingdom, and put the Wodeyars back on Mysore's throne.

The Wodeyars continued to rule Mysore state until Independence when they were pensioned off. They were enlightened and progressive rulers, so popular with their subjects that the maharaja became the first governor of the post-Independence state. The boundaries of Mysore state were redrawn on linguistic grounds in 1956 and the extended Kannada-speaking state of Greater Mysore was established. This was renamed Karnataka in 1972.

Under Nehru's premiership, vast irrigation schemes and dams were initiated in Karnataka, but since the dams tap two of the major rivers which flow into Tamil Nadu, the respective state governments have been involved in a protracted and bitter dispute over water rights which remains unresolved.

The state's modest national profile was increased temporarily when Kannada-speaking HD Deve Gowda became India's prime minister in 1996.

Southern Karnataka

BANGALORE

Pop: 5.2 million   Tel Area Code: 080

The capital of Karnataka state is a thriving modern business centre, dubbed the 'Silicon Valley' of India, whose gracious garrison town features are being remodelled in the image of India's mall-loving middle class. It likes to think it's more in tune with Mumbai and Manhattan rather than the rest of Karnataka, and has been scathingly described as a city 'in search of a soul'.

The pace of life, like the intellectual and political climate, is brisk. Hardly a day goes by without some new controversy boiling over across the front pages of its newspapers or onto the streets. It's also regarded as one of India's most progressive and liberal cities, as far as social attitudes go.

Tourist brochures call Bangalore the 'Garden City', but nothing could be further from the truth. Its attractions are limited, but it does have a congenial climate and good transport connections, and it's a useful place to arrange trips to Karnataka's national parks and wildlife sanctuaries. If you need a break from life on the road, its bars and restaurants can provide some much-needed light relief. While you're sinking a few beers and munching on pizza, you can contemplate the pros and cons of modern India's confused but headlong rush into the 21st century.

History

Bangalore is said to have received its name after an old woman living near here served a humble dish of boiled beans to a lost Hoysala king. The 'town of boiled beans' was formally

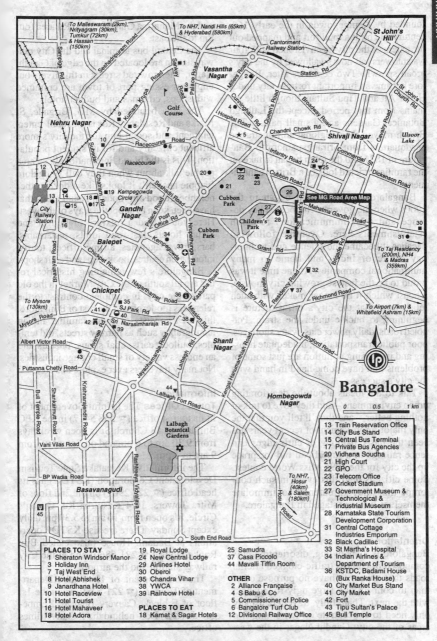

Bangalore

0   0.5   1 km

13	Train Reservation Office
14	City Bus Stand
15	Central Bus Terminal
17	Private Bus Agencies
20	Vidhana Soudha
21	High Court
22	GPO
23	Telecom Office
26	Cricket Stadium
27	Government Museum & Technological & Industrial Museum
28	Karnataka State Tourism Development Corporation
31	Central Cottage Industries Emporium
32	Black Cadillac
33	St Martha's Hospital
34	Indian Airlines & Department of Tourism
36	KSTDC, Badami House (Bux Ranka House)
40	City Market Bus Stand
41	City Market
42	Fort
43	Tipu Sultan's Palace
45	Bull Temple

PLACES TO STAY
1	Sheraton Windsor Manor
3	Holiday Inn
7	Taj West End
8	Hotel Abhishek
9	Janardhana Hotel
10	Hotel Raceview
11	Hotel Tourist
16	Hotel Mahaveer
18	Hotel Adora
19	Royal Lodge
24	New Central Lodge
29	Airlines Hotel
30	Oberoi
35	Chandra Vihar
38	YWCA
39	Rainbow Hotel

PLACES TO EAT
18	Kamat & Sagar Hotels
25	Samudra
37	Casa Piccolo
44	Mavalli Tiffin Room

OTHER
2	Alliance Française
4	S Babu & Co
5	Commissioner of Police
6	Bangalore Turf Club
12	Divisional Railway Office

founded by Kempegowda in the early 16th century. He built a mud fort and mapped out the extent of the city he envisioned with four watchtowers (all now swallowed by the city's urban sprawl). Two centuries later, Bangalore became an important fortress city under Hyder Ali and Tipu Sultan, though little remains from this period except the Lalbagh Botanical Gardens and a small palace. The British moved their regional administrative headquarters from Srirangapatnam to Bangalore in 1831 and the town began to take on the familiar ordered look of a British cantonment.

Bangalore's rapid growth began in the 1960s when the government located key defence and telecommunications research establishments here. Over the following decades it became the science and technology centre of India, and home to many multinational companies. At one time it was proud to be the fastest-growing city in Asia, a boast which it no longer makes with such relish now that the city's infrastructure is beginning to buckle under the strain. Potholed roads, daily power cuts, water shortages, poor public transportation, inadequate housing and increasing pollution are just some of problems that have come hand in hand with the city's success.

Talk to the locals about the deteriorating urban environment – and they love to talk of nothing better – and they'll tell you that the only major improvement of recent years has been the hasty painting of curb edges and fence railings in a superficial bid to spruce up the city for the 1996 Miss World contest. Some citizens held this event in such contempt that they threatened to immolate themselves if it was staged in Bangalore.

Orientation

Bangalore is a sprawling, disorienting city, composed of endless traffic-clogged arterial roads that appear to have no purpose other than to connect one large ugly roundabout with the next. Thankfully, travellers usually only need to concentrate on fathoming two areas of the city: Gandhi Nagar in the west

and the Mahatma Gandhi (MG) Rd area four km to the east.

The Central bus terminal and the City railway station are located on the edge of Gandhi Nagar. The crowded streets in this lively but unprepossessing part of town are crammed with shops, cinemas and budget hotels.

The area bounded by MG, Brigade, St Marks and Residency Rds is the retail, entertainment and social hub for the city's more affluent citizenry and for its student population. This is the bland, internationalised area people talk about when they call Bangalore 'yuppie heaven': it looks like a dozen other neighbourhoods in modern Asian cities that have been keen to adopt the ways of the west. Here you'll find a mixture of budget and luxury hotels, fast-food joints, restaurants, bars, travel agencies, airline offices, tourist information centres, bookshops and craft shops.

Bangalore's few remaining historical relics are all south of the City Market in the old part of the city. In complete contrast to the relentless modernity of the rest of Bangalore, this area consists of more familiar Indian iconography such as narrow streets, old temples, bullock carts, chai shops, bazaars and an endless variety of small cottage industries. Not many travellers ever explore this area.

Information

Tourist Offices The helpful Government of India tourist office (☎ 558 5417) in the KFC Building at 48 Church St is open weekdays from 9.30 am to 6 pm and on Saturday from 9 am to 1 pm.

The informative Karnataka State Tourism Development Corporation (KSTDC) has its head office (☎ 221 2901) on the 2nd floor of Mitra Towers, 10/4 Kasturba Rd, Queen's Circle. It's open from 10 am to 5.30 pm daily except Sunday. There are also KSTDC operations at Badami House (also called Bux Ranka House; ☎ 221 5869) and at the City railway station and the airport.

The Government of Karnataka Department of Tourism (☎ 221 5489) is on the 1st floor of F block, Cauvery Bhavan, Kempegowda (KG) Rd – behind the Indian Airlines office.

All the tourist offices have decent free maps of Bangalore. You can also buy good city maps from bookshops on MG Rd.

The handy what's-on guide, *Bangalore This Fortnight*, can be picked up free from tourist offices and hotels. The *Deccan Herald*, Bangalore's major newspaper, is a lively read and carries advertisements for most local events.

Money Thomas Cook (☎ 558 6742) at 55 MG Rd is the best place for speedy foreign exchange. It's open Monday to Saturday from 9.30 am to 6.30 pm. The Bank of Baroda at 72 MG Rd provides cash advances on Master Card and Visa credit cards.

Post & Telecommunications The GPO on Cubbon Rd is open Monday to Saturday from 8 am to 7 pm and Sunday from 10.30 am to 1.30 pm. The efficient poste restante service is open at enquiry counter No 22 from Monday to Saturday between 10 am and 6 pm. If you're staying in the MG Rd area, there's a handy post office on Brigade Rd.

From the modern telecom office next to the GPO, you can send international faxes and make telephone calls 24 hours a day.

The swanky Coffee Day Cyber Cafe at 13-15 Brigade Rd offers email and Internet access for Rs 60 for half an hour. It can also set up a local email address for you.

Visa Extensions Apply for visa extensions at the office of the Commissioner of Police (☎ 225 6242 ext 513) on Infantry Rd, a five minute walk from the GPO. It's open Monday to Saturday from 10 am to 5.30 pm. The process usually takes two to three days.

Libraries & Cultural Centres The British Library (☎ 221 3485) on St Mark's Rd has British newspapers and magazines. It's open Tuesday to Saturday from 10.30 am to 6.30 pm.

Alliance Française (☎ 225 8762) is on Thimmaiah Rd near Cantonment railway station. It has a library with French newspapers and magazines, and is open Monday, Tuesday, Thursday and Friday between 9 am

and 1 pm and from 4 to 7 pm; open mornings only on Wednesday and Saturday. It also holds exhibitions, music evenings and video nights.

Bookshops There are several excellent bookshops in town. One of the best is the Premier Bookshop, 46/1 Church St, around the corner from Berrys Hotel. Books on every conceivable subject are piled from floor to ceiling. The owner, somehow, seems to know where everything is. Gangarams Book Bureau at 72 MG Rd is also good. There's a branch of Higginbothams a couple of doors away at No 68.

Medical Services In an emergency, phone ☎ 102. For anything less urgent, try St Martha's Hospital (☎ 227 5081), Nrupathunga Rd.

National Parks To arrange accommodation in Bandipur National Park, contact the Chief Wildlife Warden (☎ 334 1993), Aranya Bhavan, 18th Cross, Malleswaram, Bangalore.

Jungle Lodges & Resorts Ltd (☎ 559 7025; fax 558 6163) arranges accommodation in Nagarhole National Park and a number of Karnataka's other wildlife sanctuaries, including tented camps (US$60 per night) on the Kali River in the Dandeli Wildlife Sanctuary (75km east of Hubli) and in the Biligiri Rangaswamy Wildlife Sanctuary (90km south-east of Mysore). This company gets good feedback from travellers. It's located on the top floor of the Shrungar Shopping Centre on MG Rd.

Vidhana Soudha

Located at the north-western end of Cubbon Park, this massive, granite, neo-Dravidian style building is one of Bangalore's most imposing. Built in 1954, it houses both the Secretariat and the State Legislature. It's floodlit on weekend evenings and on public holidays, but is not open to the public.

Cubbon Park & Museums

This 120-hectare park, laid out in 1864, is one of the main 'lungs' of the city. It's not the most beautiful of gardens but it's a pleasant escape from the surrounding urban chaos. On its fringes are the superbly restored neo-classical High Court, the grand Public Library, two municipal museums and a dull aquarium. Also in the gardens is a huge **children's park**, which adults are wisely not allowed into unless accompanied by a minor.

The **Government Museum**, one of the oldest in India, was established in 1886 and houses a poorly presented collection of stone carvings, pottery, weapons, paintings, and some good pieces from Halebid. The museum is open daily except Monday from 10 am to 5 pm; entry is Rs 1.

The **Visvesvaraya Technological & Industrial Museum** usually has schoolchildren pressing buttons on exhibits which reflect India's technological progress. It's open daily except Monday between 9.30 am and 6.30 pm; entry is Rs 5.

Lalbagh Botanical Gardens

This pleasant 96 ha park in the southern suburbs of Bangalore was laid out in the 18th century by Hyder Ali and his son Tipu Sultan. It contains many labelled centuries-old trees, one of India's largest collections of rare tropical and subtropical plants, a glasshouse modelled on London's Crystal Palace, one of Kempegowda's watchtowers and a surreal lawn clock surrounded by Snow White and the seven dwarfs. There are major flower displays here in the week preceding Republic Day and the week before Independence Day. The gardens are open daily from sunrise to sunset.

City Market

This bustling market south-west of Cubbon Park is all you need to remind you that you're still in India if you've spent all your time on MG Rd. It contains a tarpaulin-covered fruit and vegetable bazaar, a spice market, plenty of garland sellers, cloth shops and an entire colourful street lined with hole-in-the-wall tailor shops. It's not exactly a mainstream tourist attraction, but the vendors here see few travellers and are extremely friendly.

Fort & Tipu Sultan's Palace

Kempegowda built a mud-brick defence structure on this site in 1537, and in the 18th century it was solidly rebuilt in stone by Hyder Ali and Tipu Sultan. It's a sturdy little fort, though much of it was destroyed during the wars with the British. It's worth a quick visit if you're exploring the City Market.

Tipu Sultan's modest palace is notable for its elegant teak pillars. It was begun by Hyder Ali, and completed by Tipu in 1791. The palace is a five minute walk south-west of the City Market.

Bull Temple

Situated on Bugle Hill at the southern end of Bull Temple Rd, this is one of Bangalore's oldest temples. Built by Kempegowda in the Dravidian style in the 16th century, it contains a huge granite monolith of Nandi similar to the one on Mysore's Chamundi Hill. Non-Hindus are allowed to enter the temple and the priests are friendly. It's especially interesting on weekends, when there are often musicians, wedding processions and even pujas to bless new motor cars.

Ulsoor Lake

This pretty picnic spot is on the north-eastern fringe of the city centre. You can hire rowboats for Rs 60 per hour or have a 10 minute spin around the lake in a motorised dinghy for the same price. There's a decent pool (Rs 5) here, with carefully regulated separate-sex swimming hours. One of Kempegowda's watchtowers stands nearby.

Organised Tours

The KSTDC offers a huge range of tours, which can be booked in any of their offices. They all start at Badami House (also known as Bux Ranka House). They include a city sightseeing tour, run twice daily at 7.30 am and 2 pm, which costs Rs 75. It quickly covers the city's best attractions and spends a lot of time at a government-owned silk and handicraft emporium. There's also a tour to Srirangapatnam, Mysore and Brindavan Gardens departing daily at 7.15 am and returning at 11 pm. It costs Rs 165, including all entrance fees. There are also tours to Nandi Hills, to Belur, Halebid and Sravanabelagola, and a weekend tour to Hampi.

Maharaja Tours (☎ 333 4442) offers cultural tours tailored to foreign visitors which include introductions to Indian arts, a visit to a temple, a yoga demonstration, a concert and dance, and a visit to an Indian home. They depart at 3 pm, return at 9 pm and cost Rs 800, including a vegetarian dinner.

Activities
Swimming If you fancy a swim, non-guests can use the pools at the following hotels for a fee: Holiday Inn (Rs 250), Taj West End (Rs 264) and, at the management's discretion, the Sheraton Windsor Manor. There's also a public swimming pool at Ulsoor Lake.

Horse Racing Bangalore's winter race season runs from November to February and its summer season from May to July. Races are generally held on either Friday or weekends and can be a lot of fun. Contact the Bangalore Turf Club (☎ 226 2391) for details.

Adventure Activities For activities such as trekking, rafting, caving and rock-climbing, contact the General Thimmaiah National Academy for Adventure (☎ 221 0454), State Youth Centre, Nrupathunga Rd, Bangalore.

Places to Stay – bottom end
Bus Terminal Area A dozen or more budget hotels line Subedar Chatram Rd in the heart of Gandhi Nagar, just east of the bus stands.

Royal Lodge (☎ 226 6575) at No 251 is one of the cheapest, largest and oldest. It has clean singles/doubles with common bath for Rs 90/120 and doubles with attached bathroom and hot water in the morning for Rs 195.

Hotel Adora (☎ 220 0324), almost opposite at No 47, has decent rooms with attached bath for Rs 130/200.

Hotel Mahaveer (☎ 287 3670) immediately south of the City railway station and Central bus terminal, is a spotless, modern, upmarket budget hotel with small rooms with TV, attached bath and hot water in the

morning. Rooms cost Rs 160/230 and air-con doubles cost Rs 550.

Hotel Tourist (☎ 226 2381) is a little further afield at 5 Racecourse Rd. It's good value at Rs 50/90 for rooms with attached bath and hot water in the morning.

Janardhana Hotel (☎ 225 4444), on Kumara Krupa Rd, has spacious singles/doubles/triples with balconies, attached bath and hot water for Rs 170/220/270. It's good value, but is not in a great location. Checkout time is 24 hours.

Retiring rooms at the City railway station cost Rs 75 for a dorm bed, Rs 150 for a double and Rs 250 for an air-con double. They're often full by the afternoon.

MG Rd Area The *New Central Lodge* (☎ 559 2395), 56 Infantry Rd, is an average place with basic but clean singles/doubles with common bath for Rs 110/230 and with attached bath for Rs 270/300. There's hot water from 6 to 9 am. Some rooms are a bit pokey and traffic noise is a problem in the morning.

Imperial Lodge (☎ 558 5473), 95 Residency Rd, has singles/doubles/triples with attached bath for Rs 120/205/252. It's in a handy location but on another noisy main road.

Airlines Hotel (☎ 227 3783), at 4 Madras Bank Rd, is set back from the road in its own leafy grounds and has a range of facilities including a garden restaurant – complete with drive-in service – a supermarket and a bakery. Singles/doubles/triples with attached bath and hot water in the morning cost Rs 175/250/375. Unfortunately it's so popular that you need to make a reservation 10 to 15 days in advance.

Brindavan Hotel (☎ 558 4000), 108 MG Rd, has decent rooms with attached bath for Rs 195/275 and air-con rooms for Rs 325/650. The hotel is fairly quiet since it's set back from the road, but it's also often full.

City Market Area This is the place to stay if you enjoy being in the thick of the noise, bustle and atmosphere of the bazaar. It's a 25 minute walk from the City railway station.

Chandra Vihar (☎ 222 4146), on Avenue Rd, charges Rs 130/210 for clean, decent-sized rooms with attached bath, bucket shower and hot water in the morning. There are great views of the market from some rooms.

Rainbow Hotel (☎ 6702235), on Sri Narasimharaja Rd, opposite the City Market bus stand and the big white mosque, is OK value at Rs 95/168/241 for singles/doubles/triples with attached bath, though it's not keen on unaccompanied women travellers.

YWCA (☎ 223 8574), at 40 Mission Rd, is in a quiet backstreet on the edge of this area. It takes men and women, and you don't have to be a member to stay here. Rooms with attached bath cost Rs 200/400.

Places to Stay – middle

Most of the hotels in this price range are in the MG Rd area but there are a few near the racecourse, a rather dull area that's a short auto-rickshaw ride from the City railway station and Central bus terminal.

MG Rd Area The *New Victoria Hotel* (☎ 558 4076; fax 558 4945), 47-48 Residency Rd, is a classy, established hotel set in grounds filled with huge shady trees. It's full of Raj-era charm, and its brochure strangely claims that it 'redefines life as it ought to be, a living breathing memory of a century-old value system'. It's a popular place and there are not many rooms so you need to make an advance reservation. Singles/doubles with attached bath cost Rs 250/550, deluxe rooms are Rs 650 and a suite costs Rs 750. There's a bar and restaurant with indoor and garden dining.

Curzon Court (☎ 558 2997; fax 555 0631), at 10 Brigade Rd, offers comfortable air-con rooms with TV and attached bath from Rs 650/750 to Rs 800/1000.

Nilgiris Nest (☎ 558 8401; fax 558 5348), at 171 Brigade Rd, is on the 3rd floor above a supermarket of the same name. It has clean, spacious, airy rooms with TV and attached bath for Rs 500/650, or Rs 600/750 with air-con. Checkout time is 24 hours.

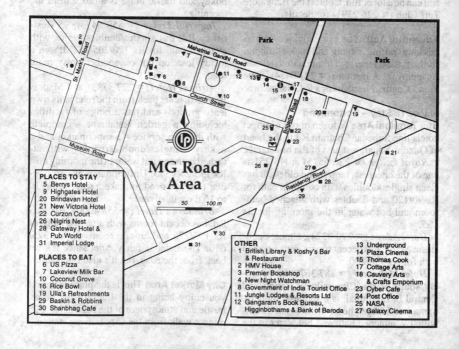

MG Road Area

0   50   100 m

PLACES TO STAY
5   Berrys Hotel
9   Highgates Hotel
20 Brindavan Hotel
21 New Victoria Hotel
22 Curzon Court
26 Nilgiris Nest
28 Gateway Hotel & Pub World
31 Imperial Lodge

PLACES TO EAT
6   US Pizza
7   Lakeview Milk Bar
10 Coconut Grove
19 Rice Bowl
19 Ulla's Refreshments
29 Baskin & Robbins
30 Shanbhag Cafe

OTHER
1   British Library & Koshy's Bar & Restaurant
2   HMV House
3   Premier Bookshop
4   New Night Watchman
8   Government of India Tourist Office
11 Jungle Lodges & Resorts Ltd
12 Gangaram's Book Bureau, Higginbothams & Bank of Baroda
13 Underground
14 Plaza Cinema
15 Thomas Cook
17 Cottage Arts
18 Cauvery Arts & Crafts Emporium
23 Cyber Cafe
24 Post Office
25 NASA
27 Galaxy Cinema

Berrys Hotel (☎ 558 7211), at 46/1 Church St, is a large, standard, mid-range establishment that's rarely full. Huge rooms with TV and attached bath cost Rs 350/400, or there are deluxe rooms for Rs 450/500. Room numbers ending in eight (eg 308, 408, etc) are the best.

Highgates Hotel (☎ 559 7172; fax 559 7799), at 33 Church St, is a tasteful, modern, three star hotel at the top of this price range. Comfortable air-con rooms with TV, fridge and attached bath cost Rs 995/1300. It has a restaurant, a lobby coffee shop and a patio. Reservations are recommended.

Racecourse Area The *Hotel Raceview* (☎ 220 3401) at 25 Racecourse Rd has doubles (no singles) for Rs 400, or Rs 600 with air-con. Keen punters may be interested to know that some of the more expensive rooms have a good view of the racetrack.

Hotel Abhishek (☎ 226 2713) at 19/2 Kumara Krupa Rd has singles/doubles with TV and attached bath for Rs 600/660, or Rs 690/750 with air-con.

Places to Stay – top end
Bangalore's importance as an industrial and business centre has resulted in a plethora of swanky hotels, most of them around MG Rd or in the more peaceful northern part of town, close to the golf and race course. The Oberoi and the Taj West End vie for the title of best hotel in town.

Gateway Hotel (☎ 558 4545; fax 558 4030), at 66 Residency Rd, is a four star member of the Taj Group. It has excellent singles/doubles from US$80/95, including breakfast. Facilities include a swimming pool and a restaurant specialising in Malabar Coast cuisine.

Holiday Inn (☎ 226 2233; fax 226 7676), at 28 Sankey Rd, has rooms from US$125/145.

Taj Residency (☎ 558 4444; fax 558 4748), 41/3 MG Rd, charges US$125/140.

Sheraton Windsor Manor (☎ 226 9898; fax 226 4941), at 25 Sankey Rd, occupies a beautiful old manor house where rooms cost from US$145/160.

Oberoi (☎ 558 5858; fax 558 5960), 37-39 MG Rd, has luxurious rooms which open onto an immense tranquil garden for US$225/255. There's a swimming pool and all the usual five star amenities.

Taj West End (☎ 225 5055; fax 220 0010), on Racecourse Rd, is a classy five star hotel occupying a carefully restored 19th century mansion and several villas set in a beautiful eight ha garden. Rooms start from US$195/215.

Places to Eat
MG Rd Area There are a huge number of places to eat around MG Rd, though most are expensive and mediocre imitations of western fast-food or pizza joints. Their attractiveness will probably be determined by how long you've been in India. Despite the burger-pizza overload, you'll find western breakfasts in very short supply.

Ulla's Refreshments, on the 1st floor of General Hall, MG Rd, is a local favourite and a great spot for snacks (Rs 15) and south Indian vegetarian dishes (Rs 20-30). It has an indoor area and a big, convivial terrace.

US Pizza, on Church St, makes the best pizzas in the city (thanks, it strangely claims, to Swedish technology). They cost around Rs 75.

Coconut Grove, also on Church St, is a friendly, semi open-air restaurant with a mouthwatering array of Keralan, Goan and Coorg regional dishes. Main courses cost between Rs 70 and Rs 85.

Rice Bowl, on Brigade Rd, is a cosy Chinese joint run by Tibetans. The food is average but it certainly comes in hearty proportions; main dishes cost around Rs 50.

Shanbhag Cafe, on Residency Rd, dishes up decent south Indian thalis for Rs 19, and a more luxurious north Indian variety for Rs 60.

New Victoria Hotel, 47-48 Residency Rd, has a nice shady garden restaurant and an old-fashioned dining hall that are both interesting eating places if you have the patience to handle the lacklustre service. The food is multi-cuisine, and there's a lunchtime buffet for Rs 75.

Casa Piccolo, 131 Residency Rd, justly receives enthusiastic raves from travellers. It's yet another western-style eatery, but it has a good atmosphere and prices are sensible – pizzas start from Rs 38, burgers from Rs 42 and steaks from Rs 52.

Lakeview Milk Bar, at 38 MG Rd, and *Baskin & Robbins*, on Residency Rd, are the places to go for ice cream.

Elsewhere The *Kamat Hotel* and *Sagar Hotel* are the two best options in Subedar Chatram Rd in Gandhi Nagar. The former dishes up south Indian veg fare, and the latter Andhra-style cuisine.

Samudra, at 25 Lady Curzon Rd, has delicious north Indian fare and more impressive fish tanks than Bangalore's aquarium. Main dishes cost Rs 50. It's a 10 minute walk north of MG Rd.

Mavalli Tiffin Room, near Lalbagh Botanic Gardens, may not look much, but it's a legendary dosa and snack joint with excellent lassis.

Paradise Island at the Taj West End is the most interesting of the five star hotel restaurants. Set in a beautiful garden pavilion, it serves excellent Thai and Chinese cuisine.

Entertainment

Bars Bangalore's affluence has bred a pub culture that wouldn't be out of place in any western country but which comes as a complete culture shock in India. Flashy bars, well-lit discos and draught beers are all the rage with well-heeled young people and office workers. Needless to say, you won't feel like a social reprobate for drinking a beer here as you might do in the 'black holes' of Tamil Nadu.

Most of the pubs are fairly undistinguishable male-dominated theme bars, and they tend to have carefully structured seating arrangements that prevent too much social interaction between strangers; women are often quarantined in 'family only' areas.

Bars are open during lunchtime and from 5 to 11 pm. Draught beer usually costs around Rs 25 for a mug or Rs 60 for a bottle. Nearly all bars serve snacks.

Pub World, next to the Gateway Hotel, is symptomatic of Bangalore's restless mimicry of the west. It manages to squeeze a British pub, German Beer Hall, Wild West saloon and Manhattan cocktail bar into one room, though you may well have a problem realising which one you're meant to be in. It's probably the plushest and most convivial of the MG Rd area pubs.

NASA, on Church St, is decked out like a spaceship and has laser shows, a young crowd, MTV and mega-decibel music. If you like this place, you'll also like the sleazy *Underground* on MG Rd, which is modelled on a London tube station.

New Night Watchman, near Berrys Hotel, has a nifty cubist park bench arrangement, a few bar stools and, thankfully, no theme decor.

Black Cadillac, at 50 Residency Rd, has quieter music, more expensive drinks and a cover charge on Friday and Saturday night (which includes the price of four drinks). Friday night is popular with Bangalore's expat community.

Concorde, on Airport Rd, is where everyone goes when the pubs close. It's a full-on nightclub with a 50-50 gender balance and no-holds-barred dancing. It's way out of town, close to the airport.

The two nicest places for a beer have nothing to do with Bangalore's pub culture: try the verandah of the *New Victoria Hotel* and the old fashioned tea-room ambience of *Koshy's Bar & Restaurant* on St Mark's Rd.

Cinema The *Plaza* on MG Rd and the *Galaxy* on Residency Rd both show first-run English-language films. Regional films are best watched at one of the many cinemas along KG Rd in Gandhi Nagar.

Things to Buy

Bangalore is a good place to purchase silk, sandalwood and rosewood items, and Lambani tribal jewellery.

The most pleasant shopping experience is to be found on Commercial St, north of MG Rd. This street is home to a number of silk, handicraft and clothes shops. Stunning, hand-embroidered saris are reasonably priced and fabric is cheaper here than in the silk emporiums lining MG Rd.

There are plenty of handicraft shops on MG Rd. Cauvery Arts & Crafts Emporium at No 23 stocks the same range of statues, jewellery, ceramics, carpets and *agarbathis* (incense) that you've seen in a thousand other tourist towns across the country. Cottage Arts at No 52 and Central Cottage Industries Emporium at No 144 also stock the usual range of artefacts.

HMV House on St Mark's Road has a selection of Hindi cassettes and CDs and a small range of western tapes.

Don't assume shops are closed because they look dark and gloomy; it's probably just one of Bangalore's frequent power cuts.

Getting There & Away

Air The Indian Airlines office (☎ 221 1914) is in the Housing Board Buildings, Kempegowda (KG) Rd. Other operators include Jet Airways (☎ 227 6617) and Sahara (☎ 558 6976).

There are daily connections to Calcutta (US$215), Calicut (US$55), Delhi (US$205), Hyderabad (US$80), Chennai (US$55) and Mumbai (US$110), plus numerous flights to Ahmedabad (US$180), Goa (US$80), Kochi (US$60), Mangalore (US$56), Pune (US$115) and Trivandrum (US$90).

There are no direct international flights to/from Bangalore, however, it does have a number of international connecting flights via Mumbai. These include services to the Gulf and to Paris, London, New York and Singapore. The advantage of these services is that you can go through customs and immigration procedures in relative peace at Bangalore airport. Facilities at Bangalore airport include foreign exchange counters and a pre-paid taxi booth.

International airlines with offices in Bangalore include:

Air France
    Sunrise Chambers, 22 Ulsoor Rd (☎ 558 7258)
Air India
    Unity Bldgs, Jayachamaraja Rd (☎ 227 7747)

British Airways
    7 St Mark's Rd (☎ 227 4034)
KLM
    West End Hotel, Racecourse Rd (☎ 226 8703)
Lufthansa
    44/2 Dickenson Rd (☎ 558 8791)
Qantas
    Westminster Bldg, Cunningham Rd
    (☎ 220 2067)
Singapore Airlines
    51 Richmond Rd (☎ 221 2822)

Bus Bangalore's huge and well-organised Central bus terminal is directly in front of the City railway station. All the regular buses within the state are operated by the Karnataka State Road Transport Corporation (KSRTC) (☎ 287 3377). Interstate buses are operated by KSRTC as well as the state transport corporation of Andhra Pradesh (APSRTC) (☎ 287 3915; platform 11), Tamil Nadu's JJTC (☎ 287 6974; platform 12) and Goa's Kadamba (near the computerised reservation booths). Computerised advance booking is available for all KSRTC superdeluxe and express buses as well as for the bus companies of neighbouring states. It's advisable to book in advance for long-distance journeys.

KSRTC operates horrifyingly fast buses to Mysore every 15 minutes from 5 am to midnight (Rs 27/41 ordinary/deluxe, three hours). It also has six daily departures to Ernakulam (16 hours), 12 to Hospet (eight hours), four to Jog Falls (eight hours), 10 to Chennai (eight hours), three to Mumbai (24 hours), three to Ooty (eight hours) and three to Panaji (15 hours).

Kadamba buses depart for Panaji at 5.30 and 6 pm (Rs 176, 13 hours). The APSRTC has plenty of buses to Hyderabad (12 hours); one departs at 7.45 am and the remainder leave in the evening. JJTC has frequent departures to Madurai (10 hours) and Coimbatore (11 hours), plus seven daily buses to Chennai (eight hours).

In addition to the various state buses, numerous private companies offer more comfortable and more expensive buses between Bangalore and the other major cities in central and southern India. The private bus fare to Goa, for example, is around Rs 200. You'll find private operators lining the street facing onto the Central bus terminal. Most private buses depart in the evening.

Train There are two railway stations in Bangalore. The main one, the City railway station, is the place to make reservations. Cantonment railway station is a useful spot to disembark if you're arriving in Bangalore and heading for the MG Rd area.

Rail reservations in Bangalore are computerised but there are no tourist quotas on any trains and bookings are heavy on most routes. On the other hand, it's usually possible for travellers to get into the emergency quota – to do so, however, you have to buy a ticket first and throw yourself on the mercy of the assistant commercial manager in the Divisional Office building immediately north of the City railway station. The reservation and enquiry office is on the left as you're facing the station and is open Monday to Saturday from 8 am to 8 pm; Sunday 8 am to 2 pm. Luggage can be left at the City railway station.

Bangalore is connected by direct daily express trains with all the main cities in southern and central India. The only lines disrupted by conversion from metre to broad gauge at the time of writing were the stretches between Mysore and Hassan, and Hassan and Mangalore.

To get to Goa, catch the daily *Ranichannamma Express* which departs at 8 pm and change trains at Londa. The journey takes 12 hours.

See the table below for a selection of major trains from Bangalore.

Getting Around
The Airport The airport is 13km east of the City railway station and about nine km east of the MG Rd area. There are prepaid taxis from the airport to the city (Rs 170); in the other direction you'll probably have to haggle for a price since drivers will be reluctant

Major Trains from Bangalore

Destination	Train Number & Name	Departure Time	Distance (km)	Duration (hours)	Fare (RS) (2nd/1st)
Calcutta	6312 *Howrah Exp*	11.30 pm Fri	2025	38.00	313/1268
Ernakulam	6526 *Kanyakumari Exp*	9.00 pm	638	13.00	163/563
Hospet	6592 *Hampi Exp*	9.55 pm	491	9.30	135/464
Hyderabad	7686 *Hyderabad Exp*	5.05 pm	790	16.30	188/656
Madras	2608 *Lalbagh Exp*	8.35 am	361	5.20	82/368
	2640 *Brindavan Exp*	2.30 pm			
	2008 *Shatabdi Exp* *	4.20 pm		4.45	370/740
Mumbai	1014 *Kurla Exp*	12.10 am	1211	24.00	247/876
	6530 *Udyan Exp*	8.30 pm			
Mysore	6222 *Kaveri Exp*	8.25 am	139	2.30	36/170
	6206 *Tippu Exp*	2.25 pm			
	6216 *Chamundi Exp*	6.15 pm			
	2007 *Shatabdi Exp* *	10.55 am		2.00	185/365
Delhi	2627 *Karnataka Exp*	6.25 pm	2444	41.45	342/1482
	2429 *Rajdhani Exp* **	6.45 am Mon		33.43	1210/3850
Thiruvananthapuram	6526 *Kanyakumari Exp*	9.00 pm	851	18.15	199/670

* Air-con only; fare includes meals and drinks; daily except Tuesday
** Air-con only

to use their meters – count on around Rs 100 for a taxi or Rs 25 for an auto-rickshaw. Bus Nos 13 and 333 go from the city to the airport for around Rs 15.

Bus Bangalore has a comprehensive local bus network. Most local buses run from the City bus stand next to the Central bus terminal; a few operate from the City Market bus stand to the south.

To get from the City railway station to the MG Rd area, catch any bus from platform 17 at the City bus stand.

Auto-Rickshaw Bangalore residents are proud to tell you that auto-rickshaw drivers are required by law to use their meters (which are properly calibrated, incidentally), and locals will *insist* on them being used. Do likewise!

The bad news is that flagging down an auto-rickshaw in Bangalore is akin to hitch-hiking, since drivers are fussy about where they want to go. This can become infuriating, but there's no sense in getting stressed out – simply find another auto-rickshaw.

Flagfall is Rs 6 and then Rs 2.80 for each extra km. Expect to pay about Rs 14 from the railway station to MG Rd. After 9 or 10 pm, you'll almost certainly have to haggle and agree on a fare.

Walking Negotiating Bangalore on foot is an unrewarding slog since the city is diffuse and the pavements wayward. Crossing the street in some parts of town is more dangerous than getting on the Bangalore-Mysore bus.

AROUND BANGALORE
Whitefield Ashram
About 20km east of Bangalore is the summer ashram of Sri Sathya Sai Baba, where he is usually in residence between March and May. His main ashram, Puttaparthi, is in neighbouring Andhra Pradesh (see that chapter for details).

Transport to both ashrams can be arranged in Bangalore at S Babu & Co (☎ 226 1351) travel agency in the Cauvery Continental Hotel, 11 Cunningham Rd. Between March

and May, half-day tours to Whitefield for either morning or evening darshan cost Rs 250. You can also get to Whitefield on bus No 333-E or 319-C from platform 17 at the City bus stand.

Bannerghatta National Park
This modest national park, 21km south of Bangalore, is home to a small population of leopards. There's also a staged 'safari' where you can see lions, tigers and elephants in a fenced-in area, plus a crocodile and snake farm. It's open daily except Tuesday; catch bus No 365 from platform 15 at the City bus stand.

Nrityagram
This dance village, 30km north-west of Bangalore, was established in the early 1990s to revive Indian classical dance. Under the auspices of well-known Odissi dancer, Protima Gauri, it offers the long-term study of classical dance and its allied subjects, such as choreography, philosophy, music, mythology and painting. The village, designed by award-winning Goan architect, Gerard Da Cunha, welcomes visitors and accommodates guests. Contact Nrityagram's Bangalore office (☎ 846 6314).

Nandi Hills
Tel Area Code: 08156
This hill station (1615m), 68km north of Bangalore, was a popular summer retreat even in Tipu Sultan's days. **Tipu's Drop**, a 600m high cliff face, not only provided a good view over the surrounding country, it was also a convenient place to dispose of enemies. There are two notable Chola temples here.

Places to Stay The *cottages* run by the Department of Horticulture are the cheapest places to stay. You can make a reservation in Bangalore (☎ 602231). The KSTDC operates the *Hotel Mayura Pine Top* (☎ 78624) which has rooms with attached bath for Rs 190/220. Book at one of the KSTDC offices in Bangalore.

Getting There & Away There are KSRTC buses to Nandi Hills (two hours) from Bangalore's Central bus terminal. Alternatively, you can visit on a KSTDC tour; see Organised Tours in the Bangalore section.

MYSORE

Pop: 735,000   Tel Area Code: 0821

This charming, easy-going city has long been a favourite with travellers – it's a manageable size, enjoys a good climate and has chosen to retain and promote its heritage rather than replace it. The city is famous for its silk and is also a thriving sandalwood and incense centre, though don't expect the air to be any more fragrant than that of the next town.

Until Independence, Mysore was the seat of the maharajas of Mysore, a princely state covering about a third of present-day Karnataka. The maharajas' walled Indo-Saracenic palace is a major attraction.

Orientation

The railway station is on the north-western fringe of the city centre, about a km from the main shopping street, Sayaji Rao Rd. The Central bus terminal is on the Bangalore-Mysore Rd, on the north-eastern fringe of the city centre. Mysore Palace occupies the entire south-eastern sector of the city centre. Chamundi Hill is an ever visible landmark to the south.

Information

Tourist Office The KSTDC tourist office (☎ 22096) is in the Old Exhibition Building on Irwin Rd and is open Monday to Saturday from 10 am to 5.30 pm. There are also counters at the railway station (☎ 30719), the Central bus terminal (☎ 54497) and a transport office (☎ 423652) next to the Hotel Mayura Hoysala.

Money The State Bank of Mysore, on the corner of Irwin and Ashoka Rds, has efficient foreign exchange facilities, as does its branch office on Sayaji Rao Rd. The Bank of Baroda on Gandhi Square provides cash advances on MasterCard and Visa credit cards.

Sandalwood City

Mysore is one of the major centres of incense manufacture in India, and scores of small, family-owned *agarbathi* (incense) factories around town export their products all over the world.

The incense sticks are handmade, usually by women and children, and a good worker can turn out at least 10,000 a day. They are made with thin slivers of bamboo, dyed red or green at one end, onto which is rolled a sandalwood putty base. The sticks are then dipped into small piles of powdered perfume and laid out to harden in the shade. ■

Post & Telecommunications The GPO is on the corner of Irwin and Ashoka Rds. It's open between 10 am and 6 pm, though the poste restante facility is only open until 4 pm. There's a handy local post office on the first floor of a building fronting KR Circle.

The central telegraph office is on the western side of the palace and is open 24 hours.

Bookshops The Ashok Book Centre is on Dhanvantri Rd, near the junction with Sayaji Rao Rd.

Medical Services The Basappa Memorial Hospital (☎ 512401) is considered the best hospital in town.

National Parks Accommodation and transport for Bandipur National Park (80km south of Mysore) should be booked with the Field Director (☎ 520901), Project Tiger, Ashokapuram, Mysore. Take an auto-rickshaw or a No 61 city bus from the City bus stand.

Mysore Palace

The beautiful profile of this walled Indo-Saracenic palace, the seat of the maharajas of Mysore, graces the city's skyline. An earlier palace burnt down in 1897 and the present one, also known as the Amba Vilas Palace, was completed in 1912 at a cost of Rs 4.2 million. The former maharaja is still in residence at the back of the palace.

Inside it's a kaleidoscope of stained glass, mirrors, gilt and gaudy colours. Some of it is

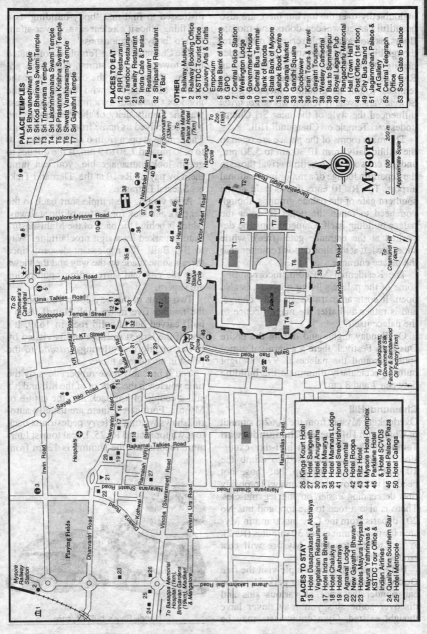

PALACE TEMPLES
T1 Sri Bhuvaneshwari Temple
T2 Sri Kodi Bhairava Swami Temple
T3 Sri Trineshvara Temple
T4 Sri Lakshmiramana Swami Temple
T5 Sri Prasanna Krishna Swami Temple
T6 Shweta Varahaswamy Temple
T7 Sri Gayathri Temple

PLACES TO EAT
12 RRR Restaurant
16 Tandoor Restaurant
21 Kwality Restaurant
29 Indra Cafe & Paras Restaurant
32 Shilpashri Restaurant & Bar

OTHER
1 Railway Museum
2 Railway Booking Office
3 KSTDC Tourist Office
4 Cauvery Arts & Crafts Emporium
5 State Bank of Mysore
6 GPO
7 Central Police Station
8 Wellington Lodge
9 Government House
10 Central Bus Terminal
14 Bank of Baroda
15 State Bank of Mysore
15 Ashok Book Centre
28 Devaraja Market
33 Gandhi Square
34 Clocktower
36 Kiran Tours & Travel
37 Gayatri Tourism
38 Wesley Cathedral
39 Bus to Somnathpur
40 Royal Legacy Pub
47 Rangacharlu Memorial Hall (Town Hall)
48 Post Office (1st floor)
49 City Bus Stand
51 Jaganmohan Palace & Art Gallery
52 Central Telegraph Office
53 South Gate to Palace

PLACES TO STAY
13 Hotel Dasaprakash & Akshaya
17 Hotel Indra Bhavan
18 Hotel Chalukya
19 Hotel Aashraya
20 Agrawal Lodge
22 New Gayathri Bhavan
23 Hotels Mayura Hoysala & Mayura Yathrinivas & KSTDC Tour Office & Indian Airlines
24 Quality Inn Southern Star
25 Hotel Metropole
26 Kings Kourt Hotel
27 Hotel Sangeeth
30 Hotel Anugraha
31 Hotel Maurya
35 Hotel Mannars Lodge
41 Hotel Sreekrishna Continental
42 Hotel Roopa
43 Ritz Hotel
44 Mysore Hotel Complex
45 Parklane Hotel & Hotel SCVDS
46 Hotel Palace Plaza
50 Hotel Calinga

Mysore

undoubtedly over the top but there are also beautiful carved wooden doors and mosaic floors, as well as a whole series of mediocre, though historically interesting, paintings depicting life in Mysore during the Edwardian Raj. The palace even has a selection of Hindu temples within its grounds, including the Shweta Varahaswamy Temple whose *gopuram* influenced the style of the later Sri Chamundeswari Temple on Chamundi Hill.

The main rooms of the palace are open to the public daily from 10.30 am to 5.30 pm, and the crowds can sometimes rival those in the departure lounge of a major international airport. The Rs 10 entry fee is paid at the southern gate of the palace grounds, though you need to retain the ticket to enter the palace building itself. Cameras must be deposited at the entrance gate (free), while shoes are left at the shoe deposit counter near the palace entrance.

The Residential Museum, incorporating some of the palace's living quarters, is also open. It costs an extra Rs 10 entry charge, and is rather dull after the magnificence of the palace itself.

On Sunday nights and during the entire Dussehra Festival, there's a carnival atmosphere around the palace as 97,000 light bulbs spectacularly illuminate the building between 7 and 8 pm.

Chamundi Hill

Overlooking Mysore from the 1062m summit of Chamundi Hill, the **Sri Chamundeswari Temple** makes a pleasant half-day excursion. Pilgrims are supposed to climb the 1000-plus steps to the top, but those not needing to improve their karma will probably find descending easier on the leg muscles. There is also a road to the top, and bus No 201 departs from the City bus stand in Mysore for the summit every 30 minutes (Rs 2). A taxi to the top from Mysore will cost around Rs 150.

Before exploring the temple visit the free **Godly Museum** near the car park. Here you can ponder the price of various sins and discover some sins you may never have thought existed. Gym enthusiasts may be distressed to find that 'body-building' is a bad thing, since it's a clear case of over-attention to 'body consciousness'.

The Chamundeswari Temple is dominated by a towering seven storey, 40m high gopuram. The statue in the car park is of the demon Mahishasura, who was one of the goddess Chamundi's victims. The goddess was the family deity of the maharajas and Mysore derived its name from Mahishasura. The temple is open from 6 am to 2 pm, 3.30 to 6.30 pm and 7.30 to 9 pm. If the queues to get in look unmanageable, you can jump them by paying Rs 10 at the 'Demand Tickets Special Entrance'.

After visiting the temple start back to the car park and look for the top of the stairway, which is behind the back of the Mahishasura statue, marked by a sign proclaiming 'Way to Big Bull'. It's a pleasant descent since there's some shade on the way and the views over the city and surrounding countryside are superb.

Two-thirds of the way down you come to the famous five metre high **Nandi** (Siva's bull) carved out of solid rock in 1659. It's one of the largest in India and is visited by bevies of pilgrims offering *prasaad* to the priest in attendance there.

You'll probably have rubbery legs by the time you reach the bottom of the hill and it's still a couple of km back into the centre of Mysore. Fortunately there are usually autorickshaws waiting to ferry pedestrians back to town for around Rs 25. Local tourist literature reports that the summit is 13km from

Nandi, Siva's bull, Mysore.

the city, but this is by the winding, switchback road; via the steps it's only about four km.

Devaraja Fruit & Vegetable Market
The Devaraja Market, stretching along the western side of Sayaji Rao Rd, south of Dhanvantri Rd, is one of the most colourful in India and provides excellent subject material for photographers.

Jaganmohan Palace & Art Gallery
The Jayachamarajendra Art Gallery in the Jaganmohan Palace, just west of Mysore Palace, has a collection of kitsch objects and Wodeyar memorabilia, including weird and wonderful musical machines, rare instruments and paintings by Raja Ravi Varma. The palace was built in 1861 and served as a royal auditorium. It's open daily; entry is Rs 5.

Mysore Zoo
Mysore has one of India's better kept zoos, set in pretty gardens on the eastern edge of the city centre. It's open daily except Friday; entry is Rs 8.

Rail Museum
Mysore's paltry **rail museum** boasts a maharani's saloon carriage, complete with royal toilet, dating from around 1899. It's east of the railway station, just across the railway track, and is open daily, though closed for lunch between 1 and 2 pm; entry is Rs 2.

Other Buildings
Mysore has several fine buildings and monuments in a variety of architectural styles. Dating from 1805, **Government House**, formerly the British Residency, is a 'Tuscan Doric' building set in 20 ha of gardens. West of Government House is **Wellington Lodge**, where Arthur Wellesley (later the Duke of Wellington) lived after the defeat of Tipu Sultan.

In front of the north gate of Mysore Palace, a 1920 **statue** of Maharaja Chamarajendar Wodeyar stands in the New Statue Circle, facing the 1927 **Silver Jubilee Clocktower**. If he glanced sideways he'd see the imposing town hall, the **Rangacharlu Memorial Hall**

of 1884. The next traffic circle west is the 1950s **Krishnaraja Circle** (KR Circle) graced by a statue of Maharaja Krishnaraja Wodeyar.

St Philomena's Cathedral, built between 1933 and 1941 in neo-Gothic style, is one of the largest churches in India. It looks rather gloomy from the outside but the whitewashed interior is airy and full of birdsong from the resident pigeons and sparrows.

Converting maharajas' palaces into hotels is a popular activity, and the grand **Lalitha Mahal Palace** of 1921, on the eastern side of town, is a prime example. It's worth driving here from the city centre (Rs 40 return by auto-rickshaw) since the road passes several exquisite colonial residences and the bougainvillea-clad **Commissioner of Police** building. The **Hotel Metropole** also started life as a guesthouse of the maharajas, and the 1910 **Chaluvamba Vilas** on Madikeri Rd was a maharaja's mansion.

The Royal City by TP Issar (INTACH, Mysore, 1991) is a comprehensive survey of the city's architecture.

Activities
Swimming The swimming pool at the Lalitha Mahal Palace Hotel is open to nonguests for Rs 150 per day; Quality Inn Southern Star charges Rs 180.

Organised Tours
The KSTDC's Mysore city tour covers the city sights plus Chamundi Hill, Somnathpur temple, Srirangapatnam and Brindavan Gardens. The tour starts daily at 7.30 am, ends at 8.30 pm and costs Rs 90. It's a pretty good tour, though some of the sights are a bit rushed.

The KSTDC also runs a Belur, Halebid and Sravanabelagola tour every Tuesday, Wednesday, Friday and Sunday (daily in the high season), starting at 7.30 am and ending at 9 pm. The cost is Rs 160. This is an excellent tour if your time is short or you don't want to go to the trouble of making your own way to these places. The time you get at each destination is sufficient for most people.

KSTDC tours can be booked through any of the city's KSTDC offices or through Dasaprakash Travel (☎ 24949), in the courtyard of the Dasaprakash Hotel.

Dussehra Festival

This 10 day festival in the first and second weeks of October is a wonderful time to visit Mysore. The palace is illuminated every night and on the last day the former maharaja leads one of India's most colourful processions. Richly caparisoned elephants, liveried retainers, cavalry, and the gaudy and flower-bedecked images of deities make their way through the streets to the sound of jazz and brass bands, and through the inevitable clouds of incense.

Places to Stay

Accommodation can be hard to find during the Dussehra Festival, so if you're arriving in October be sure to book in advance.

Places to Stay – bottom end

Mysore has plenty of budget hotels. The main areas are around Gandhi Square and in the area between Dhanvantri and Vinoba Rds.

Hotel Maurya (☎ 426677), on Hanumantha Rao St II, just off Sardar Patel Rd, is well run and excellent value. Clean singles/doubles/triples with attached bath and bucket shower cost Rs 95/175/250.

Hotel Dasaprakash (☎ 24444), near Gandhi Square, is part of a south Indian hotel chain. It's a huge, airy place built around a central courtyard with basic but acceptable rooms with attached bath from Rs 100/205 rising to Rs 175/275. Checkout is 24 hours. You get a newspaper under your door in the morning, there's an excellent vegetarian restaurant, an ice-cream parlour, a travel agent and, for emergencies, an astro-palmist on call.

Hotel Mannars Lodge (☎ 35060), off Gandhi Square towards the Central bus terminal, has modern, good-value singles/doubles/triples with attached bath for Rs 100/145/200.

Parklane Hotel (☎ 430400; fax 428424), 2720 Sri Harsha Rd, is the most popular budget hotel in the city. It's a travellers hang-out with decent rooms with attached bathroom for Rs 99/124 on the ground floor and Rs 124/149 on the upper floor. There's a courtyard bar and restaurant downstairs. You'll need to reserve a room days in advance.

Hotel Anugraha (☎ 430768), in the centre of town near the junction of Sayaji Rao and Sardar Patel Rds, is a standard Indian hotel offering adequate rooms with attached bath from Rs 70/125. Checkout is 24 hours.

Hotel Calinga (☎ 431019), opposite the City bus stand, is an old hotel with rudimentary rooms with attached bath for Rs 140/180.

There's not much to distinguish between the hotels in the Dhanvantri Rd area, which are not as good value as those around Gandhi Square. Hotels fronting onto Dhanvantri Rd can be very noisy.

New Gayathri Bhavan (☎ 421224), on Dhanvantri Rd, is a cheap, friendly, large place with a wide variety of rooms starting from Rs 50/90 for singles/doubles with common bath and Rs 145 with attached bath.

Hotel Sangeeth (☎ 424693), 1966 Narayana Shastry Rd, has clean rooms with attached bath for Rs 90/175.

Agrawal Lodge (☎ 422730), just off Dhanvantri Rd and down a side street, has rooms with attached bathroom for Rs 100/130.

Hotel Aashraya (☎ 427088), on another nearby side street, has overpriced doubles with attached bath from Rs 235 and minuscule singles for Rs 70.

Hotel Chalukya (☎ 427374) has rooms with attached bath for Rs 80/135, and deluxe doubles for Rs 275.

Hotel Indra Bhavan (☎ 423933) is a relatively clean hotel but it has seen better days. Singles/doubles/triples with attached bath cost Rs 110/140/179. There's a 'meals' hall downstairs.

Other options include the cluster of budget hotels east of the Jaganmohan Palace, though they see few foreign tourists, and the good *retiring rooms* at the railway station.

Places to Stay – middle

Ritz Hotel (☎ 422668), a few hundred metres from the Central bus terminal, is a friendly place with plenty of old-world charm. There are only four rooms: spacious doubles with mosquito nets, attached bath and 24 hour hot water are Rs 200, and a four-bed room costs Rs 322. You'll need to book a month in advance to secure a room. There's a restaurant and bar downstairs.

Hotel Mayura Hoysala (☎ 425349), 2 Jhansi Lakshmi Bai Rd, is a good KSTDC hotel on the opposite side of the city centre. It has a relaxing ambience and offers decent rooms with enormous attached bath for Rs 200/250. The hotel has its own quiet gardens, as well as a bar and restaurant.

Mayura Yathrinivas (☎ 423652), a KSTDC annexe next door, has characterless overpriced doubles with attached bath for Rs 240 and dorm beds for Rs 70.

Hotel Palace Plaza (☎ 430034), at 2716 Sri Harsha Rd, is a recommended modern hotel offering a variety of rooms ranging from Rs 275 with TV and attached bath to Rs 700 with air-con and (brace yourself) circular beds, fantasy curtains and mirrored ceilings.

Hotel SCVDS (☎ 421379), next door to the Parklane Hotel, has modern rooms with mosquito nets, TV and attached bath from Rs 199/350. It's keen to attract foreign travellers, so offers discounts of up to Rs 100 on these rates.

There are three very ordinary modern hotels, all popular with Indian tourists, south of the Central bus terminal.

Mysore Hotel Complex (☎ 426217), on the Bangalore-Nilgiri Rd, has characterless doubles with attached bath from Rs 275 or with air-con for a pricey Rs 800.

Hotel Roopa (☎ 33770), on the opposite side of road, is better value but still nothing special. Average doubles cost from Rs 200 or Rs 450 with air-con.

Hotel Sreekrishna Continental (☎ 37042), 73 Nazarbad Main Rd, has rooms with attached bath from Rs 250/300 and air-con doubles for Rs 550.

Places to Stay – top end
Hotel Metropole (☎ 420681; fax 420854), 5 Jhansi Lakshmi Bai Rd, oozes with character and charm. It was once the maharaja's guest house and is set in well-kept grounds filled with flamboyant trees. Spacious rooms with period furniture, pedestal baths and shady verandahs are superb value at Rs 900/1100 or Rs 1100/1300 with air-con. There's a pleasant bar, an elegant restaurant and an evening barbecue in the garden.

Kings Kourt Hotel (☎ 421142; fax 438384) is a large, modern establishment opposite Hotel Metropole. It charges from Rs 1190/1390 for air-con rooms, though at slack periods you may get a good reduction on this tariff.

Quality Inn Southern Star (☎ 438141; fax 421689), at 13-14 Vinoba Rd, around the corner from the Hotel Metropole, is a plush, modern hotel. It boasts a swimming pool, health club, poolside barbecue, restaurant and coffee shop. The hotel is centrally air-conditioned and rooms cost Rs 1320/2195 including breakfast.

Lalitha Mahal Palace Hotel (☎ 571265; fax 571770), six km from the city centre, is Mysore's most luxurious hotel. This huge, gleaming white structure was once one of the maharaja's palaces. Standard rooms cost US$120/140, though there are some cramped 'turret' rooms for US$50/60. The rooms in the older part of the building have the most character, but they can be gloomy and lack balconies. Facilities include a rather ordinary swimming pool, a tennis court, and a large bar with reputedly the best billiard table in India.

Places to Eat
Shilpashri Restaurant & Bar on Gandhi Square is very popular with travellers, and for good reason since the food is excellent, the prices are reasonable and the rooftop is a lovely place to dine at night. It serves western breakfasts, and Indian, Chinese and Continental mains costing between Rs 30 and Rs 50.

Akshaya Vegetarian Restaurant in the Dasaprakash Hotel has excellent 'limited' meals for Rs 20 and superb 'special meals' for Rs 30. There's also a good ice-cream parlour in the courtyard.

RRR Restaurant on Gandhi Square is a typical vegetarian place with 'meals' for between Rs 24 and Rs 40.

Parklane Hotel on Sri Harsha Rd has a convivial courtyard restaurant that's long been a travellers' favourite. It serves everything from tandoori chicken and chop suey to sandwiches and beer. The red lights above your table are for signalling the waiters not for atmosphere.

Ilapur is a clean air-con place adjacent to the Parklane Hotel. It serves north Indian and spicy Andhra food for between Rs 35 and Rs 50.

Ritz Hotel, close to the Central bus terminal, has a restaurant-bar and outdoor eating area at the back of the hotel where you can tuck into reasonably priced Indian, Chinese and Continental food.

Paras Restaurant, on Sayaji Rao Rd, is a popular local eatery serving south Indian (Rs 22) and north Indian (Rs 45) thalis at lunchtime. *Indra Cafe*, downstairs, has snacks, juices and sweets; expect to queue for a seat at lunchtime.

Tandoor Restaurant on Dhanvantri Rd is a hole-in-the-wall eatery serving Punjabi fare and cheap western breakfasts. The nearby *Bun Shop* sells tasty potato buns which make a fine light lunch for just Rs 3.

Kwality Restaurant on Dhanvantri Rd serves veg and non-veg fare as well as Chinese and tandoori specialities. Most meals are between Rs 30 and Rs 45.

Regency Restaurant, the Hotel Metropole's elegant eatery, hosts a garden barbecue every evening. The food is excellent, the service both friendly and efficient, and the prices quite reasonable for a place this grand. Count on about Rs 250 for dinner for two in the restaurant.

Lalitha Mahal Palace Hotel offers Mysore's most sumptuous dining experience, though some find the over-refined atmosphere and the baby-blue Wedgwood-style decor in the grand dining hall unsettling to the digestion. Dinner for two here will set you back around Rs 600, not including alcohol. The food is superb and there's live Indian classical music. The à la carte menu is replaced by a buffet outside the busy tourist season. The hotel travel counter can arrange a taxi back into town for around Rs 125.

Entertainment

The *Royal Legacy* on Nazarbad Main Rd, not far from the Central bus terminal, is a compact Bangalore-style pub selling beer by the mug (Rs 23), pint (Rs 46) or bottle (Rs 60). It's a popular joint with music and dancing upstairs. More relaxed places for a beer include the *Parklane Hotel* (Rs 39), *Shilpashri* (15 varieties from Rs 37 to Rs 47), Hotel Metropole's colonial-style *Planters Inn* (Rs 55), or the gentleman's club-style bar at the *Lalitha Mahal Palace Hotel* (Rs 125).

There are plenty of cinemas in the area between the Central bus terminal and Gandhi Square.

Things to Buy

Mysore is famous for carved sandalwood, inlay works, silk saris, incense and wooden toys. The best place to see the whole range is at the Cauvery Arts & Crafts Emporium on Sayaji Rao Rd. It's open daily except Sunday from 10 am to 1.30 pm and 3 to 7.30 pm. It accepts credit cards, foreign currency or travellers cheques and will arrange packing and export, though it's not cheap by Indian standards.

There are a number of other souvenir and handicraft shops in the precincts of the Jaganmohan Palace and along Dhanvantri Rd. Silk shops can be found along Devaraj Urs Rd.

You can buy silk and see weavers at work at the Government Silk Factory on Madhavacharya Rd in the southern suburb of Krishnamurthypuram. You can also visit a nearby sandalwood oil extracting plant in the suburb of Ashokapuram and purchase oil and scented incense sticks here. The factories are about two km south-east of Mysore Palace.

Getting There & Away

Air There are no flights to Mysore but Indian Airlines (☎ 421846) has an office next door to the Hotel Mayura Hoysala. It's open Monday to Saturday from 10 am to 1.30 pm and 2.15 to 5 pm.

Bus The Central bus terminal handles all of the KSRTC long-distance buses. There is a timetable in English and you can make reservations six days in advance. The City bus stand, on KR Circle, is for city and Srirangapatnam buses. Private long-distance bus agents are clustered around the road junction near the Wesley Cathedral.

Nonstop KSRTC buses hurtle off to Bangalore (Rs 27/41 ordinary/deluxe, three hours) every 15 minutes. If you're heading for Belur, Halebid or Sravanabelagola, the usual gateway is Hassan (Rs 24, three hours). Buses depart every 30 minutes. There's only one direct bus to Sravanabelagola (Rs 20, three hours), but buses depart every 30 minutes to Channarayapatana, only 10km from Sravanabelagola; you can pick up a local bus from there. Those heading to Hampi have a choice of three buses to its nearest service centre, Hospet (Rs 90/130, 12 hours). Ten buses a day head to Ooty (Rs 33, five hours) via Bandipur National Park. There are plenty of buses to Mangalore (Rs 50/70, seven hours) and Kannur (Rs 60, six hours) and three buses to Ernakulam (Rs 160, 12 hours). One bus heads to Gokarna (Rs 135, 14 hours) at 6 am and one bus heads to Chennai (Rs 110, 10 hours) at 5 pm.

In addition to the KSRTC buses, there are a number of private bus companies which run to such places as Bangalore, Mumbai, Goa, Hyderabad, Chennai, Mangalore, Ooty and Pune. Fares on these buses are more than the KSRTC buses but they are definitely more comfortable. To book tickets, try Gayatri Tourism, opposite the Ritz Hotel, and nearby Kiran Tours & Travel.

Train The booking office at the pretty pink Mysore railway station is computerised and rarely has long queues, but there's no tourist quota. The office is open Monday to Saturday from 8 am to 2 pm and 2.15 to 8 pm; Sunday, 8 am to 2 pm. There are three daily express trains to Bangalore (Rs 36 in 2nd class, three hours), plus the air-con high-speed *Shatabdi* (Rs 185, two hours) which runs daily except Tuesday. The *Shatabdi* continues on to Chennai (Rs 430, seven hours).

At the time of writing, conversion from metre to broad gauge had closed all other services from Mysore, including those to Hassan, Arsikere and Mangalore. These are optimistically expected to recommence in late 1997, when several expresses a day should undertake the journey. Until these lines reopen, to catch an express to any major Indian city requires a change in Bangalore.

Passenger services between Mysore and Bangalore stop in Srirangapatnam, an alternative to catching the bus.

Getting Around
Bus From the City bus stand, bus No 201 goes to Chamundi Hill (Rs 2) every 40 minutes. Bus Nos 150, 303 and 304 go to Brindavan Gardens (Rs 3), departing every 30 minutes. Bus Nos 125 and 313 leave every 40 minutes for Srirangapatnam (Rs 2.75). A direct private bus to Somnathpur (1½ hours) runs along Nazarabad Main Rd at around 11.45 am, but there are plenty of similar buses on this stretch heading to T Narsipur or Bannur, where you can change to another bus for Somnathpur.

Taxi & Auto-Rickshaw There are plenty of auto-rickshaws, and drivers are usually willing to use the meter. Flagfall is Rs 6 for the first km and then around Rs 3 for each subsequent km. Taxis are considerably more expensive and do not have meters so fares must be negotiated.

Car If you intend to explore the many sights around Mysore in a car, KSTDC recommended rates for car and driver hire are Rs 3.30 per km for a minimum of 250km per day. Expect to pay Rs 70 per day for the driver's expenses.

AROUND MYSORE
Somnathpur
Tel Area Code: 08227
The **Sri Channakeshara Temple** stands at the edge of the tranquil village of Somnathpur, 33km east of Mysore. Built around 1260 AD during the heyday of the Hoysala kings, it's an astonishingly beautiful, unspoilt building. It's also complete, unlike the

larger Hoysala temples at Belur and Halebid. For more details on Hoysala architecture, see the boxed section under Belur & Halebid later in this chapter.

The walls of this star-shaped temple are covered with superb sculptures in stone depicting various scenes from the *Ramayana, Mahabharata, Bhagavad Gita* and the life and times of the Hoysala kings. No two friezes are alike. The carved frieze which goes around the temple has six strips, starting with elephants at the bottom, followed by horses, a floral strip, scenes, crocodiles or lions and, finally, geese.

The temple is open daily from 9 am to 5.30 pm; entry is Rs 2

Places to Stay The only place to stay or eat in Somnathpur is the run-down KSTDC *Hotel Mayura Keshav*, just outside the temple compound. It should be an excellent place, considering its location, but it has only a couple of functional rooms (used mostly as

nesting places for sparrows) with attached bathroom for Rs 40/65. Its restaurant is very basic.

Getting There & Away Somnathpur is just a few km south of Bannur and 10km north of T Narsipur. See the earlier Mysore Getting Around section for details on public transport.

Talakad & Sivasamudram
The remains of the capital of the 4th to 5th century Ganga dynasty, built on a bank of the Cauvery River at Talakad, are now largely buried by sand. A few buildings, including a 12th century Hoysala temple, still poke through the surface. Once every 12 years this surreal temple is dug out for the performance of Panchalinga Darshan, though it doesn't take long for it to be smothered once again by the sand. Talakad is 50km south-east of Mysore.

A further 25km downstream, the Cauvery suddenly drops more than 50m at the twin waterfalls at Sivasamudram, best seen immediately after the monsoon.

Srirangapatnam
Sixteen km from Mysore on the Bangalore road stand the ruins of Hyder Ali and Tipu Sultan's capital, from which they ruled much of southern India during the 18th century. In 1799, the British finally conquered them with the help of disgruntled local leaders. Tipu's defeat marked the real beginning of British territorial expansion in southern India.

Srirangapatnam was built on a long island in the Cauvery River. There isn't much left of it since the British did a good job of demolishing the place, but ramparts and battlements and some of the gates still stand. The population of the town inside the fort is about 20,000.

The dungeon where Tipu held a number of British officers has been preserved. Inside the fortress walls there's a mosque and the **Sri Ranganathaswamy Temple**.

One km east of the fort, set in ornamental gardens, is Tipu's summer palace, known as the **Daria Daulat Bagh**. After Tipu's defeat,

Around Mysore

To Hassan Belur & Halebid

Channarayapatna

0   10   20 km

Sravanabelagola

Nagamangala

Hole Narsipur

Krishnarajpet

Basaralu

Melkote

To Bangalore

Krishnaraja Sagar

Mandya

Panadayapura

Brindavan Gardens

Srirangapatnam

To Madikeri & Mangalore

Ranganathittoo Bird Sanctuary

Bannur

Hunsur

Mysore

Somnathpur

T Narsipur

To Nagarhole National Park

Nanjangud

To Bandipur National Park & Ooty

To Kozhikode

Cauvery River

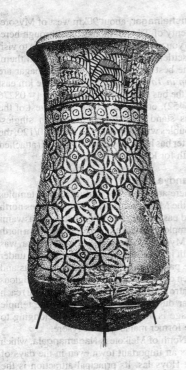
Antique pottery storage jar.

it was temporarily the home of Colonel Arthur Wellesley (later the Duke of Wellington). Its highly decorated interior now houses a museum with a motley collection of family memorabilia and paintings depicting Tipu's campaigns against the British. The museum is open daily except Friday; entry is Rs 2.

Two km further east is the impressive onion-domed **Gumbaz**, or mausoleum, of Tipu and his father, Hyder Ali.

Places to Stay The best place to stay is the KSTDC's *Hotel Mayura River View* (☎ 52114), peacefully located beside the Cauvery River, a few km from the bus stand and railway station. It has well-kept double cottages for Rs 385 (no singles) plus an indoor/outdoor restaurant-bar. Coracle rides can be arranged

with locals, but don't go for a dip unless you want to be crocodile bait.

Getting There & Away Scores of buses ply the Mysore to Bangalore road. It's also possible to get to Srirangapatnam on Mysore to Bangalore passenger trains. See the earlier Mysore Getting Around section for details.

Getting Around Walking around the sights is not really an option as the points of interest are very spread out. The best plan is to hire a bicycle on the main street in the fort, about 500m from the bus stand. All the sites are signposted so it's not difficult to find your way around. There are also tongas and auto-rickshaws for hire.

Ranganathittoo Bird Sanctuary
This sanctuary is on one of three islands in the Cauvery River, three km upstream from Srirangapatnam. It's a good place to see storks, ibises, egrets, darters, spoonbills and cormorants. It can be visited at any time of year, though it's best between July and August. Access is by a motorable road, open all year, and there are boats available.

Brindavan Gardens
Tel Area Code: 08236
These tranquil ornamental gardens, laid out below the immense Krishnaraja Sagar dam, look like they belong in a tidy central European spa resort rather than the south of India. The gardens are a popular picnic spot and crowds come each night to see the illuminated fountains. While it's probably not worth a special trip just to do either of these things, it's definitely worth coming here if you intend to soak up the surroundings by staying in the majestic Hotel Krishnaraja Sagar overlooking the gardens.

The gardens are illuminated Monday to Friday between 6.30 and 7.25 pm (7 to 7.55 pm in summer) and on weekends until 8.25 pm (to 8.55 pm in summer). Entry is Rs 5, plus Rs 15 for a camera permit. Due to fears the dam will be sabotaged, 'movie cameras, explosives and suspectable items' are prohibited. Vehicle access is also restricted to those who have a hotel booking (a 24 hour car pass costs Rs 50). If you arrive by car after 4.30 pm or without a booking, you'll have to walk the pleasant 1.5km stretch from the main gate, across the top of the dam, to the gardens and hotels.

Places to Stay The *Hotel Krishnaraja Sagar* (☎ 57322) has rooms with TV, period furniture and attached bathroom for Rs 750/1000, or Rs 1000/1200 with air-con. It's a grand, charming hotel with expansive views from its front rooms and from the common sitting area in the open-fronted hotel foyer. There's a restaurant serving Indian, Chinese and Continental dishes for around Rs 70 and also a bar. Bookings for weekend stays should be made in advance. The Hotel Metropole in Mysore handles reservations.

Hotel Mayura Cauvery (☎ 57252), nearby, is the budget alternative. Clean, basic rooms with attached bathroom and partial views of the garden cost Rs 135/168. It has a restaurant with a limited menu.

Getting There & Away The gardens are 19km north-west of Mysore, and one of the KSTDC tours stops here briefly. See the earlier Mysore Getting Around section for details on public transport.

Tibetan Settlements
There are many Tibetan refugee settlements in the low, rolling hills west of Mysore, in the area between Hunsur and Madikeri. The Tibetans are extremely friendly and generally very hospitable towards the few travellers who visit.

Bylakuppe is one of the main settlements and is the site of the monastic university, Sera Gompa. Two smaller monasteries have been established at Camp Nos 1 and 3, and the Tantric college, Gjumed Dratsang, is in Hunsur. Within the region, there are also carpet factories (where you can get Tibetan carpets made to your own design), an incense factory and various social organisations.

As there's no commercial accommodation in any of the settlements, the best place to base yourself is the small market town of **Kushalnagar**, about 90km west of Mysore. Plenty of Tibetan monks pass through here, so you may be able to get an invitation to visit a settlement and share transport with them. The best places to stay in Kushalnagar are *Top in Town*, on the main road one km east of the bus stand, and *Kodagu Plaza* (☎ 08276 74452), on the same road 250m west of the bus stand. The former has clean singles/doubles with attached bath for Rs 80/120; the latter has huge modern doubles with attached bath for Rs 250.

Mandya District
There are several beautiful Hoysala temples in the Mandya district, which stretches north and east of Mysore. The Cheluvarayaswami Temple at **Melkote**, approximately 50km north of Mysore via the town of Pandayapura, was built in the 12th century and later came under the patronage of the Mysore maharajas and even of Tipu Sultan. It's an important religious centre and there's a festival (Vairamudi) each year during March/April, when the temple image is adorned with jewels belonging to the former maharajas of Mysore.

North of Melkote is **Nagamangala**, which was an important town even in the days of the Hoysalas. Its principal attraction is the Saumyakeshava Temple, which was built in the 12th century and later added to by the Vijayanagar kings.

About 20km west of Melkote, near Krishnarajpet, is the village of **Hosaholalu**. Here you'll find the Lakshminarayana Temple, a superb example of 13th century Hoysala temple architecture which rivals in artistry the temples at Belur and Halebid.

The village of **Basaralu**, some 25km north of Mandya, is home to the exquisite 12th century Mallikarjuna Temple, executed in early Hoysala style. It's adorned with beautiful sculptures, including a 16 armed Siva dancing on Andhakasura's head, and Ravana lifting Kailasa.

Getting to any of these towns involves the use of numerous local buses; you'll have to ask around to find the right ones as the timetables are all in Kannada. Mysore is your best base for all of them except Basaralu, for which Mandya might be better. There's a range of modest accommodation in Mandya.

BANDIPUR NATIONAL PARK

Eighty km south of Mysore on the Mysore to Udhagamandalam (Ooty) road, this wildlife sanctuary covers 865 sq km and is part of a larger national park which also includes the neighbouring wildlife sanctuaries of Mudumalai in Tamil Nadu and Wynad in Kerala. This was once the Mysore maharajas' private game reserve.

The sanctuary is one of 15 selected across the country for Project Tiger, a scheme launched in 1973 by the World Wide Fund for Nature (WWF) to save the tiger and its habitat. The sanctuary is noted for its herds of gaur (Indian bison), spotted deer, elephant, sambar, sloth bears and langurs. There are also supposed to be two dozen tigers, but they are rarely seen. The best times to visit are May and June and from September to November. If there is a drought, the park may not be worth visiting because the animals migrate to the adjoining Mudumalai park for water.

Visitors must pay a fee of Rs 150 to enter the park, but this includes a one hour tour in the Forest Department's bus, which leaves hourly every day between 6 and 8 am, and 4 and 5 pm. Elephant rides are the only other means of game viewing and cost Rs 20 per person per hour. Private vehicles are not allowed to tour the park.

Bus tours and Forest Department accommodation must be booked in advance. For reservations, contact either the Chief Wildlife Warden (☎ 3341993), Aranya Bhavan, 18th Cross, Malleswaram in Bangalore or the Field Director (☎ 520901), Project Tiger, Ashokapuram, Mysore.

Places to Stay

The Forest Department's huge deluxe *bungalows* have attached bath and hot water (if there's no water shortage) and cost Rs 75. The caretaker will fix meals, and you can see chital (spotted deer) from your bedroom window. These bungalows *must* be booked and paid for in advance – if you turn up without

a reservation, it's unlikely you'll be given a room.

The KSTDC has four *cottages* located on the Mysore road, three km outside the park. They cost Rs 250 for a double and can be booked at the KSTDC transport office in Mysore (☎ 423652), or the main KSTDC office on Kasturba Rd in Bangalore (☎ 221 2901).

Bush Betta is a private resort about four km from the Bandipur reception centre, off the road to Mudumalai. It has singles/doubles for US$85/155, including all meals, an elephant ride and a jeep safari. Bookings must be made in advance at the resort's Bangalore office (☎ 5512631; fax 5593451), located at Gainnet, Raheja Plaza, Ground Floor, Richmond Rd. Resort guests are picked up at the Bandipur reception centre.

Tusker Trails resort is on the eastern edge of the park near Mangala village. It consists of six twin-bedded cottages and a swimming pool, and operates guided safaris into the forest. The resort is run by a maharaja's daughter, hence the address of its Bangalore office where bookings should be made in advance: Hospital Cottage, Bangalore Palace, Bangalore (☎ 3342862).

Getting There & Away

All buses between Mysore (2½ hours) and Ooty (three hours) stop at Bandipur. See the Getting There & Away sections of those towns for details.

NAGARHOLE NATIONAL PARK

This 643 sq km wildlife sanctuary (also known as Rajiv Gandhi National Park) is in an isolated pocket of the Coorg region, 93km south-west of Mysore. Until a few years ago, it was one of the country's finest deciduous forests and home to tigers, elephants, panthers, sloth bears, gaur, barking deer and sambar. Unfortunately, much of the forest was destroyed by fire in 1992 when tensions between officials involved in anti-poaching activities and local graziers and farmers erupted in a frenzy of arson. The destruction is no longer blatantly obvious and the forest has regenerated.

Not surprisingly, the park has seen few visitors in recent years and facilities are still minimal. Foreigners must pay a Rs 150 per day fee while in the park. The best time to visit is between October and May. Don't turn up without reserving Forest Department accommodation in advance. All enquiries and bookings should be directed to the Deputy Conservator of the Forest & Wildlife Division (☎ (08222) 2041) at Hunsur. Accommodation reservations should be made 15 days to one month in advance.

Places to Stay & Eat

At the reception centre in the heart of the sanctuary, there are two Forest Department *dormitories* with beds for Rs 20, plus a six-room *lodge* for Rs 75 per person.

Kabini River Lodge, near Karapur on the Mysore to Mananthavadi Rd, is a former Maharaja's hunting lodge. It costs US$99 per person twin share, including full board. The lodge is on the southern fringe of the park, about 65km from the sanctuary's reception centre. Bookings should be made with Jungle Lodges & Resorts Ltd (☎ 559 7025; fax 558 6163) in the Shrungar Shopping Centre, MG Rd, Bangalore.

Work on the Taj Group's planned Getaway Tusker Lodge near Murkal, about 15km north of the reception area, has been dogged by controversy and was still not completed at the time of writing. The supposedly eco-friendly resort, built on the site of old forestry cottages, has been criticised by environmentalists and has resulted in the relocation of large numbers of tribal people.

Getting There & Away

Direct buses to Nagarhole leave from Mysore's Central bus terminal at 7 am and 1.30 pm and take four hours to reach the park. Jungle Lodges & Resorts Ltd can arrange private transportation to Kabini River Lodge.

BELUR & HALEBID

Tel Area Code: 08177
The Hoysala temples at Halebid (Halebeed, Halebidu) and Belur, along with the one at

Somnathpur east of Mysore, are the cream of one of the most artistically exuberant periods of Hindu cultural development. Their sculptural decoration rivals that of Khajuraho (Madhya Pradesh) and Konark (Orissa), or the best of European Gothic art.

Construction of the **Hoysaleswara Temple** at Halebid began around 1121. Despite more than 80 years of labour, it was never completed. Nevertheless, it is easily the most outstanding example of Hoysala art. Every cm of the outside walls and much of the interior is covered with an endless variety of Hindu deities, sages, stylised animals and birds, and friezes depicting the life of the Hoysala rulers.

The temple is set in a well-tended garden, and there's a small museum adjacent to it housing a collection of sculptures. The temple is open daily from sunrise to sunset; entry is free. The museum is open daily except Friday from 10 am to 5 pm.

Halebid also has a smaller temple know as **Kedareswara** and a little-visited **Jain temple**, which has fine carvings.

The **Channekeshava Temple** at Belur is the only one at the three major Hoysala sites still in daily use. It was begun in 1116 to commemorate the Hoysala's victory over the Cholas at Talakad, and was worked on for over a century. Its exterior is not as extensively sculpted as the other Hoysala temples, but much decorative work can be found on the internal supporting pillars and lintels. It is enclosed in a paved compound, which includes a well and a bathing tank. The temple's 14th century seven storey gopuram has some sensual sculptures explicitly portraying the après-temple activities of dancing girls.

The temple is open daily from sunrise to sunset; entry is free. Non-Hindus are allowed inside but not into the inner sanctum. You can hire a spotlight to see the sculptural detail of the interior for Rs 5.

The other, lesser, Hoysala temples at Belur are the Channigaraya and the Viranarayana.

Places to Stay & Eat

Halebid The only place to stay here is the peaceful Department of Tourism *Tourist*

Cottages (☎ 3224), set in a pleasant garden next to the temple. There are just two double rooms with musty carpets, attached bath and verandahs for Rs 60/100 for one/two people. There's also a dormitory costing Rs 40 per bed but it's reserved for groups. The tiny *canteen* here has drinks, toast and omelettes and can rustle up basic meals.

Close to the temple there's a cluster of snack stands and a basic restaurant catering to Indian tourists.

Belur The *Hotel Mayura Velapuri* (☎ 22209), a spotlessly clean KSTDC operation, is the best place to stay in Belur. It's only 300m from the temple and a five minute walk from the bus stand. Excellent singles/doubles with attached bath cost Rs 168/200 in the new wing; rooms in the old wing are cheaper at Rs 135/163. Its bland canteen-bar has an uninspiring menu.

Swagath Tourist Home (☎ 22159) has basic rooms with attached bath for Rs 40/60. It's 50m before the temple on the left side of the road.

Shri Raghavendra Tourist Home (☎ 22372), to the right of the temple entrance, near the massive temple chariot, has basic rooms with common bath and mattresses on the floor for Rs 50.

Sri Vishnu Krupa (☎ 22263) is on the town's main road, a few minutes walk from the bus stand. It has fine deluxe doubles with attached bath for Rs 125 and scummy cheaper rooms with attached bath for Rs 40/100. It also has a veg restaurant.

Hotel Shankar is the most popular of the town's handful of basic restaurants. It's 200m before the temple on the left side of the road.

Getting There & Away

Halebid and Belur are only 16km apart. Crammed buses shuttle between the two towns every 30 minutes from around 6 am to 9 pm; the fare is Rs 3. If you're visiting the temples from Hassan, the last bus from the Halebid bus stand back to Hassan leaves at 5.30 pm; from Belur, the last bus goes to Hassan at 8.30 pm. There are a few buses a day from Halebid to Mysore and one dawn bus from Belur to Mysore. If you're heading to Hampi, you'll need to catch a bus from Halebid to Shimoga (three hours) and pick up a bus to Hospet (five hours) from there.

While rail services to Hassan are disrupted, Arsikere (40km north-east of Halebid) is the closest operational railhead. There are seven buses a day from Arsikere to Halebid and Belur (Rs 11, two hours). Arsikere has three passenger trains a day to Bangalore and a couple of inconveniently scheduled expresses. It also has an express connection to

---

Hoysala Architecture

The Hoysalas, who ruled this part of the Deccan between the 11th and 13th centuries, had their origins in the hill tribes of the Western Ghats and were, for a long time, feudatories of the Chalukyans. They did not become fully independent until about 1190 AD, though they first rose to prominence under their leader Tinayaditya (1047-78 AD), who took advantage of the waning power of the Gangas and Rashtrakutas. Under Bittiga (1110-52 AD), better known by his later name of Vishnuvardhana, they began to take off on a course of their own and it was during his reign that the distinctive temples at Belur and Halebid were built.

Typically, these temples are squat, star-shaped structures set on a platform to give them some height. They are more human in scale than the soaring temples found elsewhere in India, but what they lack in size they make up for in the sheer intricacy of their sculptures.

It's quickly apparent from a study of these sculptures that the arts of music and dancing were highly regarded during the Hoysala period. As with Kathakali dancing in Kerala, the arts were used to express religious fervour, the joy of a victory in battle, or simply to give domestic pleasure. It's also obvious that these were times of a relatively high degree of sexual freedom and prominent female participation in public affairs.

The Hoysalas converted to Jainism in the 10th century, but then took up Hinduism in the 11th century. This is why images of Shaivite, Vaishnavite and Jain sects co-exist in Hoysala temples. ■

Miraj (for trains to Goa) and an express four times a week to Mumbai.

KSTDC offices in Bangalore and Mysore run tours which visit both Halebid and Belur. See the Organised Tours sections in those cities for details.

SRAVANABELAGOLA

Pop: 4000   Tel Area Code: 08176

This is one of the oldest and most important Jain pilgrimage centres in India, and the site of the huge 17m high naked statue of Bahubali (Gomateshvara), said to be the world's tallest monolithic statue. It overlooks the sedate country town of Sravanabelagola from the top of the rocky hill known as Indragiri. Its simplicity and serenity is in complete contrast to the complexity and energy of the sculptural work at the temples of Belur and Halebid. The word Sravanabelagola means the Monk of the White Pond.

History

Sravanabelagola has a long historical pedigree going back to the 3rd century BC when Chandragupta Maurya came here with his guru, Bhagwan Bhadrabahu Swami, after renouncing his kingdom. In the course of time Bhadrabahu's disciples spread his teachings all over the region, firmly establishing Jainism in the south. The religion found powerful patrons in the Gangas who ruled the southern part of what is now Karnataka between the 4th and 10th centuries, and it was during this time that Jainism reached the zenith of its influence.

Information

The helpful tourist office is as the foot of the stairway climbing Indragiri Hill and is open daily except Sunday from 10 am to 5.30 pm. There's no entry fee to the site, but you are encouraged to make a donation.

Gomateshvara Statue

The statue of Bahubali was created during the reign of the Ganga king, Rachamalla. It was commissioned by a military commander in the service of Rachamalla and carved out of granite by the sculptor Aristenemi in 981 AD. Bahubali was the son of the Emperor Vrishabhadeva, who became the first Jain tirthankar, Adinath. Bahubali and his brother Bharatha competed fiercely for the right to succeed their father but, on the point of victory, Bahubali realised the futility of the struggle and renounced his kingdom. He withdrew from the material world and entered the forest, where he began to meditate in complete stillness until he attained enlightenment.

The statue depicting Bahubali in this serene state stands atop Indragiri Hill and is reached by 614 rock-cut steps. You must leave your shoes at the foot of the hill, which creates a real problem in summer since the steps become scalding. Get there before the heat of the day. If you're unable to climb the hill under your own steam, porters will carry you up in a wicker chair for Rs 75 return.

Once every 12 years, the statue of Bahubali is anointed with thousands of pots of coconut milk, yoghurt, ghee, bananas, jaggery, dates, almonds, poppy seeds, milk, saffron and sandalwood during the Mahamastakabhisheka ceremony. This will next take place in the year 2005.

Other Temples

In addition to the statue of Bahubali there are several interesting Jain *bastis* (temples) and *mathas* (monasteries) in the town and on Chandragiri Hill, the smaller of the two hills between which Sravanabelagola nestles.

Two of these, the **Bhandari Basti** and the **Akkana Basti**, are in the Hoysala style, and a third, the **Chandragupta Basti**, is believed to have been built by Emperor Ashoka. The well-preserved paintings in one of the temples are like a 600 year old comic strip of Jain stories.

Places to Stay & Eat

Nearly all of Sravanabelagola's accommodation is run by the local Jain organisation SDJMI, whose central accommodation office (☎ 57258) handles bookings for 21 guest houses in town. Most of these guest houses are efficiently-run and indistinguishable. They generally cost Rs 50 for a double, though the pick of the bunch, *Yatri Nivas*, costs Rs 100. The accommodation office is just before the bus stand, on the way into town. It's on the right-hand side, set back 50m from the road.

The friendly *Hotel Raghu* (☎ 57238), 50m from the bottom of the stairway climbing Indragiri Hill, is the only privately owned establishment. Basic but decent singles/doubles/triples with attached bath cost Rs 50/75/100. It also has a popular veg restaurant.

There is a very basic refreshment canteen in the bus stand, and chai shops and vegetarian restaurants in the street leading to the foot of Indragiri Hill.

Getting There & Away
There are four buses a day to Hassan (Rs 10, one hour); three buses to Belur (Rs 18, 2½ hours); three buses to Bangalore (Rs 28, three hours); and one to Mysore (Rs 17, 2½ hours) at 7.30 am. Nearly all long-distance buses leave in the morning or at lunchtime; there's very little transport after 2 pm. If you're having trouble making transport connections, catch a local bus 10km north-west to Channarayapatna, which is on the main Bangalore-Mangalore road.

The KSTDC operates tours from Mysore and Bangalore to Sravanabelagola; see the Organised Tours sections in those cities for details.

HASSAN
Pop: 121,000   Tel Area Code: 08172
Traditionally, Hassan has been the most convenient base from which to explore Belur, Halebid and Sravanabelagola, since it's the nearest railhead to all three sights. However, at the time of writing, virtually all rail services to Hassan had ceased while the Mysore and Mangalore lines were converted from metre to broad gauge. These lines are expected to re-open in late 1997, but don't hold your breath, since at current funding levels it's estimated that the Mangalore stretch will take 10 years to complete.

There are ample bus connections to compensate, so you'll still almost certainly pass through here. Whether you decide to stay is another matter, since there's now a fine KSTDC hotel at Belur and ample accommodation at Sravanabelagola. Hassan does have several good budget hotels, though, and the region's only upmarket establishment.

Information
The tourist office is open from 10 am to 5.30 pm. For foreign exchange, go to the State Bank of Mysore.

Places to Stay
Vaishnavi Lodging (☎ 67413), a one minute

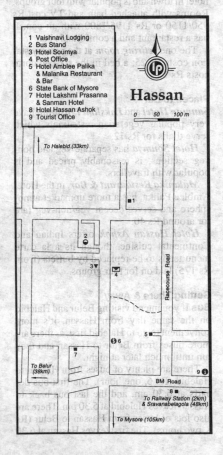

1 Vaishnavi Lodging
2 Bus Stand
3 Hotel Soumya
4 Post Office
5 Hotel Amblee Palika
   & Malanika Restaurant
   & Bar
6 State Bank of Mysore
7 Hotel Lakshmi Prasanna
   & Sanman Hotel
8 Hotel Hassan Ashok
9 Tourist Office

Hassan

0   50   100 m

To Halebid (33km)

Racecourse Road

To Belur
(38km)

BM Road

To Railway Station (2km)
& Sravanabelagola (48km)

To Mysore (105km)

walk from the bus stand, is excellent value at Rs 80/120 for clean singles/doubles with attached bath.

Hotel Lakshmi Prasanna (☎ 68391), in the centre of town, has good rooms with attached bath and bucket shower for Rs 70/110.

Hotel Amblee Palika (☎ 66307), on Racecourse Rd, has comfortable economy rooms with attached bath from Rs 205/275, though it's deluxe rooms suffer from smelly carpet syndrome.

Hotel Hassan Ashok (☎ 68731; fax 68324) on the Bangalore-Mangalore road is the best hotel in town and is popular with tour groups. Rooms with attached bath and TV cost Rs 950/1150 or Rs 1195/1800 with air-con. It has a restaurant and a comfortable bar.

The one *retiring room* at the railway station costs Rs 25; a bed in the six-bed dorm costs Rs 15.

Places to Eat

Sanman Hotel and *Lakshmi Prasanna* have very popular vegetarian restaurants which serve thalis for Rs 12.

Hotel Soumya has separate veg and non-veg sections, is reasonably priced and is popular with travellers.

Malanika Restaurant & Bar, in the Hotel Amblee Palika, has a more upmarket atmosphere and serves decent veg/non-veg fare for around Rs 40.

Hotel Hassan Ashok offers Indian and Continental cuisine, though its à la carte menu tends to be replaced by buffets (from Rs 175) laid on for tour groups.

Getting There & Away

Bus If you intend visiting Belur and Halebid on the same day from Hassan, it's more convenient to go to Halebid first, as there are more buses from Belur to Hassan and they run until much later at night.

There are plenty of buses from Hassan to Halebid (Rs 6, one hour). The first bus departs at 6.30 am, and the last bus back to Hassan leaves Halebid at 5.30 pm. There are also lots of buses from Hassan to Belur (Rs 8, two hours). The first leaves Hassan at 6.30

am and the last bus back leaves Belur at 8.30 pm.

There are four direct buses to Sravanabelagola (Rs 11, 1½ hours), but the first one doesn't leave until noon. To get an early start, catch a bus to Channarayapatna (one hour, Rs 8) and catch one of the many local buses to Sravanabelagola from there.

There are frequent buses to Mysore (Rs 24, three hours) and Bangalore (Rs 36, four hours). The first bus to both cities leaves at 5.15 am and the last at 7.45 pm.

Train The railway station is about two km from the centre of town; Rs 8 by auto-rickshaw. At the time of writing, only one train a day left Hassan and went to Arsikere (Rs 9, one hour) at 5.45 pm. Trains to Mysore and Mangalore had been suspended while the lines were converted to broad gauge. The lines are optimistically scheduled to re-open in late 1997. Note that the Mangalore line is prone to landslides during the monsoon months from June to September.

Coast & Western Ghats

MADIKERI (Mercara)

Pop: 31,200   Tel Area Code: 08272

The elevated market town of Madikeri is the capital of the Kodagu (Coorg) region, a cool green mountainous area in the south-west of Karnataka which is one of the most underrated scenic areas in India. Madikeri itself is not a particularly pretty town, but it's a good base for organising treks and is surrounded by picturesque hills where the roads are lined with hedgerows, flowering trees, spice plantations and coffee estates. The locals are a nuggetty, proud people, distinct from their lowland neighbours, and are generally encountered wrapped in multiple layers of woollen clothing.

If it seems a world apart from the rest of Karnataka, that's because Kodagu was a mini-state in its own right until 1956. Even today, there are still calls for an independent Kodagu homeland.

Orientation & Information

The town is spread out along a series of ridges, but the bus stand and most of the hotels and restaurants are together in a compact area.

There's a small tourist office (☎ 28580) in the PWD Bungalow beside the first roundabout on the Mysore road. It is open from 9.45 am to 5.45 pm daily except Sunday.

Things to See

Madikeri has a modest **fort**, containing the old palace of the Kodava kings, which is now the municipal headquarters. Nearby **St Mark's Church** is the unlikely site of a small museum with a collection of weaponry and Hindu and Jain sculptures. The austere **Omareswara Temple**, one km from the town centre back towards Mysore, is an interesting blend of Keralan and Islamic architectural styles. The view from **Raja's Seat**, the lookout close to Madikeri's KSTDC hotel, is superb and will give you some idea of what to expect when trekking. The scenic **Abbi Falls** are a 30 minute auto-rickshaw ride from the town centre; the trip costs Rs 75 return.

Trekking

The Kodagu region has superb trekking opportunities which few travellers have yet taken advantage of. Facilities are minimal and there are no detailed maps of the area, but there are several people in Madikeri who can arrange guides, food, transport and accommodation. Most treks last only two to three days, but longer treks of up to 10 days are possible. Overnight accommodation is usually in local houses or schools, though on one trek you actually get to bunk down in an old palace.

The trekking season lasts from November to March. A guide is essential since you will easily get lost in the labyrinth of forest tracks without one. Some obscure trekking routes require prior permission from the Forestry Department, which generally takes locals two days to procure. The most popular treks – to the 1700m high peaks of Tadiyendamol and Pushpagiri, and to smaller Kotebetta – do not require permission.

The man to contact in Madikeri is Mr Raja Shekhar, Project Coordinator of the YHA. He can be found at Friends Tours & Travels (☎ 29974) on College Rd, or you can contact him at home in the evenings by phoning ☎ 26272. He arranges one to three day treks with guides costing around Rs 250 per day plus food and transport. Short treks take only a day or two to prepare. Alternatively, Mr B Ganesh Aiyana at the Hotel Cauvery arranges all inclusive treks for around Rs 500 per day, but you need to make arrangements two weeks in advance. The Tadiyendamol trek can also be arranged through Apparanda Prakesh Poovana, Palace Estate, Kakkabe (☎ (08272) 571212).

Places to Stay

Hotel Cauvery (☎ 26292) is next to the cinema, close to the private bus stand. This clean and friendly place has singles/doubles with attached bath for Rs 150/250, and there is hot water in the mornings. The owner arranges treks and visits to local homes.

Hotel Chitra (☎ 27311), on the main street nearby, has very good doubles with attached bath from Rs 250.

Venayaka Lodge, in between the private and public bus stands, has dull rooms with attached bath from Rs 75/215, and views of the town sewer from the balcony.

Hotel Mayura Valley View (☎ 28387) is a KSTDC operation, 20 minutes walk from the town centre. It has rooms with attached bath for Rs 385/440. These fall to Rs 275/330 in the low season between mid-June and mid-September. It has a restaurant and stunning views.

Capital Village Resort (☎ 26929; fax 26335) is an interesting lodge, beautifully located among paddy fields and coffee, cardamom and pepper plantations. It's six km from Madikeri on the Chettali-Sidaphur Rd, off the Mysore Rd. Modern cottages with attached bath cost Rs 500 for a double; full board is available for Rs 140 extra. It's a Rs 35 auto-rickshaw ride from Madikeri.

Places to Eat

Hotel Capitol, next to the Hotel Cauvery, is mainly a bar, but it can rustle up a decent meal or acceptable egg breakfasts, and it serves superb coffee (as you would expect).

Chitra Lodge and *Hotel Mayura Valley View* have standard hotel restaurants.

Getting There & Away

The public bus stand is close to the centre of town. Buses to Mysore (Rs 24/30 ordinary/ semi deluxe, three hours) depart roughly every 30 minutes from 6.30 am until 11 pm. There are buses roughly every hour to Bangalore (Rs 50/65, six hours) and Mangalore (Rs 27/34, four hours). There are six buses to Hassan (Rs 22, 3½ hours), and also buses to Chikmagalur. The private bus stand is predominantly for local buses, though there are a few private deluxe buses to Mysore and Bangalore.

MANGALORE

Pop: 480,000   Tel Area Code: 0824

At one time Mangalore was the major seaport and shipbuilding centre of Hyder Ali's kingdom; today it's a centre for the export of coffee and cashew nuts. It has a languid tropical atmosphere and a strong Roman Catholic influence but no worthwhile attractions. If you're passing this way, it can make a convenient overnight stop – otherwise you won't miss much by avoiding it.

Orientation

Mangalore is hilly and has windy, disorienting streets. Fortunately, all the hotels and restaurants, the city bus stand and the railway station are in or around the hectic city centre. The KSRTC long-distance bus terminal is three km to the north; you'll need to take an auto-rickshaw (about Rs 10).

Information

The tourist office (no phone) is in the Hotel Indraprastha, along with the KSTDC transport office (☎ 421692) which runs tours to Udipi and Dharmastala. It's open daily except Sunday from 10.30 am to 5.30 pm.

The GPO is about 15 minutes walk downhill (south) of the city centre, just past Chetty Circle. The best place to change money is the State Bank of India, next to the Taj Manjarun Hotel. There's a Higginbothams bookshop on Lighthouse Hill Rd.

Things to See

The main remnant of the past is the **Sultan's Battery**, four km from the centre, on the headland of the old port. It really doesn't rate as one of the not-to-be-missed wonders of India. A No 16 bus from the city centre will get you there; an auto-rickshaw costs Rs 20 for the round trip.

Other possibilities include the **Shreemanthi Bai Memorial Government Museum**, just beyond the KSRTC bus terminal (bus No 19); the Keralan-style **Kadri Temple**, whose Lokeshwara statue is reputed to be one of the best bronzes in India (bus Nos 3, 4 & 6); and the painted ceiling of St Aloysius College Chapel, open from 8.30 to 10 am, 12.30 to 1 pm and 3.30 to 6 pm. If you've still got time and energy to spare, try the **Rosario Cathedral**, **Sri Gokarnanatha Temple** or the **Mangladevi Temple** which gave the town its name. For some light relief, it's worth trawling through the **old port area**, a few hundred metres downhill past the Taj Manjarun Hotel. It has plenty of fishing boats, colour and pungency.

Places to Stay – bottom end

Hotel Manorama (☎ 440306), on KS Rao Rd, has large, clean singles/doubles with attached bath from Rs 145/215. Air-con doubles go for Rs 350.

Hotel Indraprastha (☎ 425750), on Lighthouse Hill Rd, charges Rs 70/135 for big, old rooms with attached bath, and Rs 300 for air-con doubles.

Hotel Roopa (☎ 421271), on Balmatta Rd, has OK rooms with attached bath for Rs 100/140 and air-con doubles for Rs 440.

Panchami Boarding & Lodging (☎ 411986), right opposite the KSRTC bus terminal, has singles/doubles/triples with attached bath for Rs 80/120/157.

There are also *retiring rooms* and dormitories at the railway station.

Places to Stay – middle & top end
Hotel Navaratna Palace (☎ 441104) on KS Rao Rd has well-furnished singles/doubles with TV and attached bath for Rs 175/285, and air-con doubles for Rs 525

Shaan Plaza (☎ 440312), also on KS Rao Rd, has rooms for Rs 250/290 or air-con doubles for Rs 480.

Hotel Moti Mahal (☎ 441411; fax 441011), on Falnir Rd, is in a higher class, and boasts a bar, restaurant, coffee shop and swimming pool. Rooms cost Rs 450/500 or Rs 525/625 with air-con.

Taj Manjarun Hotel (☎ 420420; fax 420585), on Old Port Rd, is the best hotel in town. Air-con rooms cost Rs 1550/1675. It has a good restaurant and a swimming pool (which non-guests can use for Rs 93).

Places to Eat
Despite its fishing port and the popularity of Mangalorean-style seafood in places such as Mumbai, you'll be hard-pressed to find a decent piece of seafood in the city.

Roopa Hotel has several eateries, including

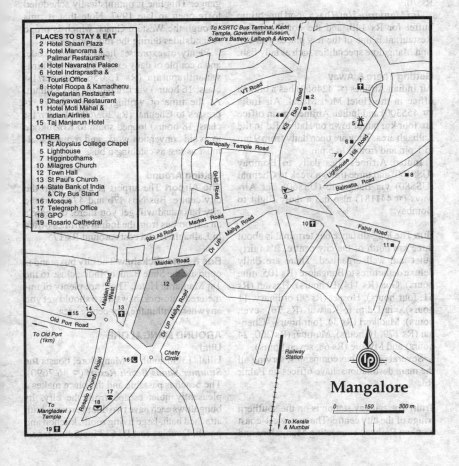

PLACES TO STAY & EAT
2 Hotel Shaan Plaza
3 Hotel Manorama &
   Palimar Restaurant
4 Hotel Navaratna Palace
6 Hotel Indraprastha &
   Tourist Office
8 Hotel Roopa & Kamadhenu
   Vegetarian Restaurant
9 Dhanyavad Restaurant
11 Hotel Moti Mahal &
   Indian Airlines
15 Taj Manjarun Hotel

OTHER
1 St Aloysius College Chapel
5 Lighthouse
7 Higginbothams
10 Milagres Church
12 Town Hall
13 St Paul's Church
14 State Bank of India
   & City Bus Stand
16 Mosque
17 Telegraph Office
18 GPO
19 Rosario Cathedral

To KSRTC Bus Terminal, Kadri
Temple, Government Museum,
Sultan's Battery, Lalbagh & Airport

VT Road
KS Rao Road
Lighthouse Hill Road
Ganapally Temple Road
GHS Road
Balmatta Road
Market Road
Bibi Ali Road
Dr UP Mallya Road
Maidan Road
Maidan Road West
Old Port Road
Rosario Church Road
Falnir Road

To Old Port
(1km)

Chetty
Circle

Railway
Station

To Mangaladevi
Temple

To Kerala
& Mumbai

Mangalore

0   150   300 m

the acceptable Shin Min Chinese Restaurant, the Kamadhenu Veg Restaurant and the Roopa Ice-Cream Parlour.

Dhanyavad, at the intersection of KS Rao and Lighthouse Hill Rds, is a popular veg restaurant serving snacks during the day and cheap 'meals' in the evening.

Palimar, beneath Hotel Manorama, is a decent veg restaurant handy for those staying on KS Rao Rd.

Mangala Restaurant at the Hotel Moti Mahal is a pseudo-plush affair kitted out in the best decor the 1970s had to offer. Indian, Chinese and Continental mains cost around Rs 70.

Taj Manjarun Hotel has a good lunchtime buffet for Rs 140, and the hotel's Galley Restaurant is one of the few places you can find Mangalore specialities such as lady fish.

Getting There & Away

Air Indian Airlines (☎ 424669) has a branch office in the Hotel Moti Mahal. Air India (☎ 455300) and Indian Airlines' main office are four km out of town on Hathill Rd in the Lalbagh area. They are open daily from 9 am to 1 pm and from 2 to 5 pm.

Indian Airlines flies daily to Bombay (US$100) and three times a week to Chennai (US$80) via Bangalore (US$60). Jet Airways (☎ 441181) also has a daily flight to Bombay.

Bus The long-distance bus terminal is about three km north of the city centre. It's fairly quiet and well organised. There are daily deluxe departures to Bangalore (Rs 105, nine hours), Goa (Rs 114, 10 hours), Hassan (Rs 51, four hours), Hospet (Rs 90 ordinary, 11 hours), via Udipi to Karwar (Rs 76, seven hours), Madikeri (Rs 34, four hours), Chennai (Rs 179, 16 hours), Mumbai (Rs 260, 24 hours) and Mysore (Rs 68, seven hours).

Several private bus companies, serving all the main destinations, have offices on Falnir Rd.

Train The railway station is on the southern fringe of the city centre. The new west-coast Konkan Railway connecting Mangalore and

Mumbai is expected to open 'some time in 1997'. At the time of writing, services were running north from Mangalore only as far as Udipi, but will eventually provide access to the entire coastal region of Karnataka and southern Maharashtra (see the boxed section in the Getting Around chapter). When this line is fully operational, Goa should be accessible in around eight hours and Mumbai in 14 hours.

At the time of writing, all rail services heading east (ie to Hassan, Mysore and Bangalore) had been suspended while the Mangalore-Hassan line was converted to broad gauge. This line is optimistically scheduled to re-open in late 1997. Note that it runs through the Western Ghats, which is prone to landslides during the monsoon season.

Plenty of expresses head to Kozhikode, and a couple of daily expresses run to Thiruvananthapuram (Rs 163/563 sleeper/1st class, 16 hours) via Ernakulam and Kollam. At the time of writing, several daily expresses to Chennai (Rs 203/697 sleeper/1st class, 18 hours) looped south to Kozhikode to avoid conversion work, and remained almost as fast as catching a bus.

Getting Around

The Airport The airport is 20km from the city centre. Bus Nos 47b and 47c from the city bus stand will get you there, or there's an airport bus from the Indian Airlines office in Lalbagh. A taxi costs around Rs 175.

Bus & Auto-Rickshaw The city bus stand is opposite the State Bank of India, close to the Taj Manjuran Hotel. There are plenty of unmetered auto-rickshaws; Rs 5 should get you anywhere within the city centre area.

AROUND MANGALORE
Ullal

Ullal, 13km south of Mangalore, boasts the *Summer Sands Beach Resort* (☎ 46 7690). The beach is passable and the place makes a pleasantly quiet escape from the city. Its bungalows each have two double rooms with attached bath, large living room, kitchen and porch. Doubles cost Rs 613 including taxes, or Rs 1040 with air-con. There's an OK restaurant and a swimming pool. Bus Nos 44a, 44c and 44d run from the city bus stand to Ullal.

Dharmastala

There are a number of Jain bastis (temples) in Dharmastala, 75km east of Mangalore, including the famous **Manjunatha Temple**. You'll also find a 14m high statue of Bahubali, which was erected in 1973. KSTDC tours from Mangalore visit here.

Venur

This town, approximately 50km north-east of Mangalore, has eight bastis and the ruins of a Mahadeva temple. An 11m high **Bahubali statue**, dating back to 1604, stands on the southern bank of the Gurupur River.

Mudabidri

There are 18 bastis in Mudabidri, 35km northeast of Mangalore. The oldest of them is the 15th century **Chandranatha Temple**, known colloquially as the 1000-pillar hall.

Karkal

A further 20km north of Mudabidri, at Karkal, are several important temples and a 13m high **Bahubali statue**, which was completed in 1432. The statue is on a small, serene hillock on the outskirts of the town. There are good views of the Western Ghats from here.

SRINGERI

Tel Area Code: 08265

The southern seat of the orthodox Hindu hierarchy is in Sringeri, a small, unspoilt town nestled among the lush coffee-growing hills of Chikmagalur, approximately 100km north-east of Mangalore. The other three centres founded by Shankaracharya are Joshimath in the Himalaya (north), Puri (east) and Dwarka (west). The interesting **Vidyashankar Temple** has zodiac pillars and a huge paved courtyard. A second temple is dedicated to Sharada, the goddess of learning. The Tunga River flows past the temple complex and

hundreds of fish gather at the ghats to be hand-fed by pilgrims. The temple complex is open from 6.30 am to 1 pm and from 5 to 8 pm.

Places to Stay & Eat

There's a range of pilgrim accommodation available; report to the reception centre (☎ 62123) next to the temple entrance to be allocated a room. The spartan rooms have attached bath and generally cost Rs 25 per person; the slightly more luxurious *Sharada* costs Rs 60.

There's are numerous nondescript veg 'meals' restaurants along the main street.

Getting There & Away

The bus stand is 200m to the right of the temple entrance. There are plenty of buses from Sringeri to virtually all points in Karnataka, including nine buses to Mangalore (5½ hours); an early morning and late evening bus to Mysore (eight hours) via Hassan (4½ hours); and several early morning and late evening buses to Bangalore (10 hours). The picturesque road to Mangalore follows the Tunga River for 10km and passes through the Kudemukh National Park.

UDIPI

Tel Area Code: 08252

The important Vaishnavaite town of Udipi (Udupi) is 58km north of Mangalore on the coastal road. It was here that the 13th century religious leader, Madhvacharya, lived and preached, and the town's **Krishna Temple** continues to draw many pilgrims. Udipi has another claim to fame since, according to local legend, the ubiquitous *masala dosa* was first created here.

There's an ordinary beach at nearby **Malpe**, which is a favourite weekend picnic spot. Boats run from Malpe's fishing port to uninhabited **St Mary's Island**, which was Vasco da Gama's first landfall on the Indian subcontinent. The island has a beach and an impressive geological formation of basalt rock pillars which form a staircase into the sea.

A boat theoretically shuttles between Malpe and St Mary's four times a day. It costs Rs 20 if you're prepared to wait for it to fill up with 30 Indian tourists; alternatively you can hire the boat for Rs 450 and have the island to yourself. You can stay overnight on the island if you take food and water, sleep rough and arrange to be picked up the following day. The trip takes one hour.

There are a handful of hotels near Udipi's bus stand. Frequent government and private buses head to Mangalore, Mysore, Bangalore and Panaji. Udipi is on the Konkan Railway, which links Mangalore with Mumbai.

MARAVANTHE

There's a decent beach at Maravanthe, approximately 10km north of Kundapura (Coondapoor), where a sand spit has formed at the Sauparnika River delta. There's another beach, known as Gudajji, close by. There are buses to Kundapura from Udipi and Mangalore; you'll need to get a taxi or a local bus to Maravanthe from there.

Turtle Bay Beach Resort (☎ (08252) 61313) is a half-baked tourist facility consisting of six tents with frame beds and a small restaurant. It's a bit of a joke, but it's right on the edge of the beach, so if you need some time out and don't mind primitive facilities, it could be OK. Tents cost Rs 200 and need to be booked a week in advance.

Hotel Sharon (☎ (08254) 20623), on the outskirts of Kundapura, has good singles/doubles from Rs 85/150, several restaurants and a bar. It's on the corner of NH17 and the Kundapura by-pass.

JOG FALLS

The Shiravati River drops 253m at Jog Falls in four separate waterfalls known as the Rani, the Rocket, the Raja and the Roarer. The falls are the highest in India and are located approximately 50km from the coast, midway between Udipi and Karwar.

The best time to see them is just after the monsoon (basically December and January), but even then they can be less than spectacular due to the controlled water flow from

the Linganamakki Dam upriver. In the wet season they're generally obscured by mist and fog, and during the dry season they almost dry up.

The view of the falls from the bus stand is impressive, but it's better from the PWD Inspection Bungalow on the opposite side of the river. You can hike to the bottom of the falls by following the steps that start close to the bus stand, but watch out for leeches during the wet season.

Because the falls are so arduous to get to, it's not worth a special journey unless you intend to hang around for a day or two to soak up the relaxing atmosphere and take some long walks. The only problem with doing this is the current shortage of accommodation – try to plan in advance.

Places to Stay & Eat

There are numerous government-run tourist homes, inspection bungalows and Forestry Department bungalows at Jog Falls but they were all dilapidated or undergoing renovation as this book went to press. The only remaining options are the unappealing dormitories at the *Youth Hostel*, one km from the falls, and the *PWD Inspection Bungalow*, which has to be booked in advance at the District Commissioners Office in Sidapur, 20km north-east of Jog Falls.

Food options are limited to the pleasant but rudimentary *chai shacks* at the bus stand. They can rustle up omelettes, noodles and snacks.

Getting There & Away

Bus Although the falls are close to the coast, they are easier to reach from inland. The best approach is via Shimoga and Sagar, which have several buses to the falls each day. The two roads between the falls and the coast are dramatic, tortuous and take several hours to negotiate: the road to Manki is more spectacular than the easier road to Bhaktal. The forests, splendid vistas and endless hairpin bends on the Manki road are best appreciated from the back seat of an Ambassador with good brakes and a careful driver, but several buses do run down to the coast. One leaves for Karwar at 1.30 pm and departs from Karwar for the return trip at 7.30 pm; another heads to Bhaktal at 4.30 pm.

Train The nearest railway station, Talguppa, is about 20km south-east of the falls, at the end of the line from Birur.

GOKARNA
Tel Area Code: 08386
The unspoilt town of Gokarna, 50km south of Karwar, attracts an unlikely mixture of Hindu pilgrims, Sanskrit scholars, beach-loving travellers and a hardcore hippy element who shifted here when things got way uncool in Goa. It's a sleepy, charming town with a single ramshackle street composed entirely of Keralan-style wooden houses. It leads to the sacred **Mahabaleshwara Temple**, home to a revered Siva lingam, and onward to the town beach. Near the temple is an enormous chariot, which is dragged along the main street amid much brouhaha on Siva's birthday in February. There's a picturesque **bathing tank** a few hundred metres south of the temple, where locals, pilgrims, and immaculately turned out Brahmins perform their ablutions next to dhobi-wallahs on the ghats.

Travellers have begun drifting into Gokarna lured by the stories of its deserted beaches, which rival anything Goa has to offer. The closest decent beach is Kudle Beach (pronounced 'kood-lee'), a 20 minute walk to the south. To reach it, follow the footpath which begins on the southern side of the Mahabaleshwara Temple and heads southwards (if you reach the bathing ghat, you've taken the wrong path).

The track soon climbs to the top of a barren headland with expansive sea views. On the southern side of the headland is the first in a series of four perfect half-moon beaches, hemmed in by headlands and backed by the foothills of the Western Ghats.

The other beaches – Om Beach, Half-Moon Beach and Paradise Beach – are a series of 30 minute walks to the south, each one becoming more and more isolated. On Kudle Beach, there's are a couple of places to rent adobe huts, a few chai stalls and a freshwater spring. There's another chai shop and a spring on Om Beach, but nothing beyond this. If you're heading for Paradise (so to speak) make sure you take adequate food and water.

Staying in Gokarna is very cheap since there are few distractions to spend money on. If you do need to change money you'll have to head for Karwar, which can take up a significant part of a day, so come prepared.

Places to Stay
The choice in Gokarna is between the rudimentary huts right on the beach or the basic but more comfortable options in town. The advantages of being on the beach are obvious and, since it's a decent hike from town, you're pretty much left to your own devices – which is highly appreciated by those travellers who like the odd spliff for breakfast.

Huts on the northern headland of Kudle Beach cost Rs 25. They're just a space to stash your gear and sleep on the floor at night, so bring a sleeping bag or a bedroll unless you want bruised hips. Padlocks are provided and the huts are secure. Communal washing and toilet facilities are primitive but there is fresh water. There's another group of huts for rent behind the centre of the beach. They cost Rs 30 and are equally primitive.

If you want to sleep on the beach, it's best to leave your belongings at Vaibhav Niwas in town for a small fee. It's not a good idea to sleep alone on the more isolated beaches.

Vaibhav Niwas (☎ 46714) is a cosy relaxed guest house set back from the town's main street. Tiny but acceptable singles/doubles with common bath cost Rs 30/50 and rooms with attached bath cost between Rs 75 and Rs 100.

New Prasad Nilaya (46250), a starkly modern hotel, whose design does not bode well for Gokarna's architectural integrity, probably has the town's best appointed rooms – though this is not saying much. They're plain, clean enough and cost Rs 100 with attached bath. The hotel is on a small side road off the main street about 500m from the temple. The manager, Chintu, is about as gregarious and welcoming as hotel operators get.

Om Lodge (☎ 46445), nearby, has basic, shabby rooms with attached bath for Rs 135 and air-con doubles for Rs 250, but the place is not well run and its bar is sleazy.

Tourist Home (46236) is a neglected KSTDC hotel on a hilltop overlooking the sea, inconveniently located some two km from town. It has three faded old rooms that look like they've been empty for years, but they're acceptably clean and spacious. Doubles with attached bath cost Rs 50 and a four-bedded room costs Rs 100.

Places to Eat

The *chai shop* which rents huts on the headland of Kudle Beach can rustle up basic snacks and meals.

Phi Restaurant, halfway along the town's main street, has cheap vegetarian light meals, good masala dosas and the coldest fridge in Karnataka.

Hotel Vinaya, also on the main street but closer to the temple, is a basic vegetarian eatery that's popular with travellers.

Shri Raghavendra Restaurant, where the side road leading to Om Lodge joins the main street, has tasty veg fare.

Om Lodge and a liquor den just east of Vaibhav Niwas are the only places in town selling alcohol since Gokarna is a sacred town.

Getting There & Away

The new Konkan Railway passes close to Gokarna. The most convenient stations for good bus connections to Gokarna are likely to be Karwar or Ankola.

Direct buses head to Karwar at 6.45 and 8 am and at 4.15 pm. Otherwise you'll have to jump on one of the more frequent private buses to Ankola and change to a local Karwar-bound bus from there. There's a direct bus to Goa at 8 am (4½ hours), otherwise head for Karwar to pick up more Goa-bound buses. There are four buses to Hubli in the morning and one just after lunch. There's a direct 6.45 am bus to Mangalore. If you miss this, catch a local bus to Kumta (25km south)

and catch one of the more frequent Mangalore buses from there.

KARWAR

Tel Area Code: 08382

Karwar is a dull, sleepy port town near the mouth of the Kali Nadi River, only a short distance south of Goa. While the town holds little of interest, the area immediately south is very picturesque since the foothills of the Western Ghats come right to the coast, forming headlands that are separated by sweeping sandy bays. Their peacefulness and beauty will change radically if a mooted new naval base in the area ever gets beyond the planning stage.

You can make boat trips up the spectacular Kali Nadi from the bridge three km north of town. A stroll to the bridge to witness the sunset and the spectacular shades of light on the surrounding Ghats is about as exciting as the local entertainment opportunities get. The bridge is a Rs 20 private auto-rickshaw ride or Rs 3 share from the town centre.

Karwar's Indian Bank is the closest bank to Gokarna that handles foreign exchange transactions. It's open weekdays from 10 am to 2 pm and on Saturday from 10 am to noon.

Places to Stay & Eat

Hotel Ashok (☎ 26418), close to the bus stand, is a reasonable place offering singles/doubles with attached bath for Rs 50/90

Anand Lodge (☎ 26156), a two minute walk from the bus stand, has acceptable doubles (only) with attached bath and balconies for Rs 90.

Hotel Bhadra (☎ 25212), near the Kali Nadi bridge, has modern doubles with attached bath for Rs 150, and air-con doubles for Rs 300. It has a veg/non-veg restaurant and a bar.

Udipi Hotel and its sister restaurant *Hotel Savita*, both on Main Rd, are clean, veg snack and 'meals' specialists.

Getting There & Away

Karwar is on the new Konkan Railway connecting Mumbai with Goa and Mangalore (see the Konkan Railway boxed section in the Getting Around chapter).

The Karwar bus stand is on the southern edge of the town centre. There are numerous buses to Panaji (four hours), Hubli (3½ hours) and Mangalore, and at least one daily departure to Sringeri, Jog Falls and Belur. Private buses shuttle between Karwar, Ankola and Gokarna. They depart from just outside the bus stand entrance. There's a direct KSRTC bus to Gokarna at 2 pm and local buses at 5 and 8 pm.

AROUND KARWAR

The nearest beaches to Karwar are **Binaga** and **Arga**, three and five km south of the town respectively. They're both scimitar-shaped swathes of sand and are generally deserted.

Krishna Rest House (☎ 27613), set back from the beach at Binaga, is a great place to stay if you want some peace and quiet. It's a basic family-run guest house with a few rooms with common bath for Rs 75/100, a double with attached bath for Rs 125 and a small cottage for Rs 125. You can either self cater or arrange food in advance with the owner. It's Rs 25 by auto-rickshaw or Rs 2 by bus from Karwar.

At the small town of **Ankola**, 37km south of Karwar, are the 15th century ruined walls of King Sarpamalika's fort and the equally old Sri Venkatraman Temple. In an unmarked mud-brick garage near the temple are two giant wooden chariots large enough to be pulled by elephants. They are carved with scenes from the *Ramayana*. There's a long deserted beach at **Belekeri**, four km north of Ankola.

Central Karnataka

HAMPI

Pop: 930   Tel Area Code: 08394
The ruins of **Vijayanagar** (see the regional highlight on p916), near the village of Hampi, are one of the most fascinating historical sites in south India. The superb ruins are set in a strange and beautiful boulder-strewn landscape which has an almost magical quality.

Hampi has become a thriving travellers' centre and most people stay at least a couple of days to soak up the atmosphere and explore the area. If you're in a hurry, you can see the main sites in one day, either by bicycle or on foot. Signposting in some parts of the site is inadequate, but you can't really get lost. It's not wise to wander around the ruins alone at dawn or dusk, since occasional muggings occur.

Orientation

There are two main points of entry to the ruins: Hampi Bazaar and the small village of Kamalapuram to the south. Most people prefer to start in Hampi Bazaar and walk or cycle to the main sites and then visit the museum at Kamalapuram. From Kamalapuram there are buses back to Hampi Bazaar (and to Hospet), or you can walk back along the road to Hampi Bazaar in about 40 minutes. There are restaurants in Hampi Bazaar and Kamalapuram, as well as a few soft-drink and snack vendors at key monuments.

Information

The tourist office (☎ 51339) is on the main street of Hampi Bazaar and is open from 10 am to 5.30 pm daily. It sells maps of the site for Rs 5 and can arrange guides for Rs 350 per day or Rs 250 for half a day. There are plenty of good books on Hampi available from Aspiration Stores, near the entrance to the Virupaksha Temple at Hampi Bazaar.

The museum at Kamalapuram is open between 10 am and 5 pm daily except Friday. It has some fine sculptures and is worth a visit.

The best place to change money is the Canara Bank in Hampi Bazaar, open between 11 am and 2 pm on weekdays from 11 am to 12.30 pm on Saturday. There are numerous authorised moneychangers offering lower rates on the main street.

Hampi Bazaar

Hampi Bazaar is a bustling village once again,

now the locals (and their animals) have re-occupied the ancient buildings lining the main street. The village has become something of a travellers' mecca, and it's a great place to stay if you're not too concerned about minor luxuries. Most of the action is at the western end of the bazaar, where the street is lined with makeshift restaurants and trinket stalls. This part of the village is dominated by the 52m high gopuram of the **Virupaksha Temple**, which dates back to the middle of the 15th century. A sign in the temple courtyard reads: 'Please keep off the Plantains from the sight of the Monkies', which translates to

something like, 'Watch out or the monkeys will pinch your bananas'.

Places to Stay

Hampi Bazaar This is the best place to soak up Hampi's special atmosphere if you don't mind basic but adequate accommodation.

Shanthi Guest House (☎ 51568) is one of the best places to stay and is a popular travellers' haunt. It charges Rs 60/80 for bare rooms, with fans and common bath, set around a garden courtyard. To get here, walk up to the entrance of the Virupaksha Temple, turn right and follow the signposts.

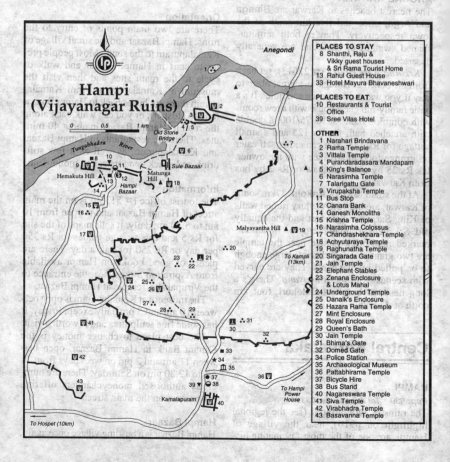

Hampi (Vijayanagar Ruins)

Anegondi

Tungabhadra River

Old Stone Bridge

Hemakuta Hill

Matunga Hill

Hampi Bazaar

Sule Bazaar

Malyavantha Hill

To Kampli (13km)

To Hampi Power House

Kamalapuram

To Hospet (10km)

PLACES TO STAY
8 Shanthi, Raju & Vikky guest houses & Sri Rama Tourist Home
13 Rahul Guest House
33 Hotel Mayura Bhavaneshwari

PLACES TO EAT
10 Restaurants & Tourist Office
39 Sree Vilas Hotel

OTHER
1 Narahari Brindavana
2 Rama Temple
3 Vittala Temple
4 Purandaradasara Mandapam
5 King's Balance
6 Narasimha Temple
7 Talarigattu Gate
9 Virupaksha Temple
11 Bus Stop
12 Canara Bank
13 Ganesh Monoliths
15 Krishna Temple
16 Narasimha Colossus
17 Chandrashekhara Temple
18 Achyutaraya Temple
19 Raghunatha Temple
20 Singarada Gate
21 Jain Temple
22 Elephant Stables
23 Zenana Enclosure & Lotus Mahal
24 Underground Temple
25 Danaik's Enclosure
26 Hazara Rama Temple
27 Mint Enclosure
28 Royal Enclosure
29 Queen's Bath
30 Jain Temple
31 Bhima's Gate
32 Domed Gate
34 Police Station
35 Archaeological Museum
36 Pattabhirama Temple
37 Bicycle Hire
38 Bus Stand
40 Nagareswara Temple
41 Siva Temple
42 Virabhadra Temple
43 Basavanna Temple

Raju Guesthouse, next door, has clean simple rooms with common bath for Rs 30/50. It has a rooftop eating area where you can relax when your room gets claustrophobic.

Vikky Guest House, nearby, has fan-cooled doubles with common bath for Rs 80. It's of a similar standard to Shanti but with less atmosphere.

Rahul Guest House is a friendly place with congenial common areas. Clean spartan rooms with mattresses on the floor cost Rs 50/60. There are common toilet and bathing facilities and some rooms have fans. The guest house is just south of the bus stand. It's the shockingly blue building in the street running parallel to the bazaar.

Sri Rama Tourist Home (☎ 51219), to the right of the temple, is popular with visiting Indians. It has the village's best appointed rooms, though they're nothing special and the place lacks any atmosphere or charm. Doubles with attached bath cost Rs 80.

If the hotels listed above are full, there are several other rudimentary guest houses where you can sleep on a mattress on the floor and have access to toilet and bathing facilities for around Rs 30.

Kamalapuram The *Hotel Mayura Bhuvaneshwari* (☎ (08394) 51574), on the northern outskirts of Kamalapuram, is a modern, well-maintained KSTDC operation. Decent singles/doubles with attached bath and mosquito nets cost Rs 200/240 or Rs 330/385 with air-con. The hotel has a veg/non-veg restaurant and a basic bar. It's a good choice for those who want to be close to the ruins but consider a comfortable bed more important than ambience.

Places to Eat
Hampi Bazaar There are plenty of simple restaurants and soft-drink stalls on the main street of Hampi Bazaar. Most of these places are half-baked, ill-equipped affairs consisting of a portable gas cooker and five or six tables, but they're congenial spots from which to observe the street life. There's very little to distinguish between them, since they all serve standard Indian fare and western stand-

bys and can all produce extensive menus from which only limited offerings are actually available.

Sri Venkateswara, on the right as you near the Virupaksha Temple, is the most established restaurant. It serves tiffin and western snacks at lunch and thalis (Rs 15) in the evening.

Geeta is the most popular alternative.

Kamalapuram This sleepy village has a few humble eateries, the most notable of which is the *Sree Vilas Hotel* opposite the bus stand. It's a rustic place serving vadai and idli for breakfast, puris for lunch and dosas in the evening. It closes at 7.30 pm. The restaurant at the *Hotel Mayura Bhuvaneshwari* serves standard KSTDC fare.

Getting There & Around
Buses run roughly hourly along the 13km stretch between Hampi Bazaar and Hospet. The first bus from Hospet is at 6.30 am, and the last one back leaves Hampi at 8.30 pm. There are also regular buses between Hospet and Kamalapuram. The first bus from Hospet leaves at 6.30 am; the last one back leaves Kamalapuram at 10 pm.

Only a few buses link Hampi Bazaar and Kamalapuram, but you can negotiate this short stretch easily in an auto-rickshaw for Rs 5 share or Rs 25 private.

You can also catch auto-rickshaws to Hampi from Hospet for Rs 50, though the return journey will cost you 50% more. A taxi for this trip costs around Rs 100 to Hampi; the price for the return leg depends largely on how desperate you look to return.

It makes a lot of sense to hire a bicycle to explore the ruins once you've seen the Vittala and Achyutaraya temples and Sule Bazaar. The entire Royal Enclosure area is navigable by bicycle since a dirt road runs through it. Once you've got up the steep hill from the bazaar, the road between Hampi Bazaar and Kamalapuram can also be used to get to the ruins; key monuments are haphazardly signposted along its length. Bicycles cost around Rs 5 per hour in Hampi Bazaar and Rs 3 per hour in Kamalapuram.

Walking is the only way to explore all the nooks and crannies of the site, but expect to cover at least seven km just to see the major ruins. If you're not fit to walk or cycle, auto-rickshaws and taxis are available for sightseeing, and will drop you as close to each of the major ruins as they can possibly get. A five hour tour costs Rs 250 by auto-rickshaw and Rs 350 by taxi.

Organised tours depart from Hospet; see that section for details.

HOSPET

Pop: 151,900   Tel Area Code: 08394

Many people who come to see the Vijayanagar ruins at Hampi use Hospet as a base. It's a fairly typical Karnataka country town whose dusty roads are clogged with bullock carts, bicycles, scooters and dilapidated buses.

Muharram Festival

For much of the year Hospet is not a particularly interesting place, but it comes alive during the festival of Muharram, which commemorates the martyrdom of Mohammed's grandson, Imam Hussain. If you're here at this time (the date varies from year to year) don't miss the fire-walkers, who walk barefoot across the red-hot embers of a fire that's been going all day and night. Virtually the whole town turns out to watch or take part and the excitement reaches fever pitch around midnight. The preliminaries, which go on all day, appear to be a bewildering hybrid of Muslim and Hindu ritual. Those who are scheduled to do the firewalking, for example, must be physically restrained from going completely berserk just before the event. ■

Information

The tourist office is open daily between 7.30 am and 7.30 pm. It has free maps and information on Hampi and sights in Northern Karnataka. Malligi Tourist Home changes travellers cheques at competitive rates.

Organised Tours

The daily KSTDC tour to the three main sites at Hampi (Hampi Bazaar, Vittala Temple and the Royal Enclosure) and to Tungabhadra

Dam departs at 9.30 am and returns at 5.30 pm; it costs Rs 60. Bookings can be made at the Hospet tourist office, Malligi Tourist Home or the Hotel Priyardarshini. If possible, book a day in advance as this tour is often full. Lunch (not included in the price) is at the KSTDC's hotel in Kamalapuram.

Places to Stay

Malligi Tourist Home (☎ 58101), 6/143 Jambunatha Rd, is an old favourite among travellers. Average doubles with attached bath and hot water start from Rs 124, rise to Rs 170 with TV, Rs 225 with air-cooling and Rs 650 with air-con in the hotel's stylish new wing. The management have an irritating but understandable tendency to try to put guests in the more expensive rooms. The hotel's foreign exchange facility, garden and restaurant are major plus points. There's also a bookshop, which has English and French books on Hampi.

Hotel Vishwa (☎ 57171), opposite the bus stand, has large, clean rooms with attached bath which are very good value at Rs 75/140, and four-bed rooms for Rs 264 including tax. The hotel is set back from the street so the rooms are quiet. There's hot water in the morning and some rooms have small balconies.

Hotel Priyardarshini (☎ 58838), on Station Rd, has rooms with attached bath for Rs 90/145, deluxe doubles for Rs 270 and air-con doubles for Rs 425. All rooms have balconies and hot water in the morning. The standard rooms are the best in town. There's a veg/non-veg garden restaurant and bar.

Hotel Sandarshan (☎ 58574), on Station Rd, has acceptable rooms with common bath for Rs 50/80 and with dank attached bath from Rs 70/100.

Hotel Shalini Lodging (☎ 58910), on Station Rd, is the town's budget option. It has basic singles/doubles/triples with bath for Rs 50/75/100. You get what you pay for.

Hotel Mayura Vijayanagar (☎ 59270) is a KSTDC operation a few km outside Hospet at Tungabhadra Dam. It has rooms with attached bath for Rs 125/160. Buses between Hospet and the dam leave every 15 minutes. It's easier to pick up a bus to Hospet from the junction at the bottom of the dam road rather than at the dam itself.

Places to Eat

Madhu Paradise, at the Malligi Tourist Home, serves reasonably priced south and north Indian veg fare and western breakfasts. Its main plus point is the attractive outdoor eating area.

Eagle Garden Bar & Restaurant, behind the Malligi, has Indian and Chinese fare and 'American' breakfasts. It's a popular spot with a thatched barn-like restaurant and tables outdoors. The food is acceptable and costs around Rs 40; Kingfishers are Rs 45.

Manasa Bar & Restaurant in the Hotel Priyardarshini serves non-veg Andhra-style dishes in a garden setting during lunchtime, and between 6 and 11 pm. The hotel also has an indoor veg restaurant open all day.

Shanthi Restaurant in the Hotel Vishwa does excellent vegetarian thalis at lunchtime for Rs 15, and snacks the rest of the day.

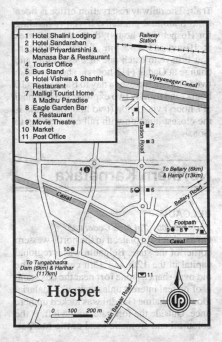

1 Hotel Shalini Lodging
2 Hotel Sandarshan
3 Hotel Priyardarshini & Manasa Bar & Restaurant
4 Tourist Office
5 Bus Stand
6 Hotel Vishwa & Shanthi Restaurant
7 Malligi Tourist Home & Madhu Paradise
8 Eagle Garden Bar & Restaurant
9 Movie Theatre
10 Market
11 Post Office

Hospet

0   100   200 m

Getting There & Away

Bus The busy bus stand in Hospet is fairly well organised, with bays marked in both English and Kannada, though buses in this part of the state are generally crowded and you'll need to fight to get on. A large backpack can make this an uncomfortable experience.

Buses to Hampi depart from Bay No 10. See the Hampi Getting There & Around section for details.

More than 10 express buses run daily to Bangalore (Rs 67/101 ordinary/deluxe, nine hours). They are nearly all morning or night departures: no Bangalore buses depart between 1 pm and 9.30 pm. There are just as many services to Hubli (Rs 31, four hours,).

There are supposedly five buses a day to Badami, but most of these pull into Hospet en route from Bangalore, so they are prone to delays and no-shows. It's much easier to get to Badami by catching one of the many buses to Gadag or Ilkal and transferring to another bus there. The journey takes five hours via Gadag and close to six hours via Ilkal.

There are four buses to Bijapur (Rs 40, six hours); five buses to Hyderabad (Rs 92, nine hours); and also daily departures to Hassan, Mangalore and Shimoga. One bus heads to Gokarna (Rs 61, eight hours) each morning at 9 am.

Train Hospet railway station is a 20 minute walk or Rs 8 auto-rickshaw ride from the centre of town. There is one direct train daily to Bangalore at 8.30 pm (Rs 135/464 in sleeper/1st class, 10½ hours). There are two expresses to Guntakal (three hours), where you can pick up many other expresses to Bangalore, and two expresses to Hubli (four hours). To get to Badami and Bijapur, you'll need to catch a Hubli train, get off at Gadag, and pick up a connection from there.

HUBLI
Pop: 728,000   Tel Area Code: 0836
Hubli is important to the traveller principally as a major railway junction on the routes from Bombay to Bangalore, Goa and northern Karnataka. At the time of writing,

services to Goa were disrupted while the line is converted from metre to broad gauge.

All the main services (hotels, restaurants, etc) are conveniently close to the railway station. The bus stand is on Lamington Rd, a 15 minute walk from the railway station.

Places to Stay
Ashok Hotel (☎ 362271) has clean, good-value singles/doubles with attached bath for Rs 130/160. Air-con doubles cost Rs 330. It's on Lamington Rd, which is parallel to the railway line, about 500m from the station.

Hotel Vipra (☎ 362336), in the same building, has equally good singles/doubles/triples with attached bath for Rs 90/140/225.

Hotel Kailash (☎ 52234), opposite the Ashok, is more upmarket. Comfortable rooms with attached bath, hot water and TV cost Rs 253/330 including tax. Air-con rooms go for Rs 385/506. There's a veg restaurant on the ground floor.

Hotel Ajanta (☎ 362216) is a short distance off the main street and visible from the railway station. It's a huge place so you'll always be able to find accommodation here. Average rooms cost Rs 50/80 with common bathroom or Rs 80/120 with attached bath. Checkout is 24 hours. There's a 'meals' restaurant on the ground floor.

Retiring rooms at the railway station cost Rs 35/60, or Rs 15 for a dorm bed.

Places to Eat
Parag Bar & Restaurant, next to the Modern Lodge, has a British pub-style restaurant and an open-air rooftop section. It serves passable veg and non-veg Indian and Chinese dishes for around Rs 40.

Royal Palace, on a sidestreet near the Ashok Hotel, is the best restaurant in this part of the city. North Indian mains cost around Rs 50.

There's a cluster of eateries at the foot of the railway station slip road offering cheap thalis, biryanis and vegetarian snacks.

Getting There & Away
Air Hubli's airport was closed for 'repairs' at the time of writing. It is expected to re-open

in late 1997 and flights to Bangalore, Chennai and Mumbai should be available. The airport is six km from the bus stand. Vipra Tours & Travels (☎ 68206) in the Vipra Hotel is an agent for several domestic airlines.

Bus Hubli has a large and busy bus stand. The KSRTC has lots of buses to Bangalore (Rs 89, nine hours) and Hospet (Rs 35, four hours). There are also four buses daily to Mumbai (Rs 120, 15 hours); three to Mysore (Rs 100, 10 hours); two to Mangalore (Rs 75, 10 hours); and at least one daily departure to Bijapur, Gokarna and Jog Falls.

There are four KSRTC buses to Panaji (Rs 42, five hours), and six slightly cheaper blue Goa government Kadamba buses, which leave from gate No 10.

Opposite the bus stand are plenty of private companies operating deluxe buses to Bangalore, Bijapur, Goa, Mangalore, Mumbai and Pune.

Train The railway reservation office is open from 8 am to 8 pm daily. If you're heading for Hospet (four hours), there are expresses at 10 am and 4.45 pm. To reach Bijapur, you'll have to catch one of these trains and change at Gadag (1½ hours). There are also two to three expresses a day to Bangalore (10 hours) and usually two expresses to Mumbai (17 hours) via Londa (two hours). Londa is the closest junction with rail connections to Goa.

Northern Karnataka

BELGAUM
Pop: 453,000   Tel Area Code: 0831
On a rather bald plateau in the north-western corner of the state, Belgaum was a regional capital in the 12th and 13th centuries. The old oval-shaped stone **fort** near the bus stand is of no real interest unless you like malarial moats. Mahatma Gandhi was locked up here once. Outside the fort gate, to the left, is the colourful and aromatic local **cattle market**.

DAVID COLLINS

DAVID COLLINS

MARK DAFFEY

PAUL BEINSSEN

Karnataka

Top: Detail of a temple at Somnathpur.
Centre Left: Gomateshvara statue,
  Sravanabelagola.

Centre Right: Tribal women in traditional
  costume.
Bottom: One of Hampi's ruined temples.

SARA-JANE CLELAND

GREG ELMS

MARK DAFFEY

Karnataka

Top Left : Domes of the Maharaja's Palace, Mysore.
Top Right: Woman washing dishes beneath the Virupaksha Temple, Hampi.
Bottom: Ruins of the Vijayanagar Kingdom, Hampi.

The **Masjid-Sata** mosque dates from 1519. There are also two interesting **Jain temples**, one with an extremely intricate roof, while the other has some fine carvings of musicians. Belgaum's **watchtower**, on Ganapath Galli in the town centre, provides a panorama of the flat countryside and distant hills. **Sunset Point**, on the old racetrack road, also offers fine views.

Places to Stay & Eat

Hotel Sheetal (☎ 429222) is about three minutes walk from the bus stand in Khade Bazaar, a pedestrian-only street that starts opposite the bus stand entrance. Clean, bright singles/doubles with attached bath cost Rs 80/160. It also has a veg restaurant.

Hotel Mayura Mallaprabha (☎ 433781), on the NH4 bypass, just behind the lake, is a modern KSTDC operation. Cottages with attached bath cost Rs 160/190.

Hotel Keerthi (☎ 423332), a tall, white establishment 500m to the right as you leave the bus stand, offers clean, comfortable rooms with attached bath from Rs 110/250. It has a veg/non-veg restaurant and a bar.

Getting There & Away

Indian Airlines (☎ 420801) has an office at the Hotel Sanman Deluxe on College Rd, but there are currently no flights from Belgaum airport. The bus stand is close to the old town area and there are buses to Mumbai, Pune, Goa, and Hubli. You'll need to catch an auto-rickshaw to the railway station, where several express trains plying between Bangalore (15 hours) and Mumbai (14 hours) stop. These trains pass through Londa (the closest rail junction with connections to Goa) and Hubli. There's also a daily express to Delhi (37 hours).

BADAMI

Pop: 18,200   Tel Area Code: 08357

Set in beautiful countryside at the foot of a red sandstone ridge, the small rural town of Badami was once the capital of the Chalukyan Empire, which covered much of the central Deccan between the 4th and 8th cen-

turies AD. Here, and at nearby Aihole and Pattadakal, you can see some of the earliest and finest examples of Dravidian temples and rock-cut caves. The forms and sculptural work at these sites provided inspiration for the later Hindu empires which rose and fell in the southern part of the peninsula before the arrival of the Muslims.

Though principally promoters of the Vedic culture, the Chalukyans were tolerant of all sects, and elements of Shaivism, Vaishnaivism, Jainism and even Buddhism can be found in many of their temples.

Badami was the Chalukyan capital from about 540 AD until 757 AD when the Chalukyans were overthrown by the Rashtrakutas. The surrounding hills are dotted with temples, fortifications, carvings and inscriptions dating not just from the Chalukyan period, but from other times when the site was occupied as a fortress. After it fell to the Rashtrakutas, Badami was occupied successively by the Chalukyans of Kalyan (a separate branch of the Western Chalukyans), the Kalachuryas, the Yadavas of Devagiri, the Vijayanagar Empire, the Adil Shahi kings of Bijapur and the Marathas.

All these various rulers have left their mark at Badami, and there's even a Pallava inscription dating back to 642 AD when their king, Narasimha Varman I, briefly overwhelmed the Chalukyans and occupied Badami for 13 years before being driven out.

Information

The tourist office is currently on the main street of Badami, between the bus and tonga stands, though it is expected to move to the new wing of the KSTDC's Hotel Mayura Chalukya once this building is completed.

Be sure to bring enough money with you to get to the next large town, since there is nowhere to change money in Badami, Pattadakal or Aihole.

Things to See

Badami This town is best known for its beautiful **cave temples**, cut into the cliff face of a red sandstone hill. They display the full range of religious sects which have developed in India. Two of them are dedicated to Vishnu, one to Siva and the fourth is a Jain temple. There's also one natural cave which is a Buddhist temple. Entry to the caves cost Rs 2.

Between the second and third cave is a stone staircase which leads to the hilltop **south fort**. If it's not locked, you can climb up here, though the steps have been cut by someone with a grudge against anyone less than three metres tall.

The caves overlook the picturesque 5th century **Agastyatirtha tank** and the peaceful waterside **Bhutanatha temples**. On the other side of the tank is the **Archaeological Museum** which houses superb examples of local sculpture, including remarkable Lajja-Gauri images of a fertility cult which flourished in the area. It's open from 10 am to 5 pm daily except Friday. The stairway behind the museum climbs through a sandstone chasm and fortified gateways to reach the various temples and ruins of the **north fort**. Anyone familiar with the landscapes of central Australia may start having flashbacks.

The fort has expansive views and overlooks the rooftops of the small friendly town of Badami. It's definitely worth exploring

Badami's narrow laneways, where you'll find old houses, tiny squares and the occasional Chalukyan ruin.

Pattadakal This village, 20km from Badami, was not only the second capital of the Badami Chalukyans, but the place where all coronations took place. It reached the height of its glory during the 7th and 8th centuries, when most of the temples here were built.

The most important monument is the Lokeshwara or **Virupaksha Temple**, a huge structure with sculptures that narrate episodes from the *Ramayana* and *Mahabharata*, as well as throw light on the social life of the early Chalukyans. The other main temple, **Mallikarjuna**, has sculptures which tell stories from the *Bhagavad Gita*. There's also an old **Jain temple** with two stone elephants. It's about a km from the village centre and is worth visiting.

Aihole This village, 43km from Badami, was the Chalukyan regional capital between the 4th and 6th centuries. Here you can see Hindu temple architecture in its embryonic stage, from the earliest **Ladkhan Temple** to the later and more complex structures like

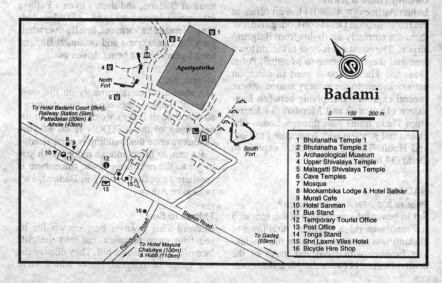

Badami

1	Bhutanatha Temple 1
2	Bhutanatha Temple 2
3	Archaeological Museum
4	Upper Shivalaya Temple
5	Malagatti Shivalaya Temple
6	Cave Temples
7	Mosque
8	Mookambika Lodge & Hotel Satkar
9	Murali Cafe
10	Hotel Sanman
11	Bus Stand
12	Temporary Tourist Office
13	Post Office
14	Tonga Stand
15	Shri Laxmi Vilas Hotel
16	Bicycle Hire Shop

Agastyatirtha

North Fort

To Hotel Badami Court (2km),
Railway Station (5km),
Pattadakal (20km) &
Aihole (43km)

South Fort

To Hotel Mayura
Chalukya (100m)
& Hubli (110km)

Station Road

Ramburg Road

To Gadag
(65km)

0   100   200 m

the **Kunligudi** and **Durgigudi** temples. The Durgigudi, a circular temple surmounted by a primitive gopuram, is particularly interesting and probably unique in India.

There are over 70 structures in and around this serene village which show the vigorous experimentation in temple architecture undertaken by the Chalukyans. Most are in a good state of preservation.

Places to Stay
Badami is the best place to base yourself, since there are several basic lodges here.

Mookambika Lodge (☎ 65067), opposite the bus stand, has clean singles/doubles with attached bath and hot water in the morning for Rs 80/140 and deluxe doubles for Rs 200.

Hotel Satkar (☎ 65017) has clean, basic rooms with attached bath and hot water in the morning from Rs 60/90. Checkout time is 24 hours.

Shri Laxmi Vilas Hotel (☎ 65077), near the tonga stand, has acceptable doubles (only) with attached bath and bucket shower for Rs 90, but it can be noisy.

Hotel Mayura Chalukya (☎ 65046) is a KSTDC hotel on Ramdurg Rd, about 400m off Station Rd. The neglected, old section has tranquil gardens and overpriced doubles/triples with mosquito nets and attached baths with dodgy plumbing for Rs 200/350. A brand new wing consists of six deluxe air-con rooms. Don't leave your room open unattended for too long as the resident monkeys are fond of pinching things.

Hotel Badami Court (☎ 65230) is easily the town's best hotel. It's two km from the town centre, on the road to the railway station. Impeccable doubles with bathtubs and TV cost Rs 750 or Rs 1092 with air-con, including tax.

The sole *retiring room* at Badami's railway station is a double costing Rs 50. Accommodation is also available at the Department of Tourism *Tourist Home*, one km from the village of Aihole on the Amingad road.

Places to Eat
Badami is the only one of the three sites with a selection of acceptable restaurants.

Hotel Sanman, close to the Badami bus stand, is popular with travellers and locals. It has cheap veg/non-veg food and cold beers.

Murali Cafe, nearby, is a basic but atmospheric veg restaurant serving thalis at lunchtime.

Hotel Mayura Chalukya has the usual KSTDC veg restaurant and beer bar; the food available is limited.

Pulikeshi Dining Room in Hotel Badami Court is an upmarket, multi-cuisine, silver service restaurant where dinner costs just under Rs 100 per head.

Getting There & Away
Bus The timetable at the bus stand in Badami is in English and Kannada but it's not particularly accurate. You'll also have to cope with the usual rugby scrum to get on a bus when it arrives. There are six buses daily to Bijapur (four hours) and Hubli (three hours), and four buses to Bangalore (12 hours). Only three buses run daily direct to Hospet (five hours), but you can catch any of the buses to Gadag (two hours) or Ilkal (two hours) to pick up a connection to Hospet.

Train The railway line through Badami is still metre gauge. Conversion work is currently disrupting services to Bangalore, and the only trains running are those shuttling between Gadag and Bijapur – nearly all of them are 2nd-class passenger trains. Tickets for passenger trains go on sale about 30 minutes before the train arrives. Five trains head to Bijapur (Rs 20, 3½ hours), the most convenient are at 11.36 am and 4.50 pm. The most convenient of the five heading to Gadag are at 7.49 am, 10.19 am and 3.49 pm. There are connections from Gadag to Hospet and Hubli. Four of the five trains to Bijapur continue on to Sholapur in Maharashtra, which is a major railway junction where you can change onto the broad-gauge system for cities such as Mumbai, Hyderabad and Bangalore.

Getting Around
Badami railway station is five km from town. Tongas congregate outside to meet the trains. A private tonga from the station into town

costs Rs 20, or is split between however many clamber aboard if it's shared. You have the choice of a tonga, auto-rickshaw (Rs 30) or taxi (Rs 50) when heading from town out to the railway station. You can hire bikes in Badami for Rs 2 per hour, which is useful if you just want to nip out to the station to check the train timetable.

The best way to explore the surrounding area is by local bus, since they're fairly frequent and run pretty much to schedule. You can easily visit both Aihole and Pattadakal in one day from Badami, but it's best to start with Aihole since the last bus from Aihole to Badami is around lunchtime; the last bus from Pattadakal to Badami is at 6 pm. There are plenty of buses from Badami to Aihole (two hours). From Aihole, there's a bus at 1 pm to Pattadakal (30 minutes), from where there are hourly buses and minibuses back to Badami. It's a good idea to take food with you.

Taxi drivers in Badami quote around Rs 450 for a day trip taking in Pattadakal and

Aihole. Mookambika Lodge can arrange a car and driver to these two places and to other local sights on the way for Rs 150 per person (minimum of two people).

BIJAPUR
Pop: 217,500   Tel Area Code: 08352
Modern Bijapur is a dull, undistinguished town blessed by the scattered ruins and still-intact gems of 15th to 17th century Muslim architecture. It is dotted with mosques, mausoleums, palaces and fortifications, including the famous Golgumbaz, whose vast dome is said to be the world's second largest. The austere grace of Bijapur's discoloured monuments is in complete contrast to the sculptural extravaganza of the Chalukyan and Hoysala temples further south. The Ibrahim Roza mausoleum, in particular, is considered to be one of the most finely proportioned Islamic monuments in India.

Bijapur was the capital of the Adil Shahi kings (1489-1686), one of the five splinter

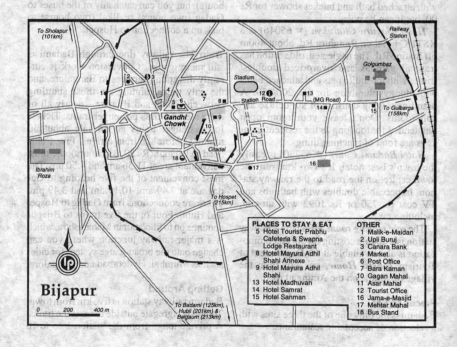

PLACES TO STAY & EAT
5 Hotel Tourist, Prabhu Cafeteria & Swapna Lodge Restaurant
8 Hotel Mayura Adhil Shahi Annexe
9 Hotel Mayura Adhil Shahi
13 Hotel Madhuvan
14 Hotel Samrat
15 Hotel Sanman

OTHER
1 Malik-e-Maidan
2 Upli Buruj
3 Canara Bank
4 Market
6 Post Office
7 Bara Kaman
10 Gagan Mahal
11 Asar Mahal
12 Tourist Office
16 Jama-e-Masjid
17 Mehtar Mahal
18 Bus Stand

Bijapur

To Sholapur (101km)
Railway Station
Golgumbaz
Stadium
Station Road
(MG Road)
To Gulbarga (158km)
Gandhi Chowk
Citadel
Ibrahim Roza
To Hospet (215km)
To Badami (125km), Hubli (201km) & Belgaum (213km)

0   200   400 m

states formed when the Bahmani Muslim kingdom broke up in 1482. The others, formed at roughly the same time, were Bidar, Golconda, Ahmednagar and Gulbarga.

Bijapur is still strongly Muslim in character, and some solo women travellers have reported being harassed here.

Orientation

The two main attractions, the Golgumbaz and the Ibrahim Roza, are at opposite ends of the town. Between them runs Station Rd (MG Rd) along which are most of the major hotels and restaurants. The bus stand is a five minute walk from Station Rd; the railway station is two km east of the centre.

Information

The useless tourist office is on Station Rd, one km east of the town centre. The post office, in the town centre, is also on Station Rd and is open Monday to Saturday from 8.30 am to 6 pm.

To change travellers cheques, head to the Canara Bank, north of the market. You'll need to provide the bank with photocopies of the pages in your passport which have your name and photograph in them.

Power cuts are frequent in Bijapur and often last for hours, so have candles handy.

Golgumbaz

Bijapur's largest and most famous monument is the Golgumbaz. Built in 1659, it's an enormous, bulky, ill-proportioned building, containing an immense hall, buttressed by octagonal seven-storey towers at each of its corners. The structure is capped by an enormous dome, 38m in diameter, said to be the world's second largest after St Peter's in Vatican City.

Around the base of the dome, high above the hall, is a gallery known as the 'whispering gallery', since the acoustics here are such that any sound made is said to be repeated 10 times over. 'Bedlam gallery' would be a more appropriate name, since it is permanently full of yelling tourists and children running amok. Access to the gallery is via a narrow staircase in the south-eastern tower

and there are views of Bijapur from the outside of the dome before you enter the gallery. The views are clearest in the early morning, which is also the best time to test the acoustics, before the school groups arrive.

The Golgumbaz is the mausoleum of Mohammed Adil Shah (1626-56), his two wives, his mistress (Rambha), one of his daughters and a grandson. Their caskets stand on a raised platform in the centre of the hall, though their actual graves are in the crypt, accessible by a flight of steps under the western doorway.

The mausoleum is open from 6 am to 6 pm; entry costs Rs 2, except on Friday, when it's free. Shoes should be left outside near the entrance to the hall.

An archaeological museum in the mausoleum's ornamental gardens is open between 10 am and 5 pm daily except Friday.

Ibrahim Roza

The beautiful Ibrahim Roza was constructed at the height of Bijapur's prosperity by Ibrahim Adil Shah II (1580-1626) for his queen. Unlike the Golgumbaz, which is impressive only for its immensity, the emphasis here is on elegance and delicacy. Its 24m high minarets are said to have inspired those of the Taj Mahal. It's also one of the few monuments in Bijapur with substantial stone filigree and other sculpturally decorative work.

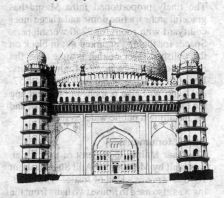

The Golgumbaz, Mohammed Adil Shah's impressive mausoleum.

Buried here are Ibrahim Adil Shah, his queen, Taj Sultana, his daughter, two sons, and his mother Haji Badi Sahiba. The entry fee is Rs 2; shoes should be left on the steps up to the platform on which the mausoleum stands.

Citadel

Surrounded by its own fortified walls and wide moat in the city centre, the citadel once contained the palaces, pleasure gardens and Durbar Hall of the Adil Shahi kings. Unfortunately, most of them are now in ruins, although some impressive fragments remain. The best is the **Gagan Mahal**, built by Ali Adil Shah I around 1561 to serve the dual purpose of a royal residence and a Durbar Hall. It looks like an opera stage set, and is completely open on one side so that an audience outside the hall had an unobstructed view of the proceedings on the raised platform inside.

Mohammed Adil Shah's seven-storey palace, the **Sat Manzil**, is nearby, but substantially in ruins. Just across the road stands the delicate **Jala Manzil**, once a water pavilion surrounded by secluded courts and gardens. On the other side of Station Rd are the graceful arches of **Bara Kaman**, the ruined mausoleum of Ali Roza.

Jama Masjid

The finely proportioned Jama Masjid has graceful arches, a fine dome and a large inner courtyard with room for 2250 worshippers. Spaces for them are marked out in black on the polished floor of the mosque. The flat roof is accessible by several flights of stairs. It was constructed by Ali Adil Shah I (1557-80), who was also responsible for erecting the fortified city walls and Gagan Mahal, and for installing a public water system.

Other Monuments

The **Asar Mahal**, to the east of the citadel, was built by Mohammed Adil Shah in about 1646 to serve as a Hall of Justice. The building was also used to house two hairs from the Prophet's beard. The rooms on the upper storey are decorated with frescoes and the front is graced with a square tank usually full of swimming kids. Women are not allowed inside. The stained but richly decorated **Mehtar Mahal** to the south serves as an ornamental gateway to a small mosque.

Upli Buruj is a 16th century, 24m high watchtower built on high ground near the western walls of the city. An external flight of stairs leads to the top, where there are a couple of hefty cannons and good views of the city and plains.

The **Malik-e-Maidan** (Monarch of the Plains) is a huge cannon measuring over four metres long, almost 1½ metres in diameter, and estimated to weigh 55 tonnes. It was cast in 1549 and brought to Bijapur as a war trophy thanks to the effort of 10 elephants, 400 oxen and hundreds of men.

Places to Stay

Hotel Tourist (☎ 20655), in the centre of town, has decent rooms with attached bath for Rs 60/100 or Rs 70/125 for the 'special' rooms, which have nothing special about them.

Hotel Mayura Adhil Shahi (☎ 20943) is a KSTDC operation where most travellers end up staying. Rooms here are set around a quiet, leafy garden courtyard which doubles as an open-air restaurant. Acceptable singles/doubles with mosquito nets, soggy attached bathrooms and hot water in the morning cost Rs 130/163 including tax.

Hotel Mayura Adhil Shahi Annexe (☎ 20401) nearby is also shrouded in greenery. It consists of four well-appointed air-con rooms with TV, attached bath and 24 hour hot water costing Rs 506 including tax.

Hotel Samrat (☎ 21620) has good rooms with attached bath and mosquito nets for Rs 90/120. It's east of the town centre on Station Rd.

Hotel Sanman (☎ 21866), opposite the Golgumbaz, has less presentable doubles/triples with attached bath for Rs 115/145. Checkout time is 24 hours.

Hotel Madhuvan (☎ 25572) is a modern hotel off Station Rd with very comfortable but overpriced doubles (only) with TV and attached bath for Rs 450 or Rs 650 with air-con.

Places to Eat
Prabhu Cafeteria, next to the Hotel Tourist, serves excellent dosas, bhelpuri, lassis and other snacks. There's nothing over Rs 12 on the menu.

Swapna Lodge Restaurant, on the 2nd floor of the same building, has good veg/non-veg food – including 63 different chicken dishes – as well as cold beer. It has an open-air terrace which is perfect for evening dining. Don't be put off by the forlorn entry to this place as both the service and food are good.

Hotel Mayura Adhil Shahi has a reasonable restaurant in the middle of its garden courtyard. It serves western breakfasts and modestly good Indian food. Of all the bars in town, this one has the most pleasant setting for an evening beer.

Hotel Madhuvan, *Hotel Sanman* and *Hotel Samrat* all have restaurants. The latter boasts what may be the world's darkest bar; it's best to light a match if you want a waiter to see you.

Getting There & Away
Bus The timetable at the bus stand is entirely in Kannada. There are daily services to Badami, Belgaum, Gulbarga, Hubli and Sholapur; four evening services to Bangalore via Hospet; four buses to Hyderabad and to Pune; and a couple to Bidar.

Train Only 10 trains currently operate from Bijapur, nearly all of them 2nd-class passenger trains. Half of these trains head to Sholapur and the other half to Gadag via Badami (Rs 20, 3½ hours). Sholapur has connections to Mumbai, Hyderabad and Bangalore; Gadag has connections to Hospet, Hubli and Bangalore. Bijapur station has a healthy quota of sleeping berths allotted to it on all major expresses passing through Sholapur and Gadag, so you should have no problem getting a berth if you're making a long-distance connection. The 12.10 pm departure to Gadag connects with the *Hampi Express* to Bangalore.

Getting Around
Bus The uncrowded local bus system has only one route: from the railway station, along Station Rd to the gate at the western end of town. Buses run every 15 minutes.

Rickshaw & Tonga Auto-rickshaw drivers charge what they think you will pay – intense haggling and Rs 15 should get you between the railway station and the town centre. To zip between the Golgumbaz and Ibrahim Roza costs the same. Tonga drivers are eager for business and will offer to take you from the railway station to the town centre for around Rs 10.

THE NORTH-EAST
Gulbarga
Pop: 349,500   Tel Area Code: 08472
This dusty, scruffy town was the Bahmani capital from 1347 until its transfer to Bidar in 1428. Later the kingdom broke up into a number of smaller kingdoms – Bijapur, Bidar, Berar, Ahmednagar and Golconda. The last of these, Golconda, finally fell to Aurangzeb in 1687.

Gulbarga's neglected **fort** is in a deteriorated state and, despite attempts to promote it as a tourist attraction, is used primarily as a public toilet. If you're feeling brave, it includes the **Jama Masjid**, reputed to have been built during the late 14th or early 15th century by a Moorish architect who is said to have imitated the great mosque in Cordoba in Spain. Gulbarga also has a number of imposing **tombs** of Bahmani kings, a shrine to an important Muslim saint and the **Sharana Basaveshwara Temple** – though the main reason why sane travellers come here these days is to make rail connections.

Places to Stay & Eat The *Hotel Mayura Bahamani* (☎ 20644) is a neglected KSTDC establishment set back off Station Rd in what is considered to be a municipal garden. Run down but clean rooms with mosquito nets, attached bath and hot water in the morning cost Rs 110/140. There's a bar and restaurant but neither have much of a clientele. The hotel is about two km from the railway station (Rs 6 by auto-rickshaw) and three km from the bus stand (Rs 8).

Hotel Aditya (☎ 24040), on the opposite side of Station Rd, has well-appointed rooms with attached bath and hot water in the morning for Rs 175/225, deluxe doubles for Rs 275 and air-con doubles for Rs 425. There's a clean veg restaurant in the hotel.

Retiring rooms at the railway station are great value at Rs 30 per bed or Rs 50 per bed in an air-con room.

If you're stuck without a room, there are a number of undistinguished budget hotels catering to Indian tourists on the road into town from the bus stand.

Getting There & Away There are plenty of government buses to Bijapur and Bidar (Rs 30, three hours), plus overnight buses to Bangalore. Four buses depart for Hyderabad, all of them in the evening.

An inordinate number of express trains pass through Gulbarga, giving it surprisingly good connections to Mumbai, Bangalore, Hyderabad and Cochin.

Bidar

Tel Area Code: 08482

This little visited, walled town in the extreme north-eastern corner of the state was the capital of the Bahmani Kingdom from 1428, and later the capital of the Barid Shahi dynasty. It's a pleasant town with a splendid 15th century **fort** containing the Ranjeenmahal, Chini Mahal and Turkish Mahal **palaces**.

The **Khwaja Mahmud Gawan Madrasa** in the middle of town has a few colourful remains of typical Islamic mosaics. The huge domed **tombs** of the Bahmani and Barid kings are also worth seeing. These abandoned structures, which dot the countryside to the west and east of town, have an enticingly desolate aura.

Bidar lent its name to the handicraft *bidriware* (for details see the Bidriware of Bidar boxed section).

Places to Stay & Eat Hotel standards in Bidar are mediocre and the choice is slim.

Hotel Ratna (☎ 27218), *Sri New Venkateshwara Lodge* (☎ 26443) and *Hotel Prince* (☎ 25747) have barely acceptable singles/doubles with attached bath for between Rs 50/80 and Rs 75/115. The first two are on the main street in the town centre, the latter is on Udgir Rd, on the way into town from the bus stand.

Hotel Mayura Barid Shahi (☎ 26571) is a KSTDC hotel on Udgir Rd which has rundown singles/doubles with attached bath for Rs 100/150. The only advantage of this place is that it has a garden restaurant where you can escape from the squalor of your room.

Hotel Mayura Restaurant, opposite the bus stand, is a clean establishment where you can get reasonable Indian food and forget your accommodation woes over a beer.

Getting There & Away Bidar has plenty of bus connections to Gulbarga and Hyderabad, plus a few buses to Bijapur and Bangalore.

The Bidriware of Bidar

During its Islamic heyday, the Persian craftsmen of Bidar came up with a form of damascening now known as *bidriware*. It involved moulding imaginative blends of blackened zinc, copper, lead and tin, which were then embossed, overlaid or inlaid with pure silver. In both design and decoration, the artefacts were heavily influenced by typical Islamic features of the time. Finely crafted pieces such as *hookahs*, goblets, *paan* boxes and bangles were exquisitely embellished with interwoven creepers and flowing floral patterns, and occasionally framed by strict geometric lines. The effect of the delicate silver filigree against the ebony-toned background was scintillating. These days artists still tap away at their craft in the backstreets of Bidar, as well as in the neighbouring city of Hyderabad. ∎

Andhra Pradesh

Andhra Pradesh was created by combining the old princely state of Hyderabad with the Telugu-speaking portions of the former state of Madras. Most of this large state stands on the high Deccan plateau, sloping down to the low-lying coastal region to the east where the mighty Godavari and Krishna rivers meet the Bay of Bengal in wide deltas.

It's one of the poorest and least developed states in India, although the final nizam (ruler) of Hyderabad was reputed to be one of the richest men in the world! New dams and irrigation projects are improving the barren, scrubby land of the plateau, but much of the state remains economically backward.

Few travellers explore Andhra Pradesh in any depth, daunted by the long distances and the poor tourist facilities, but the state has plenty of interest nonetheless. The capital, Hyderabad, is naturally a magnet for its Muslim heritage, as well as the nearby Golconda Fort and Qutb Shahi tombs. Further afield, there are the impressive ruins of the Kakatiya kingdom at Warangal, commented on by Marco Polo, and the Buddhist sites of Nagarjunakonda and Amaravathi, as well as the beautiful Kanaka Durga Temple at Vijayawada, and the famous temple complex of Tirumala in the state's extreme south-east.

During the monsoon, the deltas of the Godavari and Krishna rivers may flood, forcing trains between Calcutta and Chennai (Madras) to detour further inland through Raipur, Nagpur and Hyderabad. In October and November 1996, tropical storms and floods in eastern Andhra Pradesh killed an estimated 3000 people and severely damaged transport and communications infrastructure. Travellers to coastal areas should keep a close watch on weather patterns during and immediately following the monsoon. The worst affected months are May, October and November.

History

Andhra Pradesh was once a major Buddhist

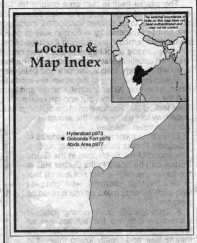

ANDHRA PRADESH AT A GLANCE

Population: 73.4 million
Area: 276,754 sq km
Capital: Hyderabad
Main Language: Telugu
Literacy Rate: 45%
Best Time to Go: October to February

Locator & Map Index

Hyderabad p973
Golconda Fort p970
Abids Area p977

Highlights

- Getting lost in the pearl bazaars of Hyderabad
- A picnic atop the ruins of Golconda Fort
- Shaving your head for *darshan* at Tirumala's Venkateshwara Temple
- Sampling the fiery Andhran cuisine

centre and part of Ashoka's empire until it broke apart. Traces of early Buddhist influence still remain in several places, particularly Amaravathi, the Sanchi of Andhra Pradesh. Later, in the 7th century, the Chalukyas held power, but they in turn fell to the Chola kingdom of the south around the 10th century.

The 13th century saw the rise of the Kakatiyas who ruled from Warangal, but by this

ANDHRA PRADESH

A REGIONAL HIGHLIGHT

Golconda Fort

Golconda is one of the most magnificent fortress complexes in India. The bulk of the ruins date from the time of the Qutb Shahi kings (16th to 17th centuries), though the origins of the fort have been traced to the earlier Hindu periods when the Yadavas and, later, the Kakatiyas ruled this part of India.

In 1512, Sultan Quli Qutb Shah, a Turkoman adventurer from Persia and governor of Telangana under the Bahmani rulers, declared independence and made Golconda his capital.

Golconda remained the capital until 1590, when the court was moved to the new city of Hyderabad. The fort subsequently came into its own again when, on two separate occasions in the 17th century, Mughal armies from Delhi were sent against the kingdom to enforce payment of tribute. Abul Hasan, the last of the Qutb Shahi kings, held out here for seven months against a Mughal army commanded by Emperor Aurangzeb before losing the fort through treachery in 1687. Following Aurangzeb's death early in the next century, his viceroys (later the nizams) made Hyderabad their capital, abandoning Golconda.

The citadel itself is built on a granite hill 120m high and is surrounded by crenellated ramparts constructed of large masonry blocks, some of them weighing several tonnes. The massive gates are studded with large pointed iron spikes, intended to prevent elephants from battering them down, and are further protected by a cordon wall to check direct attack. Outside the citadel stands another crenellated rampart, surrounding the base of the hill, with a perimeter of 11km. Outside this wall is a third wall, made up of boulders and incorporating natural defences in the landscape. All these walls are in an excellent state of preservation. The fort once had eight gates, but of these only four are still used – the Fateh, Mecca, Banjara and Balahisar gates.

Unfortunately, many of the structures inside the citadel – the palaces and harem of the Qutb Shahi kings, assembly halls, arsenal, stables and barracks – have suffered a great deal from past sieges and the ravages of time, but enough remains to give a good impression of what the place must once have looked like. Restoration of the buildings around the Balahisar Gate (the main entrance) has been underway for years – even the wrought iron work has been replaced.

One of the most remarkable features of Golconda Fort is its system of acoustics. The sound of hands clapped in the Grand Portico can be heard in the Durbar Hall at the top of the hill – a fact not lost on tour guides (or their charges), who compete with each other to make as much noise as possible!

Knowledgeable guides congregate at the entrance to the fort but are geared towards groups, asking Rs 250 for a 90 minute tour and rapidly losing interest in any offer below Rs 150. If you don't want a guide, dismiss them firmly before you enter the main gate. Alternatively, the *Guide to Golconda Fort & Qutb Shahi Tombs* may be on sale at the fort, and is a good investment if you intend to spend the day here.

The fort is open from 8 am to 6.30 pm daily, and entrance costs Rs 2 (free on Friday). To get to the fort's main entrance, Balahisar Gate, take city bus No 119 or 142 from Nampally High Rd (Public Gardens Rd), outside the public gardens. The 11km trip takes an hour and costs about Rs 2. An auto-rickshaw from Abids costs around Rs 120-150 return, including waiting charges.

An hour-long sound & light show is held daily except Monday (in English on Sunday and Wednesday only) at 6.30 pm (November-February) or 7 pm (March-October). Entry to this show costs Rs 20; children younger than five years are not permitted. ∎

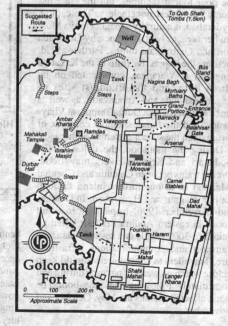

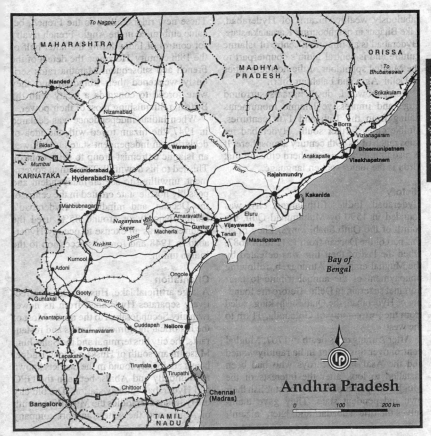

Andhra Pradesh

time Muslim power was beginning to assert itself in the form of the sultans of Delhi, who made many raids into the area and established themselves in 1323. However, their hold was tenuous and they were soon displaced by the Hindu Vijayanagar Empire.

There followed two centuries of Hindu-Muslim power struggles until, in the 16th century, the Qutb Shahi dynasty was established at Hyderabad.

It was this dynasty that built the vast and almost impregnable stone fortress of Golconda – one of India's most impressive monuments. The nearby tombs of the rulers of this Muslim dynasty rival those of the Delhi sultans and the early Mughals in size and splendour. Their reign came to an end in 1687 when the kingdom was taken over by a general of the Mughal emperor Aurangzeb. The general's successors, the nizams of Hyderabad, ruled the state right through to Independence.

HYDERABAD
Pop: 4.9 million   Tel Area Code: 040
The capital of Andhra Pradesh consists of the twin cities of Hyderabad and Secunderabad and is famous as the former seat of the

fabulously wealthy nizams of Hyderabad. Like Bijapur in neighbouring Karnataka state, Hyderabad is an important centre of Islamic culture and is central India's counterpart to the Mughal splendour of the northern cities of Delhi, Agra and Fatehpur Sikri.

Here, crowded, dusty bazaars surround huge and impressive Islamic monuments dating from the 16th and 17th centuries. Unlike cities further south, Hyderabad retains much of its 19th century atmosphere. It is also unique among southern cities in that Urdu is the major spoken language.

History

Hyderabad, India's fifth-largest city, was founded in 1590 by Muhammad Quli, the fourth of the Qutb Shahi kings. They ruled this part of the Deccan from 1512 until 1687, when the last of their line was defeated by the Mughal emperor, Aurangzeb, following nonpayment of the annual tribute to their nominal suzerain in Delhi. Before the founding of Hyderabad, the Qutb Shahi kings ruled from the fortress city of Golconda, 11km to the west.

After Aurangzeb's death in 1707, Mughal control over this part of India rapidly waned and the Asaf Jahi viceroys who had been installed to look after the interests of the Mughal Empire broke away to establish their own independent state. They gave themselves the title 'subadar' and, later, 'nizam'.

These new rulers, allied to the French, became embroiled in the Anglo-French rivalry for control of India during the latter half of the 18th century. However, the defeat of the French and subsequent Maratha raids seriously weakened their kingdom and they were forced to conclude a treaty with the British, relinquishing most of their power.

When Indian independence was declared in 1947, the nizam toyed with the idea of declaring an independent state and allowed an Islamic extremist group to seize control. This led to his downfall. The Indian government, unwilling to see an independent and possibly hostile state created in the centre of the Deccan, and mindful of Hyderabad's Hindu majority of around 85%, used the insurrection as an excuse to occupy Hyderabad in 1948 and force its accession to the Indian union.

Orientation

A large artificial lake, Hussain Sagar, effectively separates Hyderabad from its newer twin city Secunderabad to the north. Most of the historical monuments, hotels and restaurants, the city bus terminal and the Salar Jung Museum are south of Hussain Sagar. Budget hotels are mainly found in the districts known as Nampally and Abids, between the GPO and Hyderabad railway station. The old city of Hyderabad straddles the Musi River south of Abids, and the state transport company

---

Wet & Dry in Andhra Pradesh

In December 1994, just minutes after a new state government was sworn in, Andhra Pradesh became a 'dry' state. The decision to ban the sale of alcohol follows a remarkable campaign by village women who were fed up with husbands drinking away the housekeeping money. Such was the strength of their movement that the local Telugu Desam party won a resounding victory in the state election by promising to introduce prohibition.

But prohibition didn't prove the panacea its proponents might have hoped. The distilling of bootleg liquor became a major cottage industry in the villages of Andhra Pradesh, and fortunes were made in the smuggling of alcohol from neighbouring 'wet' states, leading to widespread corruption of police and officials.

In May 1997 the state government relented and legalised the sale of Indian-made foreign liquor (IMFL) throughout Andhra Pradesh (incidentally generating crores of rupees for the state coffers from licensing fees).

But despite this relaxation of prohibition, the situation in Andhra Pradesh remains 'fluid' and you should check with a tourist office before you carry liquor into the state. ∎

(APSRTC) has its bus terminal near the river in the Gowliguda area.

Secunderabad lies on the northern side of Hussain Sagar. Many trains terminate at Secunderabad railway station, though quite a few continue on to Hyderabad railway station, which is known locally as Nampally station.

The ruins of Golconda Fort and the tombs of the Qutb Shahi kings lie about 11km west of the city.

Information
Tourist Offices Andhra Pradesh Travel & Tourist Development Corporation (APTTDC)

has two offices. The Yatri Nivas Hotel office (☎ 816375) on Sardar Patel Rd in Secunderabad is primarily a booking office for APTTDC tours. It's open daily from 6.30 am to 7 pm.

The other APTTDC office (☎ 501519) is at Gangan Vihar (11th floor), Mozamjahi Rd in Hyderabad and is open Monday to Saturday from 10.30 am to 5 pm. It's pretty useless, but the small kiosk on the ground floor (6.30 am to 7 pm daily) has a basic map and brochure. The tourist information kiosks at Secunderabad railway station and at the airport are similarly useless.

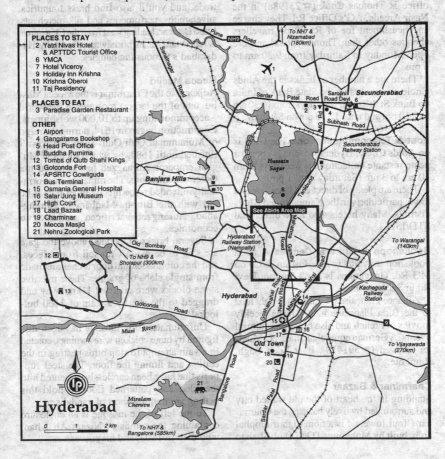

PLACES TO STAY
2 Yatri Nivas Hotel & APTTDC Tourist Office
6 YMCA
7 Hotel Viceroy
9 Holiday Inn Krishna
10 Krishna Oberoi
11 Taj Residency

PLACES TO EAT
3 Paradise Garden Restaurant

OTHER
1 Airport
4 Gangarams Bookshop
5 Head Post Office
8 Buddha Purnima
12 Tombs of Qutb Shahi Kings
13 Golconda Fort
14 APSRTC Gowliguda Bus Terminal
15 Osmania General Hospital
16 Salar Jung Museum
17 High Court
18 Laad Bazaar
19 Charminar
20 Mecca Masjid
21 Nehru Zoological Park

Hyderabad

ANDHRA PRADESH

The Government of India Tourist Office (☎ 7630037) in the Sandozi Building (2nd floor) on Himayatnagar Rd has the usual range of brochures. It's open weekdays from 6 am to 7 pm.

The useful monthly 'what's on' guide, *Channel 6* (Rs 10), can usually be tracked down at bookstores or the major hotels. The ICRISAT (International Crops Research Institute for the Semi-Arid Tropics) *Guide to Hyderabad and Secunderabad* (Rs 100) is a useful reference for long-term visitors.

Money The most efficient foreign exchange office is Thomas Cook (☎ 231988) in the Nasir Arcade, AG's Office Rd. They charge an encashment fee of Rs 20 on travellers cheques other than Thomas Cook, and are open Monday to Saturday from 9.30 am to 6 pm.

There are a number of banks in the Abids Circle area including the State Bank of India on Bank St. It's open weekdays from 10.30 am to 2.30 pm and until 12.30 pm on Saturday.

Post & Telecommunications The GPO is on Abids Circle, Hyderabad, and is open for poste restante collection on weekdays from 10 am to 3 pm (Saturday until 1 pm).

There are plenty of direct-dial kiosks around town, particularly in the Nampally and Abids districts. Many hotels also have direct dial STD/ISD.

Bookshops & Cultural Centres A good bookshop in Abids is AA Hussain & Co on MG Rd. Gangarams is at 62 Sarojini Devi Rd in Secunderabad.

Alliance Française (☎ 236646) is right next to the Birla Planetarium. It screens weekly movies in French and also organises cultural events. A German equivalent, the Max Mueller Bhavan (☎ 591410), is at Eden Bagh, Ramkote.

Charminar & Bazaar

Standing in the heart of the old walled city and surrounded by lively bazaars, the Charminar ('four towers') is a 56m high triumphal arch, built by Muhammad Quli Qutb Shah in 1591 to commemorate the end of a plague in Hyderabad. The arch is notable for its elegant balconies, stucco decorations and the small mosque, Hyderabad's oldest, on the 2nd floor. An image of the arch graces every packet of Charminar cigarettes, one of India's most popular brands. There are good views over the old city from the top of the minarets – if you can find someone to let you in. The arch is illuminated each evening from 7 to 9 pm.

The narrow streets surrounding the Charminar make up one of India's most exotic bazaars. This is the centre of India's pearl trade, and you'll also find brass foundries, silversmiths, perfumeries and silk merchants. **Laad Bazaar**, leading west from the Charminar, is renowned for its bridalware, especially Hyderabad's famous *lac* bangles.

Mecca Masjid

Adjacent to the Charminar is the Mecca Masjid, one of the largest mosques in the world – accommodating up to 10,000 worshippers. Construction began in 1614, during the reign of Muhammad Quli Qutb Shah, but wasn't finished until 1687, by which time the Mughal emperor Aurangzeb had annexed the Golconda kingdom. The minarets were originally intended to be much higher but, as he did with the Bibi-qa-Maqbara in Aurangabad, Aurangzeb sacrificed aesthetics to economics.

Several bricks embedded above the gate are said to be made with soil from Mecca, and the colonnades and door arches are made from single slabs of granite. These massive stone blocks were quarried 11km away and dragged to the site by a team of 1400 bullocks!

Unfortunately, the mosque has been disfigured by huge chicken wire awnings, erected in a vain attempt to stop birds nesting in the ceiling and liming the floor. The steel supports that have been carelessly cemented into the tiled and patterned floor to hold this netting are nothing short of vandalism.

To the left of the mosque is an enclosure containing the tombs of Nizam Ali Khan, who died in 1803, and his successors.

Life Wasn't Meant to be Wheezy

Asthma sufferers from all over India converge on a house in Hyderabad each June, on a date chosen by astrologers, to receive free and unconventional treatment.

The cure, received by some 500,000 people in 1997, is a five-centimetre-long fish, known locally as murrel, which is stuffed with a secret herbal mixture – developed by the Goud family – then swallowed live.

The family says that a Himalayan saint gave their ancestor the secret formula 152 years ago, in gratitude for the hospitality shown to him. They refuse payment for the treatment and pool their own resources to raise the Rs 40,000 needed every year to buy the herbs for the medicine. The Gouds also refuse to give anyone, even medical researchers, the formula, as the saint warned that the wriggling remedy would lose its potency if it were commercialised. ■

Birla Mandir Temple & Planetarium

This stunning Hindu temple was built of white Rajasthani marble in 1976 and graces one of the twin rocky hills overlooking the south end of Hussain Sagar. Dedicated to Lord Venkateshwara, the temple is a popular Hindu pilgrimage centre. There are excellent views over the city from the temple, especially at sunset. It's open to Hindus and non-Hindus alike, from 7 am to noon and 3 to 9 pm; there's no entry fee.

On the adjacent hill, Naubat Pahar, stand the **Birla Planetarium & Science Museum** (☎ 235081). The planetarium has presentations in English at 11 am, 4 pm and 6 pm daily. It's closed on the last Thursday of each month; admission is Rs 10. The museum is open from 10.30 am to 8.30 pm daily (closed on the last Tuesday of each month); admission is Rs 6.

Buddha Purnima & Hussain Sagar

Hyderabad, historically one of the most important Buddhist centres in India, boasts one of the largest stone Buddhas in the world. The brainchild of Telugu Desam's president, NT Rama Rao, work on the project began in 1985 at Raigir, some 50km from Hyderabad, and was completed in early 1990. The 17.5m high, 350 tonne monolith was transported to Hyderabad and loaded onto a barge for ferrying across Hussain Sagar to be erected on the dam wall.

Unfortunately, disaster struck and the statue sank into the lake taking with it eight people. There it languished for two years while ways of raising it were discussed.

Finally, in mid-1992, a Goanese salvage company raised it once more (undamaged!) and it was finally erected on a plinth in the middle of the lake.

Frequent boats make a 30 minute round trip to the statue from **Lumbini Park**, just north of Secretariat Rd, between 9 am and 6 pm for Rs 10 per head. You'll also need to pay the Rs 2 entrance fee for the park, which is a pleasant spot to enjoy Hyderabad's blood-red sunsets (open daily from 9 am to 9 pm). The **Tankbund**, which skirts the eastern shore of Hussain Sagar, has great views of the Buddha and is a popular promenade and jogging track.

Avalokitesvara, a Mahayana Buddhist bodhisattva.

ANDHRA PRADESH

Salar Jung Museum

India's answer to the Victoria & Albert Museum in London, the Salar Jung Museum's collection was put together by Mir Yusaf Ali Khan (Salar Jung III), the prime minister, or grand-vizier, of the nizam. It contains 35,000 exhibits from all corners of the world and includes sculptures, woodcarvings, religious objects, Persian miniature paintings, illuminated manuscripts, armour and weaponry. In the Jade Room you'll see the swords, daggers and clothing of the Mughal emperors and of Tipu Sultan, as well as many other objects. All this is housed in 36 rooms of one of the ugliest buildings imaginable.

The museum is open daily, except Friday, from 10 am to 5 pm, but avoid Sundays when it's bedlam. Entry is Rs 5. Bags and cameras must be deposited in the entrance hall. From Abids, bus No 7 will drop you at the Musi River bridge; just cross the river and take the first turn left.

Not far west of the Musi River bridge, facing each other across the river, are the spectacular **High Court** and **Osmania General Hospital** buildings, built in the florid Indo-Saracenic style.

Archaeological Museum

The archaeological museum is in the public gardens to the north of Hyderabad railway station. It has a small collection of archaeological finds from the area, together with copies of paintings from the Ajanta Caves in Maharashtra. Opening hours are 10.30 am to 5 pm daily, except Friday, and entry is Rs 0.50. Also worth a quick visit is the nearby **Health Museum**, which is open from 10.30 am to 1.30 pm and 2 to 5 pm; admission is free.

The gardens also feature an **aquarium** in the Jawahar Bal Bhavan. It's open daily from 10.30 am to 5 pm except Sunday.

Nehru Zoological Park

One of the largest zoos in India, the Nehru Zoological Park is spread over 1.2 sq km of landscaped gardens with animals living in large, open enclosures. They don't look any less bored than animals in zoos anywhere else in the world, but at least an effort has been made here, which is more than can be said for most Indian zoos. There's also a prehistoric animal section, a toy train around the zoo (every 15 minutes, Rs 1) and a lion safari trip (every 15 minutes, Rs 5).

The park is across the Musi River, south of the city, and is open daily except Monday from 8.30 am to 5 pm; entry costs Rs 1, or Rs 20 if you're in a private car. Once again, it's chaos here on Sundays.

Tombs of Qutb Shahi Kings

These graceful domed tombs are about 1.5km north-west of Golconda's Balahisar Gate. They are surrounded by landscaped gardens, and a number of them have beautifully carved stonework. The tombs are open daily except Friday from 9.30 am to 4.30 pm and entrance costs Rs 2, plus Rs 5 if you have a camera (Rs 25 for a video camera). Most people walk from Golconda to the tombs, but there are usually a few auto-rickshaws willing to take you for a handsome price.

Organised Tours

The APTTDC (☎ 501519) conducts daily tours of the city which pick up at 7.45 am from Yatri Nivas Hotel, 8 am from Secunderabad railway station and 8.45 am from Gangan Vihar on Mozamjahi Rd and finish at 5.30 pm at the Birla Mandir. The cost is Rs 85 plus entry charges and includes a vegetarian lunch. The tours visit Buddha Purnima, Qutb Shahi Tombs, Golconda Fort, Salar Jung Museum, Mecca Masjid, Charminar, Nehru zoo, the inevitable handicrafts emporium, Birla Mandir Temple and the Planetarium.

Brief stops are all you'll get, but if you only have a day in town the tour is good value.

An interesting alternative is the *Deccan by Dusk* tour, also operated by the APTTDC, which visits Lumbini Park and the Qutb Shahi tombs before going on to Golconda Fort for a quick tour and the sound & light show. This tour departs Yatri Nivas Hotel at 2 pm and returns at 8.45 pm and costs Rs 60 per head (including ticket for sound & light show).

ANDHRA PRADESH

Places to Stay – bottom end

The best of the cheap hotels are all in the Nampally/Abids area between Abids Circle and Hyderabad (Nampally) railway station.

Royal Lodge, Royal Home, Royal Hotel, Neo Royal Hotel and *Gee Royal Lodge* are built around a courtyard opposite the station on Nampally High Rd (Public Gardens Rd). They're all very similar – count on Rs 75/150 for singles/doubles with attached bathroom and fans. Hot water is usually only available in the mornings.

New Asian Lodge (☎ 201275) across the road is a typical, no-frills Indian boarding house, but it's adequate at Rs 75/125 with attached bathroom and fan. Bucket hot water is available.

Apsara Hotel (☎ 502663) is 10 minutes walk south-east of the station on Station Rd, and has rooms for Rs 100/150 with attached bathroom (with bucket shower), fan and hot water in the mornings, but no TV.

Nithya Lodge (☎ 595317), upstairs in a shopping arcade on Station Rd nearer Abids Circle, is friendly and is also better value. Clean, straight rooms with bucket shower are Rs 200 inclusive of taxes; Star TV will cost you Rs 25 extra. There's no restaurant, but

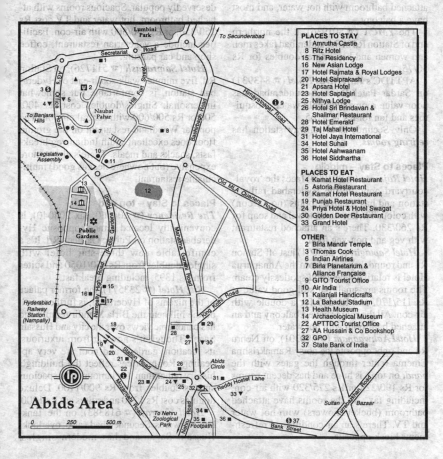

PLACES TO STAY
1 Amrutha Castle
8 Ritz Hotel
15 The Residency
16 New Asian Lodge
17 Hotel Rajmata & Royal Lodges
20 Hotel Saiprakash
21 Apsara Hotel
23 Hotel Saptagiri
25 Nithya Lodge
26 Hotel Sri Brindavan & Shalimar Restaurant
28 Hotel Emerald
29 Taj Mahal Hotel
31 Hotel Jaya International
34 Hotel Suhail
35 Hotel Aahwaanam
36 Hotel Siddhartha

PLACES TO EAT
4 Kamat Hotel Restaurant
5 Astoria Restaurant
18 Kamat Hotel Restaurant
19 Punjab Restaurant
24 Priya Hotel & Hotel Swagat
30 Golden Deer Restaurant
33 Grand Hotel

OTHER
2 Birla Mandir Temple
3 Thomas Cook
6 Indian Airlines
7 Birla Planetarium & Alliance Française
9 GITO Tourist Office
10 Air India
11 Kalanjali Handicrafts
12 La Bahadur Stadium
13 Health Museum
14 Archaeological Museum
22 APTTDC Tourist Office
27 AA Hussain & Co Bookshop
32 GPO
37 State Bank of India

Abids Area

0   250   500 m

ANDHRA PRADESH

there are plenty of places to eat quite close to the hotel.

Hotel Sri Brindavan (☎ 203970) on Station Rd near the junction with Abids Circle is also good value. It offers singles/doubles with attached bathroom for Rs 180/220. Hot water is available from 4 to 7.30 am. There are good vegetarian and non-veg restaurants. The rooms are arranged around a quiet courtyard and there's secure parking.

Hotel Suhail (☎ 510142) is clean and quiet with standard rooms for Rs 110/135, deluxe rooms for Rs 135/150 and air-con doubles for Rs 250. All the rooms have TV and attached bathroom with hot water, and most have a balcony.

The *YMCA* (☎ 801936) at the northern end of Station Rd in Secunderabad takes men and women and has singles/doubles for Rs 50/75.

APTTDC's *Yatri Nivas Hotel* (☎ 843931) on Sardar Patel Rd in Secunderabad has poor-value rooms with cold water, mosquitoes and fan for Rs 143/165.

Only Secunderabad railway station has *retiring rooms*.

Places to Stay – middle

Hotel Rajmata (☎ 201000) faces the 'royal' courtyard opposite the Hyderabad railway station and has 'deluxe' rooms (no air-con) with colour TV, hot water, towel and soap for Rs 260/330. There's an attached restaurant with veg and non-veg food.

Hotel Saptagiri (☎ 503601) just off Station Rd and round the corner from the Annapurna Hotel is relatively new and spotlessly clean. The rooms are small but still good value at Rs 115/170, and Rs 225 for a double with air-con. All the rooms have a balcony and an attached bathroom with hot water.

Hotel Aahwaanam (☎ 590301), off Nehru Rd and right opposite the noisy Ramakrishna Cinema (enter through the gates with the *nandi* on top), is huge and has decent rooms for Rs 190/225 or Rs 275/320 with air-con, including tax. All the rooms have attached bathroom (bucket showers) with hot water and TV. There's an air-conditioned refreshments kiosk opposite.

Hotel Jaya International (☎ 232929), in Reddy Hostel Lane off Bank St, has comfortable rooms for Rs 185/265 or Rs 400/500 with air-con and TV. There's no restaurant.

Hotel Siddhartha (☎ 590222), nearby on Bank St, is a quiet place with a grand foyer but lacklustre rooms. Singles/doubles cost Rs 225/275, or Rs 325/375 with air-con. There are also more expensive suites. The hotel has its own restaurant and air-conditioned coffee shop, plus secure parking.

Taj Mahal Hotel (☎ 237988), at the junction of MG and King Kothi rds, is a huge rambling place set in its own grounds and is deservedly popular. Spacious rooms with attached bathroom, hot water and TV cost Rs 250/350, or Rs 350/500 with air-con. Facilities include a vegetarian restaurant, coffee shop and car parking.

Hotel Saiprakash (☎ 511726), on Station Rd, five minutes walk south-east of Hyderabad station, is comfortable but somewhat impersonal. Singles/doubles cost Rs 400/500 or Rs 500/600 with central air-con. The popular Woodland restaurant on the ground floor does excellent south Indian veg breakfasts, snacks and meals. There's also a more expensive (but nowhere near as good) multi-cuisine restaurant.

Places to Stay – top end

The Residency (☎ 204060; fax 204040), is conveniently located almost opposite Hyderabad station on Public Gardens Rd. It's a comfortable new three-star hotel with singles/doubles from Rs 850/1050 and suites from Rs 1395, including breakfast.

Ritz Hotel (☎ 233571), the former palace of the nizams of Hyderabad, is further north on the hill near the Birla Mandir temple and has panoramic views over the city and Hussain Sagar. Though it's now far from luxurious, its location, gardens and pool are very appealing. Room prices reflect the building's history rather than its glamour, with spacious singles/doubles from Rs 900/1100. Deluxe doubles cost Rs 1200 and suites are Rs 1800.

Hotel Viceroy (☎ 618383), on the Tank-bund towards Secunderabad, also overlooks Hussain Sagar and has modern singles/

doubles for Rs 950/1150 plus suites for Rs 2300, including a buffet breakfast. This centrally air-con hotel has the usual facilities, including a pool.

Amrutha Castle (☎ 599899; fax 241850), on Secretariat Rd, must be the most bizarre hotel in India. Modelled on Mad King Ludwig's romantic Austrian folly, Neuschwanstein (by way of Disneyland and Camelot), this place has to be seen to be believed. Thoroughly modern, well-appointed rooms start at Rs 1000/2000, while suites range from Rs 1600 to Rs 3500. Facilities include fax in every room, restaurant, coffee shop, gym and a roof-top pool. As the glossy brochure exclaims, 'now its lot more than what the European Royal blue blood had exuberated'!

Most of the five-star hotels are on Road No 1 at Banjara Hills, west of Hussain Sagar. They're all centrally air-conditioned and have excellent restaurants and the full complement of facilities. All attract 20% sales tax.

Taj Residency (☎ 399999; fax 392218) is pleasantly situated on an artificial lake. Rates range from Rs 1900 to Rs 2800 in the 'executive' rooms including breakfast.

Holiday Inn Krishna (☎ 393939; fax 392682), just off Road No 1, has modern, luxurious rooms from Rs 2000 to Rs 4000.

Krishna Oberoi (☎ 392323; fax 393079) is a palatial hotel with rooms costing from Rs 2000 to Rs 8000.

Places to Eat

Hyderabad is justifiably proud of its delicious Andhran cuisine. Be warned: some of the vegetarian chilli dishes can be real tearjerkers. A few savoury specialities to look out for include *kulcha* (charcoal-baked bread), *biryani* (fragrant steamed rice with meat or vegetables), *haleen* (pounded wheat with a lightly spiced mutton sauce) and *nihari* (spiced tongue and trotters).

Grand Hotel, just around from the Hyderabad GPO, is far from grand but it has cheap non-veg local food such as biryani and mutton cutlets and is immensely popular at lunchtime.

Any *Kamat Hotel* dishes up good, cheap, south Indian vegetarian meals, with the standard fare costing from Rs 20. There's one in Secunderabad on Saronjini Devi Rd and another in Abids on AG's Office Rd opposite Indian Airlines.

Astoria Restaurant opposite the Kamat Hotel on AG's Office Rd is a popular open-air dinner spot.

Shalimar Restaurant, part of the Hotel Sri Brindavan on Station Rd, is one of the best cheap places to eat in Hyderabad. The food here is excellent and tasty. Soups are Rs 18, curries Rs 25-40 and vegetarian dishes Rs 20-40. It's open from 11 am to 11 pm daily.

Golden Deer on MG Rd, not far from Abids Circle, is more expensive, but a good choice for dinner. It specialises in Chinese/Indian meals starting around Rs 40, and is blissfully air-conditioned.

Paradise Garden Restaurant near the corner of Sardar Patel Rd and MG Rd in Secunderabad is famous for its authentic Hyderabadi cuisine. Established in 1953, this is *the* place to eat in Secunderabad, and prices are reasonable. It features two sections – an open-air patio serving both veg and non-veg fare, and a sidewalk takeaway area where you can get juicy kebabs, freshly baked rotis, oven-fresh biscuits and hot coffee.

The top-end hotels all have excellent restaurants and coffee shops, in particular the *Dakhni* at the Taj Residency and the *Firdau* at the Krishna Oberoi. These places often have entertainment to coincide with regional themes (check the ads in *Channel 6*), and it's not a bad idea to book ahead. Expect to pay at least Rs 250-500 per person. The Taj Residency's *Kabab-e-Bahar* is a less formal barbecue/kebab restaurant set outdoors on a small lake, with excellent veg and non-veg dishes for around Rs 100.

Things to Buy

Laad Bazaar near Charminar is the heart of old Hyderabad, and where you'll find Hyderabadi specialities such as pearls, glass and lac bangles, *bidri* ware and enamel jewellery. An interesting market closer to Abids is Sultan Bazaar at the end of Mahipatram Rd.

The best place to buy arts & crafts from all over India is Kalanjali on Nampally High

Rd. This shop is well laid out, has fixed prices, accepts credit cards, and will reliably send purchases anywhere round the world. It's open daily from 10 am to 8 pm. Also good is the Central Cottage Industries Emporium at 94 Minerva Complex on Sarojini Devi Rd, Secunderabad.

Getting There & Away

Air The Air India office (☎ 237243) is opposite the State Assembly on Assembly Rd. Indian Airlines (☎ 236902) is nearby on Secretariat Rd and is open daily from 10 am to 1 pm and 2 to 5.25 pm.

There are Indian Airlines flights in either direction between Hyderabad and Bangalore (daily, US$80), Mumbai (Bombay) (twice daily, US$90), Calcutta (daily except Thursday, US$170), Delhi (twice daily, US$165), Chennai (twice daily, US$80), Bhubaneswar (three times weekly, US$130), Nagpur (three times weekly, US$80) and Visakhapatnam (twice weekly, US$85).

Jet Airways (☎ 231263) flies daily to Bangalore, Mumbai and Calcutta. Skyline NEPC (☎ 243949) flies to Chennai daily (except Sunday), and to Mumbai and Visakhapatnam three times a week.

Bus Buses leave from the main APSRTC bus terminal at Gowliguda (☎ 513955) for all

Bus Services from Hyderabad

Destination	Frequency (daily)	Fare (Rs)
Aurangabad	2	120
Bangalore	9 mainly evening	175
Bidar	19	30
Mumbai	10	260
Gulbarga	7	75
Hospet	2	85
Kurnool	20	56
Chennai	1 at 4.30 pm	210
Nagpur	2	150
Nizamabad	32	50
Tirupathi	11	175
Vijayawada	30	85

parts of the state. The buses are well organised into separate bays, and there's an enquiry counter, a timetable in English and a computerised advance booking office which is open daily from 8 am to 9 pm.

There are also a number of private bus companies offering superdeluxe video services to Bangalore, Mumbai, Chennai, Nagpur and Tirupathi. Most of their offices are on Nampally High Rd close to the Hyderabad railway station entrance road; try Asian Travels (☎ 202128) inside the Asian Lodge. Most have one departure daily, usually in the late afternoon. To Bangalore or Nagpur it's Rs 220 and 12 hours; to Mumbai or Chennai it's Rs 250 and 14 hours.

Train Secunderabad is the main railway station and this is where you catch through trains (that is, all trains not originating in Hyderabad). However, trains starting at Hyderabad can be boarded here too. Bookings for any train can be made either at Hyderabad station or Secunderabad station Monday to Saturday from 8 am to 2 pm and 2.15 to 8 pm, and on Sunday from 8 am to 4 pm. Both stations have a tourist quota. For general enquiries call ☎ 131; for reservations, cancellations, availability etc call ☎ 135.

To Calcutta, you must first take a train to Vijayawada and then change to one of the east coast express trains such as the *Coromandel Express*. The fare to Calcutta is Rs 278/1062 in 2nd/1st class and the 1600km trip takes 32 hours.

Getting Around

The Airport The airport is at Begampet, about eight km north of Abids. There is no airport bus. An auto-rickshaw from Abids should cost about Rs 35 by the meter, though drivers usually refuse to use it for this ride so you'll have to haggle. Taxi drivers ask about Rs 100.

Bus Getting on any city bus in Hyderabad, other than at the terminus, is (as one traveller put it) 'like staging a banzai charge on

Guadalcanal'. He wasn't exaggerating! Buses you might find useful include:

No 2 – Secunderabad station to Charminar
No 7 – Secunderabad station to Afzalgunj and return (this is the one to catch if you're heading for Abids, as it goes down Tankbund and Nehru Rd via the GPO)
No 8 – connects Secunderabad and Hyderabad railway stations
Nos 119 & 142 – Nampally High Rd to Golconda Fort

Auto-Rickshaw & Taxi By the meter, autorickshaws cost Rs 6 for the first two km plus Rs 3 for each additional km. Most drivers need prompting to use the meter, and some may refuse, preferring a higher negotiated price. After 10 pm you may have to pay 50% of the return fare as well. A return trip to Golconda Fort by auto is around Rs 120-150, including waiting time.

Taxis cost about twice as much as autos.

Car You can rent a car and driver from the APTTDC for Rs 450 for a 6-hour day. The Krishna Oberoi will also arrange a car and driver for a half or full day for similar rates.

NAGARJUNAKONDA

Nagarjunakonda, about 150km south-east of Hyderabad on the Krishna River, was one of the largest and most important Buddhist centres in southern India from the 2nd century BC until the 3rd century AD. Known in those

days as Vijayapuri, Nagarjunakonda takes its present name from Nagarjuna, one of the most revered Buddhist monks, who governed the *sangha* for nearly 60 years around the turn of the 2nd century AD. The Madhyamika school he founded attracted students from as far afield as Sri Lanka and China.

The site was discovered in 1926. Subsequent excavations, particularly in the 1950s and 1960s, have unearthed the remains of *stupas*, *viharas*, *chaityas* and *mandapams*, as well as some outstanding examples of white marble carvings and sculptures depicting the life of the Buddha. The original site now lies under the reservoir created by the building of the enormous **Nagarjuna Sagar Dam** in 1960. But before the flooding many of the buildings were removed and reconstructed within the walls of the nearby hilltop fort, now an island in the middle of the reservoir.

As well as the reconstructed buildings, statues, friezes, coins, jewellery and prehistoric artefacts found at the site are housed in a museum on the island and give a fascinating insight into the daily lives of the ancient Buddhist city.

The **Nagarjunakonda Museum** is open daily except Friday. Launches depart from Vijayapuri, on the banks of Nagarjuna Sagar, at 9.30 am and 1.30 pm. The one hour trip costs Rs 25 per person. Each launch departs the island 30 minutes after it arrives, which is long enough for a quick whip around the

Train Services from Hyderabad

Destination	Train Number & Name	Departure Time	Distance (km)	Duration (hours)	Fare (Rs) (2nd/1st)
Aurangabad	7664 Secunderabad-Aurangabad Exp	7.05 pm S	517	13.25	139/478
Bangalore	5092 Gorakhpur-Bangalore Exp	6.20 pm S	790	15.50	185/669
Mumbai	7032 Hyderabad-Mumbai Exp	8.20 pm S	800	17.15	189/669
Calcutta	8046 East Coast Exp	6.45 am H	1591	30.00	278/1062
Chennai	7054 Hyderabad-Madras Exp	3.45 pm H	794	14.25	189/669
Delhi	2723 Andhra Pradesh Exp	6.20 am H	1397	26.20	263/965
	7021 H Nizamuddin Exp	8.00 pm H		33.30	
Tirupathi	7603 Venkatadri Exp	3.50 pm S	741	17.40	186/642

Abbreviations for train stations: S – Secunderabad, H – Hyderabad

exhibits, but to do the place justice take the morning launch out to the island and the afternoon launch back.

Places to Stay
The choice of accommodation maintained by the APTTDC includes the *Vijay Vihar Complex* (☎ (08680) 76325) close to the boat jetty at Vijayapuri, which has double rooms with air-con for Rs 300 and cottages for Rs 400 and *Project House* (☎ (08680) 76240), several km away at Hill Colony (doubles Rs 125). There's also a *youth hostel* in Hill Colony.

Getting There & Away
The easiest way to visit Nagarjunakonda from Hyderabad is to take the tour organised by the APTTDC (☎ 816375). It departs Hyderabad daily (if demand warrants it) at 6.30 am from Yatri Nivas Hotel, returns at 9.30 pm and costs Rs 170, lunch included. The tour includes visits to the Nagarjunakonda Museum (closed Friday), Pylon (an engraved granite monolith from the Buddhist period), Nagarjuna Sagar, Ethipothala Waterfalls and a working model of the dam.

If you'd prefer to make your own way there, regular buses link Hyderabad, Vijayawada and Guntur with Nagarjuna Sagar. The nearest railway station is 22km away at Macherla (a branch line running west from Guntur) from where buses leave regularly for Nagarjuna Sagar.

WARANGAL
Pop: 537,000   Tel Area Code: 08712
About 150km north-east of Hyderabad, Warangal ('one stone' hill) was once the capital of the Kakatiya kingdom which spanned the greater part of present-day Andhra Pradesh from the latter half of the 12th century until it was conquered by the Tughlaqs of Delhi early in the 14th century. The Hindu Kakatiyas were great builders and patrons of the arts, and it was during their reign that the Chalukyan style of temple architecture and decoration reached the pinnacle of its development.

If you have an interest in the various branches of Hindu temple development and have either visited or intend to visit the early Chalukyan sites at Badami, Aihole and Pattadakal in neighbouring Karnataka state, then an outing to Warangal is worthwhile. Facilities are adequate for an overnight stop, or it can be visited in a long day trip from Hyderabad.

There's a colourful **wool market** a couple of hundred metres past the bus stand.

Fort
Warangal's main attraction is the enormous, abandoned mud-brick fort, which has a terrific atmosphere and many interesting features. Carved stones from wrecked Chalukyan temples are set indiscriminately in the massive stone walls which form a distinct fortification almost a km inside the outer mud walls.

Chalukyan Temples
The most notable remaining Chalukyan temples are the **1000-Pillared Temple** on the slopes of Hanamkonda Hill (one shrine of which is still in use), the **Bhadrakali Temple** on a hillock between Warangal and Hanamkonda, and the Shambu Lingeswara or **Swayambhu Temple** (originally a Siva temple). Built in 1162, the 1000-Pillared Temple is, however, inferior to those found further south. It's in a sad state of disrepair, and looters have removed many of the best pieces and chiselled away the faces of statues.

Places to Stay & Eat
Accommodation facilities are modest. Most of the hotels are on Station Rd, which runs parallel to the railway line; turn left as you leave the station.

Vijya Lodge (☎ 25851) on Station Rd, three minutes from the railway station, is OK value at Rs 70/100.

Hotel Shanthi Krishna (☎ 25305) also on Station Rd, behind the post office, is similar.

Vikas Lodge (☎ 24194), up behind the bus stand and near the huge market, has basic rooms with bathroom for Rs 50/70.

Ashok (☎ 85491), which is on Main Rd at Hanamonda, is seven km from Warangal railway station and has single/doubles for Rs 150/200.

There are *retiring rooms* at the railway station.

Getting There & Away

Regular buses run between Warangal and Hyderabad, Nizamabad and other major centres. Local buses connect Warangal with Kazipet and Hanamkonda.

Warangal is a major railway junction and there are regular trains to Hyderabad or Secunderabad (152km, three hours, Rs 62/184 in 2nd/1st class) and to Vijayawada (209km, four hours, Rs 71/229 in 2nd/1st class).

Getting Around

The bus stand is directly opposite the entrance to the railway station. Bus No 28 will take you the five km to the fort at Mantukonda. Otherwise, it would be worth negotiating a fixed price for an auto-rickshaw to take you there and back.

VISAKHAPATNAM

Pop: 1.15 million   Tel Area Code: 0891

This coastal city is the commercial and industrial heart of Andhra Pradesh's isolated north-east corner, and is home to India's largest shipbuilding yard. Originally it was two separate towns – the northern and more urbane Waltair and the southern port town of Visakhapatnam (known as Vizag). However, as Vizag grew (and continues to rapidly do so), the pair gradually merged.

These days the twin towns have little to offer tourists and the pall of industrial smoke that hangs in the air makes them unenticing. Vizag's best known sight is the rocky promontory known as the **Dolphin's Nose** jutting into the harbour. The hilly seaside area of Waltair is edged by long beaches affording views across the Bay of Bengal and the busy Calcutta-Chennai shipping lane.

At Simhachalam Hill, 10km north of town, there's an 11th century **Vishnu temple** in fine Orissan style. The best beach is **Rishikonda**, also about 10km north.

The APSRTC (☎ 546400) operates full-day

tours of Vizag and Waltair for Rs 75 per person.

Orientation & Information

The railway station and bus stand are about 1.5km apart. Both are about 2km from the city centre, based loosely around the Poorna market area. The beach hotels are all located in Waltair, which is the most pleasant place to stay.

The tourist office in the railway station has precious little information.

Places to Stay & Eat

There's no shortage of places to stay to suit all budgets. The *retiring rooms* at the railway station include men-only dorm beds for Rs 10 and comfortable doubles at Rs 125.

City Centre A good area for cheap hotels is Main Rd near the Poorna Market.

Hotel Poorna (☎ 62344) is down an alley off Main Rd, and has clean singles/doubles with attached bathroom from Rs 70/100.

Hotel Prasanth (☎ 65282) opposite is similar with rooms for Rs 75/120.

Swagath Restaurant nearby on Main Rd has a small rooftop garden and cheap vegetarian meals and snacks.

Hotel Daspalla (☎ 564825) has rooms for Rs 300/370, or Rs 750/880 with air-con. The three-star hotel has several restaurants serving Chinese, Continental and tandoori meals as well as *dakshin*, the spicy non-veg local cuisine.

Dolphin Hotels Limited (☎ 567000) is a centrally located four-star place with a swimming pool and restaurant. Singles/doubles range from Rs 495/695 to Rs 1195/1395, and breakfast is included in rooms priced above Rs 695/895.

Beach Area

Palm Beach Hotel (☎ 554026) at the northern end of Beach Rd is old and run-down, but it's OK if you just want to be close to the beach. Rooms are Rs 200/250 or Rs 300/400 with air-con.

Park Hotel (☎ 554488; fax 554181), next door, looks old and ugly from the outside but the rooms are modern and comfortable. Air-conditioned rooms, all with a sea view, cost Rs 1150/1950. There's a swimming pool, bookshop and three restaurants, and the management is friendly.

Taj Residency (☎ 567756; fax 564370), Vizag's best, is a luxurious, tiered hotel that climbs the hill from Beach Rd. It has a swimming pool and a restaurant, and room prices range from Rs 1500 to Rs 4000 plus 20% tax.

Getting There & Away

Vizag's airport is 13km west of town; Rs 45 by auto-rickshaw. Indian Airlines (☎ 546501) flies to Calcutta (US$115) and Chennai (US$90) daily except Wednesday and Sunday, and to Hyderabad (US$85) on Monday and Saturday. NEPC Airlines (☎ 574151) flies Thursday and Saturday to Chennai (US$105) and Wednesday and Friday to Calcutta (US$125) via Bhubaneswar (US$82). Skyline NEPC (☎ 574151) flies to Mumbai (US$182) via Hyderabad (US$78) on Wednesday, Friday and Sunday.

Visakhapatnam Junction railway station is on the main Calcutta to Chennai line. To Calcutta the best train is the overnight *Coromandel Express* (879km, 15 hours, Rs 202/689 in 2nd/1st class). Heading south, the same train goes to Vijayawada (352km, 5½ hours, Rs 104/359) and Chennai Central (784km, 17 hours, Rs 189/669).

From the well-organised bus terminal, the APSRTC (☎ 546400) has services to destinations within Andhra Pradesh, as well as Puri in Orissa.

AROUND VISAKHAPATNAM

About 25km north-east of Vizag is **Bheemunipatnam**, one of the safest beaches on this part of the coast. It's also the site of the ruins of the east coast's oldest Dutch settlement. A little way inland from here is **Hollanders Green**, the Dutch cemetery.

Some 90km north of Vizag are the million-year old limestone **Borra Caves** which are filled with fascinating stalagmite and stalactite formations. A further 30km north is the **Araku Valley**, home to a number of isolated tribal communities.

VIJAYAWADA
Tel Area Code: 0866

On the banks of the mighty Krishna River, Vijayawada is a major railway junction on the east coast line from Calcutta to Chennai. About 265km east of Hyderabad, it's an important industrial centre and a fairly hectic town. Few travellers stop here but it's the most convenient place from which to visit Amaravathi.

In Vijayawada itself, there are a number of important Hindu temples including the **Kanaka Durga Temple** on Indrakila Hill, as well as two 1000 year old **Jain temples**. About eight km from Vijayawada, across the river, are the ancient Hindu cave temples of **Undavalil**.

There is a tourist information kiosk at the railway station.

Places to Stay & Eat

The noisy *retiring rooms* at the railway station cost Rs 50/100.

Modern Cafe Lodging (☎ 73171), close to the railway station on Besant Rd, has rooms from Rs 60 with the use of a very smelly common toilet.

Hanuman Dormitory at the bus terminal looks more like a hospital ward than somewhere you'd voluntarily spend the night, but it's cheap at Rs 12 for 24 hours.

Hotel Swapna Lodge (☎ 65386) on Durgaiah St near the Navrang Theatre, about two km from the railway station, offers the best value among the cheapies. It's on a quiet backstreet and is friendly and clean. Rooms cost Rs 75/100.

Sree Lakshmi Vilas Modern Cafe (☎ 62525) on Besant Rd at Governorpet, a bustling shopping district about 1.5km from the railway station, has rooms with common bathroom for Rs 65/80, or Rs 80/125 with attached bath. The hotel has a good vegetarian restaurant.

Hotel Raj Towers (☎ 61311), on Congress Office Rd, 1.5km from the railway station, has rooms with attached bathroom for Rs 200/300 and Rs 300/400 with air-con.

Hotel Manorama (☎ 77220), on MG Rd

about 500m from the new bus terminal, is similar, with rooms with attached bathroom for Rs 250/300, or Rs 300/400 with air-con.

Hotel Ilapuram (☎ 61282) on Besant Rd is one of the best value places in town. Singles/doubles are Rs 300/400, or Rs 400/500 with air-con and there are more expensive suites. The hotel has both non-veg and veg restaurants.

Most of the mid-range hotels have reasonably priced restaurants.

Hotel Nandini near the bus terminal, serves standard South Indian veg meals.

Modern Bakery & Ice-Cream Parlour on Besant Rd is OK for snacks.

Getting There & Away

Air The airport is 20km from the city. NEPC Airlines (☎ 476493) flies to Chennai and Visakhapatnam on Tuesday, Thursday and Saturday.

Bus The enormous bus terminal on Bandar Rd near the river is about 1.5km from the railway station. It's well organised and has dormitories, waiting rooms and a restaurant. From here, buses travel to all parts of Andhra Pradesh; every 30 minutes to Hyderabad (six hours), eight times daily to Warangal (six hours) and Visakhapatnam seven times daily (10 hours), as well as to Chennai twice daily (10 hours).

Train Vijayawada is on the main Chennai to Calcutta and Chennai to Delhi lines and all the express trains stop here. The quickest train from Vijayawada to Chennai is the *Coromandel Express* (seven hours, Rs 124/427 in 2nd/1st class). The same train to Calcutta (20 hours) costs Rs 251/917.

There are plenty of trains via Warangal to Hyderabad (6½ hours, Rs 109/368); one of the quickest is the *Godavari Express*. The *Tamil Nadu Express* to New Delhi (27 hours) costs Rs 293/1164 in 2nd/1st class.

To Tirupathi (nine hours), the daily *Howrah-Tirupathi Express* costs Rs 88/297 in 2nd/1st class. Heading north to Puri (Orissa), take the *Howrah-Tirupathi Express* to the junction,

Khurda Road, then a passenger train or bus for the last 44km to Puri.

There are also direct weekly trains to Kanyakumari and Bangalore, trains four times weekly to Varanasi and daily to Thiruvananthapuram (Trivandrum).

AROUND VIJAYAWADA
Amaravathi

Some 30km due west of Vijayawada, near the bank of the Krishna River, stands the ancient Buddhist centre of Amaravathi, the former capital of the Satvahanas, the successors to the Mauryas in this part of India. Here you can see the 2000 year old **stupa** with its intricately carved pillars and marble-surfaced dome which itself is equally richly carved. The carvings depict the life of the Buddha as well as scenes from everyday life. It's not as large as that at Sanchi in Madhya Pradesh but it's worth a visit if you're interested in Buddhist relics of the Hinayana era. There's a **museum** on the site containing relics found in the area.

Direct buses from Vijayawada to Amaravathi are few and far between, so it's better to take one of the hourly buses south to Guntur and then another bus from there. All up, the 65km trip takes two to three hours and costs about Rs 25. The APTTDC also organises bus tours for Rs 60 as well as boat trips for Rs 75 return. Ask at the tourist information kiosk at Vijayawada railway station or at the APTTDC's counter at the Krishnaveni Motel (☎ 426382), Sitanagaram, in Vijayawada.

TIRUMALA & TIRUPATHI
Tel Area Code: 08574

The 'holy hill' of Tirumala in the extreme south of Andhra Pradesh is one of the most important pilgrimage centres in India, and is claimed to be the busiest in the world – eclipsing Jerusalem, Rome and Mecca in its sheer number of pilgrims.

Tirumala is an engrossing place where you can easily spend a whole day just wandering around. It's one of the few temples in India which allows non-Hindus into the sanctum sanctorum but, despite this, the place sees few foreign visitors.

On the flip side, because it hosts an army of pilgrims from all over India everything at Tirumala and at its service town of Tirupathi, 20km away, is organised to keep visitors fed, sheltered and moving. Most are housed in special pilgrims' *choultries* in both Tirupathi and Tirumala. However, the private hotels and lodges are in Tirupathi, so a fleet of buses constantly ferries pilgrims up and down the hill between Tirupathi and Tirumala from before dawn until well after dusk.

Venkateshwara Temple
Pilgrims flock to Tirumala to visit the ancient temple of Venkateshwara, an avatar of Vishnu. This is the god whose picture graces the reception areas of most lodges and restaurants in southern India, with his eyes covered (since his gaze would scorch the world) and garlanded in so many flowers that only his feet are visible.

Among the powers attributed to Venkateshwara is the granting of any wish that is made in front of the idol at Tirumala; and so the millions come. There are never less than 5000 pilgrims here at any one time and, in a single day, the total is often as high as 100,000. The temple staff alone number nearly 6000!

Such popularity makes the temple one of the richest in India, with an annual income of a staggering five billion rupees. This is administered by a temple trust which ploughs the bulk of the money back into hundreds of choultries and charities such as homes for the poor, orphanages, craft training centres, schools, colleges and art academies.

It's considered auspicious to have your head shaved when visiting the temple, and if you see people with shaved heads in south India, you can be pretty sure they've recently been to Tirupathi – this applies to men, women and children.

As you face the entrance to the temple, there is a small **museum** at the top of the steps to the left. Among other things, it has a good collection of musical instruments, including a tabla-type drum called a *ubangam*! The museum is open from 8 am to 8 pm and entry is Rs 1.

Organised Tours
The APTTDC runs weekend tours to Tirupathi from Hyderabad. The tours leave at 3.30 pm on Friday and return at 7 am on Monday and include accommodation and 'special darshan'. The cost is Rs 600. It's also possible to take the bus only; this costs Rs 150 one way.

Daily tours to Tirupathi are also run from Chennai (for details see the Organised Tours section in the Chennai chapter).

Places to Stay
Tirupathi Tirupathi is the town at the bottom of the hill and the transport hub. It has plenty of hotels and lodges, so there's no problem finding somewhere to stay. A number of hotels are clustered around the main bus terminal, 500m from the centre of town and there are also *retiring rooms* at the railway station.

Special Darshan at Tirumala
After paying Rs 30 for 'special darshan', you'll be allowed to enter Tirumala's Venkateshwara Temple. Special darshan means you can go in ahead of all those who have paid nothing for their ordinary *darshan* (viewing of a god) and who have to queue – often for 12 hours or more – in the claustrophobic wire cages which ring the outer wall of the temple.

Although special darshan is supposed to get you to the front of this immense queue in two hours, on weekends when the place is much busier it can take as long as five hours, and you still have to go through the cages. A signboard at the entrance tells you how long you can expect it to take. To find the start of the queue, follow the signs to 'Sarvadarshanam', around to the left of the temple entrance.

Once inside the temple, you'll have to keep shuffling along with everyone else and, before you know it, you'll have viewed Venkateshwara and will be back outside again. ■

Vasantha Vihar Lodge (☎ 20460), 141 G Car St, is a friendly place about a minutes walk from the railway station. It has small, basic single/double rooms for Rs 45/70 with fan and attached shower.

Bhimas Hotel (☎ 25744) a block away at 42 G Car St, has rooms for Rs 65/200 and doubles with air-con for Rs 450.

Bhimas Deluxe Hotel (☎ 25521), opposite at 34-38 G Car St, is a two-star hotel with air-con rooms for Rs 400/550. All the rooms have attached bathroom and TV.

Hotel Mayura (☎ 25925; fax 25911) at 209 TP Area is a three-star hotel close to the main bus terminal. Rooms with attached bathroom cost Rs 395, or Rs 500/695 with air-con. There's a restaurant serving Indian and Mughlai cuisine.

Tirumala Most pilgrims stay in the vast *dormitories* which ring the temple – beds here are free and open to anyone. If you want to stay, check in at the accommodation reception and you'll be allocated a bed or a room. It's best to avoid weekends when the place becomes outrageously crowded.

Places to Eat
Tirupathi A good vegetarian restaurant *Lakshmi Narayana Bhavan* is opposite the main bus terminal.

The *Bhimas Hotel* also has a good vegetarian restaurant, including an air-conditioned dining hall.

The *Bhimas Deluxe Hotel's* popular basement restaurant serves north and south Indian food until late at night – the Kashmiri naan here is an extravagance to behold.

Tirumala Huge *dining halls* serve thousands of free meals daily to keep the pilgrims happy. Other than that, there are a few no-frills, banana-leaf *meals* places.

Getting There & Away
Air Tirupathi's airport has been closed for upgrading for some time but flights from here to Chennai, Hyderabad and Mumbai may now have resumed. The Indian Airlines office (☎ 22349) is in the Hotel Vishnupriya

complex, opposite the main bus terminal in Tirupathi.

Bus It's possible to visit Tirupathi on a long day trip from Chennai, but staying overnight makes it far less rushed.

Tamil Nadu's state bus company has express buses (route No 802) from the TTC/JJTC bus terminal in Chennai at 8.15 am, 3.30 and 8.30 pm. Ordinary buses are more frequent but much slower. The express buses take about four hours to do the 150km trip, cost Rs 35 and can be booked in advance in Chennai.

To Chennai, there are express buses from Tirupathi's main bus terminal at 9.45 and 11.15 am, 12.15, 2.45, 3.10 and 8.30 pm.

Most buses to Hyderabad (12 hours, Rs 175) leave in the late afternoon. There are hourly buses to Vijayawada (Rs 130) as well as plenty of services to Vellore (2½ hours, Rs 175) in neighbouring Tamil Nadu.

Train Tirupathi is well served by express trains. There are four trains daily to Chennai (147km, three hours) which cost Rs 62/181 in 2nd/1st class.

The daily *Venkatadri Express* runs to Secunderabad (741km, 17½ hours, Rs 186/642 in 2nd/1st class) and there are three daily express trains to Vijayawada (389km, nine hours, Rs 111/388). There's also an express train to Madurai (663km, 18 hours, Rs 167/590) via Vellore, Chidambaram and Tiruchirappalli, as well as a twice weekly service to Mumbai (1132km, 31 hours, Rs 242/865).

Getting Around
Bus Tirumala Link buses operate from two bus stands in Tirupathi: the main bus terminal which is about 500m from the centre of town and the Tirumala bus stand near the railway station. The 20km trip takes 45 minutes and costs Rs 10/20 one way/return on an ordinary bus, or Rs 15/30 on an 'express' bus.

To get on a bus in either Tirupathi or Tirumala, you usually have to go through a system of crowd-control wire cages which are definitely not for the claustrophobic. At busy times (weekends and festivals), it can take up to two hours to file through the cages and get onto a bus. If you're staying in Tirupathi, it's worth buying a return ticket which saves you some queuing time in the cages at the top of the hill. You can avoid going through the cages at Tirupathi by catching a bus from the main bus terminal (where there are no cages), but if you decide to leave from the Tirumala bus stand near Tirupathi railway station, you will have to go through them.

Finding the queue for the buses at the Tirumala bus stand in Tirupathi can also be a task. You must walk through a choultry to reach the cages and ticket office – the choultry is about 200m from the entry to Tirupathi railway station (turn to the right as you exit the station) opposite the bottom of the footbridge over the railway line.

The one-way road to Tirumala winds precariously upwards and the bus drivers have perfected the art of maniacal driving. The road they drive down is the old one and is very narrow and winding. It has 57 hairpin bends, which means 57 adrenalin rushes for you as the buses hurtle down – the whole experience is total lunacy.

Taxi If you're in a hurry, or don't like the cages, there are share taxis available all the time. Seats cost around Rs 40, depending on demand. A taxi to yourself costs about Rs 250 one way.

PUTTAPARTHI
Prasanthi Nilayam, the main ashram of Sri Sathya Sai Baba, is in Puttaparthi. Sai Baba's followers are predominantly Indian (and include former Prime Minister Narasimha Rao) but he also has many western devotees, among them the founder of the Hard Rock Cafe franchise.

Known as the **Abode of Highest Peace**, the ashram is spacious and beautiful with good food and accommodation – at least when the numbers aren't overwhelming. Sai Baba spends most of the year here but sometimes moves to Whitefields Ashram near Bangalore in neighbouring Karnataka or Kodaikanal in Tamil Nadu during the hot, dry season.

Getting There & Away
Puttaparthi is in the south-western corner of Andhra Pradesh, most easily reached from Bangalore (see that section in the Karnataka chapter for details). Indian Airlines flies to Puttaparthi from both Chennai (Wednesday and Sunday, US$55) and Mumbai (Monday and Thursday, US$110).

AROUND PUTTAPARTHI
If you're travelling between Puttaparthi and Bangalore, it's worth making a detour to visit the **Veerabhadra temple** at Lepakshi, built in the Vijayanagar style and notable for its beautifully executed murals and its monolithic Nandi, India's largest, which stands 4½m high and 8½m long.

Kerala

Kerala, the land of green magic, is a narrow, fertile strip on the south-west coast of India, sandwiched between the Lakshadweep Sea and the Western Ghats. The landscape is dominated by rice fields, mango and cashew-nut trees and, above all, coconut palms. The Western Ghats, with their dense tropical forests, misty peaks, extensive ridges and ravines, have sheltered Kerala from mainland invaders and encouraged maritime contact with the outside world.

People have been sailing to Kerala in search of spices, sandalwood and ivory for at least 2000 years. Long before Vasco da Gama led the Portuguese to India, the coast had been known to the Phoenicians, then the Romans, and later the Arabs and Chinese. The Arabs initially controlled the shipment of spices to Europe, which motivated the Portuguese to find a sea route to India to break the Arab monopoly. In those days Kerala was not only a spice centre in its own right, but a transhipment point for spices from the Moluccas. And it was through Kerala that Chinese products and ideas found their way to the west. Even today, local fishers use Chinese-style fishing nets.

Such long contact with people from overseas has resulted in an intriguing blend of cultures and given Malayalams (natives of Kerala) a cosmopolitan outlook, coupled with a tradition of seeking their fortunes elsewhere in India or overseas. You can generally find a Malayalam in any nook or cranny of the world.

The present-day state of Kerala was created in 1956 from Travancore, Cochin and Malabar. Malabar was formerly part of Madras State, while both Travancore and Cochin were princely states ruled by maharajas. The maharajas of Travancore and Cochin paid considerable attention to the provision of basic services and education, and it was this early concern for public welfare which resulted in the post-Independence state being one of the most progressive, literate and highly educated in India.

KERALA AT A GLANCE

Population: 33 million
Area: 38,864 sq km
Capital: Thiruvananthapuram
Main Language: Malayalam
Literacy Rate: 91%
Best Time to Go: October to March.

Locator & Map Index

The external boundaries of India on this map have not been authenticated and may not be correct.

- Kozhikode (Calicut) p1033
- Thrissur p1032
- Kochi (Cochin) p1020
- Fort Cochin p1022
- Ernakulam p1024
- Alappuzha to Kollam p1011
- Kottayam p1013
- Alappuzha (Alleppey) p1010
- Periyar Wildlife Sanctuary p1015
- Kollam (Quilon) p1008
- Varkala p1006
- Thiruvananthapuram (Trivandrum) p994
- Kovalam Beach p1000

Highlights
- Exploring the backwaters aboard a *kettuvallam* (rice-barge houseboat)
- An evening of Kathakali dance theatre
- Sun, surf and seafood on the beach at Kovalam
- An early morning cruise on Lake Periyar

Festivals
Pooram Festival – Thrissur – April/May

Another of Kerala's distinctions was that it had the first freely elected communist government in the world (elected in 1957). Communists have been in and out of office ever since

The relatively equitable distribution of land and income, found rarely to the same degree elsewhere in India, is the direct result of successive communist governments in the state. Kerala's progressive social policies have had other benefits: infant mortality in Kerala is the lowest in India, and the literacy rate of around 90% is the highest in the country.

Perhaps more than anywhere else in India, getting around Kerala can be half the fun, particularly on the backwater trips along the coastal lagoons. Even an agonisingly slow train trip can be a restful experience when you're in Kerala – watching the canals and palm trees cruising past the open windows

---

A REGIONAL HIGHLIGHT

The Backwaters

Fringing the coast of Kerala and winding far inland is a complex network of lagoons, lakes, rivers and canals. These backwaters are both the basis of a distinct lifestyle and a fascinating thoroughfare. Travelling by boat along the backwaters is one of the highlights of a visit to Kerala. The boats cross shallow, palm-fringed lakes studded with cantilevered Chinese fishing nets, and travel along narrow, shady canals where coir (coconut fibre), copra (dried coconut meat) and cashews are loaded onto boats.

Along the way are small settlements where people live on narrow spits of land only a few metres wide. Though practically surrounded by water, they still manage to keep cows, pigs, chickens and ducks and cultivate small vegetable gardens. On the more open stretches of canal, traditional boats with huge sails and prows carved into the shape of dragons drift by. The sight of three or four of these sailing towards you in the late afternoon sun is unforgettable.

Tourist Cruises The most popular backwater cruise is the eight hour trip between Kollam and Alappuzha (or vice versa). The regular public ferry service on this route has been suspended for some years due to a canal blockage at the Kollam end. Tourist boats are, however, more popular than ever. There are virtually identical daily cruises operated on alternate days by the private Alleppey Tourist Development Co-Op (ATDC) (Rs 150) and the state government District Tourism Promotion Council (DTPC) (Rs 175). Many hotels in Kollam and Alappuzha take bookings for one or other of these services.

Each cruise departs at 10.30 am and gets to the other end at 6.30 pm. A 30 minute bus ride, included in the fare, operates between Kollam and Panmana, past the canal blockage. The KTDC claims the blockage will finally be removed some time in 1997, but don't hold your breath.

Generally only two major stops are made along the way, a midday lunch stop and a brief afternoon chai stop. Ayiramthengu or the coir village of Thrikkunnappuha are popular stopping places. The crew have an ice box full of fruit, soft drinks and beer to sell, although you might want to bring along additional refreshments and snacks. Bring sunscreen and a hat as well; sitting on the roof is pleasant, but the sun can really burn.

The boat also pauses to drop visitors off at the **Matha Amrithanandamayi Mission** (☎ 0475-78) at Amrithapuri. This is the residence and headquarters of Sri Sri Matha Amrithanandamayi Devi, one of India's very few (but in this case very much revered) female gurus. Visitors should dress conservatively and there is a strict code of behaviour that all visitors are expected to adhere to.

If you want to stay at the ashram, food and accommodation are available for Rs 50, and you can pick up an onward or return cruise a day or two later. The trip also passes the **Kumarakody Temple**, where the noted Malayalam poet Kumaran Asan drowned. Close to Alappuzha, there's a glimpse of the 11th century **Karumadi Kuttan Buddha image** close to the canal bank.

Public Ferries Most passengers on the eight-hour Kollam-Alappuzha cruise will be western travellers. If you want the local experience, or you simply want a shorter trip, there are still State Water Transport boats from Alappuzha to Kottayam (six boats daily; 2½ hours; Rs 6) and Changanassery (two boats daily; three hours; Rs 8). The trip to Kottayam crosses the Vembanad Lake and then runs along a fascinating canal, making an interesting contrast to the longer trip. See the Alappuzha and Kottayam sections for more information on the public ferries.

The DTPC also runs a popular four hour cruise which departs from Alappuzha at 10 am and returns at 2 pm. This cruise is run daily during December and January, and on weekends during the rest of the year. The cost is Rs 100 or Rs 60 concession. Many people prefer this shorter trip to a full day on a boat, and it also navigates some of the narrower waterways, enabling a more intimate glimpse of backwater life.

of your carriage at 20 km/h can be bring on a state of near-spiritual inertia.

The state also has some of the best and most picturesque beaches in India: Kovalam, a little south of the capital Thiruvananthapuram (Trivandrum), is one of the most popular beaches with travellers. The new resort at Varkala beach is a lot less developed, but heading in the same direction as Kovalam – visit while it's still pleasantly understated.

Best of all, Kerala has an easy-going, relaxed atmosphere unlike the bustle you find elsewhere in India.

A REGIONAL HIGHLIGHT

Houseboats & Charters An increasingly popular, but more expensive option is to hire a houseboat, converted from a *kettuvallam* or traditional rice barge. Several of these houseboats are now available through the DTPC in Kollam and Alappuzha, catering for groups (up to eight bunks) or for couples (one or two double bedrooms). They can be hired either on a day-charter basis (Rs 3500 per boat) or overnight (Rs 5000), allowing you to make the Kollam-Alappuzha trip over two days, mooring in the backwaters overnight. Delicious traditional Keralan food can be provided (including a cook) for an additional Rs 350 per person.

The DTPC also hires four-seat speed boats for Rs 300 per hour, and slower six-seaters for Rs 200 per hour. Between a group of people, this can be a quite economical proposition and allows you to make stops and plan your own itinerary – an option not available on the public ferries or tourist cruises.

Backwater Ecology Although the backwaters have become an important tourist attraction, they are severely threatened by population growth and industrial and agricultural development. Kerala has 29 major lakes on the backwater system, seven of which drain to the sea. It's estimated that the area of these lakes has fallen from 440 sq km in 1968 to less than 350 sq km today due to legal and illegal land reclamation projects and urban development. The vast Vembanad Lake has dropped from 230 to 179 sq km. The modern backwaters are now only one-third their mid-19th century levels.

Ecological damage includes pollution, the extinction of mangroves, crocodiles and migratory fish and the destruction of oyster beds. Many migratory birds no longer visit the backwaters and destructive fishing (using dynamite, poison and very fine nets) has caused great damage. To the casual eye, the most visible danger is the unhindered spread of water hyacinth (African moss or Nile cabbage), which clogs many stretches of canal and causes great difficulties for the boat operators. ∎

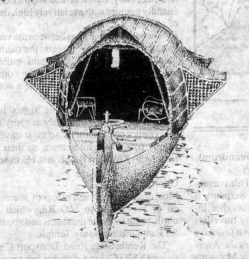

Hiring your own houseboat is one of the most relaxing ways to see the Backwaters. The Traditional rice barges have been converted into self-contained houseboats which allow you to cruise the canals at your own pace.

Name Changes

A number of towns and districts have been stripped of their anglicised names and given Malayalam names, but these are far from universally used. The major places affected include:

Old Name	New Name
Alleppey	Alappuzha
Calicut	Kozhikode
Cannanore	Kannur
Changanacherry	Changanassery
Cochin	Kochi
Palghat	Palakkad
Quilon	Kollam
Sultan's Battery	Suthanbatheri
Tellicherry	Thalasseri
Trichur	Thrissur
Trivandrum	Thiruvananthapuram

managed to retain some of the ambience characteristic of Kerala – red-tiled roofs, narrow winding lanes, intimate corner cafes, and necessary business accomplished in a friendly manner with a relatively high degree of efficiency.

When political tensions between the various factions erupt onto the streets, the calm can quickly fade and political slogans, emblems and flags – especially those of the communist and Muslim parties – become a notable feature of the urban landscape.

There is little in the way of 'sights' in the city. The famous Sri Padmanabhaswamy Temple is only open to Hindus, so most travellers simply pass through the town on their way to or from Kovalam Beach just 16km south.

Orientation

Most of the services and places of interest are on or very close to MG Rd, which runs north-south from the museums and zoo to the Sri Padmanabhaswamy Temple.

The Kerala State Road Transport Corporation (KSRTC) long-distance bus terminal, railway station, tourist reception centre and

Southern Kerala

THIRUVANANTHAPURAM (Trivandrum)

Pop: 854,000   Tel Area Code: 0471

Built over seven forested hills, Thiruvananthapuram (City of the Sacred Serpent) is small and relaxed compared with other Indian state capitals – though many travellers still find it a hot, noisy shock after a few days on the beaches of Kovalam or Varkala. Away from the transport hubs and busy Mahatma Gandhi (MG) Rd, Thiruvananthapuram has

DANCE

Folk Dancing

India has as many folk dances as it has ethnolinguistic groups. From the simple to the outlandish, India's folk dances are invariably colourful, vital displays.

Some of the best-known folk dances are the lamaist dances from the gompas of Ladakh, Sikkim and Darjeeling, the Punjab's energetic Bhangra, the stick dances of Gujarat and the Koklikatai stilt dance of Tamil Nadu. Central India's folk dances are displayed every year at the Bhagoria Dance Festival.

Classical Dance

Classical Indian dancing relates back to the Hindu god Siva's role as Nataraj, Lord of the Dance. Lord Siva's first wife was Sati and when her father, who disliked Siva, insulted him, Sati committed suicide in a sacrifice by fire that later took her name. Outraged, Siva killed his father-in-law and danced the *tandava* – the Dance of Destruction. Later, Sati reincarnated as Parvati, married Siva again and danced the *lasya*. Thus, the tandava became the male form of dance, the lasya the female form. Dancing was a part of the religious temple rituals and the dancers were known as *devadasis*. Their dances retold stories from the *Ramayana* or the *Mahabharata*.

Although temple dancing is no longer practised, classical Indian dancing is still based on its Hindu roots. Indian dance is divided into *nritta*, or rhythm; *nritya*, the combination of rhythm with expression; and *natya*, the dramatic element. Nritya is usually expressed through eye, hand and facial movements and with nritta makes up the usual dance programmes. To appreciate natya, or dance drama, you have to understand and appreciate the Hindu legends and mythology.

Classical dance is divided into four basic forms known as Bharath Natyam, Kathakali, Manipuri and Kathak. Bharath Natyam is further subdivided into three other classical forms, and is one of the most popular dances. It originated in the great temples of the south and usually tells of events in Krishna's life. Bharath Natyam dancers are usually women who, like the sculptures they take their positions from, always dance with bent knees, never standing upright, and use a huge repertoire of hand movements.

GREG ELMS

ADAM McCROW

Top: Ankle bells, like these worn by a dancer in Jaipur, add another element to traditional folk music.

Left: Folk dancers at Shilpgram, a Rajasthani village dedicated to the promotion of Indian folk arts.

Orissi, Mohini Attam and Kuchipudi are variations of Bharath Natyam which take their names from the places where they originated.

Kathakali, the second major dance form, originated in Kerala and is exclusively danced by men. It tells of epic battles of gods and demons and is as dynamic and dramatic as Bharath Natyam is austere and expressive. Kathakali dancing is noted for the elaborate make-up and painted masks which the dancers wear.

As the name indicates, Manipuri dances come from the Manipur region in the north-east. The women dancers wear hooped skirts and conical caps which are extremely picturesque, and they tell the dance's story through body and arm movements.

The final classical dance type is Kathak, which originated in the north and at first was very similar to the Bharatha Natyam school. Persian and Muslim influences later altered the dance from a temple ritual to a courtly entertainment. The dances are performed straight-legged and there are intricately choreographed foot movements to be followed. The ankle bells which dancers wear must be adeptly controlled and the costumes and themes are often similar to those in Mughal miniature paintings.

There are many opportunities to see classical Indian dancing while you are in India. The major hotels often put on performances to which outsiders as well as hotel guests are welcome.

Left: Kathakali dancers in preparation for traditional dances.

Right: The elaborate make-up and costume of a Kathakali dancer.

GREG ELMS

GREG ELMS

GREG ELMS

Kerala's Religions

The population of Kerala is roughly 60% Hindu, 20% Muslim and 20% Christian. Hindus are mainly concentrated in southern Kerala, around Thiruvananthapuram, though Muslims are also a prominent and vocal component of the population in this area. The main Muslim area is in the northern part of the state, particularly around Kozhikode (Calicut).

Kerala's main Christian area is in the central part of the state, around Kochi and Kottayam. Christianity was established here earlier than almost anywhere else in the world. In 52 AD, St Thomas the Apostle, or 'Doubting Thomas', is said to have landed on the Malabar Coast near Cranganore (now Kodungallur), where a church with carved Hindu-style columns supposedly dates from the 4th century AD. There have been Syrian Christians in Kerala since at least 190 AD, and a visitor at that time reported seeing a Hebrew copy of the gospel of St Matthew. There are 16th century Syrian churches in Kottayam. When the Portuguese arrived here 500 years ago, they were more than a little surprised to find Christianity already established along the Malabar Coast, and more than a little annoyed that these Christians had never heard of the Pope. ■

many of the budget hotels are all close together, while the municipal bus stand is 10 minutes walk south, close to the temple. It's three to four km from the southern cluster of hotels and transport facilities to Museum Rd, at the northern end of MG Rd. The large Secretariat Building, halfway along MG Rd, is a handy landmark.

Information

Tourist Offices There's a helpful Tourist Information desk at the airport as well as an accommodation booking service for both Thiruvananthapuram and Kovalam.

The Tourist Reception Centre (☎ 330031) in front of the KTDC Chaithram Hotel, near the railway station and KSRTC long-disance bus terminal, is essentially there to promote KTDC guided tours. The Tourist Facilitation Centre (☎ 61132) on Museum Rd, opposite the museum and zoo, has a colourful map, but it can handle only the most basic of enquiries.

Post & Telecommunications The GPO is tucked away down a small side street off MG Rd, about 10 minutes walk from the Central Station Rd area. Most of the counters, including poste restante, are open Monday to Saturday from 8 am to 8 pm.

The Central Telegraph Office, at the midpoint of MG Rd, is 20 minutes walk from either end. The office is open 24 hours a day.

There are numerous STD/ISD counters and kiosks around town.

Visa Extensions The office of the Commissioner of Police (☎ 60486) on Residency Rd issues visa extensions, but the process takes four days to a week. Fortunately, you don't have to leave your passport. It speeds things up if you give a Thiruvananthapuram hotel address rather than somewhere in Kovalam. The office is open every day from 10 am to 5 pm except Sunday.

Bookshops & Libraries The British Library (☎ 68716), in the YMCA grounds near the Secretariat building, is officially only open to members, but visitors are made to feel welcome. It has three-day-old British newspapers and a variety of magazines. The library is open Tuesday to Saturday from 11 am to 7 pm. Higginbothams bookshop is on MG Rd and the Continental Book Company is nearby.

Sri Padmanabhaswamy Temple

Thiruvananthapuram's most interesting temple is open to Hindus only, and even they must wear a dhoti or sari. Still, it's worth visiting – even if you're just passing through town – to see the temple's seven-storey carved gopuram reflected in the nearby sacred tank. Constructed in the Dravidian style by a maharaja of Travancore in 1733, the temple is dedicated to Vishnu, who reclines on the

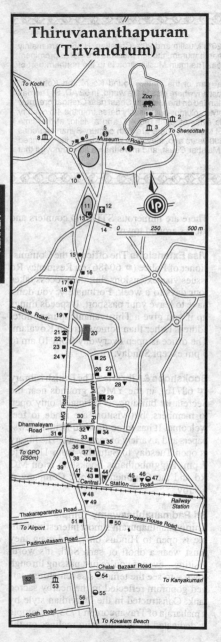

Thiruvananthapuram (Trivandrum)

PLACES TO STAY

7	Mascot Hotel
16	South Park
23	Hotel Pankaj
25	YMCA & British Library
26	Hotel Navaratna
27	Hotel Residency Tower
30	Bhaskara Bhavan Tourist Paradise
33	Sivada Tourist Home
34	Sundar Tourist Home
35	Hotel Regency
36	Vijai Tourist Home
37	Pravin Tourist Home
40	Manacaud Tourist Paradise
42	Hotel Highland
43	Hotel Ammu
45	KTD Chaithram Hotel & Tourist Reception Centre
50	Hotel Fort Manor
51	Nalanda Tourist Home
56	Hote Luciya Continental

PLACES TO EAT

18	Indian Coffee House
19	Ananda Bhavan
22	Arul Jyothi
24	Sri Ram Sweets
28	Snoozzer Ice Cream
32	Vinayak Vegetarian Restaurant
41	Hotel City Tower
44	Ambika Cafe & Prime Square
46	Maveli Cafe
48	Azad Restaurant
49	Rangoli

OTHER

1	Sri Chitra Art Gallery
2	Natural History Museum
3	Napier Museum
4	Tourist Facilitation Centre
5	State Bank of India
6	Indian Airlines
8	Science & Technology Museum & Planetarium
9	Stadium
10	State Assembly
11	Stadium
12	Church
13	Mosque
14	Connemara Market
15	Victoria Jubilee Town Hall
17	Air Maldives
20	Secretariat Building
21	Central Telegraph Office
29	Hindu Temple
31	Ayurveda College
38	Higginbothams
39	Continental Book Company
47	KSRT Long-Distance Bus Station
52	Sri Padmanabhaswamy Temple
53	Puthe Maliga Palace Museum
54	Municipal Bus Stand
55	Bus Stand No 19 (Buses & Taxis to Kovalam Beach)

sacred serpent, Ananda, which gives Thiru-vananthapuram its name.

Palace Museum

The recently opened Puthen Maliga Palace Museum, adjacent to the temple, is housed in several wings of the palace of the maharajahs of Travancore. Notable mostly for its wonderful Keralan architecture, the museum also offers a rare glimpse into the formal and private lives of one of India's most celebrated royal families. It's open from 8.30 am to 12.30 pm and from 3 to 5.30 pm; entry is Rs 5.

Museums, Gallery & Zoo

The zoo and a collection of museums are in a park in the north of the city. The museums are open Tuesday to Sunday from 10 am to 4.45 pm, but not until 1 pm on Wednesday. A single Rs 5 entry ticket covers all the museums and is obtainable from the Natural History Museum.

Housed in a whimsical, decaying, Keralan-style building dating from 1880, the **Napier Museum** displays an eclectic assortment of bronzes, historical and contemporary ornaments, temple carts, ivory carvings and life-size figures of Kathakali dancers in full costume.

The **Natural History Museum** has a rudimentary ethnographic collection as well as an interesting replica of a Nayar wooden house built in the Keralan style.

The **Sri Chitra Art Gallery** has paintings of the Rajput, Mughal and Tanjore schools, together with works from China, Tibet, Japan and Bali. There are also many modern Indian paintings, including works by Ravi Varma, Svetoslav and Nicholas Roerich.

The **Zoological Gardens** are among the best designed in Asia – set among woodland, lakes and well-maintained lawns – but some of the animal enclosures (and their inhabitants) are miserable. The zoo is open Tuesday to Saturday from 9 am to 5.15 pm. Entry is Rs 4 and there's an additional Rs 5 charge for a camera or Rs 250 for a video camera.

The **Science & Technology Museum** and **Planetarium**, about 100m west of the Mascot Hotel, cater mostly to high-school science students. The museum is open from 10 am to 5 pm daily and entry is Rs 2. The planetarium (☎ 446976) has 40 minute shows in English at noon daily (Rs 10). It's closed on Monday.

Organised Tours

The KTDC operates a variety of tours in the city and further afield. They all depart from the Tourist Reception Centre opposite the railway station.

The daily Thiruvananthapuram city tour departs at 8 am, returns at 7 pm, and costs Rs 80. The tour visits the Sri Padmanabhaswamy Temple, the museum, art gallery, zoo, Veli Lagoon and Kovalam Beach. This tour is of little interest to western visitors since

KERALA

Hindus Only

Despite Kerala's high education standards and its religious diversity, almost every Hindu temple in the state hangs out the 'No Entry' sign for non-Hindus. Don't feel left out – there's at least one temple in the state which bans many Hindus as well. Hindu or not, women between the age of 10 and 50 are not allowed in the Sabarimala Temple in central Kerala. Why? Because women of menstrual age could 'defile' the temple.

In late 1994 the temple and the state government found themselves in a tricky situation, when an investigation was launched into complaints by Sabarimala pilgrims about the standard of facilities at the temple. The Pathanamthitta District Collector was instructed to visit the temple to investigate the complaints until the horrible realisation dawned that the district collector was a 42 year old woman. The state's high court, which in 1990 had ruled that it was OK to ban women of menstrual age, hurriedly ruled that she could visit the temple, but only on her official duties – worshipping while in the temple was strictly forbidden! Although the case has focussed attention on this clear case of discrimination in a supposedly even-handed state, the rule continues. Lower caste people were also banned from temples not so many years ago. ■

the temple is off limits and there is little fascination in gawping at fellow travellers sunbathing on Kovalam Beach.

The daily Kanyakumari (Cape Comorin) tour departs at 7.30 am, returns at 9 pm, and costs Rs 150. It includes Padmanabhapuram Palace (except on Monday) and Kanyakumari, and is good value if you want to avoid public buses or staying overnight in Kanyakumari. There's also a daily tour to the Ponmudi hill resort which departs at 7.45 am, returns at 7 pm, and costs Rs 120.

Places to Stay – bottom end

There are many cheap places around Central Station Rd, near the railway station and KSRTC long-distance bus terminal, but most of them are very basic and the road is busy and noisy. The beach at Kovalam is a far more pleasant place to stay. If you have to stay overnight in Thiruvananthapuram, the best hunting ground is Manjalikulam Rd. Despite its central location, it's quiet and has a collection of cheap to mid-range hotels.

Pravin Tourist Home (☎ 330443) is a cheerful place with large singles/doubles/triples for Rs 75/135/180.

Sundar Tourist Home (☎ 330532) has simpler singles for Rs 25 to Rs 30 and doubles for Rs 60 with common bath.

Sivada Tourist Home (☎ 330320) is clean and well kept, with rooms built around a pleasant courtyard for Rs 75/120 or air-con doubles for Rs 275.

Manacaud Tourist Paradise (☎ 330360), at the Central Station Rd end of Manjalikulam Rd, has large, clean rooms with attached bathroom for Rs 75/150.

Hotel Ammu (☎ 331937), nearby, is small and popular and has doubles for Rs 180 or Rs 350 with air-con.

Nalanda Tourist Home (☎ 471864), south of the railway line, is on busy MG Rd, but the rooms at the back are not too noisy and it's cheap at Rs 60/90.

The *YMCA* (☎ 330059) is open to members only and charges Rs 30/60 or Rs 70 with attached bath.

There are *retiring rooms*, including a dormitory, at the railway station.

Places to Stay – middle

The KTDC *Chaithram Hotel* (☎ 330977) on Central Station Rd, next to the KSRTC long-distance bus terminal, is an efficient, modern hotel that's rarely full. Rooms cost Rs 350/400 or Rs 600/700 with air-con. Facilities include a bookshop, a Bank of India branch office, a coffee shop, a bright and friendly bar and veg and non-veg restaurants.

Hotel Highland (☎ 333200), on Manjalikulam Rd, is welcoming and has a good choice of rooms from Rs 180/220 or from Rs 330/400 with air-con. There's also an air-conditioned multi-cuisine restaurant.

Hotel Regency (☎ 330377), on Manjalikulam Cross Rd, has comfortable rooms for Rs 180/300 or Rs 450 with air-con, all with TV and phone. There are two restaurants, one of them on the rooftop.

Hotel Residency Tower (☎ 331661), on Press Rd, just off Manjalikulam Rd, has rooms for Rs 350/400 or Rs 690/890 with air-con. It has a bar, non-veg restaurant, direct-dial phones and TV.

Hotel Navaratna (☎ 331784), just around the corner on YMCA Rd, is a favourite of Indian business travellers and has rooms for Rs 180/220 or Rs 450/550 with air-con. The modern rooms have satellite TV and direct-dial STD, and there's a reasonable restaurant and coffee shop.

Places to Stay – top end

Hotel Lucia Continental (☎ 463443; fax 463347) is at East Fort, close to the Sri Padmanabhaswamy Temple. It's centrally air-conditioned and has rooms for Rs 1195/1395 with more expensive suites, all with satellite TV and direct-dial STD/ISD. There's also a bar, restaurant, coffee shop, bookshop, business centre and pool.

Hotel Fort Manor (☎ 462222; fax 460560) at Power House Junction, just south of the railway line, has spacious air-con rooms from Rs 1195/1495. The multi-cuisine restaurant also serves meals on the roof, which has a fabulous view over the city.

South Park (☎ 65666; fax 331861) a swank new centrally air-conditioned hotel further north on MG Rd, has rooms for

US$45/55 to US$85/95. It has one of the city's best restaurants, a coffee shop, a delicious cake shop and a bar.

The KTDC *Mascot Hotel* (☎ 438990; fax 437745), on Museum Rd north of the centre, is a pleasant hotel with a gloomy design. Rooms all have air-con and start from Rs 795/1095. There's an air-con restaurant, a coffee shop, and an open-air bar and ice-cream parlour near the pool.

Hotel Pankaj (☎ 464645), on MG Rd opposite the government Secretariat, has central air-con, rooms for Rs 859/1150 to Rs 950/1300 and suites for Rs 1800. There's a bar and two restaurants, one offering fine views from the top floor and a daily buffet lunch. Rooms have direct-dial STD and satellite TV, and there are foreign exchange and travel desks.

Places to Eat

Maveli Cafe is a bizarre, circular Indian Coffee House with a spiralling floor, next to the KSRTC long-distance bus terminal. If only the waiters wore roller skates!

Indian Coffee House should now be open about halfway along MG Rd.

Ambika Cafe at the junction of Central Station Rd and Manjalikulam Rd is a good spot for a cheap breakfast.

Prime Square, adjacent to the Ambika Cafe, has good value veg and non-veg restaurants, as well as an ice-cream parlour. It's a deservedly popular lunch spot.

Hotel City Tower on MG Rd, near the railway bridge, is also popular for lunch; thalis are Rs 15.

Central Station Rd has a number of vegetarian restaurants serving the usual 'meals' thalis, and there are several good, cheap vegetarian places opposite the Secretariat on MG Rd, including *Arul Jyothi*, *Sri Ram Sweets* and *Ananda Bhavan*.

Vinayak Vegetarian Restaurant on Dharmalayam Rd, just off Manjalikulam Rd, prepares Keralan specialities in an attractive old Keralan house.

Rangoli is south of the railway line, on MG Rd, and has a small entrance leading to

a neat and tidy air-conditioned 'family restaurant' upstairs.

Azad Restaurant a few doors north, is also clean, air-conditioned and good value.

There are restaurants in many of the hotels. *City Queen Restaurant* in the Highlands Hotel on Manjalikulam Rd, does good Chinese dishes and also serves Indian and western food.

Mascot Hotel, *Pankaj Hotel* and in particular the *South Park* all have popular lunchtime buffets.

Rooftop restaurants are all the go in Trivandrum, and from an elevated position you realise how green and park-like the city is.

Sandhya Restaurant on the 5th floor of the Pankaj Hotel has particularly fine views.

Fort Manor and the *Regency* also have top-floor restaurants.

The *Mascot* and the *Chaithram*, both KTDC hotels, have outdoor ice-cream parlours. Alternatively, try the engagingly named *Snoozzer* on Press Rd.

Getting There & Away

Air Indian Airlines (☎ 438288) is on Museum Rd, next to the Mascot Hotel; the office is open from 10 am to 5.35 pm daily, with a lunch break from 1 to 1.45 pm. Other airline contact numbers include Jet Air (☎ 61902), Air India (☎ 434837), Air Lanka (☎ 68767), Air Maldives (☎ 76341), Gulf Air (☎ 67514) and Kuwait Airways (☎ 68651).

Indian Airlines has direct connections to Bangalore (four flights weekly; US$90); Mumbai (Bombay) (daily, US$155); Chennai (Madras) (daily, US$90) and Delhi (daily, US$290). Jet Air also has daily flights to Mumbai and Chennai.

There are a number of connections to the Arabian Gulf with Air India, Gulf Air and Kuwait Airways. Air India also flies to Singapore on Monday and Saturday.

Thiruvananthapuram is a popular place from which to fly to Colombo (Sri Lanka) and Malé (Maldives). Air Lanka and Indian Airlines fly to Colombo daily for Rs 1455 one way. Air Maldives and Indian Airlines have daily flights to Malé for Rs 2045 one way.

KERALA

Bus The KSRTC bus terminal (☎ 63796), opposite the railway station, is total chaos. The law of the jungle applies each time a battered old bus comes to a screeching halt in a cloud of dust.

Buses operate regularly to destinations north along the coast, including Kollam (1½ hours, Rs 25), Alappuzha (3¼ hours, Rs 45), Ernakulam (five hours, Rs 65), and Thrissur (6¾ hours, Rs 85). Buses depart hourly for the two-hour trip to Kanyakumari. There are three buses daily for the eight-hour trip to Thekkady (for Periyar Wildlife Sanctuary).

Most of the bus services to destinations in Tamil Nadu are operated by Thiruvalluvar (the Tamil Nadu state bus service), which has its office at the eastern end of the long-distance bus terminal. It has services to Chennai (four daily, 17 hours), Madurai (10 daily, seven hours), Pondicherry (one daily, 16 hours), Coimbatore (one daily), as well as Nagercoil and Erode. KSRTC also operates several services daily to Coimbatore. Long-distance buses operate to Bangalore, but it's better to catch a train if you're going that far.

Train Although the buses are much faster than the trains, KSRTC buses, like most others in southern India, make no concessions to comfort and the drivers can be reckless. If you prefer to keep your adrenaline levels down, the train is a relaxing alternative. The reservation office, on the 1st floor of the station building, is efficient and computerised but you should reserve as far in advance as possible because long-distance trains out of Thiruvananthapuram are heavily booked. The booking office is open Monday to Saturday from 8 am to 2 pm and from 2.15 to 8 pm; Sunday from 8 am to 2 pm. If you're just making your way up the coast in short hops or to Kochi, there's no need to book.

Numerous trains run up the coast via Kollam and Ernakulam to Thrissur. Some trains branch off east and north-east at Kollam and head for Shencottah. Beyond Thrissur, many others branch off east via Palakkad to Tamil Nadu.

Trains which go all the way up the coast as far as Mangalore in Karnataka include the daily *Parsuram Express* (departs 6.05 am; 15 hours) and *Malabar Express* (departs 5.40 pm). The daily *Cannanore Express* (departs 9 pm; 12¾ hours) goes as far north as Kannur. Each of these trains travels via Kochi, and there are several additional daily expresses to Kochi including the *Venada Express* (departs 5 am), the *Kerala Express* (departs 9.40 am) and the *Vanchinad Express* (departs 5.05 pm).

It's 65km from Thiruvananthapuram to Kollam (1½ hours, Rs 21/99 in 2nd/1st class); 224km to Ernakulam (five hours, Rs 74/241); and 414km to Kozhikode (10 hours, Rs 119/410).

South of Thiruvananthapuram, it's 87km to Kanyakumari (two hours, Rs 25/128); and 427km to Coimbatore (nine hours, Rs 120/421). Coimbatore has connections to Mettupalayam and Ooty.

For long-haulers, there's the Friday-only *Himsagar Express* to Jammu Tawi which goes via Delhi.

Getting Around
The Airport The small and relaxed airport is six km from the city centre or 15km from Kovalam Beach. A No 14 local bus will take you there for around Rs 2. Prepaid vouchers for taxis cost Rs 60 to Rs 80 to destinations in the city; Rs 180 to Rs 200 to Kovalam Beach.

Local Transport Auto-rickshaws are your best bet for transport around the city. The drivers are usually willing to use their meters; flagfall is Rs 6, then around Rs 3 per km. From the railway station to the museum, it costs about Rs 15.

See the following Kovalam section for transport information from Thiruvananthapuram to the beach.

AROUND THIRUVANANTHAPURAM
Padmanabhapuram Palace
Padmanabhapuram Palace was once the seat of the rulers of Travancore, a princely state for more than 400 years, which included a large part of present-day Kerala and the western coast of Tamil Nadu.

The palace is superbly constructed of local teak and granite, and stands within the massive stone town walls which kept Tipu Sultan at bay in the 18th century. The architecture is exquisite, with ceilings carved in floral patterns, windows laid with jewel-coloured mica, and floors finished to a high polish with a special compound of crushed shells, coconuts, egg-white and the juices of local plants. The 18th century murals in the puja room on the upper floors have been beautifully preserved, and surpass even those at Mattancherry in Kochi. Ask at the curator's office for special access.

With its banqueting halls, audience chamber, women's quarters, recruiting courtyard and galleries, the palace shouldn't be missed if you are visiting this part of the country.

Padmanabhapuram is just inside Tamil Nadu, 65km south-east of Thiruvananthapuram. To get there, you can either catch a local bus from Thiruvananthapuram (or Kovalam Beach) or take one of the Kanyakumari tours organised by the KTDC; see Organised Tours in the Thiruvananthapuram section for details. The palace is closed on Monday.

KOVALAM

Tel Area Code: 0471

Thirty years ago Kovalam was a hippy idyll: a picture-perfect tropical beach; a traditional Keralan fishing village providing fresh fish, fruit and toddy (coconut beer); and about as far from decadent western civilisation as you could get and still hear Jim, Janis and Jimi. Even ten years ago, it was still a mellow backpackers' hangout with a few basic but comfortable lodges and makeshift restaurants catering for budget-minded travellers craving some rest and recreation on the long haul across the subcontinent.

But today this tiny beach is the focus of a multi-million dollar business, ferrying thousands of tourists from Britain and Europe on chartered jumbos for a two-week dose of ozone, UV and a sanitised Indian 'experience'.

The result has been an influx of some get-rich-quick merchants, chaotic beachfront development, an uncontrollable avalanche of garbage, exorbitant prices, desperate souvenir sellers and hordes of ogling sightseers. All of which threatens to destroy the ambience that made Kovalam so attractive in the first place.

But while it's far from paradise, Kovalam retains a certain charm and is still popular with sun-worshipping travellers. The beaches are generally safe and clean (though much of the rubbish is buried just under the surface), and the powerful Arabian Sea swells are inviting and invigorating. There's little local colour left in the village behind the beach, though local fishers still sail their boats out to sea each night.

Kovalam has an abundance of places to stay, ranging from cheap concrete boxes to five-star resorts, and there's an equally wide range of restaurants, many tuned in to the standard Asian travellers' menu.

Keep in mind that bold displays of naked flesh are offensive to local sensibilities, even on the beach.

Orientation

Kovalam consists of two palm-fringed coves (Lighthouse Beach and Hawah Beach) separated from less-populated beaches north and south by rocky headlands. The southern headland is marked by a prominent red-and-white striped lighthouse; the northern headland is topped by the Ashok Beach Resort. It's a 15 minute walk from one headland to the other. A maze of poorly-lit paths runs through the coconut palms behind the beach, leading to a multitude of guest houses and restaurants.

Information

There's a helpful tourist office just inside the entrance to the Ashok Beach Resort.

The Central Bank of India has a counter at the Ashok Resort which changes travellers cheques quickly and without fuss. It's only open Monday to Friday from 10.30 am to 2 pm and on Saturday from 10.30 am to noon. Up the road towards Kovalam village, Pournami Handicrafts is an authorised moneychanger, and is open from 9 am to

KERALA

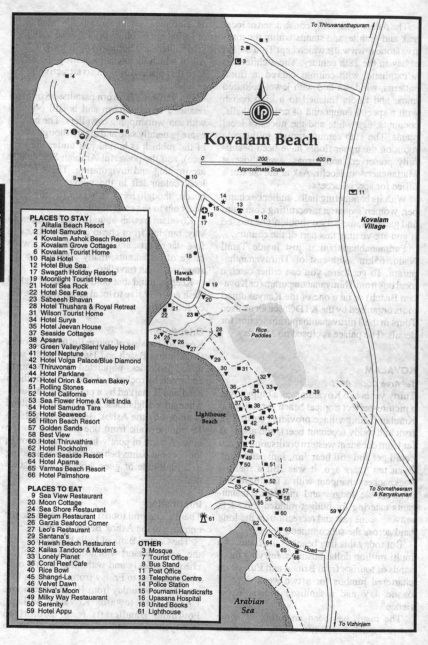

Kovalam Beach

Approximate Scale

0   200   400 m

Kovalam Village

Hawah Beach

Rice Paddies

Lighthouse Beach

Arabian Sea

To Thiruvananthapuram

To Somatheeram & Kanyakumari

To Vizhinjam

PLACES TO STAY
1 Alitalia Beach Resort
2 Hotel Samudra
4 Kovalam Ashok Beach Resort
5 Kovalam Grove Cottages
6 Kovalam Tourist Home
10 Raja Hotel
12 Hotel Blue Sea
17 Swagath Holiday Resorts
19 Moonlight Tourist Home
21 Hotel Sea Rock
22 Hotel Sea Face
23 Sabeesh Bhavan
28 Hotel Thushara & Royal Retreat
31 Wilson Tourist Home
34 Hotel Surya
35 Hotel Jeevan House
37 Seaside Cottages
38 Apsara
39 Green Valley/Silent Valley Hotel
41 Hotel Neptune
42 Hotel Volga Palace/Blue Diamond
43 Thiruvonam
44 Hotel Parklane
47 Hotel Orion & German Bakery
51 Rolling Stones
52 Hotel California
53 Sea Flower Home & Visit India
54 Hotel Samudra Tara
55 Hotel Seaweed
56 Hilton Beach Resort
57 Golden Sands
58 Best View
60 Hotel Thiruvathira
62 Hotel Rockholm
63 Eden Seaside Resort
64 Hotel Aparna
65 Varmas Beach Resort
66 Hotel Palmshore

PLACES TO EAT
9 Sea View Restaurant
20 Moon Cottage
24 Sea Shore Restaurant
25 Begum Restaurant
26 Garzia Seafood Corner
27 Leo's Restaurant
29 Santana's
30 Hawah Beach Restaurant
32 Kailas Tandoor & Maxim's
33 Lonely Planet
36 Coral Reef Cafe
40 Rice Bowl
46 Shangri-La
48 Velvet Dawn
49 Shiva's Moon
50 Milky Way Restaurant
50 Serenity
59 Hotel Appu

OTHER
3 Mosque
7 Tourist Office
8 Bus Stand
11 Post Office
13 Telephone Centre
14 Police Station
15 Upasana Hospital
16 Pournami Handicrafts
18 United Books
61 Lighthouse

6.30 pm daily. Wilson Tourist Home also has an official money changing counter.

There's a post office and a telephone centre (open 9 am to 5 pm) in Kovalam Village.

Visit India (☎ 481069), at the foot of Lighthouse Rd, is a friendly travel agent which can arrange ticketing, tours, and car and motorcycle hire.

Shops Kovalam Beach has numerous craft and carpet shops (usually of Tibetan, Kashmiri and Rajasthani origin), clothing stores (ready to wear and made to order), book exchanges, general stores selling everything from toilet paper to sunscreen, travel agents, yoga schools and even massage parlours. Just in case you thought you'd left home to immerse yourself in a different culture, western videos are shown twice a night in a number of restaurants. Beach vendors sell batik lungis, beach mats and leaf paintings, while others offer cheap (and illegal) Kerala grass.

Surfboards and boogie boards can be rented from young guys on the beach for around Rs 30 per hour.

Dangers & Annoyances Don't drink local well water at Kovalam. There are so many pit toilets adjacent to wells that you're guaranteed to get very sick if you do. Stick to bottled water.

Theft from hotel rooms, particularly cheap hotels, does occur. Ensure your room has a decent bolt and windows which lock, and stash your gear out of sight in a cupboard or under the bed. Keep an eye on any possessions you take to the beach.

Strong rips at both ends of Lighthouse Beach carry away several swimmers every year. It's safest to swim between the flags, in the area patrolled by lifeguards.

Kovalam is subject to electrical supply 'load-shedding' for 30 minutes every evening. Carry a torch after dark.

Places to Stay
There are dozens of places to stay at the bottom end of the market – the coconut groves behind the beach are littered with small lodges, houses for rent and blocks of recently constructed rooms. Shop around, but you basically get what you pay for. Ask for a reduced rate if you are staying longer than a few days.

Prices climb the closer you get to the beach, and a few minutes walk can often mean lower prices or much better rooms for the same price. Prices climb even more dramatically when the package tourists begin to arrive – November to February is the high season but some places have a peak high season over the Christmas/New Year period when prices go even higher. Outside the peak season it's a buyer's market; find the best place on the beach and bargain hard.

Places to Stay – bottom end
Most, though not all, of the cheapest places are along or just back from the beach. There are others along the road from Thiruvananthapuram and along Lighthouse Rd.

Eden Seaside Resort on Lighthouse Rd, opposite the Varmas Beach Resort, is basic but all rooms have attached bathroom; doubles cost Rs 500, dropping to half that price in the low season.

Hotel Thiruvathira (☎ 480787), almost next door, has downstairs doubles for Rs 500 and upstairs doubles with balcony and bay views for Rs 700. In the low season, prices drop to Rs 200 and Rs 250.

Green Valley/Silent Valley Hotel (☎ 480636), in a wonderfully peaceful location next to the paddy fields, has clean, neat and colourful rooms with attached bathroom for Rs 450 in the peak season and Rs 200 in the low season.

Kovalam Tourist Home (☎ 480441), a long walk back from the beach, has simple rooms with attached bathroom for just Rs 300/150 in the high/low season or Rs 400/350 with air-con. Little English is spoken.

Sabeesh Bhavan (☎ 480140), just off the Sea Rock road, is four basic rooms in a house owned by a friendly local woman for just Rs 150/75 in the high/low season.

Sandy Beach Resort (☎ 480507), behind the Apsara, has refurbished rooms for Rs 450/200 in the high/low season.

KERALA

Hotel Jeevan House (☎ 480662), right behind the Coral Reef Cafe, has a range of accommodation from Rs 250 to Rs 1200 in the high season or Rs 100 to Rs 400 off season.

Other places worth considering include the no-frills *Hotel Surya*, just back from the beach; the beachfront *Sea Flower Home* (☎ 480554), *Seaside Cottages* and *Thiruvonam*; or *Apsara*, *Ocean Park* (☎ 481402), *Rolling Stones*, *Best View* and *Hilton Beach Resort* which are all a few minutes stroll from each other and the beach.

Places to Stay – middle

The best hunting ground for mid-range hotels is Lighthouse Rd.

Hotel Seaweed (☎ 480391) is an excellent, friendly and secure place with sea breezes and bay views. There's a wide variety of rooms from Rs 500 to Rs 700 and Rs 1000 to Rs 1200 with air-con. Prices drop 25% to 30% in the low season.

Hotel Rockholm (☎ 480306), further up Lighthouse Rd, is also an excellent choice. It has great views over the small cove beyond the lighthouse. In the high season, rooms cost Rs 900/100; in the low season, there's a 25% discount.

Hotel Aparna (☎ 480950) has rooms for Rs 900/1000 in the peak season, falling to Rs 700/800 in the low season.

Varmas Beach Resort (☎ 480478) has balconies overlooking a small cove. Rooms are Rs 935 in the high season, dropping to Rs 750 in the low season.

Hotel Palmshore (☎ 481481) fronts onto the private sandy cove south of the lighthouse headland, which is a pleasant escape from the frenetic activity on Lighthouse Beach. The rooms are pleasantly designed, all with attached bathroom and a balcony facing the sea. Singles/doubles cost US$52 (US$62 with air-con) during the December/January peak, reducing to US$40/35 (US$50/45 with air-con) for the rest of the season, and falling to US$20/17 (US$25/21 with air-con) during the low season.

Golden Sands (☎ 481077) is a new hotel with large, comfortable doubles for Rs 750/350 in the high/low season.

Hotel Neptune (☎ 480222) is set back from Lighthouse Beach and has standard rooms for Rs 500, balcony rooms for Rs 550 and air-con rooms for Rs 750 over the Christmas/New Year peak. Prices in the low season fall to less than Rs 300.

Hotel Volga Palace and *Blue Diamond* (☎ 481224 for both) are of a similar standard to the Neptune.

Wilson Tourist Home (☎ 480051) is a few steps closer to the beach and slightly cheaper. It is large and friendly, with a range of rooms from Rs 400 to Rs 1500 during the season, reducing to Rs 150 to Rs 400 in the low.

Hotel Sea Rock (☎ 480422), on Hawah Beach, has been popular for years. The rooms are all doubles and have attached bathroom. Rooms with a sea view cost Rs 1200; back rooms cost Rs 550. These prices tumble to Rs 400 and Rs 300 respectively in the low season.

Hotel Thushara (☎ 480692), back in the coconut palms, has superbly built and beautifully furnished self-contained cottages and rooms for Rs 750 (Rs 200 in the low season).

Royal Retreat, next door, is a cluster of brand new air-conditioned cottages for Rs 1000/300 in the high/low season.

Moonlight Tourist Home (☎ 480375), further up this road, is popular and squeaky clean. The spacious rooms have poster beds and mosquito nets; doubles, some with small balconies, cost Rs 1000 or Rs 1500 with air-con. Prices for the rooms without air-con drop to Rs 400 in the low season.

Hotel Orion (☎ 480999) is a friendly place overlooking Lighthouse Beach just 20m from the high-tide mark, and its prime position is reflected in its tariff. Doubles are Rs 1000/600 in the high/low season and suites (with air-con and fridge) are Rs 2000/900.

Hotel Parklane (☎ 480058), a minutes walk back from the beach, is a good choice at the bottom of this range. Clean, comfortable doubles, some with a small balcony, cost Rs 700 including breakfast and taxes; rates are halved off-season. The manager is friendly and there's a pleasant rooftop restaurant.

Raja Hotel (☎ 480355), well back from the beach, has sea-facing rooms with attached bathroom for Rs 750, falling to Rs 400 in the low season. It also has a bar and a vegetarian restaurant.

Places to Stay – top end

The *Kovalam Ashok Beach Resort* (☎ 480101; fax 481522) is superbly located on the headland at the northern end of the second cove. The hotel is centrally air-conditioned and has a bar, restaurants, swimming pool, sports and massage facilities, bank and bookshop. Room prices are Rs 4000/4500 from mid-December to mid-February, dropping to Rs 3500/4000 for the other 10 months; uninspiring cottages are Rs 500 cheaper, while the Castle suite costs Rs 15,000/12,500 during the high/low season!

The KTDC *Hotel Samudra* (☎ 480089; fax 480242) is located about two km north of the main beaches but it has its own bar and restaurant. Air-con doubles cost Rs 2395, dropping to Rs 1700 in the low season.

Hotel Sea Face (☎ 418835; fax 481320) is a new resort right on Hawah Beach. Standard rooms are Rs 2000 (Rs 2400 with air-con), deluxe rooms are Rs 3000, and suites are Rs 4000 (plus 20% tax). Rates fall by 25% from June to October. All rooms have TV and direct-dial facilities, and the pool overlooks the beach.

Swagath Holiday Resorts (☎ 481148; fax 330990) is set in well-tended gardens high above the beach looking over the coconut palms to the lighthouse. Comfortable rooms cost Rs 1200 to Rs 1750 (Rs 1600 to Rs 2500 with air-con) or Rs 3500 for an air-con suite; there are no low season price reductions. There's an excellent multi-cuisine restaurant (lawn-service available), but no pool. Be warned: rooms with a view of the lighthouse are strafed with brilliant light all night long.

Places to Eat

Open-air restaurants line Lighthouse Beach and are scattered among the coconut palms behind it. Almost all the restaurants offer the standard Asian travellers' menu: porridge, muesli, eggs, toast, jam and pancakes for breakfast, and seafood with chips and salad for dinner.

At night, you stroll along the beachfront and select which fish you would like cooked from one of the many restaurants' seafood displays. The range of fresh seafood includes seer fish (delicious baked in a tandoor), barracuda, sea bass, catfish, king and tiger prawns, and crabs. Always check the prices when you order. Fish & chips and salad is typically between Rs 70 and Rs 100, depending on variety and portion size; tiger prawns will push the price beyond Rs 200.

There's plenty of competition, so don't be afraid to negotiate if the asking price is too high. The quality can vary widely from place to place and from month to month; ask other travellers or diners for their recommendations. Beer is available in most restaurants, but is expensive, even by Keralan standards.

Santana's (which has the best sound system), *Coral Reef Café*, *Velvet Dawn*, *Garzia Seafood Corner* and tiny *Leo's Restaurant* all have a reputation for quality and value. But almost without exception you must be prepared for a long wait; the length of time it takes to grill a fish is quite amazing.

Serenity, at the south end of the beach, turns out good travellers' breakfasts and recognisable 'spegatty'; and nearby *Shiva's Moon* is similar. The *Sea View Restaurant* is popular all day long, and just beyond the headland the *Sea Shore Restaurant* is a wonderful spot to sip a beer while the sun sets. For cappuccino and apple strudel, try the rooftop cafe at the *German Bakery*.

There are quite a few places back from the beach, although seafood is not the number one concern.

Lonely Planet vegetarian restaurant is nicely situated by the paddy fields, and turns out some surprisingly good South Indian food. No, we have absolutely nothing to do with it and we are not planning to open a franchised chain!

Rice Bowl Chinese restaurant, the *Shangri-La*, *Maxim's* and *Moon Cottage Restaurant* are also worth a look.

If you get tired of the interminable wait for meals at the beachside places, consider the mid-range hotels back from the beach. These places have better equipped kitchens than the beach shacks and can turn out more consistent food with much greater speed.

Lucky Coral rooftop restaurant at the Hotel Seaweed is ever-popular.

The *Rockholm's* celebrated restaurant includes a terrace overlooking the sea.

At the *Palmshore,* you can eat indoors or on the open balcony.

The *Sea Rock* has a balcony overlooking the beach.

For a splurge, head off to the *Ashok Beach Resort* or the *Swagath Holiday Resorts.*

Hotel Appu, well away from the beach, has the best cheap Indian food in Kovalam, and is packed with lunching locals from 1 to 1.30 pm.

On the beach, a number of local women sell *fruit* to sun worshippers. The ring of 'Hello. Mango? Papaya? Banana? Coconut? Pineapple?' will soon become a familiar part of your day. They'll sell you fruit at any price you're willing to pay, but you'll soon establish what the going rate is and, after that, they'll remember your face and you don't have to repeat the performance. The women rarely have any change, but they're reliable about bringing it to you later. *Toddy* (coconut beer) is available from shops in Kovalam Village.

Getting There & Away

Bus The local No 111 bus between Thiruvananthapuram and Kovalam Beach runs every 15 minutes between about 6 am and 10 pm and costs Rs 3.50. The bus leaves Thiruvananthapuram from stand 19 on MG Rd, 100m south of the municipal bus stand, opposite the Hotel Luciya Continental. Although the bus starts out ridiculously overcrowded, it rapidly empties. At Kovalam, the buses start and finish at the entrance to the Ashok Beach Resort.

There are also direct services to Emakulam and Kanyakumari (Cape Comorin, Tamil Nadu), which are good ways of avoiding the crush at Thiruvananthapuram. Kanyakumari is two hours away and there are four departures daily. One bus leaves each morning for Thekkady in the Periyar Wildlife Sanctuary.

Direct buses go to Kollam if you want to do the backwater trip.

Taxi & Auto-Rickshaw A taxi between Thiruvananthapuram and Kovalam Beach will cost Rs 150 to Rs 200, depending on where you're going to and from. Auto-rickshaws make the trip for Rs 60 to Rs 80. It's best to arrive at the lighthouse (Vizhinjam) end of the beach because this is much closer to the hotels and there usually aren't as many touts around. Pre-paid taxis from Thiruvananthapuram Airport to the beach cost around Rs 200.

AROUND KOVALAM
Vizhinjam

The small fishing village of Vizhinjam, just one km south of Kovalam Beach, is a sobering antidote to the excesses of Kovalam. Its big artificial harbour is dominated by a pink and green mosque on the northern side and a huge Catholic church to the south; from Kovalam you can sometimes hear them trading amplified calls to prayer and mass in the early hours. In recent years several villagers have died in Hindu/Muslim communal violence, and the peace is now maintained by a permanent police presence.

The beach is packed with boats which set out to fish at sunset. From the beach at night, you can see their lights strung like a necklace along the horizon.

Vizhinjam (then Vilinjam) was a capital of the 7th to 11th-century Ay kingdom, and a number of rock-cut temples have been found around the village – reminders of the period when the kingdom was under Tamil influence.

Pulinkudi & Somatheeram

At Pulinkudi, eight km south of Kovalam, there are two interesting alternatives to Kovalam's crowded beaches.

Surya Samudra Beach Garden (☎ 480413; fax 481124) is a small and very select hotel with individual cottages, many of them constructed from transplanted traditional Keralan houses. There are private beaches, a fantastic natural rock swimming pool and music, martial arts or dance performances at night. The food is superb, though expensive by local standards. From December to February, room rates range from Rs 3500/4000 to Rs 4000/4500, and gradually reduce throughout the off-season.

Somatheeram Ayurvedic Beach Resort (☎ 480600; fax 463702) a little further south on Somatheeram Beach, combines beach life with Ayurvedic medical treatment. In the peak season, most rooms are Rs 1200 to Rs 2500. Various treatment packages are available.

Pozhikkara Beach

Lagoona Beach Resort (☎ 443738) at Pachalloor village, five km north of Kovalam, is a small, basic lodge with just four rooms costing between Rs 300 and Rs 400. Compared with Kovalam, it's quiet, peaceful and authentically Keralan. Excellent Keralan meals are also available. A local ferry shuttles across the narrow lagoon to the beach, and backwater trips are made at 8 am and 4 pm daily.

VARKALA

Pop: 41,400   Tel Area Code: 0472

Varkala is an embryonic beach resort 41km north of Thiruvananthapuram. One look and it's apparent that the Keralan authorities have not learned from the mistakes which have allowed Kovalam beach to become a shambles. Several totally inappropriate developments (mostly designed to house package tourists from Britain and Europe) already mar the beach, and the garbage is piling up fast.

Orientation & Information

The town and the railway station are two km from the beach, which lies beneath towering cliffs and boasts a **mineral-water spring**. The **Janardhana Temple** is at the Beach Rd junction. One of the earliest British East India Company trading posts was established at nearby **Anjengo** in 1684.

Most places to stay are at the beach, either at the temple junction, on Beach Rd, or half a km north along the cliff tops. As at Kovalam, prices vary seasonally, and it pays to shop around. Varkala's beach can disappear almost entirely during the monsoon, gradually

reappearing in time for the tourist onslaught from November to February.

There is a currency exchange counter at the Taj Garden Retreat.

Places to Stay – bottom end

Anandan Tourist Home (☎ 602135) opposite the railway station, is neat and orderly and has rooms for Rs 60/150 or Rs 300 with air-con and TV.

JA Tourist Home (☎ 602453), nearest the temple, has basic accommodation ranging in price from Rs 75 to Rs 150.

Gratitude Inn, along Beach Rd, has five tiny rooms for just Rs 150 each. You may also be asked to purchase handicrafts from the owner's Cottage Emporium.

Beach Palace (☎ 2453), overlooking the paddy fields, is rather primitive, but cheap at Rs 70/100.

Varkala Marine Palace (☎ 603204) has rooms for Rs 150 to Rs 200 or Rs 600 with air-con. It also has an open-air tandoor overlooking the beach.

On the cliffs, 10 minutes walk north, much of the accommodation is with local families who offer rooms for Rs 75 to Rs 150. Some places to stay haven't yet acquired names, so just look for **White House, Green House** or **Red House**, all with rooms at around Rs 200 to Rs 300 in season.

Hill Top Resort has simple rooms with attached bathroom for Rs 175 to Rs 250.

Prasanthi Cliff Guest House, further around the cliffs, is run by a western couple and has three small, charmingly decorated rooms with common bath for Rs 250.

Places to Stay – middle & top end

Akshay Beach Resort (☎ 602668), on Beach Rd, has rooms for Rs 350 to Rs 400. It's basically OK, but could do with some cleaning and maintenance.

Panchavadi Beach Resort (☎ 602157), almost opposite, has eight small new rooms ranging in price from Rs 500 for standard rooms to Rs 800 for suites. There's hot water but no air-con.

Sea Pearl Chalets (☎ 660105) consists of nine new concrete wigwams on the southern

KERALA

headland overlooking the car park. It should now be open for business, as should the new four-storey monstrosity almost on the beach below the chalets. Prices were unavailable at the time of writing.

Udatha Cliff Hostel (☎ 3298), run by the genial Laila, is a spotless home on the clifftop with nine comfortable rooms, four with attached bath. Prices range from Rs 500 to Rs 800 for the rooms on the top floor. A restaurant is attached.

Taj Garden Retreat (☎ 603000; fax 602296), a gleaming new resort set among terraced gardens and coconut palms overlooking the beach, eclipses every other building in this tiny hamlet and is certainly a harbinger of future developments. It is already drawing a substantial number of charter tourists away from Kovalam. Air-con rooms are US$95/105 to US$110/120 from Christmas to the end of February and US$15 cheaper throughout the rest of the year. There's a restaurant, bar, pool, tennis courts and health club.

Places to Eat

Anandan Tourist Home, opposite the railway station, has a restaurant downstairs.

Sree Padman Restaurant perched right at the edge of the tank at the temple junction, is popular with locals.

The nearby *JA Tourist Home* advertises pizza, pasta, German bread and other unlikely goodies.

Apart from the *Kentucky Restaurant* on Beach Rd, most of the other eating places are seasonal, opening up along the cliff top at the northern part of Varkala Beach from November to February.

Sea Breeze, Sea View, Sunset Restaurant, Dreamland and others all offer similar standards (shaky tables and a diverse collection of rickety chairs), similar food (fresh

Varkala

Arabian Sea

Spring

Helipad

Rice Paddies

Beach Road

To Bureau de Change (100m) & Railway Station (2km)

Tank

Cliffs

0   50   100 m
Approximate Scale

PLACES TO STAY	
1	Prasanthi Cliff Guest House & Café Italiano
2	Hill Palace
4	Hill Top Resort
5	Red House
6	White House
8	Green House
13	Udatha Cliff Hostel
16	Varkala Marine Palace
17	Beach Palace
18	Taj Garden Retreat
19	Sea Pearl Chalets
20	Hotel
23	Panchavadi Beach Resort
24	Akshay Beach Resort
25	Gratitude Inn
29	J A Tourist Home

PLACES TO EAT	
3	Dreamland
7	Sea Breeze Restaurant & Hill View Lodge
9	Seaview Restaurant & Cliff House
10	Sun Set Restaurant
11	Vadaloram Restaurant No 1
12	Manos Restaurant
14	Sky Roof Restaurant
21	Kentucky Restaurant
26	Sree Padman Restaurant

OTHER	
15	Nature Cure Hospital
22	Tourist Helping Centre
27	Janardhana Temple
28	Temple Junction Auto-Rickshaw Stand

fish on display out the front at night) and similar service (usually incredibly slow).

Café Italiano at the Prasanthi Guest House dishes up delicious pizza, spaghetti and homemade bread with an authentic Italian touch.

Getting There & Away
Varkala is 41km north of Thiruvananthapuram (55 minutes by train, Rs 16/83 in 2nd/1st class) and just 24km south of Kollam (45 minutes, Rs 13/72). From Varkala, it's easy to get to Kollam in time for the morning backwater boat to Alappuzha. A taxi from Thiruvananthapuram direct to Varkala Beach costs about Rs 300.

Getting Around
Auto-rickshaws shuttle back and forth between the railway station and the Varkala temple junction for Rs 12 to Rs 15. A taxi to the beach costs about Rs 40.

KOLLAM (Quilon)
Pop: 374,400   Tel Area Code: 0474
Nestled among coconut palms and cashew tree plantations on the edge of Ashtamudi Lake, Kollam is a typical small Keralan market town, with old wooden houses whose red-tiled roofs overhang winding streets. It's also the southern gateway to the backwaters of Kerala.

The Malayalam era is calculated from the founding of Kollam in the 9th century. The town's later history is interwoven with the Portuguese, Dutch and English rivalry for control of the Indian Ocean trade routes and the commodities grown in this part of the subcontinent.

Information
Kollam is still referred to as Quilon, pronounced 'koy-lon'. There's a very helpful DTPC Tourist Information Centre near the KSRTC bus terminal (open Monday to Saturday from 9 am to 5.30 pm) and another at the railway station. Chani Books is in the Bishop Jerome Nagar shopping centre.

Things to See
Apart from the extraordinary **Shrine of Our Lady of Velamkanni** near the KSRTC bus terminal and Chinese fishing nets on **Ashtamudi Lake**, there are no 'sights' in Kollam – unless you count the miserable ruins of a Portuguese/Dutch fort and some 18th century churches at **Thangasseri**, three km from Kollam's centre. Otherwise, Kollam is just the starting or finishing point for the **backwater cruise** – an overnight halt at the most. Even that can easily be avoided since the burgeoning beach resort of Varkala is only 45 minutes south.

Places to Stay – bottom end
The *Govt Guest House* (☎ 70356), three km north from the centre, is a magnificent, old British Residency in colourful gardens by the water's edge on Ashtamudi Lake. Despite its superb potential, it's rather neglected and sparsely furnished, but at Rs 44/55, dirt cheap. Getting into town is the biggest drawback because it can be hard to find an auto-rickshaw.

Lakshmi Tourist Home (☎ 741067) down an alley off Main Rd, is a no-frills lodge with singles/doubles costing Rs 40/80 with attached bath.

Hotel Karthika (☎ 76240) is a large, popular place built around a central courtyard. Decent rooms are Rs 80/140 with attached bathroom or Rs 220 with air-con.

Iswarya Lodge (☎ 77801) nearby on Main Rd, is slightly cheaper at Rs 65/100.

Mahalakshmi Lodge (☎ 79440), opposite the KSRTC bus terminal, is cheap but very basic with rooms with common bathroom for just Rs 50/75.

Hotel Rail View (☎ 76918), opposite the railway station, has rooms for Rs 60/90 and an attached bar and restaurant.

There are *retiring rooms* at the station.

Places to Stay – middle
Hotel Sudarsan (☎ 744322) is good value at Rs 160/190 or from Rs 360/395 with air-con, although rooms at the front can be noisy because of the traffic. All rooms have TV and there are restaurants and a bar.

KERALA

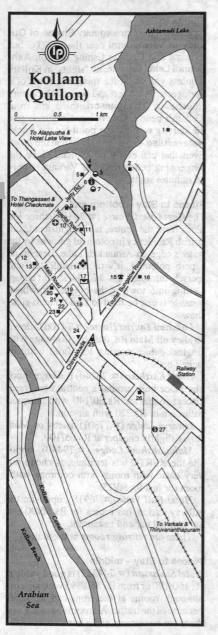

Kollam (Quilon)

Hotel Sea Bee (☎ 75371) is conveniently located on Jetty Rd and has serviceable, though sometimes unkempt rooms for Rs 150/200; Rs 500 for an air-con double.

The KTDC *Yatri Nivas* (☎ 78638) just across the inlet from the boat jetty, is large and rather lost looking. Rooms are Rs 100/150 to Rs 150/200 or Rs 300 for an air-con double. The riverside location is terrific: there's a pleasant waterfront lawn and the staff will run you across the river to the boat jetty in the hotel's speedboat if you ask nicely.

Places to Eat

Hotel Guru Prasad on Main Rd is a fairly ordinary vegetarian place where a 'meal' costs just Rs 10.

The *Azad Hotel* on the same side of the road is a rather brighter vegetarian and non-vegetarian restaurant.

Main Rd also has a decent branch of the *Indian Coffee House*.

PLACES TO STAY	
1	Govt Guest House
2	Yatri Nivas
5	Mahalakshmi Lodge
9	Hotel Sea Bee
11	Hotel Sudarsan
13	Lakshmi Tourist Home
16	Hotel Shah International
20	Iswarya Lodge
23	Hotel Karthika
26	Hotel Rail View

PLACES TO EAT	
18	Supreme Bakers
19	Indian Coffee House
21	Hotel Guru Prasad
22	Azad Hotel
24	Sree Suprabatham Restaurant

OTHER	
3	Boat Jetty
4	Jala Subhiksa Floating Restaurant
6	Tourist Information Centre
7	KSRTC Bus Terminal
8	Shrine of Our Lady of Velamkanni
10	Hospital
12	Fruit & Vegetable Market
14	Bishop Jerome Nagar Shopping Centre
15	Telegraph Office
17	Post Office
25	Clock Tower
27	State Bank of India

The *Sree Suprabatham Restaurant*, hidden away in a courtyard directly opposite the clock tower, is another typical south Indian 'meals' restaurant.

The restaurants in the *Iswarya Lodge* and the *Mahalakshmi Lodge* both have good vegetarian food.

The *Sudarsan Hotel* has a vegetarian 'meals' restaurant and a more expensive air-conditioned non-vegetarian place. It's a good spot for breakfast before a backwater cruise.

Hotel Shah International also has a reasonable restaurant.

Jala Subhiksa, a converted Keralan rice barge moored at the ferry pier, is billed as 'India's first floating restaurant'. It's a great spot for lunch or dinner, and there's an imaginative menu including such international delicacies as 'wooly chicken' and 'Taiwan squid'; mains cost around Rs 60.

Kollam is a cashew-growing centre and nuts are on sale in shops and hotels and from street vendors.

Getting There & Away
Bus Many of the buses leaving the KSRTC bus terminal are en route from somewhere else, so it's the usual pandemonium when a bus arrives. Thankfully, seats in express buses can be reserved in advance. Kollam is on the well-serviced Thiruvananthapuram-Kollam-Alappuzha-Ernakulam bus route. Superexpress services take 1½ hours to Thiruvananthapuram (Rs 25); 1¾ hours to Alappuzha (Rs 25); and 3½ hours to Ernakulam (Rs 45).

Train Kollam is 159km south of Ernakulam and the three to four-hour trip costs Rs 42/185 in 2nd/1st class. The *Trivandrum Mail* from Chennai goes through Kollam, as does the *Mumbai to Kanyakumari Express* and the Mangalore to Thiruvananthapuram coastal service.

The *Quilon Mail* between Kollam and Chennai (Egmore station) via Madurai covers the 760km in 20 hours for Rs 186/642. The trip across the Western Ghats is a delight.

Boat See The Backwaters section for information on the popular backwaters cruise to Alappuzha. Although the public ferry to Alappuzha is still not operating, there are public services across Ashtamudi Lake to Guhanandapuram (one hour) or Muthiraparam (2½ hours); fares are around Rs 6 return. The daily ATDC and DTPC tourist boats to Alappuzha can be booked at various hotels around town and start by bus from the KSRTC bus terminal.

Getting Around
The KSRTC bus terminal and the boat jetty are side by side, but the railway station is on the opposite side of town. Auto-rickshaw drivers are reasonably willing to use their meters; expect to pay around Rs 10 from the railway station to the boat jetty. The *Yatri Nivas* speedboat can be hired to explore the waterways around Kollam for Rs 300 an hour.

ALAPPUZHA (Alleppey)
Pop: 274,000   Tel Area Code: 0477
Like Kollam, this is a pleasant, easy-going market town surrounded by coconut plantations and built on the canals which service the coir industry of the backwaters. With the possible exceptions of an incongruous eight metre high concrete mermaid or the Rajiv Gandhi Memorial Old Age Home for Coir Workers, there's precious little to see for most of the year; but the annual Nehru Cup snakeboat race is an event not to be missed. Any other day of the year, the backwater trip to or from Kollam is the only reason to pass through.

Orientation & Information
The bus stand and boat jetty are conveniently close to each other, and within easy walking distance of most of the cheap hotels. The DTPC Tourist Reception Centre at the boat jetty is very helpful.

Alappuzha's water is notoriously unhealthy. Even if you drink tap water in other places, it's advisable to give Alappuzha's water a miss.

KERALA

Nehru Cup Snakeboat Race

This famous regatta takes place on the second Saturday of August each year. It's held on the lake to the east of the town. Scores of long, low-slung dugouts with highly decorated sterns compete for the cup. Each boat is crewed by up to 100 rowers shaded by gleaming silk umbrellas, all of whom are watched avidly from the banks by thousands of spectators. The annual event celebrates the seafaring and martial traditions of ancient Kerala.

Tickets for the race are available on the day from numerous ticket stands on the way to the lake where the race is held. This entitles you to a seat on the bamboo terraces which are erected for the occasion and which give an excellent view of the lake. Ticket prices range from Rs 10 for standing room to Rs 250 for the Tourist Pavilion, offering the best view at the finishing point.

Take food and drink to the race because there's little available on the lake shore. An umbrella is another necessity because the race takes place during the monsoon and the weather can alternate between driving rain and blistering sunshine.

The race is now repeated during the tourist season as the ingeniously named **Tourism Snakeboat Race**, on the third day of the Great Elephant March in mid-January.

Places to Stay – bottom end

Komala Hotel (☎ 243631), just north of the North Canal, is quite popular and has a good range of rooms. Singles/doubles/triples/quads are Rs 85/130/160/195 and air-con

To Alleppey Prince Hotel (2km)

Footbridge

North Canal

Boat Jetty Road

Mullakal Road

Cullan Road

To PWD
Guest House
& Beach

CCNB Road

South Canal

To Railway
Station

To Kollam

**Alappuzha
(Alleppey)**

0   100   200 m

PLACES TO STAY
1	Sheeba Lodge
2	Komala Hotel
7	Kuttanad Tourist Home
10	Krishna Bhavan Lodge
13	Kadambari Tourist Home
21	St George's Lodging
26	Hotel Raiban

PLACES TO EAT
9	Hotel Annapoorna
16	Hotel Aryas
17	Indian Coffee House
18	Rajas Hotel
19	Sree Durga Bhavan Restaurant
25	Indian Coffee House

OTHER
3	Mermaid Statue
4	Boat Jetty
5	DTPC Reception Centre & Restaurant
6	Bus Stand
8	Vembanad Tourist Services
11	Penguin Tourist Boat Service
12	State Bank of India
14	Temple
15	Temple
20	Temple
22	Post Office
23	Telegraph Office
24	Hospital

singles/doubles are Rs 330/440. It also has an outdoor tandoori restaurant and a bar.

Sheeba Lodge (☎ 244871), behind the Komala, is cheap and habitable at Rs 60/70, with some more expensive doubles.

Kuttanad Tourist Home (☎ 61354) is south of the North Canal, close to the bus stand. It was being completely refurbished at the time of writing, and may be worth checking out.

Krishna Bhavan Lodge (☎ 60453), opposite the boat jetty, has small, rock-bottom rooms built around a courtyard. It's OK (just) for a night at Rs 40/50 with common bath.

Kadambari Tourist Home (☎ 252216), round the corner on Mullakal Rd, is marginally better and has rooms for Rs 50/100.

St George's Lodging (☎ 61620) on CCNB Rd, opposite South Canal, is similarly dingy and similarly priced.

Places to Stay – middle & top end
Hotel Raiban (☎ 251930) is south of the South Canal, en route to the railway station. Rooms are Rs 80/125; Rs 275 for an air-con double. The attached ice-cream parlour offers some intriguing flavours like 'Apricot Quark' and 'Bunny'.

Alleppey Prince Hotel (☎ 243752), three km north of the centre on AS Rd, is centrally air-conditioned and the best place in town. It has a bar, an excellent restaurant and an inviting swimming pool. Rooms are Rs 550/650. It's popular, so book ahead. An autorickshaw from the jetty or town centre should cost Rs 15 to Rs 20; a taxi Rs 60.

Places to Eat
The *restaurant* attached to the DTPC Tourist Reception Centre on the North Canal is cheap, clean and airy and serves a wide variety of breakfasts, snacks and meals.

There's an *Indian Coffee House* branch on Mullakal Rd in the town centre and another, less well kept branch, south of the South Canal, opposite the hospital.

The *Hotel Aryas* on Mullakal Rd serves good, cheap vegetarian meals.

Hotel Komala, *Hotel Raiban*, and *Hotel Annapoorna* all have restaurants.

The *Vembanad Restaurant* at the Alleppey

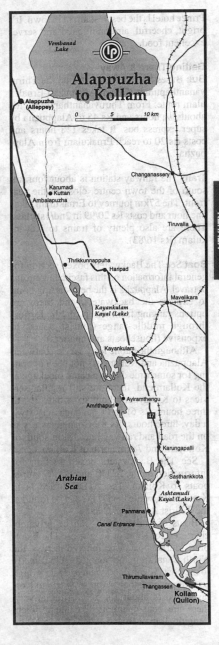

Alappuzha to Kollam

Prince hotel is the best restaurant in town. It's bright, cheerful, air-conditioned and serves excellent food.

Getting There & Away

Bus Buses operate frequently on the Thiruvananthapuram-Kollam-Alappuzha-Ernakulam route. From Thiruvananthapuram, it's about 3¼ hours and Rs 45 to Alappuzha by super express bus. It takes 1¾ hours and costs Rs 20 to reach Ernakulam from Alappuzha.

Train The railway station is about four km south of the town centre, close to the seafront. The 57km journey to Ernakulam takes one hour and costs Rs 20/99 in 2nd/1st class. There are also plenty of trains to Kayankulam (Rs 16/83).

Boat See The Backwaters boxed section for general information on this fascinating means of travel. Alappuzha is the best starting point to explore the backwaters, and there are options ranging from cheap (public ferries) through middle-range (tourist boats) to expensive (houseboats and charters).

Although the public ferry service between Alappuzha and Kollam has not been operating for some time due to a canal blockage at the Kollam end, there are still regular services to Kottayam (about six a day, 2½ to three hours, Rs 6) and Changanassery (two a day, three hours, Rs 8). Changanassery is on the road and railway line, 18km south of Kottayam and 78km north of Kollam.

See The Backwaters boxed section for information on the ATDC and DTPC tourist boats to Kollam. The ATDC office is in Komala Rd, while the DTPC can be found at the Tourist Reception Centre.

Boats of various sizes can be privately chartered for short or long trips. The baby-blue tourist boats are moored across the North Canal from the boat jetty. Go directly to the boats if you don't want to deal through an intermediary tout. A one-way trip to Kottayam costs about Rs 500. Alternatively, there are boat operators like the efficient Penguin Tourist Boat Service (☎ 61522) on Boat Jetty Rd. It has a long list of suggested backwater trips from Alappuzha. Vembanad Tourist Services (☎ 251395) and the DTPC (☎ 253308) also have boats for hire.

KOTTAYAM

Pop: 172,000   Tel Area Code: 0481

Kottayam was a focus for the Syrian Christians of Kerala. Today, it's a centre for rubber production. There are direct buses from here to Periyar Wildlife Sanctuary, and ferries to Alappuzha, so you may well find yourself passing through. The backwater trip from here to Alappuzha is a good alternative to the Alappuzha to Kollam trip.

Information

There's a private bus stand in the town centre, but the railway station two km from the city centre), ferry jetty and KSRTC bus terminal are all some distance away. The Tourist Information Centre has no information.

Temples & Churches

The **Thirunakkara Siva Temple** in the centre of town is only open to Hindus. About three km north-west of the centre are two interesting Syrian Christian churches. **Cheriapally**, St Mary's Orthodox Church or the 'small' church, has an elegant facade spoilt by tacked-on entrance porches. The interior is notable for the 400 year old vegetable dye paintings on the walls and ceiling.

Valiyapally, St Mary's Church or the 'big' church, is 100m away, and is actually smaller than its neighbour. The church was built in 1550. The altar is flanked by stone crosses, one with a Pahlavi Persian inscription. The cross on the left is probably original, but the one on the right is a copy. The guest book goes back to 1899, and was signed by Haile Selassie of Ethiopia in 1956, among others.

Places to Stay

Kaycees Lodge (☎ 563440) is centrally located on YMCA Rd, and has good rooms with attached bathroom for Rs 75/125.

The KTDC *Hotel Aiswarya* (☎ 581440) is also close to the centre, just off Temple Rd.

Rooms are Rs 150/200 to Rs 225/300; Rs 450/550 with air-con. It has the regulation restaurant and beer parlour, and suffers the usual catalogue of broken fittings and missing light bulbs.

The *Ambassador Hotel* (☎ 563293) is less conveniently located on KK Rd. Keep a sharp lookout because it's set back from the road and it's easy to miss the driveway. Singles/doubles are Rs 75/125; air-con doubles are Rs 150.

Homestead Hotel (☎ 560467), further east along KK Rd, has pleasant rooms from Rs 107/210 or Rs 450 for an air-con double, and a vegetarian restaurant.

Hotel Nisha Continental (☎ 563984) on Sastri Rd is good value at Rs 180/250 or Rs 350 for an air-con double, and has a restaurant serving traditional Keralan dishes.

Hotel Aida (☎ 568391) on MC Rd is a little more expensive with rooms for Rs 250/400 or Rs 325/500 with air-con. It has a bar, restaurant and currency exchange.

Anjali Hotel (☎ 563661; fax 563669), near the town centre, on KK Rd, is part of the excellent local Casino hotel chain. It's centrally air-conditioned and rooms range from Rs 525/875 to Rs 875/1000. It has a bar, a coffee shop and several restaurants.

Vembanad Lake Resort (☎ 564866), two km south of the town centre, has cottages in a pleasant lakeside setting for Rs 300 or Rs 500 with air-con.

Places to Eat
Indian Coffee House on TB Rd serves the usual snacks and breakfast.

The nearby *Hotel Black Stone* has basic vegetarian food.

The excellent, partly air-con *Thali Restaurant* at the Homestead Hotel on KK Rd does good thalis for Rs 20.

The Anjali Hotel's selection of restaurants includes the very efficient *Main Street* coffee bar, which has superb food.

It's worth an excursion to eat at the *Vembanad*

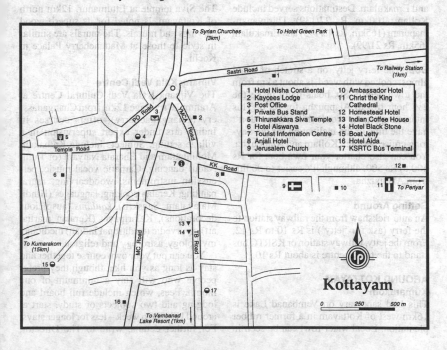

KERALA

1 Hotel Nisha Continental
2 Kaycees Lodge
3 Post Office
4 Private Bus Stand
5 Thirunakkara Siva Temple
6 Hotel Aiswarya
7 Tourist Information Centre
8 Anjali Hotel
9 Jerusalem Church
10 Ambassador Hotel
11 Christ the King Cathedral
12 Homestead Hotel
13 Indian Coffee House
14 Hotel Black Stone
15 Boat Jetty
16 Hotel Aida
17 KSRTC Bus Terminal

To Syrian Churches (3km)
To Hotel Green Park
Sastri Road
To Railway Station (1km)
PO Road
YMCA Road
Temple Road
KK Road
TB Road
MC Road
To Periyar
To Kumarakom (15km)
To Vembanad Lake Resort (1km)

Kottayam

0   250   500 m

Lake Resort's romantic lakeside evening barbecue, or in its atmospheric floating restaurant built in a converted *kettuvallam* (traditional rice barge). It's easy to hail an auto-rickshaw (Rs 20) to get back into town.

Getting There & Away

Bus There's a busy private bus stand in the centre of town, but the KSRTC bus terminal is south of the centre, on TB Rd. Most of the buses are passing through, so you may have to sharpen your elbows to get a seat. There are plenty of buses to Thiruvananthapuram via Kollam and to Kochi. It takes about four hours and costs Rs 25 to reach Thekkady in the Periyar Wildlife Sanctuary. Seven express buses daily come through from Ernakulam and either terminate at Thekkady, in the sanctuary, or continue to Madurai, a further three hours away.

Train Kottayam is well served by express trains running between Thiruvananthapuram and Ernakulam. Destinations served include Kollam (100km, Rs 27/139), Thiruvananthapuram (165km, Rs 43/193) and Ernakulam (65km, Rs 21/99).

Boat The ferry jetty, on a stretch of canal almost choked with weed, is about a km from the town centre. Six boats daily make the 2½ hour trip to Alappuzha for Rs 6. This interesting trip is worthwhile if you don't have the time or the inclination for the day-long cruise between Kollam and Alappuzha. You can also charter your own boat for Rs 400 to Rs 500, although it's easier to do this from Alappuzha.

Getting Around

An auto-rickshaw from the railway station to the ferry (ask for 'jetty') is Rs 10 to Rs 12. From the jetty, railway station or KSRTC bus stand to the town centre is about Rs 10.

AROUND KOTTAYAM
Kumarakom

This bird sanctuary on Vembanad Lake is 16km west of Kottayam in a former rubber plantation. Local water fowl can be seen in abundance, as well as migratory species like the Siberian stork. Recently, several luxury resorts have opened at Kumarakom.

Places to Stay The KTDC *Kumarakom Tourist Village* (☎ 0481-52258) has rooms in houseboats for Rs 1100 to Rs 1800.

Coconut Lagoon Resort (☎ (0481) 92491; Kochi ☎ 668221), part of the luxury Casino Group, has bungalow rooms for US$80/90 and mansion rooms for US$90/100. The setting is beautiful and there's a swimming pool.

Taj Garden Retreat (☎ (0481) 52377; Kochi ☎ 668377) is small but luxurious and is similarly priced.

Buses run regularly from Kottayam to Kumarakom. The Coconut Lagoon Resort can be reached by boat from near Kottayam, from Thanneermukkom (50km from Kochi) or all the way from Alappuzha.

Ettumanur

The Siva temple at Ettumanur, 12km north of Kottayam, is noted for its superb wood carvings and murals. The murals are similar in style to those at Mattancherry Palace in Kochi.

Vijnana Kala Vedi Centre

The Vijnana Kala Vedi Cultural Centre at Aranmula, a village 12km from Changanassery (Changanacherry), offers courses in Indian arts under expert supervision in a village setting. Subjects include Kathakali, Mohiniattam and Bharata Natyam (of Tamil Nadu) dancing, Carnatic vocal music, percussion instruments, woodcarving, mural painting, Keralan cooking, languages (Hindi, Malayalam, Sanskrit), *kaulams* (auspicious decorations), Kalaripayat (Keralan martial art), ayurvedic (traditional Indian) medicine, mythology, astrology and religion.

You can put your own course together and stay as long as you like, though they prefer people who will stay a minimum of one month. Fees, which include full board and lodging and two subjects of study, start at around US$200 a week – less for longer stays. For further details, write to The Director,

Vijnana Kala Vedi Cultural Centre, Tarayil Mukku Junction, Aranmula 689533, Kerala. Changanassery is just south of Kottayam and makes an interesting backwater trip from Alappuzha.

The Western Ghats

PERIYAR WILDLIFE SANCTUARY
Tel Area Code: 04869
Periyar is south India's most popular wildlife sanctuary, but if you go hoping to see tigers, you're almost certain to be disappointed. The great cats require an enormous amount of territory on which to lead their solitary lives and it's estimated the 777 sq km sanctuary has just 35 tigers and leopards. If, on the other hand, you treat Periyar as a pleasant escape from the rigours of Indian travel, a nice place to cruise on the lake, and an opportunity to see some wildlife and enjoy a jungle walk, then you will probably find a visit well worthwhile. The park encompasses a 26 sq km artificial lake, created by the British in 1895 to provide water to Madurai, and spreads into Tamil Nadu. It is home to bison, antelopes, sambars, wild boars, monkeys, langurs, a wide variety of birds, and some 750 elephants.

Orientation & Information
Kumily is the junction town straddling the Kerala/Tamil Nadu border just north of the park boundary. It's a small, bustling place, full of spice dealers, located about four km from Thekkady. Thekkady is the centre inside the park where the KTDC hotels and the boat jetty are located. When people refer to the sanctuary, they tend to use Kumily, Thekkady and Periyar synonymously, which can be confusing. The name 'Periyar' is used to refer to the whole park.

There's a Wildlife Information Centre near the boat jetty in Thekkady. It's advisable to bring warm clothes and waterproof clothing to Periyar. A three-day entry fee to the park

costs Rs 60 for foreigners plus Rs 10 for each additional visit.

Visiting the Park
Boat trips on the lake are the standard way of seeing the sanctuary, but spend one day at Periyar and take a midday boat trip and you're unlikely to see anything. 'As soon as a shy animal sticks its head up', reported one visitor, 'all aboard shout and scream until it goes again'. The standard two-hour boat trips cost Rs 25 on the lower deck and Rs 50 on the upper deck. There are five cruises a day: at 7, 9.30 and 11.30 am and 2 and 4 pm. The first and last departures offer the best wildlife-spotting prospects. It's better to get a small group together (the smaller the better) and charter your own boat. They're available in a variety of sizes from Rs 500 per cruise for a 12-person boat.

Jungle walks can also be interesting. A daily three-hour walk departs at 7.30 am and costs Rs 10 per person. Guides can also be arranged from the Wildlife Information Centre for walks further into the park. Curiously, they don't promote this activity, so you must ask insistently about it. Visitors are not allowed to walk in the park without an accompanying guide. Some of the guides are very knowledgeable and they're certainly cautious in areas where animals may be present.

The third way to see wildlife is to spend a night in one of the observation towers or resthouses, although these are often booked out weeks in advance. Observation towers cost Rs 160 a night plus the boat drop-off charge and you must bring your own food supplies; resthouses cost Rs 300 per night plus Rs 60 for meals. Elephant rides (Rs 30 for two people for 30 minutes) are for fun, not for serious wildlife viewing.

The best time to visit the sanctuary is between September and May. The hot season (February to May) may be less comfortable but will offer more wildlife sightings because other water sources dry up and the wildlife is forced to come down to the lakeside. Weekends are best avoided because of noisy day-trippers. What you see is a matter of luck, but even those elusive tigers do show themselves occasionally. One guide reported that in the three years he had spent at the park, he had seen tigers only twice: on one occasion, he saw a tiger swimming in the lake close to the Lake Palace Hotel.

Mangaladevi Temple

This temple, 13km from Kumily, is just a jumble of ruins but the views are magnificent. At present, the road to the temple is closed. If it reopens, it's possible to get there by rented jeep or by bicycle – although it's uphill all the way from Kumily. By jeep from Kumily, count on a three to four-hour round trip, including a lunch stop.

Organised Tours

A two-day Periyar Wildlife Sanctuary tour leaves Thiruvananthapuram most Saturdays at 6.30 am and gets back on Sunday at 9 pm. It costs Rs 300, does not include food or accommodation, and must be one of the silliest tours in India, since there's no time to see any wildlife – even if it were possible in the company of a busload of garrulous honeymooners.

Places to Stay & Eat

Outside the Sanctuary Kumily is a one-street town, but it has accommodation ranging from dirt cheap to luxurious. Although it's four km from the lake, you can catch the semi-regular bus, hire a bicycle or set off on foot; it's a pleasant, shady walk into the park.

Muckumkal Tourist Home (☎ 22070) is close to the bus stand. Avoid the back rooms, which can be noisy if the hotel's generator is switched on. Rooms with attached bathroom

To Kottayam
To Madurai
TAMIL NADU
Kumily
Bridge
To Mangaladevi
Temple (12km)
& Mullakuddy
Rest House
3 km

Periyar Wildlife Sanctuary

0   250   500 m

Thekkady

Periyar Lake

To Lake Palace

KERALA

PLACES TO STAY
4 Muckumkal Tourist Home
6 Lake Queen Tourist Home
8 Rolex Lodge
9 Woodlands Tourist Bhavan
11 Karthika Tourist Home
12 Spice Village
14 Hotel Ambadi
16 Leelapankaj
19 Periyar House
20 Aranya Nivas Hotel

PLACES TO EAT
15 Coffee Inn
22 Snack Bar

OTHER
1 Tamil Nadu Bus Terminal
2 Bus Stand & Tourist Taxis
3 Post Office
5 Mosque
7 Church
10 Hospital
13 Forest Check Point
17 Post Office
18 Park Entry Post
21 Wildlife Information Centre
23 Boat Jetty

are Rs 55/150; air-con doubles are Rs 450. The hotel's *Little Chef Restaurant* is a reasonable place to eat.

Lake Queen Tourist Home (☎ 22084), next to the Kottayam road junction, has 54 rooms from Rs 100/250. The *Lakeland Restaurant* is downstairs.

Rolex Lodge (☎ 22081), along the road to the park, has basic doubles with bathroom for Rs 100 to Rs 150.

Woodlands Tourist Bhavan (☎ 22077), close by, is a bit gloomy but cheap with doubles for Rs 100 or Rs 125 with attached bath. You might also find a cheap bed in one of the two large dorms.

Karthika Tourist Home (☎ 22146), further towards the park entrance, has rooms with bath for Rs 100/150 and a vegetarian restaurant.

Spice Village (☎ 22315) is a well-designed Casino Group resort with attractive cottages in a pleasant garden with a swimming pool. The tariff is US$80/90.

Hotel Ambadi (☎ 2219) has cottages for Rs 350 to Rs 600 and rooms for Rs 810. It's in a beautiful setting and has quite a good restaurant.

There are a few cheap *meals* places along Kumily's main drag.

Coffee Inn is a popular outdoor cafe with an eclectic selection of music and good travellers' fare (including home-made brown bread). In the tradition of travellers' restaurants in India, the food takes a *long* time to arrive. There are also a couple of small *rooms* available.

Inside the Sanctuary The KTDC has three hotels in the park. It's a good idea to make advance reservations, particularly for weekend visits. This can be done at any KTDC office or hotel.

Periyar House (☎ 22026), the cheapest of the three, is very popular. Rooms range from Rs 700 to Rs 1100, including breakfast and dinner.

Aranya Nivas (☎ 22023) has very pleasant rooms for Rs 1000/1500 and air-con suites for Rs 1150/2200. These prices drop considerably in the low season. There's a bar, garden

area, TV lounge, postal and banking facilities and a small handicrafts shop. Food in the restaurant is excellent, and most nights there's a Rs 250 buffet. Guests at the Aranya Nivas are entitled to a free morning and afternoon boat trip.

Lake Palace (bookings and reception at Aranya Nivas ☎ 22023) is well away from the noise of day-trippers. Guests are transferred to the hotel by boat and should arrive at the Thekkady boat jetty by 4 pm for the final trip of the day back to the hotel. The six suites in the palace, at one time the maharaja's game lodge, cost Rs 4000/6000 a night, including meals and boating. If you can afford it, it's a delightful place to stay and you can actually see animals from your room. With a guide, it's possible to walk to the Lake Palace from the boat jetty in about an hour.

There are *rest houses* in the sanctuary at Manakavala (eight km from Kumily), Mullakkudy (39km) and Edappalayam (five km). Not all of them may be open for visitors but you can find out and book at the Wildlife Information Centre. The rest houses cost Rs 200/300 and have a keeper who will cook for you, although you must bring your own food.

There are also *observation towers* for Rs 50, which can be booked at the Wildlife Information Centre. Although they're primitive, and you must provide all your own food and bedding, you stand the best chance of seeing animals if you rent one. One of the watchtowers is a short stroll from the Lake Palace.

Near the boat jetty in Thekkady, there's a *snack bar* offering basic food, snacks and drinks.

Getting There & Away
Bus The bus stand in Kumily is just a bit of spare land at the eastern edge of town near the state border. All buses originating or terminating at Periyar start and finish at Aranya Nivas in Thekkady, but they also stop at the Kumily bus stand.

Buses operate on the Ernakulam, Kottayam, Kumily, Madurai route. There are four express buses daily between Ernakulam and Kumily, three continuing to Madurai.

KERALA

Buses to Ernakulam take six hours and cost Rs 50.

The 110km trip from Kottayam takes about four hours and costs Rs 25. Regular buses go every half hour. The buses pass through rubber plantations and villages with pastel-coloured churches and rocket-like shrines. The road then climbs steadily through a mass of tea, coffee and cardamom plantations.

At least two direct buses daily make the eight-hour trip to Thiruvananthapuram (Rs 65). Another goes to Kovalam (nine hours), and another to Kodaikanal (6½ hours). One bus a day makes the spectacular trip to Munnar (4½ hours).

Getting Around
A bus operates between Kumily and Thekaddy every 15 minutes (or at least it's supposed to) for Rs 2. An auto-rickshaw costs Rs 30. The KTDC Periyar House and Aranya Nivas both have bicycles for rent at Rs 25 a day.

MUNNAR
Tel Area Code: 04865
Set amid southern India's most dramatic mountain scenery, the tiny hill town of Munnar (1524m) is the commercial centre of some of the world's highest tea-growing estates. The combination of craggy peaks, manicured tea estates and crisp mountain air makes Munnar a delightful alternative to the better-known hill stations of Tamil Nadu. But despite its magnificent scenery and wonderful walks, the town sees few western travellers – though it's a perennial favourite of Indian honeymooners.

Information
While the official Tourist Information Office, two km from the bus stand, is totally useless, it is more than compensated for by local eccentric Joseph Lype, who ran an electrical repair shop in the town for 40 years before becoming the town's self-appointed ambassador, tourist guide and fixer. Joseph has a booth in the bazaar, not far from the bus

stand, and can arrange accommodation, meals, tours etc according to your budget.

Walks & Views
While the **walks** out of Munnar in any direction offer spectacular views, it's worth taking an auto-rickshaw (Rs 125 return) the 16km to **Eravikulam National Park** (entrance Rs 50) where you can see the rare, but almost tame Nilgiri tahr (a type of mountain goat), or clamber over the slopes of **Anamudi** (2695m), southern India's highest peak.

A little further afield is **Top Station**, on Kerala's border with Tamil Nadu, which has spectacular views over the ghats and plains below. Regular buses form Munnar make the steep 32km climb to Top Station in around an hour, or you can hire a jeep for the return trip for around Rs 400.

Places to Stay & Eat
There's no shortage of accommodation in and around Munnar, though there's not much choice at the bottom end of the price range.

The *Govt Guest House* (☎ 30385) is a ramshackle old bungalow with rock-bottom rooms for Rs 50.

Sree Narayana Tourist Home (☎ 30212), near the Tourist Information Office, is the best cheap lodge in town and has singles/doubles starting at Rs 175/200.

Hotel Poopada (☎ 30223) nearby is a little more expensive but still good value at Rs 210/280. There's also a good, cheap *restaurant*.

Hotel Isaac's The Residency (☎ 30247), *Hotel Hill View* (☎ 30567), *Edassery Eastend* (☎ 30451) and the *Royal Retreat* (☎ 30240) are all good mid-range options with comfortable doubles in the Rs 450 to Rs 750 range. The Hill View, Eastend and Royal Retreat also have excellent *restaurants* open to non-residents.

Woodlands coffee shop in the bazaar does excellent south Indian meals and coffee.

Getting There & Away
Munnar is 130km east of Kochi via Aluva (Alwaye) and 70km north of Periyar. It's best reached by direct bus from Kochi (five daily,

4½ hours), Kottayam (five daily, five hours), Kumily (one daily, 4½ hours), Thiruvananthapuram (four daily, nine hours), Coimbatore (two daily, six hours) or Madurai (one daily, five hours).

AROUND MUNNAR
Thattekkad Bird Sanctuary
This sanctuary is 20km from Kothamangalam, on the Ernakulam to Munnar road. It's home to Malabar grey hornbills, woodpeckers, parakeets, and rarer species like the Sri Lankan frogmouth and rose-billed roller. Boat cruises are available from Boothathankettu to Thattekkad. The best time to visit is from 5 to 6 am. There's an *Inspection Bungalow* at Boothathankettu, as well as a few mid-range *hotels* in Kothamangalam.

PARAMBIKULAM WILDLIFE SANCTUARY
The Parambikulam Wildlife Sanctuary, 48km south of Palakkad, stretches around the Parambikulam, Thunakadavu and Peruvaripallam dams, and covers an area of 285 sq km adjacent to the Anamalai Wildlife Sanctuary in Tamil Nadu. It's home to elephants, bison, gaur, sloth bears, wild boars, sambars, chital, crocodiles and a few tigers and panthers. The sanctuary is open all year, but is best avoided from June to August due to the monsoon.

The sanctuary headquarters are at Thunakadavu, where the Forestry Department has an *Inspection Bungalow* and a tree-top hut (book through the Range Officer). At Parambikulam, there's a *PWD Rest House* and a Tamil Nadu government *Inspection Bungalow* (book through the Junior Engineer, Tamil Nadu PWD, Parambikulam). There are also two *watchtowers*: one at Anappadi (eight km from Thunakadavu) and another at Zungam (five km from Thunakadavu).

The best access to the sanctuary is by bus from Pollachi (40km from Coimbatore and 49km from Palakkad). There are four buses in either direction between Pollachi and Parambikulam daily. The trip takes two hours. Boat cruises operate from Parambikulam and rowboats can be hired at Thunakadavu.

Northern Kerala

KOCHI (Cochin)
Pop: 602,000   Tel Area Code: 0484
With its wealth of historical associations and its beautiful setting on a cluster of islands and narrow peninsulas, the fascinating city of Kochi perfectly reflects the eclecticism of Kerala. Here, you can see the oldest church in India, winding streets crammed with 500 year old Portuguese houses, cantilevered Chinese fishing nets, a Jewish community whose roots go back to the Diaspora, a 16th century synagogue, and a palace built by the Portuguese and given to the Raja of Cochin. The palace, which was later renovated by the Dutch, contains some of India's most beautiful murals. Another must-see is a performance of the world-famous Kathakali dance-drama.

The older parts of Fort Cochin and Mattancherry are an unlikely blend of medieval Portugal, Holland and an English country village grafted onto the tropical Malabar Coast – a radical contrast to the bright lights, bustle and big hotels of mainland Ernakulam.

Kochi is one of India's largest ports and a major naval base. The misty silhouettes of huge merchant ships can be seen anchored off the point of Fort Cochin, waiting for a berth in the docks of Willingdon Island, an artificial island created with material dredged up when the harbour was deepened. All day, ferries scuttle back and forth between the various parts of Kochi. Dolphins can often be seen in the harbour.

Orientation
Kochi consists of mainland Ernakulam; the islands of Willingdon, Bolgatty and Gundu in the harbour; Fort Cochin and Mattancherry on the southern peninsula; and Vypeen Island, north of Fort Cochin. All these areas are linked by ferry; bridges also link Ernakulam to Willingdon Island and the Fort Cochin/Mattancherry peninsula. Most hotels and restaurants are in Ernakulam, where

you'll also find the main railway station and bus terminal and the Tourist Reception Centre.

Almost all the historical sites are in Fort Cochin or Mattancherry, but accommodation and restaurant facilities are limited in these areas. The airport and two of the top hotels are on Willingdon Island.

Information
Tourist Offices The KTDC's Tourist Reception Centre (☎ 330031) on Ernakulam's Shanmugham Rd has limited information but will organise accommodation at the Bolgatty Palace Hotel and arrange conducted harbour cruises. The office is open from 8 am to 7 pm daily. The tiny Tourist Desk (☎ 371761) at Ernakulam's main ferry jetty is privately run but much more helpful. It has a good map and tourist literature and will recommend and book accommodation and tours; it's open daily from 9 am to 5 pm. If you can find a copy, *Hello Cochin* is a handy bi-monthly travel information booklet which includes timetables.

The Government of India Tourist Office (ITDC) (☎ 666045) is next to the Malabar Hotel on Willingdon Island, and offers a

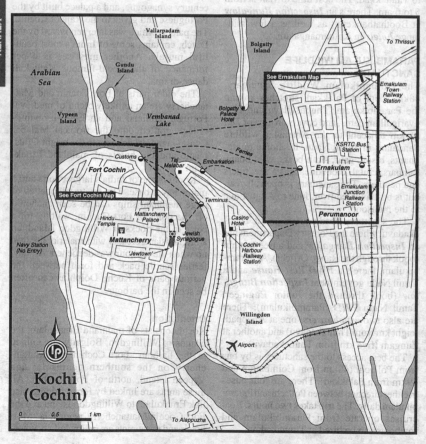

Kochi
(Cochin)

The Jews of Kochi

Kochi (Cochin) is home to a tiny, isolated and unexpected Jewish community descended from Jewish settlers who fled Palestine 2000 years ago. The first Jewish settlement was at Kodungallur (Cranganore), north of Kochi. Like the Syrian Orthodox Christians, the Jews became involved in the trade and commerce of the Malabar Coast. Preserved in the Mattancherry synagogue are a number of copper plates bearing an ancient inscription granting the village of Anjuvannam (near Kodungallur) and its revenue to a Jewish merchant, Joseph Rabban, by King Bhaskara Ravi Varman I (962-1020). You can see these plates with the permission of the synagogue guardian.

Concessions given to Joseph Rabban by Ravi Varman I included permission to use a palanquin and parasol. Palanquins and parasols in those days were the prerogative of rulers, so in effect, Ravi Varman I had sanctioned the creation of a tiny Jewish kingdom. On Rabban's death, his sons fought each other for control of the 'kingdom' and this rivalry led to its break-up and the move to Mattancherry.

The community has been the subject of much research. An interesting study by an American professor of ethnomusicology found that the music of the Cochin Jews contained strong Babylonian influences, and that their version of the Ten Commandments was almost identical to a Kurdish version housed in the Berlin Museum Archives. Of course, there has also been much local influence, and many of the hymns are similar to ragas.

The community has diminished rapidly since Indian independence and now numbers only about 20, and lacks enough adult males to perform certain rituals without outside assistance. There has been no rabbi within living memory, so all the elders are qualified to perform religious ceremonies and marriages. ∎

KERALA

range of leaflets and maps. There's a Tourist Information counter at Kochi airport during flight hours.

Post & Telecommunications The GPO (including poste restante) is at Fort Cochin, but you can have mail sent to the main post office on Hospital Rd in Ernakulam, as long as it's specifically addressed to that office. STD/ISD booths are found all over town.

Visa Extensions Apply at the office of the Commissioner of Police (☎ 360700), at the northern end of Shanmugham Rd, Ernakulam. Visa extensions can take up to 10 days to issue and you have to leave your passport at the office during that time.

Bookshops Bhavi Books on Convent Rd, Ernakulam, is a good bookshop. There are a number of bookshops along Press Club Rd, although they chiefly stock books in Malayalam. Try Cosmo Books or Current Books for titles in English. Higginbothams is on Chittoor Rd, at the junction with Hospital Rd.

Other Shops There are a number of handicraft emporiums along MG Rd, just south of

Durbar Hall Rd. A useful camera and film supplier is SP & Co on Convent Rd.

Fort Cochin

St Francis Church India's oldest European-built church was constructed in 1503 by Portuguese Franciscan friars who accompanied the expedition led by Pedro Alvarez Cabral.

The original structure was made out of wood, but the church was rebuilt in stone around the mid-16th century; the earliest Portuguese inscription found in the church is dated 1562. The Protestant Dutch captured Kochi in 1663 and restored the church in 1779. After the occupation of Kochi by the British in 1795, it became an Anglican church and it is presently being used by the Church of South India.

Vasco da Gama, the first European to reach India by sailing around Africa, died in Cochin in 1524 and was buried here for 14 years before his remains were transferred to Lisbon in Portugal. His tombstone can be seen inside the church. Rope-operated *punkahs*, or fans, are one of the unusual features of this church.

Sunday services are held in English at 8 am and in Malayalam at 9.30 am.

KERALA

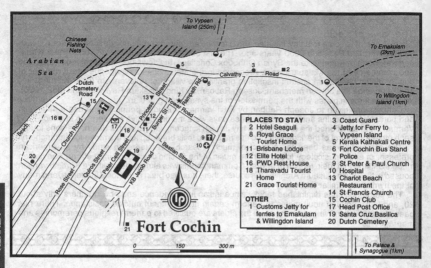

To Vypeen
Island (250m)

*Chinese
Fishing
Nets*

A r a b i a n

S e a

To Emakulam
(2km)

Dutch
Cemetery
Road

Calvathy   Road

To Willingdon
Island (1km)

Beach

To Palace &
Synagogue (1km)

Fort Cochin

0   150   300 m

PLACES TO STAY		3	Coast Guard
2	Hotel Seagull	4	Jetty for Ferry to
8	Royal Grace		Vypeen Island
	Tourist Home	5	Kerala Kathakali Centre
11	Brisbane Lodge	6	Fort Cochin Bus Stand
12	Elite Hotel	7	Police
16	PWD Rest House	9	St Peter & Paul Church
18	Tharavadu Tourist	10	Hospital
	Home	13	Chariot Beach
21	Grace Tourist Home		Restaurant
		14	St Francis Church
OTHER		15	Cochin Club
1	Customs Jetty for	17	Head Post Office
	ferries to Emakulam	19	Santa Cruz Basilica
	& Willingdon Island	20	Dutch Cemetery

Santa Cruz Basilica This large, impressive church dates from 1902, and has a fantastical pastel-coloured interior.

Chinese Fishing Nets Strung out along the tip of Fort Cochin, these fixed, cantilevered fishing nets were introduced by traders from the court of Kublai Khan. You can also see them along the backwaters between Kochi and Kottayam, and between Alappuzha and Kollam. They're mainly used at high tide, and require at least four men to operate their system of counterweights.

Mattancherry
Built by the Portuguese in 1555, **Mattancherry Palace** was presented to the Raja of Cochin, Veera Kerala Varma (1537-61), as a gesture of goodwill (and probably as a means of securing trading privileges).

The palace's alternative name, the 'Dutch Palace', resulted from substantial renovations by the Dutch after 1663. The two-storey, quadrangular building surrounds a courtyard containing a Hindu temple.

The central hall on the 1st floor was the Coronation Hall of the rajas. Their dresses, turbans and palanquins are now on display,

but more important are the astonishing **murals**, depicting scenes from the *Ramayana*, *Mahabharata* and Puranic legends connected with Siva, Vishnu, Krishna, Kumara and Durga.

These beautiful and extensive murals rarely seem to be mentioned, although they are one of the wonders of India. The staff like to keep some galleries closed (such as the ladies' bedchamber downstairs) and quietly charge extra to see it, and in some cases it's worth paying. The bedchamber is definitely worth seeing because it features a cheerful Krishna using his six hands and two feet to engage in foreplay with eight happy milk-maids.

The palace is open Saturday to Thursday from 10 am to 5 pm; entry is free but you may be asked to make a 'donation'. Photography is not permitted and there are no postcards or reproductions of the murals on sale. There are B&W photographs of the murals in the Archaeological Survey of India's *Monuments of Kerala* booklet by H Sarkar (1978), and they also appear in *Cochin Murals* by VR Chitra & TN Srinivasan (Cochin, 1940), and *South Indian Paintings* by C Sivaramamurti (New Delhi, 1968).

Jewish Synagogue Originally constructed in 1568, the synagogue was destroyed by shelling during a Portuguese raid in 1662 and was rebuilt two years later when the Dutch took over Kochi. It's an interesting little place, with hand-painted, willow-pattern floor tiles brought from Canton in China in the mid-18th century by Ezekial Rahabi, who was also responsible for the erection of the building's clock tower.

A synagogue built at Kochangadi in 1344 has since disappeared, although a stone slab from this building, inscribed in Hebrew, can be found on the inner surface of the wall which surrounds the Mattancherry synagogue.

The area around the synagogue is known as **Jewtown** and is one of the centres of the Kochi spice trade. Scores of small firms huddle together in old, dilapidated buildings and the air is filled with the pungent aromas of ginger, cardamom, cumin, turmeric and cloves. Many Jewish names are visible on business premises and houses, and there are several interesting curio shops on the street leading up to the synagogue.

The synagogue is open Sunday to Friday, from 10 am to noon and from 3 to 5 pm. Entry is Rs 1. The synagogue's guardians are friendly and keen to talk about the building and the Jewish community.

Ernakulam
Parishath Thampuram Museum This museum contains 19th century oil paintings, old coins, sculptures and Mughal paintings, but apart from some interesting temple models, it's nothing special. The museum is housed in an enormous, traditional Keralan building (previously Durbar Hall) on Durbar Hall Rd. It's open Tuesday to Sunday from 10 am to 12.30 pm and from 2 to 4.30 pm; entry is free.

Vypeen & Gundu Islands
Ferries shuttle across the narrow strait from Fort Cochin to Vypeen Island. The island boasts a lighthouse at Ochanthuruth (open from 3 to 5 pm daily), good beaches, and the early 16th century Palliport Fort (open Thursdays). Gundu, the smallest island in the

harbour, is close to Vypeen. It has a coir factory making doormats from coconut fibre. Fishers will take you to Gundu from Vypeen.

Around Kochi
The **Hill Palace Museum** is at Tripunithura, 12km south-east of Ernakulam, en route to Kottayam. The hilltop museum houses the collections of the Cochin and Travancore royal families. It's open Tuesday to Sunday from 9 am to 12.30 pm and from 2 to 4 pm; entry is Rs 1. Bus No 51 or 58 will take you there.

The **Museum of Kerala History** is at Edapally, 10km north-east of Ernakulam en route to Aluva (Alwaye) and Thrissur. It's open Tuesday to Sunday from 10 am to noon and from 2 to 4 pm; entry is Rs 2. Bus No 22 runs to Edapally.

Kathakali Performances
The origins of India's most spectacular dance-drama go back 500 years to a time when open-air performances were held in temple courtyards or in villages. There are more than 100 different arrangements, all of them

Kathakali dancers.

KERALA

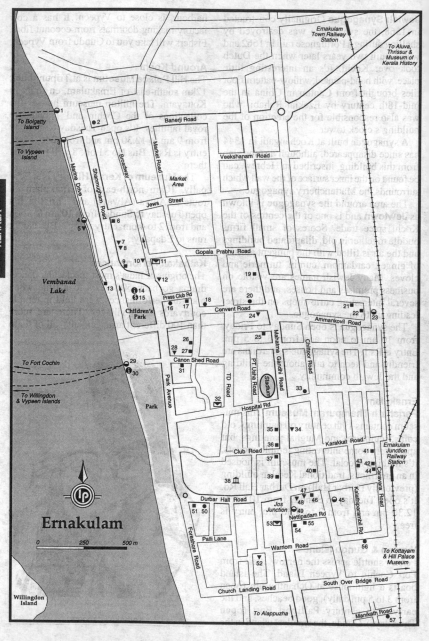

To Bolgatty
Island

To Vypeen
Island

Banerji Road

Veekshanam Road

Market
Area

Jews Street

Gopala Prabhu Road

Vembanad
Lake

Children's
Park

To Fort Cochin

To Willingdon
& Vypeen Islands

Press Club Rd

Convent Road

Ammankovil Road

Park
Avenue

Canon Shed Road

Park

Hospital Rd

Club Road

Karakkat Road

Durbar Hall Road

Jos
Junction

Nettipadam Rd

Palli Lane

Warriom Road

South Over Bridge Road

Church Landing Road

To Alappuzha

Foreshore
Road

Manikath Road

Ernakulam
Town Railway
Station

To Aluva,
Thrissur &
Museum of
Kerala History

Ernakulam
Junction
Railway
Station

Ernakulam
Junction
Railway
Station

To Kottayam
& Hill Palace
Museum

Ernakulam

0   250   500 m

Willingdon
Island

Marine Drive

Shanmugham Road

Broadway

Market Road

Chittoor Road

Mahatma Gandhi Road

PT Usha Road

TD Road

Foreshore Road

Kalathiparambil Rd

Cannava Road

based on stories from the *Ramayana* and *Mahabharata*. They are designed to continue well into the early hours of the morning. Since most visitors don't have the inclination to stay up all night, the centres which put on the dance offer shortened versions lasting about 1½ hours.

Kathakali isn't simply another form of dancing, it incorporates elements of yoga and Ayurvedic medicine. All the props are fashioned from natural materials – powdered minerals and the sap of certain trees for the bright facial make-up; the beaten bark of certain trees, dyed with fruits and spices, for wigs; coconut oil for mixing up the colours; burnt coconut oil for the black paint around the eyes; and eggplant flowers tucked under the eyelids to turn the whites of the eyes deep red. The make-up process before the dance is quite a show in its own right.

The dancers are usually accompanied by drummers and a harmonium player. A government-run school, near Palakkad in northern Kerala, teaches Kathakali dancing. Courses in Kathakali can also be taken at the Vijnana Kala Vedi Centre.

The evening starts with an explanation of the symbolism of the facial expressions, hand movements and ritualistic gestures. This is followed by an actual dance-drama lasting about one hour. All performances are Rs 50.

The See India Foundation (☎ 369471) at Devan Gurukulam, Kalathiparambil Rd, is near the Ernakulam Junction railway station. The show features an extraordinary presentation by PK Devan, who explains the dance's history and makes a plucky attempt to simplify Hinduism. Makeup begins at 6 pm, and the performance runs from 6.45 to 8 pm, with time for questions afterwards.

The Kerala Kathakali Centre stages performances at the Cochin Aquatic Club on River Rd, Fort Cochin, near the bus stand. Enthusiastic performances from young Kathakali artists nicely balance the more formal introduction to the art at the See India Foundation. Makeup begins at 5 pm, and the performance runs from 6.30 to 7.30 pm. The last ferry from Fort Cochin to Ernakulum departs after the performance at 9.30 pm.

The Cochin Cultural Centre (☎ 367866), 'Souhardham', Manikath Rd, is south of Ernakulam Junction railway station. The dance is held in a specially constructed air-conditioned theatre designed to resemble a temple courtyard. Some visitors find the introductions disappointing and extra may be charged for photography. Makeup begins at 5.30 pm and the performance runs from 6.30 to 8 pm.

KERALA

PLACES TO STAY		PLACES TO EAT			
6	Sealord Hotel	5	Ancient Mariner	11	Post Office
9	Hakoba Hotel	7	Bimbi's	14	KTDC Tourist
13	Taj Residency	8	Athul Jyoti		Reception Centre
17	Basoto Lodge	10	Bharath Coffee House	15	State Bank of India
19	Hotel Abad Plaza	12	Caravan Ice	16	Cosmo Books &
21	Hotel Luciya		Cream		Current Books
22	Ninans Tourist Lodge	24	Chariot Restaurant	18	SP & Co
25	Queen's Residency	28	Indian Coffee House	20	Bhavi Books
26	Deepak Lodge	34	Pandhal Restaurant	23	KSRTC Bus
27	Bijus Tourist Home	47	Indian Coffee House		Terminal
31	Maple Tourist Home	48	Bimbi's & Khyber	29	Main Jetty
35	Grand Hotel		Restaurant	30	Tourist Desk
36	Woodlands	52	Chinese Garden	32	Main Post Office
37	Geetha Lodge		Restaurant	33	Higginbothams
39	Anantha Bhavan			38	Parishath Thampuram
40	Hotel Sangeetha	**OTHER**			Museum
41	The Metropolitan	1	High Court Jetty &	45	Ernakulam South Bus
42	Hotel KK International		Ferry to Bolgatty		Stand
43	Paulson Park Hotel		Island	49	Bus to Fort Cochin
44	Premier Tourist Home	2	Commissioner of	50	Indian Airlines
46	Hotel Joyland		Police	53	Post Office
51	Bharat Tourist Home	3	Private Ferry to	56	See India
54	The Avenue Regent		Vypeen Island		Foundation
55	Hotel Excellency	4	Sealord Jetty	57	Cochin Cultural
					Centre

Organised Tours

The KTDC offers daily boat cruises around Kochi harbour which visit Willingdon Island, Mattancherry Palace, the Jewish Synagogue, Fort Cochin (including St Francis Church), the Chinese fishing nets and Bolgatty Island. The 3½ hour tours depart from the Sealord Boat Jetty, just north of the Tourist Reception Centre, at 9 am and 2 pm, and cost Rs 50. The KTDC Sunset Cruise from 5.30 to 7 pm costs Rs 30, but is frequently cancelled, so check early in the day to avoid disappointment.

The Tourist Desk by the Ernakulam Jetty operates three hour village backwater cruises in traditional open canoes, which include bus transport (45 minutes each way) from the jetty car park to the starting point. The trips depart at 9 am and 2 pm and cost Rs 250. They visit coir villages and coconut plantations, and give plenty of opportunity to see how life is lived along the narrow canals. Similar cruises operated by the KTDC depart at 8.30 am and 2.30 pm and cost Rs 300.

Places to Stay

Ernakulam has accommodation in all price brackets. Fort Cochin has a handful of cheap places and one in the mid-range. Bolgatty Island has one unique mid-range place and Willingdon Island has two top-end places.

Places to Stay – bottom end

Fort Cochin The choice is limited at Fort Cochin, although it's the most romantic place to stay.

Royal Grace Tourist Home (☎ 223584) is a modern new budget hotel opposite the St Peter & Paul church. Large double rooms with attached bath are Rs 125 or Rs 300 with air-con; breakfast is an additional Rs 10. Under the same management is the smaller, but similarly priced *Grace Tourist Home* on KB Jacob Rd south of the basilica.

Tharavadu Tourist Home (☎ 226897) on Quiros St is an airy and spacious traditional house with good views of the surrounding streets from the rooftop area. Doubles with bathroom are Rs 105 to Rs 135 or there's a

top-floor room for Rs 155, although it involves sharing a bathroom.

Elite Hotel (☎ 225733) on Princess St is a long-term favourite and has doubles with attached bathroom for Rs 100 to Rs 200. There's a popular restaurant downstairs.

Brisbane Lodge (☎ 225962), a couple of doors away, has three presentable rooms for Rs 100/150.

The *PWD Rest House* is nicely situated near the waterfront, but has just two double rooms for Rs 100 each.

Ernakulam

Basoto Lodge (☎ 352140) on Press Club Rd is small, simple, friendly and popular, so get there early. Singles with common bathroom cost Rs 40, while doubles with attached bathroom are Rs 90. Mosquito nets are provided.

Hakoba Hotel (☎ 353933), conveniently located on the busy Shanmugham Rd waterfront, is another good choice, although construction has spoilt the views. Doubles with attached bathroom start at Rs 160 or Rs 300 with air-con, and there's a restaurant, bar and even a (not very reliable) lift.

Maple Tourist Home (☎ 371711), on Canon Shed Rd near the main jetty, is good value with doubles for Rs 165 to Rs 220 or Rs 330 with air-con. The roof garden overlooks the jetty.

Bijus Tourist Home (☎ 369881) is a friendly place on the corner of Canon Shed and Market Rds and has rooms for Rs 125/200, with air-con doubles for Rs 360. This place is excellent value and even has hot water.

Queens Residency (☎ 365775) is a quaint Indian-style hotel with rooms for Rs 130/185 or Rs 370 with air-con.

Hotel KK International (☎ 366010), opposite the Ernakulam Junction railway station, is good value at Rs 150/200 or Rs 250/400 with air-con.

Geetha Lodge (☎ 352136) on MG Rd has simple rooms for Rs 130/200.

Anantha Bhavan (☎ 382071), nearby, has rooms for Rs 80/150 to Rs 120/230 and air-con doubles for Rs 260.

Ninans Tourist Lodge (☎ 351235) is close to the inconveniently situated KSRTC bus terminal. It's a shocker, but cheap at just Rs 50/75.

Hotel Luciya (☎ 381177), not far away, is pleasant and friendly and offers much better value at Rs 85/170 or Rs 190/275 with air-con. It has a bar, restaurant, TV lounge and laundry service.

Places to Stay – middle

Fort Cochin On Calvathy Rd, *Hotel Seagull* (☎ 228128) is right on the waterfront overlooking the harbour, and was created by converting a number of old houses and warehouses. There are doubles for Rs 200 downstairs, Rs 300 upstairs or Rs 400 with air-con. You can watch ships come and go from the bar and restaurant.

Bolgatty Island On Bolgatty Island, *Bolgatty Palace Hotel* (☎ 355003) was built in 1744 as a Dutch palace, then later became a British Residency. For years it was a wonderfully atmospheric hotel, set in lush lawns right on the harbour. Now it's run by the KTDC as just another down-at-heel middle-of-the-road government hotel with a playground and a slow restaurant. Most visitors who arrive expecting a 'palace' are disappointed, though if you lower your expectations you may find it preferable to the pre-fab hotels in Ernakulam. It's certainly worth a visit to sip a cool drink on the porch, looking out to the Chinese fishing nets at Fort Cochin.

Rooms cost from Rs 475/625 or Rs 750/950 for an air-con cottage. The air-con 'honeymoon' cottages, which are right on the water's edge, cost Rs 1200. Telephone first or enquire at the Tourist Reception Centre, Shanmugham Rd, otherwise you'll waste a lot of time if the hotel is full. Ferries (Rs 0.40) leave the High Court Jetty in Ernakulam for Bolgatty Island every 20 minutes from 6 am to 10 pm; at other times, private launches are available.

Ernakulam There are a number of mid-range places opposite the Ernakulam Junction railway station.

The Metropolitan (☎ 369931) is glossy, new and centrally air-conditioned and has rooms for Rs 500/750. There's a decent restaurant and a bar.

Paulson Park Hotel (☎ 382170), nearby, has good-value rooms for Rs 180/300 or Rs 300/480 with air-con. There's a choice of multi-cuisine or tandoori restaurants.

Hotel Sangeetha (☎ 368487) is a block west on Chittoor Rd. Rooms are Rs 220/330 to Rs 300/420 or Rs 400/450 with air-con; prices include breakfast.

Hotel Joyland (☎ 367764), nearby on Durbar Hall Rd, is well appointed and features a rooftop restaurant. Rooms are Rs 300/450 or Rs 375/525 with air-con.

Woodlands Hotel (☎ 382051), on MG Rd a little north of Club Rd, is a long-time favourite. Rooms here are Rs 250/375 or Rs 425/600 with air-con. All rooms have TV and hot water, and the hotel has a vegetarian restaurant and a roof garden.

Hotel Excellency (☎ 374001), on Nettipadam Rd south of Jos Junction, has a three-star rating and rooms for US$8/10 to US$10/12 or US$16/18 with air-con. It has good facilities, a restaurant, and even throws in 'bed coffee'.

Bharat Tourist Home (☎ 353501) is a huge place on Durbar Hall Rd next to the Indian Airlines office. It has standard rooms for Rs 370/450, or Rs 550/650 to Rs 600/700 with air-con. It has vegetarian and north Indian non-vegetarian restaurants, a coffee shop, and a marriage hall on the roof!

Places to Stay – top end

Willingdon Island The *Taj Malabar* (☎ 666811) is an impeccable five-star hotel wonderfully situated at the tip of the island, overlooking the harbour. The hotel boasts the full range of facilities, including a swimming pool. Rooms start at US$90/100, but this is a hotel where a room with a sea view (US$135-150) is worth the extra cost; deluxe suites are US$250-300.

Casino Hotel (☎ 668421) also has an excellent range of facilities, including a pool. It's much cheaper at US$65/70, but its location

KERALA

near the railway station and warehouses is no match for the Taj Malabar's.

Ernakulam On Shanmugham Rd, *Sealord Hotel* (☎ 352682) is centrally air-conditioned and excellent value. The pleasantly furnished rooms are Rs 500/600 or Rs 700/1000 for deluxe rooms. There's a rooftop restaurant with good views and a bar.

Grand Hotel (☎ 353211) on MG Rd is a spacious olde-worlde establishment with two restaurants and a 'fully illuminated lawn with fresh air'! The rooms all have air-con and cost Rs 300/350 in the old wing, Rs 400/450 in the new wing.

The Avenue Regent (☎ 372660) is a centrally air-conditioned four-star hotel on MG Rd not far from Jos Junction. Rooms range from US$34/50-42/55. There's a restaurant, bar, and round-the-clock coffee shop.

Hotel Abad Plaza (☎ 361636), further north on MG Rd, is a modern, centrally air-conditioned Indian business hotel. Rooms here are Rs 850/1050 to Rs 1000/1200. It has restaurants, a coffee shop, a health club and a rooftop swimming pool with great views over the city.

Taj Residency (☎ 371471), a more business-oriented sister to the Taj Malabar, is on the waterfront on Marine Drive. It offers all mod cons (except a swimming pool), boasts the Harbour View Bar, and charges US$80/90 or US$95/105 for rooms with a sea view.

Places to Eat
Fort Cochin Eating options in Fort Cochin are severely limited.

Elite Hotel on Princess St has fairly basic food including fish curries for around Rs 20.

Chariot Beach Restaurant just up the road, turns out uninspired Indian and western snacks and light meals, but it's a popular place to sit in the open, sip a cold drink and watch the world pass by.

Hotel Seagull on Calvetty Rd has a reasonable restaurant and a bar.

Willingdon Island In the Malabar Hotel, *Waterfront Cafe* offers a lunchtime buffet for Rs 250 (plus taxes). The Malabar's Chinese

Jade Pavilion and the plush *Rice Boats* restaurants serve excellent seafood.

Casino Hotel has a buffet in its gloomy restaurant, or there's a brighter outdoor seafood restaurant by the pool.

Ernakulam The *Indian Coffee House* on the corner of Canon Shed Rd and Park Ave opposite the Main Jetty, with its quaint waiters in cummerbunds and shabby white uniforms, offers good snacks and breakfasts. It's popular with locals and always busy.

Bimbi's is a modern, self-serve, fast-food restaurant offering both Indian and western dishes. An excellent masala dosa costs Rs 12. There's a branch on Shanmugham Rd near the Sealord boat jetty and another near Jos Junction. Each has a huge sweet store in the front and a more expensive air-conditioned restaurant upstairs.

Lotus Cascades/Jaya Cafe in the Woodlands Hotel on MG Rd, turns out excellent vegetarian thalis for Rs 30.

Pandhal Restaurant on MG Rd could easily be a modern western chain restaurant. It turns out excellent north Indian food and competent pizzas and burgers. It often has specials based around western themes.

Chinese Garden Restaurant, on Warriom Rd, just off MG Rd has good food and attentive service.

The *Ancient Mariner* is a mediocre floating restaurant on Marine Drive.

Caravan Ice Cream, near the Tourist Reception Centre, is cool and dark and has good ice cream and milkshakes (Rs 20) – try the cardamom or fig.

Athul Jyoti, on Shanmugham Rd, is a straightforward 'meals' place with basic vegetarian meals for Rs 11.

The *Bharath Coffee House* on Broadway offers similar fare.

Chariot Restaurant , with entrances on Convent Rd and Narakathara Rd, has a similar menu as the Chariot Beach Restaurant in Fort Cochin.

The 8th floor *Rooftop Restaurant* in the Sealord Hotel on Shanmugham Rd specialises in seafood.

The classy but reasonably priced *Regency Restaurant* in the Hotel Abad Plaza on MG Rd offers good Indian, Chinese and western food.

The Paulson Park Hotel, near the Ernakulam Junction railway station, has the *Moghul Hut* tandoori restaurant in its central atrium area.

The International Hotel on MG Rd boasts the classy *Restaurant du Coq D'Or*.

Getting There & Away
Hello Cochin and *Jaico Time Table* are handy booklets listing schedules, journey times and air, bus and train fares. They are usually available from bookshops and newsstands, but can be hard to track down.

Air The Indian Airlines office (☎ 141) is on Durbar Hall Rd, next to the Bharat Tourist Home. Air India (☎ 351295) is on MG Rd. Jet Airways (☎ 369879) and NEPC (☎ 381626) also fly to Kochi.

Indian Airlines has daily flights to Bangalore (US$60), Mumbai (US$135), Delhi (via Goa, US$270), Goa (US$95) and Chennai (US$90). Jet Airways also flies to Mumbai, while NEPC flies to Agatti in the Lakshadweep Islands, Bangalore and Chennai.

Bus The KSRTC bus terminal (☎ 372033) is by the railway line in Ernakulam, between the railway stations. Because the town is in the middle of Kerala, many of the buses leaving Ernakulam started their journey in places north and south of here. Although it's still often possible to get a seat on these buses, you cannot make advance reservations; you simply have to join the scrum when the bus turns up. You can make reservations up to five days in advance for many of the buses which originate in Ernakulam. The timetable is in English as well as Malayalam, and the station staff are usually quite helpful.

There are also private bus stands: the Kaloor stand is north-east of Ernakulam Town railway station, and the Ernakulam South stand is near Ernakulam Junction railway station.

The fares and times that follow are for superexpress buses unless otherwise noted.

Southbound There are two routes to Thiruvananthapuram (221km): one via Alappuzha and Kollam, and the other via Kottayam. Over 60 KSRTC buses a day take the Alappuzha to Kollam route. Superexpress buses take 4½ hours to Thiruvananthapuram for Rs 65. The intermediate distances, times and fares for superexpress buses are: Alappuzha (62km, 1½ hours, Rs 20), Kollam (150km, three hours, Rs 45), and Kottayam (76km, 1½ hours, Rs 25). There are also at least two direct buses a day to Kanyakumari (302km, 8¾ hours, Rs 85).

Eastbound At least four direct buses a day run to Madurai (324km, 9¼ hours, Rs 85). For those with phenomenal endurance, there are direct buses to Chennai (690km, 16½ hours, Rs 154).

The Madurai buses pass through Kumily, near the Periyar Wildlife Sanctuary on the Kerala/Tamil Nadu border. In addition, there are three buses direct to Kumily and Thekkady, the centre within the sanctuary (192km, six hours, Rs 46 by fast passenger bus).

Northbound There are buses every half hour to Thrissur (Trichur) (81km, two hours, Rs 25) and Kozhikode (219km, five hours, Rs 50). A couple of buses a day run right up the coast beyond Kozhikode to Kannur (Cannanore), Kasaragod and across the Karnataka state border to Mangalore.

Half a dozen interstate express buses go to Bangalore (565km, 15 hours, Rs 166) daily. The buses go via Kozhikode, Sulthanbatheri (Sultan's Battery) and Mysore.

In addition to the KSRTC state buses, there are a number of private bus companies which have superdeluxe video buses daily to Bangalore, Mumbai and Coimbatore. Check out Princy Tours (☎ 354712) in the GCDA Complex on Shanmugham Rd, opposite the Sealord Hotel. Others include Indira Travels (☎ 360693) and Conti Travels (☎ 353080) at the Jos Junction of MG Rd, and Silcon A/C Coach (☎ 394596) on Banerji Rd.

KERALA

Train Ernakulam has two stations, Ernakulam Junction and Ernakulam Town, but the one you're most likely to use is Ernakulam Junction. Note that none of the through trains on the main trunk routes go to the Cochin Harbour station on Willingdon Island.

Trains run regularly along the coast from Thiruvananthapuram via Kollam and Kottayam to Ernakulam; less frequently on to Thrissur, Kozhikode, Thalasseri and Kasaragod. Two trains daily run right through to Mangalore in Karnataka. The daily *Vanchinad Express* runs between Thiruvananthapuram and Ernakulam in just over four hours, but other services are somewhat slower.

If you're heading to/from Udhagamandalam (Ooty), there are quite a few expresses which stop at Coimbatore (198km, six hours, Rs 62/223). There are no direct trains to Goa. The fastest way to Goa is train to Mangalore and bus or the Konkan Railway from there.

Getting Around
The Airport A bus to the airport costs Rs 1.50. A taxi from Ernakulam to the airport costs around Rs 80; an auto-rickshaw is about half that.

Bus, Auto-Rickshaw & Taxi There are no convenient bus services between Fort Cochin and the Mattancherry Palace/Jewish Synagogue, but it's a pleasant half-hour walk through the busy warehouse area. Auto-rickshaws are available, though the drivers will need persuasion to use the meters – this is tourist territory.

In Ernakulam, auto-rickshaws are the most convenient mode of transport. The trip from the bus or railway stations to the tourist reception centre on Shanmugham Rd should cost about Rs 15 – a bit less on the meter. Flagfall is Rs 6, then Rs 3 a km.

Local buses are fairly good and cheap. If you have to get to Fort Cochin after the ferries stop running, catch a bus in Ernakulam on MG Rd, just south of Durbar Hall Rd. The fare is Rs 3. Auto-rickshaws will demand at least Rs 50 once the ferries stop.

Taxis charge round-trip fares between the islands, even though you only go in one direction. Ernakulam to Willingdon Island might cost Rs 150 late at night.

Boat Ferries are the main form of transport between the various parts of Kochi. Nearly all the ferry stops are named, which helps to identify them on the timetable at Main Jetty in Ernakulam. The stop on the east side of Willingdon Island is called Embarkation; the one on the west side, opposite Mattancherry, is Terminus. The main stop at Fort Cochin is known as Customs.

Major Trains from Ernakulam

Destination	Train Number & Name	Departure Time	Distance (km)	Duration (hours)	Fare (Rs) (2nd/1st)
Bangalore	6525 Bangalore Express	3.47 pm ET*	637	14.00	163/563
Mumbai CST	6332 Mumbai Express	8.45 pm EJ	1840	36.45	304/1213
Kozhikode	6307 Cannanore Express	5.00 pm EJ	190	4.15	48/217
Chennai	6320 Madras Mail	5.35 pm ET	697	13.00	172/597
Mangalore	6329 Malabar Express ET	11.00 pm	414	10:45	119/410
	6349 Parsuram Express	11.00 am ET		10.00	
Delhi	2625 Kerala Express	2.35 pm EJ	2833	48.00	382/1702
	2431 Rajdhani Express**	12.05 am Sat EJ		40.30	2390/4775
Thiruvananthapuram	6303 Vanchinad Express	5.50 am EJ	224	4.30	56/249

*Abbreviations for railway station: ET – Ernakulam Town, EJ – Ernakulam Junction
** Air-con only; catering charge additional

Getting onto a ferry at Ernakulam can sometimes involve scrambling across several ferries to get to the boat you want. If you have to do this, make sure you get onto the right ferry or you may find yourself heading for the wrong island – ask the skipper or deck hand.

Ferry fares are all Rs 2 or less.

Ernakulam to Fort Cochin/Mattancherry

There are services to Fort Cochin every 45 minutes from around 6 am to 9.30 pm. It's a pleasant 20 minute walk from the Fort Cochin pier to Mattancherry. There are also seven ferries a day direct to/from Mattancherry. The ticket office in Ernakulum opens 10 minutes before each sailing.

Ernakulam to Willingdon/Vypeen Islands

Ferries run every 20 minutes from about 6 am to 10 pm. There are also ferries to Vypeen Island (sometimes via Bolgatty Island) from the High Court Jetty on Shanmugham Rd.

Ernakulum to Bolgatty Island

Ferries for Bolgatty Island depart from the High Court Jetty every 20 minutes between 6 am and 10.20 pm. It's a five minute walk from the public jetty to Bolgatty Palace Hotel.

Fort Cochin to Willingdon Island

Ferries operate between Customs jetty and the Malabar Hotel/Tourist Office Jetty about 30 times daily, except on Sunday.

Fort Cochin to Vypeen Island

Ferries cross this narrow gap virtually nonstop from 6 am until 10 pm. There is also a vehicular ferry every half hour or so.

Hire Boats Motorised boats of various sizes can be hired from the Sealord Jetty or from the small dock adjacent to the Main Jetty in Ernakulam. They're an excellent way of exploring Kochi harbour at your leisure and without the crowds; rates start at around Rs 300 an hour. Rowboats offer to shuttle between Willingdon Island and Fort Cochin or Mattancherry for about Rs 40.

THRISSUR (Trichur)

Pop: 77,700   Tel Area Code: 0487

Famed for its murals and art work, the Hindu-only **Vadakkunathan Kshetram** temple sits atop a hill in the centre of Thrissur. There are also two impressively large churches: **Our Lady of Lourdes Cathedral** and the **Puttanpalli Church**. Skip the sad **zoo**, and the amazingly dusty and decrepit **State Museum** in the zoo grounds. However, the **Archaeological Museum**, further along Museum Road, has temple models, stone reliefs, Gandharan pieces and reproductions of some of the Mattancherry Murals. The zoo and museums are closed on Monday.

The annual **Pooram Festival**, held in April/May, is one of the biggest in the south. It includes fireworks, colourful processions and brightly decorated elephants. This festival was first introduced by Sakthan Thampuram, the maharaja of the former state of Kochi.

The Hindu-only **Sri Krishna Temple** at Guruvayoor, 33km north of Thrissur, is one of the most famous in Kerala. The temple's 40-plus elephants are kept at nearby **Punnathur Kota**.

Information

Thrissur orbits Vadakkunathan Kshetram. The encircling roads are named Round North, Round East, Round South and Round West. The Tourist Information Centre, across from the Town Hall, has minimal information.

Places to Stay

Ramanilayam Government Guest House (☎ 332300) is excellent value at Rs 100 a double, if there are rooms available. It's at the junction of Palace and Museum Rds.

The KTDC *Yatri Nivas* (☎ 332333), nearby on Stadium Rd, has rooms for Rs 100/120 or Rs 300/350 with air-con.

Chandy's Tourist Home (☎ 21167) on Railway Station Rd is close to the bus and railway stations. It has rooms for Rs 75/100.

Jaya Lodge (☎ 23258), round the corner on Kuruppam Rd, is unexciting but cheap

KERALA

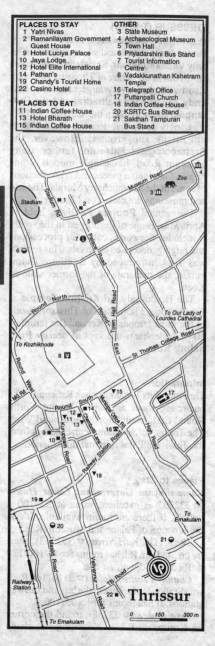

PLACES TO STAY
1 Yatri Nivas
2 Ramanilayam Government
   Guest House
9 Hotel Luciya Palace
10 Jaya Lodge
12 Hotel Elite International
14 Pathan's
19 Chandy's Tourist Home
22 Casino Hotel

PLACES TO EAT
11 Indian Coffee House
13 Hotel Bharath
15 Indian Coffee House

OTHER
3 State Museum
4 Archaeological Museum
5 Town Hall
6 Priyadarshini Bus Stand
7 Tourist Information
   Centre
8 Vadakkunathan Kshetram
   Temple
16 Telegraph Office
17 Puttanpalli Church
18 Indian Coffee House
20 KSRTC Bus Stand
21 Sakthan Tampuran
   Bus Stand

with rooms for Rs 50/80; doubles with bathroom are Rs 90.

Pathan's (☎ 25620), on Chembottil Lane just off Round South, is large and basic with rooms for Rs 85/175.

Hotel Elite International (☎ 21033), across the road, is a more comfortable option; rooms are Rs 200/250 or Rs 500/525 with air-con. It has a bar and an air-con restaurant.

Hotel Luciya Palace (☎ 24731), on Marar Rd, just off Round South, is undergoing much-needed renovations and may now be worth the asking price of Rs 250/325 or Rs 400/450 with air-con.

Casino Hotel (☎ 24699), on TB Rd, close to the bus and railway stations, is the 'best' place in town, though the claimed swimming pool does not exist and the restaurant is awful. Singles/doubles are Rs 375/400 or Rs 575/600 with air-con.

Places to Eat

A cluster of **snack stalls** sets up near the corner of Round South and Round East each evening.

There's an abundance of **Indian Coffee Houses**: you can find them on Round South; PO Rd, near Railway Station Rd; and upstairs in President Bazaar, on Kuruppam Rd.

Upstairs in **Pathan's**, at the junction of Chembottil Lane and Round South, there's a good, basic vegetarian restaurant with an air-con section.

A floor above Pathan's is the **Ming Palace** Chinese restaurant.

Further along the road, **Hotel Bharath** is a neat and clean vegetarian place.

The **Luciya Palace** has a popular outdoor bar area.

Getting There & Away

Trains to Ernakulam, 74km south, take about 1½ hours; trains to Kozhikode, 118km north, take about three hours. The railway station and KSRTC bus stand are south-west of the town centre. The large, private Sakthan Tampuran bus stand is south of the centre; the smaller, private Priyadarshini bus stand is north.

KOZHIKODE (Calicut)
Pop: 871,600   Tel Area Code: 0495
Vasco da Gama landed at Calicut in 1498, becoming the first European to reach India via the sea route around the southern cape of Africa.

His arrival heralded the period of Portuguese supremacy in India and the history of Calicut after 1498 was certainly dramatic. The Portuguese attempted to conquer the town, a centre of Malabar power under the Zamorins, or Lords of the Sea. The Portuguese attacks in 1509 and 1510 were both repulsed, although the town was virtually destroyed in the latter assault. Tipu Sultan laid the whole region to waste in 1789, and British rule was established in 1792.

Despite its colourful past, there is little of interest in the town. The central Ansari Park features musical fountains in the evening, and there's a mediocre beach two km from the town centre. Five km from town, at East Hill, the **Pazhassirajah Museum's** archae-

ological displays include copies of ancient mural paintings, bronzes, old coins and models of temples and megalithic monuments. Next door, the dusty and musty **Krishnamenon Museum** has memorabilia of the former president of India, while the **Art Gallery** has paintings of Raja Ravi Varma and Raja Raja Varma.

The three places are open Tuesday to Sunday from 10 am to 5 pm, except on Wednesday when the Krishnamenon Museum and the Art Gallery don't open until noon.

Information
If the town's banks won't change your travellers cheques, try PL Worldways, Lakhotia Computer Centre, at the junction of Mavoor and Bank Rds. Mavoor Rd is also known as Indira Gandhi Rd.

Places to Stay – bottom end
Metro Tourist Home (☎ 50029), which is at the junction of Mavoor and Bank Rds, has

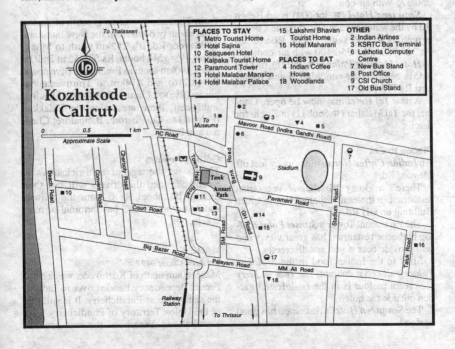

Kozhikode
(Calicut)

To Thalasseri

0   0.5   1 km
Approximate Scale

PLACES TO STAY
1 Metro Tourist Home
5 Hotel Sajina
10 Seaqueen Hotel
11 Kalpaka Tourist Home
12 Paramount Tower
13 Hotel Malabar Mansion
14 Hotel Malabar Palace
15 Lakshmi Bhavan
    Tourist Home
16 Hotel Maharani

PLACES TO EAT
4 Indian Coffee
    House
18 Woodlands

OTHER
2 Indian Airlines
3 KSRTC Bus Terminal
6 Lakhotia Computer
    Centre
7 New Bus Stand
8 Post Office
9 CSI Church
17 Old Bus Stand

To Museums

Mavoor Road (Indira Gandhi Road)

RC Road

Cherooty Road

Convent Road

Beach Road

Court Road

Town Hall Road

Bank Road

Tank

Ansari Park

Stadium

Pavamani Road

SM Road

GH Road

Stadium Road

Taluk Road

Big Bazar Road

Palayam Road

MM Ali Road

Railway Station

To Thrissur

singles/doubles for Rs 75/120 or air-con doubles for Rs 350.

Hotel Sajina (☎ 76146) on Mavoor Rd has basic rooms for Rs 60/85.

Lakshmi Bhavan Tourist Home (☎ 63927) on GH Rd is similar and costs Rs 60/90.

Hotel Maharani (☎ 61541) on Taluk Rd is slightly off the beaten track, and quiet. Rooms are Rs 140/175 or Rs 440 for an air-con double. There's a bar and a garden.

The KTDC *Hotel Malabar Mansion* (☎ 65391) is on Mananchira Square, in the centre of town, near Ansari Park. Rooms are Rs 175/200 or Rs 350 for large air-con doubles. There's a basic restaurant and bar.

Places to Stay – middle & top end

Kalpaka Tourist Home (☎ 60221) on Town Hall Rd is good-value with doubles for Rs 190 or air-con rooms for Rs 300/375. The restaurant serves south Indian food.

Paramount Tower (☎ 62731), also on Town Hall Rd, has rooms for Rs 150/250 or Rs 250/375 with air-con.

Seaqueen Hotel (☎ 366604) is on Beach Rd by the waterfront, but Kozhikode's beach is nothing to get excited about. Rooms are Rs 325/350 or Rs 350/400 with air-con.

Hotel Malabar Palace (☎ 76071), on G H Rd, is centrally air-conditioned and rooms cost Rs 775/900.

A new *Taj Hotel* may now be open. Contact the Taj Malabar (☎ 666811) in Kochi for details.

Places to Eat

An *Indian Coffee House* hides away just off Mavoor Rd.

There's a glossy *Woodlands* vegetarian restaurant in the easily spotted White Lines Building on GH Rd.

The Paramount Tower's *Sunset Point* rooftop barbecue restaurant has great views and will provide beer if you ask discreetly.

Stick to the Indian food in the *Malabar Palace's* air-con restaurant. The *Tom 'n Jerry* ice-cream parlour is in the rat-infested garden outside the hotel.

The *Seaqueen Hotel's* restaurant has good seafood.

Getting There & Away

Air The Indian Airlines office (☎ 766243) is in the Eroth Centre on Bank Rd, close to the Mavoor Rd junction. Indian Airlines flies daily to Bangalore (US$55), Mumbai (US$125) and Chennai (five days a week via Coimbatore and five days a week via Madurai, US$70), and three days a week to Goa (US$80). Jet Airways (☎ 356052) also connects daily with Mumbai.

Bus The KSRTC bus terminal is on Mavoor Rd, close to the junction with Bank Rd. There's also the New bus stand, further east along Mavoor Rd, and the Old bus stand, at the GH Rd/MM Ali Rd intersection. There are regular buses to Bangalore, Mangalore, Mysore, Ooty, Madurai, Coimbatore, Pondicherry, Thiruvananthapuram, Alappuzha, Kochi and Kottayam.

The bus to Ooty and Mysore (5½ hours) climbs over the Western Ghats and has spectacular views from the left-hand side.

Train The railway station is south of Ansari Park, about two km from the New bus stand on Mavoor Rd. It's 242km north to Mangalore (4½ to 5½ hours, Rs 57/252 in 2nd/1st class), 190km south to Ernakulam (five hours, Rs 48/216) and 414km to Thiruvananthapuram (9½ to 11 hours, Rs 88/400). Heading south-east, there are trains via Palakkad (Palghat) to Coimbatore, Bangalore, Chennai and Delhi.

Getting Around

There's no shortage of auto-rickshaws in Kozhikode, and the drivers will use their meters. It's about Rs 6 from the railway station to the KSRTC bus terminal or most hotels.

MAHÉ

Tel Area Code: 0497

Mahé, 60km north of Kozhikode, was a small French dependency handed over to India at the same time as Pondicherry. It is still part of the Union Territory of Pondicherry. Like Karaikal and Yanam on the east coast of

India, there's little French influence left and Mahé's main function seems to be supplying passing truck drivers with cheap Pondicherry beer.

The English factory established here in 1683 by the Surat presidency to purchase pepper and cardamom was the first permanent English factory on the Malabar Coast. The East India Company also had a fort here in 1708.

Places to Stay & Eat

It's far more pleasant to stay at Thalasseri, eight km north, though there are a few basic options in Mahé itself.

Government Tourist Home, near the river mouth, about one km from the bus stand, has rooms for just Rs 25, but it's generally full.

Hotel Arena (☎ 332421), nearby on Maidan Rd, has doubles for Rs 110 or Rs 270 with air-con, and an attached restaurant.

Sara Resort (☎ 332503) on Station Rd has standard doubles for Rs 150 or Rs 275 with air-con.

Getting There & Away

Mahé is too small to warrant a bus station, so buses pull up on the northern side of the bridge. There are regular buses to Mangalore and Kozhikode.

THALASSERI (Tellicherry)
Tel Area Code: 0497

Thalasseri is not worth a special detour but, if you are making your way along the coast, it's a pleasant, unhurried place to stop for a night. The town's fishing fleet returns in the late afternoon, and the beach becomes an animated fish market as people haggle over the catch.

Near the waterfront, the East India Company's 1708 **fort** is neglected but relatively intact, with a fine gateway and a modern lighthouse perched on one corner. It's right behind the fire station but the town's taxi and auto-rickshaw wallahs don't appear to know of its existence.

Logan's Rd runs from Narangapuram, near the bus and railway stations, to the town's main square.

Places to Stay

The *Brothers Tourist Home* (☎ 21558) at the Narangapuram end of Logan's Rd is cheap, with rooms for Rs 75 to Rs 100.

The nearby *Impala Tourist Home* (☎ 20484) is similar.

Further along, and also similar is the *Minerva Tourist Home* (☎ 21731).

The *Chattanchal Tourist Home* (☎ 22967), round the corner on Convent Rd, is just as cheap.

Hotel Pranam (☎ 220634) (turn left at Logan's Rd from the railway station) is more comfortable. Rooms cost Rs 100/150 to Rs 200/250 or Rs 350/375 with air-con. There's an attached restaurant.

Paris Presidency Hotel (☎ 231666), close to the end of Logan's Rd, is glossy and new with rooms for Rs 200/250 or air-con doubles for Rs 350.

Paris Lodging House (☎ 231666), adjacent, is cheaper with rooms from Rs 120/165 up to Rs 225 for an air-con double.

Places to Eat

The *Hotel New Westend* in the busy main square at the end of Logan's Rd has good non-vegetarian food – the fish curry is excellent.

The *New Surya Restaurant*, a couple of doors away, has great chilli chicken.

Kwality Sweets is one of a number of ice-cream parlours and 'cool shops' around the square.

There's an *Indian Coffee House* behind the Brothers Tourist Home.

The *Paris Presidency* has an air-con restaurant.

The *Parkview Restaurant* is near the railway crossing.

Getting There & Away

Frequent trains and buses head north along the coast to Mangalore and south to Kozhikode and Kochi. An auto-rickshaw to any of the town's hotels should cost around Rs 6.

KERALA

BEKAL & KASARAGOD
Tel Area Code: 0499

Bekal, in the far north of the state, has long, palm-fringed **beaches** and a rocky headland topped by a huge **fort** built between 1645 and 1660. There are slow-moving plans to build a large resort here, but meanwhile there's hardly a tourist in sight. You can stay inside the Bekal Fort walls at the very basic *Tourist Bungalow*. There are just two rooms for Rs 25 per person. The *Eeyem Lodge* (☎ 680343) is three km north of the fort, at the village of Palakunnu, and has rooms for Rs 60 to Rs 90.

Kasaragod is the nearest town of any size. It's about 20km north of Bekal and 47km south of Mangalore (in Karnataka). There are a number of hotels in Kasaragod along MG Rd, near the junction with NH 17. The railway station is a couple of km south of the town centre. Rooms for around Rs 50/75 can be found in places like the *Enay Tourist Home* (☎ 521164), the *Ceeyel Tourist Home* (☎ 521177) or the *Aliya Lodge* (☎ 522897), behind the post office. The *Hotel City Tower* (☎ 521324) at the bus stand end of MG Rd is a green-and-cream landmark. Rooms are Rs 250/320 or Rs 450 with air-con.

Faster trains do not stop in Bekal, which is a Rs 3 to Rs 5.50 bus ride from Kasaragod, depending on the bus and the route. It's only one to 1½ hours between Kasaragod and Mangalore by express train (Rs 17) or by the frequent superfast buses (Rs 10).

Lakshadweep

Pop: 52,750

The Lakshadweep archipelago consists of 36 islands some 200 to 300km off the Kerala coast. The islands are a northern extension of the Maldives chain. Ten of the islands are inhabited: Andrott, Amini, Agatti, Bitra, Chetlat, Kadmat, Kalpeni, Kavaratti (headquarters), Kiltan and Minicoy. The islands form the smallest of the Union Territories of India and are the country's only coral islands. The population is 93% Muslim (belonging to the Shafi school of the Sunni sect). Malayalam is spoken on all the islands except Minicoy, where the populace speaks Mahl, the language spoken in the Maldives. The main occupations of the island people are fishing and the production of copra and coir. Tourism is an emerging industry.

Legend has it that the islands were first settled by sailors from Kodungallur (Cranganore) who were shipwrecked there after going in search of their king, Cheraman Perumal, who had secretly left on a pilgrimage to Mecca. The first historical records date from the 7th century, when a *marabout* (Muslim saint) was shipwrecked on the island of Amini. Despite initial opposition to his efforts to convert the inhabitants to Islam, he eventually succeeded. When he died, he was buried on Andrott. His grave is revered to this day as a sacred site.

Even after the conversion of the entire population to Islam, sovereignty remained in the hands of the Hindu Raja of Chirakkal. It eventually passed to the Muslim rulers of Kannur in the 16th century and, in 1783, to Tipu Sultan. Following the defeat of Tipu Sultan by the British at the battle of Srirangapatnam in 1799, the islands were annexed by the East India Company. The Union Territory was constituted in 1956.

These palm-fringed coral islands with their beautiful lagoons are every bit as inviting as those in the Maldive archipelago, but until very recently they were effectively off limits. Now there are regular boat cruises and tours to the island for Indian nationals, and the resort on the uninhabited island of Bangaram is open to foreign tourists. Bangaram is in a six km by 10km lagoon with three smaller islands – Thinnakara, Parali-1 and Parali-2.

Information

There are Lakshadweep tourist offices in Kochi and in New Delhi. Foreign tourists are only allowed to visit Bangaram and stay at the Bangaram Island Resort operated by the Casino Hotel group. The Casino Hotel (☎ 0484 666821), Willingdon Island, Kochi, will obtain the necessary free permit in one or two days.

Places to Stay & Eat

Indian tourists on the regular boat cruises to the islands from Kochi usually stay on board their cruise ship. The 30 room *Bangaram Island Resort* is the only option open to foreign visitors. From mid-December to mid-June accommodation (including all meals) costs US$230/240 for singles/doubles. Prices drop to US$140/190 during the low season.

Scuba diving, snorkelling, deep-sea fishing and boat trips are extra; kayaks, catamarans and sailboats are free. Make reservations through the Manager, Bangaram Island Resort, Casino Hotel (☎ (0484) 666821; fax 0484 668001), Willingdon Island, Kochi 682003.

Getting There & Away

Air NEPC flies Kochi-Agatti on Monday and Friday for US$302 return. It costs US$30 by boat or US$80 by helicopter from Agatti to the resort.

Boat Package tours by luxury ship are arranged through SPORTS (☎ (0484) 668387; fax (0484) 668155), Lakshadweep Office, Indira Gandhi Rd, Willingdon Island, Kochi 682003. Several five or six day tours are available, ranging in price from Rs 4600 to Rs 7500. These tours are available to Indian nationals only.

Chennai (Madras)

Now officially referred to by its Tamil name, Chennai is India's fourth largest city, and the capital of Tamil Nadu state. It's an enjoyable place because it suffers far less from congestion and overcrowding than other big Indian cities. However, this is rapidly changing and it won't be long before it rivals the others for bustle, noise, and fumes. Catch it while it's still quite pleasant!

The people are zealous guardians of Tamil culture, which they regard as inherently superior to the hybridised cultures further north. They have, for instance, been among the most vociferous opponents of Hindi being made the national language. There is also a deep grass-roots sympathy for the Tamil separatist movement in neighbouring Sri Lanka, though few would have expressed support for the assassination of Rajiv Gandhi at the hands of Tamil extremists.

Although the city has long been an important centre of textile manufacturing, a great deal of industrial expansion has taken place in recent years, including the building of car-assembly plants, railway coach and truck works, engineering plants, cigarette factories, film studios and educational institutes. Chennai is the centre for Tamil film-making – the last two State Chief Ministers, Jayalalitha Jayaram and MG Ramachandran, were ex-movie stars.

The city offers a remarkably efficient range of public services. Here, it's possible to use public buses and urban commuter trains without undue discomfort (except during peak hour) and the slums and beggars are less apparent and smaller in number than in other major cities. However, the city suffers from water shortages in the summer months, especially if the last monsoon season has been a poor one.

As a tourist attraction, Chennai is something of a nonevent compared to the marvels elsewhere in the state. The main reason travellers come here is to transact business or to make a long-distance travel connection.

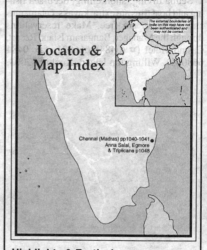

CHENNAI AT A GLANCE

Population: 5.9 million
Main Language: Tamil
Telephone Area Code: 044
Best Time to Go: January to September

Locator & Map Index

The external boundaries of India on this map have not been authenticated and may not be correct.

Chennai (Madras) pp1040-1041
Anna Salai, Egmore
& Triplicane p1048

Highlights & Festivals
Carnatic classical dance & music festival – mid-December to mid-January

History

Madras was the site of the East India Company's first settlement, founded in 1639 on land given by the Raja of Chandragiri, the last representative of the Vijayanagar rulers of Hampi. A small fort was built at a fishing settlement in 1644 and a town, which subsequently became known as George Town, grew in the area of Fort St George. The settlement became independent of Banten, Java, in 1683 and was granted its first municipal charter in 1688 by James II. It thus has the oldest municipal corporation in India, a fact which Tamil Nadu state governors are only too keen to point out at every available opportunity.

During the 18th and early 19th centuries, when the British and French competed for supremacy in India, the city's fortunes waxed and waned: it was briefly occupied by the French on one occasion. It was used by Clive of India as a base for his military expeditions during the Wars of the Carnatic, and during the 19th century, it was the seat of the Madras presidency, one of the four divisions of British Imperial India.

Orientation

Chennai is basically a conglomerate of overgrown villages. However, it can be divided into two main parts. The older section, George Town, is near the dock area north-east of Periyar EVR High Rd. In these narrow, overcrowded streets are the offices of shipping agents, some cheaper hotels and restaurants, large office buildings, bazaars and the GPO. The area's focal point is Parry's Corner – the intersection of Prakasam Rd (or Popham's Broadway as it's popularly known) and NSC Bose Rd. Many of the city buses terminate here; the Tamil Nadu state bus stand and the Thiruvalluvar (TTC) bus stand (the two long-distance bus stands) are close by on Esplanade Rd.

Street Name Changes

It's not only the city that's been renamed; many streets have had official name changes, so there is a confusing melange of names used in the vernacular. Some of them include:

Old Name	New Name
Mount Road	Anna Salai
Poonamallee High Rd	Periyar EVR High Rd
Popham's Broadway	Prakasam Rd
North Beach Rd	Rajaji Salai
South Beach Rd	Kamarajar Salai
Pycroft's Rd	Bharathi Salai
Adam's Rd	Swami Sivananda Salai
Mowbray's Rd	TTK Rd
Broadway	NSC Chandra Bose Rd

The other main part of the city is south of Periyar EVR High Rd. Through it runs Chennai's main road, Anna Salai (also known as Mount Rd), which is home to many of the city's airline offices, theatres, banks, bookshops, craft centres, consulates, tourist offices and top-end hotels and restaurants.

Egmore and Central, Chennai's two main railway stations, are close to Periyar EVR High Rd. Egmore is the departure point for most trains to destinations in Tamil Nadu. If you're going interstate, you'll probably leave from Chennai Central.

Information

Tourist Offices The Government of India tourist office (☎ 852 4295) at 154 Anna Salai is open Monday to Friday from 9.15 am to 5.45 pm, and Saturday and public holidays from 9 am to 1 pm. It's closed Sunday. This office is a good one: the staff are knowledgeable, friendly, and give out heaps of free brochures, including the monthly *Hallo! Madras* guide which lists the city's services (it's also available for Rs 5 from bookstalls around town). Bookings for ITDC tours can be made here as well. Bus No 11 or 18 from Parry's Corner or Central station will bring you here.

There are also Government of India information counters at the domestic and international airport terminals, but they have limited information.

The ITDC (☎ 827 8884) is at 29 Victoria Crescent, on the corner of C-in-C Rd. It's open from 6 am to 7 pm daily (mornings only on Sunday). This is not a tourist office as such, but all the ITDC tours can be booked, and start from, here.

Tamil Nadu Tourism Development Corporation (TTDC) have stopped providing tourist information and now concentrate on selling tours and accommodation. Their office at 143 Anna Salai has been reduced to a desk (☎ 830 3390) under the stairs selling tours (10 am to 5 pm, Monday to Friday). You can book their hotels and lodges from the office at the Hotel Tamil Nadu (☎ 582916). There are TTDC tourist booths at Central

CHENNAI

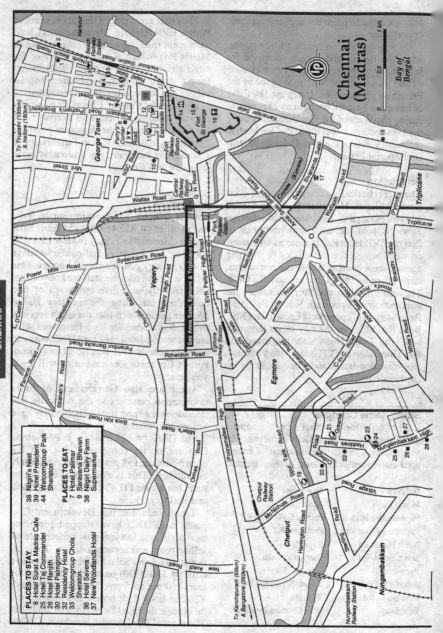

Chennai (Madras)

Harbour

North Beach Road

Beach Railway Station Road

Harbour Station Road

To Trupathi (195km) & Nellore (180km)

Rajaji Salai

Prakasam Road (Popham's Broadway)

Armenian Street

George Town

Mint Street

NSC Bose Road

Parry's Corner

Esplanade Road

Fort St George

Fort Railway Station

Central Railway Station

G H Road

Kamarajar Salai

Bay of Bengal

Waltax Road

Sydenham's Road

Power Mills Road

D'Castor Road

Farren's Road

Strahan's Road

Brick Kiln Road

Miller's Road

Ormes Road

New Avadi Road

To Kanchipuram (65km) & Bangalore (350km)

Perambur Barracks Road

Ritherdon Road

Vepery High Road

Choolai Bazar Road

Demellow's Road

Sydenham's Road

Vepery

Egmore Railway Station

See Anna Salai, Egmore & Triplicane Map

EVR Periyar High Road

Egmore

Poonamallee High Road

Chetput Railway Station

McNichols Road

Chetput

Harrington Road

Sterling Road

Village Road

Nungambakkam Railway Station

Nungambakkam

Anna Salai (Mount Road)

Cooum (Kuvam)

Swamy Sivananda Salai

Wallajah Road

Woods Road

Anna Salai (Mount Road)

Pantheon Road

Gandhi Irwin Road

C-in-C Road

Harris Road

A Nacken Street

Pycrofts Road

Bharathi Salai

White's Road

Triplicane

Park Railway Station

Spur Tank Road

College Road

Haddows Road

Greames Road

Nungambakkam High Road

0   0.5   1 km

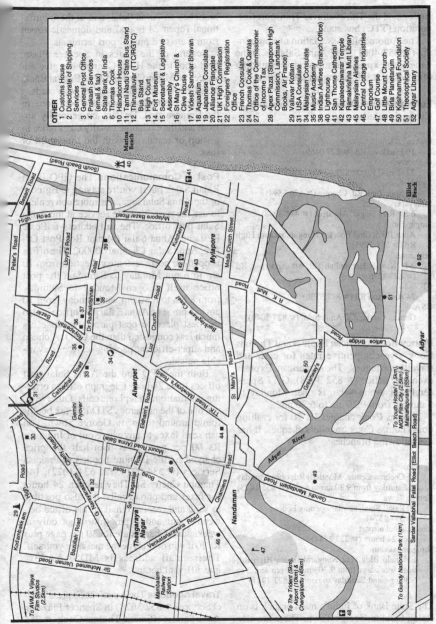

OTHER
1 Customs House
2 Directorate of Shipping Services
3 General Post Office
4 Prakash Services (email & fax)
5 State Bank of India
6 Thomas Cook
10 Handloom House
11 Tamil Nadu State Bus Stand
12 Thiruvalluvar (TTC/RGTC) Bus Stand
13 High Court
14 Fort Museum
15 Secretariat & Legislative Assembly
16 St Mary's Church & Clive House
17 Videsh Sanchar Bhavan
18 Aquarium
19 Japanese Consulate
20 Alliance Française
22 Foreigners' Registration Office
23 French Consulate
24 Thomas Cook & Qantas
27 Office of the Commissioner of Income Tax
28 Apex Plaza (Singapore High Commission, Landmark Books, Air France)
29 Valluvar Kottam
31 USA Consulate
34 Malaysian Consulate
35 Music Academy
38 Indian Airlines (Branch Office)
40 Lighthouse
41 San Thome Cathedral
42 Kapaleeshwarar Temple
43 Ramakrishna Mutt Library
45 Malaysian Airlines
46 Central Cottage Industries Emporium
47 Golf Course
48 Little Mount Church
49 Birla Planetarium
50 Krishnamurti Foundation
51 Theosophical Society
52 Adyar Library

CHENNAI

station and the Thiruvalluvar Transport Corporation (TTC) bus stand.

The Automobile Association of South India (☎ 852 4061), 187 Anna Salai, is in the American Express (administrative) Building (4th floor). It sells a national road atlas.

Foreign Consulates Foreign missions in Chennai include:

France
     16 Haddows Rd (☎ 827 0469)
Germany
     22 C-in-C Rd (☎ 827 1747)
Japan
     60 Spur Tank Rd, Chetput (☎ 826 5594)
Malaysia
     6 Sri Ram Nagar, Alwarpet (☎ 434 3048)
Singapore
     Apex Plaza (2nd floor), 3 Nungambakkam High Rd (☎ 827 3795)
Sri Lanka
     9-D Nawab Habibullah Rd, off Anderson Rd (☎ 827 2270)
UK
     24 Anderson Rd (☎ 827 3136)
USA
     Gemini Circle, 220 Anna Salai (☎ 827 3040)

Money Both American Express and Thomas Cook give competitive rates for cash and travellers cheques. The American Express exchange office (☎ 852 3638), G-17 Spencer Plaza, Anna Salai, is open Monday to Saturday from 9.30 am to 6.30 pm.

Thomas Cook charges Rs 20 for cashing non-Thomas Cook travellers cheques. It has the following branches:

Egmore
     45 Ceebros Centre, Montieth Rd; open Monday to Saturday from 9.30 am to 6 pm (☎ 855 1475)
George Town
     20 Rajaji Salai; similar opening hours (☎ 534 2374)
International airport
     open 24 hours (☎ 233 2882)
Nungambakkam
     Eldorado Bldg, 112 Nungambakkam High Rd; open weekdays from 9.30 am to 1 pm and 2 to 6.30 pm, and Saturday to noon (☎ 827 4941)

The State Bank of India's main branch is on Rajaji Salai in George Town. There are also branches on Anna Salai, and at the international (open 24 hours) and domestic (open from 5 am to 8 pm) airport terminals.

Several of the banks in Spencer Plaza, next door to the Hotel Connemara, give advances on MasterCard and Visa. Central Bank, Montieth Rd, Egmore, handles Visa cards.

Street cash transactions are best done in the Egmore area. Dealers are generally upfront and the exchange usually takes place in a shop or restaurant with the minimum of fuss.

Post & Communications The GPO is on Rajaji Salai, but if you're staying in Egmore or the Anna Salai area, it is more convenient to use the poste restante service at the Anna Salai post office. The full address is Poste Restante, Anna Salai (Mount Rd) Post Office, Anna Salai, Chennai 600002. The office is open for poste restante collection from 10 am to 6 pm Monday to Saturday; the post office itself is open Monday to Saturday from 8 am to 8.30 pm, and Sunday from 10 am to 5 pm. The Anna Salai post office is also the best place to post parcels because it's much less congested than the GPO. A cheap and super-efficient packing service is available outside.

Both the GPO and the Anna Salai post offices have 24 hour telegraph offices offering international telephone calls. Otherwise, use one of the numerous STD/ISD/fax booths found around town. In George Town, you can send faxes to anywhere out of India for Rs 60 per page (less than half the price charged by the Egmore booths) at Prakash Services (☎ 534 0214; fax 534 1022), 146 Thambu Chetty St. They're open 24 hours for faxes and phone calls. It's also possible to send and receive email at this office between 9 am and 7 pm (mornings only at weekends). Charges are Rs 30 per page plus Rs 10 if you don't type the message yourself. Their email address is MDSAAA53@ giasd01.vsnl.net.in.

Travel Agencies The American Express Travel Service (☎ 852 3628) in Spencer Plaza on Anna Salai is efficient. Thomas Cook (☎ 855

3276), 45 Ceebros Centre, Montieth Rd, is also good.

Visa Extensions & Permits The Foreigners' Registration Office (☎ 827 8210) is in the Shashtri Bhavan annexe (rear building, on the ground floor) at 26 Haddows Rd. Visa extensions (up to six months) take about one day to issue and cost Rs 725; you'll need one passport photo. The office is open weekdays from 9.30 am to 1.30 pm and 2 to 6 pm. Bus Nos 27J and 27RR from opposite the Connemara Hotel pass by.

If you're planning to visit the Andaman & Nicobar Islands by boat, you'll need a permit before buying your boat ticket (air passengers can get the permit on arrival in Port Blair).

Collect a form from the Directorate of Shipping Services (☎ 522 6873) at 6 Rajaji Salai in George Town. If you hand this form, together with two photos, into the Foreigners' Registration Office in the morning, you should be able to collect the permit on the same day between 4 and 5 pm.

Tax Clearance Income tax clearance certificates are available from the Foreign Section, Office of the Commissioner of Income Tax (☎ 827 2011 ext 4004), 121 Nungambakkam High Rd. You need to fill in form No 31 and have a copy of your passport. The procedure takes about 30 minutes.

Bookshops Landmark Books, in the basement of Apex Plaza at 3 Nungambakkam High Rd, has one of the best selections in southern India. Higginbothams at 814 Anna Salai and, to a lesser extent, The Bookshop in Spencer Plaza, have reasonable assortments of novels and coffee-table books. Higginbothams also has kiosks at Central station and the domestic airport. Giggles Book Shop, at the Connemara Hotel, is also good.

Libraries & Cultural Centres The British Council Library (☎ 852 5412) is at 737 Anna Salai. Casual visitors are not actively encouraged but you can take out temporary membership for Rs 100 a month. It's open Tuesday to Saturday from 11 am to 7 pm.

The American Center Library (☎ 827 3040), attached to the US Consulate, is open daily except Sunday from 9.30 am to 6 pm. The Alliance Française de Chennai (☎ 827 2650) at 3/4A College Rd, Nungambakkam, is open weekdays from 9 am to 1 pm and 3.30 to 6.30 pm, and on Saturday morning.

In Mylapore, the Ramakrishna Mutt Library at 16 Ramakrishna Mutt Rd, not far from the Kapaleeshwarar Temple, specialises in philosophy, mythology and Indian classics. Further south is the Krishnamurti Foundation (☎ 493 7803), 64 Greenways Rd. Across the river, in the Adyar area, is the Adyar Library (☎ 413528). It's in the grounds of the Theosophical Society and has a huge

CHENNAI

Film Capital of the World

If you're talking quantity rather than quality, then Chennai is now number one, having recently overtaken Mumbai. Last year they churned out 250 movies in the Tamil and Telugu languages alone.

Of the many film studios operating in and around the Chennai, MGR Film City is the only one that is routinely open to the public. It's also the only studio with outdoor sets – Mughal gardens, a Graeco-Roman amphitheatre and a giant concrete shark to pose before. Universal Studios it ain't but it can be quite entertaining if they're shooting outside. Entry is Rs 15 plus Rs 50 for a camera. Open daily from 8 am to 8 pm, it's near Indira Nagar about 10km south of Egmore. Bus 23C runs from Egmore, 5C from Parry's Corner.

Chennai's other big film studios, Vijaya (☎ 483 8787), Prasad (☎ 483 3715) and AVM (☎ 483 6700), are in the south-western suburb of Kodambakkam. You need the manager's permission to visit and it's not readily given.

If you've always fancied your chances as a film star, extras are occasionally needed, but studios will be more interested if you have fair hair. The Maharaja Restaurant, on Triplicane High Rd, is one place where extras have been recruited in the past, but don't just sit there waiting to be discovered – phone the studios! ■

collection of books on religion, philosophy and mysticism. Even if you're not particularly interested in their books, this is a very pleasant place to come to write letters or read. It's open Tuesday to Sunday from 8 to 11 am and 1.30 to 5 pm. To get to any of these three libraries, take bus No 5 or 19M from Anna Salai.

Medical Services For 24 hour emergency services, head to Apollo Hospital (☎ 827 6566) at 21 Greams Lane.

Fortune Teller If you're not able to get the information you require from the contacts listed above you could always try Nadi Joshim (☎ 236 6264), a popular palm leaf reader who charges Rs 250 for a session. Phone for an appointment.

Fort St George

The fort was built around 1653 by the British East India Company, but has undergone much alteration since then. It presently houses the Secretariat and the Legislative Assembly. The 46m high flagstaff at the front is actually a mast salvaged from a 17th century shipwreck.

The **Fort Museum** has a fascinating collection of memorabilia from the days of the East India Company and the British Raj. Entry is free and it's open from 9 am to 5 pm; closed Friday. Upstairs is the **banqueting hall**, built in 1802, which has paintings of Fort St George's governors and officials of the British regime.

St Mary's Church, built in 1678-80, was the first English church in Madras, and is the oldest surviving British church in India. There are reminders in the church of Clive, who was married here in 1753, and of Elihu Yale, the early governor of Chennai who went on to found the famous university bearing his name in the USA.

Opposite the church is the **pay accounts office**. It was formerly Robert Clive's house, and one downstairs room, known as Clive's Corner, is open to the public. There's little to see.

North of the fort, in the High Court Building compound, is the 1844 **lighthouse**,

superseded in 1971 by the ugly modern one on the Marina.

If you're coming to Fort St George by auto-rickshaw, ask for 'Secretariat'.

High Court Building

This red Indo-Saracenic monster at Parry's Corner is the main landmark in George Town. Built in 1892, it is said to be the largest judicial building in the world after the Courts of London. You can wander around and sit in on the sessions; court No 13 has the finest furniture and decor.

Government Museum

Well worth a visit, the government museum is on Pantheon Rd, between Egmore and Anna Salai. The buildings originally belonged to a group of eminent British citizens, known as the Pantheon Committee, who were charged with improving the social life of the British in Madras.

The main building has an excellent **archaeological section** featuring pieces from all the major southern Indian periods including Chola, Vijayanagar, Hoysala and Chalukya. It also houses a good ethnology collection.

The **bronze gallery**, in an adjacent building, has a superb collection of Chola bronze art. One of the most impressive pieces is the bronze of Ardhanariswara, the androgynous incarnation of Siva with one child-bearing hip and breast.

Next door is a poorly lit and unimpressive **art gallery**.

The museum complex is open from 9.30 am to 5 pm; closed Friday and public holidays. Entrance is Rs 3 (Rs 20 for a camera), and the ticket includes entry to the bronze gallery, which the city bus tours omit.

St Andrew's Church

Near Egmore station, St Andrew's Church was completed in 1821 in the classical style. Inside, the impressive blue dome is decorated with gold stars. There are excellent views from the 55m steeple. Services are at 9 am and 6 pm on Sunday.

Kapaleeshwarar Temple

This ancient Siva temple, off Kutchery Rd in Mylapore, was constructed in pure Dravidian style and displays the same architectural elements – *gopurams, mandapams*, a tank, etc – that are found in the more famous temple cities of Tamil Nadu. Like most other functioning temples in this state, non-Hindus are only allowed into the outer courtyard. The temple is open for *puja* from 4 am to noon and 4 to 8 pm. Bus No 21 runs here from Anna Salai or the High Court.

San Thome Cathedral

Built in 1504, then rebuilt in neo-Gothic style in 1893, this Roman Catholic church is said to house the remains of St Thomas the Apostle (Doubting Thomas). It's near Kapaleeshwarar Temple, at the southern end of Kamarajar Salai (South Beach Rd), close to the seafront.

Sri Parthasarathy Temple

This temple, on Triplicane High Rd, is dedicated to Krishna. Built in the 8th century during the reign of the Pallavas, it was subsequently renovated by the Vijayanagar kings in the 16th century.

Marina & Aquarium

The sandy stretch of beach known as the Marina extends for 13km. The guides on the city tour insist that this is the longest beach in the world!

The aquarium, on the seafront near the junction of Bharathi Salai and Kamarajar Salai, is a miserable place, worth missing just to encourage its closure.

South of the aquarium is the **Ice House**. This relic of the Raj era was used to store enormous blocks of ice cut from the Great Lakes in North America and shipped to India for refrigeration purposes.

Guindy National Park

Although there are black buck, spotted deer, civet cats, jackals, mongoose and various species of monkey here you're unlikely to see many in this large park and it's not really worth a visit. There's also a separate, uninspiring **snake park**.

Both parks are open between 8.30 am and 5 pm, though the main park is closed on Tuesday; entrance is Rs 2. The best way to get to Guindy is by urban commuter train.

Enfield Factory

The Enfield India motorcycle is manufactured by Eicher Motors in Tiruvottiyur, 17km from Chennai. It's possible to visit the factory if you phone the product manager, Ravi Lahir (☎ 543066) in advance.

Organised Tours

Tours of Chennai and the nearby temple cities are run by the TTDC and the ITDC. For details on where to book, see the Tourist Offices section at the start of this chapter. TTDC tours can also be booked at the TTC bus stand on Esplanade Rd (☎ 534 1982) between 6 am and 9 pm, or at Central station (☎ 563351).

There are a number of private travel agents around Egmore station which offer similar tours for the same price.

A few examples of tours include:

City Sightseeing Tour This includes visits to Fort St George, government museum, Valluvar Kottam, Snake Park, Kapaleeshwarar Temple and Marina Beach. The daily tours are fairly good value, although somewhat rushed. Tours run from 7.30 am to 1.30 pm, and again from 1.30 to 6 pm; the cost is Rs 65. The TTDC tour commentary is not very enlightening, but the guides are helpful.

Kanchipuram & Mamallapuram (Mahabalipuram) The daily tours go from 6.30 am to 7 pm, and cost Rs 160 or Rs 260 (air-con bus) including breakfast and lunch. It's good value if you're strapped for time, but otherwise it's a breathless dash.

Tirupathi This all-day tour to the famous Venkateshwara Temple at Tirumala in southern Andhra Pradesh is good value if you don't have time to do it yourself. Be warned that at least 12 hours are spent on the bus.

CHENNAI

The price includes 'special *darshan*' (for details, see the boxed section under Tirupathi in the Andhra Pradesh chapter). This usually takes two hours, but on weekends and holidays it can take five hours, which means the bus doesn't get back to Chennai until midnight. The daily tours officially last from 6 am to 10 pm. The fare is Rs 260 or Rs 500 (air-con), and includes breakfast, lunch and the Rs 30 special darshan fee.

Special Events

Between mid-December and mid-January, Chennai is host to the famous Carnatic Music & Dance Festival. Prestigious performances are held at various music academies, featuring some of the country's top classical dancers and musicians. Contact the Government of India tourist office for details.

Places to Stay

Egmore, on and around Kennet Lane, is the main accommodation and travel hub but competition for rooms can be fierce. Book in advance or arrive early. Two other areas for cheap hotels are George Town, between Mint St, NSC Bose Rd and Rajaji Salai; and Triplicane, a suburb to the south-east of Anna Salai, less chaotic than Egmore and preferred by many budget travellers. The top-range hotels are mainly along Anna Salai and the roads leading off this principal artery.

If you'd like to stay in a private home, contact the Government of India tourist office for a list of places offering *paying guest accommodation*. Prices range from Rs 100 to Rs 600 per person.

Hotel tax in Tamil Nadu is currently among the highest in the country – 15% on rooms

---

Festival of Carnatic Music & Dance

Chennai's Festival of Carnatic Music & Dance, which takes place from mid-December to mid-January, is one of the largest festivals of this type in the world. It's a celebration of the classical music of south India, with songs in all the main languages – Tamil, Telugu and Kannada. If you're here then, you should make a point of seeing a performance.

At each venue there's usually a lecture and demonstration in the morning, followed by several concerts, each lasting around three hours, in the afternoon and evening. Most concerts start with a *varnam*, an uptempo introduction. There are then several songs, *kirtis* or *kirtanas*, before the main number. The *raga* is the basis of Carnatic music: five, six or seven notes arranged in ascending or descending scales. There are 72 main ragas and several hundred variations of each, all organised into a complex classification.

The main instruments used are the violin, wooden flute, *veena* (a large stringed instrument), *gottuvadyam* (similar to the veena but without frets), *nagaswaram* (pipe), *thavil* (percussion instrument), *mridangam* (drum), and even a *ghatam* (a mud pot).

Performers to look out for include vocalists KV Narayanaswami, MS Subbulakshmi, T Brinda, Balamurali Krishna, TN Seshagopalan, DK Pattammal and Semmangudi Srinivasier; violinists TN Krishnan, VV Subramanian, MS Gopalkrishnan, Lalgudi Jayaraman and GLR Krishnan; veena players Gayatri and Chittibabu; flautists N Ramani, T Viswanathan and Sikkil Sisters; gottuvadyam player N Ravi Kiran; nagaswaram players Shaik Chinna Moulana Sahib and Namagiripettai; and mridangam players TK Murthy, Palghat Raghu, Vellore Ramabhadran, Umayalpuram Sivaram and TV Gopalkrishnan.

Programmes are advertised in the newspapers; it's also worth asking the tourist office for a list of venues. ■

The veena, developed 300 years ago, is found only in south India.

costing between Rs 100 and Rs 199, and 20% for anything above. The top hotels will also add a 5% to 10% service charge. Prices given below are before tax.

Places to Stay – bottom end

Egmore The *Salvation Army Red Shield Guest House* (☎ 532 1821), 15 Ritherdon Rd, is a 20 minute walk from Egmore station and welcomes both men and women. It's a clean, quiet place in leafy surroundings. A dorm bed costs Rs 40 and doubles/triples are Rs 175/200. Rooms have clean sheets and fans but bathroom facilities are communal. Checkout is 9 am.

Alarmel Lodge (☎ 825 1248), 17-18 Gandhi Irwin Rd, is across the road from Egmore station. Singles/doubles with common bathroom are just Rs 50/75 but they're usually filled with long term lodgers.

Tourist Home (☎ 825 0079), at 21 Gandhi Irwin Rd, is much more expensive and fills up quickly. Overpriced rooms, all with attached bath, start at Rs 220/250 or Rs 350 for a double with air-con.

Shri Lakshmi Lodge (☎ 825 4576), 16 Kennet Lane, is clean and quiet and has rooms with attached bathroom for Rs 150/300, or Rs 80/130 without.

Hotel Sri Durga Prasad (☎ 825 3881), nearby at 10 Kennet Lane, is similarly priced and also often full.

Dayal-De Lodge (☎ 825 1159), 486 Pantheon Rd (at the southern end of Kennet Lane), is set back from the road and quieter than some of the other hotels. There are rooms from Rs 145/199, all have attached bathrooms with 24 hour hot water. Beds have very firm mattresses.

People's Lodge (☎ 835938), Whannels Rd, is a relic which has been popular for years. It has doubles with attached bathroom from Rs 75, but you'll be lucky to find a room vacant.

The *retiring rooms* at Central and Egmore stations have doubles from Rs 145 or Rs 260 with air-con. Dorm beds are Rs 45.

TTDC Hotel Tamil Nadu (☎ 589132), at 3 Periyar EVR High Rd is a few minutes walk from Central station but some of the rooms are very noisy and badly kept. Doubles (no singles) with attached bath are Rs 250. Their 'youth hostel' here is a grubby dorm with beds for Rs 45 that you'd have to be desperate to sleep in.

Hotel Masa (☎ 825 2966), 15 Kennet Lane, is a reasonable place with rooms with bath attached from Rs 140/215/325. There are also air-con doubles/triples for Rs 400/450.

Hotel Impala Continental (☎ 825 0484), opposite Egmore station at 12 Gandhi Irwin Rd, is at the top end of the lower price bracket. Encircling a quiet courtyard, this hotel offers a range of rooms from singles/doubles at Rs 180/250 to deluxe doubles at Rs 280 and air-con doubles/triples at Rs 380/420. All the rooms have attached bathrooms and there's 24 hour hot water. A TV can be hired for Rs 35 a day. Credit cards are not accepted; checkout is 24 hours.

Hotel Imperial (☎ 825 0376; fax 825 2030) is at 6 Gandhi Irwin Rd. It's fair value, but look at a few rooms as some are far from spotless. Like the Impala, it's set around a courtyard containing shops, massage parlours, a newsstand and travel agents. Singles/doubles are Rs 160/300 or Rs 450/475 with air-con. There are also air-con suites for Rs 550/600. The hotel has two restaurants (one open-air), a nightclub and a popular bar.

Triplicane Reach this area on bus No 30, 31 or 32 from Esplanade Rd, outside the TTC bus stand, in George Town. From Egmore station, take bus No 29D, 22 or 27B.

Broadlands (☎ 854 5573), at 16 Vallabha Agraharam St, off Triplicane High Rd, opposite the Star cinema, is something of a travellers' institution, though it's now getting mixed reports, particularly because it has an unofficial policy of excluding Indians.

It's an old place set around courtyards. The simple rooms are reasonably clean and have wicker easy chairs, a table and fan. Singles are from Rs 150 with common bath, Rs 160 with bath attached. The cheapest doubles are singles with an extra bed (Rs 50). Larger doubles are Rs 340 with common bath, Rs 350 with bath attached. There are also dorm beds for Rs 50. As a rule, the higher the room

CHENNAI

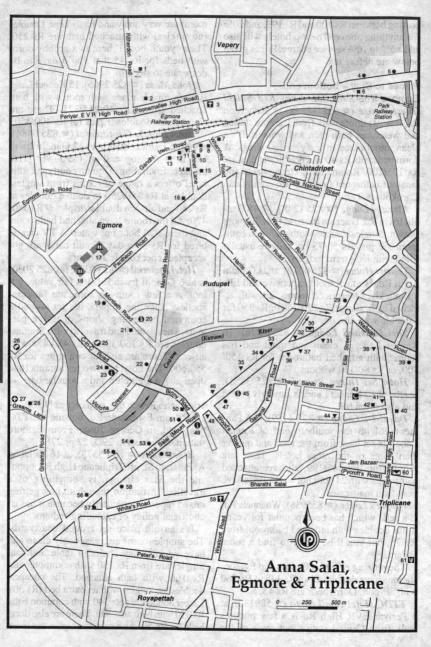

**Anna Salai,
Egmore & Triplicane**

Vepery

Ritherdon Road

Park
Railway
Station

Periyar E V R High Road (Poonamallee High Road)

Egmore
Railway Station

Gandhi Irwin Road

Kennet Lane

Wall Tax Road

Chintadripet

Arunachala Naicken Street

West Cooum Road

Egmore High Road

Egmore

Pantheon Road

Marshalls Road

Langs Garden Road

Harris Road

Pudupet

Monteith Road

Ellis Street

Wallajah Road

(Kuvam)

River

Cooum

C-in-C Road

Victoria Crescent

Binny Road

Thayar Sahib Street

General Patters Road

Anna Salai (Mount Road)

Wood's Road

Greams Road

Greams Lane

Bharathi Salai

Jam Bazaar
(Pycroft's Road)

Triplicane High Road

Triplicane

White's Road

Westcott Road

Peter's Road

Royapettah

0   250   500 m

CHENNAI

number, the better the room (Nos 43 and 44 are tops); the cheapest rooms are rather gloomy. There's a good notice board, and you can hire bicycles, but their entry policy means that if you're Indian and living abroad you'll have to show your passport to prove it.

Hotel Comfort (☎ 854 5117), 22 Vallabha Agraharam St, is near Broadlands. It's modern and characterless but the rooms are good – Rs 250/325 with attached bathroom, Rs 350/485 with air-con.

Hotel Himalaya (☎ 854 7522), 54 Triplicane High Rd, is not bad with singles, doubles and triples from Rs 250, 300 and 400 and also some air-con rooms. Exact room dimensions are prominently displayed above the door just in case you need to know them. There's a vegetarian restaurant.

George Town The *Hotel Surat* (☎ 589236), at 138 Prakasam Rd above the Madras Cafe

is not bad value – singles/doubles cost Rs 150/195 with attached bathroom, Rs 100/170 without. Avoid the rooms at the front as they are incredibly noisy.

Katheeja Mansions (☎ 535 2252), 117 Angappa Naicken St, charges Rs 100 for a single without bath and Rs 160/250 for a double/triple with bath attached. There are some air-con doubles for Rs 400. It's two blocks west of Thomas Cook, on the corner of Erablu Chetty St.

Indira Nagar The *Youth Hostel* (☎ 412882), 2nd Ave, Indira Nagar, is about 10km south of Egmore in a peaceful residential area. Dorm beds cost Rs 40 for nonmembers, Rs 20 for members, and it's possible to camp in the garden. Phone in advance for a reservation and directions, and bring a padlock for your locker. Meals are available on request (Rs 10 for a thali). If the Salvation Army Red

CHENNAI

PLACES TO STAY			
1	Salvation Army Red Shield Guest House	50	Hotel Connemara, Raintree Restaurant & Giggles Book Shop
2	YWCA International Guest House	56	Hotel Madras International
6	TTDC Hotel Tamil Nadu		
7	Hotel Vaigai	**PLACES TO EAT**	
8	People's Lodge	11	Bhoopathy Cafe
9	Hotel Chandra	15	Shaanti Restaurant
	Towers, Hotel	31	Saravanaas
	Imperial-	32	Mathura Restaurant
	Rajabhavan,	33	Manasa
	Vasanta Bhavan &	35	Dasaprakash
	Omar Khayyam		Restaurant
10	Hotel New Victoria	36	Buharis Restaurant
12	Alarmel Lodge &	37	Chungking
	Hotel Impala	38	Hotel Tirumulai
	Continental	41	Maharaja Restaurant
13	Hotel Ramprasad &	44	Srinivasa Hotel
	Tourist Home	46	Annalakshmi
14	Shri Lakshmi Lodge &	48	Aavin
	Hotel Masa	56	Yamuna Restaurant
15	Hotel Sri Durga		
	Prasad & Hotel	**OTHER**	
	Pandian	3	St Andrew's Church
16	Dayal-De Lodge	4	U-Rent (Picnic Hotel)
21	Hotel Ambassador	5	Train Reservations
	Pallava		Office
24	Hotel Kanchi	9	Sherry's Bar
28	Sindoori Hotel	17	Government Museum
40	Hotel Himalaya	18	Art Gallery
42	Broadlands & Hotel	19	British Airways
	Comfort	20	Thomas Cook

22	Indian Airlines/Air India
23	ITDC
25	German Consulate
26	Sri Lanka High Commission
27	Apollo Hospital
29	India Silk House
30	Anna Salai Post Office
34	Higginbothams
39	NEPC Airlines
43	Big Mosque
45	State Bank of India
47	TTDC Booking Office
49	Government of India Tourist Office
51	Spencer Plaza (American Express, The Bookshop, Cathay Pacific)
52	Lufthansa & Singapore Airlines
53	Victoria Technical Institute
54	Air Lanka
55	British Council Library
57	Swiss Air
58	Automobile Association of South India
59	Wesley Church
60	Triplicane Post Office
61	Sri Parthasarathy Temple

Shield Guest House (see above) is full and you don't mind the long journey to get here, for real shoestringers this is a pleasant place to stay.

Places to Stay – middle

Egmore The *YWCA International Guest House* (☎ 532 4234; fax 532 4263), 1086 Periyar EVR High Rd, is an excellent place but so popular you'll need to book well in advance. Spacious singles/doubles/triples with squeaky-clean bathrooms attached cost Rs 350/400/550, or Rs 500/550 with air-con. It accepts both men and women, but there's a transient membership fee of Rs 20 – valid for one month. The restaurant serves Indian and western food. Checkout is 24 hours.

Hotel Vaigai (☎ 834959), at 3 Gandhi Irwin Rd, is a plain hotel which has doubles at Rs 275 to Rs 325, or Rs 500 with air-con. The hotel has a veg/non-veg restaurant and a bar.

Hotel New Victoria (☎ 825 3638), 3 Kennet Lane, charges Rs 700/900 for air-con rooms with attached bath and phone conveniently located right beside the loo.

Hotel Pandian (☎ 825 2901; fax 825 8459), 9 Kennet Lane, is a popular place. It's clean and comfortable but the cheaper rooms aren't great value. Ordinary singles/doubles are Rs 350/400; air-con rooms start at Rs 650/750. The hotel has an excellent restaurant with a veg/non-veg menu, and a bar. Credit cards are accepted.

Hotel Chandra Towers (☎ 825 8171) is at 9 Gandhi Irwin Rd. It has modern but somewhat cramped singles/doubles for Rs 945/1095, and some of the doubles have double beds. There's a good restaurant, 24 hour coffee shop, and bar.

Hotel Kanchi (☎ 827 1100) is south of Egmore at 28 C-in-C Rd. Spacious singles/doubles, all with small balconies, are Rs 530/550 or Rs 700/725 with air-con. The hotel has an enclosed rooftop restaurant, a cheaper ground-floor dining hall and a bar.

Mylapore The *New Woodlands Hotel* (☎ 827 3111), 72/75 Dr Radhakrishnan Salai, has mostly air-con doubles for Rs 500. There are also some non air-con singles for Rs 250. The

hotel has a billiard room, two restaurants and a pool that nonresidents can use for Rs 60.

Nilgiri's Nest (☎ 827 5222; fax 826 0214), at 58 Dr Radhakrishnan Salai, is a good choice. Bright, modern singles/doubles cost Rs 650/900 including breakfast. It has a good restaurant and a popular adjoining supermarket.

Nungambakkam *Hotel Ranjith* (☎ 827 0521), 9 Nungambakkam High Rd, is convenient for the consulates and airline offices. There are singles/doubles for Rs 600/750, or Rs 900/1050 with air-con. There are two restaurants and a bar.

Places to Stay – top end

Many of the top-end hotels are situated in an arc which stretches from Nungambakkam High Rd, south-west of Anna Salai, through to Dr Radhakrishnan Salai. There are also a few along or just off Anna Salai itself. Unless otherwise stated, all the following hotels have central air-con, a swimming pool, multicuisine restaurants, and a bar.

Hotel Connemara (☎ 852 0123; fax 825 7361), Binny Rd, just off Anna Salai, is a Chennai institution. Owned by the Taj Group, it was recently renovated and lost a little of its old-fashioned elegance in the process. Rooms cost from US$140/160.

Hotel Ambassador Pallava (☎ 855 4476; fax 855 4492), 53 Montieth Rd, is a modern four star place which offers smart rooms from Rs 1675/2175. Nonresidents can use the pool for Rs 250.

Hotel Madras International (☎ 852 4111; fax 852 3412), 693 Anna Salai, has rooms from Rs 1120/1400. There's no pool.

Residency Hotel (☎ 825 3434; fax 825 0085), at 49 GN Chetty Rd, Theagaraya Nagar, is popular with middle-class Indian families. Singles/doubles start at Rs 1095/1400. There's no pool here, either.

Hotel Savera (☎ 827 4700; fax 827 3475), at 69 Radhakrishnan Salai has well appointed singles/doubles for Rs 1800/2400.

Hotel President (☎ 832211; fax 832299), at 16 Dr Radhakrishnan Salai has rooms from Rs 975/1275. This is a big place with

CHENNAI

spacious rooms but the atmosphere is decidedly bland.

Chennai has no shortage of five star hotels where a room will cost from US$130/150. The choice includes:

Hotel Taj Coromandel (☎ 827 2827; fax 825 7104), 17 Nungambakkam High Rd, is as luxurious as all the Taj Group hotels.

The Trident (☎ 234 4747; fax 234 6699), 1/24 G S T Rd, is the closest luxury hotel to the airport (five km) but it's a long haul from the city centre.

Welcomgroup Chola Sheraton (☎ 828 0101; fax 827 8779), 10 Cathedral Rd (the extension of Dr Radhakrishnan Salai), is closer to the centre and less expensive than the Park Sheraton.

Welcomgroup Park Sheraton (☎ 499 4101), 132 TTK Rd, Alwarpet, epitomises executive-class opulence.

Places to Eat

There are thousands of vegetarian restaurants in Chennai, ranging from the simple 'meals' restaurants where a thali lunch (rarely available in the evening) is served on a banana leaf for under Rs 20 to sumptuous spreads for 10 times that amount in the major hotels. Breakfast at the simpler restaurants, which open shortly after dawn, consists of such staples as masala dosa, idli, curd and coffee.

You'll find non-vegetarian restaurants are much thinner on the ground, and western-style breakfasts are almost impossible to find outside mid-range and top-end hotels. If you're not a vegetarian or simply want a break from south Indian cuisine, it's probably best to go for lunch or dinner at one of the larger hotels.

For excellent vegetarian meals look out for branches of the *Saravanaas/Saravana Bhavan* chain. These are clean and cheap self-service restaurants open from 6 am to 11.30 pm. There are lunchtime thalis from Rs 18 to Rs 50, masala dosas from Rs 10.50, lassis from Rs 20, and a wide range of ice creams. From 3 to 11.30 pm they serve north Indian dishes and pizzas. Pay for your meal first, then take the receipt to the serving area. Most branches also have a sit-down restaurant; the food's the same but there's a small service charge. If your meal comes to more than Rs 100 you can even pay by credit card.

George Town In this old part of town there are many vegetarian restaurants, although few stand out.

Madras Cafe on Prakasam Rd dishes out good, cheap thalis.

Saravana Bhavan (see above) has a large branch on NSC Bose Rd.

Egmore Most of the restaurants are along Gandhi Irwin Rd, in front of Egmore station.

CHENNAI

Permit Rooms

Until the early 1990s, Tamil Nadu was a 'dry' state and the capital was no exception. Anyone who wanted an alcoholic drink had to obtain a liquor permit from the tourist office before being allowed to buy a beer from a 'permit room' (bar). These permits were farcical, since they enabled patrons to purchase enough liquor to get cirrhosis of the liver.

Although prohibition has been abolished, the name 'permit room' survives and drinking alcohol in a bar in Tamil Nadu can still leave you with the feeling that you're doing something sinful. Enter a hotel (where most permit rooms, except those in the back of wine shops, are located) and ask for the bar, and unless you're in a five star hotel, the receptionist will inevitably point down – down to the basement where natural light never penetrates, and where the artificial lighting is so dim you could almost believe you're up to no good drinking alcohol.

With Tamil Nadu now boasting the highest per capita consumption of alcohol in the country, the prohibition lobby is stronger than ever. For this reason, you'll find health warnings on beer labels, dry days (such as Gandhi's birthday) and draconian government taxes on alcohol which ensure that the price of a beer in Tamil Nadu is one of the highest in India (over Rs 40 – US$1.15 at the current rate of exchange). If you're anywhere near Pondicherry while you're in the south it's worth knowing that part of the French legacy in this Union Territory is a relaxed attitude towards alcohol. Beer costs around Rs 20. ∎

Rajabhavan is a vegetarian restaurant at the entrance to the Hotel Imperial.

Bhoopathy Cafe is recommended, and directly opposite the station.

Vasanta Bhavan, on the corner of Gandhi Irwin Rd and Kennet Lane, is bustling with waiters and features an upstairs dining hall, from which you can watch the street scene below. The stall at the front sells milk-based sweets.

Raj Restaurant at the Hotel Pandian is clean and quiet and serves good non-veg dishes (Rs 55 to Rs 90). A beer costs Rs 50.

At the *Omar Khayyam* restaurant in the Hotel Imperial non-vegetarian food is good.

The *Hotel New Victoria*'s restaurant is good, too.

Triplicane The *Maharaja Restaurant*, around the corner from Broadlands, is where most backpackers seem to end up at least once. The varied vegetarian menu includes toasted sandwiches, lassis, lunchtime thalis (Rs 23), and snacks until midnight.

Hotel Tirumulai, further north, serves luscious banana-leaf thalis (Rs 25) and the biggest dosas you're ever likely to see – ask for the 'Tirumulai special dosa'.

The *Srinivasa Hotel* on Ellis St has also been recommended. There's a partitioned area for women and couples.

If you're after fruit, vegetables or spices, head south along Ellis St to the junction of Bharathi Salai, where you'll find the colourful *Jam Bazaar*.

Anna Salai Area A spotless *Saravanaas* opened recently in the forecourt of the Shanti Theatre on Anna Salai. It's a great place for a quick meal.

Mathura Restaurant, on the 2nd floor of the Tarapore Tower on Anna Salai, is an upmarket vegetarian restaurant. Their 'Madras thali' (Rs 55) comes with ice cream for dessert and is served from 11 am to 3 pm.

Buharis Restaurant, on the opposite side of the road, looks rather less impressive but serves excellent tandoori fare (Rs 40 for a half tandoori chicken). There's an air-con dining hall and an open-air terrace which is pleasant in the evening.

Chungking is an excellent and very popular Chinese restaurant near Buharis.

Manasa, near Higginbothams bookshop on Anna Salai, has also been recommended.

Dasaprakash Restaurant (also known as AVM Dasa) is an excellent upmarket cafe-style restaurant at 806 Anna Salai. It serves vegetarian fare, with some interesting choices such as broccoli crepes (Rs 80). There are fresh salads (Rs 100) and the ice creams are good.

Aavin is a stand-up milk bar a few doors from the Government of India tourist office on Anna Salai. It serves lassis, ice cream and excellent cold milk, plain or flavoured.

The Other Room, at the Hotel Ambassador Pallava, is recommended for its western dishes. Beckti Lombardia, for example, is fish stuffed with spinach and cheese, covered with mushroom sauce and reasonably priced at Rs 115.

Annalakshmi (☎ 855 0296), opened recently at 804 Anna Salai, is run by devotees of Shivanjali. It has swiftly gained the reputation of being the best vegetarian restaurant in the city. The lunch time buffet costs Rs 150 and the staff take the trouble to carefully explain what's in each dish. There's also the seven-course meal for Rs 250, beginning with Ambrosia, an Ayurvedic health drink which 'restores harmony to our modern stressed-out physical and emotional being'. It's open from noon to 3 pm, and from 7.30 to 10 pm, daily except Monday.

Hotel Connemara has a wonderful pastry shop, but for a real treat there's the Rs 354 lunchtime buffet served in the coffee shop. Also in the Connemara is the *Raintree* restaurant, which is open in the evening. The outdoor setting is superb, the service very attentive and there's live classical dancing and music some nights. It's not difficult to spend Rs 300 to Rs 400 on an à la carte meal here.

Elsewhere The *Welcomgroup Chola Sheraton* has an excellent dinner buffet for Rs 260 including taxes.

CHENNAI

New Woodlands Hotel on Dr Radhakrishnan Salai is popular with locals. The dosas, tandoori fare and milk burfis all get rave reviews.

Hotel Runs gets the prize for India's best-named restaurant. It's a cheap veg and non-veg place in Adyar, in the far south of the city, near ANZ Grindlays bank.

Self-Catering The *Nilgiri Dairy Farm* supermarket, next to the Nilgiri's Nest Hotel on Dr Radhakrishnan Salai, is a good place for dairy products, boxed tea, coffee and other edibles (closed Tuesday).

Entertainment

Outside the top-end hotels, nightlife in Chennai is pretty tame. In most cases it's early to bed and up at sparrow's fart.

Cinema There are always a few English-language movies being screened around town. Check the local papers for details.

Classical Music & Dance The Music Academy (☎ 827 5619), on the corner of TTK Rd and Dr Radhakrishnan Salai, is Chennai's most popular public venue for Carnatic classical music and Bharat Natyam dance concerts. Contact the tourist office or check the *Daily Hindu* newspaper to find out what's on and expect to pay about Rs 175 for a good seat.

Another concert venue is Kalakshetra, or the Temple of Art, which was founded in 1936 and is committed to the revival of classical dance and music, and traditional textile design and weaving. Occupying a huge campus in the southern suburb of Tiruvanmiyur, this place offers students the opportunity to study with a guru in the Indian tradition of *gurukulam*, where education is inseparable from other life experiences.

The Carnatic Music & Dance Festival takes place between mid-December and mid-January.

Bars & Nightclubs The *Hotel Connemara* has a plush bar with equally plush prices. The

beers (Rs 104) are served in gleaming tankards and are presented with a mouthwatering platter of snacks – if you polish all of these off you can forget about dinner.

Sherry's at the Hotel Imperial is a popular place and attracts a bunch of lively locals.

Maxim's is a nightclub-cum-dance show at the Hotel Imperial which closes at 11 pm.

For dance, there's the choice of *Gatsby* at the Park Sheraton, or the *Cyclone* at the Hotel President.

Things to Buy

For conventional souvenirs, there's a whole range of craft shops and various government emporia along Anna Salai. The emporia, as elsewhere in India, have more-or-less fixed prices. Also on Anna Salai is the Victoria Technical Institute, a rambling old place selling traditional crafts, handmade clothing, batik greeting cards and other bits and pieces on behalf of development groups.

The best place for quality arts and crafts is the Central Cottage Industries Emporium in Temple Towers, 476 Anna Salai, Nandanam. This place is a visual delight, with superb displays and an excellent range of works from all over India. No 18 bus along Anna Salai will drop you here.

For top-grade silks and cottons, head to either the government-sponsored Handloom House, 7 Rattan Bazaar, George Town, or the more expensive India Silk House on Anna Salai.

For musical instruments, try AR Dawood & Sons, 286 Triplicane High Rd, not far from the Broadlands Hotel.

Getting There & Away

Air Chennai is an international arrival point and an important domestic airport. The Anna international airport is well organised and not too busy, making Chennai a good entry or exit point. Next door is the relatively new domestic airport.

A departure tax of Rs 150 is payable for flights from Chennai to Sri Lanka and the Maldives, Rs 300 for other international destinations.

CHENNAI

Domestic Airlines Addresses of domestic carriers that fly into Chennai include:

East West Airlines
    9 Kodambakkam High Rd (☎ 827 7007)
Indian Airlines
    19 Marshalls Rd, Egmore; open Monday to Saturday from 8 am to 8 pm
    (☎ 855 3039; fax 855 5208)
Jet Airways
    43 Montieth Rd, Egmore (☎ 855 5353)
Modiluft
    Prestige Point (2nd floor), 16 Haddows Rd (☎ 826 0048)
NEPC Airlines
    GR Complex, 407/408 Anna Salai (☎ 434 4580)

Domestic Flights As well as the flights from Chennai listed in the table below, if they're back in business East West and Modiluft may have regular flights to Mumbai, Delhi and Hyderabad.

International Airlines Addresses of international airlines with offices in Chennai include:

Air France
    Pelican Air, Whites Rd (☎ 825 0295)
Air India
    19 Marshalls Rd, Egmore; open daily from 9.30 am to 1 pm and 1.45 to 5.30 pm (☎ 855 4477)
Air Lanka
    76 Cathedral Rd (☎ 826 1535)
British Airways
    Khaleeli Centre, Montieth Rd, Egmore (☎ 855 4680)
Cathay Pacific
    Spencer Plaza, 769 Anna Salai (☎ 825 6318)
Kuwait Airways
    55 Montieth Rd, Egmore (☎ 826 1331)
Lufthansa
    167 Anna Salai (☎ 852 5095)
Malaysian Airlines (MAS)
    Karumuttu Centre, 498 Anna Salai (☎ 434 9291)
Qantas
    112 Nungambakkam High Rd (☎ 827 8680)

Domestic Flights from Chennai

Destination	Time (hours)	IC	Fare (US$)	D2/D5	Fare (US$)	9W	Fare (US$)
Agatti	3.55	-	-	2w	256	-	-
Ahmedabad	3.35	4w	195	-	-	-	-
Bangalore	0.45	5d	55	6w	57	-	-
Bhubaneswar	4.20	3w	160	3w	175	-	-
Calcutta	2.10	2d	180	1d	200	-	-
Coimbatore	2.00	5w	70	1d	78	-	-
Delhi	2.45	3d	210	-	-	-	-
Goa	2.30	5w	110	3w	115	-	-
Hyderabad	1.00	2d	80	-	-	-	-
Kochi (Cochin)	1.35	4w	90	1d	98	-	-
Kozhikode (Calicut)	3.10	1d	70	-	-	-	-
Madurai	1.15	5w	70	1/2d	82	-	-
Mangalore	2.00	4w	80	3w	93	-	-
Mumbai (Bombay)	1.45	2d	130	6w	175	3d	132
Port Blair	2.00	3w	175	-	-	-	-
Pune	3.00	5w	140	5w	163	-	-
Puttaparthi	0.55	2w	55	-	-	-	-
Tirupathi	0.25	2w	30	-	-	-	-
Trichy	0.45	2w	85	3w	70	-	-
Trivandrum	1.45	1d	90	-	-	1d	90
Visakhapatnam	2.40	3w	90	3w	105	-	-

* Abbreviation code: IC – Indian Airlines   D2/D5 – Skyline NEPC/NEPC Airlines   9W – Jet Airways

CHENNAI

Saudia
7 Century Plaza, 560 Anna Salai (☎ 434 6157)
Singapore Airlines
167 Anna Salai (☎ 852 1872)
Swiss Air
191 Anna Salai (☎ 826 1583)
Thai
189 Anna Salai (☎ 826 9140)

International Flights There are flights to/
from Colombo (Air Lanka and Indian Air-
lines), Dubai (Air India), Frankfurt (Air
India and Lufthansa), Jakarta (Air India),
Kuala Lumpur (Malaysian Airlines, Air India
and Indian Airlines), Malé (Indian Airlines),
London (British Airways), Penang (Malay-
sian Airlines), Riyadh (Saudia), and Singapore
(Singapore Airlines, Malaysian Airlines, Air
India and Indian Airlines).

Bus The Tamil Nadu state bus company,
Thiruvalluvar Transport Corporation (TTC),
and its bus terminal (also known as the Ex-
press bus stand) are on Esplanade Rd in
George Town, around the back of the High
Court building. Interstate buses, which are
run by the affiliated Rajiv Gandhi Transport
Corporation (RGTC), also leave from here.

The TTC (☎ 534 1835) and RGTC (☎ 534
1836) reservation offices upstairs are computerised and open from 4 am to 11 pm daily.
There's a Rs 2 reservation fee, and you have
to pay Rs 0.25 for the form!

See the table below for some of the TTC/
RGTC bus services from Chennai.

The state bus stand is on the other side of
Prakasam Rd. This terminal is total chaos
and nothing is in English but an army of boys
attach themselves to every foreigner, and for
a couple of rupees they'll find your bus.

The main reason to use this stand is for
buses to Mamallapuram (Rs 10, two hours).
There are a number of services, the most
direct being No 188 and 188A/B/D/K (20
times daily). The other Mamallapuram services are Nos 19A, 19C, 119A (via Covelong,
21 times daily) and 108B (via Chennai airport and Chengalpattu, four times daily).

There are also private bus companies with
offices opposite Egmore station which run
superdeluxe video buses daily to cities such
as Bangalore, Coimbatore, Madurai and
Trichy. Prices are similar to the state buses,
although the private buses tend to be more
comfortable.

Bus Services from Chennai

Destination	Route No	Frequency (d-daily)	Distance (km)	Travel Time (hours)	Fare (Rs)
Bangalore	831, 828	20d	351	8	77
Chidambaram	300	3d	233	7	38
Hyderabad		1d	717	14	202
Kanyakumari	282	6d	700	16	132
Kodaikanal	461	2d	511	12	85
Madurai	135, 137	30d	447	10	89
Mysore	863	2d	497	11	118
Pondicherry	803, 803F	20d	162	5	27
Ooty	465, 468, 860	3d	565	15	109
Rameswaram	166	3d	570	13	89
Thanjavur	323	15d	321	18	54
Tirupathi	902/911	3d	150	4	43
Trichy	123, 124	35d	319	8	54
Trivandrum	794	6d	752	17	146
Vellore	831, 863	20d	145	4	28

Train The reservation office at Central station is on the 2nd floor of the building adjacent to the station. You can also make reservations for trains originating in most larger cities in the country. The 'Tourist Cell' here deals with Indrail Pass and tourist-quota bookings.

The reservation office (☎ 131, 132, 133) is open Monday to Saturday from 8 am to 2 pm and 2.15 to 8 pm; Sunday from 8 am to 2 pm. At Egmore the booking office is in the station itself, and keeps the same hours as the office at Central station.

See the table below for a selection of trains from Chennai.

Boat Services to the Andaman and Nicobar Islands are prone to change, so inquire about the latest schedules. There is currently one boat, the MV *Nancowry*, which sails from Chennai every 10 or so days to Port Blair (52 hours). Once a month, the boat sails via Car Nicobar. This voyage takes an extra two days; foreign nationals are not allowed to disembark at Car Nicobar. Foreigners are also not allowed to travel on the boat between May and August.

Cabin fares per person are Rs 3000 (two-berth), Rs 2480 (four-berth) and Rs 1950 (six-berth). There's also 'bunk class' for Rs 830 per person. Meals are available on board for about Rs 100 per day.

Tickets are issued at the Directorate of Shipping Services (☎ 522 6873) at 6 Rajaji Salai (opposite the Customs House, in the little office by Gate No 5) in George Town. Foreigners must get a permit for the islands before they buy a boat ticket (see the Visa Extensions & Permits section at the start of this chapter for details).

Train Services from Chennai

Destination	Train Number & Name	Departure Time	Distance (km)	Duration (hours)	Fare (Rs) (2nd/1st)
Bangalore	2007 *Shatabdi Exp***	6 .00 am MC*	356	5.00	370/740
	6007 *Bangalore Mail*	10.00 pm MC		7.00	79/359
Calcutta	2842 *Coromandel Exp*	8.10 am MC	1669	28.00	218/1116
	6004 *Howrah Mail*	10.30 pm MC		32.20	
Coimbatore	2023 *Shatabdi Exp****	3.10 pm MC	494	6.50	565/-
New Delhi	2621 *Tamil Nadu Exp*	9.00 pm MC	2194	34.00	246/1359
Hyderabad	7059 *Charminar Exp*	6.10 pm MC	794	14.20	144/669
Kochi (Cochin)	6041 *Alleppey Exp*	7.35 pm MC	700	14.30	130/597
Madurai	6717 *Pandian Exp*	6.45 pm ME	556	11.00	111/503
Mettuppalayam	6605 *Nilgiri Exp*	9.15 pm MC	630	10.00	124/556
Mumbai	6024 *Chennai Exp*	6.40 am MC	1279	24.00	191/917
	7010 *Mumbai Mail*	10.20 pm MC		30.30	
Mysore	2007 *Shatabdi Exp***	6.00 am MC	500	7.15	102/464
Rameswaram	6713 *Sethu Exp*	5.55 pm ME	656	14.30	126/574
Thanjavur	6153 *Cholan Exp*	9.25 am ME	351	9.30	79/359
Tirupathi	6057 *Saptagiri Exp*	6.25 am MC	147	2.45	38/181
Trichy	2637 *Vaigai Exp*	6.00 am ME	337	5.50	76/343
Trivandrum	6319 *Trivandrum Mail*	6.55 pm MC	921	16.45	160/712
Varanasi	6039 *Ganga Kaveri Exp*	5.30 pm MC	2144	39.00	244/1334

* Abbreviation for railway stations: MC = Madras Central; ME = Madras Egmore
** Air-con only; fare includes meals and drinks
*** Not Wednesday; air-con only; fare includes meals and drinks

Kerala
Top: Coastal Kerala's placid Backwaters.
Centre: After the crowds have gone, Kovalam.
Bottom: Chinese fishing nets, Fort Cochin.

Chennai

Top Left : Chennai is a city of traffic and billboards.

Top Right: Jaws Indian-style – Film City Studios.

Centre Right: Chennai in monsoon.

Bottom: Rooftops of Chennai at dawn.

If you need a shipping agent, try Hapag Lloyd (☎ 522 9282), 37 Rajaji Salai, George Town.

Getting Around

The Airport The domestic and international terminals are 16km south of the city centre. The cheapest way to reach them is by suburban train from Egmore to Tirusulam, which is only about 500m across the road from the terminals. The trains run from 4.15 am until 11.45 pm, the journey takes about 40 minutes, and the fare is Rs 4/72 in 2nd/1st class. These trains are not overly crowded, except during peak hours.

Public buses are not such a good bet, particularly if you've got a lot of luggage. Nos 18J, 52, 52A/B/C/D and 55A all start and finish at Parry's Corner and go along Anna Salai.

There's also a minibus service for Rs 80 (Rs 50 during the day) between the airport and the major hotels (it also drops at Broadlands) but it's a slow way to get into town because of the number of stops it makes. The booking counter is next to the taxi counters at the international terminal. If the counter's closed, the taxi drivers will try to tell you the service is no longer running; the bus should nevertheless be waiting outside and you can pay on board.

An auto-rickshaw to the airport costs Rs 70 by the meter but, since all drivers refuse to use meters on this journey, you'll need to haggle hard to pay anywhere near this. About Rs 80/120 for a day/night trip is what they'll normally charge.

A yellow-and-black taxi costs Rs 200. At the airport itself, you can buy a ticket for a taxi ride into the centre for Rs 220 at the prepaid taxi kiosk inside the international terminal. There's also a prepaid kiosk in the baggage collection area inside the domestic terminal – it's about 10% cheaper.

Bus The bus system in Chennai is less over-burdened than those in the other large Indian cities, although peak hour is still best avoided. The seats on the left-hand side and the rear seat are generally reserved for women. Some useful routes include:

Nos 16, 23C, 27, 27B, 27D, 29, & 29A – Egmore (opposite People's Lodge) to Anna Salai
Nos 31, 32 & 32A – Triplicane High Rd (Broadlands) to Central station and Parry's Corner. The No 31 continues on to Rajaji Salai (for the GPO and the Directorate of Shipping Services)
Nos 22, 27B & 29A – Egmore to Wallajah Rd (for Broadlands)
Nos 9, 9A, 9B, 10, 17D, 17E, 17K – Parry's Corner to Central and Egmore stations
Nos 11, 11A, 11B, 11D, 17A, 18 & 18J – Parry's Corner to Anna Salai

Train The suburban train is an excellent way to get between Egmore and Central station (Rs 2), Egmore and George Town (Rs 2), to Guindy (Rs 4) or the airport (Rs 4). There are relatively uncrowded ladies' compartments.

Motorcycle If you're feeling brave you can hire a moped from U-Rent (☎ 567398) at the Picnic Hotel, 1132 Periyar EVR High Rd. They charge Rs 150 per day but a year's membership of their rental scheme is also required (Rs 250). Helmets and insurance cost Rs 25 per day. An international driving licence is needed but they may accept your home licence.

Taxi Rates are Rs 25 for the first 1.5km and Rs 4 for each subsequent km. Most drivers will attempt to quote you a fixed price rather than use the meter, so negotiate.

Auto-Rickshaws On the meter it's Rs 5 for the first km, and then Rs 2.50 per km. Again, persuasion may be required before drivers will use the meter. There's a pre-paid booth outside Central station.

Tamil Nadu

The southern state of Tamil Nadu is the most 'Indian' part of India. The Aryans never brought their meat-eating influence to the far south, so this is the true home of Indian vegetarianism. The early Muslim invaders and the later Mughals made only quick forays into the region, so Hindu architecture is at its most vigorous and Muslim architecture is virtually nonexistent. Even the British influence was a minor one, despite the fact that Madras (now Chennai) was their earliest real foothold on the subcontinent.

There were a number of early Dravidian kingdoms in the south. The Pallavas, with their capital at Kanchipuram, were superseded by the Cholas, centred at Thanjavur (Tanjore). Further south, the Pandyas ruled from Madurai, while in Karnataka the Chalukyans were the main power.

Tamil Nadu is the home of Dravidian art and culture, characterised best by the amazingly ornate temples with their soaring towers known as *gopurams*. A trip through Tamil Nadu is a temple hop between such places as Kanchipuram, Chidambaram, Kumbakonam, Tiruchirappalli, Thanjavur, Madurai, Kanyakumari and Rameswaram. There are also earlier temples in Tamil Nadu, notably the ancient shrines of Mamallapuram. A special tourist train service – similar to Rajasthan's Palace on Wheels – is planned to operate between many of these temple towns.

In addition, Tamil Nadu has important wildlife reserves, some fine beaches and a number of pleasant hill stations, including the well-known Udhagamandalam (Ooty).

Budget accommodation is good value but mid-range and upmarket hotels can be quite pricey in Tamil Nadu on account of the hefty hotel tax, currently among the highest in the country. It's 15% on rooms costing between Rs 100 and Rs 199, and 20% for anything above. The top hotels will also add a 5% to 10% service charge. When you ask the price of a room make sure they give you a figure

TAMIL NADU AT A GLANCE

Population: 61.5 million
Area: 130,069 sq km
Capital: Chennai (Madras)
Main Language: Tamil
Literacy Rate: 64%
Best Time to Go: January to September

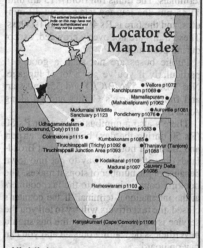

Highlights

- Temple towns, Madurai in particular
- Mamallapuram's rock-cut temples and beach
- Kodaikanal – peaceful hill station
- The former French colony of Pondicherry

Festivals

Mamallapuram Dance Festival – Mamallapuram – January
Car Festivals – Kanchipuram; January, April & May – Chidambaram; April/May, December/January – Tiruvarur; March – Tiruchirappalli; January
Natyanjali Dance Festival – Chidambaram – February
Our Lady of Good Health Festival –Velanganni – September
Vaikunta Ekadasi – Tiruchirappalli – December
Chithirai – Madurai – April/May
Teppam Festival – Madurai – January/February
Thai Pusam Festival – Palani – January

which includes the tax to avoid a nasty surprise when you check out. Prices given below are before tax.

Tamil Nadu is India's vegetarian state *par excellence*. Tamils seem to devour their thalis in acts of physical indulgence, and the food is good and consistently great value.

Unfortunately, you'll rarely have the same pleasure drinking alcohol (to find out why, see the boxed section on Permit Rooms in the Chennai chapter) and, if you like a beer with your meal, it's good to remember that most non-vegetarian restaurants will serve alcohol while exclusively vegetarian restaurants will not. Keep in mid that taxes on beer are high, too.

The people of Tamil Nadu, the Tamils, are familiar faces far from their home state, many having emigrated to Singapore, Malaysia and Sri Lanka. Despite their reputation as hard workers, the state has an easy-going and relaxed feel.

A REGIONAL HIGHLIGHT

Sri Meenakshi Temple, Madurai

Every day, the Meenakshi Temple attracts pilgrims in their thousands from all over India. Its enormous gopurams, covered with gaily coloured statues, dominate the landscape and are visible from all over Madurai. The temple is named after the legendary daughter of a Pandyan king, who was born with three breasts. The king was told that the extra breast would disappear when she met the man she was to marry, and this duly happened when she met Siva on Mt Kailasa. Siva told her to return to Madurai and, eight days later, arrived there himself in the form of Lord Sundareshwara to marry her.

Designed in 1560 by Vishwanatha Nayak, the present temple was substantially built during the reign of Tirumalai Nayak (1623-55 AD), but its history goes back 2000 years to the time when Madurai was the capital of the Pandya kings. There are four entrances to the temple, which occupies six hectares. It has 12 towers, ranging in height from 45 to 50m, and four outer-rim nine-storey towers, the tallest of which is the 50m high southern tower. The hall of 1000 columns actually has 985.

Depending on the time of day, you can bargain for bangles, spices or saris in the bazaar between the outer and inner eastern walls of the temple, watch pilgrims bathing in the tanks, listen to temple music in front of the Meenakshi Amman Shrine (the music is relayed through the whole complex on a PA system), or wander through the interesting though decidedly dilapidated museum.

This museum, known as the **Temple Art Museum**, is housed in the 1000-pillared hall and contains some beautiful stone and brass images, examples of ancient south Indian scripts, friezes and various attempts to explain the Hindu pantheon and the many legends associated with it, as well as one of the best exhibits on Hindu deities anywhere. Unfortunately, many of the labels are missing. Entrance costs Rs 1, plus Rs 10 for a camera. It's open from 7 am to 7 pm.

On most evenings at 9 pm, temple music – mantras, fiddle, squeeze box, tabla and bells – is played outside the Meenakshi Amman Shrine.

The temple is usually open between 5 am and 12.30 pm and again between 4 and 9.30 pm. If you want to take photos you need to buy a permit (Rs 30), which you will be asked to show inside anytime one of the priests notices your camera. Leave your shoes at any of the four entrances, where 'Footwear Safe Custody' stalls will mind them for a small fee.

Many of the priests inside are very friendly and will take the trouble to show you around and explain what's happening. Licensed guides charge negotiable rates. There are also 'guides' who will show you around for a very reasonable fee as long as you agree to visit their tailor shop afterwards.

At 9 pm each evening, there's a closing ceremony. An image of Siva is carried to Meenakshi's bedroom (it's taken back at about 6 o'clock the next morning). The ceremony starts inside the temple, at the Sri Sundareshwara Shrine near the east gopuram. ∎

A detail of the Sri Meenakshi Temple's lively sculpture.

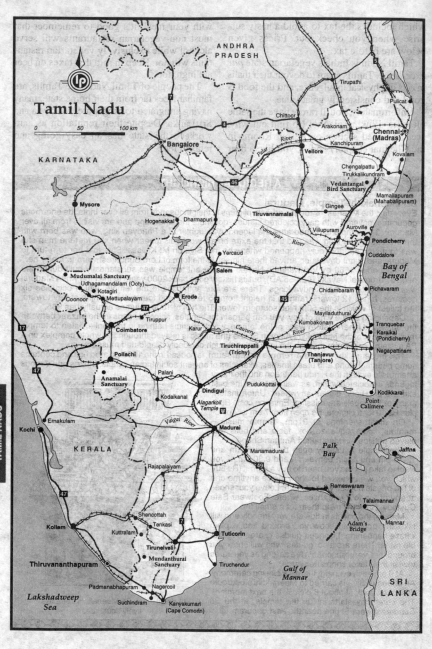

Tamil Nadu

0   50   100 km

ANDHRA
PRADESH

KARNATAKA

Bangalore

Mysore

Hogenakkal   Dharmapuri

Mudumalai Sanctuary
Udhagamandalam (Ooty)
Coonoor   Kotagiri
Mettupalayam
Coimbatore   Tiruppur

Pollachi

Anamalai
Sanctuary

Ernakulam

Kochi

KERALA

Thiruvananthapuram

Lakshadweep
Sea

Padmanabhapuram
Suchindram

Chittoor

Tirupathi

Pulicat

Arakonam
Kanchipuram   Chennai
(Madras)

Vellore   Kovalam

Chengalpattu
Tirukkalikundram
Vedantangal
Bird Sanctuary
Mamallapuram
(Mahabalipuram)

Tiruvannamalai   Gingee

Villupuram   Auroville
Pondicherry

Cuddalore

Yercaud   Bay of
Salem   Bengal

Chidambaram   Pichavaram

Erode   Mayiladuthurai

Kumbakonam   Tranquebar
Karur   Karaikal
(Pondicherry)
Tiruchirappalli   Nagapattinam
(Trichy)
Thanjavur
(Tanjore)

Palani   Pudukkottai   Kodikkarai
Point
Kodaikanal   Calimere
Dindigul
Alagarkoil
Temple

Madurai
Manamadurai   Palk
Bay   Jaffna

Rajapalaiyam   Rameswaram   Talaimannar
Adam's   Mannar
Shencottah   Bridge
Tenkasi
Kuttralam   Tuticorin
Tirunelveli
Mundanthurai   Tiruchendur   Gulf of
Sanctuary   Mannar   SRI
LANKA
Nagercoil
Kanyakumari
(Cape Comorin)

Palar   River

Ponnaiyar   River

Cauvery   River

Vaigai River

TAMIL NADU

Northern Tamil Nadu

The coast road from Chennai to Mamallapuram follows the old Buckingham Canal, now disused. Twenty-one km from Chennai is **Dakshinachitra**, an arts and crafts village currently under construction. It's an ambitious project; eventually there will be buildings to house craftspeople from Tamil Nadu, Kerala, Karnataka and Andhra Pradesh, as well as a theatre, shops, library and archives. The first two sections are now complete.

Kovalam, also known as Covelong, is a fishing settlement with a fine beach, 38km south of Chennai. The remains of a fort have been converted into the Taj group's luxurious *Fisherman's Cove Resort* (☎ (04128) 2304) where there are rooms from US$105/115, and sea-facing cottages from US$150 (all plus 30% taxes).

MAMALLAPURAM (Mahabalipuram)

Pop: 13,300   Tel Area Code: 04114

World famous for its shore temple, Mamallapuram was the second capital and sea port of the Pallava kings of Kanchipuram, the first Tamil dynasty of any real consequence to emerge after the fall of the Gupta Empire.

Though the dynasty's origins are lost in the mists of legend, it was at the height of its political power and artistic creativity between the 5th and 8th centuries AD, during which time the Pallava kings established themselves as the arbiters and patrons of early Tamil culture. Most of the temples and rock carvings here were completed during the reigns of Narasimha Varman I (630-668 AD) and Narasimha Varman II (700-728 AD). They are notable for the delightful freshness and simplicity of their folk-art origins, in contrast to the more grandiose monuments built by later larger empires such as the Cholas. The shore temple in particular strikes a very romantic theme and is one of the most photographed monuments in India. It and all the other places of interest in Mamallapuram are floodlit each night.

The wealth of the Pallava Kingdom was based on the encouragement of agriculture, as opposed to pastoralism, and the increased taxation revenue and surplus produce which could be raised through this settled lifestyle. The early Pallava kings were followers of the Jain religion, but the conversion of Mahendra Varman I (600-630 AD) to Shaivism by the saint Appar was to have disastrous effects on the future of Jainism in Tamil Nadu, and explains why most temples at Mamallapuram (and Kanchipuram) are dedicated to either Siva or Vishnu.

The sculpture here is particularly interesting because it shows scenes of day-to-day life – women milking buffaloes, pompous city dignitaries, young girls primping and posing at street corners or swinging their hips in artful come-ons. In contrast, other carvings throughout the state depict gods and goddesses, with images of ordinary folk conspicuous by their absence. Stone carving is

Cobra-headed serpent deity, Naga.

TAMIL NADU

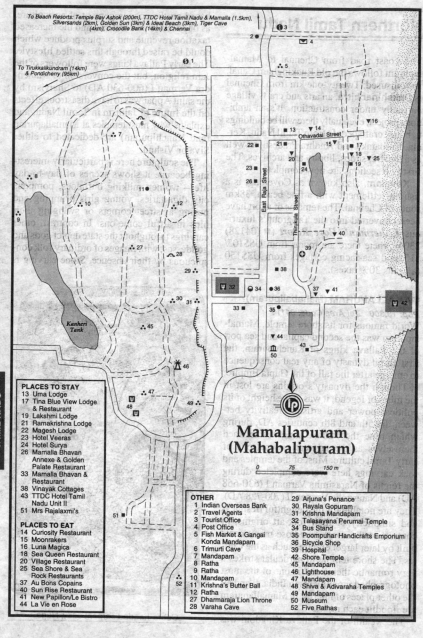

To Beach Resorts: Temple Bay Ashok (200m), TTDC Hotel Tamil Nadu & Mamalla (1.5km), Silversands (2km), Golden Sun (3km) & Ideal Beach (3km), Tiger Cave (4km), Crocodile Bank (14km) & Chennai

To Tirukkalikundram (14km) & Pondicherry (95km)

Othavadai Street

East Raja Street

Thirukula Street

Kanheri Tank

Mamallapuram
(Mahabalipuram)

0   75   150 m

TAMIL NADU

PLACES TO STAY
13 Uma Lodge
17 Tina Blue View Lodge
    & Restaurant
19 Lakshmi Lodge
21 Ramakrishna Lodge
22 Magesh Lodge
23 Hotel Veeras
24 Hotel Surya
26 Mamalla Bhavan
    Annexe & Golden
    Palate Restaurant
33 Mamalla Bhavan &
    Restaurant
38 Vinayak Cottages
43 TTDC Hotel Tamil
    Nadu Unit II
51 Mrs Rajalaxmi's

PLACES TO EAT
14 Curiosity Restaurant
15 Moonrakers
16 Luna Magica
18 Sea Queen Restaurant
20 Village Restaurant
25 Sea Shore & Sea
    Rock Restaurants
37 Au Bons Copains
40 Sun Rise Restaurant
41 New Papillon/Le Bistro
44 La Vie en Rose

OTHER
1   Indian Overseas Bank
2   Travel Agents
3   Tourist Office
4   Post Office
5   Fish Market & Gangai
    Konda Mandapam
6   Trimurti Cave
7   Mandapam
8   Ratha
9   Ratha
10 Mandapam
11 Krishna's Butter Ball
12 Ratha
27 Dharmaraja Lion Throne
28 Varaha Cave
29 Arjuna's Penance
30 Rayala Gopuram
31 Krishna Mandapam
32 Talasayana Perumai Temple
34 Bus Stand
35 Poompuhar Handicrafts Emporium
36 Bicycle Shop
39 Hospital
42 Shore Temple
45 Mandapam
46 Lighthouse
47 Mandapam
48 Shiva & Adivaraha Temples
49 Mandapam
50 Museum
52 Five Rathas

still very much a living craft in Mamallapuram, as a visit to any of the scores of sculpture workshops in and around town testifies.

Positioned at the foot of a low-lying, boulder-strewn hill where most of the temples and rock carvings are to be found, Mamallapuram is a pleasant little village and very much a travellers' haunt. Here you can find an excellent combination of cheap accommodation, mellow restaurants catering to western tastes, a good beach, handicrafts *and* the fascinating remains of an ancient Indian kingdom. Accommodation, however, gets very booked up in January, during the Mamallapuram Dance Festival.

Orientation & Information

The tourist office (☎ 42232) is staffed by helpful and enthusiastic people. They have a range of leaflets as well as a list of bus times and can tell you where to make bookings for trains out of Chennai. It's open daily from 9.45 am to 5.45 pm.

You can change most travellers cheques at the Indian Overseas Bank. It is open on weekdays from 10 am to 2 pm and Saturday until noon.

If you need a doctor, Dr Gladys Indhira has been recommended. Her surgery is behind Arafath Medicals, near the bank.

If it's reopened, visit the lighthouse to orient yourself. There are good views but photography has always been forbidden for 'security reasons' – there's a nuclear power station visible on the coast, a few km south.

Arjuna's Penance

Carved in relief on the face of a huge rock, Arjuna's Penance is the mythical story of the River Ganges issuing from its source high in the Himalaya. The panel (27m by 9m) depicts animals, deities and other semi-divine creatures, fables from the *Panchatantra*, and Arjuna doing a penance to obtain a boon from Siva. Another school maintains that the scene depicts Bhagiratha's Penance. Whoever it depicts, it's one of the freshest, most realistic and unpretentious rock carvings in India.

Mandapams

There are eight mandapams (shallow, rock-cut halls) scattered over the main hill, two of which have been left unfinished. They are mainly of interest for their internal figure sculptures.

One of the earliest rock-cut temples is the **Krishna Mandapam**. It features carvings of a pastoral scene showing Krishna lifting up the Govardhana mountain to protect his kinsfolk from the wrath of Indra.

South of the bus stand, there's a small **museum** of local finds plus some misplaced gloss-painted statuettes. Open daily, entry is Rs 2.

Shore Temple

This beautiful and romantic temple, ravaged by wind and sea, represents the final phase of Pallava art and was built in the late 7th century during the reign of Rajasimha. The temple's two spires, containing one shrine for Vishnu and another for Siva, were modelled after the Dharmaraja Ratha, but with considerable modification. Such is the significance of the shore temple that it was given World Heritage listing some years ago. Following that, a huge rock wall was constructed on the ocean side to minimise further erosion.

The temple is approached through paved forecourts, with weathered perimeter walls supporting long lines of bulls, and entrances guarded by mythical deities. Although most of the detail of the carvings has disappeared over the centuries, a remarkable amount remains, especially inside the shrines.

Entry (Rs 5) also allows you to visit the Five Rathas.

Five Rathas

These are the architectural prototypes of all Dravidian temples, demonstrating the imposing gopurams and *vimanas*, multi-pillared halls and sculptured walls which dominate the landscape of Tamil Nadu. The *rathas* are named after the Pandavas, the heroes of the *Mahabharata* epic, and are full-size models of different kinds of temples known to the Dravidian builders of the 7th

---

Dravidian Temples
The Dravidian temples of the south, found principally in Tamil Nadu, are unlike the classically designed temples located further north. The central shrine of a Dravidian temple is topped by a pyramidal tower of several storeys known as the *vimana*. One or more entrance porches, the *mandapams*, lead to this shrine. Around the central shrine, there is a series of courts, enclosures and even tanks. Many of the larger temples have '1000-pillared halls' although, in fact, there are rarely actually 1000 pillars. At Madurai, there are 985 pillars; the Sri Ranganathaswamy Temple in Tiruchirappalli (Trichy) has 940, while at Tiruvarur there are only 807.

The whole complex, which often covers an enormous area, is surrounded by a high wall with entrances through towering *gopurams*. These rectangular, pyramidal towers are the most notable feature of Dravidian design. They are often over 50m high, but their interest lies not only in their size – most are completely covered with sculptures of gods, demons, mortals and animals. The towers positively teem with life, as crowded and busy as any Indian city street. Furthermore, many are painted in such a riot of colours that the whole effect is that of a Hindu Disneyland. This is no recent development – like classical Greek statues, they were all painted at the one time. ■

---

century AD. With one exception, the rathas depict structural types which recall the earlier architecture of the Buddhist temples and monasteries. Though they are popularly known as the Five Rathas, there are actually eight of them.

Beach
The village itself is only a couple of hundred metres from the wide beach, north of the shore temple, where local fishers pull in their boats. The local toilet is also here, and a walk along the beach is an exercise in sidestepping the turds. South of the shore temple, or 500m or so north, it becomes cleaner.

Special Events
From early January for four weeks there's the **Mamallapuram Dance Festival**. Dances from all over India are staged here including Bharatha Natyam (Tamil Nadu), Kathakali (Kerala), Kuchipudi (Andhra Pradesh) as well as tribal dances, puppet shows and classical/traditional music. Pick up a leaflet of events at the tourist office in Chennai.

Places to Stay – bottom end
If you don't mind roughing it a bit, it's possible to stay with families in the area around the Five Rathas, a 15 minute walk from the bus stand. Rooms are generally nothing more than thatched huts, with electricity and fan if you're lucky, and basic washing facilities.

Touts who hang around the bus stand will find you accommodation in the village but, of course, you'll pay more if you use them. The usual cost is around Rs 250 per week (more if a tout takes you) and if you stay for less than a week the cost is about Rs 50 per day. Competition among the locals offering this sort of service is fierce.

Mrs Rajalaxmi's place is still the best. Her rooms have fans and electricity, and there's a communal toilet and bucket shower. Meals are available on request. Like many villagers, she decorates her doorstep each morning with white chalk designs known as *rangolis*.

Lakshmi Lodge (☎ 42463), near the beach and very popular with backpackers, was once a brothel. There are light, airy rooms with fans from Rs 80/100 to Rs 170/200. Indian and western food is served on 'private terraces' or you can dine on the roof under the stars and the sweeping beam of the lighthouse. A 'jealousy stone' is suspended above the entrance of this hotel; it will fall on the head of anyone envious of this hotel's success at attracting foreign travellers!

Tina Blue View Lodge & Restaurant (☎ 42319), near Lakshmi Lodge, is run by the friendly Xavier and has more of a family-style atmosphere. Singles with bathroom cost Rs 75 and doubles are Rs 100 to Rs 200. There's also a four-bed cottage. The upstairs restaurant, which catches the sea breeze, is a great place to eat or linger over a cold beer.

Uma Lodge (☎ 42322), in the same area, has clean doubles at Rs 60/90 with common/attached bathroom, and larger rooms with toilets for between Rs 120 and Rs 200. The Pumpernickel Bakery is here.

Mamalla Bhavan (☎ 42250), opposite the bus stand, has simple doubles (no singles) with bathroom and mosquitoes for Rs 60.

Magesh Lodge (☎ 42201), 129 East Raja St, has basic, clean doubles for Rs 100, and deluxe rooms for Rs 250.

Vinayak Cottages (☎ 42445), entered from either East Raja St or Thirukula St, boasts four lovely cottages (all doubles) set in a garden. They're good value at Rs 150 for a square cottage, or Rs 200 for a larger round one. All have mosquito nets and private bathroom. There are also clean double rooms in the main building for Rs 150.

Ramakrishna Lodge (☎ 42431), 8 Othavadai St, is clean, friendly and justifiably popular. Rooms are Rs 75/150 with attached bath, and there's a pleasant roof terrace. You may need to book ahead in the high season.

Places to Stay – middle & top end
Government hotel tax currently adds 20% to rooms priced at Rs 200 and above.

Mamalla Bhavan Annexe (☎ 42260), 105 East Raja St, is very popular and sometimes booked out with tour groups. All rooms are doubles with attached bathrooms and fan; they charge Rs 250, Rs 325 for air-con, and Rs 450 for deluxe rooms. There's an excellent veg restaurant. Credit cards are accepted.

Hotel Veeras (☎ 42288), near the Mamalla Bhavan Annexe and similar, has comfortable doubles for Rs 250, or Rs 400 with air-con and fridge. There's a restaurant and bar.

La Vie en Rose (☎ 42068), better known as a restaurant, has a few pleasant, clean rooms for Rs 200/250.

Hotel Surya (☎ 42292), Thirukula St, has several cottages, from Rs 250, some with air-con, in shady surroundings overlooking the small lake.

TTDC Hotel Tamil Nadu Unit II (☎ 42287), situated in its own shady grounds near the shore temple, has overpriced double cottages at Rs 250 to Rs 450 depending on position and amenities. All have an attached bathroom and fan. Facilities include a bar and restaurant.

The other mid-range and top-end hotels are scattered for several km along the road north to Chennai, with more hotels under

Finding an Indian Voice
It was more than music. Learning classical singing in south India (Carnatic Sangeetam) meant becoming a disciple of a master musician, and being accepted into a Brahmin family as a daughter. Classes were three times a week, but every few months there were festivals, such as Ganesh Chaturthi and Deepavali. These festivals entailed giving ritual offerings to my teacher, as well as to anyone who worked for me. At my Brahmin family's house I would participate in cooking for the family. In south Indian society, this was a very great honour.

I first started singing bhajans in the ashram of a world famous guru. It was the best thing there – everything else was gender segregated eating halls and bookshops and a dour and rigid discipline. But the devotional music had a great spirit of joy and invocation of the deity. Later on I went to visit the sacred mountain Arunachala in Tiruvannamalai, and there I was introduced to my music guru. I had to be formally inducted on an auspicious day at an auspicious hour; the almanac was consulted. Here I learned some of the intricacies of a music tradition that is at least a thousand years old and is passed on orally in an old fashioned guru-disciple relationship. It has no indigenous notation.

From the basic rhythm patterns I progressed to memorising 14 varanams over three years, and many other songs and smaller works. The vocal music is taught with incredible precision, and every slide and quaver has to be reproduced and memorised. Once enough complex musical works are mastered, then the ultimate achievement is in improvisation. Here you take the note forms that are particular to the raga and create new music.

To become accomplished in the tradition takes about six years – I gave it only three. Still, that was long enough to be able to find my Indian voice, which I can call on at will, anywhere in the world.

Di Cousens (Sunyata)

construction. Each is positioned on its own narrow strip of land, about 300m from the road and as close as possible to the beach. All of these so-called beach resorts offer a range of facilities which usually include a swimming pool, bar, restaurant(s) and credit card facilities.

Temple Bay Ashok Beach Resort (☎ 42251; fax 42257), is 200m from the edge of town. Air-con superdeluxe singles/doubles cost Rs 1700/2400 in either the main block or the detached cottages. Nonresidents can use the small pool for Rs 100 per day.

TTDC Hotel Tamil Nadu Beach Resort (☎ 42235) is 1.5km north. This place has the best setting of all the resorts – a forested garden and swimming pool – but it's very shabby. Doubles in sea-facing cottages, all of them with attached bathroom and balcony, cost from Rs 350 (Rs 700 with air-con).

Mamalla Beach Resort (☎ 42375) is further north, but not as close to the sea. It's a good place with clean doubles from Rs 250 downstairs and Rs 300 upstairs. There's no restaurant, but there is efficient room service provided by friendly staff.

Silversands (☎ 42228) has a plethora of inland rooms and cottages, but only the expensive suites and three-bed villas (Rs 2700) are on the beachfront. It's overpriced for what it offers, with seasonal rates ranging from Rs 300/400 to Rs 600/800 for normal singles/doubles.

Golden Sun Beach Resort (☎ 42245) is three km from Mamallapuram. Singles/doubles here start at Rs 500/600, or Rs 700/800 with air-con, and there are sea-facing rooms from Rs 900/1000. This place is often full on weekends, when there's a beachside disco. There's also a health club and pool.

Ideal Beach Resort (☎ 42240; fax 42243), three km from town, is one of the best. This place is small enough to retain the owner's intended warm and intimate atmosphere and, as such, is popular with expats and foreigners. Rooms/cottages cost Rs 425/500. An air-con cottage costs Rs 600. All have mosquito nets and are well furnished. There's a nice pool which nonresidents can use for Rs 50, and good food.

Places to Eat

Mamallapuram has, as you might expect, beachside restaurants serving attractively presented seafood in relaxing settings. Most will show you the fresh fish, prawns, crabs and squid before cooking them so you can make your choice. Be sure, however, to ask the price before giving the go-ahead as some items, king prawns for example, can be very expensive. Beer usually costs Rs 50 at the beach bars and Rs 35 in the numerous wine shops.

Sea Shore Restaurant, on the beach, offers excellent fresh seafood. Tiger prawns are Rs 250 and there's also lobster and crab. Grilled prawns and salad costs Rs 40, and the grilled baby shark is delicious. There are a couple of similar beach places next door.

Luna Magica, also on the beach, has a tank full of live lobster and prawns at prices similar to the Sea Shore. Coconut milk prawn curry is Rs 55; fried fish with chips and salad costs Rs 25.

Moonrakers, on Othavadai St, attracts travellers like moths to a lamp. It's run by three friendly brothers. The food's quite good and there's a good collection of western magazines and tapes. Prawns in garlic sauce costs Rs 50.

Village Restaurant, one of the first in town, is still very popular. It has an indoor section plus an intimate garden terrace where you can dine under coconut palms overlooking a small lake.

Tina Blue View is a good place to eat, especially in the heat of the day, as the shady upstairs area catches any breeze that might be around. The service is slow but the mellow atmosphere makes up for that. Cold beers are available.

Sea Queen Restaurant, next to Tina Blue, is reliable for good seafood.

Pumpernickel Bakery, at Uma Lodge, is part German run and does a wonderful range of bread and cakes. You can also get full meals, and there's beer and good music.

New Papillon/Le Bistro on the road to the shore temple is a tiny place run by an enthusiastic crew, and cold beers are available.

Au Bons Copains, also on the road to the

shore temple, is a friendly little cafe. Prawn fried rice is Rs 30.

Sun Rise Restaurant, behind the New Papillon and across the playing field, has a wide range of fish dishes that are good value.

Curiosity Restaurant does good breakfasts and other tasty dishes but prices are a little high.

La Vie en Rose, on the 1st floor of a building at the southern end of East Raja St, is partly French run. This lovely little place offers a different non-vegetarian menu each day and has main course meals for about Rs 70, and good coffee.

Mamalla Bhavan, opposite the bus stand, is an excellent place for south Indian vegetarian food. You can eat well at standard Indian 'meals' prices here. Around the back of the main restaurant, the special thali section serves different thalis every day for Rs 20 – it's definitely above average, but at lunchtime only. The main restaurant's also open for dinner.

Golden Palate Restaurant in the Mamalla Bhavan Annexe is the top vegetarian restaurant in town. The eggplant masala fry with special cashew gravy (Rs 25) is excellent.

Things to Buy

Mamallapuram has revived the ancient crafts of the Pallava stonemasons and sculptors, and the town wakes every day to the sound of chisels chipping away at pieces of granite. Some excellent work is turned out. The yards have contracts to supply images of deities and restoration pieces to many temples throughout India and Sri Lanka. Some even undertake contract work for the European market. You can buy examples of this work from the Poompuhar Handicrafts Emporium (fixed prices – in theory) or from the craft shops which line the roads down to the shore temple and to the Five Rathas (prices negotiable).

Exquisite soapstone images of Hindu gods, woodcarvings, jewellery and other similar products are also for sale. There are several Kashmiri shops, too.

If you want a hammock, this is quite a good place to buy one. For a book exchange service, try Himalaya Handicrafts on the main street.

Getting There & Away

The most direct route to/from Chennai (58km, two hours, Rs 10) is on bus Nos 188 and 188A/B/D/K of which there are 20 daily. Bus Nos 19C and 119A go to Chennai via Kovalam and there are 21 buses daily. To Chennai via the airport you need to take No 108B of which there are nine daily.

To Pondicherry (95km, 3½ hours, Rs 15) take bus No 188 or 188A of which there are eight daily. There are five daily buses (Nos 212A/H) to Kanchipuram (65km, two hours, Rs 10) via Tirukkalikundram and Chengalpattu (Chingleput). Alternatively, take a bus to Chengalpattu and then another bus from there to Kanchipuram.

Taxis are also available from the bus stand but long-distance trips require hours of haggling before the price gets anywhere near reasonable. It's about Rs 350 to Chennai airport.

Getting Around

Bicycles are available for hire if you want to visit some of the places of interest around Mamallapuram. Bikes (Rs 15 per day) and mopeds (Rs 125 a day, petrol extra) can be rented from Lakshmi Lodge, and there's also a bicycle shop next to Merina Lodge opposite the bus stand.

Auto-rickshaws are also available but, since this is a tourist town, they won't use meters and negotiation is essential.

AROUND MAMALLAPURAM
Tiger Cave

This shady and peaceful place is four km north of Mamallapuram and signposted off to the right of the road. It's more a clump of boulders than a cave – its name comes from the shrine (dedicated to Durga) at the entrance which features a crown of carved tiger heads. It's a popular picnic spot on weekends.

Tirukkalikundram

Fourteen km from Mamallapuram, this popular pilgrimage centre is also known as Tirukazhukundram, which means Hill of the Holy Eagles. Its hilltop temple is famous as the place where two eagles come each day, just before noon, to be fed by a priest. Legend has it that they come from Varanasi (Benares) and are en route to Rameswaram. Reality has it that they often don't even turn up. Five hundred very steep steps lead to the top of the hill; some less-fit visitors get themselves carried up in baskets. The actual village is at the base of the hill and surrounds an amazing temple complex with enormous gopurams. You can get here from Mamallapuram by bus or by bicycle.

Crocodile Bank
This successful breeding farm was set up to augment the crocodile populations of India's wildlife sanctuaries. Visitors are welcome and you can see crocs (some 5000 of them) of all sizes. There's also a snake farm where anti-venene is produced.

The farm is about 15km from Mamallapuram on the road to Chennai. You can get there by bicycle or on the 119A bus. It's open daily from 8.30 am to 5.30 pm, but it's best to be there at feeding time (4.30 pm).

KANCHIPURAM
Pop: 184,000   Tel Area Code: 04112
Sometimes known as Siva Vishnu Kanchi, Kanchipuram is one of the seven sacred cities of India and was, successively, capital of the kingdoms of the Pallavas, Cholas and rajas of Vijayanagar. During Pallava times, it was briefly occupied by the Chalukyans of Badami, and by the Rashtrakutas when the battle fortunes of the Pallava kings reached a low ebb.

Kanchipuram is a spectacular temple city and its many gopurams can be seen from a long way away. Of the original 1000 temples, there are still about 125 left spread out across the city. Many of them are the work of the later Cholas and of the Vijayanagar kings.

As it's a famous temple city visited by plenty of pilgrims and tourists, there is usually an army of hangers-on. Have plenty of small change handy to meet various demands for baksheesh from 'temple watchmen', 'shoe minders', 'guides' and assorted priests. All the temples are closed between noon and 4 pm.

Kanchi is also famous for its hand-woven silk fabrics. This industry originated in Pallava times, when the weavers were employed to produce clothing and fabrics for the kings. The shops which sell silk fabrics, such as those along the road to the Devarajaswami Temple, are used to busloads of Indian tourists in a hurry and prices are consistently higher than in Chennai. To get any sort of bargain you need to know your silk well and have done some legwork on prices in Chennai.

Other than the temples, Kanchipuram is a dusty and fairly nondescript town and there's precious little to see or do except when the temple car festivals take place (January, April and May).

Kailasanatha Temple
Dedicated to Siva, Kailasanatha is one of the earliest temples. It was built by the Pallava king, Rayasimha, in the late 7th century, though its front was added later by his son, King Varman III. It is the only temple at Kanchi which isn't cluttered with the more recent additions of the Cholas and Vijayanagar rulers, and so reflects the freshness and simplicity of early Dravidian architecture.

Fragments of the 8th-century murals which once graced the alcoves are a visible reminder of how magnificent the temple must have looked when it was first built.

The temple is run by the Archaeology Department and is very interesting. Quite unusually, non-Hindus are allowed into the inner sanctum.

Vaikunta Perumal Temple
Parameshwara and Nandi Varman II built this temple between 674 and 800 AD, shortly after the Kailasanatha Temple. It is dedicated to Vishnu. The cloisters inside the outer wall consist of lion pillars and are representative of the first phase in the architectural evolution

of the grand 1000-pillared halls of later temples.

Sri Ekambaranathar Temple

The Sri Ekambaranathar Temple is dedicated to Siva and is one of the largest temples in Kanchipuram, covering nine hectares. Its 59m high gopuram and massive outer stone wall were constructed in 1509 by Krishna Devaraja of the Vijayanagar Empire, though construction was originally started by the Pallavas and the temple was later extended by the Cholas. Inside are five separate enclosures and a 1000-pillared hall (which actually contains 540 differently decorated pillars).

The temple's name is said to be a modified form of Eka Amra Nathar – the Lord of the Mango Tree – and in one of the enclosures is a very old mango tree, with four branches representing the four Vedas. The fruit of each of the four branches is said to have a different taste, and a plaque nearby claims that the tree is 3500 years old. The tree is revered as a

manifestation of the god and is the only 'shrine' that non-Hindus are allowed to walk around. You can also partake of the sacred ash (modest contributions gratefully accepted). As this is still a functioning Hindu temple, non-Hindus cannot enter the sanctum sanctorum. With the permission of the temple priest, it's possible to climb to the top of one of the gopurams.

A 'camera fee' of Rs 5 goes towards the upkeep of the temple. The visit could cost you more, however, as this is undoubtedly one of the worst temples for hustlers.

Kamakshi Amman Temple

Dedicated to the goddess Parvati, this imposing temple is the site of the annual Car Festival, held on the 9th lunar day in February/March. When not in use, the ornately carved wooden car is kept partially covered in corrugated iron halfway up Gandhi Rd. The temple has a golden gopuram in the centre.

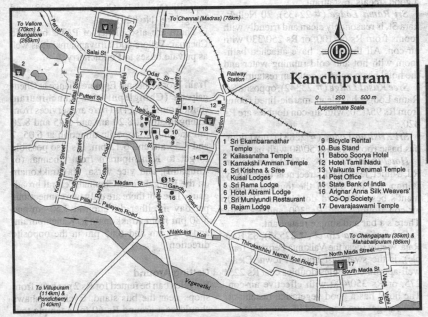

Kanchipuram

1 Sri Ekambaranathar Temple
2 Kailasanatha Temple
3 Kamakshi Amman Temple
4 Sri Krishna & Sree Kusal Lodges
5 Sri Rama Lodge
6 Hotel Abirami Lodge
7 Sri Muniyundi Restaurant
8 Rajam Lodge
9 Bicycle Rental
10 Bus Stand
11 Baboo Soorya Hotel
12 Hotel Tamil Nadu
13 Vaikunta Perumal Temple
14 Post Office
15 State Bank of India
16 Arignar Anna Silk Weavers' Co-Op Society
17 Devarajaswami Temple

TAMIL NADU

Devarajaswami Temple

Like the Sri Ekambaranathar Temple, this is an enormous monument with massive outer walls and a beautifully sculptured, 1000-pillared (actually only 96) hall. One of its most notable features is a huge chain carved from a single piece of stone. The temple is dedicated to Vishnu and was built by the Vijayanagar kings. Entrance is Rs 1 and there is a camera fee of Rs 5.

Places to Stay

Most of the cheap (and noisy) lodges are clustered in the centre of town, just a few minutes walk from the bus stand.

Rajam Lodge (☎ 22519), 9 Kamarajar St and next to the restaurant of the same name, is close to the bus stand. It's a friendly place which has basic singles/doubles/triples with attached bathroom for Rs 50/80/130.

Hotel Abirami Lodge (☎ 20797), 109 Kamarajar St, has spotless rooms from Rs 80/120, but most have no outside windows. Those at the back are quietest. The hotel has a good 'meals' restaurant.

Sri Rama Lodge (☎ 22435), 20 Nellukkara St, is reasonably clean and friendly with rooms from Rs 60/100, or Rs 250/330 with air-con. All the rooms have attached bathroom with hot and cold running water and the hotel has a good vegetarian restaurant.

Sree Kusal Lodge (☎ 23342), opposite Sri Rama Lodge, has clean, marble-lined rooms from Rs 95/150; with air-con doubles are Rs 320.

Sri Krishna Lodge (☎ 22831), next door, has basic rooms for Rs 50/80 with bath.

Hotel Tamil Nadu (☎ 22552) is on Station Rd, a quiet, leafy back street near the railway station. It's not one of the tourism department's best. Standard doubles are Rs 250, air-con doubles are Rs 300 and Rs 350. There's a bar and simple restaurant.

Baboo Soorya Hotel (☎ 22555), 85 East Raja Veethy (near the Vaikunta Perumal Temple), is the swankiest hotel in town. Clean, well-appointed singles/doubles cost Rs 225/275, or Rs 350/400 with effective air-con. The hotel has a good vegetarian restaurant. You can get non-veg food in your room.

Places to Eat

There are many small vegetarian places in the vicinity of the bus stand where you can buy a typical plate meal for around Rs 12. Try the *Hotel Abirami Lodge*, Kamarajar St.

Sri Muniyundi Restaurant (there's no English sign), Kamarajar St does reasonable non-veg food.

Baboo Soorya Hotel has a good vegetarian restaurant. Thalis are Rs 23, veg spring rolls cost Rs 16.

Getting There & Away

Bus As elsewhere, the timetable at the bus stand is in Tamil, but there is no problem finding a bus in the direction you want to go. Look for Point-to-Point buses; they're the fastest – No 76B runs to Chennai (1½ hours, Rs 11.25). There are five direct buses daily to Mamallapuram (No 212A, about two hours, Rs 10). Alternatively, take one of the more frequent buses to Chengalpattu and then catch another one from there to Mamallapuram.

There are direct TTC buses to Tiruchirappalli (No 122), Chennai (No 828) and Bangalore (No 828).

There are also plenty of PATC buses to Chennai, Vellore and Tiruvannamalai, as well as private buses to Pondicherry.

Train From Chennai Egmore change at Chengalpattu (Chingleput) for Kanchipuram (three hours, Rs 14). There are services from Chengalpattu at 8.20 am and 5.45 and 8.20 pm and in the opposite direction at 6.05, 7 and 8.33 am and 6.13 pm. It's also possible to get to Kanchipuram from Chennai (or Tirupathi), and vice versa, via Arakkonam on the Bangalore to Chennai Central broadgauge line but there are only two connections per day in either direction at 7.50 am and 5.30 pm from Arakkonam to Kanchipuram, and 9.23 am and 6.55 pm in the opposite direction.

Getting Around

Bicycles can be rented for Rs 2 per hour from shops near the bus stand. Cycle-rickshaws should cost around Rs 60 for a temple tour but they'll try for Rs 150. Auto-rickshaws are also available.

VEDANTANGAL BIRD SANCTUARY

About 35km south of Chengalpattu, this is one of the most spectacular water-bird breeding grounds in India. Cormorants, egrets, herons, storks, ibises, spoonbills, grebes and pelicans come here to breed and nest for about six months from October/November to March, depending on the monsoons. At the height of the breeding season (December and January), there can be up to 30,000 birds at once. The best times to visit are early morning and late afternoon. Entry is Rs 1.

The only place to stay is the three-roomed *Forest Department Rest House* at Vedantangal village. Reservations must be made in advance with the Wildlife Warden (☎ (044) 413947), 50 4th Main Rd, Adyar, Chennai.

Getting to Vedantangal is not all that easy. From Chengalpattu there are occasional buses to Vedantangal village. Another alternative is to get a bus to Madurantakam, the closest town of any size, and then hire transport to take you the last eight km.

VELLORE

Pop: 330,200   Tel Area Code: 0416

Vellore, 145km from Chennai, is a dusty, semirural bazaar town. For tourists, it is noteworthy only for the Vijayanagar fort and its temple, which are in an excellent state of preservation and worth visiting.

The town has a modern church built in an old British cemetery, which contains the tomb of a captain who died in 1799 'of excessive fatigue incurred during the glorious campaign which ended in the defeat of Tipoo Sultaun'. Here, too, is a memorial to the victims of the little known 'Vellore Mutiny' of 1806. The mutiny was instigated by the second son of Tipu Sultan, who was incarcerated in the fort at that time, and was put down by a task force sent from Arcot.

Vellore is now best known for its hospital, one of the best in the country. The people who come here from all over India for medical care give this humble town a cosmopolitan feel.

Vellore Fort

The fort is constructed of granite blocks and surrounded by a moat which is supplied by a subterranean drain fed from a tank. It was built in the 16th century by Sinna Bommi Nayak, a vassal chieftain under the Vijayanagar kings, Sada Sivaraja and Sriranga Maharaja. Later, it became the fortress of Mortaza Ali, the brother-in-law of Chanda Sahib who claimed the Arcot throne, and was taken by the Adil Shahi sultans of Bijapur. In 1676, it passed briefly into the hands of the Marathas until they, in turn, were displaced by the nawab Daud Khan of Delhi, in 1708. The British occupied the fort in 1760, following the fall of Srirangapatnam and the death of Tipu Sultan. It now houses various public departments and private offices, and is open daily.

The small **museum**, near the church inside the fort complex, contains sculptures and hero stones dating back to Pallava and Chola times. Shoes must be taken off before entering. It's closed on Friday.

Jalakanteshwara Temple

This temple was built about the same time as the fort (around 1550) and, although it doesn't compare with the ruins at Hampi, it is still a gem of late Vijayanagar architecture and has some stunning carvings in the *mandapam*. During the invasions by the Adil Shahis of Bijapur, the Marathas and the Carnatic nawabs, the temple was occupied as a garrison and desecrated. Following this, it ceased to be used. It is open daily from 6 am to 1 pm and 3 to 8 pm, and it costs Rs 0.25 to leave your shoes.

Places to Stay

Vellore's cheap hotels are concentrated along the roads south of and parallel to the hospital.

Srinivasa Lodge (☎ 26389), 14 Beri Bakkali St, is a clean place run by friendly people. All rooms have bathroom attached and they cost from Rs 70/100.

VDM Lodge (☎ 24008), 13 Beri Bakkali St,

has a range of rooms. Ordinary rooms are Rs 60/90, deluxe rooms with TV cost Rs 130/150.

Nagha International Lodge (☎ 26731), 13 KVS Chetty St, is a large, modern hotel with rooms from Rs 66/109 to Rs 330 for an air-con double.

Hotel River View (☎ 25251) is one km north on Katpadi Rd. It's modern and clean, but where's the view? Rooms cost Rs 300/375 with bathroom, Rs 450/550 with air-con, and there are three restaurants, a bar and a garden.

There are several more hotels to suit a range of budgets on Filterbed Rd in the south.

Places to Eat

Dawn Bakery, Gandhi Rd, has freshly baked biscuits and bread.

Simla Ice Cream Bar, Ida Scudder St, is one of many 'meals' restaurants on this street. Despite the name it's not an ice cream bar but an excellent little north Indian vegetarian cafe with a tiny tandoori oven which churns out piping-hot naan.

Hotel Anand, Ida Scudder St, is an up-market vegetarian restaurant with an air-con room.

Chinatown, opposite Natraj Travels on Gandhi Rd, does passable Chinese meals.

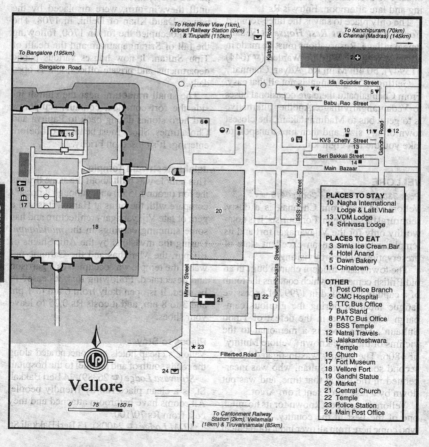

PLACES TO STAY
10 Nagha International Lodge & Lalit Vihar
13 VDM Lodge
14 Srinivasa Lodge

PLACES TO EAT
3 Simla Ice Cream Bar
4 Hotel Anand
5 Dawn Bakery
11 Chinatown

OTHER
1 Post Office Branch
2 CMC Hospital
6 TTC Bus Office
7 Bus Stand
8 PATC Bus Office
9 BSS Temple
12 Natraj Travels
15 Jalakanteshwara Temple
16 Church
17 Fort Museum
18 Vellore Fort
19 Gandhi Statue
20 Market
21 Central Church
22 Temple
23 Police Station
24 Main Post Office

Vellore

0   75   150 m

To Hotel River View (1km),
Katpadi Railway Station (5km)
& Tirupathi (110km)

To Bangalore (195km)

Bangalore Road

Katpadi Road

To Kanchipuram (70km)
& Chennai (Madras) (145km)

Ida Scudder Street

Babu Rao Street

KVS Chetty Street

Beri Bakkali Street

Main Bazaar

Gandhi Road

BSS Koil Street

Chunambukara Street

Minny Street

Filterbed Road

To Cantonment Railway
Station (2km), Vellaimalai
(18km) & Tiruvannamalai (85km)

Tum Yum soup is Rs 20, main dishes cost around Rs 40.

Lalit Vihar, KVS Chetty St, has Gujarati meals for Rs 20 including all-you-can-eat chapatis.

River Room, is one of three restaurants at the Hotel River View. Fish & chips is Rs 60, pepper steak costs Rs 70.

Getting There & Away

Bus As elsewhere in Tamil Nadu, the area is serviced by the regional bus company, (in this case PATC), and the statewide Thiruvalluvar Transport Corporation (TTC). The dusty bus terminal is chaotic and nothing is in English.

TTC buses run to Chennai (Nos 139 and 280, Rs 28), Tiruchirappalli (No 104, Rs 50) and Madurai (Nos 168, 866 and 983, Rs 66). All these buses originate in Vellore and can be booked in advance. Others, which pass through en route (and may be full), go to Bangalore, Tirupathi (2½ hours), Thanjavur and Ooty.

PATC has 26 buses a day to Kanchipuram (2½ hours, Rs 8) from 5 am. They also have buses to Chennai (30 daily, Rs 28), Tiruchirappalli and Bangalore.

Train Vellore's main railway station is five km north at Katpadi. This is the junction of the broad-gauge line from Bangalore to Chennai, and the metre-gauge Tirupathi to Madurai line (which runs via Tiruvannamalai, Villupuram, Chidambaram, Thanjavur and Tiruchirappalli). The smaller Cantonment station, two km south of town, is on the metre-gauge line only.

The 228km trip from Katpadi to Bangalore (4½ hours) costs Rs 56/249 in 2nd/1st class. To Chennai (130km, two hours) it's Rs 34/160. The daily train to Madurai (15 hours) leaves at 7.10 pm; to Tirupathi (105km, three hours) it's at the unsociable hour of 1.05 am or there's a passenger train (5½ hours) leaving at 9.15 am.

Buses wait outside Katpadi station for trains to arrive and the journey into Vellore (Rs 1.20) takes anything from 15 to 30 minutes. Auto-rickshaws charge Rs 30.

AROUND VELLORE

Vellamalai (18km)

The temple of Vellamalai is dedicated to Siva's son, Kartikkaya (Murga in Tamil). There's a temple at the bottom of the hill but the main temple, carved from a massive stone, is at the top. Shoes must be removed at the base of the hill. There's a good view of the bleak countryside around Vellamalai – the ground is stony and strewn with boulders. The cloth knots you will see tied to trees are requests that wishes be granted. The one-hour trip from Vellore on bus No 20 (hourly) costs Rs 5.

TIRUVANNAMALAI

Tel Area Code: 04175

The temple town of Tiruvannamalai, 85km south of Vellore, is an important Shaivite town. Of the 100 or more temples, the most outstanding is the Siva-Parvati Temple of Arunachaleswar, which is said to be the largest in India. The main gopuram is 66m and 13 storeys high, and there is a 1000-pillared hall.

Places to Stay

Park Lodge has basic singles/doubles for Rs 40/60.

Udipi Brindavan Lodge (☎ 22693) on Anna Salai has simple rooms for Rs 60 and two air-con rooms for Rs 230.

Hotel Trishul (☎ 22219), 6 Kanakaraya Mudali St, has rooms for Rs 250/320 and some air-con rooms. It's a three minute walk from the temple.

GINGEE (Senji)

Gingee (pronounced 'shingee') is 37km east of Tiruvannamalai. There is an interesting fort complex here, constructed mainly in the 16th century during the Vijayanagar Empire (though some of the structures date back to 1200 AD). The fort is built on three separate hills, joined by three km of fortified walls. The buildings – a granary, audience hall, Siva temple and a mosque – are fairly ordinary, but the boulder-covered mountain landscape is impressive.

Gingee is pleasantly free of postcard sellers and the like; in fact it's deserted. You can easily spend a whole day here exploring at will. There's an uneven staircase of stone slabs up Krishnagiri Hill, but the route to Rajagiri Fort is much more difficult to follow.

There are buses almost every hour from Tiruvannamalai. Ask to be let off at the fort, which is before the town.

PONDICHERRY

Pop: 593,000   Tel Area Code: 0413

Pondicherry, the former French colony settled in the early 18th century, is a charming and enduring pocket of French culture set beside the sea. Together with the other former French enclaves of Karaikal (also in Tamil Nadu), Mahé (Kerala) and Yanam (Andhra Pradesh), it now forms the Union Territory of Pondicherry.

Unlike Goa, where the only firm reminders of the Portuguese are the cathedrals, here there are hints of the previous owners everywhere, despite the fact that the French relinquished control of their colony over 40 years ago. The Tricolore flutters over the grand French Consulate, there's a Hôtel de Ville (town hall); red kepis (caps) and belts are worn by the local police, and you even occasionally hear French being spoken on the streets.

Extensive restoration work of the buildings in the centre has been undertaken by the Aurobindo Ashram, the Alliance Française, and other bodies. Many houses and institutions in the streets between the waterfront and the old canal are now very chic and gentrified, their gardens ablaze with flowering trees and bougainvillea, and their entrances adorned with shiny brass plates. The overall impression is one of gleaming whitewashed residences and a concern for maintaining standards rarely encountered elsewhere in India. Yet, beyond the canal, Pondicherry is as Indian as anywhere else.

The French influence is also reflected, as one might expect, in the food. There are some excellent restaurants serving every-

thing from authentic bouillabaisse to crème caramel to die for. As in their other colonies the French soon sought out a good source of mineral water, and bottled Pondicherry water is by far the best in India. Hotels are excellent value since Tamil Nadu's punitive taxes do not apply here. And the beer's only Rs 25!

You may come expressly to see the Sri Aurobindo Ashram and its offshoot, Auroville, 10km outside town, but you'll probably stay a lot longer than you'd intended.

Orientation

Pondicherry is laid out on a grid plan surrounded by a congested semicircular boulevard. A north-south canal (now covered) divides the eastern side from the larger western part. In colonial days, the canal separated Pondicherry's European and Indian sections. The French residential area was near the present-day harbour.

The Aurobindo Ashram, its offices, schools and guest houses, as well as the French institutions and many restaurants, are all on the eastern side while most, but not all, of the hotels are west of the canal. The railway station is at the southern edge of town, while the bus stands are west along the main drag, Lal Bahabhur St.

Information

The tourist office (☎ 39497) on Goubert Ave is open daily from 8 am to 1 pm and 2 to 6 pm. They have a free leaflet but little else. You can arrange dolphin-watching cruises here (if the cruises are running again). The office also runs city sightseeing tours (Rs 25).

The Indian Overseas Bank, in the courtyard of the Hôtel de Ville (town hall), accepts most travellers cheques. There's also a Canara Bank just off Nehru St. Both banks are open weekdays from 10 am to 2 pm and Saturday until noon.

The GPO, on Rangapillai St, is open from 10 am to 7.30 pm, Monday to Saturday. Next door is the 24 hour telegraph office.

The French Consulate (☎ 34058), on Compagnie St, is open weekdays from 8 am to noon.

Clinic Nallam (☎ 35463), 74 ID Koil St, is a recommended place to go if you need a doctor.

Bookshops The Vak Bookshop, 15 Nehru St, specialises in books on religion and philosophy. Equally good (if you read French) are the Kailash French Bookshop on Lal Bahabhur St and the French Bookshop on Suffren St next to Alliance Française. There's a branch of Higginbothams on Gingy St. For secondhand books there is also Kitab on Dupuy St.

Sri Aurobindo Ashram
Founded by Sri Aurobindo in 1926, this ashram is one of the most popular in India with westerners, and is also one of the most affluent. Its spiritual tenets represent a synthesis of yoga and modern science. After Aurobindo's death, spiritual authority passed to one of his devotees, a French woman known as The Mother, who herself died in 1973, aged 97. These days, the ashram underwrites and promotes a lot of cultural and educational activities in Pondicherry, though there is a certain tension between it and the local people because it owns virtually everything worth owning in the Union Territory but is reluctant to allow local participation in the running of the society.

The main ashram building is on Marine St and is surrounded by other buildings given over to the various educational and cultural activities of the Aurobindo Society. The ashram is open every day from 8 am to noon and 2 to 6 pm and you can be shown around on request. The flower-festooned *samadhi* (tomb) of Aurobindo and The Mother is under the frangipani tree in the central courtyard. Their old black Humber sits rusting in the garage just off the courtyard.

Opposite the main building is the educational centre where you can sometimes catch a film, slide show, play or lecture (forthcoming events are announced on the ashram's notice board). There's usually no entry charge, but a donation may be collected.

Other Attractions
Furniture polish is desperately needed by some of the French period exhibits in **Pondicherry Museum**. Endearingly arranged in the style of a junk shop there's everything from Pallava sculptures to a bed slept in by Dupleix, the colony's most famous governor. This interesting museum is at 1 Romain Roland St and is open from 10 am and 5 pm, Tuesday to Sunday. Entry is free. There's also a small **police museum**, at the police station.

There are several large churches and cathedrals around the town, including the striking brown and white **Sacred Heart Church** on South Boulevard. Nearby are the peaceful, extensive **Botanical Gardens**, opened in 1740.

The **Alliance Française**, the French cultural centre (☎ 38146), at 38 Suffren St, runs French, English and Tamil classes as well as a library, and computer centre. Its small monthly newsletter, *Le Petit Journal*, details forthcoming courses and events. The library (☎ 34351) is open from 9 am to noon and 4 to 7 pm. Temporary membership (valid for 15 days) is Rs 50.

Places to Stay – bottom end
Amala Lodge (☎ 38910), 92 Rangapillai St, is clean, excellent value, popular with travellers and run by a friendly family. There are singles/doubles for Rs 40/70 with common bath, Rs 45/75 with attached bath.

Surya Swastika Guest House (☎ 43092), is a spotless little guesthouse at 11 ID Koil St. There are rooms for Rs 40/70 with common bath, Rs 45/75 with bath attached. The only drawback is that you have to be in by 9.30 pm.

Aristo Guest House (☎ 36728), 50A Mission St, is clean and friendly and has singles/doubles for Rs 70/100 as well as a few air-con doubles for Rs 550. All the rooms have attached bathrooms.

Victoria Lodge (☎ 36366), 79 Nehru St, is shabby but clean enough, and has rooms for Rs 60/125 with attached bathroom.

Hotel Kanchi (☎ 35540), Mission St, looks like a mid-range hotel until you see the

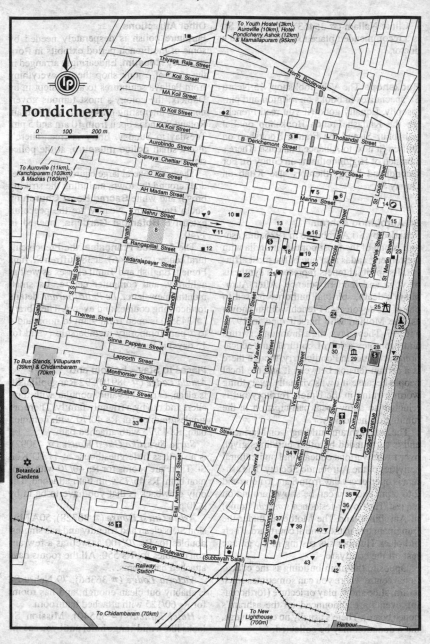

Pondicherry

To Youth Hostel (3km),
Auroville (10km), Hotel
Pondicherry Ashok (12km)
& Mamallapuram (95km)

Thiyaga Raja Street

P Koil Street

MA Koil Street

ID Koil Street

KA Koil Street

Aurobindo Street

Supraya Chettiar Street

C Koil Street

AH Madam Street

Nehru Street

Rangapillai Street

Nidarajapayer Street

St Theresa Street

Sinna Pappara Street

Lapporth Street

Monthorsier Street

C Mudhaliar Street

Lal Bahabhur Street

South Boulevard

North Boulevard

L Thollandal Street

B Derichemont
Street

Dupuy Street

Marine Street

St Louis Street

Compagnie Street

St Martin Street

France Martin Street

Mission Street

Canteen Street

Capt Xavier Street

Gingy Street

Victor Simonel Street

Suffren Street

Romain Roland Street

Dumas Street

Goubert Avenue

Covered Canal

Labourdonnais Street

Ellai Amman Koil Street

Mahatma Gandhi Road

Barathi Street

SS Illai Street

Anna Salai

To Auroville (11km),
Kanchipuram (103km)
& Madras (160km)

To Bus Stands, Villupuram
(39km) & Chidambaram
(70km)

Botanical
Gardens

To Chidambaram (70km)

Railway
Station

Subbayah Salai

To New
Lighthouse
(700m)

Harbour

0   100   200 m

rooms. It is, however, clean and quiet and some of the large, tiled rooms have a balcony. Singles/doubles with attached bathroom start at Rs 90/125.

Bar Qualithé Hotel (☎ 34325), on Government Square, is predominantly a pub but it does have six rooms lining the 1st floor verandah. All four-bedded with attached bath, they're overpriced at Rs 350.

Railway retiring rooms cost Rs 30/60 and are pretty quiet – the only action around is cows grazing on the grass growing over the train tracks.

Places to Stay – middle & top end

Ashram Guest Houses The best places to stay by far in Pondy are the guest houses run by the Aurobindo Ashram. They're all immaculately maintained and in the most attractive part of town and, although classified here as mid-range, some offer rooms which are cheaper than those in the budget hotels mentioned above. The only drawback with ashram accommodation is the 10.30 pm curfew, though arrangements can usually be made with the doorkeeper to allow you to come back later. Smoking and alcoholic drinks are banned in all ashram guest houses.

Park Guest House (☎ 34412) on Goubert Ave has the best facilities and all the rooms

on the front side face the sea and have a balcony. However, unlike the other ashram guest houses, the proprietors here prefer taking devotees rather than visiting tourists. Unless they're full, it's unlikely you'll be turned away, however you may get a slightly cool reception. Singles/doubles range from Rs 150/200 to Rs 250/300 and all have private bathroom. There's a vegetarian restaurant here.

International Guest House (☎ 36699) is on Gingy St. The cheapest rooms here are in the old wing where singles/doubles start at Rs 60/80. Doubles in the new wing cost Rs 100, and Rs 300 with air-con. All the rooms have attached bathrooms with hot water on request.

Sea Side Guest House (☎ 36194), 14 Goubert Ave, is the third of the ashram guesthouses and has a far less institutional feel to it. This old house has eight very spacious rooms all with private bathroom. When it reopens after renovation rooms are likely to be in the Rs 250 to Rs 400 range, some with air-con.

Other Hotels Attached to the restaurant/bar of the same name, **Ajantha Guest House** (☎ 38898), 22 Goubert Ave, is not a great place: all the rooms here are on the ground floor so there are no ocean views. There are

TAMIL NADU

no singles, and doubles cost Rs 250, or Rs 400 with air-con.

Hotel Surguru (☎ 39022), SV Patel Salai, is popular with businesspeople. There are rooms from Rs 330/420, and Rs 490/620 with air-con, all with attached bathrooms and Star TV. The hotel has a good vegetarian restaurant.

Ananda Inn (☎ 30711; fax 31241), SV Patel Salai, is a flashy neo-classical place, the top hotel in town. The comfortable air-con rooms are Rs 850/1050, there are good non-veg and veg restaurants, and even a 'men's beauty parlour'!

Hotel Pondicherry Ashok (☎ 605160) is a Portuguese villa-style hotel 12km north of town on the coastal road. Rooms here start at Rs 1195/1800. It's already starting to look rather run down and service is reportedly very poor. Typical government-run hotel, really.

Places to Eat

Pondicherry has some excellent places to eat, some open-air, and most serve cheap beer. If you purchase a meal ticket (Rs 15) in advance from the ashram, you can eat lunch or dinner in their dining-room.

West Side The *Hotel Aristo* has a very popular rooftop restaurant. It has a 198 item Indian menu with everything made to order, so expect to wait at least 20 minutes for your food to arrive. Most main dishes are Rs 30 to Rs 50 and there are some interesting choices, such as walnut chicken with brown rice (Rs 50). Food is cheaper and served faster in the ground-floor restaurant (closed Friday).

India Coffee House on Nehru St is good value for breakfast and snacks.

East Side Near the ashram, *Bliss Restaurant* serves straightforward thalis for Rs 15, but is closed on Sundays.

Le Café, which is opposite the French Consulate on Marine St, is a former garage turned snack bar which offers good tea and samosas. It's not to be confused with the seafront *Le Café* on Goubert Ave, a crumbly old place that is frequented by the locals after their evening promenade. Basic south

Indian food is available and you can dine with the waves crashing below.

Bar Qualithé Hotel, overlooking Government Square on Labourdonnais St, is an old refurbished place with comfy wicker chairs and bags of atmosphere. Have a plate of beef fry (Rs 25) with your beer (Rs 26). There's a range of more substantial dishes for around Rs 35.

Seagulls Restaurant at 19 Dumas St, is right by the sea and serves quite good food. Beer's available.

Blue Dragon Chinese Restaurant at 33 Dumas St serves good Chinese food as does *China Town* on Suffren St.

La Terrasse, 5 Subbish Salai, is an excellent French-run pizza restaurant, open evenings only. Pizzas cost from Rs 45 to Rs 65.

Rendezvous, at 30 Suffren St, is a lovely place with decor straight out of rural France – wicker chairs, gingham tablecloths, and shutters. It's open 8 to 11 am, noon to 3 pm and 6 to 10.30 pm. Bouillabaisse (Rs 60), lobster and mushroom quiche (Rs 90) and grilled prawns (Rs 150) are some of the excellent dishes on offer. They also do good tandoori food, and there's an attractive roof terrace.

Satsanga is just down the street from Rendezvous. French-run, the food's as good as it sounds – soupe de poisson (Rs 45), terrine de lapin (Rs 50), salade provencal (Rs 45), poulet piment vert et frites (Rs 65). The coffee's superb, as is the creme caramel, and you can sit out in the garden. There's a range of jams, pickles and peanut butter for sale. There's a pricey art gallery, and they also have a couple of rooms for rent. It's closed on Thursday.

Le Club, 33 Dumas St, is the most expensive restaurant in town. The cuisine is French, the decor peachy and the service immaculate. Wine and beer are available, both French and English are spoken, and it's open for breakfast (7.30 to 9.30 am), lunch (noon to 2 pm) and dinner (7 to 10 pm) every day except Monday. Expect to pay Rs 150 for a glass of wine, around Rs 60 for an entree, and Rs 150 for a main course. You could follow this with a plate of profiteroles (Rs 65) and a cognac (Rs 175). There's a cheaper tandoori restaurant, *Le Bistro*, in the garden.

Entertainment

There's not a great deal to do in Pondy in the evenings other than dining out in one of the restaurants or strolling along the promenade. The *Bar Qualithé Hotel* and the *Ajantha Bar* stay open until 10.30 pm.

Things to Buy

Pottery, clothing, shoes and a whole range of other Auroville products can be found in La Boutique d'Auroville on Nehru St. Incense and other handicrafts are also sold at Cottage Industries on Rangapillai St.

Getting There & Away

Bus The TTC/RGTC bus stand is by the roundabout on the road to Villupuram, to the west of the centre. It's quiet and well organised, with a computerised reservation service (Rs 2). There are buses to Chennai (4½ hours, Rs 27) at least once an hour, and buses four times daily to Madurai (7½ hours, Rs 54), Bangalore, Tirupathi and Coimbatore.

From the chaotic new bus stand, 500m to the west, there are regular buses to Bangalore (twice daily), Chidambaram (every half hour), Kanchipuram (four times daily), Karaikal (ten times daily), Kumbakonam (five times daily), Chennai (10 times daily), Mamallapuram (four times daily), Nagapattinam (three times daily), Tiruchirappalli (five times daily), Tiruvannamalai (nine times daily), Vellore (five times daily) and Villupuram.

Train Pondicherry's railway station is not very busy as most people go by bus. There are four daily passenger trains to Villupuram (38km, one hour, Rs 7) on the Chennai to Madurai line which leave Pondicherry at 5.10 and 8 am, and 5.15 and 9.30 pm. From Villupuram, many expresses go in either direction. The computerised booking service at the station covers all trains on the southern railway.

Getting Around

Large three-wheelers shuttle between the bus stations and Gingy St for Rs 2, but they're so overcrowded you might not want to use them. There are also plenty of cycle and auto-rickshaws. Auto-rickshaws are meterless and although official fares (starting at Rs 6 for up to two km) are posted near the main stands, you'll have to haggle.

Most people, however, hire a bicycle during their stay. This is also a good idea if you plan to visit Auroville. At many of the bikehire shops on MG Rd, Mission St and South Blvd, you may be asked for Rs 300 or your passport as a deposit. The only way around this is to have proof of which hotel you are staying in (they may check this, too). The usual rental is Rs 2 per hour, or around Rs 20 per day.

Mopeds can be rented from Vijay Arya (☎ 36179), 9 Aurobindo St (no sign), for Rs 80 a day. You need to leave some ID (passport or driving licence).

AUROVILLE

Tel Area Code: 0413

Just over the border in Tamil Nadu, Auroville is the brainchild of The Mother and was designed by French architect Roger Anger. It was conceived as 'an experiment in international living where men and women could live in peace and progressive harmony with each other above all creeds, politics and nationalities'. Its opening ceremony on 28 February 1968 was attended by the President of India and representatives of 121 countries, who poured the soil of their lands into an urn to symbolise universal oneness.

The project has 70 settlements spread over 20km, and about 1200 residents (two thirds of whom are foreigners), including children. The settlements include: Forecomers, involved in alternative technology and agriculture; Certitude, working in sports; Aurelec, devoted to computer research; Discipline, an agricultural project; Fertile, Nine Palms and Meadow, all engaged in tree planting and agriculture; Fraternity, a handicrafts community working in cooperation with local Tamil villagers; and Aspiration, an educational, health care and village industry project.

While most visitors attempt to 'see' Auroville in a day, you will not get the feel of the place unless you spend at least a few days here. Day-trippers and casual tourism are not actively encouraged, although visitors with a genuine interest in Auroville will not be made unwelcome. As the Aurovillians put it: 'Auroville is very much an experiment, that is in its early stages, and it is not at all meant to be a tourist attraction'.

Information
In Pondicherry, La Boutique d'Auroville (☎ 27264) has information on the community. At Auroville itself, there is a visitor's centre (☎ 62239) near Bharat Nivas. This centre has a permanent exhibition of the community's activities and the helpful staff will address any queries. It's open daily from 9.30 am to 5.30 pm. Next door is an Auroville handicrafts shop and a restaurant.

Matrimandir
The Matrimandir was designed to be the spiritual and physical centre of Auroville. Its construction has been very much a stop-start affair because the flow of funds has been less than steady. However, the meditation chamber and the main structure are now complete leaving only the finishing touches (metal discs) to be added to the external skin. Likewise, the extensive landscaping associated with the project is well under way with the help of a small army of local labourers.

The meditation chamber is lined with white marble and houses a huge, solid glass sphere. Sun rays are beamed into this sphere from a tracking mirror located in the roof. On cloudy days, solar lamps do the job.

While the Matrimandir is undoubtedly a remarkable edifice and certainly the focal point of the community, many of the more pragmatic Aurovillians would have preferred the money spent on community infrastructure and on projects of a more tangible nature. Others claim that without any such physical manifestation of Auroville's (and, therefore, The Mother's) spiritual ideal, the

The Battle for Auroville
For a time after Auroville's opening in 1968, idealism ran high and the project attracted many foreigners, particularly from France, Germany, the UK, the Netherlands and Mexico. Construction of living quarters, schools, and an enormous meditation hall known as the Matrimandir began, and dams, reafforestation, orchards and other agricultural projects were started. The amount of energy and effort invested in Auroville in those early days – and since – should be immediately obvious to anyone, and the idealism with which the place began is still tangible.

Unfortunately, the death in 1973 of The Mother, undisputed spiritual and administrative head of the Sri Aurobindo Society and Auroville, resulted in an acrimonious power struggle between the Society and the Aurovillians for control of Auroville. On two occasions in 1977 and 1978, violence led to police intervention.

Though the Aurovillians retained the sympathy of the Pondicherry administration, the odds were stacked against them. All funds for the project were channelled through the society, which had the benefit of powerful friends in the Indian government. In a demonstration of their hold over Auroville, the society began to withhold funds; and construction work, particularly on the Matrimandir, had to be temporarily abandoned.

The Aurovillians reacted resourcefully to this takeover bid, pooling their assets to take care of the food and financial needs of residents and setting up 'Auromitra', a friends-of-Auroville fund-raising organisation. Nevertheless, in early 1976, things became so serious that the ambassadors of France, Germany and the USA were forced to intervene with offers of help from their governments to prevent the residents from starving.

Finally, an Indian government committee recommended that the powers of the Aurobindo Society be transferred to a committee made up of representatives of the various interest groups, including the Aurovillians, with greater local participation. In 1988, under the Auroville Foundation Act, the administration of Auroville was taken over by a body of nine eminent persons who act as intermediaries between the central government and the Aurovillians. The government has actually gone so far as to nationalise Auroville, but the long-term future of the place still seems unclear. ■

community may have splintered long ago, particularly in view of the financial and physical hardships endured by many of its less affluent members.

You can wander round the gardens between 9.30 am and 3.30 pm. Only between 3.45 and 4.45 pm are visitors allowed inside the Matrimandir, but you need to get a ticket (free) in advance from the visitor centre, before 4 pm.

Places to Stay & Eat

Palms Beach Cottage Centre is by the big Pepsi sign in the village of Chinna Mudaliarchavadi on the way to Auroville from Pondy. Not quite what the name suggests, it's a good 15 minutes from the beach. Clean toilets and showers are shared, and there's an open-air gazebo for eating and relaxing in. Meals are available, main dishes cost around Rs 45. Singles/doubles cost Rs 50/100.

Cottage Guest House is a little further on, down the lane on the right opposite the turn-off

to Auroville. It offers basic singles/doubles with mosquito nets in a thatched-roof, semi-concrete block for Rs 50/100 with shared bathroom. Doubles with attached bathroom in the new block are Rs 150. There's a communal dining area and all meals are available.

You can also stay with virtually every one of the 33 community groups here, however, they prefer people to stay at least a week and, although work isn't obligatory, it's very much appreciated. You come here, after all, to get to know people involved in Auroville. You should note that none of these community groups will offer free accommodation in exchange for work. For most groups, money is tight. Conditions, facilities and costs vary a great deal. Some places are quite primitive with minimal facilities; others have the lot. Prices range from Rs 80 to Rs 350, with some accommodation in the *Centre Guest House* (☎ 62155), very close to the Matrimandir.

The only place in Auroville where casual visitors will find a meal – and it's a good one

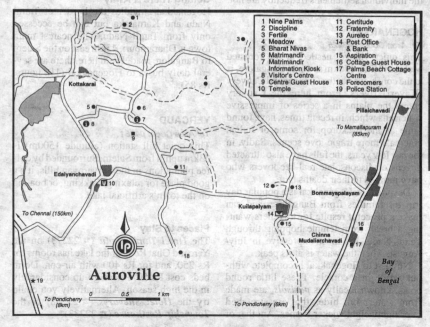

– is the brightly decorated cafeteria next to the visitor's centre. It's open daily for lunch (Rs 20 for a healthy meal of the day) as well as for dinner on Friday and Saturday night. Savoury snacks, cakes, tea and coffee are sold as well.

Getting There & Away
The best way to enter Auroville is from the coast road, at the village of Chinna Mudaliarchavadi. Ask around as it's not well signposted. It's also possible to enter from the main Pondicherry to Chennai road at Promesse. The turn-off, one km after the police station, is signposted.

Once at Auroville, you'll need something other than your feet to get around as everything is very spread out. If you rent a bike or scooter in Pondicherry, you can count on cycling at least 30km there and back. It's mostly tarmac roads or good gravel tracks. Most of the community centres (eg Matrimandir, Bharat Nivas, etc) are signposted but the individual settlements frequently are not.

HOGENAKKAL
Tel Area Code: 043425
This quiet village, nestled in the forested Melagiri Hills, 170km south of Bangalore, is at the confluence of the Chinnar and Cauvery (Kaveri) rivers. From here the Cauvery enters the plains in a series of impressive waterfalls which, in recent times, have found fame as the backdrop for some of Indian cinema's more tragic love scenes. Sadly, in the last few years, the falls have also attracted dozens of disconsolate real-life lovers who have jumped to their deaths here.

Despite this, Hogenakkal is a popular day trip for families from Bangalore, and can make a peaceful respite for travellers wanting a break from temple hopping through Tamil Nadu. It's most impressive in July/August, when the water is at its peak.

No visit to Hogenakkal is complete without a ride in a coracle. These little round boats, known locally as *parisals*, are made from waterproof hides that are stretched over lightweight wicker frames. Another of Hogenakkal's treats is an oil massage – more than 100 masseurs ply their trade here so you shouldn't have to queue.

Places to Stay & Eat
Private homes, near the police station (to the right just as you enter the village) have rooms to let. The stalls at the bus stand all sell tasty fried fish.

Hotel Tamil Nadu (☎ 447) has doubles for Rs 225, or Rs 360 with air-con including tax, plus about 30% at weekends. The large, airy rooms have monkey-proof balconies. Dorm beds (men only) in the attached *youth hostel* are Rs 50. The hotel has an uninspiring restaurant where you can get a thali for Rs 15. Non-vegetarian food should be ordered several hours in advance.

Tourist Rest House and *Tourist Home* next to the bus stand both offer basic rooms for between Rs 60 and Rs 100.

Getting There & Away
Hogenakkal straddles the border of Tamil Nadu and Karnataka but can be accessed only from Tamil Nadu. The nearest main town is Dharampuri, 45km east on the Salem to Bangalore road. From here, there are several daily buses to Hogenakkal (1¼ hours, Rs 85).

YERCAUD
Tel Area Code: 04281
This quiet hill station (altitude 1500m) is 33km uphill from Salem. Surrounded by coffee plantations in the Servaroyan hills, it's a good place for relaxing, trekking, or boating on the town's artificial lake.

Places to Stay
The *Hotel Tamil Nadu* (☎ 22273) on the Yercaud Ghat Rd near the lake has rooms for Rs 250, and for Rs 400 with air-con. Dorm beds cost Rs 50. Prices go up considerably in the high season. Alternatively you could try the *Hotel Shevarys* (☎ 22288) or the *Township Resthouse* (☎ 22233).

TAMIL NADU

Central Tamil Nadu

CHIDAMBARAM

Tel Area Code: 04144

Sixty km south of Pondicherry, Chidambaram's great temple complex of Nataraja, the dancing Siva, is another of Tamil Nadu's Dravidian architectural highlights.

The best time to be here is during one of the many festivals. The two largest are the 10 day car festivals, the dates for which usually fall in April/May and December/January. In February the Natyanjali dance festival attracts performers from all over the country.

The tourist office (☎ 22739) is at the Hotel Tamil Nadu.

Nataraja Temple

Chidambaram was a Chola capital from 907 to 1310 and the Nataraja Temple was erected during the reign of Vira Chola Raja (927-997). The complex is said to be the oldest in southern India. It covers 13 hectares and has four gopurams, the north and south ones towering at 49m high. Two of the gopurams are carved with the 108 classical postures of Nataraja, Siva in his role as the cosmic dancer.

Other notable features of the temple are the 1000-pillared hall, the Nritta Sabha court carved out like a gigantic chariot, and the image of Nataraja himself in the inner sanctum. There are other lesser temples in the complex, including ones dedicated to Parvati, Subrahmanya and Ganesh, and a newer Vishnu temple.

The Nataraja Temple courtyard with its many shrines is open from 4 am to noon and 4.30 to 9 pm. The special *puja* ceremony, held at 5 pm every Friday evening, is certainly spectacular with fire rituals and the clashing of bells and drums. Every other night, at the same time, lesser puja ceremonies are conducted. Although non-Hindus are not allowed right into the inner sanctum, there are usually priests around who will take you in – for a fee, of course.

Places to Stay

Railway retiring rooms at the station are good value at Rs 60/90 for a double/triple with attached bath.

Star Lodge (☎ 22743) on South Car St has clean and habitable rooms for Rs 40/60 with attached bathrooms. The rooms have grilles in the windows (no glass) but it's a friendly place and there's a good restaurant downstairs.

Shameer Lodge (☎ 22983), Venugopal Pillai St, is good value at Rs 45/60/90 for rooms with attached bathroom and clean sheets.

Hotel Murugan (☎ 20419) is one of several similar places on West Car St. There are basic rooms with attached bath for Rs 45/88, and an air-con double for Rs 201.

TTDC Hotel Tamil Nadu (☎ 22323) gets varied reports. Recently-cleaned rooms are fine and cost Rs 120/180, or Rs 300 for a double with air-con, plus Rs 50 for Star TV. There are dorm beds for Rs 45 in the attached 'youth hostel' but you'd be better off in one of the cheap hotels.

1 Tillai Kali Amman Temple
2 Post Office
3 Indian Overseas Bank
4 Hotel Murugan
5 Hotel Akshaya
6 Nataraja Temple
7 Bike Hire
8 State Bank of India
9 Shameer Lodge
10 Star Lodge & Babu Restaurant
11 Hotel Saradharam & Restaurant
12 Bus Stand
13 Hospital
14 TTDC Hotel Tamil Nadu & Tourist Office

To Cuddalore (50km), Pondicherry (71km) & Chennai (232km)

North Car Street
West Car Street
East Car Street
South Car Street
Pillaiyar Koil Street

To Annamalai University (1.5km) & Pichavaram (15km)

To Kumbakonam (69km)

Railway Station

0   200   400 m
Approximate Scale

Chidambaram

TAMIL NADU

Hotel Akshaya (☎ 20192), 17 East Car St, is fairly new but already looking a bit shabby. Rooms are Rs 140/160/200, air-con for Rs 300/370/420.

Hotel Saradharam (☎ 22966), 19 VGP St, near the bus stand, is the best place in town with ordinary rooms with fan and TV for Rs 250/275 and air-con rooms from Rs 425/450. There's a bar and veg and non-veg restaurants.

Places to Eat
The choice of restaurants here is rather limited.

Babu Restaurant, on the ground floor of the Star Lodge, offers good vegetarian meals in full south Indian style – banana leaves, sauce buckets and rock-bottom prices.

TTDC Hotel Tamil Nadu has veg and non-veg restaurants plus a very pleasant rooftop bar (beer is Rs 45).

Hotel Saradharam is a good place to eat. It's not expensive (butter chicken masala is Rs 38) but you need to get there early for lunch or dinner as it's very popular.

Getting There & Away
The railway station is a 20 minute walk south-east of the Nataraja Temple, or Rs 10 by cycle-rickshaw. Express and passenger trains leave for Chennai (four times daily), Kumbakonam, Thanjavur (twice daily), Tiruchirappalli and Madurai.

The bus stand, used by both TTC and local buses, is more central. Point-to-Point bus No 157 (seven per day) is quickest to Chennai. Services for Pondicherry continue to Chennai every half hour (Nos 300, 324 and 326, seven hours, Rs 35) and go to Madurai (No 521, eight hours, Rs 50).

There's a bike hire shop on South Car St (Rs 1.50 per hour).

AROUND CHIDAMBARAM
Pichavaram
The seaside resort of Pichavaram, with its backwaters and mangrove forest, is 15km east of Chidambaram. A Marine Research Institute is at nearby Parangipettai (Porto Novo), a former Portuguese and Dutch port.

The TTDC's *Aringar Anna Tourist Complex* (☎ (041445) 89232) charges Rs 45 for a dorm bed and Rs 125 for a cottage.

KUMBAKONAM
Tel Area Code: 0435
This bustling south Indian town, nestled along the Cauvery River some 37km north-east of Thanjavur, is noted for its many temples with their colourful semi-erotic sculpture. The most important are **Sarangapani**, **Kumbeshwara** and **Nageshwara**, the largest of which is second in size only to the Meenakshi Temple at Madurai. They are all closed between noon and 4.30 pm.

Once every 12 years, the waters of the Ganges are said to flow into Kumbakonam's **Mahamaham Tank** and thousands of devotees flock here to a festival held at that time. According to legend, a *kumbh* (pitcher) came to rest here after a big flood (hence the town name). Siva broke the pot with his arrow, and its spilled contents formed this sacred tank. The next festival will be held in early 2004.

Kumbakonam also makes an excellent base from which to visit the very interesting nearby temple towns of Dharasuram and Gangakondacholapuram.

Places to Stay
New Diamond Lodge (☎ 30870), 93 Ayikulam Rd, has basic singles/doubles for Rs 40/65 with common bath, Rs 50/75 with bath attached. It's fine but you should use your own padlock on the door. Rooms at the back have a great view over Nageshwara Temple.

Hotel Siva/VPR Lodge (☎ 21949) share the same reception at 104-105 TSR Big St in the main bazaar area. VPR Lodge offers excellent budget accommodation – Rs 65/90 for very clean rooms. The Siva has huge, spotless doubles with attached bathroom, constant hot water, and a choice of Indian squat and western sit-down toilets (sometimes both in the same bathroom!) for Rs 200, Rs 300 with air-con.

Pandiyan Hotel (☎ 30397), 52 Sarangapani East St, is popular and often full. All rooms have bath attached and cost Rs 55/100.

Femina Lodge (☎ 20369), 8 Post Office Rd, is a small new place with spotless doubles with attached bath for Rs 115. If standards are maintained it's excellent value.

Hotel ARR (☎ 21234) is a large place at 21 TSR Big St. There are doubles for Rs 175 (Rs 350 with air-con).

Hotel Athitya (☎ 23262), Ayikulam Rd, has a range of good rooms from Rs 250/275 (ordinary) to Rs 370/395 (air-con). There's a veg and non-veg restaurant.

Hotel Raya's (☎ 22545), 28-29 Post Office Rd, offers well-furnished doubles/triples (no singles) from Rs 300/400, or Rs 400/550 with air-con. Room 101 (Rs 600) is the 'lovers' room' – there are mirrors on every surface, including the ceiling above the bed!

Places to Eat

Arul Restaurant, opposite Hotel Pandiyan, is an excellent vegetarian place with a range of lunch-time thalis from Rs 10 to Rs 45 and an air-con dining hall upstairs.

PRV Lodge, next to Hotel Raya's and not to be confused with VPR Lodge, has a good vegetarian restaurant with meals from Rs 12, Rs 17 for specials. The naan are very good.

Hotel Raya's has a non-veg restaurant; main dishes are Rs 35 to Rs 45.

Getting There & Away

The bus stand and nearby railway station are about two km east of the town centre (Rs 10 by cycle-rickshaw)

TTC has four buses a day to Chennai (No 303, seven hours, Rs 49) and there are frequent departures to Thanjavur via Dharasuram and to Gangakondacholapuram. Other buses pass through here on their way to Madurai, Coimbatore, Bangalore, Tiruvannamalai, Pondicherry and Chidambaram. Bus No 459 connects Kumbakonam with Karaikal.

There are at least four daily express trains via Chidambaram to Chennai, and three services to Thanjavur and Tiruchirappalli.

AROUND KUMBAKONAM

A copy of the booklet *Chola Temples* (for details see the later Brihadishwara Temple section in Thanjavur) may be useful when visiting the following places.

Dharasuram

The small town of Dharasuram is four km west of Kumbakonam. Set behind the village,

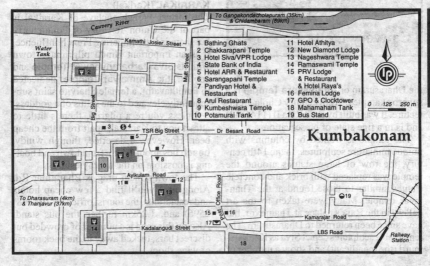

Kumbakonam

1 Bathing Ghats
2 Chakkarapani Temple
3 Hotel Siva/VPR Lodge
4 State Bank of India
5 Hotel ARR & Restaurant
6 Sarangapani Temple
7 Pandiyan Hotel & Restaurant
8 Arul Restaurant
9 Kumbeshwara Temple
10 Potamurai Tank
11 Hotel Athitya
12 New Diamond Lodge
13 Nageshwara Temple
14 Ramaswami Temple
15 PRV Lodge & Restaurant & Hotel Raya's
16 Femina Lodge
17 GPO & Clocktower
18 Mahamaham Tank
19 Bus Stand

Cauvery River
To Gangakondacholapuram (35km) & Chidambaram (69km)
Kamathi Josier Street
Water Tank
Big Street
Mutt Street
TSR Big Street
Dr Besant Road
Ayikulam Road
To Dharasuram (4km) & Thanjavur (37km)
Kadalangudi Street
Post Office Road
Kamarajar Road
LBS Road
Railway Station

0   125   250 m

TAMIL NADU

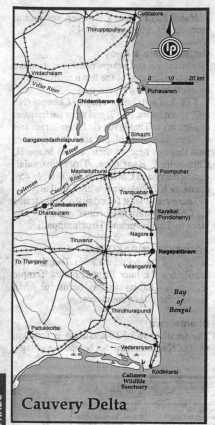

Cauvery Delta

the Dharasuram or **Airatesvara Temple** is a superb example of 12th century Chola architecture. It was built by Raja Raja II (1146-63) and is in a fine state of preservation.

The temple is fronted by columns with unique miniature sculptures. In the 14th century, the row of large statues around the temple was replaced with brick and concrete statues similar to those found at the Thanjavur temple. Many were taken to the art gallery in the Raja's palace at Thanjavur, but have since been returned to Dharasuram. The remarkable sculptures depict Siva as Kankala-murti (the mendicant) and show a number of

sages' wives standing by, dazzled by his beauty. The Archaeological Survey of India has done quite a bit of restoration here.

Although the temple is used very little at present, there is a helpful and knowledgeable priest who is an excellent English-speaking guide as well. He is available (for a small consideration) from 8 am to 8 pm daily.

Gangakondacholapuram

The gopurams of this enormous temple, 35km north of Kumbakonam, dominate the surrounding landscape. It was built by the Chola emperor, Rajendra I (1012-44), in the style of the Brihadishwara Temple (built by his father) at Thanjavur, and is dedicated to Siva. Many beautiful sculptures adorn the walls of the temple and its enclosures. You'll also see a huge tank into which were emptied vessels of water from the Ganges, brought to the Chola court by vassal kings. Like the temple at Dharasuram, this one is visited by few tourists and is no longer used for Hindu worship.

Apart from the temple and a small museum, there's very little in this small village. The temple is closed between noon and 4 pm.

KARAIKAL (Karikal)

The former French enclave of Karaikal is part of the Union Territory of Pondicherry but there is little lingering French influence. It is an important Hindu pilgrimage town with its Siva **Darbaranyeswar Temple** and another, the **Ammaiyar Temple**, dedicated to Punithavathi, a female Shaivite saint subsequently elevated to the status of a goddess.

Unless you're a pilgrim, there's little to attract you to Karaikal, apart from the cheap beer. However, a deserted, though windy, **beach** lies about 1.5km from town and boating is possible on the nearby estuary.

The town's main drag is Bharathiar Rd. Along here you'll find a few cheap hotels and restaurants, the tourist office (☎ (04368) 2596) and, 1.25km further, the bus stand. Also on this road is a number of crowded but discreet bars, tucked away in the back rooms of wine shops.

AROUND KARAIKAL

Poompuhar

Only a small village now stands at the mouth of the Cauvery River north of Karaikal but it was here that the rulers of the Chola Empire conducted trade with Rome and with centres to the east. The name of this old Chola seaport has also been given to the TTDC's chain of craft emporia. There's a fine beach, a *rest house* (☎ via Seerkashi 39) with cottages for Rs 150 and a restaurant.

Tranquebar (Tharangambadi)

Fourteen km north of Karaikal, Tranquebar was a Danish trading post in the 17th and 18th centuries and has a church built by the Lutherans. Later, it came under British rule. The impressive **Danesborg Fort** still looks out to sea, and there are some fine old colonial houses.

Nagore (Nagur)

The Andavar Dargah is an important Muslim pilgrimage centre at the village of Nagore, 12km south of Karaikal.

Velanganni

Velanganni, 35km south of Karaikal near the town of Nagapattinam, is the site of the famous Roman Catholic Church of Our Lady of Good Health. People of all religions flock to the church, many donating gold or silver models of cured bodily parts! A major festival is held here at the start of September.

CALIMERE WILDLIFE SANCTUARY

Also known as Kodikkarai, this coastal sanctuary is 90km south-east of Thanjavur in a wetland which juts out into the Palk Strait separating India and Sri Lanka. It is noted for the vast flocks of migratory water fowl, especially flamingos, which congregate here every winter. The best time to visit is between November and January when the tidal mud flats and marshes are covered with teals, shovellers, curlews, gulls, terns, plovers, sandpipers, shanks, herons and up to 3000 flamingoes at one time. In the spring, a different set of birds – koels, mynas and barbets

– are drawn here by the profusion of wild berries. Black buck, spotted deer and wild pig also congregate here. From April to June there's very little activity; the main rainy season is between October and December.

The easiest way to get to Calimere is by bus from Vedaranyam, which is the nearest town linked by frequent bus services to Nagapattinam or Thanjavur. There's a *Forest Department Rest House* with cheap, basic but adequate rooms, though all meals will have to be arranged with the staff. It's best to make a reservation for the rest house with the Forest Officer in Thanjavur.

THANJAVUR (Tanjore)

Pop: 217,000   Tel Area Code: 04362

Thanjavur was the ancient capital of the Chola kings whose origins, (like those of the Pallavas, Pandyas and Cheras with whom they shared the tip of the Indian peninsula), go back to the beginning of the Christian era. Power struggles between these groups were a constant feature of their early history, with one or other gaining the ascendancy at various times. The Cholas' turn for empire building came between 850 and 1270 AD and, at the height of their power, they controlled most of the Indian peninsula south of a line drawn between Mumbai and Puri, including parts of Sri Lanka and, for a while, the Srivijaya Kingdom of the Malay peninsula and Sumatra.

Probably the greatest Chola emperors were Raja Raja (985-1014), who was responsible for building the Brihadishwara Temple (Thanjavur's main attraction), and his son Rajendra I (1014-44), whose navy competed with the Arabs for control of the Indian Ocean trade routes and who was responsible for bringing Srivijaya under Chola control.

Thanjavur wasn't the only place to receive Chola patronage. Within easy reach of Thanjavur are numerous enormous Chola temples – main are at Thiruvaiyaru, Dharasuram near Kumbakonam and Gangakondacholapuram (for details see the Around Thanjavur and Around Kumbakonam sections). The Cholas also had a hand in building the enormous temple complex at Srirangam near Tiruchirappalli – probably India's largest.

TAMIL NADU

Thanjavur is also famous for its distinctive art style, which is usually a combination of raised and painted surfaces. Krishna is the most popular of the gods depicted; and in the Thanjavur school his skin is white, rather than the traditional blue-black.

Orientation

The enormous gopurams of the Brihadishwara Temple dominate Thanjavur. The temple itself, between the Grand Anicut Canal and the old town, is surrounded by fortified walls and a moat. The old town, too, used to be similarly enclosed, but most of the walls

have now disappeared. What remains are winding streets and alleys and the extensive ruins of the palace of the Nayaks of Madurai.

Gandhiji Rd, which runs between the railway station and the bus stand at the edge of the old town, has most of the hotels and restaurants, and the Poompuhar Arts & Crafts Emporium.

Information

The tourist office (☎ 23017), in Jawans Bhavan opposite the GPO, is open from 10 am to 5.45 pm. There's also a counter at the TTDC Hotel Tamil Nadu.

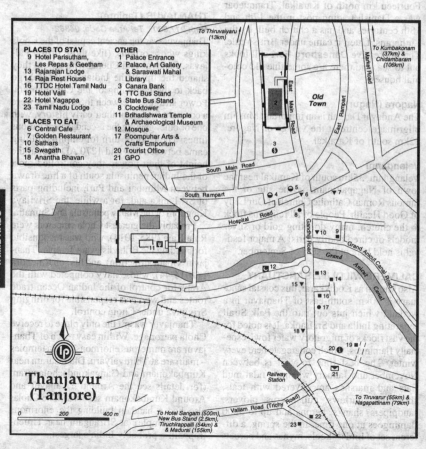

PLACES TO STAY
9 Hotel Parisutham,
   Les Repas & Geetham
13 Rajarajan Lodge
14 Raja Rest House
16 TTDC Hotel Tamil Nadu
19 Hotel Valli
22 Hotel Yagappa
23 Tamil Nadu Lodge

PLACES TO EAT
6 Central Cafe
7 Golden Restaurant
10 Sathars
15 Swagath
18 Anantha Bhavan

OTHER
1 Palace Entrance
2 Palace, Art Gallery
   & Saraswati Mahal
   Library
3 Canara Bank
4 TTC Bus Stand
5 State Bus Stand
8 Clocktower
11 Brihadishwara Temple
   & Archaeological Museum
12 Mosque
17 Poompuhar Arts &
   Crafts Emporium
20 Tourist Office
21 GPO

To Thiruvaiyaru
(13km)

To Kumbakonam
(37km) &
Chidambaram
(106km)

Old
Town

Market Road

East Main Road

East Rampart

South Main Road

South Rampart

Hospital Road

Gandhiji Road

Grand Anicut Canal Road

Grand Anicut Canal

Railway
Station

Vallam Road (Trichy Road)

To Tiruvarur (55km) &
Nagapattinam (79km)

To Hotel Sangam (500m),
New Bus Stand (2.5km),
Tiruchirappalli (54km) &
& Madurai (155km)

Thanjavur
(Tanjore)

0   200   400 m

TAMIL NADU

Tamil Nadu

Top Left: Mamallapuram's shore temples.
Top Right: The hill station of Kodaikanal.

Centre Right: Fishing boat pulled up
on Mamallapuram beach.
Bottom: Arjuna's Penance, Mamallapuram.

Detail of the colourful sculptures on a Hindu temple in Madurai, Tamil Nadu.

The Canara Bank on South Main Rd changes travellers cheques. The Hotel Parisutham does this too, but at a lousy rate.

The GPO, near the railway station, is open daily from 10 am to 4 pm; Sunday from noon. The telegraph office next door is open 24 hours.

Brihadishwara Temple & Fort
Built by Raja Raja, the Brihadishwara Temple is the crowning glory of Chola temple architecture. This superb and fascinating monument is one of only a handful in India with World Heritage listing and is worth a couple of visits. On top of the apex of the 63m high temple, a dome encloses an enormous Siva lingam (Hindus only). Constructed from a single piece of granite weighing an estimated 81 tonnes, the dome was hauled into place along a six km earthwork ramp in a manner similar to that used for the Egyptian pyramids. It has been worshipped continuously for more than 1000 years.

The gateway to the inner courtyard is guarded by an elephant and one of the largest Nandis in India measuring 6m long by 3m high, and fashioned from a single piece of rock. The carved stonework of the temple, gopurams and adjoining structures is rich in detail and reflects not only Shaivite influences, but also Vaishnavaite and Buddhist themes. In all, there are 250 lingams in the shrines along the outer walls. The frescoes adorning the walls and ceilings of the inner courtyard have been dated to Chola times and were executed using techniques similar to those used in European fresco work.

The well-arranged **Archaeological Museum**, on the southern side of the courtyard, has some interesting sculptures and photographs showing how the temple looked before much of the restoration work was done, as well as charts and maps detailing the history of the Chola Empire. The museum is open daily from 9.30 am to 1 pm and 3 to 7 pm. It sells an interesting little booklet titled *Chola Temples* by C Sivaramamurti for Rs 10 (it can also be bought at Chennai's Fort St George Museum) which describes the three temples at Thanjavur, Dharasuram and Gangakondacholapuram.

In June 1997 part of the temple was damaged by a fire that killed 39 people and injured 200 others.

The temple is open daily from 6 am to 1 pm and 3 to 8 pm. There is no admittance charge but at the entrance donations are solicited by a bored elephant. As this is still a functioning Hindu temple, non-Hindus cannot enter the sanctum sanctorum.

Thanjavur Palace & Museums
The huge corridors, spacious halls, observation and arsenal towers and shady courtyards of this vast labyrinthine building in the centre of the old town were constructed partly by the Nayaks of Madurai around 1550, and partly by the Marathas. Due to years of neglect many sections are in ruins, although restoration is now underway.

The poorly marked entrance is a wide break in the eastern wall, which leads past a school and a police station. The palace entrance is off to the left at the first junction, through the arched tunnel.

Follow the signs up to the **Royal Museum** which has an eclectic collection of regal memorabilia, most of it dating from the early 1800s when Serfoji II ruled. There are the raja's slippers, headresses and hunting weapons. The museum is open daily from 9 am to 6 pm. Admission is Rs 1. More signs lead you from the courtyard to the magnificent **Durbar Hall**, one of two such halls in the palace where audiences were held with the king. It's as yet unrestored but still in quite good condition.

An **art gallery** occupies the Nayak Durbar Hall. It has a superb collection of Chola bronze statues from the 9th to 12th centuries. The gallery is open from 9 am to 1 pm and 3 to 6 pm. Entry costs Rs 3. Nearby is the **Bell Tower**, reopened recently after some particularly unsympathetic restoration that does not bode well for the rest of the buildings requiring repair. It's worth the climb (Rs 2) for the overall views, however.

The **Saraswati Mahal Library** is next door to the gallery. Established around 1700 AD, the library contains a collection of over 30,000 palm-leaf and paper manuscripts in Indian and European languages. The library itself is closed to the public but you can visit the interesting **museum**. There's everything from the whole of the *Ramayana* written on a palm leaf to a set of explicit prints of prisoners under Chinese torture. Entry is free and it's open daily (except Wednesday) from 10 am to 1 pm and 1.30 to 5.30 pm.

Places to Stay – bottom end

Raja Rest House (☎ 30515), down a quiet side street off Gandhiji Rd, is the best value in town. The large, basic rooms are arranged around three sides of a huge courtyard, and cost Rs 45/75 with bathroom and fan. The staff are very friendly.

Rajarajan Lodge, nearby, has basic rooms for Rs 40/80 but is on noisy Gandhiji Rd, and often full.

Tamil Nadu Lodge (☎ 31088) is behind the railway station, just off Trichy Rd. The rooms have a cell-like ambience but are otherwise OK and good value at Rs 65/100. However, it's somewhat inconvenient for the centre of town.

Hotel Yagappa (☎ 30421), just off Trichy Rd and near the station, has 11 doubles at Rs 175 (Rs 395 with air-con). There's an enormous restaurant and a very pleasant bar.

Railway Retiring Rooms at the station cost Rs 60 for a double, or Rs 120 with air-con. They're often full.

Hotel Valli (☎ 31584), MK Rd, offers clean rooms with bathroom attached from Rs 120/140, or Rs 180 for a double with TV. Air-con doubles cost Rs 320. There are also rooms with three, four and seven beds.

Places to Stay – middle & top end

TTDC Hotel Tamil Nadu (☎ 31421), Gandhiji Rd, is a good place to stay but not the bargain it once was. Rooms in this former raja's guesthouse are spacious and clean with constant hot water in the attached bathrooms. The rooms surround a quiet leafy courtyard, and the staff are helpful. Doubles cost Rs 300, and Rs 500 with air-con. A TV in the ordinary rooms is an extra Rs 50. There is an attached restaurant, and a bar with cold beers.

Hotel Parisutham (☎ 31801; fax 30318), by the canal at 55 Grand Anicut Canal Rd, is the most pleasant place to stay. It has a beautiful swimming-pool, manicured lawns, two restaurants and a bar. The rooms cost US$37/67. They're all air-con and very well appointed with a fridge and a second phone strategically placed by the toilet.

Hotel Sangam (☎ 25151; fax 24895), is a large flashy hotel that opened recently on Trichy Rd. Rooms cost US$37/52. As yet there's no pool.

Places to Eat

There are plenty of simple vegetarian restaurants with 'leaf meals' (thalis served on a banana leaf) for Rs 10 near the bus stand and on Gandhiji Rd.

Anantha Bhavan is one that is recommended.

Central Cafe on the corner of Hospital and Gandhiji Rds is good for snacks, but it closes at 4 pm.

Golden Restaurant on Hospital Rd does good vegetarian meals (Rs 10).

Sathars is a good non-vegetarian restaurant which has an extensive range of dishes and is open until midnight.

Swagath, near the roundabout on Gandhiji Rd, does non-veg food that's good value. Chicken curry is Rs 21; thalis are Rs 15.

Hotel Yagappa has a large restaurant with reasonable food. Ginger chicken is Rs 40. The bar here is a very pleasant place to drink; beers are Rs 48.

Hotel Parisutham has the best restaurants in town – the non-veg *Les Repas* serves Indian and Chinese dishes (around Rs 50), and the *Geetham* offers vegetarian food. The bar is a popular place for a late evening beer with complimentary peanuts.

Getting There & Away

Bus The TTC bus stand is fairly well organised but, as usual, there is no timetable in English. The computerised reservation office is open from 7.30 am to 9.30 pm. There are 24 buses a day for Chennai, the fastest and most expensive being the No 323FP Bye-Pass Rider (7½ hours, Rs 68). Other buses that can be booked here include Tirupathi (No 851, daily, Rs 81), Ooty (No 725, Rs 62) and Pondicherry (No 928, once daily at midnight, 177km). There are also numerous buses passing through on their way to Tiruchirappalli and Madurai.

Most state buses now use the new bus stand, 3.5km south of the centre. Some still stop at the chaotic old state bus stand (beside the TTC bus stand), such as those for Tiruchirappalli (54km, 1½ hours, Rs 9.50) and Kumbakonam (37km, one hour). There are departures for both every 15 minutes.

Train To Chennai (351km), the overnight *Rameswaram Express* takes nine hours and costs Rs 82/359 in 2nd/1st class. Alternatively, the *Cholan Express* takes eight hours and travels through the day. To Villupuram (for Pondicherry), the 192km trip takes six hours and costs Rs 48/217. To Tiruchirappalli (50km, one hour) it costs Rs 17/92. The trip to Kumbakonam takes one hour, and it's 2½ hours to Chidambaram.

AROUND THANJAVUR

Many of the smaller towns in the Thanjavur area are well known for their impressive Chola temples. The distances of each from Thanjavur are in brackets.

Thirukandiyur (10km)
The temples here, Brahma Sirakandeshwara and Harsaba Vimochana Perumal, are noted for their fine sculptural work.

Thiruvaiyaru (13km)
The famous temple here is dedicated to Siva and is known as Panchanatheshwara. Accommodation is completely booked out every January, when an eight day music festival is held in honour of the saint, Thiagaraja.

Tiruvarur (55km)
The Thyagararajaswami Temple at Tiruvarur, between Thanjavur and Nagapattinam, boasts an 807-pillared hall and the largest temple chariot in Tamil Nadu. It's dragged

through the streets during the 10 day car festival in March. There are numerous cheap places to stay around the bus stand.

TIRUCHIRAPPALLI (Trichy, Tiruchy)
Pop: 770,800   Tel Area Code: 0431
The most famous landmark of this bustling town is the Rock Fort Temple, a spectacular monument perched on a massive rocky outcrop which rises abruptly from the plain to tower over the old city. It is reached by a flight of steep steps cut into the rock and from its summit you get a fantastic view of the town plus its other main landmark, the Sri Ranganathaswamy Temple (Srirangam). Shrouded in a haze of coconut palms away to the north, Sri Ranganathaswamy is one of the largest and most interesting temple complexes in India, built on an island in the middle of the Cauvery River and covering a staggering 2.5 sq km! There is also another huge temple complex nearby – the Sri Jambukeshwara Temple.

Trichy itself has a long history going back to the centuries before the Christian era when it was a Chola citadel. During the 1st millennium AD, it changed hands between the Pallavas and Pandyas many times before being taken by the Cholas in the 10th century AD. When the Chola Empire finally decayed, Trichy passed into the hands of the Vijayanagar kings of Hampi and remained with them until their defeat, in 1565 AD, by the forces of the Deccan sultans.

The town and its fort, as it stands today, was built by the Nayaks of Madurai. It was one of the main centres around which the wars of the Carnatic were fought in the 18th century during the British-French struggle for supremacy in India.

Monuments aside, the city offers a good range of hotels and an excellent local bus system which doesn't demand the strength of an ox and the skin of an elephant to use.

Orientation
Trichy is scattered over a considerable area. Although you will need transport to get from one part to another, most of the hotels and

TAMIL NADU

restaurants, the bus stand, railway station, tourist office and GPO are within a few minutes walk of each other in what is known as the junction (or cantonment) area. The Rock Fort Temple is about 2.5km north of here, near the Cauvery River.

Information

The tourist office (☎ 460136), 1 Williams Rd, is open weekdays only. They have a free leaflet but little else. There are also branch offices at the railway station and the airport.

The GPO on Dindigul Rd is open Monday to Saturday from 8 am to 7 pm.

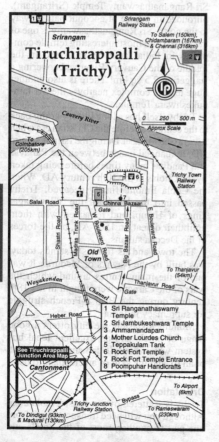

Tiruchirappalli (Trichy)

1 Sri Ranganathaswamy Temple
2 Sri Jambukeshwara Temple
3 Ammamandapam
4 Mother Lourdes Church
5 Teppakulam Tank
6 Rock Fort Temple
7 Rock Fort Temple Entrance
8 Poompuhar Handicrafts

Rock Fort Temple

The Rock Fort Temple tops an 83m high outcrop. This smooth rock was first hewn by the Pallavas who cut small cave temples into the southern face, but it was the Nayaks who made use of its naturally fortified position.

It's a stiff climb up the 437 steps cut into the stone to the top but well worth it for the views. Non-Hindus are not allowed into the Vinayaka Temple at the summit nor the bigger Sri Thayumanaswamy Temple dedicated to Siva, halfway up. Occasionally (and for a small fee) temple priests waive this regulation.

The monument is open daily from 6 am until 8 pm. Entry is Rs 0.50, plus Rs 10 if you have a camera. Leave your shoes at the entrance near the temple elephant which passes each monotonous day blessing devotees in exchange for money.

Sri Ranganathaswamy Temple (Srirangam)

This superb temple complex at Srirangam, about three km from the Rock Fort, is surrounded by seven concentric walls with 21 gopurams and is probably the largest in India. Most of it dates from the 14th to 17th centuries, and many people have had a hand in its construction, including the Cheras, Pandyas, Cholas, Hoysalas and Vijayanagars. The largest gopuram in the first wall on the southern side (the main entrance) was completed as recently as 1987, and now measures an astounding 73m.

The temple complex is very well preserved, with excellent carvings throughout and numerous shrines to various gods, though the main temple is dedicated to Vishnu. Even the Muslims are said to have prayed here after the fall of the Vijayanagar Empire. Non-Hindus are, of course, not allowed into the gold-topped sanctum, but this is no major loss since the whole place is fascinating, and non-Hindus can go as far as the sixth wall. Bazaars and Brahmins' houses fill the space between the outer four walls, and you don't have to take your shoes off or deposit your bicycle until you get to the fourth wall (Rs 0.50). If you have a camera, you'll be charged Rs 10 at this point.

Just past the shoe deposit is an information centre, where you buy the Rs 2 ticket to climb the wall for a panoramic view of the entire complex. A temple guide will unlock the gates and tell you what's what. It's worth engaging one of these guides (fee negotiable) as there is much to see and you could easily spend all day wandering around the complex. There's also a small **museum** containing sculptures. The area within the fourth wall is closed daily from 10 pm to 6 am.

An annual **Car Festival** is held here in January during which a decorated wooden chariot is pulled through the streets between the various walls. In mid-December, the **Vaikunta Ekadasi**, or Paradise Festival, takes place. At this time the temple's northern entrance is opened and, for one day, pilgrims from all over India flock through in the hope of auspicious merit.

Sri Jambukeshwara Temple

The nearby Sri Jambukeshwara Temple is

dedicated to Siva and has five concentric walls and seven gopurams. It's built around a Siva lingam partly submerged in water that comes from a spring in the sanctum sanctorum. Non-Hindus are not allowed in this part of the temple. The complex was built around the same time as the Sri Ranganathaswamy Temple. It's open daily between 6 am and 1 pm and between 4 and 9.30 pm, and there's the usual Rs 10 camera fee.

St John's Church

Trichy also has some interesting Raj-era monuments. Built in 1812, St John's Church has louvred side doors which can be opened to turn the church into an airy pavilion. Rouse the doorkeeper to let you in. The surrounding cemetery is also interesting.

Places to Stay – bottom end

Noise from the bus stand can be a significant problem in many hotels, particularly in non air-con rooms at the front.

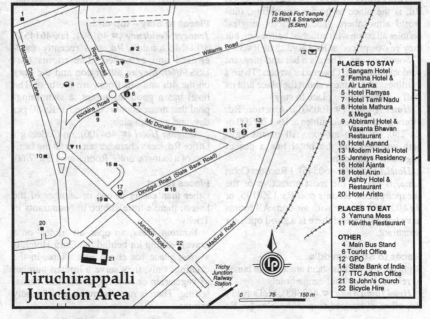

To Rock Fort Temple
(2.5km) & Srirangam
(5.5km)

PLACES TO STAY
1 Sangam Hotel
2 Femina Hotel & Air Lanka
5 Hotel Ramyas
7 Hotel Tamil Nadu
8 Hotels Mathura & Mega
9 Abbirami Hotel & Vasanta Bhavan Restaurant
10 Hotel Aanand
13 Modern Hindu Hotel
15 Jenneys Residency
16 Hotel Ajanta
18 Hotel Arun
19 Ashby Hotel & Restaurant
20 Hotel Aristo

PLACES TO EAT
3 Yamuna Mess
11 Kavitha Restaurant

OTHER
4 Main Bus Stand
6 Tourist Office
12 GPO
14 State Bank of India
17 TTC Admin Office
21 St John's Church
22 Bicycle Hire

Williams Road
Royal Road
Racquet Court Lane
Rockins Road
Mc Donald's Road
Dindigul Road (State Bank Road)
Junction Road
Madurai Road

Trichy Junction Railway Station

Tiruchirappalli Junction Area

0   75   150 m

TAMIL NADU

Modern Hindu Hotel (☎ 460758), 6B McDonald's Rd, is a cheapie that is not too noisy, if not absolutely spotless. Singles/doubles with common bath are Rs 60/100, doubles/triples with bath attached are Rs 150/250. Note that 'brothal and bad character women are not allowed'.

Railway Retiring Rooms at the railway station have dorm beds for Rs 30 and double rooms without/with air-con for Rs 100/150.

Hotel Aristo (☎ 461818), at 2 Dindigul Rd, is a friendly place that's an excellent choice. It has a laid-back atmosphere and a quiet leafy garden. Singles/doubles cost Rs 100/150, quads are Rs 250 and there are also air-con double cottages at Rs 350. All the rooms have attached bathrooms and most rooms join a large shaded terrace.

Hotel Arun (☎ 461421), at 24 Dindigul Rd, is another good place that's set back from the road, though it lacks the character of the Aristo. Singles/doubles are Rs 130/175 with bath attached. Air-con rooms are Rs 250/350. A thali in the restaurant costs Rs 11.

Ashby Hotel (☎ 460652), at 17A Junction Rd, is the place to go for crumbling, old-world atmosphere. The spacious singles/doubles all come with attached bathroom, but they're overpriced at Rs 150/225 or Rs 350/475 with air-con. There's a bar and pleasant outdoor restaurant. One reader wrote: 'There's a stillness and sadness about the place and its staff – a memorable place to stay'.

Hotel Ajanta (☎ 460501), Junction Rd, offers good singles/doubles at Rs 120/200 or Rs 280/380 with air-con. All rooms have bath attached and the hotel has a decent vegetarian restaurant.

Hotel Aanand (☎ 460545), 1 Racquet Court Lane, is one of the most attractive of the cheaper places. Rooms cost Rs 150/195, or Rs 400 for a double with air-con. All rooms have bathrooms and there is a good open-air restaurant.

Places to Stay – middle
Right outside the bus stand are a whole bunch of relatively new mid-range hotels.

Hotel Tamil Nadu (☎ 460383), McDonald's Rd, offers overpriced singles/doubles for Rs 175/300. The air-con rooms are better value at Rs 300/400.

Hotel Ramyas (☎ 461128), 13 Williams Rd, is excellent value with spotless rooms (some with a balcony) for Rs 225/275, or Rs 450/550 with air-con and Star TV. Room service is good and credit cards are accepted. The basement bar is open until 11 pm.

Hotel Mega (☎ 463092), 8 Rockins Rd, has good doubles for Rs 170, or Rs 325/375 for a single/double air-con.

The *Hotel Mathura*, next door, is similarly priced.

Abbirami Hotel (☎ 460001), 10 McDonald's Rd and almost opposite the Hotel Tamil Nadu, is a characterless place that has good-value air-con rooms for Rs 340/390 and cheaper ordinary rooms.

Femina Hotel (☎ 461551; fax 460615), 14C Williams Rd, is a huge place offering rooms at Rs 225/350, or Rs 425/600 with air-con. There are also more expensive deluxe rooms and suites. The facilities include a restaurant offering south and north Indian, Continental and Chinese cuisine, but no bar.

Places to Stay – top end
Jenneys Residency (☎ 461301; fax 461451), 3/14 McDonald's Rd, was recently modernised and extended. The rooms cost US$34/60; they're all air-con and the ones on the 4th and 5th floors are the best. The hotel has a good restaurant, a swimming-pool that nonresidents can use for Rs 50 per day, and a health club.

Sangam Hotel (☎ 464700), on Collector's Office Rd, lacks character but has all the facilities of a four-star hotel. Rooms are US$37/60.

Places to Eat
Other than eating at one or another of the hotels, there's little choice in restaurants in Trichy.

Yamuna Mess, an open-air 'diner' on a gravel parking lot behind the Guru Hotel, is a great place for cheap eats. Here, in the evenings only, they serve a limited number of vegetarian or non-veg dishes in a casual setting. There's mellow music and friendly service.

Sangeetha Restaurant, at the Hotel Aanand, is also a good place for dinner. In the open-air restaurant most dishes (eg chilli gobi fry) are Rs 13.

Vasanta Bhavan is a very busy vegetarian restaurant at the Abbirami Hotel. Meals are Rs 15.

Kavitha Restaurant does excellent, elaborate veg thalis (lunchtime only) for Rs 15, and has an air-con room.

The Peaks of Kunlun, at Jenneys Residency, is one of the best restaurants in town. Honey soy chicken (Rs 110) is delicious; chicken Manchurian (Rs 55) will blow the roof off your mouth. There are also well presented western and Indian dishes. Beer costs Rs 60.

Getting There & Away
Air The Indian Airlines office (☎ 462233) is at 4A Dindigul Rd. They have flights twice a week to Chennai (US$60).

Air Lanka has a flight to Colombo on Tuesday and Sunday for Rs 1525. The airline's office (☎ 460844) is at the Femina Hotel.

Bus The state, TTC and RGTC buses use the main bus stand, although a few buses still leave from the TTC admin office on Junction Rd.

Services to most places are frequent and tickets are sold by the conductor as soon as the bus arrives. Services include Thanjavur (every 15 minutes, 54km, 1½ hours, Rs 8) and Madurai (every half hour, 128km, four hours, Rs 21).

The TTC/RGTC buses can be computer-booked in advance at their offices. For Chennai the fastest bus is the Bye-Pass Rider (7½ hours, Rs 67). Other destinations include: Bangalore (three daily, Rs 76), Coimbatore (twice daily, Rs 32), and Tirupathi via Vellore (two daily, 9½ hours, Rs 60).

Private companies like Jenny Travels, opposite the Hotel Tamil Nadu, or KPN Travels, below the Hotel Mathura, also have superdeluxe day/night services to Chennai for Rs 95/105 and Bangalore for Rs 110/125.

Train Trichy is on the main Chennai to Madurai and Chennai to Rameswaram lines. Some trains run directly to/from Chennai while others go via Chidambaram and Thanjavur. The quickest trains to Chennai (337km, 5¼ hours) are the *Vaigai Express* and the *Pallavan Express* which cost Rs 76/343 in 2nd/1st class. The fastest service to Madurai (155km) is on the *Vaigai Express* which leaves at 11.56 am and 5.45 pm, takes 2¼ hours and costs Rs 41/184 in 2nd/1st class. The trip to Rameswaram (265km, seven hours) costs Rs 62/283 in 2nd/1st class.

For Mamallapuram, take a Chennai train as far as Chengalpattu and a bus on from there. For Mysore, take the 6 am train (No 587) to Erode Junction (four hours, Rs 25), an auto-rickshaw from Erode railway station to the bus station (Rs 25) and the 1.30 pm bus to Mysore (five hours, Rs 35).

Getting Around
The Airport Into town it's Rs 130 for a taxi, Rs 40 for an auto-rickshaw.

Bus Trichy's local bus service is excellent. Take a No 7, 59, 58 or 63 bus to the airport (seven km, 30 minutes). The No 1 (A or B) bus from the state bus stand plies frequently between the railway station, GPO, the Rock Fort Temple, the main entrance to Sri Ranganathaswamy Temple and close to Sri Jambukeshwara Temple.

Bicycle The town lends itself well to cycling as it's dead flat. There are a couple of places on Junction Rd where you can hire bicycles for Rs 1.50 per hour. Note that the incredibly busy Big Bazaar Rd is a one-way road (heading north).

Southern Tamil Nadu

MADURAI
Pop: 1.23 million   Tel Area Code: 0452
Madurai is an animated city packed with pilgrims, beggars, businesspeople, bullock

carts and legions of underemployed rick-shaw-wallahs. It is one of southern India's oldest cities, and has been a centre of learning and pilgrimage for centuries.

Madurai's main attraction is the famous **Sri Meenakshi Temple** (see the regional highlight on p1059) in the heart of the old town, a riotously baroque example of Dravidian architecture with gopurams covered from top to bottom in a breathless profusion of multicoloured images of gods, goddesses, animals and mythical figures. The temple seethes with activity from dawn till dusk, its many shrines attracting pilgrims from every part of India and tourists from all over the world. It's been estimated that there are 10,000 visitors here on any one day!

Madurai resembles a huge, continuous bazaar crammed with shops, street markets, temples, pilgrims' choultries, hotels, restaurants and small industries. Although one of the liveliest cities in the south, it's small enough not to be overwhelming and is very popular with travellers.

History
Madurai's history can be divided into roughly four periods, beginning over 2000 years ago when it was the capital of the Pandyan kings. Then, in the 4th century BC, the city was known to the Greeks via Megasthenes, their ambassador to the court of Chandragupta Maurya. In the 10th century AD, Madurai was taken by the Chola emperors. It remained in their hands until the Pandyas briefly regained their independence in the 12th century, only to lose it again in the 14th century to Muslim invaders under Malik Kafur, a general in the service of the Delhi Sultanate. Here, Malik Kafur established his own dynasty which, in turn, was overthrown by the Hindu Vijayanagar kings of Hampi. After the fall of Vijayanagar in 1565, the Nayaks ruled Madurai until 1781 AD. During the reign of Tirumalai Nayak (1623-55), the bulk of the Meenakshi Temple was built, and Madurai became the cultural centre of the Tamil people, playing an important role in the development of the Tamil language.

Madurai then passed into the hands of the British East India Company, which took over the revenues of the area after the wars of the Carnatic in 1781. In 1840, the company razed the fort, which had surrounded the city, and filled in the moat. Four broad streets – the Veli streets – were built on this fill and define the limits of the old city to this day.

Orientation
The old town on the south bank of the Vaigai River has most of the main points of interest, some of the transport services, mid-range and budget hotels, restaurants, the tourist office and the GPO.

On the north bank of the river in the cantonment area are top-end hotels, the Gandhi Museum and one bus stand. The Mariamman Teppakkulam Tank and temple stand on the south bank of the Vaigai, several km east of the old city.

Information
Tourist Offices The tourist office (☎ 34757), 180 West Veli St, is open weekdays from 10 am to 5.45 pm. The staff are helpful and hand out free maps. There are also counters at Madurai railway station and the airport.

Post & Telecommunications The post office is at the northern end of West Veli St and is open from 7 am to 7.30 pm (Sunday from 10 am to 5 pm). The poste restante counter (No 8) is open daily from 10 am to 5 pm. You can make phone calls and send faxes in the same building.

The central telegraph office and another post office are across the river in the Cantonment area – look for the telecommunications mast.

Tirumalai Nayak Palace
About 1.5km from the Meenakshi Temple, this Indo-Saracenic palace was built in 1636 by the ruler whose name it bears. Much of it has fallen into ruin, and the pleasure gardens and surrounding defensive wall have disappeared. Today, only the entrance gate, main hall and dance hall remain. The palace was partially restored by Lord Napier, the governor of Madras, in 1866-72, and further

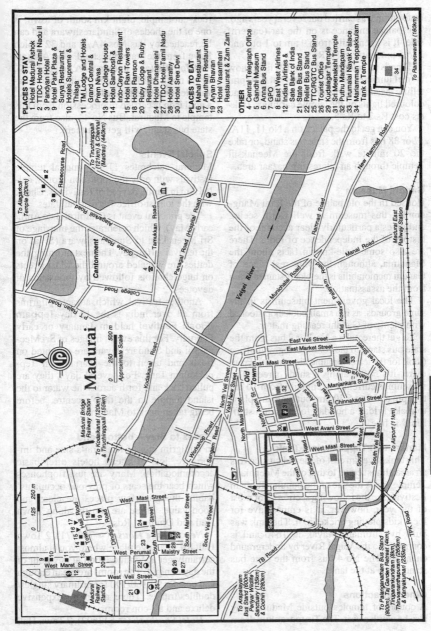

PLACES TO STAY
1 Hotel Madurai Ashok
2 TTDC Hotel Tamil Nadu II
9 Pandyan Hotel
9 Hotel Park Plaza & Surya Restaurant
10 Hotels Supreme & Thilaga
11 TM Lodge and Hotels Grand Central & Prem Nivas
13 New College House
14 Hotel Santhosh & Indo-Ceylon Restaurant
15 Hotel Ravi Towers
18 Hotel Ramson
20 Ruby Lodge & Ruby Restaurant
24 Hotel Dhanamani
27 TTDC Hotel Tamil Nadu
28 Hotel Aarathy
30 Hotel Sree Devi

PLACES TO EAT
16 Mahal Restaurant
17 Amutham Restaurant
19 Aryan Bhavan
23 Hotel Vasanthani Restaurant & Zam Zam

OTHER
4 Central Telegraph Office
5 Gandhi Museum
6 Anna Bus Stand
7 GPO
8 East West Airlines
12 Indian Airlines & Sate Bank of India
21 State Bus Stand
22 Relief Bus Stand
25 TTC/RGTC Bus Stand
26 Tourist Office
29 Kudalagar Temple
31 Sri Meenakshi Temple
32 Puthu Mandapam
33 Tirumalai Nayak Palace
34 Mariamman Teppakkulam Tank & Temple

Madurai

To Alagarkoil Temple (20km)
To Kodaikanal (120km) & Truchirappalli (155km)
To Truchirappalli (127km) & Chennai (Madras) (440km)
To Rameswaram (160km)

Racecourse Road
Alagarkoil Road
Gokale Road
College Road
Tamukkan Road
Panagal Road (Hospital Road)
Kodaikanal Road
Kadaikanal Road
Cantonment
Vaigai River

Madurai Bridge Railway Station

0   250   500 m
Approximate Scale

New Ramad Road
Ramnad Road
Manal Road
Munichalai Road
Old Kosavu Palayam Road
Madurai East Railway Station

East Veli Street
East Market Street
East Masi Street
Mahliya dampokki St.
Manjankara St.
Chinnakadai St.
North Avani St. Town
North Veli Street
Vakil New Street
North Masi Street
West Avani Street
West Masi Street
Town Hall Road
Dindigul Road
Workshop Road
Sangam Road
South Avani Street
South Masi Street
South Market Street
South Veli Street

See Inset

To Airport (11km)
To TPK Road
TB Road

TAMIL NADU

Inset:
250 m
125   250 m

West Masi Street
West Masi Street
West Maret Street
West Perumal Street
West Veli Street
Town Hall Road
Dindigul Road
South Masi Street
South Market Street
Maistry Street

Madurai Railway Station

To Arapalayam Bus Stand (600m), Vaidiyanathan Sanctuary (135km) & Cochin (280km)
To Palanganatham Bus Stand (800m), Taj (Garden Retreat) (4km), Thiruvananthapuram (250km), & Kanyakumari (235km)

restoration was carried out several years ago. The palace entrance is on the far (eastern) side. It is open daily from 9 am to 1 pm and 2 to 5 pm; entry costs Rs 1.

There's an entertaining sound & light show (son et lumière) in English, daily at 6.30 pm, telling Madurai's history using sound and coloured lights on the temple carvings. Tickets cost Rs 2 to Rs 5.

You can get to the palace on a No 11, 11A, 17 or 38 bus from the state bus stand, or take the 20 minute walk from the Meenakshi Temple through an interesting bazaar area.

Gandhi Museum

Housed in the old palace of the Rani Mangammal, this museum is well worth seeing and gives a particularly clear account of the history of the independence of India. There are also some little-known facts about the Mahatma, although the only real piece of Gandhi memorabilia is the blood-stained *dhoti* from the assassination.

The local government museum is in the same grounds, as is a small bookshop stocked with plenty of Gandhi reading matter.

To get there, take a No 1 or 2 bus from the state bus stand to the central telegraph office (look for the telecommunications mast). From there, it's 500m along a shady street. The museum is currently open daily from 10 am to 1 pm and 2 to 5.30 pm, but there are plans to make Friday a holiday for museum staff. Entry is free.

Mariamman Teppakkulam Tank

This tank, five km east of the old city, covers an area almost equal to that of the Meenakshi Temple and is the site of the popular Teppam Festival (see the following section). For most of the year, however, it is empty save for local kids playing cricket in it. The tank was built by Tirumalai Nayak in 1646 and is connected to the Vaigai River by underground channels. The No 4 bus from the state bus stand stops at the tank.

Other Attractions

A couple of temples outside Madurai may also be worth a visit. The **Tiruparankundram**

rock-cut temple, eight km south of town, is one of the abodes of Sundareshwara and can be reached by bus Nos 4A, 5 and 32 which leave from the state bus stand. The **Alagarkoil Temple** (also known as Azhagar Koil), 21km north of Madurai, is a hilltop Vaishnavaite temple. During the festival of Chithirai, a gold icon is carried in procession from this temple to Madurai. Bus No 44, also from the state bus stand, will get you there.

Special Events

Madurai celebrates 11 big annual temple festivals with only the monsoon month, called Ani in Tamil, devoid of festivities. Check with the tourist office for festival dates.

The principal event is **Chithirai** (late April/early May), which celebrates the marriage of Sri Meenakshi to Sundareshwara (Siva) on the festival's 10th day. The next morning, the deities are wheeled around the Masi streets on huge chariots followed by thousands of devotees.

Another festival which attracts pilgrims from all over India is the 12 day **Teppam (Float) Festival** held in January or early February. For this event, images of Sri Meenakshi and Sundareshwara are mounted on floats and taken to the Mariamman Teppakkulam Tank. For several days, they are pulled back and forth across the water to the island temple in the tank's centre, before being taken back to Madurai.

Places to Stay – bottom end

In a pilgrim city of Madurai's size and importance, lots of cheap hotels offer basic accommodation. Many are just flophouses which bear the scars of previous occupants' habits, though a few places are clean and good value. These are mostly along Town Hall and Dindigul Rds.

New College House (☎ 742971), 2 Town Hall Rd, is a huge place where you'll almost certainly get accommodation at any hour of the day or night. The rooms are clean enough and cost Rs 90/160/190 for ordinary singles/doubles/triples. There are more expensive deluxe and air-con rooms.

Hotel Santhosh (☎ 543692), 7 Town Hall

Rd, has basic rooms with attached bathrooms for Rs 50/80.

Hotel Ravi Towers (☎ 741961), 9 Town Hall Rd, is a good choice, with spotless rooms for Rs 125/165 with attached bath. A TV costs Rs 30 extra. There are also good air-con rooms for Rs 195/300.

Hotel Ramson (☎ 740407), 9 Permal Tank St, looks expensive but isn't at Rs 50/70 for rooms with attached bathroom. It's often full, though.

Hotel Sree Devi (☎ 747431) is at 20 West Avani St. The view of the temple from the roof is the best you'll get in the whole city (of course, this is not news to the owners who are charging an exorbitant Rs 650 for the air-con rooftop double room). The rooms (no singles) are OK and start at Rs 150 for a double with bathroom, or from Rs 350 with air-con.

Ruby Lodge (☎ 742253), 92 West Perumal Maistry St, has rooms with attached bathrooms (bucket showers only) for Rs 70/90. The hotel has its own pleasant outdoor restaurant and bar.

Hotel Grand Central (☎ 743940), 47 West Perumal Maistry St, is one of several hotels in this area that look more expensive than they are. It has good sized rooms for Rs 125/175, air-con doubles for Rs 350.

Hotel Dhanamani (☎ 742701), 20 Sunnambukara St, has singles with common bath for Rs 85, singles/doubles with attached bath for Rs 95/150, and good-value air-con doubles with Star TV for Rs 250.

Railway Retiring Rooms are noisy and cost Rs 50/95; dorm beds are just Rs 15.

Places to Stay – middle

Hotel Aarathy (☎ 31571), 9 Perumal Koil West Mada St, just a few minutes walk from the bus stands, is a good place to stay although it lacks atmosphere. It's very popular with foreigners – you may need to book ahead. All rooms have bathrooms and cost Rs 175/250, or Rs 250/350 for air-con. Towels, soap and toilet paper are provided, the rooms are comfortable and secure, and most have a small balcony with a great view over the neighbouring temple. Rouse yourself out of

bed for sunrise – it's superb! There's a pleasant open-air veg restaurant in the courtyard which is frequented daily (6 am and 4 pm) by Mahalakshmi, the temple elephant from next door.

TTDC Hotel Tamil Nadu (☎ 37471), West Veli St, is not bad for a government-run place. The rooms are clean and cost from Rs 125/195 with attached bath, Rs 260/360 with air-con and TV. There's a restaurant and bar.

TTDC Hotel Tamil Nadu II (☎ 537461), across the river on Alagarkoil Rd, is nothing special. Ordinary doubles cost Rs 250, or Rs 350 with air-con (plus Rs 75 for a TV). There's also a restaurant and bar, where it's Rs 60 for a beer.

Hotel Prem Nivas (☎ 742532), 102 West Perumal Maistry St, is popular with businesspeople and has rooms for Rs 140/240 and air-con doubles at Rs 340. Facilities are excellent and the hotel has its own air-con vegetarian restaurant.

TM Lodge (☎ 741651), 50 West Perumal Maistry St, is a reasonable place. Rooms with attached bathrooms are Rs 150/230 and air-con rooms with TV are Rs 335/360. The upper rooms are lighter and airier.

Hotel Supreme (☎ 742637), 110 West Perumal Maistry St, has doubles (no singles) at Rs 310, or Rs 530 with air-con, plus more expensive suites. Although the rooms are dark, the facilities are good and there's an excellent rooftop veg restaurant.

Hotel Thilaga (☎ 740762), 111 West Perumal Maistry St, is clean and good value. Rooms with attached bath, constant hot water, and TV cost Rs 150/175. Air-con doubles are Rs 300.

Hotel Park Plaza (☎ 742112), 114 West Perumal Maistry St, is similar to the Supreme but a little smarter. It has comfortable rooms from Rs 625/800 with air-con, and a rooftop restaurant.

Places to Stay – top end

Madurai's three top hotels are well out of the town centre.

Hotel Madurai Ashok (☎ 537531; fax 537530), Alargakoil Rd, is somewhat overpriced at Rs 1195/1800 for plain rooms but it does have a nice swimming-pool (Rs 75 for nonresidents). An auto-rickshaw out here should cost no more than Rs 25, although the price generally doubles when they hear where you want to go! A taxi charges Rs 65. City buses No 2, 16 or 20 are on this route.

Pandyan Hotel (☎ 537090), also on Alagarkoil Rd, is a little cheaper than the Ashok, at Rs 1175/1500. It's also fully air-con and with restaurant and bar. There's a pleasant garden but no pool.

Taj Garden Retreat (☎ 601020), four km south of town at Pasumalai Hill, ranks as Madurai's best hotel. Rooms come in three varieties: standard at US$90/105 a single/double; old-world (part of the original colonial villa) for US$100/115; and deluxe (new cottages with private terraces and excellent views) at US$125/140. Facilities include a multi-cuisine restaurant, swimming pool (for guests only), a tennis court, manicured gardens and a bar. Bus No 5D from the relief bus stand in Madurai stops at the main gate. From here it's still 1.5km up to the hotel (if you're walking, take the shortcut path leading off to the left about a third of the way up the road). An auto-rickshaw from town costs Rs 60, or Rs 20 from the main gate.

Places to Eat

There are many typical south Indian vegetarian restaurants around the Meenakshi Temple and along Town Hall Rd, Dindigul Rd and West Masi St. On Town Hall Rd, there are several places where you can get decent non-vegetarian food – try the *Indo-Ceylon Restaurant* at No 6, the *Mahal* which is popular with backpackers, or the *Amutham Restaurant*, near the corner of West Masi St.

New College House has a popular vegetarian dining hall and the thalis are good value.

Aryan Bhavan on the corner of West Masi St and Dindigul Rd, does astoundingly large dosa.

Ruby Restaurant, next to the Ruby Lodge on West Perumal Maistry St, is the only garden restaurant in Madurai. Delicious non-veg food is served and the menu makes good reading. You could choose a mutton bullet

(Rs 50), a mutton lever (Rs 20) or a chicken lollipop (Rs 45) but the tandoori items are best. You can also get a beer for Rs 40 – it's a popular place for a drink, and stays open until after midnight.

Hotel Vasanthani on West Perumal Maistry St is good for cheap thalis and tiffin and the upstairs section is great for watching the busy street scene.

Zam Zam, nearby, is a popular shop for sweet or savoury snacks.

Surya Restaurant, on the roof of the Hotel Supreme, has a superb view and catches any breeze. It serves Indian, Chinese and Continental vegetarian food in the evening only (5 pm to midnight) – the tandoori dishes are very good. Most items are around Rs 40. It's also open for breakfast from 6 to 11 am, and they do upmarket thalis for Rs 40 at lunchtime.

Temple View Roof Top Restaurant, in the Hotel Park Plaza, serves non-veg dishes with the same view as the Surya, a few doors down. Chicken garlic fry is Rs 40, and there are good-value vegetarian dishes, too.

Taj Garden Retreat is the place to go for a splurge. There are excellent à la carte meals in the multi-cuisine restaurant. On Saturday and Sunday evenings there's a buffet for Rs 200.

Things to Buy

Madurai has long been a textile centre and the streets around the temple still teem with cloth stalls and tailors' shops. A great place to buy locally manufactured cottons as well as the batiks loved by many travellers is Puthu Mandapam, an old, stone-pillared hall just along from the eastern entrance to Sri Meenakshi Temple. Here you'll find lines of textile stalls opposite rows of tailors, each busily treadling away and capable of whipping up a good replica of whatever you're wearing in an hour or two.

If you're buying cloth to get garments made up, it's wise to know how much material you'll need as some merchants will talk you into buying way too much only to strike a deal with the tailor who makes your clothes to keep the leftovers. The owner of the Krishnamoorthy Cloth Store (stall No 108)

is reliable and gives fair prices for material. In addition, he refuses to pay the commissions demanded by the many street touts who'll offer to take you to their 'brother's shop' at Puthu Mandapam.

Getting There & Away

Air The Indian Airlines office (☎ 37234) is on West Veli St. There are five flights weekly to Chennai (US$70) and Calicut (US$50), and three per week to Mumbai (US$150). NEPC Airlines (☎ 741644) has an office in the Supreme Hotel. It flies at least once daily to Chennai.

Bus Madurai has five bus stands and three of them are several km from the town centre. You'll need to use either a city bus or a rickshaw to get to these terminals.

The state bus stand is centrally located on West Veli St. It is the principal local bus stand, however, there is also the 'relief' bus stand for some of these services which is situated across the street.

The TTC/RGTC bus stand is also on West Veli St and is for long-distance/interstate buses. Seats on buses originating in Madurai (for details see the Bus Services from Madurai table) can be reserved in advance at the booking office (open daily from 7 am to 10 pm) and there's a timetable in English. Plenty of other TTC/RGTC buses stop in Madurai on their way through and though these can't be reserved in advance, it's not usually a problem to get a seat. TTC does not run buses

to Kodaikanal – for that you must go to the Arapalayam bus stand.

The Anna bus stand, across the river to the north, services destinations to the north-east such as Thanjavur and Trichy, as well as Rameswaram. If your bus terminates here, bus No 3 will take you to the state bus stand in town, or you can catch a cycle-rickshaw for Rs 10.

The dusty Arapalayam bus stand (take bus No 7A or JJ from the relief bus stand) is for points north-west including Coimbatore, Kodaikanal or Bangalore. There are about eight departures daily to Kodaikanal and the four-hour trip costs Rs 18. During heavy monsoon rain, the road to Kodaikanal sometimes gets washed away and the buses go via Palani, adding an hour or two to the journey.

The Palanganatham bus stand to the southwest of town is for buses heading south to destinations such as Kanyakumari and southern Kerala. Bus Nos 7, 7J and JJ7 from the relief bus stand in town will get you there.

There are several private bus companies which offer superdeluxe video buses to such places as Chennai and Bangalore. Tickets for these are sold by agencies near the state bus stand. However, beware of buying a ticket for any destination other than the above major cities. All of them will sell you a ticket to virtually anywhere (such as Kodaikanal or Rameswaram) but you'll find yourself dumped on a state bus and they'll have sold you a ticket for it at double the price you could have paid yourself.

TTC/RGTC Bus Services from Madurai					
Destination	*Route Number*	*Frequency (d-daily)*	*Distance (km)*	*Duration (hours)*	*Fare (Rs)*
Bangalore	846	14d	550	15	98
Chennai	137, 491	50d	447	10	89
Coimbatore	660	2d	227	6	29
Ernakulam	826	2d	324	10	87
Kanyakumari	566	3d	253	6	47
Pondicherry	847	2d	329	8	51
Thiruvananthapuram	865	2d	305	7	58
Tirupathi		4d	595	16	104

Train Services from Madurai

Destination	Train Number & Name	Departure	Distance (km)	Duration (hours)	Fare (Rs) (2nd/1st)
Coimbatore	6116 *Coimbatore Exp*	10.05 pm	229	6.15	74/249
Chennai	6718 *Pandian Exp*	7.35 pm	556	11.10	143/441
	2636 *Vaigai Exp*	6.45 am		7.35	117/285
Rameswaram	6115 *Rameswaram Exp*	6.00 am	164	5.10	24/175

Train The railway station is on West Veli St, a few minutes walk from the main hotel area.

If you're heading to Kollam (Quilon) in Kerala, you can take the No 721 passenger train from Madurai at 6.50 am to Virudunagar (one hour). The 6105 *Chennai-Quilon Mail* passes through Virudunagar at 9 am, reaching Kollam (225km) at 4.10 pm. The line crosses the Western Ghats through some spectacular mountain terrain, and there are some superb gopurams to be seen at Srivili-putur (between Sivakasi and Rajapalaiyam) and Sankarayinarkovil.

Getting Around

The Airport The airport is 11km south of town and a taxi charges an extortionate Rs 150 to the centre. If you can find an auto-rickshaw they'll try for around Rs 80. Alternatively, bus No 10A from the state bus stand goes to the airport but don't rely on it being on schedule.

Bus Some useful local buses include No 3 to the Anna bus stand, Nos 1 and 2 to near the Gandhi Museum, and Nos 4 and 4A to Mariamman Teppakkulam Tank. All these buses depart from the state bus stand.

Auto-Rickshaw Drivers are extremely re-luctant to use the meters and will quote whatever they think you will pay. If you can't agree, they usually won't budge.

RAMESWARAM

Pop: 35,750   Tel Area Code: 04573

Known as the Varanasi of the south, Rames-waram is a major pilgrimage centre for both Shaivites and Vaishnavaites as it was here

that Rama (an incarnation of Vishnu in the Indian epic the *Ramayana*) offered thanks to Siva. At the town's core is the Ramana-thaswamy Temple, one of the most important temples in southern India.

Rameswaram is on an island in the Gulf of Mannar, connected to the mainland at Mandapam by rail, and by one of India's engineering wonders, the Indira Gandhi Bridge. The bridge took 14 years to build and was opened by Rajiv Gandhi late in 1988.

The town lies on the island's eastern side and used to be the port from which the ferry to Talaimannar (Sri Lanka) departed before passenger services were suspended more than a decade ago. As a result, there are now very few foreign visitors.

Orientation & Information

Most of the hotels and restaurants in this small and dusty town are clustered around the Ramanathaswamy Temple. The bus stand, two km to the west, is connected by frequent shuttle buses to the town centre.

The tourist office (☎ 21371), on East Car St, has a leaflet and can give information on boat trips; there's also a tourist counter at the railway station. On the east side of the temple there's a temple information centre.

Ramanathaswamy Temple

A fine example of late Dravidian architecture, this temple is most renowned for its magnificent corridors lined with massive sculptured pillars, noted for their elaborate design, style and rich carving. Legend has it that Rama sanctified this place by worshipping Siva here after the battle of Sri Lanka. Construction of the temple began in the 12th century AD and additions were made over the centuries by various rulers, so that today its gopuram is 53m high. Only Hindus may enter the inner sanctum. The temple is open from 5 am to noon and 3 to 9 pm.

Just in case you had any ideas about sleeping in, excessively loud, distorted music is blasted from the temple during festivals, from about 4.30 am.

Kothandaraswamy Temple & Dhanushkodi

Twelve km from town, this temple was the only structure to survive the 1964 cyclone which washed the rest of the village away. Legend states that Vibishana, brother of Sita's kidnapper Ravana, surrendered to Rama at this spot.

Buses from the local bus stand opposite the tourist office on East Car St will take you down there. They continue two km beyond the temple and then it's a four km walk to Dhanushkodi. There's little here now but a few ruined houses (which make good sun shelters) and a lovely bathing pool. The walk right to the tip of the peninsula can be very hot but is well worth it.

Adam's Bridge

Adam's Bridge is the name given to the chain of reefs, sandbanks and islets that almost connects Sri Lanka with India. According to legend, this is the series of stepping stones used by Hanuman to follow Ravana, in his bid to rescue Sita.

Other Attractions

The **Gandamadana Parvatham**, on a hill three km north-west of town, is a shrine containing Rama's footprints. Devotees generally visit here at sunrise and sunset (it's closed from 11.30 am to 3.30 pm).

For a **beach**, Dhanushkodi is best. Closer to town, try the one in front of the Hotel Tamil Nadu. Most of the time you'll have it to yourself as the pilgrims prefer to do their

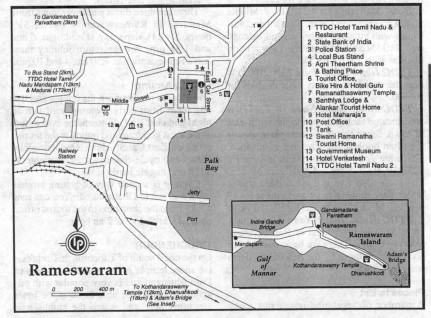

1 TTDC Hotel Tamil Nadu & Restaurant
2 State Bank of India
3 Police Station
4 Local Bus Stand
5 Agni Theertham Shrine & Bathing Place
6 Tourist Office, Bike Hire & Hotel Guru
7 Ramanathaswamy Temple
8 Santhya Lodge & Alankar Tourist Home
9 Hotel Maharaja's
10 Post Office
11 Tank
12 Swami Ramanatha Tourist Home
13 Government Museum
14 Hotel Venkatesh
15 TTDC Hotel Tamil Nadu 2

Rameswaram

TAMIL NADU

auspicious wading at **Agni Theertham**, the seashore closest to the temple.

Places to Stay

Hotels are all fairly basic, mainly geared towards pilgrims. Accommodation is tight during festivals.

Santhiya Lodge (☎ 21329), on West Car St, has rather grubby doubles from Rs 60 to Rs 90 (with bath attached). Triples are Rs 125.

Alankar Tourist Home (☎ 21216), West Car St, has basic doubles with attached bath for Rs 75.

Swami Ramanatha Tourist Home (☎ 21217), near the museum, has clean doubles with attached shower for Rs 110.

Railway Retiring Rooms are available at the railway station. They're not bad and, being away from the temple, reasonably peaceful. Doubles/triples with attached bath are Rs 95/120; dorm beds are Rs 15.

Hotel Venkatesh (☎ 21296), South Car St, has doubles/triples with attached bathroom for Rs 110/170 and four-bed rooms for Rs 200. Air-con doubles are Rs 250.

Hotel Maharaja's (☎ 21271), 7 Middle St, is a good choice. Clean, pleasant doubles/triples with attached bathroom and balcony cost Rs 155/200 and there are a few air-con doubles with TV for Rs 350.

TTDC Hotel Tamil Nadu 2 (☎ 21071) is near the station and offers basic doubles for Rs 100.

TTDC Hotel Tamil Nadu (☎ 21277) is well-located facing the sea to the north-east of town. Since this is the best place to stay it's often booked out – reserve in advance. There are good double/triple rooms for Rs 225/250, Rs 375 for a double with air-con. There are also five and six bedded rooms which they sometimes let as dorms at Rs 45 per bed. Most of the rooms have a sea view.

TTDC Hotel Tamil Nadu Mandapam (☎ 41512) is 12km west of Ramaswaram, over the bridge. There are basic doubles for Rs 150 in cottages by the beach, and dorm beds for Rs 45.

Places to Eat

A number of vegetarian restaurants along West Car St serve typical south Indian thalis, all of a pretty dismal standard.

Hotel Guru on East Car St next to the tourist office is the best place for a thali.

TTDC Hotel Tamil Nadu has the only real 'restaurant' in town, serving quite reasonable veg and non-veg food. There's also an excellent bar with pleasant sea views.

Getting There & Away

Bus TTC buses run four times daily to Madurai (four hours, Rs 28) and Kanyakumari, and three times daily to Chennai (13 hours, Rs 89) and Trichy (273km). Local buses run to Madurai more often and take longer but are marginally cheaper. There are also buses to Pondicherry and Thanjavur via Madurai.

Train There are two express trains to/from Chennai daily – the *Sethu Express* and the *Rameswaram Express*. The 666km trip takes 15 hours and costs Rs 167/583 in 2nd/1st class. Neither of these trains go through Madurai – they take the direct route through Manamadurai and Trichy.

There are three direct passenger trains from Madurai to Rameswaram (164km, 5½ hours, Rs 24), departing at midnight, 6 am and 1.55 pm. For the return journey they leave Rameswaram at 7.30 am, 4 and 10 pm.

Getting Around

Town buses ply between the temple and the bus stand from early morning until late at night and cost Rs 1. In town, the buses stop at the west gopuram and opposite the tourist office on East Car St. Unmetered auto-rickshaws and cycle-rickshaws are available at all hours; haggle hard!

Cycling is a good way of getting around town and out to Dhanushkodi. You can rent a bike from the shop next to the tourist office on East Car St for Rs 2 an hour.

TIRUCHENDUR

On the coast south of Tuticorin, this impressive shore temple is one of the six abodes of Lord Murugan and is very popular with pilgrims. You may be able to enter the inner sanctums here and watch the enthusiastic proceedings. Be careful if they offer you a gulp of the holy water – pouring it over your hands and rubbing them together joyously is an acceptable substitute for drinking it!

KANYAKUMARI (Cape Comorin)

Pop: 18,900   Tel Area Code: 04652

Kanyakumari is the 'Land's End' of India. Here, the Bay of Bengal meets the Indian Ocean and the Arabian Sea and, at Chaitrapurnima (the Tamil name for the full moon day that generally falls in April), it is possible to enjoy the unique experience of seeing the sun set and the moon rise over the ocean simultaneously. It's a popular day-trip for people staying at Kovalam Beach in Kerala.

Kanyakumari is also a popular pilgrimage destination and of great spiritual significance to Hindus. It is dedicated to the goddess Devi Kanya, the Youthful Virgin, who is an incarnation of Devi, Siva's wife. The pilgrims who come here from all over the country represent a good cross section of India.

Otherwise, Kanyakumari is highly overrated, with its trinket stalls, a lousy beach and one of those places with megaphones at the end of each street which, during festival times, rip your eardrums apart between 4 am and 10 pm.

Orientation & Information

The railway station is almost a km to the north of town, while the bus stand is 500m to the west. The tourist office (☎ 71276) is open weekdays from 10 am to 5.30 pm.

Kumari Amman Temple

Picturesquely situated overlooking the shore, this temple and the nearby ghat attract pilgrims from all over India to worship and to bathe. According to legend, Devi did penance here to secure Siva's hand in marriage. When she was unsuccessful, she vowed to remain a virgin *(kanya)*. The temple is open daily from 4.30 to 11.45 am and from 5.30 to 8.30 pm, but non-Hindus are not allowed into the inner sanctum. Men must remove their shirts, and everyone their shoes, on entering this temple.

Gandhi Memorial

Next to the Kumari Amman Temple, this striking memorial stored the Mahatma's ashes until they were immersed in the sea. It resembles an Orissan temple and was designed so that on Gandhi's birthday (2 October), the sun's rays fall on the place where his ashes were kept. It's open daily from 7 am to 12.30 pm and 3 to 7 pm.

Vivekananda Memorial

This memorial is on two rocky islands projecting from the sea about 400m offshore. The Indian philosopher Swami Vivekananda came here in 1892 and sat on the rock, meditating, before setting out as one of India's most important religious crusaders. The mandapam which stands here in his memory was built in 1970 and reflects architectural styles from all over India. The ferry to the island (half-hourly) costs Rs 6, plus a Rs 3 entry fee to the memorial, which is open from 7 to 11 am and 2 to 5 pm.

Suchindram Temple

This temple, 13km north-west of Kanyakumari at Suchindram, is noted for its 'musical' columns and its impressive 3m tall statue of Hanuman, the monkey god.

Places to Stay

Although hotels are mushrooming in Kanyakumari, demand remains high and everything is heavily booked on weekends and during festivals. Some hotels have seasonal rates so you may find that, during April/May and October to December, room prices are 100% up on what is quoted here.

Gopi Nivas Lodge has basic singles/ doubles at Rs 80/100.

Hotel Saagar (☎ 71325), South Car St, is a good place with doubles (no singles) from Rs 100 to Rs 175.

TTDC Youth Hostel, at the entrance to the Hotel Tamil Nadu, charges Rs 45 per dorm bed and is rarely full.

Railway Retiring Rooms at the railway station include a six-bed dorm at just Rs 15 per bed and singles/doubles for Rs 40/80

Vivekas Tourist Hotel (☎ 71192) has clean,

colourful rooms all with bath and shower from Rs 100/180 for a double/triple.

Manickhan Tourist Home (☎ 71387) has doubles without/with a sea view for Rs 180/250.

Kerala House (☎ 71229), on the hill just west of the temple, claims to be the south-ernmost house on the subcontinent. It is run by the Kerala Tourism Development Corpo-ration and was opened in 1956. Since then it has seen many prominent visitors, including the Dalai Lama. It's now a bit run down but there are large rooms with sea views for Rs 240/360 with attached bath.

Hotel Tamil Nadu (☎ 71257) has basic doubles for Rs 90 with common bath, and much better doubles with attached bath for Rs 325, or Rs 500 with air-con. Rooms are clean and most have a private balcony with great views of the Gandhi Memorial.

Hotel Samudra (☎ 71162) near the tem-ple has doubles from Rs 300 to Rs 500, and a well-appointed air-con double with good views for Rs 800.

Places to Eat

Hotel Saravana near the temple has a well-loaded vegetarian menu but many of the

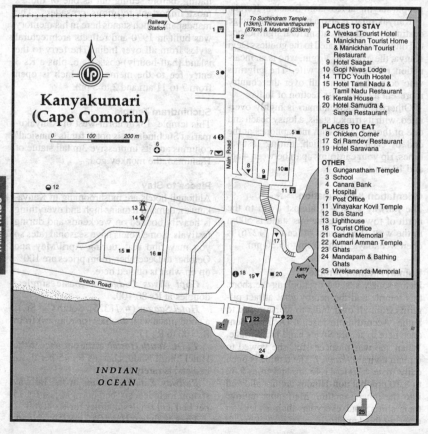

Kanyakumari (Cape Comorin)

To Suchindram Temple
(13km), Thiruvananthapuram
(87km) & Madurai (235km)

Railway Station

Main Road

Beach Road

INDIAN OCEAN

Ferry Jetty

0   100   200 m

PLACES TO STAY
2 Vivekas Tourist Hotel
5 Manickhan Tourist Home & Manickhan Tourist Restaurant
9 Hotel Saagar
10 Gopi Nivas Lodge
14 TTDC Youth Hostel
15 Hotel Tamil Nadu & Tamil Nadu Restaurant
16 Kerala House
20 Hotel Samudra & Sanga Restaurant

PLACES TO EAT
8 Chicken Corner
17 Sri Ramdev Restaurant
19 Hotel Saravana

OTHER
1 Gunganatham Temple
3 School
4 Canara Bank
6 Hospital
7 Post Office
11 Vinayakar Kovil Temple
12 Bus Stand
13 Lighthouse
18 Tourist Office
21 Gandhi Memorial
22 Kumari Amman Temple
23 Ghats
24 Mandapam & Bathing Ghats
25 Vivekananda Memorial

items are never available. Still, it offers south Indian and Chinese (of sorts) and is one of the town's most popular eateries. The paper dosas are excellent.

Sri Ramdev Restaurant just up the road offers a mean range of north Indian vegetarian fare on its tiny open-air terrace.

Sanga Restaurant is an upmarket vegetarian place in Hotel Samudra.

Chicken Corner does what it says at reasonable prices.

Manickhan Tourist Home has perhaps the best non-veg restaurant in town; their vegetarian food is also excellent.

Getting There & Away
Bus The bus stand is a dusty five-minute walk from the centre. It has timetables in English, restaurants and waiting rooms. The reservation office is open from 7 am to 9 pm.

TTC has frequent buses to Madurai (253km, six hours, Rs 47) and Chennai (679km, 16 hours, Rs 132) as well as buses to Thiruvananthapuram (Trivandrum, four times daily, three hours) and Rameswaram (four times daily, nine hours).

Local buses go to Nagercoil, Padmanabhapuram (for the palace of the former rulers of Travancore – see the Around Thiruvananthapuram section in the Kerala chapter for details), Thiruvananthapuram and Kovalam, among other places.

Train The one daily passenger train to Thiruvananthapuram leaves Kanyakumari at 5 pm and does the 87km in a dazzling two hours (Rs 25 in 2nd class).

The *Kanyakumari Express* travels to Mumbai daily in just under 48 hours, departing Kanyakumari at 5 am. The 2155km trip costs Rs 324/1340 in 2nd/1st class. This train will also take you to Thiruvananthapuram and Ernakulam (eight hours).

For the real long-haulers, the weekly *Himsagar Express* runs all the way to Jammu Tawi (in Jammu & Kashmir), a distance of 3734km, taking 74 hours. It's the longest single train ride in India, and leaves from Kanyakumari on Friday at 12.50 am and from Jammu Tawi on Monday at 10.45 pm.

This train also passes through Coimbatore (12 hours), Vijayawada (29 hours) and Delhi (60 hours).

MUNDANTHURAI TIGER SANCTUARY
Mundanthurai is in the mountains near the border with Kerala. The closest railway station is at Ambasamudram, about 25km to the north-east, and buses run from here to Papanasam, the nearest village, from where you can catch another bus to the Forest Department Rest House.

As the name implies, this is principally a tiger sanctuary though it's also noted for chital, sambar and the rare lion-tailed macaque. The best time to visit is between January and March, though it is open any time of the year. The main rainy season is between October and December. Tiger sightings are extremely infrequent and, in addition, the *Forest Rest House* is very basic.

KUTTRALAM (Courtallam)
About 135km north-west of Kanyakumari at the base of the Western Ghats, the village of Kuttralam is a popular 'health retreat' for Indian families who come to stand and wash under waterfalls believed to be rich in minerals and capable of curing almost anything.

Of the nine waterfalls, the only one in the village itself is the 60m high **Main Falls**, a five-minute walk from the bus stand. Its sheer rock face is carved with old Hindu insignia that is visible only during the dry months of January and February. Other falls, mostly accessed by shuttle buses, are up to eight km away.

Kuttralam offers only very basic lodging houses which are usually full in 'the season' (June to August). For a less humble abode you'll have to stay in Tenkasi, five km to the north. Here the *Krishna Tourist Home* (☎ 23125), next to the Tenkasi bus stand, has doubles for Rs 180 and some air-con rooms.

Tenkasi is the closest railway station to Kuttralam but trains on the main Kollam to Madurai line stop six km east at Shencottah (Sengottai) from where there's one express daily in either direction. Faster and more frequent buses also ply these routes.

The Western Ghats

KODAIKANAL

Pop: 31,200   Tel Area Code: 04542

Of the three main hill stations in the south – Udhagamandalam (Ootacamund, or Ooty), Kodaikanal and Yercaud – Kodaikanal is undoubtedly the most beautiful and, unlike Ooty, the temperature here rarely drops to the point where you need to wear heavy clothing, even in winter.

On the southern crest of the Palani Hills about 120km north-west of Madurai at an altitude of 2100m, Kodaikanal – better known as Kodai – is surrounded by thickly wooded slopes, waterfalls and precipitous rocky outcrops. The journey up and back down again is breathtaking, although there's no toy train. In the town, there are lookouts with spectacular views of the south within easy walking distance of the town centre.

Kodai has the distinction of being the only hill station in India to be set up during the Raj by Americans, though it didn't take long before they were joined by the British. American missionaries established a school for European children here in the mid-1840s, the legacy of which is the Kodaikanal International School – one of the most prestigious private schools in the country.

Kodaikanal is not just for those who want to get away from the heat and haze of the dusty plains during the summer months, but also for those seeking a relaxing place to put their feet up for a while and do some occasional hiking in the quiet *sholas* (forests). In the surrounding hills you'll find plantations of Australian blue gums which provide the eucalyptus oil sold in Kodai's many street stalls. Here too is the Kurinji, a shrub with light, purple-blue-coloured blossoms which flowers only every 12 years (the next will be in 2004, though there are always a few whose natural clocks seem to be out of time).

April to June or August to October are certainly the best times to visit Kodaikanal. April to June is the main season, whereas the peak of the wet season is November/ December. Temperatures here are mild, ranging between 11°C and 20°C in summer and 8°C and 17°C in winter.

Orientation

For a hill station, Kodai is remarkably compact. The main street is Bazaar Rd (Anna Salai), and the bottom-end hotels, restaurants and the bus stand are all in this area. Most, though not all, of the better hotels are some distance from the bazaar, but usually not more than about 15 minutes walk.

Information

The tourist office (☎ 41675), close to the bus stand, has precious little information. It's open Monday to Saturday, and they operate local tours in season. If you want literature about Kodai, try the CLS bookshop more or less opposite.

The State Bank of India, near the post office, is the best place to cash travellers cheques.

Astrophysical Laboratory

Built in 1889, this laboratory stands on the highest point in the area, three km uphill from Kodai's lake. It houses a small **museum** which is open Friday from 10 am to noon and 3 to 5 pm. The buildings with the instruments are off limits. It's a hard 45 minute uphill walk pushing a bicycle, but it only takes five minutes to coast down (you'll need good brakes).

Flora & Fauna Museum

Also worth a visit is the Flora & Fauna Museum at the Sacred Heart College at Shembaganur. It's a six km hike and all uphill on the way back. The museum is open from 10 am to noon and 3 to 5 pm; closed Sunday. Entry costs Rs 1.

Parks & Falls

Near the start of Coaker's Walk is **Bryant Park**, a botanical park laid out, landscaped and stocked over many years by the British officer after whom it is named. At **Chettiar Park**, about three km uphill from town near the Kurinji Andavar Temple, you may be able to see some Kurinji flowers.

There are numerous waterfalls in the area – the main one, **Silver Cascade** is on the road up to Kodai.

Activities

Walking & Cycling The views from Coaker's Walk which has an observatory with telescope, and from Pillar Rocks, a seven km hike (one way), are two of the most spectacular in southern India.

For more serious trekking, head to the District Forest Office, on a winding road down (north) towards Hotel Tamil Nadu. Here you can buy a pamphlet called *Kodaikanal Beauty in Wilderness* which describes 17 local treks ranging from eight km ambles to 27km hikes. It costs Rs 15 and includes a rough map plus estimates of the time required to complete each walk and the relative degree of difficulty. This office is open weekdays from 10 am to 1 pm and 2 to 6 pm.

Although the roads are rarely flat there are some nice bike rides in the area. One reader recommended going to Moir Point (10km) via the Astrophysical Laboratory, then taking the Monnar road 14km to Berijam Lake

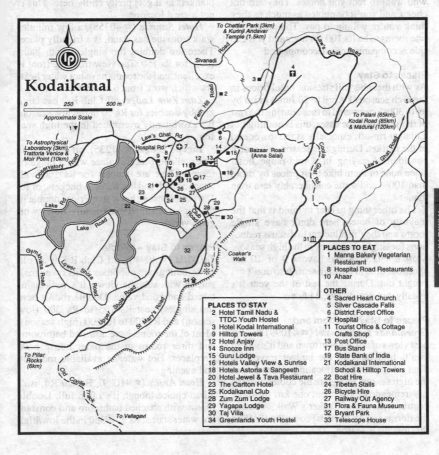

Kodaikanal

Approximate Scale
0   250   500 m

To Chettiar Park (3km) & Kurinji Andavar Temple (1.5km)

To Palani (65km), Kodai Road (85km) & Madurai (120km)

To Astrophysical Laboratory (3km), Trattoria Venice & Moir Point (10km)

Bazaar Road (Anna Salai)

Coaker's Walk

To Pillar Rocks (6km)

To Vellagavi

PLACES TO STAY
2 Hotel Tamil Nadu & TTDC Youth Hostel
3 Hotel Kodai International
9 Hilltop Towers
12 Hotel Anjay
14 Snooze Inn
15 Guru Lodge
16 Hotels Valley View & Sunrise
18 Hotels Astoria & Sangeeth
20 Hotel Jewel & Tava Restaurant
23 The Carlton Hotel
25 Kodaikanal Club
28 Zum Zum Lodge
29 Yagapa Lodge
30 Taj Villa
34 Greenlands Youth Hostel

PLACES TO EAT
1 Manna Bakery Vegetarian Restaurant
8 Hospital Road Restaurants
10 Ahaar

OTHER
4 Sacred Heart Church
5 Silver Cascade Falls
6 District Forest Office
7 Hospital
11 Tourist Office & Cottage Crafts Shop
13 Post Office
17 Bus Stand
19 State Bank of India
21 Kodaikanal International School & Hilltop Towers
22 Boat Hire
24 Tibetan Stalls
26 Bicycle Hire
27 Railway Out Agency
31 Flora & Fauna Museum
32 Bryant Park
33 Telescope House

TAMIL NADU

passing Silent Valley and Caps Valley Viewpoint. From December to June the Monnar road is closed because of the danger from fires but you can get special permission to cycle here from the District Forest Office.

Boating & Riding The lake at Kodai has been wonderfully landscaped, and boats can be hired from below the Carlton Hotel. They're cheapest at the Kodaikanal Boat & Rowing Club (from Rs 10 for a two-seater), but the tourist department also has a range of rowboats and pedal boats for rent nearby. Around here you'll be accosted by people who want to rent you horses. They are not cheap, and you'll be quoted as much as they think you're willing to pay. The prevailing rate seems to be Rs 100 per hour and you can ride accompanied or unaccompanied.

Places to Stay

As with the other hill stations, hotel prices in the high season (1 April to 30 June) jump by up to 300% compared to those during the rest of the year. In some cases, this is nothing but a blatant rip-off, especially at the lower end of the market. During this season, it's worth considering staying in a mid-range hotel since none of them hike their prices by more than 100% and some considerably less than that.

The other thing to bear in mind is that the majority of hotels here don't have single rooms and they're reluctant to discuss reductions for single occupancy in the high season. Most hotels in Kodai have a 9 or 10 am checkout time in the high season so don't get caught out. During the rest of the year it's usually, but not always, 24 hours.

Places to Stay – bottom end

Greenlands Youth Hostel (☎ 41099) has the best views of any hotel in town and it's where you'll find most of the budget travellers. That said, it can be suffocatingly crowded in the high season, though in the cooler months it's tremendous. It's about one km from the centre, at the end of Coaker's Walk. A bed in the dorms (six to 15 beds) costs Rs 40/45 in the low/high season. There are also eight

double rooms (four have fireplaces) with attached bathrooms for Rs 130 to Rs 160 in the low season and Rs 160 to Rs 190 in the high season. There's hot water from 7 to 9 am. Breakfast – either Indian or toasted brown bread with jam – and snacks are available.

TTDC Youth Hostel, beside the Hotel Tamil Nadu, has beds for Rs 45 but lacks atmosphere.

Guru Lodge is one of several very basic hotels strung out along the steep Bazaar Rd. Doubles are Rs 60 and facilities are absolutely minimal – make sure they give you blankets as it gets pretty chilly here. This is not a great location.

Hotel Sunrise (☎ 40358), a few minutes walk from the bus stand, is a friendly place. There are doubles (no singles) with bathroom for Rs 150. The view from the front is excellent, and the rooms have hot water heaters which work from 6 am to 6 pm.

Zum Zum Lodge, off Club Rd, has large grubby doubles for Rs 60 in the low season. It's exorbitantly overpriced in the high season.

Yagapa Lodge (☎ 41235), off Club Rd, is an excellent, peaceful place with a range of rooms. There are doubles for Rs 160 with attached bath and hot water in buckets, or Rs 180 with constant hot water. Prices double in the high season. It's a friendly hotel with good views.

Places to Stay – middle

Taj Villa (☎ 40940), off Club Rd, is an old stone-built group of houses in its own small garden with sublime views. It's well-maintained and good value. Double rooms here (no singles) cost Rs 195 to Rs 300 (low season) and Rs 400 to Rs 600 (high season). Most of the rooms have attached bathrooms and three rooms in the older house have fireplaces. Hot water is available morning and evening.

Hotel Anjay (☎ 41089), Bazaar Rd, isn't a bad choice though it's often full. Double rooms with attached bathroom and constant hot water start at Rs 170/350 in the low/high season.

Snooze Inn (☎ 40837) has clean rooms with TV and running hot water. Doubles (there are no singles) cost Rs 275/500 in low/high season.

Hotel Sangeeth (☎ 40456) is good value at Rs 195/325 for a double in the low/high season. All the rooms have attached bathrooms with hot and cold running water, but there are no views.

Hotel Astoria (☎ 40524) is next door to the Sangeeth. It has ordinary/deluxe doubles at Rs 300/325 in the low season and Rs 625/650 in the high. Its restaurant serves north and south Indian dishes.

Trattoria Venice, is an excellent Italian restaurant with two doubles for Rs 250. It's three km from the centre near the Astrophysical Laboratory.

Hotel Jewel (☎ 41029), Hospital Rd, is good value at Rs 275/300 for ordinary/deluxe doubles in the low season or Rs 450/650 in the high. All the rooms are well furnished with wall-to-wall carpeting and colour TV.

Hotel Tamil Nadu (☎ 41336) on Fern Hill Rd is a long walk from the centre and somewhat run-down. In the low/high season doubles cost Rs 250/425 and cottages are Rs 400/650. It has a restaurant and one of the few bars in Kodai.

Hilltop Towers (☎ 40413), on Club Rd opposite the Kodai International School, is a flashy place that's centrally located. The staff are keen and friendly and double rooms/suites cost Rs 350/450 in the low season and Rs 725/875 in the high.

Places to Stay – top end
Kodaikanal Club (☎ 41341) is set in manicured grounds close to the lake on Club Rd. Established in 1887, this colonial-style clubhouse has a library, video room, badminton and billiard tables, four 'mud' tennis courts, a bar (with cheap beers) and dining room. It offers 16 large double rooms for Rs 700/800 in the low/high season, plus 15% service charge. This room rate includes the obligatory temporary membership fee (Rs 50 per day which entitles you to use all the facilities), breakfast (Indian or Continental) and 'bed tea'

(served in your room between 6 and 7 am). The rooms are quaint and have an adjoining sitting room, bathroom, TV, heater, wicker chairs and 24 hour hot water. Don't expect to get a room here in the high season as it's booked out months ahead.

Valley View Hotel (☎ 40181) is a large modern hotel on Post Office Rd. The rooms are well appointed and those at the front have a wonderful view of the valley. It's a bargain in the low season at Rs 300/450 for singles/doubles. High season rates are Rs 1100/1400 but this includes all meals. There's a good vegetarian restaurant.

Hotel Kodai International (☎ 40649; fax 40753) is overpriced and badly located. Double rooms/cottages cost Rs 975/1155 in the low season or Rs 1500/1750 in the high.

The Carlton Hotel (☎ 40071), Lake Rd, is Kodai's most prestigious hotel and a lovely place to stay. Overlooking the lake, this hotel used to be a colonial-style wooden structure but was completely rebuilt a few years ago and is simply magnificent. In the low season, rooms cost Rs 1590/2450 with breakfast and dinner; in the high season it's Rs 1840/3600 including all meals. There are also more expensive suites and cottages. There's an excellent restaurant and a bar.

Places to Eat
Hospital Rd is the best place for cheap restaurants and it's here that most of the travellers and students from the Kodai International School congregate. There's a whole range of different cuisines available and which restaurant you choose on any particular day is largely a question of personal choice and who you find yourself with. They're all pretty good.

Tava Restaurant, below the Hotel Jewel, offers vegetarian Indian food.

Hotel Punjab does excellent tandoori food.

Ahaar is a little vegetarian place.

Silver Inn Restaurant is a good place for breakfasts and also does pizzas and other western dishes.

Wang's Kitchen has Chinese and western food at reasonable prices.

TAMIL NADU

Tibetan Brothers Restaurant is a popular place with westernised Tibetan food.

Chefmaster has continental, Chinese and Keralan dishes.

Hot Breads is a classy bakery and coffee shop in the supermarket complex on Hospital Rd. Apple pie is Rs 25, eclairs are Rs 12.

Eco Nut, also in the supermarket complex on Hospital Rd, has a wide range of health food – brown bread, cheese, essential oils etc. Try their Nutri Balls (Rs 10), which are a mixture of jaggery, peanuts, coconut and moong dal.

Little Silver Star is upstairs in the large building opposite the tourist office. They do probably the best tandoori chicken in Kodai – Rs 75 for half a chicken.

Manna Bakery Vegetarian Restaurant, Bear Shola Falls Rd, is well worth the long walk to reach it. It's run by Israel Booshi, who, as well as being a superb chef, is an active environmentalist and an interesting guy to talk to. His brown bread (available after 4 pm) is legendary, as is the apple pie (Rs 15). The open sandwiches are also good – fried egg, tomato and cheese is Rs 12. Breakfast is from 7.30, and lunch runs until 5 pm. Dinner is at 7 pm but needs to be ordered before 3 pm.

Trattoria Venice is even further out, near the Astrophysical Laboratory (follow the signs). Part Italian owned, there's pizza, pasta (Rs 40), and lasagne (Rs 45), plus superb tiramisu (Rs 45).

The Carlton Hotel is the place for a splurge. Here, they put on an excellent evening buffet from 7.30 to 10 pm for Rs 270 including tax. You can relax in the bar after eating though drinks are a little on the expensive side compared with elsewhere in Kodaikanal.

Things to Buy

The Cottage Crafts shop on Bazaar Rd opposite the post office has some excellent bits and pieces for sale. It is run by Corsock, the Co-ordinating Council for Social Concerns in Kodai. This organisation, staffed by volunteers, sells crafts on behalf of development groups, using the commission charged to help the needy. Corsock also runs the Good-

will Centre, Hospital Rd, which sells clothing and rents books, with the proceeds again going to indigent causes.

The road down to the lake (alongside the Kodaikanal Club) is lined with stalls run by Tibetans selling warm clothing, shawls and other fabrics. Their prices are very reasonable.

Kodai is a lush orchard area and, depending on the season, you'll find various fruits – pears, avocados, guavas, durians and grapefruit – in the street stalls around the bus stand.

Getting There & Away

Bus Kodai's bus stand is basically a patch of dirt opposite the Hotel Astoria and you won't find many timetables nor direction indicators on the buses in English. State buses run eight times a day to Madurai (121km, 3½ hours, Rs 18), once daily to both Tiruchirappalli (197km) and Kanyakumari (356km), and twice a day to both Coimbatore (244km) and Chennai (513km, Rs 87). As well, there are more frequent buses to Palani (65km, three hours, Rs 15), Dindigul and Kodai Road (the railway station). There's also a KSRTC semideluxe bus daily to Bangalore for Rs 105 which leaves at 6 pm and takes 12 hours (480km).

Deluxe minibuses operate in the high season between Kodaikanal and Udhagamandalam (Ooty) but they are suspended in the monsoon. They cost Rs 150 to Rs 200 and take all day to cover the 332km. Enquire at midrange hotels for departure times.

Train The nearest railway stations are Palani to the north (on the Coimbatore-Madurai-Rameswaram line), and Kodai Road on the Madurai-Trichy-Chennai line to the east. Both are about three hours away by bus.

There's a railway out-agency, up from the bus stand, where you can book seats on express trains to Chennai.

Getting Around

Taxis in Kodaikanal are very expensive compared with elsewhere even though half of them stand idle most of the day. The minimum charge is Rs 50. There are no rickshaws of any description.

The stall outside the Carlton Hotel rents mountain bikes for Rs 5/40 per hour/day. The bicycle stall near the corner of Bazaar and Club Rds has ordinary bikes for Rs 20 per day (negotiable). The hills can present quite a problem but, as you'd be walking up them anyway, it's not that much extra hassle to push a bike and at least you can coast down!

AROUND KODAI
Palani

There are fine views of the plains and scattered rock outcrops on the bus ride from Kodaikanal to Palani. The town's hill temple, **Malaikovil**, is dedicated to Lord Muruga, and an electric winch takes devotees to the top. Some 200,000 pilgrims gather at this temple for the Thai Pusam Festival in January.

There are several places to stay but *Hotel Modern Home*, Railway Feeder Rd, is far enough from the centre to be reasonably peaceful. Rooms are Rs 75/95 with attached bath.

See the earlier Getting There & Away section under Kodaikanal for information on getting to Palani.

ANAMALAI WILDLIFE SANCTUARY

This is one of the three wildlife sanctuaries on the slopes of the Western Ghats along the border between Tamil Nadu and Kerala. Though recently renamed the Indira Gandhi Wildlife Sanctuary, most people still refer to it by its original name. It covers almost 1000 sq km and is home to elephant, gaur (Indian bison), tiger, panther, spotted deer, wild boar, bear, porcupine and civet cat. The Nilgiri tahr, commonly known as ibex, can also be spotted, as can many birds.

In the heart of this beautiful forested region is the Parambikulam Dam which has formed an immense plain of water that spreads way into Kerala. The rights to this water, used mainly for irrigation and energy purposes in Tamil Nadu, are the source of one of the area's bitter disputes.

Information

The reception centre and most of the lodges are at Topslip, about 35km south-west of Pollachi. All accommodation, however, should be booked in advance in Pollachi at the Wildlife Warden's Office (☎ 4345) on Meenkarai Rd. The entrance fee is Rs 5 at Topslip but if you go on to Parambikulam on the park's Keralan side you must pay Rs 25.

The sanctuary can be visited at any time (it's best from February to June) though without your own transport you're not likely to see much. Tours are rarely run as the Forest Department's sole wildlife-viewing vehicle is perpetually in disrepair, and the public bus that plies daily between Pollachi

Wildlife Sanctuaries

There are six wildlife sanctuaries in Tamil Nadu, three close to the east coast and the others in the richly forested mountains on the borders of Kerala and Karnataka. The Guindy National Park, within the metropolitan boundaries of Chennai, is the smallest.

All the sanctuaries except Guindy offer accommodation in pretty basic Forest Rest Houses. At Mudumalai there are also more comfortable private lodges. It is possible to turn up at the government rest houses without making prior arrangements, but, it's advisable to book in advance: rooms cannot be allocated to unannounced guests until late in the evening when there's no further possibility of anyone arriving with a booking.

On the whole, transport facilities are very limited – some of the parks don't even have a vehicle for animal-viewing. This means getting to the remote parts of the sanctuaries, where you're far more likely to see animals, is all but impossible unless you have your own vehicle. And even with a private vehicle you may not get too far as in some parks (Mudumalai for example) private vehicles have been banned from touring. Some of the sanctuaries offer elephant rides through the forest which should be booked in advance if you don't want to be queuing for hours. Despite all these apparent drawbacks, visiting one of Tamil Nadu's wildlife sanctuaries can be a very rewarding experience. ■

and Parambikulam scares away everything but monkeys.

Places to Stay & Eat

Accommodation is available at three places. At Topslip, there is a dormitory and four lodges, the best of which is **Ambuli Illam** two km from the reception centre. There's a canteen here, about the only place in the park where you'll get a half decent meal. Topslip, at 740m, can get cool at night in winter.

About 24km east of Topslip near the Varagaliar River and a remote elephant camp is the **Varagaliar Rest House**. It's accessible by 4WD only and you'll need to take your own food. At Parambikulam, the very basic **rest house** has no catering facilities and only a few 'meals' places nearby.

Getting There & Away

Anamalai is between Palani and Coimbatore. Regular buses from both these places stop at the nearest large town, Pollachi, which is also on the Coimbatore to Dindigul train line. From Pollachi, there are buses twice daily to the sanctuary via the township of Anamalai. A taxi from Pollachi is Rs 400 one way.

COIMBATORE

Pop: 1.23 million   Tel Area Code: 0422

Coimbatore is a large, dirty, industrial city known for textile manufacturing and engineering goods, and is full of 'suitings and shirtings' shops. It can make a convenient overnight stop if you're heading up to Ooty or the other Nilgiri hill stations.

Orientation & Information

The two main bus stands are close to each other but about two km from the railway station. Some buses from Kerala and southern Tamil Nadu arrive at a third stand, Ukkadam, south of the railway station. Frequent city buses ply the route from here into town.

The GPO is open for poste restante collection from 10 am to 3 pm, Monday to Saturday.

Places to Stay – bottom end

Hotel Sivakami (☎ 210271), Davey & Co Lane, is friendly and helpful and has basic rooms with bathroom for Rs 80/125. There are several other similar places on this relatively peaceful street that is opposite the railway station.

Railway Retiring Rooms at the station include doubles for Rs 120, or Rs 175 with air-con. The dorm beds (men only) are Rs 35.

Hotel Shree Shakti (☎ 234225), 11/148 Sastri Rd, is a large hotel near the bus station. Staff are friendly; rooms have a fan and bathroom and cost Rs 130/180 for singles/doubles.

Zakin Hotel, Sastri Rd, has basic rooms for Rs 80/110.

Sri Ganapathy Lodge, also on Sastri Rd, has reasonable rooms with attached bath for Rs 125/185.

Places to Stay – middle & top end

Hotel Blue Star (☎ 230635) on Nehru St has well-appointed rooms for Rs 195/270 with bathroom. The rooms out the back are quieter. There's a basement bar and both a veg and non-veg restaurant.

Hotel Tamil Nadu (☎ 236311), conveniently located near the state bus stand, is surprisingly good. There are ordinary rooms for Rs 195/250 with attached bath, and air-con rooms for Rs 350/400.

Hotel City Tower (☎ 230681; fax 230103), Sivasamy Rd, is a modern place popular with businesspeople. The rooms (all doubles) cost Rs 600 with Star TV and attached baths, or Rs 900 with air-con. The hotel has two excellent restaurants.

Nilgiri's Nest (☎ 217247; fax 217131), 739 Avanashi Rd, is a pleasant, well-run hotel near the racecourse. Bed and breakfast costs Rs 695/880 in comfortable air-con rooms.

Hotel Surya International (☎ 217751; fax 216110), 105 Racecourse Rd, has luxurious rooms for Rs 700/900.

Places to Eat

There are numerous 'meals' restaurants in the railway station area serving thalis from around Rs 10.

Royal Hindu Restaurant, just north of the railway station, is a huge place offering good vegetarian meals.

Hotel Top Form on Nehru St serves non-vegetarian food at reasonable prices.

Hotel City Towers has a very pleasant rooftop restaurant, a good place for a splurge.

Annalakshmi, by the Hotel Surya International at 106 Racecourse Rd, is the top vegetarian restaurant. Run by devotees of Shvanjali, it's an interesting place to eat and the food, though expensive, is very well prepared. There are set meals from Rs 100, and it's open daily for dinner from 6.45 to 9.45 pm and Monday to Saturday for lunch from noon to 3 pm. There's another branch in Chennai.

Getting There & Away

Air The airport is 10km east of town. Indian Airlines (☎ 212208) and Air India (☎ 213393) offices are on Trichy Rd. There are Indian Airlines flights between Coimbatore and Mumbai (six times weekly, US$120), Chennai (five times weekly, US$70), Calicut (four times weekly, US$30), and Madurai (three times weekly, US$40).

Additionally, Jet Airways (☎ 212034) and Skyline NEPC (☎ 216741) both fly daily to Mumbai and NEPC Airlines has a daily flight to Chennai.

Bus The large and well-organised state bus stand only has timetables in Tamil, except for buses to Bangalore and Mysore. Buses to Bangalore (twice daily, 312km, nine hours, Rs 75) and Mysore (three times daily, 205km, Rs 44) can be booked at the reservation office (open from 9 am to 9 pm) on Bay 1. The ordinary buses to Ooty (90km, three hours, Rs 16) leave every half hour from opposite the reservation office.

The TTC/RGTC bus stand is on Cross Cut Rd, five minutes walk from the state bus stand. The reservations office is open from 7 am to 9 pm. There are services to Mysore via

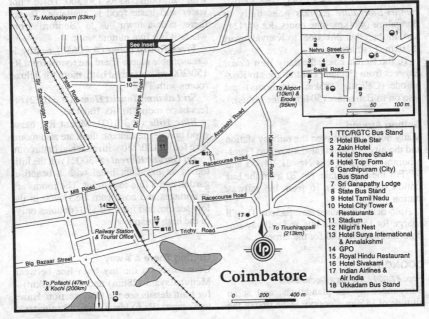

Coimbatore

1 TTC/RGTC Bus Stand
2 Hotel Blue Star
3 Zakin Hotel
4 Hotel Shree Shakti
5 Hotel Top Form
6 Gandhipuram (City) Bus Stand
7 Sri Ganapathy Lodge
8 State Bus Stand
9 Hotel Tamil Nadu
10 Hotel City Tower & Restaurants
11 Stadium
12 Nilgiri's Nest
13 Hotel Surya International & Annalakshmi
14 GPO
15 Royal Hindu Restaurant
16 Hotel Sivakami
17 Indian Airlines & Air India
18 Ukkadam Bus Stand

To Mettupalayam (53km)
See Inset
Nehru Street
Sastri Road
To Airport (10km) & Erode (95km)
Sir Shanmugan Road
Palai Road
Dr Nanjappa Road
Avanashi Road
Kamaraj Road
Racecourse Road
Racecourse Road
Mill Road
To Tiruchirappalli (213km)
Railway Station & Tourist Office
Trichy Road
Big Bazaar Street
To Pollachi (47km) & Kochi (200km)

Ooty (20 buses daily between 4 am and 11 pm), to Chennai (six daily, 11½ hours), Madurai (Nos 660 & 626, six hours), and Trichy (No 720, 13 daily, 5¼ hours).

Train Coimbatore is a major rail junction. For Ooty, catch the daily *Nilgiri Express* at 6.25 am; it connects with the miniature railway at Mettupalayam. The whole trip takes 4½ hours and costs Rs 41/184 in 2nd/1st class.

There are numerous daily trains between Coimbatore and Chennai Central (494km), the fastest being the new *Shatabdi Express* service which takes just under seven hours. Departure times are 7.25 am from Coimbatore, 3.10 pm from Chennai. Air-con chair car costs Rs 470. The *Kovai Express* takes 7½ hours and costs Rs 102/464 in 2nd/1st class. From Coimbatore it leaves at 2.20 pm; from Chennai it leaves at 6.15 am. Other trains take up to nine hours.

The daily *Rameswaram Express* at 10.45 pm goes via Madurai (229km, six hours, Rs 56/249 in 2nd/1st class) to Rameswaram (393km, 13 hours, Rs 85/395). The *Kanyakumari-Bangalore Express* goes daily to Bangalore (424km, nine hours, Rs 91/421) and, in the other direction, to Kanyakumari (510km, 12½ hours).

To the Kerala coast, the daily *West Coast Express* from Chennai Central goes to Kozhikode (Calicut) (185km, 4½ hours) and also on to Bangalore (504km, nine hours).

Getting Around

Many buses ply between the railway station and the city bus stand (also known as Gandhipuram) including bus Nos JJ, 24, 55 and 57. For the airport take No 20 from the bus station or Nos 10 or 16 from the railway station.

Auto-rickshaw wallahs are rapacious. They'll charge Rs 15 between bus and railway stations and over Rs 100 for the airport.

COONOOR

Pop: 47,000   Tel Area Code: 0423

Surrounded by tea plantations, and at an altitude of 1850m, Coonoor is the first of the three Nilgiri hill stations – Udhagamandalam (Ooty), Kotagiri and Coonoor – that you come to when leaving behind the southern plains. Like Ooty, it's on the toy train line from Mettupalayam.

While Kotagiri had the Kotas, and Ooty the Todas, so Coonoor was home to the Coon hill tribe. (The suffix, 'oor', means village.) This now bustling town appears rather squashed between the hills, and it's only after climbing up out of the busy market area with the bus and train terminals that you'll get a sense of what hill stations were originally all about. For this reason, too, most of the better accommodation is in Upper Coonoor.

Places to Stay & Eat

YWCA Guest House (☎ 34426) in Upper Coonoor is the best budget option but it's often full – phone in advance. Open to men and women, it's a handsome old colonial house with two wooden terraces and views over Coonoor. Large clean singles/doubles with bathroom cost Rs 150/300. There's hot water and basic food is available. To get there, take a town bus to 'Bedford' from where it is a five minute walk.

Vivek Tourist Home (☎ 30658), nearby, is a reasonable place. There are rooms from Rs 150/200 with attached bath, more for deluxe rooms with TV.

Sri Lakshmi Tourist Home (☎ 31022) offers basic rooms for Rs 100/150.

Blue Hills (☎ 30103), Mount Rd, has a good non-veg restaurant; there are also rooms here for Rs 130/250 with attached bathroom.

Taj Garden Retreat (☎ 30021) on the hilltop is an excellent hotel with a beautiful garden and a fine restaurant. The rooms are in cottages and cost from US$38/60 in the low season, and from US$90 (doubles only) in the high season.

Getting There & Away

Coonoor is on the toy train line between Mettupalayam (28km) and Ooty (18km) – for train details see the Ooty section. Buses to Kotagiri (Rs 6) leave every 15 minutes.

TAMIL NADU

KOTAGIRI

Pop: 25,600   Tel Area Code: 0423

Kotagiri (Line of Houses of the Kotas) is a small, quiet village about 28km east of Ooty, at an altitude of 1950m. Though the oldest of the three Nilgiri hill stations – the British started building houses here in 1819 – it is much less touristed than Ooty and calmer than Coonoor. Life is now concentrated around tea production. The road to Ooty winds along hills denuded of their original cover in favour of bright green tea plantations and dotted with Kota settlements.

From Kotagiri you can visit **Catherine Falls** eight km away near the Mettupalayam road (the last three km by foot only), **Elk Falls** (six km) and **Kodanad View Point** (22km), where there is a fine panoramic view over the Coimbatore plains, the Mysore plateau and the eastern slopes of the Nilgiris.

In town, there's a Women's Cooperative near Ramchand Square which sells local handicrafts.

Places to Stay & Eat

There are a few basic lodges in town such as the *Majestic Lodge*, the *Blue Star* and the *Hotel Ramesh Vihar*. In all, double rooms with attached bathroom start at around Rs 100. There are several 'meals' restaurants. The vegetarian *Kasturi Paradise Restaurant*, opposite the Women's Cooperative, is OK.

The nicest place to stay, for its homeliness and wonderful setting is the *Queenshill Christian Guest House*, one km uphill behind the bus stand and past the Women's Cooperative. However, this place may not be open much longer. If it is, Miss Ruth Rose, the friendly, mellow-natured lady who runs the place, offers well-furnished rooms for Rs 110 per person including breakfast. Meals are served, when possible, with all guests around one table.

Getting There & Away

There are regular buses to Ooty (Rs 6) which cross one of Tamil Nadu's highest passes. Buses to Mettupalayam (Rs 5.50) leave every 30 minutes and to Coonoor every 15 minutes.

UDHAGAMANDALAM

(Ootacamund, Ooty)

Pop: 89,000   Tel Area Code: 0423

This famous hill station in the Nilgiri Hills was founded by the British in the early part of the 19th century to serve as the summer headquarters of the Madras government. Before that time, the area was inhabited by the Todas, the tribal people of which today only about 1500 remain. They were polygamists and worshipped buffaloes, and you can see their animist shrines in various places.

Until about two decades ago, 'snooty' Ooty (altitude 2240m) resembled an unlikely combination of southern England and Australia: single-storey stone cottages, bijou fenced flower gardens, leafy, winding lanes, and tall eucalypt stands covering the otherwise barren hilltops. The other main reminders of the British period are the stone churches, the private schools, the Ooty Club, various maharajas' summer palaces, and the terraced botanical gardens.

But while parts of Ooty still exude a fading atmosphere of leafy seclusion, especially on the lake's western and southern margins, elsewhere hoteliers and real estate developers and the influx of tourist hordes with their city habits have totally transformed it.

These days, at least in the high season, it's a dreadful place full of vacuous yuppies and day-trippers with their ghetto blasters, throwing litter everywhere. The sewage system, too, is incapable of dealing with the demand placed on it. It's important to remember, should you be thinking of boating, that all this untreated filth flows directly into the lake.

All in all, Ooty is best avoided these days unless you can afford to stay in one of the former palaces. The only things it has going for it is the journey up there on the 'toy' train and the fact that it's cool when the plains down below are unbearably hot. In the winter months and during the monsoon you will need warm clothing as the overnight temperature occasionally drops to 0°C.

Orientation

Ooty is spread over a large area amongst rolling hills and valleys. Between the lake

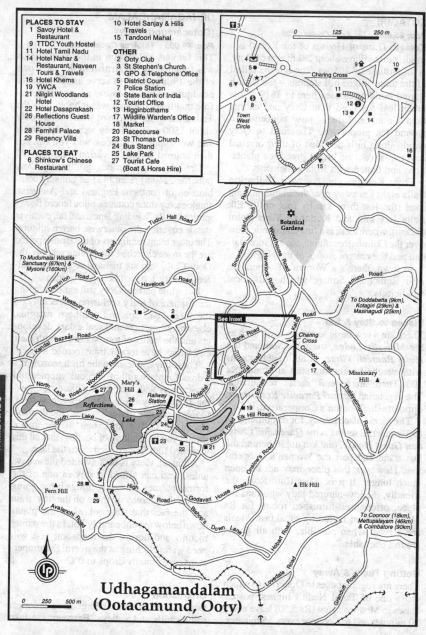

PLACES TO STAY
1 Savoy Hotel & Restaurant
9 TTDC Youth Hostel
11 Hotel Tamil Nadu
14 Hotel Nahar & Restaurant, Naveen Tours & Travels
16 Hotel Khems
19 YWCA
21 Nilgiri Woodlands Hotel
22 Hotel Dasaprakash
26 Reflections Guest House
28 Fernhill Palace
29 Regency Villa

PLACES TO EAT
6 Shinkow's Chinese Restaurant

10 Hotel Sanjay & Hills Travels
15 Tandoori Mahal

OTHER
2 Ooty Club
3 St Stephen's Church
4 GPO & Telephone Office
5 District Court
7 Police Station
8 State Bank of India
12 Tourist Office
13 Higginbothams
17 Wildlife Warden's Office
18 Market
20 Racecourse
23 St Thomas Church
24 Bus Stand
25 Lake Park
27 Tourist Cafe (Boat & Horse Hire)

Charing Cross

Town West Circle

Botanical Gardens

Tudor Hall Road

Havelock Road

To Mudumalai Wildlife Sanctuary (67km) & Mysore (160km)

Snowdown Road

Marlimund Road

Woodhouse Road

Havelock Road

Kodappamund Road

To Doddabetta (9km), Kotagiri (29km) & Masinagudi (25km)

See Inset

Bank Road

Charing Cross

Coonoor Road

Missionary Hill

Commercial Road

Ettines Road

Kandal Bazaar Road

Westbury Road

Dewin ton Road

Havelock Road

North Lake Road

Woodcock Road

Mary's Hill

Reflections Lake

South Lake Road

Railway Station

Hospital Road

Thalayattimund Road

To Coonoor (18km), Mettupalayam (46km) & Coimbatore (90km)

Fern Hill

Avalanchi Road

High Level Road

Godavari House Road

Bishop's Down Lane

Elk Hill Road

Onslow's Road

Elk Hill

I Hobart Road

Grandduff Road

Lovedale Road

Udhagamandalam (Ootacamund, Ooty)

0   250   500 m

Blue Mountain Railway

Like Darjeeling and Matheran, Ooty has a miniature railway connecting it with the lowlands. The trains, with their quaint yellow-and-blue carriages, are not quite as small as the Darjeeling toy train, but they're still tiny. Some of the railway scenes from *A Passage to India* were filmed on this train.

The unique feature of this line is the toothed central rail onto which the locomotives lock on the steeper slopes. Also unusual is the little locomotive, which is at the back pushing rather than pulling from the front. Each of the three or four carriages has its own brakeman, who sits on a little platform of each carriage and, whenever appropriate, waves a red or green flag.

The railway starts at Mettupalayam, north of Coimbatore, and goes via Coonoor to Ooty, en route affording some spectacular views of the precipitous eastern slopes of the rainforest-covered Nilgiris. Views are best from the left on the way up and from the right on the way down. ■

and the racecourse are the railway station and bus stand. From either of these it's a 10 minute walk to the bazaar area and 20 minutes to Ooty's real centre, Charing Cross (the junction of Coonoor, Kelso and Commercial roads).

Information

Tourist Office The tourist office (☎ 43977), on Commercial Rd, is open weekdays from 10 am to 1 pm and 2 to 5.45 pm. The staff give out leaflets on Ooty and book visitors on tours.

The GPO above Town West Circle is open Monday to Saturday from 9 am to 5 pm. The telegraph office (open 24 hours) is also here.

Higginbothams bookshop, next to the tourist office, has a decent range of books.

Mudumalai Park Office If you intend visiting Mudumalai Wildlife Sanctuary, it's wise to arrange accommodation and elephant rides in advance. Book at the Wildlife Warden's office (☎ 44098) in the Mahalingam Building on Coonoor Rd. It's open weekdays from 10 am to 1 pm and 2 to 5.30 pm.

Things to See & Do

Ooty is the place for outdoor activities. For walks see the boxed hiking section. If you'd prefer to go **horseback riding** (alone or with a guide) hire a horse at the Tourist Cafe on the north side of the lake. Haggle hard! A fair price is about Rs 95 an hour.

Boats for use on the lake can be rented from the Tourist Cafe but, be warned, this is where the tourist hordes are at their worst.

Prices start from Rs 35 for a two-seater pedal boat.

There's a surprisingly well-kept **botanical garden**. During the monsoon season, **horse races** are held at the racecourse but the betting is pretty tame.

Organised Tours

Naveen Tours & Travels (☎ 43747), opposite the tourist office, and Hills Travels (☎ 42090) at Hotel Sanjay, are among several private operators who run a range of tours. Avoid the tour of Ooty and Mudumalai Wildlife Sanctuary as there's no time to see any wildlife.

Places to Stay

Since Ooty is a sellers' market in the high season (1 April to 15 June), hoteliers double their prices during this time. This is clearly a rip-off since prices don't necessarily equate with quality, but there are few options. Note that many hotels are fully booked in the high season and that the checkout time (usually noon) at any hotel can be as early as 9 am.

Places to Stay – bottom end

Budget hotels in the bazaar area are very poor value and only for the desperate.

TTDC Youth Hostel (☎ 43665), Charing Cross, offers dorm beds at Rs 50, and doubles for Rs 190/375 in the low/high season.

YWCA (☎ 42218), Ettines Rd, is also reasonable value but it's often full. A dorm bed costs Rs 77 and doubles with attached bathrooms are Rs 250 (low season) and Rs 325 (high season). There are also some cottages which are a little cheaper. Meals are available

(Rs 83) and there is a loungeroom with an open fire in winter.

Reflections Guest House (☎ 43834), North Lake Rd, is an enjoyable place with good views over the lake and doubles at Rs 200 (Rs 300 in the high season). There are only six rooms, but all have hot water and the atmosphere is homely. Good breakfasts and a range of snacks can be brought to your room or are served on the grassy terrace. The friendly owner, Mrs Dique, is a good source of information on the region's history.

Places to Stay – middle

Hotel Tamil Nadu (☎ 44370) on the hill above the tourist office, is a good place in this range. Doubles with attached bathroom cost Rs 275/475 in the low/high season, plus Rs 50 for a TV. There's a restaurant but no bar.

Hotel Khems (☎ 44188), Shoreham Palace Rd, is very well appointed and good value. Standard/superior doubles are Rs 275 /475 (low season) and Rs 450/675 (high season). The hotel has its own restaurant.

Nilgiri Woodlands Hotel (☎ 42551; fax 42530), Ettines Rd, is a traditional-style hotel dating from colonial days, with clean rooms in the main building and a number of detached cottages. In the low season, doubles with attached bathroom cost Rs 200, cottages are Rs 400 and suites Rs 500. In the high season they range from Rs 300 to Rs 800.

Hotel Dasaprakash (☎ 42434) is another long-established hotel, clean and reasonable value. Doubles with attached bathroom range from Rs 300 in the low season; Rs 540 in the high season.

Regency Villa (☎ 42555) is a wonderfully atmospheric place to stay, although it's getting a little shabby around the edges. There are potted plants, wicker chairs and faded photographs of the Ooty Hunt. Cows, grazing on the lawn, add to the peacefulness of this timewarped hotel. The best rooms are ultra spacious and have bay windows, fully tiled Victorian bathrooms (with hot water) and a sitting corner by an open fire. The staff are amiable and simple meals can be arranged in advance. In the main building doubles cost Rs 550 to Rs 900; in the cottage they're Rs 350 to Rs 750.

Hotel Nahar (☎ 42173) is a huge place at Charing Cross. Doubles with attached bathroom and TV cost from Rs 450 to Rs 650 (low season), and Rs 700 to Rs 900 (high season).

Places to Stay – top end

Savoy Hotel (☎ 44142; fax 43318) at 77 Sylks Rd, is very comfortable. Part of the Taj Group, this place has doubles for US$85 in the low season and US$130 in the high. It has manicured lawns, clipped hedges, rooms with bathtubs, wooden furnishings and working fireplaces, a 24 hour bar and an excellent multi-cuisine dining room.

Fernhill Palace (☎ 43910), which is now owned by the Taj Group and closed for renovations, was built in the days when expense

---

Hikes around Ooty & the Nilgiri Hills

There are numerous long walks in the area with some superb views over Ooty and the Nilgiris.

Kotagiri Pass, on the road to Kotagiri, is an excellent starting point for treks over and along the wooded hill crests and has great views down the Nilgiris' northern slopes. About three km east of this pass is the highest peak in Tamil Nadu, **Doddabetta** (2623m), from where Coonoor, Wellington, Coimbatore, Mettupalayam and, on a clear day, even Mysore are visible. Doddabetta is 10km from Ooty.

Longer treks which pass through protected forest areas are worthwhile but difficult to arrange as you need to get permission from the Forest Department in Ooty (☎ 43968). They can suggest routes and help arrange guides, but making the preparations and getting permission could take you anything from a week to a month! It's also worth contacting the Nilgiris Trekking Association, 31 Bank Rd, Ooty.

One good four-day trek runs via Parsans Valley, Mukurti Dam, Pandiar Hills, Pykara Falls, and Mudumalai (plus a couple of days to get to and from the start and finish). ■

was of no concern and master artisans didn't command fortunes. This former retreat of the Maharaja of Mysore is in a quiet forest setting. When it reopens in 1998 prices should be similar to the Savoy and it'll probably be the best place to stay in Ooty.

Places to Eat

There are plenty of basic vegetarian 'meals' places on Commercial Rd and Main Bazaar.

Hotel Nahar has two veg restaurants and a popular snack bar serving ice cream and milk shakes.

Hotel Sanjay is a big, bustling place with generous servings of veg and non-veg fare.

Tandoori Mahal, on Commercial Rd, has tasty dishes for around Rs 60. The service is good, and the beer cold.

Shinkow's Chinese Restaurant (also known as the Zodiac Room) at 30 Commissioner's Rd has some really good food. It's run by a Chinese family so its dishes (around Rs 50) are fairly authentic.

Hotel Savoy is the place for a splurge. Buffet lunch or dinner costs Rs 250 (plus tax) for all you can eat. A beer is Rs 78.

Getting There & Away

Bus The state bus companies all have reservation offices at the bus stand, most open daily from 9 am to 5.30 pm. There are 20 buses a day to Mysore (five hours, Rs 33) and many continue to Bangalore (eight hours, Rs 70). There are buses every 30 minutes to Coimbatore (three hours, Rs 16), three buses a day to Chennai (15 hours, Rs 108), and also direct services to Kanyakumari (14 hours), Thanjavur (10 hours) and Tirupathi (14 hours).

Most of the private companies are clustered around Charing Cross. Their buses are a little more expensive than the state buses, but worth it.

For Mudumalai Wildlife Sanctuary (67km, 2½ hours, Rs 14), take one of the Mysore buses or one of the small buses which go via the narrow and twisting Sighur Ghat road. Most of these rolling wrecks travel only as far as Masinagudi, from where there are five buses a day to Theppakadu.

Local buses leave every 20 minutes for Kotagiri (one hour, Rs 5) and hourly to Coonoor (one hour, Rs 5).

Train The miniature railway is the best way to get here. Departures and arrivals at Mettupalayam usually connect with those of the *Nilgiri Express* which runs between Mettupalayam and Chennai. It departs Chennai at 9 pm and arrives in Mettupalayam at 7.25 am. From Mettupalayam, it leaves at 7.25 pm. Tickets cost Rs 163/563 in 2nd/1st class. You can catch this train from Coimbatore at 6.25 am.

The miniature train leaves Mettupalayam for Ooty (46km, Rs 19/139 in 2nd/1st class) at 7.45 am and arrives in Ooty at noon. From Ooty the train leaves at 3 pm. The trip down takes about 3½ hours.

During the high season, there's an extra departure in each direction daily, from Mettupalayam at 9.10 am and from Ooty at 2 pm. There are also two extra services between Ooty and Coonoor at this time – they leave Ooty daily at 9.30 am and 6 pm.

The track is sometimes washed out during the monsoon.

Getting Around

There are plenty of unmetered auto-rickshaws in Ooty, based outside the bus stand. In the high season, the drivers quote outrageous fares, even between the bus stand and Charing Cross. Haggling might get you around 20% off the first price quoted but nothing more, so it's worth walking. In the low season, their fares become more reasonable. Normal taxis are also available.

You can hire a bicycle at the market but many of the roads are steep so you'll end up pushing them uphill (great on the way down though!).

MUDUMALAI WILDLIFE SANCTUARY

Tel Area Code: 0423

In the luxuriantly forested foothills of the Nilgiris, this 321 sq km sanctuary is part of a much larger reserve (3000 sq km) which includes Bandipur and Wynad in neighbouring Karnataka and Kerala. The larger reserve

TAMIL NADU

ranges in vegetation from semi-evergreen forests to swamps and grasslands. In Mudumalai, the mostly dense forest is home to chital (spotted deer), gaur (Indian bison), tiger, panther, wild boar and sloth bear. Otters and crocodiles inhabit the Moyar River. The park's wild elephant population, one of the largest in the country, supposedly numbers about 600, however you're more likely to see their domesticated brethren carrying out logging duties.

The best time to visit Mudumalai is between February and June. Heavy rain is common in October and November and the park may be closed during the dry season (February to March).

Orientation & Information

The main service area in Mudumalai is Theppakadu, on the main road between Udhagamandalam (Ooty) and Mysore, where you'll find the park's reception centre (☎ 56235) open daily from 6.30 am to 6 pm. There is some accommodation and an elephant camp here, and sometimes you can see spotted deer and wild boar. You can also stay in private lodges at Masinagudi or Bokkapuram, both east of Theppakadu, however they're relatively inaccessible if you don't have your own transport.

Book sanctuary accommodation in advance with the Wildlife Warden (☎ 44098), Coonoor Rd, Ooty. Entry fees are Rs 5/2 for adults/children, plus Rs 10/50 for a still/movie camera.

Wildlife Tours

Tours of the park are limited to the sanctuary's minibuses, jeep and elephants. Private vehicles are not allowed to make tours. Minibus tours (morning and afternoon) cost Rs 25 per person for 45 minutes, and they go about 15km into the jungle. The one-hour elephant rides (Rs 140) are very popular and can be booked in advance at the Wildlife Warden's office in Ooty or direct at the Theppakadu Reception Centre.

Places to Stay & Eat

The Forest Department maintains three *dormitories* (Rs 10 per bed) and five *lodges* (Rs 50 for a double) throughout the park, each with a cook-cum-housekeeper.

Theppakadu On the river, *Forest Department Log House* is about five minutes walk from the reception centre and the best option here. The three double rooms have polished timber furnishings and there's a verandah where you can sit and while away a day or two. Unfortunately, the staff do not seem keen to rent this place and will tell you that it is occupied when it's not.

Forest Department Sylvan Lodge is right next door and next best. It looks out over the river but it's older and not quite as charming.

Forest Department Dormitory is at the reception centre.

TTDC Youth Hostel, close to Sylvan Lodge, has dorm beds for Rs 25 but the rooms are

---

Puja or Penance at Mudumalai?

It was 5 pm and Mudumalai's newest attraction, the Elephant Puja Ceremony, was about to begin. The audience, having each paid the Rs 20 entry fee, had gathered to watch the show on a grassy area across the river from the reception centre. There was an air of excitement as the matriarch, a big old girl whose skin hung loose, lead the troop of 12, predominantly young, elephants into the open-air arena. Each performer, draped in colourful cloth and with ears and trunk brightly painted, was ridden by a turbaned mahout who commanded his charge to line up facing the small gathering.

On cue, the smallest elephant picked up a small brass bell and shook it slowly. The chimes rang out as the elephant bowed onto its two front knees before a tiny statue of Ganesh, the elephant-headed god, that had been placed on the grass. A few seconds passed before it rose and, in doing so, announced the end of the puja and the start of the obscene tricks – balancing acts, walking a plank, and so on – that were to make up the bulk of this so-called ceremony. 'Circus or wildlife sanctuary?', we questioned, trying to reconcile the fact that the authorities of a national park had reduced their charges to objects of jest and ridicule. Boycott this nonsensical show if you will, simply to discourage its continuation.

Leanne Logan & Geert Cole

musty, and large groups often stay here and party into the night.

Masinagudi & Bokkapuram Masinagudi is a small village eight km east of Theppakadu. Accommodation options in the village itself are pretty poor, just the old *Belleview Resort* (☎ 56351) with rooms at Rs 100/250 and dorm beds for Rs 50, the cheaper *Travellers Bungalow*, and *Mountania Lodge* (☎ 56237) which is more expensive. South-east of Masinagudi and in Bokkapuram (five km from Masinagudi) there are several much better options.

Bamboo Banks (☎ 56222), is 1.5km from Masinagudi down a signposted turn-off to the right. It's one of the region's oldest private lodges and is very much a family affair – two of the six rooms are actually inside the family home. Rooms cost Rs 700/820, and a buffet lunch/dinner is Rs 160/200.

Blue Valley Resorts (☎ 56244), Bokkapuram, has well-appointed cottages from Rs 625 and all have a small terrace with a view of the mountains. The restaurant offers à la carte Indian and Continental food.

Jungle Hut (☎ 56240) is 500m further down the same dirt road. This family-run

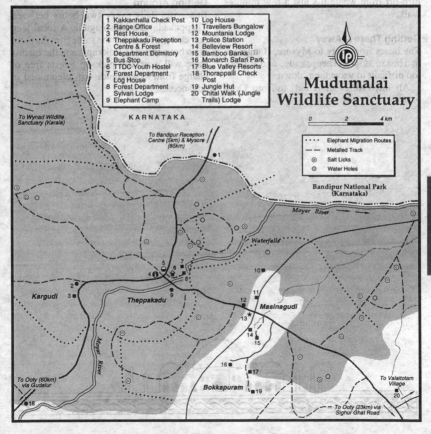

1 Kakkanhalla Check Post
2 Range Office
3 Rest House
4 Theppakadu Reception Centre & Forest Department Dormitory
5 Bus Stop
6 TTDC Youth Hostel
7 Forest Department Log House
8 Forest Department Sylvan Lodge
9 Elephant Camp
10 Log House
11 Travellers Bungalow
12 Mountania Lodge
13 Police Station
14 Belleview Resort
15 Bamboo Banks
16 Monarch Safari Park
17 Blue Valley Resorts
18 Thorappalli Check Post
19 Jungle Hut
20 Chital Walk (Jungle Trails) Lodge

Mudumalai Wildlife Sanctuary

0   2   4 km

To Wynad Wildlife Sanctuary (Kerala)

KARNATAKA

To Bandipur Reception Centre (5km) & Mysore (85km)

Bandipur National Park (Karnataka)

Moyar River

•••• Elephant Migration Routes
– – – Metalled Track
⊚ Salt Licks
◎ Water Holes

Waterfalls

Kargudi

Theppakadu

Masinagudi

Moyar River

To Ooty (60km) via Gudalur

Bokkapuram

To Ooty (23km) via Sighur Ghat Road

To Valaitotam Village

TAMIL NADU

place has 12 rooms in three bungalows and charges Rs 600/800. All meals, except breakfast, must be ordered in advance.

Monarch Safari Park (☎ 56243) is over the hill from Jungle Hut. Built by a Bengali movie star, this place has stilt cottages, all with TV, and exudes a very contrived atmosphere. Singles/doubles are Rs 700/900 and à la carte meals are available.

Chital Walk (Jungle Trails) Lodge (☎ 56256), eight km east of Masinagudi, is a good place if you have a keen interest in wildlife. It offers doubles at Rs 400 and good meals are available. The Sighur Ghat buses to/from Ooty can drop you at the Valaitotam turn-off from where it's just a few minutes walk.

Getting There & Away
The buses from Ooty to Mysore, Bangalore or Hassan stop at Theppakadu, and it's not too difficult to wave them down.

An interesting 'short cut' to/from Ooty (36km, 1½ hours) involves taking one of the small government buses which make the trip up (or down) the tortuous Sighur Ghat road. The bends are so tight and the gradient so steep that large buses can't use it. In fact, there's a sign on the road leaving Masinagudi warning that 'you will have to strain your vehicle much to reach Ooty'. Therefore most buses take the longer route via Gudalur which is equally interesting but not quite as steep (67km, 2½ hours).

You can also visit the sanctuary on tours from Ooty, but you're likely to see nothing more than tame elephants.

Getting Around
Buses run daily every two hours between Theppakadu and Masinagudi. A local jeep taxi charges Rs 50 for the same trip. As there is no bus service to Bokkapuram, the resorts there will generally pick up guests free of charge from Masinagudi – if telephoned in advance.

Andaman & Nicobar Islands

This string of over 300 richly forested tropical islands in the Bay of Bengal lies between India and Myanmar (Burma) and stretches almost to the tip of Sumatra. Ethnically, the islands are not part of India, and until fairly recently, they were inhabited only by indigenous tribal people.

The majority of the Andaman & Nicobar Islands are uninhabited. Most are surrounded by coral reefs, and have white sandy beaches and incredibly clear water – the perfect tropical paradise. This is an excellent place for snorkelling and scuba diving, and several dive centres have opened recently. An extension to the runway at Port Blair Airport should be completed before the year 2000. Until then, however, the islands will continue to be protected from mass tourism.

While Indian tourists may roam freely, foreigners are constrained by a 30 day permit allowing travel on only some Andaman islands; foreigners are not allowed to visit any islands in the Nicobar group. The tourist office says this is for our own protection ('some of the tribal people are very aggressive'), but the naval base here may have more to do with it. The government is certainly trying to promote the Andamans as a tourist destination so it's worth checking to see if the permit situation has been relaxed – several more areas were opened in 1997. There's even talk of a new air route between here and Bangkok (only 350km from Port Blair), but this will not happen until the airport extension is completed.

History

Very little of the early history of the Andaman & Nicobar Islands is known, but Marco Polo was among the first western visitors. In the early 18th century, the islands were the base of the Maratha admiral Kanhoji Angre, whose navy harassed and frequently captured British, Dutch and Portuguese merchant vessels. In 1713, Angre even managed to capture the yacht of the British governor of

Bombay, releasing it only after delivery of a ransom of powder and shot. Though attacked by the British and, later, by a combined British/Portuguese naval task force, Angre remained undefeated until his death in 1729.

The islands were finally annexed by the British in the 19th century and used as a penal colony for Indian freedom fighters. Construction of the notorious 'cellular jail'

ANDAMAN & NICOBAR ISLANDS AT A GLANCE

Population: 340,000
Area: 824 sq km on 319 islands
Capital: Port Blair
Main Languages: Hindi, Bengali, Tamil & tribal languages
Literacy Rate: 73%
Best Time to Go: mid-November to early April

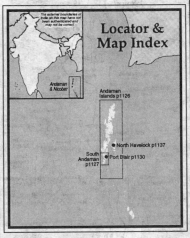

Highlights

- Island hopping
- Deserted beaches
- Superb snorkelling
- Dive centres offering PADI courses

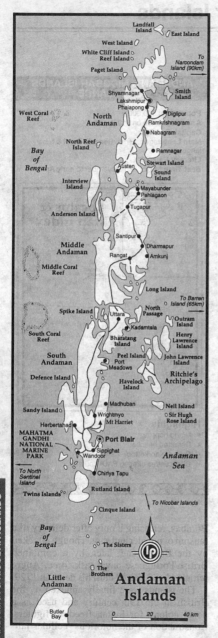

Andaman & Nicobar Islands

Andaman Islands

Landfall Island
East Island
West Island
White Cliff Island
Reef Island
Paget Island
To Narcondam Island (90km)
Shyamnagar
Lakshmipur
Phalapong
Smith Island
Diglipur
North Andaman
Ramkrishnagram
Nabagram
West Coral Reef
North Reef Island
Ramnagar
Bay of Bengal
Austen
Stewart Island
Sound Island
Interview Island
Mayabunder
Pahlagaon
Anderson Island
Tugapur
Santipur
Middle Andaman
Dharmapur
Rangat
Amkunj
Middle Coral Reef
Long Island
To Barren Island (65km)
Spike Island
North Passage
Uttara
Outram Island
Kadamtala
Henry Lawrence Island
South Coral Reef
Bharatang Island
Peel Island
Port Meadows
John Lawrence Island
South Andaman
Ritchie's Archipelago
Defence Island
Havelock Island
Sandy Island
Madhuban
Nell Island
Wrightmyo
Sir Hugh Rose Island
Herbertabad
Mt Harriet
MAHATMA GANDHI NATIONAL MARINE PARK
Port Blair
Sippighat
Wandoor
Andaman Sea
To North Sentinel Island
Chiriya Tapu
Twins Islands
Rutland Island
To Nicobar Islands
Cinque Island
Bay of Bengal
The Sisters
Little Andaman
The Brothers
Butler Bay
0   20   40 km

began in the last decade of the 19th century and was finished in 1908. Many of the jail's inmates were executed, either judicially or clandestinely. During WWII, the islands were occupied for a time by the Japanese, but they were not welcomed as liberators and local tribes initiated guerrilla activities against them. The islands were incorporated into the Indian Union when independence came to India in 1947.

In an effort to develop the islands economically, the government has disregarded the needs and land rights of the tribes and has encouraged massive transmigration from the mainland – mainly of Tamils expelled from Sri Lanka. The population has increased from 50,000 to over 300,000 in just 20 years, and the indigenous island cultures are being swamped. It's not only the people who have suffered in the name of 'development': vast tracts of forest were felled in the 1960s and 70s. There has been some replanting of the land with 'economic' timber like teak, but much of it has been turned into rubber plantations.

The islands are administered as a Union Territory, although the people are currently campaigning for statehood and greater control of the way their islands are managed. At present, administrators fly out from Delhi on a two-year 'hardship' posting, make a few nominal changes in the name of progress and fly home. Some of these hare-brained schemes have included a velodrome (one of only four in India), a high-tech swimming pool (still empty) and the Grand Trunk Rd (dubbed the Road to Nowhere, cutting through a tribal reserve and linking destinations already well served by sea). The islands may look like paradise to the visitor but they can be a frustrating place to live and work.

Climate

There is little seasonal variation in the climate. Continuous sea breezes keep temperatures within the 23°C to 31°C range and the humidity at around 80% all year. The south-west monsoons come to the islands between mid-May and October, and the north-east monsoons between November and January. The best time to visit is between mid-November and early April. December and the early part of January are the high seasons.

Environment & Tourism

The Indian government continues to destructively mismanage both the tribal people and the unique ecology of the Andaman & Nicobar Islands.

The major issues which need to be addressed are the rights and privacy of the indigenous tribes, and the development of controlled timber farming to halt forest clearing.

Tourism may have a positive role to play in all this. There are over 250 uninhabited islands in this area, most with superb beaches and coral reefs ideal for divers. Looking to the Maldives, where a few uninhabited islands have been developed exclusively for tourism, the Indian government is considering following the same example. This could compensate for the earnings lost from reduced tree-felling and would place a value-tag on the preservation of the environment. Anything would be preferable to the mass deforestation and decimation of tribes that is happening now.

Permits

Foreigners need a permit to visit the Andaman Islands. (The Nicobar Islands are off limits to non-Indian tourists.) The permit allows foreigners to stay in South Andaman, Middle Andaman, Little Andaman (tribal reserves on these islands are out of bounds), Bharatang, North Passage, Neil, Havelock and Long islands. On North Andaman foreigners may stay only in Diglipur.

Day trips are permitted to Ross, Viper, Cinque, Narcondum, Interview, Brother and Sister islands, but currently there are regular boats only to Ross and Viper islands. Boats are allowed to stop at volcanic Barren Island, but disembarkation is not allowed and, as yet, there are no regular services. All the islands of the Mahatma Gandhi National Marine Park are open except Boat, Hobday, Twin, Tarmugli, Malay and Pluto.

The permit is valid for up to 30 days. If

you have a good excuse you might be able to get a two or three-day extension, but nothing longer than that.

Permits are issued at the airport in Port Blair. If you arrive with an unconfirmed return flight, you'll probably initially be given a permit of only 10 to 15 days, but this can be extended to allow a 30 day stay. Travellers arriving by ship are usually required to obtain a permit before being issued with a ticket. The permit is available from the Foreigners' Registration Office in either Chennai (Madras) or Calcutta (allow a couple of hours), or from any Indian embassy overseas.

If you arrive here by ship, you must immediately report to the deputy superintendent of police in Port Blair (opposite the Ananda Restaurant in Aberdeen Bazaar) or when departing you could have problems proving that you've not been here longer than 30 days. Your permit will be stamped again when you depart.

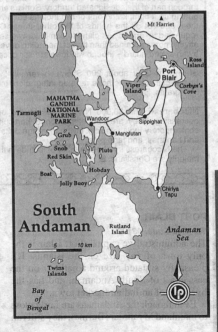

Tribal People

The islands' indigenous tribal people are victims of the Indian government's continuing policy of colonisation and development. They now constitute less than 10% of the present population and, in most cases, their numbers are falling. The negroid Onge, Sentinelese, Andamanese and Jarawa are all resident in the Andaman Islands. The group on the Nicobar Islands is of Mongoloid descent, and includes the Shompen and Nicobarese.

Onge An anthropological study made in the 1970s suggested that the Onge were declining because they were severely demoralised by loss of territory. Two-thirds of the Onges' island of Little Andaman was taken over by the Forest Department and 'settled' in 1977. The 100 or so remaining members of the Onge tribe are confined to a 100 sq km reserve at Dugong Creek. The Indian government has allowed further development – including the building of roads, jetties and a match factory – and even built tin huts to house these nomadic hunter-gathers.

Sentinelese The Sentinelese, unlike the other tribes in these islands, have consistently repulsed any attempts by outsiders to make contact with them. Every few years, contact parties arrive on the beaches of North Sentinel Island with gifts of coconuts, bananas, pigs and red plastic buckets, only to be showered with arrows. About 120 Sentinelese remain, and North Sentinel Island is their exclusive territory. It's almost as if they understand that their only hope of survival is by avoiding contact with the outside world.

Andamanese Numbering only 30 people, it seems impossible that the Andamanese can escape extinction. There were almost 5000 Andamanese when the British arrived in the mid-19th century. Their friendliness to the colonisers was their undoing and, by the end of the century, most of the population had been swept away by measles, syphilis and influenza epidemics. Their decline continues, although they've now been resettled on tiny Strait Island.

Jarawa The 250 remaining Jarawa occupy the 750 sq km reserve on South and Middle Andaman Islands. Around them, forest clearance continues at a horrific rate and the Andamans Trunk Rd runs through part of their designated territory. Settlers are encroaching on their reserve, but the Jarawa are putting up a fight, killing one or two Indians each year. In 1996 they caught five loggers, killed two of them and cut off the hands of the other three. Considering that in 1953 the Chief Commissioner requested an armed sea plane to bomb Jarawa settlements, the Jarawas' response seems comparatively more restrained than that of the Indian government. All Trunk Rd buses are now accompanied by an armed guard – though windows are still occasionally shattered by Jarawa arrows.

Shompen Only about 200 Shompen remain living in the forests on Great Nicobar. They are hunter-gatherers who have resisted integration, tending to shy away from areas occupied by Indian immigrants.

Nicobarese The 30,000 Nicobarese are the only indigenous people whose numbers are not decreasing. They are fair-complexioned horticulturalists who have been partly assimilated into contemporary Indian society. Living in village units led by a headman, they cultivate coconuts, yams and bananas, and farm pigs.

The Nicobarese inhabit a number of islands in the Nicobar group, centred on Car Nicobar, and the majority are Christians. ∎

PORT BLAIR

Tel Area Code: 03192

The administrative capital, Port Blair is the only town of any size on the islands. It's pleasantly situated around a harbour on the east coast of South Andaman, and has the lively air of an Indian market town.

Even though the Andamans are fairly close to mainland Myanmar (Burma), they still run on Indian time. This means that it's dark by 6 pm and light by 4 am.

Orientation

The town is spread over a couple of hills, but most of the hotels, the bus terminal, passenger dock and Shipping Corporation of India office are in the main bazaar area, known as Aberdeen Bazaar. The airport is a few km south of town, and the nearest beach is at Corbyn's Cove, seven km south of Aberdeen Bazaar.

Information

Tourist Offices For up-to-date information on places in the Andamans now open to foreigners, visit the very helpful Government of India tourist office (☎ 21006). Open weekdays only, from 8.30 am to 5 pm, it's above Super Shoppe, a short distance from the centre of town.

The Andaman & Nicobar tourist office (☎ 20694) is diagonally opposite Indian Airlines.

The library, near the GPO, has a small collection of books on the history, geography, flora & fauna, and tribal people of the islands. The reference section is on the 1st floor.

Money Travellers cheques and cash can be exchanged (very slowly) at the State Bank of India. It opens and closes an hour earlier than is usual on the mainland (9 am to 1 pm during the week and 9 to 11 am on Saturday). Most visitors use the efficient service at Island Travels, near Sampat Lodge, where you can change money daily between 2 and 4 pm (sometimes until 6 pm) except Sunday. The larger hotels also have foreign exchange facilities. Note that there's currently nowhere to get credit card advances on the islands.

Post & Telecommunications The GPO is 750m south of Aberdeen Bazaar. The cheapest place to send and receive faxes is at the telegraph office (fax 21318) next door, open from 10 am to 5 pm, Monday to Saturday. International telephone calls can be made from here, as well as from a number of places in Aberdeen Bazaar.

Cellular Jail National Memorial

Built by the British at the beginning of this century, the cellular jail is now a major tourist attraction, preserved as a shrine to India's freedom fighters. It originally consisted of seven wings radiating from a central tower, but only three remain today. It still gives a fair impression of the terrible conditions in which the detainees were incarcerated. It's open daily from 9 am to noon and 2 to 5 pm; there's no entry charge.

If it's running again, don't miss the excellent sound & light show. The English-language show (Rs 10) was held daily except Sunday at 7 pm.

Samudrika Marine Museum

Run by the navy, this interesting museum is divided into five galleries covering the history and geography of the islands, their people, marine life and archaeology. There are also good displays of shells and coral, though the museum could do with a few signs informing visitors how slowly coral grows and how easily it is damaged. It's open Tuesday to Sunday from 9 am to noon and 2 to 5.30 pm; entry is Rs 5.

Fisheries Museum

This interesting aquarium and museum displays some of the 350 species found in the Andaman Sea; at the time of writing, however, it was closed for major renovations.

Anthropological Museum

This small museum has displays of tools, dress and photographs of the indigenous tribes. The captions to some of the photos are poignant but telling. 'Why don't you leave us alone?' runs the caption under a photo of some Sentinelese people. The museum is open from 9 am to noon and 1 to 4 pm daily except Sunday; there's no entry charge.

Mini Zoo & Forest Museum

Over 200 indigenous animal species are found nowhere in the world but here. Some can be seen at the mini zoo, including the Nicobar pigeon and Andaman pig. The zoo's saltwater-crocodile breeding programme has been very successful and many have been returned to the wild. Fortunately, their natural habitat is dense mangrove swamps, and there have been no reports locally of crocodiles attacking swimmers. The zoo is open from 8 am to 5 pm Tuesday to Sunday; entry is Rs 0.50.

ANDAMAN & NICOBAR ISLANDS

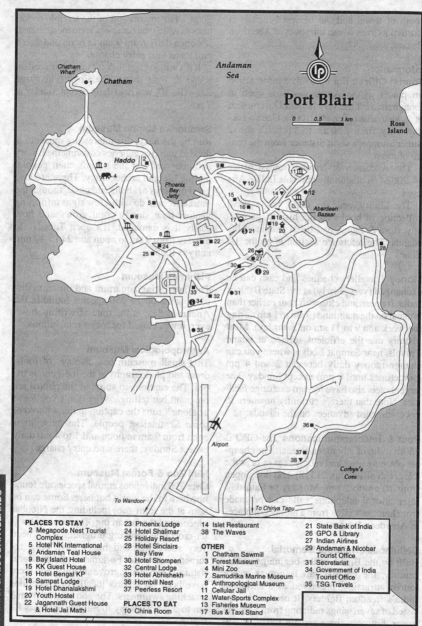

Andaman Sea

Chatham Wharf
● 1 **Chatham**

Haddo

Phoenix Bay Jetty

Port Blair

0   0.5   1 km

Ross Island

Abardeen Bazaar

Corbyn's Cove

Airport

To Wandoor

To Chiriya Tapu

PLACES TO STAY
2 Megapode Nest Tourist Complex
5 Hotel NK International
6 Andaman Teal House
9 Bay Island Hotel
15 KK Guest House
16 Hotel Bengal KP
18 Sampat Lodge
19 Hotel Dhanalakshmi
20 Youth Hostel
22 Jagannath Guest House & Hotel Jai Mathi

23 Phoenix Lodge
24 Hotel Shalimar
25 Holiday Resort
28 Hotel Sinclairs Bay View
30 Hotel Shompen
32 Central Lodge
33 Hotel Abhishekh
36 Hornbill Nest
37 Peerless Resort

PLACES TO EAT
10 China Room

14 Islet Restaurant
38 The Waves

OTHER
1 Chatham Sawmill
3 Forest Museum
4 Mini Zoo
7 Samudrika Marine Museum
8 Anthropological Museum
11 Cellular Jail
12 Water-Sports Complex
13 Fisheries Museum
17 Bus & Taxi Stand

21 State Bank of India
26 GPO & Library
27 Indian Airlines
29 Andaman & Nicobar Tourist Office
31 Secretariat
34 Government of India Tourist Office
35 TSG Travels

ANDAMAN & NICOBAR ISLANDS

Nearby is the small Forest Museum, which has a display of locally-grown woods, including padauk, which has both light and dark colours occurring in the same tree. Elephants are still used at some of the lumber camps. The museum is open from 8 am to noon and 2.30 to 5 pm daily except Sunday; entry is free.

Chatham Sawmill

It's possible to visit the sawmill, seasoning chambers and furniture workshop of one of Asia's largest wood processors, on the island of Chatham, five km north-west of Aberdeen Bazaar. As the government tourist literature enthuses, you'll see 'some of the rare species of tropical timber like padauk'. If the timbers are acknowledged as rare, you wonder what they're doing in a sawmill. The sawmill is open from 6.30 am to 2.30 pm daily except Sunday.

Water-Sports Complex

At the water-sports complex, by the Fisheries Museum, you can rent rowboats, windsurfing equipment and sailing dinghies. Water-skiing costs Rs 50 for 15 minutes; windsurfing is Rs 30 for half an hour. You can rent snorkels here for Rs 15 per hour, but you can't take them anywhere else.

Organised Tours

A range of tours are offered by A&N Tourism at Andaman Teal House (☎ 20642); Shompen Travels (☎ 20360) in the Hotel Shompen; Island Travels (☎ 21358) in Aberdeen Bazaar; and the larger hotels. However, apart from visits to Jolly Buoy, Red Skin and Cinque islands, independent sightseeing is easy enough.

Every afternoon at 3 pm, a boat leaves from the Phoenix Bay jetty for a 1½ hour harbour cruise. The trip costs Rs 20 and stops briefly at Viper Island, where the remains of the gallows tower built by the British still stand.

Places to Stay

There are currently no additional taxes on hotel prices. Watch for checkout times, though, most of which are around 7 am.

Since all the places to stay are quite spread out, it's worth hiring a bicycle or scooter to get around.

Places to Stay – bottom end

The *Youth Hostel* has dorm beds for Rs 20 (Rs 40 for nonmembers) and a few double rooms. There's a good restaurant for residents.

Central Lodge (☎ 21632), Middle Point, is a basic wooden building set back from the road. It's the most popular of the cheapies, with rooms from Rs 40/60 with common bath and Rs 80 for a double with bath attached. You can camp in the garden for Rs 20.

Sampat Lodge, Aberdeen Bazaar, is basic but friendly with rooms for Rs 40/80. The nearby *KK Guest House* is run-down and has tiny rooms for Rs 30/60. *Hotel Bengal KP* charges Rs 70/120/170 for singles/doubles/triples with attached bathrooms.

Jagannath Guest House (☎ 20148) is a good choice, with spotless rooms for Rs 80/125/200, all with attached bathroom. Run by a friendly manager, it's convenient for the bus terminal and Phoenix Bay jetty.

Hotel Jai Mathi (☎ 30836), near Jagannath Guest House but not quite so good, is well priced at Rs 75/100 for rooms with bathroom attached.

Places to Stay – middle

Most of the places in the mid-range bracket can usually be bargained down if they're not full.

Holiday Resort (☎ 30516), Prem Nagar, is fairly new, very clean and a good place to stay. Rooms are Rs 200/280, or Rs 300/360 with air-con; all rooms have bathroom attached.

Hotel Abhishekh (☎ 21565) is quite good and has clean rooms with attached bathroom for Rs 200/250/310; more for air-con. It has its own restaurant and bar but service is painfully slow.

Hotel Shalimar (☎ 21963) is on the road to Haddo. The advertised price for rooms is Rs 150/190/250 with attached bathroom, Rs

300 for an air-con double, but they might offer you a discount.

Hotel Dhanalakshmi (☎ 21953), right in Aberdeen Bazaar, has rooms with bathroom attached for a high Rs 200/300, or Rs 400/500 with air-con (the rooms at the back are the quietest). It also has a restaurant.

Hotel Shompen (☎ 20360) is overpriced at the quoted rate of Rs 350 or Rs 750 with air-con. The hotel has a restaurant and a travel agency.

Hotel NK International (☎ 20113) is convenient for the Phoenix Bay jetty, though not in a particularly attractive location. Rooms cost Rs 200/300, or Rs 300/400 with air-con.

Hornbill Nest Yatri Niwas (☎ 20018) is run by A&N Tourism. It's about one km north of Corbyn's Cove and has sea views. This is an excellent location but the place is not particularly well run. Rooms with two/four/six beds and attached bath are Rs 250/300/400. Mosquito nets are provided. There's a basic restaurant but some dishes need to be ordered in advance.

Andaman Teal House (☎ 20642) is also run by the tourist office, but is poorly located on the road to Haddo. Doubles with attached bath cost Rs 250, or Rs 400 with air-con.

Megapode Nest Tourist Complex (☎ 20207) at Haddo, on the hill above the bay, is good value at Rs 500 for a large double with attached bath, air-con and Star TV. For upmarket, air-con accommodation, the **Nicobari Cottages**, part of the same complex, are recommended at Rs 800 for a double with attached bath and tub. There's a good restaurant and great views over the bay.

Places to Stay – top end

Hotel Sinclairs Bay View (☎ 21159; fax 20038) is on the road towards Corbyn's Cove. All rooms have a sea view and cost Rs 950/1200, or Rs 1100/1400 with air-con. Although it's right on the coast there's no beach. It's a pleasant place, however, and the restaurant does excellent Indian dishes. The Samudra Diving Centre is based here.

Peerless Resort (☎ 21462; fax 21463) at Corbyn's Cove is excellently located in a very quiet part of the island, just across the road from the beach. Air-con rooms in the main block are Rs 1180/2000; rooms in the very pleasant air-con cottages cost Rs 1800/2500; discounts are negotiable outside the peak season. There's a bar, restaurant, foreign exchange facilities and a boat for hire.

Bay Island Hotel (☎ 20881; fax 21389), which has sea views, is the top hotel in Port Blair. The rooms are a little overpriced at Rs 2900/4300 – although this does include all meals. No singles are available in December and January. There's an excellent restaurant and an open-air bar which is good for a quiet beer. This beautifully designed hotel is to be commended for its attempts at eco-tourism. The swimming pool is filled with sea water, and guests are reminded not to waste water in bathrooms or damage coral when swimming. At the bottom of the hill, a private pier with a 'human aquarium' extends into the bay. The aquarium enables visitors to climb down into a glass-windowed chamber to view the multicoloured fish that congregate here to be fed.

Places to Eat

Most of the hotels have restaurants, but you may have to order seafood in advance. There are numerous small restaurants in Aberdeen Bazaar.

Ananda Restaurant, just south of Hotel Dhanalakshmi, is a good place with thalis for Rs 15, chicken masala for Rs 25 and some tandoori dishes. The air-con dining room is only Rs 1 extra.

Dhanalakshmi Restaurant, in the hotel of the same name, stays open late; main dishes are around Rs 40.

Delhi Cafeteria, opposite Mountbatten Talkies (near the Hotel Shompen), is a basic place that does good tandoori chicken dishes and excellent naan.

New India Cafe, below Hotel Jai Mathi, does thalis for Rs 15, coconut chicken for Rs 32 and prawn dishes from Rs 34 to Rs 69. It's open early for breakfast and the coffee's good.

Islet Restaurant, near the cellular jail, offers tasty veg and non-veg dishes, and it has views of the bay. If you don't like your food heavily spiced, they'll oblige. *New Lighthouse Restaurant*, beside the Fisheries Museum, has a pleasantly cool dining area upstairs and does good fish dishes – prices vary according to the size of the fish. Their 'Fish 65' costs Rs 35. *The Waves*, on Corbyn's Cove, is a good place for a drink or a meal, with tables under the coconut palms. The garlic chicken is excellent and they also do good veg dishes. A beer costs Rs 50.

The *China Room* (☎ 30759), run by a delightful Burmese couple, is an excellent place to eat. It's really just a small outdoor area and the front room of their house, but the quality of the seafood they serve is superb. Lemon fish is Rs 60, garlic prawns Rs 80 and, given 24 hours notice, you can have Szechuan-style lobster for Rs 250 or Peking duck for Rs 200.

Mandalay Restaurant at the Bay Island Hotel is the other place for a splurge. The open-air dining area catches the breeze and has pleasant views over the bay. Main dishes are around Rs 100, prawns cost Rs 150 and a beer is Rs 100. Friendly minah birds looking for scraps descend on tables as diners leave.

Getting There & Away

Air Indian Airlines (☎ 21108) has flights from Calcutta (US$175) on Monday, Wednesday and Friday to Port Blair, continuing on to Chennai (US$175). On Tuesday, Thursday and Saturday, flights run from Chennai to Port Blair, then on to Calcutta. The 25% youth discount is applicable on these fares. The flights can also be included on the US$500/750, two/three-week flight pass. The two-hour flights leave the mainland soon after dawn.

The Indian Airlines office is round the corner from the GPO. The staff here are very friendly and the office has a computer link. Flights can be heavily booked and you need to have a confirmed ticket to be sure of a seat; passengers on waiting lists usually miss out. The office is open from 9 am to 1 pm, and 2 to 4 pm daily except Sunday.

Train There's a railway out-agency at the Secretariat.

Boat There are usually two to four sailings a month between Port Blair and Chennai or Calcutta on vessels operated by the Shipping Corporation of India (SCI). There's also a monthly sailing on the route between Visakhapatnam (Andhra Pradesh) and Port Blair. Contact SCI for the latest information on the erratic schedules. It's better to arrange tickets for the journey from Port Blair back to the mainland in Calcutta or Chennai.

The trip takes three to four days on the Chennai route, and sometimes one day longer on the Calcutta route. Foreigners usually have to travel 2nd class (four or six-berth), 1st class (two or four-berth) or deluxe (two-berth). Tickets cost Rs 2243/2852/3450 per berth. Some ships have an air-con dorm for Rs 1449. If you can get a ticket for bunk class, it costs Rs 955. Prices are the same for both the Calcutta and Chennai routes. Food costs around Rs 100 per day and is usually thalis for breakfast, lunch and dinner, so you will want to bring something (fruit in particular) if you feel the need to supplement this boring diet.

The SCI may insist that you have a permit before selling you a ticket. However, if you do get your permit in advance, you must still register with the deputy superintendent of police on arrival in Port Blair.

The Port Blair SCI office for the Calcutta boat is in Aberdeen Bazaar (☎ 21347), across the road from the Hotel Dhanalakshmi. For the Chennai boat, you may be directed to the office at Phoenix Bay. Bookings for the Calcutta boat open only a few days before the boat arrives; for the Chennai boat, you can book further in advance.

In Calcutta, the SCI office (☎ 284 2354) is on the 1st floor at 13 Strand Rd. In Chennai, the SCI (☎ 522 6873) is at Jawahar Building, Rajaji Salai (opposite the Customs House). In Visakhapatnam, the office where you can find out if this route is operating is AV Bhanoji (☎ 56266), opposite the main gate at the port. Two photos and a lot of form-filling and trudging backwards and forwards between offices is required. You'll need to be organised, because bookings close four days before sailing.

Getting Around

Port Blair has numerous taxis, one auto-rickshaw and no cycle-rickshaws. Taxis have meters (and charts, since the meters need recalibrating) but drivers need a lot of persuasion to use them. From the airport, the trip to Aberdeen Bazaar should cost Rs 30 to Rs 40, and a little less to Corbyn's Cove; Rs 50 is what drivers quote for most local trips. Some of the hotels offer their guests free transport to and from the airport; the tourist office airport bus will take you to any hotel in Port Blair for Rs 15.

From the bus stand in Port Blair, there are regular departures to Wandoor (Rs 5.50, 1½ hours). See the sections below for other bus information.

It's best to have your own transport to explore parts of the island. You can hire bicycles in Aberdeen Bazaar for Rs 20 per day. An even better way to get around is by moped or motorcycle. Roads are not bad and certainly very quiet. TSG Travels (☎ 20894) rents motorcycles (Suzuki 100s) and scooters for Rs 120 per day. A deposit of Rs 500 is required. Jagannath Guest House also has a few motorcycles for hire (Rs 120).

Private boats can be hired from the tour operators but charges are high – around Rs 10,000 per day.

AROUND PORT BLAIR
Mt Harriet & Madhuban

Mt Harriet (365m) is across the inlet, north of Port Blair. There's a nature trail up to the top and, with permission from the Forest Department, it may be possible to stay in the comfortable *Forest Guest House*. To reach Mt Harriet, take the vehicle or passenger ferry from Chatham Wharf to Bamboo Flat (Rs 1, 10 minutes). From there, a road runs seven km along the coast and up to Mt Harriet.

To the north is Mt Harriet National Park and Madhuban, where elephants are sometimes trained for the logging camps. Madhuban is also accessible by boat; the tourist office and travel agencies organise occasional trips.

Ross Island

A couple of km east of Port Blair is Ross Island, chosen by the British for their administrative headquarters. In the early part of this century there would have been manicured lawns leading up to the ballroom, umbrellas round the swimming pool and daily services in the churches, but the place has been deserted since the British left during WWII. Now the jungle has taken over, and peacocks and spotted deer forage among the ruined buildings. On the top of the hill stand the remains of the Anglican church, its tower strangled by roots and vines.

Ross Island is a distinctly eerie and rather sad place, but well worth a visit. There are ferries from Phoenix Bay jetty at 8.30 and 10.30 am, 12.30 and 2 pm daily except on Wednesday. From Ross Island, there are departures at 8.45 and 10.40 am, and 12.40, 2.10 and 4.40 pm. The journey takes 20 minutes and a return ticket costs Rs 13, plus Rs 5 entry fee. You must sign in on arrival at Ross since the island is in the hands of the navy. Visit the museum near the jetty before exploring the island to get an idea of how the place once looked.

Corbyn's Cove

Corbyn's Cove is the nearest beach to Port Blair. It's seven km south of the town and four km east of the airport. There are a couple of places to stay here and a snack bar by the beach.

Nearby Snake Island is surrounded by a coral reef. You can sometimes catch a ride to the island in a fishing boat, but it's inadvisable to swim out to it because of the strong current.

It's a long, though pleasant, cliff-top walk to Corbyn's Cove from Port Blair. Taxis cost about Rs 40 each way.

Sippighat Farm

On the road to Wandoor, 15km from Port Blair, is the government experimental farm, where tour groups often stop. New types of spices, such as cinnamon, pepper, nutmeg and cloves, are being tested here.

Wandoor

The Mahatma Gandhi National Marine Park at Wandoor covers 280 sq km and comprises 15 islands. The diverse scenery includes mangrove creeks, tropical rainforest and reefs supporting 50 types of coral. Boats leave from Wandoor village, which is 29km southwest of Port Blair, at around 10 am daily (except Monday) for visits to Jolly Buoy or Red Skin islands. Although it's well worth going along to see the coral (they usually have a few snorkels for hire), only a couple of hours are spent at the islands. It is very frustrating to get to such a stunningly beautiful place only to have to turn around and leave so soon. On Jolly Buoy, for the best coral go to the left of the landing spot, not to the right as directed. Watch out for powerful currents.

The trip costs Rs 75 (Rs 50 in the low season when boats go only as far as Red Skin). An entry permit (Rs 10) for the park must first be purchased at the kiosk by the jetty.

You can reach Wandoor by bus from Port Blair (1½ hours, Rs 5.50) or by joining a tour. There are a number of good, sandy beaches at Wandoor and some excellent snorkelling, but you should take care not to walk on the coral exposed at low tide. Unfortunately, part of this reef has already been damaged.

Snorkelling & Diving

Surrounded by coral reefs and incredibly clear water, the Andaman Islands offer some of the best snorkelling and diving in the world. However, organised diving is still very much in its infancy here and dive centres open and close each year. Sensing that there might be money to be made from this sport, the government is keen to be involved. Its initial foray, which offered cut-price PADI courses from a centre at Wandoor, folded in 1995 but their new dive school may open in late 1997. Their charges will probably be similar to those offered by the centres below.

At present the choice is between three dive centres. **Samudra** (☎ 21159, 20937; fax 20038) is very well run and based in an old Japanese bunker at the Hotel Sinclairs Bay View. They charge Rs 2000 for a couple of dives in the Port Blair area or Rs 3200 beyond (Wandoor etc). If you wish to dive in the national park itself there's an additional Rs 1000 charge (payable directly to the park). They offer the PADI Open Water course (four to five days) for Rs 14,000, and the advanced PADI course for Rs 8000. These courses lead to internationally recognised certification. They also offer a day's 'Discover Scuba Diving' for Rs 2500.

Prices are similar at the other professional outfit, **Port Blair Underwater** (☎ 85389, 21358; fax (040) 339 2718), which is also PADI registered. They are based at the Peerless Resort at Corbyn's Cove.

Slightly cheaper rates are available at **Andaman Adventure Sports** (☎ /fax 30295), near the Anthropological Museum in Port Blair. They have some reasonable equipment and the owner is quite experienced, but as he's not PADI registered (or recognised by any other diving organisation) this place is probably best only if you really know what you're doing.

You can rent snorkels from tour operators and hotels but these are expensive (around Rs 70 per day) and often substandard – it's best to bring your own. The Jagannath Guest House rents snorkels for Rs 40.

Considerations for Responsible Diving

- Avoid touching living marine organisms. Some can be damaged by even the gentlest contact. Never stand on coral, even if it looks solid and robust. Some of the coral off Wandoor Beach has already been damaged by careless tourists.
- Be conscious of your fins. Even without contact the surge from heavy fin strokes near the reef can cause damage.
- Practise and maintain proper buoyancy control. Major damage can be done by divers descending too fast and colliding with the reef.
- Resist the temptation to collect or buy corals or shells.
- Dispose of your rubbish sensibly, including litter you find.
- Minimise your disturbance of marine animals.

Chiriya Tapu

Thirty km south of Port Blair is Chiriya Tapu, a tiny fishing village with beaches and mangroves. It's possible to arrange boats from here to Cinque Island. There's a beach a couple of km south of Chiriya Tapu which has some of the best snorkelling in the area. There's a bus to the village every two hours from Port Blair (1½ hours, Rs 5.50).

OTHER ISLANDS

The A&N Tourism Department has targeted half a dozen beaches for development but the tourist infrastructure is currently very limited and you shouldn't expect too much. In 1997 Bharatang (between South and Middle Andaman) and nearby North Passage were added to the list of islands fully open to visitors. Narcondam, Interview, Brother and Sister islands have just been opened for day visits only, but currently no regular boats visit these places. It's possible to charter a boat to visit volcanic Barren Island but disembarkation is not allowed.

Until the tourist complexes on the islands to be developed are built, the only other accommodation is in Andaman PWD (APWD) or Forest Guest Houses (typically Rs 60 per bed in a double room). These should be reserved in advance in Port Blair, either at the APWD (near Hotel Shompen) or the Forest Department in Haddo.

Some people bring tents or hammocks (made up by tailors in Aberdeen Bazaar) and camp out on the beaches. In Port Blair, you can rent two-person tents for Rs 40 per day from the Andaman Teal House. Other useful items include a bucket and a large knife. If you do camp, make sure you bury your rubbish. Fires are not allowed so bring a stove and kerosene with you. On the islands, kerosene supplies are usually reserved for locals.

Neil Island

Forty km north-east of Port Blair is Neil Island, which is populated by Bengali settlers. There's excellent snorkelling but some of the coral has been damaged by dynamiting for fish. Beaches are numbered: No 1 beach, a 40 minute walk west of the jetty and village,

is popular with campers who set up hammocks under the trees. There's a well nearby for fresh water. The snorkelling is best around the point at the far end of the beach, where you may also see very large fish. At low tide it's difficult getting over the coral into the water from the beach.

Places to Stay & Eat In the village there's a market, a few shops and a couple of basic restaurants serving dosas, fried fish, veg and rice. They often run out of mineral water and soft drinks.

Hawabill Nest Yatri Niwas offers four-bed rooms for Rs 250 and air-con doubles for Rs 400. Reserve in advance at the A&N tourist office in Port Blair. The *APWD Guest House* has just two rooms.

Getting There & Away On Wednesday and Friday at 6.30 am, ferries leave Phoenix Bay for Neil (three hours, Rs 7/13 for deck/upper class), continuing to Havelock. Occasionally they visit Havelock first.

Havelock Island

Fifty-four km north-east of Port Blair, Havelock covers 100 sq km and is inhabited by Bengali settlers. There are picture-postcard white-sand beaches, turquoise waters and good snorkelling. Although there are coral reefs, it's the marine life here – dolphins, turtles and very large fish – that make it interesting.

Only the northern third of the island is settled, and each village is referred to by a number. Boats dock at the jetty at No 1; the main bazaar is a couple of km south at No 3.

Having your own transport is useful – bring a bike from Port Blair or rent one for Rs 40 per day in No 3 village or from the paan shop outside the entrance to the Dolphin Yatri Niwas. A few scooters (Rs 150) are available from the Narayan paan store in No 3 village. A local bus connects the villages on an hourly circuit and also runs out to No 7 beach. A tourist bus meets the ferry.

Places to Stay & Eat You need to make a reservation in advance at the A&N tourist office in Port Blair to stay in the Dolphin Yatri Niwas or the Tent Resorts.

Dolphin Yatri Niwas Complex offers pleasant accommodation in cottages beside a beautiful secluded beach; there's no snorkelling here. Charges are Rs 200 for an ordinary double, Rs 300 for a deluxe room and Rs 800 for an air-con double, all with bath attached. Good but basic meals are served in the restaurant.

A&N tourism's ***Tent Resort***, beside No 7 beach, has eight roomy tents (twin beds) set up under the trees. They cost Rs 100 for a double and there's a maximum stay of four days. There's a couple of toilets but no washing facilities other than the wells. Basic fish thalis (Rs 25) and drinks (tea, coffee, soft drinks and mineral water) are available. Some people bring their own tents or hammocks and camp by the beach. The police come by occasionally to check that people aren't making fires or stripping off and indulging in 'hippy behaviour'. There's good snorkelling here.

and the idyllic beach stretches for several km. The only drawback is the sandflies, which make sunbathing an impossibility.

A second ***Tent Resort*** opened recently near No 5 beach, and you can use the restaurant at the Dolphin Yatri Niwas if you stay here.

MS Guest House is half a km west of the jetty and has basic rooms with attached bath for Rs 100; Rs 40 for a dorm bed.

Gauranga Lodge is the green wooden building without a sign between villages Nos 1 and 3. It has doubles for Rs 45. The bathroom here contains an Indonesian-style mandi.

Getting There & Away Ferries depart early in the morning usually on Tuesday, Wednesday, Friday and Saturday from the Phoenix Bay harbour in Port Blair. The four-hour journey to Havelock costs Rs 7/13 on the lower/upper deck. The ferries return from Havelock to Port Blair one day later.

Long Island

This little island off the south-east coast of Middle Andaman has one small village and several sandy beaches that are perfect for camping. The only accommodation is the ***Forest Rest House***, although a ***Yatri Niwas*** is planned for Lalaji Bay.

On Wednesday and Saturday, the ferry from Port Blair and Havelock calls at Long Island (eight hours, Rs 9/20 for lower/upper deck) before reaching Rangat. Bicycles are the main form of transport on the island.

Middle Andaman

The Andaman Trunk Rd runs from Port Blair north to Bharatang Island and Middle Andaman, which are linked by frequent ferries. Since this road runs beside Jarawa reserves on the west coasts of South and Middle Andaman, buses carry armed guards. Having lost land to Indian settlers, the Jarawa are hostile to any outsiders and independent travel is inadvisable. If you try to take a motorbike up here you'll probably be stopped at the checkpost about 40km outside Port Blair. There's tourist accommodation in Rangat and Mayabunder, but the entire island is now open to foreigners.

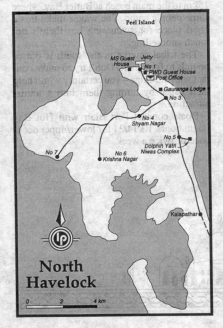

You can get to **Rangat** from Port Blair via the Havelock, Neil or Long island ferries (nine hours, Rs 12/28 for lower/upper deck) or by bus (six hours, Rs 44). There's basic accommodation at the *Hare Krishna Lodge*, and the *PWD Guest House*. A bus runs out to Cuthbert Bay for A&N Tourism's new *Hawksbill Nest* (Rs 75 per bed in a four-bed dorm, Rs 400 for an air-con double). Bookings for the Hawksbill Nest must be made in advance at the tourist office in Port Blair.

Mayabunder, 71km north of Rangat, is linked by the daily bus from Port Blair (nine hours, Rs 55) and also by occasional ferries. There's an 18-bed *APWD Guest House* here. A *Yatri Niwas* is under construction at Karmatang Bay, 10km north-east of Mayabunder, and should be open in late 1997.

North Andaman

Diglipur is the only place on North Andaman where foreigners may spend the night. It's served by a weekly ferry from Port Blair and daily ferries from Mayabunder. There's a 12-bed *APWD Guest House*, and a *Yatri Niwas* is under construction near Kalipur Beach; it's set to open in late 1997. Bookings should be made through the tourist office in Port Blair.

Cinque Island

Uninhabited North and South Cinque are part of the national park south of Wandoor. Surrounded by pristine coral reefs, they are among the most beautiful islands in the Andamans.

Only day visits are allowed and, unless you're going on one of the day trips occasionally organised by travel agents, you need to get permission from the Forest Department. The islands are two hours by boat from Chiriya Tapu or three hours from Phoenix Bay.

Little Andaman

The 100 remaining members of the Onge tribe are confined to a reserve in the south of this island. As the northern part of Little Andaman has been settled, and was opened to foreigners in 1997, time has probably run out for the Onges.

Ferries land at Hut Bay on the east coast. Basic supplies are available in the village two km to the north. Another km north brings you to the new *APWD Guest House*, which is the only accommodation (reserve bookings in Port Blair). Just under two km north of the guest house is the police station where you must register on arrival, then it's about 15km to the main beach at Butler Bay, where some people camp. The waves make this a good place for swimming but there's not much snorkelling.

The tribal reserve in the south is out of bounds to foreigners. Don't try to make contact with the Onge – you certainly won't help their cause by turning them into a tourist attraction.

Boats connect Port Blair with Hut Bay (eight hours, Rs 14/31 for lower/upper deck) once or twice a week.

Glossary

Indian English is full of interesting everyday expressions. Whereas in New York you might get robbed by a mugger, in India it will be a *dacoit* who relieves you of your goods. Politicians may employ strong-arm heavies known in India as *goondas*. There is a plethora of Indian terms for strikes and lock-ins – Indians can have *bandhs, hartaals* and *gheraos*, for example. Then there are all those Indian servants – children get looked after by *ayahs*, your house (and your *godown* or warehouse) is guarded by a *chowkidar*, and when the toilet needs cleaning there is no way your *bearer* is going to do it.

Then there are all the religious terms, the numerous Hindu gods, their attendants, consorts, vehicles and symbols. The multiplicity of religions in India also provides a wide series of terms for temples, shrines, tombs or memorials.

It's surprising how many Indian terms have crept into English usage. We can sit on a *verandah* and drink *chai* (hence 'charlady'), wear *pyjamas* or *sandals* and *dungarees* (which may well be *khaki*), *shampoo* our hair, visit the *jungle*, or worry about protecting our *loot* – they're all Indian words.

The glossary that follows is just a sample of words you may come across during your Indian wanderings. See Food in the Facts for the Visitor chapter for lots more.

abbi – waterfall.

Abhimani – eldest son of Brahma.

Abhimanyu – son of Arjuna.

acha – OK or 'I understand'.

acharya – revered teacher; originally a spiritual guide.

adivasi – tribal person.

agarbathi – incense.

Agasti – legendary sage, highly revered in the south as he is credited with introducing Hinduism as well as with developing the Tamil language.

Agni – fire, a major deity in the *Vedas*; mediator between men and the gods.

ahimsa – discipline of non-violence.

AIR – All India Radio, the national broadcaster.

Amir – Muslim nobleman.

amrita – immortality.

ananda – happiness. Ananda was the name of the Buddha's cousin and favourite disciple.

Andhaka – a 1000-headed demon, killed by Siva.

angrezi – foreigner.

anikut – dam.

anna – a 16th of a rupee; it's no longer legal tender but is occasionally referred to in marketplace parlance. (Eight annas are the equivalent of Rs 0.50.)

Annapurna – form of Durga; worshipped for her power to provide food.

apsaras – heavenly nymphs.

arak – liquor distilled from coconut milk, potatoes or rice.

Aranyani – goddess of forests.

Ardhanari – Siva in half-male, half-female form.

Arishta – A *daitya* (giant) who, having taken the form of a bull, attacked Krishna and was killed by him.

Arjuna – *Mahabharata* hero and military commander who married Krishna's sister (Subhadra), took up arms against and overcame all manner of demons, had the *Bhagavad Gita* related to him by Krishna, led Krishna's funeral ceremony at Dwarka and finally retired to the Himalaya.

Aryan – Sanskrit word for 'noble'; refers to those who migrated from Persia and settled in northern India.

ashram – spiritual community or retreat.

astrology – more than mere entertainment, astrological charts are commonly consulted before any major event, for example marriage, elections, important business trips.

attar – an essential oil made from flowers and used as a base for perfumes.

auto-rickshaw – small, noisy, three-wheeled, motorised contraption for transporting passengers short distances. Found throughout the country, and cheaper than taxis.

Avalokitesvara – one of the Buddha's most important disciples.

avataar – incarnation of a deity, usually Vishnu.

ayah – children's nurse or nanny.

Ayurveda – Indian herbal medicine.

azan – Muslim call to prayer.

baba – religious master, father, and a term of respect.

babu – lower level clerical worker (derogatory).

bagh – garden.

bahadur – brave or chivalrous; honorific title.

baksheesh – tip, bribe or donation.

Balarama – brother of Krishna and viewed by some as the seventh incarnation (avataar) of Vishnu.

bandar – monkey.

bandh – general strike.

banian – T-shirt or undervest.

baniya – moneylender.

banyan – Indian fig tree.

baoli – well, particularly a step-well with landings and galleries, found in Rajasthan and Gujarat.

baradari – summer house.

barra – big, important.

basti – Jain temple.

bazaar – market area. A market town is called a bazaar.

bearer – rather like a butler.

begum – Muslim woman of high rank.

betel – nut of the betel tree; the leaves and nut are mildly intoxicating and are chewed as a stimulant and digestive.

Bhadrakali – another name for Durga.

Bhagavad Gita – Song of the Divine One; Krishna's lessons to Arjuna, the main thrust of which was to emphasise the philosophy of *bhakti* (faith); part of the *Mahabharata*.

Bhairava – the Terrible; refers to the eight incarnation of Siva in his demonic form.

bhakti – surrendering to the gods.

bhang – dried leaves and flowering shoots of the marijuana plant.

bhang lassi – a blend of lassi with bhang (a drink with a kick).

Bharat – Hindi for India.

Bharata – half-brother of Rama; ruled for Rama while the latter was in exile.

bhavan – house, building.

Bhima – another *Mahabharata* hero, brother of Hanuman and renowned for his great strength.

bhisti (bheesti) – water carrier.

bhojnalya – simple eatery.

bidi (beedi) – small, hand-rolled cigarette; really just a rolled-up leaf.

bindi – forehead mark.

black money – undeclared, untaxed money. There's lots of it in India.

Bodhisattva – one who has almost reached nirvana, but who renounces it in order to help others attain it; literally 'one whose essence is perfected wisdom'.

bodhi tree – *ficus religiosa*, the tree under which the Buddha attained enlightenment.

Brahma – source of all existence and also worshipped as the creator in the Hindu triad.

Brahma is depicted as having four heads (a fifth was burnt by Siva's 'central eye' when Brahma spoke disrespectfully). His vehicle is a swan or goose and his consort is Saraswati.

Brahmanism – early form of Hinduism which evolved from Vedism; named after the Brahmin priests and the god Brahma.

Brahmin – a member of the priest caste, the highest Hindu caste.

Buddha – Awakened One; originator of Buddhism who lived in the 5th century BC; regarded by Hindus as the ninth reincarnation of Vishnu.

bugyal – meadow.

bund – embankment or dyke.

burkha – one-piece garment used by Muslim women to cover them from head to toe.

bustee – slum.

cantonment – administrative and military area of a Raj-era town.

caste – one's hereditary station in life.

chaat – general term for a snack.

chai – tea.

chaitya – Buddhist temple. Also prayer room or assembly hall.

chakra – focus of one's spiritual power; disc-like weapon of Vishnu.

chalo, chalo, chalo – 'let's go, let's go, let's go'.
Chamunda – form of the goddess Durga. A real terror, armed with a scimitar, noose and mace, and clothed in elephant hide. Her mission was to kill the demons Chanda and Munda, from whence comes the name.
chance list – waitlist on Indian Airlines flights.
Chanda – another manifestation of the goddess Durga.
Chandra – the moon, or the moon as a god.
Chandragupta – important ruler of India in the 3rd century BC.
chang – Tibetan rice beer.
chapati – unleavened Indian bread.
chappals – sandals.
charas – resin of the marijuana plant; also referred to as hashish.
charbagh – formal Persian garden, divided into quarters (literally: four gardens).
charpoy – Indian rope bed.
chauri – fly whisk.
chedi – *see* pagoda.
chela – pupil or follower, as George Harrison was to Ravi Shankar.
chhatri – a small, domed Mughal kiosk (literally: umbrella).
chikan – embroidered cloth.
chillum – pipe of a hookah; commonly used to describe the pipes used for smoking ganja.
chinkara – gazelle.
chital – spotted deer.
choli – sari blouse.
chorten – Tibetan word for stupa.
chota – small, spirit drink measure (as in 'chota peg').
choultry – *dharamsala* (pilgrim accommodation) in southern India.
chowk – a town square, intersection or marketplace.
chowkidar – nightwatchman.
Cong (I) – Congress Party of India.
country liquor – locally produced liquor.
CPI – Communist Party of India.
CPI (M) – Communist Party of India (Marxist).
crore – 10 million.
curd – milk with acid or rennet added to solidify it.
cutcherry/kachairri – office or building for public business.

dacoit – robber, particularly armed robber.
dagoba – *see* pagoda.
dahin – yoghurt.
daityas – demons and giants who fought against the gods.
dak – staging post.
Dalit – preferred term for India's casteless class; *see* Untouchable.
Damodara – another name for Krishna.
dargah – shrine or place of burial of a Muslim saint.
darshan – offering or audience with someone; viewing of a deity.
darwaza – gateway or door.
Dasaratha – father of Rama in the *Ramayana*.
Dattatreya – a Brahmin saint who embodied the Hindu triad.
deul – temple sanctuary
devadasi – temple dancer.
Devi – Siva's wife. She has a variety of forms.
dhaba – hole-in-the-wall restaurant or snack bar. Boxed lunches delivered to office workers.
dhal – lentil soup; what most of India lives on.
dharma – Hindu-Buddhist moral code of behaviour.
dharna – non-violent protest.
dhobi – person who washes clothes.
dhobi ghat – the place where clothes are washed.
dholi – covered litter or stretcher. You may still see elderly tourists being carried around in a dholi.
dhoti – like a lungi, but the cloth is then pulled up between the legs; worn by Hindu men.
dhurrie – rug.
digambara – sky-clad; a Jain sect whose followers demonstrate their disdain for worldly goods by going naked.
dikpalas – temple guardians
diwan – principal officer in a princely state; royal court or council.
Diwan-i-Am – Hall of Public Audience.
Diwan-i-Khas – Hall of Private Audience.
dosa – paper-thin pancakes made from lentil flour (curried vegetables wrapped inside a dosa make it a *masala dosa*).

dowry – money and goods given by a bride's parents to their son-in-law's family; it's illegal but no arranged marriage – and most marriages are arranged – can be made without it.

Draupadi – wife of the five Pandava princes in the *Mahabharata*.

Dravidian – a member of one of the aboriginal races of India, pushed south by the Indo-Europeans and now mixed with them. The Dravidian languages include Tamil, Malayalam, Telugu and Kannada.

dun – valley.

dupatta – scarf worn by Punjabi women.

durbar – royal court; also used to describe a government.

Durga – the Inaccessible; a form of Siva's wife Devi, a beautiful but fierce woman riding a tiger; major goddess of the Sakti cult.

dwarpal – doorkeeper; sculpture beside the doorways to Hindu or Buddhist shrines.

elatalam – small hand-held cymbals.

election symbols – identifying symbols for the various political parties, used because so many voters are illiterate.

Emergency – the period during which Indira Gandhi suspended many rights. Some observers assumed she intended establishing a dictatorship.

Eve-teasing – sexual harassment.

export gurus – gurus whose followers are mainly Westerners.

fakir – a Muslim who has taken a vow of poverty, but also applied to sadhus and other Hindu ascetics.

feni – liquor distilled from coconut milk or cashews; found in Goa.

filmee – music or other aspect of Indian movies

firman – a royal order or grant.

freaks – westerners wandering India.

gaddi – throne of a Hindu prince.

Ganesh – god of wisdom and prosperity. Elephant-headed son of Siva and Parvati and probably the most popular god in the Hindu pantheon.

Ganga – Ganges River; said to flow from the toe of Vishnu; goddess representing the sacred Ganges River.

ganj – market.

ganja – dried flowering tips of marijuana plant; highly potent form of cannabis.

gaon – village.

garh – fort.

gari – vehicle; motor gari is a car and rail gari is a train.

Garuda – man-bird vehicle of Vishnu.

gaur – Indian bison.

Gayatri – sacred verse of the *Rig-Veda*, repeated mentally by Brahmins twice a day.

ghat – steps or landing on a river; range of hills, or road up hills.

ghazal – Urdu songs derived from poetry; sad love themes.

ghee – clarified butter.

gherao – industrial action where the workers lock-in their employers.

giri – hill.

Gita Govinda – erotic poem by Jayadeva relating Krishna's early life as Govinda the cowherd.

godmen – commercially minded gurus; *see* export gurus.

godown – warehouse.

gompa – Tibetan-Buddhist monastery.

Gonds – aboriginal Indian race, now mainly found in the jungles of central India.

goondas – ruffians or toughs. Political parties often employ gangs of goondas.

gopis – milkmaids. Krishna was very fond of them.

gopuram – soaring pyramidal gateway tower of a Dravidian temple.

govinda – cowherd.

gram – legumes.

gumbad – a dome on a tomb or mosque.

gurdwara – Sikh temple.

guru – teacher or holy person (in Sanskrit, literally *goe* – darkness – and *roe* – to dispel).

Haji – a Muslim who has made the pilgrimage *(haj)* to Mecca.

hammam – Turkish bath.

Hanuman – monkey god, prominent in the *Ramayana*, follower of Rama.

Hara – one of Siva's names.

haram – prayer room in mosque.

Hari – another name for Vishnu.

Harijan – name given by Gandhi to India's Untouchables. This term is, however, no longer considered acceptable. *See* Dalit and Untouchable.

hartaal – strike.

hathi – elephant.

haveli – traditional mansions with interior courtyards, particularly in Rajasthan and Gujarat.

havildar – army officer.

hijra – eunuch.

Hinayana – small-vehicle Buddhism.

hindola – swing.

Hiranyakasipu – Daitya king killed by Vishnu in the man-lion (Narasimha) incarnation.

hookah – water pipe.

howdah – seat for carrying people on an elephant's back.

hypothecated – Indian equivalent of leased or mortgaged. You often see small signs on taxis or auto-rickshaws stating that the vehicle is 'hypothecated' to some bank or other.

idgah – open enclosure to the west of a town where prayers are offered during the Muslim festival of Id-ul-Zuhara.

idli – south Indian rice dumpling.

imam – Muslim religious leader.

imambara – tomb of a Shi'ite Muslim holy man.

IMFL – Indian Made Foreign Liquor; beer or spirits produced in India.

Indo-Saracenic – style of colonial architecture that integrated Western designs with Muslim, Hindu and Jain influences.

Indra – the most important and prestigious of the Vedic gods of India. God of rain, thunder, lightning and war. His weapons are the *vajra* (thunderbolt), bow, net and *anka* (hook).

Ishwara – Lord; a name given to Siva.

Jagadhatri – Mother of the World; another name for Siva's wife.

Jagganath – Lord of the World; a form of Krishna. The centre of worship is at Puri (Orissa).

jaggery – hard, brown-sugar-like sweetener made from kitul palm sap.

Jalasayin – literally: sleeping on the waters; a name for Vishnu as he sleeps on his couch over the water during the monsoon.

jali – carved marble lattice screen.

Janaka – father of Sita (Rama's wife in the *Ramayana*).

janata – literally: people. The Janata Party is the People's Party.

Jatakas – tales from the Buddha's various lives.

jauhar – ritual mass suicide by immolation, traditionally performed by Rajput women at times of military defeat to avoid being dishonoured by their captors.

jawan – policeman or soldier.

jheel – swampy area.

jhuggi – shanty settlement. *See* bustee.

ji – honorific that can be added to the end of almost anything; thus Babaji, Gandhiji.

juggernauts – huge, extravagantly decorated temple 'cars' dragged through the streets during Hindu festivals.

jumkahs – earrings.

jyoti lingam – the most important Siva shrines in India, of which there are 12.

kachairri – *see* cutchery.

kachauri – Indian-style breakfast of puris and vegetables.

Kailasa – a mountain in the Himalaya, home of Siva.

Kali – the Black; a terrible form of Siva's wife Devi. Depicted with black skin, dripping with blood, surrounded by snakes and wearing a necklace of skulls.

Kalki – the White Horse. Future (10th) incarnation of Vishnu which will appear at the end of Kali-Yuga, when the world ceases to be. Kalki has been compared to Maitreya in Buddhist cosmology.

Kama – the god of love.

kameez – woman's shirt.

Kanishka – important king of the Kushana Empire who reigned in the early Christian era.

Kanyakumari – the Virgin Maiden; another name for Durga.

karma – principle of retributive justice for past deeds.

karmacharlo – workers.

Kartikiya – god of war, Siva's son.

kata – Tibetan prayer shawl, traditionally given to a lama when pilgrims are brought into his presence.

Kedarnath – a name of Siva and one of the 12 important lingams.

khadi – homespun cloth; Mahatma Gandhi encouraged people to spin khadi rather than buy English cloth.

Khalistan – Sikh secessionists' name for an independent Punjab.

khan – Muslim honorific title.

khur – Asiatic wild ass.

kibla – direction in which Muslims turn in prayer, often marked with a niche in the mosque wall.

koil – Hindu temple.

kompu – C-shaped, metal trumpet.

kot – fort.

kothi – residence, house or mansion.

kotwali – police station.

Krishna – Vishnu's eighth incarnation, often coloured blue; a popular Hindu deity, he revealed the *Bhagavad Gita* to Arjuna.

kulfi – pistachio-flavoured sweet similar to ice cream.

kumbh – pitcher.

kund – lake.

kurta – shirt.

Kusa – one of Rama's twin sons.

lakh – 100,000. *See* crore.

Lakshmana – half-brother and aide of Rama in the *Ramayana*.

Lakshmi (Laxmi) – Vishnu's consort, goddess of wealth; sprang forth from the ocean holding a lotus. Also referred to as Padma (lotus).

lama – Tibetan-Buddhist priest or monk.

lassi – refreshing yoghurt and iced-water drink.

lathi – large bamboo stick; what Indian police hit you with if you get in the way of a lathi charge.

lenga – long skirt with a waist cord.

lingam – phallic symbol; symbol of Siva.

lok – people.

loka – realm.

Lok Dal – political party; one of the components of the Janata Party.

Lok Sabha – lower house in the Indian parliament, comparable to the House of Representatives or House of Commons.

lungi – like a sarong.

madrasa – Islamic college.

Mahabharata – Great *Vedic* epic of the Bharata Dynasty; an epic poem, containing about 10,000 verses, describing the battle between the Pandavas and the Kauravas.

Mahabodhi Society – founded in 1891 to encourage Buddhist studies in India and abroad.

Mahadeva – the Great God; a name of Siva.

Mahadevi – the Great Goddess; a name of Devi, Siva's wife.

Mahakala – Great Time; a name of Siva the destroyer, and one of the 12 sacred linga (at Ujjain in Madhya Pradesh).

mahal – house or palace.

maharaja, maharana, maharao – king.

maharani – wife of a princely ruler or a ruler in her own right.

mahatma – literally: great soul.

Mahavir – the last tirthankar (Jain teacher).

Mahayana – greater-vehicle Buddhism.

Mahayogi – the Great Ascetic; another name for Siva.

Maheshwara – Great Lord; Siva again.

mahout – elephant rider/master.

maidan – open grassed area in a city.

Makara – mythical sea creature and Varuna's vehicle; also a crocodile.

mali – gardener.

mandala – circle; symbol used in Hindu and Buddhist art to symbolise the universe.

mandapam – pillared pavilion in front of a temple.

mandi – market.

mandir – Hindu or Jain temple.

mani stone – stone carved with the Tibetan-Buddhist mantra 'Om mani padme hum' or 'Hail to the jewel in the lotus'.

mantra – sacred word or syllable used by Buddhists and Hindus to aid concentration; metrical psalms of praise found in the *Vedas*.

Mara – Buddhist god of death; has three eyes and holds the wheel of life.

Maratha (Mahratta) – warlike central Indian people who controlled much of India at various times and who fought the Mughals.

marg – major road.
Maruts – the storm gods.
masjid – mosque. Jama Masjid is the Friday Mosque or main mosque.
mata – mother.
math – monastery.
maund – now largely superseded unit of weight (about 20 kg).
mela – a fair.
memsahib – married European lady (from 'madam-sahib'). More widely used than you'd think.
mendi – henna; ornate henna patterns painted on women's hands and feet for important festivals, particularly in Rajasthan. Beauty parlours and bazaar stalls will do it for you.
Meru – mythical mountain found in the centre of the earth; on it is Swarga, the heaven of Indra.
mihrab – *see* kibla.
mithuna – pairs of men and women; often seen in temple sculpture.
Moghul – alternative spelling for Mughal. The Muslim dynasty of Indian emperors from Babur to Aurangzeb.
Mohini – Vishnu in his female incarnation.
moksha – salvation.
momos – Tibetan fried dumplings with vegetables or meat.
monsoon – rainy season between June and October.
morcha – mob march or protest.
mudra – ritual hand movements used in Hindu religious dancing.
muezzin – one who calls Muslims to prayer from the minaret.
mullah – Muslim scholar, teacher or religious leader.
mund – village (eg Ootacamund).
munshi – writer, secretary or teacher of languages.

nadi – river.
Naga – mythical snake with a human face; a person from Nagaland in north-east India.
namaz – Muslim prayers.
namkin – prepackaged spicy nibbles.
Nanda – the cowherd who raised Krishna.
Nandi – bull, vehicle of Siva. Nandi's images are usually found at Siva temples.

Narasimha (Narsingh) – man-lion incarnation of Vishnu.
Narayan – an incarnation of Vishnu the creator.
Nataraja – Siva as the cosmic dancer.
nautch girls – dancing girls; a nautch is a dance.
nawab – Muslim ruling prince or powerful landowner.
Naxalites – ultra-leftist political movement. Began in Naxal Village, West Bengal, as a peasant rebellion. Characterised by extreme violence. Still exists in Uttar Pradesh, Bihar and Andhra Pradesh.
Nilakantha – form of Siva. His blue throat is a result of swallowing poison that would have destroyed the world.
nilgai – antelope.
nirvana – the ultimate aim of Buddhist existence, final release from the cycle of existence.
niwas – house, building
nizam – hereditary title of the rulers of Hyderabad.
noth – the Lord (Jain).
NRI – Non-Resident Indian, the sub-continent's version of Overseas Chinese and of equal economic importance for modern India.
nullah – ditch or small stream.
numda – Rajasthani rug.

Om – sacred invocation representing the absolute essence of the divine principle. For Buddhists, if repeated often enough with complete concentration, it should lead to a state of emptiness.

pacha – green, pure.
padma – lotus.
padyatra – 'foot journey' made by politicians to raise support at the village level.
pagoda – Buddhist religious monument composed of a solid hemisphere topped by a spire, containing relics of the Buddha; also known as a dagoba, stupa or chedi.
pakoras – bite-size pieces of vegetable dipped in chickpea-flour batter and deep fried.
palanquin – box-like enclosure carried on poles on four men's shoulders; the occupant sits inside on a seat.

Pali – derived from Sanskrit; the original language in which the Buddhist scriptures were recorded. Scholars still refer to the original Pali texts.

palia – memorial stone.

palli – village.

pan – betel nut and leaves plus chewing additives such as lime.

pandit – expert or wise person. Sometimes used to mean a bookworm.

Parasurama – Rama with the Axe; the sixth incarnation of Vishnu.

Parsi – adherent of the Zoroastrian faith.

Parvati – the Mountaineer; another form of Siva's wife.

patachitra – Orissan cloth paintings

peepul – fig tree, especially a bo tree.

peon – lowest grade clerical worker.

pinda – funeral cake

pinjrapol – animal hospital maintained by Jains.

POK – Pakistan Occupied Kashmir.

pradesh – state.

pranayama – study of breath control.

prasad – food offering.

puja – literally: respect; offering or prayers.

pukkah – proper; very much a Raj-era term.

punkah – cloth fan, swung by pulling a cord.

Puranas – set of 18 encyclopaedic Sanskrit stories, written in verse, relating to the three gods, dating from the period of the Guptas (5th century AD).

purdah – custom among some Muslims of keeping women in seclusion.

puri – flat pieces of dough that puff up when deep fried.

qila – fort.

Radha – the favourite mistress of Krishna when he lived as Govinda (or Gopala) the cowherd.

raga – any of several conventional patterns of melody and rhythm that form the basis for freely interpreted compositions.

railhead – station or town at the end of a railway line; termination point.

raj – rule or sovereignty.

raja – king.

Rajput – Hindu warrior castes, royal rulers of central India.

rakhi – amulet.

Rama – seventh incarnation of Vishnu. His life story is the central theme of the *Ramayana*.

Ramayana – the story of Rama and Sita and their conflict with Ravana. One of India's best-known legends, it is retold in various forms throughout almost all South-East Asia.

rangoli – a chalk design.

rani – female ruler or wife of a king.

ras gullas – sweet little balls of cream cheese flavoured with rose water.

rasta roko – roadblock for protest purposes.

rath – temple chariot or car used in religious festivals.

rathas – rock-cut Dravidian temples at Mahabalipuram.

Ravana – demon king of Lanka (modern-day Sri Lanka). He abducted Sita, and the titanic battle between him and Rama is told in the *Ramayana*.

rawal – nobleman.

rickshaw – small, two-wheeled passenger vehicle. Only in Calcutta and one or two hill stations do the old human-powered rickshaws still exist. Bicycle rickshaws are more widely used.

Rig-Veda – the original and longest of the four main *Vedas*, or holy Sanskrit texts.

rishi – originally a sage to whom the hymns of the *Vedas* were revealed; these days any poet, philosopher or sage.

road – railway town which serves as a communication point to a larger town off the line; eg, Mt Abu and Abu Road, Kodaikanal and Kodai Road.

Rukmini – wife of Krishna; died on his funeral pyre.

sabzi – curried vegetables.

sadar – main.

sadhu – ascetic, holy person, one who is trying to achieve enlightenment; usually addressed as 'swamiji' or 'babaji'.

sagar – lake, reservoir.

sahib – 'lord', title applied to any gentleman and most Europeans.

Saivaite (Shaivaite) – follower of Lord Siva.

Saivism – the worship of Siva.

salai – road.

salwar – trousers worn by Punjabi women.

samadhi – an ecstatic state, sometimes defined as 'ecstasy, trance, communion with God'. Also a place where a holy man has been cremated; usually venerated as a shrine.

sambar – deer.

sangam – meeting of two rivers.

Sankara – Siva as the creator.

sanyasin – like a sadhu.

Saraswati – wife of Brahma, goddess of speech and learning; usually sits on a white swan, holding a veena (a stringed instrument).

Sati – wife of Siva. Became a sati ('honourable woman') by immolating herself. Although banned more than a century ago, the act of sati is occasionally performed.

satsang – discourse by a swami or guru.

satyagraha – non-violent protest involving a fast, popularised by Gandhi. From Sanskrit, literally: insistence on truth.

Scheduled Castes – official term for Untouchables or Dalits.

sepoy – formerly an Indian solider in British service.

serai – accommodation for travellers. Caravanserai catered to camel caravans.

shakti – creative energies perceived as female deities; devotees follow the cult of Shaktism.

shikar – hunting expedition.

shikara – gondola-like boat used on Srinagar's lakes in Kashmir.

shirting – the material shirts are made from.

shola – virgin forest.

sikhara – Hindu temple-spire or temple.

singh – literally: lion; name of the Rajput caste and adopted by Sikhs as a surname.

sirdar (sardar) – leader or commander.

Sita – in the *Vedas* the goddess of agriculture. More commonly associated with the *Ramayana*, in which Sita, Rama's wife, is abducted by Ravana and carted off to Lanka.

sitar – Indian stringed instrument.

Siva – (Shiva) the destroyer; also the Creator, in which form he is worshipped as a *lingam* (a phallic symbol).

Skanda – another name for Kartikiya, the god of war.

soma – intoxicating drink derived from the juice of a plant and which features prominently in the *Rig-Veda*. Raised to the status of a deity for its power to heal, provide wealth and impart immortality. In the *Puranas* it symbolises the moon.

sonam – karma built up in successive reincarnations.

sonf – aniseed seeds; come with the bill after a meal and used as a digestive.

sri (sree, shri, shree) – honorific; these days the Indian equivalent of Mr or Mrs.

stupa – *see* pagoda.

Subhadra – Krishna's incestuous sister.

Subrahmanya – another name for Kartikiya, god of war.

sudra – low Hindu caste.

sufi – ascetic Muslim mystic.

suiting – the material that suits are made from.

Surya – the sun; a major deity in the *Vedas*.

sutra – string; a list of rules expressed in verse. Many exist, the most famous being the *Kama Sutra*.

swami – title given to initiated monks; means 'lord of the self'. A title of respect.

swaraj – independence.

sweeper – lowest caste servant, who performs the most menial of tasks.

syce – groom.

tabla – a pair of drums.

taluk – district.

tank – reservoir.

Tantric Buddhism – Tibetan-Buddhism with strong sexual and occult overtones.

tatty – woven grass screen which is soaked in water and hung outside windows in the hot season to cool the air.

tempo – noisy three-wheeler public transport vehicle; bigger than an auto-rickshaw.

thakur – Hindu caste.

thali – traditional south Indian and Gujarati 'all-you-can-eat' vegetarian meal.

thangka – rectangular Tibetan painting on cloth.

Theravada – small-vehicle Buddhism.

thiru – holy.

thug – follower of Thuggee; ritual murderers centred in Madhya Pradesh in the last century.

thukpar – Tibetan soup.

tiffin – snack, particularly around lunchtime.

tika – a mark devout Hindus put on their foreheads with *tika* powder.

tirthankars – the 24 great Jain teachers.

toddy – alcoholic drink, tapped from palm trees.

tola – 11.6 grams.

tonga – two-wheeled horse or pony carriage.

tope – grove of trees, usually mangoes.

topi – pith helmet; widely used during the Raj era.

torana – architrave over a temple entrance.

toy train – narrow-gauge railway, usually for getting to hill stations such as Darjeeling.

Trimurti – Triple Form; the Hindu triad – Brahma, Siva and Vishnu.

Tripitaka – classic Theravada Buddhist scriptures, which are divided into three categories (hence the name the Three Baskets).

tripolia – triple gateway.

Uma – light; Siva's consort.

Untouchable – lowest caste or 'casteless' for whom the most menial tasks are reserved. The name derives from the belief that higher castes risk defilement if they touch one. Formerly known as *Harijan*, now *Dalit*.

Upanishads – Esoteric Doctrine; ancient texts forming part of the *Vedas* (although of a later date), they delve into weighty matters such as the nature of the universe and the soul.

Valmiki – author of the *Ramayana*.

Vamana – the fifth incarnation (avataar) of Vishnu, as the dwarf.

varna – the concept of caste.

Varuna – supreme Vedic god.

Vedas – the Hindu sacred books; a collection of hymns composed in pre-classical Sanskrit during the second millennium BC and divided into four books: *Rig-Veda*, *Yajur-Veda*, *Sama-Veda* and *Atharva-Veda*.

vihara – part of monastery; resting place, garden, cave with cells.

vimana – principal part of a Hindu temple.

Vishnu – the third in the Hindu trinity of gods along with Brahma and Siva. The Preserver and Restorer, who so far has nine avataars: the fish Matsya; the tortoise Kurma; the wild boar Naraha; the man-lion Narasimha; the dwarf Vamana; the Brahmin Parashu-Rama; Rama (of *Ramayana* fame); Krishna; the Buddha.

wallah – man. Can be added onto almost anything, thus dhobi-wallah (clothes washer), taxi-wallah, Delhi-wallah.

wazir – chief minister.

yagna – self-mortification.

yakshi – maiden.

yantra – a geometric plan thought to create energy.

yatra – pilgrimage.

yatri – tourist.

yoni – vagina; female fertility symbol.

zamindar – landowner.

zenana – area in an upper-class Muslim house where the women are secluded.

Index

ABBREVIATIONS

MAPS

TEXT

Map references are in **bold** type.

INDEX

BOXED TEXT

INDEX

THANKS

Thanks to the following travellers and others (apologies if we've misspelt your name) who took the time to write to us about their experiences of India:

Jennifer Abbott, Alexander Abusinov, Sam Adam, Omar Ahmed, Simon Aitken, Bill Aitken, Thomas Aldefeld, Beverly Aldridge, Abira Ali, Cherie Allan, P Allen, Ann Allen, Stewart-Lee Allen, Altair De Almeida, Efrat Amir, Ory Amitay, David Andrews, Bianco Anna, Graham Anshaw, D Anthony, Christina Apostolidi, Matthew Aquilina, Dr J Aranclo, Toby Archer, Susan Armfield, Robert Arnett, Catherine Arnold, L & P Arrowsmith, Mary Atkinson, L Aurrekoetxea, M Avraham, Ronnie Aye-Maung

Nancy Babb, Martin Badley, Verena Bahler, Sabina Bailey, S Bamford, Achal Bindra Ban, Dr Sanjoy Banerjee, Warren Bannister, James Barbar, Ed Barber, Alison & Bob Barbour, John Baring, Omri Barkay, Christopher Barnett, Martin Barr, J C Barrett, Christopher Barthel, Rebecca Bartow, Bonnie Baskin, David Bassett, Claudio Bassetti, Sandy Bastyan, Elisabeth Batchelor, Alison Batten, M Bayer, Oliver Bayne, Stephanie Beasley, Katherine Beaton, Josselin Beaulieu, Bernd Becker, C Beebe, Asaf Begerano, Josee Belanger, Anina Belhadj-Corral, J Bellerose, Adi Ben-Israel, Pat Bennett, Andrew Bennett, R Berge, David Bernardini, Paul Bett, Debbie Beveridge, Hajra Bhamji, Jiwanand Bhanot, N Govinda Bhat, K Bhumeshwar, S Bhundia, Anna Bianco, Andrew Bickle, Hvanden Biggelaar, I Bilsen, Richard Bitot, Jamie Bixby, Ryan Blair, Tatjana Blanchet, Laura Bloomgarden, John Blunden, Rachel Blythe, Eckhard Bokamper, L Boland, Jenny & John Bolger, Alan Boniface, Alistair Bool, A Booth, Bruno Bosch, F Boucarut, Laura Boutelle, Ellen Bouwer, Jeffrey Bowe, Amanda Bowen, Erroll Bowyer, C Boxall, Edward Boyapati, Anna Brady, Eric Brady, A Brager, D Brannan, Karen & Paul Breger, F Bregnard, John Breitweiss, Jennifer Brewer, Emmanuel Bricoyne, Chele Bridger, David Brodie, Sarah Bronzite, R Brooks, Heather Brown, Mary Brown, Jan & Geoff Brown, Maya Brown, Jeff Brown, M & S Browning, Roberto Bruneri, Dr Stephen Bubert, M & R Buckhorn, Eugene Buhler, Richard Bullock, Stephanie Burch, H Burema, K Burgess, Angela & Abi Burke, Lenny & Wendy Burnett, S Burns, K Burton, D Busby, Gordon Buss, Peter Buszjager, Joyce Butcher

Paul Caffrey, Laura Cain, T Callaghan, Erika Calzaferri, Denis Cameron, Duncan Campbell, M E Campbell, Jack Carbone, Amanda Carlson, Grisel Carreira, La Casey, P Cashman, Anita Cassidy, Tom Cassidy, John Casson, Matt Chabott, Agnes Chague,

Emma Chamberlain, Brenda Chandler, Anna Chapple, Dee Charlton, Keith Charlton, Katherine Charsley, T Chatterji, Helen Chia, Joseph Chinnock, Sandeep Chopra, Andrew Christensen, John Church, Paul Cina, Alex Clark, L Clarke, S Clarkson, Hans Clemensen, A Clemes, Mario Cleovoulou, Vanessa Clothier, R Cochrane, Jennifer Coffin, Ben Cohen, Rebecca Colclasire, Zachary Cole, C Colinet, Jon Collins, Dave Compton, Alec Connah, Iain Connor, F Connors, J A Cook, John Cook, Jenny & Julian Cook, Phillip Cook, Sarah & David Cooke, John Coombs, Peter Cornelis, Miles Cort, Stan Cory, Ally Couchman, Gerald Coulter, C Covelli, Roy Cox, Dr Peter Cox, Betty Cox, Rob Craig, Alma Cristina, Maggi Culver, Stef & Lis Cumine, Simon Cumming, T A Cunningham, Michael Cunningham, Raphaelle Curis, D Curtis

S Dacher, Catherine Daeues, Rod Daldry, L Dallal, T A S Damouk, Pat Daniel, Mr Daniels, Attila Danko, Paul Dargie, Rachael Davey, Katy Davies, Des Davies, Allen Davies, Erin Davis, Harry Davis, Jan Dawson, Isaac Day, C Day, Roger Day, Manish Dayal, Yigal Dayan, Steven De Backer, Natasha Deighton, Gus DellaPorta, M Denison, Tom Dennehy, Catherine Denny, Giuliana Dettori, Papan Devnani, Maria Deza, D Dhaliwal, John Diamandis, C Diechx, Magdalena Diehl, M Dilbury, Ann Ez El Din, John Dingey, Michael Dixon, Cathy & Steve Dodge, Tsering Dolkar, T M Donohue, Nell Doughrty, C Douglas, J Downs, D Doyle, Ellen Drake, Helene Dubreuil, Benoit Dubuisson, Liz & George Duff, Dr R Dufour, Laura Duncan, Michael Dunn, Joan Dunphy, Nicki Dyson

Julian & Peter Eades, Damien Eastman, Marion Eckert, Mr & Mrs Edwards, Merkis Irma Eeli, Robert Eidschun, Russell Eisgrub, S Eklund, Ulf Ellervik, Dave Ellis, Tarek El Sawy, J L M Elsberg, Daniel & Helen Elton, John & Gill Ely, Carole Emmerson, E Engels, Jeremy Engineer, Stewart Ennis, Damon Enoka, Susan Erk, Jason Erwin, Tagel Etgar, Mark & Karen Evans, Janet Evans, Laurence Everard, Andrew Ewart, Tim Eyres

Marcus Fairs, Y Fan, Jude Fapani, Eugenia Farkas, T T Farrell, Steve Farrell, Sydney Felder, Pia Feldman, Roland Felgentraeger, Brian Fenn, Una Ferguson, Gary Ferguson, Carol Ferris, Sarah Ferris-Browne, Deborah Filcoff, H Filgate, J C Filmore, C Filthuth, Gerald Fimberger, Emma Flatt, T Fletcher, Ralph Flores, Mark Follett, Quentin Ford, Yann Forget, Charlie Forman, Alberto Forneris, T Foster, William Fox, Jon Fox, Michael Foy, Elsa Frances, V Francisco, Luanne Frank, Sue & Steve Frary, Yvonne Freid, Margret Frenz, Jose Fribarren, Yvonne Fried, Kate Frost, Duncan & Elisabeth Fry, Sabrina Fry, Salvador Fuensanta

Aitor Gabilondo, Harun Gadatia, Katherine Gadd, Dipesh Gadher, Yeela Gal, Michael Galea, Fergus Gallagher, Nancy Gallagher, Ian Galloway, Maritza-Adriana Garcia, G Gardner, George Gardner, Simon Garrett, Justin Garrick, E Garrido, Piotr Gaszynski, Robert Gatt, Stephanie Gavin-Brown, Brian Gee, Gerd Geissendorfer, Stuart Geltner, Henriuk Gemal, L Gerard, Andreas Gerner, Anne Giannini, Robert Gibbons, James Gilbert, Warwick Gilbert, Ruth Giles, Mike Giles, M Gillett, F Gishen, D & L Gladis, Gesine Glaeser, Ian Gleave, Jeannine Glista, David Godfrey, Diane Godfrey, Richard Goding, Jean-Marie Godot, D & R Godrey, Mariana Goetz-Quintana, V Gogolya, Joachim Gohlicke, Ella Going, Martin Golder, David Gomeze, Nigel & Savi Goodall, Kate Goodden, Julian Goode, Allen Goodreds, Kerry Goodwin, P Gordon, Stephen Gough, Eric Govers, Mary Gow, L Gower, Jennie Gozdz, Erich Grader, Jane & Brian Graham, Dr D E Granger, Dr Travers Grant, Steve & Lisa Gray, Phil Gray, John Green, David Green, Tom Grimm, Michael Grimmer, Jurek Grobosz, Jan & Arne Groner, David Grossblat, I Guillon, Lena Gustavsson, Anni Gyumolcs

Dr Joachim Hacker, F Haegeleer, Brigitte Haehnle, Bill & Pat Haigh, Katy Haire, Judy Hall, Malcolm Hall, Derek Hall, Ruth Hall, David Hall, Larry Hallock, Colin Hallward, Sheila Hally, Remi Hamel, Allen Hammack, Mark Hammond, Annette Handley, Fiona Handley, Don Hanlon, Sheila Hannon, Nina Hansen, Anne Harding, Robert Harding, Paul Hardy, Fran Harley, C Harper, Maxine Harris, Amy Harris, Mark Harrison, Michael Hartnett, I Hartog, Michael Hartz, B Harvey, Dina Hashem, D Hashem, Robert Hastie, Jim Hastings, D Hatch, David Hatzkevich, Ted Haver, M E Hawkes, Paul Hawkie, Heather Hawkins, Suzanne Hayano, W G Heap, Alan Heathes, Phyllis Hegeman, Philip Heinemann, Andreas Heitman, Hanne & Angus Hellawell, Gudrun Heller, H H Hellin, Krystyna Hellstroem, Schuyler Henderson, Daniel Henderson, Dr Peggy Henderson, Richard Henke, Andrew Henshaw, David Herman, Ingel Hernbdndez, A Herrero, Jon & Keith Hewitt, Sophie Hewlett, Pam & Alan Hey, Claire Hickson, Rachel Higgens, C Higgins, Sam Hill, Debbie Hill, Clare Hitchen, Casper Hjorth-Knudson, Martin Ho, Shiela Hocking, Pvander Hofstad, Peter Holdforth, Michael Holloway, M & E Holmann, Mark Holmes, C & A Holmes, Annelii Holmguist, Anna Homs-Torras, Kenton Hoover, Douglas Hosdale, Emma Hoskins, Hugo Houppermans, Jonathan Howard, Ken & Anne Hoy, Esther Huber, Tracey Hudson, Jeremy & Ellen Hughes, Paul Hughes-Smith, Guy Humphreys, J S Huntley, R & M Hurford, Ashfak Hussain, J Hutchinson, A Huycke

Hussein Ibrahim, G Ilan, Steven Ireland, Kevin Isfeld, Eli Itin, Renae Ivany

L Jaarsma, Markus Jaaskelainen, Miki Jablowska, Anna Jablowska, Paul & Claire Jackson, Spencer Jackson, Graeme Jackson, W Jackson, Dean Jackson, A M Jacobsen, Astrid Jacobsen, Alain Jacquemin, Andre Jacques, Vivek Jain, A Jain, Birgit Jaki, Julia Jakubovics, Kate James, Izabela Jankowska, Ton Janusch, Joy & Paul Jarman, Eila Jarvinen, Rajah Jayendran, Brendon Jaynes, Yvonne & Anne Jeffrey, E Jeffries, Dot Jellinek, T Jellings, A Jennings, E Jensen, Axelvon Jentzkowski, Jay Jessen, Eirik Magne Johansen, Matt Johnson, Andy Johnson, R Johnson, Dennis Johnson, Stephen Johnson, R Johnson, Angela Johnson, Kev Johnston, Elaine & Frank Johnston, Don & Reggie Johnston, Frank Jones, Nick Jones, Owen Jones, Larry Jones, Emily Jones, Geoffrey Jones, Mark Jowett, M & B Jozsy

Katie Kabler, J & T Kalaitzis, Lindy Kandohla, Stephanie Kaplan, C Kaplan, Lisbethvande Kar, Judith Karmen, Halina Kapowicz, Hormuzd Katki, Damien Kearns, Laura Keller, Roy Kellett, Adam Kelley, R Kelly, Iona Kelly, Glenn Kelly, Dave Kelshaw, Treena Kennedy, Clare Kenny, Deborah Kerr, J Kerwick, Jorg Kessel, Damian Khan, Devan Khurmi, Richard Kidby, Guido Kies, Steve King, Marie Kingsbury, Stefan Kintrup, Frank & Liz Kirk, Z Kittler, Tracey Kitzman, Eddy Klijnen, L Klinger, Josef Kloiser, Christoph Klug, Tania Knight, Oliver Knowles, Marianne Kohler, Tony&Hana Korab, Manfred Korell, Bill&Yvonne Kornrich, Katarina Koskinen, Tine Kratzer, Charlie Kregel, M Kreiger, Tim Krick, Sue Krishnan, G Krishnan, M Krogh, Nicole & Michael Kropf, Robert Krumm, Judith Kuiperi, Peter Kunkel

Stephane La-Branche, Jordan Lacey, Dr Rolf Peter Lacher, Ray & Michelle Ladbury, P Van Laeren, Stephanie Lafer, J L Lal, Ashlee Lambe, Miss Lammin, Ronald Lance, Georges Landry, Kevin Lang, Kristine Lang, Phil De Lange, Veronique Langelier, Kim Langford, Romina Lanzani, Christy Lanzl, Bjorn Larsen, M L Lathia, Tricia Laudato, A C Lavenex, Mark Lazarus, Heather & John Lberg, Toby & Esther Leach, J League, Gerd Ledermann, Denise Lee, Sarah Lee, Stephen-Andrew Lee, Bronwyn Leece, Alan Leedham, Dr G A Lekhi, C Leland, Helen Leuschner, Paz Lev, David Levingston, Ron Levis, V Levitan, Stephen Lewis, G Liardet, Eva-Maria Lill, Katy Lindstrom, David Linton, Cormal Little, Brendan Lo, Sophie Logan, Michael Long, Su Loong, Ramon Lopez, Richard Lorand, Maria Lotriet, Chris Lovell, Marion Lowden, Monica Lowenberg, M Lowry, E Luiken, Michel & Jo Luinthogen, Lisa & Troy Lum, Nicholas Lux, Susan Lynn, Patricia Lyon, J Lys

H & R MacIntosh, Melissa MacKenzie, Dr J MacKinnon, Katie Macks, Chris Madden, Jan Magnusson, Rai Mahimapati-Ray, Leon Mahoney, Nick Male, La Malloy, Anita Mallya, Alex Marcovitch, Anne Margarethe, Dan Margolis, D Marjanovic, Mike Marqusee, D Marsden, Luis Marseleuno, T Martin, Tracey & Paul Martin, Fay Martin, Jane Mason, Gary Mason, Avander Mast, N X Mathew, Swati Mathur, Jan Matthe, Mr & Mrs R Matthews, Andreas Matthiess, Cera Maugey, Marjorie Maxwell, Ashley May, Clara Mazzi, Neil McAllister, Scott McCallum, Mary McCann, C McCann, Peter McCarthy, Pauline McConville, Mike McDougall, Helen McElroy, Nick McGhee, I McIntyre, Lachlan McLaine, Dana McLaughlin, Andrew McLellan, Tom McMillan, Kerry McPherson, Annie McStay, Sander Meijsen, Helen & Marvin Meistrich, Kristine Meldal, Celina Mendore, Angelo Mercure, J Merino, Jacqueline Merino, J Merino, Patrick Mertens, Simon Meyer, Heather Michaud, Karen Michel, Elaine Michelson, David Miclo, Francis Middel, Paul Middleton, C Mikton, Tiffeny Millbourn, Phil Miller, Danna Millett, Bruce Mills, Anthea Mitchell, Bruce Mitchell, Noel Mitchell, Kaye Mitchell, Betty Moen, Vik Moharir, L Monica, John Moon, David Moor, Adam Moore, Simon Moore, Ralph Morelot, Willie Moreschi, Graham & Jay Morgan, Kate Morley, Dan Morris, David Morse, Tony Mortlock, Clemens Mosch, Jane & Mick Mosco, Jennifer Moss, Dave Mountain, Suzanne Mrozik, Praveen Muhandas, Robin Mukherjee, Monica Mukherji, Rianda Mulder, Susan Mulholland, Yunus Mulla, Manuel Muller, Volker Muller, Graham Muller, Bryan Mullumby, P Murphy, Catriona Murray, J F Murray, Rosemary Murton, Peter Myers

Angela Nair, Chigusa Nakai, Valerie Nash, Caroline Nass, Joanna Nathan, Deborah Neal, Helen Neil, Stephen Nelson, Daniela Nessi, C Netzest, Paul & Susan Newby, Ian Nicholls, M S Nielsen, Richard Nimmo, Ellie Noij, Peter Norbury, Kirsty Norman, Tracy Norton, Phil & Liz Norton, K Norton, Edo Nyland

R O'Connell, PG O'Neill, Karen O'Rourke, Stephen O'Rourke, Sue Oatley, Cvan Oever, Maggie Offerhaus, Arun Ohri, Quinn Okamoto, Elisabeth Olsen, Daniel Ontell, G Opstad, Chris & Jenny Owen, Jenny Oxley

Bradley Page, Mr & Mrs Page, John Page, Helen Pagliero, Yudi Palkova, C Palmer, Sonia Park, Bryan Parkin, David Pascoe, Dr Manubhai Patel, Dhruv Patel, Endrich Patel, S Patel, Gary Patterson, Claire Patterson, Stephen Pattinson, Hazel Chris & Paul, Mike Pearce, David Pearce, D & C Pearlman, Josh Pedersen, E Pelisson, Alex Pennell, Eda Peredes, Olivia Perks, Sylvain Perron, Jacqueline Perry, S Peters, Jack Petersen, Tony Phillips, Danny Phillips, Nick Phillips, Thomas Phng, Robin Pick, Anne-Marie

Piedot, Martin Pinke, Tony Pitman, Gregory Placonouns, Brigitte Plank, R A Platt, Lidy van der Ploeg, Robert Pocknell, Dinesh Poddar, Dr Bauke van der Pol, Stefan Polanyk, Florence Polliand, B B Pontin, Neil Popat, A R A Pope, Renee Porte, S Posingis, Henry Posner, Uta Potthast, Matt Powell, Robin Prager, Shyam Prasad, Dawn Price, E E & P J Priest, Michael Owen Prior, Hilary Pugh, Deborah Purdon, P & T Purgaric, Christa Purnell, D Putney, S & V Puttock

Meg Quinn, Michel Racine, Colleen Rains, Sub Lt Rajiv, T & M Ramon, Bruce Ramsay, John Rand, Stuart Randell, M V Rarhe, Peter Ras, R & J Rawlinson, Paul Reardon, James Redfern, Geoff Rees, Joanna & Tom Reid, Lynette & Anthea Reid, Edward Reilly, Anders Restrop, Michael Reynolds, Gina Rhodes, Scott Riach, Tali Ricci, Robert Richardson, Matt Richardson, Barrie Ridout, Anton Rijsdijk, Sue Riley, J Riley, I J Riley, Soren Rindal-Nielsen, D Rios, Catherine Ripou, SandroDe Riu, Alexandra Robak, Damien Robbins, E S Robert, J M Robinson, Jimmy Robinson, David Robinson, Martin Robinson, Jean Robinson, Jackie Robson, Stephen Rock, Gwen Rodenburg, Eb Roell, Soren & Camilla Roesen, D Roessli, Andreas Rogall, Jeff Rogers, Lee Rogerson, Anne Rogiers, Kalus Romer, Simonetta Roncaglia, L Ronesi, Neils Ronnest, Anne & Michel Ropion, H Rose, Ruth Rose, John Rosley, Sian Rosser, Christian Rosset, Margareta Rossing, Mike Rothbart, Boaz Rottem, Gerard Round, Helen Rouse, Terry Rowe, Elizabeth Rowe, Amanda-Joy Rubin, Don & Sue Rudalevige, Francoise Ruffie, Daniel Rule, Simon Runnalls, Dell Russell

O Sabbing, Sudhir Sahay, Ravi Sahay, Alex Salmon, Premila Sami, H C Sampat, Donna Sanders, Martin Sands, Niranjan Sarja, Gregory Satir, Volker Sauer, Diana Saunders, R Schaafsma, Dr Walter Schaffer, Bryan Scheideck, S & U Schlippert, C Scholes, R Schrauwen, Pieter Schunselaar, C Schussler, Peter Schwarzkopf, Helene & Otto Schwelb, Anthony Scibberas, Arthur Scott, Antonio Scotti, Joni Seager, Ole See, Y Sella, Martin Semler, E Septier, Derek Severn, S Shah, A P Sharma, S Sharp, Andrew Sharpe, Jill Sharpe, Amy Shavelson, Jennifer Shaw, Timothy Shaw, Andrew Shaw, Jennifer Shaw, C Shaw, Brendan Shaw, Denis Shelton, S Shepherd, Rajendra Shepherd, Nicky Sherriff, A Short, Merav Shrira, Beth Sidaway, Annabelle Sidhu, Chaman Sidhu, Bryan Siegfried, Bryan Siegfried, Christopher Sigmond, Petr Silhanek, Steve Silk, A Sim, Wilfried Simons, Brian & Jo Simpson, J Simpson, Trevor Simpson, Lynn Simson, Amitojj Singh, Krishna Singh, Alan Sirulnikoff, Michel Slinger, Dylon Smallwood, John Smart, Ian & Allie Smith, Simon Smith, Fiona Smith, H Smith, J Smith, Michelle Helen Smith, Peter Smith, Gregory-Dale Smith,

Joanna Snaith, Kaja Snedler, Lynn De Snoo, Douglas Snyder, Dr Angela Sodan, Sam Solomon, Peter Somani, Ann Sorrel, David Spain, Jonathon Spear, Matthew Spears, Helen Speekley, Richard Spencer, Barbara Spencer, Paul Spencer, Richard Spencer, A Spignesi, Tony & Linda Spooner, Ian St Lawrence, Peter & Heike Stadler, Marilyn Staib, Katrina Stalker, Tony Stanford, William Stanley, Michelle Stanton, Paul Starkey, K Starr, Jan Steibert, Ursula Steiger, Sergio Stern, John Stevens, Jane Stevens, Greg & Darlene Stevens, Michael Stevenson, Vanessa Stewart, Jan Stiebert, Joanna Still, Richard Stocker, Mirjam Stolwyk, Brian Stone, Sue & Mark Strangeways, Debbie Strout, Sabrina Stryker, Dany Surralles, Beth & Pete Sutch, Jane Sutherland, Robert Svoboda, David Swait, Wanda & Barry Syner

Godfrey Talbot, Richard Tanner, Zolton Tarodi, EllaJo Tarot, Les Tate, David Taussig, Jan & Dave Taylor, Tansy Tazewell, Kylie Terrell, Dr James Terry, Sebastiande Terssac, C Thacker, JulesVan Thieler, David Thomas, David & Mary Thomas, Robert Thomason, Ted Thompson, D Thornber, J Thorne, Rick Thorngate, Drs A & R Thrift, Herby Thurn, Rob Thwaites, Leon Toland, T & S Tolfrenstau, Christine Townend, Luca Tramontin, Henri Tran, Eliezer Traub, Stephen Travers, Pamela Treanor, Duncan Trew, Ross Tucker, Stella Tuft, Michael Turinski, Ethel & Bob Turner, Dick & Liz Turner, Blair Turner, Dylan Turner, Daniel Tuslain, Pauline Twigg, Chris Tyler, Debra Tyler, Gill Tyson

Susanne Ulrich, David Ure

A & I Vadis-Heim, Saskiavander Valk, Chris Vanderoye, Zinne Vandevelde, Francis Vanlangendonck, Gwynneth Varner, D Veale, Roy Verbrigge, Bart Vermeiren, Stefan Vermuelen, HansPeter Vetter, Daniel Vetter, C Veyret-Abran, Jonathan Vince, David Vinkers, Ann Virgin, Frank Visakay, Josephine Vliegen, J Vlietinck, Brandon Robert Vogt

Dirk Wagener, Nic Walker, F Walker, Pamela Walpole, Maureen Walters, Sally & Rik Walton, Dr Andrew Warmington, James Watson, K Weber, Duncan Webster, Werner Weick, Don Welch, Patrick Wellaert, Juliet Wells, Joanna & Nicholas West, Peter Westgate, Andy & Emma Whatson, Jonathan Wheatley, Natalie Wheatley, E Wheeler, Lisa Wheeler, Murdo White, Tony White, Andrew White, Claire Whitefield, Yvonne Whiteman, M Whitfrew, Frank Whitling, Sharon Whitwham, Johnny Whitwright, I Widlund, J Wigh, Jackie Wigh, Stuart Wilber, Manfred Wilde, Mary Wilde, Susanne Wildi, Larissa Will, V Willems, Ines Williams, G Williams, Neil Williams, Sarah Williams, Chris Williams, Michelle Wilse, Anne Wilshin, Margaret Wilson, P Wilson, Ian Wilson, Simon Winfried, Phil Wingfield, Catherine Winter, Pamela Winton, C Wishbone, J P Wispelaere, Chris & Marion Witt, John & Lisa Wittch, Andy Wolton, Andrew & Helen Wood, D Wood, Chris Woodhouse, O Woodhouse, Simon Woolrych, Julian Woonton, Lindsay Wright, Sara Wyborn, Dick Wyckmans, M Wyszymska

Keiji Yamaguchi, R Yishai, Gideon Yoffe, Elad YomTov, Lim Yoong-Hwee, Cathy Young, Lo Yuchun

Justin Zaman, Esther Zaragoza, Tom Zarzecki, R Van Zeelst, Wolfgang Zilm

LONELY PLANET PHRASEBOOKS

Building bridges,
Breaking barriers,
Beyond babble-on

Listen for the gems

Speak your own words

Ask your own
questions

Master of
your
own
image

- handy pocket-sized books
- easy to understand Pronunciation chapter
- clear and comprehensive Grammar chapter
- romanisation alongside script to allow ease of pronunciation
- script throughout so users can point to phrases
- extensive vocabulary sections, words and phrases for every situations
- full of cultural information and tips for the traveller

'...vital for a real DIY spirit and attitude in language learning' – Backpacker

'the phrasebooks have good cultural backgrounders and offer solid advice for challenging situations in remote locations' – San Francisco Examiner

'...they are unbeatable for their coverage of the world's more obscure languages' – The Geographical Magazine

---

Arabic (Egyptian)
Arabic (Moroccan)
Australia
  Australian English, Aboriginal and
  Torres Strait languages
Baltic States
  Estonian, Latvian, Lithuanian
Bengali
Burmese
Brazilian
Cantonese
Central Europe
  Czech, French, German, Hungarian,
  Italian and Slovak
Eastern Europe
  Bulgarian, Czech, Hungarian, Polish,
  Romanian and Slovak
Egyptian Arabic
Ethiopian (Amharic)
Fijian
French
German
Greek

Hindi/Urdu
Indonesian
Italian
Japanese
Korean
Lao
Latin American Spanish
Malay
Mandarin
Mediterranean Europe
  Albanian, Croatian, Greek, Italian,
  Macedonian, Maltese, Serbian,
  Slovene
Mongolian
Moroccan Arabic
Nepali
Papua New Guinea
Pilipino (Tagalog)
Quechua
Russian
Scandinavian Europe
  Danish, Finnish, Icelandic, Norwegian
  and Swedish

South-East Asia
  Burmese, Indonesian, Khmer, Lao,
  Malay, Tagalog (Pilipino), Thai and
  Vietnamese
Spanish
Sri Lanka
Swahili
Thai
Thai Hill Tribes
Tibetan
Turkish
Ukrainian
USA
  US English, Vernacular Talk,
  Native American languages and
  Hawaiian
Vietnamese
Western Europe
  Basque, Catalan, Dutch, French,
  German, Irish, Italian, Portuguese,
  Scottish Gaelic, Spanish (Castilian)
  and Welsh

LONELY PLANET JOURNEYS

JOURNEYS is a unique collection of travel writing – published by the company that understands travel better than anyone else. It is a series for anyone who has ever experienced – or dreamed of – the magical moment when they encountered a strange culture or saw a place for the first time. They are tales to read while you're planning a trip, while you're on the road or while you're in an armchair, in front of a fire.

JOURNEYS books catch the spirit of a place, illuminate a culture, recount a crazy adventure, or introduce a fascinating way of life. They always entertain, and always enrich the experience of travel.

IN RAJASTHAN
Royina Grewal

Indian writer Royina Grewal's travels in Rajasthan take her from tribal villages to flamboyant palaces. Along the way she encounters a multitude of characters: snake charmers, holy men, nomads, astrologers, dispossessed princes, reformed bandits . . . And as she draws out the rarely told stories of farmers' wives, militant maharanis and ambitious schoolgirls, the author skilfully charts the changing place of women in contemporary India. The result is a splendidly evocative mosaic of life in India's most colourful state.

Royina Grewal lives on a farm in Rajasthan, where she and her husband are working to evolve minimal-impact methods of farming. Royina has published two monographs about the need for cultural conservation and development planning. She is also the author of *Sacred Virgin*, a travel narrative about her journey along the Narmada River, which was published to wide acclaim.

SHOPPING FOR BUDDHAS
Jeff Greenwald

Here in this distant, exotic land, we were compelled to raise the art of shopping to an experience that was, on the one hand, almost Zen – and, on the other hand, tinged with desperation like shopping at Macy's or Bloomingdale's during a one-day-only White Sale.

Shopping for Buddhas is Jeff Greenwald's story of his obsessive search for the perfect Buddha statue. In the backstreets of Kathmandu, he discovers more than he bargained for . . . and his souvenir-hunting turns into an ironic metaphor for the clash between spiritual riches and material greed. Politics, religion and serious shopping collide in this witty account of an enlightening visit to Nepal.

Jeff Greenwald is also the author of *Mister Raja's Neighborhood* and *The Size of the World*. His reflections on travel, science and the global community have appeared in the *Los Angeles Times*, the *Washington Post*, *Wired* and a range of other publications. Jeff lives in Oakland, California.

PLANET TALK

Lonely Planet's FREE quarterly newsletter

We love hearing from you and think you'd like to hear from us.

When...is the right time to see reindeer in Finland?
Where...can you hear the best palm-wine music in Ghana?
How...do you get from Asunción to Areguá by steam train?
What...is the best way to see India?

For the answer to these and many other questions read PLANET TALK.

Every issue is packed with up-to-date travel news and advice including:

* a letter from Lonely Planet co-founders Tony and Maureen Wheeler
* go behind the scenes on the road with a Lonely Planet author
* feature article on an important and topical travel issue
* a selection of recent letters from travellers
* details on forthcoming Lonely Planet promotions
* complete list of Lonely Planet products

To join our mailing list contact any Lonely Planet office.

Also available: Lonely Planet T-shirts. 100% heavyweight cotton.

LONELY PLANET ONLINE

Get the latest travel information before you leave or while you're on the road

Whether you've just begun planning your next trip, or you're chasing down specific info on currency regulations or visa requirements, check out Lonely Planet Online for up-to-the minute travel information.

As well as travel profiles of your favourite destinations (including maps and photos), you'll find current reports from our researchers and other travellers, updates on health and visas, travel advisories, and discussion of the ecological and political issues you need to be aware of as you travel.

There's also an online travellers' forum where you can share your experience of life on the road, meet travel companions and ask other travellers for their recommendations and advice. We also have plenty of links to other online sites useful to independent travellers.

And of course we have a complete and up-to-date list of all Lonely Planet travel products including guides, phrasebooks, atlases, Journeys and videos and a simple online ordering facility if you can't find the book you want elsewhere.

www.lonelyplanet.com
or
AOL keyword: lp

LONELY PLANET PRODUCTS

Lonely Planet is known worldwide for publishing practical, reliable and no-nonsense travel information in our guides and on our web site. The Lonely Planet list covers just about every accessible part of the world. Currently there are eight series: *travel guides, shoestring guides, walking guides, city guides, phrasebooks, audio packs, travel atlases* and *Journeys* – a unique collection of travel writing.

EUROPE

Amsterdam • Austria • Baltic States phrasebook • Britain • Central Europe on a shoestring • Central Europe phrasebook • Czech & Slovak Republics • Denmark • Dublin • Eastern Europe on a shoestring • Eastern Europe phrasebook • Estonia, Latvia & Lithuania • Finland • France • French phrasebook • German phrasebook • Greece • Greek phrasebook • Hungary • Iceland, Greenland & the Faroe Islands • Ireland • Italian phrasebook • Italy • Mediterranean Europe on a shoestring • Mediterranean Europe phrasebook • Paris • Poland • Portugal • Portugal travel atlas • Prague • Russia, Ukraine & Belarus • Russian phrasebook • Scandinavian & Baltic Europe on a shoestring • Scandinavian Europe phrasebook • Slovenia • Spain • Spanish phrasebook • St Petersburg • Switzerland • Trekking in Greece • Trekking in Spain • Ukrainian phrasebook • Vienna • Walking in Britain • Walking in Switzerland • Western Europe on a shoestring • Western Europe phrasebook

Travel Literature: The Olive Grove: Travels in Greece

NORTH AMERICA

Alaska • Backpacking in Alaska • Baja California • California & Nevada • Canada • Florida • Hawaii • Honolulu • Los Angeles • Mexico • Miami • New England • New Orleans • New York City • New York, New Jersey & Pennsylvania • Pacific Northwest USA • Rocky Mountain States • San Francisco • Southwest USA • USA phrasebook • Washington, DC & the Capital Region

CENTRAL AMERICA & THE CARIBBEAN

Bermuda • Central America on a shoestring • Costa Rica • Cuba • Eastern Caribbean • Guatemala, Belize & Yucatán: La Ruta Maya • Jamaica

SOUTH AMERICA

Argentina, Uruguay & Paraguay • Bolivia • Brazil • Brazilian phrasebook • Buenos Aires • Chile & Easter Island • Chile & Easter Island travel atlas • Colombia • Ecuador & the Galápagos Islands • Latin American Spanish phrasebook • Peru • Quechua phrasebook • Rio de Janeiro • South America on a shoestring • Trekking in the Patagonian Andes • Venezuela

Travel Literature: Full Circle: A South American Journey

ANTARCTICA

Antarctica

ISLANDS OF THE INDIAN OCEAN

Madagascar & Comoros • Maldives • Mauritius, Réunion & Seychelles

AFRICA

Africa - the South • Africa on a shoestring • Arabic (Moroccan) phrasebook • Cape Town • Central Africa • East Africa • Egypt • Egypt travel atlas • Ethiopian (Amharic) phrasebook • Kenya • Kenya travel atlas • Malawi, Mozambique & Zambia • Morocco • North Africa • South Africa, Lesotho & Swaziland • South Africa, Lesotho & Swaziland travel atlas • Swahili phrasebook • Trekking in East Africa • West Africa • Zimbabwe, Botswana & Namibia • Zimbabwe, Botswana & Namibia travel atlas

Travel Literature: The Rainbird: A Central African Journey • Songs to an African Sunset: A Zimbabwean Story

MAIL ORDER

Lonely Planet products are distributed worldwide. They are also available by mail order from Lonely Planet, so if you have difficulty finding a title please write to us. North American and South American residents should write to Embarcadero West, 155 Filbert St, Suite 251, Oakland CA 94607, USA; European and African residents should write to 10 Barley Mow Passage, Chiswick, London W4 4PH; and residents of other countries to PO Box 617, Hawthorn, Victoria 3122, Australia.

NORTH-EAST ASIA

Beijing • Cantonese phrasebook • China • Hong Kong • Hong Kong, Macau & Guangzhou • Japan • Japanese phrasebook • Japanese audio pack • Korea • Korean phrasebook • Mandarin phrasebook • Mongolia • Mongolian phrasebook • North-East Asia on a shoestring • Seoul • Taiwan • Tibet • Tibet phrasebook • Tokyo

Travel Literature: Lost Japan

INDIAN SUBCONTINENT

Bangladesh • Bengali phrasebook • Delhi • Hindi/Urdu phrasebook • India • India & Bangladesh travel atlas • Indian Himalaya • Karakoram Highway • Nepal • Nepali phrasebook • Pakistan • Rajasthan • Sri Lanka • Sri Lanka phrasebook • Trekking in the Indian Himalaya • Trekking in the Karakoram & Hindukush • Trekking in the Nepal Himalaya

Travel Literature: In Rajasthan • Shopping for Buddhas

SOUTH-EAST ASIA

Bali & Lombok • Bangkok • Burmese phrasebook • Cambodia • Ho Chi Minh City • Indonesia • Indonesian phrasebook • Indonesian audio pack • Jakarta • Java • Laos • Lao phrasebook • Laos travel atlas • Malay phrasebook • Malaysia, Singapore & Brunei • Myanmar (Burma) • Philippines • Pilipino phrasebook • Singapore • South-East Asia on a shoestring • South-East Asia phrasebook • Thailand • Thailand travel atlas • Thai phrasebook • Thai audio pack • Thai Hill Tribes phrasebook • Vietnam • Vietnamese phrasebook • Vietnam travel atlas

MIDDLE EAST & CENTRAL ASIA

Arab Gulf States • Arabic (Egyptian) phrasebook • Central Asia • Iran • Israel & the Palestinian Territories • Israel & the Palestinian Territories travel atlas • Istanbul • Jerusalem • Jordan & Syria • Jordan, Syria & Lebanon travel atlas • Middle East • Turkey • Turkish phrasebook • Turkey travel atlas • Yemen

Travel Literature: The Gates of Damascus • Kingdom of the Film Stars: Journey into Jordan

ALSO AVAILABLE:

Travel with Children • Traveller's Tales

AUSTRALIA & THE PACIFIC

Australia • Australian phrasebook • Bushwalking in Australia • Bushwalking in Papua New Guinea • Fiji • Fijian phrasebook • Islands of Australia's Great Barrier Reef • Melbourne • Micronesia • New Caledonia • New South Wales & the ACT • New Zealand • Northern Territory • Outback Australia • Papua New Guinea • Papua New Guinea phrasebook • Queensland • Rarotonga & the Cook Islands • Samoa • Solomon Islands • South Australia • Sydney • Tahiti & French Polynesia • Tasmania • Tonga • Tramping in New Zealand • Vanuatu • Victoria • Western Australia

Travel Literature: Islands in the Clouds • Sean & David's Long Drive

THE LONELY PLANET STORY

Lonely Planet published its first book in 1973 in response to the numerous 'How did you do it?' questions Maureen and Tony Wheeler were asked after driving, bussing, hitching, sailing and railing their way from England to Australia.

Written at a kitchen table and hand collated, trimmed and stapled, *Across Asia on the Cheap* became an instant local bestseller, inspiring thoughts of another book.

Eighteen months in South-East Asia resulted in their second guide, *South-East Asia on a shoestring*, which they put together in a backstreet Chinese hotel in Singapore in 1975. The 'yellow bible', as it quickly became known to backpackers around the world, soon became *the* guide to the region. It has sold well over half a million copies and is now in its 9th edition, still retaining its familiar yellow cover.

Today there are over 240 titles, including travel guides, walking guides, language kits & phrasebooks, travel atlases and travel literature. The company is the largest independent travel publisher in the world. Although Lonely Planet initially specialised in guides to Asia, today there are few corners of the globe that have not been covered.

The emphasis continues to be on travel for independent travellers. Tony and Maureen still travel for several months of each year and play an active part in the writing, updating and quality control of Lonely Planet's guides.

They have been joined by over 70 authors and 170 staff at our offices in Melbourne (Australia), Oakland (USA), London (UK) and Paris (France). Travellers themselves also make a valuable contribution to the guides through the feedback we receive in thousands of letters each year and on our web site.

The people at Lonely Planet strongly believe that travellers can make a positive contribution to the countries they visit, both through their appreciation of the countries' culture, wildlife and natural features, and through the money they spend. In addition, the company makes a direct contribution to the countries and regions it covers. Since 1986 a percentage of the income from each book has been donated to ventures such as famine relief in Africa; aid projects in India; agricultural projects in Central America; Greenpeace's efforts to halt French nuclear testing in the Pacific; and Amnesty International.

'I hope we send people out with the right attitude about travel. You realise when you travel that there are so many different perspectives about the world, so we hope these books will make people more interested in what they see. Guidebooks can't really guide people. All you can do is point them in the right direction.'

– Tony Wheeler

LONELY PLANET PUBLICATIONS

Australia
PO Box 617, Hawthorn 3122, Victoria
tel: (03) 9819 1877 fax: (03) 9819 6459
e-mail: talk2us@lonelyplanet.com.au

USA
Embarcadero West, 155 Filbert St, Suite 251,
Oakland, CA 94607
tel: (510) 893 8555 TOLL FREE: 800 275-8555
fax: (510) 893 8563
e-mail: info@lonelyplanet.com

UK
10 Barley Mow Passage, Chiswick,
London W4 4PH
tel: (0181) 742 3161 fax: (0181) 742 2772
e-mail: lonelyplanetuk@compuserve.com

France:
71 bis rue du Cardinal Lemoine, 75005 Paris
tel: 1 44 32 06 20 fax: 1 46 34 72 55
e-mail: 100560.415@compuserve.com

World Wide Web: http://www.lonelyplanet.com
or AOL keyword: lp